The Grants Register®

2005

Twenty-third Edition

palgrave
macmillan

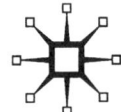
The editor of *The Grants Register* cannot undertake any correspondence in relation to grants listed in this volume.

While every care has been taken in compiling the information contained in this publication, the publisher and editor do not accept any responsibility for any errors or omissions therein.

The authors have asserted their rights to be identified as the authors of this work in accordance with the Copyright, Designs and Patent Act 1988.

This edition published 2004 by
PALGRAVE MACMILLAN
Houndmills, Basingstoke, Hampshire RG21 6XS and
175 Fifth Avenue, New York, N.Y. 10010
Companies and representatives throughout the world.

PALGRAVE MACMILLAN is the global academic imprint of the Palgrave Macmillan division of St. Martin's Press, LLC and of Palgrave Macmillan Ltd. Macmillan™ is a registered trademark in the United States, United Kingdom and other countries. Palgrave is a registered trademark in the European Union and other countries.

ISBN 1-4039-2116-4
ISSN 0072-5471

This book is printed on paper suitable for recycling and made from fully managed and sustained forest sources.

A catalogue record for this book is available from the British Library.

A catalog record for this book is available from the Library of Congress.

10 9 8 7 6 5 4 3 2 1
13 12 11 10 09 08 07 06 05 04

Printed in China

PREFACE

The twenty-third edition of *The Grants Register* provides a detailed, accurate and comprehensive survey of awards intended for students at or above the postgraduate level, or those who require further professional or advanced vocational training.

Student numbers around the world continue to grow rapidly, and overseas study is now the first choice for many of these students. *The Grants Register* provides comprehensive, up-to-date information about the availability of, and eligibility for, non-refundable postgraduate and professional awards worldwide.

We remain grateful to the institutions which have supplied information for inclusion in this edition, and would also like to thank the International Association of Universities for continued permission to use their subject index within our Subject and Eligibility Guide to Awards.

The Grants Register database is updated continually in order to ensure that the information provided is the most current available. Therefore, if your details have changed or you would like to be included for the first time, please contact The Reference Administrator (The Grants Register), at address below. If you wish to obtain further information relating to specific application procedures, please contact the relevant grant-awarding institution, rather than the publisher.

The Grants Register
Palgrave Macmillan
Houndmills
Basingstoke
RG21 6XS
United Kingdom
Tel: +44 (0)1256 329242
Fax: +44 (0)1256 357268

Website: http://www.palgrave.com
Email: grants.register@palgrave.com

LIST OF CONTENTS

HOW TO USE THE GRANTS REGISTER

For ease of use, *The Grants Register 2005* is divided into five sections:

- *The Grants Register*
- Subject and Eligibility Guide to Awards
- Index of Awards
- Index of Discontinued Awards
- Index of Awarding Organisations

The Grants Register

Information in this section is supplied directly by the awarding organisations. Entries are arranged alphabetically by name of organisation, and awards are listed alphabetically within the awarding organisation. This section includes details on subject area, eligibility, purpose, type, numbers offered, frequency, value, length of study, study establishment, country of study, and application procedure. Full contact details appear with each awarding organisation and also appended to individual awards where additional addresses are given.

Subject and Eligibility Guide to Awards

Awards can be located through the Subject and Eligibility Guide to Awards. This section allows the user to find an award within a specific subject area. *The Grants Register* uses a list of subjects endorsed by the International Association of Universities (IAU), the information centre on higher education, located at UNESCO, Paris (please see pp. 719-720 for the complete subject list). It is further subdivided into eligibility by nationality. Thereafter, awards are listed alphabetically within their designated category, along with a page reference where full details of the award can be found.

Index of Awards

All awards are indexed alphabetically with a page reference.

Index of Discontinued Awards

This Index lists awards previously included within *The Grants Register* which are no longer being offered, have been replaced by another programme, or are no longer relevant for inclusion in the publication.

Index of Awarding Organisations

A complete list of all awarding organisations, with country name and page reference.

ACADIA UNIVERSITY

Wolfville, NS, B4P 2R6, Canada

Tel: (1) 902 585 1498
Fax: (1) 902 585 1096
Email: elaine.schofield@acadiau.ca
www: http://www.acadiau.ca
Contact: Ms Elaine Schofield, Office Manager

Acadia University is an institution providing a liberal education based on the highest standards. The University provides a scholarly community that aims to ensure a broadening life experience for students, faculty and staff.

Acadia Graduate Teaching Assistantships

Subjects: English, political science, sociology, biology, chemistry, computer science, geology, psychology, education and recreation management, mathematics and statistics.
Purpose: To financially support students.
Eligibility: Open to those registered as full-time graduate students at Acadia University.
Level of Study: Postgraduate.
Type: Other.
Value: Up to Canadian $8,000.
Length of Study: One or two years.

ENGINEERING

GENERAL

Any Country

Alberta Research Council Karl A Clark Memorial Scholarship, 617
Andrew Stratton Scholarship, 632
Association for Women in Science Educational Foundation Predoctoral Awards, 104
Predoctoral Awards, 117
AUC Assistantships, 84
AUC Laboratory Instruction Graduation Fellowships in Engineering and Computer Science, 85
AUC University Fellowships, 86
Berthold Leibinger Innovationspreis, 125
BFWG: M H Joseph Prize, 143

THE GRANTS REGISTER

A-T CHILDREN'S PROJECT

668 South Military Trail, Deerfield Beach, FL 33442, United States of America
Tel: (1) 954 481 6611
Fax: (1) 954 725 1153
Email: info@atcp.org
www: http://www.atcp.org
Contact: Dr Cynthia Rothblum-Oviatt, Science Co-ordinator

The A-T Children's Project is a non-profit organisation that raises funds to support and co-ordinate biomedical research projects, scientific conferences and a clinical centre aimed at finding a cure for ataxia-telangiectasia, a lethal genetic disease that attacks children, causing progressive loss of muscle control, as well as cancer and immune system problems.

Direct Research on Ataxia-Telangiectasia

Subjects: ATM biology.
Purpose: To accelerate first rate, international scientific research in the area of ATM biology to help find a cure or life improving treatments for children with ataxia-telangiectasia.
Eligibility: Open to all ages and nationalities.
Level of Study: Research.
Type: Grant.
Value: Up to US$75,000.
Length of Study: One-two years.
Frequency: Annual.
Application Procedure: Applicants must visit the website.
Closing Date: There are no deadlines for submission of grant proposals.
Funding: Private.

AARON SISKIND FOUNDATION

c/o School of Visual Arts, MFA Photography, 214 East, 21st Street, New York, NY 10010, United States of America
Tel: (1) 609 348 5650
Fax: (1) 609 572 1243
Email: info@aaronsiskind.org
www: http://www.aaronsiskind.org

The foundation works to preserve and protect Aaron Siskind's artistic legacy, and foster knowledge of and appreciation of his art.

Individual Photographer's Fellowship

Subjects: Photography-based art. Eligible work must be based on the idea of the lens-based still image, but grant recipients work in forms as diverse as digital imagery, video, installations documentary projects and photo-generated print media.
Purpose: To stimulate excellence and the promise of future achievement in the photographic field. Postgraduate only.
Eligibility: Applicants must be citizens or permanent residents of the USA. Applications sent from outside USA not accepted.
Level of Study: Postgraduate.
Type: Fellowship.
Value: Up to US$5,000.
Country of Study: United States of America.
Application Procedure: Please send an application form, 10 x 35 mm slides of your work, a slide list, self-addressed return envelope together with your resumé and statement of plans for intended work to main address.
Closing Date: October 1st.
Funding: Private.
Additional Information: Applications procedure is explicit and applicants are advised to check the website.

AAUW EDUCATIONAL FOUNDATION

1111 16 Street North West, Washington, DC 20036, United States of America
Tel: (1) 202 728 7602
Email: foundation@aauw.org
www: http://www.aauw.org
Contact: Tara McLoughlin, Director of Programs

The AAUW Educational Foundation is composed of three corporations. These are the Association, a 150,000 member organisation with more than 1,500 branches nationwide which lobbies and advocates for education and equity; the AAUW Educational Foundation, which funds pioneering research on girls and education, community action projects, and fellowships and grants for outstanding women around the globe; and the AAUW Legal Advocacy Fund, which provides funds and a support system for women seeking judicial redress for sexual discrimination in higher education.

AAUW Community Action Grants

Subjects: All subjects.
Purpose: To provide seed money to individual women, local community based non-profit organisations, AAUW branches and AAUW state organisations for innovative programmes or non degree research projects that engage girls in maths, science and technology.
Eligibility: Applicants must be women who are United States citizens or permanent residents. Special consideration will be given to AAUW members and AAUW branch and state applicants who seek partners for collaborative projects. Collaborators can include local schools or school districts, businesses and other community based organisations. Two year grants are restricted to projects focused on girls' achievement in mathematics, science or technology. Projects must involve community and school collaboration. The fund supports planning and coalition building activities during the first year and implementation and evaluation the following year.
Type: Grant.
Value: US$2,000-7,000 for one year projects and US$5,000-10,000 for two year projects.
Length of Study: One or two years.
Frequency: Annual.
No. of awards offered: Only 5 two-year awards will be granted for the 2004-2005 cycle.
Application Procedure: Applicants must write for an application form, which is also available from the website.
Closing Date: January 15th.
Funding: Private.
Additional Information: Two types of grant are available. One year grants are for short term projects. Topic areas are unrestricted but should have a clearly defined educational activity. Two year grants are for longer term programmes and are restricted to projects focused on K-12 girls' achievement in maths, science, and/or technology. Funds support planning activities and coalition building during the first year and implementation and evaluation the following year.

For further information contact:

2201 North Dodge Street, Iowa City, IA 32243-4030, United States of America

AAUW Educational Foundation American Fellowships

Subjects: All subjects.
Purpose: To offset a scholars living expenses while she completes her final year of dissertation writing, or to increase the number of women in tenure track faculty positions and promote equality for women in higher education.
Eligibility: Open to women who are citizens or permanent residents of the United States.
Level of Study: Doctorate, Postdoctorate, Research.
Type: Fellowship.
Value: US$20,000 for the Dissertation Award, US$30,000 for the Postdoctoral Research Leave Award and US$6,000 for the Research Publication Grant.
Length of Study: One year for dissertation and postdoctoral summer for research publication grant.
Frequency: Annual.
Country of Study: United States of America or other countries if appropriate.
No. of awards offered: 77.
Application Procedure: Applicants must write for an application package or download materials on www.aauw.org. They must then return the application form, a narrative autobiography, a curriculum vitae, a statement of project, transcripts, three letters of recommendation and a filing fee. Applications may be downloaded from the

website or requested from the Customer Service office via the website.
Closing Date: Postmarked November 15th.
Funding: Private.
No. of awards given last year: 77.
No. of applicants last year: 704.

For further information contact:

c/o Customer Service Center Department 141 2201 North Dodge Street, Iowa City, IA 52243-4030, United States of America
Tel: (1) 317 337 1716

AAUW Eleanor Roosevelt Teacher Fellowships
Subjects: Gender equality.
Purpose: To support professional development for teachers, educational opportunities for girls and the advancement of gender equity in the classroom, school or district.
Eligibility: Open to all public school, K-12 women teachers who are United States citizens or permanent residents. Applicants must be committed to teaching for three years including the fellowship year.
Level of Study: Professional development.
Type: Fellowship.
Value: US$5,000.
No. of awards offered: Approx. 25.
Application Procedure: Applicants must write for an application form, which is also available from the website.
Closing Date: January 10th.
Funding: Private.

For further information contact:

2201 North Dodge Street, Iowa City, IA 52243-4030, United States of America

AAUW International Fellowships Program
Subjects: All subjects.
Purpose: To support women studying at the graduate or postgraduate level at a United States Institute of Higher Education.
Eligibility: Open to women who are not United States citizens or permanent residents who hold a United States Bachelor's degree or equivalent. Applicants must be planning to return to their home country upon completion of degree and/or research. English proficiency is required.
Level of Study: Doctorate, Graduate, Postdoctorate, Postgraduate, Predoctorate, Research.
Type: Fellowship.
Value: US$30,000 for the Postdoctoral Fellowship, US$20,000 for the Doctoral Fellowship and US$18,000 for the Master's Fellowship.
Length of Study: One year.
Frequency: Annual.
Study Establishment: Any accredited institution.
Country of Study: United States of America.
No. of awards offered: 57.
Application Procedure: Applicants must complete an application for each year applying. Applications must be obtained from the customer service centre or the AAUW website between August 1st and December 15th. Three letters of recommendation, transcripts and a minimum score of 550 on the Test Of English as a Foreign Language (213 computer-based) are also required.
Closing Date: Postmarked December 15th.
Funding: Private.
No. of awards given last year: 57.
No. of applicants last year: 1200 + .
Additional Information: These awards are non renewable.

For further information contact:

c/o Customer Service Center, 2201 North Dodge Street, Department 141, Iowa City, IA 52243-4030, United States of America

AAUW University Scholar-in-Residence
Subjects: Educational equity for women and girls.
Purpose: To enable a female Scholar to undertake and disseminate research on gender equality for women and girls.

Level of Study: Postdoctorate, Research.
Type: Grant.
Value: Not to exceed US$100,000 for a two year project.
Length of Study: Two years.
Frequency: Annual.
Country of Study: United States of America.
No. of awards offered: One.
Application Procedure: Institutional applicants must submit a proposal including both activities on gender and educational equity, and dissemination of findings. Successful proposals will be crafted to achieve impact across the institution or among departments or schools, rather than in a single department programme. Proposals must also include confirmation by an authorised institutional official confirming the institutions commitment to the project and cost share provided.
Closing Date: October 15th.
Funding: Private.
No. of awards given last year: One.
No. of applicants last year: 22.
Additional Information: Applicants should contact the Foundation for proposal guidelines or visit website www.aauw.org/fga.

THE ABBEY AWARDS

43 Carson Road, London, SE21 8HT, United Kingdom
Tel: (44) 20 8761 7980
Email: administrator@abbey.org.uk
www: http://www.abbey.org.uk
Contact: Ms Jane Reid, Administrator

The Abbey Awards provide opportunities for painters to live and work in excellent studios at the British School at Rome.

Abbey Fellowships in Painting
Subjects: Painting.
Purpose: To enable mid-career painters with an established record of achievement to live and work at the British School at Rome.
Eligibility: Open to United Kingdom and United States of America citizens only; also to citizens of other Countries provided that they have been and are currently living in the UK or the US for at least five years. There are no age restrictions. Fellowships are for painters only.
Level of Study: Graduate, Professional development.
Type: Fellowship.
Value: All expenses and spending money.
Length of Study: Three months.
Frequency: Annual.
Study Establishment: The British School at Rome.
Country of Study: Italy.
No. of awards offered: Usually three.
Application Procedure: Applicants must send for an application form enclosing a stamped addressed envelope, alternatively applicants can download application forms from the website.
Closing Date: Mid January.
Funding: Private.
Contributor: The Incorporated Edwin Austin Abbey Memorial Scholarships.
No. of awards given last year: 3.
No. of applicants last year: 62.

Abbey Scholarship in Painting
Subjects: Painting.
Purpose: To enable an exceptionally promising emergent painter to live and work in the British School at Rome.
Eligibility: Open to United Kingdom and United States of America citizens only; also to citizens of other countries provided that they have been and are currently living the UK or the US for atleast 5 years. There are no age restrictions. Awards are for painters only.
Level of Study: Graduate, Postgraduate.
Type: Scholarship.
Value: All expenses and spending money.
Length of Study: Nine months.
Frequency: Annual.
Study Establishment: The British School at Rome.

Country of Study: Italy.
No. of awards offered: One.
Application Procedure: Applicants must send for an application form enclosing a stamped addressed envelope. Alternatively, applicants can download application forms from the website.
Closing Date: Mid January.
Funding: Private.
Contributor: The Incorporated Edwin Austin Abbey Memorial Scholarships.
No. of awards given last year: One.
No. of applicants last year: Approx. 74.

THE ABBEY HARRIS MURAL FUND

43 Carson Road, London, SE21 8HT, United Kingdom
Tel: (44) 20 8761 7980
Email: administrator@abbey.org.uk
www: http://www.abbey.org.uk
Contact: Ms Jane Reid, Administrator

The Abbey Harris Mural Fund supports the creation of murals in public places in the UK.

Abbey Harris Mural Fund
Subjects: Mural painting.
Purpose: To provide grants to artists who have been commissioned to create murals in public places or in charitable institutions in the United Kingdom.
Eligibility: Awards are for painters and the work must be carried out in the UK. No other restrictions.
Level of Study: Unrestricted.
Type: Grant.
Value: Approx. UK£3,000.
Frequency: Annual.
Country of Study: United Kingdom.
No. of awards offered: Two.
Application Procedure: Send for particulars, enclosing a stamped and addressed envelope. Particulars can also be sent by e-mail.
Closing Date: Applications are accepted at any time. Decisions may be made at twice yearly meetings of the Trustees in May and November.
Funding: Private.
Contributor: E A Abbey Memorial Trust Fund for Mural Painting in Great Britain and E Vincent Harris Fund for Mural Decoration.
No. of awards given last year: Two.
No. of applicants last year: 6.

ABDUS SALAM INTERNATIONAL CENTRE FOR THEORETICAL PHYSICS (ICTP)

Strada Costiera 11, Trieste, I-34014, Italy
Tel: (39) 040 224 0111
Fax: (39) 040 224 163
Email: sci_info@ictp.trieste.it
www: http://www.ictp.trieste.it
Contact: Public Information Officer

The Abdus Salam International Centre for Theoretical Physics (ICTP) is an institution for research and high level training in physics and mathematics, mainly for scientists from developing countries. It also maintains a network of associate members and federated institutes.

Abdus Salam ICTP Fellowships
Subjects: Physics and mathematics.
Purpose: To enable qualified applicants to pursue research in the fields of condensed matter physics, mathematics and high energy physics.
Eligibility: Open to qualified applicants of any nationality, who have a PhD in physics or mathematics.
Level of Study: Postdoctorate.

Type: Fellowship.
Value: Monthly stipend, round trip expenses where applicable and allowances according to the length of the visit.
Length of Study: Up to one year.
Frequency: Dependent on funds available.
Study Establishment: ICTP.
Country of Study: Italy.
No. of awards offered: Varies.
Application Procedure: Applicants must request appropriate application forms from the secretariat, or visit the ICTP website.
Closing Date: Applications are accepted at any time.
Funding: Government.
Contributor: The Italian government, IAEA and UNESCO.

ACADEMY OF MOTION PICTURE ARTS AND SCIENCES

1313 N. Vine Street, Los Angeles, CA 90028, United States of America
Tel: (1) 310 247 3010
Fax: (1) 310 247 2600
Email: nicholl@oscars.org
www: http://www.oscars.org/nicholl
Contact: Mr Greg Beal, Programme Co-ordinator

The Academy of Motion Picture Arts and Sciences annually presents Academy Awards for motion picture artistic achievement. The Academy Film Archive is a leader in preservation and restoration and the Academy's Margaret Herrick Library holds a vast array of film related materials. The Student Academy Awards honours achievements by talented student film makers.

Don and Gee Nicholl Fellowships in Screenwriting
Subjects: Screenwriting.
Purpose: To foster the development of new writers.
Eligibility: Open to writers in English who have not sold or optioned a screen or teleplay and to those who have not sold or optioned a story for a screen or teleplay.
Level of Study: Unrestricted.
Type: Fellowship.
Value: US$30,000.
Length of Study: One year.
Frequency: Annual.
Country of Study: Any country.
No. of awards offered: Up to five.
Application Procedure: Applicants must complete an application form. This is available after January 1st and can be obtained by sending a written request via post or email or by visiting the website.
Closing Date: May 1st.
Funding: Private.
No. of awards given last year: Five.
No. of applicants last year: 6,048.
Additional Information: In addition to the Academy Awards or Oscars and the Nicholl Fellowships, the Academy offers Student Film Awards for films completed by students at an accredited college or university.

For further information contact:

1313 N. Vine Street, Los Angeles, CA 90028, United States of America

ACADEMY OF NATURAL SCIENCES

1900 Benjamin Franklin Parkway, Philadelphia, PA 19103-1195, United States of America
Tel: (1) 215 299 1000
Fax: (1) 215 299 1028
Email: daeschler@acnatsci.org
www: http://www.acnatsci.org/research/jessupinfo.html
Contact: Dr Edward Daeschler, Assistant Curator

The Academy of Natural Sciences, an international museum of natural history operating since 1812, undertakes research and public education that focuses on the environment and its diverse species. The Academy's mission is to expand knowledge of nature through discovery and to inspire stewardship of the environment.

Jessup and McHenry Awards

Subjects: The Jessup award is for zoology and the McHenry award is for botany.
Purpose: To assist predoctoral and postdoctoral students working with biological collections at the Academy of Natural Sciences in Philadelphia.
Eligibility: Students commuting within the Philadelphia area are ineligible, otherwise eligibility is unrestricted.
Level of Study: Doctorate, Postdoctorate, Postgraduate, Predoctorate.
Type: Fellowship.
Value: The stipend for subsistence is US$300 per week. Fellowships may include round trip travel costs of up to a total of US$500 for North American applicants, including Mexico and the Caribbean, and US$1,000 for applicants from other parts of the world. This is not guaranteed.
Length of Study: 2-12 weeks.
Frequency: Annual.
Study Establishment: The Academy of Natural Sciences.
Country of Study: United States of America.
Application Procedure: Applicants must send queries, requests for information and supporting information to the given address.
Closing Date: March 1st or October 1st.
Funding: Private.
No. of awards given last year: Three.
Additional Information: The provision of scientific supplies and equipment is the responsibility of the student and the sponsoring curator.

ACADIA UNIVERSITY

Wolfville, NS, B4P 2R6, Canada
Tel: (1) 902 585 1498
Fax: (1) 902 585 1096
Email: elaine.schofield@acadiau.ca
www: http://www.acadiau.ca
Contact: Ms Elaine Schofield, Office Manager

Acadia University is an institution providing a liberal education based on the highest standards. The University provides a scholarly community that aims to ensure a broadening life experience for students, faculty and staff.

Acadia Graduate Teaching Assistantships

Subjects: English, political science, sociology, biology, chemistry, computer science, geology, psychology, education and recreation management, mathematics and statistics.
Purpose: To financially support students.
Eligibility: Open to those registered as full-time graduate students at Acadia University.
Level of Study: Postgraduate.
Type: Other.
Value: Up to Canadian $8,000.
Length of Study: One or two years.
Frequency: Annual.
Study Establishment: The Division of Research and Graduate Studies at Acadia University.
Country of Study: Canada.
No. of awards offered: Limited.
Application Procedure: Applicants must write for details.
Closing Date: February 1st.
Additional Information: Recipients of a graduate teaching assistantship should expect to undertake certain duties during the academic year (up to a maximum of 10 hours per week and a maximum of 100 hours per semester) as a condition of tenure of the award. The specific duties will be established by agreement at the beginning of each academic year.

ACTION CANCER

1 Marlborough Park, Belfast, BT9 6XS, Northern Ireland
Tel: (44) 28 9080 3344
Fax: (44) 28 9080 3356
Email: info@actioncancer.org
www: http://www.actioncancer.org
Contact: Ms Nicola Nicholls, Director of Development & Policy

Action Cancer is a Northern Ireland cancer charity, funded entirely by voluntary donations. Founded in 1973, it offers awareness and health promotion, free early detection clinics for men and women concerned about cancer and a support service for cancer patients and their families. Action Cancer also provides funding for research at local universities.

Action Cancer Project Grant

Subjects: Cancer related projects.
Purpose: To help researchers in Northern Ireland carry out significant cancer-related projects by contributing to salaries, the purchase of materials and equipments, and to other appropriate costs.
Eligibility: Researchers must be working in Northern Ireland.
Level of Study: Postdoctorate
Type: Project grant.
Value: Up to UK£45,000 per annum for up to three years.
Length of Study: Three years.
Frequency: Every three years.
Country of Study: United Kingdom.
No. of awards offered: One.
Application Procedure: Awards are advertised in the local press in March. Applicants must submit a form and a decision is taken by the Action Cancer Scientific and Research Committee who take advice from external reviewers.
Closing Date: Early May.
Funding: Private.
Contributor: Voluntary donations.
No. of awards given last year: One.
No. of applicants last year: 13.

Action Cancer Research Grants

Subjects: Cancer related projects.
Purpose: To help researchers in Northern Ireland carry out cancer related projects by contributing to the cost of equipment or materials. Preference will be given to the support of individuals early in their career.
Eligibility: Researchers must be working in Northern Ireland.
Level of Study: Postdoctorate.
Type: Grant.
Value: UK£10,000.
Length of Study: One year.
Frequency: Annual.
Country of Study: United Kingdom.
No. of awards offered: Five.
Application Procedure: Awards are advertised in the local press in March. Applicants must submit an application form and a decision is made by the Scientific and Research Committee.
Closing Date: Early April.
Funding: Private.
Contributor: Voluntary donations.
No. of awards given last year: Five.
No. of applicants last year: 19.

Action Cancer Research Studentship

Subjects: Cancer related projects.
Purpose: To provide an opportunity for an outstanding graduate in an appropriate chemical, biological or biomedical science, to work on a cancer related research project and undergo research training with a view to being awarded a PhD from the Queen's University of Belfast or the University of Ulster.
Eligibility: Supervisors must be researchers in Northern Ireland.
Level of Study: Doctorate.
Type: Studentship.
Value: Approx. UK£17,800 per year.
Length of Study: Three years.

Frequency: Annual.
Country of Study: United Kingdom.
No. of awards offered: One.
Application Procedure: Awards are advertised in the local press in December. Supervisors must submit an application form and on receipt of the award must advertise for an appropriate student. Applications are reviewed externally and a decision is taken on the award by Action Cancer's Scientific and Research Committee.
Closing Date: Early January.
Funding: Private.
Contributor: Voluntary donations.
No. of awards given last year: One.
No. of applicants last year: Seven.

ACTION MEDICAL RESEARCH

Vincent House, Horsham, West Sussex, RH12 2DP, England
Tel: (44) 1403 210406
Fax: (44) 1403 210541
Email: info@action.org.uk
www: www.action.org.uk

Action Medical Research is a national research charity dedicated to preventing and treating disabling diseases. The charity supports a broad spectrum of research with the objective of preventing disease and disability, regardless of age group, and alleviating physical handicap. Emphasis is placed on clinical research, or research at the clinical and basic interface.

Action Medical Research Project Grants
Subjects: Preventing disease and disability regardless of cause or age group and alleviating physical handicap. The exceptions are cancer, cardiovascular, HIV and AIDS research.
Purpose: To support one precisely formulated line of research.
Eligibility: Open to researchers based in the United Kingdom. Grants are not awarded to MRC units, other charities or for higher education.
Level of Study: Unrestricted.
Type: Grant.
Value: Varies.
Length of Study: Up to three years, assessed annually.
Frequency: Dependent on funds available, See website.
Study Establishment: Hospitals, universities and recognised research establishments.
Country of Study: United Kingdom.
No. of awards offered: Varies.
Application Procedure: Applicants must submit a one page outline of the project before an application form can be issued. Full details and outline proposals are available on the website.
Closing Date: Please contact the Charity or visit the website.
Funding: Private.
Contributor: Voluntary income.
No. of awards given last year: 15.
No. of applicants last year: 110.

Action Medical Research Training Fellowship
Subjects: Preventing disease and disability regardless of cause or age group and alleviating physical handicap. The exceptions are cancer, cardiovascular, HIV and AIDS research.
Purpose: To enable the training of young medical and non medical graduates in research techniques and methodology in areas of interest to Research Action.
Eligibility: Open to medical and non medical graduates, preferably between 23 and 32 years old, as this is a training position. Although it is not limited to United Kingdom citizens, those who do not hold United Kingdom citizenship must be able to show that they have all the required statutory documentation, eg. work permits, to cover the period of the fellowship. No grants are made purely for higher education.
Level of Study: Doctorate, Postdoctorate, Postgraduate.
Type: Fellowship.
Value: Varies.
Length of Study: Up to three years.
Frequency: Annual, Depending on funds available, See Website.
Study Establishment: A hospital or university department.

Country of Study: United Kingdom.
No. of awards offered: Varies.
Application Procedure: Applicants must submit a one page outline of the project before an application form can be issued. Full details and outline proposal forms are available on the website.
Closing Date: Please contact the Charity or visit the website.
Funding: Private.
Contributor: Voluntary income.
No. of awards given last year: Four.
No. of applicants last year: 58.
Additional Information: Fellowships are advertised separately each year in late November.

THE ACTUARIAL FOUNDATION

475 North Martingale Road, Suite 600, Schaumburg, IL 60173-2226, United States of America
Tel: (1) 847 706 3535
Fax: (1) 847 706 3599
Email: eileen.streu@actfnd.org
www: http://www.actuarialfoundation.org
Contact: Business Manager

The Actuarial Foundation carries out research and education projects in actuarial science and studies specific projects that could be advanced under this mechanism.

The Actuarial Foundation Individual Grants Competition
Subjects: Actuarial science.
Purpose: To produce publications which will advance actuarial science, especially with regard to practical applications.
Eligibility: Proposals are invited from members of the seven sponsoring actuarial organisations (AAA, ASPA, CIA, CAS, CONAC, CCA and SoA), from faculty members of universities or colleges who have teaching and research responsibilities in the actuarial or related field, and by others who are qualified by knowledge and experience to contribute to their goals.
Level of Study: Unrestricted.
Type: Grant.
Value: Varies, approx. US$10,000.
Length of Study: Projects should generally be of less than one year in duration.
Frequency: Annual.
Country of Study: Any country.
No. of awards offered: Varies.
Application Procedure: Applicants must submit a letter of intent and an application form.
Funding: Private.
Contributor: The Actuarial Foundation and the Canadian Institute of Actuary and individuals.
Additional Information: The project may be either theoretical or empirical in nature. A key criteria is that the project should have the potential to contribute significantly to the advancement of knowledge in actuarial science. The Actuarial Foundation gives preference to projects relating to current policy issues or having direct applications and those that further the basic or continuing education of actuaries. Proposals for innovative developments in actuarial education are also considered by The Actuarial Foundation. More information is available from the website.

ADELPHI UNIVERSITY

1 South Avenue, Garden City, New York, NY 11530,
Tel: 516 877 4670
Email: admissions@adelphi.edu
www: http://www.adelphi.edu

The oldest institution of higher education for liberal arts and sciences on Long Island.

Adelphi University Graduate Assistantships
Subjects: Relevant employment in a university department as part of post-graduate study.

Purpose: To offer graduate assistance as remuneration for employment by a university department.
Eligibility: Employment must be relevant to study.
Level of Study: Postgraduate.
Type: Assistantship.
Value: Variable.
Frequency: Annual.
Study Establishment: Adelphi University.
Country of Study: United States of America.
Application Procedure: Students must apply via their academic department.
Funding: Private.
Contributor: Adelphi University.

Adelphi University Scholarships

Subjects: Post graduate study in business or social work.
Purpose: To offer scholarship opportunities ranging up to $3,000 to students pursing postgraduate study in the School of Business or the School of Social Work.
Level of Study: Postgraduate.
Type: Scholarship.
Value: Up to US$3,000.
Frequency: Annual.
Study Establishment: Adelphi University.
Country of Study: United States of America.
Application Procedure: Contact the School of Business (1) 516 877 4670 or the School of Social Work for more information.
Funding: Private.

ADHA INSTITUTE FOR ORAL HEALTH

Suite 3400, 444 North Michigan Avenue, Chicago, IL 60611, United States of America
Tel: (1) 312 440 8900
Email: institute@adha.net
www: http://www.adha.org/institute
Contact: Ms Linda Caradine, Executive Administrator

The ADHA Institute for Oral Health administers scholarship programmes for full-time dental hygiene students at Baccalaureate and graduate levels. ADHA Institute Scholarship awards invest in the future careers of dental hygiene students.

ADHA Institute Minority Scholarship

Subjects: Dental hygiene.
Purpose: To aid members of minority groups who are currently under represented in dental hygiene programmes.
Eligibility: Open to full-time students at Baccalaureate, graduate and doctoral levels who are African American, Hispanic, Asian or Native American. Scholars must currently be enrolled as full-time students in a dental hygiene programme in the United States of America, have completed a minimum of one year with a grade point average of at least 3.0 and be able to demonstrate financial need.
Level of Study: Postgraduate.
Type: Scholarship.
Value: A maximum of US$1,250.
Frequency: Dependent on funds available.
Country of Study: United States of America.
No. of awards offered: Two.
Application Procedure: Applicants must write for details or refer to the website.
Closing Date: June 1st.
Funding: Private.
Additional Information: This is a designated scholarship and is awarded on the basis of how well the applicant demonstrates the goal or achievement described.

ADHA Institute Scholarship Program

Subjects: Dental hygiene.
Purpose: To invest in the future careers of dental hygiene students.
Eligibility: Open to full-time students at Baccalaureate, graduate and doctoral levels. Scholars must currently be enrolled as full-time students in a dental hygiene programme in the United States of America,

have completed a minimum of one year with a grade point average of at least 3.0 and be able to demonstrate financial need. Additional requirements vary depending upon degree level.
Level of Study: Doctorate, Graduate, Postgraduate.
Type: Scholarship.
Value: A maximum of US$1,500.
Length of Study: One year, non renewable.
Frequency: Annual.
Country of Study: United States of America.
No. of awards offered: Approx. 20.
Application Procedure: Applicants must write for details or refer to the website.
Closing Date: June 1st.
Funding: Private.
Additional Information: Specific areas of this scholarship programme include the Certificate or Associate Scholarship Program, Baccalaureate Scholarship Program and Graduate Scholarship Program.

Colgate 'Bright Smiles, Bright Futures' Minority Scholarships

Subjects: Dental hygiene.
Purpose: To assist members of minority groups currently under represented in dental hygiene programmes.
Eligibility: Open to male African Americans, Hispanics, Asians and Native Americans who are full-time students at Baccalaureate, graduate and doctoral levels. Scholars must currently be enrolled as full-time students in a dental hygiene programme in the United States of America, have completed a minimum of one year with a grade point average of at least 3.0 and be able to demonstrate financial need.
Level of Study: Postgraduate.
Type: Scholarship.
Value: A maximum of US$1,500.
Frequency: Dependent on funds available.
Country of Study: United States of America.
No. of awards offered: Two.
Application Procedure: Applicants must write for details or refer to the website.
Closing Date: June 1st.
Funding: Commercial.
Contributor: Colgate Palmolive Company.
Additional Information: This is a designated scholarship and is awarded on the basis of how well the applicant demonstrates the goal or achievement described.

Dr Alfred C Fones Scholarship

Subjects: Dental hygiene.
Purpose: To assist a Scholar in the baccalaureate or graduate degree categories who intends to become a dental hygiene teacher or educator.
Eligibility: Open to full-time students at Baccalaureate, graduate and doctoral levels. Scholars must currently be enrolled as full-time students in a dental hygiene programme in the United States of America, have completed a minimum of one year with a grade point average of at least 3.0 and be able to demonstrate financial need. Additional requirements vary depending upon degree level.
Level of Study: Graduate.
Type: Scholarship.
Value: A maximum of US$1,500.
Frequency: Dependent on funds available.
Country of Study: United States of America.
No. of awards offered: One.
Application Procedure: Applicants must write for details or refer to the website.
Closing Date: June 1st.
Funding: Private.
Additional Information: This is a designated scholarship and is awarded on the basis of how well the applicant demonstrates the goal or achievement described.

Dr Harold Hillenbrand Scholarship

Subjects: Dental hygiene.

Purpose: To assist a Scholar who demonstrates specific academic excellence and outstanding clinical performance, in addition to having a minimum dental hygiene cumulative grade point average of 3.5 on a 4.0 scale.

Eligibility: Open to full-time students at Baccalaureate, graduate and doctoral levels. Scholars must currently be enrolled as full-time students in a dental hygiene programme in the United States of America, have completed a minimum of one year with a grade point average of at least 3.0 and be able to demonstrate financial need.

Level of Study: Postgraduate.

Type: Scholarship.

Value: A maximum of US$1,500.

Frequency: Dependent on funds available.

Country of Study: United States of America.

No. of awards offered: One.

Application Procedure: Applicants must write for details or refer to the website.

Closing Date: June 1st.

Funding: Private.

Additional Information: This is a designated scholarship and is awarded on the basis of how well the applicant demonstrates the goal or achievement described.

Irene E Newman Scholarship

Subjects: Dental hygiene.

Purpose: To assist an applicant who demonstrates strong potential in public health or community dental health.

Eligibility: Open to full-time students at Baccalaureate graduate and doctoral levels. Scholars must currently be enrolled as full-time students in a dental hygiene programme in the United States of America, have completed a minimum of one year with a grade point average of at least 3.0 and be able to demonstrate financial need.

Level of Study: Postgraduate.

Type: Scholarship.

Value: Maximum US$1,500.

Frequency: Dependent on funds available.

Country of Study: United States of America.

No. of awards offered: One.

Application Procedure: Applicants must write for details or refer to the website.

Closing Date: June 1st.

Funding: Private.

Margaret E Swanson Scholarship

Subjects: Dental hygiene.

Purpose: To financially assist an applicant who demonstrates exceptional organisational leadership potential.

Eligibility: Open to full-time students at Baccalaureate, graduate and doctoral levels. Scholars must currently be enrolled as full-time students in a dental hygiene programme in the United States of America, have completed a minimum of one year with a grade point average of at least 3.0 and be able to demonstrate financial need.

Level of Study: Postgraduate.

Type: Scholarship.

Value: A maximum of US$1,500.

Frequency: Dependent on funds available.

Country of Study: United States of America.

No. of awards offered: One.

Application Procedure: Applicants must write for details or refer to the website.

Closing Date: June 1st.

Funding: Private.

Additional Information: This is a designated scholarship and is awarded on the basis of how well the applicant demonstrates the goal or achievement described.

Sigma Phi Alpha Graduate Scholarship

Subjects: Dental hygiene.

Purpose: To aid an outstanding applicant pursuing a degree in dental hygiene or a related field.

Eligibility: Open to full-time students at graduate and doctoral levels. Scholars must currently be enrolled as full-time students in a dental hygiene programme in the United States of America, have completed

a minimum of one year with a grade point average of at least 3.0 and be able to demonstrate financial need.

Level of Study: Graduate.

Type: Scholarship.

Value: A maximum of US$1,500.

Frequency: Dependent on funds available.

Country of Study: United States of America.

No. of awards offered: One.

Application Procedure: Applicants must write for details or refer to the website.

Closing Date: June 1st.

Funding: Private.

Contributor: The Sigma Phi Alpha Dental Hygiene Society.

Additional Information: This is a designated scholarship and is awarded on the basis of how well the applicant demonstrates the goal or achievement described.

ADOLPH AND ESTHER GOTTLIEB FOUNDATION, INC.

380 West Broadway, New York, NY 10012, United States of America
Tel: (1) 212 226 0581
Fax: (1) 212 226 0584
Email: sross@gottliebfoundation.org
www: http://www.gottliebfoundation.org
Contact: Grants Manager

The Adolph and Esther Gottlieb Foundation is a non-profit corporation registered with the state of New York. It was established to award financial aid to mature creative painters, sculptors and printmakers.

Gottlieb Foundation Emergency Assistance Grants

Subjects: Painting, sculpture and printmaking.

Purpose: To provide interim financial assistance to creative visual artists whose need is the result of unforeseen catastrophic incident.

Eligibility: Open to painters, sculptors and printmakers who can demonstrate a minimum of 10 years of involvement in a mature phase of their work and who do not have the resources to meet the costs incurred by a catastrophic event eg. fire, flood or emergency medical expenses. The disciplines of film, photography or related forms are not eligible unless the work involves directly, or can be interpreted as, painting or sculpture.

Level of Study: Unrestricted.

Type: Grant.

Value: Up to US$10,000. US$4,000 is typical on a one time basis only.

Frequency: Dependent on funds available.

Country of Study: Any country.

No. of awards offered: Varies.

Application Procedure: Applicants must complete and submit an application form which is available from the Foundation throughout the year and may be requested by telephone. Second party requests are honoured only when the applicant is physically unable to communicate with the Foundation.

Closing Date: Please write for details.

Funding: Private.

Contributor: An endowment.

Additional Information: 'Maturity' is based on the level of technical, intellectual and creative development of the artist. The programme does not cover general indebtedness, dental work, unemployment, capital improvements, long-term disabilities or project funding. Review procedures for completed applications begin as soon as they are received. Full review generally takes about four weeks from the time an application is complete. Situations with imminent deadlines will receive priority. When a situation warrants it, reviews can be completed within 24 to 48 hours.

Gottlieb Foundation Individual Support Grants

Subjects: Painting, sculpture and printmaking.

Purpose: To recognise and support serious, fully committed painters, sculptors and printmakers who are in financial need.

Eligibility: Open to creative painters, sculptors and printmakers who have been in a mature phase of their work for at least 20 years and require financial assistance to continue this work. United States residency is not required. The Gottlieb Foundation does not provide funding for organisations, projects of any type, educational institutions, students, graphic artists or those working in crafts. The disciplines of photography, film, video or related forms are not eligible unless the work directly involves, or can be interpreted as, painting or sculpture.

Level of Study: Unrestricted.
Type: Grant.
Value: Varies.
Length of Study: One year.
Frequency: Annual.
Country of Study: Any country.
No. of awards offered: 10.
Application Procedure: Applicants must include a current application form, available from the Foundation, and a small group of slides of the artist's work which illustrates the progressive development of the art for at least a twenty year period. These slides must be properly labelled and dated. Applicants must also include a written statement in narrative form. This statement should include outside jobs which have helped support the artist's career, changes in artistic approach that have occurred, and other facts which can aid the review panel in forming an accurate picture. All aspects of artistic history, i.e. education, exhibitions, etc., should be described, and dates must be provided for all information. Financial disclosure, which entails completing a disclosure page and submitting a copy of a federal tax return for the past year, is necessary in the determination of financial need. A stamped self addressed envelope for the return of supplementary materials must also be included.
Closing Date: December 15th. Awards are distributed the following March.
Funding: Private.
Contributor: An endowment.
Additional Information: Artists who have been awarded a grant must allow one year to elapse before reapplication. Only first person written requests for application forms will be honoured.

AFRICA EDUCATIONAL TRUST

38 King Street, London, WC2E 8JS, England
Tel: (44) 20 7836 5075
Fax: (44) 20 7379 0090
Email: aet@boltblue.com
www: www.africaed.org
Contact: Director

The Africa Educational Trust has a free educational advice service to students, refugees and asylum seekers who have come from Africa.

Africa Educational Trust Emergency Small Grants
Subjects: All subjects.
Purpose: To provide one off grants on an emergency basis to students from Africa studying in the United Kingdom on student visa.
Eligibility: Open to students from Africa studying in the United Kingdom. The applicant must have run into unexpected difficulties at the end of his or her course for which the small level of the grant will, by itself or in conjunction with other grants, solve the problem. Most awards are made on a humanitarian basis. Academic considerations are more important at the postgraduate and research levels. Students should be studying on student visas.
Level of Study: Unrestricted.
Type: Other.
Value: UK£350 average.
Length of Study: Final year.
Frequency: Monthly.
Country of Study: United Kingdom.
No. of awards offered: 30.
Application Procedure: Apply by letter for application form.
Closing Date: Open all year.
Additional Information: Emergency Grants are provided at any time of year.

AFRICAN NETWORK OF SCIENTIFIC AND TECHNOLOGICAL INSTITUTIONS (ANSTI)

PO Box 30592, Nairobi, Kenya
Tel: (254) 2 622 619
Fax: (254) 2 622 750
Email: info@ansti.org
www: http://www.ansti.org
Contact: Administrative Assistant

The African Network of Scientific and Technological Institutions (ANSTI), is an organ of co-operation that embraces institutions engaged in the fields of science and technology. To date it has 87 member institutions in 33 countries in sub Saharan Africa.

ANSTI Postgraduate Fellowships
Subjects: Basic and engineering sciences.
Purpose: To enable students to pursue Master's and PhD courses in the basic and engineering sciences.
Eligibility: Open to African nationals only, who are staff members of ANSTI member institutions. Applicants must possess a good Bachelor's degree and must be below 36 years of age.
Level of Study: Postdoctorate, Postgraduate.
Type: Fellowship.
Value: Varies, approx. US$12,000.
Length of Study: Varies, approx. 18 months.
Frequency: Annual.
Study Establishment: ANSTI member institutions.
Country of Study: Other.
Application Procedure: Applicants must complete an application form, available by contacting ANSTI by mail, fax or email or visit our website www.ansti.org.
Closing Date: 31st March.
Funding: Government.
Contributor: DAAD/UNESCO.
No. of awards given last year: 5.
No. of applicants last year: 20.
Additional Information: The applicant is responsible for gaining admission into the university of his or her choice. Preference is given to graduates with a few years of experience.

For further information contact:

PO Box 30592, Nairobi, Kenya

AFRO-ASIAN INSTITUTE (AAI) IN VIENNA AND CATHOLIC WOMEN'S LEAGUE OF AUSTRIA

Student Division, Türkenstraβe 3, Vienna, A-1090, Austria
Tel: (43) 310 5145
Fax: (43) 310 5145 213
Email: studium@aai-wien.at
www: http://www.aai-wien.at
Contact: Mr Markus St Clair Osorno, Study Advisor

The Afro-Asian Institute (AAI)'s major function is to aid students from the developing countries of Africa, Asia and Latin America. Presently the AAI provides services for more than 5,000 students from developing countries which counts as an acknowledged contribution to Austrian development aid.

One World Scholarship Program
Subjects: All subjects.
Purpose: To promote cultural exchange, international development and international co-operation aid.
Eligibility: Open to nationals of developing countries in Africa, Asia and Latin America aged 18-35 years who have had adequate previous study or vocational practice in the specific field for which the scholarship is applied. Preference is given to candidates who are able to speak German. Only those in financial need will be considered, and the applicability of the special branch of study or training in the ap-

plicant's home country is essential. It is expected that Scholars will return to their home country after studying. Good, and sometimes excellent, study results are also required. Preference is given to applicants from the least developed countries. It is a requirement that applicants have already started their studies in Austria.

Level of Study: Doctorate, Graduate, Unrestricted.
Type: Scholarship.
Value: £475-510 per Month.
Frequency: Annual.
Study Establishment: Universities.
Country of Study: Austria.
No. of awards offered: Varies.
Application Procedure: Applicants must complete an application form, which is available from the Institute. Only personal applications will be considered. Postal applications from abroad will not be answered.
Closing Date: Please contact the organisation.
Funding: Government, Private.
Contributor: The Catholic Church.
Additional Information: It is one of AAI's essential aims to establish a 'partnership' contact between assisted students and the Scholarship donor which continues beyond the termination of studies. Only about 10 per cent of applicants can be accepted.

For further information contact:

Türkenstraße 3, Wie A-1090, Austria
Contact: Mr St Clair Osorno, Afro-Asian Institute

AGE-IN-ACTION

1st Floor, 36-on-Long, Long Street, Cape Town, Western Cape 8001, South Africa
Tel: (27) 21 426 4280
Fax: (27) 21 426 4290
Email: saca@iafrica.com
www: http://www.age-in-action.co.za
Contact: Mrs Wil Bryan, Chief Executive Officer

Zerilda Steyn Memorial Trust
Subjects: The needs and care of the aged.
Purpose: To advance postgraduate research in South Africa.
Eligibility: Open to researchers in all disciplines caring for the aged.
Level of Study: Postgraduate.
Type: Project grant.
Value: Rand 1,500 per year.
Length of Study: One year, renewable only in exceptional circumstances.
Frequency: Annual.
Study Establishment: Universities.
Country of Study: South Africa.
No. of awards offered: Several grants are made for a variety of small and large projects.
Application Procedure: Applicants must submit an application form to the trustees. A six monthly progress report is required.
Closing Date: January 30th.
Funding: Private.
Contributor: Private trust.
No. of applicants last year: 26.
Additional Information: In exceptional cases a second grant can be awarded, but this would require substantial motivation.

AGRICULTURAL HISTORY SOCIETY

Center for Agricultural History, 618 Ross Hall, Iowa State University, Ames, IA 50011-1202, United States of America
Tel: (1) 515 294 5620
Fax: (1) 515 294 6390
Email: rdhurt@iastate.edu
www: http://www.iastate.edu/~history_info/aghistry.htm
Contact: Editor

The Agricultural History Society recognises the roles of agriculture and agri-business in shaping the political, economic, social and historical profiles of different countries worldwide. Since 1927, the Society's publication, Agricultural History, has been the international journal for the field and publishes innovative research on agricultural and rural history.

Everett E Edward Awards in Agricultural History
Subjects: Agricultural and rural history.
Purpose: To encourage and reward scholarly work in the field. The award was established in 1953 in memory and recognition of the outstanding services of Everett Eugene Edwards, a long time agricultural historian and editor of Agricultural History from 1931 to 1951.
Eligibility: Open to any graduate or doctoral student submitting an article to Agricultural History during the calendar year.
Level of Study: Graduate.
Type: Award.
Value: US$200 plus publication in the journal.
Frequency: Annual.
Country of Study: Any country.
No. of awards offered: One.
Application Procedure: Applicants must submit three copies of their manuscript, prepared in accordance with the latest edition of the 'Chicago Manual of Style', to the Editor.
Closing Date: December 31st.
Additional Information: The award is presented annually to the author of the winning article at the Agricultural History Society's Presidential Luncheon. In addition the winning submission is published in the Fall issue of Agricultural History. Further information is available on request.

Gilbert C Fite Dissertation Award
Subjects: Agricultural and rural history.
Purpose: To award the best dissertation.
Eligibility: Open to any doctoral student who has completed a PhD dissertation.
Level of Study: Doctorate.
Type: Award.
Value: US$300.
Frequency: Annual.
Country of Study: Any country.
No. of awards offered: One.
Application Procedure: Applicants must complete forms and send three copies to the Editor.
Closing Date: Please contact the organisation.
Additional Information: Further information is available on request.

Theodore Saloutos Award
Subjects: Agricultural and rural history in the United States of America.
Purpose: To award the best book published annually in the United States of America on the subject of agricultural history.
Eligibility: Open to nationals of any country. Books must be based on substantial primary research and should represent a major new scholarly interpretation or reinterpretation of agricultural history scholarship.
Level of Study: Unrestricted.
Type: Prize.
Value: US$500.
Frequency: Annual.
Country of Study: Any country.
Application Procedure: Applicants must send four copies of the book to the Editor. Books may be nominated by their authors, the publisher, a member of the award committee, or a member of the Society.
Closing Date: Please contact the organisation.
Additional Information: Further information is available on request.

Vernon Carstenson Award in Agricultural History
Subjects: Agricultural and rural history.
Purpose: To promote research and publication. The award was established in 1980 to recognise Vernon Carstenson's services to agricultural history by his former students.
Eligibility: Open to any author published in the quarterly journal Agricultural History during the calendar year.

Level of Study: Doctorate, Postdoctorate.
Type: Award.
Value: US$200.
Frequency: Annual.
Country of Study: Any country.
No. of awards offered: One.
Application Procedure: All published articles per issue and year are considered.
Closing Date: The Autumn issue of the journal each year.
Additional Information: Vernon Carstensen served as editor of Agricultural History from 1953 to 1957 and as president of the Agricultural History Society from 1957 to 1958. Further information is available on request.

AIDS ACTION

1906 Sunderland Place NW, Washington, DC 20036, United States of America
Tel: (1) 202 830 5030 X 3040
Email: zamora@aidsaction.org
www: www.aidsaction.org

AIDS Action, founded in 1004, is the National AIDS Organization dedicated to the development, analysis, cultivation, and encouragement of sound policies and programs in response to the HIV epidemic.

The Pedro Zamora Public Policy Fellowship
Subjects: Research into a variety of public health and civil rights issues related to HIV prevention, treatment and care.
Purpose: To fund both undergraduate and post graduate students seeking experience in public policy and government affairs focussed on HIV/AIDS issues.
Level of Study: Graduate, Postgraduate.
Type: Fellowship.
Value: Stipend plus expenses.
Length of Study: 26 weeks.
Frequency: Three times per year.
Country of Study: United States of America.
Application Procedure: Apply with covering letter, resumé, writing sample and essay. Check website for up to date details.
Closing Date: November 1st, March 15th, July 15th.
Funding: Private.

THE AIREY NEAVE TRUST

PO Box 36800, 40 Bernard Street, London, WC1N 1WJ, England
Tel: (44) 207 833 4440
Email: hanthoc@aol.com
Contact: The Trustees

Initiated in 1989, the Airey Neave Trust provides fellowships towards both books and papers.

The Airey Neave Research Fellowships
Purpose: To support serious research connected with national and international law and human freedom.
Level of Study: Postgraduate.
Type: Fellowship.
Length of Study: Up to 3 years.
Frequency: Annual.
Study Establishment: Preferably attached to a particular university in Britain.
Country of Study: United Kingdom.
Application Procedure: Contact organisation for more details.

ALBERT ELLIS INSTITUTE

45 East 65th Street, New York, NY 10021, United States of America
Tel: (1) 212 535 0822
Fax: (1) 212 249 3582
Email: info@rebt.org
www: http://www.rebt.org
Contact: Fellowships Office

The Albert Ellis Institute is a non-profit training and therapy institute chartered by the regents of the University of the State of New York, specialising in cognitive behaviour therapy and rational emotive behaviour therapy.

Albert Ellis Institute Clinical Fellowship
Subjects: Psychology and counselling.
Purpose: To provide in depth, hands on training in cognitive behavioural therapy and rational emotive behaviour therapy.
Eligibility: Applicants must be in a doctoral program, hold a PhD, MSW, MD or RN and be license eligible in their place of practice. There are no other restrictions.
Level of Study: Postdoctorate, Postgraduate, Predoctorate.
Type: Fellowship.
Value: US$6,000.
Length of Study: Two years.
Frequency: Annual.
Country of Study: United States of America.
No. of awards offered: Varies.
Application Procedure: Applicants must obtain applications and further information by writing to the Institute.
Closing Date: February 15th.
Funding: Private.
No. of awards given last year: 5.
Additional Information: The programme begins in mid-July.

ALBERTA HERITAGE FOUNDATION FOR MEDICAL RESEARCH (AHFMR)

1500 Bell Tower, 10104-103 Avenue, Edmonton, AB, T5J 4A7, Canada
Tel: (1) 780 423 5727
Fax: (1) 780 429 3509
Email: postmaster@ahfmr.ab.ca
www: http://www.ahfmr.ab.ca
Contact: Dr Jacques Magnan, Vice President, Programmes

The Alberta Heritage Foundation for Medical Research (AHFMR) supports a community of researchers who generate knowledge that improves the health and quality of life of Albertans and people throughout the world. The Foundation's long-term commitment is to fund basic patient and health research based on international standards of excellence and carried out by new and established investigators and researchers in training.

Alberta Heritage Clinical Fellowships
Subjects: Medical research.
Purpose: To provide an opportunity for research training to candidates who have completed clinical sub-speciality training requirements.
Eligibility: Open to candidates who hold an MD or DDS and who have received a significant portion of postgraduate training in Alberta.
Level of Study: Postgraduate.
Type: Fellowship.
Value: Canadian $3,000 research allowance plus stipend.
Length of Study: Two years, with a possibility of renewal for a further year.
Frequency: Twice a year.
Study Establishment: An appropriate institution, usually in Alberta.
Country of Study: Canada.
No. of awards offered: Approx. 10.
Application Procedure: Applicants must complete an application form.
Closing Date: March 1st or October 1st.
Funding: Government.
No. of awards given last year: 14.
No. of applicants last year: 18.

Alberta Heritage Clinical Investigatorships
Subjects: Medical research.
Purpose: To provide funding for highly qualified clinicians to further their research experience beyond the fellowship level in a

setting that provides guidance and supervision by an established scientist.

Eligibility: Open to candidates who hold an MD or DDS, have completed all requirements for clinical speciality recognition and who are eligible to hold a full-time position in a clinical department of the sponsoring institution.

Level of Study: Professional development.

Type: Other.

Value: A stipend plus an establishment grant. Values are negotiated individually.

Length of Study: Three years, with a possibility of renewal for a further three years.

Frequency: Annual.

Study Establishment: A university, an affiliated hospital or institution in Alberta.

Country of Study: Canada.

No. of awards offered: Varies.

Application Procedure: Applicants must complete an application form.

Closing Date: September 15th.

Funding: Government.

No. of awards given last year: Five.

No. of applicants last year: 10.

Alberta Heritage Full-Time Fellowships

Subjects: Medical research.

Purpose: To enable doctoral graduates to prepare for careers as independent investigators.

Eligibility: Open to graduates of science programmes relevant to AHFMR objectives or to health professional programmes who have received a PhD not more than five years prior to application. Professional health degrees should not have been received more than 10 years prior to application.

Level of Study: Postdoctorate.

Type: Fellowship.

Value: Canadian $3,000 research allowance plus stipend.

Frequency: Twice a year.

Study Establishment: Usually at a university in Alberta.

Country of Study: Canada.

No. of awards offered: Varies.

Application Procedure: Applicants must complete an application form.

Closing Date: March 1st or October 1st.

Funding: Government.

No. of awards given last year: 35.

No. of applicants last year: 113.

Alberta Heritage Full-Time Studentship

Subjects: Medical sciences.

Purpose: To enable academically superior students to undertake full-time research training in a discipline relevant to the objectives of the Foundation.

Eligibility: Open to candidates sponsored by a faculty supervisor. The supervisor must have a record of productive health orientated research and sufficient competitively acquired research funding to ensure the satisfactory conduct of the student's research during the term of the award. Students must be engaged in, or accepted into, a full-time university graduate programme in a health related discipline leading to a Master's or doctoral degree. Applicants must also hold a record of superior academic performance in studies relevant to the proposed training.

Type: Studentship.

Value: Please write for details.

Length of Study: Two years with the possibility to renewal to a of maximum of five years' support.

Frequency: Annual.

Study Establishment: A university in Alberta.

Country of Study: Canada.

No. of awards offered: Approx. 40-60.

Application Procedure: Applicants must submit, in full, the original application to the Foundation's offices by either of the deadlines.

Closing Date: March 1st or October 1st.

Funding: Government.

No. of awards given last year: 92.

No. of applicants last year: 260.

Alberta Heritage Health Research Studentship

Subjects: Medical sciences.

Purpose: To enable academically superior students engaged in, or accepted on to, a full-time university programme to undertake full-time research training.

Value: Please write for details.

Length of Study: Two years with a possibility of renewal, to a maximum of five years' support.

Frequency: Annual.

Study Establishment: A university in Alberta.

Country of Study: Canada.

No. of awards offered: Varies, approx. 10.

Application Procedure: Applicants must submit the original application to the Foundation's offices by either of the deadlines. They must be completed in full to be entered into the competition.

Closing Date: March 1st or October 1st.

Funding: Government.

No. of awards given last year: 10.

No. of applicants last year: 35.

Alberta Heritage Medical Scholarships

Subjects: Medical research.

Purpose: To assist in the recruitment and establishment of scientists in Alberta.

Eligibility: Open to investigators who have recently completed their postdoctoral research training and demonstrate the ability to initiate and conduct independent as well as collaborative research. They must exhibit ability in training future research scientists. Candidates must hold a MD, DDS, DVM, PhD or the equivalent, and must have established a record of excellence in independent research over several years as a faculty member. Candidates must also show an interest in training Alberta's future research scientists.

Level of Study: Professional development.

Type: Scholarship.

Value: A stipend plus an establishment grant, negotiated individually.

Length of Study: Five years.

Frequency: Annual.

Study Establishment: A university in Alberta or affiliate.

Country of Study: Canada.

No. of awards offered: Varies.

Application Procedure: Applicants must complete an application form.

Closing Date: September 15th.

Funding: Government.

No. of awards given last year: 15 to Scholars and 10 to senior Scholars.

No. of applicants last year: 40 for Scholars, 15 for senior Scholars.

Alberta Heritage Medical Scientist Awards

Subjects: Medical research.

Purpose: To assist in the recruitment and establishment of nationally or internationally recognised medical scientists in Alberta.

Eligibility: Open to candidates who hold an MD, DDS, DVM or PhD or equivalent in a discipline important to AHFMR objectives. Applicants must be eligible for a full-time appointment at the sponsoring institution.

Level of Study: Professional development.

Type: Award.

Value: A stipend plus an establishment grant, negotiated individually.

Length of Study: Five years, renewable.

Frequency: Annual.

Study Establishment: A university in Alberta or affiliate.

Country of Study: Canada.

No. of awards offered: Varies.

Application Procedure: Applicants must complete an application form.

Closing Date: September 15th.

Funding: Government.

No. of awards given last year: Five.
No. of applicants last year: 15.

Alberta Heritage Part-Time Fellowships

Subjects: Medical research.
Purpose: To enable continuing active participation in research during professional education.
Eligibility: Open to graduates holding a PhD in a science relevant to AHFMR objectives or who are registered in a health professional programme in Alberta.
Level of Study: Postdoctorate.
Type: Fellowship.
Value: Pro-rated on full-time fellowship stipend and dependent on the amount of time spent in research.
Length of Study: One year, renewable.
Frequency: Twice a year.
Study Establishment: A university in Alberta.
Country of Study: Canada.
No. of awards offered: Approx. five.
Application Procedure: Applicants must complete an application form.
Closing Date: March 1st or October 1st.
Funding: Government.
No. of awards given last year: Five.
No. of applicants last year: Six.

Alberta Heritage Part-Time Studentship

Subjects: Medical research.
Purpose: To enable full-time degree students to continue research training on a part-time basis.
Eligibility: Open to students enrolled in a full-time professional degree programme who wish to continue research training on a part-time basis during the academic year.
Type: Studentship.
Value: Pro-rated on full-time stipend rate of Canadian $16,500 and dependent on the amount of time spent in research.
Length of Study: Two years, to a maximum of five years' support.
Frequency: Twice a year.
Study Establishment: A university in Alberta.
Country of Study: Canada.
No. of awards offered: Approx. five.
Application Procedure: Applicants must complete an application form.
Closing Date: March 1st or October 1st.
Funding: Government.
No. of awards given last year: One.
No. of applicants last year: One.

Dr Lionel E Mcleod Health Research Scholarship

Subjects: Health.
Purpose: To enable academically superior students engaged in, or accepted on to, a full-time university programme to undertake full-time research training.
Eligibility: Open to Canadian citizens or permanent residents who attend the Universities of Alberta, Calgary or British Columbia.
Level of Study: Postgraduate.
Type: Scholarship.
Value: Please write for details.
Frequency: Annual.
Country of Study: Canada.
No. of awards offered: One.
Application Procedure: Applicants must write for details.
Funding: Government, Private.

Heritage Health Research Career Renewal Awards

Subjects: Epidemiology, biostatistics, psychosocial sciences or clinical experimental method and design.
Purpose: To enable carefully selected Alberta faculty members with a demonstrated interest in clinical or health research to obtain training.
Eligibility: Open to candidates proposed and sponsored by an Alberta institution, which is prepared to ensure an adequate environment for the candidate on their return to the province. This environment should encompass fostering the development of a group

of scientists to be capable of independent research and to be able to assist others in the design of patient based and population based research.
Level of Study: Postdoctorate.
Value: Please write for details.
Frequency: Annual.
Country of Study: Canada.
No. of awards offered: Varies.
Application Procedure: Applicants must write for details.
Closing Date: March 1st or October 1st.
Funding: Government.
No. of awards given last year: One.
No. of applicants last year: Three.

Heritage Population Health Investigators

Subjects: Population health.
Purpose: To assist in the recruitment and establishment in Alberta of well trained investigators in population health research.
Eligibility: Open to applicants who have recently completed post MD or PhD research training but have not yet established an independent research record.
Level of Study: Postdoctorate.
Value: Please write for details.
Length of Study: Three years, renewable.
Frequency: Annual.
Country of Study: Canada.
No. of awards offered: 10.
Application Procedure: Applicants must write for details.
Closing Date: September 15th.
Funding: Government.
No. of awards given last year: 10.
No. of applicants last year: 20.

ALCOHOL BEVERAGE MEDICAL RESEARCH FOUNDATION

1122 Kenilworth Drive, Suite 407
Baltimore, MD 21204
United States of America
Tel: (1) 410 821 7066
Fax: (1) 410 821 7065
Email: info@abmrf.org
www: http://www.abmrf.org
Contact: Dr Robin A Kroft, Vice President

The Alcohol Beverage Medical Research Foundation is a non-profit independent research organisation that provides support for scientific studies on the use of alcoholic beverages. It awards grants to study changes in drinking patterns, effects of moderate use of alcohol on health and well being and the mechanisms underlying the behavioural and biomedical effects of alcohol.

Alcohol Beverage Medical Research Foundation Research Project Grant

Subjects: Medical and behavioural sciences.
Purpose: To support new knowledge in order to prevent alcohol related problems.
Level of Study: Doctorate.
Type: Other.
Value: Up to US$50,000 per year.
Length of Study: Up to two years.
Frequency: Twice a year.
Study Establishment: Non-profit universities and research institutions.
Country of Study: United States of America or Canada.
No. of awards offered: 30-40.
Application Procedure: Applicants must complete an application form, available on request or from the website.
Closing Date: February 1st or September 1st.
Funding: Private.
No. of awards given last year: 40.
No. of applicants last year: 150.

ALEXANDER GRAHAM BELL ASSOCIATION FOR THE DEAF AND HARD OF HEARING

3417 Volta Place North West, Washington, DC 20007, United States of America
Tel: (1) 202 337 5220
Fax: (1) 202 337 8314
Email: info@agbell.org
www: http://www.agbell.org
Contact: Ms Lisa Ruffin Schauf, Development & Donor Relations Administrator

The Alexander Graham Bell Association for the Deaf and Hard of Hearing was established in 1890 to empower hearing impaired persons to function independently by promoting universal rights and optimal opportunities to learn to use, maintain and improve all aspects of their verbal communications, including their abilities to speak, speech read, use residual hearing, and process both spoken and written language.

Alexander Graham Bell Scholarship Awards
Subjects: All subjects.
Purpose: To encourage severely or profoundly hearing impaired students to attend regular hearing colleges. A G Bell offers financial aid and scholarships through four major programmes which are parent-infant (0-6 years), school age, arts and sciences and college scholarships.
Eligibility: Open to auditory oral students born with profound hearing loss, 80 dB loss in the better ear, average, or a severe hearing loss, 60-80 dB loss, who experienced such a loss before acquiring language. Candidates must use speech and residual hearing and/or speech reading as their preferred customary form of communication and demonstrate a potential for leadership. In addition, applicants must have applied to, or already be enrolled in, a regular full-time college or university programme for hearing students.
Level of Study: Unrestricted.
Type: Scholarship.
Value: US$250-2,000.
Frequency: Annual.
Country of Study: United States of America.
No. of awards offered: Varies.
Application Procedure: Applicants must request an application form in writing September 1st thru January 1st. Fax copies or telephone applications will not be accepted. Applicants may visit the website or send an e-mail to financialaid@agbell.org for current information.
Closing Date: March 1st.
Funding: Private.
Contributor: Members and donors.
No. of awards given last year: 20.
No. of applicants last year: Approx. 100.

ALEXANDER S ONASSIS PUBLIC BENEFIT FOUNDATION

56 Amalias Avenue, Athens, GR-10558, Greece
Tel: (30) 210 371 3000
Fax: (30) 210 371 3013
Email: pubrel@onassis.gr
www: http://www.onassis.gr
Contact: Deputy Director, Human Resource Manager

The Alexander S Onassis Public Benefit Foundation establishes and supports public benefit projects, offers services and makes contributions to other public benefit institutions for medical care, education, literature, religion, science, research, journalism, art, cultural matters, history, archaeology and sport. It also awards prizes, grants and scholarships to both Greeks and foreigners.

Onassis Foreigners' Fellowship Programme Educational Scholarships Category B
Subjects: Greek language, Greek literature, Greek history and civilisation.

Purpose: To render possible the acquaintance, collaboration and exchange of information between the scholarship recipients and their Greek colleagues in Greek schools, education or other relevant departments of Greek universities.
Eligibility: Open to active elementary or high school foreign teachers who teach the Greek language, modern or ancient, Greek literature, Greek history and Greek civilisation. Only persons of other than Greek nationality are eligible. However, persons of Greek descent, second generation and on, are also eligible providing they are permanently residing and working abroad or currently studying in foreign universities.
Type: Scholarship.
Value: A monthly allowance plus hotel accommodation and a round trip air ticket.
Length of Study: A maximum of two months.
Frequency: Annual.
Country of Study: Greece.
No. of awards offered: Five.
Application Procedure: Copies of the Announcement and the relevant nomination and application forms are available daily at the Foundation's Secretariat or from the website.
Closing Date: Please contact the organisation.
Additional Information: The programme presupposes that the scholarship recipients will continue offering their services to their country of origin after they have completed their training in Greece.

Onassis Foreigners' Fellowship Programme Educational Scholarships Category C
Subjects: All subjects.
Purpose: To render possible the acquaintance, collaboration and exchange of information between the scholarship recipients and their Greek colleagues in Greek schools, education or other relevant departments of Greek universities.
Eligibility: Open to foreign postgraduate students and PhD candidates up to 40 years of age who pursue studies in universities, scholarly or research centres or fine art schools either outside Greece or in Greece.
Level of Study: Doctorate, Postgraduate.
Type: Scholarship.
Value: A monthly allowance plus hotel accommodation and a round trip air ticket.
Length of Study: 5-10 months.
Frequency: Annual.
Country of Study: Greece.
No. of awards offered: 17.
Application Procedure: Copies of the Announcement and the relevant nomination and application forms are available daily at the Foundation's Secretariat or from the website.
Closing Date: Please contact the organisation.
Additional Information: The programme presupposes that the scholarship recipients will continue offering their services to their country of origin, after they have completed their training in Greece.

Onassis Foreigners' Fellowships Programme Research Grants Category AI
Subjects: Humanistic sciences eg. philology, literature, translation, linguistics, theology, history, archaeology, philosophy, educational studies and psychology, political sciences such as sociology, anthropology, public administration, international relations and mass media, law, economics, architecture and the arts eg. visual arts, music, dance, theatre, photography and film studies.
Purpose: To enable full members of national academies and full university professors whose scholarly or artistic work has been widely acclaimed and who wish to visit Greece in order to conduct scholarly research or to collaborate with educational institutions, research institutions or organisations.
Eligibility: Only persons of other than Greek nationality are eligible. However, persons of Greek descent, second generation and on, are also eligible providing they are permanently residing and working abroad or currently studying in foreign universities. Applicants must have had a professional academic career of at least 10 years.
Level of Study: Postdoctorate.
Type: Research grant.

Value: A monthly allowance plus a round trip air ticket and A' class hotel accommodation.
Length of Study: One month.
Frequency: Annual.
Country of Study: Greece.
No. of awards offered: 10.
Application Procedure: Copies of the Announcement and the relevant nomination and application forms are available daily at the Foundation's Secretariat or from the website.
Closing Date: Please contact the organisation.
Additional Information: Any person wishing to apply under this programme should specify the category in which they want to be considered in order to receive the relevant nomination and application form. Only one application form for one of the categories can be submitted.

Onassis Foreigners' Fellowships Programme Research Grants Category All

Subjects: All subjects.
Purpose: To enable university or equivalent institutions' faculty, researchers, PhD holders, artists and musicians, and translators of Greek literature who wish to come to Greece either for scholarly research co-operation with a Greek university, research centre or institute or for their artistic creation or translation.
Eligibility: Only persons of other than Greek nationality are eligible. However, persons of Greek descent, second generation and on, are also eligible providing they are permanently residing and working abroad or currently studying in foreign universities. Applicants must have had a professional academic career of at least 10 years.
Level of Study: Postdoctorate.
Type: Fellowship.
Value: A monthly allowance plus hotel accommodation and a round trip air ticket.
Length of Study: Up to six months.
Frequency: Annual.
Country of Study: Greece.
No. of awards offered: 15.
Application Procedure: Copies of the Announcement and the relevant nomination and application forms are available daily at the Foundation's Secretariat or from the website.
Closing Date: Please contact the organisation.
Additional Information: Any person wishing to apply under this programme should specify the category in which they want to be considered in order to receive the relevant nomination and application form. Only one application form for one of the categories can be submitted.

ALEXANDER VON HUMBOLDT FOUNDATION

Jean-Paul Straße 12, Bonn, Bad Godesberg, D-53173, Germany
Tel: (49) 228 833 0
Fax: (49) 228 833 199
Email: post@avh.de
www: http://www.humboldt-foundation.de
Contact: Dr Babara Sheldon

The Alexander von Humboldt Foundation grants research fellowships to foreign scholars who hold doctorates and have not yet reached the age of 40. The Foundation also offers research awards to internationally recognised foreign scholars of any age, enabling them to spend lengthy periods of research in Germany.

Federal Chancellor Scholarship

Subjects: All subjects, but preference is given to the humanities, law, social and economic sciences, and to the arts.
Purpose: To maintain and foster a close relationship between Germany and the United States of America and the Russian Federation respectively by sponsoring individuals who demonstrate the potential of playing a pivotal role in the future development of this relationship.
Eligibility: Open to citizens of the United States of America and Russian Federation only.

Level of Study: Postgraduate.
Type: Scholarship.
Value: Please contact the organisation.
Length of Study: One year.
Frequency: Annual.
Study Establishment: Different kinds of institutions on the academic, cultural private, public and non-profit sector.
Country of Study: Germany.
No. of awards offered: 10 to the United States of America and 10 to Russian Federation citizens.
Application Procedure: Applicants must complete an application form.
Closing Date: October 31st scholarship period starting September 1st the following year.
Funding: Government.
No. of awards given last year: 10 to the United States of America and 10 to Russian Federation citizens.

Feodor Lynen Research Fellowships for German Scholars

Subjects: All subjects.
Purpose: To enable highly qualified scholars to conduct research of their choice at home institutions of non German recipients of Humboldt fellowships and awards.
Eligibility: Open to German nationals or those who have been living and working in Germany for more than five years.
Level of Study: Postdoctorate.
Type: Fellowship.
Value: Please contact the organisation.
Length of Study: One-four years.
Frequency: Annual.
Study Establishment: Research institutions or universities.
Country of Study: Other.
No. of awards offered: Up to 150.
Application Procedure: Applicants must complete an application form, available from the Bonn office.
Closing Date: February 10th, June 10th or October 10th.
Funding: Government.
No. of awards given last year: 110.
No. of applicants last year: 216.

Friedrid Wilhelm Bessel Research Award for Foreign Scientists and Scholars

Subjects: All subjects.
Purpose: To enable internationally recognised foreign scientists and scholars upto the age of 45 to conduct research on a project of their choice in Germany.
Eligibility: Open to all scholars and scientists from abroad.
Level of Study: Research.
Type: Prize.
Value: Up to €55,000.
Length of Study: 6-12 months.
Frequency: Annual.
Study Establishment: Universities and research institutions.
Country of Study: Germany.
No. of awards offered: Up to 10.
Application Procedure: Applicants are nominated by eminent German Scientists and Scholars directly to the Foundation in Bonn. Direct applications are not accepted.
Closing Date: Nominations are accepted throughout the year.
Funding: Government.
No. of awards given last year: 20.
No. of applicants last year: ca. 50.
Additional Information: Selection committee meetings are held twice a year in March and October.

Georg Forster Research Fellowships

Subjects: Any subject with emphasis on transfer of knowledge and methods to fellows home countries.
Purpose: To provide opportunities for highly qualified scholars from developing countries up to the age of 45 to carry out research projects of their own choice in Germany.

Eligibility: Open to highly qualified foreign academics from developing countries who are up to 45 years of age, have obtained a PhD degree or equivalent, can furnish proof of independent research through academic publications in internationally recognized journals. Since fellowships are designed to promote the transfer of knowledge and methods to contribute to further development in fellow's home countries, the fellowships are focused on humanities and social sciences, political science and economics, projects in the public health sector and in the fields of agriculture, forestry and geosciences, and interdisciplinary projects relating to environmental and resource protection. Candidates in the humanities should possess sound German language ability if it is needed to carry out the project successfully. German language courses at the Goethe Institute in Germany of two-four months may be available prior to commencement of the research fellowship. Those in the natural, medical and engineering sciences should possess English language ability. Candidates should already have established relations with a German research institute where the project can be realised. The fellowship is open to nationals of developing countries. A respective list of eligible countries is available at http://www.avh.de/en/programme/stip_aus/doc/gf/laenderliste.doc.
Level of Study: Postdoctorate.
Type: Fellowship.
Value: €2,100-3,000 per month.
Length of Study: 6-12 months with the possibility of extension for up to 24 months.
Frequency: Annual, 3 selections per annum.
Study Establishment: Universities or research institution.
Country of Study: Germany.
No. of awards offered: 30 per annum.
Closing Date: Applications are accepted at any time.
Funding: Government.
Contributor: Federal Ministry for Economic co-operation and Development.
No. of awards given last year: 25.
No. of applicants last year: 94.
Additional Information: Applications should be forwarded directly to the foundation or through diplomatic or consular offices of the Federal Republic of Germany in the candidates respective countries.

Humboldt Research Award for Foreign Scientists and Scholars

Subjects: All subjects.
Purpose: To enable internationally recognised foreign scientists and scholars to conduct research on a project of their choice in Germany.
Eligibility: Open to all scholars and scientists from abroad.
Level of Study: Research.
Type: Prize.
Value: Up to €75,000.
Length of Study: 6-12 months.
Frequency: Annual.
Study Establishment: Universities and research institutions.
Country of Study: Germany.
No. of awards offered: Up to 100.
Application Procedure: Applicants are nominated by eminent German Scholars directly to the Foundation in Bonn. Direct applications are not accepted.
Closing Date: Nominations are accepted throughout the year.
Funding: Government.
No. of awards given last year: 75.
No. of applicants last year: 190.
Additional Information: Selection committee meetings are held twice a year in March and October.

JSPS Research Fellowships

Subjects: All subjects.
Purpose: To enable highly qualified scholars to carry out research projects of their own choice in Japan.
Eligibility: Open to German nationals only.
Level of Study: Postdoctorate.
Type: Fellowship.
Value: Yen 392,000 per month plus travel and housing allowance.
Length of Study: One-two years.

Frequency: Annual.
Study Establishment: A university or other research institution.
Country of Study: Japan.
No. of awards offered: 40.
Application Procedure: Applicants must complete an application form.
Closing Date: February 10th, June 10th or October 10th.
Funding: Government.
No. of awards given last year: 11.
No. of applicants last year: 15.

Konrad Adenauer Research Award

Subjects: Humanities and social sciences.
Purpose: To promote academic relations between Canada and Germany.
Eligibility: Open to highly qualified Canadian Scholars, whose research work in the humanities or in the social sciences has brought them international recognition and who belong to the group of leading Scholars in their respective area of specialisation. The award will be made regardless of age, race, religion or sex.
Level of Study: Research.
Type: Prize grant.
Value: Up to €75,000.
Length of Study: One year.
Frequency: Annual.
Study Establishment: Universities and research institutions.
Country of Study: Germany.
No. of awards offered: One.
Application Procedure: Applicants must be nominated by their universities and their dossiers sent to the Awards Co-ordinator. Nomination forms and information may also be requested from the Awards Co-ordinator. Direct application are not accepted.
Closing Date: January 31st.
Funding: Government.
No. of awards given last year: One.
No. of applicants last year: One.
Additional Information: Nominations will be made jointly by the Royal Society of Canada and the University of Toronto and submitted to the Humboldt Foundation.

For further information contact:

Awards Co-ordinator The Royal Society of Canada, 283 Sparks Street, Ottawa, ON K1R 7X9 1P9, Canada
Contact: Mrs Geneviere Gouin

Max Planck Reseach Award - International Research Award of the Alexander von Humboldt Foundation and the Maxplanck Society

Subjects: On an annually - alternating basis : (2004:) bio-informatics.
Purpose: To enable internationally recognised foreign and German scientists and scholars to conduct long-term research.
Eligibility: Open to Scientists and Scholars of all nationalities.
Level of Study: Research.
Type: Prize.
Value: Up to €750,000.
Length of Study: Three-five years.
Frequency: Annual.
Study Establishment: Universities and research institutions.
Country of Study: Germany / Abroad.
No. of awards offered: 2;1 to a German national and 1 to a non German scientist or scholar.
Application Procedure: Nominations have to be initiated in Germany and may be submitted by the President/Vice Chancellors and Deans of any academic institution of higher education, the heads of the Academies of Science, the Fraunhofer Society, the Hermann von Helmholtz Association of German Research Centres, the Max Planck Society, the caesar Foundation and the Scientific Association Gottfried Wilhelm Leibniz, the former winners of the Leibniz Award, the Max Planck Research Award or the Wolfgang Paul Award award working in Germany, the chairpersons of specialist of German Research Foundation committees in closely-related disciplines.
Closing Date: End of November 2003.

Funding: Government.
Additional Information: Selection occurs once per year.

Postdoctoral Humboldt Research Fellowships

Subjects: Any subject.
Purpose: To provide opportunities for young, highly qualified scholars to carry out research projects of their own choice in Germany.
Eligibility: Open to young, highly qualified foreign academics, who are up to 40 years of age, have obtained a PhD degree or equivalent, can furnish proof of independent research through academic publications in internationally recognised journals. Candidates in the humanities should possess sound German language ability if it is needed to carry out the project successfully. German language courses at the Goethe Institute in Germany of two-four months may be available prior to commencement of the research fellowship. Those in the natural, medical and engineering sciences should possess English language ability. Candidates should already have established relations with a German research institute where the project can be realised.
Level of Study: Postdoctorate.
Type: Fellowship.
Value: €2,100-3,000 per month.
Length of Study: 6-12 months with the possibility of extension for up to 24 months.
Frequency: Annual, 3 Selections each year.
Study Establishment: Universities or research institutions.
Country of Study: Germany.
No. of awards offered: Approx. 500 per annum.
Application Procedure: Information regarding the application procedure is available at http://www.humboldt-foundation.de.co humboldt-fellow.select@avh.de.
Closing Date: Applications are accepted at any time.
Funding: Government.
No. of awards given last year: 394.
No. of applicants last year: 1238.
Additional Information: Applications should be forwarded directly to the Foundation or through diplomatic or consular offices of the Federal Republic of Germany in the candidates' respective countries.

Roman Hertog Research Fellowships

Subjects: All subjects/fields of law, economics and social sciences are particularly welcome.
Purpose: To enable young highly qualified scholars from central and south-east Europe (incl. the Baltic states) to carry out research projects of their own choice in Germany.
Eligibility: The research fellowship programme is open to candidates up to 35 years of age who hold doctorate degrees, can furnish proof of equivalent research achievements or are approaching their doctorate degrees, can furnish proof of independent research work through recognized academic publications and, in addition, have proven outstanding leadership qualities in research and teaching or through non-academic activities. This programme is eligible to nationals of the following countries: Albania, Bosnia-Herzegovina, Bulgaria, Estonia, Croatia, Latvia, Lithuania, Macedonia, Poland, Romania, Serbia and Montenegro, Slovenia, The Slovak Republic, The Czech Republic and Hungary.
Level of Study: Predoctorate.
Type: Fellowship.
Value: €1,600-2,100/month.
Length of Study: 6-12 months with the possibility of extension for up to 18 months.
Frequency: Annual, 2 selections per year.
Study Establishment: Universities or research institutions.
Country of Study: Germany.
No. of awards offered: 12 per year.
Application Procedure: Information regarding the application procedure is available at www.humboldt-foundation.de or hertog.select@auh.de.
Closing Date: Applications may be submitted at any time.
Funding: Government.
Contributor: GHS (non-profit Hetie Foundation).
No. of awards given last year: 11.
No. of applicants last year: 28.

Sofja Koralerskaja Award for Foreign Scientists and Scholars (programme is subject to confirmation in the course of an ongoing parliamentary procedure)

Subjects: All subjects.
Purpose: To enable successful outstanding young scientists and scholars from abroad upto the age of 35 to establish working groups and to conduct research on a project of their choice in Germany.
Eligibility: Open to all scholars and scientists from abroad.
Level of Study: Research.
Type: Prize.
Value: Up to €1,2 million.
Length of Study: 4 years.
Frequency: Every two years.
Study Establishment: Universities and research institutions.
Country of Study: Germany.
No. of awards offered: 10.
Application Procedure: Applicants may apply directly to the Humboldt Foundation.
Closing Date: March 15, 2004.
Funding: Government.
No. of awards given last year: 29 (2001).
No. of applicants last year: 110 (2001).
Additional Information: Selection committee meetings are held once every two years in September.

ALFRED BRADLEY BURSARY AWARD

c/o BBC Radio Drama, Room 2129, New Broadcasting House, Oxford Road, Manchester, Lancashire M60 1SJ, England
Tel: (44) 161 244 4255
Fax: (44) 161 244 4248
Contact: The Coordinator

Established in 1992. Biennial award in commemoration of the life and work of the distinguished radio producer Alfred Bradley.

Alfred Bradley Bursary Award

Subjects: Drama.
Purpose: To encourage and develop new radio writing talent in the BBC North region.
Eligibility: Entrants must live in the North region.
Level of Study: Professional development.
Value: Up to UK£6,000 and a BBC Radio drama commission.
Length of Study: Two years.
Frequency: Every two years.
Country of Study: United Kingdom.
Application Procedure: Contact the coordinator.
Funding: Private.
Additional Information: There is a change of focus for each award, e.g. previous years have targeted comedy, drama, verse drama etc.

ALFRED P SLOAN FOUNDATION

630 Fifth Avenue, Suite 2550, New York, NY 10111, United States of America
Tel: (1) 212 649 1649
Fax: (1) 212 757 5117
www: www.sloan.org

The Alfred P. Sloan Foundation, a philanthorpic nonprofit institution, was established in 1934 by Alfred P. Sloan Jr., then President and Chief Executive Officer's of the General Motors Corporation.

Sloan Research Fellowships

Subjects: Chemistry, computational and evolutionary molecular biology, computer science, economics, mathematics, neuroscience, physics.
Purpose: To enhance the careers of the very best young faculty members in specified fields of science.
Level of Study: Postdoctorate.
Type: Fellowship.
Frequency: Annual.
No. of awards offered: 116.

Application Procedure: Please check the website for detailed procedure.
Closing Date: September 15th.

ALICIA PATTERSON FOUNDATION

1730 Pennsylvania Avenue NW, Suite 850, Washington, DC 20006, United States of America
Tel: (1) 202 393 5995
Fax: (1) 301 951 8512
Email: info@aliciapatterson.org
www: http://www.aliciapatterson.org
Contact: Ms Margaret Engel, Executive Director

The Alicia Patterson Foundation gives grants to professional print reporters and photo-journalists to investigate a subject of their choice. Their reports are published in a quarterly magazine, the Alicia Patterson Foundation Reporter, and on the Foundation's website.

Alicia Patterson Journalism Fellowships
Subjects: Journalism.
Purpose: To give working print journalists a chance to spend a year researching and writing on a topic of their choosing.
Eligibility: Open to print journalists eg. reporters, editors, photographers with at least five years of full-time professional experience, who are United States citizens.
Level of Study: Professional development.
Type: Fellowship.
Value: US$35,000.
Length of Study: One year.
Frequency: Annual.
Country of Study: Any country.
No. of awards offered: Five-nine.
Application Procedure: Applicants must use the Alicia Patterson Foundation application form and are also required to submit a three page proposal, a two page autobiographical essay, three clips, four letters of reference and a budget.
Closing Date: Postmarked October 1st.
Funding: Private.
No. of awards given last year: Six.
No. of applicants last year: 231.

ALL SAINTS EDUCATIONAL TRUST

St Katherine Cree Church, 86 Leadenhall Street, London, EC3A 3DH, England
Tel: (44) 20 7283 4485
Fax: (44) 20 7621 9758
Email: enquiries@aset.org.uk
www: http://www.aset.org.uk
Contact: Mr Richard C Poulton, Clerk to the Trustees

The funds of the All Saints Educational Trust are dedicated to the formal training, or the better qualification, of teachers and to educational advance by other means eg. research or improvement in communication. There is particular emphasis within the fields of religious education, home economics or related subjects.

All Saints Educational Trust Corporate Awards
Subjects: Religious education, home economics and kindred subjects, as well as multi-cultural and inter-faith education.
Purpose: To offer assistance to individuals and institutions within certain specified terms of reference.
Level of Study: Unrestricted.
Type: Award.
Value: Varies. UK£100,000 over 3 years is the maximum awarded.
Length of Study: Up to five years.
Frequency: Dependent on funds available.
Country of Study: United Kingdom.
No. of awards offered: Two-six.
Application Procedure: Applicants must complete an application form, available on request from the Clerk to the Trust.

Closing Date: Applications are accepted at any time. March 31st is the deadline for ensuing academic year.
Funding: Private.
No. of awards given last year: Four new and three ongoing.
No. of applicants last year: 14.
Additional Information: The award must be used or applied in the United Kingdom. Further information is available on request or from the website.

All Saints Educational Trust Personal Awards
Subjects: Religious education, home economics and multicultural education.
Purpose: To give support to persons who work in certain capacities associated with education.
Eligibility: Open to individuals over 18 years of age who are, or who intend to become, teachers. Grants for research are open to individuals.
Level of Study: Unrestricted.
Type: Grant.
Value: Varies, usually UK£500-UK£10,000 but occasionally more.
Length of Study: One-three years.
Frequency: Annual.
Study Establishment: Recognised educational institutions in the United Kingdom.
Country of Study: United Kingdom.
No. of awards offered: Dependent on availability of funds.
Application Procedure: Applicants must complete an application form, available on request from the Clerk to the Trust or from the website.
Closing Date: March 31st.
Funding: Private.
No. of awards given last year: 50.
No. of applicants last year: 150.
Additional Information: Enquiries should not be delayed until the offer of a place on a course of study has been confirmed. Late applications cannot be considered.

THE ALLEN FOUNDATION, INC.

PO Box 1606, Midland, MI 48641-1606, United States of America
Tel: (1) 989 832 5678
Fax: (1) 989 696 3445
Email: d-baum@tamu.edu
www: http://www.allenfoundation.org
Contact: Dale Baum, Secretary

Established in 1975 by agricultural chemist William Webster Allen, the Allen Foundation makes grants to projects that benefit human nutrition in the areas of education, training and research.

Allen Foundation Grants
Subjects: Human nutrition in the areas of health, education, training and research.
Purpose: To assist in the field of human nutrition, to fund relevant nutritional research and to encourage the dissemination of information regarding healthful nutritional practices and habits.
Eligibility: Open to non-profit organisations which must be able to provide a copy of their federal Internal Revenue Service certification of tax-exempt status. If applying from outside the United States of America, applicants must send their country's counterpart or equivalent of the tax-exempt form. Individuals, non-profit organisations without a current exempt status, conferences, seminars, symposia, sponsorship events, fund raising events and religious organisations without a secular community designation are not eligible for the award. If a grant proposal involves primarily academic research, the grant should be conducted under the leadership of a full-time, principal investigator who is a regular faculty member with tenure or on tenure tract.
Level of Study: Research.
Type: Grant.
Country of Study: United States of America.
No. of awards offered: One.
Application Procedure: Applicants must submit an application form via email only. Application forms and further information can be obtained from the website.

Closing Date: January 1st.

Additional Information: Any applications received after this deadline will be reviewed for the following year's applications. The Board of Trustees will announce their decision for successful applicants in June. Because of the number of proposals received and the limited resources of the Foundation, applicants should never view possible declinations to fund their proposals or delays in reviewing their proposals as judgements on their actual merits of their proposals. The Foundation does not directly administer the programmes which it funds. For further information, visit the website or contact the Allen Foundation Inc.

ALZHEIMER'S ASSOCIATION

Medical & Scientific Affairs, 225 North Michigan Avenue, Suite 1700, Chicago, IL 60601, United States of America

Tel: (1) 312 335 5779
Fax: (1) 312 335 4034
Email: grants@alz.org
www: http://www.alz.org
Contact: Grants Co-ordinator

The Alzheimer's Association aims to be a source of information support and assistance on issues related to Alzheimer's disease. It seeks to provide leadership in attempting to eliminate Alzheimer's disease through the advancement of research, while enhancing care and support services for the individuals concerned and their families. To this end, the Association funds select projects for biomedical, social and behavioural research, as well as promoting, developing and disseminating educational programmes and training guidelines for health and social service professionals.

Alzheimer's Association Investigator-Initiated Research Grants

Subjects: Alzheimer's disease and related disorders.
Purpose: To build on the success of established investigators by providing sustained support for independent research projects.
Eligibility: Investigators from all stages of research career development are encouraged to apply.
Level of Study: Doctorate, Postdoctorate, Postgraduate.
Type: Research grant.
Value: Please contact the organisation.
Frequency: Annual.
Country of Study: Any country.
No. of awards offered: Varies.
Application Procedure: Applicants must, before preparing an application for any of the research grant programmes, send a one page letter of intent by email. Each letter must include the name and contact information of the principal investigator, institutions involved in the research proposal, the title of the investigation and its specific aims, presented in bullet format. The application will be available upon approval of the letter of intent. Applicants should visit the website for details. It is the responsibility of the applicant to ensure and to verify that the application is received by the Alzheimer's Association prior to the receipt date deadline and that the application is complete and correct prior to submission.
Funding: Private.
Additional Information: Multiple submissions of the same research grant application in a single fiscal year will not be accepted. An investigator may not submit more than one application per programme during the research grant competition and each application must be a separate and distinct research proposal with non overlapping aims. Applicants may revise and resubmit applications which were previously submitted, which will then be treated as new. Efforts will be made to provide some continuity in reviewers. Animal welfare and human subject protection assurances are not required at the time of submission.

Alzheimer's Association New Investigator Research Grants

Subjects: Alzheimer's disease and related disorders.
Purpose: To enable new and established investigators to test the feasibility of new ideas on a small scale, and to allow investigators to generate pilot data to support proposals to NIH foundations or the Association for larger grants.
Eligibility: Open to investigators who have had less than 10 years of research experience, including postdoctoral fellowships or residencies, after receipt of the doctoral degree. This 10 year period is taken from the submission date of the grant application. Applications from graduate and doctoral students for research projects, which will be used for the thesis or dissertation, will be accepted and judged by the usual scientific criteria.
Level of Study: Postgraduate.
Type: Research grant.
Value: Please contact the organisation.
Length of Study: Up to two years.
Frequency: Annual.
Country of Study: Any country.
No. of awards offered: Varies.
Application Procedure: Applicants must visit the website for details.
Additional Information: This award was formally known as the Pilot Research Grant. Annual progress and financial reports are required. Future, non competitive continuation funding is contingent on the timely receipt of scientific and financial reports.

Alzheimer's Association Pioneer Awards for Alzheimer's Disease Research

Subjects: Alzheimer's disease.
Purpose: To offer investigators the unique opportunity of obtaining substantial research and research support funding. The goal of the award is to support a dual effort in the investigator's laboratory, to work on a focused research project aimed at questions surrounding the interventions for Alzheimer's disease and flexible research support which will allow rapid mid-course adjustments in the ongoing research programme.
Eligibility: Investigators who have made important, ground breaking contributions to Alzheimer's disease are encouraged to apply. It is anticipated that successful applicants will hold senior academic rank, have international recognition of their research contributions, have lengthy records of peer reviewed publications in major scientific journals and have long track records of substantial funding from the National Institutes of Health or other national funding agencies. Investigators who have been Directors of Alzheimer's Disease Centers (P50 and P30), principal investigators on NIH sponsored programme projects grants (P01) or LEAD awardees are eligible, but members of the Medical and Scientific Advisory Council and of the National Board of the Alzheimer's Association are not.
Type: Award.
Value: Please contact the organisation.
Frequency: Annual.
No. of awards offered: One.
Application Procedure: Applicants must visit the website for details.
Funding: Private.
Additional Information: Biannual progress and financial reports are required. Future non competitive continuation funding is contingent on the timely submission of interim scientific and financial reports.

Senator Mark Hatfield Award for Clinical Research in Alzheimer's Disease

Subjects: Alzheimer's disease and related disorders.
Purpose: To honour Senator Hatfield's long commitment to Alzheimer's disease research in general and clinical research in particular. The award is designed to focus on the Senator's interests in clinical research and support of new investigators.
Eligibility: Open to investigators who received their doctoral degree less than 10 years prior to submission of the application.
Type: Award.
Value: Please contact the organisation.
Frequency: Annual.
No. of awards offered: One.
Application Procedure: Applicants must visit the website for details.
Funding: Private.
Additional Information: Annual progress and financial reports are required. Future non competitive continuation funding is contingent on the timely receipt of scientific progress and financial reports.

Zenith Awards

Subjects: Alzheimer's disease.
Purpose: To provide major support to qualified scientists in basic biomedical research who have already made substantial contributions in the field of Alzheimer's, or have made significant contributions to other areas of science and are now beginning to focus more directly on problems related to Alzheimer's disease and are likely to make substantial contributions to Alzheimer research in the future.
Eligibility: Open to projects that will test new and innovative ideas likely to lead to fundamental findings related to the biology of Alzheimer's disease. The proposed research must be on the cutting edge of basic, biomedical research and therefore may not fit current conventional scientific wisdom or may challenge prevailing orthodoxy. The proposed research should address fundamental problems related to the early detection, aetiology, pathogenesis, treatment and prevention of Alzheimer's disease. Previous recipients of Zenith Awards, Alzheimer's Disease Centre directors, Medical and Scientific Advisory Council members and members of the national board of the Alzheimer's Association are ineligible to apply.
Type: Award.
Value: Please contact the organisation.
Frequency: Annual.
Country of Study: Any country.
No. of awards offered: Five.
Application Procedure: Applicants must visit the website for details.
Additional Information: Applications will be evaluated by an expert panel of senior scientists, already well recognised for their own accomplishments in Alzheimer's research. Annual progress and financial reports are required. Future non competitive continuation funding is contingent on the receipt of scientific progress and financial statue reports.

ALZHEIMER'S RESEARCH TRUST

Livanos House, Granham's Road, Cambridge, Cambridgeshire, CB2 5LQ, England
Tel: (44) 01223 843899
Fax: (44) 01223 843325
Email: enquiries@alzheimers-research.org.uk
www: http://www.alzheimers-research.org.uk
Contact: Ms Harriet Millward, Acting Chief Executive

Alzheimer's Research Trust is the leading UK research charity for dementia. It funds work in any area of research that promises to further understanding of the basic disease process in Alzheimer's and related dementias, or that is directed to early detection, identifying risk factors, or offers progress towards effective treatments.

Alzheimer's Research Trust Clinical Research Training Fellowship

Subjects: The basic disease process is Alzheimer's disease and related dementias directed towards identifying risk factors and progress towards more effective early diagnosis and/or treatments.
Purpose: To support clinical research by a medically qualified applicant in the field of dementia.
Type: Fellowship.
Value: Full salary + Research Expenses of UK£2,000.
Length of Study: Up to 3 years.
Frequency: Twice a year.
Country of Study: United Kingdom.
No. of awards offered: 1.
Application Procedure: Applicants must submit a brief description of the proposal plus other information as laid down in the 'Guidelines for applicants'. There is no application form. Visit http://www.alzheimers-research.org.uk/scientists for full details.
Closing Date: January 2004, then March and November annually.
Contributor: Charitable Sources.
No. of awards given last year: Not awarded last year.

Alzheimer's Research Trust Emergency Support Grant

Subjects: The basic disease processes in Alzheimer's disease and related dementias directed towards identifying risk factors or progress towards more effective early diagnosis and/or treatments.

Purpose: To Bridge Funding Shortfalls in Research.
Eligibility: Members of Alzheimer's Research Trust Network only.
Level of Study: Research.
Type: Grant.
Value: Up to UK£30,000.
Length of Study: few weeks - 24 months.
Frequency: As necessary.
No. of awards offered: As necessary.
Application Procedure: Applicants must submit proposal as laid down in the guidelines. There is no application form. Visit http://www.alzheimers-research.org.uk/scientists for full details.
Closing Date: Can submit at any time.
Contributor: Charitable Sources.
No. of awards given last year: None - New Grant.

Alzheimer's Research Trust Network Project Co-operation Grant

Subjects: The basic disease process in Alzheimer's disease and related dementias directed towards identifying risk factors or progress towards more effective early diagnosis and/or treatments.
Purpose: To promote collaborative research between members of the Trust's Network.
Eligibility: Lead applicant must be network member, but application can include non-network and non-UK researchers.
Level of Study: Research.
Type: Grant.
Value: UK£5,000-UK£50,000.
Frequency: Twice a year if appropriate.
Country of Study: United Kingdom or elsewhere.
No. of awards offered: One or more.
Application Procedure: Lead applicants must submit a research proposal as laid down in the 'Guidelines for applicants'. There is no application form. Visit http://www.alzheimers-research.org.uk/scientists for full details.
Closing Date: Can be submitted at any time.
Contributor: Charitable Sources.
No. of awards given last year: New Grant.

Alzheimer's Research Trust PhD Studentships

Subjects: The basic disease processes in Alzheimer's disease and related dementias directed towards identifying risk factors or progress towards more effective early diagnosis and/or treatments.
Purpose: To contribute towards research in the field, and to help ensure that bright young graduates are inducted into this area.
Level of Study: Postgraduate.
Type: Scholarship.
Value: UK£63,000 or UK£67,000 in London.
Length of Study: Three years.
Frequency: Annual.
Country of Study: United Kingdom.
No. of awards offered: Up to Five.
Application Procedure: Applications must be submitted by individual or joint prospective supervisors. These should consist of a brief description of the proposed project, a curriculum vitae of proposed supervisors, a brief statement on the research and training environment, and confirmation that the application has the approval of the institution. Please visit http://www.alzheimers-research.org.uk/scientists for full details. There is no application form.
Closing Date: November prior to commencement in October of the following year.
Contributor: Charitable sources.
No. of awards given last year: Three.

Alzheimer's Research Trust Pilot Project Grant

Subjects: The basic disease process in Alzheimer's disease and related dementias directed towards identifying risk factors or progress towards more effective early diagnosis and/or treatments.
Purpose: To fund innovative research projects and pilot studies.
Level of Study: Research.
Type: Grant.
Value: Up to UK£30,000.
Length of Study: Up to 2 years.
Frequency: Twice a year.

Country of Study: United Kingdom.
No. of awards offered: One or more.
Application Procedure: Applicants must submit a research proposal of not more than 4 sides of A4, plus other information as laid down in the 'Guidelines for applicants'. There is no application form. Visit http://www.alzheimers-research.org.uk/scientists for full details.
Closing Date: November and March annually.
Contributor: Charitable Sources.
No. of awards given last year: None - new grant for 2004.

Alzheimer's Research Trust Research Equipment Grant

Subjects: The basic disease processes in Alzheimer's disease and related dementias directed towards identifying risk factors or progress towards more effective early diagnosis and/or treatments.
Purpose: To speed up and increase the accuracy and efficiency of research.
Level of Study: Research.
Type: Grant.
Value: UK£10,000-100,000.
Frequency: Twice a year.
No. of awards offered: One or more.
Application Procedure: Applicants must submit no more than four sides of A4 paper listing the equipment to be purchased should the grant be given and setting out the exact purpose to which the equipment would be put to use to benefit research. A brief specification of the equipment should be provided with appropriate costings. There is no application form. See 'Guidelines for applicants' or http://www.alzheimers-research.org.uk/scientists.
Closing Date: January and June.
Contributor: Charitable sources.
No. of awards given last year: Six.

Alzheimer's Research Trust Research Fellowships

Subjects: The basic disease process is Alzheimer's disease and related dementias directed towards identifying risk factors and progress towards more effective early diagnosis and/or treatments.
Purpose: To allow junior postdoctoral researchers of demonstrated ability and high potential to carry out further research.
Level of Study: Postdoctorate.
Type: Fellowship.
Value: Full salary plus contribution towards research and travel costs.
Length of Study: 3 years.
Frequency: Twice a year.
Country of Study: United Kingdom.
No. of awards offered: Up to five annually.
Application Procedure: Applicants must submit a research proposal of not more than 5 pages plus other information as laid down in the 'Guidelines for applicants'. There is no application form. Visit http://www.alzheimers-research.org.uk/scientists for full details.
Closing Date: January 2004, then March & November Annually.
Contributor: Charitable Sources.
No. of awards given last year: None - a new grant for 2004.

Alzheimer's Research Trust Research Major Programme Project Grants

Subjects: The basic disease processes in Alzheimer's disease and related dementias directed towards identifying risk factors or progress towards more effective early diagnosis and/or treatments.
Purpose: To support imaginative and high quality research.
Level of Study: Research.
Type: Grant.
Value: UK£150,000-UK£1,000,000.
Length of Study: Three-five years.
Frequency: Twice a Year.
Country of Study: United Kingdom.
No. of awards offered: One or more.
Application Procedure: Applicants must submit a preliminary application consisting of a curriculum vitae of each candidate, a research proposal of not more than four sides of A4, a brief statement of the candidate's major achievements in research in the last five years and a brief outline of the host institution. There is no application form visit http://www.alzheimers-research.org.uk/scientists for full details.

Closing Date: Preliminary applications are due in November or March. Full submissions are due in March or September.
Contributor: Charitable sources.
No. of awards given last year: Three.

ALZHEIMER'S SOCIETY

Gordon House, 10 Greencoat Place, London, SW1P 1PH, England
Tel: (44) 20 7692 1495
Fax: (44) 870 132 0292
Email: qrd@alzheimers.org.uk
www: http://www.alzheimers.org.uk
Contact: Dr Richard Harvey, Director of Research

The Alzheimer's Society is the leading care and research charity for people with all forms of dementia, their families and carers.

Alzheimers Society Research Grants

Subjects: All forms of dementia, particularly Alzheimer's disease.
Purpose: To support research into the cause, cure and care of dementia.
Eligibility: Awards may only be held by United Kingdom institutions. Non United Kingdom researchers may be sub-contractors.
Level of Study: Postdoctorate, Research.
Value: UK£1,000,000 per year is committed to research. Fellowship grants are approx. UK£250,000, project grants are approx. UK£650,000 and innovation grants are approx. UK£100,000.
Length of Study: Up to five years.
Frequency: Other.
Country of Study: United Kingdom.
No. of awards offered: Varies.
Application Procedure: Applicants must complete an application form, available from the website.
Closing Date: The deadline for Fellowship Grants is in March and September. There are no deadlines for Project Grants and Innovation Grants.
Funding: Commercial, Government, Private.
No. of awards given last year: 15.
No. of applicants last year: 45.
Additional Information: Further information is available on request or from the website.

For further information contact:

Alzheimers Society Quality Research in Dementia, 45-46 Lower Marsh, London, SE1 7RG, England

AMERICA-ISRAEL CULTURAL FOUNDATION (AICF)

32 Allenby Road, Tel Aviv, 63325, Israel
Tel: (972) 3 517 4177
Fax: (972) 3 517 8991
Email: aicf@netvision.net.il
www: http://aicf.webnet.org
Contact: Mr Gideon Paz, Executive Director

The America-Israel Cultural Foundation (AICF) has been promoting and supporting the arts in Israel for over 60 years. While in the past it has supported numerous cultural performing organisations and institutions, it is now focusing its support almost exclusively on the education of artists. Through its Sharett Scholarship Program, the AICF grants hundreds of study scholarships each year to Israeli students of the arts, music, dance, the visual arts, film and television, and theatre, mainly for studies in Israel. AICF also provides short-term fellowships to artists and art teachers and financially supports various projects in art schools, workshops, master classes etc.

Sharett Scholarship Program

Subjects: Performing arts, visual arts, design, film or television.
Eligibility: Open to Israeli citizens only.
Level of Study: Unrestricted.
Type: Scholarship.

Value: US$750-2,000.
Length of Study: Varies.
Frequency: Annual.
Country of Study: Any country.
No. of awards offered: Approx. 500 scholarships, fellowships and grants.
Application Procedure: Applicants must complete and submit an application form with recommendations and pre-required repertoire. Application forms are available from February 1st of each year.
Closing Date: March 10th.
Funding: Private.
Contributor: America-Israel Cultural Foundation.
No. of awards given last year: 960.
No. of applicants last year: 1,600.
Additional Information: The programme is revised on an annual basis. For more detailed information please contact the Foundation after February 1st.

AMERICAN ACADEMY OF ARTS AND LETTERS

633 West 155th Street, New York, NY 10032-7599, United States of America
Tel: (1) 212 368 5900
Fax: (1) 212 491 4615
Contact: Executive Director

Richard Rodgers Awards for the Musical Theatre

Subjects: Musical theatre.
Purpose: To encourage the development of musical theatre by subsidising productions and staged readings by a non-profit theatre in the city of New York of works by American composers and writers who are not already established in the field.
Eligibility: Open to United States citizens or permanent residents. Awards are given to professional level works. Musicals being entered should be ready for reading or production by a theatre company in New York.
Level of Study: Professional development.
Type: Award.
Value: Subsidised reading or production of original musical.
Frequency: Annual.
Country of Study: United States of America.
No. of awards offered: Varies.
Application Procedure: Applicants must send a stamped addressed envelope accompanying requests for applications. Applications are available in the Spring. Composers and authors must include tapes and scripts with their applications.
Closing Date: November 1st.
Funding: Private.
Contributor: Richard Rodgers' bequest.

AMERICAN ACADEMY OF CHILD AND ADOLESCENT PSYCHIATRY

3615 Wisconsin Avenue North West, Washington, DC 20016, United States of America
Tel: (1) 202 966 7300
Fax: (1) 202 966 2891
Email: crenner@aacap.org
www: http://www.aacap.org
Contact: Deputy Director of Research & Training

The American Academy of Child and Adolescent Psychiatry is a national, professional medical association established in 1953 as a non-profit organisation to support and improve the quality of life for children, adolescents and families affected by mental illnesses.

AACAP/Pfizer Travel Grants

Subjects: Child and adolescent psychiatry.
Purpose: To help defray the cost of attending the AACAP's Annual Meeting in San Francisco, California in October.

Eligibility: Applicants must be child and adolescent psychiatry residents at the time of the AACAP Annual Meeting and must be currently enrolled in a residency programme in the United States. All awardees must attend the Young Leaders Awards Luncheon and other stated events and serve as a monitor for one day at the Anniversary Meeting.
Level of Study: Postdoctorate.
Type: Travel grant.
Value: US$800.
Country of Study: United States of America.
No. of awards offered: 50.
Application Procedure: Applicants must submit a copy of their curriculum vitae and a one or two page, double spaced description of why they would like to attend the AACAP Annual Meeting and what they hope to get out of the experience. They must also include a letter of recommendation from their Training Director, including a statement that they are in good standing.
Contributor: Pfizer Pharmaceuticals.

Jeanne Spurlock Minority Medical Student Clinical Fellowship in Child and Adolescent Psychiatry

Subjects: Psychiatry and mental health.
Purpose: To support work during the Summer with a child and adolescent psychiatrist mentor.
Eligibility: Applications are accepted from African American, Asian American, Native American, Alaskan Native, Mexican American, Hispanic and Pacific Islander students in accredited United States medical schools.
Level of Study: Graduate.
Type: Fellowship.
Value: Up to US$2,500.
Frequency: Annual.
Country of Study: United States of America.
No. of awards offered: Up to 14.
Funding: Government.

Jeanne Spurlock Research Fellowship in Drug Abuse and Addiction for Minority Medical Students

Subjects: Psychiatry and mental health.
Purpose: To support work during the Summer with a child and adolescent psychiatrist research mentor.
Eligibility: Applications are accepted from African American, Asian American, Native American, Alaskan Native, Mexican American, Hispanic and Pacific Islander students in accredited United States medical schools. All applications must relate to substance abuse research.
Level of Study: Graduate.
Type: Fellowship.
Value: Up to US$2,500.
Frequency: Annual.
Country of Study: United States of America.
No. of awards offered: Up to five.
Funding: Government.

Presidential Scholar Award

Subjects: Child and adolescent psychiatry.
Purpose: To recognise specialised competence among child and adolescent psychiatry residents in research, public policy and innovative service systems.
Eligibility: Awardees must be AACAP resident members by the time of the Annual Meeting.
Level of Study: Research.
Type: Award.
Value: Up to US$2,500 for travel and lodging for one week's tutorial and exchange in the specified area of study. Travel and hotel expenses for participation in the Academy's Annual Meeting are also paid.
Country of Study: United States of America.
Application Procedure: Nominations must be made by programme or training directors and must include a statement in support of the nomination, the nominee's curriculum vitae and a statement from the nominee about his or her specific area of interest, be it research, public policy, administration or other, plans for the tutorial and exchange, and plans for the presentation to the home programme. While

applicants are responsible for contacting their potential mentors, the Program Director for this award can help locate potential mentors for those awardees who need assistance.
Funding: Private.
Contributor: Bristol-Myers Squibb.

THE AMERICAN ACADEMY OF FACIAL PLASTIC AND RECONSTRUCTIVE SURGERY (AAFPRS) FOUNDATION

310 Henry Street, Alexandria, VA 22314, United States of America
Tel: (1) 703 299 9291
Fax: (1) 703 299 8898
Email: info@aafprs.org
www: http://www.aafprs.org
Contact: Research Program

The American Academy of Facial Plastic and Reconstructive Surgery (AAFPRS) Foundation represents 2,700 facial plastic and reconstructive surgeons throughout the world. Its main mission is to promote the highest quality facial plastic surgery through education, dissemination of professional information and the establishment of professional standards. The AAFPRS was created to address the medical and scientific issues confronting facial plastic surgeons.

Leslie Bernstein Grant
Subjects: Facial plastic and reconstructive surgery.
Purpose: To encourage original research projects which will advance facial plastic and reconstructive surgery.
Eligibility: Open to AAFPRS fellow members.
Level of Study: Professional development.
Type: Research grant.
Value: US$25,000.
Length of Study: Three years.
Frequency: Varies.
Study Establishment: The recipient's practice or institution.
Country of Study: United States of America.
No. of awards offered: One.
Application Procedure: Applicants must submit an application form and other documentation including a curriculum vitae and research proposal. Application forms and guidelines are available on the web www.entlink.net//research/grant/foundation.funding-opportunities.cfm.
Closing Date: January 15th.
Funding: Private.
Contributor: Dr. Leslie Bernstein.
No. of awards given last year: 0.
No. of applicants last year: 1.
Additional Information: All applications must be submitted through the Centralized Otolaryngology Research Efforts (C.O.R.E) Program. (see website listed above for information and application).

For further information contact:

www: http://www.entlink.net/research/grant/Foundation-Funding-Opportunities.cfm

Leslie Bernstein Investigator Development Grant
Subjects: Facial plastic surgery, clinical or laboratory research.
Purpose: To support the work of a young faculty member in facial plastic surgery conducting significant clinical or laboratory research, as well as the training of resident surgeons in research.
Eligibility: Open to AAFPRS members who are involved in the training of resident surgeons.
Level of Study: Postgraduate.
Type: Research grant.
Value: US$15,000.
Length of Study: Two years.
Frequency: Annual.
Study Establishment: The recipient's institution.
Country of Study: United States of America.
No. of awards offered: One.
Application Procedure: Applicants must submit an application form and other documentation including a curriculum vitae and research

proposal. Application forms and guidelines are available on the web, www.entlink.net//research/grant/foundation-funding-opportunities.cfm.
Closing Date: January 15th.
Funding: Private.
Contributor: Leslie Bernstein, MD, DDS.
No. of awards given last year: 1.
No. of applicants last year: 2.
Additional Information: All applications must be submitted through the Centralized Otolaryngology Research Efforts (C.O.R.E) program. (see website listed above for information and application).

For further information contact:

www: http://www.entlink.net/research/grant/Foundation-Funding-Opportunities.cfm

Leslie Bernstein Resident Research Grants
Subjects: Facial plastic surgery.
Purpose: To stimulate resident research in projects that are well conceived and scientifically valid.
Eligibility: Open to AAFPRS members. Residents at any level may apply even if the research work will be done during their fellowship year. All applicants are required to have sponsorship and oversight of the department chair or by an AAFPRS member as mentor.
Level of Study: Postgraduate.
Type: Research grant.
Value: US$5,000.
Length of Study: Two years.
Frequency: Annual.
Study Establishment: The recipient's institution.
Country of Study: United States of America.
No. of awards offered: Up to two.
Application Procedure: Applicants must submit an application form and other documentation including a curriculum vitae and research proposal. Application forms and guidelines are available on the web, www.entlink.net//research/grant/foundation-funding-opportunities.cfm.
Closing Date: January 15th.
Funding: Private.
Contributor: Leslie Bernstein, MD, DDS.
No. of awards given last year: 2.
No. of applicants last year: 6.
Additional Information: Residents are encouraged to enter early in their training so that their applications may be revised and resubmitted if not accepted the first time. All applications must be submitted through the Centralized Otolaryngology Research Efforts (C.O.R.E) program (see website listed above for information and application).

For further information contact:

www: http://www.entlink.net/research/grant/Foundation-Funding-Opportunities.cfm

THE AMERICAN ACADEMY OF FIXED PROSTHODONTICS

Department of Restorative Dentistry, The University of Illinois at Chicago, Chicago, IL 60612-7212, United States of America
Tel: (1) 312 413 1181
Fax: (1) 312 996 3535
Email: kentk@uic.edu
www: http://www.prosthodontics.org/forum/aafp/index.html
Contact: Chairman of the Tylman Research Programme

The American Academy of Fixed Prosthodontics consists of over 500 specialists around the world, dedicated to the pursuit of knowledge, truth and competency in research, in teaching, and in the clinical practice of crown and bridge prosthodontics.

Tylman Research Program
Subjects: Dentistry.
Purpose: To promote and support research in the field of fixed prosthodontics by graduate students.

Eligibility: Open to full-time students in the United States and Canada enrolled in any graduate or postgraduate programme who are conducting research pertinent to fixed prosthodontics. Proposals must be endorsed by the programme director of an accredited prosthodontic programme. Priority will be given to students in prosthodontic programmes. Predoctoral dental students are not eligible.
Level of Study: Postgraduate.
Type: Grant.
Value: Please contact the organisation.
Frequency: Annual.
Country of Study: United States of America.
Application Procedure: Applicants must submit the protocol of the research project to the Academy Research Committee. The six best protocols are funded. The student must submit progress reports and a final manuscript of the completed project.
Funding: Private.

THE AMERICAN ALPINE CLUB (AAC)

710 Tenth Street, Suite 100, Golden, CO 80401, United States of America
Tel: (1) 303 384 0110
Fax: (1) 303 384 0111
Email: getinfo@americanalpineclub.org
www: http://www.americanalpineclub.org
Contact: Corporate Support Co-ordinator

The American Alpine Club (AAC) is a national non-profit organisation that has represented mountaineers and rock climbers for almost a century. Since its inception in 1902, the AAC has been the only national climbers' organisation devoted to the exploration and scientific study of high mountain elevations and polar regions of the world, and the promotion and dissemination of knowledge about the mountains and mountaineering through its meetings, publications and libraries. It is also dedicated to the conservation and preservation of mountain regions and other climbing areas and the representation of the interests and concerns of the American climbing community.

AAC Mountaineering Fellowship Fund Grants
Subjects: Rock climbing.
Purpose: To encourage young American climbers to visit remote areas and seek out climbs more technically demanding than they would normally undertake.
Eligibility: Applicants must be 25 years of age or under, American citizens and experienced climbers. Membership of the American Alpine Club is not a prerequisite. Members of a single expedition may apply individually, but organised groups or expeditions are ineligible. Grants are not available for the purpose of climbing instruction.
Level of Study: Unrestricted.
Type: Grant.
Value: Usually between US$300 and US$800.
Frequency: Twice a year.
Country of Study: United States of America.
No. of awards offered: 5-16.
Application Procedure: Applicants must write for application forms which are also available from the website.
Closing Date: April 1st and November 1st.
Funding: Private.
Additional Information: Grants will be based on the excellence of the proposed project and evidence of mountaineering experience. A report must be written upon project completion.

AAC Research Grants
Subjects: Scientific research focusing on mountain and polar areas.
Purpose: To recognise a specific contribution to scientific endeavour germane to mountain regions and alpine research projects.
Eligibility: There are no restrictions on eligibility, but grants will not be awarded for academic tuition. Applications are considered in terms of their scientific or technical quality and the purposes for which the funds and the AAC are established.
Level of Study: Postgraduate.
Type: Research grant.
Value: US$200-500.

Frequency: Annual.
Country of Study: Any country.
No. of awards offered: Varies.
Application Procedure: Applicants must write for application forms which are also available from the website.
Closing Date: March 1st.
Funding: Private.
Additional Information: A report must be submitted upon completion of the project.

AMERICAN ANTIQUARIAN SOCIETY (AAS)

185 Salisbury Street, Worcester, MA 01609-1634, United States of America
Tel: (1) 508 755 5221
Fax: (1) 508 754 9069
Email: cfs@mwa.org
www: http://www.americanantiquarian.org
Contact: Ms Caroline F Scoat, Director of Scholarly Programmes

The American Antiquarian Society (AAS) is a learned society, founded in 1812 in Worcester, Massachusetts. The Society maintains a research library of American history and culture up to 1876 in order to collect, preserve, and make available for study the printed record of the United States.

'Drawn to Art' Fellowship
Subjects: American art, visual culture or other projects that will make substantial use of graphic materials as primary sources.
Purpose: To support research.
Eligibility: Applicants are selected on the basis of their scholarly qualifications, the scholarly significance of the project and the appropriateness of the proposed study to the Society's collections.
Level of Study: Doctorate, Postdoctorate.
Type: Fellowship.
Value: US$1,000.
Length of Study: One month.
Frequency: Annual.
Study Establishment: The Society's Library in Worcester, Massachusetts.
Country of Study: United States of America.
No. of awards offered: One.
Application Procedure: Applicants must request an application packet which provides full details of the fellowships, including certain restrictions that apply for some categories. Applicants must phone or email with any enquiries and requests for application materials. Alternatively applicants must visit the website.
Closing Date: January 15th.
Funding: Private.
Contributor: Diana Korzenik.
No. of awards given last year: One.
Additional Information: Further information is available from the website www.americanantiquarian.org.

AAS American Society for Eighteenth-Century Studies Fellowships
Subjects: American eighteenth-century studies.
Eligibility: Open to suitably qualified Scholars. Degree candidates are not eligible. Membership in the American Society for Eighteenth-Century Studies is required upon taking up an award, but not for making an application.
Level of Study: Postdoctorate.
Type: Fellowship.
Value: US$1,000 per month.
Length of Study: One-two months.
Frequency: Annual.
Study Establishment: The Society's Library in Worcester, Massachusetts.
Country of Study: United States of America.
No. of awards offered: One-two.
Application Procedure: Applicants must request an application packet which provides full details of the fellowships, including certain

restrictions that apply for some categories. Applicants must phone or email with any enquiries and requests for application materials. Alternatively applicants must visit the website.

Closing Date: January 15th.
Funding: Private.
Contributor: The American Society for Eighteenth-Century Studies and the AAS.
No. of awards given last year: Two.
Additional Information: www.americanantiquarian.org.

AAS National Endowment for the Humanities Visiting Fellowships

Subjects: Early American history and culture.
Purpose: To make the Society's research facilities more readily available to qualified Scholars.
Eligibility: Fellowships may not be awarded to degree candidates or for study leading to advanced degrees, nor may they be granted to foreign nationals unless they have been resident in the United States of America for at least three years immediately prior to receiving the award.
Level of Study: Postdoctorate.
Type: Fellowship.
Value: The maximum stipend available is US$40,000.
Length of Study: Either six-twelve months or four-five months.
Frequency: Annual.
Country of Study: United States of America.
No. of awards offered: More than two.
Application Procedure: Applicants must request an application packet which provides full details of the fellowships, including certain restrictions that apply for some categories. Applicants must phone or email with any enquiries and requests for application materials. Alternatively applicants must visit the website.
Closing Date: January 15th.
Funding: Government.
Contributor: The National Endowment for the Humanities.
No. of awards given last year: 3.
Additional Information: Fellows may not accept teaching assignments or undertake any other major activities during the tenure of the award. Other major fellowships may be held concurrently www.americanantiquarian.org.

AAS Northeast Modern Language Association Fellowship

Subjects: American literary studies.
Purpose: To support research.
Eligibility: Applicants are selected on the basis of their scholarly qualifications, the scholarly significance of the project and the appropriateness of the proposed study to the Society's collections.
Level of Study: Postdoctorate.
Type: Fellowship.
Value: US$1,000 per month.
Length of Study: One-three months.
Frequency: Annual.
Study Establishment: The Society's Library in Worcester, Massachusetts.
No. of awards offered: At least two.
Application Procedure: Applicants must request an application packet which provides full details of the fellowships, including certain restrictions that apply for some categories. Applicants must phone or email with any enquiries and requests for application materials. Alternatively applicants must visit the website.
Closing Date: January 15th.
Funding: Private.
Contributor: Jointly funded by the Northeast Modern Language Association and AAS.
No. of awards given last year: One.
Additional Information: Further information is available on request www.americanantiquarian.org.

ACLS Frederick Burkhardt Fellowship

Subjects: All subjects supported by the AAS library.
Purpose: To support research.
Eligibility: Applicants must be recently tenured humanists selected on the basis of their scholarly qualifications, the scholarly significance

of the project and the appropriateness of the proposed study to the Society's collections.
Level of Study: Postdoctorate.
Type: Fellowship.
Value: A maximum stipend of US$65,000.
Length of Study: One year.
Frequency: Annual.
Study Establishment: The Society's Library in Worcester, Massachusetts.
Country of Study: United States of America.
Application Procedure: Applicants must request an application packet which provides full details of the fellowships, including certain restrictions that apply for some categories. Applicants must phone or email with any enquiries and requests for application materials. Alternatively applicants must visit the website, http://www.acls.org/burkguid.
Closing Date: October 2nd.
Funding: Private.
Contributor: The Andrew W Mellon Foundation and ACLS.
No. of awards given last year: Eight, 1 at AAS.
Additional Information: www.americanantiquarian.org.

American Historical Print Collectors Society Fellowship

Subjects: American prints of the eighteenth- and nineteenth-centuries.
Purpose: To support research or projects using prints as primary documentation.
Eligibility: Applicants are selected on the basis of their scholarly qualifications, the scholarly significance of the project and the appropriateness of the proposed study to the Society's collections.
Level of Study: Doctorate, Postdoctorate.
Type: Fellowship.
Value: US$1,000 monthly.
Length of Study: One month.
Frequency: Annual.
Study Establishment: The Society's Library in Worcester, Massachusetts.
Country of Study: United States of America.
Application Procedure: Applicants must request an application packet which provides full details of the fellowships, including certain restrictions that apply for some categories. Applicants must phone or email with any enquiries and requests for application materials. Alternatively applicants must visit the website.
Closing Date: January 15th.
Funding: Private.
Contributor: The American Historical Print Collectors Society and the American Antiquarian Society.
No. of awards given last year: 1.
Additional Information: www.americanantiquarian.org.

Joyce Tracy Fellowship

Subjects: Early American history and culture.
Purpose: To support research on newspapers or magazines for projects using these resources as primary documentation.
Eligibility: Applicants are selected on the basis of their scholarly qualifications, the scholarly significance to the project and the appropriateness of the proposed study to the Society's collections.
Level of Study: Doctorate, Postdoctorate.
Type: Fellowship.
Value: US$1,000 per month.
Length of Study: One-two months.
Frequency: Annual.
Study Establishment: The Society's Library in Worcester, Massachusetts.
Country of Study: United States of America.
No. of awards offered: One.
Application Procedure: Applicants must write for further information or visit the website.
Closing Date: January 15th.
Contributor: An endowment established in memory of Joyce Tracy.
No. of awards given last year: One.
Additional Information: Further information is available from the website www.americanantiquarian.org.

Kate B and Hall J Peterson Fellowships

Subjects: Early American history to 1876.

Purpose: To enable persons, who might not otherwise be able to do so, to travel to the Society in order to make use of its research facilities.

Eligibility: Open to individuals engaged in scholarly research and writing, including foreign nationals and persons at work on doctoral theses.

Level of Study: Doctorate, Postdoctorate.

Type: Fellowship.

Value: US$1,000 per month.

Length of Study: One-three months.

Frequency: Annual.

Study Establishment: The Society's Library in Worcester, Massachusetts.

Country of Study: United States of America.

No. of awards offered: 6-10.

Application Procedure: Applicants must request an application packet which provides full details of the fellowships, including certain restrictions that apply for some categories. Applicants must phone or email with any enquiries and requests for application materials. Alternatively applicants must visit the website.

Closing Date: January 15th.

Funding: Private.

Contributor: The late Hall J Peterson and his wife Kate B Peterson.

No. of awards given last year: 12.

Additional Information: Further information is available on request www.americanantiquarian.org.

Mellon Postdoctoral Research Fellowships

Subjects: All subjects.

Purpose: To provide support for residence in the Society's library.

Eligibility: Applicants are selected on the basis of their scholarly qualifications, the scholarly significance of the project and the appropriateness of the proposed study to the Society's collections.

Level of Study: Postdoctorate.

Type: Fellowship.

Value: A maximum stipend of US$40,000.

Length of Study: An academic year, 9 or 10 months in residence at the Society's Library.

Frequency: Annual.

Study Establishment: The Society's Library in Worcester, Massachusetts.

Country of Study: United States of America.

Application Procedure: Applicants must request an application packet which provides full details of the fellowships, including certain restrictions that apply for some categories. Applicants must phone or email with any enquiries and requests for application materials. Alternatively applicants must visit the website.

Closing Date: January 15th.

Contributor: The Andrew W Mellon Foundation.

No. of awards given last year: One.

Additional Information: www.americanantiquarian.org.

Reese Fellowship

Subjects: American bibliography and the history of the book in America through to 1876.

Purpose: To support research.

Eligibility: Applicants are selected on the basis of their scholarly qualifications, the scholarly significance of the project and the appropriateness of the proposed study to the Society's collections.

Level of Study: Doctorate, Postdoctorate.

Type: Fellowship.

Value: US$1,000.

Length of Study: One month.

Frequency: Annual.

Study Establishment: The Society's Library in Worcester, Massachusetts.

Country of Study: United States of America.

No. of awards offered: One.

Application Procedure: Applicants must request an application packet which provides full details of the fellowships, including certain restrictions that apply for some categories. Applicants must phone or

email with any enquiries and requests for application materials. Alternatively applicants must visit the website.

Closing Date: January 15th.

Contributor: The William Reese Company, New Haven, Connecticut.

No. of awards given last year: One.

Additional Information: www.americanantiquarian.org.

Stephen Botein Fellowship

Subjects: The history of the book in American culture to 1876.

Eligibility: Open to suitably qualified Scholars.

Level of Study: Doctorate, Postdoctorate.

Type: Fellowship.

Value: US$1,000 per month.

Length of Study: Up to two months.

Frequency: Annual.

Study Establishment: The Society's Library in Worcester, Massachusetts.

Country of Study: United States of America.

No. of awards offered: One-two.

Application Procedure: Applicants must request an application packet which provides full details of the fellowships, including certain restrictions that apply for some categories. Applicants must phone or email with any enquiries and requests for application materials. Alternatively applicants should visit the website.

Closing Date: January 15th.

Funding: Private.

Contributor: An endowment established by the family and friends of the late Mr Botein.

No. of awards given last year: Two.

Additional Information: www.americanantiquarian.org.

AMERICAN ASSOCIATION FOR CANCER RESEARCH (AACR)

615 Chestnut Street, 17th Floor, Philadelphia, PA 19106-4404, United States of America
Tel: (1) 215 440 9300
Fax: (1) 215 440 9372
Email: awards@aacr.org
www: http://www.aacr.org
Contact: Ms Sheri Ozard, Program Co-ordinator

The American Association for Cancer Research (AACR) is a scientific society of over 17,000 laboratory and clinical cancer researchers. It was founded in 1907 to facilitate communication and dissemination of knowledge among scientists and others dedicated to the cancer problem, and to foster research in cancer and related biomedical sciences. It is also dedicated to encouraging the presentation and discussion of new and important observations in the field, fostering public education, science education and training, and advancing the understanding of cancer etiology, prevention, diagnosis and treatment throughout the world.

AACR - Minority Scholar Awards in Cancer Research

Subjects: To encourage the scientific achievements of underrepresented ethnic groups in the area of cancer research.

Purpose: To recognise and support the achievements of underrepresented ethnic groups in the field of cancer research.

Eligibility: Scientists considered underrepresented in cancer research by the National Cancer Institute, i.e., African American/ Black, Alaskan Native, Hispanic American, Native American and Native Pacific Islander.

Level of Study: Doctorate, Graduate, Postdoctorate, Postgraduate, Predoctorate.

Type: Travel grant.

Value: Varies.

Length of Study: Varies.

Frequency: Annual.

Country of Study: United States of America.

Application Procedure: Contact the AACR office for further information or to receive an official application form.

Closing Date: November 7th in the preceding year.

Funding: Private.
Additional Information: Those eligible for awards are graduate and medical students, residents, clinical and postdoctoral fellows, and junior faculty, who are either engaged in cancer research or who have training and the potential to make contributions in the field.

AACR - Thomas J. Bardoo Science Education Awards for Undergraduate Students

Subjects: The education and training of the next generation of able and dedicated scientists and to facilitating and nurturing careers in cancer research or cancer-related biomedical science.
Purpose: To inspire young science students to enter the field of cancer research.
Eligibility: Applicants must be full-time, third-year undergraduates majoring in science. Awardees will be selected on the basis of their qualifications and interest in research references from their mentors, and the selection committee's evaluation of the potential professional benefit of the award to the candidates.
Type: Waiver of registration fee and a stipend.
Value: From US$1,500.
Length of Study: Two years.
Frequency: Annual.
Study Establishment: Any establishment appropriate for full time, third year undergraduates majoring in science.
Country of Study: United States of America.
Application Procedure: Applicants must have submitted an abstract for presentation at AACR annual meeting and must submit the official award application.
Closing Date: December 5th of year preceding.
Funding: Private.

AACR Career Development Awards in Cancer Research

Subjects: Cancer research.
Purpose: To support cancer research by junior faculty.
Eligibility: Open to junior faculty. Candidates must have completed productive postdoctoral research and demonstrated independent, instigator initiated research. Employees of national government or private industry are not eligible.
Level of Study: Postdoctorate, Research.
Type: Grant.
Value: US$50,000 per year.
Length of Study: Two years.
Frequency: Annual.
Study Establishment: Universities or research institutions.
Country of Study: Any country.
No. of awards offered: Varies.
Application Procedure: Applicants must be nominated by a member of AACR and must be an AACR member or applying for membership by the time the application is submitted. Associate members may not be nominators. Application forms can be downloaded from AACR website.
Closing Date: Fall of each year.
Funding: Private.
Contributor: The Cancer Research and Prevention Foundation, the Susan G Komen Breast Cancer Foundation, Genentech Inc and the Pancreatic Cancer Action Network.
No. of awards given last year: Six.
No. of applicants last year: 75.
Additional Information: For further information, please contact the organisation or refer to the website.

AACR Gertrude B Elion Cancer Research Award

Subjects: Cancer research.
Purpose: To foster meritorious basic, clinical or translational cancer research.
Eligibility: Open to tenure tracked scientists at the level of assistant professor at an institution worldwide, who have completed their postdoctoral studies or clinical research by July 1st of the award year, and ordinarily not more than five years earlier. Candidates must be

members of the AACR or apply for membership by the time the applications are submitted.
Level of Study: Postdoctorate, Research.
Type: Research grant.
Value: US$50,000.
Length of Study: One year.
Frequency: Annual.
Study Establishment: Universities or research institutions.
Country of Study: Any country.
No. of awards offered: One.
Application Procedure: Applicants must be nominated by a member of the AACR. Application forms can be downloaded from the website.
Closing Date: Varies, but is usually Fall of each year.
Funding: Private.
Contributor: GlaxoSmithKline.
No. of awards given last year: One.
No. of applicants last year: 25.
Additional Information: For further information please contact the organisation or refer to the website.

AACR Minority Serving Institutions Faculty Award in Cancer Research

Subjects: Cancer research.
Purpose: To increase the scientific knowledge base of faculty members at minority-serving institutions, and to encourage them and their students to pursue careers in the field.
Eligibility: Open to scientists at the level of assistant professor or above at an HBCU who are engaged in meritorious basic, clinical or translatorial cancer research. Candidates must be citizens of the United States or Canada, or permanent residents of these countries.
Level of Study: Postdoctorate.
Type: Travel grant.
Value: US$1,800.
Length of Study: Varies.
Frequency: Annual.
Study Establishment: AACR conferences.
Country of Study: United States of America.
No. of awards offered: Varies.
Application Procedure: Applicants must submit an application which includes the candidate's curriculum vitae, a list of publications, a statement from the candidate describing the benefits he or she expects to derive from attending the conference and at least one letter of reference.
Closing Date: Abstracts must be submitted by November 7th in preceding year. Please refer to website for application details, which may vary from year to year.
Funding: Private.
Additional Information: For further information about this award programme please contact Robin E Felder, Manager of Membership and Constituency Programs at the AACR office, on extension 124, or via email to constituencies@aacr.org.

AACR Research Fellowships

Subjects: Cancer research.
Purpose: To foster meritorious cancer research.
Eligibility: Candidates must have completed a PhD or other doctoral degree and currently be a postdoctoral or clinical research Fellow. Academic faculty holding the rank of assistant professor or higher, graduates and medical students, medical residents, permanent government employees and employees of private industry are not eligible.
Level of Study: Postdoctorate.
Type: A variable number of fellowships.
Value: US$30,000 per year.
Length of Study: One, two and three year fellowships.
Frequency: Annual.
Study Establishment: Universities or research institutions.
Country of Study: Any country.
No. of awards offered: Varies.
Application Procedure: Applicants must be nominated by a member of the AACR or apply for membership by the time the application is

submitted. Application forms can be accessed from the AACR website.

Closing Date: Varies but is usually fall of each year.
Funding: Private.
Contributor: Amgen, Inc., Astra Zeneca, Bristol-Myers Squibb Oncology and the Cancer Research and Prevention Foundation, Weinstein Foundation, William S. Graham Foundation for Melanoma Research.
No. of awards given last year: Seven.
No. of applicants last year: 125.
Additional Information: For further information, please contact the organisation or refer to the website.

AACR Scholar-in-Training Awards

Subjects: Cancer research.
Purpose: To allow individuals to attend the AACR Annual Meeting and Special Conference.
Eligibility: Open to first authors of an abstract submitted for presentation at the AACR Annual Meeting or Special Conference. Eligible candidates are graduate students, medical students and residents, clinical fellows or equivalent and postdoctoral fellows.
Level of Study: Doctorate, Graduate, Postdoctorate, Postgraduate, Predoctorate.
Type: Travel grant.
Value: US$400-2,000.
Frequency: Annual.
No. of awards offered: Varies.
Application Procedure: No application is needed. Qualified persons who want to be considered should follow the instructions included in the abstract submission materials for the AACR Annual Meetings or Special Conference. If a candidate is eligible based on the above criteria, a certification form confirming his or her status will be requested at a later date.
Closing Date: Varies, please contact AACR for details.
Funding: Private.
Contributor: AFLAC, Incorporated AstraZeneca, Aventis, Bristol-Myers Squibb Oncology, Genentech, GlaxoSmithKline, ILEX, ITO EN Limited, Novartis Pharmaceuticals, the Avon Foundation, Inglenook Vineyards, Susan Co. Komen Breast Cancer Foundation, Pezcoller Foundation.
No. of awards given last year: Approx. 400.
No. of applicants last year: Approx. 2,000.

AACR Women in Cancer Research Brigid G Leventhal Scholar Awards

Subjects: Cancer research.
Purpose: To enhance the education and training of early cancer scientists by providing financial support for their participation in the AACR meeting.
Eligibility: Candidates must be women in cancer Research members. Candidates must be full time scientists in training who are graduate students, medical students, residents, clinical fellows or equivalent or post doctoral fellows. Candidates must be first authors on abstracts submitted for consideration for presentation at the AACR meeting.
Level of Study: Doctorate, Postgraduate, Predoctorate.
Type: Travel grant.
Value: Travel costs and a subsistence allowance.
Length of Study: Varies.
Frequency: Annual.
Study Establishment: The AACR Annual Meeting.
Country of Study: United States of America.
No. of awards offered: Varies.
Application Procedure: Applicants must have submitted an abstract for presentation at AACR Annual Meeting and must submit the official award application.
Closing Date: December 5th in the year preceding.
Funding: Private.
Additional Information: For further information about this award programme, please contact Robin E Felder, Manager of Membership and Constituencies, at the AACR office, extension 124 or via email to felder@aacr.org.

AMERICAN ASSOCIATION FOR DENTAL RESEARCH (AADR)

1619 Duke Street, Alexandria, VA 22314-3406, United States of America
Tel: (1) 703 299 8094
Fax: (1) 703 548 1883
Email: erika@iadr.org
www: http://www.dentalresearch.org
Contact: Ms Erika Lopez-Tello, Meetings/Awards Co-ordinator

The American Association for Dental Research (AADR) plans and organises research meetings where dentists and dental scientists come together to share cutting edge research. The Association also publishes research journals.

AADR Student Research Fellowships

Subjects: Oral health.
Purpose: To encourage dental students to consider careers in the field.
Eligibility: Open to students enrolled in an accredited DDS, DMD or hygiene programme at a dental or health associated institution based within the United States of America. Applicants must be sponsored by a faculty member at that institution and should not have received their degree, nor should they be due to receive their degree, in the year of the award. Applicants may have an advanced degree in a basic science subject.
Level of Study: Postgraduate.
Type: Fellowship.
Value: US$2,100 plus US$300 for supplies.
Length of Study: Two years.
Frequency: Annual.
Country of Study: United States of America.
No. of awards offered: Varies.
Application Procedure: Applicants must submit a research proposal. Application guidelines are available on request.
Closing Date: January 15th.
Contributor: Dental product companies, pharmaceutical companies and AADR members.
No. of awards given last year: 23.
No. of applicants last year: 52.
Additional Information: Recipients will present their research at the AADR meeting by submitting abstracts for poster or oral presentations.

AMERICAN ASSOCIATION FOR RESPIRATORY CARE

9425 N. MacArthur Blvd, Suite 100, Irving, TX 75063-4706, United States of America
Tel: (1) 972 243 2272
Fax: (1) 972 484 2720
Email: info@aarc.org
www: http://www.aarc.org
Contact: Administrative Assistant

The American Respiratory Care Foundation is dedicated to the art, science, quality and technology of respiratory care. It is a non-profit organisation formed for the purpose of supporting research, education and charitable activities and to promote prevention, quality treatment and management of respiratory related diseases.

NBRC/AMP Gareth B Gish, MS RRT Memorial Postgraduate Recognition Award

Subjects: Respiratory care and prevention.
Purpose: To assist qualified individuals in the pursuit of training leading to an advanced degree.
Eligibility: Open to professional respiratory therapists who have at least a Baccalaureate degree with a 3.0 cumulative grade point average or better on a 4.0 scale or equivalent. Candidates must be able to provide proof of acceptance into an advanced degree programme of

a fully accredited school and proof that the applicant is a candidate for degree.
Level of Study: Postgraduate, Professional development.
Type: Award.
Value: Up to $1,500 plus airfare, a certificate of recognition, one night's lodging and registration for the AARC International Respiratory Congress.
Frequency: Annual.
Country of Study: United States of America.
No. of awards offered: One.
Application Procedure: Applicants must return a completed, signed and notarised application form, provide three letters of reference attesting to the applicant's character, academic ability and professional commitment, and supply an essay of at least 1,200 words. This must describe how the award will assist the applicant in reaching the objective of an advanced degree and the candidate's ultimate goals of leadership in healthcare. Application forms can be downloaded and printed out from the website.
Closing Date: May 31st.

Parker B Francis Respiratory Research Grant

Subjects: Respiratory care and related topics.
Purpose: To provide financial assistance for research programmes.
Eligibility: Open to qualified investigators in the field of respiratory care. The principal investigator may be a physician or respiratory therapist. However, a respiratory therapist must be the co-principal investigator if a physician is the principal applicant for the award.
Level of Study: Professional development.
Type: Research grant.
Value: The award is at the discretion of the Board of Trustees and is dependent on the quality of the proposal.
Frequency: Annual.
Country of Study: United States of America.
Application Procedure: Applicants must apply directly to the Foundation Executive Office. Complete details can be found in the Application for Research Grant packet available from the Foundation.
Funding: Private.
Contributor: Parker B Francis Foundation.
Additional Information: In 1993, the Parker B Francis Foundation provided an endowment to the American Respiratory Care Foundation to make funds available to provide financial assistance for research programmes.

William F Miller, MD Postgraduate Education Recognition Award

Subjects: Respiratory care and prevention.
Purpose: To assist a professional therapist pursuing postgraduate education which will lead to an advanced degree.
Eligibility: Open to professional respiratory therapists who have at least a Baccalaureate degree with a 3.0 cumulative grade point average or better on a 4.0 scale or equivalent. Candidates must be able to provide proof of acceptance into an advanced degree programme of a fully accredited school and proof that the applicant is a candidate for degree.
Level of Study: Postgraduate, Professional development.
Type: Research grant.
Value: Up to US$1,500 plus airfare, certificate of recognition, one night lodging and registration to the International AARC Respiratory Congress.
Frequency: Annual.
Country of Study: United States of America.
No. of awards offered: One.
Application Procedure: Applicants must return a completed, signed and notarised application form, provide three letters of reference attesting to the applicant's character, academic ability and professional commitment and supply an essay of at least 1,200 words. This must describe how the award will assist the applicant in reaching the objective of an advanced degree and the candidate's ultimate goals of leadership in healthcare.
Closing Date: May 31st.
Funding: Private.

AMERICAN ASSOCIATION FOR THE HISTORY OF NURSING (AAHN)

PO Box 175, Lanoka Harbor, NJ 08734
United States of America
Tel: (1) 609 693 7250
Fax: (1) 609 693 1037
Email: aahn@aahn.org
www: http://www.aahn.org
Contact: Executive Secretary

The American Association for the History of Nursing (AAHN) is a professional organisation accessible to everyone interested in the history of nursing. Originally founded in 1978 as a historical methodology group, the Association was briefly named the International History of Nursing Society. The Association's purpose is to foster the importance of history in understanding the present and guiding the future of nursing.

AAHN Student Research Award

Subjects: The history of nursing.
Purpose: To support research.
Eligibility: Open to students enrolled in an accredited Master's or doctoral programme who are members of the AAHN. Selection criteria include the scholarly merit of the proposal, consideration of the student's preparation for this study, the advisor's qualification for guiding the study and the project's potential for contributing to scholarship in the field of nursing history. If the study involves sources requiring approval by an institutional review board protecting human subjects, funds will not be awarded until documentation is received.
Level of Study: Doctorate.
Type: Grant.
Value: US$1,000 + Conference registration & travel.
Frequency: Annual.
No. of awards offered: Dependent on submissions.
Application Procedure: Applicants must submit four copies of a proposal which should include a title page, narrative, objectives of research, significant background information on the research, primary source availability, methods to be used, facilities to be used and a curriculum vitae. The address to which applications should be sent changes each year and applicants should check the website for the correct address.
Closing Date: May 15th.
Funding: Private.
No. of awards given last year: 2.
No. of applicants last year: 2.

For further information contact:

See brochure or website.

Post doctoral award to honor Cadet Nurse Corps

Subjects: The history of nursing.
Purpose: To support research at post doctoral level.
Eligibility: Open to members of the AAHN with a doctoral degree.
Level of Study: Postdoctorate.
Value: US$2,000 + Conference registration.
Frequency: Annual.
No. of awards offered: 1.
Application Procedure: Applicants must submit four copies of a proposal, of no more than five pages, which should include a title page, narrative, objects of research, significant background information on the research, primary source availability, methods to be used, facilities to be used and a curriculum vitae. The address to send application material changes each year so candidates should visit the website for an updated address and further details.
Closing Date: May 15th.
Funding: Private.
No. of awards given last year: 3.
No. of applicants last year: 3.

For further information contact:

Please see website

AMERICAN ASSOCIATION FOR WOMEN RADIOLOGISTS (AAWR)

820 Jorie Boulevard, Oak Brook, IL 60523, United States of America
Tel: (1) 630 590 7712
Fax: (1) 630 571 7837
Email: admin@aawr.org
www: http://www.aawr.org
Contact: AAWR Account Manager

Alice Ettinger Distinguished Achievement Award
Subjects: Radiology.
Purpose: To recognise outstanding residents on the basis of contributions to clinical care, teaching, research or public service.
Eligibility: Open to residents in the field of radiation oncology who are members of the AAWR as of January 1st of the year of the award.
Level of Study: Unrestricted.
Type: Award.
Frequency: Annual.
Country of Study: Any country.
No. of awards offered: One.
Application Procedure: Applicants must submit an application including a nominating letter from the residency director, a letter of concurrence from the department chair, a curriculum vitae and a personal statement.
Closing Date: July 1st.
Funding: Private.
Contributor: Membership dues.
Additional Information: Expenses to accept the award will be provided to the winner.

Eleanor Montague Distinguished Resident Award in Radiation Oncology
Subjects: Radiation oncology.
Purpose: To honour a resident radiation oncologist on the basis of outstanding contributions to clinical care, teaching, research and/or public service.
Eligibility: Open to residents in the field who are members of the AAWR as of January 1st of the year of the award.
Level of Study: Unrestricted.
Value: US$500 and reimbursement of expenses including travel and lodging per diem.
Frequency: Annual.
Country of Study: Any country.
No. of awards offered: One.
Application Procedure: Applicants must submit an application including a letter of nomination, a letter of concurrence and a curriculum vitae.
Closing Date: July 1st.
Funding: Private.

Lucy Frank Squire Distinguished Resident Award in Diagnostic Radiology
Subjects: Radiology.
Purpose: To honour a resident diagnostic radiologist on the basis of outstanding contributions to clinical care, teaching, research and/or public service.
Eligibility: Open to residents in the field of diagnostic radiology who are members of the AAWR as of January 1st of the year of the award.
Level of Study: Unrestricted.
Value: US$500 and reimbursement of expenses including travel and lodging per diem.
Frequency: Annual.
Country of Study: Any country.
No. of awards offered: One.
Application Procedure: Applicants must submit an application including a curriculum vitae, a letter of nomination and a letter of concurrence.
Closing Date: July 1st.
Funding: Private.
Contributor: Membership dues.

Marie Curie Award
Subjects: Radiology.
Purpose: To honour an individual who has made an outstanding contribution to the field.
Eligibility: There are no nationality restrictions and nominees need not be members of the AAWR.
Level of Study: Unrestricted.
Type: Award.
Frequency: Annual.
Country of Study: Any country.
No. of awards offered: One.
Application Procedure: Applicants must submit an application including a letter of nomination, at least one letter of support and a curriculum vitae.
Closing Date: July 1st.
Funding: Private.
Contributor: Membership dues.
Additional Information: Expenses to accept the award will be provided to the winner.

AMERICAN ASSOCIATION OF CRITICAL-CARE NURSES (AACN)

101 Columbia, Aliso Viejo, CA 92656-1491
United States of America
Tel: (1) 800 899 2226
Fax: (1) 949 362 2020
Email: info@aacn.org
www: http://www.aacn.org
Contact: Research Department

The American Association of Critical-Care Nurses (AACN) is the world's largest nursing speciality organisation with approximately 68,000 members worldwide. The AACN is committed to providing the highest quality resources to maximise nurses' contributions to caring and improving the healthcare of critically ill patients and their families.

AACN - Datex Ohmeda Grant
Subjects: Nutritional assessment in the critically ill patient.
Purpose: To provide research support for a study to be conducted by a critical care nurse.
Eligibility: Principal investigators must be nurses holding current AACN membership. Investigators who have received funding from the AACN are ineligible to receive additional funding during the lifetime of their original award. They may apply for a new award when their original award obligations have been met. Research conducted in fulfilment of an academic degree is acceptable.
Type: Grant.
Value: Up to US$5,000.
Application Procedure: Applicants must submit completed application materials and proposals. Details are available directly from the organisation or from the website.
Closing Date: February 1st.

AACN Certification Corporation Research Grant
Subjects: Certified practice including, but not limited to, studies focusing on continued competency, the Synergy Model, the value of certification as it relates to patient care and/or nursing practice, and credentialing concepts.
Purpose: To fund research.
Eligibility: Applicants need not be members of the AACN. The proposed research may be used to meet the requirements of an academic degree.
Value: Up to US$10,000.
No. of awards offered: Up to four.
Application Procedure: Applicants must submit completed application materials and proposals. Details are available directly from the organisation or from the website.
Closing Date: February 1st.
Additional Information: For more information regarding AACN Certification Corporation and the Synergy Model, visit the website http://www.certcorp.org.

AACN Clinical Practice Grant

Subjects: The AACN clinical research properties.
Purpose: To support research.
Eligibility: Principal investigators must be nurses holding current AACN membership. Investigators who have received funding from the AACN are ineligible to receive additional funding during the lifetime of their original award. They may apply for a new award when their original award obligations have been met. Research conducted in fulfilment of an academic degree is acceptable.
Level of Study: Research.
Type: Grant.
Value: Up to US$6,000.
Frequency: Annual.
No. of awards offered: Varies.
Application Procedure: Applicants must submit completed application materials and proposals. Details are available directly from the organisation or from the website.
Closing Date: October 1st.

AACN Critical Care Grant

Subjects: Critical care nursing practice.
Purpose: To fund research.
Eligibility: Principal investigators must be nurses holding current AACN membership. Investigators who have received funding from the AACN are ineligible to receive additional funding during the lifetime of their original award. They may apply for a new award when their original award obligations have been met. The proposed research may not be used to meet the requirements of an academic degree.
Level of Study: Research.
Type: Research grant.
Value: Up to US$15,000.
Frequency: Annual.
No. of awards offered: Varies.
Application Procedure: Applicants must submit completed application materials and a proposal. Details and forms are available directly from the organisation or from the website.
Closing Date: February 1st.

AACN Mentorship Grant

Subjects: Clinical research.
Purpose: To provide research support for a novice researcher with limited or no research experience working under the direction of a mentor.
Eligibility: Principal investigators must be nurses holding current AACN membership. Investigators who have received funding from the AACN are ineligible to receive additional funding during the lifetime of their original award. They may apply for a new award when their original award obligations have been met. The novice researcher may be conducting the research to meet the requirements for an academic degree but the mentor may not. The mentor must show strong evidence of research and expertise in the proposed area. The mentor may not be a mentor on another AACN Mentorship Grant in two consecutive years.
Level of Study: Research.
Type: Grant.
Value: Up to US$10,000.
Frequency: Annual.
No. of awards offered: Varies.
Application Procedure: Applicants must submit completed application materials and a proposal. Details and forms are available directly from the organisation or from the website.
Closing Date: February 1st.
Additional Information: The novice researcher will be the principal investigator and will receive the award.

AACN Sigma Theta Tau Critical Care Grant

Subjects: Critical care nursing.
Purpose: To fund research.
Eligibility: Applicants must either a member of Sigma Theta Tau or AACN.
Level of Study: Research.
Type: Grant.
Value: US$10,000.

Frequency: Annual.
No. of awards offered: Varies.
Application Procedure: Applicants must submit completed application materials and a proposal. Details are available directly from the organisation or from the website.
Closing Date: October 1st.
Contributor: Co-sponsored by the AACN and Sigma Theta Tau International.

American Nurses Foundation Research Grant

Subjects: Clinical research.
Purpose: To encourage the research career development of nurses.
Eligibility: Principal investigators must be nurses holding current AACN membership. Investigators who have received funding from the AACN are ineligible to receive additional funding during the lifetime of their original award. They may apply for a new award when their original award obligations have been met.
Level of Study: Research.
Type: Research grant.
Value: Up to US$5,000 is awarded by the American Nurses Foundation.
No. of awards offered: Varies.
Application Procedure: Applicants must obtain information and application forms from the American Nurses Foundation, and should see the website for further details.
Closing Date: May 1st.
Contributor: The AACN.

For further information contact:

The American Nurses Foundation/NRG00600 Maryland Avenue SWSuite 100W, Washington, DC 20024-2571, United States of America
Tel: (1) 202 651 7298
Email: anf@ana.org
www: http://www.nursingworld.org/anf

AMERICAN ASSOCIATION OF LAW LIBRARIES (AALL)

Scholarship Committee, Suite 940, 53 West Jackson Boulevard, Chicago, IL 60604, United States of America
Tel: (1) 312 939 4764
Fax: (1) 312 431 1097
Email: aallhq@aall.org
www: http://www.aallnet.org

The American Association of Law Libraries (AALL) was founded in 1906 to promote and enhance the value of law libraries to legal and public communities, to foster the profession of law librarianship, and to provide leadership in the field of legal information. Today the AALL represents law librarians and related professionals who are affiliated with a wide range of institutions including law firms, law schools, corporate legal departments and courts, and local, state and federal government agencies.

AALL and West George A Strait Minority Scholarship Endowment

Subjects: Law librarianship.
Eligibility: Open to degree candidates in an accredited library or law school. Preference is given to individuals with previous service to, or interest in, law librarianship and who intend to have a career in law librarianship. Applicants must be members of a minority group as defined by the current United States of America government guidelines.
Level of Study: Graduate.
Type: Scholarship.
Value: Up to US$3,500 for tuition and school related expenses.
Frequency: Annual.
Study Establishment: Accredited library schools or accredited law schools.
Country of Study: Any country.
No. of awards offered: Varies.

Application Procedure: Applicants must write for details or download an application form from the website.
Closing Date: April 1st.

James F. Connolly Lexisnexis Academic and Library Solutions Scholarship

Subjects: Law librarianship.
Eligibility: Awarded to library school graduates with law library experience who are presently attending an accredited law school with the intention of having a career as a law librarian. Preference will be given to individuals who have demonstrated an interest in government documents.
Level of Study: Graduate.
Type: Scholarship.
Value: Up to US$2,000 for tuition and school related expenses.
Frequency: Annual.
Study Establishment: ABA - Accredited Law Schools.
Country of Study: Any country.
No. of awards offered: Varies.
Application Procedure: Applicants must write for details or download an application form from the web site.
Closing Date: April 1st.

Law Librarians in Continuing Education Courses (Type V)

Subjects: Law librarianship.
Purpose: To assist Law Librarians who are registrants in continuing education courses.
Eligibility: Open to members of the AALL. Preference is given to permanent residents of the United States of America and Canada. Applicants must have a degree from an accredited library or law school and be registrants in continuing education courses related to law librarianship.
Level of Study: Postgraduate, Professional development.
Type: Scholarship.
Value: Up to US$500 for tuition.
Frequency: Three times each year.
Country of Study: Any country.
No. of awards offered: Varies.
Application Procedure: Applicants must write for details or download an application form from the website.
Closing Date: April 1st, October 1st or February 1st.
Funding: Private.

LexisNexis/John R. Johnson Memorial Scholarship Endowment

Subjects: Law librarianship.
Eligibility: Candidates who apply for AALL educational scholarships, type I-IV, become automatically eligible to receive the LexisNexis/John R. Johnson Memorial Scholarship. No separate application is needed.
Level of Study: Graduate.
Type: Scholarship.
Value: Up to US$2,000 for tuition and school related expenses.
Frequency: Annual.
Study Establishment: ALA - Accredited library schools or ABA - Accredited Law Schools.
Country of Study: Any country.
No. of awards offered: Varies.
Application Procedure: Applicants must writed for details or download an application form from the web site.
Closing Date: April 1st.

Library Degree for Law School Graduates (Type I)

Subjects: Law librarianship.
Eligibility: Open to law graduates who have the intention of following a career as a law librarian and who are candidates for a library degree in an accepted library school. Preference is given to all members and persons with meaningful law library experience. Evidence of financial need must be submitted.
Level of Study: Graduate.
Type: Scholarship.
Value: Up to US$2,000 for tuition and school related expenses.

Frequency: Annual.
Study Establishment: ALA - Accredited library schools.
Country of Study: Any country.
No. of awards offered: Varies.
Application Procedure: Applicants must write for details or download an application form from the web site.
Closing Date: April 1st.

Library Degree for Non-Law School Graduates (Type III)

Subjects: Law librarianship.
Purpose: To assist persons with meaningful law library experience.
Eligibility: Open to degree graduates who hold an award from an accredited library school. The candidate should have the intention of following a career path as a law librarian. Preference is given to applicants working for degrees with an emphasis on courses in law librarianship.
Level of Study: Graduate.
Type: Scholarship.
Value: Up to US$2,000 for tuition and school related expenses.
Frequency: Annual.
Study Establishment: ALA - Accredited library schools.
Country of Study: Any country.
No. of awards offered: Varies.
Application Procedure: Applicants must write for details or download an application form from the website.
Closing Date: April 1st.

Library School Graduates Attending Law School (Type II)

Subjects: Law.
Eligibility: Open to library school graduates working towards a degree in an accredited law school who have no more than 36 semester credit hours remaining before qualifying for the law degree, who have law library experience and who have the intention of having a career as a law librarian. Preference is given to members of the AALL.
Level of Study: Graduate.
Value: Up to US$2,000 for tuition and school related expenses.
Frequency: Annual.
Study Establishment: ABA - Accredited law schools.
Country of Study: Any country.
No. of awards offered: Varies.
Application Procedure: Applicants must write for details or download an application form from the website.
Closing Date: April 1st.

Library School Graduates seeking a Non-Law Degree (Type IV)

Subjects: Law librarianship.
Eligibility: Awarded to library school graduates who are degree candidates in an area, other than law, that will be beneficial to the development of a professional career in law librarianship and who intend to have a career as a law librarian. Scholarship restricted to members of AALL. Evidence of financial need must be submitted.
Level of Study: Graduate.
Type: Scholarship.
Value: Up to US$2,000 for tuition and school related expenses.
Frequency: Annual.
Country of Study: Any country.
No. of awards offered: Varies.
Application Procedure: Applicants must write for details or download an application form from the web site.
Closing Date: April 1st.

AMERICAN ASSOCIATION OF NEUROLOGICAL SURGEONS (AANS)

5550 Meadowbrook Drive, Rolling Meadows, IL 60008, United States of America
Tel: (1) 847 378 0500
Fax: (1) 847 378 0600
Email: info@aans.org
www: www.aans.org
Contact: Laurie Singer

Founded in 1931 as the Harvey Cushing Society, the American Association of Neurological Surgeons (AANS) is a scientific and educational association with more than 6,500 members worldwide. The AANS is dedicated to advancing the speciality of neurological surgery in order to provide the highest quality of neurosurgical care to the public. All active members of the AANS are certified by the American Board of Neurological surgery, The Royal College of Physicians and Surgeons (Neurosurgery) of Canada or the Mexican Council of Neurological Surgery, AC. Neurological surgery is the medical speciality concerned with the prevention, diagnosis, treatment and rehabilitation of disorders that affect the entire nervous system including the spinal column, spinal cord, brain and peripheral nerves.

NREF Research Fellowship

Subjects: Any field of neurosurgery.
Purpose: To provide training for neurosurgeons who are preparing for academic careers as clinician investigators.
Eligibility: Open to MDs who have been accepted into, or who are in, an approved residency training programmes in neurological surgery in North America.
Level of Study: Postdoctorate.
Type: Fellowship.
Value: US$40,000 for a one year fellowship and US$70,000 for a two year fellowship.
Length of Study: One-two years.
Frequency: Annual.
Country of Study: Other.
Application Procedure: Applicants must send a completed application, sponsor statement, programme director comments and letters of recommendation. Responses to questions 1-9, a curriculum vitae and photographic images must also be submitted. Applications available at www.aans.org.
Closing Date: October 31st.
Funding: Private.
Contributor: Corporations and membership.
No. of awards given last year: Five.
No. of applicants last year: 25.
Additional Information: Notification of awards will be made by February 28th. After notification of the award, the applicant must indicate acceptance, in writing, no later than April 1st. If unwilling to accept the award by that date, funds will be awarded to the first runner-up. A report of findings and accounting of funds will be expected at the halfway point and upon completion of the fellowship. Normally, no more than one award per year will be made to any one institution. Individuals who accept a grant from another source, NIH or private, for the same research project will become ineligible for the award. A budget must be prepared by the applicant and the sponsor indicating how the grant funds will be expended. It is the policy of the NREF to fund only direct costs involved with the research awards. This means no fringe benefits, publication costs or travel expenses. The signature representing the applicant's institution's financial officer on page four should be that of their chief financial officer or grants and contracts manager. The award will be made payable to the institution and disbursed by it according to its institutional policy.

NREF Young Clinician Investigator Award

Subjects: Any field of neurosurgery.
Purpose: To fund pilot studies that provide preliminary data used to strengthen applications for more permanent funding from other sources.
Eligibility: Applicants must be neurosurgeons who are full-time faculty in teaching institutions in North America and in the early years of their careers.
Level of Study: Postdoctorate.
Type: Fellowship.
Value: US$40,000.
Length of Study: One year.
Frequency: Annual.
Country of Study: Other.
Application Procedure: Applicants must send a completed application, sponsor statement, programme director comments and letters of recommendation. Responses to questions 1-9, a curriculum vitae and photographic images must also be submitted. Applications available at www.aans.org.
Closing Date: October 31st.
Funding: Private.
Contributor: Corporations and membership.
No. of awards given last year: Three.
No. of applicants last year: 20.
Additional Information: Notification of awards will be made by February 28th. After notification of the award, the applicant must indicate acceptance, in writing, no later than April 1st. If unwilling to accept the award by that date, funds will be awarded to the first runner-up. A summary report and an accounting of funds will be expected upon completion of the award. Normally, no more than one award per year will be made to any one institution. Individuals who accept a grant from another source, NIH or private, for the same research project will become ineligible for the award. The award is for those budget items necessary to pursue proper research. It may be used entirely, or in part, for stipend. A budget must be prepared by the applicant and sponsor indicating how the award funds will be expended. It is the policy of the NREF to fund only direct costs involved with the research awards. This means no fringe benefits, publication costs or travel expenses.

William P. VanWagenen Fellowship

Subjects: Any field on Neurosurgery.
Purpose: To fund quality research in which the plan for a period abroad has been designed, personal attributes and the quality of the research environment.
Eligibility: All senior Neurological residents in approved Neurosurgery residency programs.
Level of Study: Postdoctorate.
Type: Traveling fellowship.
Value: US$45,000.
Length of Study: 6 to 12 months.
Frequency: Annual.
Country of Study: Country of study must be different than the country of residence.
No. of awards offered: 1.
Application Procedure: Application should be submitted with letters of reference, including one from the applicant's Program Director. A letter from the proposed sponsor and documentation of intent to pursue an academic career, while not required, will strengthen the application.
Closing Date: October 1st.
Funding: Private.
Contributor: William P. VanWagenen.
No. of awards given last year: 1.
No. of applicants last year: 6.
Additional Information: By December 31st, the Chairman of the Van Wagenen Selection Committee will notify the winning applicant, who will be expected to implement the fellowship within six months following notification. A formal announcement of the award will be made at the Annual Meeting of the American Association of Neurological Surgeons.Applications and additional information regarding the William P. Van Wagenen Fellowship can be located at www.aans.org.

THE AMERICAN ASSOCIATION OF PETROLEUM GEOLOGISTS (AAPG) FOUNDATION

125 West 15th Street, Tulsa, OK 74119, United States of America
Tel: (1) 918 560 2644
Fax: (1) 918 560 2642
Email: gia@aapg.org
www: http://www.aapg.org/foundation/gia/forms.html
Contact: Ms Rebecca Griffin, Grants Co-ordinator

Established by the American Association of Petroleum Geologists (AAPG) in 1967, the AAPG Foundation is a public foundation, qualified to receive gifts which are tax deductible to United States taxpayers, in support of worthwhile educational and scientific programmes or projects related to the geosciences.

American Association of Petroleum Geologists Foundation Grants-in-Aid

Subjects: Earth and geological sciences.

Purpose: To support students whose research can be applied to the search for, and development of, petroleum and energy-minerals resources, and to related environmental geology issues.

Eligibility: Open to graduate and doctorate students of any nationality.

Level of Study: Doctorate, Graduate.

Type: Grant.

Value: A maximum of US$2,000.

Frequency: Annual, Dependent on funds available.

Country of Study: Any country.

No. of awards offered: Varies.

Application Procedure: Applicants must complete an application form and submit certified college academic transcripts or signed statements from professors commenting on the applicant's academic credentials and endorsements.

Closing Date: January 31st.

Funding: Private.

No. of awards given last year: 97.

No. of applicants last year: 315.

Additional Information: Grants are to be applied to expenses directly related to the student's thesis work, such as Summer field work, analytical analyses etc. Funds are not to be used to purchase capital equipment, or to pay salaries, tuition or room and board during the school year.

AMERICAN BAR FOUNDATION (ABF)

750 North Lake Shore Drive, Chicago, IL 60611, United States of America
Tel: (1) 312 988 6580
Fax: (1) 312 988 6579
Email: fellowships@abfn.org
www: http://www.abf-sociolegal.org
Contact: Erin Eckhoff

The American Bar Foundation (ABF) is an independent research institute and has an interdisciplinary staff of research fellows trained in law, sociology, psychology, political science, economics, anthropology and history. Current research areas include professionalism and the transformation of the legal profession in the United States of America and abroad, the impact of civil rights on the economic progress of minorities, hate speech and its regulation, the influence of family and environmental factors on juvenile delinquency, the impact of public policy on the spread of the Internet, jury decision making, historical analyses of labour and regulatory law, public interest lawyering, social reform and sentencing judgement, and the effect of victim impact evidence.

ABF Fellowships in Law and Social Science

Subjects: Socio-legal studies or social scientific approaches to law, the legal profession or legal institutions.

Purpose: To encourage original and significant research in law, the legal profession and legal institutions.

Eligibility: Applications are invited from outstanding students who are candidates for PhD degrees in the social sciences, or have completed their PhD within the past two years. The research must address significant issues in the field and show promise of a major contribution to social scientific understanding of law and legal processes. Applicants must, at minimum, have been admitted to a candidacy for a PhD before the commencement of the fellowship. In exceptional circumstances, candidates with a JD who have substantial social science training may also be considered. Minority applicants are especially encouraged to apply.

Level of Study: Doctorate, Postdoctorate.

Type: Other.

Value: US$30,000.

Frequency: Annual.

Study Establishment: The ABF.

Country of Study: United States of America.

No. of awards offered: Varies, but usually two to three.

Application Procedure: Applications must include a letter of application, a statement describing research interests, achievements to date, plans for the fellowship period, two letters of reference, a curriculum vitae, a transcript of graduate records and a sample of written work eg. a conference paper, dissertation chapter or published article. PhD candidates should include a copy of their dissertation proposal.

Closing Date: February 1st.

Funding: Private.

No. of awards given last year: Four fellowships.

No. of applicants last year: Approx. 50.

Additional Information: Further information is available on request.

AMERICAN CHEMICAL SOCIETY (ACS)

The Petroleum Research Fund (PRF), 1155 Sixteenth Street North West, Washington, DC 20036, United States of America
Tel: (1) 202 872 4481
Fax: (1) 202 872 6319
Email: prfinfo@acs.org
www: http://chemistry.org/prf
Contact: Dr Laurence Funke, Program Director

The Petroleum Research Fund (PRF) was established in 1944 by seven major oil companies. The American Chemical Society (ACS) must use the funds for advanced scientific education and fundamental research in the petroleum field, which may include any field of pure science that affords a basis for subsequent research directly connected with the petroleum field. Since the first ACS/PRF grants were approved in 1954, several grant programmes have evolved to serve segments of the scientific community. ACS/PRF does not support scholarships or scholarships. PRF funding commitments in 2002 totalled US$28 million.

ACS/PRF Scientific Education Grants

Subjects: Scientific education and fundamental research in the petroleum field.

Purpose: To provide partial funding for foreign speakers at major symposia.

Eligibility: Open to non-profit institutions throughout the United States of America and worldwide for speakers coming to conferences in the United States of America, Canada and Mexico and speaking within the PRF Trust.

Level of Study: Unrestricted.

Type: Grant.

Value: Up to US$1,200 per speaker or up to US$3,600 per symposium.

Frequency: Annual.

Country of Study: United States of America.

No. of awards offered: Varies.

Application Procedure: Applicants must use a PRF 'SE' form.

Closing Date: Applications are accepted at any time.

Funding: Private.

Contributor: A private trust.

ACS/PRF Type AC Grants

Subjects: Chemistry, the earth sciences, chemical engineering and related fields such as polymers and materials science.

Eligibility: Open to non-profit institutions in the United States of America and other countries. Grants are made in response to proposals. Recently, PRF support has been restricted to faculty holding tenure or a tenure track appointment. This is the largest PRF grant programme and usually funds proposals from graduate departments.

Level of Study: Professional development.

Type: Grant.

Value: Up to US$120,000 over three years. Most AC grants provide US$80,000 over two years. The budget may include stipends for graduate students, postdoctoral fellows, research supplies, conference travel costs, fieldwork related expenses and a US$500 annual departmental allocation. No overhead costs may be charged to the grant. Conference travel may be reimbursed up to US$2,000 per year. This limit does not apply to fieldwork related travel. Principal investigators may receive no more than US$7,500 per year in Summer salary and benefits. As PRF prefers to support people rather than purchase capital equipment, there is a limited budget for such equipment and funding will only be supplied if requested funds are matched by institutional funds.

Frequency: Annual.
Country of Study: Any country.
No. of awards offered: Varies.
Application Procedure: Applicants must use a PRF 'AC' form.
Closing Date: Applications are accepted at any time.
Funding: Private.
Contributor: A private trust.
No. of awards given last year: 201.
No. of applicants last year: 627.
Additional Information: Most grants begin on September 1st, but an earlier start can be negotiated. The PRF Advisory Board normally meets to review proposals in February, May and October. Prospective applicants should check the PRF website for current information on dates of submission and consideration.

ACS/PRF Type B Grants

Subjects: Chemistry, the earth sciences, chemical engineering and related fields such as polymers and materials science.
Eligibility: Open to non-profit institutions in the United States of America and other countries. Grants are made in response to proposals. Recently, PRF support has been restricted to faculty holding tenure or a tenure track appointment. Type B grants are restricted to departments which do not award PhDs. Grants are intended for research involving undergraduates. Graduate or postdoctoral students may not be supported by Type B funds.
Level of Study: Professional development.
Type: Grant.
Value: Up to US$50,000 which may be used to fund undergraduate student stipends, Summer faculty salary, supplies and equipment, conference travel, fieldwork and a US$500 annual departmental allocation. No overhead costs may be charged to the grant. Conference travel may be reimbursed up to US$2,000 per year. This limit does not apply to fieldwork related travel. Principal investigators may receive no more than US$7,500 per year in Summer salary and benefits. As PRF prefers to support people rather than purchase capital equipment, there is a limited budget for such equipment and funding will only be supplied if requested funds are matched by institutional funds.
Length of Study: Three years.
Frequency: Annual.
Country of Study: Any country.
No. of awards offered: Varies.
Application Procedure: Applicants must use a PRF 'B' form.
Closing Date: Applications are accepted at any time.
Funding: Private.
Contributor: A private trust.
No. of awards given last year: 50.
No. of applicants last year: 123.
Additional Information: Most grants begin on September 1st, but an earlier start can be negotiated. The PRF Advisory Board normally meets to review proposals in February, May and October. Prospective applicants should check the PRF website for information on dates of submission and consideration.

ACS/PRF Type G 'Starter' Grants

Subjects: Chemistry, the earth sciences, chemical engineering and related fields such as polymers and materials science.
Eligibility: Open to non-profit institutions in the United States of America only. Grants are made in response to proposals. These grants are intended for new faculty within the first three years of teaching and without extensive postdoctoral research experience eg. more than five years.
Level of Study: Professional development.
Type: Grant.
Value: US$35,000 over two years, which may be used to fund student stipends, faculty Summer salary, supplies and equipment, conference travel and field work costs. Travel may be reimbursed up to US$2,000 per year, though this limit does not apply to fieldwork related travel. Principal investigators may receive no more than US$7,500 per year in Summer salary and benefits. As PRF prefers to support people

rather than purchase capital equipment, there is a limited budget for such equipment and funding will only be supplied if requested funds are matched by institutional funds. No overhead costs may be charged to the grant.

Length of Study: Two years.
Frequency: Annual.
Country of Study: United States of America.
No. of awards offered: Varies.
Application Procedure: Applicants must use a PRF 'G' form.
Closing Date: Applications are accepted at any time.
Funding: Private.
Contributor: A private trust.
No. of awards given last year: 125.
No. of applicants last year: 352.
Additional Information: Most grants begin on September 1st, but an earlier start can be negotiated. The PRF Advisory Board normally meets to review proposals in February, May and October. Prospective applicants should check the PRF website for information on dates of submission and consideration. A detailed budget is not required.

AMERICAN COLLEGE OF OBSTETRICIANS AND GYNECOLOGISTS (ACOG)

409 12th Street South West
PO Box 96920, Washington
DC 20090-6920, United States of America
Tel: (1) 202 863 2577
Fax: (1) 202 554 3490
Email: lcassidy@acog.org
www: http://www.acog.org
Contact: Ms Lee Cassidy, Director of Development

The American College of Obstetricians and Gynecologists (ACOG) is a membership organisation of obstetrician gynaecologists dedicated to the advancement of women's health through education, advocacy, practice and research.

ACOG/3M Pharmaceuticals Research Awards in Lower Genital Infections

Subjects: Gynecology and obstetrics. One grant is awarded in the area of vulvar disease due to human papilomavirus (HPV). Examples may include pathogenesis, mechanisms of transmission, diagnosis, treatment, histology, immunology, and preventive measures.
Purpose: To provide seed grant funds to junior investigators for clinical research.
Eligibility: Applicants must be ACOG Junior Fellows or Fellows who are in an approved obstetrics or gynaecology residency programme, or are within three years of post residency. Applicants must be United States of America or Canadian citizens.
Level of Study: Postgraduate.
Type: Research grant.
Value: US$7,500 plus a US$1,000 travel stipend to attend the ACOG Annual Clinical Meeting.
Length of Study: One year.
Frequency: Annual.
Country of Study: United States of America or Canada.
No. of awards offered: One.
Application Procedure: Applicants must submit six copies of a proposal consisting of a hypothesis, objectives, specific aims, background and significance, and experimental design and methods. These must not exceed six type written pages in total. A curriculum vitae, letter of support from the programme director, departmental chair or laboratory director, references and a one page budget must also be submitted.
Closing Date: October 1st.
Funding: Commercial.
Contributor: 3M Pharmaceuticals.
No. of awards given last year: One.
No. of applicants last year: Five.

Additional Information: Further information can be found on the member side of the website www.acog.org.

ACOG/Berlex Laboratories Research Award in PMS/PMDD

Subjects: The basic focus of the research should include one or more of the following: effective diagnosis and treatment of PMS and PMDD and/or overall impact of PMS/PMDD on quality of life. Suggested topics include, but are not limited to: development and validation of a retrospective screen for diagnosis of PMS/PMDD; qualification of socio-economic impact of PMS/PMDD; or, impact of treatments (DRSP/EE Ocs, SSRIs and/or calcium) in improving PMS/PMDD patient's quality of life.

Purpose: To provide seed grant funds to a junior investigator for clinical research in the area of PMS/PMDD.

Eligibility: Applicants must be ACOG Junior Fellows or Fellows who are in an approved obstetrics/gynaecology residency program, or within three years post-residency.

Level of Study: Postdoctorate.

Type: Research grant.

Value: US$25,000 plus $1,000 travel stipend to attend the ACOG Annual Clinical Meeting.

Length of Study: One year.

Frequency: Annual.

Study Establishment: 2004.

Country of Study: United States of America or Canada.

No. of awards offered: One.

Application Procedure: Applicants must submit six copies of a proposal consisting of a hypothesis; objectives, specific aims, background and significance, and experimental design, and references. A one-page budget is required, applicant's curriculum vitae and a letter of support from the program director, departmental chair, or laboratory director.

Closing Date: October 1st.

Funding: Commercial.

Contributor: Berlex Laboratories Inc.

No. of awards given last year: 0.

No. of applicants last year: 2.

Additional Information: Further information can be found on the member side of the website www.acog.org.

For further information contact:

Same as main organization address.

ACOG/Berlex Laboratories Research Award in PMS/PMDD

Subjects: Obstetrics and gynecology, focusing in the area of PMS/PMDD.

Purpose: To provide seed grant funds to junior investigators for clinical research.

Eligibility: Applicants must be ACOG Junior Fellows or Fellows in an approved ob/gyn residency program or within 3 years postresidency.

Level of Study: Postgraduate.

Type: Research grant.

Value: US$25,000 plus a US$1,000 travel stipend to attend the ACOG Annual Clinical Meeting.

Length of Study: 1 year.

Frequency: Annual.

Study Establishment: 2004.

Country of Study: United States of America or Canada.

No. of awards offered: 1.

Application Procedure: Applicants must submit six copies of a proposal consisting of a hypothesis, objectives, specific aims, background and significance, and experimental design and methods. These must not exceed six typewritten pages in total. A curriculum vitae, letter of support form the program director, departmental chair or laboratory director, references and a one page budget must also be submitted.

Closing Date: October 1.

Funding: Commercial.

Contributor: Berlex Laboratories.

No. of awards given last year: New award.

Additional Information: Further information can be found on the website.

ACOG/Cytyc Corporation Research Award for the Prevention of Cervical Cancer

Subjects: Gynaecology and obstetrics, focusing on the prevention of cervical cancer.

Purpose: To provide seed grant funds to junior investigators for clinical research.

Eligibility: Open to ACOG Junior Fellows or Fellows who are in an approved obstetrics or gynaecology residency programme or within three years of post residency.

Level of Study: Postgraduate.

Type: Research grant.

Value: US$15,000 plus travel expenses to attend the ACOG Annual Clinical Meeting.

Length of Study: One year.

Frequency: Annual.

Country of Study: United States of America or Canada.

No. of awards offered: One.

Application Procedure: Applicants must submit six copies of a proposal consisting of a hypothesis, objectives, specific aims, background and significance, and experimental design and methods. These must not exceed six type written pages in total. A curriculum vitae, letter of support from the programme director, departmental chair or laboratory director, references and a one page budget must also be submitted.

Closing Date: October 1st.

Funding: Commercial.

Contributor: The Cytyc Corporation.

No. of awards given last year: One.

No. of applicants last year: 5.

Additional Information: Further information can be found on the member side of the website www.acog.org.

ACOG/Kenneth Gottesfeld-Charles Hohler Memorial Foundation Research Award in Ultrasound

Subjects: Obstetrics and gynecology. Grant funds intended to provide junior investigators with the opportunity to perform research or receive advanced training that is ultrasound specific and dedicated to a practical clinical use in a new or unique approach.

Purpose: To provide grant funds to junior investigator s for to support research or advanced training that is ultrasound specific.

Eligibility: Applicants must be ACOG Junior Fellows or Fellows in an approved ob/gyn residency program or within 5 years completion of his/her residency or fellowship.

Level of Study: Postgraduate.

Type: Research grant.

Value: One grant of US$10,000 or two grants of US$5,000 plus a US$1,000 travel stipend to attend the ACOG Annual Clinical Meeting.

Length of Study: 1 year.

Frequency: Annual.

Study Establishment: 2003.

Country of Study: United States of America or Canada.

No. of awards offered: 1 or 2.

Application Procedure: Applicants must submit six copies of a research proposal consisting of a hypothesis, objectives, specific aims, background and significance, and experimental design and methods. These must not exceed eight typewritten pages in total. A curriculum vitae, references and a one page budget must also be submitted. An advanced training proposal must be eight pages or less and include the site, the dates, the proposed curriculum and the individuals responsible for the training.

Closing Date: October 1st.

Funding: Private.

Contributor: Kenneth Gottesfeld-Charles Hohler Memorial Foundation.

No. of awards given last year: New award.

Additional Information: Further information can be found on the website.

ACOG/Kenneth Gottesfeld-Charles Hohler Memorial Foundation Research Award in Ultrasound

Subjects: To provide grant funds to a junior investigator to support research or advanced training that is ultrasound specific and dedicated to a practical clinical use in a new or unique approach.

Purpose: To provide grant funds to support work in ultrasound and it's application to obstetrics and gynaecology.
Eligibility: Applicants must be ACOG Junior Fellows or Fellows who are in an approved obstetrics/gynaecology residency program, or within five years completion of their residency or fellowship.
Level of Study: Postdoctorate.
Type: Research grant.
Value: One grant of US$10,000 or two grants of US$5,000 will be provided at the discretion of the review committee plus US$1,000 travel stipend to attend the ACOG Annual Clinical Meeting.
Length of Study: One year.
Frequency: Annual.
Study Establishment: 2003.
Country of Study: United States of America or Canada.
No. of awards offered: One or two.
Application Procedure: Applicants must submit six copies of a proposal or eight pages or less consisting of a hypothesis; objectives, specific aims, background and significance, and experimental design, and references. A advanced training proposal must be eight pages or less and include the site, the dates, the proposed curriculum and the individuals responsible for the training. A one-page budget is required and applicant's curriculum vitae.
Closing Date: October 1st.
Funding: Foundation.
Contributor: Kenneth Gottesfeld Charles Hohler Memorial Foundation,
No. of awards given last year: 2.
No. of applicants last year: 10.
Additional Information: Further information can be found on the member side of the website www.acog.org.

ACOG/Organon, Inc. Research Award in Contraception

Subjects: Obstetrics and gynaecology, focusing on the area of contraception such as estrogen supplementation during the traditional hormone free interval.
Purpose: To provide seed grant funds to junior investigators for clinical research in the area of contraception such as oestrogen supplementation during the traditional hormone free interval.
Eligibility: Applicants must be ACOG Junior Fellows or Fellows who are in an approved obstetrics or gynaecology residency programme or within three years of post residency.
Level of Study: Postgraduate.
Type: Research grant.
Value: US$25,000 plus funds for travel expenses to attend the ACOG Annual Clinical Meeting.
Length of Study: One year.
Frequency: Annual.
Country of Study: United States of America or Canada.
No. of awards offered: One.
Application Procedure: Applicants must submit six copies of a proposal consisting of a hypothesis, objectives, specific aims, background and significance, and experimental design and methods. These must not exceed six type written pages in total. A curriculum vitae, letter of support from the programme director, departmental chair or laboratory director, references and a one page budget must also be submitted.
Closing Date: October 1st.
Funding: Commercial.
Contributor: Organon, Inc.
No. of awards given last year: One.
No. of applicants last year: 8.
Additional Information: Further information can be found on the member side of the website www.acog.org.

ACOG/Ortho-McNeil Academic Training Fellowships in Obstetrics and Gynaecology

Subjects: Gynaecology and obstetrics.
Purpose: To provide opportunities for especially qualified residents or Fellows to spend an extra year involved in responsibilities which will train them for academic positions in the speciality.
Eligibility: Open to ACOG Junior Fellows or Fellows who have completed at least one year of training, and are considered by the director of their residency programme to be especially fitted for a career in medical education or academic obstetrics and gynaecology.
Level of Study: Postgraduate.
Type: Research grant.
Value: US$30,000 stipend plus travel expenses to attend the ACOG Annual Clinical Meeting.
Length of Study: One year.
Frequency: Annual.
Country of Study: United States of America or Canada.
No. of awards offered: Two.
Application Procedure: Applicants must submit six copies of a proposal consisting of a hypothesis, objectives, specific aims, background and significance, and experimental design and methods. These must not exceed six type written pages in total. A curriculum vitae, letter of support from the programme director, departmental chair or laboratory director, references and a one page budget must also be submitted.
Closing Date: October 1st.
Funding: Commercial.
Contributor: Ortho-McNeil Pharmaceutical.
No. of awards given last year: Two.
No. of applicants last year: 21.
Additional Information: Further information can be found on the member side of the website www.acog.org.

ACOG/Solvay Pharmaceuticals Research Award in Menopause

Subjects: Gynaecology and obstetrics focusing on issues related to the menopause. Relevant subjects include the physiological changes of the post reproductive woman, hormonal receptor site distribution, or other investigation deemed appropriate to furthering the basic understanding of the menopause.
Purpose: To advance knowledge in the field through encouraging basic research.
Eligibility: Open to ACOG Fellows or Junior Fellows who are in an approved obstetrics or gynaecology residency programme or are within three years of post residency.
Level of Study: Postgraduate.
Type: Research grant.
Value: US$25,000 plus a US$1,000 travel stipend to attend the ACOG Annual Clinical Meeting.
Length of Study: One year.
Frequency: Annual.
Country of Study: United States of America or Canada.
No. of awards offered: One.
Application Procedure: Applicants must submit six copies of a proposal consisting of a hypothesis, objectives, specific aims, background and significance, and experimental design and methods. These must not exceed six type written pages in total. A curriculum vitae, letter of support from the programme director, departmental chair or laboratory director, references and a one page budget must also be submitted.
Closing Date: October 1st.
Funding: Commercial.
Contributor: Solvay Pharmaceuticals, Inc.
No. of awards given last year: One.
No. of applicants last year: 6.
Additional Information: Further information can be found on the member side of the website www.acog.org.

Warren H Pearse/Wyeth Pharmaceuticals Women's Health Policy Research Award

Subjects: Gynaecology and obstetrics focusing on an aspect of policy that either defines, assists or restricts the ability of the physician to deliver health care to women in general or in a specific area.
Purpose: To provide funds to support research.
Eligibility: The principal or co-principal investigator must be an ACOG Junior Fellow or Fellow. Proposals will be considered with regards to innovation, potential utility of the research, ability to generalise results and demonstrated capability of the investigator.
Level of Study: Postgraduate.

Type: Research grant.
Value: US$15,000 plus travel expenses to attend the ACOG Annual Clinical Meeting.
Length of Study: One year.
Frequency: Annual.
Country of Study: United States of America or Canada.
No. of awards offered: One.
Application Procedure: Applicants must submit six copies of a proposal consisting of a hypothesis, objectives, specific aims, background and significance, and experimental design and methods. These must not exceed six type written pages in total. A curriculum vitae, letter of support from the programme director, departmental chair or laboratory director, references and a one page budget must also be submitted.
Closing Date: October 1st.
Funding: Commercial.
Contributor: Wyeth Pharmaceuticals.
No. of awards given last year: One.
No. of applicants last year: 5.
Additional Information: Further information can be found on the member side of the website www.acog.org.

AMERICAN COUNCIL OF LEARNED SOCIETIES (ACLS)

228 East 45th Street, New York, NY 10017
United States of America
Fax: (1) 212 949 8058
Email: grants@acls.org
www: http://www.acls.org
Contact: Grants Management Officer

ACLS American Research in the Humanities in the People's Republic of China

Subjects: The humanities.
Purpose: To enable scholars to carry out research in the People's Republic of China.
Eligibility: Open to United States citizens and permanent residents. Applicants must hold a PhD or equivalent.
Level of Study: Postdoctorate.
Type: Research grant.
Value: Monthly stipend and travel allowance.
Length of Study: 4-12 months.
Frequency: Annual.
Study Establishment: A university or research institute.
Country of Study: China.
No. of awards offered: Approx. five.
Application Procedure: Applicants must write for details.
Closing Date: November 15th.
Contributor: The National Endowment for the Humanities.

ACLS Charles A Ryskamp Research Fellowships

Subjects: Humanities or social sciences.
Purpose: To enable faculty members to conduct research under optimum conditions by providing time and resources.
Eligibility: Open to tenure track assistant professors who have successfully passed their institution's review for re-appointment or the equivalent, but have not yet been reviewed for tenure. Applicants must be employed at institutions in the United States of America and must remain so for the duration of the fellowship.
Level of Study: Postgraduate.
Type: Fellowship.
Value: US$60,000 plus US$2,500 for research and travel.
Length of Study: One academic year with the possibility of an additional Summer's support.
No. of awards offered: Up to 15.
Application Procedure: Applicants must contact the organisation.
Closing Date: October 10th.
Funding: Private.
Contributor: The Andrew W Mellon Foundation.
Additional Information: Further information is available on request.

ACLS Chinese Fellowships for Scholarly Development

Subjects: Social sciences or the humanities.
Purpose: To support scholars undertaking research.
Eligibility: Open to Chinese Scholars with an MA, PhD or equivalent from a Chinese institution who have not previously visited the United States for five months or more. Scholars involved in a degree programme are not eligible. Applicants must currently reside in China.
Level of Study: Graduate, Postdoctorate.
Type: Fellowship.
Value: Living allowance, health insurance and international airfare.
Length of Study: Up to one year.
Frequency: Annual.
Study Establishment: Approved universities or research institutions.
Country of Study: United States of America.
No. of awards offered: Approx. eight.
Application Procedure: Applicants must be nominated by the United States host. Chinese Scholars cannot apply directly.
Closing Date: November 15th.
Contributor: The Starr Foundation and the Li Foundation.
Additional Information: Further information is available on the website.

ACLS Dissertation Fellowships in East European Studies

Subjects: Social sciences and humanities relating to Albania, Bulgaria, the Czech Republic, Hungary, Poland, Romania, Slovakia, and the former Yugoslavia.
Purpose: To support dissertation research and writing.
Eligibility: Open to United States citizens or permanent legal residents.
Level of Study: Doctorate.
Type: Fellowship.
Value: Up to US$15,000.
Length of Study: One academic year.
Frequency: Annual.
Study Establishment: Any approved university or research institution.
Country of Study: Other.
No. of awards offered: Approx. 10.
Application Procedure: Applicants must write for details or consult the website.
Closing Date: November 1st.
Additional Information: The product of the proposed work must be disseminated in English. Further information is available on the website.

ACLS East European Language Training Grants

Subjects: Any Eastern European language except for the languages of the Commonwealth of Independent States.
Purpose: To support summer language training for students and scholars who cannot receive such training at their home institutions.
Eligibility: Open to United States citizens or permanent residents who are graduate students, or postdoctoral Scholars.
Level of Study: Doctorate, Postdoctorate, Postgraduate.
Type: Grant.
Value: Up to US$2,500.
Frequency: Annual.
Study Establishment: Any Institute of Higher Education.
Country of Study: United States of America.
No. of awards offered: Varies.
Application Procedure: Applicants must consult the website.
Closing Date: January 31st.
Additional Information: Further information is available on request.

ACLS Fellowships for Postdoctoral Research in East European Studies

Subjects: Social sciences and humanities relating to Albania, Bulgaria, the Czech Republic, Hungary, Poland, Romania, Slovakia and the former Yugoslavia.
Purpose: To allow Scholars to undertake a period of full-time research.
Eligibility: Open to United States citizens and permanent residents only.
Level of Study: Postdoctorate.

Type: Fellowship.
Value: Up to US$25,000. The funds are intended primarily as salary replacements and may be used to supplement sabbatical salaries or awards from other sources, provided they would intensify or extend the contemplated research.
Length of Study: At least six months.
Frequency: Annual.
Study Establishment: Approved universities or research institutions.
Country of Study: Other.
No. of awards offered: Approx. five-seven.
Application Procedure: Applicants must write for details.
Closing Date: November 1st.
Additional Information: The product of the proposed work must be disseminated in English. Further information is available on request.

ACLS Frederick Burkhardt Residential Fellowships for Recently Tenured Scholars

Subjects: Arts, humanities or social sciences.
Purpose: To support long-term, unusually ambitious projects.
Eligibility: Open to recently tenured humanists at institutions in the United States of America and Canada. Applicants must also be citizens of these countries.
Level of Study: Postgraduate.
Type: Fellowship.
Value: A stipend of US$65,000.
Length of Study: One academic year.
Frequency: Annual.
Study Establishment: Residential research centres.
Country of Study: United States of America or Canada.
No. of awards offered: Up to 11.
Application Procedure: Applicants must write for details or visit the website.
Closing Date: October 1st.
Funding: Private.
Contributor: The Andrew W Mellon Foundation, with additional funding from the Rockefeller Foundation.
Additional Information: Further information is available from the website.

ACLS Henry Luce Foundation/ACLS Dissertation Fellowships in American Art

Subjects: Art history, focusing on a topic in the history of the visual arts of the United States.
Purpose: To assist students at any stage of PhD dissertation research or writing.
Eligibility: Applicants must be United States citizens and have completed all requirements for a PhD except the dissertation before beginning tenure. They must also be in a department of art history. A student whose degree will be granted by another department may be eligible if the principal dissertation advisor is in a department of the history of art. In all cases the dissertation topic should be object orientated. Students preparing theses for the Master of Fine Arts Degree are not eligible.
Level of Study: Graduate, Predoctoral.
Type: Fellowship.
Value: US$20,000.
Length of Study: One year, non renewable.
Country of Study: United States of America.
No. of awards offered: 10.
Application Procedure: Applicants must contact the organisation.
Closing Date: November 15th.
Contributor: The Henry Luce Foundation.
Additional Information: Further information is available from the website.

ACLS Library of Congress Fellowships in International Studies

Subjects: Arts, humanities or social sciences.
Purpose: To support research using the foreign language collections of the Library of Congress.
Eligibility: Applicants must hold a PhD and preference will be given to those at an early stage in their careers ie. within seven years of their degree. Applicants must also be United States citizens or permanent residents as of the application deadline and may be affiliated with any academic institution. Independent Scholars are also welcome to apply.
Level of Study: Postdoctorate.
Type: Fellowship.
Value: US$3,500 per month.
Length of Study: Four-nine months.
Frequency: Annual.
No. of awards offered: Up to 10.
Application Procedure: Applicants must write to the organisation or visit the website.
Closing Date: November 1st.
Contributor: The Andrew W Mellon Foundation, the Association of American Universities and the Library of Congress. The Henry Luce Foundation has enabled the Library of Congress to provide funding for research concerning East or South East Asia.
Additional Information: Applicants must demonstrate the need for use of the Library of Congress foreign language holdings, and must document competence in the appropriate language at a level that would suffice to conduct research, and present a record of work that promises a high quality research work of a publishable nature. Applicants will be asked to submit a general overview of the material they expect to consult, a timetable for the completion of their research and anticipated outcomes such as publications and presentations.

ACLS/Andrew W Mellon Fellowships for Junior Faculty

Subjects: Humanities or social sciences.
Eligibility: Open to citizens of America or permanent residents only. Applicants must have at least two years of teaching experience and a PhD. However, an established Scholar who can demonstrate the equivalent of a PhD in publications and professional experience may also qualify. Scholars currently enrolled for any degree are not eligible.
Level of Study: Postdoctorate, Postgraduate.
Type: Fellowship.
Value: Varies.
Length of Study: 6-12 months.
No. of awards offered: 22.
Application Procedure: Applicants must write for details.
Closing Date: October 1st.
Additional Information: Further information is available on request.

ACLS/New York Public Library (NYPL) Fellowships

Subjects: Arts, humanities or social sciences.
Purpose: To explore the rich and diverse collections of the NYPL Humanities and Social Sciences Library.
Eligibility: Applicants must be citizens or permanent residents of the United States of America as of the application deadline date, and hold a PhD degree. However, an established Scholar who can demonstrate the equivalent of a PhD in publications and professional experience may also qualify. Applicants will be asked to identify specific resources and benefits to be gained from affiliation with the Center. Scholars currently enrolled for any degree are not eligible.
Level of Study: Postdoctorate.
Type: Fellowship.
Value: Up to US$50,000 for full professor and equivalent, US$40,000 for associate professor and equivalent and US$30,000 for assistant professor and equivalent.
Length of Study: 6-12 months.
No. of awards offered: Up to 15.
Application Procedure: Applications must be made to the ACLS Fellowship Program. Note that applications must also be made to the competition for residential fellowships administered separately by the NYPL Center for Scholars and Writers.
Closing Date: Please consult the organisation.
Additional Information: More information about the NYPL is available at http://www.nypl.org. It is possible that an application may have any one of the following outcomes: a fellowship awarded solely by the NYPL Center for Scholars and Writers, an ACLS Fellowship awarded solely by the ACLS or a joint NYPL/ACLS Residential Fellowship awarded by both organisations together.

For further information contact:

Center for Scholars & Writers, The New York Public LibraryHumanities & Social Sciences Library, Fifth Avenue & 42nd Street, New York, NY 10018-2788, United States of America
Email: csw@nypl.org

ACLS/SSRC/NEH International and Area Studies Fellowships

Subjects: The societies and cultures of Asia, Africa, the Near and Middle East, Latin America and the Caribbean, Eastern Europe and the former Soviet Union.
Purpose: To encourage humanistic research in area studies.
Eligibility: Applicants must be citizens or permanent residents of the United States as of the application deadline date, and hold a PhD degree. However, an established Scholar who can demonstrate the equivalent of a PhD in publications and professional experience may also qualify. Scholars pursuing research and writing on the societies and cultures of Asia, Africa, the Near and Middle East, Latin America and the Caribbean, East Europe and the Former Soviet Union are eligible. Scholars currently enrolled for any degree are not eligible.
Level of Study: Postdoctorate.
Type: Fellowship.
Value: Up to US$50,000 for full professor and equivalent, US$40,000 for associate professor and equivalent and US$30,000 for assistant professor and equivalent.
Length of Study: 6-12 months.
No. of awards offered: Approx. 10.
Application Procedure: Applications must be made to the ACLS Fellowship Program and all requirements and provisions of that programme must be met. The Fellow must submit a final report to both NEH and ACLS. Note that applications must also be made to the competition for residential fellowships administered separately by the NYPL Center for Scholars and Writers.
Closing Date: Please consult the organisation.
Additional Information: Further information is available on request.

For further information contact:

Center for Scholars & Writers, The New York Public Library Humanities & Social Sciences Library, Fifth Avenue & 42nd Street, New York, NY 10018-2788, United States of America
Email: csw@nypl.org

AMERICAN COUNCIL OF THE BLIND (ACB)

1155 15th Street North West, Suite 1004, Washington, DC 20005, United States of America
Tel: (1) 202 467 5081
Fax: (1) 202 467 5085
Email: tpacheco@acb.org
www: http://www.acb.org
Contact: Mrs Terry Pacheco

The American Council of the Blind (ACB) is a membership organisation that promotes the effective participation in all aspects of society of people who are blind.

ACB Scholarship Program

Subjects: All subjects.
Purpose: To provide scholarships to legally blind postsecondary students.
Eligibility: Open to United States citizens or resident aliens who are legally blind in both eyes.
Level of Study: Doctorate, Postgraduate.
Type: Scholarship.
Value: US$500-4,000.
Length of Study: One year.
Frequency: Annual.
Country of Study: United States of America.
No. of awards offered: 25-30.

Application Procedure: Applicants must submit an application form, a two page autobiographical sketch, transcripts, a letter of recommendation and proof of legal blindness.
Closing Date: March 1st.
Funding: Private.
Contributor: Public donations.
No. of awards given last year: 26.
No. of applicants last year: 325.

AMERICAN COUNCIL ON RURAL SPECIAL EDUCATION (ACRES)

Utah State University, 2865 Old Main Hill, Logan, UT 84322-2865, United States of America
Tel: (1) 785 532 2737
Fax: (1) 785 532 7732
Email: acres@ksu.edu
www: http://www.ksu.edu/acres
Contact: Headquarters Co-ordinator

ACRES Scholarship

Subjects: Special education in the areas of the handicapped, those with specific learning disabilities and the socially disadvantaged.
Purpose: To give a rural teacher an opportunity to pursue education and training not otherwise affordable within his or her district.
Eligibility: Applicants must be United States citizens, currently employed by a rural school district as a certified teacher in regular or special education, working with students with disabilities or with regular education students and retraining to a special education career.
Level of Study: Postgraduate.
Type: Scholarship.
Value: Up to US$1,000.
Length of Study: One year.
Frequency: Annual.
Country of Study: United States of America.
No. of awards offered: One.
Application Procedure: Applicants must complete and submit an application form with an essay and two letters of recommendation.
Closing Date: December 10th.
Funding: Private.
Additional Information: The award will be announced at the March ACRES symposium

AMERICAN DIABETES ASSOCIATION (ADA)

1701 North Beauregard Street, Alexandria, VA 22311, United States of America
Tel: (1) 703 549 1500
Fax: (1) 703 549 1715
Email: research@diabetes.org
www: http://www.diabetes.org/research
Contact: Research Department

The American Diabetes Association (ADA) is the nation's leading non-profit health organisation providing diabetes research, information and advocacy. The mission of the organisation is to prevent and cure diabetes, and to improve the lives of all people affected by diabetes. To fulfil this mission, the ADA funds research, publishes scientific findings and provides information and other services to people with diabetes, their families, health care professionals and the public.

ADA Career Development Awards

Subjects: Diabetes related research.
Purpose: To allow exceptionally promising new investigators to conduct research.
Eligibility: Open to United States citizens, permanent residents or those who have applied for permanent resident status who have MD or PhD degrees or, in the case of other health professions, an appropriate health or science related degree. Applicants must hold an assistant professorship or provide documentation that he or she will receive this position upon receipt of this award. At the time of the

award applicants must have at least two, but not more than five years of postdoctoral or post fellowship research experience in a diabetes related field with relevant accomplishments and publications.

Level of Study: Postdoctorate.

Type: Award.

Value: Up to US$150,000 per year and an additional 15 per cent for indirect costs. The funds are to be divided by the recipient between the salary of the principal investigator and other grant support. Each year of funding, after the first, is contingent upon approval by the ADA of the recipient's research progress report, and the availability of funds.

Length of Study: Five years, non renewable.

Frequency: Twice a year.

Country of Study: United States of America.

No. of awards offered: Varies, depending on funds available.

Application Procedure: Applicants must write for details.

ADA Clinical Research Grants

Subjects: Diabetes related research. For the purpose of this programme, clinical research is defined as research involving humans directly.

Purpose: To support patient orientated research.

Eligibility: Open to United States citizens, permanent residents or those who have applied for permanent resident status, who have MD or PhD degrees or, in the case of other health professions, an appropriate health or science related degree, and who hold full-time faculty positions or the equivalent at university affiliated institutions within the United States and its possessions. Support will be provided for studies that focus on intact human subjects in which the effects of a change in the individual's external or internal environment is evaluated.

Level of Study: Postdoctorate.

Type: Research grant.

Value: Up to US$100,000 per year for three years. Up to US$20,000 per year may be used for principal investigator salary support, and up to 15 per cent for indirect costs. Each year of funding after the first is contingent upon approval by the ADA of the recipient's research progress report, and the availability of funds.

Length of Study: Three years.

Frequency: Twice a year.

Country of Study: United States of America.

No. of awards offered: Varies, depending on funds available.

Closing Date: February 1st for July 1st funding and August 1st for January 1st funding.

ADA Junior Faculty Awards

Subjects: Diabetes.

Purpose: To support investigators who are establishing their independence as diabetes researchers.

Eligibility: Open to United States citizens or permanent residents, or those who have applied for permanent resident status, who have an MD or PhD degree or an appropriate health or science related degree. Applicants can hold any level of faculty appointment at university affiliated institutions within the United States and United States' possessions.

Level of Study: Postdoctorate.

Type: Award.

Value: Up to US$120,000 per year, plus up to US$10,000 per year towards repayment of the principle on loans for a doctoral degree such as the MD or PhD.

Length of Study: Three years.

Country of Study: United States of America.

No. of awards offered: Varies, depending on funds available.

Application Procedure: Applicants must write for details.

Closing Date: February 1st for July 1st funding and August 1st for January 1st funding.

ADA Medical Scholars Program

Subjects: Diabetes.

Purpose: To produce leaders in the fields of research, teaching and patient care, by giving physicians in training the opportunity to contribute to the process of discovery in basic and clinical research laboratories. The Medical Scholars Program will supply a unique opportunity to effectively integrate medical students into the process of discovery.

Eligibility: Open to institutions within the United States and United States possessions. The application must be initiated by the student, and the student must have a qualified sponsor. The student must have completed at least one year of medical school and the sponsor must hold a faculty position within an accredited medical school in the United States and be a United States citizen or permanent resident.

Level of Study: Postgraduate.

Type: Scholarship.

Value: Support for one year in a clinical or basic science research environment. The award will be up to US$30,000 per student, US$20,000 for the student's support, and US$10,000 for materials, supplies and travel to the Association's scientific sessions.

Frequency: Annual.

Country of Study: United States of America.

No. of awards offered: Varies.

Closing Date: February 1st for July 1st funding.

ADA Mentor-Based Postdoctoral Fellowship Program

Subjects: Diabetes.

Purpose: To support the training of scientists in an environment most conducive to beginning a career in research. An award will also be given to an established and active investigator in diabetes research for the annual stipend support of a postdoctoral Fellow to work closely with the mentor.

Eligibility: There are no citizenship requirements for the Fellow. However, the investigator must be a United States citizen or permanent resident, and must also hold an appointment at a United States research institution and have sufficient research support to provide an appropriate training environment for the Fellow. The Fellow selected by the investigator must hold a MD or PhD degree and must not be serving an internship or residency during the fellowship period. The Fellow must not have more than three years of postdoctoral research experience in the field of diabetes or endocrinology at the commencement of this fellowship.

Level of Study: Postdoctorate.

Type: Fellowship.

Value: Up to US$35,000.

Length of Study: Up to three years.

Frequency: Annual.

Country of Study: United States of America.

No. of awards offered: Varies, depending on funds available.

Application Procedure: Applicants must complete an application form.

Closing Date: October 1st for July 1st funding.

ADA Physician/Scientist Training

Subjects: Diabetes.

Purpose: To provide support for the doctoral portion of an MD or PhD degree.

Eligibility: Open to students who have a qualified sponsor and are in good academic standing. Students already enrolled in an MSTP programme are not eligible to apply for this award.

Level of Study: Postgraduate.

Type: Scholarship.

Value: Up to US$30,000 per year.

Length of Study: Three years.

Frequency: Annual.

Country of Study: United States of America.

No. of awards offered: Varies, depending on funds available.

Application Procedure: Applicants must write for details. Applications must be initiated by the student.

Closing Date: February 1st for July 1st funding.

ADA Research Awards

Subjects: Aetiology and pathophysiology of diabetes.

Purpose: To assist investigators, new or established, who have a particularly novel and exciting idea for which they need support.

Eligibility: Open to United States citizens or permanent residents or those who have applied for permanent resident status who have MD or PhD degrees, or, in the case of other health professions, an appropriate health or science related degree. Applicants must hold full-time faculty positions or the equivalent at university affiliated institutions within the United States and its possessions.

Level of Study: Postdoctorate.

Type: Research grant.
Value: US$20,000-100,000 per year, for a maximum of three years, of which a maximum of US$20,000 can be used for principal investigator salary support, and up to 15 per cent for indirect costs. Each year of funding after the first is contingent upon approval by the ADA of the recipient's research progress report, and the availability of funds.
Length of Study: Up to three years.
Frequency: Twice a year.
Country of Study: United States of America.
No. of awards offered: Varies, depending on funds available.
Closing Date: February 1st for July 1st funding and August 1st for January 1st funding.

LCIF Equipment Grant Program

Subjects: Clinical research in diabetic retinopathy.
Purpose: To enable investigators to purchase equipment in order to conduct clinical research projects.
Eligibility: Open to holders of an MD or PhD degree, or, in the case of other health professions, an appropriate health or science related degree. The applicant must hold a faculty level appointment at a research institution.
Level of Study: Postdoctorate.
Type: Other.
Value: US$25,000 for the purchase of equipment. One payment is made in July.
Frequency: Annual.
Country of Study: Any country.
No. of awards offered: Varies, depending on funds available.
Application Procedure: Applicants must submit a detailed justification of the need to purchase the equipment and an explanation of its intended use.
Closing Date: February 1st for July 1st funding.
Additional Information: This programme is part of the Lions Sight-first Diabetic Retinopathy Research Program, funded by the Lions Club International Foundation. Applicants must submit the final disposition within six months of receipt of the award.

LCIF Training Grant Program

Subjects: Diabetic retinopathy.
Purpose: To enable foreign investigators to visit American research institutions and receive training in clinical research, the implementation of public health programmes eg. screening or epidemiology. The programme also aims to enable United States investigators to visit foreign institutions, particularly institutions in underdeveloped countries, to conduct training programmes in clinical research and implement public health programmes.
Eligibility: Open to United States citizens who have an MD or PhD degree, or, in the case of other health professions, an appropriate health or science related degree, and hold a faculty level appointment at a United States research institution. The programme is also open to non United States citizens who have an MD or PhD degree.
Level of Study: Postdoctorate.
Value: Up to US$40,000.
Length of Study: Two years.
Frequency: Annual.
Study Establishment: An approved institution.
Country of Study: Any country.
No. of awards offered: Varies, depending on funds available.
Closing Date: February 1st for July 1st funding.
Additional Information: This programme is part of the Lions Sight-first Diabetic Retinopathy Research Program, funded by the Lions Club International Foundation.

AMERICAN FEDERATION FOR AGING RESEARCH (AFAR)

70 West 40th Street, 11th Floor, New York, NY 10018, United States of America
Tel: (1) 212 703 9977
Fax: (1) 212 997 0330
Email: grants@afar.org
www: http://www.afar.org
Contact: Grants Administrator

The American Federation for Aging Research (AFAR) is a leading non-profit organisation supporting biomedical ageing research. Since its founding in 1981, AFAR has provided some US $70 million to more than 1,900 new investigators and students conducting cutting edge biomedical research on the ageing process and age related diseases. The important work AFAR supports leads to a better understanding of the ageing process and to improvements in the health of all Americans as they age.

AFAR Research Grants

Subjects: Biomedical and clinical topics.
Purpose: To help junior faculty to carry out research that will serve as the basis for longer term research efforts.
Level of Study: Postdoctorate, Research.
Type: Research grant.
Value: US$60,000 for junior faculty and US$50,000 to postdoctoral fellows.
Length of Study: One-two years.
Frequency: Annual.
Country of Study: United States of America.
No. of awards offered: Approx. 25.
Application Procedure: Applicants must complete and return the application by the annual deadline. These are available from the website.
Closing Date: December.
Funding: Private.
Contributor: AFAR and the Glenn Foundation for Medical Research.

AFAR/Pfizer Research Grants in Metabolic Control and Late Life Diseases

Subjects: Metabolic control and ageing.
Purpose: To address specific areas of research that focus on the ageing process and age related diseases.
Eligibility: Applicants must be United States citizens or permanent residents.
Level of Study: Research.
Type: Grant.
Value: US$60,000.
Length of Study: One-two years.
Frequency: Annual.
Country of Study: United States of America.
No. of awards offered: Up to four.
Application Procedure: Applicants must complete and return the application by the annual deadline. These are available from the website.
Closing Date: December 14th.
Funding: Private.
Contributor: Pfizer Pharmaceuticals, Inc.
Additional Information: Projects may involve basic, clinical or epidemiological research.

Beeson Career Development Award

Subjects: Medical sciences.
Purpose: To bolster the current severe shortage of academic physicians who have the combination of medical, academic and scientific training relative to caring for other people.
Eligibility: Applicants must be United States citizens or permanent residents, be full-time faculty members with clear potential for long-term faculty appointments, and, at the time of application, have received their MD degree in 1990 or later.
Level of Study: Professional development, Research.
Type: Grant.
Value: US$600,000-US$800,000.
Length of Study: Three-Five years.
Frequency: Annual.
Country of Study: United States of America.
No. of awards offered: Up to 11.
Application Procedure: Applicants must complete and return the application by the annual deadline. These are available from the website (below).
Closing Date: December 17, 2003.
Funding: Government, Private.

Contributor: The National Institute on Aging, The John A Hartford Foundation, the Commonwealth Fund, Atlantic Philanthropies and the Starr Foundation.

For further information contact:

www: http://grants1.nih.gov/grants/guide/rfa-files/RFA-AG-04-004.html

Ellison Medical Foundation/AFAR Senior Postdoctoral Research Program

Subjects: The fundamental mechanisms of ageing.
Purpose: To encourage and further the careers of postdoctoral fellows.
Eligibility: Open to MDs and PhDs with at least three and no more than five years of prior postdoctoral training at the time of the award.
Level of Study: Postdoctorate.
Type: Research grant.
Value: US$100,000.
Length of Study: Two years.
Frequency: Annual.
Country of Study: United States of America.
No. of awards offered: Up to three.
Closing Date: December 12, 2003.
Funding: Private.

Glenn/AFAR Research Grant Program for Postdoctoral Fellows

Subjects: Ageing.
Eligibility: Open to MDs and PhDs with at least two and no more than five years of prior postdoctoral training at the time of the award.
Level of Study: Postdoctorate.
Type: Research grant.
Value: US$50,000.
Frequency: Annual.
Country of Study: United States of America.
No. of awards offered: Up to four.
Application Procedure: Applicants must obtain a copy of the AFAR Research Grant application guidelines.
Closing Date: December 12, 2003.
Funding: Private.

Glenn/AFAR Scholarships for Research in the Biology of Aging

Subjects: Biomedical research.
Purpose: To attract potential scientists to ageing research and provide students with the opportunity to conduct a research project.
Eligibility: Open to students completing MD or PhD degrees.
Level of Study: Doctorate, Research.
Type: Scholarship.
Value: US$6,000.
Length of Study: Three months.
Frequency: Annual.
No. of awards offered: Up to 25.
Application Procedure: Applicants should submit one original and four copies of the application and of all supporting materials, including academic transcripts from all institutions attended, Graduate Record Examination and/or MCAT scores, and a biographical sketch and endorsing letter of the designated mentor. In addition, one letter of reference is also required.
Closing Date: February 26, 2004.
Funding: Private.
Contributor: The Glenn Foundation for Medical Research.

Merck/AFAR Junior Investigator Award in Geriatric Clinical Pharmacology

Subjects: Geriatric clinical pharmacology.
Purpose: To address the critical need of developing more physicians.
Eligibility: Applicants must be United States citizens or permanent residents. At the time of application, candidates must be within four years of having completed postdoctoral or fellowship training. Previous training in geriatrics or clinical pharmacology is not required, but one or the other is highly desirable.

Level of Study: Professional development, Research.
Type: Grant.
Value: US$120,000.
Length of Study: Two years.
Frequency: Annual.
Country of Study: United States of America.
No. of awards offered: Two.
Application Procedure: Applications must be submitted by an institution on behalf of an individual candidate. Institutions may submit multiple applications, but only one application per institution will be funded. The application form itself must be completed by both an official of the institution and the candidate it proposes. It must be accompanied by letters of reference from two individuals who know the candidate, the candidate's curriculum vitae and a biographical sketch for the person appointed by the institution to supervise the candidate's work. An original and four copies of the application and all supporting documents must be submitted.
Closing Date: November 3, 2003.
Funding: Private.
Contributor: The Merck Company Foundation.

RPS FAR Medical Student Geriatric Scholars Program

Subjects: Geriatrics.
Purpose: To encourage medical students, particularly budding researchers, to consider a career in academic geriatrics.
Eligibility: Applicants must be United States citizens or permanent residents and have completed at least one year of medical school by the start date of the award.
Level of Study: Doctorate.
Type: Scholarship.
Value: US$4,000.
Length of Study: Eight weeks.
Frequency: Annual.
Country of Study: United States of America.
No. of awards offered: 40-60.
Application Procedure: Applicants must complete and return the application by the annual deadline. Applications are available from the website.
Closing Date: February 6, 2004.
Funding: Private.
Contributor: Anonymous donor.

AMERICAN FOUNDATION FOR AGEING RESEARCH (AFAR)

Biochemistry Department, North Carolina State University, Campus Box 7622, Polk Hall, Raleigh, NC 27695, United States of America
Tel: (1) 919 515 5679
Fax: (1) 919 515 2047
Email: afar@bchserver.bch.ncsu.edu
www: http://www4.ncsu.edu/unity/users/a/agris/afar/afar.htm
Contact: Dr Paul F Agris, President

The American Foundation for Ageing Research (AFAR) aims to promote and support research that will elucidate the basic processes involved in the biology of ageing and age associated disease, by awarding scholarships and fellowships to young, motivated scientists.

Wilson-Fulton and Robertson Awards in Ageing Research, Cecille Gould Memorial Fund Award in Cancer Research, Richard Shepherd Fellowship

Subjects: Ageing and cancer research.
Purpose: To encourage young people to pursue research in age related health problems and the biology of ageing.
Eligibility: Open to graduates enrolled in degree programmes eg. MS, PhD, MD or DDS at institutions within the United States of America. They must be working on specific projects in the fields of ageing or cancer. Sociological and psychological research is not accepted in these programmes.
Level of Study: Doctorate, Graduate, Postgraduate.
Type: Fellowship.

Value: US$500-1,000 per semester or summer. The award is renewable.
Length of Study: Between four months and one year.
Frequency: Annual.
Study Establishment: Educational institutions.
Country of Study: United States of America.
No. of awards offered: 5-10.
Application Procedure: Applicants must undertake the two levels of review: a pre-application form to determine eligibility, and a full application. Applicants should submit a request for a pre-application. A cheque or money order to AFAR for US$3 to cover handling and postage should be included with the completed pre-application. There is no charge for the submission of the full application.
Closing Date: There is no deadline.
Funding: Private.
No. of awards given last year: Three.
No. of applicants last year: 115.
Additional Information: AFAR is a national, tax-exempt, non-profit, educational and scientific charity not affiliated with North Carolina State University.

AMERICAN FOUNDATION FOR PHARMACEUTICAL EDUCATION (AFPE)

One Church Street, Suite 202, Rockville, MD 20850-4158, United States of America
Tel: (1) 301 738 2160
Fax: (1) 301 738 2161
Email: afpe@worldnet.alt.net
www: http://www.afpend.org
Contact: Administrative Assistant

AAPS/AFPE Gateway Scholarships

Subjects: Pharmaceutics.
Purpose: To encourage graduates from any discipline to pursue a PhD in a pharmacy graduate programme.
Eligibility: Open to students who are enrolled in the last three years of a Bachelor of Science or PharmD programme at a United States school or college of pharmacy, or Baccalaureate degree programme in a related field of scientific study at any college. Candidates must have a demonstrated interest in, and potential for, a career in any of the pharmaceutical sciences and be enrolled for at least one full academic year following the award of the scholarship. United States citizenship or permanent resident status is not required.
Level of Study: Postgraduate, Professional development.
Type: Scholarship.
Value: Please contact the organisation.
Frequency: Annual.
Country of Study: United States of America.
No. of awards offered: Six.
Application Procedure: Applicants must write for details.

AFPE Clinical Pharmacy Post-Pharm D Fellowships in the Biomedical Research Sciences Program

Subjects: Pharmacology including topics such as cost benefit and cost effectiveness of pharmaceuticals, the impact of current or future legislation on drug innovation and healthcare in the nation, the economics of healthcare and the quality of life in changing patterns of healthcare delivery systems, the contribution of the pharmaceutical industry, the economic impact of research and new drugs, and healthcare cost containment issues.
Eligibility: Open to all pharmacy faculty members who have a strong record of research.
Level of Study: Postdoctorate.
Type: Fellowship.
Value: Please contact the organisation.
Frequency: Annual.
Study Establishment: An Institute of Higher Education.
Country of Study: United States of America.
No. of awards offered: Three.
Application Procedure: Applicants must complete an application form and should write for details.

AFPE Gateway Research Scholarship Program

Subjects: Pharmacology.
Purpose: To encourage individuals in a pharmacy college to pursue a PhD within a pharmacy college.
Eligibility: Open to students who are enrolled in the last three years of a Bachelor of Science or PharmD programme at a United States school or college of pharmacy, or Baccalaureate degree programme in a related field of scientific study at any college. Candidates must have a demonstrated interest in, and potential for, a career in any of the pharmaceutical sciences and will be enrolled for at least one full academic year following the award of the scholarship. United States citizenship or permanent resident status is not required.
Level of Study: Postgraduate, Professional development.
Type: Scholarship.
Value: Please contact the organisation.
Frequency: Annual.
Study Establishment: An approved college of pharmacy.
Country of Study: United States of America.
No. of awards offered: 12.
Application Procedure: Applicants must write for details.

AFPE Predoctoral Fellowships

Subjects: Any of the pharmaceutical sciences, including pharmaceutics, pharmacology, manufacturing pharmacy and medicinal chemistry.
Purpose: To offer fellowship support leading to a PhD degree.
Eligibility: Open to students who have completed at least three semesters of graduate study and who have no more than three years remaining to obtain a PhD degree in a graduate programme in the pharmaceutical sciences administered by, or affiliated with, a United States school or college of pharmacy. The award is also open to students enrolled in joint PharmD and PhDs, if a PhD degree will be awarded within three additional years. Applicants must be United States citizens or permanent residents.
Level of Study: Doctorate, Postgraduate.
Type: Fellowship.
Value: Please contact the organisation.
Length of Study: One year, renewable for two additional years.
Frequency: Annual.
Study Establishment: An appropriate university.
Country of Study: United States of America.
No. of awards offered: Approx. 80.
Application Procedure: Applicants must write for details.

AMERICAN FOUNDATION FOR SUICIDE PREVENTION (AFSP)

120 Wall Street, 22nd Floor, New York, NY 10005, United States of America
Tel: (1) 212 363 3500
Fax: (1) 212 363 6237
Email: inquiry@afsp.org
www: http://www.afsp.org
Contact: Administrative Assistant

The American Foundation for Suicide Prevention (AFSP) is dedicated to preventing suicide through its support of research, treatment initiatives and professional and public education. The Foundation also offers programmes for those who have lost a family member or friend to suicide.

AFSP Distinguished Investigation Awards

Subjects: The clinical, biological or psychosocial aspects of suicide.
Level of Study: Postdoctorate, Research.
Type: Grant.
Value: Up to US$100,000.
Length of Study: One-two years.
Frequency: Annual.
Country of Study: United States of America.
No. of awards offered: Varies.
Application Procedure: Applicants should consult the website or contact the organisation for full details.
Closing Date: December 15th.

Funding: Private.
Additional Information: Decisions regarding awards are made in May and funding begins in July.

AFSP Pilot Grants

Subjects: The clinical, biological or psychosocial aspects of suicide.
Level of Study: Postdoctorate, Research.
Type: Grant.
Value: Up to US$20,000.
Length of Study: One-two years.
Frequency: Three times each year.
Country of Study: United States of America.
No. of awards offered: Varies.
Application Procedure: Applicants should consult the website or contact the organisation for full details go to www.afsp.org.
Closing Date: December 15th.
Funding: Private.
Additional Information: Decisions regarding awards are made three times a year. April 15th; August 15th; December 15th.

AFSP Postdoctoral Research Fellowships

Subjects: The clinical, biological or psychosocial aspects of suicide.
Eligibility: Applicants must have received a PhD three years prior to application for the fellowship.
Level of Study: Postdoctorate, Research.
Type: Fellowship.
Value: A progressive stipend from US$42,000-US$46,000.
Length of Study: Up to 2 years.
Frequency: Annual.
Country of Study: United States of America.
No. of awards offered: Varies.
Application Procedure: Applicants should consult the website or contact the organisation for full details go to www.afsp.org.
Closing Date: December 15th.
Funding: Private.
Additional Information: Decisions regarding awards are made in May and funding begins in July.

AFSP Standard Research Grants

Subjects: The clinical, biological or psychosocial aspects of suicide.
Level of Study: Postdoctorate, Research.
Type: Grant.
Value: Up to US$60,000.
Length of Study: Two years.
Frequency: Annual.
Country of Study: United States of America.
No. of awards offered: Varies.
Application Procedure: Applicants should consult the website or contact the organisation for full details go to www.afsp.org.
Closing Date: December 15th.
Funding: Private.
Additional Information: Decisions regarding awards are made in May and funding begins in July.

AFSP Young Investigator Award

Subjects: The clinical, biological or psychosocial aspects of suicide.
Level of Study: Research.
Type: Award.
Value: Up to US$70,000.
Length of Study: Up to 2 years.
Frequency: Annual.
Country of Study: United States of America.
No. of awards offered: Varies.
Application Procedure: Applicants should consult the website or contact the organisation for full details go to www.afsp.org.
Closing Date: December 15th.
Funding: Private.
Additional Information: Decisions regarding awards are made in May and funding begins in July. Investigators should be at the level of assistant professor or lower.

AMERICAN GEOPHYSICAL UNION (AGU)

2000 Florida Avenue North West, Washington, DC 20009, United States of America
Tel: (1) 202 462 6900
Fax: (1) 202 328 0566
www: http://www.agu.org
Contact: Director, Outreach and Research Support

The American Geophysical Union (AGU) is an international scientific society with more than 36,000 members, primarily research scientists, dedicated to advancing the understanding of the earth and solar system and making the results of the AGU's research available to the public.

Horton (Hydrology) Research Grant

Subjects: Hydrology including its physical, chemical or biological aspects.
Purpose: To support research.
Eligibility: There are no eligibility restrictions.
Level of Study: Postdoctorate.
Type: Grant.
Value: US$10,000.
Frequency: Annual.
No. of awards offered: Two.
Application Procedure: Applicants must submit four copies of the application form, an executive summary, a statement of purpose, a detailed budget and two letters of recommendation. Applicants should contact the Union for further details.
Closing Date: March 1st.
No. of awards given last year: Two.
No. of applicants last year: 27.

AMERICAN HEAD & NECK SOCIETY

11300 W. Olympic Boulevard, Suite 600
Los Angeles, CA 90064
United States of America
Tel: (1) 310 437 0559
Fax: (1) 310 437 0585
Email: admin@ahns.info
www: www.headandneckcancer.org
Contact: Mr Tom Fise, Research Grants Enquiries

The purpose of the American Head and Neck Society is to promote and advance the knowledge of prevention, diagnosis, treatment and rehabilitation of neoplasms and other diseases of the head and neck.

AHNS Career Development Award

Subjects: Diseases of the Head and Neck.
Purpose: To facilitate research in connection with career development.
Eligibility: Must be a member or candidate member of AHNS.
Level of Study: Postgraduate.
Type: Award.
Value: US$40,000 per year.
Length of Study: Two years.
Frequency: Annual.
Study Establishment: A university in the United States.
Country of Study: United States of America.
Application Procedure: Please check website.
Funding: Private.

AHNS Pilot Research Grant

Subjects: Diseases of the Head and Neck.
Purpose: To support students who wish to try a pilot project in head and neck related research.
Eligibility: Open to residents, fellows in the junior faculty.
Level of Study: Doctorate, Postgraduate.
Type: Award.
Value: US$10,000.

Length of Study: 1 year.
Frequency: Annual.
Study Establishment: A university in the United States.
Country of Study: United States of America.
No. of awards offered: 1.
Application Procedure: Check the website.
Funding: Private.

Surgeon Scientist Career Development Award

Subjects: Cancer and other diseases of the head and neck.
Purpose: To support research in the pathogenesis, pathophysiology, diagnosis, prevention or treatment of head and neck neoplastic disease.
Eligibility: Open to surgeons beginning a clinician-scientist career.
Level of Study: Postdoctorate.
Type: Award.
Value: US$35,000 per year.
Length of Study: Two years.
Frequency: Annual.
Study Establishment: A university in the United States.
Country of Study: United States of America.
No. of awards offered: 1.
Application Procedure: Please check website.
Funding: Private.

The Young Investigator Award

Subjects: Cancer and other diseases of the head and neck.
Purpose: To support research in neoplastic disease of the head and neck.
Eligibility: Candidate must be a member of AHNS.
Level of Study: Doctorate.
Type: Award.
Value: US$10,000 per year.
Length of Study: Up to 2 years.
Frequency: Annual.
Study Establishment: A university in the United States.
Country of Study: United States of America.
No. of awards offered: 1.
Application Procedure: Check the website.
Funding: Private.

AMERICAN HEALTH ASSISTANCE FOUNDATION (AHAF)

15825 Shady Grove Road, Rockville, MD 20850, United States of America
Tel: (1) 301 948 3244
Fax: (1) 301 258 9454
Email: sgarfinkel@ahaf.org
www: http://www.ahaf.org
Contact: Dr Susan Garfinkel, Director of Research Grants

The American Health Assistance Foundation (AHAF) is a non-profit charitable organisation that funds research and public education on age related and degenerative diseases including: Alzheimer's disease, macular degeneration, glaucoma and heart and stroke diseases. The organisation also provides emergency financial assistance to Alzheimer's disease patients and their care givers.

AHAF Alzheimer's Disease Research Grant

Subjects: Neurology, biomedicine, biochemistry, biophysics, molecular biology and pharmacology.
Purpose: To enable basic research on the causes of and treatments for Alzheimer's disease.
Eligibility: The principal investigator must hold the rank of assistant professor or equivalent, or higher.
Level of Study: Doctorate.
Type: Grant.
Value: Up to US$200,000 for two years or US$100,000 for two years in the Pilot programme.
Length of Study: One-two years.
Frequency: Annual.
Study Establishment: Non-profit institutions and organisations.

Country of Study: Any country.
No. of awards offered: Varies.
Application Procedure: Applicants must complete an application form. The current application form should be requested for each year or can be downloaded from the website.
Closing Date: October 15th.
Funding: Private.
No. of awards given last year: 13.
No. of applicants last year: 89.
Additional Information: Further information is available on request.

AHAF Macular Degeneration Research

Subjects: Ophthalmology, biomedicine, biochemistry, biophysics, genetics, molecular biology and pharmacology.
Purpose: To enable basic research on the causes of, or the treatment for, macular degeneration.
Eligibility: The principal investigator must hold a tenure track or tenured position and the rank of assistant professor or higher.
Type: Grant.
Value: Up to US$50,000. Grants may be renewed on a competitive peer review basis.
Length of Study: One year.
Frequency: Annual.
Study Establishment: Non-profit institutions and organisations.
Country of Study: Any country.
No. of awards offered: Varies.
Application Procedure: Applicants must complete an application form. The current application form should be requested for each year or can be downloaded from the website.
Closing Date: Letters of intent due July 16th. Application due October 23rd.
Funding: Private.
No. of awards given last year: Five.
No. of applicants last year: 31.
Additional Information: Further information is available on request.

AHAF National Glaucoma Research

Subjects: Ophthalmology, biomedicine and pharmacology.
Purpose: To enable basic research on the causes of, or treatments for, glaucoma.
Eligibility: The principal investigator must hold the rank of assistant professor or equivalent, or higher.
Level of Study: Doctorate.
Type: Grant.
Value: Up to US$35,000 per year for up to two years.
Length of Study: One-two years.
Frequency: Annual.
Study Establishment: Non-profit institutions and organisations.
Country of Study: Any country.
No. of awards offered: Varies.
Application Procedure: Applicants must complete an application form. The current application form should be requested for each year and can also be downloaded from the website.
Closing Date: November 15th.
Funding: Private.
No. of awards given last year: Eight.
No. of applicants last year: 28.
Additional Information: Further information is available on request.

AHAF National Heart Foundation

Subjects: Cardiology, biomedicine, physiology and pharmacology.
Purpose: To provide start up grants for new investigators into the causes of, or treatments for, cardiovascular disease and stroke.
Eligibility: Open to young investigators who are beginning independent research careers at the assistant professor level and are head of an independent research laboratory group.
Level of Study: Professional development.
Type: Grant.
Value: Up to US$25,000 may be requested for one year.
Length of Study: One year, renewable for a further year.
Frequency: Annual.
Study Establishment: Non-profit institutions and organisations.
Country of Study: Any country.

No. of awards offered: Varies.
Application Procedure: Applicants must complete an application form. The current application form should be requested for each year or can be downloaded from the website.
Closing Date: November 4th.
Funding: Private.
No. of awards given last year: Two.
No. of applicants last year: 18.
Additional Information: Further information is available on request.

AMERICAN HEART ASSOCIATION, INC. (AHA)

National Center, 7272 Greenville Avenue, Dallas, TX 75231-4596, United States of America
Tel: (1) 214 706 1187
Fax: (1) 214 706 1341
Email: juanita.morales@heart.org
www: http://www.americanheart.org/research
Contact: Ms Juanita Morales, Manager Promotions & Electronic Services

The American Heart Association (AHA) is a non-profit, voluntary health organisation funded by private contributions. Its mission is to reduce disability and death from cardiovascular diseases and stroke. To support this goal, the Association has given more than US$2 billion to heart and blood vessel research since 1949.

AHA National Established Investigator Award
Subjects: Cardiovascular function and disease, stroke or related basic science, clinical, bioengineering or biotechnology and public health problems.
Purpose: To support mid-term investigators with unusual promise.
Eligibility: Open to Assistant Professor level or equivalent faculty or staff investigators with between four and nine years since their first faculty/staff appointment, who have demonstrated a commitment to the cardiovascular or cerebrovascular science area as indicated by prior publication history and accomplishments. At the time of application candidates must be citizens of the United States of America or foreign nationals holding the relevant immigration visas. Non citizens must submit proof of possession of a relevant immigration visa, or permanent resident status. Applicants may not hold another association award concurrently and applicants from current or past recipients of association advanced investigatorships are not eligible.
Level of Study: Postdoctorate.
Type: Grant.
Value: US$100,000 each year for salary, fringe benefits, indirect costs and project costs.
Length of Study: Five years, non renewable.
Frequency: Annual.
Study Establishment: Non-profit institutions or hospitals.
Country of Study: United States of America.
Application Procedure: Applicants must obtain an application form from the website.
Funding: Private.
No. of awards given last year: 30.
No. of applicants last year: 171.
Additional Information: The most up to date information is available from the website. The relevant immigration visas are permanent resident, exchange visitor (J1), temporary worker in a speciality occupation (H1B), Canadian or Mexican citizen engaging in professional activities (TN) or temporary worker with extraordinary abilities in the sciences (O1).

AHA National Scientist Development Grant
Subjects: Cardiovascular function and disease, stroke or related basic science, clinical, bioengineering or biotechnology and public health problems.
Purpose: To support highly promising beginning scientists in their progress toward independence by encouraging and adequately funding research projects that can serve to bridge the gap between completion of research training and readiness for successful competition as an independent investigator.

Eligibility: Open to candidates at Assistant Professor level or its equivalent who are citizens of the United States of America or foreign nationals holding the relevant immigration visa at the time of application. Non citizens must submit proof of possession of one of the relevant immigration visas. Also, at the time of application, candidates should be initiating independent research careers, have an MD, PhD, DO or equivalent doctoral degree and meet institutional requirements for grant submission. No more than four years will have elapsed since an applicant's first faculty or staff appointment at the Assistant Professor level. Applicants cannot hold or have held any other national award.
Level of Study: Postdoctorate.
Type: Grant.
Value: US$65,000 each year for salary, fringe benefits, indirect costs and project costs. At least US$35,000 must be used for the project.
Length of Study: Four years, non renewable.
Frequency: Twice a year.
Study Establishment: Non-profit institutions or hospitals.
Country of Study: United States of America.
Application Procedure: Applicants must obtain an application form from the website. Applications may be submitted for review in the final year of a postdoctoral research fellowship or in the initial years of the first faculty or staff appointment.
Closing Date: January and July.
Funding: Private.
Contributor: Public donations.
No. of awards given last year: 111.
No. of applicants last year: 426.
Additional Information: The most up to date information is available from the website. The relevant immigration visas are exchange visitor (J1), temporary worker in a speciality occupation (H1B), Canadian or Mexican citizen engaging in professional activities (TN) or temporary worker with extraordinary abilities in the sciences (O1).

AMERICAN HERPES FOUNDATION

433 Hackensack Avenue, 9th Floor
Hackensack, NJ NJ07601
United States of America
Tel: (1) 201 883 5852
Fax: (1) 201 342 7555
www: http://www.herpes-foundation.org
Contact: Dr Jennifer Warf, Program Manager

American Herpes Foundation is a nonprofit organization dedicated to improving the management of herpesvirus infections. Our initiatives focus primarily on clinician education and awareness.

American Herpes Foundation Investigator Award
Subjects: Research areas include HSV1 and 2, VZV, EBV, CMV, and HHV6 and 8.
Purpose: To recognize and encourage newer researchers who have completed significant research in the herpes virus area.
Eligibility: Residents, fellows or junior faculty up to the 5th year of faculty appointment.
Type: Cash prize.
Value: US$5,000 case prize - 2 offered in 2004.
Frequency: Annual.
No. of awards offered: 2.
Application Procedure: Candidates must submit a letter of nomination, completed application form, CV, biographical sketch and documentation of research.
Closing Date: Call for details.
Funding: Private.
Contributor: Glaxo Smithkline.
No. of awards given last year: 1.
No. of applicants last year: 12.

For further information contact:

Tel: (201) 342 4441
www: www.herpes-foundation.org

AMERICAN HISTORICAL ASSOCIATION

400 A Street South East, Washington, DC 20003, United States of America
Tel: (1) 202 544 2422
Fax: (1) 202 544 8307
Email: ddoyle@theaha.org
www: http://www.theaha.org
Contact: Convention & Administrative Assistant

Albert J Beveridge Grant
Subjects: The history of the United States, Latin America or Canada, from 1492 to the present.
Purpose: To promote and honour outstanding historical writing.
Eligibility: Open to American Historical Association members only.
Level of Study: Doctorate, Postdoctorate, Postgraduate.
Type: Grant.
Value: A maximum of US$1,000.
Frequency: Annual.
Country of Study: Any country.
No. of awards offered: Varies.
Application Procedure: Applicants must contact the American Historical Association for details.
Closing Date: February 1st.
Funding: Private.

Bernadotte E Schmitt Grants
Subjects: The history of Europe, Asia and Africa.
Purpose: To support research.
Eligibility: Open to American Historical Association members only.
Level of Study: Doctorate, Postdoctorate, Postgraduate.
Type: Grant.
Value: Up to US$1,000.
Frequency: Annual.
Country of Study: Any country.
No. of awards offered: Varies.
Application Procedure: Applicants must contact the American Historical Association for details.
Closing Date: September 15th.
Funding: Private.

J Franklin Jameson Fellowship
Subjects: The collections of the Library of Congress.
Purpose: To support significant scholarly research by new historians.
Eligibility: Applicants must hold a PhD degree or equivalent, must have received this degree within the past seven years, and must not have published or had accepted for publication a book length historical work. The fellowship will not be awarded to complete a doctoral dissertation.
Level of Study: Postdoctorate, Postgraduate.
Type: Fellowship.
Value: US$5,000.
Length of Study: One term.
Frequency: Annual.
Country of Study: United States of America.
No. of awards offered: One.
Application Procedure: Applicants must contact the American Historical Association for details.
Closing Date: February 15th.
Funding: Government, Private.

Littleton-Griswold Research Grant
Subjects: American legal history, law and society.
Purpose: To support research.
Eligibility: Open to American Historical Association members only.
Level of Study: Doctorate, Postdoctorate, Postgraduate.
Type: Research grant.
Value: Up to US$1,000.
Frequency: Annual.
Country of Study: Any country.
No. of awards offered: Varies.
Application Procedure: Applicants must contact the American Historical Association for details.

Closing Date: February 1st.
Funding: Private.

AMERICAN INSTITUTE FOR CANCER RESEARCH (AICR)

1759 R Street North West, Washington, DC 20009, United States of America
Tel: (1) 202 328 7744
Fax: (1) 202 328 7226
Email: aicrweb@aicr.org
www: http://www.aicr.org
Contact: Associate Director for Research

The American Institute for Cancer Research (AICR) is the only major charitable organisation in the United States that fosters research on diet and cancer prevention and educates the public about the results.

AICR Investigator Initiator Grants
Subjects: Cancer research and nutrition.
Purpose: To support research that is at the forefront of the areas of diet, nutrition and cancer.
Eligibility: The principal investigator of a grant must be an assistant professor or higher, with a PhD, MD or equivalent degree.
Level of Study: Postdoctorate, Professional development.
Type: Grant.
Value: A maximum of US$165,000.
Length of Study: Two years.
Frequency: Twice a year.
Country of Study: Any country.
No. of awards offered: Varies.
Application Procedure: Applicants must forward applications to the AICR.
Closing Date: December 17th or July 1st.
Funding: Private.
Additional Information: The AICR also awards Postdoctoral Award Grants and Matching Grants. Interested applicants should contact the Institute for further information.

AMERICAN INSTITUTE FOR ECONOMIC RESEARCH (AIER)

PO Box 1000, Great Barrington, MA 01230, United States of America
Tel: (1) 413 528 1216
Fax: (1) 413 528 0103
Email: info@aier.org
www: http://www.aier.org
Contact: Ms Susan J Gillette, Assistant to the President

The American Institute for Economic Research (AIER), founded in 1933, is an independent scientific educational organisation. The Institute conducts scientific enquiry into general economics with a focus on monetary issues. Attention is also given to business cycle analysis and forecasting, as well as monetary economics.

AIER Summer Fellowship
Subjects: Scientific procedures of inquiry and monetary economics. Business cycle analysis and forecasting also receive attention.
Purpose: To further the development of economic scientists.
Eligibility: Open to graduating seniors who are either entering doctoral programmes in economics, or those enrolled in doctoral programmes in economics for no longer than one year. The programme is not designed for those enrolling into business school.
Level of Study: Postgraduate.
Type: Fellowship.
Value: US$250 weekly stipend plus room and full board.
Length of Study: Two four week sessions.
Frequency: Annual.
Study Establishment: The AIER.
Country of Study: United States of America.
No. of awards offered: 10-12.

Application Procedure: Applicants must submit a completed application form, curriculum vitae, personal statement, writing sample, an outline of proposed course of study and official transcripts. Scholastic references should be sent directly to the director from the referees.
Closing Date: March 31st.
Funding: Private.
No. of awards given last year: Seven.
No. of applicants last year: 32.

AMERICAN INSTITUTE OF INDIAN STUDIES (AIIS)

1130 East 59th Street, Chicago, IL 60637, United States of America
Tel: (1) 773 702 8638
Fax: (1) 773 702 6636
Email: aiis@uchicago.edu
www: http://www.indiastudies.org
Contact: Ms Elise Auerbach, Administrator

The American Institute of Indian Studies (AIIS) is a consortium of American colleges and universities that support the understanding of India, its people and cultures. AIIS offers a range of fellowships for research in India. It also supports individuals studying the performing arts, operates language programmes in India and offers research facilities to scholars in India.

AIIS Junior Research Fellowships
Subjects: India, its people and culture.
Purpose: To support the advancement of knowledge and understanding.
Eligibility: Open to doctoral candidates at United States colleges and universities.
Level of Study: Doctorate.
Length of Study: Up to 11 months.
Frequency: Annual.
Study Establishment: An Indian university.
Country of Study: India.
Application Procedure: Applicants must write for further information.
Closing Date: July 1st.

AIIS Senior Performing and Creative Arts Fellowships
Subjects: Performing and creative arts.
Eligibility: Open to accomplished practitioners of the performing arts of India and creative artists who demonstrate that study in India would enhance their skills, develop their capabilities to teach or perform in the United States of America, enhance American involvement with India's artistic traditions and strengthen their links with peers in India.
Level of Study: Unrestricted.
Type: Fellowship.
Frequency: Annual.
Country of Study: India.
Application Procedure: Applicants must write for further information.
Closing Date: July 1st.

AIIS Senior Research Fellowships
Subjects: South Asian studies.
Purpose: To enable Scholars to pursue further research in India.
Eligibility: Open to Scholars who hold a PhD or its equivalent and are either United States citizens or resident aliens teaching full-time at United States colleges and universities.
Level of Study: Postdoctorate.
Type: Fellowship.
Length of Study: Up to nine months.
Frequency: Annual.
Country of Study: India.
Application Procedure: Applicants must write for further information.
Closing Date: July 1st.

AIIS Senior Scholarly/Professional Development Fellowships
Subjects: India, its people and culture.
Purpose: To support the advancement of knowledge and understanding.

Eligibility: Open to established Scholars who have not previously specialised in Indian studies and to established professionals who have not previously worked or studied in India.
Level of Study: Professional development.
Type: Fellowship.
Length of Study: Six-nine months.
Frequency: Annual.
Country of Study: India.
No. of awards offered: Varies.
Application Procedure: Applicants must write for further information.
Closing Date: July 1st.

AMERICAN JEWISH ARCHIVES

3101 Clifton Avenue, Cincinnati, OH 45220, United States of America
Tel: (1) 513 221 1875
Fax: (1) 513 221 7812
Email: aja@cn.huc.edu
www: http://www.americanjewisharchives.org
Contact: Mr Kevin Proffitt, Director Fellowship Programmes

The Marcus Centre of the American Jewish Archives was founded by Dr Jacob Rader Marcus in 1947 in the aftermath of World War II and the Holocaust. It is committed to preserving a documentary heritage of the religious, organisational, economic, cultural, personal, social and family life of American Jewry. It contains nearly 5,000 linear feet of archives, manuscripts, newprint materials, photographs, audio and video tapes, microfilm, and genealogical materials.

Bernard and Audre Rapoport Fellowships
Subjects: American Jewish studies.
Eligibility: Open to postdoctoral candidates of any nationality.
Level of Study: Postdoctorate.
Type: Fellowship.
Value: Award is determined at the discretion of the selection committee.
Length of Study: One month.
Study Establishment: The Archives.
Country of Study: Any country.
Application Procedure: Applicants must provide an up to date curriculum vitae, a research proposal, evidence of published research and two recommendations from academic colleagues.
Closing Date: March 1st.

Ethel Marcus Memorial Fellowship
Subjects: American Jewish studies.
Eligibility: Open to ABDs.
Level of Study: Postgraduate.
Type: Fellowship.
Value: Award is determined at the discretion of the selection committee.
Length of Study: One month.
Study Establishment: The Archives.
Country of Study: Any country.
Application Procedure: Applicants must provide an up to date curriculum vitae, a research proposal and three faculty recommendations, including dissertation supervisors.
Closing Date: March 1st.

The Joseph and Eva R. Dave Fellowship
Subjects: American Jewish studies- preserving a documentary heritage of the religious, organisational, economic, cultural, personal, social and family and imparting it to the next generation.
Purpose: To facilitate research and writing using the vast collection at the American Jewish Archives.
Eligibility: Open to ABDs.
Level of Study: Doctorate, Postdoctorate, Postgraduate, Predoctorate, Senior or independent scholars.
Type: Fellowship.
Value: Award is determined at the discretion of the selection committee.
Length of Study: One month.
Frequency: Annual.

Study Establishment: The Archives.
Country of Study: Any country.
No. of awards offered: One.
Application Procedure: Applicants must provide an up-to-date curriculum vitae which details the precise nature of the applicant's research interests, and demonstrates clearly how the resources and holdings of the American Jewish archives are vital to the applicant's research. proposals should be more than five double-spaced, typewritten pages. Applicants must provide two recommendations. PhD students should include one from the dissertation supervisor.
Closing Date: March 18th in year of proposed study.
Funding: Private.

Loewenstein-Wiener Fellowship Awards

Subjects: American Jewish studies.
Eligibility: Open to ABDs who have completed all but the dissertation requirement, and to postdoctoral candidates.
Level of Study: Doctorate, Postdoctorate, Postgraduate.
Type: Fellowship.
Value: Award is determined at the discretion of the selection committee.
Length of Study: One month.
Study Establishment: The Archives.
Country of Study: Any country.
Application Procedure: Applicants must provide an up to date curriculum vitae, a research proposal and evidence of published research where possible. ABDs must provide three faculty recommendations including dissertation supervisors and postdoctoral candidates must provide two recommendations from academic colleagues. These will constitute the application.
Closing Date: March 1st.

Marguerite R Jacobs Memorial Award

Subjects: American Jewish studies.
Eligibility: Open to postdoctoral candidates of any nationality.
Level of Study: Doctorate, Postdoctorate, Postgraduate, Predoctorate, Senior or independent scholars.
Value: Award is determined at the discretion of the selection committee.
Length of Study: One month.
Frequency: Annual.
Study Establishment: The Archives.
Country of Study: Any country.
No. of awards offered: One.
Application Procedure: Applicants must provide an up to date curriculum vitae, a research proposal, evidence of published research, where possible, and two recommendations from academic colleagues.
Closing Date: March 1st.
Funding: Private.

The Natalie Field Memorial Fellowship

Subjects: American Jewish studies-preserving a documentary heritage of the religious, organisational, economic, cultural, personal, social and family to the next generation.
Purpose: A bequest from the will of Natalie field. To facilitate research and writing using the vast collection at the American Jewish Archives.
Eligibility: Open to ABDs.
Level of Study: Doctorate, Postdoctorate, Postgraduate, Predoctorate, Senior or independent scholars.
Type: Fellowship.
Value: Award is determined at the discretion of the selection committee.
Frequency: Annual.
Study Establishment: The Archives.
Country of Study: Any country.
No. of awards offered: One.
Application Procedure: Applicants must provide an up-to-date curriculum vitae which details the precise nature of the applicant's research interests, and demonstrates clearly how the resources and holdings of the American Jewish archives are vital to the applicant's research. Proposals should be no more than five

double-spaced, typewritten pages. Applicants must provide two recommendations. PhD students should include one from the dissertation supervisor.
Closing Date: March 18th in year of preceding study.
Funding: Private.

Rabbi Frederic A Doppelt Memorial Fellowship

Subjects: American Jewish studies-preserving a documentary heritage of the religious, organisational, economic, cultural, personal, social and family life of American Jewry and imparting it to the next generation.
Purpose: To honour Rabbi Doppelt by providing fellowships for research and writing the vast collection at the American Jewish Archives.
Eligibility: Open to ABDs. Preference will be given to candidates from Eastern Europe or those working on a topic related to East European Jewry in the American context.
Level of Study: Postdoctorate, Postgraduate, Predoctorate, Senior or independent scholars.
Type: Fellowship.
Value: Award is determined at the discretion of the selection committee.
Length of Study: One month.
Frequency: Annual.
Study Establishment: The Archives.
Country of Study: Any country.
No. of awards offered: One.
Application Procedure: Applicants must provide an up to date curriculum vitae, which details the preuse nature of the applicant's research interests, and demonstrates clearly how the resources and holdings of the American Jewish Archives are vital to the applicant's research. Proposals should be no more than five double-spaced, typewritten pages. Applicants must provide two recommendations. PhD students should include one from the dissertation supervisor.
Closing Date: March 18th in year of proposed study.
Funding: Private.

The Rabbi Harold D. Hahn Memorial Fellowship

Subjects: American Jewish studies preserving a documentary heritage of the religious, organisational, economic, cultural, personal, social and family life of American Jewry and imparting it to the next generation.
Purpose: A perpetual scholarship created to enable scholars to conduct independent research in subject areas relating to the history of North American Jewry.
Eligibility: Open to ABDs.
Level of Study: Doctorate, Postdoctorate, Postgraduate, Predoctorate, Senior or independent scholars.
Type: Fellowship.
Value: Award is determined at the discretion of the Selection Committee.
Length of Study: One month.
Frequency: Annual.
Study Establishment: The Archives.
Country of Study: Any country.
No. of awards offered: One.
Application Procedure: Applicants must provide an up-to-date curriculum vitae which details the precise nature of the applicant's research interests, and demonstrates clearly how the resources and holdings of the American Jewish archives are vital to the applicant's research. Proposals should be no more than five double-spaced, typewritten pages. Applicants must provide two recommendations. PhD students should include one from the dissertation supervisor.
Closing Date: March 18th in year of proposed study.
Funding: Private.

The Rabbi Joachin Prinz Memorial Fellowship

Subjects: American Jewish studies-preserving a documentary heritage of the religious, organisational, economic, cultural, personal, social and family life of American Jewry, and imparting it to the next generation.

Purpose: To enable the recipient to conduct an extensive study of the Dr. Joachin Prinz collection in preparation for a doctoral dissertation or other scholarly publication.
Eligibility: Open to ABDs.
Level of Study: Doctorate, Senior or independent scholars.
Type: Fellowship.
Value: Award is determined at the discretion of the selection committee.
Length of Study: One month.
Frequency: Annual.
Study Establishment: The Archives.
Country of Study: Any country.
No. of awards offered: One.
Application Procedure: Applicants must provide an up-to-date curriculum vitae which details the precise nature of the applicant's research interests, and demonstrates clearly how the resources and holdings of the American Jewish Archives are vital to the applicant's research. Proposals should be no more than five double-spaced, typewritten pages. Applicants must provide two recommendations. PhD students should include one from the dissertation supervisor.
Closing Date: March 18th in year of proposed study.
Funding: Private
Contributor: Deutsche Bank American Foundation.

Rabbi Levi A Olan Memorial Fellowship

Subjects: American Jewish studies.
Eligibility: Open to ABDs.
Level of Study: Postgraduate.
Type: Fellowship.
Value: Award is determined at the discretion of the selection committee.
Length of Study: One month.
Study Establishment: The Archives.
Country of Study: Any country.
Application Procedure: Applicants must provide an up to date curriculum vitae, a research proposal and three faculty recommendations, including dissertation supervisors.
Closing Date: March 1st.

Rabbi Theodore S Levy Tribute Fellowship

Subjects: American Jewish studies.
Eligibility: Open to ABDs.
Level of Study: Doctorate, Postdoctorate, Postgraduate, Predoctorate, Senior or independent scholars.
Type: Fellowship.
Value: Award is determined at the discretion of the selection committee.
Length of Study: One month.
Frequency: Annual.
Study Establishment: The Archives.
Country of Study: Any country.
No. of awards offered: One.
Application Procedure: Applicants must provide an up to date curriculum vitae, a research proposal and three faculty recommendations, including dissertation supervisors.
Closing Date: March 1st.
Funding: Private.

Starkoff Fellowship

Subjects: American Jewish studies.
Eligibility: Open to ABDs.
Level of Study: Postgraduate.
Type: Fellowship.
Value: Award is determined at the discretion of the committee.
Length of Study: One month.
Study Establishment: The Archives.
Country of Study: United States of America.
Application Procedure: Applicants must provide an up to date curriculum vitae, a research proposal and three faculty recommendations, including dissertation supervisors.
Closing Date: March 1st.

AMERICAN LIBRARY ASSOCIATION (ALA)

50 East Huron Street, Chicago, IL 60611, United States of America
Tel: (1) 800 545 2433 ext. 3247
Fax: (1) 312 944 6131
Email: awards@ala.org
www: http://www.ala.org/work/awards
Contact: Ms Cheryl Malden, ALA Awards Co-ordinator

Each year the American Library Association (ALA) and its member units sponsor awards to honour distinguished service and foster professional growth.

3M/NMRT Professional Development Grant

Subjects: Library studies.
Purpose: To allow librarians to attend the annual conference of the ALA.
Eligibility: Open to members of the ALA and the New Members Round Table.
Level of Study: Professional development.
Type: Grant.
Value: Airfare, hotel, conference registration and US$250.
Frequency: Annual.
Country of Study: Any country.
No. of awards offered: Three.
Application Procedure: Applicants must submit nominations to NMRT Professional Development Grant at ALA.
Closing Date: December 15th.
Funding: Commercial.
Contributor: 3M.

AASL Frances Henne Award

Subjects: Library media.
Purpose: To enable an individual to attend an AASL national conference or ALA Annual Conference for the first time.
Eligibility: Open to school library media specialists with less than five years in the profession.
Level of Study: Unrestricted.
Type: Grant.
Value: US$1,250.
Frequency: Annual.
Country of Study: Any country.
No. of awards offered: One.
Application Procedure: Applicants must write for details.
Funding: Commercial.
Contributor: R R Bowker.

AASL Highsmith Research Grant

Subjects: Library science.
Purpose: To enable an individual to conduct innovative research aimed at measuring and evaluating the impact of school library media programmes on learning and education.
Eligibility: Open to qualified researchers of any nationality.
Level of Study: Professional development.
Type: Research grant.
Value: Up to US$5,000.
Frequency: Annual.
Country of Study: Any country.
No. of awards offered: One.
Application Procedure: Applicants must write for details.
Funding: Commercial.
Contributor: The Highsmith Company.

AASL Information Technology Pathfinder Award

Subjects: Library media.
Purpose: To recognise and honour a school library media specialist for demonstrating vision and leadership through the use of information technology to build lifelong learners.
Eligibility: Open to school library media specialists, supervisors or educators.
Level of Study: Professional development.
Type: Scholarship.

Value: US$1,000 to the specialist and US$500 to the library, a citation and travel expenses to ALA Annual Conference.
Frequency: Annual.
Country of Study: Any country.
No. of awards offered: One.
Application Procedure: Applicants must write for details.
Funding: Commercial.
Contributor: Information Plus.

ALA/Information Today Library of the Future Award

Subjects: Library science.
Purpose: To honour an individual library, library consortium, group of librarians or support organisation for innovative planning for applications of, or development of, patron training programmes about information technology in a library setting.
Type: Award.
Value: US$1,500 and a citation.
Frequency: Annual.
No. of awards offered: One.
Application Procedure: Applicants must write for details.
Funding: Private.
Contributor: Information Today, Inc.

Beta Phi Mu Award

Subjects: Education for librarianship.
Purpose: To recognise distinguished service.
Eligibility: Open to library school faculty members or others in the library profession.
Level of Study: Professional development.
Value: US$500 and a citation.
Frequency: Annual.
No. of awards offered: One.
Application Procedure: Applicants must submit six copies of nominations to the ALA Awards Programme Office.
Closing Date: December 1st.
Funding: Private.
Contributor: The Beta Phi Mu International Library Science Honorary Society.
No. of awards given last year: One.

Bogle-Pratt International Library Travel Fund

Subjects: Library science.
Purpose: To enable ALA members to attend their first international conference.
Eligibility: Open to ALA members.
Level of Study: Professional development.
Type: Travel grant.
Value: US$1,000.
Frequency: Annual.
Country of Study: Any country.
No. of awards offered: One.
Application Procedure: Applicants must write for details.
Closing Date: January 1st.
Funding: Private.
Contributor: The Bogle Memorial Fund.
No. of awards given last year: 1.

Bound to Stay Bound Book Scholarships

Subjects: Library science.
Purpose: To support study in the field of library service to children in an ALA accredited programme.
Eligibility: Open to qualified applicants of any nationality who have not started the programme.
Level of Study: Postgraduate.
Type: Scholarship.
Value: US$6,000 each.
Frequency: Annual.
Country of Study: United States of America or Canada.
No. of awards offered: Two.
Application Procedure: Applicants must write or email for details.
Closing Date: March 1st.
Funding: Commercial.
Contributor: Bound to Stay Bound Books, Inc.

Carroll Preston Baber Research Grant

Subjects: Library service.
Purpose: To encourage innovative research that could lead to an improvement in library services to any specified group or groups of people.
Level of Study: Unrestricted.
Type: Research grant.
Value: Up to US$3,000.
Frequency: Annual.
Country of Study: Any country.
No. of awards offered: One.
Application Procedure: Applicants must submit an application including a research proposal.
Funding: Private.
Contributor: Eric R Baber.
No. of awards given last year: 1.
No. of applicants last year: Five.
Additional Information: The project should aim to answer a question that is of vital importance to the library community and the researchers should plan to provide documentation of the results of their work. The jury would welcome proposals that involve innovative uses of technology and proposals that involve co-operation between libraries and other agencies, or between librarians and persons in other disciplines.

Christopher J Hoy/ERT Scholarship

Subjects: Library and information studies.
Purpose: To allow individuals to attend an ALA accredited programme of library and information studies.
Eligibility: Open to applicants who will be attending an American Library Association accredited programme of library and information studies leading to a Master's degree.
Level of Study: Postgraduate.
Type: Scholarship.
Value: US$3,000.
Frequency: Annual.
Country of Study: Any country.
No. of awards offered: One.
Application Procedure: Applicants must write for details.
Funding: Private.
Contributor: The family of Christopher J Hoy.

David H Clift Scholarship

Subjects: Library science.
Purpose: To enable a worthy candidate to begin a Master's degree.
Eligibility: Open to qualified Canadian or United States citizens pursuing a Master's degree in library science in an ALA accredited programme.
Level of Study: Postgraduate.
Type: Scholarship.
Value: US$3,000.
Frequency: Annual.
Country of Study: Any country.
No. of awards offered: One.
Application Procedure: Applicants must write for details.

David Rozkuska Scholarship

Subjects: Library science.
Purpose: To provide financial assistance to an individual who is currently working with government documents in a library.
Eligibility: Open to applicants currently completing a Master's programme in library science.
Level of Study: Postgraduate.
Type: Scholarship.
Value: US$3,000.
Frequency: Annual.
Country of Study: Any country.
No. of awards offered: One.
Application Procedure: Applicants must write for details.

EBSCO ALA Conference Sponsorship

Subjects: Library science.
Purpose: To allow librarians to attend the ALA Annual Conference.
Eligibility: Open to librarians.

Level of Study: Professional development.
Type: Travel grant.
Value: Up to US$1,000 for expenses.
Frequency: Annual.
Country of Study: Any country.
No. of awards offered: 10.
Application Procedure: Applicants must write for details.
Closing Date: December 1st.
Funding: Commercial.
Contributor: EBSCO Subscription Services.

Eli M Oboler Memorial Award

Subjects: Intellectual freedom and freedom to read.
Purpose: To award the best published work in the field.
Eligibility: There are no eligibility restrictions.
Level of Study: Unrestricted.
Type: Award.
Value: US$1,500.
Frequency: Every two years.
Country of Study: Any country.
No. of awards offered: One.
Application Procedure: Applicants must submit the nominated documents with nominating form.
Closing Date: December 1st.
Funding: Private.

Elizabeth Futas Catalyst for Change Award

Subjects: Library science.
Purpose: To recognise and honour a librarian who invests time and talent to make positive changes in the profession of librarianship by taking risks to further the cause, helping new librarians grow and achieve, working for change within the ALA or other library organisations and inspiring colleagues to excel or make the impossible possible.
Type: Award.
Value: US$1,000 and a citation.
Frequency: Annual.
No. of awards offered: One.
Application Procedure: Applicants must write for details.
Contributor: An endowment administered by the ALA.
No. of awards given last year: One.

Equality Award

Subjects: Pay equity, affirmative action, legislative work and non sexist education.
Purpose: To recognise an outstanding contribution towards the promotion of equality in the library profession. The contribution may be either a sustained one or a single outstanding accomplishment.
Eligibility: Open to members of the library profession.
Level of Study: Professional development.
Value: US$500 plus a citation.
Frequency: Annual.
No. of awards offered: One.
Application Procedure: Applicants must submit six copies of nominations to the ALA Awards Program Office.
Funding: Commercial.
Contributor: The Scarecrow Press.
No. of awards given last year: One.

Facts on File Grant

Subjects: Library science.
Purpose: To award a library for imaginative programming which would make current affairs more meaningful to an adult audience. Programmes, bibliographies, pamphlets, and innovative approaches of all types and in all media will apply.
Eligibility: Open to adult librarians.
Level of Study: Professional development.
Type: Grant.
Value: US$2,000.
Frequency: Annual.
Country of Study: Any country.
No. of awards offered: One.

Application Procedure: Applicants must submit a proposal accompanied by a statement of objective, identification of the current issues, the target audience and the extent of community involvement planned, an outline of planned activities for conducting and promoting the project, a budget summary and details of how the project will be evaluated.
Funding: Commercial.
No. of awards given last year: One.

Frances Henne/YALSA/VOYA Research Grant

Subjects: Library science.
Purpose: To provide seed money to an individual, institution or group for a project to encourage research on library service to young adults.
Eligibility: Open to applicants of any nationality.
Level of Study: Unrestricted.
Type: Research grant.
Value: US$500 minimum.
Frequency: Annual.
Country of Study: Any country.
No. of awards offered: One.
Application Procedure: Applicants must write for details.

Frederick G Melcher Scholarships

Subjects: Library service to children.
Purpose: To provide financial assistance for the professional education of men and women who intend to pursue children's librarianship.
Eligibility: Open to qualified young persons who have been accepted for admission to an appropriate school.
Level of Study: Graduate.
Type: Scholarship.
Value: US$5,000.
Frequency: Annual.
Study Establishment: An ALA accredited school.
Country of Study: United States of America or Canada.
No. of awards offered: Two.
Application Procedure: Applicants must write or email for details.
Closing Date: April 1st.
Funding: Private.

Grolier Foundation Award

Subjects: Library work with children and young people to high school age.
Purpose: To recognise a librarian whose unusual contribution to the stimulation and guidance of reading by children and young people exemplifies outstanding achievement in the profession. The award is given either for outstanding for continuing service, or in recognition of one particular contribution of lasting value.
Eligibility: Open to community and school librarians.
Level of Study: Professional development.
Value: US$1,000 plus a citation.
Frequency: Annual.
No. of awards offered: One.
Application Procedure: Applicants must submit six copies of the application to the ALA Awards Program Office.
Funding: Commercial.
Contributor: Grolier Publishing Company.
No. of awards given last year: One.

H W Wilson Library Staff Development Grant

Subjects: Library science.
Purpose: To award a library organisation whose application demonstrates greatest merit for a programme of staff development designed to further goals and objectives of the library organisation.
Type: Grant.
Value: US$3,500 and a citation.
Frequency: Annual.
No. of awards offered: One.
Application Procedure: Applicants must submit six copies of the application and documentation to the ALA Awards Program Office.
Contributor: The H W Wilson Company.
No. of awards given last year: One.

Jesse H Shera Award for Excellence in Doctoral Research

Subjects: Library science.
Level of Study: Doctorate.
Type: Prize.
Value: US$500, multiple authors will divide the award.
Frequency: Annual.
Country of Study: Any country.
No. of awards offered: One.
Application Procedure: Applicants must send three copies of the paper, together with a cover letter stating that you own copyright to it.
Closing Date: Postmarked no later than February 15th.
Funding: Private.
Additional Information: The text of any submitted research paper must not exceed 10,000 words. Research papers should be drawn from work completed in pursuit of doctoral studies.

Jesse H Shera Award for Research

Subjects: Library science.
Purpose: To honor an outstanding and original paper reporting the results of research related to libraries.
Eligibility: Authors of nominated articles need not be Library Research Round Table (LRRT) members but the nominations must be made by LRRT members. All entries must be research articles published in English during the calendar year previous to the competition. All nominated articles must relate in at least a general way to library and information studies.
Level of Study: Unrestricted.
Type: Prize.
Value: US$500.
Frequency: Annual.
Country of Study: Any country.
No. of awards offered: One.
Application Procedure: Applicants wishing to nominate research articles for this award should send three copies of each article together with a covering letter stating that they are a current member of LRRT or that they are acting in their role as journal editor.
Closing Date: February 15th.
Funding: Private.
No. of awards given last year: 1.
No. of applicants last year: 12.

John Philip Immroth Award for Intellectual Freedom

Subjects: Intellectual freedom.
Purpose: To recognise a notable contribution to intellectual freedom fuelled by personal courage.
Eligibility: Open to intellectual freedom fighters.
Level of Study: Unrestricted.
Type: Award.
Value: US$500 plus a citation.
Frequency: Annual.
Country of Study: Any country.
No. of awards offered: One.
Application Procedure: Applicants must submit a detailed statement showing why the nominator believes that the nominee should receive the award. Nominations should be submitted to IFRT Staff Liaison at the ALA.
Closing Date: December 1st.
Funding: Private.

Joseph W Lippincott Award

Subjects: Participation in the activities of professional library associations, notably published professional writing or other significant activity on behalf of the profession and its aims.
Purpose: To recognise distinguished service in the profession of librarianship including outstanding participation in professional library activities, notable published professional writing or other significant activities.
Eligibility: Open to librarians.
Level of Study: Professional development.
Type: Award.
Value: US$1,000 plus a citation.
Frequency: Annual.
No. of awards offered: One.
Application Procedure: Applicants must submit six copies of nominations to the ALA Awards Program Office.
Funding: Private.
Contributor: The late Joseph W Lippincott.
No. of awards given last year: One.

Ken Haycock Award for Promoting Librarianship

Subjects: Library Science.
Purpose: Honors an individual for contributing significantly to the public recognition and appreciation of librarianship through professional performance, teaching and or writing.
Type: Award.
Value: US$1,000 and a citation.
Frequency: Annual.
No. of awards offered: One.
Funding: Private.
Contributor: Kenneth Haycock, PhD.

Lexis/Nexis/GODORT/ALA Documents to the People Award

Subjects: Library science.
Purpose: The NewsBank/Readex/GODORT/ALA Catharine J. Reynolds Award provides funding for research in the field of documents librarianship, or in a related area that would benefit the individual's performance as a documents librarian or make a contribution to the field. This award, established in 1987, is named for Catharine J. Reynolds, former Head of Government Publications at the University of Colorado, Boulder. It is supported by an annual contribution of $2,000 from the NewsBank/Readex Corporation. Applications for the NewsBank/Readex/GODORT/ALA Catharine J. Reynolds Awards are accepted from documents librarians. The awards support research in all areas of government information, U.S., foreign, international, state, regional, or local. The grant can be used to finance research costs, such as computer time or including travel. Recipients are selected on the basis of a well-defined proposal, potential ability to complete the project, promise of future contributions to the profession, financial need, and activity to the profession. Preference is given to GODORT members. Two confidential letters of recommendation should accompany the application form.
Eligibility: Open to individuals and libraries, organisations and other appropriate non commercial groups.
Level of Study: Unrestricted.
Type: Award.
Value: US$3,000.
Frequency: Annual.
Country of Study: Any country.
No. of awards offered: One.
Application Procedure: Applicants must submit nominations to GODORT Staff Liaison at the ALA.
Funding: Commercial.
Contributor: Lexis/Nexis.

Library Research Round Table Research Award

Subjects: Library science.
Purpose: To encourage excellence in research.
Eligibility: Open to library science researchers.
Level of Study: Unrestricted.
Type: Research grant.
Value: US$1,000.
Frequency: Annual.
Country of Study: Any country.
No. of awards offered: One.
Application Procedure: Please request guidelines from ALA.
Closing Date: February 2nd.
No. of awards given last year: One.
No. of applicants last year: Four.
Additional Information: Papers must not exceed 50 pages in length and will be judged on the definition of the research problem, application of research methods, clarity of reporting and the significance of conclusions. Research papers completed in pursuit of an academic degree are not eligible. Candidates should submit their entries to the jury chair, whose name is available each year from ALA.

Loleta D Fyan Public Library Research Grant

Subjects: Library service.
Purpose: To facilitate the development and improvement of public libraries and the services they provide.
Eligibility: Applicants can include but are not limited to local, regional or state libraries, associations or organisations including units of the ALA, library schools or individuals.
Level of Study: Unrestricted.
Type: Research grant.
Value: Up to US$10,000.
Frequency: Annual.
Country of Study: Any country.
No. of awards offered: One or more.
Application Procedure: Applicants must submit an application form in addition to a proposal and budget.
Closing Date: Applications are accepted at any time.
Funding: Private.
No. of awards given last year: 1.
No. of applicants last year: 10.
Additional Information: The project must result in the development and improvement of public libraries and the services they provide, have the potential for broader impact and application beyond meeting a specific local need, should be designed to effect changes in public library services that are innovative and responsive to the future, and should be capable of completion within one year.

Marshall Cavendish Excellence in Library Programming

Subjects: Library Science.
Purpose: To recognize a school or public library for programs that have community impact and respond to community needs.
Type: Award.
Value: US$3,000 and a citation.
Frequency: Annual.
No. of awards offered: One.
Funding: Corporation.
Contributor: Marshall Cavendish Corporation.

Mary V Gaver Scholarship

Subjects: Library science.
Purpose: To assist library support staff specialising in youth services.
Eligibility: Open to library support staff who are United States or Canadian citizens who are pursuing a Master's degree in library science.
Level of Study: Unrestricted.
Type: Scholarship.
Value: US$3,000.
Frequency: Annual.
Country of Study: Any country.
No. of awards offered: One.
Application Procedure: Applicants must write for details.
Closing Date: March 1.
No. of awards given last year: One.

Melvil Dewey Medal

Subjects: Library science.
Purpose: To award an individual or group for recent creative professional achievement in library management, training, cataloguing, classification and the tools and techniques of librarianship.
Type: Award.
Value: Medal and citation.
Frequency: Annual.
No. of awards offered: One.
Application Procedure: Applicants must write for details.
Contributor: The OCLC Forest Press.
No. of awards given last year: One.

Miriam L Hornback Scholarship

Subjects: Library science.
Purpose: To assist an individual pursuing a Master's degree.
Eligibility: Open to ALA or library support staff who are pursuing a Master's degree in library science and who are citizens of the United States or Canada.

Level of Study: Postgraduate.
Type: Scholarship.
Value: US$3,000.
Frequency: Annual.
No. of awards offered: One.
Application Procedure: Applicants must write for details.
Closing Date: March 1.
No. of awards given last year: Two.

New Leaders Travel Grant

Subjects: Library science.
Purpose: To enhance professional development and improve the expertise of individuals new to the field by making possible their attendance at major professional development activities.
Eligibility: Open to qualified public librarians.
Level of Study: Professional development.
Type: Travel grant.
Value: Plaque and travel grant of up to US$1,500 per applicant.
Frequency: Annual.
Country of Study: Any country.
No. of awards offered: One.
Application Procedure: Applicants must write for details.

NMRT/EBSCO Scholarship

Subjects: Library science.
Purpose: To enable an individual to begin an MLS degree in an ALA accredited programme.
Eligibility: Open to United States and Canadian citizens.
Level of Study: Postgraduate.
Type: Scholarship.
Value: US$1,000.
Frequency: Annual.
Country of Study: Any country.
No. of awards offered: One.
Application Procedure: Applicants must write for details.
Closing Date: April 1st.

Penguin Putnam Books for Young Readers Award

Subjects: Library science.
Purpose: To allow children's librarians to attend the Annual Conference of the ALA.
Eligibility: Open to members of the Association for Library Service to Children with between 1-10 years of experience who have never attended an ALA annual conference.
Level of Study: Professional development.
Type: Award.
Value: US$600.
Frequency: Annual.
Country of Study: Other.
No. of awards offered: Four.
Application Procedure: Applicants must write or email for details Phone: 800 545 2433, ext. 2163, Email: alsc@ala.org.
Closing Date: December 1st.
Funding: Commercial.
Contributor: Penguin Group, USA.
No. of awards given last year: Four.

Primark Student Travel Award

Subjects: Library science.
Purpose: To enable a student interested in a career as a business librarian to attend an ALA Annual Conference.
Eligibility: Open to qualified Master's students in an ALA accredited programme.
Level of Study: Postgraduate.
Type: Travel grant.
Value: US$1,000.
Frequency: Annual.
Country of Study: Any country.
No. of awards offered: One.
Application Procedure: Applicants must write for details.
Funding: Commercial.
Contributor: Disclosure, Inc.

Samuel Lazerow Fellowship for Research in Acquisitions or Technical Services

Subjects: Acquisitions or technical services.
Purpose: To foster advances in acquisitions or technical services by providing a fellowship for travel or writing in those fields.
Eligibility: Open to qualified librarians.
Level of Study: Professional development.
Type: Fellowship.
Value: US$1,000 plus a citation.
Frequency: Annual.
Country of Study: Any country.
No. of awards offered: One.
Application Procedure: Applicants must write for details refer to the awards section of the ACRL website, www.ala.org/acrl.
Closing Date: Early December - see website for more details.
Contributor: Thomson ISI.
No. of awards given last year: One.

Schneider Family Book Award

Subjects: Library Science.
Purpose: The Schneider Family Book Awards honor an author or illustrator for a book that embodies an artistic expression of the disability experience for child and adolescent audiences. Three annul awards each consisting of US$5000 and a framed plaque, will be given annually in each of the following categories: birth through grade school (age 0-10), middle school (age 11-13) and teens (age 13-18). (Age groupings are approximations). The book must emphasize the artistic expression of the disability experience for children and or adolescent audiences. The book must portray some aspect of living with a disability or that of a friend or family member, whether the disability is physical, mental or emotional.
Type: Award.
Value: US$5,000 and a citation for each winner.
Frequency: Annual.
No. of awards offered: Three.
Funding: Private.
Contributor: Katherine Schneider, PhD.

Shirley Olofson Memorial Awards

Subjects: Library science.
Purpose: To allow individuals to attend ALA conferences.
Eligibility: Open to members of the ALA who are also current or potential members of the New Members Round Table. Applicants should not have attended any more than five conferences.
Level of Study: Unrestricted.
Type: Award.
Value: US$1,000.
Frequency: Annual.
Country of Study: Any country.
No. of awards offered: Varies.
Application Procedure: Applicants must write for details.
Closing Date: December 15th.

SIRSI Leader in Library Technology Grant

Subjects: Library Science.
Purpose: To encourage and enable continued advancements in quality library services for a project that makes creative or groundbreaking use of technology to deliver exceptional services to its community. Eligible libraries are public, academic, school and special (i.e., medical, law, government, corporate, or museum).
Type: Grant.
Value: US$10,000 and a citation.
Frequency: Annual.
No. of awards offered: One.
Funding: Corporation.
Contributor: SIRSI Corporation.

Spectrum Initiative Scholarship Program

Subjects: Library and information studies.
Purpose: To encourage admission to an ALA recognised Master's degree programme by the four largest underrepresented groups.
Eligibility: Open to United States or Canadian citizens only, from one of the largest underrepresented groups. These are African American or African Canadian, Asian or Pacific Islander, Latino or Hispanic and native people of the United States of America or Canada.
Level of Study: Postgraduate.
Type: Scholarship.
Value: US$5,000.
Frequency: Annual.
Country of Study: United States of America or Canada.
No. of awards offered: 50.
Application Procedure: Applicants must request details via fax on demand or visit the website.
Closing Date: April 1st.

Sullivan Award for Public Library Administrators Supporting Services to Ch

Subjects: Library Science.
Purpose: To an individual who has shown exceptional understanding and support of public library service to children while having general management/supervisory/administrative responsibility that has included public library service to children in its scope.
Type: Award.
Value: Citation and commemorative gift.
Frequency: Annual.
No. of awards offered: One.
Funding: Private.
Contributor: Peggy Sullivan, PhD.

Tom C Drewes Scholarship

Subjects: Library science.
Purpose: To assist a library support staff person.
Eligibility: Open to library support staff pursuing a Master's degree who are United States or Canadian citizens.
Level of Study: Postgraduate.
Type: Scholarship.
Value: US$3,000.
Frequency: Annual.
Country of Study: Any country.
No. of awards offered: One.
Application Procedure: Applicants must write for details.

W. Y. Boyd Literary Award

Subjects: The writing and publishing of outstanding war related fiction.
Purpose: To award an author who has written a military novel that honours the service of American veterans and military personnel during a time of war, 1861-1865, 1914-1918 or 1939-1945.
Type: Award.
Value: US$5,000 and a citation.
Frequency: Annual.
No. of awards offered: One.
Application Procedure: Applicants must write for details.
Closing Date: December 1st.
Funding: Private.
Contributor: William Young Boyd II.

YALSA/Baker and Taylor Conference Grants

Subjects: Library science.
Purpose: To allow young adult librarians who work directly with young adults in either a public library or a school library, to attend the Annual Conference of the ALA.
Eligibility: Open to members of the Young Adult Library Services Association with between one and ten years of library experience who have never attended an ALA annual conference.
Level of Study: Professional development.
Type: Grant.
Value: US$1,000.
Frequency: Annual.
Country of Study: Any country.
No. of awards offered: Two.
Application Procedure: Applicants must submit applications to the Young Adult Library Services Association, ALA.
Closing Date: December 1st.
Additional Information: The American Library Association offers a number of other awards in various fields related to library science,

including the following medals and citations with no cash prizes: the Randolph Caldecott Medal, the James Bennett Childs Award, the Dartmouth Medal, the Melvil Dewey Medal, the John Newberry Medal, the Laura Ingalls Wilder Medal, the ASCLA Exceptional Service Award, the Armed Forces Librarians Achievement Citation, the Francis Joseph Campbell Citation, the Margaret Mann Citation, the Isadore Gilbert Mudge Citation, the Esther J Piercy Award, the Distinguished Library Service Award for School Administrators and the Trustees Citations. A full list of awards is available from the ALA.

AMERICAN MATHEMATICAL SOCIETY (AMS)

PO Box 6248, Providence, RI 02940-6248
United States of America
Tel: (1) 401 455 4107
Fax: (1) 401 455 4004
Email: ams@ams.org
www: http://www.ams.org
Contact: Ms Karen Butler, Executive Assistant

The American Mathematical Society (AMS) was created to further mathematical research and scholarship. Founded in 1888, it now has approximately 30,000 members, including mathematicians throughout the United States and around the world. It continues to fulfil its mission with programmes that promote mathematical research, increase the awareness of its value to society and foster excellence in mathematics education.

AMS Centennial Fellowship
Subjects: Mathematics.
Purpose: To help further the research careers of outstanding mid-career mathematicians.
Eligibility: Open to candidates who have held a doctoral degree for at least three and not more than 12 years at the inception of the award. The primary selection criteria is the excellence of the candidate's research. Preference will be given to candidates who have not had extensive fellowship support in the past. Recipients may not hold the fellowship concurrently with another research fellowship such as the Sloan or NSF Postdoctoral fellowship. Under normal circumstances, the fellowship cannot be deferred. Applications will be accepted from those currently holding a tenured, tenure track, postdoctoral or comparable position, at the discretion of the selection committee, from an institution in North America.
Level of Study: Postdoctorate.
Type: Fellowship.
Value: A stipend of US$60,000 plus an expense allowance of US$1,700.
Frequency: Annual.
Study Establishment: An institution in North America.
Country of Study: United States of America.
No. of awards offered: At least one, dependent on funds available.
Application Procedure: Applicants must submit an application including a cogent plan indicating how the fellowship will be used. The plan should include travel to at least one other institution and should demonstrate that the fellowship will be used for more than reduction of teaching at the candidate's home institution. The selection committee will consider the plan in addition to the quality of the candidate's research, and will try to award the fellowship to those for whom the award would make a real difference in the development of their research careers. Information and application forms are available on the website. Completed application forms and reference forms should be sent to the American Mathematical Society.
Closing Date: December 1st.
Funding: Private.
No. of awards given last year: One or two.

For further information contact:

AMS Centennial Fellowship, Membership & Programmes Department, American Mathematical Society, 201 Charles Street, Providence, RI 02904, United States of America

AMERICAN MUSIC CENTER, INC.

30 West 26th Street, Suite 1001, New York, NY 10010-2011, United States of America
Tel: (1) 212 366 5260
Fax: (1) 212 366 5265
Email: center@amc.net
www: http://www.amc.net
Contact: Mr Philip Rothman, Manager of Grantmaking Programs

The American Music Center is a non-profit membership and service organisation. The Center's mission is to build a national community for new American music.

Composer Assistance Program
Subjects: Music.
Purpose: To support individual composers to realize their music in performance.
Eligibility: American composers in good standing of the AMC.
Level of Study: Professional development.
Type: Fellowship.
Value: Up to US$5,000.
Length of Study: Variable.
Frequency: Annual.
Country of Study: United States of America.
Application Procedure: Download guidelines from website.
Closing Date: February 1st, May 1st, October 1st.
Funding: Private.
Contributor: The Helen F. Whitaker Fund.

Margaret Fairbank Jory Copying Assistance Program
Subjects: Musical composition.
Purpose: To assist composers with copying expenses for a première performance.
Eligibility: Open to American composers who are members of the American Music Center and in good standing at the time of application. The performance must advance the professional career of the composer. Performers, presenters or ensembles are not eligible to apply. Funds are available for copying parts for the première performance of large scale works for four or more instrumental and/or vocal parts. The composer must have a written commitment for at least one public performance of the work by a professional ensemble of recognised artistic merit.
Level of Study: Professional development.
Type: Grant.
Frequency: Three times each year.
Country of Study: Any country.
No. of awards offered: Approx. 75.
Application Procedure: Applicants must complete an application form and submit this with supporting materials. These include a brief statement of the significance of this performance to the composer's career, a brief professional curriculum vitae with a list of other recent performances, written confirmation of the exact premiere performance date, background on the performing organisation, a list of estimated expenses that totals the amount requested, and the for which support is requested.
Closing Date: February 1st, June 1st or October 1st.
Funding: Private.
Contributor: The Mary Flager Cary Charitable Trust, the Helen F Whitaker Fund, JPMorgan Chase, the Arts Alive Foundation and individuals.
No. of awards given last year: Approx. 75.
No. of applicants last year: Approx. 200.
Additional Information: Applicants should visit the website for further information.

THE AMERICAN MUSIC SCHOLARSHIP ASSOCIATION, INC. (AMSA)

441 Vine Street, Suite 1030, Cincinnati, OH 45202, United States of America
Tel: (1) 513 421 5342
Fax: (1) 513 421 2672
Email: info@amsa-wpc.org
www: http://www.amsa-wpc.org
Contact: Chief Executive Officer

The American Music Scholarship Association (AMSA) produces the annual world piano competition in Cincinnati. AMSA also provides outreach programmes to Cincinnati children (eg. The Bach, Beethoven, and Brahms Club) and worldwide performances. The young artist division winners perform at Carnegie Hall and the gold medallist of the artist division performs at Lincoln Center's Alice Tully Hall.

AMSA World Piano Competition

Subjects: Musical performance on the piano.
Purpose: To encourage the careers of aspiring young pianists and expose them to the performances of great musicians.
Eligibility: Open to piano students of any nationality who are between the ages of 5 and 30.
Level of Study: Unrestricted.
Type: Scholarship.
Value: The Artist Division's first prize is US$10,000 plus a fully managed debut recital at the Lincoln Center in New York. The second prize is US$3,000, the third US$2,000, the fourth US$1,000, the fifth US$500 and the sixth US$300. The Young Artists Division grand prize at levels 9-12 is US$1,500.
Frequency: Annual, if funds are available.
Country of Study: Any country.
Application Procedure: Applicants must apply in compliance with the full competition rules and regulations, which are available on request and on the website.
Closing Date: Please refer to the website.
Funding: Private.

AMERICAN MUSICOLOGICAL SOCIETY (AMS)

Department of Music, 201 South 34th Street, Philadelphia, PA 19104-6313, United States of America
Tel: (1) 215 898 8698
Fax: (1) 215 573 3673
Email: ams@sas.upenn.edu
www: http://www.ams-net.org
Contact: Executive Director

The American Musicological Society (AMS) was founded in 1934 as a non-profit organisation, with the aim of advancing research in the various fields of music as a branch of learning and scholarship. In 1951 the Society became a constituent member of the American Council of Learned Societies.

Alfred Einstein Award

Subjects: Musicology.
Purpose: To honour a musicological article of exceptional merit by a Scholar in the early stages of his or her career.
Eligibility: Open to citizens or permanent residents of Canada or the United States.
Level of Study: Professional development.
Type: Prize.
Value: Varies.
Frequency: Annual.
No. of awards offered: One.
Application Procedure: Applicants must be nominated. The committee will entertain articles from any individual, including eligible authors who are encouraged to nominate their own articles. Nominations should include the name of the author, the title of the article and the name and year of the periodical or other collection in which it was published. A curriculum vitae is also required.
Closing Date: June 1st.
Funding: Private.
Additional Information: Further information is available on request.

Alvin H Johnson 50 Dissertation One Year Fellowship

Subjects: Any field of musical research.
Purpose: To encourage research in the various fields of music as a branch of learning and scholarship.

Eligibility: Open to full-time students registered for a doctorate at a North American university, in good standing, who have completed all formal degree requirements except the dissertation at the time of full application. Open to all students without regard to nationality, race, religion or gender.
Level of Study: Doctorate, Postgraduate.
Type: Fellowship.
Value: US$14,000.
Length of Study: One year.
Frequency: Annual.
Country of Study: United States of America or Canada.
No. of awards offered: Five-six.
Application Procedure: Application forms will be sent via the Directors of Graduate Study at all doctorate granting institutions in North America. They will also be available directly from the Society and the website. Applications must include a curriculum vitae, certification of enrolment and degree completed, and two supporting letters from faculty members, one of whom must be the principal adviser of the dissertation. A detailed dissertation prospectus and a completed chapter or comparable written work on the dissertation should accompany the full application. All documents should be submitted in triplicate.
Closing Date: January 15th.
Funding: Private.
Additional Information: Any submission for a doctoral degree in which the emphasis is on musical scholarship is eligible. The award is not intended for support of early stages of research and it is expected that a recipient's dissertation will be completed within the fellowship year. An equivalent major award from another source may not normally be held concurrently unless the AMS award is accepted on an honorary basis.

AMS Subventions for Publications

Subjects: Any field of musicology.
Purpose: To help individuals with expenses involved in the publication of works of musical scholarship, including books, articles and works in non print media.
Eligibility: Open to younger Scholars and Scholars in the early stages of their careers. Proposals for projects that make use of newer technologies are welcomed.
Level of Study: Professional development.
Type: Grant.
Value: US$500 2,000 with a maximum of US$2,500 available.
Frequency: Twice a year.
Application Procedure: Applicants must submit a short written abstract of up to 1,000 words describing the project and its contribution to musical scholarship, a copy of the article or other equivalent sample, a copy of a contract or letter of agreement from the journal editor or publisher indicating final acceptance for publication, and a detailed budget and explanation of the expenses to which the subvention would be applied. Wherever possible expenses should be itemised. If the publication is a book a representative chapter should be submitted.
Closing Date: March 15th or September 15th.
Additional Information: No individual can receive a subvention more than once in a three year period.

Howard Mayer Brown Fellowship

Subjects: Musicology.
Purpose: To increase the presence of minority scholars and teachers in musicology.
Eligibility: Open to candidates who have completed at least one year of academic work at an institution with a graduate programme in musicology and who intend to complete a PhD in the field. Applicants must be members of a group historically underrepresented in the discipline, including African Americans, Native Americans, Hispanic Americans and Asian Americans. Candidates will normally be citizens or permanent residents of the United States of America or Canada. There are no restrictions on age or gender.
Level of Study: Postgraduate.
Type: Fellowship.
Value: US$12,000.
Length of Study: One year.
Frequency: Annual.

Study Establishment: An institution which offers a graduate programme in musicology.
Country of Study: United States of America or Canada.
Application Procedure: Applicants must be nominated. Nominations may come from a faculty member of the institution at which the student is enrolled, from a member of the AMS at another institution, or directly from the student. Supporting documents must include a letter summarising the candidate's academic background, letters of support from three faculty members and samples of the applicant's work such as term papers or any published material.
Closing Date: April 1st of the year in which the fellowship is awarded.
Funding: Private.
Additional Information: The AMS encourages the institution at which the recipient is pursuing his or her degree to offer continuing financial support. Further information is available on request.

Noah Greenberg Award

Subjects: Musicology.
Purpose: To provide a grant-in-aid to stimulate active co-operation between scholars and performers by recognising and fostering outstanding contributions to historical performing practices.
Eligibility: Both Scholars and performers may apply. Applicants need not be members of the Society.
Level of Study: Professional development.
Type: Award.
Value: Varies.
Frequency: Annual.
No. of awards offered: One-two.
Application Procedure: Applicants must submit three copies of a description of the project, a detailed budget and supporting materials such as articles or tapes of performances which are relevant to the project. Applications must be sent to the chair of the Noah Greenberg Award Committee.
Funding: Private.

Otto Kinkeldey Award

Subjects: Musicology.
Purpose: To award the work of musicological scholarship such as a major book, edition or other piece of scholarship that best exemplifies the highest quality of originality, interpretation, logic, clarity of thought and communication.
Eligibility: The work must have been published during the previous year in any language and in any country by a Scholar who is a citizen or permanent resident of Canada or the United States.
Level of Study: Professional development.
Type: Prize.
Value: Varies.
Frequency: Annual.
Application Procedure: Applicants must write for details.
Funding: Private.
Additional Information: Further information is available on request.

Paul A Pisk Prize

Subjects: Any field of musicology.
Purpose: To encourage scholarship.
Eligibility: Open to graduate students whose abstracts have been submitted to the Program Committee of the Society and papers accepted for inclusion in the Annual Meeting. Open to all students without regard to nationality, race, religion or gender.
Level of Study: Graduate.
Type: Prize.
Value: US$1,000.
Frequency: Annual.
Country of Study: United States of America or Canada.
No. of awards offered: One.
Application Procedure: Applicants must submit three copies of the complete text paper to the chair of the Pisk Prize Committee. The submission must be accompanied by a statement from the student's

academic adviser affirming the graduate student status of the applicant.
Closing Date: September 1st.
Funding: Private.
Additional Information: Further information is available on request.

Philip Brett Award

Subjects: Musicology.
Purpose: To honour an exceptional musicological work such as a published article, book, edition, annotated translation, a paper read at a conference or teaching materials in the field of gay, lesbian, bisexual, transgender or transsexual studies.
Eligibility: Work must be completed during the previous two academic years, ending June 30th, in any country and in any language.
Type: Award.
Value: A monetary prize and a certificate.
Frequency: Annual.
Country of Study: Any country.
No. of awards offered: One.
Application Procedure: Applicants must be nominated. Nominations are accepted from any individual and should include five copies of the name of the scholar, a description of the work and a statement to the effect that the work was completed during the previous two academic years.
Closing Date: July 1st.
Funding: Private.

AMERICAN NUCLEAR SOCIETY (ANS)

555 North Kensington Avenue, LaGrange Park, IL 60525, United States of America
Tel: (1) 708 352 6611
Fax: (1) 708 352 0499
Email: outreach@ans.org
www: http://www.ans.org
Contact: Scholarship Programme

The American Nuclear Society (ANS) is a non-profit, international, scientific and educational organisation. It was established by a group of individuals who recognised the need to unify the professional activities within the diverse fields of nuclear science and technology.

Alan F Henry/Paul A Greebler Scholarship

Subjects: Reactor physics.
Purpose: To aid students pursuing studies in the field.
Eligibility: Open to full-time graduate students at a North American university engaged in Master's or PhD research in the area of nuclear reactor physics or radiation transport. Applicants may be of any nationality.
Level of Study: Graduate, Postdoctorate.
Type: Scholarship.
Value: Varies.
Length of Study: Varies.
Frequency: Annual.
Study Establishment: An accredited institution.
Country of Study: United States of America.
No. of awards offered: 1.
Application Procedure: Applicants must complete an application form available from the organisation. An official grade transcript and three completed confidential reference forms are also required.
Closing Date: February 1st.
Additional Information: Further information is available either on request or from the website.

American Nuclear Society Undergraduate Scholarship

Subjects: Student must be enrolled in a course of study relating to a degree in nuclear science or nuclear engineering in a U.S. institution.

Eligibility: Applicant must be a U.S. citizen or permanent resident.
Level of Study: Graduate, Sophomore.
Type: Non-renewable.
Value: US$2,000.
Length of Study: Varies.
Frequency: Annual.
Country of Study: United States of America.
No. of awards offered: 4.
Application Procedure: Separate application required - see website to download.
Closing Date: February 1st.
Additional Information: Further information available on request. One scholarship is the James R Vogt Scholarship - for an undergraduate or graduate student enrolled in or proposing to undertake research in radio-analytical chemistry or analytical applications of nuclear science. One scholarship is the Pittsburgh Local Section Scholarship - for an under-graduate or graduate student living in Western Pennsylvania.

Everitt P Blizard Scholarship

Subjects: Radiation protection and shielding.
Purpose: To aid students pursuing studies in the field of radiation protection and shielding.
Eligibility: Open to full-time graduate students in a programme leading to an advanced degree in nuclear science, nuclear engineering or a nuclear related field. Applicants must be United States citizens or permanent residents and be enrolled in an accredited institution in the United States.
Level of Study: Graduate.
Type: Scholarship.
Value: Varies.
Length of Study: Varies.
Frequency: Annual.
Study Establishment: An accredited institution.
Country of Study: United States of America.
No. of awards offered: 1.
Application Procedure: Applicants must complete an application form available from the organisation. An official grade transcript and three completed confidential reference forms are also required.
Closing Date: February Ist.
Additional Information: Further information is available either on request or from the website.

James F Schumar Scholarship

Subjects: Materials science and technology for nuclear applications.
Eligibility: Open to United States citizens or holders of a permanent resident visa who are full-time graduate students enrolled in a pro-gramme leading to an advanced degree.
Level of Study: Graduate.
Type: Scholarship.
Frequency: Annual.
Study Establishment: An accredited institution.
Country of Study: United States of America.
No. of awards offered: One.
Application Procedure: Applicants must submit a request for an application form which should include the name of the university the candidate will be attending, the year the candidate will be in during the Autumn of the award, the major course of study and a stamped self-addressed envelope. Completed applications must include a grade transcript and three confidential reference forms. Candidates must be sponsored by an ANS section, division, student branch, committee, member, or organisation member. The applicant should indicate on the nomination form that he or she is applying for the MSTD Schol-arship.
Closing Date: February 1st.
No. of awards given last year: 1.
Additional Information: Further information is available either on request or from the website.

John and Muriel Landis Scholarship Awards

Subjects: Nuclear physics and engineering.
Purpose: To help students who have greater than average financial need.
Eligibility: Candidates should be planning to pursue a career in nuclear engineering or a nuclear related field. Candidates must have greater than average financial need, and consideration will be given to conditions or experiences that render the student disadvantaged. Applicants need not be United States citizens.
Level of Study: Graduate.
Type: Scholarship.
Value: Varies.
Frequency: Annual.
Study Establishment: An accredited institution.
Country of Study: United States of America.
No. of awards offered: Up to eight.
Application Procedure: Applicants must request an application form and include the name and a letter of commitment from the university the candidate will be attending, the year the candidate will be in the Autumn of the award, the major course of study and a stamped addressed envelope. Completed applications must include a grade transcript and three confidential reference forms. Candidates must be sponsored by an American Nuclear Society section, division, student branch, committee, member or organisation member.
Closing Date: February 1st.

John Randall Scholarship

Subjects: Nuclear physics and engineering, particularly in the areas of science and engineering related to the nuclear fuel cycle and ra-dioactive waste management.
Eligibility: Open to full-time graduate students in a programme leading to an advanced degree in nuclear science, nuclear engineering or a nuclear related field. Applicants must be United States citizens or permanent residents and be enrolled in an accredited institution in the United States.
Level of Study: Graduate.
Type: Scholarship.
Frequency: Annual.
Study Establishment: An accredited institution.
Country of Study: United States of America.
No. of awards offered: 1
Application Procedure: Applicants must complete an application form available from the organisation. An official grade transcript and three completed confidential reference forms are also required.
Closing Date: February 1st.
Additional Information: Further information is available either on request or from the website.

Robert A Dannels Memorial Scholarship

Subjects: Nuclear science or nuclear engineering.
Eligibility: Open to United States citizens or holders of a permanent resident visa who are full-time graduate students enrolled in a pro-gramme leading to an advanced degree. Handicapped persons are encouraged to apply.
Level of Study: Graduate.
Type: Scholarship.
Frequency: Annual.
Study Establishment: An accredited institution.
Country of Study: United States of America.
No. of awards offered: One.
Application Procedure: Applicants must submit a request for an application form which should include the name of the university the candidate will be attending, the year the candidate will be in during the Autumn of the award, the major course of study and a stamped self-addressed envelope. Completed appli-cations must include a grade transcript and three confidential refer-ence forms. Candidates must be sponsored by an ANS section, division, student branch, committee, member, or organisation member.
Closing Date: February 1st.

Robert A Dannels Scholarship

Subjects: Nuclear science and engineering.
Eligibility: Open to full-time graduate students in a programme leading to an advanced degree. Applicants must be United States citizens or permanent residents and must be enrolled in an accredited institution in the United States. Handicapped persons are encouraged to apply.
Level of Study: Graduate.
Type: Scholarship.
Value: Varies.
Length of Study: Varies.
Frequency: Annual.
Country of Study: United States of America.
No. of awards offered: 1.
Application Procedure: Applicants must complete an application form available from the organisation. An official grade transcript and three completed confidential reference forms are also required.
Closing Date: February 1st.
Additional Information: Further information is available either on request or from the website.

Verne R Dapp Memorial Scholarship

Subjects: Nuclear science or nuclear engineering.
Eligibility: Open to United States citizens or holders of a permanent resident visa who are full-time graduate students enrolled in a programme leading to an advanced degree.
Level of Study: Graduate.
Type: Scholarship.
Frequency: Every two years.
Study Establishment: An accredited institution.
Country of Study: United States of America.
No. of awards offered: One.
Application Procedure: Applicants must submit a request for an application form which should include the name of the university the candidate will be attending, the year the candidate will be in during the Autumn of the award, the major course of study and a stamped self-addressed envelope. Completed applications must include a grade transcript and three confidential reference forms. Candidates must be sponsored by an ANS section, division, student branch, committee, member, or organisation member.
Closing Date: February 1st.

Verne R Dapp Scholarship

Subjects: Nuclear physics and engineering.
Eligibility: Open to full-time graduate students in a programme leading to an advanced degree in nuclear science, nuclear engineering or a nuclear related field. Applicants must be United States citizens or permanent residents and be enrolled in an accredited institution in the United States.
Level of Study: Graduate.
Type: Scholarship.
Value: Varies.
Length of Study: Varies.
Frequency: Every two years.
Study Establishment: An accredited institution.
Country of Study: United States of America.
No. of awards offered: 1.
Application Procedure: Applicants must complete an application form available from the organisation. An official grade transcript and three completed confidential reference forms are also required.
Closing Date: February 1st.

Walter Meyer Scholarship

Subjects: Nuclear physics and engineering.
Eligibility: Open to full-time graduate students in a programme leading to an advanced degree in nuclear science, nuclear engineering or a nuclear related field. Applicants must be United States citizens or permanent residents and be enrolled in an accredited institution in the United States.
Type: Scholarship.

Value: Varies.
Length of Study: Varies.
Frequency: Every two years.
Study Establishment: An accredited institution.
Country of Study: United States of America.
No. of awards offered: 1.
Application Procedure: Applicants must complete an application form available from the organisation. An official grade transcript and three completed confidential reference forms are also required.
Closing Date: February 1st.
Additional Information: Further information is available either on request or from the website.

AMERICAN NUMISMATIC SOCIETY (ANS)

Broadway at 155th Street
New York, NY 10032
United States of America
Tel: (1) 212 234 3130
Fax: (1) 212 234 3381
Email: info@amnumsoc.org
www: http://www.amnumsoc.org
Contact: Dr VTE Wartenberg, Executive Director

The mission of the American Numismatic Society (ANS) is to be the pre-eminent national institution advancing the study and appreciation of coins, medals and related objects of all cultures as historical and artistic documents. It aims to do this by maintaining the foremost numismatic collection and library, supporting scholarly research and publications, and sponsoring educational and interpretative programmes for diverse audiences.

Donald Groves Fund

Subjects: Early American numismatics involving material dating no later than 1800.
Purpose: To promote publications in the field.
Level of Study: Postgraduate, Research.
Value: Varies. Funding is available for travel and other expenses in association with research as well as for publication costs.
Frequency: Annual.
Country of Study: United States of America.
No. of awards offered: Varies.
Application Procedure: Applicants must address applications to the Secretary of the Society and must include an outline of the proposed research, the method of accomplishing the research, the funding requested and the specific use to which the funding will be put. Applications will be reviewed periodically by the Donald Groves Fund Committee.
Closing Date: Applications are accepted at any time.
Funding: Private.

Frances M Schwartz Fellowship

Subjects: Numismatic methodology and museum practice.
Purpose: To assist the Fellow in the study of Greek and Roman fields relevant to the subject.
Eligibility: Open to students of numismatics who possess a Bachelor of Arts or equivalent degree.
Level of Study: Graduate, Postgraduate.
Type: Fellowship.
Value: Up to US$2,000.
Frequency: Annual.
Country of Study: United States of America.
No. of awards offered: Varies.
Application Procedure: Applicants must write for details.
Closing Date: March 1st.
Funding: Private.
Additional Information: Further information is available by emailing metcalf@amnumsoc.org.

Grants for ANS Summer Seminar in Numismatics

Subjects: Numismatics.
Purpose: To provide a selected number of graduate students with a deeper understanding of the contribution that this subject makes to other fields.
Eligibility: Open to applicants who have had at least one year's graduate study at a university in the United States of America or Canada and who are students of classical studies, history, near eastern studies or other humanistic fields.
Level of Study: Postgraduate.
Type: Grant.
Value: US$2,000.
Length of Study: Nine weeks during the Summer.
Frequency: Annual.
Study Establishment: ANS.
Country of Study: United States of America.
No. of awards offered: Approx. 10.
Application Procedure: Applicants must write well in advance for details of the application process.
Closing Date: March 1st.
Funding: Private.
No. of awards given last year: 12.
No. of applicants last year: 21.
Additional Information: One or two students from overseas are usually accepted to the seminar but will not receive a grant.

Shaykh Hamad Fellowship in Islamic Numismatics

Subjects: Islamic research.
Purpose: To support training in museum practice and research on Islamic coinage.
Eligibility: Open to candidates who have some graduate level training in medieval Near Eastern history or related field and some knowledge of Arabic.
Level of Study: Postgraduate.
Type: Fellowship.
Value: The stipend is US$3,000, and the student will receive training for the equivalent of one day a week for the academic year.
Frequency: Dependent on funds available.
Country of Study: Any country.
No. of awards offered: Varies.
Application Procedure: Applicants must write for details.
Closing Date: March 1st.
Funding: Private.

AMERICAN ORCHID SOCIETY

16700 AOS Lane, Delray Beach
West Palm Beach, FL 33446-4351
United States of America
Tel: (1) 561 404 2000
Fax: (1) 561 404 2100
Email: theaos@aos.org
www: http://orchidweb.org
Contact: Ms Pamela Giust, Awards Registrar

Grants for Orchid Research

Subjects: Orchid research.
Purpose: To advance scientific study of orchids in every respect and to assist in the publication of scholarly and popular scientific literature on orchids.
Eligibility: There are no eligibility restrictions.
Level of Study: Postgraduate.
Type: Grant.
Value: US$500-12,000.
Length of Study: Up to three years.
Country of Study: Any country.
No. of awards offered: Varies.
Application Procedure: Applicants must write for guidelines.
Closing Date: January 1st and July 1st.

AMERICAN ORIENTAL SOCIETY

Hatcher Graduate Library, University of Michigan, Ann Arbor, MI 48109-1205, United States of America
Tel: (1) 734 747 4760
Email: jrodgers@umich.edu
www: http://www.umich.edu/~aos
Contact: Grants Management Officer

The American Oriental Society is primarily concerned with the encouragement of basic research in the languages and literatures of Asia.

Louise Wallace Hackney Fellowship

Subjects: Chinese art, with special relation to painting, and the translation into English of works on the subject.
Purpose: To remind scholars that Chinese art, like all art, is not a disembodied creation, but the outgrowth of the life and culture from which it has sprung. It is requested that scholars give special attention to this approach in their study.
Eligibility: Open to United States citizens who are doctoral or postdoctoral students and have successfully completed at least three years of Chinese language study at a recognised university, and have some knowledge or training in art. In no case shall a fellowship be awarded to Scholars of well recognised standing, but shall be given to either men or women who show aptitude or promise in the said field of learning.
Level of Study: Doctorate, Postdoctorate.
Type: Fellowship.
Value: US$8,000.
Length of Study: One year.
Frequency: Annual.
Study Establishment: Any institution where paintings and adequate language guidance is available.
Country of Study: Any country.
No. of awards offered: One.
Application Procedure: Applicants must submit the following materials in duplicate: a transcript of their undergraduate and graduate course work, a statement of personal finances, a four page summary of the proposed project to be undertaken including details of expense, and no less than three letters of recommendation.
Closing Date: March 1st.
Funding: Private.
Additional Information: It is possible to apply for a renewal of the fellowship, but this may not be done in consecutive years.

AMERICAN OSTEOPATHIC ASSOCIATION (AOA)

142 East Ontario Street, Chicago, IL 60611, United States of America
Tel: (1) 312 202 8000
Fax: (1) 312 202 8200
Email: mwhitehead@aoa-net.org
www: http://www.aoa-net.org
Contact: Administrator, Research Services

The American Osteopathic Association (AOA) is organised to advance the philosophy and practice of osteopathic medicine by promoting excellence in education and research and the delivering of quality, cost effective healthcare in a distinct, unified profession.

AOA Research Grants

Subjects: Osteopathy.
Purpose: To support clinical and basic science projects that lead to a better understanding and a more effective application of the philosophy and concepts of osteopathic medicine.
Eligibility: Open to an osteopathic physician who holds a faculty or staff appointment at an AOA accredited, affiliated, or approved osteopathic institution, or a biomedical researcher who demonstrates evidence of professional training and experience as appropriate for his or her individual discipline and who holds a faculty or staff appointment at an AOA accredited, affiliated or approved osteopathic institution. Osteopathic physicians who hold a faculty or staff appointment at an

academic or healthcare institution having accreditation, affiliation or approval as appropriate for that institution's activities are also eligible. Applicants must be United States citizens.
Level of Study: Doctorate.
Type: Research grant.
Value: Varies.
Length of Study: One-two years.
Frequency: Annual.
Study Establishment: A university or hospital.
Country of Study: United States of America.
No. of awards offered: Dependent on availability of funds.
Application Procedure: The AOA Osteopathic Research Handbook contains grant applications and describes the programmes and eligibility requirements in greater detail. The Handbook is available from the Association.
Closing Date: December 1st.
Funding: Private.

For further information contact:

www: http://www.AOA-net.org

AMERICAN OTOLOGICAL SOCIETY RESEARCH FUND

UCSD Otolaryngology-Head & Neck Surgery, 200 West Arbor DriveSuite 8895, San Diego, CA 92103-8895, United States of America
Tel: (1) 619 543 7896
Fax: (1) 619 543 5521
Email: jpharris@emory.org
www: http://itsa.ucsf.edu/~ajo/AOS/AOS.html
Contact: Dr Jeffrey P Harris, Secretary & Treasurer

The purposes of the American Otological Society are to advance and promote medical and surgical otology including the rehabilitation of the hearing impaired. The Society also encourages and promotes research in otology and related disciplines, conducts an annual meeting of the members for the presentation and discussion of scientific papers and the transaction of business affairs of the Society, and publishes the papers and discussion presented during the scientific programme and the proceedings of the business meetings.

American Otological Society Research Grants
Subjects: All aspects of otosclerosis, Meniere's disease and related disorders.
Eligibility: Open to physicians and doctorate level investigators.
Level of Study: Postdoctorate, Postgraduate.
Type: Research grant.
Value: Up to US$40,000 per year. No funding is provided for the investigator's salary.
Length of Study: One year, renewable.
Frequency: Annual.
Country of Study: United States of America or Canada.
No. of awards offered: Varies.
Closing Date: January 31st.
Funding: Private.
No. of awards given last year: Three.
No. of applicants last year: 10.

American Otological Society Research Training Fellowships
Subjects: All aspects of otosclerosis, Meniere's disease and related disorders.
Purpose: To support research.
Eligibility: Open to physicians, residents and medical students in the United States of America and Canada.
Level of Study: Postgraduate.
Type: Fellowship.
Value: Up to US$40,000 depending on position and institutional norms.
Length of Study: One-two years.
Frequency: Annual.

Country of Study: United States of America or Canada.
No. of awards offered: Varies.
Closing Date: January 31st.
No. of awards given last year: One.
No. of applicants last year: One.
Additional Information: The organisation requires institutional documentation that facilities and faculty are appropriate for the requested research.

AMERICAN PHILOSOPHICAL ASSOCIATION (APA)

University of Delaware, 31 Amstel Avenue, Newark, DE 19716, United States of America
Tel: (1) 302 831 1112
Fax: (1) 302 831 8690
Email: apaonline@udel.edu
www: http://www.apa.udel.edu/apa
Contact: Dr Michael Kelly, Executive Director

The American Philosophical Association (APA) was founded in 1900 to promote the exchange of ideas among philosophers, to encourage creative and scholarly activity in philosophy, to facilitate the professional work and teaching of philosophers and to represent philosophy as a discipline.

APA Book and Article Prizes
Subjects: Philosophy.
Purpose: To award a book prize and an article prize.
Eligibility: Open to any author of a book or article on philosophy published in the two years preceding the award year provided they qualify as a younger Scholar ie. is 40 years of age or younger in the year of the volume, or has received his or her PhD 10 years or less before that year.
Type: Prize.
Value: The Book Prize is US$4,000 and the Article Prize is US$2,000.
Frequency: Annual.
No. of awards offered: One.
Application Procedure: Applicants must write for details or visit the website.
Funding: Private.
Additional Information: Awarded with the help of the Matchette Foundation. The award alternates each year.

Baumgardt Memorial Lecture
Subjects: Philosophy.
Eligibility: Open to candidates of any nationality, working in any country, whose work has some bearing on the philosophical interests of the late David Baumgardt.
Level of Study: Postgraduate.
Value: US$5,000.
Frequency: Every five years.
Country of Study: Any country.
No. of awards offered: One.
Application Procedure: Applicants must write for details or visit the website.
Funding: Private.

Frank Chapman Sharp Memorial Prize
Subjects: The philosophy of war and peace.
Purpose: To recognise unpublished work in philosophy.
Eligibility: Open to writers of unpublished essays or monographs on the philosophy of war and peace.
Level of Study: Postgraduate.
Value: US$1,500.
Frequency: Every two years in odd numbered years.
Country of Study: Any country.
No. of awards offered: One.
Application Procedure: Applicants must write for details or visit the website.
Funding: Private.
No. of awards given last year: One.
No. of applicants last year: Eight.

Rockefeller Prize

Subjects: Philosophy.
Purpose: To recognise unpublished work in philosophy.
Eligibility: Open to non academically affiliated philosophers, including those that teach part-time.
Level of Study: Postgraduate.
Value: US$1,000.
Frequency: Every two years.
Country of Study: Any country.
No. of awards offered: One.
Application Procedure: Applicants must write for details or visit the website.
Funding: Private.
Contributor: The Rockefeller Foundation.

AMERICAN PHILOSOPHICAL SOCIETY

104 South Fifth Street, Philadelphia, PA 19106-3387, United States of America
www: http://www.amphilsoc.org
Contact: Eleanor Roach, Research Administrator

The American Philosophical Society is an eminent scholarly organisation of international reputation, and promotes useful knowledge in the sciences and humanities through excellence in scholarly research, professional meetings, publications, library resources, and community outreach.

Daland Fellowships in Clinical Investigation

Subjects: Medicine, neurology, paediatrics, psychiatry or surgery.
Purpose: To award a limited number of fellowships for research in clinical medicine including the fields of internal medicine. For the purpose of this award, the committee emphasises patient orientated research.
Eligibility: Candidates are expected to have held the MD degree for less than six years. The fellowship is intended to be the first post-clinical fellowship, but each case will be decided on its merits. Preference is given to candidates who have less than two years of postdoctoral training. Applicants must expect to perform their research at an institution in the United States, under the supervision of a scientific adviser.
Level of Study: Research.
Type: Fellowship.
Value: US$50,000 for the first year and US$50,000 for the second year.
Length of Study: The term of the fellowship is one year, with renewal for a further year if satisfactory progress is demonstrated. Requests for renewal are due on the first Friday of January. Payments are made on July 15th and January 15th.
Frequency: Annual.
Application Procedure: Applicants must complete an application form. Information and forms are available from the website. If electronic access is denied, forms can be requested by mail and must indicate when the MD degree was awarded. Candidates must be nominated by their department chairman in a letter providing assurance that the nominee will work with the guidance of a scientific adviser of established reputation who has guaranteed adequate space, supplies, etc. for the Fellow. The adviser need not be a member of the department nominating the Fellow, nor need the activities of the Fellow be limited to the nominating department. As a general rule, no more than one fellowship will be awarded to a given institution in the same year of competition. Application forms must be sent to the Daland Fellowship Committee.
Closing Date: September 1st.
Funding: Private.
No. of awards given last year: Two.
No. of applicants last year: 20.

Franklin Research Grant Program

Subjects: Scholarly research.
Purpose: To contribute towards the cost of scholarly research in all areas of knowledge except those in which support by government or corporate enterprise is more appropriate. Scholarly research, as the term is used here, covers most kinds of scholarly inquiry by individuals leading to publication. It does not include journalistic or other writing for general readership, the preparation of textbooks, case books, anthologies, or other materials for use by students, or the work of creative and performing artists.
Eligibility: Applicants are normally expected to have a doctorate, but applications are considered from persons whose publications display equivalent scholarly achievement. Grants are rarely made to persons who have held the doctorate less than a year, and never for predoctoral study or research. It is the Society's long standing practice to encourage younger Scholars. The Committee will seldom approve more than two grants to the same person within any five year period. Applicants may be residents of the United States, American citizens on the staffs of foreign institutions, and foreign nationals whose research can only be carried out in the United States. Institutions are not eligible to apply. Applicants expecting to conduct interviews in a foreign language must possess sufficient competence in that language, and must be able to read and translate all source materials.
Level of Study: Research.
Type: Grant.
Value: The maximum grant is US$6,000. The budget year corresponds to the calendar year, not the academic year. If an applicant receives an award for the same project from another granting institution, the Society will consider limiting its award to costs that are not covered by the other grant.
Frequency: Annual.
Country of Study: United States of America.
Application Procedure: Applicants must complete an application form. Information and forms are available from the website. If electronic access is denied, forms can be requested by mail. These must indicate the eligibility of both applicant and project, state the nature of the research eg. laboratory, archival or fieldwork and proposed use of the grant eg. travel or purchase of microfilm. Foreign nationals must specify the objects of their research, only available in the United States eg. indigenous plants, archival materials or architectural sites. A stamped addressed envelope should also be included. If forms are downloaded from the website, applicants must ensure that the page format is maintained and must print enough copies of the form for the letters of support.
Closing Date: October 1st for a January decision and December 1st for a March decision.
Funding: Private.
Additional Information: If an award is made and accepted, the recipient is required to provide the Society with a 250 word report on the research accomplished during tenure of the grant, and a one page financial statement.

Library Resident Research Fellowships

Subjects: Library collections research.
Purpose: To support research in the APS library's collections.
Eligibility: Scholars who reside beyond a 75 mile radius of Philadelphia. The fellowships are open to both United States citizens and foreign nationals who are holders of a PhD or equivalent, PhD candidates who have passed their preliminary exams and independent Scholars. Applicants in any relevant field of scholarship may apply.
Level of Study: Research.
Type: Fellowship.
Value: US$2,000 per month.
Length of Study: A minimum of one month and a maximum of three months.
Frequency: Annual.
Application Procedure: Applicants must submit the following, a cover sheet stating the name, title of project, expected period of residence, institutional affiliation, mailing address, telephone numbers, and email if available, social security number, a letter (not to exceed three single spaced pages) which briefly describes the project and how it relates to existing scholarship stating the specific relevance of the American Philosophical Society's collections to the project, and indicating expected results of the research such as publications. A curriculum vitae and one letter of reference (doctoral candidates must use their dissertation advisor) must also be included. Published guides to the Society's collections are available in most research libraries.

Applicants are strongly encouraged to consult the Library staff by mail or phone regarding the collections. A list of these guides and further information can be found on the website.
Closing Date: March 1st for a decision by May.
Funding: Private.
No. of awards given last year: 23.
No. of applicants last year: 90.

Phillips Fund Grants for Native American Research

Subjects: Native American linguistics and ethnohistory.
Eligibility: Open to graduate students who have passed their qualifying examinations for either the Master's or doctorate degrees. Postdoctoral applicants are eligible.
Level of Study: Research.
Value: The average award is approx. US$2,000 and grants rarely exceed US$3,000. This is to cover travel, tapes and informants' fees and is not for general maintenance or the purchase of permanent equipment.
Length of Study: Ordinarily for one year.
Frequency: Annual.
Application Procedure: Applicants must complete an application form. A complete application includes all information requested on the form, the correct number of copies and three confidential letters supporting the application. It is the applicant's responsibility to verify that all materials reach the Society on time. Information and forms are available from the website. If electronic access is denied, forms can be requested by mail. These must indicate eligibility of both applicant and project, and state whether the field of research is linguistics or ethnohistory. Applications should be addressed to Phillips Fund for Native American Research at the main address.
Closing Date: March 1st.
Funding: Private.
Additional Information: If an award is made and accepted, the recipient is required to provide the Society's Library with a brief formal report and copies of any tape recordings, transcriptions, microfilms, etc. which may be acquired in the process of the grant funded research, and a release for scholarly use.

Sabbatical Fellowship for the Humanities and Social Sciences

Subjects: Humanities and social sciences.
Purpose: To support the second half of an awarded sabbatical year.
Eligibility: Open to mid career faculty of universities and four year colleges in the United States which have been granted a sabbatical or research year, but for whom financial support from the parent institution is available for only the first half of the year. Candidates must not have had a financially supported leave during the three years prior to date of application. At the discretion of the review panels, the fellowship may be used to supplement another external award of similar purpose. The total external support cannot exceed the half year salary. The Society encourages candidates to use the resources of the American Philosophical Society Library, but this is not a requirement of the fellowship. There is no restriction on where the Fellow resides during the fellowship year, but an indication of the appropriateness of the available library resources should be given. A PhD must have been awarded no fewer than five and no more than 25 years prior to date of application.
Level of Study: Research.
Type: Award.
Value: US$40,000.
Length of Study: Tenure of the fellowship is for the second half of the academic year.
Frequency: Annual.
Application Procedure: Applicants must submit an application form. Information and forms are available from the website. If electronic access is denied, applicants can request forms by mail, but must be sure to state the date that their PhD was awarded, the end date of last financially supported leave, and beginning date of sabbatical.
Closing Date: November 1st.
Funding: Private.
No. of awards given last year: 20.
No. of applicants last year: More than 250.

AMERICAN PHYSIOLOGICAL SOCIETY (APS)

9650 Rockville Pike, Bethesda, MD 20814-3991, United States of America
Tel: (1) 301 634 7118
Fax: (1) 301 634 7242
Email: info@the-aps.org
www: http://www.the-aps.onawards.html
Contact: Ms Linda Jean Dresser, Executive Assistant

The American Physiological Society (APS) is a non-profit scientific society devoted to fostering education, scientific research and the dissemination of information in the physiological sciences. By providing a spectrum of physiological information, the Society strives to play a role in the progress of science and the advancement of knowledge. The Society has integrated a prestigious awards programme providing funding to outstanding APS members, young investigators and scientists in need of funding to continue their research in physiology. Through its functions and activities, the Society plays an important role in the progress of science and the advancement of knowledge. The Society maintains staff and offices on the campus of the Federation of American Societies for Experimental Biology (FASEB) in Bethesda, Maryland.

AAAS Mass Media Science and Engineering Fellowship

Subjects: Physiology or any related subject.
Purpose: To enable promising young scientists to work in the newsroom of a newspaper, magazine, radio or television station, sharpening their ability to communicate complex scientific issues to non scientists and helping to improve public understanding of science.
Eligibility: Open to graduate or postgraduate students of physiology, or a related subject, preferably with a background in scientific writing.
Level of Study: Graduate, Postgraduate.
Type: Studentship.
Value: Subsistence and travel costs.
Length of Study: 10 weeks.
Frequency: Annual.
Study Establishment: The newsroom of a newspaper, magazine or radio or television station.
Country of Study: United States of America.
No. of awards offered: One.
Application Procedure: Applicants must complete an application form, available from Alice Ra'anan, Public Affairs Office, American Physiological Society.
Closing Date: January 15th.
No. of awards given last year: One.
Additional Information: For further details, please contact the APS or refer to the website.

APS Conference Student Award

Subjects: Biology and physiology.
Purpose: To encourage the participation of young scientists in training at the APS conferences.
Eligibility: Open to graduate students wishing to present a contributed paper at an APS conference.
Level of Study: Graduate.
Type: Award.
Value: Cash award and complimentary conference registration.
Length of Study: The duration of the conference.
Frequency: Dependent upon Conference Schedule.
Study Establishment: Any APS conference.
Country of Study: United States of America.
No. of awards offered: Varies.
Application Procedure: Applicants must submit an abstract to APS. Candidates must indicate on the abstract page a desire to be considered for the award and should contact the APS for further details.
Closing Date: Please write for details.

APS Minority Travel Fellowship Awards

Subjects: Biology and physiology.
Purpose: To increase the participation of predoctoral and postdoctoral minority students in the physiological sciences.

Eligibility: Open to advanced predoctoral and postdoctoral students. Students in the APS Porter Physiology Development programme are also eligible. Minority faculty members at MBRS and MARC eligible institutions may also submit applications.
Level of Study: Postdoctorate, Predoctorate.
Type: Travel grant.
Value: Funds for travel to attend either the Experimental Biology meeting or one of the APS Conferences.
Length of Study: The duration of the conference or meeting.
Frequency: Dependent upon meetings scheduled.
Country of Study: United States of America.
No. of awards offered: Varies.
Application Procedure: Applicants must contact the Education Office of the APS for further details.
Closing Date: Please write for details.
Contributor: NIDDK and NIGMS.

Caroline tum Suden/Frances Hellebrandt Professional Opportunity Awards

Subjects: Biology and physiology.
Purpose: To provide funds for junior physiologists to attend and fully participate in the Experimental Biology meeting.
Eligibility: Open to graduate students or postdoctoral fellows who are APS members or sponsored by an APS member.
Level of Study: Graduate, Postdoctorate.
Type: Award.
Value: US$500 per award, complimentary registration for the Experimental Biology meeting.
Length of Study: The duration of the conference.
Frequency: Annual.
Study Establishment: An APS Experimental Biology meeting.
Country of Study: United States of America.
No. of awards offered: 36.
Application Procedure: Applicants must submit an abstract to APS and should contact the Education Office for further details.
Closing Date: Please write for details.
No. of awards given last year: 36.
Additional Information: Recipients are obliged to attend the Experimental Biology meeting and present a paper.

Procter and Gamble Professional Opportunity Awards

Subjects: Biology and physiology.
Purpose: To provide funds to predoctoral students allowing them to fully participate in the Experimental Biology meeting.
Eligibility: Open to predoctoral students who are within 12-18 months of completing a PhD degree and wish to present a paper at the meeting. Applicants must be student members of the APS or have an adviser or supporting sponsor who is an APS member.
Level of Study: Predoctorate.
Type: Award.
Value: US$500 per award, complementary registration for the Experimental Biology meeting.
Length of Study: The duration of the conference.
Frequency: Annual.
Study Establishment: The APS Experimental Biology meeting.
Country of Study: United States of America.
No. of awards offered: Varies.
Application Procedure: Applicants must submit an abstract to APS and should contact the Education Office for further details.
Closing Date: Please write for details.
No. of awards given last year: 9.

William T Porter Fellowship Award

Subjects: Biology and physiology.
Purpose: To support the training of talented students entering careers in physiology by providing predoctoral fellowships for underrepresented students (African Americans, Hispanics, Native Americans, Native Alaskans, and Native Pacific Islanders).
Eligibility: Open to underrepresented ethnic minority applicants ie. African American, Hispanics, Native Americans, Native Alaskans or Native Pacific Islanders, who are citizens or permanent residents of the United States of America or its territories.
Level of Study: Graduate, Postdoctorate, Predoctorate.
Type: Fellowship.
Value: Annual Stipend of US$18,000.
Length of Study: Varies.
Frequency: Annual.
Study Establishment: Universities or research establishments.
Country of Study: United States of America.
No. of awards offered: Varies.
Application Procedure: Applicants must contact the Education Office of the APS for further details.
Closing Date: January 15th and June 15th.
No. of applicants last year: Varies.

AMERICAN PLANNING ASSOCIATION

Fellowships and Council Administration
122 South Michigan Avenue, Suite 1600
Chicago, IL 60605
United States of America
Tel: (1) 312 431 9100
Fax: (1) 312 431 9985
Email: kblank@planning.org
www: http://www.planning.org
Contact: Assistant for Divisions

The American Planning Association and its professional institute, the American Institute of Certified Planners, are organized to advance the art and science of planning and to foster the activity of planning, physical, economic, and social, at the local, regional, state, and national levels. The objective of the Association is to encourage planning that will contribute to public well being by developing communities and environments that meet the needs of people and of society more effectively.

APA Planning Fellowships

Subjects: Planning and the rational and equitable distribution of resources and opportunities.
Purpose: To encourage students of certain minority backgrounds to enter the planning profession and to help such students who would otherwise be unable to continue their studies in planning.
Eligibility: Open to United States citizens who are African American, Hispanic or Native American students enrolled in a PAB accredited graduate planning programme. The programme is open to first and second year graduate students. First year students who receive fellowships are eligible to compete for an award the following year as well. Preference will be shown to full-time students. Candidates must be able to document the need for financial assistance.
Level of Study: Graduate.
Type: Fellowship.
Value: US$1,000-5,000 paid to the school in two equal instalments.
Frequency: Annual.
Country of Study: United States of America.
No. of awards offered: Varies.
Application Procedure: Applicants must submit an application, available from the website including a two-five page personal and background statement, describing how the student's graduate education will be applied to career goals and why planning was chosen as a career. A curriculum vitae, which is optional if the information is supplied in the student's personal statement should also be included, as well as a letter of recommendation, a completed APA financial aid application form, and official transcripts of all previous collegiate and graduate academic work which should be sent directly from the office of the registrar. A photocopy of the university's letter indicating that the student has been accepted for graduate study in planning, written verification from the university's financial officer or copies of a school publication indicating the average cost of one academic year of graduate school are also required.
Closing Date: April 30th.

AMERICAN POLITICAL SCIENCE ASSOCIATION (APSA)

1527 New Hampshire Avenue North West, Washington, DC 20036, United States of America
Tel: (1) 202 483 2512
Fax: (1) 202 483 2657
Email: cfp@apsanet.org
www: http://www.apsanet.org
Contact: Programme Assistant

The American Political Science Association (APSA) is the major professional society for individuals engaged in the study of politics and government. APSA brings together political scientists from all fields of enquiry, regions and occupational endeavours. While most members teach and conduct research in universities, a quarter work outside academia in government, research organisations, consulting firms, the news media or private enterprises.

APSA Congressional Fellowship Program for Political Scientists

Subjects: Legislative process.
Purpose: To allow participants to learn about the field through direct participation.
Eligibility: Open to mid career political scientists with a PhD completed within the past 15 years or near completion who can show scholarly interest in Congress and the policy making process. Minorities are encouraged to apply.
Level of Study: Postdoctorate.
Type: Fellowship.
Length of Study: 10 months.
Frequency: Annual.
Country of Study: United States of America.
No. of awards offered: Varies.
Application Procedure: Applicants must contact APSA for details. All information is available from the website.
Funding: Private.

APSA Congressional Fellowships for Journalists

Subjects: Legislative process.
Purpose: To allow participants to learn more about the field through direct participation.
Eligibility: Open to mid career professionals with a Bachelor's degree and an interest in Congress. Preference is given to candidates with a background in political reporting but without extensive experience in Washington. Candidates should have an absolute minimum of two years of full-time professional level experience in newspaper, magazine, radio or television reporting at the time of application. Candidates with more than 10 years of experience will not be considered.
Level of Study: Professional development.
Type: Fellowship.
Value: US$38,000.
Length of Study: 10 months.
Frequency: Annual.
Country of Study: United States of America.
No. of awards offered: Varies.
Application Procedure: Applicants must visit the website for further information.
Funding: Private.
Additional Information: Applicants not currently living in the United States must be able to fund their own transportation for an interview should they be selected as finalists.

AMERICAN PSYCHOLOGICAL ASSOCIATION (APA)

Minority Fellowships Program (MFP), 750 First Street North East, Washington, DC 20002-4242, United States of America
Tel: (1) 202 336 6127
Fax: (1) 202 336 6012
Email: mfp@apa.org
www: http://www.apa.org/mfp
Contact: Administrative Assistant

The American Psychological Association Minority Fellowships Program's (APA/MFP) objective is to increase the knowledge of issues related to ethnic minority mental health and to improve the quality of mental health and substance abuse treatment delivered to ethnic minority populations as consistent with Healthy People 2010, the Surgeon General's report on mental health, and other federal initiatives to reduce health disparities. This is done by providing financial support and professional guidance to individuals pursuing doctoral degrees in psychology and neuroscience.

Diversity Program in Neuroscience

Subjects: Behavioural neuroscience, cellular neurobiology, cognitive neuroscience, computational neuroscience, developmental neurobiology, membrane biophysics, molecular neurobiology, neuroanatomy, neurobiology of ageing, neurobiology of disease, neurochemistry, neurogenetics, neuroimmunology, neuropathology, neuropharmacology, neurophysiology, neurotoxicology or systems neuroscience.
Purpose: To increase the number of ethnic minorities in neuroscience who conduct research in areas of importance to the National Institute of Mental Health.
Eligibility: Open to those with American citizenship or permanent residency and a PhD or MD degree and prior graduate training in neuroscience or other basic science.
Level of Study: Predoctorate.
Type: Fellowship.
Frequency: Annual.
Application Procedure: Applicants should see the web page.

Diversity Program in Neuroscience Postdoctoral Fellowship

Subjects: Behavioural neuroscience, cellular neurobiology, cognitive neuroscience, computational neuroscience, developmental neurobiology, membrane biophysics, molecular neurobiology, neuroanatomy, neurobiology of ageing, neurobiology of disease, neurochemistry, neurogenetics, neuroimmunology, neuropathology, neuropharmacology, neurophysiology, neurotoxicology or systems neuroscience.
Purpose: To increase the number of ethnic minorities in neuroscience who conduct research in areas of importance to the National Institute of Mental Health.
Eligibility: Open to those with American citizenship or permanent residency and a PhD or MD degree and prior graduate training in neuroscience or in other basic sciences.
Level of Study: Postdoctorate, Predoctorate.
Type: Fellowship.
Frequency: Annual.
Application Procedure: Applicants must visit the web page.
Closing Date: January 15th.
Additional Information: Benefits include travel funds to visit universities being considered for postdoctoral training, travel funds to attend the Society for Neuroscience's annual meeting and opportunities for mentoring and networking with neuroscientists.

Diversity Program in Neurosciences

Subjects: Behavioural neuroscience, cellular neurobiology, cognitive neuroscience, computational neuroscience, developmental neurobiology, membrane biophysics, molecular microbiology, neuroanatomy, neurobiology, neurobiology of ageing, neurobiology of disease, neurochemistry, neurogenetics, neuroimmunology, neuropathology, neurophysiology, neurotoxicology or systems neuroscience.
Purpose: To increase the representation of underrepresented ethnic minorities in neuroscience, as well as increasing the pool of researchers and teachers whose work focuses on ethnic minority persons and issues.
Eligibility: Applicants must be American citizens or permanent residents who are enrolled full-time in a doctoral programme. An important goal of the programme is to increase representation of black or African American, Alaskan Native, American Indian, Asian American, Hispanic or Latino and Pacific Islander students within neuroscience. However, the programme welcomes applications from all students, especially those interested in increasing the representation of underrepresented ethnic minorities in neuroscience, as well as increasing the pool of researchers and teachers in the field.
Level of Study: Doctorate.

Type: Fellowship.
Frequency: Annual.
Country of Study: United States of America.
Application Procedure: Applicants must submit a completed application, essay, references, transcripts, and Graduate Record Examination scores. Further information and application forms are available on request.
Closing Date: January 15th.
Funding: Government.
Contributor: The National Institute of Mental Health.

MFP Mental Health and Substance Abuse Services

Subjects: Clinical, counselling and school psychology.
Purpose: To improve the quality of mental health treatment and research on issues of concern to ethnic minority populations by providing financial support and professional guidance to individuals pursuing doctoral degrees in psychology and by increasing the knowledge of issues related to ethnic minority health.
Eligibility: Applicants must be American citizens or permanent residents enrolled full-time in an APA accredited doctoral programme at the time the fellowship is awarded. An additional factor among many considered is one's ethnic minority group including, but not limited to, blacks or African Americans, Alaskan Natives, American Indians, Asian Americans, Hispanics or Latinos and Pacific Islanders, and/or those who can demonstrate commitment to a career in psychology related to ethnic minority health.
Level of Study: Doctorate.
Type: Fellowship.
Frequency: Annual.
Country of Study: Any country.
Application Procedure: Applicants must submit a completed application, essay, references, transcripts, and Graduate Record Examination scores. Further information and application forms are available on request.
Closing Date: January 15th.
Funding: Government.
Contributor: The Substance Abuse and Mental Health Administration.

AMERICAN PUBLIC POWER ASSOCIATION (APPA)

2301 M Street North West, Washington, DC 20037, United States of America
Tel: (1) 202 467 2960
Fax: (1) 202 467 2992
Email: DEED@appanet.org
www: http://www.appanet.org/DEED
Contact: Ms Michelle Ghosh, DEED Administrator

The American Public Power Association (APPA) is the national trade association representing more than 2,000 municipal and other state and local government owned electric utilities. APPA provides the necessary leadership in the evolution of the electric utility industry by advancing the principles of community ownership, promoting the development of a viable and sustainable competitive wholesale power market and protecting the public interest against the abuse of market power. The Demonstration of Energy-Efficiency Developments (DEED) programme was established in 1980 by APPA and is the only research and development programme funded by and for public power.

DEED (Demonstration of Energy-Efficient Developments) Scholarship

Subjects: Engineering, mathematics or computer science.
Purpose: To promote the involvement of students studying in energy related disciplines in the public power industry and to provide host utilities with technical assistance.
Eligibility: Open to students studying related disciplines at accredited colleges and universities in a country with at least one DEED member. Applicants will not be discriminated against on the basis of sex, race, religion, national origin or citizenship.
Level of Study: Doctorate, Graduate, Postdoctorate, Postgraduate.

Type: Scholarship.
Value: US$4,000.
Frequency: Annual.
Country of Study: United States of America.
No. of awards offered: 10.
Application Procedure: Applications must be completed, sponsored and submitted by a DEED member utility, with the required signatures. An official transcript must accompany the application or be sent separately to the attention of the DEED administrator by the deadline. A second copy of the application must be sent to the local DEED Board regional director. A listing of addresses for these are available on the website.
Closing Date: January 15th and July 15th.
Funding: Private.
No. of awards given last year: 10.
Additional Information: Currently only the United States of America has DEED members. Applicants should visit the website for a listing of members.

AMERICAN RESEARCH CENTER IN EGYPT (ARCE)

Emory Briarcliff Campus, 1256 Briarcliff Road, North East, Building A, Suite 423W, Atlanta, GA 30306, United States of America
Tel: (1) 404 712 9854
Fax: (1) 404 712 9849
Email: arce@emory.edu
www: http://www.arce.org
Contact: Dr Susanne Thomas, Co-ordinator of US Operations

The American Research Center in Egypt (ARCE) is the professional society in the United States for specialists on Egypt of all periods. It is also a consortium of universities and museums that support archaeological and academic research in Egypt via fellowships, and whose membership is open to the public.

ARCE Fellowships

Subjects: Arts and humanities, Near East studies and humanistic social sciences.
Purpose: To support research in Egypt.
Eligibility: Open to citizens of the United States of America who are predoctoral candidates. Postdoctoral candidates should be nationals of the United States of America or foreign nationals who have been teaching at an American university for three years or more.
Level of Study: Doctorate, Postdoctorate, Museum carators.
Type: Fellowship.
Value: Varies.
Length of Study: 3-12 months.
Frequency: Annual.
Study Establishment: ARCE.
Country of Study: Egypt.
No. of awards offered: 10-17.
Application Procedure: Applicants must write for materials or download them from the website.
Closing Date: January 5th.
Funding: Government.
No. of awards given last year: 17.
No. of applicants last year: 31.

AMERICAN RESEARCH INSTITUTE IN TURKEY (ARIT)

c/o University Museum, 33rd & Spruce Streets, Philadelphia, PA 19104-6324, United States of America
Tel: (1) 215 898 3474
Fax: (1) 215 898 0657
Email: leinwand@sas.upenn.edu
www: http://ccat.sas.upenn.edu/ARIT
Contact: Administrative Assistant

The American Research Institute in Turkey's (ARIT) main aim is to support scholarly research in all fields of the humanities and social sciences in Turkey through administering fellowship programmes at the doctoral and postdoctoral level and through maintaining research centres in Ankara and Istanbul.

ARIT - Bosphorus University Language Fellowships
Subjects: Turkish language.
Purpose: To provide students with the opportunity of studying advanced Turkish language.
Eligibility: Open to graduate students enrolled in a degree programme or postdoctoral. Applicants must be United States citizens or permanent residents and have at least two years of college level Turkish language study or its equivalent.
Level of Study: Postgraduate.
Type: Fellowship.
Value: Tuition, travel and a maintenance stipend of varying amounts.
Frequency: Annual.
Study Establishment: Bosphorus University, Istanbul.
Country of Study: Turkey.
Application Procedure: Applicants must submit an application form, statement and references.
Funding: Government, Private.

ARIT - National Endowment for the Humanities for Advanced Fellowships for Research in Turkey
Subjects: All subjects of the humanities and interdisciplinary approaches of art, archaeology, language and history.
Purpose: To support research on ancient, medieval or modern times.
Eligibility: Open to Scholars who hold a PhD or who have completed their professional training. Applicants are expected to have an affiliation with educational institutions in the United States or Canada and must be either United States of America citizens or have resided in the United States for three years.
Level of Study: Postdoctorate, Professional development.
Type: Fellowship.
Value: Stipends generally range from US$13,335-40,000.
Length of Study: 4-12 months.
Frequency: Annual, if funds are available.
Study Establishment: In either of ARIT's two research establishments in Ankara or Istanbul.
Country of Study: Turkey.
No. of awards offered: Two-four.
Application Procedure: Applicants must submit an application form, project statement and references.
Closing Date: November 15th.
Funding: Government.
Contributor: The United States Information Agency.

ARIT Humanities and Social Science Fellowships
Subjects: All fields of the humanities and social sciences.
Purpose: To encourage research on Turkey in ancient, medieval and modern times.
Eligibility: Open to Scholars and advanced graduate students engaged in research in the field. Student applicants must have fulfilled all requirements for the doctorate except the dissertation. Applicants must be United States citizens and/or be members in good standing of educational institutions in the United States or Canada. While grants for tenures of up to one year will be considered, some preference is given to projects of shorter duration.
Level of Study: Doctorate, Postdoctorate.
Type: Fellowship.
Value: Varies, depending on the length of the study period.
Length of Study: One year, though preference is given to shorter periods of study.
Frequency: Annual.
Study Establishment: In either of ARIT's two research establishments in Ankara or Istanbul.
Country of Study: Turkey.
Application Procedure: Applicants must submit six copies of an original application. Student applicants must provide a copy of their graduate transcript. Please visit the website for further details.
Closing Date: November 15th.
Funding: Government, Private.
Contributor: The United States Information Agency.

Additional Information: Hostel, research and study facilities are available at ARIT's branch centres in Istanbul and Ankara.

Mellon Postdoctoral Fellowships In Turkey For East European Scholars
Subjects: Humanities and social sciences.
Purpose: To bring Eastern and Central European scholars to Turkey to carry out research.
Eligibility: Open to Bulgarian, Czech, Slovak, Polish, Hungarian and Romanian nationals, now includes Estonia, Latvia, Lithnania. Preference will be given to scholars in the early stages of their careers who have not had the opportunity for extensive travel.
Level of Study: Postdoctorate.
Type: Fellowship.
Value: Up to US$11,500.
Length of Study: Two-three months.
Frequency: Annual.
Study Establishment: In either of ARIT's two research establishments in Ankara or Istanbul.
Country of Study: Turkey.
No. of awards offered: Three-four.
Application Procedure: Applicants must submit an application form, project statement and references.
Closing Date: March 5th.
Funding: Private.
Contributor: The Mellon Foundation.
Additional Information: Further information is available on request or from the website http://www.mellon.org.

Samuel H Kress Foundation Graduate Fellowships in Archaeology and the History of Art
Subjects: The history of art and archaeology.
Purpose: To fund doctoral dissertation research in the field.
Eligibility: Applicants must be degree candidates who have completed all preliminary requirements for a PhD in art history and/or archaeology and who are enrolled at United States or Canadian institutions.
Level of Study: Doctorate.
Type: Fellowship.
Value: Up to US$15,000.
Length of Study: One academic year. Awards for shorter periods of time are also available.
Frequency: Annual.
Study Establishment: In either of ARIT's two research establishments in Ankara or Istanbul.
Country of Study: Turkey.
No. of awards offered: Two-four.
Application Procedure: Applicants must submit an application form accompanied by three letters of recommendation.
Closing Date: November 15th.
Funding: Private.
Contributor: The Samuel H Kress Foundation.
No. of awards given last year: 2.
No. of applicants last year: 14.

AMERICAN SCHOOL OF CLASSICAL STUDIES AT ATHENS (ASCSA)

6-8 Charlton Street, Princeton, NJ 08540-5232, United States of America
Tel: (1) 609 683 0800
Fax: (1) 609 924 0578
Email: ascsa@ascsa.org
www: http://www.ascsa.edu.gr
Contact: Ms Mary E Darlington, Assistant to the Executive Vice President

Established in 1881, the American School of Classical Studies at Athens (ASCSA) offers both graduate students and Scholars the opportunity to study Greek civilisation, first hand, in Greece. The ASCSA supports and encourages the teaching of archaeology, art, history, language and literature of Greece from early times to the present.

Advanced Fellowships

Subjects: Classical art history, history of architecture, study of pottery.
Eligibility: Open to students from the United States of America or Canadian institutions who have completed one year at the school.
Level of Study: Postgraduate, Predoctorate.
Type: Fellowship.
Value: Varies.
Length of Study: One academic year.
Frequency: Annual.
Study Establishment: The ASCSA.
Country of Study: Greece.
No. of awards offered: One.
Application Procedure: Applicants must write to the director of the school in Athens for further information.
Closing Date: February 22nd.
Funding: Private.
No. of awards given last year: 6.
No. of applicants last year: 20.
Additional Information: School Advanced Fellowships.Several fellowships are available to students who have completed the Regular Program or one year as a Student Associate Member. They are awarded by the Director of the School in consultation with the faculty and are given only if candidates meet a standard acceptable to the Director and the Committee. Applications should contain a detailed description of the project to be pursued, an updated curriculum vitae, and one letter of recommendation from the applicant's advisor.These Fellowships include: the Samuel H. Kress Fellowships in art history; the Gorham Phillips Stevens Fellowship in the history of architecture; the Homer A. and Dorothy B. Thompson Fellowship in the study of pottery and three Fellowships unrestricted as to field: the Edward Capps, the Doreen Canaday Spitzer and the Eugene Vanderpool Fellowships.The application should be sent to professor Stephen V. Tracy, Director of the School, c/o the office in Athens, and postmarked no later than February 22nd, 2004.

For further information contact:

The American School of Classical Studies at Athens 54 Soudias Street, Athens, GR-10676, Greece
Tel: (30) 011 30 210
Fax: (30) 011 30 310
www: http://www.ascsa.edu.gr
Contact: School Director

ASCSA Fellowships

Subjects: Classical philology and archaeology, post classical Greek studies or a related field.
Eligibility: Open to students at colleges or universities in the United States of America or Canada who hold a Bachelor of art degree but not a PhD, and who are preparing for an advanced degree in classical studies or a related field. Applicants must be affiliated with a college or university of the United States of America or Canada.
Level of Study: Graduate, Postgraduate, Predoctorate.
Type: Fellowship.
Value: US$8,840 stipend plus fees, room and partial board.
Length of Study: One academic year.
Frequency: Annual.
Study Establishment: The ASCSA.
Country of Study: Greece.
No. of awards offered: Eleven.
Application Procedure: Applicants must complete an official application, either available on request or from the website. Applications are judged on the basis of credentials and competitive examinations in Greek language, history and archaeology. Fulbright Fellowships are also sometimes available for work at the School. Application to the School must be made simultaneously with the application for a Fulbright grant. Two fellowships may not be held concurrently.
Closing Date: January 15th.
Funding: Private.
No. of awards given last year: 13.
No. of applicants last year: 21.

Additional Information: Further information is available on request or from the website.

For further information contact:

www: http://www.ascsa.edu.gr

ASCSA Research Fellow in Environmental Studies

Subjects: Earth sciences, geological sciences and archaeological sciences.
Purpose: To support research on studies from archaeological contexts in Greece.
Eligibility: Applicants must write for details.
Level of Study: Doctorate, Postdoctorate, Postgraduate.
Type: Fellowship.
Value: US$13,000-25,000 stipend depending on seniority and experience.
Length of Study: One academic year.
Frequency: Annual.
Study Establishment: The Malcolm H Wiener Research Laboratory for Archaeological Science at the ASCSA.
Country of Study: Greece.
No. of awards offered: One.
Application Procedure: Applicants must contact the Chair of the Wiener Laboratory by fax or email. Alternatively, they should contact Dr Sherry C Fox by fax on 011-30 210 725 0584, or by email on sfox@ascsa.edu.gr for application guidelines and further information.
Closing Date: January 15th.
Funding: Private.
No. of awards given last year: One.
No. of applicants last year: Eight.

For further information contact:

www: http://www.ascsa.edu.gr

ASCSA Research Fellow in Faunal Studies

Subjects: Biological sciences, life sciences and archaeological sciences.
Purpose: To study faunal remains from archaeological contexts in Greece.
Eligibility: Applicants must write for details.
Level of Study: Doctorate, Postdoctorate, Postgraduate.
Type: Fellowship.
Value: A stipend of US$13,000-25,000 depending on seniority and experience.
Length of Study: One academic year.
Frequency: Annual.
Study Establishment: The Malcolm H Wiener Research Laboratory for Archaeological Science at the ASCSA.
Country of Study: Greece.
No. of awards offered: One.
Application Procedure: Applicants must contact the Chair of the Wiener Laboratory by fax or email. Alternatively, they should contact Dr Sherry C Fox by fax on 011-30 210 725 0584, or by email on sfox@ascsa.edu.gr for application guidelines and further information.
Closing Date: January 15th.
Funding: Private.
No. of awards given last year: One.
No. of applicants last year: Seven.
Additional Information: Further information can be found on the website.

For further information contact:

www: http://www.ascsa.edu.gr

ASCSA Research Fellow in Geoarchaeology

Subjects: Earth sciences, geological sciences and archaeological sciences.
Purpose: To support research on a geo-archaeological topic in Greece.
Eligibility: Applicants must write for details.
Level of Study: Doctorate, Postdoctorate, Postgraduate.
Type: Fellowship.

Value: A stipend of US$13,000-25,000 depending on seniority and experience.
Length of Study: One academic year.
Frequency: Annual.
Study Establishment: The Malcolm H Wiener Research Laboratory for Archaeological Science at the ASCSA.
Country of Study: Greece.
No. of awards offered: One.
Application Procedure: Applicants must contact the Chair of the Wiener Laboratory by fax or email. Alternatively, they should contact Dr Sherry C Fox by fax on 011-30 210 725 0584, or by email on sfox@ascsa.edu.gr for application guidelines and further information.
Closing Date: January 15th.
Funding: Private.
No. of awards given last year: One.
No. of applicants last year: Eight.

For further information contact:

www: http://www.ascsa.edu.gr

ASCSA Summer Sessions

Subjects: Archaeology, with emphasis on the topography and antiq uities of Special program in 2004 for one year in Turkey.
Purpose: To aid those who wish to become acquainted with Turkey and its antiques in a limited time, and to improve their understanding of the relationship between the country, its monuments, landscape, climate, history, literature and culture.
Eligibility: Open to graduate students, high school teachers and college teachers.
Level of Study: Graduate, Postdoctorate, Postgraduate, Professional development.
Type: Scholarship.
Value: Tuition, room and partial board up to US$2,950.
Length of Study: $3\frac{1}{2}$ weeks.
Frequency: Annual.
Study Establishment: The ASCSA.
Country of Study: Turkey.
No. of awards offered: 5, Funding ranges from US$500-US$2,000.
Application Procedure: Applicants must submit a completed application form, transcripts and letters of recommendation. Applications should be made to the Committee on the Summer Sessions.
Closing Date: January 15th.
Funding: Private.
No. of awards given last year: 13.
No. of applicants last year: 83.
Additional Information: Further information can be found on the website.

For further information contact:

www: http://www.ascsa.edu.gr

J Lawrence Angel Fellowship in Human Skeletal Studies

Subjects: Biological sciences, life sciences and archaeological sciences.
Purpose: To study human skeletal remains from archaeological contexts in Greece.
Eligibility: Applicants must write for details.
Level of Study: Doctorate, Postdoctorate, Postgraduate.
Type: Fellowship.
Value: A stipend of US$13,000-25,000 depending on seniority and experience.
Length of Study: One academic year.
Frequency: Annual.
Study Establishment: The Malcolm H Wiener Research Laboratory for Archaeological Science at the ASCSA.
Country of Study: Greece.
No. of awards offered: One.
Application Procedure: Applicants must contact Dr Sherry C Fox by fax on 011-30-210 301 725 0584, or by email on sfox@ascsa.edu.gr for application guidelines and further information.
Closing Date: January 15th.
Funding: Private.

Contributor: The Malcolm H Wiener Research Laboratory for Archaeological Sciences at the American School at Athens.
No. of awards given last year: One.
No. of applicants last year: Six.
Additional Information: Further information can be found on the website.

For further information contact:

www: http://www.ascsa.edu.gr

Jacob Hirsch Fellowship

Subjects: Pre-classical, classical or post classical archaeology.
Purpose: To support individuals completing a project which requires a lengthy residence in Greece.
Eligibility: Open to graduate students of American or Israeli institutions who are writing a dissertation and to recent PhD graduates completing a project such as a dissertation for publication. Applications will be judged on the basis of appropriate credentials including referees.
Level of Study: Postdoctorate, Postgraduate, Predoctorate.
Type: Fellowship.
Value: US$8,840 stipend plus room, board and waiver of fees.
Length of Study: One academic year, non renewable.
Frequency: Annual.
Study Establishment: The ASCSA.
Country of Study: Greece.
No. of awards offered: One.
Application Procedure: Applicants must submit three letters of recommendation, transcripts and a detailed description of projects to be pursued in Greece. Applicants must apply for membership at the school simultaneously with application for the fellowship.
Closing Date: January 15th.
Funding: Private.
No. of awards given last year: One.
No. of applicants last year: 12.
Additional Information: Further information can be found on the website.

M Alison Frantz Fellowship in Post-Classical Studies at the Gennadius Library (formerly known as the Gennadeion Fellowship)

Subjects: Post classical studies in late antiquity, Byzantine studies, post Byzantine studies and modern Greek studies.
Eligibility: Open to PhD candidates. Applicants from institutions in the United States of America or Canada must be recent PhD candidates and all candidates must show a need to use the Gennadius Library.
Level of Study: Doctorate, Postdoctorate, Predoctorate.
Type: Fellowship.
Value: US$8,840 stipend plus room, board and waiver of fees.
Length of Study: One academic year.
Frequency: Annual.
Study Establishment: The Gennadius Library.
Country of Study: Greece.
No. of awards offered: One.
Application Procedure: Applicants must submit a curriculum vitae, project description and two letters of support to the Chair of Gennadius Library Committee.
Closing Date: January 15th.
Funding: Private.
No. of awards given last year: One.
No. of applicants last year: 6.
Additional Information: Further information can be found on the website.

For further information contact:

www: http://www.ascsa.edu.gr

NEH Fellowships

Subjects: Ancient, classical and post classical studies, including but not limited to history, philosophy, language, art and archaeology of Greece and the Greek world, art history, literature, philology, architecture, archaeology, anthropology, metallurgy and environmental studies from prehistoric times to the present.

Eligibility: Open to doctoral and postdoctoral Scholars who are citizens of the United States of America or foreign nationals with three years residency in the United States of America immediately preceding the application deadline.
Level of Study: Doctorate, Postdoctorate.
Type: Fellowship.
Value: A maximum stipend of US$17,500 for a five month project and US$35,000 for a 10 month project.
Length of Study: One academic year.
Frequency: Annual.
Study Establishment: The ASCSA.
Country of Study: Greece.
No. of awards offered: Two-five.
Application Procedure: Applicants must write for details or visit the website.
Closing Date: November 15th.
Funding: Government.
No. of awards given last year: Two.
No. of applicants last year: 14.
Additional Information: Further information can be found on the website.

For further information contact:

www: http://www.ascsa.edu.gr

AMERICAN SCHOOLS OF ORIENTAL RESEARCH (ASOR)

Boston University, 656 Beacon Street, 5th Floor, Boston, MA 02215-2010, United States of America
Tel: (1) 617 353 6570
Fax: (1) 617 353 6575
Email: asor@bu.edu
www: http://www.asor.org
Contact: Ms Britt Hartenberger, Program Co-ordinator

The American Schools of Oriental Research's (ASOR) mission is to initiate, encourage and support research into, and public understanding of, the peoples and cultures of the Far East from the earliest times, by fostering original research, archaeological excavations and explorations and by encouraging scholarship in the basic languages, cultural histories and traditions of the Far Eastern world

AIAR Annual Professorship

Subjects: Near Eastern archaeology, geography, history and biblical studies.
Purpose: To support studies in Near Eastern archaeology, geography, history and biblical studies.
Eligibility: Open to qualified applicants of any nationality. American citizens are eligible for the entire award. Non-United States citizens may apply but, by United States law, are only eligible for non governmental funds.
Level of Study: Postdoctorate.
Type: Other.
Value: A stipend of US$30,000. This consists of US$14,200 plus US$15,800 for room and half board for appointee and spouse at the Institute. The entire award is available via USIA for an appointee who is an United States citizen. Non governmental funds for non United States citizens total US$15,000.
Length of Study: 10 months.
Frequency: Annual.
Study Establishment: The W F Albright Institute of Archaeological Research in Jerusalem.
Country of Study: Israel.
No. of awards offered: One.
Application Procedure: Applicants must write for details.
Closing Date: October 15th.
No. of awards given last year: One.
No. of applicants last year: Five.
Additional Information: The professorship period should be continuous, without frequent trips outside the country. Residence at the Institute is required.

For further information contact:

Department of Religious Studies John Carroll University, 20700 North Park Boulevard, University Heights, OH 44118, United States of America
Email: spencer@jcu.edu
Contact: Dr John R Spencer

Andrew W Mellon Foundation Fellowships

Subjects: Humanities.
Purpose: To support Eastern European Scholars.
Eligibility: Open to Bulgarian, Czech, Hungarian, Polish, Romanian and Slovak Scholars who have obtained a doctorate by the time the fellowship is awarded. Candidates should not be permanently resident outside the six countries concerned.
Level of Study: Postdoctorate.
Type: Fellowship.
Value: US$34,500 in total.
Length of Study: Three months.
Frequency: Annual.
Study Establishment: The W F Albright Institute of Archaeological Research in Jerusalem.
Country of Study: Israel.
No. of awards offered: Three.
Application Procedure: Applicants must write for details.
Closing Date: April 2nd.
No. of awards given last year: Three.
No. of applicants last year: 15.
Additional Information: Fellows are expected to reside at the Albright if room is available. The three month periods are September 1st-November 30th, December 1st-February 29th and March 1st-May 31st. The research period should be continuous without frequent trips outside the country.

For further information contact:

Department of Religious Studies John Carroll University, 20700 North Park Boulevard, University Heights, OH 44118, United States of America
Email: spencer@jcu.edu
Contact: Dr John R Spencer

ASOR Mesopotamian Fellowship

Subjects: Mesopotamian civilisation.
Purpose: To support field research.
Eligibility: Open to predoctoral and postdoctoral Scholars. Research projects such as museum or archival research related to ancient Mesopotamian studies may also be considered. Applicants must be affiliated with an institution that is a corporate member of ASOR or must obtain individual membership in ASOR.
Level of Study: Doctorate, Postdoctorate, Predoctorate.
Type: Fellowship.
Value: US$7,000.
Length of Study: Three-six months.
Frequency: Annual.
Country of Study: Any country.
No. of awards offered: One.
Application Procedure: Applicants must write for details and an application form.
Closing Date: April 1st.
Funding: Private.
No. of awards given last year: One.
No. of applicants last year: Five.
Additional Information: A recipient who does not use the fellowship for at least three months must forfeit and return a pro-rated amount of the stipend. Fellowship time should be continuous without frequent trips outside of the Middle East.

Council of American Overseas Research Centers (CAORC) Fellowships

Subjects: Humanities, social sciences and natural sciences.
Purpose: To support the study of topics contributing to the scholarship of Near Eastern studies.

Eligibility: Open to predoctoral students and postdoctoral Scholars of United States nationality.
Level of Study: Doctorate, Graduate, Postdoctorate, Postgraduate, Predoctorate, Professional development.
Type: Fellowship.
Value: US$17,000 maximum for fellowships.
Length of Study: Two-six months.
Frequency: Annual.
Study Establishment: The American Center of Oriental Research, Amman.
Country of Study: Jordan.
No. of awards offered: More than six.
Application Procedure: Applicants must write for details.
Closing Date: February 1st.
Funding: Government.

Council of American Overseas Research Centers (CAORC) Fellowships for Advanced Multi-Country Research

Subjects: Multi-country significance in the fields of humanities, social sciences and related natural sciences in countries in the Near and Middle East and South Asia.
Eligibility: Open to doctoral candidates applying as individuals or in teams and established Scholars with United States citizenship.
Level of Study: Doctorate.
Type: Fellowship.
Value: Up to US$6,000 plus an additional US$3,000 for travel.
Frequency: Annual.
Study Establishment: The W F Albright Institute of Archaeological Research in Jerusalem.
Country of Study: Other.
No. of awards offered: Eight.
Application Procedure: Applicants must write for details.
Closing Date: December 31st.
Additional Information: Preference will be given to candidates examining comparative or cross-regional questions requiring research in two or more countries.

For further information contact:

CAORCS mithsonian Institution, 1c 3123 MRC 705, Washington, DC 20560, United States of America
Email: siwp01.ic.bwack@ic.si.edu
www: http://www.caorc.org
Contact: Grants Management Officer

Council of American Overseas Research Centers (CAORC) Senior (Postdoctoral) Fellowships

Subjects: Anthropology, economics, history, international relations, journalism and political science.
Purpose: To support research or publication projects in disciplines relating to the Near East.
Eligibility: Open to United States citizens only.
Level of Study: Postdoctorate.
Type: Fellowship.
Value: US$25,000 maximum.
Length of Study: Two-six months.
Frequency: Annual.
Study Establishment: The American Center of Oriental Research, Amman.
Country of Study: Jordan.
No. of awards offered: Two or more.
Application Procedure: Applicants must write for details.
Closing Date: February 1st.
Funding: Government.

Cyprus American Archaeological Research Institute (CAARI) Anita Cecil O'Donovan Fellowship

Subjects: Archaeology.
Purpose: To assist with expenses for research to be conducted in Cyprus or a field relevant to Cypriot archaeology.
Level of Study: Graduate.
Type: Fellowship.

Value: Up to US$750.
Length of Study: Three-six weeks.
Frequency: Annual.
Study Establishment: The Cyprus American Archaeological Research Institute.
Country of Study: Cyprus.
No. of awards offered: One.
Application Procedure: Applicants must submit a description of their project outlining its purpose, importance, budget and duration, and a curriculum vitae listing their name, address, education, field experience and relevant publications. Two letters of recommendation should also be submitted directly from the referees.
Closing Date: February 1st.
Funding: Private.
Additional Information: Residency at CAARI is mandatory.

Cyprus American Archaeological Research Institute (CAARI) Stuart Swiny & Helena Wylde Grant

Subjects: Archaeology.
Purpose: To support participation in any phase or aspect of a project in Cyprus which has been approved by ASOR's Committee on Archaeological Policy (CAP).
Eligibility: Open to Scholars of any nationality.
Level of Study: Graduate.
Type: Fellowship.
Value: US$750.
Length of Study: Three-six weeks.
Frequency: Annual.
Study Establishment: CAARI.
Country of Study: Cyprus.
No. of awards offered: One.
Application Procedure: Applicants must submit a description of their project outlining its purpose, importance, budget and duration, and a curriculum vitae listing their name, address, education, field experience and relevant publications. Two letters of recommendation should also be submitted directly from the referees.
Closing Date: February 1st.
Funding: Private.
Additional Information: Residency at CAARI is mandatory.

Harrell Family Fellowship

Subjects: Archaeology.
Purpose: To support participation in an ACOR supported project or an ACOR funded research project.
Eligibility: Open to enrolled graduate students of any nationality.
Level of Study: Graduate.
Type: Fellowship.
Value: US$1,500.
Frequency: Annual.
Country of Study: Jordan.
No. of awards offered: One.
Application Procedure: Applicants must write for details.
Closing Date: February 1st.

Jennifer C Groot Fellowship

Subjects: Archaeology.
Purpose: To support beginners in fieldwork who have been accepted as staff members on projects with ASOR/CAP affiliation in Jordan.
Eligibility: Open to United States and Canadian citizens who are graduate students and have been accepted as staff members on archaeological projects.
Level of Study: Graduate.
Type: Fellowship.
Value: US$1,500.
Frequency: Annual.
Country of Study: Jordan.
No. of awards offered: Three.
Application Procedure: Applicants must write for details.
Closing Date: February 1st.
Funding: Private.
Additional Information: Further information is available on request.

Kress Fellowship in the Art and Archaeology of Jordan

Subjects: History of art, to include art history, archaeology, architectural history, and in some cases classical studies. Topics should be focused on some aspect of the artistic legacy of a specific culture, site or period.
Purpose: To support students completing dissertation research in an art history topic.
Eligibility: Applicants must be American PhD candidates or those matriculated at United States institutions.
Level of Study: Predoctorate.
Type: Fellowship.
Value: Up to US$14,000. The amount is dependent on funding available.
Length of Study: Three-six months.
Frequency: Annual.
Study Establishment: The American Center of Oriental Research, Amman.
Country of Study: Jordan.
No. of awards offered: More than one.
Application Procedure: Applicants must write for details.
Closing Date: February 1st.
Funding: Private.

NEH Fellowship

Subjects: Archaeology, anthropology, geography, ancient history, philology, epigraphy, Biblical studies, Islamic studies, religion, art history, literature, philosophy or related disciplines.
Eligibility: Open to Scholars in Near Eastern studies holding a PhD as of January 1st 2003, who are United States citizens or alien residents residing in the country for the last three years. Research projects must have a clear humanities focus.
Level of Study: Postdoctorate.
Type: Fellowship.
Value: US$40,000 for 12 months. A total of US$60,000 is to be available for one and a half awards.
Length of Study: 4-12 months.
Frequency: Annual.
Study Establishment: The W F Albright Institute of Archaeological Research in Jerusalem.
Country of Study: Israel.
Application Procedure: Applicants must write for details.
Closing Date: October 17th.
Funding: Government.
No. of awards given last year: Two.
No. of applicants last year: Eight.
Additional Information: The research period should be continuous, without frequent trips outside the country. Residence at the Institute is preferred.

For further information contact:

Department of Religious Studies John Carroll University, 20700 North Park Boulevard, University Heights, OH 44118, United States of America
Email: spencer@jcu.edu
Contact: Dr John R Spencer

NEH Postdoctoral Research Award

Subjects: Modern and classical languages, linguistics, literature, history, jurisprudence, philosophy, archaeology, comparative religion, ethics, the history, criticism, and theory of the arts.
Purpose: To support postdoctoral scholars.
Eligibility: Open to United States citizens or foreign nationals who have lived in the United States of America for three years immediately preceding the application deadline.
Level of Study: Postdoctorate.
Type: Fellowship.
Value: US$20,000 maximum.
Length of Study: Four months.
Frequency: Annual.
Study Establishment: The American Center of Oriental Research, Amman.
Country of Study: Jordan.
No. of awards offered: One.

Application Procedure: Applicants must write for details.
Closing Date: February 1st.
Funding: Government.

Pierre and Patricia Bikai Fellowship

Subjects: Archaeology.
Eligibility: Open to participants on an archaeological research project operating in Jordan.
Level of Study: Graduate.
Type: Fellowship.
Value: Room and board at ACOR and a monthly stipend of US$400.
Length of Study: One-two months.
Frequency: Annual.
Country of Study: Jordan.
No. of awards offered: One.
Application Procedure: Applicants must write for details and an application form or download it from the website.
Closing Date: February 1st.
Funding: Private.
Additional Information: This fellowship may be combined with the Groot or Harrell Fellowships.

AMERICAN SOCIETY FOR ENGINEERING EDUCATION (ASEE)

Suite 600, 1818 North Street North West, Washington, DC 20036, United States of America
Tel: (1) 202 331 3500
Fax: (1) 202 265 8504
Email: projects@asee.org
www: http://www.asee.org
Contact: Mr Michael More, Projects Department

The American Society for Engineering (ASEE) is committed to furthering education in engineering and engineering technology. This mission is accomplished by promoting excellence in instruction, research, public service, and practice, exercising worldwide leadership, fostering the technological education of society, and providing quality products and services to members.

Army Research Laboratory Postdoctoral Fellowship Program

Subjects: Science and engineering.
Purpose: To significantly increase the involvement of creative and highly trained scientists and engineers from academia and industry in scientific and technical areas of interest and relevance to the Army.
Eligibility: Open to United States citizens and permanent residents. Applicants must present evidence of having received a PhD, ScD or other earned research doctoral degree recognised in American academic circles as equivalent to a PhD.
Level of Study: Postdoctorate.
Type: Fellowship.
Value: Varies.
Frequency: Annual.
Study Establishment: The Army Research Laboratory.
Country of Study: United States of America.
Application Procedure: Applicants must submit a research proposal with a completed application form.
Funding: Government.
Contributor: The United States government.
Additional Information: Participants will be permitted to carry out research pending completion of security clearance.

Helen T Carr Fellowship Program

Subjects: Engineering.
Purpose: To increase the number of engineering professors for the historically black engineering colleges by providing financial aid for doctoral study in engineering.
Eligibility: Open to African American faculty members, graduate students and other African Americans who have completed at least the equivalent of one academic year of full-time engineering graduate

study. Candidates must be sponsored by the Dean of one of the historically black engineering colleges at which they later intend to teach.

Level of Study: Graduate.

Value: Up to US$10,000.

Length of Study: One year, renewable as funding allows.

Frequency: Annual.

Country of Study: United States of America.

Application Procedure: Applicants must first submit a letter to the Dean of a historically black engineering college asking to be sponsored. Transcripts of undergraduate and graduate course credits and at least three references testifying to intellectual capacity and educational attainments which give promise of satisfactory performance in advanced study must then be submitted to the ASEE. A covering letter from the sponsoring Dean is required, and a single copy of each of these documents is to be sent to the committee through its secretary at ASEE headquarters.

Closing Date: Applications for fellowships to begin in August or September should be submitted by January 15th, and by May 15th for fellowships to begin the following January or February.

Funding: Government, Commercial, Private.

Contributor: The Allied-Signal Foundation, the AMOCO Foundation, AT&T-Bell Laboratories, El Dupont De Numours & Co, the Exxon Education Foundation, the General Electric Foundation, the IBM Corporation, the Mobil Oil Corporation, NASA, RCA and the Union Carbide.

AMERICAN SOCIETY FOR MICROBIOLOGY (ASM)

1752 N Street North West, Washington, DC 20036-2904, United States of America

Tel: (1) 202 942 9225

Fax: (1) 202 942 9353

Email: awards@asmusa.org

www: www.asm.org/academy/index.asp?bid = 2099

Contact: Ms Peggy McNult, Manager, Awards Programme

The American Society for Microbiology (ASM) is the oldest and largest single life science membership organization in the world. With 43,000 members throughout the world. The ASM represents all disciplines of microbiological specialization including microbiology education. The ASM's mission is to promote research and research training in the microbiological sciences and to assist communication between scientists, policymakers and the public to improve health, the environment and economic well being.

Abbott Laboratories Award in Clinical and Diagnostic Immunology

Subjects: Clinical or diagnostic immunology.

Purpose: To honour a distinguished scientist in the field.

Eligibility: There are no eligibility restrictions.

Level of Study: Unrestricted.

Type: Honorific.

Value: US$2,000 cash prize, a commemorative piece and domestic travel to the ASM General Meeting where the laureate serves as the Division V lecturer.

Frequency: Annual.

Country of Study: Any country.

No. of awards offered: One.

Application Procedure: Self nominations will not be accepted. Nominations must consist of a nomination cover page, that includes a specific description of the nominee's contributions, a curriculum vitae including a list of the nominee's publications and two additional supporting letters.

Closing Date: October 1st.

Funding: Commercial.

Contributor: Abbott Laboratories, Diagnostic Division.

No. of awards given last year: One.

No. of applicants last year: Five.

Additional Information: ASM awards are granted at the discretion of award selection committees and may not be awarded every year.

Abbott-ASM Lifetime Achievement Award

Subjects: Microbiology.

Purpose: To honour a distinguished scientist for a lifetime of outstanding contributions in fundamental research in any of the microbiological sciences.

Eligibility: Open to mature scientists, both active and retired, from all relevant areas of microbiology.

Level of Study: Unrestricted.

Type: Honorific.

Value: A US$20,000 cash prize, a commemorative medal and travel to the ASM General Meeting where the laureate delivers the Abbott-ASM Lifetime Achievement Award lecture.

Frequency: Annual.

Country of Study: Any country.

No. of awards offered: One.

Application Procedure: Self nominations will not be accepted. Nominations must consist of a nomination cover page, that includes a description of the nominee's outstanding research accomplishments, a curriculum vitae including a list of nominee's publications and two additional letters of support.

Closing Date: October 1st.

Funding: Commercial.

Contributor: Abbott Laboratories.

No. of awards given last year: One.

No. of applicants last year: 15.

Additional Information: ASM awards are granted at the discretion of the awards selection committees and may not be awarded every year.

ASM Graduate Microbiology Teaching Award

Subjects: Microbiology.

Purpose: To recognise an individual for distinguished teaching and mentoring of students at the graduate and postgraduate level and for encouraging them to subsequent achievement.

Eligibility: Nominees must be currently teaching microbiology in a recognised college or university and have devoted a substantial portion of their time during the past five years to teaching graduate students in microbiology and have a minimum of ten years of total teaching experience. Nominees may have engaged in research or other concerns, provided that teaching graduate students remained a substantial activity.

Level of Study: Unrestricted.

Type: Honorific.

Value: A US$2,000 cash prize, a commemorative piece and travel to the ASM General Meeting, where the laureate is honored.

Frequency: Annual.

Country of Study: Any country.

No. of awards offered: One.

Application Procedure: Self nominations will not be accepted. Nominations must consist of a nomination cover form, that specifically addressing how the nominee fulfils the award eligibility, including a record of teaching responsibilities, manifests of distinguished teaching, innovations, publications, special awards or other pertinent information, a curriculum vitae including a list of the nominee's publications and two additional supporting letters.

Closing Date: October 1st.

Funding: Private.

No. of awards given last year: One.

No. of applicants last year: Eight.

Additional Information: ASM awards are granted at the discretion of award selection committees and may not be awarded every year.

Aventis Pharmaceuticals Award

Subjects: Microbiology.

Purpose: To stimulate research in anti-microbial chemotherapy and honour outstanding sustained achievement.

Eligibility: Nominees must be actively engaged in research involving development of new agents, investigation of anti-microbial action or resistance to anti-microbial agents and the pharmacology, toxicology or clinical use of those agents. They must not have served on an ICAAC Program Committee within the past two years.

Level of Study: Unrestricted.

Type: Honorific.

Value: A US$20,000 cash prize, a commemorative medal and travel for the laureate to the ICAAC conference.

Frequency: Annual.
Country of Study: Any country.
No. of awards offered: One.
Application Procedure: Self nominations will not be accepted. Nominations must consist of a nomination cover page, that includes a specific description of the research on which the nomination is based, a curriculum vitae including a list of publications and two additional supporting letters.
Closing Date: April 1st.
Funding: Commercial.
Contributor: Aventis Pharmaceuticals.
No. of awards given last year: One.
No. of applicants last year: 15.
Additional Information: ASM awards are granted at the discretion of award selection committees and may not be awarded every year.

BD Award for Research in Clinical Microbiology

Subjects: Clinical microbiology.
Purpose: To honour a distinguished microbiologist for outstanding research accomplishments, clinical or non clinical, leading to or forming the foundation for important applications in the field.
Eligibility: Open to clinical microbiologists.
Level of Study: Unrestricted.
Type: Honorific.
Value: US$2,000 cash prize, a commemorative piece and travel expenses to the ASM General Meeting where the laureate serves as the Division C lecturer.
Frequency: Annual.
Country of Study: Any country.
No. of awards offered: One.
Application Procedure: Self nominations will not be accepted. Nominations must consist of a nomination cover page, that describes the nominee's activities and accomplishments pertinent to the award, a curriculum vitae including a list of publications and two additional supporting letters.
Closing Date: October 1st.
Funding: Commercial.
Contributor: BD Biosciences.
No. of awards given last year: One.
No. of applicants last year: Four.
Additional Information: ASM awards are granted at the discretion of award selection committees and may not be awarded every year.

bioMérieux Sonnenwirth Award for Leadership in Clinical Microbiology

Subjects: Microbiology.
Purpose: To honour a distinguished microbiologist who has exhibited exemplary leadership, recognises the promotion of innovation in clinical laboratory science, and demonstrates high dedication and commitment to ASM and to the advancement of clinical microbiology as a profession.
Eligibility: Open to distinguished microbiologists.
Level of Study: Unrestricted.
Type: Honorific.
Value: A US$2,000 cash prize, communerative prize and travel to the ASM general meeting.
Length of Study: Commemoratic piece travel.
Frequency: Annual.
Country of Study: Any country.
No. of awards offered: One.
Application Procedure: Self nominations will not be accepted. Nominations must consist of a nomination cover page, that describing the nominee's activities and accomplishments pertinent to the award, a curriculum vitae including a list of publications and two additional supporting letters.
Closing Date: October 1st.
Funding: Commercial.
Contributor: bioMérieux, Inc.
No. of awards given last year: One.
No. of applicants last year: Seven.
Additional Information: ASM awards are granted at the discretion of award selection committees and may not be awarded every year.

Carski Foundation Distinguished Teaching Award

Subjects: Science education.
Purpose: To recognise a mature individual for distinguished teaching of microbiology to pre-baccalaureate students and who has encouraged them to subsequent achievements.
Eligibility: Nominees must be currently teaching microbiology in a recognised college or university. A substantial portion of his or her time during the past five years must have been devoted to teaching undergraduate students in microbiology and a minimum of ten years total teaching experience is required. Nominees may have engaged in research or other concerns, provided that teaching undergraduates remained a substantial activity.
Level of Study: Unrestricted.
Type: Honorific.
Value: A US$2,000 cash prize, commemorative piece and travel to the ASM General Meeting where the laureate delivers the Carski Award lecture.
Frequency: Annual.
Country of Study: Any country.
No. of awards offered: One.
Application Procedure: Self nominations will not be accepted. Nominations must consist of a nomination cover page, a nominating letter detailing teaching responsibilities, manifests of distinguished teaching, innovations, publications and special awards, also a curriculum vitae and two additional supporting letters.
Closing Date: October 1st.
Funding: Private.
Contributor: The Carski Foundation.
No. of awards given last year: One.
No. of applicants last year: 11.
Additional Information: ASM awards are granted at the discretion of award selection committees and may not be awarded every year.

Dade MicroScan Young Investigator Award

Subjects: Microbiology.
Purpose: To recognise research excellence and potential and to further the educational or research objectives of an outstanding young clinical scientist.
Eligibility: There are no eligibility restrictions.
Level of Study: Postdoctorate.
Type: Honorific.
Value: A US$2,000 cash prize, a commemorative piece and travel to the ASM General Meeting.
Frequency: Annual.
Country of Study: Any country.
No. of awards offered: One.
Application Procedure: Self nominations will not be accepted. Nominations must consist of a nomination cover page, a curriculum vitae including a list of publications, abstracts and manuscripts in preparation, a one or two page statement from the nominee which describes how educational or research objectives will be enhanced by the award, and two additional supporting letters documenting the nominee's research excellence and anticipated impact of the award on achievement of the nominee's career objectives.
Closing Date: October 1st.
Funding: Commercial.
Contributor: Dade MicroScan.
No. of awards given last year: One.
No. of applicants last year: Eight.
Additional Information: ASM awards are granted at the discretion of award selection committees and may not be awarded every year.

Eli Lilly and Company Research Award

Subjects: Microbiology and immunology.
Purpose: To reward fundamental research of unusual merit.
Eligibility: Nominees must be working in the United States or Canada at the time of application and must be actively involved in the line of research for which the award is to be made. They must not have reached their 40th birthday by April 30th of the year the award is given.
Level of Study: Unrestricted, Under the age of 40.
Type: Honorific.
Value: A US$5,000 cash prize, a commemorative medal and travel expenses to the ASM General Meeting where the laureate delivers the Eli Lilly Award lecture.

Frequency: Annual.
Country of Study: Any country.
No. of awards offered: One.
Application Procedure: Self nominations will not be accepted. Nominations must consist of a nomination cover page, a nominating letter that includes a specific description of the research on which the nomination is based, verification of the date of birth, ie. a photocopy of driver's licence, passport or birth certificate, a curriculum vitae including a list of publications and two additional supporting letters.
Closing Date: October 1st.
Funding: Commercial.
Contributor: Lilly Research Laboratories.
No. of awards given last year: One.
No. of applicants last year: Five.
Additional Information: ASM awards are granted at the discretion of award selection committees and may not be awarded every year.

ICAAC Young Investigator Award

Subjects: Microbiology including the discovery and application of chemotherapeutic agents and other sciences associated with infectious diseases.
Purpose: To recognise and reward young investigators for excellence and research.
Eligibility: Nominees must have completed postdoctoral research training in microbiology or infectious diseases no more than three years prior to presentation of the award, must reside in North America and have performed significant research in North America.
Level of Study: Doctorate, Postdoctorate.
Type: Honorific.
Value: A US$2,500 cash prize which supports travel to the Interscience Conference on Antimicrobial Agents and chemotherapy.
Frequency: Annual.
Country of Study: Any country.
No. of awards offered: Up to two.
Application Procedure: Self nominations will not be accepted. Nominations must consist of a nomination cover page including a specific description of research, a curriculum vitae including a list of publications and two additional supporting letters.
Closing Date: April 1st.
Funding: Commercial.
Contributor: The Human Health Division of Merck US.
No. of awards given last year: Two.
No. of applicants last year: 12.
Additional Information: ASM awards are granted at the discretion of award selection committees and may not be awarded every year.

Procter and Gamble Award in Applied and Environmental Microbiology

Subjects: Environmental microbiology, Applied microbiology.
Purpose: To recognise distinguished achievement in research and development.
Eligibility: Nominees must show outstanding accomplishment in research or development in the appropriate field. They must be actively engaged in research or development at the time that the award is presented.
Level of Study: Unrestricted.
Type: Honorific.
Value: A US$2,000 cash prize, a commemorative piece and travel to the ASM General Meeting where the laureate delivers the Proctor and Gamble Award lecture.
Frequency: Annual.
Country of Study: Any country.
No. of awards offered: One.
Application Procedure: Self nominations will not be accepted. Nominations must consist of a nomination cover page which describes the work that has stimulated the nomination, a curriculum vitae including a list of publications and awards, and two additional supporting letters.
Closing Date: October 1st.
Funding: Commercial.
Contributor: Procter & Gamble.
No. of awards given last year: One.
No. of applicants last year: 10.

Additional Information: ASM awards are granted at the discretion of award selection committees and may not be awarded every year.

Promega Biotechnology Research Award

Subjects: Biotechnology.
Purpose: To honour outstanding contributions to the application of biotechnology through fundamental research, developmental research or reduction to practice.
Eligibility: An outstanding contribution can be a single exceptionally significant achievement or the aggregate of a number of exemplary achievements.
Level of Study: Unrestricted.
Type: Honorific.
Value: A US$5,000 cash prize, a commemorative piece and travel to the ASM General Meeting where the laureate delivers the Promega Biotechnology Research Award lecture.
Frequency: Annual.
Country of Study: Any country.
No. of awards offered: One.
Application Procedure: Self nominations will not be accepted. Nominations must consist of a nomination cover page, a nominating letter that includes a description of the nominee's research, a curriculum vitae including a list of publications and two additional supporting letters.
Closing Date: October 1st.
Funding: Private.
Contributor: The Promega Corporation.
No. of awards given last year: One.
No. of applicants last year: 15.
Additional Information: ASM awards are granted at the discretion of the selection committee and may not be awarded every year.

William A Hinton Research Training Award

Subjects: Microbiology.
Purpose: To honour an individual who has made outstanding significant contributions toward fostering the research training of underrepresented minorities in microbiology.
Eligibility: Nominees must have contributed to the research training of undergraduate students, graduate students, postdoctoral Fellows or health professional students. Their efforts must have led to the increased participation of underrepresented minorities in microbiology.
Level of Study: Unrestricted.
Type: Honorific.
Value: A US$2,000 cash prize, a commemorative piece and travel to the ASM General Meeting.
Frequency: Annual.
Study Establishment: American Society for Microbiology (ASM).
Country of Study: Any country.
No. of awards offered: One.
Application Procedure: Self nominations will not be accepted. Nominations must consist of a cover page, a nominating letter highlighting the nominee's activities and accomplishments pertinent to the award, a curriculum vitae and two additional supporting letters.
Closing Date: October 1st.
Funding: Private.
Contributor: ASM.
No. of awards given last year: One.
No. of applicants last year: Three.
Additional Information: ASM awards are granted at the discretion of award selection committees and may not be awarded every year.

AMERICAN SOCIETY FOR NUTRITIONAL SCIENCES

Suite L-4500, 9650 Rockville Pike, Bethesda, MD 20814-3990, United States of America
Tel: (1) 301 530 7050
Fax: (1) 301 571 1892
Email: meyersa@asns.faseb.org
www: http://www.nutrition.org
Contact: Executive Assistant

The American Institute for Nutritional Sciences is a non-profit membership organisation.

Bio-Serv Award in Experimental Animal Nutrition

Subjects: Nutrition.
Purpose: To recognise meritorious research.
Eligibility: Open to investigators who have received a doctoral degree in the 10 years preceding the award.
Level of Study: Postdoctorate.
Value: US$1,000 plus an engraved plaque.
Frequency: Annual.
Country of Study: Any country.
No. of awards offered: One.
Application Procedure: Applicants must be nominated. Nominations should include a letter stating the basis for nomination, a selected bibliography which supports the nomination, and a reprint or series of reprints on which the nomination is based.
Closing Date: September 1st.
Funding: Commercial.
Contributor: Bio-Serv, Inc.

Cenrium Center for Nutritional Science Award

Subjects: Nutrition science.
Purpose: To recognise investigative contributions to the understanding of human nutrition.
Eligibility: Preference is given to scientists from the Western hemisphere.
Level of Study: Professional development.
Value: US$1,500 plus an engraved plaque.
Frequency: Annual.
Country of Study: Any country.
No. of awards offered: One.
Application Procedure: Applicants must be nominated. Nominations should include a letter stating the significance of the work, a selected bibliography that supports the nomination and a reprint or series of reprints reporting such research.
Closing Date: September 1st.
Contributor: Wyeth.

Conrad A Elvehjem Award for Public Service in Nutrition

Subjects: Nutrition science.
Purpose: To recognise distinguished service to the public through the science of nutrition.
Eligibility: Open to qualified candidates of any nationality.
Level of Study: Unrestricted.
Value: US$1,500 plus an engraved plaque.
Frequency: Annual.
Country of Study: Any country.
No. of awards offered: One.
Application Procedure: Applicants must be nominated. Nominations must include a letter stating the basis for nomination, a selected bibliography indicating the candidate's contributions to public service and the candidate's curriculum vitae.
Closing Date: September 1st.
Contributor: Kraft Food, Inc.

E L R Stokstad Award

Subjects: Nutrition science.
Purpose: To recognise outstanding fundamental research in nutrition.
Eligibility: Preference is given to scientists at relatively early stages in their careers.
Level of Study: Unrestricted.
Type: Award.
Value: US$2,500 plus an engraved plaque.
Frequency: Annual.
Country of Study: Any country.
No. of awards offered: One.
Application Procedure: Applicants must be nominated. Nominations should include a letter stating the basis for the nomination, a selected bibliography indicating the candidate's contributions to public service, and a reprint or series of reprints supporting the research.
Closing Date: September 1st.
Funding: Commercial.
Contributor: An endowment from the family of E L R Stokstad.

Mead Johnson Award

Subjects: Nutrition.
Purpose: To recognise a single outstanding piece of research.
Eligibility: Open to outstanding investigators of any nationality.
Level of Study: Postgraduate.
Value: US$2,500 plus an inscribed scroll.
Frequency: Annual.
Country of Study: Any country.
No. of awards offered: One.
Application Procedure: Applicants must be nominated. Nominations should include a letter stating the significance of the work, a selected bibliography that supports the nomination, and a reprint or series of reprints supporting this research.
Closing Date: September 1st.
Contributor: Mead Johnson Nutritionals.

Osborne and Mendel Award

Subjects: Nutrition.
Purpose: To recognise outstanding basic research accomplishments.
Eligibility: Applicants need not be members of the Institute. The awards are usually made to professionally active nutrition scientists.
Level of Study: Unrestricted.
Value: US$2,500.
Frequency: Annual.
Country of Study: Any country.
No. of awards offered: One.
Application Procedure: Applicants must be nominated. Nominations should include a letter stating the significance of the work, a selected bibliography of all papers relating to the research on which the nomination is based, and a reprint or series of reprints reporting this research. Five copies plus the original nomination material must be submitted.
Closing Date: September 1st.
Contributor: ILSI, North America.

AMERICAN SOCIETY OF CIVIL ENGINEERS (ASCE)

1801 Alexander Bell Drive, Reston, VA 20191-4400, United States of America
www: http://www.civil.nwu.edu/asce
Contact: Student Services

Trent R Dames and William W Moore Fellowship

Subjects: Geotechnical engineering or the earth sciences.
Eligibility: Open to practising engineers or earth scientists, professors or graduate students. Membership of the Society is not required. The fellowship may be awarded to a co-researcher in a single project or divided among multiple projects. Previous fellowship holders are eligible to reapply.
Level of Study: Graduate, Professional development.
Type: Fellowship.
Value: US$5,000-10,000.
Frequency: Every two years.
Study Establishment: An approved institution.
No. of awards offered: One.
Application Procedure: Applicants must include a completed application form, a personal essay of no more than 500 words highlighting why the applicant chose to become a civil engineer, specific ASCE Student Chapter involvement, any special financial needs, and long-term goals and plans along with a detailed financial statement stating the purposes for which the funds will be used and how they will assist the applicant. Applicants must also include a description of the proposed research and its objectives, as well as a statement from the institution at which the research is to be conducted indicating that the applicant and proposed research are acceptable to the institution. A minimum of two letters of recommendation must be included, one of which must be from a faculty member. Applicants must include one sealed official transcript with each application, and a one to two page curriculum vitae, including honours, activities, organisations, ASCE activities (including any offices held) and any work experience.
Closing Date: Please consult the organisation.

AMERICAN SOCIETY OF HEATING, REFRIGERATING AND AIR CONDITIONING ENGINEERS, INC. (ASHRAE)

1791 Tullie Circle North East, Atlanta, GA 30329, United States of America
Tel: (1) 404 636 8400
Fax: (1) 404 321 5478
Email: mvaughn@ashrae.org
www: http://www.ashrae.org
Contact: Mr Michael R Vaughn, Manager of Research and Technical Services

The American Society of Heating, Refrigerating and Air Conditioning Engineers (ASHRAE) is an international organisation of 50,000 people with chapters all over the world. The Society is organised for the sole purpose of advancing the arts and sciences of heating, ventilation, air conditioning and refrigerating for the public's benefit through research, standards writing, continuing education and publications.

ASHRAE Grants-in-Aid for Graduate Students

Subjects: Heating, refrigeration, air conditioning and ventilation.
Purpose: To stimulate interest through the encouragement of original research.
Eligibility: Open to graduate engineering students capable of undertaking appropriate and scholarly research.
Level of Study: Doctorate, Postgraduate.
Type: Grant.
Value: Up to US$7,500 depending upon the needs and nature of request.
Length of Study: Usually for one year or less, non renewable.
Frequency: Annual.
Study Establishment: The grantee's institution.
Country of Study: Any country.
No. of awards offered: Usually 12-18.
Application Procedure: Applicants must complete an application form, available from the website. An application form must also be returned by the faculty advisor.
Closing Date: December 15th.
Funding: Private.
No. of awards given last year: 18.
No. of applicants last year: 48.

AMERICAN SOCIETY OF INTERIOR DESIGNERS (ASID) EDUCATIONAL FOUNDATION, INC.

608 Massachusetts Avenue North East, Washington, DC 20002-6006, United States of America
Tel: (1) 202 546 3480
Fax: (1) 202 546 3240
Email: education@asid.org
www: http://www.asid.org
Contact: Education Department

The American Society of Interior Designers (ASID) Educational Foundation represents the interests of more than 30,500 members including interior design practitioners, students and industry and retail partners. ASID's mission is to be the definitive resource for professional education and knowledge sharing, advocacy of interior designers' right to practice and expansion of interior design markets.

ASID/Joel Polsky-Fixtures Furniture Academic Achievement Award

Subjects: Interior design.
Purpose: To recognise an outstanding student's interior design research or thesis project.
Eligibility: Open to applicants of any nationality. Research papers or doctoral and Master's theses should address such interior design

topics as educational research, behavioural science, business practice, design process, theory or other technical subjects.
Level of Study: Postgraduate.
Type: Prize.
Value: US$1,000.
Frequency: Annual.
Country of Study: Any country.
No. of awards offered: One.
Application Procedure: Applicants must write for details.
Closing Date: March 28th.
Additional Information: Entries will be judged on actual content, breadth of material, comprehensive coverage of topic, innovative subject matter and bibliography or references.

ASID/Joel Polsky-Fixtures Furniture Prize

Subjects: Interior design.
Purpose: To recognise outstanding academic contributions to the discipline of interior design through literature or visual communication.
Eligibility: Entries should address the needs of the public, designers and students on topics such as educational research, behavioural science, business practice, design process, theory or other technical subjects.
Level of Study: Unrestricted.
Type: Prize.
Value: US$1,000.
Frequency: Annual.
Country of Study: Any country.
No. of awards offered: One.
Application Procedure: Applicants must write for details.
Closing Date: March.
Additional Information: Material will be judged on innovative subject matter, comprehensive coverage of topic, organisation, graphic presentation and bibliography or references.

ASID/Mabelle Wilhelmina Boldt Memorial Scholarship

Subjects: Interior design.
Eligibility: Applicants must have been practising designers for a period of at least five years prior to returning to graduate level. Preference will be given to those with a focus on design research. The scholarship will be awarded on the basis of academic or creative accomplishment, as demonstrated by school transcripts and a letter of recommendation.
Level of Study: Graduate.
Type: Scholarship.
Value: US$2,000.
Frequency: Annual.
Study Establishment: A degree granting institution.
Country of Study: Any country.
No. of awards offered: One.
Application Procedure: Applicants must write for details.
Closing Date: March 20th.

AMERICAN SOCIETY OF MECHANICAL ENGINEERS (ASME INTERNATIONAL)

Three Park Avenue, New York, NY 10016, United States of America
Tel: (1) 212 591 8131
Fax: (1) 212 591 7143
Email: oluwanifiset@asme.org
www: http://www.asme.org/education/enged/aid
Contact: Administrative Assistant

Founded in 1880 as the American Society of Mechanical Engineers (ASME International), today ASME International is a non-profit educational and technical organisation serving a worldwide membership.

ASME Graduate Teaching Fellowship Program

Subjects: Mechanical engineering.
Purpose: To encourage outstanding students, especially women and minorities, to pursue a doctorate in mechanical engineering teaching and to encourage the engineering education as a profession.
Eligibility: Open to PhD students in mechanical engineering, with a demonstrated interest in a teaching career. A Master's degree or

passage of qualifying exam is required as is a lecture responsibility teaching assistantship commitment from the applicant's department. In addition, the applicant should be a United States citizen or permanent resident, with an undergraduate degree from an ABET accredited programme, and a student member of ASME. The student must also study in the United States.

Level of Study: Doctorate, Postgraduate.
Type: Fellowship.
Value: US$5,000 per year.
Length of Study: Two years.
Frequency: Annual.
Country of Study: United States of America.
No. of awards offered: Four.
Application Procedure: Applicants must submit an undergraduate grade point average, Graduate Record Examination scores, two letters of recommendation from faculty or their MS committee, a graduate transcript, transcripts of all academic work, a statement about faculty career and a current curriculum vitae.
Closing Date: October 20th.
No. of awards given last year: 4.
No. of applicants last year: 10.
Additional Information: In the terms of the fellowship, the awardee must teach at least one lecture course. The applicant's department head must certify, prior to the award or continuation notice, the commitment of a teaching assistantship and the lecture assignment anticipated.

Elisabeth M and Winchell M Parsons Scholarship

Subjects: Mechanical engineering.
Purpose: To assist ASME student members working towards a doctoral degree.
Eligibility: Selection is based on academic performance, character, need and ASME participation. Applicants must be United States citizens and be enrolled in a United States school in an ABET accredited mechanical engineering department. No student may receive more than one auxiliary scholarship or loan in the same academic year.
Level of Study: Doctorate.
Type: Grant.
Value: US$2,000.
Frequency: Annual.
Country of Study: United States of America.
No. of awards offered. Approx. two.
Application Procedure: Application forms are available from the website.
Closing Date: March 15th.
Additional Information: Further information is available on request.

For further information contact:

102 Meadowridge Drive, Lynchburg, VA 24503-3829, United States of America
Tel: (1) 434 384 1057
Email: mrsnyder@aol.com

Marjorie Roy Rothermel Scholarship

Subjects: Mechanical engineering.
Purpose: To assist students working toward a Master's degree.
Eligibility: Selection is based on academic performance, character, need and ASME participation. Applicants must be United States citizens and must be enrolled in a United States school in an ABET accredited mechanical engineering department. No student may receive more than one auxiliary scholarship or loan in the same academic year.
Level of Study: Graduate.
Type: Scholarship.
Value: US$2,000.
Frequency: Annual.
Country of Study: United States of America.
No. of awards offered: Six-eight.
Application Procedure: Application forms are available from the website.
Closing Date: March 15th.
Additional Information: Further information is available on request.

For further information contact:

332 Valencia Street, Gulf Breeze, FL 32561, United States of America
Tel: (1) 850 932 3698
Email: eprocha340@aol.com

Rice-Cullimore Scholarship

Subjects: Mechanical engineering.
Purpose: To aid a foreign student while doing graduate work for a Master's or doctoral degree in the United States.
Eligibility: Open to candidates from any country except the United States. Selection is based on academic performance, character, need and ASME participation. No student may receive more than one auxiliary scholarship or loan in the same academic year.
Level of Study: Doctorate.
Type: Scholarship.
Value: US$2,000.
Length of Study: One year.
Frequency: Annual.
Country of Study: United States of America.
Application Procedure: Applicants must apply in their home country through the local institute of International Education Embassy (IEE) or Education Offices at the United States Embassy. Only applications received from the IEE will be considered.
Closing Date: Please contact the organisation.
Additional Information: Further information is available on request.

AMERICAN SOCIETY OF NAVAL ENGINEERS (ASNE)

1452 Duke Street, Alexandria, VA 22314-3458, United States of America
Tel: (1) 703 836 6727
Fax: (1) 703 836 7491
Email: scholarship@navalengineers.org
www: http://www.navalengineers.org
Contact: Mr Dennis A Pignotti, Operations Manager

The American Society of Naval Engineers (ASNE) is the leading professional engineering society representing scientists, engineers and allied professionals who conceive design, develop, test, construct, outfit, operate and maintain naval and maritime surface and subsurface ships, air vehicles, and their associated systems and subsystems. ASNE also serves the educators who train the professionals, researchers who renew the technology and students who bring forth new concepts. Society work helps to support the United States Navy, the United States Coast Guard, the United States Army, the United States Marine Corps and the Merchant Marines.

ASNE Scholarships

Subjects: Engineering or physical sciences.
Purpose: To encourage students to enter the field of naval engineering and to support naval engineers seeking advanced education.
Eligibility: Open to citizens of the United States of America who are about to enter one year of graduate study leading to a designated engineering or physical science degree. Scholarships will not be awarded to doctoral candidates who already have an advanced degree. Candidates must also prove demonstrable, genuine interest in a career in naval engineering.
Level of Study: Postgraduate.
Type: Scholarship.
Value: US$3,500 per year for graduate students.
Length of Study: One year.
Frequency: Annual.
Study Establishment: An accredited college or university.
Country of Study: United States of America.
No. of awards offered: Varies, usually 18-22.
Application Procedure: Applicants must submit an application form, transcripts and letters of recommendation.
Closing Date: February 15th.
Funding: Private.
Contributor: ASNE membership.
No. of awards given last year: 19.

No. of applicants last year: 87.

Additional Information: Selection criteria is based on the candidate's academic record, work history, professional promise, interest in naval engineering and extracurricular activities, as well as the recommendations of college faculty, employers and other character references. Financial need may also be considered. The programmes which apply as valid courses for this award include naval architecture, marine, ocean, mechanical, civil, aeronautical, electrical and electronic engineering, the physical sciences, as well as other programmes leading to careers with both military and civilian organisations requiring these educational backgrounds.

AMERICAN SOCIETY OF NEPHROLOGY (ASN)

1725 I Street NW, Suite 510, Washington, DC 20006, United States of America
Tel: (1) 202 659 0599
Fax: (1) 202 659 0709
Email: email@asn-online.org
www: http://www.asn-online.org
Contact: Grants Co-ordinator

The American Society of Nephrology (ASN) was founded in 1967 as a non-profit corporation to enhance and assist the study and practice of nephrology, to provide a forum for the promulgation of research, and to meet the professional and continuing education needs of its members.

ASN-ASP Junior Development Grant in Geriatric Nephrology

Subjects: Geriatric and gerontologic aspects of nephrology.
Purpose: To support developing academic subspecialists interested in careers in the field.
Eligibility: Open to individuals who are within the first three years of a faculty appointment. Candidates must have completed a subspeciality internal medicine fellowship leading to certification in nephrology by the American Board of Internal Medicine. All candidates must have United States citizenship or permanent resident status classification in the United States.
Type: Grant.
Value: US$75,000 per year. The funding can support the salary of the recipient and/or the purchase of supplies, the salaries of technical personnel, and other resources necessary for the completion of the research project. The funding cannot be used for indirect costs or the costs of administrative or clerical support. The award will also include a one time travel grant of US$3,000, which must be used to attend the meetings of the American Geriatrics Society and the ASN during the second year of the award.
Length of Study: Two years.
Frequency: Annual.
Application Procedure: Applicants must submit four copies of the grant application, available online, which must include the department chairman's letter, division director's letter, if applicable, and three letters of reference. The letters from the chairman and division director should explicitly document commitment of 75 per cent or more time to research, plans for faculty appointment, availability of space and resources, and promotion of scientific independence. Applicants must also provide four copies of their curriculum vitae (with a publication list) and a research proposal organised under the headings of specific aims, background, preliminary data, specific experiments, methods and relevant references. The portion of the application comprising these components shall be no longer than 10 pages, excluding figures and reprints.
Contributor: The Association of Subspeciality Professors (ASP) and the ASN.

Carl W Gottschalk Research Scholar Award

Subjects: Biomedical research related to nephrology.
Purpose: To foster the independent careers of young investigators.
Eligibility: Open to active ASN members who hold an MD, PhD or equivalent degree. At the time of the initiation of the award the applicant must have a full-time faculty appointment and no more than

eight years shall have elapsed since the beginning of the applicant's nephrology fellowship or first postdoctoral training.
Level of Study: Postdoctorate.
Type: Award.
Value: US$100,000, each year = US$200,000 total beginning July 1st, to cover salaries and supplies related to the candidate's research proposal. A maximum of 10 per cent may be used to cover indirect costs at the candidate's sponsoring institution. A maximum of US$40,000 may be applied to the investigator's salary, including fringe benefits.
Length of Study: Two years.
Frequency: Annual.
Country of Study: Any country.
Application Procedure: Applicants must submit four copies of the grant application, available online, which must include the department chairman's letter, division director's letter, if applicable, and three letters of reference. The letters from the chairman and division director should explicitly document commitment of 75 per cent or more time to research, plans for faculty appointment, availability of space and resources, and promotion of scientific independence. Applicants must also provide four copies of their curriculum vitae (with a publication list) and a research proposal organised under the headings of specific aims, background, preliminary data, specific experiments, methods and relevant references. The portion of the application comprising these components shall be no longer than 10 pages, excluding figures and reprints.
Closing Date: March.
Additional Information: The Carl W Gottschalk Research Scholar Award will provide support for a specific set of studies that are not supported by other funds. A progress report is required for non competitive renewal of the grant for the second year. The award is for continuous support and interruptions in the period of support will require prior written approval from the ASN. Research Scholars are required to devote at least 75 per cent of their time to research. Awardees shall be known as Carl W Gottschalk Research Scholars of the American Society of Nephrology and shall acknowledge ASN's support in publications resulting from their proposed work. The Carl W Gottschalk Research Scholar Award may be transferred from one institution to another only with the prior approval of the ASN.

John Merrill Transplant Scholar Grant

Subjects: Biomedical research related to transplantation.
Purpose: To foster the independent careers of young investigators.
Eligibility: Open to active members of both the ASN and AST who hold an MD, PhD or equivalent degree. At the time of the initiation of the award the applicant must have a full-time faculty appointment and no more than seven years shall have elapsed since the beginning of the applicant's nephrology fellowship or first postdoctoral training. The applicant should not have substantial independent funding, such as a career development award, at the time of initiation.
Level of Study: Postdoctorate.
Type: Grant.
Value: US$100,000 annually to cover salaries and supplies related to the candidate's research proposal. A maximum of 10 per cent may be used to cover indirect costs at the candidate's sponsoring institution. A maximum of US$40,000 may be applied to the investigator's salary, including fringe benefits.
Length of Study: Two years.
Frequency: Annual.
Application Procedure: Applicants must submit four copies of the grant application, available online, which must include the department chairman's letter, division director's letter, if applicable, and three letters of reference. The letters from the chairman and division director should explicitly document commitment of 75 per cent or more time to research, plans for faculty appointment, availability of space and resources, and promotion of scientific independence. Applicants must also provide four copies of their curriculum vitae (with a publication list) and a research proposal organised under the headings of specific aims, background, preliminary data, specific experiments, methods and relevant references. The portion of the application comprising these components shall be no longer than 10 pages, excluding figures and reprints.
Contributor: American Society of Transplantation.
Additional Information: A progress report is required for non competitive renewal of the grant for the second year. The award is for

continuous support, and interruptions in the period of support will require prior written approval from the ASN and AST. Awardees shall be known as John Merrill Transplant Scholars and shall acknowledge the ASN and AST's support in publications resulting from their proposed work. The John Merrill Transplant Scholar Grant may be transferred from one institution to another only with the prior approval of the ASN and AST.

M James Scherbenske Grant (formerly the ASN Career Enhancement Grant)
Subjects: Nephrology.
Purpose: To support investigators' meritorious research applications that did not receive NIH funding. These awards are designed only for those investigators who lack sufficient funds to maintain their laboratory efforts for the period needed to submit a revised grant proposal.
Eligibility: Applicants, who must be active ASN members, must have submitted an NIH grant proposal in the field of nephrology that was favourably reviewed and close to the funding range, but did not receive support. Applicants shall not have more than US$50,000 in other substantial research funding for the specific unfunded proposal or other projects for which they are the principal investigator. In addition, applicants shall have a full-time academic appointment at the time the award is initiated.
Type: Grant.
Value: US$50,000 to cover salaries and supplies. Payments will be made quarterly. A maximum of 10 per cent may be used to cover indirect costs at the applicant's sponsoring institution.
Length of Study: One year.
Frequency: Three times each year.
Country of Study: Any country.
No. of awards offered: Three-six.
Application Procedure: Applicants must submit four copies of the grant application form, available online, along with the NIH summary sheet and NIH grant proposal. Applications shall be reviewed by a committee appointed by the President of the American Society of Nephrology. The applicant's priority percentile score will strongly influence the committee's decision.
Closing Date: Mid-March, mid-June and mid-November.
Additional Information: The grant is not renewable. The grantee must inform the ASN immediately if an NIH or similar grant is funded during the tenure of this award.

AMERICAN SOCIOLOGICAL ASSOCIATION (ASA)

1307 New York Avenue North West, Suite 700, Washington, DC 20005-4701, United States of America
Tel: (1) 202 383 9005 ext. 321
Fax: (1) 202 638 0882
Email: minority.affairs@asanet.org
www: http://www.asanet.org/student/mfp.html
Contact: Dr Jean H Shin, Interim Director, MAP

The American Sociological Association (ASA), founded in 1905, is a non-profit membership association dedicated to advancing sociology as a scientific discipline and profession serving the public good. With over 13,200 members, ASA encompasses sociologists who are faculty members at colleges and universities, researchers, practitioners and students. About 20 per cent of the members work in government, business or non-profit organisations.

ASA Minority Fellowship Program
Subjects: Sociological research on mental health and mental illness including attention to prevention and to causes, consequences, adaptations and interventions.
Purpose: To support the development and training of minority sociologists, to attract talented minority students interested in mental health issues and to facilitate their placement, work and success in an appropriate graduate programme.
Eligibility: Open to citizens or non citizen nationals of the United States, or those who have been lawfully admitted to the United States for permanent residence and have in their possession an alien registration card. Applicants must have been accepted or enrolled in a full-time sociology doctoral programme in the United States. In addition, applicants must be members of a racial and ethnic group, including black or African American, Latino eg. Chicano, Cuban, Puerto Rican, American Indian or Alaskan Native, Asians eg. Chinese, Japanese, Korean, or Southeast Asian, or Pacific Islanders eg. Hawaiian, Guamanian, Samoan or Filipino. Seniors in colleges or universities, students in Masters only programmes who have been accepted by, or who are applying to, doctoral programmes and have strong interests in the sociology of mental health are encouraged to apply. If, however, a candidate is selected for an award, but not enrolled in an appropriate doctoral programme by the time the funding year begins, he or she will not be eligible to receive the award. Students already enrolled in a graduate programme can apply, provided that they fulfil the eligibility criteria and demonstrate research interests in mental health and mental illness.
Level of Study: Graduate, Predoctorate.
Type: Fellowship.
Value: US$18,156.
Length of Study: One year, renewable for up to three years.
Frequency: Annual.
Study Establishment: Varies.
Country of Study: United States of America.
No. of awards offered: Varies.
Application Procedure: Applicants must submit their complete application package to the Minority Fellowship Program in one package. The complete application package consists of a fellowship application, essays, three letters of recommendation, official transcripts and other optional supporting documents such as a curriculum vitae, published research papers and Graduate Record Examination scores.
Closing Date: January 31st for announcement by April 15th.
Funding: Government, Private.
Contributor: NIMH.
No. of awards given last year: Eight.
No. of applicants last year: 60.
Additional Information: Dissertation support is available through an NIMH Dissertation Research Grant to Fellows who have completed all course work and who have advanced to degree candidacy.

AMERICAN TINNITUS ASSOCIATION (ATA)

PO Box 5, Portland, OR 97207-0005, United States of America
Tel: (1) 503 248 9985
Fax: (1) 503 248 0024
Email: cheryl@ata.org
www: http://www.ata.org
Contact: Ms Cheryl D McGinnis

The American Tinnitus Association's (ATA) mission is to silence tinnitus through education, advocacy, research and support.

ATA Scientific Research Grants
Subjects: Tinnitus.
Purpose: To identify the mechanisms of tinnitus, to improve treatments, and to identify a cure.
Level of Study: Postdoctorate.
Type: Research grant.
Value: Varies, maximum US$50,000 standard; up to US$100,000 per year for exceptional projects.
Length of Study: 1,2, & 3 year grants awarded.
Frequency: Twice a year.
Country of Study: Any country.
No. of awards offered: Varies.
Application Procedure: Applicants must write for grant application policies and a procedures brochure. These documents can also be downloaded from the website.
Closing Date: Proposals may be sent at any time for deadlines of June 30th and December 31st.
Funding: Private.
Contributor: Sufferers of tinnitus.
No. of awards given last year: Six.
No. of applicants last year: 13.

THE AMERICAN UNIVERSITY IN CAIRO (AUC)

PO Box 2511113, Sharia Kasr El Aini, Cairo, 11511, Egypt
Tel: (20) 2 794 2964
Fax: (20) 2 795 7565
Email: aucgrad@aucegypt.edu
www: http://www.aucegypt.edu/graduate
Contact: Mrs Sawsan Mardini, Office of Graduate Studies & Research

The American University in Cairo (AUC) provides quality higher and continuing education for students from Egypt and the surrounding region. The University is an independent, non-profit, apolitical, non sectarian and equal opportunity institution. English is the primary language of instruction. The University is accredited in the United States of America by the Commission of Higher Education of the Middle States Association of Colleges and Schools.

AUC African Graduate Fellowship

Subjects: Arts, humanities, business administration, engineering or information science.
Purpose: To enable outstanding young men and women from Africa to study for a Master's degree.
Eligibility: Open to African nationals, not including Egyptians, with Bachelor's degrees, an academic record of not less than 'Very Good' and an overall grade point average of 3.0 on a 4.0 scale or the equivalent. Candidates must also show proficiency in the English language by either submitting a Test of English as a Foreign Language with TWE score of 550 or above, or taking the AUC's ELPET exam.
Level of Study: Graduate.
Type: Fellowship.
Value: A waiver of tuition, incidental and graduation fees, health insurance on the AUC plan, a monthly stipend and, if needed, a housing allowance or accommodation at the University's residence.
Length of Study: Two academic years and the intervening Summer session.
Frequency: Annual.
Study Establishment: AUC only.
Country of Study: Egypt.
No. of awards offered: Five.
Application Procedure: Applicants must complete an application form available from the Office of Graduate Studies and Research.
Closing Date: February 1st.
Funding: Private.
No. of awards given last year: Three.
No. of applicants last year: 45.

AUC Arabic Language Fellowships

Subjects: All subjects.
Purpose: To award fully admitted international graduate students who need to satisfy their degree requirement.
Eligibility: Open to candidates from any country except Egypt. Candidates must be full-time graduate students who need to take Arabic language classes in order to satisfy their requirements at AUC and would like to enrol in the Arabic Language Institute's (ALI) full-time Summer Arabic programme or take ALING classes up to 6 credits of Arabic Language not towards a degree.
Level of Study: Graduate, Postgraduate.
Type: Fellowship.
Value: 50 per cent waiver of tuition fees for the ALI intensive Arabic summer programme or 50% of up to six credits of ALING classes (non-credit classes) diving the academic year.
Length of Study: One Summer session or two courses during the academic year.
Frequency: Annual, every semester.
Study Establishment: AUC.
Country of Study: Egypt.
No. of awards offered: Five.
Application Procedure: Applicants must submit a completed application form which can be found on the website at:http://www.auc-egypt.edu/academic/gradstudies/Fellowship/arabic.html.

Closing Date: February 1st for the Summer session, November 1st for Spring and June 1st for Fall.
No. of awards given last year: Three.
No. of applicants last year: Three.
Additional Information: Fellows are assigned five hours per week of related academic or administrative work.

AUC Assistantships

Subjects: Arts, humanities, business administration, engineering or information science.
Purpose: To support graduate level teaching or research assistants who do not receive tuition waivers.
Eligibility: Fully accepted graduate students enrolled in two or more courses or actively engaged in thesis work are given preference over those not enrolled in the graduate programme. Applicants who have completed their MA or MS, are preparing for a PhD, and have or are receiving academic degree training may also receive assistantships as post-master assistants.
Level of Study: Graduate.
Type: Award.
Value: Holders of a Master's degree receive monthly stipends of Egyptian £35 per hour of load per week. Bachelor's degree holders receive monthly stipends of Egyptian £29 per hour of load per week.
Length of Study: One semester, renewable.
Frequency: Three times each year.
Study Establishment: AUC.
Country of Study: Egypt.
Application Procedure: Applications must be made to the relevant department.
Closing Date: September 7th, February 2nd or June 7th. First week of every semester and summer session.

AUC Graduate Merit Fellowships

Subjects: Business, communication, computer science, social and behavioural sciences.
Purpose: To recognise and award outstanding new or continuing graduate students who wish to pursue full-time study in one of the graduate programmes.
Eligibility: Open to students who are fully admissible to one of the graduate programmes at AUC and who have a BA or BSc degree with a minimum overall grade point average of 3.4 on a 4.0 scale and a minimum of 3.5 in their major. Students who are already enrolled in one of AUC's graduate programmes and have a minimum grade point average of 3.7 in their graduate courses are also eligible to apply.
Level of Study: Graduate.
Type: Fellowship.
Value: A waiver of tuition, student services and activities fees of approx. US$4,320 per year and a monthly stipend of Egyptian £532 for 11 months.
Length of Study: One year, though the award may be renewed for a second year with the approval of the school Dean.
Frequency: Annual.
Study Establishment: AUC.
Country of Study: Egypt.
No. of awards offered: 18.
Application Procedure: Applicants must write to the Office of Graduate Studies and Research or the Dean's offices downloadable from the web under fellowships at:http://www.aucegypt.edu/academic/gradstudies/Fellowships/merit.html.
Closing Date: Mid May.
Contributor: AUC.
No. of awards given last year: 18.
No. of applicants last year: 100.
Additional Information: Please note the Merit Fellowship provides partial tution waiver to international students.

AUC International Graduate Fellowships in Arabic Studies, Middle East Studies and Sociology-Anthropology

Subjects: Arabic studies, Middle East studies, Sociology or Anthropology.
Purpose: To recognise and award outstanding new international graduate students who wish to pursue full-time study.

Eligibility: Open to candidates from any country except Egypt. Candidates must have completed an appropriate undergraduate degree with a minimum overall grade point average of 3.4 on a 4.0 scale or equivalent.
Level of Study: Graduate, Postgraduate.
Type: Fellowship.
Value: A waiver of tuition fees, a monthly stipend and housing allowance or accommodation in the University's residence. The award also includes medical insurance.
Length of Study: Two years.
Frequency: Annual.
Study Establishment: AUC.
Country of Study: Egypt.
No. of awards offered: Two.
Application Procedure: Applicants must complete an application form, available from the website.
Closing Date: February 1st.
No. of awards given last year: 2.
No. of applicants last year: 30.
Additional Information: Fellows are assigned 18 hours per week of related academic or administrative work.

AUC Laboratory Instruction Graduate Fellowships in Engineering and Computer Science

Subjects: Computer science and engineering.
Purpose: To recognise and support outstanding graduate students who wish to pursue full-time study in either engineering or computer science.
Eligibility: Students must have a BSc degree with a minimum overall grade point average of 3.2 on a 4.0 scale or its equivalent. Students already enrolled in one of these graduate programmes with a minimum grade point average of 3.2 are also eligible.
Level of Study: Graduate.
Type: Fellowship.
Value: A waiver of tuition, student services and activities fees of approx. US$3,200 per year and a monthly stipend of Egyptian £460 for 10 months.
Length of Study: Reviewed every semester and may be renewed for a maximum period of two years. The fellowship may cover a Summer session.
Frequency: Annual.
Study Establishment: AUC.
Country of Study: Egypt.
No. of awards offered: 13.
Application Procedure: Application forms are available from the Departments of Engineering and Computer Science as well as the Office of Graduate Studies and Research downloadable from the web site under Tution and financial opportunities under Fellowships at:http://www.aucegypt.edu/academic/gradstudies/Fellowships/lab.html.
Closing Date: Mid May.

AUC Nadia Niazi Mostafa Fellowship in Islamic Art and Architecture

Subjects: Islamic art and architecture.
Purpose: To recognise and award outstanding Egyptian graduate students who wish to pursue full-time study in the programme. The award is for second year Egyptian students already enrolled in the program.
Eligibility: Open to Egyptians. Candidates must be second year students enrolled in the graduate programme in Islamic art and architecture and have completed 12 credit hours with a minimum grade point average of 3.2.
Level of Study: Postgraduate.
Type: Fellowship.
Value: A waiver of tuition fees of up to US$4,320 and a monthly stipend over a period of 10 months.
Length of Study: One academic year.
Frequency: Annual.
Study Establishment: AUC.
Country of Study: Egypt.
No. of awards offered: One.
Application Procedure: Application forms are available from the Office of Graduate Studies and Research or the Department of Arabic Studies.

Closing Date: May 15th.
Funding: Private.
No. of awards given last year: One.
Additional Information: Fellows are assigned 12 hours per week of related academic or administrative work.

AUC Ryoichi Sasakawa Young Leaders Graduate Scholarship

Subjects: Arts, humanities or social sciences.
Purpose: To educate outstanding young men and women who have demonstrated a high potential for future leadership in international affairs, public life and private endeavour.
Eligibility: Applicants must have a Bachelor's degree with a grade point average of 3.2 or above and have actively participated in extra-curricular activities. Preference is given to those students who require four semesters to complete their degree. The award is contingent upon full admission to one of AUC's graduate programmes in the humanities and social sciences.
Level of Study: Graduate.
Type: Scholarship.
Value: A waiver of tuition, incidental and AUC medical service fees, a textbook allowance and a stipend towards living expenses of US$1,600 per year for Egyptians and US$3,600 for non Egyptians.
Length of Study: Two years.
Frequency: Annual.
Study Establishment: AUC only.
Country of Study: Egypt.
No. of awards offered: Three.
Application Procedure: Graduate application forms are available from the Office of Graduate Studies and Research or can be downloaded from the website.
Closing Date: February 1st.
Funding: Private.
Contributor: The Tokyo Foundation.
No. of awards given last year: 3.
No. of applicants last year: 25.

AUC Sheikh Kamal Adham Fellowship

Subjects: Television journalism.
Purpose: To assist students undertaking postgraduate study.
Eligibility: Open to non Egyptian graduate students who are MA candidates in the journalism and mass communication department, specialising in television journalism. Selection is made on the basis of financial need and academic performance. Professional experience is also considered where applicable.
Level of Study: Graduate.
Type: Fellowship.
Value: A partial waiver of tuition fees of US$5,000 per year.
Length of Study: One year, with the possibility of one renewal.
Frequency: Annual.
Country of Study: Egypt.
No. of awards offered: One.
Application Procedure: Applicants must write to the director of the Kamal Adham Center for Television Journalism for details, or telephone (20) 2 797 5424.
Closing Date: Mid May.
No. of awards given last year: One.
Additional Information: Applicants must serve as an assistant in the Adham Center for 40 hours per month during the academic year.

AUC Teaching Arabic as a Foreign Language Fellowships

Subjects: Arabic, education and teacher training.
Purpose: To acquire language teaching skills.
Eligibility: Open to individuals who have Teaching Arabic as a Foreign Language experience or excellent qualifications in the Arabic language.
Level of Study: Graduate.
Type: Fellowship.
Value: A tuition waiver of US$4,320 and a monthly stipend of Egyptian £607 and medical insurance.
Length of Study: Two academic years and the intervening Summer session.

Frequency: Annual.
Study Establishment: AUC.
Country of Study: Egypt.
No. of awards offered: 3.
Application Procedure: Applicants must write to the Office of Graduate Admissions and the Arabic Language Institute.
Closing Date: February 1st.
Contributor: AUC.
No. of awards given last year: 3.
No. of applicants last year: 10.

AUC Teaching English as a Foreign Language Fellowships

Subjects: Education.
Purpose: To acquire language teaching experience.
Eligibility: Special consideration is given to applicants with previous Teaching English as a Foreign Language experience and/or excellent qualifications in the English language.
Level of Study: Graduate.
Type: Fellowship.
Value: A waiver of tuition fees and a monthly stipend of Egyptian £550 and medical insurance. Non-residents of Egypt are provided with accommodation in the University dormitory or with a monthly housing allowance of Egyptian £620 and one way home travel.
Length of Study: Two academic years and the intervening Summer session.
Frequency: Annual.
Study Establishment: AUC.
Country of Study: Egypt.
Application Procedure: Applicants must write to the English Language Institute in Cairo or the New York office on aucegypt@aucnyo.edu the downloadable application for the TEFL fellowship is available at:http://www.aucegypt.edu/academic/gradstudies/Fellowships/tefl.html#apply.
Closing Date: February 1st.
Contributor: AUC.
No. of awards given last year: 10.
No. of applicants last year: 50.

AUC University Fellowships

Subjects: Art and humanities, business administration and management, engineering, mass communication and information, mathematics and computer science, social and behavioural sciences.
Purpose: To assist new and continuing graduate students who display superior performance in their academic endeavours and who wish to pursue full-time study.
Eligibility: Students must have a BSc or a BA degree with a minimum overall grade point average of 3.2 on a 4.0 scale or its equivalent. Students already enrolled in one of these graduate programmes with a minimum grade point average of 3.2 are also eligible. Preference is given to outstanding already enrolled graduate students.
Level of Study: Graduate.
Type: Fellowship.
Value: A waiver of tuition, student services and activities fees of approx. US$4,320 per year and a monthly stipend of Egyptian £197 for 10 months.
Length of Study: Reviewed every semester and may be renewed for a maximum period of two years. The fellowship may cover a Summer session.
Frequency: Annual.
Study Establishment: AUC.
Country of Study: Egypt.
Application Procedure: Applicants must complete applications, available from the chosen department in May.
Closing Date: June.
Contributor: AUC.
No. of awards given last year: 18.
No. of applicants last year: 123.
Additional Information: Fellows are assigned 10-12 hours per week of work with faculty members in teaching and research activities.

AUC Writing Center Graduate Fellowships

Subjects: English, grammar, education and native language, literacy education, teaching and learning.
Purpose: To provide outstanding students with valuable teaching, academic experience and to involve them as tutors in AUC's Writing Center.
Eligibility: Open to students who are fully admissible to the graduate programme in English and Comparative Literature at AUC and who have a Bachelor of Arts degree with a minimum overall grade point average of 3.2 on a 4.0 scale or its equivalent. Students already enrolled in one of these graduate programmes with a minimum grade point average of 3.4 are also eligible.
Level of Study: Graduate.
Type: Fellowship.
Value: Up to US$4,320 waiver of tuition, student services and activities fee and a monthly stipend of Egyptian £242 for 10 months.
Length of Study: Reviewed every semester and may be renewed for a maximum period of two years. The fellowship may cover a Summer session.
Frequency: Annual.
Study Establishment: AUC.
Country of Study: Egypt.
No. of awards offered: 1.
Application Procedure: Applicants must write for details to the Chair of the Department of English and comparative literature, and the Office of Graduate Studies and Research.
Closing Date: The end of April.
Contributor: AUC.
No. of awards given last year: 1.
No. of applicants last year: 5.
Additional Information: As part of their fellowship and in support of their professional training, Fellows are assigned 10 hours of work per week in the Writing Center.

AMERICAN WATER WORKS ASSOCIATION (AWWA)

6666 West Quincy Avenue, Denver, CO 80235, United States of America
Tel: (1) 303 347 6206
Fax: (1) 303 794 6303
Email: acarabetta@awwa.org
www: http://www.awwa.org
Contact: Administrative Assistant

The American Water Works Association (AWWA) is an international non-profit scientific and educational society dedicated to the improvement of drinking water quality and supply. The Association has more than 57,000 members who represent the full spectrum of the drinking water community eg. treatment plant operators and managers, scientists, environmentalists, manufacturers, academics, regulators and others who have a genuine interest in water supply and public health.

AWWA Abel Wolman Fellowship

Subjects: Water supply and treatment.
Purpose: To encourage and support promising students from countries with AWWA sections to pursue advanced training and research.
Eligibility: Open to candidates who anticipate completing the requirements for their PhD degree within two years of the award. Applicants must be citizens of a country that has an AWWA section ie. the United States of America, Canada or Mexico. Applicants will be considered without regard to colour, gender, race, creed or country of origin.
Level of Study: Doctorate.
Type: Fellowship.
Value: Up to US$20,000.
Length of Study: Initially one year, renewable for one further year on submission of evidence of satisfactory progress and approval by a review committee.
Frequency: Annual.
Country of Study: Other.
No. of awards offered: One.

Application Procedure: Applicants must submit an official application form, official transcripts of all university education, official copies of Graduate Record Examination scores, three letters of recommendation, a proposed curriculum of study, and brief plans of dissertation research study.
Closing Date: January 15th.
Funding: Private.

AWWA Academic Achievement Award

Subjects: Water supply and treatment.
Purpose: To encourage academic excellence by recognising contributions to the field.
Eligibility: Open to all Master's theses and doctoral dissertations that are relevant to the water supply industry. The manuscript must reflect the work of a single author and be submitted during the competition year in which it was submitted for the degree. The competition is open to students majoring in any subject provided the work is directly related to the drinking water supply industry.
Level of Study: Doctorate, Postgraduate.
Type: Award.
Value: US$3,000 for first place and US$1,500 for second place.
Frequency: Annual.
Country of Study: Any country.
No. of awards offered: Four. Two are for doctoral dissertations and two are for Master's theses.
Application Procedure: Applicants must submit an entry form with the names of the author, school and department, major professor, the degree sought, a one page abstract of the manuscript plus a letter of endorsement from the major professor or department chair. Manuscripts submitted to the Academic Achievement Award Committee should be unbound.
Closing Date: October 1st.
Funding: Commercial.
Contributor: AWWA.
Additional Information: Further information is available on request.

AWWA Holly A Cornell Scholarship

Subjects: Water supply and treatment.
Purpose: To encourage and support outstanding students to pursue advanced training in the field.
Eligibility: Open to female and/or minority Master's students. Applicants must be United States citizens.
Level of Study: Postgraduate.
Type: Scholarship.
Value: US$5,000.
Frequency: Annual.
Country of Study: Any country.
No. of awards offered: One.
Application Procedure: Applicants must submit an official application form, official transcripts of all university education, official copies of Graduate Record Examination scores, three letters of recommendation, a proposed curriculum of study and a brief statement describing the student's career objectives.
Closing Date: January 15th.
Funding: Commercial.

AWWA Larson Aquatic Research Support

Subjects: Including, but not limited to, corrosion control, treatment and distribution of domestic and industrial water supplies, aquatic chemistry, analytical chemistry and environmental chemistry.
Purpose: To provide support and encouragement to outstanding students preparing for a career in one of the fields of science or engineering to which Dr Thurston E Larson made significant contributions and who will provide leadership in efforts to improve water quality.
Eligibility: Open to candidates pursuing a Master's or PhD, at an Institute of Higher Education located in Canada, Guam, Puerto Rico, Mexico or the United States of America. The requirements for the degree must be completed in the year of the award. Selection of scholarship recipients is based upon the excellence of their academic record and their potential to provide leadership in one of the fields served by Dr Larson.
Level of Study: Doctorate, Postdoctorate.

Type: Scholarship.
Value: US$5,000 for Master's students and US$7,000 for PhD students.
Frequency: Annual.
Country of Study: Other.
No. of awards offered: Two.
Application Procedure: Applicants must submit an official application form, a curriculum vitae, official transcripts of all post secondary education, official copies of Graduate Record Examination scores, three letters of recommendation, a proposed plan of study, and a statement of educational plans and career objectives demonstrating or declaring an interest in an appropriate field of endeavour, or, if applicable, a research plan.
Closing Date: January 15th for the MS for receipt in the following year and January 15th for the PhD for receipt in the same year.
Funding: Private.
Contributor: Private donations.
Additional Information: Scholarship recipients will be publicly recognised at the annual conference of the American Water Works Association in June.

AWWA Thomas R Camp Scholarship

Subjects: Water supply and treatment.
Purpose: To support and encourage outstanding students undertaking applied research in the drinking water field.
Eligibility: Open to doctoral students in even years and to Master's students in odd years. Applicants will be considered without regard to colour, gender, race, creed or country of origin.
Level of Study: Doctorate, Postgraduate.
Type: Scholarship.
Value: US$5,000.
Frequency: Annual.
Country of Study: Other.
No. of awards offered: One.
Application Procedure: Applicants must submit a completed application form, a curriculum vitae, official transcripts of all post secondary education, official copies of Graduate Record Examination scores, quantitative, verbal and analytical, three letters of recommendation, a one page statement of educational plans and career objectives demonstrating or declaring an interest in the drinking water field, and a two page proposed plan of research.
Closing Date: January 15th.
Funding: Commercial.
Contributor: Camp Dresser and McKee, Inc.
Additional Information: Further information is available on request.

THE AMERICAN-SCANDINAVIAN FOUNDATION (ASF)

58 Park Avenue, New York, NY 10016, United States of America
Tel: (1) 212 879 9779
Fax: (1) 212 249 3444
Email: grants@amscan.org
www: http://www.amscan.org
Contact: Director of Fellowships & Grants

The American-Scandinavian Foundation (ASF) is a publicly supported, non-profit organisation that promotes international understanding through educational and cultural exchange with Denmark, Finland, Iceland, Norway and Sweden. Through its awards programmes the ASF encourages lasting academic, professional and personal ties between the United States of America and Scandinavia.

ASF Fellowships and Grants for Advanced Study in the USA

Subjects: All subjects.
Purpose: For Scandinavians to undertake study or research programmes in the United States of America.
Eligibility: Applicants must be citizens of Denmark, Finland, Iceland, Norway or Sweden.
Level of Study: Doctorate, Graduate, Postdoctorate, Postgraduate, Predoctorate, Professional development, Research.
Type: Fellowship or Grant.

Value: Varies.
Length of Study: Up to one year.
Frequency: Annual.
Country of Study: United States of America.
No. of awards offered: 50-75
Application Procedure: Applicants must be recommended to the ASF by a co-operating organisation. Please contact one of these organisations for details.
Closing Date: Details are available on request.
Funding: Private.
No. of awards given last year: 60.

For further information contact:

The Denmark-America Foundation, Fiolstraße 24. 3 sal, 1171, Copenhagen, Denmark.

The League of Finnish-American Societies, Mechelininkatu 10A, Helsinki, FIN-00100, Finland.

The Iclandic-American Society, Ravdaravstigur 25, 150 Keykjavik, Iceland.

The Norway-America Association, Radhusgt 23B, Oslo, N-0158, Norway

The Sweden-America Foundation, Box 5280, Stockholm, S-10246, Sweden.

ASF Grants and Fellowships for Advanced Study or Research in Denmark, Finland, Iceland, Norway and Sweden

Subjects: All subjects.
Purpose: To encourage advanced study and research, and increase understanding between the United States of America and Scandinavia.
Eligibility: Applicants must be United States citizens or permanent residents who have a well defined research or study project that makes a stay in Scandinavia essential. Team projects are eligible but each member must apply as an individual. Some ability in the language of the host country is desirable. Priority will be given to applicants who have not previously received an ASF award.
Level of Study: Doctorate, Graduate, Postdoctorate, Postgraduate, Predoctorate, Professional development, Research.
Type: Fellowship.
Value: Grants are usually US$3,000. Fellowships are up to US$18,000.
Length of Study: A maximum of one year.
Frequency: Annual.
Country of Study: Denmark, Finland, Iceland, Norway or Sweden.
No. of awards offered: 25-30
Application Procedure: Applicants must complete an official application form and submit this with an application fee of US$10.
Closing Date: November 1st.
Funding: Private.
No. of awards given last year: 15 grants and 10 fellowships.
No. of applicants last year: 125.
Additional Information: For further information please contact Ellen McKey via email or visit the website.

ASF Translation Prize

Subjects: Translation.
Purpose: To award the best English translation of poetry, fiction, drama or literary prose written by a Scandinavian author since 1800.
Eligibility: Open to translators of any nationality.
Level of Study: Unrestricted.
Type: Translation prize.
Value: US$2,000, plus publication of an excerpt in an issue of Scandinavian Review and a commemorative bronze medallion.
Frequency: Annual.
No. of awards offered: One.
Application Procedure: Applicants must submit four copies of the translation, including a title page and a table of contents for the proposed book of which the manuscript submitted is a part, one copy of the work(s) in the original language, a separate sheet containing the

name and contact details of the translator and the title and author of the manuscript with the original language specified. A letter or other document signed by the author, the author's agent or the author's estate granting permission for the translation to be entered in this competition and published in Scandinavian Review must also be included.
Closing Date: June 1st.
Funding: Private.
Contributor: The American-Scandinavian Foundation.
No. of awards given last year: 2.
No. of applicants last year: 21.
Additional Information: The Inger Sjoberg Prize of US$1,000 will be offered annually for the Honorable Mention entry.

AMFAR

120 Wall Street, 13th floor, New York, NY 10005-3908, United States of America
Tel: (1) 212 806 1600
Fax: (1) 212 806 1601
www: http://www.amfar.org

Leading non-profit organization dedicated to the support of AIDS research, AIDS prevention, treatment education, and the advocacy of sound AIDS - related policy.

AMFAR Basic Research Grant

Subjects: The prevention of HIV infection and the disease and death associated with it and protection of the human rights of all people threatened by the epidemic of HIV/AIDS.
Purpose: To support a researcher in the various financial obligations incurred in the course of an HIV/AIDS - related investigation.
Eligibility: Applicants must be working with a suitable not-for-profit organization.
Level of Study: Postdoctorate.
Type: Grant.
Frequency: Apply as needed.
Study Establishment: Suitable not-for-profit institution.
Country of Study: United States of America.
No. of awards offered: 100 per year approx.
Application Procedure: Write to the organization for detailed guidelines. Applicants projects subject to peer-review.
Funding: Private.
Additional Information: The committee will assess scientific merit, relevance of the research to the control of the epidemic or to the benefit of patients with AIDS or AIDS related conditions, the qualifications, experience and productivity of the investigators, the facilities available.

AMFAR Clinical Research Fellowship

Subjects: The prevention of HIV infection and the disease and death associated with it and protection of the human rights of all people threatened by the epidemic of HIV/AIDS.
Purpose: To support a post doctoral investigator with limited experience in the field of HIV/AIDS to redirect or embark on a career in biological, clinical or psychosocial HIV/AIDS research.
Eligibility: Applicants must be working with a suitable not-for-profit organization.
Level of Study: Postdoctorate.
Type: Grant.
Frequency: Apply as needed.
Study Establishment: Suitable not-for-profit institution.
Country of Study: United States of America.
No. of awards offered: 100 per year approx.
Application Procedure: Write to the organization for detailed guidelines. Applicants projects subject to peer-review.
Funding: Private.
Additional Information: The committee will assess scientific merit, relevance of the research to the control of the epidemic or to the benefit of patients with AIDS or AIDS related conditions, the qualifications, experience and productivity of the investigators, the facilities available.

ANGLO-AUSTRIAN MUSIC SOCIETY

Richard Tauber Prize for Singers, Committee 158 Rosendale Road, London, SE21 8LG, England
Tel: (44) 20 8761 0444
Fax: (44) 20 8766 6151
Email: info@aams.org.uk
www: http://www.aams.org.uk
Contact: Jane Avery, Secretary

The Anglo-Austrian Music Society promotes lectures and concerts and is closely associated with its parent organisation, the Anglo-Austrian Society, which was founded in 1944 to promote friendship and understanding between the people of Great Britain and Austria through personal contacts, educational programmes and cultural exchanges.

Richard Tauber Prize
Subjects: Vocal musical performance.
Purpose: A public recital in London and prize of UK£3,000 (Three thousand pounds).
Eligibility: Open to British and Austrian resident singers. Male applicants must be aged 21-32 years and female applicants aged 21-30 years. All applicants must ordinarily be resident in the United Kingdom or Austria. Application from any country so long as resident in UK or Austria.
Level of Study: Postgraduate.
Type: Prize.
Value: UK£3000 plus public recital in London.
Frequency: Every two years.
Country of Study: Any country.
No. of awards offered: One.
Application Procedure: Applicants must complete an application form.
Closing Date: January 31st.
Funding: Private.
Additional Information: Preliminary auditions are held in London and Vienna in March. Applicants must attend these auditions at their own expense. A public final audition is held in London in June.

ANGLO-BRAZILIAN SOCIETY

32 Green Street, London, W1K 7AU, England
Tel: (44) 20 7493 8493
Email: info@anglobraziliansociety.org
www: http://www.anglobraziliansociety.org
Contact: Ms Eliane Dell'Aglio, Secretary

The Anglo-Brazilian Society was formed in 1943 to promote close and friendly relations between Brazil and the United Kingdom and to further in the United Kingdom a knowledge of Brazil, its people and its culture, with the participation of Brazilians resident in the United Kingdom.

Anglo-Brazilian Society Scholarship
Subjects: Any aspect of Brazil including the culture, history, geography, literature, economy and medicine.
Purpose: To promote close and friendly relations between Brazil and the United Kingdom by providing a contribution to the cost of a working and/or research visit to Brazil.
Eligibility: Open to British nationals normally resident in the United Kingdom.
Level of Study: Graduate, Postgraduate.
Type: Scholarship.
Value: UK£1,000.
Frequency: Annual.
Country of Study: Brazil.
No. of awards offered: One.
Application Procedure: Applicants must contact the Society and are selected by means of an essay competition and presentation of an outline of their proposed study in Brazil. The outline must be approximately 3,000 words. Recipients travel to Brazil later in the same year and are expected to deliver a lecture to the Society on their return. Final selection is by interview in London through March.

Closing Date: February 1st.
Funding: Private.
Contributor: Events run by the Anglo-Brazilian Society.
No. of awards given last year: One.
No. of applicants last year: Three.

THE ANGLO-DANISH SOCIETY

Danewood, 4 Daleside, Gerrards Cross, Buckinghamshire, SL9 7JF, England
Tel: (44) 1753 884846
Contact: Mrs Anne-Marie Eastwood, Secretary

The Anglo-Danish Society exists to promote closer understanding between the United Kingdom and Denmark. It provides a forum in which Britons and Danes can meet one another.

Anglo-Danish (London) Scholarships
Subjects: Anglo Danish cultural and scientific interests.
Purpose: To promote Anglo Danish relations.
Eligibility: Open to graduates of Danish and British nationality.
Level of Study: Doctorate, Postdoctorate, Postgraduate, Professional development.
Type: Scholarship.
Value: UK£175 per month.
Length of Study: A maximum of six months.
Frequency: Dependent on funds available.
Study Establishment: Universities.
Country of Study: Other.
No. of awards offered: Four-six.
Application Procedure: Applicants must complete an application form, available from October 1st to December 31st. Applicants should enclose a stamped addressed envelope or international reply coupons.
Closing Date: January 12th.
Funding: Commercial, Private.
No. of awards given last year: Six.
No. of applicants last year: 80.

Anglo-Danish Society Scholarships Denmark Liberation Scholarship Awards
Subjects: All subjects.
Purpose: To promote Anglo Danish friendship.
Eligibility: Only open to British (UK) students wishing to study in Denmark.
Level of Study: Doctorate, Other, Postgraduate, Advanced student.
Type: Scholarship.
Value: One at UK£9,000 and several at UK£6,000.
Length of Study: A minimum of six months.
Frequency: Annual.
Study Establishment: The Universities of Copenhagen, Odense or Aarhus or another approved institution.
Country of Study: Denmark.
No. of awards offered: Varies. Please note this will be the final year that these scholarships will be available.
Application Procedure: Application form must be completed.
Closing Date: January 12th.
Funding: Private.
No. of awards given last year: 2.
No. of applicants last year: 12.
Additional Information: Successful applicants will be required to submit a report on work undertaken to the Society at the end of the study period.

Denmark Liberation Scholarships
Subjects: Anglo Danish cultural and scientific interests.
Purpose: To promote Anglo Danish relations.
Eligibility: Open to graduates of British nationality only.
Level of Study: Doctorate, Postdoctorate, Postgraduate, Professional development.
Type: Scholarship.
Value: One major award of UK£9,000 and others at UK£6,000 each.
Length of Study: A minimum of six months.

Frequency: Annual, Please note that this will be the final year that these scholarships will be available.
Study Establishment: A Danish university or other approved institution.
Country of Study: Denmark.
No. of awards offered: Four-six.
Application Procedure: Applicants must complete an application form, available from the Secretary between October 1st and December 31st. Applicants should include a stamped addressed envelope or international reply coupons.
Closing Date: January 12th.
Funding: Private.
No. of awards given last year: Four.
No. of applicants last year: 12.

ANGLO-ISRAEL ASSOCIATION

Suite 4, St Albans House, St Albans Lane, London, NW11 7QE, England
Tel: (44) 44 208 458 1284
Fax: (44) 44 208 458 3484
Email: info@angloisraelassociation.com
Contact: Mr R Saunders, Administrator

Established in 1949, the Anglo-Israel Association aims to engender a wider understanding of Israel in the United Kingdom by means of educational programmes, to foster goodwill between the two countries and to support exchanges at every level designed to promote a positive image of Israel in the United Kingdom.

Wyndham Deedes Travel Scholarships to Israel

Subjects: Life in Israel such as the sociological, scientific, cultural and economic aspects.
Purpose: Travel Scholarship to Israel.
Eligibility: Open to citizens of the United Kingdom who have graduated from a British university or Institute of Higher Education, or who are experienced, qualified professionals in their field who intend to reside permanently in the United Kingdom.
Level of Study: Graduate.
Type: Scholarship.
Value: Up to UK£2,000 to contribute towards the cost of direct travel to and from Israel and residence in Israel.
Length of Study: A minimum period of six weeks.
Frequency: Annual.
Country of Study: Israel.
No. of awards offered: Varies.
Application Procedure: Applicants must complete an application form. Successful applicants will then be invited for an interview.
Closing Date: March 31st.
Funding: Private.
No. of awards given last year: Six.
No. of applicants last year: 200.
Additional Information: A large stamped addressed envelope should accompany all enquiries. Upon returning from Israel award recipients must submit a report of a minimum 5,000 words on their project. The Association has the right to publish these reports.

ANGLO-JEWISH ASSOCIATION

Suite 5, 107 Gloucester Place, London, W1U 6BY, England
Tel: (44) 20 7486 5055
Fax: (44) 20 7486 5155
Email: info@anglojewish.co.uk
www: http://www.anglojewish.co.uk
Contact: Cynthia Stewer, Administrator

Anglo-Jewish Association Bursary

Subjects: All subjects.
Purpose: To assist students in full-time education who are in financial need.
Eligibility: Open to Jewish students of any nationality.
Level of Study: Doctorate, Graduate, Postgraduate.
Type: Bursary.

Value: Up to UK£2,000 per year.
Frequency: Annual.
Country of Study: United Kingdom.
No. of awards offered: 100-120.
Application Procedure: Applicants must write a formal letter of application in the first instance.
Closing Date: April.
Funding: Private.
No. of awards given last year: 130.
No. of applicants last year: 950.

AORN FOUNDATION

2170 South Parker Road, Suite 300, Denver, CO 80231, United States of America
Tel: (1) 303 755 6300
Email: nharbin@aorn.org
www: www.aorn.org
Contact: Grants Enquiries

The AORN Foundation is a charitable and educational foundation created in 1992 by the Association of preoperative Registered Nurses. Its mission is to secure resources and administer assets that provide support for the aim of preparing a new generation of surgical nurses.

AORN Doctoral Degree Scholarship

Subjects: Nursing or complimentary medicine.
Purpose: To provide scholarships to registered nurses who are interested in and committed to preoperative nursing to pursue a doctoral degree.
Eligibility: Applicant must have been a member of AORN for 12 months and have a current license to practice nursing.
Level of Study: Doctorate.
Type: Scholarship.
Frequency: Annual.
Study Establishment: Suitable accredited institution.
Country of Study: United States of America.
Application Procedure: Please check the detailed guidelines on the website or obtain a copy from the Foundation's offices.
Closing Date: May 1st

AORN Master's Degree Scholarship

Subjects: Nursing or complimentary medicine.
Purpose: To provide Scholarships to registered nurses who are interested in and committed to preoperative nursing to pursue a Master's degree.
Eligibility: Applicant must have been a member of AORN for 12 months and have a current license to practice nursing.
Level of Study: Postgraduate.
Type: Scholarship.
Frequency: Annual.
Study Establishment: Suitable accredited institution.
Country of Study: United States of America.
Application Procedure: Please check the detailed guidelines on the website or obtain a copy from the Foundation's offices.
Closing Date: May 1st

THE APEX FOUNDATION FOR RESEARCH INTO INTELLECTUAL DISABILITY LIMITED

PO Box 311, Mount Evelyn, VIC 3796, Australia
Tel: (61) 3 9736 1261
Email: morrish@c031.aone.net.au
Contact: Secretary

The Apex Foundation for Research into Intellectual Disability supports research into the prevention and treatment of intellectual disability utilising the funds raised some years ago by the Association of Apex Clubs. The Foundation manages these funds and makes annual research grants in support of selected research projects.

Apex Foundation Annual Research Grants
Subjects: Disability.
Purpose: To support research projects which are concerned with the causes, diagnosis, prevention or treatment of intellectual disability.
Eligibility: Open to suitably qualified researchers of any nationality, but the research must be carried out within the Commonwealth of Australia.
Level of Study: Research.
Type: Research grant.
Value: Varies. The total annual funds available are approx. Australian $60,000.
Length of Study: Varies.
Frequency: Annual.
Country of Study: Australia.
No. of awards offered: Varies.
Application Procedure: Applicants must complete an application form, available from the Secretary of the Foundation.
Closing Date: July 31st in each year.
Funding: Private.
No. of awards given last year: 4.
No. of applicants last year: 13.

APPRAISAL INSTITUTE

550 West Van Buren Street, Suite 1000, Chicago, IL 60607, United States of America
Tel: (1) 312 335 4129
Fax: (1) 312 335 4200
Email: sdavila@appraisalinstitute.org
www: http://www.appraisalinstitute.org
Contact: Sylvia Davila, Education Trust

Educating real estate appraisers for over 60 years, the Appraisal Institute is the acknowledged leader in residential and commercial appraisal education, research, publishing and professional membership designation programmes. Appraisal Institute members are identified by their experience and knowledge of real estate valuation, and adhere to a strictly enforced code of professional ethics and standards of professional appraisal practice.

Appraisal Institute Education Trust Scholarship
Subjects: Real estate appraisal, land economics, real estate and allied fields.
Purpose: The Education Trust Scholarship is awarded on the basis of academic excellence and is intended to help finance the education endeavors of individuals concentrating in the fields listed.
Eligibility: Full time college, United States University or community College. United States citizens, graduate and undergraduate students majoring in real estate appraisal, land economics, real estate or allied fields.
Level of Study: Graduate, Postgraduate.
Type: Scholarship.
Value: Undergraduates US$2,000, Graduates US$3,000.
Length of Study: One year.
Frequency: Annual.
Country of Study: United States of America.
No. of awards offered: Varies.
Application Procedure: Applicants must submit a written statement from the Dean of the candidate's college. This should consist of a signed statement regarding the candidate's general activities and intellectual interests, their college training eg. college attended, number of years of attendance, degree secured or to be secured within the next year, activities and employment outside college for the past four years or longer, their contemplated line of study for a degree, and the career that the candidate expects to follow. This statement should not exceed 1,000 words. Official copies of all collegiate grade records, the proposed study programme, including a brief description of each course the candidate plans to pursue in working toward the degree indicated, and a certificate of approval of this programme, should also be included. Letters from two individuals regarding the candidate's qualifications and character are also required. Students must also submit 4 copies of all information (1 original and 3 copies).
Closing Date: March 15th.

Funding: Private.
Additional Information: Applications are available in November. If you would like to receive further information or request an application to be sent via email or mail. Please write to the attention of Olivia Carreon, Project Coordinator at the Appraisal Institute at the address listed, or email ocarreon@appraisalinstitute.org or call 312-335-4100.

Minorities and Women Educational Scholarship Program
Subjects: Real estate appraisal, land economics, real estate and allied fields.
Purpose: The Minority and Women Educational Scholarship is geared toward college students working toward a degree in real estate appraisal or a related field. The scholarship is to help offset the cost of tution.
Eligibility: Open to United States citizens. Applicant must be a member of a racial, ethnic or gender group underrepresented in the appraisal profession. Must be a full or part-time student enrolled in real estate related courses within a degree granting college/university or junior college/university. Individuals must have a proof a cumulative grade point average of no less than 2.5 on 4.0 scale, and have demonstrated financial need.
Level of Study: Graduate, Postgraduate.
Type: Scholarship.
Value: Minimum of US$1,000 per person.
Frequency: Annual.
Country of Study: United States of America.
No. of awards offered: Varies.
Application Procedure: Applicants must provide an official student transcript, a 500 word written essay stating why they should be awarded the scholarship, an attestation that the scholarship will be applied towards tuition and book expenses and two letters of recommendation from previous employers and/or college professors. Students must also submit 3 copies of all information (1 original and 2 copies).
Closing Date: April 15th.
Funding: Private.
Additional Information: If you would like to receive further information or request an application to be sent via email or mail, please write to the attention of Shella Barnes at the Appraisal Institute at the address listed, or email sbarnes@appraisalinstitute.org or call 312-335-4100.

ARAB-BRITISH CHAMBER CHARITABLE FOUNDATION (ABCCF)

Longmead, Benhall Green, Saxmundham, Suffolk, IP17 1HU, United Kingdom
Tel: (44) 1728 603359
Fax: (44) 1728 603359
Email: abccf@abcc.org.uk
www: http://www.abcc.org.uk
Contact: Mr Michael Payne, Secretary to the Trustees

The Arab-British Chamber Charitable Foundation (ABCCF) provides funding for Arab postgraduate students studying at British universities.

ABCCF Student Grant
Subjects: Agriculture, forestry and fishery, architecture and town planning, business administration and management, education and teacher training, engineering, mathematics and computer science, mass communication and information science, social sciences or transport.
Purpose: To assist Arab nationals in financial need whilst they are at United Kingdom universities to undertake studies in subjects of potential value to the Arab world.
Eligibility: Open to nationals of an Arab League State. The maximum age is 40 and applicants must have United Kingdom student visa status. Applicants must show a commitment to return to the Arab world on completion of the postgraduate programme.
Level of Study: Doctorate, Postgraduate.
Type: Grant.
Value: Up to UK£2,000 per academic year.
Length of Study: Three-four years.

Frequency: Annual.
Study Establishment: A university in the United Kingdom.
Country of Study: United Kingdom.
No. of awards offered: Up to 30.
Application Procedure: Applicants must complete an application form which is sent only to applicants who have confirmed that their circumstances meet with the ABCCF's criteria. Other supportive documentation is required, eg. transcripts of degrees, academic references, citizenship and visa status, university acceptance or registration and a written undertaking to return to the Arab world after graduation.
Closing Date: None.
Funding: Commercial.
Contributor: The Arab-British Chamber of Commerce, London.
No. of awards given last year: 30.
No. of applicants last year: 200.

THE ARC OF THE UNITED STATES

1010 Wayne Avenue, Suite 650, Silver Spring, MD 20910, United States of America
Tel: (1) 301 565 3842
Fax. (1) 301 565 5342
Email: info@thearc.org
www: http://www.thearc.org
Contact: Dr Sharon Davis, Professional & Family Services Director

The Arc of the United States works to include all children and adults with cognitive, intellectual and developmental disabilities in every community.

Distinguished Research Award
Subjects: The prevention or improvement of mental retardation.
Purpose: To reward an individual or individuals whose research has had a significant impact on the prevention or improvement of mental retardation.
Type: Award.
Value: The recipient of the award will receive a plaque, US$1,000 and a trip to speak at the Research and Prevention Luncheon of The Arc's National Convention.
Frequency: Every two years.
No. of awards offered: One.
Application Procedure: Applicants must send the original and five copies of a nomination to the Arc.
Closing Date: April 15th.
Funding: Private.
No. of awards given last year: One.
No. of applicants last year: Three.

ARCTIC INSTITUTE OF NORTH AMERICA (AINA)

The University of Calgary, 2500 University Drive North West, Calgary, AB, T2N 1N4, Canada
Tel: (1) 403 220 7515
Fax: (1) 403 282 4609
Email: wkjessen@ucalgary.ca
www: http://www.ucalgary.ca/aina
Contact: Ms Karla Jesson Williamson, Executive Director

Created in 1945, the Arctic Institute of North America (AINA) is a non-profit membership organisation and a multidisciplinary research institute for the University of Calgary.

Jennifer Robinson Memorial Scholarship
Subjects: Northern biology.
Purpose: To award a graduate who best exemplifies the qualities of scholarship that the late Jennifer Robinson brought to her studies at the Kluane Lake Research Station. The scholarship committee looks for evidence of Northern relevance and a commitment to field orientated research.
Eligibility: Applicants should contact the organisation for eligibility details and guidelines.

Level of Study: Graduate.
Type: Scholarship.
Value: Canadian $5,000.
Frequency: Annual.
Application Procedure: Applicants must submit a brief description, at two-three pages, of the proposed research, including a clear hypothesis, relevance, title and statement of the purpose of the research, the area and type of study, the methodology and plan for evaluation of findings. Any collaborative relationship or work should be briefly identified. Three academic reference letters, a complete curriculum vitae with copies and a separate sheet of paper listing current sources and amounts of research funding including scholarships, grants and bursaries should also be submitted. Applicants are requested to include their email address upon submitting applications, if they have one. There is no application form.
Closing Date: January 10th for applications. The winning applicant will be notified by the selection committee in February.
Funding: Private.
No. of awards given last year: One.

Jim Bourque Scholarship
Subjects: Education, environmental studies or traditional knowledge of telecommunications.
Purpose: To financially support those in post secondary training.
Eligibility: Open to Canadian Aboriginal mature or matriculating students who are enrolled in post secondary training in the relevant subject areas.
Type: Scholarship.
Value: Canadian $1,000.
Frequency: Annual.
Country of Study: Canada.
No. of awards offered: One.
Application Procedure: There is no application form. Applicants must submit, in 500 words or less, a description of their intended programme of study and the reasons for their choice. In addition applicants must include a copy of their most recent college or university transcript, a signed letter of recommendation from a community leader eg. Town or Band Council, Chamber of Commerce, Metis Local, a statement of financial need indicating funding already received or expected and a proof of enrolment into, or application for, a post secondary institution. Applications are evaluated based on need, relevance of study, achievements, return of investment and overall presentation of the application.
Closing Date: July 15th.
Additional Information: Further information is available on request.

Lorraine Allison Scholarship
Subjects: Canadian issues.
Purpose: To promote the study of Northern issues.
Eligibility: Open to any student enrolled at a Canadian university in a programme of graduate study related to Northern issues, whose application best addresses academic excellence, a demonstrated commitment to Northern research and a desire for research results to be beneficial to Northerners, especially Native Northerners. Candidates in biological science fields will be preferred, but a social science topic will also be considered. Scholars from Yukon, the North West Territories and Nunavut are encouraged to apply.
Level of Study: Graduate.
Type: Scholarship.
Value: Canadian $2,000.
Length of Study: One year with the possibility of renewal following receipt of a satisfactory progress report and reapplication.
Frequency: Annual.
Country of Study: Canada.
Application Procedure: Applicants must submit a two page description of the Northern studies programme and relevant projects being undertaken, three letters of reference from the applicant's current or past professors, a complete curriculum vitae with academic transcripts and a separate sheet of paper listing current sources and amounts of research funding, including scholarships, grants and bursaries. There is no application form.
Closing Date: January 10th.
Additional Information: The selection committee will notify the winning applicant in February.

ARD INTERNATIONAL MUSIC COMPETITION

Bayerischer Rundfunk, Munich, 80300
Germany
Tel: (49) 89 5 900 2471
Fax: (49) 89 5 900 3573
Email: ard.musikwettbewerb@brnet.de
www: http://www.ard-musikwettbewerb.de

The International Music Competition, held annually in September, covers various categories and is open to all nationalities. The 2004 competition is for flute, viola, harp and string quartet categories. The International Music Competition is part of all German ns Broadcast stations, situated in Munich, Germany.

International Music Competition of the ARD
Subjects: Music. Categories vary annually.
Purpose: To support and reward a selection of young musicians who are at concert standard.
Eligibility: Open to musicians of any nationality. Age restrictions apply.
Level of Study: Graduate.
Type: Competition.
Frequency: Annual.
Study Establishment: Conservatories, university schools of music and music academies, but also includes advanced private studies.
Country of Study: Any country.
No. of awards offered: The competition includes either four or five categories. For each category three prizes are offered.
Application Procedure: Applicants must complete and submit an application form, an application fee and an audio cassette. There is an entry fee of €80 per soloist, €100 for duos, €130 for trios, €150 for quartets, and €175 for quintets.
Closing Date: The end of April.
Funding: Commercial.
Contributor: Public radio stations in Germany.
No. of awards given last year: 21.
No. of applicants last year: 247.
Additional Information: Further information can be found in the brochure, which is available on request.

Prize Winner of the ARD International Music Competition Munich
Subjects: Music. Categories in previous years have been singing, clarinet, trumpet, double bass.
Purpose: To support and reward a selection of young musicians who are at concert standard.
Eligibility: Open to musicians of any nationality. Age restrictions apply. Further information can be found in the brochure which is available on request and on the website.
Level of Study: Graduate.
Type: Prize.
Value: €155,000 in cash awards per year but please contact the organisation for details.
Frequency: Annual.
Study Establishment: Conservatories, university schools of music and music academies, but also includes advanced private studies.
Country of Study: Any country.
No. of awards offered: The competition includes either four or five categories. For each category three prizes are offered.
Application Procedure: Applicants must complete and submit an application form, an application fee and an audio cassette.
Closing Date: April 30th.
Funding: Commercial.
Contributor: Public radio stations in Germany.
No. of awards given last year: 16 + 23 special prizes and stipends.
No. of applicants last year: 467, but accepted 208.
Additional Information: Categories in 2005 violin, violoncello, Horn, Piano duo.

ARISTOTLE UNIVERSITY OF THESSALONIKI

School of Modern Greek Language, University Campus, Thessaloniki, 541 24, Greece
Tel: (30) 2310-994168, 996772
Fax: (30) 2310-995112
Email: dps@rect.auth.gr
www: http://www.auth.gr
Contact: Studies Department

Aristotle University of Thessaloniki Scholarships
Subjects: Theology, Pastoral and Social Theology, Philogy, History and Archaeology, Philosophy and Education, Psychology, English Language and Literature, French Language and Literature, German Language and Literature, Italian Language and Literature, Mathematics, Physics, Chemistry, Biology, Geology, Informatics, Law, Economic Sciences, Political Sciences, Agriculture, Forestry & the Environment, Veterinary Medicine, Medicine, Dentistry, Pharmacy, Civil Engineering, Architecture, Rural and Surveying Engineering, Mechanical Engineering, Electrical & Computer Engineering, Chemical Engineering, Visual and Applied Arts, Music Drama, Pre-School Education, Primary Education, Physical Education and Athletics, Journalism and Mass Media Studies.
Purpose: Highlight the University's academic tradition and promote its social profile abroad.
Eligibility: Registered Full-time students of The Aristotle University Foreign citizens of non-greek origin.
Level of Study: Doctorate, Postgraduate, Undergraduate.
Value: Please contact the University.
Length of Study: 1 year subject to renewal until completion of studies.
Frequency: Annual.
Study Establishment: The Aristotle University of Thessaloniki.
Country of Study: Greece.
No. of awards offered: 5 undergraduate (First-year), 12 undergraduate (intermediate-year), 10 postgraduate (masters & doctorate).
Application Procedure: 1-15 November each academic year.
Closing Date: November 15th.
Funding: Government.
Contributor: The Aristotle University of Thessaloniki.
No. of awards given last year: 11 for undergraduate studies, 20 for postgraduate studies.
No. of applicants last year: 44.

For further information contact:

Applications are given & received only on site. No application handling through mail.

Aristotle University of Thessaloniki Scholarships
Subjects: Modern Greek language.
Purpose: To encourage foreigners to learn the language. To diffuse Greek language and civilization.
Eligibility: Open to foreign citizens of any origin.
Level of Study: Unrestricted.
Type: Scholarship.
Value: Please contact the University.
Length of Study: Approximately one month, dates between 16 August-15 September.
Frequency: Annual.
Study Establishment: The Aristotle University of Thessaloniki.
Country of Study: Greece.
No. of awards offered: 70.
Application Procedure: Applicants must complete an application form, available on request from the Studies Department or from the internet http://www.auth.gr/services/admin/studies_department.en.php3. Completed application form & supporting documents must be sent to the Department of Studies by surface mail.
Closing Date: February 28th.
Funding: Government.
Contributor: The Aristotle University of Thessaloniki.
No. of awards given last year: 70.

No. of applicants last year: 243.
Additional Information: Information leaflet & application form available via email also. Email: dps@rect.auth.gr.

For further information contact:

Aristotle University of Thessaloniki, Department of Studies, University Campus, Thessaloniki, 54124, Greece

ARMAUER HANSEN RESEARCH INSTITUTE (AHRI)

PO Box 1005, Addis Ababa, Ethiopia
Tel: (251) 1 710 288
Fax: (251) 1 711 390
Email: ahri@telecom.net.et
www: http://www.telecom.net.et/~ahri
Contact: Dr Fisseha Haile Meskal, Acting Director

The Armauer Hansen Research Institute (AHRI) is an international biomedical research institute mainly devoted to work on bacterial infections, notably tuberculosis and leprosy. It is supported by the Ethiopian, Norwegian and Swedish Governments.

AHRI African Fellowship

Subjects: Medical sciences, parasitology or tropical medicine.
Purpose: To promote biomedical science in Africa.
Eligibility: Open to African researchers who hold an MSc, MD or PhD. Women applicants are especially encouraged to apply.
Level of Study: Doctorate.
Type: Fellowship.
Value: Accommodation and salary costs are covered.
Length of Study: One year.
Frequency: Annual.
Study Establishment: AHRI.
Country of Study: Ethiopia.
No. of awards offered: One.
Application Procedure: Applicants must contact the AHRI for details.
Closing Date: Usually October 1st.
Funding: Government.
No. of awards given last year: One.
No. of applicants last year: One.

ARTHRITIS NATIONAL RESEARCH FOUNDATION (ANRF)

200 Oceangate, Suite 830, Long Beach, CA 90802, United States of America
Tel: (1) 800 588 2873
Fax: (1) 562 983 1410
Email: anrf@ix.netcom.com
www: http://www.curearthritis.org
Contact: Ms Helene Belisle, Executive Director

The Arthritis National Research Foundation (ANRF) provides funding for highly qualified postdoctoral researchers associated with major research institutes, universities and hospitals seeking to discover new knowledge for the prevention, treatment and cure of arthritis and related rheumatic diseases. The ANRF receives no government funding, operating solely through the generosity of individual contributions. Each year ANRF's Scientific Advisory Board determines which research studies may have the most lasting impact in the fight against the 100 forms of arthritis which afflict over 43 million Americans. The Scientific Advisory Board members, renowned scientists and physicians from the fields of rheumatology and immunology, have committed their collective expertise to furthering the principles and goals of the organisation. These scientists believe that ANRF fills a much needed niche in the field of rheumatic disease research by providing support for young postdoctoral investigators, often providing the first major funding in their research careers.

ANRF Research Grants

Subjects: Arthritis.
Purpose: To support research focusing on high-incidence diseases, such as osteoarthritis and rheumatoid arthritis.
Eligibility: Applicants must hold an MD and/or PhD degree. Applicants need not be United States citizens, but must conduct their research at United States institutions. Applications will be accepted from postdoctorates and faculty members, with priority going to those scientists who do not already hold awards from the NIH or from the Arthritis Foundation.
Level of Study: Postdoctorate, Research.
Type: Research grant.
Value: Grants may range from US$20,000-50,000.
Length of Study: One year.
Frequency: Annual.
Study Establishment: Qualifying non-profit institutions in the United States of America.
Country of Study: United States of America.
No. of awards offered: 10-15.
Application Procedure: Applicants must visit the website for further information or request copy of grants guidelines via Phone or e-mail.
Closing Date: January 15th.
Funding: Private.
No. of awards given last year: 10.
No. of applicants last year: 36.

ARTHRITIS RESEARCH CAMPAIGN (ARC)

Copeman House, St Mary's Court, St Mary's Gate, Chesterfield, S41 7TD, England
Tel: (44) 1246 558033
Fax: (44) 1246 558007
Email: info@arc.org.uk
www: http://www.arc.org.uk
Contact: Mr Michael Patnick, Head of Research & Education Funding

The Arthritis Research Campaign (arc) is the fourth largest medical research charity in the United Kingdom, and the only charity in the country dedicated to finding the cause of and cure for arthritis, relying entirely upon voluntary donations to sustain its wide ranging research and educational programmes.

arc Clinical Research Fellowships

Subjects: Rheumatology, musculoskeletal disease or a related subject.
Purpose: To encourage young physicians to enter into a career in clinical academic rheumatology.
Eligibility: Open to medical graduates of the United Kingdom who are at the registrar or senior registrar level. Candidates will be expected to register for a higher degree eg. MD or PhD.
Level of Study: Postgraduate, Professional development, Research.
Type: Fellowship.
Value: Fellow's salary plus reasonable laboratory expenses.
Length of Study: Two-three years.
Frequency: Twice a year.
Study Establishment: A university department, hospital or recognised research institution.
Country of Study: United Kingdom.
No. of awards offered: Varies.
Application Procedure: Applicants must complete an application form, available from the website.
Closing Date: January and September as advertised.
Funding: Private.
Contributor: Charitable voluntary donations.
No. of awards given last year: 6.
No. of applicants last year: 25.

arc Clinician Scientist Fellowship

Subjects: Rheumatology, musculoskeletal disease or a related subject.
Purpose: To provide a period of clinical training with a period of postdoctoral research.

Eligibility: Open to medical graduates who have completed their first period of research training and, in most cases, have obtained a PhD.
Level of Study: Postdoctorate, Professional development, Research.
Type: Fellowship.
Value: Fellow's salary plus supporting technician, running costs and essential equipment.
Frequency: Annual.
Study Establishment: A university, hospital or recognised research institute.
Country of Study: United Kingdom.
No. of awards offered: Varies.
Application Procedure: Applicants must complete an application form, available from the website.
Closing Date: March, as advertised.
Funding: Private.
Contributor: Charitable voluntary donations.
No. of awards given last year: 2.
No. of applicants last year: 3.

arc Educational Project Grants

Subjects: Rheumatology, musculoskeletal disease or a related subject.
Purpose: To encourage education work in the field of Arthritis and Musculoskeletal disease.
Eligibility: Open to medical, scientific or educational professionals with an interest in relevant educational research.
Level of Study: Professional development, Research.
Type: Project grant.
Value: Varies.
Length of Study: Varies.
Frequency: Three times each year.
Study Establishment: A university, hospital or recognised research institute.
Country of Study: United Kingdom.
No. of awards offered: Varies.
Application Procedure: Applicants must complete an intent form in the first instance, available from the website.
Closing Date: The last Monday in February, June and October.
Funding: Private.
Contributor: Charitable voluntary contributions.
No. of awards given last year: Five.
No. of applicants last year: 12.

arc Educational Research Fellowships

Subjects: Rheumatology, musculoskeletal disease or a related subject.
Purpose: To provide an opportunity for an individual to gain training in educational research methodology and/or medical education.
Eligibility: Open to clinicians, allied health professionals and non clinicians in institutions within the United Kingdom.
Level of Study: Postgraduate, Professional development, Research.
Type: Fellowship.
Value: Fellow's salary with lecturership scale, plus supporting technician, running costs and essential equipment.
Length of Study: Two or three years full-time or part-time.
Frequency: Twice a year.
Study Establishment: A university, hospital or recognised research institute.
Country of Study: United Kingdom.
No. of awards offered: Varies.
Application Procedure: Applicants must complete an application form, available from the website.
Closing Date: January and September, as advertised.
Funding: Private.
Contributor: Charitable voluntary contributions.
No. of awards given last year: None.
No. of applicants last year: None.

arc Educational Travel/Training Bursaries

Subjects: Rheumatology, musculoskeletal disease or a related subject.
Purpose: To promote awareness and understanding of Rheumatology among allied health professionals through research, practical experience, presentation of research and formal education by attending a National/ International Congress or a short training course.
Eligibility: Open to state registered allied health professionals committed to the care of patients with rheumatic diseases. Applicants must have at least three year of post registration work experience and one year of experience in rheumatology.
Level of Study: Postgraduate, Professional development, Unrestricted.
Type: Bursary.
Value: 90 per cent of fares, registration, accommodation and subsistence.
Length of Study: Short courses only.
Frequency: Three times each year.
Study Establishment: A recognised training establishment, a national or an international congress.
Country of Study: United Kingdom.
No. of awards offered: Varies.
Application Procedure: Applicants must complete an application form, available from the website.
Closing Date: April, July and December.
Funding: Private.
Contributor: Charitable voluntary donations.
No. of awards given last year: 12.

arc Equipment Grants

Subjects: Rheumatology, muscoskeletal disease or a related subject.
Purpose: To fund major items of equipment costing in excess of UK£20,000 which will facilitate multiple projects and make a lasting impact on rheumatological research over many years.
Eligibility: Open to established units with a track record of research in Arthritis and Musculoskeletal Disease.
Level of Study: Research.
Type: Grant.
Value: Varies.
Length of Study: Up to three years.
Frequency: Three times each year.
Study Establishment: A university, hospital or recognised research institute.
Country of Study: United Kingdom.
No. of awards offered: Varies.
Application Procedure: Applicants must complete an application form, available from the website.
Closing Date: The last Monday of February, June and October.
Funding: Private.
Contributor: Charitable voluntary contributions.
No. of awards given last year: 4.

arc Non-clinical Career Development Fellowships

Subjects: Rheumatology, musculoskeletal disease or a related subject.
Purpose: To attract and retain talented scientists in rheumatological research.
Eligibility: Open to Candidates working in institutions in the UK who should normally have between 3 and 6 years of postdoctoral research experience.
Level of Study: Postdoctorate, Professional development, Research.
Type: Fellowship.
Value: Fellow's salary usually within 1A or II range plus reasonable running costs.
Length of Study: Up to five years, with a possibility of renewal subject to satisfactory review.
Frequency: Annual.
Study Establishment: A university department or similar research institute preferably within a multidisciplinary research group.
Country of Study: United Kingdom.
No. of awards offered: Varies.
Application Procedure: Applicants must complete an application form, available from the website.
Closing Date: April and November as advertised.
Funding: Private.
Contributor: Charitable voluntary contributions.
No. of awards given last year: 0.
No. of applicants last year: 8.

arc PhD Studentships

Subjects: Rheumatology, musculoskeletal disease or a related subject.

Purpose: To encourage the best young science graduates to embark on a research career in rheumatology.

Eligibility: Open to university departments allied to rheumatology.

Level of Study: Doctorate, Postgraduate, Professional development, Research.

Type: Studentship.

Value: Incremental stipend, United Kingdom tuition fees and limited running costs.

Length of Study: Three years.

Frequency: Annual.

Study Establishment: A university, hospital or recognised research institute.

Country of Study: United Kingdom.

No. of awards offered: Varies.

Application Procedure: Applicants must complete an application form, available from the website.

Closing Date: August, as advertised.

Funding: Private.

Contributor: Charitable voluntary donations.

No. of awards given last year: Five

No. of applicants last year: 28.

arc Postgraduate Training Bursaries

Subjects: Rheumatology, musculoskeletal disease or a related subject.

Purpose: To promote the training of allied health professionals by financing a higher degree course.

Eligibility: Open to state registered, allied health professionals committed to the care of patients with Arthritis and Musculoskeletal Disease. Candidates must have at least three years of relevant postgraduate experience.

Level of Study: Postgraduate, Professional development.

Type: Bursary.

Value: Fees.

Length of Study: Various, full-time or part-time.

Frequency: Twice a year.

Study Establishment: A university, hospital or recognised research institute.

Country of Study: United Kingdom.

No. of awards offered: Varies.

Application Procedure: Applicants must complete an application form, available from the website.

Closing Date: May and September as advertised.

Funding: Private.

Contributor: Charitable Voluntary donations.

No. of awards given last year: 6.

arc Programme Grants

Subjects: Rheumatology, musculoskeletal disease or a related subject.

Purpose: To support work that cannot be carried out in the short-term, to attract and maintain high quality staff in an effective research team, and to enable established research workers of proven ability to concentrate their efforts in a specific area.

Eligibility: Established groups undertaking research relevant to the aims of the arc, and which have a substantial research track record based either on arc support or peer reviewed funding from other sources.

Level of Study: Research.

Type: Other.

Value: Varies.

Length of Study: Up to three years.

Frequency: Annual.

Study Establishment: A university, hospital or recognised research institute.

Country of Study: United Kingdom.

No. of awards offered: Varies.

Application Procedure: Applicants must submit an outline proposal form in the first instance, available from the website.

Closing Date: June.

Funding: Private.

Contributor: Charitable voluntary contributions.

No. of awards given last year: 3.

No. of applicants last year: 6.

Additional Information: Applicants should note that up to one year should be allowed for the full process of programme grant evaluation to take place.

arc Project Grants

Subjects: Rheumatology, musculoskeletal disease or a related subject.

Purpose: To further research into Arthritis and Musculoskeletal Disease.

Eligibility: Open to candidates working within institutions of the United Kingdom. Candidates must have previous experience of investigation and research.

Level of Study: Professional development, Research.

Type: Project grant.

Value: Varies.

Length of Study: Up to three years.

Frequency: Three times each year.

Study Establishment: A university, hospital or recognised research institute.

Country of Study: United Kingdom.

No. of awards offered: Varies.

Application Procedure: Applicants must complete an application form, available from the website.

Closing Date: The last Monday of February, June and October.

Funding: Private.

Contributor: Charitable voluntary contributions.

No. of awards given last year: 36.

No. of applicants last year: 150.

Additional Information: Grants are made in support of specific research projects.

arc Senior Research Fellowships

Subjects: Rheumatology, musculoskeletal disease or a related subject.

Purpose: To further research into Arthritis and Musculoskeletal diseases and to attract high flying medical or scientific researchers into rheumatology.

Eligibility: Open to Medical or Scientific Graduates with between 6 and 12 years of postdoctoral research experience. Candidates should have proven ability in establishing an independent research programme.

Level of Study: Professional development, Research.

Type: Fellowship.

Value: Fellow's salary with lecturer B or senior lectureship scale, plus supporting technician, running costs and essential equipment.

Length of Study: Up to five years, with a possibility of renewal subject to satisfactory review.

Frequency: Annual.

Study Establishment: A university, hospital or recognised research institute.

Country of Study: United Kingdom.

No. of awards offered: Varies.

Application Procedure: Applicants must complete an application form, available from the website.

Closing Date: March, as advertised.

Funding: Private.

Contributor: Charitable voluntary contributions.

No. of awards given last year: One.

No. of applicants last year: 2.

arc Travelling Fellowships

Subjects: Rheumatology, musculoskeletal disease or a related subject.

Purpose: To provide training and experience for doctors committed to a career in clinical rheumatology.

Eligibility: Open to doctors up to and including senior registrar status and postdoctoral scientists.

Level of Study: Professional development, Research.

Type: Fellowship.

Value: Fellow's salary and travelling costs.
Length of Study: One year.
Frequency: Annual.
Study Establishment: A research centre of the Fellow's choice, subject to the campaign's approval.
Country of Study: Any country.
No. of awards offered: Various.
Application Procedure: Applicants must complete an application form, available from the website.
Closing Date: September as advertised.
Funding: Private.
Contributor: Charitable voluntary contributions.
No. of awards given last year: One.
No. of applicants last year: One.

THE ARTHRITIS SOCIETY

393 University Avenue, Suite 1700, Toronto
ON, M5G 1E6, Canada
Tel: (1) 416 979 7228
Fax: (1) 416 979 1149
Email: mellis@arthritis.ca
www: http://www.arthritis.ca
Contact: Ms Marie Ellis, Manager, Medical & Scientific Programs

The Arthritis Society is Canada's only non-profit agency dedicated solely to funding and promoting arthritis research and care.

Arthritis Society Industry Program

Subjects: Arthritis.
Purpose: To foster new collaborative efforts through shared funding between The Arthritis Society and industry in relevant research.
Eligibility: Applicants should write to the Society for details or refer to the website: www.arthritis.ca.
Level of Study: Postdoctorate, Research.
Type: Research grant.
Length of Study: 1-3 Years.
Frequency: Annual.
Country of Study: Canada.
No. of awards offered: Varies.
Application Procedure: Applicants must write to the Society for details.
Closing Date: September 15th or March 15th.
Funding: Private.
Contributor: Public donors.

Arthritis Society Research Fellowships

Subjects: Arthritis.
Purpose: To provide financial support so that candidates can pursue full-time research.
Eligibility: Open to highly qualified candidates with preference given to candidates intending to embark on a research career in Canada. Candidates must hold a PhD, MD, DDS, DVM, DPharm or the equivalent.
Level of Study: Postdoctorate.
Type: Fellowship.
Value: Based on institution scales.
Length of Study: Two years, usually beginning on July 1st with a possibility of renewal.
Frequency: Annual.
Study Establishment: Ordinarily, universities. Out of country training may be arranged in order to obtain specific expertise.
Country of Study: Canada.
No. of awards offered: Varies.
Application Procedure: Applicants must complete and submit an application form with further documentation as outlined in the regulations.
Closing Date: November 1st.
Funding: Private.
Contributor: Public donors.
No. of awards given last year: Seven.
No. of applicants last year: 13.

Additional Information: Fellowships are awarded by the Society on the advice of the Review Panel. The Society reserves the right to approve or decline any application without stating its reasons.

Arthritis Society Research Grants

Subjects: Arthritis.
Purpose: To promote and support the research operations of investigators.
Eligibility: Open to investigators holding staff appointments at Canadian universities or institutions where the research is deemed relevant to arthritis. Candidates must be Canadian citizens or permanent residents.
Level of Study: Postdoctorate, Research.
Type: Research grant.
Value: Research costs. Grant funds may not be used for the remuneration of grantees.
Length of Study: Usually three years. In some cases the Panel may request a progress report after one year.
Frequency: Annual.
Study Establishment: Canadian institutions.
Country of Study: Canada.
No. of awards offered: Varies.
Application Procedure: Applicants must submit an application form and other documentation as outlined in the regulations.
Closing Date: September 15th or March 15th.
Funding: Private.
Contributor: Public donors.
No. of awards given last year: 27.
No. of applicants last year: 81.

Geoff Carr Lupus Fellowship

Subjects: Lupus.
Purpose: To provide advanced training to a rheumatologist.
Eligibility: Open to nationals of any country specialising in lupus at an Ontario lupus clinic.
Level of Study: Postdoctorate.
Type: Fellowship.
Value: Canadian $55,000.
Length of Study: One year.
Frequency: Annual.
Study Establishment: An approved Ontario lupus clinic.
Country of Study: Canada.
No. of awards offered: One.
Application Procedure: Applicants must submit an application with three letters of recommendation and a letter of acceptance from a proposed supervisor. The letter of acceptance must include an outline proposed training programme and a certified transcript of their undergraduate record.
Closing Date: November 1st.
Funding: Private.
Contributor: The Ontario Lupus Association.
Additional Information: Please see the website for further information.

Metro A Ogryzlo International Fellowship

Subjects: Clinical rheumatology.
Purpose: To provide advanced training to individuals from a developing country.
Eligibility: The successful candidate will have completed his or her training in general medicine and have a substantial prospect of returning to an academic position in his or her own country. Canadian citizens or landed immigrants are not eligible.
Level of Study: Postdoctorate.
Type: Fellowship.
Value: Up to a maximum of Canadian $31,000 per year.
Length of Study: One year, non renewable.
Frequency: Annual.
Study Establishment: A rheumatic disease unit or arthritis centre.
Country of Study: Canada.
No. of awards offered: One.
Application Procedure: Applicants must submit an application including letters of recommendation from three sponsors, letter of acceptance from the proposed supervisor, to include an outline of the

proposed training programme, and a certified transcript of their undergraduate record.

Closing Date: November 1st.

Funding: Private.

Contributor: Public donors.

Additional Information: Fellows may not receive remuneration for any other work or hold a second major scholarship, except that, with the approval of their supervisors, they may engage in and accept remuneration for such departmental activities as are conducive to their development as clinicians, teachers or investigators. Ordinarily, a Fellow who is not a graduate of a medical school in the United States, the United Kingdom, Republic of Ireland, Australia, New Zealand or South Africa must take the Medical Council of Canada evaluating examination to obtain the Medical Council of Canada certificate before an education licence can be issued.

ARTHUR RUBINSTEIN INTERNATIONAL MUSIC SOCIETY

12 Huberman Street, Tel Aviv, 64075, Israel
Tel: (972) 3 685 6684
Fax. (972) 3 685 4924
Email: competition@arims.org.il
www: http://www.arims.org.il
Contact: Ms Idith Zui, Director

The Arthur Rubinstein International Music Society was founded by Jan Jacob Bistritzky in 1980 in tribute to the artistry of Arthur Rubinstein (1887-1982) and to maintain his spiritual and artistic heritage in the art of the piano. The Society organises and finances the Arthur Rubinstein International Piano Master Competition and the Hommage à Rubinstein worldwide concert series and festivals, awards scholarships, runs music courses and master classes, organises lectures and memorial festivals, and issues publications and recordings.

Arthur Rubinstein International Piano Master Competition

Subjects: Piano.

Purpose: To reward talented pianists with the capacity for multifaceted creative interpretation of composers, ranging from the pre-classic to the contemporary era.

Eligibility: Candidates must be 18-32 years of age.

Level of Study: Professional development.

Type: Prize.

Value: The first prize is a competition gold medal plus US$25,000, the second prize is a competition silver medal plus US$15,000 and the third prize is a competition bronze medal plus US$10,000. The fourth, fifth and sixth prizes are US$3,000 each. Additional prizes, the Audience Favourite Prize and concert engagements will be announced in future bulletins.

Frequency: Every three years.

Country of Study: Any country.

No. of awards offered: 10.

Application Procedure: Applicants must complete an application form according to the rules stipulated in the prospectus of the Arthur Rubinstein International Piano Master Competition. Details are available from the organisation.

Closing Date: September 1st.

Funding: Government, Private.

No. of applicants last year: 185.

ARTIST TRUST

1402 3rd Avenue, Suite 404, Seattle, WA 98101-2118, USA
Tel: (1) 206 4678734
Fax: (1) 206 4679633
Email: info@artisttrust.org
www: http://www.artisttrust.org
Contact: Mr Joel Lee, Business Manager

Artist trust is a non-profit organization whose sole mission is to support and encourage individual artists working in all disciplines in order to enhance community life throughout Washington State.

Fellowship Program

Subjects: Award is given to practising professional artists of exceptional talent and demonstrated ability. Fellowship is a ment based, not project based award.

Level of Study: Unrestricted.

Type: Fellowship.

Value: US$4,000.

Length of Study: N/A.

Frequency: Annual, Craft/Media/Music/Literature and Dance/Design/Theatre Visual Arts Rotate every other year.

Study Establishment: N/A.

No. of awards offered: Varies each year.

Funding: Commercial, Government, Private.

Contributor: Washington State Arts Commission.

No. of awards given last year: 21.

No. of applicants last year: 416 in Craft, Literature, Media & Music.

GAP (Grants for Artists Projects) Program

Subjects: GAP grants provide support for artist-generated projects, which can include (but are not limited to) the development, completion or presentation of new work. All disciplines & inter-disciplinary projects are eligible.

Eligibility: All applicants must be 18 years or older, a Washington State resident.

Level of Study: Unrestricted.

Type: Grant.

Value: GAP awards offer a maximum of US$1,400 for projects.

Length of Study: N/A.

Frequency: Annual.

Study Establishment: N/A.

No. of awards offered: Number of grants awarded each year varies. 34 grants were awarded in 2003.

Application Procedure: Application form required (available online) work sample proof of WA State Residency Resume & work sample description.

Closing Date: Due in February of each year.

Funding: Commercial, Government, Private.

Contributor: See above.

No. of awards given last year: 34.

No. of applicants last year: 772.

Twining Humbe Award for Lifetime Aritistic Achievement

Eligibility: Artists must be nominated (by themselves or others) nominees must be female, over the age of 60, a WA State Resident, and a usual artist.

Level of Study: Unrestricted.

Type: Lifetime Artistic Achievement.

Value: US$10,000.

Length of Study: N/A.

Frequency: Annual.

Study Establishment: N/A.

No. of awards offered: 1.

Application Procedure: Nomination forms are available by mail or online.

Closing Date: Deadline is in January of each year.

Funding: Commercial, Government, Private.

ARTS AND HUMANITIES RESEARCH BOARD (AHRB)

Postgraduate Awards Division, Whitefriars, Lewins Mead, Bristol, BS1 2AE, England
Tel: (44) 117 987 6543
Fax: (44) 117 987 6544
Email: pgaenq@ahrb.ac.uk
www: http://www.ahrb.ac.uk
Contact: Vijay Chandy, Head of Postgraduate Division

The Arts and Humanities Research Board (AHRB) funds postgraduate study and research within the UK's higher education institutions. The AHRB supports master's courses and doctoral research within a huge subject domain ranging from history, modern languages and english literature, to music and the creative and performing arts. The AHRB makes awards on the basis of academic excellence.

AHRB Doctoral Awards Scheme

Subjects: Archaeology, classics and ancient history, communications, cultural and media studies, English language and literature, history of art, architecture, law, linguistics, modern languages, music, drama, dance and performing arts, philosophy or religious studies, art and design, creative writing, musical performance.
Purpose: To support full-time and part-time study by students undertaking a doctoral degree in the humanities.
Eligibility: Applicants must be resident in the United Kingdom or the European Union and be graduates of a recognised Institute of Higher Education or be expecting to graduate by July 31st preceding the start of the course. Applicants should refer to the AHRB guide for full details.
Level of Study: Doctorate.
Type: Studentship.
Value: A maintenance grant of UK£11,000 per year for London based students and UK£9,000 per year for students based elsewhere. Tuition fees up to UK£2,940 per year. In addition a study visit and conference costs (for the 2003/4 academic year).
Length of Study: Up to three years full-time and five years part-time.
Frequency: Annual.
Study Establishment: Any approved Institute of Higher Education.
Country of Study: United Kingdom.
No. of awards offered: Varies.
Application Procedure: Applicants must download and complete an application form available on the website.
Closing Date: May 3rd 2005.
Funding: Government.
No. of awards given last year: A detailed report on the statistics for each competition is published on the website in December.
No. of applicants last year: In 2003, 6,000 approx applications were received for 1,500 awards in total, across all competitions.
Additional Information: For further information please visit the website www.ahrb.ac.uk.

Professional Preparation Master's Scheme

Subjects: Art and design, practice based drama and media studies, interpreting and translation, librarianship, archives and information management, museum studies and heritage management or creative writing.
Purpose: To provide funding to allow students to undertake a master's or postgraduate diploma courses that focus on developing high-level skills and competencies for professional practice.
Eligibility: Applicants must be resident in the United Kingdom or the European Union and be graduates of a recognised Institute of Higher Education or be expecting to graduate by July 31st preceding the start of the course. Applicants should refer to the AHRB guide for full details.
Level of Study: Postgraduate.
Type: Studentship.
Value: UK£5,360 in London, UK£4,520 elsewhere plus tuition fees of up to UK£2,940. These amounts are subject to change so please consult the organisation (for the 2003/4 academic year).
Length of Study: Nine months-one year.
Frequency: Annual.
Study Establishment: An Institute of Higher Education.
Country of Study: United Kingdom.
No. of awards offered: Varies.
Application Procedure: Applicants must download and complete an application form and guide from the website.
Closing Date: May 3rd 2005.
Funding: Government.
No. of awards given last year: A detailed report on the statistics for each competition is published on the website in December.
No. of applicants last year: In 2003 6,000 approx applications were received for 1,500 awards in total across all competition.
Additional Information: For further information please visit the website www.ahrb.ac.uk.

Research Preparation Master's Scheme

Subjects: Archaeology, classics and ancient history, communications, cultural and media studies, English language and literature, history of art, architecture, law, linguistics, modern languages, music, drama, dance and performing arts, philosophy or religious studies.
Purpose: To support students undertaking master's courses that focus on advanced study and research training explicitly intended to provide a foundation for further research at doctoral level.
Eligibility: Applicants must be resident in the United Kingdom or the European Union, be graduates of a recognised Institute of Higher Education or be expecting to graduate by July 31st preceding the start of the course. Applicants should refer to the AHRB guide for full details.
Level of Study: Postgraduate.
Type: Studentship.
Value: A maintenance grant of UK£9,900 per year for London based students and UK£7,900 per year for students based elsewhere. Tuition fees up to UK£2,940 per year (for the 2003/4 academic year).
Length of Study: One-two years.
Frequency: Annual.
Study Establishment: An approved institute of higher education.
Country of Study: United Kingdom.
No. of awards offered: Varies.
Application Procedure: Applicants must download and complete an application form available on the website.
Closing Date: May 3rd 2005.
Funding: Government.
No. of awards given last year: A detailed report on the statistics for each competition is published on the website in December.
No. of applicants last year: In 2003, 6,000 approx applications were received for 1,500 awards in total across all competitions.
Additional Information: For further information please visit the website www.ahrb.ac.uk.

ARTS COUNCIL OF NORTHERN IRELAND

MacNeice House, 77 Malone Road, Belfast, BT9 6AQ, Northern Ireland
Tel: (44) 28 9038 5200
Fax: (44) 28 9066 1715
Email: creative@artscouncil-ni.org
www: http://www.artscouncil-ni.org
Contact: Awards

The Arts Council of Northern Ireland is the prime distributor of public support for the arts. In addition to providing funding for the arts its principal functions are to develop the knowledge, appreciation and practice of the arts, to increase public access to and participation in the arts, and to advise government departments on matters relating to the arts.

Arts Council of Northern Ireland General Arts Award

Subjects: Visual arts, literature, traditional arts, drama, dance, music, jazz, community arts.
Purpose: To enable the artist to achieve objectives for specific projects. Awards may also be made for travel, attending master classes, short-term training courses.
Eligibility: Open to artists who contribute regularly to the artistic activities of the community, with residency in Northern Ireland of at least one year. Open to previous award holders. Registered students are not eligible to apply for visual arts awards. There are no stipulated age limits. Not intended for courses of vocational training leading to professional qualifications.
Level of Study: Professional development.
Type: Bursary.
Value: Approx. UK£12,000.
Frequency: Annual.
Country of Study: Any country.
No. of awards offered: Varies.
Application Procedure: Applicants must complete an application form and produce slides for visual arts, published text for literature, audio for traditional arts or any other relevant materials.
Closing Date: March 25th.
Contributor: Arts Council of Northern Ireland.

British School at Rome Fellowship

Subjects: Painting, sculpture.
Purpose: To provide working and living accommodation for visual arts scholars at the British School at Rome.
Eligibility: Open to artists resident in Northern Ireland for a period of at least one year, or domiciled elsewhere but contributing regularly to the artistic activity of the community. There is no stipulated age limit.
Level of Study: Professional development.
Type: Fellowship.
Value: UK£10,000 from the Arts Council to the British School to cover costs, UK£4,500 of this to the Fellow as stipend and for materials allowance and travel expenses within Italy.
Length of Study: Nine months.
Frequency: Dependent on available studio space.
Study Establishment: The British School at Rome.
Country of Study: Italy.
No. of awards offered: One.
Application Procedure: Applicants must complete an application form and submit this with up to 12 slides and curriculum vitae. A portfolio with photographs and other relevant material such as video, catalogues and reviews, may also be submitted. Videos must be labelled and be no more than five minutes running time.
Closing Date: April.
Funding: Government.
Contributor: Arts Council of Northern Ireland, The British School at Rome.
No. of awards given last year: One.
No. of applicants last year: Nine.
Additional Information: The School is a residential centre for the practice of the fine arts and for research in the humanities.

International Studio Programme at PS 1

Subjects: Visual arts.
Purpose: To establish workspace for professional artists in the United States of America which, in turn, offers valuable exposure for these artists.
Eligibility: Open to artists resident in Northern Ireland or the Republic of Ireland for a period of at least one year, or domiciled elsewhere but contributing regularly to the artistic activity of the community. There is no stipulated age limit.
Level of Study: Professional development.
Type: Fellowship.
Value: To cover stipend, airfare and studio rent.
Length of Study: One year.
Frequency: Annual.
Study Establishment: PS 1 Museum in Long Island City.
Country of Study: United States of America.
No. of awards offered: Two.
Application Procedure: Applicants must complete an application form and produce slides.
Closing Date: Under Review.
Funding: Government.
Contributor: Arts Councils, The Irish-American Cultural Institute.

Tyrone Guthrie Centre at Annaghmakerrig

Subjects: All fields of the arts.
Purpose: For residential use by artists from all parts of Ireland.
Eligibility: Open to all serious creative artists from both North and South of Ireland.
Level of Study: Professional development.
Type: Residency.
Value: Varies, bursary covers costs of residential accommodation.
Length of Study: Usually for two-five weeks.
Frequency: Other.
Study Establishment: The Tyrone Guthrie Centre.
Country of Study: Ireland.

For further information contact:

The Tyrone Guthrie Centre, Annaghmakerrig, Newbliss, Co Monaghan Ireland
Contact: Resident Director

ARTS COUNCIL OF WALES

Museum Place, Cardiff, CF10 3NX, Wales
Tel: (44) 29 2037 6500
Fax: (44) 29 2022 1447
Email: information@ccc-acw.org.uk
www: http://www.artswales.org.uk
Contact: Mrs Angela Blackburn, Information Officer

The Arts Council of Wales is the national organisation with specific responsibility for the funding and development of the arts in Wales. Most of its funds come from the National Assembly for Wales, but it also distributes National Lottery funds to the arts in Wales.

ACW Capital Grants

Subjects: Performing arts and related subjects.
Purpose: To aid the construction or refurbishment of buildings, to purchase equipment such as musical instruments and for staging and public art, sound and lighting equipment.
Type: Grant.
Country of Study: Wales.
Application Procedure: Applicants must contact the Lottery Division, Cardiff, Carmarthen and Colwyn Bay offices for more details.
Closing Date: Applications are accepted at any time but please check before applying.
Additional Information: Grants are also available for feasibility and development studies. All applications over UK£50,000 need to be pre-registered with the Lottery Division.

ACW Community Touring Night Out

Subjects: Performing arts.
Purpose: To support community based organisations throughout Wales with access to suitable premises, who wish to promote occasional professional performing arts events for their locality.
Eligibility: Eligibility for promoters of events is restricted to community organisations within Wales. Schools and colleges may participate if offering a service to the wider community which is beyond this normal educational role. Eligibility for performers governed by this ability to provide a professional service at an affordable price regardless of nationality and location.
Type: Fees to Performers.
Value: Variable.
Frequency: all the years round (No deadlines).
Country of Study: Wales.
No. of awards offered: 370.
Application Procedure: Applications may be submitted at any time to the Community Touring Manager, Access Development Division in Cardiff and must come from the local promoters of the event. The single page application form is obtainable from the unit by post or may be found on the website www.nightout.org.uk.
Closing Date: Six weeks before the proposed event.
Funding: Government.
Contributor: National Assembly of Wales.
No. of awards given last year: 370.
No. of applicants last year: 143.
Additional Information: Community based organisations dedicated to the arts, who wish to plan more than five events in a year or more than six months ahead should seek advice from their local ACW office or the Community Touring Manager. This scheme assists community organisations by making professional performances available at a fraction of their real price. It covers all aspects of the performing arts.

For further information contact:

Community Touring Managers, Community Touring Unit, Arts Council of Wales Museum Place, Cardiff, CF10 3NX, United Kingdom

ACW Inter-Recce

Subjects: The arts.
Purpose: To encourage contact with producers and presenters in countries outside the United Kingdom with a view to future collaborations.
Value: Financial assistance.
Country of Study: Other.

Application Procedure: Applicants must contact the Wales Arts International Office in Cardiff for further information.
Closing Date: Applications may be submitted throughout the year.

ACW Lottery Film Grants
Subjects: Film production and development.
Purpose: To support the development of scripts and production of films in Wales and to contribute to the growth of a sustainable indigenous film industry reflecting Wales' society and culture.
Eligibility: Standard awards must be applied for by a registered production company and the proposed project must be capable of qualifying as a British film under schedule 1 of the Films Act 1985 (amended 1999). Funding is available for film production companies seeking funding for the development of feature length scripts or the production of short films or features for theatrical release.
Frequency: Other.
No. of awards offered: Varies.
Application Procedure: Applicants must contact the Capital Unit in Cardiff or the Production Department at Sgrin Cymru Wales for more details. Applicants must request and complete the appropriate application forms.
Closing Date: Applications can be submitted at any time but applicants are advised to contact ACW or Sgrin officers for advice on the timing of funding rounds.

For further information contact:

Sgrin Cymru Wales The Bank 10 Mount Stuart Square, Cardiff, CF10 5EE, Wales
Tel: (44) 029 2033 3300

ARTS INTERNATIONAL

251 Park Avenue South, 5th Floor, New York, NY 10010-7302, United States of America
Tel: (1) 212 674 9744
Fax: (1) 212 674 9092
Email: info@artsinternational.org
www: http://www.artsinternational.org
Contact: Mr Adam Bernstein, Director, Advised Funds & Regranting Programs

Arts International is an independent, non-profit, contemporary arts organisation dedicated to global, cultural interchange. It carries out its work through developing global networks and partnerships, information services and grant making opportunities.

The Artists Exploration Fund
Subjects: The development or expansion of creative relationships with artists and art organizations, the exploration of artistic forms or the creation.
Purpose: To enable individual performing artists to pursue opportunities abroad that further their artistic development.
Eligibility: Artists must be performing artist, working at a professional level who make a substantial portion of their living through their work as performing artists, with a minimum three year history.
Level of Study: Professional development.
Type: Grant.
Value: US$1,000-3,000.
Frequency: Annual.
Country of Study: Any country.
Application Procedure: Applicants must refer to the website for guidelines and application details.
Funding: Private.

Cintas Fellowships
Subjects: Architecture, photography, visual arts, music composition and literature.
Eligibility: Open to creative artists of Cuban citizenship or descent, working in the above mentioned fields, who are currently living outside Cuba.
Level of Study: Professional development.
Type: Fellowship.
Value: Up to US$10,000.

Frequency: Annual.
Country of Study: Any country.
No. of awards offered: Five-eight.
Application Procedure: Applicants must contact Arts International for an application form.
Closing Date: To be determined.
Funding: Private.
Additional Information: Cintas fellowships are intended to acknowledge demonstrated creative accomplishments and to encourage the professional development of talented creative artists in the fields listed. The fellowships are not awarded towards the furtherance of academic study, research or writing, nor are they offered to performing artists.

FACE Croatia
Subjects: FACE Croatia is designed to provide grants to support the broadening of public awareness of and appreciation for Croatian art and culture, and to encourage the growth of Croatian arts philanthropy in both Croatia and the United States.
Purpose: To increase awareness and appreciation and Croatian arts and culture through exchange opportunities and direct support of cultural projects in Croatia.
Eligibility: Artists must US citizens, Croatian citizens or Croatian artists permanently resident in the US. They must be sponsored by a non-profit making arts organisation.
Level of Study: Unrestricted.
Type: Arts discipline or cultural activity.
Value: Variable.
Length of Study: Variable.
Frequency: Four times per year.
Study Establishment: As approved. Typically museum, art gallery, theatre.
Country of Study: USA and Croatia.
Application Procedure: Proposals must include a narrative and budget; an organizational narrative and budget; evidence of non-profit status; three letters of recommendation from professionals in the field.
Closing Date: There is no deadline. Project proposals may be submitted at any time and will be reviewed by an advisory committee on a quarterly basis.
Funding: Private.
Contributor: Heathcote Art Foundation.

For further information contact:

'FACE Croatia Arts International' at main organisation address.
Email: facecroatia@artsinternational.org

The Fund for US Artists
Subjects: Music, theatre and dance.
Purpose: To support US artists invited to participate in major international performing arts festivals and recurring visual arts exhibitions, where their creative and professional development would be enhanced by such participation.
Eligibility: Citizens of United States who must be performing artists working at a professional level.
Level of Study: Professional development.
Type: Grant.
Value: US$1,000-15,000. Will not exceed US$25,000.
Country of Study: Any country.
Application Procedure: Applicants must refer to the website for guidelines and application details.
Closing Date: January 16, May 3, September 7.
Contributor: The Doris Duke Charitable Foundation.

INROADS
Subjects: Music, drama and dancing.
Purpose: To encourage the development of collaborative projects between United States artists and African, Asian, or Latin American performing artists.
Level of Study: Professional development.
Type: Grant.
Value: Not specified.
Frequency: Annual.
Country of Study: United States of America.

Application Procedure: Applicants must direct enquiries to Cheryl Katz, Programme Manager.
Funding: Private.
No. of awards given last year: 15.
No. of applicants last year: 35.

James R Vogt Scholarship
Subjects: Nuclear Science, radio-analytical chemistry, analytical chemistry, analytical applications of science.
Purpose: To support an undergraduate or a graduate student enrolled in or proposing to undertake research in radio-analytical chemistry or analytical applications of nuclear science.
Eligibility: Open to United States citizens or permanent residents who are enrolled in an accredited institution in the United States.
Level of Study: Graduate, Postgraduate.
Type: Scholarship.
Value: US$2,000.
Length of Study: Variable.
Frequency: Annual.
Country of Study: United States of America.
No. of awards offered: 4.
Application Procedure: Applicants must complete an application form, available on request.
Closing Date: February 1st.

THE ASCAP FOUNDATION

One Lincoln Plaza, New York, NY 10023, United States of America
Tel: (1) 212 621 6327
Fax: (1) 212 621 6504
Email: frichard@ascap.com
www: http://www.ascap.com
Contact: Administrative Assistant

The American Society of Composers, Authors and Publishers (ASCAP) is a membership association of over 120,000 composers, songwriters, lyricists and music publishers. ASCAP's function is to protect the rights of its members by licensing and paying royalties for the public performances of their copyrighted works.

ASCAP Foundation Morton Gould Young Composer Awards
Subjects: Music composition.
Purpose: To encourage talented young composers by providing recognition, appreciation and monetary awards.
Eligibility: Open to United States citizens or permanent residents who have not reached their 30th birthday by March 1st in the year of competition. Original concert music of any style will be considered. However, works which have previously earned awards or prizes in any other national competition are ineligible. Arrangements are also ineligible.
Level of Study: Unrestricted.
Type: Award.
Value: US$30,000 in total.
Frequency: Annual.
No. of awards offered: Varies from year to year.
Application Procedure: Applicants must complete an application form and other materials.
Closing Date: Postmarked March 1st.
Funding: Private.

ASHRIDGE MANAGEMENT COLLEGE

Berkhamsted, Hertfordshire, HP4 1NS, England
Tel: (44) 1442 841143
Fax: (44) 1442 841144
Email: jane.tobin@ashridge.org.uk
www: http://www.ashridge.org.uk
Contact: Ms Jane Tobin, MBA Admissions Manager

Ashridge Business School's expertise, built up through many years experience as a provider of executive development, have deliberately shaped their mission to help practising and experienced managers become even more effective as leaders and in so doing, fulfil their individual potential and that of the organisation.

Ashridge Business School MBA Programme
Eligibility: Degree, 3-5 years business experience, Interview, GMAT or Ashridge test, 2 references.
Level of Study: MBA.
Length of Study: One-two years.
Country of Study: United Kingdom.
Application Procedure: Applicants must submit a form, with two references and either a Graduate Management Admission Test score or an Ashridge Test Score. Finally, all candidates are asked to interview.
Closing Date: Places are offered on a first-come, first-serve basis after interview.
Funding: Commercial, Private.

Ashridge Entrepreneurial Bursary
Subjects: Business.
Purpose: To support self-funded participants who plan to use the project process of the programme to start a new business.
Eligibility: Open to candidates planning to start up a new business upon graduation of their MBA.
Level of Study: MBA.
Type: Bursary.
Value: 50 per cent of tuition fees plus living expenses.
Length of Study: 1 year.
Frequency: Annual.
Study Establishment: Ashridge Management College, Hertfordshire.
Country of Study: United Kingdom.
No. of awards offered: Two.
Application Procedure: Applicants must submit a 750 word maximum synopsis outlining how they think studying an MBA at Ashridge could help their entrepreneurial aspirations. Applicants must also submit an application form and two references, preferably from supervisors or managers at the applicants current workplace. For further information, visit the website.
Closing Date: December 1st.
Funding: Commercial.
Contributor: Natwest Bank, the Bank of Scotland and the Association of MBAs.
No. of awards given last year: Two.
No. of applicants last year: 15.
Additional Information: Ashridge also awards two bursaries per annum (50% of tuition and 50% of accommodation fee) to suitable applicants who are employed in the charity sector provided the applicants carry out their project work for their employing charitable organisation.

For further information contact:

AMBA15 Duncan Terrace, London, N1 8BZ, England
Tel: (44) 20 7837 3375
Fax: (44) 20 7278 3634
www: http://www.mba.org.uk

ASIAN CULTURAL COUNCIL (ACC)

437 Madison Avenue, 37th Floor, New York, NY 10022, United States of America
Tel: (1) 212 812 4300
Fax: (1) 212 812 4299
Email: acc@accny.org
www: http://www.asianculturalcouncil.org
Contact: Mr Ralph Samuelson, Director

The Asian Cultural Council (ACC) supports cultural exchange in the visual and performing arts between the United States and the countries of Asia. The emphasis of the ACC's programme is on providing individual fellowships to artists, scholars and specialists from Asia undertaking research, study, and creative work in the United States of America. Grants are also made to United States citizens pursuing similar work in Asia.

ACC Fellowship Grants Program

Subjects: Visual and performing arts.
Purpose: To provide fellowship opportunities for research, training, travel and creative work.
Eligibility: Open to individuals from East and Southeast Asia, Burma to Japan, and citizens or permanent residents of the United States of America. Artists seeking aid for personal exhibitions or performances cannot be considered.
Level of Study: Doctorate, Postdoctorate, Postgraduate, Professional development.
Value: Varies.
Length of Study: One month to one year.
Frequency: Annual.
Country of Study: Other.
No. of awards offered: Approx. 130.
Application Procedure: Applicants must send a brief project description to the Council. If the proposal falls within the Council's guidelines, application forms will be forwarded to individual candidates or more detailed information will be requested from institutional applicants.
Closing Date: February 1st or August 1st.
Funding: Private.
No. of awards given last year: 120.
No. of applicants last year: 800.

ASSOCIATED BOARD OF THE ROYAL SCHOOLS OF MUSIC

24 Portland Place, London, W1B 1LU
England
Tel: (44) 20 7636 5400
Fax: (44) 20 7637 0234
Email: abrsm@abrsm.ac.uk
www: http://www.abrsm.ac.uk
Contact: Director of Finance & Administration

The Associated Board of the Royal Schools of Music is the world's leading provider of graded music examinations with over 500,000 candidates each year in over 80 countries. It is also a major music publisher and a provider of professional development courses and seminars for music teachers.

Associated Board of the Royal Schools of Music Scholarships

Subjects: Instrumental and vocal performance.
Purpose: To enable exceptionally talented young musicians to study at one of the four Royal Schools of Music.
Eligibility: Candidates should normally be at least 21 years of age by January 31st in the year of entry. Entries can be received from any of the countries where the Associated Board organises examinations. Candidates must have a good standard of general education and must normally have qualified by passing, with distinction, Grade 8 in a practical examination of the Board's, the Advanced Certificate or the LRSM diploma, plus one other practical examination of the Board's above Grade 5.
Level of Study: Postgraduate, Professional development.
Type: Scholarship.
Value: Full course fees, a contribution to air travel and UK£3,000 per year towards living expenses.
Length of Study: From one term to four years, according to designated course.
Frequency: Annual.
Study Establishment: The Royal Academy of Music, the Royal College of Music, the Royal Northern College of Music or the Royal Scottish Academy of Music and Drama.
Country of Study: United Kingdom.
No. of awards offered: Varies.
Application Procedure: Applicants must submit an application form, health certificate, examination marks, forms, testimonials, and an authenticated cassette tape of recent performance. Candidates should apply to the Board's representative in their own country or directly to the Board in London.

Closing Date: December 31st of the year preceding year of entry.
Funding: Private.

ASSOCIATION FOR SPINA BIFIDA AND HYDROCEPHALUS (ASBAH)

ASBAH House, 42 Park Road
Peterborough, Cambridgeshire
PE1 2UQ, England
Tel: (44) 1733 555988
Fax: (44) 1733 555985
Email: lynr@asbah.org
www: http://www.asbah.org
Contact: Mrs L Rylance, Secretary to the Directorate

The Association for Spina Bifida and Hydrocephalus (ASBAH) is a voluntary organisation which works for people with spina bifida and/or hydrocephalus. The charity lobbies for improvements in legislation and provides advisory and support services to clients and their families or carers, in addition to supplying information to professionals and sponsoring medical, social and educational research.

ASBAH Bursary Fund

Subjects: Any course that will improve the chances of employment for people with spina bifida, hydrocephalus or both.
Purpose: To help with expenses of further or higher education courses approved by, but not organised by, ASBAH.
Eligibility: Open to individuals with spina bifida and hydrocephalus resident in England, Wales and Northern Ireland.
Level of Study: Unrestricted.
Type: Bursary.
Value: Course fees and other expenses.
Frequency: Dependent on funds available.
Study Establishment: Varies.
Country of Study: Other.
No. of awards offered: Varies.
Application Procedure: Applicants must complete an application form, available from Mrs M Malcolm, the Assistant Director of Services.
Closing Date: Applications are accepted at any time.
Funding: Private.
Contributor: Charitable donations.
No. of awards given last year: Two.
No. of applicants last year: Six.
Additional Information: Applicants are normally visited by an ASBAH Area Adviser prior to an award being considered.

ASBAH Research Grant

Subjects: Medical sciences, natural sciences, education and teacher training, recreation, welfare and protective services.
Purpose: To support research in an area directly related to spina bifida and/or hydrocephalus, and to explore ways of improving the quality of life for people with these conditions, those being medical, scientific, educational and social research.
Eligibility: Applicants must be resident in the United Kingdom.
Level of Study: Postgraduate.
Type: Research grant.
Value: Varies.
Length of Study: Varies.
Frequency: Dependent on funds available.
Study Establishment: Varies.
Country of Study: United Kingdom.
No. of awards offered: Varies.
Application Procedure: Applicants must make an initial enquiry to the Executive Director. If the proposed research is considered to be interesting, the applicant will be asked to complete an application form. Applications should be made in good time for submission to the committees which meet in February and September to October.
Closing Date: January 1st and August 1st.
Funding: Private.
Contributor: Charitable donations.

ASSOCIATION FOR WOMEN IN SCIENCE EDUCATIONAL FOUNDATION

7008 Richard Drive, Bethesda, MD 20817-4838, United States of America
Tel: (1) 202 326 8940
Fax: (1) 202 326 8960
Email: awisedfd@awis.org or awisedfd@aol.com
www: http://www.awis.org/ed-foundation.html
Contact: Dr Barbara Filner, President

The Association for Women in Science Educational Foundation provides fellowships to assist women students studying the sciences.

Association for Women in Science Educational Foundation Predoctoral Awards

Subjects: Life, physical, behavioural or social science and engineering.
Purpose: To promote the participation of women in engineering and the sciences.
Eligibility: Open to female students enrolled in any physical, behavioural or social science or engineering programme, leading to a PhD degree. Applicants must be within two years of completion of their PhD.
Level of Study: Doctorate, Predoctorate.
Value: Varies, usually US$100-1,000.
Frequency: Annual.
Study Establishment: An Institute of Higher Education.
Country of Study: Anywhere for U.S. Citizens; in the United States for others.
No. of awards offered: Varies.
Application Procedure: Applicants must submit an application including a basic form, a five page summary of the candidate's dissertation research, two recommendation report forms and official transcripts of all coursework conducted at post secondary institutions. Forms available at www.awis.org/ed_foundation.html.
Closing Date: Mid January.
Funding: Private.
No. of awards given last year: 7 awards and 4 citations of merit.
No. of applicants last year: Over 200.
Additional Information: Winners are notified by email in June and announced publicly in the Autumn issue of the AWIS Magazine.

ASSOCIATION OF AMERICAN GEOGRAPHERS (AAG)

1710 Sixteenth Street North West, Washington, DC 20009-3198, United States of America
Tel: (1) 202 234 1450
Fax: (1) 202 234 2744
Email: ekhater@aag.org
www: http://www.aag.org
Contact: Ms Ehsan Khater, Executive Assistant

The Association of American Geographers (AAG) is a non-profit organisation founded in 1904 to advance professional studies in geography and to encourage the application of geographic research in business, education and government. The AAG was amalgamated with the American Society of Professional Geographers (ASPG) in 1948.

AAG Dissertation Research Grants

Subjects: Geography.
Purpose: To support dissertation research.
Eligibility: Open to candidates without a doctorate at the time of the award, who have been AAG members for at least one year at the time of application and who have completed all PhD requirements except the dissertation by the end of the semester or term following the approval of the award. The candidates' dissertation supervisor must certify eligibility and proposals should demonstrate high standards of scholarship.
Level of Study: Postdoctorate.
Type: Research grant.

Value: A maximum of US$500.
Frequency: Dependent on funds available.
Country of Study: United States of America.
No. of awards offered: Three.
Application Procedure: Applicants must complete an application form, available on request from Ehsan M. Khater. Also, applicants must submit seven copies of a dissertation proposal of no more than 1,000 words and seven copies of the completed forms. The proposal should describe the problem that is to be solved, outline the methods and data to be used and summarise the results expected to be found. Budget items should also be included within the body of the proposal.
Closing Date: December 31st.
Funding: Private.
Contributor: Members.
No. of awards given last year: Six.
No. of applicants last year: Eight.
Additional Information: By accepting an AAG dissertation grant, awardees agree to submit a copy of the dissertation, and a report that documents expenses charged to the grant, to the AAG Executive Director. AAG support must also be acknowledged in presentations and publications. The awards include the Robert D Hodgson Memorial PhD Dissertation Fund, the Paul Vouras Fund, and the Otis Paul Starkey Fund. Please visit the website for any further information.

AAG General Research Fund

Subjects: Geography.
Purpose: To support research and field work expenses.
Eligibility: Open to candidates who have been AAG members for at least two years at the time of application. Proposals that, in the opinion of the committee, offer the prospect of obtaining substantial subsequent support from private foundations or federal agencies and that address questions of major import to the discipline will be given preference.
Level of Study: Postdoctorate, Professional development.
Type: Research grant.
Value: Between US$500-1,000.
Frequency: Annual, if funds are available.
Country of Study: Any country.
No. of awards offered: Varies.
Application Procedure: Applicants must complete and send seven application forms, available on request from the executive assistant, Ehsan M Khater. Successful award applicants will be announced on or about March 31st.
Closing Date: December 31st.
Funding: Private.
Contributor: AAG members.
No. of awards given last year: Five.
No. of applicants last year: Eight.
Additional Information: No awards are made if proposals are not suitable or for Master's and doctoral dissertation research. Guidelines are printed in the AAG Newsletter.

Anne U White Fund

Subjects: Geochemistry.
Purpose: To enable people, regardless of any formal training in geography, to engage in useful field studies and to have the joy of working alongside their partners.
Eligibility: Open to candidates who have been AAG members for at least two years at the time of application. Proposals that, in the opinion of the committee, best meet the purposes for which Anne and Gilbert White set up the funds will be given preference.
Level of Study: Professional development.
Type: Research grant.
Value: Between US$1,000-5,500 each.
Frequency: Annual.
Application Procedure: Applicants must complete seven application forms, available from the website or by request from the executive assistant, Ehsan M Khater. Successful applicants will be announced on or about March 31st.
Closing Date: December 31st.
Funding: Private.
No. of awards given last year: Six.
No. of applicants last year: Nine.

Additional Information: By accepting the Anne U White grant, awardees agree to submit a two page report that summarises results and documents expenses underwritten by the grant to the AAG Executive Director. In 1989, Gilbert and Anne White donated a sum of money to the Association of American Geographers to establish the Anne U White Fund. Gilbert White and other donors have subsequently added substantially to the original gift.

The George & Viola Hoffman Fund
Subjects: Historical, contemporary, systematic or regional geographic studies.
Purpose: To provide financial support towards a master's thesis or doctoral dissertation on a geographical subject in Eastern Europe.
Level of Study: Doctorate, Postgraduate.
Type: Grant.
Value: US$500.
Length of Study: One year.
Frequency: Annual.
No. of awards offered: 1.
Application Procedure: Obtain application forms and precise guidelines from main organisation, or to the chair of the Hoffman Award, Michelle Behr, Western New Mexico University, behrm@cs.
Closing Date: October 31st.

IGU Travel Grant
Subjects: Geography.
Purpose: To provide travel grants to the IGU conference.
Eligibility: US Scholars & citizens.
Level of Study: Professional development.
Type: Grant.
Value: US$1,000-1,750.
Frequency: Annual.
Country of Study: As applicable.
No. of awards offered: 20.
Application Procedure: Apply to the main organisation address or download a form from the website.

The Otis Paul Starkey Fund
Subjects: Geography.
Purpose: To support dissertation research within the U.S.A. and its possessions.
Level of Study: Doctorate.
Value: Up to US$1,900.
Length of Study: One year.
Frequency: Annual.
Country of Study: United States of America.
Application Procedure: Obtain application forms and precise guidelines from main organisation.
Closing Date: December 31st.

The Paul Vouras Fund
Subjects: Research in geography.
Purpose: To support doctoral dissertation research in geography.
Eligibility: Preference is given to minority students.
Level of Study: Doctorate.
Type: Research Grant.
Value: Up to US$1900.
Length of Study: One year.
Frequency: Annual.
Application Procedure: Application forms and precise guidelines from main organisation.
Closing Date: December 31st.
Contributor: Dr. Paul Vouras.

Robert D Hodgson Memorial PhD Dissertation Fund
Subjects: Geography, especially geographic aspects of the law of the sea and maritime boundaries.
Purpose: To provide financial support to candidates preparing doctoral dissertations in geography.
Eligibility: Applicants must demonstrate high standards of Scholarship and must be AAG members.
Level of Study: Predoctorate.
Type: Fellowship.

Value: US$500.
Length of Study: One year.
Frequency: Annual.
No. of awards offered: 1.
Application Procedure: Obtain application forms and precise guidelines from main organisation.
Closing Date: December 31st.
Additional Information: Dr. Hodgson believed that broader understanding of geographic principles would reduce international conflicts and the committee tries to favour this preference when evaluating proposals.

Visiting Geographical Scientist Program
Subjects: Geography.
Purpose: To stimulate interest in geography.
Level of Study: Professional development.
Type: Grant.
Value: US$500.
Frequency: Annual.
Study Establishment: Institution with an active chapter of Gamma Theta Upsilon.
Country of Study: United States of America.
Application Procedure: To Oscar Laron, VGSP Coordinator at main organisation address. Further details from website.

Warren Nystrom Fund Awards
Subjects: Geography.
Purpose: To support a paper based upon recent dissertations in geography.
Eligibility: Open to AAG members who have received their doctorate within the last two years. The paper submitted should be based on the student's dissertation.
Level of Study: Doctorate, Postdoctorate.
Value: Varies.
Frequency: Annual.
Country of Study: Any country.
No. of awards offered: Varies.
Application Procedure: Applicants must apply to the Association for information.
Closing Date: Mid September for the following year.
Funding: Private.
Contributor: AAG members.
No. of awards given last year: One.
No. of applicants last year: 15.
Additional Information: Awards are made for papers presented at the annual meeting of the Association.

ASSOCIATION OF CLINICAL PATHOLOGISTS

189 Dyke Road, Hove, East Sussex, BN3 1TJ, England
Tel: (44) 1273 775700
Fax: (44) 1273 773303
Email: info@pathologists.org.uk
Contact: Administrative Assistant

The Association of Clinical Pathologists promotes the practice of clinical pathology by running postgraduate education courses and national scientific meetings and has a membership of 2,000 worldwide.

Association of Clinical Pathologists Intercalated BSc Scholarship
Purpose: To support medical students undertaking BSc degrees in any pathology discipline and contribute to their living expenses during their year of study.
Type: Scholarship.
Value: Up to UK£5,000.
Frequency: Annual.
Contributor: Association of Clinical Pathologists.
No. of awards given last year: One.
No. of applicants last year: Three.

THE ASSOCIATION OF COMMONWEALTH UNIVERSITIES (ACU)

John Foster House, 36 Gordon Square, London, WC1H 0PF, England
Tel: (44) 20 7387 8572
Fax: (44) 20 7387 2655
Email: info@acu.ac.uk
www: http://www.acu.ac.uk
Contact: Awards Division

Founded in 1913, the Association of Commonwealth Universities (ACU) is the oldest international association of universities in the world. The ACU's aim is to promote contact and co-operation between its member institutions by encouraging and supporting the movement of academic and administrative staff between Commonwealth countries, providing information about universities, organising meetings and hosting a higher education management service.

ACU Quality of Life Awards

Subjects: Health studies, environmental management, distance education or transferable technology.
Purpose: To enhance the role that universities play both in providing higher education in the face of increasing demands for access, and in addressing the wider social issues of their countries.
Eligibility: Open to staff of ACU member universities or of a Commonwealth inter-university organisation. Those working in non governmental organisations, charities, industry, commerce or the public sector in a Commonwealth country are also eligible.
Type: Fellowship.
Value: Up to UK£5,000.
Length of Study: A maximum of six months.
Frequency: Annual.
Country of Study: Other.
No. of awards offered: Up to 20.
Application Procedure: Applicants must be nominated by an executive head or university in ACU membership. Each executive head may make two nominations.
Closing Date: March 31st for receipt of nominations in London.
Funding: Private.
Contributor: ACU.
Additional Information: Awards are given to support innovative projects which deal with the creation and dissemination of knowledge to the benefit of civil society in general and with disadvantaged groups in particular. Special consideration will be given to projects which take place in and give benefit to the developing Commonwealth. Projects will ideally utilise personnel or expertise from at least two Commonwealth countries, and the ACU are particularly interested in receiving proposals involving South-South collaboration.

ACU Titular Fellowships

Subjects: All subjects, but preference is given to fields in which the needs of developing countries are great.
Purpose: To enable the universities to develop the human resources of their institutions and countries, and to do so through the interchange of people, knowledge, skills and technologies.
Eligibility: Open to staff of universities in ACU membership, of Commonwealth inter-university organisations or those working in industry, commerce or public service in a Commonwealth country. Candidates must be aged between 28 and 50 years. The award is not intended for degree courses or immediately postdoctoral programmes, nor simply for the pursuit of personal research. Small scale conference attendance within a study programme is allowed, but applications will not be considered where major conference attendance is the primary or sole purpose.
Level of Study: Professional development.
Type: Fellowship.
Value: Up to UK£5,000 for travel, board, insurance and all fees other than bench fees.
Length of Study: Up to six months.
Frequency: Annual.
Study Establishment: An ACU member university or, for staff of an ACU member university, in industry, commerce or public service.
Country of Study: Other.

No. of awards offered: Up to 20.
Application Procedure: Applicants must be nominated by an executive head of university in ACU membership or by a chief executive officer of a Commonwealth inter university organisation.
Closing Date: May 31st.
Contributor: Member institutions of the ACU.
Additional Information: The ACU is especially keen to receive nominations of women candidates and for programmes intended to enhance the status & role of women in its member universities.

British Academy/ACU Grants for International Collaboration

Subjects: Humanities and social sciences.
Purpose: To support international joint activities, involving British Scholars in collaboration with Commonwealth partners. Priority is given to new programmes with an expectation of continued collaboration or a defined outcome such as planned joint publications.
Eligibility: Open to staff of Associated Commonwealth University member universities for advanced research. Support will not be offered for an open ended programme involving wide spread international participation or a programme of benefit primarily to the British partner.
Level of Study: Postdoctorate.
Type: Other.
Value: Up to UK£5,000 per year for research expenditure, travel and living costs in the partner country or countries. Awards are not intended to cover institutional overheads or permanent staff costs.
Length of Study: One year.
Frequency: Annual.
Country of Study: Other.
No. of awards offered: Up to 20.
Application Procedure: Applications should be submitted by the British partner. Applications received directly by overseas partners will not be considered.
Closing Date: May 31st.
Contributor: Funded jointly by the British Academy and ACU.
Additional Information: Applications must be for projects involving genuine collaborative work between a defined group of Scholars in one, or possibly two, Commonwealth countries. Priority is given to new programmes with an expectation of continued collaboration or a defined outcome such as planned joint publications.

Canada Memorial Foundation Scholarships

Subjects: All subjects.
Purpose: To offer awards to very able students so that they may study at a Canadian university for one year. By this means, the Canada Memorial Foundation hopes to strengthen the close association between Canada and the United Kingdom and to provide a practical, living memorial.
Eligibility: Open to citizens of the United Kingdom who are holders of a minimum Upper Second Class (Honours) Degree or equivalent. Candidates should normally be under 30 years of age.
Level of Study: Postgraduate.
Type: Scholarship.
Value: A maintenance allowance, return air fare, approved fees, a book, thesis, travel and health insurance allowance.
Length of Study: One year.
Frequency: Annual.
Study Establishment: Any university or other appropriate institution subject to the approval of the Canada Memorial Foundation.
Country of Study: Canada.
No. of awards offered: Up to two.
Application Procedure: Applications must be made through ACU, addressed to CMF Competition, Commonwealth Awards Division.
Closing Date: The third Friday in October.
Contributor: The Canada Memorial Foundation.
Additional Information: Intended for persons of high intellectual promise and of leadership potential who will play a full part in the life of the Canadian community which they visit and will return to play a full part in their own country. The Foundation welcomes candidates who have left university but wish to return to academic studies with a view to enhancing their career prospects in business or industry. In all cases candidates will need to show, beside excellent academic

qualifications, a record of participative activities, and to give convincing reasons why they wish to study in Canada together with some knowledge of Canada and of its institutions. The Foundation also particularly wishes to encourage applications from students wishing to pursue an MBA in Canada. The Canada Memorial Foundation also offers similar awards to Canadians so that they may study in the United Kingdom. Additional information and enquiries can be requested from the Canada Memorial Foundation, c/o PO Box 2235, Romford RM5 3NN.

DFID Shared Scholarship Scheme

Subjects: The economic and social development of the Scholar's country of origin.

Eligibility: Open only to students from developing Commonwealth countries for study in the United Kingdom, who are not already living in and have not already studied in, a developed country. Employees of a government department or parastatal organisation are ineligible. Candidates are required to hold, or be expected to attain, a First Class or Upper Second Class (Honours) Degree. Priority is given to candidates from poorer developing countries and to those aged under 30. Candidates should normally be aged under 35.

Level of Study: Postgraduate.

Type: Scholarship.

Value: The full cost of study, including a return airfare, maintenance and a thesis allowance.

Length of Study: One year.

Frequency: Annual.

Study Establishment: A university. A list of participating institutions available from the ACU website.

Country of Study: United Kingdom.

No. of awards offered: Up to 175.

Application Procedure: Applicants must complete an application form and send it to participating institutions,not directly to ACU.

Closing Date: March-April. Candidates should check with individual institutions for precise dates.

Contributor: Funded jointly by the Department for International Development (DFID) and participating institutions in the United Kingdom as part of the British aid programme to developing countries.

ASSOCIATION OF CONSULTING ENGINEERS

Alliance House, 12 Caxton Street, London, SW1H 0QL, England
Tel: (44) 20 7222 6557
Fax: (44) 20 7222 0750
Email: consult@acenet.co.uk
www: http://www.acenet.co.uk
Contact: Administrative Officer

The Association of Consulting Engineers (ACE) is the United Kingdom's leading trade association for engineering, technical and management consultancies. Membership is open to companies which advise on consulting engineering and related services. ACE has around 650 member firms, ranging from sole practitioners to large multidisciplinary consultancy companies.

Young Consulting Engineer of the Year

Subjects: Engineering projects and the engineering profession in general.

Purpose: To encourage younger members of the profession in their work and to make them think about their role in society.

Eligibility: Open to engineering consultants under the age of 30.

Level of Study: Unrestricted.

Value: UK£1,000 plus a medal. There are certificates for finalists.

Frequency: Annual.

Country of Study: Any country.

No. of awards offered: One.

Application Procedure: Applicants must complete an application form and submit this with other required documents.

Funding: Private.

ASSOCIATION OF RHODES SCHOLARS IN AUSTRALIA

University of Melbourne
VIC 3010, Australia
Tel: (61) 3 8344 6937
Fax: (61) 3 9347 6739
Email: g.swafford@unimelb.edu.au
www: http://www.unimelb.edu.au/research
Contact: Dr Glenn Swafford, Director, Melbourne Research & Innovation Office

Association of Rhodes Scholars in Australia Scholarship

Subjects: All subjects.

Purpose: To enable an overseas Commonwealth student to undertake research in Australia.

Eligibility: Open to graduates of a Commonwealth university approved by the committee administering the bursary. Graduates must currently be enrolled as research higher degree students at their home university, be Commonwealth citizens and may not be graduates of an Australian or New Zealand university.

Level of Study: Postgraduate, Research.

Type: Scholarship.

Value: Currently Australian $20,000 including travel expenses and a monthly stipend.

Length of Study: Six months.

Frequency: Dependent on funds available.

Study Establishment: A university.

Country of Study: Australia.

No. of awards offered: One.

Application Procedure: Applicants must apply for information and application forms, available through the website.

Closing Date: As advertised.

Funding: Private.

Contributor: Charitable donations from former Australian Rhodes Scholars.

No. of awards given last year: One.

No. of applicants last year: 14.

Additional Information: URL: www.research.unimelb.edu.au/admin/rhodes/arsa.html.

ASSOCIATION OF SURGEONS OF GREAT BRITAIN AND IRELAND

c/o The Royal College of Surgeons of England
35-43 Lincoln's Inn Fields
London, WC2A 3PN, England
Tel: (44) 20 7973 0300
Fax: (44) 20 7430 9235
Email: admin@asgbi.org.uk
www: http://www.asgbi.org.uk
Contact: Mrs Nechema Lewis, Administrative Assistant

The founding objectives of the Association of Surgeons of Great Britain and Ireland, in 1920, were the advancement of the science and art of surgery and the promotion of friendship among surgeons. As other surgical specialists developed, the Association came to represent general surgery, encompassing breast, colorectal, endocrine, laproscopic, transplant, upper gastrointestinal and vascular surgery.

Moynihan Travelling Fellowship/Dinwoody Trust Travelling Scholarships

Subjects: General surgery.

Purpose: To enable specialist registrars or consultants to broaden their education, and to present and discuss their contribution to British or Irish surgery overseas.

Eligibility: Open to either specialist registrars coming towards the end of their higher surgical training or consultants in general surgery within three years of appointment after the closing date for applications. Candidates must be nationals of and residents of the United Kingdom or the Republic of Ireland but need not be Fellows or Affiliate Fellows of the Association. They may be engaged in general surgery or a sub-speciality thereof.

Level of Study: Postdoctorate.

Type: Fellowship.

Value: The value of the Moynihan Travelling Fellowship is up to UK£4,000, and the Dinwoody Trust Travelling Scholarships are available up to UK£1,500.

Frequency: Annual.

Country of Study: Any country.

No. of awards offered: Three.

Application Procedure: Applicants must submit 12 copies of an application which must include a full curriculum vitae giving details of past and present appointments and publications, a detailed account of the proposed programme of travel, costs involved and the object to be achieved. Applications must be addressed to the Honorary Secretary at the Association of Surgeons.

Closing Date: October 1st.

Funding: Private.

Contributor: Charitable association funds and the Dinwoody Trust.

No. of awards given last year: Three.

No. of applicants last year: Seven.

Additional Information: Shortlisted candidates will be interviewed by the Scientific Committee of the Association who will pay particular attention to the originality, scope and feasibility of the proposed journey. The successful candidate will be expected to act as an ambassador for British and Irish surgery and should therefore be fully acquainted with the aims and objectives of the Association of Surgeons in its role in surgery. After the visit the Fellow will be asked to address the Association at its annual general meeting. A critical appraisal of the centres visited should form the basis of the report.

THE ASSOCIATION OF TEACHERS AND LECTURERS (ATL)

7 Northumberland Street
London, WC2N 5RD
England
Tel: (44) 20 7930 6441
Fax: (44) 20 7930 1359
Email: info@atl.org.uk
www: http://www.askatl.org.uk
Contact: Ms Thelma Meredith, Personal Assistant to General Secretary

The Association of Teachers and Lecturers (ATL) is the leading professional organisation and trade union for teachers and lecturers with over 150,000 members in England, Wales and Northern Ireland. The Association is committed to protecting and promoting the interests of its members and maintaining the highest quality professional support for them.

Walter Hines Page Scholarships

Subjects: Observation and study of teaching and the educational system in the United States of America.

Purpose: To promote the exchange of educational ideas between the United Kingdom and the United States of America.

Eligibility: Open to British teachers who are members of the ATL and who wish to visit the United States of America.

Level of Study: Professional development.

Type: Scholarship.

Value: UK£1,100 plus full hospitality.

Length of Study: Two weeks.

Frequency: Annual.

Country of Study: United States of America.

No. of awards offered: Two.

Application Procedure: Applicants must write, phone or email the ATL for details.

Closing Date: November 30th.

No. of awards given last year: Two.

No. of applicants last year: 15.

Additional Information: These awards are given in conjunction with the English speaking Union of the Commonwealth.

ASSOCIATION OF THE GREAT ORGAN OF CHARTRES

Concours international d'orgue, 75 rue de Grenelle, Paris, F-75007, France
Tel: (33) 1 45 48 3174
Fax: (33) 1 45 49 1434
Email: orgues.chartres@free.fr
www: http://orgues.chartres.free.fr
Contact: Ms Colette Morillon, Director

Under the patronage of the President of the Republic, the Association of the Great Organ of Chartres has been active for the past 30 years. After saving the great organ of the cathedral, the Association has since taken charge of the artistic life around it. The Association's aims are: to help in the regular maintenance of the instrument, to organise the international organ competition called the Grand Prix of Chartres, to organise each Summer the International Organ Festival of Chartres, to encourage and promote creation of new organ music through commissions for the Grand Prix de Chartres and to favour the diffusion of organ music in general.

International Organ Competition 'Grand Prix de Chartres'

Subjects: Organ performance in two categories of interpretation and improvisation.

Purpose: To recognise and promote young, talented organists.

Eligibility: Open to organists of any nationality who are 35 years of age or under in the year of the competition. Any contestant who has previously been awarded a second prize may compete but they must succeed in all rounds of the competition.

Level of Study: Unrestricted.

Type: Prize.

Value: The first prize is €5,000, the second prize is €3,100 and the public prize is €1,525. The winners are offered approx. 70 concerts in the most famous places in France and abroad.

Frequency: Every two years.

Country of Study: France.

No. of awards offered: Two.

Application Procedure: Applicants must send the following documents to the secretariat: a completed registration form, curriculum vitae and a certificate from the institution (national or private conservatory, academy or other institution) where the applicant studied music and indicating the honours obtained. If studies have taken place partially or wholly under private tuition, the applicant must produce a certificate signed by their teacher. Any documents such as programmes, reviews or press articles giving evidence of the applicant's musical ability, an official document establishing the applicant's age, nationality and place of residence, two passport sized photographs and the non refundable registration fee of €65 should also be included. In a separate envelope applicants should also submit an anonymous sound recording of the highest possible quality on audiocassette, DAT, CD or minidisk. It must contain only the performance of the requested works and not any other sounds (words or acoustical references), and must not be edited in any fashion. A detailed description of the specializations of the instruments used for the recording, without indicating where the organs are located and a statement on the applicant's honour stipulating that they are indeed the performer on the recorded works must be sent with this.

Closing Date: April 15th.

Funding: Government, Private.

No. of awards given last year: Three.

No. of applicants last year: 62.

Additional Information: The contestants selected for the final round who are not prize winners will receive a finalist's certificate and a medal, but are not allowed to claim the title prize winner. Contestants may not claim any other award than the one they actually received. Unjustified claims for titles will be denied and the Board of Directors of the Association will prosecute such claimants according to the common law.

ASSOCIATION OF UNIVERSITIES AND COLLEGES OF CANADA (AUCC)

International & Canadian Programs Division
350 Albert Street, Suite 600
Ottawa, ON, K1R 1B1, Canada
Tel: (1) 613 563 1236
Fax: (1) 613 563 9745
Email: awards@aucc.ca
www: http://www.aucc.ca
Contact: Ms Julie Levac, Canadian Awards Program

The Association of Universities and Colleges of Canada (AUCC) is a non-profit, non governmental association that represents Canadian universities at home and abroad. The Association's mandate is to foster and promote the interests of higher education in the firm belief that strong universities are vital to the prosperity and wellbeing of Canada.

AUCC Cable Telecommunications Research Fellowship

Subjects: The cable television industry.
Purpose: To encourage students at the Master's or PhD level to tackle topics in the engineering of communications systems for video, voice and data signals or for computer applications to cable TV requirements.
Eligibility: Open to Canadian citizens or permanent residents who are enrolled or planning to enrol in a graduate degree programme at a university in Canada. Applicants must intend to use the fellowship to assist them in completing a graduate degree which includes a thesis on a topic in the engineering of broadband communication systems or computer application to cable TV.
Level of Study: Graduate.
Type: Fellowship.
Value: Canadian $5,000.
Length of Study: One year, with the possibility of renewal for a further year.
Frequency: Annual.
Study Establishment: Any university which is a member, or affiliated to a member, of the AUCC.
Country of Study: Canada.
No. of awards offered: Two.
Application Procedure: Applicants must complete an application form. Further information and application forms available on request or from the website.
Closing Date: March 28th.
Additional Information: Further information is available on request or from the website.

Canadian Wireless Telecommunications Association (CWTA) Graduate Scholarship

Subjects: Wireless communications including, but not limited to, engineering or business.
Purpose: To benefit students at the Master's or PhD level.
Eligibility: Candidates must be Canadian citizens or permanent residents of Canada and enrolled or planning to enrol in a graduate degree programme at a university in Canada. They must also intend to use the Scholarship to assist them in completing a graduate degree which includes a thesis on a topic related to the noted fields of study. Awards are granted on the basis of academic standing and demonstrated potential for advanced study and research.
Level of Study: Postdoctorate, Postgraduate.
Type: Scholarship.
Value: Canadian $10,000.
Length of Study: One year, with the option to renew.
Frequency: Annual.
Study Establishment: Any university or college which is a member, or affiliated to a member, of the AUCC.
Country of Study: Canada.
No. of awards offered: Up to 10.
Application Procedure: Applicants must contact the organisation for details.
Closing Date: June 1st.

Department of National Defence Security and Defence Forum Internship Program

Subjects: Studies relating to current and future Canadian national security and defence issues including their political, international, historical, social, military, industrial and economic dimensions.
Purpose: To help recent MA graduates with a background in security and defence studies to obtain work experience.
Eligibility: Open to Canadian citizens or permanent residents who hold a Master's degree before taking up the award.
Level of Study: Doctorate, Postgraduate.
Type: Internship.
Value: Up to Canadian $24,000.
Length of Study: Up to one year, non renewable.
Frequency: Annual.
Study Establishment: In the private sector or non governmental organisations.
Country of Study: Canada.
No. of awards offered: Approx. six.
Application Procedure: Applicants must apply for information, available on request or from the website.
Closing Date: Postmarked February 1st.
Additional Information: On completion of the award a reasonable detailed account of the internship and any research undertaken must be submitted to the AUCC who will forward it to the Department of National Defence. Further information is available on request or from the website.

Department of National Defence Security and Defence Forum MA Scholarship Program

Subjects: Current and future Canadian national security and defence issues including their political, international, historical, social, military, industrial and economic dimensions.
Eligibility: Open to Canadian citizens or permanent residents who, as a minimum requirement, hold a Bachelor's (Honours) Degree or its equivalent before taking up the award.
Level of Study: Doctorate, Postgraduate.
Type: Scholarship.
Value: Up to Canadian $8,000.
Length of Study: At least one year, with possible renewal for a further year if evidence of satisfactory academic achievement is found.
Frequency: Annual.
Country of Study: Canada.
No. of awards offered: Approx. eight.
Application Procedure: Applicants must apply for information, available on request or from the website.
Closing Date: Postmarked February 1st.
Additional Information: Successful applicants may not hold more than one award from the federal government.

Frank Knox Memorial Fellowships at Harvard University

Subjects: Arts and sciences including engineering, business administration, design, divinity studies, education, law, public administration at the John F Kennedy School of Government, medicine, dental medicine and public health.
Eligibility: Open to Canadian citizens or permanent residents who have recently graduated or who are about to graduate from an institution in Canada which is a member or affiliated to a member of the AUCC. Applications from students presently studying in the United States of America will not be considered, although applications will be considered from recent graduates who are working in the United States of America and will be applying to the MBA programme.
Level of Study: MBA, Postgraduate.
Type: Fellowship.
Value: US$17,000 plus tuition fees and student health insurance.
Length of Study: One academic year.
Frequency: Annual.
Study Establishment: Harvard University.
Country of Study: United States of America.
No. of awards offered: Up to three.
Application Procedure: Applicants must apply directly to the graduate school of their choice. Applicants are responsible for gaining admission to Harvard University by the deadline set by the various

faculties. Further information and application forms are available on request or from the website.

Closing Date: December 31st.

Additional Information: Holders of this award may not accept any other grant for the period of this fellowship unless approved by the Committee on General Scholarships and the Sheldon Fund of Harvard University.

Frederick T Metcalf Award Program

Subjects: Disciplines related to new media companies and delivering cable communications services such as business finance and marketing, economics, television production, mass communications and engineering.

Purpose: To support students pursuing a Master's degree in a programme related to the cable communication services.

Eligibility: Open to qualified full-time students pursuing a Master's degree in a field directly related to the development and delivery of cable in Canada.

Level of Study: Postgraduate.

Type: Scholarship.

Value: Canadian $5,000.

Length of Study: One year, non renewable.

Frequency: Annual.

Study Establishment: Any university which is a member of the AUCC, or affiliated to a member of the AUCC.

Country of Study: Canada.

No. of awards offered: One.

Application Procedure: Applicants must complete an application form, which are available on request or from the website.

Closing Date: March 28th.

Office of Critical Infrastructure Protection and Emergency Preparedness (EPC) Research Fellowship in Honour of Stuart Nesbitt White

Subjects: All aspects of disaster and emergency studies as outlined in the EPC Annual Report, and especially urban and regional planning, economics, geography, risk analysis and management, systems science, social sciences, business, health administration and civil engineering.

Purpose: To encourage disaster research and emergency planning in Canada by developing a greater number of qualified professionals in this field.

Eligibility: Open to Canadian citizens or permanent residents. Preference will be given to applicants who hold a Master's degree and who would normally be pursuing doctoral studies. However, applicants with a First Class (Honours) Degree will also be considered. Acceptance into a doctoral programme is normally, but not necessarily, a prerequisite.

Level of Study: Doctorate.

Type: Fellowship.

Value: Canadian $13,500 per year.

Length of Study: One year, with a possibility of renewal for a further two years.

Frequency: Annual.

Country of Study: Canada.

No. of awards offered: Varies.

Application Procedure: Applicants must write for details or refer to the website.

Closing Date: March 28th.

Additional Information: Further information is available on request or from the website.

Paul Sargent Memorial Linguistic Scholarship Program

Subjects: All fields at the Master's level, preferably with previous exposure to an Oriental, Middle Eastern or Eastern European language.

Purpose: To assist postgraduate level students in languages.

Eligibility: Applicants must be Canadian citizens or permanent residents at the time of application and must hold a Bachelor's degree at either the major or minor level, in the language concerned, with a high record of academic achievement. Applicants must have at least an intermediate level of competence in an Oriental, Middle Eastern or

Eastern European language. The minimum proficiency required would be a consistent A in language courses.

Level of Study: Postgraduate.

Type: Scholarship.

Value: Canadian $12,000.

Length of Study: Two years.

Study Establishment: Any university which is a member, or affiliated with a member, of the AUCC.

No. of awards offered: Two.

Application Procedure: Applicants must apply for information, available on request or from the website.

Closing Date: March 14th.

Petro-Canada Graduate Research Award Program

Subjects: Sciences, engineering, social sciences and business administration.

Purpose: To recognise academic excellence and to support and encourage graduate research in specialised fields of study relating to the petroleum industry.

Eligibility: Open to Canadian citizens or permanent residents who are working towards a Master's or doctoral degree on a full-time basis on a subject related to the oil and gas industry. Awards are granted on the basis of academic standing and demonstrated potential for advanced study and research.

Level of Study: Doctorate, Postgraduate.

Type: Research grant.

Value: Canadian $10,000.

Length of Study: One year. Award holders may reapply.

Frequency: Annual.

Study Establishment: A university or college which is a member, or affiliated to a member, of the AUCC.

Country of Study: Canada.

No. of awards offered: Up to four.

Application Procedure: Applicants must apply for information, available on request or from the website.

Closing Date: Postmarked February 1st.

Additional Information: There is no restriction on the number or value of other awards that can be held concurrently by a student. However, recipients must be able to accept at least 75 per cent of the Petro-Canada award in instances where restrictions apply to other awards received.

Security and Defence Forum PhD Scholarship Program Including the Dr Ronald Baker Doctoral Scholarship

Subjects: Studies relating to current and future Canadian national security and defence issues including their political, international, historical, social, military, industrial and economic dimensions.

Eligibility: Applicants must be Canadian citizens or permanent residents at the time of application and, as a minimum requirement, hold a Master's degree or its equivalent before taking up the award.

Level of Study: Graduate.

Value: Up to Canadian $16,000. The Dr Ronald Baker Doctoral Scholarship is up to Canadian $17,000.

Country of Study: Canada.

No. of awards offered: Approx. four.

Application Procedure: Applicants must apply for information, available on request or from the website.

Closing Date: Postmarked February 1st.

Additional Information: On completion of the scholarship one copy of the dissertation or a reasonable detailed account of the research undertaken must be submitted to the AUCC who will forward it to the Department of National Defence.

Security and Defence Forum Postdoctoral Fellowship Program including the R B Byers Postdoctoral Fellowship

Subjects: Studies relating to current and future Canadian national security and defence issues including their political, international, historical, social, military, industrial and economic dimensions.

Eligibility: Open to Canadian citizens or permanent residents who hold a PhD or its equivalent before taking up the award. Individuals who hold a tenure or tenure track appointment at any level are not eligible.

Level of Study: Doctorate, Postgraduate.
Type: Fellowship.
Value: Up to Canadian $27,000.
Length of Study: One year, non renewable.
Frequency: Annual.
Country of Study: Canada.
No. of awards offered: Approx. three.
Application Procedure: Applicants must apply for information, available on request or from the website http://www.dnd.ca/eng/dp/index_e.htm.
Closing Date: Postmarked February 1st.
Additional Information: On completion of the award period a reasonably detailed account of the research undertaken, as well as copies of publications and unpublished conference presentations resulting from the award, are to be submitted to the AUCC who will forward them to the Department of National Defence. Successful applicants may not hold more than one award from the federal government.

THE ASTHMA FOUNDATION OF NEW SOUTH WALES

Unit 2/100, Pacific Highway, St Leonards, NSW 2065, Australia
Tel: (61) 2 9906 3233
Fax: (61) 2 9906 4493
Email: ask@asthmansw.org.au
www: http://www.asthmansw.org.au
Contact: Executive Director

The vision of the Asthma Foundation of New South Wales is to eliminate asthma as a major cause of illness and disruption within the New South Wales community. Fundraising efforts assist with the promotion and funding of research activities that are aimed at helping the Foundation to achieve this vision.

Ann J Woolcock Research Fellowship

Subjects: Asthma research.
Purpose: To provide an outstanding researcher in biomedical science with an opportunity for independent research.
Eligibility: Open to Australian citizens or permanent residents who hold a PhD or equivalent doctorate in a health related field of research. Applicants must also have a demonstrated ability in research in the form of publications, and an intention to remain active in research. Candidates should have been actively engaged in research, in Australia or overseas, within the two years prior to application, and should normally have no more than eight years of postdoctoral experience from the date that the doctoral thesis was passed.
Level of Study: Postdoctorate.
Type: Fellowship.
Value: Up to Australian $100,000. This sum includes salary and up to Australian $15,000 for equipment, running expenses and travel. The value of a part-time fellowship will be adjusted on a prorata basis.
Length of Study: Applicants may elect to carry out research full or part-time with remaining time spent in clinical practice. The full-time fellowship is for a period of up to three years and the part-time fellowship is for up to four years.
Frequency: Every three years.
Study Establishment: A recognised and approved institution, teaching hospital or university in New South Wales or the Australian Central Territories.
Country of Study: Australia.
Application Procedure: All applications must be submitted on the correct application form, which together with details of the conditions associated with the fellowship, can be found on the website.
Funding: Private.
Contributor: Private Donors.

Asthma Foundation of New South Wales Medical Research Project Grant

Subjects: Medical, scientific and clinical research into asthma, its causes, triggers and impact.
Purpose: To expand the body of knowledge towards the causes of asthma and its possible cure.

Level of Study: Postdoctorate, Postgraduate.
Type: Project grant.
Value: Au $50,000.
Length of Study: One year.
Frequency: Annual, Dependent of funds available.
Country of Study: Australia.
No. of awards offered: Varies.
Application Procedure: Applicants must complete application forms. Short listed candidates will be interviewed.
Closing Date: Mid November.
Funding: Private.
Contributor: Private donors.
No. of awards given last year: Four.
No. of applicants last year: Eleven.

Biomedical and Medical Postgraduate Research Scholarships

Subjects: Medical, scientific and clinical research into asthma, its causes, triggers and impact.
Purpose: To expand the body of knowledge towards the causes of asthma and its possible cure.
Level of Study: Postdoctorate, Postgraduate.
Type: Scholarship.
Value: Au $20,000.
Length of Study: One year.
Frequency: Annual, Dependent on funds available.
Country of Study: Australia.
No. of awards offered: Varies.
Application Procedure: Applicants must complete application forms. Short listed candidates will be interviewed.
Closing Date: Mid October.
Funding: Private.
Contributor: Private donors.
No. of awards given last year: Two.
No. of applicants last year: Three.

ATAXIA UK

10 Winchester House, Kennington Park, London, SW9 6EJ, England
Tel: (44) 20 7820 3900
Fax: (44) 20 7582 9444
Email: office@ataxia.org.uk
www: http://www.ataxia.org.uk
Contact: Ms Julia Greenfield, Research Liaison Officer

Ataxia UK is the leading charity in the United Kingdom working with and for people with ataxia. It will support research projects and related activities in order to enhance scientific understanding of ataxia, develop and evaluate therapeutic and supportive strategies and encourage wider involvement with ataxia research.

Ataxia UK Research Studentships

Subjects: Any aspect of both inherited and sporadic progressive ataxias, including Friedreich's and other cerebellar ataxias.
Purpose: To enhance scientific understanding of ataxia, to develop and evaluate therapeutic and supportive strategies. To increase awareness of ataxia in the research community.
Eligibility: Proposals are accepted from academic institutions, private sector research companies and suitably qualified individuals. There are no restrictions on age, nationality or residency.
Level of Study: Doctorate.
Type: Studentship.
Value: Standard PhD studentship grant.
Length of Study: Three years.
Frequency: Dependent on funds available.
Study Establishment: Any academic institution.
Country of Study: Any country.
No. of awards offered: Not more than two per year.
Application Procedure: Applicants must complete an application form available from Ataxia UK's Research Liaison Officer at research@ataxia.org.uk.
Closing Date: December 1st and April 1st.
Funding: Commercial, Private.

Additional Information: There are a number of priority areas of research and these can be obtained from the Research Liaison Officer.

Ataxia UK Travel Award

Subjects: Any aspect of both inherited and sporadic progressive ataxias including Friedreich's and other cerebellar ataxias.
Purpose: To enable researchers to present their ataxia research at national and international conferences.
Eligibility: Proposals are accepted from academic institutions, private sector research companies and suitably qualified individuals. There are no restrictions on age, nationality or residency.
Level of Study: Unrestricted.
Type: Travel grant.
Value: Dependent on the conference.
Frequency: Dependent on funds available.
Country of Study: Any country.
No. of awards offered: Varies.
Application Procedure: Applicants must complete an application form available from Ataxia's Research Liaison Officer on research@ataxia.org.uk.
Closing Date: December 1st and April 1st.
Funding: Commercial, Private.
Additional Information: There are a number of priority areas of research and these can be obtained from the Research Liaison Officer.

Project Grant

Subjects: Any aspect of both inherited and sporadic progressive ataxias including Friedreich's and other cerebellar ataxias.
Purpose: To enhance scientific understanding of ataxia and to develop and evaluate therapeutic and supportive strategies.
Eligibility: Proposals are accepted from academic institutions, private sector research companies and suitably qualified individuals. There are no restrictions on age, nationality or residency.
Level of Study: Research.
Type: Other.
Value: Varies - but maximum of UK£50,000 per year for not more than three years.
Length of Study: Up to three years.
Frequency: Dependent on funds available.
Study Establishment: Any academic institution or private sector company.
Country of Study: Any country.
No. of awards offered: Varies.
Application Procedure: Applicants must complete an application form available from Ataxia's Research Liaison Officer on research@ataxia.org.uk.
Closing Date: December 1st and April 1st.
Funding: Commercial, Private.
Additional Information: There are a number of priority areas of research and these can be obtained from the Research Liaison Officer.

Satellite Meeting at Major Symposium on Related Disorders

Subjects: Any aspect of both inherited and sporadic progressive ataxias including Friedreich's and other cerebellar ataxias.
Purpose: To raise awareness of ataxia research and enhance collaboration with researchers within the ataxia field and in related disciplines.
Eligibility: Proposals are accepted from academic institutions, private sector research companies and suitably qualified individuals. There are no restrictions on age, nationality or residency.
Level of Study: Research.
Type: Award.
Value: Dependent on the meeting.
Frequency: Dependent on funds available.
Country of Study: Any country.
No. of awards offered: Varies.
Application Procedure: Applicants must complete an application form available from Ataxia's Research Liaison Officer on research@ataxia.org.uk.
Closing Date: December 1st and April 1st.
Funding: Commercial, Private.

Additional Information: There are a number of priority areas of research and these can be obtained from the Research Liaison Officer.

ATHENAEUM INTERNATIONAL CULTURAL CENTRE

3 Adrianou Street, Athens, GR-105 55, Greece
Tel: (30) 210 321 1987
Fax: (30) 210 321 1196
Email: athenm@attglobal.net
www: http://www.athenaeum.ids.gr
Contact: Mrs Irene Mega, Executive Secretary

The Athenaeum International Cultural Centre is a non-profit association dedicated to preserving the memory of Maria Callas. The organisation was founded in 1974 by a group of inspired artists who wanted to contribute to the development and evolution of musical education and culture in Greece.

Maria Callas Grand Prix

Subjects: Singing and the piano.
Purpose: To recognise outstanding artists.
Eligibility: Open to nationals from any country.
Level of Study: Unrestricted.
Type: Competition.
Value: Please contact the organisation.
Frequency: Other.
Country of Study: Any country.
No. of awards offered: One for each category.
Application Procedure: Applicants must complete an application form and submit this with the documentation as detailed in the prospectus of the Grand Prix. There is a registration fee of €120.
Closing Date: December 31st.
Funding: Government, Private.
No. of awards given last year: Two in opera and one in piano.
No. of applicants last year: 32 for opera and 23 for piano.
Additional Information: Concert appearances are arranged for the winners.

Maria Callas Grand Prix for Opera and Oratorio-Lied

Subjects: Opera and oratorio-lied.
Purpose: To recognise outstanding singers.
Eligibility: Open to singers of any nationality. Female singers should not be older than 30 years of age and male singers not older than 32 years of age.
Level of Study: Unrestricted.
Type: Competition.
Value: Please contact the organisation.
Frequency: Every two years.
Country of Study: Any country.
No. of awards offered: One for each category and then second and third prize.
Application Procedure: Applicants must complete an application form and pay the registration fee of €120. Candidates must contact the Centre for further details.
Closing Date: December 31st.
Funding: Government, Private.
No. of awards given last year: Two.
No. of applicants last year: 32.
Additional Information: Concert appearances are arranged for the winners.

Maria Callas Grand Prix for Pianists

Subjects: Musical performance on the piano.
Purpose: To recognise outstanding pianists.
Eligibility: Open to pianists of any nationality, up to 32 years of age.
Level of Study: Unrestricted.
Type: Competition.
Value: Please contact the organisation.
Frequency: Every two years.
Country of Study: Any country.
No. of awards offered: Three.

Application Procedure: Applicants must contact the Centre for details. There is a registration fee of €120.
Closing Date: December 31st.
Funding: Government, Private.
No. of awards given last year: One.
No. of applicants last year: 40.
Additional Information: Concert appearances are arranged for the Grand Prix winner.

Maria Callas International Music Competition
Subjects: Musical performance, although disciplines vary with each competition. Singing such as opera, oratorio or lied and the piano.
Purpose: To recognise outstanding artists.
Eligibility: Open to musicians of all nationalities.
Level of Study: Unrestricted.
Type: Competition.
Value: Please contact the organisation.
Frequency: Other.
Country of Study: Any country.
No. of awards offered: Varies according to the discipline.
Application Procedure: Applicants must request full details and application procedures or consult the website. There is a registration fee of €120.
Closing Date: December 31st.
Funding: Government, Private.
No. of awards given last year: Two in opera and one in piano.
No. of applicants last year: 32 for singing and 23 for the piano competition.
Additional Information: Concert appearances are arranged for the winners.

ATLANTIC SALMON FEDERATION (ASF)

PO Box 5200, St Andrews, NB, E5B 3S8, Canada
Tel: (1) 506 529 4581
Fax: (1) 506 529 4438
Email: asfres@nbnet.nb.ca
www: http://www.asf.ca/awards/awards.html
Contact: Ms Ellen Merrill, Executive Assistant

The Atlantic Salmon Federation (ASF) is an international, non-profit organisation which promotes the conservation and management of the Atlantic salmon and its environment. ASF has a network of seven regional councils, a membership of over 150 river associations and 40,000 volunteers. Regional offices cover the salmon's freshwater range in Canada and the United States of America.

Olin Fellowship
Subjects: A wide range of endeavours including salmon management, graduate study and research.
Purpose: To support individuals seeking to improve their knowledge or skills in advanced fields while looking for solutions to current problems in Atlantic salmon biology, management and conservation.
Eligibility: Open to citizens and legal residents of the United States of America or Canada. Applicants need not be enrolled in a degree programme to be eligible.
Level of Study: Unrestricted.
Type: Fellowship.
Value: Canadian $1,000-3,000.
Frequency: Annual.
Study Establishment: Any accredited university, research laboratory or active management programme.
Country of Study: United States of America or Canada.
No. of awards offered: Varies.
Application Procedure: Applicants must complete an application form, available on request or from the website.
Closing Date: March 15th for notification by May 15th.
Funding: Private.
Contributor: Memberships and foundation grants.
No. of awards given last year: 5.
No. of applicants last year: 7.

For further information contact:

Executive Assistant, PO Box 807, Calais, ME 04619-0807, United States of America
Tel: (1) 506 529 1021
Fax: (1) 506 529 4985
Email: asfres@nb.aibn.com
Contact: Ms Ellen Merrill

ATLANTIC SCHOOL OF THEOLOGY

660 Fracklyn Street, Halifax
NS, B3H 3B5, Canada
Tel: (1) 902 423 6939
Fax: (1) 902 492 4048
Email: dmaclachlan@astheology.ns.ca
www: http://www.astheology.ns.ca
Contact: Mr David MacLachlan, Academic Dean

The Atlantic School of Theology is an ecumenical university committed to excellence in graduate level theological education and research. The School is also committed to the provision of information for Christian ministries, both lay and ordained, in church and society, primarily in Atlantic Canada.

Evelyn Hilchie Betts Memorial Fellowship
Subjects: Theology.
Purpose: To enable ordained clergy from the Third World to study at the School and thereby to introduce persons from other Christian communities to the church and theological education in Canada and to share their context with the School.
Eligibility: Open to ordained clergy from developing countries. Applicants must be interested in theological education in an ecumenical atmosphere, be able to speak and write in English, be interested in living and working in a Christian community and be willing to share their work and experiences with the Canadian church.
Level of Study: Postgraduate.
Type: Fellowship.
Value: Approx. Canadian $15,000 for transportation, tuition, room and board.
Length of Study: One academic year.
Frequency: Dependent on funds available.
Study Establishment: The Atlantic School of Theology.
Country of Study: Canada.
No. of awards offered: One.
Application Procedure: Applicants must submit a completed application form and letters of reference to the Betts Memorial Fellowship Committee.
Closing Date: December 31st.
Funding: Private.
No. of awards given last year: None.
No. of applicants last year: None.
Additional Information: Due to a shortage of funds for the scholarship no award will be possible until further notice.

AUSTRALIAN ACADEMY OF THE HUMANITIES (AAH)

GPO Box 93, Canberra, ACT 2601, Australia
Tel: (61) 2 6248 7744
Fax: (61) 2 6248 6287
Email: aah.office@anu.edu.au
www: http://www.humanities.org.au
Contact: Administration Officer

The Australian Academy of the Humanities (AAH) was established under Royal Charter in 1969 for the advancement of the scholarship, interest in and understanding of the humanities. Humanities disciplines include, but are not limited to, history, classics, English, European languages and cultures, Asian studies, philosophy, the arts, linguistics, prehistory and archaeology, and cultural and communications studies.

AAH Travelling Fellowships

Subjects: Humanities.

Purpose: To enable short-term study abroad.

Eligibility: Open to Scholars resident in Australia working in the field of humanities. Fellows of the Academy are ineligible for awards. Preference shall be given to scholars in the earlier stages of their careers, and who are not as well placed to receive funding from other sources. They should have a project going forward which requires a short visit overseas for its completion or advancement, and be near to that stage. The proposed work should not form part of the requirement for a higher degree. The fellowships are paid as a contribution to the cost of one return airfare between the applicant's place of employment in Australia and the centre of research abroad. The Academy will not award fellowships to attend conferences, to study overseas, or to students enrolled for higher degrees. The fellowship must be taken up within twelve months of the award.

Level of Study: Unrestricted.

Type: Fellowship.

Value: Australian $2,500 each.

Length of Study: At least six weeks.

Frequency: Annual.

Study Establishment: An appropriate research centre.

Country of Study: Other.

No. of awards offered: Five.

Application Procedure: Applicants must write for details.

Closing Date: July 30th.

Funding: Government.

Additional Information: Research projects should be near completion.

AUSTRALIAN EARLY CHILDHOOD ASSOCIATION, INC. (AECA)

PO Box 105, Watson
ACT 2602, Australia
Tel: (61) 2 6241 6900
Fax: (61) 2 6241 5547
Email: national@aeca.org.au
www: http://www.aeca.org.au
Contact: National Director

The Early Childhood Australia (ECA) is the national non government organisation for the interests of children from birth to eight years of age and for older children in care. ECA promotes the provision of high quality services for young children and their families and supports the role of parents in caring for their children.

Alice Creswick and Sheila Kimpton Foundation Scholarship

Subjects: A wide range of areas of interest concerning policy, practice and research in the early childhood field.

Purpose: To provide the opportunity for travel, observation and/or major study in the early childhood field.

Eligibility: Open to Australian citizens currently employed in positions which have a direct relationship with early childhood education and care and who have qualifications in the research of early childhood or related fields.

Level of Study: Unrestricted.

Type: Scholarship.

Value: Varies.

Frequency: Dependent on funds available.

Country of Study: Any country.

No. of awards offered: One.

Application Procedure: Applications will be called at appropriate times by AECA.

Funding: Private.

Additional Information: The successful applicant will be required to undertake certain commitments including the preparation of a written report and speaking engagements as required by ECA.

AUSTRALIAN FEDERATION OF UNIVERSITY WOMEN - VICTORIA

PO Box 816, Mount Eliza
VIC 3930, Australia
www: http://home.vicnet.net.au/~afuwvic
Contact: Ms Margaret James, Treasurer

AFUW Victoria Endowment Scholarship, Lady Leitch Scholarship

Subjects: All subjects.

Purpose: To assist and encourage independent research at postgraduate level which will be of practical benefit to mankind.

Eligibility: Open to women graduates who are members of the Australian Federation of University Women, or its international affiliates who are graduates of Australian Universities (Endowment Scholarship). Lady Leitch is open to AFUW/IFUW members. Only those with excellent academic records should apply.

Level of Study: Doctorate, Postdoctorate, Postgraduate, Professional development.

Type: Scholarship

Value: Approx. Australian $6,000 for each award.

Length of Study: One year.

Frequency: Annually for the AFUW Victoria and every two years for the Lady Leitch.

Country of Study: Any country.

No. of awards offered: Two.

Application Procedure: Applicants must complete an application form, with documentation on university qualifications, names of three referees, and membership of AFUW or affiliate. A stamped addressed large envelope should be included. Alternatively, application forms are available on the website.

Closing Date: March 1st.

Funding: Private.

Contributor: AFUW Victoria and Lady Leitch bequest.

No. of awards given last year: Two.

No. of applicants last year: 50.

THE AUSTRALIAN FEDERATION OF UNIVERSITY WOMEN, SOUTH AUSTRALIA, INC. TRUST FUND (AFUW-SA, INC.)

GPO Box 634, Adelaide
SA 5001, Australia
www: http://www.afuw-sa-bursaries.mx.com.au
Contact: Ms Heather Latz, Fellowships Trustee

The Australian Federation of University Women's (AFUW) main activity is assisting women in tertiary education in Australia via bursaries. Funds for the bursaries are raised through volunteer work, academic dress hire, donations and bequests.

AFUW-S, Inc. Trust Fund Bursary

Subjects: All subjects.

Purpose: To assist women to complete coursework postgraduate degrees.

Eligibility: Open to women enrolled for coursework postgraduate degrees at any Australian university. Applicants must not be in full-time paid employment or on fully paid study leave during the tenure of the bursary.

Level of Study: Doctorate, Postgraduate.

Type: Bursary.

Value: Australian $3,000.

Length of Study: The bursary must be used within one year of the date of the award.

Frequency: Annual.

Study Establishment: A recognised Australian tertiary institution.

Country of Study: Australia.

No. of awards offered: One.

Application Procedure: Applicants must complete an application form and submit this with evidence of enrolment at the institution at which the qualification is to be obtained, as well as copies of official transcripts, curriculum vitae and list of publications. Application forms can be downloaded from the website and sent by post.
Closing Date: March 1st.
Funding: Private.

Barbara Crase, Doreen McCarthy, Cathy Candler and Brenda Nettle Bursaries

Subjects: All subjects.
Purpose: To assist in the completion of a Master's or PhD research degree.
Eligibility: Open to men and women any nationality. Applicants must have completed one year of postgraduate research excluding the honours year, and must be enrolled at a University in South Australia.
Level of Study: Doctorate, Postgraduate.
Type: Bursary.
Value: Australian $3,000.
Length of Study: The bursary must be used within one year of the date of the award.
Frequency: Annual.
Study Establishment: A South Australian university.
Country of Study: Any country.
No. of awards offered: Four.
Application Procedure: Candidates should complete an application form and submit this with evidence of enrolment at the institution at which the qualification will be obtained, as well as copies of official transcripts, curriculum vitae and a list of publications. Application forms can be downloaded from the website and sent by post.
Closing Date: March 1st.
Funding: Private.

Diamond Jubilee Bursary

Subjects: All subjects.
Purpose: To assist in the completion of a coursework postgraduate degree.
Eligibility: Open to men or women of any nationality, who are enrolled in a postgraduate degree by course work at a South Australian University.
Level of Study: Doctorate, Postgraduate.
Type: Bursary.
Value: Australian $3,000.
Length of Study: The bursary must be used within one year of the date of the award.
Frequency: Annual.
Study Establishment: A South Australian university.
Country of Study: Australia.
No. of awards offered: One.
Application Procedure: Candidates should complete an application form and submit this with evidence of enrolment at the institution at which the qualification will be obtained, as well as copies of official transcripts and curriculum vitae. Application forms can be downloaded from the website and sent by post.
Closing Date: March 1st.
Funding: Private.

Padnendadlu Bursary

Subjects: All subjects.
Purpose: To assist in the completion of a postgraduate degree.
Eligibility: Applicants must be Australian indigenous women undertaking postgraduate degrees at South Australian Universities.
Level of Study: Doctorate, Postgraduate.
Type: Bursary.
Value: Australian $3,000.
Frequency: Annual.
Study Establishment: A South Australian university.
Country of Study: Australia.
No. of awards offered: One, however, runners up may be awarded less than the bursary amount.
Application Procedure: Candidates should complete an application form and submit this with evidence or enrolment at the institution at which the qualification will be obtained, as well as copies of official transcripts and curriculum vitae. Application forms can be downloaded from the website and sent by post.
Closing Date: March 1st.
Funding: Private.
Additional Information: Eligible applicants undertaking a postgraduate degree by coursework must apply for the Diamond Jubilee Bursary and those undertaking a postgraduate degree by research must apply for the Doreen McCarthy, Barbara Crase, Cathy Candler and Brenda Nettle Bursaries. In each case, completion of a declaration of indigenous status will ensure that applicants are considered for the Padnendadlu Bursary.

Thenie Baddams Bursary, Jean Gilmore Bursary and Daphne Elliott Bursary

Subjects: All subjects.
Purpose: To assist women to complete a Master's or PhD degree by research.
Eligibility: Open to female graduates who are enrolled in an Australian tertiary institution and have completed at least one year of postgraduate research, excluding their Honours year. Applicants must hold a good Honours Degree or equivalent, and must not be in full-time paid employment or study leave during tenure.
Level of Study: Doctorate, Postgraduate.
Type: Bursary.
Value: Up to Australian $5,000 each, however runners-up can be awarded a lesser amount.
Length of Study: The bursary must be used within one year of the date of the award.
Frequency: Annual.
Study Establishment: A recognised Australian Institute of Higher Education.
Country of Study: Any country.
No. of awards offered: Three.
Application Procedure: Applicants must complete an application form and submit this with evidence of enrolment at the institution at which the qualification is to be obtained, as well as copies of official transcripts, curriculum vitae and list of publications. There is an Australian $12 lodgement fee. Application forms can be downloaded from the website and sent by post.
Closing Date: March 1st.
Funding: Private.

Winifred E Preedy Postgraduate Bursary

Subjects: Dentistry or a related field.
Purpose: To assist women in the completion of a higher degree.
Eligibility: Open to females who are past or present students of the Faculty of Dentistry at the University of Adelaide, who are enrolled as graduate students in dentistry or some allied field at the University of Adelaide or to such other institution of tertiary education as the trustees may approve. The applicant must have completed one year of her postgraduate degree.
Level of Study: Doctorate, Postgraduate.
Type: Bursary.
Value: Australian $4,000.
Length of Study: The bursary must be used within one year of the date of the award.
Frequency: Annual.
Study Establishment: Anywhere if the applicant is a past student at the University of Adelaide's Dental Faculty in Australia. Otherwise the applicant must be a current student at the University of Adelaide Dental Faculty.
Country of Study: Other.
No. of awards offered: One.
Application Procedure: Applicants must complete an application form and submit this with evidence of enrolment at the institution at which the qualification will be obtained, as well as copies of official transcripts, curriculum vitae and list of publications. Application forms can be downloaded from the website and sent by post.
Closing Date: March 1st.
Funding: Private.

AUSTRALIAN INSTITUTE OF ABORIGINAL AND TORRES STRAIT ISLANDER STUDIES (AIATSIS)

GPO Box 553, Canberra, ACT 2601, Australia
Tel: (61) 2 6246 1157
Fax: (61) 2 6261 4285
Email: grants@aiatsis.gov.au
www: http://www.aiatsis.gov.au
Contact: Mr Peter Veth, Research Administration Team

The Australian Institute of Aboriginal and Torres Strait Islander Studies (AIATSIS) is a federally funded organisation central in Aboriginal and Torres Strait Islander research. Its principal function is to promote Australian Aboriginal and Torres Strait Islander studies. A staff of 60, directed by the Principal, engages in a range of services through the Research Programme, the Research Grants Programme, the archives and production team, and the library.

AIATSIS Research Grants

Subjects: Health, human biology, social anthropology, linguistics, ethnomusicology, material culture, rock art, prehistory, ethnobotany, psychology, education and Aboriginal history including oral history, native title and indigenous land use agreements.
Purpose: To promote research into Aboriginal and Torres Strait Islander Studies.
Eligibility: Open to nationals of any country.
Level of Study: Unrestricted.
Type: Research grant.
Value: No predetermined value.
Length of Study: Up to one year.
Frequency: Annual.
Country of Study: Australia.
No. of awards offered: Varies.
Application Procedure: Applicants must complete an application form, available from the website.
Closing Date: January 31st.
Funding: Government.
Contributor: The Australian Federal Government.
Additional Information: Permission to conduct research projects must be obtained from the appropriate Aboriginal or Torres Strait Island community or organisation.

AUSTRALIAN INSTITUTE OF NUCLEAR SCIENCE AND ENGINEERING (AINSE)

Private Mail Bag 1, Menai, NSW 2234, Australia
Tel: (61) 2 9717 3376
Fax: (61) 2 9717 9268
Email: ainse@ansto.gov.au
Contact: Dr Dennis Mather, Scientific Secretary

Established in 1958, the Australian Institute of Nuclear Science and Engineering (AINSE) is a consortium of Australian universities and the University of Auckland, New Zealand, in partnership with the Australian Nuclear Science and Technology Organisation (ANSTO). Its aims are to assist research and training in nuclear science and engineering and to make the facilities of the Lucas Heights Research Laboratories available to research staff and students from member institutions.

AINSE Awards

Subjects: Nuclear science and engineering.
Eligibility: Open to member organisations of AINSE which are undertaking projects in an appropriate field.
Level of Study: Unrestricted.
Type: Grant.
Value: Assistance is available mainly in the form of credits enabling university researchers to meet costs associated with the use of facilities, travel to and from Lucas Heights, and accommodation during periods of attachment. Direct grants for small items of equipment and materials may also be considered.
Length of Study: One year.

Frequency: Annual.
Study Establishment: Lucas Heights Science and Technology Centre.
Country of Study: Australia.
No. of awards offered: Varies.
Application Procedure: Applicants must contact the Scientific Secretary, AINSE or Research Office at member universities.
Closing Date: September 23rd.
Funding: Government.
No. of awards given last year: 179.
No. of applicants last year: 232.

AINSE Postgraduate Research Awards

Subjects: Nuclear physics, neutron scattering and accelerator science including AMS, radiation biology, chemistry and physics, advanced materials, engineering and nuclear technology, environmental science, biomedicine and health and any field of research using nuclear techniques of analysis in general.
Eligibility: Open to postgraduate students whose research projects are associated with nuclear science and technology and who require access to the unique national facilities at the Lucas Heights Laboratories. Candidates must be nominated by the Australian university and the University of Auckland where PhD enrolment is held or proposed.
Level of Study: Postgraduate.
Type: Research grant.
Value: Australian $7,500 per year for research supplements plus Australian $5,500 for research expenses.
Length of Study: One year.
Frequency: Annual.
Study Establishment: Lucas Heights Science and Technology Centre.
Country of Study: Australia.
Application Procedure: Applicants must contact the Scientific Secretary, AINSE or Research Office at member universities.
Closing Date: April 15th.
Funding: Government.
No. of awards given last year: 15.
No. of applicants last year: 39.

AUSTRALIAN KIDNEY FOUNDATION

82 Melbourne Street, Adelaide, SA 5006, Australia
Tel: (61) 8 8334 7555
Fax: (61) 8 8334 7540
Email: teresa.taylor@adelaide.kidney.org.au
www: http://www.kidney.org.au
Contact: National Communications Manager

Founded in 1968, the Australian Kidney Foundation's mission is to be recognised as the leading non-profit national organisation providing funding for, and taking the initiative in, the prevention of kidney and urinary tract diseases.

Australian Kidney Foundation Medical Research Grants & Scholarships

Subjects: The functions and disease of the kidney, urinary tract and related organs.
Purpose: To support medical research.
Eligibility: Open to Australian citizens who are graduates of Australian medical schools or overseas graduates who are eligible for Australian citizenship and for registration as medical practitioners in Australia.
Level of Study: Doctorate, Postgraduate.
Type: Scholarship.
Value: Please contact the organisation.
Length of Study: One year.
Frequency: Annual.
Study Establishment: Any approved medical centre, university or research institute.
Country of Study: Australia.
No. of awards offered: Up to six.
Application Procedure: Applicants must complete an application form.

Australian Kidney Foundation Seeding and Equipment Grants

Subjects: The functions or diseases of the kidney, urinary tract and related organs, or relevant problems, dialysis, transplantation, organ donation and research.
Purpose: To provide financial support for research projects related to the kidney and urinary tract.
Eligibility: Open to Australian citizens connected with Australian universities or medical centres with requisite research facilities.
Level of Study: Unrestricted.
Type: Grant.
Value: Up to Australian $15,000 per year.
Frequency: Annual.
Study Establishment: Any medical centre, university or research institute.
Country of Study: Australia.
No. of awards offered: 30-35.
Application Procedure: Applicants must contact the Foundation for details.
Closing Date: June 30th.

AUSTRALIAN MUSICAL FOUNDATION

Richards Butler, Beaufort House
15 St Botolph Street, London
EC3A 7EE, England
Tel: (44) 20 7247 6555
Fax: (44) 20 7257 5091
Contact: Mr John Emmott, Secretary

AMF Award

Subjects: Any aspect of musical study, except composition.
Purpose: To finance further studies.
Eligibility: Open to Australian singers and instrumentalists under 30 years of age who are resident in Australia or Europe.
Level of Study: Unrestricted.
Value: UK£12,000.
Length of Study: Two years, the second year being subject to assessment.
Frequency: Annual.
Country of Study: Other.
No. of awards offered: Up to three.
Application Procedure: Applicants must complete an application form and submit this with a demonstration cassette.
Closing Date: The end of April.
Funding: Private.
No. of awards given last year: One.
No. of applicants last year: 35.
Additional Information: Applications are considered in the first instance by the Foundation Committee, with a panel of adjudicators making the final choice. It is stressed that this award is intended for musicians of merit and ability. The Foundation will also take into account how applicants propose to use the award, should they win, to further their careers.

AUSTRALIAN NATIONAL UNIVERSITY (ANU)

Building 11, Canberra
ACT 0200, Australia
Tel: (61) 2 6249 5949
Fax: (61) 2 6125 5931
Email: ressch.enq@anu.edu.au
www: http://www.anu.edu.au
Contact: Research & Scholarships Office

The Australian National University (ANU) was founded by the Australian Government in 1946 as Australia's only completely research orientated university. It comprises eight research schools, six teaching faculties, a graduate school and over a dozen other academic schools or centres.

ANU Aboriginal and Torres Strait Islander Scholarship

Subjects: All subjects.
Purpose: To assist an Aboriginal or Torres Strait Islander to undertake a graduate diploma, Master's degree course, or a course leading to a PhD.
Eligibility: Open to indigenous Australians who are Aborigines or Torres Strait Islanders.
Level of Study: Postgraduate.
Type: Scholarship.
Value: Benefits accord with those of the ANU PhD or Master degree scholarships and tenure is dependent upon the programme for which the scholarship is awarded.
Frequency: Annual.
Country of Study: Australia.
No. of awards offered: One.
Application Procedure: Applicants must complete an application form, available on request or from the website.
Closing Date: October 31st.
Contributor: The Australian National University.

ANU Alumni Association PhD Scholarships

Subjects: All subjects.
Purpose: To assist international students with study in Australia.
Eligibility: Open to nationals from Hong Kong, Japan, Malaysia, Thailand and Singapore.
Level of Study: Doctorate.
Type: Scholarship.
Value: Approx. Australian $17,609 per year, tax free, payment of the programme fee for the duration of the stipend, an additional allowance for dependent children of married scholars, travel to Canberra, and a grant for the reimbursement of some removal expenses. A thesis reimbursement allowance is also available.
Length of Study: Normally tenable for three years, renewable for six months.
Country of Study: Australia.
No. of awards offered: One each for nationals of eligible countries.
Application Procedure: Applicants must complete an application form, available on request or from the website.
Closing Date: Published through the Alumni Association of each country.
Contributor: The Australian National University.
Additional Information: Initial correspondence concerning graduate courses and scholarships should be sent to the main address or sent by email. Coursework enquiries from Australian students should be emailed to admiss.enq@anu.edu.au. All other enquiries from Australian students should be sent to the main email address. International students should send all enquiries to info.ieo@anu.edu.au or visit the website http://www.anu.edu.au/ieo.

ANU Graduate School Scholarships

Subjects: All subjects.
Purpose: To fund postgraduate study.
Eligibility: Open to individuals who are permanent residents of Australia. They need not necessarily have been resident in Australia for twelve months prior to the closing date. Applicants who have been in receipt of a PhD scholarship funded in the University for one year or more are ineligible.
Level of Study: Doctorate.
Type: Scholarship.
Value: A stipend of Australian $17,609 per year tax free, travel to Canberra from within Australia and a grant for the reimbursement of some removal expenses is available.
Length of Study: Three years in the first instance, with a possible extension of six months.
Frequency: Annual.
Country of Study: Australia.
Application Procedure: Applicants must complete an application form, available on request or from the website.
Contributor: The Australian National University.

ANU Master's Degree Scholarships (The Faculties)
Subjects: All subjects.
Purpose: To assist study in most graduate school programmes for courses leading to a Master's degree by research, by coursework or by a combination of the two.
Eligibility: Open to candidates holding a Bachelor's degree with at least Upper Second Class (Honours), and, if wishing to undertake a degree by research only, applicants must have a proven capability for research.
Level of Study: Postgraduate.
Type: Scholarship.
Value: Basic stipend of Australian $17,609 per year tax free, an additional allowance for dependent children of married international scholars, travel to Canberra, excluding the international part of the airfare for those recruited from overseas, and a grant for the reimbursement of some removal expenses.
Length of Study: One year, but may be extended.
Frequency: Annual.
Study Establishment: The Faculties.
Country of Study: Australia.
No. of awards offered: Varies.
Application Procedure: Applicants must complete an application form, available on request or from the website.
Contributor: The Faculties.

ANU PhD Scholarships
Subjects: All subjects.
Purpose: To assist research.
Eligibility: Applicants should write for details.
Level of Study: Doctorate.
Type: Scholarship.
Value: A stipend of Australian $17,609 per year tax free, and if applicable, an additional allowance for dependent children of unmarried international scholars plus economy travel to Canberra and a grant for the reimbursement of some removal expenses.
Length of Study: Three years, renewable for six months.
Country of Study: Australia.
No. of awards offered: Varies.
Application Procedure: Applicants must complete an application form, available on request or from the website.
Closing Date: October 31st for citizens or permanent residents of Australia and New Zealand, and August 30th for international applicants.
Additional Information: Initial correspondence concerning graduate courses and scholarships should be sent to the main address or sent by email. Coursework enquiries from Australian students should be emailed to admiss.enq@anu.edu.au. All other enquiries from Australian students should be sent to the main email address. International students should send all enquiries to info.ieo@anu.edu.au or visit the website http://www.anu.edu.au/ieo.

ANU Re-entry Scholarships for Women
Subjects: All subjects.
Purpose: To assist women graduates to resume their studies.
Eligibility: Open to women graduates who have taken a break from their studies of at least three years since formal enrolment in a university course, the break normally being due to fulfilment of family obligations. Applicants must be Australian citizens or permanent residents. The scholarship may be awarded to undertake a graduate diploma, a Master's degree course or a PhD and applicants must hold qualifications appropriate to the level of course for which they wish to apply.
Level of Study: Doctorate, Postgraduate.
Type: Scholarship.
Value: Benefits accord with those of ANU PhD or Master's degree scholarships and tenure is dependent upon the programme for which the scholarship is awarded.
Length of Study: Tenure is dependent upon the course to which the scholarship applies.
Frequency: Annual.
Country of Study: Australia.
No. of awards offered: One or two.

Application Procedure: Applicants must submit a completed application form with a letter setting out the applicant's case for award of the scholarship and indicating their circumstances in terms of the eligibility criteria. Application forms are available on request or from the website.
Contributor: The Australian National University.

Australian Development Scholarships (ADS)
Subjects: All subjects.
Level of Study: Graduate.
Type: Scholarship.
Value: Return air fare to Australia, tuition fees, an establishment allowance and a living allowance are available.
Country of Study: Australia.
Application Procedure: Applicants must write to the Australian Diplomatic Mission or the Australian Education Centre in their home country.
Closing Date: Varies.

AUSTRALIAN RESEARCH COUNCIL (ARC)

GPO Box 2702, Canberra, ACT 2601, Australia
Tel: (61) 2 6284 6600
Fax: (61) 2 6284 6601
Email: ncgp@arc.gov.au
www: http://www.arc.gov.au
Contact: Grants Management Officer

The Australian Research Council (ARC) plays a key role in the Australian Government's investment in the future prosperity and well being of the Australian community. Its mission is to advance Australia's capacity to undertake quality research. ARC has various funding programs under the umbrella of the National Competitive Grants Program.

ARC Discovery Projects Australian Research Fellow/ Queen Elizabeth II Fellow (ARF/QEII)
Subjects: All areas of science except clinical medicine or dentistry.
Purpose: To strengthen Australia's national research and development capability by providing opportunities for established researchers to undertake research of national and international significance.
Eligibility: Open to candidates with a PhD and an excellent academic record. Applicants should have more than three years but not more than eight years of professional experience since the awarding of their PhD.
Level of Study: Postdoctorate.
Type: Fellowship.
Value: Australian Research Fellows are awarded Australian $79,071 and Queen Elizabeth II Fellows are awarded Australian $93,848. This includes 26 per cent on costs.
Length of Study: Five years.
Frequency: Annual.
Country of Study: Australia.
No. of awards offered: Approx. 15 of each.
Application Procedure: Applicants must submit applications through an Australian host institution. It is the responsibility of the applicant to approach potential host institutions.
Closing Date: March 8th.
Funding: Government.
No. of awards given last year: 30.
No. of applicants last year: 216.
Additional Information: Candidates must obtain Australian citizenship or temporary residency status at the time of commencing the fellowship. Further information is available from the website.

ARC Discovery Projects Postdoctoral Fellow (APD)
Subjects: All areas of science except clinical medicine or dentistry.
Purpose: To strengthen Australia's national research and development capability by providing opportunities for researchers to undertake research of national and international significance and to broaden their research experience.

Eligibility: Applicants must have submitted their PhD thesis before commencement of the fellowship. No more than three years should have elapsed since the awarding of their PhD and an excellent academic record is required.
Level of Study: Postdoctorate.
Type: Fellowship.
Value: Australian $62,523, including 26 per cent on costs.
Length of Study: Three years.
Frequency: Annual.
Country of Study: Australia.
No. of awards offered: Approx. 55.
Application Procedure: Applicants must submit applications through an Australian host institution. It is the responsibility of the applicant to approach potential host institutions.
Closing Date: March 8th.
Funding: Government.
No. of awards given last year: 110.
No. of applicants last year: 449.
Additional Information: Candidates must obtain Australian citizenship or temporary residency status at the time of commencing the fellowship. Further information is available from the website.

ARC Projects - Professional Fellow (APF)
Subjects: All areas of science except clinical medicine or dentistry.
Purpose: To provide opportunities for outstanding researchers with proven international reputations to undertake research which is both of major importance in its field and of significant benefit to Australia. Senior Research Fellowships are the premier fellowships offered by the Australian Research Council and, consequently, are highly sought after and extremely competitive.
Eligibility: Open to researchers who normally have more than eight years of professional experience since the awarding of their PhD and extremely high profile expatriate Australians and non Australian researchers who wish to pursue their research in Australia.
Level of Study: Postdoctorate.
Type: Fellowship.
Value: Australian $103,511-126,098 including 26 per cent on costs.
Length of Study: Five years.
Frequency: Annual.
Country of Study: Australia.
No. of awards offered: Approx. 15.
Application Procedure: Applicants must submit applications through an Australian host institution. It is the responsibility of the applicant to approach potential host institutions.
Closing Date: March 8th.
Funding: Government.
No. of awards given last year: 23.
No. of applicants last year: 165.
Additional Information: Further information is available from the website.

Australian postgraduate Award to Industry
Subjects: This Scholarship is awarded under the Linkage projects Scheme to Australian Universities by the Australian Research Council in all areas of study other than clinical medicine, public health research and dental medicine.
Purpose: To provide industry based research training to prepare high-calibre postgraduate research students and to produce a national pool of world-class researchers to meet the needs of Australian industry.
Level of Study: Doctorate.
Type: Award.
Value: Australian $24,148 per year.
Length of Study: 3 years.
Frequency: Twice per year.
Study Establishment: Australian Universities.
Country of Study: Australia.
No. of awards offered: Variable, typically several hundred per year.
Application Procedure: Applications are submitted according to the Linkage-projects funding rules available on the ARC website (www.arc.gov.au).
Closing Date: Typically in May and November (See Funding Rules available on the ARC website).

Funding: Government.
No. of awards given last year: 461.
No. of applicants last year: 1012.

AUSTRALIAN-AMERICAN FULBRIGHT COMMISSION

PO Box 9541, Deakin, ACT 2600, Australia
Tel: (61) 2 6260 4460
Fax: (61) 2 6260 4461
Email: judithgamble@fulbright.com.au
www: http://www.fulbright.com.au
Contact: Ms Judith Gamble, Program Manager

The Australian-American Fulbright commission is a bi-national commission. The major objective of the commission is to further mutual understanding between the peoples of Australia and the United States through educational exchanges. The commission also provides information for Australians wishing to study in the United States.

Coral Sea Business Administration Scholarship
Subjects: Business or industry.
Purpose: To investigate a problem or opportunity relevant to Australian business or industry in the United States of America.
Eligibility: Open to resident Australian citizens who hold a degree or diploma. Candidates should have relevant business or industry experience. Applications are encouraged from those with a record of achievement poised for advancement in their professional field.
Level of Study: Professional development.
Type: Scholarship.
Value: Up to Australian $13,000.
Length of Study: Up to three months.
Frequency: Annual.
Country of Study: United States of America.
No. of awards offered: One.
Application Procedure: Applicants must complete and submit an application form along with three reference reports, already included in the application pack and documentation of citizenship and qualifications. Further information and application packs are available from the website.
Closing Date: August 31st.
Funding: Commercial.

Fulbright Awards
Subjects: All subjects.
Eligibility: Open to Australian postgraduate and postdoctoral students, senior Scholars and professionals.
Level of Study: Doctorate, Postdoctorate, Postgraduate, Professional development.
Value: Postgraduate students receive up to Australian $40,000 and postdoctoral fellows receive up to Australian $40,000. Senior scholars receive up to Australian $30,000 and professionals up to Australian $20,000.
Length of Study: Varies.
Frequency: Annual.
Country of Study: United States of America.
No. of awards offered: Up to 13.
Application Procedure: Applicants must complete and submit an application form along with three reference reports, already included in the application pack, documentation of citizenship and qualifications. Further information and application packs are available from the website.
Closing Date: August 31st.
Funding: Commercial, Government.

Fulbright Postdoctoral Fellowships
Subjects: All subjects.
Purpose: To enable those who have recently completed their PhD to conduct postdoctoral research, further their professional training or lecture at a university.
Eligibility: Open to Australian citizens by birth or naturalisation. Those holding dual United States of America and Australian citizenship are not eligible. Applicants should have recently completed their

PhD, normally less than three years prior to application, although those who have completed their PhD four or five years prior to application will be considered.
Level of Study: Postdoctorate.
Type: Fellowship.
Value: Up to Australian $40,000.
Length of Study: 3-12 months.
Frequency: Annual.
Study Establishment: A university, college, research establishment or reputable private practice.
Country of Study: United States of America.
No. of awards offered: One.
Application Procedure: Applicants must complete and submit an application form along with three reference reports, already included in the application pack, documentation of citizenship and qualifications. Further information and application packs are available from the website.
Closing Date: August 31st.
Funding: Government.

Fulbright Postgraduate Student Award for Engineering

Subjects: Engineering.
Purpose: To enable candidates to undertake an approved course of study for an American higher degree, or engage in research relevant to an Australian higher degree.
Eligibility: Open to Australian citizens. Those with dual United States of America and Australian citizenship are not eligible.
Level of Study: Doctorate, Postgraduate.
Value: Up to Australian $40,000.
Length of Study: 8-12 months funded or up to four years unfunded.
Frequency: Annual, if funds are available.
Study Establishment: An accredited institution.
Country of Study: United States of America.
No. of awards offered: One.
Application Procedure: Applicants must complete and submit an application form along with three reference reports, already included in the application pack, documentation of citizenship and qualifications. Further information and application packs are available from the website.
Closing Date: August 31st.
Funding: Commercial, Government.
Contributor: Clough Engineering Limited.

Fulbright Postgraduate Student Award for Science and Engineering

Subjects: Science and engineering.
Purpose: To enable candidates to undertake an approved course of study for an American higher degree, or to engage in research relevant to an Australian higher degree.
Eligibility: Open to Australian citizens. Those with dual United States of America and Australia citizenship are not eligible.
Level of Study: Doctorate, Postgraduate.
Value: Up to Australian $40,000.
Length of Study: 8-12 months funded or up to four years unfunded.
Frequency: Annual.
Study Establishment: An accredited institution.
Country of Study: United States of America.
No. of awards offered: One.
Application Procedure: Applicants must complete and submit an application form along with three reference reports, already included in the application pack, documentation of citizenship and qualifications. Further information and application packs are available from the website.
Closing Date: August 31st.
Funding: Commercial, Government.
Contributor: Billiton Pvt ltd.

Fulbright Postgraduate Student Award for the Visual and Performing Arts

Subjects: Fine and applied arts.
Purpose: To enable candidates to undertake a higher degree, or carry out research towards an Australian higher degree.

Eligibility: Open to Australian citizens. Those with dual United States of America and Australian citizenship are not eligible.
Level of Study: Doctorate, Postgraduate, Professional development.
Value: Up to Australian $40,000.
Length of Study: 8-12 months funded or up to four years unfunded.
Frequency: Annual.
Country of Study: United States of America.
No. of awards offered: One.
Application Procedure: Applicants must complete and submit an application form along with three reference reports, already included in the application pack, documentation of citizenship and qualifications. Further information and application packs are available from the website.
Closing Date: August 31st.
Funding: Commercial, Government.
Contributor: Anthony Joseph Pratt.

Fulbright Postgraduate Studentships

Subjects: All subjects.
Purpose: To enable students to undertake an approved course of study for an American higher degree or its equivalent, or to engage in research relevant to an Australian higher degree
Eligibility: Open to Australian citizens by birth or naturalisation. Those holding dual United States of America and Australian citizenship are not eligible.
Level of Study: Doctorate, Postgraduate.
Type: Studentship.
Value: Up to Australian $40,000.
Length of Study: 8-12 months funded, renewable for up to five years unfunded.
Frequency: Annual.
Study Establishment: An accredited institution.
Country of Study: United States of America.
No. of awards offered: Up to 15.
Application Procedure: Applicants must complete an application form and submit this with three reference reports, already included in the application pack, and documentation of citizenship and qualifications. Naturalised citizens must provide a certificate of Australian citizenship with their application, and native-born Australians must provide a copy of their birth certificate. Further information and application packs are available from the website.
Closing Date: August 31st.
Funding: Government.
Additional Information: As the award does not include any provision for maintenance payments, applicants must be able to demonstrate that they have sufficient financial resources to support themselves and any dependants during their stay in the United States of America.

Fulbright Professional Award

Subjects: All professional fields. Programmes should include an academic as well as a practical aspect.
Purpose: To support applicants undertaking a programme of professional development.
Eligibility: Open to resident Australian citizens with a record of achievement poised for advancement to a senior management or policy role. Those holding dual United States of America and Australian citizenship are not eligible.
Level of Study: Professional development.
Type: Award.
Value: Up to Australian $20,000.
Length of Study: Three-four months. Programmes of longer duration may be proposed but without additional funding.
Frequency: Annual.
Country of Study: United States of America.
No. of awards offered: One.
Application Procedure: Applicants must complete and submit an application form along with three reference reports, already included in the application pack, documentation of citizenship and qualifications. Further information and application packs are available from the website.
Closing Date: August 31st.
Funding: Government.

Fulbright Professional Award for Vocational Education and Training

Subjects: All subjects.
Purpose: To enable candidates to visit institutions or organisations and people in the United States of America from their own field.
Eligibility: Open to Australian citizens employed in the vocational education and training sector. Those holding dual United States of America and Australian citizenship are not eligible.
Level of Study: Professional development.
Value: Up to Australian $20,000.
Length of Study: Three-four months funded.
Frequency: Annual.
Country of Study: United States of America.
No. of awards offered: One.
Application Procedure: Applicants must complete and submit an application form along with three reference reports, already included in the application pack, documentation of citizenship and qualifications. Further information and application packs are available from the website.
Closing Date: August 31st.
Funding: Government.
Contributor: The Australian National Training Authority.
No. of awards given last year: 1.

Fulbright Senior Awards

Subjects: All subjects.
Purpose: To allow candidates to teach, undertake research, be an invited speaker or visit institutions within their field.
Eligibility: Open to Australian citizens by birth or naturalisation. Those holding dual United States of America and Australian citizenship are not eligible. Applicants should be either Scholars of established reputation working in an academic institution, who intend to teach or research in the United States of America, leaders in the arts eg. music, drama, visual arts or senior members of the academically based professions who are currently engaged in the private practise of their profession.
Level of Study: Professional development.
Value: Up to Australian $30,000.
Length of Study: Four-six months.
Frequency: Annual.
Study Establishment: A university, college, research establishment or reputable private organisation.
Country of Study: United States of America.
No. of awards offered: Two.
Application Procedure: Applicants must complete an application form and submit this with three reference reports, already included in the application pack, documentation of citizenship and qualifications. Further information and application packs are available from the website. Naturalised citizens must provide a certificate of Australian citizenship with their application, and native-born Australians must provide a copy of their birth certificate.
Closing Date: August 31st.
Funding: Government.

AUSTRIAN ACADEMY OF SCIENCES

Institute of Limnology, Mondseestraβe 9, A-5310, Mondsee, A-5310, Austria
Tel: (43) 623 240 79
Fax: (43) 623 235 78
Email: ipgl.mondsee@oeaw.ac.at
www: http://www.oeaw.ac.at/ipgl
Contact: Mr Gerold Winkler, IPGL Course Administrator

The Institute of Limnology of the Austrian Academy of Sciences performs ecological research on inland waters. The overall research goal is to understand the structure, function and dynamics of freshwater ecosystems. Although the Institute primarily conducts basic research, aspects of applied research are also considered. The Institute at Mondsee, located next to Salzburg, was established in 1981 and has a staff of 31, including 16 scientists. Currently the Institute's main fields of research are tropic interactions and food web structure in lakes.

Austrian Academy of Sciences MSc Course in Limnology and Wetlands Ecosystems

Subjects: Aquatic systems.
Purpose: To give an overall insight into aquatic systems through lectures, laboratory exercises, appropriate technology, group work, role play and field studies.
Eligibility: Open to candidates from developing countries who are 25-35 years of age, have a good working knowledge of English and have an academic degree in science, agriculture or veterinary medicine from a university or other recognised Institute of Higher Education. Applicants should have practical experience in at least one special subject in their field of professional training.
Level of Study: Postgraduate.
Type: Scholarship.
Value: US$626 paid monthly to cover food, lodging and personal needs plus free tuition, health insurance, study material and equipment for laboratory work, field work and travelling expenses.
Length of Study: 18 months.
Frequency: Annual.
Study Establishment: Institute for Limnology, Mondsee, Institute IHE, Delft, The Netherlands, Makerere University, Kampala, Uganda and Egerton University, Kenya, Czech Academy of Sciences, Trebon, Czech Republic, Austrian Universities and Federal Institutes.
Country of Study: Other.
No. of awards offered: Four.
Application Procedure: Applicants must obtain application forms and further information from the Austrian Diplomatic Mission, Cultural Attaché or Cultural Institute in the applicant's home country, or from the address shown. Application forms are also available from the website.
Closing Date: October 30th.
Funding: Government.
Contributor: The Austrian Development Co-operation.
No. of awards given last year: Four.
No. of applicants last year: 50.
Additional Information: No provisions are made for dependants. It is strongly advised that dependants do not accompany Fellows due to frequent moves during the course. Fellows must also provide their own transportation to and from Austria. Participants originating from certain developing countries will be further assisted by the Austrian Government so that travel expenses will be fully covered.

Austrian Academy of Sciences Postgraduate Course in Limnology

Subjects: Physical and chemical properties and processes in lakes and rivers, the role of bacteria, protozoa, phytoplankton, epilithic algae, water plants, zooplankton, macro-microbenthos and fish in aquatic ecosystems, system-ecological aspects for different aquatic systems, quantitative approaches, food web structures, tropic interactions and carbon and nitrogen budgets, the assessment of human impacts and their effect on the ecological integrity of aquatic systems, biological indicators, methods of fish stock assessment, estimation of fish growth and fish pond management, the sustainable use of tropical and temperate wetlands, the structure and function of groundwater ecosystems eg. groundwater pollution, protection and management, biomonitoring, reconstructing the history of lakes from paleolimnological investigations, the fundamentals of water quality assessment and control, bacteriological methods for examination of water and wastewater, and water as a source of disease for men and animals.
Purpose: To assist students studying the functioning of freshwater ecosystems.
Eligibility: Open to candidates from developing countries who are 25-35 years of age, have a good working knowledge of English and have an academic degree either in science, agriculture or veterinary medicine from a university or other recognised Institute of Higher Education. Applicants should have practical experience within at least one special subject in their field of professional training.
Level of Study: Postgraduate.
Type: Scholarship.
Value: US$626 paid monthly to cover food, lodging and personal needs plus free tuition, health insurance, study material and equipment for laboratory work, field work and travelling expenses.
Length of Study: Six months.

Frequency: Annual.
Study Establishment: Institute for Limnology, Mondsee Austrian Academy of Sciences, Czech Academy of Sciences, Federal Institutes of the Ministry of Agriculture, University of Agricultural Sciences in Vienna, the Technical University in Vienna and the University of Vienna.
Country of Study: Other.
No. of awards offered: Eight.
Application Procedure: Applicants must obtain application forms and further information from the Austrian Diplomatic Mission, Cultural Attaché or Cultural Institute in the applicant's home country, or from the address shown. Application forms are also available from the website.
Closing Date: November 30th.
Funding: Government.
Contributor: The Austrian Development Co-operation.
No. of awards given last year: Nine.
No. of applicants last year: 130.
Additional Information: No provisions are made for dependants. It is strongly advised that dependants do not accompany Fellows due to frequent moves during the course. Fellows must also provide their own transportation to and from Austria. Participants originating from certain developing countries will be further assisted by the Austrian Government so that travel expenses will be fully covered.

Institute of Limnology Postgraduate Training Fellowships

Subjects: Limnology.
Purpose: To give Fellows an overall insight into the various problems of limnology so that they may be better equipped to implement necessary research in their home countries in order to find solutions to their practical problems.
Eligibility: Open to candidates from developing countries who are 25-35 years of age, have a good working knowledge of English and have an academic degree either in science, agriculture or veterinary medicine from a university or other recognised Institute of Higher Education. Applicants should have practical experience within at least one special subject in their field of professional training.
Level of Study: Postgraduate.
Type: Fellowship.
Value: Please contact the organisation.
Length of Study: Six months.
Frequency: Annual.
Country of Study: Austria.
No. of awards offered: 12.
Application Procedure: Applicants must obtain application forms and further information from the Austrian Diplomatic Mission, Cultural Attaché or Cultural Institute in the applicant's home country, or from the address shown. Application forms are also available from the website.
Closing Date: November 30th.
Additional Information: No provisions are made for dependants. It is strongly advised that dependants do not accompany Fellows due to frequent moves during the course. Fellows must also provide their own transportation to and from Austria. Participants originating from certain developing countries will be further assisted by the Austrian Government so that travel expenses will be fully covered.

AUSTRIAN SCIENCE FUND (FWF)

Weyringergasse 35, Vienna, A-1040, Austria
Tel: (43) 150 567 40
Fax: (43) 150 567 39
Email: office@fwf.ac.at
www: http://www.fwf.ac.at
Contact: Scientific Administrator

The Austrian Science Fund (FWF) is Austria's central body for the promotion of basic research. It is equally committed to all branches of science and in all its activities is guided solely by the standards of the international scientific community. Its mission is the promotion of high quality basic research, education and training through research and scientific culture and knowledge transfer.

Charlotte Bühler Habilitation Fellowships

Subjects: All subjects.
Purpose: To support and encourage young female scientists to become future university lecturers.
Eligibility: Open to female scientists up to the age of 40, who are residents of Austria.
Level of Study: Postdoctorate.
Type: A variable number of fellowships.
Value: Please contact the organisation.
Length of Study: One-two years.
Frequency: Six times per year.
No. of awards offered: Varies.
Application Procedure: Applicants must complete an application form, available from the Austrian Science Fund, from the website or by email.
Closing Date: Applications are accepted at any time.
Funding: Government.

Erwin Schrödinger Fellowships

Subjects: All subjects.
Purpose: To offer citizens the opportunity to work in leading foreign research institutions and research programmes.
Eligibility: Open to highly qualified Austrian citizens up to the age of 35.
Level of Study: Postdoctorate.
Type: A variable number of fellowships.
Value: Please contact the organisation.
Length of Study: At least 10 months, to a maximum two years.
Frequency: Six times per year.
Study Establishment: Universities or research institutions.
Country of Study: Other.
No. of awards offered: Varies.
Application Procedure: Applicants must complete an application form, available from the Austrian Science Fund, from the website or by email.
Closing Date: Applications are accepted at any time.
Funding: Government.

Hertha Firnberg Research Positions for Women

Subjects: All subjects.
Purpose: To support and encourage young female scientists and expand scientific career opportunities for women.
Eligibility: Open to female scientists up to the age of 40 who are residents of Austria.
Level of Study: Postdoctorate.
Value: Please contact the organisation.
Length of Study: Three years.
Frequency: Annual.
Study Establishment: Any university.
Country of Study: Austria.
No. of awards offered: 10.
Application Procedure: Applicants must complete an application form, available from the Austrian Science Fund, from the website or by email.
Closing Date: December.
Funding: Government.

Lise Meitner Fellowships

Subjects: All subjects.
Purpose: To offer foreign scientists the opportunity to carry out research in Austria and to enhance the Austrian scientific community through international contacts.
Eligibility: Open to highly qualified foreign scientists up to the age of 40.
Level of Study: Postdoctorate.
Type: Fellowship.
Value: Please contact the organisation.
Length of Study: One-two years.
Frequency: Six times per year.
Study Establishment: Universities or research institutions.
Country of Study: Austria.
No. of awards offered: Varies.

Application Procedure: Applicants must complete an application form, available from the Austrian Science Fund, from the website or by email.
Closing Date: Applications are accepted at any time.
Funding: Government.

AUSTRO-AMERICAN ASSOCIATION OF BOSTON

47 Windermere Road, Auburndale, MA 02466-2521, United States of America
Tel: (1) 617 332 4055
Email: george_hauser@hms.harvard.edu
Contact: Professor George Hauser, Chairman of Scholarship Committee

Membership of the Austro-American Association of Boston is open to any individual interested in any aspect of Austrian history, economy, culture, politics and tourism.

Austro-American Association of Boston Scholarship

Subjects: Austrian cultural studies. The project must be related to Austrian culture in the broadest sense eg. humanities, literature, music, fine and applied arts, and film.
Purpose: To promote the appreciation and dissemination of Austrian culture.
Eligibility: Students only are eligible.
Level of Study: Unrestricted.
Type: Scholarship.
Value: US$1,000.
Frequency: Dependent on funds available.
Country of Study: Other.
No. of awards offered: One.
Application Procedure: Applicants must submit a detailed description of the project including budget, a curriculum vitae and two letters of recommendation from people familiar with the applicants achievement and potential.
Closing Date: April 15th.
Funding: Private.
Contributor: Members.
No. of awards given last year: One.
No. of applicants last year: Seven.
Additional Information: The award is limited to individuals living or studying in New England. Projects funded in the past have included the preparation of musical or dramatic performances, the facilitation of appropriate publications and research trips to Austria. Culture is defined to include the humanities and the arts. The recipient is expected to present the results of the project at an event of the Austro-American Association.

B.P. CONSERVATION PROGRAMME

Birdlife International/FFI, Wellbrook Court, Girton Road, Cambridge, Cambridgeshire, CB3 0NA, England
Fax: (44) (44) 1223 277200;
Email: bp-conservation-programme@birdlife.org.uk
www: http://conservation.bp.com
Contact: The Programme Manager

Since 1985, the BP Conservation Programme has supported and encouraged international conservation projects that address global conservation priorities at a local level. This is achieved through a Comprehensive System of advice, training and awards. The programme is managed through a partnership between BP, FFI, CI, WCS and Birdlife International.

BP Conservation Programme Awards

Subjects: Awards are presented annually to innovative international student conservation projects. All projects must - address a conservation priority & global importance; have local support and collaboration; and have a majority & team members in university education.

Purpose: To Research species, sites and habitats with the highest priority for biodiversity conservation worldwide + develop the skills + networks of future generations of young professionals.
Eligibility: Project must - address a globally recognised conservation priority, involve people, have host government approval, be run by teams of atleast 3 people, student led, over 50% student registered, last for less than 1 year, take place in Africa, Asia, Pacific, Middle East, Eastern Europe, Latin America.
Level of Study: Doctorate, Graduate, Postgraduate, Undergraduate.
Type: Team.
Value: Awards range from US$7,500-75,000.
Length of Study: Projects should be less than 1 year in length.
Frequency: Annual.
Country of Study: This is a global programme.
No. of awards offered: Up to 30 per year.
Application Procedure: Application forms are available from our website. The application deadline is October 31st each year, and applications should be made electronically.
Closing Date: 31st October.
Funding: Private.
Contributor: BP P.I.C., BirdLife International, Conservation International, WildLife Conservation Society and Fauna & Floura International.
No. of awards given last year: 32.
No. of applicants last year: 360.

For further information contact:

Email: bp-conservation-programme@birdlife.org.uk
www: http://conservation.bp.com

BACKCARE

16 Elmtree Road, Teddington
Middlesex TW11 8ST, England
Tel: (44) 20 8977 5474
Fax: (44) 20 8943 5318
Email: info@backcare.org.uk
www: http://www.backcare.org.uk
Contact: Mrs Nia Taylor, Chief Executive

BackCare is a national charity dedicated to educating people about how to avoid preventable back pain and to supporting those living with back pain. BackCare provides education and information through its publications, telephone helpline, local branches and website. It also funds research and campaigns to raise the profile of issues surrounding back pain.

BackCare Research Grants

Subjects: Studies related to back pain such as cause and diagnosis, identification of those most susceptible, identification of the main environmental and occupational hazards, trials of different methods of treatment to alleviate back pain, methods of preventing back pain, reduction in back pain disability by influencing health education, lifestyles, patient behaviour and clinical practice, social and psychological factors relevant to back pain, back pain and primary care.
Purpose: To reduce the incidances of and disability from back pain and to improve its treatment by gaining, through research, a better understanding of its manifestation and causes.
Eligibility: Open to appropriately qualified and experienced persons.
Level of Study: Postgraduate.
Type: Research grant.
Value: Varies, dependent on funds available. The association is not a major funding organisation and is unable to fund educational courses, attendance at meetings or conferences or the purchase of computers.
Length of Study: Up to two years.
Frequency: Dependent on funds available.
Study Establishment: Suitable establishments.
Country of Study: United Kingdom.
Application Procedure: Applicants must refer to the website for details of the application procedure.
Closing Date: June 1st or November 1st.
No. of awards given last year: 4.
No. of applicants last year: 20.

THE BANFF CENTRE

Arts Programming, Box 1020, Station 28, Banff, AB T1L 1H5, Canada
Tel: (1) 403 762 6180
Fax: (1) 403 762 6345
Email: arts_info@banffcentre.ca
www: http://www.banffcentre.ca
Contact: Ms Jane Bateman, Information Officer

The Banff Centre is a place for artists. Dedicated to lifelong learning and professional career development in the arts, the year round continuing education facility serves as a site and catalyst for creativity and experience. The Banff Centre is a public institution dedicated to creative excellence and is open to participation from the full diversity of Canadian and World artists.

Banff Centre Financial Assistance
Subjects: Studio art, photography, ceramics, performance art, video art, theatre production and design, stage management, opera, singing, dance, drama, music, writing, creative non fiction and cultural journalism, publishing, media arts, television and video, audio recording, computer applications, research, audio engineering work study, theatre production, design stage management work study, Aboriginal arts programmes in dance training, programme publicity and theatre production work study and screenwriting.
Purpose: To provide financial assistance to deserving artists for a residency at The Banff Centre.
Eligibility: Open to advanced students who have been accepted for a residency at the Banff Centre.
Level of Study: Postgraduate.
Type: Grant.
Value: A major contribution towards tuition.
Length of Study: Varies.
Frequency: Annual.
Study Establishment: The Banff Centre, Arts Programming.
Country of Study: Canada.
No. of awards offered: Varies.
Application Procedure: Applicants must submit a completed application form, accompanied by requested documentation.
Closing Date: Varies according to programme.
Funding: Government, Private.
Contributor: Individual donations and Banff Centre revenues.
No. of awards given last year: 1,000.

BATTEN DISEASE SUPPORT & RESEARCH ASSOCIATION

120 Humphries Drive, Suite 2, Reynoldsburg, OH 43068, United States of America
Tel: (1) 740 927 4298
Email: bdsra1@bdsra.org
www: http://www.bdsra.org
Contact: Mr Lance W Johnston, Executive Director

The Batten Disease Support & Research Association provides information, education, medical referrals and support to families that have children with NCL or Batten Disease. The Association also provides funding for research into Batten Disease.

Batten Disease Support and Research Association Research Grant Awards
Subjects: NCL or Batten Disease in the areas of genetics, biochemistry, molecular biology and related areas with the eventual goal of developing a viable treatment.
Purpose: To support work that identifies genes, proteins, enzymes or additional NCLs and the development novel therapeutic treatments.
Eligibility: There are no eligibility restrictions.
Level of Study: Doctorate, Postdoctorate, Research.
Value: Up to US$40,000.
Length of Study: Research is for one year and doctorate and post-doctorate are up to three years.
Frequency: Annual.
Country of Study: Any country.

Application Procedure: Applicants must visit the website or call for details for the submission of grants.
Closing Date: June 15th.
Funding: Private.
No. of awards given last year: 15.
No. of applicants last year: 27.

BECKMANN FOUNDATION

14501 SE 51st Street, Bellevue, WA, WA 98006-3509,
Tel: (1) 425 9571812
Contact: The Chairman

The priorities of the Beckmann Foundation are:1) to support undergraduate study abroad in Asia in the social sciences, humanities and professions 2) to confer The Beckmann Foundation Awards in recognition of outstanding patient care 3) to improve patient care and enhance patient safety in the hospital setting.

The Beckmann Foundation Award for Clinical Excellence
Purpose: To recognize outstanding patient care by a healthcare provider.
Eligibility: Selection by foundation trustees.
Level of Study: Unrestricted.
Type: Monetary Award.
Value: Monetary award.
Frequency: Dependent on funds available.
No. of awards offered: Varies.
Funding: Private.

BEIT MEMORIAL FELLOWSHIPS

c/o Institute of Molecular Medicine, John Radcliffe Hospital, Headington, Oxford, Oxfordshire OX3 9DS, England
Contact: Mrs Melanie J Goble, Administrative Secretary

Beit Memorial Fellowships for Medical Research
Subjects: Medical research.
Purpose: To promote research into medicine and allied sciences.
Eligibility: Open to postdoctoral level or medically qualified applicants who are graduates of any faculty at an approved university in the United Kingdom, or in any country which is or has been since 1910 a British Dominion, Protectorate or Mandated Territory.
Level of Study: Postdoctorate, Research.
Type: Fellowship.
Value: UK Salary plus research expenses.
Length of Study: Three years.
Frequency: Annual.
Study Establishment: An approved university, research institute or medical school.
Country of Study: United Kingdom or Ireland.
No. of awards offered: Approx. 4.
Application Procedure: Applicants must write for details.
Closing Date: March 1st.

BEIT TRUST (ZIMBABWE, ZAMBIA AND MALAWI)

PO Box 76, Chisipite, Harare Zimbabwe
Tel: (263) 4 496132
Fax: (263) 4 494046
Email: beitrust@africaonline.co.zw
Contact: T M Johnson, Representative

Beit Trust Postgraduate Fellowships
Subjects: All subjects.
Purpose: To support postgraduate study or research.
Eligibility: Open to persons under 30 years of age or 35 in the case of medical doctors, who are university graduates domiciled in Zambia, Zimbabwe or Malawi. Applicants must be nationals of those countries.
Level of Study: Postgraduate.
Type: Fellowship.

Value: A variable personal allowance and fees plus book, clothing, thesis and departure allowances.
Length of Study: One to three years depending on course sought.
Frequency: Annual.
Study Establishment: Approved universities and other institutions in South Africa, Britain and Ireland.
No. of awards offered: 10.
Application Procedure: Applicants must complete an application form.
Closing Date: September 30th.
Funding: Private.
No. of awards given last year: 8.
No. of applicants last year: 400.

THE BERMUDA BIOLOGICAL STATION FOR RESEARCH, INC.

Ferry Reach, St Georges GE 01, Bermuda
Tel: (1 441) 297 1880
Fax: (1 441) 297 8143
Email: education@bbsr.edu
www: http://www.bbsr.edu
Contact: Ms Gillian Hollis, Assistant to Director

Bermuda Biological Station for Research Grant In Aid

Subjects: Oceanography, biological and life sciences.
Purpose: To provide financial assistance to help defray the costs of in house charges for visiting scientists.
Level of Study: Unrestricted.
Type: Grant.
Value: Varies, Bermuda $500-3,000.
Length of Study: As required.
Frequency: Annual.
Study Establishment: The Bermuda Biological Station for Research, Inc.
Country of Study: Bermuda.
No. of awards offered: Varies.
Application Procedure: Applicants must submit grant proposals with their curriculum vitae and a budget. Proposals should be concise and contain an abstract, background, objectives, methods and the significance of proposed research
Closing Date: March 1st.
Funding: Private.
No. of awards given last year: 10.
No. of applicants last year: 10.

BERTHOLD LEIBINGER STIFTUNG GMBH

Johann-Maus-Straße 2, Ditzingen, D-71254, Germany
Tel: (49) 715 630 31559
Fax: (49) 715 630 3208
Email: innovationspreis@leibinger-stiftung.de
www: http://www.leibinger-stiftung.de
Contact: Mr Sven Ederer, Project Manager

Berthold Leibinger Innovationspreis

Subjects: Applied laser physics.
Purpose: To promote the advancement of science.
Eligibility: Open to individuals and project groups who have completed a scientific paper on applied laser physics in given topics and have documented it with public access.
Level of Study: Unrestricted.
Type: Prize.
Value: €20,000, €10,000 and €5,000.
Frequency: Every two years.
No. of awards offered: Three.
Application Procedure: Applicants must submit a completed application form, short documentation of up to 10 pages in accordance with stipulated structure, biography and explanation describing the context of work signed by a person recognised by the scientific establishment.

Suggestions for the prize must include the reasons for the price worthyness.
Closing Date: Varying, Refer to internet: www.leibinger-stiftung.de.
Funding: Private.
Contributor: Berthold Leibinger.
No. of awards given last year: Three.
No. of applicants last year: Approx. 30.

For further information contact:

Berthold Leibinger Stiftung GmbH, Innovationspreis, Postfach, Ditzingen, D-71252, Germany

BETA PHI MU

School of Information Studies
Florida State University, Tallahassee
FL 32306-2100, United States of America
Tel: (1) 850 644 3907
Fax: (1) 850 644 9763
Email: beta_phi_mu@lis.fsu.edu
www: www.beta-phi-mu.org
Contact: Mr F William Summers, Executive Secretary

Beta Phi Mu is a library and information studies society, founded in 1948, with over 25,000 graduates of the American Library Association accredited professional programmes initiated. Beta Phi Mu was founded at the University of Illinois, by a group of leading librarians and library educators. Aware of the notable achievements of honour societies in other professions, they believed that such a society would have much to offer librarianship and library education. The first initiation was held in the spring of 1949 at the University of Illinois.

Blanche E Woolls Scholarship for School Library Media Service

Subjects: Library science.
Purpose: To assist a new student who plans to become a school media specialist.
Eligibility: Open to beginning applicants who have not completed more than 12 hours by Autumn. Applicants must be accepted into an ALA-accredited programme and have three references.
Level of Study: Graduate.
Type: Scholarship.
Value: US$1,500.
Frequency: Annual.
Study Establishment: An ALA accredited school.
Country of Study: United States of America.
Application Procedure: Applicants must send three references and a completed application form, available by sending a stamped addressed envelope to Beta Phi Mu headquarters. Further details are available from the website.
Closing Date: March 15th.
No. of awards given last year: One.

Doctoral Dissertation Fellowship

Subjects: Library science or information studies.
Purpose: To support library and information science doctoral students who are working on their dissertations.
Eligibility: Must meet your own programs requirements.
Level of Study: Doctorate.
Type: Fellowship.
Value: US$2000.
Length of Study: 1 Year.
Frequency: Annual.
Country of Study: Any country.
No. of awards offered: 1.
Application Procedure: Applicants must provide a 300 word abstract of dissertation, a letter from their Dean or Director approving topic, complete all degree requirements except for writing and defense of dissertation.
Closing Date: 15 th March.
Funding: Private.
No. of awards given last year: 1.

Eugene Garfield Doctoral Dissertation Fellowship

Subjects: Library and information science.
Purpose: To fund library and information science doctoral student who are working on their dissertations.
Eligibility: All requirements for degree except writing and defense of dissertation have been completed.
Level of Study: Doctorate.
Type: Fellowship.
Value: US$3,000.
Frequency: Annual.
Study Establishment: Florida State University.
Country of Study: United States of America.
No. of awards offered: 6.
Application Procedure: Applicants should provide a personal statement from applicant not to exceed 500 words relating to post-dissertation plans, three letters of reference, a completed application form, abstract of dissertation (300 word limit) a letter of Approval of topic from Dean or Director.
Closing Date: March 15th.
Funding: Government.

Frank B Sessa Award

Subjects: Library science or information studies.
Purpose: To enable the continuing professional education of a Beta Phi Mu member.
Eligibility: Open to Beta Phi Mu members only.
Level of Study: Professional development.
Type: Scholarship.
Value: US$1,250.
Frequency: Annual.
Country of Study: Any country.
Application Procedure: Applicants must request an application form from Beta Phi Mu. Further details are available from the website.
Closing Date: March 15th.
Funding: Private.
No. of awards given last year: One.

Harold Lancour Scholarship For International Study

Subjects: Library science.
Purpose: To assist a librarian or library school student to undertake short-term research in a foreign country.
Eligibility: Open to nationals of any country.
Level of Study: Unrestricted.
Type: Scholarship.
Value: US$1,500.
Frequency: Annual.
Country of Study: Any country.
No. of awards offered: One.
Application Procedure: Applicants must write to Beta Phi Mu for further details, enclosing a stamped addressed envelope. Further details are available from the website.
Closing Date: March 15th.
Funding: Private.
No. of awards given last year: One.
No. of applicants last year: 10.

Sarah Rebecca Reed Award

Subjects: Library and information science.
Purpose: To assist a student beginning study in library and information science at an ALA-accredited school.
Eligibility: Open to beginning students who have not completed more than 12 hours by Autumn. Applicants must also be accepted on an ALA-accredited programme and have five references. Nationals of any country can apply.
Level of Study: Graduate.
Type: Scholarship.
Value: US$2,000.
Frequency: Annual.
Study Establishment: An ALA accredited school.
Country of Study: United States of America.
No. of awards offered: One.
Application Procedure: Applicants must request an application from the address shown, enclosing a stamped addressed envelope. Further details are also available from the website.

Closing Date: March 15th.
Funding: Private.
No. of awards given last year: One.
No. of applicants last year: 30.

BFWG CHARITABLE FOUNDATION (FORMERLY CROSBY HALL)

28 Great James Street, London, WC1N 3ES, England
Tel: (44) 20 7404 6447
Fax: (44) 20 7404 6505
Email: bfwg.charity@btinternet.com
www: http://www.bcfgrants.org.uk
Contact: Ms Jean V Collett, Grants Administrator

The BFWG Charitable Foundation offers grants to help women graduates with their living expenses (not fees) while registered for study or research at an approved Institute of Higher Education in Great Britain. The criteria for awarding grants are the proven needs of the applicants and their academic calibre. Grants are not usually awarded for one year courses.

BFWG Charitable Foundation Grants and Emergency Grants

Subjects: All subjects.
Purpose: To assist female graduates who have difficulty meeting their living expenses while studying or researching at approved Institutions of Higher Education in Great Britain. Emergency grants are to assist female graduates facing financial crises which may prevent them completing an academic year's study. Foundation grants are awarded to female students in their final year of a PhD.
Eligibility: Open to female graduates who have completed their first year of graduate study, doctoral study or research. Foundation grants are awarded to female students in their final year of a PhD. There is no restriction on nationality.
Level of Study: Doctorate, Postdoctorate, Postgraduate.
Type: Grant.
Value: Foundation Grants are up to UK£2,500 and Emergency Grants are up to UK£500.
Length of Study: Courses that exceed one year full-time in length.
Frequency: Foundation grants are offered annually and emergency grants are offered three times per year.
Study Establishment: Approved Institutes of Higher Education.
Country of Study: United Kingdom.
No. of awards offered: Approx. 50-60 Foundation Grants and approx. 50-60 Emergency Grants.
Application Procedure: Applicants must complete an application form and submit this with two references, a copy of their graduate certificate, evidence of acceptance for the year, a cheque for UK£12 or for UK£5 in the case of Emergency Grants, and a brief summary of thesis, if applicable, for Foundation Grants. Requests for application forms must be by Email or download from the website. Closing Dates are: 1) Foundation main grants by 14/5/04. 2) Emergency Grants end of April 04 - Date to be clarified. 3) TBB bursaries by 31/10/04.
Closing Date: The deadline for Foundation Grants is April 22nd, and the deadlines for Emergency Grants are February 15th, May 15th and November 15th.
Funding: Private.
Contributor: Investment income.
No. of awards given last year: 31 Foundation Grants and 44 Emergency Grants.
No. of applicants last year: 286 Foundation Grants and Emergency Grants.

BIAL FOUNDATION

Avenida da Siderurgia Nacional 4745 - 457, Mamede do Coronado, Portugal
Tel: (351) 22 986 6100
Fax: (351) 22 986 6190
Email: fundacao@bial.pt
www: http://www.bial.pt
Contact: Chairman

The BIAL Foundation, a non-profit making institution, was set up in 1994 with the aim of encouraging and supporting research focused on humans. It manages the BIAL award, one of the most distinguished awards for Health in Europe, and the BIAL Fellowship Programme which focuses largely on psychophysiology and parapsychology.

BIAL Award

Subjects: Medical Sciences and Clinical Medicine.
Purpose: To award intellectual written work in the subject area of health. To award work of a high quality in clinical practice.
Eligibility: At least one of the authors must be a physician.
Level of Study: Graduate.
Type: Prize.
Value: €230.000.
Frequency: Every two years.
No. of awards offered: Eight.
Application Procedure: Applicants must submit six copies of an original written specimen in either English or Portuguese to the Foundation. Further requirements are listed on its Regulation which will be forwarded to prospective applicants on request.
Closing Date: October 31st.
Funding: Private.
Contributor: The BIAL Foundation.
No. of awards given last year: Six.
No. of applicants last year: 31.

For further information contact:

Bial Foundation À Av. Da Siderurgia Nacional 4745-457 S. Mamede do Coronado, Portugal

THE BIBLIOGRAPHICAL SOCIETY

c/o Institute of English Studies, Room 304/ Senate House, Malet Street, London, WCIE 7HU, United Kingdom
Email: secretary@BibSoc.org.uk
www: http://www.bibsoc.org.uk
Contact: The Honorary Secretary

Founded in 1892 the Bibliographical Society is the senior learned society dealing with the study of the book and its history.

Antiquarian Booksellers Award

Subjects: Book trade and history of publishing.
Purpose: To support research into the history of the book trade and publishing industry.
Eligibility: Applicants may be of any age or nationality and need not be members of the Society.
Level of Study: Research.
Type: Grant.
Value: Up to US$1,500
Frequency: Annual.
No. of awards offered: 1.
Application Procedure: Apply to the Secretary of the Fellowships and Bursaries sub-committee.
Closing Date: 1st December for preceding year.
Funding: Private.
Contributor: Antiquarian Booksellers Association award.
Additional Information: Successful applicants will be asked to report briefly on the progress of their project by December of the same year.

For further information contact:

Edinburgh University, 5 Buccleuch Place, Edinburgh, EH8 9JX, United Kingdom
Email: b.bell@ed.ac.uk
Contact: Dr Bill Bell, Department of English Literature

Barry Bloomfield Bursary

Subjects: Research.
Purpose: To support research and honour Barry Bloomfield.
Eligibility: Applicants may be of any age or nationality and need not be members of the society.
Level of Study: Research.

Type: Bursary.
Value: Up to £2,000
Frequency: Annual.
Application Procedure: Applications by letter supported by letters from two referees familiar with the applicant's work.
Closing Date: 1st December preceding year.
Funding: Private.
Additional Information: Successful applicants will be asked to report briefly on the progress of their project by December of the same year.

Bibliographical Society Small Grants

Subjects: Bibliographic research.
Purpose: To support bibliographic research projects by providing small grants for specific purposes.
Eligibility: Applicants may be of any age or nationality and need not be members of the society.
Level of Study: Research.
Type: Grant.
Value: £50-£200
Frequency: All-year-round.
Application Procedure: Application by letter. If the applicant is registered for a research degree the application should be accompanied by a letter of support from their academic supervisor.
Closing Date: All year round basis
Funding: Private.

For further information contact:

Edinburg University, 5 Buccleuch Place, Edinburgh, EH8 9JX, United Kingdom
Contact: Dr Bill Bell, Department of English Literature

Falconer Madan Award

Subjects: Any subject connected with Oxford or available to research specifically in an Oxford library.
Purpose: To support a scholar who needs to research in an Oxford library.
Eligibility: Applicants may be any age or nationality.
Level of Study: Research.
Value: Up to £500 plus eligibility for accommodation at Wolfson College, Oxford.
Frequency: At discretion of society.
Study Establishment: An Oxford library
Country of Study: United Kingdom.
Application Procedure: Application by letter supported by letters from two referees familiar with the applicant's work.
Closing Date: 1st December preceding year.
Funding: Private.
Contributor: Oxford Bibliographical Society.
Additional Information: Successful applicants will be asked to report briefly on the progress of their project by December of the same year.

For further information contact:

Edinburg University, 5 Buccleuch Place, Edinburgh, EH8 9JX, United Kingdom
Contact: Dr Bill Bell, Department of English Literature

The Fredson Bowers Award

Subjects: Bibliographic research.
Purpose: To support a bibliographic research project in the name of Fredson Bowers.
Eligibility: Applicants may be of any age or nationality and need not be members of the society.
Level of Study: Research.
Type: Award.
Value: $1,500
Frequency: Annual.
Application Procedure: Applications by letter supported by letters from two referees familiar with the applicant's work.
Closing Date: 1st December preceding year.
Funding: Private.

Contributor: The Bibliographical Society of America.
Additional Information: Successful applicants will be asked to report briefly on the progress of their project by December of the same year.

Royal Oak Foundation Bursary

Subjects: Bibliographical research.
Purpose: To support bibliographical research projects involving work on National Trust Collections.
Eligibility: Applicants may be of any age or nationality and need not be members of the society.
Level of Study: Research.
Type: Bursary.
Value: £500
Frequency: Annual.
Application Procedure: Applications by letter supported by letters from two referees familiar with the applicant's work.
Closing Date: 1st December preceding year
Funding: Private.
Contributor: The National Trust.
Additional Information: Successful applicants will be asked to report briefly on the progress of their project by December of the same year.

For further information contact:

The Libraries Curator, The National Trust, 36 Queen Anne's Gate, London, SWIH 9AS, United Kingdom

BIBLIOGRAPHICAL SOCIETY OF AMERICA (BSA)

PO Box 1537, Lenox Hill Station
New York, NY 10021
United States of America
Tel: (1) 212 452 2710
Fax: (1) 212 452 2710
Email: bsa@bibsocamer.org
www: http://www.bibsocamer.org
Contact: Ms Michele Randall, Executive Secretary

The Bibliographical Society of America (BSA) invites applications for its annual short-term fellowships, which supports bibliographical inquiry as well as research in the history of the book trades and in publishing history.

BSA Fellowship Program

Subjects: Books or manuscripts as historical evidence. Topics may include establishing a text or studying the history of book production, publication, distribution, collecting or reading. Enumerative listings do not fall within the scope of this programme.
Purpose: To support bibliographical inquiry and research in the history of the book trades and publishing.
Eligibility: This programme is open to applicants of any nationality.
Level of Study: Doctorate, Postdoctorate, Postgraduate.
Type: Fellowship.
Value: US$2,000.
Length of Study: One month.
Frequency: Annual.
Country of Study: Any country.
No. of awards offered: 10.
Application Procedure: Applicants must complete an application form. The original plus six photocopies must be posted to the Executive Secretary of the Fellowship Committee at the Bibliographical Society of America.
Closing Date: December 1st.
Funding: Private.
No. of awards given last year: 10.
Additional Information: For applications contact the Executive Secretary or visit the BSA's website.

BILKENT UNIVERSITY

Faculty of Business Administration, MBA Programme, Office of the Dean, Ankara, 06800, Turkey
Tel: (90) 312 290 1596
Fax: (90) 312 266 4958
Email: fba@bilkent.edu.tr
www: http://www.bilkent.edu.tr
Contact: MBA Admissions Officer

Bilkent University is a non-profit research university. Courses are instructed in English. The University has more than 11,000 students and an international teaching staff of 1,000.

Bilkent University MBA Scholarships

Subjects: MBA.
Eligibility: Open to students who have a cumulative grade point average of 3.00 over 4.00 or higher in their studies or to students with a minimum GMAT score of 650.
Level of Study: MBA.
Type: Scholarship.
Value: Varies from tuition waiver to providing a stipend in addition to tuition waiver.
Length of Study: Two years.
Frequency: Annual.
Study Establishment: Bilkent University.
Country of Study: Turkey.
No. of awards offered: Varies.
Application Procedure: Applicants must apply for the MBA in the usual way and upon admission to the programme, scholarships of various degrees may be awarded.
Closing Date: Please contact the organisation.
Contributor: Bilkent University.
No. of awards given last year: 15.
No. of applicants last year: 55.
Additional Information: For second year students, a tuition waiver is possible based on their academic achievement during the first year.

BINATIONAL AGRICULTURAL RESEARCH AND DEVELOPMENT FUND (BARD)

PO Box 6, Bet Dagan, 50250, Israel
Tel: (972) 3 965 5133
Fax: (972) 3 966 2506
Email: bard@bard-isus.com
www: http://www.bard-isus.com
Contact: Dr Edo Chalutz, Executive Director

The United States of America/Israel Agricultural Research and Development Fund (BARD) promotes and supports agricultural research and development for the mutual benefits of both countries. BARD's income derives from an endowment fund contributed to in equal parts by the United States and Israel.

BARD Postdoctoral Fellowship

Subjects: Agriculture.
Purpose: To enable young scientists to acquire new skills and techniques while becoming professionally established in the agricultural community.
Eligibility: Open to United States or Israeli citizens who have completed a PhD in their home country within the last three years.
Level of Study: Postdoctorate.
Type: Fellowship.
Value: US$37,000.
Length of Study: One year, with the possibility of renewal for up to a further year.
Frequency: Annual.
Study Establishment: A non-profit research organisation, university or government.
Country of Study: Other.
No. of awards offered: 8-10.

Application Procedure: Applicants must complete an application form and submit this with a written proposal. Guidelines and application forms are available from either the office or most eligible institutions.
Closing Date: January 15th.
Funding: Government.
No. of awards given last year: Eight.
No. of applicants last year: 24.

BARD Research Grant
Subjects: Agriculture.
Purpose: To support agricultural research projects of mutual interest to the United States of America and Israel. Projects cover any or all phases of research and development, including integrated research and development problems and basic and applied research.
Eligibility: Open to public or non-profit research institutions that demonstrate the necessary research and development capabilities, and whose proposals meet the objectives and criteria set down.
Level of Study: Research.
Value: US$300,000.
Length of Study: Approx. three years.
Frequency: Annual.
Study Establishment: Non-profit research organisations, universities or governments.
Country of Study: Other.
No. of awards offered: Approx. 35.
Application Procedure: Applicants must complete an application form and submit this with a written proposal. Guidelines and application forms are available from either the office or most eligible institutions and from BARD's website.
Closing Date: September 1st.
Funding: Government.
Contributor: The government of Israel and the government of United States of America.
No. of awards given last year: 27.
No. of applicants last year: 122.

For further information contact:

Liaison Office, USDA-ARS5601 Sunnyside Avenue, Beltsville, MD 20705-5134, United States of America
Tel: (1) 301 504 4584
Fax: (1) 301 504 4619

THE BIOCHEMICAL SOCIETY

59 Portland Place, London, W1N 3AJ, England
Tel: (44) 20 7580 5530
Fax: (44) 20 7637 3626
Email: alison.mcwhinnie@biochemsoc.org
www: http://www.biochemsoc.org
Contact: Assistant Director, Personnel & Administration

Serving biochemistry and biochemists since 1911, the aim of the Biochemical Society is to promote the advancement of the science of biochemistry. It does so in the context of cellular and molecular life sciences. Through its regular scientific meetings with special interest groups, its publishing company Portland Press Limited and its policy, professional and education contacts, the Society provides a forum for current research to be shared.

Biochemical Society General Travel Fund
Subjects: Biochemistry and molecular life sciences.
Purpose: To support scientists who wish to attend scientific meetings, or make short visits to other laboratories.
Eligibility: Open to applicants who have been members of the Biochemical Society for at least one year and satisfy all other requirements.
Type: Travel grant.
Value: Varies.
Frequency: Other.
Country of Study: Other.
No. of awards offered: Varies.

Application Procedure: Applicants must submit five copies of a completed form which must demonstrate that the most cost effective form of transport and accommodation are to be utilised. All parts of the form must be completed. The application needs to be supported by a copy of registration costs and an abstract of presentation. Application forms can be obtained from the Assistant Director, Personnel and Administration or via the website.
Closing Date: January 1st, March 1st, May 1st, June 1st, September 1st and November 1st.
Funding: Private.

BIOTECHNOLOGY AND BIOLOGICAL SCIENCES RESEARCH COUNCIL (BBSRC)

Polaris House, North Star Avenue, Swindon, Wiltshire, SN2 1UH, England
Tel: (44) 1793 413345
Fax: (44) 1793 413382
Email: research-grant.applications@bbsrc.ac.uk
www: http://www.bbsrc.ac.uk
Contact: Mr Gareth Macdonald, Grants and Awards

The mission of the Biotechnology and Biological Sciences Research Council (BBSRC) is to promote and support basic, strategic applied research relating to the understanding and exploration of biological systems.

BBSRC Research Grants
Subjects: Multidisciplinary with emphasis on biological sciences, biotechnology and engineering.
Purpose: To support research in United Kingdom universities, colleges and other higher education institutions. BBSRC seeks to develop and sustain high quality research within its range of interest and to encourage links between university researchers and researchers at BBSRC sponsored institutes.
Eligibility: Applicants must be resident in the United Kingdom. They must hold an appropriate appointment in a United Kingdom university, college or other similar higher education institution or BBSRC Institute.
Level of Study: Postdoctorate, Research.
Type: Research grant.
Value: Varies.
Frequency: Ongoing.
Study Establishment: A United Kingdom educational establishment, a BBSRC sponsored institute or a BBSRC academic analogue.
Country of Study: United Kingdom.
No. of awards offered: Varies.
Application Procedure: Applicants must complete an application form. Rules, procedures and application forms are available on the BBSRC website and from the BBSRC Secretariat and Liaison Branch.
Closing Date: Applications are accepted at any time.
Funding: Government.
Additional Information: Full details are available on the website.

BIRTH DEFECTS FOUNDATION

BDF Centre, Hemlock Way, Cannock, Staffordshire, WS11 7GF, England
Tel: (44) 1543 468888
Fax: (44) 1543 468999
Email: sbrown@bdfcharity.co.uk
www: http://www.bdfcharity.co.uk
Contact: Mrs Sheila Brown, Chief Executive Officer

The Births Defects Foundation (BDF) is a United Kingdom registered charity, whose mission is to improve child health, aid families and raise awareness. BDF is committed to funding basic, clinical and ethically approved research into the causes, prevention and treatment of birth defects.

Birth Defects Foundation Full and Small Grants
Subjects: The aetiology, prevention or treatment of birth defects.
Level of Study: Graduate, Postgraduate.
Type: Fellowship.

Value: Varies. Small grants up to UK£10,000, full grants up to UK£80,000.
Length of Study: Varies.
Frequency: Other.
Country of Study: Other.
No. of awards offered: Varies.
Application Procedure: Applicants must fill in an application form for the full grant. Application for the small grant is by a brief proposal and then by application form if the proposal is of interest to the Foundation.
Closing Date: For full grants, applicants should consult advertisements and the website in June and July for the closing date. There is no closing date for small grants.
Contributor: Charitable trading activity.
No. of awards given last year: 14.
No. of applicants last year: Over 30.

BLISS

68 South Lambeth Road, London, SW8 1RL, England
Tel: (44) 0870 770 0337
Fax: (44) 0870 770 0338
Email: information@bliss.org.uk
www: http://www.bliss.org.uk
Contact: Mr Rob Williams, Chief Executive

BLISS is dedicated to make sure that more babies born prematurely or sick at birth survive and that each one has the best possible quality of life.

BLISS Research Awards

Subjects: Neonatal medicine and appropriate family support, development of aids and equipment.
Purpose: To support researchers whose project work will make a practical difference to the care of premature and sick newborn babies.
Eligibility: We do not accept applicants for clinical research.
Level of Study: Research.
Type: Grant.
Value: Variable.
Length of Study: Variable.
Frequency: Apply as needed.
Study Establishment: Any suitable in the United Kingdom.
Country of Study: United Kingdom.
Application Procedure: Please contact Bonnie Green at BLISS.
Funding: Private.

BOARD OF ARCHITECTS OF NEW SOUTH WALES

3 Manning Street, Potts Point, NSW 2011, Australia
Tel: (61) 2 9356 4900
Fax: (61) 2 9357 4780
Email: mail@boarch.nsw.gov.au
www: http://boarch.nsw.gov.au
Contact: Ms Mae Cruz, Deputy Registrar

Board of Architects of New South Wales Research Grant

Subjects: Any architectural topic approved by the board.
Purpose: To provide assistance to those wishing to undertake research on a topic approved by the Board in order to contribute to the advancement of architecture.
Eligibility: Open to candidates who are registered as architects in New South Wales.
Level of Study: Professional development.
Type: Research grant.
Value: Australian $12,000.
Length of Study: One year.
Frequency: Every two years.
Country of Study: Australia.
No. of awards offered: One.
Application Procedure: Applicants must write for details.
Closing Date: July 30th.
Funding: Government.

No. of awards given last year: None.
Additional Information: A report is to be submitted upon completion of tenure.

Byera Hadley Travelling Scholarships

Subjects: Architecture.
Purpose: To allow candidates to undertake a course of study, research or other activity approved by the Board as contributing to the advancement of architecture.
Eligibility: Open to graduates or students of four accredited schools of architecture in New South Wales. Applicants must be Australian citizens.
Level of Study: Graduate, Research.
Type: Scholarship.
Value: The total value of the combined awards is Australian $65,000, comprised of two Registered Architect awards at Australian $30,000 and Australian $11,000, one graduand award at Australian $8,000 and four student awards at Australian $4,000 each.
Frequency: Annual.
Country of Study: Any country.
No. of awards offered: Seven.
Application Procedure: Applicants must write for details.
Closing Date: The deadline for all is July 30th.
Funding: Private.
Contributor: A bequest from the estate of the late Byera Hadley an Australian architect.
No. of awards given last year: Six.
No. of applicants last year: 19.
Additional Information: A report suitable for publication must be submitted within three years of the date of the award.

BOLOGNA CENTER OF THE JOHNS HOPKINS UNIVERSITY

Via Belmeloro 11, Bologna, I-40126, Italy
Tel: (39) 051 291 7811
Fax: (39) 051 228 505
Email: admission@jhubc.it
www: http://www.jhubc.it
Contact: Ms Bernadette O'Toole, Assistant Registrar

The Bologna Center is an integral part of Paul H Nitze School of Advanced International Studies (SAIS), one of the leading United States graduate schools devoted to the study of international relations. The programme seeks to merge the wisdom of universities, business and labour with the knowledge and expertise of those currently engaged in government, foreign affairs and international economic practice.

Paul H Nitze School of Advanced International Studies (SAIS) Financial Aid and Fellowships

Subjects: International economics, European studies and international relations. In addition to fundamental courses, international economics covers European economic integration, environmental and resource economics, commercial policies, corporate finance, economic development and public sector economics. European studies examines history, economics, contemporary politics and culture, as well as demographic and enlargement issues. International relations explores international law, international non governmental organisations, human rights, conflict management, ethnic conflict and security issues.
Purpose: To facilitate graduate study.
Eligibility: Open to students who have completed their first university degree. Students who are in the process of completing their first degree may apply providing they are awarded the degree prior to entry to the Bologna Center in the Autumn. All candidates must have an excellent command of written and spoken English and ideally have some background knowledge in economics, history, political or other social sciences. All fellowships and financial aid awards are based on need as well as academic merit.
Level of Study: Postgraduate.
Type: Fellowship.

Value: Varies. Grants may cover partial or, occasionally, full tuition. Maintenance stipends are rarely provided.
Frequency: Annual.
Study Establishment: The Bologna Center of the Johns Hopkins University and the Paul H Nitze School of Advanced International Studies.
Country of Study: Italy.
No. of awards offered: Varies, depending on funds available.
Application Procedure: Applicants must submit an application form and financial aid application. Certain donor organisations require a separate application. Admission and financial aid for United States citizens and permanent residents is administered by SAIS in Washington and all enquiries from United States students should be addressed to the Admissions Office in Washington. Financial aid and admission for non United States students is administered in Bologna and all enquiries from non United States students should be addressed to the Registrar's Office in Bologna.
Closing Date: The deadline for United States applicants is January 15th, and February 1st for non United States students.
Funding: Commercial, Government, Private.
No. of applicants last year: 600.
Additional Information: A few courses are also offered in United States of America foreign policy, as well as Latin American, African and Mediterranean issues. Language instruction is offered in the major Modern European languages. Special fellowships administered by the Bologna Center on behalf of other donor organisations have certain restrictions, which vary depending upon the donor. Many of the fellowships available to non United States students are provided by government ministries and other European organisations and are reserved for citizens of the country providing the fellowship.

For further information-contact:

Admissions Office1740 Massachusetts Avenue North West, Washington, DC 20036, United States of America
Email: admission@mail.jhuwash.jhu.edu

THE BOSTON SOCIETY OF ARCHITECTS (BSA)

52 Broad Street, 4th Floor, Boston, MA 02109-4301, United States of America
Tel: (1) 617 061 1133
Fax: (1) 617 951 0845
Email: kmiller@architects.org
www: http://www.architects.org
Contact: Awards Committee

The Boston Society of Architects (BSA) is the regional and professional association of over 3,000 architects and 1,000 affiliate members. The BSA's affiliate members include engineers, contractors, clients or owners, public officials, other allied professionals, students and lay people. The BSA administers many programmes that enhance the public understanding of design as well as the practice of architecture.

Rotch Traveling Scholarship
Subjects: Architecture.
Purpose: To provide young architects with the opportunity to travel and study in foreign countries.
Eligibility: Open to United States of America architects who will be under 35 years of age on March 10th of the year of the competition and who have a degree from an accredited school of architecture plus one full year of professional experience in an architectural office.
Level of Study: Professional development.
Type: Fellowship.
Value: A stipend of US$35,000.
Length of Study: Nine months.
Frequency: Annual.
Country of Study: Other.
No. of awards offered: One-two.
Application Procedure: Applicants must complete an application form, available on written request.
Closing Date: January 1st for application requests.

Funding: Private.
Additional Information: The Scholar is selected through a two stage design competition. The one year of professional experience required should be completed prior to the beginning of the preliminary competition. Scholars are required to return to the United States of America after the duration of the scholarship and submit a report of their travels.

BRADFORD CHAMBER OF COMMERCE AND INDUSTRY

Devere House, Vicar Lane, Little Germany, Bradford, Yorkshire, BD1 5AH, England
Tel: (44) 1274 772777
Fax: (44) 1274 772777
Email: john.speak@bradfordchamber.co.uk
www: http://www.bradfordchamber.co.uk
Contact: Nick Barker, Trust Administrator

The Bradford Chamber of Commerce and Industry represents member companies in the Bradford and district area. It works with local partners to develop the economic health of the district and has a major voice within the British Chamber of Commerce movement in order to promote the needs of local business on a national basis.

John Speak Trust Scholarships
Subjects: Modern languages.
Purpose: To promote British trade abroad by assisting people in perfecting their basic knowledge of a foreign language.
Eligibility: Open to British born nationals intending to follow a career connected with the export trade in the United Kingdom. Applicants must be over 18 years of age with a sound, basic knowledge of at least one language.
Level of Study: Professional development.
Type: Scholarship.
Value: Sufficient to cover reasonable living expenses plus an amount towards the cost of travel.
Length of Study: Between three months and one full academic year abroad depending on the circumstances and each candidate's level of knowledge of the language. It is non renewable.
Frequency: Three times each year.
Study Establishment: A recognised college or university.
Country of Study: Other.
No. of awards offered: 10.
Application Procedure: Applicants must complete an application form and undertake an interview.
Closing Date: February 28th, May 31st or October 31st.
Funding: Private.
No. of awards given last year: 10.
No. of applicants last year: 14.

BRAIN TUMOR SOCIETY

Post Office Box 5225, Carefree, AZ 85377, United States of America
Tel: (1) 800 770 8287
Email: grants@tbts.org
www: www.tbts.org
Contact: Cami Treadwell, Research Manager

The Brain Tumor Society exists to find a cure for brain tumors. It strives to improve the quality of life of brain tumor patients and their families. It disseminates educational information and provides access to psycho-social support. It raises funds to advance carefully selected scientific research projects, improve clinical care and find a cure.

BTS Research Grant
Subjects: Brain tumours.
Purpose: Scientific research aimed at finding cure for brain tumours, and support students working to a doctoral thesis in the subject.
Level of Study: Doctorate, Postgraduate.
Type: Scholarship.
Value: US$100,000 per year.
Length of Study: Two years.

Country of Study: United States of America.
Application Procedure: Please check website.
Closing Date: April 16th
Funding: Private.

BRANDON UNIVERSITY

School of Music, Brandon, MB, R7A 6A9, Canada
Tel: (1) 204 727 7388
Fax: (1) 204 728 6839
Email: music@brandonu.ca
www: http://www.brandonu.ca
Contact: Professor Robert Richardson, Graduate Music Programmes

Brandon University is linked to the international community through the exchange of people and ideas. At an informal level, faculty may collaborate with researchers from around the world in pursuit of knowledge in their respective disciplines. In addition, the university has a number of joint programmes and exchange opportunities with institutions in other countries.

Brandon University Graduate Assistantships
Subjects: Music education, performance and literature.
Purpose: To afford graduate students the opportunity to gain professional experience while studying and to provide monetary assistance.
Eligibility: Open to candidates with a Bachelor's degree in music or music education and with a minimum grade point average of 3.0 during their final year.
Level of Study: Graduate.
Value: Up to Canadian $6,500.
Length of Study: Normally two years.
Frequency: Annual.
Study Establishment: The School of Music, Brandon University.
Country of Study: Canada.
No. of awards offered: Four-eight.
Application Procedure: Applicants must complete an application form.
Closing Date: May 1st.
Additional Information: Candidates for the performance and literature major are also required to show, by audition, high potential as performers. For the music education major, candidates should have adequate related professional experience, preferably teaching.

BREAD LOAF WRITER'S CONFERENCE

Middlebury College, Middlebury, VT 05753, United States of America
Tel: (1) 802 443 5286
Fax: (1) 802 443 2087
Email: blwc@mail.middlebury.edu
www: http://www.middlebury.edu/blwc
Contact: Mrs Carol Knauss

The Bread Loaf Writer's Conference's central purpose is to create a community in which a dialogue of converging literary voices can be sustained.

Bread Loaf Writer's Conference Fellowships and Scholarships
Subjects: Fiction, non fiction and poetry.
Purpose: To provide recognition for both established writers and writers who show unusual promise, and an atmosphere in which writing can be discussed and criticised intensively.
Eligibility: Candidates for fellowships are assumed to have published a book or to have had a book length manuscript accepted for publication. Candidates for scholarship assistance will have had articles published in periodicals. There are no restrictions regarding nationality or citizenship. All writing must be submitted in English.
Level of Study: Unrestricted.
Type: Other.
Value: Fellowships carry no cash value but cover all regular charges at the Conference. Scholarships cover full or partial tuition.
Length of Study: 11 days.

Frequency: Annual.
Study Establishment: The Bread Loaf campus, Middlebury College, Vermont 05753.
Country of Study: United States of America.
No. of awards offered: Varies.
Application Procedure: Applicants must complete an application form and submit a writing sample.
Closing Date: March 1st.
Funding: Private.
No. of awards given last year: 35.
No. of applicants last year: 800.

For further information contact:

Bread Loaf writer's conference, Middlebury College, Middlebury, VT 05753.

BREAST CANCER CAMPAIGN

Clifton Centre, 110 Clifton Street, London, EC2A 4HT, England
Tel: (44) 20 7749 3700
Fax: (44) 20 7749 3701
Email: info@bcc-uk.org
www: http://www.breastcancercampaign.org
Contact: Grants Officer Chairman of the Trustees

The Breast Cancer Campaign is the only charity that specialises in funding independent breast cancer research throughout the United Kingdom. The organisation currently fund 42 projects, representing UK£3.5 million worth of research funds.

Breast Cancer Campaign Project Grants
Subjects: Breast cancer research including prevention, causes, diagnosis, treatment and management.
Purpose: To improve diagnosis and treatment of cancer, to achieve a better understanding of how it develops and ultimately to cure or prevent the disease.
Level of Study: Postdoctorate, Postgraduate.
Type: Grant.
Value: No more than UK£50,000 per year.
Length of Study: Up to three years.
Frequency: Twice a year.
Country of Study: United Kingdom.
No. of awards offered: Variable.
Application Procedure: Applicants must complete an application form. These can be obtained from the campaign office and the website, by email to research@bcc-uk.org or by telephoning (44) 20 7749 3732.
Closing Date: The beginning of January and July. Please contact the campaign office for the precise dates.
No. of awards given last year: 14.
No. of applicants last year: 72.

BREAST CANCER RESEARCH TRUST (BCRT)

48 Wayneflete Tower Avenue, Esher Place, Esher, Surrey, KT10 8QG, England
Tel: (44) 1372 463235
Fax: (44) 1372 463235
Email: bcrtrust@aol.com
Contact: Ms Rosemary Sutcliffe, Secretary

The Breast Cancer Research Trust (BCRT) exists solely to raise funds for breast cancer research at a scientific laboratory level into the case of breast cancer. The project has to be within a recognised medical unit as individuals are not funded.

Breast Cancer Research Grant
Subjects: Breast cancer.
Purpose: To study the causation of breast cancer.
Level of Study: Research.
Type: Research grant.

Value: Varies between UK£10,000-35,000 per year.
Length of Study: One-two years.
Frequency: Annual.
Study Establishment: A recognised medical unit.
Country of Study: United Kingdom.
Application Procedure: Applicants must request an application form.
Closing Date: The end of October.
Funding: Private.
No. of awards given last year: 4.
No. of applicants last year: 7.
Additional Information: Total spending on grants was UK£98,547.

For further information contact:

Breast Cancer Research Trust, 48 Wayneflete Tower Avenue, Esher, Surrey KT10 8Q9, England

THE BRITISH ACADEMY

10 Carlton House Terrace, London
SW1Y 5AH, England
Tel: (44) 20 7969 5200
Fax: (44) 20 7969 5300
Email: secretary@britac.ac.uk
www: http://www.britac.ac.uk
Contact: Ms Jane Lyddon, Assistant Secretary (International Relations)

The British Academy is the premier national learned society in the United Kingdom devoted to the promotion of advanced research and scholarship in the humanities and social sciences.

British Academy 44th International Congress of Americanists Fund

Subjects: Latin American studies.
Purpose: To enable British scholars to visit Latin America or Latin American scholars to visit Britain.
Eligibility: Open to British or Latin American Scholars.
Level of Study: Postgraduate.
Type: Travel grant.
Value: Awards do not generally exceed UK£1,000.
Frequency: Annual.
Country of Study: Other.
Application Procedure: Applications must be made by letter to the International Relations Department with appropriate supporting documentation.
Closing Date: Please contact the Academy.
Funding: Government, Private.

British Academy Ancient Persia Fund

Subjects: Iranian, Central Asian studies in the pre-Islamic period.
Purpose: To encourage and support the study of Iranian or Central Asian studies in the pre-Islamic period. Grants are offered towards travel costs.
Eligibility: Preference will be given to Scholars undertaking archaeological research or engaged in an archaeological project.
Level of Study: Postdoctorate.
Type: Travel grant.
Value: Awards do not generally exceed UK£500.
Length of Study: Tenable for one year.
Frequency: Annual.
Country of Study: Any country.
Application Procedure: Applicants must contact the Research Grants Department for a small research grant form. In cases where an applicant seeks both travel and other costs, a single application form should be used. Applicants should not complete two separate forms when submitting a dual application to the fund for travel and to the research grants fund for other elements of a project.
Closing Date: Please contact the Academy.
Funding: Private.
Additional Information: For United Kingdom residents, an application to this fund for travel costs may be combined with an application for a small research grant for other costs, up to a total of UK£5,000.

British Academy Archaeology Grants

Subjects: Archaeology.
Purpose: To support all archaeological fieldwork, together with related general and scientific post excavation work.
Eligibility: Open to individuals and organisations based in the United Kingdom and undertaking academic archaeological research at post-doctoral level.
Level of Study: Postdoctorate.
Type: Grant.
Value: Up to UK£20,000.
Frequency: Annual.
Country of Study: Any country.
No. of awards offered: Varies.
Closing Date: December 31st.
Funding: Government.
No. of awards given last year: 78.
No. of applicants last year: 118.

British Academy Awards

Subjects: Humanities and social sciences.
Purpose: To support individual research projects. The Academy also offers support for conference attendance, research posts and international collaborative projects.
Eligibility: Open to residents of the United Kingdom who specialise in humanities and social sciences. However, eligibility requirements vary depending on the scheme.
Level of Study: Postdoctorate.
Type: Other.
Value: From UK£400-20,000 depending on the scheme.
Frequency: Other.
No. of awards offered: Varies according to scheme.
Application Procedure: Applicants must consult the website for scheme details and application forms.
Closing Date: Please contact the Academy.
Funding: Government, Private.
No. of awards given last year: 1,200.
No. of applicants last year: 2,000.
Additional Information: Applicants should visit the website for further information.

British Academy Block Grants

Subjects: All subjects.
Purpose: The Academy will consider applications from learned societies or national subject associations for block grants to support attendance by a group of British scholars at a major international congress abroad.
Type: Travel grant.
Value: Grants are unlikely to exceed UK£10,000.
Application Procedure: Applications should be made at least one year in advance of the congress on a block grant application form.
Closing Date: Please contact the Academy.
Additional Information: A contribution will be made to travel expenses only and no contribution can be made to accommodation expenses or conference registration fees. If a block grant is approved, the learned society or subject association will make the decisions on the individual grants, but grants may only be made to those delivering a paper. The Academy will not accept applications from individual Scholars for conferences supported by a block grant.

British Academy Elie Kedourie Memorial Fund

Subjects: Middle Eastern, modern European history and political thought.
Purpose: To promote the study of Middle Eastern, modern European history or history of political thought.
Eligibility: Awards are offered to support any aspect of research, including travel and publication.
Level of Study: Postdoctorate.
Type: Research grant.
Frequency: Annual.
Country of Study: Any country.
Application Procedure: Applications must be made to the Research Grants Department on a small research grants application form, available from the Department.

Closing Date: Please contact the Academy.
Additional Information: Funds are not available to support travel to or attendance at conferences, workshops or seminars, either in the United Kingdom or elsewhere.

British Academy K C Wong Fellowhip

Subjects: Cultural studies.
Purpose: To enable outstanding Chinese scholars to undertake periods of research in British institutions in collaboration with British colleagues.
Eligibility: Candidates must be nationals of the People's Republic of China and Scholars of postdoctoral or equivalent status with a good command of spoken and written English.
Level of Study: Postdoctorate.
Type: Fellowship.
Frequency: Annual, if funds are available.
Study Establishment: Any approved United Kingdom institution.
Country of Study: United Kingdom.
Application Procedure: Applications must be made on the K C Wong Fellowship form available from institutions in China and from the Academy's International Relations Department.
Closing Date: Please contact the Academy.
Contributor: The K C Wong Education Foundation.

British Academy Larger Research Grants

Subjects: Humanities - ie. history in the widest sense (including the history of art, music, ideas, science, and of politics and economics), language and literature, law, philosophy, and religious studies.
Purpose: To support research projects at postdoctoral level which are large in scale and extended in duration.
Eligibility: Applicants must be resident in the UK.
Level of Study: Postdoctorate.
Type: Grant.
Value: Normal upper limit of UK£20,000 in any one year.
Frequency: Annual.
Country of Study: Any country.
No. of awards offered: Varies.
Closing Date: September 30th.
Funding: Government.
No. of awards given last year: 35.
No. of applicants last year: 85.

British Academy Overseas Conference Grants

Subjects: Humanities and social sciences.
Purpose: To help meet the costs of travel by British scholars to overseas conferences or similar gatherings. Awards will be contributions to travel expenses only.
Eligibility: Open to Scholars presenting an academic paper. Applicants must be resident in the United Kingdom and of postdoctoral or equivalent status. Postgraduate students are not eligible to apply.
Level of Study: Postdoctorate.
Type: Grant.
Value: Usually restricted to a maximum of UK£800.
Frequency: Four times per year.
Country of Study: Any country.
No. of awards offered: Varies.
Application Procedure: Applicants must submit applications on the prescribed form.
Closing Date: End of September, November, February and April.
Funding: Government.
No. of awards given last year: 354.

British Academy Postdoctoral Fellowships

Subjects: Teacher training.
Purpose: To enable outstanding young scholars to obtain experience of research and teaching in the University environment, which will strengthen their curriculum vitae and improve their prospects of obtaining permanent posts by the end of the fellowship.
Eligibility: Applicants must have obtained their doctorate no earlier than October 1st 1999 and must not have held an established teaching post in an Institute of Higher Education.
Level of Study: Postdoctorate.
Type: Fellowship.

Value: Salary starting at UK£18,185.
Length of Study: Tenable for three years and not renewable.
Frequency: Annual.
Country of Study: United Kingdom.
No. of awards offered: Up to 30.
Application Procedure: Applications must be made on the Postdoctoral Fellowship application form.
Closing Date: Please contact the Academy.

British Academy Reckitt Travelling Fellowships in Archaeology

Subjects: Archaeology.
Purpose: To enable scholars who have recently obtained a doctorate to broaden their archaeological horizons and expertise through travel abroad.
Eligibility: These awards are offered to candidates who have already obtained a doctorate in archaeology from a United Kingdom university. Candidates who have already been appointed to a full-time lecturing post are not excluded. Applicants must be ordinarily resident in the United Kingdom.
Level of Study: Postdoctorate.
Type: Travel grant.
Value: A stipend of UK£8,000 plus additional research expenses to cover the costs of overseas travel and maintenance, up to a maximum award of UK£12,000.
Frequency: Annual.
No. of awards offered: Two.
Application Procedure: Applications must be made to the Research Posts Department on the Reckitt application form.
Closing Date: Please contact the Academy.
Funding: Private.

British Academy Sino-British Fellowship Trust

Subjects: Cultural studies.
Purpose: To support individual or co-operative research projects.
Eligibility: Research may be conducted either in the United Kingdom or China, or in both countries and must involve person to person contact.
Type: Research grant.
Frequency: Annual, if funds are available.
Country of Study: Other.
Application Procedure: Applicants must contact the International Relations Department for advice.
Closing Date: Please contact the Academy.
Funding: Private.
Contributor: Sino-British Fellowship Trust SBFT.
Additional Information: Successful applications will be forwarded to the SBFT for approval in the Autumn of each year. It should be noted that the Academy will be unable to offer support should the SBFT decline to confirm funding.

British Academy Small Personal Research Grants

Subjects: Humanities and social sciences.
Purpose: For original research at postdoctoral level.
Eligibility: Applicants must be resident in the United Kingdom and be of postdoctoral or equivalent status. Postgraduate students are not eligible to apply.
Level of Study: Postdoctorate.
Type: Grant.
Value: Maximum UK£5,000, but on average UK£2,500. Grants are personal to the applicant, and solely for the costs of the research itself. There is no element of salary or maintenance to the applicant.
Frequency: Four times per year.
Country of Study: Any country.
No. of awards offered: Up to 500.
Application Procedure: Applicants must complete an application form, available from the British Academy. Two references are required.
Closing Date: End of September, November, February and April.
Funding: Government.
No. of awards given last year: 532.
No. of applicants last year: 430.

British Academy Special International Symposia
Subjects: All subjects.
Purpose: To support special joint symposia between the British Academy and a foreign partner institution.
Eligibility: The event should either be a single symposium, normally in the United Kingdom, but possibly abroad, or a pair of meetings, one in each country. Proposals for a longer series of meetings will not be considered. It is expected that there will be a degree of joint, although not necessarily matching, funding from the partner organisation abroad.
Type: Other.
Value: Up to UK£10,000. The maximum sum would be offered only in exceptional circumstances.
Frequency: Annual.
Country of Study: Any country.
Application Procedure: The British partner should apply on the Special International Symposium application form available from the International Relations Department.
Closing Date: Please contact the Academy.

British Academy Stein-Arnold Exploration Fund
Subjects: History, geography and the arts.
Purpose: To encourage research into the antiquities or historical geography or early history or arts of those parts of Asia which come within the sphere of the ancient civilisations of India, China and Iran, including Central Asia.
Eligibility: Research should be as far as possible by means of exploratory work. Applicants must be British or Hungarian subjects.
Type: Research grant.
Value: Awards do not generally exceed UK£2,500.
Frequency: Annual.
Application Procedure: Applications must be made to the Research Grants Department on the small research grant application form.
Closing Date: Please contact the Academy.
Funding: Private.

British Academy Visiting Professorships for Overseas Scholars
Subjects: Humanities and social sciences.
Purpose: To enable distinguished scholars from overseas to spend time in the United Kingdom to pursue their personal research.
Eligibility: Candidates for nomination must be either established Scholars of distinction or younger people who show great promise and who would benefit from time to pursue their research in the United Kingdom.
Level of Study: Postdoctorate.
Type: Other.
Value: Travel expenses to the United Kingdom and subsistence up to a maximum of UK£700 per week. Normal maximum length of visit one month, but applications for longer periods will be considered.
Frequency: Annual.
Country of Study: United Kingdom.
No. of awards offered: Varies.
Application Procedure: Applicants must submit applications on the prescribed form, by the British sponsor. Sponsors must undertake to make all administrative arrangements on behalf of the visitor. Applications are considered in March, in respect of visits to take place during the following financial year. Applications directly from foreign Scholars will not be accepted.
Closing Date: December 31st. It may be possible to entertain applications at other times of the year, but the Academy's aim is to allocate the available funds in one go.
Funding: Government.
No. of awards given last year: 42.

British Academy Worldwide Congress Grant
Subjects: Humanities and social sciences.
Purpose: To help meet the costs of organising major international congresses in Britain, but only where the congress is one of an established series and where it is clearly the British turn to host the conference.
Eligibility: Open to organisers of worldwide congresses in the United Kingdom.

Level of Study: Postdoctorate.
Type: Grant.
Value: Between UK£10,000 and UK£15,000 a year for two or three years prior to conference.
Frequency: Dependent on funds available.
Country of Study: United Kingdom.
Application Procedure: Applicants must apply on the prescribed forms, there is a two-stage consideration procedure.
Closing Date: None specified. Consult the Research Grants Department, at the British Academy, for guidance.
Funding: Government.
No. of awards given last year: One.
No. of applicants last year: One.

British Conference Grants
Subjects: Humanities and social sciences.
Purpose: To help meet the expenses of conferences held in Britain.
Eligibility: Applicants must be resident in the United Kingdom and be of postdoctoral or equivalent status.
Level of Study: Postdoctorate.
Type: Grant.
Value: Between UK£500 and UK£2,000.
Country of Study: United Kingdom.
Application Procedure: Applicants must submit applications on the prescribed form.
Closing Date: End of September, November, February and April.
Funding: Government.
No. of awards given last year: 151.

Elisabeth Barker Fund
Subjects: Recent European history, particularly of Eastern and Central Europe.
Purpose: To support research or small conferences.
Eligibility: Open to Scholars of postdoctoral or equivalent status ordinarily resident in the United Kingdom. Applicants need not be British nationals. Applications must be made by a British resident and not a foreign scholar.
Level of Study: Postdoctorate.
Value: Up to UK£1,000.
Frequency: Other.
Country of Study: Other.
No. of awards offered: Up to six.
Closing Date: September 30th, December 31st, April 30th.
Funding: Private.

Neil Ker Memorial Fund
Subjects: Western medieval manuscripts, particularly those of British interest.
Purpose: To promote the study of Western medieval manuscripts.
Eligibility: Open to both younger and established Scholars of any nationality for research at postdoctoral level.
Level of Study: Postdoctorate.
Type: Grant.
Value: Approx. UK£1,500.
Frequency: Annual.
Country of Study: Any country.
No. of awards offered: Varies, depending on funds available.
Application Procedure: Applicants must complete an application form.
Closing Date: End of February.
Funding: Private.
No. of awards given last year: Six.
No. of applicants last year: 10.

Thank-Offering to Britain Fellowships
Subjects: Topics of an economic, industrial, social, political, literary or historical character relating to the British Isles. Preference will be given to projects in the modern period.
Purpose: To fund a research fellowship.
Eligibility: Open to persons ordinarily resident in the United Kingdom and of postdoctoral status. Candidates should be in mid-career and must be employed at a United Kingdom university in an established teaching post.

Level of Study: Postdoctorate.
Type: Fellowship.
Value: Within the first two points of the Grade A university lecturers' scale. The award also pays for a replacement to undertake the teaching and administrative duties of the award holders for one year.
Length of Study: Normally for one year.
Frequency: Annual.
Country of Study: United Kingdom.
No. of awards offered: One.
Application Procedure: Applicants must submit applications on the prescribed form.
Closing Date: July 31st.
Funding: Private.
Contributor: Association of Jewish Refugees.
No. of awards given last year: One.
No. of applicants last year: 78.

BRITISH ASSOCIATION FOR AMERICAN STUDIES (BAAS)

Department of Cultural Studies, University of Central Lancashire, Preston, PR1 2HE, England
Tel: (44) 1772 893020
Fax: (44) 1772 892924
Email: hrsmacpherson@uclan.ac.uk
www: http://www.baas.ac.uk
Contact: Dr Heidi Macpherson, Secretary (STA)

The British Association for American Studies (BAAS), established in 1955, promotes research and teaching in all aspects of American studies. The Association organises annual conferences and specialist regional meetings for students, teachers and researchers. The publications produced are The Journal of American Studies with Cambridge University Press, BAAS Paperbacks with Edinburgh University Press and British Records Relating to America in Microform with Microform Publishing.

BAAS Short Term Awards
Subjects: United States of American culture and society.
Purpose: To fund travel to the United States of America for short-term research projects.
Eligibility: Open to residents in the United Kingdom. Preference is given to young postgraduates and to members of BAAS.
Level of Study: Doctorate, Postdoctorate, Postgraduate, Professional development.
Type: Award.
Value: UK£500.
Frequency: Annual.
Country of Study: United States of America.
No. of awards offered: 5-10.
Application Procedure: Applicants must complete an application form.
Closing Date: November 30th.
No. of awards given last year: Six.
No. of applicants last year: 35.
Additional Information: Further information is available on request.

BRITISH ASSOCIATION FOR CANADIAN STUDIES (BACS)

21 George Square, Edinburgh, EH8 9LD, Scotland
Tel: (44) 131 662 1117
Fax: (44) 131 662 1118
Email: jodie.robson@ed.ac.uk
www: http://www.canadian-studies.net
Contact: Ms Jodie Robson

In response to the growing academic interest in Canada, the British Association for Canadian Studies (BACS) was established in 1975. Its aim is to foster teaching and research on Canada and Canadian issues by locating study resources in Britain, facilitating travel and exchange schemes for professorial staff, and ensuring that the expertise of Canadian scholars who visit the United Kingdom is put to effective use. Principal activities include the publication of The British Journal of Canadian Studies and the BACS Newsletter, and organisation of the Association's annual multidisciplinary conference, which attracts scholars from Canada and Europe as well as from the United Kingdom.

Molson Research Awards
Subjects: Canadian studies, humanities and social sciences.
Purpose: To encourage and fund visits to Canada directly related to the applicant's actual or proposed teaching or research. The awards are intended to increase contact between academics and other scholars in Canada and the United Kingdom, and to assist in the preparation of teaching about Canada.
Eligibility: Open to academics from universities, colleges of higher education and polytechnics of the United Kingdom. Applicants must be citizens or long-term residents of the United Kingdom. Priority will be given to BACS members.
Level of Study: Doctorate, Postdoctorate.
Type: Travel grant.
Value: Up to UK£500.
Frequency: Annual
Study Establishment: Universities or research institutions.
Country of Study: Canada.
No. of awards offered: Three-five.
Application Procedure: Applicants must complete an application form and submit this with a covering letter, curriculum vitae and the names of two referees.
Closing Date: October 1st, February 1st or May 1st.
No. of awards given last year: Six.
No. of applicants last year: 20.
Additional Information: The BACS administers these awards on behalf of the Foundation for Canadian Studies in the United Kingdom.

Prix du Québec
Subjects: Humanities and social sciences.
Purpose: To assist British academics carrying out research related to Québec.
Eligibility: Open to citizens or long-term residents of the United Kingdom.
Level of Study: Doctorate, Postdoctorate, Professional development.
Type: Award.
Value: UK£1,000.
Frequency: Dependent on funds available.
Study Establishment: Universities, research institutions and schools.
Country of Study: Canada.
No. of awards offered: Two, one award to doctoral and postdoctoral students and one award to full-time teaching staff.
Application Procedure: Applicants must contact Jodie Robson, Administrative Secretary of BACS, for application guidelines.
Closing Date: March 1st.
Funding: Government.
Contributor: The Office of the Government of Québec in the United Kingdom.
No. of awards given last year: 2.
Additional Information: The award also seeks to encourage projects which incorporate Québec in a comparative approach. The Québec component must be more than 50 per cent.

BRITISH ASSOCIATION OF DERMATOLOGISTS (BAD)

19 Fitzroy Square, London, W1T 6EH, England
Tel: (44) 20 7383 0266
Fax: (44) 20 7388 5263
Email: debbie@bad.org.uk
www: http://www.bad.org.uk
Contact: Ms Debbie Senner, Fellowship Co-ordinator

Founded in 1920, the British Association of Dermatologists is the only professional organisation representing skin specialists in the United Kingdom and Ireland. The objectives of BAD are to stimulate and promote appropriate medical and scientific research into the causes, effects and treatment of skin disease, to publish the results, to collect, collate and publish information relevant to dermatology and hold conferences, meetings and seminars for the purposes of promoting and disseminating information, to publish the British Journal of Dermatology, to advise government and other professional bodies on dermatology and to relieve distress by promoting improvements in dermatological care. A key function of the BAD is the provision of both postgraduate training and continuing medical education (CME). Patient information and support is provided by printed literature, written responses to personal enquiries and the BAD's close work with the many patient support groups.

BAD Consultant Sabbatical Fellowship

Subjects: Dermatology.
Purpose: To allow consultant dermatologists in the United Kingdom to devote a period of not less than two months to study or research.
Eligibility: Open to consultant dermatologists appointed for more than five years who are members of the British Association of Dermatology. The entire duration of the fellowship must be devoted to the work proposed at the centre indicated on the application form. Applicants must obtain endorsement from the Head of Department and their proposed centre for the Sabbatical Fellowship and their consultant colleagues in the dermatology department.
Level of Study: Research.
Type: Fellowship.
Value: Up to UK£12,500.
Length of Study: More than two months.
Frequency: Annual.
Country of Study: United Kingdom.
No. of awards offered: One.
Application Procedure: Applicants must complete and submit a curriculum vitae, together with six copies of the entire application. A typewritten report of approximately 750 words must be submitted to the BAD no later than six weeks after completion of the fellowship. The proposed start and finish dates must be clearly indicated and the Association informed of any changes. All additional funds applied for or received must be disclosed on the application form and any funds subsequently received must be disclosed in the report upon completion of the fellowship.
Closing Date: March 20th.
Funding: Private.
Contributor: British Association of Dermatology (BAD).
No. of awards given last year: None.
No. of applicants last year: None.
Additional Information: Any publications arising as a result of the fellowship must give due acknowledgement to the fellowship and sponsor as applicable. The British Association of Dermatology reserves the right to vary the amount and conditions of the fellowship or to terminate the fellowship. The name of the winner will be published in the BAD or Dowling club newsletter and may be reported and recorded in the minutes of the annual general meeting.

BAD Study Fellowship

Subjects: Dermatology.
Purpose: To enable associate members, consultant dermatologists and trainee dermatologists to study or participate in research activities.
Eligibility: Open to members of the British Association of Dermatology. Trainees must obtain endorsements from their Head of Department and from the Head of Department of the proposed centre for the Study Fellowship.
Level of Study: Research.
Type: Fellowship.
Value: UK£3,750.
Length of Study: Three months.
Frequency: Annual.
Country of Study: United Kingdom.
No. of awards offered: One.
Application Procedure: Application forms must be completed and submitted with a curriculum vitae on the appropriate form together with six photocopies of the entire application. The proposed start and finish dates must be clearly indicated and the Association informed of any changes. A typewritten report of approximately 750 words must be

submitted to the BAD no later than six weeks after the completion of the Study Fellowship. All additional funds applied for or received must be disclosed on the application form and any funds subsequently received must be disclosed in the report upon completion of the study fellowship.
Closing Date: March 20th.
Funding: Private.
Contributor: British Association of Dermatologists.
No. of awards given last year: One.
No. of applicants last year: Two.
Additional Information: Any publications arising as a result of the fellowship must give due acknowledgement to the fellowship and sponsor as applicable. The British Association of Dermatology reserves the right to vary the amount and conditions of the fellowship or to terminate the fellowship. The name of the winner will be published in the BAD newsletter or Dowling club newsletter and may be reported and recorded in the minutes of the annual general meeting.

BAD/DC Travelling Fellowship

Subjects: Dermatology.
Purpose: To provide funding to attend a meeting of educational value.
Eligibility: Open to members of the British Association of Dermatology or Dowling club, trainees in dermatology, consultants or individuals of equivalent academic status working in dermatology in the United Kingdom.
Level of Study: Professional development.
Type: Fellowship.
Value: Between UK£250-UK£750.
Frequency: Twice a year.
Country of Study: Any country.
No. of awards offered: Varies.
Application Procedure: Applications must be completed and submitted with a curriculum vitae together with six copies of the entire application. A typewritten report of 200-400 words must be submitted to the British Association of Dermatology no later than one month after completion of the fellowship. Applications can be made for only one meeting for the value of the fellowship. All additional funds applied for or received must be disclosed on the application form and any funds subsequently received must be disclosed in the report upon completion of the fellowship.
Closing Date: March 20th for Spring allocations and September 20th for Autumn applications.
Funding: Commercial.
Contributor: Pharmaceutical industry.
No. of awards given last year: 10 in March and 14 in Autumn.
No. of applicants last year: 15 in March, 24 in September.
Additional Information: Any publications arising as a result of the fellowship must give due acknowledgement to the fellowship and sponsor as applicable. The British Association of Dermatology reserves the right to vary the amount and conditions of the fellowship or to terminate the fellowship. The name of the winner will be published in the BAD or Dowling club newsletter and may be reported and recorded in the minutes of the annual general meeting. There are also four awards made from the American Academy of Dermatology for applicants to attend the American Academy of Dermatology meeting.

Geoffrey Dowling Fellowship

Subjects: Dermatology.
Purpose: To encourage the attainment of evident merit before becoming established in senior academic and professional posts.
Eligibility: Open to members of the British Association of Dermatologists.
Level of Study: Research.
Type: Fellowship.
Value: UK£25,000.
Length of Study: One to two years.
Frequency: Annual.
Country of Study: Other.
No. of awards offered: One.
Application Procedure: Applicants must submit an application form with a curriculum vitae and six copies of the entire application. A typewritten report of 2,000 words must be submitted no later than one month after completion of the fellowship and all additional funds

applied for or received must be disclosed on the application form. Any funds subsequently received must be disclosed in the report upon completion of the fellowship.
Closing Date: March 20th.
Funding: Private.
Contributor: British Association of Dermatology.
No. of awards given last year: One.
No. of applicants last year: Four.
Additional Information: Any publications arising as a result of the fellowship must give due acknowledgement to the fellowship and sponsor as applicable. The British Association of Dermatology reserves the right to vary the amount and conditions of the fellowship or to terminate the fellowship. The name of the winner will be published in the BAD or Dowling club newsletter and may be reported and recorded in the minutes of the annual general meeting.

Roger Harman African Travelling Fellowship
Subjects: Dermatological education.
Purpose: To enable dermatologists in training or in permanent posts to visit Africa for educational purposes.
Eligibility: Open to members of the British Association of Dermatology.
Level of Study: Professional development.
Type: Fellowship.
Value: UK£10,000.
Frequency: Annual.
Study Establishment: Moshi or other approved centre in Africa.
Country of Study: Africa.
No. of awards offered: One.
Application Procedure: Applicants must complete and submit an application form together with a curriculum vitae and six copies of the entire application. All additional funds applied for or received must be disclosed in the report upon completion of the study fellowship.
Closing Date: March 20th.
Funding: Private.
Contributor: British Association of Dermatology.
No. of awards given last year: One.
No. of applicants last year: One.
Additional Information: Any publications arising as a result of the fellowship must give due acknowledgement to the fellowship and sponsor as applicable. The British Association of Dermatology reserves the right to vary the amount and conditions of the fellowship or to terminate the fellowship. The name of the winner will be published in the BAD or Dowling club newsletter and may be reported and recorded in the minutes of the annual general meeting.

BRITISH ASSOCIATION OF PLASTIC SURGEONS (BAPS)

The Royal College of Surgeons, 35-43 Lincoln's Inn Fields, London, WC2A 3PE, England
Tel: (44) 20 7831 5161
Fax: (44) 20 7831 4041
Email: secretariat@baps.co.uk
www: http://www.baps.co.uk
Contact: Ms Angela Rausch, Course & Committee Administrator

The British Association of Plastic Surgeons was founded in 1946 with the objects of relieving sickness and protecting and preserving public health by the promotion and development of plastic surgery. The aim of the association is to advance education in the field of plastic surgery.

BAPS Fellowship
Subjects: Plastic surgery.
Purpose: To enable senior trainees from developing countries to obtain further training and experience in plastic surgery.
Eligibility: Open to senior trainees in plastic surgery, living and working in developing countries.
Level of Study: Professional development.
Type: Fellowship.
Value: UK£500 per month.

Length of Study: Six months.
Frequency: Annual.
Study Establishment: Hospital plastic surgery units.
Country of Study: Other.
No. of awards offered: Two.
Application Procedure: Application details are available on request from the British Association of Plastic Surgeons.
Closing Date: 30 June.
Funding: Private.
Contributor: British Association of Plastic Surgery.
No. of awards given last year: 1.
No. of applicants last year: 4.

BAPS Student Bursaries
Subjects: Plastic surgery.
Purpose: To help medical students to cover expenses of travel and research related to plastic surgery.
Eligibility: Medical students in the UK.
Level of Study: Predoctorate.
Type: Bursary.
Value: UK£500.
Length of Study: Varies.
Frequency: Annual.
Study Establishment: Hospital plastic surgery units or research laboratories.
Country of Study: Any country.
No. of awards offered: 10.
Application Procedure: Application forms available on request from the British Association of Plastic Surgeons.
Closing Date: 31st December.
Funding: Private.
Contributor: British Association of Plastic Surgeons.
No. of awards given last year: 10.
No. of applicants last year: 46.

BAPS Travelling Bursary
Subjects: Plastic surgery.
Purpose: To enable a plastic surgeon in the United Kingdom to study new techniques abroad.
Eligibility: Open to members of the Association who are either specialist registrars in years four to six, enrolled in a recognised training programme or who have not had more than three years as consultant plastic surgeons.
Level of Study: Professional development.
Type: Bursary.
Value: Up to UK£5,000.
Length of Study: Varies.
Frequency: Annual.
Study Establishment: Any approved hospital plastic surgery units.
Country of Study: Other.
No. of awards offered: Three.
Application Procedure: Applicants must complete an application form and submit this with a proposed itinerary giving details of costs and reasons for wanting to attend a particular unit. A curriculum vitae of no more than two pages must also be submitted.
Closing Date: December 31st.
Funding: Private.
Contributor: The British Association of Plastic Surgeons.
No. of applicants last year: Five.

Paton/Maser Memorial Fund
Subjects: Plastic surgery.
Purpose: To provide funds towards research projects.
Eligibility: Open to consultants and specialist registrars in plastic surgery working in the British Isles.
Level of Study: Research.
Type: Research grant.
Value: UK£5,000.
Length of Study: Varies.
Frequency: Annual.
Study Establishment: A hospital or research laboratory.
Country of Study: Other.
No. of awards offered: One.

Application Procedure: Applicants must submit a letter of application with a copy of research protocol and a breakdown of costs.
Closing Date: December 31st.
Funding: Private.
Contributor: The British Association of Plastic Surgeons.
No. of awards given last year: One.
No. of applicants last year: One.

THE BRITISH COUNCIL

British Embassy, 3100 Massachusetts Avenue North West,
Washington, DC 20008, United States of America
Tel: (1) 202 588 7874
Fax: (1) 202 588 7918
Email: jonathan.bird@britishcouncil-usa.org
www: http://www.britishcouncil-usa.org
Contact: Mr Jonathan Bird, Scholarships & Exchanges Assistant

The British Council is Britain's international network for education, culture and development services. It co-ordinates the Marshall Scholarships Programme in the United States of America.

Atlantic Fellowships in Public Policy
Subjects: Any area of public policy.
Purpose: To provide United States mid-career professionals with an opportunity to study and gain practical experience in the United Kingdom in a wide variety of public policy areas. It was established in 1994 to commemorate the fiftieth anniversary of D-Day and the United States contribution to the liberation of Europe.
Eligibility: Open to United States mid course professionals, who are working in the area of public policy.
Level of Study: Professional development.
Type: Fellowship.
Value: Up to US$3,300 per month. The award covers a stipend, not intended to match Fellows' salary in the United States travel to and from the United Kingdom, institutional fees and family allowance.
Length of Study: 3-10 months.
Frequency: Annual.
Country of Study: United Kingdom.
No. of awards offered: Up to 10.
Application Procedure: Applicants must submit an application form and recommendation letters by the deadline announced in the Spring. Details are available from the website.
Closing Date: December of each year.
Contributor: The British Government.
No. of awards given last year: 12.
No. of applicants last year: 50.

BRITISH DENTAL ASSOCIATION

Dentsply Student Support Fund
64 Wimpole Street, London
W1G 8YS, England
Tel: (44) 20 7563 4174
Fax: (44) 20 7563 4556
Email: awards@bda.org
www: www.bda.org
Contact: Mr Richard Gott, Awards and Marketing Officer

The British Dental Association is the national professional association for dentists. With over 20,000 members, the Association strives to enhance the science, arts and ethics of dentistry, improve the nation's oral health and promote the interests of its members.

BDA / Dentsply Scholarship Fund
Subjects: Dentistry Maxillo-facial Surgery.
Purpose: To give financial assistance to students who are in severe financial hardship. Only open to 4th & 5th year BDS students or postgraduates.
Eligibility: Open to BDA members only.
Level of Study: Graduate, Postgraduate.
Type: Scholarship.
Value: Varies.

Frequency: Annual.
Country of Study: United Kingdom.
No. of awards offered: Varies, up to 10.
Application Procedure: Applicants must complete and submit application forms, accompanied by an academic reference or supporting letter. Application forms can be found in the student section of the BDA website.
Closing Date: 4th Jan & 1st Aug.
Funding: Commercial.
Contributor: Dentsply UK Ltd.
No. of awards given last year: 7.
No. of applicants last year: 30.

BRITISH ECOLOGICAL SOCIETY (BES)

26 Blades Court, Putney, London
SW15 2NU, England
Tel: (44) 20 8871 9797
Fax: (44) 20 8871 9779
Email: general@ecology.demon.co.uk
www: http://www.britishecologicalsociety.org
Contact: Grants Management Officer

As a learned society and registered charity, the British Ecological Society (BES) is an independent organisation receiving no outside funds. The aims of the Society are to promote the science of ecology through research, publications and conferences and to use the findings of such research to educate the public and to influence policy decisions which involve ecological matters.

Anne Keymer Prize
Subjects: Ecology.
Purpose: To award the best oral presentation by a postgraduate student at the Winter Meeting.
Eligibility: Open to current postgraduates or postgraduates who have recently finished their course and are currently presenting work undertaken when they were still a student.
Level of Study: Postgraduate.
Type: Prize.
Value: UK£200.
Frequency: Annual.
Application Procedure: Applicants must write for information or visit the website.
Additional Information: The candidate will be expected to present a paper at the BES Winter Meeting. The prize is named in memory of Anne Keymer who was one of the first winners of the prize in 1981. Anne was a member of the Editorial Board of the Journal of Animal Ecology, and was an exemplary scholar, teacher and citizen in her discipline.

Attendance at Courses and Workshops Co-sponsored by the BES
Subjects: Ecology.
Purpose: To provide support to allow participants to attend specialist courses, workshops, or meetings organised under the auspices of the European Ecological Federation or the Tropical Biology Association.
Eligibility: Eligibility is advertised in the 'Bulletin'.
Level of Study: Postgraduate, Research.
Value: Travel and accommodation expenses for participants, who should be prepared to play a full part in the meetings, including the possibility of giving a seminar on their work.
Application Procedure: Application details can be found in each of the journals.
Closing Date: Advertised in the 'Bulletin'.
Additional Information: Courses will vary from year to year and will be advertised in the Bulletin and in the EEF Newsletter as and when details become available.

BES Attendance at Conferences Run by Other Organisations
Subjects: Ecology.
Purpose: To aid attendance at the triennial European Ecological Congress and the INTECOL Congress.

Eligibility: Open to ecologists including students wishing to attend events co-sponsored by BES or for which the Society has elected to provide support. Preference is given to those individuals who are presenting a paper or poster at the conference.
Type: Travel grant.
Frequency: Every four years.
Application Procedure: Applicants must refer to the 'Bulletin' where the special application procedures are advertised.
Additional Information: Further information can be found on the website.

BES Award for the Best Paper by a Young Author

Subjects: Ecology.
Purpose: To award the best essay by a young author in each of the Society's journals.
Eligibility: Open to candidates at the start of their research career, with the normal age of eligibility being 30 or under. Applicants with papers stemming from doctoral theses are also welcomed. Authors wishing to be considered for an award should be the first named sole author of the paper.
Type: Prize.
Value: UK£100.
Frequency: Annual.
Application Procedure: Applicants will find further application details in each of the journals.
Additional Information: The Harper Prize is given for a paper in the Journal of Ecology, the Elton Prize for one in the Journal of Animal Ecology, the Southwood Prize for one in the Journal of Applied Ecology, and the Haldane Prize for one in the Journal of Functional Ecology. The journal editors decide the winner. Further information is available from the website.

BES Early Career Project Grants

Subjects: Ecology.
Purpose: To assist promising young ecologists by supporting innovative or important research of a pure or applied nature, and to provide an opportunity for ecologists recently appointed to academic posts to establish themselves.
Eligibility: Applicants must be in the early stages of their career and will normally be expected to have a PhD before applying.
Type: Grant.
Value: Up to UK£25,000.
Frequency: Annual.
Application Procedure: Applicants must complete an application form, available from the BES office.
Closing Date: January 31st.
Additional Information: Successful applicants will be expected to submit a brief report within 15 months of receipt of the award. Further information is available on request or from the website.

BES Education Innovation and Research Grants

Subjects: Ecology.
Purpose: To encourage teachers and others involved in formal education to develop new approaches in communicating ecology which promote good practice and make ecology both exciting and intellectually stimulating.
Level of Study: Professional development.
Type: Grant.
Value: Up to UK£750.
Application Procedure: Applicants must complete an application form, available from the BES office. Further information is available on request and from the website.
Closing Date: September 30th.
Additional Information: Successful applicants should be prepared to attend the Winter Meeting or some other Society meeting to give a presentation, workshop or poster display to show the Society what has been achieved. Useful outcomes should be communicated to other schools, teachers and pupils through the Teaching and Communicating Ecology Group teachers' newsletter, the internet, meetings or other appropriate ways. Any material produced should acknowledge the Society's contribution. Further information is available on request and from the website.

BES Honorary Membership of the Society

Subjects: Ecology.
Purpose: To award the Society's highest honor of honorary membership of the BES.
Eligibility: Open to candidates with great distinction in the science of ecology or its application.
Value: Honorary membership.
Frequency: Annual.
Application Procedure: The Society's Council is responsible for nominating and awarding honorary membership but BES members are welcome to put forward suggestions. Suggestions should include a brief statement of no more than 100 words outlining the individual's contribution to ecology and should be sent to the Executive Secretary.
Closing Date: January 31st.
Additional Information: Further information can be found on the website.

BES Prize for the Best Poster at the Winter Meeting

Subjects: Ecology.
Purpose: To award the best poster by a research student at the Winter Meeting.
Eligibility: Open to current postgraduates or postgraduates who have recently finished and are presenting work that was undertaken when they were still a student. The entrant must be the first author and have carried out the majority of the work presented.
Level of Study: Postgraduate.
Type: Prize.
Value: UK£200.
Frequency: Annual.
Application Procedure: Applicants must write for details.
Additional Information: A candidate eligible to enter must present a poster at the BES Winter Meeting. Further information is available on request and from the website.

BES Small Ecological Project Grants

Subjects: Ecological research and ecological survey.
Purpose: To promote all aspects of ecological research and ecological survey.
Eligibility: Open to ecological researchers. Support will not normally be given to projects forming part of an expedition proposal. All recipients will be required to submit a report on the work undertaken.
Level of Study: Professional development.
Type: Project grant.
Value: Up to UK£1,000 for travel and up to UK£1,000 for other costs.
Frequency: Four times per year.
Country of Study: Any country.
Application Procedure: Applicants must complete an application form, available from the BES office. The original form and seven copies must be submitted.
Closing Date: January 1st, April 1st, July 1st or October 1st.
Additional Information: Published papers and reports to other organisations should include an acknowledgement of the support from the BES. Other conditions may apply. The Coalbourn Trust is an independent trust which looks to the British Ecological Society to nominate suitable projects for funding. Recommendations for funding will be made from among the applicants for Small Ecological Project Grants. All applicants for Small Ecological Project Grants will automatically be eligible for funding from the Coalbourn Trust. Further information is available on request or from the website.

BES Specialist Course Grants

Subjects: Ecology.
Purpose: To help meet costs of specialist field courses.
Eligibility: Open to postgraduates and recent graduates who are not in full-time employment. The Society will not fund applicants where a specialist course is a formal part of a credit bearing programme eg. a degree, diploma, or certificate. There are a limited number of grants, which are allocated on a first come first served basis.
Level of Study: Graduate, Postgraduate.
Type: Grant.
Value: The course fee which may include accommodation.
Length of Study: Six months between May and October.
No. of awards offered: Limited.

Application Procedure: Applicants must complete an application form, available from the BES office.
Closing Date: As advertised in the Bulletin.
Additional Information: The Education, Training and Careers Committee decide upon the courses which will receive available grants. Successful applicants are bound by the booking conditions of the institution running the course and non attendance on a booked course will result in the applicants being personally liable for the cancellation fee. Grantees are required to produce a short report on the course. Further information is available from the website.

BES/Nordecol Student Support for Attendance at the Society's Winter Meeting

Subjects: Ecology.
Purpose: To enable students to attend the BES Winter Meeting.
Eligibility: Open to students from Nordic countries.
Type: Grant.
Value: Nordecol contributes to travel costs whilst the BES provides funds for the registration fee, meals and accommodation.
No. of awards offered: Limited.
Application Procedure: Applicants must refer to the website http://www.oikos.ekol.lu.se where the details are publicised each Autumn.
Additional Information: Further information can be found on the website.

Founders' Prize

Subjects: Ecology.
Purpose: To award an outstanding ecologist in his or her early career who is making a significant contribution towards the science of ecology.
Eligibility: Open to nominated outstanding ecologists, early in their careers ie. normally under 30 years of age. Candidates should be making a significant contribution towards the science of ecology.
Value: UK£500 and certificate.
Frequency: Every two years.
Application Procedure: Applicants must be nominated by letter from a proposer and seconder, giving a brief statement of the achievements that the individual has made to ecology plus their future potential. Suggestions should be submitted to the Executive Secretary at the BES office.
Closing Date: June 30th.

Marsh Award for Ecology

Subjects: Ecology.
Purpose: To recognise outstanding achievements and contributions to the science of ecology.
Eligibility: Open to distinguished ecologists. The Council seeks suggestions from members of the BES.
Type: Award.
Value: UK£1,000 plus a certificate.
Frequency: Annual.
Application Procedure: Applicants must send suggestions to the Executive Secretary. They should be no more than a single side of A4 and should contain the name and address of the individual and a brief statement outlining the achievements and contribution that they have made to ecology.
Closing Date: June 30th.
Additional Information: Further information can be found on the website.

Student Support for Attendance at BES Meetings

Subjects: Ecology.
Purpose: To support students attending the Society's Winter and Annual General Meeting, Annual Symposium and Special Symposium.
Eligibility: Open to students. Applications must be endorsed by the student's Head of Department or research supervisor. Bulk applications on behalf of a group of students are not accepted.
Level of Study: Postgraduate.
Type: Grant.
Value: 50 per cent of the cost of the registration fee plus meals and accommodation whilst at the meeting.
No. of awards offered: Varies.

Application Procedure: Applicants must complete an application form, available from the BES office.
Closing Date: October 31st for the Winter and Annual meeting. Other meetings are advertised in the Bulletin.
Additional Information: Further information can be found on the website.

Teacher Attendance at BES Meetings

Subjects: Ecology.
Purpose: To enable teachers to attend meetings and courses organised by the British Ecological Society.
Eligibility: Open to teachers in primary and secondary education, including field centre staff and others in a non school employment. Applicants must be able to show that the grant aid has been refused by the employer.
Level of Study: Professional development.
Value: Up to UK£200.
Application Procedure: Applicants must submit a letter which should specify the meeting or course to be attended, date, costs of travel and subsistence.
Closing Date: January 31st, April 30th or September 30th.
Additional Information: Further information can be found on the website.

BRITISH FEDERATION OF WOMEN GRADUATES (BFWG)

4 Mandeville Courtyard, London, SW11 4NB, England
Tel: (44) 20 7498 8037
Fax: (44) 20 7498 5213
Email: awards@bfwg.demon.co.uk
www: http://www.bfwg.org.uk
Contact: Secretary

The British Federation of Women Graduates (BFWG) promotes women's opportunities in education and public life. BFWG works as part of an international organisation to improve the lives of women and girls, fosters local, national and international friendship, and offers scholarships for final year postgraduate research.

AAUW: IFUW International Fellowships

Subjects: All subjects.
Purpose: To assist study or research which demonstrates a continued interest in the advancement of women.
Eligibility: Open to female members of BFWG or another national federation or association of the International Federation of University Women (IFUW). Candidates must have started the second year of research at least to which their application refers at the time of application and must be studying for three or more years. Taught Master's degrees do not count as research, though research done for an MPhil may count on the assumption that it will be upgraded to a PhD.
Level of Study: Postgraduate, Research.
Type: Fellowship.
Value: From US$18,000. These fellowships do not cover travel costs.
Length of Study: One year.
Frequency: Annual.
Study Establishment: An Institute of Higher Education.
Country of Study: United States of America.
No. of awards offered: Six.
Application Procedure: Applicants must apply through their respective federation or association. Applicants studying in Great Britain should write to the BFWG for details, enclosing a stamped addressed envelope. A list of IFUW national federations can be sent on request or downloaded from the IFUW website, http://www.ifuw.org.
Closing Date: December 15th in the year preceding the competition.
Funding: Private.
Additional Information: Recipients must submit a written report within six months of completing the fellowship.

For further information contact:

PO Box 4030, Iowa City, IA 52243-4030, United States of America
Contact: AAUW Fellowship Chair

AAUW: Rose Sidgwick Memorial Fellowship

Subjects: All subjects.

Purpose: To assist with study or research which demonstrates a continued interest in the advancement of women.

Eligibility: Open to female candidates from Great Britain below 30 years of age who are members of the BFWG. Candidates must have started the second year of research to which their application refers at the time of application and must be studying for three or more years. Taught Master's degrees do not count as research, although research undertaken for an MPhil may count on the assumption that it will be upgraded to a PhD. Preference will be given to women who show prior commitment to the advancement of women and girls through civic, community, or professional work.

Level of Study: Postgraduate, Research.

Type: Fellowship.

Value: From US$18,000. The fellowship does not cover travel.

Length of Study: One year.

Frequency: Annual.

Study Establishment: An Institute of Higher Education.

Country of Study: United States of America.

No. of awards offered: One.

Application Procedure: Applicants studying in Great Britain must write to the BFWG for details, enclosing a stamped addressed envelope. Overseas applicants must include two international reply coupons or download information from the BFWG website.

Closing Date: Early April in the year preceding the competition.

Funding: Private.

Additional Information: Recipients must submit a written report within six months of concluding the research.

AFUW: Australian Capital Territory Bursary

Subjects: All subjects.

Eligibility: Open to female members of the BFWG or another national federation or association of the International Federation of University Women (IFUW). Candidates must have started the second year of research at least to which their application refers at the time of application and must be studying for three or more years. Taught Master's degrees do not count as research, though research done for an MPhil may count on the assumption that it will be upgraded to a PhD.

Level of Study: Postgraduate, Research.

Type: Bursary.

Value: From Australian $1,000.

Length of Study: Three months.

Frequency: Annual.

Study Establishment: An Institute of Higher Education in Canberra.

Country of Study: Australia.

No. of awards offered: One.

Application Procedure: Applicants must apply through their respective federation or association. Applicants studying in Great Britain should write for details from the BFGW enclosing a stamped addressed envelope. A list of IFUW national federations can be sent upon request or downloaded from the IFUW website.

Closing Date: July 31st of the year preceding the competition.

Funding: Private.

Additional Information: Recipients must submit a written report within six months of concluding the bursary.

For further information contact:

AFUW (ACT), Inc., PO Box 520, Canberra, ACT 0201, Australia
www: http://www.afuw.org.au
Contact: Fellowship Convenor

AFUW: FFI-QLD Fellowship

Subjects: All subjects.

Eligibility: Open to female members of the BFWG or another international federation or association of IFUW. Candidates must have started the second year of research to which their application refers at the time of application and must be studying for more than three years. Taught Master's degrees do not count as research, though research undertaken for an MPhil may count on the assumption that it will be upgraded to a PhD.

Level of Study: Postgraduate, Research.

Type: Bursary.

Value: From Australian $20,000.

Length of Study: Three months.

Frequency: Annual.

Study Establishment: An Institute of Higher Education.

Country of Study: Australia.

No. of awards offered: One.

Application Procedure: Applicants must apply through their respective federation or association. Applicants studying in Great Britain should write to the BFWG for details, enclosing a stamped addressed envelope. A list of IFUW national federations can be sent upon request or downloaded from the IFUW website.

Closing Date: July 31st of the year preceding the competition.

Funding: Private.

Additional Information: Recipients must submit a written report within six months of concluding the research.

For further information contact:

QLD FFI, Private Bag 8, St Lucia, QLD 4067, Australia
www: http://www.afuw.org.au
Contact: Fellowship Convenor

AFUW: Georgina Sweet Fellowship

Subjects: All subjects.

Eligibility: Open to female members of BFWG. Candidates must have started the second year of research to which their application refers at the time of application and must be studying for three years or more. Taught Master's degrees do not count as research, though research undertaken for an MPhil may count on the assumption that it will be upgraded to a PhD.

Level of Study: Postgraduate, Research.

Type: Fellowship.

Value: Approx. Australian $4,500. The fellowship does not cover travel.

Length of Study: 4-12 months.

Frequency: Every two years.

Study Establishment: A university.

Country of Study: Australia.

No. of awards offered: One.

Application Procedure: Applicants must write to the BFWG for details, including a stamped addressed envelope or download information from the BFWG website.

Closing Date: Early April in the year preceding the competition.

Funding: Private.

Additional Information: Recipients must submit a written report within six months of concluding their research.

AFUW: Western Australian Bursaries

Subjects: All subjects.

Eligibility: Open to female members of BFWG or another national federation or association of the International Federation of University Women (IFUW). Candidates must have started the second year of research at least to which their application refers at the time of application and must be studying for three or more years. Taught Master's degrees do not count as research, though research done for an MPhil may count on the assumption that it will be upgraded to a PhD.

Level of Study: Postgraduate, Research.

Type: Bursary.

Value: From Australian $4,000. The bursaries do not cover travel.

Length of Study: One year.

Frequency: Annual.

Study Establishment: An Institute of Higher Education in Western Australia.

Country of Study: Australia.

No. of awards offered: More than one.

Application Procedure: Applicants must apply through their respective federation or association. Applicants studying in Great Britain should write for details from the BFWG, enclosing a stamped addressed envelope. A list of IFUW national federations can be sent upon request or downloaded from the IFUW website, http://www.ifuw.org.

Closing Date: July 31st of the year preceding the competition.

Funding: Private.

Additional Information: Recipients must submit a written report within six months of concluding the research.

For further information contact:

AFUW (WA), Inc. PO Box 48, Nedlands, WA 6909, Australia
www: http://www.afuw.org.au
Contact: Bursary Liaison Officer

BFWG Scholarships
Subjects: All subjects.
Purpose: To assist final year postgraduate research.
Eligibility: Open to female candidates, regardless of nationality, whose studies take place in Great Britain ie. England, Scotland or Wales. Research students must be in the final year of formal study towards a PhD degree. Taught Master's degrees do not count as research, though MPhil research students would need to be upgraded to a PhD during the dates of the competition.
Level of Study: Postgraduate, Research.
Type: Scholarship.
Value: From UK£1,000.
Frequency: Annual.
Study Establishment: A university or institution of university status.
Country of Study: Great Britain.
No. of awards offered: More than one.
Application Procedure: Applicants studying in Great Britain must write for details enclosing a stamped addressed envelope. Overseas applicants must include two international reply coupons, or download information from the BFWG website.
Closing Date: Early April in the year preceding the competition.
Funding: Private.
Additional Information: Recipients must submit a written report within six months of concluding the research.

BFWG: Beryl Mavis Green Scholarship
Subjects: All subjects.
Purpose: To assist final year postgraduate research.
Eligibility: Open to female candidates, regardless of nationality, whose studies take place in Great Britain. Research students must be in the final year of formal study towards a PhD degree. Taught Master's degrees do not count as research, though MPhil research students would need to be upgraded to a PhD during the dates of the competition.
Level of Study: Postgraduate, Research.
Type: Scholarship.
Value: From UK£1,000.
Frequency: Annual.
Study Establishment: A university or institution of university status.
Country of Study: Great Britain.
No. of awards offered: One.
Application Procedure: Applicants studying in Great Britain must write for details enclosing a stamped addressed envelope. Overseas applicants must include two international reply coupons, or download information from the BFWG website.
Closing Date: Early April in the year of the competition.
Funding: Private.
Additional Information: Recipients must submit a written report within six months of concluding the research.

BFWG: Elen Vanstone Scholarship
Subjects: All subjects.
Purpose: To assist final year postgraduate research.
Eligibility: Open to female candidates, regardless of nationality, whose studies take place in Great Britain. Research students will be in the final year of formal study towards a PhD degree. Taught Master's degrees do not count as research, though MPhil research students would need to be upgraded to a PhD during the dates of the competition.
Level of Study: Postgraduate, Research.
Type: Fellowship.
Value: From UK£1,000.
Frequency: Annual.
Study Establishment: A university or institution of university status.
Country of Study: Great Britain.

Application Procedure: Applicants studying in Great Britain must write to the for details enclosing a stamped addressed envelope. Overseas applicants must include two international reply coupons, or download details from the BFWG website.
Closing Date: Early April in the year of the competition.
Funding: Private.
Additional Information: Recipients must submit a written report within six months of concluding the research.

BFWG: Johnstone and Florence Stoney Studentship
Subjects: Biological, geological, meteorological or radiological science.
Purpose: To assist final year postgraduate research.
Eligibility: Open to female candidates, regardless of nationality, whose studies take place in Great Britain. Research students must be in the final year of formal study towards a PhD degree in biological, geological, meteorological or radiological science. Taught Master's degrees do not count as research, though MPhil research students would need to be upgraded to a PhD during the dates of the competition.
Level of Study: Postgraduate, Research.
Type: Studentship.
Value: From UK£1,000. The studentship does not cover travel.
Frequency: Annual.
Study Establishment: A university or institution of university status in Australia, New Zealand or South Africa.
Country of Study: Other.
No. of awards offered: One.
Application Procedure: Applicants studying in Great Britain must write for details enclosing a stamped addressed envelope. Overseas applicants must include two international reply coupons or download information from the BFWG website.
Closing Date: Early April in the year of the competition.
Funding: Private.
Additional Information: The recipient must submit a written report within six months of concluding the research. Preference is given to research undertaken in Australia, New Zealand or South Africa.

BFWG: Kathleen Hall Memorial Fellowships
Subjects: All subjects.
Purpose: To assist final year PhD research students from countries of low per capita income.
Eligibility: Open to female candidates, regardless of nationality, whose studies take place in Great Britain ie. England, Scotland or Wales. Preference is given to graduates from countries of low capita per income. Research students must be in the final year of formal study towards a PhD degree. Taught Master's degrees do not count as research, though MPhil research students would need to be upgraded to a PhD during the dates of the competition.
Level of Study: Postgraduate, Research.
Type: Fellowship.
Value: From UK£1,000.
Frequency: Annual.
Study Establishment: A university or institution of university status.
Country of Study: Great Britain.
No. of awards offered: More than one.
Application Procedure: Applicants studying in Great Britain must write for details enclosing a stamped addressed envelope. Overseas applicants must include two international reply coupons, or download information from the BFWG website.
Closing Date: Early April in the year of the competition.
Funding: Private.
Additional Information: Recipients must submit a written report within six months of concluding the research.

BFWG: M H Joseph Prize
Subjects: Architecture or engineering.
Purpose: To assist final year postgraduate research.
Eligibility: Open to female candidates not of United Kingdom nationality but whose studies take place in England, Scotland or Wales. Research students must be in the final year of formal study towards a PhD degree. Taught Master's degrees do not count as research,

though MPhil research students would need to be upgraded to a PhD during the dates of the competition.
Level of Study: Postgraduate, Research.
Type: Prize.
Value: From UK£500.
Frequency: Annual.
Study Establishment: A university or institution of university status.
Country of Study: Great Britain.
No. of awards offered: One.
Application Procedure: Applicants studying in Great Britain must write for details enclosing a stamped addressed envelope. Overseas applicants must include two international mail coupons, or download information from the BFWG website.
Closing Date: Early April in the year of the competition.
Funding: Private.
Additional Information: Recipients must submit a written report within six months of concluding the research.

BFWG: Margaret K B Day Memorial Scholarship
Subjects: All subjects.
Purpose: To assist final year postgraduate research.
Eligibility: Open to female candidates regardless of nationality, whose studies take place in Great Britain. Research students will be in the final year of formal study towards a PhD degree. Taught Master's degrees do not count as research, though MPhil research students would need to be upgraded to a PhD during the dates of the competition.
Level of Study: Postgraduate, Research.
Type: Scholarship.
Value: From UK£1,000.
Frequency: Annual.
Study Establishment: A university or institution of university status.
Country of Study: Great Britain.
No. of awards offered: One.
Application Procedure: Applicants studying in Great Britain must write for details enclosing a stamped addressed envelope. Overseas applicants must include two international reply coupons, or download information from the BFWG website.
Closing Date: Early April in the year of the competition.
Funding: Private.
Additional Information: Recipients must submit a written report within six months of concluding the research.

BFWG: Marjorie Shaw Scholarship
Subjects: All subjects.
Purpose: To assist final year postgraduate research.
Eligibility: Open to female candidates, regardless of nationality, whose studies take place in Great Britain. Research students will be in the final year of formal study towards a PhD degree. Taught Master's degrees do not count as research, though MPhil research students would need to be upgraded to a PhD during the dates of the competition.
Level of Study: Postgraduate, Research.
Type: Fellowship.
Value: From UK£1,000.
Frequency: Annual.
Study Establishment: A university or institution of university status.
Country of Study: Great Britain.
No. of awards offered: More than one.
Application Procedure: Applicants studying in Great Britain must write for details enclosing a stamped addressed envelope. Overseas applicants must include two international reply coupons, or download details from the BFWG website.
Closing Date: Early April in the year of the competition.
Funding: Private.
Additional Information: Recipients must submit a written report within six months of concluding the research.

BFWG: Mary Bradburn Scholarship
Subjects: All subjects.
Purpose: To assist final year postgraduate research.
Eligibility: Open to female candidates, regardless of nationality, whose studies take place in Great Britain. Research students will be in the final

year of formal study towards a PhD degree. Taught Master's degrees do not count as research, though MPhil research students would need to be upgraded to a PhD during the dates of the competition.
Level of Study: Postgraduate, Research.
Type: Fellowship.
Value: From UK£1,000.
Frequency: Annual.
Study Establishment: A university or institution of university status.
Country of Study: Great Britain.
Application Procedure: Applicants studying in Great Britain must write to the for details enclosing a stamped addressed envelope. Overseas applicants must include two international reply coupons, or download details from the BFWG website.
Closing Date: Early April in the year of the competition.
Funding: Private.
Additional Information: Recipients must submit a written report within six months of concluding the research.

BFWG: Ruth Bowden Scholarship
Subjects: Medical Sciences.
Purpose: To assist final year postgraduate research.
Eligibility: Open to female candidates, regardless of nationality, whose studies take place in Great Britain. Research students will be in the final year of formal study towards a PhD degree. Taught Master's degree do not count as research, though MPhil research students would need to be upgraded to a PhD during the dates of the competition.
Level of Study: Postgraduate, Research.
Type: Fellowship.
Value: From UK£1,000.
Frequency: Annual.
Study Establishment: A university or institution of university status.
Country of Study: Great Britain.
Application Procedure: Applicants studying in Great Britain must write to the for details enclosing a stamped addressed envelope. Overseas applicants must include two international reply coupons, or download details from the BFWG website.
Closing Date: Early April in the year of the competition.
Funding: Private.
Additional Information: Recipients must submit a written report within six months of concluding the research.

IFUW International Fellowships
Subjects: All subjects.
Eligibility: Open to female members of BFWG or another national federation or association of the International Federation of University Women (IFUW). Candidates must have started the second year of research at least to which their application refers at the time of application and must be studying for three or more years. Taught Master's degrees do not count as research, though research done for an MPhil may count on the assumption that it will be upgraded to a PhD.
Level of Study: Postgraduate, Research.
Type: Fellowship.
Value: Varies. The awards do not cover travel.
Length of Study: Eight months.
Frequency: Every three years.
Study Establishment: An Institute of Higher Education.
Country of Study: Any country.
No. of awards offered: More than eight.
Application Procedure: Applicants must apply through their respective federation or association. Applicants studying in Great Britain should write for details to the BFWG enclosing a stamped addressed envelope. A list of national federations can be sent on request or downloaded from the IFUW website, http://www.ifuw.org.
Closing Date: Early November in the year preceding the competition.
Funding: Private.
Additional Information: Recipients must submit a written report within six months of concluding the research.

For further information contact:

IFUW Headquarters, 8 rue de l'Ancien-Port, Geneva, CH-1201, Switzerland
Tel: (41) 22 731 2380

Fax: (41) 22 738 0440
Email: ifuw@ifuw.org
www: www.ifuw.org
Contact: Grants Management Officer

Israel International Schloarship

Subjects: Humanities, arts, sciences, bible and jewish studies and international law.
Eligibility: Open to female members of the BFWG or another international federation or association of IFUW. Candidates must have started the second year of research to which their application refers at the time of application and must be studying for more than three years. Taught Master's degrees do not count as research, though research undertaken for an MPhil may count on the assumption that it will be upgraded to a PhD.
Level of Study: Postgraduate, Research.
Type: Scholarship.
Value: From US$3,000.
Length of Study: Three months.
Frequency: Every three years.
Study Establishment: An Institute of Higher Education.
Country of Study: Israel.
No. of awards offered: One.
Application Procedure: Applicants must apply through their respective federation or association. Applicants studying in Great Britain should write to the BFWG for details, enclosing a stamped addressed envelope. A list of IFUW national federations can be sent upon request or downloaded from the IFUW website.
Closing Date: July 31st of the year preceding the competition.
Funding: Private.
Additional Information: Recipients must submit a written report within six months of concluding the research.

For further information contact:

1AUW, PO Box 8304, Jerusalem, 91074, Israel
www: http://www.ifuw.org/israel
Contact: Fellowship Convenor

JAUW International Fellowship

Subjects: All subjects.
Purpose: To assist independent research or advanced study.
Eligibility: Open to female members of BFWG or another national federation or association of the International Federation of University Women (IFUW). Candidates must have started the second year of research to which their application refers at the time of the application and must be studying for three or more years. Taught Master's degrees do not count as research, though research undertaken for an MPhil may count on the assumption that it will be upgraded to a PhD. Applications from all nations apart from Japan are welcome.
Level of Study: Postgraduate, Research.
Type: Fellowship.
Value: Yen 600,000/800,000. The fellowships do not cover travel.
Length of Study: Three months.
Frequency: Annual.
Study Establishment: An Institute of Higher Education.
Country of Study: Japan.
No. of awards offered: One.
Application Procedure: Applicants must apply through their respective federation or association. Applicants studying in Great Britain should write for details to BFWG enclosing a stamped addressed envelope. A list of IFUW national federations can be sent upon request or downloaded from the IFUW website, http://www.ifuw.org.
Closing Date: April 30th in the year preceding the competition.
Funding: Private.
Additional Information: Recipients must submit a written report within six months of concluding the research.

For further information contact:

11-6-101 Samon-cho Shinjuku-ku, Tokyo, 160-0017, Japan
Email: jauw@tky2.3webne.jp
www: http://www3.tky.3web.ne.jp/~jauw/
Contact: The Fellowship Chair, JAUW

Jeanne Chaton Award

Subjects: All subjects.
Eligibility: Open to female members of the BFWG or another international federation or association of IFUW. Candidates must have started the second year of research to which their application refers at the time of application and must be studying for more than three years. Taught Master's degrees do not count as research, though research undertaken for an MPhil may count on the assumption that it will be upgraded to a PhD.
Level of Study: Postgraduate, Research.
Type: Bursary.
Value: €300-1,500.
Length of Study: Three months.
Frequency: Annual.
Study Establishment: An Institute of Higher Education.
Country of Study: France.
No. of awards offered: One.
Application Procedure: Applicants must apply through their respective federation or association. Applicants studying in Great Britain should write to the BFWG for details, enclosing a stamped addressed envelope. A list of IFUW national federations can be sent upon request or downloaded from the IFUW website.
Closing Date: July 31st of the year preceding the competition.
Funding: Private.
Additional Information: Recipients must submit a written report within six months of concluding the research.

For further information contact:

AFFDU, 4, Rue De Chevreuse, Paris, F-75006, France
www: http://www.int-evry.fr/affud

NAUW: Ellen Gleditsch Stipendiefond

Subjects: All subjects.
Purpose: To assist independent research or advanced studies.
Eligibility: Open to female members of the BFWG or another national federation or association of the International Federation of University Women (IFUW). Candidates must have started the second year of research to which their application refers at the time of application and must be studying for three or more years. Taught Master's degrees do not count as research, though research undertaken for an MPhil may count on the assumption that it will be upgraded to a PhD.
Level of Study: Doctorate, Postdoctorate, Research.
Type: Scholarship.
Frequency: Every two years.
Study Establishment: An approved institution.
Country of Study: Norway.
No. of awards offered: One.
Application Procedure: Applicants must apply through their respective federation or association. Applicants studying in Great Britain should write to the BFWG for details, enclosing a stamped addressed envelope. A list of IFUW national federations can be sent upon request or downloaded from the IFUW website, http://www.ifuw.org.
Closing Date: Early April in the year preceding the competition.
Funding: Private.
Additional Information: Recipients must submit a written report within six months of concluding their research.

For further information contact:

PO Box 251, Bergen, N-5084, Norway
Fax: (47) 5558 9455

SAAWg International Fellowship

Subjects: All subjects.
Eligibility: Open to female members of the BFWG or another international federation or association of IFUW. Candidates must have started the second year of research to which their application refers at the time of application and must be studying for more than three years. Taught Master's degrees do not count as research, though research undertaken for an MPhil may count on the assumption that it will be upgraded to a PhD.
Level of Study: Postgraduate, Research.
Type: Fellowship.
Value: 2,500 S. African Rand.

Length of Study: Three months.
Frequency: Every two years.
Study Establishment: An Institute of Higher Education.
Country of Study: South Africa.
No. of awards offered: One.
Application Procedure: Applicants must apply through their respective federation or association. Applicants studying in Great Britain should write to the BFWG for details, enclosing a stamped addressed envelope. A list of IFUW national federations can be sent upon request or downloaded from the IFUW website.
Closing Date: July 31st of the year preceding the competition.
Funding: Private.
Additional Information: Recipients must submit a written report within six months of concluding the research.

For further information contact:

PO Box 1879, Bedfordview, 2008, South Africa
Contact: Fellowship Secretariat

Sarojini Naidu Memorial Schloarship

Subjects: All subjects.
Eligibility: Open to female members of the BFWG or another international federation or association of IFUW. Candidates must have started the second year of research to which their application refers at the time of application and must be studying for more than three years. Taught Master's degrees do not count as research, though research undertaken for an MPhil may count on the assumption that it will be upgraded to a PhD.
Level of Study: Postgraduate, Research.
Type: Scholarship.
Value: From 600 Indian Rupees per month.
Length of Study: Three months.
Frequency: Annual.
Study Establishment: An Institute of Higher Education.
Country of Study: Delhi, India.
No. of awards offered: One.
Application Procedure: Applicants must apply through their respective federation or association. Applicants studying in Great Britain should write to the BFWG for details, enclosing a stamped addressed envelope. A list of IFUW national federations can be sent upon request or downloaded from the IFUW website.
Closing Date: July 31st of the year preceding the competition.
Funding: Private.
Additional Information: Recipients must submit a written report within six months of concluding the research.

For further information contact:

Indian Federation of University Womens Association of Delhi, 6, Bhagwandas Road, New Delhi, 110 001, India
www: http://www.ifuw.org/india
Contact: Scholarship Convenor

SVA International Fellowship

Subjects: All subjects.
Eligibility: Open to female members of the BFWG or another international federation or association of IFUW. Candidates must have started the second year of research to which their application refers at the time of application and must be studying for more than three years. Taught Master's degrees do not count as research, though research undertaken for an Mphil may count on the assumption that it will be upgraded to a PhD.
Level of Study: Postgraduate, Research.
Type: Scholarship.
Value: 10,000 Swiss Francs.
Length of Study: Three months.
Frequency: Annual.
Study Establishment: An Institute of Higher Education.
Country of Study: Switzerland.
No. of awards offered: One.
Application Procedure: Applicants must apply through their respective federation or association. Applicants studying in Great Britain should write to the BFWG for details, enclosing a stamped addressed

envelope. A list of IFUW national federations can be sent upon request or downloaded from the IFUW website.
Closing Date: Spring of the year preceding the competition.
Funding: Private.
Additional Information: Recipients must submit a written report within six months of concluding the research.

For further information contact:

SVA,
www: http://www.unifemmes.ch/
Contact: Fellowship Secretariat

BRITISH HEART FOUNDATION (BHF)

14 Fitzharding Street, London, W1H 6DH, England
Tel: (44) 20 7935 0185
Email: research@bhf.org.uk
www: http://www.bhf.org.uk
Contact: Ms Jessica Gregory, Assistant Manager, Research Funds Department

The British Heart Foundation (BHF) exists to encourage research into the causes, diagnosis, prevention and advances of cardiovascular disease, to inform doctors throughout the country of advances in the diagnosis, cure and treatment of heart diseases, and to improve facilities for the treatment of heart patients where the National Health Service is unable to help.

BHF Clinical Science Fellowships

Subjects: The cardiovascular system.
Purpose: To enable training for clinicians who have demonstrated an interest in, and potential for, research.
Eligibility: Open to applicants from the European Economic Area. Applicants should be clinicians, aged approx. 25 to 30 years.
Level of Study: Professional development.
Type: Fellowship.
Value: This award reimburses for salary commensurate with seniority within the health service and carries a consumables allowance of up to UK£5,000 per year.
Length of Study: Up to seven years.
Frequency: Three times each year.
Study Establishment: A basic science department, preferably away from the sponsoring department.
Country of Study: Based in the UK, but the research training period can be spent overseas.
No. of awards offered: Varies.
Application Procedure: Applicants must submit the appropriate form with the approval of the head of department. The application must include a full research protocol and/or training programme together with the curriculum vitae of the proposed Fellow. Shortlisted applicants will normally be required to attend an interview. Application forms and further information are available on request.
Closing Date: Details are available on request.

BHF Intermediate Research Fellowships

Subjects: Basic or applied clinical cardiology.
Purpose: To enable highly qualified independent researchers to pursue their research objectives.
Eligibility: Open to applicants from the European Economic Area.
Level of Study: Professional development.
Type: Fellowship.
Value: A salary commensurate with seniority within the university and health service at registrar or first year senior registrar level, or academic equivalent. Up to UK£7,000 per year may be applied for to cover running expenses. Running expenses must be fully justified.
Length of Study: Up to three years.
Frequency: Three times each year.
Country of Study: United Kingdom.
No. of awards offered: Varies.
Application Procedure: Applicants must submit the appropriate form completed by themselves or their supervisor, with the approval of the head of department. The application must include a full research protocol together with the curriculum vitae of the proposed Fellow.

Closing Date: Details are available on request.
Additional Information: These fellowships are unlikely to be awarded to those who are unable to obtain advancement within the health services.

BHF Junior Research Fellowships

Subjects: Basic or applied clinical cardiology.
Purpose: To enable individuals to be trained in academic research.
Eligibility: Open to applicants from the European Economic Area who wish to be trained in academic research under the direct supervision of senior and experienced research workers.
Level of Study: Postgraduate.
Type: Fellowship.
Value: A salary, not to be higher than the top of the registrar scale or equivalent, and up to UK£5,000 per year to cover running expenses.
Length of Study: Two years, but subject to review at the end of the first year, dependent on the Foundation's approval and upon the head of department submitting a progress report on the candidates work to date.
Frequency: Three times each year.
Country of Study: United Kingdom.
No. of awards offered: Varies.
Application Procedure: Applicants must submit the appropriate form completed by the planned supervisor and with the approval of the head of department. The application must include a full research protocol together with the curriculum vitae of the proposed Fellow. The head of department must confirm that no additional financial support is necessary in order to carry out the project.
Closing Date: Details are available on request.

BHF Overseas Visiting Fellowships

Subjects: Basic or applied clinical cardiology.
Purpose: To enable senior overseas research workers to undertake research in the United Kingdom.
Eligibility: Open to established research workers of proven outstanding talent who are able to contribute to the work of the host department.
Level of Study: Professional development.
Type: Fellowship.
Value: The Fellow's salary and up to UK£5,000 per year as a contribution towards research expenses. The applicant must confirm that no additional financial support is necessary in order to carry out the project. Application may be made for funds to cover economy travel fares for the Fellow and one dependent, the latter only being eligible for travel funds if the Fellow is to be resident in the United Kingdom for one year or more.
Length of Study: Up to two years.
Frequency: Three times each year.
Study Establishment: A recognised research centre in the United Kingdom.
Country of Study: United Kingdom.
No. of awards offered: Varies.
Application Procedure: Applications must be made by the head of department in the United Kingdom institution on behalf of the Fellow and should include a full research protocol. The role of the Visiting Fellow in the research should be clearly stated. A curriculum vitae of the proposed Fellow and two letters of recommendation from the Fellow's country of origin should also be included.
Closing Date: Details are available on request.
Additional Information: These fellowships are not given for training.

BHF PhD Studentships

Subjects: Basic or applied clinical cardiology.
Purpose: To enable graduates to proceed to a PhD degree.
Eligibility: Open to candidates who have obtained the minimum of an Upper Second Class (Honours) Degree and who are from the European Economic Area.
Level of Study: Doctorate.
Type: Studentship.
Value: The level of stipend is set by the British Heart Foundation. Applicants may apply for funds to cover university fees. Up to UK£5,000 per year may also be applied for to cover research consumables.

Length of Study: Three years.
Frequency: Three times each year.
Study Establishment: An appropriate university.
Country of Study: United Kingdom.
No. of awards offered: Varies.
Application Procedure: Applications must be made by heads of department and may be made for named or unnamed candidates, although priority will be given to named candidates. Applications must be made on the appropriate form and must include a full research protocol and curriculum vitae of the candidate.
Closing Date: Details are available on request.

BHF Research Awards

Subjects: Cardiovascular research.
Purpose: To encourage and support research.
Eligibility: Open to applicants from the European Economic Area.
Level of Study: Postdoctorate.
Value: Varies.
Length of Study: Varies.
Frequency: Varies, according to the committee.
Study Establishment: Universities and medical schools.
Country of Study: United Kingdom.
No. of awards offered: Dependent on funding.
Application Procedure: Applicants must write for details.
Closing Date: Varies, according to the committee.
Additional Information: An annual report is available upon request.

BHF Senior Research Fellowships

Subjects: Basic or applied clinical cardiology.
Purpose: To enable researchers with an international reputation of outstanding ability to pursue their research interests.
Eligibility: Open to applicants from the European Economic Area. The applicant should have been engaged in original research for at least two years and have published results, and should show outstanding ability both in original thought and practical application. This ability should already have been recognised outside the applicant's institution by invitations to talk to societies both at home and abroad. The applicant's career plans should be academic medicine and research. Senior Research Fellowships are awarded to those thought likely to gain high office in teaching and research institutions.
Level of Study: Professional development.
Type: Fellowship.
Value: Salary is commensurate with seniority within the university and health service up to consultant level. Up to UK£10,000 per year may be applied for to cover running expenses which should be fully justified.
Length of Study: Three years initially, but it may be extended to five after submission of a progress report has been judged satisfactory by the Foundation.
Frequency: Annual.
Country of Study: United Kingdom.
No. of awards offered: Varies.
Application Procedure: Applicants must complete the appropriate form and submit this, with the approval of the head of department, together with a full research protocol and curriculum vitae of the proposed Fellow. Shortlisted applicants will be required to attend an interview.
Closing Date: Details are available on request.
Additional Information: A Senior Research Fellow may apply to the Committee for a second five year period by the end of which it would be expected that the Fellow would have secured a permanent and more senior position. In this case an interview will be required.

BHF Travelling Fellowships

Subjects: Basic or applied clinical cardiology.
Purpose: To enable established research workers to undertake research abroad, or acquire special knowledge which would assist them in their research after their return.
Eligibility: Open to applicants from the European Economic Area who are established research workers and are of proven outstanding talent. At the time of application the proposed Fellow should hold a post in a research institution or university with tenure of more than five years.

Level of Study: Professional development.
Type: Fellowship.
Value: The proposed Fellow may apply for funds to cover the cost of economy travel and a reasonable subsistence allowance at the place of work. It is expected that the Fellow's salary would continue to be paid by the university or institution in the United Kingdom during his or her absence abroad.
Length of Study: Up to six months.
Frequency: Three times each year.
Country of Study: Outside the UK.
No. of awards offered: Varies.
Application Procedure: Applicants must submit the appropriate form together with details of the purpose of the visit and what the Fellow expects to gain as a result of the visit. The applicant's curriculum vitae and a letter of acceptance by the host institution must be included in the application.
Closing Date: Details are available on request.

John Fyffe Memorial Fellowship

Subjects: Collagen disease and in particular, the causes, diagnosis, treatment including surgical techniques and the eventual elimination of the disease known as Marfan's syndrome.
Purpose: To enable researchers to visit other centres working in the field in order to acquire first hand knowledge and techniques so that they may be applied to research being undertaken in the United Kingdom.
Eligibility: Open to applicants from the European Economic Area.
Level of Study: Professional development.
Type: Fellowship.
Value: Up to UK£3,000 per year.
Frequency: Three times each year.
Country of Study: Any country.
No. of awards offered: Varies.
Application Procedure: Applicants must complete an application form. Application forms and further information are available on request.
Closing Date: Details are available on request.

BRITISH INSTITUTE IN EASTERN AFRICA

PO Box 30710, Nairobi, Kenya
Tel: (254) 2 433 30
Fax: (254) 2 433 65
Email: britinst@insightkenya.com
Contact: Dr Paul Lane, Director

The British Institute in Eastern Africa encourages research by individual scholars in African archaeology, history and cognate fields, and works closely with the universities, museums and antiquities services of the Eastern African countries. It is based in Nairobi where it maintains a centre for field research and a comprehensive reference library.

British Institute in Eastern Africa Graduate Attachments

Subjects: Pre-colonial history and archaeology in East Africa through field research.
Purpose: To provide opportunities for recent graduates in history, archaeology, anthropology and related disciplines to gain practical field experience in Eastern Africa.
Eligibility: Open to citizens of East African countries, the United Kingdom and the Commonwealth who are over 21 years of age. Candidates should have a Bachelor of Arts degree or equivalent and graduate training in African studies, archaeology, social anthropology or African history.
Level of Study: Postgraduate.
Type: Other.
Value: Varies.
Length of Study: Three-six months.
Frequency: Annual.
Study Establishment: The British Institute in Eastern Africa.
Country of Study: Other.
No. of awards offered: Varies.

Application Procedure: Applicants must submit a letter of application to the Director with the names of two academic referees and a curriculum vitae.
Closing Date: Normally May 15th.
Funding: Government.
No. of awards given last year: 12.
No. of applicants last year: 43.
Additional Information: Small grants and assistance may be offered on a discretionary basis to Scholars of other nationalities. Archaeological students may be required to assist in excavation carried out by the Institute's staff. Details of activities are published in the Archaeology Abroad bulletin, and in the Institute's annual report, copies of which are available on request.

British Institute in Eastern Africa Research Grants

Subjects: Humanities and social sciences with some emphasis on archaeology, African history, anthropology and related subjects.
Purpose: To assist Scholars undertaking original research in East Africa, broadly defined in any field of the humanities and social sciences.
Eligibility: Open to Scholars undertaking original research in East Africa and in any area of humanities or social sciences. Priority will be given to research on the urban history of East Africa and research on areas bordering Victoria Nyanza focusing on settlement history and the use of space, environmental history, management and technology and style and exchange.
Level of Study: Postgraduate.
Value: Up to UK£1,000 for Major Research Grants. Up to UK£1,000 for Minor Research Grants. Grants are normally awarded as contributions towards research costs and do not include institutional overheads or any stipendiary element.
Frequency: Dependent on funds available.
Study Establishment: The British Institute in Eastern Africa.
Country of Study: Other.
No. of awards offered: Varies.
Application Procedure: Applicants must submit references and both grant applications on the same form to the Director. Application forms can be obtained from the Director from June 1st onwards. It is the applicants responsibility to ensure that references are received by the Director before the deadline dates for each grant and to send a copy of their completed application to the referees. All application forms and references must be received by the set deadlines. Late applications will not be considered after that date and late references will put the applicant at a serious disadvantage.
Closing Date: November 30th for Minor Award Grants and May 30th or October 31st for Minor Research Grants.
No. of awards given last year: Major- 3, Minor- 8.
No. of applicants last year: Major- 5, Minor- 13.
Additional Information: Applicants must contact the Director for further information on relevant topics likely to receive support.
Those awarded grants will be required to keep the Institute regularly informed of the progress of their research, to provide a preliminary statement of accounts within 18 months of the award dates and to provide the Institute with copies of all relevant publications. They are encouraged to discuss with the Director the possibility of publishing their results in the Institute's journal Azania. Results for the Minor Grants Award may be expected within two months of either May 30th or October 31st and results for the Major Research Grants by early February.

For further information contact:

BIEA/PO Box 30710/GPO, Nairobi, Kenya
Email: pjlane@insightkenya.com

BRITISH INSTITUTE IN PARIS

11 rue de Constantine, Paris
Cedex 07, F-75340, France
Tel: (33) 1 44 11 73 91
Fax: (33) 1 45 50 31 55
Email: r.lethbridge@bipants.lon.ac.uk
www: http://www.bip.lon.ac.uk
Contact: Professor C L Campos, The Director

The British Institute in Paris is a teaching and research institute of London University specialising in English and French studies, translation and language pedagogy.

Quinn, Nathan and Edmond Scholarships
Subjects: French studies (3.5.2).
Purpose: To assist postgraduate research in France.
Eligibility: Open to citizens of the European Union and Commonwealth countries who are graduates and possess sufficient knowledge of French to pursue their proposed studies. Candidates in the early stages of doctoral research, or not engaged in research, are not eligible.
Level of Study: Doctorate, Postdoctorate, Postgraduate.
Type: A variable number of fellowships.
Value: UK£450 per month for the scholarship. UK£500 per month for the Junior Research fellowship.
Length of Study: The scholarship is for between one and three months. The Junior Research Fellowship is for up to nine months.
Frequency: Dependent on funds available.
Study Establishment: An approved institute.
Country of Study: France.
No. of awards offered: Dependent on availability of funds.
Application Procedure: Applicants must submit a written recommendation from their professor or tutor along with their application. The name of one academic referee must be given.
Closing Date: March 15th.
Funding: Private.
Contributor: Trust funds.
No. of awards given last year: One in 2003-2004.
No. of applicants last year: One in 2003, for 2003-04.
Additional Information: Scholarships cannot be held concurrently with other major awards. These scholarships are intended for research and not for those following taught courses.

BRITISH INSTITUTE OF RADIOLOGY (BIR)

36 Portland Place, London, W1B 1AT, England
Tel: (44) 20 7307 1400
Fax: (44) 20 7307 1414
Email: admin@bir.org.uk
www: http://www.bir.org.uk
Contact: Chief Executive

The British Institute of Radiology (BIR), being an independent forum, has as its aim the bringing together of all the professions in radiology, medical and scientific disciplines to share knowledge and educate the public, thereby improving the prevention and detection of disease and the management and treatment of patients.

Amersham Health Fellowship
Subjects: Radiology and pharmaceuticals in diagnostic imaging.
Purpose: To enable a diagnostic radiologist to gain in-depth experience abroad.
Eligibility: Open to diagnostic radiologists of senior registrar or junior consultant status. Preference is given to members of the Institute.
Level of Study: Postgraduate, Professional development.
Type: Fellowship.
Value: Up to UK£5,000.
Length of Study: Up to two months.
Frequency: Annual.
Study Establishment: One or more academic departments of radiology.
Country of Study: Other.
No. of awards offered: One.
Application Procedure: Applicants must submit an application letter and supporting documentation.
Funding: Commercial.
No. of awards given last year: None.
No. of applicants last year: 3.
Additional Information: The successful Scholar will be required to produce a report of up to 1,000 words for publication in the British Journal of Radiology.

BIR Travel Bursary
Subjects: Radiology.
Purpose: To enable an individual to present a paper at UKRC.
Eligibility: Open to radiographer members of the Institute who are under 35 years of age.
Level of Study: Professional development.
Type: Travel grant.
Value: UK£200.
Frequency: Annual.
Study Establishment: UKRC.
Country of Study: Any country.
No. of awards offered: 3.
Application Procedure: Applicants must complete a registration form.
Closing Date: February 2nd, 2004.
Funding: Private.
No. of awards given last year: One.
No. of applicants last year: One.

Nic McNally Prize for Cancer Research
Subjects: Radiology.
Eligibility: Open to young scientists, under 35 years of age at the time of application and employed in a scientific post. Applicants need not be members of the Institute.
Level of Study: Research.
Type: Travel grant.
Value: UK£500.
Frequency: Annual.
Study Establishment: Scientific Meeting.
Country of Study: United Kingdom.
No. of awards offered: One.
Application Procedure: Applicants must complete a registration form and submit this with supporting material.
Closing Date: February 28th, 2004.
Funding: Private.
No. of awards given last year: None.
No. of applicants last year: 16.

Stanley Melville Memorial Award
Subjects: Radiology.
Purpose: To enable a member of the Institute to visit clinics and institutions abroad.
Eligibility: Open to members of the Institute under 35 years of age.
Level of Study: Unrestricted.
Value: UK£1,000.
Frequency: Annual.
Country of Study: Any country.
No. of awards offered: One.
Application Procedure: Applicants must complete an application form and submit this with supporting documentation.
Closing Date: December 31st of the year preceding the award.
Funding: Private.
No. of awards given last year: One.
No. of applicants last year: Two.
Additional Information: While the successful applicant will not be obliged to write a formal report on their visit, it is hoped that they will submit a description of the work seen during the visit in a form suitable for publication in the Journal.

BRITISH JOURNAL OF ANAESTHESIA (BJA)

Department of Anaesthesia, LRI, Leicester, Leicestershire, LE1 5WW, England
Tel: (44) 116 258 5291
Fax: (44) 116 285 4487
Email: DGL3@le.ac.uk
Contact: Dr D G Lambert, Honorary Grants Officer (DJA/RCA)

The British Journal of Anaesthesia (BJA) is the largest journal of anaesthesia in Europe. In combination with the RCA, the professional body responsible for anaesthesia in the United Kingdom, it provides charitable funds for fellowships, project grants, writing workshops and publication of the Colleges' CEPD Journal.

BJA/Royal College of Anaesthetists Project and Fellowship Grants

Subjects: The application of basic science to anaesthesia but major clinical research projects also considered.

Purpose: To support specific research projects performed by a Fellow of the Royal College. It may be used for salaries of technical staff, research students and postdoctoral research Fellows or for the purchase of equipment.

Eligibility: Open to Fellows of the Royal College of Anaesthetists only. The work may be done in a university science department or in an academic clinical department, but preference will be given to projects involving co-operative research between a basic science department and a clinical department. Applicants will be established members of their department of anaesthesia.

Level of Study: Research.

Type: Project and fellowship grant.

Length of Study: Up to two years.

Frequency: Dependent on funds available.

Study Establishment: Departments of anaesthesia

Country of Study: Any country.

No. of awards offered: Varies.

Application Procedure: Applicants must respond to specific notices published in the BJA and submit their application on an approved application form.

Closing Date: Varies.

Funding: Private.

Contributor: British Journal of Anaesthesia and the Royal College of Anaesthetics.

No. of awards given last year: Varies.

Additional Information: The BJA/RCA will not pay institutional overheads.

BRITISH JOURNAL OF SURGERY

John Wiley & Sons Limited, The Atrium, Southern Gate, Chichester, West Sussex, PO19 8SQ, England
Tel: (44) 1243 770384
Fax: (44) 1243 770460
Email: bjs@wiley.co.uk
www: http://www.bjssoc.com
Contact: The Editor

British Journal of Surgery Research Bursaries

Subjects: Surgical research.

Purpose: To further surgical research.

Level of Study: Postgraduate.

Type: Grant.

Value: UK£10,000.

Frequency: Annual.

No. of awards offered: Up to three.

Application Procedure: Applicants must visit the website for application details.

Closing Date: July 31st.

Funding: Private.

Contributor: The British Journal of Surgery Society.

BRITISH LEPROSY RELIEF ASSOCIATION (LEPRA)

Fairfax House, Causton Road, Colchester, Essex, CO1 1PU, England
Tel: (44) 1206 562286
Fax: (44) 1206 762151
Email: lepra@lepra.org.uk
www: http://www.lepra.org.uk
Contact: Ms Debbie Sharp

The British Leprosy Relief Association (LEPRA) is a medical development charity which works to restore health, hope and dignity to those affected by leprosy.

LEPRA Grants

Subjects: Leprosy.

Purpose: To encourage and support research which is directly relevant to the understanding, prevention and care of leprosy.

Level of Study: Postgraduate.

Type: Grant.

Value: Dependent on funds available and the nature of the research or training.

Length of Study: Up to three years.

Frequency: Dependent on funds available.

Study Establishment: As appropriate to the nature of the research or training.

Country of Study: Any country.

No. of awards offered: Varies.

Application Procedure: Applicants must complete a research application pack, available on request. Applications must be submitted using the appropriate forms and should observe the time scales involved in the approvals process.

Closing Date: Applications are accepted at any time.

BRITISH LIBRARY - MAP LIBRARY

96 Euston Road, London
NW1 2DB, England
Tel: (44) 20 7412 7702
Fax: (44) 20 7412 7780
Email: maps@bl.uk
www: http://ihr.sas.ac.uk/maps/wallis.html
Contact: Mr Peter Barber, Map Librarian

Helen Wallis Fellowship

Subjects: History and the history of cartography, preferably with an international dimension.

Purpose: To promote the extended and complementary use of the British Library's book and cartographic collections in historical investigation.

Eligibility: Applicants should write for details.

Level of Study: Postdoctorate.

Type: Fellowship.

Value: Up to UK£300.

Length of Study: 6-12 months.

Frequency: Annual.

Study Establishment: British Library, London.

Country of Study: United Kingdom.

No. of awards offered: One.

Application Procedure: Applicants must submit a letter indicating the proposed period and outlining the research project together with a full curriculum vitae and the names of three references.

Closing Date: May 1st.

Funding: Private.

No. of awards given last year: One.

Additional Information: The award honours the memory of Dr Helen Wallis, OBE (1924-1995), Map Librarian at the British Museum and then the British Library between the years 1967-1986. Further information can be found on the website.

BRITISH LUNG FOUNDATION

73-75 Goswell Road, London
EC1V 7ER, United Kingdom
Tel: (44) 0207 688 5555
Fax: (44) 0207 688 5556
Email: blf@britishlungfoundation.com
www: http://www.lunguk.org
Contact: Julia Heidsta, Research Manager

The British Lung Foundation provides information to the public on lung conditions and all aspects of lung health. The Foundation provides support to those who live with a lung condition every day of their lives through the Breathe Easy Club, a nationwide network of local voluntary support groups, and finds solutions to lung disease by funding world class medical research.

British Lung Foundation Project Grants

Subjects: Respiratory diseases.
Purpose: To promote medical research into the prevention, diagnosis and treatment of all lung diseases.
Eligibility: Open to graduates working within the United Kingdom who have some experience of research. The principal applicant must be based in a research centre in the United Kingdom.
Level of Study: Doctorate, Postdoctorate, Postgraduate, Predoctorate, Professional development, Research.
Type: Project grant.
Value: Up to UK£120,000.
Length of Study: Up to three years.
Frequency: Annual.
Study Establishment: An approved research centre.
Country of Study: United Kingdom.
No. of awards offered: Approx. 10.
Application Procedure: Applicants must complete an application form, available from the British Lung Foundation.
Closing Date: TBA - Spring for preliminary applications for awards in Oct' 04.
Funding: Commercial, Private.
Contributor: Voluntary donations.
No. of awards given last year: Approx. 10.
No. of applicants last year: 132.

BRITISH MEDICAL ASSOCIATION (BMA)

Board of Science & Education, Tavistock, Square, London, WC1H
9JP, England
Tel: (44) 20 7383 6755
Fax: (44) 20 7383 6383
Email: info.sciencegrants@bma.org.uk
www: http://www.bma.org.uk
Contact: Mrs N Jayesinghe, Research Trusts (Grants)

The British Medical Association (BMA) is a professional association of doctors, representing their interests and providing services for its 122,000 plus members. It is an independent trade union, a scientific and educational body, and a publishing house.

Brackenbury Grant

Subjects: To assist research in the field of public health
Purpose: To assist and support research.
Eligibility: Open to members of the British Medical Association.
Level of Study: Research.
Type: Research grant.
Value: Approx. UK£1,250.
Length of Study: Three years.
Frequency: Every three years.
Country of Study: United Kingdom.
No. of awards offered: One.
Application Procedure: Applicants must complete an application form.
Closing Date: Mid March.
Funding: Private.
No. of awards given last year: None.
Additional Information: Grants are advertised in January.

C H Milburn Grant

Subjects: To assist research in Medical Jurisprudence and/or Forensic Medicine.
Purpose: To assist and support research.
Eligibility: Open to registered medical practitioners in the United Kingdom.
Level of Study: Research.
Type: Research grant.
Value: Approx. UK£750.
Length of Study: Three years.
Frequency: Every three years.
Country of Study: United Kingdom.
No. of awards offered: One.
Application Procedure: Applicants must complete an application form.

Closing Date: Mid March.
Funding: Private.
No. of awards given last year: None.
Additional Information: Grants are advertised in January.

Doris Hillier Grant

Subjects: To assist research into rheumatism and arthritis (every 3rd year into parkinsons disease).
Purpose: To assist and support research.
Eligibility: Open to registered medical practitioners in the United Kingdom.
Level of Study: Research.
Type: Research grant.
Value: Approx. UK£17,500.
Length of Study: Three years.
Frequency: Annual.
Country of Study: United Kingdom.
No. of awards offered: One.
Application Procedure: Applicants must complete an application form.
Closing Date: Mid March.
Funding: Private.
No. of awards given last year: One.
Additional Information: Grants are advertised in January.

Doris Odlum Grant

Subjects: To assist research into mental health.
Purpose: To assist and support research.
Eligibility: Open to medical practitioners registered in the British Commonwealth or the Republic of Ireland.
Level of Study: Research.
Type: Research grant.
Value: Approx. UK£600.
Length of Study: Three years.
Frequency: Every three years.
Country of Study: United Kingdom.
No. of awards offered: One.
Application Procedure: Applicants must complete an application form.
Closing Date: Mid March.
Funding: Private.
No. of awards given last year: None.
Additional Information: Grants are advertised in January.

Elizabeth Wherry and Charlotte Eyck Grants

Subjects: To assist kidney research.
Purpose: To assist and support research.
Eligibility: Open to registered medical practitioners in the United Kingdom.
Level of Study: Research.
Type: Research grant.
Value: Approx. UK£7,250.
Length of Study: Three years.
Frequency: Every two years.
Country of Study: United Kingdom.
No. of awards offered: One.
Application Procedure: Applicants must complete an application form.
Closing Date: Mid March.
Funding: Private.
No. of awards given last year: One.
Additional Information: Grants are advertised in January.

Geoffrey Holt, Ivy Powell and Edith Walsh Grants

Subjects: To assist research into cardiovascular disease.
Purpose: To assist and support research.
Eligibility: Open to members of the British Medical Association.
Level of Study: Research.
Type: Research grant.
Value: Approx. UK£4,000.
Length of Study: Three years.
Frequency: Every two years.
Country of Study: United Kingdom.

No. of awards offered: One.
Application Procedure: Applicants must complete an application form.
Closing Date: Mid March.
Funding: Private.
No. of awards given last year: None.
Additional Information: Grants are advertised in January.

H C Roscoe Grant

Subjects: To promote research into the elimination of the common cold and other viral diseases of the human respiratory system.
Purpose: To assist and support research.
Eligibility: Open to members of the British Medical Association and non medical scientists working in association with a British Medical Association member.
Level of Study: Research.
Type: Research grant.
Value: Approx. UK£30,000.
Length of Study: Three years.
Frequency: Annual.
Country of Study: United Kingdom.
No. of awards offered: One.
Application Procedure: Applicants must complete an application form.
Closing Date: Mid March.
Funding: Private.
No. of awards given last year: Two.
Additional Information: Grants are advertised in January.

Helen Tomkinson and Albert McMaster Grant

Subjects: To assist cancer research with the specific area of research defined on an annual basis.
Purpose: To assist and support research.
Eligibility: Open to members of the British Medical Association.
Level of Study: Research.
Type: Research grant.
Value: Approx. UK£11,750.
Length of Study: Three years.
Frequency: Every two years.
Country of Study: United Kingdom.
No. of awards offered: One.
Application Procedure: Applicants must complete an application form.
Closing Date: Mid March.
Funding: Private.
No. of awards given last year: None.
Additional Information: Grants are advertised in January.

Insole Grant

Subjects: To assist research in the causation, prevention or treatment of disease.
Purpose: To assist and support research.
Eligibility: Open to members of the British Medical Association.
Level of Study: Research.
Type: Research grant.
Value: Approx. UK£750.
Length of Study: Three years.
Frequency: Every three years.
Country of Study: United Kingdom.
No. of awards offered: One.
Application Procedure: Applicants must complete an application form.
Closing Date: Mid March.
Funding: Private.
No. of awards given last year: None.
Additional Information: Grants are advertised in January.

The James Trust

Subjects: To assist research into asthma.
Purpose: To assist and support research.
Eligibility: Open to members of the British Medical Association.
Level of Study: Research.
Type: Research grant.
Value: Approx. UK£21,000.

Length of Study: Three years.
Frequency: Annual.
Country of Study: United Kingdom.
No. of awards offered: One.
Application Procedure: Applicants must complete an application form.
Closing Date: Mid March.
Funding: Private.
No. of awards given last year: One.
Additional Information: Grants are advertised in January.

Joan Dawkins Grant

Subjects: The area of research for which the grant supports is defined on an annual basis.
Purpose: To assist and support research.
Eligibility: Open to medical practitioners. Non medical scientists may also apply. Projects must relate to the United Kingdom.
Level of Study: Research.
Type: Research grant.
Value: Approx. UK£30,000.
Length of Study: Three years.
Frequency: Annual.
Country of Study: United Kingdom.
No. of awards offered: One.
Application Procedure: Applicants must complete an application form.
Closing Date: Mid March.
Funding: Private.
No. of awards given last year: One.
Additional Information: Grants are advertised in January.

John William Clark Grant

Subjects: To assist research into the causes of blindness.
Purpose: To assist and support research.
Eligibility: Open to members of the British Medical Association.
Level of Study: Research.
Type: Research grant.
Value: Approx. UK£6,750.
Length of Study: Three years.
Frequency: Every two years.
Country of Study: United Kingdom.
No. of awards offered: One.
Application Procedure: Applicants must complete an application form.
Closing Date: Mid March.
Funding: Private.
No. of awards given last year: One.
Additional Information: Grants are advertised in January.

Katherine Bishop Harman Grant

Subjects: To assist research into the risks to womens health and life in pregnancy and childbearing.
Purpose: To assist and support research.
Eligibility: Open to medical practitioners registered in the United Kingdom or any other country which at one time formed part of the British Empire.
Level of Study: Research.
Type: Research grant.
Value: Approx. UK£1,000.
Length of Study: Three years.
Frequency: Every three years.
Country of Study: United Kingdom.
No. of awards offered: One.
Application Procedure: Applicants must complete an application form.
Closing Date: Mid March.
Funding: Private.
No. of awards given last year: None.
Additional Information: Grants are advertised in January.

Margaret Temple Grant

Subjects: To assist research into schizophrenia.
Purpose: To assist and support research.
Eligibility: Open to medical practitioners. Non medical scientists may also apply. Projects must relate to the United Kingdom.

Level of Study: Research.
Type: Research grant.
Value: Approx. UK£20,000.
Length of Study: Three years.
Frequency: Annual.
Country of Study: United Kingdom.
No. of awards offered: One.
Application Procedure: Applicants must complete an application form.
Closing Date: Mid March.
Funding: Private.
No. of awards given last year: One.
Additional Information: Grants are advertised in January.

Middlemore Grant

Subjects: To assist research in any branch of ophthalmic medicine or surgery.
Purpose: To assist and support research.
Eligibility: Open to registered medical practitioners in the United Kingdom.
Level of Study: Research.
Type: Research grant.
Value: Approx. UK£1,250.
Length of Study: Three years.
Frequency: Every three years.
Country of Study: United Kingdom.
No. of awards offered: One.
Application Procedure: Applicants must complete an application form.
Closing Date: Mid March.
Funding: Private.
Additional Information: Grants are advertised in January.

Nathaniel Bishop Harman Award

Subjects: To assist research into the outcome of treatment of a specific condition in hospital practice.
Purpose: To assist and support research.
Eligibility: Open to registered medical practitioners who are staff of a hospital in Great Britain or Northern Ireland but who are not staff of a recognised undergraduate or postgraduate medical school.
Level of Study: Research.
Type: Research grant.
Value: Approx. UK£625.
Length of Study: Three years.
Frequency: Every three years.
Country of Study: United Kingdom.
No. of awards offered: One.
Application Procedure: Applicants must complete an application form.
Closing Date: Mid March.
Funding: Private.
Additional Information: Grants are advertised in January.

Sir Charles Hastings and Charles Oliver Hawthorne Grants

Subjects: To assist research in general practice.
Purpose: To assist and support research.
Eligibility: Open to members of the British Medical Association engaged in general practice.
Level of Study: Research.
Type: Research grant.
Value: Approx. UK£2,350.
Length of Study: Three years.
Frequency: Every three years.
Country of Study: United Kingdom.
No. of awards offered: One.
Application Procedure: Applicants must complete an application form.
Closing Date: Mid March.
Funding: Private.
No. of awards given last year: One.
Additional Information: Grants are advertised in January.

T P Gunton Grant

Subjects: To assist research into public health education relating to cancer.
Purpose: To assist and support research.
Eligibility: Open to both medical and non medical scientists in the U.K.
Level of Study: Research.
Type: Research grant.
Value: Approx. UK£17,500.
Length of Study: Three years.
Frequency: Annual.
Country of Study: United Kingdom.
No. of awards offered: One.
Application Procedure: Applicants must complete an application form.
Closing Date: Mid March.
Funding: Private.
No. of awards given last year: None.
Additional Information: Grants are advertised in January.

Vera Down Grant

Subjects: To assist research into Neurological Disorders.
Purpose: To assist and support research.
Eligibility: Open to registered medical practitioners in the United Kingdom.
Level of Study: Research.
Type: Research grant.
Value: Approx. UK£10,750.
Length of Study: Three years.
Frequency: Every two years.
Country of Study: United Kingdom.
No. of awards offered: One.
Application Procedure: Applicants must complete an application form.
Closing Date: Mid March.
Funding: Private.
No. of awards given last year: One.
Additional Information: Grants are advertised in January.

BRITISH NUTRITION FOUNDATION (BNF)

High Holborn House, London, WC1V 6RQ, England
Tel: (44) 20 7404 6504
Fax: (44) 20 7404 6747
Email: postbox@nutrition.org.uk
www: http://www.nutrition.org.uk
Contact: Ceisscousins

The British Nutrition Foundation (BNF) promotes the nutritional well being of society through the impartial interpretation and effective dissemination of scientifically based nutritional knowledge and advice. It works in partnership with academic and research institutes, the food industry, educators and government. The Foundation influences all in the food chain, government, the professions and the media. The BNF is a charitable organisation which receives funds from the food industry, government and other sources.

BNF/Nestlé Bursary Scheme

Subjects: Nutritional problems associated with adults in apparent health and disease states, including special areas of maternal health and infant nutrition.
Purpose: To help selected medical students to undertake an elective concerned with nutritional problems encountered in developing countries.
Eligibility: Open to medical students at United Kingdom medical schools.
Type: Bursary.
Value: Up to UK£500 to reimburse travel and accommodation.
Frequency: Annual.
Country of Study: Other.
No. of awards offered: Up to 12.

Application Procedure: Application form needs to be completed, with an outline of the proposed study and a reference from the medical school.
Closing Date: Normally January 31st.
Funding: Commercial.
Contributor: Nestlé UK Ltd.
No. of awards given last year: 12.
No. of applicants last year: 30.
Additional Information: Two copies of a detailed report of the study are required within five months of returning to the United Kingdom.

Denis Burkitt Study Awards

Subjects: Public health and hygiene, social and preventive medicine, dietetics.
Purpose: To help medical and nutrition science students, who wish to undertake elective or other studies in developing nations on food and nutrition, and their relationship to health and disease within any age group.
Eligibility: Open to candidates from any country but they must be studying in the United Kingdom.
Type: Bursary.
Value: UK£750.
Frequency: Annual.
Country of Study: Other.
No. of awards offered: Up to 10.
Application Procedure: Applicants must complete an application form. Details are sent to medical schools in the Autumn and are also available direct from the British Nutrition Foundation at that time.
Closing Date: About January 20th - although it varies from year to year.
Funding: Commercial.
Contributor: Kellog company of Great Britain Ltd.
No. of awards given last year: 10.
No. of applicants last year: 36.

BRITISH PHARMACOLOGICAL SOCIETY

16 Angel Gate, City Road, London
EC1V 2SG, England
Tel: (44) 20 7417 0114
Email: admin@bps.ac.uk
www: http://www.bps.ac.uk
Contact: Ms Sarah-Jane Stagg, Executive Officer

The British Pharmacological Society is a learned society concerned with research into drugs and the way they work. Its members work in academia, industry and the health services, and many are medically qualified.

A J Clark Studentship

Subjects: Pharmacology.
Purpose: To enable young scientists with degrees in pharmacology or closely related subjects to carry out research.
Eligibility: Candidates should intend to follow a career in pharmacology.
Level of Study: Doctorate.
Type: Studentship.
Value: Annual stipend and contribution of £1,500 to research costs. Fees are paid at European Union student rates.
Length of Study: Three years.
Frequency: Annual.
Study Establishment: A recognised department in the United Kingdom.
Country of Study: United Kingdom.
No. of awards offered: One.
Application Procedure: Applicants must complete an application form, available from the Society website.
Closing Date: February 5th.
Funding: Private.
No. of awards given last year: One.
Additional Information: Applications must be accompanied by a covering letter from the proposed supervisor giving the agreement of the university or other organisation to accept the student if he or she receives an award. A detailed plan of the three year research project must also be submitted.

BRITISH RETINITIS PIGMENTOSA SOCIETY (BRPS)

PO Box 350, Buckingham, Buckinghamshire, MK18 1GZ, England
Tel: (44) 1280 821334
Fax: (44) 1280 815900
Email: info@brps.org.uk
www: http://www.brps.org.uk
Contact: Mrs Lynda Cantor MBE, Trustee/Honorary Secretary

The British Retinitis Pigmentosa Society (BRPS) is a membership organisation run by volunteers with 27 branches throughout the United Kingdom. The BRPS aims to raise funds for scientific research to provide treatments leading to a cure for Retinitis Pigmentosa. The Society provides a welfare support and guidance service to its members and their families.

BRPS Research Grants

Subjects: Retinitis pigmentosa.
Purpose: To financially support research into treatments leading to a cure for Retinitis Pigmentosa.
Eligibility: Please contact the Society.
Level of Study: Postgraduate.
Type: Research grant.
Value: Varies. Grants awarded to countries outside of the United Kingdom are made in sterling. Should sterling fall in value against the currency of the country in which the recipient of the grant works, the Society will not make good the shortfall. Unless otherwise stated the Research Grant will not provide for overheads or indirect expenses but are renewable annually upon recommendation of the Scientific Advisory Board.
Length of Study: Varies.
Frequency: Annual.
Country of Study: Any country.
No. of awards offered: Varies.
Application Procedure: Applicants must submit their application to the BRPS office.
Closing Date: Grant applications should be at the BRPS office at least six weeks prior to the Board of Trustees meeting. Dates of these meetings are supplied on request from the Honorary Secretary.
Additional Information: Progress reports should include a description of the work carried out for the purpose of the original project, the programme of work for the ensuing year and details of problems encountered with specific experimental methods and should cover at least two sides of an A4 sheet. At the conclusion of the project a final report must be submitted. Equipment or apparatus donated is for the purpose of RP research and should be maintained in good working order by the recipient. If a particular research project is completed, abandoned or discontinued the apparatus and equipment should be placed at the disposal of BRPS. The BRPS National Secretariat must be notified of any increase in salaries that are awarded either nationally or by the university or institution concerned at the time it is agreed. It is the responsibility of the recipient to inform the Secretariat of any relevant changes. Recipients must inform the Society of the exact date they commence work on their project.

BRITISH SCHOOL AT ATHENS

52 Souedias Street, Athens, 106 76, Greece
Tel: (30) 210 721 0974
Fax: (30) 210 723 6560
Email: admin@bsa.ac.uk
www: http://www.bsa.gla.ac.uk
Contact: Assistant Director

The British School at Athens promotes research into the archaeology, architecture, art, history, language, literature, religion and topography of Greece in ancient, medieval and modern times. It consists of the

Library, Fitch Laboratory for Archaeological Science, Archive, Museum, hostel and a second base at Knossos for research and fieldwork.

Hector and Elizabeth Catling Bursary

Subjects: Greek studies including the archaeology, art, history, language, literature, religion, ethnography, anthropology, geography of any period and all branches of archaeological science.
Eligibility: Open to researchers of British, Irish or Commonwealth nationality.
Level of Study: Doctorate, Postdoctorate, Postgraduate.
Type: Bursary.
Value: A maximum UK£500 per bursary to assist with travel and maintenance costs incurred in fieldwork, to pay for the use of scientific or other specialised equipment in or outside the laboratory in Greece or elsewhere, and to buy necessary supplies.
Frequency: Annual, if funds are available.
Study Establishment: The British School at Athens.
Country of Study: Other.
No. of awards offered: One-two.
Application Procedure: Applicants must submit a curriculum vitae and state concisely the nature of the intended work, a breakdown of budget, the amount requested from the Fund and how this will be spent. Applications should include two sealed letters of reference. Bursary holders must submit a short report to the Committee on completion of the project.
Closing Date: December 15th for notification by the end of February.
Funding: Private.
Additional Information: The bursary is not intended for publication costs, and can not be awarded to an excavation or field survey team.

BRITISH SCHOOL AT ROME (BSR)

The British Academy, 10 Carlton House Terrace
London, SW1Y 5AH, England
Tel: (44) 20 7969 5202
Fax: (44) 20 7969 5401
Email: bsr@britac.ac.uk
www: http://www.bsr.ac.uk
Contact: Dr Gillian Clark, Registrar

The British School at Rome (BSR) is an interdisciplinary research centre for the humanities, visual arts and architecture. Each year the School offers a range of awards in its principal fields of interest. These interests are further promoted by public lectures, conferences, publications, archaeological research and an excellent reference library.

Abbey Fellowships in Painting

Subjects: Painting.
Purpose: To give mid career artists the opportunity of working in Rome.
Eligibility: Open to mid career painters with an established record of achievement. Applicants must be citizens of the United Kingdom or United States of America or have been resident in either country for atleast 5 years.
Type: Fellowship.
Value: UK£700 per month plus full board and lodging.
Length of Study: Three months.
Frequency: Annual.
Study Establishment: The British School at Rome.
Country of Study: Italy.
No. of awards offered: Three.
Application Procedure: Applicants must complete an application form and pay an application fee.
Closing Date: Early to mid January.
Funding: Private.
Contributor: The Abbey Council.
No. of awards given last year: Three.

For further information contact:

Abbey Awards, 43 Carson Road, London, SE21 8HT, England

Abbey Scholarship in Painting

Subjects: Painting.
Purpose: To give exceptionally promising emergent painters the opportunity to work in Rome.
Eligibility: Open to citizens of the United Kingdom and United States of America and to those of other nationality provided resident in either country for atleast 5 years.
Level of Study: Unrestricted.
Type: Scholarship.
Value: UK£4,500 plus board and lodging.
Length of Study: Nine months.
Frequency: Annual.
Study Establishment: The British School at Rome.
Country of Study: Italy.
No. of awards offered: One.
Application Procedure: Applicants must complete an application form and pay an application fee.
Closing Date: Early to mid January.
Funding: Private.
Contributor: The Abbey Council.
No. of awards given last year: One.

For further information contact:

Abbey Awards, 43 Carson Road, London, SE21 8HT, England

Arts Council of England Helen Chadwick Fellowship

Subjects: Visual arts.
Purpose: To allow artists to pursue a project which could be made possible or enhanced by spending periods of time in Rome and Oxford.
Eligibility: Open to visual artists who have established their practices in the years following graduation. Applicants must be United Kingdom nationals or have been continuously resident in the United Kingdom since March 2001.
Level of Study: Professional development.
Type: Fellowship.
Value: UK£1,000 per month plus travel and materials allowances, and board and lodging at the British School at Rome and in Oxford.
Length of Study: Six months.
Frequency: Annual.
Study Establishment: The British School at Rome and Ruskin School of Drawing and Fine Art at the University of Oxford.
Country of Study: UK and Italy.
No. of awards offered: One.
Application Procedure: Applicants must write for details of the application procedure.
Closing Date: Early January.
Funding: Private.
Contributor: Arts Council England.
No. of awards given last year: One.

Balsdon Fellowship

Subjects: Archaeology, art history, history and literature of Italy from prehistory to the modern period.
Purpose: To enable senior scholars engaged in research to spend a period of time in Rome to further their studies.
Eligibility: Open to established Scholars normally posted in a university of the United Kingdom. Applicants must either be nationals of the United Kingdom or Commonwealth, working professionally or studying at graduate level for over three years within the United Kingdom or a Commonwealth country.
Level of Study: Postdoctorate, Professional development.
Type: Fellowship.
Value: UK£650 plus board and lodging.
Length of Study: Three months.
Frequency: Annual.
Study Establishment: The British School at Rome.
Country of Study: Italy.
No. of awards offered: One.
Application Procedure: Applicants must complete an application form.
Closing Date: Early January.

Funding: Private.
Contributor: A bequest to the British School at Rome.
No. of awards given last year: One.

Hugh Last Fellowship

Subjects: Classical antiquity.
Purpose: To enable established scholars to collect research material concerning classical antiquity.
Eligibility: Open to established Scholars normally posted at a United Kingdom university who are either United Kingdom or Commonwealth nationals, have been working professionally or who have been studying at graduate level for more than three years within the United Kingdom or a Commonwealth country.
Level of Study: Postdoctorate, Professional development.
Type: Fellowship.
Value: Board and lodging at the British School at Rome plus a research grant of UK£180 per month and a travel allowance of UK£150.
Length of Study: Three months.
Frequency: Annual.
Study Establishment: The British School at Rome.
Country of Study: Italy.
No. of awards offered: One.
Application Procedure: Applicants must complete an application form.
Closing Date: Early January.
Funding: Private.
Contributor: A bequest to the British School at Rome.
No. of awards given last year: One.

Paul Mellon Centre Rome Fellowship

Subjects: Anglo-Italian cultural and artistic relations.
Purpose: To assist research on grand tour subjects or on Anglo-Italian cultural and artistic relations.
Eligibility: Open to established Scholars in the United Kingdom, United States of America or elsewhere. Applicants should have fairly fluent Italian.
Level of Study: Postdoctorate, Professional development.
Type: Fellowship.
Value: Full board at the British School at Rome. For independent Scholars, the fellowship offers a stipend of UK£6,000 plus travel to and from Rome. For scholars in full-time university employment, the fellowship offers an honorarium of UK£2,000, travel to and from Rome and a sum of UK£6,000 towards replacement teaching costs for a term at the Fellow's home institution.
Length of Study: Four months.
Frequency: Annual.
Study Establishment: The British School at Rome.
Country of Study: Italy.
No. of awards offered: One.
Application Procedure: Applicants must contact the Paul Mellon Centre for Studies in British Art for details.
Closing Date: January.
Funding: Private.
Contributor: The Paul Mellon Centre for Studies in British Art.

For further information contact:

The Paul Mellon Centre for Studies in British Art, 16 Bedford Square, London, WC1B 3JA, England
Email: info@paul-mellon-centre.ac.uk
www: http://www.paul-mellon-centre.ac.uk/support/PDFs/4rome.pdf

Rome Awards in Archaeology, History and Letters

Subjects: Archaeology, art history, history and literature of Italy from prehistory to the modern period.
Purpose: To enable persons engaged in research, either for a higher degree or at early postdoctoral level, to spend a period in Rome to further their studies.
Eligibility: Open to United Kingdom or Commonwealth citizens and to those who have been working professionally or studying at postgraduate level for more than three years in the United Kingdom or a Commonwealth country. Applicants should normally have begun a programme of research in the general field for which the award is being sought, whether or not they are registered for a higher degree.

Normally applicants should be attached to or registered at a university in the United Kingdom.
Level of Study: Doctorate, Postdoctorate, Postgraduate.
Type: Grant.
Value: UK£150 per month plus UK£180 travel with board and lodging.
Length of Study: Up to four months.
Frequency: Annual.
Study Establishment: The British School at Rome.
Country of Study: Italy.
No. of awards offered: Varies.
Application Procedure: Applicants must complete an application form.
Closing Date: Early January.
No. of awards given last year: Two.

Rome Fellowship

Subjects: Archaeology, art history, history and literature of Italy from prehistory to the modern period.
Purpose: To enable those who have been awarded their doctorate prior to taking up the award to launch a major piece of post-doctoral research.
Eligibility: Open to United Kingdom or Commonwealth citizens and to those who have been working professionally or studying at postgraduate level for more than three years in the United Kingdom or Commonwealth. Successful applicants will need to have been awarded their doctorate prior to taking up the award. Normally applicants should be or have been attached to, registered at or working at the university in the United Kingdom.
Level of Study: Postdoctorate.
Type: Fellowship.
Value: £475 per month plus full board and lodging at the British School at Rome.
Length of Study: Nine months.
Frequency: Annual.
Study Establishment: The British School at Rome.
Country of Study: Italy.
No. of awards offered: Varies.
Application Procedure: Applicants must complete an application form.
Closing Date: Early January.
No. of awards given last year: One.

Rome Scholarship in Architecture

Subjects: Architecture and urbanism relevant to Rome and Italy.
Purpose: To encourage the pursuit of projects in architecture and urbanism relevant to Rome and Italy.
Eligibility: Open to architects, students of architecture and associated disciplines of at least post diploma level who are British or Commonwealth nationals, and to those who have been working professionally or studying at postgraduate level for more than three years in the United Kingdom or Commonwealth.
Level of Study: Postgraduate, Professional development.
Type: Scholarship.
Value: UK£500 per month plus board and lodging.
Length of Study: Three-nine months.
Frequency: Annual.
Study Establishment: The British School at Rome.
Country of Study: Italy.
No. of awards offered: One-two.
Application Procedure: Applicants must complete an application form and pay an application fee. Application forms are available from the British School at Rome Registrar.
Closing Date: Mid January.
No. of awards given last year: One.

Rome Scholarships in Ancient, Medieval and Later Italian Studies

Subjects: Archaeology, art history, history and literature of Italy from prehistory to the modern period.
Purpose: To enable persons engaged in research, at a predoctoral level, to spend a period in Rome to further their studies.

Eligibility: Open to United Kingdom or Commonwealth citizens and to those who have been working professionally or studying at postgraduate level for more than three years in the United Kingdom or Commonwealth. Applicants should normally have begun a programme of research in the general field for which the scholarship is being sought, whether or not registered for a higher degree. Normally applicants should be attached to or registered at a university in the United Kingdom.
Level of Study: Doctorate, Postgraduate.
Type: Scholarship.
Value: UK£4,000 plus board and lodging.
Length of Study: Nine months.
Frequency: Annual.
Study Establishment: The British School at Rome.
Country of Study: Italy.
No. of awards offered: Four-five.
Application Procedure: Applicants must complete an application form.
Closing Date: Early January.
No. of awards given last year: Four.

Rome Scholarships in the Fine Arts

Subjects: Painting, printmaking, sculpture and other suitable media including fine art, video and photography.
Purpose: To give emerging, early and mid-career artists the opportunity to work in Rome.
Eligibility: Open to United Kingdom or Commonwealth citizens who have been working professionally or studying at postgraduate level for more than three years in the United Kingdom or Commonwealth.
Level of Study: Postgraduate, Professional development.
Type: Scholarship.
Value: UK£500 per month plus board and lodging.
Length of Study: Three-nine months.
Frequency: Annual.
Study Establishment: The British School at Rome.
Country of Study: Italy.
No. of awards offered: Varies.
Application Procedure: Applicants must complete an application form and pay an application fee.
Closing Date: Early December.
No. of awards given last year: One.

Sainsbury Scholarship in Painting and Sculpture

Subjects: Painting and sculpture in which a commitment to drawing can be demonstrated clearly.
Purpose: To give emerging artists the opportunity to work in Rome.
Eligibility: Open to citizens of the United Kingdom and to those who have been working professionally or studying at postgraduate level for at least the last three years in the United Kingdom. Applicants must be under 28 on October 1st in the year in which they would begin to hold the scholarship.
Level of Study: Postgraduate.
Type: Scholarship.
Value: UK£750 per month plus board, lodging and a travel grant of UK£1,000.
Length of Study: Twelve months with an opportunity for a further nine months in the following academic year, at the discretion of the selection committee.
Frequency: Annual.
Study Establishment: The British School at Rome.
Country of Study: Italy.
No. of awards offered: One.
Application Procedure: Applicants must complete an application form and pay an application fee.
Closing Date: Early December.
Funding: Private.
Contributor: The Linbury Trust.
No. of awards given last year: 1.

Sargant Fellowship

Subjects: Visual Art and Architecture.
Purpose: To enable a distinguished artist or architect to research and make new work within the historical context of Rome,

awag from the pressures associated with exhibiting and deadlines.
Eligibility: Open to United Kingdom or Commonwealth citizens and to those who have been working professionally or studying at post-graduate level for more than three years in the United Kingdom or Commonwealth.
Level of Study: Postdoctorate.
Type: Fellowship.
Value: £2,000 per month plus full board and lodging at the British School at Rome.
Length of Study: Three months.
Frequency: Annual.
Study Establishment: The British School at Rome.
Country of Study: Italy.
No. of awards offered: One.
Application Procedure: Applicants must complete an application form.
Closing Date: Early January.
No. of awards given last year: None.

Tim Potter Memorial Award

Subjects: Archaeology.
Purpose: To promote the study of Italian archaeological material by those of high academic potential who have had limited previous opportunity to visit Italy.
Eligibility: Open to United Kingdom or Commonwealth citizens and to those who have been working professionally or studying at postgraduate level for more than three years in the United Kingdom or Commonwealth. Applicants must have graduated prior to taking up the Award, but will not necessarily be registered for postgraduate study. Applications are also invited from those working in museums who could benefit from studying comparable Italian material.
Level of Study: Graduate.
Type: Grant.
Value: £150 per month plus £500 travel allowance and full board and lodging at the British School at Rome.
Length of Study: Two to four months.
Frequency: Annual.
Study Establishment: The British School at Rome.
Country of Study: Italy.
No. of awards offered: Varies.
Application Procedure: Applicants must complete an application form.
Closing Date: Early January.
No. of awards given last year: New award.

Wingate Rome Scholarship in the Fine Arts

Subjects: Painting, printmaking, sculpture and other suitable media including fine art, video and photography.
Purpose: To give emerging, early and mid-career artists the opportunity to work in Rome.
Eligibility: Open to citizens of the United Kingdom and other Commonwealth countries, Ireland, Israel or citizens of another European Union country provided that they are, during the period of application and have been for at least three years, resident in the United Kingdom. All applicants must be aged 24 or over at the beginning of the academic year (i.e. on or after September 1st) in which the award falls.
Level of Study: Postgraduate, Professional development.
Type: Scholarship.
Value: UK£500 per month plus board and lodging.
Length of Study: Three or six months.
Frequency: Annual.
Study Establishment: The British School at Rome.
Country of Study: Italy.
No. of awards offered: One-two.
Application Procedure: Applicants must complete an application form and pay an application fee.
Closing Date: Early December.
Funding: Private.
Contributor: The Harold Hyam Wingate Foundation.
No. of awards given last year: One.

BRITISH SCHOOL OF ARCHAEOLOGY IN IRAQ

10 Carlton House Terrace, London, SW1Y 5AH, England
Tel: (44) 20 7969 5274
Fax: (44) 20 7969 5401
Email: bsai@britac.ac.uk
www: britac.ac.uk/institutes/iraq/
Contact: The Secretary

The British School of Archaeology in Iraq's aim is to encourage and support the study of, and research relating to, the archaeology, history and languages of Iraq and its neighbouring countries, including East Syria and the Gulf, from the earliest times.

British School of Archaeology in Iraq Grants

Subjects: Archaeology, history and the languages of Iraq and neighbouring countries from the earliest time to the eighteenth-century.
Purpose: To encourage and support research into the archaeology (and cognate subjects), history and languages of Iraq and its neighbouring countries.
Eligibility: Open to British Commonwealth citizens who are postgraduates with a knowledge of Western-Asiatic archaeology.
Level of Study: Postdoctorate, Postgraduate.
Type: Grant.
Value: Usually between UK£500-3,000, depending on the nature of the research.
Length of Study: One academic year.
Frequency: Annual.
Country of Study: Other.
No. of awards offered: Varies.
Application Procedure: The School considers applications for individual research grants twice a year in Spring and Autumn. Information and application forms are available from either the Secretary or the website. Two academic references are required.
Closing Date: April 15th and October 15th for grants of up to UK£1,000. October 15th is the preferred date for major research grants of over UK£1,000.
Funding: Government.
No. of awards given last year: Nine.
Additional Information: Details of the British School of Archaeology in Iraq are available on the website under Institutes Overseas and Sponsored Societies. Grantees will be required to provide a written report of their work and abstracts from these reports will be published in future issues of the BSAI Newsletter. Individual Research Grants are offered, as are Major Research Grants.

THE BRITISH SCHOOLS AND UNIVERSITIES FOUNDATION, INC. (BSUF)

12 Pilgrims Way, Guildford, Surrey, GU4 8AB, England
Tel: (44) 1483 575588
Contact: Mrs Sheila Wiltshire, Honorary Director

The British Schools and Universities Foundation (BSUF) makes grants to educational, scientific or literary institutes in the United Kingdom and in member nations of the British Commonwealth. The Foundation also fosters the education and academic work of United States scholars and students at British institutions and vice versa. It also provides a way for United States tax payers to make tax deductible gifts to the United Kingdom for colleges and schools.

BSUF May and Ward Scholarships (for British scholars)

Subjects: All subjects.
Purpose: To promote, foster and assist the education and academic work of British scholars and students at United States educational institutions and of United States scholars and students at British educational institutions.
Eligibility: Open to Scholars from the United States of America, United Kingdom, Australia, Canada and New Zealand.

Level of Study: Doctorate, Postgraduate, Professional development.
Type: Scholarship.
Value: US$12,500 maximum.
Length of Study: A maximum of two years.
Frequency: Annual.
Country of Study: The United States of America or the United Kingdom.
No. of awards offered: Four-six.
Application Procedure: Applicants must obtain an application form. Applicants should enclose a stamped addressed envelope with the request.
Closing Date: March 1st, for an award to commence the following September.
Funding: Private.
Contributor: Donors in the United States of America.
No. of awards given last year: Five.
No. of applicants last year: 150.

For further information contact:

BSUF, Suite 1006, 575 Madison Avenue, New York, NY 10022-2511, United States of America

May and Ward Scholarships British Schools and Universities (for United States scholars)

Subjects: All subjects.
Purpose: To support United States scholars at United Kingdom educational, literary and scientific institutions and British scholars in the United States.
Eligibility: Open to applicants attending or graduates of an accredited institute of learning.
Level of Study: Doctorate, Graduate, Postgraduate, Predoctorate, Professional development, Research.
Type: Scholarship.
Value: US$12,500 annually.
Length of Study: One-two years.
Frequency: Annual.
Study Establishment: A college, university or research establishment in the United States of America for United Kingdom applicants and educational institutions in the United Kingdom for United States applicants.
Country of Study: The United States of America or the United Kingdom.
No. of awards offered: Four-six.
Application Procedure: Applicants must obtain an application form and guidelines by writing to their BSUF representative at the London address if they are in the United Kingdom and to the New York address if they are in the United States of America.
Closing Date: March 1st.
Funding: Private.
Contributor: British Schools and Universities Foundation.
No. of awards given last year: Five.
No. of applicants last year: 150+.

For further information contact:

BSUF, Suite 1006, 575 Madison Avenue, New York, NY 10022-2511, United States of America

BRITISH SKIN FOUNDATION

19 Fitzroy Square, London
W1T 6EH, United Kingdom
Tel: (44) 0207 383 0266
Fax: (44) 0207 388 5263
Email: bsf@bad.org.uk
www: http://britishskinfoundation.org.uk
Contact: Mr James Stalley

The British Skin Foundation exist to support research and education into skin diseases. Working closely with patient support groups as well as many of the country's leading dermatology departments, the foundation aims to help the 7 million people in the UK who suffer with a serious skin condition.

Small Grants

Subjects: Available to anybody wishing to carry out UK based into skin disease or for the purchase of equipment.
Level of Study: Unrestricted.
Value: Up to £10,000.
Frequency: Annual.
Funding: Commercial, Private.

BRITISH SOCIOLOGICAL ASSOCIATION (BSA)

Units 3F/G, Mountjoy Research Centre, Stockton Road, Durham, DH1 3UR, England
Tel: (44) 191 383 0839
Fax: (44) 191 383 0782
Email: enquiries@britsoc.org.uk
www: http://www.britsoc.org.uk/index.htm
Contact: Deborah Brown, Office Manager

The British Sociological Association (BSA) is the learned society and professional association for sociology in Britain. The Association was founded in 1951 and membership is drawn from a wide range of backgrounds, including research, teaching, students and practitioners in many fields. The BSA provides services to all concerned with the promotion and use of sociology and sociological research.

BSA Support Fund

Subjects: Sociology.
Purpose: To allow members of the association to pursue their research interests, including conference attendance (BSA and non-BSA events). Photocopying and thesis binding costs.
Eligibility: Only fully paid-up members of the association are eligible to apply, who are registered under the UK Concessionary or UK Lower payment category. New members are eligible to apply, there is no holding period.
Level of Study: Unrestricted.
Type: Grant.
Value: Up to UK£150 per year, to cover costs associated with research, but not tuition fees, equipment or text book purchase.
Frequency: Annual.
Country of Study: United Kingdom.
No. of awards offered: Approx. 60.
Application Procedure: Applicants must obtain an application form from the British Sociological Association office.
Funding: Private.
No. of awards given last year: 65.
No. of applicants last year: 65.

THE BRITISH UNIVERSITIES NORTH AMERICA CLUB (BUNAC)

16 Bowling Green Lane, London, EC1R 0QH, England
Tel: (44) 20 7251 3472
Fax: (44) 20 7251 0215
Email: scholarships@bunac.org.uk
www: http://www.bunac.org
Contact: Scholarships Department

The British Universities North America Club (BUNAC) is a leader in the field of international work and travel exchange programmes. A non-profit, non political organisation offering an ever increasing range of programmes worldwide, BUNAC is dedicated to serving students and other young people everywhere by providing opportunities to live and work abroad legally overseas.

BUNAC Educational Scholarship Trust (BEST)

Subjects: All subjects. Some awards are specifically for sports and geography related courses.
Purpose: To help further Trans-atlantic understanding.
Eligibility: Open to citizens of the United Kingdom who have graduated from a United Kingdom university within the last five years.
Level of Study: Postgraduate.

Type: Scholarship.
Value: From a total of US$30,000, approx. US$3,000 per award.
Length of Study: Three months to three years.
Frequency: Annual.
Country of Study: United States of America or Canada.
No. of awards offered: Up to 10.
Application Procedure: Applicants must complete an application form, available in January of each year.
Closing Date: 19th March 2004.
Funding: Commercial.
No. of awards given last year: Eight.
No. of applicants last year: 70.

For further information contact:

Also available on-line at www.bunac.org.

BRITISH VASCULAR FOUNDATION

Fides House, 10 Chertsey Road, Woking, Surrey, GU21 5AB, England
Tel: (44) 1483 726511
Fax: (44) 1483 726522
Email: bvf@care4free.net
www: http://www.bvf.org.uk
Contact: K Lody, Office Manager

The British Vascular Foundation aims to provide research funding to find cures, better treatments and improve diagnosis of vascular disease. The Foundation also hopes to raise awareness of the disease's prevalence and impact and to provide information and support to sufferers, their families and friends.

Owen Shaw Award

Subjects: The rehabilitation of amputees.
Purpose: To devise better methods of helping patients to early mobilisation.
Eligibility: Open to all those with an interest in amputee rehabilitation.
Level of Study: Unrestricted.
Type: Other.
Value: UK£3,000.
Length of Study: One year.
Frequency: Annual.
Study Establishment: Any restricted research establishment.
Country of Study: United Kingdom.
No. of awards offered: One.
Application Procedure: Applicants must complete an outline proposal form, available from the Foundation.
Closing Date: January 31st.
Funding: Private.
Contributor: Owen Shaw.
No. of awards given last year: One.
No. of applicants last year: Eight.

BRITISH VETERINARY ASSOCIATION

7 Mansfield Street, London, W1G 9NQ, England
Tel: (44) 20 7636 6541
Fax: (44) 20 7637 4769
Email: press@bva.co.uk
www: http://www.bva.co.uk
Contact: Mrs Helena Cotton

The British Veterinary Association's chief interests are the standards of animal health, and veterinary surgeons' working practices. The organisation's main functions are the development of policy in areas affecting the profession, protecting and promoting the profession in matters propounded by government and other external bodies, and the provision of services to members.

Harry Steele-Bodger Memorial Travelling Scholarship

Subjects: Veterinary science and agriculture.
Purpose: To further the aims and aspirations of the late Harry Steele-Bodger.

Eligibility: Open to graduates of veterinary schools in the United Kingdom or the Republic of Ireland who have been qualified for not more than three years, and to penultimate or final year students at those schools.
Level of Study: Unrestricted.
Type: Scholarship.
Value: Approx. UK£1,100.
Frequency: Annual.
Study Establishment: A veterinary or agricultural research institute or some other course of study approved by the governing committee.
Country of Study: Any country.
No. of awards offered: One (or two).
Application Procedure: Applicants must complete an application form, available on request.
Closing Date: April 5th.
Funding: Private.
No. of awards given last year: Two.
No. of applicants last year: 13.
Additional Information: Recipients must be prepared to submit a record of their study abroad.

BROAD MEDICAL RESEARCH PROGRAM (BMRP)

The Eli & Edythe L Broad Foundation, 10900, Wilshire Boulevard, 12th Floor, Los Angeles, CA 90024-6532, United States of America
Tel: (1) 310 954 5091
Fax: (1) 310 954 5092
Email: info@broadmedical.org
www: http://www.broadmedical.org
Contact: Dr Daniel Hollander, Director

The Eli and Edythe L Broad Foundation was established in 1967. In 2001, the Foundation created the Broad Medical Research Program (BMRP) for Inflammatory Bowel Disease (IBD) Grants. The BMRP will fund innovative and early exploratory basic and clinical projects on the aetiology, management and prevention of IBD.

BMRP for Inflammatory Bowel Disease Grants
Subjects: Understanding and treating inflammatory bowel disease (IBD), which refers to Crohn's disease and ulcerative colitis.
Purpose: To stimulate innovative research that will lead to both the prevention and successful therapy of IBD. The BMRP's goal is to fund basic or clinical research projects that are in the early stages of exploration, that propose new directions or that are creative, novel, cutting edge and imaginative ideas and are not ready for funding by other more traditional granting agencies.
Eligibility: Open to non-profit organisations, such as universities, hospitals and research institutes. There are no other eligibility restrictions. In addition to experienced IBD researchers, the BMRP wishes to encourage applications from well trained scientists who are not currently working in IBD to apply their knowledge, expertise and techniques to IBD research. Interdisciplinary collaboration is strongly encouraged.
Level of Study: Research.
Type: Research grant.
Value: Budgets should be commensurate with the scope of the work. Those who will need significantly more than US$100,000/year should contact the BMRP before preparing their letters of interest.
Length of Study: One to two years, with possible renewal.
Frequency: Throughout the year.
Country of Study: Any country.
No. of awards offered: Varies.
Application Procedure: Applicants must submit a brief letter of interest of up to three pages. Please visit the website for further content information and application process. Investigators whose letters of interest appear to fit the BMRP's aims will be invited to submit full proposals.
Closing Date: There are no deadlines for receipt of letters of interest.
Funding: Private.
Contributor: Eli and Edythe L Broad.
No. of awards given last year: 34.
No. of applicants last year: 128.

Additional Information: IBD refers to two chronic inflammatory disorders: Crohn's disease (ileitis) and ulcerative colitis. Both diseases result in inflammation of the intestinal wall, but differ in location and depth of inflammation. It is estimated that up to two million people in the United States of America are affected with IBD, which occurs predominantly in developed areas of North America and Europe. Primary symptoms include abdominal pain, bleeding, diarrhoea, weight loss and fever. There can be secondary complications, such as joint, eye, skin and liver problems. In patients with mild symptoms, medications can control the disease. However, for those with severe IBD, hospitalisations, surgery, transfusions and intravenous feeding may be needed. Although scientific advances have been made in understanding and treating IBD, the precise cause, successful treatment and prevention of IBD remain unknown.

BROADCAST EDUCATION ASSOCIATION (BEA)

Scholarship Committee, 344 Moore Hall, Central Michigan University, Mount Pleasant, MI 48859, United States of America
Tel: (1) 989 774 3851
Fax: (1) 989 774 2426
Email: peter.b.orlik@cmich.edu
www: http://www.beaweb.org
Contact: Dr Peter B Orlik, Scholarship Chair

The Broadcast Education Association (BEA) is the professional association for professors, industry professionals and graduate students interested in teaching and research relating to television, radio and the electronic media industry.

Abe Voron Scholarship
Subjects: Radio.
Purpose: To assist study towards a career in radio.
Eligibility: Open to individuals who can show substantial evidence of superior academic performance and potential to be an outstanding electronic media professional. There should be compelling evidence that the applicant possesses high integrity and a well articulated sense of personal and professional responsibility.
Level of Study: Unrestricted.
Type: Scholarship.
Value: US$5,000.
Frequency: Annual.
Study Establishment: BEA member institutions.
Country of Study: Other.
No. of awards offered: One.
Application Procedure: Applicants must obtain an official application form from the BEA or from campus faculty. Applicants should refer to the website for more details www.beaweb.org.
Closing Date: September 15th.
Funding: Private.
Contributor: The Abe Voron Committee.
No. of awards given last year: One.
No. of applicants last year: 35.

Alexander M Tanger Scholarship
Subjects: Broadcasting.
Purpose: To assist study for a career in any area of broadcasting.
Eligibility: The applicant must be able to show substantial evidence of superior academic performance and potential to be an outstanding electronic media professional. There should be compelling evidence that the applicant possesses high integrity and a well articulated sense of personal and professional responsibility.
Level of Study: Unrestricted.
Type: Scholarship.
Value: US$5,000.
Frequency: Annual.
Study Establishment: BEA member institutions.
Country of Study: Other.
No. of awards offered: One.
Application Procedure: Applicants must obtain an official application form from the BEA or from campus faculty. Applicants should refer to the website for more details www.beaweb.org.

Closing Date: September 15th.
Funding: Private.
Contributor: Alexander M Tanger.
No. of awards given last year: One.
No. of applicants last year: 94.

Andrew M Economos Scholarship

Subjects: Radio.
Purpose: To support study towards a career in radio.
Eligibility: The applicant must be able to show substantial evidence of superior academic performance and potential to be an outstanding electronic media professional. There should be compelling evidence that the applicant possesses high integrity and a well articulated sense of personal and professional responsibility.
Level of Study: Unrestricted.
Type: Scholarship.
Value: US$3,500.
Frequency: Annual.
Study Establishment: BEA member institutions.
Country of Study: Other.
No. of awards offered: One.
Application Procedure: Applicants must obtain an official application form from the BEA or campus faculty. Applicants should refer to the website for more details www.beaweb.org.
Closing Date: September 15th.
Funding: Private.
Contributor: The RCS Charitable Foundation.
No. of awards given last year: One.
No. of applicants last year: 35.

Harold E. Fellows Scholarship

Subjects: Broadcasting.
Purpose: To assist those who are studying towards a career in broadcasting.
Eligibility: The applicant must be able to show substantial evidence of superior academic performance and potential to be an outstanding electronic media professional. There should be compelling evidence that the applicant possesses high integrity and a well articulated sense of personal and professional responsibility.
Level of Study: Unrestricted.
Value: US$1,250.
Frequency: Annual.
Study Establishment: BEA member institutions.
No. of awards offered: 4.
Application Procedure: Applicants must obtain an official application form from the BEA or campus faculty. Applicants should refer to the website for more details www.beaweb.org.
Closing Date: September 15th.
Funding: Private.
Contributor: National Association of Broadcasters.
No. of awards given last year: 4.
No. of applicants last year: 55.

Helen J. Siou Ssat/Fay Wells Scholarships

Subjects: Any area of broadcasting.
Purpose: To assist study in any area of broadcasting.
Eligibility: The applicant must be able to show substantial evidence of superior academic performance and potential to be an outstanding electronic media professional. There should be compelling evidence that the applicant possesses high integrity and a well articulated sense of personal and professional responsibility.
Level of Study: Unrestricted.
Type: Scholarship.
Value: US$1,250 each.
Frequency: Annual.
Study Establishment: BEA member institutions.
Country of Study: Other.
No. of awards offered: Two.
Application Procedure: Applicants must obtain an official application form from the BEA or campus faculty. Applicants should refer to the website for more details www.beaweb.org.
Closing Date: September 15th.
Funding: Private.

Contributor: Broadcasters' Foundation.
No. of awards given last year: Two.
No. of applicants last year: 94.

Joseph and Maria Silbergleid Scholarship

Subjects: Digital television.
Eligibility: The applicant must be able to show substantial evidence of superior academic performance and potential to be an outstanding electronic media professional. There should be compelling evidence that the applicant possesses high integrity and a well articulated sense of personal and professional responsibility.
Level of Study: Graduate.
Value: US$1,500.
Frequency: Annual.
Study Establishment: BEA member institutions.
No. of awards offered: One.
Application Procedure: Applicants must obtain an official application form from the BEA or campus faculty. Applicants should refer to the website for more details www.beaweb.org.
Closing Date: September 15th.
Funding: Private.
Contributor: Sponsored by the Silver Knight Group, West Palm Beach, Florida.
No. of awards given last year: One.
No. of applicants last year: 25.

NAB Harold E Fellows Scholarships

Subjects: Broadcasting.
Purpose: To assist study in any area of broadcasting.
Eligibility: The applicant must be able to show substantial evidence of superior academic performance and potential to be an outstanding electronic media professional. There should be compelling evidence that the applicant possesses high integrity and a well articulated sense of personal and professional responsibility. Also, the applicant must have worked for pay or college credit at an NAB-member station.
Level of Study: Unrestricted.
Type: Scholarship.
Value: US$1,250 each.
Frequency: Annual.
Study Establishment: BEA member institutions.
Country of Study: Other.
No. of awards offered: Four.
Application Procedure: Applicants must obtain an official application form from the BEA or campus faculty. Applicants should refer to the website for more details.
Closing Date: September 15th.
Funding: Private.
Contributor: The National Association of Broadcasters, Washington DC.
No. of awards given last year: Four.
No. of applicants last year: 80.

NAB Walter S Patterson Scholarships

Subjects: Radio.
Purpose: To assist study towards a career in radio.
Eligibility: The applicant must be able to show substantial evidence of superior academic performance and potential to be an outstanding electronic media professional. There should be compelling evidence that the applicant possesses high integrity and a well articulated sense of personal and professional responsibility.
Level of Study: Unrestricted.
Type: Scholarship.
Value: US$1,250 each.
Frequency: Annual.
Study Establishment: BEA member institutions.
Country of Study: Other.
No. of awards offered: Two.
Application Procedure: Applicants must obtain an official application form from the BEA or campus faculty. Applicants should refer to the website for more details www.beaweb.org.
Closing Date: September 15th.
Funding: Private.

Contributor: The National Association of Broadcasters.
No. of awards given last year: Two.
No. of applicants last year: 35.

Patrick Communications Vincent T Wasilewski Scholarship

Subjects: Broadcasting.
Purpose: To assist study in any area of broadcasting.
Eligibility: The applicant must be able to show substantial evidence of superior academic performance and potential to be an outstanding electronic media professional. There should be compelling evidence that the applicant possesses high integrity and a well articulated sense of personal and professional responsibility.
Level of Study: Graduate.
Type: Scholarship.
Value: US$2,500.
Frequency: Annual.
Study Establishment: BEA member institutions.
Country of Study: Other.
No. of awards offered: One.
Application Procedure: Applicants must obtain an official application form from the BEA or campus faculty. Applicants should refer to the website for more details www.beaweb.org.
Closing Date: September 15th.
Funding: Private.
Contributor: The Patrick Communications Corporation, Ellicott City, Mary land.
No. of awards given last year: One.
No. of applicants last year: 30.

Philo T. Farnsworth Scholarship

Subjects: Any area of broadcasting.
Purpose: To assist those who are studying towards a career in broadcasting.
Eligibility: The applicant must be able to show substantial evidence of superior academic performance and potential to be an outstanding electronic media professional. There should be compelling evidence that the applicant possesses high integrity and a well articulated sense of personal and professional responsibility.
Level of Study: Unrestricted.
Value: US$1500.
Frequency: Annual.
Study Establishment: BEA member institutions.
No. of awards offered: 94.
Application Procedure: Applicants must obtain an official application form from the BEA or campus faculty. Applicants should refer to the website for more details www.beaweb.org.
Closing Date: September 15th.
Funding: Private.
Contributor: BEA members and participating companies.
No. of awards given last year: 1.
No. of applicants last year: 94.

BROOKHAVEN NATIONAL LABORATORY

Brookhaven Women in Science, PO Box 183, Upton, NY 11973-5000, United States of America
Email: lsmart@bnl.gov
www: http://www.bnl.gov
Contact: Ms Loralie Smart

Brookhaven National Laboratory is a multi-programme national laboratory operated by Brookhaven Science Associates for the United States Department of Energy. The Laboratory's broad mission is to produce excellent science in a safe, environmentally benign manner with the co-operation, support and appropriate involvement of many communities.

Renate W Chasman Scholarship

Subjects: Natural sciences, engineering and mathematics.
Purpose: To encourage women whose education was interrupted to pursue formal studies or a career in the natural sciences, engineering or mathematics.

Eligibility: Open to re-entry women residing in Nassau County, Suffolk County, Brooklyn or Queens, who must be United States citizens or permanent residents. They must be currently enrolled in or have applied for a degree orientated programme at an accredited institution.
Level of Study: Postgraduate.
Type: Scholarship.
Value: US$2,000.
Frequency: Annual.
Country of Study: Any country.
No. of awards offered: One.
Application Procedure: Applicants must submit a completed application, academic record, letters of reference and a short essay on career goals.
Closing Date: April 1st.
Funding: Private.
No. of awards given last year: One.
Additional Information: Please write to the given address for further information. Application forms are also available in PDF on the website.

THE BROSS FOUNDATION, LAKE FOREST COLLEGE

Religion Department, 555 North Sheridan, Lake Forest, IL 60045, United States of America
Tel: (1) 847 735 5175
Fax: (1) 847 735 6192
Email: rmiller@lfc.edu
Contact: Mrs Anne Morgan, Bross Prize Assistant

The Bross Foundation at Lake Forest College was founded to present a scholarly award once every 10 years to the author who, in the opinion of a panel of judges, has written the best book or treatise on the relation between any discipline or topic of investigation and the Christian religion.

Bross Prize

Subjects: The relationship between any discipline and the Christian religion.
Purpose: To recognise scholarly work.
Eligibility: There are no eligibility restrictions.
Level of Study: Unrestricted.
Type: Prize.
Value: First prize of US$15,000, second prize of US$7,000 and third prize of US$4,000.
Frequency: Other.
Country of Study: Any country.
No. of awards offered: Three.
Application Procedure: Applicants must submit three copies of their manuscript.
Closing Date: September 1st.
Funding: Private.
Contributor: The Bross Memorial.
No. of awards given last year: Three.
No. of applicants last year: 150.
Additional Information: Manuscripts must be at least 50,000 words.

BUCKINGHAMSHIRE CHILTERNS UNIVERSITY COLLEGE

Queen Alexandra Road, High Wycombe
Bucks, HP11 2JZ, England
Tel: (44) 1494 522141
Fax: (44) 1494 605047
www: http://www.bcuc.ac.uk

Buckinghamshire Chilterns University College is committed to providing high academic standards in the arena of teaching, learning, scholarship and research. Primarily, our core vision is to create a vibrant academic community, which is respected and valued throughout the university sector.

Research Student Bursary

Subjects: Bursaries are available in the following subject areas: cardiovascular research; health psychology; telehealth; nutrition; oncology; and tissue viability.
Eligibility: Applicant must hold a first degree from a UK University or its equivalent. Applicants whose mother tongue is not English should also have a certificate of English language competence.
Level of Study: Doctorate.
Type: Bursary.
Value: £7,500 per annum.
Length of Study: 3 years.
Frequency: Dependent on funds available.
Study Establishment: Research Centre for Health Studies, Buckinghamshire Chilterns University College.
Country of Study: England.
Application Procedure: Contact faculty Research Officer for further details and application form.

For further information contact:

Faculty of Health Studies, Chalfont Campus, Gorelands Lane, Chalfont St. Giles, Buckinghamshire, HP8 4AD, England
Contact: Faculty Research Officer, BCUC

Research Student Bursary

Subjects: Bursaries are available in the subject area of art and design.
Eligibility: Applicant must hold a first degree from a UK University or its equivalent. Applicants whose mother tongue is not English should also have a certificate of English language competence.
Level of Study: Doctorate.
Type: Bursary.
Value: £7,500 per annum.
Length of Study: 3 years.
Frequency: Dependent on funds available.
Study Establishment: Material Knowledge Research Centre, Buckinghamshire Chilterns University College.
Country of Study: England.
Application Procedure: Contact faculty Research Officer for further details and application form.

For further information contact:

Faculty of Design, Queen Alexandra Road, High Wycombe, Buckinghamshire, HP11 2JZ, England
Contact: Faculty Research Officer, BCUC

Research Student Bursary

Subjects: Bursaries are available in the subject areas of business systems infrastructure; and pattern recognition, image processing and GIS.
Eligibility: Applicant must hold a first degree from a UK University or its equivalent. Applicants whose mother tongue is not English should also have a certificate of English language competence.
Level of Study: Doctorate.
Type: Bursary.
Value: £7,500 per annum.
Length of Study: 3 years.
Frequency: Dependent on funds available.
Study Establishment: Centre for Applied Computing, Buckinghamshire Chilterns University College.
Country of Study: England.
Application Procedure: Contact faculty Research Officer for further details and application form.

For further information contact:

Faculty of Technology, Queen Alexandra Road, High Wycombe, Buckinghamshire, HP11 2JZ, England
Contact: Faculty Research Officer, BCUC

Research Student Bursary

Subjects: Bursaries are available in the areas of international management; and business forecasting.
Eligibility: Applicant must hold a first degree from a UK University or its equivalent. Applicants whose mother tongue is not English should also have a certificate of English language competence.
Level of Study: Doctorate.
Type: Bursary.
Value: £7,500 per annum.
Length of Study: 3 years.
Frequency: Dependent on funds available.
Study Establishment: Business and Management Research Centre, Buckinghamshire Chilterns University College.
Country of Study: England.
Application Procedure: Contact faculty Research Officer for further details and application form.

For further information contact:

Buckinghamshire Business School, Chalfont Campus, Gorelands Lane, Chalfont St. Giles, Buckinghamshire, HP8 4AD, England
Contact: Faculty Research Officer, BCUC

Research Student Bursary

Subjects: Bursaries are available in the following subject areas: furniture design and manufacture; furniture history; furniture conservation and restoration; twentieth century furniture; and forest products technology.
Eligibility: Applicant must hold a first degree from a UK University or its equivalent. Applicants whose mother tongue is not English should also have a certificate of English language competence.
Level of Study: Doctorate.
Type: Bursary.
Value: £7,500 per annum.
Length of Study: 3 years.
Frequency: Dependent on funds available.
Study Establishment: Research Centre for Furniture Studies, Buckinghamshire Chilterns University College.
Country of Study: England.
Application Procedure: Contact faculty Research Officer for further details and application form.

For further information contact:

Faculty of Design, Queen Alexandra Road, High Wycombe, Buckinghamshire, HP11 2JZ, England
Contact: Faculty Research Officer, BCUC

Research Student Bursary

Subjects: Bursaries are available in the following areas: leisure and tourism education; and leisure and tourism organisation and society.
Eligibility: Applicant must hold a first degree from a UK University or its equivalent. Applicants whose mother tongue is not English should also have a certificate of English language competence.
Level of Study: Doctorate.
Type: Bursary.
Value: £7,500 per annum.
Length of Study: 3 years.
Frequency: Dependent on funds available.
Study Establishment: Leisure and Tourism Research Centre, Buckinghamshire Chilterns University College.
Country of Study: England.
Application Procedure: Contact faculty Research Officer for further details and application form.

For further information contact:

Faculty of Leisure & Tourism, Wellesbourne Campus, Kingshill Road, High Wycombe, Buckinghamshire, HP13 5BB, England
Contact: Faculty Research Officer, BCUC

BUDAPEST INTERNATIONAL MUSIC COMPETITION

Hungarofest, Rakoczi ut 20, Budapest, H-1072, Hungary
Tel: (36) 1 266 1459
Fax: (36) 1 266 5972
Email: liszkay.maria@hungarofest.hu
www: http://www.hungarofest.hu
Contact: Ms Maria Liszkay, Secretary

The Budapest Music Competition has been held since 1933. Competitions in different categories alternate annually.

Budapest International Music Competition
Subjects: Musical performance.
Eligibility: Open to young artists of all nationalities who are under 32 years of age.
Level of Study: Professional development.
Type: Competition.
Value: Up to US$11,000.
Frequency: Annual.
Country of Study: Any country.
No. of awards offered: Three.
Application Procedure: Applicants must complete an application form to be submitted with other required documentation and should contact the office for further information.
Closing Date: May 1st.
Funding: Government.
No. of awards given last year: Three.

THE BUSH FOUNDATION

E-900 First National Bank Building, 332 Minnesota Street, St Paul, MN 55101, United States of America
Tel: (1) 651 227 5222
Fax: (1) 651 297 6485
Email: info@bushfoundation.org
www: http://www.bushfoundation.org
Contact: Ms Kathi Polly, Program Assistant

We no longer wish to be included in their Register, but fellowships are available only to local artists and do not involve graduate study.

Bush Artist Fellows Program
Subjects: Visual arts, both two-dimensional and three-dimensional, multimedia, performance art, storytelling, music composition, film, video, scripts, literature and choreography. Categories rotate on a two year cycle. Traditional and folk arts.
Purpose: To provide artists with significant financial support to enable them to advance their work and further their contribution to their communities.
Eligibility: Applicants must be at least 25 years old, be residents and have lived for at least one year of the three years preceding the application deadlines in Minnesota, North Dakota, South Dakota or counties of North Western Wisconsin.
Level of Study: Professional development.
Type: Fellowship.
Value: Fellows receive US$44,000 divided into monthly stipends for the selected time period.
Length of Study: 12-24 months.
Frequency: Annual.
Country of Study: United States of America.
No. of awards offered: 15.
Application Procedure: Applicants must complete an application form, available on written request from the Foundation in August of each year.
Closing Date: Deadlines are each Autumn. The fellowships will be announced in mid April.
Funding: Private.
No. of awards given last year: 15.
No. of applicants last year: 510.

THE CALEDONIAN RESEARCH FOUNDATION

The Carnegie Trust for the Universities of Scotland, Cameron House, Abbey Park Place, Dunfermline, Fife, KY12 7PZ, Scotland
Tel: (44) 1383 622148
Fax: (44) 1383 622149
Email: jgray@carnegie-trust.org
www: http://www.carnegie-trust.org
Contact: Secretary & Treasurer

The Caledonian Research Foundation is a Scottish charity which has supported independent research in Scotland since 1990.

Caledonian Scholarship
Subjects: All subjects in the University curriculum. At least one scholarship each year is made in a non scientific discipline.
Purpose: To support postgraduate research in any subject.
Eligibility: Open to persons possessing a First Class (Honours) Degree from a Scottish University.
Level of Study: Postgraduate.
Type: Scholarship.
Value: UK£8,500 plus tuition fees and allowances.
Length of Study: Up to three years subject to annual renewal.
Frequency: Annual.
Study Establishment: Any university.
Country of Study: Scotland.
No. of awards offered: Two-three.
Application Procedure: Applicants must write for details.
Closing Date: March 15th.
Funding: Private.
No. of awards given last year: Three.
No. of applicants last year: 95.
Additional Information: This award is considered along with Carnegie Scholarships.

THE CAMARGO FOUNDATION

BP 75, Cassis Cedex, F-13714, France
Tel: (33) 4 42 01 11 57
Fax: (33) 4 42 01 36 57
www: http://www.camargofoundation.org
Contact: Mr Michael Pretina Jr, Executive Director

The Camargo Foundation maintains a study centre for the benefit of scholars who wish to pursue projects in the humanities and social sciences related to French and Francophone cultures. The Foundation also sponsors projects by visual artists, photographers, filmmakers, video artists, media artists, composers and writers.

Camargo Fellowships
Subjects: Humanities and social sciences. Visual arts, music composition and creative writing.
Purpose: To assist scholars who wish to pursue projects in the humanities and social sciences related to French and Francophone cultures, and to support projects by visual artists, photographers, filmmakers, video artists, media artists, composers and writers.
Eligibility: Open to members of university and college faculties who wish to pursue special studies while on leave from their institutions, independent Scholars working on specific projects, graduate students whose academic residence and general examination requirements have been met and for whom a stay in France would be beneficial in completing the dissertation required for their degree. The award is also open to writers, visual artists, photographers, filmmakers, video artists, multimedia artists and composers with specific projects to complete.
Level of Study: Doctorate, Postgraduate, Professional development.
Type: Residency.
Value: The use of furnished apartments, the reference library, darkroom, artist's studio and music composition studio, and a stipend of US$3,500.
Length of Study: Varies.
Frequency: Annual.
Study Establishment: Camargo Foundation, study centre in Cassis.
Country of Study: France.
No. of awards offered: Varies, approx. 20-26.
Application Procedure: Applicants must submit a completed application form, a curriculum vitae, a detailed description of their project of up to 1,000 words in length and three letters of recommendation by individuals familiar with the applicant's professional work. At least two of the letters should come from persons outside the applicant's own institution, though graduate students are exempt from this requirement. Artists should submit 10 slides showing samples of their work, composers should submit a score, cassette or compact disc, and

writers should send 10-20 pages of text or a copy of a published work. For further information and application forms applicants should contact the Foundation.

Closing Date: February 1st for the following academic year.
Funding: Private.
Contributor: The Jerome Hill endowment.
No. of awards given last year: 24.
Additional Information: A written report will be required at the end of the stay.

For further information contact:

Camargo Foundation, 125 Park Square Court, 400 Sibley Street, St Paul, MN 55101-1928, United States of America
Tel: (1) 202 302 7303

CAMBRIDGE COMMONWEALTH TRUST, CAMBRIDGE OVERSEAS TRUST AND ASSOCIATED TRUSTS

PO Box 252, Cambridge, Cambridgeshire, CB2 1RZ, England
Tel: (44) 1223 323322
Fax: (44) 1223 351449
Email: egs10@cam.ac.uk
www: admin.cam.ac.uk

Aola Richards Studentships for PhD Study

Subjects: Biological sciences with preference given to those whose research is in entomology.
Purpose: To financially support study towards a PhD.
Eligibility: Applicants must be citizens of Australia or New Zealand. The Trusts cannot admit students to the University or any of its colleges. Applicants for awards from the Trusts must, therefore, also apply to the University of Cambridge and be offered a place at Cambridge in the normal way. All applicants must have a First Class or High Second Class (Honours) Degree or equivalent and normally be under 26. All applicants must be successfully nominated for an Overseas Research Student (ORS) award which covers the difference between the home and overseas rate of the University Composition Fee.
Level of Study: Doctorate, Predoctorate.
Type: Studentship.
Value: The University Composition Fee at the home rate, approved college fees, a maintenance allowance sufficient for a single student and a contribution towards return economy airfare.
Length of Study: Up to three years.
Frequency: As available.
Study Establishment: The University of Cambridge.
Country of Study: United Kingdom.
No. of awards offered: One.
Application Procedure: Preliminary application forms should be sent to the address relevant to that particular country. The final application forms should be sent to the Secretary, the Board of Graduate Studies.
Contributor: Offered in collaboration with the Aola Richards Fund.
Additional Information: Further information is available on request.

For further information contact:

The Board for Graduate Studies, 4 Mill Lane, Cambridge, Cambridgeshire CB2 1RZ, England
Contact: The Secretary

Arab-British Chamber Charitable Foundation Scholarships

Subjects: All subjects.
Purpose: To financially support those undertaking postgraduate study.
Eligibility: Applicants must be citizens of Algeria, the Comoro Islands, Djibouti, Egypt, Jordan, Mauritania, Morocco, Palestine, Somalia, Sudan, Syria, Tunisia or the Yemen. The Trusts cannot admit students to the University or any of its colleges. Applicants for awards from the Trusts must, therefore, also apply to the University of Cambridge and

be offered a place at Cambridge in the normal way. All applicants must have a First Class or High Second Class (Honours) Degree or equivalent and normally be under 26.
Type: Scholarship.
Value: The University Composition Fee at the overseas rate, approved college fees, a maintenance allowance sufficient for a single student and a contribution towards return economy airfare.
Length of Study: One year.
Frequency: Annual.
Study Establishment: The University of Cambridge.
Country of Study: United Kingdom.
No. of awards offered: Five.
Application Procedure: Applicants must complete a preliminary application form, which can be obtained from local universities, offices of the British Council or the Trust. The preliminary application form can also be downloaded from http://www.admin.cam.ac.uk/univ/gsprospectus/c7/overseas/schemes.html. Completed forms must be returned to the main address. Shortlisted candidates will be sent forms for admission to the University of Cambridge.
Contributor: Offered in collaboration with the Arab-British Chamber Charitable Foundation and the Foreign and Commonwealth Office (FCO).
Additional Information: Further information is available on request.

Argentina Cambridge Scholarships for PhD Study

Subjects: All subjects, particularly those relevant to the needs of Argentina.
Purpose: To financially support and encourage individuals to complete a PhD at the University of Cambridge.
Eligibility: Open to students from Argentina. The Trusts cannot admit students to the University or any of its colleges. Applicants for awards from the Trusts must, therefore, also apply to the University of Cambridge and be offered a place at Cambridge in the normal way. All applicants must have a First Class or High Second Class (Honours) Degree or equivalent and normally be under 26. All applicants must be successfully nominated for an Overseas Research Student (ORS) award which covers the difference between the home and overseas rate of the University Composition Fee.
Level of Study: Doctorate, Predoctorate.
Type: Scholarship.
Value: The award covers the University Composition Fee at the appropriate rate, approved college fees, a maintenance allowance sufficient for a single student and a contribution towards return economy airfare.
Length of Study: Up to three years.
Frequency: Annual.
Study Establishment: The University of Cambridge.
Country of Study: United Kingdom.
No. of awards offered: Up to two.
Application Procedure: Applicants must complete a preliminary application form, which can be obtained from local universities, offices of the British Council or the Trust. The preliminary application form can also be downloaded from http://www.admin.cam.ac.uk/univ/gsprospectus/c7/overseas/schemes.html. Completed forms must be returned to the main address. Shortlisted candidates will be sent forms for admission to the University of Cambridge.
Funding: Government.
Contributor: Offered in collaboration with the Ministry of Education in Argentina.
Additional Information: Further information is available on request.

Argentina Cambridge Scholarships for Postgraduate Study

Subjects: All subjects, particularly those relevant to the needs of Argentina.
Purpose: To financially support those undertaking postgraduate study.
Eligibility: Open to students from Argentina. The Trusts cannot admit students to the University or any of its colleges. Applicants for awards from the Trusts must, therefore, also apply to the University of Cambridge and be offered a place at Cambridge in the normal way. All applicants must have a First Class or High Second Class (Honours)

Degree or equivalent and normally be under 26. All applicants must be successfully nominated for an Overseas Research Student (ORS) award which covers the difference between the home and overseas rate of the University Composition Fee.

Level of Study: Postgraduate.

Type: Scholarship.

Value: The award covers the University Composition Fee at the overseas rate, approved college fees, a maintenance allowance sufficient for a single student and a contribution towards return economy airfare.

Length of Study: One year.

Frequency: Annual.

Study Establishment: The University of Cambridge.

Country of Study: United Kingdom.

No. of awards offered: Up to five.

Application Procedure: Applicants must complete a preliminary application form, which can be obtained from local universities, offices of the British Council or the Trust. The preliminary application form can also be downloaded from http://www.admin.cam.ac.uk/univ/gspro-spectus/c7/overseas/schemes.html. Completed forms must be returned to the main address. Shortlisted candidates will be sent forms for admission to the University of Cambridge.

Funding: Government.

Contributor: Offered in collaboration with the Ministry of Education, Argentina.

Additional Information: Further information is available on request.

BAT Cambridge Scholarships for China (PhD Study)

Subjects: All subjects.

Purpose: To financially support study towards a PhD.

Eligibility: Open to students from China. The Trusts cannot admit students to the University or any of its colleges. Applicants for awards from the Trusts must therefore also apply to the University of Cambridge and be offered a place at Cambridge in the normal way. All applicants must have a First Class or High Second Class (Honours) Degree or equivalent and normally be under 26.

Level of Study: Doctorate, Postdoctorate.

Type: Scholarship.

Value: The University Composition Fee at the appropriate rate, approved college fees, a maintenance allowance sufficient for a single student and a contribution towards return economy airfare.

Length of Study: Three years.

Frequency: Annual.

Study Establishment: The University of Cambridge.

Country of Study: United Kingdom.

No. of awards offered: Varies.

Application Procedure: Applicants must complete a preliminary application form, which can be obtained from local universities, offices of the British Council or the Trust. The preliminary application form can also be downloaded from http://www.admin.cam.ac.uk/univ/gspro-spectus/c7/overseas/schemes.html. Completed forms must be returned to the main address. Shortlisted candidates will be sent forms for admission to the University of Cambridge.

Contributor: Offered in collaboration with British-American Tobacco (BAT).

Additional Information: Further information is available on request.

BAT Cambridge Scholarships for China (Postgraduate Study)

Subjects: All subjects.

Purpose: To financially support those undertaking postgraduate study.

Eligibility: Open to students from China. The Trusts cannot admit students to the University or any of its colleges. Applicants for awards from the Trusts must therefore also apply to the University of Cambridge and be offered a place at Cambridge in the normal way. All applicants must have a First Class or High Second Class (Honours) Degree or equivalent and normally be under 26.

Level of Study: Postgraduate.

Type: Scholarship.

Value: The University Composition Fee at the appropriate rate, approved college fees, a maintenance allowance sufficient for a single student and a contribution towards return economy airfare.

Length of Study: One year.

Frequency: Annual.

Study Establishment: The University of Cambridge.

Country of Study: United Kingdom.

No. of awards offered: Varies.

Application Procedure: Applicants must complete a preliminary application form, which can be obtained from local universities, offices of the British Council or the Trust. The preliminary application form can also be downloaded from http://www.admin.cam.ac.uk/univ/gspro-spectus/c7/overseas/schemes.html. Completed forms must be returned to the main address. Shortlisted candidates will be sent forms for admission to the University of Cambridge.

Contributor: Offered in collaboration with British-American Tobacco (BAT).

Additional Information: Further information is available on request.

BAT Cambridge Scholarships for Russia (PhD Study)

Subjects: All subjects.

Purpose: To financially support study towards a PhD.

Eligibility: Open to citizens of Russia. The Trusts cannot admit students to the University or any of its colleges. Applicants for awards from the Trusts must, therefore, also apply to the University of Cambridge and be offered a place at Cambridge in the normal way. All applicants must have a First Class or High Second Class (Honours) Degree or equivalent and normally be under 26. All applicants must be successfully nominated for an Overseas Research Student (ORS) award which covers the difference between the home and overseas rate of the University Composition Fee.

Level of Study: Doctorate, Predoctorate.

Type: Scholarship.

Value: The University Composition Fee at the appropriate rate, approved college fees, a maintenance allowance sufficient for a single student and a contribution towards return economy airfare.

Length of Study: Up to three years.

Frequency: Annual.

Study Establishment: The University of Cambridge.

Country of Study: United Kingdom.

No. of awards offered: Varies.

Application Procedure: Applicants must complete a preliminary application form, which can be obtained from local universities, offices of the British Council or the Trust. The preliminary application form can also be downloaded from http://www.admin.cam.ac.uk/univ/gspro-spectus/c7/overseas/schemes.html. Completed forms must be returned to the main address. Shortlisted candidates will be sent forms for admission to the University of Cambridge.

Contributor: Offered in collaboration with British-American Tobacco (BAT).

Additional Information: Further information is available on request.

BAT Cambridge Scholarships for Russia (Postgraduate Study)

Subjects: All subjects.

Purpose: To financially support those undertaking postgraduate study.

Eligibility: Open to citizens of Russia. The Trusts cannot admit students to the University or any of its colleges. Applicants for awards from the Trusts must, therefore, also apply to the University of Cambridge and be offered a place at Cambridge in the normal way. All applicants must have a First Class or High Second Class (Honours) Degree or equivalent and normally be under 26.

Level of Study: Postgraduate.

Type: Scholarship.

Value: The University Composition Fee at the appropriate rate, approved college fees, a maintenance allowance sufficient for a single student and a contribution towards return economy airfare.

Length of Study: One year.

Frequency: Annual.

Study Establishment: The University of Cambridge.

Country of Study: United Kingdom.

No. of awards offered: Varies.

Application Procedure: Applicants must complete a preliminary application form, which can be obtained from local universities, offices of the British Council or the Trust. The preliminary application form can

also be downloaded from http://www.admin.cam.ac.uk/univ/gsprospectus/c7/overseas/schemes.html. Completed forms must be returned to the main address. Shortlisted candidates will be sent forms for admission to the University of Cambridge.
Contributor: Offered in collaboration with the British American-Tobacco (BAT) Company.
Additional Information: Further information is available on request.

BP Cambridge Chevening Scholarships for Russia (Postgraduate Study)
Subjects: All subjects.
Purpose: To financially support those undertaking postgraduate study.
Eligibility: Open to citizens of Russia. The Trusts cannot admit students to the University or any of its colleges. Applicants for awards from the Trusts must, therefore, also apply to the University of Cambridge and be offered a place at Cambridge in the normal way. All applicants must have a First Class or High Second Class (Honours) Degree or equivalent and normally be under 26.
Level of Study: Postgraduate.
Type: Scholarship.
Value: The University Composition Fee at the overseas rate, approved college fees, a maintenance allowance sufficient for a single student and a contribution towards return economy airfare.
Length of Study: One year.
Frequency: Annual.
Study Establishment: The University of Cambridge.
Country of Study: United Kingdom.
No. of awards offered: Varies.
Application Procedure: Applicants must complete a preliminary application form, which can be obtained from local universities, offices of the British Council or the Trust. The preliminary application form can also be downloaded from http://www.admin.cam.ac.uk/univ/gsprospectus/c7/overseas/schemes.html. Completed forms must be returned to the main address. Shortlisted candidates will be sent forms for admission to the University of Cambridge.
Contributor: Offered in collaboration with BP and the Foreign and Commonwealth Office.
Additional Information: Further information is available on request.

BP Cambridge Scholarships for Egypt (PhD Study)
Subjects: All subjects.
Purpose: To financially support study towards a PhD.
Eligibility: Candidates must be citizens of Egypt. All applicants must apply for an Overseas Research Student (ORS) award which pays the difference between the home and overseas rate of the University Composition Fee. The Trusts cannot admit students to the University or any of its colleges. Applicants for awards from the Trusts must, therefore, also apply to the University of Cambridge and be offered a place at Cambridge in the normal way. All applicants must have a First Class or High Second Class (Honours) Degree or equivalent and normally be under 26.
Level of Study: Doctorate, Predoctorate.
Type: Scholarship.
Value: The University Composition Fee at the overseas rate, approved college fees, a maintenance allowance sufficient for a single student and a contribution towards return economy airfare.
Length of Study: Up to three years.
Frequency: Annual.
Study Establishment: The University of Cambridge.
Country of Study: United Kingdom.
No. of awards offered: Two.
Application Procedure: Applicants must complete a preliminary application form, which can be obtained from local universities, offices of the British Council or the Trust. The preliminary application form can also be downloaded from http://www.admin.cam.ac.uk/univ/gsprospectus/c7/overseas/schemes.html. Completed forms must be returned to the main address. Shortlisted candidates will be sent forms for admission to the University of Cambridge.
Contributor: Offered in collaboration with BP.
Additional Information: Further information is available on request.

BP Cambridge Scholarships for Postgraduate Study (Egypt)
Subjects: All subjects.
Purpose: To financially support those undertaking postgraduate study.
Eligibility: Open to citizens of Egypt. The Trusts cannot admit students to the University or any of its colleges. Applicants for awards from the Trusts must, therefore, also apply to the University of Cambridge and be offered a place at Cambridge in the normal way. All applicants must have a First Class or High Second Class (Honours) Degree or equivalent and normally be under 26.
Level of Study: Postgraduate.
Type: Scholarship.
Value: The University Composition Fee at the appropriate rate, approved college fees, a maintenance allowance sufficient for a single student and a contribution towards return economy airfare.
Length of Study: One year.
Frequency: Annual.
Study Establishment: The University of Cambridge.
Country of Study: United Kingdom.
No. of awards offered: Two.
Application Procedure: Applicants must complete a preliminary application form, which can be obtained from local universities, offices of the British Council or the Trust. The preliminary application form can also be downloaded from http://www.admin.cam.ac.uk/univ/gsprospectus/c7/overseas/schemes.html. Completed forms must be returned to the main address. Shortlisted candidates will be sent forms for admission to the University of Cambridge.
Contributor: Offered in collaboration with BP.
Additional Information: Further information is available on request.

Britain-Australia Bicentennial Scholarships for Postgraduate Study
Subjects: All subjects.
Purpose: To financially support those undertaking postgraduate study.
Eligibility: Candidates must be citizens of Australia. The Trusts cannot admit students to the University or any of its colleges. Applicants for awards from the Trusts must, therefore, also apply to the University of Cambridge and be offered a place at Cambridge in the normal way. All applicants must have a First Class or High Second Class (Honours) Degree or equivalent and normally be under 26.
Level of Study: Postgraduate.
Type: Scholarship.
Value: The University Composition Fee at the overseas rate, approved college fees, a maintenance allowance sufficient for a single student and a contribution towards return economy airfare.
Length of Study: One year.
Frequency: Annual.
Study Establishment: Jesus College, the University of Cambridge.
Country of Study: United Kingdom.
No. of awards offered: Two.
Application Procedure: Applicants must contact the Board of Graduate Studies.
Contributor: Offered in collaboration with the Foreign and Commonwealth Office (FCO) and Jesus College, Cambridge.
Additional Information: Further information is available on request.

For further information contact:

The Board for Graduate Studies, 4 Mill Lane, Cambridge, Cambridgeshire CB2 1RZ, England
Contact: The Secretary

British Chevening Brockmann Cambridge Scholarships
Subjects: Engineering.
Purpose: To financially support those undertaking postgraduate study.
Eligibility: Applicants must be from Mexico. The Trusts cannot admit students to the University or any of its colleges. Applicants for awards from the Trusts must, therefore, also apply to the University of Cambridge and be offered a place at Cambridge in the normal way. All applicants must have a First Class or High Second Class (Honours) Degree or equivalent and normally be under 26.

Level of Study: Postgraduate.
Type: Scholarship.
Value: The University Composition Fee at the overseas rate, approved college fees and a maintenance allowance sufficient for a single student.
Length of Study: One year.
Frequency: Annual.
Study Establishment: The University of Cambridge.
Country of Study: United Kingdom.
No. of awards offered: Up to two.
Application Procedure: Applicants must complete a preliminary application form, which can be obtained from local universities, offices of the British Council or the Trust. The preliminary application form can also be downloaded from http://www.admin.cam.ac.uk/univ/gsprospectus/c7/overseas/schemes.html. Completed forms must be returned to the main address. Shortlisted candidates will be sent forms for admission to the University of Cambridge.
Contributor: Offered in collaboration with the Brockmann Foundation and the Foreign and Commonwealth Office (FCO).
Additional Information: Further information is available on request.

British Chevening Cambridge Australia Trust Scholarships for Postgraduate Study

Subjects: All subjects.
Purpose: To financially support those undertaking postgraduate study.
Eligibility: Open to citizens of Australia. The Trusts cannot admit students to the University or any of its Colleges. Applicants for awards from the Trusts must, therefore, also apply to the University of Cambridge and be offered a place at Cambridge in the normal way. All applicants must have a First Class or High Second Class (Honours) Degree or equivalent and normally be under 26.
Level of Study: Doctorate.
Type: Scholarship.
Value: The University Composition Fee at the overseas rate, approved College fees, a maintenance allowance sufficient for a single student and a contribution towards return economy airfare.
Frequency: Annual.
Study Establishment: The University of Cambridge.
Country of Study: United Kingdom.
No. of awards offered: Two.
Application Procedure: Applicants must contact the Board of Graduate Studies.
Contributor: Offered in collaboration with the Foreign and Commonwealth Office (FCO) and the Cambridge Australia Trust.
Additional Information: Further information is available on request. For details of scholarships offered in collaboration with the Cambridge Australia Trust please see the website http://www.anu.edu/cabs/scholarships/cambridge/cambridge-austrust.html.

For further information contact:

Board of Graduate Studies, 4 Mill Lane, Cambridge, Cambridgeshire CB2 1RZ, England
Contact: The Secretary

British Chevening Cambridge Scholarship for Namibia (Postgraduate Study)

Subjects: All subjects.
Purpose: To financially support those undertaking postgraduate study.
Eligibility: Applicants must be from Namibia. The Trusts cannot admit students to the University or any of its colleges. Applicants for awards from the Trusts must, therefore, also apply to the University of Cambridge and be offered a place at Cambridge in the normal way. All applicants must have a First Class or High Second Class (Honours) Degree or equivalent and normally be under 26. All applicants must be successfully nominated for an Overseas Research Student (ORS) award which covers the difference between the home and overseas rate of the University Composition Fee.
Level of Study: Postgraduate.
Type: Scholarship.

Value: The University Composition Fee at the overseas rate, approved college fees and a maintenance allowance sufficient for a single student.
Length of Study: One year.
Frequency: Annual.
Study Establishment: The University of Cambridge.
Country of Study: United Kingdom.
No. of awards offered: One.
Application Procedure: Applicants must complete a preliminary application form, which can be obtained from local universities, offices of the British Council or the Trust. The preliminary application form can also be downloaded from http://www.admin.cam.ac.uk/univ/gsprospectus/c7/overseas/schemes.html. Completed forms must be returned to the main address. Shortlisted candidates will be sent forms for admission to the University of Cambridge.
Contributor: Offered in collaboration with the Malaysian Commonwealth Studies Centre and the Foreign and Commonwealth Office (FCO).
Additional Information: Further information is available on request.

British Chevening Cambridge Scholarship for PhD Study (Mexico)

Subjects: All subjects.
Purpose: To financially support study towards a PhD.
Eligibility: Open to citizens of Mexico. The Trusts cannot admit students to the University or any of its colleges. Applicants for awards from the Trusts must, therefore, also apply to the University of Cambridge and be offered a place at Cambridge in the normal way. All applicants must have a First Class or High Second Class (Honours) Degree or equivalent and normally be under 26. All applicants must be successfully nominated for an Overseas Research Student (ORS) award which covers the difference between the home and overseas rate of the University Composition Fee.
Level of Study: Doctorate.
Type: Scholarship.
Value: The University Composition Fee at the appropriate rate, approved college fees and a maintenance allowance sufficient for a single student.
Length of Study: Up to three years.
Frequency: Annual.
Study Establishment: The University of Cambridge.
Country of Study: United Kingdom.
No. of awards offered: One.
Application Procedure: Applicants for this scholarship must complete a preliminary application form which can only be obtained from the British Council in Mexico City.
Contributor: Offered in collaboration with the Foreign and Commonwealth Office (FCO).
Additional Information: Further information is available on request.

For further information contact:

The British Council, Maestro Antonio Caso 127, Col San Rafael, Delegacion Cuauhtemoc, Apartado postal 30-588, Mexico City, DF 06470, Mexico

British Chevening Cambridge Scholarship for PhD Study (Uganda)

Subjects: All subjects.
Purpose: To financially support study towards a PhD.
Eligibility: Open to students from Uganda. The Trusts cannot admit students to the University or any of its colleges. Applicants for awards from the Trusts must, therefore, also apply to the University of Cambridge and be offered a place at Cambridge in the normal way. All applicants must have a First Class or High Second Class (Honours) Degree or equivalent and normally be under 26. All applicants must be successfully nominated for an Overseas Research Student (ORS) award which covers the difference between the home and overseas rate of the University Composition Fee.
Level of Study: Doctorate.
Type: Scholarship.
Value: The University Composition Fee at the appropriate rate, approved college fees, a maintenance allowance sufficient for a single student and a contribution towards return economy airfare.

Length of Study: Up to three years.
Frequency: Annual.
Study Establishment: The University of Cambridge.
Country of Study: United Kingdom.
No. of awards offered: One.
Application Procedure: Applicants must complete a preliminary application form, which can be obtained from local universities, offices of the British Council or the Trust. The preliminary application form can also be downloaded from http://www.admin.cam.ac.uk/univ/gsprospectus/c7/overseas/schemes.html. Completed forms must be returned to the main address. Shortlisted candidates will be sent forms for admission to the University of Cambridge.
Contributor: Offered in collaboration with the Foreign and Commonwealth Office (FCO).
Additional Information: Further information is available on request.

British Chevening Cambridge Scholarship for Postgraduate Study (Cyprus)

Subjects: All subjects.
Purpose: To financially support those undertaking postgraduate study.
Eligibility: Open to citizens of Cyprus. Applicants must pass a medical examination. Candidates who are currently receiving, or who have received a British Award within the past three years, are not normally eligible for this scholarship. The Trusts cannot admit students to the University or any of its colleges. Applicants for awards from the Trusts must, therefore, also apply to the University of Cambridge and be offered a place at Cambridge in the normal way. All applicants must have a First Class or High Second Class (Honours) Degree or equivalent and normally be under 26.
Level of Study: Postgraduate.
Type: Scholarship.
Value: The University Composition Fee at the overseas rate, approved college fees, a maintenance allowance sufficient for a single student and a contribution towards return economy airfare.
Length of Study: One year.
Frequency: Annual.
Study Establishment: The University of Cambridge.
Country of Study: United Kingdom.
No. of awards offered: Three.
Application Procedure: Applicants must complete a preliminary application form, which can be obtained from local universities, offices of the British Council or the Trust. The preliminary application form can also be downloaded from http://www.admin.cam.ac.uk/univ/gsprospectus/c7/overseas/schemes.html. Completed forms must be returned to the main address. Shortlisted candidates will be sent forms for admission to the University of Cambridge.
Contributor: Offered in collaboration with the Foreign and Commonwealth Office (FCO) and Leventis Foundation.
Additional Information: Further information is available on request.

British Chevening Cambridge Scholarship for Postgraduate Study (East and West Africa)

Subjects: All subjects.
Purpose: To financially support those undertaking postgraduate study.
Eligibility: Applicants must be from Ghana, Sierra Leone, Tanzania or Uganda. The Trusts cannot admit students to the University or any of its colleges. Applicants for awards from the Trusts must, therefore, also apply to the University of Cambridge and be offered a place at Cambridge in the normal way. All applicants must have a First Class or High Second Class (Honours) Degree or equivalent and normally be under 26.
Level of Study: Postgraduate.
Type: Scholarship.
Value: The University Composition Fee at the overseas rate, approved college fees, a maintenance allowance sufficient for a single student and a contribution towards return economy airfare.
Frequency: Annual.
Study Establishment: The University of Cambridge.
Country of Study: United Kingdom.

No. of awards offered: Up to seven. Up to three are for students from Ghana, one is for students from Sierra Leone, one is for students from Uganda and one is for students from Tanzania.
Application Procedure: Applicants must complete a preliminary application form, which can be obtained from local universities, offices of the British Council or the Trust. The preliminary application form can also be downloaded from http://www.admin.cam.ac.uk/univ/gsprospectus/c7/overseas/schemes.html. Completed forms must be returned to the main address. Shortlisted candidates will be sent forms for admission to the University of Cambridge.
Contributor: Offered in collaboration with the Foreign and Commonwealth Office (FCO).
Additional Information: Further information is available on request.

British Chevening Cambridge Scholarships (Hong Kong)

Subjects: All subjects.
Purpose: To financially support those undertaking postgraduate study.
Eligibility: Applicants must be from Hong Kong. The Trusts cannot admit students to the University or any of its colleges. Applicants for awards from the Trusts must, therefore, also apply to the University of Cambridge and be offered a place at Cambridge in the normal way. All applicants must have a First Class or High Second Class (Honours) Degree or equivalent and normally be under 26.
Level of Study: Postgraduate.
Type: Scholarship.
Value: The University Composition Fee at the overseas rate, approved college fees, a maintenance allowance sufficient for a single student and a contribution towards return economy airfare.
Length of Study: One year.
Frequency: Annual.
Study Establishment: The University of Cambridge.
Country of Study: United Kingdom.
No. of awards offered: Up to eight.
Application Procedure: Applicants must complete a preliminary application form, which can be obtained from local universities, offices of the British Council or the main address. Completed forms must be returned to the main address. Shortlisted candidates will be sent forms for admission to the University of Cambridge and a scholarship application form. These forms must be returned to the Board of Graduate Studies at the address below.
Contributor: Offered in collaboration with the Foreign and Commonwealth Office (FCO).
Additional Information: Further information is available on request.

For further information contact:

The Board of Graduate Studies, 4 Mill Lane, Cambridge, Cambridgeshire CB2 1RZ, England
Contact: The Secretary

British Chevening Cambridge Scholarships (The Philippines)

Subjects: All subjects.
Purpose: To financially support those undertaking postgraduate study.
Eligibility: Applicants must be from the Philippines. The Trusts cannot admit students to the University or any of its colleges. Applicants for awards from the Trusts must, therefore, also apply to the University of Cambridge and be offered a place at Cambridge in the normal way. All applicants must have a First Class or High Second Class (Honours) Degree or equivalent and normally be under 26.
Level of Study: Postgraduate.
Type: Scholarship.
Value: The University Composition Fee at the overseas rate, approved college fees, a maintenance allowance sufficient for a single student and a contribution towards return economy airfare.
Length of Study: One year.
Frequency: Annual.
Study Establishment: The University of Cambridge.
Country of Study: United Kingdom.
No. of awards offered: Three.
Application Procedure: Applicants must complete a preliminary application form, which can be obtained from local universities, offices

169

of the British Council or the Trust. The preliminary application form can also be downloaded from http://www.admin.cam.ac.uk/univ/gsprospectus/c7/overseas/schemes.html. Completed forms must be returned to the main address. Shortlisted candidates will be sent forms for admission to the University of Cambridge.
Contributor: Offered in collaboration with the Foreign and Commonwealth Scholarships.
Additional Information: Further information is available on request.

British Chevening Cambridge Scholarships (Vietnam)
Subjects: All subjects.
Purpose: To financially support those undertaking postgraduate study.
Eligibility: Applicants must be from Vietnam. The Trusts cannot admit students to the University or any of its colleges. Applicants for awards from the Trusts must, therefore, also apply to the University of Cambridge and be offered a place at Cambridge in the normal way. All applicants must have a First Class or High Second Class (Honours) Degree or equivalent and normally be under 26. All applicants must be successfully nominated for an Overseas Research Student (ORS) award which covers the difference between the home and overseas rate of the University Composition Fee.
Level of Study: Postgraduate.
Type: Scholarship.
Value: The University Composition Fee at the overseas rate, approved college fees, a maintenance allowance sufficient for a single student and a contribution towards return economy airfare.
Length of Study: One year.
Frequency: Annual.
Study Establishment: The University of Cambridge.
Country of Study: United Kingdom.
No. of awards offered: Two.
Application Procedure: Applicants for these scholarships should apply directly to the British Embassy in Vietnam.
Contributor: Offered in collaboration with the Foreign and Commonwealth Office (FCO).
Additional Information: Further information is available on request.

For further information contact:

The British Embassy, 16 Ly Thuong Kiet, Hanoi, Vietnam

British Chevening Cambridge Scholarships for Mozambique (Postgraduate Study)
Subjects: All subjects.
Purpose: To financially support those undertaking postgraduate study.
Eligibility: Applicants must be from Mozambique. The Trusts cannot admit students to the University or any of its colleges. Applicants for awards from the Trusts must, therefore, also apply to the University of Cambridge and be offered a place at Cambridge in the normal way. All applicants must have a First Class or High Second Class (Honours) Degree or equivalent and normally be under 26. All applicants must be successfully nominated for an Overseas Research Student (ORS) award which covers the difference between the home and overseas rate of the University Composition Fee.
Level of Study: Postgraduate.
Type: Scholarship.
Value: The University Composition Fee at the overseas rate, approved college fees, a maintenance allowance sufficient for a single student and a contribution towards return economy airfare.
Length of Study: One year.
Frequency: Annual.
Study Establishment: The University of Cambridge.
Country of Study: United Kingdom.
No. of awards offered: Up to four.
Application Procedure: Applicants must complete a preliminary application form, which can be obtained from local universities, offices of the British Council or the Trust. The preliminary application form can also be downloaded from http://www.admin.cam.ac.uk/univ/

gsprospectus/c7/overseas/schemes.html. Completed forms must be returned to the main address. Shortlisted candidates will be sent forms for admission to the University of Cambridge.
Contributor: Offered in collaboration with the Malaysian Commonwealth Studies Centre and the Foreign and Commonwealth Office (FCO).
Additional Information: Further information is available on request.

British Chevening Cambridge Scholarships for Postgraduate Study (Australia)
Subjects: All subjects.
Purpose: To financially support those undertaking postgraduate study.
Eligibility: Open to citizens of Australia. The Trusts cannot admit students to the University or any of its colleges. Applicants for awards from the Trusts must, therefore, also apply to the University of Cambridge and be offered a place at Cambridge in the normal way. All applicants must have a First Class or High Second Class (Honours) Degree or equivalent and normally be under 26.
Level of Study: Postgraduate.
Type: Scholarship.
Value: The University Composition Fee at the overseas rate, approved college fees, a maintenance allowance sufficient for a single student and a contribution towards return economy airfare.
Length of Study: One year.
Frequency: Annual.
Study Establishment: The University of Cambridge.
Country of Study: United Kingdom.
No. of awards offered: Four.
Application Procedure: Applicants must write for information.
Contributor: Offered in collaboration with the Foreign and Commonwealth Office (FCO).
Additional Information: Further information is available on request.

For further information contact:

The Board for Graduate Studies, 4 Mill Lane, Cambridge, Cambridgeshire CN2 1RZ, England
Contact: The Secretary

British Chevening Cambridge Scholarships for Postgraduate Study (Chile)
Subjects: All subjects.
Purpose: To financially support study towards a PhD.
Eligibility: Applicants must be from Chile. The Trusts cannot admit students to the University or any of its colleges. Applicants for awards from the Trusts must, therefore, also apply to the University of Cambridge and be offered a place at Cambridge in the normal way. All applicants must have a First Class or High Second Class (Honours) Degree or equivalent and normally be under 26. All applicants must be successfully nominated for an Overseas Research Student (ORS) award which covers the difference between the home and overseas rate of the University Composition Fee.
Level of Study: Postgraduate.
Type: Scholarship.
Value: The University Composition Fee at the overseas rate, approved college fees and a maintenance allowance sufficient for a single student.
Length of Study: One year.
Frequency: Annual.
Study Establishment: The University of Cambridge.
Country of Study: United Kingdom.
No. of awards offered: One.
Application Procedure: Applicants for this scholarship must apply directly to the British Council in Chile.
Contributor: Offered in collaboration with the Foreign and Commonwealth Office (FCO).
Additional Information: Further information is available on request.

For further information contact:

The British Council, Eliodoro Yanez 832, Santiago de Chile, Chile

British Chevening Cambridge Scholarships for Postgraduate Study (Cuba)

Subjects: All subjects.

Purpose: To financially support those undertaking postgraduate study.

Eligibility: Open to citizens of Cuba. The Trusts cannot admit students to the University or any of its colleges. Applicants for awards from the Trusts must, therefore, also apply to the University of Cambridge and be offered a place at Cambridge in the normal way. All applicants must have a First Class or High Second Class (Honours) Degree or equivalent and normally be under 26.

Level of Study: Postgraduate.

Type: Scholarship.

Value: The University Composition Fee at the overseas rate, approved college fees, a maintenance allowance sufficient for a single student and a contribution towards return economy airfare.

Length of Study: One year.

Frequency: Annual.

Study Establishment: The University of Cambridge.

Country of Study: United Kingdom.

No. of awards offered: Two.

Application Procedure: Applicants must complete a preliminary application form, which can be obtained from local universities, offices of the British Council or the Trust. The preliminary application form can also be downloaded from http://www.admin.cam.ac.uk/univ/gsprospectus/c7/overseas/schemes.html. Completed forms must be returned to the main address. Shortlisted candidates will be sent forms for admission to the University of Cambridge.

Contributor: Offered in collaboration with the Foreign and Commonwealth Office (FCO).

Additional Information: Further information is available on request.

British Chevening Cambridge Scholarships for Postgraduate Study (Eastern Europe)

Subjects: All subjects.

Purpose: To financially support those undertaking postgraduate study.

Eligibility: Open to students from Poland, Romania or Yugoslavia. The Trusts cannot admit students to the University or any of its colleges. Applicants for awards from the Trusts must, therefore, also apply to the University of Cambridge and be offered a place at Cambridge in the normal way. All applicants must have a First Class or High Second Class (Honours) Degree or equivalent and normally be under 26.

Level of Study: Postgraduate.

Type: Scholarship.

Value: The University Composition Fee at the overseas rate, approved College fees, a maintenance allowance sufficient for a single student and a contribution towards return economy airfare.

Length of Study: One year.

Frequency: Annual.

Study Establishment: The University of Cambridge.

Country of Study: United Kingdom.

No. of awards offered: Up to six.

Application Procedure: Applicants must complete a preliminary application form, which can be obtained from local universities, offices of the British Council or the Trust. The preliminary application form can also be downloaded from http://www.admin.cam.ac.uk/univ/gsprospectus/c7/overseas/schemes.html. Completed forms must be returned to the main address. Shortlisted candidates will be sent forms for admission to the University of Cambridge.

Contributor: Offered in collaboration with the Foreign and Commonwealth Office (FCO).

Additional Information: Further information is available on request.

British Chevening Cambridge Scholarships for Postgraduate Study (European Union)

Subjects: All subjects.

Purpose: To financially support those undertaking postgraduate study.

Eligibility: Open to citizens of Belgium, Denmark, Finland, Germany, Greece, Ireland, Italy, Luxembourg, the Netherlands, Portugal and Sweden.

Level of Study: Postgraduate.

Type: Scholarship.

Value: Applicants must contact local offices of the British Council.

Length of Study: One year.

Frequency: Annual.

Study Establishment: The University of Cambridge.

Country of Study: United Kingdom.

No. of awards offered: Varies.

Application Procedure: Applicants must contact the local offices of the British Council for details of the application procedure. Candidates are advised to apply well in advance of their proposed date of entry to the University of Cambridge.

Contributor: Offered in collaboration with the Foreign and Commonwealth Office (FCO).

Additional Information: Further information is available on request. In Sweden these awards are known as the Prince Bertil Memorial Cambridge Scholarships.

British Chevening Cambridge Scholarships for Postgraduate Study (Hong Kong)

Subjects: All subjects.

Purpose: To financially support those undertaking postgraduate study.

Eligibility: Open to citizens of Hong Kong.

Level of Study: Postgraduate.

Type: Scholarship.

Value: The University Composition Fee at the overseas rate, approved college fees, a maintenance allowance sufficient for a single student and a contribution towards return economy airfare.

Length of Study: One year.

Frequency: Annual.

Study Establishment: The University of Cambridge.

Country of Study: United Kingdom.

No. of awards offered: Eight.

Application Procedure: Applicants must contact the organisation.

Additional Information: Further information is available on request.

British Chevening Cambridge Scholarships for Postgraduate Study (Indonesia)

Subjects: All subjects.

Purpose: To financially support those undertaking postgraduate study.

Eligibility: Applicants must be citizens of Indonesia.

Level of Study: Postgraduate.

Type: Scholarship.

Value: The University Composition Fee at the overseas rate, approved college fees, a maintenance allowance sufficient for a single student and a contribution towards return economy airfare.

Length of Study: One year.

Frequency: Annual.

Study Establishment: The University of Cambridge.

Country of Study: United Kingdom.

No. of awards offered: Three.

Application Procedure: Applicants must apply directly to the British Embassy in Indonesia.

Contributor: Offered in collaboration with the Malaysian Commonwealth Studies Centre and the Foreign and Commonwealth Office (FCO).

Additional Information: Further information is available on request.

For further information contact:

The British Embassy, Jalan M H Thamrin 75, Jakarta, 10310, Indonesia

British Chevening Cambridge Scholarships for Postgraduate Study (Malta)

Subjects: All subjects.

Purpose: To financially support those undertaking postgraduate study.

Eligibility: Applicants must be from Malta. The Trusts cannot admit students to the University or any of its colleges. Applicants for awards from the Trusts must, therefore, also apply to the University of

Cambridge and be offered a place at Cambridge in the normal way. All applicants must have a First Class or High Second Class (Honours) Degree or equivalent and normally be under 26.
Level of Study: Postgraduate.
Type: Scholarship.
Value: The University Composition Fee at the overseas rate and approved college fees.
Length of Study: One year.
Frequency: Annual.
Study Establishment: The University of Cambridge.
Country of Study: United Kingdom.
No. of awards offered: Two.
Application Procedure: Applicants must complete a preliminary application form, which can be obtained from local universities, offices of the British Council or the Trust. The preliminary application form can also be downloaded from http://www.admin.cam.ac.uk/univ/gsprospectus/c7/overseas/schemes.html. Completed forms must be returned to the main address. Shortlisted candidates will be sent forms for admission to the University of Cambridge.
Contributor: Offered in collaboration with the Foreign and Commonwealth Office (FCO).
Additional Information: Further information is available on request.

British Chevening Cambridge Scholarships for Postgraduate Study (Mexico)

Subjects: All subjects.
Purpose: To financially support those undertaking postgraduate study.
Eligibility: Applicants must be from Mexico. The Trusts cannot admit students to the University or any of its colleges. Applicants for awards from the Trusts must, therefore, also apply to the University of Cambridge and be offered a place at Cambridge in the normal way. All applicants must have a First Class or High Second Class (Honours) Degree or equivalent and normally be under 26.
Level of Study: Postgraduate.
Type: Scholarship.
Value: The University Composition Fee at the overseas rate, approved college fees and a maintenance allowance sufficient for a single student.
Length of Study: One year.
Frequency: Annual.
Study Establishment: The University of Cambridge.
Country of Study: United Kingdom.
No. of awards offered: One.
Application Procedure: Applicants for this scholarship must complete a preliminary application form which can only be obtained from the British Council, Mexico City.
Contributor: Offered in collaboration with the Foreign and Commonwealth Office (FCO).
Additional Information: Further information is available on request.

For further information contact:

The British Council, Maestro Antonio Caso 127, Col San Rafael, Delegacion Cuauhtemoc, Apartado Postal 30-588, Mexico City, DF 06470, Mexico

British Chevening Cambridge Scholarships for Postgraduate Study (Peru)

Subjects: All subjects.
Purpose: To financially support those undertaking postgraduate study.
Eligibility: Open to students from Peru. The Trusts cannot admit students to the University or any of its colleges. Applicants for awards from the Trusts must, therefore, also apply to the University of Cambridge and be offered a place at Cambridge in the normal way. All applicants must have a First Class or High Second Class (Honours) Degree or equivalent and normally be under 26. All applicants must be successfully nominated for an Overseas Research Student (ORS) award which covers the difference between the home and overseas rate of the University Composition Fee.
Level of Study: Postgraduate.
Type: Scholarship.

Value: The University Composition Fee at the appropriate rate, approved college fees, a maintenance allowance sufficient for a single student and a contribution towards return economy airfare.
Length of Study: One year.
Frequency: Annual.
Study Establishment: The University of Cambridge.
Country of Study: United Kingdom.
No. of awards offered: One.
Application Procedure: Applicants must contact the British Council in Peru.
Contributor: Offered in collaboration with the Foreign and Commonwealth Office (FCO).
Additional Information: Further information is available on request.

For further information contact:

The British Council, Calle Alberto Lynch 110, San Isidro, Lima, 27, Peru

British Chevening Cambridge Scholarships for Postgraduate Study (Thailand)

Subjects: All subjects.
Purpose: To financially support those undertaking postgraduate study.
Eligibility: Applicants must be from Thailand. The Trusts cannot admit students to the University or any of its colleges. Applicants for awards from the Trusts must, therefore, also apply to the University of Cambridge and be offered a place at Cambridge in the normal way. All applicants must have a First Class or High Second Class (Honours) Degree or equivalent and normally be under 26. All applicants must be successfully nominated for an Overseas Research Student (ORS) award which covers the difference between the home and overseas rate of the University Composition Fee.
Level of Study: Postgraduate.
Type: Scholarship.
Value: The University Composition Fee at the overseas rate, approved college fees, a maintenance allowance sufficient for a single student and a contribution to a return economy airfare.
Length of Study: One year.
Frequency: Annual.
Study Establishment: The University of Cambridge.
Country of Study: United Kingdom.
No. of awards offered: Two.
Application Procedure: Applicants must complete a preliminary application form, which can be obtained from local universities, offices of the British Council or the Trust. The preliminary application form can also be downloaded from http://www.admin.cam.ac.uk/univ/gsprospectus/c7/overseas/schemes.html. Completed forms must be returned to the main address. Shortlisted candidates will be sent forms for admission to the University of Cambridge.
Contributor: Offered in collaboration with the Cambridge Thai Foundation and the Foreign and Commonwealth Office (FCO).
Additional Information: Further information is available on request.

British Chevening Malaysia Cambridge Scholarship for PhD Study

Subjects: All subjects.
Purpose: To financially support study towards a PhD.
Eligibility: Open to students from Malaysia. The Trusts cannot admit students to the University or any of its colleges. Applicants for awards from the Trusts must, therefore, also apply to the University of Cambridge and be offered a place at Cambridge in the normal way. All applicants must have a First Class or High Second Class (Honours) Degree or equivalent and normally be under 26. All applicants must be successfully nominated for an Overseas Research Student (ORS) award which covers the difference between the home and overseas rate of the University Composition Fee.
Level of Study: Doctorate.
Type: Scholarship.
Value: The University Composition Fee at the appropriate rate, approved college fees, a maintenance allowance sufficient for a single student and a contribution towards return economy airfare.
Length of Study: Up to three years.
Frequency: Annual.

Study Establishment: The University of Cambridge.
Country of Study: United Kingdom.
No. of awards offered: One.
Application Procedure: Applicants must complete a preliminary application form, which can be obtained from local universities, offices of the British Council or the Trust. The preliminary application form can also be downloaded from http://www.admin.cam.ac.uk/univ/gsprospectus/c7/overseas/schemes.html. Completed forms must be returned to the main address. Shortlisted candidates will be sent forms for admission to the University of Cambridge.
Contributor: Offered in collaboration with the Foreign and Commonwealth Office (FCO).
Additional Information: Further information is available on request.

British Chevening Malaysia Cambridge Scholarships for Postgraduate Study

Subjects: All subjects.
Purpose: To financially support those undertaking postgraduate study.
Eligibility: Applicants must be from Malaysia. The Trusts cannot admit students to the University or any of its colleges. Applicants for awards from the Trusts must, therefore, also apply to the University of Cambridge and be offered a place at Cambridge in the normal way. All applicants must have a First Class or High Second Class (Honours) Degree or equivalent and normally be under 26.
Level of Study: Postgraduate.
Type: Scholarship.
Value: The University Composition Fee at the overseas rate, approved college fees, a maintenance allowance sufficient for a single student and a contribution towards return economy airfare.
Length of Study: One year.
Frequency: Annual.
Study Establishment: The University of Cambridge.
Country of Study: United Kingdom.
No. of awards offered: Four.
Application Procedure: Applicants must complete a preliminary application form, which can be obtained from local universities, offices of the British Council or the Trust. The preliminary application form can also be downloaded from http://www.admin.cam.ac.uk/univ/gsprospectus/c7/overseas/schemes.html. Completed forms must be returned to the main address. Shortlisted candidates will be sent forms for admission to the University of Cambridge.
Contributor: Offered in collaboration with the Foreign and Commonwealth Office (FCO).
Additional Information: Further information is available on request.

For further information contact:

Cambridge (Malaysia) Foundation, PO Box 10139, Kuala Lumpur, 50704, Malaysia
Contact: The Secretary

British Chevening Scholarships for Postgraduate Study (Pakistan)

Subjects: All subjects.
Purpose: To financially reward students of outstanding academic merit.
Eligibility: Open to citizens of Pakistan who are of outstanding academic merit. The Trusts cannot admit students to the University or any of its colleges. Applicants for awards from the Trusts must, therefore, also apply to the University of Cambridge and be offered a place at Cambridge in the normal way. All applicants must have a First Class or High Second Class (Honours) Degree or equivalent and normally be under 26.
Level of Study: Postgraduate.
Type: Scholarship.
Value: The University Composition Fee at the overseas rate, approved college fees, a maintenance allowance sufficient for a single student and a contribution towards return economy airfare.
Length of Study: One year.
Frequency: Annual.
Study Establishment: The University of Cambridge.
Country of Study: United Kingdom.
No. of awards offered: Five.

Application Procedure: Applicants must complete a preliminary application form, which can be obtained from local universities, offices of the British Council or the Trust. The preliminary application form can also be downloaded from http://www.admin.cam.ac.uk/univ/gsprospectus/c7/overseas/schemes.html. Completed forms must be returned to the main address. Shortlisted candidates will be sent forms for admission to the University of Cambridge.
Contributor: Offered in collaboration with the Foreign and Commonwealth Office (FCO).
Additional Information: Further information is available on request.

For further information contact:

The Board of Graduate Studies, 4 Mill Lane, Cambridge, Cambridgeshire CB2 1RZ, England
Contact: The Secretary

C T Taylor Studentship for PhD Study

Subjects: Biotechnology, computer science, chemical engineering, engineering, earth sciences and geography, genetics, land economy, mathematics, physics and chemistry, plant sciences and zoology.
Purpose: To financially support study towards a PhD.
Eligibility: Open to citizens of Australia, New Zealand or Canada. The Trusts cannot admit students to the University or any of its colleges. Applicants for awards from the Trusts must, therefore, also apply to the University of Cambridge and be offered a place at Cambridge in the normal way. All applicants must have a First Class or High Second Class (Honours) Degree or equivalent and normally be under 26. All applicants must be successfully nominated for an Overseas Research Student (ORS) award which covers the difference between the home and overseas rate of the University Composition Fee.
Level of Study: Doctorate.
Type: Studentship.
Value: Up to UK£5,000 towards the costs of study at Cambridge, to be determined in the light of the student's own resources.
Length of Study: Up to three years.
Frequency: Annual.
Study Establishment: The University of Cambridge.
Country of Study: United Kingdom.
No. of awards offered: One.
Application Procedure: Applicants must complete a preliminary application form and send it to the address relevant to that particular country. The final application forms must be sent to The Secretary of the Board of Graduate Studies.
Closing Date: July 31st.
Contributor: The C T Taylor Fund.
Additional Information: Further information is available on request.

For further information contact:

The Registry, The Old Schools, Cambridge, Cambridgeshire CB2 1TN, England

Cambridge DFID Scholarships for Postgraduate Study

Subjects: All subjects.
Purpose: To partly support those undertaking postgraduate study, financially.
Eligibility: Open to citizens from developing countries of the Commonwealth - The Falkland Islands, St Helena, Tristan de Cunha, Brunei, Cameroon, Gambia, Ghana, Kenya, Sierra Leone, Tanzania, Uganda, India, Malta, Mauritius, the Seychelles, Fiji, Kiribati, Nauru, Papua New Guinea, Pitcairn, the Solomon Islands, Tonga, Tuvalu, Vanuatu, Western Samoa, South Africa, Botswana, Lesotho, Malawi, Mozambique, Namibia, Swaziland, Zambia, Zimbabwe and the Commonwealth countries of the Caribbean. The Trusts cannot admit students to the University or any of its colleges. Applicants for awards from the Trusts must, therefore, also apply to the University of Cambridge and be offered a place at Cambridge in the normal way. All applicants must have a First Class or High Second Class (Honours) Degree or equivalent (if applying for a postgraduate course), be under the age of 35 on October 1st of the year they are applying for, return to their own country to work or study after completing the course, not be employed by a government department

or by a parastatal organisation, not at present be living in a developed country, and not have taken studies lasting a year or more in a developed country.
Level of Study: Postgraduate.
Type: Scholarship.
Value: The University Composition Fee at the overseas rate, approved college fees, a maintenance allowance sufficient for a single student and a contribution towards return economy airfare.
Length of Study: One year.
Frequency: Annual.
Study Establishment: The University of Cambridge.
Country of Study: United Kingdom.
No. of awards offered: 40.
Application Procedure: Applicants must complete a preliminary application form, which can be obtained from local universities, offices of the British Council or the Trust. The preliminary application form can also be downloaded from http://www.admin.cam.ac.uk/univ/gsprospectus/c7/overseas/schemes.html. Completed forms must be returned to the main address. Shortlisted candidates will be sent forms for admission to the University of Cambridge.
Contributor: Offered in collaboration with the Department for International Development (DFID).
Additional Information: Further information is available on request.

Cambridge European Trust Bursaries

Subjects: All subjects.
Purpose: To financially support those undertaking postgraduate study.
Eligibility: Open to citizens of the European Union, excluding the United Kingdom.
Level of Study: Postgraduate.
Type: Bursary.
Value: Part cost bursaries.
Length of Study: One year.
Frequency: Annual.
Study Establishment: The University of Cambridge.
Country of Study: United Kingdom.
No. of awards offered: Varies.
Application Procedure: Applicants should contact the organisation.
Additional Information: Further information is available on request.

Cambridge Foundation Scholarships for Postgraduate Study (Chile)

Subjects: All subjects, particularly those relevant to the needs of Chile.
Purpose: To financially support those undertaking postgraduate study.
Eligibility: Open to citizens of Chile. The Trusts cannot admit students to the University or any of its colleges. Applicants for awards from the Trusts must, therefore, also apply to the University of Cambridge and be offered a place at Cambridge in the normal way. All applicants must have a First Class or High Second Class (Honours) Degree or equivalent and normally be under 26. All applicants must be successfully nominated for an Overseas Research Student (ORS) award which covers the difference between the home and overseas rate of the University Composition Fee.
Level of Study: Postgraduate.
Type: Scholarship.
Value: The University Composition Fee at the appropriate rate, approved college fees, a maintenance allowance sufficient for a single student and a contribution towards return economy airfare.
Length of Study: One year.
Frequency: Annual.
Study Establishment: The University of Cambridge.
Country of Study: United Kingdom.
No. of awards offered: Varies.
Application Procedure: Applicants must complete a preliminary application form, which can be obtained from local universities, offices of the British Council or the Trust. The preliminary application form can also be downloaded from http://www.admin.cam.ac.uk/univ/gsprospectus/c7/overseas/schemes.html. Completed forms must be returned to the main address. Shortlisted candidates will be sent forms for admission to the University of Cambridge.

Contributor: Offered in collaboration with the Cambridge Foundation in Chile.
Additional Information: Further information is available on request.

Cambridge Nehru Scholarships for PhD Study

Subjects: All subjects.
Purpose: To financially support study towards a PhD.
Eligibility: Applicants must be from India. All applicants must be successful in winning an Overseas Research Student (ORS) award, which pays the difference between the home and overseas rate of the University Composition Fee. Those who have a First Class Master's Degree or it's equivalent, in addition to a First Class (Honours) Degree, may be given preference.
Level of Study: Doctorate, Predoctorate.
Type: Scholarship.
Value: The University Composition Fee at the home rate, approved college fees, a maintenance allowance sufficient for a single student and a contribution towards return economy airfare.
Length of Study: Up to three years.
Frequency: Annual.
Study Establishment: The University of Cambridge.
Country of Study: United Kingdom.
No. of awards offered: Up to eight.
Application Procedure: Applicants may obtain further details and a preliminary application form by writing before August 16th of the year before entry to the Joint Secretary of the Nehru Trust for Cambridge University at the address below giving details of academic qualifications.
Contributor: Offered in collaboration with the Nehru Trust for Cambridge University.
Additional Information: Further information is available on request.

For further information contact:

The Nehru Trust for Cambridge University, Teen Murti House, Teen Murti Marg, New Delhi, 110011, India

Cambridge Raffles Scholarships

Subjects: All subjects.
Purpose: To financially support those undertaking postgraduate study.
Eligibility: Applicants must be from Singapore. The Trusts cannot admit students to the University or any of its colleges. Applicants for awards from the Trusts must, therefore, also apply to the University of Cambridge and be offered a place at Cambridge in the normal way. All applicants must have a First Class or High Second Class (Honours) Degree or equivalent and normally be under 26.
Level of Study: Postgraduate.
Type: Scholarship.
Value: The University Composition Fee at the overseas rate, approved college fees, a maintenance sufficient for a single student and a contribution towards return economy airfare.
Length of Study: One year.
Frequency: Annual.
Study Establishment: The University of Cambridge.
Country of Study: United Kingdom.
No. of awards offered: Two.
Application Procedure: Applicants must complete a preliminary application form, which can be obtained from local universities, offices of the British Council or the Trust. The preliminary application form can also be downloaded from http://www.admin.cam.ac.uk/univ/gsprospectus/c7/overseas/schemes.html. Completed forms must be returned to the main address. Shortlisted candidates will be sent forms for admission to the University of Cambridge.
Contributor: Offered in collaboration with the Foreign and Commonwealth Office (FCO).
Additional Information: Further information is available on request.

Cambridge Thai Foundation Scholarship for PhD study

Subjects: All subjects.
Purpose: To financially support study towards a PhD.
Eligibility: Applicants must be from Thailand. The Trusts cannot admit students to the University or any of its colleges. Applicants for awards from the Trusts must, therefore, also apply to the University of

Cambridge and be offered a place at Cambridge in the normal way. All applicants must have a First Class or High Second Class (Honours) Degree or equivalent and normally be under 26. For PhD study applicants must be successfully nominated for an Overseas Research Student (ORS) award which pays the difference between the home and overseas rate of the University Composition Fee.
Level of Study: Doctorate.
Type: Scholarship.
Value: The University Composition Fee at the appropriate rate, approved college fees, a maintenance allowance sufficient for a single student and a contribution towards return economy airfare.
Length of Study: Up to three years.
Frequency: Annual.
Study Establishment: The University of Cambridge.
Country of Study: United Kingdom.
No. of awards offered: One.
Application Procedure: Applicants must complete a preliminary application form, which can be obtained from local universities, offices of the British Council or the main address. Completed forms must be returned to the main address. Shortlisted candidates will be sent forms for admission to the University of Cambridge and a scholarship application form. These forms must be returned to the Board of Graduate Studies.
Contributor: Offered in collaboration with the Cambridge Thai Foundation.
Additional Information: Further information is available on request.

Cambridge Thai Foundation Scholarship for Postgraduate Study

Subjects: All subjects.
Purpose: To financially support those undertaking postgraduate study.
Eligibility: Applicants must be from Thailand. The Trusts cannot admit students to the University or any of its colleges. Applicants for awards from the Trusts must, therefore, also apply to the University of Cambridge and be offered a place at Cambridge in the normal way. All applicants must have a First Class or High Second Class (Honours) Degree or equivalent and normally be under 26 years of age. All applicants must be successfully nominated for an Overseas Research Student (ORS) award which covers the difference between the home and overseas rate of the University Composition Fee.
Level of Study: Postgraduate.
Type: Scholarship.
Value: The University Composition Fee at the overseas rate, approved college fees, a maintenance allowance sufficient for a single student and a contribution towards return economy airfare.
Length of Study: One year.
Frequency: Annual.
Study Establishment: The University of Cambridge.
Country of Study: United Kingdom.
No. of awards offered: Two.
Application Procedure: Applicants must complete a preliminary application form, which can be obtained from local universities, offices of the British Council or the Trust. The preliminary application form can also be downloaded from http://www.admin.cam.ac.uk/univ/gsprospectus/c7/overseas/schemes.html. Completed forms must be returned to the main address. Shortlisted candidates will be sent forms for admission to the University of Cambridge.
Contributor: The Cambridge Thai Foundation.
Additional Information: Further information is available on request.

Canada Cambridge Scholarships For PhD Study

Subjects: All subjects.
Purpose: To financially support study towards a PhD.
Eligibility: Open to students from Canada. The Trusts cannot admit students to the University or any of its colleges. Applicants for awards from the Trusts must, therefore, also apply to the University of Cambridge and be offered a place at Cambridge in the normal way. All applicants must have a First Class or High Second Class (Honours) Degree or equivalent and normally be under 26. All applicants must be successfully nominated for an Overseas Research Student (ORS) award which covers the difference between the home and overseas rate of the University Composition Fee.

Level of Study: Doctorate, Predoctorate.
Type: Scholarship.
Value: The University Composition Fee at the home rate and approved college fees.
Length of Study: Up to three years.
Frequency: Annual.
Study Establishment: The University of Cambridge.
Country of Study: United Kingdom.
No. of awards offered: Up to five.
Application Procedure: Application forms for the scholarship will be sent out to eligible candidates once the completed form for admission to the University of Cambridge has reached the Board of Graduate Studies.
Additional Information: Further information is available on request.

For further information contact:

The Board of Graduate Studies, 4 Mill Lane, Cambridge, Cambridgeshire CB2 1RZ, England
Contact: The Secretary

CEU Cambridge Non-Degree Research Scholarships

Subjects: All subjects.
Purpose: To financially support the pursuit of non degree research.
Eligibility: Applicants must be current PhD students at the Central European University. They must be applying to pursue research at Cambridge in the same subject area that they are following at the Central European University.
Level of Study: Doctorate, Predoctorate.
Type: Scholarship.
Value: The University Composition Fee at the appropriate rate, approved college fees, a maintenance allowance sufficient for a single student and return economy airfare.
Length of Study: Up to one year.
Frequency: Annual.
Study Establishment: The University of Cambridge.
Country of Study: United Kingdom.
No. of awards offered: Up to six.
Application Procedure: Applicants must apply through the Scholarships Office at the Central European University.
Closing Date: December 16.
Contributor: Offered in collaboration with the Central European University (CEU).
Additional Information: Further information is available on request.

CIALS Cambridge Scholarships

Subjects: Law.
Purpose: To support study towards the Master of Law (LLM) degree.
Eligibility: Open to graduates of Canadian law schools who have completed a Bachelor of Law degree on or before June 1st. Applicants must be Canadian citizens. The Trusts cannot admit students to the University or any of its colleges. Applicants for awards from the Trusts must, therefore, also apply to the University of Cambridge and be offered a place at Cambridge in the normal way. All applicants must have a First Class or High Second Class (Honours) Degree or equivalent and normally be under 26.
Level of Study: Postgraduate.
Type: Scholarship.
Frequency: Annual.
Study Establishment: The University of Cambridge.
Country of Study: United Kingdom.
No. of awards offered: Two.
Application Procedure: Applicants must apply in writing to the Executive Director of the Canadian Institute for Advanced Legal Studies.
Closing Date: December 31st.
Contributor: Offered in collaboration with the Canadian Institute for Advanced Legal Studies (CIALS).
Additional Information: Further information is available on request.

For further information contact:

The Canadian Institute of Advanced Legal Studies, 4 Beechwood Avenue, Ottawa, ON K1L 8L9, Canada
Contact: Mr Frank E McArdle, Executive Director

Citibank Cambridge Scholarship for the MPhil degree in Management Studies

Subjects: Management studies.
Eligibility: The Trusts cannot admit students to the university or any of its colleges. Applicants for awards from the Trusts must, therefore, also apply to the University of Cambridge and be offered a place at Cambridge in the normal way. All applicants must have a First Class or High Second Class (Honours) Degree, or equivalent and normally be under 26. For students liable to pay fees at the overseas rate.
Level of Study: Postgraduate.
Type: Scholarship.
Value: University Composition Fee at the home rate, approved college fees, maintenance allowance sufficient for a single student, contribution towards return economy airfare.
Length of Study: One year.
Frequency: As available.
Study Establishment: The University of Cambridge.
Country of Study: United Kingdom.
No. of awards offered: One.
Application Procedure: Applicants must complete a Preliminary Application Form, which can be obtained from local universities, offices of the British Council or the main address. Completed application forms must be returned to the main address. Candidates short-listed will be sent forms for admission to the University of Cambridge and a scholarship application form. These forms must be returned to The Board of Graduate Studies at the address below.
Contributor: In collaboration with the Judge Institute of Management Studies.
Additional Information: Further information is available on request.

For further information contact:

The Board of Graduate Studies, 4 Mill Lane, Cambridge, Cambridgeshire CB2 1RZ, England
Contact: The Secretary

Citigroup Cambridge Scholarships

Subjects: Finance, economics or management studies.
Purpose: To financially support those undertaking postgraduate study.
Eligibility: Open to citizens of Australia, New Zealand, Sri Lanka, Brunei, Hong Kong, India, Indonesia, Malaysia, Philippines, Singapore and Thailand. The Trusts cannot admit students to the University or any of its colleges. Applicants for awards from the Trusts must, therefore, also apply to the University of Cambridge and be offered a place at Cambridge in the normal way. All applicants must have a First Class or High Second Class (Honours) Degree or equivalent and normally be under 26.
Level of Study: Postgraduate.
Type: Scholarship.
Value: The University Composition Fee at the overseas rate, approved college fees, a maintenance allowance sufficient for a single student and a contribution towards return economy airfare.
Length of Study: One year.
Frequency: As available.
Study Establishment: The University of Cambridge.
Country of Study: United Kingdom.
No. of awards offered: One.
Application Procedure: Applicants must complete a preliminary application form, which can be obtained from local universities, offices of the British Council or the Trust. The preliminary application form can also be downloaded from http://www.admin.cam.ac.uk/univ/gsprospectus/c7/overseas/schemes.html. Completed forms must be returned to the main address. Shortlisted candidates will be sent forms for admission to the University of Cambridge.
Contributor: Offered in collaboration with Citibank.
Additional Information: Further information is available on request.

Citigroup Cambridge Scholarships for Postgraduate Study (Czech Republic, Hungary, Poland and Slovakia)

Subjects: Economics or finance.
Purpose: To allow candidates to pursue a one year diploma at Cambridge, and, subject to a satisfactory performance in the diploma, to proceed to a one year MPhil degree.

Eligibility: Open to students from the Czech Republic, Hungary, Poland or Slovakia. The Trusts cannot admit students to the University or any of its colleges. Applicants for awards from the Trusts must, therefore, also apply to the University of Cambridge and be offered a place at Cambridge in the normal way. All applicants must have a First Class or High Second Class (Honours) Degree or equivalent and normally be under 26.
Level of Study: Postgraduate.
Type: Scholarship.
Value: The University Composition Fee at the overseas rate, approved college fees, a maintenance allowance sufficient for a single student and a contribution towards return economy airfare.
Length of Study: One year.
Frequency: Annual.
Study Establishment: The University of Cambridge.
Country of Study: United Kingdom.
No. of awards offered: Two.
Application Procedure: Applicants must complete a preliminary application form, which can be obtained from local universities, offices of the British Council or the Trust. The preliminary application form can also be downloaded from http://www.admin.cam.ac.uk/univ/gsprospectus/c7/overseas/schemes.html. Completed forms must be returned to the main address. Shortlisted candidates will be sent forms for admission to the University of Cambridge.
Contributor: Offered in collaboration with Citigroup.
Additional Information: Further information is available on request.

Computer Laboratory ORS Equivalent Awards

Subjects: Computer science.
Purpose: To financially support study towards a PhD.
Eligibility: Open to candidates studying for a PhD in the Computer Laboratory.
Level of Study: Postgraduate.
Type: Award.
Value: Up to the difference between the home and overseas rate of the University Composition Fee.
Length of Study: Up to three years.
Frequency: As available.
Study Establishment: The University of Cambridge.
Country of Study: United Kingdom.
No. of awards offered: One.
Application Procedure: Applicants must contact the organisation.
Additional Information: Further information is available on request.

Corpus Christi ACE Scholarship for Postgraduate Study

Subjects: Conservation, development or the environment.
Purpose: To financially support those undertaking postgraduate study.
Eligibility: Open to students from the developing world with a preference for applicants from Eastern Europe. The Trusts cannot admit students to the University or any of its colleges. Applicants for awards from the Trusts must, therefore, also apply to the University of Cambridge and be offered a place at Cambridge in the normal way. All applicants must have a First Class or High Second Class (Honours) Degree or equivalent and normally be under 26.
Level of Study: Postgraduate.
Type: Scholarship.
Value: The University Composition Fee at the overseas rate, approved college fees, a maintenance allowance sufficient for a single student and a contribution towards return economy airfare.
Length of Study: One year.
Frequency: Annual.
Study Establishment: Corpus Christi College, the University of Cambridge.
Country of Study: United Kingdom.
No. of awards offered: One.
Application Procedure: Applicants must complete a preliminary application form, which can be obtained from local universities, offices of the British Council or the Trust. The preliminary application form can also be downloaded from http://www.admin.cam.ac.uk/univ/gsprospectus/c7/overseas/schemes.html. Completed forms must be returned to the main address. Shortlisted candidates will be sent forms for admission to the University of Cambridge.

Contributor: Offered in collaboration with the Association for Cultural Exchange (ACE) and Corpus Christi College, the University of Cambridge.
Additional Information: Further information is available on request.

Cyprus Cambridge Scholarships For PhD Study

Subjects: All subjects.
Purpose: To financially support study towards a PhD.
Eligibility: Open to citizens of Cyprus. Candidates must sign an undertaking with the Cyprus State Scholarship Authority to return to work in Cyprus for a minimum of three years. This requirement may be deferred if, eg. the Scholar obtains a subsequent award for further studies. The Trust cannot admit students to the University or any of its colleges. Applicants for awards from the Trusts must, therefore, also apply to the University of Cambridge and be offered a place at Cambridge in the normal way. All applicants must have a First Class or High Second Class (Honours) Degree or equivalent and normally be under 26. Candidates must apply for an Overseas Research Student (ORS) award, which covers the difference between the home and overseas rate of the University Composition Fee.
Level of Study: Doctorate.
Type: Scholarship.
Value: The scholarships will take into account the financial resources of the applicant and will cover up to the University Composition Fee at the overseas rate, approved college fees, a maintenance allowance sufficient for a single student and a contribution towards return economy airfare.
Length of Study: Up to three years.
Frequency: As available.
Study Establishment: The University of Cambridge.
Country of Study: United Kingdom.
No. of awards offered: One.
Application Procedure: Applicants must complete a preliminary application form, which can be obtained from local universities, offices of the British Council or the Trust. The preliminary application form can also be downloaded from http://www.admin.cam.ac.uk/univ/gsprospectus/c7/overseas/schemes.html. Completed forms must be returned to the main address. Shortlisted candidates will be sent forms for admission to the University of Cambridge.
Contributor: Offered in collaboration with the Cyprus State Scholarship Authority.
Additional Information: Further information is available on request.

Developing World Education Fund Cambridge Scholarships for PhD Study

Subjects: All subjects.
Purpose: To financially support study towards a PhD.
Eligibility: Open to citizens of Bangladesh, Pakistan, China or Sri Lanka. The Trusts cannot admit students to the University or any of its colleges. Applicants for awards from the Trusts must, therefore, also apply to the University of Cambridge and be offered a place at Cambridge in the normal way. All applicants must have a First Class or High Second Class (Honours) Degree or equivalent and normally be under 26. Applicants must be successfully nominated for an Overseas Research Student (ORS) award, which covers the difference between the home and overseas rate of the University Composition Fee.
Level of Study: Doctorate.
Type: Scholarship.
Value: The University Composition Fee at the appropriate rate, approved college fees, a maintenance allowance sufficient for a single student and a contribution towards return economy airfare.
Length of Study: Up to three years.
Frequency: Annual.
Study Establishment: The University of Cambridge.
Country of Study: United Kingdom.
No. of awards offered: Varies.
Application Procedure: Applicants must complete a preliminary application form, which can be obtained from local universities, offices of the British Council or the Trust. The preliminary application form can also be downloaded from http://www.admin.cam.ac.uk/univ/gsprospectus/c7/overseas/schemes.html. Completed forms must be returned to the main address. Shortlisted candidates will be sent forms for admission to the University of Cambridge.

Contributor: Offered in collaboration with the Developing World Education Fund.
Additional Information: Further information is available on request.

Developing World Education Fund Cambridge Scholarships for Postgraduate Study (China)

Subjects: All subjects.
Purpose: To financially support those undertaking postgraduate study.
Eligibility: For students from a number of countries including China. The Trusts cannot admit students to the University or any of its colleges. Applicants for awards from the Trusts must, therefore, also apply to the University of Cambridge and be offered a place at Cambridge in the normal way. All applicants must have a First Class or High Second Class (Honours) Degree or equivalent and normally be under 26.
Level of Study: Postgraduate.
Type: Scholarship.
Value: The University Composition Fee at the overseas rate, approved college fees, a maintenance allowance sufficient for a single student and a contribution towards return economy airfare.
Length of Study: One year.
Frequency: Annual.
Study Establishment: The University of Cambridge.
Country of Study: United Kingdom.
No. of awards offered: Up to two.
Application Procedure: Applicants must complete a preliminary application form, which can be obtained from local universities, offices of the British Council or the Trust. The preliminary application form can also be downloaded from http://www.admin.cam.ac.uk/univ/gsprospectus/c7/overseas/schemes.html. Completed forms must be returned to the main address. Shortlisted candidates will be sent forms for admission to the University of Cambridge.
Contributor: Offered in collaboration with the Developing World Education Fund.
Additional Information: Further information is available on request.

Dharam Hinduja Cambridge DFID Shared Scholarships

Subjects: All subjects.
Purpose: To offer financial support.
Eligibility: Applicants must be from India. All applicants must be under the age of 35 on October 1st with priority given to those candidates under the age of 30, undertake to return to their own country to work or study after completing the course at Cambridge, not be employed by a national or local government department or by a parastatal organisation, not at present be living or studying in a developed country, nor have undertaken studies lasting a year or more in a developed country. Priority will be given to candidates wishing to pursue a course of study related to the economic and social development of their country.
Level of Study: Postgraduate.
Type: Scholarship.
Value: The University Composition Fee at the appropriate rate, approved college fees, a maintenance allowance sufficient for a single student and a contribution towards return economy airfare.
Length of Study: One year.
Frequency: Annual.
Study Establishment: The University of Cambridge.
Country of Study: United Kingdom.
No. of awards offered: Two.
Application Procedure: Applicants may obtain further details and a preliminary application form by writing before August 16th of the year before entry to the address below giving details of academic qualifications.
Contributor: Offered in collaboration with the Hinduja Cambridge Trust and the Department for International Development.
Additional Information: Further information is available on request.

For further information contact:

The Nehru Trust for Cambridge University, Teen Murti House, Teen Murti Marg, New Delhi, 110011, India
Contact: The Joint Secretary

Dharam Hinduja Cambridge Scholarships

Subjects: All subjects.

Purpose: To financially support study towards a PhD.

Eligibility: Applicants must be from India. All applicants must be successful in winning an Overseas Research Student (ORS) award, which pays the difference between the home and overseas rate of the University Composition Fee. Those who have, in addition, to a First Class (Honours) Degree, a First Class Master's Degree or its equivalent may be given preference.

Level of Study: Doctorate.

Type: Scholarship.

Value: The University Composition Fee at the home rate, approved college fees, a maintenance allowance sufficient for a single student and a contribution towards return economy airfare.

Length of Study: Up to three years.

Frequency: Annual.

Study Establishment: The University of Cambridge.

Country of Study: United Kingdom.

No. of awards offered: Two.

Application Procedure: Applicants must obtain further details and a preliminary application form by writing before August 16th of the year before entry to the address below giving details of academic qualifications

Contributor: Offered in collaboration with the Hinduja Cambridge Trust.

Additional Information: Further information is available on request.

For further information contact:

The Nehru Trust for Cambridge University, Teen Murti House, Teen Murti Marg, New Delhi, 110011, India

Contact: The Joint Secretary

Entente Cordiale Scholarships for Postgraduate Study

Subjects: All subjects.

Purpose: To financially support those undertaking postgraduate study.

Eligibility: Applicants must be citizens of France.

Level of Study: Postgraduate.

Type: Scholarship.

Value: Applicants must contact the British Council for details.

Length of Study: One year.

Frequency: Annual.

Study Establishment: The University of Cambridge.

Country of Study: United Kingdom.

No. of awards offered: Up to six.

Application Procedure: Applicants must obtain details of the application procedure from the British Council.

Contributor: Offered in collaboration with the United Kingdom's Foreign and Commonwealth Office (FCO).

Additional Information: Further information is available on request.

For further information contact:

British Council, 9-11 rue de Constantine, Paris, F-75007, France

Tel: (33) 1 49 55 73 43

Fax: (33) 1 47 05 77 02

FCO-China Chevening Fellowships for Postgraduate Study (China)

Subjects: All subjects.

Purpose: To financially support those undertaking postgraduate study.

Eligibility: Open to citizens of China. The Trust cannot admit students to the University or any of its colleges. Applicants for awards from the Trusts must, therefore, also apply to the University of Cambridge and be offered a place at Cambridge in the normal way. All applicants must have a First Class or High Second Class (Honours) Degree or equivalent and normally be under 26.

Level of Study: Postgraduate.

Type: Scholarship.

Value: The University Composition Fee at the overseas rate, approved college fees, a maintenance allowance sufficient for a single student and a contribution towards return economy airfare.

Length of Study: One year.

Frequency: Annual.

Study Establishment: The University of Cambridge.

Country of Study: United Kingdom.

No. of awards offered: Three.

Application Procedure: Applicants must complete a preliminary application form, which can be obtained from local universities, offices of the British Council or the Trust. The preliminary application form can also be downloaded from http://www.admin.cam.ac.uk/univ/gsprospectus/c7/overseas/schemes.html. Completed forms must be returned to the main address. Shortlisted candidates will be sent forms for admission to the University of Cambridge.

Contributor: Offered in collaboration with the Foreign and Commonwealth Office (FCO).

Additional Information: Further information is available on request.

First Canadian Donner Foundation Research Cambridge Scholarships for PhD Study

Subjects: All subjects.

Purpose: To financially support study towards a PhD.

Eligibility: Open to citizens of Canada who excel in sport. Candidates must gain admission to Magdalene College, Cambridge in the normal way. All applicants must be successfully nominated for an Overseas Research Student (ORS) award which covers the difference between the home and overseas rate of the University Composition Fee.

Level of Study: Doctorate, Predoctorate.

Type: Scholarship.

Length of Study: Three years.

Frequency: Annual.

Study Establishment: Magdalene College, the University of Cambridge.

Country of Study: United Kingdom.

No. of awards offered: One.

Application Procedure: Applicants must contact the Board of Graduate Studies.

Additional Information: Further information is available on request.

For further information contact:

The Board of Graduate Studies, 4 Mill Lane, Cambridge, Cambridgeshire CB2 1RZ, England

Contact: The Secretary

French Embassy Bursaries

Subjects: Engineering.

Purpose: To financially support those undertaking postgraduate study.

Eligibility: Open to citizens of France.

Level of Study: Postgraduate.

Type: Bursary.

Length of Study: One year.

Frequency: Annual.

Study Establishment: The Department of Engineering, the University of Cambridge.

Country of Study: United Kingdom.

No. of awards offered: Up to four.

Application Procedure: Applicants should contact the organisation.

Contributor: Offered in collaboration with the French Embassy in London.

Additional Information: Further information is available on request.

Guy Clutton-Brock Scholarship for PhD Study

Subjects: All subjects.

Purpose: To financially support those undertaking postgraduate study.

Eligibility: For a student from Zimbabwe who has been offered a place at Magdalene College, Cambridge. The Trusts cannot admit students to the University or any of its colleges. Applicants for awards from the Trusts must, therefore, also apply to the University of Cambridge and be offered a place at Cambridge in the normal way. All applicants must have a First Class or High Second Class (Honours) Degree or equivalent and normally be under 26. All applicants must be successfully nominated for an Overseas Research Student (ORS) award which covers the difference between the home and overseas rate of the University Composition Fee.

Level of Study: Doctorate, Predoctorate.
Type: Scholarship.
Value: The University Composition Fee at the home rate, approved college fees, a maintenance allowance sufficient for a single student and a contribution towards return economy airfare.
Length of Study: Up to three years.
Frequency: As available.
Study Establishment: Magdalene College, the University of Cambridge.
Country of Study: United Kingdom.
No. of awards offered: One.
Application Procedure: Applicants must complete a preliminary application form, which can be obtained from local universities, offices of the British Council or the Trust. The preliminary application form can also be downloaded from http://www.admin.cam.ac.uk/univ/gsprospectus/c7/overseas/schemes.html. Completed forms must be returned to the main address. Shortlisted candidates will be sent forms for admission to the University of Cambridge.
Contributor: Offered by the government of Zimbabwe in collaboration with Magdalene College, Cambridge in honour of Guy Clutton-Brock, hero of Zimbabwe.
Additional Information: Further information is available on request.

Guy Clutton-Brock Scholarship for Postgraduate Study

Subjects: All subjects.
Purpose: To financially support those undertaking postgraduate study.
Eligibility: Open to students from Zimbabwe who have been offered a place at Magdalene College, Cambridge. The Trusts cannot admit students to the University or any of its colleges. Applicants for awards from the Trusts must, therefore, also apply to the University of Cambridge and be offered a place at Cambridge in the normal way. All applicants must have a First Class or High Second Class (Honours) Degree or equivalent and normally be under 26. All applicants must be successfully nominated for an Overseas Research Student (ORS) award which covers the difference between the home and overseas rate of the University Composition Fee.
Level of Study: Postgraduate.
Type: Scholarship.
Value: The University Composition Fee at the overseas rate, approved college fees, a maintenance allowance sufficient for a single student and a contribution towards return economy airfare.
Length of Study: One year.
Frequency: As available.
Study Establishment: The University of Cambridge.
Country of Study: United Kingdom.
No. of awards offered: One.
Application Procedure: Applicants must complete a preliminary application form, which can be obtained from local universities, offices of the British Council or the Trust. The preliminary application form can also be downloaded from http://www.admin.cam.ac.uk/univ/gsprospectus/c7/overseas/schemes.html. Completed forms must be returned to the main address. Shortlisted candidates will be sent forms for admission to the University of Cambridge.
Contributor: Offered by the government of Zimbabwe in collaboration with Magdalene College at the University of Cambridge in honour of Guy Clutton-Brock, hero of Zimbabwe.
Additional Information: Further information is available on request.

Hamilton Cambridge Scholarship for PhD Study

Subjects: All subjects.
Purpose: To financially support study towards a PhD.
Eligibility: The Trusts cannot admit students to the University or any of its colleges. Applicants for awards from the Trusts must, therefore, also apply to the University of Cambridge and be offered a place at Cambridge in the normal way. All applicants must have a First Class or High Second Class (Honours) Degree or equivalent and normally be under 26. All applicants must be successfully nominated for an Overseas Research Student (ORS) award which covers the difference between the home and overseas rate of the University Composition Fee.
Level of Study: Doctorate.
Type: Scholarship.

Value: The University Composition Fee at the home rate, approved college fees, a maintenance allowance sufficient for a single student and a contribution towards return economy airfare.
Length of Study: Up to three years.
Frequency: As available.
Study Establishment: Selwyn College, the University of Cambridge.
Country of Study: United Kingdom.
No. of awards offered: One.
Application Procedure: Applicants must complete a preliminary application form, which can be obtained from local universities, offices of the British Council or the Trust. The preliminary application form can also be downloaded from http://www.admin.cam.ac.uk/univ/gsprospectus/c7/overseas/schemes.html. Completed forms must be returned to the main address. Shortlisted candidates will be sent forms for admission to the University of Cambridge.
Contributor: Offered in collaboration with Selwyn College, Cambridge.
Additional Information: Further information is available on request.

For further information contact:

The Board of Graduate Studies, 4 Mill Lane, Cambridge, Cambridgeshire CB2 1RZ, England
Contact: The Secretary

Hong Kong Cambridge Scholarships for PhD Study

Subjects: All subjects.
Purpose: To financially support study towards a PhD.
Eligibility: Preference is given to graduates of the Chinese University of Hong Kong and the University of Hong Kong. The Trusts cannot admit students to the University or any of its colleges. Applicants for awards from the Trusts must, therefore, also apply to the University of Cambridge and be offered a place at Cambridge in the normal way. All applicants must have a First Class or High Second Class (Honours) Degree or equivalent and normally be under 26.
Level of Study: Doctorate, Predoctorate.
Type: Scholarship.
Value: The University Composition Fee at the appropriate rate, approved college fees, a maintenance allowance sufficient for a single student and a contribution towards return economy airfare.
Length of Study: Up to three years.
Frequency: Annual.
Study Establishment: The University of Cambridge.
Country of Study: United Kingdom.
No. of awards offered: Up to five.
Application Procedure: Applicants must complete a preliminary application form, which can be obtained from local universities, offices of the British Council or the Trust. The preliminary application form can also be downloaded from http://www.admin.cam.ac.uk/univ/gsprospectus/c7/overseas/schemes.html. Completed forms must be returned to the main address. Shortlisted candidates will be sent forms for admission to the University of Cambridge.
Contributor: Offered in collaboration with the Malaysian Commonwealth Studies Centre.
Additional Information: Further information is available on request.

Huntsman Tioxide Cambridge Scholarship for Postgraduate Study

Subjects: Chemical engineering.
Purpose: To financially support those undertaking postgraduate study.
Eligibility: Applicants must be from Malaysia, South Africa or Singapore. The Trusts cannot admit students to the University or any of its colleges. Applicants for awards from the Trusts must, therefore, also apply to the University of Cambridge and be offered a place at Cambridge in the normal way. All applicants must have a First Class or High Second Class (Honours) Degree or equivalent and normally be under 26.
Level of Study: Postgraduate.
Type: Scholarship.
Value: The University Composition Fee at the overseas rate, approved college fees, a maintenance allowance sufficient for a single student and a contribution towards return economy airfare.
Length of Study: One year.

Frequency: Dependent on funds available.
Study Establishment: The University of Cambridge.
Country of Study: United Kingdom.
No. of awards offered: One.
Application Procedure: Applicants must complete a preliminary application form, which can be obtained from local universities, offices of the British Council or the Trust. The preliminary application form can also be downloaded from http://www.admin.cam.ac.uk/univ/gsprospectus/c7/overseas/schemes.html. Completed forms must be returned to the main address. Shortlisted candidates will be sent forms for admission to the University of Cambridge.
Contributor: Offered in collaboration with Huntsman Tioxide.
Additional Information: Further information is available on request.

Hutchison Whampoa Chevening Cambridge Scholarships

Subjects: All subjects.
Purpose: To financially support those undertaking postgraduate study.
Eligibility: Open to students from China and Hong Kong. The Trusts cannot admit students to the University or any of its colleges. Applicants for awards from the Trusts must, therefore, also apply to the University of Cambridge and be offered a place at Cambridge in the normal way. All applicants must have a First Class or High Second Class (Honours) Degree or equivalent.
Type: Scholarship.
Value: The University Composition Fee at the overseas rate, approved college fees, a maintenance allowance sufficient for a single student and a contribution towards return economy airfare.
Length of Study: One year.
Study Establishment: The University of Cambridge.
Country of Study: United Kingdom.
No. of awards offered: Up to 21.
Application Procedure: Applicants must complete a preliminary application form, which can be obtained from local universities, offices of the British Council or the Trust. The preliminary application form can also be downloaded from http://www.admin.cam.ac.uk/univ/gsprospectus/c7/overseas/schemes.html. Completed forms must be returned to the main address. Shortlisted candidates will be sent forms for admission to the University of Cambridge.
Contributor: In collaboration with Hutchison Whampoa and the Foreign and Commonwealth Office (FCO).
Additional Information: Further information is available on request.

Isaac Newton Trust European Research Studentships

Subjects: All subjects.
Purpose: To support research leading to a PhD.
Eligibility: Open to candidates from the European Union.
Level of Study: Doctorate.
Type: Studentship.
Value: UK£2,000 per year.
Length of Study: Three years.
Frequency: Annual.
Study Establishment: The University of Cambridge.
Country of Study: United Kingdom.
No. of awards offered: 33.
Application Procedure: Applicants must contact the Trust.
Contributor: Offered in collaboration with the Isaac Newton Trust and the Cambridge European Trust.
Additional Information: Further information is available on request.

Jawaharlal Nehru Memorial Fund Cambridge Scholarship for PhD Study

Subjects: The broad fields of science policy, technology, global restructuring, philosophy and history of science, comparative studies in religion and culture, international relations and constitutional studies, Indian history, civilisation and culture, interface of social change and economic development, environmental ecology and sustainable development.
Purpose: To financially support study towards a PhD.
Eligibility: Applicants must be from India. All applicants must be successful in winning an Overseas Research Student (ORS) award, which pays the difference between the home and overseas rate of the

University Composition Fee. Those who have, in addition, to a First Class (Honours) Degree, a First Class Master's Degree or its equivalent, may be given preference.
Level of Study: Doctorate, Predoctorate.
Type: Scholarship.
Value: The University Composition Fee at the home rate, approved college fees, a maintenance allowance sufficient for a single student and a contribution towards return economy airfare.
Length of Study: Up to three years.
Frequency: Annual.
Study Establishment: The University of Cambridge.
Country of Study: United Kingdom.
No. of awards offered: One.
Application Procedure: Applicants may obtain further details and a preliminary application form by writing before August 16th of the year before entry to the Joint Secretary of the Nehru Trust for Cambridge University at the address below giving details of academic qualifications.
Contributor: Offered in collaboration with the Jawaharlal Nehru Memorial Fund.
Additional Information: Further information is available on request.

For further information contact:

The Nehru Trust for Cambridge University, Teen Murti House, Teen Murti Marg, New Delhi, 110011, India
Contact: The Joint Secretary

Jawaharlal Nehru Memorial Trust Cambridge DFID Scholarships

Subjects: All subjects.
Purpose: To offer financial support.
Eligibility: Open to citizens from India. All applicants must be under the age of 35 on October 1st with priority given to those candidates under the age of 30, undertake to return to their own country to work or study after completing the course at Cambridge, not be employed by a national or local government department or by a parastatal organisation, not at present be living or studying in a developed country and not have undertaken studies lasting a year or more in a developed country. Priority will be given to candidates wishing to pursue a course of study related to the economic and social development of their country.
Level of Study: Postgraduate.
Type: Scholarship.
Value: The University Composition Fee at the overseas rate, approved college fees, a maintenance allowance sufficient for a single student and a contribution towards return economy airfare.
Length of Study: One year.
Frequency: Annual.
Study Establishment: The University of Cambridge.
Country of Study: United Kingdom.
No. of awards offered: Two.
Application Procedure: Applicants may obtain further details and a preliminary application form by writing before August 16th of the year before entry to the Joint Secretary giving details of their academic qualifications.
Contributor: Offered in collaboration with the Jawaharlal Nehru Memorial Trust and the Department of International Development (DFID).
Additional Information: Further information is available on request.

For further information contact:

The Nehru Trust for Cambridge University, Teen Murti House, Teen Murti Marg, New Delhi, 110011, India
Contact: The Joint Secretary

Jawaharlal Nehru Memorial Trust Cambridge Scholarships

Subjects: All subjects.
Purpose: To financially support study towards a PhD.
Eligibility: Open to candidates from India. All applicants must be successful in winning an Overseas Research Student (ORS) award, which pays the difference between the home and overseas rate of the University Composition Fee. Those who have, in addition to a First

Class (Honours) Degree, a First Class Master's Degree or its equivalent, may be given preference.
Level of Study: Doctorate.
Type: Scholarship.
Value: The University Composition Fee at the overseas rate, approved college fees, a contribution towards a maintenance allowance and a contribution to return economy airfare.
Length of Study: Two years.
Frequency: Annual.
Study Establishment: Trinity College, the University of Cambridge.
Country of Study: United Kingdom.
No. of awards offered: One.
Application Procedure: Applicants may obtain further details and a preliminary application form by writing before August 16th of the year before entry to the Joint Secretary of the Nehru Trust for Cambridge University at the address below giving details of academic qualifications.
Contributor: Offered in collaboration with the Jawaharlal Nehru Memorial Trust and Trinity College, Cambridge.
Additional Information: Further information is available on request.

For further information contact:

The Nehru Trust for Cambridge University, Teen Murti House, Teen Murti Marg, New Delhi, 110011, India
Contact: The Joint Secretary

Kalimuzo Cambridge DFID Scholarships

Subjects: All subjects.
Purpose: To offer a scholarship in memory of Professor Frank Kalimuzo, Former Vice-Chancellor of Makerere University.
Eligibility: Open to students from Uganda. All applicants must be under the age of 35 on October 1st with priority given to those candidates under the age of 30, undertake to return to their own country to work or study after completing the course at Cambridge, not be employed by a national or local government department or by a parastatal organisation, not at present be living or studying in a developed country, nor have undertaken studies lasting a year or more in a developed country. Priority will be given to candidates wishing to pursue a course of study related to the economic and social development of their country.
Level of Study: Postgraduate.
Type: Scholarship.
Value: The University Composition Fee at the overseas rate, approved college fees, a maintenance allowance sufficient for a single student and a contribution towards return economy airfare.
Length of Study: One year.
Frequency: Annual.
Study Establishment: The University of Cambridge.
Country of Study: United Kingdom.
No. of awards offered: Three.
Application Procedure: Applicants must complete a preliminary application form, which can be obtained from local universities, offices of the British Council or the Trust. The preliminary application form can also be downloaded from http://www.admin.cam.ac.uk/univ/gsprospectus/c7/overseas/schemes.html. Completed forms must be returned to the main address. Shortlisted candidates will be sent forms for admission to the University of Cambridge.
Contributor: Offered in collaboration with the Department of International Development (DFID).
Additional Information: Scholarships are offered in the memory of Professor Frank Kalimuzo, former Vice Chancellor of Makerere University. Further information is available on request.

Kalimuzo Cambridge Scholarship for PhD Study

Subjects: All subjects.
Purpose: To financially support study towards a PhD.
Eligibility: Open to students from Uganda. The Trusts cannot admit students to the University or any of its colleges. Applicants for awards from the Trusts must, therefore, also apply to the University of Cambridge and be offered a place at Cambridge in the normal way. All applicants must have a First Class or High Second Class (Honours) Degree or equivalent and normally be under 26. All applicants must be successfully nominated for an Overseas Research Student (ORS)

award which covers the difference between the home and overseas rate of the University Composition Fee.
Level of Study: Doctorate.
Type: Scholarship.
Value: The University Composition Fee at the appropriate rate, approved college fees, a maintenance allowance sufficient for a single student and a contribution towards return economy airfare.
Length of Study: Three years.
Frequency: Annual.
Study Establishment: The University of Cambridge.
Country of Study: United Kingdom.
No. of awards offered: One.
Application Procedure: Applicants must complete a preliminary application form, which can be obtained from local universities, offices of the British Council or the Trust. The preliminary application form can also be downloaded from http://www.admin.cam.ac.uk/univ/gsprospectus/c7/overseas/schemes.html. Completed forms must be returned to the main address. Shortlisted candidates will be sent forms for admission to the University of Cambridge.
Additional Information: The scholarship is awarded in the memory of Professor Frank Kalimuzo, former Vice Chancellor of Makerere University. Further information is available on request.

Kapitza Cambridge Scholarships

Subjects: All subjects.
Eligibility: Open to students from countries of the former Soviet Union. The Trusts cannot admit students to the University or any of its colleges. Applicants for awards from the Trusts must, therefore, also apply to the University of Cambridge and be offered a place at Cambridge in the normal way. All applicants must have a First Class or High Second Class (Honours) Degree or equivalent and normally be under 26.
Level of Study: Postdoctorate.
Type: Scholarship.
Value: The University Composition Fees at the overseas rate, approved college fees, a maintenance allowance sufficient for a single student and a contribution towards return economy airfare.
Length of Study: One year.
Frequency: Annual.
Study Establishment: The University of Cambridge.
No. of awards offered: Varies.
Application Procedure: Applicants must complete a preliminary application form, which can be obtained from local universities, offices of the British Council or the Trust. The preliminary application form can also be downloaded from http://www.admin.cam.ac.uk/univ/gsprospectus/c7/overseas/schemes.html. Completed forms must be returned to the main address. Shortlisted candidates will be sent forms for admission to the University of Cambridge.
Additional Information: Further information is available on request.

Karim Rida Said Cambridge Scholarship for PhD Study

Subjects: All subjects.
Purpose: To financially support study towards a PhD.
Eligibility: Applicants must be from Jordan, Lebanon, Palestine or Syria. Scholars must undertake to return to their home country or to another member state of the Arab League on completion of studies at Cambridge. Candidates may be up to 40 years old. The Trusts cannot admit students to the University or any of its colleges. Applicants for awards from the Trusts must, therefore, also apply to the University of Cambridge and be offered a place at Cambridge in the normal way. All applicants must have a First Class or High Second Class (Honours) Degree, or equivalent and may be up to the age of 40. Applicants must be successfully nominated for an Overseas Research Student (ORS) award which pays the difference between the home and overseas rate of the University Composition Fee.
Level of Study: Doctorate, Predoctorate.
Type: Scholarship.
Value: The University Composition Fee at the appropriate rate, approved college fees, a maintenance allowance sufficient for a single student and a contribution towards return economy airfare.
Length of Study: Up to three years.
Frequency: Annual.
Study Establishment: The University of Cambridge.

Country of Study: United Kingdom.
No. of awards offered: Two.
Application Procedure: Applicants must complete a preliminary application form, which can be obtained from local universities, offices of the British Council or the Trust. The preliminary application form can also be downloaded from http://www.admin.cam.ac.uk/univ/gsprospectus/c7/overseas/schemes.html. Completed forms must be returned to the main address. Shortlisted candidates will be sent forms for admission to the University of Cambridge.
Contributor: Offered in collaboration with the Karim Rida Said Foundation.
Additional Information: This scholarship is offered in memory of Karim Rida Said. Further information is available on request.

Karim Rida Said Cambridge Scholarship for Postgraduate Study

Subjects: All subjects.
Purpose: To financially support those undertaking postgraduate study.
Eligibility: Applicants must be from Jordan, Lebanon, Palestine or Syria. Scholars must undertake to return to their home country or to another member state of the Arab League on completion of studies at Cambridge. Candidates may be up to 40 years old. The Trusts cannot admit students to the University or any of its colleges. Applicants for awards from the Trusts must, therefore, also apply to the University of Cambridge and be offered a place at Cambridge in the normal way. All applicants must have a First Class or High Second Class (Honours) Degree or equivalent and may be up to the age of 40. Applicants must be successfully nominated for an Overseas Research Student (ORS) award which pays the difference between the home and overseas rate of the University Composition Fee.
Level of Study: Postgraduate.
Type: Scholarship.
Value: The University Composition Fee at the overseas rate, approved college fees, a maintenance allowance sufficient for a single student and a contribution towards a return economy airfare.
Length of Study: One year.
Frequency: Annual.
Study Establishment: The University of Cambridge.
Country of Study: United Kingdom.
No. of awards offered: Four.
Application Procedure: Applicants must complete a preliminary application form, which can be obtained from local universities, offices of the British Council or the Trust. The preliminary application form can also be downloaded from http://www.admin.cam.ac.uk/univ/gsprospectus/c7/overseas/schemes.html. Completed forms must be returned to the main address. Shortlisted candidates will be sent forms for admission to the University of Cambridge.
Contributor: Offered in collaboration with the Karim Rida Said Foundation.
Additional Information: This scholarship is offered in memory of Karim Rida Said. Further information is available on request.

Kenya Cambridge Scholarship for PhD Study

Subjects: All subjects.
Purpose: To financially support study towards a PhD.
Eligibility: Applicants must be citizens of Kenya. The Trusts cannot admit students to the University or any of its colleges. Applicants for awards from the Trusts must, therefore, also apply to the University of Cambridge and be offered a place at Cambridge in the normal way. All applicants must have a First Class or High Second Class (Honours) Degree or equivalent and normally be under 26. All applicants must be successfully nominated for an Overseas Research Student (ORS) award which covers the difference between the home and overseas rate of the University Composition Fee.
Level of Study: Doctorate.
Type: Scholarship.
Value: The University Composition Fee at the home rate, approved college fees, a maintenance allowance sufficient for a single student and a contribution towards return economy airfare.
Length of Study: Up to three years.
Frequency: Annual.
Study Establishment: The University of Cambridge.

Country of Study: United Kingdom.
No. of awards offered: One.
Application Procedure: Applicants must complete a preliminary application form, which can be obtained from local universities, offices of the British Council or the Trust. The preliminary application form can also be downloaded from http://www.admin.cam.ac.uk/univ/gsprospectus/c7/overseas/schemes.html. Completed forms must be returned to the main address. Shortlisted candidates will be sent forms for admission to the University of Cambridge.
Contributor: Offered in collaboration with the Kenya Cambridge Commonwealth Trust.
Additional Information: Further information is available on request.

The Laboratory of Molecular Biology (LMB) Cambridge Scholarships for PhD Study

Subjects: Molecular biology.
Purpose: To financially support study towards a PhD.
Level of Study: Doctorate, Predoctorate.
Type: Scholarship.
Value: Full maintenance allowance at the single student rate, after taking account of other awards from public sources towards maintenance for which the students are eligible and have received.
Length of Study: Up to three years.
Frequency: Annual.
Study Establishment: The Laboratory of Molecular Biology (LMB), the University of Cambridge.
Country of Study: United Kingdom.
No. of awards offered: Up to three.
Application Procedure: Applicants must apply directly to the LMB. The application form and further information about the department and potential supervisors is available from the website. Candidates can also write to the Director of Studies to request a copy of the form, details of current projects and other scholarship information.
Additional Information: Further information is available on request.

For further information contact:

The MRC Laboratory of Molecular Biology, Hills Road, Cambridge, Cambridgeshire CB2 2QH, England
www: http://www.mrc-lmb.cam.ac.uk
Contact: Director of Studies

The Laboratory of Molecular Biology (LMB) Newton Cambridge Scholarships

Subjects: Molecular biology.
Purpose: To support and encourage candidates to pursue a course of research leading to a PhD.
Eligibility: Open to candidates from the European Union.
Level of Study: Doctorate.
Type: Scholarship.
Value: Full maintenance allowance at the single student rate, after taking account of other awards from public sources towards maintenance for which the students are eligible and have received.
Length of Study: Three years.
Frequency: Annual.
Study Establishment: The Laboratory of Molecular Biology (LMB), the University of Cambridge.
Country of Study: United Kingdom.
No. of awards offered: Three.
Application Procedure: Applicants must apply directly to the LMB. The application form and further information about the department and potential supervisors is available online. Candidates can also write to request an application form, details of current projects and other scholarship information.
Contributor: Offered in collaboration with the LMB, the Isaac Newton Trust and the Cambridge European Trust.
Additional Information: Further information is available on request.

For further information contact:

The MRC Laboratory of Molecular Biology (LMB), Hills Road, Cambridge, Cambridgeshire CB2 2QH, England
www: http://www.mrc-lmb.cam.ac.uk
Contact: Director of Studies

Lady Noon Bursary

Subjects: All subjects.
Purpose: To financially support study towards a second Bachelor's degree as an affiliated student.
Eligibility: Applicants must be from Pakistan.
Level of Study: Graduate.
Type: Bursary.
Value: A substantial contribution towards the costs of study, to be determined in the light of the student's own resources.
Frequency: Annual.
Study Establishment: The University of Cambridge.
Country of Study: United Kingdom.
No. of awards offered: One.
Application Procedure: Applicants must complete a preliminary application form, which can be obtained from local universities, offices of the British Council or the Trust. The preliminary application form can also be downloaded from http://www.admin.cam.ac.uk/univ/gsprospectus/c7/overseas/schemes.html. Completed application forms must be returned to the main address. Candidates shortlisted will be sent forms for admission to the University of Cambridge and a scholarship application form. These forms must be returned to the Board of Graduate Studies at the address below.
Contributor: In association with the Lady Noon Trust.
Additional Information: Further information is available on request.

For further information contact:

The Board of Graduate Studies, 4 Mill Hill, Cambridge, Cambridge-shire CB2 1RZ, England

Lady Noon Cambridge DFID Scholarships

Subjects: All subjects.
Purpose: To financially support those undertaking postgraduate study.
Eligibility: Open to students from Pakistan. All applicants must be under the age of 35 on October 1st with priority given to those candidates under the age of 30, undertake to return to their own country to work or study after completing the course at Cambridge, not be employed by a national or local government department or by a parastatal organisation, not at present be living or studying in a developed country, nor have undertaken studies lasting a year or more in a developed country. Priority will be given to candidates wishing to pursue a course of study related to the economic and social development of their own country.
Level of Study: Postgraduate.
Type: Scholarship.
Value: The University Composition Fee at overseas rate, approved college fees, a maintenance allowance sufficient for a single student and a contribution towards return economy airfare.
Length of Study: One year.
Frequency: Annual.
Study Establishment: The University of Cambridge.
Country of Study: United Kingdom.
No. of awards offered: Varies.
Application Procedure: Applicants must complete a preliminary application form, which can be obtained from local universities, offices of the British Council or the Trust. The preliminary application form can also be downloaded from http://www.admin.cam.ac.uk/univ/gsprospectus/c7/overseas/schemes.html. Completed forms must be returned to the main address. Shortlisted candidates will be sent forms for admission to the University of Cambridge.
Contributor: Offered in collaboration with the Lady Noon Trust and the Department for International Development (DFID).
Additional Information: Further information is available on request.

Link Foundation/FCO Chevening Cambridge Scholarships for Postgraduate Study

Subjects: All subjects.
Purpose: To financially support those undertaking postgraduate study.
Eligibility: Open to citizens of New Zealand. The Trusts cannot admit students to the University or any of its Colleges. Applicants for awards from the Trusts must, therefore, also apply to the University of Cambridge and be offered a place at Cambridge in the normal way. All applicants must have a First Class or High Second Class (Honours) Degree or equivalent and normally be under 26.
Level of Study: Postgraduate.
Type: Scholarship.
Value: A substantial contribution of up to UK£10,000 towards the costs of study and a contribution of UK£1,000 towards the return airfare to the United Kingdom.
Length of Study: One year.
Frequency: Annual.
Study Establishment: The University of Cambridge.
Country of Study: United Kingdom.
No. of awards offered: Three.
Application Procedure: Applicants must contact the Board of Graduate Studies.
Contributor: Offered in collaboration with the Link Foundation for UK-New Zealand Relations (formerly known as the Waitangi Foundation) and the Foreign and Commonwealth Office (FCO).
Additional Information: Further information is available on request.

For further information contact:

The Board of Graduate Studies, 4 Mill Hill, Cambridge, Cambridge-shire CB2 1RZ, England
Contact: The Secretary

Mandela Cambridge Scholarships for PhD Study

Subjects: All subjects.
Purpose: To financially support study towards a PhD.
Eligibility: Applicants must be from South Africa. The Trusts cannot admit students to the University or any of its colleges. Applicants for awards from the Trusts must, therefore, also apply to the University of Cambridge and be offered a place at Cambridge in the normal way. All applicants must have a First Class or High Second Class (Honours) Degree or equivalent and normally be under 26. Applicants for study towards a PhD must be successfully nominated for an Overseas Research Student (ORS) award which pays the difference between the home and overseas rate of the University Composition Fee.
Level of Study: Doctorate, Predoctorate.
Type: Scholarship.
Value: The University Composition Fee at the appropriate rate, approved college fees, a maintenance allowance sufficient for a single student and a contribution to return economy airfare.
Length of Study: Up to three years.
Frequency: Annual.
Study Establishment: The University of Cambridge.
Country of Study: United Kingdom.
No. of awards offered: Up to 10.
Application Procedure: Applicants must complete a preliminary application form, which can be obtained from local universities, offices of the British Council or the Trust. The preliminary application form can also be downloaded from http://www.admin.cam.ac.uk/univ/gsprospectus/c7/overseas/schemes.html. Completed forms must be returned to the main address. Shortlisted candidates will be sent forms for admission to the University of Cambridge.
Contributor: Offered by the Malaysian Commonwealth Studies Centre, the Cambridge Local Examinations Syndicate, Trinity College, Cambridge, and the Cambridge University Press.
Additional Information: These scholarships are offered in honour of former South African President Nelson Mandela. Further information is available on request.

Mandela Cambridge Scholarships for Postgraduate Study

Subjects: All subjects.
Purpose: To financially support those undertaking postgraduate study.
Eligibility: Applicants must be from South Africa. The Trusts cannot admit students to the University or any of its colleges. Applicants for awards from the Trusts must, therefore, also apply to the University of Cambridge and be offered a place at Cambridge in the normal way. All applicants must have a First Class or High Second Class (Honours) Degree or equivalent and normally be under 26. Applicants for study towards a PhD must be successfully nominated for an Overseas Research Student (ORS) award which pays the difference between the home and overseas rate of the University Composition Fee.

Level of Study: Postgraduate.
Type: Scholarship.
Value: The University Composition Fee at the overseas rate, approved college fees, a maintenance allowance sufficient for a single student and a contribution towards return economy airfare.
Length of Study: One year.
Frequency: Annual.
Study Establishment: The University of Cambridge.
Country of Study: United Kingdom.
No. of awards offered: Up to 20.
Application Procedure: Applicants must complete a preliminary application form, which can be obtained from local universities, offices of the British Council or the Trust. The preliminary application form can also be downloaded from http://www.admin.cam.ac.uk/univ/gsprospectus/c7/overseas/schemes.html. Completed forms must be returned to the main address. Shortlisted candidates will be sent forms for admission to the University of Cambridge.
Contributor: Offered by the Malaysian Commonwealth Studies Centre, the Cambridge Local Examinations Syndicate, Trinity College, Cambridge, and the Cambridge University Press.
Additional Information: These scholarships are offered in honour of former South African President Nelson Mandela. Further information is available on request.

Mandela Magdalene College Scholarships for Postgraduate Scholarships

Subjects: All subjects.
Purpose: To financially support those undertaking postgraduate study and research.
Eligibility: Students must have been offered a place at Magdalene College, Cambridge and be citizens of South Africa. The Trusts cannot admit students to the University or any of its colleges. Applicants for awards from the Trusts must, therefore, also apply to the University of Cambridge and be offered a place at Cambridge in the normal way. All applicants must have a First Class or High Second Class (Honours) Degree or equivalent and normally be under 26.
Level of Study: Postgraduate.
Type: Scholarship.
Value: The University Composition Fee at the overseas rate, approved college fees, a maintenance allowance sufficient for a single student and a contribution to return economy airfare.
Length of Study: One year.
Frequency: Annual.
Study Establishment: Magdalene College, the University of Cambridge.
Country of Study: United Kingdom.
No. of awards offered: Up to three.
Application Procedure: Applicants must complete a preliminary application form, which can be obtained from local universities, offices of the British Council or the Trust. The preliminary application form can also be downloaded from http://www.admin.cam.ac.uk/univ/gsprospectus/c7/overseas/schemes.html. Completed forms must be returned to the main address. Shortlisted candidates will be sent forms for admission to the University of Cambridge.
Contributor: Offered in collaboration with Magdalene College, Cambridge and Mr Chris von Christierson.
Additional Information: Further information is available on request.

Mehmed Fuad Köprülü Scholarships for Turkey

Subjects: All subjects.
Purpose: To financially support study towards a PhD.
Eligibility: Applicants must be from Turkey. All applicants must apply for an Overseas Research Student (ORS) award which pays the difference between the home and overseas rate of the University composition fee. The Trusts cannot admit students to the University or any of its colleges. Applicants for awards from the Trusts must, therefore, also apply to the University of Cambridge and be offered a place at Cambridge in the normal way. All applicants must have a First Class or High Second Class (Honours) Degree or equivalent and normally be under 26.
Level of Study: Postdoctorate.
Type: Scholarship.

Value: The University Composition Fee at the appropriate rate, approved college fees, a maintenance allowance sufficient for a single student and a contribution towards return economy airfare.
Length of Study: Up to three years.
Frequency: Annual.
Study Establishment: The University of Cambridge.
Country of Study: United Kingdom.
No. of awards offered: 10.
Application Procedure: All applicants must complete an application for admission to the University of Cambridge as a graduate student and return it to the Turkish Council for Higher Education (YÖK).
Contributor: Offered in collaboration with the Turkish Council for Higher Education (YÖK).
Additional Information: Further information is available on request.

For further information contact:

The Turkish Council for Higher Education (YÖK)YÖK Binasi Bilkent, Ankara, 06539, Turkey

Michael Miliffe Cambridge Scholarships

Subjects: All subjects.
Purpose: To financially support study towards a second Bachelor's degree as an affiliated student.
Eligibility: Open to citizens of India. The Trusts cannot admit students to the University or any of its colleges. Applicants for awards from the Trusts must, therefore, also apply to the University of Cambridge and be offered a place at Cambridge in the normal way. All applicants must have a First Class or High Second Class (Honours) Degree or equivalent and normally be under 26.
Level of Study: Graduate.
Type: Scholarship.
Value: A substantial contribution of up to UK£9,000 per year towards the student's costs, to be determined in the light of the student's own resources.
Length of Study: Two years.
Frequency: Annual.
Study Establishment: Gonville and Caius College, the University of Cambridge.
Country of Study: United Kingdom.
No. of awards offered: Two.
Application Procedure: Applicants must contact the organisation.
Contributor: Offered in collaboration with the Michael Miliffe Fund and Gonville and Caius College, the University of Cambridge.
Additional Information: Further information is available on request.

Ministry of Education, Malaysia, Scholarships for Postgraduate Study

Subjects: All subjects.
Purpose: To financially support those undertaking postgraduate study.
Eligibility: Applicants must be from Malaysia. Candidates must be nominated by the Ministry of Education. The Trusts cannot admit students to the University or any of its colleges. Applicants for awards from the Trusts must, therefore, also apply to the University of Cambridge and be offered a place at Cambridge in the normal way. All applicants must have a First Class or High Second Class (Honours) Degree or equivalent and normally be under 26.
Level of Study: Postgraduate.
Type: Scholarship.
Value: The University Composition Fee at the overseas rate, approved college fees, a maintenance allowance sufficient for a single student and a contribution to return economy airfare.
Length of Study: One year.
Frequency: Annual.
Study Establishment: The University of Cambridge.
Country of Study: United Kingdom.
No. of awards offered: Four.
Application Procedure: Applicants must complete a preliminary application form, which can be obtained from local universities, offices of the British Council or the Trust. The preliminary application form can also be downloaded from http://www.admin.cam.ac.uk/univ/

gsprospectus/c7/overseas/schemes.html. Completed forms must be returned to the main address. Shortlisted candidates will be sent forms for admission to the University of Cambridge.
Contributor: Offered in collaboration with the Malaysian Commonwealth Studies Centre and the Ministry of Education, Government of Malaysia.
Additional Information: Further information is available on request.

For further information contact:

The Cambridge (Malaysia) Foundation, PO Box 10139, Kuala Lumpur, 50704, Malaysia

Ministry of Science, Technology and the Environment, Malaysia, Scholarships for Postgraduate Study

Subjects: All subjects.
Purpose: To financially support those undertaking postgraduate study.
Eligibility: Applicants must be from Malaysia. Candidates must be nominated by the Ministry of Science, Technology and the Environment. The Trusts cannot admit students to the University or any of its colleges. Applicants for awards from the Trusts must, therefore, also apply to the University of Cambridge and be offered a place at Cambridge in the normal way. All applicants must have a First Class or High Second Class (Honours) Degree or equivalent and normally be under 26.
Level of Study: Postgraduate.
Type: Scholarship.
Value: The University Composition Fee at the overseas rate, approved college fees, a maintenance allowance sufficient for a single student and a contribution to return economy airfare.
Length of Study: One year.
Frequency: Annual.
Study Establishment: The University of Cambridge.
Country of Study: United Kingdom.
No. of awards offered: Up to 10.
Application Procedure: Applicants must complete a preliminary application form, which can be obtained from local universities, offices of the British Council or the Trust. The preliminary application form can also be downloaded from http://www.admin.cam.ac.uk/univ/gsprospectus/c7/overseas/schemes.html. Completed forms must be returned to the main address. Shortlisted candidates will be sent forms for admission to the University of Cambridge.
Contributor: Offered in collaboration with the Malaysian Commonwealth Studies Centre and the Ministry of Science, Technology and the Environment, Government of Malaysia.
Additional Information: Further information is available on request.

For further information contact:

The Cambridge (Malaysia) Foundation, PO Box 10139, Kuala Lumpur, 50704, Malaysia

Nehru Centenary Chevening Cambridge Scholarships

Subjects: All subjects.
Purpose: To financially support study towards a second Bachelor's degree as an affiliated student.
Eligibility: Applicants must be from India. The Trusts cannot admit students to the University or any of its colleges. Applicants for awards from the Trusts must, therefore, also apply to the University of Cambridge and be offered a place at Cambridge in the normal way. All applicants must have a First Class or High Second Class (Honours) Degree or equivalent and normally be under 26.
Level of Study: Graduate.
Type: Scholarship.
Value: The University Composition Fee at the overseas rate, approved college fees, a contribution towards a maintenance allowance and a contribution towards return economy airfare.
Length of Study: Two years.
Frequency: Annual.
Study Establishment: The University of Cambridge.
Country of Study: United Kingdom.
No. of awards offered: Up to five.
Application Procedure: Applicants may obtain further details and a preliminary application form by writing before August 16th of the year

before entry to the Joint Secretary giving details of academic qualifications.
Contributor: Offered in collaboration with the Foreign and Commonwealth Office (FCO).
Additional Information: Further information is available on request.

For further information contact:

The Nehru Trust for Cambridge University, Teen Murti House, Teen Murti Marg, New Delhi, 110011, India
Contact: The Joint Secretary

Nehru Trust for the Indian Collections V&A Cambridge DFID Scholarship

Subjects: Archaeology, focusing on archaeological heritage and museums, or social anthropology, with special reference to the work of a museum.
Purpose: To financially support those undertaking postgraduate study.
Eligibility: Applicants must be from India. All applicants must be under the age of 35 on October 1st with priority given to those candidates under the age of 30, undertake to return to their own country to work or study after completing the course at Cambridge, not be employed by a national or local government department or by a parastatal organisation, not at present be living or studying in a developed country, nor have undertaken studies lasting a year or more in a developed country. Priority will be given to candidates wishing to pursue a course of study related to the economic and social development of their country.
Level of Study: Postgraduate.
Type: Scholarship.
Value: The University Composition Fee at the overseas rate, approved college fees, a maintenance allowance sufficient for a single student and a contribution to return economy airfare. In addition a supplementary allowance to cover a short period of practical training at the Victoria and Albert Museum, or other approved institution, will be given.
Length of Study: One year.
Frequency: Annual.
Study Establishment: The University of Cambridge.
Country of Study: United Kingdom.
No. of awards offered: One.
Application Procedure: Applicants may obtain further details and a preliminary application form by writing before August 10th of the year before entry to the Joint Secretary at the address below giving details of academic qualifications.
Contributor: Offered in collaboration with the Nehru Trust for the Indian Collections at the Victoria and Albert (V&A) Museum and the Department for International Development (DFID).
Additional Information: Further information is available on request.

For further information contact:

The Nehru Trust for Cambridge University, Teen Murti House, Teen Murti Marg, New Delhi, 110011, India
Contact: The Joint Secretary

Nepal Cambridge Scholarships

Subjects: All subjects.
Purpose: To financially support those undertaking postgraduate study.
Eligibility: Applicants must be from Nepal. The Trusts cannot admit students to the University or any of its colleges. Applicants for awards from the Trusts must, therefore, also apply to the University of Cambridge and be offered a place at Cambridge in the normal way. All applicants must have a First Class or High Second Class (Honours) Degree or equivalent and normally be under 26.
Level of Study: Postgraduate.
Type: Scholarship.
Value: The University Composition Fee at the overseas rate, approved college fees, a maintenance allowance sufficient for a single student and a contribution towards return economy airfare.
Length of Study: One year.
Frequency: Annual.
Study Establishment: The University of Cambridge.

Country of Study: United Kingdom.

No. of awards offered: One.

Application Procedure: Applicants must complete a preliminary application form, which can be obtained from local universities, offices of the British Council or the Trust. The preliminary application form can also be downloaded from http://www.admin.cam.ac.uk/univ/gsprospectus/c7/overseas/schemes.html. Completed forms must be returned to the main address. Shortlisted candidates will be sent forms for admission to the University of Cambridge.

Contributor: Offered in collaboration with the British Embassy in Kathmandu.

Additional Information: Further information is available on request.

OSI Chevening Cambridge Scholarships for Postgraduate Study

Subjects: Social sciences and humanities.

Purpose: To financially support those undertaking postgraduate study.

Eligibility: Open to students from Albania, Bosnia, Croatia, Estonia, Kosovo, Latvia, Lithuania, Macedonia, Slovenia, Ukraine or the Federal Republic of Yugoslavia. Successful applicants will be expected to return to their home country at the end of their course of study at Cambridge. Scholars should not have already spent a full academic year or more studying in a university outside Central and Eastern Europe, the former Soviet Union or Mongolia. The Trusts cannot admit students to the University or any of its colleges. Applicants for awards from the Trusts must, therefore, also apply to the University of Cambridge and be offered a place at Cambridge in the normal way. All applicants must have a First Class or High Second Class (Honours) Degree or equivalent and normally be under 26.

Level of Study: Postgraduate.

Type: Scholarship.

Value: The University Composition Fee at the overseas rate, approved college fees, a maintenance allowance sufficient for a single student and a contribution towards return economy airfare.

Frequency: Annual.

Study Establishment: The University of Cambridge.

Country of Study: United Kingdom.

No. of awards offered: Up to 24.

Application Procedure: Applicants must complete a preliminary application form, which can be obtained from local universities, offices of the British Council or the Trust. The preliminary application form can also be downloaded from http://www.admin.cam.ac.uk/univ/gsprospectus/c7/overseas/schemes.html. Completed forms must be returned to the main address. Shortlisted candidates will be sent forms for admission to the University of Cambridge.

Contributor: Offered in collaboration with the Open Society Institute (OSI) and the Foreign and Commonwealth Office (FCO).

Additional Information: Further information is available on request.

Oxford and Cambridge Society of Bombay Cambridge DFID Scholarship

Subjects: All subjects.

Purpose: To financially support those undertaking postgraduate study.

Eligibility: Open to a resident of Bombay City or the state of Maharashtra whose application is supported by the Oxford and Cambridge Society of Bombay. All applicants must be under the age of 35 on October 1st with priority given to those candidates under the age of 30, undertake to return to their own country to work or study after completing the course at Cambridge, not be employed by a national or local government department or by a parastatal organisation, not at present be living or studying in a developed country, not have undertaken studies lasting a year or more in a developed country, nor have undertaken studies lasting a year or more in a developed country. Priority will be given to candidates wishing to pursue a course of study related to the economic and social development of their country.

Level of Study: Postgraduate.

Type: Scholarship.

Value: The University Composition Fee at the overseas rate, approved college fees, a maintenance allowance sufficient for a single student and a contribution to return economy airfare.

Length of Study: One year.

Frequency: Annual.

Study Establishment: The University of Cambridge.

Country of Study: United Kingdom.

No. of awards offered: One.

Application Procedure: Applicants may obtain further details and a preliminary application form by writing before August 16th of the year before entry to the Joint Secretary giving details of academic qualifications.

Contributor: Offered in collaboration with the Department for International Development (DFID).

Additional Information: Further information is available on request.

For further information contact:

The Nehru Trust for Cambridge University, Teen Murti House, Teen Murti Marg, New Delhi, 110011, India

Contact: The Joint Secretary

Pegasus Cambridge Scholarships for Postgraduate Study

Subjects: Law.

Purpose: To financially assist students who have gained an offer of a place to read for the Master of Law degree (LLM).

Eligibility: Applicants must be from one of the following countries: Australia, New Zealand, Canada, Bermuda and the Commonwealth countries of the Caribbean, Kenya, Nigeria, Zambia, Zimbabwe, Hong Kong, Singapore or India. Applicants must have gained an offer of a place to read for the Master of Law degree (LLM). The Trusts cannot admit students to the University or any of its colleges. Applicants for awards from the Trusts must, therefore, also apply to the University of Cambridge and be offered a place at Cambridge in the normal way. All applicants must have a First Class or High Second Class (Honours) Degree or equivalent and normally be under 26. Applicants must be successful in winning an Overseas Research Student (ORS) award which pays the difference between the home and overseas rate of the University Composition Fee.

Level of Study: Postgraduate.

Type: Scholarship.

Frequency: Annual.

Study Establishment: The University of Cambridge.

Country of Study: United Kingdom.

No. of awards offered: Up to six.

Application Procedure: Applicants must complete a preliminary application form, which can be obtained from local universities, offices of the British Council or the Trust. The preliminary application form can also be downloaded from http://www.admin.cam.ac.uk/univ/gsprospectus/c7/overseas/schemes.html. Completed forms must be returned to the main address. Shortlisted candidates will be sent forms for admission to the University of Cambridge.

Closing Date: Please contact the organisation.

Contributor: Offered in collaboration with the Pegasus Scholarships Trust and the Foreign and Commonwealth Office (FCO).

Additional Information: Pegasus Scholarships are held in conjunction with other awards from the Cambridge Commonwealth Trust and other sources and entitle applicants to compete for the opportunity to spend three months in London on work placements after completing the LLM at Cambridge. The London placement will be taken between July and September. By submitting one application, candidates will automatically be considered for all the awards for which they are eligible. Further information is available on request.

President Árpád Göncz Scholarship for Postgraduate Study

Subjects: All subjects.

Purpose: To commemorate the visit of the President of Hungary to the University of Cambridge.

Eligibility: Applicants must be Hungarian nationals. The Trusts cannot admit students to the University or any of its colleges. Applicants for awards from the Trusts must, therefore, also apply to the University of Cambridge and be offered a place at Cambridge in the normal way. All applicants must have a First Class or High Second Class (Honours) Degree or equivalent and normally be under 26.

Level of Study: Postgraduate.

Type: Scholarship.
Value: The University Composition Fees at the overseas rate, approved college fees, a maintenance allowance sufficient for a single student and a contribution to return economy airfare.
Length of Study: One year.
Frequency: Annual.
Study Establishment: The University of Cambridge.
Country of Study: United Kingdom.
No. of awards offered: One.
Application Procedure: Applicants must complete a preliminary application form, which can be obtained from local universities, offices of the British Council or the Trust. The preliminary application form can also be downloaded from http://www.admin.cam.ac.uk/univ/gsprospectus/c7/overseas/schemes.html. Completed forms must be returned to the main address. Shortlisted candidates will be sent forms for admission to the University of Cambridge.
Additional Information: Further information is available on request.

President's Cambridge Scholarships for PhD Study

Subjects: All subjects.
Purpose: To financially support study towards a PhD.
Eligibility: Open to students from Ghana. The Trusts cannot admit students to the University or any of its colleges. Applicants for awards from the Trusts must, therefore, also apply to the University of Cambridge and be offered a place at Cambridge in the normal way. All applicants must have a First Class or High Second Class (Honours) Degree or equivalent and normally be under 26. All applicants must be successfully nominated for an Overseas Research Student (ORS) award which covers the difference between the home and overseas rate of the University Composition Fee.
Level of Study: Doctorate.
Type: Scholarship.
Value: The University Composition Fee at the appropriate rate, approved college fees, maintenance allowance sufficient for a single student and a contribution to a return economy airfare.
Length of Study: Up to three years.
Frequency: Annual.
Study Establishment: The University of Cambridge.
Country of Study: United Kingdom.
No. of awards offered: Up to five.
Application Procedure: Applicants must complete a preliminary application form, which can be obtained from local universities, offices of the British Council or the Trust. The preliminary application form can also be downloaded from http://www.admin.cam.ac.uk/univ/gsprospectus/c7/overseas/schemes.html. Completed forms must be returned to the main address. Shortlisted candidates will be sent forms for admission to the University of Cambridge.
Contributor: Offered in collaboration with the Malaysian Commonwealth Studies Centre.
Additional Information: Further information is available on request.

President's Cambridge Scholarships for Postgraduate Study

Subjects: All subjects.
Purpose: To financially support those undertaking postgraduate study.
Eligibility: Applicants must be from Ghana. The Trusts cannot admit students to the University or any of its colleges. Applicants for awards from the Trusts must, therefore, also apply to the University of Cambridge and be offered a place at Cambridge in the normal way. All applicants must have a First Class or High Second Class (Honours) Degree or equivalent and normally be under 26.
Level of Study: Postgraduate.
Type: Scholarship.
Value: The University Composition Fee at the appropriate rate, approved college fees, a maintenance allowance sufficient for a single student and a contribution towards return economy airfare.
Length of Study: One year.
Frequency: Annual.
Study Establishment: The University of Cambridge.
Country of Study: United Kingdom.
No. of awards offered: Up to five.

Application Procedure: Applicants must complete a preliminary application form, which can be obtained from local universities, offices of the British Council or the Trust. The preliminary application form can also be downloaded from http://www.admin.cam.ac.uk/univ/gsprospectus/c7/overseas/schemes.html. Completed forms must be returned to the main address. Shortlisted candidates will be sent forms for admission to the University of Cambridge.
Contributor: Offered in collaboration with the Malaysian Commonwealth Studies Centre.
Additional Information: Further information is available on request.

Prince of Wales (Cable & Wireless) Cambridge Scholarships

Subjects: All subjects.
Eligibility: Open to citizens of Japan. Successful applicants will be expected to return to their home country at the end of their course of study at Cambridge. The Trusts cannot admit students to the University or any of its colleges. Applicants for awards from the Trusts must, therefore, also apply to the University of Cambridge and be offered a place at Cambridge in the normal way. All applicants must have a First Class or High Second Class (Honours) Degree or equivalent and normally be under 26.
Level of Study: Postgraduate.
Type: Scholarship.
Value: The University Composition Fee at the appropriate rate, approved college fees, a maintenance allowance sufficient for a single student and a contribution towards a return economy airfare.
Length of Study: One year.
Frequency: Annual.
Study Establishment: The University of Cambridge.
Country of Study: United Kingdom.
No. of awards offered: 10.
Application Procedure: Applicants must complete a preliminary application form, which can be obtained from local universities, offices of the British Council or the Trust. The preliminary application form can also be downloaded from http://www.admin.cam.ac.uk/univ/gsprospectus/c7/overseas/schemes.html. Completed forms must be returned to the main address. Shortlisted candidates will be sent forms for admission to the University of Cambridge.
Additional Information: Further information is available on request.

Prince of Wales (Cable and Wireless) Cambridge Scholarships for PhD Study

Subjects: All subjects.
Purpose: To financially support study in subjects related to the needs of the scholar's country.
Eligibility: Open to citizens of a number of countries including Anguilla, Antigua and Barbuda, Barbados, Bermuda, the British Virgin Islands, the Cayman Islands, Dominica, Grenada, Jamaica, Montserrat, St Kitts-Nevis, St Lucia, St Vincent, Trinidad and Tobago, and the Turks and Caicos Islands. Successful applicants will be expected to return to their home country at the end of their course of study at Cambridge. The Trusts cannot admit students to the University or any of its colleges. Applicants for awards from the Trusts must, therefore, also apply to the University of Cambridge and be offered a place at Cambridge in the normal way. All applicants must have a First Class or High Second Class (Honours) Degree or equivalent and normally be under 26. All applicants must be successfully nominated for an Overseas Research Student (ORS) award which covers the difference between the home and overseas rate of the University Composition Fee.
Level of Study: Doctorate, Predoctorate.
Type: Scholarship.
Value: The University Composition Fee at the appropriate rate, approved college fees, a maintenance allowance sufficient for a single student and a contribution towards return economy airfare.
Length of Study: Three years.
Frequency: Annual.
Study Establishment: The University of Cambridge.
Country of Study: United Kingdom.
No. of awards offered: 10.
Application Procedure: Applicants must complete a preliminary application form, which can be obtained from local universities, offices

of the British Council or the Trust. The preliminary application form can also be downloaded from http://www.admin.cam.ac.uk/univ/gsprospectus/c7/overseas/schemes.html. Completed forms must be returned to the main address. Shortlisted candidates will be sent forms for admission to the University of Cambridge.
Contributor: Offered in collaboration with Cable and Wireless.
Additional Information: Further information is available on request.

Prince of Wales (Cable and Wireless) Chevening Cambridge Scholarships for Postgraduate Study
Subjects: Development studies, economics, economics and development, engineering, environment and development, finance, international relations, law or management studies.
Purpose: To financially support study in subjects related to the needs of the scholar's country.
Eligibility: Open to citizens of Anguilla, Antigua and Barbuda, Barbados, Bermuda, the British Virgin Islands, the Cayman Islands, Dominica, Grenada, Jamaica, Montserrat, St Kitts-Nevis, St Lucia, St Vincent, Trinidad and Tobago, and the Turks and Caicos Islands. Successful applicants will be expected to return to their home country at the end of their course of study at Cambridge. The Trusts cannot admit students to the University or any of its colleges. Applicants for awards from the Trusts must, therefore, also apply to the University of Cambridge and be offered a place at Cambridge in the normal way. All applicants must have a First Class or High Second Class (Honours) Degree or equivalent and normally be under 26.
Level of Study: Postgraduate.
Type: Scholarship.
Value: The University Composition Fee at the appropriate rate, approved college fees, a maintenance allowance sufficient for a single student and a contribution towards return economy airfare.
Length of Study: One year.
Frequency: Annual.
Study Establishment: The University of Cambridge.
Country of Study: United Kingdom.
No. of awards offered: 10.
Application Procedure: Applicants must complete a preliminary application form, which can be obtained from local universities, offices of the British Council or the Trust. The preliminary application form can also be downloaded from http://www.admin.cam.ac.uk/univ/gsprospectus/c7/overseas/schemes.html. Completed forms must be returned to the main address. Shortlisted candidates will be sent forms for admission to the University of Cambridge.
Contributor: Offered in collaboration with Cable and Wireless and the Foreign and Commonwealth Office (FCO).
Additional Information: Further information is available on request.

Prince of Wales Scholarships for PhD Study
Subjects: All subjects.
Purpose: To financially support study towards a PhD.
Eligibility: Candidates must be citizens of New Zealand. The Trusts cannot admit students to the University or any of its colleges. Applicants for awards from the Trusts must, therefore, also apply to the University of Cambridge and be offered a place at Cambridge in the normal way. All applicants must have a First Class or High Second Class (Honours) Degree or equivalent and normally be under 26. All applicants must be successfully nominated for an Overseas Research Student (ORS) award, which covers the difference between the home and overseas rate of the University Composition Fee.
Level of Study: Doctorate, Predoctorate.
Type: Scholarship.
Value: The University Composition Fee at the home rate, approved college fees, a maintenance allowance sufficient for a single student and a contribution to return economy airfare.
Length of Study: Up to three years.
Frequency: Annual.
Study Establishment: The University of Cambridge.
Country of Study: United Kingdom.
No. of awards offered: Up to five.
Application Procedure: Applicants must apply directly to the Scholarships Officer at their own university. Otherwise, they should apply directly to the New Zealand Vice Chancellor's Committee.

Contributor: Offered in collaboration with the New Zealand Vice Chancellor's Committee.
Additional Information: Further information is available on request.

For further information contact:

The New Zealand Vice Chancellor's Committee, PO Box 11-915, Manners Street, Wellington, New Zealand
Contact: Scholarships Officer

Prince Philip Graduate Exhibitions For PhD Study
Subjects: All subjects.
Purpose: To financially support study towards a PhD.
Eligibility: One scholarship will go to a student who has graduated from the Chinese University of Hong Kong and one will go to a student who has graduated from the University of Hong Kong. The Trusts cannot admit students to the University or any of its colleges. Applicants for awards from the Trusts must, therefore, also apply to the University of Cambridge and be offered a place at Cambridge in the normal way. All applicants must have a First Class or High Second Class (Honours) Degree or equivalent and normally be under 20. All applicants must be successfully nominated for an Overseas Research Student (ORS) award which covers the difference between the home and overseas rate of the University Composition Fee.
Level of Study: Doctorate.
Type: Scholarship.
Value: The University Composition Fee at the appropriate rate, approved college fees, a maintenance allowance sufficient for a single student and a contribution to return economy air fare.
Length of Study: Up to three years.
Frequency: Annual.
Study Establishment: The University of Cambridge.
Country of Study: United Kingdom.
No. of awards offered: Two.
Application Procedure: Applicants must complete a preliminary application form, which can be obtained from local universities, offices of the British Council or the Trust. The preliminary application form can also be downloaded from http://www.admin.cam.ac.uk/univ/gsprospectus/c7/overseas/schemes.html. Completed forms must be returned to the main address. Shortlisted candidates will be sent forms for admission to the University of Cambridge.
Contributor: Offered in collaboration with the Friends of Cambridge University in Hong Kong.
Additional Information: Further information is available on request.

QKenya Cambridge DFID Scholarship
Subjects: All subjects.
Purpose: To offer financial support to students from Kenya.
Eligibility: Open to students from Kenya. All applicants must be under the age of 35 on October 1st with priority given to those candidates under the age of 30, undertake to return to their own country to work or study after completing the course at Cambridge, not be employed by a national or local government department or by a parastatal organisation, not at present be living or studying in a developed country, nor have undertaken studies lasting a year or more in a developed country. Priority will be given to candidates wishing to pursue a course of study related to the economic and social development of their country.
Level of Study: Postgraduate.
Type: Scholarship.
Value: The University Composition Fee at the overseas rate, approved college fees, a maintenance allowance sufficient for a single student and a contribution towards return economy airfare.
Length of Study: One year.
Frequency: Annual.
Study Establishment: The University of Cambridge.
Country of Study: United Kingdom.
No. of awards offered: One.
Application Procedure: Applicants must complete a preliminary application form, which can be obtained from local universities, offices of the British Council or the Trust. The preliminary application

form can also be downloaded from http://www.admin.cam.ac.uk/univ/gsprospectus/c7/overseas/schemes.html. Completed forms must be returned to the main address. Shortlisted candidates will be sent forms for admission to the University of Cambridge.

Contributor: Offered in collaboration with the Kenya Cambridge Commonwealth Trusts and the Department of International Development (DFID).

Additional Information: Further information is available on request.

Rajiv Gandhi Cambridge Bursaries

Subjects: All subjects.

Purpose: To financially support study towards a PhD.

Eligibility: Applicants must be from India. The Trusts cannot admit students to the University or any of its colleges. Applicants for awards from the Trusts must, therefore, also apply to the University of Cambridge and be offered a place at Cambridge in the normal way. All applicants must have a First Class (Honours) Degree. Those with a First Class Master's Degree may be given preference.

Level of Study: Postgraduate.

Type: Bursary.

Value: A substantial contribution towards the student's costs, to be determined in the light of the student's own resources.

Length of Study: Two years.

Frequency: Annual.

Study Establishment: The University of Cambridge.

Country of Study: United Kingdom.

No. of awards offered: One.

Application Procedure: Applicants must contact the organisation.

Contributor: Offered in collaboration with the Rajiv Gandhi Foundation.

Additional Information: Further information is available on request. From The Joint Secretary, Nehru Trust for Cambridge University, Teen Murti House, Teen Murti Marg, New Delhi 110 011, India.

Sally Mugabe Memorial Cambridge DFID Scholarship for Postgraduate Study

Subjects: Subjects relevant to the needs of Zimbabwe, in particular the broad area of social studies relating to the welfare, education and health of women and children.

Purpose: To financially support those undertaking postgraduate study.

Eligibility: Open to female graduates from Zimbabwe. All applicants must be under the age of 35 on October 1st with priority given to those candidates under the age of 30, undertake to return to their own country to work or study after completing the course at Cambridge, not be employed by a national or local government department or by a parastatal organisation, not at present be living or studying in a developed country, nor have undertaken studies lasting a year or more in a developed country. Priority will be given to candidates wishing to pursue a course of study related to the economic and social development of their country.

Level of Study: Postgraduate.

Type: Scholarship.

Value: The University Composition Fee at the overseas rate, approved college fees, a maintenance allowance sufficient for a single student and a contribution to a return economy airfare.

Length of Study: One year.

Frequency: Annual.

Study Establishment: The University of Cambridge.

Country of Study: United Kingdom.

No. of awards offered: One.

Application Procedure: Applicants must complete a preliminary application form, which can be obtained from local universities, offices of the British Council or the Trust. The preliminary application form can also be downloaded from http://www.admin.cam.ac.uk/univ/gsprospectus/c7/overseas/schemes.html. Completed forms must be returned to the main address. Shortlisted candidates will be sent forms for admission to the University of Cambridge.

Contributor: Offered in memory of Sally Mugabe in collaboration with the Department for International Development (DFID) and the Zimbabwe Cambridge Trust.

Additional Information: Further information is available on request.

Schlumberger Cambridge Scholarships

Subjects: All subjects.

Purpose: To offer financial assistance to a student undertaking PhD study from a developing country.

Eligibility: Open to students from a developing country. The Trusts cannot admit students to the University or any of its colleges. Applicants for awards from the Trusts must, therefore, also apply to the University of Cambridge and be offered a place at Cambridge in the normal way. All applicants must have a First Class or High Second Class (Honours) Degree or equivalent and normally be under 26. All applicants must be successfully nominated for an Overseas Research Student (ORS) award which covers the difference between the home and overseas rate of the University Composition Fee.

Level of Study: Doctorate, Predoctorate.

Type: Scholarship.

Value: The University Composition Fee at the overseas rate, approved college fees, a maintenance allowance sufficient for a single student and a contribution to return economy airfare.

Length of Study: Up to three years.

Frequency: Annual.

Study Establishment: The University of Cambridge.

Country of Study: United Kingdom.

No. of awards offered: One.

Application Procedure: Applicants must complete a preliminary application form, which can be obtained from local universities, offices of the British Council or the Trust. The preliminary application form can also be downloaded from http://www.admin.cam.ac.uk/univ/gsprospectus/c7/overseas/schemes.html. Completed forms must be returned to the main address. Shortlisted candidates will be sent forms for admission to the University of Cambridge.

Contributor: Offered in collaboration with Schlumberger Cambridge Research Limited.

Additional Information: Further information is available on request.

Shell Centenary Cambridge Scholarships (Countries outside of the Commonwealth)

Subjects: Applied sciences and technology, environmental science, business management or economics.

Purpose: To financially support those undertaking postgraduate study.

Eligibility: Open to citizens from a number of non Commonwealth countries including China, Kazakhistan, Russia, Egypt, Iran, Oman, Saudi Arabia, Syria, Argentina, Brazil, Chile, Peru and Thailand. The Trusts cannot admit students to the University or any of its colleges. Applicants for awards from the Trusts must, therefore, also apply to the University of Cambridge and be offered a place at Cambridge in the normal way. All applicants must have a First Class or High Second Class (Honours) Degree or equivalent.

Level of Study: Postgraduate.

Type: Scholarship.

Value: The University Composition Fee at the overseas rate, approved college fees, a maintenance allowance sufficient for a single student and a contribution towards return economy airfare.

Length of Study: One year.

Frequency: Annual.

Study Establishment: The University of Cambridge.

Country of Study: United Kingdom.

No. of awards offered: Up to 12.

Application Procedure: Applicants must complete a preliminary application form, which can be obtained from local universities, offices of the British Council or the Trust. The preliminary application form can also be downloaded from http://www.admin.cam.ac.uk/univ/gsprospectus/c7/overseas/schemes.html. Completed forms must be returned to the main address. Shortlisted candidates will be sent forms for admission to the University of Cambridge.

Contributor: Offered in collaboration with Shell International Limited.

Additional Information: Further information is available on request.

Shell Centenary Chevening Scholarships for Postgraduate Study

Subjects: Applied sciences and technology, including environmental sciences, business management and economics.

Purpose: To financially support those undertaking postgraduate study.

Eligibility: Open to citizens of Pakistan, China, Russia, Nigeria, India, Malaysia, Singapore, Brazil and Thailand. The Trusts cannot admit students to the University or any of its colleges. Applicants for awards from the Trusts must, therefore, also apply to the University of Cambridge and be offered a place at Cambridge in the normal way. All applicants must have a First Class or High Second Class (Honours) Degree or equivalent and normally be under 26.
Level of Study: Postgraduate.
Type: Scholarship.
Value: The University Composition Fee at the overseas rate, approved college fees, a maintenance allowance sufficient for a single student and a contribution to return economy airfare.
Length of Study: One year.
Frequency: Annual.
Study Establishment: The University of Cambridge.
Country of Study: United Kingdom.
No. of awards offered: Two.
Application Procedure: Applicants must complete a preliminary application form, which can be obtained from local universities, offices of the British Council or the Trust. The preliminary application form can also be downloaded from http://www.admin.cam.ac.uk/univ/gsprospectus/c7/overseas/schemes.html. Completed forms must be returned to the main address. Shortlisted candidates will be sent forms for admission to the University of Cambridge.
Contributor: Offered in collaboration with Shell International Limited and the Foreign and Commonwealth Office (FCO).
Additional Information: Further information is available on request.

Shell Centenary Scholarships (Developing Countries of the Commonwealth)

Subjects: Applied sciences and technology, environmental science, business management or economics.
Purpose: To financially support those undertaking postgraduate study.
Eligibility: Open to citizens of developing countries of the Commonwealth, including Pakistan, Nigeria and India. The Trusts cannot admit students to the University or any of its colleges. Applicants for awards from the Trusts must, therefore, also apply to the University of Cambridge and be offered a place at Cambridge in the normal way. All applicants must have a First Class or High Second Class (Honours) Degree or equivalent. Applicants for all scholarships must be under 35 on October 1st in the year for which they are applying with priority being given to those under the age of 30, return to their own country to work or study after completing the course, not be employed by a government department (local or national) or by a parastatal organisation, not at present be living or studying in a developed country, and not have taken studies lasting a year or more in a developed country. Candidates wishing to pursue a course of study related to the economic and social development of their country will be given priority.
Level of Study: Postgraduate.
Type: Scholarship.
Value: The University Composition Fee at the overseas rate, approved college fees, a maintenance allowance sufficient for a single student and a contribution to return economy airfare.
Length of Study: Varies.
Frequency: Annual.
Study Establishment: The University of Cambridge.
Country of Study: United Kingdom.
No. of awards offered: Up to 10.
Application Procedure: Applicants must complete a preliminary application form, which can be obtained from local universities, offices of the British Council or the Trust. The preliminary application form can also be downloaded from http://www.admin.cam.ac.uk/univ/gsprospectus/c7/overseas/schemes.html. Completed forms must be returned to the main address. Shortlisted candidates will be sent forms for admission to the University of Cambridge.
Contributor: Offered in collaboration with the Department for International Development (DFID) and Shell International Limited.
Additional Information: Further information is available on request.

Shell Centenary Scholarships at Cambridge (Commonwealth Countries)

Subjects: Applied sciences and technology including environmental sciences, business management or economics.
Purpose: To financially support those undertaking postgraduate study.

Eligibility: Open to students from a number of Commonwealth countries including Malaysia, the Philippines, Singapore and South Africa. The Trusts cannot admit students to the University or any of its colleges. Applicants for awards from the Trusts must, therefore, also apply to the University of Cambridge and be offered a place at Cambridge in the normal way. All applicants must have a First Class or High Second Class (Honours) Degree or equivalent and normally be under 26.
Level of Study: Postgraduate.
Type: Scholarship.
Value: The University Composition Fee at the overseas rate, approved college fees, a maintenance sufficient for a single student and a contribution to return economy airfare.
Length of Study: One year.
Frequency: Annual.
Study Establishment: The University of Cambridge.
Country of Study: United Kingdom.
No. of awards offered: Up to 10.
Application Procedure: Applicants must complete a preliminary application form, which can be obtained from local universities, offices of the British Council or the main address. Completed forms must be returned to the main address. Shortlisted candidates will be sent forms for admission to the University of Cambridge and a scholarship application form. These forms must be returned to the Board of Graduate Studies at the address below.
Contributor: Offered in collaboration with Shell International Limited.
Additional Information: Further information is available on request.

Shell Centenary Scholarships at Cambridge (Non-OECD Countries)

Subjects: For study in applied sciences and technology including environmental sciences, business management or economics.
Purpose: To financially support those undertaking postgraduate study.
Eligibility: Open to students from a non Organisation For Economic Co-operation and Development (OECD) countries. The Trusts cannot admit students to the University or any of its colleges. Applicants for awards from the Trusts must, therefore, also apply to the University of Cambridge and be offered a place at Cambridge in the normal way. All applicants must have a First Class or High Second Class (Honours) Degree or equivalent and normally be under 26.
Level of Study: Postgraduate.
Type: Scholarship.
Value: The University Composition Fee at the overseas rate, approved college fees, a maintenance allowance sufficient for a single student and a contribution towards return economy airfare.
Frequency: Annual.
Study Establishment: The University of Cambridge.
Country of Study: United Kingdom.
No. of awards offered: Up to 22.
Application Procedure: Applicants must complete a preliminary application form, which can be obtained from local universities, offices of the British Council or the main address. Completed forms must be returned to the main address. Shortlisted candidates will be sent forms for admission to the University of Cambridge and a scholarship application form. These forms must be returned to the Board of Graduate Studies at the address below.
Contributor: Offered in collaboration with Shell International Ltd.
Additional Information: Further information is available on request.

For further information contact:

The Board of Graduate Studies, 4 Mill Lane, Cambridge, Cambridgeshire CB2 1RZ, England

Sir Patrick Sheehy Scholarships

Subjects: International relations.
Eligibility: The Trusts cannot admit students to the University or any of its colleges. Applicants for awards from the Trusts must, therefore, also apply to the University of Cambridge and be offered a place at Cambridge in the normal way. All applicants must have a First Class or High Second Class (Honours) Degree or equivalent and normally be under 26. All applicants must be successfully nominated for an

Overseas Research Student (ORS) award which covers the difference between the home and overseas rate of the University Composition Fee.
Level of Study: Doctorate, Predoctorate.
Type: Scholarship.
Value: The University Composition Fee at the appropriate rate, approved college fees, a maintenance allowance sufficient for a single student and a contribution to return economy airfare.
Length of Study: Up to three years.
Frequency: Annual.
Study Establishment: The University of Cambridge.
Country of Study: United Kingdom.
No. of awards offered: Varies.
Application Procedure: Applicants must complete a preliminary application form, which can be obtained from local universities, offices of the British Council or the Trust. The preliminary application form can also be downloaded from http://www.admin.cam.ac.uk/univ/gsprospectus/c7/overseas/schemes.html. Completed forms must be returned to the main address. Shortlisted candidates will be sent forms for admission to the University of Cambridge.
Additional Information: This award is offered to mark the retirement of Sir Patrick Sheehy, the Chairman of the British-American Tobacco (BAT) Company Limited. Further information is available on request.

Smuts MCSC Bursaries

Subjects: Commonwealth studies.
Purpose: To financially support study towards a PhD.
Level of Study: Doctorate, Predoctorate.
Type: Bursary.
Value: The value of the bursaries will be determined in the light of the financial circumstances of the applicant.
Frequency: Annual.
Study Establishment: The University of Cambridge.
Country of Study: United Kingdom.
No. of awards offered: Up to four.
Contributor: Offered in collaboration with the Malaysian Commonwealth Studies Centre.
Additional Information: Further information is available on request.

Smuts ORC Equivalent Awards

Subjects: Commonwealth studies.
Purpose: To financially support study towards a PhD.
Eligibility: The Trusts cannot admit students to the University or any of its colleges. Applicants for awards from the Trusts must, therefore, also apply to the University of Cambridge and be offered a place at Cambridge in the normal way. All applicants must have a First Class or High Second Class (Honours) Degree or equivalent and normally be under 26.
Level of Study: Postdoctorate.
Type: Award.
Value: Please contact the organisation.
Frequency: Annual.
Study Establishment: The University of Cambridge.
Country of Study: United Kingdom.
No. of awards offered: Two.
Application Procedure: Applicants must complete a preliminary application form, which can be obtained from local universities, offices of the British Council or the Trust. The preliminary application form can also be downloaded from http://www.admin.cam.ac.uk/univ/gsprospectus/c7/overseas/schemes.html. Completed forms must be returned to the main address. Shortlisted candidates will be sent forms for admission to the University of Cambridge.
Additional Information: Further information is available on request.

South African College Bursaries

Subjects: All subjects.
Purpose: To enable citizens of South and Southern Africa to take up college places at the University of Cambridge.
Eligibility: Applicants must be from South or Southern Africa. The Trusts cannot admit students to the University or any of its colleges. Applicants for awards from the Trusts must, therefore, also apply to the University of Cambridge and be offered a place at Cambridge in the normal way. All applicants must have a First Class or High Second

Class (Honours) Degree or equivalent and normally be under 26. All applicants must be successfully nominated for an Overseas Research Student (ORS) award which covers the difference between the home and overseas rate of the University Composition Fee.
Level of Study: Postgraduate.
Type: Bursary.
Value: The University Composition Fee at the overseas rate, approved college fees, a maintenance allowance sufficient for a single student and a contribution to return economy airfare.
Length of Study: One year.
Frequency: As available.
Study Establishment: The University of Cambridge.
Country of Study: United Kingdom.
No. of awards offered: Varies.
Application Procedure: Applicants must complete a preliminary application form, which can be obtained from local universities, offices of the British Council or the Trust. The preliminary application form can also be downloaded from http://www.admin.cam.ac.uk/univ/gsprospectus/c7/overseas/schemes.html. Completed forms must be returned to the main address. Shortlisted candidates will be sent forms for admission to the University of Cambridge.
Contributor: Offered in collaboration with Churchill College, Newnham College, Selwyn College, St Catherine's College and Sidney Sussex College, Cambridge.
Additional Information: The bursaries are normally held in conjunction with other awards from the Cambridge Commonwealth Trust and other sources. Further information is available on request.

St Edmund's Commonwealth and Overseas Studentships

Subjects: All subjects.
Purpose: To financially support those undertaking postgraduate study.
Level of Study: Postgraduate.
Type: Studentship.
Value: The University Composition Fee at the overseas rate, approved college fees, a maintenance allowance sufficient for a single student and a contribution towards return economy airfare.
Length of Study: One year.
Frequency: Annual.
Study Establishment: The University of Cambridge.
Country of Study: United Kingdom.
Application Procedure: Applicants must complete a preliminary application form, which can be obtained from local universities, offices of the British Council or the Trust. The preliminary application form can also be downloaded from http://www.admin.cam.ac.uk/univ/gsprospectus/c7/overseas/schemes.html. Completed forms must be returned to the main address. Shortlisted candidates will be sent forms for admission to the University of Cambridge.
Closing Date: Please contact the organisation.

Tanzania Cambridge DFID Scholarships

Subjects: All subjects.
Purpose: To offer financial support to students from Tanzania.
Eligibility: Open to candidates from Tanzania. All applicants must be under the age of 35 on October 1st with priority given to those candidates under the age of 30, undertake to return to their own country to work or study after completing the course at Cambridge, not be employed by a national or local government department or by a parastatal organisation, not at present be living or studying in a developed country, nor have undertaken studies lasting a year or more in a developed country. Priority will be given to candidates wishing to pursue a course of study related to the economic and social development of their country.
Level of Study: Postgraduate.
Type: Scholarship.
Value: The University Composition Fee at the overseas rate, approved college fees, a maintenance allowance sufficient for a single student and a contribution to return economy airfare.
Length of Study: One year.
Frequency: Annual.
Study Establishment: The University of Cambridge.
Country of Study: United Kingdom.
No. of awards offered: Up to four.

191

Application Procedure: Applicants must complete a preliminary application form, which can be obtained from local universities, offices of the British Council or the Trust. The preliminary application form can also be downloaded from http://www.admin.cam.ac.uk/univ/gsprospectus/c7/overseas/schemes.html. Completed forms must be returned to the main address. Shortlisted candidates will be sent forms for admission to the University of Cambridge.

Contributor: Offered in collaboration with the Department of International Development (DFID).

Additional Information: Further information is available on request.

Tanzania Cambridge Scholarship for PhD Study

Subjects: All subjects.

Purpose: To financially support study towards a PhD.

Eligibility: Open to students from Tanzania. The Trusts cannot admit students to the University or any of its colleges. Applicants for awards from the Trusts must, therefore, also apply to the University of Cambridge and be offered a place at Cambridge in the normal way. All applicants must have a First Class or High Second Class (Honours) Degree or equivalent and normally be under 26. Applicants must be successfully nominated for an Overseas Research Student (ORS) award, which covers the difference between the home and overseas rate of the University Composition Fee.

Level of Study: Doctorate, Predoctorate.

Type: Scholarship.

Value: The University Composition Fee at the appropriate rate, approved college fees, a maintenance allowance sufficient for a single student, and a contribution to return economy airfare.

Length of Study: Up to three years.

Frequency: Annual.

Study Establishment: The University of Cambridge.

Country of Study: United Kingdom.

No. of awards offered: One.

Application Procedure: Applicants must complete a preliminary application form, which can be obtained from local universities, offices of the British Council or the Trust. The preliminary application form can also be downloaded from http://www.admin.cam.ac.uk/univ/gsprospectus/c7/overseas/schemes.html. Completed forms must be returned to the main address. Shortlisted candidates will be sent forms for admission to the University of Cambridge.

Additional Information: Further information is available on request.

Tidmarsh Cambridge Scholarship for PhD Study

Subjects: All subjects.

Purpose: To financially support study towards a PhD.

Eligibility: Open to citizens of Canada. The Trusts cannot admit students to the University or any of its colleges. Applicants for awards from the Trusts must, therefore, also apply to the University of Cambridge and be offered a place at Cambridge in the normal way. All applicants must have a First Class or High Second Class (Honours) Degree or equivalent and normally be under 26. Applicants must have been successfully nominated for an Overseas Research Student (ORS) award, which covers the difference between the home and overseas rate of the University Composition Fee.

Level of Study: Doctorate.

Type: Scholarship.

Value: The University Composition Fee at the home rate, approved college fees and a maintenance allowance sufficient for a single student.

Frequency: As available.

Study Establishment: Trinity Hall, the University of Cambridge.

Country of Study: United Kingdom.

No. of awards offered: One.

Application Procedure: Application forms for the scholarship will be sent out to eligible candidates once the completed form for admission to the University of Cambridge has reached the Board of Graduate Studies.

Contributor: A benefaction from Mr Evan Schulman.

Additional Information: Further information is available on request.

For further information contact:

The Board of Graduate Studies, 4 Mill Lane, Cambridge, Cambridgeshire CB2 1RZ, England

Contact: The Secretary

UK Commonwealth (Cambridge) Scholarships for PhD Study

Subjects: All subjects.

Purpose: To offer the opportunity for individuals with proven academic merit to study towards a PhD at Cambridge.

Eligibility: Open to candidates from Australia, New Zealand and Canada. It is not a pre-requisite for successful United Kingdom Commonwealth Scholars to be nominated for an Overseas Research Student (ORS) award. However, candidates for a PhD will be expected to apply for an ORS award since these are competitive awards which provide evidence of proven academic merit and research potential.

Level of Study: Doctorate, Predoctorate.

Type: Scholarship.

Value: The University Composition Fee at the home rate, approved college fees, a maintenance allowance sufficient for a single student and a contribution towards return economy airfare.

Length of Study: Up to three years.

Frequency: Annual.

Study Establishment: The University of Cambridge.

Country of Study: United Kingdom.

No. of awards offered: Up to 15.

Application Procedure: Candidates must apply to the local Commonwealth Scholarship agency in their home country.

Contributor: Offered in collaboration with the Commonwealth Scholarship Commission in the United Kingdom.

Additional Information: Further information is available on request.

UK Commonwealth (Cambridge) Scholarships for PhD Study (Developing Countries)

Subjects: All subjects.

Eligibility: Open to candidates from developing countries of the Commonwealth. It is not a pre-requisite for successful United Kingdom Commonwealth Scholars to be nominated for an Overseas Research Student (ORS) award. However, candidates for a PhD will be expected to apply for an ORS award since these are competitive awards which provide evidence of proven academic merit and research potential.

Value: The University Composition Fee at the home rate, approved college fees, a maintenance allowance sufficient for a single student and a contribution towards return economy airfare.

Study Establishment: The University of Cambridge.

No. of awards offered: Varies.

Application Procedure: Candidates must apply to the local Commonwealth Scholarship agency in their home country.

Additional Information: Further information is available on request.

UK Commonwealth (Cambridge) Scholarships for Postgraduate Study

Subjects: All subjects.

Purpose: To financially support those undertaking postgraduate study.

Eligibility: Open to candidates from Australia, New Zealand and Canada. It is not a pre-requisite for successful United Kingdom Commonwealth Scholars to be nominated for an Overseas Research Student (ORS) award. However, candidates for a PhD will be expected to apply for an ORS award since these are competitive awards which provide evidence of proven academic merit and research potential.

Level of Study: Postgraduate.

Type: Scholarship.

Value: The University Composition Fee at the overseas rate, approved college fees, a maintenance allowance sufficient for a single student and a contribution towards return economy airfare.

Length of Study: One year.

Frequency: Varies.

Study Establishment: The University of Cambridge.

Country of Study: United Kingdom.

No. of awards offered: Up to 10.

Application Procedure: Candidates must apply to the local Commonwealth Scholarship agency in their home country.

Contributor: Offered in collaboration with the Commonwealth Scholarship Association in the United Kingdom.

Additional Information: Further information is available on request.

UK Commonwealth (Cambridge) Scholarships for Postgraduate Study (Developing Countries)

Subjects: All subjects.

Eligibility: Open to candidates from developing countries of the Commonwealth. It is not a pre-requisite for successful United Kingdom Commonwealth Scholars to be nominated for an Overseas Research Student (ORS) award. However, candidates for a PhD will be expected to apply for an ORS award since these are competitive awards which provide evidence of proven academic merit and research potential.

Value: The University Composition Fee at the home rate, approved college fees, a maintenance allowance sufficient for a single student and a contribution towards return economy airfare.

Study Establishment: The University of Cambridge.

No. of awards offered: Varies.

Application Procedure: Candidates must apply to the local Commonwealth Scholarship agency in their home country.

Additional Information: Further information is available on request.

W A Frank Downing Studentship in Law

Subjects: Law.

Purpose: To financially support those undertaking the Master of Law degree (LLM).

Eligibility: Open to citizens of Australia. The Trusts cannot admit students to the University or any of its colleges. Applicants for awards from the Trusts must, therefore, also apply to the University of Cambridge and be offered a place at Cambridge in the normal way. All applicants must have a First Class or High Second Class (Honours) Degree or equivalent and normally be under 26.

Level of Study: Doctorate.

Type: Studentship.

Value: The University Composition Fee at the overseas rate, approved college fees, a maintenance allowance sufficient for a single student and a contribution towards return economy airfare.

Length of Study: One academic year.

Frequency: Varies.

Study Establishment: The University of Cambridge.

Country of Study: United Kingdom.

No. of awards offered: One.

Application Procedure: Applicants must contact the Board of Graduate Studies.

Contributor: Offered in collaboration with the Cambridge Australia Trust.

Additional Information: Further information is available on request. For details of scholarships offered in collaboration with the Cambridge Australia Trust please see the website http://www.anu.edu/cabs/scholarships/cambridge/cambridge-austrust.html.

For further information contact:

The Board of Graduate Studies, 4 Mill Lane, Cambridge, Cambridgeshire CB2 1RZ, England

Contact: The Secretary

William and Margaret Brown Cambridge Scholarship for PhD Study

Subjects: Engineering, natural sciences, physical sciences or political sciences.

Purpose: To financially support study towards a PhD.

Eligibility: Open to students from Canada. The Trusts cannot admit students to the University or any of its colleges. Applicants for awards from the Trusts must, therefore, also apply to the University of Cambridge and be offered a place at Cambridge in the normal way. All applicants must have a First Class or High Second Class (Honours) Degree or equivalent and normally be under 26. All applicants must be successfully nominated for an Overseas Research Student (ORS) award which covers the difference between the home and overseas rate of the University Composition Fee.

Level of Study: Doctorate, Predoctorate.

Type: Scholarship.

Value: The University Composition Fee at the home rate and approved college fees.

Length of Study: Up to three years.

Frequency: As available.

Study Establishment: The University of Cambridge.

Country of Study: United Kingdom.

No. of awards offered: One.

Application Procedure: Application forms for the scholarship will be sent out to eligible candidates once the completed form for admission to the University of Cambridge has reached the Board of Graduate Studies.

Contributor: A benefaction from Dr Donald Pinchin.

Additional Information: Further information is available on request.

For further information contact:

The Board of Graduate Studies, 4 Mill Hill, Cambridge, Cambridgeshire CB2 1RZ, England

Contact: The Secretary

Wolfson Bursaries

Subjects: All subjects.

Eligibility: The Trusts cannot admit students to the University or any of its colleges. Applicants for awards from the Trusts must, therefore, also apply to the University of Cambridge and be offered a place at Cambridge in the normal way. All applicants must have a First Class or High Second Class (Honours) Degree or equivalent and normally be under 26.

Level of Study: Unrestricted.

Type: Bursary.

Frequency: Annual.

Study Establishment: Wolfson College, the University of Cambridge.

Country of Study: United Kingdom.

No. of awards offered: Varies.

Application Procedure: Applications should be made directly to the college.

Additional Information: Further information is available on request.

World Bank Cambridge Scholarships for Postgraduate Study

Subjects: Subjects related to development.

Purpose: To financially support those undertaking postgraduate study.

Eligibility: Candidates must be nationals of a World Bank member country, be under the age of 45, with priority given to those candidates under 35, be in good health and of good character, have or be about to obtain a First Class or High Second Class Degree from a recognised university in a development related field. Other prerequisites include two, but preferably four or five, years of recent full-time professional experience in their home country or other developing country, usually in public service. Candidates must agree to return to their home country upon completion of their studies, must not hold resident status in the United States of America or another industrialised country and must not have been given political asylum by an industrialised country. Candidates should not hold a Master's degree or diploma from an industrialised country, or at present be studying towards a Master's degree or diploma from an industrialised country.

Level of Study: Postgraduate.

Type: Scholarship.

Value: The University Composition Fee at the overseas rate, approved college fees, a maintenance allowance sufficient for a single student and a contribution towards return economy airfare.

Length of Study: One year.

Frequency: Annual.

Study Establishment: The University of Cambridge.

Country of Study: United Kingdom.

No. of awards offered: Up to 20.

Application Procedure: Applicants must contact the organisation.

Contributor: Offered in collaboration with the World Bank.

Additional Information: Further information is available on request.

Zambia Cambridge Scholarships for PhD Study

Subjects: All subjects.

Purpose: To financially support study towards a PhD.

Eligibility: Candidates must be from Zambia. The Trusts cannot admit students to the University or any of its colleges. Applicants for awards from the Trusts must, therefore, also apply to the University of Cambridge and be offered a place at Cambridge in the normal way. All

applicants must have a First Class or High Second Class (Honours) Degree or equivalent and normally be under 26. All applicants must be successfully nominated for an Overseas Research Student (ORS) award which covers the difference between the home and overseas rate of the University Composition Fee.
Level of Study: Doctorate, Predoctorate.
Type: Scholarship.
Value: The University Composition Fee at the home rate, approved college fees, a maintenance allowance sufficient for a single student and a contribution towards return economy airfare.
Length of Study: Up to three years.
Frequency: As available.
Study Establishment: The University of Cambridge.
Country of Study: United Kingdom.
No. of awards offered: One.
Application Procedure: Applicants must complete a preliminary application form, which can be obtained from local universities, offices of the British Council or the Trust. The preliminary application form can also be downloaded from http://www.admin.cam.ac.uk/univ/gsprospectus/c7/overseas/schemes.html. Completed forms must be returned to the main address. Shortlisted candidates will be sent forms for admission to the University of Cambridge.
Contributor: Offered in collaboration with the Zambia Cambridge Trust.
Additional Information: Further information is available on request.

Zambia Cambridge Scholarships for Postgraduate Study
Subjects: All subjects.
Purpose: To financially support those undertaking postgraduate study.
Eligibility: Candidates must be from Zambia. The Trusts cannot admit students to the University or any of its colleges. Applicants for awards from the Trusts must, therefore, also apply to the University of Cambridge and be offered a place at Cambridge in the normal way. All applicants must have a First Class or High Second Class (Honours) Degree or equivalent and normally be under 26. All applicants must be successfully nominated for an Overseas Research Student (ORS) award which covers the difference between the home and overseas rate of the University Composition Fee.
Level of Study: Postgraduate.
Type: Scholarship.
Value: The University Composition Fee at the appropriate rate, approved college fees, a maintenance allowance sufficient for a single student and a contribution towards return economy airfare.
Length of Study: One year.
Frequency: As available.
Study Establishment: The University of Cambridge.
Country of Study: United Kingdom.
No. of awards offered: One.
Application Procedure: Applicants must complete a preliminary application form, which can be obtained from local universities, offices of the British Council or the Trust. The preliminary application form can also be downloaded from http://www.admin.cam.ac.uk/univ/gsprospectus/c7/overseas/schemes.html. Completed forms must be returned to the main address. Shortlisted candidates will be sent forms for admission to the University of Cambridge.
Contributor: Offered in collaboration with the Zambia Cambridge Trust.
Additional Information: Further information is available on request.

Zimbabwe Cambridge Scholarships for PhD Study
Subjects: All subjects.
Purpose: To financially support study towards a PhD.
Eligibility: Applicants must be from Zimbabwe. The Trusts cannot admit students to the University or any of its colleges. Applicants for awards from the Trusts must, therefore, also apply to the University of Cambridge and be offered a place at Cambridge in the normal way. All applicants must have a First Class or High Second Class (Honours) Degree or equivalent and normally be under 26. All applicants for a PhD must be successfully nominated for an Overseas Research Student (ORS) award which pays the difference between home and overseas rate of the University Composition Fee.
Level of Study: Doctorate, Predoctorate.

Type: Scholarship.
Value: The University Composition Fee at the appropriate rate, approved college fees, a maintenance allowance sufficient for a single student and a contribution towards return economy airfare.
Length of Study: Up to three years.
Frequency: As available.
Study Establishment: The University of Cambridge.
Country of Study: United Kingdom.
No. of awards offered: One.
Application Procedure: Applicants must complete a preliminary application form, which can be obtained from local universities, offices of the British Council or the Trust. The preliminary application form can also be downloaded from http://www.admin.cam.ac.uk/univ/gsprospectus/c7/overseas/schemes.html. Completed forms must be returned to the main address. Shortlisted candidates will be sent forms for admission to the University of Cambridge.
Contributor: Offered in collaboration with the Cambridge Local Examinations Syndicate and the Zimbabwe Cambridge Trust.
Additional Information: Further information is available on request.

Zimbabwe Cambridge Scholarships for Postgraduate Study
Subjects: All subjects.
Purpose: To financially support those undertaking postgraduate study.
Eligibility: Applicants must be from Zimbabwe. The Trusts cannot admit students to the University or any of its colleges. Applicants for awards from the Trusts must, therefore, also apply to the University of Cambridge and be offered a place at Cambridge in the normal way. All applicants must have a First Class or High Second Class (Honours) Degree or equivalent and normally be under 26. All applicants for a PhD must be successfully nominated for an Overseas Research Student (ORS) award which pays the difference between home and overseas rate of the University Composition Fee.
Level of Study: Postgraduate.
Type: Scholarship.
Value: The University Composition Fee at the overseas rate, approved college fees, a maintenance allowance sufficient for a single student and a contribution towards return economy airfare.
Length of Study: One year.
Frequency: As available.
Study Establishment: The University of Cambridge.
Country of Study: United Kingdom.
No. of awards offered: One.
Application Procedure: Applicants must complete a preliminary application form, which can be obtained from local universities, offices of the British Council or the Trust. The preliminary application form can also be downloaded from http://www.admin.cam.ac.uk/univ/gsprospectus/c7/overseas/schemes.html. Completed forms must be returned to the main address. Shortlisted candidates will be sent forms for admission to the University of Cambridge.
Contributor: Offered in collaboration with the Cambridge Local Examinations Syndicate and the Zimbabwe Cambridge Trust.
Additional Information: Further information is available on request.

CAMBRIDGE UNIVERSITY LIBRARY

West Road, Cambridge, Cambridgeshire, CB3 9DR, England
Tel: (44) 1223 333047
Fax: (44) 1223 339973
www: http://www.cam.ac.uk/libraries
Contact: D J Hall, Deputy Librarian

Cambridge University Library is a university and legal deposit library.

Munby Fellowship in Bibliography
Subjects: Historical bibliography, the history of the book trade and book collecting. There is no restriction on the choice of topic within these fields, which may concern printed or manuscript material, Western or oriental, in any language, although research should normally be centred on collections in Cambridge.
Purpose: To sponsor bibliographical research.

Eligibility: Open to graduates of any university. Fellows may be of any nationality.
Level of Study: Postdoctorate.
Type: Fellowship.
Value: UK£19,279, reviewed annually.
Length of Study: One year.
Frequency: Annual.
Study Establishment: The Cambridge University Library.
Country of Study: United Kingdom.
No. of awards offered: One.
Application Procedure: Applicants must submit a completed coversheet, available from the Deputy Librarian at the Cambridge University Library, a curriculum vitae, a statement outlining the proposed research and a list of publications. There are no interviews. Selection takes place in December for the following October.
Closing Date: September 6th for October 1st the following year.
Funding: Private.
Contributor: The Munby Memorial Fund.
No. of awards given last year: Two.
No. of applicants last year: 32.

THE CANADA COUNCIL FOR THE ARTS

350 Albert Street, PO Box 1047, Ottawa, ON, K1P 5V8, Canada
Tel: (1) 613 566 4414 ext. 5060
Fax: (1) 613 566 4390
Email: lise.rochon@canadacouncil.ca
www: http://www.canadacouncil.ca
Contact: Ms Lise Rochon

The Canada Council for the Arts is a national agency which provides grants and services to professional Canadian artists and art organisations in dance, media arts, music, theatre, writing and publishing, interdisciplinary work, performance art and the visual arts.

Canada Council Grants for Professional artists

Subjects: Art: dance, music, theatre, media arts, visual arts, creative writing and publishing, inter-arts.
Purpose: To help professional Canadian artists pursue professional development independent artisitc creation or production.
Eligibility: Open to Canadian citizens or permanent residents of Canada who have finished their basic training in the arts and/or are recognized as professionals within their own disciplines.
Level of Study: Postgraduate.
Value: Amounts of Canadian $3,000 to Canadian $20,000 (or up to Canadian $34,000 for established visual artists only).
Frequency: Annual.
Country of Study: Any country.
No. of awards offered: Varies.
Additional Information: Interested individuals should request the grants to professional artists program in their arts discipline for detailed information on the financial assistance offered by the Canada Council Arts.

Canada Council Travel Grants

Subjects: Art.
Purpose: To enable Canadian artists to travel on occasions important to their professional careers.
Eligibility: Open to Canadian citizens or permanent residents of Canada who have finished their basic training in the arts and/or are recognized as professionals within their own disciplines.
Level of Study: Postgraduate, undergraduate.
Type: Travel grant.
Value: A maximum of Canadian $2,800 to cover travel costs, may include an allowance of Canadian $100 per day for up to five days to help defray living expenses.
Frequency: Annual.
Country of Study: Any country.
No. of awards offered: Varies.
Additional Information: Interested individuals should request the Travel grants program in their arts discipline for detailed information on the financial assistance offered by the Canada Council Arts.

J B C Watkins Award

Subjects: Architecture, music, theatre, media arts.
Purpose: To allow Canadian artists to pursue graduate study outside Canada in media arts, theatre, architecture and music.
Eligibility: Open to Canadian artists who are graduates of a Canadian university or postsecondary art institution or training school in the above subjects.
Level of Study: Postgraduate.
Value: Up to Canadian $5,000.
Frequency: Annual.
Country of Study: Other.
No. of awards offered: One.
Closing Date: Varies.
Additional Information: Interested individuals should request the Grants to Artists program for their arts discipline for detailed information on the financial assistance offered by the Canada Council Arts.

Killam Prizes

Subjects: Eminent research in any field.
Purpose: To promote and support distinguished Canadian Scholars who continue to be active in academia.
Eligibility: Prize winners, must have had a distinguished career and exceptional achivements.
Level of Study: Postgraduate.
Type: Prize.
Value: Canadian $100,000.
Length of Study: Variable.
Frequency: Annual.
Study Establishment: Universities, hospitals, research institutes, scientific institutes.
Country of Study: Canada.
No. of awards offered: 5.
Application Procedure: Scholars may not apply on their own behalf; three experts in their field must nominate them. All three may sign a single letter.
Closing Date: November 3rd.
Funding: Private.
Contributor: Dorothy J. Killam.
No. of awards given last year: 5.
Additional Information: Detailed guidelines for application available from main organisation.

Killam Research Fellowships

Subjects: Humanities, social sciences, natural sciences, health sciences, engineering and studies linking any of the disciplines within these broad fields.
Purpose: To support advanced research projects.
Eligibility: Open to Canadian citizens or permanent residents of Canada. Killam Research Fellowships are aimed at established scholars who have demonstrated outstanding ability through substantial publications in their fields over a period of several years.
Level of Study: Postgraduate.
Type: Fellowship.
Value: Partial or full salary replacement to a maximum of Canadian $53,000, based on actual salary for the year before tenure of the award. The Council does not object if the research Fellow's institution supplements the award during the year of tenure to reflect any salary increase.
Length of Study: Up to two years.
Frequency: Annual.
Country of Study: Other.
No. of awards offered: Varies.
Application Procedure: Applicants must submit requests on the appropriate application forms which are available from the Canada Endowment and Prize Section.
Closing Date: To be confirmed.

Robert Fleming Prize

Subjects: Composition young music composers in classical music.
Purpose: To encourage young Canadian composers.
Eligibility: It is intended to encourage the career development of young composers and is awarded to the most talented Canadian

music composer in the competition for Canada Council Grants to Professional musicians in classical music.
Level of Study: Postgraduate.
Value: Canadian $2,000.
Length of Study: Up to one year.
Frequency: Annual.
Country of Study: Any country.
No. of awards offered: One.
Closing Date: March 1st.
Additional Information: Artists may not apply for this prize. All successful candidates in the Canada Council Grants to Professional musicians in classical music are considered automatically.

Saidye Bronfman Award

Subjects: Any discipline within the fine crafts.
Purpose: To recognize excellence in the fine crafts. The award is made to a Canadian craftsperson judged to be an outstanding practitioner in their field, shown by their output over a working life, and their current level of achievement.
Eligibility: Open to Canadian citizens, or individuals who have permanent resident status. The nominee must have made a significant contribution to the development of fine crafts in Canada over a significant period of time, usually more than ten years.
Level of Study: Unrestricted.
Value: C$25,000.
Frequency: Annual.
No. of awards offered: One.
Application Procedure: Please write for details.
Closing Date: 31 January 2004.
Funding: Private.
Contributor: Samuel and Saidye Bronfman Family Foundation.

CANADA MEMORIAL FOUNDATION

The Association of Commonwealth Universities
John Foster House, 36 Gordon Square
London, WC1H 0PF, England
Tel: (44) 20 7380 6700
Fax: (44) 20 7387 2655
www: www.acu.ac.uk
Contact: Awards Division Head

Canada Memorial Foundation Scholarships

Subjects: All subjects, but clinical medicine is currently excluded.
Purpose: To fund a student taking a taught postgraduate degree at a university or other appropriate institution in Canada.
Eligibility: Open to citizens of the United Kingdom who are permanently resident in the United Kingdom and hold, or expect to hold, an Upper Second Class (Honours) Degree or equivalent qualification. Candidates should normally be under 30 years of age and must show convincing reasons as to why they wish to study in Canada. The award is not offered for study leading to a PhD.
Level of Study: Postgraduate.
Type: Scholarship.
Value: Fees, maintenance and air fares. Other allowances for books and study travel are available.
Length of Study: One year only. Candidates wishing to take a two year course will be required to show that they have funding to complete it.
Frequency: Annual.
Study Establishment: A university or other appropriate institution.
Country of Study: Canada.
No. of awards offered: Up to two a year.
Application Procedure: Applicants must complete a preliminary application form in addition to the main application form. Curriculum vitaes are not accepted. Application forms are available from June to October but are not sent out in the week prior to closing date.
Closing Date: Varies, but usually October of each year.
Funding: Private.
Contributor: The Canada Memorial Foundation.
No. of awards given last year: One.
No. of applicants last year: 40.

For further information contact:

The Association of Commonwealth Universities, John Foster House, 36 Gordon Square,

CANADIAN ACADEMIC INSTITUTE IN ATHENS/CANADIAN ARCHAEOLOGICAL INSTITUTE IN ATHENS (CAIA)

59 Queens Park Crescent, Toronto
ON, M5S 2C4, Canada
Tel: (1) 416 926 7290
Fax: (1) 416 926 7292
Contact: Grants Management Officer

1) Thompson (Homer and Dorothy) Fellowship 2) Elisabeth Alfolate Fellowship

Subjects: 1) Modern Greek, classical languages and literatures, history, archaeology, history of art and music 2) Hellenistic to early Byzantine studies.
Purpose: To support the studies of a person who needs to work in Greece.
Eligibility: Open to Canadian citizens or landed immigrants.
Level of Study: Doctorate, Graduate, Postdoctorate, Postgraduate, Predoctorate.
Type: Fellowship.
Value: Canadian $4,000 (approximately) plus reduced rent in the CAIA hostel for the period of the fellowship.
Length of Study: One year.
Frequency: Every two years, the two awards alternate.
Study Establishment: The Canadian Archaeological Institute at Athens.
Country of Study: Greece.
No. of awards offered: One.
Application Procedure: Applicants must write enclosing a curriculum vitae and an outline of the proposed research. Applicants must also arrange for three referees to send letters to the Canadian address.
Closing Date: March 15th.
Funding: Private.
No. of awards given last year: One.
Additional Information: In addition to studies the Fellow will assist the director of CAIA with office work for 10 hours per week, therefore some previous experience in Greece and some modern Greek is recommended.

CANADIAN ASSOCIATION OF BROADCASTERS (CAB)

PO Box 627, Station B, Ottawa
ON, K1P 5S2, Canada
Tel: (1) 613 233 4035
Fax: (1) 613 233 6961
Email: cab@cab-acr.ca
www: http://www.cab-acr.ca
Contact: Administrative Assistant

The Canadian Association of Broadcasters (CAB) is the collective voice of Canada's private radio and television stations and speciality services. The CAB develops industry wide strategic plans, works to improve the financial health of the industry, and promotes private broadcasting's role as Canada's leading programmer and local service provider.

BBM Scholarship

Subjects: Statistical and quantitative research methodology.
Purpose: To ensure that there is an investment in the development of individuals, skilled and knowledgeable in research, who may be of future benefit to the Canadian broadcasting industry.
Eligibility: Open to students enrolled in a graduate studies programme, or in the final year of an Honours Degree with the intention of entering a graduate programme, anywhere in Canada. Candidates will have demonstrated achievement in, and knowledge of, statistical

and/or quantitative research methodology in a course of study at a Canadian university or post secondary institution.
Level of Study: Graduate.
Type: One scholarship.
Value: Canadian $4,000.
Frequency: Annual.
Country of Study: Canada.
No. of awards offered: One.
Application Procedure: Applicants must complete an application form and submit a 250 word essay outlining their interest in audience research. Application forms are available from the website. Three references should be attached to the completed application form, including one from the course director.
Closing Date: June 30th.
Funding: Private.
Contributor: The BBM Bureau of Measurement and the Canadian Association of Broadcasters.

CANADIAN BAR ASSOCIATION (CBA)

Carling Ave. Suite 500/865, Ottawa, ON, K1S 5S8, Canada
Tel: (1) 613 237 2925
Fax: (1) 613 237 0185
Email: info@cba.org
www: http://www.cba.org/abc
Contact: Senior Director of Communications

The Canadian Bar Association (CBA) is the essential ally and advocate of all members of the legal profession. It is the voice of, and for, all members of the profession and its primary purpose is to serve its members. It is also the premier provider of personal and professional development and support to all members of the legal profession, promoting fair justice systems, facilitating effective law reform and promoting equality in the legal profession. The CBA is devoted to the elimination of discrimination.

Viscount Bennett Fellowship
Subjects: Law.
Purpose: To encourage a high standard of legal education, training and ethics.
Eligibility: Open to Canadian citizens only.
Level of Study: Postgraduate.
Type: Fellowship.
Value: Canadian $20,000.
Length of Study: One year.
Frequency: Annual.
Study Establishment: An approved institution.
Country of Study: Any country.
No. of awards offered: One.
Application Procedure: Applicants must write for an application form.
Closing Date: November 15th.

CANADIAN BLOOD SERVICES (CBS)

1800 Alta Vista Drive, Ottawa, ON, K1G 4J5, Canada
Tel: (1) 613 739 2408
Fax: (1) 613 739 2426
Email: cilla.perry@bloodservices.ca
www: http://www.bloodservices.ca
Contact: Ms Cilla Perry, Manager, Research & Development

Canadian Blood Services (CBS) is a non-profit, charitable organisation whose sole mission is to manage the blood system for Canadians. CBS collects approximately 740,000 units of blood annually and processes it into components and products that are administered to thousands of patients each year.

CBS Graduate Fellowship Program
Subjects: Blood transfusion science focusing on aspects of the collection and preparation of blood from volunteer donors, as well as on the biological materials derived from blood or their substitutes obtained through biotechnology. Research may encompass a broad

variety of disciplines including, but not restricted to, epidemiology, surveillance, social sciences, blood banking, immunohaematology, haematology, infectious diseases, immunology, genetics, protein chemistry, molecular and cell biology, clinical medicine, laboratory sciences, virology, bioengineering, process engineering or biotechnology.
Purpose: To attract and support young investigators to initiate or continue training in the field of blood or blood products research.
Eligibility: Open to graduate students who are undertaking full-time research training leading to a PhD degree. Students registering solely for a Master's degree will not be considered and only those demonstrating acceptance into a PhD programme will receive continued support. Candidates must have completed sufficient academic work to be admitted in good standing to a graduate school by the time the award is to take effect, or be already engaged in a PhD programme. Applicants possessing a medical degree but not licensed to practice medicine in Canada are eligible to apply for this award providing they meet the above criteria.
Level of Study: Graduate.
Value: Canadian $20,000 per year plus a yearly research and travel allowance of Canadian $1,000 per year.
Length of Study: Up to four years. The initial term is for two years, with the option for a two year renewal. Renewals must be requested in the form of a complete new application.
Frequency: Twice a year.
Country of Study: Canada.
Application Procedure: Candidates are required to submit a completed application form (GFP-01) that is available either from the website, by or the main address.
Closing Date: July 31st or November 15th.
Funding: Government.
No. of awards given last year: Six.
No. of applicants last year: 12.

CBS Postdoctoral Fellowship (PDF)
Subjects: Transfusion science. The CBS has active research programmes within transfusion science emphasising platelets, stem cells, plasma proteins, infectious disease, epidemiology and chemical transfusion practice.
Purpose: To support Fellows working with CBS affiliated research and development groups across Canada and to foster careers related to transfusion science in Canada.
Eligibility: Candidates must hold a recent PhD or equivalent research degree or an MD, DDS, DVM, plus a recent research degree in an appropriate health field (minimum of a MSc) or equivalent research experience, must not be registered for a higher degree at the time of acceptance of the award, nor undertake formal studies for such a degree during the period of appointment.
Level of Study: Postdoctorate, Professional development.
Type: Fellowship.
Value: The value of each fellowship is related to the major degree(s) and experience that the applicant holds. The fellowship offers a stipend based on current Medical Research Council rates for each of the three years as well as a first year research allowance of Canadian $10,000.
Length of Study: One-three years.
Frequency: Annual.
Country of Study: Canada.
No. of awards offered: Six.
Application Procedure: Applicants must complete CBS Form RD40. Applications must be made through and with the support of a CBS affiliated scientist. Application forms and guidelines are available from any of the CBS Centres or from the main address.
Closing Date: July 1st.
Funding: Government.
No. of awards given last year: Six.
No. of applicants last year: Seven.

CBS Research and Development Program Individual Grants
Subjects: Blood.
Purpose: To carry out research into all areas of the collection, testing, processing and therapeutic use of blood and blood products in order to

maximise effectiveness, to minimise risk to the health of donor and recipient, to minimise cost of products and service and to ensure that all applicable and validated scientific advances in blood transfusion therapy and related fields are incorporated in a timely fashion for the benefit of the public.

Eligibility: Available to principal investigators who are staff members at one of the CBS centres or head office.

Type: Grant.

Value: Materials, supplies, equipment, travel and laboratory personnel.

Length of Study: One-three years.

Frequency: Annual.

Country of Study: Canada.

Application Procedure: Applicants must complete CBS form RD10. Application forms and guidelines are available from any of the Canadian Blood Service Centres or from the main address.

Closing Date: The deadline for the letter of intent is December 16th, and the deadline for the full application is March 14th.

Funding: Government.

No. of awards given last year: Nine.

No. of applicants last year: 31.

CBS Research and Development Program Major Equipment Grants

Subjects: Blood.

Purpose: To carry out research into all areas of the collection, testing, processing and therapeutic use of blood and blood products in order to maximise effectiveness, to minimise risk to the health of donor and recipient, to minimise cost of products and service and to ensure that all applicable and validated scientific advances in blood transfusion therapy and related fields are incorporated in a timely fashion for the benefit of the public.

Eligibility: Open to principal investigators who are staff members at one of the CBS centres or head office.

Type: Grant.

Value: To cover the purchase of specific items of permanent and otherwise unavailable equipment costing more than Canadian $10,000 necessary for research relevant to the CBS research and development programme. Less expensive items of equipment are provided for under the Individual and Group Grants and the Request for Proposal.

Frequency: Annual.

Country of Study: Canada.

Application Procedure: Applicants must complete CBS form RD30. Application forms and guidelines are available from any of the Canadian Blood Service Centres or from the main address.

Closing Date: The deadline for the letter of intent is December 16th, and the deadline for the full application is March 14th.

Funding: Government.

No. of awards given last year: None.

No. of applicants last year: One.

CBS Research Fellowship In Hemostasis (RFH)

Subjects: Haemostasis management.

Purpose: To fund an original research proposal.

Eligibility: Generally open to individuals who are within four years of completion of graduate or clinical fellowship training in an appropriate speciality. The proposed research will contribute to further understanding of the processes of haemostasis and may be of a basic, pre-clinical or clinical nature.

Level of Study: Postdoctorate, Professional development.

Type: Fellowship.

Value: Canadian $70,000.

Length of Study: One year.

Frequency: Annual.

No. of awards offered: One.

Application Procedure: Candidates for this fellowship are required to complete a NNCI/CBS RFH application form (RFH-2001). Application forms and guidelines are available from the main address, as well as in electronic format on the CBS website.

Closing Date: November 1st.

Funding: Commercial.

Contributor: Novo Nordisk Canada, Inc.

No. of awards given last year: One.

No. of applicants last year: Two.

Additional Information: Although it is not a requirement of the award, the fellowship may include some active participation in a clinical programme within a Canadian healthcare facility.

CBS Small Projects Fund

Subjects: Any area of relevance to the CBS.

Purpose: To provide funding for Centre staff, including medical staff, to participate in the CBS research and development effort. Projects may address any area of obvious relevance to the mandate of CBS.

Eligibility: Projects must be based in CBS Blood Centres. Project leaders must be CBS staff members but co-applicants may be from other institutions. Designation as project leader implies that the individual is actively engaged in conducting the study or project and assumes the major responsibility and leadership for the project. CBS scientists (associate scientist, scientist, senior scientists or adjunct scientist) are not eligible to apply to this programme as project leaders and are directed to the Intramural Grants Program.

Value: Up to Canadian $15,000.

Length of Study: One year.

Frequency: Twice a year.

Study Establishment: CBS Blood Centres.

Country of Study: Canada.

Application Procedure: Requests for funding must be submitted as a completed application form (SPF-01) that is available from the main address or by email.

Closing Date: July 31st or November 15th.

Funding: Government.

No. of awards given last year: Four.

No. of applicants last year: Five.

CBS Transfusion Medicine Fellowship Awards

Subjects: Transfusion medicine.

Purpose: To provide support for physicians to acquire training in transfusion medicine through exposure to the work carried out in CBS Centres and Hospital Transfusion Services. The Royal College of Physicians and Surgeons of Canada has recently approved a submission to recognise this programme as a sub-speciality within the category 'Accreditation without certification'. It is intended that successful candidates will have some commitment to transfusion medicine in their future career plans.

Eligibility: Candidates must be in the final year of preparation for certifying examinations by the Royal College of Physicians and Surgeons of Canada, or should be newly qualified in a speciality of the Royal College. Priority will be given to those with interest and experience in areas of infectious diseases, epidemiology, public health, blood utilisation and the clinical practice of transfusion medicine.

Type: Fellowship.

Value: A stipend based on the current level of house staff salaries appropriate to the level of training, provided for in the provincial scale of the province in which the fellowship is awarded, as well as a research and travel allowance of Canadian $10,000.

Length of Study: Two years.

Frequency: Annual.

Country of Study: Canada.

No. of awards offered: Four.

Application Procedure: Applicants must complete an application form. Applications must be made through and with the support of the medical directors of the Centre and the programme director of the university or hospital at which the applicant intends to work. Application forms are available on request from medical directors at CBS Centres across Canada, or from the main address.

Closing Date: December 6th.

Funding: Government.

No. of awards given last year: One.

No. of applicants last year: One.

CANADIAN BREAST CANCER RESEARCH INITIATIVE (CBCRI)

10 Alcorn Avenue, Suite 200, Toronto, ON, M4V 3BI, Canada
Tel: (1) 416 961 9406
Fax: (1) 416 961 4189
Email: cbcri@cancer.ca
www: http://www.breast.cancer.ca
Contact: Ms Pat McAulay

Established in 1993, the Canadian Breast Cancer Research Initiative (CBCRI) is Canada's primary funder of breast cancer study. As a unique partnership of groups from the public, private and non-profit sectors, CBCRI is committed to reducing the incidence of breast cancer, increasing survival, and enhancing the lives of those affected by the disease.

CBCRI Feasibility Grants
Subjects: Oncology.
Type: Grant.
Value: Varies.
Closing Date: October 15th.
Additional Information: For the most up to date information on eligibility, application procedure and grant values, applicants should refer to the website.

CBCRI Research Grants Competition
Subjects: Oncology.
Purpose: To provide research support to individuals formally affiliated with Canadian universities or institutes.
Eligibility: Applicants must write for details or refer to the website.
Type: Grant.
Value: Varies.
Application Procedure: Applicants must complete Form 801. Candidates must write for further details and a form or refer to the website.
Closing Date: October 15th.

CBCRI Special Programs/Idea Grants
Subjects: Oncology.
Purpose: To support initiative and new research ideas that are speculative but have the potential to advance scientific knowledge.
Frequency: Twice a year.
No. of awards offered: 6-12.
Additional Information: For the most up to date information on eligibility, application procedure and grant values, applicants should refer to the website.

CBCRI Special Programs/Streams of Excellence Grants
Subjects: Oncology.
Purpose: To move research findings forward towards translational application and ultimate impact on clinical care and the treatment of breast cancer.
Eligibility: Applicants must write for details or refer to the website.
Type: Grant.
Value: The total per year is approx. canadian $1,500,000.
Length of Study: Four years with possible renewal for a further year.
Frequency: Annual.
Application Procedure: Applicants must write for details or refer to the website.

CANADIAN BUREAU FOR INTERNATIONAL EDUCATION (CBIE)

220 Laurier Avenue West, Suite 1100, Ottawa, ON, K1P 5Z9, Canada
Tel: (1) 613 237 4820
Fax: (1) 613 237 1073
Email: gbeaudoin@cbie.ca
www: http://www.cbie.ca
Contact: Grazyna Beaudoin, Grants Management Officer

The Canadian Bureau for International Education (CBIE) is a national non-profit association comprising educational institutions, organisations and individuals dedicated to internal education and intercultural training. CBIE's mission is to promote the free movement of learners and trainees across national borders. Activities include advocacy, research and information services, training programmes, scholarship management, professional development for international educators and a host of other services for members and learners.

CIDA Awards Program for Canadians
Subjects: Fields related to international development.
Purpose: To give individuals the opportunity to contribute to the implementation of CIDA's development priorities and to enhance the professional, technical and cross cultural skills of those who wish to develop expertise in international development.
Eligibility: Open to Canadian citizens and permanent residents of Canada who are registered in a recognised graduate programme at the time of application. They must have relevant qualifications and substantive work experience related to the requirements of the proposed development project and must demonstrate a commitment to international development. The project is to be carried out in collaboration with an organisation in a country eligible under Canada's Official Development Assistance (ODA) programme and must address a specific field of endeavour within CIDA's Aid Policy. The programme offers awards in three categories. These are the Innovative Research Awards, which allow Master's students to undertake field research related to their thesis or programme, the Professional Leadership Awards which are for individuals with professional experience who wish to undertake a volunteer research or service project in international development, and the International Enterprise Co-operation Awards which are intended for Master's students in business, commerce and management programmes to undertake an international internship or an internship combined with a semester of study in a developing country.
Level of Study: Graduate, Professional development.
Value: The maximum level of award has been established at Canadian $10,000 and for projects in Africa at Canadian $15,000.
Length of Study: Up to one year.
Frequency: Annual.
Country of Study: Canada.
No. of awards offered: Approx. 50.
Application Procedure: Applicants must provide a completed application form, a personal information sheet, a curriculum vitae, proof of registration in a Master's programme, a letter of support from the host institution, a letter of support from the project advisor, a letter of reference and proof of Canadian citizenship or permanent resident status. Three sets of these documents must be provided.
Closing Date: February 17th.
Funding: Government.
Contributor: The Canadian International Development Agency.
No. of awards given last year: 55.

J Armand Bombardier Internationalist Fellowships
Subjects: All subjects.
Eligibility: Open to Canadians and permanent residents of Canada who hold at least one university degree, or are in the final year of a programme. Post secondary level college graduates holding a recognised Bachelor's degree are also eligible. The latest degree must have been awarded no longer than five years from the date of application and applicants must have achieved a high academic standing.
Level of Study: Doctorate, Graduate.
Type: Fellowship.
Value: Canadian $10,000, non renewable.
Length of Study: A minimum of eight consecutive months including at least four taught months of study courses.
Frequency: Annual.
Country of Study: Any country.
No. of awards offered: 25.
Application Procedure: Applicants must complete an application form, available on the website. To receive printed or electronic versions applicants should either write to the main address or email smelanson@cbie.ca. Applicants must submit a completed application form, a letter of intent outlining the proposed study programme abroad, a curriculum vitae, academic transcripts and two letters of reference, one academic and one personal.

Closing Date: March 1st. This date is subject to change so please confirm before applying.
Funding: Private.
No. of awards given last year: 25.

CANADIAN CYSTIC FIBROSIS FOUNDATION (CCFF)

2221 Yonge Street, Suite 601, Toronto, ON, M4S 2B4, Canada
Tel: (1) 416 485 9149
Fax: (1) 416 485 0960
Email: kethier@cysticfibrosis.ca
www: http://www.cysticfibrosis.ca
Contact: Manager, Research Programs

Since 1960, the Canadian Cystic Fibrosis Foundation (CCFF) has worked to provide a brighter future for every child born with cystic fibrosis. Through its research and clinical programmes, the Foundation helps to provide outstanding care for affected individuals, while pursuing the quest for a cure or control.

CCFF Clinic Incentive Grants
Subjects: Medical sciences.
Purpose: To enhance the standard of clinical care available to Canadians with cystic fibrosis, by providing funds to initiate a comprehensive programme for patient care, research and teaching or to strengthen an existing programme.
Eligibility: Canadian hospitals and medical schools are eligible to apply. Applicants must demonstrate the regional need for specialised clinical care for cystic fibrosis, the need of the institution for assistance and its plans to attract complementary funding from other sources to develop a complete cystic fibrosis programme, the potential for the development of a comprehensive programme for care, clinical research and teaching, and the desire to collaborate with the CCFF and other Canadian cystic fibrosis clinics.
Level of Study: Research.
Type: Grant.
Length of Study: One year, renewable on an annual basis.
Frequency: Annual.
Country of Study: Canada.
Application Procedure: Applicants must complete an application form. Late applications will be subject to a penalty equal to 10 per cent of the value of the award. This penalty will be deducted from the clinic director's honorarium.
Closing Date: October 1st.

CCFF Fellowships
Subjects: Research into areas pertinent to cystic fibrosis.
Purpose: To support basic or clinical research training in areas of the biomedical or behavioural sciences pertinent to cystic fibrosis.
Eligibility: Equitable consideration will be given to Fellowship applicants from outside of Canada, who intend to return to their own country on completion of a Fellowship.
Level of Study: Postgraduate.
Type: Fellowship.
Value: Dependent upon academic qualifications and research experience.
Length of Study: Two years.
Frequency: Annual, Twice per year.
Study Establishment: An approved university department, hospital or research institute in Canada.
Country of Study: Canada.
Application Procedure: Applicants must arrange to have three letters of recommendation, one of which should be from the applicant's current or most recent supervisor.
Closing Date: 1 October, 1 April.

CCFF Research Grants
Subjects: Cystic fibrosis.
Purpose: To facilitate scientific investigation.
Eligibility: A principal investigator should hold a recognised, full-time faculty appointment in a relevant discipline at a Canadian university or hospital. Under exceptional circumstances and at the discretion of the Research Subcommittee, applications from other individuals may be evaluated on a case by case basis.
Level of Study: Doctorate.
Type: Research grant.
Value: Determined by the Medical or Scientific Advisory Committee following a detailed review of the applicant's proposed budget.
Length of Study: Usually one or two years or, in a limited number of instances, three years.
Frequency: Annual.
Study Establishment: A Canadian institution.
Country of Study: Canada.
Application Procedure: Applicants must write for details. Incomplete or late applications will be returned to the applicant.
Closing Date: October 1st.
Additional Information: Investigators are eligible to hold more than one research grant. No more than one initial application may be submitted to a single competition, and it is a requirement that the focus of a second grant be clearly delineated from the first one. The specific aims of a second grant should represent new approaches to the cystic fibrosis problem and not an extension of an existing research programme.

CCFF Scholarships
Subjects: Cystic fibrosis.
Purpose: To provide salary support for a limited number of exceptional investigators, offering them an opportunity to develop outstanding cystic fibrosis research programmes, unhampered by heavy teaching or clinical loads. It is intended to attract gifted investigators to cystic fibrosis research.
Eligibility: Open to holders of an MD or PhD degree who are sponsored by the chairman of the appropriate department and by the Dean of Faculty. They may recently have completed training or be established investigators wishing to devote major research effort to cystic fibrosis. The beginning investigator should have demonstrated promise of ability to initiate and carry out independent research and the established investigator should have a published record of excellent scientific research.
Level of Study: Doctorate, Postgraduate.
Type: Scholarship.
Value: Salary support, which is dependent on the qualifications and experience of the successful candidate, will be determined by prevailing Canadian scholarship rates and the nominating university. The salary of the Scholar may be supplemented by the institution or by clinical income and up to 50 per cent of the salary will be paid by the Foundation.
Length of Study: Three years, renewable for an additional two years on receipt of a satisfactory progress report. In no case will an award be for more than five years.
Frequency: Annual.
Study Establishment: Any approved university, hospital or research institute.
Country of Study: Canada.
No. of awards offered: Varies, subject to availability of funds.
Application Procedure: Applicants must write for details.
Closing Date: October 1st.

CCFF Senior Scientist Research Training Award
Subjects: Research into cystic fibrosis.
Purpose: To provide support to a limited number of C.F. investigators by offering them an opportunity to obtain additional training that will enhance their capacity to conduct research directly relevant to C.F.
Eligibility: Applicants must have held a recognized, full-time faculty appointment in a relevant discipline at a Canadian University or hospital for at least six years.
Level of Study: Postgraduate.
Type: Training award.
Value: Canadian $30,000.
Length of Study: 3 months to 1 year.
Frequency: Annual.
Study Establishment: An approved university department or hospital in Canada.
Country of Study: Canada.

Application Procedure: Applications must be received by the Foundation no later than 1st October. Incomplete or late applications will be returned to the applicant.
Closing Date: 1st October.
Additional Information: This award can be used for Sabbatical support for qualified individuals.

CCFF Small Conference Grants
Subjects: Medical sciences.
Purpose: To support small conferences which are focused on subjects of direct relevance to cystic fibrosis and to facilitate the exchange of special expertise between larger university based cystic fibrosis clinics and smaller, more remote clinics.
Eligibility: Open to clinic directors and CCFF funded investigators.
Level of Study: Professional development.
Type: Grant.
Value: Grants to conferences will be up to a maximum of Canadian $2,500 and grants for the exchange of expertise will not normally exceed Canadian $1,000.
No. of awards offered: Dependent on availability of funds.
Application Procedure: Applicants must make applications in the form of a letter. For medical and/or scientific conferences, the application should indicate who is organising and attending the conference, and the specific topics and purpose of the conference. For inter-clinic exchanges, the application should specify the proposed arrangements for, and the specific purpose of the exchange.
Closing Date: Applications may be submitted at any time, but the Foundation should be consulted in advance with respect to the availability of funds.
Additional Information: Grants are available on a first come, first served basis. Frequency of application from any particular individual or group should be reasonable.

CCFF Studentships
Subjects: Research into cystic fibrosis.
Purpose: To support highly qualified graduate students who are registered for a higher degree, and who are undertaking full-time research training in areas of the biomedical or behavioural sciences relevant to cystic fibrosis.
Eligibility: Equitable consideration given to Studentship applicants from outside of Canada who intend to return to their own country on completion of a studentship.
Level of Study: Doctorate, Postgraduate.
Type: Studentship.
Value: Salary + cost-of-living award at discretion of Medical/Scientific Advisory Committee.
Length of Study: 1 - 5 years.
Frequency: Three times per year.
Study Establishment: Studentships are tenable only at Canadian Universities.
Country of Study: Canada.
Application Procedure: The Foundation sponsors a studentships competition in October and April. Candidates for initial awards are eligible to apply to either competition. Like all CCFF grants, studentships are subject to the availability of funds, and the availability of funds is generally more certain with respect to the October competition.
Closing Date: 1 April, 1 July, 1 October.
Additional Information: Studentships are awarded for studies at the master's or doctoral level. If a student receiving support for studies leading to a master's degree elects to continue to a doctorate degree, he or she must reapply for an initial CCFF Studentship at the doctoral level.

CCFF Transplant Centre Incentive Grants
Subjects: Medical sciences.
Purpose: To enhance the quality of care available to cystic fibrosis transplant candidates by providing eligible centres with supplementary funding.
Eligibility: Open to any Canadian lung transplant centre which currently has one or more individuals with cystic fibrosis listed for transplant. Please note that under no circumstances will funding be provided to more than one transplant centre in the same city.

Applicants must demonstrate how funds awarded would serve to enhance the quality of care available to patients in their centre.
Level of Study: Research.
Type: Grant.
Value: Determined in accordance with a formula which takes account of the number of patients assessed, accepted and followed pre-operatively, transplanted and followed post-operatively in a given centre during the calendar year ending December 31st of the year preceding the application.
Length of Study: One year.
Frequency: Annual.
Country of Study: Canada.
Application Procedure: Applicants must contact the Foundation. Applicants must provide a rationale for the funding request and a detailed report on patient care and research within the lung transplant programme. All applications will be adjudicated by the Clinic Sub-committee of the Canadian Cystic Fibrosis Foundation.
Closing Date: October 1st.
Additional Information: Late applications will be subject to a penalty equal to 10 per cent of the value of the award.

CCFF Visiting Scientist Awards
Subjects: Biomedical and behavioural sciences relevant to the study of cystic fibrosis.
Purpose: To enable senior investigators to travel to Canada from abroad who are invited to engage in cystic fibrosis research at a Canadian institution or to assist junior or senior investigators who wish to work in another laboratory in Canada or abroad. This experience should, in some way, benefit the Canadian cystic fibrosis research effort.
Eligibility: A senior investigator can be considered such if he or she has attained at least the position of an associate professor, or has six years of equivalent experience.
Level of Study: Doctorate, Professional development.
Type: Travel grant.
Value: Varies.
Length of Study: Varies.
Frequency: Dependent on funds available.
Country of Study: Any country.
No. of awards offered: A limited number.
Application Procedure: Applicants must send an application letter, accompanied by supporting letters from the head of the appropriate department of the host university. Supporting letters should also be provided by the head of the department and the Dean of the faculty of the applicant's own university.

Special Travel Allowances
Subjects: Study of cystic fibrosis.
Purpose: To support fellows and students to attend and participate in scientific meetings related to cystic fibrosis.
Eligibility: Fellows and other CCFF supported scientists.
Level of Study: Doctorate, Postgraduate.
Type: Award.
Value: Travel + meal allowance.
Length of Study: As determined by seminar length.
Frequency: Annual.
Study Establishment: Appropriate seminar.
Country of Study: Any country.
Application Procedure: Applications should be made in the form of a letter and must be submitted prior to travel.
Closing Date: Any time but the Foundation must be consulted.

Visiting Scientist Awards
Subjects: To study cystic fibrosis.
Purpose: To support senior investigators from abroad who are invited to engage in CF research at a Canadian institution; or Canadian investigators who wish to work in another laboratory in Canada or abroad.
Level of Study: Doctorate, Postdoctorate.
Type: Grant.
Frequency: Any time, result dependent on funds available.
Study Establishment: Suitable research institution.

Country of Study: Any but the research should benefit the Canadian research effort.

Application Procedure: Applications should be in the form of a letter, accompanied by a supporting letter from the head of the appropriate department of the host university. A supporting letter signed by the head of the department and the dean of the faculty of the applicant's own university should be provided.

CANADIAN EMBASSY (USA)

501 Pennsylvania Avenue North West, Washington, DC 20001, United States of America
Tel: (1) 202 682 1740
Fax: (1) 202 682 7791
Email: webmaster@canadianembassy.org
www: http://www.canadianembassy.org
Contact: Academic Relations Office

Canadian Embassy (USA) Faculty Enrichment Program

Subjects: Priority topics include bilateral trade and economics, Canada United States border issues, cultural policy and values, environment, natural resources, energy issues and security as operation, projects that examine Canadian politics, economics, culture and society as well as Canada's role in international affairs.

Purpose: To provide faculty members with the opportunity to develop or redevelop courses with substantial Canadian content that will be offered as part of their regular teaching load, or as a special offering to select audiences in continuing or distance education.

Eligibility: Open to full-time, tenured or tenure track faculty members at accredited four year United States colleges and universities. Candidates should be able to demonstrate that they are already teaching, or will be authorised to teach, courses with substantial Canadian content (33 per cent or more). Team teaching applications are welcome. Applicants are ineligible to receive the same grant in two consecutive years or to receive two individual category Canadian Studies grants in the same grant period.

Value: Up to US$4,500.

Frequency: Annual.

Country of Study: United States of America.

No. of awards offered: Varies.

Application Procedure: Applicants must contact the organisation for an application form.

Additional Information: The Embassy especially encourages the use of new Internet technology to enhance existing courses, including the creation of instructional websites, interactive technologies and distance learning links to Canadian Universities.

Canadian Embassy (USA) Graduate Student Fellowship Program

Subjects: Business and economic issues, Canadian values and culture, communications, environment, national and international security or natural resources eg. energy, fisheries, forestry and trade.

Purpose: To offer graduate students the opportunity to conduct part of their doctoral research in Canada.

Eligibility: Open to full-time doctoral students at accredited four year colleges and universities in the United States or Canada whose dissertations are related in substantial part to the study of Canada, Canada and the United States or Canada and North America. Candidates must be citizens or permanent residents of the United States and should have completed all doctoral requirements except the dissertation when they apply for a grant.

Level of Study: Graduate.

Type: Fellowship.

Value: A maximum amount of US$850 per month may be awarded for a designated period of up to nine months.

Frequency: Annual.

Study Establishment: An accredited four year college or university.

Country of Study: Other.

Application Procedure: Applicants must provide six copies of the following in the order listed: the completed application form, a concise letter of three to four pages which will explain clearly the present status of the candidate's doctoral studies, describe the candidate's study plans in Canada, list Canadian contacts such as Scholars, research institutes, academic institutions or libraries, state clearly the exact number of months for which financial support is needed, provide a complete and detailed budget, indicate what other funding sources are available, give the names and addresses of two referees, one of which must be the dissertation advisor, contain the dissertation prospectus which must identify the key issues or the main theoretical problem, justify the methodology and indicate clearly the nature of the dissertation's contribution to the advancement of Canadian Studies. An unofficial transcript of grades, a curriculum vitae and proof of United States citizenship or permanent residency must also be included. Application forms are available on request.

Closing Date: October 31st.

Funding: Government.

Additional Information: The Graduate Student Fellowship Program promotes research in the social sciences and humanities with a view to contributing to a better knowledge and understanding of Canada and its relationship with the United States or other countries of the world.

Canadian Embassy (USA) Research Grant Program

Subjects: Business and economic issues, Canadian values and culture, communications, environment, national and international security or natural resources eg. energy, fisheries, forestry and trade.

Purpose: To assist individual scholars or a group of scholars in writing an article length manuscript of publishable quality and reporting their findings in scholarly publications.

Eligibility: Open to full-time faculty members at accredited four year United States colleges and universities, as well as scholars at American research and policy planning institutes who undertake significant research projects concerning Canada, Canada and the United States, or Canada and North America. Recent PhD recipients who are citizens or permanent residents of the United States are also eligible to apply.

Level of Study: Postgraduate.

Type: Research grant.

Value: Individual applicants may request funding for up to US$10,000. The principal investigator, on behalf of a group, may request funding for up to US$15,000.

Frequency: Annual.

Study Establishment: An accredited four year college or university.

Country of Study: United States of America.

Application Procedure: Applicants must provide six copies of the following in this order: the completed application form, a concise proposal of four-eight pages which will identify all members of the research team, if a team project, and specify each member's affiliation and role in the study, identify the key issues or the main theoretical problem, describe and justify the appropriate methodology, present a general schedule of research activities, indicate clearly both the nature and scope of the projects contribution to the advancement of Canadian Studies, include a detailed budget including all other funding sources and a description of anticipated expenditures. A curriculum vitae, and the names and addresses of two scholars from whom the applicants will solicit recommendations should also be included. Application forms are available on request.

Closing Date: September 30th.

Funding: Government.

Additional Information: The Research Grant Program promotes research in the social sciences and humanities with a view to contributing to a better knowledge and understanding of Canada and its relationship with the United States or other countries of the world.

Canadian Embassy (USA) Senior Fellowship Program

Subjects: Canadian studies, Canada or United States topics, social, political or economic issues that impact on these relationships.

Purpose: To provide senior scholars with an opportunity to complete and publish a major study which will significantly benefit the development of Canadian Studies in the United States.

Eligibility: Open to full-time tenured faculty members at accredited four year United States colleges and universities who are fully involved in Canadian Studies. These 'Canadianists' should be in the process of completing research for a book or major monograph. The study must be on a subject of widespread interest to the Canadian Studies community in the United States as well as in Canada. This fellowship

is awarded only once to any one recipient and is in recognition of an academic career dedicated to the promotion of Canadian Studies.
Level of Study: Postdoctorate, Postgraduate.
Type: Fellowship.
Value: Funding not to exceed US$3,000 per month may be awarded for a period of up to six months.
Frequency: Every two years.
Study Establishment: An accredited four year college or university.
Country of Study: United States of America.
Application Procedure: Applicants must provide six copies of the following in the order listed: a completed application form, a concise narrative of the research project which should include a statement outlining the applicant's background, field(s) of specialisation, particular areas of interest in Canadian Studies and courses taught in Canadian Studies, a presentation of the book's key issues, main theoretical problem, methodology, table of contents and a clear statement of both the nature and scope of the author's intended contribution to the advancement of knowledge, a detailed budget including all other funding sources, a description of anticipated expenditures and a statement of the exact number of months for which financial support is requested. Appendices to the narrative must include: a letter from the applicant's department chairperson, Dean, or academic vice president attesting that the applicant will be relieved of his or her regular teaching duties throughout the designated period of time an award is sought, a curriculum vitae, and the names and addresses of two referees. Application forms are available on request.
Closing Date: June 15th.
Funding: Government.

CANADIAN FEDERATION OF UNIVERSITY WOMEN (CFUW)

251 Bank Street, Suite 600, Ottawa, ON, K2P 1X3, Canada
Tel: (1) 613 234 2732; (1) 613 214 8252
Fax: (1) 613 234 8221
Email: cfuwfls@rogers.com
www: http://www.cfuw.org
Contact: Betty A. Dunlop, Fellowships Programme Manager

Found in 1919, the Canadian Federation of University Women (CFUW) is a voluntary, non-partisan, non-profit, self funded bilingual organisation of 10,000 women university graduates. CFUW members are active in public affairs, working to raise the social, economic, and legal status of women, as well as to improve education, the environment, peace, justice, and human rights.

1989 Polytechnique Commemorative Award
Subjects: All subjects.
Purpose: To provide partial funding for graduate study.
Eligibility: Open to women who hold at least a Bachelor's degree or equivalent from a recognised university, who are Canadian citizens or who have held landed immigrant status for at least one year and are able to justify the relevance of their work to women.
Level of Study: Postgraduate.
Value: Canadian $2,800.
Frequency: Annual.
Study Establishment: A recognised university.
Country of Study: Any country.
No. of awards offered: One.
Application Procedure: Applicants must complete an application form, available from the website.
Closing Date: November 1st.
Funding: Private.
No. of awards given last year: One.
No. of applicants last year: 57.
Additional Information: The candidate must be able to justify the relevance of their work to women.

Alice E Wilson Awards
Subjects: All subjects.
Purpose: To assist women's study. Special consideration is given to candidates returning to study after at least three years.

Eligibility: Open to female Canadian citizens or women who have held landed immigrant status for at least one year prior to submitting an application. Candidates should have a Bachelor's degree or its equivalent from a recognised university, not necessarily in Canada. Special consideration is given to candidates returning to study after at least three years. Candidates must have been accepted into the proposed programme of study.
Level of Study: Postgraduate.
Value: Canadian $4,000 each award.
Frequency: Annual.
Study Establishment: A recognised university.
Country of Study: Any country.
No. of awards offered: Three.
Application Procedure: Applicants must complete an application form, available from the Federation website.
Closing Date: November 1st.
Funding: Private.
No. of awards given last year: One.
No. of applicants last year: 100.

Beverley Jackson Fellowship
Subjects: All subjects.
Purpose: To provide partial funding for graduate study.
Eligibility: Open to women who are over the age of 35 at the time of application and are enrolled in graduate work at an Ontario university. Candidates should hold at least a Bachelor's degree or equivalent from a recognised university and be either a Canadian citizen or have held landed immigrant status for at least one year prior to the submission of an application. Candidates must have been accepted into the proposed programme of study.
Level of Study: Postgraduate.
Type: Fellowship.
Value: Canadian $2,500.
Frequency: Annual.
Study Establishment: A recognised university in Ontario.
Country of Study: Canada.
No. of awards offered: One.
Application Procedure: Applicants must complete an application form, available from the Federation website.
Closing Date: November 1st.
Funding: Private.
Contributor: UWC North York.
No. of awards given last year: One.
No. of applicants last year: 21.

CFUW Memorial Fellowship
Subjects: Science, mathematics or engineering.
Purpose: To provide partial funding for graduate study at the Master's degree level.
Eligibility: Open to female Canadian citizens or women who have held landed immigrant status for at least one year prior to submitting an application. Candidates should hold a Bachelor's degree or its equivalent from a recognised university and should be looking to pursue graduate work at Master's degree level. Candidates must have been accepted into a proposed programme of study.
Level of Study: Postgraduate.
Type: Fellowship.
Value: Canadian $5,500 paid in instalments twice a year.
Frequency: Annual.
Study Establishment: A recognised university.
Country of Study: Any country.
No. of awards offered: One.
Application Procedure: Applicants must complete an application form, available from the Federation website.
Closing Date: November 1st.
Funding: Private.
No. of awards given last year: One.
No. of applicants last year: 42.
Additional Information: The fellowship is not renewable.

Dr Marion Elder Grant Fellowship
Subjects: All subjects.
Purpose: To provide partial funding for full-time graduate study.

Eligibility: Open to women who have a Bachelor's degree or equivalent from a recognised university, who are Canadian citizens or who have held landed immigrant status for at least one year prior to the submission of an application and have been accepted into the proposed programme of study. Candidates must be enrolled in the second year of a first Master's degree or the first year of a second Master's degree. Any level of doctoral programme is acceptable but preference will be given to holders of an Acadia University degree.

Level of Study: Postgraduate.
Type: Fellowship.
Value: Canadian $9,000.
Frequency: Annual.
Study Establishment: A recognised university.
Country of Study: Any country.
No. of awards offered: One.
Application Procedure: Applicants must complete an application form, available from the Federation website and provide a letter of reference from their graduate supervisor.
Closing Date: November 1st.
Funding: Private.
Contributor: CFUW/Wolfville.
No. of awards given last year: One.
No. of applicants last year: 166.

Georgette Lemoyne Award

Subjects: All subjects.
Purpose: To provide partial funding for graduate study.
Eligibility: Open to women who have a Bachelor's degree or equivalent from a recognised university and who are Canadian citizens or have held landed immigrant status for at least one year prior to the submission of an application. Candidates must have been accepted into the proposed programme of study.
Level of Study: Postgraduate.
Value: Canadian $5,000.
Frequency: Annual.
Study Establishment: A Canadian university where French is one of the languages of instruction.
Country of Study: Canada.
No. of awards offered: One.
Application Procedure: Applicants must complete an application form, available from the Federation website.
Closing Date: November 1st.
Funding: Private.
No. of awards given last year: One.
No. of applicants last year: 31.

Margaret Dale Philp Biennial Award

Subjects: The humanities or social sciences with special consideration given to candidates who wish to specialise in Canadian history.
Purpose: To provide partial funding for graduate study.
Eligibility: Open to female Canadian citizens or women who have held landed immigrant status for at least one year prior to the submission of an application. Candidates should hold a Bachelor's degree or its equivalent, reside in Canada and should wish to embark on, or continue, a programme leading to an advanced degree. Candidates should also have been accepted into the proposed programme of study.
Level of Study: Postgraduate.
Value: Please contact the Federation.
Frequency: Every two years.
Study Establishment: A recognised university.
Country of Study: Canada.
No. of awards offered: One.
Application Procedure: Applicants must complete an application form, available from the Federation website.
Closing Date: November 1st.
Funding: Private.
Contributor: CFUW/Kitchener-Waterloo.
No. of awards given last year: One.
No. of applicants last year: 40.

Margaret McWilliams Predoctoral Fellowship

Subjects: All subjects.
Purpose: To provide funding for full-time doctoral study.
Eligibility: Open to female Canadian citizens or women who have held landed immigrant status for at least one year prior to the submission of an application. Candidates should hold a Bachelor's degree or its equivalent from a recognised university, not necessarily in Canada, and be a full-time student at an advanced stage ie. at least one year into her doctoral programme.
Level of Study: Doctorate.
Type: Fellowship.
Value: Canadian $10,000 paid in two six monthly instalments.
Frequency: Annual.
Study Establishment: A recognised university.
Country of Study: Any country.
No. of awards offered: One.
Application Procedure: Applicants must complete an application, available from the Federation website.
Closing Date: November 1st.
Funding: Private.
No. of awards given last year: One.
No. of applicants last year: 119
Additional Information: The fellowship is not renewable.

CANADIAN FORESTRY FOUNDATION

185 Somerset Street West, Suite 203, Ottawa, ON, K2P 0J2, Canada
Tel: (1) 613 232 1815
Fax: (1) 613 232 4210
Email: lemkay@canadianforestry.com, cfa@canadianforestry.com
www: http://www.canadianforestry.com
Contact: Administrative Assistant

The Canadian Forestry Foundation is a registered charity whose purpose is to support the educational programmes of the Canadian Forestry Association in promoting understanding and co-operation in the wise use and environmentally sound sustainable development of Canada's forests.

Canadian Forestry Foundation Forest Capital of Canada Award

Subjects: Forestry awareness.
Purpose: To recognise, annually, one community in Canada which is distinct because of its commitment to, and dependence on, the forest (past, present and future) and the civic minded recognition of the importance of the forest to the community.
Eligibility: Open to forest communities in Canada which fulfil the terms of the purpose of the award.
Level of Study: Unrestricted.
Type: Award.
Length of Study: One year.
Frequency: Annual.
Country of Study: Canada.
No. of awards offered: Three.
Application Procedure: Applicants must write for details.
Closing Date: December 31st.
Additional Information: Information on annual recipients is available on the website.

Canadian Forestry Foundation Forest Education Scholarship

Subjects: Forest education and communication.
Purpose: To encourage students to consider a career in the education and communications side of forestry.
Eligibility: Open to Canadian citizens currently enrolled in a graduate forestry programme at a recognised Canadian university. Applicants with backgrounds in communications or education who are registered in a forestry technical school may also be considered. Students with a formal forestry background who are currently studying education at the university level may also apply.
Level of Study: Postgraduate.
Type: Scholarship.
Value: Canadian $500.

Length of Study: One academic year.
Frequency: Annual.
Study Establishment: A recognised Canadian university or forestry technical school.
Country of Study: Canada.
No. of awards offered: One.
Application Procedure: Applicants must submit applications in writing.
Closing Date: May 30th.

CANADIAN FOUNDATION FOR THE STUDY OF INFANT DEATHS

Suite 308, 586 Eglinton Avenue East, Toronto, ON, M4P 1P2, Canada
Tel: (1) 416 488 3260
Fax: (1) 416 488 3864
Email: sidsinfo@sidscanada.org
www: http://www.sidscanada.org
Contact: Executive Director

The Canadian Foundation for the Study of Infant Deaths is a federally incorporated charitable organisation which was set up in 1973 to respond to the needs of families experiencing a sudden and unexpected infant death. It is the only organisation in Canada solely dedicated to finding the causes of Sudden Infant Death Syndrome, its effect on families, and to the education of the public.

Dr Sydney Segal Research Grants
Subjects: Any discipline eg. medical, psychological, nursing, biological, sociological, which is concerned with the causes, effects or prevention of Sudden Infant Death Syndrome.
Purpose: To enable students to pursue full-time higher degree studies researching into the possible causes, effects and/or prevention of Sudden Infant Death Syndrome.
Eligibility: Open to suitably qualified graduate students who are undertaking full-time training in research in the health sciences leading to an MSc or PhD or the equivalent and to suitably qualified persons who are undertaking higher level training in research into Sudden Infant Death Syndrome.
Level of Study: Doctorate, Postdoctorate, Postgraduate.
Type: Research grant.
Value: Determined in accordance with current MRC stipends for studentships and fellowships.
Length of Study: Normally one year.
Frequency: Annual.
Study Establishment: A Canadian university or teaching hospital.
Country of Study: Canada.
No. of awards offered: Up to 20.
Application Procedure: Applicants must complete an application form, available from the Foundation. Completed forms should be submitted together with references from the Head of Department of the university or teaching hospital where the applicant wishes to conduct research and other documents, details of which can be found on the application form.
Closing Date: June 1st.
Contributor: Private donations.
Additional Information: Grants will be considered only for research that is directly related to Sudden Infant Death Syndrome.

CANADIAN FRIENDS OF THE HEBREW UNIVERSITY

3080 Yonge Street, Suite 5024, Toronto, ON, M4N 3N1, Canada
Tel: (1) 416 485 8000
Fax: (1) 416 485 8565
Email: admissions@cfhu.org
Contact: Director

Canadian Friends of the Hebrew University Awards
Subjects: Arts and humanities.
Purpose: To enable Canadian students to attend the Hebrew University of Jerusalem.

Eligibility: Open to Canadian citizens or landed immigrants.
Level of Study: Doctorate, Graduate.
Type: Bursary.
Value: At the discretion of the Academic Affairs Committee.
Length of Study: One year.
Frequency: Annual.
Study Establishment: Hebrew University of Jerusalem.
Country of Study: Israel.
No. of awards offered: Varies.
Application Procedure: Applicants must write for details.
Funding: Private.

CANADIAN HIGH COMMISSION

Academic Relations Unit, Canada House, Trafalgar Square, London, SW1Y 5BJ, England
Tel: (44) 20 7258 6692
Fax: (44) 20 7258 6476
Email: vivien.hughes@dfait-maeci.gc.ca
www: http://www.dfait-maeci.gc.ca/london
Contact: Ms Vivien Hughes, Canadian Studies Project Officer

Canadian Department of Foreign Affairs Faculty Enrichment Program
Subjects: Social sciences and humanities including architecture and town planning, business administration and management, education and teacher training, fine art, law, mass communication and information, transport and communication, recreation, welfare and protection, politics, international relations, history, geography, Canadian literature in English, Canadian literature in French, sociology, etc.
Purpose: To assist in the undertaking of studies relating to Canada or comparative Canada United Kingdom topics in order to devise a new course on Canada or to modify or extend significantly the Canadian component of an existing course.
Eligibility: Open to full-time, permanent teaching members of staff from a recognised Institution of Higher Education within the United Kingdom.
Value: Up to a maximum of Canadian $4,600 paid in two instalments.
Length of Study: Three-four weeks.
Frequency: Annual.
Country of Study: Canada.
No. of awards offered: Varies.
Application Procedure: Applicants must complete an application form, available from the Academic Relations Unit at the Canadian High Commission.
Closing Date: October 31st.
Funding: Government.

Canadian Department of Foreign Affairs Faculty Research Program
Subjects: Social sciences and humanities in relation to Canada, comparative Canada-United Kingdom topics or aspects of its bilateral relations with the United Kingdom. Purely scientific subjects are ineligible.
Purpose: To promote research about Canada, comparative Canada United Kingdom topics or aspects of Canada's bilateral relations with the United Kingdom, leading to the publication of articles in the scholarly press.
Eligibility: Open to full-time academic staff members and professors emeritus of universities, colleges of higher education or equivalent degree granting institutes of the United Kingdom. Scholars at research and policy planning institutions who undertake significant Canadian, or comparative Canadian-United Kingdom projects or Canada's bilateral relations research projects may also apply.
Value: Up to a maximum of Canadian $4,600, paid in two instalments.
Length of Study: Three-four weeks.
Frequency: Annual.
Country of Study: Canada.
No. of awards offered: Varies.

Application Procedure: Applicants must complete an application form, available from the Academic Relations Unit at the Canadian High Commission.
Closing Date: October 31st.
Funding: Government.

Canadian Department of Foreign Affairs Institutional Research Program

Subjects: Canadian topics within the social sciences and humanities, comparative studies and aspects of Canada's bilateral relations with the United Kingdom.
Purpose: To assist Institutions of Higher Education to undertake, under the direction of a designated principal researcher, major team research about Canada, comparative Canada United Kingdom topics or on aspects of Canada's bilateral relations with the United Kingdom, leading to the publication of a substantial work.
Eligibility: Open to recognised Institutes of Higher Education, research and policy planning institutes or other established research institutions in the United Kingdom. There is a minimum of three full-time British academics.
Level of Study: Professional development.
Value: Up to Canadian $12,000.
Frequency: Annual.
Country of Study: Canada.
No. of awards offered: Varies.
Application Procedure: Applicants must complete an application form, available from the Academic Relations Unit at the Canadian High Commission.
Closing Date: 1st December.
Funding: Government.

CANADIAN HOME ECONOMICS ASSOCIATION (CHEA)

307-151 Slater Street, Ottawa
ON, K1P 5H3, Canada
Tel: (1) 613 238 8817
Fax: (1) 613 238 8972
Email: general@chea-acef.ca
www: http://www.chea-acef.ca
Contact: Ms Lisa Pearson, Administration Assistant

The Canadian Home Economics Association (CHEA) is the national organisation for home economics professionals and has worked to improve life in Canadian homes and communities since 1939. More than 60 years later, CHEA continues to be an advocate for positive change in the home both across Canada and abroad.

Mary A Clarke Memorial Scholarship, Silver Jubilee Scholarship and Fiftieth Anniversary Scholarship

Subjects: Home economics, human ecology, textiles or consumer science.
Purpose: To promote study towards an advanced degree in home economics or an allied field such as human ecology, textiles, family and consumer science.
Eligibility: Open to Canadian citizens or landed immigrants who are registered Master's or doctoral students in home economics, human ecology or a discipline related to human development and relationships, financial and resource management, consumer foods and nutrition, clothing and textiles, housing and shelter and aesthetics. Candidates must show professional commitment to improve the quality of life of individuals, families and their communities in Canada and the developing world. Applicants must also be registered students in a relevant academic programme in September and have been members of the Canadian Home Economics Association for at least two years. Proof of acceptance to a graduate programme must be available. The awards will be based on scholarship, personal qualities, past or potential contribution to the profession of home economics and financial considerations.
Level of Study: Doctorate, Postgraduate.
Type: Scholarship.

Value: Canadian $2,000.
Length of Study: One year.
Frequency: Annual, if funds are available.
Study Establishment: An appropriate institution.
Country of Study: Any country.
No. of awards offered: Three.
Application Procedure: Applicants must complete an application form, available through faculty offices or from CHEA.
Closing Date: Postmarked no later than March 31st.
Funding: Private.
Contributor: The Canadian Home Economics Association.
No. of awards given last year: Three.
No. of applicants last year: 20.
Additional Information: The award was established as a tribute to Mary Clarke, a valued member of CHEA and 1952-54 President.

Robin Hood Multifoods Scholarship

Subjects: Home economics.
Purpose: To financially support individuals planning a career in business, consumer service, food or food service management.
Eligibility: Open to Canadian citizens or landed immigrants who are Master's or doctoral students planning a career in business related consumer food services or food service management. Applicants must have been members of the Canadian Home Economics Association for at least two years and proof of acceptance to a graduate programme must be available. The award is based on academic achievement, personal qualities and past or potential contribution to the home economics profession. The applicant must be registered in a relevant academic programme in September.
Level of Study: Doctorate, Postgraduate.
Type: Scholarship.
Value: Canadian $1,000.
Frequency: Annual.
Study Establishment: An appropriate institution.
Country of Study: Any country.
No. of awards offered: One.
Application Procedure: Applicants must complete an application form, available through faculty offices or from CHEA.
Closing Date: Postmarked no later than March 31st.
Funding: Commercial.
Contributor: Robin Hood Multifoods Inc.
No. of awards given last year: One.
No. of applicants last year: 20.

Ruth Binnie Scholarship

Subjects: Home economics or home economics education.
Eligibility: Open to Canadian citizens who are graduates in either home economics, human ecology or consumer studies. Applicants must have been members of the Canadian Home Economics Association for at least two years. Proof of acceptance to a graduate programme must be available. First consideration will be given to applicants proceeding towards a Master's in education on a full-time basis and second consideration will go to part-time students. The awards will be based on scholarship, personal qualities, contributions toward home economics education in junior or senior high school and potential in the education field. All candidates should have a high commitment to the teaching profession and home economics education.
Level of Study: Doctorate, Postgraduate.
Type: Scholarship.
Value: Canadian $2,500.
Frequency: Annual.
Study Establishment: An appropriate institution.
Country of Study: Any country.
No. of awards offered: Two.
Application Procedure: Applicants must complete an application form, available through faculty offices or from CHEA.
Closing Date: Postmarked no later than March 31st.
Funding: Private.
Contributor: The Ruth Binnie Bequest to the Canadian Home Economics Association.
No. of awards given last year: Three.
No. of applicants last year: 20.

CANADIAN INSTITUTE FOR ADVANCED LEGAL STUDIES

Suite 2034 Beechwood Avenue, Ottawa, ON, K1L 8L9, Canada
Tel: (1) 613 744 6166
Fax: (1) 613 744 5766
Contact: Mr Frank McArdle, Executive Director

The Canadian Institute for Advanced Legal Studies conducts legal seminars for judges and lawyers in Cambridge, England and Strasbourg, France.

Right Honorable Paul Martin Scholarship
Subjects: Law.
Purpose: To study for an LLM at the University of Cambridge.
Eligibility: Open to graduates of Canadian faculties of law at the time of application, law students in their articling year at the time of application, or to students registered in their Bar Admission course at the time of application.
Level of Study: Postgraduate.
Type: Scholarship.
Value: Canadian $14,000.
Length of Study: One year.
Frequency: Annual.
Study Establishment: The University of Cambridge.
Country of Study: England.
No. of awards offered: Two.
Application Procedure: Applicants must submit a letter of application, undergraduate and faculty of law transcripts and no more than three letters of recommendation. There is no application form.
Closing Date: December 31st.
Funding: Private.
No. of awards given last year: Two.
No. of applicants last year: 36.
Additional Information: The scholarship may be held with another small award as approved by the Institute.

CANADIAN INSTITUTE OF UKRAINIAN STUDIES (CIUS)

University of Alberta, 450 Athabasca Hall, Edmonton, AB, T6G 2E8, Canada
Tel: (1) 780 492 2972
Fax: (1) 780 492 4967
Email: cius@ualberta.ca
www: http://www.ciusa.ca/
Contact: Ms Khrystyna Jendyk, Administrator

The Canadian Institute of Ukrainian Studies (CIUS) is part of the University of Alberta under the jurisdiction of the University's Vice President of Research. It was founded in 1976 in order to provide an institutional home and to develop Ukrainian scholarship and Ukrainian language education in Canada. It also supports such studies internationally, through organising research and scholarship in Ukrainian and Ukrainian and Canadian studies, by publishing books and a scholarly journal, developing materials for Ukrainian language education, largely for the bilingual school programme, and organising conferences, lectures and a seminar series. Policy is developed by the director in consultation with a CIUS unit, programme directors and an advisory council.

Canadian Institute of Ukrainian Studies Research Grants
Subjects: Ukrainian or Ukrainian and Canadian studies in history, literature, language, education, social sciences and library sciences.
Eligibility: Please write for details.
Level of Study: Postdoctorate, Research.
Type: Research grant.
Value: Up to Canadian $8,000.
Length of Study: One year.
Frequency: Annual.
Country of Study: Any country.
No. of awards offered: One.

Application Procedure: Applicants must request an application form and guide either from the main address given, by email or downloaded from the website.
Closing Date: March 1st.
Funding: Private.

Helen Darcovich Memorial Doctoral Fellowship
Subjects: Ukrainian or Ukrainian and Canadian topic in education, history, law, humanities, social sciences, women's studies or library sciences.
Purpose: To aid students to complete a thesis on a Ukrainian or Ukrainian and Canadian topic in education, history, law, humanities, social sciences, women's studies or library sciences.
Eligibility: Open to qualified applicants of any nationality. For non Canadian applicants, preference will be given to students enrolled at the University of Alberta.
Level of Study: Doctorate.
Type: Fellowship.
Value: Up to Canadian $12,000.
Length of Study: One academic year.
Frequency: Annual.
Study Establishment: Any approved Institute of Higher Education.
Country of Study: Any country.
No. of awards offered: One.
Application Procedure: Applicants must write to the main address for details. Application forms can be downloaded from the website and returned by email.
Closing Date: March 1st.
Funding: Private.
Contributor: The Helen Darcovich Memorial Endowment Fund.
No. of awards given last year: 3.
Additional Information: Only in exceptional circumstances may an award be held concurrently with other awards.

Marusia and Michael Dorosh Master's Fellowship
Subjects: Ukrainian or Ukrainian and Canadian topic in education, history, law, humanities, social sciences, women's studies or library sciences.
Purpose: To aid a student to complete a thesis on a Ukrainian or Ukrainian and Canadian topic in education, history, law, humanities, social sciences, women's studies or library sciences.
Eligibility: Open to qualified applicants of any nationality. For non Canadian applicants, preference will be given to students enrolled at the University of Alberta.
Level of Study: Postgraduate.
Type: Fellowship.
Value: Up to Canadian $8,000.
Length of Study: One academic year.
Frequency: Annual.
Study Establishment: Any approved Institute of Higher Education.
Country of Study: Any country.
No. of awards offered: One.
Application Procedure: Applicants must write to the main address for details. Information and application forms can be obtained by email and downloaded from the website.
Closing Date: March 1st.
Funding: Private.
Contributor: The Marusia and Michael Dorosh Endowment Fund.
No. of awards given last year: 1.
Additional Information: Only in exceptional circumstances may an award be held concurrently with other awards.

Neporany Research and Teaching Fellowship
Subjects: Ukrainian studies.
Purpose: To teach one course and conduct research in Ukrainian studies.
Eligibility: Applicants must hold a doctorate, or have equivalent professional achievement, in Ukrainian studies.
Level of Study: Postdoctorate.
Type: Fellowship.
Value: Up to Canadian $20,000.
Length of Study: One term, eg. half of the academic year.
Frequency: Annual.

Study Establishment: Any university with research facilities at which the Fellow's academic Ukrainian studies speciality may be pursued and the Fellow enabled to teach a course related to the speciality.
Country of Study: Any country.
No. of awards offered: One.
Application Procedure: Applicants must write for further details to the main address. Information can be obtained by email or downloaded from the website.
Closing Date: March 1st.
Funding: Private.
Contributor: The Osyp and Josaphat Neporany Educational Fund.
No. of awards given last year: 1.

CANADIAN INSTITUTES OF HEALTH RESEARCH (CIHR)

9th Floor, 410 Laurier Avenue West, Ottawa
ON, K1A 0W9, Canada
Tel: (1) 613 941 2672
Fax: (1) 613 954 1800
Email. info@cihr.ca
www: http://www.cihr.ca
Contact: Awards Officer

CIHR Canadian Graduate Scholarships Doctoral Awards
Purpose: To provide special recognition and support to students who are pursuing a doctoral degree in a health related field in Canada.
Eligibility: These candidates are expected to have an exceptionally high potential for future research achievement and productivity.
Level of Study: Doctorate.
Value: Canadian $30,000 annual stipend and Canadian $5,000 annual research allowance.
Frequency: Annual.
Study Establishment: A Canadian Institution.
Country of Study: Canada.
Application Procedure: Applicants must complete an application form in accordance with program guidelines, available on the website.
Closing Date: October 15th.
Funding: Government.

CIHR Doctoral Research Awards
Subjects: General medical sciences and health sciences.
Purpose: To provide recognition and funding to students early in their academic research career, providing them with an opportunity to gain research experience. To provide a reliable supply of higly skilled and qualified researchers.
Eligibility: Open to students engaged in full-time research training in a graduate school, who, at the time of application, have completed at least 12 months of graduate study at Master's or PhD level but have been registered for no more than 26 months as a full-time student in a doctoral program. Candidates must be Canadian citizens or permanent residents of Canada and have an exceptionally high potential for future research achievement and productivity. Individuals with a health professional degree who seek support for Doctoral research training are eligible to apply, but should also consult the guidelines for the CIHR Fellowship program.
Level of Study: Graduate.
Type: Award.
Value: An annual stipend of Canadian $20,000 for awards held inside Canada and Canadian $25,000 for awards held outside Canada, Awards are valued in Canadian dollars and are taxable.
Length of Study: A maximum of three years.
Frequency: Annual.
Study Establishment: Universities or research institutions.
Country of Study: Canada and abroad.
No. of awards offered: Varies.
Application Procedure: Applicants must complete an application form in accordance with programme guidelines, available on the CIHR website.
Closing Date: October 15th.

Funding: Government.
Contributor: CIHR.
No. of awards given last year: 121.
No. of applicants last year: 561.
Additional Information: Please consult the CIHR website for the complete program description.

CIHR Fellowships Program
Subjects: Applicants must hold, or be completing, a PhD, health professional degree or equivalent. The health professional degree must be in a field such as medicine, dentistry, pharmacy, optometry, veterinary medicine, chiropractic, nursing or rehabilitative science.
Purpose: To provide support for highly qualified candidates to add to their experience by engaging in health research either in Canada or abroad.
Eligibility: Open to Canadian citizens, permanent residents of Canada and citizens of other countries. Foreign candidates may only apply for awards to be held in Canada.
Level of Study: Doctorate, Graduate, Postdoctorate.
Type: Fellowship.
Value: Depending on the experience, a stipend of Canadian $20,000 per annum to Canadian $47,500 per annum including a further and travel allowance of Canadian $3,500 per annum. Recipients holding the award outside Canada will receive an annual stipend supplement of Canadian $5,000.
Length of Study: Five years maximum for the completion of a Health Professional PhD, four years maximum for the completion of a Health Professional Master's degree or non degree and three years maximum for PhD holders.
Frequency: Twice a year.
Study Establishment: Universities or research institutions.
Country of Study: Any country.
No. of awards offered: Varies.
Application Procedure: Applicants must submit a training module, a curriculum vitae module for both the candidate and the supervisor(s), official transcripts of the candidate's graduate and/or professional training including proof of any degrees completed, proof of Canadian licensure, three assessments from persons under whom the candidate has studied and a letter of support from the proposed supervisor of foreign candidates.
Closing Date: February 1st and October 1st.
Funding: Government.
No. of awards given last year: 160.
No. of applicants last year: 914.
Additional Information: Consult the CIHR website, www.cihr-irsc.gc.ca for the full program description.

CIHR MD/PhD Studentships
Subjects: General medical sciences.
Purpose: To promote promising students embarking on a combined MD or PhD programme at approved Canadian Universities.
Eligibility: Candidates for this Studentship Award must be enrolled in a combined MD/PhD programme at one of the approved Canadian institutions. Research supervisors should normally be holders of operating grants or salary funding obtained through a CIHR peer review process.
Level of Study: Doctorate, Graduate, Research.
Type: Studentship.
Value: A stipend of Canadian $20,000 per year plus a yearly research allowance of Canadian $500 is provided.
Length of Study: Six years maximum.
Study Establishment: The universities of British Columbia, Calgary, Dalhousie, Manitoba, McGill, Memorial, Montreal, Toronto, Western Ontario, Alberta, Sherbrooke.
Country of Study: Canada.
Application Procedure: Applicants must be nominated by the director of the MD/PhD programme at each institution.
Closing Date: Please write for details.
Funding: Government.
Contributor: CIHR.
Additional Information: For further information please contact the CIHR or refer to the website.

CANADIAN LIBRARY ASSOCIATION

Scholarships & Awards Committee, CLA, Membership Services
328 Frank Street, Ottawa
ON K2P 0X8, Canada
Tel: (1) 613 232 9625
Fax: (1) 613 563 9895
Email: info@cla.ca
www: http://www.cla.ca
Contact: B Shields, Member Services

The Canadian Library Association works to maintain a tradition of commitment to excellence in library education and to advance continuing research in the field of library and information science.

CLA Dafoe Scholarship

Subjects: Library science.
Eligibility: Open to Canadian citizens and landed immigrants.
Level of Study: Postgraduate.
Type: Scholarship.
Value: Canadian $3,000.
Length of Study: One year.
Frequency: Annual.
Study Establishment: An accredited library school.
Country of Study: Canada.
No. of awards offered: One.
Application Procedure: Applicants must complete an application form, available on request. Applicants must submit transcripts, references and proof of admission to a library school.
Closing Date: May 1st.
Funding: Commercial.
No. of awards given last year: One.
Additional Information: Consideration is given to both academic standing and financial need.

CLA Research and Development Grants

Subjects: Library and information science.
Purpose: To support theoretical and applied research in library and information science.
Eligibility: Open to Canadian citizens and landed immigrants who are personal members of the CLA.
Level of Study: Unrestricted.
Type: Research grant.
Value: One or more grants totalling Canadian $1,000.
Length of Study: One year.
Frequency: Annual.
Country of Study: Canada.
No. of awards offered: More than one.
Application Procedure: Applicants must apply for application guidelines, available on request.

H W Wilson Scholarship

Subjects: Library science.
Eligibility: Open to Canadian citizens or landed immigrants. Scholarship candidates must be commencing studies for their first professional library or information studies degree.
Level of Study: Postgraduate.
Type: Scholarship.
Value: Canadian $2,000.
Length of Study: One year.
Frequency: Annual.
Study Establishment: An accredited library school.
Country of Study: Canada.
No. of awards offered: One.
Application Procedure: Applicants must write, phone or visit the website for further information.
Closing Date: May 1st.
Funding: Private.
Contributor: The H W Wilson Company.
No. of awards given last year: One.
Additional Information: Consideration is given to both academic standing and financial need. The CLA acknowledges, with thanks, the generous support of the H W Wilson Company for their sponsorship of this award.

World Book Graduate Scholarship in Library Science

Subjects: Library science.
Eligibility: Open to Canadian citizens or landed immigrants with a BLS or MLS degree. In exceptional circumstances, the scholarship may be given to an outstanding candidate with a degree in another discipline who wishes to obtain a BLS or MLS degree.
Level of Study: Postgraduate.
Type: Scholarship.
Value: Canadian $2,500.
Length of Study: One year.
Frequency: Annual.
Study Establishment: An accredited library school.
Country of Study: United States of America or Canada.
No. of awards offered: One.
Closing Date: May 1st.
Funding: Private.
Contributor: World Book Incorporated.
No. of awards given last year: One.
Additional Information: Consideration is given to both academic standing and financial need. The scholarship is given for study leading to a further library degree or related to library work in which the candidate is currently engaged, or to library work which will be undertaken upon completion of the studies. The CLA gratefully acknowledges the support of World Book Incorporated for their continuing sponsorship of this award.

CANADIAN LIVER FOUNDATION

2235 Sheppard Avenue East, Suite 1500, Toronto, ON, M2J 5B5,
Canada
Tel: (1) 416 491 3353
Fax: (1) 416 491 4952
Email: clf@liver.ca
www: http://www.liver.ca
Contact: National Director of Health Promotion and Patient

The Canadian Liver Foundation provides support for research and education into the causes, diagnosis, prevention and treatment of diseases to the liver.

Canadian Liver Foundation Graduate Studentships

Subjects: Hepatology.
Purpose: To enable academically superior students to undertake full-time studies in a Canadian university in a Discipline relevant to the objectives of the Foundation.
Eligibility: Candidates must be accepted onto a full-time university graduate science programme in a medically related discipline related to a Master's or doctoral degree and hold a record of superior academic performance in studies relevant to the proposed training.
Level of Study: Doctorate, Postgraduate.
Type: Studentship.
Value: Canadian $16,500 per year.
Length of Study: Two years, renewable once.
Frequency: Annual.
Country of Study: Canada.
No. of awards offered: Dependent on availability of funds.
Application Procedure: Applicants must submit application forms along with supporting documents.
Closing Date: March 15th.
Funding: Private.
No. of awards given last year: Two.
No. of applicants last year: 24.
Additional Information: A student supported by the Foundation must not hold a current stipend award from another granting agency.

Canadian Liver Foundation Operating Grant

Subjects: Hepatology.
Purpose: To support research projects directed towards a defined objective.
Eligibility: Open to hepatobiliary research investigators who hold an academic appointment in a Canadian university or affiliated institution.
Level of Study: Research.
Type: Grant.
Value: Up to Canadian $60,000 per year.

Length of Study: Two years, after which time renewal may be sought.
Frequency: Annual.
Country of Study: Canada.
No. of awards offered: Dependent on availability of funds.
Application Procedure: Applicants must submit application forms along with supporting documentation.
Closing Date: March 15th.
Funding: Private.
No. of awards given last year: Five.
No. of applicants last year: 25.

THE CANADIAN NATIONAL INSTITUTE FOR THE BLIND (CNIB)

1929 Bayview Avenue, Toronto, ON, M4G 3E8, Canada
Tel: (1) 416 480 7707
Fax: (1) 416 480 7000
Email: marueen.young@cnib.ca
www: http://www.cnib.ca
Contact: Ms Maureen Young, Executive Assistant

The Canadian National Institute for the Blind (CNIB) is a voluntary non-profit rehabilitation agency that provides services for people who are blind, visually impaired or deafblind. The CNIB provides consultation in safe and efficient travel training, Braille, tape and electronic information, employment, environmental accessibility, government and community entitlements, technology, sight enhancement, eye banks and community integration. Through the EA Baker Foundation it provides fellowships and research grants into blindness prevention.

E A Baker Fellowship/Grant
Subjects: Ophthalmology and optometry.
Purpose: To further the prevention of blindness in Canada.
Eligibility: Open to Canadians for research or study in Canada, or abroad if returning to practice in Canada, with priority given to university teaching.
Level of Study: Professional development, Research.
Type: Other.
Value: Canadian $40,000.
Length of Study: Two years.
Frequency: Annual.
Country of Study: Any country.
No. of awards offered: Varies.
Application Procedure: Applicants must visit the website for information and an application form.
Closing Date: December 1st.
Funding: Private.
No. of awards given last year: 11.
No. of applicants last year: 15.
Additional Information: Award is co-funded with the Canadian Institute of Health Research.

CANADIAN NURSES FOUNDATION (CNF)

50 Driveway, Ottawa, ON, K2P 1E2, Canada
Tel: (1) 613 237 2133
Fax: (1) 613 237 3520
Email: cnf@cna-nurses.ca
www: http://www.cna-nurses.ca/cnf
Contact: CNF Scholarship Co-ordinator

The Canadian Nurses Foundation (CNF) is a registered charity founded in 1962. It is committed to promoting the health of Canadians through the advancement of the nurses' profession by financially supporting Canadian nurses in pursuing further education, research, or certification in their speciality. The CNF is funded through donations from corporations, nursing associations and individuals.

CNF Scholarships and Fellowships
Subjects: All nursing specialities. Several awards are identified for neurosurgical, oncology, community health nursing, epidemiology, gerontology, child or family healthcare, nursing administration, occupational health, dialysis nursing, home care nursing and aplastic anaemia.

Purpose: To assist Canadian nurses pursuing further education and research.
Eligibility: Open to Canadian nurses who are members of the Foundation.
Level of Study: Doctorate, Graduate, Postgraduate, Predoctorate, Professional development, Research, Baccalaureate.
Type: Scholarships, Fellowships, Bursaries.
Value: Please consult the organisation.
Length of Study: One year.
Frequency: Annual, Dependent on funds available.
Country of Study: Canada.
No. of awards offered: Varies.
Application Procedure: Applicants must visit the website for the application forms, criteria and requirements.www.canadiannurses-foundation.com.
Closing Date: 16th April 2004.
Funding: Private.
Contributor: Corporations, other foundations, individuals.
No. of awards given last year: 35.
Additional Information: Recipients must submit a summary of any thesis, study or major paper undertaken as part of the course to the CNF.

CANADIAN NURSES' RESPIRATORY SOCIETY (CNRS)

The Lung Association National Office 3, Raymond Street, Suite 300, Ottawa, ON, K1R 1A3, Canada
Tel: (1) 613 569 6411
Fax: (1) 613 569 8860
Email: info@lung.ca
www: http://www.lung.ca
Contact: President

The Canadian Nurses' Respiratory Society (CNRS) is a special nursing interest group of the Lung Association concerned with promoting a high quality of respiratory care through respiratory nursing education and research. CNRS believes in the provision of high quality respiratory nursing care which promotes respiratory health and prevents or manages respiratory illness so enhancing the quality of life for the individual, family and communities. CNRS's objectives are to promote respiratory nursing care, advance nursing education in respiratory health and disease, encourage nurses to engage in research related to respiratory health and disease, collaborate with provincial respiratory nursing societies, further the objectives of the Canadian Lung Association within the scope of the nursing profession, act as an advisory body to the Lung Association on nursing matters and maintain an affiliation with the Canadian Nurses Association and the International Council of Nurses.

CNRS Fellowships
Subjects: Respiratory nursing.
Purpose: To enable registered nurses to pursue postgraduate education with a major component of the programme involving respiratory nursing practice.
Eligibility: Applicants must be Canadian citizens or permanent Canadian residents, be a registered nurse, be enrolled or accepted for full-time studies in a graduate programme at the Master's or doctorate level and be a member of the Canadian Nurses Respiratory Society.
Level of Study: Postgraduate.
Type: Fellowship.
Value: Canadian $5,000-10,000.
Length of Study: One year.
Frequency: Annual.
Country of Study: Canada.
Application Procedure: Applicants must submit an application form available from the Canadian Lung Association or the website.
Closing Date: November 1st.
Contributor: Public funds via the Canadian Lung Association.

CNRS Research Grants
Subjects: Respiratory disease and symptoms.
Purpose: To enable registered nurses to undertake research investigations related to nursing management of patients with respiratory disease and symptoms.

Eligibility: The principal investigator must be a Canadian citizen or permanent resident, be a registered nurse, hold an appointment in, or have an affiliation with, a healthcare agency, education institution or other organisation in Canada that can administer funds in an approved manner, and be a member of the Canadian Nurses Respiratory Society.
Level of Study: Postgraduate, Research.
Type: Research grant.
Value: Up to Canadian $30,000.
Length of Study: One year.
Frequency: Annual.
Country of Study: Canada.
Application Procedure: Applicants must submit an application form, available from the Canadian Lung Association or the website.
Closing Date: November 1st.
Contributor: Public funds via the Canadian Lung Association.

CANADIAN OSTEOPATHIC EDUCATIONAL TRUST FUND

RR 2, Forest Ontario, N0N 1J0, Canada
Tel: (1) 519 786 6444
Fax: (1) 519 786 2915
Contact: Ms Patricia Rose Roper

Canadian Osteopathic Educational Trust Fund Financial Assistance

Subjects: Osteopathy.
Purpose: To encourage training of Osteopathic Physicians from Canada who will return to Canada on completion of their training.
Eligibility: Applicants must be Canadian citizens.
Value: Canadian $15,000 per year.
Length of Study: Four years.
Frequency: Annual.
Application Procedure: Applicants must submit a completed application form, recent photograph, four letters of recommendation (including one from a faculty member of the applicant's pre-professional college and one from either an Osteopathic physician or clergyman), and a statement of intent to practice in Canada upon completion of their education.
Closing Date: April 15th.
Funding: Private.
Additional Information: The award is conditioned upon the agreement of the applicant to practice in Canada for one year for each year of financial support following completion of their professional education. Further information is available on request.

CANADIAN PHYSIOTHERAPY CARDIO-RESPIRATORY SOCIETY (CPCRS)

Head Office, 3 Raymond Street, Suite 300, Ottawa, ON, K1R 1A3, Canada
Tel: (1) 613 569 6411
Fax: (1) 613 569 8860
Email: info@lung.ca
www: http://www.lung.ca
Contact: Ms Valoree McKay

The Canadian Physiotherapy Cardio-Respiratory Society (CPCRS) offers fellowships and Research Grants. The purpose of the CPCRS research programme is to pursue increased scientific knowledge in the area of cardiorespiratory physiotherapy practice. By supporting physiotherapists to pursue advanced degrees or by supporting the completion of research studies, the number of individuals with expertise in the cardiorespiratory area will increase, which ultimately will have a positive impact in the community, and for the cardiorespiratory client.

CPCRS Fellowships

Subjects: Cardiorespiratory physiotherapy.
Purpose: To pursue increased scientific knowledge in the area of cardiorespiratory physiotherapy practice.
Eligibility: Applicants must be physiotherapists pursuing postgraduate training, with respiratory research as the major component.

Level of Study: Postgraduate.
Type: Fellowship.
Value: Canadian $6,000-12,000.
Length of Study: One year.
Frequency: Annual.
Country of Study: Canada.
Application Procedure: Applicants must submit an application form, available from the Canadian Lung Association.
Closing Date: November 1st.

CPCRS Research Grants

Subjects: Cardiorespiratory physiotherapy practice.
Purpose: To pursue increased scientific knowledge in the area of cardiorespiratory physiotherapy practice.
Eligibility: Open to physiotherapists pursuing investigations related to the management of patients with respiratory disease. The principal investigator must be a Canadian citizen or a permanent Canadian resident, be a registered physiotherapist, hold an appointment in or have an affiliation with a healthcare agency, educational institution or other organisation in Canada that can administer funds in an approved manner, and be a member of the Canadian Physiotherapy Cardio-Respiratory Society. There must be only one principal investigator responsible for the study, although there may be several co-investigators.
Level of Study: Professional development, Research.
Type: Research grant.
Value: Canadian $12,000-20,000.
Length of Study: One year.
Frequency: Annual.
Country of Study: Canada.
Application Procedure: Applicants must submit an application form, available from the Canadian Lung Association.
Closing Date: November 1st.
Contributor: Public funds via the Canadian Lung Association.

CANADIAN SOCIETY FOR CHEMICAL TECHNOLOGY

130 Slater Street, Suite 550, Ottawa, ON, K1P 6E2, Canada
Tel: (1) 613 232 6252 ext. 235
Fax: (1) 613 232 5862
Email: jtrohon@cheminst.ca
www: http://www.cheminst.ca
Contact: Ms Julie Trohan, Conferences and Awards Co-ordinator

The Canadian Society for Chemical Technology is the national technical association of chemical and biochemical technicians and technologists with members across Canada who work in industry, government or academia. The purpose of the Society is the advancement of chemical technology, the maintenance and improvement of practitioners and educators and the continual evaluation of chemical technology in Canada. The Society hopes to maintain a dialogue with educators, government and industry, to assist in the technology content of the education process of technologists, to attract qualified people into the professions and the Society, to develop and maintain high standards and enhance the usefulness of chemical technology to both the industry and the public.

CSCT Norman and Marion Bright Memorial Award

Subjects: Chemical technology.
Purpose: To reward an individual who has made an outstanding contribution in Canada to the furtherance of Chemical Technology.
Eligibility: Open to chemical sciences technologists or persons from outside the field who have made significant or noteworthy contributions to its advancement.
Type: Award.
Value: An engraved medallion and a cash prize.
Frequency: Annual.
Country of Study: Canada.
No. of awards offered: One.
Application Procedure: Applicants must complete a nomination form.
Closing Date: October 31st.
Funding: Corporation.
Additional Information: Award winners are welcome to submit papers at either the CSC or CSChE conferences.

CANADIAN SOCIETY FOR CHEMISTRY (CSC)

130 Slater Street Suite 550, Ottawa, ON, K1P 6E2, Canada
Tel: (1) 613 232 6252 ext. 235
Fax: (1) 613 232 5862
Email: jtrohon@cheminst.ca
www: http://www.cheminst.ca
Contact: Ms Julie Trohon, Conferences and Awards Co-ordinator

The Canadian Society for Chemistry (CSC), one of three constituent societies of The Chemical Institute of Canada, is the national scientific and educational society of chemists. The purpose of the CSC is to promote the practice and application of chemistry in Canada.

Ichikizaki Fund for Young Chemists

Subjects: Synthetic organic chemistry.
Purpose: To provide financial assistance to young chemists who are showing unique achievements in basic research by facilitating their participation in international conferences or symposia.
Eligibility: Open to members of the Canadian Society for Chemistry who have not passed their 34th birthday as of December 31st of the year in which the application is submitted, who have a research speciality in synthetic organic chemistry and are scheduled to attend an international conference or symposium directly related to synthetic organic chemistry within one year.
Level of Study: Doctorate, Postdoctorate, Postgraduate, Professional development.
Value: The maximum value of any one award is Canadian $10,000. Successful applicants may re-apply in subsequent years, provided the cumulative total of all awards does not exceed Canadian $15,000.
Frequency: Annual.
Country of Study: Any country.
Application Procedure: Applicants must submit an application including a curriculum vitae, copies of recent research papers, the title and brief description of the conference the applicant wishes to attend, the title and abstract, if available, of the research paper the applicant intends to present and a proposed budget. Applications from graduate students must be accompanied by a letter of reference from the research supervisor.
Closing Date: December 31st for conferences scheduled between January 1st and December 31st of the following year.
Funding: Private.
Additional Information: The number of applicants to be recommended by the Society is limited to 10 per year. Although the awards are intended primarily for established researchers, applications from postgraduate students and postdoctoral fellows will be considered. However, only one application per year from a graduate student can be recommended to the Fund.

THE CANADIAN SOCIETY FOR CLINICAL INVESTIGATION (CSCI)

774 Echo Drive, Ottawa, ON, K1S 5N8, Canada
Tel: (1) 613 730 6240
Fax: (1) 613 730 8194
Email: csci@rcpsc.edu
www: www.csci-sctc.medical.org
Contact: Mrs C Frewer, Executive Director

CSCI Distinguished Scientist Award

Subjects: Medical.
Purpose: For significant contributions to new knowledge.
Eligibility: A medical scientist generally recognised in his or her field as expert, innovative and in the forefront of research.
Level of Study: Postdoctorate.
Value: Canadian $2,000 + plaque.
Frequency: Annual.
Country of Study: Canada.
No. of awards offered: One.
Application Procedure: This award is by nomination only.

Closing Date: Please write for details.
Funding: Private.
Additional Information: The recipient delivers a lecture.

CSCI Trainee Awards

Subjects: Medical.
Purpose: Given to selected trainees who have been involved in programs of research which have led to the development of an abstract for submission to the Annual Meeting of the Society.
Level of Study: Postgraduate.
Value: Canadian $500 + certificate and one year complimentary CSCI associate membership, the trainee must be present at at the Annual Meeting and deliver their paper or present their poster in person. The trainee's supervisor is responsible for the cost of the awardee to attend the meeting.
Frequency: Annual.
Country of Study: Any country.
No. of awards offered: One.
Application Procedure: Please write for details.
Funding: Private.

CSCI/CIHR Resident Research Awards

Subjects: Medical research.
Purpose: Prizes will be awarded annually for the best resident research project conducted during an RCPSC/CFPC training programme at each Canadian Medical School.
Level of Study: Postdoctorate.
Value: Canadian $500/resident/medical school + certificate and two year complimentary CSCI membership. In addition, up to C$500 support is provided for each awardee's travel expenses to the CSCI annual meeting (if he or she chooses to attend).
Frequency: Annual.
Study Establishment: Canadian Medical Schools.
Country of Study: Canada.
Application Procedure: Candidates will be selected by each faculty following the criteria outlined by the CSCI and submitted by them to the CSCI.
Funding: Private.

CSCI/RCPSC/PAIRO Canadian Specialty Resident Research Awards

Subjects: Medicine and surgery.
Purpose: To provide national recognition for original work by postgraduate trainees.
Level of Study: Postgraduate.
Value: Canadian $2,000 each and a certificate.
Frequency: Annual.
Country of Study: Any country.
No. of awards offered: Varies.
Application Procedure: Please write for details.
Funding: Private.
Additional Information: These awards are adjudicated by the CSCI. The winners will present their work at one of the scientific sessions of the Annual Meeting of the Royal College or CSCI or a relevant speciality meeting.

Joe Doupe Young Investigators Award

Subjects: Medical.
Purpose: For a significant and/or innovative piece of work.
Eligibility: Open to a new young investigator within five years of having completed formal research training or still engaged in that training.
Level of Study: Postdoctorate.
Value: Canadian $1,000 + plaque.
Frequency: Annual.
Country of Study: Any country.
No. of awards offered: One.
Application Procedure: Please write for details.
Funding: Private.
Contributor: Nickerson Trust Fund/University of Manitoba.

CANADIAN SOCIETY FOR MEDICAL LABORATORY SCIENCE (CSMLS)

PO 2830, LCD1, Hamilton, ON, L8N 3N8, Canada
Tel: (1) 905 528 8642
Fax: (1) 905 528 4968
Email: memserv@csmls.org
www: http://www.csmls.org
Contact: Administration Director

The Canadian Society for Medical Laboratory Science (CSMLS) is the certifying body and professional association for laboratory technologists in Canada. Its purpose is to promote and maintain a nationally accepted standard of medical laboratory technology by which other health professionals and the public are assured of effective and economical laboratory services and to promote, maintain and protect the professional identity and interest of medical laboratory technologists and of the profession.

CSMLS Founders' Fund Award

Subjects: Medical laboratory technology.
Purpose: To assist members with costs of professional continuing education.
Eligibility: Open to certified members in good standing at the time of application.
Level of Study: Professional development.
Type: Grant.
Value: Varies, at the discretion of the Founders' Fund Committee.
Frequency: Dependent on funds available.
Country of Study: Canada.
No. of awards offered: Varies.
Application Procedure: Applicants may submit applications at any time during the year and will be dealt with at the next scheduled meeting of the Founders' Fund Committee. These are held in conjunction with the meetings of the Board of Directors, usually in February, June, September, November and December. The decision to grant an award and the actual amount of the award shall be at the discretion of the Founders' Fund Committee. Applicants may only apply for one award for any activity.
Funding: Private.
Contributor: A member supported trust fund.

Quebec CE Fund Grants

Subjects: Medical technology.
Purpose: To promote continuing education among medical laboratory technologists who are Francophones.
Eligibility: Open to any person or group who is able to establish or co-ordinate the continuing education programmes for Francophone members of the CSMLS. This would include individual CSMLS members, an affiliated society or branch, the Ordre Professionnelle des Technologistes Médicaux du Québec (OPTMQ) and institutions which teach medical technology.
Level of Study: Postgraduate.
Type: Grant.
Value: Varies.
Country of Study: Canada.
No. of awards offered: Varies.
Application Procedure: Applicants must request an application form. All applications must include the amount of the grant requested from the fund, an outline of the proposed programme, a comprehensive budget including a breakdown of expenses, a statement of other support to be received or being applied for, development times and the dates that progress reports will be submitted during development, evidence of the need for the programme, and a signed statement declaring that CSMLS members will be permitted to participate in the finished programme at no increased differential fee.
Funding: Private.
Additional Information: It is the policy of CSMLS that continuing education programmes should normally be financially self-supporting through the fees charged for the programme. However, there are some situations in which a programme is needed in a particular location, but the programme cannot be self-supporting without charging unacceptably high fees. There may also be a need to fund development costs for certain types of programmes. All requests for the use of the Quebec CE funds shall be reviewed and approved or rejected by the Quebec CE Fund Committee and then considered for ratification at the next CSMLS Board of Directors meeting.

CANADIAN THORACIC SOCIETY (CTS)

The Lung Association, National Office 3, Raymond Street Suite 300, Ottawa, ON K1R 1A3, Canada
Tel: (1) 613 569 6411
Fax: (1) 613 569 8860
Email: info@lung.ca
www: http://www.lung.ca/cts
Contact: Grants Management Officer

The Canadian Thoracic Society (CTS) is the medical section of the Canadian Lung Association. It advises the Association on scientific matters and programmes including policies regarding support for research and professional education. The CTS provides a forum whereby medical practitioners and investigators may join in the study of thoracic diseases and other medical fields which may come within the scope of the Lung Association. The CTS's objectives are to maintain the highest professional and scientific standards in all aspects of respiratory diseases, to collect, interpret and distribute scientific information, to encourage epidemiological, clinical and other scientific studies in the prevention, diagnosis and treatment of respiratory diseases, and to stimulate and support undergraduate, postgraduate and continuing medical education in respiratory diseases.

CTS Fellowships

Subjects: Pulmonary disease.
Purpose: To support research training in pulmonary disease.
Eligibility: Applicants must be Canadian citizens or permanent residents of Canada. Candidates for the award must have obtained an MD or PhD degree or the equivalent and must not hold a university level academic position. Those expected to receive a PhD degree within the following year are eligible to apply but may not begin the fellowship until the PhD requirements have been completed. CLA Fellows may not work on projects that have not been approved by the appropriate institutional ethics committees.
Level of Study: Postdoctorate, Postgraduate.
Type: Fellowship.
Length of Study: Two years, with a possibility of renewal for a further year.
Frequency: Annual.
Country of Study: Canada.
Application Procedure: Applicants must submit applications on CIHR forms.
Closing Date: November 1st.
Funding: Commercial, Government.
Contributor: The Canadian Lung Association, the Canadian Institutes of Health Research, Industry Partners eg. Glaxo Smithkline Inc, Merck Frosst Can, Bayer Inc, Boehringer Ingelheim and Astrazeneca.
Additional Information: Recipients are selected based on priority ratings provided by the CIHR and are subject to the approval of the Canadian Thoracic Society and the Canadian Lung Association (CLA) Board of Directors. Applicants are screened to ensure proposed research areas are appropriate to the goals of the CLA. Fellowships are awarded in each case for research training in a specific institution, and may not be transferred without the explicit approval of both institutions involved.

For further information contact:

Canadian Institutes of Health Research, 410 Laurier Avenue West, 9th Floor, Address Locator 4209A, Ottawa, ON KIA 0W9, Canada
www: http://www.cihr.ca

Canadian Institutes of Health Research410 Laurier Avenue West9th FloorAddress Locator 4209A, Ottawa, ON KIA 0W9, Canada
www: http://www.cihr.ca

CANADIAN TOBACCO CONTROL RESEARCH INITIATIVE (CTCRI)

Toronto, ON, M4V 3BI, Canada
Tel: (1) 416 934 5968
Fax: (1) 416 961 4189
Email: yuliay@ctcri.ca
www: http://www.ctcri.ca
Contact: Dr Yulia Yerofeyeva, Administrator, CTCRI

The Canadian Tobacco Control Research Initiative (CTCRI) is a national partnership of research organizations working to increase capacity and innovation in research relevant to tobacco control policies and programs. The goal of the CTCRI is to provide strategic leadership to catalyze, coordinate and sustain research that has a direct impact on programs and policies aimed at reducing toacco abuse and nicotine addiction.

CTCRI Best Knowledge Synthesis grants RFA

Subjects: Tobacco related cancer research (formely Better Practices Research Grants) (up to $80,000 for 1 year plus $5,000 to successful Letters of Intent) are intended to support interdisciplinary teams of researchers and practitioners/decision-makers to conduct collaborative reviews of evidence for particular tobacco control interventions. Outcomes of the reviews are expected to be: (1) guidelines for practice in the relevant area(s); (2) priorities for further research; and (3) feedback on use of the Better Practices model associated with RFA. Deadlines are: Letter of Intent-September 22, 2003, and April 1, 2004; Full proposal - April 1, 2004 and Sep 1, 2004; http://www.ctcri.ca/en-pages/ks(bp)-grants.htm.
Purpose: To aid interdisciplinary research teams of researchers, practitioners and decision makers to conduct collaborative reviews of evidence for particular tobacco control interventions.
Eligibility: Open to applicant teams which include both researchers and those responsible for tobacco policy or programmes. International Co-applicants are welcome.
Value: Up to Canadian $80,000.
Length of Study: One year.
Frequency: Twice a year.
Country of Study: Canada.
No. of awards offered: Up to 4.
Application Procedure: Applicants must visit the website for application details.
Closing Date: September 1st and April 1st.
Contributor: Canadian Career Society/National Cancer Institute of Canada & Canadian Institutes of Health Research.
No. of awards given last year: Three.
No. of applicants last year: Seven.
Additional Information: Further information is available upon request.

Idea Grants

Subjects: Tobacco related research
Purpose: To support innovative research and young researchers within the health and social sciences in the area of tobacco control (Up to Canadian $50,000, one-time grants for 1 year) are designed to encourage unique to original research that has the potential to advance knowledge in this area. Grants will allow investigators with novel ideas and observations to conduct pilot studies, perform secondary analysis of data sets or gather new evidence necessary to determine the viability of novel research directions or hypotheses. Deadlines: October 1, 2003 and April 1, 2004 http://www.ctcri.ca/en-pages/idea-grants.htm.
Eligibility: Open to Canadian citizens or those residing legally in Canada. Applicants will have to sign a waiver affirming lack of support from tobacco companies International applicants welcome in all grant programs.
Level of Study: Graduate, Research.
Value: Up to Canadian $50,000.
Frequency: Twice a year.
Country of Study: Canada.
Application Procedure: Applicants must visit the website for details.
Closing Date: April 1st and October 1st.
Funding: Government.

Contributor: NCIC.
Additional Information: Further information is available upon request.

Research Planning Grants

Subjects: Tobacco related research, literature review or other background information gathering (Up to Canadian $15,000 for one year) are offered for the purpose of bringing together new, interdisciplinary research teams to construct research proposals for submission to traditional funding streams. Planning Grants are intended to defray the costs of preparing quality proposals that will score high in both relevance and scientific merit. Deadlines are: August 30, 2003, February 28, 2004, May 30, 2004, November 20, 2003 http://www.ctcri.ca/en-pages/planning-grants.htm.
Purpose: To aid the development of new interdisciplinary research teams for the purpose of developing a well-formed and competitive research proposal for submission to traditional funding sources in tobacco control.
Eligibility: Open to Canadian citizens or permanent residents living legally in Canada. Applicants will be required to sign a waiver affirming lack of support from tobacco companies.
Level of Study: Professional development, Research.
Value: Up to Canadian $15,000
Frequency: Four times per year.
Country of Study: Canada.
No. of awards offered: Eight.
Application Procedure: Applicants must visit the website for details.
Closing Date: February 28th, 30th May, 30th August and 30th November.
Funding: Government.
Contributor: National Cancer Institute of Canada/Canadian Cancer Society.
No. of awards given last year: 4.
No. of applicants last year: 10.
Additional Information: Further information is available upon request.

Researcher Travel Grant

Subjects: Tobacco related cancer, social, behavioural research (Up to Canadian $3,000 except in the case of certain international events) are offered to individuals to present results of his/her research at scientific meetings. There is a rolling deadline for this program, but applications must be received at least 30 days in advance of the event. www.ctcri.ca/en-pages/travel-grants.htm.
Purpose: To support travel for a student or member of a non-profit community group to attend a conference or similar event and present results of their research or high quality evaluation.
Eligibility: Open to students or members of community groups who are not affiliated with a university, government or business.
Level of Study: Graduate, Postgraduate, Professional development, Research.
Value: Up to Canadian $3,000.
Frequency: Four times per year.
Country of Study: Canada.
No. of awards offered: 10.
Application Procedure: Applicants must visit the website for details.
Closing Date: September 30th, January 10th, April 1st and June 30th.
Funding: Government, Private.
Contributor: National Cancer Institute of Canada/Canadian Cancer Society.
No. of awards given last year: 18.
No. of applicants last year: 20.
Additional Information: Further information is available upon request.

Student Research Grant

Subjects: Tobacco control research (Up to $10,000 for one year) provide grants to support students or trainees to conduct research under the supervision of a seasoned investigator. Deadlines are: September 30, 2003, December 30, 2003, March 30, 2004, June 30, 2004 www.ctcri.ca/en-pages/studentresearch-grants.htm.
Purpose: To support graduate research training in the health and social sciences, specifically in the area of tobacco control research.
Eligibility: Open to students enrolled at an accredited university in Canada. Candidates must be Canadian citizens living legally in Canada and will be expected to sign a waiver affirming lack of support from a tobacco company.

Value: Up to Canadian $10,000.
Frequency: Four times per year.
Country of Study: Canada.
No. of awards offered: 16.
Application Procedure: Applicants must visit the website for details.
Closing Date: March 30th, June 30th, September 30th and December 20th.
Funding: Government, Private.
Contributor: CCS/WCIC.
Additional Information: Further information is available upon request.

CANCER ASSOCIATION OF SOUTH AFRICA (CANSA)

PO Box 2000, Johannesburg, Braamfontein 2000, South Africa
Tel: (27) 11 616 7662
Fax: (27) 11 622 3424
Email: rbotha@cansa.org.za
www: http://www.cansa.org.za
Contact: Research Administrator

We will substantially reduce the impact of cancer by promoting health in all communities within South Africa, through advocacy and the sustainable facilitation or research, prevention, early detection and care.

CANSA Research Grants
Subjects: All aspects of the cancer problem, particularly those aspects which have a South African significance and can be investigated locally.
Purpose: To assist professional staff with the purchase of major or specialised equipment, laboratory running expenses, skilled or unskilled laboratory or other assistants and to assist with printing and/or publishing the results of all types of research which fall within the Association's scope.
Eligibility: Open to medical graduates, biochemists, graduates in social science, etc., who are in full-time employment and can show distinct evidence of a capacity for original research or, in the case of BSc graduates, have won distinctions during their undergraduate studies. Candidates should be residents of South Africa.
Level of Study: Postgraduate.
Type: Research grant.
Value: Varies, according to merit.
Length of Study: One-three calendar years.
Frequency: Annual.
Study Establishment: A university or research institution.
Country of Study: South Africa.
No. of awards offered: Varies.
Application Procedure: Applicants must complete an application form.
Closing Date: May 31st.
Funding: Private.
Contributor: Public and corporate donors.
No. of awards given last year: 52.
No. of applicants last year: 65.
Additional Information: All major equipment will remain the property of the Association. Specific details of the types of research which fall within the Association's scope as well as other additional information is available from the Association.

CANSA Travel and Subsistence (Study) Grants
Subjects: Cancer projects.
Purpose: To assist workers in the cancer field to improve their academic and/or technical qualifications and experience for the furtherance of cancer research and education, and for the improvement of diagnostic and/or treatment services to cancer patients in South Africa.
Eligibility: Open to suitably qualified applicants in some aspect of the cancer field who are in full-time employment. Applicants must be South African citizens.
Level of Study: Postgraduate.
Value: Not to exceed 50 per cent of the minimum costs on condition that the applicant, through his own institution or by other means, pays the balance of the minimum costs. Minimum costs are calculated on the basis of an economy class air fare to the furthest point of travel with such deviations as may be approved by the Association,

plus a subsistence allowance appropriate to the geographical area concerned.
Frequency: Throughout the year.
Country of Study: Any country.
No. of awards offered: Varies.
Application Procedure: Applicants must complete and forward the Travel Grant application form to the executive committee for approval.
Closing Date: A minimum of two months before the departure date.
Funding: Private.
Contributor: The Cancer Association of South Africa.
No. of awards given last year: 10.
No. of applicants last year: 16.
Additional Information: Travel Grants are awarded to suitable applicants to enable them to attend national or international conferences in the cancer field. Study Grants are awarded to suitable applicants who, by study at specialised centres, will be able to increase their knowledge in the cancer field with a view to its subsequent application in South Africa. Grantees are required to return to South Africa within a period of six months after expiration of the period for which the Grant was awarded and to continue for a period of two years in the service in which they were employed at the time of the award. Extensions will be considered on application. Grants may not be used for the purpose of studying for or obtaining degrees or diplomas. The Association also offers support to certain foreign medical scientists in the cancer field who are invited to visit South Africa to participate in scientific meetings and congresses, or for particular purposes as the need may arise.

Lady Cade Memorial Fellowship
Subjects: The cause, diagnosis or treatment of cancer.
Purpose: To encourage professional development in cancer research.
Eligibility: Open to medical graduates of senior status who are resident in South Africa and to South African nationals who are domiciled in the British Commonwealth, or in some cases, elsewhere. Preference is given to those holding senior posts at approved universities or other institutions to which the Fellows will be expected to return within six months of the termination of the fellowship and work there for a period of not less than two years.
Level of Study: Doctorate.
Type: Fellowship.
Value: Rand 150,000 from the organisation and Rand 150,000 from the Cancer Research Campaign in the United Kingdom.
Length of Study: Three months to one year.
Frequency: Other.
Study Establishment: A university or research institution.
Country of Study: United Kingdom.
No. of awards offered: One.
Application Procedure: Applicants must complete and submit an application form with a curriculum vitae.
Closing Date: Approx. six months prior to commencement of the fellowship.
Funding: Private.
Contributor: Public and corporate donors.
No. of awards given last year: 1.
No. of applicants last year: 1.
Additional Information: South Africans in the United Kingdom may apply through the Cancer Research Campaign.

For further information contact:

Cancer Research UK, PO Box 123, 61 Lincoln's Inn Fields, London, WC24 3PX, England

THE CANCER COUNCIL SOUTH AUSTRALIA

202 Grenhill Road, Eastwood, SA 5063, Australia
Tel: (61) 8 8291 4111
Fax: (61) 8 8291 4122
Email: msmith@cancersa.org.au
www: http://www.cancersa.org.au
Contact: Ms Margaret Smith, PA to Executive Director

The Cancer Council South Australia is a community based charity independent of government control that has developed since 1928 with the support of South Australians. The Foundation's mission is to pursue the eradication of cancer through research and education on the prevention and early detection of cancer and thus enhancing the quality of life for people living with cancer.

Cancer Council South Australia Research Grants

Subjects: Any scientific or medical field directly concerned with the cause, diagnosis, prevention and treatment of cancer.
Purpose: To assist postgraduate research workers undertaking research into cancer.
Eligibility: Open to postgraduate research workers who show promise of establishing themselves or to those who have already established themselves in the field of cancer research.
Level of Study: Postdoctorate.
Type: Research grant.
Value: Varies according to the needs of the proposed research project and available funds.
Length of Study: One-two years.
Frequency: Annual.
Study Establishment: An appropriate research organisation.
Country of Study: Australia.
No. of awards offered: Approx. 20.
Application Procedure: Applicants must write for details.
Closing Date: June.
Funding: Private.
Contributor: South Australian community.
No. of awards given last year: 23.
No. of applicants last year: 64.

THE CANCER RESEARCH CAMPAIGN

10 Cambridge Terrace, London
NW1 4JL, England
Tel: (44) 20 7224 1333
Fax: (44) 20 7487 4302
Email: scientific@crc.org.uk
www: http://www.crc.org.uk
Contact: Scientific Department

Please refer to our website for full details.

Cancer Research UK

Subjects: The vision of Cancer Research UK is to conquer cancer through world-class research. Through research into the causes, prevention, treatement and cure of cancer.
Purpose: To support cancer research.
Eligibility: Applications will be accepted from scientists, clinicians or healthcare workers who possess suitable academic qualifications, and have the support of the head of department in the proposed place of work. Grants are normally available to applicants who have been resident in the United Kingdom for at least three years.
Level of Study: Doctorate, Postdoctorate, Research.
Type: Research grant.
Value: Salaries, running expenses and equipment.
Length of Study: Three-five years.
Frequency: Annual.
Study Establishment: Appropriate universities, medical schools, hospitals and some research institutions. The host institution is responsible for administering the grant.
Country of Study: United Kingdom.
No. of awards offered: Varies.
Application Procedure: Applicants must obtain applications from the Research Management and Planning Directorate at Cancer Research UK.
Funding: Private.
Contributor: Public donations.

THE CANCER RESEARCH SOCIETY, INC.

625 Avenue du President-Kennedy, Suite 402, Montréal, QC, H3A 3S5, Canada
Tel: (1) 514 861 9227
Fax: (1) 514 861 9220
Email: grants@cancerresearchsociety.ca
www: http://www.cancerresearchsociety.ca
Contact: Ms Louise Langlois, Executive Director

The Cancer Research Society, founded in 1945, is a national organisation which devotes its funds exclusively to research on cancer. The Society is committed to funding basic cancer research or seed money for original ideas. The funds are allocated in the form of grants and fellowships to universities and hospitals across Canada.

Cancer Research Society, Inc. (Canada) Postdoctoral Fellowships

Subjects: Basic medical sciences.
Purpose: To provide financial support to recent PhD and MD's.
Eligibility: Open to holders of a PhD or MD degree of any nationality.
Level of Study: Postdoctorate.
Type: Fellowship
Value: Canadian $35,000.
Frequency: Annual.
Study Establishment: Universities and their affiliated institutions.
Country of Study: Canada.
No. of awards offered: Varies.
Application Procedure: Applicants must visit the website for details.
Closing Date: February 15th.
Funding: Commercial, Private.
No. of awards given last year: Three.
No. of applicants last year: 50.

Cancer Research Society, Inc. (Canada) Research Grants

Subjects: Fundamental research on cancer.
Purpose: To provide support for new or continuing research activities by independent scientists or groups of investigators in the field of cancer.
Eligibility: Candidates must hold an academic position on the staff of a Canadian university.
Level of Study: Professional development.
Type: Research grant.
Value: Canadian $30,000-60,000 to cover the cost of research. No equipment or travel is permitted.
Frequency: Annual.
Study Establishment: Universities and their affiliated institutions.
Country of Study: Canada.
No. of awards offered: Varies.
Application Procedure: Applicants must visit the website for details of application procedures.
Closing Date: February 15th.
Funding: Private, Commercial.
No. of awards given last year: 60.
No. of applicants last year: 110.

CANCER RESEARCH UK

London Research Institute, PO Box 123, Lincoln's Inn Fields, London, WC2A 3PX, England
Tel: (44) 20 7269 3090
Fax: (44) 20 7269 3585
www: http://www.cancerresearch.org
Contact: Dr Manickas Ingham, Administration Manager

Cancer Research UK London Research Institute is part of CR-UK which is a registered United Kingdom charity dedicated to saving lives through research into the causes, prevention, treatment and cure of cancer.

Cancer Research Clinical Research Fellowships

Subjects: All areas of cancer research.
Purpose: To enable research training.
Eligibility: Open to medical graduates of registrar or senior registrar status. Applicants must have obtained MRCP, FRCS or other higher medical qualifications.
Level of Study: Doctorate, Postdoctorate.

Type: Fellowship.
Value: remuneration based on current National Health Service salary scales.
Length of Study: Up to four years.
Frequency: Annual.
Study Establishment: Cancer Research UK London Research Institute laboratories.
Country of Study: United Kingdom.
No. of awards offered: Approx. three.
Application Procedure: Applicants must refer to the advertisements which list procedure information or alternatively, make direct applications to laboratory heads.
Additional Information: Fellowships are advertised in scientific and medical journals.

Cancer Research UK LRI Graduate Studentships

Subjects: All areas of cancer research.
Purpose: To enable research training.
Eligibility: Open to candidates who have normally been resident in the United Kingdom for more than three years and have obtained, or are about to obtain, a First or Upper Second Class (Honours) Degree in science. Applicants must also be aged 25 years or younger. Non residents are not excluded from consideration.
Level of Study: Doctorate.
Type: Studentship.
Value: Approx. UK£13,206-14,256 per year, depending on location.
Length of Study: Three years.
Frequency: Annual.
Study Establishment: Cancer Research UK, London Research Institute laboratories.
Country of Study: United Kingdom.
No. of awards offered: Approx. 20.
Application Procedure: Applicants must refer to the advertisements which list procedure information.

Cancer Research UK LRI Research Fellowships

Subjects: All areas of cancer research.
Purpose: To assist postdoctoral research.
Eligibility: Applicants must have been awarded a PhD or equivalent or must be able to show written proof of having submitted their thesis.
Level of Study: Postdoctorate.
Type: Fellowship.
Value: The starting salary is approx. UK£19,945-26,839 plus location allowances per year depending on experience.
Length of Study: Up to three years.
Frequency: Every two months.
Study Establishment: Cancer Research UK, London Research Institute laboratories.
Country of Study: United Kingdom.
No. of awards offered: Approx. 30.
Application Procedure: Applicants must refer to the advertisements which list procedure information or alternatively make direct applications to laboratory heads.

THE CANON FOUNDATION IN EUROPE

NL 2334 BA, Rijnsburgerweg 3, Leiden, Netherlands
Tel: (31) 71 515 6555
Fax: (31) 71 515 7027
Email: foundation@canon-europe.com
www: http://www.canonfoundation.org
Contact: Secretary

The Canon Foundation is a non-profit, grant making philanthropic organisation founded to promote, develop and spread science, knowledge and understanding, in particular between Europe and Japan.

Canon Foundation Award

Subjects: Academic education and cultural understanding in particular between Europe and Japan.
Purpose: To contribute to scientific knowledge and international understanding through a teaching assignment which can be combined with collaborative research.
Eligibility: Open to Japanese and European nationals only.

Level of Study: Postdoctorate, Professional development, Research.
Type: Award.
Value: A maximum award of €3,780 per month.
Length of Study: One-three months.
Frequency: Annual.
Country of Study: Other.
No. of awards offered: One-three.
Application Procedure: The host institution must complete a nomination form which is to be submitted with a curriculum vitae, a list of papers and two photographs.
Closing Date: October 15th.
Funding: Private.
Contributor: Canon Europa NV.
No. of awards given last year: One.
No. of applicants last year: Five.

Canon Foundation Research Fellowships

Subjects: All subjects.
Purpose: To contribute to scientific knowledge and international understanding in particular between Europe and Japan.
Eligibility: Open to Japanese and European nationals only.
Level of Study: Doctorate, Postdoctorate, Postgraduate, Research.
Type: Fellowship.
Value: A maximum of award of €27,500.
Length of Study: One year maximum.
Frequency: Annual.
Country of Study: Other.
No. of awards offered: 10-15.
Application Procedure: Applicants must complete an application form which is to be submitted with two reference letters, a curriculum vitae, a list of papers, two photographs and copies of certificates of higher education.
Closing Date: October 15th.
Funding: Private.
Contributor: Canon Europa N V.
No. of awards given last year: Nine.
No. of applicants last year: 85.

CANTERBURY BUSINESS SCHOOL

University of Kent, Canterbury, Kent, CT2 7PE, England
Tel: (44) 1227 827726
Fax. (44) 1227 761187
Email: cbs_admissions@ukc.ac.uk
www: http://www.ukc.ac.uk/cbs
Contact: Mr Bernard J Kemp, MBA Admissions Officer

Canterbury Business School Scholarships

Subjects: MBA.
Purpose: To assist students to pursue an MBA at the Canterbury Business School.
Eligibility: Applicants must have been accepted to one of the Canterbury Business School's MBA programmes.
Level of Study: MBA.
Type: Scholarship.
Frequency: Annual.
Study Establishment: Canterbury Business School.
Country of Study: England.

CANTERBURY HISTORICAL ASSOCIATION

c/o History Department, University of Canterbury, Private Bag, Christchurch, New Zealand
Fax: (64) 3 364 2003
Email: g.rice@hist.canterbury.ac.nz
Contact: Dr G W Rice, Secretary

The Canterbury Historical Association (founded 1922, but in recess between 1940 and 1953) aims to foster public interest in all fields of history, by holding meetings for the discussion of historical issues and to promote historical research and writing through its administration of the J M Sherrard Award in New Zealand local and regional history.

J M Sherrard Award

Subjects: New Zealand regional and local history writing.
Purpose: To foster high standards of scholarship in New Zealand regional and local history.
Eligibility: Open to qualified applicants from New Zealand only. Major awards are normally restricted to substantial monograph length publications which meet scholarly standards. Small scale works, biographies and family histories are not eligible.
Level of Study: Unrestricted.
Type: Prize.
Value: New Zealand $1,000.
Frequency: Dependent on funds available.
Country of Study: New Zealand.
No. of awards offered: Varies.
Application Procedure: No application is required as judges assess all potential titles appearing in the New Zealand National Biography.
Funding: Private.
No. of awards given last year: Three major awards.
No. of applicants last year: 45 works considered, 10 are shortlisted.
Additional Information: The prize money is often divided among two or three finalists. A commendation list is also published.

CARDIFF UNIVERSITY

Postgraduate Liaison office, 42-43 Park Place, Cardiff, CF10 3BB, Wales
Tel: (44) 29 2087 4587
Fax: (44) 29 2087 4622
Email: graduate@cardiff.ac.uk
www: http://www.cf.ac.uk

The university was founded in 1883 and is one of Britain's leading research and teaching universities.

EPSRC Studentships

Subjects: Chemistry.
Purpose: To support students working to an MSc in Chemistry.
Eligibility: The minimum requirement is a good degree in Chemistry or a related discipline.
Level of Study: Postgraduate.
Value: £8,000 pa stipend.
Frequency: Annual.
Study Establishment: Cardiff University
Country of Study: Wales.
No. of awards offered: 10.
Application Procedure: Contact Dr.Janie Platts by email @ platts@cf.ac.uk or check the website.

ERDF PhD Studentship

Subjects: Willow root ecology in relation to biomass and bioengineering uses of the crop.
Purpose: To support students working to a PhD in Biosciences
Level of Study: Doctorate.
Type: Studentship.
Value: £10,000 stipend per annum.
Study Establishment: Cardiff University
Country of Study: Wales.
Funding: Private.
Contributor: European Regional Development Fund.

MA Studentship in History & Archaeology

Subjects: History and archaeology
Purpose: To support students working to an MA in History and/or Archaeology.
Level of Study: Postgraduate.
Type: Studentship.
Value: $3,000 per year.
Length of Study: One year.
Frequency: Annual.
Study Establishment: Cardiff University
Country of Study: Wales.
No. of awards offered: Variable.
Application Procedure: Students should submit an application form which should include a research proposal and the names of two referees.
Closing Date: 1st June

Additional Information: Masters applicants should outline the proposed area of study and their plans for the dissertation.

MA/Msc Studentship in European Studies

Subjects: European studies.
Purpose: To support research into European Literatures, Political Theory, Public Policy, Welsh Politics and European Studies.
Eligibility: Students should be accepted into the School of European studies first.
Level of Study: Postgraduate.
Type: Studentship.
Value: Tuition fees
Length of Study: Two years.
Frequency: Annual.
Study Establishment: Cardiff University
Country of Study: Wales.
No. of awards offered: 3.
Application Procedure: Download forms from the website.
Closing Date: 30th June

PhD Studentship in European Studies

Subjects: The literatures, cultures, societies, politics and policies of Europe.
Purpose: To support students working towards a thesis in European Studies.
Eligibility: All students accepted by the School of European studies to study for a postgraduate research degree are automatically considered.
Level of Study: Doctorate.
Type: Studentship.
Value: Full tuition fee plus stipend.
Frequency: Annual.
Study Establishment: Cardiff University
Country of Study: Wales.
No. of awards offered: 1.
Application Procedure: Apply by checking guidelines on postgraduate webpages.
Closing Date: 30th June.

PhD Studentship in Psychology

Subjects: Biological psychology, cognitive psychology and social and developmental psychology.
Purpose: To support students working to a PhD in Psychology.
Eligibility: Applicants must have, or expect to obtain, at least an upper-second class honours degree.
Level of Study: Doctorate.
Type: Studentship.
Frequency: Annual.
Study Establishment: Cardiff University
Country of Study: Wales.
No. of awards offered: 10.
Application Procedure: Application forms, a post graduate prospectus and the post graduate research opportunities booklet may be obtained from LandegLA@cardiff.ac.uk
Closing Date: 15th March
Additional Information: Details about current research interests can be accessed from the website at "Studying for a PhD in the School of Psychology".

For further information contact:

School of Psychology, Cardiff University, PO Box 901, Cardiff, CF10 3YG, Wales
Contact: Mr Lesley Landeg

PhD Studentship in Visual Biophysics

Subjects: Biophysics and biochemistry in the field of optometry and vision Sciences.
Purpose: To support students working towards a PhD in visual Biophysics.
Level of Study: Doctorate.
Type: Studentship.
Frequency: Annual.
Study Establishment: Cardiff University
Country of Study: Wales.

PhD Studentship within the Welsh School of Pharmacy

Subjects: Pharmacy
Purpose: To support students working to a doctorate in pharmacy.
Level of Study: Doctorate.
Type: Studentship.
Value: £9,000 per year stipend.
Frequency: Annual.
Study Establishment: Cardiff University
Country of Study: Wales.
No. of awards offered: Variable.

For further information contact:

Postgraduate Admissions, Welsh School of Pharmacy, Cardiff University, Redwood Building, Cardiff, CF10 3XF, Wales
Contact: Mrs Lynne Terret

PhD Studentships in Biosciences

Subjects: Biosciences
Purpose: To support a student working to a PhD in Biosciences.
Eligibility: Candidates must have or expect to obtain a relevant 2.1 honours degree in a relevant subject.
Level of Study: Doctorate.
Type: Studentship.
Frequency: Annual.
Study Establishment: Cardiff University
Country of Study: Wales.
Application Procedure: Attend an open day or download an application form. Details on website.

PhD Studentships in History & Archaeology

Subjects: History and archaeology
Purpose: To support students working towards a PhD in history and archaeology.
Eligibility: Applicants must be accepted into the school of History and Archaeology first.
Level of Study: Doctorate.
Type: Studentship.
Value: $3000 per year.
Length of Study: Up to 3 years.
Frequency: Annual.
Study Establishment: Cardiff University
Country of Study: Wales.
Application Procedure: Applicants must give the proposed title for their thesis and an explanation of the scope and significance of the proposed research.
Closing Date: 1st June
Additional Information: It is not possible to hold a studentship in addition to a full award from a separate funding body.

PhD Studentships in Social Sciences

Subjects: Social Sciences.
Purpose: To support students working towards their PhD in Social Sciences.
Level of Study: Doctorate.
Type: Studentship.
Frequency: Annual.
Study Establishment: Cardiff University
Country of Study: Wales.
Application Procedure: Please apply to university for guidelines.

PhD Studentships within Clinical Investigation and Visual Function Research Group

Subjects: Clinical investigation and visual function.
Purpose: To support students working towards a PhD in the vision Sciences.
Eligibility: Students must have or expect to obtain a minimum 2.1 honours degree in a relevant subject.
Level of Study: Doctorate.
Frequency: Annual.
Study Establishment: Cardiff University.
Country of Study: Wales.
Application Procedure: Please contact Professor John wild or email WildJM@cardiff.ac.uk or check the website.

Postgraduate Research Scholarships in Law

Subjects: Law.
Purpose: To support a student working towards an MPhil or PhD in Law.
Eligibility: Students must be accepted by the Law school first.
Level of Study: Doctorate, Postgraduate.
Type: Studentship.
Value: Tuition fees and living expeness.
Frequency: Annual.
Study Establishment: Cardiff University
Country of Study: Wales.
No. of awards offered: 6.
Application Procedure: Contact the postgraduate office, Law School, Cardiff University or check the website.
Closing Date: 30th June.
Additional Information: Applicants will be interviewed and the interviews will be held in Cardiff.

Studentship in City and Regional Planning

Subjects: City planning.
Purpose: To sponsor students working to an Msc in City & Regional Planning.
Eligibility: Available to UK Students wish to work in housing policy, research or practice in Wales.
Level of Study: Postgraduate.
Type: Studentship.
Value: University fees and maintenance grant.
Length of Study: 18 months.
Frequency: Annual.
Study Establishment: Cardiff University.
Country of Study: Wales.
No. of awards offered: 12.
Application Procedure: Contact Pauline Card by email CardPD@cardiff.ac.uk or check the website.
Contributor: ESRC, Welsh Assembly Government, Welsh Local authorities.
Additional Information: Students have to meet employment criteria as well as academic criteria.

Studentships in Cell & Molecular Biology

Subjects: Cell biology, molecular biology and neurobiology.
Purpose: To support postgraduate students researching into cell and molecular biology.
Eligibility: Students must have a minimum of a 2.1 honours degree in cell biology, biochemistry, molecular biology or related subjects.
Level of Study: Doctorate.
Type: Studentship.
Frequency: Annual.
Study Establishment: Cardiff University
Country of Study: Wales.
Application Procedure: Apply to Professor Mike Boulton or check the website.

Studentships in Engineering

Subjects: Civil engineering, water engineering, structural engineering, geoenvironmental engineering.
Purpose: To support a student working towards an MSc in engineering.
Eligibility: All international students applying for MSc Engineering courses are automatically eligible.
Type: Studentship.
Value: Up to £1500
Frequency: Annual.
Study Establishment: Cardiff University.
Country of Study: Wales.
Application Procedure: Check the website.

Studentships in Geoenvironmental Engineering

Subjects: Engineering.
Purpose: To support students working to an MSc in Geoenvironmental Engineering.
Eligibility: Students must have been resident in the UK for at least 3 years.
Level of Study: Postgraduate.
Type: Studentship.
Value: £6800 stipend plus tuition fee.

Frequency: Annual.
Study Establishment: Cardiff University
Country of Study: Wales.
No. of awards offered: 6.
Contributor: EPSRC.
Additional Information: This course is intended for graduates in specialist areas in civil engineering, earth sciences and biology, who wish to enhance their skills across the three disciplines.

CARNEGIE INSTITUTION OF WASHINGTON

1530 P Street North West, Washington, DC 20005-1910, United States of America
Tel: (1) 202 939 1120
Fax: (1) 202 387 8092
Email: tmcdowell@pst.ciw.edu
www: http://www.carnegieinstitution.org
Contact: Ms Tina McDowell, Editor

The Carnegie Institution of Washington is a private, non-profit organisation engaged in basic research and advanced education in biology, astronomy, and the earth sciences. It was founded by Andrew Carnegie in 1902 and incorporated by Act of Congress in 1904. Andrew Carnegie, who provided an initial endowment of US$10 million and later gave additional millions, conceived the institution's purpose to encourage, in the broadest and most liberal manner, investigation, research, and discovery, and the application of knowledge to the improvement of mankind. Today there are six research departments: the department of terrestrial magnetism, the geophysical laboratory, the department of plant biology, the observatories, the department of global ecology and the department of embryology.

Carnegie Institution of Washington Fellowships
Subjects: Biology, astronomy and the earth sciences.
Purpose: To support advanced education.
Eligibility: Candidates are selected on an objective and non discriminatory basis through a careful process that includes assessment of the research proposal, confidential appraisal of the candidate by three or more scientists, review and comparative evaluation of each individual's qualifications and promise, review of the director's recommendations by the president of the institution, and appointment of Fellows and associates by the president. Important considerations are a candidate's apparent potential for growth and the extent that his or her development can be fostered by residence at the institution. In certain departments, a staff member agrees to act as a sponsor before a candidate is selected.
Level of Study: Doctorate, Postdoctorate, Postgraduate, Predoctorate.
Type: Fellowship.
Value: Varies.
Length of Study: Varies.
Frequency: Annual.
Study Establishment: The Carnegie Institution of Washington.
Country of Study: United States of America.
Application Procedure: Applicants must apply directly to the department of his or her interest. Procedures are explained on the website.
Closing Date: Please contact the organisation.
Additional Information: The Carnegie Institution of Washington is committed to equality of opportunity and non discrimination in all its activities, including the selection of fellows and associates. Efforts are made to recruit qualified women and minorities to help overcome the effects of past conditions that may have limited their participation in opportunities for scientific education and research.

CARNEGIE TRUST FOR THE UNIVERSITIES OF SCOTLAND

Cameron House, Abbey Park Place, Dunfermline, Fife, KY12 7PZ, Scotland
Tel: (44) 1383 622148
Fax: (44) 1383 622149
Email: jgray@carnegie-trust.org
www: http://www.carnegie-trust.org
Contact: Ms Jackie Gray, Assistant Secretary

The Carnegie Trust for the Universities of Scotland, founded in 1901, is one of the many philanthropic agencies established by Andrew Carnegie. The trust aims to offer assistance to students, to aid the expansion of the Scottish universities and to stimulate research.

Carnegie Grants
Subjects: All subjects in the Universities curriculum.
Purpose: To support personal research projects or aid in the publication of books likely to benefit the universities of Scotland.
Eligibility: Open to graduates of Scottish universities and to full-time members of staff of Scottish universities.
Level of Study: Postgraduate, Professional development.
Type: Grant.
Value: Varies according to requests but the maximum is usually UK£2,000.
Length of Study: Up to three months.
Frequency: Throughout the year.
Country of Study: Any country.
No. of awards offered: Varies.
Application Procedure: Applicants must complete an application form, available from the Trust office.
Closing Date: January 15th, May 15th or October 15th prior to Executive Committee meetings in February, June and November.
Funding: Private.
No. of awards given last year: 235.
No. of applicants last year: 262.

Carnegie Scholarships
Subjects: All subjects in the Universities curriculum.
Purpose: To support postgraduate research.
Eligibility: Open to candidates possessing a First Class (Honours) Degree from a Scottish university.
Level of Study: Postgraduate.
Type: Scholarship.
Value: UK£10,000 per year plus tuition fees and allowances.
Length of Study: Up to three years, subject to annual review.
Frequency: Annual.
Study Establishment: Any university.
Country of Study: United Kingdom.
No. of awards offered: 12.
Application Procedure: Applicants must be nominated by a senior member of staff at a Scottish university and an application form completed, available from the Trust office.
Closing Date: March 15th.
Funding: Private.
No. of awards given last year: 12.
No. of applicants last year: 95.

CASS BUSINESS SCHOOL (CUBS)

106, Bunhill Row, London, EC1Y 8TZ, England
Tel: (44) 20 7040 8607
Fax: (44) 20 7040 8898
Email: cass-mba@city.ac.uk
www: http://www.cass.city.ac.uk
Contact: Rachel Lawrence, MBA Marketing

Cass Business School has always taken pride in its academic credentials. Annually rated among the world's top business schools, it is also accredited by the Association of MBAs (AMBA) and EQUIS. Located in the City of London, it is at the heart of one of the world's most dynamic business centres. The MBA programme provides extraordinary flexibility to tailor the content of programmes to suit students' goals and future plans.

CUBS MBA Studentships
Subjects: MBA.
Eligibility: Open to candidates who have demonstrated considerable ability in their previous studies and work experience and have gained or expect to gain high scores in the Graduate Management Admissions Test.
Level of Study: MBA, Postgraduate.
Type: Studentship.

Value: Up to full fees.
Length of Study: One year.
Frequency: Annual.
Study Establishment: CASS.
Country of Study: England.
Application Procedure: Applicants must print out an application form from the website or contact the admissions office.
Contributor: In collaboration with leading companies worldwide.

CATCHING THE DREAM

8200 Mountain Road North East, Suite 203, Albuquerque, NM 87110, United States of America
Tel: (1) 505 262 2351
Fax: (1) 505 262 0534
Email: nscholarsh@aol.com
Contact: Director of Recruitment

The Mathematics, Education, Science, Business, Engineering and Computer Science (MESBEC) provides scholarships to Native Americans studying in those fields. The Native American Leadership in Education (NALE) program helps Native Americans to complete their college degrees and earn teaching credentials, administrative certification and counsellor certification. The Tribal Business management program provides scholarships to native students in the business fields.

Catching The Dream Scholarships
Subjects: All subjects.
Purpose: To provide scholarships to high potential Native American students in the fields that are critical for the political, economic, social and business development of American Indian tribes.
Eligibility: Restricted to United States of America citizens of Native American Indian and Alaskan Native ancestry. Students must be more than a quarter American Indian and enrolled with their tribe.
Level of Study: Unrestricted.
Type: Scholarship.
Length of Study: Four years.
Frequency: Annual.
Study Establishment: An accredited college or university.
Country of Study: United States of America.
No. of awards offered: 230.
Application Procedure: Applicants must complete an application form, available on written request and apply for all other sources of funds.
Closing Date: September 15th for Spring, April 15th for Autumn and March 15th for Summer.
Funding: Private.
No. of awards given last year: 230.
No. of applicants last year: 150.

CATHERINE MCCAIG'S TRUST

Clerk to the Governors, c/o McLeish Carswell, 29 St Vincent Place, Glasgow, G1 2DT, Scotland
Tel: (44) 141 248 4134
Fax: (44) 141 226 3118
Contact: Ms Anne F Wilson

McCaig Postgraduate Scholarships
Subjects: Gaelic studies.
Eligibility: Bursaries are open to students enrolling in a course of Gaelic studies at any Scottish university. Postgraduate Scholarships are open to MA students of any Scottish university who have studied Gaelic among their course subjects.
Level of Study: Postgraduate.
Type: Scholarship.
Value: UK£250 per year for bursaries for the entire course of study, UK£750 per year for the postgraduate scholarships.
Length of Study: One-three years.
Frequency: Annual.
Country of Study: United Kingdom.

Application Procedure: Applicants must complete an application form available from the Clerk.
Closing Date: May.
Funding: Private.
No. of awards given last year: One.
No. of applicants last year: Three.

CATHOLIC LIBRARY ASSOCIATION (CLA)

100 North Street, Suite 224, Pittsfield, MA 01201-5109, United States of America
Tel: (1) 413 443 2252
Fax: (1) 413 442 2252
Email: cla@clatha.org
www: http://www.cathla.org
Contact: Jean R Bostley, SSJ, Executive Director

The Catholic Library Association (CLA) represents all segments of the library community. Members strive to initiate, foster and encourage any activity or library programme that will promote literature and libraries, not only of a Catholic nature, but also of an ecumenical spirit.

Rev Andrew L Bouwhuis Memorial Scholarship
Subjects: Library science.
Purpose: To encourage promising and talented individuals to enter librarianship and to foster advanced study in the library profession.
Eligibility: Open to individuals who have been accepted into a graduate school programme, show promise of success based on collegiate record and who demonstrate the need for financial aid.
Level of Study: Graduate, Postgraduate.
Type: Scholarship.
Value: US$1,500.
Frequency: Annual.
Country of Study: United States of America.
No. of awards offered: One.
Application Procedure: Applicants must complete an application form, available on request. Please send a stamped addressed envelope.
Closing Date: February 1st.
Funding: Private.
No. of awards given last year: One

World Book, Inc. Grant
Subjects: Continuing education in school or children's librarianship.
Purpose: Establish scholarships for continuing education in school or children's librarianship.
Eligibility: Open to national members of the CLA.
Level of Study: Postgraduate, Professional development.
Type: Grant.
Value: US$1,500 to be divided among no more than three recipients.
Frequency: Annual.
Study Establishment: Special workshops, institutes, or seminars and summer sessions at Institutes of Higher Education.
Country of Study: Any country.
No. of awards offered: One-three.
Application Procedure: Applicants must send a stamped addressed envelope for details.
Closing Date: March 15th.
Funding: Commercial.
No. of awards given last year: Three.
Additional Information: This award may not be used for study leading to a degree in library science.

CAUZ GROUP

PO Box 777, Randwick NSW 2031, Australia
Tel: (61) 02 9332 1559
Fax: (61) 02 9332 1298
Email: trustawards@cauzgroup.com.au
www: www.trust.com.au
Contact: Mr Petrea Salter, Director

Cauz Group is the Administrator and PR Agency for number of high profile awards and scholarships. These include the Miles Franklin Literary Award; Kathleen Mitchell Award (literary); Portia Geach Memorial Award (for female artists); the Sir Robert Askin Operatic Travelling Scholarship (for male singers); the Lady Mollie Askin Ballet Travelling Scholarship; and the Marten Bequest Travelling Scholarship (categories include singing, instrumental music, ballet, acting, painting, poetry & prose).

Lady Mollie Askin Ballet Travelling Scholarship

Subjects: Dancing or classical ballet.
Purpose: To support the advancement of culture and education in Australia and elsewhere. To reward Australian citizens of outstanding ability and promise in ballet.
Eligibility: Open to Australian citizens who are aged 17-30 at the closing date for entries for the award.
Level of Study: Unrestricted.
Type: Scholarship.
Value: Australian $15,000.
Length of Study: More than two years.
Frequency: Every two years.
Country of Study: Any country.
No. of awards offered: One.
Application Procedure: Applicants must complete an application form to be submitted with specified documents and enclosures.
Closing Date: The last Friday in April.
Funding: Private.
Contributor: The estate of Lady Mollie Askin.
No. of awards given last year: One.
No. of applicants last year: 30.

Marten Bequest Travelling Scholarships

Subjects: Instrumental music, painting, singing, sculpture, architecture, ballet, prose, poetry or acting.
Purpose: To augment a Scholar's own resources towards affording them a cultural education by means of a travelling scholarship.
Eligibility: Applicants must have been born in Australia, and be aged 21-35, or 17-35 for ballet.
Level of Study: Unrestricted.
Type: Scholarship.
Value: Australian $18,000 over two years.
Length of Study: Two years.
Frequency: Annual.
Country of Study: Any country.
No. of awards offered: Six.
Application Procedure: Applicants must complete an application form and submit this with a study outline and supporting material as required.
Closing Date: The last Friday in October of the year preceding the award.
Funding: Private.
Contributor: The Estate of the late John Chisholm Marten.
No. of awards given last year: Six.
No. of applicants last year: 200.

Miles Franklin Literary Award

Subjects: Authorship. The prize is directed to be awarded for the novel of the year which is of the highest literary merit and which presents Australian life in any of its phases.
Purpose: To award a novel or play first published in the year preceding the award.
Eligibility: Genres not eligible for the award are farce, musical comedy, biographies, collections of short stories, poetry and children's books.
Level of Study: Unrestricted.
Type: Award.
Value: Australian $28,000.
Frequency: Annual.
Country of Study: Any country.
No. of awards offered: One.

Application Procedure: Applicants must complete an application form and enter their novel.
Closing Date: December 15th in the year preceding the awards.
Funding: Private.
Contributor: The estate of the late Miss S M S Miles Franklin.
No. of awards given last year: One.
No. of applicants last year: 55.
Additional Information: If there is no novel worthy of the prize the award may be given to the author of a play.

Portia Geach Memorial Award

Subjects: Fine and applied arts.
Purpose: To award the best portraits painted from life of some man or woman distinguished in art, letters or the sciences by any female artists.
Eligibility: Entrants must be female Australian residents who are either Australian or British born or naturalised. Works must be executed entirely in the previous year.
Type: Award.
Value: Australian $18,000. The winning portrait and selected works are exhibited for one month at the S H Ervin Gallery in Sydney, Australia.
Frequency: Annual.
No. of awards offered: One.
Application Procedure: Applicants must complete an application form and submit this with an entry fee and the works.
Closing Date: The last Friday in August.
Funding: Private.
Contributor: The estate of the late Miss Florence Kate Geach.
No. of awards given last year: One.
No. of applicants last year: 315.

Sir Robert Askin Operatic Travelling Scholarship

Subjects: Operatic singing.
Purpose: To support the advancement of culture and education in Australia and elsewhere. To reward male Australian citizens of outstanding ability and promise as an operatic singer.
Eligibility: Applicants must be male Australian citizens and be aged 18-30 at the time of application.
Level of Study: Unrestricted.
Type: Scholarship.
Value: Australian $15,000.
Length of Study: Two years.
Frequency: Every two years.
Country of Study: Any country.
No. of awards offered: One.
Application Procedure: Applicants must complete an application form to be submitted along with specified documents and enclosures.
Closing Date: The last Friday in September.
Funding: Private.
Contributor: The estate of Sir Robert Askin.
No. of awards given last year: One.
No. of applicants last year: 30.

CDS INTERNATIONAL, INC.

871 United Nations Plaza
New York, NY 10017-1814
United States of America
Tel: (1) 212 497 3513
Fax: (1) 212 497 3535
Email: rdelfino@cdsintl.org
www: http://www.cdsintl.org
Contact: Ms Anna F Oberle, Programme Officer

CDS International, Inc. is a non-profit organisation which administers work exchange programmes. CDS International's goal is to further the international exchange of knowledge and technological skills, and to contribute to the development of a pool of highly trained and interculturally experienced business, academic and government leaders.

Congress Bundestag Youth Exchange for Young Professionals

Subjects: Business, technical, computer science, social and service fields.

Purpose: To foster the exchange of knowledge and culture between German and American youth while providing career enhancing theoretical and practical work experience.

Eligibility: Open to citizens of the United States of America and permanent residents aged between 18 and 24 years who have well defined career goals and related part or full-time work experience. Applicants must be able to communicate and work well with others, have maturity enabling them to adapt to new situations, an intellectual curiosity and a sense of diplomacy.

Level of Study: Professional development.

Type: Fellowship.

Value: International air fare and partial domestic transportation, language training and study at a German professional school, seminars, including transportation and insurance.

Length of Study: Seven months of study and a five month internship.

Frequency: Annual.

Study Establishment: A field specific postsecondary professional school.

Country of Study: Germany.

No. of awards offered: Approx. 60.

Application Procedure: Applicants must complete an application form, available on request by mail, email or from the website.

Closing Date: December 1st.

Funding: Government.

No. of awards given last year: 60.

No. of applicants last year: 300.

Additional Information: Participants must have US$300-350 pocket money per month. During their year, American exchange's will have the opportunity to improve their skills through formal study and work experience. The programme also includes intensive language instruction and housing with a host family or in a dormitory.

CENTER FOR ADVANCED STUDY IN THE BEHAVIORAL SCIENCES

75 Alta Road, Stanford, CA 94305,
United States of America
Tel: (1) 650 321 2052
Fax: (1) 650 321 1192
Contact: Mr Mark Turner, Associate Director

Center for Advanced Study in the Behavioral Sciences Postdoctoral Residential Fellowships

Subjects: Behavioural sciences, biological sciences and the humanities.

Eligibility: There are no restrictions with regard to race or nationality but applicants must hold a PhD.

Level of Study: Postdoctorate.

Type: Fellowship.

Value: Equal to up to half of a nine month university salary with an informal cap, plus travel allowance to and from the Center for recipients and their families.

Length of Study: 9-12 months.

Frequency: Annual.

Study Establishment: The Center for Advanced Study in the Behavioural Sciences.

Country of Study: United States of America.

No. of awards offered: Approx. 42.

Application Procedure: Applicants must contact the Center for details.

Funding: Government, Private.

No. of awards given last year: 42.

Additional Information: Fellows should be nominated by academic officers or distinguished scholars and are expected to seek additional sources of support to share in fellowship costs. All names submitted will be kept for reviews at two year intervals. Persons authorised for fellowships are invited to indicate the year which would best suit their programme.

CENTER FOR DEFENSE INFORMATION (CDI)

1779 Massachusetts Avenue North West, Washington, DC 20036,
United States of America
Tel: (1) 202 332 0600
Fax: (1) 202 462 4559
Email: info@cdi.org
www: http://www.cdi.org
Contact: Development Director

The Center for Defense Information (CDI) provides responsible, non partisan research and analysis on the social, economic, environmental, political and military components of national and global security and aims to educate the public and inform policy makers about these issues. The organisation is staffed by retired senior government officials and knowledgeable researchers and is directed by Dr. Bruce G. Blair.

CDI Internship

Subjects: Weapons proliferation, military spending, military policy, diplomacy and foreign affairs.

Purpose: To support the work of CDIs senior staff while gaining exposure to research, issues and communications related to national security and foreign policy.

Eligibility: There are no eligibility restrictions. Paid internships are for United States of America nationals or legal immigrants.

Level of Study: Unrestricted.

Type: Internship.

Value: US$1,000 per month. Up to US$3,000-5,000 in total.

Length of Study: Three-five months.

Frequency: Three times each year.

Study Establishment: CDI.

Country of Study: Any country.

No. of awards offered: Four per trimester, 12 per year.

Application Procedure: Applicants must submit a curriculum vitae, covering letter, brief writing sample, transcript and two letters of recommendation.

Closing Date: July 1st for the Autumn deadline, October 15th for the Spring deadline and March 15th for the Summer deadline.

Funding: Private.

No. of awards given last year: 12.

No. of applicants last year: 200.

CENTER FOR HELLENIC STUDIES

3100 Whitehaven Street North West, Washington, DC 20008, United States of America
Tel: (1) 202 745 4400
Fax: (1) 202 332 8688
Email: chs@fas.harvard.edu
www: http://www.chs.harvard.edu
Contact: Programs Officer

The Center for Hellenic Studies (Trustees for Harvard University) offers residential research fellowships for professional scholars in ancient Greek studies.

Center for Hellenic Studies Junior Fellowships

Subjects: Ancient Greek studies, primarily literature, language, philosophy, history, religion, archaeology and art history, with restrictions.

Purpose: To provide selected classics scholars fairly early in their careers with an academic year free of other responsibilities to work on a publishable project.

Eligibility: Open to Scholars and teachers of Ancient Greek studies with a PhD degree or equivalent qualification and some published work.

Level of Study: Postdoctorate.

Type: Fellowship.

Value: Up to US$24,000, plus private living quarters and a study at the Center building. Limited funds for research expenses and research related travel are available.

Length of Study: Nine months from September-June, not renewable.

Frequency: Annual.

Study Establishment: The Center for Hellenic Studies in Washington.

Country of Study: United States of America.
No. of awards offered: 12.
Application Procedure: Applicants must submit an application form, curriculum vitae, description of research project, samples of publications and three letters of recommendation. Enquiries about eligibility and early applications are encouraged. Applicants who are unable to stay for the full academic year may apply for a one semester fellowship and should include a note explaining the circumstances that make this necessary with their application.
Closing Date: October 15th.
Funding: Private.
Additional Information: Residence at the Center is required.

CENTER FOR INTERNATIONAL STUDIES, UNIVERSITY OF MISSOURI-ST LOUIS

St Louis, MO 63121-4499, United States of America
Tel: (1) 314 516 5753
Fax: (1) 314 516 6757
Email: jglassman@umsl.edu
www: http://www.umsl.edu
Contact: Mr Robert Baumann, Assistant Director

The Center for International Studies supports a wide range of academic programmes designed to promote research and interest in international studies and to improve the teaching of international affairs. The Center's Office of International Student and Scholar Services coordinates and provides services for the University's international students and scholars, including admissions and immigration.

Theodore Lentz Postdoctoral or Sabbatical Fellowship in Peace and Conflict Resolution Research
Subjects: International relations.
Purpose: To provide an opportunity for the recipient to conduct research projects in peace and conflict resolution and to teach an introductory peace studies course in the Autumn semester and one course in the Spring semester.
Eligibility: A completed PhD is required and preference is given to graduates of university programmes in peace studies and conflict resolution. Graduates of political science, international relations and other social science programmes who specialise in peace and conflict resolution are also invited to apply.
Level of Study: Postdoctorate.
Type: Fellowship.
Value: Approx. US$23,400 plus university benefits and US$1,000 travel and expense allowance.
Length of Study: Nine months.
Frequency: Annual.
Study Establishment: The University of Missouri, St Louis.
Country of Study: United States of America.
No. of awards offered: One.
Application Procedure: Applicants must submit a curriculum vitae, a letter of application, evidence of completion of PhD, three letters of recommendation and a research proposal of approximately 750 words.
Closing Date: April 15th.
Funding: Private.
Contributor: The Lentz Peace Research Association.
No. of awards given last year: One.
No. of applicants last year: 18.
Additional Information: Supported in part by the Lentz Peace Research Association.

CENTRAL QUEENSLAND UNIVERSITY (CQU)

Research Services Office, Rockhampton, QLD 4702, Australia
Tel: (61) 7 4923 2602
Fax: (61) 7 4923 2600
Email: research-enquiries@cqu.edu.au
www: http://www.cqu.edu.au
Contact: Ms Jennifer Brett, Research Higher Degrees Officer

Central Queensland University's (CQU) higher degree research programmes are characterised by open and flexible learning opportunities which provide a distinctive postgraduate research experience for students. With particular strengths in sustainable regional development and resource utilisation, industrially relevant engineering, contemporary communication and innovative teaching, learning and professional practice, the focus of higher degree programmes is the conduct of cutting edge research in areas which challenge boundaries of the traditional disciplines.

CQU Postgraduate Research Award
Subjects: Arts, health and sciences, business and law, education and creative arts, engineering and physical systems, informatics or communication.
Purpose: To enable scholars to proceed as a full-time candidate to a research Master's or doctorate.
Eligibility: Candidates must be eligible for admission to a research higher degree at CQU.
Level of Study: Doctorate, Postgraduate, Research.
Type: Scholarship.
Value: Australian $18,009 living allowance plus Australian $2,000 research support per year.
Length of Study: Two-three years.
Frequency: Annual.
Study Establishment: Central Queensland University.
Country of Study: Australia.
No. of awards offered: 15.
Application Procedure: Applicants must complete an application as prescribed. Certified academic transcripts and certified citizenship status are required. All enquiries from overseas should be directed to the CQU International Office.
Closing Date: October 31st.
Funding: Government.
No. of awards given last year: Eight.
No. of applicants last year: 40.

CENTRE DE RECHERCHE EN SCIENCES NEUROLOGIQUES

Faculté de Médecine, Université de Montréal
CP 6128, Succ Centre-ville, Montréal
QC H3C 3J7, Canada
Tel: (1) 514 343 6366
Fax: (1) 514 343 6113
Email: chantal.nault@umontreal.ca
www: http://www.crsn.umontreal.ca
Contact: Dr Serge Rossignol, Director

Founded in 1975, the Centre de Recherche en Sciences Neurologiques is a multidisciplinary unit based in the Department of Physiology, Faculty of Medicine, at the Université de Montreal. Educational activities at the Centre include an international symposium each spring, open to all neuroscientists, weekly research seminars in neuroanatomy, neurophysiology and neurochemistry, and the HH Jasper and the JP Cordeau Postdoctoral Fellowships.

Herbert H Jasper Fellowship
Subjects: Neurology and neurosciences.
Purpose: To enable the use of the exceptional research facilities of the Center for Research in Neurological Sciences of the Université de Montréal.
Eligibility: Open to Canadian citizens or permanent residents.
Level of Study: Postdoctorate.
Type: Fellowship.
Value: Canadian $25,000-30,000 per year.
Length of Study: One year.
Frequency: Annual.
Study Establishment: Centre de Recherche en Sciences Neurologiques, Université de Montréal.
Country of Study: Canada.
No. of awards offered: One.

Application Procedure: Applicants must complete an application form which can be obtained from the website at http://www.crsn.umontreal.ca/bourses_jc.html or by writing to the Fellowship Committee.
Closing Date: December 31st.
Funding: Government.
No. of awards given last year: One.
No. of applicants last year: 20.
Additional Information: The fellowship provides the opportunity for the recipient to work closely with the investigator of his or her choice within a large active group of neuroscientists who are members of the Center.

JP Cordeau Fellowship

Subjects: Neurology and neurosciences.
Purpose: To enable the use of the exceptional research facilities of the Center for Research in Neurological Sciences of the Université de Montréal.
Eligibility: Open to Canadian citizens or permanent residents.
Level of Study: Postdoctorate.
Type: Fellowship.
Value: Canadian $25,000-30,000.
Length of Study: One year.
Frequency: Annual.
Study Establishment: Centre de Recherche en Sciences Neurologiques, Université de Montréal.
Country of Study: Canada.
No. of awards offered: One.
Application Procedure: Applicants must complete an application form which can be obtained from the website at http://www.crsn.umontreal.ca/bourses_jc.html or by writing to the Fellowship Committee.
Closing Date: December 31st.
Funding: Commercial, Government.
No. of awards given last year: One.
No. of applicants last year: 20.
Additional Information: The fellowship also provides the opportunity for the recipient to work closely with the investigator of his or her choice within a large active group of neuroscientists who are members of the Center.

CENTRE FOR ADDICTION AND MENTAL HEALTH

250 College Street, Toronto, ON, M5T 1R8, Canada
Tel: (1) 416 535 8501 ext. 4568
Fax: (1) 416 979 4695
Email: elizabeth_cordeiro@camh.net
www: http://www.camh.net
Contact: Ms Elizabeth Cordeiro, Manager Research Grants and Awards

The Centre for Addiction and Mental Health was formed in early 1998 and involved the amalgamation of the Addiction Research Foundation, Clarke Institute, Donwood Institute and Queen Street Mental Health Centre. As a teaching hospital and research institute fully affiliated with the University of Toronto, the Centre is in a unique position to contribute to one common goal that being the better understanding, prevention and care for mental health.

Postdoctoral Training Programme in Addiction and Mental Health

Subjects: Addiction and mental health.
Purpose: To provide Fellows with a comprehensive training programme in the fields of addiction and mental health with training in research techniques.
Eligibility: Candidates must have a PhD or MD or equivalent at the time of taking up the appointment. Preference is given to Canadian citizens and permanent residents. Other successful applicants must obtain an appropriate visa. The successful applicant is expected to be located at the CAMH during the period of appointment. Applicants must obtain sponsorship of a supervisor at the Centre who holds an appointment as associate or full professor.

Level of Study: Postdoctorate.
Type: Fellowship.
Value: Postdoctoral salary varies depending on experience: Canadian $35,000-40,000, based on CIHR salary scale.
Length of Study: One year, subject to renewal for a second year.
Frequency: Annual.
Study Establishment: The Centre for Addiction and Mental Health.
Country of Study: Canada.
No. of awards offered: Varies.
Application Procedure: Applicants must submit 10 copies of the application cover sheet, a description of the proposed programme of research relevant to the mission of the Centre, agreed upon by the proposed supervisor, not exceeding two pages single spaced, a curriculum vitae and two letters of reference to be sent directly to Elizabeth Cordeiro, Manager, Research Grants and Awards at the Centre for Addiction and Mental Health. Graduate School transcripts, two papers of sample writing, and a two page biosketch of the proposed supervisor including current funding should also be sent.
Closing Date: December 5th-(First Friday in December).
Funding: Government, Private.
Contributor: The Centre for Addiction and Mental Health Foundation and the Ontario Ministry of Health.
No. of awards given last year: Two.
No. of applicants last year: Varies.

CENTRE FOR INTERNATIONAL MOBILITY (CIMO)

PO Box 343, Hakaniemenkatu 2, Helsinki, FIN-00531, Finland
Tel: (358) 9 7747 7033
Fax: (358) 9 7747 7064
Email: cimoinfo@cimo.fi
www: http://www.cimo.fi
Contact: Ms Tarja Mäkelä, Exchanges Co-ordinator

The Centre for International Mobility (CIMO) is a service sector organisation whose expertise is geared to the promotion of cross cultural communication in education, training and international mobility with the focus on education and training, work and young people. CIMO gathers, processes and distributes information and co-ordinates international education and training programmes.

CIMO Scholarships for advanced studies of Finnish Language at a Finnish University

Purpose: To support degree students of Finnish language and literature at universities outside Finland.
Eligibility: Open to nationals of any country. Applicants should not be over 35.
Level of Study: Postgraduate.
Type: Scholarship.
Value: €725 per month.
Length of Study: One academic semester.
Frequency: Annual.
Study Establishment: A Finnish University.
Country of Study: Finland.
Application Procedure: Applicants must make an application, preferably in Finnish, on CIMO's application forms. These are available at Finnish embassies and consulates abroad and should be sent to CIMO.
Closing Date: Applicants are accepted at any time, but applicants should allow three months before the intended scholarship period.
Funding: Government.

CIMO Scholarships for Post-graduate Studies at a Finnish University

Subjects: Finnish language, Finno Ugric linguistics, ethnology and folklore.
Purpose: To support postgraduate research and advanced studies of Finnish language, Finnish literature, Finno-Ugric linguistics, ethology and folklore.
Eligibility: Open to nationals of any country. Applicants should not be over 35.

Level of Study: Doctorate, Postgraduate.
Type: Scholarship.
Value: €760 per month.
Length of Study: Four-nine months.
Frequency: Annual.
Study Establishment: A Finnish university.
Country of Study: Finland.
Application Procedure: Applicants must make an application, preferably in Finnish, on CIMO's application forms. These are available at Finnish embassies and consulates abroad and should be sent to CIMO.
Closing Date: Applications are accepted at any time, but applicants should allow three months before the intended scholarship period.
Funding: Government.

Finnish Government Scholarship Pool

Subjects: All subjects.
Eligibility: Open to applicants from Australia, Austria, Belgium, Bulgaria, China, Cuba, the Czech Republic, Denmark, Egypt, France, Germany, Greece, Hungary, Iceland, India, the Republic of Ireland, Israel, Italy, Japan, Luxembourg, Mexico, Mongolia, the Netherlands, Norway, Poland, Portugal, the Republic of Korea, Romania, Slovakia, Spain, Sweden, Switzerland, Turkey
Level of Study: Postgraduate.
Type: Scholarship.
Value: The bilateral scholarships usually consist of a monthly allowance. For short-term visitors there is a daily allowance, the amount of which is determined annually. Accommodation is provided for short-term visitors. There are no travel grants to or from Finland.
Length of Study: Postgraduate research of three-nine months.
Frequency: Annual.
Study Establishment: A Finnish university.
Country of Study: Finland.
Application Procedure: Applicants must make an application to the appropriate authority in the applicant's country and students can contact the CIMO in Finland for further information. It is necessary that applicants establish contact with the receiving institution prior to application.
Closing Date: 1st February.
Funding: Government.

CENTRE FOR THE HISTORY OF SCIENCE, TECHNOLOGY AND MEDICINE

Mathematics Tower, The University, Manchester, M13 9PL, England
Tel: (44) 161 275 5850
Fax: (44) 161 275 5699
Email: chstm@man.ac.uk
www: http://www.chstm.man.ac.uk

The Centre maintains teaching and research programmes of the highest standards. It acts as a focus for the history of science, technology and medicine in the Northwest of England. CHSTM houses a Welcome Unit for the History of Medicine and the National Archive for the History of Computing.

AHRB Studentships

Subjects: The history of science, technology and medicine.
Purpose: To support students working for their MSc in History of Science, Technology and Medicine.
Level of Study: Postgraduate.
Type: Studentship.
Frequency: Annual.
Study Establishment: Centre for the History of Science, Technology and Medicine.
Application Procedure: The AHRB deadline is 1 May. In order to ensure completion of paperwork and prompt submission of applications, the CHSTM deadline for AHRB forms is 12 April. We expect to work closely with applicants as they complete the forms, so early contact with CHSTM staff is advisable.
Closing Date: 12 April in any given year.
Funding: Government, Private.
Contributor: Arts and Humanities Research Board.

ESRC Studentships

Subjects: This new Master degree has a significant emphasis on research methods and is more closely focused on developing a PhD project.
Purpose: To fund students working for the MSc in Research Methods in History of Science, Technology and Medicine.
Eligibility: Open to applicants for our MSc in Research methods in History of Science, Technology and Medicine.
Level of Study: Postgraduate.
Type: Studentship.
Frequency: Annual.
Study Establishment: Centre for the History of Science, Technology and Medicine.
Country of Study: England.
Application Procedure: The deadline for receipt of application is 1 May. In order to ensure completion of paperwork and prompt submission of applications, the CHSTM deadline for receipt of ESRC forms is 12 April. We expect to work closely with applicants as they complete the forms so early contact with CHSTM staff is advisable.
Closing Date: 12 April in any given year.
Funding: Government.
Contributor: Economic and Social Research Council.

Ph.D Studentship in the History of 20th C. Biology

Subjects: Any research topic proposed within the broad ambit of 20th C biology, or candidates may choose from 1) The history of bacteriology/microbiology, 2) Cancer biology, 3) The reorganisation of the Life Sciences since 1960, 4) The decline of Botany, 5) The history of applied botany/plant pathology.
Purpose: To fund a Ph.D project on any aspect of the biological sciences.
Eligibility: Applicants should have a good first degree and/or as appropriate Masters degree, with some university - level knowledge of the biological sciences and training in the history of science, technology and medicine.
Level of Study: Doctorate.
Type: Studentship.
Value: Fees, a maintenance grant of GBP 9,000 linked to Research Council levels and research expenses.
Length of Study: Three years.
Frequency: Annual.
Study Establishment: Centre for the History of Science, Technology and Medicine.
Country of Study: England.
Application Procedure: Applicants should send a curriculum vitae, a covering letter and the names of two referees to The Secretary.
Closing Date: 1 May each year.
Funding: Government, Private.
Contributor: Williamson Bequest.

Wellcome Ph.D Studentship in History of Medicine

Subjects: The history of medical technology.
Purpose: To allow the student to benefit from the combined strengths of the Manchester unit in the history of modern medical technologies and the Thackray collections of surgical instruments, prostheses, hearing aids and the medical supply trade.
Eligibility: Applicants should have a Masters in history of medicine or a related field.
Level of Study: Doctorate.
Frequency: Annual.
Study Establishment: Centre for the History of Science, Technology and Medicine.
Country of Study: England.
Application Procedure: Applicants should send a curriculum vitae (including the names of two referees) and a letter outlining their relevant interests, training and career plans to the address below.
Closing Date: 4 April of relevant year.
Funding: Private.
Contributor: Wellcome Trust.

For further information contact:

Informal enquiries and requests for further particulars should be made to Professor Michael Worboys (Michael.worboys@man.ac.uk), otherwise to main organisation address.

Wellcome Trust Studentships

Subjects: The history of medicine.
Purpose: To support applicants whose main interests are in the history of medicine.
Level of Study: Research.
Type: Studentship.
Frequency: Annual.
Study Establishment: Centre for the History of Science, Technology and Medicine.
Country of Study: England.
No. of awards offered: Variable according to academic merit and research potential and is subject to ratification by the Wellcome Trust.
Application Procedure: Applicants must complete the university application form (with 2 references), the Wellcome Trust Studentship application form and submit a CV and samples of written work.
Closing Date: 1 May in each year.
Funding: Government, Private.
Contributor: Wellcome Trust.
Additional Information: Applicants are encouraged to discuss their application informally with Professor Michael Worboys and to submit their applications as soon as possible.

CENTRO DE INVESTIGACIÓN Y ESTUDIOS AVANZADOS DEL IPN (CINVESTAV-IPN)

Departmento De Matemáticas Del CINVESTAV, Apartado Postal 14-740, Mexico City, 07000, Mexico
Tel: (52) 55747 3867
Fax: (52) 55747 3876
Email: matemat@math.cinvestav.mx
www: http://www.math.cinvestav.mx
Contact: Dr Enrique Ramirez de Arellano, Head

The Mathematics Department of the Centro de Investigación y Estudios Avanzados Del IPN (CINVESTAV-IPN) offers the Solomon Lefschetz Instructorships to young mathematicians with doctorates who show definite promise in research.

Solomon Lefschetz Instructorships

Subjects: Mathematics and statistics.
Purpose: To support young mathematicians.
Eligibility: Open to applicants with a doctoral degree. Some knowledge of Spanish is also desirable.
Level of Study: Postdoctorate.
Type: Fellowship.
Value: The salary is equivalent to that of an assistant professor in the mathematics department. An allowance for moving expenses is also provided.
Length of Study: One year, with a possibility of renewal for an extra year.
Frequency: Annual, if funds are available.
Country of Study: Mexico.
No. of awards offered: Two.
Application Procedure: Applicants must submit a curriculum vitae, a short one-three page research statement and arrange for at least three letters of recommendation to be sent to the centre.
Closing Date: February 28th.
Funding: Government.
Contributor: The Mexican Office of Education.
Additional Information: Teaching duties generally include one course per semester.

CEREBRA FOUNDATION

Principality Buildings, 13 Guildhall Square, Carmarthen, SA31 1PR, Wales
Tel: (44) 126 724 4200
Fax: (44) 126 724 4201
www: www.cerebra.org

Cerebra works to ensure that up-to-date evidence-based knowledge is available and applied for the prevention of brain damage and for proven treatments.

Cerebra Research Grant

Subjects: Paediatric neurology.
Purpose: To support research relating to the prevention, detection, early diagnosis, subsequent treatment, therapy and management of paediatric neurological disorders.
Eligibility: Please read all guidelines from the website.
Level of Study: Postgraduate.
Value: Variable.
Length of Study: Variable.
Frequency: When needed.
Study Establishment: Suitable reputable Institution.
Application Procedure: Write a letter of proposal. Full details from the website.
Closing Date: No specific closing date.
Funding: Private.

CERIES (CENTRE DE RECHERCHES ET D'INVESTIGATIONS EPIDERMIQUES ET SENSORIELLES)

20 rue Victor Noir, Neuilly-sur-Seine
Cedex 92521, France
Tel: (33) 1 46 43 49 00
Fax: (33) 1 46 43 46 00
Email: contact@ceries.com
www: http://www.ceries.com

CERIES (Centre de Recherches et d'Investigations Epidermiques et Sensorielles or Centre for Epidermal and Sensory Research and Investigation) is the healthy skin research centre of Chanel.

CERIES Research Award

Subjects: The biology and physiology of healthy skin and/or its reactions to environmental factors.
Purpose: To honour a scientific researcher for a fundamental or clinical research project in the field of healthy skin
Eligibility: There are no eligibility restrictions.
Level of Study: Research.
Value: €40,000.
Length of Study: Two years.
Frequency: Annual.
Country of Study: Any country.
Application Procedure: Applicants must consult the website.
Closing Date: June 2nd.
Funding: Private.
Contributor: Chanel.
No. of awards given last year: One.
No. of applicants last year: 26.

CERN EUROPEAN LABORATORY FOR PARTICLE PHYSICS

Human Resources Division, Geneva
CH-1211, Switzerland
Tel: (41) 22 767 2735
Fax: (41) 22 767 2750
Email: recruitment.service@cern.ch
www: http://www.cern.ch/jobs
Contact: Administrative Assistant

CERN European Laboratory for Particle Physics is the world's leading laboratory in its field, that being the study of the smallest constituents of matter and of the forces that hold them together. The laboratory's tools are its particle accelerators and detectors, which are among the largest and most complex scientific instruments ever built.

CERN Doctoral Student Programme

Subjects: Applied physics, electrical, electronic, mechanical or civil engineering, mathematics, computing, geotechnics, materials science, radiation protection and ultra-high vacuum.

Purpose: To assist students who are preparing a thesis at the doctoral level in a technical field.

Eligibility: Open to nationals of one of the CERN member states. Applicants must be enrolled in a doctoral programme at a university in one of these countries. Specialists in theoretical or experimental particle physics are not eligible.

Level of Study: Doctorate.

Type: Research grant.

Value: Swiss franc 3,913 per month.

Length of Study: Two years, which can be extended to three.

Frequency: Three times each year.

Study Establishment: The European Laboratory for Particle Physics.

Country of Study: Switzerland.

No. of awards offered: Varies.

Application Procedure: Applicants must submit a completed application form with two references. Forms are available on request and from the website.

Closing Date: February 10th, July 17th or October 13th.

No. of awards given last year: Approx. 40.

No. of applicants last year: Approx. 80.

Additional Information: Selected students join a team working at CERN, and usually spend two years at the laboratory. CERN member states include Austria, Belgium, Bulgaria, the Czech Republic, Denmark, Finland, France, Germany, Greece, Hungary, Italy, the Netherlands, Norway, Poland, Portugal, Slovakia, Spain, Sweden, Switzerland and the United Kingdom.

CERN Fellowships

Subjects: Particle physics, applied science, computing or engineering.

Purpose: To support research in particle physics and development work in applied science, computing and engineering.

Eligibility: Applicants must be aged less than 33 and be nationals from Austria, Belgium, Bulgaria, the Czech Republic, Denmark, Finland, France, Germany, Greece, Hungary, Italy, the Netherlands, Norway, Poland, Portugal, Slovakia, Spain, Sweden, Switzerland or the United Kingdom. Fellows working in research in experimental or theoretical physics should normally hold a PhD, while Fellows in applied science, computing and engineering should usually hold a Master's degree. Candidates may apply a few months before obtaining their diploma.

Level of Study: Postdoctorate, Postgraduate.

Type: Fellowship.

Length of Study: One year, normally extended for a second year.

Frequency: Twice a year.

Study Establishment: The European Laboratory for Particle Physics.

Country of Study: Switzerland.

No. of awards offered: Approx. 100.

Application Procedure: Applicants must submit a completed application form, a curriculum vitae, a list of publications and three letters of recommendation.

Closing Date: The beginning of either March or September.

Funding: Government.

No. of awards given last year: Approx. 100.

No. of applicants last year: Approx. 430.

CERN Technical Student Programme

Subjects: Accelerator physics, computing, mathematics, engineering, geotechnics, instrumentation for accelerators and particle physics experiments, low temperature physics and superconductivity, materials science, radiation protection, environmental and safety engineering, solid state, surface physics and ultra-high vacuum.

Purpose: To provide placements for students who are specialising in different technical fields.

Eligibility: Open to applicants attending an educational establishment in a CERN member state and following a full-time course in one of the subjects listed in the subject index, at university or advanced technical level. Students must have completed at least 18 months of full-time studies or studies and training periods. Students must be less than 30 years of age at the time of the Selection Committee meeting. Candidates must be nationals of the member states of CERN. Students specialising in theoretical or experimental particle physics are not eligible for the programme.

Value: A subsistence allowance of swiss franc 3,130 per month to cover the expenses of a single person in the Geneva area. Students will also be covered for medical costs arising from illnesses and accidents of a professional and non professional nature. Travel expenses equivalent to a second class return rail fare to Geneva for one person may be paid.

Length of Study: Appointments will last for six consecutive months, but most one year appointments can start throughout the year.

Frequency: Three times each year.

Study Establishment: The European Laboratory for Particle Physics.

Country of Study: Switzerland.

No. of awards offered: Approx. 80-90.

Application Procedure: Applicants must submit a completed application form and separate assessments by two referees. The official CERN report on candidate form, duly completed by the supervisor of the student at the educational establishment, must be used as one of the assessments. Any additional academic information, eg. academic records, as well as a curriculum vitae would be welcome. Candidates should write for further information.

Closing Date: February 18th, July 17th or October 13th.

Funding: Government.

No. of awards given last year: Approx. 80-90.

No. of applicants last year: Approx. 240.

Additional Information: The official languages of CERN are English and French. A good knowledge of at least one of these languages is essential. CERN member states include Austria, Belgium, Bulgaria, the Czech Republic, Denmark, Finland, France, Germany, Greece, Hungary, Italy, the Netherlands, Norway, Poland, Portugal, Slovakia, Republic, Spain, Sweden, Switzerland and the United Kingdom.

CEU GRADUATE SCHOOL OF BUSINESS

NADOR UTCA 21, Budapest, 1051, Hungary
Tel: (36) 1 235 6117
Fax: (36) 1 327 3282
Email: tokat@gsb.ceu.hu
www: www.gsb.ceu.hu
Contact: Admissions Co-ordinator

CEU Graduate School of Business is the business school of the Central European University a private graduate school with its campus in Budapest, Hungary. Our American MBA degree is offered on a full and part-time basis. Our school also has an executive MBA and an MSc in it management.

Soros Scholarship

Subjects: MBA.

Purpose: To provide partial tuition scholarships to qualified candidates for the MBA degree from Central and Eastern Europe.

Eligibility: Open to candidates from the following countries: Albania, Armenia, Azerbaijan, Bulgaria, Croatia, Czech Republic, Estonia, Georgia, Hungary, Kazakhstan, Kyrgyzstan, Latvia, Lithuania, Moldova, Mongolia, Poland, Romania, the Russian Federation, Slovakia, Republic, Slovenia, Tajikistan, Turkmenistan, Ukraine, Uzbekistan or Yugoslavia.

Level of Study: MBA.

Type: Scholarship.

Value: Up to 66 per cent of tuition fees.

Length of Study: Up to four semesters.

Frequency: Dependent on funds available.

Study Establishment: The CEU Graduate School of Business.

Country of Study: Hungary.

Application Procedure: Applicants must complete an application form, available from the website.

Closing Date: Please contact the organisation.

Funding: Private.

Additional Information: Applicants should visit the website for further information www.gsb.ceu.hu.

For further information contact:

CEU Admissions Office, Nádor U. 9, Budapest, 1051, Hungary

CFS RESEARCH FOUNDATION

2 The Briars, Sarratt, Rickmansworth
WD3 6AU, England
Tel: (44) 1923 268641
Fax: (44) 1923 260352
Contact: Anne Faulkner, Honorary Director

The CFS Research Foundation was officially launched in 1993 to bring together the best minds to meet the challenge presented by chronic fatigue syndrome.

CFS Research Award
Subjects: Chronic Fatigue Syndrome.
Purpose: To support high quality research into chronic fatigue syndrome.
Level of Study: Postdoctorate.
Value: Variable.
Length of Study: Variable.
No. of awards offered: Variable.
Application Procedure: A brief synopsis should be sent to the Hon. Director (2x A4). If this falls within the remit the applicant will be sent an application form Research projects subject to peer review.
Closing Date: Apply any time.
Funding: Private.

THE CHARITABLE ASSISTANCE ADA FOUNDATION

211 East Chicago Avenue, Chicago, IL 60611-2678, United States of America
Tel: (1) 312 440 2567
Fax: (1) 312 440 2822
www: http://www.ada.org
Contact: Director

The purpose of the ADA Foundation Charitable Assistance Programs to provide a measure of financial assistance to certain groups of individuals who have a financial hardship, whether due to educational needs, chemical dependency, disability or disaster.

ADA Foundation Allied Dental Health Scholarship (Dental Hygiene, Dental Assisting, Dental Laboratory Technology)
Subjects: Dental hygiene, dental assisting and dental laboratory technology.
Purpose: To defray study expenses which include tuition, fees, books, supplies and living expenses.
Eligibility: Open to United States citizens only. Applicants must either be entering their first year (Dental Assisting) or final year (Dental Laboratory Technology and Dental Hygiene). Applicants must have a minimum grade point average of 3.0 based on a 4.0 scale and show financial need of at least US$1,000.
Level of Study: Professional development.
Type: Scholarship.
Value: US$1,000.
Frequency: Annual.
Country of Study: United States of America.
No. of awards offered: 15 dental hygiene, 10 dental assisting and five dental laboratory technology.
Application Procedure: Application forms are available from the dental hygiene, dental laboratory technology and dental assisting Programme Directors, and are distributed by school officials. Application forms must be original, typed, completed and signed with the assistance of school officials. Applicants must submit a completed application form, including the Academic Achievement Record Form and Financial Needs Assessment Form signed by school officials, two typed reference forms sealed and noted on the back of the envelopes by the referees and a typed biographical sketch.
Closing Date: August 15th for Dental Hygiene and Dental Laboratory Technology or September 15th for Dental Assisting.
Funding: Private.
Contributor: The ADA Foundation.
No. of awards given last year: 15 for dental hygiene, 10 for dental assisting and five for dental lab technology.
Additional Information: This scholarship is not renewable.

ADA Foundation Dental Student Scholarship
Subjects: Dentistry.
Purpose: To defray school expenses which include tuition, fees, books, supplies and living expenses.
Eligibility: Open to United States citizens only. Applicants must be full-time entering second year students enrolled in a dental school accredited by the Commission on Dental Accreditation of the American Dental Association. Applicants must have a minimum grade point average of 3.0 based on a 4.0 scale and show financial need of at least US$2,500.
Level of Study: Postgraduate.
Type: Scholarship.
Value: US$2,500.
Frequency: Annual.
Country of Study: United States of America.
No. of awards offered: 15-25.
Application Procedure: Application forms are available only at dental schools and are distributed by school officials. Forms must be original, typed, completed and signed with the assistance of school officials. Applicants must submit a completed application form, including the Academic Achievement Record Form and Financial Needs Assessment Form signed by school officials, two typed reference forms sealed and noted on the back of the envelopes by the referrers and a typed biographical sketch.
Closing Date: July 31st.
Funding: Private.
Contributor: The ADA Foundation.
No. of awards given last year: 25.
No. of applicants last year: 83.
Additional Information: This scholarship is not renewable.

ADA Foundation Minority Dental Student Scholarship
Subjects: Dentistry.
Purpose: To defray school expenses which include tuition, fees, books, supplies and living expenses.
Eligibility: Open to United States citizens only. Applicants must be a member of one of the following groups: black African American, Native American or Hispanic. Applicants must be full-time entering second year students enrolled in a dental school accredited by the Commission on Dental Accreditation of the American Dental Association. Applicants must have a minimum grade point average of 3.0 based on a 4.0 scale and show financial need of at least US$2,500.
Level of Study: Postgraduate.
Type: Scholarship.
Value: US$2,500.
Frequency: Annual.
Country of Study: United States of America.
No. of awards offered: 15-25.
Application Procedure: Application forms are available only at dental schools and are distributed by school officials. Forms must be original, typed, completed and signed with the assistance of school officials. Applicants must submit a completed application form, including the Academic Achievement Record Form and Financial Needs Assessment Form signed by school officials, two typed reference forms sealed and noted on the back of the envelopes by the referrers and a typed biographical sketch.
Closing Date: July 31st.
Funding: Private.
Contributor: Corporate sponsors and the ADA Foundation.
No. of awards given last year: 25.
No. of applicants last year: 45.
Additional Information: This scholarship is not renewable.

THE CHARLES A AND ANNE MORROW LINDBERGH FOUNDATION

2150 Third Avenue North Suite 310, Anoka, MN 55303-2200, United States of America
Tel: (1) 763 576 1596
Fax: (1) 763 576 1664
Email: info@lindberghfoundation.org
www: http://www.lindberghfoundation.org
Contact: Ms Shelley Nehl, Grants Co-ordinator

The Charles A and Anne Morrow Lindbergh Foundation is dedicated to furthering a balance between technological advancement and environmental preservation which was the Lindbergh's shared vision.

Lindbergh Grants

Subjects: Adaptive technology, waste minimisation and management, agriculture, aviation, aerospace, conservation of natural resources, humanities, education, arts, intercultural communication, exploration, biomedical research, health and population sciences.
Purpose: To provide grants to individuals whose initiative in a wide spectrum of disciplines seeks to actively further a better balance between technology and the natural environment.
Eligibility: Open to nationals of any country.
Level of Study: Research.
Type: Research grant.
Value: A maximum of US$10,580.
Length of Study: One year.
Frequency: Annual.
Country of Study: Any country.
No. of awards offered: Approx. 10.
Application Procedure: Applicants must complete an application form.
Closing Date: The second Tuesday in June.
Funding: Private.
Contributor: Individuals, corporations and foundations.
No. of awards given last year: 9.
No. of applicants last year: 163 o/c.

CHARLES BABBAGE INSTITUTE (CBI)

University of Minnesota, 211 Andersen Library, 222 21st Avenue South, Minneapolis, MN 55455, United States of America
Tel: (1) 612 624 5050
Fax: (1) 612 625 8054
Email: cbi@tc.umn.edu
www: http://www.cbi.umn.edu
Contact: Associate Director

The Charles Babbage Institute (CBI) is a research centre dedicated to promoting the study of the history of computing, its impact on society and preserving relevant documentation. CBI fosters research and writing in the history of computing by providing fellowship support, archival resources and information to scholars, computer scientists and the general public.

Adelle and Erwin Tomash Fellowship in the History of Information Processing

Subjects: The history of computing.
Purpose: To advance the professional development of historians in the field.
Eligibility: Open to graduate students whose dissertations deal with a historical aspect of information processing.
Level of Study: Doctorate.
Type: Fellowship.
Value: US$10,000 stipend plus up to US$2,000 to be used for tuition, fees, travel and other research expenses.
Length of Study: One year.
Frequency: Annual.
Country of Study: Any country.
No. of awards offered: One.
Application Procedure: Applicants must send their curriculum vitae, a five page statement and justification of the research problem, and a discussion of methods, research materials and evidence of faculty support for the project. Applicants should also arrange for three letters of reference and certified transcripts of graduate school credits to be sent directly to the Institute.
Closing Date: January 15th.
Funding: Private.

CHARLES DARWIN UNIVERSITY (CDU)

Research Branch, Darwin, NT 0909, Australia
Tel: (61) 8 8946 6405
Fax: (61) 8 8946 7075
Email: charles.webb@ntu.edu.au
www: http://www.ntu.edu.au
Contact: Professor Charles Webb

The Charles Darwin University (CDU) offers programmes from PhD to certificate level, incorporating the full range of vocational education courses. CDU has a distinctive research profile, reflecting the priorities appropriate to its location. It is a participating member of several CRCs and hosts the Centre for Indigenous and Natural Cultural Resource Management and the ARC Key Centre for Tropical Wildlife Management.

CDU Senior Research Fellowship

Subjects: Indigenous resource management, alternative energy, Aboriginal education, geographic information systems or remote sensing, tropical and desert environmental science including ecophysiology and environmental chemistry, tropical plant science, Southeast Asian studies, Aboriginal legal issues, Southeast Asian law, education in diverse contexts, tourism and hospitality, tropical aquaculture, tropical built environment, visual and performing arts of the Asia Pacific region and indigenous health and culture.
Purpose: To provide opportunities for outstanding researchers with proven international reputations to undertake research which is of both major importance in its field and of benefit to Australia.
Eligibility: All applicants must have an outstanding track record in a relevant field of research.
Level of Study: Postdoctorate.
Type: Fellowship.
Value: Australian $66,178-76,308 per year plus allowances, and Australian $20,000 establishment grant.
Length of Study: Three years.
Frequency: Dependent on funds available.
Study Establishment: CDU.
Country of Study: Australia.
Application Procedure: Applicants must contact the Research Branch at the University for application forms, which are also available from the website.
Closing Date: As advised.
Funding: Private.
Contributor: The University.

CDU Three Year Postdoctoral Fellowship

Subjects: Indigenous resource management, and desert alternative energy, Aboriginal education, geographic information systems or remote sensing, tropical and desert environmental science including ecophysiology and environmental chemistry, tropical plant science, Southeast Asian studies, Aboriginal legal issues, Southeast Asian law, education in diverse contexts, tourism and hospitality, tropical aquaculture, tropical built environment, visual and performing arts of the Asia Pacific region and indigenous health and culture.
Purpose: To foster research in designated areas of research strength and developing priority.
Eligibility: All applicants must have completed their PhD within five years of the date of application.
Level of Study: Postdoctorate.
Type: Fellowship.
Value: Australian $47,809-51,321 per year plus allowances, and Australian $3,500 per year research support.
Length of Study: Three years.
Frequency: Dependent on funds available.
Study Establishment: CDU.

Country of Study: Australia.
Application Procedure: Applicants must contact the Research Branch at the University for application forms, which are also available from the website.
Closing Date: As advised.
Funding: Private.
Contributor: The University.

CHARLES H HOOD FOUNDATION

95 Berkeley Street, Suite 201, Boston, MA 02116, United States of America
Tel: (1) 617 695 9439
Fax: (1) 617 423 4619
Email: mail@tmfnet.org
www: http://www.tmfnet.org/guidelines.html
Contact: Ms Gay Lockwood, Grants Administrator

Charles H Hood Foundation Child Health Research Grant
Subjects: The initiation and furtherance of medical research which will help to diminish health problems affecting large numbers of children.
Purpose: To assist junior faculty who are initiating independent research in paediatrics health and have limited federal grant experience.
Eligibility: Awards can be given to the New England states of Maine, Vermont, New Hampshire, Massachusetts, Rhode Island and Connecticut only.
Level of Study: Research.
Type: Research grant.
Value: US$75,000 per year or US$150,000 over two years.
Length of Study: Two years.
Frequency: Annual.
Country of Study: United States of America.
No. of awards offered: 10 per year.
Application Procedure: These must be completed and submitted along with letters of recommendation, a curriculum vitae, a non technical summary, a scientific summary and an itemised budget. Applicants should visit the website for further information www.tmfnet.org/guidelines.html.
Closing Date: April and October. Exact dates vary each year.
Funding: Private.
Contributor: The Charles H Hood Foundation.
No. of awards given last year: 10.
No. of applicants last year: 52.

CHAUTAUQUA INSTITUTION

Box 1098, Department Schools Office, Chautauqua, NY 14722, United States of America
Tel: (1) 716 357 6233
Fax: (1) 716 357 9014
www: http://www.ciweb.org
Contact: Vice President of Programming

The Chautauqua Institution was founded in 1874. It is a is a non-profit organisation which offers nine week summer schools for the arts, education, religion and recreation.

Chautauqua Institution Awards
Subjects: Instrumental piano and vocal music, theatre, art and dance.
Purpose: To assist talented advanced students enrolled in the Chautauqua summer programme of fine and performing arts.
Eligibility: Open to candidates of any gender, nationality and age who participate in the Chautauqua Summer Schools.
Level of Study: Postgraduate.
Type: Award.
Value: US$400-3,000.
Length of Study: Seven-eight weeks.
Frequency: Annual.
Study Establishment: The Chautauqua Institution.
Country of Study: United States of America.
No. of awards offered: Varies.

Closing Date: 10 days before the live audition, March 1st for taped auditions, and April 1st for art portfolio of slides.
Funding: Private.
Contributor: Various.
Additional Information: Walk ins are accepted for the live auditions. Most scholarships are given in music. No travel grants are provided.

CHEMICAL HERITAGE FOUNDATION (CHF)

315 Chestnut Street, Philadelphia, PA 19106-2702, United States of America
Tel: (1) 215 925 2222
Fax: (1) 215 925 1954
Email: fellowships@chemheritage.org
www: http://www.chemheritage.org
Contact: Mr Josh McIlvain, Staff Researcher & Fellowship Co-ordinator

The Beckman Center for the History of Chemistry is the historical unit of the Chemical Heritage Foundation (CHF), which is located in Philadelphia. The center is devoted to preserving, making known, and applying the history of the chemical and molecular sciences technologies, and associated industries.

Charles C Price Fellowship
Purpose: Open to scholars pursuing research on the history of the chemical sciences; preference given to projects in the history of polymers.
Type: Fellowship.
Length of Study: 1 Academic year.
No. of awards offered: 1.
Application Procedure: Please visit: www.chemheritage.org.
Closing Date: January 15, 2004.

Edelstein International Fellowship
Subjects: The history of chemical sciences and technology.
Purpose: To support study in the field.
Eligibility: Open to established Scholars.
Level of Study: Postgraduate.
Type: Fellowship.
Value: Varies.
Length of Study: One academic year.
Frequency: Annual.
Study Establishment: CHF and the Edelstein Centre for History and Philosophy of Science, Technology and Medicine in Jerusalem.
No. of awards offered: 1.
Application Procedure: Applicants must submit a letter of application which demonstrates how the CHF collection, other Philadelphia resources and the Edelstein Collection are relevant to the applicant's research. All applications must be sent to Josh McIlvain at the main address.
Closing Date: January 15th.
Funding: Private.

Edelstein International Studentship
Subjects: The history of the chemical sciences and technology.
Purpose: To support dissertation research and writing.
Eligibility: Candidates must have completed all requirements for a PhD except the dissertation.
Level of Study: Predoctorate.
Type: Studentship.
Length of Study: One academic year.
Frequency: Annual.
Study Establishment: CHF and the Edelstein Centre for History and Philosophy of Science, Technology and Medicine in Jerusalem.
No. of awards offered: 1.
Application Procedure: Applicants must send letters of application that demonstrate how the CHF collection, other Philadelphia resources and the Edelstein Collection are relevant to the applicant's research. Each application must include a budget for the project. All applications must be addressed to Josh McIlvain at the main address.
Closing Date: January 15th.

Glenn E and Barbara Hodsdon Ullyot Scholarship

Subjects: The history of science.
Purpose: To advance understanding of the importance of the chemical sciences to the public's welfare.
Level of Study: Postgraduate.
Type: Scholarship.
Length of Study: A minimum of two months.
Frequency: Annual.
No. of awards offered: 1.
Application Procedure: Applicants must submit a completed application form, a one page description of the proposed research and an outline of a specific product as an outcome of the scholarship. Application forms are available on request.
Closing Date: January 15th.

Gordon Cain Fellowship

Subjects: The history of the development of the chemical industries. The outcome of the research should further the understanding of the relationship between technology, policy, management and entrepreneurship and should shed light on the complex development of modern society and commerce.
Purpose: To support historical research.
Eligibility: Open to a scholar with a PhD who will carry out historical research on the development of the chemical industries.
Level of Study: Postgraduate.
Type: Fellowship.
Value: Varies.
Length of Study: One academic year.
Frequency: Annual.
Application Procedure: Applications must include a proposal of no more than 1,000 words outlining the applicant's research project with specific reference to how the work advances scholarship and how the outcome might be published. All applications must be sent to Josh McIlvain at the main address.
Closing Date: January 15th.

Société de Chimie Industrielle (American Section) Fellowship

Subjects: The history of science.
Purpose: To stimulate public understanding of the chemical industries, using both terms in their widest sense.
Eligibility: Applications are encouraged from writers, journalists, educators and historians of science, technology and business.
Level of Study: Postgraduate.
Type: Fellowship.
Length of Study: A minimum of three months.
Frequency: Annual.
Study Establishment: Chemical Heritage Foundation.
Country of Study: United States of America.
No. of awards offered: 1.
Application Procedure: Applicants must submit a one page research proposal outlining the specific project to be completed while in residence at CHF, and showing how the project will further public understanding of the chemical industries.
Closing Date: February 15th.
Funding: Private.

CHEMICAL INSTITUTE OF CANADA

Suite 550, 130 Slater Street, Ottawa
ON, K1P 6E2, Canada
Tel: (1) 613 232 6252 ext. 235
Fax: (1) 613 232 5862
Email: jtrohon@cheminst.ca
www: http://www.cheminst.ca
Contact: Ms Julie Trohon, Conferences & Awards Co-ordinator

The Chemical Institute of Canada (CIC) is an umbrella organisation for three constituent societies namely the Canadian Society for Chemistry, the Canadian Society for Chemical Engineering and the Canadian Society for Chemical Technology. The purpose of the Institute is to promote common scientific and technical interests and to provide service to all its members.

CIC Award for Environmental Improvement

Subjects: Environmental pollution, treatment and remediation.
Purpose: To award a company, individual, team or organisation in Canada for a significant achievement in pollution prevention, treatment or remediation in Canada.
Level of Study: Professional development.
Type: Award.
Value: A plaque and certificate for each nominated individual and travel assistance of up to Canadian $500.
Frequency: Annual, if funds are available.
Country of Study: Canada.
No. of awards offered: One.
Application Procedure: Applicants must be nominated.
Closing Date: July 1st.
Funding: Private.
Contributor: The Environment Division.

CIC Catalysis Award

Subjects: Chemistry.
Purpose: To recognise an individual who has made a distinguished contribution to the field of catalysis while resident in Canada.
Level of Study: Professional development.
Type: Award.
Value: A rhodium plated silver medal and travel expenses to present the Award Lecture.
Frequency: Every two years.
Country of Study: Canada.
No. of awards offered: One.
Application Procedure: Applicants must be nominated.
Closing Date: October 1st.
Funding: Private.

CIC Macromolecular Science and Engineering Lecture Award

Subjects: Macromolecular science or engineering.
Purpose: To recognise an individual who has made a distinguished contribution to macromolecular science or engineering.
Level of Study: Professional development.
Type: Award.
Value: A framed scroll, a cash prize of Canadian $1,500 and travel expenses.
Frequency: Annual.
Country of Study: Canada.
No. of awards offered: One.
Application Procedure: Applicants must be nominated.
Closing Date: July 1st.
Funding: Private.
Contributor: NOVA Chemicals Limited.
No. of awards given last year: One.

CIC Medal

Subjects: Chemistry and chemical engineering.
Purpose: To recognise a person who has made an outstanding contribution to the science of chemistry or chemical engineering in Canada.
Level of Study: Professional development.
Type: Award.
Value: A palladium medal and travel expenses.
Frequency: Annual.
Country of Study: Canada.
No. of awards offered: One.
Application Procedure: Applicants must be nominated.
Closing Date: July 1st.
Funding: Private.
Contributor: INCO Limited.
No. of awards given last year: One.

CIC Montreal Medal

Subjects: Chemistry and chemical engineering.
Purpose: To honour a person who has shown significant leadership in or has made an outstanding contribution to the profession of chemistry or chemical engineering in Canada.

Eligibility: Open to administrative contributions within the Chemical Institute of Canada and other professional organisations which contribute to the advancement of the professions of chemistry and chemical engineering. Contributions to the sciences of chemistry and chemical engineering are not considered.
Level of Study: Professional development.
Type: Award.
Value: A medal and travel expenses if required.
Frequency: Annual.
Country of Study: Canada.
No. of awards offered: One.
Application Procedure: Applicants must be nominated.
Closing Date: July 1st.
Contributor: Montreal CIC Local Section.

CIC Pestcon Graduate Scholarship

Subjects: Any area of pesticide research including alternative pest control strategies.
Purpose: To support postgraduate work.
Eligibility: Open to Canadian citizens, including landed immigrants, for graduate study in any area of pesticide and contaminant research. Preference will be given to students already in their second year of a PhD programme.
Level of Study: Postgraduate.
Type: Scholarship.
Value: Canadian $3,000 in two instalments.
Length of Study: One year.
Frequency: Annual.
Country of Study: Canada.
No. of awards offered: One.
Application Procedure: Applicants must submit a written application including a curriculum vitae and a brief description of no more than 500 words of the research programme undertaken and the progress to date. Applications must be accompanied by an official transcript of the candidate's academic records, the names of their supervisors and a second academic referee.
Closing Date: July 1st.
Contributor: The fifth International Congress of Pesticide Chemistry.

CIC The Bayer, Inc. Award for High School Chemistry Teachers

Subjects: Chemistry.
Purpose: To recognise excellence in the teaching of chemistry at secondary level. This award pays tribute to outstanding contributions in high school chemistry teaching, stimulates interest in the CIC among teachers and facilitates the Institute's efforts to improve chemistry teaching at the high school level.
Level of Study: Professional development.
Type: Award.
Value: A cash prize of Canadian $500 and one year of membership of the CIC.
Frequency: Annual.
Study Establishment: Any secondary school.
Country of Study: Canada.
No. of awards offered: Up to two.
Application Procedure: Applicants must be nominated.
Closing Date: December 1st.
Funding: Private.
Contributor: Bayer, Inc.

CIC Union Carbide Award for Chemical Education

Subjects: Chemistry and chemical engineering.
Purpose: To recognise a person who has made outstanding contributions in Canada to education at any level in the field of chemistry or chemical engineering.
Level of Study: Professional development.
Type: Award.
Value: A framed scroll, a cash prize of Canadian $1,000 and up to Canadian $400 travel expenses.
Frequency: Annual.
Country of Study: Canada.
No. of awards offered: One.

Application Procedure: Applicants must be nominated.
Closing Date: July 1st.
Funding: Private.

THE CHICAGO TRIBUNE

Tribune Books, 435 North Michigan Avenue, Chicago, IL 60611, United States of America
Tel: (1) 312 222 4429
Fax: (1) 312 222 3751
www: http://www.chicagotribune.com
Contact: Nelson Algren Awards

The Chicago Tribune is the midwest's leading newspaper. The Chicago Tribune literary Awards are part of a continued dedication to readers, writers and ideas.

Heartland Prizes

Subjects: A novel and a book of non fiction embodying the spirit of the nation's heartland.
Purpose: To recognise works that reinforce and perpetuate the values of heartland America.
Eligibility: The awards are not limited to Mid Western writers or regional subjects.
Level of Study: Professional development.
Type: Prize.
Frequency: Annual.
Country of Study: United States of America.
Application Procedure: Applicants must write for details.
Funding: Corporation.

Nelson Algren Awards

Subjects: Short fiction.
Purpose: To award writers of short fiction.
Eligibility: Submissions must be written by an American, be unpublished and 2,500-10,000 words in length.
Level of Study: Unrestricted.
Type: Award.
Frequency: Annual.
Country of Study: Any country.
No. of awards offered: Four.
Application Procedure: Applicants must send a self addressed, postage paid envelope, with a request for written guidelines. The competition will begin accepting entries from November 1st.
Funding: Corporation.

CHIHUAHUAN DESERT RESEARCH INSTITUTE

Box 905, Fort Davis, TX 79734, United States of America
Tel: (1) 915 364 2499
Fax: (1) 915 364 2504
Email: manager@cdri.org
www: http://www.cdri.org
Contact: Executive Director

The Chihuahuan Desert Research Institute is a non-profit scientific and educational organisation.

W Frank Blair Award

Subjects: The natural sciences and the Chihuahuan Desert Region.
Purpose: To support and promote excellence in written data presentation.
Eligibility: Students must be enrolled when the application is made.
Level of Study: Doctorate, Graduate, Postgraduate.
Type: Prize.
Value: US$500.
Frequency: Annual.
No. of awards offered: One.
Application Procedure: Applicants must contact the Institute for application instructions or see the website for more details.
Funding: Private.

CHILDREN'S LITERATURE ASSOCIATION (CHLA)

PO Box 138, Battle Creek, MI 49016-0138, United States of America
Tel: (1) 269 965 8180
Fax: (1) 269 965 3568
Email: kkiessling@childlitassn.org
www: http://www.childlitassn.org
Contact: Ms Kathryn Kiessling, Administrator

The Children's Literature Association (ChLA) is a non-profit organisation devoted to promoting serious scholarship and criticism in children's literature.

ChLA Beiter Scholarships for Graduate Students

Subjects: Children's literature.
Purpose: To fund proposals of original scholarship with the expectation that the undertaking will lead to a publication or a conference presentation and contribute to the field.
Eligibility: Winners must be, or become, members of the Children's Literature Association. Students of the ChLA Executive Board members or Scholarship Committee members are not eligible to apply. Previous recipients are not eligible to reapply until the third year from the date of the first award.
Level of Study: Doctorate, Graduate, Postdoctorate.
Type: Scholarship.
Value: From US$250-1,000 which may be used to purchase supplies and materials eg. books and videos, and as research support eg. photocopying, or to underwrite travel to special collections or libraries.
Frequency: Annual.
Country of Study: Any country.
No. of awards offered: One-four.
Application Procedure: Applicants must send five copies of their contact details including email address, academic institution and status, the expected date of their degree, a detailed description of the research proposal, a curriculum vitae and three letters of reference, one of which must be from the applicant's dissertation or thesis advisor.
Closing Date: February 1st.
Funding: Private.
No. of awards given last year: One.
No. of applicants last year: Five.
Additional Information: Applicants should visit the website for further details. If applicants wish to receive guidelines by mail, a stamped addressed envelope must be provided.

ChLA Research Fellowships and Scholarships

Subjects: Children's literature.
Purpose: To award proposals dealing with criticism or original scholarship with the expectation that the undertaking will lead to publication and make a significant contribution to the field of children's literature in the area of scholarship or criticism.
Eligibility: Applicants must be, or become, members of the Children's Literature Association.
Level of Study: Unrestricted.
Type: Other.
Value: Up to US$1,000. Individual awards may range from US$250-1,000 and may be used only for research related expenses such as travel to special collections or materials and supplies. Funds are not intended for work leading to the completion of a professional degree.
Frequency: Annual.
Country of Study: Any country.
No. of awards offered: One-four.
Application Procedure: Applicants must send five copies of the application in English including three letters of reference and a curriculum vitae. Applications must include the applicant's name, address, telephone number and email address, details of the academic institution the applicant is affiliated with and a detailed description of the research proposal, not exceeding three single spaced pages, and indicating the nature and significance of the project, where it will be carried out and the expected date of completion.
Closing Date: February 1st.
Funding: Private.

No. of awards given last year: One.
No. of applicants last year: Two.
Additional Information: In honour of the achievement and dedication of Dr Margaret P Esmonde, proposals that deal with critical or original work in the areas of science fantasy or science fiction for children or adolescents will be awarded the Margaret P Esmonde Memorial Scholarship. Applicants should visit the website for further details. If applicants wish to receive guidelines by mail, a stamped addressed envelope must be provided.

CHILDREN'S LIVER DISEASE FOUNDATION

36 Great Charles Street
Birmingham, B3 3JY, England
Tel: (44) 121 212 3839
Fax: (44) 121 212 4300
Email: cldf@childliverdisease.org
www: http://www.childliverdisease.org
Contact: The Grants Administrator

In 1980, the Children's Liver Disease Foundation was the first charity to be established concerned with liver disease. Today it leads the field in caring for babies and children with liver disease and their families.

CLDF Research Grant

Subjects: Liver disease, including medical and social.
Purpose: To support postgraduate research into liver disease in children.
Eligibility: All medical professionals.
Level of Study: Postdoctorate, Postgraduate, Research.
Type: Grant.
Value: Maximum £170,000.
Frequency: Annual.
Country of Study: United Kingdom.
No. of awards offered: Variable.
Application Procedure: Applicants are strong by advised to check the guidelines for relevant funding policies at the time of application.
Funding: Private.

CHILDREN'S MEDICAL RESEARCH INSTITUTE

Locked Bag 23, Wentworthville
NSW 2145, Australia
Tel: (61) 2 9687 2800
Fax: (61) 2 9687 2120
Email: prowe@cmri.usyd.edu.au
www: http://www.cmri.com.au
Contact: Professor P B Rowe, Director

The Children's Medical Research Institute is an independent research institute affiliated with the University of Sydney and the New Children's Hospital. Supported by grants and a state government infrastructure grant, it conducts basic research in the fields of vertebrate development, cellular immortalisation and oncogenesis, cellular signalling and gene therapy.

Childrens Medical Research Institute Graduate Scholarships and Postgraduate Fellowships

Subjects: Muscle genetics, the exploration of the role of genetic control systems in myogenesis and cytoarchitecture, neurosciences, the study of the physical properties and genetic control of neuronal development, oncogenesis, the role of oncogenes in leukaemogenesis and mechanisms of cellular immortalisation, embryology, cell fate designation at gastrulation, gene imprinting, gene therapy, genevector design for the treatment of inherited and acquired disease, cell signalling and membrane biology in neurotransmission.
Purpose: To allow individuals to undertake research.
Eligibility: Open to Australian permanent residents with suitable qualifications, usually an Honours Degree for postgraduate studies.

Level of Study: Postdoctorate, Postgraduate.
Type: Other.
Value: The award value is based on the National Health and Medical Research Council of Australia scale together with a Sydney loading.
Length of Study: Three-five years.
Frequency: Annual.
Study Establishment: A biomedical research institute affiliated to the University of Sydney.
Country of Study: Australia.
No. of awards offered: Up to four postgraduate scholarships and two postdoctoral fellowships.
Application Procedure: Applicants must submit a letter outlining their background, interests and referees. No application form is required.
Closing Date: Enrolment is in January or August.
Funding: Government, Private.
Contributor: An investment trust.
No. of awards given last year: Six.
No. of applicants last year: 32.
Additional Information: There are no course requirements.

Childrens Medical Research Institute Postdoctoral Fellowship

Subjects: Biophysics and molecular biology, embryology and reproduction biology, genetics and neurosciences.
Purpose: To allow individuals to obtain further professional training in their field of interest.
Eligibility: Open to qualified applicants of any nationality, who must meet temporary visa requirements. Knowledge of English is essential.
Level of Study: Postdoctorate.
Type: Fellowship.
Value: Varies depending on experience, but is generally Australian $47,000 for a first year PhD.
Length of Study: Up to three years.
Frequency: Dependent on funds available.
Study Establishment: A research centre.
Country of Study: Australia.
No. of awards offered: Two.
Application Procedure: Applicants must submit a letter of intent with a curriculum vitae, transcript, references and any other appropriate documentation.
Closing Date: Applications are accepted at any time.
Funding: Government, Private.
Contributor: Investment Trust.
No. of awards given last year: Two.
No. of applicants last year: 20.

Childrens Medical Research Institute Postgraduate Scholarship

Subjects: Biophysics and molecular biology, embryology and reproduction biology, genetics and neurosciences.
Purpose: To support research based study for the award of degrees of PhD or MSc (Med) at the University of Sydney.
Eligibility: Open to Australian residents only.
Level of Study: Doctorate, Postgraduate.
Type: Scholarship.
Value: More than Australian $18,500 per year.
Length of Study: Three-four years.
Frequency: Dependent on funds available.
Study Establishment: A research centre.
Country of Study: Australia.
No. of awards offered: Up to four.
Application Procedure: Applicants must submit a letter of interest with a curriculum vitae, transcript, references and any other appropriate support documents. There is no application form.
Closing Date: Enrolment takes place twice a year in January and August.
Funding: Government, Private.
Contributor: Investment Trust.
No. of awards given last year: Four.
No. of applicants last year: 12.

CHINESE AMERICAN MEDICAL SOCIETY (CAMS)

281 Edgewood Avenue, Teaneck, NJ 07666, United States of America
Tel: (1) 201 833 1506
Fax: (1) 201 833 8252
Email: hw5@columbia.edu
www: http://www.camsociety.org
Contact: Dr H H Wang, Executive Director

The Chinese American Medical Society (CAMS) is a non-profit, charitable, educational and scientific society that aims to promote the scientific association of medical professionals of Chinese descent. It also aims to advance medical knowledge and scientific research with emphasis on aspects unique to the Chinese and to promote the health status of Chinese Americans. The Society makes scholarships available to medical dental students and provides summer fellowships for students conducting research in health problems related to the Chinese.

CAMS Scholarship

Subjects: Medical or dental studies.
Purpose: To help defray the cost of study.
Eligibility: Open to Chinese Americans, or Chinese who are residing in the United States of America. Applicants must be full-time medical or dental students at approved schools within the United States of America and must be able to show academic proficiency and financial hardship.
Level of Study: Doctorate.
Type: Scholarship.
Value: US$1,000-1,500.
Frequency: Annual.
Country of Study: United States of America.
No. of awards offered: Three-five.
Application Procedure: Applicants must complete an application form and send it together with a letter for the Dean of Students verifying good standing, two to three letters of recommendation, a personal statement, a curriculum vitae and a financial statement.
Closing Date: March 31st.
Funding: Private.
Contributor: Membership and fund-raising.
No. of awards given last year: Five.
No. of applicants last year: 30.

CHOIRS ONTARIO

112 St Clair Avenue West Suite 403, Toronto, ON, M4V 2Y3, Canada
Tel: (1) 416 923 1144
Fax: (1) 416 929 0415
Email: choirs.ontario@sympatico.ca
www: http://www.choirsontario.org
Contact: General Manager

Choirs Ontario serves and supports those who gather together to sing. It is dedicated to the promotion of choral activities regardless of genre, language of performance or size of vocal ensemble. The organisation aims to provide services to choirs, conductors, choristers, composers, administrators and educators, and all those who have a passion for choral music.

Leslie Bell Prize

Subjects: Choral music, particularly conducting.
Purpose: To reward an emerging new conductor.
Eligibility: Open to Canadian citizens or landed immigrants who are permanent residents of the province of Ontario.
Level of Study: Postgraduate.
Type: Prize.
Value: Canadian $7,000.
Frequency: Every two years (even-numbered years), .
Country of Study: Any country.
No. of awards offered: One.
Closing Date: There are various deadlines.

Ruth Watson Henderson Choral Composition Competition

Subjects: Choral music, particularly composition.
Purpose: To award new choral composition.
Eligibility: Candidates must be Canadian citizens or landed immigrants who are permanent residents of Ontario.
Level of Study: Postgraduate.
Type: Prize.
Value: Canadian $1,000.
Frequency: Every two years (even-numbered years), .
Country of Study: Any country.
No. of awards offered: One.
Closing Date: There are various deadlines.
Funding: Private.

CHRISTOPHER REEVE PARALYSIS FOUNDATION (CRPF)

500 Morris Avenue, Springfield, NJ 07081, United States of America
Tel: (1) 973 379 2690
Fax: (1) 973 912 9433
Email: dlandsman@crpf.org
www: http://www.ChristopherReeve.org
Contact: Ms Jennifer L Newman, Director of Individual Grants

The Christopher Reeve Paralysis Foundation (CRPF) is committed to funding research that develops treatments and cures for paralysis caused by spinal cord injury and other central nervous system disorders. The Foundation also vigorously works to improve the quality of life for people living with disabilities through its grants programme, paralysis resource centre and advocacy efforts.

CRPF Research Grant

Subjects: Spinal Cord Injury related research.
Purpose: To fund research which will lead to effective treatments and ultimately a cure for spinal cord injury.
Eligibility: Open to American and international investigators located at institutions that have clearly established lines of accountability and fiscal responsibility. Institutional assurances regarding animal research and human subjects are required.
Level of Study: Postdoctorate, Research.
Type: Research grant.
Value: US$75,000 per year for a total maximum of US$150,000.
Length of Study: A maximum of two years.
Frequency: Annual, Semi-annual (2 × /year).
Country of Study: Any country.
No. of awards offered: Usually 40 per year. Varies from year to year depending on the level of science and the amount of funds available.
Application Procedure: Applicants must complete an application form and forward 7 copies of it to the Foundation. Forms are available from the website.
Closing Date: December 15th and June 15th.
Funding: Private.
Contributor: Private sector donations.
No. of awards given last year: 40.
No. of applicants last year: 200.
Additional Information: The intent of these awards is to promote innovative and ground breaking work, not to provide ongoing long-term support. CRPF funds activities that hold promise of identifying therapies for paralysis. Areas of research that are the focus of current CRPF emphasis and funding include strategies that may promote neural growth and survival, encourage the formation of synapses, enhance production of myelin, conduction capabilities, or may otherwise lead to restoration of the compromised circuitry in the acutely and chronically injured CNS. Research that evaluates the efficiency of drugs and other interventions that protect against secondary injury or provides insight into the mechanisms causing such damage, and defines anatomical characteristics of SCI in well defined animal models and in the human spine is also encouraged as is work that specifically documents the neural systems that are most vulnerable to SCI and functional losses occurring as a result, biological mechanisms underlying approaches to improve function, eg. bladder function and sexual function, and alleviates chronic pain and spasticity.

CHRONIC DISEASE RESEARCH FOUNDATION (CDRF)

St Thomas' Hospital, 1st Floor, South Wing, Lambeth Palace Road, London, SE1 7EH, England
Tel: (44) 20 7633 9990
Fax: (44) 20 7922 8154
Email: christel.barnetson@cdrf.org.uk
www: http://www.cdrf.org.uk
Contact: Ms Christel Barnetson, Chief Administrator

The Chronic Disease Research Foundation (CDRF) was set up to look at new ways of exploring the genetics of diseases associated with ageing. Its mission is to target those common diseases such as osteoporosis, arthritis, back pain, migraine, asthma and diabetes which we inherit from our parents, and prevent and alleviate them now and for future generations. Its principle focus is on comparative studies of identical and non identical twins, undertaken at the Twin Research Unit of St Thomas' Hospital.

CDRF Project Grants

Subjects: The genetic basis of diseases associates with ageing.
Purpose: To carry out comparative studies of identical and non identical twins to pinpoint the genetic cause of common diseases associated with ageing.
Level of Study: Postgraduate, Research.
Type: Project grant.
Value: UK£30,000-150,000.
Length of Study: Two-three years.
Frequency: Dependent on funds available.
Country of Study: United Kingdom.
No. of awards offered: Dependent on availability of funds.
Application Procedure: Applicants must submit a preliminary proposal of no more than one side of A4 including an outline of the proposal, a list of principle aims and objectives, and scale of funding. Provided the CDRFs panel of experts consider the project to be of relevance, applicants must then submit a full grant proposal.
Funding: Private.
No. of awards given last year: None.

CDRF Research Fellowship

Subjects: The genetic basis of disease associated with ageing.
Purpose: To promote postgraduate education and enable the charity to carry out further research projects.
Level of Study: Postgraduate, Research.
Type: Fellowship.
Value: UK£30,000-175,000.
Length of Study: Two-five years.
Frequency: Dependent on funds available.
Country of Study: United Kingdom.
No. of awards offered: Dependent on availability of funds.
Application Procedure: Applicants must submit a preliminary proposal of no more than one side of A4 including an outline of proposal, a list of principal aims and objectives, and scale of funding. If CDRFs panel of experts consider the project to be of relevance, applicants must then submit a full grant proposal.
Funding: Private.
No. of awards given last year: 2.

CHRONIC GRANULOMATOUS DISORDER (CGD) RESEARCH TRUST

Manor Farm, Wimborne St Giles
Dorset, BH21 5NL, England
Tel: (44) 1725 517977
Fax: (44) 1725 517977
Contact: Ms Rosemary Rymer, General Secretary

The Chronic Granulomatous Disorder (CGD) Research Trust exists to boost research that will lead to improved treatments and a cure for this rare, genetic blood disorder. The Trust encourages the dissemination of knowledge among medical professionals. It produces information for professionals and for affected people, provides moral support and a point of contact for affected people, and works to raise public awareness.

CGD Research Trust Grants

Subjects: Topics pertaining to the cause, inheritance, management and symptoms of chronic granulomatous disorder.
Purpose: To support thorough research which aims to increase understanding of the cause, inheritance, management and symptoms of chronic granulomatous disorder and to disseminate the useful results of such research.
Level of Study: Doctorate, Postgraduate, Predoctorate, Research.
Type: Other.
Value: Varies according to type.
Length of Study: Usually one-three years depending on the programme.
Frequency: Annual.
Application Procedure: Grants are advertised annually every April in Nature. Applicants must initially submit a one page outline. A number of these are then invited to complete full applications. These are then subject to a peer review. The medical panel then make recommendations and trustees announce grant offers the following January.
Closing Date: Usually the end of August.
Funding: Private.
Contributor: Voluntary donations.
No. of awards given last year: Three.
No. of applicants last year: Eight.

CIIT - CENTERS FOR HEALTH RESEARCH

Human Resources, PO Box 12137
Research Triangle Park, NC 27709
United States of America
Tel: (1) 919 558 1331
Fax: (1) 919 558 1430
Email: bramlage@ciit.org
www: http://www.ciit.org
Contact: Rusty Bramlage, Human Resources

Founded in 1974, the CIIT - Centers for Health Research is a non-profit toxicology research institute dedicated to providing an improved scientific basis for understanding and assessing the potential adverse effects of chemicals, pharmaceuticals and consumer products on human health. Many CIIT researchers are on the faculties of the University of North Carolina at Chapel Hill, North Carolina State University in Raleigh, and Duke University in Durham, the three institutions that form North Carolina's Research Triangle. CIIT is supported by 36 major companies and the American Chemistry Council.

CIIT - Centers for Health Research Postdoctoral Fellowships

Subjects: Toxicology, including genetic toxicology, biochemical toxicology, pathology, teratology, carcinogenesis, inhalation toxicology, risk assessment and molecular biology.
Purpose: To support persons during further training in toxicology.
Eligibility: Open to those who hold a recently awarded PhD degree in a discipline related to toxicology. Applicants holding a recently awarded DVM or MD degree are expected to have substantial research experience. Candidates on the J-1 Exchange Visitor Program are approved.
Level of Study: Postdoctorate.
Type: Fellowship.
Value: Varies, from US$40,000 depending upon the number of years of experience.
Length of Study: Two-three years.
Frequency: Annual.
Study Establishment: CIIT.
Country of Study: United States of America.
No. of awards offered: Varies.

Application Procedure: Applicants must apply for information, available on request or from the website.
Closing Date: Applications are accepted at any time.
Funding: Private.
Contributor: CIIT.
No. of awards given last year: 8.
No. of applicants last year: 19.
Additional Information: Fellowships are granted only for conduct of research at the Institute's facility in Research Triangle Park, NC.

CIIT - Centers for Health Research Predoctoral Traineeships

Subjects: Fields related to toxicology including biochemistry, pharmacology, chemistry, zoology and biology, etc.
Purpose: To support persons enrolled in a programme of study leading to a doctoral degree. Trainees will pursue a Ph.D. while conducting dissertation research at CIIT.
Eligibility: Open to persons who have been accepted into a course of graduate study in a subject related to toxicology by a degree granting institution.
Level of Study: Predoctorate.
Type: Fellowship.
Value: US$8,000-12,000 per year, plus tuition and fees.
Length of Study: Three-four years.
Frequency: Annual.
Study Establishment: The University of North Carolina at Chapel Hill, North Carolina State University or Duke University in the Research Triangle area, for the duration of the programme.
Country of Study: United States of America.
No. of awards offered: Four-six.
Application Procedure: Applicants must apply for information, available on request or from website.
Closing Date: Applications are accepted at any time.
Funding: Private.
Contributor: CIIT.
No. of awards given last year: 2.
No. of applicants last year: 9.
Additional Information: Preference is given to individuals who wish to conduct their dissertation research at CIIT in conjunction with local university programmes of study.

CLARA HASKIL COMPETITION

Case postale 234, rue du Conseil 31, 1800 Vevey, CH-1800, Switzerland
Tel: (41) 21 922 6704
Fax: (41) 21 922 6734
Email: clara.haskil@bluewin.ch
www: http://www.regart.ch/clara-haskil
Contact: Mr Patrick Peikert, Director

The Clara Haskil Association exists to recognise and help a young pianist whose approach to piano interpretation is of the same spirit which constantly inspired Clara Haskil, and that she illustrated so perfectly.

Clara Haskil Competition

Subjects: Piano performance.
Purpose: To recognise and financially help a young pianist.
Eligibility: Open to pianists of any nationality and either sex, who are no more than 27 years of age.
Level of Study: Postgraduate.
Type: Prize.
Value: Swiss franc 20,000.
Frequency: Every two years.
Country of Study: Any country.
No. of awards offered: One.
Application Procedure: Applicants must pay an entry fee of swiss franc 250.
Closing Date: 20 May 2005.
Additional Information: The competition is usually held during the last weeks of August or the beginning of September.

CLAUDE HARRIS LEON FOUNDATION

PO Box 13187, Mowbray
Cape Town, Western Cape 7705
South Africa
Tel: (27) 21 531 6910
Fax: (27) 21 531 6910
Email: tanya@conferencewise.co.za
www: http://www.leonfoundation.co.za
Contact: Mrs T Stone, Administration Officer

The Claude Harris Leon Foundation is a charitable trust resulting from a bequest by Claude Leon (1184-1972). The Foundation offers postdoctoral fellowships which are awarded for research to be conducted at universities and technikons in South Africa in the faculties of science, engineering and medical sciences.

Claude Harris Leon Foundation Postdoctoral Fellowship Award

Subjects: Science, engineering and medical sciences.
Purpose: To improve the building of research capacity at South African universities and technikons.
Eligibility: Open to South African and foreign nationals. The fellowships are awarded on a competitive basis, taking the applicant's academic achievements and potential as a researcher into account.
Level of Study: Postdoctorate.
Type: Fellowship.
Value: Rand 90,000 per year.
Length of Study: Two years.
Frequency: Annual.
Study Establishment: Universities and technikons.
Country of Study: South Africa.
No. of awards offered: More than 15.
Application Procedure: Applicants must complete an application form.
Closing Date: May.
Funding: Private.
Contributor: The Claude Harris Leon Foundation.
No. of awards given last year: 17.
No. of applicants last year: More than 16.

CLEMSON UNIVERSITY

MBA Office, Admissions Office, 124 Sirrine Hall, Clemson, SC 29634-1315, United States of America
Tel: (1) 864 656 3975
Fax: (1) 864 656 0947
Email: mba@clemson.edu
www: http://www.clemson.edu
Contact: Associate Director

Clemson Graduate Assistantships

Subjects: MBA.
Eligibility: Decisions regarding the awarding of these assistantships and the duties and work period assigned are separately determined by each university department or office that employs graduate assistants.
Level of Study: MBA.
Value: The assistantships pay stipends starting at US$6.18 per hour. The pay depends upon job duties and candidate qualifications. In addition, graduate assistants are granted partial remission of academic fees and enjoy some benefits provided to University faculty and staff.
Frequency: On an annual or nine month basis.
Study Establishment: Clemson University.
Country of Study: United States of America.
No. of awards offered: Varies.
Application Procedure: Applicants must contact the various university departments or offices for information, or submit a general application with a curriculum vitae to the MBA office.
Additional Information: Due to the heavy course load required of full-time MBA students, MBAs with graduate assistantships are limited to working 10 hours per week.

Clemson University Fellowships

Subjects: MBA.
Eligibility: Candidates must be full-time first year graduate students. The fellowships will be awarded based on academic scores and departmental recommendations.
Level of Study: MBA.
Type: A variable number of fellowships.
Frequency: Annual.
Study Establishment: Clemson University.
Country of Study: United States of America.
No. of awards offered: One or two.

CLEVELAND INSTITUTE OF MUSIC

11201 East Boulevard, Cleveland, OH 44106, United States of America
Tel: (1) 216 791 5000 xt. 262
Fax: (1) 216 795 3141
Email: kxg26@ewru.edu
www: http://www.cim.edu
Contact: Kristie Gripp, Director of Financial Aid

The Cleveland Institute of Music's mission is to provide talented students with a professional, world class education in the art of music. The Institute ranks among the top tier music schools across the nation, granting degrees up to the doctoral level. More than 80 per cent of the Institute's alumni perform in major national and international orchestras and opera companies, while others hold prominent teaching positions.

Cleveland Institute of Music Scholarships and Accompanying Fellowships

Subjects: Music.
Eligibility: Candidates for the Accompanying Fellowships should have a Bachelor of music degree or equivalent and must be proficient in English.
Level of Study: Graduate, Postgraduate.
Type: Other.
Value: US$1,000-20,000 for scholarships and U$1,000-3,000 for accompanying fellowships. No travel grants are provided.
Length of Study: One academic year for scholarships or from August to the following May for accompanying fellowships. Scholarships are renewable.
Frequency: Annual.
Study Establishment: The Cleveland Institute of Music.
Country of Study: United States of America.
No. of awards offered: Approx. 350 scholarships and 15 accompanying fellowships.
Application Procedure: Applicants must apply online.
Closing Date: March 1st.
Funding: Private.

COLT FOUNDATION

New Lane, Havant, Hampshire, PO9 2LY, England
Tel: (44) 23 9249 1400
Fax: (44) 23 9249 1363
Email: jackie.douglas@uk.coltgroup.com
www: http://www.coltfoundation.org
Contact: Ms Jacqueune Douglas, Director

The primary interest of the Colt Foundation is the promotion of research into medical and environmental problems created by commerce and industry and is aimed particularly at discovering the cause of illnesses arising from conditions at the place of work. The Foundation also makes grants to students taking higher degrees in related subjects.

Colt Foundation PhD Fellowship

Subjects: Medical and natural sciences including public health and hygiene, sports medicine, biological and life sciences, physiology or toxicology.
Purpose: To encourage the young scientists of the future.

Eligibility: Open to any student proposing to take a PhD in the correct subject area.
Level of Study: Doctorate.
Type: Fellowship.
Value: UK£46,500.
Length of Study: Three years.
Frequency: Annual.
Application Procedure: Applicants must visit the website where details are posted in August each year.
Closing Date: Normally October 31st.
No. of awards given last year: Two.

THE COMMONWEALTH FUND OF NEW YORK

Harkness House, 1 East 75th Street, New York, NY 10021-2692,
United States of America
Tel: (1) 212 606 3809
Fax: (1) 212 606 3875
Email: ro@cmwf.org
www: http://www.cmwf.org
Contact: Ms Robin Osborn, International Programs in Health Policy Director

The Commonwealth Fund is a philanthropic foundation established in 1918. The Fund's national programme areas include improving health care services, bettering the health of minorities, advancing the well being of elderly people, and developing the capacities of children and youth. The Fund's international programme seeks to build a network of policy orientated health researchers to stimulate innovative policies.

Australian-American Health Policy Fellowships

Subjects: Health - policy issues in Australia and the United States of America, and shared lessons of both policies.
Purpose: To offer outstanding, mid-career U.S. health policy researchers to spend up to 10 months in Australia conducting original research and working with leading Australian health policy experts on issues relevant to both countries.
Eligibility: Accomplished, mid-career health policy researchers and practitioners including academics, physicians, decision makers in managed care and other private organizations, federal and state health officials and journalists.
Level of Study: Research.
Type: Fellowship.
Value: Australian $50,000 plus family allowance.
Length of Study: Up to 10 months.
Frequency: Annual.
Study Establishment: Suitable establishment in Australia.
Country of Study: Australia.
Application Procedure: Applicants must submit a formal application, including a project proposal that falls within an area of mutual policy interest, such as: health care quality and safety, the private/public mix of insurance and providers, the fiscal sustainability of health systems, the health care workforce, and investment in preventive care strategies.
Closing Date: August 15th for the year following.
Funding: Government.

The Commonwealth Fund / Harvard University Fellowship in Minority Health Policy

Subjects: Health policy, public health, and management with special program activities on minority health issues.
Purpose: To create physician-leaders who will pursue careers in minority- health and health policy.
Level of Study: Postgraduate, Research.
Type: Fellowship.
Length of Study: One year.
Frequency: Annual.
Study Establishment: Harvard Medical School.
Country of Study: United States of America.
Application Procedure: There is no official application form. Applicants are encouraged to submit letters of inquiry via e-mail.
Closing Date: There are no deadlines.

Harkness Fellowships in Health Care Policy

Subjects: Health care policy and health services research.
Purpose: To encourage the professional development of promising health care policy researchers and practitioners whose multinational experience and outlook will contribute to innovation in health care policy and practice in the United States of America and their home countries.
Eligibility: Open to individuals who have completed a Master's degree or PhD in health services or health policy research. Applicants must also have shown significant promise as a policy orientated researcher or practitioner, eg. physicians or health services managers, journalists and government officials, with a strong interest in policy issues. Candidates should also be at the research fellow to senior lecturer level, if academically based, be in their late 20s to early 40s, and have been nominated by their department chair or the director of their institution.
Level of Study: Postgraduate, Professional development.
Type: Fellowship.
Value: Basic expenses of travel, residence and research, up to a maximum of US$75,000.
Length of Study: One year. A minimum of four months must be spent in the United States of America.
Frequency: Annual.
Study Establishment: An academic or other institution.
Country of Study: United States of America.
No. of awards offered: Two for Australia, two for New Zealand and four-five for the United Kingdom.
Application Procedure: Applicants must complete a formal application and should write to the correct country address for further information. Applicants in the United Kingdom should apply to the main address in New York.
Closing Date: October 1st.
Funding: Private.
Contributor: The Commonwealth Fund.
Additional Information: Successful candidates will have a policy orientated research project, ideally involving cross-national comparisons, on a topic relevant to the Fund's national programme areas. Projects will be supervised by senior researchers and each Fellow will be expected to produce a publishable report contributing to a better understanding of health policy issues.

For further information contact:

Associate Professor & Director (Australia), Center for Health Economics Research & Evaluation, University of Sydney, Mallett Street Campus, 88 Mallett Street, Level 6, Building F, Camperdown, NSW 2050, Australia
Tel: (61) 2 9351 0900
Fax: (61) 2 9351 0930
Email: sylviab@pub.health.usyd.edu.au
Contact: Dr Jane Hall

Policy Representative, Executive Director (New Zealand), New Zealand-United States Educational Foundation, PO Box 3465, Wellington, New Zealand
Tel: (64) 4 722 065
Fax: (64) 4 995 364
Email: jennifer@fulbright.org.nz
Contact: Ms Jennifer M Gill

Ian Axford (New Zealand) Fellowships in Public Policy

Subjects: Public policy.
Purpose: To provide American professionals with the opportunity to study, travel, and gain practical experience in public policy in New Zealand, including first hand knowledge of economic, social and political reforms, and management of the government sector.
Eligibility: Open to mid career professionals active in any part of the public, business or non-profit sectors. Applicants must be citizens of the United States of America with at least five years of experience in their professions. There are no formal age limits, but the focus of the fellowships is on mid career development and successful candidates are likely to be in their late 20s to early 40s.
Level of Study: Professional development.
Type: Fellowship.

Value: Where possible the candidates are expected to obtain paid leave. The basic award is not intended to match Fellows' United States salaries. Fellows on paid leave will receive an allowance of New Zealand $1,700 per month on top of their salaries and will be entitled to family and other allowances. Fellows unable to obtain paid leave will receive a living allowance of New Zealand $4,000 per month, intended to cover basic expenses of residence in New Zealand, and will be entitled to family and other allowances. Eligibility for the family allowance is based on a Fellow's family status at the time of the interview and will remain unchanged throughout the tenure.
Length of Study: Six-nine months.
Frequency: Annual.
Country of Study: New Zealand.
Application Procedure: Applicants must complete a formal application, including a project proposal. Candidates should show that their proposed project will inform policy in New Zealand and the United States and contribute something of value to the policy of their field.
Closing Date: March 15th.
Funding: Commercial, Government.
Additional Information: Applications are welcome equally from men and women, from members of any ethnic group and regardless of physical disabilities.

COMMONWEALTH SCHOLARSHIP COMMISSION IN THE UNITED KINGDOM

c/o Association of Commonwealth Universities, John Foster House, 36 Gordon Square, London, WC1H 0PF, England
Tel: (44) 20 7380 6700
Fax: (44) 20 7387 2655
Email: info@acu.ac.uk
www: http://www.acu.ac.uk
Contact: Awards Administrator

The Commonwealth Scholarship Commission in the United Kingdom was set up as the body responsible for the United Kingdom's participation in the Commonwealth Scholarship and Fellowship Plan in 1959. It is responsible for the selection and placement of recipients coming to the United Kingdom and for the selection of candidates from the United Kingdom to be put forward for awards in other Commonwealth countries.

Commonwealth Academic Staff Scholarships

Subjects: All subjects.
Purpose: To help universities in the developing countries of the Commonwealth to increase the numbers and enhance the experience of their locally born staff. The scholarships are intended to enable promising staff members from universities and similar institutions in the developing Commonwealth to obtain experience in a university or other appropriate institution in the United Kingdom.
Eligibility: Open to Commonwealth citizens or British protected persons permanently resident in a developing country of the Commonwealth, who have completed or are about to complete, a degree or equivalent qualification. Candidates should already hold a teaching appointment in a university or similar institution or have the assurance of such an appointment on their return. Candidates should also be under 42 years of age at the time the award is taken up and have sufficient competence in English to profit from the proposed study. These awards are not given to Indian nationals.
Level of Study: Postgraduate.
Type: Scholarship.
Value: Return air fare to the United Kingdom, approved tuition, laboratory and examination fees, a personal maintenance allowance, a grant for books and equipment, a grant towards the expense of preparing a thesis or dissertation, where applicable, a grant for approved travel within the United Kingdom, an initial clothing allowance in special cases, and in certain circumstances a marriage and child allowance. The emoluments are not subject to United Kingdom income tax.
Length of Study: One-three years.
Frequency: Annual.
Study Establishment: A university or comparable institution.

Country of Study: United Kingdom.
No. of awards offered: 45-50.
Application Procedure: Applicants must be nominated by the vice chancellor of a United Kingdom university or the vice chancellor of the university on whose permanent staff the applicant is to serve. Heads of Bangladeshi universities should send their nominations to the University Grants Commission in Dhaka and applications from Pakistan should be channelled through the Educational Secretary, Government of Pakistan, International Co-operation Manager, Ministry of Education, Islamabad.
Closing Date: December 31st for receipt of nominations in London.
Additional Information: Scholars are required to sign an undertaking to return to and resume their academic post in their own country on completion of the scholarship.

Commonwealth Fellowships

Subjects: All subjects.
Purpose: To help universities in developing countries of the Commonwealth to increase the numbers and enhance the experience of their locally born staff. The fellowships are intended to enable promising staff members from universities and similar institutions in the developing Commonwealth to receive training and experience in a university or other appropriate institution in the United Kingdom.
Eligibility: Open to Commonwealth citizens and British protected persons permanently resident in a developing Commonwealth country. Preference is given to candidates aged 28-50. Candidates must have completed a doctoral degree more than five but not more than 10 years ago, and should have had at least two years of experience as a staff member of a university or similar institution in their own country.
Level of Study: Postdoctorate.
Type: Fellowship.
Value: UK£943 per month or UK£1,132 for those studying at institutions in the London Metropolitan area, approved airfares to and from the host country, a grant for books and equipment, a grant for approved travel within the United Kingdom, an initial clothing allowance in special cases and in certain circumstances a marriage and child allowance. The emoluments are not subject to United Kingdom income tax.
Length of Study: 6 months.
Frequency: Annual.
Study Establishment: A university or comparable institution.
Country of Study: United Kingdom.
No. of awards offered: Approx. 70.
Closing Date: December 31st for receipt of nominations in London.
Funding: Government.
Additional Information: Fellows are required to sign an undertaking to return to and resume their academic post in their country on completion of the fellowships. Candidates must be nominated by the vice chancellor of the university on whose permanent staff the applicant serves. Heads of Indian universities should send their nominations to the University Grants Commission in New Delhi, heads of Pakistani universities to the Ministry of Education in Islamabad, heads of SriLankan universities to the Ministry of Higher Education in Colombo and heads of Bangladeshi universities to the University Grants Commission in Dhaka. The fellowship may not be held concurrently with other awards or with paid employment.

Commonwealth Scholarships

Subjects: All subjects.
Purpose: To enable students of high intellectual promise to pursue studies in Commonwealth countries other than their own so that on their return home they can make a distinctive contribution to life in their own countries and to advance mutual understanding in the Commonwealth.
Eligibility: Open to Commonwealth citizens under 35 years of age who are normally resident in some part of the Commonwealth other than the particular awarding country. Applicants must be graduates of high intellectual promise who are expected to make a significant contribution to their own countries on their return from postgraduate study overseas. Candidates should have graduated from a first or Master's degree within the last ten years at the time of nomination.
Level of Study: Postgraduate.
Type: Scholarship.

Value: The emoluments for scholarships include fares to and from the United Kingdom, payment of tuition fees, allowances for books, special clothing, local travel and a personal maintenance allowance.
Length of Study: One-three academic years.
Frequency: Annual.
Study Establishment: Universities, colleges and other educational institutions.
Country of Study: Designated Commonwealth countries other than candidates own.
No. of awards offered: Approx. 250 per year.
Application Procedure: Applicants must apply to the appropriate national scholarship agency in their country of normal residence. These agencies distribute prospectuses and application forms for the various awards and will usually be the best local centres to obtain information. For detailed application procedures and appropriate contact addresses visit the website, http://www.csfp-online.org.
Closing Date: Varies according to the country in which the candidate applies, usually some 12-18 months before the intended period of study.
Funding: Government.
Additional Information: Award holders must undertake to return to their own countries on completion of their studies overseas. Commonwealth Split-Site Doctoral Scholarships are available and intended for junior faculty or students of developing institutions who are studying for a doctoral degree at their home institution and would benefit from one year of full-time study in the United Kingdom (or, in exceptional circumstances, for two six month periods) as part of their PhD programme. Candidates must be nominated in the context of a departmental or institutional link with a United Kingdom institution already in operation or currently under negotiation and at the time of application be registered for a PhD or have been accepted to undertake PhD research at a home institution.

CONCORDIA UNIVERSITY

École des études supérieures, 1455 Boulevard de Maisonneuve, Montréal, QC, H3G 1M8, Canada
Tel: (1) 514 848 3809
Fax: (1) 514 848 2812
Email: verret@vax2.concordia.ca
www: http://www.concordia.ca
Contact: Ms Patricia Verret, Graduate Awards Manager

Concordia University is the result of the 1974 merger between Sir George Williams University and Loyola College. The University incorporates superior teaching methods with an inter-disciplinary approach to learning and is dedicated to offering the best possible scholarship to the student body and to promoting research beneficial to society.

Bank of Montréal Pauline Varnier Fellowship
Subjects: Business and administration management.
Eligibility: Open to women with two years of cumulative business experience who are Canadian citizens or landed immigrants intending to pursue a full-time course of study for the MBA. This is an entrance fellowship.
Level of Study: MBA.
Type: Fellowship.
Value: Canadian $10,000 per year.
Length of Study: Two years.
Frequency: Annual.
Study Establishment: Concordia University.
Country of Study: Canada.
No. of awards offered: One.
Application Procedure: Applicants must submit a completed application form, three letters of recommendation and official transcripts of all university studies by the closing date.
Closing Date: April 30th.
Funding: Private.
No. of awards given last year: One.
Additional Information: Academic merit is the prime consideration in the granting of the awards.

Concordia University Graduate Fellowships
Subjects: All subjects.
Eligibility: Open to graduates of any nationality. Candidates must be planning to pursue full-time Master's or doctoral study at the University.
Level of Study: Postgraduate.
Type: Fellowship.
Value: Canadian $2,900 per term for Master's level and Canadian $3,600 per term for doctoral level.
Length of Study: A maximum of four terms at the Master's level and nine terms at the doctoral level, calculated from the date of entry into the programme.
Frequency: Annual.
Study Establishment: Concordia University.
Country of Study: Canada.
No. of awards offered: Varies.
Application Procedure: Applicants must submit a completed application form, three letters of recommendation and official transcripts of all university studies by the closing date.
Closing Date: December 15th.
Funding: Government, Private.
No. of awards given last year: 25.
No. of applicants last year: 1050.
Additional Information: Academic merit is the prime consideration in the granting of the award.

David J Azrieli Graduate Fellowship
Subjects: All subjects.
Eligibility: Open to Master's or doctoral students of any nationality. Candidates must be planning to pursue full-time Master's or doctoral study at the University.
Level of Study: Postgraduate.
Type: Fellowship.
Value: Canadian $17,500 per year.
Length of Study: One year, non renewable.
Frequency: Annual.
Study Establishment: Concordia University.
Country of Study: Canada.
No. of awards offered: One.
Application Procedure: Applicants must submit a completed application form, three letters of recommendation and official transcripts of all university studies by the closing date.
Closing Date: December 15th.
Funding: Private.
No. of awards given last year: One.
No. of applicants last year: 1050.
Additional Information: Academic merit is the prime consideration in the granting of the award.

J W McConnell Memorial Fellowships
Subjects: All subjects.
Eligibility: Open to Canadian citizens and permanent residents of Canada who are planning to pursue full-time Master's or doctoral study at the University. Fellowships are awarded on academic merit.
Level of Study: Postgraduate.
Type: Fellowship.
Value: Canadian $2,900 per term at the Master's level and Canadian $3,600 per term at the doctoral level.
Length of Study: A maximum of four terms at the Master's level and nine terms at the doctoral level, calculated from the date of entry into the programme.
Frequency: Annual.
Study Establishment: Concordia University.
Country of Study: Canada.
No. of awards offered: Varies.
Application Procedure: Applicants must submit a completed application form, three letters of recommendation and official transcripts of all university studies by the closing date.
Closing Date: December 15th.
Funding: Private.
No. of awards given last year: 15.
No. of applicants last year: 800.

Additional Information: Academic merit is the prime consideration in the granting of the awards.

John W O'Brien Graduate Fellowship

Subjects: All subjects.
Eligibility: Open to full-time graduate students of any nationality. Candidates must be planning to pursue full-time Master's or doctoral study at the University.
Type: Fellowship.
Value: Canadian $3,300 per term at the Master's level and Canadian $4,000 per term at the doctoral level.
Length of Study: A maximum of three terms.
Frequency: Annual.
Study Establishment: Concordia University.
Country of Study: Canada.
No. of awards offered: One.
Application Procedure: Applicants must submit a completed application form, three letters of recommendation and official transcripts of all university studies by the closing date.
Closing Date: December 15th.
Funding: Private.
No. of awards given last year: One.
No. of applicants last year: 1050.
Additional Information: Academic merit is the prime consideration in the granting of awards.

Stanley G French Graduate Fellowship

Subjects: All subjects.
Eligibility: Open to graduates of any nationality. Candidates must be planning to pursue full-time Master's or doctoral study at the University.
Level of Study: Postgraduate.
Type: Fellowship.
Value: Canadian $3,300 per term for Master's level and Canadian $4,000 per term for doctoral level.
Length of Study: A maximum of three terms.
Frequency: Annual.
Study Establishment: Concordia University.
Country of Study: Canada.
No. of awards offered: One.
Application Procedure: Applicants must submit a completed application form, three letters of recommendation and official transcripts of all university studies by the closing date.
Closing Date: December 15th.
Funding: Private.
No. of awards given last year: One.
No. of applicants last year: 1050.
Additional Information: Academic merit is the prime consideration in the granting of awards.

CONSORTIUM FOR GRADUATE STUDY IN MANAGEMENT

5585 Pershing Avenue, Suite 240, St Louis, MO 63112, United States of America
Tel: (1) 314 877 5500
Fax: (1) 314 877 5505
Email: frontdesk@cgsm.org
www: http://www.cgsm.org
Contact: Executive Assistant to CEO

The aim of the Consortium for Graduate Study in Management is to provide fellowships to African Americans, Hispanic Americans and Native Americans, in order to increase the percentage of these underrepresented minority groups in corporate America.

Consortium for Graduate Study in Management Fellowships for Minorities

Subjects: Business administration.
Purpose: To hasten the entry of African Americans, Hispanic Americans and Native Americans into management positions in business by enabling them to obtain a Master's degree.

Eligibility: Open to United States citizens who are African American, Hispanic American or Native American and who hold a Bachelor's degree in any academic discipline.
Level of Study: MBA, Postgraduate.
Type: Fellowship.
Value: Full tuition and required fees over two years of full-time MBA study. Additional financial aid may also be available.
Length of Study: Two years.
Frequency: Annual.
Study Establishment: Graduate schools of management at the following universities: Indiana, Michigan, New York, North Carolina, Rochester, Southern California, Texas at Austin, Virginia, Washington, Wisconsin-Madison, Carnegie Mellon, Emory and Dartmouth.
Country of Study: United States of America.
Application Procedure: Applicants must write for details.
Closing Date: January 15th.
Funding: Private.
No. of awards given last year: 284.
No. of applicants last year: 848.

COOLEY'S ANEMIA FOUNDATION

Suite 203, 129-09 26th Avenue, Flushing, NY 11354, United States of America
Tel: (1) 718 321 2873
Fax: (1) 718 321 3340
Email: info@cooleysanemia.org
www: http://www.cooleysanemia.org
Contact: Ms Sophie Buicynski, Accounting Department

The Cooley's Anemia Foundation is dedicated to serving people afflicted with various forms of Thalarsemia, most notably the major form of this genetic blood disease, Cooley's anemia/thalarsemia major.

Cooley's Anemia Foundation Research Fellowship Grant

Subjects: Clinical or basic research related to thalarsemia. Applications on topics such as cardiac and endocrine complications of iron overload, hepatitis C, osteoporsis, bone marrow transplantation, iron chelation and gene therapy are encouraged.
Purpose: To offer medical fellowship awards to qualified applicants.
Level of Study: Postgraduate.
Type: Fellowship.
Value: US$40,000.
Length of Study: 1 year.
Frequency: Annual.
Study Establishment: Any suitable establishment.
Country of Study: Any country.
No. of awards offered: 15.
Application Procedure: Qualified applicants should download an application form from the website or apply for one from the main organisation address.
Closing Date: 1st March in each year.
Funding: Private.
Additional Information: The foundation seeks to make an extraordinary commitment towards recruiting doctors to pursue a career investigating thalarsemia, especially due to the relatively small patient base in the U.S.

CORNELL UNIVERSITY

Center for the Humanities, Andrew D White House, 27 East Avenue, Ithaca, NY 14853-1101, United States of America
Tel: (1) 607 255 9274
Email: humctr-mailbox@cornell.edu
www: http://www.arts.cornell.edu/sochum
Contact: Program Administrator

Cornell University is a learning community that seeks to serve society by educating the leaders of the future and extending the frontiers of knowledge. The university aims to pursue understanding beyond the limitations of existing knowledge, ideology and disciplinary structure and to affirm the value of the cultivation and enrichment of the human mind to individuals and society.

Mellon Postdoctoral Fellowships

Subjects: Arts and humanities.
Eligibility: Open to citizens of the United States of America and Canada and permanent residents who have completed requirements for a PhD before the application deadline and within the last four-five years.
Level of Study: Postdoctorate.
Type: Fellowship.
Value: US$35,000.
Length of Study: Nine months.
Frequency: Annual.
Study Establishment: Cornell University.
Country of Study: United States of America.
No. of awards offered: Three-four.
Application Procedure: Applicants must write for details.
Closing Date: Postmarked January 3rd.
No. of awards given last year: Five.
No. of applicants last year: 200.
Additional Information: While in residence at Cornell, postdoctoral Fellows have department affiliation, limited teaching duties and the opportunity for scholarly work. Areas of specialisation change each year.

Society for the Humanities Postdoctoral Fellowships

Subjects: Humanities.
Eligibility: Open to holders of a PhD degree who have at least one or two years of teaching experience at the college level. Applicants should be Scholars with interests that are not confined to a narrow humanistic speciality and whose research coincides with the focal theme for the year. Fellows of the Society devote most of their time to research writing, but they are encouraged to offer a weekly seminar related to their special projects.
Level of Study: Postdoctorate.
Type: Fellowship.
Value: US$35,000.
Length of Study: One academic year.
Frequency: Annual.
Study Establishment: Cornell University.
Country of Study: United States of America.
No. of awards offered: 8-10.
Application Procedure: Applicants must contact the office to receive information on the theme and application materials.
Closing Date: Postmarked on or before October 21st.
No. of awards given last year: 10.
No. of applicants last year: 180.
Additional Information: Information about this year's theme is available upon request.

THE CORPORATION OF YADDO

Box 395, Saratoga Springs, NY 12866, United States of America
Tel: (1) 518 584 0746
Fax: (1) 518 584 1312
Email: yaddo@yaddo.org
www: http://www.yaddo.org
Contact: Ms Lesley M Leduc, Public Affairs Co-ordinator

The Corporation of Yaddo is an artists' community located on a 400 acre estate in Saratoga Springs, New York. Its mission is to nurture the creative process by providing an opportunity for artists to work without interruption in a supportive environment. Yaddo awards approximately 200 residences per year of between two weeks to two months in length and is among the United States' first and most acclaimed artists communities.

Yaddo Residency

Subjects: Choreography, film, literature, musical composition, painting, performance art, photography, printmaking, sculpture and video.
Purpose: To provide uninterrupted time and space for creative artists to think, experiment and create.
Eligibility: Open to all artists who are working at the professional level in their fields. Applications are welcomed from artists from the United States of America and abroad. Open to visual artists, writers, composers and artists working in film and/or video, choreography and performance art. An abiding principle at Yaddo is that applications for residency are judged on the quality of the artists' work and professional promise.
Level of Study: Professional development.
Type: Residency.
Value: Room, board and studio space. There is no stipend. Limited help toward travel expenses available.
Length of Study: From two weeks to two months.
Frequency: Annual.
Study Establishment: Yaddo.
Country of Study: United States of America.
No. of awards offered: Approx. 200.
Application Procedure: Applicants must send a large stamped self addressed envelope to the Admissions Department. The requirements include a completed application form, letters from two sponsors, copies of a professional curriculum vitae, work samples and the US$20 non-refundable application fee.
Closing Date: January 15th or August 1st.
Funding: Private.
Contributor: Endowment.
No. of awards given last year: 204.
No. of applicants last year: 1,170.

THE COSTUME SOCIETY OF AMERICA (CSA)

55 Edgewater Drive, PO Box 73, Earleville, MD 21919, United States of America
Tel: (1) 410 275 1619
Fax: (1) 410 275 8936
Email: national.office@costumesocietyamerica.com
www: http://www.costumesocietyamerica.com
Contact: Administrative Assistant

The Costume Society of America (CSA) advances the global understanding of all aspects of dress and appearance. The Society seeks as members those who are involved in the study, education, collection, preservation, presentation and interpretation of dress and appearance in past, present, and future societies.

CSA Adele Filene Travel Award

Subjects: Cultural heritage, museum studies and related areas.
Purpose: To assist students members in their travel to the CSA national symposia to present an accepted paper or poster.
Eligibility: Open to current students with CSA membership who have been accepted to present a juried paper or poster at the CSA national symposium.
Level of Study: Unrestricted.
Type: Travel grant.
Value: Up to US$500.
Frequency: Annual.
Country of Study: United States of America.
No. of awards offered: One-three.
Application Procedure: Applicants must send three letters of support with a copy of the juried abstract and a one page letter of application.
Closing Date: Approx. two months before the event.
No. of awards given last year: Four.
No. of applicants last year: Three.

CSA Stella Blum Research Grant

Subjects: North American costume.
Purpose: Support for research projects on North American costume by CSA Student members.
Eligibility: Open to student members of the Society, who are enrolled on a degree programme at an accredited institution.
Level of Study: Doctorate, Graduate, Postdoctorate, Postgraduate, Predoctorate.
Type: Grant.
Value: Up to US$3,500. Allowable costs include transportation to and from the research site, living expenses at the research site, supplies such as film, photographic reproductions, books, paper, computer disks, postage and telephone and services such as typing, computer

searches and graphics. In addition, up to US$500 is available for travel and related expenses to present a paper based on research at the Annual Meeting and Symposium.

Frequency: Annual.
Study Establishment: An accredited institution.
Country of Study: United States of America.
No. of awards offered: One.
Application Procedure: Applicants must complete an application form, available upon request.
Closing Date: May 1st.
No. of awards given last year: One.
No. of applicants last year: Four.
Additional Information: The award will be given based on merit rather than need. Judging criteria will include creativity and innovation, specific awareness of and attention to costume matters, impact on the broad field of costume, awareness of the interdisciplinary nature of the field, ability to successfully implement the proposed project in a timely manner and faculty adviser recommendation.

CSA Travel Research Grant

Subjects: Textile and fashion design, museum studies and related areas.
Purpose: To allow an individual to travel to collections for research purposes.
Eligibility: Applicants must be current, non student CSA members and must have held membership for two years or more. Applicants must give proof of work in progress and indicate why the particular collection is important to the project.
Level of Study: Professional development.
Type: Research grant.
Value: Up to US$1,500.
Frequency: Annual.
Country of Study: Any country.
No. of awards offered: One.
Application Procedure: Applicants must send a letter of application of no more than two pages and include the name of the collection and projected date of visit, a description of the project underway, evidence of work accomplished to date, reasons for visiting the designated collection, projected completion date of project, what audience the project will be directed to, as well as a current curriculum vitae.
Closing Date: September 1st.
No. of awards given last year: One.
No. of applicants last year: Three.

COUNCIL FOR BRITISH ARCHAEOLOGY (CBA)

Bowes Morrell House, 111 Walmgate, York, YO1 9WA, England
Tel: (44) 1904 671417
Fax: (44) 1904 671384
Email: info@britarch.ac.uk
www: http://www.britarch.ac.uk
Contact: Finance Director

The Council for British Archaeology (CBA) has been campaigning for the better care of Britain's archaeology for over 50 years. It works to improve awareness and enjoyment of archaeology for the benefit of all. The Council is the leading point of contact for information about the United Kingdom's historic environment.

CBA Challenge Funding

Subjects: Archaeology.
Purpose: To encourage voluntary effort in making original contributions to the study and care of Britain's historic environment.
Eligibility: Open to residents of the United Kingdom. Academic qualifications are not required.
Level of Study: Unrestricted.
Type: Research grant.
Frequency: Varies.
Country of Study: United Kingdom.
No. of awards offered: Varies.
Application Procedure: Applicants must request further details.
Closing Date: Varies.

CBA Grant for Publication

Subjects: British archaeology.
Purpose: To finance archaeological publications which contribute significantly to research on problems of national or special regional significance.
Eligibility: Open to the general public, except those already in receipt of a direct government grant.
Level of Study: Unrestricted.
Type: Grant.
Value: Usually no more than UK£1,000 but on average UK£400.
Frequency: Three times each year.
Country of Study: United Kingdom.
No. of awards offered: 10-15.
Application Procedure: Applicants must request an application form.
Closing Date: April 1st, July 1st or December 1st.
Additional Information: No grant will be made for the publication of records or of publications based exclusively on records, or for the publication of excavation reports where the excavation has been financed by government agencies. Grants will not normally be given to finance reports other than final excavation reports.

THE COUNCIL FOR BRITISH RESEARCH IN THE LEVANT (CBRL)

c/o The British Academy, 10 Carlton House Terrace, London, SW1Y 5AH, England
Tel: (44) 20 7969 5296
Fax: (44) 20 7969 5401
Email: cbrl@britac.ac.uk
www: http://www.britac.ac.uk/institutes/cbrl

In 1998 the British Institute at Amman for Archaeology and History and the British School of Archaeology in Jerusalem amalgamated to create the Council for British Research in the Levant (CBRL). The CBRL promotes the study of the humanities and social sciences as relevant to the countries of the Levant (Cyprus, Israel, Jordan, Lebanon, Palestinian Territories and Syria).

CBRL Research Grant

Subjects: Humanities and social sciences subjects, eg. archaeology, economics, geography, historical studies, legal studies, languages and literature, linguistics, music, philosophy, politics, social anthropology, sociology and theology or religious studies.
Purpose: To support research projects from initial exploratory work through to publication.
Eligibility: Applicants must be of British nationality or a citizen of the European union or ordinarily resident in the United Kingdom, Isle of Man or the channel Islands.
Level of Study: Postdoctorate.
Type: Research grant.
Value: Please contact the organisation.
Frequency: Annual.
Study Establishment: Council for British Research in the Levant.
Country of Study: Other.
No. of awards offered: Varies.
Application Procedure: Applicants must complete an application form, available from the United Kingdom Secretary at the main address.
Closing Date: December 2004.
Funding: Government.
Contributor: The British Academy.
No. of awards given last year: 17.
No. of applicants last year: 22.

CBRL Travel Grant

Subjects: Humanities and social sciences subjects, eg. archaeology, economics, geography, historical studies, legal studies, languages and literature, linguistics, music, philosophy, politics, social anthropology, sociology and theology or religious studies.
Purpose: To cover the travel and subsistence costs of students, academics and researchers undertaking reconnaissance tours or smaller research projects in the countries of the Levant.

Eligibility: Applicants must be of British nationality or a citizen of the European Union or ordinarily resident in the United Kingdom, Isle of Man or the channel Islands.
Level of Study: Unrestricted.
Type: Travel grant.
Value: The maximum level of a travel grant is UK£600.
Frequency: Annual.
Study Establishment: Council for British Research in the Levant.
Country of Study: Other.
No. of awards offered: Varies.
Application Procedure: Applicants must complete an application form, available from the United Kingdom Secretary at the main address.
Closing Date: 30 January 2004.
Funding: Government.
Contributor: The British Academy.
No. of awards given last year: 15.
No. of applicants last year: 22.

COUNCIL FOR INTERNATIONAL EXCHANGE OF SCHOLARS (CIES)

3007 Tilden Street North West, Suite 5L, Washington, DC 20008-3009, United States of America
Tel: (1) 202 686 4000
Fax: (1) 202 362 3442
Email: apprequest@cies.iie.org
www: http://www.cies.org
Contact: Ms Judy Pehrson, Director of External Relations

The Council for International Exchange of Scholars (CIES) is a private, non-profit organisation that facilitates international exchanges in higher education. Under a co-operative agreement with the United States Department of State Bureau of Educational and Cultural Affairs, it assists in the administration of the Fulbright Scholar Program for faculty and professionals. CIES is affiliated with the Institute of International Education.

Fulbright Distinguished Chairs Program

Subjects: American studies (history, politics and literature), humanities, law, social sciences, computer science and e-commerce, business and management, fine arts, mass communications and journalism.
Purpose: To increase mutual understanding between the people of the United States and other countries and to promote international educational co-operation.
Eligibility: Open to citizens of the United States of America who hold a PhD or equivalent qualification. Candidates should have a prominent record of scholarly achievement.
Level of Study: Postdoctorate.
Value: Varies by country.
Length of Study: From three months to one academic year.
Frequency: Annual.
Country of Study: Other.
No. of awards offered: Approx. 40.
Application Procedure: Applicants must submit a letter of interest and an eight page curriculum vitae, and should telephone CIES or visit the website for more information.
Closing Date: May 1st.
Funding: Government, Private.
No. of awards given last year: 37.
No. of applicants last year: 300.
Additional Information: Applicants must contact Dario Teutonico at dteutonico@cies.iie.org for more information.

Fulbright Postdoctoral Research and Lecturing Awards for Non-US Citizens

Subjects: All subjects.
Eligibility: Open to nationals of countries and territories holding United States diplomatic or consular posts, who have a doctoral degree or equivalent qualification. Preference is given to those persons who have not had extensive previous experience within the United States of America.
Level of Study: Postdoctorate.
Type: Grant.
Value: A maintenance allowance and international travel expenses.
Length of Study: From three months to one academic year.
Frequency: Annual.
Country of Study: United States of America.
No. of awards offered: Varies, approx. 800.
Application Procedure: Applicants must make applications to the Binational Educational Commission, or the United States embassy or consulate in their home country.
Closing Date: Varies depending on the country.
Funding: Government, Private.
Contributor: The United States government and the Fulbright Commission.
No. of awards given last year: More than 800.

Fulbright Scholar Awards for Research and Lecturing Abroad for United States Citizens

Subjects: All subjects.
Purpose: To increase mutual understanding between the people of the United States of America and the people of other nations, strengthen the ties that unite the United States of America with other nations, and promote international co-operation for educational and cultural advancement.
Eligibility: Open to United States citizens with a PhD or comparable professional qualifications. University or college teaching experience is normally expected for lecturing awards. For selected assignments, proficiency in a foreign language may be required.
Level of Study: Postdoctorate, Professional development.
Type: Award.
Value: Varies by country.
Length of Study: From two months to one academic year.
Frequency: Annual.
Country of Study: Other.
No. of awards offered: 800.
Application Procedure: Applicants must complete an application, available on request from CIES or from the website.
Closing Date: August 1st.
Funding: Government, Private.
No. of awards given last year: 800.
No. of applicants last year: 2,500.
Additional Information: Individual countries' programmes are described in the Council's publication and online. Applicants must email apprequest@cies.iie.org for more information.

Fulbright Scholar Program for United States Citizens

Subjects: The humanities, social sciences, applied, natural and physical sciences and professional fields such as architecture, business, law, museum work and creative arts, etc. Clinical medicine is excluded.
Purpose: To increase mutual understanding between the United States of America and other countries of the world.
Eligibility: Open to citizens of the United States of America.
Level of Study: Postdoctorate.
Type: Grant.
Value: A maintenance allowance and international travel expenses.
Length of Study: From three months to one academic year.
Frequency: Annual.
No. of awards offered: Approx. 800.
Closing Date: August 1st.
No. of awards given last year: 800.
Additional Information: Applicants should visit the website for further information.

Fulbright Senior Specialists Program

Subjects: Anthropology, archaeology, business administration, communications and journalism, economics, education, environmental science, information technology, law, library science, political science, public administration, sociology, social work, United States studies and urban planning.
Purpose: To offer short-term grants and encourage new types of activities in the Fulbright context. The programme also aims to

advance mutual understanding, establish long-term co-operation and create opportunities for institutional linkages.

Eligibility: Open to United States citizens with a PhD or comparable professional qualifications.

Level of Study: Postdoctorate, Professional development.

Type: Grant.

Value: An honorarium and international travel expenses.

Length of Study: From two-six weeks.

Frequency: Annual.

Country of Study: Other.

No. of awards offered: Varies.

Application Procedure: Applicants must complete the application, available on the CIES website.

Closing Date: Applications and grants are processed on a rolling basis.

Funding: Government.

Additional Information: Successful candidates are expected to lecture, lead seminars, work with foreign counterparts on curriculum, programme and institutional development. Applicants must contact fulspec@cies.iie.org for more information.

COUNCIL FOR THE ADVANCEMENT OF SCIENCE WRITING, INC. (CASW)

PO Box 910, Hedgesville, WV 25427, United States of America
Tel: (1) 304 754 5077
Fax: (1) 304 754 5076
Email: diane@casw.org
www: http://www.casw.org
Contact: Ms Diane McGurgan, Administration Secretary

Taylor/Blakeslee Fellowships for Graduate Study in Science Writing

Subjects: Journalism.

Purpose: To support graduate study in science writing.

Eligibility: Applicants must have degrees in science or journalism and must convince the CASW selection committee of their ability to pursue a career in writing science for the general public.

Level of Study: Postgraduate.

Type: Fellowship.

Value: A maximum US$2,000.

Length of Study: One year.

Frequency: Annual.

Country of Study: United States of America.

No. of awards offered: Two-four.

Application Procedure: Applicants must submit four collated sets of a completed application form, a curriculum vitae, a transcript of undergraduate studies if a student, three faculty recommendations or employer recommendations, three samples of writing on 8.5 by 11 inch sheets only, and a short statement of career goals.

Closing Date: July 1st.

Funding: Private.

No. of awards given last year: Four.

No. of applicants last year: 16.

Additional Information: Science writing is defined as writing about science, medicine, health, technology and the environment for the general public via the mass media.

COUNCIL OF LOGISTICS MANAGEMENT (CLM)

2805 Butterfield Road, Suite 200, Oak Brook, IL 60523-1170, United States of America
Tel: (1) 630 574 0985
Fax: (1) 630 574 0989
Email: clmadmin@clm1.org
www: http://www.clm1.org
Contact: Graduate Scholarship Programme

The Council of Logistics Management (CLM) is a non-profit organisation of business personnel who are interested in improving their logistics management skills. CLM works in co-operation with private industry and various organisations to further the understanding and development of the logistics concept. This is accomplished through a continuing programme of organised activities, research and meetings designed to develop the theory and understanding of the logistics process, promote the art and science of managing logistics systems, and foster professional dialogue and development within the profession.

CLM George A Gecowets Graduate Scholarship Program

Subjects: Logistics management.

Purpose: To acknowledge the importance of logistics in a tangible way, while emphasising the Council's commitment to promote the art and science of managing logistics systems.

Eligibility: Applicants must be planning to pursue a career in logistics management, be a senior at an accredited four year college or university, and already be enrolled in the first year of a logistics or logistics related Master's degree programme.

Level of Study: Graduate.

Type: Scholarship.

Frequency: Annual.

Application Procedure: Applicants must submit a completed application, official college transcripts, Graduate Record Examination scores or Graduate Management Admission Test scores, and notification of any changes in address, school enrolment, or other pertinent information. The Citizens' Scholarship Foundation of America (CSFA) will then send a complete application package upon request.

Closing Date: Postmarked April 1st.

Funding: Private.

Contributor: The Council of Logistics Management.

Additional Information: The Council wishes to make high potential students aware of the tremendous opportunities and challenges that can await them in a career in logistics management, as the last 10 years have seen an exponential increase in the importance of the logistics manager.

For further information contact:

Council of Logistics Management, George A Gecowets Graduate Scholarship Program, Scholarship Management Services CSFA, 1505 Riverview Road, PO Box 297, St Peter, MN 56082, United States of America

COUNCIL ON FOREIGN RELATIONS (CFR)

Membership & Fellowship Affairs, 58 East, 68th Street, New York, NY 10021, United States of America
Tel: (1) 212 434 9489
Fax: (1) 212 434 9801
Email: fellowships@cfr.org
www: http://www.cfr.org
Contact: Ms Elise Carlson Lewis, Vice President, Membership & Fellowship Affairs

The Council on Foreign Relations (CFR) is dedicated to increasing America's understanding of the world and contributing ideas to United States foreign policy. The Council accomplishes this mainly by promoting constructive debates and discussions, clarifying world issues and publishing Foreign Affairs, the leading journal on global issues.

CFR International Affairs Fellowship Programme in Japan

Subjects: International relations.

Purpose: To cultivate American understanding of Japan and to strengthen communication between emerging leaders of the two nations.

Eligibility: Open to United States citizens aged 27-45 who have not had prior substantial experience in Japan. Fellows will be drawn from academia, government institutions, the business community and the media. The programme does not fund pre or postdoctoral scholarly research, work towards a degree, nor the completion of projects on which substantial progress has been made prior to the fellowship period. Knowledge of the Japanese language is not a requirement.

Level of Study: Professional development.

Type: Fellowship.
Value: Living expenses in Japan plus international transportation, health and travel insurance and necessary research expenses.
Length of Study: From three months to one year.
Frequency: Annual.
Country of Study: Japan.
No. of awards offered: Two-five.
Application Procedure: Application is primarily by invitation, on the recommendation of individuals in academic, government and other institutions who have occasion to know candidates particularly well suited for the experience offered by this fellowship. Others who enquire directly and who meet preliminary requirements may also be invited to apply without formal nomination. Those invited to apply will be forwarded application materials.
Closing Date: September 15th is the deadline for nominations and October 31st is the application deadline. Nominations and applications will also be accepted out of cycle.
Funding: Private.
Contributor: Hitachi Limited.
No. of awards given last year: Three-five.
No. of applicants last year: 10.
Additional Information: While the Fellow is not required to produce a book, article or report, it is hoped that some written output will result.

CFR International Affairs Fellowships

Subjects: Important problems in international affairs and their implications for the interests and policies of the United States of America, foreign states or international organisations.
Purpose: To bridge the gap between analysis and action in foreign policy by supporting a variety of policy studies and active experiences in policy making.
Eligibility: Open to United States citizens aged 27-35. While a PhD is not a requirement, successful candidates should generally hold advanced degrees and possess a solid record of work experience. The programme does not fund pre or postdoctoral research, work towards a degree, or the completion of projects for which substantial progress has been made prior to the fellowship period.
Level of Study: Professional development, Research.
Type: Fellowship.
Value: Determined according to individual budget statements in consultation with the programme administration. The programme will attempt to meet the major portion of a Fellow's current income, up to a maximum of US$60,000. The programme does not provide support for research assistance. Fellows may receive a travel grant of up to US$3,000.
Length of Study: One year.
Frequency: Annual.
Country of Study: Any country.
No. of awards offered: 8-12.
Application Procedure: Application is primarily by invitation, on the recommendation of individuals in academic, government and other institutions who have occasion to know candidates particularly well suited for the experience offered by this fellowship. Others who enquire directly and who meet preliminary requirements may also be invited to apply without formal nomination. Those invited to apply will be forwarded application materials.
Closing Date: September 15th is the deadline for nominations and October 31st is the application deadline.
Funding: Private.
No. of awards given last year: 12.
No. of applicants last year: 50.
Additional Information: While the Fellow is not required to produce a book, article or report, it is hoped that some written output will result.

Edward R Murrow Fellowship for Foreign Correspondents

Subjects: Issues in international affairs and their implications for the interests and policies of the United States, foreign states or international organisations.
Purpose: To help the Fellow increase his or her competency in reporting and interpreting events abroad and to give him or her a period of nearly a year of sustained analysis and writing, free from the daily pressures that characterise journalistic life.

Eligibility: Open to any correspondent, editor or producer for radio, television, a newspaper or a magazine widely available in the United States of America who has covered international news.
Level of Study: Professional development.
Type: Fellowship.
Value: A stipend equivalent to the salary relinquished, not to exceed US$65,000 for nine months.
Length of Study: Normally a period of nine months.
Frequency: Annual.
Study Establishment: The Council headquarters in New York City.
No. of awards offered: One.
Application Procedure: Application is primarily by nomination. A nomination letter must be submitted to the main address. The nomination letter may be submitted by a Council member, a former or current Murrow Fellow, the candidate's employer, or the candidates themselves. The nomination letter should confirm the candidate's eligibility as well as provide a brief description of their background and why the nominator believes the candidate to be an appropriate prospect for the Fellowship. For those candidates who choose to nominate themselves, their letter should address the same aforementioned issues in addition to providing a copy of their most recent curriculum vitae. Nominees who meet the criteria of the programme will then be forwarded an application form.
Closing Date: February.
Funding: Private.
No. of awards given last year: One.
No. of applicants last year: 12.
Additional Information: Further information is available on request.

COUNCIL ON SOCIAL WORK EDUCATION (CSWE)

1725 Duke Street, Suite 500, Alexandria, VA 22314-3457, United States of America
Tel: (1) 703 683 8080
Fax: (1) 703 683 8099
Email: eafrancis@cswe.org
www: http://www.cswe.org
Contact: Dr E Aracelis Francis, Director, Minority Fellowship Programmes

The Council on Social Work Education (CSWE) provides national leadership and a forum for collective action designed to ensure the preparation of competent and committed social work professionals. Founded in 1952, CSWE is a non-profit, tax exempt, national organisation representing 2,600 individual members and 119 graduate and 417 undergraduate programmes of professional social work education in major colleges and universities in the United States. CSWE's goals include improving the quality of social work education, preparing competent human service professionals and developing new programmes to meet the demands of the changing services delivery systems.

CSWE Doctoral Fellowships in Social Work for Ethnic Minority Students Preparing for Leadership Roles in Mental Health and/or Substance Abuse

Subjects: Mental health or substance abuse.
Purpose: To equip ethnic minority individuals for the provision of leadership, teaching, consultation, training, policy development and administration in mental health or substance abuse programmes and to enhance the development and dissemination of knowledge requisite for the provision of relevant clinical and social services to ethnic minority individuals and communities.
Eligibility: Applicants must be American citizens or permanent residents, including, but not limited to, persons who are American Indian or Alaskan Native, Asian or Pacific Islander, eg. Chinese, East Indian and other South Asians, Filipino, Hawaiian, Japanese, Korean or Samoan, black or Hispanic, eg. Mexican or Chicano, Puerto Rican, Cuban, Central or South American. This programme is open to students who have a Master's degree in social work and who will begin full-time study leading to a doctoral degree in social work or who are currently enrolled as full-time students in a doctoral social work programme.

Level of Study: Doctorate.
Type: Fellowship.
Value: Monthly stipends to help defray living expenses. Some tuition support may be provided depending upon the availability of funds.
Length of Study: One year.
Frequency: Annual, dependent on funds available, up to 3 years.
Study Establishment: Doctoral programs in schools of social work.
Application Procedure: Applicants must write to the CSWE for an application pack and further information, or alternatively visit the website.
Closing Date: February 28th.
Funding: Government.
Contributor: The Substance Abuse and Mental Health Services Administration.
No. of awards given last year: 21.
Additional Information: Applicants should demonstrate potential for assuming leadership roles, as well as potential for success in doctoral studies and commitment to a career in providing mental health and/or substance abuse services to ethnic minority clients and communities.

CSWE Doctoral Fellowships in Social Work for Ethnic Minority Students Specialising in Mental Health

Subjects: Mental health research.
Purpose: To educate leaders of the nation's next generation of mental health researchers.
Eligibility: Applicants must be American citizens or permanent residents, including, but not limited to, persons who are American Indian or Alaskan Native, Asian or Pacific Islander, eg. Chinese, East Indian and other South Asians, Filipino, Hawaiian, Japanese, Korean or Samoan, black or Hispanic, eg. Mexican or Chicano, Puerto Rican, Cuban, Central or South American. This programme is open to students who have a Master's degree in social work and who will begin full-time study leading to a doctoral degree in social work or are currently enrolled as full-time students in a doctoral social work programme.
Level of Study: Doctorate.
Type: Fellowship.
Value: Monthly stipends to help defray living expenses. Tuition support provided is the NIH tuition format.
Length of Study: One year, although the award is renewable upon reapplication if the Fellow maintains satisfactory progress towards degree objectives and funding is available.
Frequency: Annual, if funds available, up to 3 years.
Study Establishment: Doctoral Programs in Schools of Social Work.
Country of Study: United States of America.
No. of awards offered: 20.
Application Procedure: Applicants must write to the CSWE for an application pack and further information, or alternatively visit the website.
Closing Date: February 28th.
Funding: Government.
Contributor: The Division of Epidemiology and Services Research, National Institute of Mental Health.
No. of awards given last year: 22.
No. of applicants last year: 50.
Additional Information: Applicants should demonstrate potential for, and interest in, mental health research, as well as potential for success in doctoral studies and commitment to a career in mental health research.

CSWE Minority Fellowship Program

Subjects: Social work.
Purpose: To equip ethnic minority individuals for the provision of leadership, teaching, consultation, training, policy, development and administration in mental health or substance abuse programmes and to enhance the development and dissemination of knowledge necessary for the provision of relevant clinical and social services to ethnic minority individuals and communities.
Eligibility: Applicants must have Master's degree in social work and must be United States citizens.
Level of Study: Doctorate.
Type: Fellowship.

Value: US$10,008 per year, with a possible US$1,800 available towards tuition costs.
Length of Study: Renewable for up to three years.
Frequency: Dependent on funds available.
Study Establishment: Approved schools of social work.
Country of Study: United States of America.
No. of awards offered: 12.
Application Procedure: Applicants must request application materials.
Closing Date: February 28th.
Funding: Government.
No. of awards given last year: 14.
No. of applicants last year: 45.

THE COUNTESS OF MUNSTER MUSICAL TRUST

Wormley Hill, Godalming
Surrey, GU8 5SG, England
Tel: (44) 1428 685427
Fax: (44) 1428 685064
Email: munstertrust@compuserve.com
www: http://www.munstertrust.org.uk
Contact: Mrs Gillian Ure, Secretary

The Countess of Munster Musical Trust provides financial assistance towards the cost of studies and maintenance of outstanding postgraduate students who merit further training at home or abroad. Each year the Trust is able to offer a small number of interest free loans for instrument purchase.

Countess of Munster Musical Trust Awards

Subjects: Musical studies.
Purpose: To enable students, selected after interview and audition, to pursue a course of specialist or advanced performance studies.
Eligibility: Open to United Kingdom or British Commonwealth citizens, who are aged 18-24 years for instrumentalists and composers or under 28 for singers, who show outstanding musical ability and potential. Conductors are not considered.
Level of Study: Doctorate, Postgraduate, Professional development.
Type: Grant.
Value: By individual assessment to meet tuition fees and maintenance according to need, usually between UK£500-5,000.
Length of Study: One year, with the possibility of renewal.
Frequency: Annual.
Country of Study: Any country.
No. of awards offered: Approx. 100 per year.
Application Procedure: Applicants must complete an application form and will have to attend an audition and interview.
Closing Date: Application forms must be received between January and the second week of February for awards to go through in September.
Funding: Private.
No. of awards given last year: 62.
No. of applicants last year: 221.

CRANFIELD UNIVERSITY

Silsoe, Bedfordshire, MK45 4DT, England
Tel: (44) 1525 863319
Fax: (44) 1525 863399
Email: studentenquiries.silsoe@cranfield.ac.uk
www: http://www.silsoe.cranfield.ac.uk
Contact: Sue O'Neill, Recruitment Manager

Cranfield University at Silsoe is the hub of the university's environmental, medical and life sciences activity. The school has built its renowned track record in the management of the earth's natural resources and diagnostics by maintaining excellence in research, excellence in teaching and excellent partnerships with industrial and public sector sponsors.

Silsoe Awards

Subjects: Any MSc programme option offered by Cranfield University in the area of natural resources, earth observation, soil and water management, environmental diagnostics, medical diagnostics, bioinformatics and land reclamation.
Purpose: To assist postgraduate study.
Eligibility: Open to European Union citizens who are graduates with good United Kingdom (Honours) Degree or equivalent and have been offered a place on a one year MSc programme at Cranfield University at Silsoe.
Level of Study: Predoctorate.
Type: Bursary.
Value: Tuition fees or half of tuition fees.
Length of Study: One year.
Frequency: Annual.
Study Establishment: Cranfield University at Silsoe.
Country of Study: United Kingdom.
No. of awards offered: Approx. 20.
Application Procedure: Applicants must apply direct to the university.
Closing Date: July.
Contributor: Cranfield University at Silsoe.
No. of awards given last year: 45.
No. of applicants last year: 250.

CRANFIELD UNIVERSITY, SCHOOL OF MANAGEMENT

Cranfield, Bedfordshire, MK43 0AL, England
Tel: (44) 1234 751122
Fax: (44) 1234 751806
Email: m.williams@cranfield.ac.uk
www: http://www.cranfield.ac.uk/som
Contact: Ms Maureen Williams, Senior Marketing Executive

Cranfield School of Management is a postgraduate institution and a faculty of Cranfield University. The School offers Master's and doctoral programmes for graduates with work experience, an extensive range of management short courses and customised executive development. It also has an extensive programme of applied research.

Chevening Scholarships

Subjects: MBA.
Purpose: To enable young professionals of outstanding academic merit and leadership potential to pursue the full-time Cranfield MBA.
Eligibility: Applicants must be resident in their home country at the time of their application, and must return to that country on completion of the programme.
Level of Study: MBA.
Type: Scholarship.
Length of Study: One year.
Frequency: Annual.
Study Establishment: Cranfield School of Management.
Country of Study: England.
Application Procedure: Applications must be made in the first instance to the appropriate British Council.
Funding: Commercial, Government.
Contributor: The Foreign & Commonwealth Office and a number of leading United Kingdom companies.
No. of awards given last year: 7.
No. of applicants last year: 25.

Executive MBA (Modular) Feeshare Scholarships

Subjects: MBA.
Purpose: To assist students who are fully self-funded.
Eligibility: Applicants must apply to the MBA programme in the normal way and have been offered a place before they can be considered for a scholarhip.
Level of Study: MBA.
Type: Scholarship.
Value: Up to UK£12,500 towards tuition fees.
Length of Study: Two years.
Frequency: Annual.

Study Establishment: Cranfield School of Management.
Country of Study: England.
Application Procedure: All successful self-funded candidates are considered for a scholarship. It is not necessary to submit a separate scholarship application.
Closing Date: Places are offered on a rolling basis from September. Early application is advisable.
Funding: Private.
No. of awards given last year: 3.
No. of applicants last year: 7.

Executive MBA (Part-time) Feeshare Scholarships

Subjects: MBA.
Purpose: To assist students who are fully self-funded.
Eligibility: Applicants must apply to the MBA programme in the normal way and have been offered a place before they can be considered for a scholarship.
Level of Study: MBA.
Type: Scholarship.
Value: Up to UK£12,500 towards tuition fees.
Length of Study: Two years.
Frequency: Annual.
Study Establishment: Cranfield School of Management.
Country of Study: England.
Application Procedure: All successful self-funded candidates are considered for a scholarship. It is not necessary to submit a separate scholarship application.
Closing Date: November 1st.
Funding: Private.
No. of awards given last year: Five.
No. of applicants last year: 15.

Feeshare 69

Subjects: MBA.
Purpose: To assist exceptional students.
Eligibility: Applicants must apply to the MBA programme in the normal way and have been offered a place before they can be considered for a scholarship.
Level of Study: MBA.
Type: Scholarship.
Value: Up to 50% of the tuition fees (UK£12,500).
Length of Study: One year.
Frequency: Annual.
Study Establishment: Cranfield School of Management.
Country of Study: England.
Application Procedure: All successful candidates are considered for a scholarship. It is not necessary to submit a separate scholarship application.
Closing Date: June 1st.
Funding: Private.
No. of awards given last year: Two.
No. of applicants last year: 4.

Full-time MBA Feeshare Scholarships

Subjects: MBA.
Purpose: To assist exceptional students wishing to persue a full-time MBA course.
Eligibility: Applicants must apply to the MBA programme in the normal way and have been offered a place before they can be considered for a scholarship.
Level of Study: MBA.
Type: Scholarship.
Value: Up to 50% of the tuition fees (UK £12,500).
Length of Study: One year.
Frequency: Annual.
Study Establishment: Cranfield School of Management.
Country of Study: England.
No. of awards offered: 25.
Application Procedure: All successful candidates are considered for a scholarship it is not necessary to submit a separate scholarship application.
Closing Date: Places are offered on a rolling basis from January. Early application is advisable.

Funding: Private.
No. of awards given last year: 21.
No. of applicants last year: 276.

James Stuckey Scholarship

Subjects: MBA.
Purpose: To assist individuals wishing to pursue a full-time MBA course.
Eligibility: Open to anyone of New Zealand origin applying to the full-time MBA, who intends to return to work in New Zealand.
Level of Study: MBA.
Type: Scholarship.
Value: UK£10,000.
Length of Study: One year.
Frequency: Annual.
Study Establishment: Cranfield School of Management.
Country of Study: England.
Application Procedure: Applicants must include a covering letter with their MBA application, stating that they wish to be considered for the award.
Closing Date: May 1st.
Funding: Private.
No. of awards given last year: One.
No. of applicants last year: Two.

CRIMINOLOGY RESEARCH COUNCIL (CRC)

GPO Box 2944, Canberra
ACT 2601, Australia
Tel: (61) 2 6260 9295
Fax: (61) 2 6260 9201
Email: crc@aic.gov.au
www: http://www.aic.gov.au/crc
Contact: Administrator

The Criminology Research Council (CRC) funds methodologically sound research in the areas of sociology, psychology, law, statistics, police, judiciary, corrections, mental health, social welfare, education and related fields. The research to be conducted is policy orientated, and research outcomes should have the potential for application nationally or in other jurisdictions.

CRC Grants

Subjects: Criminological research in the areas of sociology, psychology, law, statistics, police, judiciary and corrections, etc. From time to time the Council will call for research in specific areas.
Eligibility: Open to Australian residents or visitors (actual or intending) who are pursuing or intend to pursue studies of consequence to the furtherance of criminological research in Australia. Grants are not likely to be given for assistance with research leading to the award of postgraduate degrees.
Level of Study: Doctorate, Postdoctorate.
Type: Grant.
Value: Usually Australian $25,000 paid in three instalments.
Length of Study: Usually one year, with a possibility of renewal for up to three years.
Frequency: Annual.
Country of Study: Australia.
No. of awards offered: Approx. six.
Application Procedure: Applicants must complete an application form, available from CRC.
Closing Date: Twelve weeks prior to meetings.
Funding: Government.
No. of awards given last year: Seven.
No. of applicants last year: 27.
Additional Information: The Council does not ordinarily consider applications involving travelling expenses outside of Australia. Meetings are held in March, July and November. The November meeting is for general grants funding in any area the council deems relevant.

THE CROHN'S AND COLITIS FOUNDATION OF AMERICA, INC.

386 Park Avenue South 17th Floor, New York, NY 10016-8804,
United States of America
Tel: (1) 212 685 3440
Fax: (1) 212 779 4098
Email: info@ccfa.org
www: http://www.ccfa.org
Contact: Ms Carol M Cox, Research Co-ordinator

The Crohn's and Colitis Foundation of America, Inc. is a non-profit, voluntary health organisation dedicated to improving the quality of life for persons with Crohn's disease or ulcerative colitis. It supports basic and clinical scientific research to find the causes and cure for these diseases, provides educational programmes for patients, medical and healthcare professionals, and the general public, alongside offering supportive services to patients, their families and friends.

Crohn's and Colitis Foundation Career Development Awards

Subjects: Crohn's disease and ulcerative colitis.
Purpose: To encourage the development of young outstanding scientists and help them prepare for careers of independent research into inflammatory bowel disease.
Eligibility: Open to candidates with research potential working in American laboratories who have had at least five years of postdoctoral experience, two years of which must be in research relevant to inflammatory bowel disease, prior to the start date of the award and not more than 10 years prior to the attainment of the doctoral degree. Research projects must be in the field of inflammatory bowel disease. Individuals already well established in the field are not eligible. Proof of legal work status within the United States of America is required at the time of application.
Level of Study: Postdoctorate.
Value: Up to US$40,000 salary and US$20,000 for supplies etc. plus fringe benefits not to exceed 25 per cent of the salary award.
Length of Study: Two years.
Frequency: Every two years.
Study Establishment: Approved research institutions.
Country of Study: United States of America.
No. of awards offered: Varies.
Application Procedure: Applicants must complete an application form in accordance with the guidelines, available from the Foundation.
Closing Date: January 14th or July 1st.
Funding: Private.
No. of awards given last year: Four.
Additional Information: The awards are made to eligible institutions on behalf of qualified candidates and each awardee is directly responsible to the institution to which the award is made.

Crohn's and Colitis Foundation First Award

Subjects: Crohn's disease and ulcerative colitis.
Purpose: To underwrite the first independent investigative efforts of an individual, to provide a reasonable opportunity to demonstrate creativity, productivity and further promise and to help in the transition to traditional types of research project grants.
Eligibility: The applicant must be independent of a mentor yet at the same time must be at the beginning stages of his or her research career, with no more than five years of research experience since completing postdoctoral research training. The applicant must hold an MD, PhD or equivalent and be employed by an institution within the United States of America engaged in healthcare at the time of application.
Level of Study: Postdoctorate.
Value: A maximum of US$60,000 in direct costs per year and indirect costs at 15 per cent of direct cost.
Length of Study: A maximum of three years.
Frequency: Annual.
Study Establishment: Approved research institutions.
Country of Study: United States of America.
No. of awards offered: Varies.

Application Procedure: Applicants must complete an application form in accordance with the guidelines. Please write for details.
Closing Date: January 14th or July 1st.
Funding: Private.
No. of awards given last year: Four.

Crohn's and Colitis Foundation Research Fellowship Awards

Subjects: Crohn's disease and ulcerative colitis.
Purpose: To encourage the development of young outstanding scientists and help them prepare for careers of independent research into inflammatory bowel disease.
Eligibility: Open to candidates with research potential working in American laboratories who have had at least two years of postdoctoral experience prior to the start date of the award, one year of which must have been in research relevant to inflammatory bowel disease. Candidates must have demonstrated an interest and capability in research. Research projects must be in the field of inflammatory bowel disease and individuals who are already well established in the field are not eligible. Proof of legal work status within the United States of America will be required at the time of application.
Level of Study: Postdoctorate.
Value: US$30,000 per year for salary plus fringe benefits not to exceed 25 per cent of the salary award.
Length of Study: One-three years.
Frequency: Every two years.
Study Establishment: Approved research institutions.
Country of Study: United States of America.
No. of awards offered: Varies.
Application Procedure: Applicants must complete an application form in accordance with the guidelines.
Closing Date: January 14th or July 1st.
Funding: Private.
No. of awards given last year: Four.

Crohn's and Colitis Foundation Research Grant Program

Subjects: Inflammatory bowel disease including its cause, pathogenesis or treatment.
Purpose: To provide financial support for innovative basic and clinical research.
Eligibility: Open to qualified investigators in the United States of America and abroad.
Level of Study: Postdoctorate.
Type: Research Grant.
Value: A maximum of US$100,000 for direct costs. Requests for purchases of major equipment totalling more than US$5,000 are not generally considered and the maximum amount allowed for overhead is 15 per cent of total direct costs.
Length of Study: Two years with a possibility of renewal for a further year.
Frequency: Every two years.
Country of Study: Any country.
No. of awards offered: Varies.
Application Procedure: Applicants must complete an application form in accordance with the guidelines.
Closing Date: January 14th or July 1st.
Funding: Private.
No. of awards given last year: 13.

THE CROSS TRUST

PO Box 17, 25 South Methven Street, Perth, Perthshire, PH1 5ES, Scotland
Tel: (44) 1738 620451
Fax: (44) 1738 631155
Contact: Mrs Dorothy Shaw, Assistant Secretary

The aim of the Cross Trust is to provide opportunities to young people of Scottish birth or parentage to extend the boundaries of their knowledge of human life. Proposals are to be of demonstrable merit from applicants with a record of academic distinction.

Cross Trust Grants

Subjects: Any approved subject.
Purpose: To enable young people to extend the boundaries of their knowledge and experience or to encourage performance and participation in drama or opera. The Trust may support the pursuit of studies or research.
Eligibility: Open to graduates of Scottish universities, Scottish secondary school pupils or graduates of central institutions in Scotland. Applicants must be of Scottish birth or parentage.
Level of Study: Other.
Type: Varies.
Value: Varies.
Length of Study: Varies.
Study Establishment: Any approved institute.
Country of Study: Any country.
No. of awards offered: Varies.
Application Procedure: Applicants must complete an application form.
Closing Date: There is no deadline.
Funding: Private.
No. of awards given last year: 166.
No. of applicants last year: 408.
Additional Information: Awards will only be considered from postgraduate students who have part funding in place from another organisation. The Trust may support the pursuit of studies or research.

THE CROUCHER FOUNDATION

Suite 501, Nine Queen's Road Central, Hong Kong
Tel: (852) 2 736 6337
Fax: (852) 2 730 0742
Email: info@croucher.org.hk
www: http://www.croucher.org.hk
Contact: Ms Elaine Sit, Administrative Officer

Founded to promote education, learning and research in the areas of natural science, technology and medicine, the Croucher Foundation operates a scholarship and fellowship scheme for individual applicants wishing to pursue doctoral or postdoctoral research. The Foundation otherwise makes grants to institutions only.

Croucher Foundation Fellowships and Scholarships

Subjects: Natural science, medicine and technology.
Purpose: To enable selected students of outstanding promise to devote themselves to full-time postgraduate study or research in approved academic institutions outside Hong Kong.
Eligibility: Open to permanent residents of Hong Kong. Fellowships are intended for recent PhD graduates and not for the funding of career vacancies in universities. Scholarships are intended for those undertaking a research degree, such as a PhD programme.
Level of Study: Doctorate, Postdoctorate.
Type: Scholarships, Fellowships.
Value: UK £16,080 per year for fellowships and UK£9,000 per year for scholarships. A maintenance allowance is available, as well as assistance towards airfares and tuition fees for Scholars. Married Fellows or Scholars will be given a special spouse allowance including assistance towards airfares if spouses are dependent and accompanying the holders of the award. In addition, a child allowance will be provided if they are residing with the Fellow or Scholar. If the successful applicant is on paid study leave during the tenure of the award the maintenance allowance will not apply. A one-off grant for books will be given during the first year of tenure. An allowance for thesis expenses will be given to final year PhD students on application against receipts. Fellows and Scholars will be expected to devote their whole time to the objects of their award. Fellows and Scholars are not expected to hold another position of emolument but if, at the date of application, they hold such a position or are appointed to it at a later date, or receive concurrently any scholarship or award with monetary value, they must notify the Foundation and obtain prior approval. The Trustees may, at their discretion, modify the value of the fellowship or scholarship.
Length of Study: One-two years for fellowships. One-three years for scholarships.

Country of Study: Outside Hong Kong.
No. of awards offered: Approx. 20-25.
Application Procedure: Applicants must write requesting an application form stating whether they are applying for a scholarship or fellowship, and enclose a 7 x 10 inch stamped addressed envelope for 50 grams, or download an application form from the website (www.croucher.org.hk).
Closing Date: 20 Nov 2003. Applicants should visit the website for the exact date every year.
Funding: Private.
No. of awards given last year: 30.
No. of applicants last year: 120.

CYSTIC FIBROSIS FOUNDATION (CFF)

Office of Grants Management 6931 Arlington Road, Bethesda, MD 20814, United States of America
Tel: (1) 301 951 4422
Fax: (1) 301 951 6378
Email: grants@cff.org
www: http://www.cff.org
Contact: Grants Division

The mission of the Cystic Fibrosis Foundation (CFF) is to assure the development of the means to cure and control cystic fibrosis and to improve the quality of life for those with the disease.

CFF Research Programmes in Cystic Fibrosis
Subjects: Cystic fibrosis.
Purpose: To offer competitive awards for research.
Eligibility: Some programmes have United States citizenship or permanent resident status requirements.
Level of Study: Doctorate, Professional development.
Type: Research grant.
Value: Please contact the organisation.
Frequency: Annual.
Country of Study: Any country.
No. of awards offered: Eight programmes.
Additional Information: The names of the awards are as follows: Therapeutics Development Grants, Pilot Feasibility Awards, Research Grants, Leroy Matthews Physician/Scientist Award, Harry Shwachman Clinical Investigator Award, Clinical Research Grants, CFF/NIH Funding Award and Special Research Awards. Applicants are advised to email the foundation for further information as grants are currently under review.

CFF Training Programmes in Cystic Fibrosis
Subjects: Cystic fibrosis.
Purpose: To support individuals interested in careers related to cystic fibrosis research and care.
Eligibility: Open to United States citizens and permanent residents only.
Level of Study: Doctorate, Professional development.
Type: Varies.
Value: From US$1,500-45,000.
Frequency: Annual.
Country of Study: Any country.
No. of awards offered: Four programmes.
Application Procedure: Applicants must write for an application form.
Additional Information: The names of the specific awards are: Postdoctoral Research Fellowships, Clinical Fellowships, Student Traineeships and Summer Scholarships in Epidemiology. Applicants are advised to email the foundation for further information as grants are currently under review.

CYSTIC FIBROSIS TRUST (CFT)

11 London Road, Bromley, Kent, BR1 1BY, England
Tel: (44) 20 8464 7211
Fax: (44) 20 8313 0472
Email: cpendry@cftrust.org.uk
www: http://www.cftrust.org.uk
Contact: Research Manager

The Cystic Fibrosis Research Trust (CFRT) funds medical and scientific research aimed at understanding, treating and curing cystic fibrosis, and ensuring that sufferers receive the best possible care and support in all aspects of their lives.

CFT Research Grants
Subjects: Cystic fibrosis.
Purpose: To find a cure for cystic fibrosis and also to improve the management, care and treatment of those suffering from the disease.
Eligibility: Open to suitably qualified persons from the United Kingdom.
Level of Study: Doctorate, Postgraduate, Research.
Type: Grants and studentships.
Value: Grants are made to cover such matters as salaries, expenses and equipment.
Length of Study: Up to three years, subject to annual renewal.
Frequency: Twice a year.
Country of Study: United Kingdom.
No. of awards offered: Varies.
Application Procedure: Applicants must submit an application form and include justification of the support requested. Forms are only available by email.
Closing Date: Please contact the organisation.
Funding: Private.
Contributor: Charitable donations.

CYSTIC FIBROSIS WORLD-WIDE

Bosbes 12, 5708 DA, Helmond, Netherlands
Tel: (31) 492 520 241
Fax: (31) 492 599 068
Email: info@cfww.org
www: http://www.cfww.org
Contact: Mrs Gina Steenkamer, Administration Office

Cystic Fibrosis worldwide works to promote access to appropriate care and education to those people living with the disease in developing countries and to improve the knowledge of CF among medical professionals and governments worldwide.

CF Worldwide Scholarships
Subjects: Cystic Fibrosis.
Purpose: To support individuals working in the field of clinical CF care wishing to improve their knowledge by undertaking research.
Eligibility: Normally the applicant will come from a country or region where CF research is in need of improvement.
Level of Study: Postgraduate.
Type: Scholarship.
Value: Variable.
Frequency: Annual.
Application Procedure: Please download details from the website.
Funding: Private.

DAMON RUNYON CANCER RESEARCH FOUNDATION

675 Third Avenue, New York, NY 10017, United States of America
Tel: (1) 212 455 0520
Email: awards@drcrf.org
www: http://www.drcrf.org

The Damon Runyon Cancer Research Foundation identifies and supports extraordinary young scientists across the nation who are committed to discovering the causes and cures for cancer.

Damon Runyon Cancer Research Foundation Fellowship Award
Subjects: Understanding the causes and mechanisms of cancer and developing more effective cancer therapies and preventions.
Purpose: To encourage all theoretical and experimental research relevant to the study of cancer and the search for cancer causes, mechanisms, therapies and prevention.

Eligibility: Legal residents of USA or US citizens research abroad. Candidates must be at the beginning of their first full-time post-doctoral fellowship.
Level of Study: Postdoctorate.
Type: Fellowship.
Value: US$39,000-57,000 per year.
Length of Study: 3 years.
Frequency: 3 × per year.
Study Establishment: Suitable accredited establishment within USA.
Country of Study: USA / US citizen working outside USA.
No. of awards offered: 50-60 per year.
Application Procedure: Applicants should download an application from www.drcrf.org. Fellowship awards to be approved by the Board of Directors of the Damon Runyon Cancer Research Foundation acting upon the recommendation of the Scientific Advisory Committee.
Funding: Private.
No. of awards given last year: 53.
No. of applicants last year: 477.

Damon Runyon Scholar Award

Subjects: Understanding the causes and mechanisms of cancer and developing more effective cancer therapies and preventions.
Purpose: To support the development of outstanding scientists as independent investigators in the cancer field by helping foster their research productivity during the first few years of their first faculty position.
Eligibility: Researchers must show exceptional promise within the first three years of their assistant professors appointment.
Level of Study: Postdoctorate, Professional development.
Type: Grant.
Value: US$100,000 per year.
Length of Study: 3 years.
Frequency: Annual.
Country of Study: USA / US citizen working outside USA.
No. of awards offered: 5.
Application Procedure: The application must be made with three years of the initial faculty appointment. The institution and department must guarantee, in written form, a commitment to the individual and the development of their laboratory and career.
Closing Date: July 1.
Funding: Private.
No. of awards given last year: 5.
No. of applicants last year: 87.
Additional Information: The award will be allocated to the awardee's institution, with the understanding that it is to be used for the awardee's salary, technical support and/or equipment. The award may not be used for institutional overhead or indirect costs.

The Damon Runyon-Lilly Clinical Investigator Award

Subjects: Understanding the causes and mechanisms of cancer and developing more effective cancer therapies and preventions.
Purpose: To support young physician-scientists conducting patient-oriented cancer research.
Eligibility: This award is specifically intended to provide outstanding young physicians with the resources and training structure essential to becoming independent clinical investigators.
Level of Study: Professional development, Research.
Type: Grant.
Value: Stipend US$100,000, Research allowance US$75,000, mentor stipend US$30,000 payment of medical student debt up to US$100,000.
Length of Study: Up to 5 years.
Frequency: Annual.
Study Establishment: Suitable facilities within USA.
Country of Study: USA / US citizen working outside USA.
No. of awards offered: 5.
Application Procedure: Forms may be downloaded from www.drcrf.org.
Closing Date: March 1.
Funding: Private.
Contributor: Eli-Lilly.
No. of awards given last year: 5.
No. of applicants last year: 41.

DANISH CANCER SOCIETY

Strandboulevarden 49, Copenhagen
DK-2100, Denmark
Tel: (45) 3525 7500
Fax: (45) 3525 7701
Email: info@cancer.dk
www: http://www.cancer.dk
Contact: Ms Birgit Christensen, Head Secretary

The Danish Cancer Society's mission is to fight cancer and its consequences through research, preventative measures and support for patients and their families. Patient's interests in relation to authorities are also represented.

Danish Cancer Society Psychosocial Research Award

Subjects: Psychology.
Eligibility: Only cancer related projects will be granted.
Level of Study: Research.
Type: Research grant.
Length of Study: Up to five years.
Frequency: Annual.
Country of Study: Denmark.
Application Procedure: Applicants should visit the website for details.
Funding: Private.
Contributor: Legacies and testamentary gifts, and investment income lotteries.
No. of awards given last year: 30.
No. of applicants last year: 49.

Danish Cancer Society Scientific Award

Subjects: Medical and natural sciences.
Eligibility: Only cancer related projects will be granted.
Level of Study: Research.
Type: Research grant.
Length of Study: Up to five years.
Frequency: Annual.
Country of Study: Denmark.
Application Procedure: Applicants should visit the website for details.
Funding: Private.
Contributor: Legacies and testamentary gifts, and investment income lotteries.
No. of awards given last year: 179.
No. of applicants last year: 370.

DAPHNE JACKSON TRUST

Department of Physics, University of Surrey, Guildford, Surrey, GU2 7XH, England
Tel: (44) 1483 689166
Fax: (44) 1483 689166
Email: djmft@surrey.ac.uk
www: http://www.daphnejackson.org
Contact: Mrs Jennifer Woolley, Trust Director

The Daphne Jackson Trust offers sponsored fellowships to qualified scientists, engineers and computing specialists wishing to return to their profession after having taken a career break for family reasons. Fellowships are held in universities and industrial laboratories throughout the United Kingdom.

Daphne Jackson Fellowship

Subjects: Science, engineering or computing.
Eligibility: Open to United Kingdom residents who have a minimum of a First Degree and have taken a career break of at least three years.
Level of Study: Research.
Type: Fellowship.
Length of Study: Two years.
Country of Study: United Kingdom.
No. of awards offered: Approx. 12 per year.

Application Procedure: Applicants must send a curriculum vitae along with the names of at least two referees.
Closing Date: Applications are accepted at any time.
Funding: Commercial, Private.
No. of awards given last year: Twelve.

DEBRA

DEBRA House, 13 Wellington Business Park, Dukes Ride, Crowthorne, Berkshire, RG45 6LS, England
Tel: (44) 01344 771961
Fax: (44) 01344 762661
Email: debra@debra.org.uk
www: http://www.debra.org.uk

DEBRA UK is the National charity working on behalf of people with the genetic skin blistering condition, Epidermolysis Bullosa (EB).

DEBRA UK Research Grant Scheme
Subjects: EB is a rare genetic condition causing skin blistering and other disability. DEBRA's main research interests are 1) genetic therapies in EB, 2) cancers in EB, 3) wound healing in EB and 4) clinical research to accurate symptoms.
Purpose: To find research into Epidermolysis Bullosa (EB).
Eligibility: Successful applicants are likely to be productive postdocs, usually with a track record as a PI.
Level of Study: Postdoctorate.
Type: Project grant mainly.
Value: Average UK£40-50,000 pa.
Length of Study: Grants for projects are usually for 1-3 years.
Frequency: Twice a year.
No. of awards offered: Varies.
Application Procedure: Application form can be downloaded from www.debra-international.org or from the DEBRA UK Office.
Closing Date: 1 April & 1 October each year.
Funding: Private.
Contributor: Charitable funding.
No. of awards given last year: 11.
No. of applicants last year: 15.

DELTA SOCIETY

580 Naches Ave Sw #101, Renton, WA 98055-2297, United States of America
Tel: (1) 425 226 7357
Fax: (1) 425 235 1076
Email: info@deltasociety.org
www: http://www.deltasociety.org
Contact: Administrative Assistant

The Delta Society's mission is to improve human health through service and therapy animals. The Society does this by expanding awareness of the positive effects animals can have on family health and human development, reducing barriers to the involvement of animals in everyday life, delivering animal assisted therapy to more people and by increasing the availability of well trained service dogs.

James M Harris/Sarah W Sweatt Student Travel Grant
Subjects: Veterinary medicine, general medical sciences and general education.
Purpose: To provide an annual grant for transportation costs for a student to attend the Delta Society Training Conference.
Eligibility: Open to students who are enrolled full-time in a veterinary or human health professional training programme pursuing a Master's or doctoral degree.
Level of Study: Postgraduate.
Type: Travel grant.
Value: Transportation costs.
Frequency: Annual.
Country of Study: United States of America.
No. of awards offered: One.

Application Procedure: Applicants must contact the Society for details.
Closing Date: Changes year to year.

DEMOCRATIC NURSING ORGANISATION OF SOUTH AFRICA (DENOSA)

PO Box 1280, Pretoria, 0001, South Africa
Tel: (27) 12 343 2315
Fax: (27) 12 344 0750
Email: info@denosa.org.za
www: http://www.denosa.org.za
Contact: Executive Director

The Democratic Nursing Organisation of South Africa (DENOSA) is a professional organisation and labour union for nurses in South Africa.

DENOSA Bursaries, Scholarships and Grants
Subjects: Nursing.
Purpose: To encourage post basic studies at a South African teaching institution.
Eligibility: Open to members of the organisation in good standing who hold the required registered nursing qualifications.
Level of Study: Doctorate, Graduate, Postgraduate, Professional development.
Type: Bursary.
Value: Varies.
Study Establishment: A South African teaching institution.
No. of awards offered: Varies.
Application Procedure: Applicants must complete an application form.
Closing Date: January 31st.
Funding: Private.
Contributor: Donor funding.
No. of awards given last year: 125.
No. of applicants last year: 158.
Additional Information: Further information is available on request.

THE DENMARK-AMERICA FOUNDATION

Fiolstraede 24, 3rd Floor, Copenhagen, DK-1171, Denmark
Tel: (45) 3312 8323
Fax: (45) 3332 5323
Email: daf-fulb@daf-fulb.dk
www: http://www.daf-fulb.dk
Contact: Ms Marie Monsted, Executive Director

The Denmark-America Foundation was founded in 1914 as a private foundation, and today its work remains based on donations from Danish firms, foundations and individuals. The Foundation offers scholarships for studies in the United States of America at the graduate and postgraduate university level and has a trainee programme.

Denmark-America Foundation Grants
Subjects: All subjects.
Purpose: To further understanding between Denmark and the United States of America.
Eligibility: Open to Danes and Danish-American citizens (Dual).
Level of Study: Graduate, MBA, Postdoctorate, Postgraduate, Professional development.
Type: Bursary.
Value: Varies.
Length of Study: Between three months and one year.
Frequency: Annual.
Country of Study: United States of America.
No. of awards offered: Varies.
Application Procedure: Applicants must complete a special application form, available by contacting the secretariat.
Funding: Private.
No. of awards given last year: 40.
No. of applicants last year: 300.

DENTISTRY CANADA FUND/FONDS DENTAIRE CANADIEN (DCF)

427 Gilmour Street, Ottawa
ON, K2P 0R5, Canada
Tel: (1) 613 236 4763
Fax: (1) 613 236 3935
Email: information@dcf-fdc.ca
www: http://www.dcf-fdc.ca
Contact: Co-ordinator Administration

The Dentistry Canada Fund (DCF) is the national charitable foundation dedicated to assisting in the encouragement of optimal oral health in Canada through education, research and promotion.

DCF Biennial Research Award

Subjects: Dentistry.
Purpose: To encourage research.
Eligibility: Open to graduate or postgraduate students who have conducted their research in association with a Canadian dental faculty. Applicants must either be in their graduating year or the ensuing year.
Level of Study: Graduate, Postgraduate.
Type: Research grant.
Value: Canadian $2,000 plus a commemorative plaque.
Frequency: Every two years.
Country of Study: Canada.
No. of awards offered: One.
Application Procedure: Applicants must submit one typewritten double spaced copy, not exceeding 25 pages and four copies of an original research project in the form of a paper must be submitted. The manuscript should not be a previously published paper of the candidate's graduate work currently in press or already published in a scientific journal. Each applicant must also send a current curriculum vitae.
Closing Date: October 1st.
Additional Information: Each entry will be reviewed by three referees appointed by the CDA Committee on Dental Materials and Devices. The decision of the Committee is final.

DCF Fellowships for Teacher/Researcher Training

Subjects: Dentistry.
Purpose: To provide financial assistance to students who wish to pursue a career in dentistry research or teaching at graduate level.
Eligibility: Applicants must be Canadian citizens or permanent residents who have completed a course in dentistry, a dental hygiene programme or a programme in science and also be eligible for admission to a graduate or other advanced education programme.
Level of Study: Postgraduate.
Type: Fellowship.
Country of Study: Canada.
Application Procedure: Applicants must submit an application including official transcripts of previous post secondary education and letters of recommendation from a faculty member of the applicant's post secondary institution and from the administrative head of the institution and department where he or she expects to be employed. All applications must include a curriculum vitae.
Closing Date: February 1st.

DCF/Wrigley Dental Student Research Awards

Subjects: Oral biology.
Purpose: To enable applicants to undertake research projects in oral biology. Preference is given to research or community education projects concerned with the benefits of salivary stimulation and caries reduction.
Eligibility: Open to students enrolled in Canadian dental schools.
Level of Study: Graduate.
Type: Research grant.
Frequency: Annual.
Country of Study: Canada.
No. of awards offered: Up to three.

Application Procedure: Applicants must submit an application including background on the subject matter, the research objectives, the proposed hypothesis, the research approach and the project's timetable and budget.
Closing Date: February 1st.

DEPARTMENT FOR EMPLOYMENT AND LEARNING

Adelaide House, 39-49 Adelaide Street, Belfast, BT2 8FD, Northern Ireland
Tel: (44) 28 9025 7710
Fax: (44) 28 9025 7747
Email: del@nics.gov.uk
www: http://www.delni.gov.uk
Contact: Mrs Siobhan Woods

The Department for Employment and Learning makes available research and advanced course studentships to provide for both the payment of approved fees and the maintenance of students who are being trained in methods of research and undertaking approved postgraduate courses of instruction.

DEL Postgraduate Studentships and Bursaries for Study in Northern Ireland

Subjects: Science, technology, social sciences and humanities.
Purpose: To provide students ordinarily resident in the United Kingdom with bursaries similar to those given by the Arts and Humanities Research Board, the Engineering and Physical Sciences Council, the Economic and Social Research Council and the Natural Environment Research Council for attendance at courses in Northern Ireland.
Eligibility: Open to United Kingdom and European Union residents only. Applicants for studentships must have at least an Upper Second Class Degree. Bursaries are open to United Kingdom residents who must be ordinarily resident in Northern Ireland on the date of the application for an award and hold a university degree or qualification regarded by the department as equivalent to a degree.
Level of Study: Postgraduate.
Type: Other.
Value: In line with the other United Kingdom awarding bodies.
Length of Study: Varies.
Frequency: Annual.
Study Establishment: Appropriate institutions.
Country of Study: Northern Ireland.
No. of awards offered: Varies, determined by universities.
Application Procedure: Applicants must complete an application form, available from universities in Northern Ireland.
Closing Date: Deadlines are determined by the institution concerned.
Funding: Government.

For further information contact:

Queen's University Belfast, University Road, Belfast, Northern Ireland

University of Ulster, Crorore Road, Coleraine, Co London Derry

DEPARTMENT OF EDUCATION AND SCIENCE (IRELAND)

International Section, Training College Building, Marlborough Street, Dublin, 1, Ireland
Tel: (353) 1 889 2426
Fax: (353) 1 889 2376
Email: dolores_ronane@education.gov.ie
www: http://www.education.gov.ie
Contact: Ms Dolores Ronane, International Section

The Department of Education and Science's (Ireland) International Section deals with International Scholarships from foreign governments with whom Ireland has a cultural agreement. The awards are distributed between October and March.

Department of Education and Science (Ireland) Exchange Scholarships and Postgraduate Scholarships Exchange Scheme

Subjects: All subjects.
Purpose: To allow students to pursue study or research in Ireland.
Eligibility: Open to Australian, Austrian, Belgian, Chinese, Finnish, German, Greek, Italian, Japanese, Dutch, Norwegian, Russian Federation, Spanish and Swiss nationals who are university graduates and have completed at least three years of academic study. A good knowledge of English or Irish is necessary, depending on the course taken.
Level of Study: Graduate, Postgraduate.
Type: Scholarship.
Value: Please contact the association for details.
Length of Study: Eight months.
Frequency: Annual.
Study Establishment: An Irish University or Institute of Higher Education.
Country of Study: Ireland.
No. of awards offered: 28.
Application Procedure: Applicants must apply to the appropriate institution in their home country.
Closing Date: April 30th.
Funding: Government.
No. of awards given last year: 25.

Department of Education and Science (Ireland) Summer School Exchange Scholarships

Subjects: All subjects.
Purpose: To allow European students to attend a summer school in Ireland.
Eligibility: Open to Belgian, French, Finnish, German, Hungarian, Italian, Dutch, Czech Republic, Russian Federation and Spanish nationals who are university graduates. A good knowledge of English or Irish is necessary, depending on the course taken.
Level of Study: Unrestricted.
Type: Scholarship.
Value: Please contact the association for details.
Length of Study: Two weeks-one month.
Frequency: Annual.
Study Establishment: Summer schools at University College Dublin, University College Galway or University College Cork.
Country of Study: Ireland.
No. of awards offered: 34.
Application Procedure: Applicants must apply to the appropriate institution in their home country.
Closing Date: April 30th.
Funding: Government.
No. of awards given last year: 20.
No. of applicants last year: 20.

DESCENDANTS OF THE SIGNERS OF THE DECLARATION OF INDEPENDENCE

DSDI Scholarship Committee, PO 7 Colby Court, Unit 4-144, Bedford, NH 03110, United States of America
Contact: Mrs Phillip F Kennedy

Descendants of the Signers of the Declaration of Independence Scholarships

Subjects: All subjects.
Purpose: Financially to assist Descendants of the Signers of the Declaration of Independence (those who prove eligibility and become members of this Society) to pursue their goals in higher education.
Eligibility: Open to proven direct lineal descendants of a signer of the Declaration of Independence. Proof of lineage must be established before an application is sent. Applicants must give the name of their ancestor signer in their first communication or they will not receive a reply. Applicants must be attending an accredited four year college or university course full-time, in graduate or undergraduate study.
Level of Study: Unrestricted.

Type: Scholarship.
Value: US$3,000, paid directly to the institution. Funds may be applied toward any costs chargeable to the students college account, ie. room, board, books, fees, tuition.
Frequency: Annual.
Country of Study: United States of America.
No. of awards offered: 3.
Closing Date: March 15th.
Funding: Private.
No. of awards given last year: 3.
No. of applicants last year: 25.
Additional Information: Only those with proven descent (a Society member number) will receive an application. Competition among eligible applicants is based on merit, need, and length of time to graduation.

DEUTSCHE FORSCHUNGSGEMEINSCHAFT (DFG)

Kennedyallee 40, Bonn
D 53176, Germany
Tel: (49) 228 885 1
Fax: (49) 228 885 2777
Email: postmaster@dfg.de
www: http://www.dfg.de
Contact: Administrative Assistant

The Deutsche Forschungsgemeinschaft (DFG) is the central organisation for academic research in Germany. DFG supports research projects in German universities and institutions, promotes co-operation between scientists and forges support links between German academic science and industry, and with partners in foreign countries. DFG gives special attention to the education of young scientists and scholars.

Albert Maucher Prize

Subjects: Geosciences.
Purpose: To promote outstanding young scientists and scholars in the field of geosciences.
Eligibility: Open to promising young scientists and scholars up to the age of 35 who are German nationals or permanent residents of Germany.
Level of Study: Postdoctorate.
Type: Award.
Value: Please contact the organisation.
Length of Study: Varies.
Frequency: Every two years.
Study Establishment: Approved universities or research institutions.
Country of Study: Germany.
Application Procedure: Applicants must write for details or visit the website. Application is by nomination.
Closing Date: Please write for details.

DFG Collaborative Research Grants

Subjects: All subjects.
Purpose: To promote long-term co-operative research in universities and academic research.
Eligibility: Open to promising groups of German nationals and permanent residents of Germany.
Level of Study: Postdoctorate, Research.
Type: A variable number of grants.
Value: Dependent on the requirements of the project.
Length of Study: 3-15 years.
Study Establishment: Universities and academic institutions.
Country of Study: Germany.
No. of awards offered: Varies.
Application Procedure: Applicants must write or visit the website for further information. Applications must be formally filed by the universities.
Closing Date: Please write for details.
Additional Information: A list of collaborative research centres is available in Germany only from the DFG.

DFG Individual Grants

Subjects: All subjects.

Purpose: To foster the proposed research projects of promising academic scientists or scholars.

Eligibility: Open to promising researchers and scholars who are German nationals or permanent residents of Germany.

Level of Study: Postdoctorate, Postgraduate, Predoctorate, Research.

Type: A variable number of grants.

Value: Dependent on the requirements of the project.

Length of Study: Two-three years with the option of applying for renewal.

Frequency: Throughout the year.

Study Establishment: Universities.

Country of Study: Any country.

No. of awards offered: Varies.

Application Procedure: Applicants must submit a proposal for a research project. Applicants must write for more details or visit the website.

Closing Date: Applications are accepted at any time.

DFG Joint Research Projects

Subjects: All subjects.

Purpose: To foster co-operation between German scientists and scientists in Middle and Eastern European countries and countries of the former Soviet Union.

Eligibility: Open to German Scholars and Scholars from any participating Eastern European country.

Level of Study: Postdoctorate, Research.

Type: A variable number of grants.

Value: Dependent on the length of the research project and the number of participants.

Length of Study: Varies.

Frequency: Annual.

Study Establishment: Universities.

Country of Study: Any country.

No. of awards offered: Varies.

Application Procedure: Applications must be submitted by researchers from German research institutes. Applicants must write for details or visit the website.

Closing Date: Please write for details.

DFG Research Training Groups

Subjects: All subjects.

Purpose: To promote high quality graduate studies at doctoral level through the participation of graduate students recruited through country wide calls in research programmes.

Eligibility: Open to highly qualified graduate and doctoral students of any nationality.

Level of Study: Postgraduate, Predoctorate.

Type: A variable number of fellowships.

Length of Study: Up to nine years.

Study Establishment: Any approved university.

Country of Study: Germany.

No. of awards offered: Varies.

Application Procedure: Applications should be submitted in response to calls. For further information applicants must visit the website.

Closing Date: Please write for details.

Additional Information: A list of graduate colleges presently funded is available (in Germany only) from the DFG.

DFG Research Units

Subjects: All subjects.

Purpose: To promote intensive co-operation between highly qualified researchers in one or several institutions in fields of high scientific promise.

Eligibility: Open to interested groups of German nationals and permanent residents of Germany.

Level of Study: Postdoctorate, Research.

Type: Research grant.

Value: Dependent on the requirements of the project.

Length of Study: Up to six years.

Frequency: Annual.

Study Establishment: An approved university.

Country of Study: Germany.

No. of awards offered: Varies.

Application Procedure: Applicants must submit proposals to the Senate of the DFG. Applicants must write or visit the website for further information.

Closing Date: Please write for details.

Additional Information: A list of currently operating research groups is available in Germany only from the DFG.

Emmy Noether-Programme

Subjects: All subjects.

Purpose: To give outstanding young scholars the opportunity to obtain the scientific qualifications needed to be appointed as a lecturer.

Eligibility: Open to promising young postdoctoral scientists up to the age of approximately 30, who are German nationals or permanent residents of Germany and are within five years of receiving their PhD.

Level of Study: Postdoctorate.

Type: Project grant.

Value: For the two years of research spent abroad the candidate will receive a project grant in keeping with the requirements of the project including an allowance for subsistence and travel. For the three years of research spent at a German university or research institution the candidate will receive a project grant.

Length of Study: Five years.

Frequency: Annual.

Study Establishment: Universities or research institutions.

Country of Study: Any country.

No. of awards offered: 100.

Application Procedure: Applicants must complete an application form. For further information applicants must write or visit the website.

Closing Date: Please write for details.

Eugen and Ilse Seibold Award

Subjects: Arts and humanities.

Purpose: To promote outstanding young scientists and scholars who have made significant contributions to the scientific interchange between Japan and Germany.

Eligibility: Open to outstanding young German or Japanese Scholars.

Level of Study: Postdoctorate.

Type: Award.

Value: Please contact the organisation.

Length of Study: Varies.

Frequency: Every two years.

Study Establishment: Universities or research institutions.

Country of Study: Other.

No. of awards offered: Two.

Application Procedure: Applicants must write for details or visit the website. Application is by nomination.

Closing Date: Please write for details.

Gottfried Wilhelm Leibniz Prize

Subjects: All subjects.

Purpose: To promote outstanding scientists and Scholars in German universities and research institutions.

Eligibility: Open to outstanding Scholars in German universities.

Level of Study: Predoctorate, Research.

Type: Research grant.

Value: Please contact the organisation.

Length of Study: Five years.

Frequency: Annual.

Study Establishment: Any approved university or research institution.

Country of Study: Germany.

No. of awards offered: Varies.

Application Procedure: Applicants must write for details or visit the website. Application is by nomination. Nominations are restricted to selected institutions such as DFG member organisations or individuals eg. former prize winners or chairpersons of DFG review committees.

Closing Date: Please write for details.
Additional Information: A list of prize winners is available in Germany only from the DFG.

Guest Professorships

Subjects: All subjects.
Purpose: To support stays of foreign scientists at German universities.
Eligibility: Open to foreign scientists whose individual research is of special interest to research and teaching in Germany.
Level of Study: Postdoctorate.
Type: A variable number of fellowships.
Value: Dependent on the duration of the stay.
Length of Study: 3-12 months.
Frequency: Annual.
Study Establishment: German universities.
Country of Study: Germany.
No. of awards offered: Varies.
Application Procedure: Applicants must submit a proposal by the university intending to host the guest professor.
Additional Information: Further information is available on the website.

Heinz Maier-Leibnitz Prize

Subjects: All subjects.
Purpose: To promote outstanding young scientists at doctorate level.
Eligibility: Open to promising young Scholars up to the age of 33, who are German nationals or permanent residents of Germany.
Level of Study: Doctorate, Postdoctorate.
Type: Award.
Value: Please contact the organisation.
Length of Study: Varies.
Frequency: Annual.
Study Establishment: Any approved university or research institution.
Country of Study: Germany.
No. of awards offered: Six.
Application Procedure: Applicants must write for details or visit the website. Application is by nomination.
Closing Date: Please write for details.

Heisenberg Programme

Subjects: All subjects.
Purpose: To promote outstanding young scientists.
Eligibility: Open to high calibre young scientists up to the age of 35 years who are German nationals or permanent residents of Germany.
Level of Study: Postdoctorate.
Type: Scholarship.
Value: Varies.
Length of Study: Five years.
Frequency: Annual.
Study Establishment: Any approved university or research institution.
Country of Study: Germany.
No. of awards offered: Varies.
Application Procedure: Applicants must submit a research proposal, a detailed curriculum vitae, copies of degree certificates, a copy of the thesis, a letter explaining the choice of host institution, a list of all previously published material and a letter outlining financial requirements in duplicate. For further information applicants must contact DFG.
Closing Date: Applications are accepted at any time.

Priority Programs

Subjects: All subjects.
Purpose: To promote proposals made by interested groups of scientists in selected fields.
Eligibility: Open to interested groups of scientists from Germany or any country participating in the scheme.
Level of Study: Postdoctorate, Research.
Type: A variable number of grants.

Value: The Senate decides on the financial ceiling for each programme.
Length of Study: Up to six years.
Frequency: Annual.
Study Establishment: Universities or academic establishments.
Country of Study: Any country.
No. of awards offered: Varies.
Application Procedure: Applicants must write or visit the website for further information. Priority Programs are operated through calls for proposals, with all applications subject to open panel review, usually after discussion with the applicants.
Closing Date: Please write for details.

DIABETES RESEARCH & WELLNESS FOUNDATION

Office 101-102, Northney Marina, Hayling Island, Hampshire, PO11 0NH, England
Tel: (44) 23 9263 7808
Fax: (44) 23 9263 6137
Email: drwf@diabeteswellnessnet.org.uk
www: http://www.diabeteswellnessnet.org.uk
Contact: Mr James Rogers, Executive Director

The Diabetes Research & Wellness Foundation was established in 1998 to fund research into finding a cure for diabetes. Each year this goal becomes more important as the number of people diagnosed continues to rise. The organisation hopes to make diabetes a thing of the past, and, until then, alleviate its awful complications.

DRWF Research Fellowship

Subjects: Endocrinology or diabetes.
Purpose: To encourage research.
Eligibility: Open to suitable candidates who are working at an institution within the United Kingdom in an established position.
Level of Study: Doctorate, Postdoctorate, Research.
Type: Fellowship.
Value: Up to UK£120,000 for the non clinical fellowship and up to UK£100,000 for the clinical fellowship.
Length of Study: Up to three years for the non clinical fellowship and up to two years for the clinical fellowship.
Frequency: Annual.
Study Establishment: A recognised institution or research group in the United Kingdom.
Country of Study: United Kingdom.
No. of awards offered: One.
Application Procedure: Applicants must undergo a three stage selection procedure starting with a pre-application. This is a single sheet of A4 with single line spacing, using a clearly readable font in 11 or 12 point. The pre-application must include the applicant's name, qualifications, contact details and present post. The pre-application must also include the name of the head of the group where the grant will be held, the post held or expected post to be held within the group and the relevant contact details of the group. There should also be a 300 word abstract of the proposal research work including the title, research question of approximately 300 words, relevance to diabetes, expected outcome and any additional information to support the application, but no references. Lastly, a brief curriculum vitae of the applicant on a separate single sheet of A4. Successful applicants at the pre-selection stage are required to submit a full application by August.
Closing Date: April 30th.
Funding: Commercial, Private.
No. of awards given last year: One.
No. of applicants last year: 22.
Additional Information: Fellowships are alternated between clinical and non clinical, year by year. Final interviews of selected candidates are held in October. The recipient of the fellowship is expected to take it up early in the following year.

DIABETES UK

10 Parkway, London, NW1 7AA, England
Tel: (44) 20 7424 1833
Fax: (44) 20 7424 1082
Email: eleanor.kennedy@diabetes.org.uk
www: http://www.diabetes.org.uk
Contact: Dr Eleanor Kennedy, Research Manager

Diabetes UK's overall aim is to help and care for both people with diabetes and those closest to them, to represent and campaign for their interests, and to fund research into diabetes. Diabetes UK continues to encourage research into all areas of diabetes.

Diabetes UK Equipment Grant

Subjects: Endocrinology, Diabetes and subjects relevant to diabetes.
Purpose: To enable the purchase of equipment which is required only for a single project or programme and is solely concerned with diabetes research.
Eligibility: Open to suitably qualified members of the medical or scientific professions who are resident in the United Kingdom.
Level of Study: Postdoctorate.
Type: Grant.
Value: More than UK£5,000.
Frequency: Annual.
Country of Study: United Kingdom.
No. of awards offered: Varies.
Application Procedure: Applicants must complete an application form which will be assessed by a peer review. Please write or telephone for details. Details can be found on the website.
Closing Date: April 1st, August 1st and December 1st.
Funding: Private.
Contributor: Voluntary contributions.
No. of awards given last year: Three.

Diabetes UK Project Grants

Subjects: Endocrinology, Diabetes or subjects relevant to diabetes.
Purpose: To provide funding for a well defined research proposal of timeliness and promise which, in terms of the application, may be expected to lead to a significant advance in our knowledge of diabetes.
Eligibility: Open to suitably qualified members of the medical or scientific professions who are resident in the United Kingdom.
Level of Study: Postdoctorate.
Type: Project grant.
Value: A maximum UK£50,000 per year.
Length of Study: One-three years.
Frequency: Annual.
Country of Study: United Kingdom.
No. of awards offered: Varies.
Application Procedure: Applicants must complete an application form which will be assessed by a peer review and should write or telephone for details. Details can be found on the website.
Closing Date: April 1st, August 1st, December 1st.
Funding: Private.
Contributor: Voluntary contributions.

Diabetes UK Research Fellowships

Subjects: Diabetes mellitus, Diabetes or subjects relevant to diabetes.
Eligibility: Open to suitably qualified members of the medical or scientific professions who are resident in the United Kingdom.
Level of Study: Postdoctorate.
Type: Varies.
Value: Varies.
Length of Study: Two-three years.
Frequency: Annual.
Country of Study: United Kingdom.
Application Procedure: Applicants must complete an application form and should write or telephone for details. Detail can be found on the website.
Closing Date: September.
Funding: Private.

Contributor: Members' donations & subscriptions.
No. of awards given last year: Five.
No. of applicants last year: 25.
Additional Information: Availability is advertised annually in the scientific and medical press.

Diabetes UK Research Studentships

Subjects: Endocrinology, Diabetes or subjects relevant to diabetes.
Purpose: To train basic scientists in diabetes research.
Eligibility: Open to potential supervisors in single departments or in collaborative projects between departments, pre-clinical or clinical. Applicants must be resident in the United Kingdom.
Level of Study: Postgraduate.
Type: Studentship.
Value: In London UK£11,500 maintenance and UK£5,000 laboratory expenses. Outside London UK£10,500 maintenance and UK£5,000 laboratory expenses.
Length of Study: Three years.
Frequency: Annual.
Country of Study: United Kingdom.
No. of awards offered: Varies.
Application Procedure: Applicants must complete an application form. Please write or telephone for details. Details can be found on the website.
Closing Date: September.
Funding: Private.
Contributor: Voluntary contributions.
No. of awards given last year: 15 (awarded in 2002).
Additional Information: Availability is advertised annually in the scientific and medical press.

Diabetes UK Small Grant Scheme

Subjects: Endocrinology, Diabetes or subjects relevant to diabetes.
Purpose: To enable research workers to develop new ideas in the field of diabetes research.
Eligibility: Open to suitably qualified members of the medical or scientific professions who are resident in the United Kingdom.
Level of Study: Postdoctorate.
Type: Grant.
Value: A maximum of UK£10,000.
Length of Study: Varies.
Frequency: Other.
Country of Study: United Kingdom.
No. of awards offered: Varies.
Application Procedure: Applicants must complete an application form which will be assessed by a peer review within six to eight weeks. Please write or telephone for details. Details can also be found on the website.
Closing Date: Applications are accepted at any time.
Funding: Private.
Contributor: Voluntary contributions.
No. of awards given last year: 14.
No. of applicants last year: 30.

THE DIGESTIVE DISORDERS FOUNDATION

3 St Andrew's Place, Regent's Park
London, NW1 4LB, England
Tel: (44) 20 7486 0341
Fax: (44) 20 7224 2012
Email: julia@digestivedisorders.org.uk
www: http://www.digestivedisorders.org.uk
Contact: Ms Julia Young, Research Grants Administrator

The Digestive Disorders Foundation (formerly the British Digestive Foundation) supports research into the cause, prevention and treatment of digestive disorders, including digestive cancers, ulcers, irritable bowel syndrome, inflammatory bowel disease, diverticulitis, liver disease and pancreatitis. The Foundation also provides information for the public explaining the symptoms and treatment of these and other common digestive conditions.

Digestive Disorders Foundation Fellowships and Grants
Subjects: Gastroenterology such as basic or applied clinical research into normal and abnormal aspects of the gastrointestinal tract, liver and pancreas, the prevention of and treatment for digestive disorders.
Purpose: To provide funding for gastroenterological research.
Eligibility: Open to applicants resident within the United Kingdom. Fellowship projects must contain an element of basic science training.
Level of Study: Doctorate, Postdoctorate, Postgraduate, Research.
Type: Other.
Value: Up to UK£10,000 for Research Grants and up to UK£2,000 for Travel Grants. For fellowships, payment of a full-time salary up to specialist registrar grade if medically qualified is available.
Length of Study: One, two or three years.
Frequency: Dependent on funds available.
Study Establishment: A recognised and established research centres.
Country of Study: Other.
No. of awards offered: Approx. 10.
Application Procedure: Applicants must complete an application form for consideration in a research competition. Competitions are advertised in December and July each year. Details are available from the website.
Funding: Commercial, Private.
Contributor: Charitable donations.
No. of awards given last year: 5.
No. of applicants last year: Varies.
Additional Information: Conditions are advertised in the medical press. Research grants are awarded for specific projects in the same field of interest. Travel grants are awarded to assist researchers by enabling them to visit overseas institutions with the aim of learning new techniques or otherwise advancing their own research.

DIRKSEN CONGRESSIONAL CENTER

2815 Broadway, Pekin, IL 61554, United States of America
Tel: (1) 309 347 7113
Fax: (1) 309 347 6432
Email: fmackaman@dirksencenter.org
www: www.dirksencenter.org
Contact: Executive Director

The Dirksen Congressional Center sponsors educational and research programmes to help people understand better the United States Congress, its members and leaders, and the public policies it produces.

Dirksen Congressional Research Grants Program
Subjects: Political science and government.
Purpose: To fund the study of the United States Congress and its leaders.
Eligibility: Open to United States citizens or residents. Awards are to individuals only. No institutional overhead charges are permitted.
Level of Study: Doctorate, Postdoctorate, Professional development.
Type: Research grant.
Value: Up to US$3,500.
Length of Study: Not defined.
Frequency: Annual.
Study Establishment: Unrestricted.
Country of Study: United States of America.
No. of awards offered: Varies.
Application Procedure: Applicants should visit the Centers website for application information.
Closing Date: February 1st.
Funding: Private.

Robert H Michel Civic Education Grants
Subjects: Education and teacher training. Areas of interest include designing lesson plans, creating student activities and applying instructional technology in the classroom.
Purpose: To help teachers, curriculum developers and others improve the quality of civic instruction, with priority on the role of Congress in the United States of America Federal Government.

Eligibility: Open to United States citizens or residents. Awards are given to individuals only. No institutional overhead charges are permitted.
Level of Study: Professional development.
Type: Grant.
Value: Varies, up to US$5,000.
Frequency: Annual.
Study Establishment: Unrestricted.
Country of Study: United States of America.
No. of awards offered: Varies.
Application Procedure: Applicants should visit the Center's website for application information.
Closing Date: May 1st.
Funding: Private.

DONATELLA FLICK ASSOCIAZIONE

5 Coutts Crescent, St. Albans Road, London, NW5 IRF, England
Tel: (44) 20 7792 2885
Fax: (44) 20 7792 2574
Email: administrator@conducting.org
www: http://www.conducting.org
Contact: Administrator

The Donatella Flick Associazione organises the Donatella Flick Conducting Competition which, in association with the London Symphony Orchestra, aims to help advance career opportunities for young conductors. The award subsidises study and concert engagements for the winner who will work as Assistant Conductor with the London Symphony Orchestra for one year.

Donatella Flick Conducting Competition
Subjects: Conducting.
Purpose: To assist a young conductor in establishing an international conducting career.
Eligibility: Open to conductors who are citizens of member states of the European Community and aged under 35.
Level of Study: Professional development.
Type: Prize.
Frequency: Every two years.
Study Establishment: London Symphony Orchestra.
Country of Study: Any country.
Application Procedure: Applicants must complete an application form and submit this with references specific to the competition, as well as videos and other supporting documentation such as other prizes, reviews and curriculum vitae etc.
Funding: Private.
Contributor: Mrs Donatella Flick.
Additional Information: Entry is by recommendation, documentation and supporting video. Finalists are then selected for audition, and three finalists conduct a public concert. The course of study of entrants must be approved by the organising committee.

DOW JONES NEWSPAPER FUND, INC.

PO Box 300, Princeton, NJ 08543-0300, United States of America
Tel: (1) 609 452 2820
Fax: (1) 609 520 5804
Email: newsfund@wsj.dowjones.com
www: http://djnewspaperfund.dowjones.com
Contact: Grants Management Officer

The Dow Jones Newspaper Fund is a private foundation that promotes careers in journalism.

DJ Newspaper Fund Editing Intern Program
Subjects: Communication studies and journalism.
Purpose: To encourage careers in copy editing.
Eligibility: Open to citizens of the United States of America only.
Level of Study: Graduate, Postgraduate.
Type: Other.
Value: US$1,000 scholarship for interns returning to school at the end of the Summer.

Length of Study: Summer programme.
Frequency: Annual.
Country of Study: United States of America.
No. of awards offered: Up to 110.
Application Procedure: Applicants must complete an application form and submit this with a curriculum vitae, list of grades or courses, essays and tests. Candidates will only be considered if an application form is submitted with the required materials. Application forms are available between July 15th-September 28.
Closing Date: All materials must be postmarked by November 1.
Funding: Private.
No. of awards given last year: 100.
No. of applicants last year: 600.
Additional Information: This is a United States national competition.

DR HADWEN TRUST FOR HUMANE RESEARCH

84A Tilehouse Street, Hitchin, Hertfordshire, SG5 2DY, England
Tel: (44) 1462 436819
Fax: (44) 1462 436844
Email: info@drhadwentrust.org.uk
www: http://www.drhadwentrust.org.uk
Contact: Dr Carol Newman, Scientific Officer

The Dr Hadwen Trust for Humane Research is a registered charity, established in 1970, to promote research into techniques and procedures to replace the use of living animals in biomedical research, teaching and testing.

Dr Hadwen Trust for Humane Research Grants

Subjects: Scientific research to develop humane alternative methods to the use of living animals in biomedical research and testing.
Purpose: To advance medical progress and replace animal experiments.
Eligibility: Open to nationals from any country, but research must be based in the United Kingom.
Level of Study: Doctorate, Postdoctorate, Postgraduate.
Type: Grant.
Value: Varies according to need and to funds available. Payments are usually made quarterly, and may be used as salary for the researcher, for technical assistance, for expenses incurred during the research, purchase of equipment or attendance at meetings.
Length of Study: A maximum of three years, interim progress reports are required. Renewal past three years is awarded only in exceptional circumstances.
Frequency: Dependent on funds available.
Country of Study: United Kingdom.
No. of awards offered: Varies.
Application Procedure: Official application form must be completed.
Closing Date: Applications are accepted at any time.
Funding: Private.
Contributor: Public donations.
No. of awards given last year: Nine.
Additional Information: Recipients are required to sign an agreement not to use Trust funds for any procedure using living animals or animal tissues. Applications must be signed by the candidate's head of department and administrative authority.

Dr Hadwen Trust for Humane Research Plus PhD Studentship

Subjects: Developing alternatives to animal experiments in biomedical fields.
Purpose: To encourage young graduates with good honours degrees to train in non animal methods.
Eligibility: Open to applicants resident in the United Kingdom.
Level of Study: Postgraduate.
Type: Studentship.
Value: Outside London UK£8,600 per year, in London UK£11,210 plus an allowance for consumables.
Length of Study: Three years.
Frequency: Dependent on funds available.
Country of Study: United Kingdom.

No. of awards offered: Varies.
Application Procedure: Applicants must make initial enquiries in writing to the scientific adviser, Dr G Langley. Applications must be submitted by the project supervisor.
Funding: Private.
Contributor: Donations from the general public.

Dr Hadwen Trust Research Assistant or Technician

Subjects: The development, validation or implementation of a technique or procedure which would replace one currently using living animals.
Purpose: To provide additional scientific or technical support for a research project.
Eligibility: Open to applicants resident in the United Kingdom.
Value: Salary for research assistant or technician plus an allowance for consumables.
Length of Study: Three years.
Frequency: Dependent on funds available.
Study Establishment: Varies.
Country of Study: United Kingdom.
No. of awards offered: Varies.
Application Procedure: Applicants must make initial enquiries in writing to the scientific adviser, Dr G Langley. Applications must be made by the senior researcher who will oversee the work.
Funding: Private.

Dr Hadwen Trust Research Fellowship

Subjects: The development, validation or implementation of a technique or procedure which would replace one currently using living animals.
Purpose: To attract and retain talented young scientists in non animal research fields. The funds provide personal support and a contribution to direct research costs.
Eligibility: Open to applicants resident in the United Kingdom.
Level of Study: Postdoctorate.
Type: Fellowship.
Value: Salary on research analogous salary scale grade 1A, up to spinal point 9 plus a London allowance where appropriate and an allowance for consumables.
Length of Study: Three years.
Frequency: Dependent on funds available.
Study Establishment: Varies.
Country of Study: United Kingdom.
No. of awards offered: Varies.
Application Procedure: Applicants must make initial enquiries in writing to the scientific adviser, Dr G Langley. Application forms must be submitted by a senior researcher who will oversee the work.
Funding: Private.
Contributor: Public donations.

DR M AYLWIN COTTON FOUNDATION

c/o Albany Trustee Company Ltd, PO Box 232, Pollet House, St Peter Port, GY1 4LA, Guernsey
Tel: (44) 1481 724136
Fax: (44) 1481 710478
Email: info@cotton-foundation.org
www: http://www.cotton-foundation.org
Contact: Administrator

Cotton Research Fellowships

Subjects: Archaeology, architecture, history, language and the arts of the Mediterranean.
Eligibility: Open to senior Scholars.
Level of Study: Professional development.
Type: Fellowship.
Value: Up to UK£10,000, to cover the costs of accommodation, travel, photography, photocopying and all other expenses relating to the work for which the fellowship is awarded.
Frequency: Annual.
Country of Study: Any country.
No. of awards offered: Varies.

Application Procedure: Applicants must submit a curriculum vitae and an outline of the research they intend to undertake.
Closing Date: February 28th.
Funding: Private.
Contributor: Dr M Aylwin Cotton.
Additional Information: The Foundation also provides grants annually to finance the publication costs of a completed work or a work due for publication in the immediate future.

DR WILLIAMS'S TRUST

14 Gordon Square, London, WC1H 0AR, England
Tel: (44) 20 7387 3727
Contact: The Director

The Dr Williams's Trust gives further education grants to Protestant Dissenting Ministers in the United Kingdom. It also owns the Dr Williams's Library in London.

Glasgow Bursary

Subjects: Religious studies, theology, Christian history, etc.
Purpose: To support an educated nonconformist ministry.
Eligibility: Open to graduate Protestant Dissenting ministers for research leading to the degree of PhD.
Level of Study: Postgraduate.
Type: Bursary.
Value: Approx. UK£14,500 per year plus fees paid each term.
Length of Study: One year, renewable for a second year.
Frequency: Dependent on funds available.
Study Establishment: The University of Glasgow Faculty of Divinity.
Country of Study: United Kingdom.
No. of awards offered: One.
Application Procedure: Applicants must contact the Director of the Trust for details.
Closing Date: March 31st.
Funding: Private.
No. of awards given last year: One.
No. of applicants last year: Six.

DUBLIN INSTITUTE FOR ADVANCED STUDIES

10 Burlington Road, Dublin, 4, Ireland
Tel: (353) 1 668 0748
Fax: (353) 1 668 0561
Email: registrar@admin.dias.ie
www: http://www.dias.ie
Contact: Ms Ruth Graham, Administrative Assistant

The Dublin Institute for Advanced Studies is a statutory corporation established in 1940 under the Institute for Advanced Studies Act of that year. It is a publicly funded independent centre for research in basic disciplines. Research is currently carried out in the fields of Celtic studies and cosmic physics including astronomy, astrophysics, geophysics and theoretical physics.

Dublin Institute for Advanced Studies Scholarship in Astronomy, Astrophysics and Geophysics

Subjects: Astronomy, astrophysics or geophysics.
Purpose: To enable training in advanced research methods in the fields of astronomy, astrophysics and geophysics.
Eligibility: Open to candidates from any country.
Level of Study: Doctorate, Graduate, Postdoctorate, Postgraduate, Predoctorate.
Type: Scholarship.
Value: Please contact the Institute for details.
Length of Study: One year.
Frequency: Annual.
Study Establishment: The Dublin Institute for Advanced Studies.
Country of Study: Ireland.
No. of awards offered: Three.
Application Procedure: Applicants must complete an application form, available upon request.

Closing Date: Please write for details.
Funding: Government.
Contributor: State funded.
No. of awards given last year: Two.
No. of applicants last year: 12.

Dublin Institute for Advanced Studies Scholarship in Celtic Studies

Subjects: Celtic studies, futurology or anthropology.
Purpose: To enable training in advanced research methods in the field of Celtic studies.
Eligibility: Open to nationals of any country.
Level of Study: Doctorate, Postdoctorate, Postgraduate.
Type: Scholarship.
Value: Please contact the Institute for details.
Length of Study: One year.
Frequency: Annual.
Study Establishment: The Dublin Institute for Advanced Studies.
Country of Study: Ireland.
No. of awards offered: Three.
Application Procedure: Applicants must complete an application form, available upon request.
Closing Date: Applications are accepted at any time.
Funding: Government.
No. of awards given last year: Three.
No. of applicants last year: 10.

Dublin Institute for Advanced Studies Scholarship in Theoretical Physics

Subjects: Physics.
Purpose: To enable training in advanced research methods in the field of theoretical physics.
Eligibility: Open to candidates of any country.
Level of Study: Postdoctorate.
Type: Scholarship.
Value: Please contact the Institute for details.
Length of Study: One year.
Frequency: Annual.
Study Establishment: The Dublin Institute for Advanced Studies.
Country of Study: Ireland.
No. of awards offered: Five.
Application Procedure: Applicants must complete an application form, available upon request.
Closing Date: Please write for details.
Funding: Government.
Contributor: State funded.
No. of awards given last year: Three.
No. of applicants last year: 30.

DUMBARTON OAKS: TRUSTEES FOR HARVARD UNIVERSITY

1703 32nd Street North West, Washington, DC, 20007, United States of America
Tel: (1) 202 339 6410
Email: DumbartonOaks@doaks.org
www: http://www.doaks.org
Contact: Ms Carol A Sellery, Fellowship Program Manager

Dumbarton Oaks houses important research and study collections in the areas of Byzantine and Medieval studies, landscape architecture studies and pre-Columbian studies. While the gallery holds exhibitions and the gardens are open to the public, the research facilities exist primarily to serve scholars who hold appointments at Dumbarton Oaks.

Dumbarton Oaks Fellowships and Junior Fellowships

Subjects: Byzantine civilisation in all its aspects, including the late Roman and Early Christian period and the Middle Ages generally, studies of Byzantine cultural exchanges with the Latin West, Slavic and Near Eastern Countries, pre-Columbian studies and Garden and Landscape Studies.

Purpose: To promote study and research or to support writing of doctoral dissertations.

Eligibility: Junior Fellowships are open to persons of any nationality who have passed all preliminary examinations for a higher degree and are writing a dissertation. Candidates must have a working knowledge of any languages required for the research. Fellowships are open to Scholars of any nationality holding a PhD or relevant advanced degree and wishing to pursue research on a project of their own at Dumbarton Oaks.

Level of Study: Doctorate, Postdoctorate.

Type: Fellowship.

Value: US$14,260 per year for junior fellowships, US$25,990 per year for fellowships. Both junior and regular Fellows receive furnished accommodation or a housing allowance and US$1,950, if needed, to assist with the cost of bringing and maintaining dependants in Washington plus an expense account of US$925 for approved research expenditure during the academic year. Fellows are also provided with travel assistance.

Length of Study: Up to one academic year of full-time study, non renewable.

Frequency: Annual.

Study Establishment: Dumbarton Oaks.

Country of Study: United States of America.

No. of awards offered: 10-11 fellowships in Byzantine studies and three-four in each of the other fields.

Application Procedure: Applicants must contact Dumbarton Oaks for the current application brochure.

Closing Date: November 1st of the academic year preceding that for which the fellowship is required.

No. of awards given last year: 35.

No. of applicants last year: 200.

Additional Information: Dumbarton Oaks also awards a limited number of Summer Fellowships.

DUQUESNE UNIVERSITY, DEPARTMENT OF PHILOSOPHY

Pittsburgh, PA 15282, United States of America
Tel: (1) 412 396 6500
Fax: (1) 412 396 5353
Email: thompson@duq.edu
www: http://www.duq.odu
Contact: Ms Joan Thompson, Administrative Assistant

The PhD programme in the Department of Philosophy at Duquesne University emphasises continental philosophy, ie. phenomenology and twentieth-century French and German philosophy, as well as the history of philosophy.

Duquesne University Graduate Assistantship

Subjects: Philosophy.

Purpose: To provide a stipend to enable students to obtain a PhD in philosophy.

Eligibility: Open to holders of a Bachelor's degree in philosophy or its equivalent, who have a grade point average of at least 3.7 and an excellent Graduate Record Examination score. Candidates should have knowledge of a second language.

Level of Study: Doctorate.

Type: Other.

Value: A stipend of approximately US$9,700 plus all tuition for coursework.

Length of Study: Five-six years.

Frequency: Annual.

Study Establishment: McAnulty College and Graduate School of Liberal Arts.

Country of Study: United States of America.

No. of awards offered: 13 including 2 for first year students, 13 1/2 - this includes 2 for new incoming students.

Application Procedure: Applicants must complete an application form including a statement of intent, three letters of recommendation, Graduate Record Examination scores, application fee and Test of English as a Foreign Language scores.

Closing Date: February 15th before the Autumn term.

Funding: Private.

Contributor: Duquesne University.

No. of awards given last year: 13 1/2.

No. of applicants last year: 75.

DYSTONIA SOCIETY

46-47 Britton Street, London, EC1M 5UJ, England
Tel: (44) 20 7490 5671
Fax: (44) 20 7490 5672
www: http://www.dystonia.org.uk
Contact: Administrative Assistant

The Dystonia Society exists to support people with any form of the neurological movement disorder or dystonia, and their families, through the promotion of awareness, research and welfare.

Jackie Deakin Dystonia Prize Essay Competition

Subjects: Neurology, movement disorders and dystonia.

Purpose: To promote awareness and understanding of dystonia among tomorrows medical profession.

Eligibility: Open to third, fourth and fifth year students at United Kingdom medical schools.

Type: Prize.

Value: The first prize is UK£1,000, the second is UK£500 and there are six further prizes of UK£250 each.

Frequency: Every two years.

Study Establishment: Medical schools.

Country of Study: United Kingdom.

No. of awards offered: Eight.

Application Procedure: Applicants must refer to the website or contact the Society directly.

Closing Date: Registration must be completed by by November 30th 2004 and completion and submission of the essay must take place by January 15th 2005.

Funding: Private.

Contributor: Voluntary donations.

No. of awards given last year: Eight.

No. of applicants last year: 24.

EARLY AMERICAN INDUSTRIES ASSOCIATION

1324 Shallcross Avenue, Wilmington, DE 19806, United States of America
Tel: (1) 302 652 7297
Email: eaiainfo@worldnet.att.net
www: http://www.eaiainfo.org
Contact: Ms Justine J Mataleno, Co-ordinator

The Early American Industries Association seeks to encourage the study and better understanding of early American industries in the home, in the shop, on the farm and on the sea. It also wishes to discover, identify, classify and exhibit obsolete tools, implements and mechanical devices which were used in early America.

Early American Industries Association Research Grants Program

Subjects: Early American industrial development, including craft practices, industrial technology and identification and use of obsolete tools, implements and mechanical devices used prior to 1900.

Purpose: To encourage research leading to a publication, exhibition or audio-visual material for educational purposes.

Eligibility: Open to citizens or permanent residents of the United States of America. Individuals may be either sponsored by an institution or engaged in self directed projects.

Level of Study: Doctorate, Graduate, Postdoctorate, Postgraduate, Predoctorate, Research.

Type: Grant.

Value: Up to US$2,000.

Length of Study: One year, non renewable.

Frequency: Annual.
Country of Study: United States of America.
No. of awards offered: Three-five.
Application Procedure: Applicants must submit a completed application form plus three letters of recommendation.
Closing Date: March 15th.
Funding: Private.
Contributor: Membership dues and donations.
No. of awards given last year: 3.
No. of applicants last year: 14.
Additional Information: Awards may be used to supplement existing financial awards. Successful applicants are required to file a project report on forms supplied by the Association. These are not scholarship funds.

EARTHWATCH INSTITUTE

Research Program, 3 Clock Tower Place, Suite 100, Maynard, MA 01754, United States of America
Tel: (1) 978 461 0081
Fax: (1) 978 461 2332
Email: research@earthwatch.org
www: http://www.earthwatch.org/research

Earthwatch Institute supports diverse research projects of high scientific merit worldwide, which address critical environmental and social issues at local, national and international levels. Researchers are given both funding and field assistance from layperson volunteers. Volunteers are recruited by Earthwatch, who pay for the opportunity to assist them in the field.

Earthwatch Education Awards
Subjects: Science education, historical and cultural education.
Purpose: To give teachers and students the opportunity to experience field research first hand and share this experience with their students and local communities.
Level of Study: Professional development.
Type: Fellowship.
Length of Study: Two-three weeks.
Frequency: Annual.
Country of Study: Any country.
No. of awards offered: 265.
Application Procedure: Applicants must complete an application form and submit it with the other requested documents. Incomplete applications will not be considered. Letters of recommendation are required and should explain how long and in what respect they know the applicant. There is an application fee of US$20.
Closing Date: Applications are accepted on an ongoing basis.
Funding: Private.
Contributor: Over 40 donors including foundations and corporations.
No. of awards given last year: 250.
No. of applicants last year: 700.
Additional Information: Recipients are limited to two Education Awards and cannot receive an award in two consecutive years.

Earthwatch Field Research Grants
Subjects: Disciplines include, but are not limited to, anthropology, archaeology, biology, botany, cartography, conservation, ethnology, folklore, geography, geology, hydrology, marine sciences, meteorology, musicology, nutrition, ornithology, restoration, sociology and sustainable development.
Purpose: To provide grants for field research projects that can constructively utilise teams of non specialist field assistants in accomplishing their research goals.
Eligibility: There are no residency requirements or nomination processes. Preference is given to applicants who hold a PhD and have both field and teaching experience, however, support is also offered for outstanding projects by younger postdoctoral scholars and, in special cases, graduate students. Women and minority applicants are encouraged. Research teams must include qualified volunteers from the Earthwatch Institute.
Level of Study: Doctorate, Postdoctorate.
Type: Grant.

Value: Varies. The normal range of support is US$7,000-130,000. Grants are awarded on a per capita basis, depending upon the number of volunteer participants who are recruited by Earthwatch.
Length of Study: Teams last for two-three weeks and projects can go on all year.
Frequency: Annual.
Study Establishment: Research sites.
Country of Study: Any country.
No. of awards offered: Approx. 140.
Application Procedure: Applicants must complete an application form, which can be obtained from the Earthwatch headquarters or by visiting the website. Preliminary proposals must be submitted 13 months prior to field dates.
Closing Date: There is no deadline.
Funding: Private.
Contributor: Volunteers' contributions.
No. of awards given last year: 130.
No. of applicants last year: 400.
Additional Information: Further information is available on request.

EAST LOTHIAN EDUCATIONAL TRUST

Finance Department, John Muir House, Haddington, East Lothian EH41 3HA, Scotland
Tel: (44) 1620 827436
Fax: (44) 1620 827446
Contact: Kim Brand, Clerk

The East Lothian Educational Trust provides grants to individuals who are undertaking studies, courses or projects of an educational nature, including scholarships abroad and educational travel. Applicants must be residents of East Lothian.

East Lothian Educational Trust General Grant
Subjects: All subjects, but must be of an educational nature.
Purpose: To provide supplementary support to individuals who undertake studies.
Eligibility: Open to residents of East Lothian, excluding Musselburgh, Wallyford and Whitecraig.
Level of Study: Unrestricted.
Type: Grant.
Value: Variable.
Length of Study: Unrestricted.
Frequency: Annual.
No. of awards offered: Variable.
Application Procedure: Applicants must complete an application form.
Closing Date: August 20th and November 20th each year.
Funding: Private.

EASTMAN SCHOOL OF MUSIC OF THE UNIVERSITY OF ROCHESTER

26 Gibbs Street, Rochester, NY 14604, United States of America
Tel: (1) 585 274 1060
Fax: (1) 585 232 8601
Email: admissions@esm.rochester.edu
www: http://www.rochester.edu/eastman
Contact: Mary Ellen Nugent, Director of Financial Aid

In its 16 year history the Eastman School of Music has remained faithful to its founding mission to develop articulate and literate musicians. The breadth and depth of the accomplishments of its graduates is testimony to the strength and value of an Eastman education.

Eastman School of Music Graduate Awards
Subjects: Music.
Purpose: To support the School's academic programmes.
Eligibility: Open to nationals of all countries. Candidates should have the qualifications necessary for admission to the Eastman School of Music. Non United States citizens are usually offered service scholarships in ensemble work at graduate level.
Level of Study: Doctorate, Postgraduate.

Type: Award.
Value: Up to US$25,685.
Length of Study: One academic year, renewable.
Frequency: Annual.
Study Establishment: At the School.
Country of Study: United States of America.
No. of awards offered: Approx. 200.
Application Procedure: Applicants must complete an application form. In addition, most awards require an interview in Rochester.
Closing Date: January 1st.
Funding: Private.
Contributor: The Institution.
No. of awards given last year: 214.
No. of applicants last year: 735.
Additional Information: Further information is available on request.

THE EBB AND FLOW CHARITABLE TRUST

28 Northmoor Road, Oxford, OX2 6UR, England
Tel: (44) 1865 513100
Fax: (44) 1865 513100
Contact: Mrs Alison Bickmore, Trust Secretary

The Ebb and Flow Charitable Trust is a small family trust largely concerned with the needs of disabled children and adults. The Trust would like to make more awards in the field of specialist therapies eg. music, art, occupational etc. The Trust also supports work for the homeless and educational enterprises outside statutory provision.

Ebb & Flow Grant

Subjects: Any subject, the practice of which is calculated to benefit the development and/or welfare of disabled or handicapped persons of any age.
Purpose: To assist students with the expenses of the additional year of study usually required for acquiring professional skills as therapists.
Eligibility: Grants are only given for studies undertaken in the United Kingdom.
Level of Study: Postgraduate, Professional development.
Type: Grant.
Value; UK£200-UK£400.
Length of Study: One year.
Frequency: Dependent on funds available.
Country of Study: United Kingdom.
No. of awards offered: One-three at each half yearly meeting of the trustees when suitable applicants offer themselves.
Application Procedure: Applicants must submit a completed application form from the Secretary.
Closing Date: January 14th and July 14th.
Funding: Private.
Contributor: Income from investments.
No. of awards given last year: 7 for postgraduate work.
No. of applicants last year: 95 across all areas of the Trust's interests.
Additional Information: The Ebb and Flow Trust also funds grants to groups and organisations whose work focuses on homelessness and mental and physical disabilities.

ECONOMIC AND SOCIAL RESEARCH COUNCIL (ESRC)

Polaris House, North Star Avenue, Swindon, Wiltshire, SN2 1UJ, England
Tel: (44) 1793 413000
Fax: (44) 1793 413056
Email: ptd@esrc.ac.uk
www: http://www.esrc.ac.uk
Contact: Ms Zoë Grimwood, Research Trg-development

The Economic and Social Research Council (ESRC) is an independent, government funded body set up by royal charter. The mission of ESRC is to promote and support, by any means, high quality basic, strategic and applied research and related postgraduate training in the social sciences. It also aims to advance knowledge and provide trained social scientists who meet the needs of users and beneficiaries, thereby contributing to the economic competitiveness of the United Kingdom, the effectiveness of public services and policy, and quality of life. ESRC also provides advice, disseminates knowledge and promotes public understanding of the social sciences.

ESRC 1+3 Awards & +3 Awards

Subjects: Social sciences.
Purpose: To promote social science research and postgraduate training. The ESRC aims to provide continuous support for high quality postgraduate training and research on issues of importance to business, the public sector and government.
Eligibility: Open to United Kingdom or European Community nationals with a First or Upper Second Class (Honours) Degree in any subject, or a United Kingdom professional qualification acceptable to the ESRC as of degree standard plus three years of subsequent full-time, relevant professional work experience. Candidates must have ordinarily been resident in Great Britain throughout the three year period preceding the date of application but should not have been resident during any part of that period wholly or mainly for the purpose of receiving full-time education.
Level of Study: Postgraduate.
Type: Studentship.
Value: ESRC 1+3 awards cover fees and/or maintenance, depending on the student's situation, circumstances and the type of award.
Length of Study: Up to three years.
Frequency: Annual.
Study Establishment: ESRC recognised Institutional outlets and courses.
Country of Study: United Kingdom.
No. of awards offered: Varies.
Application Procedure: Applicants must complete an application form. Information sheets and application forms are available from February each year and must be collected from the social science department of any university or Institute of Higher Education or career guidance outlet.
Closing Date: May 1st.
Funding: Government.
No. of awards given last year: 669.
No. of applicants last year: 1809.
Additional Information: The 1 refers to the one year Master's and the 3 refers to the 3 year PhD.

ECONOMIC HISTORY ASSOCIATION (EHA)

University of Kansas, Department of Economics, 226A Summerfield Hall, Lawrence, KS 66049, United States of America
Tel: (1) 785 864 2847
Fax: (1) 785 864 5270
Email: eha@ky.edu
www: http://www.eh.net/eha
Contact: Mr Thomas Weiss, Executive Director

The Economic History Association (EHA) was founded in 1940. Its mission is to stimulate interest in the study of economic history, to encourage research in economic history and ideas, to co-operate with societies devoted to the study of agricultural, industrial, technological or business history and to collaborate with economists, historians, statisticians, geographers and all other students of economic change.

Arthur H Cole Grants-in-Aid

Subjects: Economic history.
Purpose: To support research.
Eligibility: Applicants must have completed a PhD and be members of the EHA.
Level of Study: Postdoctorate.
Type: Other.
Value: Typically US$1,500 award.
Frequency: Annual.
Country of Study: Any country.

No. of awards offered: 3-4.
Application Procedure: Applicants must supply seven copies of the following: a description of the project of no more than five pages, a curriculum vitae and a brief budget for the project. Applications must be marked for the attention of Professor Chiaki Moriguchi. Electronic submissions preferred.
Closing Date: April 1st.
Funding: Private.
Contributor: EHA Members.
No. of awards given last year: 4.
No. of applicants last year: 9.
Additional Information: Membership enquiries should be addressed to the office of the Executive Director or at www.ch.net/EHA.

For further information contact:

Northevestern N,
Email: chiaki@northevestern.edu
Contact: Professor Chiaki Moriguchi

EDMUND NILES HUYCK PRESERVE, INC.

PO Box 189, Rensselaerville, NY 12147, United States of America
Tel: (1) 518 797 3440
Fax: (1) 518 797 3440
Email: rlwyman@capital.net
www: http://www.huyckpreserve.org/ggl.htm
Contact: Mr Richard Wyman, Executive Director

The Edmund Niles Huyck Preserve is a 2,000 acre nature preserve and biological research station with a newly expanded laboratory and housing for 20. The habitat is the north eastern hardwood hemlock forest with lakes, streams, bogs and plantations.

Edmund Niles Huyck Preserve, Inc. Graduate and Postgraduate Grants

Subjects: Ecology, behaviour, evolution and natural resources of the area, and conservation biology.
Purpose: To promote scientific research on the flora and fauna of the Huyck Preserve and vicinity.
Eligibility: Open to all nationalities. Awards are made without regard to sex, colour, religion, ethnic origin or academic affiliation of the applicant and support is based solely on the quality of the proposed research and its appropriateness to the natural resources and facilities of the Preserve.
Level of Study: Doctorate, Graduate, Postdoctorate, Postgraduate.
Type: Grant.
Value: A maximum of US$2,500 plus laboratory space and lodging. Grants are renewable.
Length of Study: Varies.
Frequency: Annual.
Study Establishment: At the Preserve.
Country of Study: United States of America.
No. of awards offered: 10.
Application Procedure: Applicants must complete an application form, available on written request. Proposals must contain an abstract of not more than 200 words describing the background and significance of the proposal. A literature cited section should be included and an up to date curriculum vitae provided. The researcher should submit three references that deal specifically with their proposed work.
Closing Date: February 1st.
Funding: Private.
No. of awards given last year: Six.
No. of applicants last year: 12.
Additional Information: Further information is available from the website.

EDUCATIONAL TESTING SERVICE (ETS)

Rosedale Road, Princeton, NJ 08541-0001, United States of America
Tel: (1) 609 734 1806
Fax: (1) 609 734 1755
Email: ldelauro@ets.org
www: http://www.ets.org
Contact: Ms Linda J DeLauro

The Educational Testing Service (ETS) is a non-profit organisation whose goal is to help advance quality and equity in education by providing valid assessments, research, projects and services.

ETS Postdoctoral Fellowships

Subjects: Psychology, education, sociology of education, psychometrics, statistics, computer science, policy research or special education, minority issues in education, literacy.
Purpose: To provide research opportunities to individuals who hold a doctorate in education and related fields, and to increase the number of women and minority professionals conducting research in educational measurement.
Eligibility: The applicant should hold a doctorate in educational measurement or related field. A background in second language education and assessment is highly desirable. The applicant should show evidence of a commitment to research, especially research, and to achieving excellence in this field. Recommendations from established Scholars in measurement and educational research would be highly valued.
Level of Study: Postdoctorate.
Type: Fellowship.
Value: US$60,000. In addition, limited relocation expenses, consistent with ETS guidelines, will be reimbursed upon presentation of receipts.
Length of Study: Two years, second year renewable upon successful completion of 1st year, and mutual consent.
Frequency: Annual.
Country of Study: United States of America.
No. of awards offered: Up to three.
Application Procedure: Applicants must submit a curriculum vitae, a five page typed research proposal, a description of relevant work, interests and experience, publications and other relevant documents and materials, official transcripts of undergraduate and graduate studies and letters of recommendation from three people who are familiar with the applicant's work. There is no formal application form.
Closing Date: Materials must be postmarked by February 1st.
Funding: Private.
Contributor: The Educational Testing Service.
No. of awards given last year: 5.
No. of applicants last year: 39.

ETS Summer Program in Research for Graduate Students

Subjects: Psychology, education, teaching, learning, psychometrics, statistics, computer science, linguistics, literacy, psycholinguistics, educational technology, minority issues, testing issues, including alternate forms of assessment for special populations, testing issues associated with new forms of assessment, or policy research.
Purpose: To increase the number of women and minority professionals in educational measurement and related fields and to provide students with the opportunity to conduct independent research under the mentorship of an ETS researcher.
Eligibility: Open to graduate students who are pursuing a doctorate in a relevant discipline. The main criteria for selection will be scholarship and the match of applicant interests with participating ETS staff. Affirmative action goals will also be considered.
Level of Study: Predoctorate.
Value: US$5,000 for the two month period. Participants will be reimbursed for limited travel to and from Princeton, consistent with the ETS travel policy.
Length of Study: June-July.
Frequency: Annual.
Country of Study: United States of America.
No. of awards offered: Up to 16.
Application Procedure: Applicants must submit an application including a statement of interest, a curriculum vitae, letters of reference from two individuals who are familiar with the applicant's academic work and official transcripts of undergraduate and graduate studies.
Closing Date: February 1, 2004.
Funding: Private.
Contributor: The ETS.
No. of awards given last year: 29.
No. of applicants last year: 137.

Additional Information: To request applications email- internships@ets.org or apply on line at www.ets.org\research\fellowships\html.

For further information contact:

Applicants must submit application online at ETS website. www.ets.org\research\fellowships\html,

ETS Sylvia Taylor Johnson Minority Fellowship Educational Measurement

Subjects: Educational research, Educational measurement, Policy research, Minority issues in education, Assessment: Universal access to PRE-K Assessment, Teacher education & achievement.
Purpose: To promote excellence, as well as to encourage original and significant research for early career scholars. Studies focused on issues concerning the education of minority students are especially encouraged.
Eligibility: Open to applicants who have received their doctoral degree within the past ten years and who are United States citizens or permanent residents. Selections will be based on the applicants record of accomplishment and proposed topic of research. Applicants should have a commitment to education and an independent body of scholarship that signals the promise of continuing outstanding contributions to educational measurement.
Level of Study: Postdoctorate.
Type: Fellowship.
Value: The stipend will be set in relation to the successful applicant's compensation at the home institution. In addition, limited relocation expenses, consistent with ETS guidelines, will be reimbursed.
Length of Study: One year, renewal upon successful completion of first year by mutual consent.
Frequency: Annual.
Country of Study: United States of America.
No. of awards offered: 1.
Application Procedure: Applicants must submit a letter of interest, a current curriculum vitae, a detailed proposal of the research the applicant will conduct while at ETS, letters of reference from three individuals who are familiar with the applicant's work and samples of published research. Notification to applicants of results will be returned by March 1st.
Closing Date: February 1.
Funding: Private.
Contributor: ETS.
No. of awards given last year: 1.
No. of applicants last year: 11.
Additional Information: Through her research, extensive writings and service to the educational community as an educator, editor, counsellor, committee member, and a collaborator during her lifetime, Sylvia Taylor Johnson had a significant influence in educational measurement and assessment nationally. In honour of Dr Johnson's important contributions to the field of education, the ETS has established the Sylvia Taylor Johnson Minority Fellowship in Educational Measurement.

For further information contact:

Email: fellowships@ets.org
www: www.ets.org/research/fellowships.html

THE EDWARD F ALBEE FOUNDATION, INC.

14 Harrison Street, New York, NY 10013, United States of America
Tel: (1) 212 226 2020
Email: albeefdtn@aol.com
www: http://www.pipeline.com/~jtnyc/albeefdtn.html
Contact: Mr Jacob Holder, Foundation Secretary

The Edward F Albee Foundation provides residence and working space to writers and visual artists at its facilities in Montauk, New York. The residency is offered at no charge to the participants and imposes no obligations, except diligent application to their work and respect for the privacy of others.

William Flanagan Memorial Creative Persons Center
Subjects: Writing, painting, sculpting and musical composition.
Purpose: To provide accommodation.
Eligibility: Open to artists and writers in need who have displayed evidence of their talent.
Level of Study: Unrestricted.
Value: Accommodation only.
Length of Study: Four months between June 1st and October 1st.
Frequency: Annual.
Study Establishment: The William Flanagan Memorial Creative Persons Center in Montauk, Long Island.
Country of Study: United States of America.
No. of awards offered: 20 places.
Application Procedure: Applicants must complete an application form. Forms are available upon request and should be accompanied by a pre-paid return envelope. Other materials are also required, and applicants should write for further details.
Closing Date: January 1st to April 1st.
Funding: Private.
No. of awards given last year: 20.
No. of applicants last year: 300.
Additional Information: The environment is communal and residents are expected to do their share in maintaining the conditions of the Center.

THE ELECTROCHEMICAL SOCIETY, INC.

65 South Main Street, Pennington, NJ 08534, United States of America
Tel: (1) 609 737 1902
Fax: (1) 609 737 2743
Email: ecs@electrochem.org
www: http://www.electrochem.org
Contact: Erin Goudwin, Electrochemical Society, Inc.

The Electrochemical Society is an international non-profit educational organisation concerned with a broad range of phenomena relating to electrochemical and solid state science and technology. The Society has more than 8,000 individual members worldwide as well as roughly 100 corporations and laboratories which hold contributing membership.

Electrochemical Society Summer Fellowships
Subjects: Electrochemical and solid state science.
Purpose: To fund a student's research through the Summer months.
Eligibility: Open to nationals of any country who are enrolled in either an American or Canadian university or college.
Level of Study: Unrestricted.
Type: Fellowship.
Value: US$4,000.
Length of Study: Three months over one Summer.
Frequency: Annual.
Study Establishment: International.
Country of Study: United States of America or Canada.
No. of awards offered: Four.
Application Procedure: Applicants must submit an application and supporting materials.
Closing Date: January 1st.
Funding: Private.
No. of awards given last year: Four.
No. of applicants last year: Four.

ELIZABETH GREENSHIELDS FOUNDATION

1814 Sherbrooke Street West, Suite 1, Montréal, QC, H3H 1E4, Canada
Tel: (1) 514 937 9225
Fax: (1) 514 937 0141
Email: greenshields@bellnet.ca
Contact: Ms Isabelle Lalonde, Administrative Assistant

The purpose of the Elizabeth Greenshields Foundation is to aid artists in the early stages of their careers. Awards are limited to candidates working in the areas of painting, drawing, printmaking, and sculpture. Work must be figurative or representational, as abstract art is precluded by the terms of the Foundation's charter.

Elizabeth Greenshields Grant

Subjects: Painting, drawing, printmaking and sculpture.
Purpose: To assist talented artists in the early stages of their careers.
Eligibility: Open to nationals of any country. There is no age limit but candidates must have started or completed training at an established school of art or demonstrate, through past work and future plans, a commitment to making art a lifetime career. The Foundation will not accept applications from commercial artists, photographers, video artists, filmmakers, craftmakers or any artist whose work falls primarily into these categories. Applicants may reapply to the Foundation, whether or not they have previously received a grant, but candidates who have previously been declined must wait for a period of two years before reapplying. Grantees may reapply for a second grant one year after the first grant was awarded.
Level of Study: Unrestricted.
Type: Grant.
Value: Canadian $12,500.
Frequency: Throughout the year.
Country of Study: Any country.
No. of awards offered: 45-55 per year.
Application Procedure: Applicants must complete an application form and submit this with six slides, 12 for sculptors, completed no longer than three years ago. Requests for application forms can be made in writing with return postage paid or by phone, fax or email.
Closing Date: Grants are awarded throughout the year.
Funding: Private.
No. of awards given last year: 50.
No. of applicants last year: 1500.
Additional Information: Application forms are sent to individuals only. The Foundation is not a school or a gallery.

EMBLEM CLUB SCHOLARSHIP FOUNDATION

PO Box 712, San Luis Rey, CA 92068, United States of America
Tel: (1) 619 757 0619
Fax: (1) 619 757 0619
Email: perky2@home.com
www: http://www.emblemclub.org
Contact: Administrative Secretary

Emblem Club Scholarship Foundation Grant

Subjects: Education and teacher training.
Purpose: To assist teachers who are working towards their Master's degree and accreditation in order to teach the deaf and hearing impaired. This does not include audiology or speech therapy.
Eligibility: Applicants must be United States citizens of no more than 50 years of age, and must agree to teach within the United States of America. There are no other restrictions as to minority, religion or language.
Level of Study: Postgraduate.
Type: Grant.
Value: Varies.
Frequency: Four times per year.
Country of Study: United States of America.
Application Procedure: Applicants must apply to the schools concerned.
Closing Date: March 1st, June 1st, September 1st or January 1st.
Funding: Private.

ÉMIGRÉ MEMORIAL GERMAN INTERNSHIP PROGRAMS (EMGIP)

PO Box 345, Durham, NH 03824, United States of America
Email: gkr@hopper.unh.edu
Contact: Professor George K Romoser, Director

The Emigré Memorial German Internship Programs (EMGIP) rest on the co-operation of North American and German affairs specialists with German government offices. Interns are placed in German offices to encourage training for future specialists on Germany and to cultivate German United States of America contacts. EMGIP is independent of governments and universities.

Émigré Memorial German Internship Programs

Subjects: Government service and social sciences.
Purpose: To promote professional study and work on German government and society.
Eligibility: Open to North American students or those studying in a North American institution who are advanced graduate students and are not native German speakers. A high standard of written and spoken German and evidence of study in the social sciences or humanities, including languages, at higher education level is required.
Level of Study: Graduate, Postgraduate, Predoctorate, Professional development.
Type: Work Study.
Value: A stipends ranging from housing aid to between €600-1,000 per month depending on location. No travel costs are paid.
Length of Study: Up to three months.
Frequency: Dependent on funds available.
Study Establishment: Parliamentary offices in government institutions.
Country of Study: Germany.
No. of awards offered: 8-11.
Application Procedure: Applicants must complete and return five copies of answers to selected questions from the organisation, five copies of all university/colleges attended, a recent photo and a fee of US$200 by United States cheque or money order, payable to German Internships. Applications must only be sent by mail and not by email, express or special mail.
Closing Date: 23 Feb.
Funding: Government.
Contributor: German offices and the German Academic Exchange Service.
No. of awards given last year: 11.
No. of applicants last year: 21.

ENGINEERING AND PHYSICAL SCIENCES RESEARCH COUNCIL (EPSRC)

Polaris House, North Star Avenue, Swindon, Wiltshire, SN2 1ET, England
Tel: (44) 1793 444239
Fax: (44) 1793 444007
Email: jan.tucker@epsrc.ac.uk
www: http://www.epsrc.ac.uk
Contact: Ms Jan Tucker, Peer Review Operations

The Engineering and Physical Sciences Research Council (EPSRC) promotes and supports high quality, basic, strategic and applied research and related postgraduate training in engineering and physical sciences. It aims to advance knowledge and technology by providing trained scientists and engineers, in order to meet the needs of users and beneficiaries, and thereby contribute to economic competitiveness and quality of life.

EPSRC Advanced Research Fellowships

Subjects: Engineering, Mathematics, Physics, Chemistry, Materials and Information Technology; with Life Sciences Interface.
Purpose: To support outstanding young academic research workers in order that they may devote themselves to full-time research projects.
Eligibility: Open to candidates holding a PhD or equivalent standing in their profession along with at least three years of experience at the postdoctoral level upon the expected start date of the fellowship. Candidates should be within 10 years of completing their PhD by the time the award commences, with a minimum of three years postdoctoral experience.
Level of Study: Postdoctorate.
Type: Fellowship.

Value: Funding for basic salary costs which includes National Insurance and superannuation contributions. Successful candidates also receive a Fellowship Support Fund (FSF) of UK£4,000 per year. The use of the FSF, which is at the discretion of the Fellow, will vary according to the nature of the research programme, but may include small items of equipment including computers, software, travel and subsistence expenses, such as visits to collaborators and conferences, and small amounts of research and technical effort. Up to UK£2,000 may be used in the first year to cover relocation and removal costs associated with taking up the fellowship. The FSF must not be used to meet any university overheads or indirect or unspecified costs. A full account of the use of the FSF will be required at the end of the fellowship. Please note that payments of salary and relevant FSF for all fellowships are administered via the university hosting the award. The salary is paid on an 'age for wage' basis.

Length of Study: A maximum of five years.

Frequency: Annual.

Study Establishment: Any academic institution acceptable to the Council.

Country of Study: United Kingdom.

No. of awards offered: Up to 40.

Application Procedure: Applicants must complete an application form, available on the website. After initial sitting by EPSRC the subject area panel shortlists those candidates to be invited for interview. The interviewees are usually the top ranked 25-33 per cent of candidates. The remaining candidates not selected for interview are informed of this decision as soon as possible. Applicants are limited to one per year.

Closing Date: November.

Funding: Government.

No. of awards given last year: 41.

No. of applicants last year: Approx. 300.

Additional Information: A degree of mobility during the course of a fellowship may be beneficial. Any proposal to transfer the fellowship to a different organisation would need to be discussed with the existing and proposed organisations. If the new organisation agrees to host the fellowship, the EPSRC will normally be agreeable to a transfer. In such cases the original award would be closed down and a new award issued for the balance of the funding period. Fellows are expected to devote their whole working time to research. Up to one day a week may, however, be spent on teaching and demonstrating. The period of the fellowship may also be extended to compensate for an agreed abeyance, sick leave in excess of three months and maternity leave. At the end of the fellowship, a complete account of the research undertaken is required. The Individual Grant Review Fellowships (IGR) should also include a report on how the FSF was spent. Submission of the form is required within three months of the termination date of the fellowship. Any request to extend the IGR submission date must be made in writing and agreed by the EPSRC. EPSRC will not consider further applications from Fellows who are in default of submitting an IGR. For further information applicants should visit the website.

EPSRC Doctoral Training Grants (DTGs)

Subjects: Engineering, mathematics, information technology, materials, chemistry or physics.

Purpose: To provide funds directly to universities to support doctoral training in subjects which lie broadly within the remit of the EPSRC.

Eligibility: Open to candidates at a university whose standards of training, supervision and career advice meet those set by the EPSRC. Students must meet eligibility requirements of the education (fees and awards) regulations 1997.

Level of Study: Doctorate, Postgraduate, Predoctorate.

Type: Grant.

Value: Payments will be profiled over the first three years, save an element held back to the final quarter pending reconciliation of actual expenditure against payments made. A separate grant will be awarded for each subsequent annual output from the research algorithm. Funds can be used for the following types of expenditure: fees, consumables, part-time study and industrial placements, extended support and broadening skills training and career advice. Funds must not be used for academic salaries, premises costs, administration charges, indirect costs or overheads. The level of DTG funding is determined on the basis of the EPSRC research grants held by the university.

Length of Study: Three years to provide flexibility over the duration of research studentships and to allow for late and deferred starts and breaks through illness.

Frequency: Annual.

Study Establishment: United Kingdom universities.

Country of Study: United Kingdom.

Application Procedure: Applicants are selected in accordance with the university's postgraduate admission requirements and should approach the university at which they wish to study.

Funding: Government.

Additional Information: Students are selected and paid by the university. Further information is available from the website.

EPSRC Postdoctoral Fellowships in Mathematics

Subjects: Mathematics.

Purpose: To provide support for outstanding individuals at various stages of their careers to give them the freedom to pursue their research interests full-time, free from the burden of academic duties.

Eligibility: Candidates should be within three years of completing their PhD and should not hold permanent academic posts nor have more than four years of postdoctoral experience. This fellowship is open to European Union citizens.

Level of Study: Postdoctorate.

Type: Fellowship.

Value: The successful candidate receive funding for basic salary costs on an 'age for wage' basis, plus appropriate employers National Insurance and superannuation. There is a Fellowship Support fund (FSF) which is UK£6000 per year, to be used at the discretion of the Fellow. The use will vary according to the nature of the research programme, but may include small items of equipment including computers and software, travel and subsistence expenses, such as visits to collaborators and conferences, and small amounts of technical effort. Up to UK£2000 may be used in the 1st year to cover relocation and removal costs associated with taking up the fellowship. The FSF must not be used to meet any university overheads or indirect or unspecified costs. A full account of the use of the FSF will be required at the end of the fellowship. Please note that payment of the salary and relevant FSF for all fellowships are administered via the university hosting the award.

Length of Study: Three years.

Frequency: Annual.

Study Establishment: Normally universities or research institutions in the United Kingdom.

Country of Study: Other.

No. of awards offered: 10.

Application Procedure: Applicants must complete an application form, available on the website. The subject area panel shortlists those candidates to be invited for interview. The interviewees are usually the top ranked 25-33 per cent of candidates and interviews are usually held in December or January. The remaining candidates not selected for interview are informed of this decision as soon as possible. Applications are limited to one per year and applications for more than one type of fellowship will not be accepted.

Closing Date: January 8th.

Funding: Government.

No. of applicants last year: 50.

Additional Information: A degree of mobility during the course of a fellowship may be beneficial. Any proposal to transfer the fellowship to a different organisation would need to be discussed with the existing and proposed organisations. If the new organisation agrees to host the fellowship, the EPSRC will normally be agreeable to a transfer. In such cases the original award would be closed down and a new award issued for the balance of the funding period. Fellows are expected to devote their whole working time to research. Up to one day a week may, however, be spent on teaching and demonstrating. The period of the fellowship may also be extended to compensate for an agreed abeyance, sick leave in excess of three months and maternity leave. At the end of the fellowship, a complete account of the research undertaken is required. The format of the fellowship final report is likely to change in the near future. In due course these will be known as the

Individual Fellowship Report (IFR). The IFR format will allow a report of the outcomes of the research undertaken by the Fellow and will also include an element for reporting how the FSF was spent. Submission of the form is required within three months of the termination date of the fellowship. Any request to extend the submission date must be made in writing and agreed by the EPSRC. EPSRC will not consider further applications from Fellows who are in default of submitting an IFR.

EPSRC Postdoctoral Theory Fellowship in Physics

Subjects: Physics.

Purpose: To provide support for outstanding individuals at the start of their careers to give them the freedom to pursue their research interests full-time, normally shortly or immediately after completing a PhD.

Eligibility: Candidates should be within three years of completing their PhD at the time of the submission deadline and should not hold permanent academic posts. This fellowship is open to European Union citizens.

Level of Study: Postdoctorate.

Type: Fellowship.

Value: The successful candidate receive funding for basic salary costs on an 'age for wage' basis, plus appropriate employers National Insurance and superannuation. There is a Fellowship Support fund (FSF) which is UK£6000 per year, to be used at the discretion of the Fellow. The use will vary according to the nature of the research programme, but may include small items of equipment including computers and software, travel and subsistence expenses, such as visits to collaborators and conferences, and small amounts of technical effort. Up to UK£2000 may be used in the 1st year to cover relocation and removal costs associated with taking up the fellowship. The FSF must not be used to meet any university overheads or indirect or unspecified costs. A full account of the use of the FSF will be required at the end of the fellowship. Please note that payment of the salary and relevant FSF for all fellowships are administered via the university hosting the award.

Length of Study: Three years.

Frequency: Annual.

Study Establishment: Normally universities or research institutions in the United Kingdom.

Country of Study: Other.

No. of awards offered: Approx. four.

Application Procedure: Applicants must complete an application form, available on the website and are required to ensure their personal referees submit their comments on the correct forms. Note letters of support are not accepted. Short listing of candidates for interview is carried at on the basis of referees (personal and those chosen by EPSRC) reports. The interviewees are usually the top ranked 25-33 per cent of candidates and interviews are usually held in February. The remaining candidates not selected for interview are informed of this decision as soon as possible. Applications are limited to one per year and applications for more than one type of fellowship will not be accepted.

Closing Date: January 8th

Funding: Government.

No. of applicants last year: 20.

Additional Information: A degree of mobility during the course of a fellowship may be beneficial. Any proposal to transfer the fellowship to a different organisation would need to be discussed with the existing and proposed organisations. If the new organisation agrees to host the fellowship, the EPSRC will normally be agreeable to a transfer. In such cases the original award would be closed down and a new award issued for the balance of the funding period. Fellows are expected to devote their whole working time to research. Up to one day a week may, however, be spent on teaching and demonstrating. The period of the fellowship may also be extended to compensate for an agreed abeyance, sick leave in excess of three months and maternity leave. At the end of the fellowship, a complete account of the research undertaken is required. The format of the fellowship final report is likely to change in the near future. In due course these will be known as the Individual Fellowship Report (IFR). The IFR format will allow a report of the outcomes of the research undertaken by the Fellow and will also include an element for reporting how the FSF was spent. Submission of the form is required within three months of the termination date

of the fellowship. Any request to extend the submission date must be made in writing and agreed by the EPSRC. EPSRC will not consider further applications from Fellows who are in default of submitting an IFR.

EPSRC Senior Research Fellowships

Subjects: Engineering, mathematics, physics, chemistry, materials and information technology and life sciences interface.

Purpose: To enable outstanding established scientists and engineers at the peak of their capabilities to devote themselves to full-time research free of the restrictions imposed by their normal academic duties.

Eligibility: Open to scientists and engineers who are already established in their careers, having proved their exceptional research and interpretative ability. Applicants must be members of permanent staff of United Kingdom universities, technical colleges or similar United Kingdom academic institutions. Must be at level of Senior Lecturer/Reader/Professor or equivalent. Fellows are expected to return to their normal employment at the termination of the fellowship.

Level of Study: Professional development.

Type: Fellowship.

Value: Replacement of the Fellow's basic academic salary, excluding the superannuation and National Insurance contributions, as these must be covered by the academic host institution. The fellowship will include a Fellowship Support Fund (FSF) which is a fixed sum of UK£4000 per annum over the period of the award. Use of the FSF is at the discretion of the Fellow but may not be used to meet any university overheads or indirect or unspecified costs. Full details of use of the FSF will be required at the end of the fellowship. Please note that payment of salary and relevant FSF is administered via the university hosting the award.

Length of Study: A maximum of five years.

Frequency: Annual.

Study Establishment: Any academic institution acceptable to the Council.

Country of Study: United Kingdom.

No. of awards offered: Three.

Application Procedure: Applicants must complete an application form, available on the EPSRC website. The application forms can be downloaded via the links. An applicant is limited to one application for a fellowship each year. Applications for more than one type of fellowship will not be accepted.

Closing Date: November 2003 for 2004 round of awards. May after for subsequent rounds.

Funding: Government.

No. of awards given last year: Three.

No. of applicants last year: 60.

Additional Information: A degree of mobility during the course of a fellowship may be beneficial. Any proposal to transfer the fellowship to a different organisation would need to be discussed with the existing and proposed organisations. If the new organisation agrees to host the fellowship, the EPSRC will normally be agreeable to a transfer. In such cases the original award would be closed down and a new award issued for the balance of the funding period. Fellows are expected to devote their whole working time to research. Up to one day a week may, however, be spent on teaching and demonstrating. The period of the fellowship may also be extended to compensate for an agreed abeyance, sick leave in excess of three months and maternity leave. At the end of the fellowship, a complete account of the research undertaken is required. The Individual Grant Review(IGR) should also include a report on how the FSF was spent. Submission of the form is required within three months of the termination date of the fellowship. Any request to extend the IGR submission date must be made in writing and agreed by the EPSRC. EPSRC will not consider further applications from Fellows who are in default of submitting an IGR. For further information applicants should visit the website.

MOD Joint Grants Scheme

Subjects: All subjects.

Purpose: To support high quality research that has relevance to defence.

Eligibility: Open to anyone eligible for research council funding and is particularly suited to the development of new research links. Funding

is available to jointly support high quality basic and strategic research of relevance to defence needs.
Type: Research grant.
Value: Varies.
Length of Study: Varies.
Frequency: Dependent on funds available.
Study Establishment: Universities and similar institutions.
Country of Study: United Kingdom.
No. of awards offered: Varies.
Application Procedure: Applicants must visit the Defence Science and Technology Laboratory (Dstl) website, http://www.dstl.gov.uk where further details can be found about the scheme, contacts and MoD areas of interest.
Closing Date: There is no closing date.
Funding: Government.

ENGLISH-SPEAKING UNION (ESU)

Dartmouth House, 37 Charles Street, London, W1J SED, England
Tel: (44) 20 7529 1550
Fax: (44) 20 7495 6108
Email: esu@esu.org
www: http://www.esu.org
Contact: Cultural Affairs Officer

The English Speaking Union (ESU) is an independent, non political educational charity with members throughout the world, promoting international and human achievement through the worldwide use of the English language.

ESU Chautauqua Institution Scholarships
Subjects: Art (painting, ceramics and sculpture), music education, literature and international relations and drama.
Purpose: To enable British teachers to study at the Chautauqua Summer School.
Eligibility: Open to British teachers with a particular interest in the arts, aged 25-35.
Level of Study: Professional development.
Type: Scholarship.
Value: UK£850 plus board, room, tuition and lecture sessions at the Summer School.
Length of Study: Six weeks.
Frequency: Annual.
Study Establishment: Chautauqua Institution's Summer School in Chautauqua, New York.
Country of Study: United States of America.
No. of awards offered: Two.
Application Procedure: Applicants must write for details.
Closing Date: November.
Funding: Private.

ESU Music Scholarships
Subjects: Music.
Purpose: To enable musicians of outstanding ability to study at summer schools in the United States, Canada, France, United Kingdom, Czech Republic or Hungary.
Eligibility: Candidates must be aged 30 or under, and be students or graduates from a recognised United Kingdom conservatory or university music department.
Level of Study: Professional development.
Type: Scholarship.
Value: Tuition, board and lodging and relevant flight costs.
Length of Study: Two-nine weeks, depending on the particular scholarship.
Frequency: Annual.
Study Establishment: Summer school.
Country of Study: Other.
No. of awards offered: 10.
Application Procedure: Applications must be supported by a teacher's reference.
Funding: Commercial, Private.
Contributor: Private trust funds.

ESU Travelling Librarian Award
Subjects: Library science.
Purpose: To encourage United States and United Kingdom contacts in the library world and establish links between pairs of libraries.
Eligibility: Open to professionally qualified United Kingdom and American librarians.
Level of Study: Professional development.
Type: Travel grant.
Value: Board and lodging and relevant flight costs.
Length of Study: A minimum of three weeks.
Frequency: Annual.
Country of Study: Other.
No. of awards offered: One.
Application Procedure: Applicants must submit a curriculum vitae and covering letter explaining why they are the ideal candidate for the award.
Closing Date: Please write for details.
Funding: Commercial, Private.
Additional Information: Applicants should contact the Librarian by telephoning or emailing library@esu.org.

Lindemann Trust Fellowships
Subjects: Astronomy, chemistry, engineering, geology, geophysics, mathematics, physics and biophysics.
Eligibility: Open to United Kingdom and Commonwealth citizens who are graduates of a United Kingdom university and to United Kingdom and Commonwealth citizens who are pursuing postgraduate research at a United Kingdom university, although are not graduates of that institution. Preference is given to those who have demonstrated their capacity for original research and who will be under 30 years of age on September 1st of the fellowship year, but candidates up to 35 years of age are not debarred.
Level of Study: Postdoctorate, Postgraduate.
Type: Fellowship.
Value: A stipend of US$30,000.
Length of Study: One year.
Frequency: Annual.
Study Establishment: A university.
Country of Study: United States of America.
No. of awards offered: Two.
Application Procedure: Applicants must write for details.
Closing Date: October.
Funding: Private
Additional Information: Fellows are not required to work for an American degree but are expected to be attached to a university, college or seat of advanced learning and technical repute in the United States of America. The place of study and research programme must be approved by the Committee. A limited amount of teaching as an adjunct to research activities is not excluded.

ENTENTE CORDIALE SCHOLARSHIPS

French Cultural Department, 23 Cromwell Road, London, SW7 2EL, England
Tel: (44) 20 7073 1300
Fax: (44) 20 7073 1326
Email: entente.cordiale@ambafrance.org.uk
www: http://www.francealacarte.org.uk/entente
Contact: Administrative Officer

Launched by an agreement between the United Kingdom and French governments in 1995, the Entente Cordiale Scholarships enable outstanding British postgraduates to study or carry out research on the other side of the Channel, with a view to dispel preconceived ideas and promote good relations between the two countries.

Bourses Scholarships
Subjects: All subjects.
Purpose: To allow individuals to study or carry out research in France.
Eligibility: Open to British citizens.
Level of Study: Postgraduate.
Type: Scholarship.

Value: UK£8,000 for students living in Paris and UK£7,500 for those studying outside Paris.
Length of Study: One academic year.
Frequency: Annual.
Study Establishment: Approved universities or grande écoles.
Country of Study: France.
No. of awards offered: 10.
Application Procedure: Applicants must complete an application form, available from the website.
Closing Date: March 19th.
Funding: Private.
Contributor: Blue Circle (Lafarge), BP, Kingfisher plc, London Electricity, UBS Warburg, Xerox, Paul Minet Sir Patrick Sheeny Schlumberger, French Embassy.
No. of awards given last year: 9.
No. of applicants last year: 60.
Additional Information: Scholarships are also awarded to French postgraduates to study in the United Kingdom. Interested parties should contact the British Council in Paris.

EPILEPSY ACTION

New Anstey House, Gate Way Drive, Yeadon, Leeds, LS19 7XY, England
Tel: (44) 0113 2108800
Fax: (44) 0113 3910300
Email: research@epilepsy.org.uk
www: http://www.epilepsy.org.uk
Contact: Dr Margaret Rawnsley, Research Administration Officer

Epilepsy Action is the largest member led epilepsy organisation in Britain. As well as campaigning to improve epilepsy services + raise awareness of the condition, we offer assistance to people in a number of ways including a national network of branches, volunteers + free phone + e-mail helpline.

Postgraduate Research Bursaries

Subjects: Epilepsy Action encourages all non-laboratory research into epilepsy. These bursaries will be awarded to studies researching into the social, health care + psychological aspects of epilepsy.
Purpose: To support Postgraduate research in the social, + medical aspect of epilepsy.
Eligibility: Students should be registered for a postgraduate degree/study at a UK University.
Level of Study: Doctorate, Postdoctorate, Postgraduate, Predoctorate.
Type: Bursary.
Value: UK£1,500.00.
Length of Study: Open.
Frequency: Annual.
Study Establishment: 2003.
Country of Study: United Kingdom.
No. of awards offered: 3.
Application Procedure: Contact Research Administration Office at contact info.
Closing Date: Sept 2004.
Funding: Private.
Contributor: Organisation's own funds.
No. of awards given last year: 3.
No. of applicants last year: 7.

EPILEPSY FOUNDATION (EF)

4351 Garden City Drive, Landover, MD 20785, United States of America
Tel: (1) 301 459 3700
Fax: (1) 301 577 2684
www: http://www.epilepsyfoundation.org
Contact: Ms Cassandra Richard, Research Coordinator

The Epilepsy Foundation (EF) is a national, charitable organisation, founded in 1968 as the Epilepsy Foundation of America. It is the only organisation wholly dedicated to the welfare of people with epilepsy and to working on their behalf through research, education, advocacy and service.

Behavioral Sciences Research Training Fellowship

Subjects: Epilepsy research relative to the behavioural sciences. Appropriate fields of study include sociology, social work, psychology, anthropology, nursing, political science and others relevant to epilepsy research and practice.
Purpose: To offer qualified individuals the opportunity to develop expertise in epilepsy research through a training experience or involvement in an epilepsy research project.
Eligibility: Open to individuals who have received their doctoral degree in a field of the behavioural sciences by the time the fellowship commences and desire additional postdoctoral research experience in epilepsy. Applications from women and minorities are encouraged.
Level of Study: Postdoctorate.
Type: Fellowship.
Value: A stipend of up to US$30,000, depending on the experience and qualifications of the applicant and the scope and duration of the proposed project.
Length of Study: One year.
Frequency: Annual.
Study Establishment: An approved facility.
Country of Study: United States of America.
No. of awards offered: One.
Application Procedure: Applicants must complete an application form, available from the Foundation. Applicants may also visit the website research page for details.
Closing Date: February 1st.
Funding: Private.
No. of awards given last year: One.
Additional Information: The closing date for applications may vary from year to year. Applicants should email cmorris@efa.org for details.

Dreifuss International Travel Programme

Subjects: Epilepsy.
Purpose: To provide an opportunity for a visiting professor to spend time at a host institution to promote the exchange of medical and scientific information and expertise on epilepsy between the United States of America and other countries.
Eligibility: Either the visitor or the host institution must be from the United States of America.
Level of Study: Professional development.
Type: Travel grant.
Value: Travel expenses and minor incidental expenses.
Length of Study: Three-six weeks.
Frequency: Throughout the year.
Study Establishment: An approved facility.
Country of Study: Any country.
No. of awards offered: Up to 10 depending on funds available.
Application Procedure: Applicants must complete an application form, available from the Foundation. Applicants may also visit the website research page for details.
Closing Date: There is no deadline.
Funding: Private.

Research Grants

Subjects: Basic biomedical, behavioural and social science with particular encouragement given to applications in the behavioural sciences.
Purpose: To support basic and clinical research which will advance the understanding, treatment and prevention of epilepsy.
Eligibility: Open to United States researchers. Priority is given to investigators just entering the field of epilepsy, to new or innovative projects or to investigators whose research is relevant to developmental or paediatric aspects of epilepsy. Applications from women and minorities are encouraged, whilst applications from established investigators with other sources of support are discouraged. Research grants are not intended to provide support for postdoctoral Fellows.
Level of Study: Postdoctorate, Postgraduate.
Value: Up to US$40,000 support, but this may vary.
Length of Study: One year.
Frequency: Annual.

Country of Study: United States of America.
No. of awards offered: Varies.
Application Procedure: Applicants must complete an application form, available from the Foundation. Applicants may also visit the website research page for details.
Closing Date: September 1st.
Funding: Private.
Additional Information: The closing date for applications may vary from year to year. Applicants should email cmorris@efa.org for details.

Research Training Fellowships

Subjects: Basic or clinical epilepsy.
Purpose: To offer qualified individuals the opportunity to develop expertise in epilepsy research through involvement in an epilepsy research project.
Eligibility: Open to physicians and PhD neuroscientists who desire postdoctoral research experience. Preference is given to applicants whose proposals have a paediatric or developmental emphasis. Research must address a question of fundamental importance. A clinical training component is not required. Applications from women and minorities are encouraged.
Level of Study: Postdoctorate.
Type: Fellowship.
Value: A stipend of US$40,000.
Length of Study: One year.
Frequency: Annual.
Study Establishment: A facility where there is an ongoing epilepsy research programme.
Country of Study: United States of America or Canada.
No. of awards offered: Varies.
Application Procedure: Applicants must complete an application form, available from the Foundation. Applicants may also look at the website research page for details.
Closing Date: September 1st.
Funding: Private.

Research/Clinical Training Fellowships

Subjects: Basic or clinical epilepsy, with an equal emphasis on clinical training and clinical epileptology.
Purpose: To offer qualified individuals the opportunity to develop oxpertico in opilopcy recearch through training and involvement in an epilepsy research project.
Eligibility: Open to individuals who hold an MD degree and have completed their residency training. Applications from women and minorities are encouraged.
Level of Study: Postdoctorate, Postgraduate.
Type: Fellowship.
Value: A stipend of US$40,000.
Length of Study: One year.
Frequency: Annual.
Study Establishment: A facility where there is an ongoing epilepsy research programme.
Country of Study: United States of America.
No. of awards offered: Varies.
Application Procedure: Applicants must complete an application form, available from the Foundation. Applicants may also visit the website research page for details.
Closing Date: September 1st.
Funding: Private.
Additional Information: These fellowships include the Merrit-Putnam Fellowship.

EPILEPSY RESEARCH FOUNDATION

Research & Information Executive, PO Box 3004, London, W4 1XT, England
Tel: (44) 20 8400 6108
Fax: (44) 20 8995 4781
Email: info@erf.org.uk
www: http://www.erf.org.uk
Contact: L Slocombe, Executive Director

The Epilepsy Research Foundation promotes and supports basic and clinical scientific research into epilepsy. It seeks to identify medical research needs in epilepsy and raise money for independent research to be carried out by the best available research teams.

Epilepsy Research Foundation Research Grant

Subjects: Epilepsy.
Purpose: To promote and support basic and clinical research into epilepsy.
Eligibility: Open to researchers resident in the United Kingdom.
Level of Study: Research, Unrestricted.
Type: Research grant.
Value: A maximum of UK£60,000.
Length of Study: One-three years.
Frequency: Annual.
Country of Study: United Kingdom.
Application Procedure: Applications are invited by advertisements in scientific journals. A one page summary is requested initially.
Closing Date: The end of October.
Funding: Private.
No. of awards given last year: 4.
No. of applicants last year: 40.

EPISCOPAL CHURCH FOUNDATION

815 Second Avenue, New York, NY 10017
United States of America
Tel: (1) 212 697 2858
Fax: (1) 212 297 0142
Email: all@episcopalfoundation.org
www: http://www.episcopalfoundation.org
Contact: Fellows Program Manager

The Episcopal Church Foundation is an independent, lay led organisation which offers innovative programmes in leadership development, education and philanthropy for the clergy and laity of the Episcopal Church. It does not accept on solicited grant proposals or extend aid to individuals.

Episcopal Church Foundation Graduate Fellowship Program

Subjects: Theological studies.
Purpose: To support doctoral study for Episcopalians planning teaching careers in theological education in the Episcopal church in the United States.
Eligibility: Open to recent graduates of an accredited seminary who have been nominated by one of the 11 Episcopal seminaries, by Harvard Divinity School or the Union Theological Seminary of New York. Scholars who are not graduates of these institutions may seek nomination through the Fellows Forum. Neither ordination nor a Master of Divinity degree is required. Priority consideration is given to applicants who are in the early stages of their doctoral studies.
Level of Study: Doctorate.
Type: Fellowship.
Value: US$10,000 regardless of financial need.
Length of Study: One year, renewable for a further two years.
Frequency: Annual.
Study Establishment: At accredited institutions in the United States of America and abroad.
Country of Study: Any country.
No. of awards offered: Four.
Application Procedure: Applicants must contact the Deans office at any of the 11 accredited Episcopal seminaries, the Harvard Divinity School or the Union Theological Seminary for application materials.
Funding: Private.
Additional Information: Applicants must be communicants of the Episcopal Church in the United States of America and show demonstrated evidence of commitment to this church.

THE ERIC THOMPSON TRUST

c/o The Royal Philharmonic Society, 10 Stratford Place, London, W1C
1BA, England
Tel: (44) 20 7491 8110
Fax: (44) 20 7493 7463
Email: ett@royalphilharmonicsociety.org.uk
www: http://www.etorgantrust.co.uk
Contact: Mr David Lowe, Clerk to The Trustees

The Eric Thompson Trust aims to provide modest grants to help aspiring professional organists. Preference will be given to students seeking assistance towards specific projects, rather than continuing academic tuition eg. summer schools or special lessons in addition to normal studies and opportunities to play on historical instruments in the context of further study.

Eric Thompson Charitable Trust for Organists
Subjects: The organ.
Purpose: To provide aspiring professional organists with financial assistance for special studies such as summer schools, travel and subsistence for auditions or performance, or other incidental costs incurred in their work.
Eligibility: Some professional training as an organist is required.
Level of Study: Professional development.
Type: Other.
Value: Determined by the Trustees but normally limited to a contribution towards costs.
Frequency: Twice a year.
Country of Study: Any country.
No. of awards offered: Varies.
Application Procedure: Applicants must send full details of their needs together with information on their training and career, two written references from organists of good standing in the profession and other relevant material to the Clerk to the Trustees.
Closing Date: December 31st or June 30th for consideration in January and July respectively.
Funding: Private.
Contributor: Personal and corporate donors.

ESADE

MBA Office, Avenue d'espluges 92-96, Barcelona, E-08034, Spain
Tel: (34) 93 495 2088
Fax: (34) 93 495 3828
Email: mba@esade.edu
www: http://www.esade.edu
Contact: Ms Nuria Guilera, MBA Admissions Director

Established in 1958, ESADE is a private non-profit institution of higher education with a distinctly international outlook. It consists of three schools: the Business School, the Law School and the Language School. Located in one of Barcelona's most attractive residential areas, ESADE's three buildings provide a total of 26,850 square metres of space for teaching and study.

ESADE MBA Scholarships
Subjects: MBA.
Purpose: To assist full-time MBA students with tuition fees.
Eligibility: Scholarships are awarded on the basis of applicants' academic records, professional experience, personal merits and how well they fit the required profile of the programme.
Level of Study: MBA.
Type: Scholarship.
Value: The scholarship covers up to 50 per cent of the programme tuition fees.
Length of Study: 18 months.
Frequency: Annual.
Study Establishment: ESADE.
Country of Study: Spain.
Application Procedure: Applicants must apply for a scholarship along with their course application. Scholarship applications are reviewed once candidates have been admitted to the MBA programme by the admissions committee.
Closing Date: May.

ESTHER A AND JOSEPH KLINGENSTEIN CENTER FOR INDEPENDENT EDUCATION

Box 125, Teachers College, Columbia University, New York, NY
10027, United States of America
Tel: (1) 212 678 3156
Fax: (1) 212 678 3254
Email: njames@tc.columbia.edu
www: http://www.klingenstein.org
Contact: Grants Management Officer

The mission of the Esther A and Joseph Klingenstein Center for Independent Education is to improve the quality of independent school education by strengthening leadership among teachers and administrators who work in, and with, independent schools. The Center aims to attract educators who have demonstrated outstanding accomplishment or potential for excellence. The goal is to equip these educators with the knowledge, skills and values necessary for informed practice using the resources of Colombia University and drawing upon a wide range of experts in education.

Esther A and Joseph Klingenstein Fellowship Awards
Subjects: Education, administrative or academic disciplines.
Purpose: To foster educational leadership skills for teachers and administrators in independent elementary, middle and secondary schools.
Eligibility: Open to qualified applicants who have at least five years of teaching experience in grades 5 to 12 in an independent school and who plan to return to their home school following the fellowship year.
Level of Study: Professional development.
Type: Fellowship.
Length of Study: One academic year.
Frequency: Annual.
Study Establishment: The Klingenstein Center, Teachers College, Columbia University.
Country of Study: United States of America.
Application Procedure: Applicants must complete an application form.
Funding: Private.

Klingenstein Summer Institute
Subjects: Educational science.
Purpose: To provide professional development for teachers in independent elementary, middle and secondary schools.
Eligibility: Open to teachers currently employed in independent secondary schools with two-five years of experience in grades 9 to 12.
Level of Study: Graduate, Professional development.
Type: Fellowship.
Value: Room and board totalling approx. US$2,820, plus four graduate credits from the Teachers College.
Length of Study: Two weeks.
Frequency: Annual.
Study Establishment: A residential boarding school.
Country of Study: United States of America.
No. of awards offered: 70.
Application Procedure: Applicants must telephone for application materials.
Funding: Private.

EUROPEAN MOLECULAR BIOLOGY ORGANISATION (EMBO)

Postfach 1022.40, Heidelberg, D-69012, Germany
Tel: (49) 622 188 910
Fax: (49) 622 188 91200
Email: embo@embo.org
www: http://www.embo.org
Contact: Dr Ellen Peerenboom, Press and Public Relations Officer

The European Molecular Biology Organisation (EMBO) was established in 1962 and is an international academy focusing on molecular biology in its broadest sense, responding to developing scientific areas that use molecular biology to describe biological events at the molecular level. EMBO's aim is to promote biosciences in Europe.

EMBO Award for Communication in the Life Sciences
Subjects: Public communication of science.
Purpose: To promote and reward public communication of the life sciences and their applications by practising scientists in Europe.
Eligibility: Open to scientists working in active research in an area of life sciences at the time of nomination. Candidates must be working in either Europe or Israel, and the criterion for consideration is excellence in public communication of science via any medium or activity. If written works are to be judged with the application, these must have been published in printed form in Europe or Israel by the time of nomination. Works published in any European language will be considered. However, if a published English translation of the work exists, this should be submitted in preference. Books or book chapters will not be considered for the award, but they may be mentioned in support of the application. Scientists who are already widely regarded as professional communicators are not eligible, rather the award is intended for scientists who have, while remaining active in laboratory research, risen to the challenge of communicating science to a non scientific audience. Above all, the jury looks for imagination and originality.
Type: Monetary Award & Medal.
Value: €5,000.
Frequency: Annual.
No. of awards offered: One.
Application Procedure: Applicants must apply using the forms available on the website.
Closing Date: August 31st.
Funding: Private.
Contributor: EMBO.
No. of awards given last year: One.
No. of applicants last year: 27.
Additional Information: For further information email Dr Andrew Moore at scisoc@embo.org.

For further information contact:

Meyerhofstraβe 1, Heidelberg, D-69117, Germany
Tel: (49) 622 188 91119
Fax: (49) 622 188 91200
Email: embo@embo.org
www· http://www.embo.org

EMBO Long-Term Fellowships in Molecular Biology
Subjects: Molecular biology and disciplines relying on molecular biology.
Purpose: To promote the development of research in Europe and Israel.
Eligibility: Open to holders of a doctoral degree. EMBO fellowships are not awarded for exchanges between laboratories within any one country. Applicants must be nationals from a European Molecular Biology Conference (EMBC) member state or be wishing to travel from one EMBC member state to another.
Level of Study: Postdoctorate.
Type: Fellowship.
Value: A return travel allowance for the Fellow and any dependants plus a stipend and dependants' allowance.
Length of Study: One year, renewable for a further year.
Frequency: Twice a year.
Study Establishment: A suitable laboratory.
Country of Study: Any country.
No. of awards offered: Varies.
Application Procedure: Further information is available on the website www.embo.org.
Closing Date: February 15th and August 15th.
Funding: Government.
Contributor: The 24 EMBC member states.
No. of awards given last year: 177.
No. of applicants last year: 789.
Additional Information: The following countries form the European Molecular Biology Conference (EMBC): Austria, Belgium, Croatia, the Czech Republic, Denmark, Finland, France, Germany, Greece, Hungary, Iceland, Ireland, Israel, Italy, the Netherlands, Norway,

Poland, Portugal, Slovenia, Spain, Sweden, Switzerland, Turkey and the United Kingdom. Special provision is also made for applications involving Cyprus. For further information email fellows@embo.org.

EMBO Restart Fellowship
Subjects: Molecular biology and disciplines relying on molecular biology.
Purpose: To promote the development of research in Europe and Israel.
Eligibility: Open to candidates holding a PhD degree with some postdoctoral training, a proven track record and at least one first author paper. Applicants must have a research plan for the duration of the award and the support of a host laboratory which will provide space and facilities for the duration of the fellowship. As well, the candidate must have taken a break from research for childcare for at least one year and the post previously held terminated during pregnancy or maternity leave.
Level of Study: Postdoctorate.
Type: Fellowship.
Value: A return travel allowance for the fellow and any dependants plus a stipend and dependants' allowance.
Length of Study: Two years.
Frequency: Annual.
Study Establishment: A suitable laboratory.
Country of Study: Other.
No. of awards offered: Eight.
Application Procedure: Applicants must visit the website for further information.
Closing Date: August 15th.
Funding: Government.
Contributor: The 24 EMBC member states.
No. of awards given last year: Six.
No. of applicants last year: 27.
Additional Information: The following countries form the European Molecular Biology Conference (EMBC): Austria, Belgium, Croatia, the Czech Republic, Denmark, Finland, France, Germany, Greece, Hungary, Iceland, Ireland, Israel, Italy, the Netherlands, Norway, Poland, Portugal, Slovenia, Spain, Sweden, Switzerland, Turkey and the United Kingdom. Special provision is also made for applications involving Cyprus. For further information, email women@embo.org.

EMBO Short-Term Fellowships in Molecular Biology
Subjects: Molecular biology and disciplines relying on molecular biology.
Purpose: To promote the development of research in Europe and Israel.
Eligibility: Open to nationals from a European Molecular Biology Conference (EMBC) member state or to those wishing to travel from one EMBC member state to another. EMBO Fellowships are not awarded for exchanges between laboratories within any one country.
Level of Study: Doctorate, Postdoctorate, Postgraduate, Predoctorate, Research.
Type: Fellowship.
Value: The return travel for the Fellow only for the duration of the fellowship.
Length of Study: One week to three months.
Frequency: Throughout the year.
Study Establishment: A suitable laboratory.
Country of Study: Other.
No. of awards offered: Varies.
Application Procedure: Applicants must visit the website for information.
Closing Date: There is no deadline.
Funding: Government.
Contributor: The 24 EMBC member states.
No. of awards given last year: 141.
No. of applicants last year: 252.
Additional Information: The following countries form the European Molecular Biology Conference (EMBC): Austria, Belgium, Croatia, the Czech Republic, Denmark, Finland, France, Germany, Greece, Hungary, Iceland, Ireland, Israel, Italy, the Netherlands, Norway, Poland, Portugal, Slovenia, Spain, Sweden, Switzerland, Turkey and the United Kingdom. Special provision is also made for applications involving Cyprus. For further information, email fellows@embo.org.

EMBO World Programme Fellowships

Subjects: Molecular Biology and disciplines relying on Molecular Biology.

Purpose: The aim is to further collabration and intraction between Scientists Worldwide.

Eligibility: Open to scientists who have the aim of furthering collaboration and interaction worldwide. Preference will be given to applicants from developing countries and emerging economies.

Level of Study: Doctorate, Postdoctorate.

Type: Fellowship.

Value: A monthly stipend plus return travel allowance.

Length of Study: Six to nine months.

Frequency: Annual.

Study Establishment: A suitable laboratory.

Country of Study: Other.

No. of awards offered: Varies.

Application Procedure: Applicants must visit the website for further information or email world@embo.org.

Closing Date: March 1st.

Funding: Government.

Contributor: The 24 EMBC member states.

No. of awards given last year: 7.

No. of applicants last year. 95.

Additional Information: The following countries form the European Molecular Biology Conference (EMBC): Austria, Belgium, Croatia, the Czech Republic, Denmark, Finland, France, Germany, Greece, Finland, Iceland, Israel, Italy, the Netherlands, Norway, Poland, Portugal, Slovenia, Spain, Switzerland, Turkey and the United Kingdom. Special provision is also made for applications involving Cyprus.

EMBO Young Investigator

Subjects: Molecular biology and disciplines relying on molecular biology.

Purpose: To promote the development of research in Europe and Israel.

Eligibility: Open to leading members of an independent laboratory for at least one and not more than three years in a European Molecular Biology Conference (EMBC) member country. Leading members must have two-eight years of post PhD scientific experience and an excellent track record. Applicants must also have demonstrated physical mobility and have enough funds to run their laboratories.

Level of Study: Postdoctorate.

Value: €15,000.

Length of Study: Three years.

Frequency: Annual.

Study Establishment: The applicant's own independent laboratory.

Country of Study: Other.

No. of awards offered: Varies.

Application Procedure: Applicants must visit the website.

Closing Date: April 1st.

Funding: Government.

Contributor: The 24 EMBC member states.

No. of awards given last year: 23.

No. of applicants last year: 169.

Additional Information: The following countries form the European Molecular Biology Conference (EMBC): Austria, Belgium, Croatia, the Czech Republic, Denmark, Finland, France, Germany, Greece, Hungary, Iceland, Ireland, Israel, Italy, the Netherlands, Norway, Poland, Portugal, Slovenia, Spain, Sweden, Switzerland, Turkey and the United Kingdom. Special provision is also made for applications involving Cyprus. For further information, email yip@embo.org.

EUROPEAN SOCIETY OF SURGICAL ONCOLOGY (ESSO)

Av. E. Mounier 83, Brussels, 1200, Belgium
Tel: (32) 2 537 3106
Fax: (32) 2 539 0374
Email: esso@esso-surgeonline.be
www: http://www.esso-surgeonline.be
Contact: Ms Fabienne Pilkiewicz, ESSO Administrator

E.S.S.O. was founded to advance the art, science and practice of surgery for the treatment of cancer. ESSO endeavour to ensure that the highest possible standard of surgical treatment is available to cancer patients throughout Europe by organising congresses, granting fellowships and publishing the EJSO.

ESSO Fellowships

Subjects: Surgical oncology.

Purpose: To allow young surgeons the chance to spend time in another specialist centre to either expand their experience or learn new techniques.

Eligibility: Please see in chapter Education of the ESSO website (www.ESSO-surgeonline.be)

Level of Study: Postdoctorate.

Type: Fellowship.

Value: €2,500 for European fellowships and €10,000 for the major international training fellowship.

Length of Study: Two-three weeks for fellowships and three months for the major training fellowship.

Frequency: Annual.

Country of Study: Any country.

No. of awards offered: Four fellowships and one major training fellowship.

Application Procedure: Applicants must submit a full curriculum vitae with their application, together with a note of their career intentions. Applicants should also outline what they hope to gain from the training fellowship, including what specific experience is sought and how this will fit in with the applicant's career development. Applicants should provide details as to which institution they wish to visit, together with details of the clinical or research training opportunities that the department can offer. A letter of support from the applicant's head of department must be included and this can be in the form of a reference. A letter of support from the head of the department they wish to visit must also be supplied, indicating that the department to be visited will be in a position to provide the experience required by the applicant.

Closing Date: August 31st.

Additional Information: Applicants must be or become ESSO members.

For further information contact:

Department of Surgery - University Hospital, UMEA, S 90185, Sweden
Contact: Dr Peter Naredi

EUROPEAN SOUTHERN OBSERVATORY (ESO)

Karl-Schwarzschild-Straße 2, Garching bei Muenchen, D-85748, Germany
Tel: (49) 893 200 60
Fax: (49) 893 202 362
Email: vacancy@eso.org
www: http://www.eso.org
Contact: Mr Roland Block, Head of Personnel Department

The European Southern Observatory (ESO) is an intergovernmental organisation for research in astronomy. At present ESO is operating the Very Large Telescope (VLT) at Cerro Paranal in Chile, the world's most powerful facility for optical astronomy, and La Silla Observatory.

ESO Fellowship

Subjects: Astronomy and astrophysics.

Purpose: To provide a unique opportunity to learn and participate in the process of observational astronomy while pursuing a research programme.

Level of Study: Postdoctorate.

Type: Fellowship.

Value: A basic monthly salary of not less than €2,918, to which is added an expatriation allowance as well as some family allowances, if applicable. The Fellow will also have an annual travel budget for scientific meetings, collaborations and observing trips.

Length of Study: One year, with a possible extension to three years in Garching. Fellowships in Chile are for one year with a possible extension to four years.
Frequency: Annual.
Study Establishment: The European Southern Observatory.
Country of Study: Other.
No. of awards offered: Six-nine.
Application Procedure: Applicants must visit the ESO website for an application form and further information.
Closing Date: October 15th.
Funding: Government.
Contributor: Belgium, Denmark, France, Germany, Italy, Netherlands, Portugal, Sweden, Switzerland and the United Kingdom.
Additional Information: Fellowships begin between April and October of the year in which they are awarded. Selected Fellows can join ESO only after having completed their doctorate.

EUROPEAN SYNCHROTRON RADIATION FACILITY (ESRF)

BP 220, Grenoble, F-38043, France
Tel: (33) 4 76 88 20 00
Fax: (33) 4 76 88 20 20
Email: stuck@esrf.fr
www: http://www.esrf.fr
Contact: Ms Elizabeth Moulin

The European Synchrotron Radiation Facility (ESRF) supports scientists in the implementation of fundamental and applied research on the structure of condensed matter in fields such as physics, chemistry, crystallography, earth science, biology, medicine, surface science and materials science.

ESRF Postdoctoral Fellowships

Subjects: Physics, biology, chemistry, mineralogy and crystallography, computer engineering and accelerators science.
Purpose: To enable postdoctoral fellows to develop their own research programme. In addition, they should be motivated to collaborate with external users.
Eligibility: Preference is given to member country nationals but other nationals may be accepted for the postdoctoral positions.
Level of Study: Postdoctorate.
Value: €2,975 each month, plus a possible relocation allowance of up to €371 each month. These amounts correspond to a gross remuneration and are subject to social charges and income tax in France.
Length of Study: Two-three years.
Frequency: Dependent on funds available.
No. of awards offered: Up to 20.
Application Procedure: Applicants must complete an application form, available on request from the personnel department of the ESRF.
Closing Date: Individual deadlines exist for each position. Please contact the organisation.
Funding: Private.
Contributor: Public funds from 16 countries, mostly European.
No. of awards given last year: 25.
No. of applicants last year: 304.
Additional Information: Member countries are Belgium, Denmark, Finland, France, Germany, Italy, the Netherlands, Norway, Spain, Sweden, Switzerland and the United Kingdom. New associated members are the Czech Republic, Israel, Portugal and the Republic of Hungary. Further information can be found on the website.

ESRF Thesis Studentships

Subjects: Physics, biology, chemistry, mineralogy and crystallography, computer engineering and accelerators science. The ESRF proposes subjects related to the use of synchrotron radiation or synchrotron or storage ring technology.
Purpose: To enable grant holders to prepare a PhD at the ESRF and to enable young scientists to acquire knowledge of the use of Synchrotron Radiation or its generation.

Eligibility: Preference is given to member country nationals but other nationals may be accepted for the postdoctoral positions.
Level of Study: Doctorate.
Value: €1,959 per month. These amounts correspond to a gross remuneration and are subject to social charges and income tax in France.
Length of Study: Two-three years.
Frequency: Dependent on funds available.
Study Establishment: Universities.
Country of Study: Other.
No. of awards offered: Up to 10.
Application Procedure: Applicants must complete an application form, available on request from the personnel department of the ESRF.
Closing Date: There is an individual deadline for each position.
Funding: Private.
Contributor: Public funds from 16 countries, mainly European.
No. of awards given last year: 12.
No. of applicants last year: 202.
Additional Information: Member countries are Belgium, Denmark, Finland, France, Germany, Italy, the Netherlands, Norway, Spain, Sweden, Switzerland and the United Kingdom. Newly associated members are the Czech Republic, Israel, Portugal and the Republic of Hungary. Further information can be found on the website.

EUROPEAN UNIVERSITY INSTITUTE (EUI)

Via dei Roccettini 9, 50016 San Domenico di Fiesole
Florence, Italy
Tel: (39) 055 468 51
Fax: (39) 055 468 5444
Email: applyres@iue.it
www: http://www.iue.it
Contact: Mr Kenneth Hulley, Assistant Administrator (Academic Service)

The European University Institute's (EUI) main aim is to make a contribution to the intellectual life of Europe. Created by the European Union Member States, it is a postgraduate research institution, pursuing interdisciplinary research programmes on the main issues confronting European society and the construction of Europe.

EUI Postgraduate Scholarships

Subjects: History and civilisation, economics, law or political and social sciences.
Purpose: To provide the opportunity for study leading to the doctorate degree or Master's from the Institute.
Eligibility: Open to nationals of the 15 European Union member states. Candidates must possess a good Honours Degree or its equivalent, and have full written and spoken command of at least two of the Institute's official languages. Under certain conditions, nationals of countries other than the European Union may be admitted to the Institute and eligible for a scholarship.
Level of Study: Doctorate, Postgraduate.
Type: Scholarship.
Value: Varies but approx. €1,060 per month.
Length of Study: One year, renewable for up to an additional three years.
Frequency: Annual.
Study Establishment: The EUI.
Country of Study: Italy.
No. of awards offered: Approx. 115-125.
Application Procedure: An on-line web form must be completed and a set of application forms (available from EUI and the website) sent in by mail.
Closing Date: January 15th.
Funding: Government.
Contributor: The Member States of the European Union.
No. of awards given last year: 125.
No. of applicants last year: 1,400.

Additional Information: The scholarships are granted, by the governments of the 15 European Union member states to nationals of their own countries. The awards are currently distributed as follows: Federal Republic of Germany 29, France 25, Italy 29, United Kingdom 26, Spain 25, the Netherlands 15, Denmark 10, Belgium 10, the Republic of Ireland 10, Greece 10, Luxembourg 5, Portugal 11, Austria 12, Finland 6 and Sweden 10.

Jean Monnet Fellowships

Subjects: Humanities and social sciences, with special attention to problems related to the European Community and to the development of Europe's cultural and academic heritage.
Purpose: To encourage postdoctoral research.
Eligibility: Open mainly to candidates with a doctoral degree at an early stage of their academic career.
Level of Study: Postdoctorate.
Type: Fellowship.
Value: €12,000-20,000 per year, depending on age. It also covers allowances for dependants, travel and medical insurance.
Length of Study: One year (10 months), possibly renewable for a further year.
Frequency: Annual.
Study Establishment: The EUI.
Country of Study: Italy.
No. of awards offered: 40-50.
Application Procedure: Applicants must complete an application form available by contacting the office at the EUI via the Internet or by contacting the Jean Monnet Fellowships Officer.
Closing Date: October 25th.
Funding: Government.
Contributor: Member States of the European Union.
No. of awards given last year: 50.
No. of applicants last year: 370.
Additional Information: Further information is available from the website.

EVANGELICAL LUTHERAN CHURCH IN AMERICA (ELCA)

Division for Ministry, 8765 West Higgins Road
Chicago, IL 60631-4195
United States of America
Tel: (1) 773 380 2873
Fax: (1) 773 380 2829
Email: pwilder@elca.org
www: http://www.elca.org
Contact: Pat Wilder, Executive Secretary

ELCA Educational Grant Program

Subjects: Theological studies.
Eligibility: Open to members of the Evangelical Lutheran Church in America who are enrolled in an accredited graduate institution for study in a PhD, Ed.D., or ThD programme in a theological area appropriate to seminary teaching. Priority is given to women and minority students.
Level of Study: Doctorate.
Type: Grant.
Value: US$250-5,000. Funds are distributed according to need and the contribution the applicant will make towards the future of the church.
Length of Study: Grants are awarded for a maximum of four years with a fifth year award for the dissertation.
Frequency: Annual.
Country of Study: United States of America.
No. of awards offered: 40-65.
Application Procedure: Applications are available online at http://www.elca.org/dm/te/grants.html in January. Two recommendations are required for each applicant.
Closing Date: March 15th.
Funding: Private.
No. of awards given last year: 65.
No. of applicants last year: 72.

EVRIKA FOUNDATION

PO Box 6151, Patriarch Evtimii Boulevard
Sofia, BG-1000, Bulgaria
Tel: (359) 2 981 5181
Fax: (359) 2 981 5483
Email: evrika@einet.bg
www: http://www.evrika.org
Contact: Mr Vassil Velev, Executive Director

The Evrika Foundation was established in 1990 by state and public organisations to promote the development of youth technical and scientific creativity, and to encourage youth economic enterprise and to assist youth education, specialisation and training. The Evrika Foundation is a non governmental, non religious and apolitical organisation.

Evrika Foundation Awards

Subjects: Agriculture and farm management, management systems and techniques, engineering or natural sciences.
Purpose: To support young people with proven abilities and skills.
Eligibility: Open to Bulgarian nationals only, up to the age of 35. Scholarships are available to postgraduate students and grants and awards are reserved for Scholars who hold a Master's degree or PhD.
Level of Study: Doctorate, Graduate.
Type: Other.
Value: Dependent on the type of award.
Frequency: Annual.
Country of Study: Other.
No. of awards offered: Three-four.
Application Procedure: Applicants must complete and submit an application form with references.
Closing Date: December 15th.
Funding: Private.
No. of awards given last year: Three.
No. of applicants last year: 285.

EXETER COLLEGE

Oxford, Oxfordshire, OX1 3DP, England
Tel: (44) 1865 279660
Fax: (44) 1865 279630
Email: joan.himpson@exeter.ox.ac.uk
www: http://www.exeter.ox.ac.uk
Contact: Ms Joan Himpson, Academic Administrator

Exeter College is one of the University of Oxford's oldest Colleges. Founded in 1314, the College currently has 461 students, of which 307 are undergraduates and 154 are postgraduate students.

Exeter College Senior Scholarship in Theology

Subjects: Theology or theology and philosophy.
Purpose: To support a graduate who wishes to read for the Final Honour School of theology or philosophy and theology.
Eligibility: Applicants must hold by the time of admission at least a Second Class (Honours) Degree in a subject other than theology.
Level of Study: MBA.
Type: Scholarship.
Value: A minimum value of UK£200 which may be supplemented up to a maximum of all college fees, university fees to the amount charged to home and European Union students, and maintenance to the current maximum Local Education Authority maintenance grant.
Length of Study: Two years.
Frequency: Every three years.
Study Establishment: Exeter College, the University of Oxford.
Country of Study: United Kingdom.
No. of awards offered: One.
Application Procedure: Applicants must apply in writing to the Academic Administrator, with a curriculum vitae and the names of two academic references.
Funding: Private.

Contributor: Endowment.
No. of awards given last year: None.
No. of applicants last year: None.

Monsanto Senior Research Fellowship
Subjects: Molecular biology, cellular biology or biochemistry.
Purpose: To support research.
Eligibility: Open to qualified applicants of any nationality.
Level of Study: Postdoctorate.
Type: Fellowship.
Value: A stipend of between UK£17,626 and UK£26,491 per year. Fellows are entitled to free lunch and dinner, free rooms in the college if unmarried, and a housing allowance if not resident in the college.
Length of Study: Three-five years.
Frequency: Every three-five years.
Study Establishment: Exeter College, the University of Oxford.
Country of Study: United Kingdom.
No. of awards offered: One.
Application Procedure: Applicants must address enquiries to the Academic Administrator.
Funding: Private.
No. of awards given last year: One.
No. of applicants last year: 76.
Additional Information: The next award is not expected to be given until 2007.

Queen Sofia Research Fellowship
Subjects: Peninsular Spanish literature.
Purpose: To support research.
Eligibility: Applicants should be close to completing doctoral or postdoctoral work and must be under 31 at the time of taking up the fellowship. They must also be fluent in Spanish.
Level of Study: Doctorate, Postdoctorate.
Type: Fellowship.
Value: A stipend of up to UK£12,000 per year. Fellows are entitled to free lunch and dinner, free rooms in the college if unmarried, and a housing allowance if not resident in the college.
Length of Study: Two-three years.
Frequency: Every three years.
Study Establishment: Exeter College, the University of Oxford.
Country of Study: United Kingdom.
No. of awards offered: One.
Application Procedure: Applicants must address enquiries to the Academic Administrator.
Funding: Private.
Contributor: Endowment.
No. of awards given last year: One.
No. of applicants last year: 30.

Staines Medical Research Fellowship
Subjects: Medical science.
Purpose: To support research into medical science.
Eligibility: Applicants should be close to completing doctoral or postdoctoral work and must be under 31 at the time of taking up the fellowship.
Level of Study: Doctorate, Postdoctorate.
Type: Fellowship.
Value: A stipend of between UK£300 and UK£10,240 per year. Fellows are entitled to free lunch and dinner, free rooms in the college if unmarried and a housing allowance if not resident in the college.
Length of Study: Two-three years.
Frequency: Every 5 years.
Study Establishment: Exeter College, the University of Oxford.
Country of Study: United Kingdom.
No. of awards offered: One.
Application Procedure: Applicants must address enquiries to the Academic Administrator.
Funding: Private.
Contributor: Endowment.
No. of awards given last year: One.
No. of applicants last year: 65.

F BUSONI FOUNDATION
Conservatorio Statale di Musica 'C Monteverdi' Piazza Domenicani 25, Bolzano, I-39100, Italy
Tel: (39) 047 197 6568
Fax: (39) 047 197 3579
Email: info@concorsobusoni.it
www: http://www.concorsobusoni.it
Contact: Ms Maria Pia Venturi, Secretary

The Busoni International Piano Competition was first held in 1949 to commemorate the 25th anniversary of the death of composer Ferruccio Busoni. The aim of the competition is to create a forum for Busoni's music as well as for promising young pianists.

Foundation Busoni International Piano Competition
Subjects: Piano performance.
Purpose: To award excellence in piano performance.
Eligibility: Open to pianists of any nationality aged between 16-28 years.
Level of Study: Unrestricted.
Type: Prize.
Value: The first prize is €22,000 plus 60 important concert contracts, the second prize is €10,000, the third prize is €5,000, the fourth prize is €4,000, the fifth prize is €3,000 and the sixth prize is €2,500. There are also other special prizes.
Frequency: Every two years.
Country of Study: Italy.
No. of awards offered: 10.
Application Procedure: Applicants must complete and submit an application form with a birth certificate, reports or certificates of study, a brief curriculum vitae and documentation of any artistic activity. Three recent photographs, the entrance fee and written evidence of any prizes and international competitions should also be included.
Closing Date: May 31st.
Funding: Commercial, Government, Private.
Contributor: The municipality of Bolzano.
No. of awards given last year: 10.
No. of applicants last year: 150.
Additional Information: The competition lasts for two years, with the preselection phase taking place in the first year. The next preselection phase takes place in 2004.

FANCONI ANEMIA RESEARCH FUND, INC.
1801 Willamette Street, Suite 200, Eugene, OR 97401, United States of America
Tel: (1) 541 687 4658
Fax: (1) 541 687 0548
Email: info@fanconi.org
www: http://www.fanconi.org
Contact: Ms Mary Ellen Eiler, Executive Director

To support research into effective treatments and a cure for Fanconi anaemia.

Fanconi Anemia Research Award
Subjects: Fanconi anaemia.
Purpose: To support research into effective treatments and a cure for Fanconi anaemia.
Eligibility: There are no restrictions on eligibility in terms of nationality, residency, age, gender, sexual orientation, race, religion or politics.
Level of Study: Doctorate, Postdoctorate.
Value: US$5,000-1,000,000.
Length of Study: One-two years.
Frequency: Other.
Country of Study: Any country.
No. of awards offered: Unlimited.
Application Procedure: Applicants must email to obtain information about the application process and to complete an application form.
Closing Date: There is no closing date.

Funding: Commercial, Government, Private.
No. of awards given last year: Seven.
No. of applicants last year: 10.
Additional Information: The Internal Revenue Service has confirmed that the funds are not a private foundation for the purposes of tax exempt donations but a public charitable organisation under 501(c) 3 of the Internal Revenue Code.

FANNIE AND JOHN HERTZ FOUNDATION

2456 Research Drive, Livermore, CA 94550, United States of America
Tel: (1) 925 373 1642
Email: askhertz@aol.com
www: http://www.hertzfoundation.org
Contact: Ms Linda Kubiak, Fellowship Administrator

The Fannie and John Hertz Foundation runs a national competition for graduate fellowships in the applied physical sciences.

Fannie and John Hertz Foundation Fellowships
Subjects: Applied physical and biophysical sciences.
Purpose: To promote the education and enhancement of the technological stature of the United States, by aiding in the education of the most capable students, working for PhDs in the applied physical and biophysical sciences.
Eligibility: Open to citizens or permanent residents of the United States of America who have received a Bachelor's degree by the start of tenure and who propose to complete a programme of graduate study leading to a PhD. Students who have commenced graduate study are also eligible. The Foundation does not support candidates pursuing joint PhD and professional degree programmes.
Level of Study: Doctorate.
Type: Fellowship.
Value: US$25,000 per nine month academic year, plus up to US$15,000 towards the cost of tuition.
Length of Study: One academic year and may be renewed annually for up to five years.
Frequency: Annual.
Study Establishment: Specific universities listed on the website.
Country of Study: United States of America.
No. of awards offered: 20.
Application Procedure: Applicants must complete a Hertz application form, four reference reports on the supplied specific forms and official transcripts of all college work must be submitted. The application form is available from the Foundation's website.
Closing Date: The first Friday in November.
Funding: Private.
No. of awards given last year: 15.
No. of applicants last year: Approx. 550.

THE FEDERATION OF AMERICAN SOCIETIES FOR EXPERIMENTAL BIOLOGY (FASEB)

9650 Rockville Pike, Bethesda, MD 20814-3998, United States of America
Tel: (1) 301 530 7020
Fax: (1) 301 571 0699
www: http://www.faseb.org/marc
Contact: Ms Cheryl Wright, Programme Co-ordinator

The Federation of American Societies for Experimental Biology (FASEB) provides travel award opportunities for a variety of activities to support the training of faculty, scientists and students in the biomedical and behavioural sciences. There are available travel awards for Annual FASEB Societies Selected Scientific Meetings, Summer Research Opportunity Programmes, Career Development Seminars, Grantmanship Training Programmes, Summer Conferences and more.

Minority Scientist Scholarships to FASEB Summer Research Conferences
Subjects: Biological and life sciences.
Purpose: To provide an opportunity for individuals to attend FASEB Summer Research Conferences.
Eligibility: Open to full-time minority faculty members at academic or research institutions in the United States of America.
Level of Study: Doctorate, Postdoctorate.
Type: Travel grant.
Value: Conference registration, travel costs and a subsistence allowance.
Length of Study: Varies.
Frequency: Annual.
Study Establishment: FASEB Summer Research Conferences.
Country of Study: United States of America.
No. of awards offered: 30.
Application Procedure: Applicants must complete an application form available from the organisation.
Closing Date: Please write for details.
Funding: Government.
No. of awards given last year: 339.
No. of applicants last year: 450
Additional Information: Further information is available on the website.

FEDERATION OF EUROPEAN MICROBIOLOGICAL SOCIETIES (FEMS)

Keverling Buismanweg, 4, Delft, 2628 CL, Netherlands
Tel: (31) 15 269 3920
Fax: (31) 15 269 3921
Email: fems@fems-microbiology.org
www: http://www.fems-microbiology.org
Contact: Dr D Van Rossum, Executive Officer

The Federation of European Microbiological Societies (FEMS) is devoted to the promotion of microbiology in Europe. FEMS advances research and education in the science of microbiology within Europe, for example, by encouraging joint activities and facilitating communication among microbiologists, supporting meetings and laboratory courses and publishing books and journals.

FEMS Fellowship
Subjects: Microbiology.
Purpose: To foster transnational research in microbiology and to support young scientists to pursue a short-term research project in another European country.
Eligibility: The award is restricted to members of FEMS member societies.
Level of Study: Doctorate, Graduate, Postdoctorate, Postgraduate, Predoctorate, Professional development, Research.
Type: Fellowship.
Value: A maximum of €3,500.
Length of Study: A maximum of three months.
Frequency: Twice a year.
No. of awards offered: Approx. 50.
Application Procedure: Applicants must complete and submit an application form to a society which is a member of FEMS. The delegate of the member society will handle the application and submit it to the Federation for funding. FEMS will then make a decision on the application. Addresses of the Federations delegates are published on the website.
Closing Date: December 1st and June 15th.
Funding: Private.
No. of awards given last year: 44.

THE FIELD PSYCH TRUST

301 Dixie Street, Carrollton, GA 30117, United States of America
Tel: (1) 770 834 8143
Email: arichard@westga.edu
www: http://www.fieldpsychtrust.org
Contact: Dr Anne C Richards, Trustee

The Field Psych Trust is a charitable trust honouring the professional life and contributions of psychologist/educator Dr Arthur W Combs. It provides grant funding to encourage graduate student research grounded in perceptual (field) psychology perspectives. It also supports publication of manuscripts related to Dr Combs' professional life and work.

Field Psych Trust Grant

Subjects: As a psychological theory, perceptual (field) psychology is applicable to any subject area in which links between human experience, meaning and/or perception and human behaviour can be explored. Those which explore the history, contributions and further development of perceptual (field) psychology as related to the research and writings of Arthur W Combs will be favoured.
Purpose: To encourage research.
Eligibility: Open to graduate students in good standing through a competitive review process.
Level of Study: Doctorate, Graduate, Postdoctorate, Predoctorate.
Type: Research grant.
Value: Varies according to the itemised budget request of successful applicants and their projects. Awards range from US$500-1,500.
Length of Study: Varies, although one year is preferable.
Frequency: Twice a year.
Study Establishment: An accredited Institution of Higher Education.
Country of Study: Any country.
No. of awards offered: Two.
Application Procedure: Applicants must complete an application form and submit references. Application forms can be found on the website. Applications are judged with respect to the relevance of the proposed project to the mission of the Field Psych Trust, substance, conceptual quality and clarity of the proposal, significance of the project in addressing matters of consequence to the human condition, and the degree of confidence that the prospective grant recipient has the ability to produce the proposed project.
Closing Date: January 31st and October 5th of each year.
Funding: Private.
Contributor: The estate of Arthur W Combs.
No. of awards given last year: Review process incomplete at this time.
No. of applicants last year: 1.
Additional Information: Awards are subject to conditions which are described and include an obligation to submit a final report upon conclusion of the project, which can take the form of a completed Master's thesis, research project report, doctoral dissertation or published manuscript. More information is available from the website, or by contacting Anne Richards at the main address.

FINE ARTS WORK CENTER IN PROVINCETOWN, INC.

24 Pearl Street, Provincetown, MA 02657, United States of America
Tel: (1) 508 487 9960
Fax: (1) 508 487 8873
Email: info@fawc.org
www: http://www.fawc.org
Contact: Mr Hunter O'Hanian, Executive Director

Established in 1968, the Fine Arts Work Center offers seven month fellowships to emerging visual artists and creative writers. Housing, studios and monthly stipends are provided to create a community of peers as a catalyst for artistic growth.

Fine Arts Work Center in Provincetown Fellowships

Subjects: Visual arts and creative writing in fiction and poetry.
Purpose: To give artists and writers the opportunity to work in a congenial and stimulating environment and to devote most of their time to art and writing.
Eligibility: Open to all, but preference is given to emerging artists of outstanding promise. Applicants are accepted on the basis of work submitted.
Level of Study: Unrestricted.
Type: Fellowship.
Value: US$375-650 per month, plus housing and studio space.

Length of Study: Seven months.
Frequency: Annual.
Study Establishment: Provincetown, Massachusetts.
Country of Study: United States of America.
No. of awards offered: 10 for visual arts and 10 for writing.
Application Procedure: Applicants must send a stamped addressed envelope for applications, the fee for which is US$35. Alternatively, application forms can be downloaded from the website.
Closing Date: February 1st for visual artists and December 1st for writers.
Funding: Government, Private.
No. of awards given last year: 20.
No. of applicants last year: 1,000.
Additional Information: The Centre is a working community not a school.

FIRST (FLORICULTURE INDUSTRY RESEARCH AND SCHOLARSHIP TRUST)

PO Box 280, East Lansing, MI 48826-0280, United States of America
Tel: (1) 517 333 4617
Fax: (1) 517 333 4494
Email: willbrandt@firstinfloriculture.org
www: http://www.firstinfloriculture.org
Contact: Mr William Willbrandt, Executive Director

FIRST (Floriculture Industry Research and Scholarship Trust) is a leading organisation for funding research and education in floriculture to improve the production and marketability of plants.

FIRST Scholarship Program

Subjects: Horticulture and the horticultural industry.
Eligibility: Open to students who are studying horticulture or have a career interest in any aspect of the horticultural industry. Further information is available on request.
Type: Scholarship.
Value: Varies.
Frequency: Annual.
Study Establishment: An accredited college or university.
Country of Study: United States of America.
No. of awards offered: Varies.
Application Procedure: Applicants must contact FIRST directly to obtain the latest scholarship application form which lists all of the current scholarships and requirements. Application forms are available from January 1st to May 1st from the website or by sending a stamped addressed envelope or printed self addressed mailing label to the main address.
Closing Date: May 1st.
Additional Information: Applicants are requested to contact the Foundation directly for information on individual scholarships. Information regarding the Foundation's research grant programme is also available from the website.

FONDATION FYSSEN

194 Rue de Rivoli, Paris, F-75001, France
Tel: (33) 1 42 97 53 16
Fax: (33) 1 42 60 17 95
Email: secretariat@fondation-fyssen.org
www: http://www.fondation-fyssen.org
Contact: Mrs Nadia Ferchal, Director

The aim of the Fyssen Foundation is to encourage all forms of scientific enquiry into cognitive mechanisms, including thought and reasoning, that underlie animal and human behaviour; their biological and cultural bases, and phylogenetic and ontogenetic development.

Fondation Fyssen Postdoctoral Study Grants

Subjects: Disciplines relevant to the aims of the Foundation such as ethology, palaeontology, archaeology, anthropology, psychology, epistemology, logic or the neurosciences.
Purpose: To fund scientific research.

Eligibility: Open to French research scientists who wish to work in laboratories abroad and foreign research scientists who wish to work in French laboratories, under 35 years of age.
Level of Study: Postdoctorate.
Type: Grant.
Value: €20,000.
Length of Study: Two years for researchers of neurobiology who are coming from the United States of America to France and one year for all others.
Frequency: Annual.
Application Procedure: Applicants must complete an application form, available from the secretariat of the Foundation or from the website.
Closing Date: The end of March.
Funding: Private.
No. of awards given last year: 43.
No. of applicants last year: 152.

FOOD AND DRUG LAW INSTITUTE (FDLI)

1000 Vermont Avenue NW, Suite 200, Washington, DC 20005 1000, United States of America
Tel: (1) 202 371 1420
Fax: (1) 202 371 0649
Email: ccommentst@fdli.org
www: http://www.fdli.org
Contact: Ms M Cathryn Butler, Academic Programs

The Food and Drug Law Institute (FDLI) is a non-profit educational association dedicated to advancing the public health by providing a neutral forum for critical examination of the laws, regulations and policies related to drugs, medical devices, other healthcare technologies and food.

H Thomas Austern Memorial Writing Competition - Food and Drug Law

Subjects: Current issues relevant to the food and drug field including a relevant case law, legislative history and other authorities, particularly where the United States Food and Drug Administration is involved. Additional topic possibilities are available from the website.
Purpose: To encourage law students interested in the areas of law affecting foods, drugs, devices, cosmetics and biologics.
Eligibility: Entrants must currently be enrolled in a JD programme at any of the United States law schools.
Level of Study: Postgraduate.
Value: Two first prizes of US$1,500, two second prizes of US$1,000.
Frequency: Annual.
Country of Study: United States of America.
No. of awards offered: Four.
Application Procedure: Applicants must submit a typewritten, double spaced paper on 81/2 × 11 inch paper. The cover sheet must list the applicant's full name, address and telephone number, law school and year, and the date of submission of the paper. Papers must not exceed 40 pages in length, including footnotes - for shorter paper competition. There is no page limit for papers >41 pgs. For longer paper competition.
Closing Date: June 15.
Funding: Private.
Contributor: Association funds and Association member dues.
No. of awards given last year: Four & One Hon. Mention.
No. of applicants last year: Approx. 75.
Additional Information: Winning papers will be considered for publication in the Food and Drug Law Journal.

FOREST ROBERTS THEATRE

Northern Michigan University, 1401, Presque Isle, Marquette, MI 49855-5364, United States of America
Tel: (1) 906 227 2559
Fax: (1) 906 227 2567
www: http://www.nmu.edu/theatre/
Contact: Ms Lindsey Harman, Award Co-ordinator

Mildred and Albert Panowski Playwriting Award
Subjects: Playwriting.
Purpose: To encourage and stimulate artistic growth among educational and professional playwrights.
Eligibility: Open to amateur, pre-professional and professional playwrights. There is no restriction as to theme or genre but plays must be written in English and entries must be original, full length plays. One act plays and previously submitted works are unacceptable as are submissions which have not been previously produced or published. Story adaptations and translations are eligible.
Level of Study: Unrestricted.
Value: US$2,000 cash award and production of the winning script plus travel costs and a one week summer workshop.
Frequency: Annual.
Country of Study: United States of America.
No. of awards offered: One.
Application Procedure: Applicants must send a stamped addressed envelope to receive rules and an application form.
Closing Date: November 15th.
Funding: Private.
Contributor: Dr James Panowski.
No. of awards given last year: One
No. of applicants last year: 350.

FOULKES FOUNDATION

37 Ringwood Avenue, London, N2 9NT, England
Tel: (44) 20 8444 2526
Fax: (44) 20 8444 2526
www: http://www.foulkes-foundation.org
Contact: M Foulkes, The Registrar

The aim of the Foulkes Foundation Fellowship is to promote medical research by providing financial support for postdoctoral science graduates who need a medical degree before they can undertake medical research, and similarly for medical graduates who need a science PhD degree.

Foulkes Foundation Fellowship
Subjects: All aspects of medical research, especially in the areas of molecular biology and biological sciences.
Purpose: To promote research by providing financial support.
Eligibility: Open to recently qualified scientists and medical graduates who intend to contribute to medical research and who have a PhD or equivalent or proven research ability.
Level of Study: Postdoctorate.
Type: Fellowship.
Value: Varies depending on individual need, but the scale for the basic SRC Studentship is used as a guideline. Fellowships do not cover fees.
Length of Study: Up to three years.
Frequency: Annual.
Country of Study: United Kingdom.
No. of awards offered: Varies.
Application Procedure: Applicants must send a stamped addressed envelope to the Registrar for additional information and an application form.
Closing Date: March 15th.
Funding: Private.
No. of awards given last year: Five.
No. of applicants last year: 75.

FOUNDATION FOR ANESTHESIA EDUCATION AND RESEARCH (FAER)

Charlton Building 1-128, Mayo Clinic, 200 First Street, South West, Rochester, MN 55905, United States of America
Tel: (1) 507 266 6866
Fax: (1) 507 284 0120
Email: todd.kerry@mayo.edu
www: http://www.faer.org
Contact: Ms Kerry Todd, Assistant Director

The Foundation for Anesthesia Education and Research (FAER) strives to foster progress in anaesthesiology, critical care, pain and all areas of perioperative medicine. The organisation aims to generate new knowledge that advances health and patient care by facilitating the career development of anaesthesiologists dedicated to research and education. FAER offers four types of grants to anaesthesiologists. They range from US$25,000-US$175,000. A 20 member committee consisting of both clinical and basic science anaesthesiologists reviews proposals. Clinical and outcomes projects are encouraged.

FAER Research Education Grant

Subjects: Anaesthesiology.
Purpose: To improve the quality and productivity of education and research.
Eligibility: Open to anaesthesiology residents or faculty.
Level of Study: Postgraduate.
Type: Grant.
Value: US$25,000.
Length of Study: Two years.
Frequency: Annual.
Application Procedure: Applicants must visit the website.
Closing Date: February 15th and August 15th.
Additional Information: Further information is available on request.

FAER Research Fellowship Grant

Subjects: Anaesthesiology.
Purpose: To provide significant training in research techniques and scientific methods.
Eligibility: Open to anaesthesiology residents after CA-1 training and six months of Clinical Scientist Track.
Level of Study: Postdoctorate.
Type: Fellowship.
Value: US$50,000.
Length of Study: One year.
Frequency: Annual.
Application Procedure: Applicants must visit the website.
Closing Date: February 15th or August 15th.
Additional Information: Further information is available on request.

FAER Research Starter Grants

Subjects: Anaesthesiology.
Purpose: To support and initiate a project for which investigator will seek further support.
Eligibility: Applicants must be instructors or assistant professors who are within five years of their initial appointment.
Level of Study: Postdoctorate.
Type: Grant.
Value: US$35,000 in the first year and US$50,000 in the second.
Length of Study: Two years.
Frequency: Annual.
Application Procedure: Applicants must visit the website.
Closing Date: February 15th or August 15th.
Additional Information: Further information is available on request.

FAER Research Training Grant (RTG)

Subjects: Anaesthesiology.
Purpose: To allow the applicant to become an independent investigator.
Eligibility: Applicants must be instructors or assistant professors who are within five years of their initial appointment.
Level of Study: Postdoctorate.
Type: Grant.
Value: US$75,000 in the first year and US$100,000 in the second.
Length of Study: Two years.
Frequency: Annual.
Application Procedure: Applicants must visit the website.
Closing Date: February 15th or August 15th.
Additional Information: Further information is available on request.

FOUNDATION FOR DIGESTIVE HEALTH AND NUTRITION

4930 Del Ray Avenue, Bethesda, MD 20814, United States of America
Tel: (1) 301 222 4005
Fax: (1) 301 222 4010
Email: desta@gastro.org
www: http://www.fdhn.org
Contact: Ms Desta L Wallace, Research Awards Manager

The Foundation for Digestive Health and Nutrition is the foundation of the American Gastroenterological Association (AGA), the leading professional society representing gastroenterological and heptatologists worldwide. It is separately incorporated and governed by a distinguished board of AGA physicians and members of the lay public. The Foundation raises funds for research and public education in the prevention, diagnosis, treatment and cure of digestive diseases. Along with the AGA, it conducts public education initiatives related to digestive diseases. The Foundation also administers the disbursement of grants on the behalf of the AGA and other funders.

AGA Astra Zeneca Fellowship/Faculty Transition Awards

Subjects: Medical science, specifically gastroenterology and hepathology.
Purpose: To prepare and support physicians for independent research careers in digestive diseases.
Eligibility: Applicants must be MDs currently in a gastroenterology related fellowship at an accredited United States or Canadian institutions and be committed to academic careers. They will have completed two years of research training at the start of this award. The additional training could be considered the equivalent of practical training ordinarily involved in a PhD programme. Therefore, individuals who hold a PhD are ineligible. Please note that non United States or Canadian citizens based at United States or Canadian institutions are eligible to apply. Women and minority investigators are strongly encouraged to apply. Applicants must be AGA members or sponsored by an AGA member.
Level of Study: Postgraduate.
Type: Award.
Value: US$36,000 per year.
Length of Study: Two years.
Frequency: Annual.
Country of Study: The United States of America, Canada or Mexico.
No. of awards offered: Four.
Application Procedure: Applicants must visit the website.
Closing Date: September 5th.
Funding: Private.
Contributor: The AGA.
Additional Information: At the end of the award, the recipient will be required to indicate how the funds were used, the accomplishments made during the training project and how this training has contributed to his or her research career development. A complete financial statement and scientific progress report are required annually and upon completion of the programme. All publications arising from work funded by this programme must acknowledge support of the award.

AGA Elsevier Research Initiative Award

Subjects: Medical science, specifically gastroenterology and hepathology.
Purpose: To provide non salary funds for new investigators to help them establish their research careers and to support pilot projects that represent new research directions for established investigators. The intent is to stimulate research in gastroenterology or hepatology related areas by permitting investigators to obtain new data that can ultimately provide the basis for subsequent grant applications of more substantial funding and duration.
Eligibility: Investigators must possess an MD, PhD or equivalent and must hold a faculty positions at accredited United States or Canadian institutions. They may not hold awards on similar a topic from other agencies. Applicants must be members of the AGA. Women and

minorities are strongly encouraged to apply. Applicants for this award may not simultaneously apply for the AGA/Miles and Shirley Fiterman Foundation Basic Research Award.
Level of Study: Postdoctorate, Postgraduate, Predoctorate.
Type: Award.
Value: US$25,000.
Length of Study: One year.
Frequency: Annual.
Country of Study: The United States of America, Canada or Mexico.
No. of awards offered: One.
Application Procedure: Applicants must visit the website.
Closing Date: January 7th.
Funding: Private.
Contributor: The AGA.

AGA June and Donald O Castell, MD Esophageal Clinical Research Award

Subjects: Oesophageal diseases.
Purpose: To support investigators who have demonstrated a high potential to develop an independent, productive research career.
Eligibility: Applicants must have an MD or PhD equivalent to hold a full-time faculty position at a United States or Canadian university or professional institute and be members of the AGA. The recipient must be at or below the level of assistant professor, and his/her initial appointment to the faculty position must have been within seven years of the time of application. This award is not intended for fellows, but for juniors who have demonstrated unusual promise, have some record of accomplishment in research and have established independent research programmes at the time of the award. Candidates must devote atleast 50 per cent of their efforts to research related to oesophageal function or diseases. Applicants may not simultaneously apply for an AGA Research Scholar Award, AGA Fiterman Foundation Basic Research Award or AGA/Elsevier Research Initiative Award.
Level of Study: Graduate.
Type: Research grant.
Value: US$35,000.
Length of Study: One year.
Frequency: Annual.
Country of Study: United States of America.
No. of awards offered: One.
Application Procedure: Applicants must visit the website.
Closing Date: January 7th.
Funding: Private.

AGA Merck Clinical Research Career Development Award

Subjects: Gastroenterology or hepathology.
Purpose: To provide salary support to junior faculty members performing clinical research at the outset of their career in order to develop an independent and productive career as a clinical investigator.
Eligibility: Applicants must hold full-time faculty positions at United States or Canadian universities or professional institutes at the time of application. Applicants must be members of the AGA. The research performed must be based upon, or otherwise include, direct patient contact or medical records analysis. The award may be used to support a fully trained investigator at the outset of his/her career or junior faculty seeking to obtain additional training, such as working with a defined mentor. This award is not meant to support advanced training or junior faculty acquiring additional procedural skills.
Level of Study: Graduate.
Type: Award.
Value: US$25,000 per year.
Length of Study: Two years.
Frequency: Annual.
Country of Study: United States of America.
No. of awards offered: One.
Application Procedure: Applicants must visit the website.
Closing Date: January 7th.
Funding: Private.

Additional Information: A complete financial statement and scientific progress report are required annually and upon completion of the programme. All publications arising from work funded by this programme must acknowledge support of this award.

AGA Miles and Shirley Fiterman Foundation Basic Research Awards

Subjects: Medical science, specifically gastroenterology and hepathology.
Purpose: To provide research or salary support for junior faculty members involved in basic research in any area of gastrointestinal, liver function or related diseases.
Eligibility: Applicants must hold faculty positions at an accredited United States or Canadian university or professional institute and must hold an MD, PhD or equivalent. Applicants must be individual members of the AGA. The recipient must be at or below the level of assistant professor and his/her appointment to the faculty position must have been within seven years of the time of application. This award is not intended for fellows, but for junior faculty who have demonstrated unusual promise, have some record of accomplishment in research and have established an independent research programme at the time of the award. Candidates must devote atleast 70 per cent of their efforts to research related to the gastrointestinal tract or the liver. Applicants for this award may not simultaneously apply for the AGA Research Scholar Award or the AGA/Elsevier Research Initiative Award.
Level of Study: Postgraduate.
Type: Award.
Value: US$35,000.
Length of Study: One year.
Frequency: Annual.
Country of Study: The United States of America, Canada or Mexico.
No. of awards offered: Two.
Application Procedure: Applicants must visit the website.
Closing Date: January 8th.
Funding: Private.
Contributor: The Miles & Shirley Fiterman Foundation.

AGA Miles and Shirley Fiterman Foundation Clinical Research in Gastroenterology or Hepatology/Nutrition Awards

Subjects: Medical science, specifically gastroenterology and hepathology.
Purpose: To recognise excellence in clinical research and to help support the clinical research of the recipients.
Eligibility: The award is not meant to be one that solely recognises past achievements by a senior member of the academic gastroenterology community. The recipients of these awards should be active investigators whose research is ongoing. Nominees must be members of the AGA.
Type: Award.
Value: US$35,000.
Frequency: Annual.
Country of Study: The United States of America, Canada or Mexico.
No. of awards offered: Two.
Application Procedure: Applicants must visit the website.
Closing Date: January 7th.
Funding: Private.
Contributor: The Miles & Shirley Fiterman Foundation.
Additional Information: Two awards are offered: the Joseph B Kirsner Award in Gastroenterology and the Hugh R Butt Award in Hepathology or Nutrition. The award defines clinical research as studies related to patients or disease processes having direct contact between the principal investigator and humans.

AGA R Robert and Sally D Funderburg Research Scholar Award in Gastric Biology Related to Cancer

Subjects: Gastric mucosal cell biology, regeneration and regulation of cell growth.
Purpose: To support an active established investigator working on novel approaches in the field of gastric cancer and who consequently

enhances the fundamental understanding of gastric cancer pathobiology in order to ultimately develop a cure for the disease.
Eligibility: Applicants must hold faculty positions at accredited United States or Canadian Institutions and must have established themselves as independent investigators in the field of gastric biology. Women and minority investigators are strongly encouraged to apply. Applicants must be individual members of the AGA.
Level of Study: Postgraduate.
Type: Award.
Value: US$25,000.
Length of Study: Two years.
Frequency: Annual.
Country of Study: The United States of America, Canada or Mexico.
No. of awards offered: One.
Application Procedure: Applicants must visit the website.
Closing Date: September 5th.
Contributor: The AGA, the late R Robert and the late Sally D. Funderburg.

AGA Research Scholar Awards

Subjects: Gastroenterology and hepathology.
Purpose: To ensure that a major proportion of young investigators' time is protected for research. The overall objective is to enable young investigators to develop independent and productive research careers in related fields and to support physicians or investigators who have the potential to develop independent, productive research careers.
Eligibility: Applicants must hold full-time faculty positions at United States or Canadian universities or professional institutes at the time of application and be members of the AGA. The award is not intended for Fellows, but for young faculty who have demonstrated unusual promise and have some record of accomplishment in research. Candidates should be in the beginning years of their careers. Those who have been at the assistant professor level or equivalent for more than five years at the time the award would begin are not eligible. Candidates must hold an MD, PhD or equivalent degree. Candidates must devote at least 70 per cent of their efforts to research related to the gastrointestinal tract or liver. Women and minority investigators are strongly encouraged to apply.
Level of Study: Graduate.
Type: Research grant.
Value: US$65,000 per year.
Length of Study: Three years.
Frequency: Annual.
Country of Study: United States of America.
No. of awards offered: Six.
Application Procedure: Applicants must visit the website.
Closing Date: September 5th.
Funding: Private.
Additional Information: A complete financial statement and scientific progress report are required upon completion of the programme. All publications arising from work funded by this programme must acknowledge the support of the award. Awardees must submit their work for presentation at Digestive Disease Week during the last year of the award.

AGA Student Research Fellowship Awards

Subjects: Medical science, specifically gastroenterology and hepathology.
Purpose: To stimulate interest in research careers in digestive diseases by providing salary support for research projects.
Eligibility: Candidates may be medical or graduate students, who are not yet engaged in their thesis research, at accredited United States or Canadian institutions. Candidates holding advanced degrees must be enrolled as medical or graduate students and they may not hold any similar support from other agencies, eg. American Liver Foundation, Crohn's and Colitis Foundation of America. Women and minority students are strongly encouraged to apply.
Level of Study: Graduate, Postgraduate, Professional development.
Type: Award.
Value: From US$2,000-3,000.
Length of Study: A minimum of 10 weeks.
Frequency: Annual.

Country of Study: The United States of America, Canada or Mexico.
No. of awards offered: Up to 20.
Application Procedure: Applicants must visit the website.
Closing Date: March 3rd.
Funding: Private.
Contributor: The AGA.

FOUNDATION FOR HIGH BLOOD PRESSURE RESEARCH

PO Box 13F, Monash University, VIC 3800, Australia
Tel: (61) 3 9905 2555
Fax: (61) 3 9905 2566
Email: fhbpr@med.monash.edu.au
Contact: Ms Jan Morrison, Administrative Officer

The Foundation for High Blood Pressure Research was established to support research into any aspects of blood pressure, hypertension and associated cardiovascular diseases.

Foundation for High Blood Pressure Research Postdoctoral Fellowship

Subjects: The understanding of the causes, prevention, treatment or effects of hypertension.
Purpose: To fund a scientist to perform research.
Eligibility: Open to applicants from Australia or New Zealand, who have a degree in medicine or science, with an appropriate PhD.
Level of Study: Postdoctorate.
Type: Fellowship.
Value: Salary and associated costs, plus project maintenance.
Length of Study: Two years.
Frequency: Annual.
Study Establishment: An approved institute, university or hospital.
Country of Study: Australia.
No. of awards offered: One.
Application Procedure: Applicants must complete and submit an application with a curriculum vitae and relevant publications.
Closing Date: Please consult the Foundation.
Funding: Private.
Contributor: The Foundation.
No. of awards given last year: One.
No. of applicants last year: 10.
Additional Information: The award is advertised in Australia and overseas. Interested applicants should contact the Honorary Secretary for further information.

ISH Postdoctoral Award

Subjects: The understanding of the causes, prevention, treatment or effects of hypertension.
Purpose: To fund an international scientist to perform research at an Australian research institution.
Eligibility: Open to applicants who have a degree in medicine or science, or appropriate PhD.
Level of Study: Postdoctorate.
Type: Fellowship.
Value: Some assistance is provided to the employing institution comprising of part salary only.
Length of Study: Two years.
Frequency: Every two years.
Study Establishment: An approved institute, university or hospital.
Country of Study: Australia.
No. of awards offered: One.
Application Procedure: Applicants must complete and submit an application with a curriculum vitae and relevant publications.
Closing Date: Please consult the Foundation.
Funding: Private.
Contributor: The Foundation.
No. of awards given last year: One.
No. of applicants last year: Four.
Additional Information: Details are advertised in Australia and overseas. Interested applicants should contact the Honorary Secretary for further information.

FOUNDATION FOR PHYSICAL THERAPY

1111 North Fairax Street, Alexandria, VA 22314, United States of America
Tel: (1) 800 999 2782 ext. 8505
Fax: (1) 703 706 8519
Email: foundation@apta.org
www: http://www.apta.org/foundation
Contact: Ms Lucy Dickson, Scientific Review Administrator

The Foundation for Physical Therapy is a national, independent, non-profit corporation founded to support the physical therapy profession's research needs in the areas of scientific research, clinical research and health services research.

FPT Research Grants

Subjects: Physical therapy, rehabilitation medicine, neuroscience, sports medicine, pediatrics, medical sciences and social or preventative medicine.
Purpose: To support emerging investigators by funding research studies in specified areas.
Eligibility: Applicants must be nationals of the U.S.A and fulfil specific requirements with regard to previous research experience. Please check the website.
Level of Study: Postgraduate.
Value: US$40,000
Length of Study: One year.
Frequency: Annual.
Country of Study: United States of America.
No. of awards offered: Varies.
Application Procedure: Please check the website.
Closing Date: 15th October.
Funding: Private.
No. of awards given last year: 2.
No. of applicants last year: 12.

McMillan Doctoral Scholarships

Subjects: Physical therapy, rehabilitation medicine, neuroscience, sports medicine, pediatrics, medical sciences and social or preventative medicine.
Purpose: To assist physical therapists with outstanding potential for doctoral studies in the first year of study towards a doctorate.
Eligibility: Open to candidates who possess a license to practice physical therapy in the United States and fulfil specific requirements with regard to research experience. Please check the website.
Level of Study: Doctorate.
Type: Scholarship.
Value: US$5,000
Length of Study: One year.
Frequency: Annual.
Country of Study: United States of America.
Application Procedure: Please check the website.
Closing Date: 15th October.
Funding: Private.

New Investigator Fellowships Training Initiative (NIFTI)

Subjects: Physical therapy, rehabilitation medicine, neuroscience, sports medicine, pediatrics, medical sciences and social or preventative medicine.
Purpose: To fund doctorally prepared physical therapists as developing researchers and improve their competitiveness in securing external funding for future research.
Eligibility: Open to candidates who possess a licence to practice physical therapy in the United States of America, have received the required post professional doctoral degree no earlier than five years prior to the year of application and have completed a research experience as part of their post professional doctoral education.
Level of Study: Postdoctorate.
Type: Fellowship.
Value: US$30,000.
Length of Study: One year.
Frequency: Annual.
Country of Study: United States of America.
No. of awards offered: Varies.

Application Procedure: Applicants must complete an application form.
Closing Date: January 15th.
Funding: Private.
No. of awards given last year: One.
No. of applicants last year: Six.

Promotion of Doctoral Studies (PODS)

Subjects: Physical therapy, rehabilitation medicine, neuroscience, sports medicine, pediatrics, medical sciences and social or preventative medicine.
Purpose: To fund doctoral students who, having completed one full year of coursework, wish to continue their coursework or enter the dissertation phase.
Eligibility: Open to candidates who possess a licence to practice physical therapy in the United States of America and who are enrolled as students in a regionally accredited postprofessional, doctoral programme. The content of this programme should have a demonstrated relationship to physical therapy. Applicants must also be able to demonstrate continuous progress towards the completion of their post professional doctoral programme in a timely fashion and with a commitment to further the physical therapy profession through research and teaching within the United States and its territories.
Level of Study: Doctorate.
Type: Scholarship.
Value: Two levels at US$7,500 or US$15,000.
Length of Study: One year.
Frequency: Annual.
Country of Study: United States of America.
No. of awards offered: Varies.
Application Procedure: Applicants must complete an application form.
Closing Date: January 15th.
Funding: Private.
No. of awards given last year: 14.
No. of applicants last year: 53.

Research Grants

Subjects: Physical therapy, rehabilitation medicine, neuroscience, sports medicine, pediatrics, medical sciences and social or preventative medicine.
Purpose: The purpose of Foundation's Research Grant program is to fund research studies in specific areas initiated by emerging investigators.
Eligibility: Open to all those who possess a license to practice physical therapy in the U.S. or its territories, must be a U.S. citizen or permanent resident. Projects to be completed in fulfillment of requirements for an academic degree are not eligible to be funded by a Foundation research grant. A doctoral student in the latter stage of the dissertation phase of his/her program may submit an application, but must provide evidence of completion of the degree by October 15, 2003. If this evidence is not provided by this date, the proposed project will not be funded. Studies that are to be completed for an academic degree are not eligible for Foundation research grant funding. In addition, the proposed study must differ substantially from any thesis research being conducted by graduate assistant(s) to be supported by this research grant.
Level of Study: Research.
Type: Grant.
Value: US$40,000.
Frequency: Annual.
Country of Study: United States of America.
No. of awards offered: Varies.
Application Procedure: Applicants must complete an application form.
Closing Date: August 13, 2004.
Funding: Private.
No. of awards given last year: 2.
No. of applicants last year: 12.
Additional Information: Guidelines and application forms are available on line in the spring at http://www.apta.org/Foundation/applications online. A paper version of the RFP is available from the Foundation.

FOUNDATION FOR SCIENCE AND DISABILITY, INC.

503 North West, 89 Street, Gainesville, FL 32607, United States of America
Tel: (1) 352 374 5774
Fax: (1) 352 374 5781
Email: rmankin@gainesville.usda.ufl.edu
www: http://www.as.wvu.edu˜scidis/organizations
Contact: Dr Richard Mankin, Grants Committee Chair

The Foundation for Science and Disability aims to promote the integration of scientists with disabilities into all activities of the scientific community and of society as a whole, and to promote the removal of barriers in order to enable students with disabilities to choose careers in science.

Foundation for Science and Disability Student Grant Fund

Subjects: Engineering, mathematics, medicine, computer science and natural sciences, or computer science.
Purpose: To increase opportunities in science for physically disabled students at the graduate or professional level.
Eligibility: Open to candidates from the United States of America.
Level of Study: Doctorate, Postdoctorate, Postgraduate.
Type: Grant.
Value: US$1,000.
Length of Study: One year.
Frequency: Annual.
Country of Study: United States of America.
No. of awards offered: One-three.
Application Procedure: Applicants must submit a completed application form, copies of official college transcripts, a letter from the research or academic supervisor in support of the request and a second letter from another faculty member.
Closing Date: December 1st.
Funding: Private.
No. of awards given last year: Two.
No. of applicants last year: Eight.
Additional Information: The award may be used for an assistive device or instrument, or as financial support to work with a professor, or on an individual research project, or for some other special need.

FOUNDATION FOR THE ADVANCEMENT OF MESOAMERICAN STUDIES, INC. (FAMSI)

268 South Suncoast Boulevard, Crystal River, FL 34429-5498, United States of America
Tel: (1) 352 795 5990
Fax: (1) 352 795 1970
Email: famsi@famsi.org
www: http://www.famsi.org
Contact: Dr Sandra Noble, Executive Director

The Foundation for the Advancement of Mesoamerican Studies (FAMSI) was created in 1993 to foster increased understanding of ancient Mesoamerican cultures. The Foundation assists qualified scholars who might otherwise be unable to complete their programmes of research and synthesis. FAMSI provides Research Funds and Research Materials online.

FAMSI Research Grant

Subjects: Mesoamerican studies, focusing on investigations concerning the ancient pre-Columbian cultures of Mexico, Guatemala, Belize, Honduras and El Salvador.
Purpose: To support scholarly works with the potential for significant contributions to the understanding of ancient Mesoamerican cultures and to provide monies for projects that might otherwise not continue.
Eligibility: Open to recent graduates, degree candidates or active professionals who are involved in fully developed programmes of

Mesoamerican study. FAMSI does not provide funds for equipment, salary or stipends and does not fund other institutions.
Level of Study: Unrestricted.
Value: General research grants provide a maximum of US$10,000, and contingency grants a maximum of US$2,000.
Length of Study: One year.
Frequency: Annual.
Study Establishment: Unrestricted.
Country of Study: Other.
No. of awards offered: 25-35.
Application Procedure: Applicants must complete a current application form and submit this with three letters of reference, a curriculum vitae, a budget, a statement of purpose and an abstract in English. Application forms are available on written request or from the website.
Closing Date: September 15th.
Funding: Private.
Contributor: Anonymous individuals.
No. of awards given last year: 35.
No. of applicants last year: 105.
Additional Information: Online Research Materials at www.famsi.org include an interactive Maya Hieroglyphic Dictionary, a Bibliography of Mesoamerican Volumes with more than 65,000 entries, an Introduction to Ancient Cultures of Mesoamerica, 3000 color photographs of ancient objects and monuments.

FOUNDATION OF THE AMERICAN COLLEGE OF HEALTHCARE EXECUTIVES

Suite 1700, One North Franklin Street, Chicago, IL 60606-4425, United States of America
Tel: (1) 312 424 9388
Fax: (1) 312 424 9405
Email: membershipl@ache.org
www: http://www.ache.org
Contact: Membership Marketing Representative

It is the mission of the Foundation of the American College of Healthcare Executives to be the professional membership society for healthcare executives; to meet its members' professional, educational and leadership needs; to promote high ethical standards and conduct; and to advance healthcare leadership and management excellence.

Albert W. Dent Graduate Student Scholarship

Subjects: Healthcare management.
Purpose: To help minority students better prepare themselves for a career in healthcare management.
Eligibility: Open to United States and Canadian citizens who are Student Associates of the American College of Healthcare Executives and are in good standing. Applicants must be minority students enrolled for full-time study for the upcoming fall term, which is didactic final year of work in a healthcare management graduate program, be able to demonstrate financial need, and must not be previous recipients.
Level of Study: Graduate.
Type: Scholarship.
Value: US$3,500.
Frequency: Annual.
Country of Study: United States of America or Canada.
No. of awards offered: Varies.
Application Procedure: Applicants must complete an application form, available from their programme director or the main address.
Closing Date: Applications are accepted between January 1st-March 31st.

Foster G. McGaw Graduate Student Scholarship

Subjects: Healthcare management.
Purpose: To help students better prepare themselves for a career in healthcare management.
Eligibility: Open to United States and Canadian citizens who are Student Associates of the American College of Healthcare Executives and are in good standing. Applicants must be enrolled in full-time

study for the upcoming fall term, which is the final year of didactic work in a healthcare management graduate program, be able to demonstrate financial need and must not be previous recipients.
Level of Study: Graduate.
Type: Scholarship.
Value: US$3,500.
Frequency: Annual.
Country of Study: United States of America or Canada.
No. of awards offered: Varies.
Application Procedure: Applicants must complete an application form, available from their programme director or the main address.
Closing Date: Applications are accepted between January 1st-March 31st.

FOUNDATION PRAEMIUM ERASMIANUM

Jan van Goyenkade 5, Amsterdam, NL-1075 HN, Netherlands
Tel: (31) 20 676 0222
Fax: (31) 20 675 2231
Email: spe@erasmusprijs.org
www: http://www.erasmusprijs.org
Contact: Y C Goester, Secretary

The Foundation Praemium Erasmianum operates internationally in the fields of social studies and the arts and humanities, through the awarding of the Erasmus Prize and other activities.

ERASMUS Prize
Subjects: Arts, humanities or social studies.
Purpose: To honour persons who have made an exceptional contribution to European culture.
Eligibility: There are no eligibility restrictions.
Level of Study: Unrestricted.
Type: Money prize.
Value: €150,000.
Frequency: Annual.
Country of Study: Any country.
No. of awards offered: One.
Application Procedure: Applications by third parties only are considered.
Funding: Private.

Foundation Praemium Erasmianum Study Prize
Subjects: Humanities or social sciences.
Purpose: To honour young academics who have written an excellent thesis in the field of humanities or social sciences.
Eligibility: Open to students of Dutch universities.
Level of Study: Postdoctorate.
Type: Money prize.
Value: €3,000.
Frequency: Annual.
Country of Study: Any country.
No. of awards offered: Five.
Application Procedure: Relevant faculties or universities nominate candidates, from which the Foundation selects five winners.
Closing Date: July 15th.
Funding: Private.
No. of awards given last year: Five.
No. of applicants last year: 21.

FRANCIS CHAGRIN FUND

c/o Society for the Promotion of New Music (SPNM), 4th Floor 18-20 Southwark Street, London, SE1 1TJ, England
Tel: (44) 20 7407 1640
Fax: (44) 20 7403 7652
Email: spnm@spnm.org.uk
www: http://www.spnm.org.uk
Contact: Ms Jo-Anne Naish, Administrator

From contemporary jazz, classical and popular music to that written for film, dance and other creative media, the SPNM is one of the main advocates of new music in the United Kingdom today.

Francis Chagrin Fund
Subjects: Composition.
Purpose: To help cover the costs of photocopying incurred by composers in reproducing performance materials for unpublished works awaiting their first performance.
Eligibility: Applicants must be British composers or composers resident in the United Kingdom. Their works must be unpublished.
Level of Study: Unrestricted.
Type: Grant.
Value: UK£250 maximum.
Frequency: Dependent on funds available.
No. of awards offered: Unlimited.
Application Procedure: Applicants must submit an application form, curriculum vitae, two references and relevant invoices. Application forms are available from the SPNM.
Closing Date: There is no deadline.
Funding: Private.
Additional Information: The committee meets once per month.

FRANK KNOX MEMORIAL FELLOWSHIPS

3 Birdcage walk, Westminster, London, SW1H 9JJ, England
Tel: (44) 20 7222 1151
Fax: (44) 20 7222 7189
www: http://www.frankknox.harvard.edu
Contact: Ms Anna Mason, Secretary

The Frank Knox Memorial Fellowships were established at Harvard University in 1945 by a gift from Mrs Annie Reid Knox, widow of the late Colonel Frank Knox, to allow students from the United Kingdom to participate in an educational exchange programme.

Frank Knox Fellowships at Harvard University
Subjects: Arts, sciences including engineering and medical sciences, business administration and management, design, divinity, education, law, public administration and public health.
Eligibility: Open to citizens of the United Kingdom who, at the time of application, have spent at least two of the last four years at a university or university college in the United Kingdom and who will have graduated by the start of tenure. Fellowships are not awarded for postdoctoral study and no application will be considered from persons already in the United States of America. A period of full-time work since graduation is necessary prior to embarking on the MBA programme.
Level of Study: Postgraduate.
Type: Fellowship.
Value: US$18,500 plus tuition fees. Unmarried Fellows may be accommodated in one of the university dormitories or halls.
Length of Study: One academic year. Depending on the availability of sufficient funds fellowships may be renewed for those Fellows registered for a degree programme of more than one year.
Frequency: Annual.
Study Establishment: Harvard University.
Country of Study: United States of America.
No. of awards offered: Six.
Application Procedure: Applicants must file an admissions application directly with the graduate school of their choice at an early date. Harvard University will try to arrange a suitable course for each individual.
Closing Date: October 27th.
Funding: Private.
Contributor: The estate of the late Frank Knox.
No. of awards given last year: Six.
No. of applicants last year: 110.
Additional Information: Travel grants are not awarded, although in cases of extreme hardship applications can be made to Harvard University for travel cost assistance.

FRANKLIN AND ELEANOR ROOSEVELT INSTITUTE

Franklin D Roosevelt Library, 4079 Albany Post Road, Hyde Park, NY 12538, United States of America
Tel: (1) 845 486 1150
Fax: (1) 845 486 1150
www: http://www.feri.org
Contact: Chairman, Grants Committee

The Franklin and Eleanor Roosevelt Institute is a private non-profit corporation dedicated to preserving the legacy and promoting the ideals of Franklin and Eleanor Roosevelt.

Roosevelt Institute Research Grant
Subjects: The Roosevelt years and clearly related subjects.
Purpose: To encourage younger scholars to expand their knowledge and understanding of the Roosevelt period and to give continued support to more experienced researchers who have already made a mark in the field.
Eligibility: Open to qualified researchers of any nationality with a viable plan of work. Proposals are recommended for funding by an independent panel of Scholars which reports to the Institute Board.
Level of Study: Doctorate, Graduate, Postdoctorate.
Type: Research grant.
Value: Up to US$2,500.
Frequency: Twice a year.
Study Establishment: The Franklin D Roosevelt Library, Hyde Park in New York.
Country of Study: United States of America.
No. of awards offered: 15-20.
Application Procedure: Applicants must submit two copies of each of the following: an application front sheet, research proposal, relevance of holdings, travel plans, time estimate, curriculum vitae, three letters of reference and budget. Application forms and guidelines are available from the website or by emailing, faxing, or writing to the Roosevelt Institute.
Closing Date: February 15th and September 15th.
Funding: Private.

FRAXA RESEARCH FOUNDATION

45 Pleasant Street, Newburyport, MA 01950, United States of America
Tel: (1) 978 462 1866
Fax: (1) 978 463 9985
Email: info@fraxa.org
www: http://www.fraxa.org
Contact: Ms Katherine Clapp, President

The FRAXA Research Foundation funds postdoctoral fellowships and investigator initiated grants to support medical research aimed at the treatment of Fragile X Syndrome. FRAXA is particularly interested in preclinical studies of potential pharmacological and genetic treatments and studies aimed at understanding the function of the FMRI gene.

FRAXA Grants and Fellowships
Subjects: The treatment of Fragile X Syndrome, and potential pharmacological and genetic treatments and studies aimed at understanding the function of the FMRI gene.
Purpose: To promote research aimed at finding a specific treatment for Fragile X syndrome.
Eligibility: There are no eligibility restrictions.
Level of Study: Postdoctorate, Research.
Type: Other.
Value: Up to US$35,000 for postdoctoral fellowships. No limit for investigator initiated grants.
Length of Study: One year, renewable.
Frequency: Twice a year.
Country of Study: Any country.
No. of awards offered: 25-35 each year.
Application Procedure: Applicants must complete an application form, available from the FRAXA Research Foundation or from the website. Potential applicants are welcome to submit a one page initial inquiry letter describing the proposed research before submitting a full application.
Closing Date: May 1st or December 1st.
Funding: Private.
No. of awards given last year: 36.
No. of applicants last year: 60.
Additional Information: Further information is available on request.

THE FREDERIC CHOPIN SOCIETY

Ostrogski Castle, Ul Okolnik 1, Warsaw, PL 00-368, Poland
Tel: (48) 22 826 81 90
Fax: (48) 22 827 95 99
Email: konkurs@chopin.pl
www: http://www.konkurs.chopin.pl
Contact: Administrative Assistant

The Frederic Chopin Society organises the International Chopin Piano Competition, the Scholarly Piano Competition for Polish Pianists, the Grand Prix du Disque Frederic Chopin, courses in Chopin's music interpretation and Chopin music recitals, as well running as a museum and collection.

International Frederic Chopin Piano Competition
Subjects: Piano performance of Chopin's music.
Purpose: To recognise the best artistic interpretation of Chopin's music and to encourage professional development.
Eligibility: Open to pianists of any nationality, born between 1977 and 1988.
Level of Study: Unrestricted.
Type: Prize.
Value: US$25,000 for the first prize, US$20,000 for the second prize, US$15,000 for the third prize, US$11,000 for the fourth prize, US$8,000 for the fifth prize, US$6,000 for the sixth prize and six remaining finalists shall be awarded mentions of US$2,000 each.
Frequency: Every five years.
Country of Study: Any country.
No. of awards offered: Six.
Application Procedure: Applicants must complete and submit an application form attached with the rules.
Closing Date: March 1st.
Funding: Government, Private.
No. of awards given last year: 14 (Competition 2000).

FREDERICK DOUGLASS INSTITUTE FOR AFRICAN AND AFRICAN-AMERICAN STUDIES

University of Rochester, 302 Morey Hall, Rochester, NY 14627-0440, United States of America
Tel: (1) 585 275 7235
Fax: (1) 585 256 2594
Email: fdi@troi.cc.rochester.edu
www: http://www.cc.rochester.edu/college/aas
Contact: G R Radegonde-Eison, Administrative Assistant

The Frederick Douglass Institute for African and African-American Studies was established in 1986 to promote the development of African and African-American studies and graduate education through advanced research at the University of Rochester. It has served as an interdisciplinary centre, with its focus on the social sciences, though not excluding the humanities and the natural sciences.

Frederick Douglass Institute Postdoctoral Fellowship
Subjects: Historical and contemporary topics on the economy, society, politics and culture of Africa and its diaspora. Broadly conceived projects on human and technological aspects of energy development and agriculture in Africa are welcomed.
Purpose: To support the completion of a project.
Eligibility: Open to Scholars who hold a PhD degree in a field related to the African and African American experience.

Level of Study: Postdoctorate.
Type: Fellowship.
Value: A stipend of US$35,000 as well as full access to the university's facilities and office space in the Institute. It also supports the completion of a research project for one academic year.
Frequency: Annual.
Country of Study: Any country.
No. of awards offered: One.
Application Procedure: Applicants must submit a completed application, a curriculum vitae, a three-five page description of the project plus a short bibliography and a sample of published or unpublished writing on a topic related to the proposal. Three letters of recommendation that comment upon the value and feasibility of the work proposed are to be sent by referees.
Closing Date: January 31st.
Additional Information: All Fellows receive office space in the Institute and opportunities to interact and collaborate with Scholars of their respective disciplines within the University. Fellows must be in full-time residence during the tenure of their awards and are expected to be engaged in scholarly activity on a full-time basis. They must be available for consultation with students and professional colleagues, make at least two formal presentations based upon their research and contribute generally to the intellectual discourse on African and African-American Studies.

Frederick Douglass Institute Predoctoral Dissertation Fellowship

Subjects: Historical and contemporary topics on the economy, society, politics and culture of Africa and its diaspora. Broadly conceived projects on human and technological aspects of energy development and agriculture in Africa are welcomed.
Purpose: To support the completion of a dissertation.
Eligibility: Open to graduate students of any university who study aspects of the African and African American experience. Applicants must have completed and passed all required courses, any qualifying oral and/or written exams and have written at least one chapter of the dissertation, which then becomes part of the application package, to qualify for this award.
Level of Study: Predoctorate.
Type: Fellowship.
Value: A stipend of US$18,000 as well as full access to the university's facilities and office space in the institute.
Frequency: Annual.
Country of Study: Any country.
Application Procedure: Applicants must complete and send the FDI fellowship application form, a curriculum vitae, an official transcript showing completion of all preliminary coursework and qualifying examinations, the dissertation prospectus, a sample chapter from the dissertation, three letters of recommendation to be sent out by the referees, including one from the dissertation supervisor assessing the candidate's prospects for completing the project within a year.
Closing Date: January 31st.
Additional Information: All Fellows receive office space in the Institute and opportunities to interact and collaborate with Scholars of their respective disciplines within the University. Fellows must be in full-time residence during the tenure of their awards and are expected to be engaged in scholarly activity on a full-time basis. They must be available for consultation with students and professional colleagues, make at least two formal presentations based upon their research and contribute generally to the intellectual discourse on African and African-American Studies.

FRENCH EMBASSY, LINGUISTIC SECTION

6 Perth Avenue, Yarralumla, Canberra, ACT 2600, Australia
Tel: (61) 2 6216 0100
Fax: (61) 2 6216 0156
Email: language@france.net.au
www: http://www.france.net.au/language/program
Contact: Mr Christian Marmidin, Attaché de Co-opération pour le Français

French Government Postgraduate Scholarships

Subjects: French language, literature and civilisation.
Eligibility: Open to Australian citizens who hold a Bachelor of Arts degree and who have completed three years at a university.
Level of Study: Postgraduate.
Type: Scholarship.
Value: €730 monthly maintenance allowance plus medical cover.
Length of Study: One year.
Frequency: Annual.
Study Establishment: An approved university.
Country of Study: France.
No. of awards offered: Two.
Application Procedure: Applicants must submit an application after their admission to the postgraduate programme of a French university. Application forms are available from the French departments of universities.
Closing Date: December 31st.
Funding: Government.
No. of awards given last year: Two.

Language Assistantships in Australia

Subjects: French language studies.
Purpose: To enable French assistants to take up positions supporting the teaching of French in Australian schools.
Eligibility: Open to French citizens only.
Level of Study: Postgraduate.
Type: Other.
Value: Please contact the organisation.
Length of Study: One year, non renewable.
Frequency: Annual.
Country of Study: Australia.
No. of awards offered: 26.
Application Procedure: Applicants must apply to the French Ministry of Education in Paris or through the CIEP (Centre International d'Etudes Pédagogiques), 1 Avenue León-Journault, 92318 Sèvres Cedex, www.ciep.fr.
Funding: Government.
No. of awards given last year: 20.
Additional Information: These awards are organised by the Bureau de Co-opération pour le Francais of the Embassy of France in Australia (BCLE).

Language Assistantships in France and New Caledonia

Subjects: French language studies.
Purpose: To enable graduates who intend to teach French in the future or beginning teachers of French to improve their language skills.
Eligibility: Open to young Australian graduates only.
Level of Study: Graduate.
Type: Other.
Value: €902 living allowance plus medical cover in France, between €1250-1350 in overseas 'Départements' and between €1400-1600 in New Caledonia.
Length of Study: Seven months.
Frequency: Annual.
Study Establishment: Any approved high school.
Country of Study: Other.
No. of awards offered: 80 in France and four in New Caledonia.
Application Procedure: Applicants must write for details.
Closing Date: October 20th for New Caledonia, December 19th for Metropolitan France and overseas 'Départements'
Funding: Government.
No. of awards given last year: 36.
Additional Information: These awards are organised by the Bureau de Co-opération pour le Francais (BCF) of the Embassy of France in Australia. Successful applicants will conduct English conversation classes with small groups of students for 12 hours per week.

Ministry of Foreign Affairs (France) International Teaching Fellowships

Subjects: French language education.
Purpose: To enable experienced teachers of French to spend time at a French primary school, a French 'college', a French Lycée.

Eligibility: Open to Australian teachers of French employed by state education authorities.
Level of Study: Professional development.
Type: Fellowship.
Length of Study: One year.
Frequency: Annual.
Study Establishment: A lycée, collège, primary school or Institut Universitaire de Formation de Maîtres (IUFM).
Country of Study: France.
No. of awards offered: Two.
Application Procedure: Applicants must complete an application form, available from state departments of education.
Closing Date: April 30th.
Funding: Government.
No. of awards given last year: Two.
Additional Information: These awards are organised by the Bureau de Co-opération pour le Francais of the Embassy of France in Australia (BCF).

Ministry of Foreign Affairs (France) Stage de Nouméa (Three Week Course)

Subjects: French language and French and Melanesian culture.
Purpose: To enable primary and secondary teachers of French to refresh and consolidate their knowledge of French, to improve their teaching skills and to increase their knowledge of French and Melanesian cultures.
Eligibility: Open to primary and secondary school teachers of French.
Level of Study: Professional development.
Value: Australian $4,000.
Length of Study: Three weeks.
Frequency: Annual.
Study Establishment: CREIPAC, Nouméa (New-Caledonia).
Country of Study: Other.
No. of awards offered: Up to 30.
Application Procedure: Applicants from state schools must apply through their local Department of Education. Teachers from Catholic or Independent schools must refer to their State authorities.
Closing Date: August 1st. Applicants from state schools must check with the Department.
Funding: Government.
No. of awards given last year: 12.

Ministry of Foreign Affairs (France) Stage de Paris/Toulon

Subjects: French.
Eligibility: Open to experienced primary and secondary teachers of French, especially those holding positions of responsibility in language departments.
Level of Study: Professional development.
Value: Varies.
Length of Study: Four weeks.
Frequency: Annual.
Study Establishment: The Centre International d'Etudes Pédagogiques (CIEP) de Sévres and the Campus International de Toulon.
Country of Study: France.
No. of awards offered: Between 10 and 15.
Application Procedure: Applicants must write for details.
Closing Date: August 1st.
Funding: Government.
No. of awards given last year: 11.

Ministry of Foreign Affairs (France) Support for Associations of Independent Schools and Catholic

Subjects: French.
Purpose: To financially assist independent schools which have a particular project related to the teaching of French.
Eligibility: Open to French teachers from independent schools and catholic.
Level of Study: Professional development.
Type: Grant.
Value: Varies.
Frequency: Annual.
Country of Study: Australia.
No. of awards offered: 12.

Application Procedure: Applicants must submit their projects to their State Association. Each State Association of Independent Schools will then sort the projects according to its own priorities and forward them along with the statement of priorities to the Linguistic Section of the French Embassy.
Closing Date: May 15th for project submissions from teachers. May 31st for forwarded projects and priorities list from Associations.
Funding: Government.
No. of awards given last year: 12.

Ministry of Foreign Affairs (France) Support for FATFA (Federation of the Association of Teachers of French in Australia)

Subjects: French.
Purpose: To support initiatives in the teaching of French.
Eligibility: Open to Australian associations of French teachers.
Level of Study: Professional development.
Type: Grant.
Value: Varies.
Frequency: Annual.
No. of awards offered: 1.
Application Procedure: Applicants must write for details.
Closing Date: May 15th.
Funding: Government.
No. of awards given last year: None.

Ministry of Foreign Affairs (France) Tertiary Studies in French Universities (Baudin Travel Grants)

Subjects: French language.
Purpose: To encourage graduate and postgraduate students to study for at least one semester at a French university.
Eligibility: Open to graduate or postgraduate students with a double major in French and another subject.
Level of Study: Graduate, Postgraduate.
Type: Grant.
Value: Australian $2,000 + Medical cover (worth $2,000).
Length of Study: More than one semester.
Frequency: Annual.
Study Establishment: A university.
Country of Study: France.
No. of awards offered: 16.
Application Procedure: Applicants must complete an application form, available on request from every Australian university's department or section of French studies. Students must apply for a course of study approved for credit by their home institution.
Closing Date: May 15th.
Funding: Government.
No. of awards given last year: 16.

Ministry of Foreign Affairs (France) University Study Tours (Nouméa)

Subjects: French language.
Purpose: To assist French language students to attend a two week course in Nouméa (New-Caledonia).
Eligibility: Open to French language students in Australian Universities.
Level of Study: Graduate.
Value: Australian $500.
Length of Study: Two weeks.
Frequency: Annual.
Study Establishment: CREIPAC, Nouméa.
Country of Study: Other.
No. of awards offered: 30.
Application Procedure: Applicants must write for details.
Closing Date: April 30th.
Funding: Government.
No. of awards given last year: 20.
Additional Information: The tours are currently organised at different times of the year by the French departments of the James Cook University of North Queensland, the Australian National University, Flinders University, Macquarie University, Melbourne and Monash

Universities. Students from other universities are entitled to join one of these groups. Please contact the relevant French department for further information.

FRIENDS OF FRENCH ART

100 Vanderlip Drive, Villa Narcissa, Rancho Palos Verdes, CA 90275, United States of America
Tel: (1) 310 377 4444
Fax: (1) 310 377 4584
Email: villacisssa@aol.com
Contact: Ms Elin Vanderlip, President

Friends of French Art restore art in peril, both in France and the United States of America.

Summer Art Restoration Program
Subjects: Art restoration and conservation.
Purpose: To give graduate students in the field of art conservation the opportunity to spend the summer in France.
Eligibility: Open to graduate students in the field of art restoration.
Level of Study: Postgraduate
Value: Approx. US$5,000 air fare to France and accommodation while working on a specific project.
Length of Study: Summer programme.
Frequency: Annual.
Country of Study: France.
No. of awards offered: Varies.
Application Procedure: Applicants should contact the organisation for details.
Funding: Private.
Contributor: Private donations through the Friends of French Art.

For further information contact:

University of Delaware, Winterthur Art Conservation Department, Winterthur, DE 19735, United States of America

FRIENDS OF ISRAEL EDUCATIONAL FOUNDATION

Academic Study Group, PO Box 7545
London, NW2 20B, England
Tel: (44) 20 7435 6803
Fax: (44) 20 7794 0291
Email: info@foi-asg.org
Contact: Mr John D A Levy

The Friends of Israel Educational Foundation and its sister operation, the Academic Study Group, aim to encourage a critical understanding of the achievements, hopes and problems of modern Israel, and to forge new collaborative working links between the United Kingdom and Israel.

Friends of Israel Educational Foundation Academic Study Bursary
Subjects: All subjects.
Purpose: To provide funding for British academics planning to pay a first research or study visit to Israel.
Eligibility: Open to research or teaching postgraduates. The Academic Study Group will only consider proposals from British academics who have already linked up with professional counterparts in Israel and agreed terms of reference for an initial visit.
Level of Study: Postdoctorate.
Type: Bursary.
Value: UK£300 per person.
Frequency: Annual.
Country of Study: Israel.
No. of awards offered: 30.
Application Procedure: Applicants must contact the organisation, there is no application form.
Closing Date: November 15th or March 15th.
Funding: Private.

Contributor: Trusts and individual donations.
No. of awards given last year: Five.
No. of applicants last year: 50 + .

Friends of Israel Educational Foundation Young Artist Award
Subjects: Fine arts.
Purpose: To enable a promising British artist to pay a working visit to Israel and prepare work for an exhibition on Israeli themes in the United Kingdom.
Eligibility: Open to promising young British painters, print makers and illustrators.
Level of Study: Postgraduate, Professional development.
Type: Award.
Value: Airfares, accommodation and basic living costs.
Length of Study: A minimum of two months.
Frequency: Annual.
Study Establishment: A kibbutz.
Country of Study: Israel.
No. of awards offered: One-two.
Application Procedure: Applicants must submit a personal curriculum vitae, an academic letter of reference, a statement of reasons for wishing to visit Israel, and a representative selection of work.
Closing Date: May.
Funding: Private.
Contributor: Individual donations.
Additional Information: Shortlisted candidates will be interviewed and artwork examined by a distinguished panel of judges.

Jerusalem Botanical Gardens Scholarship
Subjects: Botany and horticulture.
Purpose: To provide opportunities for botanists and horticulturists to work at the Jerusalem Botanical Gardens.
Eligibility: Preference is given to permanent residents of the United Kingdom who hold a degree in a relevant subject. Landscape architects with practical, hands on plant skills are also eligible.
Level of Study: Postgraduate, Professional development.
Type: Scholarship.
Value: Return air passage to Israel, subsidised accommodation in the vicinity of the Hebrew University campus and a subsistence allowance which covers the full placement. Participants receive no formal salary.
Length of Study: 6-12 months.
Frequency: Annual.
Study Establishment: The Jerusalem Botanical Gardens.
Country of Study: Israel.
No. of awards offered: Varies.
Application Procedure: Applicants must submit a curriculum vitae, an academic letter of reference, a statement of reasons for wishing to work in Jerusalem, two passport sized photographs and a hand written covering letter.
Closing Date: March 31st.
Funding: Private.
Contributor: Trusts and individual donations.

FRIENDS OF JOSE CARRERAS INTERNATIONAL LEUKEMIA FOUNDATION

1100 Fairview Avenue North, D5-100, Seattle, WA 98109-1024, United States of America
Tel: (1) 206 667 7108
Fax: (1) 206 667 6124
Email: friendsjc@fhcrc.org
www: http://www.carrerasfoundation.org
Contact: Administrator

Friends of Jose Carreras International Leukemia Foundation Fellowship
Subjects: Medical sciences or leukaemia.
Purpose: To support research in the field of leukaemia or related haematological disorders.

Eligibility: Candidates must hold an MD or PhD degree and have completed at least three years of postdoctoral training but must be less than 10 years past their first doctoral degree when the award begins.
Type: Fellowship.
Value: US$50,000.
Length of Study: One year, renewable for an additional two years.
Frequency: Annual.
Study Establishment: A suitable institution with the academic environment to provide adequate support for the proposal project.
Country of Study: Any country.
No. of awards offered: One.
Application Procedure: Applicants must complete an application form, available from the website. All applications must be typed, single spaced, in English and must follow the format specified in the application packet. Award announcements will be made by letter in January. Please do not contact the Foundation for results. Reapplication by unsuccessful candidates will be necessary for the following year.
Closing Date: October.

THE FRINK SCHOOL OF FIGURATIVE SCULPTURE

Old Court, Roundwell Street, Tunstall, Stoke-on-Trent, Staffordshire
ST6 5AN, England
Tel: (44) 1782 816430
Email: info@frinkschool.org
www: http://www.frinkschool.org
Contact: The Administrator

Sculpture School, teaching the traditional art of sculpture not taught in mainstream education today.

Frink School Bursary
Subjects: Teaching the traditional art of sculpture, working with clay, steel, stone, cement, polystyrene. Life drawing is also taught.
Purpose: Up to 1/3 of fees subject to your circumstances.
Eligibility: Dependent upon applicants financial circumstances.
Level of Study: Other, Fellow Frink.
Type: Bursary up to 1/3 of school fees.
Value: Up to UK£1,500 dependent on funds available.
Length of Study: One year.
Frequency: Dependent on funds available.
Study Establishment: 1995.
Country of Study: United Kingdom.
No. of awards offered: Dependent on funds available.
Application Procedure: Written applications or via email.
Closing Date: September.
Funding: Private.
Contributor: Fubber Trust.
No. of awards given last year: 4.
No. of applicants last year: 10.

FROMM MUSIC FOUNDATION

c/o Department of Music, Harvard University, Cambridge, MA 02138,
United States of America
Tel: (1) 617 495 2791
Fax: (1) 617 496 8081
Email: moncrieff@fas.harvard.edu
www: http://www.fas.harvard.edu
Contact: Ms Jean Moncrieff

Fromm Foundation Commission
Subjects: Music composition.
Purpose: To support compositions by young and lesser known composers. The award includes a stipend for premiere performance of commissioned work.
Eligibility: There are no eligibility restrictions.
Level of Study: Unrestricted.
Frequency: Annual.
Country of Study: Any country.

No. of awards offered: Up to 12.
Application Procedure: Applicants must obtain guidelines from the Fromm Music Foundation.
Closing Date: June 1st.
Funding: Private.
No. of awards given last year: 12.
No. of applicants last year: 150.

FULBRIGHT COMMISSION (ARGENTINA)

Viamonte 1653, 2 Piso, Buenos Aires, Capital Federal 1055,
Argentina
Tel: (54) 11 4814 3561
Fax: (54) 11 4814 1377
Email: gabarca@fulbright.com.ar
www: http://www.fulbright.edu.ar
Contact: Programme Officer, Educational Advisor

The Fulbright Programme is an educational exchange programme which sponsors awards for individuals approved by the J William Fulbright Board. The programme's major aim is to promote international co-operation and contribute to the development of friendly, sympathetic and peaceful relations between the United States and other countries in the world.

Fulbright Commission (Argentina) Awards for US Lecturers and Researchers
Subjects: All subjects except medical science.
Purpose: To enable United States lecturers to teach at an Argentine university for one semester, and to enable United States researchers to conduct research at an Argentine institution for three months.
Eligibility: Open to United States researchers and lecturers. Applicants must be proficient in spoken Spanish.
Level of Study: Professional development.
Value: Varies according to professional experience.
Length of Study: Three months.
Frequency: Annual.
Country of Study: Argentina.
Funding: Government.
Contributor: The United States of America and the Argentine government.

Fulbright Commission (Argentina) Master's Program
Subjects: All subjects except medical science.
Purpose: To support Argentines pursuing a Master's degree in the United States of America.
Eligibility: Open to Argentines only.
Level of Study: Postgraduate.
Length of Study: Two years.
Frequency: Annual.
Country of Study: United States of America.
Application Procedure: Applicants must contact the Fulbright Commission in Argentina between February 1st and April 30th.
Funding: Government, Private.
Contributor: The Binational Commission ie. between the United States of America and Argentina, and private sources.

Fulbright Commission (Argentina) US Students Research Grant
Subjects: All subjects except medical science.
Purpose: To enable American students to study in Argentina.
Eligibility: Open to United States of America citizens who hold a Bachelor's degree, are writing a Master's thesis or PhD dissertation and are proficient in Spanish.
Level of Study: Doctorate, Graduate, Postgraduate.
Type: Research grant.
Length of Study: Eight months.
Frequency: Annual.
Country of Study: Argentina.
No. of awards offered: 10-12.

Application Procedure: Applicants must complete an application form.
Funding: Government.
Contributor: The United States of America and Argentine government.

FULBRIGHT TEACHER AND ADMINISTRATOR EXCHANGE

600 Maryland Avenue, SW Room 320, Washington, DC 20024, United States of America
Tel: (1) 202 314 3527
Fax: (1) 202 479 6806
Email: fulbright@grad.usda.gov
www: http://www.fulbrightexchanges.org
Contact: Administrative Officer

Sponsored by the United States Department of State, the Fulbright Teacher and Administrator Exchange arranges direct one to one classroom exchanges to over 30 countries for teachers at the elementary, secondary, two year and four year college levels. Administrators may participate in six week seminars in eleven countries.

Fulbright Teacher and Administrator Exchange
Subjects: Education or cultural exchange.
Purpose: To promote cultural understanding between peoples of other countries and the people of the United States of America through educational exchange.
Eligibility: Open to administrators and teachers of all subjects and levels from elementary through to community college. Applicants must be United States citizens, be fluent in English, have a current full-time academic position, be in at least their third year of teaching and hold a Bachelor's degree.
Level of Study: Professional development.
Type: Grant.
Value: Varies by country.
Length of Study: Six weeks to one year.
Frequency: Annual.
Study Establishment: K-12 Schools, two year colleges and four year colleges.
Country of Study: Any country.
No. of awards offered: Varies.
Application Procedure: Applicants must submit a basic application which includes a two page essay, three letters of recommendation, administrative approval and a peer interview.
Closing Date: October 15th.
Funding: Government.
No. of awards given last year: 250.
No. of applicants last year: 800.

FUND FOR THEOLOGICAL EDUCATION, INC.

825 Houston Mill, RoadSuite 250, Atlanta, GA 30329, United States of America
Tel: (1) 404 727 1450
Fax: (1) 404 727 1490
Email: fte@thefund.org
www: http://www.thefund.org
Contact: Ms Sharon Watson Fluker, Director

The Fund for Theological Education (FTE) exists to promote excellence in the profession of ministry and scholarship by inspiring, recruiting and supporting gifted women and men from diverse backgrounds in their theological formation. The mission of FTE is to respond to the continuing need for outstanding persons for Christian leadership as pastors, educators and citizens.

Expanding Horizons - Dissertation Fellowship for African Americans
Subjects: Religion and theology.
Purpose: To support African American students in PhD and ThD programmes in the final writing stage of their dissertation.

Eligibility: Open to African American students in the writing stages of their dissertation. The dissertation proposal must have been approved prior to application.
Level of Study: Doctorate.
Type: Fellowship.
Value: Up to US$15,000.
Length of Study: One year, non renewable.
Frequency: Annual.
Study Establishment: Graduate or theological schools.
Country of Study: United States of America.
No. of awards offered: Up to 10 per year.
Application Procedure: Applicants must complete an application form, available from the programme office or the website.
Closing Date: February 1st.
Funding: Private.
Contributor: Lilly Endowment, Inc.
No. of awards given last year: Nine.
No. of applicants last year: Varies.

Expanding Horizons - Doctoral Fellowship for African Americans
Subjects: Religion and theology.
Eligibility: Open to African American students entering the first year of a PhD or ThD programme and studying at an ATS (Association of Theological Schools) accredited school or in another accredited graduate programme.
Level of Study: Doctorate.
Type: Fellowship.
Value: Up to US$15,000.
Length of Study: One year, with a possibility of renewal for a second year.
Frequency: Annual.
Study Establishment: Graduate or theological schools.
Country of Study: United States of America.
No. of awards offered: Up to 10.
Application Procedure: Applicants must complete an application form, available from the programme office or website.
Closing Date: March 1st.
Funding: Private.
Contributor: Lilly Endowment, Inc.
No. of awards given last year: Seven.
No. of applicants last year: Varies.

Ministry Fellowship
Subjects: Religion, theology and divinity.
Purpose: To enrich theological education in a Master of Divinity degree programme.
Eligibility: Open to applicants aged 35 or younger and entering a Master of Divinity degree programme in the Autumn semester. The award is to be used for the design and implementation of creative projects during the Summer.
Level of Study: Postgraduate.
Type: Fellowship.
Value: US$5,000 plus conference attendance.
Frequency: Annual.
Study Establishment: A school accredited by the Association of Theological Schools of North America.
Country of Study: United States of America or Canada.
No. of awards offered: 40.
Application Procedure: Applicants must complete and submit an application form together with supporting documentation. Forms are available from the website or by request.
Closing Date: April 1st.
Funding: Private.
No. of awards given last year: 39.
No. of applicants last year: 125.

North American Doctoral Fellowship
Subjects: Religion and theology.
Purpose: To support students from African American, Asian American, Hispanic American and Native American populations already in doctoral programmes leading towards completion of a PhD or ThD.

Eligibility: Open to students from targeted racial or ethnic groups at any point in their graduate programme, though preference is given to students further along in their programmes. Students must be currently enrolled in programmes of religion or theology.
Level of Study: Doctorate.
Type: Fellowship.
Value: US$5,000.
Length of Study: One year.
Frequency: Annual.
Country of Study: United States of America.
No. of awards offered: 10-12 per year.
Application Procedure: Applicants must complete an application form, available from the programme office or website.
Closing Date: March 1st.
Funding: Private.
No. of awards given last year: 10.
No. of applicants last year: Varies.

FUND FOR UFO RESEARCH, INC.

PO Box 277, Mount Rainier, MD 20712, United States of America
Tel: (1) 703 684 6032
Fax: (1) 703 684 6032
Email: swiman@pop.dn.net
www: http://www.fufor.com
Contact: Mr Donald L Berliner, Chairman

The Fund for UFO Research is a non-profit corporation established in 1979 to raise funds to support scientific research and public education related to the mystery of unidentified flying objects. The Fund takes no stand on any proposed explanation, but is convinced that unexplained, high performance craft have long been in the skies.

Fund for UFO Research Grants

Subjects: Topics include analysis of sighting reports, physical trace and photographic cases, government involvement in UFOs and abduction cases.
Purpose: To provide financial assistance for scientific research and public education projects relating to the phenomenon of unidentified flying objects.
Eligibility: Open to anyone wishing to undertake scientific research or public education projects related to UFOs. There are no restrictions, except that reports must be written in English.
Level of Study: Unrestricted.
Type: Research grant.
Value: Awards can cover not only personal expenses, but also supplies, equipment, publication costs and fees for services in the case of professional consultants.
Length of Study: Varies.
Frequency: Dependent on funds available.
Country of Study: Any country.
No. of awards offered: Unlimited.
Application Procedure: Applicants must complete an application form, available upon request.
Closing Date: Applications are accepted at any time.
Funding: Private.
Contributor: Individuals.
No. of awards given last year: Four.
No. of applicants last year: 10.

FUNGAL RESEARCH TRUST

27 Regina Terrace, London, W13 9HY, England
Tel: (44) 020 8567 2939
Email: jutta@beep.net
www: http://www.fungalresearchtrust.org
Contact: Secretary

The Fungal Research Trust is a small charity that funds small research and travel grants and the aspergillus website (http://www.aspergillus.man.ac.uk). The website is the most comprehensive source of data on the aspergillus fungus and the diseases it causes.

Fungal Research Trust Travel Grants

Subjects: Fungal diseases and fungi.
Purpose: To enable researchers to attend the national and international fungal meetings.
Eligibility: There are no restrictions.
Level of Study: Doctorate, Postdoctorate, Postgraduate, Professional development, Research.
Type: Travel grant.
Value: UK£750.
Length of Study: Up to one week.
Frequency: Dependent on funds available.
No. of awards offered: Up to three.
Application Procedure: Applicants must submit a letter of application.
Closing Date: Applications are considered at any time, but three months notice before travel is required.
Funding: Commercial, Private.
Contributor: Numerous.
No. of awards given last year: Two.
No. of applicants last year: Two.
Additional Information: Advertisements for other awards are placed in the Lancet.

GENERAL BOARD OF HIGHER EDUCATION AND MINISTRY

PO Box 340007, Nashville, TN 37203-0007, United States of America
Tel: (1) 615 340 7388
Fax: (1) 615 340 7377
Email: bkohler@gbhem.org
Contact: Reverend Robert F Kohler

The General Board of Higher Education and Ministry of the United Methodist Church prepares and assists those whose ministry in Christ is exercised through ordination, the diaconate, licensing or certification. It also provides general oversight and care for united Methodist institutions of higher education and campus ministries as well as financial resources for students to attend Institutions of Higher Education through church offerings and investments.

Dempster Fellowship

Subjects: Theology
Purpose: To increase the effectiveness of teaching in United Methodist schools of theology by assisting worthy PhD candidates who are committed to serving the church through theological education.
Eligibility: Open to members of The United Methodist Church who plan to teach in seminaries, or to teach religion and related subjects in universities or colleges. The applicant must have received the Master of Divinity degree or its equivalent from one of the United Methodist Seminaries, or be in a PhD programme or its equivalent at one of these schools at the time of application. Verification of study towards a PhD or an equivalent degree is required prior to the distribution of the stipend. A person already holding a PhD degree is not excluded from candidacy.
Level of Study: Doctorate.
Type: Fellowship.
Value: Up to US$10,000.
Length of Study: One year, with a possibility of renewal at the discretion of the Committee on Awards.
Frequency: Annual.
Country of Study: Any country.
No. of awards offered: Five.
Application Procedure: Applicants must submit a completed application form, transcripts of all previous academic work, secure letters of reference, term or other paper of essay length, results of the Graduate Record Examination scores, summary statement of academic plans and a curriculum vitae. Further information is available on request.
Closing Date: February 1st.
Funding: Private.
Contributor: The United Methodist Church.
No. of awards given last year: Five.
No. of applicants last year: 20.

GENERAL SOCIAL CARE COUNCIL

Goldings House, 2 Hay's Lane
London, SE1 2HB, England
Tel: (44) 20 7397 5100
Fax: (44) 20 7397 5101
Email: info@bursaries.gscc.org.uk
Contact: Administrative Officer

The General Social Care Council is the first ever regulatory body for the social care profession in England. It was set up to establish codes of conduct and practice for social care workers, a register of practising professionals and to regulate and support social work, education and training. It takes forward some of the work of the Central Council for Education and Training in Social Work, which closed on September 28th 2001. Similar councils exist for Northern Ireland, Scotland and Wales.

General Social Care Council Postgraduate Bursary

Subjects: Social work.
Purpose: To support those seeking the qualifications required for social work.
Eligibility: Open to graduates who are aged 22 on completion of the course, who have ordinarily been resident in the United Kingdom for three years and comply with the LEA regulations for Mandatory Awards.
Level of Study: Postgraduate.
Type: Bursary.
Length of Study: Two years.
Frequency: Annual.
Country of Study: United Kingdom.
No. of awards offered: Approx. 1,000.
Closing Date: June 7th. Late applications must be received by October 31st.
Funding: Government.
Contributor: The Department of Health.
No. of awards given last year: 1,000.

GEOLOGICAL SOCIETY OF AMERICA (GSA)

3300 Penrose Place, PO Box 9140, Boulder, CO 80301-9140, United States of America
Tel: (1) 303 357 1028
Fax: (1) 303 357 1070
Email: dlorenz@geosociety.org
www: http://www.geosociety.org
Contact: Ms Diane C Lorenz, Program Officer Grants, Awards and Medals

Established in 1888, the Geological Society of America (GSA) is a non-profit organisation dedicated to the advancement of the science of geology. GSA membership is for the generalist and the specialist in the field of geology and offers something for everyone.

Gladys W Cole Memorial Research Award

Subjects: Investigation of the geomorphology of semi-arid and arid terrain in the United States of America and Mexico.
Purpose: To provide financial support for research.
Eligibility: Open to GSA members or Fellows aged 30-65 who have published one or more significant papers on geomorphology. Funds cannot be used to pay for work already accomplished, but previous recipients may reapply if additional support is needed to complete their work. All qualified applicants are urged to apply.
Level of Study: Postdoctorate.
Type: Research grant.
Value: US$8,000.
Frequency: Annual.
Country of Study: Other.
No. of awards offered: One.
Application Procedure: Applicants must complete an application form available from the website.
Closing Date: February 1st.
Funding: Private.

Contributor: Dr W Storrs Cole.
No. of awards given last year: One.

GSA Research Grants

Subjects: Earth science.
Purpose: To provide partial support for Master's and doctoral thesis research.
Eligibility: Open to students attending colleges and universities within the United States of America, Canada, Mexico and Central America. Applicants must be members of the GSA in order to apply.
Level of Study: Graduate.
Type: Research grant.
Value: There are no set limits.
Length of Study: One year, renewable.
Frequency: Annual.
Country of Study: Other.
No. of awards offered: Varies.
Application Procedure: Applicants must complete current application forms.
Closing Date: February 1st.
Funding: Government, Private.
Contributor: GSA's Penrose and Pardee endowments, the National Science Foundation, industry, individual GSA members through the GEOSTAR and Research Grants funds, and numerous dedicated research funds that have been endowed at the GSA Foundation by members.
No. of awards given last year: 251.
No. of applicants last year: 571.
Additional Information: Grants are awarded on the basis of the scientific merits of the problem, the capability of the investigator and the feasibility of the budget, and as an aid to a research project, not to sustain the entire cost.

W Storrs Cole Memorial Research Award

Subjects: Invertebrate micropalaeontology.
Purpose: To support research into invertebrate micropalaeontology.
Eligibility: Open to GSA members or Fellows aged 30-65 who have published one or more significant papers on micropalaeontology. Funds cannot be used for work already accomplished but recipients of previous awards may reapply if additional support is needed to complete their work. All qualified applicants are urged to apply.
Level of Study: Postdoctorate.
Type: Research grant.
Value: US$7,300.
Frequency: Annual.
Application Procedure: Applicants must write for further details and an application form or visit the website.
Closing Date: Applications must be postmarked before February 1st.
Funding: Private.
Contributor: Dr W Storrs Cole.
No. of awards given last year: One.

GEORGE WALFORD INTERNATIONAL ESSAY PRIZE (GWIEP)

12 Bloomfield Road, London, N6 4ET, England
Email: richenda@gwiep.net
www: http://www.gwiep.net
Contact: Ms Richenda Walford, Trustee

The George Walford International Essay Prize (GWIEP) is a registered charity which awards a cash prize each year to the winner of an essay on the subject of systematic ideology.

George Walford International Essay Prize (GWIEP)

Subjects: Systematic ideology seeks to understand the origin and development of ideologies, how ideologies and ideological groups work together, and the possibilities of guiding the development of ideologies on a global scale.
Purpose: To award prize to the best essay on systematic ideology.
Eligibility: Everyone is eligible, with the exception of the trustees and judges themselves. There are no bars regarding age, race, nationality or gender.

Level of Study: Unrestricted.
Type: Prize.
Value: UK£3,000.
Length of Study: Varies.
Frequency: Annual.
Country of Study: Any country.
No. of awards offered: One.
Application Procedure: Applicants must contact GWIEP for details. Information can be requested by mail though communication via email and the website is greatly preferred.
Closing Date: May 31st.
Funding: Private.
Contributor: The family of the late George Walford.
No. of awards given last year: One.
Additional Information: For more information about the prize and systematic ideology please visit the website.

GEORGIA LIBRARY ASSOCIATION (GLA)

c/o GLA Administrative Services, 1438 W Peachtree Street North West, Suite 200, Atlanta, GA 30309-2955, United States of America
Tel: (1) 770 961 3520
Fax: (1) 404 892 7879
Email: kendalls@cobbcat.org
www: http://wwwlib.gsu.edu/gla
Contact: Scholarship Committee Chair

The Georgia Library Association's (GLA) mission is to provide an understanding of the place that libraries should take in advancing the educational, cultural and economic life of the state, to promote the expansion and improvement of library service and to stimulate activities toward these ends.

Hubbard Scholarship

Subjects: Library science.
Purpose: To recruit excellent librarians for Georgia and provide financial assistance toward completing a degree in library science.
Eligibility: Open to United States citizens accepted for admission to a Master's programme at an American Library Association (ALA) accredited library school, who intend to complete the course of study within two years.
Level of Study: Postgraduate.
Type: Scholarship.
Value: US$3,000, paid in equal instalments at the beginning of each term, semester or quarter.
Length of Study: Two years.
Frequency: Annual.
Study Establishment: An ALA accredited school.
Country of Study: United States of America.
No. of awards offered: One.
Application Procedure: Applicants must submit an official form of application, proof of acceptance in an accredited library school and official transcripts of all academic work sent directly from each institution of higher education. Three letters of reference must also be sent directly from the referee.
Closing Date: May 1st.
Additional Information: The Scholar is required to work in a library or library related capacity in Georgia for one year following completion of the programme, or agree to pay back a pro-rated amount of the scholarship plus interest within a two year period.

GERMAN ACADEMIC EXCHANGE SERVICE (DAAD)

871 United Nations Plaza, New York, NY 10017, United States of America
Tel: (1) 212 758 3223
Fax: (1) 212 755 5780
Email: fu@daad.org
www: http://www.daad.org
Contact: Grants Management Officer

The German Academic Exchange Service is the New York office of the Deutscher Akademischer Austauschdienst (DAAD), a private, publicly funded self governing organisation of the Institutes of Higher Education in Germany. The DAAD promotes international academic relations especially through the exchange of students and faculty. The New York office assists residents of the United States of America or Canada who are enrolled or employed full time at an Institute of Higher Education and would like to study or conduct research in Germany.

DAAD Alexander von Humboldt Foundation

Subjects: Topics as selected by young U.S. citizens who show outstanding.
Purpose: To promote international cooperation in research.
Eligibility: Applicants must hold a bachelor's degree and be under 35 years of age. Prior knowledge of German is not a requirement.
Level of Study: Postgraduate.
Type: Scholarship.
Value: €2,000 to €3,000 per month plus expenses including German language course.
Frequency: Annual.
Study Establishment: Study centre or other suitable institute.
Country of Study: Germany.
No. of awards offered: 10.
Application Procedure: Download application forms and guidelines from the website.
Closing Date: October 31st.
Funding: Private.

DAAD German Studies Research Grant

Subjects: The cultural, political, historical, economic and social aspects of modern and contemporary German affairs.
Purpose: To promote study in the field from an interdisciplinary and multidisciplinary perspective.
Eligibility: Open to Master's and PhD candidates working on a Certificate in German Studies and PhD candidates doing preliminary dissertation research. Nominees must have completed two years of college level German and a minimum of three German studies courses by the deadline. Support cannot be provided for stays in Germany in the context of study abroad programmes.
Type: Grant.
Value: To offset possible additional research costs or summer earnings requirements.
Country of Study: North America or Germany
Application Procedure: Department and/or programme chairs should nominate candidates to the DAAD. Applicants must visit the website for further information.
Closing Date: November 1st or May 1st.

DAAD Graduate Scholarship for Research in Germany

Subjects: Any subject other than dentistry, medicine, pharmacy and veterinary medicine.
Purpose: To support highly qualified Graduate students, Ph.D candidates and post-doctoral researchers to research in Germany.
Eligibility: Applicants must have a well-defined project that makes a stay in Germany essential.
Level of Study: Doctorate, Postdoctorate, Postgraduate.
Type: Scholarship.
Value: €795 to €975 per month.
Length of Study: 1-10 months.
Study Establishment: A university or research institute in Germany.
Country of Study: Germany.
Application Procedure: Download application forms and guidelines from website.
Closing Date: Performing musicians/fine artists November 1st. All other subjects November 15th.
Funding: Private.

DAAD International Lawyers: Study and Training Program

Subjects: German law.
Purpose: To give young lawyers the opportunity to gain a unique insight into the structure and function of German law. Through this programme the DAAD aims to support and encourage closer inter-

national links in the area of law and to improve mutual knowledge of the legal systems in other countries.

Eligibility: Open to applicants from the United Kingdom, France, Belgium, the Netherlands, Luxembourg, Poland, the Commonwealth of Independent States, Japan, South Korea, the United States and Canada. The DAAD encourages applications from North American lawyers who hold JD or LLB degrees and who have or will have passed the bar examination by the beginning of the scholarship period, proof of which is required prior to departure to Germany. The importance of gaining a knowledge of German law should be evident from the applicant's stated professional or research goals. Applicants must have a very good command of German, which would enable them to take an active part in all lectures and discussions. In general, applicants should be younger than 30 years of age. Students currently in their last year of law school who will obtain a JD or LLB and will have passed the bar examination by the beginning of the scholarship period may apply. Applicants should preferably have some relevant professional experience.

Level of Study: Postgraduate.

Type: Scholarship.

Value: A monthly stipend to cover board and a single room in university housing.

Length of Study: Eight months

Country of Study: Germany.

Application Procedure: Applicants must complete an application form, available from the website.

DAAD Leibniz Scholarships for Doctoral Candidates and post-Docs

Subjects: Humanities and education, economic and social sciences, life sciences, physical sciences and evironmental research.

Purpose: To provide young academics and scientist with an opportunity to complete a research project.

Eligibility: Applicants must be excellently-qualified university graduates who hold a Master's degree or PhD.

Level of Study: Doctorate, Postdoctorate, Postgraduate.

Type: Scholarship.

Value: €800 to €1,800 plus expenses, rent subsidy and family allowance.

Frequency: Annual.

Study Establishment: One of the Leibniz Institutes.

Country of Study: Germany.

Application Procedure: Download application forms and guidelines from website.

Closing Date: July 31st.

Funding: Private.

DAAD Study Visit Research Grants for Faculty

Subjects: All subjects.

Purpose: To allow scholars to pursue research at universities and other institutions in Germany.

Eligibility: Open to individuals with at least two years of teaching or research experience after a PhD or equivalent and a research record in the proposed field.

Level of Study: Postdoctorate, Professional development.

Type: Grant.

Value: A monthly maintenance allowance.

Length of Study: One-three months.

Frequency: Annual.

Country of Study: Germany.

No. of awards offered: Varies.

Application Procedure: Applicants must obtain forms from the DAAD New York office or download them from the website.

Closing Date: August 1st for visits during the first half of the year and February 1st for visits during the second half of the year.

Additional Information: Grants are awarded for specific research projects and cannot be used for travel only, attendance at conferences or conventions, editorial meetings, lecture tours or extended guest professorships. Further information is available from the website.

DAAD Summer Language Courses at Goethe-Institutes

Subjects: All subject, but the fields of English and German or any other modern languages or literatures are not eligible.

Purpose: To allow students to attend intensive eight week language courses.

Eligibility: Open to students pursuing full-time study at any accredited graduate or professional school in the United States or Canada, with the exception of those in the fields of English, German or any other modern languages or literatures. As a rule, applicants must be citizens of the United States of America or Canada. Foreign nationals may be eligible if they have been full-time graduate students at an American or Canadian university for at least one academic year at the time of application. Preference will be given to students who are under 33 years of age. Applicants must have completed three semesters of college level German or have an equivalent level of language proficiency. Applicants should not have previously studied in a German speaking country for more than two months or been granted a German language course scholarship by the DAAD or any other organisation within the last three years. Recipients of the scholarships are selected on the basis of an outstanding academic record and potential, as well as a demonstrated need for acquiring a better proficiency in the German language for their future studies and research.

Level of Study: Postgraduate.

Type: Scholarship.

Value: Tuition and fees, room and partial board.

Length of Study: Eight weeks.

Frequency: Annual.

Study Establishment: Goethe Institutes.

Country of Study: Germany.

Application Procedure: Applicants must obtain forms from the DAAD New York office or download them from the website.

Closing Date: January 31st.

Additional Information: Further information is available from the website.

DAAD-AICGS Grant

Subjects: Post war Germany.

Eligibility: Open to PhD candidates, recent PhDs and junior faculty members.

Level of Study: Doctorate, Postdoctorate.

Type: Fellowship.

Value: Funds for summer residency.

Frequency: Annual.

Study Establishment: The American Institute for Contemporary German Studies (AICGS).

Country of Study: United States of America.

No. of awards offered: One.

Application Procedure: Applicants must write for details.

Closing Date: April 15th.

Additional Information: Further information is available from the website.

For further information contact:

AICGS, 1400 16th Street North West, Suite 420, Washington, DC 20036-2217, United States of America

Tel: (1) 202 332 9312

Fax: (1) 202 265 9531

Email: info@aicgs.org

www: http://www.aicgs.org

Hochschulsommerkurse at German Universities

Subjects: German studies and language courses.

Purpose: To provide a broad range of language courses with an integrated thematic focus on literary, cultural, political and economic aspects of modern and contemporary Germany.

Eligibility: Open to graduate students in all disciplines, enrolled full-time and between 18 and 32 years of age. Two years of college level German or equivalent at the time of application are a prerequisite.

Level of Study: Graduate, Postgraduate.

Type: Scholarship.

Value: Tuition, room and board in whole or in part and a small international travel subsidy.

Length of Study: Three-four weeks.

Frequency: Annual.

Study Establishment: Universities.

Country of Study: Germany.
Application Procedure: Applicants must obtain a course catalogue, available from the DAAD New York office or from the website. Applicants must specify the national category.
Closing Date: January 31st.

Leo Baeck Institute-DAAD Grants

Subjects: The social, communal and intellectual history of German speaking Jewry.
Purpose: To assist students in their research.
Eligibility: Open to American doctoral students and recent PhDs.
Level of Study: Doctorate, Postdoctorate.
Type: Fellowship.
Value: Varies.
Frequency: Annual.
Study Establishment: The Leo Baeck Institute.
Country of Study: United States of America or Germany.
No. of awards offered: Six.
Application Procedure: Applicants must write for details.
Closing Date: November 1st.
Additional Information: Further information is available from the website.

For further information contact:

The Leo Baeck Institute, 129 East 73rd Street, New York, NY 10021, United States of America
Tel: (1) 212 744 6400
Fax: (1) 212 988 1305
Email: lbi1@lbi.com

GERMAN HISTORICAL INSTITUTE

1607 New Hampshire Avenue North West
Washington, DC 20009
United States of America
Tel: (1) 202 387 3355
Fax: (1) 202 483 3430
Email: info@ghi-dc.org
www: http://www.ghi-dc.org
Contact: Mr Christof Mauch, Director

The German Historical Institute is an independent research institute dedicated to the promotion of historical research in the Federal Republic of Germany and the United States. The Institute supports and advises German and American historians and political scientists and encourages co-operation between them.

Fritz Stern Dissertation Prize

Subjects: German history, history of German in America, German-American relations.
Purpose: Each year the friends of the GHI awards the Fritz Stern Dissertation Prize for the two best doctoral dissertations submitted in German history, German-American relations, or the history of Germans in North America. The winners are invited to the GHI to present their research at the annual symposium of the Friends each November. Candidates are nominated by their dissertation at a North American university during the previous academic year. The prizewinners recieve an award of US$2,000 and reimbursement for travel to Washington, D.C.
Eligibility: Open to American Ph.D's.
Level of Study: Doctorate.
Type: Prize.
Value: 2 x US$2,000.
Frequency: Annual.
Country of Study: United States of America.
No. of awards offered: 2.
Application Procedure: Applicants must refer to website for further information.
Closing Date: May 1.
Funding: Private.
Contributor: Friends of the German Historical Institute.
No. of awards given last year: 2.

German Historical Institute Collaborative Research Programme for Postdoctoral Scholars

Subjects: German and United States post World War II history, transatlantic studies and comparative studies in social, cultural and political history.
Purpose: To support a research programme for postdoctoral Scholars on the topic of continuity, change and globalisation in post war Germany and the United States.
Eligibility: Open to German and United States postdoctoral students. Applications from women and minorities are especially encouraged.
Level of Study: Postdoctorate.
Type: Fellowship.
Value: US$20,000-40,000 dependent on length of study.
Length of Study: 6-12 months.
Frequency: Dependent on funds available.
Country of Study: United States of America.
Application Procedure: Applicants must refer to the website for details.
Closing Date: Refer to Website.
Funding: Government.
Contributor: The National Endowment for Humanities.
No. of awards given last year: 1.

German Historical Institute Courses in German Handwriting and Archives

Subjects: German handwriting, German archives, German history and transatlantic studies.
Purpose: To introduce students to German handwriting of previous centuries by exposing them to a variety of German archives, familiarising them with major research topics in German culture, history, and encouraging the exchange of ideas among the next generation of United States Scholars.
Eligibility: Open to United States doctoral students. Applications from women and minorities are especially encouraged.
Level of Study: Doctorate.
Type: Scholarship.
Value: US$2,500.
Length of Study: Two weeks.
Frequency: Annual.
Country of Study: Germany.
Application Procedure: Applicants must refer to the website for details.
Closing Date: December 31st.
Funding: Government.
No. of awards given last year: 13.

German Historical Institute Doctoral and Postdoctoral Fellowships

Subjects: Humanities and social sciences, comparative studies in social, cultural and political history, and studies of German American relations and transatlantic studies.
Purpose: To give support to German and United States doctoral and postdoctoral students working on topics related to the Institute's general scope of interest.
Eligibility: Open to German and United States doctoral students. Applications from women and minorities are especially encouraged.
Level of Study: Doctorate, Postdoctorate.
Type: Fellowship.
Value: US$1,350 for doctoral students, US$2,650 for postdoctoral students.
Length of Study: Up to six months.
Frequency: Annual.
Country of Study: United States of America.
No. of awards offered: Open.
Application Procedure: Applicants must refer to the website for details.
Closing Date: May 31st.
Funding: Government.
No. of awards given last year: 14.
No. of applicants last year: 50.
Additional Information: All candidates are expected to evaluate source material in the United States of America that is important for

their research on German history. At the end of the scholarship they are required to report on their findings or give a presentation at the GHI.

German Historical Institute Transatlantic Doctoral Seminar in German History

Subjects: German history and transatlantic studies.
Purpose: To bring together young Scholars from Germany and the United States who are nearing completion of their doctoral degrees. It provides an opportunity to debate doctoral projects in a transatlantic setting.
Eligibility: Open to German and United States doctoral students. Applications from women and minorities are especially encouraged.
Level of Study: Doctorate.
Type: Scholarship.
Value: US$2,000.
Length of Study: Four days.
Frequency: Annual.
Country of Study: Other.
Application Procedure: Applicants must refer to the website for details.
Closing Date: December 1st
Funding: Government.
No. of awards given last year: 16.

Kade-Heideking Fellowship

Subjects: Same as Thyssen-Heideking Fellowship.
Purpose: Funded by the Annete Kade Charitable Trust, the Kade-Heideking Fellowship is awarded annually to a German doctoral student working in one of the three area to which the late Jürgen Heideking made significant contributions: American history and German-American relations from the early modern period to the present; international history of the nineteenth twentieth centuries, including the history of international relations and the comparative history of conical systems and societies; and twentieth-century German history, with emphasis on America's influence on German society between 1918 and 1949. This is a residential fellowship of twelve months' duration, and the recipient is expected to divide his or her time between the GHI and the University of Wisconsin in Madison.
Eligibility: Open only to German doctoral students.
Level of Study: Doctorate.
Type: Fellowship.
Value: US$30,000.
Length of Study: 12 months.
Frequency: Annual.
Country of Study: United States of America.
No. of awards offered: 1.
Application Procedure: Applicants must refer to website for details.
Closing Date: November 15.
Funding: Private.
Contributor: Annete Kade Charitable Trust Fund.
No. of awards given last year: 1.

Medieval History Seminar

Subjects: Medieval History.
Purpose: The Medieval History Seminar is devoted to the latest research in the field of European medieval studies. Like the Transatlantic Doctoral Seminar, this program invites sixteen doctoral students from Europe and North America to discuss their dissertation projects with peers and senior scholars from both sides of the Atlantic. This seminar is held every other fall, alternating between venues in Europe and the United States. The annual deadline for applications is May 1.
Eligibility: Open to American and European citizens.
Level of Study: Doctorate.
Type: Grant.
Value: US$2,000.
Length of Study: Four days.
Frequency: Every two years.
Country of Study: USA and Europe.
No. of awards offered: 16.

Application Procedure: Applicants must refer to the website for details.
Funding: Government.
No. of awards given last year: 16.

Thyssen Heideking Fellowship

Subjects: American history, German history in the 20th century, comparative international history, German-American relations.
Purpose: The German historical Institute invites applications for a one-year postdoctoral fellowship in memory of the late Jürgen Heideking. The fellowship, supported by the Fritz Thyssen Foundation, is intended for American scholars working in one of the three years to which Professor Heideking made important contributions: American history and German-American relations from the early modern period to the present; international history of the nineteenth and twentieth centuries, including the history of international relations and the comparative history of colonial systems and societies; and twentieth-century German history, with emphasis on America's influence on German society between 1918 and 1949. The Hiedeking Fellow will recieve a stipend of €21,250 (plus a family allowance if applicable) for a fellowship period of six to twelve months in residence at the University of Cologne. The fellow will be expected to give one public lecture on his/her research.
Eligibility: Open only to American scholars.
Level of Study: Postdoctorate.
Type: Fellowship.
Value: €21,250.
Length of Study: 6 months to 1 year.
Frequency: Annual.
Country of Study: Germany.
No. of awards offered: 1.
Application Procedure: Applicants must refer to the website for details.
Closing Date: November 15.
Funding: Private.
Contributor: Fritz Thyssen Foundation.
No. of awards given last year: 1.

Young Scholars Forum

Subjects: Humanities and social sciences, comparative studies in social cultural and political history, studies of German-American relation, German history, European history.
Purpose: This annual forum gathers together American and European Ph.D. candidates and recent Ph.D. recipients who work in the fields of German, German-American, or European history. For one weekend in the spring young scholars have the opportunity to present their work to peers and distinguished academics from both sides of the Atlantic. The forum is conducted in English, and its topic varies yearly, spanning the Middle Ages to the present. The annual deadline for application is November 1.
Eligibility: Open to Americans, and Europeans, Germans in particular.
Level of Study: Doctorate, Postdoctorate.
Type: Grant.
Value: US$2,000.
Length of Study: Three days.
Frequency: Annual.
Country of Study: United States of America.
Application Procedure: Applicants must refer to website for details.
Closing Date: January 10.
Funding: Government.
No. of awards given last year: 15.

GERMAN MARSHALL FUND OF THE UNITED STATES (GMF)

11 Dupont Circle North West, Suite 750, Washington, DC 20036, United States of America
Tel: (1) 202 745 3950
Fax: (1) 202 265 1662
Email: info@gmfus.org
www: http://www.gmfus.org
Contact: Administrative Assistant

The German Marshall Fund of the United States (GMF) is an American institution that stimulates the exchange of ideas and promotes co-operation between the United States and Europe in the spirit of the post war Marshall Plan. GMF was created in 1972 by a gift from Germany as a permanent memorial to Marshall Plan Aid.

GMF Research Fellowships Program

Subjects: Comparative analysis of a specific issue in more than one country or the exploration of an issue in a single country in ways that can be expected to have relevance to other countries. The geographical scope of the programme includes Western, Central and Eastern Europe, including Russia and Turkey as they relate to Europe, but not the Central Asian countries that were formerly part of the Soviet Union.
Purpose: To support research projects that seek to improve the understanding of significant contemporary economic, political and social developments involving the United States of America and Europe.
Eligibility: Open to citizens of the United States and permanent residents only. Special consideration will be given to applicants seeking support for dissertation fieldwork in one or more European countries and to projects involving parallel or collaborative research by both established and younger Scholars, including projects designed on a transatlantic basis.
Level of Study: Doctorate, Postdoctorate, Postgraduate.
Type: Fellowship.
Value: For dissertation fieldwork in Europe the grants are worth US$20,000. The support for advanced research grants will not exceed US$40,000.
Length of Study: For dissertation fieldwork in Europe up to one year, and for advanced research support not less than one semester and not greater than one year.
Frequency: Annual.
Study Establishment: There is no restriction on the place of tenure.
Country of Study: Other.
No. of awards offered: Approx. 20.
Application Procedure: Applicants must visit the website for information and downloadable application forms.
Closing Date: November 15th for dissertation or advanced research.
No. of awards given last year: 22.
No. of applicants last year: 120.
Additional Information: All award recipients are responsible for arranging their own housing, insurance, benefits and travel, including a visa if applicable. Submissions will be reviewed by a committee of established Scholars from various disciplines. An independent selection committee of Scholars will make recommendations to the Fund.

GERMANISTIC SOCIETY OF AMERICA

Institute of International Education, 809 United Nations Plaza, New York, NY 10017, United States of America
Tel: (1) 212 984 5330
www: http://www.iie.org
Contact: W Jackson, Manager

Germanistic Society of America Fellowships

Subjects: German language, literature, philosophy, history, art history, political science, economics and banking, international law and public affairs.
Purpose: To support research or study in Germany.
Eligibility: Open to United States citizens who have a good academic record and the capacity for independent study. Preference is given to candidates with a Masters degree.
Level of Study: Postgraduate.
Type: Fellowship.
Value: US$12,000.
Length of Study: One academic year of nine months.
Frequency: Annual.
Country of Study: Germany.
No. of awards offered: Four.

Application Procedure: Applicants must apply for information, available on request.
Closing Date: October 25th.
Funding: Private.
No. of awards given last year: Four.
No. of applicants last year: 30.
Additional Information: Candidates selected will be considered for Fulbright Travel Grants.

THE GETTY GRANT PROGRAM, J PAUL GETTY TRUST

1200 Getty Center Drive, Suite 800, Los Angeles, CA 90049-1685, United States of America
Tel: (1) 310 440 7320
Fax: (1) 310 440 7703
Email: researchgrants@getty.edu
www: http://www.getty.edu/grants
Contact: Senior Programme Officer

The Getty Grant Program is part of the J Paul Getty Trust, a private operating foundation dedicated to the visual arts and the humanities. The Grant Program supports a wide range of projects that promote research in the history of art related fields, advancement of the understanding of art and the conservation of cultural heritage.

Collaborative Research Grants

Subjects: History of art or related fields.
Purpose: To provide opportunities for teams of Scholars to collaborate on interpretative research projects that offer new explanations of art and its history.
Eligibility: Collaborative Research Grant teams must consist of two or more art historians, or of an art historian and one or more Scholars from other disciplines. Funding is also available for the research and planning of scholarly exhibitions. Teams for these projects must include Scholars from both museums and universities.
Level of Study: Postdoctorate.
Type: Research grant.
Value: Varies according to the needs of the project.
Length of Study: One-two years.
Frequency: Annual.
Country of Study: Any country.
No. of awards offered: Varies.
Application Procedure: Applicants must complete an application form. Additional information, detailed guidelines and application forms are available from the website or by contacting the Getty Grant Program Office.
Closing Date: November 1st.
Funding: Private.
Additional Information: Further information is available on request.

Curatorial Research Fellowships

Subjects: History of art or related fields.
Purpose: To support the professional scholarly development of curators by providing them with time off from regular museum duties to undertake short-term research or study projects.
Eligibility: Open to full-time curators who have a minimum of three years of professional experience and are employed at museums with art collections.
Level of Study: Professional development.
Type: Fellowship.
Value: Please contact the organisation.
Length of Study: One-three months.
Frequency: Annual.
Country of Study: Any country.
No. of awards offered: Varies.
Application Procedure: Applicants must complete an application form. Additional information, detailed guidelines and application forms are available from the website or by contacting the Getty Grant Program Office.
Closing Date: November 1st.
Funding: Private.
Additional Information: Further information is available on request.

Postdoctoral Fellowships
Subjects: History of art or related fields.
Purpose: To provide support for outstanding Scholars in the early stages of their careers to pursue interpretative research projects that make a substantial and original contribution to the understanding of art and its history.
Eligibility: Open to Scholars of all nationalities who have earned a doctoral degree within the past six years.
Level of Study: Postdoctorate.
Type: Fellowship.
Value: Please contact the organisation.
Length of Study: One year.
Frequency: Annual.
Country of Study: Any country.
Application Procedure: Applicants must complete an application form. Additional information, detailed guidelines and application forms are available from the website or by contacting the Getty Grant Program Office.
Closing Date: November 1st.
Funding: Private.
Additional Information: Further information is available on request.

Residential Grants at the Getty Center
Subjects: Arts and humanities.
Purpose: To provide support for established scholars to undertake research related to a specific theme while in residence at the Getty Center in Los Angeles.
Eligibility: Open to established Scholars who are working on projects which address the given scholarly theme.
Level of Study: Postdoctorate, Research.
Type: Grant.
Value: Please contact the organisation.
Frequency: Annual.
Country of Study: Any country.
No. of awards offered: Varies.
Application Procedure: Applicants must complete an application form. Additional information, detailed guidelines and application forms are available from the website or by contacting the Getty Grant Program office.
Closing Date: November 1st.
Funding: Private.

GÉZA ANDA FOUNDATION

Bleicherweg 18, Zurich, CH-8002, Switzerland
Tel: (41) 1 205 1423
Fax: (41) 1 205 1429
Email: info@gezaanda.org
www: http://www.gezaanda.org
Contact: Ms Ruth Bossart

The Géza Anda Foundation was established in 1977 in memory of the pianist, Géza Anda. It holds the Géza Anda Concours, an international piano competition every three years awarding three prize winners, special prizes and provides the opportunity for the laureates to appear as soloists in concerts and recitals.

International Géza Anda Piano Competition
Subjects: Piano playing.
Purpose: To sponsor young pianists in the musical spirit of Géza Anda.
Eligibility: Open to pianists born after June 8th, 1974.
Level of Study: Unrestricted.
Type: Prize.
Value: Cash prizes of swiss franc 60,000 and other benefits such as free concert management services for three years.
Frequency: Every three years.
Country of Study: Switzerland.
No. of awards offered: Three.
Application Procedure: Applicants must complete four rounds in the competition: an audition, a recital, Mozart and a final concert with orchestra.
Closing Date: March 1st.

Funding: Private.
No. of awards given last year: Three official awards and four special awards.
Additional Information: Dates of 10th Géza Anda Piano Competition: 8th-20th June 2006.

GILBERT MURRAY TRUST

5 Warnborough Road, Oxford, OX2 6HZ, England
Tel: (44) 1865 556633
Contact: Mrs Mary Bull, Secretary, International Studies Committee

Gilbert Murray Trust Junior Awards
Subjects: International affairs or international law.
Purpose: To study the purposes and work of the United Nations.
Eligibility: Open to persons of any nationality who are, or who have been, students at a university or similar institution in the United Kingdom. Candidates should currently be taking or should have taken part in a course of international affairs or international law and must not be over 25 years of age, although consideration will be given to those over that age in special cases
Level of Study: Postgraduate.
Type: Award.
Value: UK£300.
Frequency: Annual.
Country of Study: Any country.
No. of awards offered: 10.
Application Procedure: Applicants must submit five copies, in typed form and on one side only, of a letter of application, a curriculum vitae, an outline of their intention with regards to a future career, full particulars of the purpose for which the award would be used and a supporting testimonial from a person capable of judging the candidate's ability to use the award profitably.
Closing Date: April 1st in the year of the award.
Funding: Private.
Contributor: Small individual contributions.
No. of awards given last year: 10.
No. of applicants last year: 25.
Additional Information: Awards are only given to support a specific project, such as a research visit to the headquarters of an international organisation, or to a particular country, or a short research course at an institution abroad, which will assist the applicant in his or her study of international affairs in relation to the purpose and work of the United Nations. The Junior Awards are not intended as general financial support for the study of international affairs.

GILCHRIST EDUCATIONAL TRUST (GET)

Mary Trevelyan Hall, 10 York Terrace East, London, NW1 4PT, England
Tel: (44) 20 7631 8300 ext. 773
Contact: Mrs Everidge, Secretary

GET Grants
Subjects: All subjects.
Purpose: To promote the advancement of education and learning.
Eligibility: Open to: (1) Students in the United Kingdom who are within sight of the end of a course and who are facing unexpected financial difficulties which may prevent completion of their studies. Individuals entitled to student loans are not eligible; (2) Students who are required to open a short period outgoing abroad as part of their course; (3) British expeditions proposing to carry out scientific research in another country.
Level of Study: Doctorate, Postgraduate.
Type: Grant.
Frequency: Dependent on funds available.
Study Establishment: Any university.
Country of Study: United Kingdom.
No. of awards offered: Varies.
Application Procedure: Expeditions are required to complete an application form. Eligible individuals are sent a list of information required.

Closing Date: February 28th for expeditions. There is no deadline for applications from individuals.
Funding: Private.

Gilchrist Fieldwork Award

Subjects: All scientific subjects.
Purpose: To fund a period of fieldwork by established scientists or academics.
Eligibility: Open to teams wishing to undertake a field season of over six weeks in relation to one or more scientific objectives. Teams should not consist of more than 10 members most of whom should be British and holding established positions in research departments at universities or similar establishments. The proposed research must be original and challenging, achievable within the timetable and preferably of benefit to the host country or region.
Type: Grant.
Value: UK£12,000.
Frequency: Every two years.
Country of Study: Any country.
No. of awards offered: One.
Application Procedure: Applicants must write for details.
Closing Date: March 15th in even-numbered years.
Funding: Private.
Additional Information: The award is competitive.

GILROY AND LILLIAN P ROBERTS CHARITABLE FOUNDATION

10 Presidential Boulevard, Suite 250, Bala Cynwyd, PA 19004-1136, United States of America
Tel: (1) 610-668-1998
Contact: Mr Stanley Merves, Grants Enquiries

Private foundation funded under the will of Gilroy Roberts, designer of the obverse of the Kennedy half-dollar when he was Chief Engraver of the U.S. Mint.

Gilroy Roberts Art of Engraving Fellowship

Purpose: Gain knowledge in BAS Relief and Engraving.
Eligibility: Students with art background.
Level of Study: Unrestricted.
Type: Tuition, Room & Board and a small Stipend.
Value: US$2,000.
Length of Study: One week.
Frequency: Annual.
Study Establishment: Colorado College.
Country of Study: United States of America.
No. of awards offered: 5.
Application Procedure: Application form available thru: American Numismatic Association, 919 North Cascade, Colorado Springs, Co.
Closing Date: As stated on application (changes annually).
Funding: Private.
Contributor: Gilroy and Lillian P. Roberts Charitable Foundation.
No. of awards given last year: 5.
No. of applicants last year: 15.
Additional Information: Course is given annually.

For further information contact:

American Numismatic Association, 919 North Cascade, Colorado Springs, Co.

GLADYS KRIEBLE DELMAS FOUNDATION

521 Fifth Avenue, Suite 1612, New York, NY 10175-1699, United States of America
Tel: (1) 212 687 0011
Fax: (1) 212 687 8877
Email: info@delmas.org
www: http://www.delmas.org
Contact: Ms Shirley Lockwood

The Gladys Krieble Delmas Foundation promotes the advancement and perpetuation of humanistic enquiry and artistic creativity by encouraging excellence in scholarship and in the performing arts, and by supporting research libraries and other institutions that preserve the resources which transmit this cultural heritage.

Gladys Krieble Delmas Foundation Grants

Subjects: The history of Venice, the former Venetian empire and contemporary Venetian society and culture. Disciplines of the humanities and social sciences are eligible areas of study including, but not limited to art, architecture, archaeology, theatre, music, literature, political science, economics and law.
Purpose: To promote research into Venice and the Veneto.
Eligibility: Open to citizens and permanent residents of the United States of America who have some experience in advanced research. Graduate students must have fulfilled all doctoral requirements except for completion of the dissertation. The dissertation proposal must, however, have been approved by the time of application for the grant. There is also a programme for Scholars from Commonwealth countries.
Level of Study: Postdoctorate, Predoctorate.
Type: Grant.
Value: US$500-16,500 depending on length of study. At the discretion of the trustees and advisory board of the Foundation, funds may be made available for aid on the publication of results.
Length of Study: Up to one academic year.
Frequency: Annual.
Country of Study: Italy.
No. of awards offered: Usually 15-25.
Application Procedure: Applicants must complete an application form. Instruction sheets and forms are available from the Foundation.
Closing Date: December 15th.
Funding: Private.

For further information contact:

2 Lansdowne Circus, Leamington Spa, Warwickshire CV32 4SW, England
Contact: Professor M E Mallett

GLASGOW EDUCATIONAL AND MARSHALL TRUST

21 Beaton Road, Glasgow, G41 4NW, Scotland
Tel: (44) 141 423 2169
Fax: (44) 141 424 1731
Contact: R R McLean, Administrator

The Glasgow Educational and Marshall Trust is a charitable trust which meets quarterly and awards bursaries to, amongst others, mature students and postgraduate students, and to aid travel and school trips.

Glasgow Educational and Marshall Trust Bursary

Subjects: All subjects.
Purpose: To offer financial support to those living within the Glasgow Municipal Boundary.
Eligibility: Applicants must have a minimum of five years of residence within the Glasgow Municipal Boundary, as it was prior to 1975. Years spent within the Boundary purely for the purpose of study do not count.
Level of Study: Unrestricted.
Type: Bursary.
Value: UK£100-1,000.
Frequency: Annual.
Country of Study: Other.
Application Procedure: Applicants must complete and submit an application form together with two written references prior to the start of the course. No retrospective awards are available.
Closing Date: July 31st.
Funding: Private.
No. of awards given last year: 68.
No. of applicants last year: 240.
Additional Information: Further information is available on request.

GLAUCOMA RESEARCH FOUNDATION

490 Post street, Suite 1427, San Francisco, CA 94102, United States
of America
Tel: (1) 415 986 3162
Fax: (1) 415 986 3763
Email: research@glaucoma.org
www: http://www.glaucoma.org
Contact: Ms Jennifer Rulon, Research Manager

The Glaucoma Research Foundation is a national non-profit organisation working to protect the sight and independence of people with glaucoma, through research and education.

Pilot Project Grants Program

Subjects: Glaucoma.
Purpose: To provide funds for research.
Eligibility: Applicants must hold a graduate degree.
Level of Study: Postgraduate.
Type: Research grant.
Value: US$15,000-50,000.
Length of Study: One year.
Frequency: Annual,
Country of Study: United States of America.
No. of awards offered: Varies.
Application Procedure: Applicants must write, phone or visit the website for details.
Closing Date: December 1st.

GLAXOSMITHKLINE

Medicines Research Centre, Gunnels Wood Road, Stevenage, SG1
2NY, England
Tel: (44) 1438 763280
Fax: (44) 1438 763276
Email: ms3845@gsk.com
www: http://www.glaxosmithkline.co.uk
Contact: Director, European Academic Liaison

GlaxoSmithKline is a pharmaceutical and health care company, committed to improving the quality of human life by enabling people to do more, feel better and live longer. The focus of the company is health care, treatment, prevention and diagnosis including the concept of proactive health living. GlaxoSmithKline is comprised of three integrated businesses: pharmaceuticals, consumer health care and clinical diagnostics.

GlaxoSmithKline Collaborative Research Projects

Subjects: Pharmaceuticals, consumer healthcare and clinical diagnostic services.
Purpose: To target people whose research activities fit into the company's own research programme.
Eligibility: Open to groups who are carrying out relevant research activities. Speculative approaches are also welcome from the academic sector.
Level of Study: Doctorate, Graduate.
Type: Studentship.
Value: Please contact the organisation.
Length of Study: One-three years.
Frequency: Annual.
Study Establishment: Any university.
Country of Study: Any country.
Application Procedure: Applicants must write for details.
Closing Date: Applications are accepted at any time.
Funding: Commercial, Government.
Contributor: The majority of studentships are jointly funded with the Research Councils and a small number are totally funded by them.

Services to Academia

Subjects: Pharmacology, chemistry, biotechnology and toxicology.
Eligibility: Open to students excelling in the listed subject areas during their studies.
Level of Study: Professional development.
Type: Other.

Value: Varies.
Frequency: Annual.
Country of Study: Any country.
No. of awards offered: Varies.
Application Procedure: Organisations must approach the company in writing.
Closing Date: Applications are accepted at any time.
Funding: Commercial.

THE GOLDA MEIR MOUNT CARMEL INTERNATIONAL TRAINING CENTRE (MCTC)

PO Box 6111, Haifa, 31060, Israel
Tel: (972) 4 837 5904
Fax: (972) 4 837 5913
Email: mctc@mctc.co.il
Contact: Mrs Mazal Renford, Director

The Golda Meir Mount Carmel International Training Centre (MCTC) devotes its resources to training women and men from developing countries and societies in transition. Its underlying philosophy stresses the importance of grassroots development and recognition of women's contribution. It conducts courses and workshops at the MCTC and abroad in three key areas: community development, early childhood education and management of microenterprises.

MCTC Assistance for Courses

Subjects: Courses in community organisation and management of human services, pre school education, organisation and management of income generating projects and small scale industries, and management of non governmental organisations (NGOs).
Purpose: To assist developing countries and transitional societies in training personnel engaged in socio-economic development.
Eligibility: Open mainly to women aged 25-45 years of age from developing countries. Male students are also accepted. Participants must have completed at least 12 years of schooling, have undergone relevant professional training and have work experience. A good knowledge of the language in which the course will be given is essential.
Level of Study: Postgraduate, Professional development.
Value: Tuition, lodging and board
Length of Study: Three or six weeks.
Frequency: Annual.
Study Establishment: MCTC.
Country of Study: Israel.
No. of awards offered: 28.
Application Procedure: Applicants must apply to the Israeli diplomatic representative in their country for admission to the course.
Closing Date: Three months prior to the commencement of the course.
Funding: Government.
Contributor: MASHAV - Centre for International Cooperation Ministry of Foreign Affairs, Israel.
No. of awards given last year: 400.
No. of applicants last year: 1,400.
Additional Information: Courses are given in English, French or Spanish and include lectures, discussion groups, study tours and fieldwork.

MCTC Tuition and Maintenance Scholarships

Subjects: Community organisation and management of human services, pre-school education, organisation and management of income generating projects and small-scale industries or management of non governmental organisations (NGOs).
Eligibility: Open to nationals of developing countries and transitional societies.
Level of Study: Postgraduate, Professional development.
Type: Scholarship.
Value: US$3,000 per month.
Length of Study: 3 or 6 weeks.
Frequency: Annual.

Study Establishment: MCTC.
Country of Study: Israel.
No. of awards offered: 28.
Application Procedure: Applicants must complete an application form including a health form and copies of their diplomas. Forms can be obtained from the nearest Israeli diplomatic representative.
Closing Date: Three months prior to the course start date.
Funding: Government.
Contributor: MASHAV - Centre for International Cooperation Ministry of Foreign Affairs, Israel.
No. of awards given last year: 400.
No. of applicants last year: 1,400.
Additional Information: Courses are given in English, French or Spanish and includes lectures, discussion groups, study tours and fieldwork.

GOLDEN KEY NATIONAL HONOR SOCIETY

International Headquarters, 1189 Ponce de Leon Avenue NE, Atlanta, GA 30306-4624, United States of America
Tel: (1) 404 377 2400
Fax: (1) 404 373 4033
Email: scholarships@goldenkey.gsu.edu
www: http://goldenkey.gsu.edu
Contact: Mr Luke Anderson, Co-ordinator of Scholarships and Awards

Golden Key National Honor Society is a non-profit academic honours organisation that recognises the top 15 per cent of juniors and seniors in all undergraduate fields. Membership of the Society is by invitation only and there are various benefits available to members. The Society has a five part mission to recognise scholastic achievement and excellence in all undergraduate fields of study, unite collegiate faculty and administrators with students to foster a network of scholars, to award scholarships for the pursuit of knowledge, to serve the campus and community for personal growth and leadership development and to connect members with career opportunities.

Golden Key National Honor Society Art International

Subjects: Painting, drawing, photography, sculpture, computer generated art, graphic design and illustration, applied art such as jewellery, textiles, ceramics and set design, printmaking and mixed media.
Purpose: To recognise and reward the creative talents of members and to reward their superlative works of art through their visual arts scholarship programme.
Eligibility: Open to Golden Key members.
Level of Study: Unrestricted.
Type: Scholarship.
Value: US$1,000 to one winner in each of the eight categories.
Frequency: Annual.
No. of awards offered: Eight.
Application Procedure: Applicants must contact the Golden Key organisation for application material.
Closing Date: April 1st.
Funding: Private.
Contributor: Society members.
No. of awards given last year: Eight.
No. of applicants last year: 400.
Additional Information: Winning entries may be displayed at the Golden Key International Convention and may be published in Concepts, the society's award winning annual magazine.

Golden Key National Honor Society Business Achievement Awards

Subjects: Business administration and management.
Purpose: To honour students for their excellence in the field of business study.
Eligibility: Open to Golden Key members.
Level of Study: Unrestricted.
Type: Scholarship.

Value: The winner will receive a US$1,000 award, the second place applicant will receive US$750 and the third place applicant will receive US$500.
Length of Study: Varies.
Frequency: Annual.
No. of awards offered: Three.
Application Procedure: Applicants will be asked to respond to a problem posed by an honorary member within the discipline.
Closing Date: March 1st.
Funding: Private.
Contributor: Society members.
No. of awards given last year: Three.
No. of applicants last year: 25.
Additional Information: Further information is available from the website.

Golden Key National Honor Society Earth Ethics Award

Subjects: All subjects.
Purpose: To recognise a member who exhibits exemplary dedication to environmental awareness and responsibility.
Eligibility: Open to Golden Key members.
Level of Study: Unrestricted.
Type: Scholarship.
Value: US$1,000.
Frequency: Annual.
No. of awards offered: One.
Application Procedure: Applicants must complete a specific assignment, details of which are available from the organisation. Applicants must send the essay along with their contact details to the society.
Closing Date: February 15th.
Funding: Private.
Contributor: Society members.
No. of awards given last year: One.
No. of applicants last year: 120.
Additional Information: The winning earth ethics essay will be published in Concepts magazine.

Golden Key National Honor Society Education Achievement Awards

Subjects: Education.
Purpose: To honour students for excellence in the field.
Eligibility: Open to Golden Key members.
Level of Study: Unrestricted.
Type: Scholarship.
Value: The winner will receive a US$1,000 award, the second place applicant will receive US$750 and the third place applicant will receive US$500.
Frequency: Annual.
No. of awards offered: Three.
Application Procedure: Applicants are asked to complete a specific assignment, details of which are available by contacting the organisation. The thematic unit must be accompanied by an application form, an academic transcript and a letter of recommendation from a professor in the discipline.
Closing Date: March 1st.
Contributor: Society members.
No. of awards given last year: Three.
No. of applicants last year: 30.

Golden Key National Honor Society Engineering Achievement Award

Subjects: Engineering.
Purpose: To honour students for excellence in the field.
Eligibility: Open to Golden Key members.
Level of Study: Unrestricted.
Type: Scholarship.
Value: The winner will receive a US$1,000 award, the second place applicant will receive US$750 and the third place applicant will receive US$500.
Frequency: Annual.
No. of awards offered: Three.

Application Procedure: Applicants must provide a solution to a design problem. A range of topics are available by contacting the Society.
Closing Date: March 1st.
Funding: Private.
Contributor: Society members.
No. of awards given last year: Three.
No. of applicants last year: 20.

Golden Key National Honor Society Excellence in Speech and Debate Awards

Subjects: All subjects.
Purpose: To recognise talented members for their oratory skills.
Eligibility: Open to Golden Key members.
Level of Study: Unrestricted.
Type: Scholarship.
Value: Varies.
Frequency: Annual.
No. of awards offered: Two.
Application Procedure: Applicants must submit a videotaped monologue of no more than five minutes in length.
Closing Date: April 1st.
Funding: Private.
Contributor: Society members.
No. of awards given last year: Two.
No. of applicants last year: 30.

Golden Key National Honor Society GEICO Adult Scholar Awards

Subjects: All subjects.
Purpose: To recognise academic achievement in students from all backgrounds and from all disciplines.
Eligibility: Candidates must have completed at least 12 credit hours since their return to the university and be enrolled at the time of application. Candidates must be working towards a Baccalaureate degree.
Level of Study: Unrestricted.
Type: Scholarship.
Value: US$1,000.
Frequency: Annual.
No. of awards offered: 10.
Application Procedure: Applicants must submit an official application form, an academic transcript and a personal essay of no more than 500 words describing their educational goals, their other commitments and the obstacles they have overcome to achieve academic excellence. Candidates must submit a letter of recommendation either from an employer or from a professor in their major field of study.
Closing Date: April 1st.
Funding: Commercial.
Contributor: GEICO Insurance.
No. of awards given last year: 10.
No. of applicants last year: 200.
Additional Information: The Society recognises that returning students are an important component of their member population and this award hopes to reward motivated students for their commitment to maintaining academic excellence while balancing additional responsibilities.

Golden Key National Honor Society Information Systems Achievement Awards

Subjects: Information systems.
Purpose: To honour students for excellence in their field.
Eligibility: Open to Golden Key members.
Level of Study: Unrestricted.
Type: Scholarship.
Value: Varies from US$500-1,000.
Frequency: Annual.
No. of awards offered: Three.
Application Procedure: Applicants are asked to respond a specific assignment, the details of which can be obtained from the organisation. This solution must be accompanied by an application form, an academic transcript and a letter of recommendation from a professor in the discipline. Applications will be judged by honorary members in the field of information systems based on the creativity and viability of the response.
Closing Date: March 1st.
Funding: Private.
Contributor: Society members.
No. of awards given last year: Three.
No. of applicants last year: 15.

Golden Key National Honor Society International Student Leader

Subjects: All subjects.
Purpose: To recognise a talented member for outstanding commitment to Golden Key, as well as for campus and community leadership and academic achievement.
Eligibility: Open to Golden Key members who are in good standing and are currently enrolled in an accredited graduate programme.
Level of Study: Unrestricted.
Type: Scholarship.
Value: US$1,000.
Frequency: Annual.
No. of awards offered: One.
Application Procedure: Applicants must submit an official application form, a personal statement of no more than 1,000 words explaining why the student feels that he or she should receive the award, a detailed list of Golden Key involvement, a list of extracurricular activities listing involvement in other organisations, honours and awards received, community service activities and work experience, and a letter of recommendation from the Golden Key chapter advisor.
Closing Date: May 1st.
Funding: Private.
Contributor: Society members.
No. of awards given last year: One.
No. of applicants last year: 50.
Additional Information: The award will be presented at the international convention.

Golden Key National Honor Society Literary Achievement Awards

Subjects: Fiction, non fiction, poetry and news writing.
Purpose: To recognise and encourage members' literary talents.
Eligibility: Open to Golden Key members. Each entry must be an original composition and previously published works will not be accepted. Only one composition per member, per category will be accepted.
Level of Study: Unrestricted.
Type: Scholarship.
Value: US$1,000.
Frequency: Annual.
No. of awards offered: Four.
Application Procedure: Entries must be accompanied by a separate Literary Achievement Awards application form. The applicant's name or other identification must not appear on any page other than the application as a numbering system will be used to track entries and applications.
Closing Date: April 1st.
Funding: Private.
Contributor: Society members.
No. of awards given last year: Four.
No. of applicants last year: 500.
Additional Information: Winning entries will be published in Concepts, the Society's award winning annual magazine.

Golden Key National Honor Society Performing Arts Showcase

Subjects: Dance, drama, film making, instrumental performance, original musical composition and vocal performance.
Purpose: To recognise and encourage creative talents.
Eligibility: Open to Golden Key members. Only one entry per member, per category will be accepted.
Level of Study: Unrestricted.
Type: Scholarship.
Value: US$1,000.
Frequency: Annual.

No. of awards offered: Six.
Application Procedure: Each entry must be accompanied by a separate Performing Arts Showcase application form, available from the Society. Entries must be submitted on VHS videotape and may not exceed ten minutes in length.
Closing Date: March 1st.
Funding: Private.
Contributor: Society members.
No. of awards given last year: Six.
No. of applicants last year: 175.

Golden Key National Honor Society Research Travel Grants

Subjects: All subjects.
Purpose: To assist students who need funding to pursue field research related to an honours thesis.
Eligibility: Open to Golden Key members. The student must be able to show that they have been invited to present their research at a specific conference.
Level of Study: Unrestricted.
Type: Grant.
Value: US$500.
Frequency: Annual.
Country of Study: Any country.
No. of awards offered: 10.
Application Procedure: The student must submit documentation supported by the thesis advisor that the trip is highly relevant to the research to be conducted, as well as a documented budget that summarises the overall cost of attending the conference or of travelling to undertake necessary research. Applications must include a statement of personal particulars, details of Golden Key activities, a description of the proposed research presentation and documented evidence that the applicant has been invited to present at a specified professional association conference or research symposia, or a documented research proposal related to progress in the applicant's honours thesis, a brief statement of the relevance of this request signed by the applicant's academic departmental chairperson or thesis advisor, and a recent academic transcript.
Closing Date: October 15th and April 15th.
Funding: Private.
Contributor: Society members.
No. of awards given last year: 10.
No. of applicants last year: 50.

Golden Key National Honor Society Service Award

Subjects: All subjects.
Purpose: To recognise an individual for outstanding commitment to community service.
Eligibility: Open to a Golden Key member who has been enrolled as a student during the previous academic year.
Level of Study: Unrestricted.
Type: Scholarship.
Value: US$500.
Frequency: Annual.
No. of awards offered: One.
Application Procedure: The application packet must include an official application form, a 250-500 word statement describing the service project and the applicant's philosophy of community service, two letters of recommendation from the applicant's chapter advisor and one from a representative of the beneficiary of the service.
Closing Date: February 15th.
Funding: Private.
Contributor: Society members.
No. of awards given last year: One.
No. of applicants last year: 75.

Golden Key National Honor Society Student Scholastic Showcase

Subjects: All subjects.
Purpose: To highlight the research of Society members across the broad spectrum of academic disciplines.

Eligibility: Open to Golden Key members. Alumni are eligible. Only one entry per member is permitted. Winners of the Golden Key Scholar Award are not eligible.
Level of Study: Unrestricted.
Type: Scholarship.
Value: US$1,000.
Frequency: Annual.
No. of awards offered: Four.
Application Procedure: Applicants must submit an abstract, not to exceed 250 words, which describes the nature of the study. The abstract should be written in language that is suitable for a reader who is unfamiliar with the discipline. Each entry must contain a complete copy of the paper or research and a letter of support from a faculty member related to, or familiar with, the research project, and be accompanied by an official Student Scholastic Showcase application.
Closing Date: March 1st.
Funding: Private.
Contributor: Society members.
No. of awards given last year: Four.
No. of applicants last year: 100.

Golden Key Scholar Award

Subjects: All subjects.
Purpose: To support members' graduate study at accredited universities.
Eligibility: Open to lifetime members of the Golden Key who are in good standing at the time of the application, have graduated no earlier than five years prior to the application deadline from an institution with an active chapter of the Golden Key International Honor Society, hold Baccalaureate degrees or the equivalent by the time they receive their scholarships or enrol in a post Baccalaureate programme of study at an accredited Institute of Higher Education during the academic year of application as a full-time student.
Level of Study: Graduate.
Type: Scholarship.
Value: US$10,000.
Frequency: Annual.
Study Establishment: Any accredited university.
Country of Study: Any country.
No. of awards offered: 12.
Application Procedure: Applicants must submit an application form and four sets of the required documents to the Society's headquarters.
Closing Date: January 15th.
Funding: Private.
Contributor: Society members.
No. of awards given last year: 12.
No. of applicants last year: 100.

THE GOLDSMITHS' COMPANY

Goldsmiths' Hall Foster Lane, London, EC2V 6BN, England
Tel: (44) 20 7606 7010
Fax: (44) 20 7606 1511
Contact: The Assistant Clerk

One of the Great Twelve Livery Companies, committed to promoting excellence in the design and craftsmanship of silver and precious metal jewellery. Actively involved in fostering aspects of Education considered to be in greatest need of encouragement.

Goldsmiths Company Science for Society Courses

Subjects: Medical physics, Genetics, Particle Physics, Complementary Medicine, Astrophysics, Sustainable Development.
Purpose: To provide teachers of A levels with first hand practical experience of the theory which they teach.
Eligibility: Open to United Kingdom science teachers of secondary age children, but other disciplines are accepted.
Level of Study: Professional development.
Value: Free tuition, accommodation and travel after joining.
Length of Study: One week in July.
Frequency: Annual.
Study Establishment: Various locations around the United Kingdom.
Country of Study: United Kingdom.

No. of awards offered: Approx. 120 vacancies each year.
Application Procedure: Please write for details.
Closing Date: Vacancies are on a first come, first served basis.
Funding: Private.

Goldsmiths' Travelling Grants for Schoolmasters and Schoolmistresses

Subjects: Refreshment study in a field different from their professional expertise.
Purpose: To enable schoolmasters and schoolmistresses to pursue an interest as far removed as possible from their classroom duties.
Eligibility: Open to primary and secondary teachers in schools, in both the private and maintained sectors. They should have had at least 10 years teaching experience and should not normally be over 55 years of age.
Level of Study: Professional development.
Type: Travel grant.
Value: Up to UK£5,000 to include supply cover for the candidate granted leave who is expected to receive his or her normal salary during absence.
Length of Study: One-two months.
Frequency: Annual.
Country of Study: Any country.
No. of awards offered: Up to 8.
Application Procedure: The applicant should complete the application form (available from the Company) with his or her personal details, education, qualifications and teaching experience, provide a letter of application setting out, on not more than three sides but with as much detail as possible, the proposal for the period of leave, outline itinerary and estimate of expenses, and forward the application to his or her Head. The Head should complete the appropriate part of the application form with an assessment of the merit of the application and a recommendation of the candidate. The Employer (who may be the Head acting on behalf of the Governors or Local Education Authority) should complete the statement on the application form agreeing to the candidate's leave of absence, indicating whether or not the candidate will be paid on full salary during his or her leave of absence, and should then ensure that the letter of application is attached to the application form and forward both to the Clerk of the Goldsmiths' Company at the address shown.
Closing Date: December 1st.
Funding: Private.
No. of awards given last year: 7.
No. of applicants last year: 65.

GRADUATE INSTITUTE OF INTERNATIONAL STUDIES, GENEVA

Institut Universitaire de Hautes Études Internationales, Case Postale 36132 rue de Lausanne, Geneva, CH-1211, Switzerland
Tel: (41) 22 908 5700
Fax: (41) 22 908 5710
Email: info@hei.unige.ch
www: http://heiwww.unige.ch
Tel: 412 151 Pax Ch
Contact: Mr Simon Wermelinger, Secretary General

The Graduate Institute of International Studies is a teaching and research establishment devoted to the scientific study of contemporary international relations. The international character of the Institute is emphasised by the use of both English and French as working languages. Its plural approach, which draws upon the method of history and political science, law and economics, reflects its aim to promote a broad approach and in depth understanding of international relations.

Graduate Institute of International Studies (HEI-Geneva) Scholarships

Subjects: History and international politics, international economics, international law and political science.

Eligibility: Open to any applicant who can prove sound knowledge of the French language and sufficient prior study in political science, economics, law or modern history through the presentation of a college or university degree.
Level of Study: Doctorate, Postgraduate.
Type: Scholarship.
Value: Swiss franc 1,000 per month.
Length of Study: One year, possibly renewable.
Frequency: Annual.
Study Establishment: Graduate Institute of International Studies, Geneva.
Country of Study: Switzerland.
No. of awards offered: 24.
Application Procedure: Applicants must contact the Institute for details.
Closing Date: March 1st.
Funding: Government.
Contributor: The Canton of Geneva and the Swiss Confederation.
No. of awards given last year: 24.
No. of applicants last year: 49.
Additional Information: Scholarships are normally awarded to more advanced students of the Institute. As a general rule, they are not granted during the first year of studies. Scholars are exempt from Institute fees, but not from the obligatory fees of the University of Geneva which confers the doctorate (doctorat en relations internationales).

GRAINS RESEARCH AND DEVELOPMENT CORPORATION (GRDC)

PO Box E6, Kingston, ACT 2604, Australia
Tel: (61) 2 6272 5525
Fax: (61) 2 6271 6430
Email: grdc@grdc.com.au
www: http://www.grdc.com.au
Contact: Mrs Katie Poidomani, Program Co-ordinator

The Grains Research and Development Corporation's (GRDC) mission is to invest in research and development for the greatest benefit to its stakeholders, grain growers and the Commonwealth. The GRDC links innovative research with industry needs. The Corporation's vision is for a profitable, internationally competitive and ecologically sustainable grains industry.

GRDC Grains Industry Research Scholarships

Subjects: Fields of high priority to the grains industry.
Eligibility: Open to permanent Australian residents who hold academic qualifications equivalent to a First Class (Honours) Degree or have otherwise demonstrated a high level of postgraduate achievement in research, teaching or extension activities.
Level of Study: Doctorate, Postgraduate.
Type: Fellowship.
Value: A tax free stipend of Australian $25,000 with no allowances for dependants. An additional grant of up to Australian $5,000 per year may be provided to the host organisation to support the work.
Length of Study: Up to three years.
Frequency: Annual.
Study Establishment: Any university with a record of achievement for full-time research in the subject area leading to a DPhil.
Country of Study: Australia.
No. of awards offered: Up to six.
Application Procedure: Applicants must complete an application form, available on request. Applications (6 copies) should include the curriculum vitae of the applicant and the report of at least two referees. Evidence that the university and collaborating organisations will provide facilities and supervision of the project must also be supplied.
Closing Date: October for the following year.
Funding: Government.
Contributor: The government and Australian grain growers.
No. of awards given last year: 10.
No. of applicants last year: Approx. 50.

Additional Information: The Corporation's five year research and development plan outlines the objectives and programmes to be covered. Copies of this may be obtained from the Secretariat.

GRDC In-Service Training

Subjects: Grains research and development.
Purpose: To support training on an industry wide basis by funding younger scientists, technical staff or other persons engaged in work relevant to the Corporation's objectives who may not be eligible for other forms of support. Funds may be provided for travel, secondment or interchange between institutions.
Eligibility: Open to permanent Australian residents only.
Level of Study: Unrestricted.
Type: Grant.
Value: Personal travel costs, including economy class air fares and contribution to living expenses for a maximum of six months.
Length of Study: Up to six months.
Frequency: Annual.
Country of Study: Any country.
Application Procedure: Applicants must submit 6 copies of a curriculum vitae, details of the proposed in-service training, the names, positions and locations of the proposed collaborators and training venue, and approximate dates for the programme, which must fall within the appropriate funding year. Details of any travel directly related to the proposed programme, a proposed budget, including the cost of travel and expected accommodation and living expenses, an indication of other forms of support available to the applicant, evidence that the proposed collaborators are agreeable to the training programme, supporting comments from two referees, and a covering letter should also be included.
Closing Date: October for the following year.
Contributor: The government and Australian grain growers.
Additional Information: On completion of their award, trainees must provide the Board with a report.

GRDC Industry Development Awards

Subjects: Grains research and development.
Purpose: To fund study tours or for other purposes approved by the Corporation.
Eligibility: Open to permanent Australian residents who are experienced growers, processors or other contributors to the work of the Corporation who are not engaged in research and development activity.
Level of Study: Unrestricted.
Type: Award.
Value: Up to a total of Australian $15,000 towards personal travel costs, including economy class air fares and contribution to living expenses.
Frequency: Annual, Twice Yearly.
Country of Study: Any country.
Application Procedure: Applicants must submit five copies of the nominee's curriculum vitae, details of the proposed programme, the names, positions and locations of the proposed collaborators, approximate dates for the programme, and details of any internal travel directly related to the proposed programme. A proposed budget, including the cost of international and internal travel, and expected accommodation and living expenses, an indication of other forms of support available to the nominee, evidence that the proposed collaborators are agreeable to the programme, supporting comments from two referees, and a covering letter should also be included.
Closing Date: End of March & September each year.
Contributor: The government and Australian grain growers.
Additional Information: On completion of the award, a report must be given to the Board. Preference may be given to applicants who have access to matching funds.

GRDC Senior Fellowships

Subjects: Grains research and development.
Purpose: To allow experienced research and development personnel to enhance their experience and their potential to contribute to the work of the Corporation by working at an institution in Australia or overseas.
Eligibility: Open to permanent Australian residents only.
Level of Study: Unrestricted.
Type: Fellowship.
Value: Up to a total of Australian $50,000 towards personal travel costs, including economy class air fares and a contribution to living expenses.
Length of Study: Up to one year.
Frequency: Annual.
Country of Study: Any country.
Application Procedure: Applicants must submit 6 copies of the following documentation: the nominee's curriculum vitae, including a list of publications, details of the nominee's research project and its relationship to the host institution's programme of research (this should include evidence that the host institution already has an interest and competence in the area of research proposed by the applicant and that it is relevant to the Corporation's objectives), the names, positions and major publications of the proposed collaborators, together with a letter of invitation from the Head of the host institution. They should also include approximate dates for the programme, which must fall within the appropriate funding year, details of any internal travel directly related to the proposed programme, a proposed budget, including the cost of international and internal travel, and expected accommodation and living expenses, an indication of other forms of support available to the applicant, evidence that the host institution has available the necessary facilities and is willing to accept the Fellow, supporting comments from two referees, and a covering letter. On completion of their award Fellows must furnish the Board with a report. Preference may be given to applicants who have access to matching funds.
Closing Date: October for the following year.
Funding: Government.
Contributor: The government and Australian grain growers.

GRDC Visiting Fellowships and Industry Awards

Subjects: Grains research and development.
Purpose: To give support and stimulus to research programmes supported by the Corporation by funding visits by overseas personnel who could enhance those programmes.
Eligibility: Open to candidates of any nationality.
Level of Study: Postgraduate.
Type: Fellowship.
Value: The Corporation will consider paying the nominee's personal travel costs, contributing to living expenses and providing some support to the host institution or company. The maximum total level of support will normally be Australian $17,500.
Length of Study: Up to one year.
Frequency: Annual.
Country of Study: Australia.
Application Procedure: Applicants must submit 6 copies of the following documentation: the nominee's curriculum vitae, details of the nominee's research project or itinerary for study and its relationship to the host institution's or company's programme of research, development or other industry contribution, the name, position and industry contributions of the person proposing the nominee, together with a letter of support from the Head of the host institution or company, where appropriate, the names, positions and institutions of collaborators of the proposed project or study tour. They should also include approximate dates for the programme, which must fall within the appropriate funding year, details of any travel directly related to the proposed programme, a proposed budget, including the cost of international and internal travel, and expected accommodation and living expenses, an indication of other forms of support available to the nominee, including those from the home institution or company, evidence that the host institution or company has accepted the nomination, supporting comments from two referees, and a covering letter.
Closing Date: October for the following year.
Contributor: The government and Australian grain growers.

Additional Information: On completion of the award, a report must be given to the Board. Preference may be given to nominees who have access to matching funds.

GRIFFITH UNIVERSITY

Nathan Campus, QLD 4111, Australia
Tel: (61) 7 3875 6596
Fax: (61) 7 3875 3885
Email: m.mitchell@griffith.edu.au
www: http://www.gu.edu.au/postgrad
Contact: Postgraduate Scholarships Officer

In the pursuit of excellence in teaching, research and community service, Griffith University is committed to innovation, bringing disciplines together, internationalisation, equity and social justice and life-long learning, for the enrichment of Queensland, Australia and the international community.

Griffith University Postgraduate Research Scholarships
Subjects: All subjects.
Purpose: To provide financial support for candidates undertaking full-time research leading to the award of the degree of Doctor of Philosophy or Master of Philosophy.
Eligibility: Open to any person, irrespective of nationality, holding or expecting to hold a First Class (Honours) Degree or equivalent, from a recognised institution. Applicants must demonstrate proficiency in the English language by scoring an overall score of 6.5 in the IELTS test, or have a score of at least 580 on the Teaching English As a Foreign Language test or hold a test score of 237 (new Teaching English As a Foreign Language) with an essay rating of 5.0.
Level of Study: Postgraduate.
Type: Scholarship.
Value: Australian $18,484 per year tax exempt.
Length of Study: Up to two years for Research Master's and up to three years for PhD candidates, with a possible extension of up to six months for the PhD, subject to satisfactory progress.
Frequency: Annual.
Study Establishment: Griffith University.
Country of Study: Australia.
No. of awards offered: Varies.
Application Procedure: Applicants must complete an application form.
Closing Date: October 31st.
Additional Information: The scholarship does not cover the cost of tuition fees which range from Australian $15,000-19,000 per year.

Jackson Memorial Fellowship
Subjects: The application of the social, political, economic, environmental or technological sciences to the analysis and resolution of substantial policy issues at the national or regional levels.
Purpose: To consolidate links with a variety of institutions in South East Asia and to provide funding to facilitate visits to Griffith University by faculty staff of the Association of South East Asian Institution of Higher Learning (ASAIHL) member institutions.
Eligibility: Open to senior members of faculty staff of the ASAIHL member institutions.
Level of Study: Professional development.
Type: Fellowship.
Frequency: Annual.
Study Establishment: A faculty of Griffith University.
Country of Study: Australia.
Application Procedure: Applicants must apply through the heads of their employing institutions.
Closing Date: 15th September.
Funding: Private.
No. of awards given last year: 1.
No. of applicants last year: Varies.

Sir Allan Sewell Visiting Fellowship
Subjects: All faculties of Griffith University.
Purpose: To commemorate the distinguished service of Sir Allan Sewell to Griffith University by offering awards to enable visits by distinguished scholars engaged in academic work who can contribute to the research and teaching in one or more areas of interest to a faculty or college of the university.
Eligibility: Open to researchers of any nationality.
Level of Study: Professional development.
Type: Fellowship.
Frequency: Annual.
Study Establishment: Griffith University.
Country of Study: Australia.
Application Procedure: Applicants must be invited to apply by faculties or colleges of the University.
Closing Date: 15th September.
Funding: Private.
No. of awards given last year: Varies.
No. of applicants last year: Varies.

THE GRUNDY EDUCATIONAL TRUST

Springhill Cottage, Shirley Holms, Lymington, Hampshire, SO41 8NG, England
Tel: (44) 1590 672130
Fax: (44) 1590 677846
Email: pggrundy@aol.com
Contact: Mr P G Grundy, Secretary to the Trustees

Grundy Educational Trust
Subjects: Technologically or scientifically based disciplines in industry, commerce or the professions.
Purpose: To assist in covering maintenance costs whilst obtaining postgraduate or second degrees.
Eligibility: Open to United Kingdom citizens under 30 years of age.
Level of Study: Doctorate, Postgraduate.
Type: Award.
Value: Up to UK£3,000.
Length of Study: One-three years.
Frequency: Annual.
Study Establishment: Birmingham, Loughborough, Imperial College, Southampton, Surrey, UMIST or Nottingham.
Country of Study: United Kingdom.
No. of awards offered: 10-12.
Application Procedure: Applicants must apply through the seven selected universities only.
Closing Date: May 31st.
Funding: Private.
No. of awards given last year: 11.
No. of applicants last year: 25.

GUIDE DOGS FOR THE BLIND ASSOCIATION

Hillfields Burghfield Common, Reading, Berkshire, RG7 3YG, England
Tel: (44) 118 983 5555
Fax: (44) 118 983 5433
Email: guidedogs@guidedogs.org.uk
www: http://www.guidedogs.org.uk
Contact: Ms Fiona Reilly, Ophthalmic Research Officer

Founded in 1931, the Guide Dogs for the Blind Association's mission is to provide guide dogs, mobility and other rehabilitation services that meet the needs of blind and partially sighted people. The Association also supports other activities which enhance the quality of life of visually impaired people, including funding research into eye conditions.

Guide Dogs Ophthalmic Research Fellowship Grant
Subjects: The retina.
Purpose: To promote high quality research into the causes, treatment, prevention and cure of sight threatening diseases and conditions.
Eligibility: Applicants must be resident in the United Kingdom.
Level of Study: Research.
Type: Fellowship.
Value: Salary and other running costs.

Length of Study: Three years.
Frequency: Annual.
Study Establishment: Specialist ophthalmic departments or organisations.
Country of Study: United Kingdom.
No. of awards offered: Dependent on availability of funds.
Application Procedure: Applicants must submit an application in accordance with Guide Dogs Ophthalmic Research Fellowship Grant application guidelines.
Closing Date: The last Friday in February.
Funding: Private.
Contributor: Donations to the Guide Dogs for the Blind Association.
Additional Information: The Guide Dogs for the Blind Association is committed to avoiding the use of experimental animals or tissues from laboratory animals in funded research and will not accept any application which involves these procedures.

Guide Dogs Ophthalmic Research Grant

Subjects: The causes, treatment, prevention and cure of sight threatening diseases and conditions, more especially those that involve large numbers of people, require improved therapeutic regimens or that are likely to lead to a clinical application.
Purpose: To promote high quality research into the causes, treatment, prevention and cure of sight threatening diseases and conditions.
Eligibility: Applicants and any research workers must be resident in the United Kingdom. The principal applicant must be in a tenured post for the duration of the requested grant.
Level of Study: Research.
Type: Research grant.
Value: Up to UK£50,000 per year.
Length of Study: Three years.
Frequency: Annual.
Study Establishment: Specialist ophthalmic departments or organisations.
Country of Study: United Kingdom.
No. of awards offered: 6-10 depending of funds.
Application Procedure: Applicants must submit an application in accordance with Guide Dogs Ophthalmic Research Fellowship Grant application guidelines.
Closing Date: The last Friday in February.
Funding: Private.
Contributor: Donations to the Guide Dogs for the Blind Association.
No. of awards given last year: Six.
No. of applicants last year: 50.
Additional Information: The Guide Dogs for the Blind Association is committed to avoiding the use of experimental animals or tissues from laboratory animals in funded research and will not accept any application which involves these procedures.

GUILLAIN-BARRÉ SYNDROME SUPPORT GROUP

Lincolnshire County Council, Council Offices Eastgate, Sleaford, Lincolnshire, NG34 8NR, England
Tel: (44) 1529 300328
Fax: (44) 1529 300328
Email: admin@gbs.org
Contact: Ms Glennys Sanders, Honorary President

The Guillain-Barré Syndrome Support Group provides emotional support, personal visits and comprehensive literature to patients and their relatives and friends. The Group also educates the public and the medical community about the Support Group and maintains their awareness of the illness. The Group fosters research into the cause, treatment and other aspects of the illness and encourages fund raising and support for its activities.

Guillain-Barré Syndrome Support Group Research Fellowship

Subjects: Any aspect of Guillain-Barré syndrome (GBS) or related diseases including chronic inflammatory demyelinating polyradiculoneuropathy (CIDP).

Purpose: To advance research into the prevention and cure of GBS and CIDP.
Level of Study: Doctorate, Postgraduate, Professional development, Research.
Type: Fellowship.
Value: Up to UK£65,000.
Length of Study: Up to three years.
Frequency: Dependent on funds available.
Study Establishment: Any suitable hospital or university laboratory or department.
Country of Study: Other.
No. of awards offered: One.
Application Procedure: Applicants must write for an application form.
Closing Date: Please contact the organisation.
Contributor: Members' donations, fund raising and trust funds.
No. of awards given last year: One.
Additional Information: Further information is available on request.

THE GYPSY LORE SOCIETY

5607 Greenleaf Road, Cheverly, MD 20785
United States of America
Tel: (1) 301-341-1261
Fax: (1) 301-341-1261
Email: headquarters@gypsyloresociety.org
www: http://www.gypsyloresocieity.org
Contact: Ms Sheila Shako, Treasurer

The Gypsy Lore Society, an international association of persons interested in Gypsy Studies, was formed in Great Britain in 1888. The Gypsy Lore Society, North American Chapter, was founded in 1977 in the United States and since 1989 has continued as the Gypsy Lore Society. Society goals include promotion of the study of the Gypsy peoples and analogous itinerant or nomadic groups, dissemination of information aimed at increasing understanding of Gypsy culture in its diverse forms, and establishment of closer contacts among Gypsy scholars.

Gypsy Lore Society Young Scholar's Prize in Romani Studies

Subjects: Any Topic in Romani (Gypsy) Studies.
Purpose: To recognize outstanding work by young scholars in Romani (Gypsy) Studies.
Eligibility: Unpublished paper not under consideration for publication. Self-contained scholarly articles of publishable quality that treat a relevant topic in an interesting and insightful way.
Level of Study: Doctorate, Graduate, Postdoctorate, Graduate students beyond first year of study + PhD holders no more than 3 years beyond degree.
Type: Cash prize.
Value: US$300.
Frequency: Annual, if worthy work is submitted. Committee reserves right not to award prize in a given year.
Study Establishment: Any.
Country of Study: Any country.
No. of awards offered: One.
Application Procedure: Submit 4 copies of paper along with an abstract of fewer than 250 words, and a cover sheet with the title of the paper, the author's name, affiliation, mailing address, e-mail address, telephone + fax numbers, date of entrance into an appropriate graduate program or awarding of the PhD, and US Social Security number, if the author has one.
Closing Date: October 30, 2004.
Funding: Private.
Contributor: Gypsy Lore Society.
No. of awards given last year: 0.

For further information contact:

Gypsy Lore Society Prize Competition, Department of Slavic Languages + Literatures, 405 Foster Hall, 1130 East, 59th Street, University of Chicago, Chicago, IL 60637, United States of America

HAGLEY MUSEUM AND LIBRARY

PO Box 3630, Wilmington, DE 19807
United States of America
Tel: (1) 302 658 2400 ext. 243
Fax: (1) 302 655 3188
Email: crl@udel.edu
www: http://www.hagley.org
Contact: Ms Carol Ressler Lockman, Center Co-ordinator

Located along the Brandywine River on the site of the first du Pont black powder works, Hagley Museum and Library provides a unique glimpse into American life at home and at work in the nineteenth-century. Set among more than 230 acres of trees and flowering shrubs, Hagley offers a diversity of restorations, exhibits and live demonstrations for visitors of all ages.

Hagley Museum and Library Grants-in-Aid of Research

Subjects: American economic and technological history and French eighteenth-century history.
Purpose: To support travel to the Hagley Library for scholarly research in the collections.
Eligibility: Open to degree candidates and advanced scholars of any nationality. Research must be relevant to Hagley's collections.
Level of Study: Doctorate, Graduate, Postdoctorate. Predoctorate.
Type: Research grant.
Value: Up to US$1,400 per month.
Length of Study: Two-eight weeks.
Frequency: Four times per year.
Study Establishment: The Library.
Country of Study: United States of America.
No. of awards offered: 25 grants in aid.
Application Procedure: Applicants must submit a completed application form with a five page proposal.
Closing Date: March 30th, June 29th or October 30th.
Funding: Private.
Contributor: Foundation funds.
No. of awards given last year: 19.
No. of applicants last year: 40.
Additional Information: Candidates may apply for research in the imprint, manuscript, pictorial and artefact collections of the Hagley Museum and Library. In addition the resources of the 125 libraries in the greater Philadelphia area will be at the disposal of the visiting scholar. The Research Fellowship is to be used only in the Hagley Library.

Hagley/Winterthur Arts and Industries Fellowship

Subjects: Business and economics, design, architecture, crafts, fine arts, technology and industrial history focusing on historical and cultural relationships between economic life and the arts.
Purpose: To support scholarly research at Hagley and Winterthur Libraries.
Eligibility: Open to advanced scholars, graduate students and independent researchers.
Level of Study: Doctorate, Postdoctorate, Professional development.
Type: Other.
Value: US$1,400 per month.
Length of Study: Up to three months.
Frequency: Annual.
Country of Study: United States of America.
No. of awards offered: Six.
Application Procedure: Applicants must submit a completed application form with a five page proposal and two recommendations.
Closing Date: December 1st.
Funding: Private.
Contributor: Foundation funds.
No. of awards given last year: Two.
No. of applicants last year: 14.
Additional Information: The scholar must travel to Delaware to use the collections at both the Hagley and Winterthur libraries.

Henry Belin du Pont Dissertation Fellowship in Business, Technology and Society

Subjects: Business and technology.
Purpose: To aid students whose research on important historical questions would benefit from the use of Hagley's research collections.
Eligibility: Open to graduate students or PhD candidates.
Level of Study: Graduate, Predoctorate.
Type: Fellowship.
Value: US$6,000, free housing, use of computer, email and internet access and an office.
Length of Study: Four months.
Frequency: Annual.
Study Establishment: The Center for the History of Business, Technology and Society at Hagley.
Country of Study: United States of America.
Application Procedure: Applicants must submit an application dossier including a dissertation prospectus, a statement concerning the relevance of Hagley's research collections to the project and at least two letters of recommendation. Writing samples are also welcome. Potential applicants are strongly encouraged to consult with Hagley staff prior to submitting their dossier.
Closing Date: November 15th.
Funding: Private.
Additional Information: Recipients are expected to have no other obligations during the term of the fellowship, to maintain continuous residence at Hagley for its duration and to participate in events organised by Hagley's Center for the History of Business, Technology and Society. Towards the end of the residency the recipient will make a presentation at Hagley based on research conducted during the Fellowship. Hagley should also receive a copy of the dissertation, as well as any publications aided by the Fellowship.

Henry Belin du Pont Fellowship

Subjects: Areas of study relevant to the Library's archival and artefact collections.
Purpose: To support access to and use of Hagley's research collections and to enable individual out-of-state scholars to pursue their own research and to participate in the interchange of ideas among the Center's scholars.
Eligibility: Open to applicants who have already completed their formal professional training. Consequently, degree candidates and persons seeking support for degree work are not eligible to apply. Applicants must not be residents of Delaware and preference will be given to those whose travel costs to Hagley will be higher. Research must be relevant to Hagley's collections.
Level of Study: Doctorate, Postdoctorate.
Type: Fellowship.
Value: US$1,500 stipend per month.
Length of Study: Two-six months.
Frequency: Annual.
Study Establishment: The Library.
Country of Study: United States of America.
No. of awards offered: Varies.
Application Procedure: Applicants must submit a completed application form with a five page proposal.
Closing Date: March 31st, June 30th or October 30th.
Funding: Private.
Contributor: Foundation funds.
No. of awards given last year: Three.
No. of applicants last year: 10.
Additional Information: Fellows must devote all their time to study and may not accept teaching assignments or undertake any other major activities during the tenure of their fellowships. At the end of their tenure, Fellows must submit a final report on their activities and accomplishments. As a centre for advanced study in the humanities, Hagley is a focal point of a community of scholars. Fellows are expected to participate in seminars which meet periodically, as well as attend colloquia, lectures, concerts, exhibits and other public programmes offered during their tenure. Research fellowships are to be used in the Hagley Library only, not as scholarships for college.

THE HAGUE ACADEMY OF INTERNATIONAL LAW

Peace Palace, Carnegieplein 2, The Hague, NL-2517 KJ, Netherlands
Tel: (31) 70 302 4154
Fax: (31) 70 302 4153
Email: hagueacademy@registration
www: http://www.hagueacademy.nl
Contact: The Secretariat

The Hague Academy of International Law's purpose is to gather together young international lawyers of a high standard from all parts of the world who will undertake original research work within the framework of the subject matter of the concerned year. The results of this research work may, if appropriate, be published collectively.

Hague Academy of International Law / Doctoral Scholarships

Subjects: International law.
Purpose: To aid individuals with the completion of their theses through the assistance of the Academy.
Eligibility: Open to doctoral candidates up to the age of 40 years from developing countries who reside in their home country and do not have access to scientific sources.
Level of Study: Doctorate.
Type: Scholarship.
Value: Please contact the Academy for details.
Length of Study: Two months from July 1st.
Frequency: Annual.
Study Establishment: The Hague Academy of International Law.
Country of Study: Netherlands.
No. of awards offered: Four.
Application Procedure: Applicants must submit their applications with a letter of recommendation from the professor under whose direction the thesis is being written. The thesis may be concerned with either private or public international law and the title should be mentioned.
Closing Date: March 1st.
Funding: Private.
Contributor: The Levi Lassen Foundation.
No. of awards given last year: Four.
No. of applicants last year: 30.

Hague Academy of International Law / Scholarships for Sessions of Courses

Subjects: International private or public law.
Purpose: To assist students with living expenses, including the registration fee, during summer courses.
Eligibility: Open to candidates aged 40 and below, who have not yet received an Academy scholarship. Applicants must have sufficient knowledge of English or French.
Level of Study: Doctorate.
Type: Scholarship.
Value: Applicants should contact the Academy for details. Scholars are exempt from registration fees and examination fees. Travelling expenses will not be refunded.
Length of Study: Three weeks.
Frequency: Annual.
Study Establishment: The Hague Academy of International Law.
Country of Study: Netherlands.
No. of awards offered: Varies.
Application Procedure: Applicants must apply personally by submitting a curriculum vitae, one photograph and a statement of evidence which the candidate considers to be of value in support of their application. Every application must be typed and accompanied by a recommendation from a professor of international law. Applicants should, if possible, attach copies of any scientific publications. As documents forwarded by applicants are not returned, university certificates or other documents must be submitted in the form of copies, duly verified by a competent authority. The teaching period for which the candidate wants to be registered should be stated clearly.
Closing Date: March 1st.

Funding: Private.
Contributor: Foundations, institutions and personalities.
No. of awards given last year: 121.
No. of applicants last year: 326.

THE HAMBIDGE CENTER

PO Box 339, Rabun Gap, GA 30568
United States of America
Tel: (1) 706 746 5718
Fax: (1) 706 746 9933
Email: center@hambidge.org
www: http://www.hambidge.org
Contact: Residency Director

The Hambidge Center's primary function is an artist residency programme with the following aims: to provide artists with time and space to pursue their work, to enhance their communities' art environment, provide public accessibility, and to protect and sustain the natural environment, land and endangered species. The Center is set in 600 acres of mountain and valley terrain with waterfalls and nature trails.

Hambidge Center Residency Program Scholarships

Subjects: Any field or discipline of creative work.
Purpose: To provide applicants with an environment for creative work in the arts and sciences.
Eligibility: Open to qualified applicants in all disciplines who can demonstrate seriousness, dedication and professionalism. International residents are welcome. The Fulton County Arts Council Fellowship is open to residents of Fulton County, Georgia only.
Level of Study: Unrestricted.
Type: Fellowship.
Length of Study: Two weeks to two months.
Frequency: Dependent on space available.
Study Establishment: The Hambidge Center.
Country of Study: United States of America.
Application Procedure: Applicants must submit an application form and a stamped addressed envelope to the centre marked for the attention of the Residency Program. The application form can be downloaded from the website. Applicants for the Fulton County Arts Council Fellowship should contact Fulton County Arts Council.
Closing Date: October 1st for residencies from March to August and May 1st for residencies from September to February.
Funding: Government, Private.
Additional Information: The scholarships that are offered by the Center are the Nellie Mae Rowe Fellowship, the Fulton County Arts Council Fellowship and teaching fellowships at public or independent schools.

For further information contact:

The Fulton County Arts Council, 121 Pryor Street South West, Atlanta, GA 30303, United States of America
Tel: (1) 404 730 5780

HAMILL FOUNDATION

1160 Dairy Ashford Suite 250, Houston, TX, TX 77079-3014, United States of America
Contact: The Trustees

French Foundation Fellowships

Subjects: Alzheimer's disease.
Purpose: To aid the development of young scientists with demonstrated promise for a research career in Alzheimer's disease.
Eligibility: Candidates who are more than six research years out from a PhD or residency are not ordinarily eligible.
Level of Study: Postdoctorate.
Type: Fellowship.
Value: US$35,000.
Length of Study: A maximum of two years.
Frequency: Annual.
Country of Study: Any country.

No. of awards offered: One.
Application Procedure: Applicants must complete an application form, available from the website.
Closing Date: November 1st.

HARRY FRANK GUGGENHEIM FOUNDATION (HFG)

527 Madison Avenue, New York, NY 10022-4301, United States of America
Tel: (1) 212 644 4907
Fax: (1) 212 644 5110
www: http://www.hfg.org
Contact: Administrative Assistant

The Harry Frank Guggenheim Foundation (HGF) sponsors scholarly research on problems of violence, aggression and dominance. The Foundation provides both research grants to established scholars and dissertation fellowships to graduate students during the dissertation writing year. The HFG review of research is published twice a year.

HFG Dissertation Fellowship

Subjects: Any discipline which includes the study of dominance, aggression and violence.
Purpose: To support a PhD candidate in the writing stage of a dissertation. Work must be relevant to HFG programme interests in the study of violence and aggression.
Eligibility: Open to PhD candidates of any nationality.
Level of Study: Doctorate.
Type: Fellowship.
Value: US$15,000.
Length of Study: One year.
Frequency: Annual.
Study Establishment: Any university.
Country of Study: Any country.
No. of awards offered: 10.
Application Procedure: Applicants must submit an application form, research proposal and letter from their adviser. Candidates should contact the Foundation for application materials.
Closing Date: February 1st.
No. of awards given last year: 10.
No. of applicants last year: 150.
Additional Information: It is mandatory that a final report is given to the Foundation. Recipients of dissertation fellowships must submit a copy of the dissertation, approved and accepted by the home university or college, within six months of the end of the award year. The award is only available in circumstances where all necessary research has been done and the dissertation will be complete within one year.

HFG Research Program

Subjects: The social, behavioural and biological sciences. Research which is related to the Foundation's programme will be considered regardless of the disciplines involved.
Purpose: To promote understanding of the human social condition through the study of the causes and consequences of dominance, aggression and violence.
Eligibility: Open to individuals or institutions in any country.
Level of Study: Postdoctorate, Postgraduate.
Type: Research grant.
Value: Up to US$35,000 per year. Applicants should contact the organisation for more details.
Length of Study: One year. Two or three year projects may be considered.
Frequency: Annual.
Country of Study: Any country.
No. of awards offered: 15-35 per year. Awards are based predominantly on merit.
Application Procedure: Applicants must submit an application form and research proposal along with a curriculum vitae and budget request. Application materials are available by contacting the Foundation.
Closing Date: August 1st.
No. of awards given last year: 46.

No. of applicants last year: 324.
Additional Information: The Foundation operates a programme of specific and innovative study and research. Proposals should be for a specific project and should describe well defined aims and methods, not general institutional support. Grants will be considered for salaries, employee benefits, research assistantships, computer time, supplies and equipment, field work, reasonable secretarial and technical help and other items necessary to the successful completion of a project. The Foundation cannot supply funds for overhead costs of institutions, travel to professional meetings, publication subsidies, self education or elaborate fixed equipment.

THE HARRY S TRUMAN LIBRARY INSTITUTE

500 West US Highway 24, Independence, MO 64050-1798, United States of America
Tel: (1) 816 833 0425
Fax: (1) 816 833 2715
Email: library@truman.nara.gov
www: http://www.trumanlibrary.org
Contact: Grants Administrator

The Harry S Truman Library Institute is a non-profit partner of the Harry S Truman Library.

Harry S Truman Library Institute Dissertation Year Fellowships

Subjects: The public career of Harry S Truman and the history of the Truman administration.
Purpose: To encourage historical scholarship in the Truman era.
Eligibility: Open to graduates who have completed their dissertation research and are ready to begin writing. Dissertations must be on some aspect of the life and career of Harry S Truman or of the public and policy issues which were prominent during the Truman years.
Level of Study: Graduate, Postgraduate.
Type: Fellowship.
Value: US$16,000, payable in two instalments.
Length of Study: One year.
Frequency: Annual.
Country of Study: United States of America.
No. of awards offered: One-two.
Application Procedure: Application forms are available from the website.
Closing Date: February 1st for notification in April.
Funding: Private.
Additional Information: Recipients will not be required to come to the Truman Library but will be expected to furnish the Library with a copy of their dissertation.

Harry S Truman Library Institute Research Grants

Subjects: The public career of Harry S Truman and the history of the Truman administration.
Purpose: To enable scholars to come to the library to use its archival facilities.
Eligibility: Open to graduate students and postdoctoral scholars who are working on a project pertaining to Truman's public career or to some facet of his administration.
Level of Study: Doctorate, Graduate, Postdoctorate, Postgraduate, Research.
Type: Research grant.
Value: Up to US$2,500, to cover round trip air fare between the applicant's home and Independence, and a modest sum to cover living expenses while working at the Library.
Length of Study: One-three weeks.
Frequency: Twice a year.
Study Establishment: The Library.
Country of Study: United States of America.
No. of awards offered: Varies.
Application Procedure: Application forms are available from the website.
Closing Date: April 1st or October 1st.
Funding: Private.

Harry S Truman Library Institute Scholar's Award

Subjects: An aspect of the life and career of Harry S Truman or of the public and foreign policy issues which were prominent during the Truman years.

Purpose: To free a scholar from teaching or other employment for a substantial period of time for the purpose of writing a book length manuscript.

Eligibility: Open to established scholars and scholars about to embark on their careers.

Level of Study: Postdoctorate.

Type: Award.

Value: Up to US$30,000.

Frequency: Every two years if funds are available.

Country of Study: United States of America.

No. of awards offered: One.

Application Procedure: Applicants must write for details.

Closing Date: December 15th.

Funding: Private.

Additional Information: The research should result in a book length manuscript intended for publication. One copy of the publication resulting from work done under the award is to be provided by the author to the Library.

THE HARRY S TRUMAN LIBRARY INSTITUTE

500 West US Hwy 24 Independence, MO 64050-1798, United States of America
Tel: (1) 816 833 0425
Fax: (1) 816 833 2715
Email: library@truman.nara.gov
www: http://www.trumanlibrary.org
Contact: Grants administrator

Dissertation Year Fellowships

Subjects: The public career of Harry S Truman and the history of the Truman administration.

Purpose: To encourage historical scholarship in the Truman era.

Eligibility: Open to individuals who have completed their disserration research and are ready to begin writing.

Level of Study: Postgraduate.

Type: Fellowship.

Value: US$16,000 payable in two installments.

Frequency: Annual.

Country of Study: United States of America.

No. of awards offered: One or Two.

Application Procedure: Please write for an application form.

Closing Date: February 1st for notification in April.

Funding: Private.

Additional Information: Recipients will not be required to come to the Truman Library but will be expected to furnish the Library with a copy of their dissertation.

Research Grants

Subjects: The career of Harry S Truman and the history of the Truman administration.

Purpose: To enable graduate students and postdoctoral scholars to come to the library for one to three weeks to use its archival facilities.

Eligibility: Open to graduate and postdoctoal scholars who are working on a project pertaining to Truman's public career or to some facet of his administration.

Level of Study: Doctorate, Graduate, MBA, Postdoctorate, Postgraduate, Predoctorate.

Type: Research grant.

Value: Up to US$2,500, to cover round-trip air fare between the applicant's home and a modest sum to cover living expenses while working at the Library.

Length of Study: One-three weeks.

Study Establishment: The Library.

Country of Study: United States of America.

No. of awards offered: Varies.

Application Procedure: Please write for details.

Closing Date: April 1st, October 1st.

Funding: Private.

Scholar's Award

Subjects: The public career of Harry S Truman or some aspect of the history of the Truman administration or the United States of America during that administration.

Eligibility: Open to established scholars and scholars about to embark on their careers.

Level of Study: Postgraduate.

Value: Based primarily on a proposed budget submitted by the applicant and may amount to as much as one-half the applicant's academic year salary.

Frequency: Every two years.

Study Establishment: Recipients will be expected to spend a major portion of their research time utilizing the resources of the Truman Library.

Country of Study: United States of America.

No. of awards offered: One.

Application Procedure: Please write for details.

Closing Date: December 15th.

Funding: Private.

Additional Information: The research should result in a book-length manuscript intended for publication, one copy of the publication resulting from work done under the award is to be provided by the author to the library.

HARRY S TRUMAN SCHOLARSHIP FOUNDATION

712 Jackson Place North West, Washington, DC 20006, United States of America
Tel: (1) 202 395 4831
Fax: (1) 202 395 6995
Email: staff@truman.gov
www: http://www.truman.gov
Contact: Administrative Assistant

The Harry S Truman Scholarship Foundation was established by Congress in 1975 as the official federal memorial to honour the 33rd President of the United States of America. The Foundation recognises President Truman's contributions to the nation, his commitment to public service and his interest in education.

Harry S Truman Scholarship Foundation Scholarships

Subjects: Public service. The Foundation defines this as employment in the following: government at any level, uniformed services, public interest organisations, non-governmental research or educational organisations, and public service oriented non-profit organisations such as those whose primary purposes are to help needy or disadvantaged persons or to protect the environment. A wide variety of fields of study can lead to public service careers, for example, agriculture, biology, engineering, environmental management, physical and social sciences, as well as traditional fields such as economics, education, government, history, international relations, law, political science, public administration, public health and public policy.

Purpose: To reward outstanding students who intend to pursue careers in public service.

Eligibility: Open to United States citizens or, in the case of nominees from American Samoa or the Commonwealth of the Northern Mariana Islands, United States nationals. Candidates should be at college or university pursuing a Bachelor's degree as full-time students. Applicants must have a college grade point average of at least B or equivalent and be in the upper fourth of their class.

Level of Study: Graduate.

Type: Scholarship.

Value: Up to US$30,000.

Frequency: Annual.

Country of Study: United States of America. Some programmes abroad are upon approval of the Executive Secretary.

No. of awards offered: 75-85.

Application Procedure: Applicants must be nominated by a faculty representative at their Institute of Higher Education. The Foundation neither solicits nor accepts direct candidate applications. Junior means a student who has one more year of full-time study to complete the requirements for a Baccalaureate degree.
Closing Date: January 29th.
Funding: Government.

HARVARD UNIVERSITY

Weatherhead Center for International Affairs, 1737 Cambridge Street, Cambridge, MA 02138, United States of America
Tel: (1) 617 495 3671
Fax: (1) 617 495 8292
Email: college@fas.harvard.edu
www: http://www.harvard.edu
Contact: CFIA Fellowship Office

Harvard University, which celebrated its 350th anniversary in 1986, is the oldest Institute of Higher Education in the United States. Founded 16 years after the arrival of the pilgrims at Plymouth, the university has grown from nine students with a single master to an enrolment of more than 18,000 degree candidates, including undergraduates and students in 10 graduate and professional schools.

Harvard Academy Program for International and Area Studies Predoctoral and Postdoctoral Fellowships

Subjects: Area studies, especially those areas of the world that require the use of difficult languages, or conversely, assisting area specialists in developing expertise in an established discipline.
Purpose: To identify young scholars at the start of their careers whose work combines disciplinary excellence in the social sciences with an in-depth grounding in particular countries or regions outside the United States or Canada.
Eligibility: Open to postdoctoral scholars and predoctoral candidates who have completed all course work and general examinations by the beginning of the year for which they seek support.
Level of Study: Doctorate, Postdoctorate, Predoctorate.
Type: Fellowship.
Value: Predoctoral awards are US$24,000, plus university facilities. Postdoctoral awards are US$34,000, plus health insurance.
Length of Study: Two years.
Frequency: Annual.
Study Establishment: The Weatherhead Center for International Affairs (WCFIA), Harvard University.
Country of Study: United States of America.
No. of awards offered: Varies, four to six for two year appointments.
Application Procedure: Applicants must contact Jeana Flahive at the Weatherhead Center for more information on (1) 617 495 2137 or email: jflahive@wcfia.harvard.edu.
Closing Date: October 15th, but please contact the organisation for confirmation.
Funding: Private.

Harvard University Graduate Student Associate Program

Subjects: Anthropology, economics, government, history, East Asian history and languages, law, Middle Eastern studies, public policy, sociology, population and international health, inner Asian and Altaic studies.
Purpose: To provide a supportive and stimulating environment in which outstanding graduate students can interact with one another as well as with faculty and fellows of the Center, as they complete their dissertations and begin the transition to a career.
Eligibility: Open to students in a PhD programme or similarly advanced degree programme at any of Harvard's academic departments or professional schools. Students who are accepted will have finished their coursework, completed general exams and have a focus relating to the core interests of the Weatherhead Center. Preference is then

given to those applicants whose work is related to current research projects at the Center.
Level of Study: Doctorate, Predoctorate.
Type: Other.
Value: Graduate student associates receive research grants of US$500-2,000 and are provided with office space equipped with computers and printers.
Length of Study: Two years.
Frequency: Annual.
Study Establishment: The Weatherhead Center for International Affairs (WCFIA), Harvard University.
Country of Study: United States of America.
No. of awards offered: 4-6.
Application Procedure: Applicants should contact Clare Putnam at the Weatherhead Center for more information on (1) 617 495 9899, or email: cputnam@wcfia.harvard.edu.
Closing Date: March 1st, but please contact the university for confirmation.
Funding: Private.
Additional Information: Selected GSAs are expected to participate in the programme's seminars and activities, including support of undergraduate associates of the Center. GSAs may renew their affiliation for up to three years. The interests of the Weatherhead Center are broadly defined to encompass research on international, transnational and comparative topics, both contemporary and historical, including rigorous policy analysis as well as the study of countries and regions other than the United States.

John M Olin Institute for Strategic Studies Predoctoral and Postdoctoral Fellowships in National Security

Subjects: The causes and conduct of war, military strategy and history, defence policy and institutions, economic security, defence economics and the defence industrial base.
Purpose: To support young scholars conducting basic research in the broad area of security and strategic affairs, including the economics of these issues.
Eligibility: Open to postdoctoral scholars and predoctoral candidates who have completed all course work and general examinations by the beginning of the year for which they seek support.
Level of Study: Doctorate, Postdoctorate.
Type: Fellowship.
Value: Predoctoral awards are up to US$20,000 plus university facilities, fees and health insurance. Postdoctoral awards are up to US$35,000 plus health insurance.
Frequency: Annual.
Study Establishment: The Weatherhead Center for International Affairs (WCFIA), Harvard University.
Country of Study: United States of America.
No. of awards offered: Up to 10 but may vary.
Application Procedure: Applicants must contact Ann Townes at the Weatherhead Center for more information on (1) 617 496 5495, or email: atownes@wcfia.harvard.edu.
Closing Date: January 15th, but please contact the organisation for confirmation.
Funding: Private.

Justice, Welfare and Economics Dissertation Fellowships

Subjects: Research on the connections between freedom, justice, economics, human welfare and development.
Purpose: To enable students to disengage from teaching for a year in order to develop or complete their dissertations.
Eligibility: Recipients must be in residence at Harvard and may not accept any other grants or teaching fellowships during the tenure of fellowship.
Level of Study: Predoctorate.
Type: Fellowship.
Value: US$20,000 which may increase to cover facilities, fees or tuition if the student's school or Department will not do so.
Length of Study: One year.
Frequency: Annual.
Study Establishment: Harvard University.
Country of Study: United States of America.
No. of awards offered: Varies.

Application Procedure: Contact Clare Putnam at the Weatherhead Center for more information or application guidelines. Telephone: (1) 617 495 9899; e-mail: cputnam@wcfia.harvard.edu.
Closing Date: Early March in year of study.
Funding: Private.

Program on US-Japan Relations Advanced Research Fellowships

Subjects: Issues or problems in contemporary United States Japanese relations, Japan's international relations and other studies of Japan that contribute to an understanding of Japan's international behaviour.
Purpose: To support the work of scholars engaged in the study of contemporary Japan and/or the relations between the United States of America and Japan.
Eligibility: Preference is given to non Japanese citizens, but others, especially from Pacific Rim countries, may apply. Applicants must hold a doctoral or other terminal degree in a discipline bearing on the study of contemporary United States of America and Japanese relations, other aspects of Japan's foreign relations, or domestic Japanese politics and policy. Applicants must demonstrate significant scholarly achievement or potential.
Level of Study: Postdoctorate.
Type: Fellowship.
Value: Up to US$40,000 plus health insurance and shared office space.
Frequency: Annual.
Study Establishment: The Weatherhead Center for International Affairs (WCFIA), Harvard University.
Country of Study: United States of America.
No. of awards offered: Two or three.
Application Procedure: Applicants must contact Frank Schwartz at the Weatherhead Center for more information on (1) 617 495 1890, or email: fschwart@wcfia.harvard.edu. Applications can also be downloaded from http://data.fas.harvard.edu/cfia/us-japan/pdapplication.htm.
Closing Date: March 1st, but please contact the organisation for confirmation.
Funding: Private.

Sidney R Knafel Dissertation Completion Grant

Subjects: The core interests of the Weatherhead Center. These interests are broadly defined as research on international, transnational and comparative topics (both contemporary and historical) including rigorous policy analysis as well as the study of countries and regions other than the United States.
Purpose: To aid a Harvard doctoral candidate who is completing a dissertation related to the core research interests of the Centre.
Eligibility: Applicants must be PhD candidates currently enrolled at Harvard University (or doctoral degree candidates from other Harvard faculties) and likely to complete their degree by the end of the academic year for which the fellowship is awarded. The recipient may not accept any other grants or teaching fellowships during the tenure of this fellowship.
Level of Study: Doctorate, Predoctorate.
Type: Fellowship.
Value: A stipend of US$20,000 plus facilities fees and individual health insurance. Office space and access to computer facilities at the Weatherhead Center will also be provided.
Length of Study: One year.
Frequency: Annual.
Study Establishment: The Weatherhead Center for International Affairs (WCFIA), Harvard University.
Country of Study: United States of America.
Application Procedure: Applicants must contact Clare Putnam at the Weatherhead Center for more information on (1) 617 495 9899, or email: cputnam@wcfia.harvard.edu.
Closing Date: February 28th, but please contact the organisation for confirmation.
Funding: Private.
Additional Information: Named after Sidney R Knafel who served as chairman of the Centre's Visiting Committee from 1991-2000.

Thyssen Postdoctoral Fellowship

Subjects: Transnational security issues.
Purpose: To assist young German scholars and to form an interdisciplinary group studying transnational security issues.
Eligibility: Applicants must be German nationals. Fellowships are offered for research conducted while in residence at the Weatherhead Center for International Affairs, Harvard University.
Level of Study: Postdoctorate.
Type: Fellowship.
Value: US$40,000 plus health insurance plus shared office space.
Frequency: Annual.
Country of Study: United States of America.
No. of awards offered: One.
Application Procedure: Applicants must contact Clare Putnam at the Weatherhead Center for more information on (1) 617 495 9899, or email: cputnam@wcfia.harvard.edu.
Closing Date: February 18th, but please contact the organisation for confirmation.
Funding: Private.

Weatherhead Center Predissertation Grants

Subjects: The core interests of the Weatherhead Center. These interests are broadly defined as research on international, transnational and comparative topics (both contemporary and historical) including rigorous policy analysis as well as the study of countries and regions other than the United States.
Purpose: To aid graduate students who have passed preliminary exams and who are exploring or beginning research on a project related to the core research interests of the Center.
Eligibility: Applicants must be currently enrolled at Harvard University and of predoctoral, or similarly advanced, degree status who will have finished their preliminary exams.
Level of Study: Predoctorate.
Type: Grant.
Value: Approx. US$3,000.
Frequency: Annual.
Study Establishment: The Weatherhead Center for International Affairs (WCFIA), Harvard University.
Country of Study: United States of America.
No. of awards offered: Up to seven.
Application Procedure: Applicants must contact Clare Putnam at the Weatherhead Center for more information on (1) 617 495 9899, or email: cputnam@wcfia.harvard.edu.
Closing Date: March. Please contact the organisation for confirmation.
Funding: Private.

Weatherhead Grants for Graduate Student Conferences

Subjects: International politics.
Purpose: To offer financial resources for graduate student conferences at Harvard that address topics relating to international affairs.
Eligibility: Open to graduates who need funds to support conferences related to international affairs that directly benefit graduate students. Preference will be given to conferences that have not been previously funded.
Level of Study: Graduate.
Type: Grant.
Value: Up to US$1,000.
Frequency: Twice a year.
Study Establishment: Harvard University.
Country of Study: United States of America.
Application Procedure: Applicants must contact Clare Putnam at the Weatherhead Center for more information on (1) 617 495 9899, or email: cputnam@wcfia.harvard.edu.
Closing Date: Mid October and mid-February.
Funding: Private.

Weatherhead Grants for Independent Scholars

Subjects: Variable subjects relating to international affairs.
Purpose: To offer undergraduates at the University financial resources to organise programs on their own that address their interests relating to international affairs and directly benefit the Harvard undergraduate community.

Eligibility: Undergraduate organisations and student groups that need funds to support activities related to international affairs that directly benefit the undergraduate community may apply.
Type: Grant.
Value: Grants up to a maximum of US$1,000 are available.
Frequency: Annual.
Study Establishment: Harvard University.
Country of Study: United States of America.
No. of awards offered: Variable.
Application Procedure: Contact Clare Putnam at the Weatherhead Centre for more informaiton or an application. Telephone: (1) 617 495 9899; e-mail: cputnam@wcfia.harvard.edu.
Closing Date: Mid-October and mid-February of relevant academic year.
Funding: Private.

HARVARD UNIVERSITY, CENTER FOR THE STUDY OF WORLD RELIGIONS

42 Francis Avenue, Cambridge, MA 02138
United States of America
Tel: (1) 617 496 5834
Fax: (1) 617 496 5411
Email: brooke_palmer@harvard.edu
www: http://www.hds.harvard.edu/cswr
Contact: Co-ordinator of Educative Planning

Harvard University, Center for the Study of World Religions fosters excellence in the study of religions of the world. Two characteristics mark the Center, the first being the international scope of its subject matter and constituency, and the second is the encouragement of multiple disciplinary approaches towards the study of religion. The Center offers no scheduled courses of instruction but rather is distinguished by the quality of scholars in residence, senior Fellows and others, affiliated faculty, and visiting lecturers.

Harvard University, Center for the Study of World Religions, Senior Fellowship

Subjects: Religious studies including the historical and comparative study of religions.
Purpose: To provide individual scholars from many nations with time for investigation and access to the resources of Harvard University. It also facilitates the exchange of ideas growing out of such research.
Eligibility: Open to postdoctoral scholars who, in their research projects, utilise multiple disciplinary approaches toward the study of religion, whether from the point of view of arts, medicine, law, music, economics or cosmological sciences.
Level of Study: Postdoctorate.
Type: Fellowship.
Value: Senior Fellowships include admission to the Director's Seminar, University library access, a US$4,000 stipend per academic year and the option of residence at the Center. In recognition of the Center's 40th Anniversary, up to four awards will be designated as 40th Anniversary Fellowships. Stipend awards for the 40th Anniversary Fellowships will range from US$25,000-50,000 per academic year, and also include a research assistant allowance of US$1,000, a relocation allowance of US$1,500, use of a shared office at the Center, and the option of residence at the Center.
Length of Study: One academic year.
Frequency: Annual.
Study Establishment: Harvard University Center for the Study of World Religions, in Cambridge Massachusetts.
Country of Study: United States of America.
No. of awards offered: Varies.
Application Procedure: Applicants must complete an application form, arrange for two letters of recommendation, the form for which is available on the website, and provide a research proposal and curriculum vitae.
Closing Date: January 15th.
Funding: Private.

THE HASTINGS CENTER

21 Malcolm Gordon Road, Garrison, NY 10524, United States of America
Tel: (1) 845 424 4040
Fax: (1) 845 424 4545
Email: visitors@thehastingscenter.org
www: http://www.thehastingscenter.org
Contact: Ms Lori P Knowles, Executive Vice President

The Hastings Center is an independent, non-profit research and educational institute that studies ethical, social and legal issues in medicine, the life sciences, health policy and environment policy.

Hastings Center International Visiting Scholars Program

Subjects: Ethical, legal and policy issues in medicine, the life sciences and the professions.
Purpose: To enable international visiting scholars to spend time at the Center for advanced study and research.
Eligibility: Open to international scholars.
Level of Study: Doctorate, Postdoctorate, Predoctorate.
Type: Grant.
Value: Some financial aid is available based on need.
Length of Study: Usually four-six weeks.
Frequency: Annual.
Study Establishment: The Hastings Center.
Country of Study: United States of America.
No. of awards offered: Varies.
Application Procedure: Applicants must visit the website for applications. A detailed description of a research topic and work plan is also required as well as a copy of a recent writing sample, a curriculum vitae and the names and addresses of two referees.
Closing Date: Applications are accepted at any time, but should be submitted at least three months prior to the proposed stay.
No. of awards given last year: 13.
No. of applicants last year: 15.
Additional Information: Participation in the ongoing activities of the Center such as conferences, seminars and workshops is encouraged.

HATTORI FOUNDATION

72E Leopold Road, London, SW19 7JQ, England
Tel: (44) 20 8944 5319
Fax: (44) 20 8946 6970
Email: admin@hattorifoundation.org.uk
www: http://www.hattorifoundation.org.uk
Contact: Ms Sarah C Hallan, Administrator

The chief aim of the Hattori Foundation is to encourage and assist exceptionally talented young instrumental soloists or chamber ensembles who are British nationals or resident in the United Kingdom, and whose talent and achievement give promise of an international career.

Hattori Foundation Awards

Subjects: Instrumental, solo performance and ensembles.
Purpose: To assist young instrumentalists of exceptional talent in establishing a solo or chamber music career at international level.
Eligibility: Open to British or foreign nationals aged 21-27 years studying full-time in the United Kingdom. Foreign applicants must have won a major prize in an international competition or won a national competition. Candidates should be of postgraduate performance level.
Level of Study: Postgraduate, Professional development.
Type: Award.
Value: No pre-determined amounts. The grant is based on the requirements of the approved project.
Length of Study: Varies.
Frequency: Annual.
Country of Study: British Nationals can study in any country. Foreign nationals must be resident in the United Kingdom only.

No. of awards offered: Up to 20.
Application Procedure: Applicants must submit a completed application form with reference forms and a 30 minute performance (recital) on cassette tape or compact disc.
Closing Date: April 30th.
Funding: Private.
Contributor: Hattori family.
No. of awards given last year: 14.
No. of applicants last year: 59.
Additional Information: Grants may be made for study, concert experience and international competitions but course fees and the purchase of instruments are not funded. Projects must be submitted for approval and discussion with the Director of Music and the trustees. Auditions take place in June and are in two stages.

HAYSTACK MOUNTAIN SCHOOL OF CRAFTS

PO Box 518, Deer Isle, ME 04627
United States of America
Tel: (1) 207 348 2306
Fax: (1) 207 348 2307
Email: haystack@haystack-mtn.org
www: http://www.haystack-mtn.org
Contact: Ms Jacqueline Michaud, Development Director

The Haystack Mountain School of Crafts studio programme in the arts offers two and three week workshops in a variety of craft and visual mediums including clay, wood, glass, metals, fibres and graphics.

Haystack Scholarship

Subjects: Instruction in fine crafts.
Purpose: To allow craftspeople of all skill levels to study at Haystack sessions for two or three week periods. Technical Assistant and work study positions as well as minority scholarships and fellowships are awarded.
Eligibility: Open to nationals of any country, who are 18 or older.
Level of Study: Unrestricted.
Type: Other.
Value: US$600-1,200.
Length of Study: Two week and three week sessions.
Frequency: Annual.
Country of Study: Any country.
No. of awards offered: 100.
Application Procedure: Applicants must include references and supporting materials in their application.
Closing Date: March 25th.
Funding: Private.
No. of awards given last year: 100.
No. of applicants last year: 300.

HEALTH RESEARCH BOARD (HRB)

73 Lower Baggot Street, Dublin, Ireland
Tel: (353) 1 676 1176
Fax: (353) 1 661 1856
Email: hrb@hrb.ie
www: http://www.hrb.ie
Contact: Research Grants Manager

The Health Research Board (HRB) is comprised of 16 members appointed by the Minister of Health, with eight of the members being nominated on the co-joint nomination of the universities and colleges. The main functions of the HRB are to promote or commission health research, to promote and conduct epidemiological research as may be appropriate at national level, to promote or commission health services research, to liase and co-operate with other research bodies in Ireland and overseas in the promotion of relevant research, and to undertake such other cognate functions as the Minister may from time to time determine.

Clinical Research Training Fellowship in Nursing and Midwifery

Subjects: Nursing and Midwifery.
Purpose: The purpose of Fellowships is to provide experienced nurses and midwives with an opportunity to carry out research in clinical nursing or midwifery, leading to a postgraduate degree at masters or doctoral level. These fellowships will provide nurses with the research experience necessary to develop their expertise as specialists in their chosen field of nursing or midwifery.
Eligibility: To be eligible for a fellowship a candidate must: be registered as a nurse or midwife; have practised professional nursing or midwifery for atleast five years; hold a post in nursing or midwifery practice or a post related to nursing or midwifery; have been employed in the Irish health services, or an Irish academic Department of Nursing and/or Midwifery, within two years prior to the closing date for application to the Fellowship; Can Confirm support approval from Head of Department in which the research study is being carried out and provide evidence of academic supervision from a suitably qualified nurse or a midwife.
Level of Study: Graduate, Postgraduate.
Type: Fellowship.
Length of Study: Up to three years.
Frequency: Annual.
Study Establishment: Fellowships are tenable by nurses or midwives employed in a recognised health service or an Irish academic Department of Nursing and/or Midwifery and registered with an academic Department of Nursing and/or Midwifery or other relevant academic department.
Country of Study: Ireland.
Application Procedure: Application form available on our website, www.hrb.ie.
Funding: Government.

Equipment Grants

Subjects: Medical sciences.
Purpose: To facilitate the purchase of medium sized items of equipment aimed at improving the quality or broadening the scope of a scientific research investigation being undertaken at an Irish academic institution in the biomedical sciences.
Eligibility: Applicants should hold a full-time academic post in an Irish university or college and be actively engaged in biomedical research in Ireland.
Level of Study: Postdoctorate, Research.
Value: Awards will be in the range UK£50,000 to UK£250,000 per piece or equipment. A contribution towards essential running and maintenance costs may be allowed in the first 3 months.
Frequency: Dependent on funds available.
Country of Study: Ireland.
No. of awards offered: Varies, depending on the quality of the applications received and the amount of funding made available from the Department of Health.
Application Procedure: Applications for equipment that is essential for the conduct of biomedical research may be made and applications will be assessed on the basis of the research case presented. Please write for further details.
Closing Date: October 10th.
Funding: Government.
Additional Information: Applications reflecting interdepartmental collaboration are particularly welcome.

For further information contact:

www.hrb.ie,

Health Research Board PhD training sites

Subjects: Medical, epidemiological, health and health services research biomedical research teams of at least 4 researchers are invited to devise a 4 year programme including structured training and rotation between labs.
Purpose: To enhance the training of post-graduates in the health-related sciences.
Eligibility: Teams of at least 4 scientists.
Level of Study: Predoctorate.
Value: Up to UK£1 million.

Length of Study: 4 Years.
Frequency: Depending on feedback.
Study Establishment: Any academic institution.
Country of Study: Ireland.
No. of awards offered: Pilot scheme 2 awards in 2004.
Application Procedure: Applicants must complete an online application form.
Closing Date: Consult the HRB website.
Funding: Government.

Health Services Research Fellowships

Subjects: Clinical, epidemiological, public health, statistics, health economics, social science, operational and management disciplines.
Purpose: To enable graduates with some appropriate relevant experience to pursue a career in health devices and research in Ireland.
Eligibility: Candidates must normally hold a primary degree in a discipline relevant to health services research, have acquired appropriate postgraduate experience in the field of health services and research, have support from an approved academic department or centre, have obtained the prior approval of a head of department for the research study being proposed, be Irish citizens or graduates from overseas with a permanent Irish resident status.
Level of Study: Graduate.
Type: Fellowship.
Value: Please consult the organisation.
Length of Study: Normally the maximum period of the award will be three years, with renewal being subject to appropriate annual review.
Frequency: Annual.
Study Establishment: Institutions approved by the Board, such as teaching hospitals, universities, research institutes and health boards in Ireland.
Country of Study: Ireland.
No. of awards offered: Varies.
Application Procedure: Applicants must complete an application form, available from the website.
Funding: Government.

For further information contact:

Online at www.hrb.ie,

HRB Clinical Research Training Fellowships

Subjects: Biomedicine.
Purpose: To enable medical and dental graduates at any stage in their career to gain specialised research training in the biomedical field in Ireland.
Eligibility: Candidates should be graduates in medicine or dentistry from post registration up to and including senior registrar or equivalent academic level.
Level of Study: Graduate, Postdoctorate, Postgraduate.
Value: Please consult the organisation.
Length of Study: Normally two years.
Frequency: Annual.
Study Establishment: At an appropriate academic department in the Republic of Ireland.
Country of Study: Ireland.
No. of awards offered: Varies.
Application Procedure: Applicants must apply with the support of the head of an appropriate sponsoring laboratory in the Republic of Ireland. Candidates may apply to remain in their current laboratory, to return to one where they have worked before, or move to a new laboratory. Applicants must write to the Research Grants Section at the Health Research Board for more information.
Funding: Government.
Additional Information: Proposals may be submitted for specialised research training or for training in a basic subject relevant to a particular clinical interest.

HRB Postdoctoral Research Fellowships

Subjects: Bench-based health sciences.
Eligibility: Applicants must be postdoctorates with less than five years of postdoctoral experience.

Level of Study: Postdoctorate.
Type: Fellowship.
Value: Please consult the organisation.
Length of Study: Up to three years.
Frequency: Annual.
Study Establishment: A university, research hospital or institute.
Country of Study: Ireland.
No. of awards offered: Varies.
Application Procedure: Applicants must complete an online application form, available from the website.
Funding: Government.

HRB Project Grants-General

Subjects: Biomedical sciences, public health and epidemiology, health services research or health research.
Purpose: To facilitate research in biomedical sciences, public health, epidemiology and health service research.
Eligibility: The principal must hold a full-time academic post in an Irish academic institution and his or her speciality should be within the range of disciplines stated in the subject index. Applicants must reside in the Republic of Ireland and grants are tenable in this country
Value: Please consult the organisation.
Length of Study: Up to 3 years.
Frequency: Annual.
Study Establishment: An Irish academic institution.
Country of Study: Ireland.
No. of awards offered: Varies.
Application Procedure: Applicants must complete an online application form, available from the website.
Funding: Government.

HRB Research Project Grants North-South Co-operation

Subjects: Biomedical sciences, public health and epidemiology, health services research or health research.
Purpose: To stimulate co-operation between research investigators in the Republic of Ireland and in Northern Ireland by making grant support available for joint health research projects of a high quality.
Eligibility: Applicants should hold a full-time academic post in an Irish university or college and be actively engaged in medical, epidemiological, health service or health research in Ireland. Irish applicants must have a co-applicant from Northern Ireland, who will be funded by the R&D office in Belfast.
Level of Study: Research.
Value: Please consult the organisation.
Length of Study: One-three years.
Frequency: Annual.
Study Establishment: Recognised academic institutions and health service centres.
Country of Study: Ireland.
No. of awards offered: Varies.
Application Procedure: Applicants must complete an online application form, available from the website.
Funding: Government.

HRB Summer Student Grants

Subjects: Medical, dental science, health service and science.
Purpose: To develop interest in research and give the student the opportunity to become familiar with research techniques.
Eligibility: Open to students from medical, dental science or health service related disciplines.
Level of Study: Graduate.
Type: Grant.
Value: Please consult the organisation.
Length of Study: Eight weeks.
Frequency: Annual.
Study Establishment: A university, research hospital or institution.
Country of Study: Ireland.
No. of awards offered: Varies.
Application Procedure: Applicants must obtain an application form, available by writing or from the website.
Funding: Government.

HEART UK

c/o Wheldon Events & Conferences, 27 Honiton Way, Aldridge, West Midlands, WS9 0JS, England
Tel: (44) 1922 457984
Fax: (44) 1922 455238
Email: natashadougall@wheldonevents.freeserve.com
www: http://www.heartuk.org.uk
Contact: Ms Natasha Dougall, Meetings Organiser

Heart UK aims to foster scientific research and good clinical practice related to the management of hyperlipidaemia in the UK. The organisation also works to promote screening for families with hypercholesterolaemia (FH) who risk premature death from coronary heart disease (CHD). They also promote the study of the causes, diagnosis and treatment of lipid disorders and associated metabolic diseases.

Sue McCarthy Travelling Scholarship

Subjects: Medical sciences.
Purpose: To support the transfer of expertise and/or patient samples between international laboratories.
Eligibility: Open to medical and scientific professionals.
Level of Study: Unrestricted.
Type: Scholarship.
Value: UK£1,500.
Frequency: Annual.
Study Establishment: A university, hospital or research institution.
Country of Study: United Kingdom.
No. of awards offered: One.
Application Procedure: Applicants must request an application form from Heart UK.
Closing Date: The end of March.
Funding: Private.
No. of awards given last year: One.
No. of applicants last year: 11.

HEBREW IMMIGRANT AID SOCIETY (HIAS)

333 Seventh Avenue, New York, NY 10001, United States of America
Tel: (1) 212 613 1358
Fax: (1) 212 967-4356
Email: scholarship@hias.org
www: http://www.hias.org
Contact: Scholarship Co-ordinator

The Hebrew Immigrant Aid Society (HIAS) is the America's oldest international and refugee resettlement agency dedicated to assisting persecuted and opressed people worldwide and delivering them to safe havens, HIAS has helped more than 4.5 million people in the 122 years of its existence.

HIAS Scholarship Awards Competition

Subjects: All subjects.
Purpose: To help HIAS-assisted refugees and asylees in pursuing higher education.
Eligibility: Open to HIAS assisted refugees and asylees in the United States and Israel. US applicants must have completed one year ie. two semesters at a United States of America college or graduate school.
Level of Study: Doctorate, Graduate, MBA, Postdoctorate, Postgraduate, Predoctorate, Professional development, Research.
Type: Scholarship.
Value: Average US$1,500.
Length of Study: One year must be completed prior and must be poised to start another academic year.
Frequency: Annual.
Country of Study: United States of America.
No. of awards offered: Varies. Approximately 100.
Application Procedure: Applicants must complete an official application. Application must be completed online. Application forms are available from mid December each year.

Closing Date: March 15th.
Funding: Private.
No. of awards given last year: 84 U.S., 62 Israel. 146 total.
No. of applicants last year: 800.
Additional Information: Applications are judged on financial need, academic scholarship and community service.

For further information contact:

www: http://www.hias.org

HEED OPHTHALMIC FOUNDATION

Cleveland Clinic Foundation, Desk I-329500 Euclid Avenue, Cleveland, OH 44195, United States of America
Tel: (1) 216 445 8145
Fax: (1) 216 444 8968
Contact: Executive Secretary

Heed Fellowship Stipend

Subjects: Diseases and surgery of the eye or research in ophthalmology.
Purpose: To provide assistance to men and women who desire to further their education or to conduct research in ophthalmology.
Eligibility: Open to United States citizens who are graduates of an institution approved by the AMA.
Level of Study: Postgraduate.
Type: Fellowship.
Value: Please contact the organisation.
Length of Study: One year, non renewable.
Frequency: Annual.
Study Establishment: ALUMNI.
Country of Study: United States of America.
No. of awards offered: Depends on availability of funds.
Application Procedure: Go to www.heed.org.
Closing Date: 1-15-2004.
Funding: Private.
No. of applicants last year: Approx. 100.

HENRY A MURRAY RESEARCH CENTER

Radcliffe Institute for Advanced Study, Harvard University, 10 Garden Street, Cambridge, MA 02138, United States of America
Tel: (1) 617 495 8140
Fax: (1) 617 496 3993
Email: mrc@radcliffe.edu
www: http://www.radcliffe.edu/murray
Contact: Programme Co-ordinator

The Henry A Murray Research Center is a centre for research on the changing lives of American women. The Center's purpose is to promote the use of existing social science data to explore human development and social change. The archive holds over 230 studies available for new research.

Adolescent and Youth Research Award

Subjects: Social and behavioural sciences.
Purpose: To support predoctoral and postdoctoral researchers who focus on adolescent development projects drawing on the Centers data.
Eligibility: Predoctoral applicants must be enrolled in a doctoral programme in a relevant field, and must have their dissertation proposal approved by an advisor or committee before the grant application is made.
Level of Study: Doctorate, Postdoctorate, Predoctorate.
Type: Research grant.
Value: Up to US$5,000 predoctoral and up to US$10,000 postdoctoral.
Frequency: Annual.
Country of Study: Any country.
Application Procedure: Applicants must submit five copies of a curriculum vitae including social security number, permanent home address and the name and address of a referee who has been asked to send a letter of recommendation directly to the programme. Also, an

application for the Use of Data form and a Computer Data Request form should be submitted if applicable, as well as six copies of a proposal that describes the intended research, and a covering page.
Closing Date: The deadline for predoctoral applications is April 1st, and for postdoctoral applications is October 15th or March 15th.
Contributor: The W T Grant Foundation.
No. of awards given last year: 7.
No. of applicants last year: Varies.

Henry A Murray Dissertation Award Program
Subjects: Social and behavioural studies.
Purpose: To enable doctoral students to undertake projects which focus on some aspect of the study of lives, concentrating on issues in human development or personality. Priority will be given to projects drawing on Center data.
Eligibility: Applicants must be enrolled in a doctoral programme in a relevant field and must have had their dissertation proposal approved by an advisor or committee before the grant application is made.
Level of Study: Doctorate, Predoctorate.
Type: Research grant.
Value: Up to US$5,000.
Length of Study: One year.
Frequency: Annual.
Country of Study: Any country.
Application Procedure: Applicants must submit six copies of a curriculum vitae including their social security number, permanent home address and the name and address of a referee who has been asked to send a letter of recommendation directly to the programme. Also, an application for the Use of Data form and a Computer Data Request form should be submitted if applicable, as well as six copies of a proposal that describes the intended research and a covering form.
Closing Date: April 1st.
Funding: Private.
Contributor: The Radcliffe Institute.
No. of awards given last year: 3.
No. of applicants last year: Varies.

Jeanne Humphrey Block Dissertation Award
Subjects: Social and behavioural studies.
Purpose: To enable a female doctoral student to undertake research on gender differences or some developmental issue of particular concern to girls or women. Projects drawing on Center data will be given priority, although this is not a requirement.
Eligibility: Female Applicants must be enrolled in a doctoral programme in a relevant field and must have had their dissertation proposal approved by an advisor or committee before the grant application is made.
Level of Study: Doctorate, Predoctorate.
Type: Award.
Value: Up to US$5,000.
Length of Study: One year.
Frequency: Annual.
Country of Study: Any country.
No. of awards offered: One.
Application Procedure: Applicants must submit six copies of a curriculum vitae including their social security number, permanent home address and the name and address of a referee who has been asked to send a letter of recommendation directly to the programme. Also, an application for the Use of Data form and a Computer Data Request form should be submitted if applicable, as well as six copies of a proposal that describes the intended research and a covering page.
Closing Date: April 1st.
Contributor: Murray Center Endowment.
No. of awards given last year: One.
No. of applicants last year: Varies.

Studying Diverse Lives
Subjects: Social sciences.
Purpose: To allow social science researchers to use the Henry A Murray Research Centers Diversity Archive.
Eligibility: Open to postdoctoral researchers looking for data with racially and ethnically diverse samples to use in their work who have received their doctorate within the last ten years.

Level of Study: Postdoctorate.
Type: Research grant.
Value: Up to US$10,000.
Frequency: Annual.
Country of Study: Any country.
Application Procedure: Applicants must submit six copies of a curriculum vitae including their social security number, permanent home address and the name and address of a referee, who has been asked to send a letter of recommendation directly to the programme, should be attached to the proposal. Also, an application for the Use of Data form and a Computer Data Request form should be submitted if applicable, as well as six copies of a proposal that describes the intended research and a covering page.
Closing Date: February 1st and October 15th.
Funding: Government.
Contributor: The National Institute of Mental Health.
No. of awards given last year: 2.
No. of applicants last year: 9.
Additional Information: Grant recipients will be required to attend one of two research meetings at Harvard to discuss their work.

THE HENRY MOORE INSTITUTE

74 The Headrow, Leeds, West Yorkshire LS1 3AA, England
Tel: (44) 113 246 7467
Fax: (44) 113 246 1481
Email: hmi@henry-moore.ac.uk
www: http://www.henry-moore-fdn.co.uk/hmi
Contact: Liz Aston

The Henry Moore Institute aims to enlarge the understanding of how sculpture makes meaning at different times and in different places through a programme of exhibitions, talks, conferences, publications and through its collection activities and research fellowship programme.

Henry Moore Institute Research Fellowship
Subjects: Sculpture, both historical and contemporary.
Purpose: To enable scholars to use the Institute's facilities which include the sculpture collection, library, archive and slide library to assist them in researching their particular field.
Eligibility: There are no restrictions.
Level of Study: Doctorate, Postdoctorate, Research.
Type: Fellowship.
Value: Accommodation, travel and daily living expenses.
Length of Study: One month.
Frequency: Annual.
Study Establishment: The Henry Moore Institute.
Country of Study: United Kingdom.
No. of awards offered: Four.
Application Procedure: To apply please send a letter of application (marked 'RF'), a proposal (1000 words max.) and a CV by 9 January 2004.
Closing Date: 9th January 2004.
Funding: Private.
Contributor: The Henry Moore Foundation.
No. of awards given last year: Four.
No. of applicants last year: 70.

THE HERB SOCIETY OF AMERICA, INC.

9019 Kirtland Chardon Road, Kirtland, OH 44094, United States of America
Tel: (1) 440 256 0514
Fax: (1) 440 256 0541
Email: herbs@herbsociety.com
www: http://www.herbsociety.org
Contact: Ms Michelle Milks, Office Administrator

The aim of the Herb Society of America is to promote the knowledge, use and delight of herbs through educational programmes, research and sharing the experience of its members with the community.

Herb Society of America Research Grant

Subjects: Herbal projects.

Purpose: To further the knowledge and use of herbs and to contribute the results of study and research to the records of horticulture, science, literature, history, art or economics.

Eligibility: Open to persons with a proposed programme of scientific, academic or artistic investigation of herbal plants.

Level of Study: Unrestricted.

Type: Research grant.

Value: Up to US$5,000.

Length of Study: Up to one year.

Frequency: Annual.

Country of Study: Any country.

Application Procedure: Applicants must submit an application clearly defining all their research in 500 words or less and a proposed budget with specific budget items listed. Requests for funds will not be considered unless accompanied by five copies of the application form and proposal.

Closing Date: January 31st.

Contributor: Members.

No. of awards given last year: Two.

No. of applicants last year: 45.

Additional Information: Finalists will be interviewed.

HERBERT HOOVER PRESIDENTIAL LIBRARY ASSOCIATION

302 Parkside Drive, PO Box 696, West Branch, IA 52358, United States of America

Tel: (1) 319 643 5327

Fax: (1) 319 643 2391

Email: info@hooverassociation.org

www: http://www.hooverassociation.org

Contact: Ms Patricia A Hand, Manager of Promotions & Academic Programs

The Herbert Hoover Presidential Library Association is a private non-profit support group for the Herbert Hoover Presidential Library Museum and National Historic Site in West Branch, Iowa.

Herbert Hoover Presidential Library Association Travel Grants

Subjects: American history, journalism, political science or economic history.

Purpose: To encourage the scholarly use of the holdings, and to promote the study of subjects of interest and concern to Herbert Hoover, Lou Henry Hoover and other public figures.

Eligibility: Open to current graduate students, postdoctoral students and qualified independent scholars. Priority is given to well developed proposals that utilise the resources of the Library, have the greatest likelihood of publication and subsequently, greatest likelihood of use from educators, students and policy makers.

Level of Study: Doctorate, Graduate, Postdoctorate, Postgraduate, Predoctorate, Professional development, Research.

Type: Travel grant.

Value: Between US$500-1,500 to cover the cost of a trip to the Library, but requests will be considered for longer research stays. There is no money available for any other purpose other than to defray the expense of travel to West Branch, Iowa.

Length of Study: Varies by individual.

Frequency: Annual.

Study Establishment: The Herbert Hoover Presidential Library-Museum in West Branch, Iowa.

Country of Study: United States of America.

No. of awards offered: Varies.

Application Procedure: Applicants must submit a completed application form, a project proposal of up to 1,200 words, and three letters of reference mailed separately. The application form can be obtained from the website.

Closing Date: March 1st.

Funding: Private.

No. of awards given last year: 10.

No. of applicants last year: 17.

Additional Information: For archival holdings information please contact the Hoover Library on (1) 319 643 5301 or at hoover.library@nara.gov Website: www.hoover.nara.gov.

HERBERT SCOVILLE JR PEACE FELLOWSHIP

110 Maryland Avenue North East, Suite 409, Washington, DC 20002, United States of America

Tel: (1) 202 543 4100

Fax: (1) 202 543 6297

Email: scoville@clw.org

www: http://www.scoville.org

The Herbert Scoville Jr Peace Fellowship was established in 1987 to provide college graduates with the opportunity to gain a Washington perspective on key issues of peace and security.

Herbert Scoville Jr Peace Fellowship

Subjects: Arms control and disarmament.

Purpose: To provide a unique educational experience to outstanding graduates, which will allow them develop leadership skills that can serve them throughout a career in arms control or a related area of public service, and to contribute to the work of the participating arms control and disarmament organisations and to continue the work of Herbert Scoville Jr.

Eligibility: Open to United States of America college graduates with experience or interest in arms control, disarmament, international security and/or peace issues. A fellowship to a foreign national from a country of proliferation concern to the United States of America is awarded periodically.

Level of Study: Postgraduate.

Type: Fellowship.

Value: Please contact the organisation.

Length of Study: Four to six months.

Frequency: Twice a year.

Country of Study: United States of America.

Application Procedure: Applicants must telephone, write or consult the website for information on application requirements.

HEREDITARY DISEASE FOUNDATION

1303 Pico Boulevard, Santa Monica, CA 90405, United States of America

Tel: (1) 310 450 9913

Fax: (1) 310 450 9532

Email: cures@hdfoundation.org

www: http://www.hdfoundation.org

Contact: Nancy S. Wexler, President

The Hereditary Disease Foundation is a non-profit, basic Science organization dedicated to the cure of genetic disease.

HDF Research Grant

Subjects: Huntington's Disease.

Purpose: To support research projects that focus on Huntington's Disease.

Level of Study: Doctorate, Postdoctorate, Postgraduate.

Type: Grant.

Value: Up to US$50,000.

Length of Study: One year with possibility of renewal.

Frequency: Annual.

Application Procedure: Complete application form and submit 35 copies.

Closing Date: February 15th, June 15th and October 15th.

Funding: Private.

Additional Information: Grants are considered seed money.

For further information contact:

Hereditary Disease Foundation, 3960 Broadway, 6th Floor, New York, NY 10032, United States of America

Contact: Carb D. Johnson

HILDA MARTINDALE EDUCATIONAL TRUST

Royal Holloway University of London, Egham, Surrey TW20 0EX, England
Tel: (44) 1784 434455
Fax: (44) 1784 437520
Contact: Miss J L Hurn, Secretary to the Trustees

The Hilda Martindale Educational Trust was set up by Miss Hilda Martindale in order to help women of the British Isles with the costs of vocational training for any profession or career likely to be of use or value to the community. Applications are considered annually by six women trustees.

Hilda Martindale Exhibitions

Subjects: Any vocational training for a profession or career likely to be of value to the community.
Purpose: To assist with the costs of vocational training.
Eligibility: Open to women of the British Isles over 21 years of age. Assistance is not given for short courses, courses abroad, elective studies, intercalated BSc years, access courses or academic research. Awards are not given to those who are eligible for grants from research councils, the British Academy or other public sources.
Level of Study: Graduate, Postgraduate, Professional development.
Type: Grant.
Value: Varies, normally UK£200-1,000.
Length of Study: One year.
Frequency: Annual.
Study Establishment: Any establishment approved by the trustees.
Country of Study: United Kingdom.
No. of awards offered: 25-35.
Application Procedure: Applicants must complete two copies of an application form, which must be obtained from and returned to the Secretary to the Trustees.
Closing Date: March 1st for the following academic year. Late or retrospective applications will not be considered.
Funding: Private.
Contributor: Private trust.
No. of awards given last year: 17.
No. of applicants last year: 128.

HILGENFELD FOUNDATION FOR MORTUARY EDUCATION

PO Box 4311, Fullerton, CA 92834, United States of America
Contact: Mr Chester Gromaki, President

Hilgenfeld Foundation Grant

Subjects: Mortuary science education.
Purpose: To support scholarships and research.
Eligibility: Open to nationals of the United States only.
Level of Study: Graduate, Postgraduate, Professional development.
Type: Other.
Length of Study: Varies.
Frequency: Annual.
Country of Study: United States of America.
No. of awards offered: Approx. 20.
Application Procedure: Applicants must submit an application on forms provided by the Hilgenfeld Foundation.
Closing Date: Applications are accepted at any time.
Funding: Private.
Contributor: The Hilgenfeld Family.
No. of awards given last year: 26.
No. of applicants last year: 100.
Additional Information: Scholarship grants are awarded through a co-operative effort between the Hilgenfeld Foundation and the American Board of Funeral Service.

For further information contact:

American Board of Funeral Service Education, 38 Florida Avenue, Portland, ME 04103, United States of America

THE HINRICHSEN FOUNDATION

10-12 Baches Street, London, N1 6DN, England
Contact: L E Adamson, Administrator

Hinrichsen Foundation Awards

Subjects: Contemporary music composition, performance and research.
Purpose: To promote the written areas of music.
Eligibility: Preference will be given to United Kingdom applicants and projects taking place in the United Kingdom. Grants are not given for recordings, for the funding of commissions, for degree or other study courses or for the purchase of instruments or equipment.
Level of Study: Unrestricted.
Value: Varies.
Frequency: Dependent on funds available.
No. of awards offered: Varies.
Application Procedure: Applicants must submit a completed application form along with two references.
Closing Date: Applications are accepted at any time.
No. of awards given last year: 52.

HISTORIC NEW ORLEANS COLLECTION

533 Royal Street, New Orleans, LA 70130, United States of America
Tel: (1) 504 523 4662
Fax: (1) 504 598 7108
Email: info@hnoc.org
www: http://www.hnoc.org
Contact: Director of Museum Programmes

The Historic New Orleans Collection was established in 1966 by General and Mrs L Kemper Williams, private collectors of Louisiana material, to maintain and expand their collection and make it available to the public through research facilities and exhibitions.

Kemper and Leila Williams Prize in Louisiana History

Subjects: History.
Purpose: To honour the best contribution to historical work about Louisiana.
Eligibility: There are no eligibility restrictions.
Level of Study: Unrestricted.
Type: Prize.
Frequency: Annual.
Country of Study: Any country.
No. of awards offered: One.
Application Procedure: Applicants must submit four copies of work and four copies of the application form.
Closing Date: January 15th for works published from the previous calendar year.
Funding: Private.
Additional Information: The administration of these prizes is determined by a committee of scholars chosen by the Louisiana Historical Association. Funding is provided by the Historic New Orleans Collection.

HISTORY OF SCIENCE SOCIETY (HSS)

Executive Office, Box 351330, University of Washington, Seattle, WA 98195, United States of America
Tel: (1) 206 543 9366
Fax: (1) 206 685 9544
Email: info@hssonline.org
www: http://www.hssonline.org
Contact: Mr Robert J Malone, Executive Director

The History of Science Society (HSS) is the world's largest society dedicated to understanding science, technology, medicine, and their interactions with society within their historical context.

HSS Travel Grant

Subjects: The history of science from ancient to modern times.
Purpose: To allow an individual to travel to the annual HSS meeting.

Eligibility: Eligibility is restricted to those who participate in the annual meeting. Preference is given to HSS members and those who have not been awarded a travel grant in the past two years.
Level of Study: Doctorate, Postdoctorate, Postgraduate.
Type: Travel grant.
Value: US$10-1,000.
Frequency: Annual.
Country of Study: United States of America.
No. of awards offered: Approx. 50.
Application Procedure: Applicants must apply to the HSS Executive Office.
Closing Date: June 1st.
Funding: Government.
Contributor: The National Science Foundation.
No. of awards given last year: 43.
No. of applicants last year: 48.
Additional Information: Applicants must book their ticket through the HSS affiliated travel agency, or show proof that a less expensive fare has been obtained. Other awards include the History of Women in Science Prize, Watson Davis and Helen Miles Davis Prize, Derek Price Award, Ida and Henry Schuman Prize, Pfizer Prize, Joseph H Hazen Education Prize.

HONDA FOUNDATION

6-20 Yaesu 2-chome, Chuo-ku
Tokyo, 104, Japan
Tel: (81) 3 3274 5125
Fax: (81) 3 3274 5103
Email: lej07727@nifty.ne.jp
www: http://www.soc.nii.ac.jp/hf/eng
Contact: Yutaka Ishihara, Secretary General

The Honda Foundation was established in December 1977 to contribute to the creation of true human civilisation on the basis of the philosophy of the late Mr Soichiro Honda, the founder of Honda Motor Company Limited.

Honda Prize
Subjects: Eco-technology.
Purpose: To recognise a distinguished achievement in the field of ecotechnology.
Eligibility: Open to individuals or an organisation, irrespective of nationality.
Type: Prize.
Value: The prize includes a donation of Yen 10,000,000 and an original medal.
Frequency: Annual.
Closing Date: March 31st every year.
Funding: Private.
Contributor: The late Mr Soichiro Honda, the founder of Honda Motor Company Limited.
No. of awards given last year: One.
No. of applicants last year: One.
Additional Information: Eco-technology is the new concept which harmonises the progress of technology and civilisation, rather than pursuing technology designed solely for efficiency and profit.

THE HOROWITZ FOUNDATION FOR SOCIAL POLICY

1247 State Road, Route 206, Corner HWY 516, Blawenbury Road, Rockey Hill Intersection, Princeton, NJ 08540-1619, United States of America
Tel: (1) 609 921 1479
Fax: (1) 732 445 3138
Email: ihorowitz@transactionpub.com
www: http://www.horowitz-foundation.org
Contact: Mr Irving Louis Horowitz, The Chairman

An independent foundation for the support and advancement of social science research.

Eli Ginzberg Award
Subjects: Targeted grants for work in major areas of the social sciences including anthropology, area studies, economics, political science, psychology, sociology and urban studies as well as newer areas such as evaluation research.
Purpose: For a project involving solutions to major urban health problems in urban settings.
Eligibility: Open to nationals of any country. Candidates may propose new projects, and they may also solicit support for research in progress, travel funds or preparing a work for publication.
Level of Study: Unrestricted, scholars in initial stage of research. Level unrestricted.
Type: Grant with additional stipend.
Value: From US$2000 to US$5000 with additional stipend.
Length of Study: One year.
Frequency: Annual.
Study Establishment: Award made to individual project on merit.
Country of Study: Open worldwide.
No. of awards offered: One.
Application Procedure: Application forms may be requested from the Horowitz Foundation or downloaded from the website. The application should be accompanied by a cover sheet listing the name of the applicant, the title of the project, a 50-word abstract stating what is to be done and why, including methodology to be used and a 50 word summary of the policy implications of the research. The application must be signed.
Closing Date: 31st December in the year preceding.
Funding: Private.

John L. Stanley Award
Subjects: Targeted grants for work in major areas of the social sciences, including anthropology, area studies, economics, political science, psychology, sociology and urban studies as well as newer areas such as evaluation research.
Purpose: For a work that seeks to expand our understanding of the political and ethical foundations of policy research.
Eligibility: Open to nationals of any country. Candidates may propose new projects and they may also solicit support for research in progress, including final work on a dissertation, supplementing research in progress, travel funds, or preparing a work for publication.
Level of Study: Unrestricted, scholars in the initial stage of research. Level unrestricted.
Type: Grant with additional stipend.
Value: From US$2000 to US$5000 with additional stipend.
Length of Study: One year.
Frequency: Annual.
Study Establishment: Award made to individual project on merit.
Country of Study: Open worldwide.
No. of awards offered: One.
Application Procedure: Application forms may be requested from the Horowitz Foundation or downloaded from the website. The application should be accompanied by a cover sheet listing the name of the applicant, the title of the project, a 50-word abstract stating what is to be done and why, including methodology to be used and a 50 word summary of the policy implications of the research. The application must be signed.
Closing Date: 31st December in the year preceding.
Funding: Private.

Joshua Feigenbaum Award
Subjects: Targeted grants for work in major areas of the social sciences, including anthropology, area studies, economics, political science, psychology, sociology and urban studies as well as newer areas such as evaluation research.
Purpose: For empirical research on policy aspects of the arts and popular culture, with special reference to mass communication.
Eligibility: Open to nationals of any country. Candidates may propose new projects, and they may also solicit support for research in progress, including final work on a dissertation, supplementing research in progress, travel funds, or preparing a work for publication.
Level of Study: Unrestricted, Scholars in the initial stage of research. Level unrestricted.
Type: Grant with additional stipend.

Value: From US$2000 to US$5000 with additional stipend.
Length of Study: One year.
Frequency: Annual.
Study Establishment: Award made to individual project on merit.
Country of Study: Open worldwide.
No. of awards offered: One.
Application Procedure: Applications forms may be requested from The Horowitz Foundation or downloaded from the website. The application should be accompanied by a cover sheet using the name of the applicant, the title of the project, a 50-word abstract stating what is to be done and why, including methodology to be used and 50-word summary of the policy implications of the research. The application must be signed.
Closing Date: 31st December in the year preceding.
Funding: Private.

Robert K. Merton Award

Subjects: Targeted grants for work in major areas of the social sciences including anthropology, area studies, economics, political science, psychology, sociology and urban studies as well as newer areas such as evaluation research.
Purpose: For studies in the relation between social theory and public policy.
Eligibility: Open to nationals of any country. Candidates may propose new projects, and they may also solicit support for research in progress, travel funds or preparing a work for publication.
Level of Study: Unrestricted, Scholars in initial stage of research.
Type: Grant with additional stipend.
Value: From US$2000 to US$5000 with additional stipend.
Length of Study: One year.
Frequency: Annual.
Study Establishment: Award made to individual project on merit.
Country of Study: Open worldwide.
No. of awards offered: One.
Application Procedure: Application forms may be requested from the Horowitz Foundation or downloaded from the website. The application should be accompanied by a cover sheet listing the name of the applicant, the title of the project, a 50-word abstract stating what is to be done and why, including methodology to be used and a 50-word summary of the policy implications of the research. The application must be signed.
Closing Date: 31st December in the year preceding.
Funding: Private.

HORSERACE BETTING LEVY BOARD (HBLB)

52 Grosvenor Gardens, London, SW1W 0AU, England
Tel: (44) 20 7333 0043
Fax: (44) 20 7333 0041
Email: vet.grants@hblb.org.uk
www: http://www.hblb.org.uk
Contact: Equine Grants Team

The Horserace Betting Levy Board (HBLB) operates in accordance with the Betting, Gaming and Lotteries Act 1963. It assesses and collects contributions from bookmakers and the Horserace Totalisator Board and uses these for the advancement of equine veterinary science and education and other improvements within the horseracing industry.

Horserace Betting Levy Board Senior Equine Clinical Scholarships

Subjects: Equine veterinary studies with emphasis on the thoroughbred.
Purpose: To support postgraduate veterinary clinical training.
Eligibility: Open to holders of degrees, registerable with the RCVS, in veterinary science or medicine who have had at least two years practical experience following graduation and who wish to undertake specialised higher clinical training in the equine veterinary field.
Level of Study: Postgraduate.
Type: Scholarship.

Value: A stipend to the holder is UK£16,810 in year one with increments for years two and three. The institution receives UK£8,080 to cover expenses directly relevant to the scholarship.
Length of Study: Up to three years, subject to satisfactory progress.
Frequency: Annual.
Study Establishment: At any of the six veterinary schools, or at any appropriate university department or research institute or veterinary practice in the United Kingdom.
Country of Study: United Kingdom.
No. of awards offered: Up to six.
Application Procedure: The study establishment must submit applications on appropriate forms.
Closing Date: March 1st.
Funding: Government.
No. of awards given last year: Two.
No. of applicants last year: Usually up to 10.
Additional Information: Awards normally commence on October 1st. The study establishment is responsible for the appointment of clinical scholars.

Horserace Betting Levy Board Veterinary Research Training Scholarship

Subjects: Equine veterinary medicine or science, with emphasis on the thoroughbred.
Purpose: To support postgraduate equine veterinary research training.
Eligibility: Open to holders of a degree, registerable with the RCVS, in veterinary medicine or science who wish to undertake full-time training in research in the equine veterinary field leading to a PhD.
Level of Study: Postgraduate.
Type: Scholarship.
Value: A stipend to the holder UK£15,400-16,810 in year one, depending on experience, with increments for years two and three. UK£6,360 (accountable) per year for fees and expenses, and UK£4,570 (unaccountable) per year to the department in which the holder works. Scales are reviewed annually.
Length of Study: Up to three years, subject to satisfactory progress.
Frequency: Annual.
Study Establishment: Any of the six veterinary schools or at any appropriate university department, research institute or veterinary practice in the United Kingdom.
Country of Study: United Kingdom.
No. of awards offered: Up to six.
Application Procedure: Applicants must submit applications on appropriate forms.
Closing Date: March 1st.
Funding: Government.
No. of awards given last year: Two.
No. of applicants last year: Usually up to 10.
Additional Information: Candidates must be nominated by a professor, lecturer, director or head of department of an eligible institution. Candidates will be interviewed by the Board's Veterinary Advisory Committee. Awards normally commence on October 1st.

HORTICULTURAL RESEARCH INSTITUTE

1000 Vermont Street North West, Suite 300, Washington, DC 20005, United States of America
Tel: (1) 202 789 2900 ext. 3014
Fax: (1) 202 789 1893
Email: hriresearch@anla.org
www: http://www.anla.org/research
Contact: Ms Teresa A Jodon, Research Communications & Grants Manager

The aim of the Horticultural Research Institute is to direct, fund, promote and communicate research which increases the quality and value of plants, improves the productivity and profitability of the nursery and landscape industry, and protects and enhances the environment.

Horticultural Research Institute Grants

Subjects: Nursery and landscape industry, especially woody and perennial landscape plants, their production, marketing, landscape, water management or the environment.
Purpose: To support necessary research for the advancement of the nursery, greenhouse and landscape industry.
Eligibility: Open to nationals and permanent residents of the United States of America and Canada. Candidates must submit an appropriate project which the Institute feels is deserving of support.
Level of Study: Unrestricted.
Type: Grant.
Value: US$5,000-30,000.
Length of Study: One year, occasionally renewable by re-application.
Frequency: Annual.
Study Establishment: At state or federal research laboratories, land grant universities, forest research stations, botanical gardens and arboreta.
Country of Study: United States of America.
No. of awards offered: 15-30.
Application Procedure: Applicants must submit the application electronically.
Closing Date: May 15th.
Funding: Private.
Contributor: Nursery and landscape firms, as well as state and regional nursery and landscape associations.
No. of awards given last year: 17.
No. of applicants last year: 160.
Additional Information: Applicants should visit the website to download an application form.

THE HOSPITAL FOR SICK CHILDREN FOUNDATION

555 University Avenue, Suite 1725, Toronto, ON M5G 1X8, Canada
Tel: (1) 416 813 6101
Fax: (1) 416 813 8142
Email: gwen.burrows@sickkids.on.ca
www: http://www.sickkids.on.ca/foundation
Contact: Grants Officer

The Hospital for Sick Children Foundation is a fund raising and granting organisation, dedicated to the betterment of the health of children. The Foundation is committed to supporting the broader aims of child health in Canada through an annual allocation to the National Grants Programme for paediatric research, health promotion, public education, postgraduate training and innovative community projects.

Duncan L Gordon Fellowships

Subjects: Paediatric healthcare, both clinical training and research training.
Purpose: To provide postdoctoral training.
Eligibility: Open to physicians and scientists wishing to obtain postdoctoral training, who are Canadian citizens or landed immigrants, are of outstanding academic achievement and can provide evidence of special aptitude for teaching and research.
Level of Study: Postdoctorate.
Type: Fellowship.
Length of Study: One-three years.
Frequency: Annual.
Study Establishment: Any agreed institution.
Country of Study: Any country.
No. of awards offered: Up to three.
Application Procedure: Applicants must be nominated by the head of the department in which they are involved. A project proposal and three letters of reference are required. Applicants should contact the office for current guidelines and application forms. Applicants must supply an outline of the course of study and detailed study plans indicating the location and facilities which will be available and the individual who would supervise his or her study. Application forms, guidelines and additional information can be found on the website.
Closing Date: October 1st.
Funding: Commercial, Private.

Contributor: A broad base of individual and corporate donors.
Additional Information: The candidate must indicate his or her objectives in paediatrics upon completion of the fellowship period.

HOSPITAL FOR SICK CHILDREN RESEARCH TRAINING CENTRE (RESTRACOMP)

Hospital for Sick Children, 555 University Avenue, Toronto, ON M5G 1X8, Canada
Tel: (1) 416 813 7781
Fax: (1) 416 813 8142
Email: nadia.ramsundar@sickkids.ca
www: http://www.sickkids.on.ca
Contact: J Rovet

RESTRACOMP Research Fellowship

Subjects: Paediatric research, biomedical research.
Purpose: To provide funds to postgraduate students or fellows seeking research training.
Eligibility: Open to those nominated by the active senior staff of the Research Institute of the Hospital for Sick Children.
Level of Study: Graduate, Postdoctorate, Postgraduate.
Type: Fellowship.
Value: Up to Canadian $30,000 per year, 2 yr. Maximum.
Length of Study: One year.
Frequency: Biannually.
Study Establishment: The Hospital for Sick Children, in Toronto.
Country of Study: Canada.
No. of awards offered: 10-12.
Application Procedure: Applicants must submit an application which is entered into a competition with other candidates.
Closing Date: Applications are accepted in mid April and mid October.
Funding: Private.

HOUBLON-NORMAN FUND

Bank of England, Threadneedle Street, London, EC2R 8AH, England
Tel: (44) 20 7601 3377
Fax: (44) 20 7601 5953
Email: jay.begum@bankofengland.co.uk
www: http://www.bankofengland.co.uk/houblonnormanfund
Contact: Ms Jay Begum, Secretary to the Houblon-Norman Fund

Houblon-Norman Fellowships/George Fellowships

Subjects: Economics and finance.
Purpose: To promote research into and disseminate knowledge and understanding of the working, interaction and function of financial and business institutions in Great Britain and elsewhere and the economic conditions affecting them.
Eligibility: Open to distinguished research workers as well as younger postdoctoral or equivalent applicants of any nationality. Preference will be given to British and European Union nationals.
Level of Study: Postdoctorate.
Type: Fellowship.
Value: The value of a fellowship is dependent on the candidate's circumstances and will be of such amount as seems necessary for undertaking the work. It might take the form of payment to the individual's employer.
Length of Study: One month-one year.
Frequency: Annual.
Study Establishment: The Bank of England.
Country of Study: United Kingdom.
No. of awards offered: Varies.
Application Procedure: Applicants must complete an application form.
Closing Date: As advertised in the press.
No. of awards given last year: Two (2003/04).
No. of applicants last year: 18.
Additional Information: Please see the website.

HUDSON RIVER FOUNDATION (HRF)

17 Battery Place, Suite 915, NY, NY 10004, United States of America
Tel: (1) 212 924 8290
Fax: (1) 212 924 8325
Email: info@hudsonriver.org
www: http://www.hudsonriver.org
Contact: Grants Management Officer

The Hudson River Foundation (HRF) supports scientific research, education and projects to enhance public access to the Hudson River. The purpose of the Foundation is to make science integral to the decision-making with regard to the Hudson River and its watershed and to support competent stewardship of this extraordinary resource.

HRF Graduate Fellowships
Subjects: The Hudson River system.
Purpose: To assist advanced graduate - students in conducting research on the Hudson River System.
Eligibility: Applicants must be enrolled in an accredited programme, have a thesis advisor and advisory committee (if appropriate to the institution), and have a thesis research plan approved by the student's institution or department.
Level of Study: Doctorate, Graduate.
Type: Fellowship.
Value: Please contact the organisation.
Frequency: Annual.
No. of awards offered: Up to six.
Application Procedure: Applicants must obtain an HRF Call for Proposals booklet, available on request or from the website. Applications must include an HRF Proposal Cover Page, letter of interest, description of the project of up to 10 pages, timetable, statement of the significance and relevance of the project to the HRF's objectives, an estimate of the cost of supplies and travel using the HRF's Proposal Budget Summary Page, and a letter from the university stating that the student will receive a tuition waiver or reimbursement for the period of the fellowship. Two letters of recommendation, sent under a separate cover are also required, one of which must be from the student's advisor and should certify the student's current status, evaluate the student's capabilities, and rate the student's project on technical merit. The original and 10 copies of the proposal must be submitted to the Science Director.
Additional Information: The award is conditional upon a full tuition waiver or reimbursement by the University.

Hudson River Expedited Grants
Subjects: Emergency situations such as unexpected natural or human - induced events, or research efforts for which additional funds are needed to enhance an existing research effort prior to the Foundation's next formal funding cycle.
Purpose: To facilitate the study of emergency situations affecting the Hudson River.
Level of Study: Postgraduate.
Type: Grant.
Value: Variable.
Length of Study: Variable.
Frequency: Dependent on need.
Application Procedure: Proposals to include propal cover, abstract, description, personnel and reasons for expedited review. Please submit an original and ten copies to the Science Director, Dennis Suszkowski, at the main organisation address.
Closing Date: None because of the nature of the award.

Hudson River Graduate Fellowships
Subjects: Research on the resources, key species, toxic substances, abundances of key organisms, dynamics of Hudson River trophic webs, hydrodynamics, sediment transport, public policy and social science of the Hudson Bay River.
Purpose: To fund research fellowships to advanced graduate students conducting research on the Hudson River System.
Eligibility: Applicants must be in an accredited doctoral program, must have a thesis advisor and a research plan approved by the applicant's institution.
Level of Study: Doctorate, Postgraduate.

Type: Full-time research fellowship.
Value: US$11,000 stipend plus US$1,000 expenses for master's and US$15,000 stipend plus US$1,000 expenses for doctorate.
Length of Study: One year.
Frequency: Annual.
Study Establishment: Any.
Country of Study: Any country.
No. of awards offered: Up to Six.
Application Procedure: Supply a description, timetable, statement of significance and relevance, estimate of the cost, resume of student and two letters of recommendation. The original and ten copies of the proposal to be forwarded to the Science Director at the main organisation address.
Closing Date: April 14th.

Hudson River Research Grants
Subjects: Research designed to compare and contrast the Hudson River with other estuarine ecosystems through literature review as well as laboratory or field experiments.
Purpose: To elucidate the dynamic interactions among the physical, chemical and biological processes that are important to the Hudson River ecosystem.
Eligibility: There are no eligibility restrictions.
Level of Study: Graduate.
Type: Grant.
Length of Study: Up to two years.
Frequency: Annual.
Study Establishment: The Foundation prefers, but does not require, that unaffiliated researchers seek some institutional affiliation for the purpose of conducting the proposed research.
Country of Study: Any country.
Application Procedure: Submit a preproposal consisting of a cover page, project description of no more than three single-spaced pages and an estimated budget. Twenty-five copies of the proposal to be submitted by 5.00 pm, September 23rd of preceding year.
Closing Date: September 23rd.
Additional Information: Hudson River Research Grants are made after a rigorous review process, including peer review.

Hudson River Travel Grants
Subjects: Research designed to compare and contrast the Hudson River with other estuarine ecosystems through literature review as well as laboratory or field experiments.
Purpose: Travel Grants are available for travel related to the research goals of the Hudson River Fund.
Level of Study: Postgraduate.
Type: Grant.
Value: As appropriate, with budget and references.
Length of Study: Variable.
Frequency: As needed.
Application Procedure: An original plus ten copies to The Science Director, Dennis Suszkowski, (1) 212-924-8290, address as main organization.
Closing Date: Any time of year, but as far in advance of anticipated need as possible.

Tibor T Polgar Fellowship
Subjects: All aspects of the environment of the Hudson River, from Troy, New York, to New York Harbor and Bight. Previous projects have studied hydrodynamics, larval fish, zooplankton, terrapins, landscape ecology, nutrients and public policy.
Purpose: To fund Summer research on the Hudson River.
Eligibility: There are no eligibility restrictions.
Level of Study: Graduate.
Type: Fellowship.
Value: US$3,800 and limited research funds.
Length of Study: From May-June to August-September.
Frequency: Annual.
Country of Study: United States of America.
No. of awards offered: Eight every Summer.
Application Procedure: Applicants must submit the original and five copies of their application which must include letters of interest from the student and of support from the sponsor, a short description of the

research project including its significance of between four and six pages, a detailed timetable for the completion of the project, a detailed budget with estimated cost of supplies, travel and other expenses, and the student's curriculum vitae. Because of the training and educational aspects of this program, each potential fellow must be sponsored by a primary advisor. The advisor must be willing to commit sufficient time for supervision of the research and to attend at least one meeting to review the progress of the research. Advisors will receive a stipend of US$500.

Closing Date: February 24th in each year.
Funding: Private.
Additional Information: The objectives of the programme are to gather important information on all aspects of the river and to train students in conducting estuarine studies and public policy research. Polgar Fellowships may be awarded for studies anywhere within the tidal Hudson estuary from the Federal Dam at Troy, to New York Harbor.

HUMANE RESEARCH TRUST

Brook House, 29 Bramhall Lane South, Bramhall, Stockport, Cheshire SK7 2DN, England
Tel: (44) 161 439 8041
Fax: (44) 161 439 3713
Email: Members@Humane.freeserve.co.uk
www: http://www.btinternet.com/~shawweb/hrt/index.htm
Contact: Mr David Greenfield, Trust Secretary

The Humane Research Trust is a national charity which funds a range of unique medical research programmes into human illness at hospitals and universities around the country. In keeping with the philosophy of the Trust, none of the research involves animals, and much of it seeks to establish and develop pioneering techniques which will replace animal intensive experiments currently undertaken elsewhere.

Humane Research Trust Grant
Subjects: Humane research.
Purpose: To encourage scientific programmes where the use of animals is replaced by other methods.
Eligibility: Open to established scientific workers engaged in productive research. Nationals of any country are considered but for the sake of overseeing, projects should be undertaken in a United Kingdom establishment.
Level of Study: Unrestricted.
Type: Grant.
Value: Varies.
Length of Study: Varies.
Frequency: Dependent on funds available.
Study Establishment: Various.
Country of Study: United Kingdom.
No. of awards offered: Varies.
Application Procedure: Applicants must complete an application form, available on request.
Closing Date: Varies. The trustees meet every three to four months.
Funding: Private.
Contributor: Supporters and legacies.
No. of awards given last year: Eight.
No. of applicants last year: 27.
Additional Information: The Trust is a registered charity and donations are encouraged.

HUMANITARIAN TRUST

27 St James Place, London, SW1A 1NR, England
Contact: Mrs M Myers, Secretary of Trustees

Set up to support general charitable purposes.

Humanitarian Trust Awards
Subjects: Awards are not made for journalism, theatre, music or any arts subjects, nursing, medical auxiliaries, midwifery, radiology, treatment techniques or medical technology 'Academic' subjects only.
Eligibility: Open to applicants already holding an original grant who can show evidence of approx. UK£200 shortfall. Candidates are only

considered when studying academic subjects and the awards cannot be used for travel, overseas courses and fieldwork.
Level of Study: Graduate, Postgraduate.
Type: Award.
Value: Approx. UK£200.
Length of Study: One year, non renewable.
Frequency: Once Only.
Study Establishment: Any approved institution.
Country of Study: United Kingdom.
No. of awards offered: Approx. 15.
Application Procedure: Applicants must write in and submit two references preferably from tutors or heads of department, a breakdown of anticipated income/expenditure and a curriculum vitae.
Funding: Private.
No. of awards given last year: 18.
No. of applicants last year: 100.

HUMANITIES RESEARCH CENTRE (HRC)

Australian National University (ANU), Canberra, ACT 0200, Australia
Tel: (61) 2 6125 2700
Fax: (61) 2 6248 0054
Email: administration.hrc@anu.edu.au
www: http://www.anu.edu.au/hrc
Contact: Ms Judy Buchanan, Assistant Office Administrator & Programme Manager

The Humanities Research Centre (HRC) was established in 1972 specifically to stimulate humanities research and debate at the Australian National University (ANU), within Australia and beyond.

HRC Visiting Fellowships
Subjects: Humanities. The HRC interprets this generously, recognising that new methods of theoretical enquiry have done much to break down the traditional distinction between the humanities and the social sciences, recognising too, the importance of establishing dialogue between the humanities and the natural and technological sciences and the creative arts.
Purpose: To provide scholars with time to pursue their own work in congenial and stimulating surroundings.
Eligibility: Open to candidates of any nationality who are at postdoctoral level.
Level of Study: Postdoctorate.
Type: Other.
Value: Return economy airfare up to Australian $2,700, plus accommodation for 12 weeks.
Length of Study: 12 weeks.
Frequency: Annual.
Study Establishment: The Humanities Research Centre at the Australian National University.
Country of Study: Australia.
No. of awards offered: Up to 20.
Application Procedure: Applicants must complete a formal application, available from the website.
Closing Date: January 31st.
Funding: Government.
No. of awards given last year: 19.
Additional Information: Fellows are required to spend all of their time in residence at the Centre, but are encouraged to visit other institutions. Please refer to the website for further information.

THE HUNTINGTON

1151 Oxford Road, San Marino, CA 91108, United States of America
Tel: (1) 626 405 2194
Fax: (1) 626 449 5703
Email: cpowell@huntington.org
www: http://www.huntington.org
Contact: Ms Carolyn Powell, Committee on Awards

Barbara Thom Postdoctoral Fellowship
Subjects: British and American history, literature, art history, or history of science.

Purpose: To support a non tenured faculty member while they are revising a manuscript for publication.
Eligibility: Preference will be given to scholars who are four or five years beyond the award of PhD.
Level of Study: Postdoctorate.
Type: Fellowship.
Value: US$40,000.
Length of Study: One year.
Frequency: Annual.
Study Establishment: The Huntington.
Country of Study: United States of America.
No. of awards offered: Two.
Application Procedure: Applicants must contact the Chair of the Committee on Awards.
Closing Date: Applications are accepted between October 1st and December 15th.
Funding: Private.

Huntington Short-Term Fellowships

Subjects: British and American history, literature, art history, or history of science.
Purpose: To enable outstanding scholars to carry out significant research in the collections of the Library and Art Gallery, by assisting in balancing the budgets of such persons, on leave at reduced pay and living away from home.
Eligibility: Open to nationals of any country who have demonstrated, to a degree commensurate with their age and experience, unusual abilities as scholars through publications of a high order of merit. Attention is paid to the value of the candidates project and the degree to which the special strengths of the Library and Art Gallery will be used.
Level of Study: Postdoctorate, Postgraduate.
Type: Fellowship.
Value: US$2,000 per month.
Length of Study: One-five months.
Frequency: Annual.
Study Establishment: The Huntington.
Country of Study: United States of America.
No. of awards offered: Approx. 100, depending on funds available.
Application Procedure: Applicants must contact the Chair of the Committee on Awards.
Closing Date: Applications are accepted between October 1st and December 15th.
Funding: Private.
Additional Information: Fellowships are available for work towards doctoral dissertations.

Mellon Postdoctoral Research Fellowships

Subjects: British and American history, literature, art history, or history of science.
Purpose: To support scholarship study in a field appropriate to the Huntingtons collections.
Eligibility: Preference will be given to scholars who have not held a major award in the three years preceding the year of this award.
Level of Study: Postdoctorate.
Type: Fellowship.
Value: US$40,000.
Length of Study: One year.
Frequency: Annual.
Study Establishment: The Huntington.
Country of Study: United States of America.
No. of awards offered: Two.
Application Procedure: Applicants must contact the Committee on Fellowships.
Closing Date: Applications are accepted between October 1st and December 15th.
Funding: Private.

National Endowment for the Humanities Fellowships

Subjects: British and American history, literature, art history, or history of science.
Purpose: To support scholarship in a field appropriate to the Huntingtons collections.

Eligibility: Preference will be given to scholars who have not held a major award in the three years preceding the year of this award.
Level of Study: Postdoctorate.
Type: Fellowship.
Value: Up to US$40,000.
Length of Study: 4-12 months.
Frequency: Annual.
Study Establishment: The Huntington.
Country of Study: United States of America.
No. of awards offered: Three.
Application Procedure: Applicants must contact the Chair of the Committee on Awards.
Closing Date: Applications are accepted between October 1st and December 15th.
Funding: Government.

W M Keck Foundation Fellowship for Young Scholars

Subjects: British and American history, literature, art history, or history of science.
Purpose: To encourage outstanding young scholars to pursue their own lines of enquiry, complete dissertation research or begin a new project in the fields of British and American history, literature, art history, and the history of science.
Eligibility: There are no restrictions on age, nationality or citizenship.
Level of Study: Postdoctorate, Postgraduate.
Type: Fellowship.
Value: US$2,300 per month.
Length of Study: One-three months.
Frequency: Annual.
Study Establishment: The Huntington.
Country of Study: United States of America.
No. of awards offered: Varies.
Application Procedure: Applicants must contact the Chair of the Committee on Awards.
Closing Date: Applications are accepted between October 1st and December 15th.
Funding: Private.

HUNTINGTON'S DISEASE ASSOCIATION

108 Battersea High Street, London, SW11 3HP, England
Tel: (44) 207 223 7000
Fax: (44) 20 7223 9489
Email: info@hda.org.uk
www: http://www.hda.org.uk
Contact: Ms Eileen Cook, The Administrator

HDA Research Project Grants

Subjects: Furthering understanding into Huntington's Disease. Improving its treatment or otherwise improving the quality of life for patients and their carers.
Purpose: To support research projects into Huntington's Disease in a direct way. Preference given to small 'pump priming grants' likely to lead to support from a major funding body.
Eligibility: Open to suitably qualified researchers of any nationality.
Level of Study: Postgraduate, Research.
Value: Up to UK£25,000.
Length of Study: 1-3 years.
Frequency: Annual.
Study Establishment: Suitable UK institution.
Country of Study: United Kingdom.
Application Procedure: Applicants should apply to the main organisation.
Closing Date: 1st March.
Funding: Private.

HDA Studentship

Subjects: Furthering understanding into Huntington's Disease. Improving its treatment or otherwise improving the quality of life for patients and their carers.
Purpose: To support a postgraduate student undertaking research into Huntington's Disease.
Level of Study: Postgraduate.

Type: Studentship.
Value: Payment of registration fees, UK£8,000 maintenance grant, contribution of UK£4,000 towards the running costs up to a maximum of UK£4,000 p.a.
Length of Study: Up to 3 years.
Frequency: Annual.
Study Establishment: Suitable U.K. academic institution.
Country of Study: United Kingdom.
Application Procedure: Applicants should apply to the main organisation.
Closing Date: 1st March.

THE HURSTON-WRIGHT FOUNDATION

6525 Belcrest Road, Suite 531, Hyalts ville, MD 20782, United States of America
Tel: (1) 301 683-2134
Email: info@hurston-wright.org
www: http://www.hurston-wright.org

The Foundation was established in September 1990 by novelist Marita Golden. Our mission is to develop, nurture and sustain the world community of writers of African descent.

The Hurston-Wright Award for College writers.
Subjects: Fiction or non-fiction writing in any genre.
Purpose: To support students of African descent enrolled full time as undergraduate or graduate students in any college or university in the United States.
Eligibility: Students of African descent from any of the diaspora.
Level of Study: Graduate, Postgraduate.
Type: Scholarship.
Value: US$1,000 or US$500.
Length of Study: Variable.
Frequency: Annual.
Study Establishment: Any suitable college or university.
Country of Study: United States of America.
No. of awards offered: 3.
Application Procedure: Submit to main organisation. Please check the website for details.
Closing Date: December 31.
Funding: Private.
No. of awards given last year: 3.

Hurston-Wright Legacy Award
Subjects: Works by published writers of African descent including any area of the diaspora.
Purpose: To support published writers of African descent in furthering their art.
Eligibility: Writers of African descent including any of the diaspora.
Level of Study: Professional development, Unrestricted.
Type: Scholarship.
Value: US$10,000 or US$5,000.
Length of Study: Variable.
Frequency: Annual.
No. of awards offered: 9.
Application Procedure: Book must be submitted by the publisher with permission of the writer.
Closing Date: December 8th.
Funding: Private.
No. of awards given last year: 9.

The Hurston-Wright Writer's week Scholarships
Subjects: Fiction or non-fiction writing in any genre.
Purpose: To support promising writers attending writer's week.
Eligibility: Students of African descent from any of the diaspora.
Level of Study: Professional development.
Type: Scholarship.
Value: Up to US$1,100.
Length of Study: Duration of workshop.
Frequency: Annual.
Study Establishment: Howard University, Washington DC.
Country of Study: United States of America.

No. of awards offered: Variable.
Application Procedure: Write a brief letter of no more than two paragraphs stating your financial situation and the amount of assistance you are requesting.
Closing Date: June 11.
Funding: Private.

For further information contact:

The Hurston-Wright Foundation, 6525 Belcrest Road, Suite 531, Hyalts Ville, MD 20782, United States of America
Tel: (1) 301 683-2134
Email: info@hurston-wright.org
www: http://www.hurston-wright.org

HYPERTENSION TRUST

127 High Street, Teddington, Middlesex, TW11 8HH, England
Tel: (44) 20 8977 0011
Fax: (44) 20 8977 0055
Email: gmccarthy@hamptonmedical.com
www: http://www.hypertensiontrust.org
Contact: Mrs G McCarthy, Administrator

The Hypertension Trust is a registered charity established to support research in hypertension and related cardiovascular conditions. Funds are available to support annual awards for Research Fellowships and Research Studentships.

Hypertension Trust Fellowship
Subjects: Hypertension and related cardiovascular conditions.
Purpose: To support research into hypertension and related cardiovascular conditions.
Eligibility: Applicants must hold a medical degree or higher degree in science eg. doctorate, and have evidence of research aptitude or clinical experience in hypertension. The fellowship is open to United Kingdom citizens or European Union nationals working in the United Kingdom.
Level of Study: Graduate, Postgraduate.
Type: Fellowship.
Value: A salary of approx. UK£20,000-30,000 per year. Up to UK£5,000 per year in expenses is available.
Length of Study: Two years.
Frequency: Annual.
Country of Study: United Kingdom.
No. of awards offered: One.
Application Procedure: Applicants must complete an application form.
Closing Date: 5th March 2004 Interviews: 27th May 2004.
Contributor: Surplus funds following the 16th Scientific Meeting of the International Society of Hypertension in June 1996.
No. of awards given last year: One.
No. of applicants last year: 13.
Additional Information: Applicants should visit the website for additional information.

Hypertension Trust Studentship
Subjects: Hypertension and related cardiovascular conditions.
Purpose: To support research into hypertension and related cardiovascular conditions.
Eligibility: Open to graduates of a European Union university or those currently working in a United Kingdom or Republic of Ireland hospital or institution.
Level of Study: Graduate, Postgraduate.
Type: Studentship.
Value: A salary based on MRC rates and PhD fees. Up to UK£5,000 in expenses.
Length of Study: Three years.
Frequency: Annual.
Country of Study: Other.
No. of awards offered: One.
Application Procedure: Applicants must complete an application form.
Closing Date: 5th March 2004 Interviews: 27th May 2004.

Contributor: Surplus funds following the 16th Scientific Meeting of the International Society of Hypertension in June 1996.
No. of awards given last year: 0.
No. of applicants last year: 3.
Additional Information: Applicants should visit the website for additional information.

IAN KARTEN CHARITABLE TRUST

The Mill House, Newark Lane, Ripley, Surrey, GU23 6DP, England
Fax: (44) 1483 222420
Email: iankarten@aol.com
Contact: Mr Tim Simon, Trustee & Administrator

The Ian Karten Charitable Trust aims to improve the quality of life and independence of people with severe physical, sensory, cognitive or learning disability by providing for them centres for computer aided training, education and communications (CTEC Centres). It also aims to support higher education by funding lectureships and studentships for postgraduate studies and research at universities in the United Kingdom.

Ian Karten Scholarship
Subjects: Most subjects, with varying levels of priority.
Purpose: To assist eligible students with the costs of postgraduate programmes of research at universities in the United Kingdom.
Eligibility: The scholarships will be available on a competitive basis for postgraduate students taking selected courses leading to Masters degrees or PhDs, and to musicians of outstanding merit for postgraduate training.
Level of Study: Doctorate, Postgraduate.
Type: Scholarship.
Value: Varies.
Frequency: Annual.
Study Establishment: United Kingdom university or conservatoire.
Country of Study: United Kingdom.
No. of awards offered: 100.
Application Procedure: Applicants must address enquiries about the availability at a particular university or conservatoire of Ian Karten Scholarships and about the procedure for applying to the institution concerned.
Closing Date: May 31st.
Funding: Private.
Contributor: Ian H Karten.
No. of awards given last year: 160.
No. of applicants last year: 500.
Additional Information: From the year 2000-2001 the Trust will provide funds for Ian Karten Scholarships directly to selected universities and conservatoires in the United Kingdom. The scholarships will be awarded by the institutions, on a basis agreed with the Trust.

IEEE (INSTITUTE OF ELECTRICAL AND ELECTRONICS ENGINEERS, INC.) HISTORY CENTER

39 Union Street, New Brunswick, NJ 08901, United States of America
Tel: (1) 732 932 1066
Fax: (1) 732 932 1193
Email: history@ieee.org
www: http://www.ieee.org/history_center
Contact: Mr Robert Colburn, Research Co-ordinator

The mission of the IEEE History Center is to preserve, research and promote the history of information and electrical technologies.

IEEE Fellowship in Electrical History
Subjects: The history of electrical engineering and computer technology.
Purpose: To support graduate work in the history of electrical engineering.
Eligibility: Open to suitably qualified graduate students.
Level of Study: Doctorate, Postdoctorate, Postgraduate.

Type: Fellowship.
Value: US$17,000 plus US$3,000 research budget.
Length of Study: One year.
Frequency: Annual.
Study Establishment: A college or university of recognised standing.
Country of Study: Any country.
No. of awards offered: One.
Application Procedure: Applicants must submit a completed application, transcripts, three letters of recommendation and a research proposal.
Closing Date: February 1st.
Funding: Corporation.
Additional Information: The fellowship is made possible by a grant from the IEEE Life Member Fund and is awarded by the IEEE History Committee. Application materials become available in October. Materials may be requested from the Center directly. Applicants should contact the IEEE Center for the History of Electrical Engineering for further information.

IMPERIAL COLLEGE OF SCIENCE, TECHNOLOGY AND MEDICINE

Exhibition Road, London, SW7 2AZ, England
Tel: (44) 20 7594 8023
Fax: (44) 20 7594 8004
Email: r.a.clay@ic.ac.uk
Contact: Ms R A Clay, Scholarships co-ordinator registry

The Imperial College of Science, Technology and Medicine is a college of the University of London and provides university education at first degree and postgraduate level in the fields of science, engineering and medicine.

John Stanley Scholarship
Subjects: Environmental technology.
Purpose: To facilitate postgraduate study or research.
Eligibility: Open to applicants undertaking a programme of postgraduate study in environmental technology at the Department of Environmental Science and Technology, Imperial College.
Level of Study: Doctorate, Postgraduate.
Type: Scholarship.
Value: Fees at the home student rate only and maintenance at the research council studentship basic rates.
Length of Study: One year, renewable for up to two additional years.
Frequency: Annual.
Study Establishment: The Department of Environmental Science and Technology, Imperial College.
Country of Study: United Kingdom.
No. of awards offered: Two.
Application Procedure: Applicants must state that they wish to apply on Section 9 of their admissions application form (PG1) and attach an additional letter asking to be considered for the award.
Closing Date: July 31st.
Funding: Private.
Contributor: Offered in collaboration with the Holly Hill Charitable Trust.
No. of awards given last year: Two.
Additional Information: Further information is available on request.

Rees Jeffreys Road Fund Bursaries
Subjects: Transport.
Purpose: To facilitate postgraduate study or research by supporting attendance on the Intercollegiate MSc.
Eligibility: Open to citizens of the United Kingdom who hold an Upper Second Class (Honours) Degree or above.
Level of Study: Postgraduate.
Type: Bursary.
Value: Fees and maintenance at the research council studentship basic rates.
Frequency: Annual.
Study Establishment: The Department of Civil Engineering, Imperial College.
Country of Study: United Kingdom.

No. of awards offered: Two, at the discretion of the Trustees.
Application Procedure: Applicants must complete an application form and submit this with two references and a short written statement.
Closing Date: June 15th.
Funding: Private.
Contributor: Rees Jeffreys Road Fund.
No. of awards given last year: Two.
Additional Information: Research into transport leading to the PhD at the University of London is also a programme eligible for support under this scheme.

Stephen and Anna Hui Fellowship

Subjects: Earth sciences defined as geology, extractive metallurgy, minerals, mining engineering, petroleum engineering, earth resources engineering and extractive metallurgy.
Purpose: To facilitate postgraduate study or research.
Eligibility: Open to graduates with a First or Upper Second Class (Honours) Degree from universities in China including Hong Kong and Taiwan.
Level of Study: Doctorate, Postgraduate.
Type: Fellowship.
Value: Fees and a maintenance allowance based on the United Kingdom's research council studentship rates.
Length of Study: One year, renewable for up to two additional years.
Frequency: Every two-three years.
Study Establishment: Imperial College.
Country of Study: United Kingdom.
No. of awards offered: One.
Application Procedure: Applicants must complete an application form and submit this with two references and a transcript or academic record.
Closing Date: January 31st.
Funding: Private.
Contributor: Stephen and Anna Hui Fellowship Trust Fund.
Additional Information: Further information is available on request.

INSEAD

Boulevard de Constance, Fontainebleau
Cedex F-77305, France
Tel: (33) 1 60 72 43 92
Fax: (33) 1 60 74 55 35
Email: mba.info@insead.fr
www: http://www.insead.edu/mba
Contact: Ms Helen Henderson, Director, Financial Aid

INSEAD is widely recognised as one of the most influential business schools in the world. With its second campus in Asia to complement its established presence in Europe, INSEAD is setting the pace in globalising the MBA. The one year intensive MBA programme is focused on international general management.

INSEAD Alumni Fund (IAF) Scholarship for the Asian campus

Subjects: MBA.
Eligibility: Open to candidates admitted and starting their course on INSEAD's Asian campus.
Level of Study: MBA.
Type: Scholarship.
Value: Varies.
Frequency: Annual.
Study Establishment: INSEAD.
Country of Study: Singapore.
No. of awards offered: Three.
Application Procedure: Applicants must complete a specific assignment, details of which are available from the organisation or from the website.
Closing Date: May 5th for the September intake of the same year and September 30th for the January intake of the following year.
Contributor: Alumni and a gift from a private individual.

INSEAD Alumni Fund (IAF) Scholarships

Subjects: MBA.
Purpose: To assist candidates admitted to the MBA programme.
Eligibility: Open to applicants from emerging or developing countries.
Level of Study: MBA.
Type: Scholarship.
Value: From €3,000-10,000.
Frequency: Annual.
Study Establishment: INSEAD.
Country of Study: Other.
No. of awards offered: Varies.
Application Procedure: Applicants must complete a specific assignment, details of which are available from the website.
Closing Date: May 5th for the September intake of the same year and September 30th for the January intake of the following year.
Contributor: Alumni.

INSEAD Antoine Rachid Irani/Bissada Scholarship

Subjects: MBA.
Purpose: To financially support MBA candidates.
Eligibility: Open to candidates of Lebanese or Egyptian nationality who are fluent in Arabic, preferably have a minimum of three years in a Lebanese university, who have obtained excellent academic and professional results and have been admitted to the INSEAD MBA programme.
Level of Study: MBA.
Type: Scholarship.
Value: Full tuition fees, but in order to lengthen the period of the scholarship, winners must pledge to repay 10 per cent of the value of the scholarship two years after graduating from INSEAD and an additional 10 per cent three years after graduating.
Frequency: Annual.
Study Establishment: INSEAD.
Country of Study: Other.
No. of awards offered: One.
Application Procedure: Applicants must complete a specific assignment, details of which are available from the organisation or from the website.
Closing Date: May 5th for the September class of the same year and September 30th for the January class of the following year.
Contributor: Bissada Management.

INSEAD Belgian Alumni and Council Scholarship Fund

Subjects: MBA.
Purpose: To assist MBA participants.
Eligibility: Open to candidates of merit of Belgian nationality and those who have lived in Belgium for at least five years. Priority will be given to admitted applicants who intend to return to Belgium after their MBA.
Level of Study: MBA.
Type: Scholarship.
Value: €6,400.
Frequency: Annual.
Study Establishment: INSEAD.
Country of Study: Other.
No. of awards offered: Two.
Application Procedure: Applicants must complete a specific assignment, details of which are available from the organisation or from the website.
Closing Date: May 5th for the September class of the same year and September 30th for the January class of the following year.
Contributor: Alumni and the Belgian Council.

INSEAD Børsen/Danish Council Scholarship

Subjects: MBA.
Purpose: To assist MBA participants.
Eligibility: Open to candidates of Danish nationality, admitted to the INSEAD MBA programme.
Level of Study: MBA.
Type: Scholarship.
Value: Please contact the organisation.
Frequency: Annual.

Study Establishment: INSEAD.
Country of Study: Other.
No. of awards offered: Two.
Application Procedure: Applicants must complete an application form, available from the website.
Closing Date: May 15th for the September class of the same year and September 15th for the January class of the following year.
Contributor: The Danish Council/Børsen.

INSEAD Canadian Foundation Scholarship

Subjects: MBA.
Purpose: To provide financial assistance and scholarships to deserving Canadians admitted to the INSEAD MBA programme.
Eligibility: Open to candidates of Canadian nationality, preferably resident in Canada, who have been admitted to the INSEAD MBA programme and are intending to return to Canada.
Level of Study: MBA.
Type: Scholarship.
Value: Up to Canadian $10,000.
Frequency: Annual.
Study Establishment: INSEAD.
Country of Study: Other.
No. of awards offered: Varies.
Application Procedure: Applicants must submit the following in support of their application, a covering letter requesting scholarship specifying which campus, a budget detailing the need for financial assistance including current and expected sources of funding, a copy of a completed INSEAD admission form with essay and supporting documents, a copy of reference letters submitted in support of application to INSEAD, a copy of Graduate Management Admissions Test results, a copy of university transcripts, and a copy of confirmation of admittance to INSEAD.
Closing Date: June 30th for candidates admitted to the September intake of the same year, and October 31st for candidates admitted to the January class of the following year.
Contributor: Alumni.
Additional Information: The Canadian INSEAD Foundation is a non-profit corporation whose purpose is to encourage Canadian students to develop an international business understanding and perspective. The Foundation's board members include many prominent Canadian business leaders and INSEAD alumni. Foundation members also act as the de facto representatives of Canada on INSEAD's International Council. The Foundation's financial assistance has to date already benefited over 50 Canadian alumni. It is hoped that this financial assistance and scholarship programme, while benefiting its Canadian recipients, will also impact favourably on the Canadian economy.

For further information contact:

The Board of Trustees, Canadian INSEAD Foundation, c/o Richard Tarte, Société générale de financement du Québec 600 de La Gauchetière Street West Suite 1700, Montréal, QC H3B 4L8, Canada
Tel: (1) 514 876 9290 ext. 2171

INSEAD Eli Lilly and Company Innovation Scholarship

Subjects: MBA.
Eligibility: Open to students of merit who demonstrate the capacity for innovative thinking and actions. Nationals from Africa, Asia, Central and Eastern Europe, Middle East, Central and South America, Turkey and Canada may apply.
Level of Study: MBA.
Type: Scholarship.
Value: Partial tuition.
Frequency: Annual.
Study Establishment: INSEAD.
Country of Study: Other.
No. of awards offered: Two per class.
Application Procedure: Applicants must complete a specific assignment, details of which are available from the organisation or from the website.
Closing Date: May 5th for the September intake of the same year and September 30th for the January intake of the following year.
Contributor: Eli Lilly Foundation.

Additional Information: Eli Lilly creates and delivers innovative pharmaceutical based healthcare solutions that enable people worldwide to live longer, healthier, more active lives.

INSEAD Elmar Schulte Diversity Scholarship

Subjects: MBA.
Purpose: To encourage diversity in the INSEAD MBA programme.
Eligibility: Open to candidates from non traditional MBA backgrounds who have been admitted to the programme.
Level of Study: MBA.
Type: Scholarship.
Value: Varies.
Frequency: Annual.
Study Establishment: INSEAD.
Country of Study: Other.
No. of awards offered: Varies.
Application Procedure: Applicants must complete an application form, available from the website.
Closing Date: May 5th for the September intake of the same year and September 30th for the January intake of the following year.
Contributor: Alumni.

INSEAD Elof Hansson Scholarship Fund

Subjects: MBA.
Purpose: To assist MBA participants.
Eligibility: Open to candidates of Swedish nationality who have been admitted to the INSEAD MBA programme.
Level of Study: MBA.
Type: Scholarship.
Value: €6,000.
Frequency: Annual.
Study Establishment: INSEAD.
Country of Study: Other.
No. of awards offered: Two.
Application Procedure: Applicants must complete an application form, available from the website.
Closing Date: May 15th for the September class of the same year and September 15th for the January class of the following year.
Contributor: The Elof Hansson Foundation.

INSEAD Freshfields Scholarship

Subjects: MBA.
Eligibility: Open to candidates of Asian nationality admitted to the INSEAD MBA programme, who will spend some time studying at INSEAD's Asian campus.
Level of Study: MBA.
Type: Scholarship.
Value: Up to €17,500.
Frequency: Annual.
Study Establishment: INSEAD.
Country of Study: Singapore.
No. of awards offered: Two.
Application Procedure: Applicants must complete an application form, available from the website.
Closing Date: May 5th for the September class of the same year and September 30th for the January class of the following year.
Contributor: Freshfields.
Additional Information: Freshfields is a major international law firm and market leader in international transactions that has an appreciation of the importance of the Asia Pacific region.

INSEAD Giovanni Agnelli Scholarship

Subjects: MBA.
Purpose: To support MBA participants.
Eligibility: Open to Italian candidates of high merit, admitted to the INSEAD MBA programme.
Level of Study: MBA.
Type: Scholarship.
Value: €1,500.
Frequency: Annual.
Study Establishment: INSEAD.
Country of Study: Other.
No. of awards offered: One-two.

Application Procedure: Applicants must complete an application form, available from the website.
Closing Date: May 5th for the September class of the same year and September 30th for the January class of the following year.
Contributor: Fiat.
Additional Information: This endowed scholarship is offered by the Fiat Group.

INSEAD Henry Grunfeld Foundation Scholarship
Subjects: MBA.
Purpose: To aid MBA students who can demonstrate a commitment to a career in investment banking.
Eligibility: Open to participants from a United Kingdom background with an interest in pursuing a career in investment banking.
Level of Study: MBA.
Type: Scholarship.
Value: Partial tuition.
Frequency: Annual.
Study Establishment: INSEAD.
Country of Study: Other.
No. of awards offered: One.
Application Procedure: Applicants must complete a specific assignment, details of which are available from the organisation or from the website.
Closing Date: May 5th for the September class of the same year and September 30th for the January class of the following year.
Contributor: The Henry Grunfeld Foundation.
Additional Information: Henry Grunfeld was a co-founder of S G Warburg, the United Kingdom investment bank that became one of the largest securities firms in the world, combining merchant banking, securities broking and market making.

INSEAD Jean François Clin MBA Scholarship
Subjects: MBA.
Purpose: To assist MBA participants from Francophone Africa.
Eligibility: Open to applicants from Burkino Faso, Guinea, Côte D'Ivoire, Mali, Niger, Senegal, Togos, Cambodia, Laos, Myanmar, Thailand and Vietnam who have already gained admission to the INSEAD MBA programme and have close ties with his or her country of origin. Candidates must have had at least secondary education in his or her country of origin although university level education may have been spent abroad. Scholarships will be awarded to candidates for either the September or January classes, on the basis of both merit and need.
Level of Study: MBA.
Type: Scholarship.
Value: Partial tuition.
Frequency: Annual.
Study Establishment: INSEAD.
Country of Study: Other.
No. of awards offered: Three.
Application Procedure: Applicants must complete a specific assignment, details of which are available from the organisation or from the website.
Closing Date: May 5th for the September intake of the same year and September 30th for the January intake of the following year.
Contributor: Jean François Clin.
Additional Information: Jean-François Clin, an alumnus of INSEAD who has a general interest in the economic development of Francophone West Africa and South East Asia, believes that managers in the region will need to be better equipped to face increasing competition, globalisation of businesses and demands on productivity.

INSEAD Judith Connelly Delouvrier Scholarship
Subjects: MBA.
Purpose: To support females undertaking the MBA.
Eligibility: Open to deserving American women admitted to the September MBA programme.
Level of Study: MBA.
Type: Scholarship.
Value: US$15,000.
Frequency: Annual.
Study Establishment: INSEAD.

Country of Study: Other.
No. of awards offered: One.
Application Procedure: Applicants must complete a specific assignment, details of which are available from the website.
Closing Date: May 5th for the September class of the same year.
Contributor: Alumni.
Additional Information: This scholarship is offered to remember Judith Connelly Delouvrier, wife of Phillippe Delouvrier, an INSEAD MBA of 1977, who was a victim of the TWA Flight 800 tragedy in 1996.

INSEAD L'Oréal Scholarship
Subjects: MBA.
Purpose: To foster creativity, diversity and entrepreneurial spirit within the MBA population.
Eligibility: Open to candidates of any nationality who demonstrate a capacity for creativity, innovation and entrepreneurial activity and who can demonstrate financial need.
Level of Study: MBA.
Type: Scholarship.
Value: Partial tuition fees.
Length of Study: One year.
Frequency: Annual.
Study Establishment: INSEAD.
Country of Study: Other.
No. of awards offered: Two per year, one per intake.
Closing Date: May 5th for the September class of the same year and September 30th for the January class of the following year.
Contributor: L'Oréal.

INSEAD Lord Kitchener National Memorial Scholarship
Subjects: MBA.
Purpose: To assist MBA participants from the United Kingdom.
Eligibility: Open to candidates who are British subjects and have served, or be the son or daughter of a parent who has at any time served or is serving on a full-time engagement in HM Armed Forces. This includes members and former members of the Territorial Army and other Reserve Forces of the Crown, and their sons and daughters, providing that the former have served an element of full-time or permanent service for a minimum consecutive period of three months.
Level of Study: MBA.
Type: Scholarship.
Value: UK£2,000 each.
Frequency: Annual.
Study Establishment: INSEAD.
Country of Study: Other.
No. of awards offered: Two per year, one per intake.
Application Procedure: Applicants must complete an application form, available from the website and send it to INSEAD with documentary evidence of either the candidates' or the candidates parent's service in the British Armed Forces.
Closing Date: May 5th for the September class of the same year and September 30th for the January class of the following year.
Additional Information: The Lord Kitchener National Memorial Fund was created in memory of the first Earl Kitchener of Khartoum who died in action in June 1916 when he went down with his ship. Earl Kitchener had a national reputation as Secretary of State for War and as the organiser of 'Kitchener's Army'. The Council of the Fund regards that the acquisition of an MBA would benefit not only the individual but also the United Kingdom as a whole as it is relevant to overseas trade and is a worthy memorial to the first Earl Kitchener, a great patriot and also a far-seeing internationalist.

INSEAD Louis Franck Scholarship
Subjects: MBA.
Eligibility: Open to candidates of United Kingdom nationality admitted to INSEAD. Financial need is neither a necessary nor a sufficient condition for being granted an award. Nevertheless, the candidate's financial position will be taken into account, and awards will not necessarily be granted to the best candidates if there is a sound candidate who is in financial need. Selected scholars are required to write a thesis or report, the subject of which to be agreed with the trustees, to be presented to the trustees within three months of graduation.
Type: Scholarship.

Value: Varies, approx. UK£5,000 each.
Frequency: Annual.
Study Establishment: INSEAD.
Country of Study: Other.
No. of awards offered: Up to eight.
Application Procedure: Applicants must complete a specific assignment, details of which are available from the website.
Closing Date: May 5th for the September class of the same year and September 30th for the January class of the following year.
Funding: Private.
Contributor: The Louis Franck Trust.
Additional Information: This scholarship was established in 1983 by Louis Franck, who served for many years on the Board of INSEAD, to mark his gratitude for the opportunities in life which the United Kingdom gave him. Louis Franck was born in Belgium in 1907 and came to work in England as a young man. He became a prominent banker in the City of London and was responsible for transforming Samuel Montagu, now part of HSBC Investment Bank, from a quiet firm of bullion and foreign exchange dealers into a leading merchant bank. During World War II, Louis Franck had a distinguished record in the British Army, including involvement in the clandestine Special Operations Executive, and was awarded the CBE in recognition of his services. Louis Franck died in Switzerland in September 1988.

INSEAD Sasakawa (SYLLF) Scholarships
Subjects: MBA.
Purpose: To encourage candidates to broaden their knowledge and enhance their career leadership through the INSEAD MBA programme.
Eligibility: Open to candidates of any nationality. The awards will be made on a competitive basis.
Level of Study: MBA.
Type: Scholarship.
Value: €3,000-11,000 depending on the number and quality of applications.
Frequency: Annual.
Study Establishment: INSEAD.
Country of Study: Other.
No. of awards offered: One or more per intake.
Application Procedure: Applicants must complete a specific assignment, details of which are available from the website.
Closing Date: May 5th for the September class of the same year and September 30th for the January class of the following year.
Funding: Private.
Contributor: The Sasakawa Young Leaders Fellowship Fund (SYLFF).

INSEAD Sisley-Marc d'Ornano Scholarship
Subjects: MBA.
Purpose: To support young graduates seeking further education in order to contribute to the economic development of Poland.
Eligibility: Open to Polish nationals admitted to the INSEAD MBA programme who demonstrate a commitment to work in Poland for three years after the INSEAD MBA programme. The winner of the scholarship will agree to take up a professional activity in Poland for at least three years, as if not, the candidate is obliged to reimburse the scholarship.
Level of Study: MBA.
Type: Scholarship.
Value: Tuition fees and a living allowance. Partial scholarships, ie. tuition fees only, may be awarded in the case of residence outside Poland.
Frequency: Annual.
Study Establishment: INSEAD.
Country of Study: Other.
No. of awards offered: One.
Application Procedure: Applicants must submit an essay addressing the following question: 'Give the main reason for your applying for the scholarship and describe your aspirations for your future career development'. Scholarship applications may be submitted with the admissions application form. Application forms are available from the website.

Closing Date: May 5th for the September intake of the same year and September 30th for the January intake of the following year.
Contributor: Sisley.
Additional Information: This scholarship is offered in memory of the late Marc d'Ornano, who lost his life in a car accident while at the start of an excellent career.

INSTITUT FRANÇAIS DE WASHINGTON

234 Dey Hall, CB 3170, UNC-CH
Chapel Hill, NC 27599-3170
United States of America
Tel: (1) 919 962 0154
Fax: (1) 919 962 5457
Email: cmaley@email.unc.edu
www: http://www.unc.edu/depts/institut
Contact: Dr Catherine A Maley, President

The purpose of the Institut Français de Washington is to promote the study of French civilisation, history, literature and art in the United States of America.

Edouard Morot-Sir Fellowship in Literature
Subjects: French studies in the areas of art, economics, history, history of science, linguistics, literature or social sciences.
Eligibility: Open to those in the final stage of a PhD dissertation, or who have held a PhD for no longer than six years before the application deadline.
Level of Study: Doctorate, Postdoctorate.
Type: Fellowship.
Value: US$1,500.
Length of Study: At least two months.
Frequency: Annual.
Country of Study: France.
Application Procedure: Applicants must write a maximum of two pages describing the research project and planned trip and enclose a curriculum vitae. A letter of recommendation from the dissertation director is also required.
Closing Date: January 15th.
Funding: Private.
No. of awards given last year: One.
No. of applicants last year: 45.
Additional Information: Awards are for maintenance during research in France and should not be used for travel.

Gilbert Chinard Fellowships
Subjects: French studies in the areas of art, economics, history, history of science, linguistics, literature or social sciences.
Eligibility: Open to those in the final stage of a PhD dissertation, or who have held a PhD for no longer than six years before the application deadline.
Level of Study: Doctorate, Postdoctorate.
Type: Fellowship.
Value: US$1,500.
Length of Study: At least two months.
Frequency: Annual.
Country of Study: France.
No. of awards offered: Three.
Application Procedure: Applicants must write a maximum of two pages describing the research project and planned trip and enclose a curriculum vitae. A letter of recommendation from the dissertation director is also required for PhD candidates.
Closing Date: January 15th.
Funding: Private.
No. of awards given last year: Two.
No. of applicants last year: 45.
Additional Information: Awards are for maintenance during research in France and should not be used for travel.

Harmon Chadbourn Rorison Fellowship
Subjects: French studies in the areas of art, economics, history, history of science, linguistics, literature or social sciences.

Eligibility: Open to those in the final stage of a PhD dissertation, or who have held a PhD for no longer than six years before the application deadline.
Level of Study: Doctorate, Postdoctorate.
Type: Fellowship.
Value: US$1,500.
Length of Study: At least two months.
Frequency: Every two years.
Country of Study: France.
No. of awards offered: One.
Application Procedure: Applicants must write a maximum of two pages describing the research project and planned trip and enclose a curriculum vitae. A letter of recommendation from the dissertation director is also required for PhD candidates.
Closing Date: January 15th.
Funding: Private.
No. of awards given last year: One.
No. of applicants last year: 45.
Additional Information: Awards are for maintenance during research in France and should not be used for travel.

THE INSTITUT MITTAG-LEFFLER

Auravägen 17, SE 18260-Djursholm, Sweden
Tel: (46) 8 6220560
Fax: (46) 8 6220589
Email: koskull@ml.kva.se
www: http://www.ml.kva.se
Contact: Marie-Louise Koskull, Administrator of the Visiting Programme

The Institut Mittag-Leffler is a Nordic research institute for mathematics, under the auspices of the Royal Swedish Academy of Sciences, created by Gösta and Signe Mittag-Leffler who donated their house, library and fortune to the Academy.

Institut Mittag-Leffler Grants
Subjects: Mathematics. The specific topics vary each year.
Eligibility: Open to recent PhDs and advanced graduate students. Preference will be given to applications for long stays.
Level of Study: Doctorate.
Type: Grant.
Value: Krona 15,000 per month or Krona 108,000 for those who stay for the full duration of the programme, plus a family allowance.
Length of Study: One academic year, from September through to June 15th.
Frequency: Annual.
Country of Study: Sweden.
No. of awards offered: Varies.
Application Procedure: Applicants must complete an application form.
Closing Date: January 31st.
Additional Information: Further information is available on request.

INSTITUTE FOR ADVANCED STUDIES IN THE HUMANITIES

University of Edinburgh, Hope Park Square, Edinburgh, EH8 9NW, Scotland
Tel: (44) 131 650 4671
Fax: (44) 131 668 2252
Email: iash@ed.ac.uk
www: http://www.ed.ac.uk/iash
Contact: Ms Anthea Taylor, Assistant to Director

The Institute for Advanced Studies in the Humanities aims to promote scholarship in the humanities, and wherever possible to foster interdisciplinary enquiries. This is achieved by means of fellowships awarded for the pursuit of relevant research and by the public dissemination of findings in seminars, lectures, conferences, exhibitions, cultural events and publications.

Andrew W Mellon Foundation Fellowships in the Humanities
Subjects: The humanities. No limitation will be placed on the area of research within the humanities, but preference will be given to Scholars from any discipline whose work concerns one of the Institute's themes eg. The New Information Order or Scotland in Europe and Europe in Scotland.
Purpose: To promote advanced research within the field of humanities and to sponsor interdisciplinary research.
Eligibility: Open to Bulgarian, Czech, Estarian, Hungarian, Latrian, Lithuanian, Polish, Romanian and Slovak scholars only. Fellows must be able to speak English and be under 45 years of age.
Level of Study: Postdoctorate.
Type: Grant.
Length of Study: Three months.
Frequency: Annual.
Study Establishment: The Institute for Advanced Studies in the Humanities at the University of Edinburgh.
Country of Study: Scotland.
No. of awards offered: Four.
Application Procedure: Applicants must complete an application form, available from the Institute.
Closing Date: March 31st.
Funding: Private.
No. of awards given last year: Four.
No. of applicants last year: 33.

Institute for Advanced Studies in the Humanities Visiting Research Fellowships
Subjects: Archaeology, history of art, classics, English literature, history, European and oriental languages and literature, linguistics, philosophy, Scottish studies, history of science, law, divinity, music and the social sciences. Preference will be given to scholars, from any discipline, whose work concerns one of the Institute's themes eg. The New Information Order, or Scotland in Europe and Europe in Scotland.
Purpose: To promote advanced research within the field and also to sponsor interdisciplinary research.
Eligibility: Open to scholars of any nationality holding a doctorate or offering equivalent evidence of aptitude for advanced studies. Degree candidates are not eligible.
Level of Study: Postdoctorate.
Type: Fellowship.
Value: Most fellowships are honorary, but limited support towards expenses is available to a small number of candidates.
Length of Study: Two-six months.
Frequency: Annual.
Study Establishment: The Institute for Advanced Studies in the Humanities at the University of Edinburgh.
Country of Study: United Kingdom.
No. of awards offered: 15.
Application Procedure: Applicants must complete an application form, available from the Institute. Candidates should advise their referees to write on their behalf directly to the Institute.
Closing Date: December 1st. Candidates should ensure that their references are received in Edinburgh before January 12th.
Funding: Private.
No. of awards given last year: 14.
No. of applicants last year: 23.
Additional Information: Fellows have the use of study rooms at the Institute, near the library and within easy reach of the National Library of Scotland, the Central City Library, the National Galleries and Museums, the Library of the Society of Antiquaries in Scotland, and the National Archives of Scotland.

INSTITUTE FOR ADVANCED STUDY

Einstein Drive, Princeton, NJ 08540, United States of America
Tel: (1) 609 734 8000
Fax: (1) 609 924 8399
Email: gwhidden@ias.edu
www: http://www.ias.edu
Contact: Ms Georgia Whidden, Public Affairs Officer

The Institute for Advanced Study is an independent, private institution whose mission is to support advanced scholarship and fundamental research in historical studies, mathematics, natural sciences, social science and theoretical biology. It is a community of scholars where theoretical research and intellectual enquiry are carried out under the most favourable conditions.

Institute for Advanced Study Postdoctoral Residential Fellowships

Subjects: Social science, history, astronomy, theoretical physics, mathematics or theoretical biology.
Purpose: To support advanced study and scholarly exploration.
Eligibility: There are no restrictions on eligibility.
Level of Study: Postdoctorate.
Type: Fellowship.
Value: US$30,000-50,000.
Length of Study: Generally one year.
Frequency: Annual.
Country of Study: United States of America.
No. of awards offered: 190.
Application Procedure: Applicants must complete an application. Materials are available from the school administrative officers.
Closing Date: Varies, but is between November 15th and December 15th.
No. of awards given last year: 190.
No. of applicants last year: 2,400.

INSTITUTE FOR ECUMENICAL AND CULTURAL RESEARCH

PO Box 6188, Collegeville, MN 53621-6188
United States of America
Tel: (1) 320 363 3366
Fax: (1) 320 363 3313
Email: iecr@iecr.org
www: http://www.iecr.org
Contact: Patrick Henry, Executive Director

The Institute for Ecumenical and Cultural Research seeks to discern the meaning of Christian identity and unity in a religiously and culturally diverse nation and world and to communicate that meaning for the mission of the church and the renewal of human community. The Institute is committed to research, study, prayer, reflection and dialogue, in a place shaped by the Benedictine tradition of worship and work.

Bishop Thomas Hoyt Jr Fellowship

Subjects: Ecumenical and cultural research.
Purpose: To provide the Institute's residency fee to a North American person of colour writing a doctoral dissertation, in order to help the churches to increase the number of persons of colour working in ecumenical and cultural research.
Eligibility: Open to a North American, Canadian, or Mexican, person of colour writing a doctoral dissertation within the general area of the Institute's concern.
Level of Study: Postgraduate.
Type: Other.
Value: US$3,400, this figure is slated to rise gradually in future years, check the web page for projections.
Length of Study: One academic year (or two if semesters).
Frequency: Annual.
Study Establishment: The Institute.
Country of Study: United States of America.
No. of awards offered: One each year (or two if for semesters).
Application Procedure: Applicants must apply in the usual way to the Resident Scholars Programme (see separate listing). If invited by the admissions committee to be a Resident Scholar, the person will then be eligible for consideration for the Hoyt Fellowship.
Closing Date: January 15th prior to intended period of stay.
Funding: Private.
No. of awards given last year: Zero.
No. of applicants last year: Zero.

INSTITUTE FOR HUMANE STUDIES (IHS)

3301 North Faifax DriveSuite 440, Arlington, VA 22201-4432, United States of America
Tel: (1) 703 993 4880
Fax: (1) 703 993 4890
Email: ihs@gmu.edu
www: http://theihs.org
Contact: Ms Keri Anderson, Student Co-ordinator

The Institute for Humane Studies (IHS) is a unique organisation that assists graduate students worldwide with a special interest in individual liberty. IHS awards over US$400,000 a year in scholarships to students from universities around the world. They also sponsor the attendance of hundreds of students at free summer seminars, and provide various forms of career assistance. Through these and other programmes, IHS and a network of faculty associates promote the study of liberty across a broad range of disciplines, encouraging understanding, open enquiry, rigorous scholarship and creative problem solving.

Charles G Koch Summer Fellowship

Subjects: Current public policy issues, career development workshops, writing projects with a professional editor and the Washington DC policy community.
Purpose: To offer intensive eight week internship experiences with Washington DC free market public policy think tanks alongside two week-long seminars.
Eligibility: Open to graduate students and recent graduates.
Level of Study: Graduate.
Type: Internship.
Value: US$1,500 plus furnished housing and travel expenses.
Length of Study: Ten weeks consisting of a full-time eight week internship and two week-long intensive seminars.
Frequency: Annual.
Application Procedure: Applicants must apply online www.the-ihs.org/intern.
Closing Date: February 15th.
Funding: Private.
No. of awards given last year: 40.

Felix Morley Journalism Competition

Subjects: Principles include inalienable individual rights eg. their protection through the institutions of private property, contract law, the rule of law, voluntarism in all human relations, the self-ordering market, free trade, free migration and peace.
Purpose: To award journalists for demonstrated ability, potential for development as a writer and appreciation of classical liberal principles evidenced in submitted publications.
Eligibility: Open to full-time students or those aged 25 and younger.
Level of Study: Unrestricted.
Type: Competition.
Value: The first prize is US$2,500, the second prize is US$1,000, the third prize is US$750 and the runners up prize is US$250.
Frequency: Annual.
Application Procedure: Applicants can download applications at www.the ihs.org/morley.
Closing Date: December 1st.
Funding: Private.

Hayek Fund for Scholars

Subjects: Social sciences, law, the humanities, journalism.
Purpose: To help offset expenses for participating in professional conferences and job interviews.
Eligibility: Open to graduate students and untenured faculty members.
Level of Study: Postgraduate.
Type: Other.
Value: US$1,000.
Frequency: Annual.
Country of Study: Any country.
Application Procedure: Visit the website (www.theihs.org) for application requirements.

For further information contact:

George Mason University, 4400 University Drive, Fairfax, VA 22030, United States of America
Tel: (1) 703 323 1055
Fax: (1) 703 425 1536
Contact: Programme Director

IHS Felix Morley Memorial Journalism Competition

Subjects: Current issues from a classical liberal perspective.
Purpose: To encourage writing that reflects an interest in the classical liberal tradition.
Eligibility: Open to fulltime students or under 25 years old.
Level of Study: Unrestricted.
Type: Other.
Value: First prize US$2,500, second prize US$1,500, third prize US$1,000, five runners-up prizes US$500.
Frequency: Annual.
Country of Study: Any country.
Application Procedure: Download an application at www.theihs.org/morley.
Closing Date: December 1st.

For further information contact:

George Mason University 4400 University Drive, Fairfax, VA 22030, United States of America
Tel: (1) 703 323 1055
Fax: (1) 703 425 1536
Contact: Keri Landerson, Programme Director

IHS Film & Fiction Scholarships

Subjects: Film making, fiction writing or playwriting.
Eligibility: Open to graduate students pursuing a Master of Fine Arts degree. Applicants should have a demonstrated interest in classical liberal ideas and their application in contemporary society. They should also demonstrate the desire, motivation and creative ability to succeed in their chosen profession.
Level of Study: Graduate.
Type: Scholarship.
Value: Up to US$10,000.
Frequency: Annual.
Application Procedure. Applicants must apply online at www.theihs.org/film&fiction.
Closing Date: January 15.
Funding: Private.

IHS Humane Studies Fellowships

Subjects: Arts and humanities, fine and applied art, law, mass communication and information, religion and theology or social and behavioural science.
Purpose: To support outstanding students with a demonstrated interest in the classical liberal tradition intent on pursuing an intellectual and scholarly career.
Eligibility: Open to graduate students with enrolled in the next academic year at accredited colleges and universities.
Level of Study: Graduate, Postgraduate.
Type: Fellowship.
Value: Up to US$12,000.
Frequency: Annual.
Country of Study: Any country.
Application Procedure: Applicants must complete and submit an application form with three completed evaluations, three essays, official test scores, official transcripts and a term paper or writing sample. Applications can be downloaded at www.theihs.org/hsf.
Closing Date: December 30th.
Funding: Private.
No. of awards given last year: 100.
No. of applicants last year: 650.

IHS Liberty & Society Summer Seminars

Subjects: Foundations of liberty, liberty and culture, liberty and current issues and liberty crisis, social change workshop and liberty society.

Purpose: To allow individuals to learn and exchange ideas.
Level of Study: Graduate.
Value: All free summer seminars include room and board, lectures and seminars, materials and books. Each seminar spot is worth approximately US$1,000.
Frequency: Annual.
Study Establishment: The IHS.
Country of Study: United States of America.
Application Procedure: Applicants must apply online at www.theihs.org.
Closing Date: The final deadline is March 30th.

IHS Summer Graduate Research Fellowship

Subjects: The humane sciences eg. history, political and moral philosophy, political economy, economic history, legal and social theory.
Purpose: To give students who share an interest in scholarly research in the classical liberal tradition the opportunity to work on a thesis chapter or a paper of publishable quality and to participate in interdisciplinary seminars under the guidance of a faculty supervisor.
Eligibility: Open to graduate students in the humanities, social sciences and law who intend to pursue academic careers and who are currently pursuing research in the classical liberal tradition.
Level of Study: Doctorate, Graduate, Postgraduate.
Type: Fellowship.
Value: US$5,000.
Frequency: Annual.
Country of Study: United States of America.
No. of awards offered: 8-10.
Application Procedure: Applicants must submit a proposal, curriculum vitae, a copy of Graduate Record Examination scores or Law School Admission Test scores and transcripts, a writing sample and reference details. Visit the website for further information.
Closing Date: February 15th.
Funding: Private.

IHS Young Communicators Fellowship

Subjects: Journalism, film, writing (fiction or non fiction), publishing or free-market oriented public policy.
Purpose: To help place Fellows in strategic positions that can enhance their abilities and credentials to pursue targeted careers.
Eligibility: Open to advanced students and recent graduates who have a clearly demonstrated interest in the classical liberal tradition of individual rights and market economies.
Level of Study: Professional development.
Type: Fellowship.
Value: US$5,000, to include stipend, housing and travel.
Frequency: Annual.
Country of Study: Any country.
No. of awards offered: Varies.
Application Procedure: Applicants must submit a proposal of 500-1,000 words explaining what specific summer position, similar short-term position, or training programme could be pursued if they were supported by a Fellowship, how the proposed opportunity would enhance the applicant's career prospects, and how the proposed opportunity could contribute to the applicant's understanding of classical liberal principles and their application to today's issues. A current curriculum vitae listing educational background, including major field and any academic honours received, current educational status, work experience, including Summer positions and internships, and citations of any publications should also be included. Candidates should also submit a writing sample or other sample of work appropriate to the intended career and provide the name, address, and phone number of an academic and/or professional reference.
Closing Date: March 15th for Summer positions and 10 weeks prior to the start of other positions.

Liberty and Society Week-Long Summer Conferences

Subjects: Classical liberal ideas.
Purpose: To introduce participants to the foundations of classical liberal thought.
Eligibility: Open to graduate and undergraduate students.
Level of Study: Unrestricted.
Type: Varies.

Value: US$1,000.
Frequency: Annual.
Country of Study: Any country.
Application Procedure: Visit www.theihs.org/seminars to apply.
Closing Date: March 31st.

For further information contact:

George Mason University, 4400 University Drive, Fairfax, VA 22030, United States of America
Tel: (1) 703 323 1055
Fax: (1) 703 425 1536
Contact: Programme Director

THE INSTITUTE FOR SUPPLY MANAGEMENT (ISM)

2055 East Centennial Circle, PO Box 22160, Tempe, AZ 85285-2160, United States of America
Tel: (1) 480 752 6276
Fax: (1) 480 752 7890
Email: jcavinato@ism.ws
www: http://www.ism.ws
Contact: Dr Joseph L Cavinato, Senior Vice President

The Institute for Supply Management (ISM) is a non-profit association that provides national and international leadership in purchasing and supply management research and education. ISM provides more than 46,000 members with opportunities to expand their professional skills and knowledge.

ISM Doctoral Grants
Subjects: Purchasing materials and supply management.
Purpose: To financially assist individuals in preparation for a career in the field, for university teaching and to encourage research.
Eligibility: Open to doctoral candidates who are pursuing a PhD or DBA in purchasing, business, logistics, management, economics, industrial engineering or a related field and who are at the dissertation stage. Applicants must be enrolled in an accredited United States university to be eligible for the award.
Level of Study: Doctorate.
Type: Grant.
Value: Up to US$10,000.
Frequency: Annual.
Country of Study: United States of America.
No. of awards offered: Four.
Application Procedure: Applicants must submit an application form and documents including letters of recommendation, transcripts and a research proposal.
Closing Date: January 31st.
Funding: Private.
Contributor: ISM.
No. of awards given last year: Four.
No. of applicants last year: 20.
Additional Information: Upon successful completion of the research, the ISM will be interested in the publication of material from the study. Nominations are invited from departments of economics, management, marketing and business administration at United States universities offering a doctoral degree in appropriate fields.

ISM Senior Research Fellowship Program
Subjects: Topics include but are not limited to the integration of purchasing with other functions, the impact of globalisation on purchasing, the role of purchasing in supply chain management, measuring purchasing effectiveness, historical analysis of trends in purchasing, objective measures of supplier performance, the application of electronic commerce in purchasing and supply, the use of purchasing as a strategic tool, the identification of educational or training tools and skills for purchasing and supply management, forecasting methods, ERP and purchasing, alliances and supplier development.
Purpose: To help support emerging, high potential scholars who teach and conduct research in purchasing and supply management.

Eligibility: Open to assistant professors, associate professors or equivalent who have demonstrated exceptional academic productivity in research and teaching. Candidates are chosen from those who can help produce useful research that can be applied to the advancement of purchasing and supply management. Candidates must be full-time faculty members within or outside the United States of America and be current or past members of ISM committees, groups, forums or affiliated organisations. An assistant professor should have three or more years of post degree experience. Previous awardees are ineligible.
Level of Study: Predoctorate.
Type: Fellowship.
Value: US$5,000.
Frequency: Annual.
Country of Study: United States of America.
No. of awards offered: Two.
Application Procedure: Applicants must submit four copies of each of the following items in one complete package: a letter of application explaining qualifications for the fellowship, a research proposal of no more than five pages including a problem statement or hypothesis, research methodology with data sources, collection and analysis, value to the field of purchasing and supply and a curriculum vitae including works in progress.
Closing Date: April 1st.
Funding: Private.
Contributor: ISM.
No. of applicants last year: 5-10.
Additional Information: It is expected that the ISM Fellows will present the results of their research at an ISM forum eg. research symposium, ISM Annual International Purchasing Conference and/or an NAPM publication such as 'The Journal of Supply Chain Management'.

THE INSTITUTE FOR THE STUDY OF AGING

767 Fifth AvenueSuite 4600, New York, NY 10153, United States of America
Tel: (1) 212 572 4086
Fax: (1) 212 572 4094
Email: tlee@aging-institute.org
www: http://www.aging-institute.org
Contact: Ms Tonya Lee, Grants Manager

The Institute for the Study of Aging is a non-profit foundation based in New York City. The Institute supports research on Alzheimer's disease and cognitive decline.

Institute for the Study of Aging Grants Program
Subjects: Early identification, prevention and treatment of Alzheimer's disease and cognitive decline. The Institute focuses its efforts in facilitating drug discovery and development in this field.
Purpose: To promote the research and development of technology and therapies to identify, treat and prevent cognitive decline, Alzheimer's disease and related dementias.
Eligibility: There are no eligibility restrictions.
Level of Study: Unrestricted.
Type: Grant.
Value: Negotiable.
Length of Study: One-three years.
Frequency: There is no funding cycle.
Study Establishment: A non-profit family foundation.
Country of Study: Any country.
Application Procedure: Applicants must submit a brief lay summary, a research proposal of up to five pages including background, aims, supporting data, experimental design and methods, a biosketch, a summary of resources and a budget with justification.
Closing Date: Applications are accepted at any time.
Funding: Private.
No. of awards given last year: 29.
Additional Information: In addition to funding research activities, the Institute sponsors and/or co-sponsors conferences, scientific and medical workshops to advance knowledge on issues related to

Alzheimer's disease and cognitive vitality. For further information please contact Lorenzo Refolo, Scientific Director, email: lrefolo@aging-institute.org or Howard Fillit, Executive Director, email: hfillit@aging-institute.org.

INSTITUTE OF ADVANCED LEGAL STUDIES (IALS)

School of Advanced Study, Charles Clore House, 17 Russell Square, London, WC1B 5DR, England
Tel: (44) 20 7862 5883
Fax: (44) 20 7862 5850
Email: dphillip@sas.ac.uk
www: http://www.ials.sas.ac.uk
Contact: Mr D E Phillips, Administrative Secretary

The Institute of Advanced Legal Studies (IALS) has a national and international role in the promotion and facilitation of legal research. It possesses one of the leading research libraries in Europe and organises a regular programme of conferences, seminars and lectures. It also offers postgraduate taught and research programmes and specialised training courses.

Howard Drake Memorial Fund
Subjects: Law and library science.
Purpose: To encourage collaboration and exchanges between legal scholars and law librarians, especially between those of different countries and to promote the study of law librarianship and the training of law librarians.
Eligibility: There are no restrictions on eligibility.
Level of Study: Professional development.
Type: Grant.
Value: Up to approx. UK£800 per grant.
Frequency: Dependent on funds available.
Study Establishment: The IALS.
Country of Study: United Kingdom.
No. of awards offered: One-two.
Application Procedure: Applicants must make applications to the Administrative Secretary. There is no official application form.
No. of awards given last year: None.
No. of applicants last year: None.

IALS Visiting Fellowship in Law Librarianship
Subjects: Law and library science.
Purpose: To enable experienced law librarians, who are undertaking research in appropriate fields, to relate their work to activities in which the Institutes own library is involved.
Eligibility: Open to experienced law librarians from any country.
Level of Study: Unrestricted.
Type: Fellowship.
Value: Non-stipendary.
Length of Study: A minimum of three months and a maximum of one year.
Frequency: Annual.
Study Establishment: The IALS.
Country of Study: United Kingdom.
No. of awards offered: One.
Application Procedure: Applicants must submit a full curriculum vitae, the names, addresses and telephone numbers of two referees and a brief statement of the research programme to be undertaken to the Administrative Secretary.
Closing Date: January 31st in respect of the following academic year.
No. of awards given last year: One.
No. of applicants last year: One.

IALS Visiting Fellowship in Legislative Studies
Subjects: Law.
Purpose: To enable individuals in the field to undertake research.
Eligibility: Open to established academics and practitioners from any country. This award is not available for postgraduate research.
Level of Study: Unrestricted.
Type: Fellowship.
Value: Non-stipendary.

Length of Study: A minimum of three months and a maximum of one year.
Frequency: Annual.
Study Establishment: The IALS.
Country of Study: United Kingdom.
No. of awards offered: One.
Application Procedure: Applicants must submit a full curriculum vitae, the names, addresses and telephone numbers of two referees and a brief statement of the research programme to be undertaken.
Closing Date: January 31st in respect of the following academic year.
No. of awards given last year: None.
No. of applicants last year: One.

IALS Visiting Fellowships
Subjects: Law.
Eligibility: Open to nationals of any country who are established legal scholars, and are undertaking research in appropriate fields.
Level of Study: Unrestricted.
Type: Fellowship.
Value: Non-stipendary.
Length of Study: A minimum of three months and a maximum of one year.
Frequency: Annual.
Study Establishment: The IALS.
Country of Study: United Kingdom.
No. of awards offered: Up to six.
Application Procedure: Applicants must submit a full curriculum vitae, the names, addresses and telephone numbers of two referees and a brief statement of the research programme to be undertaken.
Closing Date: January 31st in respect of the following academic year.
No. of awards given last year: Seven.
No. of applicants last year: 16.
Additional Information: This award is not available for postgraduate research.

INSTITUTE OF BIOLOGY

20 Queensberry Place, London, SW7 2DZ, England
Tel: (44) 20 7581 8333
Fax: (44) 20 7823 9409
Email: info@iob.org
www: http://www.iob.org
Contact: Ms Georgina Day, Education Officer

The Institute of Biology's mission is to promote biology and the biological sciences, to foster the public understanding of science, to enhance the status of the biology profession and to represent its members as a whole to government and other bodies worldwide. The Institute is the 'voice' of British biology.

Dax Copp Travelling Fellowship
Subjects: Biological sciences.
Purpose: To support overseas travel in connection with biological study, teaching or research and to aid those who would otherwise not have this opportunity.
Eligibility: Open to students in the biological sciences studying in the United Kingdom.
Level of Study: Unrestricted.
Type: Fellowship.
Value: UK£500.
Frequency: Annual.
No. of awards offered: Varies.
Application Procedure: Applicants must complete an application form, available from the Expeditions Grants Manager. Applicants are also required to produce a reasoned statement of the purpose to which the fellowship will be put, supported by three referees.
Closing Date: Mid January.
Funding: Private.
Contributor: Membership.
No. of awards given last year: One.
No. of applicants last year: 20.

Additional Information: Applicants receiving a fellowship will be expected to provide the Institute with a report within six months of the fellowship ending.

For further information contact:

Royal Geographical Society, 1 Kensington Gore, London, SW7 2AR, England
Tel: (44) 20 7591 3073
Email: grants@rsg.org
Contact: Expedition Grants Manager

THE INSTITUTE OF CANCER RESEARCH (ICR)

McElwain Laboratories15 Cotswold Road, Sutton, Surrey, SM2 5NG, England
Tel: (44) 20 8643 8901 ext. 4253
Fax: (44) 20 8643 6940
Email: joanna.richards@icr.ac.uk
www: http://www.icr.ac.uk
Contact: Ms Renate Divers, Assistant Registrar

Over the past 90 years, the Institute of Cancer Research (ICR) has become one of the largest, most successful and innovative cancer research centres in the world. The Institute and the Royal Marsden NHS Trust exist side by side in Chelsea and on a joint site at Sutton, and this close association allows for maximum interaction between fundamental laboratory work and clinical environment.

ICR Research Studentships
Subjects: Cancer research.
Eligibility: Open to applicants holding a of a First or Upper Second Class (Honours) Degree or equivalent in a relevant subject.
Level of Study: Doctorate.
Type: Studentship.
Value: A generous stipend and consumables.
Length of Study: Up to three years.
Frequency: Annual.
Study Establishment: The Institute.
Country of Study: United Kingdom.
No. of awards offered: 15-20.
Application Procedure: Applicants must complete an application form and attend an interview.
Closing Date: January.
Funding: Government.
Contributor: Cancer Research UK.
No. of awards given last year: 20.
No. of applicants last year: 212.
Additional Information: A limited number of Institute postdoctoral fellowships are offered from time to time as vacancies occur.

INSTITUTE OF CLASSICAL STUDIES

3rd Floor, Senate House, Malet Street, London, WC1E 7HU, England
Tel: (44) 20 7636 8700
Fax: (44) 20 7862 8722
Contact: Ms Margaret Packer, Institute Secretary

Michael Ventris Memorial Award
Subjects: Mycenaean studies.
Purpose: To promote the study of the Mycenaean civilisation.
Eligibility: Open to applicants from all countries who are postgraduate students or young scholars who have obtained a doctorate in the last eight years.
Level of Study: Postdoctorate, Postgraduate.
Value: UK£1,500.
Frequency: Annual.
Country of Study: Any country.
No. of awards offered: One.
Application Procedure: Applicants must send a typewritten letter with two references.
Closing Date: February 28th.

Additional Information: A second Michael Ventris Award is made annually for architecture and is administered by the Architectural Association.

INSTITUTE OF CURRENT WORLD AFFAIRS

4 West Wheelock Street, Hanover, NH 03755, United States of America
Tel: (1) 603 643 5548
Fax: (1) 603 643 9599
Email: icwa@valley.net
www: http://www.icwa.org
Contact: Administrative Assistant

Institute of Current World Affairs Fellowships
Subjects: International affairs.
Purpose: To enable young adults of outstanding promise and character to study and write about areas or issues of the world outside the United States.
Eligibility: Open to individuals under 36 who have finished their formal education. Applicants must have a good command of spoken and written English.
Level of Study: Postgraduate, Professional development.
Type: Fellowship.
Value: Full support for Fellows and their immediate families.
Length of Study: A minimum of two years.
Frequency: Annual.
Country of Study: Other.
No. of awards offered: Four.
Application Procedure: Applicants must write to the Executive Director and explain briefly the personal background and professional experience that would qualify them in the Institutes current areas of concern, details of which are available upon request. They should also describe the activities they would like to carry out during the two years overseas. This initial letter is followed by a more detailed written application process and must be completed prior to the deadline.
Closing Date: Deadlines for completed applications are April 1st for a June decision and September 1st for a December decision.
Funding: Private.
Additional Information: Fellowships are not awarded to support work toward academic degrees nor to underwrite specific studies or research projects. The Institute is also known as the Crane-Rogers Foundation.

INSTITUTE OF EUROPEAN HISTORY

Institut für Europäische Geschichte, Alte Universitätsstraße 19, Mainz, D-55116, Germany
Tel: (49) 613 1393 9360
Fax: (49) 613 1393 0154
Email: ieg2@inst-euro-history.uni-mainz.de
www: http://www.inst-euro-history.uni-mainz.de
Contact: Dr Andreas Kunz, Deputy Director

The Institute of European History in Mainz, founded in 1950, is dedicated to the promotion of historical research. Its Abteilung für Religionsgeschichte specialises in the history of occidental religion and has developed into a centre for ecumenical research on the Reformation. The Abteilung für Universalgeschichte concentrates its research on the history of Europe between the sixteenth and twentieth-centuries.

Institute of European History Fellowships
Subjects: Western religious history and modern and contemporary European history.
Purpose: To support young scientists in the completion of their doctoral work or in the execution of shorter postdoctoral projects.
Eligibility: Open to holders of a Master's degree and to Fellows in the advanced stages of graduate work, at least two years after admission to doctoral candidacy. Applicants must have successfully completed their comprehensive oral examinations.

Level of Study: Doctorate, Postdoctorate.
Type: Fellowship.
Value: A monthly stipend, a family allowance, health insurance and a travel allowance, all of which are in line with the guidelines of the German Academic Exchange Service (DAAD).
Frequency: Annual.
Study Establishment: The Institute of European History.
Country of Study: Germany.
Application Procedure: Applicants must contact either the Director of the Section of World History or the Director of the History of Occidental Religion.
Closing Date: February, June or October.
Funding: Government.
No. of awards given last year: 20.
No. of applicants last year: 100.

INSTITUTE OF FOOD TECHNOLOGISTS (IFT)

221 North LaSalle Street, Chicago, IL 60601, United States of America
Tel: (1) 312 782 8424
Fax: (1) 312 782 8348
Email: info@ift.org
www: http://www.ift.org
Contact: Scholarship Department

The Institute of Food Technologists (IFT), founded in 1939, is a non-profit scientific society with 29,000 members working in food science, technology and related professions in industry, academia and government. IFT's mission is to advance the science and technology of food through the exchange of knowledge. As the society for food science and technology, IFT brings the scientific perspective to the public discussion of food issues.

IFT Graduate Fellowships

Subjects: Food technology and food science.
Purpose: To encourage and support outstanding research.
Eligibility: Open to current graduates pursuing a course of study leading to an MS or PhD degree. Candidates must possess an above average interest in research together with demonstrated scientific aptitude.
Level of Study: Doctorate, Graduate, Postgraduate.
Type: Fellowship.
Value: Varies.
Frequency: Annual.
Study Establishment: Any educational institution that is conducting fundamental investigations in the advancement of food science and technology.
Country of Study: United States of America or Canada.
Application Procedure: Applicants must contact IFT for details.
Funding: Commercial, Private.
Contributor: Contributors include General Mills, Inc., the Coca-Cola Foundation and Proctor & Gamble Company.

INSTITUTE OF HISTORICAL RESEARCH (IHR)

Senate House, Malet Street, London
WC1E 7HU, England
Tel: (44) 20 7862 8740
Fax: (44) 20 7862 8811
Email: ihrsec@sas.ac.uk
www: http://www.ihr.sas.ac.uk
Contact: Director

The Institute of Historical Research (IHR) is the centre for advanced study in history. It is the meeting place for scholars from around the world, housing the largest open access collection of primary sources for historians in Britain, administering research and providing courses, seminars and conferences.

IHR Past and Present Postdoctoral Fellowships in History

Subjects: History.
Purpose: To provide one year of postdoctoral study.
Eligibility: Applicants may be of any nationality and their PhD may have been awarded in any country. Those who have previously held another postdoctoral fellowship will not normally be eligible. The fellowship may not be held in conjunction with any other award. Fellowships will begin on October 1st each year and it is a strict condition of these awards that a PhD thesis should have been submitted by that date.
Level of Study: Postdoctorate.
Type: Fellowship.
Value: UK£15,000.
Length of Study: One year.
Frequency: Dependent on funds available.
Study Establishment: IHR.
Country of Study: England.
No. of awards offered: One.
Application Procedure: Applicants must complete an application form, available from the Fellowship Assistant in early January.
Closing Date: April 9th.
Funding: Private.
Contributor: The Past and Present Society.
No. of awards given last year: One.

Isobel Thornley Research Fellowship

Subjects: Arts and humanities, medieval history, modern history or contemporary history.
Purpose: To help candidates at an advanced stage of a PhD to complete their doctorates.
Eligibility: Open to candidates without regard to nationality, but only to those registered for a PhD at the University of London.
Level of Study: Doctorate, Postgraduate.
Type: Fellowship.
Value: UK£6,700.
Length of Study: One year.
Frequency: Dependent on funds available.
Study Establishment: IHR.
Country of Study: United Kingdom.
No. of awards offered: One.
Application Procedure: Applicants must complete an application form, available from the Fellowship Assistant in early January.
Closing Date: March 1st.
Funding: Private.
Contributor: Isobel Thornley bequest.
No. of awards given last year: One.

Royal History Society Fellowship

Subjects: Arts and humanities, medieval history, modern history or contemporary history.
Purpose: To help candidates at an advanced stage of a PhD to complete their doctorates.
Eligibility: Open to nationals of any country.
Level of Study: Doctorate, Postgraduate.
Type: Fellowship.
Value: Approx. UK£6,700.
Length of Study: One year.
Frequency: Annual.
Study Establishment: IHR.
Country of Study: United Kingdom.
No. of awards offered: One.
Application Procedure: Applicants must complete an application form, available from the Fellowship Assistant in early January.
Closing Date: March 1st.
Funding: Private.
Contributor: The Royal Historical Society.
No. of awards given last year: 2.

Scouloudi Fellowships

Subjects: Arts and humanities, medieval history, modern history or contemporary history.
Purpose: To help candidates at an advanced stage of a PhD to complete their doctorates.

Eligibility: Only open to United Kingdom citizens or to candidates with a first degree from a United Kingdom university.
Level of Study: Doctorate, Postgraduate.
Type: Fellowship.
Value: Approx. UK£6,700.
Length of Study: One year.
Frequency: Annual.
Study Establishment: IHR.
Country of Study: United Kingdom.
No. of awards offered: Seven.
Application Procedure: Applicants must complete an application form, available from the Fellowship Assistant in early January.
Closing Date: March 1st.
Funding: Private.
Contributor: The Scouloudi Foundation.
No. of awards given last year: Seven.

INSTITUTE OF HORTICULTURE (IOH)

14/15 Belgrave Square, London
SW1X 8PS, England
Tel: (44) 20 7245 6943
Fax: (44) 20 7245 6943
Email: ioh@horticulture.org.uk
www: http://www.horticulture.org.uk
Contact: A Clarke, General Secretary

The Institute of Horticulture (IOH) is the professional institute for horticulturists of all disciplines in the industry.

Martin McLaren Horticultural Scholarship

Subjects: Horticulture, botany or landscape architecture.
Purpose: To fund one year of an MSc course at an American university.
Eligibility: Applicants must have gained a botany, horticulture or landscape architecture degree, and be in the early stages of their career. The age limit is 27 years of age.
Level of Study: Postgraduate.
Type: Scholarship.
Value: US$25,000.
Length of Study: One year.
Frequency: Annual.
Study Establishment: A university.
Country of Study: United States of America.
No. of awards offered: One.
Application Procedure: Applicants must complete an application form, available from the IOH.
Closing Date: November 10th.
Funding: Private.
Contributor: The Martin McLaren Trust.
No. of awards given last year: One.
Additional Information: The Martin McLaren Horticultural Scholarship/Garden Club of America Interchange Fellowship is one year spent in an United Kingdom or United States of America university.

INSTITUTE OF IRISH STUDIES

Queen's University Belfast, Belfast
BT9 6AW, Northern Ireland
Tel: (44) 28 9027 3386
Fax: (44) 28 9043 9238
Email: irish.studies@qub.ac.uk
www: http://www.qub.ac.uk/iis
Contact: Director

The Institute of Irish Studies at Queen's University was established in 1965 and was one of the first of its kind. It is one of the leading centres for research based teaching in Irish studies and is an internationally renowned centre of interdisciplinary Irish scholarship attracting academics from all over the world.

Institute of Irish Studies Senior Visiting Research Fellowship

Subjects: Irish studies.
Purpose: To promote research.
Eligibility: Open to established Scholars of senior standing with a strong publication record.
Level of Study: Postdoctorate.
Type: Fellowship.
Value: UK£18,267.
Length of Study: One year.
Frequency: Annual.
Study Establishment: The Institute of Irish Studies.
Country of Study: Northern Ireland.
No. of awards offered: Up to two.
Application Procedure: Awards are usually advertised in February to March.
Closing Date: Varies.

Mary McNeill Scholarship in Irish Studies

Subjects: Irish studies.
Eligibility: Open to well qualified students enrolled in the one year MA course in Irish studies at Queen's University. Applicants must be citizens of the United States or Canada and be enrolled as overseas students on this course.
Level of Study: Postgraduate.
Type: Scholarship.
Value: UK£3,000.
Length of Study: One year.
Frequency: Dependent on funds available.
Study Establishment: Queen's University of Belfast.
Country of Study: Ireland.
No. of awards offered: 1.
Application Procedure: Application form obtainable from the Secretary, Institute of Irish Studies, Queens University Belfast, Belfast BT7 1NN Tel: (028) 9027 3386 E-mail: irish.studies@qub.ac.uk.
Closing Date: May 31st.
No. of awards given last year: 1.

THE INSTITUTE OF MATERIALS, MINERALS AND MINING

Danum House, South Parade, Doncaster, South Yorkshire, DN1 2DY, England
Tel: (44) 1302 380912
Fax: (44) 1302 380900
Email: hq@imm.org.uk
www: http://www.imm.org.uk
Contact: Ms Carol MacKenzie, Professional Affairs Assistant

The Institute of Materials, Minerals and Mining is a qualifying body and learned society for individuals seeking to be recognised, or already practising as, professionals in the international minerals and materials industry.

Bosworth Smith Trust Fund

Subjects: Metal mining and non ferrous extraction metallurgy or mineral dressing.
Purpose: To assist research.
Eligibility: Open to applicants who possess a degree in a relevant subject.
Level of Study: Postgraduate.
Value: Approx. UK£5,500 to cover working expenses, visits to mines and plants in connection with research and the purchase of apparatus.
Length of Study: One year.
Frequency: Annual.
Study Establishment: An approved university.
Country of Study: United Kingdom.
No. of awards offered: Varies.
Application Procedure: Applicants must complete an application form, available on request.
Closing Date: March 15th.

Edgar Pam Fellowship

Subjects: All subjects within IMechE's field of interest ranging from explorative geology to extractive metallurgy.
Eligibility: Open to young graduates resident in Australia, Canada, New Zealand, South Africa or the United Kingdom who wish to undertake advanced study or research in the United Kingdom.
Level of Study: Postgraduate.
Type: Fellowship.
Value: UK£2,000.
Length of Study: One year.
Frequency: Annual.
Study Establishment: Approved universities.
Country of Study: United Kingdom.
No. of awards offered: One.
Application Procedure: Applicants must complete an application form, available on request.
Closing Date: March 15th.

G Vernon Hobson Bequest

Subjects: Mining geology.
Purpose: To advance the teaching and practise of geology as applied to mining.
Eligibility: Open to university staff throughout the United Kingdom.
Level of Study: Professional development.
Value: Approx. UK£1,300 to cover travel, research or other objects in accordance with the terms of the bequest.
Frequency: Annual.
Country of Study: United Kingdom.
No. of awards offered: More than one.
Application Procedure: Applicants must complete an application form, available on request.
Closing Date: March 15th.

Mining Club Award

Subjects: Mineral industry operations.
Purpose: To enable candidates to study in the United Kingdom or overseas, to present a paper at an international minerals industry conference or to assist the candidate in attending a full-time course of study related to the minerals industry outside the United Kingdom
Eligibility: Open to British citizens aged 21-35 years who are actively engaged in full or part-time postgraduate study or employment in the minerals industry.
Level of Study: Postgraduate, Professional development.
Type: Award.
Value: Approx. UK£1,500.
Frequency: Annual.
Country of Study: Any country.
No. of awards offered: Varies.
Application Procedure: Applicants must complete an application form, available on request.
Closing Date: March 15th.

Stanley Elmore Fellowships

Subjects: Extractive metallurgy and mineral processing.
Eligibility: Open to applicants who are fully qualified to undertake postdoctoral research. In general, preference will be given to applicants who are members of IMechE.
Level of Study: Postdoctorate.
Type: Fellowship.
Value: UK£12,000-16,000. Lesser amounts are available for approved short-term assignments.
Length of Study: One year, with a possibility of renewal to a maximum of three years.
Frequency: Annual.
Study Establishment: An approved university.
Country of Study: United Kingdom.
No. of awards offered: One-two.
Application Procedure: Applicants must complete an application form, available on request.
Closing Date: March 15th.

THE INSTITUTE OF SPORTS MEDICINE

Royal Free & University College Medical School, Charles Bell House, 67-73 Riding House Street, London, W1W 7EJ, England
Tel: (44) 20 7813 2832
Fax: (44) 20 7813 2832
Email: m.hobsley@ucl.ac.uk
Contact: Miss D Meynell, Secretary

The Institute of Sports Medicine is a postgraduate medical institute which was established to develop research, teaching and treatment in sports medicine. It offers national awards to medical practitioners and runs courses on different aspects of this specialist subject. Now that it is based at University College, London, the Institute hopes to work closely with the College in the fulfilment of its objectives.

Duke of Edinburgh Prize for Sports Medicine

Subjects: Sports medicine in the community.
Purpose: To promote postgraduate work and to signify standards of excellence.
Eligibility: Open to medical practitioners in the United Kingdom.
Level of Study: Postgraduate.
Type: Prize.
Value: Varies, but usually a substantial cash prize.
Frequency: Annual.
Country of Study: United Kingdom.
No. of awards offered: One.
Application Procedure: Applicants must write for an entry or nomination form in the first instance.
Closing Date: Varies annually. The exact date is specified in the conditions of entry.
Funding: Private.
No. of applicants last year: Three.

Sir Robert Atkins Award

Subjects: Sports medicine.
Purpose: To increase medical support and active involvement in the field and to recognise a doctor who has provided the most consistently valuable medical, clinical or preventive service to a national sporting organisation or sport in general.
Eligibility: Open to medical practitioners in the United Kingdom.
Level of Study: Postgraduate.
Type: Award.
Value: Varies, but usually a substantial cash prize.
Frequency: Annual.
Country of Study: United Kingdom.
No. of awards offered: One.
Application Procedure: Applicants must write for an entry or nomination form in the first instance.
Closing Date: Varies.
Funding: Private.
No. of applicants last year: One.

THE INSTITUTION OF CIVIL ENGINEERS

1-7 Great George Street, Westminster, London, SW1P 3AA, England
Tel: (44) 20 7665 2110
Fax: (44) 20 7233 0515
Email: helen.moger@ice.org.uk
www: http://www.ice.org.uk
Contact: Ms Ellen Ryan, Education Officer

QUEST C H Roberts Bequest

Subjects: Civil engineering.
Purpose: To promote the exchange of engineering graduates between the United Kingdom and Spain for the purpose of furthering their academic studies and engineering training.
Eligibility: Open to British or Spanish nationals who are members or associate members of the Institution.
Level of Study: Postgraduate.
Type: Bursary.
Value: Approx. UK£2,000.
Length of Study: Six-nine months.
Frequency: Annual.

Country of Study: Spain for United Kingdom candidates and the United Kingdom for Spanish candidate.
No. of awards offered: Two.
Application Procedure: Applicants must complete an application form, available from Ms Coverdale.
Closing Date: March 31st.
Funding: Private.
Contributor: The British Council.
Additional Information: Successful applicants are encouraged under the terms of the bequest to learn the language of the other country, some prior knowledge is essential, and to acquire a knowledge of its people by residence, study and engineering experience. They will be required to further their knowledge of the language by spending one to two hours weekly on additional language study with an approved institute or teacher, whose fees will be covered by the award. Practical experience gained in Spain under the award will be accepted towards the experience required for permission to take the professional examination.

QUEST Institution of Civil Engineers Continuing Education Award

Subjects: Civil engineering.
Purpose: To enable approved persons to undertake MSc courses after some years industrial experience.
Eligibility: Open to graduates of any nationality who hold an accredited First Class Degree in civil engineering and have been members of the Institution at any grade for not less than two years.
Level of Study: Postgraduate.
Type: Award.
Value: Up to UK£2,000.
Frequency: Annual.
Country of Study: United Kingdom.
No. of awards offered: 10-15.
Application Procedure: Applicants must complete an application form, available from Ms Coverdale.
Closing Date: March 31st.
No. of awards given last year: 13.
No. of applicants last year: 20.

QUEST Institution of Civil Engineers Overseas Travel Awards

Subjects: Civil engineering, environmental engineering, transportation and agricultural engineering.
Purpose: To support overseas travel by institution members to overseas universities, specific overseas projects and mid-career support and development.
Eligibility: Open to institution members, preference being given to postgraduate applicants proposing individual overseas projects or requiring mid career support.
Level of Study: Postgraduate.
Value: Up to UK£2,000.
Length of Study: 3-12 months.
Frequency: Annual.
Country of Study: Any country.
No. of awards offered: Approx. 15.
Application Procedure: Applicants must complete an application form, available from Mrs Coverdale.
Closing Date: March 31st.
Additional Information: Applications are not necessarily restricted to technical developments, but may be concerned with organisational, managerial or financial aspects of civil engineering. Awards will be judged on merit.

THE INSTITUTION OF ELECTRICAL ENGINEERS (IEE)

Qualifications Department, Michael Faraday House, Six Hills Way, Stevenage, Hertfordshire, SG1 2AY, England
Tel: (44) 20 7240 1871
Fax: (44) 20 7497 3633
Email: kcheung@iee.org.uk
www: http://www.iee.org.uk
Contact: Scholarships Officer

The Institution of Electrical Engineers (IEE) seeks to promote the advancement of electrical, manufacturing and information engineering and facilitate the exchange of knowledge and ideas. The IEE wishes to provide a broad range of services to members, to assist them in developing their careers by improving their capabilities as engineers, and to play their full part in contributing to society.

D H Thomas Travel Bursary

Subjects: Electrical, electronic, information engineering, manufacturing engineering and related disciplines.
Purpose: To support members undertaking research in Europe.
Eligibility: Open to IEE members undertaking personal and professional research. Preference is given to research taking place in Germany.
Level of Study: Doctorate, Postdoctorate, Postgraduate, Professional development, Research.
Type: Scholarship.
Value: UK£500.
Length of Study: Up to three years.
Frequency: Every two years.
Country of Study: Other.
No. of awards offered: One.
Application Procedure: Applicants must complete an application form. Given that there are a limited number of awards, applicants are advised to apply as early in the year as possible.
Closing Date: Applications may be received from January 1st to December 15th.
Additional Information: Further information can be found on the website.

Hudswell Bequest Travelling Fellowships

Subjects: Electrical, electronic, manufacturing, engineering and related disciplines.
Purpose: To allow members to pursue study overseas.
Eligibility: Open to IEE members undertaking postgraduate research in the United Kingdom.
Level of Study: Postgraduate.
Type: Fellowship.
Value: Up to UK£1,000.
Frequency: Annual.
Country of Study: United Kingdom.
No. of awards offered: Four.
Application Procedure: Applicants must make enquiries with the IEE. Given that there are a limited number of awards, applicants are advised to apply as early in the year as possible.
Closing Date: Applications may be received from January 1st to December 15th.
No. of awards given last year: Two.
Additional Information: Further information can be found on the website.

Hudswell International Research Scholarships

Subjects: Electrical, electronic, information technology, manufacturing engineering and related disciplines.
Purpose: To assist members of the Institution with advanced research work, leading to the award of a doctorate, to be undertaken outside the applicant's home country.
Eligibility: Open to those who have been members of the IEE for a minimum of two years before an application is submitted. It is expected that applicants should have attained Chartered Membership of the IEE, but applications may be accepted from applicants whose research studies may lead to Chartered Membership on completion of the approved doctorate.
Level of Study: Doctorate, Postgraduate.
Type: Scholarship.
Value: UK£5,000.
Length of Study: One year.
Frequency: Every two years.
Study Establishment: Internationally recognised universities or research establishments with a high reputation for research.
Country of Study: Other.
No. of awards offered: Three.

Application Procedure: Applicants must complete an application form. Given that there are a limited number of awards available, applicants are advised to apply as early as possible.
Closing Date: October 15th.
No. of awards given last year: Three.

IEE Master's Degree Research Scholarship
Subjects: Electrical, electronic, manufacturing or information engineering.
Purpose: To assist IEE members undertaking advance postgraduate research studies for MRes or MPhil degrees.
Eligibility: Applicants must be IEE members who have satisfied the IEE educational requirements for Corporate Membership, or whose course of studies will lead to Corporate Membership of the IEE. Applicants must have been an IEE member, in any class, for not less than two years.
Level of Study: Postgraduate.
Type: Scholarship.
Value: UK£2,500 for one year of full-time study or UK£1,250 per year for part-time study.
Frequency: Annual.
Country of Study: United Kingdom.
No. of awards offered: Two.
Application Procedure: Applicants must make enquiries with the IEE.
Closing Date: 15th October.
Additional Information: Given that there are a limited number of awards available, applicants are advised to apply as early as possible. This award is subject to complete revision and substantial changes in terms and conditions.

IEE Postgraduate Scholarships
Subjects: Electrical, electronic, communications, manufacturing or power engineering.
Purpose: To assist IEE members with research studies.
Eligibility: Open to research students holding qualifications which have been accepted by the IEE and to members wishing to complete a research programme that will lead to Chartered Membership. The qualifications must fulfil the IEE's educational requirements for Chartered Membership.
Level of Study: Doctorate, Postgraduate, Research.
Type: Scholarship.
Value: UK£1,250.
Length of Study: One year.
Frequency: Annual.
Country of Study: United Kingdom.
No. of awards offered: Three.
Application Procedure: Applicants must complete an application form and are advised to apply as early in the year as possible.
Closing Date: Applications may be received between January 1st and October 15th.
No. of awards given last year: Three.
Additional Information: Further details are available from the website.

IEE Prize
Subjects: Electrical, electronic and related engineering.
Eligibility: Open to graduates and students, who must be nominated by their head of department at a university.
Level of Study: Postgraduate.
Type: Other.
Value: UK£100 and two years' free membership of the IEE.
Frequency: Annual.
Country of Study: Any country.
Closing Date: September 30th (January 31st for Australia).
Additional Information: The IEE Prize is awarded by the Institution to outstanding students undergoing or having completed a course of study which has been accredited by the IEE or accredited by an overseas National Institution with which the IEE has a mutual recognition agreement.

For further information contact:

Qualifications Department ref Q(AC)Savoy Place, London, WC2R 0BL, England
Tel: (44) 20 7240 1871
Fax: (44) 20 7497 3609
Contact: Section Leader (Scholarships)

IEE Robinson Research Fellowship
Subjects: Electrical engineering.
Level of Study: Postgraduate.
Type: One fellowship.
Frequency: Every three years.
Country of Study: United Kingdom.
Application Procedure: Potential applicants should make enquiries with the IEE.
Closing Date: 15th October.
Additional Information: This award is subject to complete revision and substantial changes in terms and conditions.

IEE Undergraduate Scholarships and Grants
Subjects: Electrical and electronic engineering.
Eligibility: Open to students who are completing the final year of an IEE-accredited honours degree course and are normally resident in the UK.
Type: Scholarship.
Value: Up to UK£500, payable in instalments.
Frequency: Annual.
Study Establishment: Universities or other institutions of higher education.
Country of Study: United Kingdom.
No. of awards offered: 8.
Application Procedure: Application form must be completed.
Closing Date: June 30th.

For further information contact:

Qualifications Department ref Q(SP)Savoy Place, London, WC2R 0BL, England
Tel: (44) 20 7240 1871
Fax: (44) 20 7497 3609
Contact: Section Leader (Scholarships)

IEE Younger Members Conference Bursary
Subjects: Electrical engineering and related disciplines.
Purpose: To assist IEE members with presenting papers at IEE conferences.
Eligibility: Open to members of the IEE who are full-time students and/or aged under 30, who have had papers accepted for presentation at an IEE conference. Applicants must also have no other sources of funding towards the registration fee or accommodation whilst attending the event.
Level of Study: Postgraduate, Professional development.
Type: Travel grant.
Frequency: Annual.
No. of awards offered: Two per conference.
Application Procedure: Applicants must complete an application form.
Closing Date: Two months prior to the date of the conference.
No. of awards given last year: Three.
Additional Information: This award is subject to complete revision and substantial changes in terms and conditions.

J R Beard Travelling Fund Awards
Subjects: Electrical, electronic, manufacturing and related engineering.
Purpose: To enable members of the IEE to travel overseas and thus broaden their professional experience.
Eligibility: Open to IEE members intending to expand their experience in the field of manufacturing techniques conducted overseas. Applicants must currently be studying in the United Kingdom. Grants are available to assist, in particular, younger IEE members to broaden their professional experience through overseas travel.
Level of Study: Unrestricted.

Type: Travel grant.
Value: Up to UK£500.
Frequency: Annual.
Country of Study: Any country.
No. of awards offered: Six.
Application Procedure: Applicants must complete an application form. Given that there are a limited number of awards applicants are advised to apply as early in the year as possible.
Closing Date: Applications for these scholarships may be received from January 1st to December 15th.
Additional Information: Further information can be found on the website.

Leonard Research Grant

Subjects: Electrical, electronic, manufacturing or related engineering.
Purpose: To assist engineering graduates who might not otherwise be able to undertake or complete work leading to a higher degree.
Eligibility: Applicants should currently be resident in the United Kingdom and must have satisfied the Institution's educational requirement for corporate membership.
Level of Study: Doctorate, Postgraduate.
Type: Research grant.
Value: Please contact the organisation.
Frequency: Every 4 years.
Study Establishment: A suitable university.
Country of Study: United Kingdom.
No. of awards offered: One.
Application Procedure: Applicants must complete an application form.
Closing Date: Please contact the organisation.

Leslie H Paddle Fellowship

Subjects: Electronic or radio engineering.
Purpose: To assist IEE members with research studies.
Eligibility: Open to first year research students currently resident in the United Kingdom. Applicants must possess qualifications accepted by the IEE as fulfilling the educational requirements for Chartered Membership.
Level of Study: Doctorate, Postgraduate.
Type: Fellowship.
Value: UK£10,000.
Length of Study: Two years.
Frequency: Annual.
Study Establishment: A suitable university.
Country of Study: United Kingdom.
No. of awards offered: One.
Application Procedure: Applicants must make enquiries with the IEE. Given that there are a limited number of awards, applicants are advised to apply as early in the year as possible.
Closing Date: Applications may be received between January 1st and October 15th.
No. of awards given last year: One.
Additional Information: It is hoped that the fellowship will encourage co-operation between industry and the higher education sector and that an industrial organisation will be associated with the fellowship. Leslie H Paddle Fellowship holders who satisfactorily complete their research studies may use the appendage IEE Scholar. Further details can be found on the website.

Lord Lloyd of Kilgerran Memorial Prize

Subjects: Mobile radio or RF engineering.
Purpose: To aid a candidate who intends to undertake an MSc, MPhil or PhD in mobile radio and RF engineering.
Eligibility: Applicants should currently be resident in the United Kingdom and should have been professional, practising engineers for a minimum of three years.
Level of Study: Postgraduate.
Type: Scholarship.
Value: UK£1,000.

Length of Study: One year for full-time study, two years for part-time study.
Frequency: Annual.
Study Establishment: A suitable university.
Country of Study: United Kingdom.
No. of awards offered: One.
Application Procedure: Applicants must complete an application form.
Closing Date: 31st December.
No. of awards given last year: Two.

Princess Royal Scholarship

Subjects: Engineering work commensurate with the activities of the IEE.
Purpose: To enable an IEE member to use his or her professional knowledge and experience in a way that is beneficial to an under-privileged community in a developing country.
Eligibility: Open to applicants undertaking a specific programme of work with a charitable organisation. The nature of the work must be commensurate with the activities of the IEE. The programme must be undertaken for a period of not less than three months and conducted in co-operation with an organisation in the receiving country.
Level of Study: Postgraduate.
Type: Scholarship.
Value: UK£1,000.
Frequency: Annual.
Country of Study: Other.
No. of awards offered: One.
Application Procedure: Applicants must complete an application form. Given that there are a limited number of awards, applicants are advised to apply as early in the year as possible.
Closing Date: Applications may be received between January 1st and October 15th.
No. of awards given last year: One.
Additional Information: Further information can be found on the website.

Robinson Research Scholarship

Subjects: Electrical, electronic, communications, information or manufacturing engineering and related disciplines.
Purpose: To assist IEE members with research leading to the award of a PhD or postdoctoral qualification.
Eligibility: Open to first year research students currently resident in the United Kingdom. Applicants must possess qualifications which have been accepted by the IEE as fulfilling the educational requirements for Chartered Management. If not already a member, the candidate must apply for admission to the class of Associate Member (AMIEE) of the IEE.
Level of Study: Doctorate, Postdoctorate, Postgraduate.
Type: Scholarship.
Value: UK£1,250 per year.
Length of Study: Two years.
Frequency: Annual.
Study Establishment: A suitable university or research establishment.
Country of Study: United Kingdom.
No. of awards offered: Two.
Application Procedure: Applicants must complete an application form.
Closing Date: October 15th.
No. of awards given last year: Two.
Additional Information: Given that there are a limited number of awards available, applicants are advised to apply as early as possible.

Vodafone Scholarships

Subjects: Mobile telecommunications and related subjects.
Eligibility: Open to members of the Institution of any class.
Level of Study: Postgraduate.
Type: Scholarship.
Value: UK£1,250 per year.
Frequency: Annual.

Country of Study: United Kingdom.
No. of awards offered: 2.
Closing Date: 15th October.
Additional Information: The Scholarships are sponsored by the Vodafone Group plc.

For further information contact:

Qualifications Department ref Q(SP)Savoy Place, London, WC2R 0BL, England
Tel: (44) 20 7240 1871 ext. 2211
Fax: (44) 20 7497 3633
Email: twalter@iee.org
Contact: Mr T Walter, Senior Assistant, Scholarships & Prizes

William Morley Bursary

Subjects: Electrical, electronic, manufacturing or information engineering.
Purpose: To support needy electrical, electronic, manufacturing or information engineering students who are citizens of either Zimbabwe or the United Kingdom.
Eligibility: Candidates must be studying or have offers of places at a university to study a degree course in Zimbabwe, or an IEE accredited course in South Africa, or a degree course accredited by the Engineering Council of South Africa, or an IEE accredited United Kingdom degree course.
Value: Variable, UK£500-1000 per year dependent on student need and location of study.
Length of Study: Up to three years.
Frequency: Annual.
Study Establishment: At a United Kingdom, Zimbabwean or South African University.
Country of Study: Other.
No. of awards offered: Varies, four-six awards annually.
Application Procedure: Applicants must complete an application form.
Closing Date: Applications may be received throughout the year.

INSTITUTION OF FIRE ENGINEERS

148 Upper New Walk, Leicester
Leicestershire, LE1 7QB, England
Tel: (44) 116 255 3654
Fax: (44) 116 247 1231
Email: info@ife.org.uk
www: http://www.ife.org.uk
Contact: Mr D Newman, Examinations Secretary

Institution of Fire Engineers Scholarships

Subjects: Fire fighting, fire engineering, fire protection or fire research.
Purpose: To assist men and women in the profession of fire engineering who wish to carry out research or further their studies in some particular aspect of the field.
Eligibility: Applicants should be residents of and working in the UK.
Level of Study: Unrestricted.
Type: Scholarship.
Value: UK£1,000 for United Kingdom scholarships, UK£2,000 for International scholarships.
Length of Study: Approx. one year.
Frequency: Annual.
Country of Study: United Kingdom - United Kingdom, International - Anywhere.
No. of awards offered: Two.
Application Procedure: Applicants must write for details.
Closing Date: Notified in the Fire Prevention and Fire Engineers Journal.
Funding: Private.
No. of awards given last year: Two.
Additional Information: Selection for both scholarships will be made on the merit of the project and its relevance and value to fire fighting, fire engineering, fire protection or fire research.

INSTITUTION OF MECHANICAL ENGINEERS (IMECHE)

Northgate Avenue, Bury St Edmunds, Suffolk, IP32 6BN, England
Tel: (44) 1284 718617
Fax: (44) 1284 765172
Email: prizesandawards@imeche.org.uk
www: http://www.imeche.org.uk
Contact: The Prizes and Awards Officer

The Institution of Mechanical Engineers (IMechE) was founded in 1847 by engineers. They formed an institution to promote the exchange of ideas and encourage individuals or groups in creating inventions that would be crucial to the development of the world as a whole. Now, over 150 years later, IMechE is one of the largest engineering institutions in the world with over 88,000 members in 120 countries.

Donald Julius Groen Prizes

Subjects: Engineering.
Purpose: To award the author of outstanding papers or for outstanding achievements in the group's sphere of activity.
Eligibility: Open to authors of papers or those who have achievements of a sufficiently high standard to warrant the award of an IMechE prize. As a general rule, but with certain exceptions, grants are normally awarded only to members of the Institution.
Type: Prize.
Value: UK£250.
Frequency: Annual.
No. of awards offered: 14.
Application Procedure: Applicants must contact the Institution of Mechanical Engineers for details.
Funding: Private.

Flatman Grants

Subjects: Mechanical engineering.
Purpose: To help individuals to further their education or to obtain special experience overseas.
Eligibility: Open to IMechE members under 30 years of age.
Level of Study: Postgraduate, Professional development.
Type: Grant.
Value: Up to UK£750
Frequency: Annual.
Country of Study: Any country.
No. of awards offered: Approx. 10.
Application Procedure: Applicants must submit a completed application form with three references.
Closing Date: Three months before a decision is required.
Funding: Private.
Additional Information: A report is required within three months of completion of project.

James Bates Grants

Subjects: Engineering.
Purpose: To promote mechanical engineering and the professional development of young members of the Institution.
Eligibility: Open to young members of IMechE.
Type: Grant.
Value: 50 per cent of the cost of travel, accommodation, meals and appropriate fees will be made to applicants who attend the railway division technical meetings and industrial visits arranged by young members' panels.
Frequency: Annual.
No. of awards offered: Varies.
Application Procedure: Applicants must contact the Institution of Mechanical Engineers for details.
Funding: Private.

James Bates Prize

Subjects: Engineering.
Purpose: To award technical contributions submitted by young members of IMechE.

Eligibility: Open to members of the Institution under the age of 31. Certain exceptions are made.
Type: Prize.
Value: The first prize is UK£100 and the second prize is UK£50.
Frequency: Annual.
No. of awards offered: region/branch (First & Second Prize).
Application Procedure: Applicants must contact the Institution of Mechanical Engineers for details.
Funding: Private.
Contributor: James Bates.
Additional Information: Awards are given for technical contributions submitted by graduates or students and read before a local meeting of the Institution providing that the paper or contribution is of sufficient merit.

James Clayton Awards

Subjects: Mechanical engineering.
Purpose: To enable the recipient to pursue advanced postgraduate studies or programmes of research.
Eligibility: Open to IMechE members who hold an accredited engineering degree or who have satisfied the academic requirements for IMechE membership by other means. Applicants must not have had less than two years of acceptable professional training in mechanical engineering.
Level of Study: Postgraduate.
Type: Grant.
Value: Up to UK£1,000 per year.
Length of Study: Up to three years.
Frequency: Annual.
Study Establishment: An approved centre.
Country of Study: United Kingdom.
No. of awards offered: Approx. 10.
Application Procedure: Applicants must complete and submit an application form with three references.
Closing Date: Three months before a decision is required.
Funding: Private.
Additional Information: A report is required within three months of completion of the project.

James Clayton Lectures

Subjects: Mechanical engineering.
Purpose: To provide for the expenses of the person presenting the lecture which is to take place at an ordinary meeting of the Institution on a subject relating to mechanical engineering science, research, invention or experimental work.
Level of Study: Postgraduate.
Type: Grant.
Value: UK£500.
Frequency: Annual.
Country of Study: United Kingdom.
No. of awards offered: One.
Application Procedure: Applicants must write for details.
Funding: Private.

James Clayton Overseas Conference Travel for Senior Engineers

Subjects: Mechanical engineering.
Purpose: To assist members of the Institution who have been invited to contribute in some way to a conference or who could be expected to make a significant contribution to the aims of a conference by their attendance.
Eligibility: Open to IMechE members over the age of 40 years.
Level of Study: Professional development.
Type: Travel grant.
Value: Up to UK£1,000.
Country of Study: Any country.
No. of awards offered: Varies.
Application Procedure: Applicants must submit a completed application form with three references.
Funding: Private.
Additional Information: A report is required three months after the conference.

James Clayton Postgraduate Hardship Award

Subjects: Mechanical engineering.
Purpose: To assist outstanding postgraduates who experience hardship while undertaking courses of advanced study, training or research work on a course approved by the Institution.
Eligibility: Open to candidates who have completed a degree course in mechanical engineering accredited by IMechE and who have gained graduate membership of IMechE.
Level of Study: Postgraduate.
Type: Grant.
Value: Up to UK£1,000.
Length of Study: One year.
Frequency: Annual.
Country of Study: United Kingdom.
No. of awards offered: Up to three.
Application Procedure: Applicants must complete and submit an application form with three references.
Closing Date: Three months before a decision is required.
Funding: Private.
Additional Information: A report is required three months after the activity has been completed.

James Watt International Medal

Subjects: Mechanical engineering.
Purpose: To award an eminent engineer who has attained worldwide recognition in mechanical engineering.
Eligibility: Open to United Kingdom engineers and those nominated from overseas.
Type: Prize.
Frequency: Odd numbered years.
No. of awards offered: One.
Application Procedure: Applicants must write for details.
Funding: Private.
Additional Information: This award is the premier international award of the Institution.

Labrow Grants

Subjects: Mechanical engineering.
Purpose: To support research in the science or practice of mechanical engineering.
Eligibility: Open to members of IMechE. Applicants should have no less than two years of acceptable practical training in mechanical engineering.
Level of Study: Unrestricted.
Type: Grant.
Value: Up to UK£7,000.
Frequency: Varies.
Country of Study: Any country.
No. of awards offered: Varies.
Application Procedure: Applicants must submit a completed application form with three references.
Funding: Private.
Additional Information: A report is required three months after the activity has been completed.

Neil Watson Grants

Subjects: Mechanical engineering, power generation or internal combustion engines.
Purpose: To enable young engineers to attend conferences and seminars, to study engineering practices overseas or to attend suitable training courses in the field of power generation and in particular, internal combustion engines.
Eligibility: Usually only open to non corporate members of IMechE, under the age of 31.
Level of Study: Postgraduate.
Type: Grant.
Value: UK£500.
Frequency: Annual.
Country of Study: Any country.
No. of awards offered: Varies.
Application Procedure: Applicants must complete and submit an application form with three references.

Funding: Private.
Additional Information: A report is required three months after the activity has been completed.

Solids Handling Award

Subjects: Bulk solids technology.
Purpose: To recognise an individual's professional excellence in the field.
Eligibility: Open to people from any nationality. The award is either for a paper published by the Institution, for research, design or development work in the field or in recognition of an individual's professional excellence. Applicants do not have to be members of IMechE.
Type: Award.
Value: UK£250 and a plaque.
Frequency: Annual.
No. of awards offered: One.
Application Procedure: Nominations for the award are made by the Bulk Materials Handling Committee and are approved by the Process Industries Division Board.
Funding: Commercial.
Contributor: Ajax Equipment Limited.

Spencer Wilks Scholarship/Fellowship

Subjects: Mechanical engineering.
Purpose: To promote or encourage the study of automobile engineering.
Level of Study: Postgraduate.
Type: Scholarship.
Value: Up to UK£10,000.
Frequency: Annual.
Country of Study: Any country.
No. of awards offered: One.
Application Procedure: Applicants must write for details.
Funding: Private.

Thomas Andrew Common Grants

Subjects: Areas related to mechanical engineering.
Purpose: To provide assistance to IMechE members to attend conferences.
Eligibility: Open to members under the age of 40 who have been invited to contribute in some way to a conference or who could be expected to make a significant contribution to the aims of a conference by their attendance.
Level of Study: Postgraduate, Professional development.
Type: Grant.
Value: Up to UK£1,000.
Frequency: Varies.
Study Establishment: Approved conferences.
Country of Study: Any country.
No. of awards offered: Approx. 35.
Application Procedure: Applicants must complete and submit an application form with three references.
Closing Date: Three months before a decision is required.
Funding: Private.
Additional Information: A report is required within three months of return from the conference.

INSTITUTO NACIONAL DE METEOROLOGIA (INM)

Camino de las MorenasS/N Ciudad Universitaria
Madrid, E-28040
Spain
Tel: (34) 91 581 9860
Fax: (34) 91 581 9892
Email: carlos.legaz@inm.es
www: http://www.inm.es
Tel: 2247 LEMMC
Contact: Dr Carlos Garcia-Legaz Martinez

INM Fellowship for Curso Internacional de Técnico en Meteorologia General Applicada

Subjects: Atmospheric sciences and meteorology.
Eligibility: Candidates should have a background of training and professional experience in sciences, engineering or meteorology. A good knowledge of the Spanish language is required.
Level of Study: Professional development.
Type: Fellowship.
Value: Please contact the organisation for details.
Length of Study: 21 months.
Frequency: Every two years.
Study Establishment: INM training centre.
Country of Study: Spain.
No. of awards offered: 15-20.
Application Procedure: Applicants must complete an application form, distributed by the INM. Candidates should be supported by a meteorological or academic authority. Applications can be submitted through the WMO in Geneva.
Funding: Government.
No. of awards given last year: 15.
No. of applicants last year: 60.

INM Short-term Fellowship

Subjects: Atmospheric sciences and meteorology.
Purpose: To support on the job training in different departments of the INM.
Eligibility: Candidates must be staff of the meteorological service in their country. A good knowledge of English or the Spanish language is required.
Level of Study: Professional development.
Type: Fellowship.
Value: Please contact the association for details.
Length of Study: Two months.
Frequency: Annual.
Study Establishment: INM technical departments.
Country of Study: Spain.
No. of awards offered: 10-15.
Application Procedure: Applicants must complete an application, but no form is required, through the permanent representatives of their countries with WMO expressing their support of the candidate.
Closing Date: The beginning of June for fellowships to be initiated in the second semester.
Funding: Government.
No. of awards given last year: 15.
No. of applicants last year: 100.

INTENSIVE CARE SOCIETY (ICS)

29B Montague Street, London, WC1B 5BH, England
Tel: (44) 20 7291 0690
Fax: (44) 20 7580 0689
Email: admin@ics.ac.uk
www: http://www.ics.ac.uk
Contact: Chair of Research Committee

The Intensive Care Society (ICS) is a charitable organisation promoting advances in the care of the critically ill. This is largely accomplished through educational means and promoting research activity.

ICS Research Grants

Subjects: Any aspect of intensive care medicine and care of the critically ill.
Purpose: To promote research.
Eligibility: Applicants must be ICS members.
Level of Study: Unrestricted.
Type: Research grant.
Value: Please contact the organisation.
Frequency: Dependent on funds available.
Country of Study: Any country.
No. of awards offered: Varies.
Application Procedure: Applicants must complete an application form, available from the website.

Closing Date: Please contact the organisation.
Funding: Private.
Additional Information: Further information is available on the Society's website.

INTER AMERICAN PRESS ASSOCIATION (IAPA)

IAPA Scholarship Fund, Inc.2911 North West 39th Street, Miami, FL 33142, United States of America
Tel: (1) 305 376 3522
Fax: (1) 305 376 8950
Email: info@sipiapa.org
www: http://www.sipiapa.org
Contact: Scholarships Director

The Inter-American Press Association (IAPA) was established in 1942 to defend and promote the right of the peoples of the Americas to be fully and freely informed through an independent press.

IAPA Scholarship Fund, Inc.

Subjects: Journalism in the print media.
Purpose: To help develop more rounded journalists through cultural exposure and study in a foreign country.
Eligibility: Open to natives of North America, Latin America and the West Indies who are 21-35 years of age and are either professional journalists with at least three years of experience in the print media, or graduates of a school of journalism.
Level of Study: Postgraduate, Professional development.
Type: Scholarship.
Value: US$13,000.
Length of Study: Nine months.
Frequency: Annual.
Study Establishment: An American or Canadian university school of journalism approved by the Fund for Latin American and West Indian candidates, or an approved university or field work in a Latin American country for United States and Canadian candidates.
Country of Study: Other.
No. of awards offered: Four-six.
Application Procedure: Applicants must complete an application form, available from the Scholarships Director.
Closing Date: December 31st.
Additional Information: Candidates should have good command of the language of the country they intend to visit. United States and Canadian Scholars must take a minimum of three university courses, participate in the Fund's Reporting Program, and undertake a major research project. The Association also gives IAPA awards of US$500-1,000 and a scroll or plaque to Latin American and American journalists.

INTERNATIONAL AGENCY FOR RESEARCH ON CANCER (IARC)

150 cours Albert Thomas, Lyon
Cedex 08 F-69372, France
Tel: (33) 4 72 73 84 48
Fax: (33) 4 72 73 80 80
Email: fel@iarc.fr
www: http://www.iarc.fr
Tel: 380 023
Contact: Ms Eve Elakroud, Administrative Assistant IARC Fellowship Programme

The International Agency for Research on Cancer (IARC) is part of the World Health Organisation. IARC's mission is to co-ordinate and conduct research into the causes of human cancer and the mechanisms of carcinogenesis, and to develop scientific strategies for cancer control. The Agency is involved in both epidemiological and laboratory research and disseminates scientific information through publications, meetings, courses and fellowships.

IARC Postdoctoral Fellowships for Training in Cancer Research

Subjects: Environmental carcinogenesis including biostatistics, epidemiology of cancer, all aspects of chemical and viral carcinogenesis, cancer prevention, molecular cell biology, molecular genetics, biochemistry, immunology, molecular pathology and mechanisms of carcinogenesis.
Purpose: To provide training in cancer research to junior scientists.
Eligibility: Open to junior scientists actively engaged in medical or allied sciences research who wish to pursue a career in cancer research. Preference will be given to applicants with a doctoral degree, PhD or MD obtained within the last five years in medicine or the natural sciences or to those who are in the final phase of completing their doctoral degree. Applications will not be considered if the applicant has previously received postdoctoral training abroad, or has started postdoctoral work at the host institute before the applicant is informed of the outcome of the application (usually by the end of May). Fellowships must be taken up by December 31st of the year of award and cannot be started before the doctoral degree is formally obtained. Applicants should have an adequate knowledge of the working language of the host laboratory as well as the ability to read and write English at a level sufficient for scientific communication.
Level of Study: Postdoctorate.
Type: Fellowship.
Value: Travel for the Fellow and for one dependent if accompanying the Fellow for at least eight months. Stipends vary according to country of tenure. An annual family allowance of US$400 for spouses and US$450 for each child is also provided.
Length of Study: One year.
Frequency: Annual.
Study Establishment: An institution of the candidate's choice in another country abroad where suitable research facilities and material exist (not tenable at the IARC in Lyon).
Country of Study: Other.
No. of awards offered: Approx. 10.
Application Procedure: Applicants must complete and submit an application form and include with it a letter of acceptance from the host laboratory. Applications must be supported by the Director of the applicant's own institution.
Closing Date: December 31st.
No. of awards given last year: 10.
No. of applicants last year: 50.
Additional Information: Applicants should provide reasonable assurance that they will return to a post in their own country at the end of the fellowship.

INTERNATIONAL AIRLINE TRAINING FUND (IATF)

IATA Centre, Route de l'Aeroport 33, PO Box 416, Geneva, CH-1215, Switzerland
Tel: (41) 22 799 2605
Fax: (41) 22 799 2682
Email: iatf@iata.org
www: http://www.iata.org
Contact: IATF Co-ordinator

The International Airline Training Fund's (IATF) mission is to provide vocational training opportunities for staff of IATA member airlines based in countries with developing economies. It does so by providing scholarships and other training opportunities to enable worthy candidates to follow vocational training courses conducted by the IATA Aviation Training & Development Institute, the Aviation MBA at Concordia University, as well as several other courses.

IATF Aviation MBA Scholarship

Subjects: Aviation law, business administration and management.
Purpose: To allow candidates to study for their global aviation MBA course.
Eligibility: Open to staff from IATA member airlines from countries with developing economies. Applications for IATF Scholarships will be considered only after the applicant has gained acceptance onto the course by Concordia University.

Level of Study: MBA, Postgraduate.
Type: Scholarship.
Value: Please contact the organisation.
Frequency: Annual.
Study Establishment: Concordia University.
Country of Study: Canada.
Application Procedure: Applicants must first complete a course application form, available from Concordia University, followed by a scholarship application form, available from the human resources director of the applicant's airline or from the IATF secretariat.
Closing Date: May 31st.
Funding: Commercial.
Contributor: IATA member airlines and aviation industry suppliers.
Additional Information: All applicants have to take the Graduate Management Admissions Test and should accordingly make timely arrangements to do so at the nearest testing point to their place of residence.

For further information contact:

Concordia University, Annex FB 801, 1455 de Maisonneuve Boulevard West, Montréal, H3G 1M8, Canada

IATF Global Aviation MBA Scholarship (GAMBA)

Subjects: Business administration and management.
Purpose: To allow candidates to study for their global aviation MBA course.
Eligibility: Open to staff from IATA member airlines from countries with developing economies.
Level of Study: MBA, Postgraduate.
Type: Scholarship.
Value: Please contact the organisation.
Frequency: Annual.
Application Procedure: Applicants must first complete a course application form, available from Concordia University. They must then complete a scholarship application form, available from the human resources director of the applicant's airline or from the IAFT secretariat.
Funding: Commercial.
Additional Information: All applicants have to take the Graduate Management Admissions Test and should accordingly make timely arrangements to do so at the nearest testing point to their place of residence. This programme is the same as the Aviation MBA but has a distance learning format and runs over two academic years.

IATF IATA Aviation Training and Development Institute (ATDI) Scholarships

Subjects: Business administration and management in the field of aviation training and development.
Purpose: To enable staff of IATA member airlines based in countries with developing economies to follow short courses of specialist vocational training provided under the auspices of the IATA Aviation Training & Development Institute (ATDI).
Eligibility: Open to staff from IATA member airlines from countries with developing economies.
Level of Study: Postgraduate.
Type: Scholarship.
Value: Please contact the organisation.
Frequency: Throughout the year.
Country of Study: Switzerland, the United States of America or Singapore.
No. of awards offered: Varies.
Application Procedure: Applicants must channel applications through the human resources director of the IATA member airline which employs the applicant for an IATF-IATDI scholarship.
Funding: Commercial, Private.
Contributor: IATA member airlines and aviation industry suppliers.
Additional Information: The scholarship committee meets quarterly to assess accumulated applications as of that date and to make awards. The ATDI seeks to offer skills training for managers, supervisors and other airline industry specialist staff who wish to add to their

professional knowledge and ability. The range of courses taught is wide, with courses in heavy demand being repeated during the course of the year.

INTERNATIONAL ASSOCIATION FOR THE STUDY OF INSURANCE ECONOMICS

53 Route de Malagnou, Geneva
CH-1208, Switzerland
Tel: (41) 22 707 6600
Fax: (41) 22 736 7536
Email: secretariat@genevaassociation.org
www: http://www.genevaassociation.org
Contact: Professor Patrick Liedtke, Secretary General

The International Association for the Study of Insurance Economics was established in 1973 for the purpose of promoting economic research in the sector of risk and insurance.

Ernst Meyer Prize

Subjects: Risk and insurance economics.
Purpose: To recognise research work which makes a significant and original contribution.
Eligibility: Open to professors, researchers or students of economics.
Level of Study: Unrestricted.
Type: Prize.
Value: Swiss franc 5,000.
Frequency: Annual.
Country of Study: Any country.
No. of awards offered: One.
Application Procedure: Applicants must write for details.
Closing Date: September 30th.
Funding: Private.
No. of applicants last year: 7.

Geneva Association

Subjects: Topics of interest in risk management or insurance.
Purpose: To defray printing costs of university theses.
Eligibility: Open to authors of university theses already submitted.
Level of Study: Doctorate, Postdoctorate.
Type: Grant.
Value: Swiss franc 3,000 to help defray printing costs.
Frequency: Annual.
Application Procedure: Applicants must write for further information.
Closing Date: September 30th.
Funding: Private.

International Association for the Study of Insurance Economics Research Grants

Subjects: Risk management and insurance economics.
Purpose: To promote economic research.
Eligibility: Open to graduates involved in research for a thesis leading to a doctoral degree in economics.
Level of Study: Postgraduate.
Type: Research grant.
Value: Swiss franc 10,000.
Length of Study: 10 months.
Frequency: Annual.
Country of Study: Any country.
No. of awards offered: Two.
Application Procedure: Applicants must submit an application accompanied by a personal history, a description of the research undertaken and a letter of recommendation from two professors of economics.
Closing Date: September 30th.
Funding: Private.
Additional Information: The Association reserves the right to support research on other subjects which may be submitted. The Association also grants authors of university theses already submitted, dealing in depth with a subject in the field of risk and insurance economics, a subsidy of up to swiss franc 3,000 towards printing costs.

INTERNATIONAL ASSOCIATION FOR THE STUDY OF OBESITY

231 North Gower Street, London
NW1 2NS, United Kingdom
Tel: (44) 207 691 1900
Fax: (44) 7387 6033
Email: kate.Baillie@iaso.org
www: http://www.iaso.org
Contact: Kate Baillie, Director

The International Association for the study of obesity is the leading global professional organization concerned with obesity operating in more than 50 countries around the world.

The IASO New Investiagtor Award
Subjects: Obesity research.
Purpose: To support investigation who wish to study obesity for masters or doctoral thesis.
Level of Study: Doctorate, Postgraduate.
Type: Award.
Value: Variable.
Length of Study: Variable.
Frequency: Annual.
Study Establishment: Open.
Country of Study: Open.
Application Procedure: Please check website.

INTERNATIONAL ASSOCIATION OF FIRE CHIEFS (IAFC) FOUNDATION

Box 1818, Windermere, FL 341759
United States of America
Tel: (1) 717 846 9705
Contact: Ms Sue Hawkins

Each year the International Association of Fire Chiefs (IAFC) Foundation co-ordinates a scholarship programme made possible through the generosity of corporations throughout the United States, as well as donations from individuals and persons sponsoring a scholarship as a memorial to a friend or colleague.

IAFC Foundation Scholarship
Subjects: All subjects.
Purpose: To assist fire service personnel towards college degrees.
Eligibility: Open to any person who is an active member of a state, county, provincial, municipal, community, industrial or federal fire department who has demonstrated proficiency as a member. Dependants of members are not eligible.
Level of Study: Graduate, Postdoctorate, Professional development.
Type: Scholarship.
Value: US$250-4,000.
Frequency: Annual.
Country of Study: Any country.
No. of awards offered: 30.
Application Procedure: Applicants must complete an application form. This includes a 250 word statement outlining reasons for applying for assistance and an explanation as to why the candidate thinks that the course will be useful in their chosen field.
Closing Date: August 1st.
Funding: Commercial, Private.
No. of awards given last year: 17.
No. of applicants last year: 219.
Additional Information: In evaluating the applications, preference will be given to those demonstrating need, desire and initiative.

For further information contact:

4025 Fair Ridge Dr, Fairfax, VA 22033-2868, United States of America
Tel: (1) 703-273-0911

INTERNATIONAL ASTRONOMICAL UNION (IAU)

98bis boulevard Arago, Paris, 75014, France
Tel: (33) 1 43 25 83 58
Fax: (33) 1 43 25 26 16
Email: iau@iap.fr
www: http://www.iau.org
Contact: Administrative Assistant

The mission of the International Astronomical Union (IAU), founded in 1919, is to promote and safeguard the science of astronomy in all its aspects through international co-operation. The IAU, through its 12 scientific divisions and 40 commissions covering the full spectrum of astronomy, continues to play a key role in promoting and co-ordinating worldwide co-operation in astronomy.

IAU Travel Grant
Subjects: Astronomy and astrophysics.
Purpose: To provide funds to qualified individuals to enable them to visit institutions abroad. It is intended that the visitors have ample time and opportunity to interact with intellectual life of the host institution. It is a specific objective of the programme that astronomy in the home country is enriched after the applicant returns.
Eligibility: Open to faculty members, staff members, postdoctoral Fellows or graduate students at any recognised educational or research institution.
Level of Study: Graduate, Postdoctorate, Postgraduate, Research.
Value: One return economy fare between home and host institutions.
Length of Study: Approx. more than three months at a single host institution.
Country of Study: Any country.
No. of awards offered: 12-15 per year.
Application Procedure: Applicants must submit an application including a curriculum vitae, a plan of scientific activity, letters of support from the home and host institutions, information on responsibility for subsistence at the host institution, and information on the lowest available fare. Applications should be submitted in time for the Officers of the Commission to consult by post.
Closing Date: There is no deadline.
Contributor: Academy of sciences of our 70 national members.
No. of awards given last year: 15.
No. of applicants last year: 30.

For further information contact:

Univ Virginia - Univ Station, Box 3818, Charlottesville, VA 22903 0818, United States of America
Tel: (1) 4349247494
Fax: (1) 4349243104
Email: crt@viginia.edu
Contact: Dr Charles R. Tolbert, President

Univ Toronto, Erindale College, Mississauga, ON L5l 1C6, Canada
Tel: (1) 905 828 5351
Fax: (1) 905 828 5328
Email: jpercy@credit.erin.utoronto.ca
Contact: Prof John R. Percy, Vice-President

INTERNATIONAL BANK FOR RECONSTRUCTION AND DEVELOPMENT

1818 H Street North West, Washington, DC 20433, United States of America
Tel: (1) 202 473 1817
Fax: (1) 202 522 4036
Email: jjwbgsp@worldbank.org
www: http://www.worldbank.org/wbi/scholarships
Contact: Mr Abdul-Monen Al-Mashat, Scholarships Administrator

Joint Japan/World Bank Graduate Scholarship Program (JJ/WBGSP)

Subjects: Development related fields.
Purpose: To promote economic and social development by awarding scholarships.
Eligibility: Eligibility criteria can be found on the programme's website.
Level of Study: Postgraduate.
Type: Scholarship.
Length of Study: One-two years.
Frequency: Annual.
Study Establishment: All universities in the member countries of World Bank.
Country of Study: Other.
No. of awards offered: 402.
Application Procedure: Applicants must complete an application form and submit it along with admission letters and supporting documents.
Closing Date: April 1st.
Funding: Government.
Contributor: Japan.
No. of awards given last year: 312.
No. of applicants last year: 3,000.

INTERNATIONAL BEETHOVEN PIANO COMPETITION

Universität für Musik und darstellende Kunst Wien, Anton-Von-Webernplatz 1, Vienna, A-1030, Austria
Tel: (43) 171 155 6050
Fax: (43) 171 155 6059
Email: beethoven-comp@mdw.ac.at
www: http://www.mdw.ac.at/beethoven-competition
Contact: Ms Elga Ponzer, Secretary General

International Beethoven Piano Competition Vienna

Subjects: Piano.
Purpose: To encourage the artistic development of young pianists.
Eligibility: Open to pianists of all nationalities born between January 1st 1973 and December 31st 1988.
Level of Study: Unrestricted.
Type: Competition.
Value: The first prize is €7,122, a Bosendorfer Model 200 piano and engagements, the second prize is €5,087, the third prize is €4,069, and there are three further prizes of €1,500.
Frequency: Every four years.
Country of Study: Austria.
No. of awards offered: Six.
Application Procedure: Applicants must write for details.
Closing Date: September 30th.
Funding: Government, Private.
No. of awards given last year: Six.
No. of applicants last year: 248.
Additional Information: For more information please visit the website.

INTERNATIONAL CENTRE FOR GENETIC ENGINEERING AND BIOTECHNOLOGY (ICGEB)

Padriciano 99, Trieste, I-34012, Italy
Tel: (39) 040 375 71
Fax: (39) 040 226 555
Email: vincent@icgeb.org
www: http://www.icgeb.org
Contact: Ms Susan Vincent, Office of the Director General

The International Centre for Genetic Engineering and Biotechnology (ICGEB) is an organisation devoted to advanced research and training in molecular biology, with special regard to the needs of the developing world. The component host countries are Italy and India. The full member states of ICGEB are the following: Afghanistan, Algeria, Argentina, Bangladesh, Bhutan, Brazil, Bulgaria, Chile, China, Colombia, Costa Rica, Côte d'Ivoire, Croatia, Cuba, Ecuador, Egypt, Hungary, Iran, Iraq, Jordan, Kuwait, Macedonia, Mauritius, Mexico, Morocco, Nigeria, Pakistan, Panama, Peru, Poland, Romania, Russia, Senegal, Serbia and Montenegro,Slovakia, Slovenia, Sri Lanka, Sudan, Syria, Tanzania, Trinidad and Tobago, Tunisia, Turkey, Uruguay, Venezuela, Vietnam.

ICGEB Long-Term Postdoctoral Fellowship Programme

Subjects: The New Delhi laboratory is concerned with mammalian biology, virology, immunology, malaria, recombinant gene products, plant biology, plant molecular biology, insect resistance, and plant resistance. In Trieste molecular biology, proteomics, molecular medicine, virology, microbiology, bacteriology, protein structure and bioinformatics, molecular pathology, molecular immunology is of interest, and the Italian institutes are concerned with enzymology, human genetics, immunology, molecular biology, plant molecular biology and virology.
Purpose: To provide long-term training in genetic engineering and biotechnology for scientists from the member states and to promote state of the art academic and industrial research training in an international context. The fellowship aims to effectively contribute to the scientific development of the Fellow's home country. Training is proposed within the scope of biotechnological and genetic engineering research and offers an opportunity for individuals to broaden their scientific background or to extend their research in health, nutrition, industrial development, environmental protection and energy production.
Eligibility: Open to promising postdoctoral or established research students under the age of 35, who are nationals of one of the ICGEB Member States.
Level of Study: Postdoctorate.
Type: Fellowship.
Value: US$13,000-21,000 per Fellow per year, depending on the place of study, as well as travel costs and medical insurance.
Length of Study: One year, with the possibility of an extension for a further year.
Frequency: Annual.
Study Establishment: ICGEB laboratories in Trieste, Italy, New Delhi, India and in selected Italian research institutes.
Country of Study: Other.
No. of awards offered: Varies.
Application Procedure: Applicants must submit a completed application form through, and endorsed by, the respective National Liaison Officer in his or her country of origin.
Closing Date: June 30th for the first review and December 31st for the second review.
Additional Information: For further information please write to the main address or refer to the website.

ICGEB Short-Term Postdoctoral Fellowship Programme

Subjects: Molecular biology, proteomics, molecular medicine, virology, microbiology, bacteriology, protein structure and bioinformatics, molecular pathology, molecular immunology, mammalian biology, malaria, biotechnology, plant biology, plant molecular biology, plant transformation, insect resistance and plant resistance.
Purpose: To provide short-term training in genetic engineering and biotechnology for scientists from the member states of ICGEB, and to promote academic and industrial research in an international context.
Eligibility: Open to promising postdoctoral students, who are nationals of one of the Member States of ICGEB and have already made contact with an ICGEB research group or affiliated centres involved in an ongoing collaborative research project.
Level of Study: Postdoctorate.
Type: Fellowship.
Value: An allowance to cover travel costs as well as board and lodging.
Length of Study: A maximum of three months.
Frequency: Annual.
Study Establishment: ICGEB laboratories in Trieste, Italy, New Delhi, India and at ICGEB affiliated centres involved in an ongoing collaborative research project funded by the ICGEB.

Country of Study: Other.
No. of awards offered: Varies.
Application Procedure: Applicants must submit a completed application form through the ICGEB Liaison Officer of the applicant's country of origin. Application forms can be found on the website.
Closing Date: Applications are accepted at any time.

Predoctoral Fellowship Programme ICGEB International PhD Course

Subjects: Molecular biology, molecular medicine, virology, microbiology, bacteriology, protein structure and bioinformatics, molecular pathology, molecular immunology, proteomics, leukocyte biology, muscle molecular biology, and biotechnology development and transfer.
Purpose: To enable promising young students to attend and complete the PhD course at ICGEB Trieste in Italy. The course is in collaboration with the Scuola Normale Superiore (SNS) Pisa, Italy and is validated by the Open University, UK (Life Sciences Programme).
Eligibility: Open to promising predoctoral students under the age of 30 from any Member State of the ICGEB.
Level of Study: Predoctorate.
Type: Fellowship.
Value: €15,600.
Length of Study: Three-four years.
Frequency: Annual.
Study Establishment: ICGEB component laboratories in Trieste.
Country of Study: Italy.
No. of awards offered: Five.
Application Procedure: Applicants must submit a complete application to ICGEB Trieste.
Closing Date: April 15th for pre selection.
Additional Information: For further information please refer to the website.

Predoctoral Fellowship Programme ICGEB JNU PhD Course in Molecular Biology

Subjects: Mammalian biology, virology, immunology, malaria and biotechnology, plant biology, plant molecular biology, plant transformation, insect and plant resistance.
Purpose: To offer postgraduate training with the aim of obtaining a PhD degree in the field of molecular biology at the Jawaharlal Nehru University in New Delhi, in collaboration with the ICGEB.
Eligibility: Open to promising young students in possession of an MSc from a recognised university, who are nationals of one of the ICGEB Member States.
Level of Study: Postgraduate, Predoctorate.
Type: Fellowship.
Value: US$10,200.
Length of Study: Four-five years, depending on the academic qualification the individual student has achieved prior to embarking on the course.
Frequency: Annual.
Study Establishment: Jawaharlal Nehru University in New Delhi.
Country of Study: India.
No. of awards offered: Three-four.
Application Procedure: For details of the application process, applicants must contact Ms Vincent or one of the ICGEB Group Leaders in New Delhi, India, by faxing (91) 11 616 23 16.
Closing Date: Please write for details.
Additional Information: For more information on this course please refer to the website.

INTERNATIONAL CENTRE FOR PHYSICAL LAND RESOURCES

Geological Institute, University Ghent, Krijgslaan 281/S8, Ghent, Belgium
Tel: (32) 9 264 4626
Fax: (32) 9 264 4991
Email: plrprog.adm@rug.ac.be
www: http://allserv.rug.ac.be/~amtanghe/main.html
Contact: Professor E Van Ranst

The International Centre for Physical Land Resources has a long standing tradition in the academic formation and training in physical land resources, including soil science, soil survey, land evaluation, agricultural applications and eremology eg. dryland and desertification. Since 1997 the scope of courses has been widened with courses on the non-agricultural use and application of physical land resources.

Postgraduate Studies in Physical Land Resources Scholarship

Subjects: Fundamental soil science, soil genesis, prospection and classification, non agricultural use and applications of land and soils, geotechnical engineering, soil mechanics and hydrogeology, management of physical and land resources, agricultural applications, soil fertility, soil erosion and conservation or land evaluation.
Purpose: To provide postgraduate training opportunities to nationals from developing countries.
Eligibility: Open to nationals of the developing world or non European Union members.
Level of Study: Postgraduate.
Type: Scholarship.
Value: €500.
Length of Study: One year, with a possible maximum extension to two years.
Frequency: Annual.
Study Establishment: The University of Gent.
Country of Study: Belgium.
No. of awards offered: Approx. two.
Application Procedure: Applicants must complete an application form and submit this with certified diplomas and transcripts to the Programme Secretariat to obtain academic admission.
Closing Date: March 31st.
Funding: Government.
No. of awards given last year: One.
No. of applicants last year: 10.

INTERNATIONAL CHAMBER MUSIC COMPETITION

UFAM, 8 rue du Dôme, Paris, F-75116, France
Tel: (33) 1 47 04 76 38
Fax: (33) 1 47 27 35 03
Email: ufam@wanadoo.fr
www: http://www.infoservice.fr/ufam
Contact: Mrs Dominique Bertrand, President

Organisation of International singing and chamber music competitions.

International Chamber Music Competition

Subjects: Groups of wind and string instruments, with or without the piano.
Purpose: To enable musicians to play engagements across the world.
Eligibility: Open to groups of musicians of any nationality, who are no more than 36 years of age. The average age of the group should not exceed 34 years.
Level of Study: Postgraduate.
Type: Prize.
Value: €25,000 plus special prizes. Please contact the organisation for details.
Frequency: Every two years.
Country of Study: Any country.
No. of awards offered: Varies.
Application Procedure: Applicants must request a brochure.
Closing Date: September 12th in the year of the competition.
Funding: Private.

Paris International Singing Competition

Subjects: Singing, opera or melody.
Purpose: To help young singers in starting their career.
Eligibility: Open to female singers aged 32 years and younger and male singers aged 34 years and younger. There are no nationality restrictions.

Level of Study: Unrestricted.
Type: Prize.
Value: Please contact the organisation. There is free accommodation for competitors and winners are offered important singing engagements.
Frequency: Every two years.
Country of Study: Any country.
No. of awards offered: Eight.
Application Procedure: Applicants must request a brochure.
Closing Date: May.

INTERNATIONAL COLLEGE OF SURGEONS

1516 North Lake Shore Drive, Chicago, IL 60610-1694, United States of America
Tel: (1) 312 642 3555
Fax: (1) 312 787 1624
Email: max@icsglobal.org
www: http://www.icsglobal.org
Contact: International Executive Director

ICS Scholarship
Subjects: Medical research and surgery.
Purpose: To support education and research.
Eligibility: Open to surgeons from third world countries travelling to developed nations to further their education.
Level of Study: Doctorate, Postdoctorate, Postgraduate, Professional development.
Type: Scholarship.
Value: Please consult the organisation.
Frequency: Dependent on funds available.
Country of Study: Any country.
No. of awards offered: Varies.
Application Procedure: Applicants must send requests to ICS headquarters.
Additional Information: Further information is available on request.

INTERNATIONAL COUNCIL FOR CANADIAN STUDIES (ICCS)

75 Albert S-908, Ottawa, ON, K1P 5E7, Canada
Tel: (1) 613 789 7828
Fax: (1) 613 789 7830
Email: general@iccs-ciec.ca
www: http://www.scholarships-bourses-ca.org
Contact: Program Assistant

The International Council for Canadian Studies (ICCS) administers programmes for Canadian students (CSFP, FGA, OAS and PRA) on behalf of the Department of Foreign Affairs and International Trade (DFAIT). The ICCS is also responsible for the administration aspects of scholarships and study programmes offered to students of foreign countries, funded by DFAIT.

ICCS Canadian Commonwealth Scholarship Program
Subjects: All subjects, except medicine or introduction to languages.
Purpose: To provide opportunities for students of other Commonwealth countries to pursue advanced studies in Canada. The scholarships are intended for men and women of high intellectual promise who may be expected to make a significant contribution to their own countries on their return from study in Canada.
Eligibility: Open to members of the British Commonwealth.
Level of Study: Doctorate, Graduate, Postgraduate, Research.
Type: Scholarship.
Value: The expenses of travel, living and study for the Scholar only. No dependent allowance is payable.
Length of Study: Varies, depending on where the applicant is applying from. Scholarships are offered for one degree only. An award will not be granted for less than one semester.
Frequency: Annual.
Country of Study: Canada.
No. of awards offered: Varies.

Application Procedure: Applicants must contact the designated Commonwealth agency in their home country for application guidelines. In most countries the agency is part of the national government's Department of Ministry of Education. Citizens of New Zealand and the United Kingdom must contact different organisations. Addresses are listed on the website. Please note that the Canadian Commonwealth agency and the ICCS do not accept applications and supporting documents sent directly by applicants.
Closing Date: Varies in each country.
Funding: Government.
Contributor: The Department of Foreign Affairs and International Trade.

ICCS Commonwealth Scholarship and Fellowship Plan
Subjects: As specified by each country.
Purpose: To assist the pursuit of graduate studies or research abroad in a Commonwealth country other than Canada.
Eligibility: Open to Canadian citizens or permanent residents who are graduates of a Canadian university, and have completed a university degree or expect to graduate prior to the tenure of the award. There are no age restrictions, but preference will be given to applicants who have obtained a university degree within the last five years.
Level of Study: Doctorate, Graduate, Postgraduate, Research.
Type: Other.
Value: Most awards include the scholar's return travel from Canada to the awarding country, a monthly living allowance, tuition and compulsory academic fees and medical insurance. Various other allowances may be available, depending on the host country.
Length of Study: As specified by each country.
Frequency: Annual.
Country of Study: India, Malaysia, New Zealand, Sri Lanka, Trinidad and Tobago, Uganda, the United Kingdom or Fiji.
No. of awards offered: Varies.
Application Procedure: Applicants can download an application form from the website, apply online or pick up an application from the graduate studies or student awards office at any Canadian university.
Closing Date: Please contact the organisation.
Funding: Government.
Additional Information: The Canadian Scholarship and Fellowship Selection Committee will select nominations to be forwarded to the awarding country. The number of nominations varies, but will be approximately double the number of awards expected to be made. The decision of the Canadian Committee is final and not open to appeal. The actual offer of a scholarship will be made by the Commonwealth Scholarship Agency in the awarding country. In general, the Agency tries to place selected candidates in the institutions of their choice, however, where this is not possible, an alternative institution offering opportunities for the proposed course of study will be chosen.

ICCS Foreign Government Awards
Subjects: Most subjects, except introduction to languages.
Purpose: To assist Canadians to study or conduct research abroad.
Eligibility: Open to Canadian citizens with a working knowledge of the host country's language and a Bachelor's degree or PhD for postdoctoral fellowships, completed before the beginning of the award term.
Level of Study: Doctorate, Graduate, Postdoctorate, Postgraduate, Research.
Type: Scholarship.
Value: Generally to cover tuition fees, living allowance, transportation and medical insurance.
Frequency: Annual.
Country of Study: Chile, Colombia, Finland, France, Mexico, Korea, Germany, Italy, Japan, the Netherlands, the Phillippines, Russia, or Spain.
No. of awards offered: Varies.
Application Procedure: Applications are initially evaluated by a preselection committee of Canadian academics. The committee submits a list of recommended candidates and alternates to each host country where award recipients are chosen. A list of participating countries is available on request.
Closing Date: Varies, October to January.
Funding: Government.

INTERNATIONAL DEVELOPMENT RESEARCH CENTRE (IDRC)

Centre Training & Awards Unit, 250 Albert Street, PO Box 8500,
Ottawa, ON, K1G 3H9, Canada
Tel: (1) 613 236 6163
Fax: (1) 613 563 0815
Email: cta@idrc.ca
www: http://www.idrc.ca/awards
Contact: Ms Danielle Reinhardt, Programme Assistant

The International Development Research Centre (IDRC) is a public corporation created by the Canadian government to help communities in the developing world find solutions to social, economic and environmental problems through research.

Canadian Window on International Development

Subjects: One award is for research that explores the relationship between Canadian aid, trade, immigration and diplomatic policy, and international development and the alleviation of global poverty, and a second award will be granted for research into a problem that is common to First Nations or Inuit communities in Canada and a developing region of the world.
Eligibility: Successful candidates will propose comparative research requiring data from both Canada and a developing region of the world to better understand the common, interrelated problem or issue identified for in depth study. Selection will favour those proposals which demonstrate the relevance of the research topic for Canada and for the less developed country or countries being studied, and the close linkage between the international and national character of the topic.
Level of Study: Doctorate, Graduate, Postgraduate.
Value: Up to Canadian $20,000.
Length of Study: Three to twelve months.
Frequency: Annual.
Study Establishment: Universities.
Country of Study: Canada.
No. of awards offered: Two or three per year.
Application Procedure: Applicants must complete an application form.
Closing Date: April 1st.
Funding: Government.
No. of applicants last year: Varies.
Additional Information: Further information is available on the website (www.idrc.ca/awards).

Community Forestry: Trees and People - John G Bene Fellowship

Subjects: Forestry management.
Purpose: To assist Canadian graduate students in undertaking research on the relationship of forest resources to the social, economic and environmental welfare of people in developing countries.
Eligibility: Open to Canadian citizens and permanent residents who are registered at a Canadian university at the Master's or doctoral level. Applicants must have an academic background that combines forestry or agroforestry with social sciences.
Level of Study: Doctorate, Graduate, Postgraduate.
Type: Fellowship.
Value: Canadian $15,000.
Length of Study: Three-twelve months.
Frequency: Annual.
Study Establishment: Universities.
Country of Study: Canada.
No. of awards offered: One.
Application Procedure: Applicants must submit a summary of their research proposal, budget of proposed research, application form, curriculum vitae, two references, a letter from the institution confirming affiliation, transcripts, confirmation from their academic advisor that coursework is complete and proof of Canadian citizenship or permanent residency.
Closing Date: March 1st.
Funding: Private.
Contributor: Endowment.
No. of awards given last year: One.

Additional Information: Further information is available on the website(www.idrc.ca/awards).

Ecosystem Approaches to Human Health Awards

Subjects: The interactions between multiple determinates of health within defined ecosystems, using transdisciplinary, participatory and gender integrative approaches, moving from an exclusive health service response to an ecosystem management response to human health problems.
Purpose: To provide financial assistance to graduate students undertaking research projects which look at the relationships between the environment and human health.
Eligibility: Research questions and methods need to address the implications of gender and social differences as these relate to ecosystem approaches to human life. Awards will be granted for training and research linked to the ecosystem approaches to human health programme initiative of the centre. Priority will be given to proposals for research on ecosystems that are stressed through agriculture, urbanisation or mining activities.
Level of Study: Doctorate, Graduate, Postgraduate.
Type: Award.
Value: Up to Canadian $15,000.
Length of Study: Up to one year.
Frequency: Please check website.
Study Establishment: Universities.
Country of Study: Other.
No. of awards offered: Up to six.
Application Procedure: Applicants must write for details.
Funding: Government.
Contributor: Canadian Government.
No. of awards given last year: Five.
No. of applicants last year: 13.
Additional Information: www.idrc.ca/awards.

IDRC Doctoral Research Awards

Subjects: IDRC's research activities focus on three programme areas: social and economic equity, environment and natural resource management, information and communication techniques (ICTs) for development.
Purpose: To promote the growth of Canadian capacity in research on sustainable and equitable development from an international perspective.
Eligibility: Open to Canadian citizens and permanent residents. Applicants must be registered at a Canadian university, have a research proposal for a doctoral thesis and provide evidence of affiliation and complete coursework prior to taking on research.
Level of Study: Doctorate.
Type: Award.
Value: Up to Canadian $20,000.
Length of Study: Three-twelve months.
Frequency: Twice a year.
Study Establishment: Universities. Normally such research is conducted in Latin America, Africa, the Middle East or Asia.
Country of Study: Canada.
No. of awards offered: Varies.
Application Procedure: Applicants must complete and submit an application form with a research proposal, budget, curriculum vitae, two references, a letter from the institution of affiliation, approval of thesis by committee, transcripts, confirmation from their advisor that coursework will be complete before the start of research, and proof of Canadian citizenship or permanent residency.
Closing Date: April and November.
Funding: Government.
Contributor: The Canadian government.
No. of applicants last year: Varies.
Additional Information: Further information is available on the website(www.idrc.ca/awards).

Use of Fertility Enhancing Food, Forage and Cover Crops in Sustainably Managed Agroecosystems: The Bentley Fellowship

Subjects: Use of fertility enhancing plants such as leguminous forages, cover crops and grain legumes in subsistence tropical agriculture.

Purpose: To provide assistance to those who wish to undertake applied on-farm research in a developing country with co-operating farmers.
Eligibility: Open to Canadian or developing country students or researchers with a university degree in agriculture, forestry or biology.
Level of Study: Doctorate, Graduate, Postdoctorate, Postgraduate, Unrestricted.
Type: Fellowship.
Value: Up to Canadian $30,000.
Length of Study: 18-24 Months.
Frequency: Every two years.
Study Establishment: Universities.
Country of Study: Other.
No. of awards offered: One-two.
Application Procedure: Applicants must complete an application form, available on request.
Closing Date: October.
Funding: Private.
No. of awards given last year: One.
No. of applicants last year: 11.
Additional Information: Further information is available on the website(www.idrc.ca/awards).

INTERNATIONAL FEDERATION OF LIBRARY ASSOCIATIONS AND INSTITUTIONS (IFLA)

PO Box 95312, The Hague, NL-2509 CH, Netherlands
Tel: (31) 70 314 0884
Fax: (31) 70 383 4827
Email: ifla@ifla.org
www: http://www.ifla.org
Contact: Ms Josche Neven, Co-ordinator of Professional Activities

Established in 1927, the primary function of the International Federation of Library Associations and Institutions (IFLA) is to encourage, sponsor and promote research and development in all aspects of library activity, and to share its findings with the library community as a whole for the greater good of librarianship.

The Guust van Wesemael Literacy Prize
Subjects: Library science.
Purpose: To recognise an achievement in the field of literacy promotion in a developing country.
Eligibility: Open to candidates from developing countries.
Level of Study: Unrestricted.
Value: €2,725.
Frequency: Every two years.
Country of Study: Any country.
No. of awards offered: One.
Application Procedure: Applicants must complete an application form, available from IFLA headquarters.
Closing Date: March 1st every odd numbered year.
Funding: Private.
No. of awards given last year: Two.
Additional Information: The prize should be used for follow up activities such as purchasing targeted collections of appropriate books.

Hans-Peter Geh Grant for Conference Participation
Subjects: Library and information science.
Purpose: To sponsor a librarian to attend an IFLA seminar or conference in Germany in order to become acquainted with new developments in the field of information.
Eligibility: Applicants must be IFLA affiliates, or employees of IFLA members. Open only to librarians from the former Soviet region or the Baltic States.
Level of Study: Professional development.
Value: €1,135.
Frequency: Annual.
Country of Study: Any country.
Application Procedure: Applicants must complete an application form, available from IFLA headquarters.

Closing Date: February 1st.
Funding: Private.
No. of awards given last year: One.

INTERNATIONAL FEDERATION OF UNIVERSITY WOMEN (IFUW)

8 rue de l'Ancien-Port, Geneva
CH-1201, Switzerland
Tel: (41) 22 731 2380
Fax: (41) 22 738 0440
Email: ifuw@ifuw.org
www: http://www.ifuw.org
Contact: Grants Management Officer

The International Federation of University Women (IFUW) is a non-profit, non governmental organisation comprising of graduate women working locally, nationally and internationally to advocate the improvement of the status of women and girls at the international level, to promote lifelong education and to enable graduate women to use their expertise to effect change.

British Federation Crosby Hall Fellowship
Subjects: All subjects.
Purpose: To encourage advanced scholarship and original research.
Eligibility: Open to female applicants who are either a member of one of IFUW's national federations or associations or, in the case of female graduates living in countries where there is not yet a national affiliate, an independent member of IFUW. Applicants should be well started on a research programme and should have completed at least one year of graduate work.
Level of Study: Doctorate, Postdoctorate, Research.
Type: Fellowship.
Value: UK£2,500.
Study Establishment: An approved Institute of Higher Education.
Country of Study: United Kingdom.
No. of awards offered: One.
Application Procedure: Applicants must apply through their respective federation or association. A list of IFUW national federations can be sent upon request or obtained from the Internet. IFUW independent members and international individual members must apply directly to IFUW headquarters In Geneva.
Closing Date: Early September in the year preceding the competition.
Funding: Private.
No. of awards given last year: One.
Additional Information: Applicants in the United States and the United Kingdom should write to the addresses shown for those countries, all others should write to the main address. Further information is available from the website.

For further information contact:

AAUW/IFUW Liason, 1111 Sixteenth Street NW, Washington, DC 28036, United States of America
Fax: (1) 202 872 1425

BFWG, 4 Mandeville Courtyard, 142 Battersea Park Road, London, SW11 4NB, England
Tel: (44) 20 7498 8037
Fax: (44) 20 7498 8037

Ida Smedley Maclean, CFUW/A Vibert Douglas, IFUW and Action Fellowship
Subjects: All subjects.
Purpose: To encourage advanced scholarship and original research.
Eligibility: Open to female applicants who are either a member of one of IFUW's national federations or associations or, in the case of female graduates living in countries where there is not yet a national affiliate, an independent member of IFUW. Applicants should be well started on a research programme and should have completed at least one year of graduate work.
Level of Study: Doctorate, Postdoctorate, Postgraduate.
Type: Fellowship.

Value: The Maclean Fellowship is Swiss franc 8,000-10,000, the Douglas Fellowship is Canadian $6,000 and the SAAP Fellowship is swiss franc 8,000-10,000.
Length of Study: More than eight months.
Study Establishment: An approved Institute of Higher Education other than that in which the applicant received her education or habitually resides.
Country of Study: Any country.
No. of awards offered: One of each fellowship.
Application Procedure: Applicants must write for details enclosing a stamped addressed envelope. Applicants should apply through their respective federation or association. A list of IFUW national federations can be sent upon request or obtained from the Internet.
Closing Date: Early September in the year preceding the competition.
Funding: Private.
No. of awards given last year: One of each.
Additional Information: Applicants in the United States and the United Kingdom should write to the addresses shown for those countries, all others should write to the main address. Further information is available from the website.

For further information contact:

AAUW/IFUW Liaision, 1111 Sixteenth Street NW, Washington, DC 28036, United States of America
Fax: (1) 202 872 1425

BFWG, 4 Mandeville Courtyard, 142 Battersea Park Road, London, SW11 4NB, England
Tel: (44) 20 7498 8037
Fax: (44) 20 7498 8037

Winifred Cullis and Dorothy Leet Grants, NZFUW Grants

Subjects: All subjects.
Purpose: To enable recipients to carry out research, obtain specialised training essential to research or training in new techniques.
Eligibility: Open to female applicants who are either a member of one of IFUW's national federations or associations or, in the case of female graduates living in countries where there is not yet a national affiliate, an independent member of IFUW. Applicants should be well started on a research programme and should have completed at least one year of graduate work.
Level of Study: Doctorate, Graduate, Postdoctorate, Postgraduate.
Type: Grant.
Value: Varies, Swiss franc 3,000-6,000.
Length of Study: A minimum of two months.
Country of Study: Any country.
No. of awards offered: Varies.
Application Procedure: Applicants must write for details enclosing a stamped addressed envelope. Applicants should apply through their respective federation or association. A list of IFUW national federations can be sent upon request or obtained from the Internet. Applicants in the United States of America and the United Kingdom should write to the addresses shown for those countries and all others should write to the main address.
Closing Date: Early September in the year preceding the competition.
Funding: Private.
No. of awards given last year: 15-20.
Additional Information: Further information is available from the website.

For further information contact:

AAUW/IFUW Liason, 1111 Sixteenth Street NW, Washington, DC 28036, United States of America
Fax: (1) 202 872 1425

BFWG, 4 Mandeville Courtyard, 142 Battersea Park Road, London, DC SW11 4NB, England
Tel: (44) 20 7498 8037
Fax: (44) 20 7498 8037

INTERNATIONAL FOUNDATION FOR ETHICAL RESEARCH (IFER)

53 West Jackson Boulevard, Suite 1552, Chicago, IL 60604, United States of America
Tel: (1) 312 427 6025
Fax: (1) 312 427 6524
Email: ifer@navs.org
www: http://www.ifer.org
Contact: Mr Peter O'Donovan, Deputy Director

The International Foundation for Ethical Research (IFER) supports the development and implementation of viable, scientifically valid alternatives to the use of animals in research, product testing, and classroom education. IFER is dedicated to the belief that through new technologies and diligent research, solutions can be found that will create a better world for all, without using animals.

IFER Fellowship for Alternatives in Scientific Research

Subjects: Tissue cultures, cell cultures, organ cultures, gas chromatography, mathematical and computer models and clinical and epidemiological surveys
Purpose: To develop, validate and disseminate alternatives to the use of live animals in research, education and product testing. Alternatives are defined as methods which replace, refine or reduce the number of animals traditionally used.
Eligibility: Open to students enrolled in Master's and PhD programmes.
Level of Study: Graduate, Postgraduate.
Type: Fellowship.
Value: US$12,500 and US$2,500 for supplies.
Length of Study: One year, renewable for up to three years based on eligibility and funding.
Frequency: Annual.
Country of Study: Any country.
No. of awards offered: Varies.
Application Procedure: Applicants must write for details or refer to the website.
Funding: Private.
Additional Information: Further information can be found on the website.

INTERNATIONAL FOUNDATION FOR SCIENCE (IFS)

Karlavägen 108, 5th Floor, Stockholm, 115 26, Sweden
Tel: (46) 85 458 1800
Fax: (46) 85 458 1801
Email: info@ifs.se
www: http://www.ifs.se
Contact: Head of Finance & Administration

The International Foundation for Science (IFS) shall contribute to the strengthening of capacity in developing countries to conduct relevant and high quality research on the management, use and conservation of biological resources and the environment in which these resources occur and upon which they depend.

IFS Research Grant

Subjects: The renewable utilisation of biological resources such as projects in agriculture, forestry, natural products and aquatic resources, as well as research on the sustainable utilisation and conservation of natural ecosystems.
Purpose: To build scientific capacity in developing countries.
Eligibility: Open to scientists who are citizens of developing countries, in possession of an academic degree of not less than an MSc or the equivalent, currently working at a university or research institution in a developing country, normally under 40 at the time of their first application for a grant and at the beginning of their research careers.
Level of Study: Research.
Type: Research grant.
Value: Awards are limited to US$12,000 per research period and may be renewed twice. IFS also gives other support to help grantees further their research. IFS funding is not intended for travel or study,

but should be used for purchasing the basic tools of research such as equipment, expendable supplies and literature.

Frequency: Twice a year.
Country of Study: Other.
No. of awards offered: 200 per year.
Application Procedure: Applicants must complete an application form. This is available on request in English or French.
Closing Date: Applications are accepted at any time.
Funding: Government.
Contributor: Regular financing comes from USA, France, Germany, the Netherlands, Norway, Sweden, and Switzerland. A number of national and international development agencies contribute to the IFS granting and supporting programmes.
Additional Information: Research proposed by applicants shall be conducted in a developing country and relevant to the needs of a developing country.

INTERNATIONAL HARP CONTEST IN ISRAEL

4 Aharonowitz Street, Tel Aviv, 63566, Israel
Tel: (972) 3 528 233
Fax: (972) 3 629 9524
Email: harzimco@netvision.net.il
www: http://www.harpcontest-israel.org.il
Contact: Ms Esther Herlitz, Director

The International Harp Contest takes place in Israel every three years and is judged by a jury of internationally known musicians. It was founded in 1959 and since then harpists from all over the world gather in Jerusalem to participate in the contest, the only one of it's kind.

International Harp Contest in Israel

Subjects: Harp playing.
Purpose: To encourage excellence in harp playing.
Eligibility: Open to harpists of any nationality who are aged 35 years or younger.
Level of Study: Professional development.
Type: Prize.
Value: The first prize is a grand concert harp from the House of Lyon and Healy, Chicago, the second prize is US$6,000 and the third prize is US$4,000. The Popee Prize is US$1,500 for best performance of the required Israeli composition in stage one and the Herlitz Prize is US$1,000 for best performance of a contemporary piece in stage three. The Chamber Music Prize is US$1,000 for the best performance of Ravel's Introduction and Allegro in stage three. Board and lodging is provided by the Contest Committee. The Gulbenkian Prize for a contemporary work.
Frequency: Every three years.
Country of Study: Any country.
No. of awards offered: Seven.
Application Procedure: Applicants must complete an application form and submit this with recommendations, a record of concert experience, curriculum vitae and birth certificate. There is a registration fee of US$150.
Closing Date: April 1st.
Funding: Government, Private.
Contributor: Culture authority, the government of Israel, the Ministry of Culture, foundations and donors.
No. of awards given last year: Five.
No. of applicants last year: 36.

THE INTERNATIONAL HUMAN FRONTIER SCIENCE PROGRAM ORGANIZATION (HFSP)

12, quai Saint-Jean. BP 10034, Strasbourg, Cedex F-67080, France
Tel: (33) (0) 388215121
Fax: (33) (0) 388328897
Email: info@hfsp.org
www: http://www.hfsp.org
Contact: Dr Martin Redington Director of Scientific Affairs and Communications

The Human Frontier Science Program (HFSP) promotes basic research in the life sciences that is original, interdisciplinary and requires international collaboration, and support the basic research focused on elucidating the complex functions of living organisms. The support and training of young investigators is given special emphasis.

HFSP Career Development Award (CDA)

Subjects: Elucidation of the complete mechanisms of living organisms. Emphasis is placed on novel, innovative, interdisciplinary approaches to basic research that involve scientific exchanges across national borders.
Purpose: To promote the development of a global network of young, independent investigators throughout the world, and provide former HFSP long-term Fellows with funds to re-establish their own programme in their home country.
Eligibility: Only for HFSP long-term fellows return to their home countries.
Level of Study: Postdoctorate, Research.
Type: Award.
Value: US$180,000 in total.
Length of Study: Two or three years.
Frequency: Annual.
Country of Study: Other.
Application Procedure: Applicants must apply online via the website.
Closing Date: October or November.
Contributor: Management supporting parties including Canada, France, Germany, Italy, Japan, Switzerland, United Kingdom, United States of America and the European Union.

HFSP Long-Term Fellowships

Subjects: Interdisciplinary research in the life sciences to elucidate the complex mechanisms of living organisms.
Purpose: To provide a period of postdoctoral training for researchers who are expected to play an important role in originating and pursuing creative research. The third year of support can be used for postdoctoral research in the home country.
Eligibility: Applicants must be within 3 years of receiving their PhD at the start of the fellowship. Applicants cannot go to a country of which they are a national or in which he or she received their PhD degree. Applicants are expected to move into a new field of research and individuals with training in Physics, Mathematics, Computer Science or Engineering are encovered to utilise HFSP fellowships to obtain training in the life sciences.
Level of Study: Postdoctorate, Research.
Type: A variable number of fellowships.
Value: Approx. US$45,000 per year per Fellow.
Length of Study: Three years.
Frequency: Annual.
Study Establishment: Outstanding academic or non-profit research institutions.
Country of Study: Any country.
No. of awards offered: 90.
Application Procedure: Applicants must refer to the website.
Funding: Government.

HFSP Program Grant

Subjects: Interdisiplinary research in the life sciences to elucidate the complex mechanisms of living organisms.
Purpose: To enable the research team to develop new lines of research through the collaboration.
Eligibility: Open to teams of independent researchers at any stage of their careers.
Level of Study: Postdoctorate, Research.
Type: Project grant.
Value: Up to US$450,000 per team, per year.
Length of Study: Up to three years.
Frequency: Annual.
No. of awards offered: Varies.
Application Procedure: Applicants must first apply for the award by submitting a letter of intent online. Please visit the website for full details. Only those ranked highest by the review committee members will then be invited to submit a full application.

Closing Date: March or April.
Funding: Government.
Contributor: Management supporting parties including Canada, France, Germany, Italy, Japan, Switzerland, United Kingdom, United States of America and the European Union.
No. of awards given last year: 22.
No. of applicants last year: 454.

HFSP Short Term Fellowships

Subjects: Interdisciplinary research in the life sciences to elucidate the complex mechanisms of living organisms.
Purpose: To enable researchers to learn state of the art techniques already in use abroad or to establish new research collaborations.
Eligibility: Open to promising researchers.
Level of Study: Postdoctorate, Research.
Type: A variable number of fellowships.
Value: Dependent on the length of time spent abroad.
Length of Study: Two weeks to three months.
Frequency: Throughout the year.
Study Establishment: Laboratories.
Country of Study: Any country.
Application Procedure: Applicants must refer to the website.
Closing Date: Applications are accepted throughout the year.
Funding: Government.
Contributor: Governments or Research Councils of Canada, France, Germany, Italy, Japan, Switzerland, UK, USA and the European Union.

HFSP Young Investigators Grants

Subjects: Interdisplinary research in the life success to elucidate the complex mechanisams of living organisms.
Purpose: To enable teams of young research scientists to formulate innovative and fertile research projects that focus on problems at the forefront of life sciences.
Eligibility: Open to all nationalities. Applicants must be within the first five years of obtaining an independent position eg. Assistant Professor, Lecturer, 'Joshu' or equivalent and within 10 years of obtaining their PhD before the deadline for submission of letter of intent. The principle applicant must have their laboratory in a member country with at least one other team member located in another member country.
Level of Study: Postdoctorate, Research.
Type: Project grant.
Value: US$450,000 per team, per year.
Length of Study: Up to three years.
Frequency: Annual.
No. of awards offered: Varies.
Application Procedure: Applicants must first apply for the award by submitting a letter of intent online. Please visit the website for full details. Only those ranked highest by the review committee members will then be invited to submit a full application.
Closing Date: March or April.
Funding: Government.
Contributor: Management supporting parties including Canada, France, Germany, Italy, Japan, Switzerland, United Kingdom, United States of America and the European Union.
No. of awards given last year: 9.
No. of applicants last year: 95.
Additional Information: It is expected that outstanding young scientists in the initial period of their independent careers are in a particularly good position to formulate innovative and fertile research projects. A clear emphasis is placed on novel collaborations that bring biologists together with scientists from different disciplines eg. chemistry, physics, mathematics, computer science and engineering.

INTERNATIONAL INSTITUTE FOR MANAGEMENT DEVELOPMENT (IMD)

Chemin de Bellerive 23, PO Box 915, Lausanne, CH-1001, Switzerland
Tel: (41) 21 618 0298
Fax: (41) 21 618 0615
Email: mbainfo@imd.ch
www: http://www.imd.ch/mba
Contact: Ms Janet Shaner, Director, MBA Marketing

The International Institute for Management Development (IMD), created by industry to serve industry develops cutting edge research and programmes that meet real world needs. Their clients include dozens of leading, international companies and their experienced faculty incorporate new management practices into the small and exclusive MBA programme. With no nationality dominating IMD is truly global, practical and relevant.

IMD MBA Alumni Scholarship

Subjects: MBA.
Purpose: To financially support applicants from Africa, Latin America and Eastern Europe undertaking an MBA.
Eligibility: Candidates must have gained acceptance into the IMD MBA programme, provide evidence of financial need, demonstrate that all other financing options have been exhausted and show high potential for successful careers in private, public or governmental sectors of business.
Level of Study: Graduate, MBA.
Type: Scholarship.
Value: Swiss franc 30,000 towards tuition fees and book expenses.
Frequency: Annual.
Study Establishment: The International Institute for Management Development (IMD).
Country of Study: Switzerland.
No. of awards offered: Three.
Application Procedure: Applicants must complete and submit the IMD MBA application form for financial assistance and the MBA application form. In addition, applicants must write an essay and should contact the organisation for details.
Closing Date: September 30th.
Funding: Private.
Contributor: IMD Alumni Loan Fund.
No. of awards given last year: Three.
No. of applicants last year: Twelve.

Nestlé Scholarship for Women

Subjects: MBA.
Purpose: To financially support women undertaking a MBA.
Eligibility: Candidates must be female, have gained acceptance onto the MBA course and show financial need.
Level of Study: Graduate, MBA.
Type: Scholarship.
Value: Swiss franc 25,000 towards tuition and living expenses.
Length of Study: One year.
Frequency: Annual.
Study Establishment: IMD.
Country of Study: Switzerland.
No. of awards offered: One.
Application Procedure: Applicants must submit an additional essay of a maximum 750 words, on the topic Diversity in Management, along with their completed IMD MBA application form for financial assistance.
Closing Date: September 30th.
Funding: Commercial.
No. of awards given last year: One.
No. of applicants last year: Ten.

Staton Scholarship

Subjects: MBA.
Eligibility: Candidates must be from Argentina, Chile or Uruguay and must have already gained acceptance into the IMD MBA program.
Level of Study: Graduate, MBA.
Type: Scholarship.
Value: US$50,000 towards tuition fees and book expenses.
Length of Study: One year.
Frequency: Annual.
Study Establishment: IMD.
Country of Study: Switzerland.
No. of awards offered: One.
Application Procedure: Applicants must complete and submit the IMD MBA application form for financial assistance and the MBA application form. In addition, applicants must submit a 750 word essay

on the topic The Role of Entrepreneurship in Moving My Country Forward.
Closing Date: September 30th.
Funding: Private.
Contributor: Woods Staton.
No. of awards given last year: Zero.
No. of applicants last year: One.
Additional Information: It is a condition of the scholarship that candidates return to Argentina, Chile or Uruguay for at least three years after graduation.

Von Muralt-Lo Scholarship
Subjects: MBA.
Purpose: To financially support two candidates from China or Hong Kong.
Eligibility: Candidates must be based in China, Hong Cong or Estonia and they must have already gained acceptance into the IMD MBA program.
Level of Study: Graduate, MBA.
Type: Scholarship.
Value: Swiss franc 25,000.
Length of Study: One year.
Frequency: Annual.
Study Establishment: IMD.
Country of Study: Switzerland.
No. of awards offered: Two.
Application Procedure: Applicants must complete and submit the IMD MBA application form for financial assistance and the MBA application form. In addition, candidates must submit a 500 word essay and contact the organisation for details.
Closing Date: September 30th.
Funding: Private.
Contributor: Mr and Mrs Peter von Muralt-Lo.
No. of awards given last year: Zero.
No. of applicants last year: Two.
Additional Information: Candidates need to clearly demonstrate their desire to further contribute to China, Hong Kong or Estonia.

Wall Street Journal Europe; IMD Future Leaders Scholarships
Subjects: MBA.
Purpose: To financially support candidates who demonstrate strong leadership potential.
Eligibility: Candidates must have gained acceptance into the MBA programme.
Level of Study: Graduate, MBA.
Type: Scholarship.
Value: €20,000 towards tuition fees and book expenses.
Length of Study: One year.
Frequency: Annual.
Study Establishment: IMD.
Country of Study: Switzerland.
No. of awards offered: Three.
Application Procedure: Applicants must complete and submit the IMD MBA application form. In addition, candidates must submit an essay of a maximum of 750 words on the topic Leadership Through Difficult Times.
Closing Date: September 30th.
Funding: Commercial.
Contributor: The Wall Street Journal and IMD.
No. of awards given last year: Three.
No. of applicants last year: Forty.

INTERNATIONAL MATHEMATICAL UNION (IMU)

Institute for Advanced Study, Einstein Drive, Princeton, NJ 08540, United States of America
Tel: (1) 609 734 8200
Fax: (1) 609 683 7605
Email: imu@ias.edu
www: http://www.mathunion.org
Contact: Ms Linda Geraci

The International Mathematical Union (IMU) is an international, non governmental and non-profit making scientific organisation, with the purpose of promoting international co-operation in mathematics. It belongs to the International Council of Scientific Unions (ICSU).

IMU Fields Medals
Subjects: Mathematics.
Purpose: To reward outstanding achievements.
Eligibility: Open to young mathematicians up to 40 years old and of any nationality.
Level of Study: Unrestricted.
Type: Prize.
Frequency: Every 4 years.
Country of Study: Any country.
No. of awards offered: Two-four.
Application Procedure: Applicants must be nominated by other mathematicians.
Closing Date: 31/1/2005.
Contributor: The Fields Foundation.
No. of awards given last year: 2002 - 2 awards.

Rolf Nevanlinna Prize
Subjects: Mathematical aspects of information science.
Eligibility: Open to young mathematicians up to 40 years old and of any nationality.
Level of Study: Unrestricted.
Type: Prize.
Frequency: Every 4 years.
Country of Study: Any country.
No. of awards offered: One.
Application Procedure: Applicants must be nominated by other mathematicians.
Closing Date: 31/1/2005.
Contributor: The University of Helsinki/IMU.
No. of awards given last year: 1.

INTERNATIONAL MUSIC FESTIVAL SION-VALAIS

Case postale 1429, Sion, CH-1951, Switzerland
Tel: (41) 27 323 4317
Fax: (41) 27 323 4662
Email: Info@sion-festival.ch
www: http://www.sion-festival.com
Contact: Ms Fabienne Gapany, General Secretary

The International Music Festival Sion-Valais is a music festival held in August and September with around 15 concerts.

International Violin Competition Sion-Valais Shlomo Mintz, President of the Jury
Subjects: Violin and interpretative performance.
Purpose: To help discover a new talent, to enrich the musical experience and practice of the participants, and to encourage and support prize winners in their future careers.
Eligibility: Open to violinists of any nationality aged between 15-32 years.
Level of Study: Unrestricted.
Type: Prize.
Value: The first prize is US$15,000. The total amount available for prizes is US$35,000.
Length of Study: 10 days.
Frequency: Every two years.
Country of Study: Switzerland.
No. of awards offered: Six prizes and several special prizes.
Application Procedure: Applicants must complete an application form and submit this with three passport sized photographs, a curriculum vitae and a receipt showing payment of the entrance fee of Swiss franc 100.
Closing Date: April 15th.
Funding: Government, Private.
No. of awards given last year: 8.
Additional Information: Up to 30 candidates are invited to the Sion for the public eliminatory rounds. The first three prize winners will

perform in two or three representation concerts with a symphonic orchestra right after the competition.

INTERNATIONAL NAVIGATION ASSOCIATION (PIANC)

Graaf de Ferraris, 11th Floor, Box 3, 20 Avenue Roi Albert II, Brussels, B-1000, Belgium
Tel: (32) 2 553 7160
Fax: (32) 2 553 7145
Email: info@pianc-aipcn.org
www: http://www.pianc-aipcn.org
Contact: Secretary General

The International Navigation Association (PIANC) is a worldwide non political and non-profit making technical and scientific organisation of private individuals, corporations and national governments. PIANC's objective is to promote the maintenance and operation of both inland and maritime navigation by fostering progress in the planning, design, construction, improvement, maintenance and operations of inland and maritime waterways, ports and coastal areas for general use in industrialised and industrialising countries. Facilities for fisheries, sport and recreational navigation are included in PIANC's activities.

De Paepe - Willems Award

Subjects: The design, construction, improvement, maintenance or operation of inland and maritime waterways such as rivers, estuaries, canals, port approaches, inland and maritime ports and coastal areas, and related fields.
Purpose: To encourage young professionals to submit for presentation outstanding technical articles in the fields of interest to PIANC.
Eligibility: Open to members of PIANC or candidates sponsored by a member, who are under the age of 35.
Level of Study: Unrestricted.
Type: Award.
Value: A monetary award of €5,000 and free membership of PIANC for a five year period. Free hotel accommodation will be provided, together with a coverage of travel expenses to the venue of the General Assembly.
Frequency: Annual.
Country of Study: Any country.
No. of awards offered: One.
Application Procedure: Applicants must complete an application form, available on request from the PIANC General Secretariat or on the PIANC website, and submit this together with the article. Articles must be written by a single author, not have been previously published elsewhere, not exceed 12,000 words, be in type script, and in English or French with a summary in the same language. Articles may be accompanied by illustrations or diagrams.
Closing Date: October 31st.
Funding: Government, Private.
Additional Information: The prize will be awarded to the individual candidate who submits the most outstanding article in the calendar year preceding the Annual General Assembly at which the prize is awarded, provided the article is judged to be of sufficiently high standard. The prize winner will be invited to present a commentary on his or her article during the General Assembly of the PIANC or during the Congress. In judging the articles the jury shall take into account their technical level, originality and practical value and the quality of presentation. Candidates are advised that the Bulletin is designed for readers with a wide range of engineering interests and highly specialised articles should be written with this in mind.

INTERNATIONAL PEACE SCHOLARSHIP FUND

c/o PEO, 3700 Grand Avenue, Des Moines, IA 50312, United States of America
Tel: (1) 515 255 3153
Fax: (1) 515 255 3820
www: http://peointernational.org
Contact: Ms Carolyn J Larson, Project Supervisor

PEO International Peace Scholarship

Subjects: All subjects.
Purpose: To support international women studying for graduate degrees.
Eligibility: Any nationality may apply apart from candidates from the United States of America or Canada. Eligibility is based on financial need, nationality, degree, full-time status and residence.
Level of Study: Doctorate, Graduate, Postgraduate.
Type: Other.
Value: US$6,000 maximum per year.
Length of Study: A maximum of two years.
Frequency: Annual.
Country of Study: United States of America or Canada.
No. of awards offered: Approx. 180.
Application Procedure: Eligibility must be established before application material is sent. Candidates should write to the main address and request an eligibility form or download from our website: www.peointernational.org. GO to P.E.O_projects and find IPS>Eligibility Information, if the applicant is deemed eligible an application form is sent
Closing Date: December 15th for receipt of the eligibility form and January 31st for receipt of the application form
Funding: Private.
Contributor: PEO members.
No. of awards given last year: 180.
No. of applicants last year: 350.
Additional Information: Scholarships cannot be used for travel, research dissertations, internships or practical training. An applicant must have a contact person who is a citizen of the United States or Canada and who will act as a non academic advisor. Applicants must also have round trip return travel expense guaranteed at the time of the application and return to their own country on completion of their studies.

INTERNATIONAL READING ASSOCIATION

800 Barksdale Road, PO Box 8139, Newark, DE 19714-8139, United States of America
Tel: (1) 302 731 1600 ext. 423
Fax: (1) 302 731 1057
Email: research@reading.org
www: http://www.reading.org
Contact: Marcella Moore, Research & Policy Division

The International Reading Association seeks to promote high levels of literacy for all by improving the quality of reading instruction through studying the reading processes and teaching techniques, serving as a clearinghouse for the dissemination of reading research through conferences, journals and other publications and actively encouraging the lifetime reading habit.

Albert J Harris Award

Subjects: Reading and literacy.
Purpose: To recognise outstanding published works on the topics of reading disabilities and the prevention, assessment or instruction of learners experiencing difficulty learning to read.
Eligibility: Articles must be single or joint authored research based articles. Nominees for this award do not need to be members of the International Reading Association. Publications that have appeared in a refereed professional journal or monograph within the last 18 months are eligible and may be submitted by the author or anyone else.
Level of Study: Postgraduate.
Type: Prize.
Value: US$1,000.
Frequency: Annual.
Country of Study: Any country.
No. of awards offered: One.
Application Procedure: Applicants must obtain guidelines with specific information from the main address or by visiting the website.
Closing Date: September 15th.
Funding: Private.

Dina Feitelson Research Award

Subjects: Literacy.

Purpose: To recognise an outstanding empirical study that was published in English in a refereed journal, which specifically reports on an investigation of aspects of literary acquisition such as phonemic awareness, the alphabetic principle, bilingualism, home influences on literacy development or cross cultural studies of beginning reading.

Eligibility: Articles must have been published in a refereed journal within the past 18 months and may be submitted by the author or anyone else. Empirical studies involve the collection of original data from direct experimentation or observation, and articles that develop theory without data, secondary reviews of the literature or descriptions of the theory are not eligible for this competition. Nominees for this award do not need to be members of the International Reading Association.

Level of Study: Unrestricted.

Type: Prize.

Value: US$500.

Frequency: Dependent on funds available.

Country of Study: Any country.

No. of awards offered: One.

Application Procedure: Applicants must obtain guidelines with specific information from the main address or by visiting the website.

Closing Date: September 15th.

Funding: Private.

Additional Information: The Dina Feitelson Research Award was established to honour the memory of Dina Feitelson. This award began in 1997.

Elva Knight Research Grant

Subjects: Literacy education.

Purpose: To assist a researcher in a reading and literacy project. Research is defined as an enquiry which addresses significant questions about literacy instruction and practice.

Eligibility: Applicants must be members of the International Reading Association and projects should be completed within two years.

Level of Study: Postgraduate, Research.

Type: Research grant.

Value: Upto a maximum of US$10,000 (upto four award winners per year contingent upon available funds in any given year).

Length of Study: Two years.

Frequency: Annual.

Country of Study: Any country.

No. of awards offered: Up to four awards. It is expected that at least one award will go to a researcher outside the United States and/or Canada and at least one to a teacher-initiated research project.

Application Procedure: Applicants must obtain guidelines with specific information from the main address or by visiting the website.

Closing Date: January 15, 2004.

Funding: Private.

Additional Information: This award began in 1982.

Helen M Robinson Award

Subjects: Literacy education.

Eligibility: Open to all doctoral students at the early stages of their dissertation research worldwide who are members of the International Reading Association.

Level of Study: Doctorate.

Type: Research grant.

Value: US$1,000.

Frequency: Annual.

Country of Study: Any country.

No. of awards offered: One.

Application Procedure: Applicants must obtain guidelines with specific information from the main address or by visiting the website.

Closing Date: January 15th.

Funding: Private.

Additional Information: This award began in 1991.

International Reading Association Outstanding Dissertation of the Year Award

Subjects: Reading and literacy.

Purpose: To recognise dissertations in the field of reading and literacy.

Eligibility: Open to all doctoral students worldwide who are members of the International Reading Association.

Level of Study: Doctorate.

Type: Prize.

Value: US$1,000.

Frequency: Annual.

Country of Study: Any country.

No. of awards offered: One.

Application Procedure: Applicants must obtain guidelines with specific information from the main address or by visiting the website.

Closing Date: October 1st.

Funding: Private.

Additional Information: This award began in 1964. Should there be more than one winner the US$1,000 prize will be split.

International Reading Association Teacher as Researcher Grant

Subjects: Literacy.

Purpose: To support teachers in their enquiries about literacy learning and instruction.

Eligibility: All applicants must be members of the International Reading Association and practising pre K-12 teachers with full-time teaching responsibilities, including librarians, classroom teachers and resource teachers. Applicants are limited to one proposal per year. There must be a span of three years before past grant recipients can apply for another Teacher as Researcher Grant.

Level of Study: Research.

Type: Research grant.

Value: Up to US$5,000 maximum, but priority is given to smaller grants of between US$1,000-2,000.

Frequency: Annual.

Country of Study: Any country.

No. of awards offered: Several.

Application Procedure: Applicants must obtain guidelines with specific information from the main address or by visiting the website.

Closing Date: January 15th.

Funding: Private.

Additional Information: This award began in 1997.

Jeanne S Chall Research Fellowship

Subjects: Reading and literacy.

Purpose: To encourage and support doctoral research investigating issues in beginning research, readability, reading difficulty and stages of reading development.

Eligibility: Open to doctoral students who are members of the International Reading Association and are planning or beginning dissertations.

Level of Study: Doctorate, Research.

Type: Fellowship.

Value: US$6,000 maximum.

Frequency: Annual.

Country of Study: Any country.

No. of awards offered: One.

Application Procedure: Applicants must obtain guidelines with specific information from the main address or by visiting the website.

Closing Date: January 15th.

Funding: Private.

Additional Information: This award began in 1997.

Nila Banton Smith Research Dissemination Support Grant

Subjects: Reading and literacy.

Purpose: To facilitate the dissemination of literacy research to the educational community.

Eligibility: Open to all members of the International Reading Association worldwide.

Level of Study: Professional development, Research.

Type: Grant.

Value: US$5,000.

Length of Study: 2-10 months.

Frequency: Annual.

No. of awards offered: One.

Application Procedure: Applicants must obtain guidelines with specific information from the main address or by visiting the website.
Closing Date: January 15th.
Additional Information: This award began in 1991.

Reading/Literacy Research Fellowship
Subjects: Literacy education.
Purpose: To provide support to a researcher who has shown exceptional promise in reading or literacy research.
Eligibility: Open to any International Reading Association member outside the United States or Canada.
Level of Study: Postdoctorate.
Type: Fellowship.
Value: US$1,000.
Frequency: Annual.
Country of Study: Other.
No. of awards offered: One.
Application Procedure: Applicants must obtain guidelines with specific information from the main address or by visiting the website.
Closing Date: January 15th.
Funding: Private.
Additional Information: This award began in 1974

INTERNATIONAL RESEARCH AND EXCHANGE BOARD (IREX)

2121 K Street North West, Suite 700, Washington, DC 20037, United States of America
Tel: (1) 202 628 8188
Fax: (1) 202 628 8189
Email: irex@irex.org
www: http://www.irex.org
Contact: Ms Michelle Duplissis, Senior Program Officer

IREX (the International Research and Exchanges Board) is the premier United States non-profit organisation specialising in education, independent media, internet development and civil society programmes in the United States, Europe, Eurasia, the Near East and Asia. Since its founding in 1968, IREX has supported over 15,000 students, scholars, policymakers, business leaders, journalists and other professionals. IREX serves as a major resource for universities, governments and the corporate sector in understanding international political, social, economic and business developments.

ECA/IREX/FSA Contemporary Issues Fellowship Program
Subjects: Business administration, civic education, educational policy, economics, energy policy, environmental policy, human rights, international relations, the internet, journalism and media, law enforcement, military/security issues, non governmental organisation development and management, political science, public administration (government), public health policy, rule of law and social welfare.
Purpose: To provide opportunities for experienced professionals and specialists to conduct policy orientated research in the United States of America.
Eligibility: Open to citizens and residents of Armenia, Azerbaijan, Belarus, Georgia, Kazakhstan, Kyrgyzstan, Moldova, the Russian Federation, Tajikistan, Turkmenistan, Ukraine or Uzbekistan. Candidates must be aged 25 to 55, have an academic degree at least equivalent to a United States Master's degree, have at least three years experience in the listed topic of research and possess a high level of proficiency in written and spoken English. Applicants must not have participated in a United States government sponsored grant of more than six weeks in the past two years.
Level of Study: Professional development.
Type: Fellowship.
Value: Travel, housing, a stipend, medical insurance, a research allowance and return trip transportation from the home city to the placement city.
Length of Study: Four months.
Frequency: Annual.
Study Establishment: A university, research centre, government institution or non governmental organisation.
Country of Study: United States of America.

No. of awards offered: 100.
Application Procedure: Applicants must submit a completed application form, research proposal, two letters of recommendation, curriculum vitae, and a short personal biography. All applications must contain developed and focused research projects that are policy-driven with practical application in Eurasia. Please contact the organisation for further details.
Closing Date: November.
Funding: Government.
Contributor: The Bureau of Cultural and Educational Affairs, at the United States Department of State.
No. of awards given last year: 100.
No. of applicants last year: 1000.
Additional Information: Prospective applicants are encouraged to contact IREX's Eurasia field offices and educational advising centres before submitting an application. Further information and field office contacts are available on the website.

IREX Individual Advanced Research Opportunities
Subjects: Humanities or social sciences.
Purpose: To provide opportunities for United States scholars wishing to pursue research in the humanities and social sciences, policy research and development and cross-disciplinary studies with a strong focus on Europe and Eurasia.
Eligibility: Open to citizens and three year permanent residents of the United States of America. Applicants must hold a PhD or other terminal graduate degree or be pursuing a PhD or Master's degree. Doctoral candidates must have completed all requirements for the PhD except for the dissertation. Master's candidates are eligible for grants of one to three months to conduct policy relevant research for a thesis or comparable project. Normally, command of the host country's language sufficient for advanced research is required of all applicants. Further details can be found on the website.
Level of Study: Doctorate, Graduate, MBA, Postdoctorate, Postgraduate, Predoctorate, Professional development, Research.
Type: Grant.
Value: Up to a maximum of US$40,000. Covers travel and visa fees, dollar stipend and a housing allowance.
Length of Study: Two-nine months.
Frequency: Annual.
Study Establishment: Appropriate institutions.
Country of Study: Other.
No. of awards offered: Varies.
Application Procedure: Applicants must visit the website for application forms and further information or email: iaro@irex.org.
Closing Date: November 1st.
Funding: Government, Private.
Contributor: The United States Department of State (Title 8), National Endowment for the Humanities (NEH) and the IREX Scholar Support Fund.
No. of awards given last year: 25.
Additional Information: Applicants must study in one of the following countries: Albania, Armenia, Azerbaijan, Belarus, Bosnia and Herzegovina, Bulgaria, Croatia, Czech Republic, Estonia, Georgia, Hungary, Iran, Kazakhstan, Kyrgyzstan, Latvia, Lithuania, Macedonia, Moldova, Mongolia, Romania, Russia, Serbia and Montenegro, Slovakia, Slovenia, Tajikistan, Turkey, Turkmenistan, Ukraine and Uzbekistan. Further information is available on request, however please contact IREX for programme information well in advance of the deadline.

IREX John J and Nancy Lee Roberts Fellowship Program
Subjects: Social sciences concerned with Europe, Eurasia, the Near East and Asia. Applicants should refer to the website as there will be a theme each year limiting the geographical focus and the eligible fields of research.
Purpose: To provide a single grant for research.
Eligibility: Open to citizens and three year permanent residents of the United States of America. Applicants must hold a PhD or other terminal graduate degree at the time of application. Collaborative research programmes involving international colleagues are strongly encouraged.
Level of Study: Postdoctorate, Postgraduate.

Type: Grant.
Value: Up to US$30,000.
Length of Study: Up to 12 months.
Frequency: Annual.
Country of Study: Other.
No. of awards offered: One.
Application Procedure: Applicants must contact IREX or visit the website for application forms.
Closing Date: March 15th.
Funding: Private.
Contributor: John J and Nancy Lee Roberts.
No. of awards given last year: One.
Additional Information: Applicants must study in one of the following countries: Afghanistan, Albania, Armenia, Azerbaijan, Belarus, Bosnia and Herzegovina, Bulgaria, China, Czech Republic, Estonia, Georgia, Hungary, Iran, Kazakhstan, Kyrgyzstan, Latvia, Lithuania, Macedonia, Moldova, Mongolia, North Korea, Pakistan, Poland, Romania, Russia, Serbia and Montenegro, Slovakia, Slovenia, Tajikistan, Turkey, Turkmenistan, Ukraine and Uzbekistan. Further information is available on request. The program is limited to a specific Geographic area each year. Please visit the website for more information.

IREX Short-Term Travel Grants

Subjects: Policy-Relevant Research.
Purpose: To advance the public cultural and historical knowledge of Europe and Eurasia.
Eligibility: Open to citizens and permanent residents of the United States of America who have a PhD or other Terminal Graduate Degree and need project support.
Level of Study: Postdoctorate, Postgraduate.
Type: Travel grant.
Value: Up to US$3,500 travel expenses. Airfare on a United States flag carrier is provided through IREX Travel as well as per diem for food, lodging and local transport. The grant may also cover incidental expenses such as visa fees, photocopying and medical evacuation insurance.
Length of Study: Up to 60 days.
Frequency: Annual.
Country of Study: Eastern Europe and Eurasia.
No. of awards offered: Varies.
Application Procedure: Applicants must contact Amy Schulz, Program officer, on stg@irex.org for details or application guidelines. Application forms are available to download from the website.
Closing Date: February 1st.
Funding: Government.
Contributor: The United States Department of State's Title VIII Program.
No. of awards given last year: Approx. 40.
No. of applicants last year: Varies.
Additional Information: Applicants will be notified of award decisions approximately eight weeks after the application deadline. Applicants must study in one of the following countries: Albania, Armenia, Azerbaijan, Belarus, Bosnia and Herzegovina, Bulgaria, Croatia, Czech Republic, Estonia, Georgia, Hungary, Kazakhstan, Kyrgyzstan, Latvia, Lithuania, Macedonia, Moldova, Poland, Romania, Russia, Serbia and Montenegro, Slovakia, Tajikistan, Turkmenistan, Ukraine or Uzbekistan.Country of Study: Eastern Europe and Eurasia.

THE INTERNATIONAL SCHOOL FOR ADVANCED STUDIES (SISSA)

Via Beirut 2-4, Trieste, I-34014, Italy
www: http://www.sissa.it
Contact: Scientific Secretariat

The International School for Advanced Studies (SISSA) is a centre for research and postgraduate studies leading to the PhD degree (equivalent to the Italian Dottore di Ricerca) in the fields of astrophysics, mathematics, neuroscience, elementary particles and condensed matter physics and functional and structural genomics.

SISSA Fellowships

Subjects: Applied mathematics, astrophysics, functional and structural genomics, mathematical analysis, mathematical physics, statistical and biological physics, neurosciences, theory of elementary particles or the theory of computational physics of condensed matter.
Purpose: To financially support PhD studies.
Eligibility: Open to candidates over the age of 30 at the beginning of the academic year.
Level of Study: Doctorate.
Type: Fellowship.
Value: Please contact the School for details.
Frequency: Annual.
Study Establishment: The International School for Advanced Studies (SISSA).
Country of Study: Italy.
No. of awards offered: 58.
Application Procedure: Applicants must complete the application form which can be found on the website.
Funding: Government.
Contributor: The Italian Government.

INTERNATIONAL SCHOOL OF CRYSTALLOGRAPHY, E MAJORANA CENTRE

c/o Dip to Scienze Della Terra Geo Ambientoli, Pza Porta San Donato 1, Bologna, I-40126, Italy
Tel: (39) 051 209 4912
Fax: (39) 051 209 4904
Email: riva@geomin.unibo.it
www: http://www.geomin.unibo.it
Contact: Professor L Riva Di Sanseverino

The International School of Crystallography is an international organising committee which offers, once a year, short advanced courses of 10-13 days on frontier topics in crystallography, solid state chemistry, materials science, structure activity relationship, molecular biology and biophysics.

International School of Crystallography Grants

Subjects: Frontier topics in crystallography eg. high pressure crystallography, polymorphism and drug design via crystallography.
Purpose: To enable postgraduates to attend short high level courses held at Erice once a year.
Eligibility: Open to all who have scientific interests related to the topic chosen each year at a PhD or postdoctoral level. English language is mandatory.
Level of Study: Doctorate, Postdoctorate, Postgraduate.
Type: Grant.
Value: Fees, board and lodging during the course.
Length of Study: 8-12 days.
Frequency: Annual.
Study Establishment: E Majorana Centre, Erice, Sicily, Italy.
Country of Study: Italy.
No. of awards offered: Approx. 30-40.
Application Procedure: Applicants must submit a letter of recommendation stating their financial needs, personal data and details of scientific interests. Further details can be found at http://www.crystalerice.org.
Closing Date: The end of November.
Funding: Government.
Contributor: NATO, the European Commission and the Italian National Research Council.
No. of awards given last year: 70.
No. of applicants last year: 250.

For further information contact:

Department of Organic Chemistry, Via Marzolo 1, Padova, I-35131, Italy
Tel: (39) 049 827 5275

Fax: (39) 049 827 5239
Email: paola@chor00.unipd.it
Contact: Dr Paola Spadon

INTERNATIONAL SOCIETY OF NEPHROLOGY

Global Headquarters, Avenue Gaulois
7, Brussels, 1040, Belgium
Tel: (32) 2 743 1546
Fax: (32) 2 743 1550
Email: info@isn-online.org
www: http://www.isn-online.org

The International Society of Nephrology (ISN) pursues the goal of worldwide advancement of education, science and patient care in nephrology. ISN achieves this through its journal Kidney International, organising international congresses, symposia, specific programmes and fellowships. As a result ISN helps to improve renal science and renal patient care worldwide especially in emerging countries.

ISN Fellowship Awards

Subjects: Nephrology.
Purpose: To offer training opportunities to young nephrologists in emerging countries with the ultimate goal of improving the standards of their home institutions upon their return.
Eligibility: Open to young nephrologists from emerging countries, as defined by World Bank criteria. Applicants must have received sufficient training in internal medicine or other fields to pass all host country examinations that are necessary for the care of patients. Fellowships are primarily offered for clinical training in nephrology, but in some circumstances research training may be allowed.
Level of Study: Postdoctorate, Predoctorate.
Type: Fellowship.
Value: US$22,500 for one year and less for shorter periods. If the host country is contributing funds then this is subtracted from the standard fund.
Length of Study: Short-term fellowships are for three months and long-term fellowships are for one-two years.
Frequency: Annual.
Study Establishment: Any suitable university, scientific institution or hospital.
No. of awards offered: Up to 55 each year.
Application Procedure: Applicants must complete an application form for both full-time fellowship and the short-term fellowship award. Applicants must provide evidence of a guaranteed position in a medical institution upon return to their home country. The applicant must agree to return to their home country upon completion of the training, if not then the recipient will have to refund the ISN fellowship in full.
Closing Date: Deadlines are the end of January and the end of July each year. The selection is made in May and November each year.
Funding: Commercial, Private.
Contributor: Offered in collaboration with sister societies and industry, the American Society of Nephrology, the Japanese Society of Nephrology, the National Kidney Research Fund in the United Kingdom and Fresenius in Germany.
No. of awards given last year: 44.
No. of applicants last year: 62.
Additional Information: The selection procedure has three parts: data verification, where information provided by applicants is verified and evaluated through correspondence, then evaluation, where five members of the Committee, one from each Continent, score each application according to standard format, and finally selection, which is largely based on the aforementioned scores but also considers the geographical balance, urgent needs in certain regions and the preference of certain sponsors.

For further information contact:

International Society of Nephrology, Global Headquarters, Avenue Gaulois, 7, Brussels, 1040, Belgium
Tel: (32) 2 743 1546

Fax: (32) 2 743 1550
Email: an@associationhg.com
Contact: An Devriese

ISN Travel Grants

Subjects: Nephrology.
Purpose: To encourage young physicians and scientists to attend conferences especially those from emerging countries. Travel grants are offered to facilitate attendance at the ISN International Congress and the ISN Forefronts Commission Conference.
Eligibility: Applicants must have training and experience in an area of research relevant to the conference and an infrastructure at their home institutions to allow the pursuit of techniques and approaches discussed at the conference. Young physicians and scientists are preferred as are ISN fellows. A portion of the grants are reserved for applicants from emerging countries.
Level of Study: Doctorate, Postdoctorate, Postgraduate, Research.
Type: Travel grant.
Value: The size of the grant is decided according to each conference and congress.
Length of Study: Varies.
Frequency: Other.
No. of awards offered: 120 travel grants for each International Congress of Nephrology and six travel grants for young scientists from emerging countries to attend each ISN Forefront Conference.
Application Procedure: Applicants must complete an application form which can be downloaded from the ISN website or requested from the ISN Secretary General a year prior to the Congress. Applications can also be obtained from the Directors of the ISN Forefront Programmes.
Closing Date: Please contact the organisation.
Funding: Commercial, Private.
Contributor: Offered in collaboration with sponsors of ISN.
No. of awards given last year: 120.
No. of applicants last year: 395.
Additional Information: Further information is available on request.

For further information contact:

ISN Secretary General, Cairo Kidney Centre3 Hussein El-Memar Street, Antikhana, PO Box 91, Bab El-Louk, Cairo, 11513, Egypt
Tel: (20) 2 579 0267
Email: lsn@rusys.eg.net
Contact: Dr Rashad Barsoum

ISN Visiting Scholars Program

Subjects: Nephrology.
Purpose: To improve the long-term quality of patient care, education and research in fields relevant to the kidney at the host institution, and enable senior physicians or scientists who are experts in nephrology and related disciplines to spend between six weeks and three months at an institution in the developing world.
Eligibility: Applicants must focus primarily on hands-on activities which are the focus of this award eg. the establishment of a new clinical programme, research programme or laboratory technique. ISN visiting scholars should spend the duration of their study time at an institution in the developing world. Applicants must be experts in nephrology and related disciplines.
Level of Study: Postdoctorate, Research.
Type: Scholarship.
Value: US$25,000, inclusive of travel and expenses, for three months or a pro rata amount for a shorter period of time.
Length of Study: Six weeks to three months.
Frequency: At the discretion of the ISN.
No. of awards offered: At the discretion of the ISN but usually up to two scholarships per year.
Application Procedure: Applicants must send a description of the programme, its objectives, personal references and a letter of acceptance from the host institution to the ISN Secretary General. Applicants must be members of the ISN.
Closing Date: Please contact the organisation.
Funding: Commercial, Private.
No. of awards given last year: Two.

No. of applicants last year: Two.
Additional Information: Further information is available on request.

For further information contact:

Cairo Kidney Centre, 3 Hussein El-Memar Street Antikhana, PO Box 91Bab El-Louk, Cairo, 11513, Egypt
Tel: (20) 2 579 0267
Email: isn@rusys.eg.net

THE INTERNATIONAL SPINAL RESEARCH TRUST (ISRT)

Unit 8a, Bramley Business Centre, Station Road, Bramley, Guildford, Surrey, GU5 0AZ, United Kingdom
Tel: (44) 1483 898786
Fax: (44) 1483 898763
Email: research@spinal-research.org
www: http://www.spinal-research.org
Contact: Head of Research

The International Spinal Research Trust (ISRT) organises fundraising to support research projects that have the aim of repairing or restoring the loss of function that occurs as a result of injury to the spinal cord. A structured research strategy has been developed to target funds towards relevant research topics.

ISRT Project Grant
Subjects: Furthering the understanding of mammalian spinal cord injury and approaches towards the repair and restoration of function.
Purpose: To provide support for laboratory or clinically based projects.
Eligibility: Open to suitably qualified and experienced principal investigators.
Level of Study: Postdoctorate, Research.
Type: Grant.
Value: Please contact the organisation.
Length of Study: Up to three years.
Frequency: Dependent on funds available.
Study Establishment: An appropriate university or research institution.
Country of Study: Any country.
No. of awards offered: According to funds available.
Application Procedure: Calls for proposals on a specific theme will be advertised periodically. Short listed applicants will be required to complete a full application form.
Closing Date: Varies, as advertised.
Funding: Private.
Additional Information: Each call for proposals is on a specific theme. Proposals must be within the charity's remit.

Nathalie Rose Barr PhD Studentship
Subjects: Topics relevant to ISRT's research strategy.
Purpose: To support basic and clinical students while working towards a research based PhD degree.
Eligibility: Applicants must hold relevant positions at a United Kingdom university or research establishment.
Level of Study: Postgraduate.
Type: Studentship.
Value: Starts in line with the Wellcome Trust.
Length of Study: Four years for the basic research studentship, and three years for the clinical research fellowship.
Frequency: Annual.
Study Establishment: Universities.
Country of Study: United Kingdom.
No. of awards offered: Approx. two-four each year.
Application Procedure: Following advertisement, supervisors will submit project proposals on an ISRT application form. Supervisors of successful projects will then advertise for students.
Closing Date: As advertised, usually August.
Funding: Private.
Additional Information: The advertisement is for supervisors to submit project proposals, not for PhD students themselves.

INTERNATIONAL UNION AGAINST CANCER (UICC)

Fellowships Department, 3 rue de Conseil-Général, Geneva, CH-1205, Switzerland
Fax: (41) 22 809 1810
Email: bbaker@uicc.org
www: http://fellows.uicc.org
Contact: Mr Brita M Baker, Head

The International Union Against Cancer (UICC) Fellowships Programme provides long, medium and short-term fellowships abroad to qualified investigators, clinicians, and nurses, who are actively involved in cancer research, clinical oncology or oncology nursing.

UICC Asia-Pacific Cancer Society Training Grants (APCASOT)
Subjects: Non-medical aspects of cancer society work, such as fundraising, media relations, organisation and managerial skills, surveillance of cancer statistics, behavioural research, advocacy, non medical patient services, prevention and early detection education programmes.
Purpose: To support the training of qualified individuals in non medical aspects of cancer society work.
Eligibility: Open to staff and accredited volunteers from cancer societies in the Asia-Pacific region.
Level of Study: Unrestricted.
Type: Grant.
Value: US$1,800 to the least expensive round trip fare or other appropriate form of transport and to living costs. Extra costs for visa, passports, airport taxes and insurance are the responsibility of the grant recipient. No financial support is provided for dependants.
Length of Study: One-two weeks.
Frequency: Annual.
Study Establishment: Cancer Society.
Country of Study: Any Country in the Asia Pacific region.
No. of awards offered: Five.
Application Procedure: Applicants must complete an application form, available from the Fellowships Department or from the website.
Closing Date: September 1st for December selection.
Funding: Private.
Contributor: The William Rudder Memorial Fund (Australia).
No. of awards given last year: Three.
No. of applicants last year: Seven.

UICC International Cancer Research Technology Transfer Fellowships (ICRETT)
Subjects: Cancer control and prevention, epidemiology and cancer registration, public education and behavioural sciences.
Purpose: To enable recipients to learn or teach up to date research techniques, transfer appropriate technology or acquire advanced clinical management, diagnostic and therapeutic skills.
Eligibility: Open to qualified investigators and experienced clinicians.
Level of Study: Professional development.
Type: Fellowship.
Value: The average stipend is US$3,000.
Length of Study: Up to three months with stipend support for one month.
Frequency: Annual.
Country of Study: Any country.
No. of awards offered: 156.
Application Procedure: Applicants are normally notified of their success within 60 days of the registration of a complete application. Application forms can be obtained from the Fellowships Department or downloaded from the website.
Closing Date: Applications are accepted at any time.
Funding: Government, Commercial, Private.
No. of awards given last year: 112.
No. of applicants last year: 300.
Additional Information: The fellowships are funded by the National Cancer Institute, USA, Cancer Research UK, Swedish Cancer Society, National Cancer Institute of Canada/Cancer Society of Canada, Italian Cancer Research Foundation, Dutch Cancer Society, French

National League Against Cancer, Dr Mildred Scheel Foundation Deutsche Krebshilfe, Germany, Cancer Society of Finland, Australian Cancer Society Inc., Israel Cancer Association, Cancer Association of South Africa, Association of UICC Fellows.

UICC International Cancer Technology Transfer Fellowships (ICRETT) for Bilateral Exchanges Between Indonesia and the Netherlands

Subjects: Cancer control and prevention, epidemiology and cancer registration, public education or behavioural sciences.

Purpose: To foster the acquisition of up to date clinical management, diagnostic and therapeutic expertise, exchange knowledge and enhance skills in cancer control and prevention and facilitate rapid transfer of cancer research and technology.

Eligibility: Eligible to nationals of Indonesia and experts from any country who have been invited to teach these specialised skills at institutes abroad. Qualified cancer investigators should be in the early stages of their careers whilst clinicians should be fully established in their oncology practise.

Level of Study: Postdoctorate, Postgraduate, Professional development, Research.

Type: Fellowship.

Value: One month stipend and travel of US$3,000. Home and/or host institutions are expected to cover living costs for any additional periods. UICC also contributes to the least expensive international return air fares or other appropriate form of transport. Travel estimates should not include costs for internal travel within the home and/or host countries. These and extra costs for visa, passports, airport taxes and insurance are the responsibility of the Fellow. No allowances are made for accompanying dependants.

Length of Study: A maximum of three months.

Frequency: Annual.

Study Establishment: A suitable host institution.

Country of Study: Netherlands.

No. of awards offered: 10.

Application Procedure: Applicants must complete an application form, available from the Fellowships Department or from the website.

Closing Date: Applications are accepted at any time.

Funding: Private.

No. of awards given last year: Three.

No. of applicants last year: Six.

UICC International Fellowships for Beginning Investigators (ACSBI)

Subjects: Epidemiology, prevention, cause, detection, diagnosis, treatment and psycho-oncology.

Purpose: To enable investigators and clinicians who are in the early stages of their careers to carry out basic, translational or clinical projects and to develop, acquire and apply advance research procedures and techniques that foster a bi-directional flow of knowledge, experience, expertise and innovation to and from the United States of America.

Eligibility: Open to candidates in the early stages of their careers. Applications that are geared to the development of specific cancer control measures in developing, central and East European countries are particularly encouraged. Candidates should hold assistant professorships or similar positions at their home institutes and must ordinarily have a minimum of two years and maximum of 10 years of postdoctoral experience after obtaining their MD or PhD degrees or equivalents. Awards are conditional on the Fellow returning to the home institute at the end of the fellowship and on the availability of appropriate facilities and resources to apply newly acquired skills. Candidates who are physically present at the proposed host institute whilst their applications are under consideration are not eligible for UICC fellowships.

Level of Study: Postdoctorate, Professional development, Research.

Type: Fellowship.

Value: Average value of US$40,000 for travel and stipend support. Calculation of travel and stipend awards are based on the candidate's estimates which are adjusted, if need be, to published fares and UICC scales. Travel awards contribute to least expensive international return air fares or other appropriate forms of transport. Travel estimates should not include costs for internal travel within the home and/or host

countries. These and extra costs for visa, passports, airport taxes and insurance, are the responsibility of the Fellow. No allowances are made for accompanying dependants.

Length of Study: One year, extendable by a further year at no additional cost to UICC.

Frequency: Annual.

Country of Study: Any country.

No. of awards offered: 8-10.

Application Procedure: Applicants must submit completed applications with all supporting documentation to reach the UICC by the application closing date. Application forms may be obtained from the fellowships department or from the website.

Closing Date: December 1st. Applicants are notified in mid April of the following year.

Funding: Private.

Contributor: The American Cancer Society.

No. of awards given last year: Eight.

No. of applicants last year: 25-36.

UICC Translational Cancer Research Fellowships (TCRF)

Subjects: Areas that connect cell and molecular biologists to the patients in the clinic.

Purpose: To accelerate the translation of basic, experimental and applied research insights for solid tumours into their clinical or population applications through the form of new ideas, drugs and treatments.

Eligibility: The fellowships are subject to the UICC general conditions for fellowships.

Level of Study: Research.

Type: Fellowship.

Value: Approx. US$55,000.

Length of Study: One year.

Frequency: Annual.

Country of Study: Any country.

No. of awards offered: Three.

Application Procedure: Applicants must complete an application form, available from the fellowships department or from the website.

Closing Date: December 1st.

Funding: Commercial.

Contributor: Novartis Pharma AG (Switzerland) and AstraZeneca (UK).

No. of awards given last year: Three.

No. of applicants last year: 20.

Additional Information: Further information is available on request.

UICC Trish Greene International Oncology Nursing Fellowships

Subjects: Training for nursing cancer patients.

Purpose: To support nurses who are actively engaged in the care of cancer patients and who come from developing and Eastern European countries.

Eligibility: Open to English or French speaking nurses who are actively engaged in the care of cancer patients in their home institutes and who come from developing or East European countries where specialist cancer nurse training is not yet widely available.

Level of Study: Professional development.

Type: Fellowship.

Value: The average stipend is US$2,800.

Length of Study: One-three months with stipend support for one month.

Frequency: Annual.

Study Establishment: The Comprehensive Cancer Centre.

Country of Study: Any country.

No. of awards offered: 15.

Application Procedure: Applicants must submit applications complete with supporting documentation to the UICC Geneva Office by the application closing date. Application forms can be obtained from the Fellowships department or the website.

Closing Date: November 1st for notification in mid February.

Funding: Private.

Contributor: The Oncology Nursing Society (USA) and the Norwegian Cancer Society.

No. of awards given last year: 15.

No. of applicants last year: 24.

UICC Yamagiwa-Yoshida Memorial International Cancer Study Grants

Subjects: Cancer research.
Purpose: To enable cancer investigators from any country to carry out bilateral research projects which exploit complementary materials or skills, including advanced training in experimental methods or special techniques.
Eligibility: Open to appropriately qualified investigators from any country who are actively engaged in cancer research. Candidates who are already physically present at the proposed host institute are not eligible.
Level of Study: Professional development.
Type: Grant.
Value: The average stipend is US$9,000. If a Fellow's return home is delayed beyond the extra approved period, 50 per cent of the travel award, the return portion has to be reimbursed to the UICC. Calculation of travel and stipend awards are based on the candidate's estimates which are adjusted, if need be, to published fares and UICC scales. Travel awards contribute to the least expensive international return air fares or other appropriate form of transport. Travel estimates should not include costs for internal travel within the home or host countries. These and extra costs for visa, passports, airport taxes and insurance are the responsibility of the Fellow. No financial support is provided for dependants.
Length of Study: Three months. May be extended by their original duration, subject to written approval of the home and host supervisors. Funding for these additional periods may be secured from other funding agencies.
Frequency: Annual.
Country of Study: Any country.
No. of awards offered: 15.
Application Procedure: Applicants must complete an application form, available from the Fellowships Department or from the website.
Closing Date: January 1st for notification by mid April, July 1st for notification by mid October.
Funding: Commercial, Private.
Contributor: Kyowa Hakko Kyoga Company Limited, Toray Industries, Inc. and the Japan National Committee for UICC.
No. of awards given last year: 14.
No. of applicants last year: 16.

INTERNATIONAL UNION FOR VACUUM SCIENCE AND TECHNOLOGY (IUVSTA)

7 Mohawk, Nepean, ON, K2H 7G7, Canada
Tel: (1) 613 829 5790
Fax: (1) 613 829 3061
Email: bill@thinkfilms.ca
www: http://www.iuvsta.org
Contact: Dr William D Westwood, Secretary General

The International Union for Vacuum Science and Technology (IUVSTA) is a non-government organisation whose member societies represent all vacuum scientists, engineers and technologists in their country.

Welch Foundation Scholarship

Subjects: Vacuum science.
Purpose: To encourage promising scholars who wish to study vacuum science, techniques or their application in any field.
Eligibility: Open to applicants of any nationality who hold the minimum of a Bachelor's degree, although preference is given to those holding a doctoral degree.
Level of Study: Doctorate, Postdoctorate, Postgraduate.
Type: Scholarship.
Value: US$15,500.
Length of Study: One year.
Frequency: Annual.
Study Establishment: An appropriate laboratory.
Country of Study: Any country.
No. of awards offered: One.
Application Procedure: Applicants must complete and submit an application form with a research proposal, a curriculum vitae and two letters of reference. More information and application forms can be obtained from the website under Welch headings.
Closing Date: April 15th.
Funding: Private.
Contributor: IUVSTA.
No. of awards given last year: One.
No. of applicants last year: Four.

For further information contact:

Canadian Photorics Fabrication Centre, Institute for Microstructural Sciences, National Research Council, Building M-50, Montreal Rd., Ottawa, ON K1A 0R6, Canada
Email: frsims@nortelnetworks.com
Contact: Dr FR Shepherd Administrator Technical Manager

INTERNATIONALER ROBERT-SCHUMANN-WETTBEWERB ZWICKAU

Organisationsbüro, Münzstraße 12, Zwickau, D-08056, Germany
Tel: (49) 375 212 636
Fax: (49) 375 834 130
Email: kulturbuero@zwickau.de
www: http://www.zwickau.de/robert-schumann.htm
Contact: Ms Hannelore Heil

International Robert Schumann Competition

Subjects: Piano performance or individual singing.
Purpose: To support the interpretation of the work of Robert Schumann.
Eligibility: Open to pianists up to the age of 30 and to individual singers up to the age of 32.
Level of Study: Professional development.
Type: Competition.
Value: Please contact the organisation.
Country of Study: Any country.
No. of awards offered: 10.
Application Procedure: Applicants must write for further details.
Funding: Commercial, Government.

IOWA STATE UNIVERSITY

Iowa State University, Ames, IOWA 50011, United States of America
Tel: (1) 515 2944111
www: http://www.iastate.edu
Contact: Dr James R Bloedell, Dean

Iowa State University of Science & Technology is a public band-grant institution serving the people of Iowa, the nation and the world.

Accountemps student Scholarship

Subjects: Accounting, finance or information systems.
Purpose: To support a full-time declared student of accounting towards post graduate study and a career in accounting.
Eligibility: Not eligible to students who have already gained their CPA.
Level of Study: Postgraduate.
Type: Scholarship.
Value: $2,500
Frequency: Annual.
Study Establishment: Iowa State University
Country of Study: United States of America.
No. of awards offered: 2.
Closing Date: April 1st
Funding: Private.
Contributor: AICPA.

For further information contact:

Program, AICPA-Team 046, 1211 Avenue of the America, New York, NY 100 36-8775,
Contact: Accountemps Student Scholarship program

Air and Waste Management Association Midwest Section Scholarship Award

Subjects: Environment-related studies.
Purpose: To support a postgraduate student pursuing a course of study and research leading to a career in environment related studies.
Level of Study: Postgraduate.
Type: Scholarship.
Length of Study: One year.
Frequency: Annual.
Study Establishment: Iowa State University.
Country of Study: United States of America or Canada.
Closing Date: June 1st
Funding: Commercial.
Contributor: Air and Waste Management Association.

For further information contact:

A&WMA-Midwest Section, RMK consultants, Karsas city, MO 64113, United States of America
Tel: (1) 515 294 4111
www: http://www.iastate.edu
Contact: Ralph Keller, Scholarship Program

AMBUCS Scholarship

Subjects: Physical therapy, Occupational therapy, speech language pathology or hearing audiology.
Purpose: To provide financial assistance to needy postgraduate students studying therapy.
Eligibility: Candidates must document financial need and express intent to enter clinical produce in the relevant discipline.
Level of Study: Postgraduate.
Type: Scholarship.
Frequency: Annual.
Study Establishment: Iowa State University.
Country of Study: United States of America.
Closing Date: April 15th
Funding: Private.
Contributor: AMBUCS.

For further information contact:

AMBUCS Resource Center, PB 5127, High Point, NC 27262,
Contact: National Scholarships Committee

American Electroplaters and Surface Finishers Society Scholarship

Subjects: Metallurgy, metallurgical engineering, materials Science or engineering, chemistry, chemical engineering environmental engineering.
Purpose: To support post-graduate students to continue their studies in metallurgical engineering and related disciplines.
Eligibility: Must intend to study full-time for the year of the scholarship
Level of Study: Postgraduate.
Type: Scholarship.
Length of Study: One year.
Frequency: Annual.
Study Establishment: Iowa State University.
Country of Study: United States of America.
Closing Date: April 15th
Funding: Private.
Contributor: AESFS.

For further information contact:

Central Florida Research Park 12644 Research Parkway, Orlando, FL 32826-3298,
Contact: Scholarship Committee AFSFS

American Society of Naval Engineers Scholarship

Subjects: Naval engineering.
Purpose: To support a post-graduate student for one year of full-time study leading to a designated engineering or physical science degree.

Eligibility: The candidate must be a U.S. citizen and have demonstrated or expressed a genuine interest in a career in naval engineering.
Level of Study: Postgraduate.
Type: Scholarship.
Value: $3,500
Length of Study: One year.
Frequency: Annual.
Study Establishment: Iowa State University.
Application Procedure: Selection criteria will be based on the candidate's academic record, work history, professional promise and interest in naval engineering.
Closing Date: February 15th
Funding: Private.
Contributor: American Society of Naval Engineers.

For further information contact:

1452 Duke Street, Alexandria, VA 22314-3458,
Contact: The American Society of Naval Engineers

Charles and Kathleen Manatt Democracy Studies

Subjects: International relations, political science, public administration.
Purpose: To support students who have completed their undergraduate studies and who are working towards a graduate degree.
Level of Study: Postgraduate.
Type: Fellowship.
Value: $1,800
Length of Study: 6 weeks.
Frequency: Annual.
Study Establishment: Iowa State University
Country of Study: United States of America.
No. of awards offered: 2.
Closing Date: May 22nd
Funding: Private.

For further information contact:

1101 15th Street NW Third Floor, Washington DC, 20005,
Contact: Mr Dorin Tudoran, Director of Research & Communications

Charles E. Fahmey Education Foundation Scholarship

Subjects: Any subject as approved by Iowa State University.
Purpose: To support a graduate student who is a resident of Wapello Country.
Eligibility: Selection is made without regard to sex, race, age, religion or marital status.
Level of Study: Postgraduate.
Type: Scholarship.
Value: $2,500
Frequency: Annual.
Study Establishment: Iowa State University.
Country of Study: United States of America.
Closing Date: February 15th
Funding: Private.
Contributor: Charles E. Fahmey Foundation.

For further information contact:

Firstar Bank, NA 123 East Third Street, Ottumwa, IA 52501-8003, United States of America
Contact: Trust Department

John L. Carey Scholarship

Subjects: Accountancy.
Purpose: To support a graduate student with a liberal arts degree who are interested in pursuing a C.P.A. certificate.
Level of Study: Postgraduate.
Type: Scholarship.
Value: $5,000 per year.
Length of Study: Two years.
Frequency: Annual.
Study Establishment: Iowa State University
Country of Study: United States of America.

No. of awards offered: 5.
Application Procedure: Candidates must supply two letters of recommendation as well as transcripts from both undergraduate and graduate entrance tests.
Closing Date: April 1st
Funding: Private.
Contributor: American Institute of Certified Public Accountants.
Additional Information: Students must maintain scholartic progress in order to quality for the second year.

For further information contact:

A.I.C.P.A. , 1211 Avenue of the American, New York, United States of America
Contact: AICPA Carey Scholarships Program

IRIS FUND FOR PREVENTION OF BLINDNESS

York House199, Westminster Bridge Road, London, SE1 7UT, England
Tel: (44) 20 7928 7743
Fax: (44) 20 7928 7919
Email: info@irisfund.org.uk
www: http://www.irisfund.org.uk
Contact: Executive Director

The Iris Fund for Prevention of Blindness supports nationwide research into the prevention, treatment and cure of all forms of blindness and serious eye disorders, whether inherited, congenital or acquired. The Fund also focuses on current needs by sponsoring screening programmes and helping ophthalmology departments purchase vital innovative equipment when funds are unavailable from other sources.

Iris Fund Grants for Research and Equipment (Ophthalmology)
Subjects: Ophthalmology.
Purpose: To prevent and cure blindness and serious eye disorders.
Eligibility: Open to suitably qualified individuals. Applications must be submitted by qualified consultant ophthalmologists or equivalent for research under his or her supervision. Research projects can only take place in the United Kingdom.
Level of Study: Unrestricted.
Type: Grant.
Value: As funds become available.
Length of Study: Usually for a maximum of three years.
Frequency: Annual.
Country of Study: United Kingdom.
No. of awards offered: Varies.
Application Procedure: Applicants must submit eight copies of the application form as well as supporting paperwork.
Funding: Commercial, Private.

IRISH-AMERICAN CULTURAL INSTITUTE (IACI)

1 Lackawanna Place, Morristown, NJ 07960, United States of America
Tel: (1) 973 605 1991
Fax: (1) 973 605 8875
Email: info@iaci-usa.org
www: www.iaci-usa.org

The Irish American Cultural Institute (IACI), a non-profit educational institute, is dedicated to preserving and promoting the highest standards of artistic development, education, research and entertainment in fostering the cultural understanding of Irish heritage in America. With international headquarters in Morristown, New Jersey, the Institute has a long history of supporting the arts and humanities through grants and awards as well as through programming. The Institute is strictly non-political and non-sectarian. Founded in 1962, the IACI is the sole United States of America organisation with the distinction of having the President of Ireland as patron.

IACI Visiting Fellowship in Irish Studies at National University of Ireland, Galway
Subjects: Irish studies.
Purpose: To allow scholars to spend a semester at the University of Ireland, Galway and whose work relates to any aspect of Irish studies.
Eligibility: Open to Scholars who normally reside in the United States of America, and whose work relates to any aspect of Irish studies.
Level of Study: Postgraduate.
Type: Fellowship.
Value: A stipend of US$13,000 plus transatlantic transportation.
Length of Study: A period of not less than four months.
Frequency: Annual.
Country of Study: Ireland.
No. of awards offered: One.
Application Procedure: Applicants must complete an application form and submit this with a current curriculum vitae and list of publications. Application forms are available on request.
Closing Date: December 31st for the forthcoming academic year.
Contributor: Jointly funded with University College Galway (UCG).
Additional Information: The holder of the fellowship will be provided with services appropriate to a visiting faculty member during his or her time at UCG. There are certain relatively minor departmental responsibilities expected of the holder during his or her time at UCG, and certain other expectations regarding publication, upon completion of the fellowship.

Irish Research Funds
Subjects: All subjects. Historical research has predominated, but other areas of research will be considered equally.
Purpose: To promote scholarly enquiry and publication regarding the Irish American experience.
Eligibility: Open to individuals of any nationality. Media production costs and journal subventions will not be considered for funding.
Level of Study: Postgraduate.
Type: Grant.
Value: US$1,000-5,000.
Frequency: Annual.
Country of Study: Any country.
No. of awards offered: Varies.
Application Procedure: Applicants must complete an application form. Further information is available on request.
Funding: Private.

ISMA CENTRE

The University of Reading, Whiteknights Park, PO Box 242, Reading, Berkshire, RG6 6BA, England
Tel: (44) 118 378 8239
Fax: (44) 118 931 4741
Email: admin@ismacentre.rdg.ac.uk
www: http://www.ismacentre.rdg.ac.uk
Contact: Ms Julie Stewart, Marketing & Recruitment Manager

The ISMA Centre at the University of Reading is a leader in the research and education of applied securities and investment banking education. Its graduate study opportunities include Master's degrees and doctoral research programmes. The Centre is part of the School of Business at the University, but is housed in its own facilities with two financial dealing rooms.

ISMA Centre Doctoral Scholarship
Subjects: A topic relating to behavioural finance, corporate finance, credit risk, equity investment, strategies and risk management.
Purpose: To support research in the field.
Eligibility: Open to candidates with an excellent academic background who have completed, or who are in the process of completing, a Master's degree with grade averages at distinction level, in a course containing a significant proportion of finance.
Level of Study: Doctorate.
Type: Scholarship.
Value: UK£10,000 paid quarterly plus PhD fee waiver.
Length of Study: Three years.
Frequency: Annual.

Study Establishment: ISMA Centre, University of Reading.
Country of Study: United Kingdom.
No. of awards offered: Three.
Application Procedure: Applicants must complete an application form, available from the Centre.
Funding: Commercial.
Contributor: ISMA Centre and the University of Reading.
No. of awards given last year: Three.
No. of applicants last year: 120.

ITALIAN INSTITUTE FOR HISTORICAL STUDIES

Via Benedetto Croce 12, Naples, I-80134, Italy
Tel: (39) 081 551 7159
Fax: (39) 081 551 2390
Email: instituto@iiss.unina.it
www: http://www.iiss.unina.it
Contact: Ms Marta Herling, Secretary

The Italian Institute for Historical Studies is a postgraduate institute for the study of history and philosophy. The study of history is seen in connection with the disciplines of philosophy, the arts, economics and literature. The Institute offers two annual scholarships for non-Italian postgraduates specialising in humanities and social sciences.

Adolfo Omodeo Scholarship
Subjects: History and philosophy. The study of history is seen in connection with the disciplines of philosophy, the arts, economics and literature.
Purpose: To allow students to participate in life at the Institute while completing a personal research project with the assistance of its staff.
Eligibility: Open to any nationality. Applicants must possess a Bachelor's degree.
Level of Study: Postgraduate.
Type: Scholarship.
Value: Please contact the Institute for details.
Length of Study: Eight months.
Frequency: Annual.
Study Establishment: The Italian Institute for Historical Studies.
Country of Study: Italy.
No. of awards offered: One.
Application Procedure: Applicants must submit an application including birth certificate, proof of citizenship, university diploma, scholarly work, curriculum vitae, programme of research, letters of reference and copies of publications.
Closing Date: September 30th.
Funding: Government, Private.
No. of awards given last year: Two.
No. of applicants last year: Two.

Frederico Chabod Scholarship
Subjects: History and philosophy. The study of history is seen in connection with the disciplines of philosophy, the arts, economics and literature.
Purpose: To allow students to participate in life at the Institute, while completing a personal research project with the assistance of its staff.
Eligibility: Open to nationals of all countries. Applicants must possess a Bachelor's degree.
Level of Study: Postgraduate.
Type: Scholarship.
Value: Please contact the Institute for details.
Length of Study: Eight months.
Frequency: Annual.
Study Establishment: The Italian Institute for Historical Studies.
Country of Study: Italy.
No. of awards offered: One.
Application Procedure: Applicants must submit an application including birth certificate, proof of citizenship, university diploma, scholarly work, curriculum vitae, programme of research, letters of reference, and copies of publications.
Closing Date: September 30th.

Funding: Government, Private.
No. of awards given last year: Two.
No. of applicants last year: Two.

IWHM BERNARD BUTLER TRUST FUND

37 Oasthouse Drive, Fleet, Hampshire GU51 2UL, United Kingdom
Tel: (44) 01252 627748
Fax: (44) 01252 627748
Email: info@iwhm-trust.co.uk
www: http://www.iwhm-trust.co.uk
Contact: The Secretary

The trust was established in 1998 from the assets of the Institution of Works and Highways Management after the merger of its professional activities with the Institution of Civil Engineers in 1994.

The Bernard Butler Trust Fund
Subjects: To encourage men and women engaged in the engineering field to improve their education, training and professional standing together with aiding and promoting individuals/organisations to advance engineering training, safety & methods of working.
Purpose: To promote the ideals first established in 1938 and to ensure their legacy is perpetuated for the benefit of those to come.
Eligibility: Those who can show practical and personal qualities needed to promote engineering.
Level of Study: Graduate, Postgraduate, Professional development, Research.
Type: Training, Education and Research grants.
Frequency: Dependent on funds available.
Study Establishment: Variable.
Application Procedure: Download an application form from the website.
Funding: Private.
Contributor: Institution of works and highways Management.
No. of awards given last year: 13.
No. of applicants last year: 13.

THE J B HARLEY RESEARCH FELLOWSHIPS TRUST

76 Ockendon Road, London, N1 3NW, England
Tel: (44) 20 7359 6477
Email: t.campbell@ockendon.clara.co.uk
www: http://www.maphistory.info/harley.html
Contact: Mr Tony Campbell

J B Harley Research Fellowships in the History of Cartography
Subjects: The history of cartography.
Purpose: To promote the use of the great wealth of historical and cartographical material available in London.
Eligibility: Open to anyone pursuing advanced research in the history of cartography, irrespective of nationality, discipline or profession. Advanced research is taken to mean work towards a doctorate, postdoctoral research or work of an equivalent level regardless of the applicants formal qualifications. Preference will be given to interpretative studies in map history, irrespective of area, theme or period.
Level of Study: Doctorate, Postdoctorate.
Type: Grant.
Value: Normally UK£250 per week.
Length of Study: Up to four weeks.
Frequency: Annual.
Study Establishment: London libraries.
Country of Study: United Kingdom.
No. of awards offered: Three.
Application Procedure: Applicants must consult the website for details.
Closing Date: 1st November [each year].
Funding: Private.
No. of awards given last year: Three.
No. of applicants last year: 12.

Additional Information: See 'Harley Fellows: listing, with analysis of awards and applicant numbers (1994)' http://www.maphistory.info/harlflws.html.

J N TATA ENDOWMENT

Bombay House, 24 Homi Mody Street, Bombay, Mumbai 400001, India
Tel: (91) 022 5665 7643
Fax: (91) 022 2204 5432
Email: gjkerawalla@tata.com
Contact: Chief Executive Officer

The J N Tata Endowment awards one time loan scholarships to Scholars of conspicuous distinction for postgraduate, PhD or post-doctoral studies abroad in all fields. Mid career professionals with an outstanding academic background and experience in the field going abroad for further specialisation are also considered for the scholarship.

J N Tata Endowment Loan Scholarship
Subjects: All subjects.
Purpose: To provide an opportunity to the gifted to pursue higher studies abroad in all disciplines.
Eligibility: Open only to Indian nationals. Applicants must be graduates of a recognized Indian university with a sound academic and extracurricular record. Deserving mid-career professionals are also eligible.
Level of Study: Doctorate, MBA, Postdoctorate, Postgraduate, Professional development.
Type: Loan scholarship.
Value: Please contact the organisation.
Length of Study: Minimum one year. Minimum six months for Mid-Career Professionals.
Frequency: Annual.
Country of Study: Any Country except India.
No. of awards offered: 100+.
Application Procedure: Applicants must complete an application form. Forms are issued against an application fee of Indian Rupees One Hundred only.
Closing Date: February 15th for the Autumn and Spring semesters.
Funding: Private.
Contributor: Tata Trusts.
No. of awards given last year: 115.
No. of applicants last year: 1201.
Additional Information: The award is primarily for the Autumn semester. The selection of Scholars is made on the basis of a personal interview which assesses the student's competence in the field of graduation, general knowledge, maturity and suitability for the proposed field of study. Interviews are conducted between March and June for the Autumn and Spring semesters.

For further information contact:

Administrative Office, J N Tata Endowment, Mulla House, 4th Floor, 51 MG Road, Bombay, Mumbai 400001, India

JACOB'S PILLOW DANCE FESTIVAL, INC.

Box 287, Lee, MA 01238, United States of America
Tel: (1) 413 637 1322
Fax: (1) 413 243 4744
Email: info@jacobspillow.org
www: http://www.jacobspillow.org
Contact: Ms J R Glover, Education Director

The Jacob's Pillow Dance Festival seeks to nurture and sustain artistic creation, presentation, education and preservation, and engage and deepen public appreciation and support for dance. Founded in 1932 by modern dance pioneer Ted Shawn, the school provides rigorous dance training and education for some 100 pre-professionals, artists and teachers seeking professional development in a residential artist community.

Jacob's Pillow Education Fund Scholarship
Subjects: Dance traditions, techniques, repertory and theory. Classes are offered in all forms of dance and vary from year to year. Ballet, modern, jazz and cultural traditions are four core school programmes offered annually. In addition, one or two programmes with an emphasis on choreographic development are part of each summer's offerings.
Purpose: To allow advanced dancers an opportunity to participate in summer dance workshops with world renowned faculty and artists.
Eligibility: Open to United States of America and foreign nationals who are over 16 years of age, have advanced dance training and complete application requirements for the programme the applicant wishes to attend.
Level of Study: Unrestricted.
Type: Scholarship.
Value: Room, board, tuition and performance tickets. There is no travel allowance.
Length of Study: Varies, usually one-three weeks.
Frequency: Annual.
Study Establishment: The School at Jacob's Pillow Dance Festival.
Country of Study: United States of America.
No. of awards offered: 50-60 per cent of students are provided with partial scholarships.
Application Procedure: Applicants must contact the School after December 1st for audition requirements for the upcoming Summer programme. Applicants can write, phone or visit the website for details.
Closing Date: The deadline for videotaped auditions is March 22nd.
Funding: Private.
Contributor: Private contributions.
No. of awards given last year: Approx. 100.
No. of applicants last year: Varies.
Additional Information: Scholarships are only offered to enable dancers to attend the School at Jacob's Pillow Dance Festival and are non transferable. Scholarship awards apply towards the total programme fee which includes tuition, room and board and access to performances.

For further information contact:

(For UPS/Express Mail) The School at Jacob's Pillow, 358 George Carter Road, Becket, MA 01233, United States of America

JAMES AND GRACE ANDERSON TRUST

32 Wardie Road, Edinburgh, EH5 3LG, England
Tel: (44) 131 552 4062
Fax: (44) 131 467 1333
Email: tim.straton@virgin.net
Contact: Mr Tim Straton, Trustee

The James and Grace Anderson Trust funds research into the cure or alleviation of cerebral palsy.

James and Grace Anderson Trust Research Grant
Purpose: To advance by investigation, research or otherwise in any way, knowledge with regard to the causes of cerebral palsy and related conditions and, if possible, curing or alleviating the same.
Eligibility: The Trust does not make travel awards.
Level of Study: Research.
Type: Grant.
Value: Maximum UK£25,000.
Length of Study: One to three years.
Frequency: Twice a year.
Country of Study: Scotland.
Application Procedure: Application must be made in writing, giving full details of the research being carried out and the anticipated value. A copy of the ethical approval, if granted, should also be included.
Closing Date: 15th April and 15th October.
Funding: Private.
No. of awards given last year: 1.
No. of applicants last year: One.

JAMES COOK UNIVERSITY

Graduate Research School, Townsville, QLD 4811, Australia
Tel: (61) 7 4781 4575
Fax: (61) 7 4781 6204
Email: ResearchHigherDegrees@jcu.edu.au
www: http://www.jcu.edu.au
Contact: Ms Susan Meehan, Manager

James Cook University prides itself on its international reputation for research and discovery and the teaching is enhanced and enlivened by that research activity. Students will experience at first hand the process of producing new knowledge, which will provide them with the confidence and the ability to become the entrepreneurs and innovators of tomorrow.

James Cook University Postgraduate Research Scholarship

Subjects: All Disciplines.
Purpose: To encourage full-time postgraduate research leading to a Master's or PhD degree.
Eligibility: Open to any student who has attained at least an Upper Second Class (Honours) Bachelor's Degree.
Level of Study: Postgraduate.
Type: Scholarship.
Value: Australian $18,009 per year. The award does not cover annual tuition fees for overseas students.
Length of Study: Three years with a possible additional six months in exceptional circumstances for the PhD, or two years for the Master's programme.
Frequency: Annual.
Study Establishment: James Cook University.
Country of Study: Australia.
No. of awards offered: Up to seven.
Closing Date: October 31st.

Noel and Kate Monkman Postgraduate Award

Subjects: Marine biology.
Purpose: To encourage full-time study towards an MSc or PhD degree in marine biology.
Eligibility: Open to Australian citizens or those with permanent resident status in Australia, who hold or are expecting to hold an Upper Second Class (Honours) Degree, or its equivalent, in marine biology or a related science.
Level of Study: Postgraduate.
Type: Scholarship.
Value: To be determined.
Length of Study: Three years for the PhD or two years for the Master's programme.
Frequency: Dependent on funds available.
Study Establishment: James Cook University.
Country of Study: Australia.
No. of awards offered: One.

JAMES MADISON MEMORIAL FELLOWSHIP FOUNDATION

2000 K Street, North West, Suite 303, Washington, DC 20006, United States of America
Tel: (1) 202 653 8700
Fax: (1) 202 653 6111
Email: madison@act.org
www: http://www.jamesmadison.com
Contact: Mr Lewis F Larsen, Director of Programs

The mission of the James Madison Memorial Fellowship Foundation is to strengthen secondary school teaching of the principles, framing and development of the United States of America Constitution.

James Madison Fellowship Program

Subjects: History, political science or education.
Eligibility: Applicants must be United States of America citizens.
Level of Study: Graduate.

Type: Fellowship.
Value: Up to US$24,000.
Length of Study: Up to five years.
Frequency: Annual.
Country of Study: United States of America.
No. of awards offered: Up to 60.
Application Procedure: Applicants must obtain an application form by calling (1) 800 525 6928. Applications may also be downloaded from the Foundation's website.
Closing Date: March 1st.
Funding: Government, Private.
No. of awards given last year: 70.

JAMES PANTYFEDWEN FOUNDATION

9 Market Street, Aberystwyth, Ceredigion SY23 1DL, Wales
Tel: (44) 1970 612806
Fax: (44) 1970 612806
Email: pantyfedwen@btinternet.com
Contact: Mr Richard H Morgan, Executive Secretary

James Pantyfedwen Foundation Grants

Subjects: All subjects.
Purpose: To promote mainly postgraduate research.
Eligibility: Open to Welsh nationals, especially those who wish to train as ministers of religion of any denomination. The qualifying criteria for this is defined by benefactor.
Level of Study: Postgraduate.
Type: Grant.
Value: Varies, usually up to a maximum of UK£6,000.
Length of Study: Up to three years.
Frequency: Annual.
Country of Study: United Kingdom.
No. of awards offered: Varies.
Application Procedure: Applicants must submit applications on the appropriate forms, accepted on an ongoing basis. Closing date for students in each year is 31st July.
Closing Date: Please contact the organisation 31st July in each year.
Funding: Private.
Contributor: Exclusive to private investment portfolio.
No. of awards given last year: 45.
No. of applicants last year: 176.

JANSON JOHAN HELMICH OG MARCIA JANSONS LEGAT

Blommeseter, Norderhov, Hönefoss, N-3512, Norway
Tel: (47) 3 213 5465
Fax: (47) 3 213 5626
Email: janlegat@online.no
www: http://www.jansonslegat.no
Contact: Mr Reidun Haugen, Manager

Janson Johan Helmich Scholarships and Travel Grants

Subjects: All subjects.
Purpose: To support practical or academic training.
Eligibility: Open to qualified Norwegian postgraduate students with practical experience for advanced study abroad.
Level of Study: Doctorate, MBA, Postgraduate, Professional development, Research.
Type: Scholarship.
Value: A maximum of norwegian krone 75,000.
Frequency: Annual.
Country of Study: Any country.
No. of awards offered: 30.
Application Procedure: Applicants must complete an application form.
Closing Date: March 15th.
No. of awards given last year: 25.
No. of applicants last year: 198.

JAPAN SOCIETY FOR THE PROMOTION OF SCIENCE (JSPS)

Jochi Kioizaka Building, 6-26-3 Kioi-cho
Chiyoda-ku, Tokyo
102-0094, Japan
Tel: (81) 3 3263 9094
Fax: (81) 3 3263 1854
www: http://www.jsps.go.jp/e-home.htm
Contact: Administrative Assistant

The Japan Society for the Promotion of Science (JSPS) is a quasi-governmental organisation established by a national law for the purpose of contributing to the advancement of science. JSPS plays a key role in the administration of various scientific and academic programmes.

JSPS Invitation Fellowship Programme for Research in Japan

Subjects: All fields of the humanities, social sciences, natural sciences, engineering or medicine.
Purpose: To promote international co-operation and mutual understanding in scientific research.
Eligibility: Open to university professors and associate and assistant professors, senior scientists, and other persons with substantial professional experience.
Level of Study: Professional development.
Type: Fellowship.
Value: Please consult the organisation.
Length of Study: The short-term programme is for between 14 and 60 days and the long-term programme is 2-10 months.
Frequency: Annual.
Study Establishment: Universities and research institutions.
Country of Study: Japan.
No. of awards offered: Varies.
Application Procedure: Applications must be submitted to JSPS by the inviting scientist in Japan.
Funding: Government.
Additional Information: A short-term programme is also available with a fellowship period of 14-60 days, and a reduced award amount.

JSPS Postdoctoral Fellowships for Foreign Researchers

Subjects: Humanities, social sciences, natural sciences, engineering or medicine.
Purpose: To assist promising and highly qualified young foreign researchers wishing to conduct research in Japan.
Eligibility: Open to citizens of countries which have diplomatic relations with Japan. Applicants must have a doctoral degree.
Level of Study: Postdoctorate.
Type: Fellowship.
Value: Please contact the organisation.
Length of Study: Two years but a minimum of one year.
Frequency: Annual.
Study Establishment: Universities and research institutions.
Country of Study: Japan.
No. of awards offered: Varies.
Application Procedure: Applicants must write for details. Application must be submitted to JSPS by the host researcher in Japan.
Funding: Government.

JAPANESE AMERICAN CITIZENS LEAGUE (JACL)

1765 Sutter Street, San Francisco, CA 94115, United States of America
Tel: (1) 415 921 5225
Fax: (1) 415 931 4671
Email: jacl@jacl.org
www: http://www.jacl.org
Contact: Scholarships Officer

The Japanese American Citizens League (JACL) was founded in 1929 to fight discrimination against people of Japanese ancestry. It is the largest and one of the oldest Asian American organisations in the United States. The JACL has over 24,500 members in 112 chapters located in 25 states, Washington DC, and Japan. The organisation operates within a structure of eight district councils, with headquarters in San Francisco, California.

JACL Scholarship and Award Program

Subjects: Creative or performing arts.
Purpose: To recognise education as a key to greater opportunities for JACL members.
Eligibility: Open to members of the JACL. Applicants must be enrolled or planning to enrol full-time in an accredited school for the following semester. Membership of the JACL is not race restrictive. Only applicants that exhibit severe financial need will be considered for the student aid award (Hagiwara).
Level of Study: Doctorate, Graduate, Postdoctorate.
Type: Scholarship and Award.
Value: Awards vary between US$1,000-5,000.
Frequency: Annual.
Study Establishment: Any accredited college, university, trade school, business school, law school, art school or other Institute of Higher Education.
Country of Study: Any country.
No. of awards offered: Eight for the graduate programme, two for the law programme, one for the student aid award and two for the performing arts programme.
Application Procedure: Applicants must request an application form from the JACL, enclosing a stamped addressed envelope, and stating the category which they would like to apply for, or download an application form and eligibility information from the website.
Closing Date: April 1st.
Funding: Private.
Additional Information: Selection is based upon scholastic achievement, community involvement, extracurricular activities, personal statement and letters of recommendation. For the Student Aid award a Financial Aid Statement is required, for the creative and performing arts award sample works are required.

JAPANESE GOVERNMENT

Embassy of Japan, 112 Empire Circuit, Yarralumla, ACT 2600, Australia
Tel: (61) 2 6273 3244
Fax: (61) 2 6273 1848
Email: cultural@japan.org.au
www: http://www.japan.org.au
Contact: Ms Eriko Prior, Monbukagakusho Scholarship Co-ordinator

Japanese Government (Monbukagakusho) Scholarships In-Service Training for Teachers Category

Subjects: Teacher training.
Eligibility: Open to Australians under 35 years of age who are university or teacher training graduates currently in active service in primary or secondary schools, or who are on the staff at teacher training institutions or educational administrative institutions. Applicants must have at least five years of experience in their terms of service. University academic staff members should not be selected as grantees.
Level of Study: Postgraduate.
Type: Scholarship.
Value: Return air fare plus yen 184,000 per month.
Length of Study: 18 months.
Frequency: Annual.
Study Establishment: A Japanese university.
Country of Study: Japan.
No. of awards offered: One-two.
Application Procedure: Applicants must complete an application form available from the Embassy of Japan in their own country. Applications are not available from the main organisation.
Closing Date: Late March.
Funding: Government.

No. of awards given last year: Two.
No. of applicants last year: Six.
Additional Information: Applicants must be willing to study the Japanese language.

Japanese Government (Monbukagakusho) Scholarships Research Category

Subjects: Humanities, social sciences, literature, history, aesthetics, law, politics, economics, commerce, pedagogy, psychology, sociology, music and fine arts, natural sciences, pure science, engineering, agriculture, fisheries, pharmacology, medicine, dentistry or home economics.
Eligibility: Open to Australian graduates under 35 years of age.
Level of Study: Doctorate, Postgraduate.
Type: Scholarship.
Value: Return air fare plus yen 184,000 per month.
Length of Study: 18-24 months.
Frequency: Annual.
Study Establishment: A Japanese university.
Country of Study: Japan.
No. of awards offered: Approx. 17.
Application Procedure: Applicants must complete an application form available from the Embassy of Japan in their own country. Applications are not available from the main organisation.
Closing Date: June.
Funding: Government.
No. of awards given last year: 17.
No. of applicants last year: 50.
Additional Information: Applicants must be willing to study the Japanese language.

JEAN SIBELIUS INTERNATIONAL VIOLIN COMPETITION

PB 31, Helsinki, Finland
Tel: (358) 9 4114 3443
Fax: (358) 10 850 4760
Email: violin.competition@kolumbus.fi
www: http://www.siba.fi/sibeliuscompetition
Contact: Mr Harri Pohjolainen, Competition Secretary

The International Jean Sibelius Violin Competition is organised by the Sibelius Society. The first competition was held in 1965 to mark the 100th anniversary of the Maestro's birth.

Jean Sibelius International Violin Competition

Subjects: Musical performance on the violin.
Purpose: To recognise and reward exceptional young violinists.
Eligibility: Open to violinists of any nationality born in 1975 or later.
Level of Study: Unrestricted.
Type: Prize.
Value: The first prize is €20,000, the second prize is €15,000, the third prize is €10,000 plus five prizes of €2,000.
Frequency: Every five years.
Country of Study: Any country.
No. of awards offered: Eight.
Application Procedure: Applicants must refer to the competition brochure for the rules, application forms and programme which is published in May of the preceding year. The brochure will be sent to schools around the world, but can also be sent directly on request. Applicants should contact the competition Secretary.
Closing Date: August 18th.
Funding: Government.
Contributor: The Ministry of Education.
No. of awards given last year: 12.
No. of applicants last year: 121.
Additional Information: For further information please contact the Competition Secretary.

JEWISH COMMUNITY CENTERS ASSOCIATION (JCC)

15 East, 26th Street, New York, NY 10010-1579, United States of America
Tel: (1) 212 532 4949 ext. 246
Fax: (1) 212 481 4174
Email: info@jcca.org
www: http://www.jccworks.com
Contact: Ms Naomi Marks, Scholarships Co-ordinator

The Jewish Community Centers Association (JCCA) of North America is the leadership network of, and central agency for, over 275 Jewish Community Centers, YM-YWHAs and camps in the United States and Canada, which annually serve more than one million members. The Association offers a wide range of services and resources to enable its affiliates to provide educational, cultural and recreational programmes to enhance the lives of North American Jewry. The JCC Association is also the United States government accredited agency for serving the religious and social needs of Jewish military personnel, their families and patients, in Virginia hospitals through JWB Chaplains Council.

JCC Association Scholarships

Subjects: Social work, Jewish education, health, physical education, recreation, education and non-profit business administration.
Purpose: To provide scholarships for graduate study at the Master's level in areas leading to full-time professional employment at a Jewish Community Center.
Eligibility: Open to applicants who have obtained a BA (Honours) Degree with a grade point average of at least 3.0 and a strong commitment to the Jewish Community Center Movement. It is preferred that applicants have knowledge of Jewish community practises, customs, rituals and organisation.
Level of Study: Graduate.
Type: Scholarship.
Value: Up to US$10,000 for tuition costs.
Length of Study: One year, renewable for one extra year based on satisfactory academic performance.
Frequency: Annual.
Country of Study: United States of America or Canada.
No. of awards offered: 8-10.
Application Procedure: Applicants must submit an application, reference letters, personal statement and transcripts. Application forms and information are available on the website.
Closing Date: February 1st.
Funding: Private.
No. of awards given last year: Eight.
No. of applicants last year: 50.
Additional Information: Candidates must make the commitment of working at a JCC following completion of graduate work.

JEWISH FOUNDATION FOR EDUCATION OF WOMEN

135 East, 64th Street, New York, NY 10021, United States of America
Tel: (1) 212 288 3931
Fax: (1) 212 288 5798
Email: fdnscholar@aol.com
www: http://www.jfew.org
Contact: Ms Marge Goldwater, Executive Director

The Jewish Foundation for Education of Women is a private, non sectarian organisation. It provides scholarship assistance for higher education to women with financial need within a 50 mile radius of New York City through several specific programmes.

Fellowship Programme for Émigrés Pursuing Careers in Jewish Education

Subjects: Religious education and Jewish studies.
Purpose: To provide fellowships for graduate work to women who are interested in pursuing careers in Jewish education.
Eligibility: Women must be residents of New York city or a 50 mile radius thereof. Students entering or enrolled in full-time rabbinical and

cantorial programmes, or Master's and doctoral programmes in Jewish education or Jewish studies are eligible.
Level of Study: Doctorate, Graduate, Professional development.
Type: Fellowship.
Value: US$10,000-20,000 per year.
Length of Study: Two years for the Master's degree and four years for the rabbinical, cantorial programmes and PhD.
Frequency: Annual.
Country of Study: United States of America.
No. of awards offered: 5-10.
Application Procedure: Applicants must request an application in writing or by email. In the application request the candidate must indicate their current educational status and the programme for which financial aid is required.
Closing Date: March 15th.
Funding: Private.
Additional Information: The Foundation also provides recipients with the opportunity to meet with the programme supervisor for enriched learning on a monthly basis and to productively share experiences as a means of learning how to teach more effectively.

Scholarships for Émigrés in the Health Professions

Subjects: Medicine, dentistry, nursing, pharmacy, occupational therapy, physical therapy, physician assistant and dental hygiene.
Eligibility: Applicants must be female émigrés from the former Soviet Union, who live within a 50 mile radius of New York city and demonstrate financial need.
Level of Study: Graduate.
Type: Scholarship.
Value: US$5,000 per year.
Frequency: Annual.
Study Establishment: Schools within a 50 mile radius of New York City.
Country of Study: United States of America.
No. of awards offered: Approx. 80.
Application Procedure: Applicants must request an application in writing or email the Federation Scholar. Application forms are available in late October.
Closing Date: May 15th.
Funding: Private.

JILA (FORMERLY JOINT INSTITUTE FOR LABORATORY ASTROPHYSICS)

440 UCB, University of Colorado, Boulder, CO 80309-0440, United States of America
Tel: (1) 303 492 7789
Fax: (1) 303 492 5235
Email: jilavf@jila.colorado.edu
www: http://jilawww.colorado.edu
Contact: Programme Assistant

JILA's interests at present are research and applications in the fields of laser technology, opto-electronics, precision measurement, surface science and semiconductors, information and image processing, and materials and process science, as well as basic research in atomic, molecular and optical physics, precision measurement, gravitational physics, chemical physics, astrophysics, and geophysical measurements. To provide an opportunity for persons actively contributing to these fields, JILA operates the Visiting Fellowship Programme as well as the Postdoctoral Research Associate Programme.

JILA Postdoctoral Research Associateship and Visiting Fellowships

Subjects: Natural sciences.
Purpose: To support additional training beyond the PhD and sabbatical research.
Eligibility: There are no restrictions other than those which might be required by the grant which supports the research.
Level of Study: Postdoctorate, Professional development.
Type: Fellowship.
Value: Varies.

Length of Study: Visiting Fellowships are for between 4 and 12 months. Postdoctoral Research Associateships are for one year or more.
Frequency: Annual.
Country of Study: United States of America.
No. of awards offered: Varies.
Application Procedure: Applicants must complete an application form available from the website.
Funding: Government.
Contributor: Varies.

JOHN CARTER BROWN LIBRARY AT BROWN UNIVERSITY

Box 1894, Providence, RI 02912, United States of America
Tel: (1) 401 863 2725
Fax: (1) 401 863 3477
Email: jcbl_fellowships@brown.edu
www: http://www.jcbl.org
Contact: Ms Nan Sumner-Mack, Programme Administration

The John Carter Brown Library, an independently funded and administered institution for advanced research in history and the humanities, is located on the campus of Brown University. The Library supports research focused on the colonial history of the Americas, including all aspects of the European, African and Native American involvement.

Alexander O Vietor Memorial Fellowship

Subjects: European and American maritime history between 1450 and 1800.
Purpose: To assist students conducting research into early maritime history.
Eligibility: Open to Scholars engaged in predoctoral, postdoctoral or independent research. Graduate students must have passed their preliminary or general examinations at the time of application.
Level of Study: Doctorate, Postdoctorate, Predoctorate.
Type: Fellowship.
Value: US$1,400 per month.
Length of Study: Two-four months.
Frequency: Annual.
Country of Study: United States of America.
No. of awards offered: One.
Application Procedure: Applicants must complete an application form. Candidates should write to or email the Director.
Closing Date: January 15th.
Funding: Private.
No. of awards given last year: One.
Additional Information: Further information is available on request.

Barbara S Mosbacher Fellowship

Subjects: All aspects of the discovery, exploration, settlement and development of the new world and the related history of Europe and Africa prior to 1825.
Purpose: To assist Scholars in any area of research related to the Library's holdings.
Eligibility: Open to Scholars engaged in predoctoral, postdoctoral or independent research. Graduate students must have passed their preliminary or general examinations at the time of application.
Level of Study: Postdoctorate, Predoctorate, Research.
Type: Fellowship.
Value: US$1,400 per month.
Length of Study: Two-four months.
Frequency: Annual.
Country of Study: United States of America.
No. of awards offered: Varies.
Application Procedure: Applicants must complete an application form. Candidates should write to or email the Director.
Closing Date: January 15th.
Funding: Private.
No. of awards given last year: One.
Additional Information: Further information is available on request.

Center for New World Comparative Studies Fellowship

Subjects: The early history of the Americas from the late fifteenth-century to 1830 and all aspects of the discovery, exploration, settlements and development of the new world.

Purpose: To enable research with a definite comparative dimension relating to the history of the Americas prior to 1825.

Eligibility: Open to Scholars engaged in predoctoral, postdoctoral or independent research. Graduate students must have passed their preliminary or general examinations at the time of application.

Level of Study: Doctorate, Postdoctorate, Predoctorate.

Type: Fellowship.

Value: US$1,400 per month.

Length of Study: Two-four months.

Frequency: Annual.

Country of Study: United States of America.

No. of awards offered: Two.

Application Procedure: Applicants must complete an application form. Candidates should write to or email the Director.

Closing Date: January 15th.

Funding: Private.

No. of awards given last year: One.

Charles H Watts Memorial Fellowship

Subjects: All aspects of the discovery, exploration, settlement and development of the new world and the related history of Europe and Africa prior to 1825.

Purpose: To assist Scholars in any area of research related to the Librarys holdings.

Eligibility: Open to Scholars engaged in predoctoral, postdoctoral or independent research. Graduate students must have passed their preliminary or general examinations at the time of application.

Level of Study: Postdoctorate, Predoctorate, Research.

Type: Fellowship.

Value: US$1,400 per month.

Length of Study: Two-four months.

Frequency: Annual.

Country of Study: United States of America.

No. of awards offered: Varies.

Application Procedure: Applicants must complete an application form. Candidates should write to or email the Director.

Closing Date: January 15th.

Funding: Private.

No. of awards given last year: One.

Helen Watson Buckner Memorial Fellowship

Subjects: All aspects of the discovery, exploration, settlement and development of the New World and the related history of Europe and Africa prior to 1825.

Purpose: To assist Scholars in any area of research related to the Librarys holdings.

Eligibility: Open to Scholars engaged in predoctoral, postdoctoral or independent research. Graduate students must have passed their preliminary or general examinations at the time of application.

Level of Study: Postdoctorate, Predoctorate, Research.

Type: Fellowship.

Value: US$1,400 per month.

Length of Study: Two-four months.

Country of Study: United States of America.

No. of awards offered: Varies.

Application Procedure: Applicants must complete an application form. Candidates should write to or email the Director.

Closing Date: January 15th.

Funding: Private.

No. of awards given last year: One.

Additional Information: Further information is available on request.

JCB William Reese Company Fellowship

Subjects: The discovery, exploration, settlement and development of the new world and the related history of Europe and Africa prior to 1825.

Purpose: To enable the study of American bibliography and the history of the book in the Americas.

Eligibility: Open to Scholars engaged in predoctoral, postdoctoral or independent research. Graduate students must have passed their preliminary or general examinations at the time of application.

Level of Study: Postdoctorate, Predoctorate, Research.

Type: Fellowship.

Value: US$1,400 per month.

Length of Study: Two-four months.

Frequency: Annual.

No. of awards offered: One.

Application Procedure: Applicants must contact the organisation for details.

Closing Date: January 15th.

Funding: Commercial.

No. of awards given last year: 25.

No. of applicants last year: 46.

Jeannette D Black Memorial Fellowship

Subjects: The early history of the Americas from the late fifteenth-century to 1830 and all aspects of the discovery, exploration, settlements and development of the new world.

Purpose: To enable research into the history of cartography or a closely related area.

Eligibility: Open to Scholars engaged in predoctoral, postdoctoral or independent research. Graduate students must have passed their preliminary or general examinations at the time of application.

Level of Study: Doctorate, Postdoctorate, Predoctorate.

Type: Fellowship.

Value: US$1,400 per month.

Length of Study: Two-four months.

Frequency: Annual.

Country of Study: United States of America.

No. of awards offered: One.

Application Procedure: Applicants must write to or email the Director.

Closing Date: January 15th.

Funding: Private.

No. of awards given last year: One.

John Carter Brown Library at Brown University Long Term Fellowships

Subjects: All aspects of the discovery, exploration, settlement and development of the new world, including the related history of Europe and Africa prior to 1825.

Purpose: To assist Scholars in any area of research related to the Librarys holdings.

Eligibility: Open to American citizens or those who have been resident in the United States of America for three years immediately preceding the term of the fellowship. Those living within commuting distance, classed as within approx. 50 miles of the library, are ordinarily not eligible for JCB fellowships.

Level of Study: Postdoctorate, Research.

Type: Fellowship.

Value: US$3,500 per month.

Length of Study: 5-10 months.

Frequency: Annual.

Study Establishment: The John Carter Brown Library.

Country of Study: United States of America.

No. of awards offered: Approx. four.

Application Procedure: Applicants must complete an application form. Candidates should write to or email the Director.

Closing Date: January 15th.

Funding: Government, Private.

Contributor: The Andrew W Mellon Foundation and the National Endowment for the Humanities.

No. of awards given last year: Four.

No. of applicants last year: 14.

Additional Information: Recipients are expected to relocate to Providence and be in continuous residence at the John Carter Brown Library for the entire term of the award.

Library Associates Fellowship

Subjects: All aspects of the discovery, exploration, settlement and development of the new world and the related history of Europe and Africa prior to 1825.

Purpose: To assist Scholars in any area of research related to the Librarys holdings.
Eligibility: Open to Scholars engaged in predoctoral, postdoctoral or independent research. Graduate students must have passed their preliminary or general examinations at the time of application.
Level of Study: Postdoctorate, Predoctorate, Research.
Type: Fellowship.
Value: US$1,400 per month.
Length of Study: Two-four months.
Frequency: Annual.
Country of Study: United States of America.
No. of awards offered: One.
Application Procedure: Applicants must complete an application form. Candidates should write to or email the Director.
Closing Date: January 15th.
Funding: Private.
Contributor: Associates of the John Carter Brown Library.
Additional Information: Further information is available on request.

Maria Elena Cassiet Fellowships

Subjects: The history of the colonial period of the Americas.
Purpose: To sponsor historical research relating to Spanish America.
Eligibility: Open to Scholars who are permanent residents of countries in Spanish America only and who are engaged in predoctoral, postdoctoral or independent research. Graduate students must have passed their preliminary or general examinations at the time of application.
Level of Study: Postdoctorate, Predoctorate, Research.
Type: Fellowship.
Value: US$1,400 per month.
Length of Study: Two-four months.
Frequency: Annual.
Study Establishment: The John Carter Brown Library.
Country of Study: United States of America.
No. of awards offered: One-two.
Application Procedure: Applicants must complete an application form. Candidates should write to or email the Director.
Closing Date: January 15th.
Funding: Private.
No. of awards given last year: One.

Paul W McQuillen Memorial Fellowship

Subjects: All aspects of the discovery, exploration, settlement and development of the new world and the related history of Europe and Africa prior to 1825.
Purpose: To assist scholars in any area of research related to the Librarys holdings.
Eligibility: Open to Scholars engaged in predoctoral, postdoctoral or independent research. Graduate students must have passed their preliminary or general examinations at the time of application.
Level of Study: Postdoctorate, Predoctorate, Research.
Type: Fellowship.
Value: US$1,400 per month.
Length of Study: Two-four months.
Frequency: Annual.
Country of Study: United States of America.
No. of awards offered: Varies.
Application Procedure: Applicants must complete an application form. Candidates should write to or email the Director.
Closing Date: January 15th.
Funding: Private.
No. of awards given last year: One.
Additional Information: Further information is available on request.

Ruth and Lincoln Ekstrom Fellowship

Subjects: The history of women and the family in the Americas prior to 1825, including the question of cultural influences on gender formation.
Purpose: To sponsor historical research.

Eligibility: Open to Scholars engaged in predoctoral, postdoctoral or independent research. Graduate students must have passed their preliminary or general examinations at the time of application.
Level of Study: Postdoctorate, Predoctorate, Research.
Type: Fellowship.
Value: US$1,400 a month.
Length of Study: Two-four months.
Frequency: Annual.
Country of Study: United States of America.
No. of awards offered: One-two.
Application Procedure: Applicants must complete an application form. Candidates should write to or email the Director.
Closing Date: January 15th.
Funding: Private.
No. of awards given last year: One.
Additional Information: Further information is available on request.

Touro National Heritage Trust Fellowship

Subjects: Some aspect of the Jewish experience in the Western hemisphere pre-1830.
Purpose: To sponsor historical research.
Eligibility: Open to graduates of any nationality engaged in predoctoral, postdoctoral or independent research. Applicants must have passed their preliminary or general examinations at the time of application.
Level of Study: Doctorate, Postdoctorate, Predoctorate.
Type: Fellowship.
Value: US$1,400 per month.
Length of Study: Two-four months.
Frequency: Annual.
Country of Study: United States of America.
No. of awards offered: One.
Application Procedure: Applicants must complete and submit an application form. Candidates should write to or email the Director.
Closing Date: January 15th.
Funding: Private.
No. of awards given last year: One.
Additional Information: The Touro Fellow will be selected by an academic committee consisting of representatives from Brown University, the American Jewish Historical Society, Brandeis University, the Newport Historical Society and the John Carter Brown Library, as well as a representative of the Executive Committee of the Touro National Heritage Trust. The Touro Fellow must be prepared to participate in symposia or other academic activities organised by these institutions and may be called upon to deliver one or two public lectures.

JOHN DOUGLAS FRENCH ALZHEIMER'S FOUNDATION (JDFAF)

11620 Wiltshire Boulavard, Suite 270, Los Angeles, CA 90025, United States of America
Tel: (1) 310 445 4654
Fax: (1) 310 479 0516
www: http://www.jdfaf.org
Contact: Fellowship Administrator

French Foundation Fellowships

Subjects: Alzheimer's disease.
Purpose: To aid the development of young scientists with demonstrated promise for a research career in Alzheimer's disease.
Eligibility: Candidates who are more than six research years out from a PhD or residency are not ordinarily eligible.
Level of Study: Postdoctorate.
Type: Fellowship.
Value: US$35,000.
Length of Study: A maximum of two years.
Frequency: Annual.
Country of Study: Any country.
No. of awards offered: One.
Application Procedure: Applicants must complete an application form, available from the website.
Closing Date: November 1st.

JOHN E FOGARTY INTERNATIONAL CENTER (FIC) FOR ADVANCED STUDY IN THE HEALTH SCIENCES

Division of International Training & Research Building 31, Room B2C39, Fogarty International Center, 31 Center Drive, MSC 2220, Bethesda, MD 20892, United States of America
Tel: (1) 301 496 1653
Fax: (1) 301 402 0779
Email: ficinfo@nih.gov
www: http://www.nih.gov/fic/programs.html
Contact: Program Officer

The John E Fogarty International Center (FIC) for Advanced Study in the Health Sciences, a component of the National Institutes of Health (NIH), promotes international co-operation in the biomedical and behavioural sciences. This is accomplished primarily through long and short-term fellowships, small grants and training grants. This compendium of international opportunities is prepared by the FIC with the hope that it will stimulate scientists to seek research enhancing experiences abroad.

AIDS International Training and Research Programme (AITRP)

Subjects: Biomedical and behavioural research related to AIDS.
Purpose: To enable scientists from developing countries to increase their proficiency to undertake biomedical and behavioural research related to AIDS and HIV, related TB infections and to develop these acquired skills in clinical trials, prevention and related research.
Eligibility: Decisions about whom to accept for training are made by the programme directors. All current programme directors have developed collaborative activities with specific countries. The relevant United States programme director should be contacted for country specific information, necessary qualifications, eligibility and application procedures. Scientists from the participating countries are eligible to apply for these training programmes.
Level of Study: Research.
Type: Research grant.
Frequency: Annual.
No. of awards offered: Varies.
Application Procedure: Applications are accepted from United States institutions in response to a specific request for applications. Individuals who wish to become trainees must apply to the project director of an awarded grant. Application forms are available from the website.
Funding: Government.

Fogarty International Research Collaboration Award (FIRCA)

Subjects: Biomedical and behavioural sciences.
Purpose: To foster international research partnerships between NIH supported United States scientists and their collaborators in regions of the developing world.
Eligibility: Open to principal investigators of a United States based NIH sponsored research project grant that will be active for at least one year beyond the submission date of the FIRCA application. It is also open to scientists affiliated with public and private research institutions in Africa, Asia, (except Japan, Singapore, South Korea and Taiwan), Central and Eastern Europe, Russia and the Newly Independent States of the Former Soviet Union, Latin America and the non United States Caribbean, the Middle East and the Pacific Islands except Australia and New Zealand. The United States scientist will apply as principal investigator with a colleague from a single laboratory or research site in an eligible country.
Level of Study: Unrestricted.
Type: Research grant.
Value: Up to US$32,000 in direct costs per year are available for up to three years. Additional funds are available for the purchase of supplies and equipment necessary to the collaborative research project, for the foreign collaborator's laboratory only, funds for travel for the United

States principal investigator, the foreign collaborator and/or their research associates. In addition up to US$2,000 is allowed for conference travel for the foreign collaborator. No salaries are offered under these awards, but a stipend of up to US$5,000 may be allocated for the foreign collaborator, if justified.
Length of Study: One-three years.
Frequency: Three times each year.
Study Establishment: The foreign collaborator's research site.
Country of Study: Other.
No. of awards offered: Approx. 35 depending on funds available.
Application Procedure: Applicants must submit applications on the grant application form PHS 398. Special instructions and conditions apply. Please refer to the website for further information.
Closing Date: March 25th, July 25th or November 25th.
Funding: Government.

HIV-AIDS and Related Illnesses Collaboration Award (AIDS-FIRCA)

Subjects: HIV and AIDS research
Purpose: To support co-operative research between NIH grant recipients and foreign institutions throughout the world.
Eligibility: Open to principal investigators of a United States based NIH sponsored research project grant that will be active during the proposed grant award period. The award is also open to scientists affiliated with public and private research institutions in other countries, who serve as co-investigators.
Type: Grant.
Value: Up to US$32,000 in direct costs per year, for a maximum of three years to support direct costs. Funds are also available for supplies and equipment necessary to support the collaborative studies at the foreign and United States sites and for travel for the principal investigator, the foreign collaborator and/or their research associates. In addition, up to US$2,000 is allowed for conference travel for a foreign collaborator from a developing country. No salaries are offered under these awards, but a stipend of up to US$50,000 may be allocated for a foreign collaborator from a developing country, if required.
Length of Study: Up to three years.
Application Procedure: Applicants must refer to the website for further information and application details.
Closing Date: September 1st, January 2nd or May 1st.

John E Fogarty International Research Scientist Development Award

Subjects: Medical research.
Purpose: To forge working relationships between future heads of health research programmes in the United States of America and established researchers in developing countries that will lead to ongoing collaborations in the study of health problems of mutual interest.
Eligibility: Applicants must be American citizens or permanent residents, have a doctoral or medical degree, or the equivalent, in a health science field earned within the last seven years. Applicants must have a demonstrated commitment and competence in health research, and have an invitation from a sponsor affiliated with an internationally recognised research facility in Africa, Asia (except Japan, Singapore, South Korea and Taiwan), Central and Eastern Europe, Russia and the Newly Independent States of the Former Soviet Union, Latin America and the non United States Caribbean, the Middle East and the Pacific Islands except Australia and New Zealand. Applications to work in institutions in Sub-Saharan Africa are especially encouraged. Applicants must have a United States sponsor or mentor at a research institution with ongoing collaborative research funding in one of the eligible countries listed above.
Value: Up to US$50,000 based on the level of experience, an allowance of up to US$20,000 for materials and an administrative supplement of up to US$20,000 during the third year if the candidate is promoted to junior faculty status upon return. An economy class round trip airfare is also provided.
Application Procedure: Applicants must refer to the website for further information and application forms.
Closing Date: February 13th.

JOHN F AND ANNA LEE STACEY SCHOLARSHIP FUND

c/o National Cowboy Hall of Fame, 1700 North East 63rd Street, Oklahoma City, OK 73111, United States of America
Tel: (1) 405 478 2250
Email: emuno@nationalcowboymuseum.org
Contact: Mr Ed Muno

In accordance with the will of the late Anna Lee Stacey, a trust fund has been created for the education of young men and women who aim to make art their profession.

John F and Anna Lee Stacey Scholarships
Subjects: Painting and drawing in the classical tradition of western culture.
Purpose: To foster a high standard in the study of form, colour, drawing, painting, design, and technique, as these are expressed in modes showing patent affinity with the classical tradition of western culture.
Eligibility: Open to United States citizens only of 18-35 years of age who are skilled in, and devoted to, the classical or conservative tradition of Western culture.
Level of Study: Postgraduate.
Type: Scholarship.
Value: A total of approx. US$5,000.
Length of Study: One year.
Frequency: Annual.
Country of Study: Any country.
No. of awards offered: One-Five.
Application Procedure: Applicants must complete and submit an application form with up to 10 35mm slides of their work. Slides and completed application forms should be sent by United States mail, not rail or air express. Applicants should also enclose a recent photograph, a letter outlining plans and objectives and at least four letters of reference. No more than 10 slides.
Closing Date: February 1st.
Funding: Private.
Contributor: A bequest from the John F and Anna Lee Stacey Foundation.
No. of awards given last year: Five.
No. of applicants last year: 100.
Additional Information: The Committee does not maintain storage facilities, so applicants must not send slides or any materials before October 1st. Each successful competitor will be required to submit a brief quarterly report together with 35mm slides of their work and a more complete report at the termination of the scholarship.

JOHN SIMON GUGGENHEIM MEMORIAL FOUNDATION

90 Park Avenue, New York, NY 10016, United States of America
Tel: (1) 212 687 4470
Fax: (1) 212 697 3248
Email: fellowships@gf.org
www: http://www.gf.org
Contact: Assistant Secretary

The John Simon Guggenheim Memorial Foundation is concerned with encouraging and supporting scholars and artists to engage in research in any field of knowledge and creation within the arts. The Foundation was established by United States Senator Simon Guggenheim and his wife as a memorial to their son who died April 26th, 1922.

Guggenheim Fellowships to Assist Research and Artistic Creation (Latin America and the Caribbean)
Subjects: Sciences, humanities, social sciences and creative arts.
Purpose: To further the development of scholars and artists by assisting them to engage in research in any field of knowledge and creation in any of the arts, under the freest possible conditions irrespective of race, colour or creed.
Eligibility: Open to citizens and permanent residents of countries of Latin America and the Caribbean who have demonstrated an exceptional capacity for productive scholarship or exceptional creative ability in the arts.
Level of Study: Postdoctorate, Professional development.
Type: Fellowship.
Value: Grants will be adjusted to the needs of Fellows, taking into consideration their other resources and the purpose and scope of their plans. The average grant in 2003 was US$31,081.
Length of Study: Ordinarily for one year, but in no instance for a period shorter than six consecutive months.
Frequency: Annual.
Country of Study: Any country.
No. of awards offered: 37 in 2003.
Application Procedure: Applicants must complete an application form. Further information is available on the Foundation's website.
Closing Date: December 1st.
Funding: Private.
Contributor: The Foundation.
No. of awards given last year: 37 in 2003.
No. of applicants last year: 737.
Additional Information: Members of the teaching profession receiving sabbatical leave on full or part salary are eligible for appointment, as are holders of other fellowships and of appointments at research centres. Fellowships are awarded by the Trustees upon nominations made by a committee of selection.

Guggenheim Fellowships to Assist Research and Artistic Creation (USA and Canada)
Subjects: Sciences, humanities, social sciences and creative arts.
Purpose: To further the development of scholars and artists by assisting them to engage in research in any field of knowledge and creation in any of the arts, under the freest possible conditions irrespective of race, colour or creed.
Eligibility: Open to citizens and permanent residents of the United States of America and Canada who have demonstrated an exceptional capacity for productive scholarship or exceptional creative ability in the arts.
Level of Study: Postdoctorate, Professional development.
Typo: Fellowship
Value: Grants will be adjusted to the needs of Fellows taking into consideration their other resources and the purpose and scope of their plans. The average grant in 2003 was US$36,685.
Length of Study: Ordinarily for one year, but in no instance for a period shorter than six consecutive months.
Frequency: Annual.
Country of Study: Any country.
No. of awards offered: 184 in 2003.
Application Procedure: Applicants must complete an application form. Further information is available on the Foundation's website.
Closing Date: October 1st.
Funding: Private.
Contributor: The Foundation.
No. of awards given last year: 184 in 2003.
No. of applicants last year: 282.
Additional Information: Members of the teaching profession receiving sabbatical leave on full or part salary are eligible for appointment, as are holders of other fellowships and of appointments at research centres. Fellowships are awarded by the Trustees upon nominations made by a committee of selection.

JOHNS HOPKINS UNIVERSITY

Bloomberg School of Public Health, Center for Alternatives to Animal Testing, 111 Market Place, Suite 840, Baltimore, MD 21202, United States of America
Tel: (1) 410 223 1692
Fax: (1) 410 223 1603
Email: caat@jhsph.edu
www: http://caat.jhsph.edu
Contact: Grants Co-ordinator

The vision of the Johns Hopkins Center for Alternatives to Animal Testing is to be a leading force in the development and use of reduction, refinement and replacement alternatives in research, testing and education to protect and enhance the health of the public.

CAAT Research Grants

Subjects: Alternatives to current testing methods to replace, reduce and refine the use of animals.
Purpose: To serve as starter grants.
Eligibility: There are no eligibility restrictions.
Level of Study: Unrestricted.
Type: Research grant.
Value: A maximum of US$20,000.
Length of Study: One year.
Frequency: Annual.
Country of Study: United States of America.
No. of awards offered: Approx. 12.
Application Procedure: Applicants must complete a preproposal. After review, those which are applicable are invited to submit a full application.
Closing Date: The preproposal deadline is March 15th
Funding: Private.
No. of awards given last year: 12.
No. of applicants last year: 30.

JOSEPH COLLINS FOUNDATION

787 7th Avenue, Room 3950, New York, NY 10019-6099, United States of America
Fax: (1) 212 728 8111
Contact: Secretary & Treasurer

The Joseph Collins Foundation was established in 1951 as the result of a bequest by the late Dr Joseph Collins, physician and pioneer neurologist, for the purpose of allowing needy medical students to complete their medical education with an MD degree without sacrificing all other interests in the broad field of learning.

Joseph Collins Foundation Grants

Subjects: Medicine.
Purpose: To aid needy medical students with broad cultural interests who wish to receive an adequate medical education and obtain an MD degree without sacrificing other interests.
Eligibility: Open to anyone attending an accredited medical school in the United States of America, located east of the Mississippi River, who intends to specialise in neurology, psychiatry or general practice. Applicants must have successfully completed their first year at an accredited medical school. No grants are available to students attending medical schools West of the Mississippi River. Awards are not made to pre-medical or postgraduate medical students or to chiropractor, osteopathic or podiatry students.
Level of Study: Postgraduate.
Type: Grant.
Value: Varies, up to a maximum of US$10,000 annually, to be used towards tuition.
Length of Study: One year, renewable at the discretion of the Foundation.
Study Establishment: Any accredited medical school, located east of the Mississippi River.
Country of Study: United States of America.
No. of awards offered: Varies.
Application Procedure: Applicants must complete an application form, available to accredited medical schools upon request by the medical school authorities. Applicants must obtain and return application forms from the medical school authorities for forwarding to the Foundation. Application forms must be accompanied by a separate letter from the Dean or other officer of the medical school, approving the application on the basis of qualification, merit and need. This letter must contain a specific recommendation as to the amount of financial assistance required by the student to enter or continue in medical school.
Funding: Private.

JUNE BAKER TRUST

5 Forest Road, Kintore, Aberdeenshire, AB51 0US, Scotland
Tel: (44) 1467 632337
Email: ramseyph@lineone.net
Contact: Mrs Priscilla Ramsey, Chairman

June Baker collected, refurbished and arranged a collection of artefacts in her domestic environment. In 1990 her friends established the Trust, in memory of her life and death, to help individuals in the conservation of historic and artistic artefacts in Scotland, or those training with the intention to do so.

June Baker Trust Awards

Subjects: Conservation of historic and artistic artefacts.
Purpose: To assist with travel, training and equipment.
Eligibility: Open to individuals from Scotland working or training in conservation in Scotland.
Type: Grant.
Value: Up to UK£500 towards travel, training and purchase of equipment.
Frequency: Annual.
Country of Study: Scotland.
No. of awards offered: One-Four.
Application Procedure: Applicants must complete an application form, available from the Chairman.
Closing Date: June 1st.
Funding: Private.
Contributor: Trust investments.
No. of awards given last year: Three.
No. of applicants last year: Eight.
Additional Information: Applicants must work, or intend to work in Scotland.

KAY KENDALL LEUKAEMIA FUND

Allington House, 1st Floor, 150 Victoria Street, London, SW1E 5AE, England
Tel: (44) 20 7410 7045
Fax: (44) 20 7410 0332
Email: liz.storer@sfct.org
Contact: Ms Elizabeth Storer, Trust Secretary

Kay Kendall Leukaemia Fund Research Fellowship

Subjects: Aspects of leukaemia or relevant studies on related haematological malignancies.
Purpose: To encourage researchers new to the field of leukaemia research to submit applications on their own account.
Eligibility: Open to applicants of any nationality but intending to work mainly in the United Kingdom. Applicants must hold a recognised higher degree but need not be medically qualified.
Level of Study: Postdoctorate.
Type: Fellowship.
Value: Salary and laboratory expenses.
Length of Study: Three years.
Frequency: Annual.
Country of Study: United Kingdom.
No. of awards offered: Two-three.
Application Procedure: Applicants must submit a research proposal form and support from the intended United Kingdom institution.
Closing Date: January.
Funding: Private.
No. of awards given last year: Two.
Additional Information: Further information is available on request.

KAZAN STATE TECHNICAL UNIVERSITY (KSTU)

10 K Marx Street, Kazan, Tatarstan 420111, Russia
Tel: (7) 843 238 5044
Fax: (7) 843 236 6032
Email: agishev@kai.ru
www: http://www.kai.ru
Contact: Professor Ravil R Agishev, Head of International Co-operation

The Kazan State Technical University (KSTU) aims to support joint international research projects relating to scientific and technical issues, as well as training a young generation of local scientists and technicians.

KSTU Rector's Grant

Subjects: Scientific research.
Purpose: To support joint research on scientific and technical issues and to invite eligible applicants to deliver lectures on new scientific branches of mutual interest.
Eligibility: Applicants must be proficient in Russian or English, have a PhD or DSc and not be more than 45 years of age.
Level of Study: Postdoctorate, Professional development.
Type: Research grant.
Value: US$1,500 plus the monthly loan of the KSTU Professor.
Length of Study: Three-six months.
Frequency: Annual.
Study Establishment: KSTU.
Country of Study: Russia.
No. of awards offered: Two.
Application Procedure: Applicants must complete an application form. An abstract must also be submitted including four pages of curriculum vitae with research aims and recommendations from three professors.
Closing Date: August 31st.
Funding: Government.
No. of awards given last year: 2.
No. of applicants last year: 11.

KENNAN INSTITUTE FOR ADVANCED RUSSIAN STUDIES

Woodrow Wilson International Center for Scholars, One Woodrow Wilson Plaza, 1300 Pennsylvania Avenue North West, Washington, DC 20004-3027, United States of America
Tel: (1) 202 691 4100
Fax: (1) 202 691 4247
Email: kiars@wwic.si.edu
www: http://www.wilsoncenter.org
Contact: Ms Jennifer Giglio, Program Associate

The Kennan Institute for Advanced Russian Studies sponsors advanced research on the successor states to the USSR, and encourages Eurasian studies with its public lecture and publication programmes, maintaining contact with scholars and research centres abroad. The Institute seeks to function as a forum where the scholarly community can interact with public policymakers.

Kennan Institute Research Scholarship

Subjects: Social sciences and humanities. Research proposals examining topics in Eurasian studies are eligible, with those topics relating to regional Russia, the NIS and contemporary issues especially welcome.
Purpose: To offer support to junior scholars studying the former Soviet Union, allowing them time and resources in the Washington DC area to work on their first published work, or to continue their research.
Eligibility: Open to academic participants in the early stages of their career before tenure, or Scholars whose careers have been interrupted or delayed. For non academics, an equivalent degree or professional achievement is expected.
Level of Study: Postdoctorate.
Type: Scholarship.
Value: US$3,000 per month plus research facilities, word processing support and some research assistance.
Length of Study: Three-nine months.
Frequency: Dependent on funds available.
Study Establishment: The Kennan Institute.
Country of Study: Other.
No. of awards offered: Four.
Application Procedure: Applicants must complete an application form. The application must include project proposal Publications list, bibliography, biographical data and three letters of recommendation

specifically in support of the research to be conducted at the Institute. Applications received by fax or email will not be accepted.
Closing Date: All materials must be received by December 1st.
Funding: Government.
No. of awards given last year: Three.
No. of applicants last year: 25.

Kennan Institute Short Term Grants

Subjects: Eurasian studies in the social sciences and humanities.
Purpose: To support scholars in need of the academic and archival resources of the Washington DC area in order to complete their research.
Eligibility: Open to academic participants with a doctoral degree or those who have nearly completed their dissertations. For non academic participants, an equivalent level of professional development is required. Applicants can be citizens of any country, but must note their citizenship when applying.
Level of Study: Doctorate, Postdoctorate.
Type: Scholarship.
Value: US$100 per day.
Length of Study: Up to 31 days.
Frequency: Dependent on funds available.
Study Establishment: The Kennan Institute.
Country of Study: Other.
No. of awards offered: Four are available to non United States citizens and four to United States citizens.
Application Procedure: Applicants must submit a concise description of his or her research project of 700-800 words, a curriculum vitae, a statement on preferred dates of residence in Washington DC and two letters of recommendation specifically in support of the research to be conducted at the institute. No application form is required for short-term grants.
Closing Date: March 1st, June 1st, September 1st and December 1st.
Funding: Government, Private.
No. of awards given last year: 40.
No. of applicants last year: 230.

KENNEDY MEMORIAL TRUST

3 Birdcage walk, Westminster, London, SW1H 9JJ, England
Tel: (44) 20 7222 1151
Fax: (44) 20 7222 7189
www: http://www.kentrust.demon.co.uk
Contact: Ms Anna Mason, Secretary

As part of the British national memorial to President Kennedy, the Kennedy Memorial Trust awards scholarships to British postgraduate students for study at Harvard University or the Massachusetts Institute of Technology. The awards are offered annually following a national competition and cover tuition costs and a stipend to meet living expenses.

Kennedy Scholarships

Subjects: All fields of arts, science, social science or political studies.
Purpose: To enable students to undertake a course of study in the United States of America.
Eligibility: Open to resident citizens of the United Kingdom who have been wholly or mainly educated in the United Kingdom. At the time of application, candidates must have spent at least two of the last five years at a university or university college in the United Kingdom and must either have graduated by the start of tenure in the following year or have graduated not more than three years prior to the commencement of studies. No application will be considered from persons already in the United States of America. Scholarships for the study of an MBA will only be granted in exceptional circumstances and candidates must have completed two years of employment in business or public service since graduation. An independent application to Harvard or MIT is necessary.
Level of Study: Postgraduate.
Type: Scholarship.

Value: US$18,500 to cover support costs, special equipment and some travel in the United States of America, plus tuition fees and travelling expenses to and from the United States.
Length of Study: One year. In certain circumstances, students who are applying for PhD or two year Master's programmes may be considered for extra funding to help support a second year of study.
Frequency: Annual.
Study Establishment: Harvard University and the Massachusetts Institute of Technology (MIT) in Cambridge, Massachusetts.
Country of Study: United States of America.
No. of awards offered: 12.
Application Procedure: Applicants must submit a form, statement of purpose, references and a letter of endorsement from the applicant's university. Completed applications should be sent via the applicant's university.
Closing Date: November 3rd.
Funding: Private.
Contributor: Public donation.
No. of awards given last year: 10.
No. of applicants last year: 160.
Additional Information: Scholars are not required to study for a degree in the United States of America but are encouraged to do so if they are eligible and able to complete the requirements for it.

KOREA FOUNDATION

Fellowship Programme Team, Seocho PO Box 227, Diplomatic Center Building, 1376-1, Seocho-2-Dong, Seocho-gu, Seoul, 137-072, Korea, Republic (South)
Tel: (82) 2 3463 5614
Fax: (82) 2 3463 6075/6076
Email: fellow@kf.or.kr
www: http://www.kf.or.kr
Contact: Ms Hyejong Chang, Programme Officer

The Korea Foundation seeks to improve awareness and understanding of Korea worldwide as well as to foster co-operative relationships between Korea and foreign countries through a variety of exchange programmes.

Korea Foundation Advanced Research Grant

Subjects: Korean related research in the humanities and social sciences, culture and arts, and comparative research related to Korea.
Purpose: To support scholarly research and writing activities of Korean studies students during their sabbatical leave to advance scholarship in Korean studies.
Eligibility: Open to overseas Korean studies Scholars with a PhD degree in a subject related to Korea, who are currently engaged in Korea related teaching and research activities. In the case of Korean nationals, only those with foreign residency status and regular faculty positions at foreign universities are eligible to apply. Candidates who are receiving support from other programmes administered by the Korea Foundation are not eligible to receive this grant at the same time.
Level of Study: Postdoctorate, Professional development, Research.
Type: Research grant.
Value: The grant amount is designed to be flexible to satisfy the various circumstances of Korean studies scholars at different stages in their careers to supplement a scholar's sabbatical compensation.
Length of Study: 6-12 months.
Frequency: Annual.
Country of Study: Other.
Application Procedure: Applicants must complete an application form. Application forms are available from the Foundation or the website.
Closing Date: February 28th.
Additional Information: Further information is available from the website.

Korea Foundation Fellowship for Field Research

Subjects: Korean related research in the humanities and social sciences, culture and arts, and comparative research related to Korea.

Purpose: To promote Korean studies and support professional researchers in Korean studies by facilitating their research activities in Korea.
Eligibility: Open to university professors and instructors, doctoral candidates, researchers and other professionals. Candidates must be proficient in Korean or English. In the case of Korean nationals, only those with foreign residency status and regular faculty positions at foreign universities are eligible to apply. Fellows in this programme must concentrate on their research and may not enroll in any language courses or other university courses during the fellowship period. Candidates who are receiving support from other organisations or programmes administered by the Korea Foundation are not eligible to receive this fellowship at the same time.
Level of Study: Doctorate, Postdoctorate, Professional development, Research.
Type: Fellowship.
Value: The grant amount will be determined by the Foundation according to the Fellow's research experience and current position. Awards range between US$1,000 and US$1,600 monthly. The Foundation will also provide an international economy class airline ticket for round trip transportation between the airport nearest to the Fellow's residence and Korea. Travellers' insurance is also provided.
Length of Study: Three months to one year.
Frequency: Annual.
Country of Study: Korea.
No. of awards offered: Varies.
Application Procedure: Applicants must complete an application form. Application forms are available from the Foundation and the website.
Closing Date: July 31st.
No. of awards given last year: 38.
No. of applicants last year: 80.
Additional Information: Further information is available from the website.

Korea Foundation Fellowship for Graduate Studies

Subjects: Korean related research in the humanities and social sciences, culture and arts, and comparative research related to Korea.
Purpose: To promote Korean studies and foster young scholars in this field by providing graduate students majoring in Korean studies with scholarships for their coursework and/or research while enrolled at their home institutions.
Eligibility: Open to MA or PhD level students majoring in Korean studies at any university in the United States of America, Canada, Europe, Australia, New Zealand, China and Japan. Korean nationals are eligible to apply only if they have permanent residency status overseas. Candidates who are receiving support from other programmes administered by the Korea Foundation are not eligible to receive this fellowship at the same time.
Level of Study: Doctorate, Graduate, Postgraduate, Predoctorate.
Type: Scholarship.
Value: A stipend intended to cover living expenses and/or tuition costs, of an amount to be determined based on the country, region, institution and academic level of applicants.
Length of Study: One academic year.
Frequency: Annual.
Country of Study: USA, Canada, Europe, Australia, New Zealand, China, Japan.
No. of awards offered: Up to 110.
Application Procedure: Applicants must complete an application form available from the Foundation or from the website.
Closing Date: Varies according to the region. Please contact the Foundation for details.
No. of awards given last year: 20.
No. of applicants last year: 200.
Additional Information: Further information is available from the website.

Korea Foundation Fellowship for Korean Language Training

Subjects: Korean studies related to the humanities, culture and arts, social sciences or comparative research.

Purpose: To provide foreign scholars and graduate students who need systematic Korean language education with the opportunity to enroll in a Korean language programme at a language institute affiliated to a Korean university.

Eligibility: Candidates must have a basic knowledge of, and an ability to communicate in, the Korean language. In the case of Korean nationals, only those with foreign residency status are eligible to apply. Candidates who are receiving support from other organisations or programmes administered by the Korea Foundation are not eligible to receive this fellowship at the same time.

Level of Study: Graduate, Postgraduate.

Type: Fellowship.

Value: The grant amount will be determined by the Foundation according to the Fellow's academic experience and current position. Awards range between US$700 and US$850. The tuition for language training will be paid by the Foundation directly to the Korean language institute that the Foundation designates. Travel insurance is also provided. Please note that the cost of an international round trip airline ticket is not covered under this fellowship.

Length of Study: Six months, nine months or one year.

Frequency: Annual.

Study Establishment: A language institute affiliated to a Korean university.

Country of Study: Korea.

No. of awards offered: Varies.

Application Procedure: Applicants must complete an application form. Application forms are available from the Korean Foundation. Applicants must request an application form by supplying their curriculum vitae including Korean language ability and previous study of Korean.

Closing Date: May 31st.

No. of awards given last year: 64.

No. of applicants last year: 109.

Additional Information: Further information is available from the website.

Korea Foundation Postdoctoral Fellowship

Subjects: Korean related research in the humanities and social sciences, culture and arts, and comparative research related to Korea.

Purpose: To provide promising and highly qualified PhD recipients with the opportunity to conduct research at leading universities in the field of Korean studies so that they can further develop their scholarship as well as have their dissertations published as manuscripts.

Eligibility: Open to non Korean Scholars who have received a PhD degree in a subject related to Korea within five years of their application but do not currently hold a regular faculty position. Korean nationals with permanent resident status in foreign countries may apply. Candidates who are receiving support from other programmes administered by the Korea Foundation are not eligible to receive this fellowship at the same time.

Level of Study: Postdoctorate.

Type: Fellowship.

Value: A stipend support for a 12 month period, of an amount to be determined based on the country, region and institution where the fellow will conduct his or her research.

Length of Study: One year.

Frequency: Annual.

Country of Study: Any country.

No. of awards offered: Four.

Application Procedure: Applicants must complete an application form. Application forms are available from the website.

Closing Date: December 31st preceding the fellowship year.

Additional Information: Further information is available from the website.

KOSCIUSZKO FOUNDATION

15 East, 65th Street, New York, NY, 10021-6595, United States of America
Tel: (1) 212 734 2130
Fax: (1) 212 628 4552
Email: thekf@aol.com
www: http://www.kosciuszkofoundation.org
Contact: Mr Thomas J Pniewski, Director Cultural Affairs

The Kosciuszko Foundation, founded in 1925, is dedicated to promoting educational and cultural relations between the United States and Poland, and to increasing American awareness of Polish culture and history. In addition to its grants and scholarships, which total more than US$1 million annually, the Foundation presents cultural programmes including lectures, concerts and exhibitions, promoting Polish culture in the United States, and nurturing the spirit of multicultural co-operation.

Chopin Piano Competition

Subjects: Piano performance of Chopin or other composers.

Purpose: To encourage highly talented students of piano to study and play works of Chopin and other Polish composers.

Eligibility: Open to students between the ages of 16 and 22 who are United States citizens or full-time international students in the United States with a valid visa who wish to pursue a career in piano performance.

Level of Study: Unrestricted.

Type: Prize.

Value: First prize of US$2,500, a second prize of US$1,500 and a third prize of US$1,000. Scholarships may be awarded in the form of shared prizes.

Frequency: Annual.

Country of Study: United States of America.

No. of awards offered: Three.

Application Procedure: Applicants must complete an application form, available in December via the Kosciuszko Foundation's Cultural Department. Applications should be marked Chopin Piano Competition.

Closing Date: The first week of March.

Additional Information: The required repertoire is as follows: Chopin: one mazurka of the contestant's choice, two major works chosen from the following Ballades, scherzi, sonatas, f-sharp minor polonaise, a-flat major polonaise-fantasy, andante spianato and grande polonaise, barcarolle, f-minor fantasy, introduction and rondo op 16, allegro de concert, op 46, a group of 3 consecutive etudes, Szymanowski: one mazurka of the contestant's choice, a major work by Bach, excluding The Well-Tempered Clavier, a complete sonata by Beethoven, Hadyn, Mozart or Schubert, a major nineteenth-century work (including Debussy, Ravel, Prokofiev, Rachmaninoff but excluding those already mentioned) and a substantial work by an American, Polish or Polish-American composer written within the last 75 years. All works are to be complete and played from memory. The competition is held on three consecutive days in mid April.

Kosciuszko Foundation Graduate and Postgraduate Studies and Research in Poland Program

Subjects: All subjects.

Purpose: To enable American students to pursue a course of graduate or postgraduate study and research in Poland for an academic year or semester.

Eligibility: Open to United States graduate and postgraduate students who wish to pursue a course of graduate or postgraduate study and research at institutes of higher education in Poland. University faculty members who wish to spend a sabbatical pursuing research in Poland are also eligible. All entrants must have the requisite Polish language ability commensurate with the proposed research project.

Level of Study: Graduate, Postgraduate.

Type: Grant.

Value: Housing, plus a monthly stipend from the Polish Ministry in Polish currency for living expenses, and additional funding of US$250 per month from the Foundation for expenses. Transportation to and from Poland is not included.

Length of Study: One academic year or semester.

Frequency: Annual.

Country of Study: Poland.

No. of awards offered: Varies.

Application Procedure: Applicants must complete application forms, available in the Autumn by mail or from the website.

Closing Date: January 15th.

Contributor: The Foundation and the Polish Ministry of National Education.

Additional Information: Applicants must have a working knowledge of the Polish language and are reviewed based on academic background, motivation for pursuing graduate studies and/or research in Poland, and the proposal of studies and research in Poland. Applicants must have the agreement of a university and must be under the advice of a Polish university academic advisor. If the applicant is required to pay tuition for a study programme it is their responsibility to secure a tuition waiver as this grant does not cover tuition. Students must also pass a medical.

Kosciuszko Foundation Tuition Scholarships

Subjects: Polish-American related issues and activities.
Purpose: To provide financial aid to students in the United States of America and Poland.
Eligibility: Open to United States citizens of Polish descent for graduate studies in any field of study at an institution in the United States or Polish citizens who are legal permanent residents for graduate studies in any field at a United States Institute of Higher Education, or United States citizens who are pursuing a major in polish studies on graduate level. All entrants must have a grade point average of 3.0.
Level of Study: Graduate.
Type: Scholarship.
Value: US$1,000-5,000.
Length of Study: One academic year, renewable for a further academic year.
Frequency: Annual.
Country of Study: United States of America.
No. of awards offered: Varies.
Application Procedure: Applicants must write for details or visit the website.
Closing Date: January 15th.
Additional Information: Information and guidelines are available all year round. A student can receive funding through the Tuition Scholarship programme no more than twice. Only one member per immediate family may receive a Tuition Scholarship during a given academic year.

The Kosciuszko Foundation Year Abroad Program at the Jagiellonian University in Krakow

Subjects: Polish language, history, literature, and culture.
Eligibility: Open to United States citizens who are students in an MA or PhD programme, though not at the dissertation level.
Level of Study: Doctorate, Graduate, Postgraduate.
Type: Grant.
Value: Tuition and housing, plus a monthly stipend in Polish currency for living expenses from the Polish Ministry of National Education plus a monthly stipend of US$150 from the Foundation.
Length of Study: One year.
Frequency: Annual.
Study Establishment: Polonia Institute at Jagiellonian University in Krakow.
Country of Study: Poland.
No. of awards offered: Varies.
Application Procedure: Applicants must complete application forms, available in the Autumn by mail, or from the website.
Closing Date: January 16th.
No. of awards given last year: 12.
Additional Information: Candidate should mention the Year Abroad Program in their request letter. Applicants must complete a physician's certificate as part of the application procedure.

The Polish American Club of North Jersey Scholarships

Subjects: All subjects.
Purpose: To financially aid full-time graduate students in the United States.
Eligibility: Applicants must be United States citizens or permanent residents of Polish descent, active members of the Polish American Club of North Jersey, have a minimum grade point average of 3.0 and be children or grandchildren of Polish American Club of North Jersey members.
Level of Study: Postgraduate, Predoctorate.
Type: Scholarship.

Value: US$1,000.
Length of Study: One year only.
Frequency: Annual.
Country of Study: United States of America.
Application Procedure: Applicants must complete an application form, available on the website from October to the end of December, on the website with the full application procedure.
Closing Date: January 15th.
Additional Information: Only one member per immediate family may receive a Polish American Club of North Jersey Scholarship during any given academic year.

KPMG FOUNDATION

3 Chestnut Ridge Road, Montvale, NJ 07645, United States of America
Tel: (1) 201 307 7932
Fax: (1) 201 307 7093
Email: tperino@kpmg.com
www: http://www.kpmgfoundation.org
Contact: Grant Support Programme

Minority Accounting Doctoral Scholarship Program

Subjects: Accounting.
Purpose: To support African Americans, Hispanic Americans and Native Americans studying for a PhD in Accounting.
Eligibility: Candidates must be African American, Hispanic American or Native American and studying full-time for a doctorate degree in accountancy.
Level of Study: Doctorate.
Type: Scholarship.
Value: US$10,000 per year, renewable for a total of five years.
Length of Study: Up to five years.
Frequency: Annual.
Study Establishment: A full-time AACSB accredited university.
Country of Study: United States of America.
No. of awards offered: Up to 15.
Application Procedure: Applicants must visit the website for further information and application forms.
Closing Date: May 1st.
Funding: Private.
Additional Information: The awards are to be announced in May.

KURATORIUM FÜR DIE VERLEIHUNG DES HEINRICH WIELAND PREISES

Pettenkoferstraße 8a, Munich
80336, Germany
www: http://www.boehringer-ingelheim.com/corporate/home/home.asp
Contact: Professor Nepomuk Zöllner, Chairman

Heinrich Wieland Prize

Subjects: Medical sciences.
Purpose: To recognise achievements in the areas of chemistry, biochemistry, physiology and medicine of lipids.
Eligibility: Open to nationals of any country.
Level of Study: Unrestricted.
Type: Prize.
Value: €25,000 and a medal.
Frequency: Annual.
Country of Study: Any country.
No. of awards offered: One.
Application Procedure: Applications must be sent to the Chairman. They must include a curriculum vitae, bibliography, a two-three page description of recent results and copies of recent publications. German and English applications will be considered.
Closing Date: February 29th.
Funding: Commercial.
Contributor: Boehringer Ingelheim.
No. of awards given last year: One.

For further information contact:

www: http://www.boehringer-ingelheim.com/corporate/research/heinrich_wieland_prize.htm

THE KURT WEILL FOUNDATION FOR MUSIC

7 East, 20 Street, 3rd Floor, New York, NY 10003, United States of America
Tel: (1) 212 505 5240
Fax: (1) 212 353 9663
Email: kwfinfo@kwf.org
www: http://www.kwf.org
Contact: Mr Brian Butcher, Office Manager

The Kurt Weill Foundation for Music is a non-profit, private foundation chartered to preserve and perpetuate the legacies of the composer Kurt Weill (1900-1950) and his wife, singer and actress Lotte Lenya (1898-1981). The Foundation awards grants and prizes, sponsors print and online publications, maintains the Weill-Lenya Research Center and administers Weill's copyrights.

Kurt Weill Foundation for Music Grants Program
Subjects: Any subject related to the perpetuation of Kurt Weill's artistic legacy. This includes performances or recordings of his compositions in their original form, scholarly projects focusing on Kurt Weill and other related activities as outlined in the printed guidelines.
Purpose: To fund projects that aim to perpetuate Kurt Weill's artistic legacy.
Eligibility: There are no eligibility restrictions.
Level of Study: Doctorate, Postdoctorate, Postgraduate, Professional development.
Value: College and university production performances maximum US$5,000 otherwise no restrictions on requested amounts.
Frequency: Annual.
Country of Study: Any country.
No. of awards offered: Varies.
Application Procedure: Applicants must complete an application form for all but performances over US$5,000. Guidelines and forms are available from the website or from the Foundation directly.
Closing Date: November 1st. There is no deadline for professional proposals over US$5,000.
Funding: Private.

Kurt Weill Prize
Subjects: Music theatre of the twentieth-century.
Purpose: To encourage scholarship focusing on musical theatre in the twentieth-century.
Eligibility: Open to nationals of any country.
Level of Study: Unrestricted.
Type: Prize.
Value: US$2,500 for books, US$500 for articles.
Frequency: Every two years.
Country of Study: Any country.
No. of awards offered: Two.
Application Procedure: Applicants must submit five copies of their published work. Works must have been published within the two years preceding the award year.
Closing Date: April 30th.
Funding: Private.

KUWAIT FOUNDATION FOR THE ADVANCEMENT OF SCIENCE (KFAS)

PO Box 25263, Safat, Kuwait City 13113, Kuwait
Tel: (965) 242 5912
Fax: (965) 240 3912
Email: prize@kfas.org.kw
www: http://www.kfas.org
Contact: Dr Ali A Al-Shamlan, Director General

The Kuwait Foundation for the Advancement of Science (KFAS) aims to support efforts for modernisation and scientific development within Kuwait by sponsoring basic and applied research, awarding grants to support and encourage research, and awarding grants, prizes and recognition to enhance intellectual development. The KFAS also grants scholarships and fellowships for academic or training purposes, holds symposiums and scientific conferences, and encourages, supports and develops research projects and scientific programmes.

Islamic Organisation for Medical Sciences Prize
Subjects: Medical practice addressing professional and well documented clinical and laboratory experiments, appropriate documentation of Islamic medical heritage including Islamic jurisprudence.
Purpose: To support and promote scientific research in the field of Islamic medical sciences.
Level of Study: Unrestricted.
Type: Prize.
Frequency: Every two years.
No. of awards offered: Two.
Application Procedure: Nominations must be proposed by universities, scientific institutes, international organisations, individuals, past recipients of the prize and academic bodies.
Closing Date: December 31st.
Funding: Private.
Contributor: KFAS.
No. of awards given last year: No awards were given last year as the award given every two years.

KFAS Kuwait Prize
Subjects: Basic sciences, applied sciences, economics and social sciences, arts and letters, and Arabic and Islamic scientific heritage.
Purpose: To recognise the scientific achievements of outstanding Arab and Kuwaiti researchers and scientists worldwide.
Level of Study: Unrestricted.
Type: Prize.
Value: Kuwaiti dinar 30,000 which is approx. US$100,000 for each prize. The combined value of the prizes is more than US$1 million.
Frequency: Annual.
No. of awards offered: 10.
Application Procedure: Applicants must apply themselves or through non political organisations and may also be recommended by Search Committees.
Closing Date: October 31st.
Funding: Private.
Contributor: KFAS.
No. of awards given last year: 2.
No. of applicants last year: 80.
Additional Information: Further information is available on request.

L S B LEAKEY FOUNDATION

PO Box 29346, San Francisco, CA 94129-9911, United States of America
Tel: (1) 415 561 4646
Fax: (1) 415 561 4647
Email: info@leakeyfoundation.org
www: http://www.leakeyfoundation.org
Contact: Ms Cary Roloson, Grants Manager

The Leakey Foundation was formed to further research into human origins. Recent priorities include research into the environments, archaeology and human palaeontology of the Miocene, Pliocene, and Pleistocene. Other concerns are the behaviour, morphology and ecology of the great apes and other primate species when it contributes to the development or testing of models of human evolution, and the behavioural ecology of contemporary hunter gatherers.

L S B Leakey Foundation General Research Grant
Subjects: Human evolution.
Eligibility: There are no age, nationality, or residency restrictions. Research must be at least at the graduate level of studies.
Level of Study: Doctorate, Postdoctorate, Postgraduate, Research.
Type: Grant.

Value: The majority of the Foundation's general research grants to doctoral students are between US$3,000-12,000. However, larger grants, especially to postdoctoral students and senior scientists, may be funded up to US$20,000.

Length of Study: Varies with field season.

Frequency: Twice a year.

Country of Study: Any country.

No. of awards offered: Approx. 70.

Application Procedure: Applicants must complete an application form. Application guidelines and forms are available on request from the Foundation or from the website.

Closing Date: January 5th or August 15th.

Funding: Private.

Contributor: Charitable donations.

No. of awards given last year: Approx. 60.

No. of applicants last year: Approx. 160.

Additional Information: Website www.leakeyfoundation.org. E-mail grants@leakeyfoundation.org.

LA TROBE UNIVERSITY

Bundoora Campus, Melbourne, VIC 3083, Australia
Tel: (61) 3 9479 2971
Fax: (61) 3 9479 1464
Email: c.cocks@latrobe.edu.au
www: http://www.latrobe.edu.au/rgso
Contact: Scholarships & Candidature Co-ordinator

La Trobe University is one of the leading research universities in Australia. The University has internationally regarded strengths across a diverse range of disciplines. It offers a detailed and broad research training programme and provides unique access to technology transfer and collaboration with end users of its research and training via its Research and Development Park.

Australian Postgraduate Awards

Subjects: Health sciences, humanities, social sciences, science, technology, engineering, law or management.

Purpose: To support research leading to Master's or doctoral degrees.

Eligibility: Open to applicants who have completed at least four years of tertiary education studies at a high level of achievement eg. First Class (Honours) Degree or equivalent at an Australian university. Applicants must be Australian citizens or have permanent resident status and have lived in Australia continuously for the year prior to the closing date for application. Applicants who have previously held an Australian Government Award (APA, APRA or CPRA) for more than three months are not eligible for an APA and applicants who have previously held an Australian Postgraduate Course Award (APCA) may apply only for an APA to support PhD research. The awards may be held concurrently with other non Australian government awards.

Level of Study: Doctorate, Postgraduate, Research.

Type: Award.

Value: Australian $18,009 per year full-time which is tax exempt plus allowances and Australian $9,620 per year part-time, which is taxable plus allowances.

Length of Study: The Master's is two years and the PhD is three years in length. Periods of study already undertaken towards the degree will be deducted from the tenure of the award.

Frequency: Annual.

Study Establishment: Bundoora Campus, La Trobe University.

Country of Study: Australia.

No. of awards offered: 41.

Application Procedure: Applicants must write for application kits, available from the school in which the candidate wishes to study. Applications must be submitted in duplicate to the Research and Graduate Studies Office.

Closing Date: October 31st.

Funding: Government.

No. of awards given last year: 44.

Additional Information: APA holders are required to pay the annual General Service Fee of Australian $357 for the Bundoora Campus or Australian $310 for the Bendigo Campus. Paid work may be permitted for up to a maximum of eight hours per week for the full-time award or up to four hours per week for the part-time award.

International Postgraduate Research Scholarships (IPRS)

Subjects: Health sciences, humanities, social sciences, science, technology, engineering, law or management.

Purpose: To attract top quality overseas postgraduate students to areas of research in Institutes of Higher Education and to support Australia's research efforts.

Eligibility: Open to suitably qualified overseas graduates (excluding New Zealand) eligible to commence a doctoral or Master's degree by research. The IPRS may be held concurrently with a university research scholarship and applicants for an IPRS are advised to apply for La Trobe University Postgraduate Research Scholarship (LTUPRS). Applicants who have already commenced a Master's or PhD candidature or applicants for Master's candidature by coursework and minor thesis are not eligible to apply for an IPRS. IPRSs are awarded on the basis of academic merit and research capacity alone.

Level of Study: Doctorate, Postgraduate.

Type: Scholarship.

Value: Tuition fees plus basic healthcare cover.

Length of Study: Two years for the Master's and three years for the PhD.

Frequency: Annual.

Study Establishment: Bundoora Campus, La Trobe University.

Country of Study: Australia.

No. of awards offered: 9.

Application Procedure: Applicants must submit the application form for international candidates available from the International Programmes Office. Email international@latrobe.edu.au for further information.

Contributor: The Australian government.

Additional Information: Applicants in most instances will become members of a research team working under the direction of senior researchers.

La Trobe University Postdoctoral Research Fellowship

Subjects: All subjects.

Purpose: To advance research activities on the various campuses of the university by bringing to or retaining promising scholars in Australia.

Eligibility: Open to students who have been awarded their doctorates within the last five years. Applicants must hold a doctoral degree or equivalent at the date of appointment. The University may also take into account the proposed area of research having regard to the University's research promotion and management strategy policies.

Level of Study: Postdoctorate.

Type: Fellowship.

Value: Australian $48,400 to $51,954 per year, plus air fares and a resettlement allowance.

Length of Study: Two years.

Frequency: Annual.

Country of Study: Australia.

No. of awards offered: One or more, subject to funding.

Application Procedure: Applicants must complete an application form available from the website, requested in writing or via email. The administrative contact is Dr Barbara Murray, Co-ordinator, Grants and Fellowships, telephone (61) 3 9479 2049, fax (61) 3 9479 1464, or email b.murray@latrobe.edu.au.

Closing Date: August.

Funding: Government.

No. of awards given last year: Four.

No. of applicants last year: 55.

Additional Information: A project must be proposed by the applicant in collaboration with a La Trobe University research worker or team. The approved project will be designated in the letter of offer and the major objectives of a Fellow's project shall not be altered without the written approval of the university.

La Trobe University Postgraduate Scholarship

Subjects: Aboriginal studies, accountancy, agriculture, archaeology, art history, Asian studies, Australian studies, behavioural health sciences, biochemistry, botany, chemistry, cinema studies, communication disorders, computer science, drama, economic history, economics, econometrics, education, electronic and communication sciences, English, genetics and human variation, geology, gerontology, health administration, health education, history, history and philosophy of science, Italian, legal studies, linguistics, Latin American studies, mathematics, microbiology, nursing, occupational therapy, orthoptics, pacific studies, peace studies, philosophy, philosophy of science, physics, physiotherapy, podiatry, politics, prosthetics and orthotics, psychology, religious studies, revolutionary studies, romance languages, social work, sociology, statistics, Spanish, women's studies or zoology.

Purpose: To provide financial assistance.

Eligibility: Open to applicants of any nationality having qualifications deemed to be equivalent to an Australian First Class (Honours) Degree.

Level of Study: Doctorate, Postgraduate.

Type: Scholarship.

Value: Approx. Australian $16,832 per year. There is no spouse allowance but Australian $919 per year is available per dependent child, along with a thesis allowance, partial removal and travel allowance. All amounts are dependent on funds available.

Length of Study: Up to two years for Master's candidates and up to three years for PhD candidates.

Frequency: Annual.

Country of Study: Australia.

No. of awards offered: Approx. 50.

Application Procedure: Applicants must complete an application form, available directly from the department offering the relevant course of study.

Closing Date: September 30th for overseas applicants, October 31st for Australian citizens and permanent residents.

THE LADY DAVIS FELLOWSHIP TRUST

Hebrew University, Givat Ram, Jerusalem, 91904, Israel
Tel: (972) 2 658 4723 / (972) 2 651 2306
Fax: (972) 2 566 3848
Email: LDFT@vms.huji.ac.il
www: http://ldft.huji.ac.il
Contact: Mr M Mark Sopher, Executive Secretary

The Lady Davis Trust Doctoral Student Fellowships

Subjects: All subjects.

Purpose: To advance the interests of international scholarship and Israeli higher education.

Eligibility: Applicants must be enrolled in a recognised doctoral programme at a university outside of Israel and have an academic sponsor.

Level of Study: Doctorate.

Type: Fellowship.

Frequency: Annual.

No. of awards offered: Varies.

Application Procedure: Applicants must write for details or visit the website.

Closing Date: January 31st.

Additional Information: Further information is available from the website.

The Lady Davis Trust Postdoctoral Research Fellowship

Subjects: All subjects.

Purpose: To advance the interests of international scholarship and Israeli higher education.

Eligibility: Applicants must have received their doctorate no earlier than October 1st 1999.

Level of Study: Postdoctorate.

Type: Fellowship.

Frequency: Annual.

No. of awards offered: Varies.

Application Procedure: Applicants must write for details or visit the website.

Closing Date: December 31st.

Additional Information: Further information is available from the website.

The Lady Davis Trust Visiting Professorships

Subjects: All subjects.

Purpose: To advance the interests of international scholarship and Israeli higher education.

Eligibility: Open to full or associate professors.

Level of Study: Doctorate, Postdoctorate, Postgraduate.

Type: Fellowship.

Frequency: Annual.

Study Establishment: The Hebrew University in Jerusalem, or the Israel Institute of Technology in Haifa.

Country of Study: Israel.

Application Procedure: Applicants must write for details or visit the website.

Closing Date: November 30th.

Additional Information: Similar awards are available to promising students of the Hebrew University or the Technikon to study or undertake research in outstanding institutions abroad. Further information is available from the website.

LADY TATA MEMORIAL TRUST

Academic Department of Haemotology & Cytogenetics
The Royal Marsden Hospital, Fulham Road
London, SW3 6JJ, England
Tel: (44) 20 7352 8171
Fax: (44) 20 7351 6420
Contact: Secretary

Lady Tata Memorial Trust Scholarships

Subjects: Leukaemia.

Purpose: To encourage study and research in diseases of the blood, with special reference to leukaemias and furthering knowledge in connection with such diseases.

Eligibility: Open to qualified applicants of any nationality.

Level of Study: Postdoctorate.

Type: Scholarship.

Value: Ranging between UK£15,000-20,000 per year.

Length of Study: One-two years.

Frequency: Annual.

Country of Study: Any country.

No. of awards offered: Normally 10.

Application Procedure: Applicants must submit eight copies of the application, including form, summary of proposed research, and two letters of reference.

Funding: Private.

LALOR FOUNDATION

c/o Grants Management Associates, 77 Summer Street, 8th Floor, Boston, MA 02110, United States of America
Tel: (1) 617 426 7122
Fax: (1) 617 426 5441
Email: lalorfoundation@grantsmanagement.com
www: http://www.lalorfound.org
Contact: Administrative Assistant

The Lalor Foundation was incorporated in Delaware in 1935 under bequests from members of the Lalor family. A major objective of the Foundation has been to give assistance and encouragement to capable, young investigators who have embarked on teaching and research careers in universities and colleges.

Lalor Foundation Postdoctoral Fellowships

Subjects: Reproductive biology as related to the regulation of fertility.

Purpose: To promote intensive research and to assist and encourage able young investigators in academic positions to follow research careers in reproductive physiology.

Eligibility: Open to tax exempt institutions within or outside the United States of America. Candidates should apply for details. The individual nominated by the institution for the postdoctoral fellowship may be a citizen of any country and should have training and experience at least equal to PhD or MD level. People who have held a doctoral degree for less than five years are preferred. The institution applying

can nominate a Fellow either from its own staff or from elsewhere but, qualifications being equal, candidates external to the institution may carry modest preference. The institution nominating the candidate must provide the name and performance record of the nominated candidate on the application form.
Level of Study: Postdoctorate.
Type: Fellowship.
Value: Up to US$35,000 per year to cover a fellowship stipend, institutional overheads and miscellaneous expenses.
Frequency: Annual.
Study Establishment: An institution which is tax exempt.
Country of Study: Any country.
No. of awards offered: Approx. 30.
Application Procedure: Applicants must submit an application form, available from the website or on request.
Closing Date: January 15th.
Funding: Private.
No. of awards given last year: Approx. 30.
No. of applicants last year: Approx. 75.

LANCASTER UNIVERSITY

Student Support Office, University House, Bailrigg, Lancaster, LA1 4YW, England
Tel: (44) 1524 65201
Fax: (44) 1524 594294
Email: pgadmissions@lancaster.ac.uk
www: http://www.lancs.ac.uk
Contact: Ms Susan Gara, College Secretory

A campus University dedicated to excellence through teaching and research, offering a wide range of internationally recognised postgraduate courses.

Cartmel College Scholarship Fund
Subjects: All subjects offered by the University.
Purpose: To assist students unable to obtain adequate grants from other bodies.
Eligibility: Open to candidates of any nationality who have a place at Lancaster University. Priority is given to members of Cartmel College and new students.
Level of Study: Graduate, Postgraduate.
Type: Scholarship.
Value: UK£300-500 not including fees.
Frequency: Annual.
Study Establishment: Lancaster University.
Country of Study: United Kingdom.
No. of awards offered: Varies.
Application Procedure: Applicants must write to the Student Support Office for details.
Closing Date: June 1st.
Funding: Government.
No. of awards given last year: Four.

Lancaster University County College Awards
Subjects: All subjects offered by the University.
Purpose: To assist students whose course of study will lead to financial hardship.
Eligibility: Open to candidates of any nationality who have a place at Lancaster University. Candidates must be former members of the County College.
Level of Study: Postgraduate.
Value: Up to UK£1000.
Frequency: Annual.
Study Establishment: Lancaster University.
Country of Study: United Kingdom.
No. of awards offered: Varies.
Application Procedure: Applicants must write to the Student Support Office for further application details.
Closing Date: June 1st.
Funding: Government.
No. of awards given last year: Three.

Lancaster University International Bursaries
Subjects: All subjects.
Purpose: To offer financial support.
Eligibility: Open to nationals of India, Mexico and Thailand who have not previously studied at Lancaster University.
Level of Study: Postgraduate.
Type: Bursary.
Value: UK£2,000, offset against fees.
Length of Study: One year or more.
Frequency: Annual.
Study Establishment: Lancaster University.
Country of Study: United Kingdom.
No. of awards offered: Three.
Application Procedure: Applicants must complete an application, available on request from the International Office.
Closing Date: June 2nd 2004.
Funding: Government.

For further information contact:

International Office, University House, Lancaster University, LA1 4YW.

Peel Awards
Subjects: All subjects offered by the University.
Purpose: To enable students who are unable to secure finance from other sources to study at Lancaster University.
Eligibility: Open to candidates of any nationality who have a place at Lancaster University and who will be over 21 years of age at the commencement of the course.
Level of Study: Postgraduate, Undergraduates over 21 years old.
Value: Varies but does not cover fees UK£500-1750.
Frequency: Annual.
Study Establishment: Lancaster University.
Country of Study: United Kingdom.
No. of awards offered: 20-30.
Application Procedure: Applicants must complete an application form, available on request from the Student Support Office.
Closing Date: June 1st.
Funding: Private.
Contributor: Peel (Dowager Corntess Eleanor) Trust.
No. of awards given last year: 21.

LANCASTER UNIVERSITY, THE MANAGEMENT SCHOOL

MBA Office, Lancaster University Management School, Lancaster, LA1 4YX, UK
Tel: (44) (0) 1524 594068
Fax: (44) (0) 1524 592417
Email: mba@lancaster.ac.uk
www: http://www.lums.lancs.ac.uk
Contact: Angela Graves

Lancaster University Management School (LUMS) is one of only 2 UK business schools of carry to coveted 6-star (6*) rating for Research Quality and has been rated "Excellent" for Teaching Quality by the Higher Education Funding Council for England and Wales. LUMS is EQUIS accredited and its MBA Programmes are AMBA accredited and winners of the Association of MBAs Student of the Year Award twice. In the Financial Times MBA rankings 2004, LUMS was placed joint 69th in the world, placing the Lancaster MBA 8th in the UK and 16th in Europe.

Lancaster MBA 40th Anniversary Bursaries
Subjects: Full Time MBA.
Purpose: To celebrate Lancaster University's 40th Birthday, we have a number of bursaries to assist candidates to pursue the Full Time MBA.
Eligibility: These bursaries are open to applicants from any part of the world and will be awarded on the basis of exceptional ability and need.
Value: In the range of UK£1000-5000.

Length of Study: 12 months.
Frequency: Annual.
Study Establishment: Lancaster University Management School.
Country of Study: United Kingdom.
No. of awards offered: Dependent on demand.
Application Procedure: Applicants should contact the MBA Office for full details. Candidates should send a 1000 word statement demonstrating how, through their ideas and achievements, they will be an asset to the programme. Cases of exceptional need will also be considered. We can only consider applications from candidates who already hold an offer of a place on the programme.
Closing Date: 31st May 2004.
Funding: Private.
No. of awards given last year: N/A.
No. of applicants last year: N/A.

Lancaster MBA Scholarships

Subjects: Full Time MBA.
Purpose: In line with the increasing calibre of our MBA class, we are offering five company-sponsored scholarships to assist exceptional candidates to pursue the Full Time MBA.
Eligibility: Students who meet specific academic and professional criteria, which are above our standard admissions requirements. Candidates must contact the MBA Office for details.
Level of Study: Postgraduate, Full Time MBA.
Type: Scholarship.
Value: UK£7,500.
Length of Study: 12 months.
Frequency: Annual.
Study Establishment: Lancaster University Management School.
Country of Study: United Kingdom.
No. of awards offered: 5.
Application Procedure: Applicants must contact the MBA Office for full details. Candidates send us a 1000 word statement demonstrating significant achievement in their career to date and outlining how their career plan can benefit from the Lancaster MBA. We can only consider applications from candidates who already hold an offer of a place on the programme.
Closing Date: 31st May 2004.
Funding: Private.
No. of awards given last year: N/A.
No. of applicants last year. N/A.

LAW AND JUSTICE FOUNDATION OF NEW SOUTH WALES

GPO Box 4264, Sydney, NSW 2001, Australia
Tel: (61) 2 9221 3900
Fax: (61) 2 9221 6280
Email: if@lawfoundation.net.au
www: http://www.lawfoundation.net.au
Contact: Ms Catherine Lloyd, Grants Manager

The Law and Justice Foundation's objectives are to contribute to the development of a fair and equitable justice system which addresses the legal needs of the community, and to improve access to justice by the community, in particular by economically and socially disadvantaged people.

Law and Justice Foundation of New South Wales Grants Program

Subjects: Law.
Purpose: To promote community understanding of, and access to, the legal system in New South Wales. The Law Foundation invests in community based projects that promote research into, and the understanding of, the legal system.
Type: Grant.
Value: Varies.
Frequency: Dependent on funds available.
Country of Study: Australia.
No. of awards offered: Varies.
Application Procedure: Applicants must seek grant guidelines, which are available from the website.

Closing Date: Please contact the Foundation.
Funding: Government.
Contributor: Users of legal services in New South Wales.
No. of awards given last year: 21.
No. of applicants last year: 75.

LEEDS INTERNATIONAL PIANOFORTE COMPETITION

Piano Competition Office, The University of Leeds, Leeds, West Yorkshire, LS2 9JT, England
Tel: (44) 113 244 6586
Fax: (44) 113 244 6586
Email: admin@leedspiano.bdx.co
www: http://www.leedspiano.com
Contact: Office Manager

The aim of the Leeds International Pianoforte Competition is to offer talented young professional pianists of all nationalities the chance to be recognised by the musical world and the media and to help them build their professional careers.

Leeds International Pianoforte Competition. 6th-23rd September (2006)

Subjects: Piano competition.
Purpose: To promote the careers of talented professional pianists.
Eligibility: Open to professional pianists of all nationalities who were born on or after September 1st 1976. This is for the next competition in September 2006.
Level of Study: Professional development.
Type: Money and engagements in the UK and Worldwide.
Value: Total prize fund in excess of UK£60,000 and a number of national and international engagements.
Frequency: Every three years.
Country of Study: Any country.
No. of awards offered: 36.
Application Procedure: Applicants must complete an application form.
Closing Date: 10th February 2006.
Funding: Private, Commercial.
Contributor: The Halifax.
No. of awards given last year: At the 2003 competition- 35.
No. of applicants last year: 228.

LENTZ PEACE RESEARCH ASSOCIATION (LPRA)

c/o University of Missouri-St Louis, 8001 Natural Bridge Road, St Louis, MO 63121-4499, United States of America
Tel: (1) 314 516 5798
Fax: (1) 314 516 6757
Email: bob.baumann@umsl.edu
Contact: Mr Robert Baumann, Board Member

The Lentz Peace Research Association (LPRA) was established in 1930 in St Louis as the Character Research Association by Dr Theodore F Lentz with an aim towards conducting scientific research on the causes of war and conditions for peace. In 1993 LPRA initiated the Lentz Fellowship in Peace and Conflict Resolution Research in residence at the University of Missouri-St Louis.

Theodore Lentz Fellowship in Peace and Conflict Resolution Research

Subjects: International relations.
Purpose: To support research projects in peace and conflict resolution and to enable the recipient to teach an introductory peace studies course in the fall semester and one course in the Spring semester at the University of Missouri-St Louis.
Eligibility: A completed PhD is required and preference is given to graduates of university programmes in peace studies and conflict resolution. Graduates of political science, international relations and other social science programmes who specialise in peace and conflict

resolution are also invited to apply. Post-doctoral or Sabbatical fellowship.
Level of Study: Postdoctorate.
Type: Fellowship.
Value: Approx. US$23,400 plus university benefits and US$1,000 travel and expense allowance.
Length of Study: Nine months.
Frequency: Annual.
Study Establishment: The University of Missouri-St Louis.
Country of Study: United States of America.
No. of awards offered: One.
Application Procedure: Applicants must send a curriculum vitae, a letter of application, evidence of completion of the PhD, three letters of recommendation and a research proposal of approximately 750 words to the Center for International Studies.
Closing Date: April 15th.
Funding: Private.
Contributor: The Lentz Peace Research Association.
No. of awards given last year: One.
No. of applicants last year: 18.
Additional Information: The fellowship is supported in part by the University of Missouri-St Louis.Fellow must serve in residence at University of Missouri-St Louis.

LEO BAECK INSTITUTE (LBI)

15 West 16th Street, New York, NY 10011-6301, United States of America
Tel: (1) 212 744 6400
Fax: (1) 212 988 1305
Email: lbaeck@lbi.cjh.org
www: http://www.lbi.org
Contact: Secretary

The Leo Baeck Institute (LBI) is a research, study and lecture centre, a library and repository for archival and art materials. It is devoted to the preservation of original materials pertaining to the history and culture of German speaking Jewry.

David Baumgardt Memorial Fellowship
Subjects: Modern intellectual history of German speaking Jewry.
Purpose: To provide financial support to scholars whose research projects are connected with the writings of Professor David Baumgardt or his scholarly interests.
Level of Study: Doctorate, Postdoctorate, Postgraduate.
Type: Fellowship.
Value: US$3,000.
Length of Study: One year.
Frequency: Annual.
Study Establishment: The Leo Baeck Institute.
Country of Study: United States of America.
No. of awards offered: One.
Application Procedure: Applicants must submit an application form, a curriculum vitae and a full description of the research project. Doctoral students must submit official transcripts of graduate and undergraduate work, written evidence that they are enrolled in a PhD programme and two letters of recommendation, one by their doctoral advisor and one by another Scholar familiar with the work. Postdoctoral candidates must submit evidence of their degree of which transcripts are not required, and two letters of recommendation from two colleagues familiar with their research.
Closing Date: November 1st.
Funding: Private.
Contributor: The Leo Baeck Institute.

Fritz Halbers Fellowship
Subjects: Culture and history of German speaking Jewry.
Purpose: To provide financial assistance to scholars whose projects are connected with the culture and history of the German speaking Jewry.
Level of Study: Doctorate, Graduate, Postdoctorate, Postgraduate, Predoctorate.
Type: Fellowship.

Value: US$3,000.
Length of Study: One year.
Frequency: Annual.
Country of Study: United States of America.
No. of awards offered: More than one.
Application Procedure: Applicants must submit an application form, curriculum vitae and a full description of the research project. Doctoral students must submit official transcripts of graduate and undergraduate work, written evidence that they are enrolled in a PhD programme and two letters of recommendation, one by their doctoral adviser and one by another Scholar familiar with the work. Postdoctoral candidates must submit evidence of their degree of which transcripts are not required and two letters of recommendation from two colleagues familiar with their research.
Closing Date: November 1st.
Funding: Private.
Contributor: The Leo Baeck Institute.

LBI/DAAD Fellowship for Research at the Leo Baeck Institute, New York
Subjects: Social, communal and intellectual history of German speaking Jewry.
Purpose: To provide assistance to students for dissertation research and to academics for writing a scholarly essay or book.
Level of Study: Doctorate, Graduate, Postdoctorate.
Type: Fellowship.
Value: US$2,000.
Length of Study: One year.
Frequency: Annual.
Study Establishment: The Leo Baeck Institute.
Country of Study: United States of America.
No. of awards offered: Two.
Application Procedure: Applicants must submit an application form, a curriculum vitae and a full description of the research project. Doctoral students must submit official transcripts of graduate and undergraduate work, written evidence that they are enrolled in a PhD programme and two letters of recommendation, one by their doctoral advisor and one by another Scholar familiar with the work. Postdoctoral candidates must submit evidence of their degree of which transcripts are not required, and two letters of recommendation from two colleagues familiar with their research.
Closing Date: November 1st.
Funding: Private.
Contributor: The Leo Baeck Institute.
Additional Information: The fellowship holders agree to submit a brief report on their research activities after the period for which the fellowship was granted.

LBI/DAAD Fellowships for Research in the Federal Republic of Germany
Subjects: Social, communal and intellectual history of German speaking Jewry.
Purpose: To provide financial assistance to doctoral students doing research for their dissertation and to academics in the preparation of a scholarly essay or book.
Eligibility: Applicants must be United States citizens and PhD candidates or recent PhDs who have received their degrees within the preceding two years.
Level of Study: Doctorate, Postdoctorate.
Type: Fellowship.
Value: Please contact the organisation.
Length of Study: One year.
Frequency: Annual.
Country of Study: Germany.
No. of awards offered: One-two.
Application Procedure: Applicants must submit an application form, a curriculum vitae and a full description of the research project. Doctoral students must submit official transcripts of graduate and undergraduate work, written evidence that they are enrolled in a PhD programme and two letters of recommendation, one by their doctoral advisor and one by another Scholar familiar with the work. Postdoctoral candidates must submit evidence of their degree of

which transcripts are not required, and two letters of recommendation from two colleagues familiar with their research.
Closing Date: November 1st.
Funding: Private.
Contributor: The Leo Baeck Institute.
Additional Information: The fellowship holders agree to submit a brief report on their research activities upon conclusion of their fellowship. These awards are in conjunction with awards offered by the German Academic Exchange Service (DAAD) in New York, United States of America.

LEUKAEMIA RESEARCH FUND

43 Great Ormond Street, London, WC1N 3JJ, England
Tel: (44) 20 7405 0101
Fax: (44) 20 7242 1488
Email: info@lrf.org.uk
www: http://www.lrf.org.uk

The Leukaemia Research Fund is devoted exclusively to leukaemia, Hodgkin's disease and other lymphomas, myeloma, myelodysplastic syndromes, aplastic anaemia and the myeloproliferative disorders. The Fund is committed to finding causes, improving and developing new treatments and diagnostic methods, as well as supplying free information booklets and answering written and telephone enquiries.

Gordon Piller Studentships

Subjects: All life science disciplines. The research topic must be applicable to leukaemia.
Purpose: To train graduates in life sciences in research and allow them to submit for a PhD degree.
Eligibility: Open to graduates of any nationality who work and reside in the United Kingdom.
Level of Study: Postgraduate.
Type: Studentship.
Value: Varies.
Length of Study: Three years.
Frequency: Annual.
Study Establishment: Universities, medical schools and research institutes.
Country of Study: United Kingdom.
No. of awards offered: Four.
Application Procedure: Applicants must be invited to apply and must complete the appropriate form.

Leukaemia Research Fund Clinical Research Training Fellowships

Subjects: All life science disciplines. The research topic must be applicable to leukaemia.
Purpose: To train registrar grade clinicians in research and allow them to submit for a higher degree.
Eligibility: Open to researchers of any nationality who work and reside in the United Kingdom.
Level of Study: Research.
Type: Fellowship.
Value: Varies.
Length of Study: Three years.
Frequency: Annual.
Study Establishment: Universities, medical schools, research institutes and teaching hospitals.
Country of Study: United Kingdom.
Application Procedure: Applicants must complete an application form.

Leukaemia Research Fund Clinical Training Fellowship

Subjects: Haematology, oncology.
Purpose: To train registrar grade clinicians in the care and treatment of patients with a haematological malignancy.
Eligibility: Open to researchers of any nationality who work and reside in the United Kingdom.
Level of Study: Other, Clinical.
Type: Fellowship.

Value: Varies.
Length of Study: Two years.
Frequency: Three times each year.
Study Establishment: Any United Kingdom centre of excellence for leukaemia medicine.
Country of Study: United Kingdom.
No. of awards offered: 11.
Application Procedure: Applicants must complete an application form.
Closing Date: Available on request.
No. of awards given last year: Five.
No. of applicants last year: 15.

Leukaemia Research Fund Grant Programme

Subjects: All life science disciplines.
Purpose: To give long-term support to research groups studying the causes and treatment of haematological malignancies.
Eligibility: Open to researchers who work and reside in the United Kingdom.
Level of Study: Unrestricted.
Type: Research grant.
Value: Varies.
Length of Study: Varies.
Frequency: Three times each year.
Study Establishment: Universities, medical schools, research institutes and teaching hospitals.
Country of Study: United Kingdom.
No. of awards offered: Varies.
Application Procedure: Applicants must complete an application form only after discussion with the Scientific Director.
Closing Date: Available on request.

LEUKEMIA AND LYMPHOMA SOCIETY

1311 Mamoroneck Avenue, White Plains, NY 10605, United States of America
Tel: (1) 914 821 8843
Fax: (1) 914 949 6691
Email: researchprograms@lls.org
www: http://www.lls.org
Contact: Director of Research Administration

The Leukemia and Lymphoma Society is a national voluntary health agency dedicated to the conquest of leukaemia, lymphoma and myeloma through research. Through its research programme, the Society hopes to encourage and promote research activity of the highest quality. In addition, the Society also supports patient aid, public and professional education and community service programmes.

Career development program

Subjects: Leukaemia, lymphoma, Hodgkin's disease and myeloma research.
Purpose: To provide support for individuals pursuing careers in basic, clinical or translational research.
Eligibility: Applications may be submitted by individuals working in domestic or non-profit organisations such as universities, hospitals or units of state and local governments. International applicants are welcome to apply.
Level of Study: Postdoctorate.
Type: Fellowship.
Value: Between US$45,000 and 100,000 per year.
Length of Study: Three-five years, based on experience and training.
Frequency: Annual.
Study Establishment: International and domestic non-profit organisations, including hospitals, universities and research institutes.
Country of Study: Worldwide.
No. of awards offered: Varies.
Application Procedure: Applicants may visit the website for details of the Career Development Award Application Packet. Web address is http://www.lls.org/cdp.
Closing Date: Preliminary application: 9/15. Full application: 10/1.
Funding: Private.

Translational Research Program

Subjects: Leukemia, lymphoma, Hodgkin's disease and myeloma research.

Purpose: To encourage and provide early stage support for clinical research.

Eligibility: Open to individuals working in domestic or foreign non-profit organisations such as universities, hospitals or units of state and local governments. International Applicants are Welcome to Apply.

Level of Study: Postdoctorate, Research.

Value: Up to US$130,000 per year.

Length of Study: Three years, with the possibility of two additional years.

Frequency: Annual.

Study Establishment: International and domestic non-profit organisations, including Hospitals, Universities and Research Institutes.

Country of Study: Other.

No. of awards offered: Varies.

Application Procedure: Applicants must contact the Society or visit the website for details web address is: http://www.lls.org/trp.

Funding: Private.

LEUKEMIA RESEARCH FUND OF CANADA (LRFC)

936 The East Mall, Toronto, ON, M9B 6J9, Canada
Tel: (1) 416 661 9541
Fax: (1) 416 661 7799
Email: administration@leukemia.ca
www: http://www.leukemia.ca
Contact: CEO

LRFC is a non-profit organization whose mission is to raise money to support research in leukemia, lymphoma (Hodgkin & non-Hodgkin) and myeloma.

LRFC Awards

Subjects: Leukemia, lymphoma (Hodgkin & non-Hodgkin) and myeloma.

Purpose: To support peer-reviewed research and fellowships in leukemia, lymphoma (Hodgkin & non-Hodgkin) and myeloma.

Eligibility: Open to applicants with a faculty appointment at a Canadian university.

Level of Study: Postdoctorate, Research.

Type: Fellowships, operating grants.

Value: Varies.

Length of Study: One year. Fellowships are renewable for one further year.

Frequency: Annual.

Country of Study: Canada.

No. of awards offered: Varies.

Application Procedure: Applicants must complete an official application. Applications are available from Deans of medicine, the LRFC office, the website (www.leukemia.ca), by contacting (1) 877-668-8326 or via email grants@leukemia.ca.

Closing Date: February 1st.

Funding: Private.

Additional Information: A special grant is available for the study of CLL.

THE LEVERHULME TRUST

Research Awards Advisory Committee, 1 Pemberton Row, London,
EC4A 3BG, England
Tel: (44) 20 7822 6964
Fax: (44) 20 7822 5084
Email: jcater@leverhulme.org.uk
www: http://www.leverhulme.org.uk
Contact: Mrs Bridget Kerr, Grants Administrative Officer

The Leverhulme Trust awards grants mainly for research but also, to a limited extent, for the support of students and areas of educational activity.

Leverhulme Trust Emeritus Fellowships

Subjects: All subjects.

Purpose: To assist experienced researchers in the completion of research already begun.

Eligibility: Open to individuals who have retired in the last three years or who are about to retire. Applicants must hold, or have recently held, teaching and/or research posts in universities or institutions of similar status in the United Kingdom. Applicants must also have an established record of research and be aged 59 or over at the age of retirement.

Level of Study: Postdoctorate.

Type: Fellowship.

Value: Up to UK£20,000 by individual assessment. The awards are to meet incidental costs and do not provide a personal allowance or pension supplementation.

Length of Study: Between three months and two years.

Frequency: Annual.

Country of Study: Other.

No. of awards offered: Approx. 30.

Application Procedure: Applicants must complete an application form. Requests for application forms must be accompanied by an A4 sized stamped addressed envelope.

Closing Date: February 10th.

Funding: Private.

No. of awards given last year: 37.

No. of applicants last year: 119.

Leverhulme Trust Research Fellowships

Subjects: All subjects.

Purpose: To assist experienced researchers pursuing investigations who are prevented by routine duties or other causes, from undertaking or completing a research programme.

Eligibility: Open to persons educated in the United Kingdom or the Commonwealth or who are permanent members of the United Kingdom scholarly community and who are normally resident in the United Kingdom. Awards are not normally made to those aged under 30 and are not made to those registered for first or higher degrees, professional or vocational qualifications.

Type: Fellowship.

Value: Up to UK£21,000 by individual assessment.

Length of Study: Three months to two years.

Frequency: Annual.

Country of Study: Any country.

No. of awards offered: Approx. 120.

Application Procedure: Applicants must complete an application form. Requests for application forms must be accompanied by an A4 sized stamped addressed envelope.

Closing Date: Mid November.

Funding: Private.

No. of awards given last year: 120.

No. of applicants last year: 660.

Leverhulme Trust Study Abroad Studentships

Subjects: All subjects.

Purpose: To fund advanced study or research at a centre of learning.

Eligibility: Open to candidates who have obtained a first degree from a United Kingdom university at the time of application or who are able to show evidence of equivalent education in the United Kingdom. Applicants must also have been educated at a school or schools in the United Kingdom or other part of the Commonwealth. They must be normally resident in the United Kingdom and under 30 years of age on June 1st. If older than this, candidates must make a strong and appropriate case for special consideration. Students wishing only to improve knowledge of modern languages are not eligible.

Level of Study: Doctorate, Postdoctorate, Postgraduate, Professional development.

Type: Studentship.

Value: UK£13,500 per year plus return airfare and other allowances at the discretion of the Committee.

Length of Study: One or two years.

Frequency: Annual.

Study Establishment: Any centre of learning.

Country of Study: Other.

No. of awards offered: Approx. 20.
Application Procedure: Applicants must complete an application form. Requests for application forms must be accompanied by an A4 sized stamped addressed envelope.
Closing Date: January 9th.
Funding: Private.
No. of awards given last year: 20.
No. of applicants last year: 119.

LEWIS & CLARK COLLEGE

Lewis & Clark College, Graduate School of Education, 0615 S.W. Palatine Hill Road, Portland, Oregon 97219-7899,
Tel: 503 768 7090
Email: sfcelclark.edu
www: http://www.lclark.edu
Contact: Ms The Bursar

The College was founded by Presbyterian pioneers as Albary Collegiate Institute in 1867. The school moved to the former Lloyd Frank estate in Portland's southwest hills in 1942 and took the name Lewis Clark College.

Mary Stuart Rogers Scholarship

Subjects: Any subject approved by the university.
Purpose: To support postgraduate students by funding study at Masters Degree or PhD level.
Level of Study: Postgraduate.
Value: US$3,000.
Frequency: Annual.
Study Establishment: Lewis & Clark College.
Country of Study: United States of America.
No. of awards offered: Variable.
Application Procedure: Contact the teacher, education department.

LEWIS WALPOLE LIBRARY

154 Main Street, Farmington, CT 06032-2958, United States of America
Tel: (1) 860 677 2140
Fax. (1) 860 677 6369
Email: walpole@yale.edu
www: http://www.library.yale.edu/Walpole
Contact: Dr Margaret K Powell, The Librarian

The Lewis Walpole Library is a research centre for the study of all aspects of English eighteenth-century studies and is a prime centre for the study of Horace Walpole and Strawberry Hill.

Lewis Walpole Library Fellowship

Subjects: Eighteenth-century British studies including history, literature, theatre, drama, art, architecture, politics, philosophy or social history.
Purpose: To fund study into any aspect of the Library's collection of eighteenth-century British prints, paintings, books and manuscripts.
Eligibility: Applicants should normally be pursuing an advanced degree or must be engaged in postdoctoral research or equivalent research.
Level of Study: Doctorate, Postdoctorate, Postgraduate, Research.
Type: Fellowship.
Value: US$1,800 plus travel expenses and on-site accommodation.
Length of Study: One month.
Frequency: Annual.
Study Establishment: Lewis Walpole Library, Yale University.
Country of Study: United States of America.
No. of awards offered: More than two.
Application Procedure: Applicants must submit a curriculum vitae, a brief outline of research proposal of up to three pages and two confidential letters of recommendation.
Closing Date: January 15th.
Funding: Private.
No. of awards given last year: 13.
No. of applicants last year: 35.

LIBRARY AND INFORMATION TECHNOLOGY ASSOCIATION (LITA)

50 East Huron Street, Chicago, IL 60611, United States of America
Tel: (1) 312 280 4270
Fax: (1) 312 280 3257
Email: lita@ala.org
www: http://www.lita.org
Contact: Grants Management Officer

The Library and Information Technology Association (LITA) provides a forum for discussion, an environment for learning and a programme for actions on the design, development and implementation of automated and technological systems in the library and information science field.

LITA/Christian Larew Memorial Scholarship in Library & Information Technology

Subjects: Library and information science, with an emphasis on information technology.
Purpose: To encourage the entry of qualified people into the library and information technology field.
Eligibility: Open to students at the Master's degree level in an ALA accredited programme.
Level of Study: Postgraduate.
Type: Scholarship.
Value: US$3,000.
Frequency: Annual.
Study Establishment: An ALA accredited programme.
Country of Study: United States of America.
No. of awards offered: One.
Application Procedure: Candidates must send a statement indicating their previous experience in the field and what he or she can bring to the profession. Application forms and instructions are available from the website.
Contributor: The Electronic Business and Information Services (EBIS), a unit of Baker & Taylor, Inc.
Additional Information: Factors considered in awarding the scholarship are academic excellence, leadership, evidence of commitment to a career in library automation and information technology, and prior activity and experience in those fields.

LITA/LSSI Minority Scholarship in Library and Information Technology

Subjects: Library science and information technology.
Purpose: To encourage the entry of qualified persons into the library automation field.
Eligibility: Open to United States or Canadian citizens, who are qualified members of a principal minority group: American Indian or Alaskan native, Asian or Pacific Islander, African American or Hispanic.
Level of Study: Postgraduate.
Type: Scholarship.
Value: US$2,500.
Frequency: Annual.
Study Establishment: An ALA accredited programme.
Country of Study: United States of America.
No. of awards offered: One.
Application Procedure: Applicants must write, phone or visit the website for application forms.
Funding: Commercial.
Contributor: Library Systems and Service, Inc.

LITA/OCLC Minority Scholarship in Library & Information Technology

Subjects: Library information science, with an emphasis on library automation.
Purpose: To encourage the entry of qualified minority persons into the library automation field who plan to follow a career in that field and who evidence potential leadership in, and a strong commitment to, the use of automated systems in libraries.
Eligibility: Open to United States or Canadian citizens, who are qualified members of a principal minority group: American Indian or

Alaskan native, Asian or Pacific Islander, African American or Hispanic.
Level of Study: Postgraduate.
Type: Scholarship.
Value: US$3,000.
Frequency: Annual.
Study Establishment: An ALA accredited programme.
Country of Study: United States of America.
No. of awards offered: One.
Application Procedure: Applicants must write, phone or visit the website for application forms.
Funding: Commercial.
Contributor: Online Computer Library Center.
Additional Information: Factors considered in awarding the scholarship are academic excellence, leadership, evidence of commitment to a career in library automation and information technology, and prior activity and experience in those fields.

LITA/SIRSI Scholarship in Library and Information Technology

Subjects: Library information science, with an emphasis on library automation.
Purpose: To encourage the entry of qualified persons into the library automation field who plan to follow a career in that field.
Eligibility: Open to beginning students at the Master's degree level in an ALA accredited programme.
Level of Study: Postgraduate.
Type: Scholarship.
Value: US$2,500.
Frequency: Annual.
Study Establishment: An ALA accredited programme.
Country of Study: United States of America.
No. of awards offered: One.
Application Procedure: Applicants must write, telephone or visit the website for application forms. Applicants must illustrate their qualifications for this scholarship with a statement indicating the nature of their previous experience, letters of reference and a personal statement.
Funding: Commercial.
Contributor: SIRSI.
Additional Information: Factors considered in awarding the scholarship are academic excellence, leadership, evidence of commitment to a career in library automation and information technology, and prior activity and experience in those fields.

LIBRARY COMPANY OF PHILADELPHIA

1314 Locust Street, Philadelphia, PA 19107, United States of America
Tel: (1) 215 546 3181
Fax: (1) 215 546 5167
Email: jgreen@librarycompany.org
www: http://www.librarycompany.org
Contact: Fellowship Office

Founded in 1731, the Library Company of Philadelphia was the largest public library in America until the 1850s and contains printed materials on aspects of American culture and society in that period. It is a research library of 450,000 books, pamphlets, newspapers and periodicals, 75,000 prints, maps and photographs and 150,000 manuscripts.

Library Company of Philadelphia and Historical Society of Pennsylvania Research Fellowships in American History and Culture

Subjects: Eighteenth-century and nineteenth-century American social and cultural history, African American history, literary history or the history of the book in America.
Purpose: To offer short-term fellowships for research in residence in their collections.
Eligibility: The fellowship supports both postdoctoral and dissertation research. The project proposal should demonstrate that the Library Company and/or the Historical Society of Pennsylvania has a primary source central to the research topic. Candidates are encouraged to

enquire about the appropriateness of a proposed topic before applying.
Level of Study: Doctorate, Postdoctorate.
Type: Fellowship.
Value: US$1,750.
Length of Study: One month.
Frequency: Annual.
Study Establishment: An independent research library.
Country of Study: United States of America.
No. of awards offered: Usually 25-30.
Application Procedure: Applicants must send four copies each of a curriculum vitae, a description of the proposed project of two-four pages in length and a letter of reference.
Closing Date: March 1st. Fellows may take up residence at any time from the following June to May of the next year.
Funding: Private.
Contributor: The Andrew W Mellon Foundation, the Barra Foundation and McLean Contributionship.
No. of awards given last year: 34.
No. of applicants last year: 120.
Additional Information: Fellows will be assisted in finding reasonably priced accommodation. International applications are especially encouraged since two fellowships, jointly sponsored with the Historical Society of Pennsylvania, are reserved for Scholars whose residence is outside the United States of America. A partial catalogue of the Library's holdings is available through the website. This programme includes fellowships offered by the Library Company's programme in Early American Economy and Society and by the Balch Institute for Ethnic studies.

Library Company of Philadelphia Program in Early American Economy and Society

Subjects: Pre-1860 American economic and business history.
Purpose: To promote scholarship by offering long-term dissertation and advanced research fellowships.
Eligibility: The fellowship supports both postdoctoral and dissertation research in the collections of the Library Company and often Philadelphia repositories.
Level of Study: Postdoctorate, Research.
Type: Fellowship.
Value: US$17,500-35,000.
Length of Study: Three months.
Frequency: Annual.
Study Establishment: An independent research library.
Country of Study: United States of America.
No. of awards offered: Two.
Application Procedure: Applicants must send four copies each of a curriculum vitae, a description of the proposed project of two-four pages in length, two letters of recommendation and a relevant writing sample of up to 24 pages in length. Candidates are encouraged to enquire about the appropriateness of a proposed topic before applying.
Closing Date: March 1st. Fellows may take up residence at any time from the following September to May of the next year.
Funding: Private.
No. of awards given last year: Four.
Additional Information: Further information can be found on the website.

LIFE COURSE CENTRE

University of Minnesota, Twin Cities, Department of Sociology, 1014A Social Sciences Building, 267-19 Avenue S, Minneapolis, MN 55455, United States of America
Tel: (1) 612 624 4064
Fax: (1) 612 624 7020
Email: morti002@atlas.socsci.umn.edu
www: http://www.soc.umn.edu
Contact: Dr Jeylan T Mortimer

The Life Course Centre at the University of Minnesota supports scholarly enquiry related to the life course. Through research, seminars and courses offered by Centre faculty and visiting scholars, the

Center provides an intellectual forum that enriches the research and educational activities of a broad range of faculty and students, as research assistants, in the department of sociology, as well as in other units of the University.

National Research Service Award Mental Health and Adjustment in the Life Course

Subjects: Topics include early work experience, mental health and the transition to adulthood, the joint development of autonomy and intimacy, the sources of competence and resilience in the face of adversity, physical and relational aggression, the life course consequences of victimisation, cognitive and emotional factors in decision making in criminal, delinquent and work behaviour, perceptions of criminal sanctions and their efficacy in inhibiting offending, and female inmates' adaptations to prison life as a function of prior life experience or trajectories of deviance and reintegration.

Purpose: To provide opportunities for students to carry out longitudinal research into the psychosocial determinants of mental health and adjustment, with an emphasis on childhood, adolescence, and the transition to adulthood.

Eligibility: Open to United States citizens or residents. Postdoctoral candidates must have received a PhD in a social science discipline or an equivalent degree such as an MD, public health or nursing degree.

Level of Study: Postdoctorate.

Type: Fellowship.

Value: A stipend in accordance with NRSA guidelines, providing tuition, fees and medical insurance.

Length of Study: A maximum of two years. This award is subject to review at the end of the first year.

Frequency: Every two years.

Study Establishment: The University of Minnesota.

Country of Study: United States of America.

No. of awards offered: Four, one of which is postdoctoral.

Application Procedure: Applicants must provide a letter describing current research interests, a complete curriculum vitae, a university transcript, three letters of recommendation and samples of written work.

Closing Date: November 1st. Applications will be accepted until the position is filled.

Funding: Government.

Contributor: The National Institute of Mental Health.

Additional Information: The University of Minnesota is committed to the policy that all persons shall have equal access to its programmes, facilities and employment without regard to race, colour, creed, religion, national origin, sex, age, marital status, disability, public assistance status or sexual orientation.

LIFE SCIENCES RESEARCH FOUNDATION (LSRF)

Lewis Thomas Laboratories, Princeton University, Washington Road, Princeton, NJ 08544, United States of America
Tel: (1) 609 258 3551
Email: sdirenzo@molbio.princeton.edu
www: http://www.lsrf.org
Contact: Assistant Director

The Life Sciences Research Foundation (LSRF) solicits monies from industry, foundations and individuals to support postdoctoral fellowships in the life sciences. The LSRF recognises that discoveries and the application of innovations in biology for the public's good will depend upon the training and support of the highest quality young scientists in the very best research environments. The LSRF awards fellowships across the spectrum of life sciences: biochemistry, cell, developmental, molecular, plant, structural, organismic population and evolutionary biology, endocrinology, immunology, microbiology, neurobiology, physiology and virology.

LSRF Three Year Postdoctoral Fellowships

Subjects: Biological and life sciences.

Purpose: To offer research support for aspiring scientists.

Eligibility: Open to researchers of any nationality, who are graduates of medical or graduate schools in the biological sciences and who hold an MD or PhD. Awards will be based solely on the quality of the individual applicant's previous accomplishments and on the merit of the proposal for postdoctoral research.

Level of Study: Postdoctorate.

Type: Fellowship.

Value: US$50,000 per year. The salary scale begins at US$30,000 for a first year postdoctoral and a five per cent raise thereafter. The Fellow will control expenditure of the remainder. It can be used for fringe benefits, travel to the host institution, travel to visit the sponsor and to the LSRF annual meeting. However, its main purpose is to support the Fellow's research expenses.

Length of Study: Three years.

Frequency: Annual.

Study Establishment: Appropriate research institutions.

Country of Study: Other.

No. of awards offered: 16-18.

Application Procedure: Applicants must submit a form, a curriculum vitae, not exceeding three pages, a five page research proposal, a letter from the sponsoring laboratory supervisor, three sealed letters of reference and a stamped addressed envelope. One application plus three copies are to be submitted. The entire proposal must be printed in standard size type ie. 10-12 point. No condensed print is allowed. Application information and forms are available from the website.

Closing Date: October 1st.

Funding: Private.

No. of awards given last year: 16.

No. of applicants last year: 535.

Additional Information: LSRF Fellows must carry out their research at non-profit institutions. The fellowship cannot be used to support research that has any patent commitment or other kind of agreement with a commercial profit making company.

LIGHT WORK

316 Waverly Avenue, Syracuse
NY 13244, United States of America
Tel: (1) 315 443 1300
Fax: (1) 315 443 9516
Email: jjhoone@syr.edu
www: http://www.lightwork.org
Contact: Anisha Joseph

Light Work is an artist run space which focuses on providing direct support for artists working in photography through its Artist-in-Residence Program, exhibitions and publications.

Light Work Artist-in-Residence Program

Subjects: Photography.

Purpose: To support and encourage the production of new work by emerging and mid career artists.

Eligibility: Open to artists of any nationality working in photography with experience and demonstrable, serious intent in the field. Students are not eligible.

Level of Study: Professional development.

Type: Residency.

Value: US$2,000 stipend plus a darkroom and apartment.

Length of Study: One month, not renewable.

Frequency: Annual.

Country of Study: United States of America.

No. of awards offered: 15.

Application Procedure: Applicants must send a letter of intent describing in general terms the project or type of work they would like to accomplish while in residence. In addition, 20 slides of work, a curriculum vitae and a short statement about the work must be included with a stamped addressed envelope for the return of materials. There are no application forms.

Closing Date: Applications are accepted at any time.

Funding: Government, Private.

No. of awards given last year: 15.

No. of applicants last year: 300.

Additional Information: Residencies are non academic. Artists will be asked to give one informal lecture about their work and to contribute work produced in Syracuse to the Light Work collection. Work by participating artists is published in the Contact Sheet. Light Work also curates two photography galleries at Syracuse University.

THE LISTER INSTITUTE OF PREVENTIVE MEDICINE

The White House, 70 High Road, Bushey Heath, Hertfordshire, WD23 1GG, England
Tel: (44) 20 8421 8808
Fax: (44) 20 8421 8818
Email: secretary@lister-institute.org.uk
www: http://www.lister-institute.org.uk
Contact: Mr Keith Cowey, Secretary

Now the Lister Institute of Preventive Medicine originally founded in 1891, operates as a medical research charity whose sole function is to award Research Prizes to young clinical and non-clinical scientists working in the biological, biomedical sciences. The prizes are awarded on the basis of the proposed researching quality and potential implication

Lister Institute Research Prizes

Subjects: Biomedical and biological science.
Purpose: To promote biomedical excellence in the UK through the support of postdoctoral scientific research into the causes and prevention of disease in man, thereby enhancing the state of public health.
Eligibility: Open to residents of the United Kingdom who have obtained a PhD, DPhil, MD or MB BCh with membership of the Royal College of Physicians. Candidates must have a minimum of three and maximum of ten years postgraduate research experience. Applicants must have guaranteed support for the period of the award. The bulk of the work should be UK based.
Level of Study: Postdoctorate, Research.
Type: Research prize.
Value: UK£150,000 to be spent in Support of the recipients research for a period of three years. The only restriction is "no personal salaries".
Length of Study: Three years.
Frequency: Annual.
Study Establishment: An employing UK University, research institute unit, hospital or charity laboratory.
Country of Study: United Kingdom.
No. of awards offered: Two-Three.
Application Procedure: Applicants must complete and submit an application form, curriculum vitae and two letters of reference.
Closing Date: The end of the second week in January.
Funding: Private.
Contributor: Investment income.
No. of awards given last year: New scheme.
Additional Information: Research topics are of the applicant's own choosing but are primarily laboratory based and targeted at generating understanding and underpinning knowledge through fundamental research. Epidemeological, bioinformatics and small clinical projects would also be considered but not social research. Projects are assessed on scientific merit and potential. The awards are personal and are transferable within the United Kingdom. There are no priority diseases or scientific disciplines, provided that the proposed research has implications for preventive medicine. Epidemeological, bioinformatics small clinical projects would also be considered but not social research.

LONDON ARTS

2 Pear Tree Court, London, EC1R 0DS, England
Tel: (44) 20 7608 6100
Fax: (44) 20 7608 4100
Email: info@lonab.co.uk
www: http://www.arts.org.uk/londonarts
Contact: Mr David Edwards, Public Affairs Administrator

London Arts joined with the other regional arts boards and the Arts Council of England on 1st April 2002 to create a new, single arts funding and development organisation.

Awards and Schemes for Artists Arts Council England, London

Subjects: The arts.
Purpose: To help artists in the London area to reach a new and wider audience.
Eligibility: Open to individual writers, artists, composers and photographers who wish to undertake an arts project in London. Arts council England, London is unable to offer fees or grants for any individual undertaking education in the statutory further or higher education sectors.
Level of Study: Professional development.
Type: Award.
Value: Varies.
Length of Study: Varies.
Frequency: Rolling application process.
Country of Study: United Kingdom.
No. of awards offered: Varies.
Application Procedure: Applicants must submit an application form.
Closing Date: Please write for details.
Funding: Government.
Additional Information: For information on the awards and schemes administered by Arts Council England, please contact the listed address.

For further information contact:

Grants Unit, Arts Council England, London, 2 Pear Tree Ct, London, EC1R ODS,

THE LONDON CHAMBER OF COMMERCE AND INDUSTRY EXAMINATIONS BOARD (LCCIEB)

Athena House, 112 Station Road, Sidcup, Kent, DA15 7BJ, England
Tel: (44) 20 8302 0261
Fax: (44) 20 8309 1473
Email: custserv@iccieb.org.uk
www: http://www.lccieb.com
Contact: Ms Valerie Brasier

The London Chamber of Commerce and Industry Examinations Board (LCCIEB) is a leading international awarding body for business, information technology, secretarial, financial and marketing qualifications. Established over a century ago the Board is active today in more than 125 countries worldwide and is a leading NVQ awarding body in the United Kingdom.

LCCIEB Examinations Board Scholarships

Subjects: Business studies, marketing or finance.
Purpose: To award scholarships to qualified candidates wishing to take higher level qualifications or desiring to pursue LCCIEB qualifications.
Eligibility: Open to suitable candidates of any nationality. Candidates must have passed at least one LCCIEB qualification.
Level of Study: Unrestricted.
Type: Scholarship.
Value: Varies according to student requirements.
Length of Study: Unrestricted.
Frequency: Annual.
Study Establishment: Unrestricted but preference is normally given to candidate undertaking LCCIEB qualifications at LCCIEB registered training centres.
Country of Study: Any country.
Application Procedure: Applicants must complete an application form subject to recommendation from a registered LCCIEB centre. The LCCIEB centre must process the application on the applicants behalf.
Closing Date: Unrestricted.
Funding: Private.

Contributor: London Chamber of Commerce and Industry Commercial Education Trust.
No. of awards given last year: 20.
No. of applicants last year: 50.
Additional Information: Awards do not usually exceed UK£1,500 per application.

For further information contact:

Application forms can be downloaded from website www.LCCIEB.com or LCCICET, Julie Robinson, The old School, Holly Walk Leamington SPA, Warwickshire, CV32 4GL,
Tel: 01926 458 661

LONDON STRING QUARTET FOUNDATION

110 Gloucester Avenue, London, NW 1 8HX, England
Tel: (44) 20 7591 4847
Fax: (44) 20 8727 2372
Email: info@playquartet.com
www: http://www.lsqf.com
Contact: Administrator

The London String Quartet Foundation is a registered charity whose purpose is to promote the discovery and development of talent and audiences for the string quartet. The main activity of the Foundation is organising the triennial London International String Quartet Competition.

London International String Quartet Competition
Subjects: Musical performance.
Purpose: To encourage young string quartets to develop further on the world stage and take part in this prestigious competition.
Eligibility: There are no restrictions except that each musician in the quartet must be under 35 years on 9th April.
Level of Study: Unrestricted.
Value: Prizes total UK£28,000, and are split into five different awards of differing amounts and a menu of development prizes for three prize winners. Concerts are also organised for the first three prize winners
Frequency: Every three years.
Country of Study: Any country.
No. of awards offered: Six.
Application Procedure: Applicants must complete an application form, available on the website.
Closing Date: October 1st in the year preceding the award.
Funding: Commercial, Private.

LORD DOWDING FUND FOR HUMANE RESEARCH

261 Goldhawk Road, London, W12 9PE, England
Tel: (44) 20 8846 9777
Fax: (44) 20 8846 9712
Email: info@ldf.org.uk
www: http://www.ldf.org.uk
Contact: Head of Research

The Lord Dowding Fund for Humane Research is a department of the National Anti-Vivisection Society. It aims to support, sponsor and fund better methods of research for testing products and curing disease, which work towards replacing the use of laboratory animals.

Lord Dowding Fund for Humane Research
Subjects: Medical research, veterinary science, toxicology and teaching. A wide range of techniques are supported, including cell, tissue or organ culture, computer simulation mathematical modelling, quantum pharmacology chemical analysis, epidemiology, genetic or tissue engineering, virology and pain research.
Purpose: To support research aimed at replacing the use of laboratory animals.

Eligibility: Applications on behalf of junior scientists must be made by a senior scientist eg. a PhD supervisor or Head of Research. Projects must not involve the use of animals and applicants must not hold a Home Office licence.
Level of Study: Research.
Type: Award.
Value: Up to UK£75,000.
Length of Study: Up to three years.
Frequency: Four times per year.
Study Establishment: Academic departments or hospitals.
Country of Study: United Kingdom.
No. of awards offered: Varies.
Application Procedure: Applicants must complete an application form and submit a project proposal. An information pack can be requested from the organisation, or is available by visiting the website. Applications are peer-reviewed.
Closing Date: February 1st, May 1st, August 1st and November 1st each year.
Funding: Private.
Contributor: Private subscribers, legacies and fund raising events.
No. of awards given last year: 3 (2002).
No. of applicants last year: 19.

LOREN L ZACHARY SOCIETY FOR THE PERFORMING ARTS

2250 Gloaming Way, Beverly Hills, CA 90210, United States of America
Tel: (1) 310 276 2731
Fax: (1) 310 275 8245
Contact: Mrs Nedra Zachary, National Vocal Competition Director

The Loren L Zachary Society for the Performing Arts was founded in 1972 by the late Dr Loren L Zachary and Nedra Zachary. The purpose of the organisation is to help further the careers of young opera singers by providing financial assistance. The National Vocal Competition, now in its 32nd year, has helped over 80 singers to embark on international careers. The Director of the competitor is Mrs. Nedra Zachary.

Loren L Zachary Society National Vocal Competition for Young Opera Singers
Subjects: Operatic singing.
Purpose: To assist in the careers of young opera singers through competitive auditions and monetary awards.
Eligibility: Open to female singers between 21-33 years of age and male singers between 21-35 years of age who have completed operatic training and are fully prepared to pursue professional stage careers. Applicants must reside in the United States of America, Mexico, or Canada.
Level of Study: Professional development.
Type: Competition.
Value: US$10,000 for the top winner. A round trip flight to Europe for opera auditioning purposes may be awarded to a finalist. Approx. US$45,000 is distributed amongst the finalists and the minimum award is US$1,000.
Frequency: Annual.
Country of Study: Any country.
No. of awards offered: 10.
Application Procedure: Applicants must complete an application form accompanied by proof of age and an application fee of US$35. For application forms and exact dates, singers should send a stamped addressed business sized envelope to the Society in November. Faxed requests will not be accepted.
Closing Date: The deadline for the New York preliminary auditions is in January and the Los Angeles deadline is in March.
Funding: Private.
No. of awards given last year: 10.
No. of applicants last year: 200.
Additional Information: Applicants must be present at all phases of the auditions. Tapes are not acceptable. Preliminary and semi final auditions take place in New York in February, and in Los Angeles in April. The grand final and awards distribution occurs on May 23, 2004.

LOWE SYNDROME ASSOCIATION (LSA)

222 Lincoln Street, West Lafayette, IA 47906-2732, United States of America
Tel: (1) 765 743 3634
Email: info@lowesyndrome.org
www: http://www.lowesyndrome.org
Contact: Ms Kaye McSpadden, Director of Public & Scientific Affairs

The Lowe Syndrome Association (LSA) is an international non-profit organisation made up of families, friends and professionals dedicated to helping children with Lowe Syndrome and their families. Its main purposes are to foster communication among families, provide information and support research.

LSA Medical Research Grant

Subjects: Understanding and treatment of Lowe Syndrome.
Purpose: To support research projects that will lead to a better understanding of the metabolic basis of Lowe Syndrome, better treatments of the major complications of the disease and the prevention of and/or a cure for it.
Eligibility: Open to researchers who are affiliated with a non-profit institution.
Level of Study: Unrestricted.
Type: Grant.
Value: Varies. The most recent was US$30,000.
Length of Study: One year.
Frequency: Dependent on funds available.
No. of awards offered: Varies.
Application Procedure: Applicants must submit their application in writing. Specific instructions are available in the grant proposal guidelines document.
Closing Date: Varies.
Funding: Private.
Contributor: Members of the LSA and fund raising events.
No. of awards given last year: One.
No. of applicants last year: One.

THE MACDOWELL COLONY

100 High Street, Peterborough, NH 03458, United States of America
Tel: (1) 603 924 3886
Fax: (1) 603 924 9142
Email: info@macdowellcolony.org
www: http://www.macdowellcolony.org
Contact: Ms Courtney Bethel, Admissions Co-ordinator

The MacDowell Colony was founded in 1907 to provide creative artists with uninterrupted time and seclusion to work and enjoy the experience of living in a community with gifted artists. Residences are up to eight weeks for writers, composers, film and video makers, visual artists, architects and interdisciplinary artists. Artists in residence receive room, board and the exclusive use of a studio. There are no residency fees. A travel grant and limited writer's aid grant are available to artists in residence.

MacDowell Colony Residencies

Subjects: Creative writing, visual arts, musical composition, film or video making, architecture and interdisciplinary arts.
Purpose: To provide a place where creative artists can take advantage of uninterrupted work time and seclusion in which to work and enjoy the experience of living in a community of gifted artists.
Eligibility: Open to established and emerging artists in the fields specified.
Level of Study: Unrestricted.
Type: Residency.
Value: Up to US$1,000 for writers in need of financial assistance plus limited travel grants.
Length of Study: Usually four weeks.
Frequency: Three times each year.
Study Establishment: The Colony.
Country of Study: United States of America.
No. of awards offered: A total of 32 studios are available each application period for individual residencies.

Application Procedure: Applicants must write, telephone or refer to the website for information and an application.
Closing Date: January 15th, April 15th and September 15th for residencies to become tenable in the Summer, Autumn and Winter-Spring respectively.
Funding: Private.
No. of awards given last year: 240 residencies.
No. of applicants last year: 1400+ applications.
Additional Information: The studios are offered for the independent pursuit of the applicant's art. No workshops or courses are given and there are no stipends. Requests for information should be accompanied by a stamped addressed envelope.

MACKENZIE KING SCHOLARSHIP TRUST

Mackenzie King Scholarship Selection Committee, Faculty of Law, University of British Columbia, 1822 East Mall, Vancouver, BC, V6T 1Z1, Canada
Tel: (1) 604 822 4564
Fax: (1) 004 822 8108
Email: blom@law.ubc.ca
www: http://www.mkingscholarships.ca
Contact: Professor Joost Blom, Chair

The Mackenzie King Scholarship Trust consists of two funds established under the will of the Right Honourable William Lyon Mackenzie King (1874-1950). Both scholarships are to support postgraduate study by graduates of Canadian universities.

Mackenzie King Open Scholarship

Subjects: All subjects.
Eligibility: Open to graduates of any Canadian university. Applicants should be persons of unusual worth or promise as awards are determined on the basis of academic achievement, personal qualities and demonstrated aptitudes. Consideration is also given to the applicant's proposed programme of postgraduate study.
Level of Study: Postgraduate.
Type: Scholarship.
Value: Canadian $7,500.
Length of Study: One year, non renewable.
Frequency: Annual.
Country of Study: Any country.
No. of awards offered: One.
Application Procedure: Applicants must complete an application form available from the Faculty of Graduate Studies at each Canadian university and from the website. Applications must be submitted to the Dean of Graduate Studies at the Canadian university from which the candidate most recently graduated.
Closing Date: February 1st.
Funding: Private.
No. of awards given last year: One.

Mackenzie King Travelling Scholarships

Subjects: International or industrial relations, including international aspects of law, history, politics and economics.
Purpose: To give Canadian students the opportunity to broaden their outlook and sympathies and to contribute in some measure to the understanding of the problems and policies of other countries.
Eligibility: Open to graduates of any Canadian university who propose to engage in postgraduate studies in the given fields in the United States or the United Kingdom.
Level of Study: Postgraduate.
Type: Scholarship.
Value: Canadian $10,000.
Length of Study: One year, non renewable.
Frequency: Annual.
Study Establishment: Suitable institutions.
Country of Study: UK / USA.
No. of awards offered: Four.
Application Procedure: Applicants must complete an application form available from the Faculty of Graduate Studies in each Canadian university or from the website. Applications must be submitted to the

Dean of Graduate Studies at the Canadian university from which the candidate most recently graduated.
Closing Date: February 1st.
Funding: Private.
No. of awards given last year: Four.

THE MACQUARIE BANK

Recruitment and Careers, GPO Box 4294, Sydney, NSW 1164, Australia
Tel: (61) 2 8232 3333
Fax: (61) 2 8232 4544
Email: mbaschol@macquarie.com
www: http://www.macquarie.com.au
Contact: Shanan Green, Recruitment Manager

Formed in 1985 from one of the leading Australian merchant banks, Macquarie Bank Limited has been an innovator in the Australasian banking industry, offering outstanding products and services and regularly leading the field in market development initiatives. It is now Australia's leading investment bank and one of the top 25 companies listed on the Australian stock exchange. The bank employs approx. 5,000 people and has around 43 offices worldwide.

Macquarie Bank Graduate Management Scholarship
Subjects: MBA.
Purpose: To encourage and contribute to a higher standard of management education and to contribute to the effectiveness of Australasia's future managers.
Eligibility: Open to citizens or permanent residents of Australia or New Zealand who have undertaken work experience reflecting management expertise or potential. Applicants must indicate a firm intention to reside in Australia or New Zealand within a reasonable period after completion of the course and must be bonafide candidates for full-time study on an MBA course at an institution approved by the Trustees. Applicants must not yet have commenced the relevant course on either a full or part-time basis.
Level of Study: MBA, Postgraduate.
Type: Scholarship.
Value: US$35,000, payable over the study period.
Length of Study: A maximum of two years, the normal term of an MBA course.
Frequency: Annual.
Study Establishment: Any well known business school approved by the trustees.
Country of Study: Australia, the United Kingdom, Europe or the USA.
No. of awards offered: One.
Application Procedure: Applicants must complete application forms with references. These are available from the website.
Closing Date: The last Friday in October.
Funding: Commercial.
Contributor: The Macquarie Bank Foundation.
No. of awards given last year: One.
No. of applicants last year: 50-60.
Additional Information: Successful applicants will be required to attend initial and final interviews in Australia between November and December.

MAKING MUSIC, THE NATIONAL FEDERATION OF MUSIC SOCIETIES (NFMS)

7-15 Rosebery Avenue, London
EC1R 4SP, England
Tel: (44) 870 903 3780
Fax: (44) 870 903 3785
Email: info@makingmusic.org.uk
www: http://www.makingmusic.org.uk
Contact: Ms Kate Fearnley, Award Administrator

Making Music, The National Federation of Music Societies, is the leading umbrella group for the voluntary and semi-professional music sector. Making Music represents and supports over 2,000 music groups throughout the UK. Making Music groups promote over 8,000 performances, spend just over UK£8.9 million on professional artists a year and perform to audiences of around 1.5 million.

Philip & Dorothy Green Award for Young Concert Artists in association with Making Music
Subjects: Music.
Purpose: To support young musicians at the start of their professional careers.
Eligibility: Open to singers under 30 years of age and instrumentalists under 28 years of age. All applicants must be European Community citizens normally resident within the United Kingdom.
Level of Study: Professional development.
Type: Award.
Value: Up to 50 engagements with affiliated societies throughout Great Britain and Northern Ireland, shared between the winners.
Frequency: Annual.
No. of awards offered: Four-five.
Application Procedure: Applicants must submit a completed application form with their curriculum vitae.
Closing Date: As advertised in the national press and on the website.
Funding: Private.
No. of awards given last year: Six.
No. of applicants last year: 60 + .

MANHATTAN SCHOOL OF MUSIC (MSM)

120 Claremont Avenue, New York, NY 10027, United States of America
Tel: (1) 212 749 2802 ext. 449
Fax: (1) 212 749 3025
www: http://www.msmnyc.edu
Contact: Ms Amy A Anderson, Director of Financial Aid

The Manhattan School of Music (MSM) is a major national and international force in the education of professional musicians. It is the largest private conservatory in the nation offering both classical and jazz training.

MSM Scholarships
Subjects: Music.
Purpose: To recognise outstanding talent, achievements and performance.
Eligibility: Open to all students who demonstrate, through performance, that they have attained excellence in music and have the capacity for further development. Students must demonstrate financial need and provide the necessary income documents in order to qualify.
Level of Study: Doctorate, Graduate, Postgraduate.
Type: Scholarship.
Value: Tuition expenses only, ranging from US$1,000 to the full tuition costs, payable in equal instalments by semester.
Length of Study: One academic year, renewable for a total of two years.
Frequency: Annual.
Study Establishment: The MSM.
Country of Study: United States of America.
No. of awards offered: Approx. 375.
Application Procedure: United States citizens and permanent residents must submit a completed PROFILE and FAFSA form. For international students an international application in house form must be submitted.
Closing Date: March 15th for March auditions and April 15th for May auditions.
Funding: Private.
No. of awards given last year: 335.
No. of applicants last year: 1000.

MARCH OF DIMES BIRTH DEFECTS FOUNDATION

1275 Mamaroneck Avenue
White Plains, NY 10605
United States of America
Tel: (1) 914 997 4555
Fax: (1) 914 997 4560
Email: research-grants@modimes.org
www: http://www.modimes.org
Contact: Grants Administration

Four major problems threaten the health of America's babies: birth defects, infant mortality, low birth weight and lack of prenatal care. The goal of the March of Dimes Birth Defects Foundation is to eliminate these problems so that all babies can be born healthy.

Basil O'Connor Starter Scholar Research Award Program

Subjects: The broader aspects of pregnancy outcome eg. factors underlying the birth and survival of a healthy infant, the cognitive development of low birth weight infants, as well as the function of chromosomes, their subunits, genes or supporting structures.
Purpose: To support young scientists who are just embarking on their independent research careers.
Eligibility: Open to young investigators holding MDs or PhDs, who are interested in undertaking independent research after the completion of their doctoral and postdoctoral training. Applicants may not be recipients of a major grant exceeding US$100,000 at the time of their application.
Level of Study: Doctorate, Postdoctorate.
Type: Research grant.
Value: Up to US$75,000 per year. This award is not intended to cover the applicant's salary but to provide support for technical help and supplies.
Length of Study: Two years.
Frequency: Annual.
Study Establishment: An appropriate institution.
Country of Study: Any country.
No. of awards offered: Varies.
Application Procedure: Applicants must be nominated. Nominations must be accompanied by the candidate's full name, appointment, full mailing address, telephone and fax numbers, email designation, curriculum vitae and an abstract of the proposed research. A hard copy should not be submitted if the application is transmitted by fax.
Closing Date: An abstract is due by February 15th, with the full application due on May 31st.
Additional Information: Further information is available on request.

March of Dimes Research Grants

Subjects: Basic biological processes governing development, genetics, clinical studies, studies of reproductive health, environmental toxicology, and social or behavioural studies.
Purpose: To encourage research directed at the prevention of birth defects.
Eligibility: Open to qualified scientists from universities, hospitals and research institutions.
Level of Study: Research.
Type: Research grant.
Value: Approx. US$70,000 per year.
Length of Study: Two or three years.
Frequency: Annual.
Study Establishment: An appropriate institution.
Country of Study: Any country.
No. of awards offered: Varies.
Closing Date: Letters of intent are due on April 30th, and the full application is due on September 30th.
Additional Information: Further information is available on request.

MARGARET MCNAMARA MEMORIAL FUND (MMMF)

1818 H Street NWMSN H2-204, Washington, DC 20433, United States of America
Tel: (1) 202 473 8751
Fax: (1) 202 522 3142
Email: mmmf@worldbank.org
www: http://www.worldbank.org/yournet
Contact: Chairman of the MMMF Selection Committee

The Margaret McNamara Memorial Fund (MMMF) was established in 1981 to honour the late Margaret McNamara and her commitment to the well being of women and children in developing countries.

MMMF Grants

Subjects: All subjects.
Purpose: To support the education of women from developing countries who are committed to improving the lives of women and children in their home countries.
Eligibility: Open to women who are nationals of a developing country which is a current borrower from the World Bank. Applicants must be residing in the United States, but not as permanent residents. Candidates must already be enrolled in an accredited educational institution in the United States where the grant will be used. They must be at least 25 years old and must not be related to any World Bank Group staff member or their spouse.
Level of Study: Postgraduate, Professional development, Research, All.
Type: Grant.
Value: US$11,000. This amount is revised annually.
Length of Study: Two years or more.
Frequency: Annual.
Study Establishment: Universities or research institutions.
Country of Study: United States of America & Canada.
No. of awards offered: Up to six.
Application Procedure: Applicants must write or email for application forms. These must be submitted along with two recommendations and an academic transcript.
Closing Date: February 1st.
Funding: Private.
Contributor: Private donations.
No. of awards given last year: Five.
No. of applicants last year: 250.
Additional Information: Website: - www.worldbank.org/yournet click on MMMI Grants for Women from Developing Countries.

MARINE CORPS HISTORICAL CENTER

History & Museums Division, Building 58, 901 M Street South East, Washington Navy Yard, Washington, DC 20374-5040, United States of America
Tel: (1) 202 433 4244
Fax: (1) 202 433 7265
Contact: Grants & Fellowships Co-ordinator

The Marine Corps Historical Center houses the History and Museums Divisions. The Historical branch provides reference services to the public and government agencies, maintains the Marine Corps' archives and oral history collection, and produces official histories of Marine activities, units and bases. The Museums branch maintains the artefact and personal papers collection, and operates the Marine Corps Museum and the Air-Ground Museum.

Beeler-Raider Fellowship

Subjects: United States military and naval history, as well as history and history based studies in the social and behavioural sciences with a direct relationship to the United States Marine Corps.
Purpose: To encourage graduate level and advanced study of the combat contributions of enlisted Marines.
Eligibility: The competition is limited to citizens or nationals of the United States of America. While the programme concentrates

on graduate students, fellowships are available to other qualified persons.

Level of Study: Postgraduate.
Type: Fellowship.
Value: Please consult the organisation.
Frequency: Annual.
No. of awards offered: One.
Application Procedure: Applicants must submit a preliminary application to the Director of Marine Corps History and Museums outlining their qualifications, and either proposing a specific topic or requesting a suggested topic based on the applicant's interests and qualifications. If the evaluation of the preliminary application is favourable, the applicant will be asked to make a formal application on a form provided by the Center. The applicant is responsible for insuring that all required documentation is mailed before the closing date.
Funding: Private.
Contributor: The Marine Corps Heritage Foundation.
Additional Information: The Director of Marine Corps History and Museums will notify all applicants individually of their decision not later than mid July.

Marine Corps Historical Center College Internships

Subjects: History.
Purpose: To offer opportunities for college students to participate on a professional level in the Marine Corps Historical Center many historical and museum activities. The intent of the programme is to give promising and talented student interns a chance to earn college credits while gaining meaningful experience in fields in which they might choose to seek employment after school or pursue a vocational interest.
Eligibility: Applicants must be registered students at a college or university which will grant academic credit for work experience as interns in subject areas related to the student's course of study. While there are no restrictions on individuals applying for intern positions, it has been found that mature and academically superior students are most successful. The agreement of the academic institution to the internship for credit is essential.
Level of Study: Professional development.
Type: Internship.
Value: A small grant of daily expense money is provided. Any other costs of the internship must be made by the student.
Study Establishment: Internships are served either at the Marine Corps Historical Center or the Marine Corps Air Ground Museum, Marine Corps Development and Education Command in Quantico, Virginia.
Country of Study: United States of America.
No. of awards offered: Varies.
Application Procedure: Applicants must contact the Chief Historian at the Center for further details.
Closing Date: Please contact the organisation.
Funding: Private.

Marine Corps Historical Center Dissertation Fellowships

Subjects: Topics in United States military and naval history, as well as history and history based studies in the social and behavioural sciences with a direct relationship to the United States Marine Corps.
Purpose: To award a qualified graduate student working on a doctoral dissertation relevant to Marine Corps history.
Eligibility: Applicants must be citizens of the United States, enrolled in a recognised graduate school, have completed by September all requirements for the doctoral degree except the dissertation and have an approved, pertinent dissertation topic. A fellowship will not be awarded to an applicant who has held or accepted an equivalent fellowship from any other Department of Defence agency, however, recipients of the Marine Corps' Master's Thesis Fellowships may apply.
Level of Study: Doctorate.
Type: Fellowship.
Value: Please consult the organisation.
Frequency: Annual.
No. of awards offered: One.
Application Procedure: Applicants must complete an application form, available from the Chairman of the History Department of the applicant's university, or by writing to the Director of the Marine Corps

History and Museums at the Center. The applicant is responsible for insuring that all required documentation is mailed before the closing date.
Closing Date: 1st May
Funding: Private.
Contributor: The Marine Corps Heritage Foundation.
No. of awards given last year: 1.
No. of applicants last year: 1.
Additional Information: Evaluation of applicants is on the basis of academic achievements, faculty recommendations, and demonstrated research and writing ability. The nature of the topic must be of benefit to the study and understanding of Marine Corps history. All awards will be based on merit, without regard to race, creed, colour, or sex. The Director of Marine Corps History and Museums will notify all applicants individually of their decision not later than mid July.

Marine Corps Historical Center Master's Thesis Fellowships

Subjects: Topics in United States military and naval history, as well as history and history based studies in the social and behavioural sciences, with a direct relationship to the United States Marine Corps. This programme gives preference to projects covering the pre-1975 period where records are declassified or can be most readily declassified and made available to scholars.
Purpose: To award a number of fellowships to qualified graduate students working on topics pertinent to Marine Corps history.
Eligibility: Applicants must be actively enrolled in an accredited Master's degree programme which requires a Master's thesis. The competition is limited to citizens or nationals of the United States of America. A fellowship will not be awarded to anyone who has held or accepted an equivalent fellowship from any other Department of Defence agency.
Level of Study: Postgraduate.
Type: Fellowship.
Value: Please consult the organisation.
Frequency: Annual.
No. of awards offered: 2.
Application Procedure: Applicants must complete an application form, available from the chairman of the history department of the applicant's university, or by writing to the Director of the Marine Corps History and Museums, at the Center. The applicant is responsible for insuring that all required documentation is mailed before the closing date.
Closing Date: 1st May
Funding: Private.
Contributor: The Marine Corps Heritage Foundation.
No. of awards given last year: 1.
No. of applicants last year: 2.
Additional Information: The Director of Marine Corps History and Museums will notify all applicants individually of their decision not later than mid July.

Marine Corps Historical Center Research Grants

Subjects: Topics in United States military and naval history, as well as history and history based studies in the social and behavioural sciences, with a direct relationship to the United States Marine Corps. This programme gives preference to projects covering the pre-1975 period where records are declassified or can be most readily declassified and made available to scholars.
Purpose: To encourage research.
Eligibility: While the programme concentrates on graduate students, grants are available to other qualified persons. Applicants for grants should have the ability to conduct advanced study in those aspects of American military history and museum activities related to the United States Marine Corps.
Level of Study: Research.
Type: Grant.
Value: Please contact the organisation.
Frequency: Annual.
Application Procedure: Applicants must submit a preliminary application to the Director of Marine Corps History and Museums outlining their qualifications, and either proposing a specific topic or requesting a suggested topic based on the applicant's interests and

qualifications. If the evaluation of the preliminary application is favourable, the applicant will be asked to make a formal application on a form provided by the Center.
Closing Date: Please contact the organisation.
Funding: Private.
Contributor: The Marine Corps Heritage Foundation.

MARQUETTE UNIVERSITY, GRADUATE SCHOOL

PO Box 1881, Milwaukee, WI 53201-1881, United States of America
Tel: (1) 414 288 7137
Fax: (1) 414 288 1902
Email: mugs@marquette.edu
www: http://www.grad.marquette.edu
Contact: Mr Thomas Marek, Student Services Co-ordinator

Marquette University is a private, Jesuit university situated about 100 miles north of Chicago. It is a graduate research institution with 18 doctoral and over 40 Master's and certificate programmes.

Alpha Sigma Nu Graduate Scholarship
Subjects: All subjects.
Purpose: To offer tuition scholarships for members of Alpha Sigma Nu.
Eligibility: Open to first year graduate students who are members of Alpha Sigma Nu.
Level of Study: Graduate.
Type: Scholarship.
Value: US$10,800.
Length of Study: Two years.
Frequency: Annual.
Country of Study: United States of America.
No. of awards offered: Two.
Application Procedure: Applicants must send a letter of application to the Graduate School.
Closing Date: February 15th.
Funding: Private.
No. of awards given last year: Two.

Johnson's Wax Research Fellowship
Subjects: Engineering, chemistry or biology.
Eligibility: Applicants must be admitted to a doctoral programme in engineering, biology or chemistry.
Level of Study: Doctorate.
Type: Fellowship.
Value: US$5,500 stipend.
Length of Study: One year.
Frequency: Annual.
No. of awards offered: One.
Application Procedure: Qualified applicants will be contacted by their department.
Closing Date: February 15th.
Funding: Private.
No. of awards given last year: One.
Additional Information: The award is offered to a different programme each year.

Marquette University Women's Club Fellowship
Subjects: All subjects.
Purpose: To support students who received their Baccalaureate degrees from Marquette University.
Eligibility: Applicants must be admitted to a degree programme and have received a Bachelor's degree from Marquette University.
Level of Study: Graduate.
Type: Fellowship.
Value: US$2,000 stipend.
Length of Study: One year.
Frequency: Annual.
No. of awards offered: One.
Application Procedure: Qualified students will be contacted by their department.
Closing Date: February 15th.

Funding: Private.
No. of awards given last year: One.
Additional Information: The award is offered to a different graduate programme each year.

Marquette University's Graduate Assistantship
Subjects: All subjects.
Purpose: To support teaching and research.
Eligibility: Open to full-time Master's and doctoral students.
Level of Study: Graduate.
Type: Other.
Value: Stipends range from US$10,835-16,120 plus an 18 credit tuition scholarship, the value of which is approx. US$22,000.
Length of Study: One year.
Frequency: Annual.
No. of awards offered: 289.
Application Procedure: Applicants must submit an application to graduate school by the deadline. Please see the graduate bulletin for details or visit the website.
Closing Date: February 15th for the Autumn deadline and November 15th for the Spring deadline.
Funding: Private.
Contributor: Marquette University.
No. of awards given last year: 289.

Milwaukee Foundation's Frank Rogers Bacon Research Assistantship
Subjects: Electrical engineering.
Purpose: To provide research support for students.
Eligibility: Open to full-time Master's and doctoral students.
Level of Study: Graduate.
Type: Fellowship.
Value: US$10,835 stipend.
Length of Study: Varies.
Frequency: Annual.
Country of Study: United States of America.
No. of awards offered: Varies depending on funds.
Application Procedure: Applicants must contact the Department of Electrical and Computer Engineering at the University.
Closing Date: February 15th.
Funding: Private.
No. of awards given last year: Seven.

R A Bournique Memorial Fellowship
Subjects: Chemistry.
Eligibility: Open to graduate students in chemistry.
Level of Study: Graduate.
Type: Fellowship.
Value: US$1,250 stipend.
Length of Study: For the Summer.
Frequency: Annual.
No. of awards offered: Two.
Application Procedure: Applicants must contact the Department of Chemistry.
Funding: Private.
No. of awards given last year: Two.

MARSHALL AID COMMEMORATION COMMISSION

c/o ACU, John Foster House, 36 Gordon Square, London, WC1H 0PF, England
Tel: (44) 20 7380 6700
Fax: (44) 20 7387 2655
Email: info@marshallscholarship.org
www: http://www.marshallscholarship.org
Contact: Administrative Assistant

The Marshall Aid Commemoration Commission is responsible for the selection and placement of recipients of Marshall scholarships from the United States of America to the United Kingdom. The first awards were presented in 1954.

Marshall Scholarships

Subjects: All subjects.

Purpose: To provide intellectually distinguished young Americans with the opportunity to study in the United Kingdom, and thus to understand and appreciate the British way of life.

Eligibility: Open to United States citizens, who have graduated with a minimum grade point average of 3.7 or A- from an accredited United States college not more than two years previously. Recipients are required to take a degree at their United Kingdom university. Preference is given to candidates who combine high academic ability with the capacity to play an active part in the United Kingdom university.

Level of Study: Postgraduate.

Type: Scholarship.

Value: Approximately UK£19,000 per year, which comprises tuition fees, residence, travel and related costs.

Length of Study: Two academic years, with a possible extension for a third year.

Frequency: Annual.

Study Establishment: Any suitable institution.

Country of Study: United Kingdom.

No. of awards offered: 40.

Application Procedure: Applicants must submit an application form, university or college endorsement, and four references. Information and application forms can be obtained from the various consulate addresses. Full details on application procedures can be obtained from the website.

Closing Date: October annually.

Funding: Government.

No. of awards given last year: 40.

No. of applicants last year: 800.

For further information contact:

Cultural Department, British Embassy, 3100 Massachusetts Avenue NW, Washington, DC 20008, United States of America

British Consulate-General, 33 North Dearborn Street, Chicago, IL 60602, United States of America

British Consulate-General, 1 Memorial Drive, Suite 1500, Cambridge, MA 02142, United States of America

British Consulate-General, 1 Sansome Street, San Francisco, CA 94104, United States of America

British Consulate-General, 11766 Wiltshire Boulevard, Suite 400, Los Angeles, CA 90025, United States of America

British Consulate-General, Wells Fayo Plaza, 1000 Louisiana No 1900, Houston, TX 77002, United States of America

British Consulate-General, Georgia Pacific Center, Suite 3400, 134 Peachtree Street NE, Atlanta, GA 30303, United States of America

MARY ROBERTS RINEHART FUND

MSN 3E4, English Department, George Mason University, 4400 University Drive, Fairfax, VA 22030-4444, United States of America
Tel: (1) 703 993 1180
Email: bgompert@gmu.edu
www: http://www.gmu.edu/departments/writing/rinehart.htm
Contact: Mr William Miller, Director of Graduate Writing Program

The Mary Roberts Rinehart Fund is housed within a public university and was established to support and encourage unpublished writers.

Mary Roberts Rinehart Awards

Subjects: Writing eg. works of fiction, poetry, biography, autobiography or history with a strong narrative quality.

Purpose: To encourage developing writers who need financial assistance, not otherwise available, to complete works in progress.

Eligibility: Open to new and relatively unknown writers, without regard to citizenship, sex, colour or creed. Published writers are ineligible. Applicants from any country are eligible, although only works in English will be read and awards will only be made in United States dollars.

Level of Study: Unrestricted.

Type: Competition.

Value: US$2,000.

Frequency: Annual.

Country of Study: Any country.

No. of awards offered: Three.

Application Procedure: There are no formal application forms. The only way to have a work considered is to have it nominated by a sponsoring writer, agent, writing teacher or editor who is familiar with the author. Candidates are requested to provide their address and telephone number with their submission and should also include brief biographical information.

Closing Date: November 30th for announcement in the following March.

Funding: Private.

Contributor: The Mary Roberts Rinehart Foundation.

No. of awards given last year: Three.

No. of applicants last year: 500 + .

MARYLAND INSTITUTE COLLEGE OF ART (MICA)

1300 West Mount Royal Avenue, Baltimore, MD 21217, United States of America
Tel: (1) 410 225 2255
Fax: (1) 410 225 2408
Email: graduate@mica.edu
www: http://www.mica.edu
Contact: Mr Scott G Kelly, Director of Graduate Studies

The Maryland Institute College of Art (MICA) offers a Master of Fine Arts (MFA) degree in painting, sculpture, mixed media, photography, graphic design and digital imaging. It also offers excellent art education degrees such as an MAT, MA, and an MFA for art educators. The college has private studios, a strong visiting artists programme, housing and excellent exhibition opportunities. A new MA degree in digital arts is also available.

MICA Fellowship

Subjects: Arts.

Purpose: To serve as a tuition scholarship.

Level of Study: Graduate.

Type: Fellowship.

Value: US$5,000-12,000 per year.

Length of Study: One-two years.

Frequency: Annual.

Study Establishment: MICA.

Country of Study: United States of America.

No. of awards offered: 10.

Application Procedure: All accepted applicants are automatically considered.

Closing Date: February 15th.

Funding: Private.

Contributor: MICA.

No. of awards given last year: 10.

No. of applicants last year: 525.

MICA International Fellowship Award

Subjects: Fine and applied arts.

Purpose: To serve as a tuition scholarship.

Eligibility: Open to all international students accepted to the Institute.

Level of Study: Graduate.

Type: Fellowship.

Value: US$12,000 per year.

Length of Study: One-two years.

Frequency: Annual.

Study Establishment: MICA.

Country of Study: Any country.

No. of awards offered: One.

Application Procedure: All accepted applicants are automatically considered.
Closing Date: February 15th.
Funding: Private.
Contributor: MICA.
No. of awards given last year: One.
No. of applicants last year: 35.

MASSEY UNIVERSITY

National Student Administration & Teaching Support, Private Bag 11-222, Palmerston North, New Zealand
Tel: (64) 6 350 5799 ext. 2909
Fax: (64) 6 350 2263
Email: scholarships@massey.ac.nz
www: http://www.massey.ac.nz
Contact: Scholarships Officer

Massey University has over 30,000 students, 12,000 of which study on campus with the remaining 18,000 studying by correspondence. The five colleges of business, education, science, humanities and social sciences, and design, fine arts and music provide a comprehensive range of undergraduate and graduate degrees and diplomas all tailored to meeting national and international needs.

Massey Doctoral Scholarship

Subjects: Agriculture, forestry, town planning, arts and humanities, business administration and management, education and teacher training, engineering, commercial law, media studies, mathematics and computer science, nursing, midwifery, natural sciences, social welfare and social work, environmental studies, religious studies, tourism, social and behavioural studies and air transport, design, fine arts or music.
Purpose: To fund research towards a PhD degree.
Eligibility: Open to those with a minimum qualification of a First Class (Honours) Degree.
Level of Study: Doctorate.
Type: Scholarship.
Value: Please contact the organisation.
Length of Study: Three years.
Frequency: Annual.
Study Establishment: The University.
Country of Study: New Zealand.
No. of awards offered: 20-30.
Application Procedure: Applicants must complete an application form, available from the University. Further details can be found on the website.

THE MATSUMAE INTERNATIONAL FOUNDATION

4-14-46 Kamiogi, Suginami-ku, Tokyo, 167-0043, Japan
Tel: (81) 3 3301 7600
Fax: (81) 3 3301 7601
Email: contact@matsumae-if.org
www: http://www.matsumae-if.org
Contact: Mr S Nakajima

Matsumae International Foundation Research Fellowship

Subjects: Engineering, mathematics, medicine, natural sciences or agriculture.
Purpose: To provide the opportunity for foreign scientists to conduct research at Japanese institutions.
Eligibility: Open to applicants under 40 years of age, of non Japanese nationality, who hold a doctorate or have two years of research experience after receipt of a Master's degree, and who have not been to Japan previously.
Level of Study: Postdoctorate, Professional development.
Type: Fellowship.
Value: An air ticket, personal accident or sickness insurance and a research stipend plus yen 300,000 on arrival in addition to yen 200,000 monthly.

Length of Study: Three-six months.
Frequency: Annual.
Study Establishment: Unrestricted.
Country of Study: Japan.
No. of awards offered: 20.
Application Procedure: Applicants must obtain the current issue of the fellowship announcement from the Foundation.
Closing Date: July 31st.
Funding: Private.
Contributor: Charitable donations from individuals.
No. of awards given last year: 17.
No. of applicants last year: 116.
Additional Information: Priority will be given to the fields of science, engineering and medicine.

MCDONNELL CENTER FOR THE SPACE SCIENCES

Washington University, Campus Box 1169, One Brookings Drive, St Louis, MO 63130-4899, United States of America
Tel: (1) 314 935 5332
Fax: (1) 314 935 7361
Email: phillips@wustite.wustl.edu
www: http://wurtzite.wustl.edu
Contact: Professor Roger J Phillips, Director

The McDonnell Center for the Space Sciences exists to encourage scholarship and to promote collaborative research by Washington University scientists on space science related problems.

McDonnell Center Astronaut Fellowships in the Space Sciences

Subjects: Space sciences, physics, earth sciences, astronomy, chemistry and planetary studies.
Purpose: To encourage scholarship and research in accepted Washington University graduate students with an interest in space science.
Eligibility: Open to citizens of the United States of America who have applied for and been accepted into a graduate programme in the departments of physics, earth and planetary sciences or chemistry at Washington University, St Louis. Candidates must have an excellent academic background and a particular interest in the space sciences.
Level of Study: Doctorate.
Type: Fellowship.
Value: Full tuition plus stipend.
Length of Study: Nine months, one academic year, or three years.
Frequency: Annual.
Study Establishment: Washington University.
Country of Study: United States of America.
No. of awards offered: Three.
Application Procedure: Applicants must apply to one of the standard science or engineering departments at the University.
Closing Date: January 15th.
Funding: Private.
No. of awards given last year: 1.

McDonnell Graduate Fellowship in the Space Sciences

Subjects: Space sciences, physics, earth sciences, astronomy, chemistry and planetary studies.
Purpose: To encourage graduate scholarship and research.
Eligibility: Open to candidates who have applied for and been accepted into a graduate program in the department of physics or earth and planetary sciences at Washington University in St Louis. Candidates must have an excellent academic background and a particular interest in the space sciences.
Level of Study: Doctorate.
Type: Fellowship.
Value: Full tuition plus a stipend.
Length of Study: Three years.
Frequency: Annual.
Study Establishment: Washington University.
Country of Study: United States of America.
No. of awards offered: Four-six.

Application Procedure: Applicants who have been accepted into a Washington University graduate programme in physics, earth and planetary sciences, chemistry, biology or electrical engineering and who have exhibited an interest in the space sciences are automatically considered for a McDonnell Center Fellowship.
Closing Date: January 15th.
Funding: Private.
No. of awards given last year: Four.

MCGILL UNIVERSITY

3644 Peel Street, Montréal, QC, H3A 1W9, Canada
Tel: (1) 514 398 6604
Fax: (1) 514 398 4659
www: http://www.law.mcgill.ca
Contact: Ms Linda Coughlin, Secretary

Maxwell Boulton QC Fellowship
Subjects: Law, especially with significance to the Canadian legal system and legal community.
Purpose: To provide younger scholars with an opportunity to pursue a major research project or to complete the research requirements for a higher degree.
Eligibility: Open to candidates who have completed the residency requirements for a doctoral degree in law.
Level of Study: Doctorate, Postdoctorate.
Type: Fellowship.
Value: Canadian $30,000-35,000 per year.
Length of Study: One year.
Frequency: Annual.
Country of Study: Canada.
No. of awards offered: Two.
Application Procedure: Applicants must write for details.
Closing Date: February 1st.
No. of awards given last year: Two.
No. of applicants last year: 20.

MEDICAL LIBRARY ASSOCIATION (MLA)

65 East Wacker Place, Suite 1900, Chicago, IL 60601, United States of America
Tel: (1) 312 419 9094
Fax: (1) 312 419 8950
Email: mlapd2@mlahq.org
www: http://www.mlanet.org
Contact: Professional Development Department

The Medical Library Association (MLA) is organised exclusively for scientific and educational purposes, and is dedicated to the support of health sciences research, education and patient care. MLA fosters excellence in the professional achievement and leadership of health sciences library and information professionals to enhance the quality of health care, education and research.

Cunningham Memorial International Fellowship
Subjects: Medical librarianship.
Purpose: To provide a foreign medical librarian with the opportunity to observe and perform specialised work in the United States of America or Canada.
Eligibility: Open to those with a Baccalaureate degree and a library degree who are working in a medical library. The applicant must submit a signed statement from a home country official stating that he or she is guaranteed a position in a medical library upon returning home. A satisfactory score must be achieved on the Test of English as a Foreign Language competency examination. Nationals of the United States of America or Canada are not eligible.
Level of Study: Professional development.
Type: Fellowship.
Value: US$8,000 to cover living expenses and travel within the United States of America and Canada.
Length of Study: Three months.
Frequency: Annual.
Study Establishment: Medical libraries.
Country of Study: United States of America or Canada.
No. of awards offered: One.
Application Procedure: Applicants must submit a completed application form with three letters of reference in English, a project overview, certificate of health, Test of English as a Foreign Language examination result, and audio or video tape.
Closing Date: December 1st.
Funding: Private.
No. of awards given last year: One.

For further information contact:

www: http://www.mlanet.org/awards/grants/

MLA Continuing Education Grants
Subjects: The theoretical, administrative and technical aspects of library and information science.
Purpose: To provide professional health science librarians with the opportunity to continue their education.
Eligibility: Open to United States or Canadian citizens, or permanent residents who are medical librarians with a graduate degree in library science and at least two years of work experience at the professional level.
Level of Study: Professional development.
Type: Fellowship.
Value: US$100-500.
Length of Study: One year.
Frequency: Annual.
Country of Study: United States of America.
No. of awards offered: Usually one.
Application Procedure: Applicants must complete and submit an application form along with three references. Candidates should also identify a continuing education programme.
Closing Date: December 1st.
Funding: Private.
No. of awards given last year: One.
Additional Information: The award is not to support work towards a degree or certificate.

For further information contact:

www: http://www.mlanet.org/awards/grants/

MLA Doctoral Fellowship
Subjects: Medical librarianship or information science.
Purpose: To encourage superior students to conduct doctoral work in the field of health sciences librarianship or information sciences.
Eligibility: Open to citizens or permanent residents of the United States of America or Canada who are graduates of an ALA accredited library school and are in a PhD programme with an emphasis on biomedical and health related information science.
Level of Study: Doctorate.
Type: Fellowship.
Value: US$2,000.
Length of Study: One year, non renewable.
Frequency: Every two years.
Country of Study: United States of America or Canada.
No. of awards offered: One.
Application Procedure: Applicants must submit a completed application form with two letters of reference, transcripts of graduate work completed, a summary of the project and a detailed budget plus a signed statement of terms and conditions.
Closing Date: December 1st.
Contributor: Thomson ISI.
No. of awards given last year: One.
Additional Information: The award supports research or travel applicable to the candidate's study and may not be used for tuition.

For further information contact:

www: http://www.mlanet.org/awards/grants/

MLA Research, Development and Demonstration Project Award

Subjects: Health science librarianship or the information sciences.

Purpose: To provide support for research, development or demonstration projects that will help to promote excellence in the field of health sciences librarianship.

Eligibility: Open to members of the Association who have a graduate degree in library science, are practising medical librarians with at least two years of experience at the professional level and are citizens or permanent residents of the United States of America or Canada. Grants will not be given to support an activity which is only operational in nature or which has only local usefulness.

Level of Study: Postgraduate.

Type: Award.

Value: US$100-1,000.

Length of Study: One year.

Frequency: Annual.

Country of Study: United States of America or Canada.

No. of awards offered: Usually one.

Application Procedure: Applicants must submit a completed application form with three references, detailed description of project design and budget.

Closing Date: December 1st.

Funding: Private.

No. of awards given last year: One.

For further information contact:

www: http://www.mlanet.org/awards/grants/

MLA Scholarship

Subjects: Library science.

Purpose: To provide an opportunity to study at an ALA accredited library school.

Eligibility: Open to citizens and permanent residents of the United States of America or Canada who are entering an ALA accredited library school or who have at least one half of the academic requirements of the programme to finish in the year following the granting of the scholarship.

Level of Study: Graduate.

Type: Scholarship.

Value: US$5,000.

Length of Study: One full academic year.

Frequency: Annual.

Country of Study: United States of America or Canada.

No. of awards offered: One.

Application Procedure: Applicants must contact submit a completed application form with two letters of reference, official transcripts and a statement of career objectives.

Closing Date: December 1st.

Funding: Private.

No. of awards given last year: One.

For further information contact:

www: http://www.mlanet.org/awards/grants/

MLA Scholarship for Minority Students

Subjects: Medical librarianship.

Purpose: To provide a minority student with the opportunity to begin or continue graduate study in the field of library and information science.

Eligibility: Open to Black, Hispanic, Asian, Pacific Island or Native American students who are entering an ALA accredited library school and have at least one half of the academic requirements of the programme to finish in the year following the granting of the scholarship.

Level of Study: Graduate.

Type: Scholarship.

Value: US$5,000.

Length of Study: One academic year.

Frequency: Annual.

Study Establishment: An ALA accredited school.

Country of Study: United States of America or Canada.

No. of awards offered: One.

Application Procedure: Applicants must submit a completed application form with two letters of reference, official transcripts and a statement of career objectives.

Closing Date: December 1st.

No. of awards given last year: One.

For further information contact:

www: www.mlanet.org/awards/grant

MEDICAL RESEARCH COUNCIL (MRC)

20 Park Crescent, London, W1B 1AL, England
Tel: (44) 20 7636 5422
Fax: (44) 20 7670 5002
Email: robert.hay@headoffice.mrc.ac.uk
www: http://www.mrc.ac.uk
Contact: Mr Robert Hay, Fellowships Administrator

The Medical Research Council (MRC) offers support for talented individuals who want to pursue a career in the biomedical sciences, public health and health services research. It provides its support through a variety of personal award schemes that are aimed at each stage in a clinical or non clinical research career.

Collaborative Career Development Fellowship in Stem Cell Research

Subjects: Biomedical Sciences.

Purpose: To provide specialised training in Stem Cell Research to support Fundamental Stem Cell Biology or work towards new Stem Cell Derived Treatments for major diseases and disabilities.

Eligibility: Applications are normally expected to have a PhD/DPhil in a relevant discipline or hold a relevant research oriented masters degree and have undertaken a period of not less than three years appropriate research training.

Level of Study: Postdoctorate.

Type: Fellowship.

Value: An appropriate clinical or academic salary along with a fixed sum for research expenses and a travel allowance for attendance at scientific conferences.

Length of Study: Up to three years.

Frequency: Annual.

Study Establishment: A suitable university or similar institution.

Country of Study: United Kingdom.

No. of awards offered: Varies.

Application Procedure: Applications must submit a personal application. Forms and further details are available from the MRC.

Closing Date: Usually around February but applicants are advised to check the website for details.

Funding: Government.

No. of awards given last year: Up to 6.

No. of applicants last year: 19.

Additional Information: Awards may be joint funded with the MRC, or funded by bodies other than the MRC. Please contact the fellowships section at the MRC for further details.

MRC Career Development Award

Subjects: Biomedical sciences.

Purpose: To award outstanding researchers who wish to consolidate and develop their research skills and make the transition from post-doctoral research and training to becoming independent investigators, but who do not hold established positions.

Eligibility: It is expected that all applicants will hold a PhD or MPhil in a basic science and will have at least three years of postdoctoral research experience.

Level of Study: Postdoctorate, Research.

Type: Fellowship.

Value: Competitive personal salary support plus research support staff at technical level, research expenses, capital equipment and a travel allowance for attendance at scientific conferences.

Length of Study: Up to four years.

Frequency: Annual.

Study Establishment: A suitable university department or similar institution.

Country of Study: United Kingdom.
No. of awards offered: Up to eight.
Application Procedure: Applicants must submit a personal application. Forms and further details are available from the MRC.
Closing Date: Usually around November, but applicants are advised to check the website for details.
Funding: Government.
No. of awards given last year: 9.
No. of applicants last year: 78.
Additional Information: Awards may occasionally be joint funded with other bodies. Please contact the fellowships section at the MRC for further details.

MRC Clinical Research Training Fellowships
Subjects: Biomedical sciences.
Purpose: To provide an opportunity for specialised or further research training leading to the submission of a PhD, DPhil or MD.
Eligibility: Open to hospital doctors, dentists, general practitioners, nurses, midwives and Allied Health Professionals. Residence requirements apply.
Level of Study: Postgraduate, Research.
Type: Fellowship.
Value: An appropriate clinical academic salary will be provided along with a fixed sum for research expenses and a travel allowance for attendance at scientific conferences.
Length of Study: Up to three years.
Frequency: Twice a year.
Study Establishment: A suitable university department or similar institution.
Country of Study: United Kingdom.
No. of awards offered: Up to 32.
Application Procedure: Applicants must submit a personal application. Forms and further details are available from the MRC.
Closing Date: Round one is August/September, and round two is January/February, but applicants are advised to check the website for details.
Funding: Government.
No. of awards given last year: 31.
No. of applicants last year: 218.
Additional Information: In addition to this scheme, the MRC also offers Joint Training Fellowships with the Royal Colleges of Surgeons of England and Edinburgh and the Royal College of Obstetricians and Gynaecologists. These awards are aimed at individuals whose long-term career aspirations involve undertaking academic clinical research. Fellowships may also be jointly funded with the MS Society, or the Prior Group. Please contact the Fellowships Section at the MRC for further details.

MRC Clinician Scientist Fellowship
Subjects: Biomedical sciences.
Purpose: To provide an opportunity for outstanding clinical researchers who wish to consolidate their research skills and make the transition from postdoctoral research and training to becoming independent investigators.
Eligibility: The scheme is open to hospital doctors, dentists, general practitioners, nurses, midwives and Allied Health Professionals. All applicants must have obtained their PhD or MD in a basic science or clinical project, or expect to have received their doctorate by the time they intend to take up an award and must not hold tenured positions.
Level of Study: Postdoctorate, Research.
Type: Fellowship.
Value: Competitive personal salary support plus research support staff at the technical level, research expenses, capital equipment and a travel allowance for attendance at scientific conferences.
Length of Study: Up to four years.
Frequency: Annual.
Study Establishment: A suitable university department or similar institution.
Country of Study: United Kingdom.
No. of awards offered: Up to seven.
Application Procedure: Applicants must submit a personal application. Forms and further details are available from the MRC.

Closing Date: August to December, but applicants are advised to check the website for details.
Funding: Government.
No. of awards given last year: 7.
No. of applicants last year: 55.
Additional Information: For 2004/05 Fellowships may also be jointly funded with the Limbury Trust . Please contact the Fellowships section at the MRC for further details.

MRC Collaborative/Industrial Collaborative Studentships
Subjects: Any biomedical science.
Purpose: To enhance links between academia and industry in the provision of high quality research training.
Eligibility: Candidates should have graduated with a good Honours Degree from a United Kingdom academic institution in a subject relevant to the MRC's scientific remit. This should be an Upper Second Class Degree or higher. The MRC will however consider qualifications or a combination of qualifications and experience which demonstrates equivalent ability and attainment eg. a Lower Second Class Degree can be enhanced by a Master's degree. A copy of the regulations governing residence eligibility may be obtained from the Council.
Level of Study: Postgraduate.
Value: A tax free maintenance stipend depending on United Kingdom location, university tuition fees up to the current DFEE recommended limit plus college fees, where applicable. Awards also include a fixed sum for conference travel expenses and a support grant to the university department to help cover incidental costs of students' training. As a measure of interest and involvement the industrial company is expected to make a financial contribution to the cost of the studentship.
Length of Study: Up to three years.
Frequency: Annual.
Study Establishment: Universities, medical schools, industry and other academic institutions.
Country of Study: United Kingdom.
No. of awards offered: Approx. 50.
Application Procedure: The MRC does not make awards directly to students. Awards are made to departments who apply for studentships by application. Departments will then advertise for students to apply for their awards. Students who wish to apply for a studentship are advised to contact the department where they wish to study to see if it has an allocation of awards.
Closing Date: Departments should submit student nomination forms to the MRC no later than July 31st each year.
Funding: Commercial.
No. of awards given last year: Approx. 50.
Additional Information: The industrial company is expected to make a contribution.

MRC Masters Studentships
Subjects: Any biomedical science.
Purpose: To enable students to undertake early research training relevant to strategic research or strategic employment in a research related capacity in academia or industry.
Eligibility: Candidates should have graduated with a good Honours Degree. A copy of the regulations governing residence eligibility may be obtained from the Council.
Level of Study: Postgraduate.
Type: Studentship.
Value: Tax free maintenance stipend, depending on United Kingdom location, and university tuition fees up to the current DFEE recommended limit. Awards also include a fixed sum for conference travel expenses.
Length of Study: One year.
Frequency: Annual.
Study Establishment: Universities, medical schools and other academic organisations.
Country of Study: United Kingdom.
No. of awards offered: Approx. 90.
Application Procedure: The MRC does not make awards directly to students. Awards are made to departments who apply for studentships by application. Departments will then advertise for students to apply for their awards. Students who wish to apply for a studentship

are advised to contact the department where they wish to study to see if it has an allocation of awards.

Closing Date: Departments must submit student nomination forms to the MRC no later than July 31st each year.

Funding: Government.

No. of awards given last year: Approx. 90.

Additional Information: The MRC also has awards in strategic scientific priority areas from time to time. Further details are available from the MRC website. Studentship awards will be replaced by Doctoral Training Accounts (DTA) for October 2004 awards. Further details can be obtained from the MRC website www.mrc.ac.uk.

MRC Patient Oriented Clinician Scientist Fellowship

Subjects: Biomedical sciences.

Purpose: To allow outstanding clinical researchers to consolidate their research skills and make the transition from postdoctoral research and training to becoming independent investigators. These awards allow for a greater proportion of time (up to 40 per cent) to be spent in clinical work, at least some of which should be of direct relevance to the project.

Eligibility: Open to hospital doctors, dentists, general practitioners, nurses, midwives and Allied Health Professionals who have already secured a PhD in a basic science subject.

Level of Study: Postdoctorate, Research.

Type: Fellowship.

Value: Competitive personal salary support plus research support staff at technical level, research expenses, capital equipment and a travel allowance for attendance at scientific conferences.

Length of Study: Up to five years.

Frequency: Annual.

Study Establishment: A suitable university department or similar institution.

Country of Study: United Kingdom.

No. of awards offered: Up to four.

Application Procedure: Applicants must submit a personal application. Forms and further details are available from the MRC.

Closing Date: August to December, but applicants are advised to check the website for details.

Funding: Government.

No. of awards given last year: 2.

No. of applicants last year: 12.

MRC Research Studentships

Subjects: Any biomedical science.

Purpose: To enable individuals to undertake a training programme under the guidance of named supervisors that includes a research project plus training in research methods and personal key skills.

Eligibility: Candidates should have graduated with a good Honours Degree from a United Kingdom academic institution in a subject relevant to the MRC's scientific remit. This should be an Upper Second Class Degree or higher. The MRC will however consider qualifications or a combination of qualifications and experience which demonstrates equivalent ability and attainment eg. a Lower Second Class Degree can be enhanced by a Master's degree. A copy of the regulations governing residence eligibility may be obtained from the Council.

Level of Study: Predoctorate.

Type: Other.

Value: A tax free maintenance stipend depending on United Kingdom location, university tuition fees up to the current DFEE recommended limit plus college fees, where applicable. Awards also include a fixed sum for conference travel expenses and a support grant to the university department to help cover incidental costs of students' training.

Length of Study: Most studentships are three years, but they can be linked to a Master's course, making it a four year programme.

Frequency: Annual.

Study Establishment: Universities, medical schools, MRC research establishments and other academic organisations.

Country of Study: United Kingdom.

No. of awards offered: 390 including studentships in strategic capacity building areas.

Application Procedure: The MRC does not make awards directly to students. Awards are made to departments who apply for studentships by application. Departments will then advertise for students to

apply for their awards. Students who wish to apply for a studentship are advised to contact the department where they wish to study to see if it has an allocation of awards.

Closing Date: Departments must submit student nomination forms to the MRC no later than July 31st each year.

Funding: Government.

Additional Information: Studentship awards will be replaced by Doctoral Training Accounts (DTA) for October 2004 awards. Further details can be obtained from the MRC website www.mrc.ac.uk.

MRC Royal College of Obstetricians and Gynaecologists (RCOG) Training Fellowship

Subjects: Biomedical sciences.

Purpose: To provide members of the Royal College with an opportunity for specialist or further research training in a basic science relevant to obstetrics and gynaecology leading to the submission of a PhD, a DPhil or an MD.

Eligibility: Open to members of the RCOG wishing to pursue research at PhD or MD level. Applicants must have a minimum of one year of experience in clinical obstetrics and gynaecology and hold part one membership of the college. Residence requirements apply.

Level of Study: Postgraduate, Research.

Type: Fellowship.

Value: An appropriate clinical academic salary will be provided along with a fixed sum for research expenses and a travel allowance for attendance at scientific conferences.

Length of Study: Up to three years.

Frequency: Annual.

Study Establishment: A suitable university or similar institution.

Country of Study: United Kingdom.

No. of awards offered: One a year.

Application Procedure: Applicants must contact the Fellowships Section, Research Career Awards of the MRC for details.

Closing Date: Applicants are advised to check the MRC website for details.

Funding: Government.

No. of awards given last year: 0.

No. of applicants last year: 6.

MRC Royal College of Surgeons of Edinburgh Training Fellowship

Subjects: Biomedical sciences.

Purpose: To provide an opportunity for specialised or further research training within the United Kingdom leading to the submission of a PhD, DPhil or MD.

Eligibility: Open to members of the Royal College of Surgeons of Edinburgh wishing to pursue research at the PhD or MD level. Residence requirements apply.

Level of Study: Postgraduate, Research.

Type: Fellowship.

Value: An appropriate clinical academic salary will be provided along with a fixed sum for research expenses and a travel allowance for attendance at scientific conferences.

Length of Study: Up to three years.

Frequency: Annual.

Study Establishment: A suitable university department or similar institution.

Country of Study: United Kingdom.

No. of awards offered: One-two a year.

Application Procedure: Applicants must submit a personal application. Forms and further details are available from the MRC.

Closing Date: Applicants are advised to check the MRC website for details.

Funding: Government.

No. of awards given last year: 1.

No. of applicants last year: 22.

MRC Royal College of Surgeons of England Training Fellowship

Subjects: Biomedical sciences.

Purpose: To provide an opportunity for specialised or further research training within the United Kingdom leading to the submission of a PhD, DPhil or MD.

Eligibility: Open to members of the Royal College of Surgeons of England wishing to pursue research at the PhD or MD level. Residence requirements apply.
Level of Study: Postgraduate, Research.
Type: Fellowship.
Value: An appropriate clinical academic salary will be provided along with a fixed sum for research expenses and a travel allowance for attendance at scientific conferences.
Length of Study: Up to three years.
Frequency: Annual.
Study Establishment: A suitable university department or similar institution.
Country of Study: United Kingdom.
No. of awards offered: Up to two a year.
Application Procedure: Applicants must submit a personal application. Forms and further details are available from the MRC.
Closing Date: Round one is August/September, and round two is in January/February, but applicants are advised to check the website for details.
Funding: Government.
No. of awards given last year: 2.
No. of applicants last year: 32.

MRC Senior Clinical Fellowship
Subjects: Biomedical sciences.
Purpose: To provide an opportunity for clinical researchers of exceptional ability to concentrate on a period of research.
Eligibility: Open to nationals of any country. Applicants are expected to have proven themselves to be independent researchers, be well qualified for an academic research career and demonstrate the promise of becoming future research leaders. The scheme is open to hospital doctors, dentists, general practitioners, nurses, midwives and Allied Health Professionals. Applicants must hold a PhD or MD in a basic science or clinical project and have at least three years of postdoctoral research experience.
Level of Study: Postdoctorate, Research.
Type: Fellowship.
Value: Competitive personal salary support is provided plus research support staff at the technical and postdoctoral level, research expenses, capital equipment and a travel allowance for attendance at scientific conferences.
Length of Study: Up to five years, with a possibility of renewal through open competition for a further five years.
Frequency: Annual.
Study Establishment: A suitable university department or similar institution.
Country of Study: United Kingdom.
No. of awards offered: Up to four.
Application Procedure: Applicants must complete a personal application. Forms and further details are available from the MRC.
Closing Date: Usually around August, but applicants are advised to check the website for details.
Funding: Government.
No. of awards given last year: 3.
No. of applicants last year: 16.

MRC Senior Non-Clinical Fellowship
Subjects: Biomedical sciences.
Purpose: To provide support for non clinical scientists of exceptional ability to concentrate on a period of research.
Eligibility: Open to nationals of any country. Applicants are expected to have proven themselves to be independent researchers, be well qualified for an academic research career and demonstrate the promise of becoming future research leaders. It is expected that all applicants will hold a PhD or DPhil in a basic science project, have at least six years of relevant postdoctoral research experience and not hold a tenured position.
Level of Study: Postdoctorate, Research.
Type: Fellowship.
Value: Competitive personal salary support is provided plus research support staff at the technical and postdoctoral level, research expenses, capital equipment and a travel allowance for attendance at scientific conferences.

Length of Study: Up to five years, with a possibility of renewal through open competition for a further five years.
Frequency: Annual.
Study Establishment: A suitable university department or similar institution.
Country of Study: United Kingdom.
No. of awards offered: Up to six.
Application Procedure: Applicants must complete a personal application. Forms and further details are available from the MRC.
Closing Date: Usually around September, but applicants are advised to check the website for details.
Funding: Government.
No. of awards given last year: 5.
No. of applicants last year: 34.

MRC Special Training Fellowships in Bioinformatics, Neuroinformatics and Computational Biology
Subjects: Biomedical sciences.
Purpose: To provide specialist, multidisciplinary research training at the doctoral or postdoctoral level. Fellows may undertake a Master's degree during the first part of their fellowship, followed by a period of specialist research training.
Eligibility: The scheme is aimed at individuals from a variety of backgrounds such as non biological as well as biological, non clinical as well as clinical, and individuals with PhDs or MDs or with informatics research experience at the predoctoral level.
Level of Study: Postgraduate, Research.
Type: Fellowship.
Value: An appropriate academic salary will be provided along with a fixed sum for research expenses and a travel allowance for attendance at scientific conferences.
Length of Study: Up to four years.
Frequency: Annual.
Study Establishment: A suitable university department or similar institution.
Country of Study: United Kingdom.
No. of awards offered: Up to Four.
Application Procedure: Applicants must complete a personal application. Forms and further details are available from the MRC.
Closing Date: Applicants are advised to check the website for details.
Funding: Government.
No. of awards given last year: 5.
No. of applicants last year: 23.
Additional Information: Award holders are encouraged to apply for a PhD or MD if they do not already have one.

MRC Special Training Fellowships in Health Services and Health of the Public Research
Subjects: Biomedical sciences in health services research and health of the public. Applications must be within the health services and health of the public remit as defined by the MRC.
Purpose: To provide support for researchers wishing to gain further training in multidisciplinary research to address problems of direct relevance to the health services within the United Kingdom.
Eligibility: Open to non medical graduates, hospital doctors, dentists, general practitioners, nurses, midwives and allied health professionals who are seeking a research career in health services and research.
Level of Study: Postdoctorate, Research.
Type: Fellowship.
Value: An appropriate academic salary will be provided along with a fixed sum for research expenses and a travel allowance for attendance at scientific conferences.
Length of Study: Up to four years.
Frequency: Annual.
Study Establishment: A suitable university department or similar institution.
Country of Study: United Kingdom.
No. of awards offered: Up to 15.
Application Procedure: Applicants must complete a personal application. Forms and further details are available from the MRC.
Closing Date: Usually around September/October, but applicants are advised to check the website for details.
Funding: Government.

No. of awards given last year: 14.
No. of applicants last year: 46.
Additional Information: Some awards are jointly funded with the Department of Health.

MRC/Academy of Medical Sciences Tenure Track Clinician Scientist Fellowship

Subjects: Biomedical sciences.
Purpose: To allow outstanding clinical researchers to consolidate their research skills and make the transition from postdoctoral research and training to becoming independent investigators, and to support career development and promote recruitment into clinical academic medicine.
Eligibility: Open to hospital doctors, dentists and general practitioners.
Level of Study: Postdoctorate, Research.
Type: Fellowship.
Value: Competitive personal salary support plus research support staff at the technical level, research expenses, capital equipment and a travel allowance for attendance at scientific conferences.
Length of Study: Up to five years.
Frequency: Annual
Study Establishment: A suitable university department or similar institution.
Country of Study: United Kingdom.
No. of awards offered: Varies.
Application Procedure: Applicants must submit a personal application. Forms and further details are available from the MRC.
Closing Date: August-December, but applicants are advised to check the website for details.
Funding: Government.
No. of awards given last year: 4.
No. of applicants last year: 8.

MEET THE COMPOSER, INC.

75 Ninth Avenue, 3R Suite C, New York, NY 10011, United States of America
Tel: (1) 212 645 6949
Fax: (1) 212 645 9669
Email: mtrevino@meetthecomposer.org
www: http://www.meetthecomposer.org
Contact: Mr Edward Ficklin, Director of Programmes

Meet The Composer's mission is to increase artistic and financial opportunities for American composers by fostering the creation, performance, dissemination and appreciation of their music.

Commissioning Music/USA

Subjects: Music commissioning.
Purpose: To support the commissioning of new works.
Eligibility: Open to United States citizens only. Organisations that have been producing or presenting for at least three years are eligible and may be dance, chorus, orchestra, opera, theatre and music-theatre companies, festivals, arts presenters, public radio and television stations, internet providers, soloists and small performing ensembles of all kinds eg. jazz, chamber, new music etc.
Level of Study: Professional development.
Value: A single organisation may apply for up to US$15,000 and a consortium for up to US$30,000.
Frequency: Annual.
Country of Study: United States of America.
Application Procedure: Individuals cannot apply themselves. Host organisations must submit completed application forms and accompanying materials.
Closing Date: January 15th.
Contributor: Offered in partnership with the National Endowment for the Arts.
No. of awards given last year: 20-30.
No. of applicants last year: 150-200.
Additional Information: Further information is available on request.

JPMorganChase Regrant Program for Small Ensembles

Subjects: Musical performance.
Purpose: To support small New York city based ensembles and music organisations with a commitment to performing work of living composers and contemporary music.
Eligibility: Applicants must write for details.
Level of Study: Professional development.
Type: Award.
Value: US$1,000-5,000.
Frequency: Annual.
Country of Study: United States of America.
Application Procedure: Applicants must contact the organisation.
Closing Date: April 30th.
Funding: Commercial.
Contributor: In partnership with JPMorganChase.
No. of awards given last year: 15-20.
No. of applicants last year: 75-100.
Additional Information: Further information is available on request.

Meet The Composer Fund

Subjects: Musical performance.
Purpose: To enable composers to participate actively in performances of their work and consequently build audiences for new music. Participation may include performing, conducting, speaking with the audience, presenting workshops, giving interviews and coaching performances.
Eligibility: Open to United States citizens only. Organisations may be choruses, dance, opera, theatre and music theatre companies, symphonies, arts presenters, musical organisations, festivals, television production companies, radio stations and performing ensembles of all kinds eg. jazz, chamber, new music etc. Awards are based solely on the overall quality of the application which includes merit of composer participation, level of audience or community involvement and general strength of the compositions.
Level of Study: Professional development.
Value: Up to US$250-1,000 per composer.
Frequency: Four times per year.
Country of Study: United States of America.
Application Procedure: Varies from region to region but individuals cannot apply themselves, as performing organisations apply on behalf of the composer. Interested parties should contact the organisation for further details.
Closing Date: Application deadlines are quarterly: January 2nd, April 1st, June 1st and October 1st.
No. of awards given last year: 85 per cent.
No. of applicants last year: 800-1,000.
Additional Information: Further information is available on request.

Music Alive

Subjects: For professional composers to work with teachers, students and their families, nurturing creativity in the classroom while writing works for students to play and sing.
Purpose: To support composer residencies.
Eligibility: Open to all American Symphony Orchestra League and youth member orchestras.
Level of Study: Professional development.
Type: Residency.
Value: A composer's fee of US$2,500 per residency week, composer's expenses of up to one round trip for every two week residency and up to US$175 per day for food and lodging, and orchestra expenses of up to US$1,000 per residency week.
Length of Study: Two-eight week residencies.
Frequency: Annual.
Country of Study: United States of America.
Application Procedure: Individuals cannot apply themselves, as performing organisations apply on behalf of the composer.
Closing Date: August 16th.
Contributor: Offered in partnership with the American Symphony Orchestra League.
Additional Information: Further information is available on request.

Music Alive: Composers and Orchestras Together

Subjects: Musical performance.

Purpose: To financially support orchestras.

Eligibility: Open to all American Symphony Orchestra league professional and youth member orchestras. The residencies must be scheduled in conjunction with performances of the composer's work. The works may be a world premiere or an existing work by a living American composer. Performance of a world premiere or commissioned work is not a requirement of the programme. Residency weeks may be scheduled contiguously or divided into multiple visits but must be of a one week minimum duration.

Level of Study: Professional development.

Type: Grant.

Value: A composer's fee of up to US$2,500 per residency per week, composer's expenses of up to one round trip for every two week residency and up to US$175 per day for food and lodging, and orchestra expenses of up to US$1,000 per residency week.

Length of Study: Two-eight weeks.

Frequency: Annual.

Country of Study: United States of America.

Application Procedure: Individuals cannot apply themselves. Performing organisations must apply on behalf of the composer.

Closing Date: August 16th.

Additional Information: Further information is available on request.

MELVILLE TRUST FOR CARE AND CURE OF CANCER

c/o Tods Murray WS, 66 Queen Street, Edinburgh, EH2 4NE,
Scotland
Tel: (44) 131 226 4771
Fax: (44) 131 225 3676
Email: maildesk@todsmurray.com

Melville Trust for Care and Cure of Cancer Research Fellowships

Subjects: The care and cure of cancer.

Purpose: To fund innovative research work.

Eligibility: Applicants need not necessarily hold a medical qualification or have experience of research.

Level of Study: Research.

Type: Fellowship.

Length of Study: Up to two years.

Frequency: Annual.

Study Establishment: One of the clinical or scientific departments in Lothian, Borders, Fife or Dundee.

Application Procedure: Applicants must complete an application form and then be interviewed.

Closing Date: March 31st.

No. of awards given last year: Two.

No. of applicants last year: Four.

Melville Trust for Care and Cure of Cancer Research Grants

Subjects: The care and cure of cancer.

Eligibility: Applicants need not necessarily hold a medical qualification or have experience of research.

Level of Study: Research.

Type: Grant.

Value: Up to UK£25,000.

Length of Study: Up to two years.

Frequency: Annual.

Study Establishment: One of the clinical or scientific departments in Lothian, Borders, Fife or Dundee.

Application Procedure: Applicants must complete an application form.

Closing Date: March 31st.

Funding: Private.

No. of awards given last year: Five.

No. of applicants last year: Seven.

MEMORIAL FOUNDATION FOR JEWISH CULTURE

50 Broadway, 34th Floor, New York, NY 10004, United States of
America
Tel: (1) 212 425 6606
Fax: (1) 212 425 6602
Email: office@mfjc.org
www: http://www.mfjc.org
Contact: Dr Jerry Hochbaum, Executive Vice President

The Memorial Foundation for Jewish Culture was established in 1965 to help assure a creative future for Jewish life throughout the world. The Foundation encourages Jewish scholarship, Jewish cultural creativity, and makes possible the training of professionals to serve in communities deprived of a large Jewish presence.

Memorial Foundation for Jewish Culture Grants for Jewish Research and Publication

Subjects: Jewish studies.

Purpose: To facilitate research and publication and the preparation of textbooks and educational literature for children and youth.

Eligibility: Open to universities, Jewish educational organisations and recognised scholarly bodies.

Level of Study: Unrestricted.

Type: Grant.

No. of awards offered: Varies.

Application Procedure: Please consult the organisation.

Memorial Foundation for Jewish Culture International Doctoral Scholarships

Subjects: Jewish studies.

Purpose: To assist in the training of future Jewish scholars for careers in Jewish scholarship and research and to enable religious, educational and other Jewish communal workers to obtain advanced training for leadership positions.

Eligibility: Open to graduate students of any nationality who are specialising in a Jewish field. Applicants must be officially enrolled or registered in a doctoral programme at a recognised university.

Level of Study: Doctorate.

Type: Scholarship.

Value: US$2,000-7,500 per year but varies depending on the country where study is undertaken.

Length of Study: One academic year, renewable for a maximum of four years.

Frequency: Annual.

Study Establishment: A recognised university.

Country of Study: Any country.

No. of awards offered: Varies.

Application Procedure: Applicants must write requesting an application.

Closing Date: October 31st.

Memorial Foundation for Jewish Culture International Fellowships in Jewish Studies

Subjects: A field of Jewish specialisation which will make a significant contribution to the understanding, preservation, enhancement or transmission of Jewish culture.

Purpose: To allow well qualified individuals to carry out independent scholarly, literary or artistic projects.

Eligibility: Open to recognised or qualified Scholars, researchers or artists of any nationality who possess the knowledge and experience to formulate and implement a project in a field of Jewish specialisation.

Level of Study: Unrestricted.

Type: Fellowship.

Value: US$2,000-7,500 but varies depending on the country in which the project is undertaken.

Length of Study: One academic year, in exceptional cases renewable for a further year.

Frequency: Annual.

Country of Study: Any country.

No. of awards offered: Varies.

Application Procedure: Applicants must write requesting an application.
Closing Date: October 31st.

Memorial Foundation for Jewish Culture International Scholarship Programme for Community Service

Subjects: The rabbinate, Jewish education, communal service or religious functionaries, eg. shohatim, mohalim.
Purpose: To assist well qualified individuals for career training.
Eligibility: Open to any individual who is planning or who is currently undertaking training in his or her chosen field in a recognised Yeshiva, teacher training seminary, school of social work, university or other educational institution.
Level of Study: Unrestricted.
Type: Scholarship.
Value: US$1,000-4,000 but varies depending on the country in which the recipient is trained and other considerations.
Length of Study: One year, renewable.
Frequency: Annual.
Study Establishment: Diaspora Jewish communities in need of such personnel.
Country of Study: Other
No. of awards offered: Varies.
Application Procedure: Applicants must write for details.
Closing Date: November 30th.
Additional Information: Recipients must commit themselves to serve a community of need. They should also be knowledgeable in the language and culture of that country or be prepared to learn it.

Memorial Foundation for Jewish Culture Scholarships for Post-Rabbinical Students

Subjects: Jewish studies.
Purpose: To assist in the training of future Jewish religious scholars and leaders and to assist newly ordained rabbis to obtain advanced training for careers as head of Yeshivot, as Dayanim and in other leadership positions.
Eligibility: Open to recently ordained rabbis engaged in full-time studies at a Yeshiva, Kollel or rabbinical seminaries.
Level of Study: Unrestricted.
Type: Scholarship.
Value: US$1,000-4,000.
Length of Study: One year.
Frequency: Annual.
Country of Study: Any country.
No. of awards offered: Varies.
Application Procedure: Applicants must write for details.
Closing Date: November 30th.
Additional Information: The Foundation also provides grants to bolster Jewish educational programmes in areas of need. Grants are awarded on the understanding that the recipient institution will assume responsibility for the programme following the initial limited period of Foundation support. Grants are made only for team or collaborative projects.

MENINGITIS RESEARCH FOUNDATION

Midland Way, Thornbury, Bristol, BS35 2BS, England
Tel: (44) 1454 281811
Fax: (44) 1454 281094
Email: lindaglennie@meningitis.org
www: http://www.meningitis.org
Contact: Mrs Joy Pepper, Research Administrator

The Meningitis Research Foundation is a registered charity that supports an international programme of independently peer reviewed research into the prevention, detection and treatment of meningitis and septicaemia. The Foundation also provides information for the public and health professionals, runs medical and scientific meetings and provides support to people affected by the disease.

Meningitis Research Foundation Project Grant

Subjects: Meningitis and associated infections that focus on prevention, including vaccine directed research, improving the speed and

accuracy of diagnosis, improving treatment and outlook for patients, in particular development of more effective therapies, and epidemiology and disease surveillance. The charity's trustees particularly welcome well-designed applications for research relating to the development of a serogroup B meningococcal vaccine.
Purpose: To fight death and disability from meningitis and septicaemia by supporting research with the potential to produce results in immediate problem areas. This may include basic research that contributes to understanding their pathophysiology or epidemiology but priority is given to work that is likely to bring clinical or public health benefits.
Eligibility: There are no eligibility restrictions.
Level of Study: Research.
Type: Project grant.
Value: Up to UK£150,000 per year.
Length of Study: Up to five years.
Frequency: Twice a year.
Study Establishment: Universities, research institutes and teaching hospitals.
No. of awards offered: Two.
Application Procedure: Applicants must submit a two or three page outline proposal by email summarising the work planned, the approximate cost and the duration of the project. The Foundation will decide whether to request a full application based on this outline proposal according to whether it conforms to the Charity's objectives and research strategy, its feasibility and whether there is overlap with projects already funded. At this stage there is no scientific assessment of the proposed research. Researchers who are invited to submit a full application are sent grant application forms and other documents to refer to when completing their application. Full applications are assessed by structured peer review, according to the Association of Medical Research Charities' principles of accountability, balance, independence, rotation of advisers, and impartiality. A minimum of two independent external referees provide detailed written comments and an overall score on the application. The Scientific Advisory Panel then meets to decide on proposals to recommend, with reference to referee reviews. Final decisions are made by the Foundation's Trustees on applications recommended by the Panel. Meningitis Research Foundation grants are highly competitive and are awarded primarily on the basis of clear relevance to the Charity's aims and scientific merit.
Closing Date: February 28th or 31st August.
Funding: Private.
Contributor: Voluntary donations from the public.
No. of awards given last year: Four.
No. of applicants last year: 42.

Meningitis Research Foundation Small Project Grant

Subjects: Meningitis and associated infections that focus on prevention, including vaccine directed research, improving the speed and accuracy of diagnosis, improving treatment and outlook for patients, in particular, development of more effective therapies, and epidemiology and disease surveillance. The Charity's Trustees particularly welcome well-designed applications for research relating to the development of a serogroup B meningococcal vaccine.
Purpose: To fight death and disability from meningitis and septicaemia by supporting research with the potential to produce results in immediate problem areas. This may include basic research that contributes to understanding their pathophysiology or epidemiology but priority is given to work that is likely to bring clinical or public health benefit.
Eligibility: There are no eligibility restrictions.
Level of Study: Research.
Type: Small Project Grant.
Value: Up to UK£30,000 per year.
Length of Study: Up to three years.
Frequency: Twice a year.
Study Establishment: Universities, research institutes and teaching hospitals.
No. of awards offered: Two.
Application Procedure: Applicants must submit a two or three page outline proposal by email summarising the work planned, the approximate cost and the duration of the project. The Foundation will decide whether to request a full application based on this outline

proposal according to whether it conforms to the Charity's objectives and research strategy, its feasibility and whether there is overlap with projects already funded. At this stage there is no scientific assessment of the proposed research. Researchers who are invited to submit a full application are sent grant application forms and other documents to refer to when completing their application. Full applications are assessed by structured peer review, according to the Association of Medical Research Charities' principles of accountability, balance, independence, rotation of advisers, and impartiality. A minimum of two independent external referees provide detailed written comments and an overall score on the application. The Scientific Advisory Panel then meets to decide on proposals to recommend, with reference to referee reviews. Final decisions are made by the Foundation's Trustees on applications recommended by the Panel. Meningitis Research Foundation grants are highly competitive and are awarded primarily on the basis of clear relevance to the Charity's aims and scientific merit.

Closing Date: February 28th or August 31st.
Funding: Private.
Contributor: Voluntary donations from the public.
No. of awards given last year: Nil.
No. of applicants last year: Six.

MENINGITIS TRUST

Fern House, Bath Road, Stroud
Gloucestershire, GL5 3TJ, England
Tel: (44) 1453 768000
Fax: (44) 1453 768001
Email: support@meningitis-trust.org.uk
Contact: Ms Sarah Booker, Education & Research Co-ordinator

The Meningitis Trust is an internationally respected charity with a strong community focus. It has three main aims which are to provide care and support for people affected by meningitis, to educate both public and professionals and to fund life saving medical research. The strategic aim of the Trust is to work towards the eradication of meningitis as a serious medical condition. Research priorities have been reviewed in relation to progress with development of serogroup B meningococcal vaccine.

Meningitis Trust Research Award

Subjects: The after effects of meningitis, the aftercare of patients and families who have been affected by meningitis, recognition, diagnosis and management of meningitis.
Purpose: To contribute to the funding of research into all types of meningitis whether bacterial or viral.
Eligibility: Please contact the Trust for eligibility requirements. Generally funding is given to postgraduate study but applications from those studying for a doctorate will be considered.
Level of Study: Unrestricted.
Type: Research grant.
Value: Up to UK£400,000 per year.
Frequency: Dependent on funds available.
Application Procedure: Applicants must submit a précis and if accepted they will be required to submit a completed full application.
Closing Date: Please contact the organisation.

MENZIES CENTRE FOR AUSTRALIAN STUDIES

28 Russell Square, London, WC1B 5DS, England
Tel: (44) 20 7862 8854
Fax: (44) 20 7580 9627
Email: menzies.centre@kcl.ac.uk
www: http://www.kcl.ac.uk/menzies
Contact: Ms Kirsten McIntyre

The Menzies Centre for Australian Studies is located at King's College, University of London. There are six broad areas of activity which form the core of the Centre's operations. These are teaching, postgraduate seminars, public lectures, conferences, research and external lecturing. The Centre also offers scholarship and fellowship programmes.

Australian Bicentennial Scholarships and Fellowships

Subjects: All subjects.
Purpose: To promote scholarship, intellectual links, mutual awareness and understanding between the United Kingdom and Australia. The awards also aim to enable United Kingdom graduates to study in approved courses or undertake approved research in Australia and to enable Australian graduates to study in approved courses or undertake approved research in the United Kingdom.
Eligibility: Open to holders of a good postgraduate degree or similar who are seeking to further their education or professional experience without taking a further degree. Candidates must either be registered as postgraduate students at a British tertiary institution or eligible for registration at an Australian tertiary institution and usually resident in the United Kingdom.
Level of Study: Postdoctorate, Postgraduate, Professional development.
Type: Scholarships + Fellowships.
Value: Up to UK£4,000.
Frequency: Annual.
Study Establishment: Any approved Institute of Higher Education.
Country of Study: Other.
No. of awards offered: One-four.
Application Procedure: Applicants must submit a completed application form, three references and a letter of acceptance from the proposed host institution.
Closing Date: June 7th for United Kingdom applicants and October 29th for Australian applicants.
Funding: Private.
Contributor: The Australian Bicentennial Trust.

Menzies Centre for Australian Studies Postgraduate Visiting Fellowship

Subjects: No restriction, but usually modern languages and literatures.
Purpose: To allow postgraduate students from European universities to travel to Britain to consult material essential to their research on Australian topics.
Level of Study: Postgraduate.
Type: Fellowship.
Value: UK£600.
Frequency: Dependent on funds available.
Study Establishment: Any UK tertiary institution.
Country of Study: United Kingdom.
No. of awards offered: Up to two.
Application Procedure: Letter of application to Head of Centre and two references submitted.
Closing Date: May 10th (variable).
No. of awards given last year: Two.
No. of applicants last year: Six.

Menzies Centre for Australian Studies Visiting Fellowships European

Subjects: Modern languages and literatures, political science and government, international relations, sociology, women's studies, area and cultural studies.
Purpose: To encourage the teaching of Australian studies in Europe.
Eligibility: Applicants should take courses with Australian content or be prepared to introduce a significant and on-going Australian component into their teaching at a European university.
Level of Study: Professional development.
Type: Fellowship.
Value: UK£600-1,200.
Frequency: Dependent on funds available.
Country of Study: UK / Australia.
No. of awards offered: Variable.
Application Procedure: Letter of application must be completed and two or three references submitted.
Closing Date: Variable.
No. of applicants last year: Seven.

Northcote Graduate Scholarship

Subjects: All subjects.
Purpose: To enable students to undertake a higher degree at an Australian university.
Eligibility: Open to applicants resident in the United Kingdom who are under 30 years of age.
Level of Study: Postgraduate.
Type: Scholarship.
Value: An allowance of Australian $20,000 per year plus return economy airfare and payment of compulsory fees.
Length of Study: Up to three years.
Frequency: Annual.
Study Establishment: Any approved tertiary institution.
Country of Study: Australia.
No. of awards offered: Up to two.
Application Procedure: Applicants must complete and submit an application form, two references and a letter of acceptance from their chosen Australian university.
Closing Date: August 31st.
Funding: Private.
Contributor: The Northcote Trust.
No. of awards given last year: Two.
No. of applicants last year: 30.

THE METROPOLITAN MUSEUM OF ART

1000 Fifth Avenue, New York, NY 10028-0198, United States of America
Tel: (1) 212 650 2763
Fax: (1) 212 570 3782
Email: communications@metmuseum.org
www: http://www.metmuseum.org
Contact: Internship Programmes & Education

The Metropolitan Museum of Art is one of the world's largest and finest art museums. Its collections include more than two million works of art spanning 5,000 years of world culture, from prehistory to the present, and from every part of the world. As one of the greatest research institutions in the world, the Metropolitan Museum welcomes the responsibility to train future scholars and museum professionals. The Museum offers opportunities for students at several stages in their academic careers, from high school to the postgraduate level. Internships and apprenticeships can be either paid or unpaid, full or part-time and can last from nine weeks to an academic year.

The Metropolitan Museum of Art Annette Kade Art History Fellowship

Subjects: Fine art.
Purpose: To allow foreign students to study in the United States, who would not otherwise be able to do so.
Eligibility: Open to French & German predoctoral art history students.
Level of Study: Predoctorate.
Type: Fellowship.
Length of Study: One year.
Frequency: Annual.
Study Establishment: The Metropolitan Museum of Art, New York.
Country of Study: United States of America.
No. of awards offered: One.
Application Procedure: Applicants must submit a typed application in triplicate should include the contact details of the applicant, a curriculum vitae, details of professional experience, a statement not exceeding 1,000 words describing what the applicant expects to accomplish in the fellowship period and how the Museum's facilities can be utilised to achieve these objectives, a tentative schedule of work to be accomplished, proposed start and end dates, and three letters of recommendation, at least one of which should be professional and one academic. Master's degree and predoctoral applicants should only send the original plus two copies of their official undergraduate and graduate transcripts.
Closing Date: November.
Funding: Private.
Contributor: Annette Kade.

Additional Information: Predoctoral Fellows will generally be expected to assist the hosting curatorial departments with projects that complement and are incidental to their approved scholarly subject. They will be asked to give a gallery talk during their fellowship term and be expected to participate in a Fellows' colloquiam in the second half of their term, in which they will give a 20 minute presentation on their work in progress. Senior Fellows will also be invited to participate in these activities.

Metropolitan Museum of Art Lifchez/Stronach Curatorial Internship

Subjects: Art history.
Purpose: To support a student interested in a curatorial career.
Eligibility: The student should come from a background of financial need or other disadvantage that might jeopardise his or her pursuing such a career without this support.
Level of Study: Graduate.
Type: Internship.
Value: Please contact the organisation for details.
Length of Study: Nine months from mid September to early June and the possibility of participation in the summer orientation programme.
Frequency. Annual.
Study Establishment: The Metropolitan Museum of Art.
Country of Study: United States of America.
No. of awards offered: Varies.
Application Procedure: Applicants must submit a typed application including their name and address, a full curriculum vitae, two academic recommendations, official transcripts, a list of art history or other relevant courses taken, and an essay or letter of not more than 500 words describing their career goals, interest in museum work and their reasons for applying. There are no application forms.
Closing Date: Please contact the Museum.
Funding: Private.
Contributor: Judith Lee Stronach and Raymond Lifchez.
Additional Information: The intern is assigned to a curatorial department to work on projects appropriate to his or her academic background, professional skills and career goals.

Metropolitan Museum of Art Roswell L Gilpatric Internship

Subjects: Museum studies.
Purpose: To support students showing an interest in museum careers.
Eligibility: Open to graduate students showing special interest in museum careers.
Level of Study: Graduate.
Type: Internship.
Value: Please contact organisation for details.
Length of Study: Nine weeks from mid June to mid August.
Frequency: Annual.
Study Establishment: The Metropolitan Museum of Art.
Country of Study: United States of America.
No. of awards offered: Varies.
Application Procedure: Applicants must submit a typed application including their name and address, a full curriculum vitae, two academic recommendations, official transcripts, a list of art history or other relevant courses taken, and an essay or letter of not more than 500 words describing their career goals, interest in museum work and their reasons for applying. There are no application forms.
Closing Date: Please contact the Museum.
Funding: Private.
Contributor: The Thorne Foundation.

Metropolitan Museum of Art Six Month Internship

Subjects: Art history or related fields.
Purpose: To promote greater diversity in the national pool of future museum professionals.
Eligibility: Open to candidates of any nationality.
Level of Study: Graduate, Postgraduate.
Type: Internship.
Value: Please contact the organisation for details.
Length of Study: Six months full-time from June-December and participation in the summer orientation programme.

Frequency: Annual.
Study Establishment: The Metropolitan Museum of Art.
Country of Study: United States of America.
No. of awards offered: Varies.
Application Procedure: Applicants must submit a typed application including their name and address, a full curriculum vitae, two academic recommendations, official transcripts, a list of art history or other relevant courses taken, and an essay or letter of not more than 500 words describing their career goals, interest in museum work and their reasons for applying. There are no application forms.
Closing Date: Please contact the Museum.
Funding: Private.
Additional Information: Interns are placed in one of the museum's departments, where they work on projects that suit their academic background, professional skills and career goals.

Metropolitan Museum of Art Summer Internships for College Students

Subjects: Art history or related fields.
Purpose: To support students showing an interest in museum careers.
Eligibility: Open to recent graduates who have not yet entered graduate school. Candidates should have a strong background in art history and intend to pursue careers in art museums. It is not always possible to obtain a visa for foreign nationals.
Level of Study: Graduate.
Type: Internship.
Value: Varies.
Length of Study: 10 weeks full-time from June to August including two weeks of orientation.
Frequency: Annual.
Study Establishment: The Metropolitan Museum of Art.
Country of Study: United States of America.
No. of awards offered: Varies.
Application Procedure: Applicants must submit a typed application including their name and address, a full curriculum vitae, two academic recommendations, official transcripts, a list of art history or other relevant courses taken, and an essay or letter of not more than 500 words describing their career goals, interest in museum work and their reasons for applying. There are no application forms.
Closing Date: Please contact the Museum
Funding: Private.
Contributor: The Lebensfeld Foundation, The Billy Rose Foundation, The Solow Art and Architecture Foundation, and the Ittleson Foundation, Inc.

Metropolitan Museum of Art Summer Internships for Graduate Students

Subjects: Art history or related fields.
Purpose: To support students showing an interest in museum careers.
Eligibility: Open to individuals who have completed at least one year of graduate work in art history or an allied field and who intend to pursue careers in art museums. It is not always possible to obtain a visa for foreign nationals.
Level of Study: Graduate.
Type: Internship.
Value: US$3,250.
Length of Study: 10 weeks full-time.
Frequency: Annual.
Study Establishment: The Metropolitan Museum of Art.
Country of Study: United States of America.
No. of awards offered: Varies.
Application Procedure: Applicants must submit a typed application including their name and address, a full curriculum vitae, two academic recommendations, official transcripts, a list of art history or other relevant courses taken, and an essay or letter of not more than 500 words describing their career goals, interest in museum work and their reasons for applying. There are no application forms.
Closing Date: Please contact the Museum.
Funding: Private.

Contributor: The Lebensfeld Foundation, The Billy Rose Foundation, Francine LeFrak Friedburg, the Solow Art and Architecture Foundation, and the Ittleson Foundation, Inc.
Additional Information: Graduate interns work on projects related to the Museum's collection or to a special exhibition as well as administrative areas.

MICHIGAN SOCIETY OF FELLOWS

University of Michigan, 3572 Rackham Building, 915 E Washington Street, Ann Arbor, MI 48109-1070, United States of America
Tel: (1) 734 763 1259
Email: society.of.fellows@umich.edu
www: http://www.rackham.umich.edu/Faculty/society.html
Contact: Administrative Assistant

The Michigan Society of Fellows, founded in 1970, promotes academic and creative excellence in the humanities and the arts, the social, physical and life sciences and the professions. The objective of the Society is to provide financial and intellectual support for individuals selected for outstanding achievement, professional promise and interdisciplinary interests.

Michigan Society of Fellows Postdoctoral Fellowships

Subjects: All subjects offered by the University of Michigan.
Purpose: To provide financial and intellectual support for individuals selected for outstanding achievement, professional promise and interdisciplinary interests.
Eligibility: Applicants must be near the beginning of their professional careers and have completed a PhD or comparable professional or artistic degree three years prior to application.
Level of Study: Postdoctorate.
Type: Fellowship.
Value: A stipend of US$44,558 per year.
Length of Study: Three years.
Frequency: Annual.
Study Establishment: The University of Michigan.
Country of Study: United States of America.
No. of awards offered: Four.
Application Procedure: Applicants must complete an application form available from the website.
Closing Date: Postmarked the first Friday in October.
Funding: Private.
Contributor: The University of Michigan.
No. of awards given last year: Four.
No. of applicants last year: 336.

MIGRAINE TRUST

45 Great Ormond Street, London, WC1N 3HZ, England
Tel: (44) 20 7831 4818
Fax: (44) 20 7831 5174
Email: research@migrainetrust.org
www: http://www.migrainetrust.org

Established in 1965, the Migraine Trust is a research charity. The Trust aims to fund and promote research into migraine, improve the diagnosis and treatment of migraine and provide information and advice on managing migraine.

Migraine Trust Grants

Subjects: All aspects of migraine and associated headaches.
Purpose: To fund research.
Eligibility: Grants are awarded on merit and not according to predetermined criteria.
Level of Study: Doctorate, Postdoctorate, Postgraduate.
Type: Grants, fellowships and studentships.
Value: Varies.
Length of Study: Up to three years.
Frequency: Annual.
Study Establishment: Approved universities or research institutions.
Country of Study: Unrestricted, except for the studentships which must be taken in the UK only.

No. of awards offered: Varies.
Application Procedure: Applicants must write for an application form and research grant conditions in the first instance. Studentship applications must be made by the host institution and not directly by the student.
Closing Date: Please contact the Foundation.
Funding: Private.
Contributor: Migraine sufferers.
No. of awards given last year: None.
No. of applicants last year: None.

THE MILLAY COLONY FOR THE ARTS, INC. (MCA)

East Hill Road, PO Box 3, Austerlitz, NY 12017-0003, United States of America
Tel: (1) 518 392 3103
Email: application@millaycolony.org
www: http://www.millaycolony.org
Contact: Ms Martha Hodewell, Executive Director

The Millay Colony for the Arts, Inc. (MCA) provides fully funded one month residencies to writers, visual artists and composers at Steepletop, the national historic landmark home of poet Edna St Vincent Millay.

MCA Residencies

Subjects: Visual arts, musical composition and creative writing.
Eligibility: Open to visual artists, composers and writers. Applicants are invited to the Colony strictly on the basis of artistic merit.
Level of Study: Unrestricted.
Type: Residency.
Value: Room, board and studio space for one month. The Millay Colony does not provide financial assistance of any kind.
Length of Study: One month.
Frequency: Monthly from April to November.
Study Establishment: Steepletop, the former home of Edna St Vincent Millay.
Country of Study: United States of America.
No. of awards offered: 48 residencies per year.
Application Procedure: Applicants must complete an application form available on request with a stamped addressed envelope or via email.
Closing Date: November 1st.
Funding: Government, Private.
No. of awards given last year: 48-50.
No. of applicants last year: 600.
Additional Information: Applications are reviewed by selection committees comprised of professional artists.

MINISTRY OF EDUCATION, SCIENCE AND CULTURE (ICELAND)

Sölvhůlsgata 4, Reykjavik, IS-150, Iceland
Tel: (354) 545 9500
Fax: (354) 562 3068
Email: postur@mrn.stjr.is
www: http://www.ministryofeducation.is
Contact: Mrs Thůrunn Bragadůttir, Division for Higher Education, Science & Research

Ministry of Education, Science and Culture (Iceland) Scholarships in Icelandic Studies

Subjects: Icelandic for foreign students (Icelandic language, literature and history).
Eligibility: Citizens of following countries: Austria, Belgia, Bulgaria, Canada (if Icelandic origin), China, Croatia, Czech Republic, Denmark, Estonia, Faroe Islands, Finland, France, Germany, Greenland, Holland, Hungary, Ireland, Italy, Japan, Latvia, Lithuania, Norway, Poland, Russia, Slovakia, Slovenia, Spain, Sweden, Switzerland, Taiwan, United Kingdom, United States of America.

The scholarships are intended for students of language and literature. Preference will, as a rule, be given to a candidate under 35 years of age.
Level of Study: Unrestricted.
Type: Scholarship.
Value: Krona 550,000 plus tuition.
Length of Study: Eight months.
Frequency: Annual.
Study Establishment: The University of Iceland, Reykjavik.
Country of Study: Iceland.
No. of awards offered: 27/28.
Application Procedure: The scholarship authorities of each co-operating country are invited to present applications for up to 2-3 candidates. Applicants must therefore apply to the relevant government department in their own country. United States candidates should apply to the Institute of International Education. United Kingdom candidates should apply to the Icelandic Embassy. Candidates of Icelandic origin from Canada or the United States should apply to the Icelandic National League of North America, 103-94 Ist Avenue, Gimli, MB, ROC 1 B 1.
Closing Date: Nomination of candidates must reach the Ministry of Culture and Education, Iceland, before May Ist.
Funding: Government.
No. of awards given last year: 26.
Additional Information: As from the academic year 2003-2004 the total scholarship scheme has been revised and the quota for each country has been abolished. A budget of Icel. Kr. 20,000,000 will be available for approximately 28 applicants to receive a scholarship for eight months, september 1st 2004 to April 30th 2005 for study of Icelandic for Foreign Students at the University of Iceland, Faculty of Humanities.The scholarship authorities of each co-operating country are invited to present applications for up to 2-3 candidates. All applications must have been evaluated and forwarded to the Icelandic Ministry of Education, Science and Culture through the home country scholarship authorities.A special committee in Iceland will decide on the outcome of the applications and its evaluation will ben announced to the candidates in June/July 2004.

For further information contact:

Icelandic Embassy, 2A Hans Street, London, SW1X 0JE, England
Email: icemb.london@utn.stjr.is
www: http://www.iceland.org/uk

MINISTRY OF FOREIGN AFFAIRS (ITALY)

Italian Cultural Institute, 39 Belgrave Square, London, SW1X 8NX, England
Tel: (44) 20 7235 1461
Fax: (44) 20 7235 4618
Email: ici@italcultur.org.uk
www: http://www.italcultur.org.uk
Contact: Ms Lina Panetta, Cultural & Education Officer

The Italian Cultural Institute is the official Italian government agency for the promotion of cultural exchanges between Great Britain and Italy. The Institute promotes collaboration between universities, academies and learned societies in the two countries and assists in the organisation of major Italian cultural events in Britain.

Italian Government Scholarships

Subjects: Any subject connected with Italian culture.
Purpose: To further cultural exchanges in the frame of the cultural agreement between Italy and the United Kingdom.
Eligibility: Open to British nationals who are final year university students, researchers or musicians with good academic records. Applicants must be under 38 years of age.
Level of Study: Doctorate, Postgraduate, Professional development, Research.
Type: Scholarship.

Value: Approx. €620 per month. This amount is to be confirmed each year.
Length of Study: Four-eight months starting in November.
Frequency: Annual.
Study Establishment: Universities, institutions or research centres.
Country of Study: Italy.
No. of awards offered: Dependent on availability of funds.
Application Procedure: Applicants must complete an application form available from the library of the Italian Cultural Institute in London.
Closing Date: Usually the end of February.
Funding: Government.
No. of awards given last year: 10.
No. of applicants last year: 26.
Additional Information: Further information is available on request.

MINTEK

Human Resources Division, Private Bag X3015, Randburg, 2125, South Africa
Tel: (27) 11 709 4648
Fax: (27) 11 709 4465
Email: bobt@mintek.co.za
www: http://www.mintek.co.za
Contact: Head of Academic Support

Mintek is the partially state funded South African metallurgical research organisation. Its mission is to serve the national interest through high calibre research, development and technology transfer that promotes mineral technology, and fosters the establishment of small, medium and large industries in the field of minerals and products derived from them.

Mintek Bursaries
Subjects: Chemical engineering, electrical engineering, light current and electronics, metallurgical engineering, chemistry, with the emphasis on inorganic, physical or analytical chemistry, metallurgy, extraction and physical, mineralogy, geology or physics.
Purpose: To promote the training of research workers for the minerals industry in general and to meet its own needs for technically trained people.
Eligibility: Open to graduates of any nationality who possess an appropriate four year degree or higher qualification. A knowledge of English is essential. Preference is given to South African citizens. Merit and excellence are the criteria for selection. The project should be a promising development that will contribute to Mintek's activities and is in line with its strategic purpose, the student must have a strong academic background and show the potential to develop expertise that would benefit Mintek, and the institution where the project is carried out should be a centre of excellence in the subject.
Level of Study: Postgraduate.
Type: Bursary.
Value: Rand 32,400 per year for a MSc degree and Rand 40,200 per year for a PhD degree.
Length of Study: Up to two years. Extension of this period can be granted by the President of Mintek.
Frequency: Annual.
Study Establishment: Any university or technikons in fields that complement its own activities.
Country of Study: South Africa.
No. of awards offered: 10-15.
Application Procedure: Applicants must write for details.
Closing Date: There is no deadline.
Funding: Government.
Additional Information: Candidates are requested to sign a contract before starting their project. Usually Mintek insists on a service commitment from the bursar on completion of his or her studies on a year for year basis. Bursars are paid a monthly bursary-salary and Mintek pays the institution an amount to cover the project's running costs.

MIZUTANI FOUNDATION FOR GLYCOSCIENCE

Sen-I Kaikan Suite 5F, 3-1-11 Nihonbashi-honcho, Chuo-ku, Tokyo, 103-0023, Japan
Tel: (81) 3 3246 0224
Fax: (81) 3 3246 1265
Email: info@mizutanifdn.or.jp
www: http://www.mizutanifdn.or.jp
Contact: Keiichi Yoshida, Executive Secretary

The Mizutani Foundation for Glycoscience undertakes major programmes such as the worldwide distribution of research grants to qualified glycoscientists for their outstanding basic research, assistance of international exchanges between Japanese and foreign glycosciences, contributions to glycoscience related meetings in Japan and practice of other activities that are necessary to achieve the aim of the Foundation.

Mizutani Foundation for Glycoscience Research Grants
Subjects: Glycoscience.
Purpose: To contribute to human welfare through the enhancement of glycoscience by awarding grants for creative research into glycoscience conducted by domestic and overseas researchers, and awarding grants for international exchanges and for convening conferences in the field of glycoscience.
Eligibility: Open to those with a doctorate corresponding to a PhD or MD in the United States of America in a field relevant to the proposed project, who have documented capability of performing independent studies and are a member of a scientific institution where he or she can carry out the proposed study. An applicant who has been awarded the grant previously may reapply after five years.
Level of Study: Postgraduate.
Type: Research grant.
Value: Yen 3,000,000-10,000,000.
Length of Study: One year.
Frequency: Annual.
Country of Study: Any country.
No. of awards offered: 10-15.
Application Procedure: Applicants must download an application form from the website.
Closing Date: July 1st to September 1st.
Contributor: The Seikagaku Corporation.
No. of awards given last year: 14.
No. of applicants last year: 100.
Additional Information: Further information is available on request.

MMA HEALTHSERVE

First Floor, 106-110 Watney Street, London, E1W 2QE, England
Tel: (44) 20 7790 1336
Fax: (44) 20 7790 1384
Email: laura@healthserve.org
www: http://www.healthserve.org
Contact: Dr Peter Armon, Medical Director

The MMA HealthServe is developing a health resource centre to promote Christian medical mission. Other support includes elective days, a refresher course, overseas update publications and grants.

MMA Grants
Subjects: Medical mission, church related or Christian healthcare.
Purpose: To assist doctors, nurses and other paramedics to gain a postgraduate qualification.
Eligibility: Open to committed Christians based in the United Kingdom who have spent at least one tour working in a church or mission related medical post and who will be going back to continue this work for at least one further tour of three years.
Level of Study: Postgraduate.
Type: Grant.
Value: Up to UK£750.
Frequency: Varies.
Country of Study: The UK or developing world countries.

Application Procedure: Applicants must complete an application form available on written request.
Closing Date: At least six months before the course is due to start.
Funding: Private.
No. of awards given last year: Three.
No. of applicants last year: Three.
Additional Information: Each request is discussed on its own merit.

MODERN LANGUAGE ASSOCIATION OF AMERICA (MLA)

26 Broadway 3rd Floor, New York, NY 10004-1789, United States of America
Tel: (1) 646 576 5141
Fax: (1) 646 458 0030
Email: awards@mla.org
www: http://www.mla.org
Contact: Ms Annie Reiser, Co-ordinator, MLA Book Prizes

The Modern Language Association of America (MLA) is a non-profit membership organisation that promotes the study and teaching of language and literature in English and foreign languages.

Aldo and Jean Scaglione Prize for a Translation of a Literary Work
Subjects: Translation.
Purpose: To award an outstanding translation into English of a book length literary work.
Eligibility: Open to translations published in the year preceding the year in which the award is given.
Type: Prize.
Value: US$2,000.
Frequency: Every two years.
No. of awards offered: One.
Application Procedure: Applicants must send six copies of the work. For detailed information about specific prizes, applicants should contact the MLA.
Closing Date: April 1st.
Funding: Private.

Aldo and Jeanne Scaglione Prize for Comparative Literary Studies
Subjects: Comparative literary and cultural studies involving at least two literatures.
Purpose: To recognise outstanding scholarly work in comparative literary studies.
Eligibility: Open to books published in the year before the award is given. Authors must be members of the MLA.
Level of Study: Postdoctorate.
Type: Prize.
Value: US$2,000.
Frequency: Annual.
No. of awards offered: One.
Application Procedure: Applicants must send four copies of the work. For detailed information about specific prizes, applicants should contact the MLA.
Closing Date: May 1st.
Funding: Private.

Aldo and Jeanne Scaglione Prize for French and Francophone Literary Studies
Subjects: French and Francophone linguistic or literary studies.
Purpose: To recognise outstanding scholarly work.
Eligibility: Open to books published in the year before the prize is given. Authors must be members of the MLA.
Level of Study: Postdoctorate.
Type: Prize.
Value: US$2,000.
Frequency: Annual.
No. of awards offered: One.

Application Procedure: Applicants must send four copies of the work. For detailed information about specific prizes, applicants should contact the MLA.
Closing Date: May 1st.
Funding: Private.

Aldo and Jeanne Scaglione Prize for Italian Studies
Subjects: Italian literature, culture or comparative literature involving Italian.
Purpose: To award an outstanding scholarly work.
Eligibility: Open to books published in the year before the award is to be given. Authors must be members of the MLA.
Level of Study: Postdoctorate.
Type: Prize.
Value: US$2,000.
Frequency: Every two years.
No. of awards offered: One.
Application Procedure: Applicants must send four copies of the work. For detailed information about specific prizes, applicants should contact the MLA.
Closing Date: May 1st.
Funding: Private.

Aldo and Jeanne Scaglione Prize for Studies in Germanic Languages and Literatures
Subjects: The linguistics or literatures of any of the Germanic languages including Danish, Dutch, German, Norwegian, Swedish or Yiddish.
Purpose: To recognise an outstanding scholarly work.
Eligibility: Authors must be members of the MLA. Books must have been published in the two years preceding the year of the award.
Level of Study: Postdoctorate.
Type: Prize.
Value: US$2,000.
Frequency: Every two years.
No. of awards offered: One.
Application Procedure: Applicants must send four copies of the work. For detailed information about specific prizes, applicants should contact the MLA.
Closing Date: May 1st.
Funding: Private.

Aldo and Jeanne Scaglione Prize for Studies in Slavic Languages and Literatures
Subjects: Linguistic or literary study of a work in a Slavic language.
Purpose: To recognise an outstanding scholarly work.
Eligibility: Open to books published in the year or two before the prize is given. Authors need not be members of the MLA.
Level of Study: Postdoctorate.
Type: Prize.
Value: US$2,000.
Frequency: Every two years.
No. of awards offered: One.
Application Procedure: Applicants must send four copies of the work. For detailed information about specific prizes, applicants should contact the MLA.
Closing Date: May 1st.
Funding: Private.

Aldo and Jeanne Scaglione Prize for Translation of a Scholarly Study of Literature
Subjects: Translation.
Purpose: To recognise an outstanding translation into English of a book length work of literary history, literary criticism, philology or literary theory.
Eligibility: Open to books published in the year or two before the prize is given. Authors need not be members of the MLA.
Level of Study: Postdoctorate.
Type: Prize.
Value: US$2,000.
Frequency: Every two years.
No. of awards offered: One.

Application Procedure: Applicants must send four copies of the work. For detailed information about specific prizes, applicants should contact the MLA.
Closing Date: May 1st.
Funding: Private.

Fenia and Yaakov Leviant Memorial Prize
Subjects: English translation of a Yiddish literary work and/or Yiddish literature and culture.
Purpose: To recognise an outstanding translation into English or an outstanding scholarly work in the field of Yiddish.
Eligibility: The prize is awarded alternatively to a translational or scholarly work in the field of Yiddish. In 2004 the prize will be awarded to a scholarly work in English translation from between 1999 and 2003. Cultural studies, critical biographies, edited works in the field of Yiddish folklore or linguistic studies are eligible.
Level of Study: Postdoctorate.
Type: Prize.
Value: US$500.
Frequency: Every two years.
No. of awards offered: One.
Application Procedure: Applicants must send four copies of the work. For detailed information about specific prizes, applicants should contact the MLA.
Closing Date: May 1st.
Funding: Private.

Howard R Marraro Prize
Subjects: Italian literature or comparative literature involving Italian.
Purpose: To award an outstanding scholarly work.
Eligibility: Authors must be members of the MLA.
Level of Study: Postdoctorate.
Type: Prize.
Value: US$1,000.
Frequency: Every two years.
No. of awards offered: One.
Application Procedure: Applicants must send four copies of the work. For detailed information about specific prizes, applicants should contact the MLA.
Closing Date: May 1st.
Funding: Private.

James Russell Lowell Prize
Subjects: Literary theory, media, cultural history or interdisciplinary topics.
Purpose: To recognise an outstanding literary or linguistic study, a critical edition of an important work or a critical biography.
Eligibility: Open to books published the year before the award is due to be given. Authors must be current members of the MLA.
Level of Study: Postdoctorate.
Type: Prize.
Value: US$1,000.
Frequency: Annual.
No. of awards offered: One.
Application Procedure: Applicants must send six copies of the work. For detailed information about specific prizes, applicants should contact the MLA.
Closing Date: March 1st.
Funding: Private.

Katherine Singer Kovacs Prize
Subjects: Latin American or Spanish literatures and cultures.
Purpose: To recognise an outstanding book published in English in the field.
Eligibility: Open to books published in the year before the prize is given. Competing books should be broadly interpretative works that enhance understanding of the interrelations among literature, the arts and society.
Level of Study: Postdoctorate.
Type: Prize.
Value: US$1,000.
Frequency: Annual.
No. of awards offered: One.

Application Procedure: Applicants must send six copies of the work. For detailed information about specific prizes, applicants should contact the MLA.
Closing Date: May 1st.
Funding: Private.

Kenneth W Mildenberger Prize
Subjects: Teaching foreign languages and literatures.
Purpose: To support work in the field of teaching foreign languages and literatures.
Eligibility: Authors need not be members of the MLA. Open to books published in the year prior to the prize being given.
Level of Study: Postdoctorate.
Type: Prize.
Value: US$1,000.
Frequency: Annual.
No. of awards offered: One.
Application Procedure: Applicants must send four copies of the work. For detailed information about specific prizes, applicants should contact the MLA.
Closing Date: May 1st.
Funding: Private.
Additional Information: The prize is give for a research article in odd numbered years and a book in even numbered years.

Lois Roth Award for a Translation of Literary Work
Subjects: Translation.
Purpose: To recognise an outstanding translation into English of a book length literary work.
Eligibility: Open to translations published in the year before the prize is given. Translators need not be members of the MLA.
Level of Study: Postdoctorate.
Type: Prize.
Value: US$1,000.
Frequency: Every two years.
No. of awards offered: One.
Application Procedure: Applicants must send six copies of the work. For detailed information about specific prizes, applicants should contact the MLA.
Closing Date: April 1st.
Funding: Private.

Mina P Shaughnessy Prize
Subjects: Teaching English language, literature, rhetoric and composition.
Purpose: To recognise a research publication in the field of teaching English language, literature, rhetoric and composition.
Eligibility: Open to books published in the year prior to the prize being given. Authors need not be members of the MLA.
Level of Study: Postdoctorate.
Type: Prize.
Value: US$1,000.
Frequency: Annual.
No. of awards offered: One.
Application Procedure: Applicants must send four copies of the work. For detailed information about specific prizes, applicants should contact the MLA.
Closing Date: May 1st.

MLA Prize for a Distinguished Bibliography
Subjects: Bibliography.
Purpose: To award an outstanding enumerative or descriptive bibliography.
Eligibility: Editors need not be members of the MLA. Open to books published in the two years prior to the prize being given.
Level of Study: Postdoctorate.
Type: Prize.
Value: US$1,000.
Frequency: Every two years.
No. of awards offered: One.
Application Procedure: Applicants must send four copies of the work. For detailed information applicants should contact the MLA.
Closing Date: May 1st.
Funding: Private.

MLA Prize for a Distinguished Scholarly Edition

Subjects: Works in any of the modern languages.
Purpose: To recognise an outstanding scholarly edition.
Eligibility: At least one volume must have been published in the year or two prior to the award being given. Editors need not be members of the MLA. Editions may be single or multiple volumes.
Level of Study: Postdoctorate.
Type: Prize.
Value: US$1,000.
Frequency: Every two years.
No. of awards offered: One.
Application Procedure: Applicants must send four copies of the work. For detailed information about specific prizes, applicants should contact the MLA.
Closing Date: May 1st.
Funding: Private.

MLA Prize for a First Book

Subjects: Literary theory, media, cultural history or interdisciplinary topics.
Purpose: To recognise an outstanding literary or linguistic study, a critical edition of an important work, or a critical biography.
Eligibility: Open to books published in the year before the prize is given as the first book length publication of a current MLA member.
Level of Study: Postdoctorate.
Type: Prize.
Value: US$1,000.
Frequency: Annual.
No. of awards offered: One.
Application Procedure: Applicants must send six copies of the work. For detailed information about specific prizes, applicants should contact the MLA.
Closing Date: April 1st.
Funding: Private.

MLA Prize for Independent Scholars

Subjects: English or other modern languages and literatures.
Purpose: To award a scholarly book in the field of modern language.
Eligibility: Open to books published the year before the prize is given. At the time of publication of the book the author must not be enrolled in a programme leading to an academic degree or hold a tenured, tenure accruing or tenure track position in post secondary education. Authors or publishers must request an application form from the MLA. Authors need not be members of the MLA.
Level of Study: Postdoctorate.
Type: Prize.
Value: US$1,000.
Frequency: Annual.
No. of awards offered: One.
Application Procedure: Applicants must send six copies of the work. For detailed information about specific prizes, applicants should contact the MLA.
Closing Date: May 1st.
Funding: Private.

MLA Prize in United States, Latina and Latino or Chicana and Chicano Literacy and Cultural Studies

Subjects: Chicana and Chicano, Latina and Latino literary or cultural studies.
Purpose: To award an outstanding scholarly study.
Eligibility: Open to authors who are members of the MLA.
Level of Study: Postdoctorate.
Type: Prize.
Value: US$1,000.
Frequency: Annual.
No. of awards offered: One.
Application Procedure: Applicants must send four copies of their work. For detailed information about specific prizes, applicants should contact the MLA.
Closing Date: May 1st.
Funding: Private.

Morton N Cohen Award for A Distinguished Edition of Letter

Subjects: Edition of letters in any of the modern languages.
Eligibility: At least one volume must have been published in the year or two prior to the award being given. Editors need not be members of the MLA. Editions may be single or multiple volumes.
Level of Study: Postdoctorate.
Type: Award.
Value: US$1,000.
Frequency: Every two years.
No. of awards offered: One.
Application Procedure: Applicants must send four copies of the work. For detailed information about specific prizes, applicants should contact the MLA.
Closing Date: May 1st.
Funding: Private.

William Sanders Scarborough Prize

Subjects: Black American literature and culture.
Purpose: To recognise an outstanding book in the field of Black American literature or culture.
Eligibility: Books that are primarily translation will not be considered.
Level of Study: Postdoctorate.
Type: Prize.
Value: US$1,000.
Frequency: Annual.
No. of awards offered: One.
Application Procedure: Applicants must send four copies of the work. For detailed information about specific prizes, applicants should contact the MLA.
Closing Date: May 1st.

MONASH UNIVERSITY

Wellington Road, Clayton, VIC 3168, Australia
Tel: (61) 3 9905 3009
Fax: (61) 3 9905 5042
Email: mrgs@adm.monash.edu.au
www: http://www.monash.edu.au/phdschol
Contact: Monash Research Graduate School

Monash University is one of Australia's largest universities with 10 faculties covering every major area of intellectual activity, six campuses in Australia and an increasing global presence. Research at Monash covers the full spectrum from fundamental to applied and ranges across the arts and humanities, social, natural, health and medical sciences and the technological sciences. The University is determined to preserve its strength in fundamental research, which underpins its successes in applied research and to continue to make a distinguished contribution to intellectual and cultural life.

Monash International Postgraduate Research Scholarship (MIPRS)

Subjects: All subjects.
Purpose: To provide support for supervised full-time research at Master's and doctoral level.
Eligibility: Open to graduates of any Australian or overseas university, who should hold a First Class (Honours) Bachelor's Degree or equivalent.
Level of Study: Doctorate.
Type: Scholarship.
Value: The award meets the full cost of international tuition fees.
Length of Study: Up to two years for the Master's degree, and up to three years with the possibility of an additional six month extension for the doctoral degree.
Frequency: Annual.
Study Establishment: Monash University.
Country of Study: Australia.
No. of awards offered: Nine.
Application Procedure: Applicants must complete an application kit, which is available four months before closing date.

Closing Date: October 31st.
Additional Information: International students must meet English language proficiency requirements.

Monash University Silver Jubilee Postgraduate Scholarship

Subjects: Medicine or pharmacy.
Purpose: To provide supervised full-time research at Master's and doctoral level.
Eligibility: Open to graduates of any Australian or overseas university, who should hold a First Class (Honours) Bachelor's Degree or equivalent.
Level of Study: Doctorate.
Type: Scholarship.
Value: Australian $23,294 per year plus establishment, relocation, incidentals and thesis allowance.
Length of Study: Up to two years for the Master's degree, and up to three years with the possibility of an additional six month extension for the doctoral degree.
Frequency: Annual.
Study Establishment: Monash University.
Country of Study: Australia.
No. of awards offered: One.
Application Procedure: Applicants must complete an application kit, which is available four months before the closing date.
Closing Date: October 31st.
Additional Information: International students must meet English language proficiency requirements.

Sir James McNeill Foundation Postgraduate Scholarship

Subjects: Engineering, medicine, music or science.
Purpose: To enable a PhD Scholar to pursue a full-time programme of research which is both environmentally responsible and socially beneficial to the community.
Eligibility: Open to graduates of any Australian or overseas university, who should hold a First Class (Honours) Bachelor's Degree or equivalent.
Level of Study: Doctorate.
Type: Scholarship.
Value: Australian $23,271 per year, plus allowances.
Length of Study: Up to three years, with the possibility of an additional six months extension.
Frequency: Annual.
Study Establishment: Monash University.
Country of Study: Australia.
No. of awards offered: One.
Application Procedure: Applicants must complete an application kit, which is available four months before the closing date.
Closing Date: October 31st.
No. of awards given last year: One.
No. of applicants last year: 400.
Additional Information: International students must meet English language proficiency requirements.

Vera Moore International Postgraduate Research Scholarships

Subjects: All subjects.
Purpose: To provide support for supervised full-time research at Master's and doctoral level.
Eligibility: Open to graduates of any Australian or overseas university, who should hold a First Class (Honours) Bachelor's Degree or equivalent.
Level of Study: Doctorate.
Type: Scholarship.
Value: The full cost of tuition fees plus a research allowance of Australian $550 per year.
Length of Study: Up to two years for the Master's degree, and up to three years with the possibility of an additional six month extension for the doctoral degree.
Frequency: Annual.
Study Establishment: Monash University.
Country of Study: Australia.
No. of awards offered: One.

Application Procedure: Applicants must complete an application kit, which is available four months before the closing date.
Closing Date: October 31st.
Additional Information: International students must meet English language proficiency requirements.

THE MONGOLIA SOCIETY, INC.

Hangin Scholarship Committee, 322 Goodbody HallIndiana University, Bloomington, IN 47405-7005, United States of America
Tel: (1) 812 855 4078
Fax: (1) 812 855 7500
Email: monsoc@indiana.edu
www: http://www.indiana.edu/~mongsoc
Contact: Ms Susie Drost

The Mongolia Society was founded in late 1961 as a private, non-profit, non political organisation interested in promoting and furthering the study of Mongolia, its history, language and culture. The aims of the Society are exclusively scholarly, educational and charitable.

Dr Gombojab Hangin Memorial Scholarship

Subjects: All subjects.
Purpose: To give a student a chance to pursue studies in the United States of America.
Eligibility: Open to students of Mongolian heritage, defined as an individual of Mongolian ethnic origin who has permanent residency in the Mongolian People's Republic, the People's Republic of China or the former Soviet Union.
Level of Study: Unrestricted.
Type: Scholarship.
Value: Up to US$2,400. The award does not include transportation from the recipient's country to the United States, nor does it include board and lodging at the university where the recipient will study.
Length of Study: One year.
Frequency: Annual.
Country of Study: United States of America.
No. of awards offered: One.
Application Procedure: Applicants must request the scholarship application form in English and return it written in English, accompanied by a photocopy of the applicant's identification card and passport, complete with photograph, and a curriculum vitae. Letters of recommendation should also be enclosed.
Closing Date: January 1st.
Funding: Private.
Additional Information: Upon conclusion of the award year, the recipient must write a report of his or her activities which resulted from receipt of the scholarship.

MONTESSORI ST NICHOLAS CENTRE

24 Prince's Gate, London, SW7 1PT, England
Tel: (44) (44) 207 584 9987
Fax: (44) (44) 207 589 3764
Email: centre@montessori.org.uk
www: http://www.montessori.org.uk
Contact: The Chief Executive

Montessori. St Nicholas offer grants and awards under a scholarship scheme for Post Graduate Students carrying out research or training in Montessori teaching. Annual awards total UK£60,000 on average.

The Birts Scholarship

Purpose: To recognise and encourage research into Montessori teaching.
Eligibility: UK Citizens holding a UK recognised degree.
Level of Study: Graduate.
Type: Scholarship.
Value: UK£4-6,000.
Length of Study: 2 years.
Frequency: Annual.
Country of Study: United Kingdom.

No. of awards offered: 1 annually at Postgraduate Level, 60 below this.
Application Procedure: By application form from the charity and interview.
Closing Date: 1st July annually.
Funding: Private.
No. of awards given last year: 1.
No. of applicants last year: 12.

MONTREAL NEUROLOGICAL INSTITUTE

McGill University, 3801 University Street, Montréal, QC, H3A 2B4, Canada
Tel: (1) 514 398 8998
Fax: (1) 514 398 8248
Email: fil@mni.lan.mcgill.ca
www: http://www.mcgill.ca/mni
Contact: Ms Filomena Lumia, Personnel Liaison Officer

The Montreal Neurological Institute is dedicated to the study of the nervous system and neurological disorders. Its 70 principal researchers hold teaching positions at McGill University. The Institute is characterised by close interaction between basic science researchers and the clinicians at its affiliated hospital.

Jeanne Timmins Costello Fellowships
Subjects: Neurology, neurosurgery, neuroscience research and study.
Purpose: To support research.
Eligibility: Open to candidates of any nationality who have an MD or PhD degree. Those with MD degrees will ordinarily have completed clinical studies in neurology or neurosurgery.
Level of Study: Doctorate, Postgraduate.
Type: Fellowship.
Value: Canadian $25,000 per year.
Length of Study: One year, with the possibility of renewal for a further year.
Frequency: Annual.
Study Establishment: The Montréal Neurological Institute.
Country of Study: Canada.
No. of awards offered: Four.
Application Procedure: Applicants must write for details.
Closing Date: October 15th.
Funding: Private.
Contributor: Jean Timmins Costello.
No. of awards given last year: Four.

Preston Robb Fellowship
Subjects: Neurology, neurosurgery or neuroscience.
Purpose: To support research.
Eligibility: Open to researchers of any nationality.
Level of Study: Doctorate, Postdoctorate, Postgraduate.
Type: Fellowship.
Value: Canadian $25,000.
Length of Study: One year.
Frequency: Annual.
Country of Study: Canada.
No. of awards offered: One.
Application Procedure: Applicants must write for details.
Closing Date: October 15th.
Funding: Private.
Contributor: Preston Robb.
No. of awards given last year: One.

MOTOR NEURONE DISEASE ASSOCIATION

PO Box 246, Northampton, Northamptonshire, NN1 2PR, England
Tel: (44) 1604 250505
Fax: (44) 1604 638289
Email: research@mndassociation.org
Contact: Mrs M D Reicale, Research Administrator

The Motor Neurone Disease Association supports research on fundamental aspects of motor neurone disease (MND) and on its management and alleviation. It provides information and advice to patients and carers and runs a nationwide care service. MND paralyses selectively or generally and is fatal, irreversible and at present, incurable.

MND PhD Studentship Award
Subjects: Research on all aspects of MND in all relevant disciplines.
Purpose: To stimulate interest in MND research by encouraging young scientists into the field.
Eligibility: Restricted to United Kingdom laboratories.
Level of Study: Postdoctorate.
Type: Studentship.
Value: Approx. UK£65,000.
Length of Study: Three years.
Frequency: Annual.
Country of Study: United Kingdom.
No. of awards offered: One-two.
Application Procedure: Applicants must submit a summary of their proposal that is first considered by three members of the Research Advisory Panel (RAP). Full applications are invited thereafter and application forms provided. Full applications are submitted to two or more independent referees and then to the RAP for consideration.
Closing Date: Summary applications must be received by May 7th 2004.
No. of awards given last year: One.
No. of applicants last year: Four.
Additional Information: The studentships are awarded on the basis of scientific merit and the value of research training offered.

MND Research Project and Pump Pricing Grants
Subjects: Research into all aspects of MND in all disciplines.
Purpose: To understand and research the cause and effective treatments of MND.
Eligibility: Overseas applicants must have a project that is unique in concept or design, that involves some aspect of collaboration with a United Kingdom institute.
Type: Grant.
Value: Cappers at UK£50,000 per annum. Approx. UK£60,000 per year.
Length of Study: One-three years.
Frequency: Twice a year.
Study Establishment: A research institution.
No. of awards offered: Varies.
Application Procedure: Applicants must submit a summary of their proposal that is first considered by three members of the Research Advisory Panel (RAP). Full applications are invited thereafter and application forms provided. Full applications are submitted to two or more independent referees and then to the RAP for consideration.
Closing Date: Summary applications must be received by November 5th 2004.
No. of awards given last year: Five.
No. of applicants last year: 22.

MOTT MACDONALD CHARITABLE TRUST

St Anne House, Wellesley Road, Croydon, Surrey, CR9 2UL, England
Tel: (44) 20 8774 2000
Fax: (44) 20 8681 5706
Email: s1b@mm-croy.mottmac.com
www: http://www.mottmac.com/careers/vacanci2.htm
Contact: Secretary

Mott MacDonald Charitable Trust Scholarships
Subjects: Disciplines of the Mott MacDonald Group.
Purpose: To enable a recipient to pursue studies and thus, contribute to the advancement of engineering technology.
Eligibility: Open to engineering students who wish to further their academic training at postgraduate level. Students returning to academic training after a period of employment are preferred.

Level of Study: Postgraduate.
Type: Scholarship (MSc).
Value: Please consult the organisation.
Frequency: Annual.
Study Establishment: Any university.
Country of Study: United Kingdom.
No. of awards offered: Varies.
Application Procedure: Applicants must complete an application form, available on request from the main address.
Closing Date: 31st March.
Funding: Commercial.
No. of awards given last year: 4.
No. of applicants last year: 129.

MOUNT DESERT ISLAND BIOLOGICAL LABORATORY

PO Box 35, Department NIA, Old Bar Harbor Road, Salsbury Cove,
ME 04672, United States of America
Tel: (1) 207 288 3605
Fax: (1) 207 288 2130
Email: phand@mdibl.org
www: http://www.mdibl.org
Contact: Ms Patricia Hand, Administrative Director

The Mount Desert Island Biological Laboratory is a marine and bio-medical research laboratory which uses unique models such as shark, skate and flounder to solve questions related to human and environmental health.

Mount Desert Island New Investigator Award

Subjects: Biological and life sciences.
Purpose: To support independent investigators spending one-two months in the Summer doing physiological research on marine animals at the Mount Desert Island Biological Laboratory.
Eligibility: Open to scientists at all stages of their career who wish to use marine systems for research studies at MDIBL.
Level of Study: Postdoctorate, Professional development.
Type: Fellowship.
Value: US$1,000-12,000. Special awards from the Salisbury Cove Research Fund (Thomas H Maren Foundation) are available for up to US$20,000 depending on need and potential long-term commitment to the laboratory.
Length of Study: Two-three months.
Frequency: Dependent on funds available.
Study Establishment: Mount Desert Island Biological Laboratory.
Country of Study: United States of America.
No. of awards offered: 15-20.
Application Procedure: Applicants must obtain an application form from the organisation. Please visit the website for application information www.mdibl.org.
Closing Date: February 1st.
Funding: Government, Private.
No. of awards given last year: 18.
No. of applicants last year: 23.
Additional Information: The Mount Desert Island Biological Laboratory, located in Salisbury Cove, Maine is a 105 year old research institution and an international centre for comparative physiology, toxicology, tissue culture biology and marine functional genomics studies. Awards can be used to defray the cost of laboratory space, housing, equipment fees and other costs depending on individual needs. Additional information can be found on the website.

MRS GILES WHITING FOUNDATION

Writers' Program, 1133 Avenue of the Americas, New York, NY
10036-6710, United States of America
Tel: (1) 212 336 2138
www: http://www.whitingfoundation.org
Contact: Ms Kellye Rosenheim, Associate Director

Whiting Fellowships in the Humanities

Subjects: Humanities.
Purpose: To recognise and award outstanding doctoral candidates in the humanities during the final year of dissertation writing.
Eligibility: Open to students selected by their participating institutions which consist of Bryan Mar, the University of Chicago, Columbia, Harvard, Princeton, Stanford and Yale.
Level of Study: Doctorate.
Type: Fellowship.
Value: Varies. The amount of the stipend is set by each school, but is usually US$17,500.
Frequency: Annual.
Country of Study: Any country.
No. of awards offered: Varies.
Application Procedure: Direct applications are not accepted by the Foundation.
Funding: Private.

Whiting Writers' Awards

Subjects: Writing.
Purpose: To identify and support emerging writers of exceptional promise.
Eligibility: Open to writers of fiction, poetry or non fiction, essayists, literary Scholars, playwrights, novelists, poets or critics. Selections are based on the quality of the nominee's writing accomplishment and the likelihood of outstanding future work. The programme places special emphasis on promising emerging talent. To qualify, writers need not be young, given that new talent may emerge at any age.
Level of Study: Unrestricted.
Type: Award.
Value: US$35,000.
Frequency: Annual.
Country of Study: Any country.
No. of awards offered: 10.
Application Procedure: Direct applications and informal nominations are not accepted by the Foundation. Recipients are nominated by writers, educators and editors from communities across the United States of America whose experience and vocations bring them into contact with individuals of unusual talent. The nominators and selectors are appointed by the Foundation and serve anonymously. Nominees are not informed of their candidacies.
Funding: Private.

MULTIPLE SCLEROSIS SOCIETY OF CANADA (MSSC)

250 Bloor Street East, Suite 1000, Toronto, ON, M4W 3PG, Canada
Tel: (1) 416 967 3001
Fax: (1) 416 967 3040
Email: jackie.munroe@mssociety.ca
www: http://www.mssociety.ca
Contact: Ms Jackie Munroe, Research Grants Programme Manager

The mission of the Multiple Sclerosis Society of Canada (MSSC) is to be a leader in finding a cure for multiple sclerosis and enabling people affected by the disease to enhance their quality of life.

MSSC Career Development Award

Subjects: Multiple sclerosis.
Purpose: To encourage full-time research.
Eligibility: Open to individuals holding a doctoral degree who have recently completed their training in research and are capable of carrying out independent research relevant to multiple sclerosis on a full-time basis.
Level of Study: Postdoctorate.
Value: The salary scale, conditions of remuneration and allowable involvement in non research activities will be similar to Medical Research Council (MRC) scholarships.
Length of Study: Three years initially, with the opportunity for renewal twice.

Frequency: Annual.
Study Establishment: A Canadian school of medicine.
Country of Study: Canada.
No. of awards offered: Limited.
Closing Date: October 1st.
Funding: Private.
No. of awards given last year: None.
No. of applicants last year: None.

MSSC Postdoctoral Fellowship

Subjects: Multiple sclerosis and allied diseases.
Purpose: To encourage research.
Eligibility: Open to qualified persons holding an MD or PhD degree and intending to pursue research work relevant to multiple sclerosis and allied diseases. The applicant must be associated to an appropriate authority in the field he or she wishes to study.
Level of Study: Postdoctorate.
Type: Fellowship.
Value: Salary scales will be similar to those suggested by the Canadian Institutes for Health Research.
Length of Study: Three years, but may be extended for one additional year under exceptional circumstances.
Frequency: Annual.
Study Establishment: A recognised institution which deals with problems relevant to multiple sclerosis.
Country of Study: Other.
No. of awards offered: Varies.
Closing Date: October 1st.
Funding: Private.
No. of awards given last year: 10.
No. of applicants last year: 12.

MSSC Research Grant

Subjects: Multiple sclerosis.
Purpose: To fund research projects.
Eligibility: Open to researchers working in Canada or intending to return to Canada.
Level of Study: Postgraduate.
Type: Research grant.
Value: Varies.
Length of Study: One, two or three years. If further funding is requested reapplication must be made in full.
Frequency: Annual.
Study Establishment: An approved institution.
Country of Study: Any country.
No. of awards offered: Limited.
Closing Date: October 1st.
Funding: Private.
No. of awards given last year: Nine.
No. of applicants last year: 14.

MSSC Research Studentship

Subjects: Multiple sclerosis research.
Purpose: To provide further training in a specialised area related to research in multiple sclerosis and allied diseases.
Eligibility: Open to qualified persons holding an MD or PhD degree. Applications directed towards understanding the pathogenesis and potential treatment of multiple sclerosis will receive priority.
Level of Study: Postgraduate.
Type: Studentship.
Value: Salary scales will be similar those suggested by the Canadian Institutes for Health Research.
Length of Study: Four years, but may be extended under exceptional circumstances. Renewal must be obtained each year.
Frequency: Annual.
Study Establishment: A recognised institution.
Country of Study: Other.
No. of awards offered: Varies.
Closing Date: October 1st.
No. of awards given last year: 26.
No. of applicants last year: 27.

MULTIPLE SCLEROSIS SOCIETY OF GREAT BRITAIN AND NORTHERN IRELAND

372 Edgware Road, London, NW2 6ND, England
Tel: (44) 20 8438 0700
Email: researchadmin@mssociety.org.uk
www: http://www.mssociety.org.uk
Contact: Assistant Information Officer

The Multiple Sclerosis Society of Great Britain and Northern Ireland is the United Kingdom's largest charity for people affected by multiple sclerosis (MS). The study funds research, runs holiday homes and respite care, provides grants, education and training, publishes various publications and runs a freephone specialist helpline.

Multiple Sclerosis Society of Great Britain and Northern Ireland Research Grants

Subjects: Multiple sclerosis.
Purpose: To promote medical research into the cause and treatment of multiple sclerosis
Eligibility: Open to nationals of all countries.
Level of Study: Doctorate, Postdoctorate.
Type: Research grant.
Value: Research Grants may be awarded in the form of fellowships and PhD studentships, to provide remuneration for research workers. They may also be awarded for the provision of scientific assistance in connection with some particular aspect of research by a qualified medical or graduate scientist, to meet the entire or part cost of technical laboratory assistance, equipment and materials.
Length of Study: Innovative Awards are for one year, PhD and Junior Fellowships are for four years, Project Grants are for two years and Senior Fellowships are for five years.
Frequency: Twice a year.
Study Establishment: Suitable institutions.
Country of Study: Any country.
No. of awards offered: Varies.
Application Procedure: Applicants must complete an application form.
Closing Date: Please contact the Society.
Funding: Commercial, Private.
Contributor: Charitable donations.
Additional Information: Applications should, where applicable, be sponsored by the Head of the hospital department or laboratory in which the work is to be carried out.

MUSCULAR DYSTROPHY ASSOCIATION (MDA)

Research Department, 3300 East Sunrise Drive, Tucson, AZ 85718, United States of America
Tel: (1) 520 529 2000
Fax: (1) 520 529 5300
Email: grants@mdausa.org
www: http://www.mdausa.org
Contact: Grants Manager

The Muscular Dystrophy Association (MDA) supports research into over 40 diseases of the neuromuscular system to identify the causes of, and effective treatments for, the muscular dystrophies and related diseases including spinal muscular atrophies and motor neuron diseases, peripheral neuropathies, inflammatory myopathies, metabolic myopathies and diseases of the neuromuscular junction.

MDA Grant Programs

Subjects: The muscular dystrophies and related diseases.
Purpose: To support research into over 40 diseases of the neuromuscular system, and to identify the causes of, and effective treatments for, the muscular dystrophies and related diseases.
Eligibility: Open to persons who are professional or faculty members at appropriate educational, medical or research institutions, qualified to conduct and supervise program of original research, who have

access to institutional resources necessary to conduct the proposed research project, and who hold a MD, PhD.

Level of Study: Postdoctorate.
Type: Grant.
Value: Please contact the Association.
Length of Study: One year, renewable for a further two and three years.
Frequency: Annual.
Country of Study: Any country.
No. of awards offered: Varies.
Application Procedure: Applicants must complete the Request for Research Grant Application.
Closing Date: Pre-applications are due no later than December 15th or June 15th.
Funding: Private.
Contributor: Voluntary contributions.
Additional Information: Proposals from applicants outside the United States of America will only be considered for projects of highest priority to the MDA. Other conditions apply. Research is sponsored under the following grant programmes: Neuromuscular Disease Research and Neuromuscular Disease Research Development. Further information is available from the website.

MUSCULAR DYSTROPHY CAMPAIGN OF GREAT BRITAIN AND NORTHERN IRELAND

Research Department, 7-11 Prescot Place, London, SW4 6BS, England
Tel: (44) 20 7720 8055
Fax: (44) 20 7498 0670
Email: research@muscular-dystrophy.org
www: http://www.muscular-dystrophy.org
Contact: Ms Nicola King, Head of Research

The Muscular Dystrophy Campaign is a United Kingdom based charity funding medical research and support services for people with muscular dystrophy and related conditions.

Muscular Dystrophy Research Grants

Subjects: Muscular dystrophy and allied neuromuscular conditions.
Purpose: To provide continuity of funding for high quality research of central importance to the Muscular Dystrophy Campaign's research objectives.
Eligibility: Only fund UK research. Grant holders must have a tenured and salaried position.
Level of Study: Postdoctorate, Research.
Value: Salary of research staff, equipment and consumables. Salary of grant holder is not funded.
Length of Study: 1-3 Years.
Frequency: Annual.
Study Establishment: Universities, hospitals or research institutions.
Country of Study: United Kingdom.
No. of awards offered: Varies.
Application Procedure: Applicants must contact the Head of Research with an A4 summary of proposed research.
Closing Date: October 2004.
Funding: Private.
No. of awards given last year: 10.
No. of applicants last year: 30.

MUSEUM OF COMPARATIVE ZOOLOGY

26 Oxford Street, Cambridge, MA 02138, United States of America
Tel: (1) 617 495 2460
Fax: (1) 617 496 8308
Email: ernstmayrgrant@oeb.harvard.edu
www: http://www.mcz.harvard.edu
Contact: Ms Andrea Prill, Assistant to the Director

The Museum of Comparative Zoology was founded in 1859, through the efforts of Louis Agassiz (1807-1873). Agassiz, a zoologist from Neuchatel, Switzerland, served as the Director of the Museum from 1859 until his death in 1873. A brilliant lecturer and scholar, he established the Museum and its collections as a centre for research and education.

Ernst Mayr Grants

Subjects: Animal Taxonomy.
Purpose: To enable systematists to make short visits to museums in order to undertake research needed for the completion of taxonomic revisions and monographs.
Eligibility: There are no restrictions on eligibility. Preference is given to studies that use the Museum of Comparative Zoology's collections, although applications to work at other museums will be considered.
Level of Study: Unrestricted.
Type: Travel grant.
Value: Typical expenses that may be covered by this award include travel, lodging and meals for up to a few weeks while conducting research, services purchased from the host institution and research supplies.
Length of Study: Varies, short visits.
Frequency: Twice a year.
Study Establishment: Museums.
Country of Study: Any country.
No. of awards offered: Varies.
Application Procedure: Applicants must submit a short project description, itinerary, budget, curriculum vitae and three letters of support. No proposal forms are required or provided. Proposals may be submitted through standard mail or electronically. Submissions through standard mail must include four copies of all materials and be received by the closing date. Proposals submitted electronically must be created in Microsoft Word or plain ASCII text format. For additional information see http://www.oeb.harvard.edu/files_grants/may-rgra.cfm.
Closing Date: April 15th and September 15th.
Funding: Private.
Contributor: Endowment.
No. of awards given last year: 17.
No. of applicants last year: 29.
Additional Information: Announcements of awards will be made within two months of the closing date.

MUSICIANS BENEVOLENT FUND (MBF)

16 Ogle Street, London, W1W 6JA, England
Tel: (44) 20 7636 4481
Fax: (44) 20 7637 4307
Email: education@mbf.org.uk
www: http://www.mbf.org.uk
Contact: Ms Susan Dolton, Education Administrator

The Musicians Benevolent Fund is the music business's own charity-the largest of its kind in the UK. Last year it helped about 1,500 people of any age and in any area of the music business who were in need as a result of illness, accident or other misfortune and spent over UK£2 million on its benevolent work. The MBF also plays a significant role in education and this role is fulfilled through various award schemes, run by the MBF and guided by a committee made up of eminent musicians and advisers. In 2003, more than 240 individuals benefited from awards totalling more than UK£340,000. In addition, almost UK£225,000 was awarded to organisations, which provide advanced training and performance opportunities to outstanding young musicians.

Guilhermina Suggia Gift

Subjects: Musical performance of the cello.
Purpose: To assist with the studies of an outstanding cellist.
Eligibility: Open to cellists under the age of 21 years of any nationality.
Level of Study: Professional development.
Value: Up to UK£3,000.
Frequency: Annual.
Country of Study: Any country.
No. of awards offered: One.

Application Procedure: Applicants must complete an application form and provide two references.
Closing Date: Autumn 2004.
Funding: Private.
No. of awards given last year: One.
No. of applicants last year: 18.

Ian Fleming Charitable Trust Music Education Awards

Subjects: Musical performance.
Purpose: To help exceptionally talented young musicians.
Eligibility: Open to singers and instrumentalists possessing the potential to become first class performers, who have been resident in the United Kingdom for three years. Instrumentalists must be under 25 years of age, female singers under 27 and male singers under 28.
Level of Study: Postgraduate, Professional development.
Value: Varies, to cover tuition, maintenance and the purchase of instruments. Awards range from UK£2,000-5,000.
Frequency: Annual.
Country of Study: Any country.
No. of awards offered: Approx. 10.
Application Procedure: Applicants must complete application forms and provide two references.
Closing Date: February 11th.
Funding: Private.
No. of awards given last year: 8.
No. of applicants last year: 307.
Additional Information: Selected applicants will be asked to audition in March/April.

Manoug Parikian Award

Subjects: Musical performance on the violin.
Purpose: To assist the studies of an outstanding young violinist.
Eligibility: Open to violinists under the age of 21 years of any nationality.
Level of Study: Professional development.
Value: UK£3,000.
Frequency: Annual.
Country of Study: Any country.
No. of awards offered: One.
Application Procedure: Applicants must complete an application form and provide two references.
Closing Date: Autumn 2004.
Funding: Private.
No. of awards given last year: One.
No. of applicants last year: 19.
Additional Information: The Manoug Parikian Award is run in conjunction with the RPS Emily Anderson Prize. The Award must be used for study costs or instrument purchase.

MBF Awards for Accompanists and Repetiteurs

Subjects: Musical performance.
Purpose: To assist accompanists and repetiteurs.
Eligibility: Open to postgraduates, accompanists under the age of 27 and repetiteurs under 30. Applicants should have been resident in the United Kingdom for three years.
Level of Study: Postgraduate, Professional development.
Value: Up to UK£3,500 each.
Frequency: Annual.
Country of Study: Any country.
No. of awards offered: 5-10.
Closing Date: May 7th 2004.
Funding: Private.
No. of awards given last year: Seven.
No. of applicants last year: 22.
Additional Information: Selected students will be asked to audition. The Sir Henry Richardson Scholarship of UK£3,500 will be awarded to the most outstanding musician heard in each discipline.

MBF Music Education Awards

Subjects: Musical performance.
Purpose: To help exceptionally talented young musicians.
Eligibility: Open to singers and instrumentalists possessing the potential to become first class performers, who have been resident in the

United Kingdom for three years. Instrumentalists must be under 25 years of age, female singers under 27 and male singers under 28 years old.
Level of Study: Postgraduate, Professional development.
Value: Varies, to cover tuition maintenance and the purchase of instruments. Awards range from UK£1,000-5,000.
Frequency: Annual.
Application Procedure: Applicants must complete an application form and provide two references.
Closing Date: Feb 11th 2004.
Funding: Private.
No. of awards given last year: 50.
No. of applicants last year: 307.
Additional Information: The following major awards are also available through these auditions: Ian Fleming Charitable Trust Music Education Awards, Professor Charles Leggett Awards, Emily English Scholarship and Maidment Scholarships.

Miriam Licette Scholarship

Subjects: Musical performance and song.
Purpose: To assist a female student of French song.
Eligibility: Open to soprano, mezzo soprano or contralto singers for advanced study. Applicants should be in full-time study or in their first 12 months in the profession and be under 30 years of age.
Level of Study: Postgraduate, Professional development.
Type: Scholarship.
Value: UK£3,000.
Frequency: Annual.
Country of Study: Any country.
No. of awards offered: One, but there may be further discretionary awards.
Application Procedure: Selected students will be asked to audition. An application form must be completed and two references provided.
Closing Date: December 1st 2003.
Funding: Private.
No. of awards given last year: Three.
No. of applicants last year: 54.
Additional Information: The award is run in conjunction with the Maggie Teyte Prize.

For further information contact:

Maggie Teyte Prize 20 Beaumont Street, London, W1G 6DG, England
Contact: Administrator

Myra Hess Trust

Subjects: Musical performance on strings and piano.
Purpose: To give assistance for the purchase of instruments, for tuition, maintenance and towards the cost of first recitals.
Eligibility: Open to outstanding young instrumentalists between 20 and 27 years of age inclusive. Preference is given to those entering a professional career as a soloist. Open to piano, violin, viola, cello and double bass students.
Level of Study: Postgraduate, Professional development.
Value: Up to UK£3,000 each.
Frequency: Annual.
Country of Study: Any country.
No. of awards offered: 5-15.
Application Procedure: Applicants must complete an application form and provide two references. Selected applicants are asked to audition in June/July.
Closing Date: May 20th 2004.
Funding: Private.
No. of awards given last year: 13.
No. of applicants last year: 98.

Peter Whittingham Award

Subjects: Jazz.
Purpose: To promote both composition and performance through an innovative jazz project.
Eligibility: Open to individuals, ordinarily resident in the United Kingdom to work independently or with a project group. The project should be in creation or performance in the field of cutting edge jazz.

Money is not given for course fees. All applicants should be under 26 years old.
Level of Study: Graduate, Postgraduate, Professional development.
Value: UK£4,000.
Frequency: Annual.
No. of awards offered: One.
Application Procedure: A written description of the project must be provided together with a budget and a reference, and a recording demonstrating composition and/or performance.
Closing Date: October 2004.
Funding: Private.
No. of awards given last year: 1.
No. of applicants last year: 13.
Additional Information: Selected applicants will be asked to attend an interview.

Sybil Tutton Awards

Subjects: Musical performance in opera.
Purpose: To assist exceptionally talented students on a recognised course of operatic study.
Eligibility: Open to opera students under 30 years of age who have been resident in the United Kingdom for three years.
Level of Study: Postgraduate, Professional development.
Value: Up to UK£3,000 each.
Frequency: Annual.
Country of Study: Any country.
No. of awards offered: 5-10.
Application Procedure: Applicants must complete an application form and provide two references.
Closing Date: May 14th 2004.
Funding: Private.
No. of awards given last year: Six.
No. of applicants last year: 42.
Additional Information: Selected students will be asked to audition in June.

THE MYASTHENIA GRAVIS FOUNDATION OF AMERICA

1821 University Ave W Ste 8256, St Paul, MN 55104, United States of America
Tel: (1) 800 541 5454
Fax: (1) 615 917 1835
Email: mgfa@myasthenia.org
www: http://www.myasthenia.org
Contact: Ms Debora K Boelz, Chief Executive

The MGFA mission is to facilitate the timely diagnosis and optimal care of individuals affected by myasthenia gravis and to improve their lives through programs of patient services public information, medical research, professional education, advocacy and patient care.

Henry R Viets Medical/Graduate Student Research Fellowship

Subjects: The scientific basis of myasthenia gravis or related neuromuscular conditions.
Purpose: To promote research into the cause and cure of myasthenia gravis.
Eligibility: There are no eligibility restrictions.
Level of Study: Doctorate, Postgraduate, Research.
Type: Fellowship.
Value: US$3,000.
Length of Study: Short-term.
Frequency: Annual.
Country of Study: Any country.
No. of awards offered: Four-eight.
Application Procedure: Applicants must briefly describe, in abstract form, the question proposed for study, its association to myasthenia gravis or related neuromuscular conditions and research methodology. Further information may then be requested by the Foundation.
Closing Date: March 15th.

Funding: Private.
No. of awards given last year: Three.
No. of applicants last year: Eight.

Myasthenia Gravis Nursing Research Fellowship

Subjects: Myasthenia gravis.
Purpose: To fund research specific to myasthenia gravis.
Eligibility: There are no eligibility restrictions.
Level of Study: Postgraduate, Research.
Type: Fellowship.
Value: US$3,000.
Length of Study: Short-term.
Frequency: Annual.
Country of Study: Any country.
No. of awards offered: Two-three.
Application Procedure: Applicants must contact the Foundation for further details.
Closing Date: Applications are accepted at any time.
Funding: Private.
No. of awards given last year: One.
No. of applicants last year: Three.

Osserman/Sosin/McClare Research Fellowship

Subjects: Research pertinent to myasthenia gravis, concerned with neuromuscular transmission, immunology, molecular cell biology of the neuromuscular synapse, the aetiology or pathogenesis, diagnosis or treatment of the disease.
Purpose: To investigate the fundamental nature of myasthenia gravis.
Eligibility: There are no eligibility restrictions.
Level of Study: Postdoctorate.
Type: Fellowship.
Value: US$50,000.
Length of Study: One year.
Frequency: Annual.
Country of Study: Any country.
No. of awards offered: Two-four.
Application Procedure: Submit 10 page proposal, lay summary, budget, applicants's and preceptors curriculum vitae, letters of recommendation.
Closing Date: October 1.
Funding: Private.
No. of awards given last year: Two.
No. of applicants last year: Five.

NANTUCKET HISTORICAL ASSOCIATION (NHA)

PO Box 1016, Nantucket, MA 02554
United States of America
Tel: (1) 508 228 1655
Fax: (1) 508 325 7968
Email: library@nha.org
www: http://www.nha.org
Contact: Cristin Merck, Campaign Associate

The Nantucket Historical Association (NHA) is the principal repository of Nantucket history, with extensive archives, collections of historic properties and art and artefacts that broadly illustrate Nantucket's past. The Research Library at the NHA contains a rich collection of primary and secondary sources that document all facets of Nantucket's cultural, social, economic and spiritual history for more than three centuries. More than 400 manuscript collections relate to Nantucket individuals and families, ships, businesses and trades, churches, schools and organisations. Searchable inventories of the library's manuscript, map and book holdings can be accessed via the NHA website. The NHA art and artefacts collections include paintings, drawings, prints, baskets, silver, whaling tools, scrimshaw, furniture and textiles. The particular strengths of the collection lie in artefacts that document Nantucket's whaling industry.

E Geoffrey and Elizabeth Thayer Verney Research Fellowship

Subjects: History.

Purpose: To enhance the public's knowledge and understanding of the heritage of Nantucket, Massachusetts.

Eligibility: Open to graduate students and independent Scholars in any field to conduct research in the collections of the NHA.

Level of Study: Graduate.

Type: Residency.

Value: The NHA will provide housing in the historic property, Thomas Macy House. Housing is available January-May or October-December. The NHA will also provide a weekly stipend of US$200 for up to three weeks.

Length of Study: Three-four weeks.

Frequency: Annual.

Study Establishment: The NHA.

Country of Study: United States of America.

No. of awards offered: One.

Application Procedure: Applicants must send a full description of the proposed project, a preliminary bibliography and a complete curriculum vitae. An account of travel expenses must also be included with the anticipated time and duration of stay. Applications must be addressed to the Library Director.

Closing Date: November 21st.

No. of awards given last year: One.

Additional Information: Applicants will be notified by December 22nd.

NANYANG TECHNOLOGICAL UNIVERSITY (NTU)

Nanyang Business School MBA Office, Nanyang Avenue, Singapore

Tel: (65) 6790 4899
Fax: (65) 6791 3561
Email: nbsmba@ntu.edu.sg
www: http://www.nanyangmba.ntu.edu.sg
Contact: Administrative Officer

The Nanyang Business School is one of Asia's top business schools. Its flagship programme is the Nanyang MBA, which has consistently been ranked one of the top in Asia. The programme has gained a strong foothold in the business world through a unique blend of academic rigour and industry relevance.

NTU Alumni Scholarship

Subjects: MBA.

Purpose: To provide financial support to alumni of Nanyang Technological University admitted to the MBA programme on full-time basis.

Eligibility: Open to alumni of Nanyang Technoligical University admitted to the MBA programme on full-time basis. Recipients of other scholarships or bursaries are not eligible to apply.

Level of Study: MBA.

Type: Scholarship.

Value: A lump sum of S$3,000 per annum.

Length of Study: Each scholarship shall be tenable only for the academic year in which it is awarded.

Frequency: Annual.

Study Establishment: NTU.

Country of Study: Singapore.

No. of awards offered: Two for MBA.

Application Procedure: The completed form (copies available at http://ww.ntu.edu.sg/alumni2/forms/postgradform.pdf) must be submitted.

Closing Date: End July.

Funding: Private.

Contributor: NTU Alumni Fund.

No. of awards given last year: 0.

For further information contact:

Nanyang Technological University Level 5, Administrative Annexe 42 Nanyang Avenue, Singapore

Contact: The Director, Alumni and Endowment Office.

NTU APEC Scholarship

Subjects: MBA.

Purpose: To allow outstanding candidates from the APEC member economies to pursue the Master of Business Administration Programme at NTU on a full-time basis.

Eligibility: Open to nationals from the following APEC member economies (except Singapore) to pursue a full-time MBA programme at NTU: Australia, Brunei Darussalam, Canada, Chile, Chinese Taipei, Indonesia, Japan, Malaysia, Mexico, New Zealand, Papua New Guinea, People's Republic of China, Peru, Philippines, Republic of Korea, Russia, Thailand, United States, Vietnam. Singaporeans and Singapore Permanent Residents and recipients of other scholarships or bursaries are not eligible to apply.

Level of Study: MBA.

Type: Scholarship.

Value: Monthly stipend of S$1,400; book allowance of S$500; tuition fees, health insurance, examination fees and other approved fees, allowances and expenses; cost of one overseas Business Study Mission; cost of travel from home country to Singapore on award of the scholarship; and cost of travel from Singapore to home country on successful completion of the Masters programme. Each scholarship is tenable for a period of four trimesters only.

Length of Study: Full-time for 16 months.

Frequency: Annual.

Study Establishment: NTU.

Country of Study: Singapore.

No. of awards offered: Two.

Application Procedure: Application forms (copies available at http://ww.ntu.edu.sg/GradStudies/Coursework+Programmes) and supporting documents are required.

Closing Date: December 31st.

Funding: Government.

Contributor: NTU.

No. of awards given last year: Two.

No. of applicants last year: 50.

Additional Information: Applications open in September/October and closed on 31st December each year. Invitations for applications will be placed in the newspapers in the capital cities of the APEC countries on the University's website at http://www.ntu.edu.sg/GradStudies/Coursework+Programmes. International students have to apply for a Student's Pass from Singapore immigration in order to pursue a full-time course of study in Singapore. The University will assist successful international applicants in their applications for the Student's Pass.

NTU ASEAN Postgraduate Scholarship

Subjects: MBA.

Purpose: To allow outstanding candidates from the ASEAN (Association of South East Asian Nations) member economies, except Singapore to pursue the Master of Business Administration programme at NTU on a full-time basis.

Eligibility: Open to nationals of the following member countries of ASEAN (Brunei Darussalam, Cambodia, Indonesia, Laos, Malaysia, Myanmar, Philippines, Thailand and Vietnam) to pursue a designated full time Masters degree by coursework at NTU. Singaporeans and Singapore permanent residents and recipients of other scholarships or bursaries are not eligible to apply.

Level of Study: MBA.

Type: Scholarship.

Value: Monthly stipend of S$1,350; book allowance of S$500; tuition fees, health insurance, examination fees and other approved fees, allowances and expenses; cost of one overseas Business Study Mission; cost of travel from home country to Singapore on award of the scholarship; and cost of travel from Singapore to home country on successful completion of the Masters programme. Each scholarship is tenable for a period of four trimesters only.

Length of Study: Full-time for 16 months.

Frequency: Annual.

Study Establishment: NTU.

Country of Study: Singapore.

No. of awards offered: One to Two.

Application Procedure: Application forms (copies available at http://ww.ntu.edu.sg/GradStudies/Coursework+Programmes) and supporting documents are required.

Closing Date: December 31st.
Funding: Government.
No. of awards given last year: One.
No. of applicants last year: 50.
Additional Information: Applications open in September/October and close on 31st December each year. Invitations for applications will be placed in the newspapers in the capital cities of the ASEAN countries on the University's website at http://www.ntu.edu.sg/Grad-Studies/Coursework + Programmes. International students have to apply for a Student's Pass from Singapore Immigration in order to pursue a full-time course of study in Singapore. The University will assist successful international applicants in their applications for the Student's Pass.

NTU MBA Scholarship

Subjects: MBA.
Purpose: To enable outstanding overseas candidates to pursue the MBA programme on a full-time basis.
Eligibility: Open to international applicants to pursue a full-time MBA Programme at NTU. Singaporeans and Singapore Permanent Residents and recipients of other scholarships or bursaries are not eligible to apply.
Level of Study: MBA.
Type: Scholarship.
Value: S$24,000 to cover the tuition fees of a full-time programme.
Length of Study: Full-time for 16 months.
Frequency: Annual.
Study Establishment: NTU.
Country of Study: Singapore.
No. of awards offered: Four.
Application Procedure: Application forms (copies available at http://www.nanyangmba.ntu.edu.sg/scholarships.pdf or the MBA office) and application for admission to the MBA programme with supporting documents are required.
Closing Date: End of February.
Funding: Private.
No. of awards given last year: Four.
No. of applicants last year: 81.
Additional Information: Applications open in October each year and close on end February each year. International students have to apply for a Student's Pass from Singapore Immigration in order to pursue a full-time course of study in Singapore. The University will assist successful international applicants in their applications for the Student's Pass.

NTU SCCCF Business Scholarship

Subjects: MBA.
Purpose: To provide financial support to Singaporeans and permanent residents of Singapore who are admitted onto the MBA programme on either a full-time or part-time basis.
Eligibility: Open to Singaporeans and Singapore permanent residents admitted to the MBA programme on either a full-time or part-time basis. Recipients of other scholarships or bursaries are not eligible to apply.
Level of Study: MBA.
Type: Scholarship.
Value: A lump sum of S$5,000.
Length of Study: Full-time is 16 months and part-time is 24-32 months.
Frequency: Annual.
Study Establishment: NTU.
Country of Study: Singapore.
No. of awards offered: Three.
Application Procedure: Applicants must apply in September and October each year. Invitations for applications will be placed on the notice boards of the MBA Office and the Office of Academic Services (Graduate Branch).
Closing Date: To be decided by the donor, usually end October.
Funding: Commercial.
Contributor: The Singapore Chinese Chamber of Commerce Foundation Business Scholarship.
No. of awards given last year: 0.
No. of applicants last year: 0.

THE NATIONAL ACADEMY OF EDUCATION

New York University, School of Education, 726 Broadway, 5th Floor, New York, NY 10003-9580, United States of America
Tel: (1) 212 998 9035
Fax: (1) 212 995 4435
Email: nae.info@nyu.edu
www: http://www.nae.nyu.edu
Contact: Ms Danielle Samalin, Fellowship Co-ordinator

The National Academy of Education consists of up to 125 members who are elected on the basis of outstanding scholarship or contributions to education. From its establishment in 1965, the Academy has sponsored a variety of commissions and study panels that have published proceedings and reports. Since 1986, the National Academy of Education has administered a Postdoctoral Fellowship Programme designed to support young scholars.

National Academy of Education Spencer Postdoctoral Fellowships

Subjects: All subjects encouraged for education and educational research.
Purpose: To ensure the future of research in education by supporting young scholars working in critical areas of educational scholarship. The Academy seeks to fund proposals which promise to make significant scholarly contributions to the field of education as well as to advance the careers of its recipients.
Eligibility: Open to candidates who have obtained doctoral degrees in the past five years and are conducting research relevant to the improvement of education in all its forms. United States citizenship is not required.
Level of Study: Postdoctorate.
Type: Fellowship.
Value: US$50,000.
Length of Study: One academic year full-time or two academic years part-time.
Frequency: Annual.
Study Establishment: Any establishment.
Country of Study: Any country.
No. of awards offered: Up to Twenty(20).
Application Procedure: Applicants must complete an application form. Please visit the website for a more detailed description and to download application forms.
Closing Date: See website: http://www.nae.nyu.edu.
Funding: Private.
Contributor: The Spencer Foundation.
No. of awards given last year: 30.
No. of applicants last year: 200.
Additional Information: The fellowship is non residential. Research must relate to education in all its forms.

NATIONAL AIR AND SPACE MUSEUM, CEPS SMITHSONIAN (NASM)

Room 3757, Washington, DC 20560, United States of America
Tel: (1) 202 633 2471
Fax: (1) 202 786 2566
Email: zimbelmanj@nasm.si.edu
www: http://www.nasm.edu/ceps

The Smithsonian Institution's National Air and Space Museum (NASM) maintains the largest collection of historic air and spacecraft in the world. It is also a vital centre for research into the history, science and technology of aviation and space flight.

CEPS Fellowship

Subjects: Geological and geophysical investigations of the history of planetary surfaces, including studies of processes responsible for generating the surface land forms.
Purpose: To assist postdoctoral candidates interested in scientific research in planetary and terrestrial geological and geophysical studies.

433

Eligibility: There are no eligibility restrictions.
Level of Study: Postdoctorate.
Type: Fellowship.
Value: Competitive with the National Research Council Awards.
Length of Study: One-two years.
Frequency: Dependent on funds available.
Study Establishment: In residence at the NASM.
Country of Study: United States of America.
No. of awards offered: One.
Application Procedure: Applicants must complete an application form.
Closing Date: Please contact the organisation.
Funding: Private.
Contributor: Smithsonian Restricted Funds.
No. of awards given last year: One.
No. of applicants last year: 21.

For further information contact:

Center for Earth and Planetary Studies, Room 3757, Washington, DC 20560-0315, United States of America
Contact: Chairman

Daniel and Florence Guggenheim Fellowship

Subjects: Aviation History.
Purpose: To promote research into, and writing about, the history of aviation and space flight.
Eligibility: Predoctoral applicants should have completed preliminary coursework and examinations and be engaged in dissertation research postdoctoral applicants should have received their Ph.D within the past seven years.
Level of Study: Postdoctorate, Predoctorate, Non-academic investigators.
Type: Fellowship.
Value: US$20,000 for predoctoral candidates, US$30,000 for postdoctoral candidates.
Length of Study: 3-12 months.
Frequency: Annual.
Study Establishment: Smithsonian Institution.
Country of Study: United States of America.
Application Procedure: Download an application form from the website or mail a written application to: Ms Collette Williams Fellowship Coordinator Rm 3313, MRC 312, PO Box 37012, National Air and Space Museum, Smithsonian Institution, Washington D.C. 20013-7012.
Closing Date: Mail in November please. Applicants will be notified April 15th to begin between June 1st and October 1st same year.
Funding: Private.
Contributor: The Daniel & Florence Guggenheim Foundation.
Additional Information: All candidates are encouraged to pursue programs of research and writing that support publication of works that are scholarly in tone and substance, and/or addressed to an audience with broad interests. Outstanding manuscripts resulting from this program may be offered to the Smithsonian Institution press for publication.

NATIONAL ALLIANCE FOR RESEARCH ON SCHIZOPHRENIA AND DEPRESSION (NARSAD)

60 Cutter Mill Road, Suite 404, Great Neck, NY 11021, United States of America
Tel: (1) 516 829 5576
Fax: (1) 516 487 6930
Email: amoran@narsad.org
www: http://www.narsad.org
Contact: Ms Audra Moran, Director, Research Grants Programme

The National Alliance for Research on Schizophrenia and Depression (NARSAD) raises and distributes funds for scientific research into the causes, cures, treatments and prevention of neurobiological disorders, primarily the schizophrenias, depression and bipolar disorders. NARSAD is the largest donor supported organisation devoted exclusively to supporting scientific research on psychiatric brain disorders in the world.

NARSAD Distinguished Investigator Awards

Subjects: Schizophrenia, major affective disorders or other serious mental illnesses including bipolar disease, borderline disorders with depression or suicide plus research with children's psychiatric disorders.
Purpose: To encourage experienced scientists to pursue innovative projects in diverse areas of neurobiological research.
Eligibility: Open to senior researchers at the rank of professor or equivalent and who maintain their own laboratory.
Level of Study: Postdoctorate, Research.
Type: Grant.
Value: Up to US$100,000.
Length of Study: One year.
Frequency: Annual.
Country of Study: Any country.
No. of awards offered: Varies.
Application Procedure: Applicants must refer to the website for guidelines and a face sheet.
Closing Date: May 15th.
Funding: Private.
Contributor: Donors.
No. of awards given last year: 15.
No. of applicants last year: 159.
Additional Information: Further information is available from the website.

NARSAD Independent Investigator Awards

Subjects: Schizophrenia, major affective disorders or other serious mental illnesses including bipolar disease, borderline disorders with depression or suicide plus research with children's psychiatric disorders.
Purpose: To facilitate innovative research opportunities in diverse areas of neurobiological research.
Eligibility: Open to scientists at the academic level of associate professor or equivalent. Candidates must have won national competitive support as a principal investigator.
Level of Study: Postdoctorate, Research.
Type: Grant.
Value: Up to US$50,000 maximum per year.
Length of Study: Two years.
Frequency: Annual.
Country of Study: Any country.
No. of awards offered: Varies.
Application Procedure: Applicants must refer to the website for guidelines and a face sheet.
Closing Date: March 5th.
Funding: Private.
Contributor: Donors.
No. of awards given last year: 45.
No. of applicants last year: 229.
Additional Information: Further information is available from the website.

NARSAD Young Investigator Awards

Subjects: Schizophrenia, major affective disorders or other serious mental illnesses including bipolar disease, borderline disorders with depression or suicide plus psychiatric research with children's psychiatric disorders.
Purpose: To enable promising investigators to either extend their research fellowship training or to begin careers as independent research faculty.
Eligibility: Open to investigators who have attained a doctorate or equivalent degree, are affiliated with a specific research institution and who have a mentor or senior collaborator who is performing significant research in an area relevant to schizophrenia, depression or other serious mental illnesses. Candidates should be at the postdoctoral to assistant professor level.
Level of Study: Postdoctorate, Research.
Type: Grant.
Value: Up to US$30,000 maximum per year.

Length of Study: Up to two years.
Frequency: Annual.
Country of Study: Any country.
No. of awards offered: Varies.
Application Procedure: Applicants must refer to the website for guidelines and a face sheet.
Closing Date: July 25th.
Funding: Private.
Contributor: Donors.
No. of awards given last year: 175.
No. of applicants last year: 673.
Additional Information: This award is intended to support only advanced Fellows and assistant professors or their equivalent. Further information is available from the website.

NATIONAL ASSOCIATION OF BROADCASTERS (NAB)

1771 N Street NW, Washington, DC 20036-2800, United States of America
Tel: (1) 202 429 5489
Fax: (1) 202 429 4199
Email: nab@nab.org
www: http://www.nab.org/research/grants/grants.asp
Contact: Research Information

The National Association of Broadcasters (NAB) aims to make high quality academic research available to industry practitioners as well as other researchers.

NAB Grants for Research in Broadcasting

Subjects: Broadcast research, especially research on economic, business, social or policy issues of importance to the United States of America's commercial broadcast industry.
Purpose: To stimulate interest in broadcast research.
Eligibility: Open to all academic personnel working in disciplines that relate to the social, cultural, political and economic aspects of broadcasting. Graduate students are invited to submit proposals.
Level of Study: Doctorate, Graduate, Postdoctorate, Postgraduate.
Type: Grant.
Value: US$5,000 average.
Length of Study: One year.
Frequency: Annual.
Country of Study: United States of America.
No. of awards offered: Varies.
Application Procedure: Applicants must complete an application form available on written request or from the website.
Closing Date: Please write for details.
No. of awards given last year: Six.
No. of applicants last year: 41.

NATIONAL ASSOCIATION OF COMPOSERS

PO Box 49256, Barrington Station, Los Angeles, CA 90049, United States of America
Tel: (1) 310 541 8213
Fax: (1) 310 373 3244
Email: bia@flash.net
www: http://www.music-usa.org/nacusa
Contact: President

The National Association of Composers presents concerts of the members' music throughout the United States, mainly the West Coast (Los Angeles and San Francisco) and the East Coast (New York, Philadelphia and Boston).

National Association of Composers Young Composers Competition

Subjects: Music composition.
Purpose: To foster the creation of new American concert hall music.

Eligibility: Open to nationals of any country between the ages of 18 and 30.
Level of Study: Postdoctorate, Postgraduate.
Type: Competition.
Value: Please contact the organisation.
Frequency: Annual.
Country of Study: Any country.
No. of awards offered: Two.
Application Procedure: Applicants must send in their music as there are no application forms.
Closing Date: October 30th.
Funding: Private.

NATIONAL ASSOCIATION OF DENTAL ASSISTANTS

900 South Washington Street, G-13, Falls Church, VA 22046, United States of America
Tel: (1) 703 237 8616
Fax: (1) 703 533 1153
Contact: Scholarship Department

National Association of Dental Assistants Annual Scholarship Award

Subjects: Dental assistant certification, recertification, dental training, continuing dental education seminars or any course that is related to, or required in, the dental degree programme.
Purpose: To enable dental assistants to further their education.
Eligibility: Open to dental assistants who have a minimum of two years of membership in good standing. Applicants may also be a member's dependent, spouse or grandchild. All courses must be approved by the board.
Level of Study: Unrestricted.
Type: Scholarship.
Value: US$250 - Varies.
Frequency: Annual.
Study Establishment: Appropriate institutions.
Country of Study: Any country.
No. of awards offered: One-two.
Application Procedure: Applicants must submit one recommendation from their current or previous employer, one recommendation from someone other than a member, if a member's dependent, such as a school counsellor or another dental assistant, a completed application form and an updated student transcript.
Closing Date: May 31st.
Funding: Commercial.
No. of awards given last year: Two.
No. of applicants last year: Approx. 10.

NATIONAL ASSOCIATION OF SCHOLARS (NAS)

221 Witherspoon Street
2nd Floor, Princeton, NJ 08542-3215
United States of America
Tel: (1) 609 683 1437
Fax: (1) 609 683 0316
Email: brasor@nas.org
www: http://www.nas.org
Contact: G C Brasor, Associate Director

The National Association of Scholars (NAS) is an organisation of professors, graduate students, college administrators and independent scholars committed to rational discourse as the foundation of academic life in a free democratic society. The NAS works to enrich the substance and strengthen the integrity of scholarship and teaching, convinced that only through an informed understanding of the western intellectual heritage and the realities of the contemporary world, can citizen and scholar be equipped to sustain civilisation's achievements.

Barry R Gross Memorial Award

Subjects: Academic reform.
Purpose: To reward an NAS member for outstanding service, through the medium of the organisation or responsible citizenship, to the cause of academic reform.
Eligibility: Candidates must be NAS nominated.
Type: Award.
Value: US$1,000, a plaque and travel expenses to attend the national conference and present a speech.
Frequency: Every 18 months.
Application Procedure: No applications are accepted.
Funding: Private.
Additional Information: Established to honour the memory of Barry R Gross.

Peter Shaw Memorial Award

Subjects: Writing on issues pertaining to higher education and American intellectual culture.
Purpose: To recognise exemplary writing on issues pertaining to higher education and American intellectual culture.
Eligibility: Candidates must be NAS nominated.
Type: Award,
Value: US$1,000, a plaque and travel expenses to attend the national conference and present a speech.
Frequency: Every 18 months.
Application Procedure: No applications are accepted.
Funding: Private.
Additional Information: Established to honour the memory of Peter Shaw.

Sidney Hook Memorial Award

Subjects: The defence of academic freedom and integrity of academic life.
Purpose: To award an individual for distinguished contributions to the defence of academic freedom and the integrity of academic life.
Eligibility: Candidates must be NAS nominated.
Type: Award.
Value: US$2,500, a plaque and travel expenses to attend the national conference and present a speech.
Frequency: Every 18 months.
Application Procedure: No applications are accepted.
Funding: Private.
Additional Information: The award was established to honour the memory of Sidney Hook.

NATIONAL ASTHMA CAMPAIGN

Providence House, Providence Place, London, England
Tel: (44) 20 7226 2260
Fax: (44) 20 7704 0740
Email: pmajor@asthma.org.uk
www: http://www.asthma.org.uk
Contact: Office for Funding

The National Asthma Campaign is the independent United Kingdom charity dedicated to conquering asthma. It funds asthma research, offers help and advice and campaigns for a better deal for people with asthma.

National Asthma Campaign Project Grants

Subjects: The study of asthma including causation and mechanisms, diagnosis and management, evaluation of therapies, organisation of care and the translation of laboratory findings into clinical settings.
Purpose: To fund applied, basic or clinical research relevant to asthma or a related allergy.
Eligibility: Open to tenured individuals working in the United Kingdom.
Level of Study: Research.
Type: Project grant.
Value: Varies.
Length of Study: A maximum of three years.
Frequency: Annual.
Country of Study: Other.

No. of awards offered: 20-25 per year.
Application Procedure: Applicants must complete an application form, available directly from the website.
Closing Date: Late November.
Funding: Private.
No. of awards given last year: 21.
No. of applicants last year: 83.
Additional Information: The charity runs an annual, competitive project grant round, taking advice on funding priorities from its research committee. A statement of the charities research strategy and links to the strategy documents can be found on the website.

NATIONAL ATAXIA FOUNDATION

2600 Fernbrook Lane, Suite 119, Minneapolis, MN 55447, United States of America
Tel: (1) 763 553 0020
Fax: (1) 763 553 0167
Email: naf@mail.ataxia.org
www: http://www.ataxia.org
Contact: Executive Director

The National Ataxia Foundation is dedicated to improving the lives of persons affected by ataxia through support, education and research.

Ataxia Research Grant

Subjects: Neurology and genetics in relation to the study of ataxia.
Purpose: To support research projects.
Eligibility: There are no eligibility restrictions.
Level of Study: Unrestricted.
Type: Research grant.
Value: US$5,000-35,000.
Length of Study: One year.
Frequency: Annual.
Country of Study: Any country.
No. of awards offered: Approx. nine.
Application Procedure: Applicants must apply for application forms and guidelines, available on request or from the website.
Closing Date: August 15th.
Funding: Private.
Contributor: Members of the Foundation.
No. of awards given last year: 15.
No. of applicants last year: 15.

NATIONAL BRAIN TUMOR FOUNDATION (NBTF)

414 Thirteenth Street, Suite 700, Oakland, CA 94612-2603, United States of America
Tel: (1) 510 839 9777
Fax: (1) 510 839 9779
Email: nbtf@braintumor.org
www: http://www.braintumor.org
Contact: Director of Patient Services

Charles B Wilson Brain Tumor Research Excellence Grant

Subjects: Neuro oncology and neuroscience.
Purpose: To provide funding for general research.
Eligibility: Preference is given to translational research but all types of applications are accepted.
Level of Study: Research.
Type: Research grant.
Value: A total value of US$100,000.
Country of Study: United States of America or Canada.

NABTC/NABTT Research Grant

Subjects: Brain tumours.
Purpose: To fund research.
Eligibility: Applicants must be researchers at a member institution of the North American Brain Tumor Consortium (NABTC) or New Approaches to Brain Tumor Therapy (NABTT).

Level of Study: Research.
Type: Grant.
Value: US$100,000.
Study Establishment: A member institution of the North American Brain Tumor Consortium (NABTC) or New Approaches to Brain Tumor Therapy (NABTT).
Country of Study: United States of America or Canada.
No. of awards offered: One.
Application Procedure: Applicants must visit the website for further information.

NBTF Quality of Life Research Grant

Subjects: Brain tumours.
Purpose: To provide support for research into quality of life issues affecting both brain tumour patients and their caregivers.
Level of Study: Research.
Type: Research grant.
Value: US$15,000.
Country of Study: United States of America or Canada.
No. of awards offered: One.
Application Procedure: Applicants must visit the website for further information.

Oligo Brain Tumor Fund

Subjects: Neurology.
Purpose: To support research into oligodendroglioma tumours.
Level of Study: Research.
Type: Research grant.
Value: US$50,000.
Country of Study: United States of America or Canada.
No. of awards offered: Varies.
Application Procedure: Applicants must visit the website for further information.
Closing Date: February.
Funding: Private.
Contributor: The Jeffrey Bein Family.

NATIONAL CANCER INSTITUTE OF CANADA (NCIC)

Suite 200, 10 Alcorn Avenue, Toronto, ON, M4V 3B1, Canada
Tel: (1) 416 961 7223
Fax: (1) 416 961 4189
Email: ncic@cancer.ca
www: http://www.ncic.cancer.ca
Contact: Dr Michael A Wosnick, Executive Director

The National Cancer Institute of Canada (NCIC) is the largest non government funder of cancer research in Canada. In concert with its partner, the Canadian Cancer Society, and with the Terry Fox Foundation, the NCIC provides support for research and related programmes undertaken at Canadian universities, hospitals and other research institutions.

CCS Feasibility Grants

Subjects: Cancer research.
Purpose: To provide a modest level of funding as the NCIC recognises that it is difficult to submit a full application for a research grant without having first conducted preliminary studies.
Eligibility: This programme is open to all applicants but priority will be given where it is apparent that no other resources are available. These grants will not be awarded to support travel to conduct planning meetings. These funds will also not be awarded for conference travel or for the purchase of permanent equipment.
Level of Study: Postgraduate.
Type: Grant.
Value: Up to Canadian $35,000.
Length of Study: One year, but funds may be spent over a two year period.
Frequency: Annual.
Country of Study: Canada.
No. of awards offered: Varies.

Application Procedure: Applicants must write for details or refer to the website.
Closing Date: Please contact the organisation.
Funding: Private.
Contributor: The Canadian Cancer Society.
Additional Information: Further information is available from the website.

NCIC Clinical Research Fellowships

Subjects: Clinical cancer research.
Purpose: To assist outstanding individuals who hold a doctoral degree in medicine and who seek specialised training.
Eligibility: Open to Canadian citizens or residents who possess a doctoral degree in medicine from a recognised institution and be licensed to practice in Canada. Preference will be given to those who can demonstrate research commitment by having completed, or being enrolled in, a relevant graduate course.
Level of Study: Postdoctorate, Professional development.
Type: Fellowship.
Value: Minimum Canadian $35,000 rising for each year of postdoctoral experience to a maximum of Canadian $47,500 per year.
Length of Study: Up to three years.
Frequency: Annual.
Study Establishment: A teaching hospital.
Country of Study: Canada, or abroad as approved.
No. of awards offered: Varies.
Application Procedure: Applicants must write for details or refer to the website.
Closing Date: February 1st.
Funding: Private.
Contributor: The Terry Fox Foundation and the Canadian Cancer Society.
No. of applicants last year: One.
Additional Information: Further information is available from the website. Stipends are subject to annual review. Recipients of these fellowships are eligible to apply for a contribution of Canadian $1,200 towards the cost of conference travel per award year.

NCIC Equipment Grants for New Investigators

Subjects: Cancer research.
Purpose: To make it possible for new investigators to set up cancer research facilities in Canada. The award is designed to assist young investigators beginning their career.
Eligibility: Applicants should be new investigators who have no more than two years of experience as an independent investigator and have not received an operational research grant from the National Cancer Institute or another comparable agency.
Level of Study: Postgraduate.
Type: Grant.
Value: Up to Canadian $75,000, plus an additional Canadian $75,000.
Frequency: Dependent on funds available.
Country of Study: Canada.
No. of awards offered: Varies.
Application Procedure: Applicants must write for details or refer to the website.
Closing Date: Please contact the organisation.
Funding: Private.
Contributor: The Terry Fox Foundation.
Additional Information: The award is not intended to facilitate the relocation of individuals from one laboratory to another. Further information is available from the website.

NCIC Post-PhD and Post-MD Research Fellowships

Subjects: Cancer research.
Purpose: To provide training in cancer research for outstanding candidates who plan a career in Canada in this field of investigation.
Eligibility: Candidates must be graduates of a university recognised by the NCIC and must be accepted for postdoctoral training in the field of cancer research in an academic environment also recognised. If the fellowship is to be taken outside Canada the applicant must be either a Canadian citizen or Canadian landed immigrant. Post MD candidates must be licensed to practice in Canada. For applicants with both PhD

and MD degrees, the degree obtained most recently will determine the fellowship category for which they should apply.

Level of Study: Postgraduate.

Type: Fellowship.

Value: Minimum Canadian $35,000 rising for each year of postdoctoral experience to a maximum of Canadian $47,500 per year.

Length of Study: Up to a maximum of three years.

Frequency: Annual.

Study Establishment: A Canadian institute or abroad if the applicant is Canadian or a Canadian landed immigrant.

Country of Study: Canada or abroad.

No. of awards offered: Varies.

Application Procedure: Applicants must refer to the website.

Closing Date: February 1st.

Funding: Private.

Contributor: The Terry Fox Foundation and the Canadian Cancer Society.

No. of awards given last year: 20.

No. of applicants last year: 60.

Additional Information: Further information is available from the website.

NCIC Research Grants for New Investigators

Subjects: Cancer research.

Purpose: To facilitate the greatest possibility for new investigators to obtain grant support for cancer research. The award is designed to assist new investigators who are beginning a career in cancer research.

Eligibility: Applicants should be new investigators who have no more than two years of experience as an independent investigator and have not previously received a research grant from the National Cancer Institute of Canada or another comparable agency.

Level of Study: Postgraduate.

Type: Research grant.

Value: Varies.

Frequency: Annual.

Study Establishment: An approved institution.

Country of Study: Canada.

No. of awards offered: Varies.

Application Procedure: Applicants must write for details or refer to the website.

Closing Date: October 15th.

Funding: Private.

Contributor: The Terry Fox Foundation.

No. of awards given last year: Six.

No. of applicants last year: 26.

Additional Information: Grantees are asked to play a direct role in the Institute's efforts to provide more funds for research in the future. Recipients of the award are expected to acknowledge the support of the Institute and its financial partners in all scientific communications and press releases related to the award.

NCIC Research Grants to Individuals

Subjects: Cancer research.

Purpose: To stimulate Canadian investigators in a very broad spectrum of research.

Eligibility: Open to a researcher who is designated as the principal investigator and must be based in, or formally affiliated with, but not necessarily receive salary support from, an eligible Canadian host institution such as a university, research institute or healthcare agency. Graduate students, postdoctoral Fellows, research associates, technical support staff, or investigators based outside of Canada are not eligible to be a principal investigator.

Level of Study: Postgraduate.

Type: Research grant.

Value: Awards will be granted for the purchase and maintenance of animals, for expendable supplies, minor items of equipment, for payment of graduate students, postdoctoral Fellows and technical and professional assistants, and for research travel and permanent equipment. An allocation for conference travel will be added automatically by the NCIC. These grants do not provide for personal salary support of the principal investigator and/or co-applicants nor for institutional overhead costs.

Length of Study: Three years in the first instance, with possible renewals for periods of one-five years.

Frequency: Annual.

Study Establishment: Universities or other institutions.

Country of Study: Canada.

No. of awards offered: Varies.

Application Procedure: Applicants must complete an application form. Further details are available on request or from the website.

Closing Date: Please contact the organisation.

Funding: Private.

Contributor: The Terry Fox Foundation and the Canadian Cancer Society.

No. of awards given last year: 116.

No. of applicants last year: 358.

Additional Information: Further information is available from the website. Grants will be awarded to projects deemed worthy of support, provided that the basic equipment and research facilities are available in the institution concerned and that it will provide the necessary administrative services. Grants are made only with the consent and knowledge of the administrative head of the institution at which they are to be held and applications must be countersigned accordingly.

NCIC Research Scientist Awards

Subjects: Cancer research.

Purpose: To provide a career development opportunity for individuals committed to a high standard of cancer research.

Eligibility: Applicants must hold a PhD, MD or comparable degree and be conducting research in a field relevant to cancer or cancer control. An intention to remain in Canada is required. Candidates must have a minimum of three years of postdoctoral training in research and may not have more than five years of research experience calculated from the beginning of their independent research career. Applicants must also hold a nationally peer reviewed research grant relevant to cancer at the time of application.

Level of Study: Postdoctorate.

Type: Research grant.

Value: The initial salary will depend on the experience and competence of the individual. The University must be willing to provide space and two years of salary at the end of the award.

Length of Study: A maximum of six years.

Frequency: Annual.

Study Establishment: An approved university or research establishment.

Country of Study: Canada.

No. of awards offered: Varies.

Application Procedure: Applicants must refer to the website for details. Applications are made by the university in which the candidate will hold an academic appointment, and not directly from the applicants themselves.

Closing Date: Please contact the organisation.

Funding: Private.

Contributor: The Canadian Cancer Society.

No. of awards given last year: Seven.

No. of applicants last year: Nine.

Additional Information: Further information is available from the website.

NCIC Research Studentships

Subjects: Cancer research.

Purpose: To award outstanding PhD students who plan a career in cancer research in Canada.

Eligibility: Applicants must be Canadian residents enrolled in a PhD programme at a Canadian institute. Applicants must have completed atleast two years of research training at graduate level or have equivalent research experience.

Level of Study: Postgraduate.

Type: Research grant.

Value: Canadian $21,500 per year.

Length of Study: A maximum of four years.

Frequency: Annual.

Study Establishment: An approved institution.

Country of Study: Canada.

No. of awards offered: Varies.

Application Procedure: Applicants must refer to the website for details and application forms.
Closing Date: Please contact the organisation.
Funding: Private.
Contributor: The Terry Fox Foundation and the Canadian Cancer Society.
No. of awards given last year: 16.
No. of applicants last year: 48.
Additional Information: Further information is available from the website. The NCIC invite all members of the research community to identify and approach qualified individuals, and encourage them to apply.

NCIC Travel Awards for Senior Level PhD Students

Subjects: Cancer research.
Purpose: To provide financial assistance by helping to defray the travel costs associated with making a scientific presentation at a conference, symposium or other appropriate professional gathering.
Eligibility: Applicants must be students enrolled in a PhD or MD programme at a Canadian institution and be in the final phase of their studies. Candidates must be attending a conference for the purpose of presenting data from a cancer related project on a first author basis.
Level of Study: Postgraduate.
Type: Travel grant.
Value: Up to Canadian $1,500.
Frequency: Three times each year.
Country of Study: Canada.
No. of awards offered: Up to 20 per calendar year.
Application Procedure: Applicants must refer to the website.
Closing Date: April 1st, September 1st or December 1st.
Funding: Private.
Contributor: The Canadian Cancer Society.
No. of awards given last year: 13.
No. of applicants last year: 20.
Additional Information: Further information is available from the website.

NATIONAL CENTER FOR ATMOSPHERIC RESEARCH (NCAR)

PO Box 3000, Advanced Study Programme, Boulder, CO 80307-3000, United States of America
Tel: (1) 303 497 1601
Fax: (1) 303 497 1646
Email: barbm@ucar.edu
www: http://www.asp.ucar.edu/asp
Contact: Ms Barbara Hansford, Co-ordinator

The National Center for Atmospheric Research (NCAR) is a national research center focused on atmospheric science.

NCAR Postdoctoral Appointments in the Advanced Study Program

Subjects: Atmospheric sciences.
Purpose: To assist and support research.
Eligibility: Open to those who have recently received their PhD and scientists with no more than four years of applicable experience since receiving their PhD. Foreign nationals may also apply.
Level of Study: Postdoctorate.
Type: Fellowship.
Value: US$45,000 per year for recent PhDs, US$47,000 for appointees in the second year at NCAR/ASP. All appointees are eligible for life and health insurance and travel expenses to the center are reimbursed for the appointee and family. Fellows living abroad will have round trip travel expenses for themselves and their families paid up to a maximum of US$2,500. A small allowance for moving and storing personal belongings is provided. Scientific travel and registration fees that cost up to US$1,500 per year are normally available.
Length of Study: Up to one year, with a possibility of renewal for a further year.
Frequency: Annual.
Study Establishment: The Center.
Country of Study: United States of America.

No. of awards offered: 8-10.
Application Procedure: Applicants must send transcripts of graduate university courses, a curriculum vitae including any scientific work experience, an abstract of doctoral thesis, four references, a short statement describing the applicant's interest in the atmospheric sciences and the work he or she would like to do during their visit to the National Center for Atmospheric Research. Applications should be addressed to Barbara Hanford at the main address or sent by express mail to the address below.
Closing Date: January 5th.
Funding: Government.
No. of awards given last year: 9.
No. of applicants last year: 120.
Additional Information: NCAR is an equal opportunity employer with an affirmative action programme.

For further information contact:

1850 Table Mesa Drive, Boulder, CO 80305, United States of America.

THE NATIONAL COLLEGIATE ATHLETIC ASSOCIATION

700 West Washington Avenue, PO Box 6222, Indianapolis, IN 46206-6222, United States of America
Tel: (1) 317 917 6222
Fax: (1) 317 917 6888
www: http://www.ncaa.org
Contact: Administrative Assistant

The National Collegiate Athletic Association is the organisation through which the nation's colleges and universities speak and act on athletics matters at the national level. It is a voluntary association of more than 1,200 institutions, conferences, organisations and individuals devoted to the sound administration of intercollegiate athletics.

NCAA Postgraduate Scholarship

Subjects: All subjects.
Purpose: To honour outstanding student athletes who are also outstanding scholars.
Eligibility: Open to student athletes enrolled at an NCAA member institution, in the last year of intercollegiate competition and with a minimum grade point average of 3,200 on a 4,000 scale or its equivalent.
Level of Study: Postgraduate.
Type: Grant.
Value: One time grant of US$6,900. This is not earmarked for a specific area of postgraduate study but the awardee must use it as a full-time graduate student in a graduate or professional school of an academically accredited institution, part-time or full-time within three years of winning the award.
Frequency: This grant is not renewable.
Country of Study: Any country.
No. of awards offered: 174.
Application Procedure: Applicants must be nominated by their faculty athletics representative or director of athletics.
Closing Date: There are three deadlines which may vary slightly each year.
Funding: Private.

THE NATIONAL EDUCATION ASSOCIATION (NEA) FOUNDATION FOR THE IMPROVEMENT OF EDUCATION

1201 16th Street North West, Suite 234, Washington, DC 20036-7840, United States of America
Tel: (1) 202 822 7840
Fax: (1) 202 822 7779
Email: cchirichella@nea.org
www: http://www.nfie.org
Contact: Ms Christine Chirichella, Communications Officer

NEA Foundation Fine Arts Grant Program

Subjects: Art, music, theatre, dance, design, media or folk arts.
Purpose: To enable teachers to create and implement fine arts programmes that promote learning by students at risk of school failure.
Eligibility: Open to NEA member teachers of art, music, theatre, dance, design, media or folk arts is designated to implement the grant work.
Type: Grant.
Value: US$2,000.
Length of Study: One year.
No. of awards offered: 10.
Application Procedure: Applications must be submitted by local affiliates of the NEA. The local affiliate accepts the grant and administers the project.
Closing Date: Please contact the organisation.

NEA Foundation Innovation Grants

Subjects: Education.
Purpose: To promote collaborative, innovative ideas that lead to student achievement of high standards.
Eligibility: Open to teams of two or more practising United States public school teachers in grades K-12, public school education support personnel, public higher education faculty and staff. Preference will be given to National Education Association members, and to educators who serve economically disadvantaged and/or underserved students.
Level of Study: Postgraduate.
Type: Grant.
Value: US$1,000-3,000.
Length of Study: 18 months.
Frequency: Annual.
Country of Study: United States of America.
Application Procedure: Applicants must consult the organisation for details.
Closing Date: Applications may be submitted at any time.

NEA Foundation Learning and Leadership Grants

Subjects: All subjects.
Purpose: To support high quality professional development that addresses specific student learning needs. Recipients must also exercise professional leadership by sharing their new learning with their colleagues.
Eligibility: Open to practising public school classroom teachers, public school education support personnel and faculty and staff of public higher education institutions. Two or more collaborating educators may also apply for a group grant. Preference will be given to members of the NEA.
Level of Study: Professional development.
Type: Grant.
Value: Up to 75 individual grants of US$1,000 each and up to 10 group grants of US$3,000 each.
Length of Study: One year.
Frequency: Annual.
Country of Study: United States of America.
No. of awards offered: Up to 75.
Application Procedure: Applicants should consult the organisation for details.
Closing Date: Applications are accepted at any time.

NATIONAL FEDERATION OF THE BLIND (NFB)

Scholarship Committee, 805 Fifth Avenue, Grinnell, IA 50112, United States of America
Tel: (1) 641 236 3366
Email: epc@roudley.com
www: http://www.nfb.org
Contact: Chairman

Founded in 1940, the National Federation of the Blind (NFB) is the nation's largest and most influential membership organisation of blind people. With 50,000 members, the NFB has affiliates in all 50 states plus Washington DC and Puerto Rico, and over 700 local chapters. As a consumer and advocacy organisation, the NFB is considered the leading force in the blindness field today.

NFB Computer Science Scholarship

Subjects: Computer science.
Eligibility: Open to legally blind persons pursuing, or planning to pursue, a full-time post secondary course of training. The scholarship is awarded on the basis of academic excellence, service to the community and financial need. Candidates need not be members of the Federation.
Level of Study: Unrestricted.
Type: Scholarship.
Value: US$3,000.
Frequency: Annual.
Country of Study: United States of America.
No. of awards offered: One.
Application Procedure: Applicants must complete an application form, available on request.
Closing Date: March 31st.
Funding: Private.

NFB E U Parker Scholarship

Subjects: All subjects.
Purpose: To honour a long time leader of the National Federation of the Blind whose participation in the organisation stood for strong principles and strong support of the Federation's work.
Eligibility: Open to legally blind persons pursuing, or planning to pursue, a full-time post secondary course of training. The scholarship is awarded on the basis of academic excellence, service to the community and financial need. Candidates need not be members of the Federation.
Level of Study: Unrestricted.
Type: Scholarship.
Frequency: Annual.
Country of Study: United States of America.
No. of awards offered: One.
Application Procedure: Applicants must complete an application form, available on request.
Closing Date: March 31st.
Funding: Private.

NFB Educator of Tomorrow Award

Subjects: Teaching.
Eligibility: Open to legally blind persons pursuing, or planning to pursue, a full-time post secondary course of training. The winner must be planning a career in elementary, secondary or post secondary teaching. The Scholarship is awarded on the basis of academic excellence, service to the community and financial need. Candidates need not be members of the Federation.
Level of Study: Unrestricted.
Type: Scholarship.
Value: US$3,000.
Frequency: Annual.
Country of Study: United States of America.
No. of awards offered: One.
Application Procedure: Applicants must complete an application form, available on request.
Closing Date: March 31st.
Funding: Private.

NFB Hermione Grant Calhoun Scholarship

Subjects: All subjects.
Eligibility: Open to legally blind women pursuing, or planning to pursue, a full-time post secondary course of training. The scholarship is awarded on the basis of academic excellence, service to the community and financial need. Candidates need not be members of the Federation.
Level of Study: Unrestricted.
Type: Scholarship.
Value: US$3,000.
Frequency: Annual.
Country of Study: United States of America.
No. of awards offered: One.

Application Procedure: Applicants must complete an application form, available on request.
Closing Date: March 31st.
Funding: Private.
Additional Information: Dr Isabelle Grant endowed this scholarship in memory of her daughter.

NFB Howard Brown Rickard Scholarship

Subjects: Law, medicine, engineering, architecture or the natural sciences.
Eligibility: Open to legally blind persons pursuing, or planning to pursue, a full-time post secondary course of training. The scholarship is awarded on the basis of academic excellence, service to the community and financial need. Candidates need not be members of the Federation.
Level of Study: Unrestricted.
Type: Scholarship.
Frequency: Annual.
Country of Study: United States of America.
No. of awards offered: One.
Application Procedure: Applicants must complete an application form, available on request.
Closing Date: March 31st.
Funding: Private.

NFB Jennica Ferguson Memorial Scholarship

Subjects: All subjects.
Purpose: To keep the memory of Jennica Ferguson alive, a young woman who dealt with her blindness and terminal illness with a grace and strength she frequently assured others she drew from the Federation and from her faith in God.
Level of Study: Unrestricted.
Type: Scholarship.
Frequency: Annual.
Country of Study: United States of America.
No. of awards offered: One.
Application Procedure: Applicants must complete an application form, available on request.
Funding: Private.

NFB Kenneth Jernigan Scholarship

Subjects: All subjects.
Purpose: To keep fresh and current in the twenty first-century the understandings that Kenneth Jernigan brought to the field. To do this, the NFB has endowed this scholarship dedicated to his memory and to the continuation of the work he began.
Eligibility: Open to legally blind persons pursuing, or planning to pursue, a full-time post secondary course of training. The scholarship is awarded on the basis of academic excellence, service to the community and financial need. Candidates need not be members of the Federation.
Level of Study: Unrestricted.
Type: Scholarship.
Value: US$12,000.
Frequency: Annual.
Country of Study: United States of America.
No. of awards offered: One.
Application Procedure: Applicants must complete an application form, available on request.
Closing Date: March 31st.
Funding: Private.
Additional Information: Given by the American Action Fund for Blind Children and Adults, a non-profit making organisation which works to assist blind persons, in memory of the man who changed perceptions regarding the capabilities of the blind in this country and throughout the world. Kenneth Jernigan is viewed as the most important figure in the twentieth-century in the lives of blind persons.

NFB Kuchler-Killian Memorial Scholarship

Subjects: All subjects.
Eligibility: Open to legally blind persons pursuing, or planning to pursue, a full-time post secondary course of training. The scholarship is awarded on the basis of academic excellence, service to the community and financial need. Candidates need not be members of the Federation. There are no additional restrictions.
Level of Study: Unrestricted.
Type: Scholarship.
Value: US$3,000.
Frequency: Annual.
Country of Study: United States of America.
No. of awards offered: One.
Application Procedure: Applicants must complete an application form, available on request.
Closing Date: March 31st.
Funding: Private.
Additional Information: Given in loving memory of her parents, Charles Albert Kuchler and Alice Helen Kuchler, by Junerose Killian, a dedicated member of the National Federation of the Blind in Connecticut.

NFB Michael and Marie Marucci Scholarship

Subjects: All subjects that involve study abroad.
Eligibility: Open to candidates studying a foreign language or comparative literature pursuing a degree in history, geography or political science with a concentration in international studies, or majoring in any other discipline that involves study abroad. The winner's file must also show evidence of competence in a foreign language.
Level of Study: Unrestricted.
Type: Scholarship.
Frequency: Annual.
Country of Study: United States of America.
No. of awards offered: 1.
Funding: Private.
Additional Information: Given by two dedicated and valued members of the National Federation of the Blind of Maryland.

NFB Scholarships

Subjects: All subjects.
Eligibility: Open to legally blind persons pursuing, or planning to pursue, a full-time post secondary course of training. The scholarship is awarded on the basis of academic excellence, service to the community and financial need. Candidates need not be members of the Federation. There are no additional restrictions, except that one scholarship may be given to a person working full-time who is attending or planning to attend a part-time course of study which will result in a new degree and broader opportunities in present or future work if a suitable candidate applies.
Level of Study: Unrestricted.
Type: Scholarship.
Value: US$3,000.
Frequency: Annual.
Country of Study: United States of America.
No. of awards offered: 13.
Application Procedure: Applicants must complete an application form, available on request.
Closing Date: March 31st.
Funding: Private.

NATIONAL FOUNDATION FOR INFECTIOUS DISEASES (NFID)

4733 Bethesda Avenue, Suite 750, Bethesda, MD 20814, United States of America
Tel: (1) 301 656 0003
Fax: (1) 301 907 0878
Email: info@nfid.org
www: http://www.nfid.org
Contact: Mr Charlotte Lazrus, Grants Manager

The National Foundation for Infectious Diseases (NFID) is a non-profit, non governmental organisation whose mission is public and professional education and promotion of research on the causes, treatment and prevention of infectious diseases.

Colin L Powell Minority Postdoctoral Fellowship in Tropical Disease Research

Subjects: Tropical diseases.

Purpose: To encourage and assist a qualified minority researcher to become a specialist and investigator in the field of tropical disease research.

Eligibility: Open to applicants who hold a doctorate from a recognised university and who are permanent residents or citizens of the United States of America. Each applicant is required to have arranged for an American or foreign laboratory in which to conduct his or her research. The laboratory should be supervised by a recognised leader in tropical disease research qualified to oversee the work of the selected Fellow. The fellowship may not be awarded if the applicant has received or will be receiving a major fellowship, research grant or traineeship from the federal government or another foundation in excess of the total amount of this award.

Level of Study: Postdoctorate.

Type: Fellowship.

Value: A stipend of US$30,000, of which US$3,000 may be used for travel and supplies, at the investigator's discretion. Although it is anticipated that the award will be tax exempt, no guarantee of internal revenue service rulings can be made. No overhead to the sponsoring institution will be paid but the stipend may be supplemented by other monies up to US$30,000 to achieve salary levels consistent with other Fellows within the supporting institution.

Length of Study: One year.

Frequency: Annual.

No. of awards offered: One.

Application Procedure: Applicants must submit the original application and four copies no later than the deadline. The application should be addressed to the Grants Manager.

Closing Date: January.

Funding: Private.

Contributor: NFID, GlaxoSmithKline.

Additional Information: Minority in the context of this fellowship refers to underrepresented minorities in the biomedical sciences eg. Black, Hispanic, American Indian, or Alaskan Native and Asian or Pacific Island from the United States Bureau of the Census.

John P Utz Postdoctoral Fellowship in Medical Mycology

Subjects: Medical mycology.

Purpose: To encourage and assist a qualified physician to become a specialist and an investigator in medical mycology.

Eligibility: Open to physicians who are citizens of the United States of America. Applicants must demonstrate aptitude and training in research and must confirm arrangements for conduct of the proposed research in a recognised host laboratory. The applicant must be sponsored by a university affiliated medical center. The fellowship may not be awarded if the applicant has received or will receive a major fellowship, research grant or traineeship from the Federal government or another foundation in excess of the amount of this award.

Level of Study: Postdoctorate.

Type: Fellowship.

Value: A stipend of US$40,000 plus US$1,000 for travel and supplies. Although it is anticipated that the award will be tax exempt, no guarantee of internal revenue service rulings can be made. No overhead will be paid to the sponsoring institution.

Length of Study: One year.

Frequency: Annual.

Study Establishment: Approved research institutions.

Country of Study: United States of America.

No. of awards offered: One.

Application Procedure: Applicants must submit four copies of an original application including a letter from the laboratory director, curriculum vitae, description of applicant's proposed research project and a signed statement indicating that the applicant will acknowledge support received from the grant. Postmarked no later than January 6, 2004.

Closing Date: January.

Funding: Private.

Contributor: NFID and Pfizer, Inc.

No. of awards given last year: One.

NFID New Investigator Matching Grants

Subjects: Infectious diseases, microbiology, clinical medicine, epidemiology, and nursing. Those topics included in the top ten infectious diseases problems as recognised by the NFID will receive highest priority for funding, as follows, HIV and AIDS, antimicrobial resistance and emerging infections, vaccine preventable diseases, hospital acquired and opportunistic infections, viral hepatitis, gastrointestinal, diarrhoeal and foodborne diseases, sexually transmitted diseases, tuberculosis, zoonotic diseases and tropical infectious diseases biological warfare.

Purpose: To assist new investigators who are beginning their research.

Eligibility: Open to young investigators, defined as individuals with full-time junior faculty (Instructor or Assistant Professor) status, at a recognised and accredited institute of higher learning. Priority will be given to those who do not have research grants and whose studies represent pilot work with intent to further develop their research.

Level of Study: Postgraduate.

Type: Grant.

Value: US$2,000. Each application must be accompanied by an agreement from the applicant's sponsoring institution to match the award with equal funds. No indirect costs may be included

Frequency: Annual.

Country of Study: United States of America or Canada.

No. of awards offered: Varies.

Application Procedure: Applicants must complete a four page application proposal available from the NFID or downloadable from the website.

Closing Date: February 14th.

Funding: Private.

Contributor: NFID.

NFID Postdoctoral Fellowship in Emerging Infectious Diseases

Subjects: Epidemiology research.

Purpose: To encourage and assist a qualified physician to become a recognised authority on emerging infectious diseases and epidemiology.

Eligibility: Open to physicians who are citizens of the United States of America and who have completed an infectious diseases fellowship.

Level of Study: Postdoctorate.

Type: Fellowship.

Value: US$50,000.

Length of Study: One year.

Frequency: Annual.

Study Establishment: The National Center for Infectious Diseases, CDC Atlanta, Georgia.

Country of Study: United States of America.

No. of awards offered: One.

Application Procedure: Applicants must submit four copies of an original application including a letter from the laboratory director, curriculum vitae, description of applicant's proposed research project and a signed statement indicating that the applicant will acknowledge support received from the grant.

Closing Date: January.

Funding: Private.

Contributor: NFID, Centers for Disease Control and Prevention.

No. of awards given last year: One.

NFID Postdoctoral Fellowship in Nosocomial Infection Research and Training

Subjects: Medical research into nosocomial infections.

Purpose: To encourage and assist a qualified physician researcher to become a specialist and an investigator in the field of nosocomial infections.

Eligibility: Open to physicians in training who are citizens of the United States of America. Applicants must demonstrate aptitude or accomplishments in laboratory or epidemiologic research and must confirm arrangements for the site of the proposed research in a recognised host laboratory. Applicants who have received or who are about to receive grants in the same academic year in excess of the amount of this award are not eligible for funding.

Level of Study: Postdoctorate.

Type: Fellowship.
Value: A stipend of US$40,000 of which US$1,000 may be used for travel and supplies at the investigator's discretion. Although it is anticipated that the award will be tax exempt, no guarantee of internal revenue service rulings can be made. No overhead to the sponsoring institution will be paid.
Length of Study: One year.
Frequency: Annual.
Country of Study: United States of America.
No. of awards offered: One.
Application Procedure: Applicants must submit four copies of an original application including a letter from the laboratory director, curriculum vitae, description of applicant's proposed research project and a signed statement indicating that the applicant will acknowledge support received from the grant. Postmarked no later than January 6, 2004.
Closing Date: January.
Funding: Private.
Contributor: NFID.
No. of awards given last year: One.

NATIONAL HEADACHE FOUNDATION

428 West Saint James Place, 2nd Floor, Chicago, IL 60614, United States of America
Tel: (1) 773 388 6399
Fax: (1) 773 525 7357
Email: info@headaches.org
www: http://www.headaches.org
Contact: Executive Director

The National Headache Foundation disseminates information, funds research, sponsors public and professional education programmes and has a nationwide network of support groups, with 20,000 members. The Foundation is the recognised authority in headache and head pain, and offers the award winning newsletter NHF Head Lines, patient education brochures, and audio and video tapes.

National Headache Foundation Research Grant
Subjects: Treatment and causes of headache.
Purpose: To encourage better understanding and treatment of headache and head pain.
Eligibility: Open to researchers in neurology and pharmacology departments in medical schools throughout the United States of America. Submissions from other departments and individual investigators are also welcome.
Level of Study: Doctorate, Postdoctorate, Postgraduate.
Type: Research grant.
Value: Dependent on funds available. Grants only cover direct costs of carrying out research and do not cover overheads or salaries.
Frequency: Annual.
Country of Study: United States of America.
No. of awards offered: Varies, depending on funds available and the number of worthy projects submitted.
Application Procedure: Applicants must complete an application form.
Closing Date: December 1st for notification by the following March.
Funding: Private.
Contributor: Dues and donations.
No. of awards given last year: Seven.
No. of applicants last year: 10.

NATIONAL HEALTH AND MEDICAL RESEARCH COUNCIL (NHMRC)

Centre for Research Management (MDP 33), GPO Box 9848, Canberra, ACT Australia
Tel: (61) 2 6213 4153
Fax: (61) 2 6289 9132
Email: research@nhmrc.gov.au
www: www.nhmrc.gov.au
Contact: Administrative Assistant

The National Health and Medical Research Council (NHMRC) (Australia) consolidates within a single national organisation the often independent functions of research funding and development of advice. One of its strengths is that it brings together and draws upon the resources of all components of the health system, including governments, medical practitioners, nurses and allied health professionals, researchers, teaching and research institutions, public and private programme managers, service administrators, community health organisations, social health researchers and consumers.

Australian Clinical Research Postdoctoral Fellowship
Subjects: Scientific research, including the social and behavioural sciences, which can be applied to any area of clinical or community medicine.
Purpose: To provide training in scientific research methods.
Eligibility: Open to Australian citizens or graduates from overseas with permanent Australian resident status, who are not under bond to any foreign government. Candidates should hold a doctorate in a health related field of research or have submitted a thesis for such by December of the year of application and be actively engaged in such research in Australia or overseas and have no more than two years' postdoctoral experience at the time of application.
Level of Study: Postdoctorate.
Type: Fellowship.
Value: Aus$59K + Aus$5K pa.
Length of Study: Four years.
Frequency: Annual.
Study Establishment: Institutions approved by the NHMRC, such as teaching hospitals, universities and research institutes.
Country of Study: Australia.
No. of awards offered: Varies.
Application Procedure: Application forms are available from www.nhmrc.gov.au.
Closing Date: First Friday in July each year.
Funding: Government.
No. of awards given last year: 5.
No. of applicants last year: 14.

Biomedical (Dora Lush) and Public Health Postgraduate Scholarships
Subjects: Biomedical sciences & Public Health.
Purpose: To encourage science honours or equivalent graduates of outstanding ability to gain full-time medical research experience.
Eligibility: Open to Australian citizens who have already completed a science honours degree (or equivalent) at the time of submission of the application, science honours graduates and unregistered medical or dental graduates from overseas, who have permanent resident status and are currently residing in Australia. The scholarship shall be held within Australia.
Level of Study: Postgraduate.
Type: Scholarship.
Value: Varies.
Length of Study: One year, renewable for up to two further years.
Frequency: Annual.
Study Establishment: Institutions approved by the NHMRC, such as teaching hospitals, universities and research institutes.
Country of Study: Australia.
No. of awards offered: Varies.
Application Procedure: www.nhmrc.gov.au/funding/schlorships.htm.
Closing Date: First Friday of August each year.
Funding: Government.
No. of awards given last year: 85.
No. of applicants last year: 176.

Burnet Fellowships
Subjects: Any field of health and medical sciences.
Purpose: To attract back to Australia health and medical researchers of a high calibre who have spent considerable time overseas and who have not returned because of the lack of suitable opportunities.

Eligibility: Open to Australian citizens or permanent residents who are not under bond to any foreign government. Candidates should have a current academic or hospital appointment overseas (for at least seven years) equivalent to an Australian Professor or Associate Professor, be actively engaged in research and apply in conjunction with a host institution which must undertake to provide infrastructural support and administer the award. Normal access procedures for receipt of NHMRC funds will apply.

Level of Study: Professional development.

Type: Fellowship.

Value: Allocation of Aus$400,000 per year.

Length of Study: Five years.

Frequency: Dependent on funds available.

Study Establishment: Australian research institutions.

Country of Study: Australia.

No. of awards offered: Varies.

Application Procedure: Applicants must submit applications in writing with a curriculum vitae attached. There is no application form.

Closing Date: Applications are accepted at any time.

Funding: Government.

Additional Information: Enquiries should be directed to the Fellowships Office at the main address or by telephone on (61) 2 6289 9119 or by fax on (61) 2 6289 9131.

C J Martin Fellowships (Overseas Biomedical)

Subjects: Biomedical sciences.

Purpose: To enable Fellows to develop their research skills and work overseas on specific research projects within the biomedical sciences under nominated advisers.

Eligibility: Open to Australian citizens or graduates from overseas with permanent Australian resident status who are not under bond to any foreign government. Candidates should hold a doctorate in a medical, dental or related field of research, be actively engaged in such research in Australia and have no more than two year's post-doctoral experience at the time of application.

Level of Study: Postdoctorate.

Type: Fellowship.

Value: Varies.

Length of Study: Four years, the first two of which are to be spent overseas and the final two in Australia.

Frequency: Annual.

Study Establishment: Institutions approved by the NHMRC, such as teaching hospitals, universities and research institutes.

Country of Study: Any country.

No. of awards offered: Varies.

Application Procedure: Application forms available from www.nhmrc.gov.au.

Closing Date: First Friday in July each year.

Funding: Government.

No. of awards given last year: 28.

No. of applicants last year: 73.

Career Development Awards

Subjects: Help researchers develop leadership ability in research. Any human health-related research area.

Purpose: Help researchers to conduct research that is internationally competitive. Help research develop a capacity for independent research.

Eligibility: Australian citizens or permanent residents. Normally between 3 & 9 years post-doc.

Type: Fellowship.

Value: Varies.

Length of Study: Five years.

Frequency: Annual.

Study Establishment: Institutions approved by NHMRC, such as teaching hospitals, universities and research institutes.

Country of Study: Australia.

No. of awards offered: Varies.

Application Procedure: Application forms available from : www.nhmrc.gov.au.

Closing Date: Second Friday in April early year.

Funding: Government.

No. of awards given last year: 42.

No. of applicants last year: 95.

Howard Florey Centenary Fellowship

Subjects: Any human health-related research area.

Purpose: To evalute Australian researchers working overseas to return Australia to pursue medical research.

Eligibility: Australian citizens currently researching overseas. Between 2-5 years post-doc.

Type: Fellowship.

Value: Aus$70K + Aus$10K pa.

Length of Study: Two Years.

Frequency: Annual.

Study Establishment: Institutions approved by the NHMRC, such as teaching hospitals, universities and research institutes.

Country of Study: Australia.

No. of awards offered: Varies.

Application Procedure: Application forms available at www.nhmrc.gov.au.

Closing Date: First Friday in July early year.

Funding: Government.

No. of awards given last year: 7

No. of applicants last year: 15.

Industry Fellowships

Subjects: Human Health-Related Field.

Purpose: Enable Australian researchers to gain experience in industrial research. Increase knowledge of commercial aspects of R & D within research institutions.

Eligibility: Australian citizens or permanent residents. Ordinarily with 3-9 years post-doc experience in Medical Research.

Type: Fellowship.

Value: Aus$87K pa.

Length of Study: 4 years.

Frequency: Annual.

Study Establishment: Institutions approved by the NHMRC, such as teaching hospitals, universities and research institutes.

Country of Study: Any country.

No. of awards offered: Varies.

Application Procedure: Application forms available from www.nhmrc.gov.au.

Closing Date: Last Friday in June early year.

Funding: Government.

No. of awards given last year: 8.

No. of applicants last year: 21.

Neil Hamilton Fairley Fellowships (Overseas CCINICAC)

Subjects: Scientific research, including the social and behavioural sciences, which can be applied to any area of clinical or community medicine.

Purpose: To provide training in scientific research methods.

Eligibility: Open to Australian citizens or graduates from overseas with permanent Australian resident status who are not under bond to any foreign government. Candidates should hold a doctorate in a health related field of research or have submitted a thesis for such by December of the year of application and be actively engaged in such research in Australia and have no more than two year's postdoctoral experience at the time of application.

Level of Study: Postdoctorate.

Type: Fellowship.

Value: Varies.

Length of Study: Four years, the first two of which are to be spent overseas and the final two in Australia.

Frequency: Annual.

Study Establishment: Institutions approved by the NHMRC, such as teaching hospitals, universities and research institutes.

Country of Study: Any country.

No. of awards offered: Varies.

Application Procedure: Application form available from www.nhmrc.gov.au.

Closing Date: First Friday in July each year.

Funding: Government.

No. of awards given last year: 2.

No. of applicants last year: 5.

NHMRC Medical and Dental and Public Health Postgraduate Research Scholarships

Subjects: Medical or dental research.
Purpose: To encourage medical and dental graduates to gain full-time research experience.
Eligibility: Open to Australian citizens who are medical or dental graduates registered to practice in Australia, with the proviso that medical graduates can also apply during their intern year and that dental postgraduate research scholarships may be awarded prior to graduation provided that the evidence of high quality work is shown. Also open to medical and dental graduates from overseas who hold a qualification that is registered for practice in Australia and who have permanent resident status and are currently residing in Australia. Evidence of residence status must be provided. The scholarship shall be held within Australia.
Level of Study: Postgraduate.
Type: Scholarship.
Value: Varies.
Length of Study: One year, renewable for up to two further years.
Frequency: Annual.
Study Establishment: Institutions approved by the NHMRC such as teaching hospitals, universities and research institutes.
Country of Study: Australia.
No. of awards offered: Varies.
Application Procedure: Available from www.nhmrc.gov.au/funding/scholarships.htm.
Closing Date: First Friday of August each year.
Funding: Government.
No. of awards given last year: 70.
No. of applicants last year: 115.

NHMRC/INSERM Exchange Fellowships

Subjects: Biomedical sciences.
Purpose: To enable Australian Fellows to work overseas on specific research projects in INSERM labs in France & vice versa.
Eligibility: Open to Australian citizens and permanent residents, who are not under bond to any foreign government, who hold a doctorate in a medical, dental or related field of research or have submitted a thesis for such by December in the year of application, are actively engaged in such research in Australia and have no more than two year's postdoctoral experience at the time of application.
Level of Study: Postdoctorate.
Type: Fellowship.
Value: Varies.
Length of Study: Four years, the first two of which are to be spent in France and the final two in Australia.
Frequency: Annual.
Study Establishment: Institutions approved by the NHMRC, such as teaching hospitals, universities and research institutes, and INSERM laboratories in France.
Country of Study: France / Australia.
No. of awards offered: One.
Application Procedure: Applications forms available from www.nhmrc.gov.au.
Closing Date: First Friday of July each year.
Funding: Government.
No. of awards given last year: 1.
No. of applicants last year: 1.
Additional Information: This fellowship is awarded in association with l'Institut National de la Santé et de la Recherche Médicale (INSERM), France.

Peter Doherty Fellowships

Subjects: Biomedical sciences.
Purpose: To provide a vehicle for training in clinical and basic research in Australia, and to encourage persons of outstanding ability to make medical research a full-time career.
Eligibility: Open to Australian citizens or graduates from overseas with permanent Australian resident status who are not under bond to any foreign government. Candidates should hold a doctorate in a medical, dental or related field of research or have submitted a thesis for such by December in the year of application, be actively engaged

in such research in Australia or overseas and have no more than two year's postdoctoral experience at the time of application.
Level of Study: Postdoctorate.
Type: Fellowship.
Value: Aus$59K + Aus$5K pa.
Length of Study: Four years.
Frequency: Annual.
Study Establishment: Institutions approved by the NHMRC, such as teaching hospitals, universities and research institutes.
Country of Study: Australia.
No. of awards offered: Varies.
Application Procedure: Application forms available from www.nhmrc.gov.au.
Closing Date: First Friday in July each year.
Funding: Government.
No. of awards given last year: 25.
No. of applicants last year: 54.

Public Health Fellowship

Subjects: Public Health.
Purpose: To provide full time training in public health research in Australia.
Eligibility: Hold a doctorate in a health-related field of research or have submitted PhD by December in year of application. No more than 2 year post-doc. Australian citizens or permanent residents.
Type: Fellowship.
Value: Aus$59K + Aus$5K.
Length of Study: Four years.
Frequency: Annual.
Study Establishment: Institutions approved by the NHMRC, such as teaching hospitals, universities and research institutes.
Country of Study: Australia.
No. of awards offered: Varies.
Application Procedure: Application forms available from www.nhmrc.gov.au.
Closing Date: First Friday in July each year.
Funding: Government.
No. of awards given last year: 11.
No. of applicants last year: 31.

Sidney Sax Fellowship (Overseas Public Health)

Subjects: Public Health.
Purpose: To provide full-time training in public health research overseas in Australia.
Eligibility: Hold a Doctorate in a Health-Related field of Research or have submitted PhD by December in year of application. No more than 2 years Post-Doc. Australian citizens or permanent resident.
Type: Fellowship.
Value: Varies.
Length of Study: Four years.
Frequency: Annual.
Study Establishment: Institutions approved by the NHMRC, such as teaching hospitals, universities and research institutes.
Country of Study: Any country.
No. of awards offered: Varies.
Application Procedure: Application forms avaliable from www.nhmrc.gov.au.
Closing Date: First Friday in July early year.
Funding: Government.
No. of awards given last year: 3.
No. of applicants last year: 7.

Training Scholarship for Indigenous Health Research.

Purpose: To encourage research with relevance to the health well being of Aboriginal & Torres Strait Islander people.
Eligibility: Open to Australian Citizens or Australian permanent residents enrolling in a diploma, certificate, an undergraduate degree or a postgraduate degree at a fully accredited institution which will enable the applicant to persue research relevant to Aboriginal & Torres Strait Islander Health, health care, health care delivery or health research in the area of Aboriginal & Torres Strait Islander health.
Level of Study: Postdoctorate.
Type: Scholarship.

Length of Study: One year, renewable up to further 2 years.
Frequency: Annual.
Country of Study: Australia.
Application Procedure: Avalable from www.nhmrc.gov/funding/scholarships.htm.
Closing Date: First Friday of August.
Funding: Government.
No. of awards given last year: 9.
No. of applicants last year: 17.

NATIONAL HEART FOUNDATION (USA) (NHF)

22512 Gateway Centre Drive, Clarksburg, MD 20871, United States of America
Tel: (1) 301 948 3244
Fax: (1) 301 248 4403
Email: smonahan@ahaf.org
www: http://www.ahaf.org
Contact: Research Grants Department

AHAF's National Heart Foundation (NHF) programme was established in 1976 to fund research on and educate the public about coronary heart disease. As the programme has grown and changed over the years, its name has changed accordingly, from Atherosclerosis Research Fund to Coronary Heart Disease Research Project to Coronary Heart Disease Research to its current name, National Heart Foundation. The programme became the National Heart Foundation in 1992 to reflect its expanded mission to fund research on stroke and all cardiovascular diseases.

NHF Grant
Subjects: Cardiology, biomedicine, physiology, or pharmacology.
Purpose: To provide start up grants for new investigators in cardiovascular disease and stroke.
Eligibility: The principal investigator must hold the academic rank of assistant professor or the equivalent.
Level of Study: Professional development.
Type: Grant.
Value: Up to US$25,000 may be requested for one year.
Length of Study: One year, renewable for a further year by competitive review.
Frequency: Annual.
Country of Study: Any country.
No. of awards offered: Varies.
Application Procedure: Applicants must complete an application form, available on request or from the website.
Closing Date: November 1st or the following Tuesday if it falls on a weekend or Monday.
Funding: Private.
Contributor: Many small contributions.
No. of awards given last year: Two.
No. of applicants last year: 18.

NATIONAL HEART FOUNDATION OF AUSTRALIA

411 King Street, West Melbourne
VIC 3003, Australia
Tel: (61) 3 9329 8511
Fax: (61) 3 9326 3190
Email: research@heartfoundation.com.au
www: http://www.heartfoundation.com.au
Contact: Research Manager

The National Heart Foundation of Australia is a non government, non-profit health organisation funded mostly by public donation. The Foundation's mission is to prevent early death and disability from heart disease and stroke. The Foundation funds biomedical research, provides clinical leadership and develops health promotion strategies and initiatives.

National Heart Foundation of Australia Career Development Fellowship
Subjects: Cardiovascular disease and related disorders.
Purpose: To enable a senior Australian researcher of exceptional merit and proven record in the cardiovascular field to undertake independent research.
Eligibility: Open to Australian citizens and permanent residents only.
Level of Study: Research.
Type: Fellowship.
Value: Please contact the organisation.
Length of Study: Five years, non renewable.
Frequency: Annual.
Study Establishment: Universities, hospitals or research institutions.
Country of Study: Australia.
Application Procedure: Applicants must be nominated by the head of the host department or institution.
Funding: Private.

National Heart Foundation of Australia Clinical Research Fellowship
Subjects: Cardiovascular disease and related disorders.
Purpose: To award graduates who have demonstrated expertise and significant achievement in cardiovascular research.
Eligibility: Open to Australian citizens and permanent residents only.
Level of Study: Postdoctorate.
Type: Fellowship.
Value: Please contact the organisation.
Frequency: Annual.
Study Establishment: Universities, hospitals or research institutions.
Country of Study: Australia.
No. of awards offered: One.
Funding: Private.

National Heart Foundation of Australia Overseas Research Fellowships
Subjects: Clinical or basic medical sciences related to cardiovascular disease and related disorders.
Purpose: To allow Fellows to obtain skills in cardiovascular research.
Eligibility: Open to Australian citizens or permanent residents who are actively engaged in research in Australia on December 31st of the year prior to application.
Level of Study: Postdoctorate.
Type: Fellowship.
Value: Please contact the organisation.
Length of Study: Three years.
Frequency: Annual.
Study Establishment: Approved institutions.
Country of Study: Other.
Application Procedure: Applicants must be nominated by the head of the host department or institution.
Funding: Private.
Additional Information: Fellowships are awarded on the understanding that the Fellow will return to Australia to continue his or her career upon completion of the fellowship.

National Heart Foundation of Australia Postgraduate Biomedical Research Scholarship
Subjects: Cardiovascular disease and related disorders.
Purpose: To allow graduates to undertake a period of training in research under the full-time supervision and tuition of a responsible investigator.
Eligibility: Open to Australian citizens and permanent residents only.
Level of Study: Postgraduate.
Type: Scholarship.
Value: Please contact the organisation.
Length of Study: Up to three years.
Frequency: Annual.
Study Establishment: Universities, hospitals or research institutions.
Country of Study: Australia.

Application Procedure: Applicants must submit an application outlining a research proposal accompanied by the supervisor's reference and backing.
Funding: Private.

National Heart Foundation of Australia Postgraduate Clinical Research Scholarship

Subjects: Cardiovascular disease.
Purpose: To enable medical graduates to undertake a period of training in research under the full-time supervision and tuition of a responsible investigator.
Eligibility: Open to Australian citizens and permanent residents only.
Level of Study: Postgraduate.
Type: Scholarship.
Value: Please contact the organisation.
Length of Study: Three years.
Frequency: Annual.
Study Establishment: Universities, hospitals and research institutions.
Country of Study: Australia.
No. of awards offered: Varies.
Application Procedure: Applicants must submit an application outlining a research proposal accompanied by the supervisor's reference and backing.
Funding: Private.

National Heart Foundation of Australia Postgraduate Public Health Research Scholarship

Subjects: Cardiovascular research and related disorders.
Purpose: To allow graduates to undertake a period of training in research under the full-time supervision and tuition of a responsible investigator.
Eligibility: Open to Australian citizens and permanent residents only.
Level of Study: Postgraduate.
Type: Scholarship.
Value: Please contact the organisation.
Length of Study: Up to three years.
Frequency: Annual.
Study Establishment: Universities, hospitals or research institutions.
Country of Study: Australia.
Application Procedure. Applicants must submit an application outlining a research proposal accompanied by the supervisor's reference and backing.
Funding: Private.

National Heart Foundation of Australia Research Grants-in-Aid

Subjects: Basic, clinical or public health research.
Purpose: To support research in the cardiovascular field.
Eligibility: Open to Australian citizens and permanent residents only.
Level of Study: Research.
Type: Grant.
Value: Please contact the organisation.
Length of Study: Up to two years.
Frequency: Annual.
Study Establishment: An approved institution.
Country of Study: Australia.
Application Procedure: Applicants must submit an application outlining research proposal. References are also required.
Funding: Private.

NATIONAL HEART FOUNDATION OF NEW ZEALAND

PO Box 17-160, Greenlane, Newmarket, Auckland, New Zealand
Tel: (64) 9 571 9191
Fax: (64) 9 571 9190
Email: helens@nhf.org.nz
www: http://www.nhf.org.nz
Contact: Ms Helen Stewart, Research Grants Administrator

The National Heart Foundation of New Zealand aims to promote good health and to reduce suffering and premature death from diseases of the heart and circulation.

National Heart Foundation of New Zealand Fellowships

Subjects: Any aspect of cardiovascular disease including rehabilitation and education.
Purpose: To promote the aims of the National Heart Foundation of New Zealand.
Eligibility: Normally open to New Zealand graduates only.
Level of Study: Postgraduate.
Type: Other.
Value: Varies, according to the determination of the Scientific Committee and within an annual budget.
Frequency: Annual.
Country of Study: Other.
No. of awards offered: Varies.
Application Procedure: Applicants must apply to the Foundation for the publication 'A Guide to Applicants for Research and Other Grants'.
Closing Date: June 1st.
Funding: Private.
No. of awards given last year: Five.

National Heart Foundation of New Zealand Limited Budget Grants

Subjects: Any aspect of cardiovascular disease including rehabilitation and education. Priority areas include modification of lifestyle with regards to cardiovascular disease, the socio-economic determinants of heart disease, Maori health and Pacific Island health, diagnosis and management of patients with cardiovascular disease.
Purpose: To further the aims of the National Heart Foundation of New Zealand.
Eligibility: Normally open to New Zealand graduates only.
Level of Study: Postgraduate.
Type: Grant.
Value: Varies, according to the determination of the Scientific Committee and within an annual budget.
Frequency: Three times each year.
Country of Study: New Zealand.
No. of awards offered: Varies.
Application Procedure: Applicants must write for details.
Closing Date: February 1st, June 1st or October 1st.
Funding: Private.
No. of awards given last year: Fourteen.
Additional Information: These grants cover small projects eg. less than New Zealand $15,000 and grants-in-aid.

National Heart Foundation of New Zealand Maori Cardiovascular Research Fellowship

Subjects: Cardiovascular health.
Purpose: To financially support graduates who propose to engage in research to improve Maori cardiovascular health.
Eligibility: Open to medical graduates or to non medical graduates enrolled for a higher degree. Preference will be given to those with a working knowledge of Te Reo Maori and who are committed to Maori health.
Level of Study: Doctorate, Postgraduate, Predoctorate.
Type: Fellowship.
Value: New Zealand $30,000.
Length of Study: Two years.
Frequency: Annual.
Country of Study: New Zealand.
No. of awards offered: One.
Application Procedure: Applications will be considered at the annual meeting of the Scientific Committee.
Closing Date: February 1st.
Funding: Private.
No. of awards given last year: One.

National Heart Foundation of New Zealand Project Grants

Subjects: Any aspect of cardiovascular disease including rehabilitation and education. Priority areas include modification of lifestyle with

447

regards to cardiovascular disease, the socio-economic determinants of heart disease, Maori health and Pacific Islander health, diagnosis and management of patients with cardiovascular disease.

Purpose: To provide short-term support for a single individual or small group working on a clearly defined research project which will promote the aims of the National Heart Foundation of New Zealand.

Eligibility: Normally open to New Zealand graduates only.

Level of Study: Postgraduate.

Type: Grant.

Value: Varies, according to the determination of the scientific committee and within an annual budget.

Frequency: Annual.

Country of Study: Other.

No. of awards offered: Varies.

Application Procedure: Applicants must write for details.

Closing Date: March 1st.

Funding: Private.

No. of awards given last year: Seven.

National Heart Foundation of New Zealand Senior Fellowship

Subjects: Cardiovascular disease.

Purpose: To support graduates from New Zealand who have trained as cardiologists or other scientists working in the field of cardiovascular research.

Eligibility: Applicants must possess an appropriate postgraduate degree or diploma. The maximum age for appointment will normally be 40 years.

Level of Study: Postgraduate.

Type: Fellowship.

Value: Up to New Zealand $1,500 to enable research work to commence. In subsequent years, Senior Fellows may apply for working expenses not exceeding New Zealand $1,000 annually with no single item to exceed New Zealand $500.

Length of Study: Up to three years.

Frequency: Other.

Country of Study: New Zealand.

No. of awards offered: One.

Application Procedure: Applicants should follow the format outlined in the revised 'A Guide to Applicants for Research and Other Grants,' which is available from the website. Applications should be sent to Professor Norman Sharpe, Medical Director.

Closing Date: June 1st.

Funding: Private.

Additional Information: The fellowship must be taken up within 12 months of the award. Further research funding will require an application for project grant funds from the Foundation. Funding for conference expenses must be applied for separately.

National Heart Foundation of New Zealand Travel Grants

Subjects: Any aspect of cardiovascular disease including education. Priority areas include modification of lifestyle with regards to cardiovascular disease, the socio-economic determinants of heart disease, Maori health and Pacific Island health, diagnosis and management of patients with cardiovascular disease.

Purpose: To enable medical or non medical workers to travel in New Zealand or overseas for short-term study or to attend conferences.

Eligibility: Normally open to New Zealand graduates only.

Level of Study: Postgraduate.

Type: Grant.

Value: Varies, according to the determination of the scientific committee and within an annual budget.

Frequency: Three times each year.

Country of Study: Any country.

No. of awards offered: Varies.

Application Procedure: Applicants must write for details.

Closing Date: February 1st, June 1st or October 1st.

Funding: Private.

No. of awards given last year: 4.

NATIONAL HEART RESEARCH FUND

Suite 12D Joseph's Well, Leeds
LS3 1AB, England
Tel: (44) 113 2347474
Fax: (44) 113 297 6208
Email: mail@heartresearch.org.uk
www: http://www.heartresearch.org.uk

Since 1967 the National Heart Research Fund has provided a lifeline of support for research into the prevention, treatment and cure of heart disease.

National Heart Research Fund Medical Research Grant

Subjects: Research projects into ways to fight and treat heart disease for patients of all ages.

Purpose: To fund medical research into fighting heart disease.

Level of Study: Research.

Value: Average UK£45,000.

Length of Study: 1 year.

Frequency: Annual.

Country of Study: United Kingdom

No. of awards offered: Approx. 50.

Application Procedure: Send 10 copies of application, outlining aims and objectives, to the National Heart Research Fund Medical Review Panel.

Closing Date: 30th March and 30th September.

Funding: Private.

No. of awards given last year: 55.

NATIONAL HISTORICAL PUBLICATIONS AND RECORDS COMMISSION (NHPRC)

Room 111, National Archives & Records Administration, 700 Pennsylvania Avenue North West, Washington, DC 20408-0001, United States of America
Tel: (1) 202 501 5605 ext. 253
Fax: (1) 202 501 5601
Email: nhprc@nara.gov
www: http://www.nara.gov
Contact: Director for Communications & Outreach

The National Historical Publications and Records Commission (NHPRC) is the grant making affiliate of the National Archives and Records Administration (NARA). The Commission has defined its purpose to carry out its statutory mission to ensure understanding of the nation's past by promoting, nationwide, the identification, preservation and dissemination of essential historical documentation.

NHPRC Fellowship in Archival Administration

Subjects: Library and archive studies.

Purpose: To provide experience in management and administration for archivists.

Eligibility: Open to individuals who must have spent two-five years working as an archivist, and be United States of America citizens. While not required, it is desirable that applicants have the equivalent of two semesters of full-time graduate training in a programme containing an archival education component.

Level of Study: Professional development.

Type: Fellowship.

Value: A stipend of US$35,000 plus an additional US$7,000 for fringe benefits.

Length of Study: 9-12 months.

Frequency: Annual.

Country of Study: United States of America.

No. of awards offered: One.

Application Procedure: Applicants must contact the Commission for guidelines and host institution information. This information is available before December of the preceding year.

Closing Date: Postmarked March 15th.

Funding: Government.

NHPRC Fellowship in Documentary Editing

Subjects: Documentary editing.
Purpose: To provide individuals with training in the field of historical documentary editing.
Eligibility: Open to applicants who hold PhD or have completed all requirements for the doctorate except the dissertation. Applicants may be working on their dissertation and must be United States of America citizens.
Level of Study: Doctorate, Postdoctorate.
Type: Fellowship.
Value: US$41,250 including funds for fringe benefits.
Length of Study: 11 months.
Frequency: Annual.
Country of Study: United States of America.
No. of awards offered: One.
Application Procedure: Applicants must contact the Commission for guidelines and host institution information. This information is available before December of the preceding year.
Closing Date: Postmarked March 15th.
Funding: Government.
Additional Information: Further information is available from the website.

NATIONAL HUMANITIES CENTER (NHC)

PO Box 12256, Research Triangle Park, NC 27709-2256, United States of America
Tel: (1) 919 549 0661
Fax: (1) 919 990 8535
Email: nhc@ga.unc.edu
www: http://www.nhc.rtp.nc.us
Contact: Deputy Director

The National Humanities Center (NHC) is a residential institute for advanced study in history, languages and literature, philosophy and other fields of the humanities. Each year it awards approximately 35 to 40 fellowships to Scholars of demonstrated achievement and to promising younger Scholars.

NHC Fellowships

Subjects: History, philosophy, languages and literature, classics, religion, history of the arts and other fields in the liberal arts.
Purpose: To support advanced postdoctoral scholarship in the humanities.
Eligibility: Open to Scholars of any nationality. Social scientists, natural scientists, or professionals whose work has a humanistic dimension may also apply. Applicants must hold a doctorate or have equivalent professional accomplishments. Fellowships are awarded to senior Scholars of recognised accomplishment and to promising young Scholars engaged in research beyond the revision of their dissertations.
Level of Study: Postdoctorate.
Type: Fellowship.
Value: Ranges from US$30,000 to US$50,000. Fellowships are individually determined in accordance with the needs of each Fellow and the Center's ability to meet them. As the Center cannot in most instances replace full salaries, applicants are urged to seek partial funding in the form of sabbatical salaries or grants from other sources. In addition to stipends, the Center provides round trip travel expenses for Fellows and their immediate families to and from North Carolina.
Length of Study: One academic year, although a few fellowships may be awarded for a single semester.
Frequency: Annual.
Study Establishment: The Center.
Country of Study: United States of America.
No. of awards offered: 40.
Application Procedure: Applicants must submit the Center's form supported by their curriculum vitae, a 1,000 word project proposal and three letters of recommendation.
Closing Date: Postmarked October 15th.
Funding: Private.
Contributor: Private foundation grants, income from the Center's endowment and the National Endowment for the Humanities.

NATIONAL INSTITUTE OF GENERAL MEDICAL SCIENCES (NIGMS)

45 Center Drive, MSC 6200, Bethesda, MD 20892-6200, United States of America
Tel: (1) 301 496 7301
Fax: (1) 301 402 0224
Email: pub_info@nigms.nih.gov
www: http://www.nigms.nih.gov
Contact: Ms Susan J Athey, Public Affairs

The National Institute of General Medical Sciences (NIGMS) is a component of the National Institutes of Health, the principal biomedical research agency of the United States government. NIGMS supports basic biomedical research that is not targeted to specific diseases, but that increases the understanding of life processes and lays the foundation for advances in disease diagnosis, treatment and prevention.

MARC Faculty Predoctoral Fellowships

Subjects: Biomedical or behavioural sciences.
Purpose: To provide an opportunity for faculty who lack the PhD degree or equivalent to obtain the research doctorate.
Eligibility: Open to full-time, permanent faculty members in a biomedically related science or mathematics programme and have been at the minority or minority serving institution for at least three years at the time of application. Candidates must be enrolled in, or have been accepted into, a PhD or combined MD-PhD training programme in the biomedical or behavioural sciences. Candidates must intend to return to the minority institution at the end of the training period.
Level of Study: Postgraduate.
Type: Fellowship.
Value: An applicant may request a stipend equal to his or her annual salary, but not to exceed the stipend of a level one postdoctoral Fellow, currently at US$36,108. The applicant may also request tuition and fees as determined by the training institution as well as an allowance of US$2,750 per year for training related costs.
Frequency: Annual.
Country of Study: United States of America.
No. of awards offered: Varies.
Application Procedure: Applicants must write to the main address for details or telephone Dr Adolphus Toliver, on (1) 301 594 3900. Further details are also available from the website www.nigms.nih.gov.
Funding: Government.

NIGMS Fellowship Awards for Minority Students

Subjects: Biomedical or behavioural sciences.
Purpose: Awards support research training leading to a Ph.D or equivalent research degree, a combined M.D-Ph.D degree or another combined professional doctorate-research Ph.D.
Eligibility: Open to highly qualified students who are members of minority groups that are under represented in the biomedical or behavioural sciences in the United States. These groups include African Americans, Hispanic Americans, Native Americans, including Alaska Natives, and natives of the United States Pacific Islands.
Level of Study: Postgraduate, Predoctorate.
Type: Fellowship.
Value: An annual stipend of US$19,968, a tuition and fee allowance, and an annual institution fee of US$2,750, which may be used for travel to scientific meetings and for laboratory and other training expenses.
Length of Study: Up to five years.
Frequency: Annual.
Country of Study: United States of America.
No. of awards offered: Varies.
Application Procedure: Applicants must write to the main address for details or telephone Dr Adolphus Toliver, on (1) 301 594 3900. Further details are also available from the website http://www.nigms.nih.gov.
Funding: Government.

NIGMS Fellowship Awards for Students With Disabilities

Subjects: Biomedical or behavioural sciences.
Purpose: To address the problem of the low participation rate of Americans with disabilities in biomedical research.These awards provide up to 5 years of support for research training leading to a PhD or equivalent research degree, combined M.D-PhD degree or another combined professional doctorate research PhD degree in the biomedical or behavioral science.
Eligibility: Open to principal investigators at domestic institutions holding an active NIGMS research grant, programme project grant, centre grant or co-operative agreement research programme with a reasonable period of research support remaining.
Level of Study: Doctorate, Graduate, Postdoctorate, Postgraduate, Predoctorate.
Type: Fellowship.
Value: Varies.
Length of Study: Two years or more.
Frequency: Annual.
Country of Study: United States of America.
No. of awards offered: Varies.
Application Procedure: Applicants must write to the main address for details or telephone Dr Anthony René, on (1) 301 594 3833. Further details are also available from the website, http:// www.nigms.nih.gov.
Funding: Government.

NIGMS Postdoctoral Awards

Subjects: Biomedical or behavioural sciences.
Purpose: NIGMS welcomes NRSA applications from eligible individuals who seek postdoctoral biomedical research training in areas related to the scientific programs of the Institute.
Eligibility: Open to applicants who have received the doctoral degree (domestic or foreign) by the beginning date of the proposed award.
Level of Study: Postdoctorate.
Type: Research grant.
Value: Up to US$50,808 per year, based on the salary of the applicant at the time of the award.
Frequency: Annual.
Study Establishment: The institutional setting may be domestic or foreign, public or private.
Country of Study: Any country.
No. of awards offered: Varies.
Application Procedure: Applicants must write to the main address for details or telephone Dr Alison Cole, on (1) 301 594 3349. Further details are also available from the website, http://www.nigms.nih.gov.
Funding: Government.

NIGMS Research Project Grants

Subjects: Biomedical or behavioural sciences.
Purpose: To support a discrete project related to the investigator's area of interest and competence.
Eligibility: Research grants may be awarded to non-profit organisations and institutions, governments and their agencies, and occasionally to individuals who have access to adequate facilities and resources for conducting the research, as well as profit making organisations. Foreign institutions and international organisations are also eligible to apply for these grants.
Level of Study: Postgraduate.
Value: These grants may provide funds for reasonable costs of the research activity, as well as for salaries, equipment, supplies, travel and other related expenses.
Frequency: Annual.
Country of Study: United States of America.
No. of awards offered: Varies.
Application Procedure: Applicants must contact the Office of Extramural Outreach and Information Resources for details.
Funding: Government.

For further information contact:

Office of Extramural Outreach & Information Resources, NIH, 6701 Rockledge Drive, MSC 7910, Room 6207, Bethesda, MD 20892-7910, United States of America

Tel: (1) 301 435 0714
Email: grantsinfo@nih.gov

NIGMS Research Supplements for Underrepresented Minorities

Subjects: Biomedical or behavioural sciences.
Purpose: To help minority scientists and students develop their capabilities for independent research careers. Supplements are avaliable to high school students, undergraduate students, post baccalaureate and post master's degree and predoctoral students as well as minority individuals in postdoctoral training and minority staff and faculty.
Eligibility: Open to principal investigators at domestic institutions holding an active NIGMS research grant, programme project grant, centre grant or co-operative agreement research programme with a reasonable period of research support remaining.
Level of Study: Unrestricted.
Type: Grant.
Value: Varies.
Length of Study: Two years or more.
Frequency: Annual.
Study Establishment: An institution in the United States.
Country of Study: United States of America.
No. of awards offered: Varies.
Application Procedure: Applicants must write to the main address for details or telephone Dr Anthony René, on (1) 301 594 3833. Further details are also available from the website, http://www.nigms.nih.gov.
Funding: Government.

NATIONAL INSTITUTE ON AGING

GW 218, Bethesda, MD 20892
United States of America
Tel: (1) 301 496 9322
Fax: (1) 301 402 2945
Email: mk46u@nih.gov
www: http://www.nih.gov
Contact: Dr Miriam Kelty, Associate Director

The National Institute on Aging conducts and supports research and research training in all areas of biological ageing, the neuroscience and neuropsychology of ageing, geriatrics and the social and behavioural sciences of ageing.

NIH Research Grants

Subjects: The biology of ageing neuroscience and neuropsychology of ageing, geriatrics and the social and behavioural sciences of ageing.
Purpose: To support research and training in biological, clinical, behavioural and social aspects of ageing mechanisms and processes.
Eligibility: Varies, depending on mechanism, but generally open to United States citizens only.
Level of Study: Postdoctorate, Professional development.
Type: Grants, fellowships, career development awards and institutional training awards.
Value: Varies.
Length of Study: One-five years.
Frequency: Annual.
Country of Study: The United States of America or others depending on mechanisms.
No. of awards offered: Varies.
Application Procedure: Applicants must download the application form PHS 398 on the website.
Closing Date: Deadlines are staggered. Please see form PHS 398.
Funding: Government.
Contributor: The United States government.
Additional Information: Some award mechanisms are limited to citizens and permanent residents of the United States of America. Others are open to applicants from any country. Further information is available on the website.

NATIONAL KIDNEY RESEARCH FUND (NKRF)

King's Chambers, Priestgate, Peterborough, Cambridgeshire PE1
1FG, England
Tel: (44) 1733 704658
Fax: (44) 1733 704685
Email: grants@nkrf.org.uk
www: http://www.nkrf.org.uk
Contact: Mrs Elaine Davies, Grants Administration Manager

The National Kidney Research Fund (NKRF) aims to advance and promote research into kidney and renal disease. These may include epidemiological, clinical or biological approaches to relevant problems. All research must be carried out in the United Kingdom.

NKRF Research Project Grants

Subjects: Renal medicine.
Purpose: To support both basic scientific and clinical research projects, improving the understanding of renal disease, its causes, treatment and management.
Eligibility: Open to suitably qualified researchers of any nationality. Work must be carried out in the United Kingdom.
Level of Study: Unrestricted.
Type: Project grant.
Value: Up to UK£100,000 over one-three years for a full research project, and up to UK£30,000 over one-two years for a start up research project.
Length of Study: One-three years.
Frequency: Twice a year.
Study Establishment: Any institution.
Country of Study: United Kingdom.
No. of awards offered: Varies.
Application Procedure: Applicants must complete an application form available from the Grants Department or website.
Closing Date: Provisional dates to 2004: March 5th for round one, August 27th to round two.
Funding: Private.
Contributor: Public donations.
No. of awards given last year: Ten.
No. of applicants last year: 61.

NKRF Senior Fellowships

Subjects: Renal medicine and related scientific studies.
Eligibility: Open to postdoctoral researchers in the biomedical field with evidence of independent research or academic clinicians or those building towards this senior role. Applicants may be of any nationality but project work must be carried out in the United Kingdom.
Level of Study: Postdoctorate, Professional development, Research.
Type: Fellowship.
Value: Up to UK£285,000 over a maximum of five years. Salary will be at the Consultant/Senior Registrar level or an established academic at the appropriate university scale. Includes a UK£12,000 per year bench allowance for consumables, minor equipment and technical support.
Length of Study: Three-five years, subject to review in the third year.
Frequency: Annual.
Study Establishment: Any institution.
Country of Study: United Kingdom.
No. of awards offered: Varies.
Application Procedure: Applicants must complete an application form available from the Grants Department or website.
Closing Date: November 28th provisional 26th November 2004.
Funding: Private.
Contributor: Public donations.
No. of awards given last year: One (2003).
No. of applicants last year: Six.

NKRF Special Project Grants

Subjects: Renal disease.
Purpose: To provide support for substantial projects in scientific disciplines related to renal disease and its management.
Eligibility: Open to suitably qualified researchers of UK or EU residency nationality.
Level of Study: Professional development, Research.

Type: Grant.
Value: Up to UK£150,000.
Length of Study: Three years.
Frequency: Dependent on funds available.
Country of Study: United Kingdom.
No. of awards offered: Varies.
Application Procedure: Applicants must complete application forms, available from the Grants Department and also via the website or email.
Closing Date: Please see the website.
Funding: Commercial, Government.
No. of awards given last year: 2.
No. of applicants last year: 12.

NKRF Studentships

Subjects: Renal medicine.
Purpose: To enable postgraduates to start a career in renal medicine by completing a course of training including submitting a PhD thesis.
Eligibility: Open to applicants of any nationality. Work must take place in the United Kingdom.
Level of Study: Postgraduate.
Type: Studentship.
Value: Up to UK£50,000. University fees are met by the NKRF and a bench fee is available to the host institution.
Length of Study: Three years, subject to a satisfactory annual report.
Frequency: Annual.
Study Establishment: Any institution.
Country of Study: United Kingdom.
No. of awards offered: Varies.
Application Procedure: Applicants must complete an application form available from the Grants Department or website.
Closing Date: November 28th, provisional date 26th November 2004.
Funding: Private.
Contributor: Public donations.
No. of awards given last year: Two.
No. of applicants last year: 9.

NKRF Training Fellowships

Subjects: Renal medicine and related scientific studies.
Purpose: To enable medical or scientific graduates to undertake specialised training in renal research.
Eligibility: Open to medical candidates of immediate post registration to registrar level and to science candidates with a PhD or DPhil and at least two years of postdoctoral experience. Project work must be carried out in the United Kingdom.
Level of Study: Postdoctorate, Professional development, Research.
Type: Fellowship.
Value: Up to UK£150,000. The level of financial support will be based on an appropriate point on current NHS or university pay scales and includes a UK£5,000 per year United Kingdom bench allowance with fees where applicable.
Length of Study: One-three years, subject to annual review.
Frequency: Annual.
Study Establishment: Any institution.
Country of Study: United Kingdom.
No. of awards offered: Varies.
Application Procedure: Applicants must complete an application form available from the Grants Department, the website or via email.
Closing Date: November 28th 2003. Provisional 26th November 2004.
Funding: Private.
Contributor: Public donations.
No. of awards given last year: Three (2003).
No. of applicants last year: 24.

NATIONAL LEAGUE OF AMERICAN PEN WOMEN, INC. (NLAPW)

1300 17th Street NW, Washington, DC 20036-1973, United States of America
Tel: (1) 202 785 1997
Fax: (1) 202 452 6868
Email: nlapw1@juno.com
Contact: Ms Mary Jane Hillery, National Scholarship Chairperson

The National League of American Pen Women (NLAPW) exists to promote women in the creative arts including art, writing and music.

NLAPW Grants for Mature Women
Subjects: Art, writing and music.
Purpose: To advance creative purpose in art, writing and music.
Eligibility: Open to women over 35 years of age who wish to pursue special work in their field of art, letters or music. Applicants must be citizens of the United States of America. Current and past recipients are not eligible for this award.
Level of Study: Unrestricted.
Type: Grant.
Value: US$1,000. The award may be used for college, framing, research or any creative purpose that furthers a career in the creative arts.
Frequency: Every two years.
Country of Study: United States of America.
No. of awards offered: One in each category.
Application Procedure: Applicants must send a letter stating their age, background and creative purpose and include proof of their citizenship. There are no application forms but no applications will be accepted by telephone or email.
Closing Date: October 1st of even numbered years.
Funding: Private.
Contributor: NLAPW.
No. of awards given last year: Three.
No. of applicants last year: 1000+.
Additional Information: Interested parties must send a stamped addressed envelope to receive current information.

For further information contact:

66 Willow Road, Sudbury, MA 01776-2663, United States of America

NATIONAL LIBRARY OF AUSTRALIA

Canberra, ACT 2600, Australia
Tel: (61) 2 6262 1258
Fax: (61) 2 6262 1516
Email: g.powell@nla.gov.au
Contact: Mr Graeme Powell, Manuscript Librarian

The National Library of Australia is responsible for developing and maintaining a comprehensive collection of Australian library materials, a strong collection of non Australian publications, and for administering and co-ordinating a range of national bibliographical activities.

Harold White Fellowships
Subjects: There are few subject limitations but most fellowships fall within the categories of arts and humanities, fine and applied arts or social sciences.
Purpose: To promote the Library as a centre of scholarly activity and research, to encourage scholarly and literary use of the collection and the production of publications based on them, to publicise the Library's collections.
Eligibility: Open to established Scholars, writers and librarians from any country. Fellowships are not normally offered to candidates working for a higher degree.
Level of Study: Unrestricted.
Type: Fellowship.
Value: Australian $700 per week.
Frequency: Annual.
Study Establishment: The National Library of Australia.
Country of Study: Australia.
No. of awards offered: Three-five.
Application Procedure: Applicants must complete an application form available from the National Library.
Closing Date: April 30th.
Funding: Government.
No. of awards given last year: Four.
No. of applicants last year: 35.
Additional Information: Normally Fellows will be expected to give a public lecture and at least one seminar during their tenure on the

subject of their research. At least three quarters of the fellowship time should be spent in Canberra.

NATIONAL MARFAN FOUNDATION

22 Manhasset Avenue, Port Washington, NY 11050, United States of America
Tel: (1) 516 883 8712 ext. 17
Fax: (1) 516 883 8040
Email: research@marfan.org
www: http://www.marfan.org
Contact: Ms Josephine Grima, Director of Research

The National Marfan Foundation was founded in 1981 by people who have Marfan syndrome and their families. It is a voluntary organisation that has three objectives: to disseminate accurate and timely information about Marfan syndrome to patients, family members and physicians, to provide a network of communications for patients and relatives to share experiences, support one another and improve their medical care, and to support and foster research. In 1995, the Foundation's mission was expanded to include Marfan syndrome and related connective tissue disorders. These genetic disorders of connective tissue affect approximately 200,000 people in the United States and strike men and women of any race or ethnic group without discrimination.

National Marfan Foundation Research Grant
Subjects: Marfan syndrome and related connective tissue disorders. Areas include basic, translational and clinical research in genetics, cardiology, ophthalmology and orthopaedic issues of Marfan syndrome.
Purpose: To provide financial support for investigators (scientists and physicians) studying any or all disciplines involved in Marfan syndrome research.
Eligibility: The principal investigator must hold an MD, DO, PhD, ScD, DDS, DVM or equivalent degree. The investigator must have proven ability to pursue independent research as evidenced by original research publications in peer reviewed journals.
Level of Study: Doctorate, Postdoctorate, Research.
Type: Research grant.
Value: US$50,000-100,000.
Length of Study: One or two years.
Frequency: Annual.
Country of Study: Any country.
No. of awards offered: Three-four.
Application Procedure: Applicants must complete an application form, available from the website.
Closing Date: July 2nd.
Funding: Private.
Contributor: Private donors.
No. of awards given last year: Three.
No. of applicants last year: 10.

THE NATIONAL MULTIPLE SCLEROSIS SOCIETY

733 Third Avenue, New York, NY 10017, United States of America
Tel: (1) 212 986 3240
Fax: (1) 212 986 7981
Email: nat@nmss.org
www: http://www.nationalmssociety.org
Contact: Grants Management Officer

The National Multiple Sclerosis Society is dedicated to ending the devastating effects of multiple sclerosis.

National Multiple Sclerosis Society Junior Faculty Awards
Subjects: Neurosciences related to multiple sclerosis.
Purpose: To enable highly qualified persons who have concluded their research training and have begun academic careers as independent investigators to undertake independent research.

Eligibility: Open to citizens of the United States of America holding a doctoral degree, and who have had sufficient research training at the pre or postdoctoral levels to be capable of independent research. Individuals who have already carried out independent research for more than five years are not eligible.
Level of Study: Professional development.
Value: Approx. US$75,000 per year.
Length of Study: Five years.
Frequency: Annual.
Study Establishment: An approved university, professional or research institute.
Country of Study: United States of America.
No. of awards offered: Varies.
Application Procedure: Applicants must complete an application form.
Closing Date: February 1st for awards on August 1st.
Funding: Private.
No. of awards given last year: 2.
No. of applicants last year: 5.
Additional Information: The candidate will not be an employee of the Society but rather of the institution. It is expected that the institution will develop plans for continuing the candidate's appointment and for continued salary support beyond the five year period of the award. Fellows may not supplement their salary through private practise or consultation, nor accept another concurrent award. The grantee institution holds title to all equipment purchased with award funds.

National Multiple Sclerosis Society Pilot Research Grants

Subjects: Multiple sclerosis.
Purpose: To provide limited short-term support of novel high risk research.
Eligibility: Open to suitably qualified investigators.
Level of Study: Research.
Type: Research grant.
Value: Up to US$40,000 in direct costs may be requested.
Length of Study: One year.
Frequency: Dependent on funds available.
Country of Study: Any country.
No. of awards offered: Varies.
Application Procedure: Applicants must complete an application form.
Closing Date: Applications are accepted at any time.
Funding: Private.
No. of awards given last year: 38.
No. of applicants last year: 70.
Additional Information: Grants are awarded to an institution to support the research of the principal investigator. Progress reports are required.

National Multiple Sclerosis Society Postdoctoral Fellowships

Subjects: Multiple sclerosis.
Purpose: To provide postdoctoral training which will enhance the likelihood of performing meaningful and independent research relevant to multiple sclerosis.
Eligibility: Open to unusually promising recipients of MD or PhD degrees. Foreign nationals are welcome to apply for fellowships in the United States of America only. The Society will consider applications from established investigators who seek support to obtain specialised training in some field in which they are not expert, when such training will materially enhance their capacity to conduct more meaningful research. United States citizenship is not required for training in United States institutions but applicants who plan to train in other countries must be citizens of the United States of America. These fellowships are awarded to support training in research and are not awarded to support clinical training directed towards the completion of internship or speciality board certification. Similarly, they cannot be used to provide support for individuals whose primary responsibility is teaching or service, although Fellows are encouraged to spend a reasonable amount of their time, up to 10 per cent, in teaching.
Level of Study: Postdoctorate.
Type: Fellowship.

Value: Varies according to professional status, previous training, accomplishments in research and the pay scale of the institution in which the training is provided. Fellowships may be supplemented by other forms of support, with prior approval.
Length of Study: One-three years.
Frequency: Annual.
Study Establishment: An institution of the candidate's choice.
Country of Study: Other.
No. of awards offered: Varies.
Application Procedure: Applicants must complete an application form.
Closing Date: February 1st for grants on August 1st or thereafter.
Funding: Private.
No. of awards given last year: 22.
No. of applicants last year: 64.
Additional Information: Fellows are not considered employees of the Society but rather of the institution where the training is provided. The fellowship is to be administered in accordance with the prevailing policies of the sponsoring institution. It is the responsibility of the applicant to make all the necessary arrangements for their training with the mentor and institution of their choice.

National Multiple Sclerosis Society Research Grants

Subjects: Multiple sclerosis, the cause, prevention, alleviation and cure.
Purpose: To stimulate, co-ordinate and support fundamental or applied clinical or non clinical research.
Eligibility: Open to suitably qualified investigators.
Level of Study: Professional development.
Type: Research grant.
Value: Funds may be used to pay the salaries of associated professional personnel, technical assistants and other non professional personnel in proportion to their time spent directly on the project, in whole or in part. Salaries are made in accordance with the prevailing policies of the grantee institution. If requested, other expenses such as travel costs and fringe benefits may also be paid.
Length of Study: Three years.
Country of Study: Any country.
No. of awards offered: Varies.
Application Procedure: Applicants must complete an application form.
Closing Date: February 1st for grants on October 1st, August 1st for grants on April 1st.
Funding: Private.
No. of awards given last year: 53.
No. of applicants last year: 163.
Additional Information: Grants are awarded to an institution to support the research of the principal investigator. Scientific equipment and supplies bought with grant funds become the property of the grantee institution. Progress reports are required and appropriate publication is expected.

NATIONAL ORCHESTRAL INSTITUTE

2110 Clarice Smith Performing Arts Center, University of Maryland, College Park, MD 20742-1620, United States of America
Tel: (1) 301 405 2317
Fax: (1) 301 314 9504
Email: noi@accmail.umd.edu
www: http://www.nationalorchestralinstitute.com

National Orchestral Institute Scholarships

Subjects: Orchestral performance and chamber music.
Purpose: To provide an intensive three week orchestral training programme to enable musicians to rehearse and perform under internationally acclaimed conductors and study with principal musicians of the United States' foremost orchestras in preparation for careers as orchestral musicians.
Eligibility: Open to advanced musicians between 18-28 years of age, primarily students and postgraduates of United States universities, conservatories and colleges. Others, however, are welcome to apply but must appear at an audition centre. String players, including

harpists, who live more than 100 miles away from an audition centre may audition by tape.
Level of Study: Unrestricted.
Type: Scholarship.
Value: Full tuition, room and board.
Length of Study: Three weeks.
Frequency: Annual.
Study Establishment: The University of Maryland.
Country of Study: United States of America.
No. of awards offered: Approx. 100.
Application Procedure: Applicants must submit an application, a fee of US$40, curriculum vitae and letter of recommendation.
Closing Date: Before the regional auditions.
Funding: Government.
Contributor: The University of Maryland.
No. of awards given last year: 100.
No. of applicants last year: 800.
Additional Information: Personal auditions are required at one of the audition centers throughout the country.

THE NATIONAL ORGANIZATION FOR RARE DISORDERS (NORD)

PO Box 1968, 55 Kenosia Avenue, Danbury, CT 06813-1968, United States of America
Tel: (1) 203 744 0100
Fax: (1) 203 798 2291
Email: lcataldo@rarediseases.org
www: http://www.rarediseases.org
Contact: Ms Linda M Cataldo, Field Services Co-ordinator

The National Organization for Rare Disorders (NORD) is a federation of voluntary health organisations dedicated to helping people with rare (orphan) diseases and assisting the organisations that serve them. NORD is committed to the identification, treatment and cure of rare disorders through programmes of advocacy, education, research and service. For more information on current research funding opportunities please visit the research section of the website.

NORD Clinical Research Grants
Subjects: Seed money grants to Academic scientists studying new treatments or diagnostic tests for rare diseases.
Purpose: To support small clinical trials.
Eligibility: Open to academic scientists in the United States of America, Canada and Europe, or any country that adheres to the most recent guidelines for human subject protection as set forth by the NIH.
Level of Study: Doctorate, Postdoctorate, Research.
Type: Research grant.
Value: US$30,000 per year.
Length of Study: 1 year.
Frequency: Annual.
Country of Study: Other.
No. of awards offered: 6-12.
Application Procedure: Applicants must submit an application form, letter of intent and proposals. Forms are available from the website.
Closing Date: Enquiries are accepted at any time for future announcements and should be sent by email.
Funding: Private.
Contributor: Public donations.
No. of awards given last year: 22.
No. of applicants last year: 100.
Additional Information: Funding opportunities are announced January-March.

NORD/ROSCOE BRADY Lysosomal Storage Diseases Fellowships
Subjects: Genetics, new treatments and diagnostics, and/or epidemiology of lysosomal storage diseases in general, or for a specific lysosomal storage disease.
Purpose: To assist physicians who desire to establish careers in lysosomal storage diseases and clinical medicine.

Eligibility: Open to all countries that adhere to the most recent guidelines for human subject protection as set forth by the NIH. Applicants will have an MD or MD/PhD earned in or after 1994.
Level of Study: Doctorate, Postdoctorate, Research.
Type: Fellowship.
Value: US$50,000-70,000 per year.
Length of Study: One year but renewable for a second year.
Frequency: Annual.
Country of Study: Other.
No. of awards offered: One.
Application Procedure: Application forms and required attachments may be obtained directly from the website.
Closing Date: March 25th.
Funding: Private.
Contributor: Public donations.
No. of awards given last year: Three.
No. of applicants last year: 14.

NATIONAL OSTEOPOROSIS FOUNDATION (NOF)

1232 22nd Street North West, Washington, DC 20037-1292, United States of America
Tel: (1) 202 223 2226
Fax: (1) 202 223 2237
Email: rita@nof.org
www: http://www.nof.org
Contact: Co-ordinator

NOF Scholar's, Foundation and Mazess Research Grants
Subjects: Epidemiology, pathogenesis and osteoporosis.
Purpose: To support clinical or basic research related to the epidemiology, pathogenesis, diagnosis and treatment of osteoporosis.
Eligibility: Applicants must have an MD, PhD or equivalent degree, United States citizenship or permanent resident status, and be affiliated with non profit institutions within the United States, its territories or the Commonwealth of Puerto Rico. Federal agencies and their employees are not eligible.
Level of Study: Postdoctorate, Research.
Type: Research grant.
Value: US$57,000.
Length of Study: One year.
Frequency: Annual.
Country of Study: United States of America.
No. of awards offered: Five.
Application Procedure: Applicants must visit the website for further information.
Closing Date: December 1st for next year.
Funding: Private.
No. of awards given last year: 5.
No. of applicants last year: 48.

NOF Student Fellowship Grants
Subjects: Epidemiology, pathogenesis and osteoporosis.
Purpose: To support of clinical or basic research.
Level of Study: Graduate.
Type: Fellowship.
Value: US$3,000.
Length of Study: Eight weeks to four months.
Country of Study: Other.
No. of awards offered: Five.
Application Procedure: Applicants must visit the website for further information.
Closing Date: 12/15 of previous year.
Funding: Private.
No. of awards given last year: 5.
No. of applicants last year: 15.
Additional Information: Postdoctoral fellowships may be awarded to individuals who have received a doctoral degree under special circumstances, such as graduate students or house officers who wish to spend an elective in a research setting devoted to basic or clinical research on osteoporosis.

NATIONAL OSTEOPOROSIS SOCIETY (NOS)

Camerton, Bath, BA2 0PJ, England
Tel: (44) 1761 471771
Fax: (44) 1761 471104
Email: info@nos.org.uk
www: http://www.nos.org.uk
Contact: Martin Stevens, Scientific Co-ordinator

The National Osteoporosis Society (NOS) is the only national charity dedicated to the diagnosis, prevention and treatment of osteoporosis and osteoporotic fractures.

Linda Edwards Memorial Studentships

Subjects: Prevention and treatment of osteoporosis.
Purpose: To support a student researching osteoporosis at doctorate level.
Level of Study: Doctorate.
Type: Studentship.
Value: UK£10,000-15,000
Length of Study: One to three years.
Frequency: Annual.
No. of awards offered: Varies.
Application Procedure: Please refer to the website.
Funding: Private.
Contributor: Donations from NOS membership.
No. of awards given last year: 2.
No. of applicants last year: 4.
Additional Information: The NOS only has limited funds to spend and often resorts to partial spending.

NOS Project Grants

Subjects: The prevention, diagnosis and treatment of osteoporosis and osteoporotic fractures.
Level of Study: Doctorate, Postdoctorate, Research.
Type: Project grant.
Value: Applications in excess of UK£50,000 over 3 year period are unlikely to be accepted for funding. Partial funding of projects may occur.
Length of Study: One-three years.
Frequency: Annual.
Country of Study: United Kingdom.
No. of awards offered: Varies.
Application Procedure: Applicants must obtain an application form from the NOS in June. They should be submitted by September for peer review. Awards are announced in January.
Closing Date: September.
Contributor: Donations from NOS Membership.
No. of awards given last year: Two projects.
No. of applicants last year: 22.

NATIONAL RADIO ASTRONOMY OBSERVATORY (NRAO)

520 Edgemont Road, Charlottesville, VA 22903-2475, United States of America
Tel: (1) 434 296 0221
Fax: (1) 434 296 0278
Email: info@nrao.edu
www: http://www.nrao.edu
Contact: Secretary

Jansky Postdoctorals

Subjects: Areas of present interest include theoretical and observational studies of discrete radio sources, galaxies, the interstellar medium, planets, millimetre wave instrumentation and research, interferometry, aperture, synthesis, large antenna arrays, radio astronomy instrumentation (HFET and SIS amplifiers, radiometer systems, cryogenics), data processing, information theory, computer system applications or digital and online techniques.

Purpose: To provide outstanding opportunities to qualified young PhDs who wish to devote themselves to full-time research.
Eligibility: Open to astronomers, physicists, electrical engineers and computer specialists. Preference will be given to recent PhD recipients.
Level of Study: Postdoctorate.
Value: US$35,000 per year, plus a liberal vacation allowance, authorised travel expenses and a moving allowance.
Length of Study: Two years, with a possibility of renewal for one further year.
Frequency: Annual.
Study Establishment: The Observatory's centres in Charlottesville, Virginia; Green Bank, West Virginia; Tucson, Arizona; and Socorro, New Mexico.
Country of Study: Any country.
No. of awards offered: Four.
Application Procedure: Applications normally commence in September or October. There is no application form. The initial letter should include a statement of the individual's research interests together with his or her own appraisal of his or her qualifications for carrying out research. Applications should be single sided with no staples. The applicant should have three letters of recommendation sent directly to the NRAO.
Closing Date: Please contact the organisation.
Funding: Government.
Contributor: The National Science Foundation.
Additional Information: Research Associates may formulate and carry out investigations either independently or in collaboration with others.

NATIONAL RESEARCH COUNCIL (NRC) OFFICE FOR CENTRAL EUROPE AND EURASIA

500 Fifth Street NW, Washington, DC 20001, United States of America
Tel: (1) 202 334 2644
Fax: (1) 202 334 2614
Email: ocee@nas.edu
www: http://www7.nationalacademies.org/dsc
Contact: Ms Kelly Robbins, Senior Programme Officer

The National Research Council (NRC) was organised by the National Academy of Sciences in 1916 to associate the broad community of science and technology with the Academy's purposes of further knowledge and advising the federal government.

NRC Twinning Program

Subjects: Fields supported by NSF. This does not include disease related topics.
Purpose: To yield significant publications and long-term sustained linkages between researchers in the United States of America and underrepresented countries in Eastern Europe.
Eligibility: Open to American citizens or permanent residents but not to employees of the United States' government. Principal investigators must hold a PhD or equivalent.
Level of Study: Postdoctorate.
Type: Travel grant.
Value: US$14,000-16,000.
Length of Study: Two years.
Frequency: Annual, if funds are available.
Country of Study: Other.
No. of awards offered: 8-12 per year.
Application Procedure: Applicants must submit five copies of a description of their proposed research, a budget, a curriculum vitae, a list of publications, a curriculum vitae of foreign counterparts, letters of support from United States applicants' institutions, correspondence with prospective twinning partner and a list of potential peer reviewers.
Closing Date: Varies.
Funding: Government.
Contributor: NSF.
No. of awards given last year: 10.

No. of applicants last year: 30.
Additional Information: Further information is available on the website.

NATIONAL RESEARCH COUNCIL OF CANADA (NRC)

Recruitment Unit, Montreal Road, M58, Ottawa, ON, K1A 0R6, Canada
Tel: (1) 613 993 9150
Fax: (1) 613 990 7669
Email: ra.coordinator@nrc.ca
www: http://www.nrc.ca/careers
Contact: Research Associates Co-ordinator

The National Research Council of Canada (NRC) is a dynamic, nationwide research and development organisation committed to helping Canada realise its potential as an innovative and competitive nation.

NRC Research Associateships
Subjects: Biological sciences, biotechnology, chemistry, molecular science, chemical engineering and process technologies, electrical engineering, astrophysics, industrial materials research, marine dynamics, construction, mechanical engineering, aeronautics, physics, photonics, microstructural sciences, plant biotechnology, biochemistry, microbiology or advanced structural ceramics.
Purpose: To give promising scientists and engineers an opportunity to work on challenging research problems in fields of interest to NRC as a stage in the development of their research careers.
Eligibility: Open to nationals of any country, although preference will be given to Canadians and permanent residents of Canada. Applicants should have acquired a PhD in natural science or a Master's degree in an engineering field within the last five years or should expect to obtain their degree before taking up the associateship. Selections will be made on a competitive basis with a demonstrated ability to perform original research of high quality in the chosen field as the main criterion.
Level of Study: Postgraduate.
Type: Other.
Value: Canadian $43,890 for a new PhD.
Frequency: Annual.
Study Establishment: Laboratories in the National Research Council of Canada.
Country of Study: Any country.
No. of awards offered: Approx. 50.
Application Procedure: Applicants must fill out an application form, available from the organisation or the website www.careers-carrieres.nrc-cnrc.gc.ca.
Closing Date: Applications are accepted at any time.
Funding: Government.
No. of awards given last year: 53.
No. of applicants last year: 400.
Additional Information: Salaries are revised annually. Further information is available from the website.

NATIONAL RESEARCH FOUNDATION (NRF)

PO Box 2600, Pretoria, 0001, South Africa
Tel: (27) 12 481 4209
Fax: (27) 12 349 1179
Email: haveline@nrf.ac.za
www: http://www.nrf.ac.za
Contact: Ms HA Michau, Manager, Student Support

The National Research Foundation (NRF) is responsible for funding South African research and other expertise in the fields of the social, natural and applied sciences, humanities, engineering and technology. The NRF is funded by the government, but also pursues joint ventures and collaboration with industry and the international community to increase the impact of its activities.

NRF Doctoral Scholarships and Postdoctoral Fellowships for Study Abroad
Subjects: Natural and applied sciences, engineering, social sciences and the humanities.
Purpose: To foster postgraduate studies and research in the fields of applied and natural sciences, engineering, social sciences and the humanities.
Eligibility: Open to South African citizens who are in the process of obtaining or who have obtained their doctoral degree. Applicants for postdoctoral fellowships should have obtained their doctorate within the last five years.
Level of Study: Doctorate, Postdoctorate, Postgraduate.
Type: Other.
Value: Scholarships are US$12,000, and postdoctoral awards are up to US$16,500.
Length of Study: Up to three years of doctoral study, or up to two years of postdoctoral research.
Frequency: Scholarships are offered annually and fellowships are offered twice a year.
Study Establishment: Approved institutions abroad for full-time study or research.
Country of Study: Other.
No. of awards offered: 20.
Application Procedure: Applicants must complete and submit an application form, full academic record, and referee's reports. Forms are available from the bursary offices of the universities and technikons or can be downloaded from the website.
Closing Date: The deadline for scholarships is July 31st of the year preceding the award, and for fellowships the deadlines are March 31st and September 30th.
Funding: Government.
No. of awards given last year: 30.
No. of applicants last year: 90.
Additional Information: Candidates should motivate their choice of overseas institution.

NRF Fellowships for Postdoctoral Research
Subjects: Natural and applied sciences, engineering, technology, social sciences and humanities.
Purpose: To foster postdoctoral research in the natural and applied sciences, engineering, social sciences and the humanities.
Eligibility: Open to any nationals who have received their PhD within the last five years.
Level of Study: Postdoctorate.
Type: Fellowship.
Value: Up to Rand 60,000 plus a contribution of Rand 10,000 towards the running cost of the project.
Length of Study: Up to two years.
Frequency: Twice a year.
Study Establishment: Any university, technikon or research institute for full-time research.
Country of Study: South Africa.
No. of awards offered: 50.
Application Procedure: Applicants must complete and submit an application form, full academic record and the names of referees. Forms are available from the bursary offices of universities and technikons or can be downloaded from the website.
Closing Date: January 31st or July 31st.
Funding: Government.
No. of awards given last year: 50.
No. of applicants last year: 150.

NRF Scholarships for Doctoral Study
Subjects: Natural and applied sciences, engineering, social sciences and the humanities.
Purpose: To foster postgraduate studies in the fields of natural and applied sciences, engineering, social sciences and the humanities.
Eligibility: Open to South African citizens studying for full-time doctoral studies at South African universities or technikons.
Level of Study: Doctorate, Postgraduate.
Type: Scholarship.
Value: Rand 50,000 per year.
Length of Study: Up to three years.

Frequency: Annual.
Study Establishment: Any university or technikon for full-time study.
Country of Study: South Africa.
No. of awards offered: Approx. 30.
Application Procedure: Applicants must complete and submit an application form, full academic record and referee's reports. Forms are available from university and technikon bursary offices.
Closing Date: July 31st of the year preceding the award.
Funding: Government.
No. of awards given last year: 45.
No. of applicants last year: 150.
Additional Information: The award of a scholarship does not bind the candidate to enter the Foundation's service. However, candidates are expected to obtain the degree for which the award was made. In addition, one contribution will be made towards travel costs during the entire duration of the study to either attend a conference, locally or abroad, with the proviso that the student will be making a contribution to the conference, and/or visit a laboratory for two to three months, provided it is linked to the student's research.

NRF Scholarships for Master's Study

Subjects: Natural and applied sciences, engineering, social sciences and the humanities.
Purpose: To foster studies in the fields of applied and natural sciences, engineering, social sciences and the humanities.
Eligibility: Open to South African citizens for full-time Master's study at South African universities or technikons.
Level of Study: Postgraduate.
Type: Scholarship.
Value: Rand 33,000 per year.
Length of Study: Two years. Where Master's registration is upgraded to PhD, the maximum period of support for Master's and doctoral study will be four years in total.
Frequency: Annual.
Study Establishment: Any university or technikon for full-time study.
Country of Study: South Africa.
No. of awards offered: 50.
Application Procedure: Applicants must complete and submit an application form, full academic record, and referee's reports. Forms are available from the bursary offices of universities and technikons.
Closing Date: July 31st of the year preceding the award.
Funding: Government.
No. of awards given last year: 50.
No. of applicants last year: 200.
Additional Information: The award of a scholarship does not bind the candidate to enter the Foundation's service. However, candidates are expected to obtain the degree for which the award was made. In addition, one contribution will be made towards travel costs during the entire duration of the study to either attend a conference, locally or abroad, with the proviso that the student will be making a contribution at the conference, or visit a laboratory for two to three months, provided it is linked to the student's research.

NATIONAL RESTAURANT ASSOCIATION EDUCATIONAL FOUNDATION

175 West Jackson Boulevard, Suite 1500, Chicago, IL 60604-2702, United States of America
Tel: (1) 312 715 5385
Fax: (1) 312 566 9726
Email: dramos@foodtrain.org
www: http://www.nraef.org
Contact: Mrs Dalilah Torres-Ramos, Scholarship Programme Specialist

The Educational Foundation of the National Restaurant Association is the educational branch of the National Restaurant Association, and is the largest provider of food service and hospitality scholarships, grants and fellowships.The National Restaurant Assocation Educational Foundation is a not-for-profit organization dedicated to fulfilling the educational mission of the National Resturant Association. Focusing on three key strategies of risk management, recruitment, and retention, the NRAEF is the premier provider of educational resources, materials, and programs which address attracting, developing, and retaining the industry's workforce.

National Restaurant Association Educational Foundation Professional Development Scholarship for educators.

Purpose: This scholarship is for restaurant and foodservice educators who want to complement classroom time with "Hands-on" operational professional development or attend one of the 2004 NRAEF summer institutes.
Eligibility: Open to United States citizens who are full-time teachers or administrators in a secondary or post secondary school. Applicants must be those who will continue to be full-time teachers or administrators in a food service or hospitality orientated programme, or those who will be full-time students pursuing an advanced degree during the next academic year.
Level of Study: Professional development.
Type: Scholarship.
Value: US$1,500.
Frequency: Annual.
Country of Study: United States of America.
No. of awards offered: Varies.
Application Procedure: Applicants must submit typed applications, available from at www.nraef.org along with a letter of recommendation on school headed paper from an immediate supervisor or programme director.
Closing Date: March 15, 2004.
Funding: Private.

NATIONAL SCIENCE FOUNDATION (NSF)

Division of Earth Sciences, 4201 Wilson Boulevard, Arlington, VA 22230, United States of America
Tel: (1) 703 292 8550
Fax: (1) 703 292 9025
Email: hzimmer@nsf.gov
www: http://www.geo.nsf.gov/ear
Contact: Division Director

The National Science Foundation (NSF) supports research in the areas of goology, geophysics, geochemistry, paleobiology and hydrology, including interdisciplinary or multidisciplinary proposals that may involve one or more of these disciplines. Proposals for research in newly emerging areas of science that may not fit easily into one of these categories are especially welcome.

NSF Division of Earth Sciences

Subjects: The earth's structure, properties, processes and evolution, including basic research in areas of practical importance. Support is provided in most fields of the earth sciences including geology, geophysics, geochemistry surfacial processes, and hydrology.
Purpose: To advance the state of knowledge in the earth sciences and enhance the ability of United States colleges and universities to conduct research and education in these fields.
Eligibility: Open to qualified research scientists at United States universities, colleges and other research institutions.
Level of Study: Unrestricted.
Value: Award sizes vary greatly depending on the project proposed.
Frequency: Annual.
Study Establishment: Appropriate sites and institutions.
Country of Study: Any country.
No. of awards offered: Varies.
Application Procedure: Applicants must consult the NSF Guide to Programs and Earth Sciences Research at NSF. Latest editions of these publications may be requested by mail from the forms and publications unit.
Funding: Government.
Additional Information: For detailed information on general application procedure, preparation of proposals and budgeting, please refer to the website http://www.nsf.gov. The Division is a participant in the National Earthquake Hazard Prevention Program and the United States of America Global Change Research Program.

NATIONAL SPACE CLUB

2000 L Street club NW, Suite 710, Washington, DC 20036, United States of America
Tel: (1) 202 973 8661
Email: jbanke@hq.space.com
www: http://www.nationalspaceclubflorida.org
Contact: Grants Management Officer

Dr Robert H Goddard Scholarship

Subjects: Science or engineering.
Purpose: To stimulate the interest of talented students in the fields of space research and exploration and therefore to help promote the advancement of scientific knowledge.
Eligibility: Open to citizens of the United States of America in the junior year of an accredited university who intend to pursue graduate study in science or engineering during the interval of the scholarship. Previous winners may re-enter. Selection is based upon official school transcripts, faculty letters of recommendation, accomplishments demonstrating personal qualities of creativity and leadership and scholastic plans leading to future participation in some phase of the aerospace sciences and technology.
Level of Study: Graduate.
Type: Scholarship.
Value: US$10,000.
Length of Study: One year, renewable for a further year if circumstances and accomplishments warrant it.
Frequency: Annual.
Country of Study: United States of America.
No. of awards offered: One.
Closing Date: January 10th, but please consult the organisation.
Funding: Commercial.
Additional Information: Personal need is considered but not as a primary criterion.

NATIONAL STRENGTH AND CONDITIONING ASSOCIATION (NSCA)

PO Box 9908, Colorado Springs, CO 80932-0908, United States of America
Tel: (1) 719 632 6722
Fax: (1) 719 632 6367
Email: foundation@nsca-lift.org
www: http://www.nsca-lift.org
Contact: Ms Karri Todd Baker, Membership Director

As the worldwide authority on strength and conditioning, we support and disseminate research-based knowledge and its practical application to improve athletic performance and fitness.

NSCA Challenge Scholarship

Subjects: Strength and conditioning.
Purpose: To financially assist members in their pursuit of a career in the field of strength and conditioning.
Eligibility: Applicants must have been NSCA members for at least one year from the application deadline and seeking a graduate degree in a strength and conditioning related field.
Level of Study: Graduate, Postgraduate.
Type: Scholarship.
Value: US$1,000.
Frequency: Annual.
Study Establishment: Unrestricted.
Country of Study: Any country.
No. of awards offered: 12.
Application Procedure: Applicants must submit a current curriculum vitae, a covering letter of application and three current letters of recommendation, an original copy of an authorised transcript from all post secondary schools attended, and an essay of no more than 500 words describing course of study, career goals and need. All material must be mailed together and postmarked by March 15th. Applicants may also apply via the website.
Closing Date: March 15th.
Funding: Private.

Contributor: Funding is made possible by the Bob Hoffman Foundation, NSCA Certification Commission and the NSCA National Office.
No. of awards given last year: 12.
No. of applicants last year: 20.

NSCA Power Systems Professional Scholarship

Subjects: Strength and conditioning.
Purpose: To financially assist members in their pursuit of a career as a strength and conditioning coach.
Eligibility: Open to any NSCA member who has been a member for at least one year from the application deadline.
Level of Study: Graduate, Postgraduate.
Type: Scholarship.
Value: US$1,000.
Frequency: Annual.
Study Establishment: Unrestricted.
Country of Study: Any country.
No. of awards offered: One.
Application Procedure: The head strength coach from the applicant's school must submit a letter of application. The applicant must submit an original, official transcript from all secondary schools attended, a current curriculum vitae and an essay of no more than 500 words describing career goals and objectives. The transcript must be mailed directly to the NSCA office by the school. To obtain an application form applicants should telephone or visit the website. Only one candidate per school is permitted.
Closing Date: All materials must be postmarked by March 15th.
Funding: Private.
Contributor: Power Systems, Inc.
No. of awards given last year: One.
No. of applicants last year: Five.

NSCA Student Research Grant

Subjects: Strength and conditioning.
Purpose: To fund graduate student research that is directed by a graduate faculty member.
Eligibility: Open to NSCA members who have been members for at least one year from the application deadline. Graduate student members who are studying in the field of are invited to apply. A graduate faculty member is required to serve as co-investigator in the study.
Level of Study: Graduate, Postgraduate, Research.
Type: Grant.
Value: Up to US$2,500.
Length of Study: One year.
Frequency: Annual.
Study Establishment: Unrestricted.
Country of Study: Any country.
No. of awards offered: Varies, dependent on the number of applications.
Application Procedure: Applicants must submit an application pack consisting of a covering letter of application, a completed application form, an original school transcript from each school attended or attending, an abstract, a proposal (including rationale, study purpose and methods), references, an itemised budget, proposed time schedule, a human consent form, proof of institutional review board approval and an abbreviated curriculum vitae of faculty co-investigator.
Closing Date: March 15th.
Funding: Private.
Contributor: The NSCA Certification Commission and NSCA National Office.
No. of awards given last year: 12.
No. of applicants last year: 20.
Additional Information: Application forms can be accessed via the website or by telephoning the organisation.

NATIONAL UNION OF TEACHERS (NUT)

Central Co-ordinating Unit, Hamilton House, Mabledon Place, London, WC1H 9BD, England
Tel: (44) 20 7380 4704
Fax: (44) 20 7387 8458
www: http://www.teachers.org.uk
Contact: Ms Angela Bush

NUT Page Scholarship

Subjects: A specific aspect of American education relevant to the recipient's own professional responsibilities.

Purpose: To promote the exchange of educational ideas between Britain and America.

Eligibility: Open to teaching members of the NUT aged 25-60 years, though 25-55 is preferred.

Level of Study: Professional development.

Type: Scholarship.

Value: Up to UK£1,700 pro-rata daily rate with complete hospitality in the United States of America provided by the English Speaking Union of the United States of America.

Length of Study: Two weeks. The scholarship must be taken during the American academic year, which is September-May.

Frequency: Annual.

Country of Study: United States of America.

No. of awards offered: One.

Application Procedure: Applicants must complete an application form. An outline and synopsis of the 1,000-1,500 word project must accompany the form along with a curriculum vitae and scholastic and personal testimonials.

Closing Date: December 22nd.

Funding: Private.

Contributor: NUT.

No. of awards given last year: One.

No. of applicants last year: 120.

Additional Information: The scholarship is limited to the individual teacher and neither the spouse nor partner can be included in the travelling, accommodation or study arrangements. Recipients are required to report on their visit to teacher groups and educational meetings in the United States of America and on their return home.

NATIONAL UNIVERSITY OF SINGAPORE (NUS)

Registrar's Office, 10 Kent Ridge Crescent, 119260, Singapore
Tel: (65) 6874 2301
Fax: (65) 6778 6371
Email: gradenquiry@nus.edu.sg
www: http://www.nus.edu.sg
Contact: Grants Management Officer

NUS Graduate Scholarships for ASEAN Nationals

Subjects: Public policy, architecture, arts in Chinese studies, arts in English studies, arts in Southeast Asian studies, arts in urban design, business administration (English or Chinese), clinical embryology, computing, dental surgery in endodontics, dental surgery in oral and maxillofacial surgery, dental surgery in orthodontics, dental surgery in periodontology, dental surgery in prosthodontics, laws, medicine in internal medicine, medicine in anaesthesia, medicine in diagnostic radiology, medicine in obstetrics and gynaecology, medicine in occupational medicine, medicine in ophthalmology, medicine in paediatric medicine, medicine in psychiatry, medicine in public health, medicine in surgery. Other subject areas include science in building science, science in chemical engineering, science in civil engineering, science in electrical engineering, science in environmental engineering, science in industrial and systems engineering, science in management of technology, science in materials science and engineering, science in mathematics, science in mechanical engineering, science in mechatronics, science in project management, science in real estate, science in safety, health and environmental technology, science in transportation systems and management, social sciences in applied psychology, social sciences in economics, social sciences in international studies, and social sciences in social work.

Purpose: To provide outstanding candidates from ASEAN* countries (except Singaporeans) with an opportunity to pursue studies (by coursework) at the NUS. *ASEAN is the abbreviation for the Association of South East Asian Nations and it comprises Brunei, Cambodia, Indonesia, Laos, Malaysia, Myanmar, Philippines, Singapore, Thailand and Vietnam.

Eligibility: Open to citizens of ASEAN member countries, except Singapore. Recipients of the scholarship may not hold any other award without approval.

Level of Study: Postgraduate.

Type: Scholarship.

Value: 1. Stipend of US$1,350 per month and Tuition fee and other approved fees at NUS. 2. A one-time book allowance of S$500. 3. Cost of economy travel directly from home country to Singapore upon award of scholarship. 4. Cost of economy travel directly from Singapore back to home country on successful completion of study.

Frequency: Annual.

Study Establishment: The NUS.

Country of Study: Singapore.

No. of awards offered: Varies.

Application Procedure: Applicants must complete and submit application forms for the designated degrees with supporting documents to the respective faculties and graduate schools.

Closing Date: Varies.

Additional Information: ASEAN is the abbreviation for the Association of South East Asian Nations and comprises the following nations in Southeast Asia: Brunei, Cambodia, Indonesia, Laos, Malaysia, Myanmar, Philippines, Singapore, Thailand and Vietnam.

For further information contact:

www: http://www.nus.edu.sg/corporate/courses
Contact: Respective Faculty/School offering the course

NUS Research Scholarship

Subjects: Engineering, science, medicine, humanities, business or law.

Purpose: To encourage qualified candidates to pursue research in their fields of interest.

Eligibility: Open to graduates with at least an Upper Second Class (Honours) Bachelor's Degree or equivalent.

Level of Study: Doctorate, Postgraduate.

Type: Scholarship.

Value: Stipend of S$1,500 per month and full research fee subsidy.

Length of Study: One-five years.

Frequency: Annual.

Study Establishment: The NUS.

Country of Study: Singapore.

No. of awards offered: Varies.

Application Procedure: Applicants must complete an application form, available on request.

Closing Date: Semester I Intake : Mid / End Dec, Semester II Intake: May / Jun.

Funding: Government.

For further information contact:

www: http://www.nus.edu.sg/registrar/prospective/graduate/application.html
Contact: Respective Faculty/School

NATURAL ENVIRONMENT RESEARCH COUNCIL (NERC)

Polaris House, North Star Avenue, Swindon, Wiltshire, SN2 1EU, England
Tel: (44) 1793 411500
Fax: (44) 1793 411501
www: http://www.nerc.ac.uk/funding
Contact: Dr A M McFarlane, Process Manager

The Natural Environment Research Council (NERC) is one of the seven United Kingdom Research Councils which fund and manage research in the United Kingdom. NERC is the leading body in the United Kingdom for research, survey, monitoring and training in the environmental sciences. NERC supports research and training in universities and in its own centres, surveys and units.

NERC Advanced Course Studentships

Subjects: Environmental sciences.

Purpose: To allow postgraduate students to undertake courses recognised by NERC, which usually lead to an MSc or MRes. These courses are essentially vocational and are designed to prepare students for employment in industry or the public sector, or to advance their study.

Eligibility: Open to persons who, at the closing date of application for an award, have been ordinarily resident in Great Britain or Northern Ireland throughout the three year period preceding that date. Ordinarily resident means that no period of the candidate's residence during those three years has been wholly, or mainly, for the purpose of receiving full-time education. Candidates must hold a First or Second Class (Honours) Degree in an appropriate branch of science or technology. NERC also accepts qualifications, or a combination of qualifications and experience, which demonstrate equivalent ability and attainment. A less than sufficient first degree may be enhanced to meet the requirements by the acquisition of: a) a Masters degree to enhance the first degree by one step, e.g. from 2(ii) to 2(i) and/or b) substantial relevant postgraduate work experience, i.e. a minimum of two and a half years full time equivalent to enhance a degree by one step, five years equivalent to enhance by two steps. The postgraduate work experience must relate to the discipline of the first degree, a subsequent Masters degree or the intended area of postgraduate study. There is no age limit for studentships but the Council reserves the right to decline an application from a candidate if it considers that an award would not represent a good investment of public funds.

Level of Study: Postgraduate, Predoctorate.

Type: Studentship.

Value: UK£7,323 maintenance grant per year for students outside London and UK£9,323 per year for students in London, payment of approved fees and assistance with travel and subsistence expenses under specified conditions eg. fieldwork.

Length of Study: One year.

Frequency: Annual.

Study Establishment: Any approved Institute of Higher Education.

Country of Study: United Kingdom.

No. of awards offered: Varies, approx. 290.

Application Procedure: Applications must be submitted by the head of the department in which the student proposes to work. Applications will not be accepted directly from individual candidates. Awards are tenable only for those courses which are currently recognised by NERC for the purposes of its studentship scheme. The number of NERC awards given to each of these courses is detailed in the display notice. A review of the portfolio of NERC supported advanced courses is undertaken every five years.

Closing Date: July 31st for student nominations.

Funding: Government.

No. of awards given last year: 349.

NERC Advanced Research Fellowships

Subjects: The sciences of the natural environment.

Purpose: To support outstanding research workers who are well qualified for academic careers but who do not hold tenured posts at the time of application.

Eligibility: Open to candidates who hold a PhD and who have had at least two years of research experience at the postdoctoral level at the time of application, though not necessarily in the United Kingdom. They must also have proven their ability as individual research workers.

Level of Study: Postdoctorate.

Type: Fellowship.

Value: Awards are based on the United Kingdom universities non clinical academic and related research staff scale and are related to age when taking up an appointment. Up to UK£10,000 per year is also available for small items of equipment, consumables and United Kingdom fieldwork. Funding for specified overseas fieldwork can also be requested.

Length of Study: Depends on the individual scheme, but it is generally up to five years with a possible extension of a further five years.

Frequency: Annual.

Study Establishment: Universities and other approved research institutes.

Country of Study: United Kingdom.

No. of awards offered: Varies.

Application Procedure: Applicants must refer to the fellowship handbook and application forms available via the NERC website.

Closing Date: November 15th.

Funding: Government.

No. of awards given last year: Nine.

Additional Information: All applications must carry the full support of the host institution, which will be expected to act as the Fellows employer. As part of NERC's commitment to promoting equal opportunities, all fellowships may be held by suitably qualified candidates on a full or part-time basis, subject to the agreement of the host institution. The NERC is particularly keen to attract applications from scientists in the areas of applied mathematics, physics or strongly quantitative disciplines wishing to develop a career in environmental science.

NERC Postdoctoral Research Fellowships

Subjects: The sciences of the natural environment.

Purpose: To enable a small number of outstanding research workers to devote the majority of their time to research so that they may further develop their research potential.

Eligibility: Candidates must hold a PhD or be able to demonstrate equivalent and relevant research experience. Applications will be accepted from PhD students but, if successful, awards may not start until NERC has received written confirmation of the outcome of the applicant's PhD viva. However, applicants are advised that some post PhD experience can be an advantage when seeking a postdoctoral fellowship.

Level of Study: Postdoctorate, Postgraduate.

Type: Fellowship.

Value: Awards are based on the United Kingdom universities non clinical academic and related research staff scale. Starting salary is related to age when taking up appointment, UK£8,500 per year is also available for the purchase of small items of equipment, consumables and UK field work. Funding for specified overseas fieldwork can also be requested.

Length of Study: Three years, with the possibility of extension for up to two further years.

Frequency: Annual.

Study Establishment: At universities and other approved research institutes.

Country of Study: United Kingdom.

No. of awards offered: Varies.

Application Procedure: Applicants must refer to the fellowship handbook and application forms available via the NERC website.

Closing Date: November 15th.

Funding: Government.

No. of awards given last year: 18.

Additional Information: All applications must carry the full support of the host institution, which will be expected to act as the Fellows employer. As part of the NERC's commitment to promoting equal opportunities, all fellowships may be held by suitably qualified candidates on a full or part-time basis, subject to the agreement of the host institution. The NERC is particularly keen to attract applications from scientists in the areas of mathematics, physics or other strongly quantitative disciplines wishing to develop a career in environmental science.

NERC Research Studentships

Subjects: Environmental sciences.

Purpose: To enable students to receive training in methods of research and to undertake research in particular scientific areas under the guidance of named supervisors.

Eligibility: Open to persons who, at the closing date of application for an award, have been ordinarily resident in Great Britain or Northern Ireland throughout the three year period preceding that date. Ordinarily resident means that no period of the candidate's residence during those three years has been wholly, or mainly, for the purpose of receiving full-time education. Candidates must hold a First or Upper Second Class (Honours) Degree in an appropriate branch of science or technology. NERC also accepts qualifications, or a combination of qualifications and experience, which demonstrate equivalent ability and attainment. A less than sufficient first degree may be enhanced to meet the requirements by the acquisition of: a) a Masters degree to enhance the first degree by one step, e.g. from 2(ii) to 2(i) and/or b) substantial relevant postgraduate work experience, i.e. a minimum of two and a half years full time equivalent to enhance a degree by one step, five years equivalent to enhance by two steps. The postgraduate work experience must relate to the discipline of the first degree, a subsequent Masters degree or the intended area of postgraduate study. There is no age limit for studentships but the Council reserves the right to decline an application from a candidate if it considers that an award would not represent a good investment of public funds.

Level of Study: Postgraduate.

Type: Studentship.

Value: A maintenance grant of UK£12,000 per year for students outside London and UK£14,000 per year for students in London, the payment of approved fees and assistance with travel and subsistence expenses under specified conditions eg. fieldwork.

Length of Study: Up to three years, part of which may be spent at an institution in Europe.

Frequency: Annual.

Study Establishment: Any approved Institute of Higher Education.

Country of Study: Other.

No. of awards offered: Varies, approx. 310.

Application Procedure: Applications must be submitted by the head of the department in which the student proposes to work. Applications will not be accepted directly from individual candidates. To encourage research students to gain additional experience outside the academic sphere some of these awards are made as Co-operative Awards in Sciences of the Environment (CASE Studentships). CASE awards involve the joint supervision of the student by a member of staff of an academic institution and a scientist from industry, a public authority or government research institute.

Closing Date: November 1st for departments to apply for quotas, July 31st for student nominations.

Funding: Government.

No. of awards given last year: 366.

Additional Information: It is expected that the awards will lead to the submission of a PhD thesis.

NATURAL HISTORY MUSEUM

Cromwell Road, London, SW7 5BD, England
Tel: (44) 20 7942 5530
Fax: (44) 20 7942 5841
Email: l.houseago@nhm.ac.uk
www: http://www.nhm.ac.uk/science
Contact: L Houseago, Liaison Officer

The Natural History Museum's mission is to maintain and develop its collections and use them to promote the discovery, understanding, responsible use and enjoyment of the natural world.

Natural History Museum Sys-Resource

Subjects: Biomedical sciences to explain the taxonomy, molecular diversity, distribution and ecology of various organisms detrimental to human and animal health, the impact of mineralogical, geochemical and human disturbances on environmental quality, earth materials, history and processes to study the properties and relationships of minerals, meteorites, rocks and fossils so as to further the understanding of the origin of the Earth. Other areas of interest are ecological patterns and processes to investigate the distribution of organisms in space and through time and the processes by which these patterns are generated, thereby providing a sound scientific basis for the conservation and management of biological diversity, fauna and flora to make known the diversity of the natural world through description and naming of animals and plants with particular emphasis on those from threatened habitats and systematics and to discover and investigate the broad patterns of biodiversity and evolution as a foundation for comparative biology and its uses.

Purpose: To provide access for researchers so that they can undertake short visits to utilise the facilities of the Natural History Museum and its associates, the Royal Botanical Gardens, Kew and the Linnean Society.

Eligibility: Open to applicants from the European Union member states, and associated and accession states.

Level of Study: Doctorate, Postdoctorate, Research.

Value: International travel, accommodation, local travel and subsistence along with all access and facility costs.

Length of Study: Up to 60 working days.

Frequency: Twice a year.

Study Establishment: The Natural History Museum, London.

Country of Study: United Kingdom.

No. of awards offered: 25 per call.

Application Procedure: Applicants must contact the Natural History Museum by telephone, email or via the website.

Closing Date: Please refer to the website.

Funding: Government.

Contributor: The European Union IHP Programme.

No. of awards given last year: 51.

No. of applicants last year: 250.

Additional Information: During the visit the user is assigned a mentor, according to their speciality. The role of the mentor is to familiarise the user with the department, collections and facilities and to give training where necessary. The visits are often collaborative in which case the mentor will work directly with the user. Please note that projects which include one of the associated institutions must be collaborative with the Natural History Museum.

NATURAL SCIENCES AND ENGINEERING RESEARCH COUNCIL OF CANADA (NSERC)

350 Albert Street, Ottawa, ON, K1A 1H5, Canada
Tel: (1) 613 995 5521
Fax: (1) 613 996 2589
Email: schol@nserc.ca
www: http://www.nserc.ca
Contact: Corporate Account Executive

NSERC is Canada's instrument for promoting and supporting university research in the natural sciences and engineering, other than the health sciences. NSERC supports both basic university research through discovery grants and project research through partnerships among universities, governments and the private sector, as well as the advanced training of highly qualified people.

NSERC Canada Graduate Scholarship

Subjects: Engineering or natural sciences.

Purpose: To provide financial support to the most outstanding scholars high calibre scholars who are or will be engaged in Master's or doctoral level studies in the natural sciences or engineering.

Eligibility: Open to Canadian citizens or permanent residents who will undertake a programme of postgraduate studies and research leading to an advanced degree. Specific eligibility conditions apply for PGS/CGS Masters and PGS Doctoral awards. Applicants must have obtained a first class average in the last two completed years of study.

Level of Study: Doctorate, Graduate, Postgraduate, Predoctorate.

Type: Scholarship.

Value: The PGS/CGS Master's is Canadian $17,500 per year for two years, and the PGS is Canadian $35,000 per year for two years.

Length of Study: Two years for the MSc or PhD, with a possibility of renewal for a further two years for PhDs only, One year for the MSc; up to three years for PhD study.

Frequency: Annual.

Study Establishment: Universities.

Country of Study: Canada.

No. of awards offered: 600 Masters, 600 Doctoral.

Application Procedure: Applicants must complete application form 200. Applicants who are, or have recently been, registered at a Canadian university must submit their application through the graduate studies office of the university. There may be an earlier deadline at the university for these applications.

Closing Date: November 15th.

Funding: Government.

Additional Information: The information provided here is subject to change. Please visit the NSERC's website for up to date information.

NSERC Doctoral Prizes

Subjects: Engineering or natural sciences.

Purpose: To recognise high quality research conducted by students completing their doctoral degree in the relevant field.

Eligibility: Open to doctoral students who have successfully defended their doctoral thesis between September 6th of the previous year and September 5th of the current year and are either Canadian citizens or permanent residents in Canada at the time of nomination. Candidates must be nominated by their university.

Level of Study: Doctorate.

Type: Prize.

Value: Canadian $10,000 per student.

Length of Study: Varies.

Frequency: Annual.

Study Establishment: Any university.

Country of Study: Canada.

No. of awards offered: Up to four.

Application Procedure: Deans of Graduate Studies at Canadian Universities can nominate one eligible candidate from each of the two categories.

Closing Date: October 2nd.

Funding: Government.

Additional Information: The information provided here is subject to change. Please visit the NSERC's website for up to date information.

NSERC Industrial Research Fellowships (IRF)

Subjects: Industrial research and development within the natural sciences and engineering disciplines.

Purpose: To encourage highly qualified scientists and engineers to seek careers in Canadian industry to promote awareness in Canadian industry of the capabilities of Canadian universities and university research; and to facilitate the transfer of technology and expertise.

Eligibility: Open to Canadian citizens or permanent residents who have recently completed a doctorate degree and who are seeking postdoctoral employment in industry in Canada for the first time.

Level of Study: Postdoctorate.

Type: Fellowship.

Value: NSERC's contribution to the Fellow's salary is Canadian $30,000 per year for two years, plus a company contribution of a minimum of Canadian $10,000 per year.

Length of Study: Two years maximum.

Frequency: Approx. every three months.

Study Establishment: Approved Canadian industrial organisations.

Country of Study: Canada.

No. of awards offered: 80 annually.

Application Procedure: Applicants must negotiate the terms of employment and proposed research with the sponsoring industrial organisation. Form 200 is to be completed by the candidate and their referees, and Form 183C must be completed by the nominating organisation. Both forms should be submitted together by the nominating organisation. Please refer to the NSERC website for further details.

Closing Date: Varies, please visit the website.

Funding: Government.

Contributor: NSERC.

No. of awards given last year: 84.

No. of applicants last year: 103.

Additional Information: There are four competitions each year. The information provided here is subject to change. Please visit the NSERC's website for up to date information.

NSERC Postdoctoral Fellowships

Subjects: Engineering or natural sciences.

Purpose: To provide support to a core of the most promising researchers at a pivotal time in their careers. The fellowships are also intended to secure a supply of highly qualified Canadians with leading edge scientific and research skills for Canadian industry, government and universities.

Eligibility: Open to Canadian citizens or permanent residents residing in Canada, who have recently received, or will shortly receive a PhD in one of the fields of research that NSERC supports.

Level of Study: Postdoctorate.

Type: Fellowship.

Value: Canadian $40,000 per year.

Length of Study: One year, renewable for one additional year.

Frequency: Annual.

Study Establishment: A university or research institution of the Fellow's choice.

Country of Study: Any country.

Application Procedure: Applicants must complete Form 200. Information is available on request.

Closing Date: November 15th. There may be earlier deadlines at the department from which you have, or will, obtain your PhD.

Funding: Government.

Additional Information: The information provided here is subject to change. Please visit the NSERC's website for up to date information.

NSERC Postgraduate Scholarships

Subjects: Engineering or natural sciences.

Purpose: To provide financial support to high calibre scholars who are or will be engaged in Master's or doctoral level studies in the natural sciences or engineering.

Eligibility: Open to Canadian citizens or permanent residents who will undertake a programme of postgraduate studies and research leading to an advanced degree. Specific eligibility conditions apply for PGS/CGS Masters' and PGS Doctoral awards. Applicants must have obtained a first class average in the last two completed years of study.

Level of Study: Doctorate, Graduate, Postgraduate, Predoctorate.

Type: Scholarship.

Value: The PGS Master's is Canadian $17,300 per year for two years, and the PGS Doctoral is Canadian $21,000 per year for two years.

Length of Study: Two years for the MSc or PhD, with a possibility of renewal for a further two years for PhDs only.

Frequency: Annual.

Study Establishment: Universities.

No. of awards offered: 1700 app.

Application Procedure: Applicants must complete application form 200. Applicants who are, or have recently been, registered at a Canadian university must submit their application through the graduate studies office of the university. There may be an earlier deadline at the university for these applications.

Closing Date: November 15th.

Funding: Government.

Additional Information: The information provided here is subject to change. Please visit the NSERC's website for up to date information.

NETHERLANDS ORGANISATION FOR INTERNATIONAL CO-OPERATION IN HIGHER EDUCATION (NUFFIC)

PO Box 29777, The Hague, NL-2502 LT, Netherlands
Email: nuffic@nuffic.nl
www: http://www.nuffic.nl
Contact: Ms Rosalien van Santen, Information Officer

Since its founding in 1952, the Netherlands Organisation for International Co-operation in Higher Education (NUFFIC) has been an independent non-profit organisation. Its mission is to foster international co-operation in higher education. Special attention is given to development co-operation.

European Development Fund Awards for Citizens of ACP Countries

Subjects: All subjects.

Eligibility: Open to citizens of African, Caribbean and Pacific countries associated with the European Union.

Level of Study: Unrestricted.

Value: Course fees, books and field trips, international travel expenses, insurance, a monthly allowance and a stipend to cover the initial expense of becoming established.

Length of Study: For the duration of the course.

Country of Study: Other.

No. of awards offered: Varies.

Application Procedure: Applicants must obtain information and application forms from the Netherlands Embassy in the candidate's country and the European Union Delegations and offices of the Commission. The application should be submitted through the candidate's employer and government.

Closing Date: Please contact the Commission for details.

Additional Information: NUFFIC does not administer these awards and will not accept applications. Delegations of the Commission can be found usually in the capital cities of Angola, Barbados and the Eastern Caribbean, Benin, Botswana, Burkina Faso, Burundi, Cameroon, Cape Verde, Central African Republic, Chad, the Democratic Republic of the Congo, the Republic of the Congo, Cûte d'Ivoire, Djibouti, the Dominican Republic, Eritrea, Ethiopia, Gabon, Gambia, Ghana, Guinea, Guinea Bissau, Guyana, Haiti, Jamaica, Kenya, Lesotho, Liberia, Madagascar, Malawi, Mali, Mauritania, Mauritius, Mozambique, Namibia, Niger, Nigeria, Papua New Guinea, Rwanda, Senegal, Sierra Leone, the Solomon Islands, Somalia, Sudan, Surinam, Swaziland, Tanzania, Togo, Trinidad and Tobago, Uganda, Zambia and Zimbabwe. Offices of the Commission can be found in Antigua and Barbuda, the Bahamas, Belize, Comoros, Equatorial Guinea, Netherlands Antilles and Aruba, New Caledonia, Samoa, Sao Tome and Principe, Seychelles, Tonga and Vanuatu.

NFP Netherlands Fellowships Programme of Development Co-operation

Subjects: All subjects offered by the Institutes for International Education in the Netherlands.

Purpose: To develop human potential through education and training mainly in the Netherlands with a view to diminishing qualitative and quantitative deficiencies in the availability of trained manpower in developing countries.

Eligibility: Open to candidates who have the education and work experience required for the course, as well as an adequate command of the language in which it is conducted. This is usually English but sometimes French. The age limit is 40 for men and 45 for women. It is intended that candidates, upon completion of training, return to their home countries and resume their jobs. When several candidates with comparable qualifications apply, priority will be given to women. Candidates for a fellowship must be nominated by their employer and formal employment should be continued during the fellowship period.

Level of Study: Postgraduate.

Type: Fellowship.

Value: Normal living expenses, fees and health insurance. International travel expenses are provided only when the course lasts three months or longer.

Length of Study: For the duration of the course.

Country of Study: Netherlands.

No. of awards offered: Varies.

Application Procedure: Applicants must contact the Netherlands Embassy in their own country for information on nationality eligibility and on the application procedure. Information on the courses for which the fellowships are available can be obtained from the website.

Funding: Government.

Additional Information: As a rule the candidate's government is required to state its formal support, except in the case of certain development orientated non government organisations. Further information is available from the website http://www.studyin.nl.

THE NETHERLANDS ORGANISATION FOR SCIENTIFIC RESEARCH (NWO)

Lann van Nieuw Oost Indie 131, PO Box 93138, The Hague, NL-2509 AC, Netherlands
Tel: (31) 70 344 0852
Fax: (31) 70 385 0971
Email: nwo@nwo.nl
www: http://www.nwo.nl
Contact: Mr Weyma, Head Of Central Programmes

The Netherlands Organisation for Scientific Research (NWO) is the central Dutch organisation in the field of fundamental and strategic scientific research. NWO encompasses all fields of scholarship and consequently plays a key role in the development of science, technology and culture in the Netherlands. NWO is an independent organisation which acts as the national research council in the

Netherlands. NWO is the largest national sponsor of fundamental scientific research undertaken in the 13 Dutch universities and provides many types of funding for research driven by intellectual curiosity.

TALENT Programme

Subjects: All subjects.

Purpose: To assist students who wish to conduct research at a reputable research institute outside the Netherlands. The programme is designed to make a major contribution to the market value of the recipients of TALENT scholarships.

Eligibility: Open to highly qualified, young postdoctoral students who are Dutch nationals or permanent residents of the Netherlands.

Level of Study: Postdoctorate.

Type: Scholarship.

Value: Varies.

Length of Study: Up to one year.

Frequency: Three times each year.

Study Establishment: A university or research institute.

Country of Study: Any country outside the Netherlands.

No. of awards offered: Varies.

Application Procedure: Applicants must contact Mr A Wiegel at the Central Programmes and Institutes Department for details, on (31) 70 344 0644.

Closing Date: January 15th, May 15th or October 15th.

Funding: Government.

No. of awards given last year: 42.

No. of applicants last year: 79.

THE NEUROBLASTOMA SOCIETY

Beverley House, Frilford, Abingdon, Oxfordshire, OX13 5NU, England
Tel: (44) 1865 391207
Email: antonya@cooperox.org.uk
www: http://www.nsoc.co.uk
Contact: Ms Antonya Cooper, Chairman

The Neuroblastoma Society was started in 1982 by a group of parents with children affected by neuroblastoma. The aim is to raise money to fund medical research towards better treatment and an eventual cure of this aggressive childhood tumour. The Society also aims to offer support to families affected by the disease.

Neuroblastoma Society Research Grants

Subjects: Paediatric oncology specifically in neuroblastoma.

Purpose: To fund clinical research towards improvements in treatment and a cure for neuroblastoma.

Eligibility: There are no age or nationality restrictions but candidates must be based in the United Kingdom.

Value: Up to UK£150,000.

Length of Study: Two-three years.

Frequency: Every two years.

Study Establishment: A reputable research institution, usually a university or hospital.

Country of Study: United Kingdom.

No. of awards offered: Usually three-four.

Application Procedure: Applicants must apply to the Society for the terms of grant application.

Closing Date: December 31st.

Funding: Private.

Contributor: Members of the Society.

No. of awards given last year: Three.

No. of applicants last year: Six.

NEW SOUTH WALES CANCER COUNCIL

PO Box 572, Kings Cross, NSW 2011, Australia
Tel: (61) 2 9334 1735
Fax: (61) 2 9326 9328
Email: gillianm@nswcc.org.au
www: http://www.cancercouncil.com.au
Contact: Ms Gillian Mackay, Programme Co-ordinator, Cancer Control Network

The New South Wales Cancer Council is one of the leading cancer charity organisation in New South Wales. Their mission is to defeat cancer and to do that they are working to build a cancer smart community. In building a cancer smart community, the Council undertakes high quality research and is an advocate on cancer issues, providing information and services to the public and raising funds for cancer programmes.

New South Wales Cancer Council Research Programme Grant

Subjects: Cancer research.
Purpose: To provide relatively long-term, flexible support for cancer researchers.
Eligibility: Open to investigators with a sufficient record of research achievement in any field of cancer research.
Level of Study: Unrestricted.
Type: Research grant.
Value: Varies, depending on requirements.
Length of Study: Three-five years, potentially renewable based on results.
Frequency: Varies, depending on other priorities.
Study Establishment: An approved institution in New South Wales.
Country of Study: Australia.
No. of awards offered: Varies.
Application Procedure: Applicants must complete an application form, available on request or from the website.
Funding: Private.
Contributor: Community fund raising.
No. of awards given last year: Three.
No. of applicants last year: 32.

New South Wales Cancer Council Research Project Grants

Subjects: All aspects of cancer which elucidate its origin, cause and control at a fundamental and applied level. Grants are open to all research disciplines relevant to cancer including behavioural, bio-medical, clinical, epidemiological, psychosocial and health services.
Eligibility: Open to Australian residents from New South Wales. Recipients of tobacco sponsorship are ineligible.
Level of Study: Unrestricted.
Type: Research grant.
Value: Varies, depending on requirements.
Length of Study: One-three years.
Frequency: Annual.
Study Establishment: An approved institution in New South Wales.
Country of Study: Australia.
No. of awards offered: Varies.
Application Procedure: Applicants must complete an application form, available on request or from the website.
Closing Date: Early May. Please visit the website for confirmation.
Funding: Private.
Contributor: Community fund raising.
No. of awards given last year: Six.
No. of applicants last year: 68.

NEW YORK STATE HISTORICAL ASSOCIATION

PO Box 800, Lake Road, Cooperstown, NY 13326-0800, United States of America
Tel: (1) 607 547 1491
Fax: (1) 607 547 1405
Email: goodwind@nysha.org
www: http://www.nysha.org
Contact: Mr Daniel Goodwin, Editor

The mission of the New York State Historical Association is to instil and cultivate, in a broad public audience, an informed appreciation of the diversity of the American past, especially as represented and exemplified by the history of New York State, in order to better understand the present.

Dixon Ryan Fox Manuscript Prize of the New York State Historical Association

Subjects: The history of New York State.
Purpose: To honour the best unpublished book length monograph.
Eligibility: Open to nationals of any country. Biographies and edited volumes may be included. Fiction and poetry are not eligible entries.
Level of Study: Doctorate, Postdoctorate, Postgraduate, Professional development.
Type: Prize.
Value: US$3,000 plus assistance in publishing.
Length of Study: Dependent on the book length.
Frequency: Annual.
Country of Study: Other.
No. of awards offered: One.
Application Procedure: Applicants must submit two copies of the manuscript, typed and double spaced with at least one inch margins.
Closing Date: January 20th.
Funding: Private.
No. of awards given last year: One.
No. of applicants last year: Fighteen

NEW ZEALAND COMMONWEALTH SCHOLARSHIPS AND FELLOWSHIPS COMMITTEE

PO Box 11-915, Wellington, New Zealand
Tel: (64) 4 381 8510
Fax: (64) 4 381 8501
Email: schols@nzvcc.ac.nz
www: http://www.nzvcc.ac.nz
Contact: Scholarships Officer

The New Zealand Commonwealth Scholarships and Fellowships Committee is a secretariat which provides administrative and policy services to the eight vice chancellors of the New Zealand Universities.

New Zealand Commonwealth Scholarships

Subjects: Study undertaken should be of developmental relevance to the candidate's home country.
Purpose: To enable persons of high intellectual promise to study in New Zealand in the expectation that they will make a significant contribution to life in their own countries on their return.
Eligibility: Open to graduates who are citizens of a Commonwealth country and who have graduated within the last five years.
Level of Study: Postgraduate.
Type: Scholarship.
Value: New Zealand $14,400 per annum plus travel and allowances.
Length of Study: Up to three years.
Frequency: Annual.
Country of Study: New Zealand.
No. of awards offered: Approx. 10.
Application Procedure: Applicants must send nominations to the appropriate agency in their home country.
Closing Date: Differs from country to country. Applications close in New Zealand on July 31st.
Funding: Government.
Contributor: NZAID-New Zealand Agency for International Development.
Additional Information: Scholarships fall within the framework of the Commonwealth Scholarship and Fellowship Plan.

NEW ZEALAND VICE-CHANCELLORS COMMITTEE (NZVCC)

PO Box 11-915, Wellington, New Zealand
Tel: (64) 4 381 8510
Fax: (64) 4 381 8501
Contact: Scholarships Officer

Claude McCarthy Fellowships

Subjects: Open.
Purpose: To enable graduates of a New Zealand university to undertake original work or research.
Eligibility: Open to any graduate of a New Zealand university.
Level of Study: Doctorate, Postgraduate.
Type: Fellowship.
Value: Varies, according to country of residence during tenure, and the project itself. Assistance for expenses incurred in travel, employment of technical staff, special equipment, etc. may be provided.
Length of Study: Usually no more than one year.
Frequency: Annual.
Country of Study: Any country.
No. of awards offered: Varies, depending upon funds available, but there is usually 12-15.
Application Procedure: Applicants must write for details.
Closing Date: August 1st.
Funding: Private.
Contributor: The Claude McCarthy Trust.
Additional Information: Further information is available on request.

Gordon Watson Scholarship

Subjects: International relationships or social and economic conditions.
Purpose: To facilitate study abroad.
Eligibility: Candidates must be New Zealand citizens or permanent residents. Open to holders of an Honours Degree, or a degree in theology from a university in New Zealand. Candidates must undertake to return to New Zealand after the scholarship period for not less than two years.
Level of Study: Postgraduate.
Type: Scholarship.
Value: New Zealand $12,000 per year.
Length of Study: Three years.
Frequency: Annual.
Study Establishment: Any approved university.
Country of Study: Other.
No. of awards offered: One per annum.
Application Procedure: Applicants must write for details.
Closing Date: October 1st.
Funding: Private.
Contributor: The Gordon Watson Trust.
Additional Information: Further information is available on request.

L B Wood Travelling Scholarship

Subjects: All subjects.
Purpose: To allow graduates to undertake doctoral studies in the United Kingdom.
Eligibility: Open to all holders of postgraduate scholarships from any faculty of any university in New Zealand, provided that application is made within three years of the date of graduation.
Level of Study: Doctorate.
Type: Scholarship.
Value: New Zealand $3,000 per year, as a supplement to another postgraduate scholarship.
Length of Study: Up to three years.
Frequency: Annual.
Study Establishment: A university or institution of university rank.
Country of Study: United Kingdom.
No. of awards offered: One.
Application Procedure: Applicants must write for details.
Closing Date: October 1st.
Funding: Private.
Contributor: The L B Wood Trust.
Additional Information: Further information is available on request.

Shirtcliffe Fellowship

Subjects: Arts, science, law, commerce or agriculture.
Purpose: To provide further aid for New Zealand doctoral students.
Eligibility: Open to graduates of New Zealand universities.
Level of Study: Doctorate.
Type: Fellowship.

Value: New Zealand $2,000 as a supplement to the postgraduate scholarship emolument.
Length of Study: Up to three years.
Frequency: Annual.
Study Establishment: A suitable Institute of Higher Education.
Country of Study: Other.
No. of awards offered: Three.
Application Procedure: Applicants must write for details.
Closing Date: October 1st.
Funding: Private.
Additional Information: Further information is available on request.

William Georgetti Scholarships

Subjects: All subjects.
Purpose: To encourage postgraduate study and research in a field which is important to the social, cultural or economic development of New Zealand.
Eligibility: Candidates must be New Zealand citizens or permanent residents. Open to graduates who have been resident in New Zealand for five years immediately before application and who are preferably aged between 21 and 28.
Level of Study: Postgraduate.
Type: Scholarship.
Value: Up to NZD$7,500 for study in New Zealand and up to NZD$15,000 for study overseas.
Frequency: Annual.
Study Establishment: Suitable universities.
Country of Study: Any country.
No. of awards offered: Varies.
Application Procedure: Applicants must write for details.
Closing Date: October 1st.
Funding: Private.
Contributor: The Georgetti Trust.
Additional Information: Further information is available on request.

NEWBERRY LIBRARY

60 West Walton Street, Chicago, IL 60610, United States of America
Tel: (1) 312 255 3666
Fax: (1) 312 255 3680
Email: research@newberry.org
www: http://www.newberry.org
Contact: Ms Krista Geier, Programme Assistant

The Newberry Library, open to the public without charge, is an independent research library and educational institution dedicated to the expansion and dissemination of knowledge in the humanities. With a broad range of books and manuscripts relating to the civilisations of Western Europe and the Americas, the Library's mission is to acquire and preserve research collections of such material, and to provide for and promote their effective use by a diverse community of users.

American Society for Eighteenth-Century Studies (ASECS) Fellowship

Subjects: Arts and humanities from 1660-1815.
Purpose: To support scholars wanting to use the Newberry's collections.
Eligibility: Open to members of the Society. The award is limited to scholars from outside the Chicago area.
Level of Study: Doctorate, Postdoctorate.
Type: Fellowship.
Value: US$1,200 per month, pro-rata.
Length of Study: One month.
Frequency: Annual.
Study Establishment: The Newberry Library.
Country of Study: United States of America.
No. of awards offered: One.
Application Procedure: Applicants must submit a completed application form, a description of the project and three letters of reference.
Closing Date: February 15th.
Funding: Private.
Contributor: ASECS.

No. of awards given last year: One.
No. of applicants last year: 28.

For further information contact:

60 W. Walton, Chicago, IL 60610, United States of America
Contact: Committee on Awards, The Newberry Library

Annette Kade Fellowship in French or German Studies in the Middle Ages or Renaissance

Subjects: Medieval or early modern French or German studies.
Eligibility: Open to applicants with a PhD at the dissertation stage enrolled at a Newberry Library Centre for Renaissance Studies consortium member university.
Level of Study: Doctorate.
Type: Fellowship.
Value: US$30,000.
Length of Study: 12 months, consisting of six months of residential research at the Library, followed by six months of tenure at a library or other archival institution in Germany or France.
Frequency: Annual.
Study Establishment: The Newberry Library.
Country of Study: Other.
No. of awards offered: One.
Application Procedure: Applicants must visit the website for application forms and details.
Closing Date: January 15th.
Funding: Private.
Contributor: The Annette Kade Charitable Trust.

For further information contact:

60 W. Walton, Chicago, IL 60610, United States of America
Contact: Committee on Awards, The Newberry Library

Arthur Weinberg Fellowship for Independent Scholars

Subjects: Humanities.
Purpose: To assist Scholars working outside the academy who have demonstrated excellence through publishing and are working in a field appropriate to the Newberry's collections.
Eligibility: Open to all Scholars but preference is given to those working on historical issues related to social justice or reform.
Level of Study: Unrestricted.
Type: Fellowship.
Value: US$1,200.
Length of Study: One month.
Frequency: Annual.
Study Establishment: The Newberry Library.
Country of Study: United States of America.
No. of awards offered: Varies.
Application Procedure: Applicants must write for details. Application forms may also be downloaded from the website.
Closing Date: February 15th.
Funding: Private.

For further information contact:

60 W. Walton, Chicago, IL 60610, United States of America
Contact: Committee on Awards, The Newberry Library

Audrey Lumsden-Kouvel Fellowship

Subjects: Late medieval or renaissance studies.
Purpose: To enable scholars to use the Newberry's extensive holdings. The fellowship is intended to encourage Scholars to pursue research at the Newberry during sabbaticals.
Eligibility: Open to postdoctoral scholars wishing to carry out extended research. Applicants must plan to be in continuous residence for at least three months. Preference will be given to projects focusing on romance cultures.
Level of Study: Postdoctorate.
Type: Fellowship.
Value: US$4,000.
Length of Study: At least three months.
Frequency: Annual.
Study Establishment: The Newberry Library.

Country of Study: United States of America.
No. of awards offered: One.
Application Procedure: Applicants must write for details. Application forms may also be downloaded from the website.
Closing Date: February 15th.
Funding: Private.
No. of awards given last year: One.
No. of applicants last year: 31.

For further information contact:

60 W. Walton, Chicago, IL 60610, United States of America
Contact: Committee on Awards, The Newberry Library

Center for Great Lakes Culture/Michigan State University Fellowship

Subjects: The cultural history and expressions of the diverse peoples of the Great Lakes or the Ohio Valley region eg. Michigan, Illinois, Wisconsin, Minnesota, Ohio, Indiana, West Virginia, Kentucky and Ontario.
Purpose: To support projects using the Newberry Library collections.
Eligibility: Open to scholars with a PhD or the equivalent or an established record of scholarly research. Candidates for degrees are not eligible. The award is limited to scholars from outside the Chicago area.
Level of Study: Postdoctorate.
Type: Fellowship.
Value: US$1,250.
Length of Study: One month.
Frequency: Annual.
Study Establishment: The Newberry Library.
Country of Study: United States of America.
No. of awards offered: Two.
Application Procedure: Applicants must write for details. Application forms may also be downloaded from the website.
Closing Date: February 15th.
Funding: Government, Private.
Contributor: The Center for Great Lakes Culture and Michigan State University.
No. of awards given last year: Two.
No. of applicants last year: Seven.

For further information contact:

60 W. Walton, Chicago, IL 60610, United States of America
Contact: Committee on Awards, The Newberry Library

Committee on Institutional Co-operation Faculty Fellowship

Subjects: American Indian studies.
Purpose: To support research at the Newberry by CIC faculty.
Eligibility: Open to faculty members of a CIC institution.
Level of Study: Postdoctorate.
Type: Fellowship.
Value: US$35,000.
Length of Study: A minimum of nine months.
Frequency: Annual.
Study Establishment: The Newberry Library.
Country of Study: United States of America.
No. of awards offered: One.
Application Procedure: Applicants must contact the CIC programme at the D'Arcy McNickle Centre for American Indian history on mcnickle@newberry.org.
Closing Date: January 6th.
Funding: Government, Private.
Contributor: The Committee on Institutional Co-operation.
Additional Information: In addition to carrying out this independent research, the CIC Faculty Fellow will lead a Spring seminar at the Library for graduate students at CIC institutions on a topic appropriate to the Newberry's collections and the expertise of the fellow.

For further information contact:

60 W. Walton, Chicago, IL 60610, United States of America
Contact: Committee on Awards, The Newberry Library

Committee on Institutional Co-operation Graduate Student Fellowship

Subjects: American Indian studies.
Purpose: To support dissertation research.
Eligibility: Open to graduate students at CIC institutions.
Level of Study: Doctorate.
Type: Fellowship.
Value: US$1,500 per month.
Length of Study: Up to three months.
Frequency: Annual.
Study Establishment: The Newberry Library.
Country of Study: United States of America.
No. of awards offered: Varies.
Application Procedure: Applicants must contact the CIC programme at the D'Arcy McNickle Centre for American Indian history at mcnickle@newberry.org.
Closing Date: January 6th.
Funding: Government, Private.
Contributor: Committee on Institutional Co-operation, Newberry Library.

For further information contact:

60 W. Walton, Chicago, IL 60610, United States of America
Contact: Committee on Awards, The Newberry Library

Frances C Allen Fellowships

Subjects: Humanities or social sciences.
Purpose: To encourage women of American Indian heritage in their studies through financial support.
Eligibility: Open to women of American Indian heritage who are pursuing an academic programme in any graduate or pre-professional field.
Level of Study: Graduate, Postgraduate.
Type: Fellowship.
Value: Varies according to need and may include travel expenses. Up to US$8,000 in approved expenses is available.
Length of Study: One month-one year.
Frequency: Annual.
Study Establishment: The Newberry Library.
Country of Study: United States of America.
No. of awards offered: Varies.
Application Procedure: Applicants must write for details. Application forms may also be downloaded from the website.
Closing Date: February 15th.
Funding: Private.
Contributor: The Frances C Allen Fund.
No. of awards given last year: Four.
No. of applicants last year: Six.
Additional Information: Allen Fellows are expected to spend a significant part of their tenure in residence at the Newberry's D'Arcy McNickle Centre for American Indian History.

For further information contact:

60 W. Walton, Chicago, IL 60610, United States of America
Contact: Committee on Awards, The Newberry Library

Herzog August Bibliothek Wolfenbüttel Fellowship

Subjects: Humanities.
Purpose: To enable a period of residence in Wolfenbüttel, Germany for study of the collections housed in the Herzog August Bibliothek.
Level of Study: Postdoctorate.
Type: Fellowship.
Value: Please contact the organisation.
Length of Study: Three months.
Frequency: Annual.
Study Establishment: The Herzog August Bibliothek in Wolfenbüttel.
Country of Study: Germany.
No. of awards offered: One.
Application Procedure: Applicants must write for details. Application forms may also be downloaded from the website.
Closing Date: January 15th for linked long-term fellowship, February 15th for linked short-term fellowship.
Funding: Private.

For further information contact:

60 W. Walton, Chicago, IL 60610, United States of America
Contact: Committee on Awards, The Newberry Library

Lester J Cappon Fellowship in Documentary Editing

Subjects: Editing and archiving.
Purpose: To support historical editing projects based on Newberry materials.
Eligibility: Open to Scholars who live outside the Chicago area.
Level of Study: Postdoctorate.
Type: Fellowship.
Value: Up to US$5,000.
Length of Study: Varies.
Frequency: Annual.
Study Establishment: The Newberry Library.
Country of Study: United States of America.
No. of awards offered: One.
Application Procedure: Applicants must write for details. Application forms may also be downloaded from the website.
Closing Date: February 15th.
Funding: Private.
Contributor: Lester J Cappon.
No. of awards given last year: One.
No. of applicants last year: Eight.

For further information contact:

60 W. Walton, Chicago, IL 60610, United States of America
Contact: Committee on Awards, The Newberry Library

Lloyd Lewis Fellowship in American History

Subjects: Any field of American history appropriate to the collections of the Newberry Library.
Eligibility: Open to established scholars, holding a PhD, who have demonstrated excellence in the field through publications. Foreign nationals may apply if they have resided in the United States for three or more years.
Level of Study: Postdoctorate.
Type: Fellowship.
Value: Up to US$40,000.
Length of Study: 6-11 months.
Frequency: Annual.
Study Establishment: The Newberry Library.
Country of Study: United States of America.
No. of awards offered: Varies.
Application Procedure: Applicants must write for details. Application forms may also be downloaded from the website.
Closing Date: January 15th.
Funding: Private.
Contributor: The Lloyd Lewis Memorial Fund.
No. of awards given last year: One.
No. of applicants last year: 24.
Additional Information: Lewis Fellows participate in the Library's scholarly community through regular participation in seminars, colloquia and other events. Lewis Fellowships may be combined with sabbaticals or other stipendiary support. Applicants may ask to be considered for NEH and Mellon Fellowships at the time of their application.

For further information contact:

60 W. Walton, Chicago, IL 60610, United States of America
Contact: Committee on Awards, The Newberry Library

Mellon Postdoctoral Research Fellowship

Subjects: Humanities.
Purpose: To support residential research and writing.
Eligibility: Open to postdoctoral scholars in any field of relevance to the Library's collection.
Level of Study: Postdoctorate.
Type: Fellowship.
Value: Up to US$40,000.
Length of Study: 6-11 months.
Frequency: Annual.

Study Establishment: The Newberry Library.
Country of Study: United States of America.
No. of awards offered: Varies.
Application Procedure: Applicants must write for details. Application forms may also be downloaded from the website. Completed applications must include three letters of recommendation.
Closing Date: January 15th.
Funding: Private.
Contributor: The Mellon Foundation.
No. of awards given last year: Four.
No. of applicants last year: 105.
Additional Information: Fellows will become part of Newberry's community of Scholars, participating in bi-weekly fellows seminars, colloquial and other events.

For further information contact:

60 W. Walton, Chicago, IL 60610, United States of America
Contact: Committee on Awards, The Newberry Library

Monticello College Foundation Fellowship for Women

Subjects: Any field appropriate to the Library's collections.
Purpose: To offer young women the opportunity to undertake work in residence at the Library and to significantly enhance their careers through research and writing.
Eligibility: Open to women who hold a PhD and are in the early stages of their academic careers. This academic award is designed for a woman whose work gives clear promise of scholarly productivity and who would benefit significantly from six months of research, writing and participation in the intellectual life of the library. Other things being equal, preference is given to the applicant whose proposed study is concerned with the study of women.
Level of Study: Postdoctorate.
Type: Fellowship.
Value: US$15,000.
Length of Study: Six months.
Frequency: Annual.
Study Establishment: The Newberry Library.
Country of Study: United States of America.
No. of awards offered: One.
Application Procedure: Applicants must write for details. Application forms may also be downloaded from the website.
Closing Date: January 15th.
Funding: Private.
Contributor: The Monticello College Foundation.
No. of awards given last year: One.
No. of applicants last year: 31.

For further information contact:

60 W. Walton, Chicago, IL 60610, United States of America
Contact: Committee on Awards, The Newberry Library

National Endowment for the Humanities (NEH) Fellowships

Subjects: Any field appropriate to the Library's collections.
Purpose: To encourage scholarly research, and to deepen and enrich the opportunities for serious intellectual exchange through the active participation of Fellows in the library community.
Eligibility: Open to United States citizens or foreign nationals who have been resident in the United States for three years, who are established Scholars at the postdoctoral level or its equivalent. Preference is given to applicants who have not held major fellowships for three years preceding the proposed period of residency.
Level of Study: Postdoctorate.
Type: Fellowship.
Value: Up to US$40,000.
Length of Study: 6-11 months.
Frequency: Annual.
Study Establishment: The Newberry Library.
Country of Study: United States of America.
No. of awards offered: Varies.
Application Procedure: Applicants must write for an application form. Completed application forms must include all letters of reference. Application forms may also be downloaded from the website.
Closing Date: January 15th.
Funding: Government.
Contributor: The NEH.
No. of awards given last year: Four.
No. of applicants last year: 54.
Additional Information: Applicants may combine this award with sabbatical or other stipendiary support. Scholars conducting research in American history may also ask to be considered for the Lloyd Lewis Fellowship at the time of their application.

For further information contact:

60 W. Walton, Chicago, IL 60610, United States of America
Contact: Committee on Awards, The Newberry Library

Newberry Library British Academy Fellowship for Study in Great Britain

Subjects: Humanities.
Purpose: To allow an individual to study in Great Britain in any field in which the Newberry's collections are strong.
Eligibility: Open to established scholars at the postdoctoral level or equivalent. Preference is given to readers and staff of the Newberry Library and to established Scholars who have previously used the Newberry Library.
Level of Study: Postdoctorate.
Type: Fellowship.
Value: A stipend of UK£1,350 per month while in the United Kingdom.
Length of Study: Up to three months.
Frequency: Annual.
Country of Study: United Kingdom.
No. of awards offered: Varies.
Application Procedure: Applicants must write for details. Application forms may also be downloaded from the website.
Closing Date: January 15th.
Funding: Private.
Contributor: The British Academy.
No. of awards given last year: Three.
No. of applicants last year: Eight.
Additional Information: The home institution is expected to continue to pay the Fellow's salary.

Newberry Library Ecole des Chartes Exchange Fellowship

Subjects: Renaissance studies.
Purpose: To enable a graduate student to study at the Ecole des Chartes in Paris.
Eligibility: Preference is given to graduate students at institutions in the Renaissance Centre Consortium.
Level of Study: Doctorate.
Type: Fellowship.
Value: Varies, but provides a monthly stipend and free tuition.
Length of Study: Three months.
Frequency: Annual.
Study Establishment: The Ecole des Chartes.
Country of Study: France.
No. of awards offered: Varies.
Application Procedure: Applicants must write for details. Application forms may also be downloaded from the website.
Closing Date: January 15th.
Funding: Private.
Contributor: The Ecole des Chartes.
No. of awards given last year: One.
No. of applicants last year: Five.
Additional Information: The Ecole des Chartes is the oldest institution in Europe specialising in the archival sciences, including palaeography, bibliography, textual editing and the history of the book.

For further information contact:

60 W. Walton, Chicago, IL 60610, United States of America
Contact: Committee on Awards, The Newberry Library

Newberry Library Short-term Resident Fellowships for Individual Research

Subjects: Any field appropriate to the Library's collections.
Purpose: To provide access to Newberry's collections for those who live beyond commuting distance from Chicago.
Eligibility: Open to nationals of any country who hold a PhD degree or have completed all requirements for the degree except the dissertation. Awards are limited to Scholars from outside the Chicago area.
Level of Study: Doctorate, Postdoctorate.
Type: Fellowship.
Value: US$1,200 per month.
Length of Study: One week-two months.
Frequency: Annual.
Study Establishment: The Newberry Library.
Country of Study: United States of America.
No. of awards offered: Varies.
Application Procedure: Applicants must write for details. Application forms may also be downloaded from the website.
Closing Date: February 15th.
Funding: Private.
No. of awards given last year: 19.
No. of applicants last year: 105.

For further information contact:

60 W. Walton, Chicago, IL 60610, United States of America
Contact: Committee on Awards, The Newberry Library

Rockefeller Foundation Fellowship in the Humanities

Subjects: American Indian studies.
Purpose: To support residential research.
Eligibility: Open to historians working in reservation based communities, tribal college faculty and librarians or curators at American Indian cultural centres or museums.
Level of Study: Unrestricted.
Type: Fellowship.
Value: US$3,000 per month plus some expenses.
Length of Study: One-three months.
Frequency: Annual.
Study Establishment: The Newberry Library.
Country of Study. United States of America
No. of awards offered: Varies.
Application Procedure: Applicants must visit the website for application forms and details.
Closing Date: January 15th, April 15th, September 15th.
Funding: Private.
Contributor: The Rockefeller Foundation.
Additional Information: Applicants' projects may culminate in a variety of formats, including but not limited to curriculum development projects, artistic works or publications.

For further information contact:

60 W. Walton, Chicago, IL 60610, United States of America
Contact: Committee on Awards, The Newberry Library

Rockefeller Foundation Postdoctoral Fellowship in the Humanities

Subjects: American Indian studies.
Purpose: To support residential research.
Level of Study: Postdoctorate.
Type: Fellowship.
Value: US$40,000.
Length of Study: A minimum of 10 months.
Frequency: Annual.
Study Establishment: The Newberry Library.
Country of Study: United States of America.
No. of awards offered: One.
Application Procedure: Applicants must visit the website for details and application forms.
Closing Date: January 15th.
Funding: Private.
Contributor: The Rockefeller Foundation.

For further information contact:

60 W. Walton, Chicago, IL 60610, United States of America
Contact: Committee on Awards, The Newberry Library

Short-term Fellowship in the History of Cartography

Subjects: The history of cartography.
Purpose: To financially support work in residence at the Newberry on projects related to the history of cartography.
Eligibility: Open to established scholars of any nationality, but limited to scholars who live outside the Chicago area.
Level of Study: Doctorate, Postdoctorate.
Type: Fellowship.
Value: US$1,200 per month.
Length of Study: One week to two months.
Frequency: Annual.
Study Establishment: The Newberry Library.
Country of Study: United States of America.
No. of awards offered: One-two.
Application Procedure: Applicants must submit an application, project description, curriculum vitae and letters of reference. Applicants must visit the website for further details and application forms.
Closing Date: February 15th.
Funding: Private.
Contributor: Arthur Holzheimer.
No. of awards given last year: One.
No. of applicants last year: 13.

For further information contact:

60 W. Walton, Chicago, IL 60610, United States of America
Contact: Committee on Awards, The Newberry Library

South Central Modern Language Association Fellowship

Subjects: Humanities.
Purpose: To support residential research at the Library by members of the South Central Modern Language Association.
Eligibility: Open to Scholars who live outside the Chicago area.
Level of Study: Doctorate.
Type: Fellowship.
Value: US$2,000.
Length of Study: One month.
Frequency: Annual.
Study Establishment: The Newberry Library.
Country of Study: United States of America.
No. of awards offered: One.
Application Procedure: Applicants must write for details. Application forms may also be downloaded from the website.
Closing Date: February 15th.
Funding: Private.
Contributor: The South Central Modern Language Association.
No. of awards given last year: One.
No. of applicants last year: One.

For further information contact:

60 W. Walton, Chicago, IL 60610, United States of America
Contact: Committee on Awards, The Newberry Library

Susan Kelly Power and Helen Hornbeck Tanner Fellowship

Subjects: American Indian heritage.
Purpose: To support residential research.
Eligibility: Open to applicants with American Indian heritage.
Level of Study: Doctorate, Postdoctorate.
Type: Fellowship.
Value: US$1,200 per month.
Length of Study: Up to two months.
Frequency: Annual.
Study Establishment: The Newberry Library.
Country of Study: United States of America.
No. of awards offered: One.
Application Procedure: Applicants must visit the website for application details and forms.

Closing Date: February 15th.
Funding: Private.

For further information contact:

60 W. Walton, Chicago, IL 60610, United States of America
Contact: Committee on Awards, The Newberry Library

Weiss/Brown Publication Subvention Award
Subjects: Humanities, particularly European civilisation before 1700 in the areas of music, theatre, French or Italian literature or cultural studies.
Purpose: To subsidise the publication of a scholarly book or books.
Eligibility: Open to authors of books already accepted for publication.
Level of Study: Unrestricted.
Type: Award.
Value: Variable, up to US$15,000.
Frequency: Annual.
No. of awards offered: Varies.
Application Procedure: Applicants must write for details. Application guidelines may also be downloaded from the website. Applicants will be asked to provide detailed information regarding the publication and the subvention request.
Closing Date: January 15th.
Funding: Private.
Contributor: Roger Weiss and Howard Brown.
No. of awards given last year: Two.
No. of applicants last year: Two.

For further information contact:

60 West Walton St., Chicago, IL 60610, United States of America
Contact: Committee on Awards, The Newberry Library

NEWBY TRUST LIMITED

Hill Farm, Froxfield, Petersfield, Hampshire, GU32 1BQ, England
Tel: (44) 1730 827557
Fax: (44) 1730 827938
www: www.newby-trust.org.uk
Contact: Miss W Gillam, Company Secretary

The Newby Trust Limited is a grant giving charity working nationally, whose principal aims are to promote medical welfare, education and training and the relief of poverty.

Newby Trust Awards
Subjects: All subjects.
Eligibility: Open to students of any nationality. Overseas students must have already started their course in the United Kingdom before applying.
Level of Study: Doctorate, Postgraduate, Professional development.
Type: Grant.
Value: Up to UK£1,000 for fees or maintenance.
Frequency: Annual.
Study Establishment: A suitable university.
Country of Study: United Kingdom.
No. of awards offered: Varies.
Application Procedure: Applicants must submit in duplicate a personal letter with a curriculum vitae, two letters of academic reference, a statement of income and expenditure including fees, and a stamped addressed envelope. Application forms are not supplied. Applications intended for the start of an academic year should be submitted at least four months in advance.
Closing Date: At least two weeks prior to Director's meetings which are usually held in March or April, July and October.
Funding: Private.
Contributor: Funds from the Trust.
No. of awards given last year: 130.
No. of applicants last year: 900.
Additional Information: Funding is not available for the CPE law exam, BSc intercalculated with a medical degree, postgraduate medical or veterinary degrees in the first or second years, courses outside the United Kingdom, adventure or volunteer courses in general, including gap year projects.

NEWCASTLE BUSINESS SCHOOL (NBS), UNIVERSITY OF NORTHUMBRIA AT NEWCASTLE

International Office, Ellison Place
Newcastle upon Tyne
NE1 8ST, England
Tel: (44) 191 227 4274
Fax: (44) 191 261 1264
Email: er.scholarships@northumbria.ac.uk
www: http://www.northumbria.ac.uk/nbs

Newcastle Business School (NBS) is part of the University of Northumbria which is widely recognised as one of the United Kingdom's leading modern universities. Quality assessors of the Higher Education Funding Council for England have rated the standard of education provided by NBS as excellent. The School offers programmes at levels from University Certificate, through first degree to Master's, MBA, DBA and PhD.

Northumbria University International Scholarships
Subjects: All subjects.
Eligibility: Open to non European Union students beginning a full-time course of at least one year's duration. This does not include English language (ELAN) courses, distance learning programmes, exchange programmes, short courses or any courses delivered outside the United Kingdom.
Level of Study: MBA, Postgraduate, Research.
Type: Scholarship.
Length of Study: At least one year.
Study Establishment: The University of Northumbria.
Country of Study: England.
No. of awards offered: Varies.
Application Procedure: Applicants must obtain application forms from the main address.
Closing Date: June, July or August.
Additional Information: Please visit the website for further information.

NEWCOMEN SOCIETY IN THE UNITED STATES

412 Newcomen Road, Exton, PA 19341
United States of America
Tel: (1) 610 363 6600
Fax: (1) 610 363 0612
Email: newcomen@libertynet.org
Contact: Ms Maureen Hayes, Controller

Harvard/Newcomen Postdoctoral Award
Subjects: Business history.
Purpose: To improve the scholar's professional acquaintance with business and economic history, to increase his or her skills as they relate to this field, and to enable him or her to engage in research that will benefit from the resources of the Harvard Business School and the Boston scholarly community.
Eligibility: Open to Scholars who have received a PhD in history, economics or a related discipline within the past 10 years, and who would not otherwise be able to attend Harvard Business School.
Level of Study: Postdoctorate.
Type: Fellowship.
Value: US$46,000.
Length of Study: One year.
Frequency: Annual.
Study Establishment: Harvard Business School in Cambridge, Massachusetts.
Country of Study: United States of America.
No. of awards offered: One.
Application Procedure: Applicants must contact Harvard University for further details.
Closing Date: March 15th.

For further information contact:

Straus Professor of Business History, Harvard University, Graduate School of Business Administration, Soldiers Field Road, Boston, MA 02163, United States of America
Tel: (1) 617 495 6354
Email: tmccraw@hbs.edu
Contact: Mr Thomas K McCraw

Newcomen Society Dissertation Fellowship in Business and American Culture

Subjects: American business history.
Purpose: To encourage students to pursue careers in studying and teaching in the field.
Eligibility: Open to United States doctoral students only.
Level of Study: Doctorate.
Type: Fellowship.
Value: US$10,000.
Length of Study: Nine months full-time.
Frequency: Annual.
Country of Study: United States of America.
No. of awards offered: One.
Application Procedure: Applicants must submit five copies of their curriculum vitae and a research programme which must not exceed 10 double spaced pages, including references. Faxed proposals cannot be accepted. University transcripts and two letters of recommendation must be sent in support of applications.
Closing Date: February 1st.

NICOLO PAGANINI INTERNATIONAL VIOLIN COMPETITION

Comune di Genova, Settore Promozione della Citta, Turismo e Spettacolo, Ufficio Conservazione, Promozione Violini Storici e Premio Paganini, Via Sottoripa 5, Genova, I-16124, Italy
Tel: (39) 010 557 4215
Fax: (39) 010 557 4326
Email: violinopaganini@comune.genova.it
www: http://www.comune.genova.it/turismo/paganini/welcome.htm
Contact: Miss Anna Rita Cero, Secretary

The Nicolo Paganini International Violin Competition is a competition for young violinists between 16 and 33 years old. It offers a first prize of €12,000 and the possibility for the winner to play Paganini's violin on October 12th, on the occasion of the closing ceremony of the Christopher Columbus celebrations.

Nicolo Paganini International Violin Competition

Subjects: Violin.
Purpose: To discover new talented young violinists and to encourage them to spread the music values which Paganini himself, and his music, stands for.
Eligibility: Open to violinists of any nationality born between April 30th 1971 and April 30th 1988.
Level of Study: Unrestricted.
Type: Prize.
Value: The first prize is €12,000, the second €7,000, the third €4,500, the fourth €2,700, the fifth €2,200 and the sixth €1,600.
Frequency: Every two years.
Country of Study: Any country.
No. of awards offered: Six and Four Special prizes.
Application Procedure: Applicants must write for an application and registration form. Registration fee of €100 to be paid only after having passed the preselection. Forms can be downloaded from the website, but must be mailed to the competition.
Closing Date: April, 30th 2004.
Funding: Government.
Contributor: Comune di Genova.
No. of awards given last year: Six and Four Special prizes.
No. of applicants last year: 95.
Additional Information: The competition is held from September 16th to 26th 2004.

For further information contact:

Segreteria del Concorso Internazionale di Violino 'Premio Paganini', c/o Comune di Genevo - Archivio Generale, S.TA S. Francesco, 4, Genova, 16124, Italy

NIEMAN FOUNDATION

1 Francis Avenue, Cambridge, MA 02138, United States of America
Tel: (1) 617 495 2238
Fax: (1) 617 495 8976
Email: nieman@harvard.edu
www: http://www.nieman.harvard.edu
Contact: Program Assistant

The Nieman Foundation's fellowships provide a mid career opportunity for journalists to spend a year of learning and reflection at Harvard University. Fellows design an individual course of study and participate in Nieman seminars.

Nieman Fellowships for Journalists

Subjects: Each Fellow is free to design an individual course of study. Some pursue courses in a reporting speciality, whereas others explore the breadth of Harvard's schools and departments.
Purpose: To provide an opportunity for journalists to spend a year at Harvard University, where Fellows experience discovery and enrichment, learning and reflection in Harvard classrooms, in Nieman seminars and from the close friendships that emerge during the Nieman year.
Eligibility: Applicants must be full-time staff or freelance journalists working for the news or editorial departments of newspapers, news services, radio, television, magazines of general public interest or internet news sites. They must also have at least five years of professional experience in the news media and their employer's consent for a leave of absence for that academic year. There are no age, nationality or residency restrictions.
Level of Study: Postgraduate, Professional development.
Type: Fellowship.
Value: Please contact the organisation.
Length of Study: One academic year.
Frequency: Annual.
Study Establishment: Harvard University.
Country of Study: United States of America.
No. of awards offered: 12 to journalists from the United States, and 12 to journalists from other countries (only funding for citizens of certain countries).
Application Procedure: Applicants must obtain information and an application form by contacting the Program Officer at the Nieman Foundation. The completed application form must include supporting materials, letters of recommendation, essays on journalism experience and proposed course of study, and work samples.
Closing Date: US citizens Jan. 31. Citizens of most other countries March 1.
Funding: Private.
No. of awards given last year: 24.
No. of applicants last year: 260.
Additional Information: No course credits are given or degrees granted. Further information is available on request.

NORTH ATLANTIC TREATY ORGANIZATION (NATO)

NATO Headquarters, Boulevard Leopold III, Brussels, B-1110, Belgium
Tel: (32) 2 707 4111
Email: natodoc@hq.nato.int
www: http://www.nato.int
Contact: Academic Affairs Officer

The North Atlantic Treaty was signed in Washington on April 4th 1949, creating an alliance of 12 independent nations committed to each other's defence. Four more European nations later acceded to the

Treaty between 1952 and 1982. On March 12th 1999, the Czech Republic, Hungary and Poland were welcomed into the Alliance, which now numbers 19 members.

Manfred Wörner Fellowship

Subjects: International relations.
Purpose: To honour the memory of the late Secretary General by focusing attention on his leadership in the transformation of the alliance, including efforts at extending NATO's relations with CEE countries and promoting the principles and image of the Transatlantic partnership.
Eligibility: Please contact the organisation.
Level of Study: Professional development.
Type: Fellowship.
Value: €20,000.
Frequency: Annual.
Country of Study: Any country.
Funding: Government.

NORTH DAKOTA UNIVERSITY SYSTEM

000 East Boulevard
Bismarck, ND 58505
United States of America
Tel: (1) 701 328 2960
Email: ndus.office@ndus.nodak.edu
www: http://www.ndus.nodak.edu
Contact: Ms Rhonda Shaver, Co-ordinator

The North Dakota University System, governed by the State Board of Higher Education, is comprised of 11 public campuses.

North Dakota Indian Scholarship

Subjects: All subjects.
Purpose: To assist Native American students in obtaining a basic college education.
Eligibility: Open to residents of North Dakota with a quarter degree of Indian blood, who are accepted for admission at an Institute of Higher Education or state vocational programme. Recipients must be enrolled full-time and have a grade point average above 2.00.
Level of Study: Doctorate, Postgraduate.
Type: Scholarship.
Value: US$700.
Frequency: Annual.
Country of Study: United States of America.
No. of awards offered: 140.
Application Procedure: Applicants must complete an application form.
Closing Date: July 15th.
Funding: Government.
Contributor: The state.
No. of awards given last year: 140.

NORTH WEST CANCER RESEARCH FUND

22 Oxford Street, Liverpool, L7 7BL, England
Tel: (44) 151 709 2919
Fax: (44) 151 708 7997
Email: nwcrf@btclick.com
www: http://www.cancerresearchnorthwest.co.uk
Contact: Mr A W Renison, General Secretary

North West Cancer Research Fund Research Project Grants

Subjects: All types of cancer, the mechanisms by which they arise and the way they exert their effects.
Purpose: To provide financial support for fundamental cancer research in North West England, North and Mid-Wales.
Eligibility: Open to candidates undertaking research at one of the universities named below in the Northwest. No grants are awarded for buildings or for the development of drugs.

Type: Grant.
Value: Approx. UK£45,000 per year.
Length of Study: Usually three years.
Frequency: Dependent on funds available.
Study Establishment: The University of Liverpool, Lancaster University and the University of Wales, Bangor.
Country of Study: North West England, North and Mid-Wales.
Application Procedure: The NWCRF Scientific Committee meet twice a year. All applications are subject to peer review.
Closing Date: April 1st and October 1st.
Funding: Private.
Contributor: Voluntary donations.
No. of awards given last year: 10.
No. of applicants last year: 50.

For further information contact:

NWCRF Scientific Committee, Department of Medicine, Duncan Building, Daulby Street, Liverpool, L69 3BX, England
Email: nwcrf@btclick.com
Contact: The Secretary

NORWEGIAN INFORMATION SERVICE IN THE UNITED STATES

825 Third Avenue, 38th Floor
New York, NY 10022-7584
United States of America
Tel: (1) 212 421 7333
Fax: (1) 212 754 0583
Email: norcons@interport.net
www: http://www.norway.org
Contact: Grants & Scholarships Department

America-Norway Heritage Fund Grant

Subjects: All subjects.
Purpose: To award special grants to Americans of Norwegian descent who have made significant contributions to American culture, enabling them to visit Norway to share the results of their work through lectures, exhibitions or performances. In this way, it is hoped that Norwegians will become better acquainted with the cultural, economic, political and religious contributions made by Norwegian-Americans in the building of America.
Eligibility: Open to Americans of Norwegian descent.
Level of Study: Unrestricted.
Type: Travel grant.
Value: Travel expenses as well as an honorarium.
Length of Study: One-two weeks. Activities should be scheduled between October-April.
Frequency: Annual.
Country of Study: Norway.
Application Procedure: Applications are not accepted. Candidates will be selected by the Board of Directors of the Fund in co-operation with its connections in the United States of America. However, proposals for possible candidates will be appreciated.
Contributor: The Lutheran Brotherhood Insurance Company.

For further information contact:

Nordmanns-Forbundet, Rådhusgt 23 B, Oslo, N-0158, Norway

American-Scandinavian Foundation (ASF)

Subjects: All subjects.
Purpose: To encourage advanced study and research in Scandinavian countries.
Eligibility: Applicants must be United States citizens or permanent residents. Team projects are eligible, but each member must apply as an individual, submitting a separate, fully documented application. First priority will be given to applicants who have not previously received an ASF award. Only in exceptional cases will a third award be considered. The ASF considers it desirable that all candidates have at

least some ability in the language of the host country, even if it is not essential for the execution of the research plan. For projects that require a command of one or more Scandinavian (or other) language, candidates should defer application until they have the necessary proficiency.
Level of Study: Postgraduate.
Type: Other.
Value: Grants are normally US$3,000, and fellowships can be up to US$18,000.
Frequency: Annual.
Country of Study: Other.
No. of awards offered: Varies.
Application Procedure: Applicants must complete an application on ASF application forms, available on request from the Foundation.
Closing Date: November 1st.

For further information contact:

American Scandinavian Foundation (ASF), 56 Park Avenue, New York, NY 10016, United States of America
Tel: (1) 212 879 9779
Fax: (1) 212 249 3444
Contact: Grants Management Officer

Fulbright Stipend

Subjects: All subjects.
Level of Study: Graduate, Postdoctorate, Postgraduate.
Length of Study: Three months to one year.
Application Procedure: Applicants must contact the organisation. Candidates with a PhD or more should contact the Council of International Exchange of Scholars.
Funding: Government.

For further information contact:

Fulbright Senior Scholars Program, Council of International Exchange of Scholars, 3007 Tilden Street North West, Suite 5M, Washington, DC 20008-3009, United States of America

John Dana Archbold Fellowship Program

Subjects: All subjects.
Purpose: To support educational exchange between the United States and Norway.
Eligibility: Open to United States citizens aged 20-35, in good health and of good character. Qualified applicants must show evidence of a high level of competence in their chosen field, indicate a seriousness of purpose, and have a record of social adaptability. There is ordinarily no language requirement.
Level of Study: Postdoctorate, Postgraduate, Professional development, Research.
Type: Fellowship.
Value: Up to US$5,000. Individual grants vary, depending on the projected costs. Note that there will be no tuition at the University of Oslo. The maintenance stipend is sufficient to meet expenses for a single person. The travel allowance covers round trip airfare to Oslo.
Length of Study: One year.
Frequency: Annual.
Study Establishment: The University of Oslo.
Country of Study: Other.
No. of awards offered: Two.
Application Procedure: Applicants must write to the Nansen Fund, Inc. for an application form.
Closing Date: January 15th.
Funding: Private.
Additional Information: The University of Oslo International Summer School offers orientation and Norwegian languages courses six weeks before the start of the regular academic year. For Americans, tuition is paid. Attendance is required. Americans visit Norway in even numbered years and Norwegians visit the United States of America in odd numbered years. For further information please contact the Nansen Fund, Inc.

For further information contact:

The Nansen Fund, Inc., 77 Saddlebrook Lane, Houston, TX 77024, United States of America
Tel: (1) 713 680 8255

Memorial Fund of May 8th 1970

Subjects: All subjects.
Purpose: To promote cultural exchange between foreign countries and Norwegian folk high schools by providing scholarships for residence. The folk high schools have no set curricula or examinations, and serve as Life Laboratories whose objective is to help prepare young people for everyday life in the community.
Eligibility: Open to candidates aged 18-22 years who do not have a permanent residence in Norway, and do not hold a Norwegian passport. Candidates must be planning to return to their home country after a year in Norway. Candidates must be aware of the kind of education the Memorial Fund bursaries cover, that being a year in a Norwegian folk high school, not admission to education on a higher level, such as a university, or specialised training.
Level of Study: Unrestricted.
Type: Scholarship.
Value: The scholarship will cover board and lodging. In addition it is possible to apply for extra funds. Applicants from some countries may apply for required books and excursions arranged by the school. Also, extra support may be provided for short study trips and short courses before or after the school year. A fixed amount towards spending money may also be given. Normally the students must pay their own travelling expenses. The folk high schools do not charge tuition fees.
Length of Study: One year.
Frequency: Annual.
Study Establishment: Norwegian folk high schools.
Country of Study: Norway.
No. of awards offered: Approx. 25.
Application Procedure: Applicants must request more information and application forms from the Memorial Fund of 8th of May 1970 or to the nearest Norwegian Embassy. Applicants who require a scholarship to attend a folk high school should not apply to a folk high school themselves. In this case, the Board will place successful applicants at a folk high school based on their hobbies and interest. Residence permits must be applied for by each individual student when a scholarship has been granted.
Closing Date: March 15th.
Funding: Government.
No. of awards given last year: 25.
No. of applicants last year: 700.
Additional Information: A folk high school is a one year independent residential school, primarily for young adults, offering many non traditional subjects of study. Each school has its own profile, but as a group, the Norwegian folk high schools teach classes covering almost all interest areas, including history, arts, crafts, music, sports, philosophy, theatre, photography etc.

For further information contact:

c/o IKF, Grensen 9a N-0159 Oslo, Norway, Oslo, N-0159, Norway
Email: ikf@ikf.no

Norwegian Emigration Fund of 1975

Subjects: Emigration history and relations between the United States of America and Norway.
Purpose: To award grants for advanced or specialised study in Norway.
Eligibility: Open to citizens and residents of the United States of America. The fund may also give grants to institutions in the United States whose activities are primarily centred on the subjects mentioned.
Level of Study: Graduate, Postgraduate.
Type: Grant.

Value: Norwegian krone 5,000-20,000.
Frequency: Annual.
Country of Study: Norway.
No. of awards offered: Varies.
Application Procedure: Applicants must complete an application form and return it clearly marked Emigration Fund to Nordmanns-Forbundet. Applications as well as enclosures will not be returned.
Closing Date: February 1st.
Funding: Government.

Norwegian Marshall Fund

Subjects: Science and humanities.
Purpose: To provide financial support for Americans to come to Norway to conduct postgraduate study or research in areas of mutual importance to Norway and the United States, thereby increasing knowledge, understanding and strengthening the ties of friendship between the two countries.
Eligibility: Open to citizens of the United States, who have arranged with a Norwegian sponsor or research institution to pursue a research project or programme in Norway. Under special circumstances, the awards can be extended to Norwegians for study or research in the United States.
Level of Study: Postgraduate, Research.
Type: Research grant.
Value: The size of the individual grants depends on the research subject, purpose and the intended length of stay in Norway. In previous years, the grants have varied from Norwegian Krone 10,000 to 30,000.
Length of Study: Varies.
Frequency: Annual.
Study Establishment: Norwegian universities.
Country of Study: Norway.
No. of awards offered: 5-15.
Application Procedure: Applicants must contact the Norway-America Association to receive an application. Application forms must be typewritten in either English or Norwegian and submitted in duplicate, including all supplementary materials. Each application must also be accompanied by a letter of support from the project sponsor or affiliated research institution in Norway. There is an application fee of Norwegian Krone 350.
Closing Date: March 23rd.
Funding: Government.

For further information contact:

The Norway-America Association, Rådhusgt 23 B, Oslo, N-0158, Norway
Fax: (47) 2 335 7160
Email: namerika@online.no
www: http://www.noram.no/index_am.html
Tel: 23 35 71 75

Norwegian Ministry of Foreign Affairs Travel Grants

Subjects: Norwegian culture and society.
Purpose: To give financial assistance to teachers and graduate students visiting Norway for study and research purposes.
Eligibility: Open to citizens and residents of the United States who are members of NORTANA. They must be university or college teachers of Norwegian or other courses in Norwegian culture or society, or graduate students who have passed their preliminary examinations in these fields.
Level of Study: Graduate, Professional development.
Type: Travel grant.
Value: US$750-1,500.
Frequency: Annual.
Country of Study: Norway.
No. of awards offered: Varies.
Application Procedure: Applicants must download an application form from the website.
Closing Date: February 15th.
Funding: Government.
Contributor: The Norwegian Ministry of Foreign Affairs.

Norwegian Thanksgiving Fund Scholarship

Subjects: Fisheries, geology, glaciology, astronomy, social medicine or Norwegian culture.
Eligibility: Open to American graduate students.
Level of Study: Graduate.
Type: Scholarship.
Value: Up to US$3,000.
Country of Study: Norway.
No. of awards offered: One.
Application Procedure: Applicants must contact the American Scandinavian Foundation.

For further information contact:

The American Scandinavian Foundation, 58 Park Avenue, New York, NY 10016, United States of America
Tel: (1) 212 879 9779
Fax: (1) 212 249 3444

NORWICH JUBILEE ESPERANTO FOUNDATION

37 Granville Court, Cheney Lane, Oxford, Oxfordshire, OX3 0HS, England
Tel: (44) 1865 245509
www: http://www.esperanto.org/uk/nojef
Contact: Dr Kathleen M Hall, Secretary to the Foundation

A registered charitable trust established in 1967 (registration number 313190) the Norwich Jubilee Esperanto Foundation was founded for the advancement of education in the study and practice of Esperanto. It can pay travelling expenses to enable young persons who have shown efficiency in the study of Esperanto to visit foreign countries. It also awards prizes and encourages research.

Norwich Jubilee Esperanto Foundation Grants-in-Aid

Subjects: Esperanto.
Purpose: To encourage thorough study of Esperanto by enabling young students to travel abroad and promote research into the teaching of Esperanto.
Eligibility: Open to citizens under 26 years of age of any country, who require financial assistance and who have a high standard of competence in Esperanto. An efficiency test may be required but there are no set academic or age requirements for research grants.
Level of Study: Unrestricted.
Type: Travel grant.
Value: Approx. UK£50-200, up to UK£1,000.
Length of Study: From one week to several months.
Frequency: Dependent on funds available.
Study Establishment: Any venue approved by the Foundation.
Country of Study: Other.
No. of awards offered: Varies.
Application Procedure: Applicants must submit a letter of application in Esperanto. An application may be completed later.
Closing Date: Applications are accepted at any time provided an adequate margin is left for processing.
Funding: Private.
Contributor: Legacies from past supporters.
No. of awards given last year: 20.
No. of applicants last year: 22.
Additional Information: Visitors to the United Kingdom will be expected to speak in Esperanto to schools or clubswww:http://www.esperanto.org/uk/nojef.

NOVARTIS FOUNDATION

41 Portland Place, London, England
Tel: (44) 20 7636 9456
Fax: (44) 20 7436 2840
Email: dchadwick@novartisfound.org.uk
www: http://www.novartisfound.org.uk
Contact: Dr D J Chadwick, Director

A scientific and educational charity, the Novartis Foundation was established in 1997 as the direct successor to the Ciba Foundation which was created in 1947 by Ciba of Basle. There are three main functions, those being the organisation of scientific meetings, the publishing of books and the provision of accommodation and hospitality for visiting scientists and their societies.

Novartis Foundation Symposium Bursaries

Subjects: Biomedicine, chemistry and related topics.
Purpose: To enable young scientists to attend Novartis Foundation symposia and, immediately following the meeting, spend time in the laboratory of one of the symposium participants.
Eligibility: Open to applicants of any nationality, aged 23-35 on the closing date for application, who are actively engaged in research on the topic covered by the symposium of their choice.
Level of Study: Doctorate, Postdoctorate.
Type: Bursary.
Value: Travel expenses, by the most economical means, bed and breakfast during the symposium, and board and lodging while in the host's laboratory.
Length of Study: One-three months, including travel, attendance at a Novartis Foundation symposium and up to twelve weeks in one of the symposium participants' laboratory or institution.
Frequency: Annual.
Country of Study: Any country.
No. of awards offered: Approx. eight.
Application Procedure: Applicants must send a full curriculum vitae and a statement of current research, stating their symposium of choice from current advertisements.
Closing Date: Please refer to advertisements.
Funding: Commercial.
Contributor: Novartis AG, Basle.
No. of awards given last year: Nine.
No. of applicants last year: 80.
Additional Information: The availability of the awards is advertised on the Foundation's web site, in the Foundation's e-mail bulletin, by circular to overseas members of the Novartis Foundation's Scientific Advisory Panel and invited symposiasts and by an advertisement in Nature, or other journals if more appropriate. Awards are advertised every three-six months and at least six months before the date of the relevant meetings. The awardee is selected by the senior staff of the Foundation, usually four months before the symposium. Offers to host an awardee are sought from symposiasts at the time of the invitation to the symposium. The successful awardee is asked to select three names from the membership list of the symposium and every effort is made by the Novartis Foundation to accommodate the awardee's choice. Successful candidates are expected to submit a short report following their return home.

NURSES' EDUCATIONAL FUNDS, INC.

555 West 57th Street, Suite 1327, New York, NY 10019, United States of America
Tel: (1) 212 399 1428
Contact: Scholarship Co-ordinator

Nurses' Educational Funds, Inc. is an independent, non-profit organisation which grants scholarships to registered nurses for graduate study. It is governed by a board of trustees of nursing and business leaders, and is supported by contributions from corporations, foundations, nurses and individuals interested in the advancement of nursing.

Nurses' Educational Funds Fellowships and Scholarships

Subjects: Administration, supervision, education, clinical specialisation and research.
Purpose: To provide the opportunity to registered nurses who seek to qualify through advanced study in a degree programme.
Level of Study: Doctorate, Graduate, Postgraduate.
Type: Fellowship.
Value: Please contact the organisation.
Frequency: Annual.

Country of Study: United States of America.
No. of awards offered: Varies.
Funding: Private.

OFFICE OF RESEARCH & GRADUATE EDUCATION PFIZER INC

A-300 HSC, Box 35640, Washington DC
United States of America
Tel: (1) 800 201 1214
Email: info@psymark.com
www: http://www.physicianscientist.com
Contact: Dr Albert Berger

Pfizer's Medical and Academic Partnerships provide support for researchers in a range of medical disciplines.

The ACCF/Pfizer Postdoctoral Fellowship Awards in Cardiovascular Medicine

Subjects: Cardiovascular medicine.
Purpose: To support physician scientists in pursuing basic biomedical research in an academic setting.
Level of Study: Postdoctorate.
Type: Fellowship.
Value: US$65,000 per year.
Length of Study: Three years.
Frequency: Annual.
Study Establishment: A U.S. medical school.
Country of Study: United States of America.
No. of awards offered: 2.
Application Procedure: Apply online from the website.
Closing Date: December 1st.
Funding: Private.
No. of awards given last year: 2.
Additional Information: The candidate's potential for future outstanding contributions to the field will be closely evaluated.

Pfizer Fellowship in Biological Psychiatry

Subjects: Biological psychiatry.
Purpose: To encourage retention of talented scientists in the field of biological psychiatry.
Level of Study: Postdoctorate.
Type: Fellowship.
Value: US$65,000 per year.
Length of Study: Three years.
Frequency: Annual.
Study Establishment: A U.S. medical school.
Country of Study: United States of America.
Application Procedure: Please apply online via the website.
Closing Date: January 30th.
Funding: Commercial.
Additional Information: The candidate's potential for future outstanding contributions to the field will be closely evaluated.

The Pfizer Fellowships in Infectious Diseases

Subjects: Research into infectious diseases.
Purpose: To encourage the retention of talented scientists in the field of infectious diseases.
Level of Study: Postdoctorate.
Type: Fellowship.
Value: US$65,000 per year.
Length of Study: Three years.
Frequency: Annual.
Study Establishment: A U.S. medical school.
Country of Study: United States of America.
No. of awards offered: 2.
Application Procedure: Online via the website.
Closing Date: January 30th.
Funding: Commercial.
Additional Information: Applications must demonstrate a strong career interest in academic infectious diseases.

The Pfizer Fellowships in Rheumatology / Immunology.
Subjects: Rheumatology and Immunology.
Purpose: To encourage retention of talented scientists in the field of Rheumatology / Immunology.
Level of Study: Postdoctorate.
Type: Fellowship.
Value: US$65,000 per year.
Length of Study: Three years.
Frequency: Annual.
Study Establishment: A U.S. medical school.
Country of Study: United States of America.
No. of awards offered: 2.
Application Procedure: Online via the website.
Closing Date: January 30th.
Funding: Commercial.
No. of awards given last year: 1.
Additional Information: The candidate's potential for future outstanding contributions to the field will be closely evaluated.

Pfizer Scholar's Grant in Clinical Epidemiology.
Subjects: Clinical epidemiology.
Purpose: To support research bridging the basic science of epidemiology with clinical medicine.
Eligibility: Applicants must have completed their clinical training and demonstrate the motivation and ability to conduct original research.
Level of Study: Postgraduate.
Type: Grant.
Value: US$65,000 per year.
Length of Study: Three years.
Frequency: Annual.
Study Establishment: A U.S. medical school.
Country of Study: United States of America.
Application Procedure: Online via the website.
Closing Date: January 9th.
Funding: Commercial.
No. of awards given last year: 2.
Additional Information: Grantees must plan to conduct their research at a U.S academic institution with an experienced mentor.

Pfizer Scholars Grants in Pain Medicine.
Subjects: Pain medicine.
Purpose: To support physician scientists who wish to pursue basic biomedical research in an academic setting.
Level of Study: Postgraduate.
Type: Scholarship.
Value: US$65,000 per year.
Length of Study: Two years.
Frequency: Annual.
Study Establishment: U.S. academic medical institution.
Country of Study: United States of America.
No. of awards offered: 2.
Application Procedure: Online via the website.
Closing Date: January 9th.
Funding: Commercial.
Additional Information: Applicants will be selected for the quality of their research proposals, mentioning program and potential for advancing pain medicine.

Pfizer Visiting Professorships
Subjects: Medical research.
Purpose: To enable selected institutions to invite a distinguished specialist for 3 days of teaching and professional exchange.
Eligibility: Applications evaluated by an independent advisory board.
Level of Study: Postdoctorate.
Type: Award.
Value: US$75,000 per visit.
Length of Study: Three days.
Frequency: Annual.
Study Establishment: U.S. medical school or teaching hospital.
Country of Study: United States of America.
No. of awards offered: 80.
Application Procedure: Online via the website.
Funding: Commercial.

The Pfizer/AGS Foundation Junior Faculty Scholars Program
Subjects: Geriatric medicine, geropsychiatry and geriatric neurology.
Purpose: To help recipients make the transition from junior faculty to independent researcher in the area of geriatric medicine.
Eligibility: Applicants must have an MD or DO degree and have completed one year of geriatric medicine.
Level of Study: Postgraduate.
Type: Scholarship.
Value: US$65,000 per year.
Length of Study: Two years.
Frequency: Annual.
Country of Study: United States of America.
No. of awards offered: 2.
Application Procedure: Online via the website.
Closing Date: December 1st.
Funding: Commercial.

OMAHA SYMPHONY GUILD

1605 Howard Street, Omaha, NE 68102, United States of America
Tel: (1) 402 342 3836
Fax: (1) 402 342 3819
Email: bravo@omahasymphony.org
www: http://www.omahasymphony.org
Contact: Volunteer Co-ordinator

The purpose of the Omaha Symphony Guild is to promote the growth and development of the Omaha Symphony Orchestra.

Omaha Symphony Guild International New Music Competition
Subjects: Music theory and composition.
Purpose: To award composers of unpublished compositions which have never been performed by a professional orchestra.
Eligibility: Open to composers aged 25 and over.
Level of Study: Postgraduate.
Type: Competition.
Value: US$3,000 award and a premiere performance.
Frequency: Annual.
Country of Study: United States of America.
No. of awards offered: One.
Application Procedure: Applicants must write for an application form. Two copies of the composition score must be submitted. Photocopies are acceptable but no tapes are accepted. The entry fee is US$30 and cheques should be made payable to the Omaha Symphony Guild. Application forms can also be downloaded from the website.
Closing Date: April 15th.
Funding: Private.
Contributor: The Omaha Symphony Guild.
Additional Information: Compositions must be no longer than 20 minutes. If applicants require the score to be returned they must include a US$10 postage and handling fee.

OMOHUNDRO INSTITUTE OF EARLY AMERICAN HISTORY AND CULTURE

PO Box 8781, Williamsburg, VA 23187-8781, United States of America
Tel: (1) 757 221 1110
Fax: (1) 757 221 1047
Email: ieahc1@wm.edu
www: http://www.wm.edu/oieahc
Contact: Ms Sally D Mason, Assistant to the Director

The Omohundro Institute of Early American History and Culture publishes books in its field of interest, the William and Mary Quarterly, and a biannual newsletter, Uncommon Sense. It also sponsors conferences and colloquia, and annually awards a two year NEH Postdoctoral Fellowship and a one year Andrew W Mellon Postdoctoral Research Fellowship.

Andrew W Mellon Postdoctoral Research Fellowship

Subjects: The history and culture of North America's indigenous and immigrant peoples during the colonial, revolutionary and early national periods of the United States of America and the related histories of Canada, the Caribbean, Latin America, the British Isles, Europe and Africa from 1500 to approx. 1815.

Purpose: To revise the applicant's book manuscript into a first book that will make a distinguished contribution to scholarship, with publication by the Institute intended.

Eligibility: Applicants must not have previously published a book or have a book under contract, and must also have received their PhD at least one year prior to the application deadline.

Level of Study: Postdoctorate.

Type: Fellowship.

Value: US$45,000.

Length of Study: One year, residential recommended.

Frequency: Annual.

Study Establishment: The Omohundro Institute of Early American History and Culture.

Country of Study: United States of America.

No. of awards offered: One.

Application Procedure: Applicants must complete an application form and submit this with a completed manuscript. Application forms are available on request and from the web pages.

Closing Date: November 1st.

Funding: Private.

Contributor: The Andrew W Mellon Foundation and the College of William and Mary.

No. of awards given last year: One.

No. of applicants last year: 14.

The National Endowment for Humanities (NEH) Institute Postdoctoral Fellowship

Subjects: The history and culture of North America's indigenous and immigrant peoples during the colonial, revolutionary and early national periods of the United States and the related histories of Canada, the Caribbean, Latin America, the British Isles, Europe and Africa from 1500 to approx. 1815.

Purpose: To revise a dissertation into a first book that will make a major contribution to the field of early American history and culture, for publication by the Institute.

Eligibility: Applicants must have been United States of America citizens for three years prior to applying.

Level of Study: Postdoctorate.

Type: Fellowship.

Value: US$40,000.

Length of Study: Two years.

Frequency: Annual.

Study Establishment: The Omohundro Institute of Early American History and Culture.

Country of Study: United States of America.

No. of awards offered: One.

Application Procedure: Applicants must complete an application form, available on written request or from the web pages.

Closing Date: November 1st.

Funding: Government.

Contributor: The NEH and the College of William and Mary.

No. of awards given last year: One.

No. of applicants last year: 21.

ONCOLOGY NURSING FOUNDATION (ONS)

125 Enterprise Drive, RIDC Park West, Pittsburgh, PA 15275-1214, United States of America
Tel: (1) 866 257 4667
Fax: (1) 877 369 5497
Email: found@ons.org
www: http://www.ons.org
Contact: Director of Research

The mission of the Oncology Nursing Society (ONS) is to promote excellence in oncology nursing and quality cancer care. The Foundation works to fulfil this mission by providing nurses and healthcare professionals with access to the highest quality educational programmes, cancer care resources, research opportunities, and networks for peer support.

ONS Foundation Research Awards

Subjects: Oncology nursing research, including research proposals related to AIDS, neuro-oncology, community health, cancer related genetics, nursing outcomes, oncology nursing education, symptom assessment and management, pain, palliative care, nausea and vomiting, neutropenia or biotherapy.

Eligibility: Open to health professionals working in the field of oncology.

Level of Study: Unrestricted.

Type: Research grant.

Value: Generally US$3,000-10,000, though some awards are up to US$100,000.

Length of Study: Two years.

Frequency: Dependent on funds available.

Country of Study: Any country.

No. of awards offered: 28.

Application Procedure: Applicants must complete an application form, available on request. They must also include a research proposal.

Closing Date: November 1st.

THE ONTARIO INSTITUTE FOR STUDIES IN EDUCATION/UNIVERSITY OF TORONTO (OISE/UT)

252 Bloor Street West, Toronto, ON, M5S 1V6, Canada
Tel: (1) 416 923 6641 ext. 8157
Fax: (1) 416 926 4765
Email: mbrennan@oise.utoronto.ca
www: http://www.oise.utoronto.ca

The Ontario Institute for Studies in Education/University of Toronto (OISE/UT) is an educational institution dedicated to the establishment of a learning society, through immersing itself in the world of applied problem solving and expanding the knowledge and capacities of individuals to lead productive lives.

OISE/UT FUNDING SUPPORT

Subjects: Adult education, applied psychology, curriculum, educational administration, higher education, history and philosophy of education, sociology in education or human development.

Purpose: To support students studying at OISE/UT.

Eligibility: Open to persons of any nationality who are suitably qualified for admission to a MA or a PhD programme in graduate studies at the OISE/UT.

Level of Study: Doctorate.

Type: Funding Support.

Value: Please contact the organisation.

Frequency: Annual.

Study Establishment: OISE/UT.

Country of Study: Canada.

Application Procedure: Applicants must not apply, as they are nominated by each OISE/UT department at the time of admission.

OISE/UT Graduate Assistantships

Subjects: Adult education, applied psychology, curriculum, educational administration, higher education, history and philosophy of education, sociology in education or human development.

Purpose: To provide remuneration and financial assistance for graduate students who are engaged in research and/or field development oriented projects contributing to their academic and professional development.

Eligibility: Open to persons of any nationality who are suitably qualified for admission to a Master's or doctoral degree programme in graduate studies at the OISE/UT. Applicants must be registered full-time students at OISE/UT.

Level of Study: Doctorate, Postgraduate.

Type: Other (employment).
Value: Please contact the organisation.
Frequency: Annual.
Study Establishment: OISE/UT.
Country of Study: Canada.
No. of awards offered: 182.
Application Procedure: Applicants must submit a completed application form.
Closing Date: December 1st.

ONTARIO MINISTRY OF EDUCATION AND TRAINING

PO Box 4500,189 Red River Road, 4th Floor, Thunder Bay, ON, P7B 6G9, Canada
Tel: (1) 807 343 7257
Fax: (1) 807 343 7278
www: http://osap.gov.on.ca
Contact: OGS Officer

Ontario Ministry of Education and Training Graduate Scholarship Programme

Subjects: All subjects.
Purpose: To encourage excellence in graduate studies.
Eligibility: Open to Canadian residents with an overall A- average or equivalent during the previous two years of study. 60 awards may be allocated to students holding a student authorisation.
Level of Study: Doctorate, Graduate, MBA.
Type: Scholarship.
Value: Approx. Canadian $5,000 per term.
Length of Study: Two or three consecutive terms of full-time graduate study.
Frequency: Annual.
Study Establishment: A university in Ontario.
Country of Study: Canada.
No. of awards offered: 2,000.
Application Procedure: Applicants currently registered at a university in Ontario must submit their applications and supporting documentation through that institution.
Closing Date: November 15th.
Funding: Government.
Contributor: The Ministry of Training, and colleges and universities.
No. of awards given last year: 2,000.
No. of applicants last year: 6,500.
Additional Information: Students may hold another award up to Canadian $10,000 and may accept research assistantships or part-time teaching or demonstrating appointments, providing that the total amount paid to the Scholar within the period of the award shall not interfere with their status as full-time graduate students. The total amount of time spent by the student in connection with such an appointment, including preparation, marking examinations, etc. must not exceed an average of 10 hours per week. Students must reapply each year and may receive a maximum of four awards.

THE OPEN GATE FOUNDATION

Emerson Hall, Havard University, Cambridge, MA 02138,
Tel: (1) 617 495 9512
Email: opengate@hglc.org
www: http://www.hglc.org/opengate
Contact: Professor Warren Goldfarb

The Open Gate Foundation was formed in 1986 to support and encourage scholarship and research in the field of sexual orientation.

Open Gate Research Grant

Subjects: Sexual orientation.
Purpose: To support scholarly projects on legal, political, medical and cultural subjects.
Level of Study: Postgraduate.
Type: Grant.
Value: US$1000-US$3000.

Frequency: Annual.
Study Establishment: Harvard University.
Application Procedure: Application in the form of a short letter. Please see website for details or email opengate@hglc.org.
Closing Date: None but allow one month for review.
Funding: Private.

OPPENHEIM-JOHN DOWNES MEMORIAL TRUST

50 Broadway, London, Westminster, SW1H OBL, United Kingdom
Contact: Grants Management Officer

The trust makes annual awards in December to deserving artists of any kind unable to pursue their vocation by reason of poverty. Awards are restricted to persons over 30, who are natural born British subjects and of parents who are both natural born British subjects (534 Race Relations Act applies).

Oppenheim-John Downes Trust Grants

Subjects: Arts.
Purpose: To assist artists, musicians, writers, inventors, singers, actors and dancers of all descriptions who are unable to pursue their vocation by reason of their poverty.
Eligibility: Open to artists over 30 years of age, born in the British Isles of British parents and grandparents born after 1900. These qualifications are mandatory and applicants who do not qualify in all respects should not apply.
Level of Study: Unrestricted.
Type: Grant.
Value: UK£50-1,500 depending on requirement.
Frequency: Annual.
Country of Study: Any country.
No. of awards offered: Approx. 30-40.
Application Procedure: Applicants must write for details.
Closing Date: 15th October.
Funding: Private.
No. of awards given last year: 38.

ORCHESTRE SYMPHONIQUE DE MONTRÉAL

260 de Maisoneurve Boulevard West, Montréal, QC, H2X 1Y9, Canada
Tel: (1) 514 842 3402
Fax: (1) 514 842 0728
Email: concoursosm@osm.ca
www: http://www.osm.ca
Contact: Associate Music Administrator

Founded in 1934, the Orchestre Symphonique de Montréal is one of the greatest orchestras in the world. Under the guidance of its Artistic Director, Maestro Charles Dutoit, it gives about 100 concerts each year and has produced more than 85 recordings.

Orchestre Symphonique de Montréal Competitions

Subjects: Piano, singing, string or wind instrument performance.
Purpose: To award the best performances.
Eligibility: Open to Canadian citizens and landed immigrants only.
Level of Study: Unrestricted.
Type: Scholarship.
Value: Canadian $30,000.
Frequency: Annual.
Country of Study: Any country.
No. of awards offered: Nine.
Application Procedure: Applicants must complete a registration form showing proof of eligibility and submit a curriculum vitae and registration fee.
Closing Date: October 4th.
Funding: Private.
Contributor: Standard Life.

ORENTREICH FOUNDATION FOR THE ADVANCEMENT OF SCIENCE, INC. (OFAS)

855 Route 301, Cold Spring, NY 10516-9802, United States of America
Tel: (1) 845 265 4200
Fax: (1) 845 265 4210
Email: ofas1@juno.com
Contact: Dr Rozlyn A Krajcik, Assistant Director Scientific Affairs

The Orentreich Foundation for the Advancement of Science (OFAS) is an operating private foundation that performs its own research and collaborates on projects of mutual interest.

OFAS Grants

Subjects: Areas of interest to the Foundation including ageing, dermatology, endocrinology and serum markers for human diseases.
Purpose: To allow an individual to conduct collaborative biomedical research or research at the Foundation.
Eligibility: Open to applicants at or above the postgraduate level in science or medicine at an accredited research institution in the United States of America. There are, however, no citizenship restrictions.
Level of Study: Postgraduate.
Type: Grant.
Value: Varies depending on the needs, nature and level of OFAS interest in the project.
Frequency: Four times per year.
Country of Study: United States of America.
Application Procedure: Applicants must submit an outline of proposed joint or collaborative research including, as a minimum, a brief overview of the current research in the field of interest, a statement of scientific objectives, a protocol summary, the curriculum vitae of the principal investigator, funding needed and total estimated project funding. Applications are reviewed at least quarterly. OFAS is usually the initiator of joint projects.
Closing Date: Applications may be submitted at any time.
Funding: Private.
Additional Information: Individuals who have a research question relating to a human disease or disease prevention factor for which there is adequate scientific basis for a serum marker to justify use of tho Sorum Treasury, should submit a brief overview of a proposal. Researchers will be asked for additional information after the initial screening process. Proposals will be evaluated on an ongoing basis. In certain cases where the research applies directly to the primary interests of OFAS in ageing, dermatology or endocrinology, limited grants to fund collaborative studies are available.

ORGANIZATION OF AMERICAN HISTORIANS (OAH)

112 North Bryan Avenue, Bloomington, IN 47408-4199, United States of America
Tel: (1) 812 855 9852
Fax: (1) 812 855 0696
Email: awards@oah.org
www: http://www.oah.org
Contact: Administrative Assistant

The Organization of American Historians (OAH) was founded in 1907 as the Mississippi Valley Historical Association and originally focused on the history of the Mississippi Valley. Now national in scope and, with approximately 11,000 members, it is a large professional organisation created and sustained for the investigation, study and teaching of American history.

ABC-Clio America History and Life Award

Subjects: American history.
Purpose: To recognise and encourage scholarship as documented in journal literature, and to advance new perspectives on accepted interpretations or previously unconsidered topics.
Eligibility: Open to entrants who have published an article in an American historical journal. Nominations and applications are welcome from both individuals and editors. Each entry must have been published during the period November 16th 2000 to November 15th 2002.
Type: Award.
Value: US$750 and a certificate.
Frequency: Every two years.
No. of awards offered: One.
Application Procedure: Applicants should visit the website for complete application requirements. There is no standard application form. Publishers are encouraged to enter one or more articles in the competition.
Closing Date: December 1st.
Contributor: OAH.
No. of awards given last year: One.
No. of applicants last year: 40.

AH Willi Paul Adams Foreign Languages Book Prize

Subjects: American history, namely the past and issues of continuity and change, as well as events or processes that began, developed or ended in what is now the United States of America.
Purpose: To award a prize to the best book published in a foreign language.
Eligibility: This prize is not open to books whose manuscripts were originally submitted for publication in English or by people for whom English is their first language.
Type: Prize.
Value: US$1,000 & certificate.
Frequency: Every two years.
No. of awards offered: One.
Application Procedure: Applicants must write a two page essay in English explaining why the book is a significant and original contribution to understanding American history. This and four copies of the book should be sent to the Willi Paul Adams Award Committee at the main address of the organization of American Historians (112 North Bryan avenue, PO Box 5457, Bloomington, IN 47408-5457). Authors of eligible books are invited to nominate their work. Scholars who know of eligible publications written by others are urged to inform those authors of the prize. Publishers are encouraged to enter one or more books in the competition. There is no standard application form.
Closing Date: May 1st in even years.
Contributor: OAH.
No. of awards given last year: One.
No. of applicants last year: 14.

Avery O Craven Award

Subjects: The coming of the Civil War, the Civil War years or the Era of Reconstruction, with the exception of works of purely military history.
Purpose: To award the most original book in the field.
Type: Award.
Value: US$500 and a certificate.
Frequency: Annual.
No. of awards offered: One.
Application Procedure: Applicants should visit the website for complete application requirements. There is no standard application form. Publishers are encouraged to enter one or more articles in the competition.
Closing Date: October 1st.
Contributor: OAH.
No. of awards given last year: One.
No. of applicants last year: 39.
Additional Information: The exception of works of purely military history recognises and reflects the Quaker convictions of Craven, President of the Organisation of American Historians 1963-64.

David Thelen award

Subjects: Past issues of continuity and change, also with events or processes that began, developed or ended in what is now the United States of America.
Purpose: To award a prize for the best article published in a foreign language.
Eligibility: Comparative and international studies that fall within these guidelines are welcomed. This prize is not open to articles whose

manuscripts were originally submitted for publication in English or by other people for whom English is their first language.

Type: Prize.

Value: The winning article will be printed in the Journal of American History and its author awarded a US$500 subvention for refining the article's English translation.

Frequency: Every two years.

No. of awards offered: One.

Application Procedure: Applicants must write a one-two page essay in English explaining why their article is a significant and original contribution to an understanding of American history. This and five copies of the article should be sent. The application must include the following information: name, mailing address, institutional affiliation, fax number and email address if available, and the language of submitted article. Authors of eligible articles are invited to nominate their work. Scholars who know of eligible publications written by others are urged to inform others of the prize. Applicants should visit the website for complete application requirements. There is no standard application form. Publishers are encouraged to enter one or more articles in the competition.

Closing Date: May 1st.

Contributor: OAH.

No. of awards given last year: One. Next one will be given in 2004.

No. of applicants last year: 12 from the award given in 2002.

For further information contact:

ChairJournal of American History, 1215 East Atwater, Bloomington, IN 47401, United States of America
Contact: Joanne Meyerowitz

Ellis W Hawley Prize

Subjects: Political economy, politics or institutions of the United States of America in its domestic or international affairs, from the Civil War to the present.

Purpose: To award the best book length historical study in the field.

Eligibility: Eligible works shall include book length historical studies, written in English and published during a given calendar year.

Type: Prize.

Value: US$500 and a certificate.

Frequency: Annual.

No. of awards offered: One.

Application Procedure: Applicants should visit the website for complete application requirements. There is no standard application form. Publishers are encouraged to enter one or more articles in the competition.

Closing Date: October 1st.

No. of awards given last year: One.

No. of applicants last year: 45.

Erik Barnouw Award

Subjects: American history.

Purpose: To recognise outstanding reporting or programming on network television, cable television or in documentary film.

Level of Study: Professional development.

Type: Award.

Value: US$500, plus a certificate.

Frequency: Annual.

No. of awards offered: One-two.

Application Procedure: Applicants should visit the website for complete application requirements. There is no standard application form. Companies are encouraged to enter one or more firms in the competition.

Closing Date: December 1st.

No. of awards given last year: One.

No. of applicants last year: 27.

Frederick Jackson Turner Award

Subjects: American history.

Purpose: To award an author's first book on some significant phase of American history and also the press that publishes it.

Eligibility: The work must be the first book length study of history published by the author. If the author has a PhD, he or she must have received it no more than seven years prior to submission of the

manuscript for publication. The work must be published in the calendar year before the award is given.

Type: Award.

Value: US$1,000 plus a medal and certificate.

Frequency: Annual.

No. of awards offered: One.

Application Procedure: Applicants should visit the website for complete application requirements. There is no standard application form. Publishers are encouraged to enter one or more books in the competition.

Closing Date: October 1st.

No. of awards given last year: One.

No. of applicants last year: 72.

Horace Samuel and Marion Galbraith Merrill Travel Grants in Twentieth Century American Political History

Subjects: Late nineteenth and twentieth-century American political history.

Purpose: To promote access of younger scholars to the Washington DC region's rich primary source collections.

Level of Study: Graduate.

Type: Travel grant.

Value: US$500-3,000.

Frequency: Annual.

Application Procedure: Applicants should visit the website for complete application requirements. There is no standard application form.

Closing Date: December 1st.

No. of awards given last year: 3.

No. of applicants last year: 34.

Huggins-Quarles Award

Subjects: History, ethnic studies, whiteness studies, Afro-Caribbean studies, cultural studies (post-colonialism), feminist studies, popular culture and media studies, immigration history, environmental studies or diplomatic history.

Eligibility: Open to minority graduate students at the dissertation research stage of their PhD.

Level of Study: Postgraduate.

Type: Award.

Value: US$1,000.

Frequency: Annual.

Application Procedure: Applicants should visit the website for complete application requirements. There is no standard application form.

Closing Date: December 1st.

No. of awards given last year: 2.

No. of applicants last year: 17.

James A Rawley Prize

Subjects: The history of race relations in the United States.

Purpose: To reward a book dealing.

Type: Prize.

Value: US$1,000 and a certificate.

Frequency: Annual.

No. of awards offered: One.

Application Procedure: Applicants should visit the website for complete application requirements. There is no standard application form. Publishers are encouraged to enter one or more books in the competition.

Closing Date: October 1st.

No. of awards given last year: Two.

No. of applicants last year: 58.

Japanese Residencies Program

Subjects: American history and culture, native Americans, the West, social, economic and political history of the twentieth-century.

Purpose: To contribute to the expansion of personal scholarly networks between Japan and the United States of America.

Eligibility: Applicants must be current members of the OAH, have a PhD, and be scholars of American history or culture. The committee invites applicants from previous competitions as well as new applicants to apply.

Level of Study: Professional development.
Type: Residency.
Value: Modest daily expenses, round trip expenses to Japan and accommodation.
Length of Study: Two weeks.
Frequency: Annual.
Country of Study: Japan.
No. of awards offered: Three.
Application Procedure: Applicants must send a two page curriculum vitae emphasising teaching experience and publications, three references, details of the institution to which the applicant wishes to apply and a personal statement no longer than two pages describing their interest in the programme and the issues that their own history teaching has addressed. For further information visit the website or contact the alumni of this programme. Postal applications must be addressed to the OAH Selection Committee. There is no standard application form. (Please visit website for additional information.).
Closing Date: December 1st.
Additional Information: The three selectees are encouraged to explore Japan before and after the end of the residency at their own expense. During the residency, selected scholars will give lectures and seminars in their speciality and provide individual consultation to Japanese scholars, graduate students and sometimes undergraduates studying American history and culture. Visitors will also participate in the collegial life of their host institutions. Each university has its own particular field of interest. Hiroshima University is concerned with environmental history, feminism, native Americans and the West; Chiba University with the social, economic and political history of the twentieth-century; and Doshisha University with cultural history. Residencies take place from 1st-14th November at Hiroshima University, late June at Chiba University and late October through to early November at Doshisha University.

La Pietra Dissertation Travel Fellowship in Transnational History

Subjects: American history.
Purpose: To provide financial assistance to graduate students whose dissertation topics deal with aspects of American history that extend beyond the United States' borders.
Eligibility: Applicants must be currently enrolled in a United States or foreign graduate programme.
Level of Study: Graduate.
Type: Fellowship.
Value: US$1,250.
Frequency: Annual.
No. of awards offered: One.
Application Procedure: Applicants must submit a two-three page project description indicating the dissertation's significance, including a statement of the major collections to be examined abroad and their relevance to the dissertation as well as two letters of recommendation including one from the dissertation advisor and a current curriculum vitae indicating language proficiency. For further application details, candidates should visit the website. There is no standard application form. (Please see website for additional information).
Closing Date: December 1st.
No. of awards given last year: One.
No. of applicants last year: 18.

Lerner-Scott Prize

Subjects: United States women's history.
Purpose: To award the best doctoral dissertation.
Level of Study: Postdoctorate.
Type: Prize.
Value: US$1,000 and a certificate.
Frequency: Annual.
No. of awards offered: One.
Application Procedure: Each application must contain a letter of support from a faculty member at the degree granting institution, along with an abstract, table of contents and sample chapter from the dissertation. Email addresses for the applicants and the adviser should also be included if available. For further application details, candidates should visit the website. There is no standard application form.

Closing Date: December 1st (Beginning in 2004, deadline will be October 1st).
No. of awards given last year: One.
No. of applicants last year: 14.

Liberty Legacy Foundation Award

Subjects: American history and the civil rights movement.
Purpose: To recognise the historical significance of the struggle for civil rights in the United States of America through awarding the best researched book on this topic.
Eligibility: Open to writers and publishers writing a book on any historical aspect of the struggle for human civil rights in the United States of America. Each entry must be published between January 1st 2002 and December 31st 2002.
Level of Study: Professional development.
Type: Competition.
Value: US$2,000 plus a certificate to the winning author and a certificate of merit to the publisher.
Frequency: Annual.
Country of Study: United States of America.
No. of awards offered: One.
Application Procedure: Applicants should visit the website for complete application requirements. There is no standard application form. Publishers are encouraged to enter one or more books in the competition.
Closing Date: October 1st.
No. of applicants last year: 54.
Additional Information: This award was inspired by OAH President Darlene Clark Hine's call in her 2002 OAH presidential address for more research on the origins of the civil rights movement in the period before 1954.

Louis Pelzer Memorial Award

Subjects: Any period or topic in the history of the United States.
Purpose: To promote and encourage strong essay writing with special emphasis on literary craftsmanship, subject significance and competent handling of evidence.
Type: Award.
Value: The winning essay will be published in the Journal of American History. The organisation offers a prize of US$500, a certificate and a medal to the winner.
Frequency: Annual.
Application Procedure: Applicants must submit five copies of essays which should not exceed 7,000 words in length (including endnotes). The footnotes at the end of the text should be triple spaced. Manuscripts are judged anonymously therefore the author's name and graduate programme should appear only on a separate cover page. For further application details, candidates should visit the website. There is no standard application form.
Closing Date: December 1st.
No. of awards given last year: One.
No. of applicants last year: 16.

For further information contact:

Committee Chair, Louis Pelzer Award Committee, Journal of American History, 1215 East Atwater Avenue, Bloomington, IN 47401, United States of America
Contact: Joanne Meyerowitz

Mary K Bonsteel Tachau PreCollegiate Teaching Award

Subjects: History.
Purpose: To recognise the contributions made by precollegiate and classroom teachers to improve history education.
Eligibility: Open to pre-collegiate teachers engaged at least half time in history teaching, whether in history or social studies. Successful candidates shall demonstrate exceptional ability in initiating or participating in projects which involve students in historical research, writing or other means of representing their knowledge of history, or in school, district, regional, state or national projects which enhance the professional development of teachers. They should also show ability in initiating or participating in projects which aim to build bridges between pre-collegiate and collegiate teachers, in working with museums, historical preservation societies or other public history

481

associations to enhance the place of public history in pre-collegiate schools, in developing innovative history criteria which foster a spirit of enquiry and emphasise critical skills, and in publishing or otherwise publicly presenting scholarship that advances education or knowledge.

Level of Study: Professional development.
Type: Award.
Value: A certificate, US$750, one year OAH membership and a one year subscription to the OAH Magazine of History. If the winner is an OAH member, the award will include a one year renewal of membership in the awardee's usual membership category. Finally, the winner's school will receive a plaque suitable for permanent public display.
Frequency: Annual.
No. of awards offered: One.
Application Procedure: Applicants must submit one application packet to each of the three committee members that includes copies of the following in the order given: a covering letter of no more than two pages written by a colleague indicating why the teacher merits the award, two letters written by former or present students of no more than two pages each, a curriculum vitae of no more than three pages, samples of the applicant's written work a narrative prepared by the applicant describing the goals and effects of the candidate's work in the classroom and elsewhere for history education of no more than three pages and the names, addresses and telephone numbers of at least three professional referees, including the writer of the covering letter, at least one of whom must be a colleague or supervisor. For further application details, candidates should visit the website. There is not standard application form.
Closing Date: December 1st.
No. of awards given last year: One.
No. of applicants last year: 2.

Merle Curti Award

Subjects: American social, intellectual, and/or cultural history.
Purpose: To recognise books in the fields of American social, intellectual, and/or cultural history.
Type: Award.
Value: US$1,000, a certificate and a medal.
Frequency: Annual.
No. of awards offered: One.
Application Procedure: Applicants must visit the website for complete application requirements. There is no standard application form. Publishers are encouraged to enter one or more books in the competition.
Closing Date: October 1st in the year the book was published.
Contributor: OAH.
No. of awards given last year: One.
No. of applicants last year: 131.

OAH Awards and Prizes

Subjects: American history.
Purpose: To recognise scholarly and professional achievement in the field of American history.
Eligibility: Open to applicants of any nationality.
Level of Study: Unrestricted.
Value: Varies, depending on award.
Frequency: Other.
Application Procedure: Applicants must obtain flyers for each award from the OAH office. The names and addresses of committee members are listed and submissions are sent directly to these members. There are no application forms to fill out and no application fees.
Closing Date: Deadlines vary.

Ray Allen Billington Prize

Subjects: American frontier history.
Purpose: To award the best book in American frontier history, defined broadly so as to include the pioneer periods of all geographical areas and comparisons between American frontiers and others.
Type: Award.
Value: US$1,000, a certificate and a medal.

Frequency: Every two years (even-numbered years), .
No. of awards offered: One.
Application Procedure: Applicants must visit the website for complete application requirements. There is no standard application form. Publishers are encouraged to enter one or more books in the competition.
Closing Date: October 1st.
Contributor: OAH.
No. of awards given last year: One.
No. of applicants last year: 61.

Richard W Leopold Prize

Subjects: Foreign policy, military affairs broadly construed, the historical activities of the federal government or biography in one of the foregoing areas.
Purpose: To improve contacts and interrelationships within the historical profession, where an increasing number of historically trained scholars hold distinguished positions in governmental agencies. It is awarded to the best book written by a historian connected with federal, state or municipal government.
Eligibility: The winner must have been employed in a government position for the last five years. If the author has accepted an academic position the book must have been published within two years from the time of the change.
Type: Prize.
Value: US$1,500 and a certificate.
Frequency: Every two years.
No. of awards offered: One.
Application Procedure: Applicants should visit the website for complete application requirements. There is no standard application form. Publishers are encouraged to enter one or more books in the competition.
Closing Date: October 7th.
No. of awards given last year: 2 for 2002 (award is biennial) next award will be given in 2004.
No. of applicants last year: 20.

White House Historical Association Fellowships

Subjects: Cultural education.
Purpose: To award teachers and scholars whose work enhances understanding of how the White House functions in all its various capacities as home, workplace, museum, structure and symbol.
Eligibility: Open to teachers and Scholars. Studies dealing primarily with political or governmental policy issues will not be considered except for ones concerning the operation of the White House as a political institution.
Level of Study: Research.
Type: Project grant.
Value: US$2,000 per month plus a travel stipend.
Length of Study: One-six months.
Country of Study: United States of America.
No. of awards offered: Three.
Application Procedure: Applicants must send a curriculum vitae, a two page summary of their project including the proposed final product of the research and timetable with three professional references. Applicants should visit the website for complete application requirements. There is no standard application form.
Closing Date: December 1st.
No. of awards given last year: 7.
No. of applicants last year: 17.

ORGANIZATION OF AMERICAN STATES (OAS)

1889 F Street North West, Washington, DC 20006-3897, United States of America
Tel: (1) 202 458 3000
Fax: (1) 202 458 3897
Email: portal@iacd.oas.org
www: http://www.oas.org
Contact: Administrative Assistant

OAS Graduate Academic Studies
Subjects: All fields except medicine and related fields and languages.
Purpose: To promote the economic, social, scientific and cultural development of the member states in order to achieve a stronger bond and better understanding among the peoples of the Americas.
Level of Study: Postgraduate.
Type: Fellowship.
Frequency: Annual.
Country of Study: Any member country of the OAS.
No. of awards offered: Varies.

ORIENTAL CERAMIC SOCIETY

30B Torrington Square, London, WC1E 7JL, England
Tel: (44) 20 7636 7985
Fax: (44) 20 7580 6749
Contact: Ms Jean Martin

The Oriental Ceramic Society was established in 1921 and aims to increase knowledge and appreciation of Asian ceramics and other arts. The Society is open to anyone interested in the arts of Asia. Membership is worldwide, and meetings, lectures and exhibitions are held regularly.

George De Menasce Memorial Trust Bursary
Subjects: Any aspect of oriental art.
Purpose: To promote research into oriental art.
Eligibility: Open to applicants of the highest calibre. The last recipient of the bursary wrote on his extensive research into Mamluk ceramics. Applicants should contact the Society for more details.
Level of Study: Postgraduate.
Type: Bursary.
Value: Up to UK£2,000.
Frequency: Every four to five years.
Country of Study: Any country.
No. of awards offered: One.
Application Procedure: Applicants must write for details and complete a form giving complete academic qualifications.
Funding: Private.
Additional Information: The recipient is required to read a paper on the research they have undertaken which is then published, so the research should be of an unusual and highly interesting nature. Research connected with a PhD degree is not normally considered adequate for the bursary.

ORTHOPAEDIC RESEARCH AND EDUCATION FOUNDATION (OREF)

6300 N River RoadSuite 700, Rosemont, IL 60018-4261, United States of America
Tel: (1) 847 698 9980
Fax: (1) 847 698 7806
Email: mcguire@oref.org
www: http://www.oref.org
Contact: Mrs Jean McGuire, Vice President Grants

In 1955, leaders of the major professional organisations in the speciality, the American Orthopaedic Association, the American Academy of Orthopaedic Surgeons and the Orthopaedic Research Society, established the Orthopaedic Research and Education Foundation (OREF) as a means of supporting research and building the scientific base of clinical practice. Today, the Foundation raises over US$5 million per year and holds a unique place in United States medicine.

Fellowship in Health Services Research
Subjects: Orthopaedics.
Purpose: To enable orthopaedic surgeons with research skills to manage health services and outcomes research.
Eligibility: Applicants must be orthopaedic surgeons in either Canada or United States of America.
Level of Study: Postdoctorate.
Type: Fellowship.
Value: US$70,000 per year.

Length of Study: Two years.
Frequency: Annual.
Study Establishment: At participating institutions.
Country of Study: United States of America.
No. of awards offered: One.
Application Procedure: Applicants must make a formal application.
Closing Date: October 1st.
Funding: Private.
Contributor: Orthopaedic surgeons.
No. of awards given last year: One.
No. of applicants last year: Five.

OREF Career Development Award
Subjects: Orthopaedic surgery.
Purpose: To encourage a commitment to scientific research in orthopaedic surgery.
Eligibility: Applicants must be orthopaedic surgeons, and are not eligible if they are holders of NIH ROI award.
Level of Study: Professional development.
Type: Award.
Value: Up to US$75,000 per year.
Length of Study: Three years.
Frequency: Annual.
Country of Study: United States of America or Canada.
No. of awards offered: One-three.
Application Procedure: Applicants must make a formal application with letters of recommendation.
Closing Date: October 1st.
Funding: Private.
Contributor: Orthopaedic surgeons.
No. of awards given last year: Two.
No. of applicants last year: 17.

OREF Clinical Research Award
Subjects: Orthopaedics.
Purpose: To recognise outstanding clinical research related to musculoskeletal disease or injury.
Eligibility: Restricted to members of the American Academy of Orthopaedic Surgeons, the Orthopaedic Research Society (ORS), the Canadian Orthopaedic Association or the Canadian Orthopaedic Research Society. Alternatively, candidates may be sponsored by a member.
Level of Study: Professional development.
Type: Award.
Value: US$20,000.
Length of Study: One year.
Frequency: Annual.
Country of Study: United States of America or Canada.
No. of awards offered: One.
Application Procedure: Applicants must submit an original manuscript.
Closing Date: July 1st.
Funding: Private.
Contributor: Orthopaedic surgeons.
No. of awards given last year: One.
No. of applicants last year: Nine.

OREF Prospective Clinical Research
Subjects: Orthopaedics.
Purpose: To provide funding for promising prospective clinical proposals.
Eligibility: Applicants must be orthopaedic surgeons.
Level of Study: Professional development.
Type: Award.
Value: Up to US$50,000 per year.
Length of Study: Three years.
Frequency: Annual.
Study Establishment: Medical centre.
Country of Study: United States of America.
No. of awards offered: One-three.
Application Procedure: Applicants must make a formal application.
Closing Date: October 1st.
Funding: Private.

Contributor: Orthopaedic surgeons.
No. of awards given last year: Two.
No. of applicants last year: 11.

OREF Research Grants

Subjects: Sports medicine, surgery, rheumatology and treatment techniques.
Purpose: To encourage new investigators by providing seed money and start up funding.
Eligibility: Open to orthopaedic surgeons who are PI or co PI. PI cannot have NIH ROI awards.
Level of Study: Postdoctorate.
Type: Research grant.
Value: Up to US$50,000 per year.
Length of Study: Two years.
Frequency: Annual.
Study Establishment: A medical centre.
Country of Study: United States of America.
No. of awards offered: 8-12.
Application Procedure: Applicants must make a formal application.
Closing Date: October 1st.
Funding: Private.
Contributor: Orthopaedic surgeons and orthopaedic corporations.
No. of awards given last year: 12.
No. of applicants last year: 65.

OREF Resident Research Award

Subjects: Orthopaedics.
Purpose: To encourage the development of research interests for residents and Fellows.
Eligibility: Applicants must be orthopaedic surgeon residents or Fellows in an approved residency programme in the United States.
Level of Study: Professional development.
Type: Award.
Value: US$15,000.
Length of Study: One year.
Frequency: Annual.
Study Establishment: Medical centre.
Country of Study: United States of America.
No. of awards offered: Up to 10.
Application Procedure: Applicants must make a formal application.
Closing Date: October 1st.
Funding: Private.
Contributor: Orthopaedic surgeons.
No. of awards given last year: 13.
No. of applicants last year: 46.

OSTEOGENESIS IMPERFECTA FOUNDATION, INC.

804 W Diamond Avenue, Suite 210, Gaithersburg, MD 20878, United States of America
Tel: (1) 301 947 0083
Fax: (1) 301 947 0456
Email: bonelink@oif.org
www: http://www.oif.org
Contact: Mr Heller An Shapiro, Executive Director

The Osteogenesis Imperfecta Foundation works to improve the quality of life for individuals affected by osteogenesis imperfecta, through research to find treatments and a cure, awareness, education and mutual support.

Michael Geisman Memorial Fellowship Grant

Subjects: Osteogenesis imperfecta.
Purpose: To encourage research scientists to develop expertise in the field.
Eligibility: Open to suitably qualified investigators with less than five years of postdoctoral research training.
Level of Study: Postdoctorate.
Type: Fellowship.

Value: US$50,000 per year salary comprised of US$35,000 per year for salary and US$15,000 per year for supplies. Second year funding may be available.
Frequency: Annual.
Country of Study: Any country.
No. of awards offered: Varies.
Application Procedure: Applicants must complete an application form, available on request or from the website.
Closing Date: Please contact the organisation for details.
Funding: Private.

Osteogenesis Imperfecta Foundation Seed Research Grant

Subjects: Osteogenesis imperfecta.
Purpose: To fund seed projects which can then be submitted to larger funding bodies.
Eligibility: Open to qualified researchers in the field.
Level of Study: Postdoctorate.
Type: Research grant.
Value: Up to US$60,000. Indirect costs and salaries will not be covered.
Length of Study: One year.
Frequency: Annual.
Country of Study: Any country.
No. of awards offered: Varies.
Application Procedure: Applicants must complete an application form, available on request or from the website.
Closing Date: Please contact the organisation for details.
Funding: Private.

PALOMA O'SHEA SANTANDER INTERNATIONAL PIANO COMPETITION

Calle Hernán Cortés 3, Santander, E-39003, Spain
Tel: (34) 94 231 1451
Fax: (34) 94 231 4816
Email: concurso@albeniz.com
www: http://www.albeniz.com
Contact: A Kaufmann, Secretariat General

The Paloma O'Shea Santander International Piano Competition is one of the best rated competitions in the world. It provides an opportunity for exceptionally talented pianists to enhance their careers. The jury is composed of renowned musicians in order to ensure that grants are made in a fair and unbiased manner.

Paloma O'Shea Santander International Piano Competition

Subjects: Piano performance.
Purpose: To give support to young pianists of exceptional talent.
Eligibility: Open to pianists of any nationality under the age of 29 years.
Level of Study: Unrestricted.
Type: Competition.
Value: Please contact the organisation for details.
Length of Study: July 25th-August 7th, 2005.
Frequency: Every three years.
Country of Study: Other.
No. of awards offered: Seven.
Application Procedure: Applicants in the United States should contact Mrs Brookes McIntyre at the address below. Applicants from all other countries must contact the Secretariat General for details at the main address.
Closing Date: October 30, 2004.
Funding: Commercial, Government, Private.
No. of awards given last year: Seven.
Additional Information: In general 20 pianists will participate in Santander. Each one will be chosen from the pre-selection phase which is recorded and filmed on video. Six participants will be selected for the semi-finals and later three participants go through to the final. The competition consists of four stages. The first is a recital and chamber music (a quintet for piano and strings), the semi finals consist

of a concerto with a chamber orchestra and recital, and the final, a concerto with a symphony orchestra.

For further information contact:

PO Box 82743, Albuquerque, NM 87198, United States of America
Tel: (1) 505 250 2341
Fax: (1) 505 265 8932
Contact: Mrs Brookes McIntyre

PAN AMERICAN HEALTH ORGANIZATION (PAHO) REGIONAL OFFICE OF THE WORLD HEALTH ORGANIZATION (WHO)

Regional Office for the Americas/Pan-American Sanitary Bureau, 525 23rd Street North West, Washington, DC 20037-2895, United States of America
Tel: (1) 202 974 3000
Fax: (1) 202 974 3663
Email: rgp@paho.org
www: http://www.paho.org
Contact: Grants Administrator

The Pan American Health Organization (PAHO) is an international public health agency working to improve health and living standards of the countries of the Americas. It serves as the specialised organisation for health of the Inter American System and as the regional office for the Americas of the World Health Organization.

PAHO Grants

Subjects: Public health studies.
Purpose: To contribute to the public health of the region of the Americas (individual programme objectives vary). Programmes include graduate thesis grants, research training grants, regional research competitions (announced yearly) and special initiatives announced via the PAHO website.
Eligibility: Open to citizens and residents of Latin America and the Caribbean.
Level of Study: Doctorate, Graduate, Postgraduate, Research.
Type: Research Grant.
Value: Please contact the organisation.
Frequency: Varies.
Study Establishment: Varies.
Country of Study: Latin America or Caribbean countries only.
No. of awards offered: Varies according to programme.
Application Procedure: Applicants must complete an application form. Guidelines and application forms are available from the website.
Closing Date: Varies according to the programme.
Funding: Government.
Contributor: Member states and their agencies.

PARALYZED VETERANS OF AMERICA, SPINAL CORD RESEARCH FOUNDATION

801 18th Street North West, Washington, DC 20006, United States of America
Tel: (1) 202 416 7652
Fax: (1) 202 416 7641
Email: foundations@pva.org
www: http://www.pva.org
Contact: Forence Montgomery, Administrative Officer

The Spinal Cord Research Foundation aims to fund innovative educational projects that enhance the quality of life of individuals with spinal cord injury or disease (SCI/D) and/or increases the knowledge and effectiveness of health professionals in the SCI/B community.

Spinal Cord Research Foundation Grants

Subjects: The basic sciences related to spinal cord injury or disease, clinical and functional studies of the medical, psychological and economic effects of spinal cord injury or disease, as well as interventions

proposed to alleviate these effects, design and development of new and improved rehabilitative and assistive devices for individuals with spinal dysfunction.
Purpose: To improve the quality of life of individuals with spinal cord injuries and to hasten the discovery of a cure for spinal cord injury.
Eligibility: Open to qualified individuals who are seeking funds to develop a project in the field of spinal cord injury. Please visit the website for further eligibility requirements.
Level of Study: Postdoctorate.
Type: Other.
Value: Please consult the organisation.
Length of Study: Two years, with a chance to resubmit after the second year is completed.
Frequency: Annual.
Application Procedure: Applicants must obtain a brochure, guidelines and applications for a grant request, which can be downloaded from the website or are available from the Foundation.
Closing Date: September 1st
Funding: Private.
Additional Information: All grant recipients must submit biannual and annual progress reports, a photo and an article in layman's language for publications in PVA's monthly publication, Paraplegia News, and other publications.

PARAPSYCHOLOGY FOUNDATION, INC.

228 East 71st Street, New York, NY 10021, United States of America
Tel: (1) 212 628 1550
Fax: (1) 212 628 1559
Email: info@parapsychology.org
www: http://www.parapsychology.org
Contact: Vice President

Established in 1951, the Parapsychology Foundation acts as a clearing house for information about parapsychology. Essentially an administrative organisation, it maintains one of the largest libraries to do with parapsychology, the Eileen J Garret Library, as well as supporting various programmes which include the library, a grant and scholarship programme, a conference and lecture programme, and a speaker's bureau and publishing programme.

D Scott Rogo Award for Parapsychological Literature

Subjects: Parapsychology.
Purpose: To provide support to authors working on a manuscript pertaining to the science of parapsychology.
Eligibility: Open to nationals of any country.
Level of Study: Unrestricted.
Type: Award.
Value: US$3,000.
Length of Study: One year.
Frequency: Annual.
Country of Study: Any country.
No. of awards offered: One.
Application Procedure: Applicants must submit a brief synopsis of the proposed contents of manuscript, a list of previous writings and a sample writing of assistance.
Closing Date: April 15th for notification on May 1st.

Eileen J Garrett Scholarship

Subjects: Parapsychology.
Purpose: To assist students attending an accredited college or university in pursuing the academic study of the science of parapsychology.
Eligibility: Open to nationals of any country.
Level of Study: Unrestricted.
Type: Scholarship.
Value: US$3,000.
Length of Study: One year.
Frequency: Annual.
Study Establishment: An accredited college or university.
Country of Study: Any country.
No. of awards offered: One.

Application Procedure: Applicants must submit samples of writings on the subject with an application form from the Foundation. Letters of reference are required from three individuals, familiar with the applicant's work and/or studies in parapsychology.

Closing Date: July 15th for notification on August 1st.

Parapsychology Foundation Grant

Subjects: Parapsychology.

Purpose: To support original study, research and experiments in parapsychology.

Eligibility: Open to nationals of any country.

Level of Study: Unrestricted.

Type: Grant.

Value: Varies.

Length of Study: One year.

Frequency: Annual.

Country of Study: Any country.

Application Procedure: Applicants must contact the organisation for details.

Closing Date: Applications are accepted at any time.

Additional Information: Funding for the Foundation Grant is limited but applicants are still welcome to submit a proposal on the off chance that the programme will be reviewed.

PARKER B FRANCIS FELLOWSHIP PROGRAM

Physiology Program, Harvard School of Public Health, Room 1411 Building 1665 Huntington Avenue, Boston, MA 02115, United States of America
Tel: (1) 617 432 4099
Fax: (1) 617 277 2382
Email: sagudelo@hsph.harvard.edu
www: http://www.hsph.harvard.edu/pbf
Contact: Ms Sylvie Agudelo, Executive Director

Parker B Francis Fellowship Program

Subjects: Pulmonary research.

Purpose: To support rising stars in the field of pulmonary research as they make the transition from postdoctoral trainee to independent researcher.

Eligibility: Open to applicants, ideally, with between two and seven years of postdoctoral research experience, published articles in leading journals and with a clear trajectory in pulmonary research.

Level of Study: Postdoctorate.

Type: Fellowship.

Value: The total budget is limited to US$38,000 for the first year, US$40,000 for the second, and US$42,000 for the third. These totals include stipend plus fringe benefits and may include travel to a maximum of US$1,500. Direct research project costs and indirect costs are not allowed. These expenses ought to be supported by research project grants which are an essential part of the application in documenting the availability of sufficient research project support to make possible fulfilment of the Fellow's research aims.

Length of Study: Three years.

Frequency: Annual.

Country of Study: United States of America or Canada.

No. of awards offered: 18.

Application Procedure: Applicants must submit a completed application form, biographical sketch and brief statement of their career goals. Also a letter from their mentor evaluating the applicant's qualifications and indicating their career goals in the field of pulmonary research, three letters of recommendation, a summary of the past training record of the primary mentor (including names of former trainees and their current positions, sources and level of support with grants pending and the extent of equipment and space for research training available to the primary mentor and trainee), signatures of the primary mentor on the face page, department or division head and the fiscal officer responsible for administering the grant.

Closing Date: Mid October.

Funding: Private.

Contributor: The Francis Families Foundation.

No. of awards given last year: 18.

No. of applicants last year: 50.

Additional Information: Further information is available from the website.

PARKINSON'S DISEASE FOUNDATION, INC. (PDF)

710 W, 168th Street, New York, NY 10032, United States of America
Tel: (1) 212 923 4700
Fax: (1) 212 923 4778
Email: info@pdf.org; sstone@pdf.org
www: http://www.pdf.org
Contact: Sharon Stone, Director - Grants & Special Programs

The Parkinson's Disease Foundation (PDF) was founded in 1957 to encourage and promote research into Parkinson's disease, a chronic, degenerative neurological disorder that exhibits itself in such symptoms as tremor, stiffness and slowness of movement. (The mission of the Parkinson's Disease Foundation is two-fold: to understand and find the cure to Parkinson's Disease and related movement disorders; and for as long as this search continues to ensure that those individuals and families who live with Parkinson's are able to achieve and maintain the best possible quality of life.)

H Houston Merritt Fellowship

Subjects: Parkinson's disease research.

Eligibility: Open to established scientists at the level of associate professor or above.

Level of Study: Postdoctorate.

Type: Fellowship.

Value: US$15,000.

Length of Study: 6-12 months.

Frequency: Annual.

Study Establishment: The College of Physicians and Surgeons, Columbia University, New York.

Country of Study: United States of America.

No. of awards offered: One.

Application Procedure: Applicants must send applications, including a curriculum vitae, directly to Dr Stanley Fahn at the Foundation. There is no application form.

Closing Date: April 1st.

Funding: Private.

Parkinson's Disease Foundation International Research Grants Program

Subjects: Parkinson's disease research.

Purpose: To support projects of highest scientific caliber from around the world that also; are directly relevant to the study of causes of and cure for Parkinson's disease, are complimentary to not duplication of other research in the field, have the potential to lead to research proposals to the National Institutes of Health (NIH) and/or other sources of government support. Both basic and clinical proposals are eligible for support. Preference will be given to scientists who are at an early stage in their professional career.

Eligibility: Open to PhDs and MDs.

Level of Study: Postgraduate.

Type: Grant.

Value: Up to US$40,000.

Length of Study: One year.

Frequency: Annual.

Study Establishment: Any institution.

Country of Study: Any country.

No. of awards offered: 12-14.

Application Procedure: Applicants must contact Sharon Stone for details on Telephone 212-923-4700 or 800-457-6676.

Closing Date: February 9th.

Funding: Private.

No. of awards given last year: 30 (but this was a special joint program - no longer doing joint program).

PDF Postdoctoral Fellowships

Subjects: Parkinson's disease research.
Eligibility: Open to physicians who have completed their residency in neurology.
Level of Study: Postdoctorate.
Type: Fellowship.
Value: US$35,000.
Length of Study: One year.
Frequency: Annual.
Study Establishment: The College of Physicians and Surgeons, Columbia University, New York.
Country of Study: United States of America.
No. of awards offered: Three.
Application Procedure: Applicants must send applications, including a curriculum vitae, directly to Dr Stanley Fahn at the Foundation. There is no application form.
Closing Date: April 1st.
Funding: Private.

PDF Summer Fellowships

Subjects: Parkinson's disease research.
Purpose: To allow students to study under the supervision of an established investigator.
Eligibility: Open to pre-medical and medical students and to doctoral candidates.
Level of Study: Doctorate, Postgraduate.
Type: Fellowship.
Value: US$1,800-2,200.
Length of Study: 10 weeks.
Frequency: Annual.
Study Establishment: Any college or university.
Country of Study: United States of America.
No. of awards offered: 10-15.
Application Procedure: Applicants must complete an application form, available from the Foundation.
Closing Date: April 1st.

THE PARKINSON'S DISEASE SOCIETY OF THE UNITED KINGDOM (PDS)

215 Vauxhall Bridge Road, London, SW1V 1EJ, England
Tel: (44) 20 7931 8080
Fax: (44) 20 7233 9908
Email: research@parkinsons.org.uk
www: http://www.parkinsons.org.uk
Contact: Ms Catherine Fleming, Research Officer

The Parkinson's Disease Society of the United Kingdom (PDS) works with people who have Parkinson's, their families, and health and social care professionals. The mission of the PDS is, through research, the conquest of Parkinson's and the alleviation of the suffering and distress it causes. The work of the PDS includes research into the cause, cure and prevention of Parkinson's, and improvements in treatments, a helpline staffed by nurses offering advice on all aspects of Parkinson's including drug treatments, surgery, therapies, social and health care rights, benefits, driving, insurance and employment. The PDS also provides a wide range of publications, audio tapes and videos, a comprehensive education and training programme and a national network of field staff, branches and welfare visitors, offering local information, support, advice and social activities.

PDS Research Project Grant

Subjects: Medical sciences, neurology, neurosciences, biochemistry, toxicology, pathology, genetics, geriatrics or pharmacy.
Purpose: To support research into the causes, cure and prevention of Parkinson's disease, and care and effective treatments.
Eligibility: Open to United Kingdom residents. The principal applicant must hold a tenured position for the duration of the award and hold suitable qualifications.
Level of Study: Postdoctorate, Professional development.
Type: Project grant.
Value: To include at least one salary plus consumables and equipment.

Length of Study: Up to three years.
Frequency: As available.
Study Establishment: A recognised research institution, university or hospital in the United Kingdom.
Country of Study: United Kingdom.
No. of awards offered: Varies.
Application Procedure: Applicants must complete an application form which is available from the Society's website.
Closing Date: Please refer to the website.
Funding: Private.
Contributor: Donations.
No. of awards given last year: 13.
No. of applicants last year: 42.
Additional Information: The Society is currently implementing a new research strategy. For further details of this please visit the Society's website.

PDS Studentships and Junior/Senior Fellows

Subjects: Medical sciences, neurology, neurosciences, biochemistry, toxicology, pathology, genetics, geriatrics or pharmacy.
Purpose: To support research into the causes, cure and prevention of Parkinson's disease, and care and effective treatments.
Eligibility: Open to United Kingdom residents with suitable qualifications and a salaried position for the duration of the award.
Level of Study: Doctorate.
Type: Fellowship.
Value: Funding ranges from UK£55,000 for non clinical to UK£105,000 for clinical.
Length of Study: Up to three years.
Frequency: As available.
Study Establishment: A recognised teaching, research or clinical institution in the United Kingdom.
Country of Study: United Kingdom.
No. of awards offered: Varies.
Application Procedure: Applicants must complete an application form which is available from the Society's website.
Closing Date: December 20th.
Funding: Private.
Contributor: Donations.
Additional Information: The Society is currently implementing a new research strategy. For further details of this please visit the Society's website.

PARTICLE PHYSICS AND ASTRONOMY RESEARCH COUNCIL (PPARC)

Polaris House, North Star Avenue, Swindon, Wiltshire, SN2 1SZ, England
Tel: (44) 1793 442026
Fax: (44) 1793 442036
Email: steve.cann@pparc.ac.uk
www: http://www.pparc.ac.uk
Contact: Mr Steve Cann, E & T Section

The mission of the Particle Physics and Astronomy Research Council (PPARC) is to pursue a programme of high quality basic research in astronomy, planetary science and particle physics which furthers the understanding of fundamental questions, trains high quality scientists and engineers, increases the United Kingdom industry's competitiveness, attracts future generations of scientists and engineers and stimulates public interest.

European Young Investigator (EVRYI) Awards

Subjects: Particle physics, astronomy or astrophysics.
Purpose: To enable and encourage outstanding young researchers from all over the world to work in a European environment for the benefit of the development of European Science and the building of the next generation of leading European researchers.
Eligibility: Open to researchers from anywhere in the world who have between 2 and up to 10 years of postdoctoral experience at the closing date of the call, taking into account career breaks.
Level of Study: Postdoctorate.
Type: Fellowship.

Value: Total value will range from UK£550K to UK£900K (UK£110K to UK£180K per year).
Length of Study: Up to five years.
Frequency: Annual.
Study Establishment: Any academic institution which is acceptable to PPARC.
Country of Study: United Kingdom.
No. of awards offered: One(1).
Application Procedure: Applicants must refer to the PPARC website for application information.
Closing Date: 15th December 2004.
Funding: Government.
Additional Information: Further information is available on request by emailing evryi@pparc.ac.uk.

PPARC Daphne Jackson Memorial Fellowships

Subjects: Particle physics or astronomy.
Purpose: To enable high level engineers and scientists to return to their professions after a career break for family or other reasons.
Eligibility: Open to promising engineers and scientists who have taken a career break.
Level of Study: Postdoctorate, Research.
Type: Fellowship.
Value: Dependent on age and experience.
Length of Study: Two years.
Frequency: Annual.
Study Establishment: Universities and research institutions.
Country of Study: United Kingdom.
No. of awards offered: Varies.
Application Procedure: Applicants must contact Dr E A Johnson, Trust Co-ordinator, or Jennifer Woolley, Administrator, for application forms and further information.
Closing Date: Please write for details.
Additional Information: The Daphne Jackson Memorial Fellowship is also administered by the BBSRC and the EPSRC.

For further information contact:

The Daphne Jackson Memorial Fellowships Trust, Department of Physics, University of Surrey, Guildford, Surrey GU2 5XH, England
Tel: (44) 1483 259166

PPARC Postdoctoral Fellowships

Subjects: Particle physics or astronomy.
Purpose: To enable less experienced researchers to devote themselves to independent and original research.
Eligibility: Applicants must have, or expect to have, a PhD.
Level of Study: Postdoctorate.
Type: Fellowship.
Length of Study: Up to three years.
Frequency: Annual.
Study Establishment: Any academic institution which is acceptable to PPARC.
Country of Study: United Kingdom.
No. of awards offered: Approx. 10.
Application Procedure: Applicants must refer to the PPARC website for application information.
Closing Date: November 1st.
Funding: Government.
Additional Information: Further information is available on request by emailing fellowships@pparc.ac.uk.

PPARC Postgraduate Studentships

Subjects: Particle physics or astronomy.
Eligibility: Open to postgraduates from the United Kingdom and European Union countries.
Level of Study: Postgraduate.
Type: Studentship.
Length of Study: Up to three years.
Frequency: Annual.
Study Establishment: Any academic institution which is acceptable to PPARC.
Country of Study: United Kingdom.
No. of awards offered: Approx. 185.

Application Procedure: Applicants must refer to the PPARC website for application information.
Closing Date: July 31st.
Funding: Government.
Additional Information: Further information is available on request by emailing studentships@pparc.ac.uk.

PPARC Research Grants in Astronomy and Particle Physics

Subjects: Particle physics or astronomy.
Eligibility: For requirements please refer to the website.
Level of Study: Postdoctorate, Research.
Type: Research grant.
Value: Varies.
Frequency: Twice a year.
Study Establishment: Any academic institution which is acceptable to PPARC.
Country of Study: United Kingdom.
No. of awards offered: Varies.
Application Procedure: Applicants must refer to the PPARC website for application information.
Funding: Government.

PPARC Royal Society Industry Fellowships

Subjects: Particle physics or astronomy.
Purpose: To enhance interaction between those in industry and the research base, to the benefit of United Kingdom industry.
Eligibility: Open to senior academic scientists and industrial employees with a project proposal central to their own research programme for which a collaborative effort would bring benefits.
Level of Study: Postdoctorate, Professional development.
Type: Fellowship.
Value: Varies.
Length of Study: Six months-two years full-time, or part-time over a period of up to four years.
Frequency: Annual.
Study Establishment: An appropriate academic institution or position in the industry.
Country of Study: United Kingdom.
No. of awards offered: Up to 15.
Application Procedure: Applicants must find a suitable industrial or academic partner to host their project before submitting an application. Applications and further information are available from the Research Appointments Department of The Royal Society.
Closing Date: June or December.
Funding: Commercial, Private.
Contributor: The Royal Society, EPSRC, BBSRC, Rolls-Royce and PPARC.
Additional Information: Apart from the Royal Society Fellowships Programme the following fellowship programmes are administered by the PPARC in collaboration with other partners: The European Organisation for Nuclear Research (CERN) Fellowships, The European Space Agency (ESA) Fellowships, The Anglo-Australian Postdoctoral Research Fellowships, and the Daphne Jackson Fellowships. Further information on these programmes is available on the PPARC website.

For further information contact:

Research Appointments Department, The Royal Society, 6 Carlton House Terrace, London, SW1Y 5AG, England
Tel: (44) 20 7451 2542
Email: ukresearch.appointments@royalsoc.ac.uk
www: http://www.royalsoc.ac.uk/gr_ifs.html

PPARC Senior Research Fellowships

Subjects: Particle physics or astronomy.
Purpose: To enable a small number of outstanding scientists at the peak of their capabilities to devote themselves full-time to research and scholarship, free of the restrictions imposed by their normal employment.
Eligibility: Open to scientists who are already established in their careers, having proved their exceptional research and interpretative ability. Applicants must be members of permanent staff of United Kingdom universities, technical colleges or similar institutions. Fellows

are expected to return to their normal employment at the termination of the fellowship.
Level of Study: Postdoctorate.
Type: Fellowship.
Value: The Council will pay the salary, but not superannuation or National Insurance contributions, as if the Fellow is continuing in his or her normal employment at his or her home institution.
Length of Study: Up to three years.
Frequency: Annual.
Study Establishment: Any academic institution which is acceptable to PPARC.
Country of Study: United Kingdom.
No. of awards offered: Up to 6.
Application Procedure: Applicants must refer to the PPARC website for application information.
Closing Date: November 1st.
Funding: Government.
Additional Information: Fellowships are not intended to replace sabbatical leave. Further information is available on request or by emailing fellowships@pparc.ac.uk.

PATERSON INSTITUTE FOR CANCER RESEARCH

Christie Hospital NHS Trust, Manchester, M20 4BX, England
Tel: (44) 161 446 3136
Fax: (44) 161 446 3109
Email: gcowling@picr.man.ac.uk
www: http://www.paterson.man.ac.uk/education
Contact: Dr Graham Cowling, Scientific Administrator

The Paterson Institute is a Cancer Research UK funded centre for cancer research and forms the research arm of a specialist cancer hospital, the Christie Hospital NHS Trust. It carries out cancer research in a large number of areas and has 16 research groups and around 200 scientists.

Paterson 4 Year Studentship

Subjects: Oncology.
Purpose: To support study towards a PhD.
Eligibility: Open to candidates who have obtained a First Class (Honours) or Second Class (Honours) Bachelor of Science Degree.
Level of Study: Doctorate, Postgraduate.
Type: Studentship.
Value: UK£11,200 per year stipend, university fees and bench fees.
Length of Study: Four years.
Frequency: Annual.
Study Establishment: The University of Manchester.
Country of Study: United Kingdom.
No. of awards offered: Two - three.
Application Procedure: Applicants are advised to visit the website for details.
Closing Date: Before January 15th.
Funding: Private.
Contributor: Paterson Institute.
No. of awards given last year: 3.
No. of applicants last year: 200.
Additional Information: All positions are advertised on the website. Self-funded students are accepted subject to qualifications and three year funding. The first nine months are spent on rotation in three research laboratories. Students must submit a final project of their choice.

PhD Studentship

Subjects: Oncology.
Purpose: To support the study towards a PhD.
Eligibility: Candidates must have a First or Upper Second Class Bachelor of Science Degree.
Level of Study: Doctorate, Postgraduate.
Type: Studentship.
Value: UK£11,200 per year stipend, university fees and bench fees.
Length of Study: Three years.
Frequency: Annual.

Study Establishment: The University of Manchester.
Country of Study: United Kingdom.
No. of awards offered: Two-six.
Application Procedure: Applicants must visit the website for details.
Closing Date: Usually before January 31st.
Funding: Government, Private.
Contributor: Cancer Research UK, other funding bodies.
No. of awards given last year: 1.
No. of applicants last year: 100.
Additional Information: All positions are advertised on the website. Self-funded students are accepted subject to qualifications and three year funding.

PAUL MELLON CENTRE FOR STUDIES IN BRITISH ART, LONDON

16 Bedford Square, London, WC1B 3JA, England
Tel: (44) 20 7580 0311
Fax: (44) 20 7636 6730
Email: info@paul-mellon-centre.ac.uk
www: http://www.paul-mellon-centre.ac.uk
Contact: Mr Brian Allen, Director of Studies

The Paul Mellon Centre for Studies in British Art is an art and architectural research institution, based in London but part of Yale University.

Paul Mellon Centre Grants

Subjects: Any aspect of British art or architecture before 1960.
Purpose: To support scholarship in British art or architecture and to disseminate knowledge through publications, exhibitions and educational programmes.
Eligibility: Open to candidates of any nationality.
Level of Study: Graduate, Postdoctorate, Postgraduate, Predoctorate, Professional development, Research.
Type: Grant.
Value: UK£500-20,000 curatorial research, publication, educational and research support grants.
Length of Study: A maximum of one academic year.
Frequency: Annual.
Country of Study: The United States of America or the United Kingdom.
No. of awards offered: Varies, usually 15-20.
Application Procedure: Applicants must submit their name, address and telephone number, an outline proposal of not more than three pages, a detailed breakdown of estimated costs, the proposed completion and/or publication date where appropriate, a curriculum vitae and three letters of recommendation. These should be sent directly to the Paul Mellon Centre in London.
Closing Date: September 15th.
Funding: Private.
No. of awards given last year: 25.
No. of applicants last year: 80.

THE PAULO CELLO COMPETITION

PL 1105, Helsinki, FIN-00101, Finland
Tel: (358) 4 0528 4876
Fax: (358) 9 2243 2879
Email: cello@paulo.fi
www: http://www.cellocompetitionpaulo.org
Contact: Administrative Assistant

The Paulo Cello Competition organises an international competition for cellists of all nations.

International Paulo Cello Competition

Subjects: Cello performance.
Eligibility: Open to cellists aged 16-33 years old.
Level of Study: Unrestricted.
Type: Competition.
Value: The first prize is €15,000, the second prize is €12,000, the third prize is €9,000 and the fourth, fifth and sixth prizes are €2,000.

Frequency: Approx. every five years.
Country of Study: Finland.
No. of awards offered: Six.
Application Procedure: Applicants must write for a brochure containing details of the application and audition pieces.
Closing Date: May 15th.
Funding: Private.
Contributor: The Paulo Foundation.
No. of awards given last year: Six, plus three special awards.
No. of applicants last year: 66.
Additional Information: Further information is available on request.

PEN AMERICAN CENTER

568 Broadway, New York, NY 10012, United States of America
Tel: (1) 212 334 1660
Fax: (1) 212 334 2181
Email: pen@pen.org
www: http://www.pen.org
Contact: Mr Stephen Motika

PEN American Center is a fellowship of writers dedicated to defending free expression and advancing the cause of literature and literacy. The American Center is the largest of 130 international PEN Centers worldwide.

PEN Writers Fund
Subjects: Writing and translation.
Purpose: To assist professional published writers facing emergency situations.
Eligibility: Open to published professional writers and produced playwrights who have a traceable record of writing and publication.
Level of Study: Unrestricted.
Type: Grant.
Value: Up to US$1,000.
Frequency: Every three months.
Country of Study: Any country.
Application Procedure: Applicants must submit an application which consists of a two page form, published writing samples, documentation of financial emergency, including bills etc., and a professional curriculum vitae.
Closing Date: Applications are accepted at any time.
Funding: Private.
Additional Information: A separate fund exists for writers and editors with AIDS who are in need of emergency assistance. The funds are not for research purposes, to enable writers to complete unfinished projects, or to fund writing publications or organisations. Grants and loans are for unexpected emergencies only, and not for the support of working writers. PEN also offers numerous annual awards to recognise distinguished writing, editing and translation. The award is for published writers.

PENN HUMANITIES FORUM

University of Pennsylvania, 3619, Locust Walk, Philadelphia, PA
19104-6213, United States of America
Tel: (1) 215 898 8220
Fax: (1) 215 746 5946
Email: humanities@sas.upenn.edu
www: http://humanities.sas.upenn.edu
Contact: Jennifer Conway, Associate Director

The Penn Humanities Forum promotes interdisciplinary collaboration across University of Pennsylvania departments and schools and between the University and the Philadelphia region. Each year, a broad topic sets the theme for a research seminar for resident and visiting scholars, courses and public events involving Philadelphia cultural institutions.

Mellon Postdoctoral Fellowships in the Humanities
Subjects: Humanities.
Purpose: To support research for untenured junior scholars.

Eligibility: Open to younger Scholars who, at the time of application, have received a PhD, but have not yet held it for more than eight years nor been granted tenure. Research proposals are invited in all areas of humanistic studies except educational curriculum building and performing arts. Preference is given to proposals that are interdisciplinary and directly related to the annual topic, and to candidates who have not previously utilised the resources of the university and whose work would allow them to take advantage of the research strengths of the institution and to make contribution to its intellectual life. The requirements are residency at the University of Pennsylvania and the teaching of one course per semester.
Level of Study: Postdoctorate.
Type: Fellowship.
Value: US$37,000 plus health insurance.
Length of Study: One academic year, non renewable.
Frequency: Annual.
Study Establishment: The University of Pennsylvania.
Country of Study: United States of America.
No. of awards offered: Five.
Application Procedure: Applicants must complete an application, available to download from the Forum's website,
Closing Date: Applications must be postmarked no later than October 15th.
Funding: Private.
No. of awards given last year: Five.
No. of applicants last year: 120.
Additional Information: Fellows may not normally hold other concurrent awards.

THE PERRY FOUNDATION

31 Rossendale, Chelmsford, Essex CM1 2UA, England
Tel: (44) 1245 260805
Fax: (44) 1245 260805
Email: david.naylor@blueyonder.co.uk
www: http://www.perryfoundation.co.uk
Contact: Mr D J Naylor, Secretary & Chief Executive

The Perry Foundation offers research awards and postgraduate scholarships in agriculture and related disciplines. Research awards are offered to universities and institutes in the United Kingdom and are normally for a three year period. Postgraduate scholarships are offered to holders of First or Second Class Degrees and are for a three year period leading to a PhD. Both research awards and postgraduate scholarships must be undertaken at a university, college or research establishment in the United Kingdom.

Perry Postgraduate Scholarships
Subjects: The production and utilisation of crops for food and non-food uses, ecologically acceptable and sustainable farming systems including, in particular, water and nutrient balances, integrated disease and pest control systems for both crops and livestock, socio-economic studies in the occupation and use of land, the rural economy and infrastructure and developments in marketing. Projects must be of definable benefit to UK agriculture.
Purpose: To enable postgraduates to undertake research and investigate work into agriculture and related fields and to build up a pool of highly competent researchers in the UK.
Eligibility: Holders of First and Upper Second Class Honours Degrees in appropriate subjects who have been offered a place at university, college or other establishment which will lead to the award of a PhD.
Level of Study: Doctorate.
Type: Postgraduate scholarships.
Value: Currently UK£12,000 maintenance stipend, UK£2,870 tuition fees, plus bench fees to a maximum of UK£2,500. All per academic year.
Length of Study: 3 years.
Frequency: Annual.
Study Establishment: Universities, colleges and research establishments and institutes in the UK.
Country of Study: United Kingdom.
No. of awards offered: 3-4 per year.

Application Procedure: Applicants must write to or e-mail the Foundation Secretary requesting an application form. Full details will be provided to suitable applicants.
Closing Date: 30th November.
Funding: Private.
No. of awards given last year: 3.
No. of applicants last year: 100 plus annually.
Additional Information: Projects must be of definable benefit to UK agriculture.

Perry Postgraduate Scholarships and Research Awards

Subjects: The production and utilisation of crops for food and non food uses, ecologically acceptable and sustainable farming systems, including in particular, water and nutrient balances, integrated disease and pest control systems for both crops and livestock, socio-economic studies in the occupation and use of land, the rural economy and infrastructure, and developments in marketing. Must be of definable benefit to UK agriculture.
Purpose: To enable postgraduates to undertake research projects and investigative work into agriculture and related fields, and to build and develop a pool of highly competent researchers in the United Kingdom.
Eligibility: Open to holders of First and Upper Second Class Degrees in appropriate subjects, gained at a university in the United Kingdom.
Level of Study: Postgraduate.
Type: Other.
Value: Currently UK£12,000 stipend, UK£2,870 tuition fees, plus bench fees to a maximum of UK£2,500 per year for postgraduate scholarships. Research awards are normally UK£15,000 per year maximum.
Length of Study: Normally three years leading to a doctorate or completion of a research award.
Frequency: Annual.
Study Establishment: Universities, colleges, institutes and research establishments in the United Kingdom.
Country of Study: United Kingdom.
No. of awards offered: Three-four depending on the availability of funds.
Application Procedure: Applicants must write to the Foundation Secretary for a brochure, containing details of procedure, and application forms. Applications submitted by individuals must be supported by their university, college, institute or other establishment.
Closing Date: November 30th for the postgraduate scholarships and October 31st for the research awards.
Funding: Private.
No. of awards given last year: 3.
No. of applicants last year: More than 100 each year.
Additional Information: Both the postgraduate scholarships and the research awards must be of definable benefit to United Kingdom agriculture.

PETERHOUSE

Cambridge, Cambridgeshire CB2 1RD, England
Tel: (44) 1223 338200
Fax: (44) 1223 766147
www: http://www.pet.cam.ac.uk
Contact: Ms Julie Petrucci, College Secretary

Friends of Peterhouse Bursary

Subjects: All subjects except clinical medicine.
Purpose: To fund study for a postgraduate one or two year taught course or an overseas affiliated student, as a registered graduate student at Peterhouse.
Eligibility: Open to those who are required to pay university fees at the overseas rate. Applicants should be under 25 years of age on December 1st in the year in which they hope to come into residence.
Level of Study: Postgraduate.
Type: Bursary.
Value: University fees only.
Length of Study: One year.
Frequency: Annual.
Study Establishment: Peterhouse only.

Country of Study: United Kingdom.
No. of awards offered: One.
Application Procedure: Applicants must complete an application form and submit this with a curriculum vitae and two references.
Closing Date: April 1st.
Funding: Private.
Contributor: The Friends of Peterhouse.
No. of awards given last year: One.
No. of applicants last year: 21.
Additional Information: Further details are available from the website www.pet.cam.ac.uk.

Peterhouse Research Fellowship

Subjects: All subjects.
Purpose: To support a young Scholar in postdoctoral research at Peterhouse.
Eligibility: Applicants must hold, or be studying for, a degree from Cambridge or Oxford universities.
Level of Study: Postdoctorate.
Type: Fellowship.
Value: Maintenance and allowances.
Length of Study: Three years.
Frequency: Annual.
Study Establishment: Peterhouse only.
Country of Study: United Kingdom.
No. of awards offered: Two-three.
Application Procedure: Applicants must complete an application form, available on request.
Closing Date: Early February.
Funding: Private.
Contributor: Peterhouse.
No. of awards given last year: Two.
No. of applicants last year: 132.

Peterhouse Research Studentship

Subjects: All subjects.
Purpose: To assist study for a PhD at Peterhouse.
Eligibility: Applicants should be under 25 years of age on December 1st in the year in which they hope to come into residence.
Level of Study: Postgraduate.
Type: Studentship.
Value: Full fees and maintenance subject to deduction of any other emoluments that may be awarded.
Length of Study: Three years.
Frequency: Annual.
Study Establishment: Peterhouse only.
Country of Study: United Kingdom.
No. of awards offered: Two-three.
Application Procedure: Applicants must complete an application form and submit this with a curriculum vitae and two references.
Closing Date: April 1st.
Funding: Private.
Contributor: Peterhouse.
No. of awards given last year: Three.
No. of applicants last year: 23.
Additional Information: Further details are available from the website www.pet.cam.ac.uk.

PETSAVERS

Woodrow House1 Telford Way, Waterwells Business Park, Quedgeley, Gloucester, Gloucestershire, GL2 4AB, England
Tel: (44) 1452 726700
Fax: (44) 1452 726701
Email: adminoff@bsava.com
www: http://www.bsava.com
Contact: M J Berriman, Administrator

Petsavers was established in 1970 to promote clinical investigations into the many unsolved diseases of dogs, cats, rabbits and other small animals. In the past 20 years Petsavers has given over UK£1 million towards numerous clinical studies, clinical research studentships and residencies. The Britist Small Animal Veterinary Association supports Petsavers with its administration costs enabling all donations to benefit pets.

Petsavers Award

Subjects: Small animal veterinary medicine and surgery.
Purpose: To advance the science of small animal medicine and surgery.
Eligibility: Open to veterinary surgeons currently working in United Kingdom universities, centres of learning or veterinary practices.
Level of Study: Postgraduate, Professional development.
Type: Award.
Value: Varies.
Length of Study: One-three years.
Frequency: Annual.
Study Establishment: Universities, veterinary schools and veterinary practices.
Country of Study: United Kingdom.
No. of awards offered: Varies.
Application Procedure: Applicants must write for details.
Funding: Private.
Contributor: Donations by practice clients.
No. of awards given last year: Nine.
No. of applicants last year: 35.
Additional Information: Projects must involve clinical cases only and no experimental animals.

PHARMACEUTICAL RESEARCH AND MANUFACTURERS OF AMERICA FOUNDATION (PHRMAF)

1615 L Street, NW Suite 1260, Washington, DC 20036, United States of America
Tel: (1) 202 572 7756
Fax: (1) 202 572 7799
Email: foundation@phrma.org
www: http://www.phrmafoundation.org
Contact: Ms Eileen M McCarron, Director of Development

The Pharmaceutical Research and Manufacturers of America Foundation (PhRMAF) is a non-profit making organisation established in 1965 to promote public health through scientific and medical research. It provides funding for research and for the education and training of scientists and physicians who have selected pharmacology, pharmaceutics, toxicology, informatics or health outcomes as a career choice.

PhRMA Medical Student Research Fellowships

Subjects: Clinical pharmacology.
Purpose: To generate interest in research careers among medical students.
Eligibility: Candidates must be sponsored by the school or university at which the research is to be conducted.
Type: Fellowship.
Value: US$18,000.
Length of Study: 3-24 months.
Frequency: Annual.
Study Establishment: A school of medicine or dentistry in the United States of America.
Country of Study: United States of America.
No. of awards offered: Four.
Application Procedure: Applicants must write for details or visit the Foundation's website.
Closing Date: September 15th.

PhRMAF Medical Student Fellowships

Subjects: Pharmacology, toxicology or clinical pharmacology.
Purpose: To support medical, dental or veterinary students who have substantial interests in research and teaching careers in pharmacology or clinical pharmacology and who are willing to work full-time in a specific research effort.

Eligibility: Open to applicants with firm commitment from a university in the United States prior to applying for a PhRMAF award. All applicants must be citizens or permanent residents of the United States of America.
Level of Study: Graduate, Postgraduate, Predoctorate.
Type: Fellowship.
Value: Up to US$18,000.
Length of Study: Three months - two years.
Frequency: Annual.
Study Establishment: An accredited school of medicine, or dentistry medicine.
Country of Study: United States of America.
Application Procedure: Applications are to be submitted by the appropriate representative of the school or university to the Director of Development at PhRMAF. Detailed application requirements are stated on the Foundation's website where the applicant can download an application form and read the specific requirements for each award.
Closing Date: September 1st.
Funding: Private.
Additional Information: Research projects involving animal subjects require a statement that the project will follow the guidelines set forth by the NIH Guide for the Care and Use of Laboratory Animals and that the project will be performed, reviewed and approved by a faculty committee of the university. The recipient school is expected to submit an annual report on the disposition of the funds awarded by PhRMAF. A final report is due within 60 days after the conclusion of the grant. These reports must be signed by the recipient's sponsor. Any publications, speeches, presentations and other materials that stem directly from the research supported by this grant must acknowledge the support of PhRMAF. Three reprints of each publication should be forwarded to PhRMAF.

PhRMAF Postdoctoral Fellowships in Health Outcomes Research

Subjects: Health outcomes research, patient reported outcomes or pharmacoeconomics.
Purpose: To support well trained graduates from PharmD, MD and PhD programmes who seek to further develop and refine their research skills through formal postdoctoral training.
Eligibility: Open to full-time students who are citizens or permanent residents of the United States of America. Applicants must have firm commitment from a university in the United States of America before applying for a PhRMAF award. The department's chair will be expected to verify the applicant's doctoral candidacy.
Level of Study: Graduate, Postdoctorate, Postgraduate.
Type: Fellowship.
Value: A stipend of US$40,000 annually.
Length of Study: One or two years.
Frequency: Annual.
Study Establishment: An accredited school of medicine, pharmacy, dentistry, public health or nursing.
Country of Study: United States of America.
No. of awards offered: Varies.
Application Procedure: Applications must include a research plan written by the applicant, the mentor's research record and a description of how the mentored experience will enhance the applicant's career development in health outcomes research. Applications are to be submitted by the appropriate representative of the school or university to the Director of Development at PhRMAF. Detailed application requirements are stated on the Foundation's website where applicants can download an application form and read the specific requirements for each award.
Closing Date: October 1st.
Funding: Private.

PhRMAF Postdoctoral Fellowships in Informatics

Subjects: Informatics.
Purpose: To support well trained graduates from PhD programmes who seek to further develop and refine their informatics research skills through formal postdoctoral training.
Eligibility: Open to full-time students who are citizens or permanent residents of the United States of America. Applicants must have firm commitment from a university in the United States of America before

applying for a PhRMAF award. The department's chair will be expected to verify the applicant's doctoral candidacy.
Level of Study: Postdoctorate.
Type: Fellowship.
Value: US$40,000 annually.
Length of Study: One or two years.
Frequency: Annual.
Country of Study: United States of America.
No. of awards offered: Varies.
Application Procedure: Applicants must submit an application including a research plan written by the applicant, the mentor's research record and a description of how the mentored experience will enhance the applicant's career development in informatics. Applications are to submitted by the appropriate representative of the school or university to the Director of Development at PhRMAF. Detailed application requirements are stated on the Foundation's website where the applicant can download an application form and read the specific requirements for each award.
Closing Date: September 1st.
Funding: Private.
Additional Information: Research projects involving animal subjects require a statement that the project will follow the guidelines set forth by the NIH Guide for the Care and Use of Laboratory Animals and that the project will be performed, reviewed and approved by a faculty committee of the university. The recipient school is expected to submit an annual report on the disposition of the funds awarded by PhRMAF. A progress report is to be submitted by the recipient ten months into the first year of funding of the fellowship. The second year of funding, when applicable, is contingent upon a satisfactory review of the report. A final report is due within 60 days after the conclusion of the grant. These reports must be signed by the recipient's sponsor. Any publications, speeches, presentations and all other materials that stem directly from the research supported by this grant must acknowledge the support of the PhRMAF. Three reprints of each publication should be forwarded to the PhRMAF.

PhRMAF Postdoctoral Fellowships in Pharmaceutics

Subjects: Pharmaceutics.
Purpose: To encourage graduates to continue to develop and refine their pharmaceutics research skills through formal postdoctoral training.
Eligibility: Open to graduates from PhD programmes in pharmaceutics. Before an individual is eligible to apply for a PhRMAF award, the applicants must first have a firm commitment from a university in the United States. Applicants must be full-time students and the department's chair is expected to verify the applicant's doctoral candidacy. All applicants must be citizens of the United States of America or permanent residents.
Level of Study: Postdoctorate, Postgraduate.
Type: Fellowship.
Value: A stipend of US$40,000 annually.
Length of Study: One or two years.
Frequency: Annual.
Study Establishment: Schools of pharmacy in the United States of America.
Country of Study: United States of America.
No. of awards offered: Varies.
Application Procedure: Applicants must visit the organisation's website where detailed application requirements are stated and application forms can be downloaded. Applications must include a research plan written by the applicant, the mentor's research record and a description of how the mentored experience will enhance the applicant's career development in pharmaceutics. Applications are to be submitted by the appropriate representative of the school or university to the Director of Development at PhRMAF.
Closing Date: October 1st.
Funding: Private.
Additional Information: Research projects involving animal subjects require a statement that the project will follow the guidelines set forth by the NIH Guide for the Care and Use of Laboratory Animals and that the project will be performed, reviewed and approved by a faculty committee of the university. The recipient school is expected to submit

an annual report on the disposition of the funds awarded by PhRMAF. A progress report is to be submitted by the recipient ten months into the first year of funding of the fellowship. The second year of funding, when applicable, is contingent upon a satisfactory review of the report. A final report is due within 60 days after the conclusion of the grant. These reports must be signed by the recipient's sponsor. Any publications, speeches, presentations, and all other materials that stem directly from the research supported by this grant must acknowledge the support of the PhRMAF. Three reprints of each publication should be forwarded to the PhRMAF.

PhRMAF Postdoctoral Fellowships in Pharmacology-Morphology

Subjects: Pharmacology-morphology, including cell biology.
Purpose: To advance understanding of drug action through discovery of specifically related cellular and tissue changes and to uncover associations between normal and abnormal function in particular tissue and cellular structures.
Eligibility: Open to full-time, postdoctoral students who are trained and qualified primarily either in pharmacology or in one of the morphologic specialities eg. anatomy, cell biology, pathology. Applicants must have firm commitment from a university in the United States of America before applying for the PhRMAF award. The department's chair is expected to verify the applicant's doctoral candidacy.
Level of Study: Graduate, Postdoctorate, Postgraduate.
Type: Fellowship.
Value: US$40,000 stipend annually.
Length of Study: One or two years.
Frequency: Annual.
Study Establishment: An accredited school of medicine.
Country of Study: United States of America.
No. of awards offered: Varies.
Application Procedure: Applicants must visit the website where detailed application requirements are stated and application forms can be downloaded. Applications must include a research plan written by the applicant, the mentor's research record and a description of how the mentored experience will enhance the applicant's career developments in pharmacology-morphology. Applications are to be submitted by the appropriate representative of the school or university to the Director of Development at PhRMAF.
Closing Date: September 1st.
Funding: Private.
Additional Information: Research projects involving animal subjects require a statement that the project will follow the guidelines set forth by the NIH Guide for the Care and Use of Laboratory Animals and that the project will be performed, reviewed and approved by a faculty committee of the university. The recipient school is expected to submit an annual report on the disposition of the funds awarded by PhRMAF. A progress report is to be submitted by the recipient ten months into the first year of funding of the fellowship. The second year of funding, when applicable, is contingent upon a satisfactory review of the report. A final report is due within 60 days after the conclusion of the grant. These reports must be signed by the recipient's sponsor. Any publications, speeches, presentations and other materials that stem directly from the research supported by this grant must acknowledge the support of PhRMAF. Three reprints of each publication should be forwarded to PhRMAF.

PhRMAF Postdoctoral Fellowships in Pharmacology/Toxicology

Subjects: Pharmacology or toxicology.
Purpose: To facilitate career entry into pharmacology or toxicology at the level of postdoctoral training and to provide funding for recent graduates from PhD programmes who seek to develop research skills through formal postdoctoral training.
Eligibility: Open to applicants with firm commitment from a university in the United States, prior to applying for a PhRMAF award. Applications must be submitted by an accredited United States school and all applicants must be citizens of the United States of America or permanent residents.
Level of Study: Postdoctorate.
Type: Fellowship.
Value: US$40,000 stipend annually.

Length of Study: One or two years.
Frequency: Annual.
Study Establishment: An accredited school of medicine, pharmacy, dentistry or veterinary medicine.
Country of Study: United States of America.
No. of awards offered: Varies.
Application Procedure: Applicants must visit the organisation's website where detailed application requirements are stated and application forms can be downloaded. Applications must be submitted by the appropriate representative of the school or university to the Director of Development at PhRMAF. An application must include a research plan written by the applicant, a mentor's research record and a description of how the mentored experience will enhance the applicant's career development on pharmacology or toxicology.
Closing Date: September 1st.
Funding: Private.
Additional Information: Research projects involving animal subjects require a statement that the project will follow the guidelines set forth by the NIH Guide for the Care and Use of Laboratory Animals and that the project will be performed, reviewed and approved by a faculty committee of the university. The recipient school is expected to submit an annual report on the disposition of the funds awarded by PhRMAF. A progress report is to be submitted by the recipient ten months into the first year of funding of the fellowship. The second year of funding, when applicable, is contingent upon a satisfactory review of the report. A final report is due within 60 days after the conclusion of the grant. These reports must be signed by the recipient's sponsor. Any publications, speeches, presentations, and all other materials that stem directly from the research supported by this grant must acknowledge the support of PhRMAF. Three reprints of each publication should be forwarded to PhRMAF.

PhRMAF Predoctoral Fellowships in Health Outcomes Research

Subjects: Health outcomes research, patient reported outcomes or pharmacoeconomics.
Purpose: To support a student's PhD doctoral programme after course work has been completed and the remaining training activity is the student's research project.
Eligibility: Open to applicants who have a firm commitment from a university in the United States. Applicants must be full-time students and the department's chair is expected to verify the applicant's doctoral candidacy. All applicants must be citizens of the United States of America or permanent residents.
Level of Study: Postgraduate.
Type: Fellowship.
Value: A stipend of US$20,000 annually. Up to US$500 per year may be used for expenses associated with thesis preparation.
Length of Study: One or two years.
Frequency: Annual.
Study Establishment: An accredited school of medicine, pharmacy, dentistry, public health or nursing.
Country of Study: United States of America.
No. of awards offered: Varies.
Application Procedure: Applications are to submitted by the appropriate representative of the school or university to the Director of Development at PhRMAF. Detailed application requirements are stated on the Foundation's website where the applicant can download an application form and read the specific requirements for each award.
Closing Date: October 1st.
Funding: Private.
Additional Information: Research projects involving animal subjects require a statement that the project will follow the guidelines set forth by the NIH Guide for the Care and Use of Laboratory Animals and that the project will be performed, reviewed and approved by a faculty committee of the university. The recipient school is expected to submit an annual report on the disposition of the funds awarded by PhRMAF. A progress report is to be submitted by the recipient ten months into the first year of funding of the fellowship. The second year of funding, when applicable, is contingent upon a satisfactory review of the report. A final report is due within 60 days after the conclusion of the grant. These reports must be signed by the recipient's sponsor. Any publications, speeches, presentations, and all other materials that stem

directly from the research supported by this grant must acknowledge the support of the PhRMAF. Three reprints of each publication should be forwarded to the PhRMAF.

PhRMAF Predoctoral Fellowships in Pharmaceutics

Subjects: Pharmaceutics.
Purpose: To support promising students during their thesis research.
Eligibility: Open to full-time students and citizens or permanent residents of the United States of America. Applicants must have firm commitment from a university in the United States of America prior to applying for a PhRMAF award and the department's chair will be expected to verify the applicant's doctoral candidacy.
Level of Study: Postgraduate.
Type: Fellowship.
Value: A stipend of US$20,000 annually. This includes up to US$500 for expenses associated with thesis research.
Length of Study: One or two years.
Frequency: Annual.
Study Establishment: A school of pharmacy.
Country of Study: United States of America.
No. of awards offered: Varies.
Application Procedure: Applicants must visit the organisation's website where detailed application requirements are stated and application forms can be downloaded. Applications must be submitted by the appropriate representative of the school or university to the Director of Development at PhRMAF.
Closing Date: October 1st.
Funding: Private.
Additional Information: Research projects involving animal subjects require a statement that the project will follow the guidelines set forth by the NIH Guide for the Care and Use of Laboratory Animals and that the project will be performed, reviewed and approved by a faculty committee of the university. The recipient school is expected to submit an annual report on the disposition of the funds awarded by PhRMAF. A progress report is to be submitted by the recipient ten months into the first year of funding of the fellowship. The second year of funding, when applicable, is contingent upon a satisfactory review of the report. A final report is due within 60 days after the conclusion of the grant. These reports must be signed by the recipient's sponsor. Any publications, speeches, presentations, and all other materials that stem directly from the research supported by this grant must acknowledge the support of the PhRMAF. Three reprints of each publication should be forwarded to the PhRMAF.

PhRMAF Predoctoral Fellowships in Pharmacology/ Toxicology

Subjects: Pharmacology or toxicology.
Purpose: To support promising students during their thesis research.
Eligibility: Open to advanced students who have completed the bulk of their pre-thesis requirements and are starting their thesis research by the time the award is activated. Students just starting graduate school should not apply. Before an individual is eligible to apply for a PhRMAF award, the applicant must have a firm commitment from a university in the United States of America. The applicant must be a citizen or permanent resident of the United States of America.
Level of Study: Predoctorate.
Type: Fellowship.
Value: A stipend of US$20,000 per year. This includes up to US$500 for expenses associated with thesis research.
Length of Study: One or two years.
Frequency: Annual.
Study Establishment: An accredited school of medicine, pharmacy, dentistry or veterinary medicine.
Country of Study: United States of America.
No. of awards offered: Varies.
Application Procedure: Applicants must visit the organisation's website where detailed application requirements are stated and application forms can be downloaded. Applications must be submitted by the appropriate representative of the school or university to the Director of Development at PhRMAF.
Closing Date: September 1st.
Funding: Private.

Additional Information: Research projects involving animal subjects require a statement that the project will follow the guidelines set forth by the NIH Guide for the Care and Use of Laboratory Animals and that the project will be performed, reviewed and approved by a faculty committee of the university. The recipient school is expected to submit an annual report on the disposition of the funds awarded by PhRMAF. A progress report is to be submitted by the recipient ten months into the first year of funding of the fellowship. The second year of funding, when applicable, is contingent upon a satisfactory review of the report. A final report is due within 60 days after the conclusion of the grant. These reports must be signed by the recipient's sponsor. Any publications, speeches, presentations and other materials that stem directly from the research supported by this grant must acknowledge the support of PhRMAF. Three reprints of each publication should be forwarded to PhRMAF.

PhRMAF Research Starter Grants in Health Outcomes Research

Subjects: Health outcomes research, patient reported outcomes or pharmacoeconomics.
Purpose: To support individuals beginning independent research careers in academia.
Eligibility: Open to applicants sponsored by the school or university at which the research is to be conducted. Applicants must be appointed to an entry level tenure track or equivalent permanent position in a department or unit responsible for pharmaceutical activities as part of its core mission. All applicants must be citizens or permanent residents of the United States of America.
Level of Study: Graduate, Postgraduate.
Type: Grant.
Value: US$30,000 annually.
Length of Study: One or two years.
Frequency: Annual.
Study Establishment: An accredited school of medicine, pharmacy, dentistry, public health or nursing.
Country of Study: United States of America.
No. of awards offered: Varies.
Application Procedure: Applicants must visit the organisation's website where detailed application requirements are stated and application forms can be downloaded. Applications must be submitted by the appropriate representative of the school or university to the Director of Development at PhRMAF. The description of an applicant's career goals and the departmental chair's description of institutional support for the applicant's salary are all important when evaluating an application.
Closing Date: October 1st.
Funding: Private.
Additional Information: Research projects involving animal subjects require a statement that the project will follow the guidelines set forth by the NIH Guide for the Care and Use of Laboratory Animals and that the project will be performed, reviewed and approved by a faculty committee of the university. The recipient school is expected to submit an annual report on the disposition of the funds awarded by PhRMAF. A progress report is to be submitted by the recipient ten months into the first year of funding of the fellowship. The second year of funding, when applicable, is contingent upon a satisfactory review of the report. A final report is due within 60 days after the conclusion of the grant. These reports must be signed by the recipient's sponsor. Any publications, speeches, presentations and all other materials that stem directly from the research supported by this grant must acknowledge the support of the PhRMAF. Three reprints of each publication should be forwarded to the PhRMAF.

PhRMAF Research Starter Grants in Informatics

Subjects: Informatics.
Purpose: To offer support to new investigators beginning their independent research careers in academia at the Faculty level.
Eligibility: Open to applicants sponsored by the school or university at which the research is to be conducted. Applicants must be appointed to an entry level tenure track or equivalent permanent position in a department or unit responsible for informatics activities as part of

its core mission. All applicants must be citizens or permanent residents of the United States of America.
Level of Study: Graduate, Postdoctorate, Postgraduate.
Type: Grant.
Value: US$30,000 annually.
Length of Study: One or two years.
Frequency: Annual.
Country of Study: United States of America.
No. of awards offered: Varies.
Application Procedure: Applicants must visit the organisation's website where detailed application requirements are stated and application forms can be downloaded. Applications must be submitted by the appropriate representative of the school or university to the Director of Development at PhRMAF. The description of an applicant's career goals and the departmental chair's description of institutional support for the applicant's salary are all important when evaluating an application.
Closing Date: September 1st.
Funding: Private.
Additional Information: Research projects involving animal subjects require a statement that the project will follow the guidelines set forth by the NIH Guide for the Care and Use of Laboratory Animals and that the project will be performed, reviewed and approved by a faculty committee of the university. The recipient school is expected to submit an annual report on the disposition of the funds awarded by PhRMAF. A progress report is to be submitted by the recipient ten months into the first year of funding of the fellowship. The second year of funding, when applicable, is contingent upon a satisfactory review of the report. A final report is due within 60 days after the conclusion of the grant. These reports must be signed by the recipient's sponsor. Any publications, speeches, presentations and all other materials that stem directly from the research supported by this grant must acknowledge the support of PhRMAF. Three reprints of each publication should be forwarded to the PhRMAF.

PhRMAF Research Starter Grants in Pharmaceutics

Subjects: Pharmaceutics.
Purpose: To offer support to new investigators beginning their independent research careers in academia.
Eligibility: Open to applicants sponsored by the school or university at which the research is to be conducted. Applicants must be appointed to an entry level tenure track or equivalent permanent position in a department or unit responsible for pharmaceutical activities as part of its core mission. All applicants must be citizens or permanent residents of the United States of America.
Level of Study: Graduate, Postdoctorate, Postgraduate.
Type: Grant.
Value: US$30,000 annually.
Length of Study: One or two years.
Frequency: Annual.
Study Establishment: Schools of pharmacy.
Country of Study: United States of America.
No. of awards offered: Varies.
Application Procedure: Applicants must visit the website where detailed application requirements are stated and application forms can be downloaded. Applications must be submitted by the appropriate representative of the school or university to the Director of Development at PhRMAF. The description of an applicant's career goals and the departmental chair's description of institutional support for the applicant's salary are all important when evaluating an application.
Closing Date: October 1st.
Funding: Private.
Additional Information: Research projects involving animal subjects require a statement that the project will follow the guidelines set forth by the NIH Guide for the Care and Use of Laboratory Animals and that the project will be performed, reviewed and approved by a faculty committee of the university. The recipient school is expected to submit an annual report on the disposition of the funds awarded by PhRMAF. A progress report is to be submitted by the recipient ten months into the first year of funding of the fellowship. The second year of funding, when applicable, is contingent upon a satisfactory

review of the report. A final report is due within 60 days after the conclusion of the grant. These reports must be signed by the recipient's sponsor. Any publications, speeches, presentations and all other materials that stem directly from the research supported by this grant must acknowledge the support of PhRMAF. Three reprints of each publication should be forwarded to PhRMAF.

PhRMAF Research Starter Grants in Pharmacology/ Toxicology

Subjects: Pharmacology or toxicology.
Purpose: To support individuals beginning independent research careers in academia.
Eligibility: Open to applicants sponsored by the school or university at which the research is to be conducted. Applicants must be appointed to an entry level tenure track or equivalent permanent position in a department or unit responsible for pharmacology or toxicology activities as part of its core mission. All applicants must be citizens or permanent residents of the United States of America.
Level of Study: Graduate, Postdoctorate, Postgraduate.
Type: Grant.
Value: US$30,000 annually.
Length of Study: One or two years.
Frequency: Annual.
Study Establishment: An accredited school of medicine, pharmacy, dentistry or veterinary medicine.
Country of Study: United States of America.
Application Procedure: Applicants must visit the website where detailed application requirements are stated and application forms can be downloaded. Applications must be submitted by the appropriate representative of the school or university to the Director of Development at PhRMAF. The description of an applicant's career goals and the departmental chair's description of institutional support for the applicant's salary are all important when evaluating an application.
Closing Date: September 1st.
Funding: Private.
Additional Information: Research projects involving animal subjects require a statement that the project will follow the guidelines set forth by the NIH Guide for the Care and Use of Laboratory Animals and that the project will be performed, reviewed and approved by a faculty committee of the university. The recipient school is expected to submit an annual report on the disposition of the funds awarded by PhRMAF. A progress report is to be submitted by the recipient ten months into the first year of funding of the fellowship. The second year of funding, when applicable, is contingent upon a satisfactory review of the report. A final report is due within 60 days after the conclusion of the grant. These reports must be signed by the recipient's sponsor. Any publications, speeches, presentations and all other materials that stem directly from the research supported by this grant must acknowledge the support of PhRMAF. Three reprints of each publication should be forwarded to PhRMAF.

PhRMAF Sabbatical Fellowships in Health Outcomes Research

Subjects: Health outcomes research, patient reported outcomes or pharmacoeconomics.
Purpose: To support faculty members at all levels with active research programmes and the opportunity to work at other institutions to learn new skills or develop new collaborations that will enhance their research and research training activities in health outcomes.
Eligibility: Open to citizens or permanent residents of the United States of America. Applicants are expected to have approval for a sabbatical leave from their home institution and to provide an endorsement from the mentor who will sponsor their visiting scientific activity. Matching funds must be provided through the university.
Level of Study: Postdoctorate, Postgraduate, Professional development.
Type: Fellowship.
Value: A stipend of up to US$40,000.
Length of Study: Six months-one year.
Frequency: Annual.
Study Establishment: An accredited school of medicine, pharmacy, dentistry, public health or nursing.
Country of Study: United States of America.

No. of awards offered: Varies.
Application Procedure: Applications are to submitted by the appropriate representative of the school or university to the Director of Development at PhRMAF. Detailed application requirements are stated on the Foundation's website where applicants can download an application form and read the specific requirements for each award.
Closing Date: October 1st.
Funding: Private.
Additional Information: Research projects involving animal subjects require a statement that the project will follow the guidelines set forth by the NIH Guide for the Care and Use of Laboratory Animals and that the project will be performed, reviewed and approved by a faculty committee of the university. The recipient school is expected to submit an annual report on the disposition of the funds awarded by PhRMAF. A progress report is to be submitted by the recipient within 30 days after the conclusion of each year of the fellowship. A final report is due within 60 days after the conclusion of the grant. These reports must be signed by the recipient's sponsor. Any publications, speeches, presentations and all other materials that stem directly from the research supported by this grant must acknowledge the support of PhRMAF. Three reprints of each publication should be forwarded to PhRMAF.

PhRMAF Sabbatical Fellowships in Informatics

Subjects: Informatics.
Purpose: To give faculty members at all levels with active research programmes an opportunity to work at other institutions and to develop new collaborations that will enhance their research and research training activities in informatics.
Eligibility: Applicants are expected to have approval for a sabbatical leave from their home institution and provide an endorsement from the mentor who will sponsor their visiting scientific activity. Matching funds must be provided through the university. All applicants must be citizens of the United States of America or permanent residents.
Level of Study: Postdoctorate, Postgraduate, Professional development.
Type: Fellowship.
Value: A stipend of up to US$40,000.
Length of Study: Six months-one year.
Frequency: Annual.
Country of Study: United States of America.
No. of awards offered: Varies.
Application Procedure: Applications are to submitted by the appropriate representative of the school or university to the Director of Development at PhRMAF. Detailed application requirements are stated on the Foundation's website where the applicant can download an application form and read the specific requirements for each award.
Closing Date: September 1st.
Funding: Private.
Additional Information: Research projects involving animal subjects require a statement that the project will follow the guidelines set forth by the NIH Guide for the Care and Use of Laboratory Animals and that the project will be performed, reviewed and approved by a faculty committee of the university. The recipient school is expected to submit an annual report on the disposition of the funds awarded by PhRMAF. A progress report is to be submitted by the recipient within 30 days after the conclusion of each year of the fellowship. A final report is due within 60 days after the conclusion of the grant. These reports must be signed by the recipient's sponsor. Any publications, speeches, presentations and all other materials that stem directly from the research supported by this grant must acknowledge the support of the PhRMAF. Three reprints of each publication should be forwarded to the PhRMAF.

PhRMAF Sabbatical Fellowships in Pharmaceutics

Subjects: Pharmaceutics.
Purpose: To enable pharmaceutics faculty members at all levels with active research programmes an opportunity to work at other institutions and to develop new collaborations that will enhance their research and research training activities in pharmaceutics.
Eligibility: Open to citizens of the United States of America or permanent residents. Applicants are expected to have approval for a sabbatical leave from their home institution and provide an

endorsement from the mentor who will sponsor their sabbatical activity. Matching funds must be provided through the university.

Level of Study: Postdoctorate, Postgraduate, Professional development.

Type: Fellowship.

Value: A stipend of up to US$40,000.

Length of Study: Six months to one year.

Frequency: Annual.

Study Establishment: An approved institute.

Country of Study: United States of America.

Application Procedure: Applicants must visit the organisation's website where detailed application requirements are stated and application forms can be downloaded. Applications must be submitted by the appropriate representative of the school or university to the Director of Development at PhRMAF.

Closing Date: October 1st.

Funding: Private.

Additional Information: Research projects involving animal subjects require a statement that the project will follow the guidelines set forth by the NIH Guide for the Care and Use of Laboratory Animals and that the project will be performed, reviewed and approved by a faculty committee of the university. The recipient school is expected to submit an annual report on the disposition of the funds awarded by PhRMAF. A progress report is to be submitted by the recipient within 30 days after the conclusion of each year of the fellowship. A final report is due within 60 days after the conclusion of the grant. These reports must be signed by the recipient's sponsor. Any publications, speeches, presentations and all other materials that stem directly from the research supported by this grant must acknowledge the support of the PhRMAF. Three reprints of each publication should be forwarded to the PhRMAF.

PhRMAF Sabbatical Fellowships in Pharmacology/ Toxicology

Subjects: Pharmacology or toxicology.

Purpose: To give faculty members at all levels with active research programmes an opportunity to work at other institutions to learn new skills or develop new collaborations that will enhance their research and research training activities in pharmacology or toxicology.

Eligibility: Open to applicants with approval for sabbatical leave from their home institution and who can provide an endorsement from the mentor who will sponsor their visiting scientific activity. Matching funds must be provided through the university. All applicants must be citizens or permanent residents of the United States of America.

Level of Study: Postdoctorate, Postgraduate, Professional development.

Type: Fellowship.

Value: Up to US$40,000 stipend.

Length of Study: Six months-one year.

Frequency: Annual.

Study Establishment: An accredited school of medicine, pharmacy, dentistry or veterinary medicine.

Country of Study: United States of America.

No. of awards offered: Varies.

Application Procedure: Applicants must visit the organisation's website where detailed application requirements are stated and application forms can be downloaded. Applications must be submitted by the appropriate representative of the school or university to the Director of Development at PhRMAF.

Closing Date: September 1st.

Funding: Private.

Additional Information: Research projects involving animal subjects require a statement that the project will follow the guidelines set forth by the NIH Guide for the Care and Use of Laboratory Animals and that the project will be performed, reviewed and approved by a faculty committee of the university. The recipient school is expected to submit an annual report on the disposition of the funds awarded by PhRMAF. A final report is due within 60 days after the conclusion of the grant. These reports must be signed by the recipient's sponsor. Any publications, speeches, presentations and all other materials that stem directly from the research supported by this grant must acknowledge the support of PhRMAF. Three reprints of each publication should be forwarded to PhRMAF.

THE PHI BETA KAPPA SOCIETY

1606 New Hampshire Avenue NW, Washington, DC 20009, United States of America
Tel: (1) 202 265 3235
Fax: (1) 202 986 1601
Email: sbeasley@pbk.org
www: http://www.pbk.org
Contact: Ms Sandra Beasley Awards Coordinator

The Phi Beta Kappa Society has pursued its mission of fostering and recognising excellence in the liberal arts and sciences since 1776.

The Jensen Fellowship

Subjects: The language and culture of France.

Purpose: To support study in France.

Eligibility: Applicants must be under the age of 40 and U.S. citizens.

Level of Study: Postgraduate.

Type: Award.

Value: US$10,000.

Length of Study: Six months.

Frequency: Annual.

Country of Study: France.

Closing Date: 31st October.

Funding: Private.

Additional Information: Preference will be given to secondary school teachers of French.

Mary Isabel Sibley Fellowship

Subjects: French language or literature in even years and Greek language, literature, history or archaeology in odd years.

Purpose: To recognise female scholars who have demonstrated their ability to carry out original research.

Eligibility: Open to unmarried women aged 25-35 who have demonstrated their ability to carry out original research. Candidates must hold the doctorate or have fulfilled all the requirements for the doctorate except the dissertation. There are no restrictions as to nationality and the award is not restricted to members of Phi Beta Kappa.

Level of Study: Doctorate, Postdoctorate, Postgraduate.

Type: Fellowship.

Value: US$20,000.

Length of Study: One year, non renewable.

Frequency: Annual.

Country of Study: Any country.

No. of awards offered: One.

Application Procedure: Applicants must complete an application form, available from Phi Beta Kappa, and submit this with transcripts and references.

Closing Date: January 15th.

Funding: Private.

No. of awards given last year: One.

No. of applicants last year: 50.

The Walter J. Jensen Fellowship for French Language, Literature, and Culture

Subjects: Each fellowship supports travel to France for six months of residence and study during the Fellowship year, during which time the fellow will submit progress reports to Phi Beta Kappa.

Purpose: To help educators and researchers improve education in Standard French language, literature, and culture and in the study of Standard French in the United States.

Eligibility: Candidates must be under the age of 40 who can certify their career is or will involve active use of the French language.

Level of Study: Postgraduate.

Type: Fellowship.

Value: US$10,000, with additional support available for airfare and, if applicable, support of dependent(s).

Length of Study: Year-long fellowship includes six months of dedicated study.

Frequency: Annual.

Study Establishment: 2001 (First award year, 2005).

Country of Study: France.

No. of awards offered: One per year.

Application Procedure: Self-managed application form must be completed including submission of academic records, references, plans for study, and proof of superior competence in French according to the standards established by the American Association for Teachers of French.
Closing Date: October 1st of each year.
Funding: Private.
Contributor: Dr. Walter J. Jensen.
No. of awards given last year: 0(first year of award).
No. of applicants last year: N/A.
Additional Information: Preference may be given to, though eligibility is not restricted to members of Phi Beta Kappa and teachers at the high school level or above. 'Standard French' is defined to exclude a focus on Creole, Quebecois, and other dialects. Natives may not be native speakers of French.

For further information contact:

Application available in downloadable format via website: www.pbk.org. Also available in hard copy upon request to the national office.

PHILHARMONIA ORCHESTRA/MARTIN MUSICAL SCHOLARSHIP FUND

'Beeches', Well Hill, Chelsfield, Kent, BR6 7PR, United Kingdom
Tel: (44) (01959) 532-299
Fax: (44) (01959) 532-299
Email: info@philharmonia.co.uk
www: http://www.philharmonia.co.uk
Contact: Mr Martyn Jones, Administrator

Emanual Hurwitz Award for Violinists of British Nationality
Subjects: Musical performance on violin only.
Purpose: To reward exceptional musical talent.
Eligibility: Open to British nationals only.
Level of Study: Postgraduate.
Type: Award.
Value: Varies.
Frequency: Annual.
Country of Study: Any country.
No. of awards offered: Varies.
Application Procedure: Applicants must write for details.
Closing Date: Please contact the organisation.
Additional Information: Further information is available on request.

Friends of the Philharmonia Award for Wood Wind Performers
Subjects: Music education.
Eligibility: Open to candidates of any nationality who are studying in the United Kingdom.
Level of Study: Postgraduate.
Type: Award.
Value: UK£1,000.
Frequency: Annual.
Country of Study: United Kingdom.
Application Procedure: Applicants must write for details.
Closing Date: February 1st.
Funding: Private.

John E Mortimer Foundation Awards
Subjects: Musical performance on all instruments.
Purpose: To reward exceptional musical talent.
Eligibility: Applicants must write for details.
Level of Study: Postgraduate.
Type: Award.
Value: Prizes are of varying value.
Frequency: Annual.
Country of Study: Any country.
No. of awards offered: Varies.

Application Procedure: Applicants must complete an application form and submit this with a stamped addressed envelope and a non returnable registration fee of UK£10.
Closing Date: December 1st.
Additional Information: Further details are available on request.

June Allison Award
Subjects: Musical performance on woodwind only.
Purpose: To assist exceptional musical talent with specialist and advanced study, and to help bridge the gap between study and fully professional status.
Eligibility: Applicants must write for details.
Level of Study: Postgraduate.
Type: Award.
Value: UK£500 plus recital.
Frequency: Annual.
Country of Study: Any country.
Application Procedure: Applicants must complete an application form and submit this with a stamped addressed envelope and a non returnable registration fee of UK£10.
Closing Date: December 1st.
Additional Information: Further details are available on request.

Lady Marga Alexander Memorial Award for Cellists
Subjects: Music education.
Eligibility: Open to students of all nationalities studying in the United Kingdom.
Level of Study: Postgraduate.
Type: Award.
Frequency: Annual.
Country of Study: United Kingdom.
Application Procedure: Applicants must write for details.
Closing Date: February 1st.
Funding: Private.

Martin Musical Scholarships
Subjects: Musical performance.
Purpose: To assist exceptional musical talent with specialist and advanced study and to help in bridging the gap between study and fully professional status.
Eligibility: Open to practising musicians as well as students who are instrumental performers, including pianists, preparing for a career on the concert platform either as a soloist or orchestral player, and are of no more than 25 years of age. Preference is given to United Kingdom citizens.
Level of Study: Postgraduate.
Type: Scholarship.
Value: Varies.
Length of Study: Two years, with a possibility of renewal.
Frequency: Annual.
Country of Study: Other.
No. of awards offered: Varies.
Application Procedure: Applicants must complete an application form.
Closing Date: October 1st.
Funding: Private.
No. of awards given last year: 50.
No. of applicants last year: 71.
Additional Information: It is not the present policy of the Fund to support organists, singers, conductors, composers, academic students or piano accompanists. Further information is available on request.

Reginald Conway Memorial Award for String Performers
Subjects: Musical performance on strings only.
Purpose: To reward exceptional musical talent.
Eligibility: Applicants must write for details.
Level of Study: Postgraduate.
Type: Award.
Value: Varies.
Frequency: Annual.
Country of Study: Any country.
Application Procedure: Applicants must write for details.

Closing Date: Please contact the organisation.
Additional Information: Further information is available on request.

Sidney Perry Scholarship
Subjects: Musical performance.
Purpose: To support postgraduate study.
Eligibility: Open to nationals of any country.
Level of Study: Postgraduate.
Type: Scholarship.
Value: Varies.
Length of Study: Up to two years.
Frequency: Annual.
Country of Study: Any country.
No. of awards offered: Varies.
Application Procedure: Applicants must complete an application form.
Closing Date: October 1st.
No. of awards given last year: Three.
Additional Information: Further information is available on request.

TotalFinaElf Ensemble Award
Subjects: Musical performance.
Purpose: To reward exceptional musical talent.
Eligibility: Open to any ensemble of three to eight performers. Applicants must be 25 years old or younger. Applicants must write for details.
Level of Study: Postgraduate.
Type: Award.
Value: Varies.
Length of Study: Varies.
Frequency: Annual.
Country of Study: United Kingdom.
Application Procedure: Applicants must write for details.
Closing Date: Please contact the organisation.
Additional Information: Further information is available on request.

TotalFinaElf in Association with Arts & Business New Partners, Outreach and Access Ensemble Award
Subjects: Musical performance.
Purpose: To reward exceptional musical talent.
Eligibility: Open to ensembles of three to eight people who are specialising in educational work. Applicants must be 25 years old or younger.
Level of Study: Postgraduate.
Type: Award.
Value: Varies.
Frequency: Annual.
Country of Study: United Kingdom.
Application Procedure: Applicants must write for details.
Closing Date: Please contact the organisation.
Additional Information: Further information is available on request.

TotalFinaElf Recital Series
Subjects: Musical performance.
Purpose: To reward exceptional musical talent.
Eligibility: Applicants must be 25 years old or younger.
Level of Study: Postgraduate.
Value: A recital series at the Royal Festival Hall.
Frequency: Annual.
Country of Study: United Kingdom.
Application Procedure: Applicants must write for details.
Closing Date: Please contact the organisation.
Additional Information: Further information is available on request.

Trevor Snoad Memorial Trust
Subjects: Music performance on the viola.
Purpose: To reward exceptional musical talent.
Eligibility: Open to outstanding viola players. There is no limit to the number of times an unsuccessful candidate may apply. Each candidate is eligible to apply for two awards.
Level of Study: Postgraduate.
Type: Award.

Value: UK£500.
Frequency: Annual.
Country of Study: Any country.
No. of awards offered: One.
Application Procedure: Applicants must complete an application form.
Closing Date: October 1st.
No. of awards given last year: One.
No. of applicants last year: Three.
Additional Information: An award is valid for two years and must be taken up within that time. Candidates are selected by audition. Preliminary auditions are held in the Autumn with final auditions in the Spring. Further information is available on request.

PHILLIPS EXETER ACADEMY

20 Main Street, Exeter, NH 03833-2460, United States of America
Tel: (1) 603 777 3405
Fax: (1) 603 777 4393
Email: beggers@exeter.edu
www: http://www.exeter.edu
Contact: Ms Barbara Eggers, Dean of Faculty

Philips Exeter Academy is a private secondary school with over 1,000 students.

George Bennett Fellowship
Subjects: Creative writing.
Purpose: To allow a person commencing a career as a writer the time and freedom from material considerations to complete a manuscript in progress.
Eligibility: Preference is given to writers who have not published a book with a major commercial publisher. Works must be in English.
Level of Study: Unrestricted.
Type: Fellowship.
Value: US$10,000 per year.
Frequency: Annual.
Study Establishment: Phillips Exeter Academy in Exeter, New Hampshire.
Country of Study: United States of America.
No. of awards offered: One.
Application Procedure: Applicants must send a manuscript, together with an application form, personal statement and US$5.
Closing Date: December 1st for the following academic year.
Funding: Private.
No. of awards given last year: One.
No. of applicants last year: 150.
Additional Information: Duties include being in residence for one academic year while working on the manuscript and informal availability to student writers. Requests for further information should be accompanied by a stamped addressed envelope. Information can also be obtained from the Academy website.

PITTSBURGH NEW MUSIC ENSEMBLE

PO Box 99476, Pittsburgh, PA 15233, United States of America
Tel: (1) 412 889 7231
Email: pnme@pnme.org
www: http://www.pnme.org
Contact: Mr Kevin Noe, Artistic Director

The Pittsburgh New Music Ensemble presents a festival of new music every summer and utilizes a resident ensemble of artists (vln, fl, cl, vc, pft, perc, baritone and dancer). Concerts incorporate lighting, visual images, film, costuming and movement to create a uniquely integrated artistic experience with music at its center.

Harvey Gaul Composition Contest
Subjects: Music composition.
Purpose: To award a commission for the Pittsburgh New Music Ensemble.
Eligibility: Open to United States citizens only.
Level of Study: Unrestricted.

Type: Competition.
Value: US$6,000.
Frequency: Every two years.
Country of Study: United States of America.
No. of awards offered: One.
Application Procedure: Applicants must complete an application form, available on request.
Closing Date: September 30th.
Funding: Private.
No. of awards given last year: One.
No. of applicants last year: 130.
Additional Information: There is a US$20 application fee.

THE PKD FOUNDATION

9221 Ward Parkway, Suite 400, Kansas City, MO 64114-3367, United States of America
Tel: (1) 800 PKD CURE or 816 931 2600
Fax: (1) 816 931 8655
Email: pkdcure@pkdcure.org
www: http://www.pkdcure.org
Contact: Administrative Assistant

The PKD Foundation is the only organisation worldwide solely devoted to promoting research into finding a cure for polycystic kidney disease and to improving the care and treatment of those affected by it.

RFA Grants
Subjects: Polycystic kidney disease research.
Purpose: To facilitate research in Polycystic kidney disease (PKD).
Eligibility: Open to qualified basic and clinical principal investigators. Applicants must have faculty status, an equipment expense less than US$10,000 and institutional approval of human experimentation procedures and animal use.
Level of Study: Postgraduate, Professional development.
Type: Grants & Fellowships.
Value: Grants - Grants of US$130,000 for two years (US$65,000 per annum) are awarded to Basic and Clinical principal investigators. Upon completion of two years an applicant may apply for a third year of funding for an approved project.Fellowships - Awards a two-year grant of up to US$50,000 per year, with the possibility of an additional third year on availability of funds.
Length of Study: Two year.
Frequency: Annual.
No. of awards offered: Dependent on availability of funds.
Application Procedure: Applicants must either visit the website or telephone the organisation to request an application form.
Closing Date: August 1st.
Contributor: Members.
No. of awards given last year: 57.
No. of applicants last year: 89.

PLASTIC SURGERY EDUCATIONAL FOUNDATION (PSEF)

444 East Algonquin Road, Arlington Heights, IL, 60005, United States of America
Tel: (1) 847 228 9900
Fax: (1) 847 228 9131
Email: ml@plasticsurgery.org
www: http://www.plasticsurgery.org
Contact: Ms Mary Lewis

The mission of the Plastic Surgery Educational Foundation (PSEF) is to develop and support domestic and international education, as well as research and public service activities of plastic surgeons.

Plastic Surgery Basic Research Grant
Subjects: Plastic surgery.
Purpose: To encourage young investigators to perform clinical research.

Eligibility: Open to plastic surgeons and holders of an MD or PhD working in plastic surgery. Residents, Fellows and non members of ASPRS or PSEF require sponsorship of a member or candidate for membership of ASPRS or PSEF or the American Society for Aesthetic Plastic Surgery.
Level of Study: Postgraduate, Professional development.
Type: Research grant.
Value: Research seed money up to US$5,000.
Length of Study: One year.
Frequency: Annual.
Country of Study: Any country.
No. of awards offered: Approx. 40.
Application Procedure: Applicants must complete an application, available on the website under medical professionals, PSEF funded programmes.
Closing Date: Mid January.
Funding: Private.
Contributor: The Plastic Surgery Educational Foundation.

Plastic Surgery Research Fellowship Award
Subjects: Any area related to plastic surgery.
Purpose: To encourage research and academic career development in plastic and reconstructive surgery.
Eligibility: Open to surgical residents or Fellows preparing for a plastic surgery residency, plastic surgery residents planning to interrupt their training for a research experience, or recent residency graduates wishing to supplement their clinical training with a research experience. Residents, Fellows and non members of ASPRS or PSEF require sponsorship of a member or candidate for membership of ASPRS or PSEF.
Level of Study: Postgraduate, Professional development.
Type: Fellowship.
Value: Each award underwrites the salary of the investigator for a one year period (US$30,000).
Length of Study: One year.
Frequency: Annual.
Country of Study: Any country.
No. of awards offered: Three, one from each contributor.
Application Procedure: Applicants must complete an application, available on the website under medical professionals, PSEF funded programmes.
Closing Date: November 15th.
Funding: Private.
Contributor: Lyndon Peer, Mercedes-Benz and LLC.
No. of awards given last year: One in each category.

PSEF Scientific Essay Contest
Subjects: Plastic surgery. One award category is to focus on theory, history, ethics, socio-economic issues relating to the art and science of plastic surgery, and three prizes on the non plastic surgeon category.
Eligibility: Open to persons involved in research in the field of plastic surgery.
Level of Study: Postgraduate, Professional development.
Type: Prize.
Value: US$500-3,000.
Length of Study: One year.
Frequency: Annual.
Country of Study: Any country.
No. of awards offered: Five.
Application Procedure: Applicants must submit manuscripts which should contain the result of original clinical or basic science research in an area of importance to plastic and reconstructive surgery. Information on essay content and format are available on the website under medical professionals, PSEF funded programmes.
Closing Date: February 15th.
Funding: Private.
Contributor: Bernard G Sarnat MD, D Ralph Millard from the Plastic Surgery Society and the Plastic Surgery Educational Foundation.

PLAYMARKET

Independent Newspapers Limited
PO Box 9767, Wellington
New Zealand
Tel: (64) 4 382 8462
Fax: (64) 4 382 8461
Email: info@playmarket.org.nz
www: http://www.playmarket.org.nz
Contact: Ms Dilys Grant, Director

Playmarket was founded in 1973 to assist New Zealand playwrights with a professional production of their scripts. For 25 years Playmarket have offered script assessment, development and agency services. Playmarket are at the heart of New Zealand theatre and its focus is playwrights.

The Bruce Mason Playwriting Award
Subjects: Playwriting.
Purpose: To recognise achievement at the beginning of a career.
Eligibility: Open to New Zealand playwrights.
Level of Study: Unrestricted.
Type: Award.
Value: New Zealand $7,000.
Length of Study: One year.
Frequency: Annual.
Country of Study: New Zealand.
No. of awards offered: One.
Application Procedure: Applicants must submit their name and address, plus two references. No scripts need to be submitted.
Closing Date: Varies annually.
Funding: Commercial.
Contributor: Independent Newspapers Limited.
No. of awards given last year: One.
No. of applicants last year: 13.
Additional Information: It is expected that the award will be used to write or complete a work for the theatre.

POLISH EMBASSY

47 Portland Place, London, W1 1JH, England
Tel: (44) 020 7580 5430
Fax: (44) 020 7637 2190
Email: milewska@bt.connect.com
www: http://www.polishembassy.org.uk
Contact: Counsellor, Science & Education

The Polish Embassy helps establish links between scientific and educational institutions in Poland and the United Kingdom. It awards Polish government scholarships (postgraduate bursaries, short-term visits and language programmes) and also offers grants within the framework of the British-Polish Research Partnership Programme which is designed to support joint scientific research.

Polish Embassy Scholarship for Polonicum, Warsaw University, Jagiellonian University, Cracow, Silesia University, Katowice, KUL, Lublin
Subjects: Polish language course.
Eligibility: Priority in the scholarship allocation will be given to applicants studying Central European or Polish history, language and literature.
Level of Study: Doctorate, Graduate, Postgraduate, Professional development.
Type: Scholarship.
Value: Students are provided with accommodation, but will have to pay for return travel to Poland.
Length of Study: Four weeks during the Summer.
Frequency: Annual.
Study Establishment: The University of Warsaw, Jagiellonian University in Cracow, the Maria Curie-Skodowska University in Lublin and the University of Silesia in Katowice.
Country of Study: Poland.
No. of awards offered: Eight.

Application Procedure: Applicants must complete an application form and submit this with a covering letter and one letter of reference to the Polish Embassy. Application forms and further information are available from the Polish Embassy.
Closing Date: February 15, 2004.
Funding: Government.
Contributor: The Polish Ministry of Education.
No. of awards given last year: Eight.

Polish Embassy Short Visits Grants
Subjects: Educational research.
Purpose: To allow academics and professionals to establish contacts, develop programmes of joint research and exchange scientific information.
Eligibility: The age limit is 50. Candidates should be experienced academics in their professional field in a way which could contribute to research in the candidate's subject area.
Level of Study: Doctorate, Postdoctorate, Postgraduate, Professional development, Research.
Type: Grant.
Value: Internal travel cost related to the visitors' itinerary plus accommodation and daily rate for subsistence. Alternatively, a lump sum grant-in-aid will be paid by the Polish side. Recipients are expected to pay their return travel to Poland.
Length of Study: One week to one month.
Frequency: Annual.
Study Establishment: Universities and other Institutes of Higher Education and research.
Country of Study: Poland.
No. of awards offered: Unspecified.
Application Procedure: Applicants must submit with their application their curriculum vitae, an explanation of the purpose of their visit and a letter of invitation from an academic institution in Poland expressing willingness to receive the visiting applicant. Applications must be sent to the Polish Embassy no later than 12 weeks prior to the proposed date of arrival in Poland.
Funding: Government.
Contributor: The Polish Ministry of Education.

Polish Government Postgraduate Scholarships Scheme
Subjects: Unrestricted. The following subjects in particular are taught to a high standard in Polish universities: sociology, mathematics, geography and geology, history of Polish architecture, music both performance and composition, the arts and scientific topics.
Purpose: To provide financial support for British students wishing to study in Poland.
Eligibility: Open to British citizens with a university degree or equivalent qualification. Priority is given to candidates who hold an Honours Degree and have had some experience of research, laboratory techniques or teaching since graduation. Married candidates must indicate whether they are prepared to go unaccompanied. Candidates wishing to study Polish philology, Slavonic languages and the history and geography of Poland must be conversant with Polish or the appropriate Slavonic language. Applicants should be under 35 years of age.
Level of Study: Doctorate, Postgraduate, Professional development.
Type: Scholarship.
Value: A monthly allowance, free accommodation in student hostels or a monthly allowance towards accommodation found privately, free meals in a student canteen or a monthly allowance in lieu, a modest book grant, exemption from tuition fees and free medical care.
Length of Study: Three-nine months.
Frequency: Annual.
Study Establishment: A university or another Institute of Higher Education.
Country of Study: Poland.
No. of awards offered: Varies.
Application Procedure: Applicants must complete an application form and submit this with a curriculum vitae, a copy of their diploma, research proposal, medical statement and two letters of recommendation. Application forms are available from the Education Officer.

Closing Date: February 15, 2004.
Funding: Government.
Contributor: The Polish Ministry of Education.
No. of awards given last year: 17.
Additional Information: This scheme is run under agreement between Poland and the United Kingdom on exchange.

POLLOCK-KRASNER FOUNDATION, INC.

863 Park Avenue, New York, NY, 10021
United States of America
Tel: (1) 212 517 5400
Fax: (1) 212 288 2836
Email: grants@pkf.org
www: http://www.pkf.org
Contact: Program Officer

The Pollock-Krasner Foundation's mission is to aid, internationally, those individuals who have worked as professional artists over a significant period of time.

Pollock-Krasner Foundation Grant
Subjects: Painting, sculpting, print making, mixed media or installation art.
Purpose: To aid, internationally, individual artists of artistic merit with financial need.
Eligibility: Applicants may be painters, sculptors, print-makers, mixed media or installation artists. The Foundation has no age or geographic limits. Commercial artists, photographers, filmmakers, craft-makers and students are not eligible.
Level of Study: Professional development.
Type: Grant.
Frequency: Annual.
Application Procedure: Applicants must write, fax or email the Foundation for an application and guidelines.
Closing Date: There is no deadline as grants are awarded throughout the year.
Funding: Private.
Additional Information: The Foundation does not fund academic study.

PONTIFICAL INSTITUTE OF MEDIEVAL STUDIES

59 Queen's Park Crescent East
Toronto, ON, M5S 2C4, Canada
Tel: (1) 416 926 7290
Fax: (1) 416 926 7276
Email: sheila.campbell@utoronto.ca
www: http://www.pims.ca

Council of the Institute Awards
Subjects: Medieval studies.
Eligibility: Open to Scholars engaged in medieval studies.
Level of Study: Postdoctorate.
Type: Bursary and scholarship.
Value: Varies depending on funds available.
Length of Study: One year.
Frequency: Annual.
Study Establishment: The Institute.
Country of Study: Canada.
No. of awards offered: Varies.
Application Procedure: Applicants must complete an application form, available on request.
Closing Date: January 15th.
Additional Information: The Institute also offers a small number of Research Associateships annually, without stipend, to postdoctoral students and senior Scholars who wish to use the Institute library for their research.

THE POPULATION COUNCIL

Policy Research Division, One Dag Hammarskjold Plaza, New York, NY, 10017, United States of America
Tel: (1) 212 339 0671
Fax: (1) 212 755 6052
Email: ssfellowship@popcouncil.org
www: http://www.popcouncil.org
Tel: 9102900660 POPCO
Contact: Ms Jude Lam-Garrison, Fellowship Co-ordinator

The Population Council is an international non-profit, non-governmental institution that seeks to improve the wellbeing and reproductive health of current and future generations around the world and to help achieve a humane, equitable and sustainable balance between people and resources. The Council conducts biomedical, social science and public health research and helps build research capacities in developing countries.

Population Council Fellowships in Population and Social Sciences
Subjects: Population studies including demography and public health in combination with a social science discipline, such as economics, sociology, anthropology, or geography, dealing with the developing world.
Purpose: To make a significant contribution to the advanced training of professionals in the broad field of population studies through the awarding of fellowships on a competitive basis, with particular emphasis on the training of nationals from developing countries.
Eligibility: Predoctoral fellowships are open to applicants who have completed all coursework requirements toward a PhD or an equivalent degree in one of the social sciences in combination with population studies. Applications requesting support for either the dissertation fieldwork or the dissertation writing period will be considered. Postdoctoral fellowships are open to persons having a PhD or equivalent degree who wish to undertake postdoctoral training and research at an institution other than the one at which they received their PhD degree. Awards are open to all qualified persons, but strong preference will be given to applicants from developing countries who have a firm commitment to return home upon completion of their training programmes. Applications by women are particularly encouraged.
Level of Study: Doctorate, Postdoctorate, Professional development.
Type: Fellowship.
Value: For predoctoral the value is US$24,000, for postdoctoral US$32,000, and for midcareer the value varies. A monthly stipend based on the type of fellowship and place of study, tuition payments and related fees, transportation expenses for the Fellow only and health insurance are also included. Some research related costs may also be part of the award. Tuition at the postdoctoral and midcareer academic levels is not included in the award.
Length of Study: Up to one year.
Frequency: Annual.
Study Establishment: A training or research institution with a strong programme in population studies, regardless of geographic location.
Country of Study: Any country.
No. of awards offered: 15-20.
Application Procedure: Applicants must submit an application and supporting documents in English. Application forms can be obtained from the website. Requests for application forms should include a brief description of candidates' academic and professional qualifications and a short statement about their research or study plans for the proposed fellowship period.
Closing Date: December 15th of each year for notification in March. If the 15th falls on a weekend or holiday then the due date is the next business day.
No. of awards given last year: 14.
No. of applicants last year: 111.
Additional Information: Selection will be based on the recommendation of the Fellowship Committee which consists of three distinguished Scholars in the field of population. Selection criteria will stress academic excellence and prospective contribution to the population field. Application for independent research funds, or for fieldwork not related to a dissertation, will not be considered. The Bernard Berelson

Fellowships are for training at The Population Council's New York office. Prior to submitting a formal application to the Fellowship Office for consideration, the Berelson applicants are required to seek sponsorship from at least one council staff member from the New York office. There are two types of Bernard Berelson Fellowships, which are postdoctoral and midcareer.

PRADER-WILLI SYNDROME ASSOCIATION UK

125a London Road, Derby, DE1 2QQ, England
Tel: (44) 1332 365676
Fax: (44) 1332 360401
Email: website@pwsa-uk.demon.co.uk
www: http://www.pwsa-uk.demon.co.uk
Contact: Administrative Assistant

PWSA (UK) Research Grants

Subjects: Some help may be offered for research into PWS, but is dependent on current financial status of the association. We can usually provide contact names and addresses for people with PWS, and other statistical data.
Purpose: To improve understanding and/or treatment of Prader-Willi Syndrome.
Level of Study: Unrestricted.
Frequency: Dependent on funds available.
Country of Study: United Kingdom.
Application Procedure: A letter or telephone call to the PWSA (UK).
Funding: Private.

PRAGUE SPRING INTERNATIONAL MUSIC COMPETITION

Hellichova 18, Prague, CS-118 00, Czech Republic
Tel: (42) 2 5732 0468
Fax: (42) 2 5731 3725
Email: info@festival.cz
www: http://www.festival.cz

Categories of the Competition are changing annually.2004 Piano, tombone.2005 - Harpsichord, string quartet 2006 - Cello, organ.

Prague Spring International Music Competition

Subjects: Music.
Purpose: To encourage and assist outstanding young musicians.
Eligibility: Open to musicians of any nationality who do not exceed the main age limit of 30.
Level of Study: Unrestricted.
Value: Prizes range from koruna 10,000-120,000. Accommodation is paid for those who qualify for the second round and final.
Frequency: Annual.
Country of Study: Czech Republic.
No. of awards offered: Three main prizes.
Application Procedure: Applicants must complete an application form, available from the website, and enclose an audio tape with a recording of the setting compositions, a copy of their birth certificate and a photograph. There is an application fee of US$100.
Closing Date: December 15th of the year preceding the award.

PREHISTORIC SOCIETY

University College London, Institute of Archaeology, 31-34 Gordon Square, London, WC1H 0PY, England
Fax: (44) 20 7383 2572
Email: prehistoric@ucl.ac.uk
Contact: Ms Tessa Machling, Administrative Assistant

The Prehistoric Society is open to professionals and amateurs alike and has over 2,000 members worldwide. Its main activities are lectures, study tours and conferences and it publishes an annual journal (PPS) and a newsletter (PAST) which is published three times a year.

Prehistoric Society Conference Fund

Subjects: Archaeology, especially prehistoric.
Purpose: To finance attendance at international conferences.
Eligibility: Preference is given first to Scholars from developing countries, whether they are members of the Society or not, then to members of the Society not qualified to apply for conference funds available to university staff. Other members of the Society are also eligible.
Level of Study: Postgraduate.
Type: Travel grant.
Value: A maximum of UK£250.
Length of Study: One year. Renewals are considered.
Frequency: Annual.
Country of Study: Any country.
No. of awards offered: Two.
Application Procedure: Applicants must contact the Honorary Secretary for an application form.
Closing Date: December 31st.
Funding: Private.
Additional Information: Recipients are required to submit a short report on the conference to PAST, the Society's newsletter and their papers for the Society's proceedings if these are not to be included in a conference volume.

Prehistoric Society Research Fund Grant

Subjects: Prehistoric archaeology.
Purpose: To further research in prehistory by excavation or other means.
Eligibility: Open to all members of the Society. The Society may make specific conditions relating to individual applications.
Level of Study: Unrestricted.
Type: Grant.
Value: At the discretion of the Society.
Length of Study: One year. Renewals are considered.
Frequency: Annual.
Country of Study: Any country.
No. of awards offered: Varies.
Application Procedure: Applicants must include the names of two referees in their application.
Closing Date: December 31st.
Funding: Private.
Additional Information: Awards are made on the understanding that a detailed report will be made to the Society as to how the grant was spent.

Prehistoric Society Research Grant Conference Award

Subjects: Prehistoric archaeology.
Purpose: To fund initial projects and visits to conferences.
Eligibility: There are no eligibility restrictions.
Level of Study: Unrestricted.
Value: Variable but usually under UK£500.
Frequency: Annual.
Application Procedure: Applicants must complete an application form.
Closing Date: January 1st.
Funding: Private.

PRESS GANEY ASSOCIATES

404 Columbia Place, South Bend, IN 46601
United States of America
Tel: (1) 800 232 8032
Fax: (1) 574 232 3485
Email: kleddy@pressganey.com
www: http://www.pressganey.com
Contact: Ms Kelly Leddy, Research Specialist

Press Ganey Associates, Inc. is the health care industry's top satisfaction measurement and improvement firm, serving more than 5,900 health care facilities and processing nearly 7,000,000 surveys annually. As the one of the industry's market leaders, the company offer one of the world's largest comparative databases and unparalleled benchmarking opportunities.

Press Ganey Best Practices Research Program
Subjects: The subject of the grant is patient satisfaction in all aspects of the healthcare industry.
Purpose: To increase the systematic and rigorous study of patient satisfaction, through the funding of applied research that will identify best practises and that can be used throughout the healthcare industry.
Eligibility: There are no eligibility restrictions.
Level of Study: Research, Unrestricted.
Value: US$10,000.
Frequency: Annual.
No. of awards offered: Five.
Application Procedure: Please visit the website or e-mail Kelly leddy at kleddy@pressganey.com for application procedures.
Closing Date: March 12, 2004.
Contributor: Press Ganey Associates.
No. of awards given last year: 5.
No. of applicants last year: 83.

PREVENT BLINDNESS AMERICA

500 East Remington Road, Schaumburg, IL 06173, United States of America
Tel: (1) 847 843 2020
Fax: (1) 847 843 8458
Email: chelton@preventblindness.org
www: http://www.preventblindness.org/research
Contact: Director, Program Services

The goal of the programme is to restore and preserve sight through research in detection, prevention, treatment and curing of visual disorders, as well as diseases leading to impaired sight and partial or total blindness.New Program:Clinical research projects focused on our mission to prevent blindness.

Prevent Blindness America Investigator Award
Subjects: Ophthalmology, vision and related sciences. New clinically based research program focused on the prevention of blindness and all related social and economic impacts.
Purpose: To award investigators who are interested in conducting research into vision or vision related sciences.
Eligibility: Open to residents of the United States of America or Canada.
Level of Study: Research.
Value: By individual assessment. A maximum of US$25-$50 K is available to help defray the cost of personnel, equipment and supplies needed for a specific research investigation.
Length of Study: One year. Support may be renewed.
Frequency: Annual.
Study Establishment: Any institution which offers research facilities suitable for the research project in question.
Country of Study: United States of America or Canada.
No. of awards offered: Approx. 20-25.
Application Procedure: Applicants must write for an application form and programme details. Written application submitted by March 1st.
Closing Date: 1st March.
Funding: Private.
Contributor: Donations from individuals.
No. of awards given last year: New program.
Additional Information: It is the responsibility of candidates to make arrangements with the institutions of their choice. Applications for support of pilot projects are welcome.

PRIMATE CONSERVATION INC

1411 Shannock Road, Charlestown, RI RI 02813-3726, United States of America
Tel: (1) 401 364 7140
Fax: (1) 401 364 6785
Email: nrowe@primate.org
www: http://www.primate.org
Contact: The Grants Administrator

PCI gives small grants and matching funds for the conservation projects and studies of the least known and most endangered primates in their natural habitat. We do not fund tuition, Laboratory work, travel to conferences, or salaries.

Primate Conservation Inc.
Subjects: Conservation and research projects on the least known and/or most endangered primates in habitat countries with wild populations.
Purpose: To protect and study the least known and/or most endangered primates in their natural habitats.
Eligibility: Competitive proposals reviewed by 2 independent reviewers and awarded by board of directors for projects which meet our mission statement.
Level of Study: Doctorate, Graduate, Postgraduate, Research.
Type: Grant for various aspects of field research & conservation projects in primate habitat countries.
Value: Average US$2500 Maximum US$5000.
Length of Study: 2 months to 2 years.
Frequency: 2 × per year.
No. of awards offered: Varies with each funding season.
Application Procedure: Application & guidelines can be downloaded from our website. All materials included in the application must be in our office by the deadline date. 6 copies of each proposal is needed plus e-mail version sent to Director nrowe@primate.org in a .doc file.
Closing Date: Sept 20th and Feb 10th.
Funding: Private.
Contributor: Private Donation.
No. of awards given last year: 20.
No. of applicants last year: 45.

PRINCETON UNIVERSITY PROCTER FELLOWSHIPS

University Registry, The Old Schools
Cambridge, Cambridgeshire, CB2 1TN
England
Tel: (44) 1223 332317
Fax: (44) 1223 332332
Email: mrf25@admin.cam.ac.uk
www: http://www.admin.cam.ac.uk
Contact: Ms Melanie Foster, Scholarships Clerk

Procter Visiting Fellowships
Subjects: The liberal arts and sciences, exclusive of professional, technical or commercial subjects.
Purpose: To support study in the liberal arts and sciences.
Eligibility: Open to Commonwealth citizens who hold a First Class (Honours) Degree or equivalent from a United Kingdom university and are able to prove exceptional scholarly power. Preference is normally given to candidates who would be in their second or third year of postgraduate research when, if elected, they take up tenure of the award.
Level of Study: Postgraduate.
Type: Fellowship.
Value: US$15,000 for 10 months plus full tuition fees and medical insurance.
Length of Study: One year.
Frequency: Annual.
Study Establishment: Princeton University, New Jersey.
Country of Study: United States of America.
No. of awards offered: Varies.
Application Procedure: Applicants must complete an application form, available on request.
Closing Date: Please write for details.
Additional Information: The fellowship is normally tenable for one year as a visiting award, but provision also exists exceptionally for a Fellow to be nominated for admission to a PhD programme at Princeton. Candidates who wish to be considered for nomination for the PhD programme should state so on the application form.

PROGRESSIVE SUPRANUCLEAR PALSY (PSP-EUROPE) ASSOCIATION

The Old Rectory, Wappenham, Towcester, Northamptonshire, NN12 8SQ, England
Tel: (44) 1327 860299
Fax: (44) 1327 861007
Email: psp.eur@virgin.net
www: http://www.pspeur.org
Contact: Administrative Assistant

Progressive Supranuclear Palsy (PSP) is a neuro-degenerative disease, involving the death of neurons above the nuclei, which control balance, movement vision, speech and ability to swallow, hence the progressive symptoms. Average life expectancy is some seven years. Prevalence across the United Kingdom is at least five per 100,000. Neuro fibrillary tangles of Tau are formed in the brain. Genetic susceptibility and the cause of this disease are being actively researched. The Progressive Supranuclear Palsy (PSP-Europe) Association is committed to promoting research worldwide into cause, effective treatment and cure of PSP. Its objectives also include engendering awareness and providing information and support for afflicted families across Europe.

PSP Research Grants
Subjects: The cause and effective treatment of PSP.
Eligibility: There are no eligibility restrictions.
Level of Study: Doctorate, Postgraduate.
Type: Research grant.
Value: Normally less than UK£100,000.
Length of Study: Two years.
Frequency: Annual.
Country of Study: Any country.
No. of awards offered: One or two.
Application Procedure: Applications are submitted initially in one A4 page summary of proposed research, length and outline cost, together with a curriculum vitae. Those considered by the Medical Advisory Panel (MAP) to be relevant are then asked to submit a full application, copies of which are forwarded to each member of the MAP, who scores the application. The applications are also put out for peer review. The Chairman of the MAP then briefs the Trustees at the following Executive Committee Meeting, where funds available are assessed and awards made. These Executive Committee Meetings are held in May and November each year.
Closing Date: August 1st and February 1st.
Contributor: Donor trusts.
No. of awards given last year: Two.
No. of applicants last year: 10.

PROSTATE RESEARCH CAMPAIGN UK

Canada House, 272 Field End Road, Eastcote (near Ruislip), Middlesex, HA6 1HP, England
Tel: (44) 0208 582 0246 or 01923 821999
Fax: (44) 0208 582 0250
Email: info@prostate-research.org.uk
www: http://www.prostate-research.org.uk
Contact: The Director

A UK Registered charity (charity number 1037063) which funds research into BOTH Prostate cancer AND benign prostate conditions. Also provides informative literature to patients and families, a website, books etc.

Prostate Research Campaign UK (Research Grants)
Subjects: Research into prostate cancer, Benign Prostatic Hyperplasia and prostatitis. Causes, prevention, understanding, treatment and ultimate cure. Investigation of genetics, stem cell research and all manner of aspects of prostate disorders.
Purpose: Research into both malignant and benign prostate diseases.
Eligibility: Available to English speaking nationals of any country, of any mature age, resident in the United Kingdom and wishing to carry out research at a recognised UK hosptital or institution into malignant or benign prostate disease. Bench space in a UK hospital/instituton must be a prior condition for work to be carried out in the UK.
Value: 3 categories: (a) 0-UK£10,000 (b) 0-UK£25,000 (c) 0-UK£50,000.
Frequency: Dependent on funds available, usually twice per annum.
Country of Study: United Kingdom.
No. of awards offered: Governed by funds available each time.
Application Procedure: Twice a year advertisements appear in The BRITISH MEDICAL JOURNAL and The BRITISH JOURNAL OF UROLOGY International inviting applicants to describe research projects they wish to undertake and to indicate the level of funding sought. Application forms not presently sought but nature of application is described in the adverts. Applications are NOT normally entertained at other times and NOT on a speculative basis.
Closing Date: This is specified in relevant advertisements.
Contributor: Charitable funds raised by Prostate Research Campaign UK.
No. of awards given last year: 20 + approx.
No. of applicants last year: 40 approx.

PYMATUNING LABORATORY OF ECOLOGY (PLE)

The University of Pittsburgh, 13142 Hartstown Road, Linesville, PA 16424, United States of America
Tel: (1) 814 683 5813
Fax: (1) 814 683 2302
Email: ple@toolcity.net
www: http://www.pitt.edu/~biology/pymatuning
Contact: Dr Gail F Johnston, Associate Director

The Pymatuning Laboratory of Ecology (PLE) is a University of Pittsburgh field station dedicated to environmental education and ecological research. Situated on the shores of the Pymatuning Reservoir in North Western Pennsylvania, PLE's land includes woods, wetlands, successional fields and experimental agricultural lands. Researchers from nine institutions conduct projects ranging from community and ecosystem ecology to evolutionary genetics and behaviour.

Darbaker Botany Prize
Subjects: Botany.
Purpose: To award funds for the pursuit of excellent graduate and recent postdoctoral research in botany at Pymatuning Laboratory of Ecology.
Level of Study: Doctorate, Postdoctorate, Postgraduate.
Type: Research grant.
Value: US$500-1,500.
Length of Study: One year.
Frequency: Annual.
Study Establishment: Pymatuning Laboratory of Ecology.
Country of Study: United States of America.
No. of awards offered: One-three.
Application Procedure: Applicants must request guidelines from the Pymatuning Laboratory of Ecology or refer to the website.
Closing Date: February 1st.
Funding: Private.
No. of awards given last year: One.
No. of applicants last year: Two.

G M McKinley Research Fund
Subjects: Ecology.
Purpose: To fund research at the graduate and recent postdoctoral level in ecological science at the Pymatuning Laboratory of Ecology.
Level of Study: Doctorate, Postdoctorate, Postgraduate.
Type: Research grant.
Value: US$500-3,000.
Length of Study: One year.
Frequency: Annual.
Study Establishment: Pymatuning Laboratory of Ecology.
Country of Study: United States of America.
No. of awards offered: One-five.
Application Procedure: Applicants must request guidelines from the Pymatuning Laboratory of Ecology or refer to the website.

Closing Date: February 1st.
Funding: Private.
Contributor: Dr G M McKinley.
No. of awards given last year: Eight.
No. of applicants last year: 10.

QUEEN ELISABETH INTERNATIONAL MUSIC COMPETITION OF BELGIUM

20 rue aux Laines, Brussels, B-1000, Belgium
Tel: (32) 2 213 4050
Fax: (32) 2 514 3297
Email: info@qeimc.be
www: http://www.qeimc.be
Contact: Secretariat

The Queen Elisabeth International Music Competition of Belgium is a non-profit association, located in Brussels, whose principal aim is to organise major international competitions for music virtuosos. In this way, the competition participates in the Belgian and international music world, and gives its support to young musicians.

Queen Elisabeth International Music Competition of Belgium

Subjects: Singing Opera + Oratorio + Lied/Melodie/Song/ 2004 + 2004: Composition, 2005: Violin, 2007: Piano.
Purpose: To provide career support for young pianists, singers, violinists and composers.
Eligibility: Open to musicians of any nationality who are at least 17 years of age and not older than 27 for violin and piano, 30 years of age for singing and 40 for composers. The competition is made up of a first round, a semi-final and a final round.
Level of Study: Unrestricted.
Value: From a total amounting to more than €80,000.
Frequency: Other.
Country of Study: Any country.
No. of awards offered: Six.
Application Procedure: Applicants must obtain an application form from the Secretariat of the Competition or via www.qeimc.be.
Closing Date: January 15th.
Funding: Private.
No. of awards given last year: 12.
No. of applicants last year: Unrestricted.
Additional Information: There are also master classes with jury members.

QUEEN MARIE JOSÉ INTERNATIONAL PRIZE FOR MUSICAL COMPOSITION

Case Postale 19, Meinier, Geneva, CH-1525, Switzerland
www: http://www.reinemariejose.ch
Contact: General Secretary

In order to encourage gifted musicians, Her Majesty Queen Marie José decided to create an international prize for musical composition.

Queen Marie José Prize International Prize for Musical Composition

Subjects: Musical composition.
Purpose: To reward a new musical composition never performed before.
Eligibility: Open to composers of all nationalities and of any age.
Level of Study: Unrestricted.
Type: Prize.
Value: Swiss franc 15,000.
Frequency: Every two years.
Country of Study: Any country.
No. of awards offered: One.
Application Procedure: Applicants must apply for information, available on request or from the website.
Closing Date: May 31st.
Funding: Private.

Contributor: Her Majesty the Queen Marie José.
Additional Information: The award winning work remains its author's exclusive property but, if possible, is performed as part of the Merlinge concerts.

QUEEN MARY UNIVERSITY OF LONDON

Admissions & Research Student Office
London, E1 4NS, England
Tel: (44) 20 7882 5511
Fax: (44) 20 7882 5588
Email: admissions@qmul.ac.uk
www: http://www.qmul.ac.uk
Contact: Mr Peter Smith, Admissions Assistant

Queen Mary is the fourth largest college in the University of London. Located on an attractive campus they have more than 8,000 students studying in four faculties plus St Bartholomew's and the Royal London School of Medicine and Dentistry. Of these, more than 1,600 are following postgraduate courses or undertaking research.

Queen Mary Research Studentships

Subjects: Arts, sciences, engineering, social sciences, law, medicine or dentistry.
Purpose: To provide the opportunity for full-time research leading towards an MPhil or PhD.
Eligibility: Open to suitably qualified candidates who hold at least an Upper Second Class (Honours) or equivalent at First Degree level.
Level of Study: Research.
Type: Studentship.
Value: Maintenance at the current research council rate plus tuition fees.
Length of Study: Three years full-time subject to a satisfactory academic report.
Frequency: Annual.
Study Establishment: Queen Mary, University of London.
Country of Study: United Kingdom.
No. of awards offered: 10 + .
Application Procedure: Applicants must contact the Admission and Recruitment Office for further application details.
Closing Date: Mid Summer.
Funding: Government.
No. of awards given last year: 30.
No. of applicants last year: 200.
Additional Information: These studentships are not available to existing Queen Mary research students.

THE QUEEN'S NURSING INSTITUTE

3 Albemarle Way, Clerkenwell
London, EC1V 4RQ, England
Tel: (44) 20 7490 4227
Fax: (44) 20 7490 1269
Email: mail@qni.org.uk
www: http://www.qni.org.uk
Contact: Miss Sarah Perry, Assistant Director

The Queen's Nursing Institute exists to promote and support the best community nursing practice in order to foster the highest possible standards of public health. Through its unique Innovation and Creative Practice Award Scheme and its new Grants Scheme it provides both professional and financial support for a range of community nurse led initiatives throughout England, Wales and Northern Ireland.

Innovation and Creative Practice Award

Subjects: Implementation of good practice, or a project or an idea, within the community.
Purpose: To support nurses in a community setting to improve patient care through the development of innovative and creative practice.
Level of Study: Graduate, Postgraduate, Professional development, Research.
Type: Grant.

Value: UK£6,000 for major projects, UK£2,000 for grants.
Length of Study: Varies, usually one year.
Frequency: Annual.
Study Establishment: Queen's Nursing Institute.
Country of Study: United Kingdom.
No. of awards offered: Varies, usually 6-10.
Application Procedure: Applicants must submit a form, application proposal and a curriculum vitae.
Closing Date: The last Friday in July for major projects and the first Monday in April and November for grants.
Funding: Private.
Contributor: National Gardens Scheme.
No. of awards given last year: Eight.
No. of applicants last year: 120.
Additional Information: Applicants are encouraged to discuss their application with a staff member before applying.

QUEEN'S UNIVERSITY OF BELFAST

Postgraduate Office, Research & Regional Services, Lanyon North, Belfast, BT7 1NN, Northern Ireland
Tel: (44) 28 9027 2585
Fax: (44) 28 9027 2570
Email: pg.office@qub.ac.uk
www: http://www.qub.ac.uk
Contact: Ms C Farrell

Queen's University has provided a stimulating environment for postgraduate students since the 1850's. It has a reputation as a centre of academic excellence, embracing the most effective technologies and techniques of the 21st century. It offers over 130 postgraduate courses and research opportunities in more than 60 different research areas.

Mary McNeill Scholarship in Irish Studies
Purpose: To fund one selected candidate on MA in Irish Studies programme.
Eligibility: Open to well qualified United States or Canadian students enrolled in the MA (Irish Studies) programme.
Level of Study: Postgraduate.
Type: Scholarship.
Value: UK£3,000.
Length of Study: One year full time.
Frequency: Annual.
Study Establishment: Queen's University, Belfast.
Country of Study: United Kingdom.
Application Procedure: For application form please contact Institute of Irish Studies, Queen's University, Belfast.
Closing Date: 31st May in proposed year of entry.

For further information contact:

Institute of Irish Studies, Queen's University, Belfast, BT7 1NN, Northern Ireland

Queen's University of Belfast Studentships
Subjects: Humanities, social sciences, engineering, medicine and science.
Purpose: Personal Research.
Eligibility: Open to candidates of any nationality who are proficient in English and have obtained a first class or upper second class honours degree or equivalent.
Level of Study: Postgraduate.
Type: Studentship.
Value: Varies from home fees only to fees plus maintenance.
Length of Study: Up to 3 years.
Frequency: Annual.
Study Establishment: Queen's University, Belfast.
Country of Study: United Kingdom.
No. of awards offered: Varies.
Application Procedure: You must complete an application form. Please write or e-mail for further information.
Closing Date: 30th April.
Contributor: Queen's University, Belfast.

Visiting Professorships
Subjects: All subjects offered by the University.
Purpose: Three Visiting Professorships are available to develop links between the university and industry, commerce or the professions. A further three Visiting Professorships are available to foster and encourage the participation of women in the candidate's field of study.
Eligibility: Applicants must be either senior scholars in universities or equivalent institutions, or have attained senior positions and established reputations in industry, commerce or the professions.
Level of Study: Professional development.
Type: Other.
Value: UK£1,600.
Length of Study: One year, with the possibility of renewal. Renewals are without Honorarium.
Frequency: Annual.
Study Establishment: Queen's University of Belfast.
Country of Study: United Kingdom.
No. of awards offered: Six.
Application Procedure: Applicants must complete an application form.
Closing Date: 31st October.

For further information contact:

Queen's University, Belfast, BT7 1NN,
Contact: Academic Council Office

THE RADCLIFFE INSTITUTE FOR ADVANCED STUDY

34 Concord Avenue, Cambridge, MA 02138, United States of America
Tel: (1) 617 495 8212
Fax: (1) 617 495 8136
Email: bunting_fellowships@radcliffe.harvard.edu
www: http://www.radcliffe.edu
Contact: Administrator of Fellowships

The Radcliffe Institute for Advanced Study is a scholarly community where individuals pursue advanced work across a wide range of academic disciplines, professions and creative arts. Within this broad purpose, the Radcliffe Institute sustains a continuing commitment to the study of women, gender and society.

Radcliffe Institute for Advanced Study Fellowship Programme
Subjects: All subjects.
Purpose: To support women and men of exceptional promise and demonstrated accomplishment who wish to pursue independent work.
Eligibility: Open to female and male scholars in any field who gained a doctorate or appropriate terminal degree at least two years prior to appointment, female creative writers and visual or performing artists with a record of significant accomplishment and equivalent professional experience. Special eligibility requirements apply to creative artists.
Level of Study: Postdoctorate, Research.
Type: Fellowship.
Value: Please consult the organisation.
Frequency: Annual.
Study Establishment: Harvard University.
Country of Study: United States of America.
Application Procedure: Applicants must visit the website.
Closing Date: Please consult the organisation.

RADIO AND TELEVISION NEWS DIRECTORS FOUNDATION (RTNDF)

1000 Connecticut Avenue North West, Suite 615, Washington, DC 20036, United States of America
Tel: (1) 202 659 6510
Fax: (1) 202 223 4007
Email: walts@rtndf.org
www: http://www.rtndf.org
Contact: Ms Walt Swanston, Senior Project Director

The mission of the Radio and Television News Directors Foundation (RTNDF) is to promote excellence in electronic journalism through research, education and professional training in four principal programme areas: journalistic ethics and practices, the impact of technological change on electronic journalism, the role of electronic news in politics and public policy, and cultural diversity in the electronic journalism profession.

Capitol Hill News Internships

Subjects: Electronic journalism.
Purpose: To provide an opportunity for students to make future contacts and learn the ropes of political coverage.
Eligibility: Open to recent college graduates whose career objective is electronic journalism. Preference is given to minority students.
Level of Study: Postgraduate.
Type: Internship.
Value: US$1,000 per month. Travel, housing and other living expenses are the responsibility of the intern.
Length of Study: Three months.
Frequency: Annual.
Country of Study: United States of America.
No. of awards offered: Four
Application Procedure: Applicants must write or email for an application form, including a curriculum vitae and a one page essay on why they are interested in this programme. Late, incomplete, or faxed applications will not be accepted.
Closing Date: The deadline for the Spring internships is January 19th and April 1st for the Summer internships.
Funding: Private.
Contributor: The Radio-Television Correspondent's Association.
Additional Information: Interns will be responsible for following newsworthy congressional activities and helping to co-ordinate these activities. Excellent writing skills are essential. Interns will get hands on experience in the House and Senate Radio or TV galleries, working with the Washington press and congressional staff to cover the political process.

RTNDF Fellowships

Subjects: Electronic journalism.
Eligibility: For young journalists in radio or television with up to 10 years of experience.
Level of Study: Postgraduate, Professional development.
Type: Fellowship.
Value: Up to US$2,500.
Frequency: Annual.
Country of Study: United States of America.
No. of awards offered: Eight.
Application Procedure: Applicants must write for application form.
Closing Date: May 4th.
Funding: Private.
Additional Information: The awards include: the Sandra Freeman Geller and Alfred Geller Fellowship, the Shirlee Barish Fellowship, the Michele Clark Fellowship for Minority News Professionals, the Jacque I Minotte Health Reporting Fellowship, the Vada and Barney Oldfield National Security Fellowship, RTNDF Environment and Science Reporting Fellowship, the Michael Burke News Management Fellowship and the NS Bienstock Fellowship for Minority Journalists.

RADIOLOGICAL SOCIETY OF NORTH AMERICA, INC. (RSNA)

820 Jorie Boulevard, Oak Brook, IL 60523-2251, United States of America
Tel: (1) 630 571 7816
Fax: (1) 630 571 7837
Email: walter@rsna.org
www: http://www.rsna.org
Contact: Mr Scott A Walter, Grant Review Process Manager

The Research and Education Foundation of the Radiological Society of North America (RSNA) provides grant support to medical students, residents, fellows and full time faculty members of departments of radiology, radiation oncology and nuclear medicine.

Institutional Fellowship in Radiological Informatics

Subjects: Radiology or related disciplines.
Purpose: To enable institutions with departments strong in information technology to provide training opportunities to young physicians in the radiologic sciences who are not yet professionally established in the area of radiologic informatics.
Eligibility: Fellows must be physicians or scientists in North America who have completed their residency or post-doctoral training.
Level of Study: Postdoctorate.
Type: Fellowship.
Value: US$50,000.
Length of Study: One year.
Frequency: Annual.
Study Establishment: Approved department of radiology within North America.
Country of Study: United States of America.
Application Procedure: By application or nomination.
Closing Date: June 1st.
Funding: Private.

Introduction to Research for International Young Academics

Subjects: Academic radiology.
Purpose: To encourage young radiologists from countries outside North America to pursue careers in academic radiology.
Eligibility: Eligible candidates must be not more than three years out of training, and must be fluent in English.
Level of Study: Postdoctorate.
Type: Fellowship.
Value: Complimentary registration and a stipend of US$1,000 to the individual's department to defray participant's travel expenses.
Length of Study: One year.
Frequency: Annual.
Study Establishment: Any approved by RSNA.
Country of Study: Seminar attendance in USA.
No. of awards offered: Fifteen.
Application Procedure: By nomination from the candidates department Chairperson or training director.
Closing Date: 15th April each year.

RSNA Derck Harwood - Nash International Fellowship

Subjects: Academic radiology.
Purpose: Supplies travel and living expenses to international scholars whose educational goals can be met most appropriately by a course of study in a North-American institution.
Eligibility: Promising international scholars who are embarking on a career in academic radiology and who demonstrate that their specific educational goals can be met most appropriately by a course of study in a North American institution.
Level of Study: Professional development.
Type: Fellowship.
Value: Up to US$10,000.
Length of Study: 1 year.
Frequency: Annual.
Study Establishment: CIRE approved academic center in North America.
Country of Study: United States of America.
Application Procedure: By application or nomination. Forms available to download from the website.
Closing Date: 15th June of each year.
No. of awards given last year: One.

RSNA Educational Scholar Program

Subjects: Radiology or related disciplines.
Purpose: To fund board certified individuals who are seeking an opportunity to develop their expertise in the discipline of education in the radiological sciences.
Eligibility: Open to board certified individuals in radiology or related disciplines who hold an MD, have a demonstrated interest in teaching and show that the pursuit of advanced training in education will impact the future education of radiologists. Applicants must be citizens of a North American country or have permanent resident status.
Level of Study: Postgraduate, Predoctorate.

Type: Grant.
Value: Up to US$75,000 per year.
Length of Study: Two years.
Frequency: Annual.
No. of awards offered: One.
Application Procedure: Applicants must complete an application form, available from the website.
Closing Date: June 1st.

RSNA Holman Pathway Research Seed Grant

Subjects: Any area of radiology-related research, including basic, clinical, developmental and health-care planning, delivery and evaluation.
Purpose: To support residents selected by the American Board of Radiology (ABR) into the B. Leonard Holman Research Pathway.
Eligibility: Applicants must be working on a new pilot project and must not have served as a principal investigator, co-principal investigator or co-investigator on grants totalling US$50,000 or more in a single calendar year.
Type: Research award.
Value: One year grant of US$30,000 or less to support a specific research project. No salary support will be provided. An application for a second year of support of up to US$30,000 may be made if the awardee shows significant progress toward the stated goals of the project.
Frequency: Annual.
Country of Study: United States of America.
Application Procedure: Applicants already have been accepted into the Leonard B. Holman Research Pathway for their residency-training program in radiology, radiation oncology or nuclear medicine. Applicants should download an application form from the RSNA website or from the main organization address.
Closing Date: 15th January each year, to begin 1st July.

RSNA Institutional Clinical Fellowship in Cardiovascular Imaging

Subjects: Cardiovascular imaging.
Purpose: To provide opportunities for radiologists early in their careers to gain experience and expertise in cardiovascular imaging.
Eligibility: Open to citizens or permanent residents of a North American country who must have completed their residency training in the radiological sciences. Fellows must also hold an MD or the equivalent as recognised by the American Medical Association and must be ACGME certified in radiology or be eligible to sit for such certification.
Type: Fellowship.
Value: US$50,000 per year paid to a department. The Foundation does not pay overhead or indirect costs.
Length of Study: Three years.
Frequency: Annual.
No. of awards offered: One.
Application Procedure: Applications must be submitted by a department in preparation for the recruitment of a Fellow into an existing cardiovascular imaging training programme. Application forms are available from the website.
Closing Date: June 1st.

RSNA International Radiology Program Educational Grant To

Subjects: Radiology or related disciplines.
Purpose: To provide an opportunity for scientists and physicians in developed countries to use or develop educational materials specifically to educate the teachers in emerging countries who will return to their respective countries to improve clinical practice and education.
Eligibility: Open to individuals in the radiological sciences in developed countries throughout the world with the facilities and institutional support to establish the programme required to successfully compete for this grant.
Level of Study: Postgraduate.
Type: Grant.
Value: Up to US$100,000 per year. Each year's funding is based on successful progress toward the stated goals of the proposal. The Foundation does not pay institutional overhead costs or indirect costs.

Length of Study: Three years.
Frequency: Annual.
No. of awards offered: One.
Application Procedure: Applicants must complete an application form, available from the website.
Closing Date: June 1st.

RSNA Medical Student Departmental Grant Program

Subjects: Diagnostic radiology, radiation oncology or nuclear medicine.
Purpose: To provide matching grants to enable departments of diagnostic radiology, radiation oncology or nuclear medicine allied with North American medical schools to offer research opportunities to medical students.
Eligibility: Open to departments of diagnostic radiology, radiation oncology or nuclear medicine who have been allied with fully accredited North American medical schools for five consecutive years.
Type: Grant.
Value: US$1,000 per month for three or more months to be matched by the department.
Frequency: Annual.
Application Procedure: Applicants must complete an application form, available from the website. Departments must describe their commitment to research, provide details of the medical student's proposed activity and participation, and identify the method by which the student will be selected. They must also designate a scientific advisor to oversee the medical student's participation in the research programme.
Closing Date: January 8th.

RSNA Medical Student/Scholar Assistant Program

Subjects: Radiology or related disciplines.
Purpose: To make radiology research opportunities available for medical students early in their training and encourage them to consider academic radiology as a career option.
Eligibility: Open to full-time medical students at an accredited North American medical school. Nominees must be citizens of a North American country or hold permanent resident status.
Type: Grant.
Value: US$5,000.
Length of Study: One year.
Frequency: Twice a year.
Application Procedure: Applicants must be nominated by a current RSNA scholar grant recipient and work with the scholar on his/her designated research project.
Closing Date: There is no specific deadline. The scholar is notified of the option to nominate a medical student. The application must be prepared with the assistance of the nominating scholar.

RSNA Research Fellow Program

Subjects: Medical sciences.
Purpose: To provide young investigators not yet professionally established in the radiological sciences an opportunity to gain further insight into scientific investigation and to develop competence in research techniques and methods.
Eligibility: Open to citizens or permanent residents of a North American country who have an MD, DO, DVM, DDS, DMD degree or the equivalent as recognised by the American Medical Association. Individuals with a PhD or ScD, in addition to the appropriate medical degree, are not eligible for this award, though MD or PhDs who have their PhDs in areas other than medical research are eligible. Applicants should be near the end of their prescribed training and/or have completed the prerequisite training to sit for qualifying exams. Preference will be given to candidates who have a commitment from a North American educational institution for a faculty appointment after the fellowship is completed.
Level of Study: Doctorate, Postdoctorate, Postgraduate, Predoctorate.
Type: Fellowship.
Value: US$45,000 for one year with US$5,000 to the institution, on request, to be applied to direct expenses. Applications for renewal for a second year at US$50,000, plus US$5,000 to the institution, on

request, will be considered. The Foundation does not pay overhead or indirect costs.

Length of Study: One or two years.

Frequency: Annual.

No. of awards offered: One.

Application Procedure: Applicants must complete an application form, available from the website.

Closing Date: January 15th.

RSNA Research Fellowship in Basic Radiologic Sciences

Subjects: Radiological sciences.

Purpose: To provide training and research opportunities for scientists who possess a PhD or equivalent degree to gain insight into scientific investigation and to develop competence in state of the art research in basic radiological sciences.

Eligibility: Fellows must be within five years of completing their doctoral training in the radiological sciences and be eligible to join a department of diagnostic radiology, radiation oncology or nuclear medicine.

Level of Study: Postdoctorate.

Type: Fellowship.

Value: US$45 salary support for one year. Application for renewal for a second year of salary support at US$50,000 will be considered based on progress toward the stated goals during the initial year. US$5,000 will be given to the institution each year to help cover direct expenses.

Length of Study: Initially one year, further year by application.

Frequency: Annual.

Study Establishment: Any which provides the necessary space, facilities and equipment.

Country of Study: United States of America.

No. of awards offered: Varies.

Application Procedure: Download an application form from the website or contact the main organization address.

Closing Date: January 15th in same year. Award starts July 1st.

Funding: Private.

Additional Information: This program is designed to promote and enhance the understanding and utilization of basic radiological sciences within departments of diagnostic radiology, radiation oncology and nuclear medicine. Research fellows must be prepared to devote 100% of their time to research under the guidance of a scientific advisor of their choice for the full term of the fellowship.

RSNA Research Resident Program

Subjects: Radiology, radiation oncology and nuclear medicine.

Purpose: To provide opportunities for individuals to gain further insight into scientific investigation, and to develop competence in research and educational techniques and methods.

Eligibility: Open to citizens or permanent residents of a North American country. Applicants should be in residency training so that the award can occur during any year after the first year of training and should have an academic degree acceptable for a radiology residency.

Level of Study: Postgraduate.

Type: Grant.

Value: US$30,000 designed to replace a portion of the resident's salary.

Length of Study: One year, non renewable.

Frequency: Annual.

No. of awards offered: One.

Application Procedure: Applicants must complete an application form, available from the website.

Closing Date: January 15th.

RSNA Scholars Program

Subjects: Medical sciences.

Purpose: To support junior clinical faculty members and allow them to gain experience in research early in their academic careers.

Eligibility: Open to citizens or permanent residents of a North American country who have completed advanced training and are within five years of an initial faculty appointment at a North American educational institution. Applicants must also be board certified or eligible to sit for certifying exams and have not served or not currently be serving as principal investigator or co-principal investigator on grants or contracts totalling US$50,000 or more in a single calendar year.

Level of Study: Doctorate, Postdoctorate.

Type: Award.

Value: US$75,000 per year, payable to the institution, to be used exclusively as a stipend for the scholar.

Length of Study: Two years. In unusual circumstances, a third year may be granted to provide bridge funding between the scholar award and additional funding obtained from other sources. A separate application is required to be considered for a third year of funding.

Frequency: Annual.

No. of awards offered: One.

Application Procedure: Scholar applicants must be nominated by their host institution. If awarded, scholars will be required to take the Advanced Grant Writing Course offered through the RSNA Office of Research Development (ORD). Personal interviews will be conducted for selected finalists. Three letters of recommendation are needed as is a budget with details of the project and all sources of support.

Closing Date: January 15th.

RSNA Seed Grant Research Program

Subjects: Diagnostic radiology, radiation oncology or nuclear medicine.

Purpose: To assist investigators in defining objectives and testing hypotheses before they apply for major grants from corporations, foundations, or government agencies.

Eligibility: Applications are accepted from any country. Applicants must hold a full-time faculty position in an educational institution at the time the award commences and be in a department of diagnostic radiology, radiation oncology or nuclear medicine having completed all advanced training. Applicants must not have served as a principal investigator, co-principal investigator, or co-investigator on grants totalling US$50,000 or more in a single calendar year. Any area of radiology related research is eligible including basic, clinical, developmental and healthcare planning, delivery and evaluation.

Type: Research grant.

Value: US$30,000 or less, payable to the recipient's department in two equal instalments.

Length of Study: One year.

Frequency: Twice a year.

Application Procedure: Applicants must complete an application form, available from the website.

Closing Date: January 15th.

RSNA World Wide Web Based Educational Program

Subjects: Radiology or related disciplines.

Purpose: To provide an opportunity for scientists and physicians to develop educational materials specifically for wide spread distribution through the Internet.

Eligibility: Open to anyone in the radiological sciences from any country. Individuals who are not in the radiological sciences such as computer or web specialists may be involved as co-investigators.

Level of Study: Postgraduate, Professional development.

Type: Grant.

Value: Up to US$75,000.

Length of Study: One year.

Application Procedure: Applicants must complete an application form, available from the website.

Closing Date: June 1st.

RAGDALE FOUNDATION

1260 North Green Bay Road, Lake Forest, IL 60045, United States of America

Tel: (1) 847 234 1063

Fax: (1) 847 234 1075

Email: ragdaleboo45@aol.com

www: http://www.ragdale.org

Contact: Ms Sylvia Brown, Marketing & Programming Director

The Ragdale Foundation is an independent, non-profit organisation whose mission is to provide a peaceful place for artists of all disciplines to work. Residences offered range from two weeks to two months.

Frances Shaw Fellowship
Subjects: Writing, particularly authorship.
Purpose: To support women over the age of 55 who are beginning to write seriously.
Eligibility: Open to women over the age of 55 only. Applicants must be United States citizens.
Level of Study: Unrestricted.
Type: Residency.
Value: US$1,500.
Length of Study: Two months.
Frequency: Annual.
Country of Study: United States of America.
No. of awards offered: One.
Application Procedure: Applicants must write for guidelines enclosing a stamped addressed envelope.
Closing Date: February 1st.
Funding: Private.
No. of awards given last year: One.
No. of applicants last year: 75.

Ragdale Foundation Residencies
Subjects: Creative writing, musical composition, film-making or the visual arts.
Purpose: To provide a peaceful place and uninterrupted time for writers and composers to do their work.
Eligibility: Open to all creative writers, Scholars, composers, film makers and visual artists. Professional recognition is helpful for admission, but it is not essential. Selections are based on the peer panel's rankings of work samples.
Level of Study: Unrestricted.
Type: Residency.
Length of Study: Periods of between two weeks and two months.
Frequency: Throughout the year, except May and December 15th to January 1st.
Study Establishment: Ragdale House and Barnhouse, Friend's Studio.
Country of Study: United States of America.
No. of awards offered: Up to 12 places at any one time, approx. 160 per year.
Application Procedure: Applicants must submit slides, tapes or samples of writing and two references.
Closing Date: January 15th for June to December and June 1st for January to April.
Funding: Private.
Contributor: Private donors and the Illinois Arts Council.
No. of awards given last year: 200.
No. of applicants last year: 600.
Additional Information: Couples are not accepted unless each qualifies independently. Ragdale is in Lake Forest, 30 miles North of Chicago on Lake Michigan. The Ragdale House and Barnhouse were designed by Howard Van Doren Shaw. Much of his landscaping also remains intact such as a garden, lanes through a meadow and prairie, a wide lawn and large trees. Ragdale is on the National Register of Historic Places and the property overlooks a large nature preserve. A new studio building was constructed in 1991.

RAMSAY MEMORIAL FELLOWSHIPS TRUST

University College London
Gower Street, London, WC1E 6BT
England
Tel: (44) 20 7380 7815
Fax: (44) 20 7380 7327
Email: g.hawes@ucl.ac.uk
Contact: Mr Gary Hawes, Executive Secretary

The Ramsay Memorial Fellowships Trust was constituted in 1920 to administer the Ramsay Fellowships which were founded in memory of the late Sir William Ramsay.

British (General) Fellowship
Subjects: Chemistry.
Purpose: To assist postdoctoral research.
Eligibility: Usually open to United Kingdom or Commonwealth citizens who have had training in research methods as evidenced by the possession of a PhD or its equivalent, preferably from a university within the United Kingdom or Commonwealth and who can demonstrate their capacity for original research in chemical science. The maximum age for candidates is 35 years.
Level of Study: Postdoctorate.
Type: Fellowship.
Value: Normally equivalent to the lower part of the lecturer scale for United Kingdom universities, plus superannuation benefits and a maximum of UK£500 for research expenses.
Length of Study: Two years.
Frequency: Annual.
Study Establishment: A university, university college or other Institute of Higher Education.
Country of Study: Other.
No. of awards offered: Approx. one-two.
Application Procedure: Applicants must complete an application form, available from August.
Closing Date: November 15th.
Funding: Private.
No. of awards given last year: Two.
No. of applicants last year: 46.
Additional Information: Recipients are encouraged to undertake a small amount of teaching work, not exceeding three hours per week.

REES JEFFREYS ROAD FUND

13 The Avenue, Chichester
West Sussex, PO19 4PX, England
Tel: (44) 1243 787013
Fax: (44) 1243 790622
Contact: Mr B Fieldhouse, Secretary

The Rees Jeffreys Road Fund makes grants for courses or research connected with roads and transportation. Within those subjects, it endows university teaching posts, pays bursaries for postgraduate students, sponsors research and contributes to research projects put forward. It has a small budget for the provision of roadside rests and improving roadside environment.

Rees Jeffreys Road Fund Bursaries
Subjects: Transport - Schlolarship and research which will lead to the better understanding of transport issues and offer the prospect of new thinking and ideas few grappling with contemporary transport issues.
Purpose: To facilitate postgraduate study or research into transport.
Eligibility: Open to candidates of any nationality who hold at least an Upper Second Class (Honours) Degree at a UK university.
Level of Study: Doctorate, Postgraduate.
Type: Bursary-full fees and maintenance lump sum contribution to PhD research.
Value: Fees and the equivalent of SERC maintenance for MSc courses in transportation.
Length of Study: 1 to 2 years.
Frequency: Annual.
Study Establishment: Universities and Research Institutions.
Country of Study: United Kingdom.
No. of awards offered: Approx. 10.
Application Procedure: Applicants must be recommended by the intended institution of study.
Closing Date: July 1st for study courses.
Funding: Private.

No. of awards given last year: Ten.
No. of applicants last year: 24.

Rees Jeffreys Road Fund Research Grants

Subjects: Transport.
Purpose: To facilitate research projects into roads and transportation.
Level of Study: Research.
Value: UK£1,000 to UK£20,000, depending on the project.
Frequency: Annual.
Study Establishment: Universities and Research Institutions.
No. of awards offered: Approx. 12 per year.
Application Procedure: Applicants must write a letter to the secretary.
Closing Date: There is no fixed deadline. Applications will be considered by the trustees at one of five meetings each year.
Funding: Private.
No. of awards given last year: 29.
No. of applicants last year: 40.

THE REID TRUST FOR THE HIGHER EDUCATION OF WOMEN

53 Thornton Hill, Exeter, Devon, EX4 4NR, England
Contact: Mrs H M Harvey, Honorary Treasurer

The Reid Trust for the Higher Education of Women was founded in 1868 in connection with Bedford College for Women for the promotion and improvement of women's education. It is administered by a small committee of voluntary trustees.

Reid Trust Awards

Subjects: All subjects.
Purpose: To assist in the higher education of women.
Eligibility: Open to women educated in the United Kingdom who have appropriate academic qualifications and who wish to undertake further training or research.
Level of Study: Unrestricted.
Value: UK£50-750.
Frequency: Annual.
Country of Study: United Kingdom.
No. of awards offered: Usually six-ten.
Application Procedure: Applicants must complete an application form available by sending a stamped addressed envelope with a request.
Closing Date: May 31st.
Funding: Private.
Contributor: Historic College Trust.
No. of awards given last year: 16.
No. of applicants last year: 200 + .

Reid Trust For the Higher Education of Women

Subjects: All subjects.
Purpose: To promote the education of women.
Eligibility: Open to female who have the appropriate academic qualifications and who wish to undertake further study or research. Open to women educated in Britain who have appropriate academic qualifications and who wish to undertake further training or research in the United Kingdom.
Level of Study: Unrestricted.
Type: Grant.
Value: UK£50-750 each.
Length of Study: Unrestricted.
Frequency: Annual.
Country of Study: United Kingdom.
No. of awards offered: Usually 10-12.
Application Procedure: Applicants must complete an application form, obtained by sending a stamped addressed envelope with a request.
Closing Date: May 31st.
Funding: Private.
No. of awards given last year: 16.
No. of applicants last year: 200.

REMEDI

The Old Rectory, Stanton Prior, Bath, BA2 9HT, England
Tel: (44) 1761 472662
Fax: (44) 1761 470662
Email: g.coles_remedi@btinternet.com
www: http://www.remedi.org.uk
Contact: P D Mesquita OBE, Director

REMEDI, founded in 1973, supports pioneering research into all aspects of disability and disease to improve the quality of life.

REMEDI Research Grants

Subjects: Diabetes, anputees, childhood eczema, osteoporosis, rehabilitation of the elderly, speech therapy, stroke, autism and head injury.
Purpose: To support pioneering research into all aspects of disability and disease. The Trustees are particularly interested in funding or part funding initial grants where applicants find it difficult to obtain funding through larger organisations.
Eligibility: Open to English speaking applicants living and working in the United Kingdom.
Level of Study: Unrestricted.
Type: Research grant.
Value: Varies.
Length of Study: One-three years.
Frequency: Twice a year.
Study Establishment: A hospital or university.
Country of Study: United Kingdom.
No. of awards offered: Varies.
Application Procedure: Applicants must email the Director with a summary including costs and start date on one side of A4 paper. If the Chairman considers the research project to be of interest the Director will email an application form to be completed. Completed applications are sent to independent referees for peer review. The Trustees normally make awards twice a year in June and November.
Closing Date: Applications are accepted at any time.
Funding: Private.
Contributor: Trusts, companies and individuals.
No. of awards given last year: 8.
No. of applicants last year: 180.
Additional Information: Grants will not be awarded for course fees, administration and university overheads. Cancer and cancer related diseases are not normally supported. Trustees have decided to reduce the number of awards, but substantially increase the size of the grants.

REPORTERS COMMITTEE FOR FREEDOM OF THE PRESS

1815 North Forte Myer Drive, Suite 900, Arlington, VA 22209-1817, United States of America
Tel: (1) 703 807 2100
Fax: (1) 703 807 2109
Email: rcfp@rcfp.org
www: http://www.rcfp.org
Contact: Ms Maria Gowen, Office Manager

The Reporters Committee for Freedom of the Press is a voluntary, unincorporated association of reporters and editors, dedicated to protecting the First Amendment interests of the news media. From its office in Arlington, Virginia, the Reporters Committee staff provide cost free legal defence and research services to journalists and their attorneys throughout the United States and also operate the FOI service centre to assist the news media with federal and state open records and open meetings issues.

Jack Nelson Legal Fellowship

Subjects: Media law.
Eligibility: To be eligible for the programme, candidates must have been granted a law degree no later than August 1999. Significant experience in print or electronic news reporting and strong legal research and writing skills are required.

Level of Study: Postgraduate, Professional development.
Type: Fellowship.
Value: US$30,000 plus fully paid health benefits.
Length of Study: One year.
Frequency: Annual.
Country of Study: United States of America.
No. of awards offered: One.
Application Procedure: Applicants must submit a covering letter, curriculum vitae, contact details of three referees, news clips and a short legal writing sample to the attention of Gregg P Leslie, Acting Executive Director. There is no application form.
Closing Date: February 1st.
Funding: Private.
No. of awards given last year: One.
No. of applicants last year: 40.
Additional Information: The Fellow will monitor significant developments in first amendment media law, assist with legal defence requirements from reporters, prepare legal memoranda, amicus briefs and other special projects. He or she will also write for The Reporter's Committee's publications, the quarterly magazines The News Media and The Law and the bi-weekly newsletter News Media Update.

Reporters Committee Legal Fellowship

Subjects: Media law.
Eligibility: Candidates must have received a law degree no later than August 2000. Strong legal research and writing skills are required and a background in news reporting is very strongly preferred.
Level of Study: Postgraduate, Professional development.
Type: Fellowship.
Value: US$30,000 plus fully paid health benefits.
Length of Study: One year, September-August.
Frequency: Annual.
Country of Study: United States of America.
No. of awards offered: One.
Closing Date: February 1st.
Funding: Private.
No. of awards given last year: One.
No. of applicants last year: 40.
Additional Information: Legal fellows monitor significant developments in first amendment media law, assist with legal defence requests from reporters, prepare legal memoranda, amicus briefs and other special projects. They write for the Committee's publications, the quarterly magazine The News Media and The Law and the bi-weekly newsletter, News Media Update.

Robert R McCormick Tribune Foundation Journalism Fellowship

Subjects: Media law.
Eligibility: Candidates must possess a law degree and be admitted to the bar of any state. They must have a minimum of two or three years of postgraduate legal experience in a law firm, public interest group, government agency, or judicial clerkship. Substantial experience in appellate brief writing is mandatory and strong legal research and writing skills is required. A background in news reporting is strongly preferred.
Level of Study: Postgraduate, Professional development.
Type: Fellowship.
Value: US$40,000.
Length of Study: One year.
Frequency: Annual.
Country of Study: United States of America.
No. of awards offered: One.
Application Procedure: Applicants must submit a covering letter, curriculum vitae and contact details of three referees, a sample appellate brief and news clips or another short non legal writing sample to Gregg P Leslie, Acting Executive Director. There is no application form.
Closing Date: February 1st.
Funding: Private.
No. of awards given last year: One.
No. of applicants last year: 10.
Additional Information: The McCormick Tribune Journalism Fellow will be responsible for ensuring that their publications are appealing to,

and understandable by, the core readers, those being journalists who do not have any special legal knowledge. The Fellow will also serve as the primary editor of the single topic guides and the daily news product, making sure the website is updated regularly. The Fellow will be responsible for helping to identify media law topics that should be addressed in analytical pieces or in enterprise reporting projects, drawing from his or her experience concerning what newsrooms need to know about developments in free press law. In addition, the journalism Fellow will write, edit and design for the Committee's flagship publications, the quarterly magazine, The News Media and The Law, and the bi-weekly newsletter, News Media Update. The Fellow will also be able to audit a course on first amendment or media law at one of the Washington area universities. The Fellow will also be expected to draft approx. six appellate amicus briefs in significant cases involving first amendment media law issues during the fellowship. The Fellow will also monitor significant developments in media law, assist with responding to legal defence requests from reporters, and prepare legal memoranda and other special projects.

Robert R McCormick Tribune Foundation Legal Fellowship

Subjects: Media law.
Eligibility: Candidates must possess a law degree and be admitted to the bar of any state. They must have a minimum of two or three years of postgraduate legal experience in a law firm, public interest group, government agency or judicial clerkship. Substantial experience in appellate brief writing is mandatory and strong legal research and writing skills is required. A background in news reporting is strongly preferred.
Type: Fellowship.
Value: US$42,000.
Length of Study: One year.
Frequency: Annual.
Country of Study: United States of America.
No. of awards offered: One.
Application Procedure: Applicants must submit a covering letter, curriculum vitae and contact details of three referees, a sample appellate brief and news clips or another short non legal writing sample to Gregg P Leslie, Acting Executive Director. There is no application form.
Closing Date: February 1st.
Funding: Private.
No. of awards given last year: One.
No. of applicants last year: 10.
Additional Information: The Fellow will be expected to draft approx. six appellate amicus briefs in significant cases involving First Amendment media law issues during the fellowship. The legal Fellow will also monitor significant developments in media law, assist with responding to legal defence requests from reporters, prepare legal memoranda and other special projects. In addition, the legal Fellow will write for the Committee's publications, the quarterly magazine The News Media and The Law and the bi-weekly newsletter News Media Update.

REPRESENTATION OF THE FLEMISH GOVERNMENT

Embassy of Belgium, 3330 Garfield Street, NW, Washington, DC 20008, United States of America
Tel: (1) 202 625 5850
Fax: (1) 202 342 8346
Email: franm@wizard.net
www: http://www.diplobel.us/
Contact: Françoise Masters, Cultural and Administrative Officer

The Government of Flandero offers bursaries to permit students to continue their studies in Flandero.

Fellowship for American College Students

Subjects: Study or research at universities, conservatories of music or art academics recognised by the Flemish community in the fields of art, music humanities, social and political sciences, law, economics, sciences and medicine.

Purpose: To enable students to continue their education in Flanders, Belgium.
Eligibility: U.S. citizens who are already studying for a first or doctoral degree.
Level of Study: Doctorate, Graduate, Postdoctorate, Postgraduate, Predoctorate.
Type: Fellowship.
Value: A monthly stipend of approximately €674.27 at a Flemish institution, reimbursement of tuition fees, health insurance and public liability insurance in accordance with Belgian law. There is no reimbursement of travel expenses.
Length of Study: Variable.
Frequency: Annual.
Study Establishment: Recognised institutes in Flanders.
Country of Study: Belgium.
No. of awards offered: Five.
Application Procedure: Download on application form from www.diplobel.us/ or contact Mrs. Francoise, Marters, Cultural Officer, at the Belgian Embassy, Washington.
Closing Date: 14th January to commence in September of the same year.
Funding: Government.
Additional Information: The decision to grant a fellowship is made by the Ministry of the Flemish community after consultation with the prospective host institution.

RESEARCH CORPORATION (USA)

101 North Wilmot Road, Suite 250, Tucson, AZ 85711, United States of America
Tel: (1) 520 571 1111
Fax: (1) 520 571 1119
Email: awards@rescorp.org
www: http://www.rescorp.org
Contact: Ms Carmen Vitello, Editor, Science Advancement Programme

The Research Corporation (USA) was one of the first United States of America foundations, and is the only one wholly devoted to the advancement of academic science. An endowed organisation, it makes grants totalling US$5-7 million annually for independently proposed research in chemistry, physics and astronomy at United States of America and Canadian colleges and universities.

Cottrell College Science Awards
Subjects: Physics, chemistry or astronomy.
Purpose: To support significant research that contributes to the advancement of science.
Eligibility: Open to faculty members at public and private institutes of higher education in the United States of America or Canada. The principal investigator must have an appointment in a department of astronomy, chemistry or physics and the department must offer at least Baccalaureate, but not doctoral degrees. The institution must demonstrate its commitment by providing facilities and opportunities for faculty and student research.
Level of Study: Doctorate.
Type: Research award.
Value: Equipment and supplies, student Summer stipends of up to US$3,500 and a faculty Summer stipend of up to US$7,500.
Length of Study: Up to five years, possibly renewable.
Frequency: Twice a year.
Study Establishment: Public and private universities with non PhD granting departments of astronomy, chemistry or physics.
Country of Study: United States of America or Canada.
No. of awards offered: 100 +.
Application Procedure: Applicants must complete an application form and should visit the website for guidelines and application request forms.
Closing Date: November 15th or May 15th.
Funding: Private.
Contributor: Foundation endowment.
No. of awards given last year: 72.
No. of applicants last year: 277.

Cottrell Scholars Awards
Subjects: Physics, chemistry or astronomy.
Purpose: To encourage excellence in both research and teaching.
Eligibility: Open to faculty in the third year of a first tenure track position.
Level of Study: Doctorate.
Type: Award.
Value: US$75,000, which may be flexibly applied in keeping with the applicants' approved programme.
Frequency: Annual.
Study Establishment: Universities with PhD granting departments of physics, chemistry and astronomy.
Country of Study: United States of America or Canada.
No. of awards offered: Varies.
Application Procedure: Applicants must complete an application form and should visit the website for guidelines and application request forms.
Closing Date: September 1st.
Funding: Private.
Contributor: Foundation endowment.
No. of awards given last year: 15.
No. of applicants last year: 99.
Additional Information: Candidates must provide both a research and teaching plan for peer review.

Research Corporation (USA) Research Opportunity Awards
Subjects: Physics, chemistry or astronomy.
Purpose: To assist mid-career faculty scientists in launching new research programmes.
Eligibility: Open to established faculty members in PhD departments in the United States of America or Canada.
Level of Study: Doctorate.
Type: Research award.
Value: Up to US$50,000.
Frequency: Twice a year.
Study Establishment: Universities with PhD granting departments of physics, chemistry and astronomy.
Country of Study: United States of America or Canada.
No. of awards offered: Varies.
Application Procedure: Applicants must be nominated by the department chair and selected nominees are invited to submit applications on the forms provided. Interested parties should visit the website.
Closing Date: May 1st or October 1st are the deadlines for nominations.
Funding: Private.
Contributor: Foundation endowment.
No. of awards given last year: 6.
No. of applicants last year: 7.
Additional Information: The chair of each PhD granting physics, astronomy and chemistry department in the United States of America or Canada may make two nominations twice a year from tenured faculty without major research funding. Applications are invited from a selected group of these nominees.

RESEARCH INTO AGEING

PO Box 32833, London, N1 9ZQ, England
Tel: (44) 20 7404 6878
Fax: (44) 20 7404 6816
Email: ria@ageing.co.uk
www: http://www.ageing.org
Contact: Dr S Sorensen, Research Manager

Research into Ageing's purpose is to advance the prevention, or improvement in treatment, of diseases and disabilities which become more common in later life. This is done by funding high quality research, supporting the education of scientists, raising awareness of the potential of research and lobbying for implementation of results.

Queen Elizabeth the Queen Mother Fellowship Award
Subjects: Geriatric medicine, gerontology, cell and molecular biology of ageing processes.

Purpose: To provide an opportunity for postdoctoral scientists or those who are medically qualified to become independent researchers and to undertake research of high quality.
Eligibility: Open to candidates who have no more than 10 years of postdoctoral experience and intend to maintain a long-term interest in ageing research. Applicants must be able to speak English. The award is only tenable at United Kingdom institutions.
Level of Study: Postdoctorate.
Type: Fellowship.
Value: Up to UK£50,000 per year for the duration of the award.
Length of Study: Three years.
Frequency: Annual.
Country of Study: United Kingdom.
No. of awards offered: Four-six.
Application Procedure: Applicants must initially submit a two page outline proposal on a form available on request. Shortlisted applicants will be sent a full application form. Fellowships are considered annually in May and November.
Closing Date: Outline proposal forms are due in Winter and Summer. Applicants should check the exact date with the Research Department. This can be found on the website.
No. of awards given last year: Four-six.
No. of applicants last year: 28.

Research into Ageing Prize Studentships

Subjects: Geriatric medicine, gerontology, cell and molecular biology of ageing processes or related disciplines.
Purpose: To ensure a flow of first class students into the field of ageing research.
Eligibility: Open to potential supervisors wishing to enable a postgraduate to obtain a further degree, usually to PhD standard, through work on a topic connected with age related illness or the ageing process. Applicants must be able to speak English and must be employed by a United Kingdom institution.
Level of Study: Postgraduate.
Type: Studentship.
Value: A stipend, university fees up to UK£3,000 per year, expenses for consumables and travel up to UK£3,000 per year.
Length of Study: Three years.
Frequency: Annual.
Study Establishment: Suitable United Kingdom establishments.
Country of Study: United Kingdom.
No. of awards offered: Four.
Application Procedure: Applicants must initially submit a two page outline proposal on a form available on request. Shortlisted applicants will be sent a full application form. Studentships are considered annually in November for start the following year.
Closing Date: Outline proposal forms must be returned between July and August. Applicants should check the exact date with the Research Department.
No. of awards given last year: Three.
No. of applicants last year: 15-20.
Additional Information: Awards should be applied for by supervisors.

Research into Ageing Programme Grants

Subjects: Geriatric medicine, gerontology or related disciplines.
Purpose: To provide support for research that cannot be carried out in the short-term. The programme is designed to enable researchers to establish longer term programmes of work and retain teams of research workers without having to repeatedly seek funds.
Eligibility: Open to individuals, groups of researchers or interdisciplinary teams. Applicants should normally hold an established post at a university or institution within the United Kingdom and have a good track record of research in the proposed field of work.
Level of Study: Postdoctorate.
Type: Programme grant.
Value: Up to UK£500,000.
Length of Study: Up to five years.
Frequency: Annual.
Study Establishment: Universities, medical colleges, hospitals and general practices.
Country of Study: United Kingdom.
No. of awards offered: Dependent on availability of funds.

Application Procedure: Applicants must initially submit a two page outline proposal on a form available on request. Shortlisted applicants will be sent a full application form. Research project grants are considered annually in May.
Closing Date: Outline applications are due in November. Applicants should check the exact date with the Research Department.
No. of awards given last year: Three.
No. of applicants last year: 36.

RESOURCES FOR THE FUTURE (RFF)

1616 P Street North West, Washington, DC 20036, United States of America
Tel: (1) 202 328 5043
Fax: (1) 202 939 3460
Email: macauley@rff.org
www: http://www.rff.org
Contact: Co-ordinator for Academic Programmes

Resources for the Future (RFF) is a non-profit and non partisan think tank located in Washington, DC that conducts independent research rooted primarily in economics and other social sciences on environmental and natural resource issues.

Gilbert F White Postdoctoral Fellowship

Subjects: Social and policy sciences, environmental studies, energy and natural resources.
Purpose: To enable postdoctoral researchers to spend a year in residence conducting research in the social or policy sciences in areas related to the environment, energy or natural resources.
Eligibility: A strong economics background, or closely related discipline in the social or policy sciences, is required. Applicants must be of postdoctorate level.
Level of Study: Postdoctorate.
Type: Fellowship.
Value: Please visit the website for details.
Length of Study: Eleven months.
Frequency: Annual.
Country of Study: United States of America.
No. of awards offered: Two.
Application Procedure: Applicants must submit a covering letter and curriculum vitae with a proposal relating to budget and three letters of recommendation. No application form is required. Application forms sent by fax or email will not be accepted.
Closing Date: February 28th.

Joseph L Fisher Dissertation Award

Subjects: Economics, policy sciences, environment and natural resources.
Purpose: To support PhD students in their last year of dissertation research in economics or other policy sciences on issues related to the environment, energy or natural resources.
Eligibility: Open to all nationalities. Students must be in the final year of dissertation research or writing.
Level of Study: Doctorate.
Type: Award.
Value: US$12,000.
Length of Study: One year.
Frequency: Annual.
Country of Study: Any country.
No. of awards offered: Varies.
Application Procedure: Applicants must submit a letter of application, a curriculum vitae, graduate transcripts, a one page abstract of the dissertation, a technical summary of the dissertation, a letter from the department chair and two letters of recommendation. Applications sent by fax or email will not be accepted.
Closing Date: February 28th.

RFF Fellowships in Environmental Regulatory Implementation

Subjects: Environmental studies and natural resources.
Purpose: To support research that documents the implementation and outcomes of environmental regulations.

Eligibility: Open to Scholars from universities and research establishments who have a doctorate or equivalent degree or professional research experience.
Level of Study: Postdoctorate.
Type: Fellowship.
Value: Negotiable stipend.
Length of Study: One-two years.
Frequency: Annual.
Country of Study: United States of America.
No. of awards offered: Two.
Application Procedure: Applicants must submit a pre-proposal containing their full name, title and address including telephone number and email address, a descriptive name or title of the project, a concise description of the research to be addressed, the importance of the problem, the product eg. book or monograph expected to result from the project, a list of the major tasks involved in conducting the project, a schedule for start and completion of the project, a brief statement of prior experience of the applicant and an estimated budget. The pre-proposal should be limited to two pages, single spaced with no smaller than 11 point font and one inch margins. Applicants whose pre-proposals are selected for further review will then be invited to submit final proposals. These are limited to ten pages and are to follow a similar format. They must include all of the information contained in the pre-proposal but should offer further detailed description of the proposed research, anticipated contribution of the project and the importance of the results. They should also include a curriculum vitae with the applicant's educational background, professional experience, a list of most relevant publications and honours and awards received. In addition, final proposals must include three letters of recommendation from fellow faculty members or colleagues and these are not included in the 10 page limit. Applications sent by fax or email will not be accepted.
Closing Date: January 6th for pre-proposals and February 28th for final proposals.
Funding: Private.

RESUSCITATION COUNCIL (UK)

5th Floor, Tavistock House, NorthTavistock Square, London, WC1H 9HR, England
Tel: (44) 20 7388 4678
Fax: (44) 20 7383 0773
Email: enquiries@resus.org.uk
www: http://www.resus.org.uk
Contact: Dr M C Colquhoun, Chairman of the Research Sub-Committee

The Resuscitation Council (UK) is the expert advisory body on the training and practise of resuscitation in the United Kingdom. It also actively pursues and promotes research in the field of resuscitation medicine.

Resuscitation Council Research Fellowships
Subjects: Any fields of resuscitation medicine.
Purpose: To support research Fellows during conduct of full-time research in approved projects.
Eligibility: Open to research Fellows carrying out work in a suitable venue in the United Kingdom. Applicants must be full or associate members of the Resuscitation Council (UK).
Level of Study: Doctorate, Postdoctorate, Postgraduate, Research.
Type: Fellowship.
Value: Basic salary level including National Insurance and Superannuation contributions. The salary would be at the appropriate point on the applicant's salary scale.
Length of Study: Up to two years.
Frequency: Dependent on funds available.
Country of Study: United Kingdom.
Application Procedure: Applicants must visit the website for application procedures.
Funding: Private.
Contributor: The Resuscitation Council (UK).
No. of awards given last year: None.
No. of applicants last year: Four.

Resuscitation Council Research Grants
Subjects: Any field of resuscitation medicine.
Purpose: To provide equipment and support for research projects in resuscitation medicine.
Level of Study: Unrestricted.
Value: Up to UK£10,000.
Frequency: Dependent on funds available.
Country of Study: United Kingdom.
Application Procedure: Applicants must visit the website for application details.
Closing Date: Please contact the organisation for details.
Funding: Private.
Contributor: The Resuscitation Council, United Kingdom.
No. of awards given last year: Nine.
No. of applicants last year: Nine.

REUTERS FOUNDATION

85 Fleet Street, London, EC4P 4AJ, England
Tel: (44) 20 7542 7015
Fax: (44) 20 7542 8599
Email: foundation@reuters.com
www: http://www.foundation.reuters.com
Contact: Mrs Julia Fuller

Reuters Foundation is an educational and humanitarian trust primarily funded by Reuters Group, the international news and information organisation. Its first purpose, when established in 1982, was to promote high standards in journalism through study and training programmes. It now also supports other educational and humanitarian projects.

Alva Clarke Memorial Fellowship
Subjects: All subjects.
Purpose: To provide the opportunity for journalists from the Caribbean to be members of the Reuters Foundation Programme at Green College, Oxford University.
Eligibility: Open to citizens of a Caribbean state who are full-time journalists or regular contributors to newspapers, magazines, radio or television in the Caribbean. Candidates are likely to be aged 28 to 45 with more than five years professional experience and a clear commitment to a career in journalism. Candidates must be fluent in English.
Level of Study: Professional development.
Type: Fellowship.
Value: Travel expenses (economy class), tuition fees and a monthly living allowance.
Length of Study: Three months.
Frequency: Annual.
Study Establishment: Green College, the University of Oxford.
No. of awards offered: One.
Application Procedure: Applicants must complete an application form and submit this with supporting material. Please write for details or view online at www.foundation.reuters.com/fellowships/oxford.asp.
Closing Date: December 31st.
No. of awards given last year: One.

Reuter Foundation Television Journalism Programme
Subjects: International television journalism.
Purpose: To bring together journalists from different countries for practical training in television news reporting.
Eligibility: Open to television journalists, under the age of 35, from developing countries or the former Soviet Bloc countries of East and Central Europe and Asia. Applicants must be fluent in English and have more than two years experience.
Level of Study: Professional development.
Value: The award covers travel expenses (economy class), tuition fees, accommodation and a modest living allowance for meals and local travel.
Length of Study: Two weeks.
Frequency: Annual.
Country of Study: Other.
No. of awards offered: Varies, up to eight.

Application Procedure: Applicants must complete an application form, available on request or on-line at www.foundation.reuters.com/journalism/television/index.htm.
Closing Date: No deadline.
No. of awards given last year: 12.

Reuters Foundation Environment in the News Research Study Programme
Subjects: Environment.
Purpose: To focus on the handling of environmental issues as news stories.
Eligibility: Open to full-time journalists or regular contributors to newspapers, news agencies, magazines, radio or television based in any country worldwide. Candidates must be proficient in written and spoken English. Successful candidates are likely to be aged 25 to 35.
Level of Study: Professional development.
Value: Travel expenses (economy class), tuition fees and a living allowance for meals and local travel.
Length of Study: Two weeks.
Frequency: Annual.
No. of awards offered: Up to 12.
Application Procedure: Applicants must complete an application form and submit this with supporting material. Please write for details or view on-line at www.foundation.reuters.com.

Reuters Foundation Fellowships
Subjects: Journalism.
Purpose: To bring together journalists from all over the world for the purpose of individual university study.
Eligibility: Open to full-time journalists employed by newspapers, news agencies, general circulation magazines, radio or television in the developing world or countries in transition. Applicants must have more than five years full-time experience and are aged approx. 28-45. They must be committed to a career in journalism in the country in which they work. English must be proficient.
Level of Study: Professional development.
Type: Fellowship.
Length of Study: Six months.
Frequency: Annual.
Study Establishment: Oxford, United Kingdom.
Country of Study: Other.
No. of awards offered: 12.
Application Procedure: Applicants must complete an application form, available on request or on-line at www.foundation.reuters.com/fellowships/oxford_applying.asp.
Closing Date: December 31st.
No. of awards given last year: 8.

Reuters Foundation Fellowships in Medical Journalism
Subjects: Medical sciences.
Purpose: To enable journalists who report on medical issues to re-search and study at the University of Oxford, England.
Eligibility: Open to specialist medical writers and broadcasters with more than five years reporting experience.
Level of Study: Professional development.
Type: Fellowship.
Value: Travel expenses, tuition fees and a cost of living stipend.
Length of Study: One term.
Frequency: Annual.
Study Establishment: Green College, Oxford University.
Country of Study: Other.
No. of awards offered: One.
Application Procedure: Applicants must complete an application form. Available on request or on-line at www.foundation.reuters.com/fellowships/oxford_applying.asp.
Closing Date: December 31st.

Reuters Foundation Journalism Training
Subjects: Journalism, writing international news and writing business news.
Purpose: To provide training for journalists. The awards are for practical work in a classroom situation, coupled with some lectures and outside visits.

Eligibility: Open to full-time journalists from developing countries or the former Soviet Bloc countries of Central and Eastern Europe and Central Asia, aged 23 to 45, with a sound working knowledge of the English language.
Level of Study: Professional development.
Length of Study: Two-four weeks.
Frequency: Annual.
Country of Study: Any country.
No. of awards offered: Varies.
Application Procedure: Applicants must complete an application form, available on request. Details of all planned course plus eligibility criteria are posted on www.foundation.reuters.com, where you will also find an on-line application form.
Closing Date: On going.
No. of awards given last year: Four courses, 12 people per course.

Reuters Foundation University Fellowship for US Journalists
Subjects: Journalism.
Purpose: To enable established journalists to spend three months studying at Oxford University.
Eligibility: Open to writers and broadcasters from the United States of America, including specialists in economic, environmental, medical and scientific subjects. Reuters staff and members of their families are not eligible for fully funded Reuter Foundation fellowships.
Level of Study: Professional development.
Type: Fellowship.
Value: Travel expenses (economy class), tuition fees and monthly living allowance.
Length of Study: Three months.
Frequency: Annual.
Study Establishment: The University of Oxford.
Country of Study: United Kingdom.
No. of awards offered: One.
Application Procedure: Applicants must complete an application form and submit this with a biography of approx. 250 words outlining the applicants career, a description of approx. 1,000 words of the intellectual and social values that shape the applicants work, a statement of up to 1,000 words explaining the applicants proposed theme of study at Oxford, and examples of work and references. Further details are available at www.foundation.reuters.com/fellow-ships/oxford.asp.
Closing Date: December 31st.
No. of awards given last year: One.

Reuters Foundation Workshops for Photojournalists
Subjects: Mass communication and information science.
Purpose: To support photojournalists throughout the world, who may not have easy access to advanced training opportunities.
Eligibility: Open to full-time journalists, photo journalists or regular contributors to newspapers, news agencies, magazines, radio or television. Candidates must be proficient in spoken and written English.
Level of Study: Professional development.
Value: Tuition fees and course materials.
Length of Study: A number of days.
Frequency: Annual.
Country of Study: Any country.
No. of awards offered: Up to twelve.
Application Procedure: Applicants must complete an application form and submit this with supporting documentation. Please write for details or view our website at www.foundation.reuters.com/journalism/index.htm for details of planned courses.

RHODES UNIVERSITY

PO Box 94, Grahamstown, 6140, South Africa
Tel: (27) 46-603, 8055
Fax: (27) 46-622, 8444
Email: research-admin@ru.ac.za
www: http://www.ru.ac.za/research
Contact: Miss Moira Pogrund, Dean of Research

Rhodes University is a small university campus in Grahamstown. The University offers excellent undergraduate and postgraduate education, provides opportunities for research and fosters personal development and leadership as well as team, social and communication skills among its diverse student body.

Allan Gray Senior Scholarship

Subjects: All subjects at the University.
Purpose: To encourage and enable previously disadvantaged South Africans to pursue their studies at Honours and Master's level.
Eligibility: Open to previously disadvantaged South African students with the appropriate qualifications.
Level of Study: Postgraduate.
Type: Scholarship.
Value: Rand 35,000.
Length of Study: One year, renewable upon reapplication.
Frequency: Annual.
Study Establishment: Rhodes University, Grahamstown.
Country of Study: South Africa.
No. of awards offered: Four.
Application Procedure: Applicants must submit a curriculum vitae and a full academic record. Shortlisted applicants will be required to complete an application form providing additional information and referee reports.
Closing Date: August 1st in the year preceding registration.
Funding: Private.
Contributor: Donor and investments.
No. of awards given last year: Four.
No. of applicants last year: 103.
Additional Information: Postgraduate Scholars must assist with teaching and/or research duties up to a maximum of six hours a week in their department of study, without additional remuneration. Awards are for full-time study in attendance at Rhodes University only.

Andrew Mellon Foundation Scholarship

Subjects: Humanities, commerce, education, law, pharmacy and science.
Purpose: To encourage and enable previously disadvantaged people to pursue their studies Honours, at Master's or doctoral level at Rhodes University, as well as to enhance the recipients' ability to contribute to higher education in South Africa.
Eligibility: Open to previously disadvantaged individuals with the appropriate qualifications.
Level of Study: Postgraduate.
Type: Scholarship.
Value: Rand 25,000 for Master's and Rand 40,000 for doctoral.
Length of Study: One year, renewable upon reapplication.
Frequency: Annual.
Study Establishment: Rhodes University, Grahamstown.
Country of Study: South Africa.
No. of awards offered: 30 at Honours level; 10 at Master's or doctoral level.
Application Procedure: Applicants must submit a curriculum vitae and a full academic record. Shortlisted applicants will be required to complete an application form providing additional information and referee reports.
Closing Date: August 1st in the year preceding registration.
Funding: Private.
Contributor: Donor and investments.
No. of awards given last year: 30 at Honours level; 10 at Masters or doctoral level.
No. of applicants last year: 250.
Additional Information: Scholars must assist with teaching and/or research duties up to a maximum of six hours a week in their department of study, without additional remuneration. Awards are for full-time study in attendance at Rhodes University only.

Guy Butler Research Award

Subjects: English language, English literature, South African English drama, South African journalism in English, and cultural studies focusing on English related topics in South Africa.
Purpose: To attract outstanding graduate students to the University, thereby extending the tradition of originality and innovation which has characterised the discipline of the University, for the benefit of South Africa.
Level of Study: Postgraduate.
Type: Scholarship.
Value: Rand 35,000 at Master's level and Rand 50,000 at doctoral level.
Length of Study: One year, renewable upon reapplication.
Frequency: Annual.
Study Establishment: Rhodes University, Grahamstown.
Country of Study: South Africa.
No. of awards offered: One.
Application Procedure: Applicants must submit a curriculum vitae and a full academic record. Shortlisted applicants will be required to complete an application form providing additional information and referee reports.
Closing Date: August 1st.
Funding: Private.
Contributor: Donor and investments.
No. of awards given last year: One.
No. of applicants last year: 40.
Additional Information: Applicants must register full-time attendance at Rhodes University. The Guy Butler Research Award must be acknowledged in the thesis and any publication derived from it.

Henderson Postgraduate Scholarships

Subjects: Mathematical, physical, earth, life and pharmaceutical sciences, accountancy or information systems.
Purpose: To encourage and enable students to pursue their studies at the Master's and doctoral levels, and to enhance recipients' research abilities and produce internationally competitive graduates with an innovative, analytical, articulate and well rounded desire to learn.
Eligibility: Open to South African citizens with appropriate qualifications.
Level of Study: Postgraduate.
Type: Scholarship.
Value: Rand 35,000 for Master's and Rand 50,000 for doctoral.
Length of Study: One year, renewable upon reapplication.
Frequency: Annual.
Study Establishment: Rhodes University, Grahamstown.
Country of Study: South Africa.
No. of awards offered: One.
Application Procedure: Applicants must submit a curriculum vitae and a full academic record. Shortlisted applicants will be required to complete an application form, providing additional information and referee reports.
Closing Date: August 1st in the year preceding registration.
Funding: Private.
Contributor: Donor and investments.
No. of awards given last year: One.
No. of applicants last year: 29.
Additional Information: Scholars must assist with teaching and/or research duties up to a maximum of six hours a week in their department of study, without additional remuneration. Awards are for full-time study in attendance at Rhodes University only.

Hobart Houghton Research Fellowship

Subjects: Economics.
Purpose: To promote work of scientific value relevant to the economic problems of the Eastern Cape Province, Republic of South Africa, which could contribute to the betterment of the people of the region.
Eligibility: Open to English speakers who hold at least a Master's degree in economics and who exhibit successful research experience.
Level of Study: Doctorate, Postdoctorate.
Type: Fellowship.
Value: Rand 25,000.
Length of Study: 2-12 months.
Frequency: Annual.
Study Establishment: Rhodes University, Grahamstown.
Country of Study: South Africa.
No. of awards offered: One.
Application Procedure: Applicants must complete an application form, available from Dean of Research. Enquiries may also be addressed to Professor H Nel, Department of Economics and Economic History, email h.nel@ru.ac.za or from the website.

Closing Date: September 30th.
Funding: Commercial.
No. of awards given last year: One.
No. of applicants last year: Four.

Hugh Kelly Fellowship
Subjects: Biochemistry and microbiology, botany, chemistry, computer science, statistics, mathematics, both pure and applied, pharmaceutical sciences, physics and electronics, zoology and entomology, ichthyology, fisheries science, geography or geology, human kinetics and ergonomics.
Purpose: To enable senior scientists to devote themselves to advanced work.
Eligibility: Open to suitable senior postdoctoral scientists. Preference is given to candidates willing to accept appointments for at least six months. Applicants must be English speakers.
Level of Study: Postdoctorate.
Type: Fellowship.
Value: Currently under review, but a package of approx. Rand 70,000. If the Fellow accepts an appointment for at least six months and is accompanied by a spouse, the spouse's air or rail fares will also be paid. University accommodation will be provided free of charge, but the provision of a telephone if available at the place of residence will be for the Fellow's personal account.
Length of Study: Up to one year.
Frequency: Every two years.
Study Establishment: Rhodes University, Grahamstown.
Country of Study: South Africa.
No. of awards offered: One.
Application Procedure: Applicants must complete an application form, available from the Dean of Research or from the website.
Closing Date: July 31st of the year preceding the award.
Funding: Private.
Contributor: Donor and investments.
No. of awards given last year: One.
No. of applicants last year: Six.
Additional Information: The Fellow will be required to present a concise report on the work completed at the conclusion of the term of the fellowship.

Hugh Le May Fellowship
Subjects: Philosophy, classics, ancient, modern or medieval history, classical, biblical, medieval or modern languages, political theory or law.
Purpose: To enable scholars to devote themselves to advanced work.
Eligibility: Open to any postdoctoral Scholars of standing, with research publications to their credit. Applicants must be English speakers.
Level of Study: Postdoctorate.
Type: Fellowship.
Value: Return economy air ticket, furnished accommodation and small monthly cash stipend.
Length of Study: Three-four months. This may be extended by mutual agreement, subject to availability of funds.
Frequency: Every two years.
Study Establishment: Rhodes University, Grahamstown.
Country of Study: South Africa.
No. of awards offered: One.
Application Procedure: Applicants must complete an application form, available from the Dean of Research or from the website.
Closing Date: July 31st of the year preceding the award.
Funding: Private.
Contributor: Donor and investments.
No. of awards given last year: One.
No. of applicants last year: Three.
Additional Information: Fellows are not expected to undertake teaching duties.

Patrick and Margaret Flanagan Scholarship
Subjects: All subjects.
Purpose: To enable South African women graduates to attend a university in the United Kingdom in order to obtain a higher postgraduate qualification.

Eligibility: Open to women graduates, preferably those who are English speaking applicants of South African descent. Selection is based initially on academic merit, as well as broader qualities of intellect and character.
Type: Scholarship.
Value: Rand 180,000 per year.
Length of Study: Two years.
Frequency: Annual.
Study Establishment: Rhodes University, Grahamstown.
Country of Study: United Kingdom.
No. of awards offered: One.
Application Procedure: Applicants must submit a curriculum vitae and full academic record. Candidates shortlisted will be sent an application form or additional information and referee reports.
Closing Date: August 1st of the year prior to registration abroad.
Funding: Private.
Contributor: Donor and investments.
No. of awards given last year: One.
No. of applicants last year: 113.

Rhodes University Postdoctoral Fellowship
Subjects: All subjects.
Purpose: To enable scholars to devote themselves to advanced work which will closely complement existing programmes in the host department.
Eligibility: Open to any postdoctoral Scholars of standing, with research publications to their credit and of exceptional merit. Applicants must be English speakers.
Level of Study: Postdoctorate.
Type: Fellowship.
Value: Rand 70,000 per year with an additional allocation of a maximum of Rand 5,000 to be used at the discretion of the head of department for running costs for the postdoctoral project or the transport of the candidate to Grahamstown.
Length of Study: One year, but may be extended by mutual agreement, subject to the availability of funds.
Frequency: Annual.
Study Establishment: Rhodes University, Grahamstown.
Country of Study: South Africa.
No. of awards offered: Two-three.
Application Procedure: Applicants must be nominated. Nominations should be made through heads of departments and directors of research institutes at Rhodes University. Nominations must include a full curriculum vitae, research proposal and the name of three referees who may be consulted. Further information may be obtained from the Dean of Research or from the website.
Closing Date: July 31st of the year preceding the award.
Funding: Private.
Contributor: Donor and investments.
No. of awards given last year: Six.
No. of applicants last year: 34.
Additional Information: Fellows are not expected to undertake teaching duties.

Rhodes University Postgraduate Scholarship
Subjects: Humanities, commerce, education, law, pharmacy or science.
Purpose: To encourage and enable students to pursue their studies at Master's and doctoral levels, enhancing recipients' research abilities and producing internationally competitive graduates with an innovative, analytical, articulate, adaptable and well rounded desire to learn.
Eligibility: Open to students with the appropriate qualifications. Academic merit will override criterion.
Level of Study: Postgraduate.
Type: Scholarship.
Value: Rand 35,000 for Master's and Rand 50,000 for doctoral.
Length of Study: One year, renewable upon reapplication.
Frequency: Annual.
Study Establishment: Rhodes University, Grahamstown.
Country of Study: South Africa.
No. of awards offered: Four.

Application Procedure: Applicants must submit a curriculum vitae and a full academic record. Shortlisted applicants will be required to complete an application form providing additional information and referee reports.
Closing Date: August 1st in the year preceding registration.
Funding: Private.
Contributor: Donor and investments.
No. of awards given last year: Four.
No. of applicants last year: 31.
Additional Information: Scholars must assist with teaching and/or research duties up to a maximum of six hours per week in their department of study, without additional remuneration. Awards are for full-time study in attendance at Rhodes University only.

RICHARD III SOCIETY, AMERICAN BRANCH

2041 Christian Street, Philadelphia, PA 19146, United States of America
Email: feedback@r3.org
www: http://www.r3.org
Contact: Ms Laura Blanchard, Schallek Fellowships

The Richard III Society was founded in 1924 in England as The Fellowship of the White Boar and was renamed the Richard III Society in 1959. The American Branch was founded in 1961. Today the Society has more than 4,000 members worldwide and American Branch membership is more than 800.

William B Schallek Memorial Graduate Fellowship Award
Subjects: Medieval history.
Purpose: To support graduate study of fifteenth-century English history and culture.
Eligibility: Applicants must be United States citizens or have made an application for first citizenship papers, or be permanent resident aliens, enrolled at a recognised educational institution.
Level of Study: Doctorate.
Type: Fellowship.
Value: US$500-2,000 depending on the need and/or quality of applicant.
Length of Study: One year, although renewals will be considered.
Frequency: Annual.
Study Establishment: Recognised and accredited degree granting institutions.
Country of Study: Any country.
No. of awards offered: Varies.
Application Procedure: Applicants must visit the website for guidelines, lists of past awards, their topics and application forms.
Closing Date: February 28th for the following academic year.
No. of awards given last year: Three.
No. of applicants last year: Seven.

RICS EDUCATION TRUST

12 Great George Street, London, SW1P 3AD, England
Tel: (44) 20 7334 3713
Fax: (44) 20 7334 3795
Email: jmacdonnell@rics.org.uk
www: http://www.rics-foundation.org
Contact: Ms Janny MacDonnell

The Royal Institution of Chartered Surveyors (RICS) is the professional institution for the surveying profession.

RICS Education Trust Award
Subjects: The theory and practice of surveying in any of its disciplines including general practice, quantity surveying, building surveying, rural practice, planning and development, land surveying or minerals surveying.
Eligibility: Open to chartered surveyors and others carrying out research studies in relevant subjects.
Level of Study: Unrestricted.
Type: Research grant.

Value: Usually up to UK£5,000.
Frequency: Twice a year.
Country of Study: Any country.
Application Procedure: Applicants must complete an application form.
Closing Date: September 30th or February 28th.
Funding: Commercial.
Contributor: RICS.
No. of awards given last year: 20.
No. of applicants last year: 40.

ROB AND BESSIE WELDER WILDLIFE FOUNDATION

PO Drawer 1400, Sinton, TX 78387, United States of America
Tel: (1) 361 364 2643
Fax: (1) 361 364 2650
Email: welderwf@aol.com
www: http://hometown.aol.com/welderwf/welderweb.html
Contact: Dr Lynn Drawe, Director

The Rob and Bessie Welder Wildlife Foundation is a private non-profit operating foundation whose mission is to conduct research and education in wildlife management and closely related fields. The Welder Foundation operates a wildlife refuge on a commercial ranch in the midst of an active oil field.

Welder Wildlife Foundation Fellowship
Subjects: Wildlife ecology and management.
Purpose: To provide support to individual graduate student research.
Eligibility: Open to United States of America citizens or aliens registered in a United States of America university for a graduate degree. Priority is given to students who wish to work at the Welder Foundation Refuge or in the Coastal Bend Region of Texas.
Level of Study: Doctorate, Graduate.
Type: Fellowship.
Value: Up to US$17,000 per year, according to individual needs.
Length of Study: The duration of a graduate degree programme.
Frequency: Annual.
Study Establishment: Any legitimate wildlife management or wildlife ecological department at any accredited university.
Country of Study: United States of America.
No. of awards offered: 15 at any given time, approx. five each year.
Application Procedure: Applicants must write for details.
Closing Date: October 1st for fellowships to begin in January.
Funding: Private.
Contributor: Private endowment.
No. of awards given last year: Five.
No. of applicants last year: 25.

ROBERT BOSCH FOUNDATION

c/o CDS International, Inc. 871 United Nations Plaza, 15th Floor, First Avenue 49th Street, New York, NY 10017-1814, United States of America
Tel: (1) 212 497 3518
Fax: (1) 212 497 3535
Email: info@cdsintl.org
www: http://www.cdsintl.org
Contact: Weingart Carolin, Program assistant

The Robert Bosch Foundation is one of the largest German industry foundations. Many of the foundation's international exchange programmes are aimed at providing young people with opportunities to improve their knowledge of other countries and cultures and to build up networks among future leaders in Europe and the United States.

Robert Bosch Foundation Fellowships
Subjects: Business administration, economics, public affairs, public policy, political science, law, journalism and mass communication.
Purpose: To promote the advancement of American and German-European relations, and to broaden the participants' professional competence and cultural horizons.

Eligibility: Open to citizens of the United States of America between the ages of 23-34 years old with a graduate or professional degree or equivalent work experience in the above subject areas. Candidates must provide evidence of outstanding professional or academic achievement and a strong knowledge of the German language. For those candidates who are outstanding in other areas but lack sufficient knowledge of German, the Foundation will provide language training prior to programme participation.
Level of Study: Postgraduate, Professional development.
Type: Fellowship.
Value: €1,800 per month stipend. Extra funding is available for family, language training and business travel.
Length of Study: Nine months from September-May.
Frequency: Annual.
Country of Study: Germany.
No. of awards offered: 20.
Application Procedure: Applicants must complete an application form and attend a personal interview. Please visit website for more details.
Closing Date: October 15th.
Funding: Private.
Additional Information: Programme participants receive internships in German institutions such as the Federal Parliament, private corporation headquarters, mass media and other elements within the framework of government or commerce. Internships will be at a high level, closely related to senior officials. The programme will follow the following schedule: an intensive course on German language, political, economic and cultural affairs, work experience, a visit to Berlin and the former East Germany, a visit to the European Economic Community and NATO headquarters in Brussels, a group visit to France for an overview of the political, economic and cultural perspective of another European country, and a final programme evaluation in Stuttgart. All activities are conducted in German.

THE ROBERT WOOD JOHNSON FOUNDATION

Route 1 & College Road East, PO Box 2316, Princeton, NJ 08543-2316, United States of America
Tel: (1) 800 734 7635
Email: hss@rwjf.org
www: http://www.rwjf.org

Established in 1972 in memory of Robert Wood Johnson, who founded Johnson & Johnson.

The Robert Wood Johnson Health & Society Scholars Program.

Subjects: A broad range of factors affecting the nation's health.
Purpose: To build the nation's capacity for research, leadership & action.
Level of Study: Postdoctorate.
Type: Scholarship.
Length of Study: Two years.
Frequency: Annual.
Study Establishment: One of six universities.
Country of Study: United States of America.
No. of awards offered: 18.
Application Procedure: Contact the Foundation or download an application form from the website.
Closing Date: October 15th.
Funding: Private.

ROBERTO LONGHI FOUNDATION

Via Benedetto Fortini 30, Florence, I-50125, Italy
Tel: (39) 055 658 0794
Fax: (39) 055 658 0794
Email: longhi@iris.firenze.it
www: http://www.iris.firenze.it/frl/borse_e.htm
Contact: Dr Silvia Meloni Trkulja, Direttoral Scientifito

The aim of the Robert Longhi Foundation is to advance art historical studies. Applications are accepted annually from prospective fellows who hold an advanced degree in art history. Fellows pursue individual and group research projects using the library and photo archive, participate in seminars and lectures by distinguished scholars at the Foundation and visit galleries, restorations and exhibitions.

Roberto Longhi Foundation Fellowships

Subjects: History of art.
Purpose: To aid those who want to seriously dedicate themselves to research in the history of art.
Eligibility: Open to citizens of Italy who possess a degree from an Italian university with a thesis in the history of art and to non Italian citizens who have fulfilled the preliminary requirements for a doctoral degree in the history of art at an accredited university or an institution of equal standing. Students who have reached their 30th birthday before the application deadline are not eligible.
Level of Study: Doctorate, Postgraduate.
Type: Fellowship.
Value: €600 per month.
Length of Study: Nine months.
Frequency: Annual.
Study Establishment: The Institute.
Country of Study: Italy.
No. of awards offered: Up to 10.
Application Procedure: Applicants must submit an application containing their biographical data including place and date of birth, domicile, citizenship, transcript of undergraduate and graduate records, a copy of the degree thesis if available and of other original works, a curriculum vitae including knowledge of foreign languages both spoken and written, letters of reference from at least two persons of academic standing who are acquainted with the applicants work, the subject of the research proposed and two passport photographs.
Closing Date: May.
Funding: Private.
Contributor: Private funds and capital endowment.
No. of awards given last year: 10.
No. of applicants last year: 19.
Additional Information: Successful candidates must give the assurance that they can dedicate their full-time to the research for which the fellowship is assigned. They may not enter into any connection with other institutions, they must live in Florence for the duration of the fellowship, excepting travels required for their research. They may not exceed the periods of vacations fixed by the Institute and are required to attend seminars, lectures and other activities arranged by the Institute. The Fellows must, in addition, submit a written report at the end of their stay in Florence relating the findings of their individual research undertaken at the Longhi Foundation. Once approved by the scientific committee the Fellows research must be published only in the Foundations annual journal Proporzioni. Non compliance with the above conditions will be considered sufficient grounds for the cancellation of a fellowship. Further information is available on request.

ROCHE RESEARCH FOUNDATION

Building 92/8.08 F Hoffmann-La Roche Limited, Basel, CH-4070, Switzerland
Tel: (41) 61 688 5227
Fax: (41) 61 688 1460
Email: research.foundation@roche.com
www: http://www.research-foundation.org
Contact: Ms Margrit Freiburghaus

The Roche Research Foundation is a charity sponsored by F Hoffmann-La Roche Limited, subsidising experimental scientific research in the life sciences.

Roche Research Foundation

Subjects: Biology, medicine or chemistry.
Purpose: To promote scientific research at Swiss universities and hospitals in the biomedical field, and to sponsor the experimental research of Swiss Fellows in biology, chemistry and medicine at universities and laboratories abroad.

Eligibility: Open to all qualified researchers for fellowships at Swiss universities or hospitals, and to qualified Swiss students for fellowships abroad.
Level of Study: Doctorate, Postdoctorate, Postgraduate.
Type: Fellowship.
Value: Living costs.
Frequency: Quarterly.
Country of Study: Any country.
Application Procedure: Applicants must complete an application form in English.
Closing Date: January 15th, April 15th, July 15th or October 15th.
Funding: Private.

ROCKEFELLER ARCHIVE CENTER

15 Dayton Avenue, Sleepy Hollow, NY 10591-1598, United States of America
Tel: (1) 914 631 4505
Fax: (1) 914 631 6017
Email: archive@mail.rockefeller.edu
www: http://www.rockefeller.edu/archive.ctr
Contact: Dr Darwin H Stapleton, Executive Director

The Rockefeller Archive Center holds the archives of the Rockefeller family and its philanthropies, and assists scholarly researchers who visit the Center to examine documents in the archives.

Rockefeller Archive Center Research Grant Program
Subjects: Developments and issues of the twentieth-century in the United States of America and throughout the world.
Purpose: To foster research in the records of the Rockefeller Foundation, Rockefeller University, the Rockefeller Brothers Fund and the Rockefeller family, as well as in the collections of vother institutions and individuals deposited at the Rockefeller Archive Center.
Eligibility: Open to applicants of any discipline, usually graduate students or postdoctoral Scholars, who are engaged in projects which require substantial use of the collections.
Level of Study: Unrestricted.
Type: Grant.
Value: Up to US$2,500 for applicants within the United States of America and Canada and US$3,000 for applicants from outside the United States of America, depending upon travel, lodging and research expenses of the applicant.
Length of Study: One to four weeks.
Frequency: Annual.
Study Establishment: The Rockefeller Archive Center.
Country of Study: United States of America.
No. of awards offered: Varies.
Application Procedure: Applicants must complete an application form.
Closing Date: November 30th for notification in March.
Funding: Private.
No. of awards given last year: 43.
No. of applicants last year: 65.

ROSL (ROYAL OVER-SEAS LEAGUE) ARTS

Over-Seas House, Park Place, St James's Street, London, SW1A 1LR, England
Tel: (44) 20 7408 0214 ext. 219
Fax: (44) 20 7499 6738
Email: culture@rosl.org.uk
www: http://www.rosl.org.uk
Contact: Ms Elaine Mitchener, Promotions Officer

The principal aim of the ROSL (Royal Over-Seas League) ARTS is to provide performance and exhibition opportunities for prize winning artists and musicians early in their careers, bringing their work to the attention of the professional arts community, the media and the general public.

ROSL Annual Music Competition
Subjects: Musical performance, in four solo classes such as strings (including the harp and guitar) woodwind / brass + percussion, keyboard, singers and an ensemble class, Biennial Award for Violists.
Purpose: To support and promote young Commonwealth musicians.
Eligibility: Open to citizens of the Commonwealth, including the United Kingdom, and former Commonwealth countries, who are no more than 28 years of age for instrumentalists or 30 years of age for singers.
Level of Study: Professional development.
Type: Competition.
Value: Over UK£30,000 in prizes, including a UK£5,000 first prize.
Frequency: Annual.
Country of Study: Any country.
No. of awards offered: Varies.
Application Procedure: Applicants must write or email for an application form.
Closing Date: January 14th.
Funding: Commercial, Private.
No. of awards given last year: 19.
No. of applicants last year: 500.

Royal Over-Seas League Travel Scholarship
Subjects: Painting and drawing, photography, print, mixed-media.
Purpose: To support and promote young UK and Commonwealth artists.
Eligibility: Open to citizens of Commonwealth, including the UK, and former Commonwealth countries, who are up to 35 years of age.
Level of Study: Unrestricted.
Value: Scholarship value UK£3,000 Art. Five Art Travel Scholarships 1 for UK artist, 4 Scholarship to commonwealth artists (Regions vary each year).
Frequency: Annual.
Country of Study: UK / Commonwealth.
No. of awards offered: Varies.
Application Procedure: Please write for application materials.
Closing Date: March.
Funding: Commercial, Private.
No. of awards given last year: 5.
No. of applicants last year: 450.
Additional Information: Each artist may be represented by one recent work only, in oil or comparable media, watercolour or mixed media, including drawings. Editioned, multiple and free standing works will not be accepted. Works must not exceed 152 cm in their largest dimension, inclusive of frame.

ROTARY FOUNDATION

One Rotary Center, 1560 Sherman Avenue, Evanston, IL 60201-3698, United States of America
Tel: (1) 847 866 3000
Fax: (1) 847 328 8554
Email: scholarshipinquiries@rotaryintl.org
www: http://www.rotary.org
Contact: Administrative Assistant

Through the Rotary Foundation, Rotarians worldwide strive to promote international understanding and relations between peoples of different nations.

Rotary Foundation Academic Year Ambassadorial Scholarships
Subjects: All subjects.
Purpose: To further international understanding and friendly relations among people of different countries.
Eligibility: Open to citizens of a country in which there are rotary clubs who have completed more than two years of college level coursework or equivalent professional experience before commencing their scholarship studies. Applicants must be proficient in the language of the proposed host country.
Level of Study: Unrestricted.
Type: Scholarship.

Value: Round trip transportation, tuition, room and board expenses, some educational supplies and one month of language training if necessary, totalling up to US$25,000 or its equivalent.
Length of Study: One academic year.
Frequency: Annual, if funds are available.
Study Establishment: A study institution assigned by the Trustees of the Rotary Foundation.
Country of Study: Other.
No. of awards offered: Varies.
Application Procedure: Applicants should contact a local Rotary club for details.
Closing Date: Varies according to the local Rotary club, but between March and July 15th. Applicants must apply over a year in advance.
Funding: Private.
Additional Information: Scholars will not be assigned to study in areas of a country where they have previously lived or studied for more than six months. During the study year, scholars are expected to be outstanding ambassadors of goodwill through appearances before Rotary clubs, schools, civic organisations and other forums. Upon completion of the scholarship, scholars are expected to share the experiences of understanding acquired during the study year with the people of their home countries. Candidates should contact local Rotary clubs for information on the availability of particular scholarships. Not all Rotary districts are able to offer scholarships. Further details are available from the website at www.rotary.org.

Rotary Foundation Cultural Ambassadorial Scholarships

Subjects: For cultural immersion and intensive language study.
Purpose: To further international understanding and friendly relations among people of different countries, and to make possible intensive language study and cultural immersion in another country.
Eligibility: Open to citizens of a country in which there are rotary clubs who have completed more than two years of college level coursework or equivalent professional experience before commencing their scholarship studies. Applicants must have completed more than one year of college level coursework or equivalent in the proposed language of study.
Level of Study: Unrestricted.
Type: Scholarship.
Value: Round trip transportation, language training expenses, and homestay living arrangements, totalling up to US$12,000 and US$19,000 respectively.
Length of Study: Three or six months.
Frequency: Annual, if funds are available.
Study Establishment: A language school assigned by the Trustees of the Rotary Foundation.
Country of Study: Any country in which there is a Rotary Club.
No. of awards offered: Varies.
Application Procedure: Applicants should contact their local Rotary club for details. Applications are considered for candidates interested in studying Arabic, English, French, German, Hebrew, Italian, Japanese, Korean, Mandarin Chinese, Polish, Portuguese, Russian, Spanish, Swahili and Swedish.
Closing Date: Varies according to the local Rotary club, but between March and July 15th. Applicants must apply over a year in advance.
Funding: Private.
Additional Information: During the study year, scholars are expected to be outstanding ambassadors of goodwill through appearances before Rotary clubs, schools, civic organisations and other forums. Candidates should contact local Rotary clubs for information on the availability of particular scholarships. Not all Rotary districts are able to offer scholarships. Further details are available from the website.

Rotary Foundation Multi-Year Ambassadorial Scholarships

Subjects: All subjects.
Purpose: To further international understanding and friendly relations among people of different countries and help defray the cost of pursuing a degree.
Eligibility: Open to citizens of a country in which there are rotary clubs who have completed more than two years of college level coursework or equivalent professional experience before commencing their scholarship studies. Applicants must be proficient in the language of the proposed host country.
Level of Study: Graduate, Postgraduate, Unrestricted, B.A.
Type: Scholarship.
Value: The award provides a flat grant of US$12,500, or its equivalent, per year to be applied towards the cost of a degree programme.
Length of Study: Two years.
Frequency: Annual, if funds are available.
Study Establishment: A foreign study institution approved by the trustees of the Rotary Foundation.
Country of Study: Any country in which there is a Rotary Club.
No. of awards offered: Varies.
Application Procedure: Applicants should contact a local Rotary club for details.
Closing Date: Varies according to the local Rotary club, but between March and July 15th. Applicants must apply over a year in advance.
Funding: Private.
Additional Information: Scholars will not be assigned to study in areas of a country where they have previously lived or studied for more than six months. During the study year, scholars are expected to be outstanding ambassadors of goodwill through appearances before Rotary clubs, schools, civic organisations and other forums. Upon completion of the scholarship, scholars are expected to share the experiences of understanding acquired during the study year with the people of their home countries. Candidates should contact local Rotary clubs for information on the availability of particular scholarships. Not all Rotary districts are able to offer scholarships. Further details are available from the website.

Rotary Grants for University Teachers

Subjects: Fields taught must have practical use to the host country.
Purpose: To build international understanding while strengthening higher education in low income countries.
Eligibility: Open to candidates who have held a college or university appointment for three or more years and are proficient in the language of their prospective host country. Rotarians and relatives of rotarians are eligible.
Level of Study: Professional development.
Type: Grant.
Value: Up to US$12,500 for three-five months or up to US$22,500 for six-ten months.
Length of Study: Three-five months or six-ten months.
Frequency: Annual, Dependent on funds available.
Study Establishment: A college/university located in a low-income country.
Country of Study: Low-income countries only.
No. of awards offered: Varies.
Application Procedure: Applicants should contact a local Rotary club for details.
Closing Date: Varies according to the local Rotary club, but between March and July 15th. Applicants must apply over a year in advance.
Funding: Private.
Additional Information: Grant recipients are expected to be outstanding ambassadors of goodwill to the people of their host and home countries through appearances to Rotary clubs. Not all Rotary districts are able to offer grants for university teachers. Further details are available from the website.

ROTARY YONEYAMA MEMORIAL FOUNDATION, INC.

8F abc Building, 2-6-3 Shiba Koen, Minato-ku, Tokyo, 105-0011, Japan
Tel: (81) 3 3434 8681
Fax: (81) 3 3578 8281
www: http://www.rotary-yoneyama.or.jp/english
Contact: Administrative Assistant

The Rotary Yoneyama Memorial Foundation, Inc. has been growing in service and organisation annually through the endorsement and co-operation of Japanese Rotaries. It awards scholarships to students not only from Asian countries but also from the rest of the world who are residents of Japan and studying or conducting research at Japanese Institutes of Higher Education.

Rotary Yoneyama Scholarship

Subjects: All subjects.
Eligibility: Open to non Japanese candidates with a 'college student' visa for the purpose of studies and research, and be under 40 years old.
Level of Study: Doctorate, Postgraduate.
Type: Scholarship.
Value: Yen 150,000 per month.
Length of Study: A maximum of two years.
Frequency: Annual.
Study Establishment: Colleges and universities.
Country of Study: Japan.
No. of awards offered: Varies.
Application Procedure: Applicants should contact the Foundation for details or visit the website.
Closing Date: Please contact the organisation.
Funding: Private.
Contributor: Rotarians in Japan.
Additional Information: It is recommended that applicants contact the Foundation directly, since requirements for certain applicants can be conditional. Selection is extremely competitive, as the number of awards is limited.

THE ROYAL ACADEMY OF ENGINEERING

29 Great Peter Street, London, SW1P 3LW, England
Tel: (44) 20 7222 2688
Fax: (44) 20 7233 0054
www: http://www.raeng.org.uk
Contact: Dr Elizabeth Horwitz, MacRobert Award Scheme

The Royal Academy of Engineering's objectives may be summarised as the pursuit, encouragement and maintenance of excellence in the whole field of engineering in order to promote the advancement of the science, art and the practice of engineering for the benefit of the public.

Exxon Mobil Teaching Fellowships

Subjects: Chemical, petroleum or mechanical engineering, Geology.
Purpose: To encourage able young engineering and earth science lecturers to remain in the education sector in their early years.
Eligibility: Open to well qualified graduates, preferably with industrial experience and must hold full-time lecturing posts at Institutes of Higher Education in the United Kingdom. They should have been in their current posts for at least one year. The post must include the teaching of chemical, petroleum, or mechanical engineering to undergraduates on courses which are accredited for registration as chartered engineers. These courses must include substantial elements of chemical, petroleum, or mechanical engineering, but need not be entirely devoted to these subjects. For applicants whose career path has been graduation at the age of 22, followed by academic or industrial posts, the age limit is generally 32 years (at the closing date). Older candidates who have taken time out, eg. for industrial experience, parenthood or voluntary service, will also be considered. Applicants should preferably be chartered engineers, or of equivalent professional status, or should be making progress towards this.
Level of Study: Postdoctorate.
Type: Fellowship.
Value: UK£9,000.
Length of Study: Four years.
Frequency: Annual.
Study Establishment: The applicant's current university in the United Kingdom.
Country of Study: United Kingdom.
No. of awards offered: Up to six.
Application Procedure: Applicants must complete an application form.
Closing Date: October 1st.

Funding: Commercial.
Contributor: Esso UK Plc.
Additional Information: A brochure is available on request. Enquiries about Esso University contacts should be made to the E-mail bowbricki@raeng.co.uk for more information.

Panasonic Trust Awards

Subjects: Engineering, particularly new engineering developments and new technologies.
Purpose: To encourage the technical updating and continuous professional development of qualified engineers through courses provided by United Kingdom Institutes of Higher Education at Master's level.
Eligibility: Open to United Kingdom citizens who are qualified to degree level in engineering or a related discipline. HND, HNC, OND, ONC or City and Guilds Full Technological Certificate qualifications are acceptable as a minimum. Applicants must be members, at any grade, of an engineering institution, working at the professional level in engineering in the United Kingdom and have several years of experience working at this level. Preference is given to those undertaking part-time modular Master's courses. The intended course of study must be relevant to the applicant's current or future career plans.
Level of Study: Professional development.
Type: Award.
Value: Usually to cover 50 per cent of course fees up to a maximum of UK£1,000.
Length of Study: The duration of the course.
Frequency: Dependent on funds available.
Country of Study: United Kingdom.
No. of awards offered: Varies.
Application Procedure: Applicants must write to the main address for application instructions, the application form and guidelines for employers and course co-ordinators.
Closing Date: Offered all year round.
Funding: Private.
Additional Information: Employers are expected to support an application in writing. The Trustees hope that the employer, once approached, might pay the full fees for the course. However, if this is not possible, a contribution from the employer is desirable. Applications must be supported by the course director or co-ordinator to confirm that the applicant is suitable for the course. Applications for grants of less than UK£1,000 should be submitted at least four weeks before the start of the course. Applications for larger grants should be submitted at least six weeks before the start of the course.

Royal Academy of Engineering Industrial Secondment Scheme

Subjects: All fields of engineering.
Purpose: To provide financial support for the secondment of academic engineering staff to industrial companies within the United Kingdom.
Eligibility: Open to permanent members of United Kingdom Institutes of Higher Education with an approved engineering qualification, teaching some aspects of engineering. Preference may be given to junior staff without previous industrial experience, or to more senior members whose industrial experience may have been some time ago.
Level of Study: Unrestricted.
Type: Grant.
Value: Varies.
Length of Study: Usually three-six months.
Frequency: Dependent on funds available.
Study Establishment: An industrial or commercial company.
Country of Study: United Kingdom.
No. of awards offered: Varies.
Application Procedure: Applicants must submit a completed application form with a curriculum vitae, personal statement outlining the nature and objectives of the proposed secondment, letter of support from the applicants head of department, statement from the applicants employer detailing the financial aspects of the application, statement from the host company confirming the agreed work programme and defining the benefits of the secondment to the company and detailing any contribution costs which the company may wish to make. Application forms are available from the main address.

Funding: Government.
No. of awards given last year: 18.
No. of applicants last year: 26.
Additional Information: The main objective is to obtain up to date industrial experience, to improve teaching capabilities and generally to foster academic industrial links. Contact Mr A Eades for further information.

Royal Academy of Engineering International Travel Grants

Subjects: Engineering, materials technology or computing.
Purpose: To facilitate study visits overseas, generally for attendance at conferences, research institutions and/or industrial sites.
Eligibility: Open to postgraduate students, postdoctoral researchers, lecturers involved in research and chartered engineers in United Kingdom Institutes of Higher Education and in United Kingdom industry. Grants are not given to Fellows of The Royal Academy of Engineering, civil servants, employees of the British Museum or other government bodies. To be eligible for funding applicants must be United Kingdom or European Union nationals or United Kingdom permanent residents. There are no age restrictions.
Level of Study: Doctorate, Postdoctorate, Postgraduate, Professional development.
Type: Travel grant.
Value: 30-50 per cent of approved costs.
Frequency: Dependent on funds available.
Country of Study: Other.
No. of awards offered: Varies.
Application Procedure: Applicants must submit a completed application form, nominating two referees of their choice, an abstract if an essay is being presented at a conference, publication list, photocopy of the personal details page form their passport, and a short paragraph of no more than 200 words, on a separate sheet of A4, justifying the relevance of the activity to their current work.
Closing Date: Applications are accepted at any time.
Funding: Government.
No. of awards given last year: Over 700.
No. of applicants last year: Over 1000.
Additional Information: Applicants are urged to submit their forms at least two months prior to the departure date to enable APEX fares to be used.

Royal Academy of Engineering MacRobert Award

Subjects: The successful development of innovation in engineering or the other physical sciences.
Purpose: To recognise and reward outstanding contributions relating to innovation in engineering.
Eligibility: Open to individuals, independent teams and teams working for a firm, organisation or laboratory. There should be no more than five members in a team.
Level of Study: Unrestricted.
Type: Award.
Value: UK£50,000 and a gold medal.
Frequency: Annual.
Country of Study: United Kingdom.
No. of awards offered: One.
Application Procedure: Applicants must submit a 200-500 word summary of the engineering achievement, supported by 15 copies of relevant technical documentation. Further details and rules and conditions are available from the Royal Academy of Engineering.
Closing Date: January 30th.
Funding: Private.
No. of awards given last year: One.

Sainsbury Management Fellowship Scheme

Subjects: Engineering.
Purpose: To enable young chartered engineers of the highest career potential to undertake MBA courses at European business schools.
Eligibility: Open to United Kingdom citizens, who hold a First or Upper Second Class (Honours) Degree in engineering or a closely allied subject, have chartered engineer status or are making substantial progress towards it, have the potential and ambition to achieve senior management responsibility at an early age, and be aged 26-34 years at the commencement of the proposed MBA course.
Level of Study: MBA, Postgraduate, Professional development.
Type: Fellowship.
Value: Course fees.
Length of Study: One year.
Frequency: Annual.
Study Establishment: Awards are normally tenable at the following business schools: North America - Harvard, MIT, Stanford, Wharton, Columbia, Kellogg, University of Chicago. In Europe: INSEAD France, IMD Switzerland, Erasmus The Netherlands, IESE Spain, SDA Bocconi Italy.
Country of Study: Any country.
No. of awards offered: 10.
Application Procedure: Applicants must complete an application form, please contact the office for details.
Closing Date: Applications are accepted at any time.
Funding: Private.
Contributor: The Gatsby Charitable Foundation.
No. of awards given last year: 10.
No. of applicants last year: 46.

ROYAL ACADEMY OF MUSIC

Marylebone Road, London, NW1 5HT, England
Tel: (44) 20 7873 7393
Fax: (44) 20 7873 7394
Email: go@ram.ac.uk
www: http://www.ram.ac.uk
Contact: Examinations Officer

The Royal Academy of Music is a music college offering courses in music at postgraduate level. The Academy is part of the University of London.

Royal Academy of Music General Bursary Awards

Subjects: All relevant branches of music education and training.
Purpose: To help defray tuition fees and general living expenses for study at the Royal Academy of Music.
Eligibility: Open to any student offered a place at the Academy.
Level of Study: Postgraduate.
Type: Bursary.
Value: According to need and availability of funds.
Length of Study: Normally for a complete academic year. Individual requirements may be imposed.
Frequency: Varies.
Study Establishment: The Royal Academy of Music.
Country of Study: United Kingdom.
No. of awards offered: Varies.
Application Procedure: Applicants must complete an application form which is sent automatically to all postgraduate students who are offered places.
Closing Date: January 31st for the following academic year.

ROYAL AERONAUTICAL SOCIETY

4 Hamilton Place, London, W1J 7BQ, England
Tel: (44) 20 7670 4300
Fax: (44) 20 7670 4309
Email: careers@raes.org.uk
www: http://www.aerosociety.com
Contact: Careers Centre Manager

The Royal Aeronautical Society was founded in 1866 and is the only professional institution which covers all aspects of the aerospace industry including research, manufacture, operations and maintenance. Society membership unlocks a host of benefits for both the individual and organisations. Membership is open to anyone with an association or interest in aerospace.

Handley Page Award

Subjects: Aeronautics. The award is for original work leading to advancement and progress in the art and science of aeronautics,

with special reference to the practical application of a device, or the long-term implications of a new concept, directed towards the safety of those who work with or travel in aircraft. The award can also be given to encourage interest in aerospace technology in university.
Purpose: To encourage the advancement of safety and reliability in air transport.
Eligibility: Open to citizens of the United Kingdom and the British Commonwealth who are suitably qualified to undertake the proposed work.
Level of Study: Professional development.
Type: Award.
Value: Approx. UK£5,000 to be awarded in whole or in part to an individual or group.
Frequency: Annual.
Country of Study: Other.
No. of awards offered: One.
Application Procedure: Applicants must complete an application form, available on request.
Closing Date: May 31st.
Funding: Private.
Contributor: The Society Trust Fund.

ROYAL AGRICULTURAL COLLEGE, SCHOOL OF BUSINESS

Cirencester, Gloucestershire, GL7 6JS, England
Tel: (44) 1285 652531
Fax: (44) 1285 650219
Email: admissions@royagcol.ac.uk
www: http://www.royagcol.ac.uk
Contact: Dean of Business

The Royal Agricultural College, School of Business, is a privately owned Higher Education Institution, established in 1845, and now publicly funded. It has strong food chain links and an excellent national and international network of companies and university partners.

Alltech Biotechnology, Inc. MSc/MBA Studentships
Subjects: Agricultural biotechnology, animal science and agrifood, agribusiness management, equine business management or wine business management.
Eligibility: Applicants should have obtained or expect to obtain, a First or Upper Second Class (Honours) Degree or equivalent in an appropriate biological science, agri-food business or business degree. Furthermore, they should be highly motivated, possess good interpersonal skills and be willing to travel. Candidates must be competent in the English language. A good command of a continental European language would also be an advantage.
Level of Study: MBA, Postgraduate.
Type: Studentship.
Value: Tuition, accommodation and subsistence.
Length of Study: Nine months.
Frequency: Annual.
Study Establishment: The Royal Agricultural College.
Country of Study: UK, USA, Netherlands, Uruguay.
Application Procedure: Applicants can apply on the website or alternatively, contact the college.

ROYAL ANTHROPOLOGICAL INSTITUTE

50 Fitzroy Street, London
WTP 5BT, England
Tel: (44) 20 7387 0455
Fax: (44) 20 7383 4235
Email: admin@therai.org.uk
www: http://www.therai.org.uk
Contact: Director of Grants

The Royal Anthropological Institute is a non-profit making registered charity. It is entirely independent, with a Director and a small staff accountable to the Council, elected annually from the Fellowship.

Council and Committee members and the editorial team of the Institute's principal journal, the Journal of the Royal Anthropological Institute (incorporating MAN), give their services without remuneration.

Emslie Horniman Anthropological Scholarship Fund
Subjects: Anthropology.
Purpose: To provide predoctoral grants for fieldwork in anthropology with a preference for research outside the United Kingdom.
Eligibility: Open to citizens of the United Kingdom, Commonwealth or Irish Republic who are university graduates or who can satisfy the trustees of their suitability for the study proposed. Preference is given to applicants whose proposals include field work outside the United Kingdom. Graduates who already hold a doctorate in anthropology are not eligible. Open to individuals only, as no grants are given to expeditions or teams.
Level of Study: Postgraduate, Predoctorate.
Type: Scholarship.
Value: UK£1,000-9,500.
Frequency: Annual.
Country of Study: Any country.
No. of awards offered: Approx. 10.
Application Procedure: Applicants must request an application form.
Closing Date: March 31st.
Funding: Private.
No. of awards given last year: 4 (Total 12,152).
Additional Information: No grants are available for library research, university fees or subsistence in the United Kingdom.

ROYAL COLLEGE OF MIDWIVES

15 Mansfield Street, London
W1G 9NH, England
Tel: (44) 20 7312 3535
Fax: (44) 20 7312 3536
Email: info@rcm.org.uk
www: http://www.rcm.org.uk
Contact: S.E. Mac Donald, Education and Research Manager

THe Royal College of Midwives is the major professional organisation for midwives in the UK, and aims to contribute to the art and science of midwifery knowledge and practice. The RCM awards and scholarships provide opportunities for the development of good practice ultimately improving the care provided to women, their babies and families.

Hospital Savings Association (HSA) Charitable Trust Scholarships
Subjects: As above.
Purpose: To provide financial support for midwives undertraining further Academic studies relevant to the improvement of practice and care.
Eligibility: Midwives who are RCM members. Employment in clinical practice in thens, or returning to NHS; or in non-profit making charity employment; Can demonstrate the contribution to health care delivery during the next 5 years; Undertaking studies of direct relevance to patient care; Studying in the UK; Have not already receives HSA funding.
Level of Study: Doctorate, Graduate, Postgraduate, Professional development.
Type: Scholarships.
Value: <UK£5000 for midwives studying for a soctorate or masters degree. <UK£3000 for midwives to study to Bsc, Diploma or certificate study. <UK£1000 for any study (except doctorate/masters)
Frequency: Annual.
Country of Study: United Kingdom.
No. of awards offered: Several.
Application Procedure: Application forms avaliable from Marlyn Gennace: Email. Marlyn.Gennace@rcm.org.ukClosing date: End of October.
Funding: Commercial.
Contributor: HSA Charitable Trust

Mary Seacole Nursing Leadership Award
Subjects: 4 different awards to midwives, nurses + health visitors to support leadership development of BME practitioners.
Purpose: To provide an opportunity for development of professional practice, service development and leadership potential of black and minority ethic midwives, nurses + health Visitors.
Eligibility: Nurse, midwife or health visitor. Application should reflect the example set by Mary Seacole.
Level of Study: Doctorate, Graduate, Professional development, Research.
Type: Leadership Awards.
Value: UK£6250
Length of Study: 1 year.
Frequency: Annual.
Country of Study: United Kingdom.
No. of awards offered: 4.
Application Procedure: Apply sending an SAE to:Mary Seacole Award,c/o Awards Officer,Royal College of Nursing,20 Cavendish Square. London wig orn.
Closing Date: End of May
Funding: Government.
Contributor: Department of Health.
No. of awards given last year: 1. (Previously 1 single award- now 4 sections according to professional area of practice.)

For further information contact:

Royal College of Nursing, 20 Cavendish Square, London, W1G 0RN, United Kingdom
Contact: Mary Seacole Award Awards Officer

RCM Midwifery Awards
Subjects: Individuals or groups can apply for one of the eleven Awards. This allows the award winner to develop a project in one of the categories.
Purpose: Is to recognise and celebrate innovation in Midwifery practice, education and research.
Eligibility: - May be individual or small group applications.- Should meet criteria of one of the eleven categories.
Value: Varies. (Up to UK£20,000 in total.)
Length of Study: N/A.
Frequency: Annual.
Country of Study: Projects Based in UK - though some (ie) student travel may involve external activity.
No. of awards offered: 11 - A range of awards which may include:- Promotion of Normality, Evidence into Practice, Reducing Social Exclusion, Working in Partnership, Excellence in Midwifery Management or Leadership, Student Travel Award, Excellence in Midwifery Education, Innovations in England, Wales, Scotland,Northern Ireland.
Application Procedure: Apply in writing or e-mail (see below). Application of 500 words.Short-listing process.- Short listed candidates attend for interview.
Closing Date: 16.7.2004
Funding: Commercial.
Contributor: Several.
No. of awards given last year: 10 awards in 5 categories.
No. of applicants last year: 110.

For further information contact:

Gothic House, 3 The Green, Richmond, Surrey, TW9 1PL,
Email: mail@chamberdunn.co.uk
Contact: Chamberlain Dunn Associates,

Ruth Davies Research Bursary
Subjects: 2 annual business of UK£5,000 which is used to building + strengthening the research amongst midwives; and to enable midwives to further develop their research knowledge and skills.
Purpose: To promote and develop midwifery research and evidence based practice.
Eligibility: Practising midwives; Members of the RCM; Practitioners with basic knowledge + skills in research; Midwives with access to research support; Midwives who have been practising for a minimum of 2 years.

Level of Study: Doctorate, Graduate, Postdoctorate, Postgraduate, Professional development, Research.
Type: Bursary.
Value: UK£10,000 in 2 UK£5,000 bursaries.
Length of Study: 1 year.
Frequency: Annual.
Country of Study: United Kingdom.
No. of awards offered: 2 awards.
Application Procedure: Succint CV to cover previous 5 years; Research proposal of no more than 2500 words; Letters of support (from manage + academic)
Closing Date: 16-7-2004
Funding: Commercial.
Contributor: RNPFN/Liverpool Victoria.
No. of awards given last year: 2.
No. of applicants last year: 10.

For further information contact:

RCM, 15 Mansfield St., London, W1G 9NH, United Kingdom
Contact: Mrs M. Gennace Ruth Davis Research Bursary Administrator

ROYAL COLLEGE OF MUSIC

Prince Consort Road, London, SW7 2BS, England
Tel: (44) 20 7591 4377
Fax: (44) 20 7591 4856
Email: cpartridge@rcm.ac.uk
www: http://www.rcm.ac.uk
Contact: Ms Celia Partridge, International & Awards Officer

The Royal College of Music, London, provides specialised musical education and professional training at the highest international level for performers and composers. This enables talented students to develop the musical skills, knowledge, understanding and resourcefulness which will equip them to contribute significantly to musical life in the United Kingdom and internationally.

Royal College of Music Scholarships
Subjects: Music performance, composition or conducting.
Purpose: To recognise merit in music performance, composition or conducting.
Eligibility: Unrestricted, but only for study at the College.
Level of Study: Unrestricted.
Type: Scholarship.
Value: Up to UK£13,200 (up to full fees).
Length of Study: One-four years.
Frequency: Annual.
Study Establishment: Music conservatoire.
Country of Study: United Kingdom.
No. of awards offered: Approx. 140.
Application Procedure: Applicants must apply only by application for a place of study.
Closing Date: October 5th.
Funding: Private.
No. of awards given last year: 90.
No. of applicants last year: 1,500.

ROYAL COLLEGE OF NURSING (RCN)

20 Cavendish Square, London, W1G 0RN, England
Tel: (44) 20 7409 3331
Fax: (44) 20 7647 3433
Email: moira.lambert@rcn.org.uk
www: http://www.rcn.org.uk
Contact: Ms Moira Lambert, Awards Officer

The Royal College of Nursing of the United Kingdom (RCN) represents nurses and nursing, promotes excellence in practice and shapes health policies.

Barbers Company Clinical Nursing Scholarship
Subjects: All subjects relating to nursing.
Purpose: To enable nurses making a career in clinical nursing to undertake further education, research or a clinical project.

Level of Study: Doctorate, Postgraduate, Predoctorate.
Type: Scholarship.
Value: UK£5,000.
Frequency: Annual.
Study Establishment: Universities.
Country of Study: United Kingdom.
No. of awards offered: Varies.
Application Procedure: Applicants must send in their curriculum vitae plus 500 words on the course/research or project.
Closing Date: February 28th.
Funding: Commercial.
Contributor: Barber Surgeons.
No. of awards given last year: Six.
No. of applicants last year: 40.

For further information contact:

Royal College of Nursing Institute, Radcliffe Infirmary, Woodstock Road, Oxford, Oxon OX2 6HE, England

Hettie C Hopkins Care of the Elderly Nursing Scholarship

Subjects: Care of the elderly.
Purpose: To promote the science and art of nursing in North Wales.
Eligibility: Open to nurses practising in Wales who hold a statutory qualification.
Level of Study: Unrestricted.
Type: Scholarship.
Value: Varies.
Length of Study: Varies.
Frequency: Annual.
Study Establishment: Various.
Country of Study: Wales.
No. of awards offered: Varies.
Application Procedure: Applicants must complete and submit an application form.
Closing Date: March 31st.
Funding: Private.
Contributor: Hettie C. Hopkins, OBE.
No. of awards given last year: One.
No. of applicants last year: One.

For further information contact:

Royal College of Nursing, Ty Maeth, King George V Drive East, Cardiff, CF14 4XZ, Wales

HSA Charitable Trust Awards For Health Care Assistants

Subjects: Nursing and midwifery.
Purpose: To fund health care assistants working towards S/NVQ level 2, 3, or 4.
Eligibility: Open to Health Care Assistants working towards S/NVQ level 2, 3 or 4.
Level of Study: Professional development.
Type: Scholarship.
Value: Up to UK£250 each.
Length of Study: Unrestricted.
Frequency: Annual.
Study Establishment: Unrestricted.
Country of Study: United Kingdom.
No. of awards offered: Approx. 20.
Application Procedure: Applicants must send a stamped addressed envelope to the Awards Officer to receive an application form. Enquiries will be dealt with all year round.
Closing Date: Considered any time.
Funding: Commercial.
Contributor: HSA Charitable Trust.
No. of awards given last year: New Award.

For further information contact:

HSA Charitable Trust Awards For Health Care Assistants c/o Awards Officer, Royal College of Nursing, 20 Cavendish Square, London, W1G 0RN, England

HSA Charitable Trust Scholarships for Nurses and Midwives

Subjects: Nursing, midwifery and health visiting.
Purpose: To fund nurses and midwives in clinical practice towards course fees on post-registration study and enrolled nurses taking conversion courses.
Eligibility: Open to nurses, midwives and health visitors in the United Kingdom working in the NHS or caring for NHS patients and enrolled nurses in the NHS or Non-profit organisations.
Level of Study: Doctorate, Graduate, Postgraduate, Predoctorate, Professional development.
Type: Other.
Value: UK£1,000-5,000 each.
Length of Study: Unrestricted.
Frequency: Annual.
Study Establishment: A university.
Country of Study: United Kingdom.
No. of awards offered: Up to 60.
Application Procedure: Applicants must request an application form by sending a stamped addressed envelope. Applications and enquiries will be dealt with between August and October each year.
Closing Date: November 1st.
Funding: Commercial.
Contributor: H S A charitable trust.
No. of awards given last year: 61.
No. of applicants last year: 131.

For further information contact:

HSA Charitable Trust Scholarships, c/o Awards Officer, 20 Cavendish Square, London, W1G 0RN, England

Johnson & Johnson/Ethicon Nurses Education Trust Fund

Subjects: Nursing, midwifery and health visiting.
Purpose: To further members' education and to enhance the standard of expertise in their chosen field of nursing.
Eligibility: Open to members of the RCN, NATN or ICNA only.
Level of Study: Professional development.
Type: Grant.
Value: Up to UK£1,000 Each.
Length of Study: Unrestricted.
Frequency: Annual.
Study Establishment: Unrestricted.
Country of Study: Any country.
No. of awards offered: Varies.
Application Procedure: Applicants must contact Fitwise for an application form.
Closing Date: April.
Funding: Commercial.
Contributor: Johnson & Johnson/Ethicon.
No. of awards given last year: 15.
No. of applicants last year: 125.

For further information contact:

Fitwise Drumcross Hall, Bathgate, EH48 4JT, England

Nuffield Trust/RCN Travelling Fellowships

Subjects: Nursing, midwifery and health visiting including public health, health policy and health education.
Purpose: To undertake a study overseas to pursue an area of innovation in health services.
Eligibility: Open to members of the RCN only.
Level of Study: Professional development.
Type: Fellowship.
Value: Up to UK£5,000 each.
Length of Study: Unrestricted.
Frequency: Annual.
Study Establishment: Unrestricted.
Country of Study: Any country.
No. of awards offered: Varies.

Application Procedure: Applicants must send a stamped addressed envelope for application requirements. Enquiries are dealt with between November and January.
Closing Date: February.
Funding: Private.
Contributor: Nuffield Trust.
No. of awards given last year: 5.
No. of applicants last year: 38.

For further information contact:

RCN/Nuffield Trust Travelling Fellowship, Royal College of Nursing, 20 Cavendish Square, London, W1G 0RN, England
Contact: Awards Officer

RCN Educational Scholarships. Hettie C. Hopkins Care of the Elderly Nursing Scholarship

Subjects: See Purpose.
Purpose: To promote the Advancement of the Art and Science of Nursing, particularly in care of the elderly.
Eligibility: RCN member holding a statutory qualification in nursing and practising in Wales and who wish to pursue a project associated with care of the Elderly.
Level of Study: Unrestricted.
Type: Scholarship.
Value: Up to UK£1,000.
Length of Study: Variable.
Frequency: Annual.
Study Establishment: Variable.
Country of Study: Wales.
No. of awards offered: Varies.
Application Procedure: Application to trustees of each fund.
Closing Date: March 31st Annually.
Funding: Private.
Contributor: Hettie C. Hopkins (Covenant).
No. of awards given last year: 1.
No. of applicants last year: 1.

RCN Educational Scholarships. The Allen Iswlyn Giles Memorial Nursing Scholarship

Subjects: See Purpose.
Purpose: To promote the advancement of the art and Science of Nursing.
Eligibility: RCN member holding a statutory qualification in Nursing and Practising in Wales.
Level of Study: Unrestricted.
Type: Scholarship.
Value: Up to UK£1,000.
Length of Study: Variable.
Frequency: Annual.
Study Establishment: Variable.
Country of Study: Wales.
No. of awards offered: Varies.
Application Procedure: Application to trustees of each fund.
Closing Date: 31st May Annually.
Funding: Private.
Contributor: Allen Iswlyn Giles (Covenant).
No. of awards given last year: 0.
No. of applicants last year: 12.

RCN Grants

Subjects: Nursing, midwifery and health visiting.
Purpose: To assist RCN members to enhance their professional skills, knowledge and competence. Pre-registration nursing students in RCN membership are also eligible.
Eligibility: Open to RCN members with two years of RCN membership for post registration nurses or one year's membership for pre-registration nursing students.
Level of Study: Professional development.
Type: A variable number of grants.
Value: Up to UK£250 each.
Length of Study: Unrestricted.
Frequency: Annual.

Study Establishment: Unrestricted.
Country of Study: Any country.
No. of awards offered: Varies.
Application Procedure: Applicants must request information by sending a stamped addressed envelope. Enquiries are dealt with between May and July.
Closing Date: August 1st.
Funding: Private.
Contributor: RCN Charitable Trust Funds.
No. of awards given last year: 34.
No. of applicants last year: 80.

For further information contact:

RCN Grants (001-532), 20 Cavendish Square, London, W1G 0RN, England
Contact: Awards Officer

RCN Margaret Parkinson Scholarships

Subjects: Nursing and midwifery.
Purpose: To encourage graduates with a non nursing degree to qualify as a nurse, and for post registration nurses to undertake study.
Eligibility: Open to graduates who have not yet started nurse training or post registration nurses and midwives in membership of Royal College of Nursing.
Level of Study: Graduate, Professional development.
Type: Scholarship.
Value: Varies.
Length of Study: Varies.
Frequency: Annual.
Study Establishment: Usually universities.
Country of Study: United Kingdom.
No. of awards offered: Varies.
Application Procedure: Applicants must send a stamped addressed envelope to the Awards Officer stating if they are a graduate or postregistration nurse. Enquiries will be dealt with between November and January.
Closing Date: February.
Funding: Private.
Contributor: Margaret Parkinson Scholarship Fund.
No. of awards given last year: One.
No. of applicants last year: One.

RCN Scholarships Fund

Subjects: Nursing, midwifery and health visiting including public health, health policy and health education.
Purpose: To provide funding for a project, study visit or course to facilitate professional development with an emphasis on education, leadership or management.
Eligibility: Open to applicants with three years RCN membership for Major scholarship and one year membership for Senior Nurse scholarship.
Level of Study: Doctorate, Graduate, MBA, Postgraduate, Predoctorate, Professional development, Research.
Type: Scholarship.
Value: Up to UK£4,000 for a Major scholarship and up to UK£1,500 for a Senior Nurse scholarship.
Length of Study: Unrestricted.
Frequency: Annual.
Study Establishment: Unrestricted.
Country of Study: Any country.
No. of awards offered: Approx. Six.
Application Procedure: Applicants must request information by sending a stamped addressed envelope. Enquiries are dealt with between February and April.
Closing Date: May 1st.
Funding: Private.
Contributor: RCN Charitable Trust Funds.
No. of awards given last year: 10.
No. of applicants last year: 26.

For further information contact:

RCN Scholarships c/o Awards Officer, Royal College of Nursing, 20 Cavendish Square, London, W1G 0RN, England

ROYAL COLLEGE OF OBSTETRICIANS AND GYNAECOLOGISTS (RCOG)

27 Sussex Place, Regent's Park, London, NW1 4RG, England
Tel: (44) 20 7772 6263
Fax: (44) 20 7772 6359
Email: rdeshmukh@rcog.org.uk
www: http://www.rcog.org.uk
Contact: The Awards Administrator

The Royal College of Obstetricians and Gynaecologists (RCOG) is dedicated to the encouragement of the study and the advancement of the science and practice of obstetrics and gynaecology.

Endometriosis Millennium Fund Award

Subjects: Endometriosis.
Purpose: To stimulate and encourage research, clinical or laboratory based, or to encourage clinicians to acquire extra clinical skills to manage patients.
Eligibility: Open to members of the College or members of the RCOG Trainees Register, who are resident and working within the British Isles.
Level of Study: Postgraduate.
Type: Research grant.
Value: Up to UK£5,000.
Frequency: Annual.
Country of Study: United Kingdom.
No. of awards offered: More than one.
Application Procedure: Applicants must submit an application on the requisite form, which can be downloaded from the website or can be obtained from the Awards Secretary at the RCOG. Applications must be accompanied by two references from supervisors or senior colleagues and written confirmation of availability of laboratory space or access for surgical training in the host institution must be provided with the application. An undertaking will be given that a structured typewritten report will be provided at the end of the grant period and that the source of grant will be acknowledged in any related publications.
Closing Date: 16th Feb 2004.
Contributor: The Endometriosis Millennium Fund.
Additional Information: The award may only be used for the purpose approved by the Assessment Committee.

RCOG Bernhard Baron Travelling Scholarships

Subjects: Obstetrics or gynaecology.
Purpose: To expand the recipient's knowledge in areas in which he or she already has some experience.
Eligibility: Open to Fellows and members of the College.
Level of Study: Postgraduate.
Type: Scholarship.
Value: Up to UK£6,000.
Frequency: Annual.
Country of Study: Any country.
No. of awards offered: One.
Application Procedure: Applicants must contact the Awards Secretary for details.
Closing Date: 20th August, 2004.
No. of awards given last year: One.
No. of applicants last year: 16.

RCOG Eden Travelling Fellowship

Subjects: Obstetrics or gynaecology.
Purpose: To enable the recipient to gain additional knowledge and experience in the pursuit of a specific research project in which he or she is currently engaged.
Eligibility: Open to medical graduates of not less than two years of standing from any approved university in the United Kingdom or Commonwealth.
Level of Study: Postgraduate.
Type: Fellowship.
Value: Up to UK£5,000, according to the project undertaken.
Length of Study: For a specified period of time.
Frequency: Annual.

Study Establishment: At another department of obstetrics and gynaecology or of closely related disciplines.
Country of Study: Any country.
No. of awards offered: One.
Application Procedure: Applicants must include information on qualifications, areas of interest and/or publications in a specified area, centres to be visited with confirmation of arrangements from the head of that centre, estimated costs and the names of two referees.
Closing Date: 20th August, 2004.
Additional Information: Further information is available on request.

RCOG Edgar Gentilli Prize

Subjects: Obstetrics or gynaecology.
Purpose: To recognise original work done on the cause, nature, recognition and treatment of any form of cancer of the female genital tract.
Eligibility: Eligibility is unrestricted.
Type: Prize.
Value: UK£750 plus book tokens to the value of UK£250.
Frequency: Annual.
No. of awards offered: One.
Application Procedure: Applicants must submit results of their research in the form of an original manuscript, adequately referenced and written in a format comparable to those used for submission to a learned journal, or by means of reprint of a published article.
Closing Date: 16th Feb 2004.
Additional Information: Further information is available on request.

RCOG Ethicon Travel Awards

Subjects: Obstetrics or gynaecology.
Purpose: To promote international goodwill in the speciality.
Eligibility: Open to RCOG members who have passed both Part I and II of the membership exams. Members from the British Isles must be trainees and overseas members must not be in independent practice.
Level of Study: Postgraduate.
Type: Travel grant.
Value: Up to UK£1000.
Frequency: Twice a year.
No. of awards offered: Up to 15.
Application Procedure: Applicants must complete an application form, available from the Awards Secretary or from the website.
Closing Date: Please see the website. 31st Jan 2004 and 31st July 2004.
Additional Information: Travel must take place within 12 months of the award being made.

RCOG Green-Armytage and Spackman Travelling Scholarship

Subjects: Obstetrics or gynaecology.
Purpose: To allow applicants to visit centres where similar work is being carried out to their own.
Eligibility: Open to Fellows and members of the College. Applicants should have shown a special interest in some particular aspect of obstetrical or gynaecological practice.
Level of Study: Postgraduate.
Type: Scholarship.
Value: Please contact the organisation.
Frequency: Every two years.
Country of Study: Any country.
No. of awards offered: One.
Application Procedure: Applicants must include information on qualifications, areas of interest and/or publications in a specified area, centres to be visited with confirmation from the head of that centre, estimated costs, and the names of two referees.
Closing Date: 20th August, 2004.
Additional Information: Further information is available on request.

RCOG Harold Malkin Prize

Subjects: Obstetrics or gynaecology.
Purpose: To award those undertaking best original work whilst holding a Specialist Registrar post in a hospital.
Eligibility: Open to RCOG members or membership candidates.
Level of Study: Professional development.

Type: Prize.
Value: The first prize is UK£250 and second prize is UK£150.
Frequency: Annual.
No. of awards offered: Two.
Application Procedure: Applicants must contact the Awards Secretary for details.
Closing Date: 16th Feb 2004.
Additional Information: Further information is available on request.

RCOG Overseas Fund
Subjects: Obstetrics or gynaecology.
Purpose: To allow individuals to travel to the United Kingdom for further training.
Eligibility: Open to RCOG members or the equivalent, working overseas.
Level of Study: Professional development.
Type: Travel grant.
Value: Up to UK£2,000.
Frequency: Annual.
No. of awards offered: Up to 8.
Application Procedure: Applicants must see the website.
Closing Date: 20th August, 2004.

RCOG Research Prize
Subjects: Obstetrics and gynaecology.
Purpose: To recognise the best research projects in any aspect of obstetrics and gynaecology.
Level of Study: Graduate.
Value: UK£500 and UK£200.
Frequency: Annual.
Country of Study: UK, Northern Ireland and Republic of Ireland.
Application Procedure: Applicants should submit no more than 1500 words outlining the research with reference to publications (if any) is required. The research must have been carried out during the undergraduate course and in a relevant department.
Closing Date: 16th February.
Funding: Private.
Additional Information: Submissions may by sent by e-mail or post (4 copies of the typewritten submission on A4 paper). Please state clearly which award you are applying for and include your Supervisor's name and address.

RCOG USA/British Isles Visiting Fellowship
Subjects: Obstetrics or gynaecology.
Purpose: To enable the recipient to visit, make contact with and gain knowledge from a specific centre offering new techniques or methods of clinical management within the speciality.
Eligibility: Open to specialist Registrars in the British Isles, junior Fellows or those in residency programmes in the United States of America.
Level of Study: Professional development.
Type: Fellowship.
Frequency: Annual.
Country of Study: Other.
No. of awards offered: One.
Application Procedure: Applicants must contact the Awards Secretary for details.
Closing Date: 20th Aug 2004.

RCOG William Blair-Bell Memorial Lectureships in Obstetrics and Gynaecology
Subjects: Obstetrics or gynaecology.
Purpose: To allow an individual to give a lecture.
Eligibility: Open to Fellows or members of not more than two years standing.
Type: Other.
Value: Honorarium of UK£500.
Frequency: Annual.
Application Procedure: Applicants must contact the Awards Secretary.
Closing Date: 16th February, 2004.

RCOG/Wyeth Historical Lecture
Subjects: Obstetrics or gynaecology with a strong historical content.
Purpose: To allow an individual to give a lecture on a current development in the field.
Eligibility: Open to RCOG Fellows and members.
Type: Other.
Value: An honorarium of UK£400. This amount may be subject to change and applicants should contact the organisation.
Frequency: Annual.
No. of awards offered: One.
Application Procedure: Applicants must contact the Awards Secretary for details.
Closing Date: 16th February, 2004.
Funding: Private.
Contributor: Wyeth Laboratories.

Tim Chard Case History
Subjects: Obstetrics and gynaecology, with specific reference to a clinical problem tackled with appropriate insight into the medical, social and psychological implications of the case.
Purpose: To mark the contribution of Professor Chard to obstetrics and gynaecology.
Level of Study: Graduate.
Value: UK£500 and UK£200.
Frequency: Annual.
Study Establishment: Accredited medical school.
Country of Study: UK, Northern Ireland and Republic of Ireland.
Application Procedure: Applicants should submit one case history with discussion. Maximum 1500 words and 10 biographical references. Include the name and address of supervisor.
Closing Date: 16th February.
Funding: Private.
Contributor: Bart's and the London School of Medicine.
Additional Information: Submissions may by sent by e-mail or post (4 copies of the typewritten submission on A4 paper). Please state clearly which award you are applying for, and make separate applications for each. Applications which do not comply with the stipulations will not be accepted.

THE ROYAL COLLEGE OF OPHTHALMOLOGISTS

17 Cornwall Terrace, London
NW1 4QW, England
Tel: (44) 20 7935 0702
Fax: (44) 20 7935 9838
Email: education@rcophth.ac.uk
www: http://www.rcophth.ac.uk
Contact: Beth Barnes, Deputy

The college is responsible for promoting high standards of professional practice, setting curricula and conducting examinations, inspecting hospital eve units for their training sutability and providing professional support and advice for opthalogists. The college runs an annual scientific congress and seminars for opthalnologists and publishes a range of clinical gudelines.

Royal College of Ophthalmologists Clinical Research Fellowships The Keeler Scholarship.
Purpose: To enable the scholar to study, research or acquire special skills, knowledge or experience at a suitable location in the United Kingdom or elsewhere for a minimum period of six months.
Eligibility: Fellows, Members and affiliate members of the college are eligble to apply for the scholarship. The trustees will give special consideration to candidates intending to make a career in ophthalmology in the United Kingdom.
Level of Study: Postgraduate.
Type: Scholarship.
Value: Up to UK£20,000.

Frequency: Every two years.
Country of Study: United Kingdom or elsewhere.
No. of awards offered: 1.
Application Procedure: An application must be completed and copied 5 times and submitted with 5 copies of the candidates's Curriculum Vitae.
Closing Date: February 20, 2004.
Funding: Commercial.
Contributor: Keeler LTD.
No. of awards given last year: 1.

Royal College of Ophthalmologists Clinical Research Fellowships The Pharmacia Ophthalmic Fellowship

Purpose: To enable the scholar to study, research or acquire special skills, knowledge or experience at a suitable location in the United Kingdom or elsewhere for a minimum period of six.
Eligibility: Applicants must be citizens of the United Kingdom and fellows, members and affiliates of the Royal College of Ophthalmologists, Those fellows, members and affiliates being in good standard.
Level of Study: Postgraduate.
Type: Fellowship
Value: Up to UK£35,000.
Frequency: Annual.
Country of Study: United Kingdom or elsewhere.
No. of awards offered: 1.
Application Procedure: An application form must be completed and copied 5 times and submitted with 5 copies of the candidate's curriculum Vitae.
Closing Date: To be arranged.
Funding: Commercial.
Contributor: Pharmacia Ltd.
No. of awards given last year: 1.

Royal College of Ophthalmologists Travel Awards Ethicon Foundation Fund.

Purpose: To prove financial assistance to members and fellows of the Royal College of Ophthalmologists who are travelling abroad for research or training purposes.
Eligibility: Applicants must be members and fellows of the Royal College of Ophthamologists.
Level of Study: Postgraduate.
Type: Travel Award.
Value: Generally UK£400-600 per Award.
Frequency: Annual.
Country of Study: Any country.
No. of awards offered: Varies.
Application Procedure: An application form must be completed and copied 5 times and submitted with 5 copies of the candidates Curriculum Vitae.
Closing Date: To be arranged.
Funding: Commercial.
Contributor: Ethicon Ltd.
No. of awards given last year: 4.

Royal College of Ophthalmologists Travel Awards Sir William Lister Award

Purpose: To provide personal travel expenses to citizens of the United Kingdom who are travelling abroad for the research or training.
Eligibility: Applicants must be citizens of the United Kingdom.
Level of Study: Postgraduate.
Type: Travel Award.
Value: Generally UK£400-600 per award.
Frequency: Annual.
Country of Study: Any country.
No. of awards offered: Varies.
Application Procedure: An application form must be completed and copied 5 times and submitted with 5 copies of the candidate's Curriculum Vitae.
Closing Date: To be arranged.
Funding: Private.

Royal College of Ophthalmologists Travel Awards The Dorey Bequest.

Purpose: To provide personal travel expenses to members and fellows of the Royal College of Ophthalmologists who are travelling abroad for the research or training.
Eligibility: Members and fellows of the Royal College of Ophthalmologists.
Level of Study: Postgraduate.
Type: Travel Award.
Value: Generally UK£400-600 per Award.
Frequency: Annual.
Country of Study: Any country.
No. of awards offered: Varies.
Application Procedure: An application form must be completed and copied 5 times and submitted with 5 copies of the candidate's Curriculum Vitae.
Closing Date: To be arranged.
Funding: Private.

ROYAL COLLEGE OF ORGANISTS (RCO)

7 St Andrew Street, Holborn, London, EC4A 3LQ, England
Tel: (44) 20 7936 3606
Fax: (44) 20 7353 8244
Contact: Senior Executive

The Royal College of Organists (RCO) is membership based. It promotes the art of organ playing as choral directing, and provides an organisation with a library, events and examinations to further that object.

RCO Grants and Travel Scholarships

Subjects: Organ playing.
Eligibility: Open to promising pupils of any nationality who are training to be organists. Some of the grants are restricted to applicants under 20 years of age.
Level of Study: Unrestricted.
Type: Grant and Travel Scholarship.
Length of Study: One year, renewable.
Frequency: Annual.
Country of Study: Any country.
No. of awards offered: Varies.
Application Procedure: Applicants must write for an application form.
Funding: Commercial, Private.

RCO Scholarships and Awards

Subjects: Organ playing.
Purpose: To assist organists with professional playing.
Eligibility: Open to members of the College. Only in exceptional circumstances will awards be made to non members. Membership is open to all upon payment of an annual subscription.
Level of Study: Unrestricted.
Type: Grant.
Length of Study: One year, renewable.
Frequency: Annual.
Study Establishment: Varies.
Country of Study: Any country.
No. of awards offered: Varies.
Application Procedure: Applicants must write for an application form.
Funding: Private.
Contributor: College trusts.

ROYAL COLLEGE OF PAEDIATRICS AND CHILD HEALTH

50 Hallam Street, London, W1W 6DE, England
Tel: (44) 20 7307 5633
Fax: (44) 20 7307 5693
Email: amanda.leighton@rcpch.ac.uk
www: http://www.rcpch.ac.uk
Contact: Miss Amanda Leighton, Conference Organiser

The Royal College of Paediatrics and Child Health works to advance the art and science of paediatrics, to raise the standard of medical care provided to children, to educate and examine those concerned with health of children, and to advance the education of the public and, in particular, medical practitioners in child health.

Heinz Visiting and Travelling Fellowships
Subjects: Paediatrics.
Purpose: To enable paediatricians from any part of the Commonwealth to visit the United Kingdom and to attend the Spring meeting of the College, or to enable British paediatricians to spend time in a developing country.
Eligibility: Open to paediatricians from the United Kingdom and Commonwealth countries. Paediatricians from any part of the Commonwealth who will benefit from meeting United Kingdom paediatricians and seeing something of their work are eligible for the Visiting Fellowship. Preference is given, in general, to applicants from developing countries who are not otherwise likely to visit the United Kingdom. Travelling Fellowships are open to United Kingdom paediatricians in the early years of their professional life.
Level of Study: Professional development.
Type: Fellowship.
Value: Air fares and living expenses.
Length of Study: Up to 12 weeks for Visiting Fellowships and up to three months for Travelling Fellowships.
Frequency: Annual.
Country of Study: United Kingdom for the visiting fellowship and upto three months for travelling fellowship.
No. of awards offered: Varies.
Application Procedure: Applicants must complete an application form, available from Amanda Leighton. The application form is to be submitted with a letter of support from the applicant's head of department.
Closing Date: Please write for details.
Funding: Private.
Contributor: H J Heinz Company.
No. of awards given last year: Three.

ROYAL COLLEGE OF SURGEONS OF ENGLAND

35-43 Lincoln's Inn Fields, London
WC2A 3PE, England
Tel: (44) 20 7869 6611
Fax: (44) 20 7869 6644
Email: research@rcseng.ac.uk
www: http://www.rcseng.ac.uk
Contact: Miss Bumbi Singh, Research Department

The Royal College of Surgeons of England is an independent professional body committed to promoting and advancing the highest standards of surgical care for patients.

Ethicon Foundation Fund
Subjects: Surgery.
Purpose: To promote international goodwill in surgery and to assist Fellows travelling abroad for research or training purposes.
Eligibility: Open to Fellows of the Royal College of Surgeons of England. Applicants should be sufficiently advanced in their training to benefit from such an experience or be within one year of their appointment as a consultant.
Level of Study: Professional development.
Type: Grant.
Value: Varies according to the number of awards and travel costs.
Length of Study: Varies.
Frequency: Twice a year.
Country of Study: Any country.
No. of awards offered: Varies.
Application Procedure: Applicants must send 10 copies of the application form to the Research Department of the College and should include a letter of support from the head of department or consultant under whom the applicant is currently working and a letter of support

from another independent referee. Application forms available from The Research Department at the main address.
Closing Date: Please contact the organisation.

For further information contact:

Research Department.

Lionel College Memorial Fellowship in Otolaryngology
Subjects: Head and neck surgery, with an emphasis on laryngology, rhinology or otology.
Purpose: To encourage research in the area of Head & Neck Surgery.
Eligibility: Open to candidates who are Fellows of the Royal College of Surgeons and between 25-35 years of age. Candidates must be senior trainees or recently appointed consultants, or of similar status in the field.
Level of Study: Professional development.
Type: Fellowship.
Value: Up to UK£3,000.
Length of Study: Varies.
Frequency: Annual.
Study Establishment: Appropriate research institutions.
Country of Study: Any country.
No. of awards offered: One.
Application Procedure: Applicants must send eight copies of applications to the Research Department of the College and should include an application form and letters of support from the applicant's present consultant and from the heads of the departments to be visited. If the applicant is already a consultant, the name of an independent referee in the United Kingdom should be submitted. Application forms available from Research Department at the main address.
Closing Date: Wednesday 30th June 2004.

Royal College of Surgeons, New York Travelling Fellowships
Subjects: Surgery or dentistry.
Purpose: To enable young surgeons and dental surgeons to visit the United States of America to observe medical procedures first hand.
Eligibility: Open to United Kingdom surgeons, usually between 30-36 years of age, who are qualified practitioners in their speciality and Fellows of the Royal College of Surgeons of England.
Level of Study: Professional development.
Type: Fellowship.
Value: Up to US$7,000.
Length of Study: At least Four-six weeks.
Frequency: Annual.
Country of Study: United States of America.
No. of awards offered: Three.
Application Procedure: Applicants must complete an application form, available from the main address, and include letters of support from the applicant's present consultant (or, if already a consultant, the name of an independent referee, in the UK), and the head of department to be visited in the USA.
Closing Date: Wednesday 30th June 2004.

ROYAL COMMISSION FOR THE EXHIBITION OF 1851

Sherfield Building, Imperial College, London, SW7 2AZ, England
Tel: (44) 20 7594 8790
Fax: (44) 20 7594 8794
Email: royalcom1851@imperial.ac.uk
www: http://www.royalcommission1851.org.uk
Contact: Mr Malcolm Shirley, Secretary

The Royal Commission for the Exhibition of 1851 is an educational trust supporting innovation and creativity in science, technology and occasionally the arts, almost always at post-graduate level. Apart from the competitive schemes listed, assistance is sometimes given to suitable charities or individuals.

1851 Industrial Fellowships
Subjects: Industry-based applied science and engineering.
Purpose: To give employed young engineers of exceptional promise the opportunity to conduct research to encourage profitable innovation and creativity in British industry.
Eligibility: Open to citizens of Great Britain.
Level of Study: Doctorate.
Type: Fellowship.
Value: Half salary up to UK£18,000 per year plus expenses.
Length of Study: Three years.
Frequency: Annual.
Study Establishment: Any approved university / British company.
Country of Study: United Kingdom.
No. of awards offered: Approx. six.
Application Procedure: Applicants must complete an application form, available from companies, the commission or from the website.
Closing Date: 30th January.
Funding: Private.
Contributor: The profits from the Great Exhibition.
No. of awards given last year: Six.
No. of applicants last year: 30.

1851 Research Fellowships
Subjects: Pure and applied sciences including mathematics and any branch of engineering.
Purpose: To give employed young scientists or engineers of exceptional promise the opportunity to conduct research.
Eligibility: Open to citizens of the Great Britain, the commonwealth, Republic of Ireland or Pakistan.
Level of Study: MBA.
Type: Fellowship.
Value: Approx. UK£21,000 in year one, UK£22,000 in year two, plus London weighting.
Length of Study: Two years.
Frequency: Annual.
Study Establishment: Any approved university.
Country of Study: Any country.
No. of awards offered: Approx. six.
Application Procedure: Applicants must complete an application form, available from all United Kingdom universities or from the website. Applications must be made by professors of United Kingdom universities on behalf of the applicants.
Closing Date: 27 February.
Funding: Private.
Contributor: The profits from the Great Exhibition.
No. of awards given last year: Six.
No. of applicants last year: 130.

Royal Commission Industrial Design Studentship
Subjects: Industrial design.
Purpose: To fund engineering and science graduates for a postgraduate industrial design course.
Eligibility: Open to United Kingdom nationals only with a first degree in engineering.
Level of Study: Postgraduate.
Type: Studentship.
Value: Approx. UK£8,500 per year plus materials and fees.
Length of Study: One-two years.
Frequency: Annual.
Study Establishment: Universities.
Country of Study: Any country.
No. of awards offered: Approx. six.
Application Procedure: Applicants must complete an application form and submit this with the required enclosures. Forms available from the commission or its web site.
Closing Date: 30th April.
Funding: Private.
Contributor: The profits from the Great Exhibition.
No. of awards given last year: Six.
No. of applicants last year: 24.

Royal Commission Industrial Fellowships
Subjects: Industrial and management engineering.
Purpose: To allow able graduates working in industry to carry out research and development leading to a higher degree or other career milestone.
Eligibility: Open to United Kingdom nationals only with a degree in science or engineering who are working in for a British company.
Level of Study: Doctorate, Postgraduate.
Type: Fellowship.
Value: 50 per cent of salary, up to a maximum of UK£18,000 per annum plus university fees and travel up to UK£3,200 per annum.
Length of Study: Three years.
Frequency: Annual.
Country of Study: United Kingdom.
No. of awards offered: Approx. six.
Application Procedure: Applicants must complete an application form.
Closing Date: January 26th.
Funding: Private.
Contributor: The profits from the Great Exhibition.
No. of awards given last year: Six.
No. of applicants last year: 30.

ROYAL GEOGRAPHICAL SOCIETY (WITH THE INSTITUTE OF BRITISH GEOGRAPHERS)

1 Kensington Gore, London, SW7 2AR, England
Tel: (44) 20 7591 3073
Fax: (44) 20 7591 3031
Email: grants@rgs.org
www: http://www.rgs.org/grants
Contact: Grants Co-ordinator

The Royal Geographical Society (with the Institute of British Geographers) is the United Kingdom's learned society for geography and geographers and a professional body. It supports and promotes many aspects of geography including geographical research, education and teaching, field training and small expeditions, the public understanding and popularisation of geography, and the provision of geographical information.

Gilchrist Fieldwork Award
Subjects: Natural sciences or geography.
Purpose: To finance an overseas research proposal which will enable original and challenging research to take place, preferably of potential applied benefit to the host country.
Eligibility: Open to teams of up to 10 members, the majority of which must be British and hold established posts in university departments.
Level of Study: Doctorate, Postdoctorate.
Type: Grant.
Value: UK£10,000.
Length of Study: More than six weeks.
Frequency: Every two years.
Country of Study: Outside the United Kingdom.
No. of awards offered: One.
Application Procedure: Applicants must submit a proposal, following the guidelines, to the Grants Co-ordinator by the closing date. There is no application form.
Closing Date: March 15th.
Funding: Commercial.

For further information contact:

The Secretary, Gilchrist Educational Trust, Mary Trevewyan Hall, 10 York Terrace East, London, NW1 4PT, England

Monica Cole Research Grant
Subjects: Earth and geological sciences.
Purpose: To enable the winner to undertake original fieldwork overseas.
Eligibility: Open to female physical geographers only. Applicants must be registered at a United Kingdom university.

Level of Study: Doctorate, Postdoctorate, Postgraduate.
Type: Grant.
Value: UK£1,000.
Frequency: Every three years.
Country of Study: Outside the United Kingdom.
No. of awards offered: One.
Application Procedure: Applicants must download guidelines from the website or contact the Grants Co-ordinator. There is no application form.
Closing Date: January 25th.
Funding: Private.

Neville Shulman Challenge Award

Subjects: The geographical sciences and exploration.
Purpose: To further the understanding and exploration of the planet, while promoting personal development through the intellectual or physical challenges involved.
Eligibility: Open to any United Kingdom national over the age of 25.
Level of Study: Unrestricted.
Type: Grant.
Value: Normally up to UK£5,000.
Length of Study: Unrestricted.
Frequency: Annual.
Country of Study: Any country.
No. of awards offered: Normally one.
Application Procedure: Applicants must submit a proposal, following the guidelines, to the Grants Co-ordinator by the closing date. There is no application form. Details are available from the website.
Closing Date: October 31st.
Funding: Private.
No. of awards given last year: One.
No. of applicants last year: 24.

Ralph Brown Expedition Award

Subjects: Natural sciences.
Purpose: To support and encourage objectives that involve the study of rivers, inland or coastal wetlands or shallow marine environments.
Eligibility: Open to applicants over 25 from any country who must be a Fellow or Associate Fellow of the Society.
Level of Study: Postgraduate, Research.
Type: Grant.
Value: UK£15,000.
Frequency: Annual.
Country of Study: Any country.
No. of awards offered: One.
Application Procedure: Applicants must contact the Grants Co-ordinator or refer to the website for detailed guidelines.
Closing Date: November 30th.
Funding: Private.
No. of awards given last year: One.
No. of applicants last year: 15.

Royal Geographical Society Expedition Research Grants

Subjects: Geographical, earth, life and human sciences.
Purpose: To support British expeditions carrying out geographical field research and exploration overseas.
Eligibility: Open to multidisciplinary teams, rather than individuals, the majority of which must be British and over 19 years of age.
Level of Study: Unrestricted.
Type: Grant.
Value: UK£750-3,000.
Length of Study: Must be over five weeks.
Frequency: Twice a year.
Country of Study: Other.
No. of awards offered: 60-70.
Application Procedure: Applicants must complete an application form. These can be obtained from the Society's website or by writing to the Grants Co-ordinator.
Closing Date: January 25th or August 25th.
Funding: Commercial, Private.
No. of awards given last year: 52.
No. of applicants last year: 61.

Slawson Awards

Subjects: Social and behavioural sciences or development studies.
Purpose: To assist students intending to carry out geographical field research in developing countries to increase knowledge, awareness and understanding of the world in which we live.
Eligibility: Applicants must normally be United Kingdom citizens, currently be registered for a PhD at a United Kingdom Institute of Higher Education and be Fellows of the Society.
Level of Study: Postgraduate.
Type: Grant.
Value: Normally up to UK£3,000.
Frequency: Annual.
Country of Study: Outside the United Kingdom, preferably in developing countries.
Application Procedure: Applicants must submit a proposal, following the guidelines, to the Grants Co-ordinator by the closing date. There is no application form and more details are available from the website.
Closing Date: February 21st.
Funding: Private.
No. of awards given last year: Two.
No. of applicants last year: 20.

Violet Cressey-Marcks Fisher Travel Scholarship

Subjects: Natural sciences or geography.
Purpose: To finance research in the field.
Eligibility: Applicants must be registered at a United Kingdom university. There is no age limit.
Level of Study: Postgraduate, Research.
Value: UK£350.
Length of Study: More than six months.
Frequency: Annual.
Country of Study: Outside the UK.
No. of awards offered: One.
Application Procedure: Applicants must submit a formal proposal following guidelines to the Grants Co-ordinator. Guidelines can be downloaded from the website. There is no application form.
Closing Date: January 25th.
Funding: Private.
No. of awards given last year: One.
No. of applicants last year: 16.

ROYAL HOLLOWAY, UNIVERSITY OF LONDON

Egham, Surrey, TW20 0EX, England
Tel: (44) 1784 443399
Fax: (44) 1784 471381
Email: liaison-office@rhul.ac.uk
www: http://www.rhul.ac.uk
Contact: Ms Claire Collingwood, Schools & International Liaison Officer

All departments of Royal Holloway, University of London seek to provide taught programmes which reflect the latest developments and are responsive to the needs of students and society, together with research and scholarship which contribute to the advancement of knowledge and the enhancement of public policy, wealth creation and the quality of life.

Royal Holloway, University of London College Overseas Entrance Scholarships

Subjects: All subjects.
Purpose: To award outstanding academic achievement.
Eligibility: Open to overseas students only for full-time Masters or research.
Level of Study: Postgraduate, Research.
Type: Scholarship.
Value: Up to a maximum of UK£10,000 depending on the number of awards available and the strength of the applicant. This award pays fees and/or some maintenance depending on level of award.
Frequency: Annual.
Application Procedure: Students who accept the offer of a place will automatically receive an application form.

Closing Date: February 1st.
Additional Information: Further details of the awards can be found on the Universitys website or in the booklet Funding Postgraduate Studies, available from the college.

Royal Holloway, University of London College Research Studentship

Subjects: All subjects.
Level of Study: Doctorate.
Type: Studentship.
Value: Tuition fees at the home rate.
Length of Study: Tenable for three years full-time or six years part-time.
Frequency: Annual.
Application Procedure: Applicants must indicate if they wish to be considered, but departments nominate their candidates.
Closing Date: Applicants should contact the relevant academic department.
Additional Information: These studentships cannot be held with a research council, AHRB or similar major award. Further details of the awards can be found on the University's website or in the booklet Funding Postgraduate Studies, available from the college.

Royal Holloway, University of London Departmental Assistantships

Subjects: All subjects.
Level of Study: Postgraduate.
Type: Other.
Value: Up to UK£4,000 per year for a maximum of six hours work per week, 48 weeks per year.
Length of Study: Tenable for one year full-time or two years part-time.
Frequency: Annual.
Application Procedure: Applicants must indicate on their application form that they wish to be considered.
Closing Date: Applicants should contact the relevant academic department.
Additional Information: These Assistantships cannot be held with a research council, AHRB or similar major award. Departmental assistantships require research students to support teaching and research in the department for up to six hours each week. Further details of the awards can be found on the University's website or in the booklet Funding Postgraduate Studies, available from the college.

Royal Holloway, University of London Endowed Postgraduate Scholarships

Subjects: All subjects.
Eligibility: This award cannot be held with a research council, AHRB or similar major award.
Level of Study: Postgraduate, Research.
Type: Scholarship.
Value: Varies.
Length of Study: Tenable for three years full-time. For part-time maintenance elements are reduced pro-rata.
Frequency: Annual.
No. of awards offered: Varies.
Application Procedure: Applicants must indicate if they wish to be considered, but departments nominate their candidates.
Closing Date: Applicants should contact the relevant academic department.
Additional Information: Availability varies from year to year and is restricted to certain departments. Interested parties should contact the academic department for availability. More details of the awards can be found on the University's website or in the booklet Funding Postgraduate Studies, available from the college.

Thomas Holloway Research Studentship

Subjects: Arts and humanities, business administration and management, music, drama, cinema and television, mathematics and computer science, natural sciences and social science or behavioural science.

Eligibility: This studentship cannot be held with a research council, AHRB or similar major award.
Level of Study: Doctorate.
Type: Studentship.
Value: Tuition fees at the home rate plus maintenance of up to UK£9,000 per year. Rates vary between departments.
Length of Study: Tenable for three years full-time. For part-time maintenance elements are reduced pro-rata.
Frequency: Annual.
Application Procedure: Applicants must indicate if they wish to be considered, but departments nominate their candidates.
Closing Date: Applicants should contact the relevant academic department.

ROYAL HORTICULTURAL SOCIETY (RHS)

Wisley, Woking, Surrey, GU23 6QB, England
Tel: (44) 1483 212381
Fax: (44) 1483 212382
Email: lindsay@rhs.org.uk
Contact: Mr Lindsay Thomson, Head of Education

The Royal Horticultural Society (RHS) is a membership charity holding a Royal Charter for horticulture. The Society promotes the science, art and practice of horticulture in all its branches through a wide range of educational, research and advisory activities. It also maintains some major gardens, shows and the internationally renowned Lindley Library.

Blaxall Valentine Trust Award

Subjects: Horticulture.
Purpose: To help finance worldwide plant collecting in natural habitats and study expeditions which will provide real benefits to horticulture.
Eligibility: Open to applicants worldwide, but preference is given to United Kingdom and Commonwealth citizens. Applicants should preferably be within the age bracket of 20-35 years and satisfy the Society that their health enables them to undertake the project proposed. Financial sponsorship will be available to both professional and amateur horticulturists and consideration for an award is not restricted to RHS members.
Level of Study: Unrestricted.
Value: Funds are limited. High cost projects are expected to receive supplementary finance from other sources, including personal contributions.
Frequency: Four times per year.
Country of Study: Any country.
Application Procedure: Applicants must complete an application form available on request. Candidates may be called for interview.
Closing Date: December 24th, March 31st, June 30th or September 30th.
Funding: Private.

Coke Trust Award

Subjects: Horticulture.
Purpose: To broaden professional gardeners' and student gardeners' knowledge, skills and experience, and to finance horticultural projects which demonstrate a distinct educational or historic value, as submitted by institutions, charities or gardens.
Eligibility: Submissions are welcomed from applicants worldwide, but preference is given to United Kingdom and Commonwealth citizens. Applicants should preferably be within the age bracket of 20-35 years and satisfy the Society that their health enables them to undertake the project proposed. Financial sponsorship will be available to both professional and amateur horticulturists and consideration for an award is not restricted to RHS members.
Value: Funds are limited. High cost projects are expected to receive supplementary finance from other sources, including personal contributions.
Frequency: Four times per year.

Country of Study: United Kingdom.
No. of awards offered: Unlimited.
Application Procedure: Applicants must complete an application form, available on request.
Closing Date: December 24th, March 31st, June 30th or September 30th.
Funding: Private.

Osaka Travel Award

Subjects: Horticultural related study or work experience will be considered.
Purpose: To allow young people from the United Kingdom and Japan to study in each other's country and benefit from a cross-cultural exchange of ideas.
Eligibility: Open to British and Japanese citizens with a horticultural background. Applicants should preferably be within the age bracket of 20-35 years. Financial sponsorship will be available to both professional and amateur horticulturists and consideration for an award is not restricted to RHS members. The awards are made to individuals, not to groups or expeditions.
Level of Study: Unrestricted.
Type: Bursary.
Value: Funds are limited. High cost projects are expected to receive supplementary finance from other sources, including personal contributions.
Frequency: Four times per year.
Country of Study: Other.
No. of awards offered: One.
Application Procedure: Applicants must complete an application form, available on request. Candidates may be called for interview.
Closing Date: December 24th, March 31st, June 30th or September 30th.
Funding: Private.
Additional Information: Recipients must submit a brief factual report within six weeks of completion, along with an outline of achievements or difficulties and an account of expenses.

Queen Elizabeth the Queen Mother Bursary

Subjects: Horticulture.
Purpose: To help finance related projects eg. study tours, horticulturally related expeditions, minor research projects possibly working with an acknowledged expert on short-term research, taxonomic studies, specialised courses and programmes of study such as specific subject symposia.
Eligibility: Submissions are welcomed from applicants worldwide but preference is given to United Kingdom and Commonwealth citizens. Applicants should preferably be within the age bracket of 20-35 years and satisfy the Society that their health enables them to undertake the project proposed. Financial sponsorship will be available to both professional and amateur horticulturists and consideration for an award is not restricted to RHS members. The awards are made to individuals, not to groups or expeditions.
Level of Study: Unrestricted.
Type: Bursary.
Value: Funds are limited. High cost projects are expected to receive supplementary finance from other sources, including personal contributions.
Frequency: Four times per year.
Country of Study: Any country.
No. of awards offered: One-three.
Application Procedure: Applicants must complete an application form, available on request. Candidates may be called for interview.
Closing Date: December 24th, March 31st, June 30th or September 30th.
Funding: Private.
Additional Information: Recipients must submit a brief factual report within six weeks of completion, along with an outline of achievements or difficulties, including any unusual problems eg. medical or political, and an account of expenses. Recipients must also be prepared to give a lecture on their project at the Society's headquarters at Vincent Square in London, within 18 months of completing the project.

RHS Financial Award

Subjects: Horticulture.
Purpose: To help finance horticulture related projects and to further the interests of horticultural education along with horticultural work experience.
Eligibility: Submissions are welcomed from applicants worldwide, but preference is given to United Kingdom and Commonwealth citizens. Applicants should preferably be within the age bracket of 20-35 years and satisfy the Society that their health enables them to undertake the project proposed. Financial sponsorship will be available to both professional and amateur horticulturists and consideration for an award is not restricted to RHS members. The awards are made to individuals, not to groups or expeditions.
Level of Study: Unrestricted.
Type: Bursary.
Value: Funds are limited. High cost projects are expected to receive supplementary finance from other sources, including personal contributions.
Frequency: Four times per year.
Country of Study: Any country.
No. of awards offered: Unlimited.
Application Procedure: Applicants must complete an application form, available on request. Candidates may be called for interview.
Closing Date: December 24th, March 31st, June 30th or September 30th.
Funding: Private.
Additional Information: Recipients must submit a brief factual report within six weeks of completion, along with an outline of achievements or difficulties, including any unusual problems eg. medical or political, and an account of expenses.

ROYAL INCORPORATION OF ARCHITECTS IN SCOTLAND (RIAS)

15 Rutland Square, Edinburgh, EH1 2BE, Scotland
Tel: (44) 131 229 7545
Fax: (44) 131 228 2188
Email: lconnolly@rias.org.uk
www: http://www.rias.org.uk
Contact: Ms Linda Connolly, Awards Administrator

Martin Jones Memorial Scholarship and Award

Subjects: Architecture.
Purpose: To support an outstanding student in pursuing a personal line of creative investigation and research.
Eligibility: Open to students and graduates of the School of Architecture in Duncan of Jordanstone College of Art, Dundee University.
Level of Study: Postgraduate.
Type: Scholarship.
Value: UK£7,500.
Frequency: Annual.
Country of Study: Any country.
No. of awards offered: One.
Application Procedure: Invitations are issued in the Autumn each year.
Closing Date: The end of January.
Funding: Private.

For further information contact:

The Martin Jones Award, c/o School of Architecture, Duncan of Jordanstone, Perth Road, Dundee, DD1 4HT, Scotland

RIAS Award for Measured Drawing

Subjects: Architecture and measured drawing.
Purpose: To encourage and recognise original hand measured drawing as essential to an architect's training.
Eligibility: Open to student members and members of the RIAS.
Level of Study: Postgraduate.
Value: The premier award for student members is UK£200 and the prize for full members is UK£100.
Frequency: Annual.
Country of Study: Any country.

No. of awards offered: One.
Closing Date: The end of January.
Additional Information: The Committee will judge competitors on the following points: the choice of architectural fabric for the measured study, such as buildings under threat, the clarity of understanding and accuracy revealed by the drawing and the elegance with which the analysis is presented. Adjudication will normally take place in March. If confirmed by the RIAS council the result of the competition will be notified to the competitors. The presentation of the award will be made at the RIAS Annual Convention. The winning drawing will form part of a travelling exhibition of RIAS Awards and Prizes and may, at the Incorporation's discretion, subsequently form part of the RIAS Archive.

RIAS John Maclaren Travelling Fellowship

Subjects: Architecture.
Purpose: To assist study at a school of architecture or engineering, or to assist an individual in taking up a paid position in practice in the country chosen for study, or to reward work which has involved study overseas.
Eligibility: Applicants must be on the Register of Registered Architects and be corporate members of the RIAS.
Level of Study: Postgraduate.
Type: Fellowship.
Value: UK£600 and a certificate.
Frequency: Every two years.
Country of Study: Other.
No. of awards offered: One.
Closing Date: The end of January.
Additional Information: It is the preference of the RIAS that the outcome of the fellowship should be a presentation of the results of the study at the RIAS Convention, with a lodgement in the RIAS library of such manuscript and slides or photographs as may be appropriate. The fellowship requires both scholarship and analysis, and submission to the RIAS of evidence of lasting value. Applicants, both in their proposal and in the subsequent presentation, are expected to have adopted an investigative and critical attitude towards their proposed subject of study in the manner of a learned society dissertation. The option of presenting the results orally at the Convention, with the deposit of the material in the library, or the simple deposit of written material in the library, will be a matter for determination between the Fellow and the RIAS Awards Committee.

Sir John Burnet Memorial Award

Subjects: Architecture.
Purpose: To test a student's skill in architectural design and communicating by drawing, prepared within a predetermined time limit, their proposals in response to a client's brief.
Eligibility: Open to student members of the RIAS who should be first year full-time post Part I.
Level of Study: Postgraduate.
Value: UK£150 and a certificate.
Frequency: Annual.
Country of Study: Any country.
No. of awards offered: One.
Additional Information: Submissions will be judged by the RIAS Awards Committee. The Committee may be assisted by distinguished critics, co-opted by the Committee. The judges will consider skills in interpreting a brief within a time deadline, flair in architectural design and skill in methods of communication and presentation. The drawings will remain the property of the RIAS.

Sir Robert Lorimer Memorial Award

Subjects: Architecture.
Purpose: To encourage students to keep sketch books or notebooks, as in Lorimer's time.
Eligibility: Open to student members and members of the RIAS under the age of 29.
Level of Study: Postgraduate.
Value: A book voucher to the value of UK£125 and a certificate.
Frequency: Annual.
Country of Study: Any country.
No. of awards offered: One.

Closing Date: The end of January.
Additional Information: The assessors prefer working sketch books, which are a record of study and travel, and will look for careful observation and sensitive draughtsmanship. Adjudication will normally take place in March. If confirmed by the RIAS Council the result of the competition will be notified to the competitors. The presentation of the award will be made at the RIAS Annual Convention.

Sir Rowand Anderson Silver Medal

Subjects: Architecture.
Purpose: To recognise the best student member in Scotland.
Eligibility: Open to student members of the RIAS within a year of passing Part II.
Level of Study: Postgraduate.
Value: A silver medal and a certificate.
Frequency: Annual.
Country of Study: Scotland.
No. of awards offered: One.
Closing Date: October 31st.
Additional Information: The RIAS Awards Committee may require to interview candidates before making their selection. The award and presentation will be made at the RIAS Annual Convention, for which the winner may be asked to make available a selection of his or her portfolio for exhibition.

Thomas Ross Award

Subjects: Architecture pertaining particularly to Scotland, Scottish architecture and environment or the study of ancient Scottish buildings or monuments.
Purpose: To recognise post qualification research.
Eligibility: Candidates must be members of the RIAS, be of graduate status or possess and produce evidence of such other qualifications as may satisfy the requirements of the RIAS.
Level of Study: Postgraduate.
Value: UK£600, a certificate and the possibility of additional help towards publication.
Frequency: Every two years.
Country of Study: Any country.
No. of awards offered: One, though the Committee, at its discretion, may make more than one award, provided that the total number of awards in a six year period does not exceed three.
Closing Date: The end of January.
Additional Information: The Committee will judge applicants upon the clarity of the proposal or completed work, upon the candidates' ability to write and to present material and upon the extent to which the study covers ground not covered by existing material. The Committee may require applicants to attend an interview.

THE ROYAL INSTITUTION OF NAVAL ARCHITECTS (RINA)

10 Upper Belgrave Street, London, SW1X 8BQ, England
Tel: (44) 20 7235 4622
Fax: (44) 20 7245 6959
Email: hq@rina.org.uk
www: http://www.rina.org.uk
Contact: Mr D Bragger, Professional Affairs Manager

The Royal Institution of Naval Architects (RINA) exists to promote and serve the interests and needs of its members, who are those involved in the design, construction, repair and operation of ships, boats and marine structures.

Froude Research Scholarship in Naval Architecture

Subjects: Hydrodynamics or other problems connected with marine technology.
Purpose: To support naval architecture research.
Eligibility: Open to applicants from any country, normally under 30 years of age, who have shown unusual promise in the study of naval architecture and are members of RINA.
Level of Study: Postgraduate.
Type: Scholarship.
Value: UK£700.

Length of Study: Two years with a possibility of renewal for a further year.
Frequency: Annual.
Study Establishment: An approved institution.
Country of Study: Any country.
No. of awards offered: Usually one.
Application Procedure: Applicants must complete an application form and submit this with a letter of support from the head of department of the applicant's university or college and evidence of the offer of a postgraduate placement. Applications should be returned to RINA. Candidates may be required to attend an interview in London. Application forms are available from the Director of Professional Affairs.
Closing Date: July 31st prior to commencement.
Funding: Private.
Contributor: Trust fund.
No. of awards given last year: Two.
No. of applicants last year: Five.
Additional Information: The holder is required to submit a report on the work done during the first year accompanied by a letter stating satisfactory progress from the head of department. The holder is also required to submit a report on satisfactory completion of the research and is not permitted to accept payment from a company in respect of work done in connection with the research for which the scholarship was awarded.

Sir William White Postgraduate Scholarship in Naval Architecture

Subjects: Marine engineering and naval architecture.
Purpose: To enable students to follow a postgraduate course or carry out research work into problems connected with the design and construction of ships.
Eligibility: Open to applicants from any country who have passed a course of study recognised by the Institute and who have at some time been employed in the marine industry.
Level of Study: Postgraduate.
Type: Scholarship.
Value: UK£1,000 payable at the commencement of first year of study.
Length of Study: One-two years.
Frequency: Annual.
Study Establishment: An approved university, college or research establishment.
Country of Study: United Kingdom.
No. of awards offered: One-two.
Application Procedure: Applicants must complete an application form and submit this with qualification certificates, a letter of support from the applicant's university and evidence of the offer of a postgraduate placement. Applications should be returned to RINA. Candidates may be required to attend an interview in London. Application forms are available from the Director of Professional Affairs.
Closing Date: July 31st prior to commencement.
Funding: Private.
Contributor: Trust fund.
No. of awards given last year: One.
Additional Information: The holder is required to submit a report on satisfactory completion of the research and is not permitted to accept payment from a company in respect of work done in connection with the research for which the scholarship was awarded.

ROYAL IRISH ACADEMY

19 Dawson Street, Dublin, 2, Ireland
Tel: (353) 1 676 2570
Fax: (353) 1 676 2346
Email: admin@ria.ie
www: http://www.ria.ie
Contact: Ms Laura Mahoney, Assistant Executive Secretary

The Royal Irish Academy is the senior institution in Ireland for both the sciences and humanities. It publishes a number of journals and monographs. It is Ireland's national representative in a large number of international unions, and through its national committees runs conferences, lectures and workshops. It also manages a number of long-term research projects. The Academy participates in the Royal Society European Science Exchange Programmes in pure and applied science, in the British Academy European Exchange Programmes in the humanities, and in the Austrian, Hungarian, or Polish academy exchange schemes in science and the humanities. Small grants for work in all disciplines are available annually from the Academy's own funds.

Eoin O'Mahony Bursary

Subjects: History.
Purpose: To assist Irish scholars undertaking overseas research on historical subjects of Irish interest.
Level of Study: Unrestricted.
Type: Bursary.
Value: Varies.
Length of Study: Varies.
Frequency: Annual.
Country of Study: Any country.
No. of awards offered: One.
Application Procedure: Applicants must complete an application form, available from the Academy.
Closing Date: End of January.
Funding: Private.
Contributor: Trust fund.
No. of awards given last year: Eight.
Additional Information: Preference will be given to projects concerning family history, in particular those which are associated with the 'Wild Geese' (genealogy). Special consideration will be given to those who have been active in local learned societies.

Royal Irish Academy Award in Biochemistry

Subjects: Biochemistry.
Eligibility: Open to anyone who is actively engaged in biochemical research in Ireland. The award may be made to scientists at any stage of their scientific career and will primarily recognise scientific work carried out in the past decade.
Level of Study: Postdoctorate, Professional development.
Value: A silver medal.
Frequency: Annual.
Country of Study: Ireland.
No. of awards offered: One.
Application Procedure: Applicants must be nominated. Nomination must be made by two scientists who also supply the names of two independent referees, one of whom must reside outside Ireland.
Closing Date: Please contact the Academy.
Funding: Private.
Contributor: Schering Plough (Brinny) Company.
No. of awards given last year: One.
Additional Information: The recipient delivers a review lecture at the Royal Irish Academy and also at a meeting of the Irish Area Section of the Biochemical Society.

Royal Irish Academy Award in Microbiology

Subjects: Microbiology.
Purpose: To recognise research contributions in referred international journals.
Eligibility: Open to people who are resident in either Northern Ireland or the Republic of Ireland. Only applicants less than 40 years of age on January 1st of the year of the award are eligible.
Level of Study: Unrestricted.
Value: A silver medal.
Frequency: Every two years.
Country of Study: Ireland.
No. of awards offered: One.
Application Procedure: Applicants must be nominated independently by two scientists who are familiar with their work.
Closing Date: February 23rd.
Funding: Private.
No. of awards given last year: One.
Additional Information: The recipient will deliver a review lecture at the Royal Irish Academy. A copy of the lecture must be deposited in the Academy's library.

Royal Irish Academy Award in Nutritional Sciences

Subjects: Dietetics or microbiology.
Purpose: To recognise research contributions in nutritional sciences in referred international journals.
Eligibility: Open to people who are resident in either Northern Ireland or the Republic of Ireland. Only applicants who are less than 45 years of age on January 1st of the year of the award are eligible.
Level of Study: Postdoctorate, Professional development.
Value: A silver medal.
Frequency: Every two-four years.
Country of Study: Ireland.
No. of awards offered: One.
Application Procedure: Applicants must be nominated independently by two scientists who are familiar with the work of the nominee.
Closing Date: Applications are accepted at any time.
Funding: Private.
Additional Information: The recipient will deliver a review lecture at the Royal Irish Academy. A copy of the lecture must be deposited in the Academy's library.

Royal Irish Academy Award in Pharmacology and Toxicology

Subjects: Pharmacology and toxicology.
Purpose: To recognise achievement.
Eligibility: Open to all those who work in or close to the areas of pharmacology and toxicology and who are resident in either Northern Ireland or the Republic of Ireland.
Level of Study: Postdoctorate, Professional development.
Value: A silver medal.
Frequency: Every two years.
Country of Study: Ireland.
Application Procedure: Applicants must be nominated by not less than two persons who will have obtained the prior agreement of the nominee.
Closing Date: Applications are accepted at any time.
Funding: Private.
Contributor: The Élan Corporation.
No. of awards given last year: One.
Additional Information: The medal will be presented at a function to be held at the Royal Irish Academy. The recipient will be required to speak on this occasion and a copy of the address must be deposited in the Academy's library.

Royal Irish Academy European Exchange Fellowship

Subjects: Humanities, social sciences or natural sciences.
Purpose: To promote academic exchange between Ireland and Austria, Great Britain, Hungary, France and Poland.
Level of Study: Postdoctorate, Professional development.
Type: Fellowship.
Value: Varies.
Length of Study: Varies.
Frequency: Annual.
Country of Study: Other.
Application Procedure: Applicants must complete an application form, available form the Academy.
Closing Date: October 30th.
Funding: Government.
No. of awards given last year: 17.

Royal Irish Academy Science Writing Competition

Subjects: Biochemistry.
Eligibility: Open to graduate students in third level institutions in either Northern Ireland or the Republic of Ireland.
Level of Study: Postgraduate, Predoctorate, Research.
Value: €1,000 for the winner and €400 for the runner-up.
Frequency: Annual.
Country of Study: Ireland.
No. of awards offered: Two.
Application Procedure: Applicants must submit five copies of the article.
Closing Date: March 26th.
Funding: Private.
Contributor: Yamanouchi Ireland and the Irish Times newspaper.

No. of awards given last year: Two.
Additional Information: The newspaper article must be suitable for a non scientific reader explaining the development of any new topic in biochemistry and its significance to medical, agricultural or industrial practices. The winner's article will appear in the Irish Times newspaper.

ROYAL PHARMACEUTICAL SOCIETY OF GREAT BRITAIN

1 Lambeth High Street, London, SE1 7JN, England
Tel: (44) 20 7735 9141
Fax: (44) 20 7735 7629
Email: enquiries@rpsgb.org.uk
www: http://www.rpsgb.org.uk/
Contact: Ms Dilys Wood, Education Division

The Royal Pharmaceutical Society of Great Britain is the regulatory and professional body for pharmacists in England, Scotland and Wales.

Galen Award

Subjects: To build research capacity in pharmacy practice.
Purpose: To fund members of the Royal Pharmaceutical Society who wish to pursue PhD, or post-doctoral research.
Eligibility: Applicants must be members of the Society.
Level of Study: Doctorate, Postdoctorate, Predoctorate.
Type: Grant.
Value: Up to UK£10,000.
Frequency: Annual.
Country of Study: United Kingdom.
Application Procedure: Download application form and guidance notes from the website.
Funding: Private.
Contributor: Bequest by Rowland Henry Wiliams.
Additional Information: The award could also be used to fund new areas of research, eg. pre-pilot and feasibility studies that would not be considered by other funding bodies.

Research Training Bursary Scheme

Subjects: Community pharmacy in everyday practice.
Purpose: To support community pharmacists who have an interest in conducting research relating to everyday practice.
Eligibility: Applications are assessed on the individual rather than the proposed project.
Level of Study: Postgraduate.
Type: Bursary.
Value: Salary, course fees, research costs up to UK£250, Conference attendance up to UK£200.
Frequency: Annual.
Country of Study: United Kingdom.
Application Procedure: Obtain contact details from the website, e-mail practiceresearch@rpsgb.org.uk, or write to main organisation.
Contributor: Leverhulme Trade Charities Trust.

Royal Pharmaceutical Society/CRISP Scholarships

Subjects: Pharmaceutical sciences.
Purpose: To allow students to take up postgraduate research on a full-time basis.
Eligibility: Open to candidates who have been awarded the Pharmaceutical Chemists' Qualifying Diploma or a United Kingdom degree in pharmacy approval for the purposes of registration in Great Britain by the Council of the Royal Pharmaceutical Society of Great Britain.
Level of Study: Doctorate.
Type: Scholarship.
Value: Minimum annual value of UK£6,520 for students attending establishments within the City of London and the Metropolitan Police District, minimum annual value of UK£5,260 for students attending any other establishment. The exact value is dependent on the student's age and experience. Payment is made in equal monthly instalments. Tuition fees up to the Home or EC student rate are paid directly to the scholar's school of pharmacy.

Length of Study: One year, renewable for up to a total of three years, subject to satisfactory progress.
Frequency: Annual.
Study Establishment: Any United Kingdom school of pharmacy.
Country of Study: United Kingdom.
No. of awards offered: Varies.
Application Procedure: Application form with sections for completion by a) the applicant, b) the applicant's proposed supervisor, c) the head of the school of pharmacy, d) the applicant's undergraduate tutor. The applicant should append a one page CV to the form.
Closing Date: March 1st.
Additional Information: Applications for the awards should be made on behalf of the candidate by the head of the school of pharmacy at which the research is to be undertaken. The awardee may not teach or engage in any other form of employment for more than six hours in a week. The awardee should submit a copy of his or her thesis not more than one year after the end of the total period of research funded by the Society. Each CRISP (Collaborative Research Investment Studentship Programme for Pharmacy) Scholarship is co-sponsored by the Royal Pharmaceutical Society and a pharmaceutical company.

Sir Hugh Linstead Fellowship

Subjects: To build research capacity in pharmacy practice.
Purpose: To support research relating to community pharmacy.
Eligibility: The applicant must be working on a project that will be of value to the community.
Level of Study: Doctorate, Postdoctorate.
Type: Fellowship.
Value: UK£20,000.
Frequency: Annual.
Country of Study: United Kingdom.
No. of awards offered: 2.
Application Procedure: Download application form and guidance notes from the website.
Funding: Private.
Contributor: Leverhulme Trade Charities Trust.

ROYAL PHILHARMONIC SOCIETY (RPS)

10 Stratford Place, London, W1C 1BA, England
Tel: (44) 20 7401 8110
Fax: (44) 20 7493 7463
Email: admin@royalphilharmonicsociety.org.uk
www: http://www.royalphilharmonicsociety.org.uk
Contact: General Administrator

The Royal Philharmonic Society (RPS) offers support for young musicians and composers, sponsorship of new music events, debate and discussion about the future of music and has an active commissioning policy. It recognises achievement through the prestigious annual RPS Music Awards and with the Society's Gold Medal. Full information is available on the RPS website.

Julius Isserlis Scholarship

Subjects: Musical performance in varying instrumental categories.
Purpose: To facilitate musical study abroad, starting within 16 months of the award being made.
Eligibility: Open to students of any nationality, permanently resident in the United Kingdom, who are 15-25 years of age.
Level of Study: Unrestricted.
Type: Scholarship.
Value: UK£25,000.
Length of Study: Two years.
Frequency: Every two years.
Country of Study: Other.
No. of awards offered: One main award with the additional possibility of smaller discretionary awards.
Application Procedure: Applicants must complete an application form. There is a UK £20 entry fee.
Closing Date: March 2005.
Funding: Private.
Additional Information: The winner must take up residence for a period of study in the country designated on the application.

RPS Composition Prize

Subjects: Musical composition.
Purpose: To encourage young composers.
Eligibility: Open to past and present registered students of any conservatoire or university within the United Kingdom, of any nationality, under the age of 29. Former winners are not eligible.
Level of Study: Postgraduate.
Type: Prize.
Value: UK£5,000 commission plus a guaranteed performance of commissioned work.
Frequency: Annual.
No. of awards offered: Two.
Application Procedure: Applicants must complete an application form. There is a UK£20 entry fee but this is free to RPS members.
Closing Date: March 31st annually.
Funding: Private.
No. of awards given last year: Two.
No. of applicants last year: 70.

THE ROYAL SCOTTISH ACADEMY (RSA)

17 Waterloo Place, Edinburgh, EH1 3BG, Scotland
Tel: (44) 131 558 7097
Fax: (44) 131 557 6417
Email: info@royalscottishacademy.org
www: http://www.royalscottishacademy.org
Contact: Secretary

Founded in 1826, the Royal Scottish Academy (RSA), Scotland's foremost body of artists, has promoted the works of leading contemporary painters, sculptors, printmakers and architects. It also gives practical and financial help to young artists through scholarships as well as the annual Student's Exhibition.

The Alastair Salvesen Art Scholarship

Subjects: Painting in any medium.
Purpose: To encourage young painters who have already made the transition from college to a working environment.
Eligibility: Open to painters who have been trained at one of four Scottish colleges of art in Aberdeen, Dundee, Edinburgh or Glasgow and be currently living and working in Scotland.
Level of Study: Postgraduate
Type: Scholarship.
Value: Up to UK£10,000 depending on the plan submitted, and an exhibition that lasts approx. three weeks to take place in November or December in a gallery.
Length of Study: Three-five months.
Frequency: Annual.
Study Establishment: Any of the main art colleges.
Country of Study: Scotland.
No. of awards offered: One.
Application Procedure: Applicants must contact the RSA.
Closing Date: The end of December.
Funding: Private.
Contributor: The Alastair Salvesen Trust.
No. of awards given last year: One.

The John Kinross Memorial Fund Student Scholarships/ RSA

Subjects: Painting, sculpture, architecture or printmaking.
Purpose: To allow young artists from the established training centres in Scotland to spend time in Italy.
Eligibility: Open to students in final or postgraduate years of study at one of the Scottish colleges of art. The architecture scholarship is open to senior students at one of the six Scottish schools of architecture presenting work which would normally be related to the requirements of RIBA Part 1 or Part 2 Syllabus. Group work is not acceptable.
Level of Study: Postgraduate.
Type: Scholarship.
Value: Varies.
Length of Study: Three months.
Frequency: Annual.

Country of Study: Italy.
No. of awards offered: Varies, usually 10-15.
Closing Date: Late April.
Funding: Private.
Contributor: The Kinross Scholarship Fund which is administered by the RSA.
No. of awards given last year: 15.
No. of applicants last year: 80.

RSA Annual Student Competition

Subjects: Painting, sculpture, architecture or printmaking.
Eligibility: Candidates should be residents of Scotland. Painting, printmaking and sculpture students should be in their final or postgraduate years of study at one of the Scottish schools of architecture or one of the main Scottish colleges of art in Aberdeen, Dundee, Edinburgh or Glasgow. Applicants should submit one work. Architecture students should be in their final year and present work normally related to the requirements of the RIBA Part II syllabus.
Level of Study: Postgraduate.
Type: Competition.
Value: More than UK£6,000 worth of prizes and awards.
Frequency: Annual.
Study Establishment: All main colleges of art and architecture.
Country of Study: Scotland.
No. of awards offered: Varies.
Application Procedure: Applicants must submit applications via their college, which must be countersigned by their tutor.
Closing Date: February.
Funding: Commercial.
Contributor: The RSA.
No. of awards given last year: 15.
No. of applicants last year: 400.
Additional Information: The Academy also sponsors an annual exhibition of painting, sculpture, printmaking and architecture, with special awards for students. Entry forms are available in January. Various monetary awards are also made from May 2nd-July 5th.

Sir William Gillies Bequest-Hospitalfield Residencies

Subjects: Painting, sculpture, architecture or printmaking.
Purpose: To provide young professional artists who are Scottish or have studied in Scotland, with a period for personal development and the exploration of new directions.
Eligibility: Applicants should have completed a period of formal study in an area of the visual arts by at least one year, have continued to practise and exhibit and wish to continue to develop ideas and concepts which they regard as important.
Level of Study: Postgraduate.
Type: Residency.
Value: Accommodation, studio space and access to the private collection of Patrick Allan-Fraser.
Length of Study: One or three months.
Frequency: Annual.
Study Establishment: Hospitalfield House, Arbroath.
Country of Study: Scotland.
No. of awards offered: Usually three.
Application Procedure: Applicants must contact the RSA.
Closing Date: The end of November.
Funding: Private.
Contributor: The Bequest Fund administered by the RSA.

THE ROYAL SOCIETY

6 Carlton House Terrace, London, SW1Y 5AG, England
Tel: (44) 20 7451 2547
Fax: (44) 20 7930 2170
Email: ukresearch.appointments@royalsoc.ac.uk
www: http://www.royalsoc.ac.uk
Contact: Research Appointments Officer

The Royal Society is an independent academy promoting the natural and applied sciences. The Society has a dual role, as the United Kingdom Academy of Science acting nationally or internationally and as the provider of a broad range of services for the scientific community in the national interest, responsive to individual demand with selection by merit, not by field. The Royal Society supports over 300 research appointments, covering all disciplines and at all levels: research professorships, senior research fellowships, research fellowships, university research fellowships, Leverhulme Trust and Amersham fellowships for one year research sabbaticals and Industry Fellowships to enhance industry academia links.

Copus Public Understanding of Science Development Fund

Subjects: All areas of science.
Purpose: To encourage and support major new initiatives which aim to improve the public understanding of science and technology.
Eligibility: Applicants must be resident in the United Kingdom.
Level of Study: Unrestricted.
Type: Grant.
Value: Up to UK£20,000.
Frequency: Annual.
Study Establishment: Varies.
Country of Study: Other.
No. of awards offered: Varies
Application Procedure: Applicants must complete an application form. Further information is available on request. Requests must quote the name of the scheme or programme. If requests are made by email applicants must include their full name and postal address.
Funding: Government.
Contributor: OST.
No. of awards given last year: Seven.
No. of applicants last year: 34.
Additional Information: Further information is available on the website or by contacting Scott Kier on (44) 20 7451 2513.

Copus Public Understanding of Science Seed Fund

Subjects: All areas of science.
Purpose: To assist pump priming activities or initiatives directly concerned with the promotion of the public understanding of science at a local level.
Eligibility: Open to residents of the United Kingdom.
Level of Study: Unrestricted.
Type: Grant.
Value: Up to UK£3,000.
Frequency: Annual.
Study Establishment: Varies.
Country of Study: United Kingdom.
No. of awards offered: Varies.
Application Procedure: Applicants must complete an application form. Further information is available from the website or by contacting Natasha Martineau on (44) 20 7451 2579. Requests must quote the name of the scheme or programme. If requests are made by email applicants must include their full name and postal address.
Funding: Government.
Contributor: OST.
No. of awards given last year: 25.
No. of applicants last year: 68.
Additional Information: Further information is available on the website or by contacting Scott Kier on (44) 20 7451 2513.

Dorothy Hodgkin Fellowships

Subjects: Natural sciences including mathematics or engineering.
Purpose: To provide the first step into a research career for excellent young scientists and engineers.
Eligibility: Open to applicants under the age of 35 years with postdoctoral status and no more than four years of postdoctoral research experience. Applicants must either be currently employed in the United Kingdom or have been resident in the United Kingdom for a continuous period of at least three years, not including time spent in full-time education. Those already holding a substantive post in a European Union university are not eligible.
Level of Study: Postdoctorate.
Type: Fellowship.
Value: Salaries at research staff IIA/II scales.
Length of Study: Four years.
Frequency: Annual.

Study Establishment: Universities and Institutes of Higher Education.
Country of Study: United Kingdom.
No. of awards offered: Varies.
Application Procedure: Applicants must complete an official application. Further information and application forms are available from the website. If any problems occur applicants should contact the Research Appointments Department on (44) 20 7451 2542 or by email. Requests must quote the name of the scheme or programme. If requests are made by email applicants must include their full name and postal address.
Closing Date: Please contact the organisation for details.
Funding: Government, Commercial, Private.
Additional Information: Further information is available on request and on the website.

James Ellis Research Fellowship
Subjects: Quantum information processing.
Purpose: To assist research focused on the practical implementation of quantum computation rather than other possible applications in the field of quantum information processing.
Eligibility: Applicants must have a PhD or equivalent research experience and two-seven years of full-time postdoctoral experience. Career breaks such as maternity leave, European Union national service and voluntary service overseas can be discounted, but teaching experience or time spent in industry since the award of a PhD should be included in the total amount of postdoctoral experience. Part-time work will be counted pro-rata.
Level of Study: Postdoctorate.
Type: Fellowship.
Value: Salaries on the university lecturers' A or B scale for non clinical academic and related staff.
Length of Study: Five years in the first instance.
Frequency: Annual.
Study Establishment: Appropriate university departments.
Country of Study: United Kingdom.
No. of awards offered: Varies.
Application Procedure: Applicants must complete an official form. Further information and application forms are available from the website.
Closing Date: Early January.
Funding: Government.

Leverhulme Trust Senior Research Fellowships
Subjects: Natural sciences including mathematics or science.
Purpose: To enable senior scientists in academia to be relieved of all teaching and administration duties to undertake full-time research.
Eligibility: Open to senior scientists at the mid career stage who hold a permanent post in Institutes of Higher Education or universities in the United Kingdom.
Level of Study: Postdoctorate.
Type: Fellowship.
Value: The Fellow's employing institution will be reimbursed for full salary costs of a younger academic employed to take over the Fellow's teaching and administration duties for the fellowship period.
Length of Study: One academic term to one academic year.
Frequency: Annual.
Country of Study: United Kingdom.
No. of awards offered: Seven.
Application Procedure: Applicants must complete an official application. Further information and application forms are available from the website. Requests must quote the name of the scheme or programme. If requests are made by email applicants must include their full name and postal address.
Closing Date: December 6th.
Funding: Private.
Additional Information: Further information is available on request and on the website.

Olga Kennard Research Fellowship Scheme
Subjects: Crystallography or structural molecular biology.
Eligibility: Open to citizens of the European Union, Norway, Israel and Switzerland. Applicants must have at least three years of postdoctoral experience and be aged between 26-40 years.

Level of Study: Postdoctorate.
Type: Fellowship.
Value: Salary with London allowance where appropriate, together with annual research expenses, travel expenses and a contribution to baggage costs for overseas applicants.
Length of Study: Five years.
Frequency: As vacancies occur.
Study Establishment: Appropriate university departments.
Country of Study: United Kingdom.
No. of awards offered: One.
Application Procedure: Applicants must complete an official application. Further information and application forms are available from the website. Requests must quote the name of the scheme or programme. If requests are made by email applicants must include their full name and postal address.
Closing Date: There is no fixed deadline.
Additional Information: Further information is available on the website.

Paul Instrument Fund
Subjects: Instrument development for pure or applied physical science.
Purpose: To assist the design, construction and maintenance of novel, unusual or much improved types of physical instruments and apparatus needed for an investigation in pure or applied physical science.
Eligibility: Open to British subjects or persons domiciled or ordinarily resident in the United Kingdom. Applicants must be employed and working in the United Kingdom.
Level of Study: Postdoctorate, Research.
Type: Grant.
Value: Varies.
Frequency: Three times each year.
Country of Study: United Kingdom.
No. of awards offered: Varies.
Application Procedure: Application forms and details are available from the Royal Society.
Closing Date: January 15th, May 15th or September 15th.
Funding: Private.

Rink Research Fellowship Scheme
Subjects: Clinical science, particularly degenerative disorders or diseases of later life.
Eligibility: Open to citizens of the European Union who are either employed in the United Kingdom or have been resident in the United Kingdom for at least three consecutive years, not including time spent in full-time education. Applicants must be medically qualified with a PhD or MD, be aged between 26-40 years and have no more than seven years of research experience. Those who hold a substantive post in such a department or in a European Union university are not eligible.
Level of Study: Postdoctorate.
Type: Fellowship.
Value: Please visit the website or contact the organisation for details.
Length of Study: Five years.
Frequency: As vacancies occur.
Study Establishment: A department in a British university or a recognised clinical research establishment.
No. of awards offered: One.
Application Procedure: Applicants must apply for information, available on request. Requests must quote the name of the scheme or programme. If requests are made by email applicants must include their full name and postal address.
Closing Date: There is no fixed deadline.
Funding: Private.
Additional Information: Further information is available on request or on the website.

Royal Society Conference Grants
Subjects: Natural and applied sciences or technology.
Purpose: To assist with expenses in participating at a conference overseas.

Eligibility: Open to non government scientists of PhD status who are normally resident in the United Kingdom. Applicants must be presenting their own paper or poster at a meeting or chairing a session. Please refer to the website for further details.
Level of Study: Postdoctorate.
Type: Grant.
Value: Varies.
Length of Study: Varies.
Frequency: Four times per year.
Country of Study: Outside the UK.
No. of awards offered: Varies.
Application Procedure: Applicants must complete an official application. Further information and forms are available from the website and on request from Sandra Goodall by telephoning (44) 20 7451 2540 or emailing sandra.goodall@royalsoc.ac.uk. Requests must quote the name of the scheme or programme.
Closing Date: March 1st, June 1st, October 1st and December 1st.
Funding: Government.

Royal Society History of Science Meetings

Subjects: The history of science.
Purpose: To support the funding of meetings.
Eligibility: Open to scientific bodies or learned societies concerned with the history of science.
Level of Study: Graduate, Postdoctorate, Postgraduate.
Type: Grant.
Value: Up to UK£5,000.
Frequency: Annual.
Country of Study: United Kingdom.
No. of awards offered: Varies.
Application Procedure: Applicants must contact Karen Peters on (44) 20 7451 2595 or by email on karen.peters@royalsoc.ac.uk. Information is also available on the website. Requests must quote the name of the scheme or programme. If requests are made by email applicants must include their full name and postal address.
Closing Date: August 15th.
Funding: Government.
No. of awards given last year: One.

Royal Society Industry Fellowships Scheme

Subjects: All areas of natural science.
Purpose: To provide opportunities for industrial scientists and engineers to carry out research or course development in a university or polytechnic. The scheme also provides similar opportunities for corresponding academic employees to undertake a project in industry.
Eligibility: Open to applicants of any nationality at the mid career stage who hold a PhD or equivalent. Applicants must hold either a substantive academic post in an Institute of Higher Education in the United Kingdom or be employed as a scientist, mathematician or engineer in an industry in the United Kingdom.
Level of Study: Postgraduate.
Type: Fellowship.
Value: The Fellow's employer will be reimbursed for the salary only.
Length of Study: Six months to two years. Part-time appointments are permitted.
Frequency: Twice a year.
Country of Study: United Kingdom.
No. of awards offered: Varies, approx. eight.
Application Procedure: Applicants must complete an official application. Further information and application forms are available from the website.
Closing Date: December or June.
Funding: Private, Commercial, Government.
Additional Information: Further information is available on request and from the website.

Royal Society Research Grants Scheme

Subjects: Any scientific or technological discipline within the remit of the Royal Society. Natural sciences including mathematics, engineering, agricultural and medical research, scientific aspects of archaeology, geography, experimental psychology and the history of science.

Purpose: To allow the purchase of specialised equipment or essential consumable materials for use in research projects of 'timeliness and promise'. The scheme aims to support those new into research, or researchers moving into a new field of research. The scheme also aims to meet the requests for support to enable a new facet of research or new directions in an existing research programme and to provide support for research in the history of science.
Eligibility: Open to academic workers in United Kingdom universities, Institutes of Higher Education and research institutions. Further information is available on request or on the website.
Level of Study: Postdoctorate, Research.
Type: Grant.
Value: Up to UK£10,000.
Frequency: Twice a year.
Country of Study: United Kingdom.
No. of awards offered: Varies.
Application Procedure: Applicants must complete an official application. Further information and application forms are available on the website or by contacting Miss Susan Moss on (44) 20 7451 2539, or by email on susan.moss@royalsoc.ac.uk. Applications cannot be accepted if sent by fax or email.
Closing Date: April 1st and November 1st.
Funding: Private.
Contributor: The public.
No. of awards given last year: 341.
No. of applicants last year: 899.

Royal Society University Research Fellowships

Subjects: Science including agriculture, medicine, mathematics, engineering or technology.
Purpose: To provide support for young, high quality research workers to work in university departments, possibly leading to a permanent post.
Eligibility: Please contact the organisation or visit the website for details.
Level of Study: Postdoctorate.
Type: Fellowship.
Value: Salaries on the university lecturers' A or B scale for non clinical academic and related staff.
Length of Study: Five years in the first instance, possibly renewable in two instalments up to a maximum of 10 years.
Frequency: Annual.
Study Establishment: Appropriate university departments.
Country of Study: United Kingdom.
No. of awards offered: Varies.
Application Procedure: Applicants must complete an official application form. Further information and application forms are available from the website.
Closing Date: Early January.
Funding: Government.
No. of awards given last year: 40.
No. of applicants last year: 300.
Additional Information: Fellowships must be held at a university in the United Kingdom.

The Royal Society-Wolfson Foundation Laboratory Refurbishment Scheme

Subjects: The natural sciences.
Purpose: To support the physical infrastructure in universities for basic research in a specific field which is chosen each year.
Eligibility: Open to scientists who hold a substantive post in a United Kingdom university.
Level of Study: Postdoctorate, Research.
Type: Grant.
Value: Varies.
Frequency: Annual.
Country of Study: United Kingdom.
No. of awards offered: Approx. 20.
Application Procedure: Applicants must submit 15 copies of the complete application. Further information is available on request or from the website. Applications cannot be accepted if sent by fax. Requests must quote the name of the scheme or programme.
Closing Date: Please contact the organisation.

Funding: Private.
Contributor: The Wolfson Foundation.
No. of awards given last year: 21.
No. of applicants last year: 48.
Additional Information: Applications and all enquiries should be addressed to Elaine Potter on (44) 20 7451 2541 or by email to elaine.potter@royalsoc.ac.uk. Enquiries made by email are preferred. Further information is available on request or on the website.

ROYAL SOCIETY FOR THE ENCOURAGEMENT OF ARTS, MANUFACTURERS AND COMMERCE (RSA)

8 John Adam Street, London, England
Tel: (44) 20 7930 5115
Fax: (44) 20 7839 5805
Email: lizzie.tulip@rsa.org.uk
www: http://rsa-afa.org.uk
Contact: Project Co-ordinator

The Royal Society for the Encouragement of Arts, Manufactures and Commerce (RSA), is an instrument of change, working to create a civilised society based on a sustainable economy. It is a charity which uses its independence and the resources of its international fellowship to stimulate discussion, develop ideas and encourage action. Its main fields of interest today are business and industry, design and technology, education, the arts and the environment.

RSA Art for Architecture

Subjects: Art and architecture.
Purpose: To encourage collaboration between design professionals, by giving grants to support the artists places in design teams at the early stage of the design process.
Eligibility: Open to visual artists who are to be employed at the earliest stage of a building project as part of the design team. The award is restricted to projects within the British Isles, but is also open to individuals of any nationality if attached to a project.
Type: Varies.
Value: UK£2,000-15,000 Awards are in the form of payment towards the design fees of artists appointed.
Frequency: Three times each year.
Country of Study: United Kingdom.
No. of awards offered: Two.
Application Procedure: Applicants must complete an application form. Other documentation such as slides, plans and letters of support should be submitted with all applications to Lizzie Tulip.
Closing Date: See the website at www.rsa-afa.org.uk.
Funding: Commercial, Government.
Contributor: The Commission for Architecture and the Built Environment (CABE).
No. of awards given last year: 8.
No. of applicants last year: 50.
Additional Information: There is also a Publication Award, intended to help fund publications that focus on issues and practice relating to collaboration.

RSA Design Directions

Subjects: A range of design projects-many encouraging cross-disciplinary working-that urge students to consider the role of design within a broad societal context.
Purpose: The awards are given as prizes to winning students in the scheme and can be used for research, travel, funding for further study, funding for internships or other purposes agreed with the RSA.
Eligibility: Open to students within the EU and studying at further or higher education level.
Level of Study: Graduate, Postgraduate.
Type: Competition.
Value: These vary from amounts beginning at UK£500 up to UK£10,000.
Length of Study: Varies.
Frequency: Annual.

Study Establishment: An appropriate institution.
Country of Study: European Union.
No. of awards offered: Varies.
Application Procedure: Applicants must visit the website for project briefs and details for application.
Closing Date: Varies according to project-applicants should check website (www.rsa-design.net).
Funding: Commercial, Government, Private.
Contributor: Commercial organisations.
No. of awards given last year: 72.
No. of applicants last year: 2,200 (Competition Entrants).
Additional Information: RSA design directions does not offer grants; it is an annual competition open to design students.

ROYAL SOCIETY OF CANADA

283 Sparks Street, Ottawa, ON, K1R 7XG, Canada
Tel: (1) 613 991 6990
Fax: (1) 613 991 6996
Email: adminrsc@rsc.ca
www: http://www.rsc.ca
Contact: Dr Andrew D Miall, FRSC Programme Chair

The primary objective of the Royal Society of Canada is to promote learning and research in the arts and sciences. It draws on the breadth of knowledge and expertise of its members from all disciplines to recognise and honour distinguished accomplishments, to advise on the state of scholarship and culture across the country, and to inform the public of newsworthy social, scientific and ethical questions of the day.

CCMS (Committee on the Challenges of Modern Society) Fellowships

Subjects: Subjects related to the natural or social environment.
Purpose: To allow Fellows to contribute to the work of the CCMS pilot studies. The purpose of these studies is to suggest, on the basis of existing knowledge, solutions to problems relating to the natural and social environment. To achieve this objective, the programme provides support to Fellows who wish to conduct research under the guidance of pilot study directors or to work as members of the CCMS pilot study teams or both.
Eligibility: Open to citizens of NATO countries who have demonstrated research interest or have experience in a subject area related to one of the ongoing CCMS pilot studies, and willingness to work under the guidance of the respective pilot study director. Candidates must have a suitable background which is acceptable to the pilot study director, a connection with a research unit or government agency having an active interest in the subject with a view to ensuring the useful application of the experience gained to the needs of the home country, and a good working knowledge of the language of the CCMS pilot study director with whom the Fellow will be working, or English or French, if either of them is sufficient and mutually convenient.
Level of Study: Postdoctorate, Professional development.
Type: Fellowship.
Frequency: Annual.
Country of Study: Any country.
No. of awards offered: Varies.
Application Procedure: Applicants must complete an application form. Application forms and a list of pilot studies are available on request. Consultation with the pilot study director prior to the preparation of the application is recommended.
Closing Date: December 31st.
Contributor: NATO.

THE ROYAL SOCIETY OF CHEMISTRY

Burlington House Piccadilly, London, W1J 0BA, England
Tel: (44) 20 7437 8656
Fax: (44) 20 7734 1227
Email: langers@rsc.org
www: http://www.rsc.org
Contact: Mr S S Langer

The Royal Society of Chemistry is the learned society for chemistry and the professional body for chemists in the United Kingdom with 46,000 members worldwide. The society is a major publisher of chemical information, supports the teaching of chemistry at all levels, organises hundreds of chemical meetings a year and is a leader in communicating science to the public. It is now the United Kingdom National Adhering Organisation (NAO) to the International Union of Pure and Applied Chemistry (IUPAC).

Corday-Morgan Memorial Fund

Subjects: Chemistry.
Purpose: To allow members of any established chemical society or institute in the Commonwealth to visit chemical establishments in another Commonwealth country.
Eligibility: Open to citizens of, and those domiciled in, any Commonwealth country.
Level of Study: Professional development.
Type: Grant.
Value: Up to UK£500. The grants will complement, where appropriate, those for visits to developing countries available from the International Committee's fund, and funding would cover the additional travel costs involved, together with appropriate subsistence. Applicants should also see the visits to developing countries awards.
Frequency: Dependent on funds available.
Country of Study: Any country.
No. of awards offered: Approx. 10.
Application Procedure: Applicants must submit applications on the official form and will normally be considered within one month of receipt.
Closing Date: Applications are accepted at any time.
No. of awards given last year: Six.
No. of applicants last year: Eight.
Additional Information: Applicants must be travelling to another country (not necessarily in the Commonwealth) and would normally stop en route to visit a third country which must be in the Commonwealth.

Hickinbottom/Briggs Fellowship

Subjects: Organic chemistry.
Purpose: To assist research.
Eligibility: Open to applicants domiciled in the United Kingdom or Republic of Ireland. Candidates must already hold a PhD or equivalent in chemistry and be not more than 36 years of age on October 31st.
Level of Study: Postdoctorate.
Type: Fellowship.
Value: Approx. UK£17,000.
Length of Study: Three years.
Frequency: Dependent on funds available.
Study Establishment: A British or Irish university or college.
Country of Study: Other.
No. of awards offered: One.
Application Procedure: Applicants must apply by application forms or be nominated.
Closing Date: June 1st.
No. of awards given last year: One.

J W T Jones Travelling Fellowship

Subjects: Chemistry.
Purpose: To promote international co-operation, to enable chemists to carry out short-term studies in well established scientific centres abroad and to learn and use techniques not accessible to them in their own country.
Eligibility: Open to members of the Royal Society of Chemistry who hold at least a Masters or PhD degree in chemistry or a related subject and are already actively engaged in research. Candidates must produce evidence that the theoretical and practical knowledge or training to be acquired in the foreign laboratory will be beneficial to their scientific development and must also return to their country of origin upon termination of the fellowship.
Level of Study: Professional development.
Type: Fellowship.

Value: A lump sum of up to UK£5,000, designed to cover part or all of an economy class air or rail ticket and a subsistence allowance. It is expected that the institution of origin and/or the host institution will contribute to defray any remaining expenses incurred by the fellowship holder.
Length of Study: Normally one-three months.
Frequency: Four times per year.
Country of Study: Any country.
No. of awards offered: Approx. six.
Application Procedure: Applicants must apply for application forms, together with full details, from the International Affairs Officer.
Closing Date: January 1st, April 1st, July 1st or October 1st.
No. of awards given last year: Four.
No. of applicants last year: Five.
Additional Information: Fellowships will not be awarded to attend scientific meetings. Applications will be considered by a Fellowship Committee and the holder will be required to submit a formal report on the work accomplished.

Royal Society of Chemistry Journals Grants for International Authors

Subjects: Chemistry.
Purpose: To allow international authors to visit other countries in order to collaborate in research, exchange research ideas and results, and to give or receive special expertise and training.
Eligibility: Open to anyone with a recent publication in any of the Society's journals. Those from the United Kingdom or Republic of Ireland are excluded.
Level of Study: Professional development.
Type: Grant.
Value: A lump sum of up to UK£2,000, designed to cover part or all of an economy class air or rail ticket and a subsistence allowance. It is expected that the institution of origin and/or the host institution will contribute to defray any remaining expenses incurred by the grant holder.
Length of Study: Normally one-three months.
Frequency: Four times per year.
Country of Study: Any country.
No. of awards offered: 100.
Application Procedure: Applicants must apply for application forms, together with full details, from the International Affairs Officer.
Closing Date: January 1st, April 1st, July 1st or October 1st.
No. of awards given last year: 83.
No. of applicants last year: 107.

Royal Society of Chemistry Research Fund

Subjects: Chemistry and chemical education.
Purpose: To provide financial support to those working in less affluent institutions.
Eligibility: Open to members of the Society.
Level of Study: Professional development.
Type: Grant.
Value: Up to UK£1,200 for the purchase of chemicals, equipment or for running expenses of research.
Length of Study: One year.
Frequency: Annual.
Country of Study: Any country.
No. of awards offered: 20-30.
Closing Date: October 31st.
No. of awards given last year: 30.
No. of applicants last year: 50.
Additional Information: Funds are limited, so preference will be given to those working in less well-endowed institutions. The Selection Committee is especially anxious to see inventive applications of a 'pump priming' nature. Members in developing countries should note particularly that additional funds have been made available by the Society's International Committee to provide grants for successful applicants from such countries. Preference will be given to those able to cite collaborative research projects with United Kingdom institutions.

Royal Society of Chemistry Visits to Developing Countries

Subjects: Chemistry.

Purpose: To promote international co-operation, specifically, to enable chemists to carry out short-term studies in well established scientific centres abroad and to learn and use techniques not accessible to them in their own country.

Eligibility: Open to members of the Society.

Level of Study: Professional development.

Type: Grant.

Value: Up to UK£500. The grants will complement, where appropriate, those for visits to Commonwealth countries, and funding would cover the additional travel costs involved, together with appropriate subsistence. Applicants should also see the Corday-Morgan Memorial Fund.

Frequency: Dependent on funds available.

Country of Study: Any country.

No. of awards offered: Approx. 10.

Application Procedure: Applicants must submit applications on the official form and will normally be considered within one month of receipt.

Closing Date: Applications are accepted at any time.

Additional Information: Applicants must be travelling to another country and would normally stop en route to visit a third country. This must be a developing country.

THE ROYAL SOCIETY OF EDINBURGH (RSE)

22-26 George Street, Edinburgh, Scotland
Tel: (44) 131 240 5000
Fax: (44) 131 240 5024
Email: resfells@royalsoced.org.uk
www: http://www.ma.hw.ac.uk/RSE
Contact: Research Awards Manager

The Royal Society of Edinburgh (RSE) is Scotland's National Academy. It is an independent body, founded in 1783 by Royal Charter for the Advancement of Learning and Useful Knowledge and governed by an elected council of Fellows.

Auber Bequest

Subjects: All subjects.

Purpose: To provide assistance for the furtherance of academic research.

Eligibility: Open to naturalised British citizens or individuals wishing to acquire British nationality who are over 60 years of age, resident in Scotland or England and are bona fide scholars engaged in academic, but not industrial, research. Applicants should not have been British nationals at birth, nor held dual British nationality, and must have since acquired British nationality.

Level of Study: Unrestricted.

Value: Varies, not normally exceeding UK£3,000.

Length of Study: Up to two years.

Frequency: Every two years.

Country of Study: Other.

No. of awards offered: Varies.

Application Procedure: Applicants must complete an application form, available from the Research Awards Manager.

Closing Date: October 31st.

Funding: Private.

Contributor: The Auber Bequest.

No. of awards given last year: Two.

No. of applicants last year: Four.

BP/RSE Research Fellowships

Subjects: Mechanical engineering, chemical engineering, control engineering, solid state sciences, information technology, non biological chemistry and geological sciences.

Purpose: To support independent research in specific fields.

Eligibility: Open to persons of all nationalities who have a PhD or equivalent qualification. Applicants should be aged under 35 on the date of appointment and must show they have a capacity for inno-

vative research and a substantial volume of published work relevant to their proposed field of study.

Level of Study: Postdoctorate.

Type: Fellowship.

Value: Salaries within the scales RGIA-2 for research and analogous staff in Institutes of Higher Education with annual increments and superannuation benefits. Financial support towards expenses involved in carrying out the research is available, including a start up grant of UK£1,000 in the first year only and a further allowance of up to UK£1,500 for travel and subsistence each year. Up to UK£2,500 is also available by competitive bid from the support fund pool each year.

Length of Study: Up to three years.

Frequency: Annual.

Study Establishment: Any Institute of Higher Education approved for the purpose by the Council of the Society.

Country of Study: Scotland.

No. of awards offered: One.

Application Procedure: Applicants must complete an application form, available from the Research Fellowships Secretary. Candidates must negotiate directly with the relevant head of department of the proposed host institution.

Closing Date: Mid March.

Funding: Private.

Contributor: British Petroleum (BP).

No. of awards given last year: One.

No. of applicants last year: 26.

Additional Information: Fellows will be expected to devote their full time to research and will not be allowed to hold other paid appointments without the express permission of the Council of the RSE.

CRF (Caledonian Research Foundation)/RSE European Visiting Research Fellowships

Subjects: Archaeology, art and architecture, economics and economic history, geography, history, jurisprudence, linguistics, literature and philology, philosophy or religious studies.

Purpose: To create a two way flow of visiting scholars in arts and letters between Scotland and continental Europe.

Eligibility: Open to members of the academic staff of a Scottish Institute of Higher Education or equivalent continental European institution. Applicants must be aged 60 or under on the date of the appointment, which is variable, but must be within 16 months of date of award. Applicants from continental Europe must be nominated by members of staff from a Scottish Institute of Higher Education.

Level of Study: Professional development.

Type: Fellowship.

Value: Up to UK£6,000 for visits of six months which is reduced prorata for shorter visits, to cover actual costs of travel, subsistence and relevant study costs.

Length of Study: Up to six months.

Frequency: Annual.

Study Establishment: A Scottish Institute of Higher Education or a recognised Institute of Higher Education in a continental European country.

Country of Study: Other.

No. of awards offered: Eight.

Application Procedure: Applicants must complete an application form, available from the Research Fellowships Secretary in August and September each year.

Closing Date: Early November.

Funding: Private.

Contributor: The CRF.

No. of awards given last year: Six.

No. of applicants last year: 10.

Additional Information: Successful applicants will be required to submit a report within two months of the end of the visit.

CRF (Caledonian Research Foundation)/RSE Personal Research Fellowships

Subjects: Biological, biochemical, physical or clinical sciences.

Purpose: To aid independent research.

Eligibility: Open to students of all nationalities who have a PhD and are aged 32 or under on the date of appointment, or who have two-six years of postdoctoral experience.

Level of Study: Postdoctorate.
Type: Fellowship.
Value: A salary according to age, qualifications and experience. Salaries are within the scales RGIA-2 for research staff in Institutes of Higher Education. Financial support towards expenses involved in carrying out the research is available, including a start up grant of UK£1,000 in the first year only. Fellows receive UK£1,000 for travel and subsistence each year.
Length of Study: Up to three years.
Frequency: Annual.
Study Establishment: Any Institute of Higher Education.
Country of Study: Scotland.
No. of awards offered: Varies.
Application Procedure: Applicants must complete an application form, available from the CRF. Candidates must negotiate with the relevant Head of Department of the proposed host institution.
Closing Date: Mid March.
Funding: Private.
Contributor: The CRF.
No. of awards given last year: Two.
No. of applicants last year: 20.
Additional Information: The fellowships are administered by the Caledonian Research Foundation (CRF). Fellows will be expected to devote their full time to research and will not be allowed to hold other paid appointments without the express permission of the Council of the RSE.

For further information contact:

The CRF (Caledonian Research Foundation), 39 Castle Street, Edinburgh, EH2 3BH, Scotland
Contact: Grants Management Officer

CRF (Caledonian Research Foundation)/RSE Support Research Fellowship

Subjects: Biology, biochemical, physical and clinical sciences related to medicine.
Purpose: To enable Fellows to take study leave, either in their own institution or elsewhere, whilst remaining in continuous employment with their present employer.
Eligibility: Open to existing members of academic staff aged 40 or under on date of appointment and employed on the lecturer scale, who have held a permanent appointment for at least five years in any Scottish Institute of Higher Education.
Level of Study: Professional development.
Type: Fellowship.
Value: The actual cost for non clinical staff will be reimbursed according to the lecturer A scale (maximum RGI-3) with the placement determined by the employer. If clinically qualified, the salary will be within clinical senior lecturer grade. A provision of UK£1,000 is made for a start up grant. There is also a grant of UK£1,000 for travel and subsistence.
Length of Study: One year.
Frequency: Annual.
Study Establishment: Any Institute of Higher Education.
Country of Study: Scotland.
No. of awards offered: One.
Application Procedure: Applicants must complete an application form, available from the CRF.
Closing Date: Mid March.
Funding: Private.
Contributor: The CRF.
No. of awards given last year: One.
No. of applicants last year: Four.

For further information contact:

The CRF (Caledonian Research Foundation), 39 Castle Street, Edinburgh, EH2 3BH, Scotland
Contact: Grants Management Officer

Henry Dryerre Scholarship

Subjects: Medical or veterinary physiology.
Purpose: To support postgraduate research.

Eligibility: Open to European citizens holding a First Class (Honours) Degree from a Scottish university.
Level of Study: Postgraduate.
Type: Scholarship.
Value: Fees, research costs and travel expenses up to UK£850 per year and a maintenance grant of UK£5,956 if living away from home.
Length of Study: Three years full-time research.
Frequency: Other..
Study Establishment: A Scottish institution.
Country of Study: Scotland.
No. of awards offered: One.
Application Procedure: Applicants must be nominated by a professor, reader or lecturer in a Scottish university.
Closing Date: March 2005.
Funding: Private.
No. of awards given last year: One.
No. of applicants last year: One.
Additional Information: The scholarships are administered by the Carnegie Trust for the Universities of Scotland.

For further information contact:

Carnegie Trust for the Universities of Scotland, Cameron House, Abbey Park Place, Dunfermline, Fife KY12 7PZ, Scotland
Tel: (44) 1383 622148
Fax: (44) 1383 622149
Email: carnegie.trust@ed.ac.uk
Contact: Miss J Gray

John Moyes Lessells Scholarships

Subjects: All forms of engineering.
Purpose: To enable well qualified engineering graduates of Scottish Institutes of Higher Education to study some aspect of their profession overseas.
Eligibility: Applicants must be graduates of a Scottish Institute of Higher Education.
Level of Study: Postgraduate, Predoctorate, Professional development.
Type: Scholarship.
Value: Normally up to UK£15,000 per year. Additional research or travel expenditure may be sanctioned.
Length of Study: Initially for one year but shorter periods or extension for a second year may be considered. Acceptance of a scholarship implies a willingness to spend at least two years in the United Kingdom following the period of tenure.
Frequency: Annual.
Country of Study: Other.
No. of awards offered: Varies.
Application Procedure: Applicants must complete an application form, available from the Research Awards Manager or the RSE website.
Closing Date: February 15th.
Funding: Private.
No. of awards given last year: Five.
No. of applicants last year: Seven.

Royal Society of Edinburgh Wellcome Research Workshops

Subjects: Biomedical science, veterinary science, history of medicine.
Purpose: To bring together research staff, academic staff and clinicians from a wide spectrum of backgrounds and levels to discuss research topics of common concern. Attendance will be by invitation of the organiser.
Eligibility: Open to academic research or clinical staff in Scottish Higher Education or Research Institutes. Joint applications welcome.
Level of Study: Doctorate, Postdoctorate, Postgraduate, Professional development, Research.
Type: Other.
Value: Up to UK£2,000 per workshop.
Frequency: Annual.
Study Establishment: In the Society's rooms or at a suitable research centre.
Country of Study: Scotland.

No. of awards offered: 3.
Closing Date: End of April.
Funding: Private.
Contributor: The Wellcome Trust.
No. of awards given last year: 3.
No. of applicants last year: 5.
Additional Information: The workshops, which may be specialist or multidisciplinary, are organised by the applicant and are restricted to a maximum of 40 participants, including five speakers. The workshops are advertised annually. They are sponsored by the Wellcome Trust.

For further information contact:

22-24 George Street, Edinburgh, EH2 2PQ, Scotland
Tel: (44) 131 225 6057
Fax: (44) 131 220 6889
Contact: Research Fellowships Secretary

Scottish Executive / RSE Support Research Fellowships

Subjects: All subjects. The fellowships are awarded in fields likely to enhance the development of industry and encourage better uses of resources in Scotland.
Purpose: To enable support Fellows to take study leave, either in their own institution or elsewhere, whilst remaining in continuous employment with their present employer.
Eligibility: Candidates must be existing members of staff who have held a permanent appointment for not less than five years in any Institution of Higher Education in Scotland. Applicants should be aged under 40 on the date of appointment (January 1st) and employed on the lecturer grade or equivalent.
Level of Study: Professional development.
Type: Fellowship.
Value: The actual cost of replacement staff will be reimbursed according to the Lecturer A scale (maximum RGI-3) with the placement determined by the employer. Superannuation costs and employer's National Insurance contributions will also be reimbursed.
Length of Study: Up to one year of full-time research.
Frequency: Annual.
Study Establishment: Any Institute of Higher Education, research institution or industrial laboratory approved for the purpose by the Council of the Society.
Country of Study: Scotland.
No. of awards offered: Four.
Application Procedure: Applicants must complete an application form, available from the Research Fellowships Secretary. Applicants must negotiate directly with the proposed host institution.
Closing Date: Mid March.
Funding: Government.
Contributor: The Scottish Executive.
No. of awards given last year: Three.
No. of applicants last year: Approx. 15.
Additional Information: Further information is available on request or on the website.

Scottish Executive Personal Research Fellowships

Subjects: All subjects. The fellowships are awarded in fields likely to enhance the development of industry and encourage better uses of resources in Scotland.
Purpose: To encourage independent research in any discipline.
Eligibility: Open to persons of all nationalities who have a PhD or equivalent qualification. Applicants must be aged 32 or under on the date of appointment (October 1st) or have between two-six years of postdoctoral experience. They must also show they have a capacity for innovative research and have a substantial volume of published work relevant to their proposed field of study.
Level of Study: Postdoctorate.
Type: Fellowship.
Value: Annual stipends are within the scales RGIA-2 for research and analogous staff in Institutes of Higher Education with annual increments and superannuation benefits. Expenses of up to UK£7,000 in year one, UK£6,000 in years two and three for travel and attendance at meetings or incidentals may be reimbursed. No support payments are available to the institution but Fellows may seek support for their research from other sources.

Length of Study: Up to three years full-time research.
Frequency: Annual.
Study Establishment: Any Institute of Higher Education, research institution or industrial laboratory approved for the purpose by the Council of the Society.
Country of Study: Scotland.
No. of awards offered: Four.
Application Procedure: Applicants must complete an application form, available from the Research Fellowships Secretary. Applicants should negotiate directly with the proposed host institution.
Closing Date: Mid March.
Funding: Government.
Contributor: The Scottish Executive.
No. of awards given last year: Four.
No. of applicants last year: Approx. 50.
Additional Information: Fellows may not hold other paid appointments without the express permission of the Council, but teaching or seminar work appropriate to their special knowledge may be acceptable.

THE ROYAL SOCIETY OF MEDICINE (RSM)

1 Wimpole Street, London, W1M 8AE, England
Tel: (44) 20 7290 2900
Fax: (44) 20 7290 2909
Email: anne-marie.fisker@roysocmed.ac.uk
www: http://www.roysocmed.ac.uk
Contact: Ms Anne-Marie Fisker, Manager

The Royal Society of Medicine (RSM) provides academic services and club facilities for its members as well as publishing a monthly journal and a quarterly bulletin, and providing over 300 educational conferences and meetings per year.

Colyer Prize

Subjects: Odontology.
Purpose: To reward the best original work in dental science completed during the previous five years.
Eligibility: Open to dental surgeons educated at a United Kingdom dental school who have not been qualified for more than 10 years.
Level of Study: Postdoctorate.
Type: Prize.
Value: Varies, at least UK£100.
Frequency: Every three years.
Country of Study: United Kingdom.
No. of awards offered: One.
Application Procedure: Further details are available from the Academic Registrar at the RSM.
Closing Date: March 31st.
No. of applicants last year: One.

John of Arderne Medal

Subjects: Coloproctology.
Purpose: To award the presenter of the best paper presented at the short papers meeting of the section of coloproctology. Applicants have to submit an abstract for presentation at the meeting.
Eligibility: Open to applicants of any nationality.
Level of Study: Professional development.
Type: Award.
Value: Approx. UK£500.
Frequency: Annual.
Study Establishment: Varies.
Country of Study: Any country.
No. of awards offered: One.
Application Procedure: Further details are available from the RSM administrator.
Closing Date: September and December.
No. of awards given last year: One.
No. of applicants last year: 80.

Karl Storz Travelling Scholarship

Subjects: Laryngology and rhinology.
Purpose: To assist with the cost of travel to overseas centres.
Eligibility: Open to senior registrars or consultants of not more than two years standing, who must be members of the section of laryngology and rhinology of the RSM.
Level of Study: Postdoctorate.
Type: Scholarship.
Value: UK£1,000.
Frequency: Annual.
Country of Study: Any country.
No. of awards offered: One.
Application Procedure: Applicants must submit a paper to the RSM section of laryngology and rhinology. Further details are available from the RSM administrator.
Closing Date: 27 February 2004.
Funding: Commercial.
Contributor: Karl Storz Endoscopy Limited.
No. of awards given last year: One.
No. of applicants last year: 25.
Additional Information: The recipient will be required to submit a brief report on the visit within three months of his or her return.

Medical Insurance Agency Prize

Subjects: Surgery.
Purpose: To enable the recipient to travel to a recognised institution to further his or her knowledge of surgery, or to attend an overseas conference in the speciality. To enable the recipient to attend the annual 'Out-of-Town' meeting of the Section of Surgery. The use of the fund to attend an alternative conference is permitted by agreement of council.
Eligibility: Open to surgeons in training, holding the post up to the grade of registrar or senior registrar.
Level of Study: Professional development.
Type: Prize.
Value: UK£500 (Varies).
Frequency: Annual.
Study Establishment: A recognised institution in the United Kingdom or overseas.
Country of Study: Any country.
No. of awards offered: One.
Application Procedure: Further details are available from the RSM administrator. Abstracts are submitted & selected papers are presented at February meeting. Papers should be laboratory based research papers.
Additional Information: The recipient will be required to submit a brief report on the visit within three months of his or her return.

For further information contact:

Section of Surgery Hon. Sec. - avail from administrator.

Mental Health Foundation Essay Prize

Subjects: Psychiatry.
Purpose: To award an essay.
Eligibility: Open to candidates practising medicine in the United Kingdom or the Republic of Ireland who are in training at any grade from senior house officer to senior registrar or equivalent. Applicants need not be members of RSM.
Level of Study: Unrestricted.
Type: Prize.
Value: Varies, approx. UK£500-£250 depending on available finance. It also includes a subscription to RSM if funds are available.
Frequency: Annual.
Country of Study: United Kingdom.
No. of awards offered: Two.
Application Procedure: Essays should be submitted in triplicate to the RSM section of psychiatry.
Closing Date: 5th January.
No. of applicants last year: One.
Additional Information: The subject is chosen by the Council. Essays should be approx. 5,000 words in length.

Nichols Fellowship

Subjects: Obstetrics and gynaecology.
Purpose: To encourage research to advance knowledge in the field.
Eligibility: Open to suitably qualified United Kingdom citizens.
Level of Study: Postdoctorate.
Type: Fellowship.
Value: UK£500 per year for two years, the second year being at the discretion of the Section Council.
Length of Study: Two years.
Frequency: Every three years.
Country of Study: Any country.
No. of awards offered: One.
Application Procedure: Applicants must apply to the academic administrator at the RSM.

Norman Gamble Fund and Research Prize

Subjects: Otology.
Purpose: To support specific research projects.
Eligibility: Open to British nationals.
Level of Study: Unrestricted.
Type: Prize.
Value: UK£100 for the research prize and UK£1,500 for the grant in aid. Awards alternate every two years.
Frequency: Other.
Country of Study: Any country.
No. of awards offered: One.
Application Procedure: Further details are available from the RSM administrator.
Closing Date: December 5th 2003.
Funding: Private.
No. of awards given last year: 1.
No. of applicants last year: 4.

Norman Tanner Medal and Prize (1st Prize) Glaxo Travelling Fellowship (2nd Prize)

Subjects: Surgery.
Purpose: To enable the recipient to travel to a recognised institution to further his or her knowledge of surgery, or to attend an overseas conference in the speciality. To enable the recipient to attend the annual 'Out-of-Town Meeting' of the section of Surgery. The use of the fund to attend an alternative conference is permitted by agreement of council.
Eligibility: Open to Surgeons in training of any nationality.
Level of Study: Professional development.
Type: Travel grant.
Value: UK£500 (1st Prize) UK£500 (2nd Prize).
Frequency: Annual.
Country of Study: Any country.
No. of awards offered: Two.
Application Procedure: Abstracts are submitted & selected papers are presented at the December meeting. Papers should be clinically orientated. Further details are available from the Academic Administrator at the RSM.
Closing Date: Early October.
Additional Information: The recipient will be required to submit a brief report on the visit within three months of his or her return.

For further information contact:

Section of Surgery Honorary Secretary - avail from administrator.

Ophthalmology Travelling Fellowship

Subjects: Ophthalmology.
Purpose: To enable British ophthalmologists to travel abroad with the intention of furthering the study or advancement of ophthalmology, or to enable foreign ophthalmologists to visit the United Kingdom for the same purpose.
Eligibility: Open to ophthalmologists in the British Isles of any nationality who have not attained an official consultant appointment, nor undertaken professional clinical work or equivalent responsibility for any substantial period before or during the execution of original work.
Level of Study: Professional development.
Type: Fellowship.
Value: UK£500-2,000.

Frequency: Twice a year.
Study Establishment: Varies.
Country of Study: Any country.
No. of awards offered: Varies.
Application Procedure: Applicants must apply to the academic administrator at RSM.
Closing Date: Entries are evaluated in December and May.
No. of awards given last year: Four.
No. of applicants last year: Six.

Royal Society of Medicine Travelling Fellowship
Subjects: Urology.
Purpose: To enable the holder to enhance his or her knowledge and experience by visiting an overseas unit.
Eligibility: Open to members of the section of urology of RSM, who should be in urological training or within three years of a consultant appointment.
Level of Study: Professional development.
Type: Fellowship.
Value: UK£1,000.
Frequency: Annual.
Country of Study: Any country.
No. of awards offered: Varies.
Application Procedure: Further details are available from the RSM administrator.
Closing Date: October 9th.

RSM Presidents Prize
Subjects: Clinical neurosciences.
Purpose: To reward summaries of cases for clinical presentation.
Eligibility: Open to applicants of any nationality.
Level of Study: Professional development.
Type: Prize.
Value: UK£100.
Frequency: Annual.
Country of Study: Any country.
No. of awards offered: One.
Application Procedure: Further details are available from the RSM administrator.
Closing Date: January.
Funding: Private.
No. of awards given last year: One.
No. of applicants last year: 12.
Additional Information: Presentations take place in April.

Sylvia Lawler Prize
Subjects: Oncology.
Purpose: To provide prizes in the field of oncology.
Eligibility: Open to medically or scientifically qualified trainees.
Level of Study: Postgraduate.
Type: Prize.
Value: Details on application.
Frequency: Annual.
Country of Study: United Kingdom.
No. of awards offered: Two.
Application Procedure: Applicants must submit an abstract of one side of A4 to the annually held Sylvia Lawler prize meeting. Abstract forms are available from the Academic Administrator at the RSM.
Closing Date: Please contact the Foundation.

ROYAL TOWN PLANNING INSTITUTE (RTPI)

41 Botolph Lane, London, EC3R 8DL, England
Tel: (44) 20 7929 9473
Fax: (44) 20 7929 8199
Email: judy.woollett@rtpi.org.uk

The Royal Town Planning Institute (RTPI) was founded in 1914 and is a registered charity. Its aim is to advance the science and art of town planning in all its aspects, including local, regional and national planning for the benefit of the public. The Institute is primarily concerned with maintaining high standards of competence and conduct within the profession, promoting the role of planning within the country's social, economic and political structures, and presenting the profession's views on current planning issues.

George Pepler International Award
Subjects: Town and country planning or some particular aspect of planning theory and practice.
Purpose: To enable young people of any nationality to visit another country for a short period to study.
Eligibility: Open to persons under 30 years of age of any nationality.
Level of Study: Professional development, Research.
Value: Up to UK£1,500.
Length of Study: Short-term travel outside the United Kingdom for United Kingdom residents or for visits to the United Kingdom for applicants from abroad.
Frequency: Every two years.
Country of Study: Any country.
No. of awards offered: One.
Application Procedure: Applicants must submit a statement showing the nature of the study visit proposed, together with an itinerary. Application forms are available on request from the RTPI.
Closing Date: March 31st 2004.
Funding: Private.
Contributor: Trust fund.
No. of awards given last year: One.
No. of applicants last year: 20.
Additional Information: At the conclusion of the visit the recipient must submit a report.

RUSSELL SAGE FOUNDATION

112 East 64th Street, New York, NY 10021, United States of America
Tel: (1) 212 750 6012
Fax: (1) 212 371 4761
Email: info@rsage.org
www: http://www.russellsage.org
Contact: Vice President of Administration

The Russell Sage Foundation is the principal American foundation devoted exclusively to research in the social sciences. Located in New York City, the Foundation is a research centre, a funding source for studies by scholars at other academic and research institutions, and an active member of the nation's social science community.

Russell Sage Foundation Visiting Scholar Appointments
Subjects: Social sciences.
Eligibility: Open to scholars in the social sciences. The Foundation particularly welcomes groups of visiting scholars who wish to collaborate on a specific project during their residence at the foundation. In order to develop these projects fully, support is sometimes provided for working groups prior to their arrival at the foundation. Awards are not made for the support of graduate degree work, nor for institutional support.
Level of Study: Doctorate, Postdoctorate.
Type: Fellowship.
Value: Varies.
Length of Study: One academic year.
Frequency: Annual.
Study Establishment: The Foundation.
Country of Study: Any country.
No. of awards offered: Varies.
Application Procedure: Applicants should consult the website or contact the organisation for details.
Closing Date: November 15th prior to the year of residence.
Additional Information: Awardees are expected to offer the Foundation the right to publish any book length manuscripts resulting from Foundation support.

RUTH ESTRIN GOLDBERG MEMORIAL FOR CANCER RESEARCH

885 Gloucester Road, Union, NJ 07083, United States of America
Tel: (1) 908 688 1725
Contact: Mrs Myrna Abramson, Past President

Ruth Estrin Goldberg Memorial for Cancer Research

Subjects: Cancer research.
Eligibility: Open to candidates from the eastern United States of America, preferably New York, New Jersey, Pennsylvania, Connecticut, Massachusetts, Delaware or Maryland.
Level of Study: Unrestricted.
Value: US$10,000-15,000.
Frequency: Annual.
Country of Study: United States of America.
No. of awards offered: Two.
Application Procedure: Applicants must write for an application form and guidelines.
Closing Date: February 28th.
Funding: Private.
Contributor: Members and friends.
No. of awards given last year: Two.
No. of applicants last year: 10-15.
Additional Information: The Ruth Estrin Goldberg Memorial for Cancer Research is a volunteer organisation.

RYAN DAVIES MEMORIAL FUND

1 Squire Court, The Marina, Swansea, SA1 3XB, Wales
Tel: (44) 1792 301500
Fax: (44) 1792 301500
Contact: Mr Michael D Evans, Secretary

The Ryan Davies Memorial Fund honours the memory of the great Welsh performer, Ryan Davies, and gives awards in the performing arts to postgraduate students of Welsh extraction.

Ryan Davies Memorial Fund Scholarship Grants

Subjects: Music, drama and all performing arts.
Purpose: To enable Welsh artists to continue studies following their formal training.
Eligibility: Open to Welsh artists or artists of Welsh extraction only.
Level of Study: Professional development.
Type: Grant.
Value: Up to UK£2,500 each.
Length of Study: Up to one year.
Frequency: Annual.
Study Establishment: Unrestricted.
Country of Study: Any country.
No. of awards offered: Up to eight.
Application Procedure: Applicants must apply by forwarding all relevant information including their reason for application, qualifications, referees and any further background information to the Secretary.
Closing Date: May 30th.
Funding: Private.
Contributor: The general public.
No. of awards given last year: Eight.
No. of applicants last year: 50.
Additional Information: The Fund was set up in memory of Ryan Davies, Wales' most versatile entertainer. Artists will be notified of their application by July 31st.

S S HUEBNER FOUNDATION FOR INSURANCE EDUCATION

430 Vance Hall, Philadelphia, PA 19104-6301, United States of America
Tel: (1) 215 898 9631
Fax: (1) 215 898 0310
Email: hcalvert@wharton.upenn.edu
www: http://www.huebnergeneva.org
Contact: Associate Director

The S S Huebner Foundation is an educational foundation with the objective of promoting education and research in risk management and insurance. It provides PhD fellowships for the study of risk management and insurance economics at the Wharton School of the University of Pennsylvania, and publishes books and working papers.

S S Huebner Foundation for Insurance Education Predoctoral Fellowships

Subjects: Managerial science and applied economics, with specialisation in risk management and insurance economics.
Purpose: To increase the supply of college professors specialising in risk management and insurance economics.
Eligibility: Open to citizens of the United States of America and Canada who hold a Bachelor's degree from an accredited United States or Canadian university or college and intend to pursue an insurance teaching career.
Level of Study: Doctorate, Postdoctorate.
Type: Fellowship.
Value: Full tuition and fees of the Wharton School of the University of Pennsylvania plus an annual living stipend of US$20,000.
Length of Study: Four years.
Frequency: Annual.
Study Establishment: The Wharton School of the University of Pennsylvania.
Country of Study: United States of America.
No. of awards offered: Varies.
Application Procedure: Applicants must apply to the Wharton Doctoral program for admission and to the Huebner Foundation for funding.
Closing Date: December 15 (Wharton Admission), January 15 (Huebner funding).
Funding: Private.
Contributor: Leading insurance companies in the United States of America and Canada.
Additional Information: Candidates are required to certify that it is their intention to follow an insurance teaching career and that they will major in insurance and risk management for a graduate degree. Applicants must take the admission test for graduate study in business. For information concerning these examinations candidates should write directly to the Educational Testing Service. Applicants should apply separately and directly to the Wharton School Doctoral Program Office for admission into the Insurance and Risk Management Doctoral Program.

SAINT ANDREW'S SOCIETY OF THE STATE OF NEW YORK SCHOLARSHIPS, THE CARNEGIE TRUST FOR THE UNIVERSITIES OF SCOTLAND

Cameron House, Abbey Park Place, Dunfermline, Fife, KY16 7PZ, Scotland
Tel: (44) 013 83 622 148
Fax: (44) 013 83 622 149
Email: jgray@carnegie-trust.org
Contact: Chairman of the Scottish Selection Commitee

Scholarships to those of Scottish descent or birth offered for study at a University in the United States, within a radius of 250 miles from New York city or the Washington area. Applicants must be first graduates of a Scottish University or Oxford or Cambridge.

St Andrew's Society of the State of New York Scholarship Fund

Subjects: All subjects.
Purpose: To support advanced study exchanges between the United States of America and Scotland.
Eligibility: Open to newly qualified graduates of a Scottish university or of Oxford or Cambridge. Candidates are required to have a Scottish background. The possession of an Honours Degree is not essential. Personality and other qualities will influence the selection.
Level of Study: Postgraduate.
Type: Scholarship.
Value: US$20,000 to cover university tuition fees, room and board, and transportation expenses.
Length of Study: One academic year.
Frequency: Annual.
Study Establishment: A university within 250 miles of New York City.
Country of Study: United States of America.

No. of awards offered: Two.
Application Procedure: Applicants must write for details. Each Scottish university will vet its own applicants and nominate one candidate to go forward to the Final Selection Committee to be held in Edinburgh in early March. Oxford and Cambridge applicants should apply directly to the Society.
Closing Date: End of January.
Funding: Private.
No. of awards given last year: Two.
No. of applicants last year: 10.
Additional Information: Only in unusual circumstances will the Society consider other locations. Thereafter, the Scholar is expected to spend a little time travelling in America before returning to Scotland.

SAMRO (SOUTHERN AFRICAN MUSIC RIGHTS ORGANISATION) ENDOWMENT FOR THE NATIONAL ARTS

PO Box 31609, Braamfontein 2017, South Africa
Tel: (27) 11 489 5000
Fax: (27) 11 403 1934
www: http://www.samro.org.za
Tel: 4 24653 SAMROSA
Contact: J C Otto, Liaison & Research Officer

SAMRO (Southern African Music Rights Organisation) is Southern Africa's Society of Composers and Lyricists, administering the public perfomance, broadcasting and diffusion service rights in their musical works. Through the SAMRO Endowment for the National Arts, it currently supports music study at home and abroad for citizens of South Africa, Botswana, Lesotho and Swaziland.

SAMRO Intermediate Bursaries for Composition Study In Southern Africa

Subjects: Music.
Purpose: To support music composition study as a major subject in either the serious or jazz popular music genres.
Eligibility: Open to citizens of South Africa, Botswana, Lesotho and Swaziland, who have met the requirements for proceeding to the third, fourth or honours year of a senior undergraduate degree or equivalent diploma course. Applicants must have been born after February 15th 1972. For entering any year of a Master's or doctorate degree, the age limit is 32. Older students are considered in special circumstances.
Level of Study: Postgraduate.
Type: Bursary.
Value: Rand 9,000 for third, fourth and honours year and Rand 6,000 for Master's or doctorate degrees.
Length of Study: One year.
Frequency: Annual.
Study Establishment: A university, technikon or other recognised statutory institute of tertiary education approved by the trustees.
Country of Study: South Africa, Botswana, Lesotho, or Swaziland.
No. of awards offered: 10.
Application Procedure: Applicants must complete an application form.
Closing Date: February 15th.
Funding: Private.
Contributor: SAMRO.
No. of awards given last year: Four.
No. of applicants last year: Five.
Additional Information: Applicants must produce an official letter of acceptance for entering any year of Master's or doctoral degrees.

SAMRO Overseas Scholarship

Subjects: Music.
Purpose: To encourage music study at postgraduate level in the serious or jazz popular music genres.
Eligibility: Open to postgraduate students who are citizens of South Africa, Botswana, Lesotho or Swaziland. The age limit is 30 years.
Level of Study: Postgraduate.
Type: Scholarship.
Value: Rand 120,000 plus travel expenses of up to Rand 10,000.

Length of Study: Two years.
Frequency: Annual.
Study Establishment: An institute or educational entity approved by the SAMRO Endowment for the National Arts.
Country of Study: UK, Europe or North America.
No. of awards offered: Two.
Application Procedure: Applicants must complete an application form.
Closing Date: April 30th.
Funding: Private.
Contributor: SAMRO.
No. of awards given last year: Two.
No. of applicants last year: 9.
Additional Information: These awards rotate on a quadrennial basis as follows: 2003 is singers, 2004 is instrumentalists and 2005 is keyboard players, 2006 is Composers.

SAMRO Postgraduate Bursaries for Indigenous African Music Study

Subjects: Music.
Purpose: To encourage the study of indigenous African music at the postgraduate level in either the traditional, serious or jazz popular music genres.
Eligibility: Open to postgraduate students who are citizens of South Africa, Botswana, Lesotho or Swaziland. The age limit is 40 years.
Level of Study: Postgraduate.
Type: Bursary.
Value: Rand 5,500.
Length of Study: Five years.
Frequency: Annual.
Study Establishment: A university or other recognised statutory institute of tertiary education approved by the trustees and situated in SAMRO's current territory of operation.
Country of Study: South Africa, Botswana, Lesotho, or Swaziland.
No. of awards offered: Six.
Application Procedure: Applicants must complete an application form.
Closing Date: February 15th.
Funding: Private.
Contributor: SAMRO.
No. of awards given last year: 3.
No. of applicants last year: 3.
Additional Information: Applicants must produce an official letter of acceptance from a recognised tertiary institute of learning. They must have acceptance into the first year, or of entry into any subsequent year, of a postgraduate degree in indigenous African music at such an institute.

SAMUEL H KRESS FOUNDATION

174 East 80th Street, New York, NY 10021, United States of America
Tel: (1) 212 861 4993
www: http://www.kressfoundation.org
Contact: Wyman Meers, Programme Associate

Over the past 75 years, the Samuel H Kress Foundation has established a record of philanthropy in three related areas: the collection and distribution of works of art from the great European traditions, the preservation of significant European monuments of art and architecture and the nurturing of professional expertise in art history and art conservation.

Kress Fellowships for Advanced Training in Fine Arts Conservation

Subjects: Specific areas of fine art conservation.
Purpose: To enable young American conservators to undertake post MA advanced internships.
Eligibility: Open to those who have completed their academic training in conservation.
Level of Study: Postgraduate.
Type: Fellowship.
Value: US$25,000.
Frequency: Annual.

Study Establishment: Appropriate institutions.
Country of Study: United States of America.
No. of awards offered: 10.
Application Procedure: Applicants must write for details. The Foundation does not accept grant materials by fax.
Closing Date: February 28th.
No. of applicants last year: Approx. 25.
Additional Information: Emphasis is on hands-on training. These grants are not for completion of degree programmes. Enquiries should be directed to Ms Ackerman or Wyman Meers.

Samuel H Kress Foundation Travel Fellowships
Subjects: Art history.
Purpose: To facilitate travel for PhD candidates in the history of art to view materials essential for the completion of dissertation research.
Eligibility: Open to predoctoral candidates at American universities.
Level of Study: Doctorate.
Type: Fellowship.
Value: Varies between US$3,500-10,000.
Frequency: Annual.
Country of Study: Any country.
No. of awards offered: 10-15.
Application Procedure: Applicants must be nominated by their art history department. There is a limit of one applicant per department and the Foundation does not accept grant materials by fax.
Closing Date: November 30th.
Funding: Private.
No. of awards given last year: 10.
No. of applicants last year: Approx. 50.

Samuel H Kress Foundation Two Year Research Fellowships at Foreign Institutions
Subjects: Art history.
Purpose: To facilitate advanced dissertation research in association with a selected institute of art history in either Florence, Jerusalem, Leiden, London, Munich, Nicosia, Paris, Rome or Zurich.
Eligibility: Open to PhD candidates in history of art for the completion of their dissertation research. Candidates must be citizens of the United States of America or matriculated at an institution in the United States of America.
Level of Study: Predoctorate.
Type: Fellowship.
Value: US$22,500 per year.
Length of Study: Two years.
Frequency: Annual.
Study Establishment: One of a number of art historical institutes in Florence, Jerusalem, Leiden, London, Munich, Nicosia, Paris, Rome or Zurich.
Country of Study: Other.
No. of awards offered: Four.
Application Procedure: Applicants must be nominated by their art history department. There is a limit of one applicant per department and the Foundation does not accept grant materials by fax.
Closing Date: November 30th.
Funding: Private.
No. of awards given last year: Four.
No. of applicants last year: Approx. 25.

SAN ANGELO SYMPHONY SOCIETY

PO Box 5922, San Angelo, TX 76902, United States of America
Tel: (1) 325 658 5877
Fax: (1) 325 653 1045
Email: grace@sanangelosymphony.org
www: http://www.sanangelosymphony.org
Contact: Grace Torres, Executive Director

The San Angelo Symphony provides the only source of classical music in a 90 mile radius. Eight concerts, a Summer pop concert, two children's concerts and the International Sorantin Competition comprise the annual season. The Symphony also supports a 300 member guild.

Sorantin Young Artist Award
Subjects: Piano performance, vocal performance or instrumental performance.
Purpose: To recognise and reward talent.
Eligibility: Open to instrumentalists and pianists under 28 years of age and vocalists under 31 years of age by November in the year of the competition.
Level of Study: Postgraduate.
Type: Competition.
Value: The overall winner receives US$3,000 includes his or her division prize and a guest appearance with the San Angelo Symphony Orchestra. The division winner receives US$1,000 and the division runner up, US$500.
Frequency: Annual.
Country of Study: Any country.
No. of awards offered: Varies.
Application Procedure: Applicants must complete an application form by the entry deadline. At the time of application, all entry fees must be paid.
Closing Date: October 6th.
Funding: Private.
Contributor: Mr and Mrs Norman Rousselot
No. of awards given last year: Six.
No. of applicants last year: 43.

SAN FRANCISCO CONSERVATORY OF MUSIC

1201 Ortega Street, San Francisco, CA 94122, United States of America
Tel: (1) 415 759 3422
Fax: (1) 415 759 3499
Email: cmk@sfcm.edu
www: http://www.sfcm.edu
Contact: Director of Studies

The San Francisco Conservatory of Music is a college of music which trains students for careers as professional symphony musicians, concert artists, opera singers, composers, conductors and teachers.

San Francisco Conservatory Performance Scholarships in Music
Subjects: Musical performance.
Purpose: To permit talented students to attend the Conservatory.
Eligibility: Open to United States and foreign nationals who will be attending the Conservatory on a full-time basis. Candidates must have had considerable experience in musical performance.
Level of Study: Graduate, Postgraduate.
Type: Scholarship.
Value: Varies. Please contact the organisation for full details.
Length of Study: One year, renewable.
Frequency: Annual.
Study Establishment: San Francisco Conservatory of Music.
Country of Study: United States of America.
No. of awards offered: Varies.
Application Procedure: Applicants should visit the website and contact the organisation for further information.
Closing Date: Please contact the organisation for information on deadlines.
Funding: Private.
Additional Information: Further information is available on request.

SAVOY FOUNDATION

PO Box 69, 230 Foch, St Jean Sur Richelieu, QC, J3B 2B2, Canada
Tel: (1) 450 358 9779
Fax: (1) 450 346 1045
Email: epilepsy@savoy-foundation.ca
www: http://www.savoy-foundation.ca
Contact: Secretary

The Savoy Foundation's main activity is to support and encourage research into epilepsy.

Savoy Foundation Post Doctoral and Clinical Research Fellowships

Subjects: Medical and behavioural science, as they relate to epilepsy.
Purpose: To support a full-time research project in the field of epilepsy.
Eligibility: Candidates must be scientists or medical specialists with a PhD or MD.
Level of Study: Postdoctorate, Postgraduate, Research.
Type: Research grant.
Value: Canadian $25,000.
Length of Study: One year, in the first instance, but will be renewable once and, exceptionally, twice upon request.
Frequency: Annual.
Country of Study: Canada.
No. of awards offered: Varies.
Application Procedure: Applicants must contact the Foundation or visit the website for application forms and further information.
Closing Date: January 15th.
Funding: Private.
Contributor: The Savoy Foundation endowments.
Additional Information: The period of support may begin at any time between May and October.

Savoy Foundation Research Grants

Subjects: Medical and behavioural science, as they relate to epilepsy.
Purpose: To support further research into epilepsy.
Eligibility: Only available to clinicians and established scientists.
Level of Study: Postdoctorate, Postgraduate, Research.
Type: Research grant.
Value: Up to Canadian $25,000.
Frequency: Annual.
Country of Study: Other.
No. of awards offered: Varies.
Application Procedure: Applicants must contact the Foundation or visit the website for application forms and further information.
Closing Date: January 15th.
Funding: Private.
Contributor: The Savoy Foundation endowments.
Additional Information: The grant is only available to Canadian citizens or for projects conducted in Canada.

Savoy Foundation Studentships

Subjects: Biomedicine, neurology and epileptology.
Purpose: To support training and research in a biomedical discipline, the health sciences or social sciences related to epilepsy.
Eligibility: Candidates must have a good university record eg. a BSc, MD or equivalent diploma and have ensured that a qualified researcher affiliated to a university or hospital will supervise his or her work. Concomitant registration in a graduate programme is encouraged. The awards are available to Canadian citizens or for projects conducted in Canada.
Level of Study: Doctorate, Postgraduate, Predoctorate.
Type: Studentship.
Value: The stipend will be Canadian $12,000 for the first year, with a Canadian $1,000 increase for each year of renewal. An annual sum of Canadian $1,000 will be allocated to the laboratory or institution as additional support for the research project.
Length of Study: One-four years.
Frequency: Annual.
Country of Study: Other.
No. of awards offered: Varies.
Application Procedure: Applicants must contact the Foundation or visit the website for application forms and further information.
Closing Date: January 15th.
Funding: Private.
Contributor: The Savoy Foundation endowments.

SCHOOL OF ORIENTAL AND AFRICAN STUDIES (SOAS)

University of London, Thornhaugh Street, Russell Square, London, WC1H 0XG, England
Tel: (44) 20 7074 5091
Fax: (44) 20 7074 5089
Email: jt26@soas.ac.uk
www: http://www.soas.ac.uk
Tel: 262433 W6876
Contact: Mrs Jean Tullett, Scholarships Officer

The School of Oriental and African Studies (SOAS) regards its role as advancing the knowledge and understanding of the cultures and societies of Asia and Africa and of the School's academic disciplines, through high quality teaching and research.

Bernard Buckman Scholarship

Subjects: Chinese studies with the emphasis on modern and contemporary China, although it is possible to study aspects of pre-modern China.
Purpose: To provide fee remission for a student taking an MA in Chinese studies.
Eligibility: Open to those candidates who qualify to pay for home or European Union tuition fees.
Level of Study: Postgraduate.
Type: Scholarship.
Value: Home or European Union postgraduate fee.
Length of Study: One year.
Frequency: Annual.
Study Establishment: SOAS.
Country of Study: United Kingdom.
No. of awards offered: One.
Application Procedure: Applicants must complete an application form, which can be obtained from the registry. Application forms can be downloaded from the website.
Closing Date: March 31st.
Funding: Private.
No. of awards given last year: One.
No. of applicants last year: Seven.

SOAS Bursary

Subjects: Oriental and African studies in archaeology area studies, economics, ethnomusicology, history, law, languages, linguistics, phonetics, politics, religious studies, social anthropology or development studies.
Purpose: To provide financial assistance to study for a Masters or postgraduate diploma.
Eligibility: There are no eligibility restrictions.
Level of Study: Postgraduate.
Type: Bursary.
Value: UK£7,345.
Length of Study: One year, non renewable.
Frequency: Annual.
Study Establishment: SOAS.
Country of Study: United Kingdom.
No. of awards offered: Eight.
Application Procedure: Applicants must complete and submit an application form obtainable from the academic registrar, with two references plus a 500 word submission. Application forms available on the website.
Closing Date: March 31st.
Funding: Government.
No. of awards given last year: Eight.
No. of applicants last year: 287.

SOAS Research Student Fellowships

Subjects: The languages and cultures of Africa, East Asia, near and Middle East, South Asia, Southeast Asia, focusing on anthropology and sociology, art and archaeology, development studies, economics, ethnomusicology, financial and management studies, history, law, linguistics, political studies and the study of religions.
Purpose: To support research study at SOAS.

555

Eligibility: There are no eligibility restrictions. Applications are invited in respect of all subject areas offered by the school but preference will be given to applications in African or Asian languages, literatures or cultures, anthropology, history, law, media studies, music, refugee and migration studies and religions.
Level of Study: Doctorate.
Type: Fellowship.
Value: UK£9,350 plus remission of home or European Union fees.
Length of Study: Three years.
Frequency: Annual.
Study Establishment: SOAS.
Country of Study: United Kingdom.
No. of awards offered: Nine.
Application Procedure: Applicants must complete and submit an application form which is obtainable from the academic registrar, with two references, a 500 word submission and five photocopies. Application forms can be downloaded from the website.
Closing Date: March 31st.
Funding: Government.
No. of awards given last year: Nine.
No. of applicants last year: 120.

SCHOOL OF VETERINARY MEDICINE, HANNOVER

Postfach 71 11 80, Hannover, D-30545, Germany
Tel: (49) 511 953 6
Fax: (49) 511 953 8050
Email: bhuesch@vw.tiho-hannover.de
www: http://www.tiho-hannover.de
Contact: Executive Member of the Board

The School of Veterinary Medicine, Hannover is a centre of teaching and research in veterinary medicine and zoology with approximately 300 scientists and 2,000 students. Among the 26 institutes and clinics is the Institute for Parasitology where the Karl-Enigk-Stiftung was founded.

Karl-Enigk-Stipendium

Subjects: Parasitology, mainly veterinary parasitology.
Purpose: To support research in experimental parasitology, mainly veterinary parasitology.
Eligibility: Applicants must not be older than 32 years and must be from European countries where German is spoken.
Level of Study: Doctorate, Postdoctorate.
Type: Scholarship.
Value: Please contact the organisation for further information.
Length of Study: Varies.
Frequency: Annual.
Country of Study: Any country.
No. of awards offered: Varies.
Application Procedure: Applicants must submit a curriculum vitae, publication list, short research proposal and references from the head of the research institute. Applications must be addressed to Karl Enigk-Stiftung c/o School of Veterinary Medicine Hannover.
Closing Date: Applications are accepted at any time.
Funding: Private.
No. of awards given last year: Three.
No. of applicants last year: Five.

SCOULOUDI FOUNDATION

c/o The Institute of Historical Research, University of London, Senate House, London, WC1E 7HU, England
Tel: (44) 20 7862 8740
Fax: (44) 20 7862 8740
www: http://www.history.ac.uk
Contact: Nicola Cowee, Fellowship Assistant

The IHR is an important resource meeting-place for scholars from all over the world. It contains an outstanding open access library, runs courses and major conferences, offers research fellowships and other awards and produces many significant research aids and tools.

Economic History Society Research Fellowships

Subjects: Economic and social history.
Purpose: To help candidates at an advanced stage of a PhD to complete their doctorates or to provide one years postdoctoral study in history.
Eligibility: Open to postdoctoral candidates who must have recently completed a doctoral degree in economic or social history or to graduates who are engaged in the completion of a doctoral degree in economic or social history and who must have completed two years, but not more than four years of full-time or eight years part-time, research on their chosen topics. Fellowships are open to citizens of the United Kingdom or to candidates with a degree from a university in the United Kingdom.
Level of Study: Doctorate, Postdoctorate, Postgraduate.
Type: Fellowship.
Value: UK£7,000.
Length of Study: One year.
Frequency: Dependent on funds available.
Study Establishment: An Institute of historical research.
Country of Study: England.
Application Procedure: Applicants must complete an application form, available from the Assistant Secretary in early January.
Closing Date: Approx. end of March.
Contributor: The Economic History Society.
No. of awards given last year: Three.

Scouloudi Foundation Historical Awards

Subjects: History or a related subject.
Purpose: To provide subsidies towards the cost of publishing a book or article in the field of history, incorporating an academic thesis or other scholarly work already accepted by a reputable publisher or learned journal, or to pay for special expenses incurred in the completion of advanced historical work such as the cost of fares and subsistence during visits to libraries or record repositories.
Eligibility: Open to graduates of United Kingdom universities who possess a relevant Honours degree or United Kingdom citizens with a similar qualification from a university outside the United Kingdom. These awards are not made for study or research towards a post-graduate qualification eg. work on theses for higher degrees are not eligible.
Level of Study: Doctorate, Postdoctorate.
Type: Varies.
Value: UK£100-1,000. Applicants should not ask for more than their minimum requirements for the year concerned.
Frequency: Annual.
Country of Study: Any country.
No. of awards offered: Varies.
Application Procedure: Applicants must complete an application form.
Closing Date: March 1st.
Funding: Private.
Contributor: The Scouloudi Foundation.

SEMICONDUCTOR RESEARCH CORPORATION (SRC)

PO Box 12053, Research Triangle Park, NC 27709, United States of America
Tel: (1) 919 941 9453
Fax: (1) 919 941 9450
Email: students@src.org
www: http://www.src.org
Contact: Fellowships Office

The Semiconductor Research Corporation (SRC) is a consortium of about 60 semiconductor manufacturers and equipment makers. The SRC manages a research portfolio in major research universities throughout the United States. At any given time it supports about 700 advanced degree students on contract research, 45 graduate Fellows and 15 Master's scholars. The SRC supports a pragmatic approach to developing student programmes and provides industry interactions, presentation and other opportunities for its students.

SRC Graduate Fellowship Program

Subjects: Electrical engineering, computer engineering, chemical engineering, mechanical engineering, materials science, physics and some related areas.

Purpose: To attract academically outstanding students to doctoral programmes in areas of interest to the semiconductor industry.

Eligibility: Open to students who have United States citizenship or permanent resident status. Students are also required to be performing their doctoral research under the guidance of an SRC funded faculty member.

Level of Study: Doctorate.

Type: Fellowship.

Value: Please contact the organisation.

Length of Study: Five years or until completion of the PhD degree, whichever comes first.

Frequency: Annual.

Study Establishment: Universities having SRC funded contracts. A list is available on the website.

Country of Study: United States of America.

No. of awards offered: Varies.

Application Procedure: Applicants must complete an application form. Applications are distributed through SRC funded faculty in November. Applications are also distributed through other venues outside the SRC community and applications are encouraged from non SRC funded colleges.

Funding: Commercial.

Contributor: The semiconductor industry.

Additional Information: Recipients are required to be associated with an SRC funded contract. Resources are available to assist qualified students in identifying suitable faculty within SRC funded universities. SRC contracts support precompetitive research areas of interest to the semiconductor industry.

SRC Master's Scholarship Program

Subjects: Electrical engineering, computer engineering, chemical engineering, mechanical engineering, materials science, physics and some related areas.

Purpose: To attract under represented minorities and women to disciplines of interest to the semiconductor industry.

Eligibility: Open to students having United States citizenship or permanent resident status. Students are also required to be from underrepresented minorities eg. African American, Native American, Hispanic or female.

Level of Study: Postgraduate.

Type: Scholarship.

Value: Please contact the organisation.

Length of Study: Two years or until completion of the Master's degree, whichever comes first.

Frequency: Annual.

Study Establishment: Universities having SRC funded contracts. A list is available on the website.

Country of Study: United States of America.

No. of awards offered: Five.

Application Procedure: Applicants must complete an application form. Applications are distributed through SRC funded faculty in November with a due date early in February. Applications are also distributed through other avenues outside the SRC community and applications are encouraged from non SRC funded colleges.

Funding: Commercial.

Contributor: The semiconductor industry.

Additional Information: Recipients are required to be associated with an SRC funded contract. Resources are available to assist qualified students in identifying suitable faculty within SRC funded universities. SRC contracts support precompetitive research in areas of interest to the semiconductor industry.

SERONO FOUNDATION FOR THE ADVANCEMENT OF MEDICAL SCIENCE

12 Chemin des Aulx, 1228 Plan-les-Quates
Geneva, Switzerland
Tel: (41) 22 706 9368
Fax: (41) 22 706 9398
Email: renee.beaudry@serono.com
www: http://www.serono-foundation.org
Contact: The Secretary

The Serono Foundation for the Advancement of Medical Science is an independent non-profit organization dedicated to support educational activities in basic and clinical research. The aim of the Foundation is to improve human health and welfare through the advancement of medical sciences. The Foundation promotes and supports scientific research-oriented investigators by fostering an open exchange of information, experience and knowledge within the scientific and medical communities. Specifically the Foundation facilitates exchange of information on relevent topics between universities, research institutes, industries, national agencies and international organizations. The Foundation accomplishes its mission by sponsoring independent scientific workshops and conferences, and by supporting peer-reviewed research fellowships, primarily in the fields of reproduction, endocrinology, immunology, neurology and oncology.

Fellowships in Biomedicine

Subjects: Topic changes each year - Neurology, reproductive endocrinology, cancer biology, etc. 2004 award is reproductive endocrinology.

Purpose: Postdoctoral Research.

Eligibility: 1) Completed PhD/MD preferably not more than 3 years prior to start of fellowship. 2) Should be changing laboratory. 3) Communicate fluently in English.

Level of Study: Postdoctorate.

Type: Fellowship.

Value: US$90,000 over 2 years.

Length of Study: 2 years.

Frequency: Annual.

Study Establishment: Any.

Country of Study: Any country.

No. of awards offered: 2-4 each year.

Application Procedure: See www.serono-foundation.org for application form & guidelines.

Closing Date: 28th February each year.

Funding: Private.

Contributor: Serono.

No. of awards given last year: 3.

SHASTRI INDO-CANADIAN INSTITUTE (SICI)

Room 1402 Education Tower, 2500 University Drive North West,
Calgary, AB, T2N 1N4, Canada
Tel: (1) 403 220 7467
Fax: (1) 403 289 0100
Email: sici@ucalgary.ca
www: http://www.ucalgary.ca/~sici
Contact: Ms Lori Mudrick-Donnon, Programme Officer

The Shastri Indo-Canadian Institute (SICI) is a unique educational enterprise that promotes understanding between Canada and India, mainly through facilitating academic activities. The Institute funds research, links institutions in the two countries and organises seminars and conferences.

557

SICI India Studies Fellowship Competition

Subjects: Subjects relating to India in the social sciences and humanities including education, law, management and the arts.
Purpose: To support candidates wishing to undertake research or training in India.
Eligibility: Applicants must be Canadian citizens or landed immigrants.
Level of Study: Doctorate, Postdoctorate, Postgraduate, Professional development, Research.
Type: Fellowship.
Value: Varies.
Length of Study: Three months to one year.
Frequency: Annual.
Study Establishment: Varies.
Country of Study: India.
No. of awards offered: Varies from year to year.
Application Procedure: Applicants must contact the Canada head office for the application procedure.
Closing Date: July 3rd.
Funding: Government.

SHEFFIELD HALLAM UNIVERSITY

Graduate Studies Team, City Campus, Howard Street, Sheffield, S1 1WB, England
Tel: (44) 114 225 5555
Fax: (44) 114 225 4055
Email: resenq@shu.ac.uk
www: http://registry.shu.ac.uk/gst
Contact: Senior Administrative Officer

Sheffield Hallam University received the highest rating of all the new universities in the 1996 Research Assessment Exercise. The university has a postgraduate population of 4,500 students and is one of the United Kingdom's major providers of postgraduate and research opportunities.

Hallam Studentships

Subjects: All subject areas covered by the University, eg. business, computing, cultural studies, education, finance, health studies, materials, sport and exercise, science, mathematics, engineering, social studies and environmental science courses.
Purpose: To support study towards a PhD degree.
Eligibility: Open to European Union nationals only.
Level of Study: Doctorate.
Type: Other.
Value: UK£10,900 maintenance award and fees (current 03/04 rate). If competition is run for the 04/05 academic year, the maintenance award will be UK£12,000.
Length of Study: Up to three years full-time.
Frequency: Annual.
Study Establishment: Sheffield Hallam University.
Country of Study: United Kingdom.
No. of awards offered: 5.
Application Procedure: Applicants must direct initial enquiries to the Graduate Studies Team. If there are studentships for the chosen area of study then an application form must be completed.
Closing Date: Applications are accepted when the St. ships are advertised. Usually from May-September.
Funding: Commercial, Government.
Contributor: Shu plus external collaborator.
No. of awards given last year: 4.

Sheffield Hallam University Research Studentships

Subjects: Structural materials, analysis and characterisation, surface engineering, materials modelling, polymers and self-assembled systems, electro-active mats and devices, computer science.
Purpose: To support study towards an MPhil or PhD at Sheffield Hallam University.
Eligibility: Open to European Union nationals only.
Level of Study: Doctorate, Postgraduate.
Type: Bursary.
Value: UK£9,000 maintenance award and fees.
Length of Study: Three years full-time.
Frequency: Annual.

Study Establishment: Sheffield Hallam University.
Country of Study: United Kingdom.
No. of awards offered: Subject to corporate review.
Application Procedure: Applicants must complete an application form. For an application pack contact Joe Rennie.
Funding: Commercial, Government.

For further information contact:

Materials Research Institute, City Campus, Howard Street, Sheffield, South Yorkshire S1 1WB, England
Tel: (44) 114 225 3010
Fax: (44) 114 225 3501
Contact: Grants Management Officer

SHELBY CULLOM DAVIS CENTER FOR HISTORICAL STUDIES

Department of History, G-13 Dickinson Hall, Princeton University, Princeton, NJ 08544-1017, United States of America
Tel: (1) 609 258 4997
Fax: (1) 609 258 5326
www: http://www.princeton.edu/~davisctr
Contact: Ms Jennifer Houle, Manager

Since 2001 the Shelby Cullom Davis Center for Historical Studies has focused on the study of migration in history.

Shelby Cullom Davis Center Research Projects, Research Fellowships

Subjects: Migration.
Eligibility: Applicants must have completed a PhD.
Level of Study: Postdoctorate.
Type: Fellowship.
Length of Study: One-two semesters.
Frequency: Annual.
Study Establishment: Shelby Cullom Davis Center.
Country of Study: United States of America.
No. of awards offered: Varies.
Application Procedure: Applicants must complete an application form.
Closing Date: December 1st.
Funding: Private.
No. of awards given last year: Seven-eight.

SIDNEY SUSSEX COLLEGE

Cambridge, Cambridgeshire CB2 3HU, England
Tel: (44) 1223 338810
Fax: (44) 1223 765744
Email: gradtutor@sid.com.ac.uk
www: http://www.sid.com.ac.uk
Contact: Tutor for Graduate Students

Founded in 1596, Sidney Sussex College admits men and women as undergraduates and graduates. The college presently has 180 graduate students, including 100 working for the PhD degree. The college has excellent sporting, dramatic, and musical facilities and can house the majority of its graduate students in college rooms during their first year only.

Evan Lewis Thomas Law Studentships

Subjects: Law.
Purpose: To support students carrying out research or taking advanced courses.
Eligibility: There are no eligibility restrictions.
Level of Study: Doctorate, Postgraduate.
Type: Studentship.
Length of Study: One-three years.
Frequency: Annual.
Study Establishment: The University of Cambridge.
Country of Study: United Kingdom.
No. of awards offered: Three-four.

Application Procedure: Applicants must obtain application forms from the tutor for graduate studies. Applicants must also apply for a postgraduate place at the University of Cambridge.
Closing Date: 1st Feb 2004.
Funding: Private.

For further information contact:

Email: gradtutor@sid.com.ac.uk

Sidney Sussex College Research Studentship

Subjects: All subjects.
Purpose: To provide full support for research leading to a PhD degree.
Eligibility: Applicants must also apply for a postgraduate place at the University of Cambridge. Preference is given to candidates under 26 years of age. Candidates must be members of Sidney Sussex College.
Level of Study: Doctorate.
Type: Studentship.
Length of Study: Three years.
Frequency: Annual.
Study Establishment: The University of Cambridge.
Country of Study: United Kingdom.
No. of awards offered: One.
Application Procedure: Applicants must complete an application form, available from the tutor for graduate studies.
Closing Date: 1st March 2004.
Funding: Private.
Contributor: Sidney Sussex College.

For further information contact:

Email: gradtutor@sid.com.ac.uk

SIGMA ALPHA IOTA

8022 Collingwood Crescent, Sarasota, FL 34201, United States of America
Tel: (1) 941 351 6825
Fax: (1) 941 351 6826
Email: barbarastaton@verizon.net
www: http://www.sai-national.org/phil/philiama.html
Contact: Ms Barbara Staton, Director

Sigma Alpha Iota, International Music Fraternity, was organised in 1903 to form chapters of music students and musicians who shall by their influence and their musical interest uphold the highest ideals of a music education, and to raise the standard of productive musical work among the women students of colleges, conservatories and universities.

Sigma Alpha Iota Inter-American Music Awards

Subjects: Musical composition but the specifications vary.
Purpose: To promote contemporary composers of the Americas and their music.
Eligibility: Open to any composer residing in North, Central or South America. Prior winners are not eligible. Applicants' previous compositions shall not have been published by nationally or internationally known music publishers.
Level of Study: Unrestricted.
Type: Award.
Value: US$1,000. Transportation to the convention and lodging for two nights will also be provided for the winning composer.
Frequency: Every three years.
Country of Study: Any country.
No. of awards offered: One.
Application Procedure: Applicants must submit a manuscript and application form. Applicants may enter more than one work for the competition and an entry fee of US$35 must accompany each manuscript submitted.
Closing Date: Please contact the Foundation.
Funding: Private.
Contributor: Organisation members.
No. of awards given last year: One.
No. of applicants last year: 38.

Additional Information: Compositions shall be for solo string instruments eg. the violin, viola and cello, and piano accompaniment is optional. They must be no longer than 10 minutes in duration and represent an advanced difficulty level for college performers. Once submitted, works shall not be announced, performed or recorded until the IAMA winner is presented at the National Convention.

SIGMA THETA TAU INTERNATIONAL

550 West North Street, Indianapolis, IN 46202, United States of America
Tel: (1) 317 634 8171
Fax: (1) 317 634 8188
Email: research@stti.iupui.edu
www: http://www.nursingsociety.org
Contact: Research Grant Programme

Sigma Theta Tau International exists to promote the development, dissemination and utilisation of nursing knowledge. It is committed to improving the health of people worldwide through increasing the scientific base of nursing practice. In support of this mission, the society advances nursing leadership and scholarship and furthers utilisation of nursing research in health care delivery as well as in public policy.

Rosemary Berkel Crisp Research Award

Subjects: Women's health, oncology and infant or child care.
Purpose: To support nursing research is the critical areas of women's health, Oncology and infant/child care.
Eligibility: Open to registered nurses with a current licence who have a Master's or higher degree, (those with Baccalaureate degrees may be co-investigators), have submitted a complete research application package, are ready to initiate the research project and are a member of the Sigma Theta Tau International. Some preference is given to applicants residing in Illinois Missouri, Arkansas, Kentucky and Tennessee.
Level of Study: Doctorate, Predoctorate.
Type: Award.
Value: US$5,000.
Frequency: Annual.
Country of Study: Any country.
No. of awards offered: One.
Application Procedure: Applicants must submit a completed Sigma Theta Tau research application and agreement
Closing Date: December 1st.
Funding: Private.
Contributor: The Harry L Crisp, II and Rosemary Berkel Crisp Foundation to Sigma Theta Tau International's Research Endowment.
No. of awards given last year: One.
No. of applicants last year: 52.
Additional Information: The allocation of funds is based upon a research project in the area of women's health, oncology or paediatrics that is ready for implementation, the quality of the proposed research, future potential of the application, appropriateness of the research budget and feasibility of the time frame.

Sigma Theta Tau International Association of Perioperative Registered Nurses Foundation Grant

Subjects: Perioperative nursing practice. All relevant topics will be considered although priority will be given to research studies that relate to the AORN research priorities, the relationship of nursing interventions to quality and cost effective outcomes, prevention of wound infections, protection from injury, thermal, electric, laser, chemical or physical, maintenance of skin integrity, patient satisfaction with care, nursing care, pain management and anxiety management. Patient and family satisfaction with communication and teaching, the relationship of staff mix, cost and length of stay to quality outcomes, the impact of technology on patient outcomes, the conduct and utilisation of research related to AORN's standards, recommendation and practice guidelines and ethical issues related to patient outcomes are also relevant subjects.
Purpose: To encourage nurses to conduct research related to perioperative nursing practice and contribute to the development of perioperative nursing science.
Eligibility: The principal investigator is required to be a registered nurse with a current license in the perioperative setting, or a registered

nurse who demonstrates interest in or significant contributions to nursing practice. The principal investigator must have, as a minimum, a Master's degree in nursing. Applicants must submit a completed AORN research application. Membership of either organisation is acceptable, but not required.

Level of Study: Postgraduate.
Type: Research grant.
Value: US$10,000. Allocation of funds is based on the quality of the research, the future promise of the applicant, and the applicant's research budget.
Frequency: Annual.
Country of Study: Any country.
No. of awards offered: One.
Application Procedure: Applicants must write to the AORN for an application form and general instructions.
Closing Date: April 1st.
Funding: Private.
Contributor: The Association of Perioperative Registered Nurses and Sigma Theta Tau International.
Additional Information: July is the funding date.

For further information contact:

Association of Perioperative Registered Nurses, 2170 South Parker Road, Suite 300, Denver, CO 80231-5711, United States of America
Tel: (1) 800 755 2676 ext. 277
Fax: (1) 303 750 2927
Email: sbeya@aorn.org
www: http://www.aorn.org

Sigma Theta Tau International Research Grant Opportunities

Subjects: Nursing.
Purpose: To encourage qualified nurses to contribute to the advancement of nursing through research. Multidisciplinary and international research is encouraged.
Eligibility: Applicants must be a registered nurse with a current licence, must have received a Master's degree, must have submitted an application package, must be ready to start the research project, and must have signed a Sigma Theta Tau research agreement. Allocation of funds is based on the quality of the proposed research, the future promise of the applicant, and the applicant's research budget. Applicants from novice researchers who have received no other national research funds are encouraged and will receive preference for funding, other aspects being equal.
Level of Study: Postgraduate.
Type: Research grant.
Value: Up to US$5,000.
Frequency: Annual.
Study Establishment: Unrestricted.
Country of Study: Any country.
No. of awards offered: 10-15.
Application Procedure: Write for information booklet and application form.
Closing Date: March 1st.
Funding: Private.
Contributor: Sigma Theta Tau.
Additional Information: Preference is given to Sigma Theta Tau International Members. Funding date is July 1st.

Sigma Theta Tau International Small Research Grants

Subjects: Nursing.
Purpose: To encourage qualified nurses to contribute to the advancement of nursing through research.
Eligibility: Open to registered nurses with a current license, who have submitted a complete research application package, have the project ready for implementation, hold a Master's degree and/or be enrolled in a doctoral programme and have signed a Sigma Theta Tau International research agreement.
Level of Study: Predoctorate.
Type: Research grant.
Value: Up to US$5,000.
Frequency: Annual.
Country of Study: Any country.

No. of awards offered: 10-15.
Closing Date: December 1st.
Funding: Private.
Additional Information: This grant has no specific focus, however, multiidisciplinary, historical, and international research is encouraged.

Sigma Theta Tau International/American Association of Critical Care Nurses

Subjects: Critical care nursing practice.
Purpose: To encourage qualified nurses to contribute to the advancement of nursing. Research must be related to critical care nursing practice.
Eligibility: Open to registered nurses with a current licence, who have received a Master's degree and submitted a grant proposal relevant to critical care nursing practice. Research must be related to critical care nursing practice.
Level of Study: Postgraduate.
Value: Up to US$10,000.
Frequency: Annual.
Study Establishment: Unrestricted.
Country of Study: Any country.
No. of awards offered: One.
Application Procedure: Applicants must write for an information booklet and application form.
Closing Date: October 1st.
Funding: Private.
Contributor: The American Association of Critical Care Nurses and Sigma Theta Tau International.
Additional Information: January 1st is the funding date.

For further information contact:

American Association of Critical Care Nurses, Department of Research, 101 Columbia, Aliso Viejo, CA 92656-1491, United States of America
Tel: (1) 949 362 2000
Fax: (1) 949 362 2020

Sigma Theta Tau International/American Association of Diabetes Educators Grant

Subjects: Diabetes education and care.
Purpose: To encourage qualified nurses to contribute to the enhancement of quality and increase the availability of diabetes education and care.
Eligibility: The principal investigator must be a registered nurse but team members may be from other disciplines. The principal investigator must also have received a Master's degree, and have the ability to complete the project in one year from funding date. Preference will be given to Sigma Theta Tau members, other qualifications being equal. The grant must be dedicated to diabetes education and care research.
Level of Study: Postgraduate.
Value: Up to US$6,000.
Frequency: Annual.
Country of Study: Any country.
No. of awards offered: One.
Application Procedure: Applicants must write for an information booklet and an application form.
Closing Date: October 1st.
Funding: Private.
Contributor: The American Association of Diabetes Educators and Sigma Theta Tau International.
Additional Information: January 1st is the funding date.

For further information contact:

AADE Foundation Awards, 100 West Monroe Street, Suite 400, Chicago, IL 60603, United States of America
Tel: (1) 312 424 2426
Fax: (1) 312 424 2427

Sigma Theta Tau International/American Nephrology Nurses Association Grant

Subjects: Nephrology nursing.
Purpose: To encourage research related to nephrology nursing practice.

Eligibility: Open to registered nurses with a current licence and a Master's degree. Preference will be given to Sigma Theta Tau members, other qualifications being equal.
Level of Study: Postgraduate.
Value: Up to US$6,000.
Frequency: Annual.
Study Establishment: Unrestricted.
Country of Study: Any country.
No. of awards offered: One.
Application Procedure: Applicants must send application forms to the American Nephrology Nurses Association and must write for an information booklet and application form.
Closing Date: October 31st.
Funding: Private.
Contributor: The American Nephrology Nurses Association and Sigma Theta Tau International.
Additional Information: April 1st is the funding date.

For further information contact:

American Nephrology Nurses' Association, East Holly Avenue, PO Box 56, Pitman, NJ 08071-0056, United States of America
Tel: (1) 856 256 2320
Fax: (1) 888 600 2662

Sigma Theta Tau International/American Nurses Foundation Grant

Subjects: Any clinical topic.
Purpose: To encourage the research career development of nurses through the support of research conducted by beginning nurse researchers, or experienced nurse researchers who are entering a new field of study.
Eligibility: Open to registered nurses with a current licence and a Master's degree, who have submitted a complete research application package, are ready to start the research project and have signed a Sigma Theta Tau research agreement. Preference will be given to Sigma Theta Tau members, other qualifications being equal.
Level of Study: Postgraduate.
Value: Up to US$7,500.
Frequency: Annual.
Study Establishment: Unrestricted.
Country of Study: Any country.
No. of awards offered: One.
Application Procedure: Applicants must write for an information booklet and application form. Proposals should be sent to the Sigma Theta Tau International headquarters in even numbered years, for which applicants should use the STTI application and to the American Nurses Foundation in odd numbered years, for which applicants should use the ANF application.
Closing Date: May 1st.
Funding: Private.
Contributor: The American Nurses Foundation and Sigma Theta Tau International.
Additional Information: Allocation of funds is based on the quality of the proposed research, the future promise of the applicant and the applicant's research budget. October is the funding date.

For further information contact:

(Odd-numbered years), American Nurses Foundation, 600 Maryland Avenue South West, Suite 100 West, Washington, DC 20024-2571, United States of America
Tel: (1) 202 651 7071
Fax: (1) 202 651 7354

Sigma Theta Tau International/Association of Operating room Nurses Foundation Grant

Subjects: Perioperative nursing.
Purpose: To encourage nurses to conduct research related to perioperative nursing practice and contribute to the development of perioperative nursing science.
Eligibility: The principal investigator should be a registered nurse with a current license in the perioperative setting and have received a

Master's degree in nursing. Membership of either funding organisation is acceptable but not required.
Level of Study: Predoctorate.
Value: US$10,000.
Frequency: Annual.
Country of Study: Any country.
No. of awards offered: One.
Application Procedure: Applicants should submit a completed application package for the relevant institution for that year.
Closing Date: April 1st.
Funding: Private.
No. of awards given last year: One.

For further information contact:

Association of Operating Room Nurses, 2170 South Parker Road, Suite 300, Denver, CO 80231-5711, United States of America
Tel: (1) 800 755 2676 ext. 277
Fax: (1) 303 750 2927
Email: sbeyea@aorn.org
www: http://www.aorn.org
Contact: Ms Suzanne Beyea

Sigma Theta Tau International/Emergency Nurses Association Foundation Grant

Subjects: Topics relating to specialised practice of emergency nursing. All relevant subjects will be considered, although priority will be given to studies which relate to ENA Research Initiatives which include, but are not limited to, mechanisms to assure effective, efficient and quality emergency nursing care delivery systems, factors affecting healthcare cost, productivity and market forces to emergency services, ways to enhance health promotion and injury prevention, and mechanisms to assure quality and cost effective educational programmes for emergency nursing.
Purpose: To support research related to the specialized practice of emergency nursing.
Eligibility: The principal investigator is required to be a registered nurse, but team members may be from other disciplines. Applicants must have a Master's degree, submit a complete application with signed research agreement and be ready to or have already started the research project.
Level of Study: Postgraduate.
Value: Up to US$6,000.
Frequency: Annual.
Study Establishment: Unrestricted.
Country of Study: Any country.
No. of awards offered: One.
Application Procedure: Applicants must write for an information booklet and application form.
Closing Date: February 1st.
Funding: Private.
Contributor: The Emergency Nursing Foundation and Sigma Theta Tau International.
Additional Information: July 1st is the funding date.

For further information contact:

ENA Foundation, 915 Lee Street, Des Plaines, IL 60016-6569, United States of America
Tel: (1) 847 460 4100
Fax: (1) 847 460 4005

Sigma Theta Tau International/Glaxo Wellcome New Investigator Mentor Grant

Subjects: Nursing issues related to medication and medication administration. Possible topics include, but are not limited to compliance issues with patients who have asthma, HIV or AIDS, medication management problems in home healthcare, interventions to increase or enhance the appropriate use of metered dose inhalers by adolescents, or administration of IV medications in nursing homes and training of personnel administering IV medications.
Purpose: To enable research focusing on nursing issues related to medication and medications and their administration in the adult clinical setting.

Eligibility: Applicants must be a registered nurse with a current licence, received a Master's degree, submitted an application package and have signed a Sigma Theta Tau research agreement.
Level of Study: Postgraduate.
Type: Research grant.
Value: US$5,500 (US$3,000 New Investigator, US$2,500 mentor).
Frequency: Annual.
Country of Study: United States of America.
No. of awards offered: One.
Application Procedure: Applicants must write for an information booklet and application form.
Closing Date: December 1st.
Funding: Commercial.
Contributor: Nursing Research Program, Clinical Applications Research and Glaxo Wellcome Inc.
Additional Information: Preference will be given to Sigma Theta Tau members, all other qualifications being equal. Allocation of funds is based on the quality of the proposed research, the future promise of the applicant, and the applicant's research budget. The funding date is in June.

Sigma Theta Tau International/Glaxo Wellcome Prescriptive Practice Grant

Subjects: Practice nursing. Topics may include, but are not limited to, current status of prescriptive privileges by state, nurses or clients' satisfaction with prescriptive authority, barriers and constraints on nursing practice related to prescribing privileges, health policy and delivery system issues in nurses prescribing, needs of specific populations and client outcomes related to nurse prescribes.
Purpose: To support research relating to the prescribing practices of advanced practice nurses.
Eligibility: The recipient must be dedicated to the prescribing practices of advanced practice nurses. Applicants must be a registered nurse with a current licence, have received a Master's degree, submitted a complete research application package, be ready to start the research project and have signed a Sigma Theta Tau research agreement.
Level of Study: Postgraduate, Professional development.
Type: Research grant.
Value: Up to US$5,000.
Frequency: Annual.
Study Establishment: Unrestricted.
Country of Study: United States of America.
No. of awards offered: One.
Application Procedure: Applicants must write for an information booklet and application form.
Closing Date: December 1st.
Funding: Commercial.
Contributor: Glaxo Wellcome.
Additional Information: Preference will be given to Sigma Theta Tau members, all other qualifications being equal. Allocation of funds is based on the quality of the proposed research, the future promise of the applicant, and the applicant's research budget. The funding date is in June.

Sigma Theta Tau International/Mead Johnson Nutritionals Perinatal Grant

Subjects: Research must be related to perinatal issues spanning the perinatal period through the first year of life. This may include, but is not limited to, low and high risk maternal and neonatal care practices and innovative patient care delivery systems.
Purpose: To encourage qualified nurses to contribute to the advancement of nursing through research.
Eligibility: Applicants must be a registered nurse with a current licence, have received a Master's degree, submitted a complete research application package, be ready to start the research project and have signed a Sigma Theta Tau research agreement. Applicants must also be a United States citizen.
Level of Study: Postgraduate.
Type: Research grant.
Value: Up to US$10,000.
Frequency: Annual.
Study Establishment: Unrestricted.

Country of Study: United States of America.
No. of awards offered: One.
Application Procedure: Applicants must write for an information booklet and application form.
Closing Date: December 1st.
Funding: Commercial.
Contributor: Mead Johnson.
Additional Information: Preference will be given to Sigma Theta Tau members, all other qualifications being equal. Allocation of funds is based on the quality of the proposed research, the future promise of the applicant and the applicant's research budget. The funding date is June 1st.

Sigma Theta Tau International/Oncology Nursing Society Grant

Subjects: Clinical oncology.
Purpose: To encourage the research career development of nurses through the support of clinically orientated oncology research.
Eligibility: Open to registered nurses who are actively involved in some aspect of cancer patient care, education or research, and hold a Master's degree. Preference will be given to Sigma Theta Tau members, other qualifications being equal.
Level of Study: Postgraduate.
Value: Up to US$10,000.
Frequency: Annual.
Study Establishment: Unrestricted.
Country of Study: Any country.
No. of awards offered: One.
Application Procedure: Applicants must send proposals for this grant to the Oncology Nursing Society and must write for an information booklet and application form.
Closing Date: November 1st.
Funding: Private.
Contributor: The Oncology Nursing Society and Sigma Theta Tau International.
Additional Information: The funding date is in May.

For further information contact:

Oncology Nursing Foundation, 501 Holiday Drive, Pittsburgh, PA 15220-2749, United States of America
Tel: (1) 412 921 7373
Fax: (1) 412 921 6565

Sigma Theta Tau International/Rehabilitation Nursing Foundation Grant

Subjects: Rehabilitation nursing.
Purpose: To encourage research related to rehabilitation nursing.
Eligibility: The principal investigator is required to be a registered nurse in rehabilitation or a registered nurse who demonstrates interest in and significant contributions to rehabilitation nursing. Proposals that address the clinical practice, educational or administrative dimensions of rehabilitation nursing are requested. Quantitative and qualitative research projects will be accepted for review. The principal investigator must have Master's degree in nursing and an ability to complete the project within two years of initial funding.
Level of Study: Postgraduate.
Value: Up to US$6,000.
Frequency: Annual.
Country of Study: Any country.
No. of awards offered: One.
Application Procedure: Applicants must write for details.
Closing Date: April 1st.
Funding: Private.
Contributor: The Rehabilitation Nursing Foundation and Sigma Theta Tau International.
Additional Information: The funding date is the following January.

For further information contact:

Rehabilitation Nursing Foundation, 4700 West Lake Avenue, Glenview, IL 60025, United States of America
Tel: (1) 847 375 4710
Fax: (1) 847 375 4710
Email: info@rehabnurse.org

Virginia Henderson/Sigma Theta Tau International Clinical Research Grant

Subjects: Clinical research.

Purpose: To encourage the research career development of clinically based nurses through support of clinically orientated research.

Eligibility: Open to registered nurses actively involved in some aspect of healthcare delivery, education or research in a clinical setting, who are members of Sigma Theta Tau International, hold a Master's degree in nursing or are enrolled in a doctoral programme. The allocation of funds is based on a research project ready for implementation, the quality of the proposed research, the future potential of the applicant, appropriateness of the research budget and feasibility of the time frame.

Level of Study: Doctorate, Postgraduate, Predoctorate.

Type: Research grant.

Value: US$5,000.

Frequency: Every two years.

Country of Study: Any country.

No. of awards offered: One.

Application Procedure: Applicants must complete a Sigma Theta Tau International research grant application.

Closing Date: December 1st in odd numbered years.

Funding: Private.

Contributor: The Virginia Henderson Clinical Research Endowment Fund.

Additional Information: June is the funding date.

SIGMA XI, THE SCIENTIFIC RESEARCH SOCIETY

Sigma Xi Headquarters, Box 13975, 99 Alexander Drive, Research Triangle Park, NC 27709, United States of America
Tel: (1) 919 549 4691
Fax: (1) 919 549 0090
Email: giar@sigmaxi.org
www: http://www.sigmaxi.org
Contact: Grant Programme Co-ordinator

Sigma Xi, The Scientific Research Society is the international honour society for scientists and engineers. Founded in 1886, its goals are to foster worldwide interactions among science, technology, and society, to encourage appreciation and support of original work in science and technology, and to honour scientific accomplishments.

Sigma Xi Grants-in-Aid of Research

Subjects: Scientific research projects in any field eg. physical sciences and engineering, behavioural and life sciences, astronomy, cell biology, chemistry, computer science, mathematics, ecology, engineering, geology, physics, psychology, anthropology, ophthalmology and blood plasma research.

Eligibility: Open to graduate students in degree programmes.

Level of Study: Doctorate, Graduate, Predoctorate, Research.

Type: Grant.

Value: Awards are made in amounts up to a maximum of US$1,000 except in the fields of astronomy and eye or vision research where special funds allow for awards up to a maximum of US$2,500. No part of an award may be used for the payment of indirect costs to the recipient's institution. All funds must be expended directly in support of the proposed investigation. Any equipment purchased shall be the property of the institution.

Frequency: Annual.

Country of Study: Any country.

No. of awards offered: Approx. 300 awards annually.

Application Procedure: Applicants must visit the website for up to date guidelines and to fill out an interactive form.

Closing Date: March 15th or October 15th.

Funding: Private.

Additional Information: The following are not granted support: educational programmes and curriculum development, stipends for applicants or assistants, manuscript preparation and publication costs, the purchase of standard equipment and supplies that should normally be available in an institutional research laboratory, travel to scientific meetings or symposia, and requests for a third year of support. The Committee attaches low priority to support for use of institutional and departmental equipment and facilities.

SIR ERNEST CASSEL EDUCATIONAL TRUST

199 West Malvern Road, Malvern, Worcestershire, WR14 4BB, England
Tel: (44) 1684 572437
Email: casseltrust@sherborn.demon.co.uk
Contact: D N Constable, Secretary

The Sir Ernest Cassel Educational Trust awards overseas research grants, through the British Academy, in the language, literature or civilisation of any country. The Trust also awards the Mountbatten Memorial Grants to Commonwealth university students in their final year of study in the United Kingdom.

Mountbatten Memorial Grants to Commonwealth Students

Subjects: All subjects.

Purpose: To assist overseas students from the Commonwealth who encounter unforeseen financial difficulties in their final year of study.

Eligibility: Open to Commonwealth students who are pursuing a course of study at postgraduate level at universities or other recognised Institutes of Higher Education within the United Kingdom.

Level of Study: Doctorate, Graduate, MBA, Postgraduate, Predoctorate.

Type: Grant.

Value: Up to UK£500.

Frequency: Annual.

Country of Study: United Kingdom.

No. of awards offered: Varies.

Application Procedure: Applicants must apply in writing and include a brief curriculum vitae.

Funding: Private.

Contributor: Cassel Trust investments.

No. of awards given last year: 75.

No. of applicants last year: 500.

Additional Information: Grants are administered and awarded on the Trust's behalf by a number of universities and other Institutes of Higher Education. Applicants should consult their university or college student welfare officer for further information. The Trust does not sponsor, pay fees or award scholarships. There are no grants for one year courses.

Sir Ernest Cassel Educational Trust Overseas Research Grants

Subjects: The language, literature or civilisation of any country.

Purpose: To help towards the expenses of approved research abroad.

Eligibility: Open to junior teaching members of university faculties and other recognised Institutes of Higher Education in the United Kingdom, regardless of the applicant's country of birth.

Level of Study: Unrestricted.

Type: Research grant.

Value: UK£100-500.

Frequency: Annual.

Country of Study: Other.

No. of awards offered: Varies.

Application Procedure: Applicants must write to the British Academy for information.

Closing Date: September 30th, December 31st, February 28th or April 30th.

Funding: Private.

Contributor: Cassel Trust investments.

No. of awards given last year: Eight.

No. of applicants last year: Unknown.

Additional Information: Grants are administered by the British Academy.

For further information contact:

10 Carlton House Terrace, London, SW1Y 5AH, England

SIR HALLEY STEWART TRUST

22 Earith Road, Willingham, Cambridge, Cambridgeshire, CB4 5LS, England
Tel: (44) 1954 260707
www: http://www.sirhalleystewart.org
Contact: Mrs Sue West, Administrator

The Sir Halley Stewart Trust has a Christian basis and is concerned with the development of body, mind and spirit, a just environment and international goodwill. The Trust aims to promote innovative research activities or developments. It emphasises the prevention rather than alleviation of human suffering. Certain priorities apply.

Sir Halley Stewart Trust Grants
Subjects: Medical, social or religious research within certain priority areas.
Purpose: To assist pioneering research.
Eligibility: Not open to general appeals, building, capital, running costs or personal education including educational and travel costs.
Level of Study: Doctorate, Postgraduate, Predoctorate, Research.
Value: Salaries and relevant costs for innovative and imaginative young researchers in the region of UK£15,000-20,000.
Length of Study: Limited to two or three years.
Frequency: Dependent on funds available.
Study Establishment: Under the auspices of a charitable institution eg. a hospital, laboratory, university department or charitable organisation.
Country of Study: Mainly UK but some overseas, Africa (west/south) gives priority.
Application Procedure: Applicants must contact the Trust for further details. There is no application form and applications will not be accepted if sent by fax or email.
Closing Date: Applications are accepted at any time.
Funding: Private.
No. of awards given last year: 54.
No. of applicants last year: 756.
Additional Information: Further information is available from the Trust office by obtaining a copy of Notes for those Seeking Grants. The website contains the most up to date details.

SIR JOHN SOANE'S MUSEUM FOUNDATION

636 Broadway, Suite 720, New York, NY 10012, United States of America
Tel: (1) 646 654 0085
Fax: (1) 646 654 0089
Email: soane@mindspring.com
Contact: Mrs Cynthia Sanford, Joint Executive Director

The Sir John Soane's Museum Foundation assists the Museum in London to further Soane's commitment to educate and inspire the general and professional public in architecture and the fine and decorative arts. Programmes have attracted students, collectors, architects, decorators and arts enthusiasts since 1991 to its events, lectures, tours and dinners.

Sir John Soane's Museum Foundation Travelling Fellowship
Subjects: Art, architecture and the decorative arts.
Purpose: To enable scholars to pursue research projects related to the work of Sir John Soane's Museum and its collections.
Eligibility: Open to candidates enrolled in a graduate degree programme in a field appropriate to the Foundation's purpose.
Level of Study: Postgraduate.

Type: Fellowship.
Value: US$4,000.
Frequency: Annual.
Study Establishment: The choice of the fellowship recipient.
Country of Study: Usually the USA or the UK.
No. of awards offered: One.
Application Procedure: Applicants must submit a formal proposal of not more than five pages describing the goal, scope and purpose of the research project, in addition to three letters of recommendation. An interview may be required.
Closing Date: February 1st.
Funding: Private.
Contributor: The Board of Directors and the Advisory Board.
No. of awards given last year: One.
No. of applicants last year: Six.
Additional Information: At the end of each research project the award recipient must submit written documentation or a sketch book on the progress of the research as outlined in the original proposal with respect to goal, scope and allocation of funds, and give a lecture on the research, arranged by the Foundation. The Scholar usually spends some time at Sir John Soane's Museum at 13 Lincoln's Inn Fields, London, studying architectural drawings, models, and paintings.

SIR RICHARD STAPLEY EDUCATIONAL TRUST

North Street Farmhouse, Sheldwich, Near Faversham, Kent, ME13 0LN, England
Email: admin@stapleytrust.org
www: http://www.stapleytrust.org
Contact: Mrs Christine Ford, Administrator

The Sir Richard Stapley Educational Trust awards grants to graduates studying for higher degrees without subject restriction the trust will support only one postgraduate degree at a university in the United Kingdom.

Sir Richard Stapley Educational Trust Grants
Subjects: Medical, dental or veterinary science and higher degrees in other subjects.
Purpose: To support postgraduate study.
Eligibility: Open to graduates holding a First Class (Honours) Degree or an Upper Second Class (Honours) Degree, who are more than 24 years of age on October 1st of the proposed academic year. Students in receipt of a substantial award from local authorities, the NHS Executive Industry, Research Councils, the British Academy or other similar public bodies will not normally receive a grant from the Trust. Courses not eligible include electives, diplomas, professional training and intercalated degrees. The Trust does not support students for full-time PhD studies beyond a third year. Applicants must already be resident in the United Kingdom at the time of application.
Level of Study: Postgraduate.
Type: Grant.
Value: From UK£300-1,000.
Length of Study: Not defined, but PhD studies are not more than three years in duration. Grants are awarded for one full academic year in the first instance.
Frequency: Annual.
Study Establishment: Any appropriate university.
Country of Study: United Kingdom.
No. of awards offered: Dependent on availability of funds.
Application Procedure: Applicants making enquiries must include a large stamped addressed envelope before 28th February. Application forms will be sent out and must be returned complete with one academic reference in sealed envelopes on or before 28th February. Applicants will be notified in June.
Closing Date: 28th February.
Funding: Commercial, Private.
No. of awards given last year: 280.
No. of applicants last year: 390.

Additional Information: Grants are only paid upon receipt of official confirmation of participation in the course as well as confirmation that a financial shortfall still exists. All matters concerning application are by email and letter only.

SIR ROBERT MENZIES MEMORIAL FOUNDATION

210 Clarendon Street, East Melbourne, VIC, Australia
Tel: (61) 3 9419 5699
Fax: (61) 3 9417 7049
Email: menzies@vicnet.net.au
www: http://www.menzies.foundation.org.au
Contact: Ms S K Mackenzie, General Manager

The Sir Robert Menzies Memorial Foundation was formed as a memorial to Sir Robert Menzies in 1979. It is a non-profit and non political organisation with two principal activities. One is directed to the health and fitness of the Australian community and the other to the promotion of academic excellence.

Sir Robert Menzies Memorial Research Scholarships in the Allied Health Sciences

Subjects: Occupational therapy, speech pathology, physiotherapy, psychology, nursing, optometry or physical education.
Purpose: To allow an outstanding applicant to carry out doctoral research work that is likely to improve the health of Australians.
Eligibility: Open to Australian citizens of at least five years standing. Applicants will generally have completed the first year of their PhD project.
Level of Study: Doctorate, Postgraduate.
Type: Scholarship.
Value: Australian $24,000 free of income tax.
Length of Study: Two years.
Frequency: Annual.
Study Establishment: A tertiary institute with appropriate facilities.
Country of Study: Australia.
No. of awards offered: One.
Application Procedure: Applicants must complete and submit an application form, academic transcripts and other documents. Further information is available on request.
Closing Date: June 30th.
Funding: Private.
Contributor: The Sir Robert Menzies Memorial Foundation.
No. of awards given last year: One.
No. of applicants last year: 30.

Sir Robert Menzies Scholarships in Law

Subjects: Law.
Purpose: To enable Australian citizens to pursue postgraduate studies in the United Kingdom, generally leading to a higher degree.
Eligibility: Open to Australian citizens of five years of standing with at least an Upper Second Class (Honours) Degree in law at the time of application.
Level of Study: Postgraduate.
Type: Scholarship.
Value: Tuition fees or a research grant equivalent, return airfare, examination and other compulsory fees, UK£300 for books and equipment in the first year and UK£150 in the second year, up to UK£120 towards the typing and binding of a thesis, a quarterly living allowance of UK£2,000 plus additional allowance of UK£150 per month for spouse and UK£30 per month for each dependent child under 16.
Length of Study: One-two years.
Frequency: Annual.
Study Establishment: The Universities of St Andrews, Edinburgh, Cambridge or Oxford and occasionally elsewhere.
Country of Study: United Kingdom.
No. of awards offered: One or two.
Application Procedure: Applicants must complete and submit an application form along with academic transcripts and other documents.
Closing Date: August 31st.
Funding: Private.

Contributor: The Trust, the Foreign and Commonwealth Office and the Foundation in Australia.
No. of awards given last year: Two.
No. of applicants last year: 40.

THE SKIDMORE, OWINGS AND MERRILL FOUNDATION

224 South Michigan Avenue, Suite 1000, Chicago, IL 60604, United States of America
Tel: (1) 312 427 4202
Fax: (1) 312 360 4551
Email: somfoundation@som.com
Contact: Ms Lisa Westerfield, Administrative Director

The mission of the Skidmore, Owings and Merrill Foundation is to help young architects and engineers broaden their professional education, instil a heightened sense of responsibility as future practitioners to improve the quality of the built and natural environments, and to encourage them to appreciate the influence of place making, culture and technology on the design of buildings and their settings.

Architecture Master's Degree Travelling Fellowship

Subjects: Architecture.
Purpose: To help young architects to broaden their education and take an enlightened view of society's need to improve the built and natural environments.
Eligibility: Open to candidates of any citizenship who are graduating from a United States of America university. For the Bachelor degree Travelling Fellowship winners must receive, prior to fellowship commencement, a Bachelor's degree in architecture. For the Master's degree fellowship winners must receive, prior to commencement of the fellowship, a Master's degree in architecture.
Level of Study: Graduate, also undergraduate.
Type: Fellowship.
Value: US$15,000.
Frequency: Annual.
Study Establishment: Accredited schools, colleges or universities.
Country of Study: United States of America
No. of awards offered: Two for Bachelor level graduating students and one for Master's level.
Application Procedure: Applicants must submit a portfolio with a proposed travel itinerary and a signed copyright release statement provided by the Foundation. Full guidelines are available on request and on the website. Students must be nominated by a United States of America school of attendance.
Funding: Private.
No. of awards given last year: Three.
Additional Information: Information is sent to schools between February and March.

Building Systems Technology Research Grant

Subjects: Topics such as energy efficient design, the application of new technologies, the appropriate use or re-use of natural resources and the integration of building systems as components of a work of architecture.
Purpose: To expand the vision and imagination of young engineers in the design and engineering of building systems.
Eligibility: The award is under the administration of the American Society of Heating, Refrigerating and Air Conditioning and adheres to all their deadline requirements, details of which can be viewed under the Student Zone at http://www.ashrae.org.
Level of Study: Graduate.
Type: Fellowship.
Value: US$7,500.
Frequency: Annual.
Study Establishment: Accredited schools in the United States of America.
Country of Study: United States of America.
No. of awards offered: One.

Application Procedure: Applicants must submit their application through the American Society of Heating, Refrigerating and Air Conditioning's Grants-in-Aid Program.
Funding: Private.

Interior Architecture Travelling Fellowship

Subjects: Architecture and design, including awareness and skilful handling of the full range of elements that support a designed interior space, including furniture and finishes, lighting and artwork.
Purpose: To encourage young designers to explore the relationship between architecture and interiors, with particular emphasis on the three dimensional modelling of space and the integration of interior spaces and elements with building architecture and systems.
Eligibility: Applicants must be graduating with a Bachelor's or Master's degree from either an accredited United States of America architectural school, the Foundation for Interior Design Education Research (FIDER) or the Association of Independent Colleges of Art and Design (AICAD). Applicants must be nominated by the faculty and endorsed by the chair of the department from which they will receive the degree.
Level of Study: Graduate, also undergraduate.
Type: Fellowship.
Value: US$7,500.
Frequency: Annual.
Study Establishment: Accredited schools in the United States of America.
Country of Study: United States of America.
No. of awards offered: One.
Application Procedure: Applicants must submit a portfolio with two copies each of a letter of recommendation, proposed travel itinerary and a signed copyright release statement provided by the SOM Foundation. Full guidelines are available on request or from the website. Students must be nominated by the United States school of attendance.
Funding: Private.
Additional Information: Information is sent to schools between February and March.

Structural Engineering Travelling Fellowship

Subjects: The role of aesthetics, innovation, efficiency and economy in the structural design of buildings, bridges and other structures.
Purpose: To foster an appreciation of the aesthetic potential inherent in the structural design of buildings, bridges and other major works of architecture and engineering.
Eligibility: Open to candidates of any citizenship who are graduating from an American school with a Bachelor's, Master's or PhD degree in civil or architectural engineering, with a specialisation in structural engineering. Applicants must be nominated by the faculty and endorsed by the chair of the department from which they will receive the degree. Applicants must intend to enter the professional practice of structural engineering in the field of buildings or bridges.
Level of Study: Doctorate, Graduate, also undergraduate.
Type: Competition.
Value: US$10,000.
Frequency: Annual.
Study Establishment: Accredited schools in the United States of America.
Country of Study: United States of America.
Application Procedure: Applicants must submit four copies of a letter of recommendation, curriculum vitae, recent graduate and undergraduate transcripts, a brief essay between two and four pages in length plus figures, a proposed travel itinerary, a computer disk containing the essay and itinerary and a signed copyright release provided by the Foundation. Full guidelines are available on request.
Funding: Private.
Additional Information: The fellowship hopes to encourage an awareness of the visual impact of structural engineering among engineering students and their schools. It also helps to strengthen the connection between aesthetics and efficiency, economy and innovation in structural design.

Urban Design Travelling Fellowship

Subjects: Pertinent urban design issues such as appropriate development character, sense of place, preservation and adaptive reuse, way finding and ease of access and movement, and sustainable patterns of densification and growth.
Purpose: To encourage young architects with an interest in urban design to broaden their knowledge of the design of modern, high density cities.
Eligibility: Open to candidates of any citizenship who are graduating from a United States school with a Bachelor's degree in architecture, landscape architecture or urban design or a Master's degree in urban design. Applicants must be nominated by the faculty and endorsed by the chair of the department from which they will receive the degree.
Level of Study: Graduate.
Type: Fellowship.
Value: US$7,500.
Frequency: Annual.
Study Establishment: Accredited schools in the United States of America.
Country of Study: United States of America.
No. of awards offered: One.
Application Procedure: Applicants must submit a portfolio with two copies each of a letter of recommendation, curriculum vitae, recent transcript, proposed travel itinerary and a signed copyright release statement provided by the Foundation. Full guidelines are available on request.
Funding: Private.
Additional Information: Information is sent to schools between February and March.

SME EDUCATION FOUNDATION

PO Box 930, Dearborn, MI 48121-0930, United States of America
Tel: (1) 313 271 1500 ext. 1702
Fax: (1) 313 240 6095
Email: quinste@sme.org
www: http://www.sme.org/foundation
Contact: Mr Steve Quinlan, Grants Program Officer

The SME Education Foundation provides the manufacturing professional with an outlet to support the development of the manufacturing workforce of the future. As one of the nation's leading organisations dedicated to advancing manufacturing education, the Foundation awards grants and scholarships and administers student outreach programmes designed in partnership with corporations, foundations, educational institutions and individual donors. Since 1998, the Foundation has awarded more than US$12 million in cash grants, scholarships and special awards.

SME Education Foundation Grants Program

Subjects: Manufacturing engineering.
Purpose: To establish a process that will stimulate the academic community to help improve the competency of the manufacturing workforce. It focuses on identifying and then closing competency gaps between industry's manufacturing workforce needs and what is currently provided by educational programmes.
Eligibility: Open to full-time university faculty representing manufacturing engineering or manufacturing engineering technology programmes which offer manufacturing courses. Applicants must be Canadian, American or Mexican.
Level of Study: Postgraduate.
Type: Grant.
Value: Funds are reimbursed upon receipt of an invoice and narrative report.
Length of Study: Two years.
Frequency: Annual.
Country of Study: USA, Canada or Mexico.
No. of awards offered: Varies.
Application Procedure: Applicants must submit a signed original application with seven copies to coincide with the request. Further information is available from the website.
Closing Date: The first Friday in December.
Funding: Private.

Contributor: SME members, chapters, regions and corporations.
Additional Information: Grants must be matched dollar for dollar by the educational institution, industry or government unit.

THE SMITH AND NEPHEW FOUNDATION

Heron House, 15 Adam Street, London, WC2N 6LA, England
Tel: (44) 20 7960 2276
Fax: (44) 20 7960 2298
Email: barbara.foster1@smith-nephew.com
www: http://www.snfoundation.org.uk
Contact: Ms Barbara Foster, Foundation Administrator

The Smith and Nephew Foundation aims to improve health care in the United Kingdom by offering awards to individuals in the nursing professions undertaking educational or research projects.

Smith and Nephew Foundation Nursing Research Studentship
Subjects: Projects which have been designed to enhance the evidence base for nursing and midwifery practice and which clearly evaluate the effectiveness and outcomes of nursing and midwifery interventions. Nursing care of patients with skin or tissue damage and vulnerability.
Purpose: To aid nursing research as part of a PhD programme.
Eligibility: Applications are invited from outstanding nurse researchers who will contribute to the evidence base for the nursing care of patients with skin or tissue damage and vulnerability.
Level of Study: Postgraduate.
Type: Studentship.
Value: Up to UK£90,000.
Length of Study: Up to three years.
Frequency: Annual.
Country of Study: United Kingdom.
No. of awards offered: One.
Application Procedure: Applicants must apply for details by telephone, email or post. The fellowships are advertised in the relevant nursing journals and on the Foundation website www.snfoundation.org.uk.
Closing Date: Advertised usually at the beginning of March with a closing date 8 weeks later.
Funding: Commercial.
Contributor: Smith & Nephew plc.
No. of awards given last year: Two.
No. of applicants last year: 10.
Additional Information: Further information is available on request.

Smith and Nephew Foundation Postdoctoral Nursing Research Fellowship
Subjects: Nursing care of patients with skin or tissue damage and vulnerability.
Purpose: To aid nursing postdoctoral research and support outstanding career nurse researchers.
Eligibility: Applications are invited from potential fellows and the proposed host research team or unit. The host research team must be a university school, faculty or department of nursing and have a proven track record of research and development in the nursing care of patients with skin damage or tissue damage or vulnerability.
Level of Study: Postdoctorate.
Type: Fellowship.
Value: UK£120,000.
Length of Study: Up to three years.
Frequency: Annual.
Country of Study: United Kingdom.
No. of awards offered: One.
Application Procedure: Applicants must apply for details by telephone, email or post. The fellowships are advertised in the relevant nursing journals and on the Foundation website www.snfoundation.org.uk.
Closing Date: Advertised usually at the beginning of March closing date usually 8 weeks later.

Funding: Commercial.
Contributor: Smith and Nephew plc.
No. of awards given last year: One.
No. of applicants last year: Seven.

SMITHSONIAN ASTROPHYSICS OBSERVATORY (SAO)

60 Garden Street, Mail Stop 47, Cambridge, MA 02138, United States of America
Email: predoc@cfa.harvard.edu
www: http://cfa-www.harvard.edu/newtop/saohome.html
Contact: Dale A Alianiello, Fellowship Program Co-ordinator

SAO Predoctoral Fellowships
Subjects: Astronomy, astrophysics, atomic and molecular physics, planetary science, radio and geoastronomy, solar and stellar physics or theoretical astrophysics.
Purpose: To allow students from other institutions throughout the world to undertake their thesis research at SAO.
Eligibility: Applicants must have completed their preliminary course work and examinations and be ready to begin dissertation research at the time of the award.
Level of Study: Predoctorate.
Type: Fellowship.
Value: A stipend of US$24,600. Some funds may also be available for relocation, travel and other expenses.
Length of Study: One year, with a possibility of renewal for up to a total of three years.
Frequency: Annual.
Study Establishment: The Smithsonian Astrophysical Observatory.
Country of Study: United States of America.
No. of awards offered: Varies.
Application Procedure: Applicants must contact directly Smithsonian scientists in their area of interest to discuss possible research topics. Applicants must complete an application form, available on request via email and downloadable from the website http://cfa-www.harvard.edu/predoc.
Closing Date: April 15th.
No. of awards given last year: Eight.
No. of applicants last year: 15
Additional Information: Further information can be found on the website.

SMITHSONIAN INSTITUTION

750 9th Street North West, Suite 9300 MRC 902, PO Box 37012, Washington, DC 20013-7012
United States of America
Tel: (1) 202 275 0655
Fax: (1) 202 275 0489
Email: siofg@.si.edu
www: http://www.si.edu/research + study
Contact: Mr Bryan T Fair, Office of Fellowships

The Smithsonian Institution was established in 1846 with funds bequeathed to the United States by James Smithson. The Institution is as an independent trust instrumentality of the United States holding some 140 million artefacts and specimens in its trust for the increase and diffusion of knowledge.

Smithsonian Institution Graduate Student Fellowships
Subjects: Animal behaviour, ecology, environmental science, anthropology, archaeology, astrophysics, astronomy, earth sciences, paleobiology, evolutionary and systematic biology, history of science and technology, history of art and folklife.
Purpose: To enable graduate students to conduct individual research under the guidance of Smithsonian staff members. Projects must be related to the research and interests of the Institution's professional staff.
Eligibility: Open to graduate students of any nationality who are formally enrolled and engaged in a graduate programme of study at a

degree granting institution and have completed at least one semester before the appointment period, and have not yet been advanced to candidacy. Projects proposed will be approved in advance by a Smithsonian staff member who will serve as the appointee's advisor. Fluency in English is required.

Level of Study: Graduate.
Type: Fellowship.
Value: US$3,700.
Length of Study: 10 weeks.
Frequency: Annual.
Study Establishment: Smithsonian Institution facilities.
Country of Study: United States of America.
No. of awards offered: Varies.
Application Procedure: Applicants must complete an application pack, available from the office or the website: www.si.edu/research + study.
Closing Date: January 15th.

Smithsonian Institution Postdoctoral Fellowships

Subjects: American social and cultural history, history of science and technology, history of art, anthropology, biological sciences, earth sciences and history of African art and culture.
Purpose: To offer appointments to those who wish to pursue postdoctoral research training at the Smithsonian Institution in collaboration with a member of the professional staff of the Institution.
Eligibility: Open to candidates of any nationality who have received a PhD or equivalent within seven years of the application date. Recipients must have completed the degree or certificate at the time the fellowship commences. Fluency in English is required.
Level of Study: Postdoctorate.
Type: Fellowship.
Value: US$30,000 per year plus research and travel allowances.
Length of Study: 3-12 months, usually one year.
Frequency: Annual.
Study Establishment: Smithsonian Institution facilities.
Country of Study: United States of America.
No. of awards offered: Varies.
Application Procedure: Applicants must complete an application form. Further information and application forms are available from the office or online at: www.si.edu/research + study.
Closing Date: January 15th.
No. of awards given last year: Varies.
No. of applicants last year: Varies.

Smithsonian Institution Predoctoral Fellowships

Subjects: Anthropology, biological sciences, earth sciences, history of art, history of science and technology, American social and cultural history, and the history of African art and culture.
Purpose: To financially support those undertaking predoctoral fellowships.
Eligibility: Open to students of any nationality who are enrolled in a university as candidates for a PhD or equivalent. At the time of appointment the university must approve the undertaking of dissertation research at the Smithsonian Institution and indicate that requirements for the doctorate, other than the dissertation, have been met. Fluency in English is required.
Level of Study: Postgraduate, Predoctorate.
Type: Fellowship.
Value: US$17,000 per year plus research and travel allowances.
Length of Study: 3-12 months.
Frequency: Annual.
Study Establishment: Smithsonian Institution facilities.
Country of Study: United States of America.
No. of awards offered: Varies.
Application Procedure: Applicants must complete an application form available from the office or online at: www.si.edu/research + study.
Closing Date: January 15th.
Additional Information: Projects proposed will be approved in advance by a Smithsonian staff member who will serve as the appointee's advisor. Projects must be related to the research and interest of the Institution's professional staff.

Smithsonian Institution Senior Fellowships

Subjects: Anthropology, biological sciences, American social and cultural history, history of science and technology, history of art, and the history of African art and culture.
Purpose: To offer appointments to senior scholars who wish to pursue research at the Smithsonian Institution. Projects must be related to the research and interests of the Institution's professional staff.
Eligibility: Open to applicants of any nationality who are seven or more years beyond the degree of PhD or equivalent. Projects proposed will be approved in advance by a Smithsonian staff member who will serve as the appointee's advisor. Fluency in English is required.
Level of Study: Postdoctorate.
Type: Fellowship.
Value: US$30,000 per year plus allowances.
Length of Study: 3-12 months.
Frequency: Annual.
Study Establishment: Smithsonian Institution facilities.
Country of Study: United States of America.
No. of awards offered: Varies.
Application Procedure: Applicants must complete an application pack, available from the office or the website: www.si.edu/research + study.
Closing Date: January 15th.

SMITHSONIAN INSTITUTION - NATIONAL AIR AND SPACE MUSEUM

Room 3313, Washington, DC 20560-0312
United States of America
Tel: (1) 202 357 2515
Fax: (1) 202 786 2447
Email: collette.williams@nasm.si.edu
www: http://www.nasm.edu/nasm/joinnasm/fellow/fellow.htm
Contact: Ms Collette Williams, Fellowships Co-ordinator

A Verville Fellowship

Subjects: The history of aviation and space flights.
Purpose: To fund the analysis of major trends, developments and accomplishments in the history of aviation or space studies.
Eligibility: Open to all interested candidates who can demonstrate skills in research and writing. An advanced degree is not a requirement.
Level of Study: Postgraduate.
Type: Fellowship.
Value: A stipend of US$45,000 with limited additional funds available for travel and miscellaneous expenses.
Length of Study: 9-12 months, normally beginning June 1st-October 1st.
Country of Study: United States of America.
No. of awards offered: One.
Application Procedure: Applicants must submit a summary description, research proposal, bibliography, estimated schedule, research budget, curriculum vitae and letters from three referees. Six copies of the complete application must be submitted. Further information and an application pack are available on request or downloadable from the website.
Closing Date: January 15th.
Additional Information: Residence in the Washington DC, Metropolitan area during the fellowship term is a requirement of this fellowship. Further information is available on the website.

The Guggenheim Fellowships

Subjects: Historical research related to aviation and space.
Purpose: To promote research into, and writing about, the history of aviation and space flight.
Eligibility: Postdoctoral fellowships are open to applicants who have received a PhD degree or equivalent within seven years of the beginning of the fellowship period. Predoctoral

fellowships are open to applicants who have completed preliminary course work and examinations and are engaged in dissertation research. All applicants must be able to speak and write fluently in English.

Level of Study: Postdoctorate, Predoctorate.
Type: Fellowship.
Value: Postdoctoral stipend US$30,000 for one year term and predoctoral stipend US$20,000 for one year term, with limited additional funds available for travel and miscellaneous expenses.
Length of Study: 3-12 months.
Frequency: Annual.
Study Establishment: A major portion of research must be conducted at the Smithsonian.
Country of Study: United States of America.
No. of awards offered: Varies.
Application Procedure: Applicants must submit a summary description, research proposal, bibliography, estimated schedule, research budget, transcripts from all graduate institutions, English training with test scores and level of proficiency in reading, conversing and writing, if English is not native language, curriculum vitae and letters from three referees. Six copies of the complete application must be submitted.
Closing Date: January 15th.
Additional Information: Residence in the Washington DC, metropolitan area during the fellowship term is a requirement of the fellowship. Further information is available on the website.

National Air and Space Museum Aviation/Space Writers Award

Subjects: Aerospace topics.
Purpose: To support research leading towards publication.
Eligibility: Applicants for NASM or Smithsonian Fellowships are encouraged to apply for the Aviation/Space Writers Award but recipients of the award need not be in residence at the National Air and Space Museum.
Type: Grant.
Value: US$5,000 to support research travel and expenses, or the publication of research.
Frequency: Every two years.
Country of Study: United States of America.
Application Procedure: Applicants must submit a letter of proposal stating the subject of their research and publication goals not exceeding five pages.
Closing Date: January 15th.
Additional Information: A specific budget indicating how the money will be used must be included.

Ramsay Fellowship in Naval Aviation History

Subjects: The history of aviation at sea and in naval service, particularly the United States Navy.
Eligibility: Open to all interested candidates who can demonstrate skills in research and writing. An advanced degree is not a requirement.
Level of Study: Postgraduate.
Type: Fellowship.
Value: A stipend of US$45,000 with additional limited funds available for travel and miscellaneous expenses.
Length of Study: 9-12 months.
Country of Study: United States of America.
No. of awards offered: One.
Application Procedure: Applicants must submit a summary description, research proposal, bibliography, estimated schedule, research budget, curriculum vitae and letters from three referees. Six copies of the complete application must be submitted. Further information and an application pack are available on request or downloadable from the website.
Closing Date: January 15th.
Additional Information: Residence in the Washington DC, Metropolitan area during the fellowship term is a requirement of this fellowship. Further information is available on the website.

THE SNOWDON AWARD SCHEME

22 City Business Centre, 6 Brighton Road, Horsham, West Sussex RH13 5BB, England
Tel: (44) 01403 211 252
Fax: (44) 01403 211 252
Email: infor@snowdonawardscheme.org.uk
www: www.snowdonawardscheme.org.uk
Contact: Laura Hanlon, Administrator

The Snowdon Award Scheme provides grants of upto UK£2,000 to physically disabled students for disability - related costs of further or higher education or training in the UK. Preferred age range 17-25 but mature students may apply, funds permitting.

Snowdon Award

Purpose: Support physically impaired students in further or higher education or training in the UK.
Eligibility: Physically impaired students.
Value: UK£250-2,000 (UK£2,500 in exceptional circumstances).
Frequency: Annual.
Study Establishment: All recognised further, higher education or training centres.
Country of Study: United Kingdom.
No. of awards offered: Up to 100 a year, depending on funds.
Application Procedure: Application form and at least four specialized references required. Application form available online.
Closing Date: 31st May annually.
Funding: Commercial, individuals, private, trusts.
Contributor: Trusts and commercial sponsors.
No. of awards given last year: 78.
No. of applicants last year: N/A.

SOCIAL SCIENCE RESEARCH COUNCIL (SSRC)

810 Seventh Avenue, New York, NY 10019, United States of America
Tel: (1) 212 377 2700
Fax: (1) 212 377 2727
Email: info@ssrc.org
www: http://www.ssrc.org
Contact: Mr John Meyers, Director of Development

Founded in 1923, the Social Science Research Council (SSRC) is an independent, non governmental, non-profit, international association devoted to the advancement of interdisciplinary research in the social sciences. The aim of the organisation is to improve the quality of publicly available knowledge around the world.

ACLS/SSRC/NEH International and Area Studies Fellowships

Subjects: Humanities.
Purpose: To encourage humanistic research in area studies.
Eligibility: Open to United States citizens who have lived in the United States for at least three years and completed their PhD more than two years prior to application.
Level of Study: Postdoctorate.
Type: Fellowship.
Length of Study: 6-12 months.
Frequency: Annual.
Country of Study: Other.
No. of awards offered: Approx. 10.
Application Procedure: Applicants must apply for information, available on request from ACLS.
Closing Date: October.
Contributor: The National Endowment for the Humanities.

For further information contact:

ACLS 633 Third Avenue, New York, NY 10017-6795, United States of America
Fax: (1) 212 697 1505
Email: grants@acls.org
www: http://www.acls.org

SSRC Abe Fellowship Program

Subjects: The social sciences and humanities relevant to any one or combination of the following themes: global issues, problems common to industrial and industrialising societies and issues that relate to United States Japanese relations.

Purpose: To develop a new generation of researchers who study policy relevant topics of long range importance and who will become members of bilateral and global research networks. The programme promotes a new level of intellectual co-operation between the Japanese and American academic and professional research communities concerned with, and trained for, advancing global understanding and problem solving.

Eligibility: Open to Japanese and American citizens and other nationals, who can demonstrate serious and long-term affiliations in Japanese or American research communities. Applicants must hold a PhD or have attained an equivalent level of professional experience as evaluated in their country of residence. Applications from researchers in non academic professions are welcome.

Level of Study: Postdoctorate.

Type: Fellowship.

Value: Research and travel expenses as necessary for completion of the research project in addition to limited salary replacement

Length of Study: Up to one year.

Frequency: Annual.

Study Establishment: An appropriate institution.

Country of Study: Other.

No. of awards offered: Approx. 14.

Application Procedure: Applicants must submit a reference and an optional language evaluation form.

Closing Date: September 1st.

Funding: Private.

Contributor: The Japan Foundation Center for Global Partnership.

No. of awards given last year: 15.

No. of applicants last year: 60-100.

Additional Information: In addition to receiving fellowship awards, Fellows will attend annual conferences and other events sponsored by the programme, which will promote the development of an international network of scholars   concerned with research on contemporary policy issues. Funds are provided by the Japan Foundation's Center for Global Partnership. Further information is available by e-mailing abe@ssrc.org.

SSRC Africa Program Advanced Research Grants

Subjects: African studies. Applicants working in literature, philosophy, religion and art history, which are previously underrepresented, are especially encouraged to apply.

Purpose: To support field research in Africa and comparative, theoretical research that proposes more than the analysis of previously gathered materials.

Eligibility: Open to citizens and permanent residents of the United States of America for at least three consecutive years, who hold a PhD or an equivalent degree.

Level of Study: Postdoctorate.

Type: Research grant.

Value: Up to US$15,000.

Frequency: Annual.

Country of Study: Africa.

No. of awards offered: Varies.

Application Procedure: Individuals/applicants should send proposals/application materials before closing date.

Closing Date: December 1st.

Additional Information: If travel to Africa is planned, applicants must try to arrange for affiliation with an African university or research institute. Grants are for Sub-Saharan regions. North Africa is included in the Near and Middle East program.

For further information contact:

Social Science Research Council, Africa Program, 810, 7th Avenue, 31st Floor, New York, NY 10019, United States of America

SSRC Africa Program Dissertation Fellowships

Subjects: The social sciences and humanities in Africa, South of the Sahara.

Eligibility: Open to full-time students, regardless of citizenship, who are enrolled in doctoral programs in the United States of America, and to United States citizens and permanent residents enrolled in full-time doctoral programs abroad.

Level of Study: Doctorate.

Type: Fellowship.

Value: Varies.

Length of Study: 9-18 months.

Frequency: Annual.

Country of Study: Africa.

No. of awards offered: Varies.

Application Procedure: Application form must be completed - requested by SSRC. Send materials before closing date.

Closing Date: November 1st.

Funding: Private.

Additional Information: Applicants are expected to have achieved a level of fluency in African and European languages sufficient to enable them to accomplish the goals of their project satisfactorily. Limited support for additional language training and dissertation write-up support may be included in awards. Please contact SSRC in May for further information.

For further information contact:

SSRC, 810, 7th Avenue, 31st Floor, New York, NY 10019, United States of America

Contact: Africa Program

SSRC Africa Program Predissertation Fellowships

Subjects: African studies.

Purpose: To support short-term field trips to Africa to encourage preliminary field activities, the identification of local scholars and contacts, and planning for students preparing for dissertation research on Africa.

Eligibility: Open to students who have completed one year of graduate study in the social sciences or humanities at a United States university, or who are United States citizens or permanent residents who have completed this study abroad, and have been accepted into a full PhD program.

Level of Study: Postgraduate.

Type: Varies.

Value: Up to US$2,500.

Frequency: Annual.

Country of Study: Africa.

Application Procedure: Send proposal/application info. before the deadline.

Closing Date: November 1st.

Funding: Private.

Additional Information: Grants are for Sub-Saharan regions. North Africa is included in the Near and Middle East program.

For further information contact:

810, 7th Avenue, 31st Floor, New York, NY 10119, United States of America

Tel: (1) 212 661 0280

Contact: Africa Program, SSRC

SSRC Berlin Programme for Advanced German and European Studies

Subjects: The economic, political and social aspects of modern and contemporary German and European affairs.

Purpose: To encourage the comparative and interdisciplinary study by supporting anthropologists, economists, political scientists, sociologists and all scholars in German social science and cultural studies fields, including historians working on the period since the mid nineteenth-century.

Eligibility: Open to citizens and permanent residents of the United States of America and Canada who have completed all requirements, except the dissertation, for a PhD at the time the fellowship begins, or postdoctorals of all levels. Postdoctoral applicants must have been residing in U.S. atleast 3 years prior to application deadline. U.S. citizenship is not required.

Level of Study: Doctorate, Postdoctorate, Predoctorate.

Value: Please contact the organisation.

Length of Study: Nine months to one year.
Frequency: Annual.
Study Establishment: The Free University of Berlin.
Country of Study: Germany.
No. of awards offered: 12.
Application Procedure: Applicants must apply for information, available.
Closing Date: December.
Funding: Government, Private.
Contributor: National Endowment for the Humanities, Freie Universität Berlin.
Additional Information: Fellows are expected to produce a research monograph dealing with one or more aspects of German or European affairs, including United States European relations. The programme is funded by the Berlin government and the German Marshall Fund of the United States. Applicants must contact the programme for further information.

For further information contact:

This fellowship no longer at SSRC. For information please contact bprogram@zedst.fu-berlin.de.

SSRC Eurasia Program Dissertation Fellowships

Subjects: Dissertation Write-up awards of US$15,000 for one academic year provide support to graduate students near the completion of their doctoral programs in the social sciences and related humanities. These fellowships are intended for applicants who have completed all formal components of their dissertation field research or data collection, and who have made significant progress in outlining emergent, innovative contributions to scholarship.
Purpose: To provide support to students who have completed research for their doctoral dissertations and expect to complete the writing of their dissertations during the next academic year.
Eligibility: Applicants for dissertation Write-up fellowships must have attained ABD status (must have completed all requirements for the Ph.D. degree except for the dissertation) by the fellowship start date. They must be US citizens or permanent residents. The fellow's home institution is expected to make a cost-sharing contribution of no less than 10 percent of the fellowship award. Detailed information on eligibility criteria and conditions of awards will be available in the application materials.
Level of Study: Doctorate, Graduate.
Type: Fellowship.
Value: Up to US$15,000.
Length of Study: Up to one year.
Frequency: Annual.
Country of Study: Eurasia (Armenia, Azerbaijan, Belarus, Georgia, Kazakhstan, Kyrgyztan, Moldova, Russia, Tajikistan, Turkmenistan, Ukraine, and Uzbekistan).
No. of awards offered: Varies.
Application Procedure: Awards are made on the basis of evaluations and recommendations by the Title VIII Program Committee, an interdisciplinary committee composed of scholars of the region. The committee rewards proposals with clarity of argument, purpose, theory, and method, written in a style accessible to readers outside the applicant's discipline. Applicants must submit a completed application, a narrative statement, transcripts, a course list and language evaluation form, and references. Full information is available online.
Closing Date: November.
Funding: Government.
Contributor: U.S. Department of state under the Program for Research and Training on Eastern Europe and the Independent States of the Former Soviet Union (Title VIII).
No. of awards given last year: 7.
No. of applicants last year: Approximately 30.
Additional Information: No funding is available for the Baltic States

For further information contact:

810, Seventh Avenue, 31st Floor, New York, NY 10019,
Tel: (212) 377-2700
Fax: (212) 377-2727

Email: eurasia@ssrc.org
www: www.ssrc.org/fellowships/eurasia
Contact: Social Science Research Council, Eurasia Fellowship Program

SSRC Eurasia Program Postdoctoral Fellowships

Subjects: Postdoctoral awards of US$24,000 are designed to improve the academic employment and tenure opportunities of recent PhD recipients (up to five years past the PhD but no more than three years into a tenure-track position at the time of application) in the social sciences and related humanities. Particular consideration is given to tenure-track faculty with heavy teaching loads, as well as to those projects that generate path-breaking interdisciplinary approaches, or those that invite conceptual boundary crossings-theoretically, methodologically, or geographically.
Purpose: To improve the academic employment and tenure opportunities of new PhDs and junior faculty.
Eligibility: Applicants for Postdoctoral fellowships must have the Ph.D. in hand at the time of application (ABD's will not be considered), must have received the degree no more than five years prior to the application deadline, and must have accumulated no more than 3 consecutive years in a tenure-track teaching position (although they need not currently be in a tenure-track position). They must be US citizens or permanent residents. Where applicable, the Postdoctoral research fellow's home institution is expected to make a cost-sharing contribution of no less than 10 percent of the fellowship award. Independent scholars, not currently affiliated with an institution, are not subject to this requirement. Detailed information on eligibility criteria and conditions of awards will be in the application materials.
Level of Study: Doctorate, Postdoctorate.
Type: Fellowship.
Value: A stipend of US$24,000 to provide two years of Summer support plus one semester free of teaching for postdoctorates.
Length of Study: Two years.
Frequency: Annual.
Country of Study: Eurasia (Armenia, Azerbaijan, Belarus, Georgia, Kazakhstan, Kyrgyztan, Moldova, Russia, Tajikistan, Turkmenistan, Ukraine, and Uzbekistan).
No. of awards offered: Varies.
Application Procedure: Awards are made on the basis of evaluations and recommendations by the Title VIII Program Committee, an interdisciplinary committee and composed of scholars of the region. The committee rewards proposals with clarity of argument, purpose, theory, and method, written in a style accessible to readers outside the applicant's discipline. Applicants must submit a completed application, a narrative statement, a CV and references. Full information is available on-line
Closing Date: November.
Funding: Government.
Contributor: U.S. Department of State under the Program for Research and Training on Eastern Europe and the Independent States of the Former Soviet Union (Title VIII).
No. of awards given last year: Approx. 3.
No. of applicants last year: Approx. 20.
Additional Information: No funding is available for the Baltic States

For further information contact:

810, Seventh Avenue, 31st Floor, New York, NY 10019, United States of America
Tel: (1) 377-2700
Fax: (1) 377-2727
Email: eurasia@ssrc.org
www: www.ssrc.org/fellowships/eurasia
Contact: Social Science Research Council, Eurasia Fellowship Program

SSRC Eurasia Program Teaching Fellowships

Subjects: Teaching Fellowships are designed to encourage faculty members who have a proven desire to push the contemporary boundaries of Eurasian studies through the creation and implementation of significantly revised or wholly new university courses and curricula. The teaching fellowship awards of US$10,000 support the creation of original and innovative course curricula within the humanities and social sciences that relate to Eurasian studies. The SSRC invites proposals with a diverse range of pedagogical and thematic approaches. These fellowships are meant to be dispersed over a period of two years.

Purpose: To encourage and support faculty members at all career levels in their efforts to impart their own knowledge and expertise to their students.

Eligibility: Applicants for the Teaching Fellowships must have the Ph.D. in hand and currently be teaching full-time in an accredited US university, and the must be US citizens or permanent residents. The home institution of the Teaching Fellowship recipient is expected to provide a letter of intent stating that the institution or relevant department intends to support the implementation of the fellow's new course into the offered curriculum at least once within a period of no more than two years. Detailed information on eligibility criteria and conditions of awards will be available in the application materials.

Level of Study: Postdoctorate.

Type: Fellowship.

Value: US$10,000.

Length of Study: Maximum two years.

Frequency: Annual.

Country of Study: Eurasia (Armenia, Azerbaijan, Belarus, Georgia, Kazakhstan, Kyrgyztan, Moldova, Russia, Tajikistan, Turkmenistan, Ukraine, and Uzbekistan).

No. of awards offered: Varies.

Application Procedure: Awards are made on the basis of evaluations and recommendations by the Title VIII Program Committee, an interdisciplinary committee and composed of scholars of the region. The committee rewards proposals with clarity of argument, purpose, theory, and method, written in a style accessible to readers outside the applicant's discipline. Applicants must submit a completed application, a narrative statement, a CV and references. Full information is available on-line.

Closing Date: November 1 (may change annually).

Funding: Government.

Contributor: U.S. Department of State (Title VIII).

No. of awards given last year: 3.

No. of applicants last year: 15.

For further information contact:

810, Seventh Avenue, 31st Floor, New York, NY 10019,
Tel: (212) 377-2700
Fax: (212) 377-2727
Email: eurasia@ssrc.org
www: http://www.ssrc.org/fellowships/eurasia/
Contact: Social Science Research Council, Eurasia Fellowship Program

SSRC Euroasia Program Predisseration Training Fellowships

Subjects: Predisseration Training awards invite graduate students in the first or second year of their doctoral programs at the time of application to enhance their research skills in Eurasian Studies. Awards of US$3,000-7,000 are intended to support skills training such as language learning at a recognized program in the US or abroad; formal training away from one's home institution to acquire analytical or methodological skills normally unavailable to the candidate; or well-defined exploratory research expressly leading to the formulation of a dissertation proposal. The ideal applicant is one who exhibits a well-honed intellectual curiosity and the ability to cross disciplinary boundaries.

Purpose: To provide graduate students with the opportunity to enhance their research skills in the field of Eurasian Studies.

Eligibility: Applicants for Predissertation training fellowships must be enrolled in a doctoral program in the social sciences or humanities or equivalent degree, but not yet advanced to the Ph.D. candidacy. ABD's are not eligible for these fellowships. They must be US citizens or permanent residents. The fellow's home institution is expected to make a cost-sharing contribution of no less than 10 percent of the fellowship award. Detailed information on eligibility criteria and conditions of awards will be available in the application materials.

Level of Study: Doctorate, Graduate.

Type: Fellowship.

Value: US$3,000-7,000.

Length of Study: Up to 9 Months.

Frequency: Annual.

Country of Study: Eurasia (Armenia, Azerbaijan, Belarus, Georgia, Kazakhstan, Kyrgyztan, Moldova, Russia, Tajikistan, Turkmenistan, Ukraine, and Uzbekistan).

No. of awards offered: Varies.

Application Procedure: Awards are made on the basis of evaluations and recommendations by the Title VIII Program Committee, an interdisciplinary committee composed of scholars of the region. The committee rewards proposals with clarity of argument, purpose, theory, and method, written a style accessible to readers outside the applicant's discipline. Applicants must submit a completed application, a narrative statement, transcripts, a course list and language evaluation form, and references. Full information is available on-line.

Closing Date: November.

Funding: Government.

Contributor: U.S. Department of State under the Program for Research and Training on Eastern Europe and the Independent States of the Former Soviet Union (Title VIII).

No. of awards given last year: 6.

No. of applicants last year: Approximately 20.

Additional Information: No funding is available for the Baltic States.

For further information contact:

810 Seventh Avenue, 31st Floor, New York, NY 10019, United States of America
Tel: (1) 377-2700
Fax: (1) 377-2727
Email: eurasia@ssrc.org
www: http://www.ssrc.org/fellowships/eurasia
Contact: Social Science Research Council, Eurasia Fellowship Program

SSRC International Dissertation Field Research Fellowship Program

Subjects: The IDRF Program is committed to scholarship that advances knowledge about cultures, socities, aesthetics, economics and/or polities outside the United States. The Program promotes work that is relevant to a particular discipline while resonating across other fields and area specializations.

Purpose: To provide support for international dissertation field research for students in the social sciences and humanities.

Eligibility: Open to candidates who will complete all PhD requirements except fieldwork before commencement of research and are able to provide evidence of language fluency adequate to complete the project.

Level of Study: Doctorate.

Type: Fellowship.

Value: Support in the field, plus travel expenses. Awards rarely exceed US$17,000.

Length of Study: 9-12 months.

Frequency: Annual.

Country of Study: Other.

No. of awards offered: Approx. 50.

Application Procedure: Applicants must complete an application form, available from the SSRC website : http://www.ssrc.org/programs/idrf.

Closing Date: November.

Funding: Private.

Contributor: The Andrew W Mellon Foundation.

Additional Information: Applicants must contact the programme for further information by emailing idrf@ssrc.org.

SSRC Japan Program Dissertation Workshop

Subjects: All subjects.

Purpose: To create a network of advanced graduate students and faculty.

Eligibility: Open to full-time advanced graduate students, regardless of citizenship, who are enrolled at United States institutions. Applicants must have an approved dissertation prospectus, but cannot have completed writing for final submission. A narrative description of the dissertation topic and a letter of reference from the student's advisor are required as part of the application.

Level of Study: Doctorate.

Value: In most cases, the SSRC will fully cover participants' travel, lodging and meals for the duration of the workshop.

Frequency: Annual.

Country of Study: Japan.

No. of awards offered: 10-12.

Application Procedure: Applicants must apply for information, available on request by emailing japan@ssrc.org.

Closing Date: October 1st.

Funding: Private.

Contributor: The Japan Foundation.

No. of awards given last year: 12.

No. of applicants last year: 33.

SSRC Japan Program JSPS Postdoctoral Fellowship Program

Subjects: Social sciences and humanities.

Purpose: To provide qualified researchers with the opportunity to conduct research with leading universities and other research institutions in Japan.

Eligibility: Open to United States citizens or permanent residents. Applicants will need proof of an affiliation with an eligible host research institution. For one to two years of study, Scholars must have received a PhD no more than six years prior to April 1st of the year for which they are applying. For 3-11 months of study, Scholars must have received a PhD no more than 10 years prior to April 1st of the year for which they are applying. Previous awardees are not eligible.

Level of Study: Postdoctorate.

Type: Fellowship.

Value: Round trip airfare, insurance coverage for accidents and illness, a monthly stipend of Yen 392,000, and a settling in allowance of Yen 200,000. Applicants will also be eligible for up to an additional Yen 1,500,000 annually for research expenses for stays of 12-24 months and a domestic travel allowance of Yen 150,000 for stays of 3-11 months.

Length of Study: One-two years.

Frequency: Annual.

Study Establishment: An approved institution.

Country of Study: Japan.

No. of awards offered: One.

Application Procedure: Applicants must apply for information, available on request by emailing japan@ssrc.org.

Closing Date: December. Please contact the SSRC for the exact date.

Funding: Private.

Contributor: The Japan Society for the Promotion of Science.

No. of awards given last year: 13.

No. of applicants last year: 34.

SSRC Latin American Program Working Group on Cuba Grant Competition

Subjects: Cuba.

Purpose: To promote academic collaboration between scholars in Cuba and North America. To promote the acquisition and transfer of information among libraries, museums and archives, the dissemination of work by Cuban researchers through the provision of funds to defray costs of publication or translation of scholarly volumes, research projects conducted jointly by scholars at institutions in the United States and Cuba, international travel by Cuban researchers to conferences and travel by North American academics invited by Cuban institutions to present lectures in Cuba.

Eligibility: Open to Scholars in Cuba and the United States.

Level of Study: Postgraduate, Professional development, Research.

Value: Varies. Usually travel grants will not exceed US$2,500 per researcher, grants in support of museums, libraries and archives will not exceed US$5,000, and awards for institutional partnerships will range from US$10,000-15,000.

Length of Study: Varies.

Frequency: Dependent on funds available.

No. of awards offered: Varies.

Application Procedure: Applicants must apply for information, available from the Latin America page on SSRC website.

Closing Date: Varies.

Funding: Private.

No. of awards given last year: 16.

Additional Information: Applicants must contact the programme for further information via email on cupaprogram@ssrc.org.

SSRC Program in Applied Economics Fellowship in Applied Economics

Subjects: Economics.

Purpose: To prepare students to write accomplished and innovative dissertations that address vital and complex economic and social issues.

Eligibility: Please consult website.

Level of Study: Doctorate, Postgraduate.

Value: Please visit the website for further details.

Frequency: Annual.

Application Procedure: Applicants must consult the website for application information and materials.

Funding: Private.

Contributor: John D and Corline T Mac A Shaw Funds.

Additional Information: For more detailed information regarding the programme, please contact the organisation or visit the website: http://www.ssrc.org/pae.

SSRC Program on Philanthropy and the Non-profit Sector Fellowships

Subjects: Philanthropy and the non-profit sector. This can include psychology, public policy, political economy, organisational demography and history.

Purpose: To provide greater visibility, coherence and direction to the study of philanthropy and the non-profit sector in the United States through annual fellowship competitions.

Eligibility: There are no citizenship requirements, but applicants must be enrolled in doctoral programmes at United States universities and must have completed all requirements for a PhD including an approved dissertation prospectus except the research component.

Level of Study: Doctorate.

Type: Fellowship.

Value: US$18,000. An additional US$5,000 for dissertation write up may be requested.

Length of Study: Nine months to one year.

Frequency: Annual.

Country of Study: United States of America.

No. of awards offered: Seven.

Application Procedure: Applicants must apply for information, available on request from Contact Program on Philanthropy and the Non-profit Sector at the main address or from the website.

Closing Date: December.

Funding: Private.

Contributor: Anonymous.

No. of awards given last year: 11 (2 partial).

No. of applicants last year: 71.

Additional Information: Fellowship winners will attend a multidisciplinary dissertation workshop. Applicants must contact the programme for further information by email on phil-np@ssrc.org.

SSRC Program on the Corporation as a Social Institution Fellowships

Subjects: Economic sociology, political economy, business history and corporate law.

Purpose: To develop a stronger, conceptually richer and potentially more interdisciplinary approach to the study of firms and other business institutions.

Eligibility: Open to graduate students from all fields conducting research in economic sociology, political economy, business history, corporate law or related fields who must be advanced by PhD candidacy before taking up the fellowship.

Level of Study: Doctorate.

Type: Fellowship.

Value: US$10,000.

Length of Study: Two years.

Frequency: Annual.

Application Procedure: Applicants must submit an approved dissertation proposal, a two page summary of the project, a budget, and two letters of recommendation to the Program on the Corporation as a Social Institution, Social Science Research Council at the main address.

Closing Date: January.

Contributor: The Alfred P Sloan Foundation.

Additional Information: Students will participate in four workshops over the course of two years with senior Scholars working in sociology, economics, law and business. Please contact program director guthrie@ssrc.org for additional information.

SSRC Sexuality Research Fellowship Program

Subjects: Human sexuality research.

Purpose: To fund social and behavioural research.

Eligibility: There are no citizenship, residency, or nationality requirements. Dissertation students must have completed all requirements for a PhD, except the dissertation, in a full-time graduate programme leading to a PhD in a social, health or behavioural science department of a nationally accredited United States college or university. Postdoctoral candidates must hold a PhD or its equivalent in a social or behavioural science from a state or nationally accredited university in the United States, or an equivalent PhD degree from an accredited non United States university.

Level of Study: Doctorate, Postdoctorate.

Type: Fellowship.

Value: US$28,000 at doctoral level and US$38,000 at postdoctoral level.

Length of Study: One year for dissertations, one-two years for postdoctorate.

Frequency: Annual.

Country of Study: United States of America.

No. of awards offered: 10 dissertation fellowships and four-six postdoctoral fellowships.

Application Procedure: Applicants must apply for information, available on request by email on srfp@ssrc.org. All application materials are available online at www.ssrc.org/programs/sexuality or by emailing srfp@ssrc.org.

Closing Date: December.

Funding: Private.

Contributor: The Ford Foundation.

No. of awards given last year: 15.

No. of applicants last year: 100.

Additional Information: Members of minority groups are especially encouraged to apply. Applicants must contact the program for further information.

SSRC South Asia Regional Fellowship Program: Fellowships for the Study of Migration

Subjects: Humanities.

Purpose: To enable successful applicants to take leave from teaching and other responsibilities to write up completed research.

Level of Study: Postdoctorate.

Funding: Private.

SSRC South Asia Regional Fellowship Program: Fellowships for the study of sexuality

Subjects: Social sciences or Humanities as related to the study of sexuality.

Purpose: The primary intent of the fellowships is to enable successful applicants to take leave from teaching and other responsibilities to write up completed research. Proposed fellowship outputs may include preparation of syllabi. Applications proposing new research seeking support for ongoing field research will not be rejected but given much lower priority.

Eligibility: Eligibility is restricted to college and university based researchers who teach in any social science, humanities or related discipline. Applicants must hold an earned Ph.D. from an accredited university. Applicants must hold a permanent, full-time position in an accredited college or university in Bangladesh, India, Nepal, Pakistan or Sri Lanka.

Level of Study: Postdoctorate.

Type: Short term fellowship.

Value: Junior scholars are eligible for a maximum fellowship amount of USD 2,200 and senior scholars are eligible for a maximum fellowship amount of USD 3,000.

Length of Study: Three - six months.

Frequency: Annual.

Study Establishment: Fellows must be affiliated with a local research center of institute during their fellowship tenure.

Country of Study: Current place of residence (Bangladesh, India, Nepal, Pakistan or Sri Lanka).

No. of awards offered: A total of twenty fellowships are available each year. Up to fifteen fellowships are reserved for junior scholars (less than Professor rank), and no more than five for senior scholars (Professor rank and above).

Application Procedure: Applicants may download application forms from www.ssrc.org/fellowships/southasia or may contact our partner institutes listed below for an application form. Applications should be sent to the partner institutes listed below for an application form. Applications should be sent to the partner institute located in the country from which you are applying. Please email all your inquiries to sur@ssrc.org.

Closing Date: May 15, 2003.

Funding: Private.

Contributor: Ford Foundation.

No. of awards given last year: 13.

No. of applicants last year: 80.

Additional Information: Applications forms are also available through our partner institutes in the region. For more information, please contact: Center for Alternatives, Bangladesh: ssrc-cfa@proshikanet.com, Center for Studies in social Sciences, Calcutta, India: ssrccal@csssc.ernet.in, Social Science Baha, Nepal: ssrc@himalassociation.org, Social Scientists' Association, Sri Lanka: ssrc-ssa@eureka.lk, Sustainable Development Policy Institute, Pakistan: ssrcpakistan@sdpi.org.

SSRC Summer Institute on International Migration

Subjects: Social Science.

Purpose: To enable attendance at a workshop/conference training young scholars in the field of migration studies.

Eligibility: Open to advanced doctoral candidates currently involved in research or writing for their dissertations and recent PhDs revising their dissertations for publication or initiating new research.

Level of Study: Postdoctorate, Postgraduate, Predoctorate.

Type: Award.

Value: Flights, meals and lodging necessary for participation in the institute are fully subsidised.

Length of Study: 1 Week.

Frequency: Dependent on funds available.

Study Establishment: The University of California at Los Angeles.

Country of Study: United States of America.

No. of awards offered: 20.

Application Procedure: TBA.

Closing Date: TBA.

Funding: Private.

Contributor: UCLA and SSRC.

No. of awards given last year: 20.

No. of applicants last year: 250.

Additional Information: The Institute is a collaboration between the SSRC and the University of California, Los Angeles.

For further information contact:

Contact: TBA

SSRC-Mellon Mays Fellowships

Subjects: The processes of migration and settlement of the USA, and the outcomes for both immigrants and native-born Americans.

Purpose: To offer intensive training to students of minority background in developing dissertation and funding proposals.

Eligibility: Applicants must be United States citizens or permanent residents who are of African, Latino, Asian, Pacific Island, or native American ancestry. Applicants have to be graduate students who are matriculated in doctoral programs in the social sciences, including

history, have taken coursework related to international migration, have completed their first year of graduate study, and have developed a preliminary research focus for their dissertation.
Level of Study: Postgraduate.
Type: Other.
Value: Transportation, room and board, and other participation costs, as well as a stipend for workshop participants.
Length of Study: Three weeks, two in June and one in August.
Frequency: Annual.
Study Establishment: A university.
Country of Study: United States of America.
No. of awards offered: 10-15.
Application Procedure: Write for further information and application materials.
Closing Date: January 10th.
Funding: Private.
Contributor: The Andrew W Mellon Foundation.
Additional Information: The awards will be announced in April.

SOCIAL SCIENCES AND HUMANITIES RESEARCH COUNCIL OF CANADA (SSHRC)

350 Albert Street, PO Box 1610, Ottawa, ON, K1P 6G4, Canada
Tel: (1) 613 992 0691
Fax: (1) 613 992 1787
Email: jta@sshrc.ca
www: http://www.sshrc.ca
Contact: Mr Joel Tatelman, English Editor

The Social Sciences and Humanities Research Council of Canada (SSHRC) is the federal agency responsible for promoting and supporting research and research training in the social sciences and humanities in Canada. SSHRC supports research on the economic, political, social and cultural dimensions of the human experience.

Aileen D Ross Fellowship
Subjects: Sociology.
Purpose: To support an outstanding SSHRC doctoral and postdoctoral fellowship holder who is conducting research in sociology, especially in poverty.
Eligibility: Open to Canadian citizens or permanent residents living in Canada at the time of application, who are not under SSHRC sanction resulting from financial or research misconduct, or already in receipt of SSHRC, NSERC or MRC (now CIHR) funding to undertake or complete a previous doctoral degree. At the time of taking up the award, applicants must have completed either a Master's degree or at least one year of doctoral study, and be pursuing either full-time studies leading to a PhD, or equivalent, with research specialisation in sociology with the intention of pursuing an academic career. Candidates wishing to study at a foreign university may only do so if one of their previous degrees was earned in Canada.
Level of Study: Doctorate, Postdoctorate.
Type: Fellowship.
Value: US$10,000 plus value of the fellowship.
Length of Study: One year.
Country of Study: Canada.
No. of awards offered: One.
Application Procedure: Applicants must indicate their interest in the doctoral or postdoctoral application form. Further details can be found on the website.
Closing Date: Postdoctoral applications are due October 1st. Doctoral application dates are set by the university.
Additional Information: Preference will be given to postdoctoral applicants.

Bora Laskin National Fellowship in Human Rights Research
Subjects: Human rights, as relevant to Canada.
Purpose: To support research, preferably of a multidisciplinary or interdisciplinary nature, and to develop Canadian expertise in the field of human rights, with an emphasis on themes and issues relevant to the Canadian human rights scene.
Eligibility: Open to Canadian citizens or permanent residents of Canada. Preference will be given to applicants with at least five years of proven research experience in their field, as this fellowship is not intended for scholars just beginning their research careers.
Level of Study: Postdoctorate, Research.
Type: Fellowship.
Value: Canadian $45,000, plus a research and travel allowance of Canadian $10,000.
Length of Study: One year, non renewable.
Frequency: Annual.
Country of Study: Other.
No. of awards offered: One.
Application Procedure: Applicants must complete an application form, available from the website.
Closing Date: October 1st.
Funding: Government.

Canada Graduate Scholarship Program (CGS): Master's Scholarship
Subjects: Social sciences and humanities.
Purpose: To support graduate students working toward a Master's degree at a Canadian University.
Eligibility: For citizens or permanent residents of Canada who are applying for, or registered in a master's program in the social sciences or humanities at a Canadian University.
Level of Study: Graduate, Predoctorate.
Type: Scholarship.
Value: CDN$17,500.
Length of Study: 1 year.
Frequency: Annual.
Country of Study: Canada.
No. of awards offered: Several hundred.
Application Procedure: Applicants must visit the website for further information.
Closing Date: Applicants must consult the program description in the website to determine their applicant status which in turn determines the application deadline.
Funding: Government.
No. of awards given last year: Hundreds.
No. of applicants last year: Thousands

The Canada Project Research Initiative.
Subjects: Social sciences and humanities.
Purpose: To support policy-relevant research on Canada's national Competitiveness and position in the world.
Eligibility: Only researchers - individuals and small terms-affiliated with postsecondary institutions are eligible to apply.
Level of Study: Research.
Type: Grant.
Value: Up to CDN$162,500.
Length of Study: 12 months.
Frequency: Annual.
Country of Study: Canada.
Application Procedure: Visit the website for application forms and instructions.
Closing Date: April.
Funding: Government.

Canadian Forest Service Graduate Supplements
Subjects: Forestry and related fields.
Purpose: To promote Canadian doctoral research into forestry, to encourage the use of Canadian Forest Service (CFS) centres and to increase contacts between CFS researchers and Canadian universities.
Eligibility: Open to SSHRC doctoral Fellows who are conducting research in an area related to forestry in Canada and who are in the third or fourth year of their programme. Candidates must have at least one CFS scientist on their supervisory committee and must carry out all or part of their research at a CFS forestry centre.
Level of Study: Doctorate, Predoctorate, Research.
Type: Other.

Value: Canadian $5,000 supplement to the Canadian $17,700 doctoral fellowship.
Length of Study: Up to two years.
Frequency: Annual.
No. of awards offered: Five.
Application Procedure: Applicants must visit the website.
Closing Date: Interested doctoral students should contact their department for the SSHRC Doctoral Fellowship application deadline.
Contributor: The Canadian Forest Service.

For further information contact:

Canadian Forest Service Graduate Supplements, Science Branch, Natural Resources Canada, 580 Booth Street, Ottawa, ON K1A 0E4, Canada
Tel: (1) 613 947 8992
Fax: (1) 613 947 9090
Email: mlamarch@nrcan.gc.ca
Contact: Program Co-ordinator

CESC-SSHRC Education Research Initiative

Subjects: Education, economics, statistics, social sciences.
Purpose: To support quantitative research in education relevant to the new economy that draws on unique Canadian data sets.
Eligibility: Open to Canadian citizens, permanent residents and qualified researchers from other countries.
Level of Study: Research.
Value: Up to Canadian $100,000.
Length of Study: Two years.
Frequency: Annual.
Study Establishment: Post secondary educational institutions, non-profit and educational organisations.
Country of Study: Canada.
Application Procedure: Applicants must complete an application form from the website.
Closing Date: January 5th.
Funding: Government.
Contributor: Canadian Education Statistics Council.
Additional Information: For further information visit the initiative on the New Economy section of the website.

Community - University Research Alliances (CURA)

Subjects: Social sciences and humanities.
Purpose: To support research projects jointly developed and undertaken by university based researchers and community organisations.
Eligibility: Open to Canadian based organisations in Canada teaming up with university based researchers to address issues of mutual interest and concern.
Level of Study: Postdoctorate, Research.
Type: Grant.
Value: Please contact the organisation.
Length of Study: Up to five years.
Frequency: Annual.
Country of Study: Canada.
Application Procedure: Applicants must visit the website for further information on the two stage application process.
Closing Date: December 8th for letter of intent and August 4th for the formal application, by invitation only.
Funding: Government.

Doctoral Awards

Subjects: Social sciences or humanities.
Purpose: To develop research skills and to assist in the training of highly qualified academic personnel by supporting students who demonstrate a high standard of scholarly achievement.
Eligibility: Open to Canadian citizens or permanent residents living in Canada at the time of application, who are not under SSHRC sanction resulting from financial or research misconduct, or already in receipt of SSHRC, NSERC, or MRC (now CIHR) funding to undertake or complete a previous doctoral degree. At the time of taking up the award applicants must have completed either a Master's degree or at least one year of doctoral study, and be pursuing either full-time studies

leading to a PhD, or equivalent. Candidates wishing to study at a foreign university may only do so if one of their previous degrees was earned in Canada.
Level of Study: Doctorate.
Type: Fellowship / Scholarship. SSHRC Doctoral Fellowships and Canada Graduate Scholarship (CGS) Program : Doctoral Scholarships.
Value: SSHRC Doctoral Fellowships: Canadian $17,700 per year, up to and including the fourth year of doctoral study (Tenable in Canada and abroad) CGS Doctoral Scholarship: CDN $35,000 per annum for 3 years (Tenable only at Canadian Universities).
Length of Study: 6-48 months.
Frequency: Annual.
Study Establishment: Recognised universities.
Country of Study: SSHRC Doctoral Fellowships : tenable in Canada or abroad; CGS Doctoral Scholarships : tenable in Canada only.
No. of awards offered: Varies.
Application Procedure: Applicants must complete an application along with a detailed description. Forms are available from the website.
Closing Date: For applicants registered at a Canadian University, the university sets the deadline; for all others, November 15th.
Funding: Government.
No. of awards given last year: 572.
No. of applicants last year: 1,521.

Essential Skills: Research and Workshop Grants

Subjects: Social sciences and humanities.
Purpose: Research Grants: to support research that will help Canadians acquire workplace and general life skills.(see overleaf).
Eligibility: University based researchers and research teams affiliated with Canadian postsecondary institutions. Workshop Grants: for holders of essential skills grants to participate in a workshop on policy-relevant research in essential skills.
Level of Study: Research.
Type: Grant.
Value: Research Grants: up to Canadian $100,000 per annum; Workshop Grants: up to Canadian $100,000 for each workshop.
Length of Study: 2 years (research grants).
Frequency: Annual.
Country of Study: Canada.
Application Procedure: Applicants must visit the website for further information on the application process.
Closing Date: Research Grants: January. Workshop Grants: April.
Funding: Government.

Geomatics for Informed Decisions (GEOIDE) Networks of Centres of Excellence Graduate Supplement Program

Subjects: Geomatics.
Purpose: To support SSHRC doctoral fellowship holders conducting research in geomatics related fields.
Eligibility: Open to applicants or holders of an SSHRC doctoral fellowship.
Level of Study: Doctorate.
Type: Other.
Value: Canadian $5,000 in addition to the value of the doctoral fellowship.
Length of Study: Up to two years.
Frequency: Annual.
Country of Study: Canada.
Application Procedure: Applicants must indicate their interest on the doctoral fellowship application form. Further details can be found on the website.
Closing Date: November 15th or date set by the applicant's university, whichever is earlier.
Funding: Government.

Homeless and Diversity Issues in Canada: Strategic Research Grants.

Subjects: Social sciences and humanities.
Purpose: To support community-and policy-relevant research on homelessness as it relates to ethnic/cultural/racial diversity.
Level of Study: Research.

Type: Grant.
Value: Up to CDN$50,000 per annum.
Length of Study: 24 months.
Frequency: Annual.
Country of Study: Canada.
Application Procedure: Visit the website for application forms and instructions.
Closing Date: March.
Funding: Government.

Image Text, Sound and Technology: Networking Summer Institute, Workshop and Conference Grants

Subjects: Social sciences and humanities.
Purpose: To help scholars especially in the humanities, apply innovative digital technologies to research on image, text and sound.
Eligibility: Researchers affiliated with Canadian postsecondary institutions.
Level of Study: Research.
Type: Grant.
Value: Up to CDN$50,000.
Length of Study: 12 Months.
Frequency: Annual.
Country of Study: Canada.
Application Procedure: Visit the website for application information and forms.
Closing Date: September.
Funding: Government.

Jules and Gabrielle Léger Fellowship

Subjects: The Crown and Governor General in a parliamentary democracy.
Purpose: To encourage research and writing on the historical and contemporary contribution of the Crown and its representatives, federal and provincial, to the political, constitutional, cultural, intellectual and social life of the country, including comparisons between Canadian and Commonwealth systems.
Eligibility: Open to Canadian citizens or permanent residents of Canada, who have proven experience in the proposed field of research and are not be under SSHRC sanction for financial or research misconduct.
Level of Study: Postdoctorate, Research.
Type: Fellowship.
Value: Canadian $40,000, plus Canadian $10,000 for research and travel costs.
Length of Study: One year, non renewable.
Frequency: Every two years.
Study Establishment: A recognised university or research institute.
Country of Study: Any country.
No. of awards offered: One.
Application Procedure: Applicants must visit the website for full application details.
Closing Date: October 1st.
Funding: Government.

Multiculturalism in Canada: Research and Workshop Grants.

Subjects: Social sciences and humanities.
Purpose: To support research on diverse issues that arise from Canada's increasingly multicultural and multi-ethnic population.
Eligibility: Researchers and research terms affiliated with Canadian postsecondary institutions.
Level of Study: Research.
Type: Grant.
Value: Research Grants: up to CDN$50,000 per annum; Workshop Grants: up to CDN$100,000.
Length of Study: 12 months.
Frequency: Annual.
Country of Study: Canada.
Application Procedure: Visit the website for application forms and instructions.
Funding: Government.

Northern Research Development Program.

Subjects: Social sciences and humanities.
Purpose: To support research in and about the Canadian North, with emphases on involving local stakeholders.
Eligibility: Applications should come from research teams made up of university-based researchers and community/not for profit organizations. See program description on website for details.
Level of Study: Research.
Type: Grant.
Value: Up to CDN$40,000.
Length of Study: Up to two years.
Frequency: Annual.
Country of Study: Canada.
Application Procedure: Visit the website for application information, forms and instructions.
Closing Date: January, May.
Funding: Government.

Queen's Fellowships

Subjects: Canadian studies.
Purpose: To assist a candidate who intends to enter a doctoral programme in the relevant field.
Eligibility: Open to Canadian citizens and permanent residents who, by the time of taking up the fellowship, will have completed one year of graduate study or all the requirements for the Master's degree beyond the Bachelor's (Honours) Degree or its equivalent, and will be registered in a programme of studies leading to a PhD or its equivalent. This award is offered to one or two outstanding successful doctoral fellowship candidates.
Level of Study: Doctorate.
Type: Fellowship.
Value: Tuition fees and travel to the main place of tenure and travel for research purposes.
Length of Study: One year, non renewable.
Frequency: Annual.
Study Establishment: A recognised university.
Country of Study: Canada.
No. of awards offered: One-two.
Application Procedure: Applicants cannot apply for this award but are automatically eligible if they intend to study Canadian studies at a Canadian university. The Queen's Fellowship is not a programme but a special award given to a doctoral Fellow.
Funding: Government.
Additional Information: Further information is available on the website.

Research/Creation Grants in Fine arts.

Subjects: Fine arts and related disciplines.
Purpose: To support programs of research/creation by artist researchers affiliated with Canadian post secondary institutions.
Eligibility: Artist-researchers affiliated with Canadian postsecondary institutions.
Level of Study: Research.
Type: Grant.
Value: Up to a total of CDN$250,000 over 3 years.
Length of Study: Up to 3 years.(36 months).
Frequency: Annual.
Country of Study: Canada.
Application Procedure: Visit the website for application forms and instructions.
Closing Date: Novemeber (but check website).
Funding: Government.

Skills Research Initiative: Research Grants.

Subjects: Social sciences and humanities.
Purpose: To support policy-relevant research on skills and highly-qualified people.
Eligibility: Only researchers affiliated with postsecondary institutions are eligible to apply. See program description on website for further details.
Level of Study: Research.
Type: Grant.
Value: Up to Canadian $25,000.

Length of Study: 12 months.
Frequency: Annual.
Country of Study: Canada.
No. of awards offered: Up to six.
Application Procedure: Visit the website for application forms and instructions.
Closing Date: March 1, 2004.
Funding: Government.

SSHRC Aid to Occasional Research Conferences and International Congresses in Canada

Subjects: Arts and humanities and social sciences.
Purpose: To encourage and facilitate the communication of research, within and between disciplines, among Canadian researchers, international experts and foreign researchers through occasional regional and national conferences and workshops, as well as through congresses of major international scholarly associations held in Canada.
Eligibility: For applicants to be eligible they must be either Canadian citizens or permanent residents of Canada at the time of application, be researchers in the social sciences or humanities, be members of the conference's or congress' organising committee. Applicants for congress grants must also be members in good standing of the international scholarly association in question, be affiliated with a Canadian university that agrees to administer the grant and not be under SSHRC sanction for financial or research misconduct. For a conference to be eligible, it must take place after the date specified for SSHRC's announcement of competition results, have a defined theme and be devoted to scholarly research issues in the social sciences or humanities, be held in Canada or at a Canadian academic institution abroad, not be receiving support for the same activity under another SSHRC programme, and not be an association's annual general meeting. Please note that a conference that is held by an association and that coincides with that association's annual general meeting is eligible only if the organisers can demonstrate that the conference is a distinct, independent and self-contained event, and that it will address an audience different from, or broader than, that of the annual general meeting. For a congress to be eligible, it must be sponsored by an international scholarly association that has as its main objective the furthering of advanced scholarly research in a discipline of the social sciences or the humanities, and that shows evidence of a membership with broad international representation, eg. a minimum of three countries, take place in Canada after the date specified for SSHRC's announcement of competition results, include a fully constituted business meeting of its members, and have a defined research theme in areas within the association's purview.
Type: Grant.
Value: The maximum value and period of tenure of a grant is Canadian $10,000 for a conference held within the 12 months following the announcement of results and Canadian $50,000 for a congress held within three years following the announcement of results. The actual amount of the grant depends on the merit of the application, the financial need and the appropriateness of the proposed budget.
Length of Study: One year.
Frequency: Twice a year.
Country of Study: Canada.
Application Procedure: Applicants must consult the organisation or visit the website.
Closing Date: May 1st or November 1st.
Funding: Government.

SSHRC Aid to Research and Transfer Journals

Subjects: Social sciences and humanities.
Purpose: To assist in the effective dissemination of original research findings and in the transfer of knowledge to practitioners. The programme offers two types of grants: General Grants, to help defray part of the costs related to the production of a journal, and Special Initiative Grants, to assist with the establishment of electronic publishing or other initiatives or improvements, and to defray the costs of initiatives of exceptional quality and interest.
Eligibility: Open to candidates who are either Canadian citizens or permanent residents of Canada at the time of application and are established researchers in the social sciences or in the humanities. They must also be a member of the sponsoring institution or organ-

isation and not be under SSHRC sanction for financial or research misconduct. A research or transfer journal must have as its main objective the publishing of the results of advanced research and scholarly work by specialists for a readership of specialists or practitioners, normally appear at least twice a year and have published a minimum of four issues in the last two years prior to the application deadline, and have as its primary focus a discipline or disciplines within SSHRC's mandate. The journal must also have a subscription level over 200, be in either English or French and be sponsored, edited and published in Canada, by a Canadian institution or a Canadian association.
Type: Grant.
Value: The maximum value of a General Grant is Canadian $30,000 per year or Canadian $90,000 over three years; the maximum value of a Special Initiative Grant is Canadian $10,000.
Frequency: Every three years.
Country of Study: Canada.
Application Procedure: Applicants must make the case for the funding requested. For full details on application visit the website.
Closing Date: June 30th.
Funding: Government.
Additional Information: Further information is available on the website.

SSHRC Aid to Scholarly Publications

Subjects: Social sciences or humanities.
Purpose: To promote the sharing of research results by assisting the publication of individual works that make an important contribution to the advancement of knowledge.
Eligibility: Candidates must consult the website for eligibility requirements.
Level of Study: Postdoctorate, Research.
Type: Grant.
Frequency: Annual.
Application Procedure: Applicants must refer to the website or email the Federation on secaspp@hssfc.ca. Applicants may apply at any time.
Funding: Government.
Additional Information: The programme is administered on behalf of SSHRC by the Humanities and Social Sciences Federation of Canada (HSSFC). Detailed information concerning application requirements, eligibility, value etc. can be obtained by contacting them.

For further information contact:

The Humanities & Social Sciences Federation of Canada (HSSFC), 151 Slater Street, Ottawa, ON K1P 5H3, Canada
Tel: (1) 613 238 6112 ext. 350
Email: secaspp@aspp.hssfc.ca
www: http://www.hssfc.ca/aspp/homee.htm

SSHRC Aid to Small Universities

Subjects: Arts, humanities or social sciences.
Purpose: To promote the focused development of social sciences and humanities research capacity in small universities by encouraging them to critically assess their most promising potential areas for research concentration, develop effective strategies for strengthening their research capabilities in these areas and to develop ongoing focal points or research centres where appropriate.
Eligibility: Open to institutions who have degree granting status for social sciences and humanities disciplines at the graduate level or beyond, and are an institutional member of the Association of Universities and Colleges of Canada (AUCC), or a member of the AUCC and be affiliated with an institution itself too large to be eligible for the ASU Program. They must also operate in an official language other than that of the larger parent institution, have fewer than 250 full-time faculty in SSHRC fields and be independent of the federal government for the purpose of faculty employment status.
Level of Study: Research.
Type: Grant.
Value: Determined using a formula based on the number of full-time social sciences and humanities faculty at the institution. Awards are usually up to Canadian $30,000 for three years.
Length of Study: Three years.

Frequency: Every three years.
Country of Study: Canada.
Application Procedure: Applicants must contact the organisation or visit the website.
Closing Date: December.
Funding: Government.

SSHRC Institutional Grants

Subjects: Social sciences or humanities.
Purpose: To help universities develop and maintain a solid base of research and research related activities.
Eligibility: Open to Canadian post secondary institutions.
Level of Study: Postgraduate.
Type: Research grant.
Value: Varies, calculated on the number of faculty in each university. Universities may award not more than Canadian $5,000 to individual researchers to help cover small research expenses, cost of travel to conferences and other similar costs. SSHRC guarantees a minimum annual grant of Canadian $2,000.
Length of Study: Three years.
Frequency: Every three years.
Country of Study: Canada.
No. of awards offered: Varies.
Application Procedure: Applicants must complete an application form, available from the website.
Closing Date: December 1st.
Funding: Government.
Additional Information: Further information is available on the website.

SSHRC Major Collaborative Research Initiatives (MCRI)

Subjects: Arts, humanities or social sciences.
Purpose: To strengthen Canadian research capacity by promoting high quality, innovative, collaborative research and unique student training opportunities in a collaborative research environment.
Eligibility: Open to leading Scholars with a solid track record and past experience in collaborative research, student training and grant management. Please consult the programme description on the website.
Level of Study: Research.
Type: Grant.
Value: Up to Canadian $500,000 per year with a minimum budget of Canadian $100,000 per year. A Canadian $20,000 development fund will also be offered to assist the research team's planning and preparation for its formal application.
Length of Study: Five years.
Frequency: Annual.
Application Procedure: Applications must be submitted by the Project Director on behalf of the research team. There is a two stage application process, the first being a letter of intent, followed by a formal application.
Closing Date: January 31st for the first stage and September 1st for the second.
Funding: Government.
Additional Information: For further information contact Pierrette Tremblay, Research Grants Co-ordinator on (1) 613 996 2994, at the organisation address or at pierrette.tremblay@sshrc.ca.

SSHRC Postdoctoral Fellowships

Subjects: Social sciences or humanities.
Purpose: To support the most promising new scholars and to assist them in establishing a research base at an important time in their research career.
Eligibility: Open to candidates who are Canadian citizens or permanent residents living in Canada at the time of application. They must also be able to demonstrate skill in research, not be under SSHRC sanction resulting from financial or research misconduct and have earned their doctorate from a recognised university no more than 36 months prior to the competition deadline or have completed their degree within six years prior to the competition deadline but have had their career interrupted or delayed for the purpose of child rearing. Candidates must also have finalised arrangements for affiliation with a university or a research institution and have applied not more than

once before for a postdoctoral fellowship. At the time of taking up the award, applicants must have completed all requirements for the doctoral degree, must intend to engage in full-time postdoctoral research and not hold a tenure or tenure track position.
Level of Study: Postdoctorate.
Type: Fellowship.
Value: Up to Canadian $35,028 per annum, plus a research allowance of up to Canadian $5,000.
Length of Study: A minimum of 12 months and a maximum of 24 months.
Frequency: Annual.
Study Establishment: For applicants who earned their doctorate at a Canadian University, there is no restriction on the location of the tenure.
Country of Study: Any country, under certain conditions.
No. of awards offered: Approx. 100.
Application Procedure: Applicants must complete an application form.
Closing Date: October 1st.
Funding: Government.
No. of awards given last year: 100.
No. of applicants last year: 380.
Additional Information: Applicants wishing to hold their award at a foreign university may do so only if their PhD was earned at a Canadian university.

SSHRC Relationships in Transition

Subjects: Public policy issues relating to law reform.
Purpose: To support the writing of research papers relevant to law reform in Canada.
Eligibility: Participants must meet SSHRC's general eligibility criteria. Proposals for interdisciplinary papers are invited from researchers and teams of researchers affiliated with Canadian postsecondary institutions. Please see the website for full details.
Level of Study: Research.
Type: Grant.
Value: Average Canadian $25,000, but up to Canadian $40,000 per paper.
Length of Study: One year.
Frequency: Annual.
No. of awards offered: Varies.
Application Procedure: Applications must consist of a research proposal and a budget proposal. Applicants must visit the website for further details.
Closing Date: Please contact the organisation.
Additional Information: Each year the focus is on one of the following four themes: economic relationships, personal relationships, social relationships and governance relationships. Successful candidates will be invited to present their papers at a conference held in the Spring. Further information is available on the website.

SSHRC Research Development Initiatives

Subjects: Humanities, the social and cognitive sciences or the educational sciences.
Purpose: To support research that defines new conceptual and methodological perspectives and challenges. Research should define new priorities to be taken into account when conducting research, disseminating research results or training new researchers. The programme supports research that both addresses and elicits the changing directions of research and the evolution of the relevant disciplines.
Eligibility: Candidates should consult the website for eligibility requirements.
Level of Study: Research.
Value: A maximum of Canadian $50,000 per year.
Length of Study: Three years.
Frequency: Annual.
Application Procedure: Applicants must visit the website for further details as there are two parts to the application process, a form and a project description. Applications must be addressed to the Strategic Programmes and Joint Initiatives Division at the main address or emailed to collaborative@sshrc.ca.
Closing Date: February 28th, July 15th or October 31st.

Funding: Government.
Additional Information: Further information is available on the website.

SSHRC Strategic Research Grants

Subjects: Social sciences and humanities.
Purpose: To support research and research related activities in areas of national importance. SSHRC offers many different programs to support research in areas and on topics deemed of importance to Canada, Always refer to the website for the latest information.
Eligibility: Applicants should visit the website for requirements.
Level of Study: Research.
Type: Grant.
Frequency: Annual.
Country of Study: Canada.
Application Procedure: Applicants must visit the website for full application details.

Standard Research Grants

Subjects: Social sciences or humanities.
Purpose: To support and develop excellence in research, with the research projects proposed by the researchers themselves.
Eligibility: Open to Scholars who are Canadian citizens or permanent residents of Canada and who are affiliated with a Canadian university or a recognised postsecondary institution.
Level of Study: Research.
Type: Research grant.
Value: Up to a maximum of Canadian $100,000 per year but not totalling more than Canadian $250,000 over a three year period. A minimum of Canadian $5,000 in at least one of the years is required unless the applicant is at an institution not receiving a General Research Grant.
Length of Study: Grants in support of research programmes will ordinarily be expected to cover three year periods.
Frequency: Annual.
Study Establishment: An approved institution.
Country of Study: Any country.
No. of awards offered: Varies.
Application Procedure: Applicants must visit the website for full application details.
Closing Date: October 15th.
Funding: Government.

Thérèse F Casgrain Fellowship

Subjects: Canadian women and social change.
Purpose: To carry out research in the field of social justice, particularly in the defence of individual rights and the promotion of the economic and social interests of Canadian women.
Eligibility: Open to Canadian citizens or permanent residents. At the time of taking up the fellowship, the successful candidate must have obtained a doctorate or an equivalent advanced professional degree, as well as have proven research experience and not be under SSHRC sanction for financial or research misconduct.
Level of Study: Postdoctorate.
Type: Fellowship.
Value: Canadian $40,000, paid in three instalments, of which up to Canadian $10,000 may be used for travel and research expenses.
Length of Study: One year, non renewable.
Frequency: Every two years.
Country of Study: Canada.
No. of awards offered: One.
Application Procedure: Applicants must complete an application form, available from the website.
Closing Date: October 1 every second year. (2004, 2006, etc.).
Funding: Private.
Contributor: The Thérèse F Casgrain Foundation.
No. of awards given last year: One.
No. of applicants last year: 21.
Additional Information: The fellowship was created by the Thérèse F Casgrain Foundation and is administered by the Social Sciences and Humanities Research Council. Affiliation with a university or an appropriate research institute or similar organisation is desirable, but is not a condition of the award. Recipients must submit a final report to

the Foundation outlining conclusions of the research, accompanied by a complete financial statement for all expenses. Further information is available on the website.

Valuing Literacy in Canada Doctoral and Postdoctoral Fellowship Supplements

Subjects: Literacy education.
Purpose: To aid fellows conducting research on adult literacy, workplace literacy or family literacy.
Eligibility: Applicants must be SSHRC doctoral or postdoctoral Fellows and therefore have satisfied the eligibility criteria.
Level of Study: Postdoctorate.
Type: Fellowship.
Value: Canadian $5,000, supplementary to the regular fellowship award.
Length of Study: Up to two years.
Frequency: Annual.
No. of awards offered: Five.
Application Procedure: Applicants must indicate their interest in this supplement on their initial application form for SSHRC's Postdoctoral Fellowships or contact the responsible programme officer, Luc Lebrun. Further details can be found on the website.
Closing Date: Please contact the organisation.

Virtual Scholar in Residence Program

Subjects: The area of study varies from year to year.
Purpose: To allow an individual to work with the Law Commission of Canada (LCC) to advance research in a particular area.
Eligibility: Open to researchers affiliated to a Canadian post secondary educational institution.
Level of Study: Research.
Type: Research grant.
Value: A maximum of Canadian $50,000 to cover a period of intensive research with the LCC. Financial details regarding this grant will be negotiated between the LCC, SSHRC and the successful applicant's institution following the second stage of the competition. In addition the Commission will also provide up to Canadian $10,000 for research expenses.
Length of Study: Eight months.
Frequency: Annual.
Country of Study: Canada.
No. of awards offered: One.
Application Procedure: Applicants must visit the website for application details.
Closing Date: December 2004. (See website for exact date).
Funding: Government.

SOCIAL WORKERS EDUCATIONAL TRUST

British Association of Social Workers, 16 Kent Street, Birmingham, West Midlands, B5 6RD, England
Tel: (44) 121 622 3911
Fax: (44) 121 622 4860
Email: swet@basw.co.uk
www: http://www.basw.co.uk/swet
Contact: Ms Gill Aslett, Honorary Secretary

The Social Workers Educational Trust offers grants to experienced social workers for post qualifying training or research, with the overall aim of improving social work practice in the United Kingdom.

Anne Cummins Scholarship

Subjects: Competitive submission of proposals for research and practice development in health related social work.
Purpose: To support study or research on health related social work practice.
Eligibility: Open to qualified social workers who have completed two years of work practice post qualification, resident in the UK.
Level of Study: Postgraduate, Professional development.
Type: Award.
Value: UK£1,000-1,500.
Frequency: Annual.

Country of Study: United Kingdom.
No. of awards offered: One.
Application Procedure: Applicants must complete an application form. Details and forms are available on written request from the Social Workers Educational Trust or from the website. Applicants should state whether their application is for a grant or scholarship.
Funding: Private.
No. of awards given last year: One.

SOCIETY FOR RENAISSANCE STUDIES

12A Manley Street, London, NW1 8LT, England
Tel: (44) 20 7862 8703
Fax: (44) 20 7862 8722
Email: richard.simpson@sas.ac.uk
www: http://www.sas.ac.uk/srs
Contact: Mr Richard Simpson

The Society for Renaissance Studies, founded in 1967, provides a forum for those interested in any aspect of the study of the Renaissance. The Society provides support for interdisciplinary teaching and research, organising and supporting conferences and lectures and publishing the journal Renaissance Studies, in conjunction with Blackwells. Topics covered in talks, articles and reviews include the history, art, architecture, philosophy, science, technology, religion, music, the literatures and languages of Europe and of countries in contact with Europe, during the Renaissance. The Society has branches in Ireland, Wales and Scotland which also organise events for members. The Society is a registered charity no. 1025890.

Renaissance Society Fellowships
Subjects: Renaissance studies.
Eligibility: Open to any postgraduate student registered in the United Kingdom. There are no age or nationality restrictions.
Level of Study: Postgraduate.
Type: Travel grant.
Value: Up to UK£1,500.
Frequency: Annual.
Country of Study: Any country.
No. of awards offered: Up to two.
Application Procedure: Applicants must submit a text of not more than 1,000 words describing the research projects to be undertaken, noting the title of the dissertation and the relationship of the proposed travel project to the dissertation and requesting a specific amount of funding. In addition, the applicant must include a short budget detailing the expenditure planned for travel, accommodation and subsistence during the trip. While the maximum amount to be awarded for a single fellowship is UK£1,500, the Society welcomes applications for projects requiring smaller sums. Applications should be sent to Dr Michelle O'Malley.
Closing Date: January 30th.
Funding: Private.
Contributor: The Society for Renaissance Studies.
Additional Information: Fellows will be required to produce a written report to the Society which will be published in the Society's 'Bulletin'. They may also be invited to give a fifteen-minute paper on their project to the Society's annual meeting or at the Society's national conference.

For further information contact:

School of Humanities, University of Sussex, Falmer, Brighton, BN1 9RQ, England
Email: m.o-malley@sussex.ac.uk
Contact: Dr Michelle O'Malley

SOCIETY FOR THE PROMOTION OF HELLENIC STUDIES

Senate House, Malet Street, London, WC1E 7HU, England
Tel: (44) 20 7862 8730
Fax: (44) 20 7862 8731
Email: hellenic@sas.ac.uk
www: http://www.sas.ac.uk/icls/hellenic
Contact: Secretary

The Society for the Promotion of Hellenic Studies, generally known as the Hellenic Society, was founded in 1879 to advance the study of Greek language, literature, history, art and archaeology in the Ancient, Byzantine and Modern periods.

Dover Fund
Subjects: Greek language and papyri.
Purpose: To further the study of the history of the Greek language in any period from the Bronze Age to the fifteenth-century AD, and to further the edition and exegesis of Greek texts from any period within those same limits.
Eligibility: Open to currently registered research students, and lecturers, teaching Fellows, research Fellows, postdoctoral Fellows and research assistants who are within the first five years of their appointment.
Level of Study: Doctorate, Postdoctorate, Postgraduate.
Type: Grant.
Value: Grants will be made for such purposes as books, photography, including microfilm and photocopying, and towards the costs of visits to libraries, museums and sites. The sums awarded will vary according to the needs of the applicant, but most grants will be in the range of UK£50-250. Larger grants may be made from time to time at the discretion of the awards committee.
Frequency: Annual.
Study Establishment: The Society for the Promotion of Hellenic Studies.
Country of Study: United Kingdom.
No. of awards offered: Varies.
Application Procedure: Applicants must complete an application form, available from the Society. Applications should be marked for the attention of the Dover Fund and sent to the main address.
Closing Date: February 14th of the year in which the award is sought.
Funding: Private.
Contributor: Membership subscriptions.
No. of awards given last year: 3.
No. of applicants last year: 8.

Dover Fund Grant
Subjects: Classical Greek.
Purpose: To further the study of the history of the Greek language, from the Bronze Age to the fifteenth-century AD.
Eligibility: Open to currently registered research students, lecturers and postdoctoral Fellows in their first five years of appointment.
Level of Study: Doctorate, Postdoctorate, Postgraduate.
Type: Grant.
Value: Usually UK£50-250.
Frequency: Annual, if funds are available.
No. of awards offered: Approx. three.
Application Procedure: Please request an application form from the Society.
Closing Date: February 14th.
Funding: Private.
No. of awards given last year: 3.
No. of applicants last year: 7.

SOCIETY FOR THE PROMOTION OF ROMAN STUDIES

Senate House, Malet Street, London, WC1E 7HU, England
Tel: (44) 20 7862 8727
Fax: (44) 20 7862 8728
Email: romansoc@sas.ac.uk
www: http://www.sas.ac.uk/icls/roman
Contact: Dr Helen M Cockle, Secretary of Society

The Society for the Promotion of Roman Studies aims to promote the study of history, architecture, archaeology, language, literature and the art of Italy and the Roman Empire, including Roman Britain, from the earliest times to about 700 AD.

Hugh Last and Donald Atkinson Funds Committee Grants
Subjects: The history, archaeology, language, literature or art of Italy and the Roman Empire including Roman Britain.

Purpose: To assist in the undertaking, completion or publication of work that relates to any of the general scholarly purposes of the Roman Society. In addition, postgraduate students may apply for small grants to visit conferences and for other research purposes.
Eligibility: Open to applicants of graduate, postgraduate or post-doctoral status or the equivalent, usually of United Kingdom nationality.
Level of Study: Graduate, Postdoctorate, Postgraduate.
Type: Grant.
Value: Varies, but usually UK£200-1,500.
Frequency: Annual.
Country of Study: Other.
No. of awards offered: 20.
Application Procedure: Applicants must ensure that two references are sent directly to the Society. Completion of an application form is not essential.
Closing Date: January 15th.
Funding: Private.
No. of awards given last year: 15.
No. of applicants last year: 24.
Additional Information: Grants for the organisation of conferences of colloquial and symposia will only be considered in exceptional circumstances.

SOCIETY FOR THE PSYCHOLOGICAL STUDY OF SOCIAL ISSUES (SPSSI)

SPSSI Central Office, 208 I Street NE, Washington, DC 20002, United States of America
Tel: (1) 202 223 5100
Fax: (1) 202 223 5555
Email: spssi@spssi.org
www: http://www.spssi.org
Contact: Ms Brenda Stanard, Administrative Associate

The Society for the Psychological Study of Social Issues (SPSSI) is an interdisciplinary, international organisation of over 3,000 social scientists who share an interest in research on the psychological aspects of important social issues. The Society's goals are to increase understanding of social issues through research and its dissemination and to support policy efforts consistent with such research.

Clara Mayo Grants
Subjects: Aspects of sexism, racism or prejudice.
Purpose: To support the writing of a Master's thesis or predissertation research.
Eligibility: Open to individuals who have matriculated in graduate programmes in psychology, applied social science and related disciplines.
Level of Study: Graduate, Postgraduate.
Type: Research grant.
Value: Up to US$1,000.
Frequency: Annual.
Country of Study: United States of America.
No. of awards offered: Varies.
Application Procedure: Applicants must send five copies of a cover sheet with the title of the thesis and address details, an abstract of no more than 100 words, a budget request and other relevant details. Further details can be found on the website.
Closing Date: May 1st or November 1st.
Funding: Private.
No. of awards given last year: Five.

Gordon Allport Intergroup Relations Prize
Subjects: Intergroup relations.
Purpose: To recognise the best paper or article of the year on intergroup relations.
Eligibility: Open to non members, as well as members of SPSSI. Graduate students are especially urged to submit papers.
Level of Study: Doctorate, Graduate, Postdoctorate, Postgraduate.
Type: Prize.
Value: US$1,000.
Frequency: Annual.

Country of Study: Any country.
No. of awards offered: One.
Application Procedure: Applicants must submit four copies of their entry. Entries can be either papers published during the current year or unpublished manuscripts. Applicants must include contact information for all authors. Entries cannot be returned.
Closing Date: November 1st.
No. of awards given last year: One.
Additional Information: Originality of the contribution, whether theoretical or empirical, will be given special weight. The research area of intergroup relations includes such dimensions as age, sex, and socio-economic status, as well as race.

Louise Kidder Early Career Award
Subjects: Social and community psychology.
Purpose: To recognise social issues researchers who have made substantial contributions to the field early in their careers.
Eligibility: Nominees should be social issues investigators who have made substantial contributions to social issues research within five years of receiving a graduate degree and who have demonstrated the potential to continue such contributions.
Level of Study: Postdoctorate, Professional development.
Type: Award.
Value: US$500 plus plaque.
Frequency: Annual.
Country of Study: Any country.
No. of awards offered: One.
Application Procedure: Applicants must send five copies of a covering letter stating the nominee's accomplishments to date and future contributions, a curriculum vitae, and three letters of support. For full details visit the website.
Closing Date: May 1st.
Funding: Private.
No. of awards given last year: One.

Otto Klineberg Intercultural and International Relations Award
Subjects: Intercultural or international relations. The originality of the contribution, whether theoretical or empirical, will be given special weight.
Purpose: To recognise the best paper or article of the year.
Eligibility: Open to non members, as well as members of SPSSI. Graduate students are especially urged to submit papers.
Level of Study: Doctorate, Graduate, Postdoctorate, Postgraduate.
Type: Prize.
Value: US$1,000.
Frequency: Annual.
Country of Study: Any country.
No. of awards offered: One.
Application Procedure: Applicants must submit five copies of their entry. Entries can be either papers published in the current year or unpublished manuscripts. Applicants must include contact details for all authors. Entries cannot be returned. Further details can be found on the website.
Closing Date: February 15th.
Funding: Private.

SPSSI Applied Social Issues Internship Program
Subjects: The application of social science principles to social issues in co-operation with a community, city or state government organisation, public interest group or other non profit entity.
Purpose: To encourage intervention projects, non partisan advocacy projects, applied research and writing and implementing policy.
Eligibility: Open to graduate students and first year postdoctorates in psychology, applied social science and related disciplines. Applicants must be SPSSI members.
Level of Study: Graduate, Postdoctorate, Postgraduate.
Type: Grant.
Value: US$300-2,500 to cover research costs, community organising, Summer stipends etc.
Frequency: Annual.
Country of Study: Any country.
No. of awards offered: Varies.

Application Procedure: Applicants must submit an application consisting of three copies of a two-five page proposal including a budget, a short curriculum vitae, a letter from a faculty sponsor or supervisor of the project, including a statement concerning protection for participants if relevant, and a letter from an organisational sponsor, though this is waived if the applicant is proposing to organise a group. Further details can be found on the website.
Closing Date: May 1st.
Funding: Private.

SPSSI Grants-in-Aid Program

Subjects: Scientific research in social problem areas related to the basic interests and goals of SPSSI and particularly those that are not likely to receive support from traditional sources.
Eligibility: Open to students at the dissertation stage of a graduate career or beyond.
Level of Study: Doctorate, Graduate, Postdoctorate, Postgraduate.
Type: Grant.
Value: Up to US$2,000. Up to US$1,000 for graduate students, which must be matched by the student's university. Funds are not normally provided for travel to conventions, travel or living expenses while conducting research, stipends of principal investigators, or costs associated with manuscript preparation.
Frequency: Twice a year.
Country of Study: Any country.
No. of awards offered: Varies.
Application Procedure: Applicants must submit four copies of a statement that includes a cover sheet stating the title of the proposal, the contact details of the investigator, an abstract of 100 words or less summarising the proposed research, project purposes, theoretical rationale and specific procedures to be employed, the relevance of research to SPSSI goals and grants-in-aid criteria, the curriculum vitae of the investigator and the specific amount requested including a budget. A faculty sponsor's recommendation must be provided if the investigator is a graduate student as support is seldom awarded to students who have not yet reached the dissertation stage. A recommended length for the entire proposal is five-seven double spaced, typed pages. The programme is sponsored in part by the Sophie and Shirley Cohen Memorial Fund and through membership contributions. Further information can be found on the website.
Closing Date: November 1st and May 1st.
Funding: Private.

SPSSI Social Issues Dissertation Award

Subjects: Social issues in psychology or in a social science with psychological subject matter.
Eligibility: Open to doctoral dissertations on a relevant topic accepted between March 1st of the year preceding that of application and March 1st of the year of application.
Level of Study: Postgraduate.
Type: Prize.
Value: First prize of US$750 and a second prize of US$500.
Frequency: Annual.
Country of Study: Any country.
No. of awards offered: Two.
Application Procedure: Applicants must visit the website for details.
Closing Date: May 1st.
Funding: Private.
No. of awards given last year: Two.

THE SOCIETY FOR THE SCIENTIFIC STUDY OF SEXUALITY (SSSS)

PO Box 416, Allentown, PA 18105, United States of America
Tel: (1) 319 895 8407
Fax: (1) 319 895 6203
Email: thesociety@inetmail.att.net
www: http://www.sexscience.org
Contact: Mr David L Fleming, Executive Director

The Society for the Scientific Study of Sexuality (SSSS) is an international organisation dedicated to the advancement of knowledge about sexuality. The Society brings together an interdisciplinary group of professionals who believe in the importance of both production of quality research and the clinical, educational and social applications of research related to all aspects of sexuality.

SSSS Student Research Grant Award

Subjects: Human sexuality from any discipline: psychology, anthropology, social work, biology, theology and medical research.
Purpose: To support research in the field of human sexuality.
Eligibility: Open to students of any nationality who are enrolled in a degree granting programme.
Level of Study: Unrestricted.
Type: Grant.
Value: US$1,000.
Frequency: Twice a year.
Study Establishment: An appropriate institution.
Country of Study: Any country.
No. of awards offered: Three.
Application Procedure: Applicants must send a stamped addressed envelope for further details and application forms.
Closing Date: February 1st or September 1st.
Funding: Private.
Contributor: The Foundation for the Scientific Study of Sexuality.
No. of awards given last year: Two.
Additional Information: The purpose of the research can be a Master's thesis or doctoral dissertation, but this is not a requirement.

SOCIETY FOR THE STUDY OF FRENCH HISTORY

Department of History, University of Stirling, Stirling, FK9 4LA, Scotland
Tel: (44) 1786 467580
Fax: (44) 1786 467581
Email: mgr1@stir.ac.uk
Contact: Dr Michael Rapport, Secretary

The Society for the Study of French History was established to encourage research into French history. It offers a forum where scholars, teachers and students can meet and exchange ideas. It also offers bursaries for research and conferences to postgraduates registered in the United Kingdom undertaking research into French history.

Society for the Study of French History Bursaries

Subjects: Any aspect of French history.
Purpose: To enable postgraduates to undertake research in French history.
Eligibility: Open to postgraduate students registered at a United Kingdom university. Students at any level A postgraduate study may apply, provided that their dissertation is on some aspect of French history.
Level of Study: Postgraduate.
Type: Bursary.
Value: Upto UK£500.
Length of Study: Dependent on the project for which the award is given.
Frequency: Annual.
Country of Study: France.
No. of awards offered: Around eight.
Application Procedure: Applicants must give details of the research being pursued and the use to which the money would be put, along with the names of two referees. There is no application form and applications by email are acceptable. Applicants are responsible for writing to their referees. Successful applicants will be required to submit, in the first instance, a brief outline of their research proposal and then, after the research trip, a synopsis of their findings, both for publication in the society's bulletin, The French Historian.
Closing Date: 1 February.
Funding: Private.
Contributor: The Society for the Study of French History.
No. of awards given last year: Three.
No. of applicants last year: Six.

Society for the Study of French History Conference Bursaries

Subjects: Any aspect of French history.
Purpose: To enable postgraduates to attend conferences related to research.
Eligibility: Open to postgraduate students registered at a United Kingdom university.
Level of Study: Postgraduate.
Type: Bursary.
Value: Up to UK£100 each.
Frequency: Annual.
Country of Study: France.
No. of awards offered: Five.
Application Procedure: Applicants must give details of the conference being attended and the use to which the money will be put, along with names of two referees. There is no application form and applications by email are acceptable.
Closing Date: There is no deadline.
Funding: Private.
Contributor: The Society for the Study of French History.
No. of awards given last year: Five.
No. of applicants last year: Five.

THE SOCIETY FOR THEATRE RESEARCH

c/o The Theatre Museum, 1E Tavistock Street, London, WC2E 7PA, England
Email: e.cottis@btinternet.com
www: http://www.str.org.uk
Contact: Research Awards Sub-Committee Chairman

The Society for Theatre Research was founded in 1948 for all interested in the history and technique of British theatre. It publishes annually one or more books, newsletters, and three issues of the journal Theatre Notebook, holds lecture meetings and other events, and gives an annual book prize as well as grants for theatre research.

Society for Theatre Research Awards

Subjects: The history and practice of the British theatre, including music hall, opera, dance and other associated performing arts. Exclusively literary topics are not eligible.
Purpose: To aid research into the history and practice of British theatre.
Eligibility: Applicants should normally be aged 18 or over but there is no other restriction on their status, nationality or the location of the research.
Level of Study: Unrestricted.
Value: From a total of approx. UK£4,000. Major awards are normally UK£1,000-1,500 and other awards are normally UK£200-500.
Frequency: Annual.
Country of Study: Any country.
No. of awards offered: Two major awards and a number of lesser awards.
Application Procedure: Applicants must write to the Chairman of the Research Awards Sub-Committee after October 1st of the preceding year for an application form and guidance notes. All applications and enquiries must be made by post to the Society's accommodation address.
Closing Date: February 1st.
Funding: Private.
Contributor: Members' subscriptions, donations, and bequests.
No. of awards given last year: Nine.
No. of applicants last year: 25.
Additional Information: While applications will need to show evidence of the value of the research and a scholarly approach, they are by no means restricted to professional academics. Many awards, including major ones, have previously been made to theatre practitioners and 'amateur' researchers, who are encouraged to apply. The Society also welcomes proposals which in their execution extend methods and techniques of historiography. In coming to its decisions, the Society will consider the progress already made by the applicants and the possible availability of other grants.

SOCIETY OF APOTHECARIES OF LONDON

Black Friars Lane, London, EC4V 6EJ, England
Tel: (44) 20 7236 1180
Fax: (44) 20 7329 3177
Email: clerk@apothecaries.org
www: http://www.apothecaries.org
Contact: R J Stringer, The Clerk

Gillson Scholarship in Pathology

Subjects: Pathology.
Purpose: To encourage original research in any branch of pathology.
Eligibility: Open to candidates under 35 years of age who are either licenciates or freemen of the Society, or who obtain the licence or the freedom within six months of election to the scholarship.
Level of Study: Postgraduate.
Type: Scholarship.
Value: UK£1,800 in total. Payments are made twice annually for the duration of the scholarship.
Length of Study: Three years, renewable for a second term of three years.
Frequency: Every three years.
Country of Study: Any country.
No. of awards offered: One.
Application Procedure: Applicants must submit two testimonials and present evidence of their attainments and capabilities as shown by any papers already published, and/or a detailed record of any pathological work already done. Candidates should also state where the research will be undertaken.
Closing Date: December 1st.
Funding: Private.
Additional Information: Preference is given to the candidate who is engaged in the teaching of medical science or in its research. Scholars are required to submit an interim report at the end of the first six months of tenure, and a complete report one month prior to the end of the third year. Any published results should also be submitted to the Society.

SOCIETY OF ARCHITECTURAL HISTORIANS (SAH)

1365 North Astor Street, Chicago, IL 60610-2144, United States of America
Tel: (1) 312 573 1365
Fax: (1) 312 573 1141
Email: info@sah.org
www: http://www.sah.org
Contact: Ms Gail Ettinger, Programme Co-ordinator

A national, non-profit, membership organisation established in 1940, the Society of Architectural Historians (SAH) promotes discussion among those interested in architecture and its related disciplines, encourages scholarly research in the history of architecture and the built environment, and supports the preservation of architectural monuments worldwide.

Carroll LV Meeks Fellowship

Subjects: Architectural history.
Purpose: To enable an outstanding student to participate in the annual SAH domestic study tour. The location of this is different every year.
Eligibility: Open to SAH members who are students engaged in graduate work in architecture, or architectural history, city planning or urban history, landscape or the history of landscape design.
Level of Study: Postgraduate.
Type: Scholarship.
Value: A surcharge on non student participants' registrations is applied toward such tour scholarships to defray the cost of the tour itself.
Frequency: Annual.
Country of Study: Any country.
No. of awards offered: One.

Application Procedure: Applicants must complete an application form, available on request by writing to SAH for guidelines or visiting the SAH website.
Closing Date: The date changes each year, please contact the organisation.
Funding: Commercial, Private.
No. of awards given last year: One.
No. of applicants last year: Four.

Edilia and François-Auguste de Montequin Fellowship in Iberian and Latin American Architecture

Subjects: Spanish, Portuguese or Ibero American architecture, including colonial architecture produced by the Spaniards in the Philippines and what is today the United States of America.
Purpose: To fund travel for research into Spanish, Portuguese or Ibero American architecture.
Eligibility: Open to SAH members who are junior Scholars, including graduate students.
Level of Study: Doctorate, Postdoctorate, Postgraduate.
Type: Fellowship.
Value: US$2,000 for junior scholars awarded each year and US$6,000 for senior scholars offered every two years.
Frequency: Annual for junior scholars and every two years for senior scholars.
Country of Study: Any country.
No. of awards offered: Two.
Application Procedure: Applicants must complete an application form, available on request by writing to SAH for guidelines or visiting the SAH website.
Closing Date: November 15th.
Funding: Private.
No. of awards given last year: One.
No. of applicants last year: Five.

Keepers Preservation Education Fund Fellowship

Subjects: Historic preservation.
Purpose: To enable a graduate student to attend the annual meeting of the Society, held each April.
Eligibility: Open to members of any nationality who are currently engaged in the study of historic preservation.
Level of Study: Postgraduate.
Type: Fellowship.
Value: Registration fee for the meeting itself is waived, plus reimbursement for travel, lodging and meals directly related to the meeting, up to a combined total of US$500.
Frequency: Annual.
Country of Study: Any country.
No. of awards offered: One.
Application Procedure: Applicants must write to SAH for application guidelines or download an application from the society's website.
Closing Date: November 15th.
Funding: Private.
No. of awards given last year: One.
No. of applicants last year: Seven.

Rosann Berry Fellowship

Subjects: Architectural history or an allied field eg. city planning, landscape architecture, decorative arts or historic preservation.
Purpose: To enable a student engaged in advanced graduate study to attend the annual meeting of the Society.
Eligibility: Open to persons of any nationality who have been members of SAH for at least one year prior to the meeting, and who are currently engaged in advanced graduate study, normally beyond the Master's level, that involves some aspect of the history of architecture or of one of the fields closely allied to it.
Level of Study: Postgraduate.
Type: Fellowship.
Value: Registration fee connected with the meeting is waived, plus reimbursement for travel, lodging and meals directly related to the meeting, up to a combined total of US$500.
Frequency: Annual.
Country of Study: Any country.
No. of awards offered: One.

Application Procedure: Applicants must complete an application form, available on request by writing to SAH for guidelines or visiting the SAH website.
Closing Date: November 15th.
Funding: Private.
No. of awards given last year: One.
No. of applicants last year: 15.

Sally Kress Tompkins Fellowship

Subjects: Architectural history and historic preservation.
Purpose: To enable an architectural history student to work as an intern on an Historic American Buildings Survey project, during the summer.
Eligibility: Open to architectural history and historic preservation students.
Level of Study: Doctorate, Postgraduate.
Type: Fellowship.
Value: US$9,200.
Frequency: Annual.
Country of Study: United States of America.
No. of awards offered: One.
Application Procedure: Applicants must submit an application including a sample of work, a letter of recommendation from a faculty member, and a United States Government Standard Form 171, available from HABS or most United States government personnel offices. Applications should be sent to the Sally Kress Tompkins Fellowship. Applicants not selected for the Tomkins Fellowship will be considered for other HABS Summer employment opportunities. For more information, please contact Catherine C Laudie, HABS/HAER Co-ordinator.
Closing Date: February 7th.
Funding: Government.
No. of awards given last year: One.
No. of applicants last year: Seven.

For further information contact:

The Sally Kress Tompkins Fellowship, c/o HABS/HAER, National Park Service, 1849C Street NW, Washington, DC 2270-20240, United States of America

Spiro Kostof Annual Meeting Fellowship

Subjects: Architectural history.
Purpose: To enable an advanced graduate student in architectural history to attend the annual meeting of the Society of Architectural Historians.
Eligibility: Open to doctoral candidates only who have been members of the SAH for at least one year.
Level of Study: Doctorate, Predoctorate.
Type: Fellowship.
Value: US$500.
Frequency: Annual.
No. of awards offered: One.
Application Procedure: Applicants must write for an application form, available after June 1st by mail or by visiting the website.
Closing Date: November 15th.
Funding: Commercial, Private.
Contributor: The Society of Architectural Historians.
No. of awards given last year: One.
No. of applicants last year: 15.

SOCIETY OF ARCHITECTURAL HISTORIANS OF GREAT BRITAIN

Flat 4, 23 London Street, Edinburgh, EH3 6LY, Scotland
Email: secretary@sahgb.org.uk
www: http://www.sahgb.org.uk
Contact: Mr Andrew Martindale, Honorary Secretary

The Society of Architectural Historians of Great Britain encourages the study and enjoyment of architectural history. It was founded in 1956. Through its membership, the Society provides a forum for the interchange of ideas and information, acting as a valuable link between architectural historians both in Great Britain and abroad. Membership is open to all who are interested in architecture and its history.

Ramsden Bursaries

Subjects: Any aspect of the history of architecture.
Purpose: To support postgraduate research in the field of architectural history.
Eligibility: Candidates may apply for a second award, but in cases of equal merit, priority will be given to the first time applicant. No one may receive more than two awards.
Level of Study: Postgraduate.
Type: Bursary.
Value: To support research expenses including travel, building survey, photography and conference attendance. Bursaries are not awarded for maintenance at home, purchase of books or equipment, secretarial help or tuition fees. The value does not normally exceed UK£500, and the maximum is UK£1,000.
Length of Study: Projects are normally to be completed within one year.
Frequency: Twice a year.
No. of awards offered: Up to five.
Application Procedure: Applicants must submit an application including the title and description of the project, a curriculum vitae, detailed estimated costs, the date of the start of the project and estimated completion date, as well as two letters of recommendation to be sent directly by referees to the Secretary. Applicants are responsible for asking their referees to write. Five copies of the application should be submitted to the Honorary Secretary of the Society with a stamped addressed envelope if acknowledgement is required.
Closing Date: April 30th or October 31st each year.
Funding: Private.
Contributor: Endowment.
Additional Information: The award decisions will be made annually in May and November, and announced in the Society's Newsletter. Payments to successful applicants will only be made after documentary evidence of each major item of expenditure has been supplied. This may be in receipt or invoice, or confirmation of travel booking or conference enrolment. The Society must be acknowledged in any published work arising out of the application. Copies of books, or in the case of shorter publications, an offprint or photocopy should be sent to the Honorary Secretary of the Society. A brief report of the use made of the grant must be submitted to the Honorary Secretary within a year of its receipt and, if the work extends beyond a year, a second report should be submitted on its completion. For further details please contact the Honorary Secretary.

Stroud Bursaries

Subjects: Any aspect of the history of architecture.
Purpose: To support publication in the field of architectural history.
Level of Study: Unrestricted.
Type: Bursary.
Value: Subsidy to defray publication costs, cost of purchase of illustrations, payment of copyright fees, contribution to the costs of mounting an exhibition. The amount does not normally exceed UK£500, and the maximum is UK£1,000.
Length of Study: Projects are normally to be completed within one year. Candidates may apply for a second award, but in cases of equal merit, priority will be given to the first time applicant. No one may receive more than two awards.
Frequency: Twice a year.
No. of awards offered: Up to five.
Application Procedure: Applicants must submit an application including the title and description of the project, a curriculum vitae, detailed estimated costs, the date of the start of the project and estimated completion date, as well as two letters of recommendation to be sent directly by referees to the Secretary. Applicants are responsible for asking their referees to write. Five copies of the application should be submitted to the Honorary Secretary of the Society with a stamped addressed envelope if acknowledgement is required.
Closing Date: April 30th or October 31st each year.
Funding: Private.
Contributor: Endowment.

Additional Information: The award decisions will be made annually in May and November, and announced in the Society's Newsletter. Payments to successful applicants will only be made after documentary evidence of each major item of expenditure has been supplied. The Society must be acknowledged in any published work arising out of the application. Copies of books, or in the case of shorter publications, an offprint or photocopy should be sent to the Honorary Secretary within a year of receipt and, if the work extends beyond a year, a second report should be submitted on its completion. For further details please contact the Honorary Secretary.

SOCIETY OF CHILDREN'S BOOK WRITERS AND ILLUSTRATORS (SCBWI)

8271 Beverly Boulevard, Los Angeles, CA 90048, United States of America
Tel: (1) 323 782 1010
Fax: (1) 323 782 1892
Email: scbwi@scbwi.org
www: http://www.scbwi.org
Contact: Mr Stephen Mooser, President

The Society of Children's Book Writers and Illustrators (SCBWI) is an organisation of 19,000 writers, illustrators, editors, agents, and publishers of children's books, television, film and multimedia.

Barbara Karlin Grant

Subjects: Children's picture books.
Purpose: To assist picture book writers in the completion of a specific project.
Eligibility: Open to both full and associate members of the Society who have never had a picture book published. The grant is not available for a project on which there is already a contract.
Level of Study: Unrestricted.
Type: Grant.
Value: The full grant is US$1,500 and the runner up grant is US$500.
Frequency: Annual.
Country of Study: Any country.
No. of awards offered: One.
Application Procedure: Applicants must write for details.
Closing Date: May 15th.
Funding: Private.
No. of awards given last year: Two.
No. of applicants last year: 75.

Don Freeman Memorial Grant-in-Aid

Subjects: Children's picture books.
Purpose: To enable picture book artists to further their understanding, training and work in the picture book genre.
Eligibility: Open to both full and associate members of the Society who, as artists, seriously intend to make picture books their chief contribution to the field of children's literature.
Level of Study: Unrestricted.
Type: Grant.
Value: The full grant is US$1,500 and the runner up grant is US$500.
Frequency: Annual.
Country of Study: Any country.
No. of awards offered: Two.
Application Procedure: Applicants must submit an application to the Society. Receipt of application will be acknowledged.
Closing Date: Application requests should be submitted by June 15th and completed applications should be submitted by February 10th.
Funding: Private.
No. of awards given last year: Two.
No. of applicants last year: 48.

SCBWI General Work-in-Progress Grant

Subjects: Children's literature.
Purpose: To assist children's book writers in the completion of a specific project.
Eligibility: Open to both full and associate members of the Society. The grant is not available for projects on which there is already a

contract. Recipients of previous grants are not eligible to apply for any further SCBWI Grants.
Level of Study: Unrestricted.
Type: Grant.
Value: The full grant is US$1,500 and the runner up grant is US$500.
Frequency: Annual.
Country of Study: Any country.
No. of awards offered: One full grant and one runner up grant.
Application Procedure: Applicants must write for details.
Closing Date: May 1st.
Funding: Private.
No. of awards given last year: Two.
No. of applicants last year: 123.

SCBWI Grant for a Contemporary Novel for Young People

Subjects: Children's literature.
Purpose: To assist children's book writers in the completion of a specific project.
Eligibility: Open to both full and associate members of the Society. The grant is not available for projects on which there is already a contract. Recipients of previous grants are not eligible to apply for any further SCBWI Grants.
Level of Study: Unrestricted.
Type: Grant.
Value: The full grant is US$1,500 and the runner up grant is US$500.
Frequency: Annual.
Country of Study: Any country.
No. of awards offered: One full grant and one runner up grant.
Application Procedure: Applicants must write for details.
Closing Date: May 1st.
Funding: Private.
No. of awards given last year: Two.
No. of applicants last year: 110.

SCBWI Grant for Unpublished Authors

Subjects: Children's literature.
Purpose: To assist children's book writers in the completion of a specific project.
Eligibility: Open to both full and associate members of the Society who have never had a book published. The grant is not available for a project on which there is already a contract. Recipients of previous grants are not eligible to apply for any further SCBWI Grants.
Level of Study: Unrestricted.
Type: Grant.
Value: The full grant is US$1,500 and the runner up grant is US$500.
Frequency: Annual.
Country of Study: Any country.
No. of awards offered: One full grant and one runner up grant.
Closing Date: May 1st.
Funding: Private.
No. of awards given last year: Two.
No. of applicants last year: 45.

SCBWI Non-Fiction Research Grant

Subjects: Children's literature.
Purpose: To assist children's book writers in the completion of a specific project.
Eligibility: Open to both full and associate members of the Society. The grant is not available for projects on which there is already a contract. Recipients of previous grants are not eligible to apply for any further SCBWI Grants.
Level of Study: Unrestricted.
Type: Grant.
Value: The full grant is US$1,500 and the runner up grant is US$500.
Frequency: Annual.
Country of Study: Any country.
No. of awards offered: One full grant and one runner up grant.
Application Procedure: Applicants must write for details.
Closing Date: May 1st.
Funding: Private.
No. of awards given last year: One.
No. of applicants last year: 75.

SOCIETY OF EXPLORATION GEOPHYSICISTS FOUNDATION (SEG)

Box 702740, Tulsa, OK 74170, United States of America
Tel: (1) 918 497 5500
Fax: (1) 918 497 5560
Email: klanigan@seg.org
www: http://www.seg.org
Contact: Ms Kathleen Lanigan

The Society of Exploration Geophysicists (SEG) began a program of encouraging the establishment of scholarship funds by companies and individuals in the field of geophysics in 1958. In 1963, the Foundation's activities were expanded to include grants-in-aid.

SEG Scholarships

Subjects: Geophysics and related earth sciences.
Purpose: To encourage careers in the exploration of geophysics and related earth sciences.
Eligibility: Open to citizens of any country who are entering graduate level and have above average grades and an aptitude for physics, mathematics and geology.
Level of Study: Unrestricted.
Type: Scholarship.
Value: Usually US$500-3,000 per academic year. Average awards are approx. US$2,000.
Length of Study: One academic year, renewable.
Frequency: Annual.
Country of Study: Any country.
No. of awards offered: Varies.
Application Procedure: Applicants must submit a completed application form accompanied by three years of transcripts and two letters of recommendation from the mathematics and science faculty.
Closing Date: March 1st of the year in which the award is made.
Funding: Commercial, Private.
No. of awards given last year: 118.
No. of applicants last year: 349.
Additional Information: Approximately US$200,000 given in scholarship to 100+ students annually.

SOCIETY OF NAVAL ARCHITECTS AND MARINE ENGINEERS

601 Pavonia Avenue Suite 400, Jersey City, NJ 07306, United States of America
Tel: (1) 201 798 4800 ext. 3029
Fax: (1) 201 798 4975
Email: efaustins@sname.org
www: http://www.sname.org/
Contact: Executive Director

The objectives of the Society of Naval Architects and Marine Engineers are to advance the state of the art, to afford facilities for the exchange of information and ideas, to disseminate the results of the research, experience and information among the members, to encourage and sponsor such research, to co-operate with educational institutions and to promote the professional integrity and status of members.

Society of Naval Architects and Marine Engineers Graduate Scholarships

Subjects: Naval architecture, marine engineering and ocean engineering, but not necessarily limited to these subjects.
Purpose: To encourage young men and women to enter marine industry related fields.
Eligibility: Open to citizens of any country who are college graduates of a recognised technical institution. Applicants must be members of the Society in good standing for one year.
Level of Study: Graduate, MBA, Predoctorate.
Type: Scholarship.
Value: Varies, usually to cover tuition costs at the selected school.
Length of Study: One year.
Frequency: Annual.

Country of Study: Any country.
No. of awards offered: Varies.
Application Procedure: 1. Open to U.S., Canadian and International applicants. 2. Society membership required one year prior to application. 3. Awards are made for one year of study leading to a Master's Degree in naval architecture, marine engineering, ocean engineering or in fields directly related to the marine industry. 4. Applicants must not receive their Master's Degree prior to September 1 of the year in which they are applying for their scholarship. 5. Graduate scholarships are awarded to an individual only once. 6. Application may be obtained by written request to the attention of the Chairman, Scholarships Committee, at the Society's address. 7. Applicants are required to provide GRE scores irregardless of graduate school admission requirements. 8. The Scholarships Committee must receive application prior to January 15th with all supporting data by February 15th for review by the Scholarships Committee. 9. Selection in April based upon recommendations of Scholarships Committee and approval by the Executive Committee.
Closing Date: February 1st.
Funding: Private.
No. of awards given last year: 9.
No. of applicants last year: 20 or more.

For further information contact:

601 Pavonia avenue, Suite 400, Jersey City, NJ 07306,
Contact: Scott C. McClure, Chairman, Scholarship

SOCIETY OF ORTHOPAEDIC MEDICINE

PO Box 223, Patchway, Bristol, BS32 4XD, England
Tel: (44) 1454 610255
Fax: (44) 1454 610255
Email: admin@soc-ortho-med.org
www: http://www.soc-ortho-med.org
Contact: Administrative Director

The Society of Orthopaedic Medicine in a non-profit making organisation offering grants for work within musculoskeletal medicine.

SOM Research Grant

Subjects: Musculoskeletal medicine.
Purpose: To assist those undertaking programmes of study that will increase knowledge in the field and enhance their professional development.
Eligibility: Applications are considered from those who may be undertaking a research degree leading to an MPhil, a research degree leading to a PhD/DProf, a pilot study or a presentation at a conference. Grants are also available for equipment.
Level of Study: Graduate, Postdoctorate, Predoctorate, Professional development.
Type: Research grant.
Value: Up to UK£5,000. UK£2000 of this allocation will be available in the form of smaller grants of up to UK£500.
Frequency: Annual.
Country of Study: United Kingdom.
No. of awards offered: Varies according to funds.
Application Procedure: An application form must be completed, available from the organisation.
Closing Date: Applications are accepted all year round.
No. of awards given last year: Five.
No. of applicants last year: Eight.

SOCIETY OF WOMEN ENGINEERS (SWE)

230 East Ohio Street, Suite 400, Chicago, IL 60611, United States of America
Tel: (1) 312 596 5223
Fax: (1) 312 596 5252
Email: hq@swe.org
www: http://www.swe.org
Contact: Ms Betty Shanahan, Executive Director

The Society of Women Engineers (SWE) was founded in 1950 and is a non-profit educational service organisation. SWE is the driving force that establishes engineering as a highly desirable career aspiration for women. SWE empowers women to succeed and advance in those aspirations and be recognized for their life changing contributions and achievements as engineers and leaders. For more information about the society please visit www.swe.org or call 312-596-5223.

BK Krenzer Memorial Re-entry Scholarship

Subjects: Engineering.
Purpose: To assist women in obtaining the credentials necessary to re-enter the job market as engineers.
Eligibility: Open to women who have been out of the job market as well as out of school for a minimum of two years. Recipients may be entering any year of an engineering programme, as full or part-time students. Preference is given to graduate engineers desiring to return to the workforce following a period of temporary retirement.
Level of Study: Graduate, Postgraduate.
Type: Scholarship.
Value: US$2,000.
Frequency: Annual.
Country of Study: United States of America.
No. of awards offered: One.
Application Procedure: Application forms are available from the website.
Closing Date: May 15th.
Funding: Private.
Additional Information: Recipients will be notified in September. Further information is available on request.

Lydia I Pickup Memorial Scholarship

Subjects: Engineering and computer science.
Purpose: To advance the applicant's career in engineering or computer science.
Eligibility: Open only to women majoring in engineering or computer science in a college or university with an ABET accredited programme.
Level of Study: Graduate.
Type: Scholarship.
Value: US$2,000.
Frequency: Annual.
Country of Study: United States of America.
No. of awards offered: One.
Application Procedure: Application forms are available from the website.
Closing Date: February 1st.
No. of awards given last year: One.

Microsoft Corporation Scholarships

Subjects: Computer science or computer engineering.
Purpose: To encourage women engineers to attain a high level of education and professional achievement.
Eligibility: Open only to women majoring in engineering or computer science in a college or university with an ABET accredited programme. Applicants must be United States citizens.
Level of Study: Graduate, Postgraduate.
Type: Scholarship.
Value: US$2,500.
Frequency: Annual.
Study Establishment: A four year college or university.
Country of Study: United States of America.
No. of awards offered: Two.
Application Procedure: Application forms are available from the website.
Closing Date: February 1st.
Funding: Commercial.
Contributor: The Microsoft Corporation.
Additional Information: Further information is available on the website.

Olive Lynn Salembier Scholarship

Subjects: Engineering and computer science.
Purpose: To aid women who have been out of the engineering market and out of school to obtain the credentials necessary to re-enter the job market as an engineer.

Eligibility: Open to women who have not practised engineering or been enrolled in an engineering or other university or college programme in the past two years. Applicants must be United States citizens. Recipients may be entering any graduate year, including doctoral programmes, as full or part-time students.
Level of Study: Doctorate, Graduate.
Type: Scholarship.
Value: US$2,000.
Frequency: Annual.
Country of Study: United States of America.
No. of awards offered: One.
Application Procedure: Application forms are available from the website.
Closing Date: May 15th.
Funding: Private.
Additional Information: Further information is available on request.

Past Presidents Scholarships

Subjects: Engineering.
Eligibility: Open only to women majoring in engineering or computer science in a college or university with an ABET accredited programme. United States citizenship is required.
Level of Study: Graduate, Postgraduate.
Type: Scholarship.
Value: US$1,500.
Frequency: Annual.
Country of Study: United States of America.
No. of awards offered: Two.
Application Procedure: Application forms are available from the website.
Closing Date: Please contact the organisation.
No. of awards given last year: Two.
Additional Information: Further information is available on request.

SWE General Motors Foundation Graduate Scholarship

Subjects: Mechanical engineering, electrical engineering, chemical engineering, industrial engineering, materials science and engineering or manufacturing engineering.
Purpose: To encourage women engineers to attain high levels of education and professional achievement.
Eligibility: Open only to women students entering the first year of a Master's degree programme. Applicants must have a career interest in the automotive industry or manufacturing, and have demonstrated leadership potential.
Level of Study: Graduate, Postgraduate.
Type: Scholarship.
Value: US$1,000, plus a travel grant of US$5,00 for each recipient to attend the SWE National Conference.
Frequency: Annual.
Country of Study: United States of America.
No. of awards offered: One.
Application Procedure: Application forms are available from the website.
Closing Date: February 1st.
Funding: Commercial.
Contributor: General Motors.
Additional Information: Further information is available on request.

SOIL AND WATER CONSERVATION SOCIETY (SWCS)

7515 Northeast Ankeny Road, Ankeny, IA 50021-9764, United States of America
Tel: (1) 515 289 2331
Fax: (1) 515 289 1227
www: http://www.swcs.org
Contact: Administrative Assistant

The Soil and Water Conservation Society (SWCS) fosters the science and the art of soil, water and related natural resource management to achieve sustainability. The SWCS promotes and practices an ethic recognising the interdependence of people and the environment.

Kenneth E Grant Research Scholarship

Subjects: Soil conservation.
Purpose: To provide financial aid to members research on a specific topic that will help SWCS carry out its mission of advocating the protection, enhancement and wise use of soil, water and related natural resources.
Eligibility: Open to members of the SWCS who have demonstrated integrity, ability and competence to complete the specified study topic.
Level of Study: Postgraduate.
Type: Research grant.
Value: Please contact the organisation.
Length of Study: One year.
Frequency: Annual.
Country of Study: Any country.
No. of awards offered: One.
Application Procedure: Applicants must submit a proposal and evidence of their ability to meet eligibility requirements. There are no specific application forms.
Funding: Private.

SONS OF THE REPUBLIC OF TEXAS

1717 8th Street, Bay City, TX 77414, United States of America
Tel: (1) 979 245 6644
Fax: (1) 979 244 3819
Email: srttexas@srttexas.org
www: http://www.srttexas.org
Contact: Administrative Assistant

Seeks to perpetuate the memory and spirit of the men and women who settled Texas and won its independence through great personal sacrifice and dedication to the cause of freedom.

Presidio La Bahia Award

Subjects: History.
Purpose: To promote suitable preservation of relics, appropriate dissemination of data, and research into Texas heritage, with particular emphasis on the Spanish colonial period.
Eligibility: Open to all persons interested in the Spanish colonial influence on Texas culture.
Level of Study: Unrestricted.
Type: Award.
Value: The first prize is a minimum of US$1,200, and second and third place prizes are the divided balance from the total amount available of US$2,000 at the discretion of the judges.
Frequency: Annual.
Study Establishment: Any suitable institution.
Country of Study: Any country.
No. of awards offered: Three.
Application Procedure: Applicants must submit four copies of published writings to the office. Galley proofs are not acceptable.
Closing Date: Entries are accepted from June 1st-September 30th.
Funding: Private.
Additional Information: Research writings have, in the past, proved to be the most successful type of entry. However, consideration will be given to other literary forms, art, architecture and archaeological discovery. For projects other than writing, contestants should furnish a description of the proposed entry, so that the Chairman may issue specific instructions.

Summerfield G Roberts Award

Subjects: History.
Purpose: To encourage literary effort and research about historical events and personalities during the days of the Republic of Texas 1836-1846, and to stimulate interest in the period.
Eligibility: Open to all writers.
Level of Study: Unrestricted.
Type: Award.
Value: US$2,500.
Length of Study: Not relevant.
Frequency: Annual.
Study Establishment: Any suitable institution.
Country of Study: Any country.

No. of awards offered: One.
Application Procedure: Manuscripts must be written or published during the calendar year for which the award is given. There is no word limit. No entry may be submitted more than one time. The manuscripts must be mailed (5 copies, for the use of the judges) to the General Office of the Sons of the Republic of Texas postmarked no later than January 14th in the year of award.
Closing Date: January 15th.
Funding: Private.
Additional Information: The award was made possible through the generosity of Mr. & Mrs. Summerfield G. Roberts.

SOROPTIMIST INTERNATIONAL OF GREAT BRITAIN AND IRELAND

127 Wellington Road South, Stockport
Cheshire, SK1 3TS, England
Tel: (44) 161 480 7686
Fax: (44) 161 477 6152
Contact: Administrative Officer

Soroptomist International of Great Britain and Ireland Golden Jubilee Fellowship

Subjects: All subjects.
Eligibility: Open to women residing within the boundaries of Soroptimist International of Great Britain and Ireland, who need not be Soroptimists. The countries are Anguilla, Antigua and Barbuda, Bangladesh, Barbados, British Virgin Islands, Cameroon, Gambia, Grenada, Guernsey, India, Isle of Man, Jamaica, Jersey, Republic of Ireland, Malawi, Malta, Mauritius, Nigeria, Pakistan, Seychelles, Sierra Leone, South Africa, Sri Lanka, St Vincent and the Grenadines, Thailand, Trinidad and Tobago, the Turks and Caicos Islands, Uganda, United Kingdom and Zimbabwe. Preference is given to women seeking to train or retrain for a business or profession as mature students. However all applications will be considered by the committee.
Level of Study: Unrestricted.
Type: Fellowship.
Frequency: Annual.
Study Establishment: Any agreed institution, providing the residential stipulation is met.
Country of Study: Any country.
No. of awards offered: Approx. 40.
Application Procedure: Applicants must enclose a stamped addressed envelope or international reply coupon for details. Applications in writing must be made on a personal basis to the Secretary.
Funding: Private.
Additional Information: Preference is given to women improving their skills or acquiring new ones to either seek employment after years in the home or to enter a field in which prospects for employment or advancement are greater.

SOUTH AFRICAN ASSOCIATION OF WOMEN GRADUATES (SAAWG)

Postsuite 495, Post Bag X9
Benmore, 2010, South Africa
Tel: (27) 11 883 4847
Fax: (27) 11 883 4847
Email: medwards@netactive.co.za
www: http://www.ifuw.org/southafrica
Contact: Miss Margaret Edwards, National President

The South African Association of Women Graduates (SAAWG) promotes the tertiary education of women and their self development over their life span. It seeks and facilitates equity for women graduates, cross cultural insights and co-operation, and societal advancement. Its great underlying purpose is world peace, brought about through education and international friendship. SAAWG is affiliated to the International Federation of University Women (IFUW) and is a member of the Federation of University Women of Africa (FUWA).

Bertha Stoneman Memorial Award for Botanical Research

Subjects: Botany or any related subject including environmental studies.
Purpose: To provide assistance for women undertaking research.
Eligibility: Open to members of the SAAWG.
Level of Study: Postgraduate.
Value: Rand 1,000.
Frequency: Annual.
Country of Study: Any country.
No. of awards offered: One.
Application Procedure: Applicants must write for application forms.
Closing Date: October 31st.
Funding: Private.
No. of awards given last year: One.
Additional Information: The award is made when a suitable applicant applies.

For further information contact:

Post suite 495, Post Bag X9, Benmore, Polo, 2010, South Africa
Contact: The fellowship secretary

Edna Machanick Award

Subjects: All subjects.
Purpose: To provide assistance to women at tertiary institutions, other than a university.
Eligibility: Open to South African women of all races who have successfully completed one year of a course of study and are in need of financial assistance to complete their studies towards a non degree qualification eg. diploma or certificate at the tertiary education level.
Level of Study: Graduate.
Type: Award.
Value: Rand 500 per year.
Frequency: Annual.
Study Establishment: Any Institute of Higher Education.
Country of Study: Any country.
No. of awards offered: Three-four.
Application Procedure: Applicants must complete an application form, available on written request.
Closing Date: October 31st.
Funding: Private.
Additional Information: The awards are generally made by the institutions concerned. SAAWG provides the funding.

Hansi Pollak Scholarship

Subjects: Any branch of the social sciences.
Purpose: To assist postgraduate study or research devoted to the practical purpose of ameliorating social conditions in South Africa.
Eligibility: Open to South African women graduates of all races who are, or have become, members of the Association.
Level of Study: Doctorate, Postgraduate.
Type: One scholarship.
Value: Rand 6,000 paid in six month instalments.
Length of Study: Two years, non renewable.
Frequency: Every two years.
Study Establishment: Any recognised university.
Country of Study: Any country.
No. of awards offered: One.
Application Procedure: Applicants must write for application forms.
Funding: Private.
No. of awards given last year: One.
No. of applicants last year: 50.
Additional Information: Fellows must spend at least two years in South Africa after completing a Master's or doctoral degree, in order to put into practice the results of the research.

For further information contact:

PO Box 6638, Johannesburg, 2000, South Africa
Email: jocelynbell@iafrica.com
Contact: Ms Jocelyn Bell

Isie Smuts Research Award

Subjects: All subjects.
Purpose: To assist postgraduate women in research.

Eligibility: Open to members of the SAAWG.
Level of Study: Postgraduate.
Type: Award.
Value: Rand 1,000.
Frequency: Annual.
Study Establishment: Any university.
Country of Study: South Africa.
No. of awards offered: One.
Application Procedure: Applicants must write to Miss V Henley.
Closing Date: October 31st.
Funding: Private.
No. of awards given last year: One.

Joan Whitmore Scholarship

Subjects: Environmental science.
Purpose: To assist postgraduate study or research in the broad field of environmental issues.
Level of Study: Postgraduate.
Type: One scholarship.
Frequency: Annual.
Study Establishment: The University of Pretoria.
Country of Study: South Africa.
Application Procedure: Applicants must contact the university showing evidence of the relevance of their study or research to the development of South Africa and of their community service.
Closing Date: January 31st.
Funding: Private.

For further information contact:

University of Pretoria, Client Service Centre, Arcadia, Pretoria, 0002 RSA, South Africa
www: http://www.up.ac.za

SAAWG International Fellowship

Subjects: All subjects.
Purpose: To assist women, who wish to study in South Africa.
Eligibility: Open to members of the International Federation of University Women, foreign students enrolled at a South African university for at least one year for postgraduate research.
Level of Study: Postgraduate.
Type: Fellowship.
Value: At least rand 1,000.
Length of Study: Not less than six months.
Frequency: Every three years.
Study Establishment: A university.
Country of Study: South Africa.
No. of awards offered: One.
Application Procedure: Applicants must write for application forms.
Closing Date: August 31st.
Funding: Private.
Additional Information: The award is made when a suitable applicant applies.

SOUTH AFRICAN COUNCIL FOR ENGLISH EDUCATION (SACEE)

PO Box 660, Pretoria 0001, South Africa
Tel: (27) 12 429 8616
Fax: (27) 12 429 8616
Email: ueng6@unisa.ac.za
www: http://www.sacee.org.za
Contact: Ms Patricia Bootland, Administrative Secretary

The South African Council for English Education's (SACEE) mission statement is to support the teaching, learning and appreciation of English. They have branches throughout South Africa, and major national projects are the English Alive publication, English olympiad, language challenge, oracy programme and plays festival.

Norah Taylor Bursary

Subjects: Speech training, oral communication and the teaching of English as a second language.

Purpose: To assist teachers to further their training.
Eligibility: Open to qualified teachers teaching English or other subjects in English, with three years of post matriculation study, and at least four years of teaching experience.
Level of Study: Graduate, Postgraduate, Professional development, Unrestricted.
Type: Bursary.
Value: Varies, depending upon the type of course taken.
Length of Study: Varies.
Frequency: Annual.
Study Establishment: Any educational institution (in South Africa).
Country of Study: South Africa.
No. of awards offered: Varies.
Application Procedure: Applicants must write for details.
Closing Date: July 31st of the year preceding that for which the bursary is required.
Funding: Private.
No. of awards given last year: One.
No. of applicants last year: 7.
Additional Information: Applicants not conforming to the requirements cannot be considered and will not be replied to.

SACEE EX-PCE Bursary

Subjects: English and subjects in English, including literature, drama or radio.
Purpose: To assist teachers in service who wish to improve their qualifications and to assist those who wish to take up postgraduate study specialising in the English language.
Eligibility: Open to nationals and residents of South Africa. Applicants' normal place of residence should be Gauteng RSA.
Level of Study: Postgraduate.
Type: Bursary.
Value: Varies, depending upon type of course taken.
Length of Study: Varies.
Frequency: Annual.
Study Establishment: Any academic institution.
Country of Study: South Africa.
No. of awards offered: Varies.
Application Procedure: Applicants must write for details.
Closing Date: Applications are accepted at any time.
Funding: Private.
No. of awards given last year: 1.
No. of applicants last year: 5.

SOUTH AFRICAN DENTAL ASSOCIATION

Private Bag 1, Houghton, Johannesburg, Braamfontein 2041, South Africa
Tel: (27) 11 484 5288
Fax: (27) 11 642 5718
Email: rswanepoel@sada.co.za
www: http://www.sadanet.co.za
Contact: Ms Rita Swanepoel, Secretary

The South African Dental Association's main objective is to promote the interests of its members in order to promote optimal oral health for all.

DDF Scholarship for the Development of a Research Technique for Dentistry/Dental Research

Subjects: Dentistry.
Purpose: To enable a qualified person to spend time in a laboratory to study a research technique.
Eligibility: Open to individuals with a proven record of research or those who are sponsored by such an individual. The applicant must undertake to live and work in South Africa for at least two years after the tenure of the scholarship or else refund the money.
Level of Study: Postgraduate.
Type: Scholarship.
Value: Rand 8,000.
Length of Study: At least one month. The scholarship must be held in the year it is awarded.

Frequency: Annual.
Country of Study: Any country.
No. of awards offered: One.
Application Procedure: Applicants must write for details.
Closing Date: April 30th.
Funding: Private.
No. of applicants last year: One.
Additional Information: This award does not render itself solely to the specific support of research nor to the study of research techniques.

THE SOUTH AFRICAN INSTITUTE OF INTERNATIONAL AFFAIRS (SAIIA)

Jan Smuts House, PO Box 31596, Johannesburg, Braamfontein 2017, South Africa
Tel: (27) 11 339 2021
Fax: (27) 11 339 2154
Email: saiiagen@global.co.za
www: http://www.wits.ac.za/saiia
Contact: Mrs Huguette Ilunga, Personal Assistant

The South African Institute of International Affairs (SAIIA) is an independent, non governmental foreign policy think tank, whose purpose is to encourage wider and more informed interest in international affairs and public education and to focus on policy relevant research.

SAIIA Bradlow Fellowship
Subjects: Social and behavioural sciences.
Purpose: To provide travel costs and a stipend to enable a senior Scholar to reside at the Institute in order to research a subject of importance to South Africa's international relations.
Eligibility: Open to senior Scholars.
Level of Study: Research.
Type: Fellowship.
Value: The stipend covers living expenses and a return economy class airfare from the candidate's place of residence.
Length of Study: Four-six months.
Frequency: Annual.
Study Establishment: SAIIA.
Country of Study: South Africa.
No. of awards offered: One.
Application Procedure: Applicants must send a curriculum vitae including a short research proposal of not more than 1,000 words to the director of studies.
Funding: Private.
Contributor: The Bradlow Foundation.
No. of awards given last year: One.

SOUTHDOWN TRUST

Hillbarn Cottage10 Nepcote Findon, Near Worthing, West Sussex BN14 0SD, England
Contact: Mr J G Wyatt, Secretary

The Southdown Trust is a small charity which gives limited help to individuals for educational purposes.

Southdown Trust Awards
Subjects: All subjects except, law, drama and music, dance and journalism, sociology, women's studies, business studies, arts, sport, IT, counselling, peace studies, PhD's Medicine only in later stages of medical studies.
Purpose: To encourage personal initiative, education and concern for others.
Eligibility: Open mainly to United Kingdom citizens but other nationalities are considered.
Value: Varies - UK£25-500.
Country of Study: United Kingdom.
No. of awards offered: Varies.
Application Procedure: Applicants must write giving full details and include a stamped addressed envelope.
Closing Date: May 1st, November 1st.

Funding: Private.
No. of awards given last year: 100.
No. of applicants last year: 2,000.

SOUTHERN CROSS UNIVERSITY

Graduate Research College, PO Box 157, Lismore, NSW 2480, Australia
Tel: (61) 2 6620 3705
Fax: (61) 2 6626 9145
Email: jrussell@scu.edu.au
www: http://www.scu.edu.au
Contact: Mr John Russell, Administrative Officer

Southern Cross University is one of Australia's most modern, creative and innovative universities founded on traditions of academic excellence, with national and international industry links. The University's courses emphasise real world skills and vocational training and are designed to give graduates a competitive edge in today's demanding employment market.

Southern Cross University Postgraduate Research Scholarships
Subjects: All subjects.
Purpose: To support a student while undertaking postgraduate research study.
Eligibility: There are no eligibility restrictions.
Level of Study: Postgraduate.
Value: Up to Australian $12,000.
Length of Study: Up to three years.
Frequency: Twice a year.
Study Establishment: Southern Cross University.
Country of Study: Australia.
No. of awards offered: 15-25.
Application Procedure: Applicants must complete an application form.
Closing Date: October 31st or May 31st.
Funding: Government.
No. of awards given last year: 23.
No. of applicants last year: 70.

SOUTHWEST MISSOURI STATE UNIVERSITY (SMSU)

College of Business Administration, 400 David D Glass Hall, Springfield, MO 65801, United States of America
Tel: (1) 417 836 5646
Fax: (1) 417 836 4407
Email: dmf603f@smsu.edu
www: http://www.coba.smsu.edu
Contact: MBA Admissions Officer

The Master of Business Administration (MBA) degree at Southwest Missouri State University (SMSU) is a College of Business Administration degree with courses taken in various departments. The programme will provide the background knowledge necessary for professional practice in the field of business. In the eyes of MBA students at SMSU, educational value is defined by a high quality programme, low tuition rates and low living costs in an attractive locale.

SMSU Carr Foundation Scholarship
Subjects: MBA.
Purpose: To assist students with expenses and enhance learning.
Eligibility: Students must be enrolled on the MBA programme and display financial need.
Level of Study: Graduate.
Type: Scholarship.
Value: US$600.
Length of Study: Varies.
Frequency: Annual, if funds are available.
Study Establishment: Southwest Missouri State University.
Country of Study: United States of America.

No. of awards offered: One.
Application Procedure: Applicants must contact the organisation for application details.
Closing Date: Please contact the organisation.

SMSU Graduate Assistantships

Subjects: All subjects.
Purpose: To assist students with expenses and to enhance learning while studying for advanced degrees at SMSU.
Eligibility: Applicants must be admitted to a graduate programme at SMSU to be eligible. A minimum grade point average of 3.00 on the last 60 hours of undergraduate course work or a minimum grade point average of 3.00 on nine or more hours of graduate course work is required. Graduate students who did not receive both their primary and secondary education where English was the primary language must meet the following requirements to qualify for graduate assistantships: successful completion of one semester of graduate studies at SMSU, during which they complete cultural orientation to prepare them for a teaching appointment and pass an SMSU juried examination in which the candidate must demonstrate his or her ability to interpret written English passages and to communicate orally in English in a classroom setting.
Level of Study: Graduate, MBA.
Type: Other.
Value: A minimum stipend of US$6,150 for the academic year. In a few situations a stipend of US$8,200 may be awarded.
Length of Study: A maximum of two years.
Frequency: Annual.
Study Establishment: SMSU.
Country of Study: United States of America.
No. of awards offered: Varies.
Application Procedure: Applicants must submit an application directly to the department in which the assistantship is sought. It is wise to check with the department before applying. Applications are available from the Graduate College and on the website http://www.smsu.edu/grad. Information from an applicant must include employment history, academic history and the addresses of referees.
Additional Information: Graduate assistantships are offered in both administrative and academic areas and involve administrative, research or teaching responsibilities. Whenever feasible, the assistantship assignment is closely related to the student's programme of study. A graduate assistant is required to complete a minimum of six hours of graduate course work during each semester of appointment. Some departments or units may require assistants to take more than six hours of course work. Graduate assistants are not eligible to work at any other paid position at SMSU during the time of their assistantship. A limited number of graduate assistantships are available during the Summer session. A graduate assistant appointed for the Summer session will receive a stipend of either US$1,537 or US$2,050. Summer graduate assistants are required to complete a minimum of three hours of graduate course work during the Summer session.

SMSU Graduate of Business Professional Honor Society Scholarship

Subjects: MBA.
Purpose: To assist students with expenses and enhance learning.
Eligibility: Applicants must be enrolled in either the MBA programme or the MAcc programme, have a grade point average of not less than 3.33, have active membership in the Graduate of Business Professional Honor Society and have been a member of the society for at least two semesters.
Level of Study: MBA.
Type: Scholarship.
Value: US$250.
Frequency: Annual.
Study Establishment: SMSU.
Country of Study: United States of America.
No. of awards offered: One.
Application Procedure: Applicants must contact the organisation for application details.
Closing Date: Please contact the organisation for details.

SMSU Robert and Charlotte Bitter Graduate Scholarship

Subjects: MBA.
Purpose: To assist students with expenses and enhance learning.
Eligibility: Applicants must have been admitted to the MBA or MAcc programme and have a Graduate Management Admissions Test score of 1,100 or higher, be enrolled in 12 hours each semester and have a grade point average of 3.33.
Level of Study: Graduate, MBA.
Type: Scholarship.
Value: US$1,200.
Length of Study: Varies.
Frequency: Annual, if funds are available.
Study Establishment: SMSU.
Country of Study: United States of America.
No. of awards offered: One.
Application Procedure: Applicants must contact the organisation for application details.
Closing Date: Please contact the organisation.

SPINAL CORD INJURY RESEARCH FOUNDATION

Paralyzed Veterans of America Education & Training Foundation, 801 18th Street North West, Washington, DC 20006, United States of America
Tel: (1) 202 416 7651
Fax: (1) 202 416 7641
Email: foundations@pva.org
www: http://www.pva.org
Contact: Administrative Officer

The Spinal Cord Injury Research Foundation aims to fund innovative educational projects that enhance the quality of life of individuals with spinal cord injury or disease (SCI/D) and/or increases the knowledge and effectiveness of health professionals in the SCI/D community.

Spinal Cord Injury Research Foundation Grants

Subjects: Spinal cord injury encompassing continuing education and training, post professional traineeships, patient or client education and conferences.
Purpose: To provide funds for grants to institutions, agencies and organisations that will improve the knowledge and abilities of health professionals, people with SC/D and those significant to them.
Eligibility: Open to suitably qualified persons working in the field.
Level of Study: Doctorate, Graduate, Postgraduate, Predoctorate.
Type: Grant.
Value: Varies.
Frequency: Annual.
Country of Study: United States of America or Canada.
No. of awards offered: Varies.
Application Procedure: Applicants should visit the website for details.
Closing Date: June 1st.
No. of awards given last year: 10.

ST ANDREW'S SOCIETY OF THE STATE OF NEW YORK

3 West 51st Street, New York, NY 10019, United States of America
Tel: (1) 212 223 4248
Fax: (1) 212 223 0748
Email: standrewsny@msn.com
Contact: Ms Kimberly Howland, Office Manager

St Andrew's Society of the State of New York's constitution states. 'For the relief of natives of Scotland and their descendants who might be in want or distress and to promote social intercourse among its members'.

St Andrew's Society of the State of New York Scholarship
Subjects: All subjects.
Purpose: To promote cultural and intellectual interchange and goodwill between Scotland and the United States of America.
Eligibility: Open to students of Scottish descent who have graduated from a Scottish University or Oxford or Cambridge University.
Level of Study: Postgraduate.
Type: Scholarship.
Value: US$10,000/US$20,000.
Length of Study: One year.
Frequency: Annual.
Study Establishment: Any University/Any University in the USA within a radius of 250 miles from New York City & also including the Washington area.
Country of Study: Scotland/United States of America.
No. of awards offered: Two/Two scholarships to USA citizens to study in Scotland. Two scholarships to Scottish students to study in the USA.
Application Procedure: Applicants must submit an application form, documentation of transcripts and letters of recommendation. The president of each college or university must recommend one student only from that institution.
Closing Date: January 30.
Funding: Private.
No. of awards given last year: Two.
No. of applicants last year: 25.

STANFORD HUMANITIES CENTER

242 Santa Theresa Street, Stanford University, Stanford, CA 94305-4015, United States of America
Tel: (1) 650 723 3052
Fax: (1) 650 723 1895
Email: sebbard@stanford.edu
www: http://shc.stanford.edu
Contact: Administrative Assistant

The Stanford Humanities Center was founded in 1980 to promote humanistic research and education, both at Stanford University and nationally. To this aim it provides fellowships, public presentations and research workshops.

External Faculty Fellowships
Subjects: Humanities.
Purpose: To offer research opportunities both to members of humanities departments as traditionally defined and to other scholars seriously interested in humanistic issues.
Eligibility: Candidates should be at least three years beyond receipt of their PhD. These fellowships are intended primarily for persons currently teaching or affiliated with academic institutions, but others may apply.
Level of Study: Postdoctorate.
Type: Fellowship.
Value: Up to US$35,000 for junior scholars and up to US$50,000 for senior scholars. In addition, up to US$12,500 will be offered as a housing or travel subsidy. Applicants are expected to seek supplementary financial support and are required to contribute this support, together with any sabbatical earnings, to their stipend.
Length of Study: One year residency, not renewable.
Frequency: Annual.
Study Establishment: Stanford Humanities Center.
Country of Study: United States of America.
No. of awards offered: Varies.
Application Procedure: Applicants must complete an application form available from the Center.
Closing Date: Please contact the organisation for details.
Funding: Government, Private.

Rockefeller Fellowships in Black Performing Arts
Subjects: Arts, humanities or the performing arts.
Purpose: To support scholars with an interest in the arts whose research examines the character and global influences of black performing arts and culture with a specific focus on performance. In addition these fellowships will support research which furthers the understanding of links between humanities, performance and arts generally within the specific area of black studies, or by placing black performance in a comparative context.
Eligibility: Please contact the organisation or consult the website for eligibility details.
Level of Study: Postdoctorate, Research.
Type: Fellowship.
Value: Up to US$25,000 for junior scholars and up to US$40,000 for senior scholars. In addition, up to US$12,500 will be offered as a housing and moving allowance. Applicants are expected to seek supplementary financial support and are required to contribute this support, together with any sabbatical earnings, to their stipend.
Frequency: Annual.
Study Establishment: Stanford Humanities Center.
Country of Study: United States of America.
No. of awards offered: Two, one to a senior and one to a junior.
Application Procedure: Applicants must complete an application form available from the Center.
Closing Date: Please contact the organisation for dates.
Funding: Private.
Contributor: The Rockefeller Foundation and the Stanford Humanities Center, in conjunction with the Stanford Committee on Black Performing Arts.

STANLEY SMITH (UK) HORTICULTURAL TRUST

Cory Lodge, PO Box 365, Cambridge, Cambridgeshire, CB2 1HR, England
Tel: (44) 1223 336299
Fax: (44) 1223 336278
Contact: Mr James Cullen, Director

The Stanley Smith (UK) Horticultural Trust supports projects which contribute to the development of the art or science of horticulture ie. garden conservation and restoration, education and training, publications and travel.

Stanley Smith (UK) Horticultural Trust Awards
Subjects: Horticulture. The Trust supports individual projects in all aspects (including training) of amenity horticulture and some aspects of commercial horticulture.
Eligibility: Open to institutions and individuals. All projects are judged entirely on merit and there are no eligibility requirements, but grants are not awarded for students to take academic or diploma courses of any kind.
Level of Study: Unrestricted.
Type: Varies.
Value: Varies.
Length of Study: Dependent on the nature of the project.
Frequency: Twice a year.
Country of Study: Any country.
No. of awards offered: Varies.
Application Procedure: Applicants must apply to the Trust. Trustees allocate awards in Spring and Autumn.
Closing Date: February 15th and August 15th.
Funding: Private.
Contributor: Donations.
No. of awards given last year: 38.
No. of applicants last year: 176.

STATE LIBRARY OF NEW SOUTH WALES

Macquarie Street, Sydney, NSW 2000, Australia
Tel: (61) 2 9273 1766
Fax: (61) 2 9273 1248
Email: library@slnsw.gov.au
www: http://www.slnsw.gov.au
Contact: State Librarian

The State Library of New South Wales is the premier reference and research library in the state. The Library consists of the State

Reference Library and the Mitchell Library which contains the famous Australian Research Collections pertaining to the history of Australia and the Southwest Pacific region.

C H Currey Memorial Fellowship
Subjects: Australian history.
Purpose: To promote the writing of Australian history from original sources.
Eligibility: Open to individuals of any nationality.
Level of Study: Unrestricted.
Type: Fellowship.
Value: Approx. Australian $20,000.
Frequency: Annual.
Country of Study: Australia.
Application Procedure: Applicants must complete an application form, available from the State Librarian.
Closing Date: Varies.
Funding: Private.

Nancy Keesing Fellowship
Subjects: Australian history, literature, life and culture.
Purpose: To encourage the use of the State Library's collections for original research.
Eligibility: Open to researchers of any nationality.
Level of Study: Unrestricted.
Type: Fellowship.
Value: Australian $10,000.
Frequency: Annual.
Study Establishment: The State Library of New South Wales.
Country of Study: Australia.
Application Procedure: Applicants must complete an application form, available on request.
Closing Date: Varies.
Funding: Private.

STATISTICAL SOCIETY OF CANADA

1485 Laperriere Avenue, Ottawa
ON, K1Z 7S8, Canada
Tel: (1) 613 725 2253
Fax: (1) 613 729 6206
Email: ssc@thewillowgroup.com
www: http://www.ssc.ca
Contact: Secretary

The Statistical Society of Canada provides a forum for discussion and interaction among individuals involved in all aspects of the statistical sciences. It publishes a newsletter, Liaison, as well as a scientific journal, The Canadian Journal of Statistics. The Society also organises annual scientific meetings and short courses on professional development.

Pierre Robillard Award
Subjects: Statistics.
Purpose: To recognise the best PhD thesis defended at a Canadian university and written in a field covered by the Canadian Journal of Statistics.
Level of Study: Doctorate.
Type: Award.
Value: A certificate, a monetary prize of Canadian $400 and one year's membership of the Society.
Frequency: Annual.
Country of Study: Canada.
No. of awards offered: Varies.
Application Procedure: Applicants must submit four copies of the thesis together with a covering letter from the thesis supervisor.
Closing Date: February 15th.
No. of awards given last year: One.
No. of applicants last year: 10.
Additional Information: The committee may decide that none of the submitted theses merits the award.

STOUT RESEARCH CENTRE, VICTORIA UNIVERSITY OF WELLINGTON

PO Box 600, Wellington, New Zealand
Tel: (64) 4 465 5305
Fax: (64) 4 463 5439
Email: stout-centre@vuw.ac.nz
www: http://www.vuw.ac.nz/stout-centre
Contact: Ms Margarita Ivanova, Administrator

J D Stout Fellowship
Subjects: New Zealand society, history or culture.
Purpose: To encourage research.
Eligibility: Open to distinguished scholars from New Zealand and abroad.
Level of Study: Postdoctorate.
Type: Fellowship.
Value: Up to New Zealand $56,000.
Length of Study: One year.
Frequency: Annual, if funds are available.
Study Establishment: The Stout Research Centre.
Country of Study: New Zealand.
No. of awards offered: One.
Application Procedure: Applicants must write for details.
Closing Date: August 1st of the year preceding the fellowship.

STROKE ASSOCIATION

Stroke House 240 City Road, London, EC1V 2PR, England
Tel: (44) 20 7566 0300
Fax: (44) 20 7490 4768
Email: research@stroke.org.uk
www: http://www.stroke.org.uk
Contact: Dr Sharon Crossen, Research Office

The Stroke Association raises funds for research, prevention, welfare, information and community services.

Stroke Association Clinical Fellowships
Subjects: The prevention, treatment or rehabilitation of strokes.
Purpose: To equip a trainee for a career in the field.
Eligibility: Open to departments that can demonstrate a track record in providing an educational training programme which may include a research project.
Level of Study: Professional development.
Type: Fellowship.
Value: UK£35,000.
Length of Study: One year.
Frequency: Annual.
Study Establishment: Suitable universities and medical schools.
Country of Study: United Kingdom.
No. of awards offered: Two.
Application Procedure: Applicants must respond to advertisements in the British Medical Journal in January of each year. Application forms are available from www.stroke.org.uk.
Closing Date: Usually March.
Funding: Private.
No. of awards given last year: 2.
Additional Information: Fellowships are assessed by peer review. Awards are made in June.

Stroke Association Therapy Research Bursaries
Subjects: Stroke research.
Purpose: To provide a research training programme and appropriate supervision to equip a trainee for a career in stroke research.
Eligibility: These bursaries are primarily intended for nurses and therapists, but consideration will be given to other health professionals. They will be awarded to departments that can demonstrate a track record and current participation in stroke research.
Level of Study: Postgraduate, Professional development.
Type: Bursary.

Value: UK£20,000 per year.
Length of Study: Up to three years.
Frequency: Annual.
Study Establishment: Suitable universities and hospitals.
Country of Study: United Kingdom.
No. of awards offered: Two.
Application Procedure: Applicants must respond to advertisements in Therapy Weekly in January of each year. Application forms are available from www.stroke.org.uk.
Closing Date: Usually March.
Funding: Private.
No. of awards given last year: 2.
Additional Information: Further information is available on request.

Stroke Research Awards

Subjects: Stroke research encompassing epidemiology, prevention, acute treatment, assessment and rehabilitation, psychology of stroke and stroke in ethnic minorities.
Purpose: To advance research into stroke.
Eligibility: Open to medically qualified and other clinically active researchers in the United Kingdom, in the relevant fields. Applications are judged by peer review on their merit without limitations of age. Applicants can be from any country but must be based in the United Kingdom.
Level of Study: Postdoctorate, Research.
Type: Project grant.
Value: Salaries for researchers and support staff, some equipment costs, consumables and essential travel. No other overheads, advertising etc. are covered. The maximum award is normally UK£60,000 per year.
Length of Study: One-three years.
Frequency: Annual.
Study Establishment: A suitable university or hospital in the United Kingdom.
Country of Study: United Kingdom.
No. of awards offered: Usually 20-30.
Application Procedure: Application forms are available from www.stroke.org.uk.
Closing Date: As advertised, usually in July and November.
Funding: Private.
Contributor: Donations.
No. of awards given last year: 11.
No. of applicants last year: 80.

THE STUDENT AWARDS AGENCY FOR SCOTLAND

Gyleview, House, 3 Redheughs Rigg, Edinburgh, EH12 9HH, Scotland
Tel: (44) 0845 111 1711
Fax: (44) 131 244 5887
Email: Leia.fitzgerald@scotland.gov.uk
www: http://www.saas.gov.uk/
Contact: Mr Victor Abela

The brief of the Student Awards Agency for Scotland is to administer the Students' Allowances Scheme, the Postgraduate Students' Allowances Scheme, No longer administered by us. This is done through the various Research Boards and the Nursing and Midwifery Bursary Scheme.

Student Awards Agency for Scotland-Postgraduate Students' Allowances Scheme

Subjects: Postgraduate professional or vocational training such as teacher training for graduates and training courses leading to diplomas and certificates in librarianship, continuing education, information technology etc.
Purpose: To allow students to attend short postgraduate courses of a vocational or professional nature.
Eligibility: Open to British nationals and nationals of a EU member state, ordinarily resident in Scotland, who are following short postgraduate courses. Applicants will be expected to have resided in Britain (ordinarily Scotland) for three years preceding the start of the

course. Residence mainly or wholly for educational purposes is not regarded as ordinary residence.
Level of Study: Postgraduate.
Type: Grant.
Value: Payment of tuition fees and a means-tested maintenance allowance.
Length of Study: One-two years.
Frequency: Annual.
Country of Study: Other.
No. of awards offered: Varies.
Application Procedure: Please write or telephone for an application form.
Closing Date: January 31st.
Funding: Government.
Contributor: Tax-payer.

STUDIEFONDS VOOR ZUIDAFRIKAANSE STUDENTEN NZAV

Studenten NZAV, Keizersgracht 141, Amsterdam, NL-1015 CK, Netherlands
Tel: (31) 20 624 9318
Fax: (31) 20 638 2596
Email: studiefonds@zuidafrikahuis.nl
www: http://www.zuidafrikahuis.nl
Contact: Dr S B I Veltkamp-Visser, Secretary

Netherlands-South Africa Study Fund

Subjects: All subjects.
Purpose: To support postgraduate study in Holland.
Eligibility: Open to nationals of South Africa.
Level of Study: Postgraduate.
Value: Please contact the organisation for details.
Length of Study: Up to one year.
Frequency: Annual.
Country of Study: Netherlands.
No. of awards offered: 5-10.
Application Procedure: Applicants must write for details.
Closing Date: May 15th or December 15th.
Funding: Private.
No. of awards given last year: 13.
No. of applicants last year: 28.

SUDAN CIVIC FOUNDATION (SCF)

SCF House, 37 Monkswell, Cambridge, Cambridgeshire, CB2 2JU, England
Tel: (44) 1223 504393
Fax: (44) 1223 501125
Email: equiano@sudan21.net
www: http://www.sudan21.net/equiano.html
Contact: Dr Salah Al Bander, Director

The Sudan Civic Foundation (SCF) is an independent non-profit making group whose purpose is to contribute to public understanding of socio-economic and political issues through research, discussion and publications. It was established in 1996 to provide, among other things, a network for those who share a common concern for better race relations.

Equiano Memorial Award

Subjects: The promotion of race relations.
Purpose: To support a person engaged in the study or promotion of tolerance and peaceful co-existence between communities, and to support research or practical field investigations, leading to a report, essay or dissertation.
Eligibility: There are no eligibility restrictions.
Level of Study: Unrestricted.
Type: Research grant.
Value: UK£2,000.
Length of Study: One year. Applicants may reapply for a second year of funding.

Frequency: Annual.
Study Establishment: An academic or professional establishment.
Country of Study: Any country.
No. of awards offered: Two.
Application Procedure: Applicants must complete an application form and should write for details.
Closing Date: March 31st.
Funding: Private.
Contributor: Dr Salah Al Bander.
No. of awards given last year: One.
No. of applicants last year: 420.
Additional Information: Applicants must be registered at a recognised educational institution. The award is based on need as well as academic merit. The area of study must fit in with research priorities of the Foundation.

THE SUSAN G KOMEN BREAST CANCER FOUNDATION

5005 LBJ Freeway, Suite 250, Dallas, TX 75244, United States of America
Tel: (1) 972 855 1656
Fax: (1) 972 855 1640
Email: grants@komen.org
www: http://www.komen.org
Contact: National Grants and Sponsored Programs Office

It is the mission of the Susan G Komen Breast Cancer Foundation to eradicate breast cancer as a life threatening disease by advancing research, education, screening and treatment.

Susan G Komen Breast Cancer Foundation Basic Clinical and Translational Breast Cancer Research

Subjects: The cause, treatment, prevention and cure of breast cancers.
Purpose: To foster investigation.
Level of Study: Research.
Type: Research grant.
Value: Up to US$250,000 combined direct and indirect costs.
Length of Study: Two or three years
Frequency: Annual.
Country of Study: Any country.
No. of awards offered: Dependent on funding per project.
Application Procedure: Applicants must register before submitting an application. Registration is available on the website. Candidates should contact the main address for more information. All applications must be submitted electronically.
Closing Date: Refer to the Komen website, www.komen.org, to view important deadlines.
Funding: Private.

Susan G Komen Breast Cancer Foundation Dissertation Research Award

Subjects: The cause, treatment, prevention and cure of breast cancers.
Purpose: To allow successful candidates to conduct dissertation research.
Level of Study: Doctorate.
Type: Award.
Value: Up to US$30,000.
Length of Study: Two years.
Frequency: Annual.
Country of Study: Any country.
No. of awards offered: Varies.
Application Procedure: Applicants must register before submitting an application. Registration is available on the website. Candidates should contact the main address for more information. All applications must be submitted electronically.
Closing Date: Refer to the komen website, www.komen.org, to view important deadlines.
Funding: Private.

Susan G Komen Breast Cancer Foundation Imaging Technology Research

Subjects: Advanced imaging technology.
Purpose: To fund research and develop new methods for early detection and diagnosis of breast cancer.
Eligibility: Applicants from any country may apply.
Type: Research grant.
Value: Up to US$250,000 combined direct and indirect costs.
Length of Study: Two or three years.
Frequency: Annual.
Country of Study: Any country.
No. of awards offered: Varies.
Application Procedure: Applicants must register before submitting an application. Registration is available on the website. Candidates should contact the main address for more information. All applications must be submitted electronically.
Closing Date: Refer to the Komen website, www.komen.org, to view important deadlines.
Funding: Private.

Susan G Komen Breast Cancer Foundation Population Specific Research Project

Subjects: Unique needs, trends and barriers to breast healthcare among populations such as African American, Asian Pacific Islander, Hispanic Latino, Native American, lesbian, low literacy, breast cancer survivors and other defined communities.
Purpose: To fund innovative research projects addressing breast cancer and epidemiology within specific populations at risk from disease.
Level of Study: Research.
Type: Research grant.
Value: Up to US$250,000 combined direct and indirect costs.
Length of Study: Two or three years.
Frequency: Annual.
Country of Study: Any country.
No. of awards offered: Varies.
Application Procedure: Applicants must register before submitting an application. Registration is available on the website. Candidates should contact the main address for more information. All applications must be submitted electronically.
Closing Date: Refer to the Komen website, www.komen.org, to view important deadlines.
Funding: Private.

Susan G Komen Breast Cancer Foundation Postdoctoral Fellowship in Breast Cancer Research, Public Health or Epidemiology

Subjects: Breast health and breast cancer.
Purpose: To encourage young scientists to begin a career in breast cancer research or to support continued research and continued independent investigations in breast health and breast cancer.
Eligibility: Applicants from any country may apply. Candidates must be no more than three years post completion of a PhD. MD candidates must be no more than three years post completion of their clinical fellowship or five years post completion of residency.
Level of Study: Postdoctorate.
Type: Fellowship.
Value: US$45,000.
Length of Study: Two or Three years.
Frequency: Annual.
Country of Study: Any country.
No. of awards offered: Varies.
Application Procedure: Applicants must register before submitting an application. Registration is available on the website. Candidates should contact the National Grants and Sponsored Programs Office at the main address for more information. All applications must be submitted electronically.
Closing Date: Refer to the Komen website, www.komen.org, to view important deadlines.
Funding: Private.

SWEDISH INFORMATION SERVICE

1 Dag Hammarskjold Plaza, 45th Floor, New York, NY 10017-2201,
United States of America
Tel: (1) 212 583 2550
Fax: (1) 212 752 4789
Email: requests@swedeninfo.com/info@swedennewyork.com
www: www.swedennewyork.com
Contact: Academic Liaison Officer

The Section for Information and Public Affairs of the Consulate General of Sweden in New York, works to promote awareness in the United States of Swedish cultural achievement and advancement in scientific research and development, and contributes to the formation of public opinion and policy in an international context.

Bicentennial Swedish-American Exchange Fund
Subjects: Priority is given to politics, public administration, working life, human environment, mass media, business and industry, education or culture.
Purpose: To provide an opportunity for those in a position to influence public opinion and contribute to the development of their society to make an intensive research trip to Sweden.
Eligibility: Applicants should be citizens or permanent residents of the United States. People who have made recurrent visits to, or resided in Sweden, will only be considered in exceptional circumstances. The grant may not be used to finance participation in conferences or regular ongoing vocational or academic courses. If co-applicants on the same project are selected, the grant will be divided between them. The grant may be used in conjunction with scholarships from other sources.
Level of Study: Research.
Type: Travel grant.
Value: Krona 25,000 or the equivalent in United States dollars to partially cover transportation and living expenses.
Length of Study: Two-four weeks intensive research.
Frequency: Annual.
Country of Study: Sweden.
No. of awards offered: Two.
Application Procedure: Application forms are available from the website or can be requested directly from the Swedish Information Service, during the month of November. Because a signature is required, application forms should be printed out and signed before sending in the post. Two letters of recommendation are also required. Email applications are not accepted. Application forms to be filled in by hand may be requested by post along with a stamped addressed envelope.
Closing Date: The first Friday in February.
Funding: Government.
Contributor: The Swedish Institute in Stockholm, Sweden.
No. of awards given last year: Five.
No. of applicants last year: 40.
Additional Information: The project must be completed within one year of receipt of the grant. Six months after the completed research trip a report must be submitted to the Swedish Information Service. Award recipients are announced during the month of May.

SWISS FEDERAL INSTITUTE OF TECHNOLOGY ZÜRICH

Eidgenössische Technische Hochschule, Zürich, Austauschdienst,
ETH Zentrum, Zurich, CH-8092, Switzerland
Tel: (41) 1 632 2141
Fax: (41) 1 632 1264
Email: doc.exchange@rektorat.ethz.ch
www: http://www.mobilitaet.ethz.ch
Contact: Silke Jonda, Student Exchange Office

ETH Zurich. The name is known throughout the world: The Swiss Federal Institute of Technology Zurich is a science and technology university with an outstanding research record. Excellent research conditions, state-of-the-art infrastructure and an attractive urban environment add up to the ideal setting for creative personalities.

Swiss Federal Institute of Technology Scholarships
Subjects: Architecture, engineering (civil, mechanical, electrical, production, rural and surveying), computer science, materials science, chemistry, physics, mathematics, biology, environmental sciences, earth sciences, pharmacy, agriculture and forestry.
Eligibility: Open primarily, but not exclusively, to nationals of Canada, Italy, Japan, Poland, Spain, the United Kingdom and the United States of America. Candidates should be 20-30 years of age, have had at least two years of university study and have a good working knowledge of German.
Level of Study: Unrestricted.
Type: Scholarship.
Value: Swiss franc 1,300-1,500 per month, plus tuition and health insurance allowance.
Length of Study: One academic year between October and July.
Frequency: Annual.
Study Establishment: The Institute.
Country of Study: Switzerland.
No. of awards offered: Eight.
Application Procedure: Applications must be made to the appropriate address.
Closing Date: February 15th.
Funding: Government.

SYMPHONY OF THE MOUNTAINS

Renaissance Center, Box 131200 East, Center Street, Kingsport, TN
37660, United States of America
Tel: (1) 423 392 8423
Fax: (1) 423 392 8428
Email: info@symphonyofthemountains.org
www: www.symphonyofthemountains.org
Contact: Ms Ann Myers, Executive Director

Elizabeth Harper Vaughn Concerto Competition
Subjects: Three categories alternate annually in the following sequence: percussion, wind instruments and brass, strings or piano.
Purpose: Sponsored by Symphony of the Mountains.
Eligibility: Open to musicians who are 26 years of age or under.
Level of Study: Postgraduate.
Type: Competition.
Value: US$1,500 plus a concert performance with the orchestra and accommodation.
Frequency: Annual.
Country of Study: Any country.
No. of awards offered: One.
Application Procedure: Applications must be accompanied by a letter of recommendation from a qualified teacher, the entrance fee of US$20, payable to Symphony of the Mountains, and a cassette tape. The tape recording must be a concerto, or work of similar importance, written with orchestral accompaniment.
Closing Date: December 1st.
Funding: Private.
Contributor: Women's Symphony Committee.
No. of awards given last year: One.
No. of applicants last year: 30.
Additional Information: The competition is held in March.

SYRACUSE UNIVERSITY

Graduate School, 303 Bowne Hall, Syracuse, NY 13244-1200, United
States of America
Tel: (1) 315 443 4492
Fax: (1) 315 443 3423
Email: grad@gwmail.syr.edu
www: http://cwis.syr.edu
Contact: Susan M Ceri, Manager, Graduate Awards

Syracuse University is a non-profit, private student research university.

Syracuse University African American Fellowship
Subjects: African American studies.
Eligibility: Open to United States citizens who are African American.

Level of Study: Unrestricted.
Type: Fellowship.
Value: US$33,580.
Length of Study: One-six years.
Frequency: Annual.
Study Establishment: Syracuse University.
Country of Study: United States of America.
No. of awards offered: Six.
Application Procedure: Applicants must apply through admission application.
Closing Date: January 10th.
Funding: Private.
Contributor: The Syracuse University Graduate School.
No. of awards given last year: Six.
No. of applicants last year: 20.

Syracuse University Fellowship

Subjects: All subjects.
Purpose: To provide a full support package during a student's term of study.
Eligibility: Open to nationals of any country.
Level of Study: Unrestricted.
Type: Fellowship.
Value: US$33,580.
Length of Study: One-six years.
Frequency: Annual.
Study Establishment: Syracuse University.
Country of Study: United States of America.
No. of awards offered: 101.
Application Procedure: Applicants must apply through admission application.
Closing Date: January 10th.
Funding: Private.
Contributor: The Syracuse University Graduate School.
No. of awards given last year: 101.
No. of applicants last year: 250.

Whitney Young Fellowships

Subjects: Social welfare and social work.
Eligibility: Open to African American students.
Level of Study: Postgraduate
Type: Fellowship.
Value: US$29,645.
Length of Study: Two-three years.
Frequency: Annual.
Study Establishment: Syracuse University.
Country of Study: United States of America.
No. of awards offered: Two.
Application Procedure: Applicants must apply through admission application.
Closing Date: August 5th.
Funding: Private.
Contributor: The Syracuse University Graduate School.
No. of awards given last year: Two.
No. of applicants last year: Six.

TEAGASC (IRISH AGRICULTURE AND FOOD DEVELOPMENT AUTHORITY)

19 Sandymount Avenue, Dublin, 4, Ireland
Tel: (353) 1 637 6000
Fax: (353) 1 668 8023
Email: corourke@hq.teagasc.ie
www: http://www.teagasc.ie
Contact: Dr C O'Rourke, Manager

Teagasc (Irish Agriculture and Food Development Authority) is the parastatal body responsible for agricultural and food research, farm advisory services and farmer education in the Republic of Ireland. Its research programme includes foods, dairy cows, beef cattle, pigs, sheep, crops, horticulture, environment and rural economics and sociology at eight research centres.

Teagasc Walsh Fellowships

Subjects: Any subject relevant to food and agriculture in Ireland eg. animal sciences, plant sciences, physical or earth sciences, environment, economics and rural development.
Purpose: To support MSc and PhD projects on topics relevant to the overall Teagasc research programme on agriculture and food.
Eligibility: Applicants must be college faculty members who, in co-operation with Teagasc researchers, submit proposals relevant to the Teagasc programme on agriculture and food in Ireland. If successful, they then select postgraduate students for MSc or PhD programmes as Walsh Fellows. Applications are not accepted from individual students, or for taught non research postgraduate courses.
Level of Study: Doctorate, Postgraduate, Research.
Type: Fellowship.
Value: €15,000 per year to cover a postgraduate stipend and all fees. A limited provision for materials and travel is also available.
Length of Study: One and a half to three years.
Frequency: Annual.
Study Establishment: Any third level college, in association with a Teagasc Research Centre.
Country of Study: Other.
No. of awards offered: Approx. 40.
Application Procedure: Applicants must apply for an information brochure which includes an application form, available on request.
Closing Date: Mid December.
Funding: Government.
Contributor: Teagasc's own resources, via the Irish government and the European Union agri-food industry.
No. of awards given last year: 40.
No. of applicants last year: 80.

THE TEXTILE INSTITUTE

1st Floor, St James's Buildings, Oxford Street, Manchester, M1 6FQ, England
Tel: (44) 870 876 0100
Fax: (44) 870 876 0700
Email: hyeowart@textileinst.org.uk
www: http://www.texi.org
Contact: Miss E H Yeowart, Professional Affairs Manager

The Textile Institute has an international membership covering almost 100 countries and spanning every sector and occupation relating to fibres and their uses. The mission of the Textile Institute is to promote professionalism in all areas associated with the textile industries, including clothing and footwear, worldwide.

Cotton Industry War Memorial Trust Scholarships

Subjects: Textile technology or design.
Purpose: To assist students who are studying or undertaking research in textile related fields.
Eligibility: All applicants must reside in the United Kingdom and undertake to be employed in, and to benefit, the United Kingdom textile industry.
Level of Study: Doctorate, Graduate, Postgraduate.
Type: Scholarship.
Value: Up to UK£1,000.
Frequency: Annual.
Country of Study: Any country.
No. of awards offered: Varies.
Application Procedure: Applicants must complete an application form.
Closing Date: Mid July.
No. of awards given last year: 10.
No. of applicants last year: 90 in total for all scholarships.

Lord Barnby Foundation Bursaries

Subjects: Textiles.
Purpose: To assist those who are or who have been employed in the textile industry and who are studying on a full-time or part-time course of study leading to a qualification in a textile related field.
Eligibility: Open to United Kingdom nationals previously employed for at least two years in the United Kingdom textile industry.

Level of Study: Unrestricted.
Type: Bursary.
Value: Varies, up to UK£500.
Frequency: Annual.
Country of Study: United Kingdom.
No. of awards offered: Two.
Application Procedure: Applicants must complete an application form.
Closing Date: Mid July.
No. of awards given last year: One.
No. of applicants last year: 90 in total for all scholarships.

Textile Institute Scholarship

Subjects: Any textile related subject.
Purpose: To assist students who are studying or undertaking research in textile related fields.
Eligibility: Open to students or professionally qualified individuals wishing to undertake further study in the fields of textile technology or design.
Level of Study: Doctorate, Graduate, Postgraduate.
Type: Scholarship.
Value: Generally UK£100-400.
Frequency: Annual.
Country of Study: Any country.
No. of awards offered: Varies.
Application Procedure: Applicants must complete an application form.
Closing Date: Mid July.
No. of awards given last year: 10.
No. of applicants last year: 90 in total for all scholarships.

Worshipful Company of Weavers' Scholarships

Subjects: All subjects relevant to weaving, including design.
Purpose: To assist students who are studying or undertaking research in textile related fields.
Eligibility: All applicants must undertake to be employed in, and to benefit, the United Kingdom textile industry. Open to United Kingdom nationals only.
Level of Study: Doctorate, Graduate, Postgraduate.
Type: Scholarship.
Value: Varies, up to UK£1,200.
Frequency: Annual.
Country of Study: United Kingdom.
No. of awards offered: Varies.
Application Procedure: Applicants must complete an application form.
Closing Date: Mid July.
No. of awards given last year: 17.
No. of applicants last year: 90 in total for all scholarships.

THIRD WORLD ACADEMY OF SCIENCES (TWAS)

c/o The Abdus Salam International Centre for Theoretical Physics, Strada Costiera 11, Trieste, I-34014, Italy
Tel: (39) 040 224 0327
Fax: (39) 040 224 559
Email: info@twas.org
www: http://www.twas.org
Contact: Mr Mohamed H A Hassan, Executive Director

The Third World Academy of Sciences (TWAS) is an autonomous international organisation promoting excellence in scientific research in the South.

CSIR (The Council of Scientific & Industrial Research)/ TWAS Fellowship for Postdoctoral Research

Subjects: Newly emerging areas of science and technology.
Purpose: To enable scholars who wish to pursue postdoctoral research to undertake research in laboratories or institutes of the CSIR.

Eligibility: The minimum qualification requirement is a PhD degree in science or technology. Applicants must be regular employees in a developing country and should hold a research assignment.
Level of Study: Postdoctorate.
Type: Fellowship.
Value: A monthly stipend of Indian rupees 11,500 for a maximum of 12 months, plus a contingency grant of Indian rupees 20,000 per year.
Frequency: Annual.
Study Establishment: CSIR research laboratories or institutes.
Country of Study: India.
No. of awards offered: Varies.
Application Procedure: Applicants must complete an application form, available on request or from the website http://www.ictp.trieste.it/~twas/CSIR.html.
Closing Date: June 1st.
Funding: Government.
Contributor: CSIR, India, the Italian Ministry of Foreign Affairs and the Directorate General for Development Co-operation.
Additional Information: CSIR is the premier civil scientific organisation of India, which has a network of research laboratories covering wide areas of industrial research. Further information is available on the website.

For further information contact:

Senior Deputy Advisor, CSIR (The Council of Scientific & Industrial Research), Anusandhan Bhavan - 2 Rafi Marg, New Delhi, 110001, India
Tel: (91) 11 331 6751
Fax: (91) 11 371 0618
Email: rprasad@csirhq.ren.nic.in
Contact: Dr B K Ramaprasad

TWAS Fellowship for Postdoctoral Research and Advanced Training

Subjects: All fields of basic sciences.
Purpose: To enhance the research of young promising scientists, specifically those at the beginning of their research career, helping them to foster links for future collaboration.
Eligibility: Open to nationals of developing countries with permanent positions in universities or research institutes in developing countries holding a PhD or equivalent. Candidates must not be older than 40 years and preference will be given to candidates from less developed countries.
Level of Study: Postdoctorate.
Type: Fellowship.
Value: Travel support and subsistence of up to US$200. Living expenses are usually obtained from local sources.
Length of Study: 6-12 months.
Frequency: Annual.
Country of Study: Developing countries.
No. of awards offered: Varies.
Application Procedure: Applicants must complete an application form, available on request or from the website.
Closing Date: October 1st.
Funding: Government.
Contributor: The Italian Ministry of Foreign Affairs and the Directorate General for Development Co-operation.
Additional Information: Further information is available on the website.

TWAS Grants for Scientific Meetings in Developing Countries

Subjects: Agricultural, biological, chemical, engineering or geological and medical sciences.
Purpose: To encourage international scientific meetings in Third World countries.
Eligibility: Open to organisers of international scientific meetings in developing countries. Special consideration is given to those meetings which are likely to benefit the scientific community in the Third World and to promote regional and international co-operation in developing science and its applications to the problems of the Third World.
Level of Study: Postgraduate, Professional development.
Type: Travel grant.

Value: Up to US$4,000 for travel expenses of principal speakers from abroad and/or participants from the region.
Frequency: Annual.
Country of Study: Developing countries.
No. of awards offered: Varies.
Application Procedure: Applicants must complete an application form, available on request or from the website.
Closing Date: June 1st for meetings held between January and June of the following year, and December 1st for meetings held between July and December of the following year.
Funding: Government.
Contributor: The Italian Ministry of Foreign Affairs and the Directorate General for Development Co-operation.
Additional Information: Further information is available on the website.

TWAS Prizes

Subjects: Medical sciences, biology, chemistry, mathematics and physics, agricultural sciences and engineering sciences.
Purpose: To recognise and support outstanding achievements made by scientists from developing countries. They are awarded to those scientists whose research work has significantly contributed to the advancement of sciences.
Eligibility: Open to nationals of developing countries who are, as a rule, working and living in these countries. Consideration is given to proven achievements judged particularly by their national and international impact. Members of TWAS are not eligible for such awards.
Level of Study: Doctorate, Postdoctorate, Postgraduate, Professional development.
Type: Prize.
Value: US$10,000 plus a plaque on which major contributions of the award winner are mentioned.
Frequency: Annual.
Country of Study: Developing countries.
No. of awards offered: Five.
Application Procedure: Applicants must be designated on the nomination form. The nomination must be accompanied by a one-two page biographical sketch of the nominee including their major scientific accomplishments, a list of 12 of the candidate's most significant publications as well as a complete list of publications and a curriculum vitae. Nominations for the awards are invited from all members of the TWAS as well as from academies, national research councils, universities and scientific institutions in developing countries and advanced countries.
Closing Date: March 1st. Nominations received after the deadline will be considered in the next year.
Funding: Government.
Contributor: The Italian Ministry of Foreign Affairs and the Directorate General for Development Co-operation.
No. of awards given last year: Eight.
Additional Information: The awards are usually presented on a special occasion, normally coinciding with the general meeting of the Academy and/or a general conference organised by the Academy. Recipients of awards are expected to give lectures about the work for which the awards have been made. Further information is available on the website.

TWAS Prizes to Young Scientists in Developing Countries

Subjects: Biology, chemistry, mathematics or physics, rotated annually.
Purpose: To enable academies and research councils in over 20 Third World countries to institute prizes and medals for young scientists in their countries.
Eligibility: Open to academies and research councils in developing countries. The age limit for prize winners is 40 years.
Level of Study: Postgraduate.
Type: Prize.
Value: Usually US$2,000.
Frequency: Annual.
Country of Study: Developing countries.
No. of awards offered: Over 20.
Application Procedure: Applicants must write for details.

Funding: Government.
Contributor: The Italian Ministry of Foreign Affairs and the Directorate General for Development Co-operation.
Additional Information: Further information is available on the website.

TWAS Research Grants

Subjects: Biology, chemistry, mathematics or physics.
Purpose: To reinforce and promote scientific research in basic sciences in the Third World, to strengthen the endogenous capacity in science and to reduce the exodus of scientific talents from the South.
Eligibility: Applicants must be nationals of developing countries with an advanced academic degree, some research experience, and must hold positions at universities or research institutions in developing countries.
Level of Study: Doctorate, Postdoctorate, Postgraduate, Professional development.
Value: Up to US$10,000. Grants are to be used to purchase scientific equipment, consumable laboratory supplies and scientific literature (textbooks and proceedings only).
Length of Study: One year.
Frequency: Annual.
Country of Study: Developing countries.
No. of awards offered: Varies.
Application Procedure: Applicants must complete an application form available on request or from the website. Applications must be submitted in English.
Closing Date: July 1st or December 1st.
Funding: Government.
Contributor: The Italian Ministry of Foreign Affairs, the Directorate General for Development Co-operation and the Swedish Agency for Research Co-operation with Developing Countries.
Additional Information: Further information is available on the website or on request.

TWAS Spare Parts for Scientific Equipment

Subjects: Biology, chemistry and physics.
Purpose: The programme has been established in response to the current difficulty faced by several laboratories in the Third World to obtain badly needed spares and replacement parts for scientific equipment which often interrupts their experimental research for long periods.
Eligibility: Applicants must be research group leaders at universities or research institutes in developing countries.
Level of Study: Professional development.
Type: Grant.
Value: Up to US$1,000 including insurance and freight charges.
Frequency: Continuous.
Country of Study: Developing countries.
No. of awards offered: Varies.
Application Procedure: Applicants must first contact the suppliers and obtain a proforma invoice, valid for three to six months, including cost, insurance and freight charges for the items they require. Applicants must submit a completed application form with the proforma invoice from the supplier. Application forms are available on request or from the website.
Closing Date: Applications are accepted at any time.
Funding: Government.
Contributor: The Italian Ministry of Foreign Affairs and the Directorate General for Development Co-operation.
Additional Information: Applications for computer parts will not be accepted. Further information is available on the website.

TWAS UNESCO Associateship Scheme

Subjects: Biology, chemistry, physics, mathematics, engineering, agricultural sciences and medical sciences.
Purpose: To alleviate the problem of isolated talented scientists in developing countries, and strengthen the research programmes of Centres of Excellence in the South.
Eligibility: Open to associates among the most eminent and promising researchers in developing countries. Special consideration is given to scientists from isolated institutions in developing countries.
Level of Study: Postdoctorate, Professional development.

Value: Travel costs plus US$200 per month for incidental local expenses. The host centre covers accommodation, food and research facilities.

Length of Study: Three years, plus the entitlement to visit the Centre twice for a period of two-three months each time. There is a possibility of renewal for a further three years depending on funds available.

Frequency: Annual.

Study Establishment: There are over 80 centres.

Country of Study: Developing countries.

No. of awards offered: Varies.

Application Procedure: Applicants must complete an application form, available on request or from the website.

Closing Date: December 1st.

Funding: Government.

Contributor: UNESCO, the Italian Ministry for Foreign Affairs and the Directorate General for Development Co-operation.

Additional Information: Further information is available on the website.

THIRD WORLD NETWORK OF SCIENTIFIC ORGANIZATIONS (TWNSO)

c/o TWAS & The Abdus Salam ICTP, Trieste, I-34014, Italy
Tel: (39) 040 224 0683
Fax: (39) 040 224 0689
Email: info@twnso.org
www: http://www.twnso.org
Contact: Secretariat

The Third World Network of Scientific Organizations (TWNSO) is a non governmental organisation founded in 1988 to promote science based sustainable economic development in the South. It was founded on the initiative of the Third World Academy of Sciences (TWAS), and by ministers of science, technology and higher education and heads of science academies and research councils in developing countries. In 1990 TWNSO acquired consultative status with UNESCO.

Celso Furtado Award

Subjects: The understanding and promotion of the socio-economic development of countries in the South.

Purpose: To give recognition, encouragement and support to outstanding work in the field of the political economy of developing countries.

Eligibility: Applicants must have worked in the field of political economy resulting in a fundamental contribution to the advancement of socio-economic development and the developing world in the global context.

Type: Prize.

Value: US$10,000 and a medallion.

Frequency: Every three years.

Country of Study: Any country.

Application Procedure: Applicants must be designated on the nomination form. The nomination should be accompanied by a one-two page profile of the nominated individual, a list of significant publications relevant to the award, a complete list of publications and a curriculum vitae of the candidate.

Closing Date: January 31st.

Funding: Government.

Contributor: The Federal Republic of Brazil.

Additional Information: Further information is available on the website. The award is named after Celso Furtado, one of the leading Latin American economists from Brazil.

TWNSO Grants to Institutions in the South for Joint Research Projects

Subjects: Biotechnology, new materials, microelectronics, information technology, space technology, new and renewable energies, soil erosion and desertification, floods and earthquakes, biodiversity, atmosphere pollution, toxic and chemical waste or fresh water resources.

Purpose: To award grants to joint research projects with well defined objectives.

Eligibility: Open to institutions in developing countries in the South. Applications must be joint proposals from two to three institutions.

Level of Study: Professional development.

Type: Grant.

Value: Up to US$30,000.

Length of Study: Up to two years.

Frequency: Annual.

Country of Study: Developing countries.

No. of awards offered: Varies.

Application Procedure: Applicants must complete and submit an application form, available on request or from the website. Applications must be submitted from two or three institutions in the South.

Closing Date: December 1st.

Funding: Government.

Contributor: The OPEC Fund for International Development.

Additional Information: Further information is available on the website.

THE THIRD WORLD ORGANISATION FOR WOMEN IN SCIENCE (TWOWS)

Enrico Fermi Building, Room 109, Via Beirut 6, Trieste, I-34014, Italy
Tel: (39) 040 224 0321
Fax: (39) 040 224 0689
Email: info@twows.org
www: http://www.twows.org
Contact: Ms Leena Mungapen, Secretariat

TWOWS Postgraduate Fellowships for Women from Sub-Saharan Africa and Least Developed Countries (LDC) at Centres of Excellence in the South

Subjects: Agriculture, engineering, mathematics and computer sciences, medical sciences and natural sciences.

Purpose: To strengthen the research efforts of qualified women scientists working and living in Third World countries and to recognise, support and encourage the scientific and technological achievements of women in the Third World. The fellowships also aim to facilitate access to educational and training opportunities for young and promising women scientists in Third World countries, and to promote the involvement of women in science and technology professions, in scientific leadership and in the decision making processes, both at the national and international level.

Eligibility: Open to female students in Sub Saharan Africa and Least Developed Countries (LDC).

Level of Study: Doctorate.

Type: Fellowship.

Length of Study: Up to three years.

Frequency: Annual.

Country of Study: Developing countries.

No. of awards offered: Up to 50.

Application Procedure: Applicants must complete an application form, available from the website.

Closing Date: May 31st.

Funding: Government.

Contributor: The Department for Research Co-operation of the Swedish International Development Co-operation Agency (Sida-SAREC).

No. of awards given last year: 50.

No. of applicants last year: 322.

THE THOMSON FOUNDATION

37 Park Place, Cardiff, CF10 3BB, Wales
Tel: (44) 29 2035 3060
Fax: (44) 29 2035 3061
Email: enquiries@thomfound.co.uk
www: http://www.thomsonfoundation.co.uk
Contact: Mr Gareth Price

The Thomson Foundation provides practical, intensive training both in the United Kingdom and abroad, along with a wide range of consultancies to journalists, managers, technicians and production staff in television, radio and the press.

Thomson Foundation Scholarship

Subjects: Journalism, radio or television broadcasting, internet publishing and photojournalism.
Purpose: To enable recipients to attend Thomson Foundation training courses in Britain.
Eligibility: Open to professional journalists and broadcasters with at least three years of full-time experience.
Level of Study: Professional development.
Type: Scholarship.
Value: Varies.
Length of Study: Varies, usually a 12 week Summer course or a shorter four week course.
Study Establishment: The Thomson Foundation.
Country of Study: United Kingdom.
No. of awards offered: Varies.
Application Procedure: Applicants must complete an application form, available from the Foundation, for the courses they wish to apply for.
Closing Date: April 15th.
Funding: Government, Private.
Contributor: The British Foreign Office Chevening Scholarship Scheme.
No. of awards given last year: Six.
No. of applicants last year: 20.
Additional Information: Annual three month courses in TV, radio and press journalism run from June-September.

THOURON-UNIVERSITY OF PENNSYLVANIA FUND FOR BRITISH-AMERICAN STUDENT EXCHANGE

University of Glasgow, Court Office, Glasgow, G12 8QQ, Scotland
Tel: (44) 141 330 5853
Fax: (44) 141 330 4920
Email: dmaddern@admin.gla.ac.uk
www: http://www.gla.ac.uk
Contact: Ms D H Maddern, Administrator

The University of Glasgow is host to the United Kingdom operation of the Thouron Awards and organises the annual competition for the selection of United Kingdom graduates applying for awards tenable at the University of Pennsylvania, Philadelphia, in the United States of America.

Thouron Awards

Subjects: All subjects.
Purpose: To promote better understanding between the people of the United Kingdom and the United States of America.
Eligibility: Open to United Kingdom citizens who are graduates, normally resident in the United Kingdom and who have followed a regular school education in the United Kingdom. Postdoctoral candidates are not eligible unless their proposed study is in a field different from that in which they undertook their previous postgraduate study. No application will be considered from a student already in the United States of America or who has previously spent an academic year at the University of Pennsylvania.
Level of Study: Postgraduate.
Type: Scholarship.
Value: US$1,376 per month plus tuition fees.
Length of Study: One-two years.
Frequency: Annual.
Study Establishment: The University of Pennsylvania, Philadelphia.
Country of Study: United States of America.
No. of awards offered: Up to 10.
Application Procedure: Applicants for the award must submit three application forms, three passport sized photographs and three referee forms. Applications for admission to individual postgraduate courses are dealt with separately and should be sent directly to the University of Pennsylvania.

Closing Date: Varies, but is around mid November each year.
Funding: Private.
Contributor: Sir John R H Thouron and the late Lady Thouron (Esther Dupont).
No. of awards given last year: Six.
No. of applicants last year: 110.
Additional Information: United States citizens interested in studying in the United Kingdom should write to the University of Pennsylvania for further details of the U.S. Thouron Award.

THRASHER RESEARCH FUND

15 East South Temple Street, Salt Lake City, UT 84150-6910, United States of America
Tel: (1) 801 240 4753
Fax: (1) 801 240 1625
Email: brownrj@thrasherresearch.org
www: http://www.thrasherresearch.org
Contact: Mr Justin Brown, Research Manager

The Thrasher Research Fund provides grants for paediatric medical research that addresses problems in children's health that are significant in terms of either magnitude or severity. Priority is given to clinical and/or translational research that has a relatively shorter distance to application. The Fund assumes that significant solutions to children's health problems remain undiscovered and invites a broad array of applications designed to remedy these deficiencies.

Food-Based Approaches to Micronutrient Malnutrition Program

Eligibility: Open to research scientists and private voluntary organisations. Applications from local, in-country organisations are encouraged.
Level of Study: Research.
Type: Grant.
Value: Typically US$100,000-300,000.
Length of Study: Up to three years.
Frequency: Rolling Cycle Quarterly Meetings.
Country of Study: Any country.
No. of awards offered: Varies.
Application Procedure: Instructions for application can be obtained by contacting, Thrasher Research Fund Details at the website www.thrasherresearch.org.
Closing Date: Applications are considered as they are received.
Funding: Private.
Contributor: Thrasher Research Fund.
No. of awards given last year: Varies. Typically 10-15 grants/year.
No. of applicants last year: Varies.

Thrasher Research and Field Demonstration Project Grants

Subjects: Paediatrics.
Purpose: To promote international and national child health research and child health related projects. The emphasis is on practical and applied interventions with the potential to improve the health of children worldwide.
Eligibility: Open to research scientists and private voluntary organisations. Pre and postdoctoral students may be employed on Thrasher funded projects, but the principal investigator is expected to take an active role in the project and assume full responsibility for it. The principal investigator must have a connection with a university, research institution or appropriate private voluntary organisation.
Level of Study: Research.
Type: Grant.
Value: Typically US$100,000-300,000.
Length of Study: Up to three years.
Frequency: Four times per year.
Country of Study: Any country.
No. of awards offered: Varies.
Application Procedure: Application guidelines are available on the Fund's website. Potential applicants are encouraged to contact Fund staff prior to a formal submission to determine how a potential project will fit with current Fund interests.

Closing Date: Proposals that have completed the external review process will be considered at the subsequent quarterly meeting.
Funding: Private.
Contributor: The Thrasher Research Fund.
Additional Information: Historically the Fund has primarily supported international research. In an effort to achieve greater balance, the Fund is currently emphasising research conducted in the United States.

TOKYU FOUNDATION FOR INBOUND STUDENTS

1-21-6 Dogenzaka, Shibuya Ku, Tokyo, 150-0043, Japan
Tel: (81) 3 3461 0844
Fax: (81) 3 5458 1696
Email: tqzaiden@246.ne.jp
www: http://www.tokyu-f.jp
Contact: Mr Takashi Izumi, Managing Director & Secretary General

The Tokyu Foundation for Inbound Students grant scholarships to postgraduate students studying in Japan from Asia Pacific areas.

Tokyu Scholarship
Subjects: All subjects.
Purpose: To promote international exchange by fostering the development of international goodwill between Japan and her neighbours in Asia and the Pacific and contributing to international co-operation and cultural exchange in the broadest possible sense.
Level of Study: Postgraduate.
Type: Scholarship.
Value: Yen 160,000 per month per student.
Length of Study: Up to two years.
Frequency: Annual.
Country of Study: Japan.
No. of awards offered: 20-25.
Application Procedure: Applicants must complete an application form.
Closing Date: Please consult the Foundation.
Funding: Commercial.
Contributor: Tokyu Corporation.
No. of awards given last year: 21.
No. of applicants last year: 869.
Additional Information: Applicants must travel to Japan at their own cost and be admitted to enter university postgraduate school.

TOURETTE SYNDROME ASSOCIATION, INC. (TSA)

42-40 Bell Boulevard, Suite 205, Bayside, NY 11361-2874, United States of America
Tel: (1) 718 224 2999
Fax: (1) 718 279 9596
Email: ts@tsa-usa.org
www: http://tsa-usa.org
Contact: Ms Sue Levi-Pearl, Vice President, Medical & Scientific Programmes

The Tourette Syndrome Association, Inc. (TSA), founded in 1972, is the only national voluntary non-profit membership organisation dedicated to identifying the cause, finding the cure and controlling the effects of Tourette Syndrome. Members include individuals with the disorder, their relatives and other interested, concerned people. The Association develops and disseminates educational material to individuals, professionals and to agencies in the fields of health care, education and government, co-ordinates support services to help people and their families cope with the problems that occur with Tourette Syndrome, and funds research that will ultimately find the cause of and cure for it and, at the same time, lead to improved medications and treatments.

TSA Research Grants
Subjects: Basic neuroscience specifically relevant to Tourette Syndrome.
Purpose: To foster basic and clinical research related to the causes or treatment of Tourette Syndrome.
Eligibility: Open to candidates who have an MD, PhD or equivalent qualifications. Previous experience in the field of movement disorders is desirable, but not essential. Fellowships are intended for young postdoctoral investigators in the early stages of their careers.
Level of Study: Doctorate, Postdoctorate.
Type: Research grant.
Value: Varies, depending upon the category and applicants' experience within that category, and is usually US$5,000-75,000. Postdoctoral is up to US$40,000.
Length of Study: One-two years.
Frequency: Annual.
Study Establishment: Any institution with adequate facilities.
Country of Study: Any country.
No. of awards offered: Varies.
Application Procedure: Applicants must submit a letter of intent briefly describing the scientific basis of the proposed project.
Closing Date: Please contact the Association.
Funding: Private.
No. of awards given last year: 16.
No. of applicants last year: 72.
Additional Information: The Association provides up to 10 per cent of overhead or indirect costs within the total amount budgeted.

TRANSPORTATION ASSOCIATION OF CANADA (TAC)

Secretariat, 2323 St Laurent Boulevard, Ottawa, ON, K1G 4J8, Canada
Tel: (1) 613 736 1350
Fax: (1) 613 736 1395
Email: gmorier@tac-atc.ca
www: http://www.tac-atc.ca
Contact: Mr Gilbert Morier

The Transportation Association of Canada (TAC) is a non-profit association of government and industry members which acts as a neutral forum for the gathering and exchanging of information on technical guidelines and best practices. Its areas of interest are roads, their links with other modes of transportation and urban transportation.

TAC Scholarships
Subjects: Road and transportation related disciplines.
Eligibility: Open to Canadian citizens and landed immigrants who hold university degrees and who are acceptable to the university at which they plan to carry out their postgraduate studies in the transportation field.
Level of Study: Postgraduate.
Type: Scholarship.
Value: Canadian $3,000-5,000.
Length of Study: One year.
Frequency: Annual.
Study Establishment: Universities.
Country of Study: Other.
No. of awards offered: Five.
Application Procedure: Applicants must submit all applications electronically via TAC's website.
Closing Date: The first working day in March. Applicants should check the website for the exact date, which varies each year.
Funding: Commercial, Government, Private.
No. of awards given last year: Five.
Additional Information: Scholarships currently offered are from the DELCAN Corporation, Stantec Consulting Limited, federal, provincial and territorial governments of Canada, ND LEA Consultants, ND LEA Engineers and Planners, and EBA Engineering Consultants Limited.

TREE RESEARCH & EDUCATION ENDOWMENT FUND

The Tree Fund, PO Box 3188, 1402 W Anthony, Campaign, IL 61826-3188, United States of America
Tel: (1) 217 239 7070
Fax: (1) 217 355 9516
Email: treefund@treefund.org
www: http://www.treefund.org
Contact: Ms Cindy Stachowski

To identify and fund projects and programmes that advance knowledge in the field of arboriculture and urban forestry which benefit people, trees and the environment.

Hyland R Johns Grant Program
Subjects: Arboricultural, urban and community forestry grants not scholarships.
Purpose: To provide funding for research.
Eligibility: Open to qualified researchers of any nationality.
Level of Study: Postgraduate.
Type: Research grant.
Value: US$7,500-25,000.
Length of Study: Two-three years.
Frequency: Annual.
Country of Study: Any country.
Application Procedure: Applicants must complete an application form.
Closing Date: May 1st.
Funding: Private.
Contributor: ISA members.
No. of awards given last year: Seven.
No. of applicants last year: 39.

John Z Duling Grant Program
Subjects: Arboricultural, urban and community forestry grants not scholarships.
Purpose: To provide money to support projects.
Eligibility: Open to qualified researchers of any nationality.
Level of Study: Postgraduate.
Typo: Research grant
Value: A maximum of US$7,500. Funds cannot be used for expenses associated with attendance at colleges and universities eg. tuition, books or laboratory fees.
Length of Study: One-three years.
Frequency: Annual.
Country of Study: Any country.
No. of awards offered: 5-10.
Application Procedure: Applicants must complete a two page application form, available from the ISA Research Trust.
Closing Date: November 1st.
Funding: Private.
Contributor: International Society of Arboriculture (ISA), National Arborist Association.
No. of awards given last year: 10.
No. of applicants last year: Approx. 60.

TROPICAL AGRICULTURAL RESEARCH AND HIGHER EDUCATION CENTER (CATIE)

CATIE Graduate School, PO Box 7170
Turrialba, Costa Rica
Tel: (506) 556 1016
Fax: (506) 556 0914
Email: posgrado@catie.ac.cr
www: http://www.catie.ac.cr
Contact: Dean of the Graduate School

The Tropical Agricultural Research and Higher Education Center (CATIE) is an international, non-profit, regional, scientific and educational institution. Its main purpose is research and education in agricultural sciences, natural resources and related subjects in the American tropics, with emphasis on Central America and the Caribbean.

CATIE Scholarships
Subjects: Ecological agriculture, biotechnology and genetic resources, management and conservation of tropical forestry and biodiversity, tropical woodlands, tropical agroforestry, tropical crop protection and improvement, integrated watershed management and protected areas and environmental socioeconomics.
Purpose: To develop specialised intellectual capital in clean technology, tropical agriculture, natural resources management and human resources in the American tropics.
Eligibility: Priority is given to citizens of Belize, Guatemala, El Salvador, Honduras, Nicaragua, Panama, Costa Rica, Mexico, Venezuela, Colombia, the Dominican Republic, Bolivia and Paraguay.
Level of Study: Doctorate, Postgraduate.
Type: Grant-loan system.
Value: Tuition and fees.
Length of Study: Two years for a Master degree and three-four years for a PhD.
Frequency: Annual.
Country of Study: Costa Rica.
No. of awards offered: 45.
Application Procedure: Applicants must undertake an admission process which constitutes 75 per cent for curricular evaluation and 25 per cent for a domiciliary examination.
Closing Date: Applications are accepted at any time, but the evaluation deadline is October.
Funding: Government.
Contributor: ASDI, DANIDA, OAS, CATIE, AID, DAAD, Russel Train (WWF), CONACYT (Mexico) and others.
No. of awards given last year: 45.
No. of applicants last year: 350.

TRUSTEES OF THEODORA BOSANQUET BURSARY

c/o 28 Great James Street, London, WC1N 3ES, England
Tel: (44) 20 7404 6447
Fax: (44) 20 7404 6505
Email: bfwg.charity@btinternet.com
www: http://www.bcfgrants.org.uk
Contact: Mrs Considine, Company Secretary

The Trustees of Theodora Bosanquet Bursary was set up to support female postgraduate students carrying out research in English literature or history requiring the use of libraries and archives in London. It provides accommodation in a hall of residence for up to four weeks between mid June and mid September.

Theodora Bosanquet Bursary
Subjects: English or history.
Purpose: To support female students carrying out research requiring the use of libraries and archives in London.
Eligibility: Open to graduate women only.
Level of Study: Doctorate, Postdoctorate, Postgraduate.
Type: Other.
Value: Up to UK£600. The award provides accommodation only in a hall of residence for up to four weeks in mid June and mid September.
Length of Study: Up to four weeks.
Frequency: Annual.
Study Establishment: London Halls of Residence.
Country of Study: United Kingdom.
No. of awards offered: One-two.
Application Procedure: Applicants must request an application form by email or download from the website. Forms should then be returned either by email or post enclosing a large stamped addressed envelope or international reply coupons. The envelope should be marked with TBB.
Closing Date: October 31st.
Funding: Private.
Contributor: Investment income.

No. of awards given last year: 3 but usually 2.
No. of applicants last year: 6.

For further information contact:

Email: bfwg.charity@btinternet.com
www: www.bcfgrants.org.uk

TURKU CENTRE FOR COMPUTER SCIENCE (TUCS)

TUCS Office, Data City, Lemminkäisenkatu 14 A, 4th Floor, Turku,
FIN-20520, Finland
Tel: (358) 2 2154 049
Fax: (358) 2 2410 154
Email: tucs@abo.fi
www: http://www.tucs.fi
Contact: Ms Pia Le Grand, Administrative Officer, Educational Affairs

TUCS is a joint centre of research and education for the three universities in Turku, Finland: University of Turku, Åbo Akademi University and Turku School of Economics and Business Administration The TUCS Graduate School offers a framework for studying for the doctoral (Ph.D) degree in Computer Science, Mathematics, Information Systems, Computer Engineering, Communication Systems, or Microelectronics.

TUCS Postgraduate Grant

Subjects: Computer science, information systems or computer engineering.
Purpose: To support students studying for a doctoral degree.
Eligibility: Open to candidates who have a Test of English as a Foreign Language score of at least 550 points or a corresponding level of English proficiency and an MSc or BSc in computer science or a related field. The Graduate Record Examination test is not required but can be sent voluntarily.
Level of Study: Postgraduate.
Type: Grant.
Value: €1,180 per month for postgraduate and €1,430 per month for postdoctoral. Both grants are tax free.
Length of Study: Four years.
Frequency: Annual.
Study Establishment: An approved graduate school.
Country of Study: Finland.
No. of awards offered: 2-4 each year.
Application Procedure: Applicants must submit an application, curriculum vitae, financing plan for studies, application for financial support, letters of recommendation with full contact details, official copies of examinations gained with official English translations, a certificate of English proficiency and a statement of research interests.
Closing Date: The deadline for studies starting in September is May 15th and for studies starting in January the deadline is September 30th.
Funding: Government.
No. of awards given last year: Three.
No. of applicants last year: 98.

UCLA CENTER FOR 17TH AND 18TH CENTURY STUDIES AND THE WILLIAM ANDREWS CLARK MEMORIAL LIBRARY

310 Royce Hall, UCLA, Los Angeles, CA 90095-1404, United States
of America
Tel: (1) 310 206 8552
Fax: (1) 310 206 8577
Email: c1718cs@humnet.ucla.edu
www: http://www.humnet.ucla.edu/humnet/c1718cs
Contact: Fellowship Co-ordinator

The UCLA Center for 17th and 18th Century Studies provides a forum for the discussion of central issues in the field of early modern studies, facilitates research and publication, supports scholarship and encourages the creation of interdisciplinary, cross cultural programmes that advance the understanding of this important period. The William Andrews Clark Memorial Library, administered by the Center, is known for its collections of rare books and manuscripts concerning seventeenth and eighteenth-century Britain and Europe, Oscar Wilde and the 1890s, the history of printing, and certain aspects of the American West.

Ahmanson and Getty Postdoctoral Fellowships

Subjects: Arts and humanities, religious studies and social sciences.
Purpose: To encourage participation by junior scholars in the centre's year long interdisciplinary core programmes.
Eligibility: Open to postdoctoral Scholars who have received their PhD in the last six years and whose research pertains to the theme as announced by the Library.
Level of Study: Postdoctorate.
Type: Fellowship.
Value: US$18,400.
Length of Study: Two consecutive academic quarters.
Frequency: Annual.
Study Establishment: UCLA and the William Andrews Clark Memorial Library
Country of Study: United States of America.
No. of awards offered: Up to four.
Application Procedure: Applicants must submit an application form, curriculum vitae, proposal statement, a bibliography and three letters of reference.
Closing Date: February 1st.
Funding: Private.
Contributor: The Ahmanson Foundation of Los Angeles and the Getty Trust.
No. of awards given last year: Four.
No. of applicants last year: 30.
Additional Information: The award is theme based and is announced each year. The series intends to be interdisciplinary, with emphasis on both literary and historical perspectives. Participating fellows will be expected to make a substantive contribution to programme seminars.

ASECS (American Society for Eighteenth-Century Studies)/Clark Library Fellowships

Subjects: The Restoration and the eighteenth-century.
Eligibility: Open to members of ASECS who are postdoctoral Scholars and hold a PhD or equivalent at the time of application. The award is also open to advanced doctoral candidates who are members of ASECS.
Level of Study: Postdoctorate.
Type: Fellowship.
Value: US$2,000.
Length of Study: One month.
Frequency: Annual.
Study Establishment: UCLA and the William Andrews Clark Memorial Library.
Country of Study: United States of America.
No. of awards offered: Varies.
Application Procedure: Applicants must submit an application form, curriculum vitae, proposal statement, a bibliography and three letters of reference.
Closing Date: February 1st.
Funding: Government.
Contributor: ASECS and the Clark Library Endowment.
No. of awards given last year: One.
No. of applicants last year: 40.

Clark Library Short-Term Resident Fellowships

Subjects: Research relevant to the Library's holdings.
Eligibility: Open to PhD Scholars or equivalent who are involved in advanced research.
Level of Study: Postdoctorate.
Type: Fellowship.
Value: US$2,000 per month.
Length of Study: One-three months.
Frequency: Annual.

Study Establishment: UCLA and the William Andrews Clark Memorial Library.
Country of Study: United States of America.
No. of awards offered: Varies.
Application Procedure: Applicants must submit an application form, curriculum vitae, proposal statement, a bibliography and three letters of reference.
Closing Date: February 1st.
Funding: Government, Private.
Contributor: The Ahmanson Foundation and the Clark Library Endowment.
No. of awards given last year: 16.
No. of applicants last year: 60.

Clark Predoctoral Fellowships

Subjects: Any area represented in the Clark's collections.
Purpose: To support dissertation research.
Eligibility: Open to advanced doctoral students at the University of California, whose dissertation concerns an area appropriate to the collections of the Clark Library.
Level of Study: Predoctorate.
Type: Fellowship.
Value: US$6,000.
Length of Study: Three months.
Frequency: Annual.
Study Establishment: UCLA and the William Andrews Clark Memorial Library.
Country of Study: United States of America.
No. of awards offered: Varies.
Application Procedure: Applicants must submit an application form, curriculum vitae, proposal statement, a bibliography and three letters of reference.
Closing Date: February 1st.
Funding: Private.
Contributor: The Ahmanson Foundation.
No. of awards given last year: Three.
No. of applicants last year: Nine.

Clark-Huntington Joint Bibliographical Fellowship

Subjects: Early modern literature and history and other areas where the sponsoring libraries have common strengths.
Purpose: To support bibliographical research.
Level of Study: Postdoctorate, Professional development.
Type: Fellowship.
Value: US$4,000.
Length of Study: Two months.
Frequency: Annual.
Study Establishment: The Clark Library and the Huntington Library.
Country of Study: United States of America.
No. of awards offered: One.
Application Procedure: Applicants must submit an application form, curriculum vitae, proposal statement, a bibliography and three letters of reference.
Closing Date: February 1st.
Funding: Private.
No. of awards given last year: One.
No. of applicants last year: 15.

For further information contact:

William Andrews Clark Memorial Library, 2520 Cimarron Street, Los Angeles, CA 90018-2098, United States of America
Contact: Fellowship Co-ordinator

Kanner Fellowship In British Studies

Subjects: British history and culture.
Eligibility: Open to both postdoctoral and predoctoral Scholars.
Level of Study: Postdoctorate, Predoctorate.
Type: Fellowship.
Value: US$6,000.
Length of Study: Three months.
Frequency: Annual.

Application Procedure: Applicants must submit an application form, curriculum vitae, proposal statement, a bibliography and three letters of reference.
Closing Date: February 1st.
Funding: Private.
Contributor: Penny Kanner.
No. of awards given last year: One.
No. of applicants last year: Five.

UCLA CENTER FOR MEDIEVAL AND RENAISSANCE STUDIES (CMRS)

Box 951485, Los Angeles, CA 90095-1485, United States of America
Tel: (1) 310 825 1880
Fax: (1) 310 825 0655
Email: cmrs@humnet.ucla.edu
www: http://www.humnet.ucla.edu/cmrs
Contact: Ms Susanne Kahle, Assistant Director

Through its activities and programmes, the UCLA Center for Medieval and Renaissance Studies (CMRS) promotes interdisciplinary and cross cultural studies of modern civilisation in its formative period from late antiquity to the middle of the seventeenth-century.

CMRS Summer Fellowship

Subjects: Medieval and early modern history, culture, literature, philosophy or religion.
Purpose: To defray expenses for a scholar conducting research at UCLA.
Eligibility: Open to candidates who have a PhD or similar degree from a recognised and accredited university.
Level of Study: Postdoctorate.
Type: Fellowship.
Value: US$500.
Length of Study: Not to exceed three months.
Frequency: Annual.
Study Establishment: CMRS.
Country of Study: United States of America.
No. of awards offered: One.
Application Procedure: Applicants must submit a curriculum vitae, a two page project description and one letter of recommendation.
Closing Date: Early February for Summer notification
No. of awards given last year: One.

UCLA INSTITUTE OF AMERICAN CULTURES (IAC)

1237 Murphy Hall, Box 951419, Los Angeles, CA 90095-1419, United States of America
Tel: (1) 310 206 2557
Fax: (1) 310 825 8099
Email: iaccoordinator@gdnet.ucla.edu
www: http://www.gdnet.ucla.edu/iacweb/iachome.htm
Contact: Dr N Cherie Francis, Co-ordinator

The UCLA Institute of American Cultures (IAC) is committed to advancing knowledge, strengthening and integrating interdisciplinary research and enriching instruction on African Americans, American Indians, Asian Americans and Chicanos. Since 1969, the IAC has been responsible for developing and expanding graduate studies, research and training in ethnic studies and is a major contributor to the academic and intellectual life of the university.

UCLA IAC Postdoctoral/Visiting Scholar Fellowships

Subjects: Arts and humanities, education and teacher training, fine arts, applied arts, law, social sciences and sciences.
Purpose: To enable PhD Scholars wishing to work in association with the American Indian Studies Center, the BUNCHE Center for African American Studies, the Asian American Studies Center and the Chicano Studies Research Center, to conduct research and publish books or manuscripts relating to ethnic studies and interdisciplinary instruction.
Eligibility: Open to United States citizens and permanent residents.

Level of Study: Postdoctorate.
Type: Fellowship.
Value: US$29,000-34,000 stipend plus health benefits and up to US$4,000 in research support.
Length of Study: Up to one year.
Frequency: Annual.
Country of Study: United States of America.
No. of awards offered: One to Two.
Application Procedure: Applicants must complete an application form, available from one of the ethnic studies centres, the IAC, or from the website.
Closing Date: December 31st.
No. of awards given last year: Four.
Additional Information: Further information is available on request or from the website.

For further information contact:

American Indian Studies Center, 3220 Campbell Hall, Box 951548, Los Angeles, CA 90095-1548, United States of America
Tel: (1) 310 825 7315
Fax: (1) 310 206 7060
Email: aisc@ucla.edu
www: http://www.sscnet.ucla.edu/indian
Contact: Fellowship Director

UNITED DAUGHTERS OF THE CONFEDERACY

328 North Boulevard, Richmond, VA 23220-4057, United States of America
Tel: (1) 804 355 1636
Fax: (1) 804 353 1396
Email: hqudc@rcn.com
www: http://www.hqudc.org
Contact: Executive Secretary

The objectives of the United Daughters of the Confederacy are historical, educational, benevolent, memorial and patriotic, to honour the memory of those who served and those who fell in the service of the Confederate States of America.

Mrs Simon Baruch University Award
Subjects: Southern United States history in or near the period of the Confederacy or bearing upon the causes that led to secession and the War Between the States. The life of an individual, a policy or a phase of life may be eligible.
Purpose: To encourage research and to assist scholars in the publication of their thesis, dissertations and other writings.
Eligibility: Open to individuals who have graduated with an advanced degree from a United States university or college within the previous 15 years, or whose thesis or dissertation has been accepted by such institutions as part of graduation requirements. Book length manuscripts should contain at least 75,000 words and monographs 25,000-50,000 words.
Level of Study: Postgraduate.
Value: US$2,000 to aid in defraying the costs of publication and US$500 to the author.
Frequency: Every two years (even-numbered years), .
Country of Study: Any country.
No. of awards offered: One.
Application Procedure: Applicants must write for details.
Closing Date: May 1st of the award year.
Funding: Private.

UNITED STATES BUSINESS SCHOOL (PRAGUE)

Truhlárská 13-15, 110 00, Prague, Veleslavín 1, Czech Republic
Tel: (42) 0 2231 6960
Fax: (42) 0 2248 14527
Email: usbsp@usbsp.com
www: http://www.usbsp.com
Contact: Ms Ondrej Vobruba, Business Development Director

The United States Business School in Prague offers one of the pre-eminent Western MBA programmes under professors from leading business colleges throughout the United States. The MBA degree is awarded by the Rochester Institute of Technology and accredited by the Association to Advance Collegiate Schools of Business (AACSB).

United States Business School (Prague) MBA Scholarships
Subjects: MBA.
Purpose: To provide financial support to exceptional students.
Eligibility: Open only to students enrolled in the full-time MBA programme.
Level of Study: MBA, Postgraduate.
Type: Scholarship.
Value: Scholarships are awarded on the basis of results of the Graduate Management Admissions Test scores. For scores of 650-699 US$1,000 is awarded and for scores of 700 or above, US$2,000 is awarded. The funds are provided as a discount from the tuition fee.
Length of Study: 10 months.
Frequency: Annual.
Study Establishment: The United States Business School Prague.
Country of Study: Czech Republic.
Application Procedure: Applicants must contact the organisation or visit the website for details.
Closing Date: July 31st.
Funding: Private.
Contributor: Czech Telecom, the Czech Insurance Company, McKinsey & Company, T-Mobile, Pilsner Urquell.
Additional Information: As the United States Business School in Prague was established to help Central and Eastern Europe in the transformation of their economies, financial support is available mainly to the citizens of these countries. For Czech and Slovak citizens up to US$8,000 is available, and for citizens of other Central and Eastern European countries up to US$7,000 is allocated. Please contact the organisation for further information.

UNITED STATES CENTER FOR ADVANCED HOLOCAUST STUDIES

United States Holocaust Memorial Museum, 100 Raoul Wallenberg Place South West, Washington, DC 20024-2126, United States of America
Tel: (1) 202 314 0378
Fax: (1) 202 479 9726
www: http://www.ushmm.org
Contact: Ms Lisa Zaid, Fellowships Office

The United States Holocaust Memorial Museum is America's national institution for the documentation, study and interpretation of Holocaust history, and serves as the country's memorial to the millions of people murdered during the Holocaust. The Center for Advanced Holocaust Studies fosters research in holocaust and genocide studies.

United States Center for Advanced Holocaust Studies Research Fellowships
Subjects: History, Political Science, Literature, Philosophy, Sociology, Religion and other disciplines as they relate to the study of the Holocaust.
Purpose: To support research and writing in the fields of Holocaust and Genocide studies.
Eligibility: Fellowships are awarded to candidates working on their dissertations (ABD), postdoctoral researches and senior scholars. Applicants must be affiliated with an academic and/or research institution when applying for a fellowship.
Level of Study: Doctorate, Postdoctorate.
Type: Fellowship.
Value: The Museum will provide a stipend, office space, postage, and access to computer, telephone, facsimile machine and photocopier. Cost sharing among other institutions is welcome.
Length of Study: 3-9 months.

Frequency: Annual.
Country of Study: United States of America.
No. of awards offered: Varies.
Application Procedure: Applicants must consult the Museum's website or contact Lisa Zaid, the Programme Assistant, for application forms and information.
Closing Date: November, please consult website for updated information about deadlines.
Funding: Government, Private.
No. of awards given last year: 25.
No. of applicants last year: 85.

For further information contact:

United States Holocaust Memorial Museum, Center for Advanced Holocaust Studies, 100 Raoul Wallenberg PL SW, Washington DC, 2024-2126, United States of America
Contact: Lisa Zaid

UNITED STATES DEPARTMENT OF STATE FULBRIGHT PROGRAMMES

Institute of International Education, 809 United Nations Plaza, New York, NY 10017-3580, United States of America
Tel: (1) 212 984 5330
Fax: (1) 212 984 5325
www: http://www.usia.gov
Contact: US Student Programmes

USIA Fulbright is an independent foreign affairs agency supporting United States foreign policy and national interests abroad. USIA conducts international educational and cultural exchanges, broadcasting, and information programmes.

Hubert H Humphrey Fellowship Programme
Subjects: Natural resources and environmental management, public policy analysis and public administration, economic development, agricultural development, agricultural economics, finance and banking, human resource management, personnel, urban and regional planning, public health policy and management, technology policy and management, educational planning, communications, journalism.
Purpose: Mid career fellowship of advanced study and professional exchange to increase mutual understanding between the people of the United States of America and the people of developing countries by means of sharing work related experience.
Eligibility: Open to mid career professionals in public service from designated developing countries and Central or Eastern Europe (low and middle income), with at least a first university degree, five years of substantive professional experience, demonstrated leadership qualities, and fluency in English (TOEFL required for all applicants). An English refresher course is available.
Level of Study: Postgraduate, Professional development.
Type: Fellowship.
Value: International and domestic travel, tuition and books, monthly stipend, professional development allowance, health insurance, leadership and professional seminars.
Length of Study: 10 months.
Frequency: Annual.
Study Establishment: Selected universities throughout the United States of America.
Country of Study: United States of America.
No. of awards offered: 137 in 2003.
Application Procedure: Applicants must submit an applications, available through United States Embassy cultural service or Fulbright Commission in home countries.
Closing Date: Between July and September each year; varies by country.
Funding: Government.
Contributor: US government.
No. of awards given last year: 148.
No. of applicants last year: 3,000.
Additional Information: Website: www.iie.org/pgms/hhh.

For further information contact:

U.S. Embassy or Fulbright Commission in the applicant's home Country.

UNITED STATES EDUCATIONAL FOUNDATION IN INDIA (USEFI)

Fulbright House, 12 Hailey Road, New Delhi, 110001, India
Tel: (91) 11 332 8944
Fax: (91) 11 332 9718
Email: info@fulbright-india.org
www: http://www.fulbright-india.org
Contact: Programme Officer

The activities of the United States Educational Foundation in India (USEFI) may be broadly categorised as the administration of the Fulbright Exchange Fellowships for Indian and United States scholars and professionals, and the provision of educational advising services to help Indian students wishing to pursue higher education in the United States.

Fulbright-CII Fellowships for Leadership in Management
Subjects: Leadership in management.
Purpose: To enable business managers to attend a management programme in the United States of America.
Eligibility: Open to Indian business managers.
Level of Study: Professional development.
Type: Fellowship.
Length of Study: 10 weeks.
Study Establishment: Usually the Graduate School of Administration, Carnegie Mellon University, Pittsburgh.
Country of Study: United States of America.
No. of awards offered: Four-five.
Application Procedure: Applicants must complete an application form, available from the CII.
Closing Date: December 31st.
Funding: Private.
Contributor: The Confederation of Indian Industry (CII) and USEFI.
No. of awards given last year: Seven.
Additional Information: For further information contact the Confederation of Indian Industry (CII).

For further information contact:

Head, USA Desk, Confederation of Indian Industry, India Habitat Centre, Corega, 4th Floor, Lodhi Road, New Delhi 110003, India
Tel: (91) 46 822 3035
Fax: (91) 46 222 2819
Email: kankana.das@ciionline.org
Contact: Ms Kankana Das

Fulbright-TATA Travel Fellowships
Subjects: Humanities, social sciences including administration, economics, education, environmental science, language and literature, population studies and women's studies. Applications in subjects that would help in the development of India and its national resources are encouraged.
Purpose: To assist academics and professionals who have invitations to visit the United States of America for either a research or teaching assignment.
Eligibility: Open to Indian citizens resident in India at the time of application who have not been to the United States of America in the previous three years. Applicants must have a high level of academic and professional achievement, proficiency in English and be in good health. Applicants must be permanent full-time faculty members at an Indian college, university or research institute, hold a PhD degree or have equivalent published work and be no more than 50 years of age. In addition, applicants must be accepted by a recognised United States university or research institution for postdoctoral research and/or as a visiting lecturer and have assurance of dollar support to cover the expenses in the United States for the duration of the assignment. The letter of acceptance must show the nature and duration of the assignment,

and must be accompanied by evidence of dollar support of not less than US$2,000 per month and not more than US$25,000 per academic year. American universities, Indian universities or research institutions could offer the evidence of dollar support in the form of a grant or fellowship. The letters of invitation or sponsorship from United States host institutions must indicate that all expenses towards room and board, local transportation, and related personal expenses will be met. No personal funding or financial support from family or friends is permitted.

Level of Study: Postdoctorate, Professional development.

Type: Travel grant.

Value: Round trip economy class airfare and health insurance.

Length of Study: Research or teaching assignments are 4-12 months and professional visits are two-six months.

Frequency: Annual.

Country of Study: United States of America.

No. of awards offered: Four.

Application Procedure: Applicants must complete an application form. Requests for application materials must state the applicant's academic and professional qualifications, date of birth, current position and grant category and be accompanied by a 7 by 10 inch stamped addressed envelope. Requests for application materials must be sent to the USEFI offices in the applicant's region or to the J N Tata Endowment (JNTE) by October 15th or downloaded from the USEFI website.

Closing Date: November 1st.

No. of awards given last year: Three.

No. of applicants last year: Seven.

Additional Information: Further information is available from the USEFI website.

For further information contact:

J N Tata Endowment (JNTE), Bombay House, 24 Homi Modi Street, Mumbai, 400001, India

Tel: (91) 20 491 31

Contact: Director

Hubert H Humphrey Fellowships

Subjects: Agriculture, planning, resource management, public health and public administration. Subject to availability of funds, fellowships may also be offered to working journalists and to medical practitioners in the area of drug abuse.

Eligibility: Open to Indian citizens resident in India at the time of application who have not been to the United States of America in the previous three years. Applicants must have a high level of academic and professional achievement, proficiency in English and be in good health. Preferably applicants will have a First Class Master's or a professional degree of at least four year's duration. Applicants must have at least five years of substantial professional experience in the respective field and not be more than 40 years of age. Applicants applying for the fellowships in drug abuse must hold a PhD or equivalent degree in the health, behavioural or social sciences or an MD.

Level of Study: Doctorate, Postgraduate, Professional development.

Type: Fellowship.

Value: Tuition and fees, a monthly maintenance allowance, modest allowance for books and supplies, round trip international travel to the host institution and domestic travel to Washington DC and/or Minnesota workshops.

Length of Study: 10 months.

Frequency: Annual.

Country of Study: United States of America.

No. of awards offered: Varies.

Application Procedure: Applicants must complete an application form. Requests for application materials must state the applicant's academic and professional qualifications, date of birth, current position and grant category and be accompanied by a 7 by 10 inch stamped addressed envelope. Requests for application materials must be sent to the USEFI offices in the applicant's region. Alternatively, applications can be downloaded from the USEFI website.

Closing Date: June 30th.

Funding: Government.

No. of awards given last year: Five.

No. of applicants last year: 57.

Additional Information: Further information is available on request.

USEFI Junior Research

Subjects: The United States of America, law, intellectual property rights and special education.

Eligibility: Open to Indian citizens resident in India at the time of application who have not been to the United States of America in the previous three years. Applicants must have a high level of academic and professional achievement, proficiency in English and be in good health. Applicants must be registered for a PhD at an Indian institution at least one year prior to application. The fellowship is also open to professionals with postgraduate degrees who are working in areas where study of IPR or special education would be helpful to their institutions.

Level of Study: Predoctorate, Professional development.

Type: Fellowship.

Value: Maintenance in the United States of America, affiliation fees, health insurance and round trip economy class airfare.

Length of Study: Up to six months.

Frequency: Annual.

Country of Study: United States of America.

No. of awards offered: Four-five.

Application Procedure: Applicants must complete an application form. Requests for application materials must state the applicant's academic and professional qualifications, date of birth, current position and grant category and be accompanied by a 7 by 10 inch stamped addressed envelope. Requests for application materials must be sent to the USEFI offices in the applicant's region. Alternatively, download information from the USEFI website.

Closing Date: June 30th.

Funding: Government.

No. of awards given last year: Six.

No. of applicants last year: 27.

Additional Information: Further information is available on request.

USEFI Postdoctoral Research Scholar Grants

Subjects: The United States of America, special education, society and development, and management.

Purpose: To provide scholars with the opportunity to undertake research on contemporary issues and concerns.

Eligibility: Open to Indian citizens resident in India at the time of application who have not been to the United States of America in the preceding three years. Applicants must have a high level of academic and professional achievement, proficiency in English and be in good health. Applicants must be employed as full-time faculty members in an Indian college, university or research institution, or as a full-time professional at an Indian non-profit organisation, hold a PhD degree or have equivalent published work and be under 50 years of age.

Level of Study: Postdoctorate.

Type: Grant.

Value: Round trip travel, monthly stipend, university affiliation fees, health insurance and a modest settling in allowance, dependent allowance and round trip travel for one dependent.

Length of Study: Up to eight months.

Frequency: Annual.

Study Establishment: A university or research institution.

Country of Study: United States of America.

No. of awards offered: Limited.

Application Procedure: Applicants must complete an application form. Requests for application materials must state the applicant's academic and professional qualifications, date of birth, current position and grant category and be accompanied by a 7 by 10 inch stamped addressed envelope. Requests for application materials must be sent to the USEFI offices in the applicant's region.

Closing Date: July 1st.

No. of awards given last year: Eight.

No. of applicants last year: 162.

Additional Information: Applicants must demonstrate the relevance of the proposed research to India and/or the United States, its applicability in India, its benefit to the applicant's institution and the need to carry it out in the United States. Further information is available on request.

USEFI Postdoctoral Travel-Only Grants

Subjects: Social sciences, humanities, fine arts or the performing arts.

Eligibility: Open to Indian citizens resident in India at the time of application who have not been to the United States of America in the preceding three years. Applicants must have a high level of academic and professional achievement, proficiency in English and be in good health. Applicants must be full-time faculty members of an Indian college, university or research institution, hold a PhD degree or have equivalent published work and be no more than 50 years of age. Applicants must be accepted by a recognised United States university or research institution for postdoctoral research and/or as a visiting lecturer and have assurance of dollar support to cover the expenses in the United States for the duration of the assignment. The letter of acceptance must show the nature and duration of the assignment, and must be accompanied by evidence of dollar support and of not less that US$2,000 per month and not more than US$25,000 per academic year. United States universities, Indian universities or research institutions could offer the evidence of dollar support in the form of a grant or fellowship. The letter(s) of invitation or sponsorship from United States host institutions must indicate that all expenses (towards room and board, local transportation, and related personal expenses) will be met.

Level of Study: Postdoctorate, Professional development.

Type: Travel grant.

Value: Round trip economy class airfare and health insurance.

Length of Study: Research or teaching assignments are 4-12 months. Inter-institutional collaboration is for two-three months and social science, humanities, fine arts or performing arts candidates are for two-three months.

Frequency: Annual.

Country of Study: United States of America.

No. of awards offered: Two.

Application Procedure: Applicants must complete an application form. Requests for application materials must state the applicant's academic and professional qualifications, date of birth, current position and grant category and be accompanied by a 7 by 10 inch stamped addressed envelope. Requests for application materials must be sent to the USEFI offices in the applicant's region or can be downloaded from the USEFI website.

Closing Date: November 1st.

Funding: Government.

No. of awards given last year: One.

No. of applicants last year: Seven.

Additional Information: Further information is available on request.

USEFI Professional Fellowships in Information Science and Technology

Subjects: Information science and technology.

Eligibility: Open to Indian citizens resident in India at the time of application who have not been to the United States of America in the preceding three years. Applicants must have a high level of academic and professional achievement, proficiency in English and be in good health. Applicants must be permanently employed as a librarian, assistant librarian, documentation officer, manager of information systems or equivalent position, hold a Master's degree in library and information science, management of information systems or other equivalent qualifications and preferably be no more than 45 years of age.

Level of Study: Professional development.

Type: Fellowship.

Value: Maintenance in the United States of America, affiliation fees, health insurance and round trip economy or excursion air fare.

Length of Study: Up to six months.

Frequency: Annual.

Country of Study: United States of America.

No. of awards offered: Three-four.

Application Procedure: Applicants must complete an application form. Requests for application materials must state the applicant's

academic and professional qualifications, date of birth, current position and grant category and be accompanied by a 7 by 10 inch stamped addressed envelope. Requests for application materials must be sent to the USEFI offices in the applicant's region or alternatively can be downloaded from the website.

Closing Date: June 30th.

Funding: Government.

No. of awards given last year: Seven.

No. of applicants last year: 65.

Additional Information: Further information is available on request from USEFI.

USEFI Professional Fellowships in Plastics and Performing Arts, Museum Studies and Arts/Culture Management

Subjects: Museum studies, arts or culture management, plastics or performing arts.

Purpose: To enable museum professionals or those employed in Arts and Culture organisations to attend non degree courses at United States of America universities or institutions in the relevant areas, and to gain practical work experience in suitable settings in the United States of America.

Eligibility: Open to Indian citizens resident in India at the time of application who have not been to the United States of America in the preceding three years. Applicants must have a high level of academic and professional achievement, proficiency in English and be in good health. Applicants must have completed their formal education, preferably having a postgraduate degree in the relevant area. Museum Studies applicants must be employed in museums in India. Arts and Culture Management applicants must be employed in Indian art and culture institutions or organisations. Plastics and performing arts applicants should have completed their formal education, or have substantial training under the auspices of the traditional Guru-Shishya Parampara. Applicants must be aged between 25 and 40 years.

Level of Study: Postgraduate, Professional development.

Type: Fellowship.

Value: Round trip travel, moderate monthly stipend, university fees, health insurance and a modest settling in allowance.

Length of Study: Two-six months.

Frequency: Dependent on funds available.

Country of Study: United States of America.

No. of awards offered: Four.

Application Procedure: Applicants must complete an application form. Requests for application materials must state the applicant's academic and professional qualifications, date of birth, current position and grant category and be accompanied by a 7 by 10 inch stamped addressed envelope. Requests for application materials must be sent to the USEFI offices in the applicant's region. Alternatively, applicants can download information from the USEFI website.

Closing Date: July 15th.

Funding: Government.

No. of awards given last year: Six.

No. of applicants last year: 58.

Additional Information: Further information is available on request from USEFI.

USEFI Visiting Lecturer Grants

Subjects: Contemporary issues significant to India and the United States of America in the fields of humanities or the social sciences.

Purpose: To allow scholars to share their expertise on contemporary issues significant to India and the United States of America.

Eligibility: Open to Indian citizens resident in India at the time of application who have not been to the United States of America in the preceding three years. Applicants must have a high level of academic and professional achievement, proficiency in English and be in good health. Applicants must be permanent full-time faculty members at an Indian college, university or research institute, hold a PhD degree or have equivalent published work, have at least 10 years of college or university level teaching experience and be no more than 50 years of age.

Level of Study: Postdoctorate.

Type: Grant.

Value: Round trip travel, monthly stipend, university fees, health insurance and a modest settling in allowance.
Length of Study: Three months.
Frequency: Annual.
Country of Study: United States of America.
No. of awards offered: Two-three.
Application Procedure: Applicants must complete an application form. Requests for application materials must state the applicant's academic and professional qualifications, date of birth, current position and grant category and be accompanied by a 7 by 10 inch stamped addressed envelope. Requests for application materials must be sent to the USEFI offices in the applicant's region or can be downloaded from the USEFI website.
Closing Date: July 15th.
No. of awards given last year: Four.
No. of applicants last year: 42.
Additional Information: Further information is available on request.

UNITED STATES FOUNDATION

15 boulevard Jourdan, Paris, Cedex 14 F-75690, France
Tel: (00) 1 53 00 00 00
Fax: (33) 1 53 80 68 99
Email: fondusa@iway.fr
Contact: Mr Terence Murphy, Director

Harriet Hale Woolley Scholarships

Subjects: Art and music.
Purpose: To support the study of visual fine arts in Paris.
Eligibility: Open to United States citizens, who are 21-29 years of age and have graduated with high academic standing from a United States college, university or professional school of recognised standing. Preference is given to mature students who have already completed graduate study. Applicants should provide evidence of artistic or musical accomplishment. Applicants should have a good working knowledge of French, sufficient to enable the student to benefit at once from study in France, good moral character, personality and adaptability and good physical health and emotional stability. Grants are for those doing painting, printmaking or sculpture and for instrumentalists, not for research in art history, musicology or composition, nor for students of dance or of theatre.
Level of Study: Graduate, Postgraduate.
Type: Scholarship.
Value: A stipend of US$8,500.
Length of Study: One academic year.
Frequency: Annual.
Country of Study: France.
No. of awards offered: Four-five.
Application Procedure: Applicants must write for details.
Closing Date: January 31st.
Funding: Private.
No. of awards given last year: Four.
No. of applicants last year: 25.

UNITED STATES INSTITUTE OF PEACE (USIP)

1200 17th Street North, WestSuite 200, Washington, DC 20036-3011, United States of America
Tel: (1) 202 429 3842
Fax: (1) 202 429 6063
Email: grant_program@usip.org
www: http://www.usip.org
Contact: Ms Cornelia Smith, Grant Programme Administration Assistant

The United States Institute of Peace (USIP) is mandated by Congress to promote education and training, research and public information programmes on means to promote international peace, and resolve international conflicts without violence. The Institute meets this mandate through an array of programmes, including grants, fellowships, conferences and workshops, library services, publications and other educational activities.

Jennings Randolph Program for International Peace Dissertation Fellowship

Subjects: A broad range of disciplines and interdisciplinary fields are eligible.
Purpose: To support dissertations that explore the sources and nature of international conflict, and strategies to prevent or end conflict and to sustain peace.
Eligibility: Open to applicants of all nationalities who are enrolled in an accredited college or university in the United States of America. Applicants must have completed all requirements for the degree except the dissertation by the commencement of the award.
Level of Study: Doctorate.
Type: Fellowship.
Value: US$17,000 which may be used to support writing or field research.
Length of Study: One year.
Frequency: Annual.
Study Establishment: The student's home university or site of fieldwork.
Country of Study: United States of America.
No. of awards offered: 10.
Application Procedure: Applicants must complete an application form, available on request from the Institute or from the website.
Closing Date: January 9th.
Funding: Government.
Additional Information: The programme does not support work involving partisan political and policy advocacy or policy making for any government or private organisation. Further information is available on the website or from Miss Jean Brodeur Administration Assistant, telephone (1) 202 429 3886, jrprogram@usip.org.

Jennings Randolph Program for International Peace Senior Fellowships

Subjects: Preventive diplomacy, ethnic and regional conflicts, peacekeeping and peace operations, peace settlements, post conflict reconstruction and reconciliation, democratisation and the rule of law, cross cultural negotiations, United States policy in the twenty first-century and related subjects.
Purpose: To use the recipient's existing knowledge and skills towards a fruitful endeavour in the international peace and conflict management field, and to help bring the perspectives of this field into the Fellow's own career.
Eligibility: Open to outstanding practitioners and Scholars from a broad range of backgrounds. The competition is open to citizens of any country who have specific interest and experience in international peace and conflict management. Candidates would typically be senior academics, but applicants who hold at least a Bachelor's degree from a recognised university will also be considered.
Type: Fellowship.
Value: A stipend, an office with computer and voicemail and a part-time research assistant.
Length of Study: Up to 10 months.
Frequency: Annual.
Study Establishment: USIP.
Country of Study: United States of America.
No. of awards offered: 10-12.
Application Procedure: Applicants must complete an application form, available on request from the Institute or from the website.
Closing Date: September 15th.
Funding: Government.
Additional Information: Miss Jean Bordeur, 202 429 3886, jrprogram@usip.org or www.usip.org for more information.

USIP Solicited Grants

Subjects: Special priority topics identified in advance by the Institute. Current grant topics can be found on the website.
Purpose: To provide financial support for research, education and training, and the dissemination of information on international peace and conflict resolution.
Eligibility: Open to non-profit organisations and individuals, both American and foreign. These include institutions of post secondary, community and secondary education, public and private education, training or research institutions and libraries. Although the Institute can

provide grant support to individuals, it prefers that an institutional affiliation be established. The Institute will not accept applications that list as participants, consultants, or project personnel members of the Institute's Board of Directors or staff. In addition, any application that lists the Institute as a collaborator in the project will not be accepted.

Level of Study: Postdoctorate, Research.
Type: Grant.
Value: Most awards fall in the range of US$25,000 to US$45,000, although somewhat larger grants are also awarded. The amount of any grant is based on the proposed budget and on negotiations with successful applicants.
Length of Study: One-two years.
Frequency: Twice a year.
No. of awards offered: Approx. 35.
Application Procedure: Applicants must complete an application form, available on request from the Institute or from the website.
Closing Date: March 1st for the Spring competition and October 1st for the Autumn competition.
Funding: Government.
No. of awards given last year: 38.
No. of applicants last year: 212.

USIP Unsolicited Grants

Subjects: Topic areas of interest to the Institute include, but are not restricted to, international conflict resolution, diplomacy, negotiation theory, functionalism and track two diplomacy, methods of third party dispute settlement, international law, international organisations and collective security, deterrence and balance of power, arms control, psychological theories about international conflict, the role of non violence and non violent sanctions, moral and ethical thought about conflict and conflict resolution, and theories about relationships among political institutions, human rights and conflict.
Purpose: To provide financial support for research, education and training, and the dissemination of information on international peace and conflict resolution.
Eligibility: The Institute may provide grant support to non-profit organisations and individuals, both American and foreign. These include institutions of post secondary, community and secondary education, public and private education, training or research institutions and libraries. Although the Institute can provide grant support to individuals, it prefers that an institutional affiliation be established. The Institute will not accept applications that list members of the Institute's Board of Directors or staff as participants, consultants or project personnel. In addition, any application that lists the Institute as a collaborator in the project will not be accepted.
Level of Study: Postdoctorate, Research.
Type: Grant.
Value: Most awards fall in the range of US$25,000-45,000, although somewhat larger grants are also awarded. The amount of any grant is based on the proposed budget and on negotiations with successful applicants.
Length of Study: One-two years.
Frequency: Twice a year.
No. of awards offered: Approx. 65.
Application Procedure: Applicants must complete an application form, available on request from the Institute or from the website.
Closing Date: October 1st or March 1st.
Funding: Government.
No. of awards given last year: 63.
No. of applicants last year: 419.

UNITED STATES TROTTING ASSOCIATION

750 Michigan Avenue, Columbus, OH 43215, United States of America
Tel: (1) 614 224 2291
Fax: (1) 614 228 1385
Email: jpawlak@ustrotting.com
www: http://www.ustrotting.com
Contact: Mr John Pawlak, Publicity/PR Director

The United States Trotting Association promotes the sport of harness racing and the Standardbred breed. It also maintains and disseminates racing information and records and serves as the registry for the breed.

John Hervey, Broadcasters and Smallsreed Awards

Subjects: Journalism, television broadcasting and photography.
Purpose: To honour the best media stories on harness racing in the categories of newspaper, magazines, television and photo journalism.
Eligibility: Stories must have been published or aired in North America.
Level of Study: Unrestricted.
Type: Prize.
Value: First prize is US$500, second prize is US$100 and third prize is US$100 in each division.
Frequency: Annual.
Country of Study: Any country.
No. of awards offered: 15.
Application Procedure: Applicants must submit entries to the address shown. There is no application form.
Closing Date: December 1st.
Funding: Private.
Contributor: The United States Trotting Association.
No. of awards given last year: 12.
No. of applicants last year: 75.
Additional Information: Articles, television programmes and photographs must be published or broadcast in North America.

UNIVERSAL ESPERANTO ASSOCIATION

Nieuwe Binneweg 176, Rotterdam
NL-3015 BJ, Netherlands
Tel: (31) 10 436 1044
Fax: (31) 10 436 1751
Email: uea@inter.nl.net
www: http://www.uea.org
Contact: Mr P Zapelli

Spreading the use of the international language Esperanto.

Universal Esperanto Association Awards

Subjects: Esperanto.
Purpose: To train young volunteer workers for the advancement of the language and literature of Esperanto.
Eligibility: Open to individuals of all nationalities who are between 18-29 years of age. A fluent knowledge of Esperanto, both written and spoken, is essential prior to qualification.
Level of Study: Unrestricted.
Type: Award.
Value: A monthly stipend of €400 plus accommodation.
Length of Study: Up to one year, non renewable.
Frequency: Annual.
Study Establishment: The Head Office of the Association.
Country of Study: Netherlands.
No. of awards offered: One-two.
Closing Date: Applications are accepted at any time.
No. of awards given last year: 3.
No. of applicants last year: 10.

UNIVERSITA' PER STRANIERI DI SIENA

Via Pantaneto N 45, Siena, I-53100, Italy
Tel: (39) 057 724 0111
Fax: (39) 057 728 3163
Email: info@unistrasi.it
www: http://www.unistrasi.it
Contact: Ms Giuseppina Grassiccia, Head of Promotions & International Division

The Universita' Per Stranieri Di Siena is a state university which undertakes research and instruction in the fields of Italian language and culture. It is located in the heart of Tuscany, Italy, and offers Italian language courses for foreigners, graduate courses related to Italian culture and language, and training courses for teachers of Italian as a foreign language.

Regional Agency for the Right to University Study (DSU) Grants

Subjects: Linguistics, philology, history, literature, education and teacher training.
Purpose: To give university students the financial means necessary to fulfil their study programme.
Eligibility: This award is restricted by merit and family or personal income.
Level of Study: Graduate.
Type: Scholarship.
Value: University fees and lodging in the students' halls of residence.
Length of Study: One year.
Frequency: Annual.
Study Establishment: The University of Siena for Foreigners.
Country of Study: Italy.
No. of awards offered: 43.
Application Procedure: Applicants must apply to the DSU after enrolment to the second year course at the university in Italy.
Closing Date: September.
Funding: Government.
No. of awards given last year: 43.

For further information contact:

Azienda Regionale per il Diritto Allo Studio, Via dei Termini 6, Siena, I-53100, Italy

Universita' Per Stranieri Di Siena CILS Grants

Subjects: Italian language and culture.
Purpose: To exempt students from the payment for the CILS Exam.
Eligibility: Open to candidates who hold a certificate of merit.
Level of Study: Unrestricted.
Type: Grant.
Value: The examination fee.
Frequency: Dependent on funds available.
Study Establishment: Conventional institutions throughout the world.
No. of awards offered: Varies.
Application Procedure: Applicants must apply for information, available on request.
Closing Date: Please write for details.
Funding: Private.
Contributor: The University of Siena for Foreigners and Bank Monte dei Paschi of Siena.
No. of awards given last year: 4.
Additional Information: The CILS (Certification of Italian as a Foreign Language) is an examination established by the University and aimed to assess student's proficiency in Italian. It is recognised by the Italian Ministry of Foreign Affairs.

For further information contact:

CILS Certification Centre, Via S Bandini 35, Siena, I-53100, Italy

Universita' Per Stranieri Di Siena Doctorate in Italian Literature, History of the Italian Language and Philology

Subjects: Language, literature and education.
Purpose: To further research into the Italian language with an intertextual approach.
Eligibility: Open to citizens of the European Union who hold a university degree equivalent to the Italian Laurea degree.
Level of Study: Doctorate.
Type: Scholarship.
Value: Established by law.
Length of Study: Three years.
Frequency: Annual.
Study Establishment: The University of Siena for Foreigners and the consorted university 'La Sapienza' of Rome.
Country of Study: Italy.
No. of awards offered: Anno 2002/2003: 10. Anno 2003/2004: 12.

Application Procedure: This is a public competition and regulations are published in the Gazzetta Ufficiale of the Italian Republic every year.
Closing Date: Usually late Spring or early Summer. Deadlines are published each year in the official document Gazzetta Ufficiale.
Funding: Government.
Contributor: The University of Siena for foreigners.
No. of awards given last year: None.

Universita' Per Stranieri Di Siena Doctorate in Linguistics and Teaching of Italian to Foreigners

Subjects: Italian language.
Purpose: To further research into the teaching of Italian to foreigners.
Eligibility: Open to citizens of the European Union who hold a university degree considered equivalent to the Italian 'Laurea' degree.
Level of Study: Doctorate.
Type: Scholarship.
Value: Established by law.
Length of Study: Three years.
Frequency: Annual.
Study Establishment: The University of Siena for Foreigners.
Country of Study: Italy.
No. of awards offered: Anno 2002/2003: 12. Anno 2003/2004: 14.
Application Procedure: This is a public competition and regulations are published in the Gazzetta Ufficiale of the Italian Republic every year.
Closing Date: Usually late Spring or early Summer. Deadlines are published each year in the official document Gazzetta Ufficiale.
Funding: Government.
Contributor: The University of Siena for Foreigners.
No. of awards given last year: Three.
Additional Information: Further information is available on request.

Universita' Per Stranieri Di Siena Socrates Erasmus Students Mobility

Subjects: Arts and humanities.
Purpose: To provide an opportunity for someone to study abroad.
Eligibility: Open to applicants who are enrolled in the University for Foreigners of Siena and are European Union citizens.
Level of Study: Graduate.
Type: Grant.
Value: €120 per month.
Length of Study: From 3-12 months.
Frequency: Annual.
Study Establishment: The University of Birmingham in the United Kingdom, Heidelberg Universität in Germany, the University of Poitiers and University of Rennes in France, The University College London (UK).
Country of Study: Other.
No. of awards offered: Varies according to the partnerships established with European universities. There are eight for students and two for teachers.
Application Procedure: Applicants must complete an application form which will be submitted to the examination of the relevant commission. Applications should be addressed to the Divisione Promozione E Relazioni Internazionali.
Closing Date: The end of May.
Contributor: The European Union and the University of Siena for Foreigners.
No. of awards given last year: 15.
No. of applicants last year: 15.
Additional Information: The grants support students abroad while they attend one or more terms at the host university, choosing courses offered there and taking the appropriate examinations.

Universita' Per Stranieri Di Siena PVS Grants

Subjects: Italian language and culture.
Purpose: To support study at regular and special Italian language courses for students coming from developing countries.
Eligibility: Open to candidates who hold a study qualification valid for admission to university level studies in their home country and are a citizen of a developing country.
Level of Study: Graduate.

Type: Scholarship.
Value: Fees and lodging.
Length of Study: One-two months.
Frequency: Annual.
Study Establishment: The University of Siena for Foreigners.
Country of Study: Italy.
No. of awards offered: 73.
Application Procedure: Applicants must apply directly to the Italian Cultural Institutes in their home country.
Closing Date: The end of February.
Funding: Private.
Contributor: The University of Siena for Foreigners and the Bank Monte dei Paschi di Siena.
No. of awards given last year: 65.
Additional Information: Further information is available on request.

Universita' Per Stranieri Di Siena Unstra Grants

Subjects: Italian language and culture.
Purpose: To support study at regular courses.
Eligibility: Open to applicants who hold a study qualification valid for admission to university level studies in their home country.
Level of Study: Graduate.
Type: Scholarship.
Value: Course fees.
Length of Study: One-three months.
Frequency: Annual.
Study Establishment: The University of Siena for Foreigners.
Country of Study: Italy.
No. of awards offered: 90.
Application Procedure: Applicants must apply directly to the Italian Cultural Institutes in their home country.
Closing Date: The end of February.
Funding: Private.
Contributor: The University of Siena for Foreigners and the Bank Monte dei Paschi di Siena.
No. of awards given last year: 67.
Additional Information: Further information is available on request.

UNIVERSITA' PER STRANIERI DI PERUGIA

Palazzo Gallenga Piazza Fortebraccio 4, Perugia, I-06122, Italy
Tel: (39) 075 574 61
Fax: (39) 075 573 0901
Email: borse@unistrapg.it
www: http://www.unistrapg.it
Contact: Anpiolo Boncompagni, Press Office

Of all the Italian institutions which conduct research into the teaching and acquisition of the Italian language and which foster the knowledge of Italian culture, the Universita' Per Stranieri Di Perugia is the oldest and the most prestigious. The University is the only Italian member of ALTE (Association of Language Testers in Europe).

University for Foreigners Scholarships

Subjects: Italian language and culture.
Eligibility: Open to foreign citizens and Italians resident abroad. Preference is given to students of Italian at schools and universities abroad, and to teachers of the Italian language.
Level of Study: Postgraduate.
Type: Scholarship.
Value: To cover one month's study and living expenses.
Length of Study: One-six months.
Frequency: Monthly.
Study Establishment: The University.
Country of Study: Italy.
No. of awards offered: 350.
Application Procedure: Applications for scholarships must be made through the Italian Institutes of Culture in the country of residence. Direct application to the University for Foreigners may be made only by applicants residing in countries where there are no Italian Institutes of Culture. Further information is available on request or from the website.

Closing Date: At least four months before the start of the course.
No. of awards given last year: 350.
No. of applicants last year: 6,000.

UNIVERSITÉ CATHOLIQUE DE LOUVAIN (UCL)

Secrétariat à la coopération internationale Place de l'Université 1, B-1348, Louvain-la-Neuve, Belgium
Tel: 10 47 30 95
Fax: 10 47 40 75
Email: info@sco.ucl.ac.be
www: http://www.sco.ucl.ac.be
Contact: Mr Duque Christian

The French speaking Université Catholique de Louvain (UCL) organises a yearly scholarship contest for postgraduate studies, medical specialisation and PhD.

UCL Co-operation Fellowships

Subjects: Any subject relevant to Third World development.
Purpose: To promote economic, social, cultural and political progress in developing countries by training graduates from these countries.
Eligibility: Open to nationals of developing countries who hold all the requirements to be admitted to UCL at postgraduate level. Applicants should have an excellent academic background and some professional experience. They should also demonstrate that their study programme is able to promote the development of their home country and that they have a good command of French ie. the Diplôme d'Études en Langue Française (DELF). Applicants must be less than 35 years of age for a PhD and 40 years of age for a specialisation. Applicants for a PhD must be members of the academic or scientific staff of a university in their own country, be able to demonstrate their intent for an academic career and prove that they will be reintegrated into their home institution upon completion of their PhD.
Level of Study: Doctorate, Postgraduate.
Type: Fellowship.
Value: Tuition, living expenses, family allowance, medical insurance and transportation costs to the recipient's home country at the end of studies.
Length of Study: Up to four years.
Frequency: Annual.
Study Establishment: The Catholic University of Louvain.
Country of Study: Belgium.
No. of awards offered: Up to 20.
Application Procedure: Applicants must first write to the Secrétariat á la coopération internationale (SCO) at UCL, including a description of the programme that they wish to undertake, a short note explaining how they comply with the eligibility and selection criteria and a detailed curriculum vitae. Application forms will then be sent to those students who are eligible.
Closing Date: October 30th for letters and December 31st for application forms.
Funding: Private.
No. of awards given last year: 21.
No. of applicants last year: 139.

UNIVERSITIES FEDERATION FOR ANIMAL WELFARE (UFAW)

The Old School, Brewhouse Hill, Wheathampstead, Hertfordshire, AL4 8AN, England
Tel: (44) 1582 831818
Fax: (44) 1582 831414
Email: ufaw@ufaw.org.uk
www: http://www.ufaw3.dircon.co.uk
Contact: Secretary

The Universities Federation for Animal Welfare (UFAW) seeks to prevent cruelty and promote humane behaviour towards all animals and encourage and promote, through education and scientific research, a proper understanding of the needs of animals.

UFAW Animal Welfare Research Training Scholarships

Subjects: UFAW is particularly keen to receive applicants for studies that may lead to significant developments in the assessment of the welfare of animals or studies aimed at providing new insight into the subjective mental experiences of animals relevant to their welfare. Applications for projects in other aspects of animal welfare science will also be considered.

Purpose: To encourage high quality science likely to lead to substantial advances in animal welfare and to enable promising graduates to start a career in animal welfare science.

Eligibility: Open to nationals of any country.

Level of Study: Doctorate.

Type: Scholarship.

Value: Science graduates: UK£12,680-13,984, and veterinary graduates: UK£13,334-15,786. In addition up to UK£8,000 research costs per year will be met.

Length of Study: Three years.

Frequency: Annual, if funds are available.

Study Establishment: Scholarships may only be held at appropriate academic departments in the United Kingdom.

Country of Study: United Kingdom.

No. of awards offered: One

Application Procedure: Applicants must complete a two stage process. Initially supervisors must submit a brief concept note using an application form available from UFAW. Selected applicants will then be invited to submit more detailed proposals prepared jointly by the supervisor and PhD candidate.

Closing Date: Concept note end of January and detailed proposal end of April.

Funding: Private.

No. of awards given last year: Two.

UFAW Research and Project Awards

Subjects: Full or part funding for self-contained projects or initial funding for studies which may lead to further investigation or welfare benefits. Awards can be used to supplement current work or to extend previous projects which promote animal welfare or to support non research projects which promote animal welfare, such as preparation and publication of books and teaching materials.

Purpose: To encourage fundamental and high quality research that is likely to lead to substantial improvements in animal welfare.

Eligibility: Open to nationals of any country.

Level of Study: Unrestricted.

Type: Grant.

Value: UK£3,500 plus (rarely in excess of UK£10,000).

Length of Study: For the duration of the approved works.

Frequency: Dependent on funds available.

Country of Study: Any country.

No. of awards offered: Varies.

Application Procedure: Applicants must submit application forms available from the Secretary.

Closing Date: Considered at approx. three month intervals.

Funding: Private.

Additional Information: Annual progress reports are required within one month of the anniversary of the start date and a final report must be submitted within three months of the completion date.

UFAW Small Project and Travel Awards

Subjects: Sciences and medicine, as they relate to the study of animal welfare.

Purpose: To support research projects and other activities for the benefit of animal welfare.

Eligibility: Open to nationals of any country.

Level of Study: Unrestricted.

Value: Up to UK£3,500.

Length of Study: For the duration of the approved works.

Frequency: Dependent on funds available.

Country of Study: Any country.

Application Procedure: Applicants must complete an application form which must show that the fullest possible account of the welfare of any animals to be used has been taken. Applications must be made on forms available from the Secretary.

Closing Date: Considered at approx. three month intervals.

Funding: Private.

Additional Information: A report is required within one month of completion of the project.

UFAW Vacation Scholarships

Subjects: Research is supported that is likely to provide new insight into the subjective mental experiences of animals relevant to their welfare and at understanding their needs and preferences, and also applied research aimed at developing practical solutions to animal welfare problems.

Purpose: To encourage students to develop their interests in animal welfare and their abilities for animal welfare research.

Eligibility: Open to nationals of any country. Candidates must be registered at a university or college in the UK. Applicants need a nominated supervisor to oversee the project.

Type: Scholarship.

Value: UK£100 subsistence and UK£20 departmental expenses for each week of study.

Length of Study: Maximum of eight weeks.

Frequency: Annual.

Country of Study: Any country.

No. of awards offered: Varies, approx. 12.

Application Procedure: Application form must be completed. Forms are available from the Secretary and must be completed prior to application.

Closing Date: February 28th.

Funding: Private.

No. of awards given last year: 12.

No. of applicants last year: 28.

Additional Information: Successful applicants must submit a written report to UFAW by November of the year the project was undertaken.

UNIVERSITY INSTITUTE OF EUROPEAN STUDIES

Via Maria Vittoria 26, Turin, I-10123, Italy
Tel: (39) 011 839 4660
Fax: (39) 011 839 4664
Email: info@iuse.it
www: http://www.iuse.it
Contact: Ms Maria Grazia Goiettina, Course Secretariat

The University Institute of European Studies promotes international relations and European integration by organising academic activities. The Institute has a comprehensive library in international law and economics. Since 1952 the Institute has been a European Documentation Centre (EDC), thus receiving all official publications of European institutions.

University Institute of European Studies Postgraduate Scholarships

Subjects: International trade law focusing on the origin and evolution of international trade, instruments and rules of the main economic international organisations, sources of law in international trade, legal aspects of international contracts in international trade, conflict of laws, modes of payment taxation, arbitration and dispute resolution.

Purpose: To allow students to attend the postgraduate course on international trade law.

Eligibility: Open to Italian and foreign graduates in law, business and economics. Candidates from Turin are not eligible.

Level of Study: Postgraduate.

Type: Scholarship.

Value: Part of the accommodation expenses.

Length of Study: Three months.

Frequency: Annual.

Study Establishment: The ILO Turin Centre.

Country of Study: Italy.

No. of awards offered: Varies.

Application Procedure: Candidates should fill in the application form obtainable from the Secretariat or the website. A copy of the degree, including a transcript of academic records and a certificate of English knowledge should be attached.

Closing Date: Mid January.

Funding: Private.
No. of awards given last year: Seven.
No. of applicants last year: 300.
Additional Information: The course aims to provide candidates with a common approach to the main legal issues in international trade law and contract drafting. Lecturers are prominent Italian and international experts, university professors or practitioners and senior officials of international institutions. The course, usually held in Spring, is in English. The number of participants is limited and full-time participation is required throughout the programme.

UNIVERSITY OF ALBERTA

Graduate Awards and Scholarships, Faculty of Graduate Studies and Research105, Administration Building, Edmonton, AB, T6G 2M7, Canada
Tel: (1) 780 492 3499
Fax: (1) 780 492 0692
Email: grad.awards@ualberta.ca
www: http://gradfile.fgsro.ualberta.ca

Opened in 1908, the University of Alberta has a long tradition of scholarly achievements and commitment to excellence in teaching, research and service to the community. It is one of Canada's five largest research intensive universities, with an annual research income from external sources of more than Canadian $112 million. It participates in all 14 of the Federal Networks of Centres of Excellence which link industry, universities and government in applied research and development.

Alberta Research Council Karl A Clark Memorial Scholarship

Subjects: Computer Engineering or Computer Science concerned with software and information technologies.
Eligibility: Open to students of any nationality who are enrolled in a graduate degree programme and engaged in thesis research at the Master's or doctoral level.
Level of Study: Doctorate, Graduate.
Type: Scholarship.
Value: Canadian $20,000.
Length of Study: One year, renewable for one further year through open competition.
Frequency: Annual.
Country of Study: Any country.
No. of awards offered: One.
Application Procedure: Application forms are available from university departments.
Closing Date: Applicants must be nominated by the department in which they plan to pursue their studies. March 1st for submission of nominations from departments. Check with the department for internal deadline.
No. of awards given last year: 1.

Grant Notley Memorial Postdoctoral Fellowship

Subjects: The politics, history, economy or society of Western Canada or related fields.
Purpose: To encourage scholars of superior research ability who graduated within the last three years.
Eligibility: Open to persons who have recently completed a PhD programme or who will do so in the immediate future. Applicants should be active and promising young scholars who will perform significantly in fields associated with Grant Notley's interests or related fields. Applicants who have received their PhD degree from the University of Alberta, who will be on sabbatical leave, or who have held or will have held postdoctoral fellowships at other institutions for two years are not eligible.
Level of Study: Postdoctorate.
Type: Fellowship.
Value: Canadian $40,000 per year, a non renewable research grant of Canadian $4,000, and return travel from the point of residence at the time of application.
Length of Study: Two years.
Frequency: Annual.

Study Establishment: The University of Alberta.
Country of Study: Canada.
No. of awards offered: One.
Application Procedure: Applicants must visit the website for application information.
Closing Date: January 2nd.
Funding: Private.
No. of awards given last year: One.
No. of applicants last year: Four.

Izaak Walton Killam Memorial Postdoctoral Fellowships

Subjects: All subjects.
Purpose: To attract scholars of superior research ability who graduated within the last three years.
Eligibility: Open to candidates of any nationality who have recently completed a PhD programme or will do so in the immediate future. Applicants who have received their PhD degree from the University of Alberta, who will be on sabbatical leave, or who have held or will have held postdoctoral fellowships at other institutions for two years are not eligible.
Level of Study: Postdoctorate.
Type: Fellowship.
Value: Canadian $40,000 per year, a non renewable research grant of Canadian $4,000 and a return airfare.
Length of Study: Two years.
Frequency: Annual.
Study Establishment: The University of Alberta.
Country of Study: Canada.
No. of awards offered: Eight.
Application Procedure: Applicants must visit the website for application information.
Closing Date: January 2nd.
Funding: Private.
No. of awards given last year: Six.
No. of applicants last year: 33.

Izaak Walton Killam Memorial Scholarships

Subjects: All subjects.
Eligibility: Open to candidates of any nationality who are registered in, or are admissible to, a doctoral programme at the University. Scholars must have completed at least one year of graduate work prior to beginning the scholarship. Applicants must be nominated by the department in which they plan to pursue their doctoral studies.
Level of Study: Doctorate.
Type: Scholarship.
Value: Canadian $20,100 per year plus a non renewable research grant of Canadian $2,000, tuition and fees.
Length of Study: Two years from May 1st or September 1st, subject to review after the first year.
Frequency: Annual.
Study Establishment: The University of Alberta.
Country of Study: Canada.
No. of awards offered: Approx. 20.
Application Procedure: Applicants must contact the university departments for application information.
Closing Date: February 1st for the submission of nominations from departments. Please check with the department for their internal deadline.
Funding: Private.
No. of awards given last year: 20.
No. of applicants last year: 137.

Province of Alberta Graduate Fellowships

Subjects: All subjects.
Eligibility: Open to Canadian citizens or permanent residents at the date of application who have completed at least one year of graduate study and who are registered in a full-time doctoral programme at the University of Alberta.
Level of Study: Doctorate.
Type: Fellowship.
Value: Canadian $10,500 for commencement in May and Canadian $7,000 for commencement in September.
Length of Study: One year from May 1st or September 1st.

Frequency: Annual.
Study Establishment: The University of Alberta.
Country of Study: Canada.
No. of awards offered: Approx. 40.
Application Procedure: Applicants must be nominated by the department in which they plan to pursue their doctoral studies.
Closing Date: February 1st for the submission of nominations from departments. Please check with the department for their internal deadline.
Funding: Government.
No. of awards given last year: 40.
No. of applicants last year: 252.
Additional Information: Recipients must carry out a full-time research programme during the Summer months.

Province of Alberta Graduate Scholarships

Subjects: All subjects.
Eligibility: Open to Canadian citizens or permanent residents who are entering or continuing, at the date of application, in a full-time Master's programme at the University of Alberta. Applicants must be nominated by the department in which they plan to pursue their studies. Students registered as qualifying graduates or probationary students are not eligible.
Level of Study: Graduate.
Type: Scholarship.
Value: Canadian $9,300 for commencement in May, Canadian $6,200 for commencement in September.
Length of Study: One year from May 1st or eight months from September 1st. Partial awards may be recommended at a reduced value and the award may be terminated earlier by either the student or the university and the amount reduced proportionately.
Frequency: Annual.
Study Establishment: The University of Alberta.
Country of Study: Canada.
No. of awards offered: Approx. 44.
Application Procedure: Applicants must complete an application form available from the relevant university department.
Closing Date: February 1st for the submission of nominations from departments. Please check with the department for their internal deadline.
Funding: Government.
No. of awards given last year: 44.
No. of applicants last year: 162.

UNIVERSITY OF BATH

Graduate Office, Claverton Down, Bath, BA2 7AY, England
Tel: (44) 1225 323234
Fax: (44) 1225 386366
Email: grad-office@bath.ac.uk
www: http://www.bath.ac.uk
Contact: Dr Lisa Isted, Assistant Registrar

The University of Bath offers taught and research postgraduate study in humanities and social sciences, engineering and design and science and management. In the 2001 Research Assessment Exercise, 71% of its research active staff achieved grades five or five, demonstrating research of international excellence. The university came fifth in The Times newspaper 2003 ranking list.The University of Bath offers taught and research programmes in Enginnering and Design, Humanities and Social Sciences, Science, Management, Health. In the 2001 Research Assessment Exercise, 71 % of its research active staff achieved grades 5 or 5, demonstrating research of international excellence. The University came fifth in the The Times newspaper 2003 Good University Guide.

University of Bath Research Studentships

Subjects: All subjects offered by the University.
Purpose: To provide funds for well qualified candidates to pursue full-time research leading to a research degree.
Eligibility: Open to candidates of any nationality with a minimum Second Class (Honours) Degree or equivalent. Candidates must have applied or been accepted for study for a research degree.

Level of Study: Doctorate, Research.
Type: Scholarship.
Value: Home fees plus a minimum annual comparable with those paid by the UK Research Councils (UK£9,000 in 2003/2004).
Length of Study: Up to three years.
Frequency: Annual.
Study Establishment: The University of Bath.
Country of Study: United Kingdom.
No. of awards offered: Approx. 20.
Application Procedure: Applicants must state that they wish to apply for the Studentship when applying for a higher degree and must contact the appropriate academic department or the graduate office.
Closing Date: August 1st.
Funding: Government.
Contributor: The University of Bath.
No. of awards given last year: 21.
Additional Information: Please contact the Graduate office for details of other awards available including Departmental Studentships, ORS awards, DFID SSS awards and United Kingdom Research Council Studentships.

UNIVERSITY OF BIRMINGHAM

Student Services & Admissions, Edgbaston, Birmingham, West Midlands, B15 2TT, England
Tel: (44) 121 414 3344
Fax: (44) 121 414 3907
www: http://www.bham.ac.uk
Tel: 333762 UOBHAM G
Contact: Ms Gillian M York, Financial Support Assistant

The University of Birmingham is a leading research institution, offering a wide range of programmes, high teaching and research standards, and excellent facilities for academic work.

Kenward Memorial Fellowship

Subjects: Engineering production.
Purpose: To provide financial assistance to those wishing to undertake research at the University of Birmingham.
Eligibility: Open to graduates in suitable disciplines.
Level of Study: Doctorate.
Type: Fellowship.
Value: Varies, but is dependent on funds available.
Length of Study: One year, possibly renewable for a further one or two years.
Frequency: Dependent on funds available.
Study Establishment: The University of Birmingham.
Country of Study: United Kingdom.
Application Procedure: Applicants must apply through recommendation by school and evidence of academic achievement.
Closing Date: Advertised with vacancies.
Funding: Private.
Contributor: Friends of the late Sir Harold Leslie Kenward.
No. of awards given last year: One.
Additional Information: The holder of the fellowship, as well as undertaking research, will undertake a limited amount of teaching in the school, not exceeding two hours each week.

Neville Chamberlain Scholarship

Subjects: Humanities subjects. Preference will be given to studies focusing on modern political, social and economic history, especially concerning Great Britain and its nineteenth-century sphere of influence.
Purpose: To provide financial assistance to students wishing to study for a higher degree.
Eligibility: Open to non United Kingdom students with a good Honours Degree who have been offered and have accepted admission to study for a higher degree in a humanities subject. Proficiency in English is essential.
Level of Study: Postgraduate.
Type: Scholarship.
Value: A supplement to student's resources should these be inadequate for taking the degree. An award may be given towards both

tuition fees and maintenance but normally should not exceed UK£7,000 per year.
Length of Study: One year, renewable as funding allows.
Study Establishment: The University of Birmingham.
Country of Study: United Kingdom.
No. of awards offered: One, depending on funds available.
Application Procedure: Applicants must be nominated by the school at which they wish to attend.
Closing Date: Mid June.
Funding: Private.
Contributor: The family of Neville Chamberlain.
No. of awards given last year: Two.
No. of applicants last year: Eight.

UNIVERSITY OF BRISTOL

Student Finance Office, Students Union, Queen's Road, Bristol, BS8 1LN, England
Tel: (44) 117 954 5785
Fax: (44) 117 954 5709
Email: std-fin@bris.ac.uk
www: http://www.bristol.ac.uk/Depts/StdFin
Contact: Ms Judith Tyler, Student Finance Officer

The University of Bristol is committed to providing high quality teaching and research in all its designated fields.

University of Bristol Postgraduate Scholarships
Subjects: Any research topic which is covered in the work of the department within the University.
Purpose: To recruit high quality research students.
Eligibility: Open to new research students with normally at least an Upper Second Class (Honours) Degree or equivalent and full-time or part-time students who are not in full-time employment. All scholars must be registered and in attendance for a research degree at the University.
Level of Study: Postgraduate.
Type: Scholarship.
Value: UK£5,000 plus home tuition fees of UK£2,950.
Length of Study: Three years.
Frequency: Annual.
Study Establishment: The University of Bristol.
Country of Study: United Kingdom.
No. of awards offered: 30.
Application Procedure: Applicants must complete the appropriate form and submit this to the department of their field of interest.
Closing Date: Normally May 1st.
Funding: Private.
Contributor: The University of Bristol.
No. of awards given last year: 30.
Additional Information: Overseas students need to find the difference between home and overseas fees. To do this they can apply for an Overseas Research Scholarship (ORS).

For further information contact:

Postgraduate Admissions, University of Bristol, Senate House, Tyndall Avenue, Clifton, Bristol, BS8 1TH, England

UNIVERSITY OF BRITISH COLUMBIA (UBC)

Faculty of Graduate Studies, 180-6371 Crescent Road, Vancouver, BC, V6T 1Z2, Canada
Tel: (1) 604 822 4556
Fax: (1) 604 822 5802
Email: graduate.awards@ubc.ca
www: http://www.grad.ubc.ca
Contact: Ms Jiffin Arboleda, Awards Administrator

The University of British Columbia (UBC) is one of North America's major research universities. The Faculty of Graduate Studies has 6,500 students and is a national leader in interdisciplinary study and research, with 98 departments, 18 interdisciplinary research units, nine interdisciplinary graduate programmes, two graduate residential colleges and one scholarly journal.

Izaak Walton Killam Postdoctoral Fellowships
Subjects: All subjects.
Purpose: To support all areas of academic research.
Eligibility: Open to candidates who show superior ability in research and have obtained, within two academic years of the anticipated commencement date of the fellowship, a doctorate at a university other than UBC. Graduates of UBC are not normally eligible.
Level of Study: Postdoctorate.
Type: Fellowship.
Value: Canadian $40,000 per year and Canadian $4,000 travel allowance for duration of the award.
Length of Study: Two years, subject to satisfactory progress at the end of the first year.
Frequency: Annual.
Study Establishment: UBC.
Country of Study: Canada.
No. of awards offered: Eight.
Application Procedure: Applicants must submit an application form, academic transcripts and three reference letters to the appropriate department. For information and application forms, please visit the website.
Closing Date: January 2nd.
Funding: Private.
No. of awards given last year: Four.
No. of applicants last year: 200.
Additional Information: Candidates are responsible for contacting the appropriate department at the University to ensure their proposed research project is acceptable and may be undertaken under the supervision of a member of the department. Candidates can email killam@mercury.ubc.ca for further details.

Izaak Walton Killam Predoctoral Fellowships
Subjects: All subjects.
Purpose: To assist doctoral students with full-time studies and research.
Eligibility: Open to students of any nationality, discipline, age or sex. This award is given at PhD level only and is strictly based on academic merit. Students must have a first class standing in their last two years of study.
Level of Study: Doctorate.
Type: Fellowship.
Value: Canadian $22,000 per year and a Canadian $1,500 travel allowance for the duration of the award.
Frequency: Annual.
Study Establishment: UBC.
Country of Study: Canada.
No. of awards offered: Approx. 15.
Application Procedure: Top ranked students are selected from the University Graduate Fellowship competition. Application forms can be obtained from departments or the Faculty of Graduate Studies or the website. Students must submit their applications to the departments, not to Graduate Studies.
Closing Date: Each department has its own internal deadline, usually in early Autumn.
Funding: Private.
No. of awards given last year: 12.
No. of applicants last year: 200.

University of British Columbia Graduate Fellowship (UGF)
Subjects: All subjects.
Purpose: To assist graduate students with their studies and research.
Eligibility: Open to students of any nationality, discipline, age or sex. This award is strictly based on academic merit and as a result applicants must be nominated by their departments based on academic merit. Students must have a first class standing in their last two years of study.
Level of Study: Graduate.
Type: Fellowship.

Value: Canadian $16,000 per year for two year fellowships, Canadian $16,000 for one year fellowships, or Canadian $8,000 for one year partial fellowships.
Frequency: Annual.
Study Establishment: UBC.
Country of Study: Canada.
No. of awards offered: Approx. 450.
Application Procedure: Applicants must submit their applications to the UBC department by the department deadline date, not to the Faculty of Graduate Studies. UGF applications are available from the website.
Closing Date: Early Autumn.
Funding: Government.
No. of awards given last year: 460.
No. of applicants last year: Approx. 2,500.
Additional Information: Please check for internal departmental deadlines.

THE UNIVERSITY OF CALGARY

Faculty of Graduate Studies, Earth Sciences Building Room 720
2500 University Drive North West, Calgary, AB, T2N 1N4, Canada
Tel: (1) 403 220 5690
Fax: (1) 403 289 7635
Email: cbusch@ucalgary.ca
www: http://www.ucalgary.ca
Contact: Ms Connie Busch, Graduate Scholarship Officer

The University of Calgary is a place of education and scholarly inquiry. Its mission is to seek truth and disseminate knowledge and it aims to pursue this mission with integrity for the benefit of the people of Alberta, Canada and the world.

Alberta Art Foundation Graduate Scholarships in the Department of Art
Subjects: Painting, printmaking, sculpture, drawing or photography.
Purpose: To support study.
Eligibility: Open to students entering the second year of the MFA programme.
Level of Study: Postgraduate.
Type: Scholarship.
Value: Canadian $6,000.
Frequency: Annual.
Study Establishment: The University of Calgary.
Country of Study: Canada.
No. of awards offered: Three.
Application Procedure: Applicants must be nominated by the department of art.
Closing Date: February 1st.

Alberta Law Foundation Graduate Scholarship
Subjects: Natural resources, energy and environmental law.
Eligibility: Open to full-time graduates who are registered in or admissible to a programme of studies leading to a Master's degree in the Faculty of Law at the University of Calgary.
Level of Study: Postgraduate.
Type: Scholarship.
Value: Canadian $13,000 each.
Length of Study: One year, non renewable.
Frequency: Annual.
Study Establishment: The University of Calgary.
Country of Study: Canada.
No. of awards offered: Two.
Application Procedure: Applicants must complete an application form, available from the director of the graduate programme at the Faculty of Law.
Additional Information: In cases where no suitable application is received no awards will be made.

Alberta Research Council Scholarship
Subjects: Agriculture, forestry, fishery, transport, communications, energy engineering, natural sciences or home economics.

Eligibility: Open to graduate students engaged in thesis research at Master's or PhD level in the relevant fields.
Level of Study: Doctorate, Postgraduate.
Type: Scholarship.
Value: Approx. Canadian $17,300 which is equal to PGS Master's level NSERC Scholarship.
Length of Study: One year. Students may apply in open competition for a subsequent year's award.
Frequency: Annual.
Study Establishment: The University of Calgary.
Country of Study: Canada.
No. of awards offered: One.
Application Procedure: Applicants must complete an application form, available from the graduate programme directors of the departments concerned.
Closing Date: February 1st.

Canadian Natural Resources Limited Graduate Scholarship
Subjects: Engineering, earth and geological sciences, home economics or MDA.
Eligibility: Open to full-time graduate students, registered or eligible to register full-time in economics, geology and geophysics, engineering or management.
Level of Study: Postgraduate.
Type: Scholarship.
Value: Up to Canadian $10,000.
Length of Study: One year.
Frequency: Annual.
Study Establishment: The University of Calgary.
Country of Study: Canada.
No. of awards offered: One.
Application Procedure: Applicants must complete an application form, available from the graduate co-ordinators of the departments concerned of the University of Calgary.
Closing Date: February 1st.

Craigie (Peter C) Memorial Scholarship
Subjects: The humanities.
Eligibility: Open to full-time registrants from any country who are registered in and have completed one term of study in a programme of studies leading to an MA degree in a department of the Faculty of Humanities. The recipient must have an outstanding scholastic record and will have been or be involved in activities contributing to the general welfare of the university committee.
Level of Study: Postgraduate.
Type: Scholarship.
Value: Canadian $5,000.
Frequency: Every two years.
Study Establishment: The University of Calgary.
Country of Study: Canada.
No. of awards offered: One.
Application Procedure: Applicants must apply to the Faculty of Humanities in the first instance. Recommendations from the Faculty will be submitted for consideration and approval by the University Graduate Scholarship Committee.
Closing Date: February 1st.

Davies (William H) Medical Research Scholarship
Subjects: Medicine.
Eligibility: Open to qualified graduates of any recognised university who will be registered in the Faculty of Graduate Studies at the University of Calgary. Successful candidates must conduct their research programme within the Faculty of Medicine.
Level of Study: Postgraduate.
Type: Scholarship.
Value: Canadian $3,000-11,000 depending on qualifications, experience and graduate programme.
Length of Study: 4-12 months, renewable in open competition.
Study Establishment: The University of Calgary.
Country of Study: Canada.
No. of awards offered: More than one.

Application Procedure: Applicants must apply to the Assistant Dean of Medical Science in the first instance. The Graduate Scholarship Committee will make the final decision based on departmental recommendations. Awards are made on the basis of academic excellence.
Closing Date: April 1st.

Honourable N D McDermid Graduate Scholarship in Law
Subjects: Law.
Eligibility: Open to graduate students enrolled on a full-time basis in the LLM programme in the Faculty of Law at the University of Calgary.
Level of Study: Postgraduate.
Type: Scholarship.
Value: Canadian $10,000.
Frequency: Annual.
Study Establishment: The University of Calgary.
Country of Study: Canada.
No. of awards offered: Two.
Application Procedure: Applicants must complete an application form, available from the Dean's office.
Closing Date: February 1st.
Additional Information: The scholarship is not renewable. In cases where no suitable applications are received the award will not be made.

Izaak Walton Killam Memorial Scholarships
Subjects: All subjects.
Eligibility: Open to qualified graduates of any university who are admissible to a doctoral programme at the University of Calgary. Applicants must have completed at least one year of graduate study prior to taking up the award.
Level of Study: Doctorate, Postgraduate.
Type: Scholarship.
Value: Canadian $20,500. If approved, award holders may also receive up to Canadian $3,000 over the full term of appointment for special equipment and/or travel in direct connection with the PhD research.
Length of Study: One year, renewable for a further year upon presentation of evidence of satisfactory progress. Further renewal is available in open competition.
Frequency: Annual.
Study Establishment: The University of Calgary.
Country of Study: Canada.
No. of awards offered: Four-five.
Application Procedure: Applicants must complete an application form, available from the graduate scholarship secretary at the university.
Closing Date: February 1st annually.
No. of awards given last year: Four-five.

Province of Alberta Graduate Scholarships and Fellowships
Subjects: All subjects.
Eligibility: Candidates must be registered in, or admissible to, a programme leading to a Master's or doctoral degree. The award is restricted to Canadian citizens and landed immigrants.
Level of Study: Doctorate, Postgraduate.
Type: Other.
Value: The scholarship consists of Canadian $9,300 per year and the fellowship of Canadian $10,500 per year.
Length of Study: One year, renewable in open competition.
Frequency: Annual.
Study Establishment: The University of Calgary.
Country of Study: Canada.
No. of awards offered: 60-70.
Application Procedure: Applicants must complete an application form, available from the directors of graduate studies of the departments concerned.
Closing Date: February 1st.
Additional Information: Students whose awards begin in May are expected to carry out a full-time research programme during the Summer months.

Robert A Willson Doctoral Management Scholarship
Subjects: MBA.
Eligibility: Open to candidates who are registered in or admissible to a full-time programme leading to a doctoral degree in management at the University of Calgary. While academic excellence is essential, candidates should also present evidence of leadership in their academic or professional background.
Level of Study: Doctorate.
Type: Scholarship.
Value: Up to Canadian $10,000.
Length of Study: One year.
Frequency: Annual.
Study Establishment: The University of Calgary.
Country of Study: Canada.
No. of awards offered: One.
Application Procedure: Applicants must apply to the Faculty of Management.
Closing Date: May 30th.

Sheriff Willoughby King Memorial Scholarship
Subjects: Prevention of family violence and the treatment of the victims of family violence.
Eligibility: Open to candidates registered in the Faculty of Graduate Studies at the University of Calgary who are pursuing a Master of Social Work Degree. Candidates must be Canadian citizens.
Level of Study: Postgraduate.
Type: Scholarship.
Value: Canadian $5,000.
Length of Study: One year.
Frequency: Annual.
Study Establishment: The University of Calgary.
Country of Study: Canada.
No. of awards offered: One to a candidate studying in the area of treatment, and one to a candidate studying in the area of prevention.
Application Procedure: Applicants must apply to the Faculty of Social Work. Recommendations from the Faculty will be considered by the University Graduate Scholarship Committee at its annual meeting. Awards are made on the basis of academic excellence.
Closing Date: February 1st.
No. of awards given last year: One to a candidate studying in the area of treatment, and one to a candidate studying in the area of.

University of Calgary Cogeco, Inc. Graduate Scholarship
Subjects: Mass communication or information sciences.
Eligibility: Open to students admissible to or registered in an Master's programme, either thesis or course based, in communication studies programmes at the University of Calgary.
Level of Study: Postgraduate.
Type: Scholarship.
Value: Canadian $5,000.
Length of Study: One year.
Frequency: Annual.
Study Establishment: The University of Calgary.
Country of Study: Canada.
No. of awards offered: One.
Application Procedure: Applicants must apply to the MA of communications studies programme.
Closing Date: February 1st.
Additional Information: The Graduate Scholarship Committee makes the final decision based on departmental recommendations. Awards will be made on the basis of academic excellence.

University of Calgary Dean's Special Entrance Scholarship
Subjects: All subjects.
Eligibility: Open to men and women admissible to the Faculty of Graduate Studies in a programme of study leading to either the Master's or doctoral degree. Applicants must be entering a first year of graduate work after an absence from full-time study at a university for more than three years for the purpose of raising children, caring for elderly parents or other demanding family responsibilities.
Level of Study: Doctorate, Postgraduate.
Type: Scholarship.

Value: Canadian $8,000.
Length of Study: One year, non renewable.
Frequency: Annual.
Study Establishment: The University of Calgary.
Country of Study: Canada.
No. of awards offered: Four.
Application Procedure: Applicants must complete the graduate scholarship application form and submit this with a description, of up to one page in length, of the family responsibilities, to the chairperson of the Graduate Scholarship Committee.
Closing Date: February 1st.

University of Calgary Dean's Special Master's Scholarship

Subjects: All subjects.
Eligibility: Open to candidates who are or will be registered in a full-time thesis based Master's programme in a relevant discipline.
Level of Study: Postgraduate.
Type: Scholarship.
Value: Canadian $5,000.
Length of Study: One year, renewable in open competition.
Frequency: Annual.
Study Establishment: The University of Calgary.
Country of Study: Canada.
No. of awards offered: Up to five.
Application Procedure: Applicants must apply to the appropriate departments at the University of Calgary.
Closing Date: February 1st.

University of Calgary Faculty of Law Graduate Scholarship

Subjects: Natural resources, energy and environmental law.
Eligibility: Open to full-time graduate students who are registered in or admissible to a programme of studies leading to a Master's degree in the Faculty of Law.
Level of Study: Postgraduate.
Type: Scholarship.
Value: Up to Canadian $10,000.
Length of Study: One year, non renewable.
Frequency: Annual.
Study Establishment: The University of Calgary.
Country of Study: Canada.
No. of awards offered: One.
Application Procedure: Applicants must complete an application form, available from the graduate programme director at the Faculty of Law. Awards will be recommended by a committee of the Faculty of Law based upon academic excellence.
Closing Date: February 1st.
Additional Information: In cases where no suitable applications are received no awards will be made.

University of Calgary Silver Anniversary Graduate Fellowships

Subjects: All subjects.
Eligibility: Open to qualified graduates of any recognised university who are registered in or admissible to a doctoral programme at the University of Calgary. The award is restricted to Canadian residents.
Level of Study: Doctorate.
Type: Fellowship.
Value: Up to Canadian $20,000 but in no case less than Canadian $16,000.
Length of Study: One year, renewable for a further year upon presentation of evidence of satisfactory progress.
Frequency: Annual.
Study Establishment: The University of Calgary.
Country of Study: Canada.
No. of awards offered: More than two.
Application Procedure: Applicants must apply to their department.
Closing Date: February 1st.
Additional Information: Awards are granted on the basis of academic standing and demonstrated potential for advanced study and research.

UNIVERSITY OF CAMBRIDGE

University Registry, The Old Schools, Cambridge, Cambridgeshire
CB2 1TN, England
Tel: (44) 1223 332317
Fax: (44) 1223 332332
Email: mrf25@admin.cam.ac.uk
www: http://www.admin.cam.ac.uk
Contact: D M Holburn, Acting Senior Tutor

The University of Cambridge is a loose confederation of faculties, colleges and other bodies. The colleges are mainly concerned with the teaching of their undergraduate students through tutorials and supervisions and the academic support of both graduate and undergraduate students, while the University employs professors, readers, lecturers and other teaching and administrative staff who provide the formal teaching in lectures, seminars and practical classes. The University also administers the University Library.

Churchill College Research Studentships

Subjects: All subjects for which research supervision can be provided at the University.
Purpose: To assist research for candidates who intend to register for the degree of PhD.
Eligibility: Open to any person who has graduated from a university or, if not a graduate, can show evidence of exceptional qualifications for research.
Level of Study: Doctorate.
Type: Studentship.
Value: University and college fees, plus maintenance based on recommended rates.
Length of Study: Three years.
Frequency: Dependent on funds available.
Study Establishment: Churchill College, University of Cambridge.
Country of Study: United Kingdom.
No. of awards offered: Varies, depending on funds available.
Application Procedure: Applicants must complete an application form, available from the Tutor for Advanced Students.
Closing Date: February 15th.
Funding: Private.
No. of awards given last year: Two.
No. of applicants last year: 60.

For further information contact:

Churchill College, Cambridge, Cambridgeshire CB3 0DS, England
Tel: (44) 1223 336157
Fax: (44) 1223 336180
Contact: Tutor for Advanced Students

Clare Hall Foundation Fellowship

Subjects: All subjects.
Purpose: To help a promising scholar.
Eligibility: Open to persons who already hold academic posts in their own country, have not previously studied in the United Kingdom or North America and are able to demonstrate that a period of study in Cambridge would be of special benefit. There is no restriction as to gender or age, although preference may be given to applicants under the age of 40. Applicants must be from either a developing country, a centrally planned economy or a country in transition to a market economy.
Level of Study: Postdoctorate.
Type: Fellowship.
Value: Normally sufficient to cover three months' residency in Cambridge.
Length of Study: Three months, although by supplementing other funds the fellowship would possibly permit a longer stay of up to six months.
Frequency: Annual.
Study Establishment: Normally Clare Hall, but probably attached to one of the university departments.
Country of Study: United Kingdom.
No. of awards offered: One.
Application Procedure: Applicants must address applications, accompanied by a curriculum vitae, to the chairman of the Fellowship

Committee at the college, to whom three referees should write directly. One reference should be from a referee whose work is recognised in the United Kingdom.
Closing Date: Applications are accepted at any time.
No. of awards given last year: One.
No. of applicants last year: Unknown.
Additional Information: The fellowship is awarded on the grounds of academic suitability.

For further information contact:

College Secretary, Clare Hall, Herschel Road, Cambridge, Cambridgeshire CB3 9AL, England
Tel: (44) 1223 332360
Fax: (44) 1223 332333
Contact: Ms Elizabeth Ramsden

Corpus Christi College Research Scholarships
Subjects: All subjects.
Purpose: To enable the successful candidate to pursue, as a member of the College, a course of study in any subject leading to a research based higher degree, normally a PhD, at the University of Cambridge.
Eligibility: Open to all those who have been offered a place at the college by June 15th.
Level of Study: Postgraduate.
Type: Scholarship.
Value: Awards are made usually in collaboration with the other funding bodies. The amount of the awards varies but substantial contributions up to UK£9,000 towards fees or maintenance costs are made.
Length of Study: Usually three years.
Frequency: Annual.
Study Establishment: Corpus Christi College.
Country of Study: United Kingdom.
No. of awards offered: 6 or more, usually in collaboration with other funding bodies.
Application Procedure: All those eligible are considered. There is no application form.
Closing Date: June 15th.
Funding: Private.
Contributor: Dr John Taylor.

For further information contact:

Corpus Christi College, Cambridge, CB2 1RH, England
Tel: (44) 1223 338038
Fax: (44) 1223 765589
Contact: Tutor for Advanced Students

Downing College Research Fellowships
Subjects: As advertised, but generally arts and science subjects in alternate years.
Purpose: To enable promising young scholars to undertake research, undistracted by other duties, to consolidate their reputations.
Eligibility: Open to graduates who have completed or are on the point of completing a PhD. Applicants must normally be under 30 on taking up the award, or if over 30, must normally not have completed more than 12 terms of research as a registered research student.
Level of Study: Postdoctorate.
Type: Fellowship.
Value: For resident pre PhD, UK£15,129 is available and for resident post PhD UK£16,150 is available. A fellow who is single is provided with free accommodation in college.
Length of Study: Three years.
Frequency: Annual.
Country of Study: United Kingdom.
No. of awards offered: One.
Application Procedure: Applicants must complete an application form, available from the Senior Tutor, following advertisements. The application form indicates that candidates must ask referees to write to the college.
Closing Date: December 1st for the following October.
Funding: Private.
Contributor: Downing College.

No. of awards given last year: One.
No. of applicants last year: 83.

For further information contact:

Tutorial Office Manager, Downing College, Cambridge, Cambridgeshire CB2 1DQ, England
Tel: (44) 1223 334811
Fax: (44) 1223 362279
Contact: Ms Jane Perks

E D Davies Scholarship
Subjects: All subjects.
Purpose: To enable graduates to undertake a course of research in any subject area.
Eligibility: Open to graduates of any university who have been admitted to a course of research.
Level of Study: Postgraduate.
Type: Scholarship.
Value: UK£1,250 per year. The award is designed to supplement funding from other sources.
Length of Study: A maximum of three years. Candidates must re-apply annually.
Frequency: Annual.
Study Establishment: Fitzwilliam College, University of Cambridge.
Country of Study: England.
No. of awards offered: One.
Application Procedure: Applicants must complete an application form, available on request.
Closing Date: Early September.
Funding: Private.
No. of awards given last year: One.
No. of applicants last year: 15.

For further information contact:

Fitzwilliam College, Cambridge, Cambridgeshire CB3 0DG, England
Tel: (44) 1223 332035
Fax: (44) 1223 332082
Contact: Dr W Alison, Tutor for Graduate Students

Evans Fund
Subjects: All aspects of anthropology and archaeology of South East Asia, especially in relation to Borneo, the Malay Peninsula, Singapore and Thailand.
Purpose: To support research.
Eligibility: Open to graduates of any university who intend to engage in research in a suitable field.
Level of Study: Doctorate, Postdoctorate, Postgraduate.
Type: Fellowship.
Value: Up to UK£6,000 per year.
Length of Study: One or two years in the first instance, up to a maximum of three years.
Frequency: Annual.
Study Establishment: The University of Cambridge.
Country of Study: Any country.
No. of awards offered: More than one.
Application Procedure: Applicants must obtain an application form from the Secretary which must be returned together with an outline of the applicant's proposed scheme of travel and research, a curriculum vitae and the names and addresses of two referees.
Closing Date: March 7th.
Funding: Private.
Contributor: Legacy.
No. of awards given last year: Five grants.
No. of applicants last year: Eight.
Additional Information: It is expected that the successful candidate will either be based in Cambridge, or will spend a substantial period of time in Cambridge during or after their period of research.

For further information contact:

Department of Social Anthropology, University of Cambridge, Free School Lane, Cambridge, Cambridgeshire CB2 3RF, England
Tel: (44) 1223 334599

Fax: (44) 1223 335993
Email: ms127@hermes.cam.ac.uk
Contact: Secretary of the Evans Fund Advisory Committee

Fitzwilliam College Graduate Scholarship

Subjects: All subjects.
Eligibility: Open to candidates who have applied for admission to Cambridge University through the Board of Admission of Graduate Studies and subsequently satisfied the conditions of admission. Preference is given to those studying arts subjects.
Level of Study: Postgraduate.
Type: Fellowship.
Value: UK£1,250.
Length of Study: A maximum of three years. Candidates must re-apply annually.
Frequency: Annual.
Study Establishment: Fitzwilliam College, University of Cambridge.
Country of Study: United Kingdom.
No. of awards offered: Varies.
Application Procedure: Applicants must write for details.
Closing Date: Early September.
Funding: Private.
No. of awards given last year: One.
No. of applicants last year: 15.
Additional Information: Preference is given to candidates conducting research in an arts subject.

For further information contact:

Fitzwilliam College, Cambridge, Cambridgeshire CB3 0DG, England
Contact: Dr W Alison, Tutor for Graduate Students

Fitzwilliam College Hirst-Player Studentship

Subjects: Theology.
Purpose: To support students who need assistance with payment of fees and who would otherwise be unable to read for a degree in Cambridge.
Eligibility: Open to graduates of any university. The awards are only available to candidates who have applied for admission to the University through the Board of Graduate Studies and subsequently satisfied the conditions of admission made by the Board. Preference is given to those intending to take holy orders in a Christian church.
Level of Study: Postgraduate.
Type: Studentship.
Value: UK£2,000 per year. The award is designed to supplement other funds.
Length of Study: One year.
Frequency: Annual.
Study Establishment: Fitzwilliam College, University of Cambridge.
Country of Study: United Kingdom.
No. of awards offered: One.
Application Procedure: Applicants must complete the application form, available on request. Candidates should also place Fitzwilliam College as first preference on the form.
Closing Date: October 1st.
Funding: Private.
No. of awards given last year: One.

For further information contact:

Fitzwilliam College, Cambridge, Cambridgeshire CB3 0DG, England
Tel: (44) 1223 332035
Fax: (44) 1223 332082
Contact: Dr W Alison, Tutor for Graduate Students

Fitzwilliam College J R W Alexander Studentship in Law

Subjects: Law.
Eligibility: Open to graduates from a British university who will have graduated by the time they come into residence.
Level of Study: Postgraduate.
Type: Studentship.
Value: UK£350. The award is designed to supplement funding from other sources.
Length of Study: One year.

Frequency: Annual.
Study Establishment: Fitzwilliam College, the University of Cambridge.
Country of Study: United Kingdom.
No. of awards offered: One.
Application Procedure: Applicants must have applied for admission to the University through the Board of Graduate Studies and subsequently satisfied the conditions of admission made by the Board. Candidates should also place Fitzwilliam College as their first preference on their application.
Closing Date: September 25th.
Funding: Private.
No. of awards given last year: One.
No. of applicants last year: Two.

For further information contact:

Fitzwilliam College, Cambridge, Cambridgeshire CB3 0DG, England
Tel: (44) 1223 332035
Fax: (44) 1223 322082
Contact: Dr W Alison, Tutor for Graduate Students

Fitzwilliam College Leathersellers' Graduate Scholarship

Subjects: Physical or biological sciences, mathematics or engineering.
Purpose: To support students who wish to undertake research.
Eligibility: Open to Home graduates from any British university who have been admitted to a course of research in one of the appropriate faculties.
Level of Study: Postgraduate.
Type: Scholarship.
Value: UK£2,000 per year. The award is designed to supplement funding from other sources.
Length of Study: Three years, subject to an annual review.
Frequency: Annual.
Study Establishment: Fitzwilliam College, the University of Cambridge.
Country of Study: United Kingdom.
No. of awards offered: One.
Application Procedure: Applicants must complete an application form, available on request.
Closing Date: June 13th.
Funding: Commercial.
No. of awards given last year: One.
No. of applicants last year: Six.

For further information contact:

Fitzwilliam College, Cambridge, Cambridgeshire CB3 0DG, England
Tel: (44) 1223 332035
Fax: (44) 1223 332082
Contact: Dr W Alison, Tutor for Graduate Students

Fitzwilliam College Research Fellowship

Subjects: All subjects. On a triennial subject iota.
Purpose: To enable scholars to carry out a programme of new research.
Eligibility: Open to candidates who are carrying out research for a PhD at any British or Irish university, or who have recently (normally defined as less than one year before the date of application) completed their course of study for this degree.
Level of Study: Doctorate.
Type: Fellowship.
Value: Varies. Non stipendiary funding is also offered (Candidates are expected to apply for the appropriate grants for the support of their research on their own initiative).
Frequency: Annual.
Study Establishment: Fitzwilliam College, the University of Cambridge.
Country of Study: United Kingdom.
No. of awards offered: Varies.
Application Procedure: Applicants must write for details.
Closing Date: January.
No. of awards given last year: 1.
No. of applicants last year: 161.

Additional Information: Fellowships are awarded for new research only and not to enable candidates to complete their PhD dissertation.

For further information contact:

Fitzwilliam College, Cambridge, Cambridgeshire CB3 0DG, England
Tel: (44) 1223 332029
Fax: (44) 1223 332074
Email: jmw65@cam.acuk
Contact: The Master's Secretary

Fitzwilliam College Shipley Studentship

Subjects: Theology.
Purpose: To enable graduates to undertake research.
Eligibility: Open to graduates of any university. The awards are only available to candidates who have applied for admission to the University through the Board of Graduate Studies and subsequently satisfied the conditions of admission made by the Board. Candidates should also place Fitzwilliam College as their first preference in their application.
Level of Study: Postgraduate.
Type: Studentship.
Value: UK£1,250 per year. The award is designed to supplement other funds.
Length of Study: One year.
Frequency: Annual.
Study Establishment: Fitzwilliam College, the University of Cambridge.
Country of Study: United Kingdom.
No. of awards offered: One.
Application Procedure: Applicants must complete an application form, available on request.
Closing Date: October 1st.
Funding: Private.
No. of awards given last year: One.
No. of applicants last year: Five.

For further information contact:

Fitzwilliam College, Cambridge, Cambridgeshire CB3 0DG, England
Tel: (44) 1223 332035
Fax: (44) 1223 332082
Contact: Dr W Alison, Tutor for Graduate Students

Gibson Studentship

Subjects: Theology, namely New Testament studies.
Purpose: To support students who wish to undertake research.
Level of Study: Postgraduate.
Type: Scholarship.
Value: UK£1,000.
Length of Study: Maximum of three years, candidates must re-apply annually.
Frequency: Annual.
Study Establishment: Fitzwilliam College, University of Cambridge.
Country of Study: England.
No. of awards offered: One.
Application Procedure: Applicants must complete an application form available on request.
Closing Date: Early September.
Funding: Private.
Additional Information: Preference will be given to those who name Fitzwilliam College as their first choice.

For further information contact:

Fitzwilliam College, Huntingdon Road, Cambridge, CB3 0DG, England
Contact: Dr W Allison, Tutor for Graduate Students

Girton College Research Fellowships

Subjects: Arts and humanities and natural sciences.
Purpose: To provide the opportunity for graduate students to conduct research in their chosen field of study.
Eligibility: Open to qualified graduates of any university who are able to provide evidence of outstanding research abilities. There is no age limit, but fellowships will normally be awarded to candidates at an early stage of their academic careers who have recently completed their PhD or are close to completion.
Level of Study: Doctorate.
Type: Fellowship.
Value: UK£13,105-15,129 per year for predoctoral Fellows and UK£14,117-16,150 per year for postdoctoral Fellows for over three years. The stipend is reviewed annually.
Length of Study: Up to three years.
Frequency: Annual.
Study Establishment: Girton College, the University of Cambridge.
Country of Study: United Kingdom.
No. of awards offered: Two-four.
Application Procedure: Applicants must submit a completed application form, which is available from the Mistress' secretary from around July or August each year for Science subjects & November December for Arts.
Closing Date: Usually the end of September to the beginning of the first week of October & beginning of January for arts.
Funding: Private.
Contributor: College endowment.
No. of awards given last year: 3.
No. of applicants last year: 300.
Additional Information: The arts and science competitions will be run in different terms.

For further information contact:

Girton College, Cambridge, Cambridgeshire CB3 0JG, England
Tel: (44) 1223 338951
Fax: (44) 1223 338896
Email: ic208@cam.ac.uk
www: http://www.cl.cam.ac.uk
Contact: Mistress' Secretary

Gonville and Caius College Gonville Bursary

Subjects: All subjects offered by the University.
Purpose: To help outstanding students from outside the EU to meet the costs of degree courses at the University of Cambridge.
Eligibility: Open to candidates who have been accepted by the College through its normal admissions procedures, and who are classified as overseas students for fees purposes. A statement of financial circumstances is required.
Level of Study: Doctorate, Postgraduate.
Type: Bursary.
Value: Reimbursement of college fees.
Length of Study: Up to three years, with a possibility of renewal, dependent on satisfactory progress.
Frequency: Annual.
Study Establishment: Gonville and Caius College, the University of Cambridge.
Country of Study: United Kingdom.
No. of awards offered: Up to six.
Application Procedure: Applicants must contact the Admissions Tutor for further information. There are no application forms.
Closing Date: Deadlines are the same as for the University's courses.

For further information contact:

Gonville & Caius College, Trinity Street, Cambridge, Cambridgeshire CB2 1TA, England
Tel: (44) 1223 332447
Fax: (44) 1223 332456
Email: admissions@cai.cam.ac.uk
www: http://www.cai.cam.ac.uk
Contact: Admissions Tutor

Gonville and Caius College W M Tapp Studentship in Law

Subjects: Law.
Purpose: To encourage the study of law.
Eligibility: Open to candidates who are not already members of the College, but who propose to register as graduate students at the University of Cambridge. Candidates must be under 30 years of age as of October 1st of the studentship year and be graduates or expect to be graduates no later than August of the same year. Preference is

given to applicants nominating Gonville and Caius College as their first choice when applying under the Cambridge Intercollegiate Graduate Application Scheme.

Level of Study: Doctorate, Postgraduate.
Type: Studentship.
Value: A stipend similar to that of a state studentship for research, plus fees and certain allowances, a dependent allowance, an allowance for a period of approved postgraduate experience, a travelling contribution for foreign students and a research allowance for research students.
Length of Study: One year, renewable for up to a maximum of three years.
Frequency: Annual.
Study Establishment: Gonville and Caius College, the University of Cambridge.
Country of Study: United Kingdom.
No. of awards offered: Approx. six.
Application Procedure: Applicants must complete an application form, available from the Admissions Tutor.
Closing Date: January 15th.

For further information contact:

Gonville & Caius College, Cambridge, Cambridgeshire CB2 1TA, England
Tel: (44) 1223 332447
Fax: (44) 1223 332456
Email: admissions@cai.cam.ac.uk
www: http://www.cai.cam.ac.uk
Contact: Admissions Tutor

Isaac Newton Studentship

Subjects: Astronomy and astronomical physics especially gravitational astronomy both theoretical and observational, including the development of instrumentation and work on any branch of physical optics that has a direct bearing on astronomy or astronomical techniques.
Purpose: To further advanced study and research.
Eligibility: Open to graduates of any university who should normally be under 26 years of age on January 1st prior to beginning tenure.
Level of Study: Postgraduate.
Type: Studentship.
Value: Approx. UK£9,200. Married students will receive an allowance under PPARC conditions. The electors may also award grants for fees, books or other expenses incurred by the student in the course of study or research.
Length of Study: Up to three years.
Frequency: Annual.
Study Establishment: The University of Cambridge.
Country of Study: United Kingdom.
No. of awards offered: More than one.
Application Procedure: Applicants must send applications to the university registry together with evidence of age and qualifications. Applicants should request that three referees send letters of recommendation by the deadline. It is recommended that an account of any work bearing on astronomy or astrophysics, and copies of the papers published on these subjects should be included, plus a clear statement of the course of study and/or research proposed for the tenure of the studentship.
Closing Date: February 12th.
No. of awards given last year: Two.
No. of applicants last year: Eight.

For further information contact:

Registrar, University Secretariat, The Old Schools, Cambridge, Cambridgeshire CB2 1TN, England

Magdalene College Leslie Wilson Research Scholarships

Subjects: All subjects offered by the University.
Purpose: To assist study for a doctorate degree.
Eligibility: Open to graduates from the United Kingdom and overseas who will be studying at Cambridge for a PhD degree. Consideration is normally restricted to those who have obtained, or who have a strong prospect of obtaining, a First Class (Honours) Bachelor's Degree.

Preference is given to those nominating Magdalene College as their first choice.

Level of Study: Doctorate.
Type: Scholarship.
Value: A maximum of approx. UK£13,854 for a Scholar who has no other sources of finance including a maintenance grant of UK£9,000, university fees of UK£2,940 and college fees of UK£1,914. Rented accommodation in or near Magdalene College will be made available during the first year of residence for unmarried Scholars. Married Scholars will be offered rented accommodation near to the college.
Length of Study: Up to three years.
Frequency: Annual.
Study Establishment: Magdalene College, the University of Cambridge.
Country of Study: United Kingdom.
No. of awards offered: One.
Application Procedure: Applicants must obtain a CIGAS form from the Board of Graduate Studies. United Kingdom candidates are expected to apply, if eligible, for State or Research Council Studentships. Overseas candidates are expected to apply for United Kingdom government support as well as Overseas Student Bursaries awarded by the University of Cambridge and administered by the Board of Graduate Studies. In addition, all candidates should obtain a Leslie Wilson Research Scholarship form from the address below.
Closing Date: May 1st.

For further information contact:

Magdalene College, University of Cambridge, Cambridge, Cambridgeshire CB3 0AG, England
Tel: (44) 1223 33 2135
Fax: (44) 1223 46 2589
Contact: Admissions Tutor for Graduates

Oliver Gatty Studentship

Subjects: Biophysical and colloid science.
Purpose: To assist full-time study and training for research.
Eligibility: Open to graduates and postdoctoral students of all universities, with preference being given to graduates of universities from outside the United Kingdom.
Level of Study: Postgraduate.
Type: Studentship.
Value: The studentship is intended to cover full costs and its value will be determined by the electors after taking into account the student's circumstances and funds available.
Length of Study: Up to three years subject to satisfactory assessment of the department's graduate committee at the end of the first year.
Frequency: Usually every three years.
Study Establishment: The University of Cambridge.
Country of Study: United Kingdom.
No. of awards offered: One.
Application Procedure: Applicants must contact Hugo Hocknell for details.
Closing Date: Usually the end of March.
Funding: Private.
No. of awards given last year: One.
No. of applicants last year: Eight.

Pembroke College Graduate Awards

Subjects: All subjects offered by the University.
Eligibility: Open to candidates of any nationality who are accepted by Pembroke College and who intend to register for a PhD degree at the University of Cambridge.
Level of Study: Doctorate, Postgraduate.
Type: Studentship.
Value: Full or Partial support.
Length of Study: Three years.
Frequency: Annual.
Study Establishment: Pembroke College, the University of Cambridge.
Country of Study: United Kingdom.

No. of awards offered: Several.
Application Procedure: All eligible applicants will be sent a form when they are offered a place. Candidates must make Pembroke their first choice college.
Closing Date: Please contact the college.
Funding: Private.
Contributor: Pembroke College.
No. of awards given last year: 12 (Partial funding).
No. of applicants last year: 25.

For further information contact:

Pembroke College, Cambridge, Cambridgeshire CB2 1RZ, England
Tel: (44) 1223 338115
Fax: (44) 1223 338163
Contact: Graduate Admissions Secretary

Queen's College Research Fellowships

Subjects: All subjects. For candidates who are not members of the college the subject areas are restricted and are specified in the advertising for the competition each year (July/August).
Purpose: To provide the opportunity for postdoctoral research in various fields of study.
Eligibility: Open to graduates of any university who should normally not have completed more than four years of research including time on research degrees.
Level of Study: Postdoctorate.
Type: Fellowship.
Value: Specified in the advertising for the competition each year.
Length of Study: Three years.
Frequency: Annual.
Study Establishment: Queen's College, the University of Cambridge.
Country of Study: United Kingdom.
No. of awards offered: Two.
Application Procedure: Applicants must complete and submit an application form and research proposal. Written work will be requested from short-listed candidates.
Closing Date: Usually October 8th.
Funding: Private.
Contributor: Endowed funds.
No. of awards given last year: Two.
No. of applicants last year: 60.
Additional Information: Interviews take place in November of the academic year prior to that in which the fellowship will commence.

For further information contact:

Queen's College, Cambridge, Cambridgeshire CB3 9ET, England
Tel: (44) 1223 335601
Fax: (44) 1223 335522
www: http://www.quns.cam.ac.uk
Contact: Clerk to the Tutors

St John's College Benefactors' Scholarships for Research

Subjects: All subjects offered by the University.
Purpose: To fund candidates for PhD and M.Phil degrees.
Eligibility: Open to candidates of any nationality with a First Class (Honours) Degree or equivalent.
Level of Study: Postgraduate.
Type: Scholarship.
Value: UK£9,000, plus approved college and university fees, a scholar's Book Grant of up to UK£100 and other expenses.
Length of Study: Up to three years.
Frequency: Annual.
Study Establishment: St John's College, the University of Cambridge.
Country of Study: United Kingdom.
No. of awards offered: Three.
Application Procedure: Applicants must see the Cambridge University graduate studies prospectus for particulars.
Closing Date: May 1st.
No. of awards given last year: Three.

For further information contact:

St John's College, Cambridge, Cambridgeshire CB2 1TP, England
Tel: (44) 1223 338612
Fax: (44) 1223 766419
Email: graduate_admissions@joh.cam.ac.uk

William Wyse Studentship in Social Anthropology

Subjects: Social anthropology.
Purpose: To support study.
Eligibility: Open to all students who wish to study for the degree of PhD.
Level of Study: Doctorate.
Type: Studentship.
Value: Varies.
Length of Study: Three years.
Frequency: Annual.
Study Establishment: The University of Cambridge.
Country of Study: United Kingdom.
Application Procedure: Applicants should contact the admissions secretary for details.
Closing Date: Please write for details.
No. of awards given last year: Five grants.
No. of applicants last year: Eight.

For further information contact:

Department of Social Anthropology, Free School Lane, Cambridge, Cambridgeshire CB2 3RF, England
Tel: (44) 1223 334599
Fax: (44) 1223 335993
Contact: Admissions Secretary

UNIVERSITY OF CAMBRIDGE

Newnham College, Sidgwick Avenue, Cambridge, Cambridgeshire
CB3 9DF, England
Tel: (44) 1223 335791
Fax: (44) 1223 357898
Email: graduate.tutor@newn.cam.ac.uk
www: http://www.cam.ac.uk
Contact: Graduate Tutor

Newnham College is for women studying at the University of Cambridge, at both undergraduate and graduate level.

Mary Ann Ewart

Subjects: Open to all subjects.
Purpose: To support an M.Phil or PhD Student.
Level of Study: Doctorate, Graduate.
Type: Scholarship.
Value: Circa £6,500 per annum.
Length of Study: Between one and three years.
Frequency: Dependent on funds available.
Study Establishment: Newnham College, Cambridge.
No. of awards offered: Varies from year to year, but usually at least two.
Application Procedure: Apply to the Graduate Tutor in the first instance.
Closing Date: 1st April.
Funding: Private.

Pelham Roberts

Subjects: Archaelogy, natural sciences or medicine.
Purpose: To support an M.Phil or PhD Student.
Level of Study: Graduate.
Type: Scholarship.
Value: Circa £5000 per annum.
Length of Study: Between one and three years.
Frequency: Dependent on funds available.
Study Establishment: Newnham College, Cambridge.
Country of Study: United Kingdom.
No. of awards offered: One.
Funding: Private.

Principal's Studentship
Subjects: Mathematics or Humanities.
Purpose: To support an M.Phil or PhD Student.
Level of Study: Graduate.
Type: Scholarship.
Value: Circa £5000.
Length of Study: Between one and three years.
Frequency: Dependent on funds available.
Study Establishment: Newnham College, Cambridge.
No. of awards offered: One.
Funding: Private.

Royalton. KISCH
Subjects: History of religion, anthropology of religion and sociology of religion.
Purpose: To support an M.Phil or PhD student.
Level of Study: Graduate.
Type: Scholarship.
Frequency: Dependent on funds available.
Study Establishment: Newnham College, Cambridge.
Country of Study: United Kingdom.
No. of awards offered: One.
Funding: Private.

Wood Whistler Prize and Medal. A prize of £2,500 for a student in their first or second year of graduate studies in English
Subjects: English Literature.
Purpose: To reward an outstanding student.
Level of Study: Graduate.
Type: Prize.
Value: Circa £2,500.
Frequency: Annual.
Study Establishment: Newnham College, Cambridge.
No. of awards offered: One.
Funding: Private.

UNIVERSITY OF CAMBRIDGE, JUDGE INSTITUTE OF MANAGEMENT

Trumpington Street, Cambridge, Cambridgeshire, CB2 1AG, England
Tel: (44) 1223 339700
Fax: (44) 1223 339701
Email: enquiries@jims.cam.ac.uk
www: http://www.jims.cam.ac.uk
Contact: Ms Louise Freckleton

The Judge Institute of Management is the University of Cambridge's business school. Founded in 1990 it offers a portfolio of management programmes, including the Cambridge MBA. Accredited by AMBA and EQUIS, the business school now hosts one of the largest concentrations of interdisciplinary business and management research activity in Europe.

Margaret Thatcher Scholarships
Subjects: MBA.
Purpose: To provide an opportunity for the business leaders of tomorrow to gain a thorough business education in an international environment at a world class university and to ensure that lessons learned in Cambridge and more broadly in Western Europe can be widely disseminated to future business leaders in Russia.
Eligibility: Open to Russian candidates with at least three years of work experience in Russia or elsewhere in the former Soviet Union. Applicants must have strong support from their current employer and have evidence of a career plan showing how they would use the skills and knowledge gained on the MBA course to develop their career within Russia. Applicants for the two year integrated programme must have a work placement set up within a work organisation.
Level of Study: MBA.
Type: Scholarship.
Value: Varies from UK£3,000-30,000.
Length of Study: One year.

Frequency: Annual.
Study Establishment: Judge Institute of Management, University of Cambridge.
Country of Study: England.
No. of awards offered: Up to five.
Application Procedure: Applicants must complete and submit an application form, together with a covering letter indicating that they would like to apply for a Margaret Thatcher Scholarship, to the Judge Institute of Management.
Closing Date: The end of March.
Funding: Private.
No. of awards given last year: Five.
No. of applicants last year: 15.

N Boustany MBA Scholarship
Subjects: MBA.
Eligibility: Open to Lebanese nationals who have obtained a good Honours Degree from a recognised university and have at least two years of full-time, real world experience. Candidates will need to demonstrate a high intellectual potential, practical common sense and the ability to put ideas into action. They also need to be highly motivated with a strong desire to learn. Applicants will be asked to take the Test of English as a Foreign Language (TOEFL) where applicable and the Graduate Management Admission Test (GMAT).
Level of Study: Graduate.
Type: Bursary.
Value: US$40,000 including full tuition and travelling expenses.
Length of Study: 2 years.
Frequency: Every two years.
No. of awards offered: One.
Application Procedure: Applicants must contact or email their curriculum vitae to Mr M Tamar.
Closing Date: May 31st.

For further information contact:

1 avenue des Citronniers, Monte Carlo, Monaco
Fax: (377) 77 93 15 05 56
Email: metropolegroup@monaco.mc
www: http://www.jims.cam.ac.uk
Contact: Mr M Tamar

Sainsbury Bursaries
Subjects: MBA.
Purpose: To support students engaged in charitable, voluntary or public sector work in areas such as housing, health and education, local economic development and social services, as it is difficult for such candidates to secure sponsorship from their employers.
Eligibility: Preference will be given to applicants from the United Kingdom but exceptional candidates working for international aid agencies based outside the United Kingdom will be given consideration. It is expected that applicants will contribute to the sectors in the United Kingdom after completion of the MBA. Candidates must have completed three years of work experience within the charitable, voluntary or public sector prior to submitting their application. The applicants for the two year integrated course must have a placement set up within an organisation in the charitable, voluntary or public sector. Candidates must also show evidence of a career plan showing how they would use skills and knowledge gained on the MBA course to develop their career within the charitable, voluntary or public sector.
Level of Study: MBA.
Type: Bursary.
Value: Ranges from UK£10,000-20,000 at the discretion of The Sainsbury Bursary Scheme Committee. The Committee is also willing to consider higher awards of up to UK£25,000 for candidates who show exceptional ability and potential.
Length of Study: One year.
Frequency: Annual.
Study Establishment: Judge Institute of Management, University of Cambridge.
Country of Study: England.
No. of awards offered: Four-seven.
Application Procedure: Applicants must complete and submit an application form for the MBA along with a covering letter indicating that

they would also like to apply for a Sainsbury Bursary, to the Judge Institute.
Closing Date: The end of March.
Funding: Private.
Contributor: The Monument Trust.
No. of awards given last year: Two.
No. of applicants last year: Five.
Additional Information: The Monument Trust is one of the Sainsbury Family Charitable Trusts.

UNIVERSITY OF CANTERBURY

Private Bag 4800, Christchurch, New Zealand
Tel: (64) 3 364 2808
Fax: (64) 3 364 2325
Email: hr@regy.canterbury.ac.nz
www: http://www.canterbury.ac.nz
Contact: Ms Hazel Reeves, Human Resources Administrator

The University of Canterbury offers a variety of subjects in a few flexible degree structures; first and postgraduate degrees in arts, commerce, education, engineering, fine arts, forestry, law, music and science. At Canterbury, research and teaching are closely related and while this feature shapes all courses it is very marked at postgraduate level.

University of Canterbury and Creative New Zealand Ursula Bethell Residency in Creative Writing
Subjects: Creative writing, fiction, poetry, scriptwriting and literary non-fiction.
Purpose: To foster New Zealand writing by providing a full-time opportunity for a writer to work in an academic environment.
Eligibility: Open to authors of proven merit who are normally resident in New Zealand and to New Zealand nationals temporarily resident overseas.
Level of Study: Unrestricted.
Type: Fellowship.
Value: Emolument at the rate of New Zealand $46,500.
Length of Study: Up to one year.
Frequency: Dependent on funds available.
Study Establishment: The University of Canterbury.
Country of Study: New Zealand.
No. of awards offered: One.
Application Procedure: Applicants must submit details of published writings and work in progress, and include a proposal of work to be undertaken during the appointment only.
Closing Date: Usually October 31st.
Funding: Government.
No. of awards given last year: 30 since 1979.
Additional Information: The appointment will be made on the basis of published or performed writing of high quality. Conditions of appointment should be obtained from the Human Resources Department before applying, available in August from: hr@regy.canterbury.ac.nz.

UNIVERSITY OF DELAWARE

Department of History, Newark, DE 19716, United States of America
Tel: (1) 302 831 8226
Fax: (1) 302 831 1538
Email: pato@udel.edu
www: http://www.udel.edu
Contact: Ms Patricia H Orendorf, Administrative Assistant

The University of Delaware maintains more than 30 research centres which provide students with the opportunity to use state of the art equipment and computing facilities while conducting research at the University. A high proportion of full-time graduates receive financial assistance through fellowships, tuition scholarships and assistantships.

E Lyman Stewart Fellowship
Subjects: History.
Purpose: To provide a programme of graduate study leading to an MA or PhD degree for students who plan careers as museum

professionals, historical agency administrators, or seek careers in college teaching and public history.
Eligibility: Open to nationals of any country.
Level of Study: Doctorate, Graduate, Postgraduate, Predoctorate.
Type: Fellowship.
Value: US$11,600 plus tuition.
Frequency: Annual.
Study Establishment: The University of Delaware.
Country of Study: United States of America.
No. of awards offered: Four-six.
Application Procedure: Applicants must submit an application form, transcripts, Graduate Record Examination (GRE) scores, Test of English as a Foreign Language (TOEFL) scores where applicable, plus three letters of recommendation and a writing sample.
Closing Date: January 15th.
Funding: Private.
No. of awards given last year: Seven.
No. of applicants last year: 22.
Additional Information: This is a residential programme.

Fellowships in the University of Delaware Hagley Program
Subjects: The history of industrialisation, broadly defined to include business, economics, labour and social history and the history of science and technology.
Purpose: To provide a programme of graduate study leading to an MA or PhD degree for students who seek careers in college teaching and public history.
Eligibility: Open to graduates of any nationality seeking degrees in American or European history or the history of science and technology.
Level of Study: Doctorate, Graduate, Postgraduate, Predoctorate.
Type: Fellowship.
Value: US$11,600 for Master's candidates and doctoral candidates. All tuition fees for university courses are paid.
Length of Study: One year, renewable once for those seeking a terminal MA and up to three times for those seeking the doctorate.
Frequency: Annual.
Study Establishment: The University of Delaware.
Country of Study: United States of America.
No. of awards offered: Approx. two-three.
Application Procedure: Fellows are selected upon Graduate Record Examination scores, recommendations, undergraduate grade index, work experience and personal interviews.
Closing Date: January 15th.
Funding: Government, Private.
No. of awards given last year: Three.
No. of applicants last year: 18.
Additional Information: This is a residential programme.

UNIVERSITY OF DUNDEE

Nethergate, Dundee, DD1 4HN, Scotland
Tel: (44) 1382 345028
Fax: (44) 1382 345343
Email: j.e.nicholson@dundee.ac.uk
www: http://www.dundee.ac.uk
Contact: Postgraduate Office

The University of Dundee believes emphatically in the traditional mission of universities, that being the pursuit of excellence in the twin activities of learning and discovery. The University is well placed to fulfil these objectives as it has an established record in teaching and research.

University of Dundee Research Awards
Subjects: Medicine, dentistry, science, engineering, law, arts, social sciences, environmental studies, town planning, architecture, management and consumer studies, nursing, fine art, television and imaging.
Purpose: To assist full-time research leading to a PhD.
Eligibility: Open to holders of a First or Upper Second Class (Honours) Degree or equivalent.

Level of Study: Doctorate, Postgraduate.
Type: Studentship.
Value: UK£7,500 plus tuition fees at the home rate.
Length of Study: One year, renewable annually for up to a maximum of two additional years.
Frequency: Dependent on funds available.
Study Establishment: The University of Dundee.
Country of Study: United Kingdom.
No. of awards offered: Dependent on availability of funds.
Application Procedure: Applicants must contact the relevant faculty office for information on the availability of awards.
Closing Date: March 2nd.
No. of awards given last year: Seven.
No. of applicants last year: 70.

UNIVERSITY OF EAST ANGLIA (UEA)

Norwich, Norfolk, NR4 7TJ, England
Tel: (44) 1603 592810
Fax: (44) 1603 507728
Email: v.striker@uea.ac.uk
www: http://www.uea.ac.uk/eas/fellowships/index.shtml
Contact: Ms Val Striker, Dean's Secretary

The University of East Anglia (UEA) is organised into 17 schools of study encompassing the sciences, humanities and social sciences, and professional studies. These are supported by central service and administration departments.

Charles Pick Fellowship

Subjects: Fictional and non fictional literature.
Purpose: To assist and support the work of a new and as yet, un-published writer of fiction or non fictional prose and to give promising writers time to devote to the development of their talent.
Eligibility: Open to all ages and nationalities who are writers of fiction or non fictional prose in English. Applicants must not yet have had a book published but all applicants must provide a reference from either an editor, agent or accredited teacher of creative writing to be sent direct to the Charles Pick Fellowship.
Level of Study: Professional development.
Type: One fellowship.
Value: UK£10,000 plus free accommodation provided on the university campus.
Length of Study: Six months starting August 1st.
Frequency: Annual.
Study Establishment: UEA.
Country of Study: United Kingdom.
No. of awards offered: One.
Application Procedure: Applicants must submit a completed application form together with a typescript of an original unpublished piece of fiction or non fiction. This should not be more than 2,500 words written in English. E-mailed and faxed applications and any application form sent without a reference will not be accepted. Late references' will also not be accepted. There will be no interviews but candidates will be judged on the quality and promise of their writing, the project they describe and their reference. They will also be expected to provide reasonable proof of writing progress on occasion during their residency.
Closing Date: January 31st.
Funding: Private.
No. of awards given last year: One.
No. of applicants last year: 81.
Additional Information: The Charles Pick Fellowship is dedicated to the memory of the distinguished publisher and literary agent, Charles Pick, whose career began in 1933 and continued until shortly before his death in January 2000. He encouraged young writers at the start of their careers with introductions to other writers as well as practical and financial help. The new fellowship seeks to continue this spirit of encouragement by giving support to the work of a new and as yet, unpublished writer of fictional or non fictional prose. Please note that for the purposes of this fellowship, non fiction prose includes, for example, biography, memoir and travel writing but not critical or historical monographs based on academic research.

David T K Wong Fellowship

Subjects: Writing.
Purpose: To support promising writers in producing a work of fiction set in the Far East.
Eligibility: Open to all writers whose projects deal with some aspect of life in the Far East.
Level of Study: Professional development.
Type: Fellowship.
Value: UK£25,000.
Length of Study: One year.
Frequency: Annual.
Study Establishment: UEA.
Country of Study: United Kingdom.
No. of awards offered: One.
Application Procedure: Applicants must obtain further information and application forms by writing to the School of English and American Studies at UEA.
Closing Date: October 31st.
Funding: Private.
Contributor: David T K Wong.
No. of awards given last year: One.
No. of applicants last year: 79.
Additional Information: The Far East is defined as China, Hong Kong, Macau, Taiwan, Japan, Korea, Mongolia, Laos, Cambodia, Vietnam, Thailand, Burma, Philippines, Singapore, Malaysia, Indonesia and Brunei.

UEA Writing Fellowship

Subjects: Creative writing.
Purpose: To enable a creative writer to work in a university atmosphere and with a regional arts board on a reciprocal basis. To teach a unit of creative writing at university undergraduate level.
Eligibility: Open to practising, published writers in fiction and poetry. Applicants must be English speaking.
Level of Study: Professional development.
Type: Fellowship.
Value: UK£7,500 plus free accommodation.
Length of Study: The Spring semester of each academic year.
Frequency: Annual.
Study Establishment: UEA.
Country of Study: United Kingdom.
No. of awards offered: One.
Application Procedure: Applicants must submit a completed application form, curriculum vitae and two examples of recent work.
Closing Date: October. Exact dates can be verified by telephoning the organisation or watching for advertisements in the press.
Funding: Government.
Contributor: UEA and Arts Council England East.
No. of awards given last year: One.
No. of applicants last year: 17.
Additional Information: Interviews take place in the United Kingdom.

THE UNIVERSITY OF EDINBURGH

Old College, South Bridge, Edinburgh, EH8 9YL, Scotland
Contact: Robert Lawrie Schorships Financial Aid Office

American Friends of the University of Edinburgh Scholarship

Subjects: All subjects.
Purpose: To foster good relations with students from United States alumni contributions and to enhance graduate study opportunities for deserving students.
Eligibility: Applicants must hold a United States passport.
Level of Study: Postgraduate.
Type: Scholarship.
Value: One at US$5,000, and two at US$1,000.
Frequency: Annual.
Country of Study: Scotland.
No. of awards offered: Three.
Application Procedure: Applicants must complete an application form, available from the Scholarship & Financial Aid Office.
Closing Date: 1st April.

Contributor: The University of Edinburgh USA Development Trust Inc.
No. of awards given last year: One.
Additional Information: www.scholarships.ed.ac.uk.

UNIVERSITY OF EDINBURGH COLLEGE OF SCIENCE AND ENGINEERING

Weir Building, The King's Buildings, Edinburgh, EH9 3JY, Scotland
Tel: (44) 131 650 5765
Fax: (44) 131 650 5738
Email: sciengmail@ed.ac.uk
www: http://www.scieng.ed.ac.uk
Contact: Administrator

University of Edinburgh College of Science and Engineering Scholarship
Subjects: Science or engineering.
Purpose: To provide funds for well qualified candidates to pursue full-time research leading to a PhD.
Eligibility: Open to individuals of any nationality with a First or Upper Second Class (Honours) Degree or its equivalent. Candidates must have applied or have been accepted to study for a research degree.
Level of Study: Doctorate.
Type: Scholarship.
Value: Please consult the organisation.
Frequency: Dependent on funds available.
Study Establishment: The University of Edinburgh.
Country of Study: United Kingdom.
No. of awards offered: Varies from year to year.
Application Procedure: Applicants must make an application for admission as a postgraduate student and indicate a wish to be considered for a scholarship.
Closing Date: Varies according to the school.
Additional Information: Further information is available from the school in which the candidate intends to study.

UNIVERSITY OF ESSEX

Postgraduate Admissions Office, University of Essex, Wivenhoe Park, Colchester, Essex, C04 3SQ, England
Tel: (44) (0) 1206 872719
Fax: (44) 1206 872808
Email: pgadmit@essex.ac.uk
www: www.essex.ac.uk
Contact: The Bursar

The University of Essex is one of the UK's leading academic institutions, ranked sixth nationally for teaching and tenth for research. It boasts two of the exceptional 6* rated research departments in Government and Sociology and 9990 of its research active staff are in departments awarded 4, 5, 5* or 6*.

Computer Science EPSRC Studentships EU Postgraduates
Subjects: Department of Computer Science.
Purpose: Support for Home and Eu Postgraduates.
Eligibility: Home and EU.
Level of Study: Postgraduate.
Type: Bursary.
Value: For Home students it covers tuition fees and a basic maintenance allowance. For EU students it covers fees.
Frequency: Annual.
Study Establishment: University of Essex.
No. of awards offered: Limited number.
Application Procedure: Indicate your wish to be considered for this award on your application form. Please contact department for any further information.
Closing Date: July.
Funding: Government.
Contributor: EPSRC.

Computer Science Overseas Research Student (ORS) Award
Subjects: Department of Computer Science.
Purpose: Support overseas candidates.
Eligibility: Overseas students.
Level of Study: Postgraduate.
Type: Bursary.
Value: ORS Award pays the difference between home and overseas fees.
Frequency: Annual.
Study Establishment: University of Essex.
No. of awards offered: Three.
Application Procedure: The department nominates 3 overseas students for this award. Please contact department for more information.
Closing Date: January.
No. of awards given last year: 3.

Giulia Mereu Scholarship
Subjects: Department of Law.
Purpose: Support a student on the LLM International Human Rights Law.
Eligibility: LLM applicant to University of Essex.
Level of Study: Postgraduate.
Type: Scholarship.
Value: Cover fee, plus a modest allowance that enables the recipient to undertake one months internship with a human rights organisation.
Length of Study: One year.
Frequency: Annual.
Study Establishment: University of Essex.
No. of awards offered: One.
Application Procedure: Please contact department for more details.
Funding: Private.

Master Training Packages (MTP)
Subjects: Department of Electronic Systems Engineering.
Purpose: Support students on MSc Physics of Laser Communications or MSc Photonics.
Eligibility: Home and EU students.
Level of Study: Postgraduate.
Type: Bursary.
Value: For home students fees and maintenance given. For EU students fees only.
Length of Study: One year.
Frequency: Annual.
Study Establishment: University of Essex.
Application Procedure: Please see departmental website.
Closing Date: Please see department for further information.
Funding: Government.
Contributor: EPSRC.

PhD Scholarships in Art History and Theory
Subjects: Department of Art History and Theory.
Purpose: Funding for Home/EU or overseas students intending to register for a PhD in the Department of Art History and Theory at the Unversity of Essex.
Eligibility: Students applying for PhD.
Level of Study: Postgraduate.
Type: Scholarship.
Value: UK£3,000 a year plus wairer on Home/EU tuition fees. Overseas students get a reduction in fees equivalent to Home/EU fee.
Frequency: Annual.
Study Establishment: University of Essex.
No. of awards offered: 2 were available for Oct 2003 entry.
Application Procedure: Description (maximum 500 words) of proposed research project and a CV. For more information, contact department.
Closing Date: April.

PhD Studentship in Political Theory
Subjects: Department of Government.
Purpose: Support a PhD student working with professor Richard Bevamy and his colleagues within the Political Theory Group.
Eligibility: Phd candidate.

Level of Study: Postgraduate.
Type: Studentship.
Value: Fees paid at EU rate.
Length of Study: PhD.
Study Establishment: University of Essex.
No. of awards offered: One.
Application Procedure: Please see departmental website.

University of Essex Foundation Scholarships

Purpose: To assist local students undertaking a full-time master programme.
Eligibility: Local students.
Level of Study: Postgraduate.
Type: Scholarship.
Value: UK£1,500.
Length of Study: Full-time Master.
Frequency: Annual.
Study Establishment: University of Essex.
No. of awards offered: 3 bursaries to Essex graduates and 3 to applicants from the local Essex/Sussex area.
Application Procedure: Please contact the department that you wish to study in.
No. of awards given last year: Six.
Additional Information: Examples of how the University of Essex foundation scholarships are awarded. The Department of History offer foundation scholarships to Essex or Sufflu residents and to current Essex graduates.

University of Essex Scholarships

Subjects: The fund is distributed to individual centers and departments at the unversity of Essex and is allocated by them.
Purpose: To support students starting a new postgraduate degree.
Eligibility: Students who have applied for postgraduate study at the University of Essex.
Level of Study: Postgraduate.
Type: Scholarship.
Value: For 2003-04 the fund was UK£350,000. This increases annually and will amount to UK£650,000 by 2005-06.
Frequency: Annual.
Study Establishment: University of Essex.
No. of awards offered: For 2003-04 the fund was UK£350,000. This was distributed to departments and centers at the university.
Application Procedure: Details given on departmental websites.
Closing Date: Please see website.
Additional Information: Examples of how University of Essex Scholarships are awarded. The department of History offers a single scholarship of UK£3,500 or two scholarships of UK£1,750 to full-time taught MA students with a 1st or high 2.1. They also offer a single scholarship of UK£10,500 or two of UK£5,250 each to full or part-time PhD students. The Department of Literature, Film, and Theatre Studies offer UK£1,000 scholarships for MA students and PhD scholarships at UK£4,000 each.

For further information contact:

See: www.essex.ac.uk/scholarships/ for more information or contact chosen department or centre directly,

UNIVERSITY OF EXETER

The Graduate School, Northcote House, The Queen's Drive, Exeter, Devon, EX4 4QJ, England
Tel: (44) 1392 263044
Fax: (44) 1392 263313
Email: gradschool@exeter.ac.uk
www: http://www.exeter.ac.uk/gradschool
Contact: Mr Dan Cook, Administrative Officer

The University of Exeter combines a reputation of national and international excellence in research with a record of established excellence in teaching. Providing a superb environment in which to live and work, the University of Exeter is representative of the best in British university education.

Andrew Stratton Scholarship

Subjects: Engineering and science.
Eligibility: Open to postgraduate students in engineering or science.
Level of Study: Postgraduate.
Type: Scholarship.
Value: UK£1,000.
Length of Study: One year.
Frequency: Dependent on funds available.
Study Establishment: The University of Exeter.
Country of Study: United Kingdom.
Application Procedure: Applicants must consult the University.
Closing Date: Please contact the organisation.
Additional Information: Further information is available on request.

Anning-Morgan Bursary

Subjects: All subjects.
Purpose: To financially support postgraduate study.
Eligibility: Open to students residing in the Duchy of Cornwall prior to entry or during their postgraduate studies.
Level of Study: Postgraduate.
Type: Bursary.
Value: Fees only.
Length of Study: A maximum of two years.
Frequency: Every two years.
Study Establishment: The University of Exeter.
Country of Study: United Kingdom.
Application Procedure: Applicants must consult the University.
Additional Information: Further information is available on request.

Anthony Parsons Memorial Scholarship

Subjects: Arabic, Islamic or Middle East studies.
Purpose: To financially support those undertaking postgraduate study.
Eligibility: Open to students conducting research.
Level of Study: Postgraduate.
Type: Scholarship.
Value: Up to UK£3,000.
Frequency: Dependent on funds available.
Study Establishment: The University of Exeter.
Country of Study: United Kingdom.
Application Procedure: Applicants must consult the University.

British Council Awards and Scholarships for International Students

Subjects: All subjects offered by the University.
Purpose: To allow international students to pursue certain postgraduate study.
Eligibility: Open to candidates for research degrees who have obtained at least an Upper Second Class (Honours) Degree or its equivalent.
Level of Study: Postgraduate.
Type: Scholarship.
Value: Varies.
Length of Study: Varies.
Frequency: Annual.
Study Establishment: The University of Exeter.
Country of Study: United Kingdom.
No. of awards offered: Varies.
Application Procedure: Applicants must obtain details from the British Council representative in the applicant's own country.
Closing Date: Please contact the organisation.
Additional Information: Further information is available on request.

Commonwealth Scholarship Plan

Subjects: All subjects.
Purpose: To allow students to pursue postgraduate study.
Eligibility: Open to students from Commonwealth countries who do not already hold scholarships from their own country.
Level of Study: Postgraduate.
Type: Scholarship.
Value: Varies but includes payment of tuition fees.
Study Establishment: The University of Exeter.
Country of Study: United Kingdom.

Application Procedure: Applicants must apply well in advance in their country of permanent residence, through the Commonwealth Scholarship Agency.
Closing Date: Please contact the organisation.
Additional Information: Further information is available on request.

Cornwall Heritage Trust Scholarship
Subjects: All subjects centring on Cornwall's heritage.
Eligibility: Open to students working towards a Master's degree on a dissertation focussing on an aspect of Cornwall's Heritage.
Level of Study: Postgraduate.
Type: Scholarship.
Value: UK£1,000.
Length of Study: One year.
Frequency: Annual.
Study Establishment: The University of Exeter.
Country of Study: United Kingdom.
No. of awards offered: One.
Application Procedure: Applicants must inform the Graduate School when applying for a place on a programme.
Closing Date: 27th August, 2004.
No. of awards given last year: 3.
No. of applicants last year: 3.
Additional Information: Further information is available on request.

University of Exeter Graduate Research Assistantships
Subjects: All subjects.
Purpose: To assist students by offering them a top quality scheme that offers excellent career development opportunities.
Eligibility: Open to M.Phil and PhD students.
Level of Study: Doctorate, Research.
Type: Other.
Value: Fees and maintenance at research council rates. This is currently set at UK£8,000 per year.
Length of Study: Four years.
Study Establishment: The University of Exeter.
Country of Study: United Kingdom.
Application Procedure: Applicants must visit the website of the school in which they wish to study.
Additional Information: Further details of this scheme are available from the website. Graduate Research Assistants are required to undertake two days a week of research for a research team in addition to their own research.

University of Exeter Graduate Teaching Assistantships (GTA)
Subjects: All subjects.
Purpose: To assist students by offering them a top quality scheme that offers excellent career development opportunities.
Eligibility: Open to MPhil and PhD students.
Level of Study: Doctorate, Research.
Type: Other.
Value: Fees and maintenance at research council rates, which are currently UK£8,000 per year.
Length of Study: Up to four years.
Study Establishment: The University of Exeter.
Country of Study: United Kingdom.
Application Procedure: Applicants must visit the website of the school in which they wish to study.
Closing Date: Please contact the organisation.
Additional Information: Further details of this scheme are available from the Graduate School website. GTAs are given full training with SEDA accreditation and are expected to teach for up to 150 hours per year.

University of Exeter Overseas Research Students Award Scheme
Subjects: All subjects.
Purpose: To assist international students of outstanding merit and research potential undertaking research degrees.
Eligibility: International students holding offers of study for research degrees.

Level of Study: Doctorate, Research.
Type: Award.
Value: The difference between the tuition fees for a home or European Union postgraduate student and that for an international postgraduate student.
Length of Study: Three years.
Frequency: Annual.
Study Establishment: The University of Exeter.
Country of Study: United Kingdom.
No. of awards offered: Varies.
Application Procedure: Application forms and details are sent to all applicants offered a place before mid January for M.Phil or PhD study.
Closing Date: 2nd February 2004.
Funding: Government.
Contributor: Universities UK.
No. of awards given last year: 5.
No. of applicants last year: 65.

University of Exeter Research Scholarships
Subjects: All subjects.
Purpose: To fund M.Phil and PhD study.
Eligibility: Open to international applicants for PhD and M.Phil/PhD programmes.
Level of Study: Doctorate.
Type: Scholarship.
Value: Full fee.
Length of Study: 3 years.
Frequency: Annual.
Study Establishment: The University of Exeter.
Country of Study: United Kingdom.
No. of awards offered: Varies.
Application Procedure: Applicants should apply for the ORS scheme. Forms will be sent to eligible offer holders. ORS applications are automatically considered for the ERS scheme.
Closing Date: 2nd February 2004.
Contributor: University of Exeter.
No. of awards given last year: New scheme.
No. of applicants last year: New scheme.
Additional Information: Further information is available on request.

University of Exeter Sports Scholarships
Subjects: Sport.
Purpose: To assist students of outstanding sporting ability who show evidence of achievement or potential at national level.
Level of Study: Graduate, Postgraduate.
Type: Scholarship.
Value: Free university residential accommodation and UK£1,000 per year for sporting expenses.
Length of Study: One year initially, but may be renewed for a further two years.
Frequency: Annual.
Study Establishment: The University of Exeter.
Country of Study: United Kingdom.
No. of awards offered: Varies.
Application Procedure: Applicants must contact the Secretary of the Sports Scholarship Board at the University.
Closing Date: February 15th.
Additional Information: Students will be provided with a mentor with whom an annual programme of training and competition will be agreed.

UNIVERSITY OF GLASGOW

Glasgow, G12 8QQ, Scotland
Tel: (44) 141 330 4575
Fax: (44) 141 330 4045
Email: sras@gla.ac.uk
www: http://www.gla.ac.uk/sras/pg.html
Contact: Graduate Assistant Director

The University of Glasgow is a major research led university operating in an international context, which aims to provide education through the development of learning in a research environment, to undertake fundamental, strategic and applied research and to sustain and add value to Scottish culture, to the natural environment and to the national economy.

James Houston Scholarship
Subjects: Veterinary medicine.
Purpose: To assist the advanced study or research into bovine animals, with particular reference to blood stock breeding and its improvement.
Eligibility: Open to university graduates of veterinary medicine and qualified veterinary surgeons.
Level of Study: Postgraduate.
Type: Scholarship.
Value: Please consult the organisation.
Frequency: Every two years.
Study Establishment: The University of Glasgow.
Country of Study: United Kingdom.
No. of awards offered: One.
Application Procedure: Applicants must write for details.
Closing Date: February.
Additional Information: Preference is given to graduates in veterinary medicine of the University of Glasgow.

For further information contact:

Faculty of Veterinary Medicine, University of Glasgow Veterinary School, Bearsden, Glasgow, G61 1QH, Scotland
Email: gvmx04@udcf.gla.ac.uk

John Crawford Scholarship
Subjects: Veterinary medicine.
Purpose: To assist the advanced study or research into equine animals, with particular reference to blood stock breeding and its improvement.
Eligibility: Open to university graduates of veterinary medicine and qualified veterinary surgeons.
Level of Study: Postgraduate.
Type: Scholarship.
Value: Please consult the organisation.
Frequency: Every two years.
Study Establishment: The University of Glasgow.
Country of Study: United Kingdom.
Application Procedure: Applicants must write for details.
Additional Information: Preference is given to graduates in veterinary medicine of the University of Glasgow.

For further information contact:

Faculty of Veterinary Medicine, University of Glasgow Veterinary School, Bearsden, Glasgow, G61 1QH, Scotland
Email: gvmx04@udcf.gla.ac.uk

University of Glasgow Postgraduate Research Scholarships
Subjects: All subjects.
Purpose: To assist with research towards a PhD degree.
Eligibility: Open to candidates of any nationality who are proficient in English and who have obtained a First or an Upper Second Class (Honours) Degree or equivalent.
Level of Study: Postgraduate.
Type: Scholarship.
Value: Please consult the organisation.
Frequency: Annual.
Study Establishment: The University of Glasgow.
Country of Study: Scotland.
Application Procedure: Applicants must refer to the University's application for graduate studies form which covers application for admission and scholarship. Please refer to the notes for applicants issued with the application form for address details.
Funding: Private.
Contributor: Endowments.
Additional Information: Scholars from outside the European Union will be expected to make up the difference between the home fee and the overseas fee.

William Barclay Memorial Scholarship
Subjects: Biblical studies, theology and church history or any subject falling within the faculty of the divinity.
Purpose: To provide an opportunity for a scholar to undertake research.
Eligibility: Open to any suitably qualified graduate of theology from a university outside the United Kingdom.
Level of Study: Postgraduate.
Type: Scholarship.
Value: Please consult the organisation.
Frequency: Annual.
Study Establishment: The Faculty of Divinity at the University of Glasgow.
Country of Study: Scotland.
Application Procedure: Applicants must request postgraduate study application material. The PG form is used for the Barclay application.
Funding: Private.

For further information contact:

Faculty of Divinity, Glasgow, G12 8QQ, Scotland
Tel: (44) 141 330 6525
Fax: (44) 141 330 4943
Email: gvmx04@udcf.gla.ac.uk

UNIVERSITY OF HAWAII

Moore Hall 416, 1890 East-West Road
Hawaii, Honolulu 96822
United States of America
Tel: (1) 808 956 5652
Fax: (1) 808 956 6345
Email: csas@hawaii.edu
www: http://www.hawaii.edu/csas/
Contact: Center for South Asian Studies

The center's academic strengths in Asian studies are complemented by a local community deeply interested in the cultural heritage as well as the contemporary affairs of Asian peoples and cultures.

The J. Watumull Scholarship for the Study of India
Subjects: Visual and performing arts, history, philosophy, religion and politics.
Purpose: To promote understanding by financing a student who presents a focussed and well developed proposal for study in India.
Level of Study: Postgraduate.
Type: Scholarship.
Value: US$5,000 per annum.
Length of Study: At least 2 months.
Frequency: Annual.
Study Establishment: A recognized Indian Institution.
Country of Study: India.
No. of awards offered: 3.
Application Procedure: Download application form from the website.
Closing Date: April 2nd
Funding: Private.
Contributor: Watumull Foundation.

UNIVERSITY OF KENT

Admissions and Partnership Services
Canterbury, Kent, CT2 7NZ
United Kingdom
Tel: (44) 1227 827272
Fax: (44) 1227 827077
Email: recruitment@kent.ac.uk
www: http://www.kent.ac.uk
Contact: The Registry

The University of Kent aims to provide higher education of excellent quality characterised by flexibility and interdisciplinarity, informed by research and scholarship, and meeting the lifelong needs of a diversity of students.

Computing Laboratory Bursary

Subjects: Our research reaches national and international standards. The main areas of research are: formal methods, programming languages (which together form the Theoretical Computer Science Group), networks and distributed system, systems engineering, applied and interdisciplinary informatics, and computers and education.
Purpose: To support postgraduate studies towards PhD.
Eligibility: Maintenance usually available only to UK/EU candidates. Fees (Home or overseas) available to all candidates.
Level of Study: Doctorate.
Type: Bursary.
Value: Up to four awards of fees plus UK£10,500 maintenance for United Kingdom and European Union applicants, and up to seven awards of fees only for home or overseas applicants, as well as the possibility of a contribution to maintenance for outstanding overseas applicants, particularly those who may be in receipt of funding from other sources.
Length of Study: Three years.
Frequency: Annual.
Study Establishment: The University of Kent.
Country of Study: United Kingdom.
No. of awards offered: Up to four maintenance and seven fees only.
Application Procedure: Applicants must enclose a covering letter and indicate their area of interest. See web site: www.cs.ukc.ac.uk/research/pg.
Closing Date: 8th June 2004.
Funding: Government.
No. of awards given last year: 3 Full (Maintenance),7 fees only.
No. of applicants last year: Approx 150.

EPSRC Grant for School of Physical Sciences

Subjects: Physical sciences.
Purpose: To support research.
Eligibility: Open to candidates who hold or expect to obtain a First Class (Honours) Degree. They should also be citizens of one of the European Union countries.
Level of Study: Postgraduate.
Type: Grant.
Value: Tuition fees plus the maintenance bursary at the same rate as provided by the EPSRC.
Length of Study: Three years.
Frequency: Annual.
Study Establishment: The University of Kent.
Country of Study: United Kingdom.
Application Procedure: Applicants must complete an application form.
Closing Date: There is no fixed closing date.
Contributor: EPSRC.
No. of awards given last year: Three.
No. of applicants last year: 15.
Additional Information: Holders of the studentships are required to undertake a small amount of teaching assistance.

EPSRC Quota for Computer Science

Subjects: Theoretical computer science, functional programming, programming languages and systems/formal methods, development of computer networks, distributed systems, communication architectures, network support for multimedia distributed systems, parallel processing, object oriented databases and expert systems, numerical computation, simulation and visualisation, information systems development methodologies, software systems and engineering, enterprise and unified modelling.
Purpose: To support postgraduate studies towards a PhD.
Eligibility: Primarily open to United Kingdom nationals although European Community citizens may qualify in special circumstances.
Level of Study: Postgraduate.
Value: Home fees plus maintenance grant of approx. UK£10,000 per year.
Length of Study: Three years.
Frequency: Annual.
Study Establishment: The University of Kent.
Country of Study: United Kingdom.
No. of awards offered: Two.

Application Procedure: Applicants must indicate their interest on postgraduate application forms.
Closing Date: June.
Funding: Government.
Contributor: EPSRC.
No. of awards given last year: Two.

Ian Gregor Scholarship

Subjects: The School of English has an International reputation in a wide variety of fields of research. The diversity of our interests range from the medieval to the postmodern, and include Amercian literature, postcolonial literature, Anglo-Irish literature, Shakespeare and renaissance studies, Dickenes and Victorian studies, modern poetry, theory and cultural ethnography.
Purpose: To support a candidate registered for the taught or research MA programmes in English.
Eligibility: Candidates are expected to hold at least an Upper Second Class (Honours) Degree or equivalent. Candidates should also have applied for an external scholarship, such as AHRB.
Level of Study: Graduate, Postdoctorate, Research.
Type: Scholarship.
Value: Home fees plus UK£500. An equivalent contribution towards fees will be made in the case of overseas students.
Length of Study: One year.
Frequency: Annual.
Study Establishment: The University of Kent.
Country of Study: United Kingdom.
No. of awards offered: One.
Application Procedure: Candidates must complete the postgraduate application form, indicating in the appropriate section that they are interested in being considered for departmental scholarships. A covering letter supporting the scholarship application should be attached.
Closing Date: May 30th.
No. of awards given last year: One.

Kent Law School Studentships and Bursaries.

Subjects: Law in its many applications.
Purpose: To provide funding for one year in the first instance, extended to a maximum of three years (for registered students only) based on satisfactory progress, (including upgrading to a PhD). The retention of the posts will be subject to a review of progress and performance in both research and teaching, after the first year.
Eligibility: Candidates should hold an Upper Second Class (Honours) Degree or a good postgraduate taught degree in law.
Level of Study: Doctorate, Postgraduate, Research.
Type: Studentship.
Value: Home fees plus the Research Council equivalent of a maintenance grant.
Length of Study: One-three years.
Frequency: Annual.
Study Establishment: The University of Kent.
Country of Study: United Kingdom.
No. of awards offered: Two.
Application Procedure: Applicants must submit to the University's recruitment and admissions office a research proposal, curriculum vitae and covering letter with an application for their chosen research degree. They should also ensure that the recruitment and admissions office receives two referees' reports by the closing date for applications.
Closing Date: 18th June 2004.
Funding: Private.
Contributor: Kent Law School.
No. of awards given last year: Two.
No. of applicants last year: 15.
Additional Information: Holders of the studentships will be expected to teach for a maximum of six hours per week in term time on an undergraduate law module, at the direction of the head of department.

Maurice Crosland History of Science Studentship

Subjects: Medieval and early modern cultural and social history, early modern ecclesiastical history, the history and cultural studies of science, the history of propaganda, the history and memory of the Great War, and the history of Kent.

Purpose: To fund research to PhD level.
Eligibility: Open to qualified applicants of any nationality.
Level of Study: Doctorate, Postgraduate, Research.
Type: Studentship.
Value: Home fees plus a maintenance bursary.
Length of Study: Three years.
Frequency: Dependent on funds available.
Study Establishment: The University of Kent.
Country of Study: United Kingdom.
No. of awards offered: One.
Application Procedure: Applicants must apply to Professor Crosbie Smith.
Closing Date: June 1st.
Funding: Private.
No. of awards given last year: Two.
No. of applicants last year: Five.

For further information contact:

Centre for History & Cultural Studies of Science, Rutherford College, University of Kent at Canterbury, Canterbury, Kent, CT2 7NX, England
Tel: (44) 1227 761000
Fax: (44) 1227 827258
Contact: Professor Crosbie Smith

University of Kent Anthropology Bursaries

Subjects: Anthropology.
Purpose: To support both research and taught programmes.
Eligibility: Candidates are expected to hold an Upper Second Class (Honours) Degree.
Level of Study: Doctorate, Postgraduate, Research.
Type: Bursary.
Value: Home fees only.
Length of Study: Three years.
Frequency: Annual.
Study Establishment: The University of Kent.
Country of Study: United Kingdom.
No. of awards offered: Three.
Closing Date: Please write for details.
No. of awards given last year: Two.
Additional Information: Applicants should contact Ms Nicola Kerry Yoxall in the department of anthropology at Eliot College via email on n.a.kerry-yoxall@ukc.ac.uk.

University of Kent Canterbury Business School

Subjects: A wide range of business and management disciplines.
Eligibility: Candidates should hold an Upper Second Class (Honours) Degree and be a citizen of one of the European Uni countries.
Level of Study: Postgraduate.
Value: Three awards at UK£4,000 for full-time students and one award at UK£2,000 for a part-time student.
Length of Study: Three years.
Frequency: Annual.
Country of Study: United Kingdom.
Application Procedure: Applications must contact Professor John Butler in the department of social and public policy, Darwin College or e-mail him at j.r.butler@ukc.ac.uk.
Closing Date: June.
Funding: Private.
Contributor: The University of Kent.

University of Kent Department of Economics Bursaries

Subjects: Labour economics, money and development, international finance and trade, migration, defence and energy economics.
Purpose: To support research.
Eligibility: Candidates must have at least a taught Master's degree in Economics.
Level of Study: Doctorate, Postgraduate, Research.
Type: Research grant.
Value: Up to the equivalent of home fees plus a maintenance grant of UK£4,150 (current rate).
Length of Study: Three years.
Frequency: Annual.

Study Establishment: The University of Kent.
Country of Study: United Kingdom.
No. of awards offered: Two.
Application Procedure: Applicants must enclose a separate letter proposing their wish to apply for the bursary along with their university PhD application form. A link to the online application form can be found on the department's website, http://www.ukc.ac.uk/economics/students/postgrad/degrees.
Closing Date: June.
Funding: Government.
No. of awards given last year: Two.
Additional Information: Candidates should note that four-six hours of teaching per week and acceptable progress in the programme of study will be expected of the student. The bursary will be subject to review each year.

University of Kent Department of Electronics Studentships

Subjects: Electronics subjects including image processing and vision embedded systems, broadband and wireless communications, medical electronics.
Purpose: To enable well qualified students to undertake research programmes within the department.
Eligibility: Candidates are expected to hold an Upper Second Class (Honours) Degree or equivalent in an appropriate subject, and be nationals of one of the European Union countries.
Level of Study: Doctorate, Postgraduate, Research.
Type: Studentship.
Value: Research Council studentships are at a fixed rate determined annually by EPSRC. Departmental bursaries depend on individual circumstances.
Length of Study: Three years.
Frequency: Annual.
Study Establishment: The University of Kent.
Country of Study: United Kingdom.
No. of awards offered: Varies.
Application Procedure: Applicants should contact the department of electronics.
Closing Date: June.
Funding: Government.
Contributor: EPSRC.

For further information contact:

Department of Electronics, University of Kent, Canterbury, Kent CT2 7NT, England
Email: m.c.fairhurst@ukc.ac.uk
Contact: Professor M C Fairhurst

University of Kent Department of Politics and International Relations Bursary

Subjects: European Studies International Relations & International Political Economy, Intergovernmental Co-operation in the EU, Political Theory and Law, Politics and Conflict Analysis.
Purpose: To support research.
Eligibility: Candidates must be citizens of one of the European Union countries. Please write for further details with regards to academic eligibility.
Level of Study: Doctorate, Postgraduate.
Type: Bursary.
Value: Home fees.
Length of Study: Three years.
Frequency: Annual.
Study Establishment: The University of Kent.
Country of Study: United Kingdom.
No. of awards offered: Approx. three.
Application Procedure: Applicants must apply by letter to the head of department after being accepted for research study.
Closing Date: Applications may be submitted at any time.
No. of awards given last year: One.
No. of applicants last year: Four.
Additional Information: A maximum of six hours of teaching per week will be required.

University of Kent Department of Psychology Studentships

Subjects: Psychology, group and intergroup processes, social cognition and interpersonal behaviour, developmental psychology, forensic psychology, psychology and law, health psychology, human-computer interaction, vision, language, cognitive neuropsychology, and work-life balance.

Purpose: To support research studies.

Eligibility: Candidates should hold or expect to obtain at least an Upper Second Class (Honours) Degree.

Level of Study: Postgraduate, Research.

Type: Studentship.

Value: Tuition fees at the United Kingdom rate plus the maintenance bursary at the same rate as provided by the ESRC.

Length of Study: Three years.

Frequency: Annual.

Study Establishment: The University of Kent.

Country of Study: United Kingdom.

No. of awards offered: Two/Three.

Application Procedure: Applicants must complete an application form.

Closing Date: The deadline changes according to when studentships are advertised. This is usually the end of July/mid August.

Funding: Private.

Contributor: The University of Kent.

No. of awards given last year: Three.

No. of applicants last year: 20-30.

Additional Information: A maximum of six hours of teaching per week will be required.

University of Kent English Scholarship

Subjects: The School of English has an international reputation in a wide variety of fields of research. The diversity of our interests range from the medieval to the postmodern, and include American literature, postcolonial literature, Anglo-Irish literature, Shakespeare and renaissance studies, Dickens and Victorian Studies, modern poetry, theory and cultural ethnography.

Purpose: To support research.

Eligibility: Candidates are expected to hold at least an Upper Second Class (Honours) Degree or equivalent. Candidates should also have applied for an external scholarship, such as AHRB.

Level of Study: Doctorate, Postgraduate, Research.

Type: Research grant.

Value: Home tuition fees and up to UK£3,500 bursary per year for up to three year's full-time study. Some undergraduate teaching or research assistance may be expected from the successful candidate.

Length of Study: Three years.

Frequency: Annual.

Study Establishment: The University of Kent.

Country of Study: United Kingdom.

No. of awards offered: One.

Application Procedure: Candidates must complete the postgraduate application form, indicating in the appropriate section that they are interested in being considered for departmental scholarships. A covering letter supporting the scholarship application should be attached.

Closing Date: May 30th.

Funding: Private.

No. of awards given last year: One.

Additional Information: Holders of the scholarship are expected to undertake a small amount of teaching or research assistance each week.

University of Kent Institute of Mathematics and Statistics (IMS) Studentships

Subjects: Mathematics or statistics.

Purpose: To support studies at the IMS.

Eligibility: Candidates for scholarships should hold a First Class (Honours) Degree in mathematics or a related subject.

Level of Study: Doctorate.

Type: Studentship.

Value: Tuition fees plus the maintenance bursary at the same rate as provided by the EPSRC.

Length of Study: Three years.

Frequency: Dependent on funds available.

Study Establishment: The University of Kent.

Country of Study: United Kingdom.

No. of awards offered: Three.

Application Procedure: Candidates should complete an application form for postgraduate study and indicate that they wish to be considered for this award.

Closing Date: April 19th.

Funding: Private.

No. of awards given last year: None.

Additional Information: Holders of the studentships are required to undertake a small amount of teaching assistance. For more information please email imspg-admiss@ukc.ac.uk.

University of Kent Research School of Biosciences

Subjects: Laboratory-based research concentrates on the five major areas of modern biology: applied and environmental microbiology, cancer research, cell biology and development, infectious diseases, and protein science.

Purpose: To support research.

Eligibility: Primarily open to United Kingdom nationals although European Union citizens may qualify in special circumstances. Candidates should hold an Upper Second Class (Honours) Degree.

Level of Study: Doctorate, Postgraduate, Research.

Value: Home tuition fees and a maintenance bursary at the same rate as that provided by the Research Councils.

Length of Study: Three years.

Frequency: Annual.

Study Establishment: The University of Kent.

Country of Study: United Kingdom.

No. of awards offered: Seven.

Application Procedure: Applicants should contact Dr Andrew MacGregor, department of biosciences for further information via email on a.n.macgregor@ukc.ac.uk.

Closing Date: July 31st.

Funding: Government.

Contributor: BBSRC.

No. of awards given last year: Seven.

University of Kent School of Drama, Film and Visual Arts Scholarships

Subjects: Drama, including performance-making process and theory, theatre history.

Purpose: To support research.

Eligibility: Candidates are expected to hold an Upper Second Class (Honours) Degree and be a citizen of one of the European Union countries.

Level of Study: Postgraduate, Research.

Type: Bursary - fees only.

Length of Study: The studentship is three years and the bursary is one year.

Frequency: Annual.

Study Establishment: The University of Kent.

Country of Study: United Kingdom.

No. of awards offered: Ten.

Application Procedure: Applicants must write for details.

Closing Date: 31st July.

No. of awards given last year: Eleven.

Additional Information: Some teaching may be required.

University of Kent School of European Culture and Language Scholarships

Subjects: The literature and culture of France, Germany, Italy and Spain and supervise research in each of these national areas.

Purpose: To support research.

Eligibility: Candidates are expected to hold an Upper Second Class (Honours) Degree and be a citizen of one of the European Union countries.

Level of Study: Postgraduate, Research.

Type: Research grant.

Value: UK£1,500.

Length of Study: Three years.

Frequency: Annual.

Study Establishment: The University of Kent.
Country of Study: United Kingdom.
No. of awards offered: Varies, up to four.
Application Procedure: Applicants must contact Professor Graham Anderson at the School of European Culture and Languages, Cornwallis West Building or by email at g.anderson@ukc.ac.uk.
Closing Date: June.
No. of awards given last year: Three.
No. of applicants last year: Seven.
Additional Information: Some part-time teaching will be required.

University of Kent School of Physical Sciences.

Subjects: The physical sciences.
Purpose: Studentship.
Eligibility: Candidates should hold an Upper Second Class (Honours) Degree or equivalent EU degree and be a citizen of one of the European Union countries or equivalent EU degree.
Level of Study: Postgraduate.
Type: Studentship.
Value: Home/EU fees plus maintenance at Research Council Rate.
Length of Study: Three years.
Frequency: Dependent on funds available.
Country of Study: United Kingdom.
No. of awards offered: 6.
Application Procedure: Applicants must contact Dr. Chris Solomon in the School of Physical Sciences at c.j.solomon@kent.ac.uk.
Closing Date: June.
Funding: Commercial, Government.
Contributor: The University of Kent.
No. of awards given last year: 5.

University of Kent Sociology and Social and Public Policy Studentships

Subjects: Sociological theory and the culture of modernity.
Purpose: To support research.
Eligibility: Candidates should hold a First Class or an Upper Second Class (Honours) Degree.
Level of Study: Doctorate, Postgraduate, Predoctorate, N.B. Not available to MA/MSc students.
Type: Studentship.
Value: Up to 4 awards at UK£9,000 for full-time students, up to 10 awards at UK£4,000 for full-time students or UK£2,000 for a part time student.
Length of Study: Three years.
Frequency: Annual.
Study Establishment: The University of Kent.
Country of Study: United Kingdom.
No. of awards offered: up to 14.
Application Procedure: Applicants must contact The Admissions Secretary, School of Social policy, Sociology or Social Research, CT2 7NF, or e-mail: socio-office@kent.ac.uk.
Closing Date: June.
Funding: Government.
No. of awards given last year: Eight.
Additional Information: A maximum of two hours of teaching per week will be required.

University of Kent Sociology Studentship

Subjects: Sociological theory and the culture of modernity.
Purpose: To support research.
Eligibility: Candidates should hold a First Class or Upper Second Class (Honours) Degree.
Level of Study: Doctorate, Postdoctorate, Postgraduate, N.B. Not available to MA/MSc students.
Type: Studentship.
Value: Up to 4 awards at UK£9,000 for full-time students, up to 10 awards at UK£4,000 for full-time students, or UK£2,000 for a part-time student.
Length of Study: Three years.
Frequency: Annual.
Study Establishment: The University of Kent.
Country of Study: United Kingdom.
No. of awards offered: Up to 14.

Application Procedure: Applicants must contact The Graduate Admissions Secretary, School of Social Research, CTZ 7NP or email: socio-office@kent.ac.uk.
Closing Date: June.
Funding: Government.
No. of awards given last year: Eight.

THE UNIVERSITY OF LEEDS

Research Degrees & Scholarships Office, Leeds, West Yorkshire LS2 9JT, England
Tel: (44) 113 233 4007
Fax: (44) 113 233 3941
Email: ajmorrison@adm.leeds.co.uk
www: http://www.leeds.ac.uk
Contact: Ms J Y Findlay, Senior Assistant Registrar

The University of Leeds aims to promote excellence and to achieve and sustain international standing in higher education teaching, learning and research and to serve a wide range of student constituencies, social and professional communities and industrial, commercial and government agencies, locally, nationally and internationally.

BEIT Trust - FCO Chevening - Leeds University Scholarships

Subjects: All subjects.
Purpose: To provide awards to students of high academic calibre from Malawi, Zambia and Zimbabwe.
Eligibility: Open to candidates who have obtained, or are about to obtain, the equivalent of a United Kingdom First or Upper Second Class (Honours) Degree. Candidates must be nationals of Malawi, Zambia and Zimbabwe and aged between 20 and 35.
Level of Study: Postgraduate.
Type: Scholarship.
Value: Academic fees, living expenses, books, equipment, arrival and departure allowance, economy return airfares and the production of a dissertation.
Length of Study: One year.
Frequency: Annual.
Study Establishment: The University of Leeds.
Country of Study: United Kingdom.
No. of awards offered: Three.
Application Procedure: Applications must be made to the BEIT Trust.
Closing Date: August to October in the year preceding the study year.
Funding: Government, Private.
No. of awards given last year: Three.
No. of applicants last year: Not known.

For further information contact:

The BEIT Trust, BEIT House, Grove Road, Woking, Surrey GU21 5JB, England

BP - FCO Chevening - Leeds University Scholarships

Subjects: Exploration geophysics, geochemistry, environmental engineering and project management, economics, finance and accounting, business administration and management, international studies, politics of international resources and development.
Purpose: To provide postgraduate scholarships to Vietnamese students of high academic calibre.
Eligibility: Open to candidates who have obtained, or are about to obtain, a United Kingdom First or Upper Second Class (Honours) Degree or equivalent. Candidates must be nationals of Vietnam and be aged between 20 and 25 years. An adequate standard of English is required.
Level of Study: Postgraduate.
Type: Scholarship.
Value: Academic fees, living expenses, books, equipment, arrival and a departure allowance, economy return airfares and the production of a dissertation.
Length of Study: One year.

Frequency: Annual.
Study Establishment: The University of Leeds.
Country of Study: United Kingdom.
No. of awards offered: Four.
Application Procedure: Applicants must apply by application form after acceptance on to a taught course. Application forms are available from the scholarships office or the British Council.
Closing Date: January 9th.
Funding: Commercial, Government, Private.
No. of awards given last year: Four.
No. of applicants last year: Not known.

For further information contact:

The British Council Information Centre, 25B Le Duan Dist 1, Ho Chi Mihn City, Vietnam

Canon Collins Educational Trust for Southern Africa (CCETSA) - FCO Chevening - Leeds University Scholarships

Subjects: All subjects from any full-time taught Master's programme.
Purpose: To provide awards to students of high academic calibre.
Eligibility: Open to candidates who have obtained or are about to obtain the equivalent of a United Kingdom First or good Second Class (Honours) Degree. Candidates must be nationals of Botswana, Lesotho, Mozambique, Namibia, South Africa or Swaziland and be aged between 20 and 35 years.
Level of Study: Postgraduate.
Type: Scholarship.
Value: Academic fees, living expenses, books, equipment, an arrival and departure allowance, economy return airfares and the production of a dissertation.
Length of Study: One year.
Frequency: Annual.
Study Establishment: The University of Leeds.
Country of Study: United Kingdom.
No. of awards offered: Up to 10.
Application Procedure: Applicants must complete an application form available on request from the CCETSA.
Closing Date: March 15th.
Funding: Government, Private.
No. of awards given last year: Six

For further information contact:

Canon Collins Educational Trust for Southern Africa (CCETSA), 22 The Ivories, 6 Northampton Street, London, N1 2HY, England

Derek Fatchett Memorial Scholarships (Palestine)

Subjects: Politics or international studies.
Purpose: To provide awards to students of high academic calibre.
Eligibility: Open to candidates who have obtained or are about to obtain the equivalent of a United Kingdom First or Second Class (Honours) Degree. Candidates must be nationals of Palestine.
Level of Study: Postgraduate.
Type: Scholarship.
Value: Academic fees, living expenses, books, equipment, arrival and departure allowance, economy return airfares and the production of a dissertation.
Length of Study: One year.
Frequency: Annual.
Study Establishment: The University of Leeds.
Country of Study: United Kingdom.
No. of awards offered: One.
Application Procedure: Application procedures are now handled by the British Council offices in Ramallah and East Jerusalem.
Closing Date: May 31st.
Funding: Private.
No. of awards given last year: None.
No. of applicants last year: Not known.

For further information contact:

British Council, 4th Floor, Tabourn Building, Al Ahliyyeh College Street, PO Box 2464, Ramallah, Israel

Hong Kong Arts Development Council - FCO Chevening - Leeds University Scholarships

Subjects: Performing and studio arts, art gallery and museum studies, social history and theory of art, art history, sculpture studies, feminist theory and practice in the visual arts, theatre studies, music, film music studies, music and liturgy, arts education or performance studies, studio practice.
Purpose: To provide awards to students of high academic calibre.
Eligibility: Open to candidates who have obtained or are about to obtain the equivalent of a United Kingdom First or Second Class (Honours) Degree in a relevant subject. Candidates must be permanent residents of Hong Kong.
Level of Study: Postgraduate.
Type: Scholarship.
Value: Academic fees, living expenses, books, equipment, arrival and departure allowance, economy return airfares and the production of a dissertation.
Length of Study: One year.
Frequency: Annual.
Study Establishment: The University of Leeds.
Country of Study: United Kingdom.
No. of awards offered: Three.
Application Procedure: Applicants must complete an application form, available from the Hong Kong Arts Development Council.
Closing Date: Mid April.
Funding: Government, Private.
No. of awards given last year: Three.
No. of applicants last year: Not known.

For further information contact:

Hong Kong Arts Development Council, HKADC Arts Scholarship, 22/F 181 Queens Road, Central, Hong Kong

Kulika Charitable Trust - FCO Chevening - University of Leeds Scholarships

Subjects: All subjects.
Purpose: To provide postgraduate scholarships to students of a high academic calibre.
Eligibility: Open to candidates who have obtained a United Kingdom First or Upper Second Class (Honours) Degree or equivalent. Candidates must be nationals of Uganda.
Level of Study: Postgraduate.
Type: Scholarship.
Value: Academic fees, living expenses, books, equipment, arrival and a departure allowance, economy return airfares and the production of a dissertation.
Length of Study: One year.
Frequency: Annual.
Study Establishment: The University of Leeds.
Country of Study: United Kingdom.
No. of awards offered: Five.
Application Procedure: Applicants must apply via an application form after acceptance on to a taught course. Application forms for the scholarship are available from the British Council in Uganda.
Closing Date: January 6th.
Funding: Government, Private.
No. of awards given last year: Five.
No. of applicants last year: Not Known.

For further information contact:

British Council in Uganda, IPS Building, Parliament Avenue, PO Box 7070, Kampala, Uganda

Open Society Institute - FCO Chevening - Leeds University Scholarship

Subjects: All subjects of any one year full-time taught Master's programme.
Purpose: To provide awards to students of high academic calibre.
Eligibility: Open to candidates who have obtained the equivalent of a United Kingdom First Class or Upper Second Class (Honours) Degree. Candidates must be nationals of Lebanon and aged between 20 and 35 years.

639

Level of Study: Postgraduate.
Type: Scholarship.
Value: Academic fees, living expenses, books, equipment, arrival and departure allowance, economy return airfares and the production of a dissertation.
Length of Study: One year.
Frequency: Annual.
Study Establishment: The University of Leeds.
Country of Study: United Kingdom.
No. of awards offered: Up to six.
Application Procedure: Applicants must contact the local SOROS Foundation or British Council offices for information and preliminary application forms.
Closing Date: 30th January.
Funding: Government, Private.
No. of awards given last year: Two.
No. of applicants last year: Not Known.

For further information contact:

The British Council, Sadat/Sidani Street, Azar Building, Ras Beirut, Lebanon

Shell centenary chevening scholarships

Subjects: Engineering Geology, Exploration Geophysics, Structural Geology with Geophysics, Geochemistry, Environmental Geochemistry, Environmental Engineering and Project Management, International Construction Management and Engineering, Engineering Project Management, Sustainable Waste Management, Combustion and Energy, Computational Fluid Dynamics, Automotive Engineering, Mechanical Engineering, Integrated Design of Chemical Plant, Fire and Explosion Engineering, Environmental Pollution Control, Mineral Resource and Environmental Geostatics, Modern Digital and Radio Frequency Wireless Communications.
Purpose: To provide postgraduate scholarships to students of high academic calibre.
Eligibility: Open to candidates who have obtained, or are about to obtain, a United Kingdom First Class (Honours) Degree or equivalent. An excellent standard of English is required. Candidates must be aged under 35. Open to all nationalities except those who are nationals of member states of the organisation for economic co-operation and development (with the exception of the Czech Republic, Hungary, Mexico, Poland, South Korea, Slovak Republic and Turkey.
Level of Study: Postgraduate.
Type: Scholarship.
Value: Academic fees, living expenses, books, equipment, arrival and a departure allowance, economy return airfares and the production of a dissertation.
Length of Study: One year.
Frequency: Annual.
Study Establishment: The University of Leeds.
Country of Study: United Kingdom.
No. of awards offered: Four.
Application Procedure: Applicants must apply by application form after acceptance on to a taught course. .
Closing Date: March 1st.
Funding: Commercial, Government, Private.
No. of awards given last year: None.
No. of applicants last year: None.

Shell Centenary Scholarships

Subjects: Engineering Geology, Exploration Geophysics, Structural Geology with Geophysics, Geochemistry, Environmental Geochemistry,Environmental Engineering and Project Management, International Construction Management and Engineering, Engineering Project Management, Sustainable Waste Management, Combustion and Energy, Computational Fluid Dynamics, Automotive Engineering, Mechanical Engineering, Integrated Design of Chemical Plant, Fire and Explosion Engineering, Environmental Pollution Control, Mineral Resource and Environmental Geostatistics, Modern Digital and Radio Frequency Wireless Communications.
Purpose: To provide postgraduate scholarships to students of high academic calibre.

Eligibility: Open to candidates who have obtained, or are about to obtain, a United Kingdom First Class (Honours) Degree or equivalent. An excellent standard of English is required. Candidates must be aged under 35. Open to all nationalities except those who are nationals of member states of the Organisation for Economic Co-operation and Development (with the exception of the Czech Republic, Hungary, Mexico, Poland, South Korea, Slovak Republic and Turkey).
Level of Study: Postgraduate.
Type: Scholarship.
Value: Academic fees, living expenses, books, equipment, arrival and a departure allowance, economy return airfares and the production of a dissertation.
Length of Study: One year.
Frequency: Annual.
Study Establishment: The University of Leeds.
Country of Study: United Kingdom.
No. of awards offered: Two.
Application Procedure: Applicants must apply by application form after acceptance on to a taught course.
Closing Date: March 1st.
Funding: Commercial, Government, Private.
No. of awards given last year: None.
No. of applicants last year: None.

Tetley and Lupton Scholarships for Overseas Students for Master's Study

Subjects: All subjects.
Purpose: To provide awards to overseas students of high academic calibre.
Eligibility: Open to candidates liable to pay tuition fees for Master's degrees at the full cost for overseas students. Applicants must be of a high academic standard.
Level of Study: Doctorate, Postgraduate.
Type: Scholarship.
Value: UK£3,000 per year towards academic fees.
Length of Study: One year.
Frequency: Annual.
Study Establishment: The University of Leeds.
Country of Study: United Kingdom.
No. of awards offered: Up to 12.
Application Procedure: Applicants must apply for a course and then a scholarship.
Closing Date: March 1st.
Funding: Private.
No. of awards given last year: 12.
No. of applicants last year: Unknown.

Tetley and Lupton Scholarships for Overseas Students for Research Study

Subjects: All subjects.
Purpose: To provide awards to international research students of high academic calibre.
Eligibility: Open to candidates liable to pay tuition fees for research degrees at the full rate for overseas students. Applicants must be of a high academic standard.
Level of Study: Doctorate, Postgraduate.
Type: Scholarship.
Value: Varies according to the programme of study but will be approximately UK£3,000 towards academic fees.
Length of Study: One year, which may be renewed for a second or third year according to duration of the course. The award may also be held concurrently with other awards, except those providing full payment of fees.
Frequency: Annual.
Study Establishment: The University of Leeds.
Country of Study: United Kingdom.
No. of awards offered: Approx. 40.
Application Procedure: Applicants must apply for a course and then a scholarship. Research candidates need to apply concurrently was national overseas research student (ORS) competition.
Closing Date: 26th January.
Funding: Private.

No. of awards given last year: 32.
No. of applicants last year: 323.

University of Leeds International Fee Bursary (Vietnam)
Subjects: Development studies, international political economy, international studies or international resources and development.
Purpose: To provide scholarships to students of high academic calibre who wish to study in the School of Politics and International Studies.
Eligibility: Applicants must already hold a degree of equivalent standard to a good Second Class (Honours) Degree. An adequate standard of English is also required. Applicants must be nationals of Vietnam.
Level of Study: Postgraduate.
Type: Scholarship.
Frequency: Annual.
Study Establishment: The University of Leeds.
Country of Study: United Kingdom.
No. of awards offered: One.
Application Procedure: Applicants must make an application in letter form to the Taught Postgraduate Secretary at Leeds University Business School.
Closing Date: June 11th.
Funding: Private.

University of Leeds International Fee Bursary (Vietnam)
Subjects: Accounting, finance, economics or human resource management.
Purpose: To provide scholarships to students of high academic calibre who wish to study in the Leeds University Business School.
Eligibility: Applicants must already hold a degree of equivalent standard to a good Second Class (Honours) Degree. An adequate standard of English is also required. Applicants must be nationals of Vietnam.
Level of Study: Postgraduate.
Type: Scholarship.
Value: Academic fees.
Length of Study: One year.
Frequency: Annual.
Study Establishment: The University of Leeds.
Country of Study: United Kingdom.
No. of awards offered: Two.
Application Procedure: Applicants must make an application in letter form to the Taught Postgraduate Secretary at Leeds University Business School.
Closing Date: June 11th.
Funding: Private.
No. of awards given last year: Two.

University of Leeds International Fee Bursary (Vietnam)
Subjects: Economics, Economics and Finance, Accounting and Finance, Human Resource Management.
Purpose: To provide scholarships to students of high academic calibre.
Eligibility: Open to nationals of Vietnam who have obtained a degree equivalent to a good Second Class (Honours) Degree. An adequate standard of English is required.
Level of Study: Postgraduate.
Type: Scholarship.
Value: Academic fees.
Length of Study: One year.
Frequency: Annual.
Study Establishment: The University of Leeds.
Country of Study: United Kingdom.
No. of awards offered: One.
Application Procedure: Applicants must address a letter of application to the Leeds University Business School.
Closing Date: June 11th.
Funding: Private.
No. of awards given last year: One.

For further information contact:

International Office, University of Leeds, Leeds, LS2 9JT, England

University of Leeds International Fee Bursary (Vietnam)
Subjects: Information Systems, Distributed Multimedia Systems, Multidisciplinary Informatics.
Purpose: To provide scholarships to students of high academic calibre.
Eligibility: Open to nationals of Vietnam who have obtained a degree equivalent to a good Second Class (Honours) Degree. An adequate standard of English is required.
Level of Study: Postgraduate.
Type: Scholarship.
Value: Academic fees.
Length of Study: One year.
Frequency: Annual.
Study Establishment: The University of Leeds.
Country of Study: United Kingdom.
No. of awards offered: One.
Application Procedure: Applicants must address a letter of application to the school of computing.
Closing Date: June 11th.
Funding: Private.
No. of awards given last year: One.

For further information contact:

International Office, University of Leeds, Leeds, LS2 9JT, England

University of Leeds International Fee Bursary (Vietnam)
Subjects: Development studies, international political economy, international studies or international resources.
Purpose: To provide scholarships to students of high academic calibre.
Eligibility: Open to nationals of Vietnam who have obtained a degree equivalent to a good Second Class (Honours) Degree. An adequate standard of English is required.
Level of Study: Postgraduate.
Type: Scholarship.
Value: Academic fees.
Length of Study: One year.
Frequency: Annual.
Study Establishment: The University of Leeds.
Country of Study: United Kingdom.
No. of awards offered: One.
Application Procedure: Applicants must address a letter of application to the school of Politics and International Studies.
Closing Date: June 11th.
Funding: Private.
No. of awards given last year: One.

For further information contact:

International Office University of Leeds, Leeds, LS2 9JT, England

University of Leeds International Fee Bursary (Vietnam)
Subjects: Information systems or multimedia systems.
Purpose: To provide scholarships to students of high academic calibre who wish to study in the school of computing.
Eligibility: Applicants must be nationals of Vietnam and must already have obtained a good Second Class (Honours) Degree. An adequate standard of English is also required.
Level of Study: Postgraduate.
Type: Scholarship.
Value: Academic fees.
Length of Study: One year.
Frequency: Annual.
Study Establishment: The University of Leeds.
Country of Study: United Kingdom.
No. of awards offered: One.
Application Procedure: Applicants must make an application in letter form to the Taught Postgraduate Secretary in the School of Computing.
Closing Date: June 11th.
Funding: Private.
No. of awards given last year: One.

University of Leeds Overseas Research Students Awards Scheme - National Competition
Subjects: All subjects.
Purpose: To provide postgraduate scholarships for international research students of high calibre.
Eligibility: Open to applicants who have obtained a United Kingdom Upper Second Class (Honours) Degree or equivalent. An adequate standard of English is required.
Level of Study: Doctorate, Postgraduate.
Type: Scholarship.
Value: Partial academic fees.
Length of Study: Up to three years.
Frequency: Annual.
Study Establishment: The University of Leeds.
Country of Study: United Kingdom.
Application Procedure: Applicants must complete an application form.
Closing Date: 26th January.
Funding: Government.
No. of awards given last year: 32.
No. of applicants last year: 323.

University of Leeds Shared Scholarship Scheme
Subjects: All subjects related to the economic, social and technological development of the student's home country.
Purpose: To provide scholarships to students of high academic calibre.
Eligibility: Applicants must already have obtained a United Kingdom Upper Second Class (Honours) degree or equivalent. An adequate standard of English is also required and candidates must be nationals of, or permanently resident in, a developing Commonwealth country.
Level of Study: Postgraduate.
Type: Scholarship.
Value: Academic fees, living expenses, books, equipment, arrival and departure allowance, economy return airfares and the production of a dissertation.
Length of Study: One year.
Frequency: Annual.
Study Establishment: The University of Leeds.
Country of Study: United Kingdom.
No. of awards offered: Up to seven.
Application Procedure: Applicants must complete an application form.
Closing Date: Please contact the organisation.
Funding: Government, Private.
No. of awards given last year: Five.
No. of applicants last year: 371.

UNIVERSITY OF LOUISIANA AT MONROE (ULM)

The College of Business Administration, 700 University Avenue, Monroe, LA 71209-1110, United States of America
Tel: (1) 318 342 1100
Fax: (1) 318 342 1101
Email: pena@ulm.edu
www: http://ele.ulm.edu/mba
Contact: Mrs Jackie W O'Neal, MBA Director

The University of Louisiana at Monroe (ULM) College of Business Administration offers an MBA programme consisting of 30 graduate semester hours, including six hours of electives. Concentrations are offered in the areas of general business, e-commerce, entrepreneurship, healthcare administration and gerontology. Courses are offered both night and day.

ULM Graduate Assistantships
Subjects: MBA.
Eligibility: Open to full-time applicants who have been accepted for admission to the MBA programme.
Level of Study: Graduate.
Type: Assistantship.

Value: Full tuition waiver and a stipend of up to US$2,500 per semester.
Length of Study: One-two years.
Study Establishment: ULM.
Country of Study: United States of America.
No. of awards offered: Varies.
Application Procedure: Applicants must submit an application form and three letters of recommendation. Forms are available by phone, fax and email from the organisation.
Funding: Government.
Additional Information: Graduate assistants must work 20 hours per week in a variety of research, educational and administrative activities.

UNIVERSITY OF MANCHESTER

Oxford Road, Manchester, M13 9PL, England
Tel: (44) 161 275 2736
Fax: (44) 161 275 2445
Email: sara.duncalf@man.ac.uk
www: http://www.man.ac.uk
Contact: Mr Nick Church, Senior Administrative Assistant

The University of Manchester is an international provider of quality research and graduate education across a variety of disciplines and has a wide range of good support facilities.

Frederick Craven Moore Awards
Subjects: Biological sciences and medicine.
Purpose: To support research.
Eligibility: Open to graduates of any approved university or to other suitably qualified persons who can furnish satisfactory evidence of their qualifications to pursue research in clinical medicine.
Level of Study: Doctorate, Postgraduate.
Type: Other.
Value: The value of the scholarship varies, but it is normally not less than the annual value of a state or research council postgraduate award in medicine. The value of the fellowship is determined on an individual basis in accordance with the qualifications and experience of the Fellow.
Length of Study: One year. The scholarships are renewable for up to a maximum of two additional years.
Frequency: Annual.
Study Establishment: Manchester University.
Country of Study: United Kingdom.
No. of awards offered: Varies.
Application Procedure: Applicants must contact the Graduate School of Science, Engineering and Medicine.
Closing Date: May 1st.

University of Manchester Research Studentships and Scholarships
Subjects: Any area of study within the purview of the graduate schools of art, social science, education, science and engineering, biological sciences or medicine, dentistry, nursing and pharmacy.
Purpose: To support research and provide funding for high quality graduates wishing to study for a PhD.
Eligibility: The University provides significant funds to support research studentships for UK, EU and overseas graduates wishing to study for a PhD. These normally provide support towards maintenance and/or payment of the home (UK) tuition fee. Awards are initially for one year but may be renewed for up to two succeeding years. Applicants should normally hold, or be expected to receive, a first or upper second class Honours degree, or equivalent.Candidates must have applied and been accepted on to a programme of study before he/she can be considered for a URS award. If eligible, candidates must also have applied for UK Research Council, AHRB or ORS award as applicable. This application (or alternatively the PhD application form) will be used to assess the candidate for University funding. Candidate in Science & Engineering, Biological Sciences, Medicine and related disciplines are automatically considered for Research Council funding by the relevant departments themselves.
Level of Study: Doctorate, Postgraduate.
Type: Other.

Value: Varies. Some full studentships including maintenance and United Kingdom fees are available as are part scholarships.
Length of Study: Three years.
Frequency: Annual.
Study Establishment: The University of Manchester.
Country of Study: United Kingdom.
No. of awards offered: Up to 50.
Application Procedure: Full details available from the Student Services Centre 0161 275 5000, www.man.ac.uk.
No. of awards given last year: Approx. 50.
No. of applicants last year: Approx. 900.

UNIVERSITY OF MARYLAND

National Orchestral Institute School of Music, 2110 Clarice Smith Performing Arts Center, College Park, MD 20742-1211, United States of America
Tel: (1) 301 405 2317
Fax: (1) 301 314 9504
www: www.umd.edu
Contact: Mr Richard Scerbo, Manager

The University of Maryland, College Park (UMCP) is the flagship institution of the University of Maryland System. As the comprehensive public research university for the state of Maryland and the original 1862 land grant institution in Maryland, UMCP has the responsibility within the University of Maryland for serving as the state's primary centre for graduate study and research, advancing knowledge through research, providing high quality undergraduate instruction across a broad spectrum of academic disciplines and extending service to all regions of the state.

International Music Competitions
Subjects: Piano (William Kapell), cello (Leonard Rose) and voice (Marian Anderson).
Purpose: To recognise and assist the artistic development of young musicians at the highest levels of achievement in piano, cello, and voice.
Eligibility: Open to musicians of all nationalities, fulfilling the following age criteria: piano 18-33 years of age, cello 18-30 years of age, and voice 21 30 years of age.
Level of Study: Professional development.
Type: Competition.
Value: Finalist prizes US$20,000, US$10,000 and US$5,000, semi-finalists US$1,000.
Frequency: Other.
Study Establishment: The University of Maryland.
Country of Study: United States of America.
No. of awards offered: Three finalist prizes and nine semi-finalist prizes.
Application Procedure: Applicants must submit an application form, fee, cassette recording, repertoire list, curriculum vitae, photos, and letters of recommendation.
Closing Date: Mid-December of the year preceding the competition.
No. of awards given last year: 12.
No. of applicants last year: 180.
Additional Information: The competition is held in late May to early June. Concurrent Festivals offer master classes, recitals and symposia.

For further information contact:

Clarice Smith Performing Arts Center, Suite 3800, University of Maryland, MD 20742, United States of America
Contact: Mr George Moquin, International Competitions Director

National Orchestral Institute Scholarships
Subjects: Orchestral performance.
Purpose: To provide an intensive three week orchestral training programme to enable musicians to rehearse and perform under internationally acclaimed conductors and study with principal musicians of the United States' foremost orchestras in preparation for careers as orchestral musicians.

Eligibility: Open to advanced musicians between 18-28 years of age. Though primarily for students and postgraduates of United States universities, conservatories and colleges. Others, however, are welcome to apply but must appear at an audition centre. String players, including harpists, who live more than 200 miles away from an audition centre may audition by tape.
Level of Study: Professional development.
Type: Scholarship.
Value: Full tuition, room and board.
Length of Study: Three weeks.
Frequency: Annual.
Study Establishment: The University of Maryland.
Country of Study: United States of America.
No. of awards offered: Approx. 100.
Application Procedure: Applicants must submit an application, fee, curriculum vitae, and letters of recommendation.
Closing Date: Before regional auditions.
No. of awards given last year: 100.
No. of applicants last year: 1000.
Additional Information: Personal auditions are required at one of the audition centres throughout the country.

For further information contact:

National Orchestral Institute, School of Music, 2110 Clarice Smith Performing Arts Center, University of Maryland, College Park, MD 20742-1211, United States of America
Tel: (1) 301 405 2317
Fax: (1) 301 314 9504
Contact: Mr Richard Scerbo, Orchestra Manager

UNIVERSITY OF MELBOURNE

Scholarships Office, VIC 3010, Australia
Tel: (61) 3 8344 8747
Fax: (61) 3 9349 1740
Email: pg-schools@unimelb.edu.au
www: http://www.services.unimelb.edu.au

The University of Melbourne has a long and distinguished tradition of excellence in teaching and research. It is the leading research institution in Australia and enjoys a reputation for the high quality of its research programmes, consistently winning the largest share of national competitive research funding.

Melbourne International Fee Remission Scholarships
Subjects: All subjects offered by the University.
Purpose: To enable graduates to undertake research in any discipline.
Eligibility: Open to international students.
Level of Study: Postgraduate, Research.
Type: Scholarship.
Value: Full tuition fees.
Length of Study: Up to two years at the Master's level and up to three years at the PhD level. A six month extension is possible at the PhD level.
Frequency: Annual.
Study Establishment: The University of Melbourne.
Country of Study: Australia.
No. of awards offered: 60. Available only to international students.
Application Procedure: Applicants must complete the scholarship application form available on request or from the website. To be considered, applicants must receive an unconditional course offer to undertake a research higher degree. To apply for admission, applicants must complete the University of Melbourne 'Admission as a Postgraduate Student' application form (available from our website).
Closing Date: A small number of scholarships may be available throughout the year subject to availability.
Funding: Government.
Contributor: Scholarship fund.
No. of awards given last year: 60.
No. of applicants last year: 500.

Additional Information: Further information is available from the website www.services.unimelb.edu.av/scholarships/pgrad.

Melbourne Research Scholarships

Subjects: All subjects offered by the University.
Purpose: To enable graduates to undertake research in any discipline.
Eligibility: Open to candidates from Australia and foreign countries.
Level of Study: Doctorate, Postgraduate, Research.
Type: Scholarship.
Value: Australian $17,455 per year, payable fortnightly (2003 rate).
Length of Study: Up to two years at the Master's level and up to three years at the PhD level. A six month extension is possible at the PhD level.
Frequency: Annual.
Study Establishment: The University of Melbourne.
Country of Study: Australia.
No. of awards offered: 210 of which approximately 90 may be awarded to international students.
Application Procedure: Applicants must complete the scholarship application form available on request or from the website.
Closing Date: October 01st for Australian citizens and residents in the main selection round, and September 15th for international students. A small number of scholarships may be available throughout the year subject to availability.
Funding: Government.
Contributor: Scholarship fund.
No. of awards given last year: 210.
No. of applicants last year: 1000.
Additional Information: Further information is available from the website www.services.unimelb.edu.av/scholarships/pgrad.

UNIVERSITY OF NEBRASKA AT OMAHA (UNO)

College of Business Adminstration, University of Nebraska at Omaha, Omaha, 6001 Dodge Street NE 68182-0048
United States of America
Tel: (1) 402 554 2341
Fax: (1) 402 554 4036
Email: cba@unomaha.edu/mba
www: http://mba.unomaha.edu
Contact: MBA Admissions Officer

The University of Nebraska at Omaha's (UNO) College of Business Administration offers a dynamic, challenging Master's programme designed to help students acquire the knowledge, perspective and skills necessary for success in the marketplace of today and tomorrow. The goal of the programme is to develop leaders who have the ability to incorporate change, use information technology to resolve problems and make sound business decisions. The curriculum focuses on results with an emphasis on how to excel in a rapidly changing world.

UNO Graduate Assistantships

Subjects: All subjects.
Eligibility: Open to qualified students who are enrolled in a graduate degree programme.
Level of Study: Graduate, MBA.
Type: Other.
Value: A waiver of tuition costs up to 12 hours of graduate credit per semester.
Study Establishment: UNO.
Country of Study: United States of America.
No. of awards offered: One-three each semester.
Application Procedure: Applicants must make enquiries in their department about the availability of assistantships, the procedures for applying, and the details of when the application and supporting credentials should be on file in the department or school for consideration.
Closing Date: June 1st.
No. of awards given last year: Three.
No. of applicants last year: 40.

UNIVERSITY OF NEVADA, LAS VEGAS (UNLV)

Graduate College, 4505 S Maryland Parkway, Box 451017, Las Vegas, NV 89154-6031, United States of America
Tel: (1) 702 895 3655
www: http://www.unlv.edu
Contact: Administrative Officer

UNLV Alumni Association Graduate Scholarships

Subjects: All subjects.
Purpose: To reward outstanding graduate students.
Eligibility: Applicants must have completed at least 12 credits of graduate study at UNLV, have a minimum undergraduate and graduate grade point average of 3.5 and enrol for six or more graduate credits in each semester of the scholarship year.
Level of Study: Graduate, MBA.
Type: Scholarship.
Value: US$1,000.
Length of Study: One year.
Frequency: Annual.
Study Establishment: UNLV.
Country of Study: United States of America.
No. of awards offered: Three.
Application Procedure: Applicants must telephone (1) 702 895 3320 or write for application forms or further information.
Closing Date: March 1st.

UNLV Graduate Assistantships

Subjects: All subjects.
Purpose: To offer financial assistance and support to students admitted to any graduate degree programme.
Eligibility: Open to students who have already been admitted to any graduate degree programme.
Level of Study: Graduate, MBA.
Type: Other.
Value: A nine month stipend of US$8,500 for Master's level assistantships plus tuition and fee waivers.
Length of Study: One year.
Frequency: Annual.
Study Establishment: UNLV.
Country of Study: United States of America.
No. of awards offered: Varies.
Application Procedure: Applicants must send applications and all supporting materials to the Dean of the graduate college.
Closing Date: March 1st or November 1st for the Spring assistantship. Applications may be accepted after this date in the event of an unexpected opening for the Autumn semester. On some rare occasions an assistantship is available for the Spring semester.
Additional Information: Graduate assistants must carry a minimum of six semester hours of credit and are expected to spend 20 hours per week on departmental duties such as instruction or research.

UNLV James F Adams/GSA Scholarship

Subjects: All subjects.
Purpose: To recognise academic achievement of graduate students.
Eligibility: Applicants must have completed at least 12 credits of graduate study at UNLV, have a minimum undergraduate and graduate grade point average of 3.5 and enrol for six or more graduate credits in each semester of the scholarship year.
Level of Study: Graduate, MBA.
Type: Scholarship.
Value: US$1,000.
Length of Study: Varies.
Frequency: Annual.
Study Establishment: UNLV.
Country of Study: United States of America.
No. of awards offered: Six.
Application Procedure: Applicants must telephone (1) 702 895 3320 or write for application forms or further information.
Closing Date: March 1st.

UNIVERSITY OF NEW ENGLAND (UNE)

Research Grants Office, Research Services, Armidale, NSW 2351, Australia
Tel: (61) 2 6773 2239
Fax: (61) 2 6773 3543
Email: aharris@metz.une.edu.au
www: http://www.une.edu.au
Contact: Manager, Research Office

The University of New England (UNE) is Australia's oldest regional university. UNE has a reputation for quality research with students undertaking research in the arts, education, environmental engineering, health studies, rural science and science. The UNE PhD is over 40 years old and has 550 PhD students currently enrolled.

Australian Postgraduate Award

Subjects: Any accepted at U.N.E.
Purpose: To support research at the level of Master's or PhD.
Eligibility: Applications must be Australian or NZ citizens or Australian permanent residents who have been accepted for admission to a PhD or research Masters at U.N.E.; full internal candidature.
Level of Study: Doctorate, Postgraduate.
Type: Award.
Value: Australian $18,484, p.a, travel, relocation and thesis expenses.
Length of Study: Masters- two years, no extension, PhD- three years, 6-months extension at discretion of U.S.
Frequency: Annual.
Study Establishment: The University of New England.
Country of Study: Australia.
Application Procedure: Please check website.
Closing Date: 31st October.

International Postgraduate Research Scholarship

Subjects: Any as accepted at UNE.
Purpose: To support research at the level of Master's of PhD.
Eligibility: Overseas Students; full-time internal candidature.
Level of Study: Doctorate, Postgraduate.
Type: Scholarship.
Value: Payment of course tuition fees, travel, relocation, dependents allowance and thesis expenses.
Length of Study: Masters- 2 years, no extension, PhD 3 years, 12 months extension at discretion of university.
Frequency: Annual.
Study Establishment: The University of New England.
Country of Study: Australia.
Application Procedure: Please check website.
Closing Date: 31st October.

University of New England Postgraduate Equity Scholarship

Subjects: Any as accepted at UNE.
Purpose: To support research at the level of Master's of PhD.
Eligibility: Australian or NZ citizens or Australian permanent Residents who have been accepted for admission to a PhD.
Level of Study: Doctorate, Postgraduate.
Type: Scholarship.
Value: Australian $18,484, travel, relocation and thesis expenses.
Length of Study: Masters- two years, no extension, PhD- three years, six months extension at discretion of university.
Frequency: Annual.
Study Establishment: The University of New England
Country of Study: Australia.
Application Procedure: Please check website.
Closing Date: 31st October.
Additional Information: Applicants must be female, Aboriginal or Torres Strait Islander, from a non-English speaking background, or have a disability.

University of New England Research Assistantship

Subjects: Any as accepted at UNE.
Purpose: To support research at the level of Master's or PhD.

Eligibility: Applicants must be accepted for admission to a PhD or research Masters at U.N.E. full-time internal candidature.
Level of Study: Doctorate, Postgraduate, Predoctorate.
Type: Assistantship.
Value: Australian $15,000 pa; travel, relocation and dependents allowance; thesis expenses.
Length of Study: PhD; three years, 6 month extension possible Master's; two years, no extension.
Frequency: Annual.
Study Establishment: The University of New England.
Country of Study: Australia.
Application Procedure: Please check website.
Closing Date: 30th April and 31st October.

UNIVERSITY OF NEW HAMPSHIRE

The Family Research Laboratory, Department of Sociology, Horton Social Science Center, Durham, NC 03824, United States of America
Tel: (1) 603 862 2594
Fax: (1) 603 862 1122
Email: murray.straus@unh.edu
www: http://www.unh.edu
Contact: Mr Murray Straus, Co-Director

The Family Research Laboratory at the University of New Hampshire conducts research studies of interest to state and national policy makers and citizens. Studies include a national survey of families and youth, and the 30 nation international dating violence study. Staff and faculty members associated with the laboratory give lectures and workshops to professionals and provide information to the public about family violence and related family issues. The Family Violence Research Program, which is part of the laboratory, is the first and only research programme concerned with all aspects of family violence and related phenomena. The laboratory maintains a library of about 2,500 books and sponsors a number of regional and national conferences.

University of New Hampshire Postdoctoral Fellowships For Research on Family Violence

Subjects: Family violence including physical, sexual and psychological maltreatment of children, partners in marital, cohabiting and dating relationships, and maltreatment of the elderly by members of their family.
Purpose: To provide training and experience in research into all aspects of family violence.
Eligibility: Open to citizens or permanent residents of the United States of America.
Level of Study: Postdoctorate.
Type: Fellowship.
Length of Study: One or two years.
Frequency: Annual.
Study Establishment: The Family Research Laboratory at the University of New Hampshire.
Country of Study: United States of America.
No. of awards offered: Four.
Application Procedure: Applicants must send a brief letter, publications and arrange for three letters of recommendation. Application required from Website www.unh.edu/fri.
Closing Date: Continuous.
Funding: Government.
Contributor: The National Institute of Mental Health.
No. of awards given last year: Four.
No. of applicants last year: 35.

THE UNIVERSITY OF NOTTINGHAM

Graduate School, University Park, Nottingham, Nottinghamshire, NG7 2RD, England
Tel: (44) 115 951 4664
Fax: (44) 115 951 4668
Email: postgraduate-enquiries@nottingham.ac.uk
www: http://www.nottingham.ac.uk/gradschool
Contact: Mr Ian Wilson, Research Policy Officer

The University of Nottingham is a community of students and staff dedicated to bringing out the best in all of its members. It aims to provide the finest possible environment for teaching, learning and research and has a well known record of success.

University of Nottingham Doctoral Training Awards
Subjects: All subjects offered by the University.
Purpose: To promote research.
Eligibility: Open to graduates of all nationalities.
Level of Study: Postgraduate, Predoctorate.
Type: Scholarship.
Value: More than UK£9,000 maintenance per year where appropriate, plus payment of fees at the home or European Union rate.
Length of Study: Three years leading to PhD submission given adequate academic progress.
Frequency: Annual.
Study Establishment: The University of Nottingham.
Country of Study: United Kingdom.
No. of awards offered: More than 75.
Application Procedure: Applicants must contact the individual schools for information.
Closing Date: Please contact the individual schools for information.
Contributor: University of Nottingham.
No. of awards given last year: Over 75.
Additional Information: The scholarships are awarded internally to the schools and/or institutes that bid for them. It is then up to those schools receiving awards to advertise the scholarship and set an application deadline.

University of Nottingham Weston Scholarships
Subjects: All subjects from a prescribed list.
Purpose: To provide promising students with full-time home and European Union fees.
Eligibility: There are no eligibility restrictions.
Level of Study: Postgraduate.
Type: Studentship.
Value: Home or European Union fees only.
Length of Study: Usually one year full-time or the part-time equivalent.
Frequency: Annual.
Study Establishment: The University of Nottingham.
Country of Study: United Kingdom.
No. of awards offered: Four.
Application Procedure: Applicants must submit applications to the individual schools and contact them for details.
Closing Date: 1 August, 2004.
No. of awards given last year: 4.
Additional Information: The scholarships are awarded internally to the schools and/or institutes that bid for them. It is then up to those schools receiving awards to advertise the scholarship and set an application deadline.

UNIVERSITY OF OTAGO

Scholarships Office, PO Box 56, Dunedin, New Zealand
Tel: (64) 3 479 1100 ext. 5291
Fax: (64) 3 479 8367
Email: pgschols@nimrodel.otago.ac.nz
www: http://www.otago.ac.nz
Contact: Mrs Margaret Sykes, Postgraduate Administrator

The University of Otago has over 17,000 students, most of whom are based at the Dunedin campus, which is the oldest campus in New Zealand. The University has four divisions: the Division of Commerce (School of Business), the Division of Health Sciences, the Division of Humanities and the Division of Science. The University has a School of Medicine in Christchurch and Wellington, and a campus in Auckland.

University of Otago Dr Sulaiman Daud 125th Jubilee International Postgraduate Scholarship
Subjects: All subjects.
Purpose: To fund research towards a PhD or Master's degree.

Eligibility: Open to citizens of Malaysia with a minimum qualification of a First Class (Honours) Degree.
Level of Study: Doctorate, Postgraduate.
Type: Scholarship.
Value: New Zealand $20,000 per year for doctoral study and New Zealand $13,000 per year for Master's study.
Length of Study: Three years for doctoral study and two years for Master's study.
Frequency: Annual.
Study Establishment: The University of Otago.
Country of Study: New Zealand.
No. of awards offered: One.
Application Procedure: Applicants must complete an application form, available from the website.
Closing Date: June 30th.

University of Otago International Scholarships
Subjects: All subjects.
Purpose: To assist with funding for study.
Eligibility: Open to all international applicants intending to study at the University of Otago.
Level of Study: Doctorate, Graduate.
Type: Scholarship.
Value: Master's scholarships US$8,500 per year for up to two years and PhD scholarships US$14,000 per year for three years.
Length of Study: Two years for Master's study and three for doctoral study.
Frequency: Annual.
Study Establishment: The University of Otago.
Country of Study: New Zealand.
No. of awards offered: Four Master's scholarships and four PhD scholarships.
Application Procedure: Applicants must complete the application for International study at the University of Otago, available from the website.
Closing Date: October 15th.

University of Otago Masters Awards
Subjects: All subjects.
Purpose: To fund research towards a Master's degree.
Eligibility: Open to permanent residents or citizens of New Zealand or Australia, and to citizens of France and Germany with a minimum qualification of a First Class (Honours) Degree who are entering the thesis year of a Master's degree.
Level of Study: Postgraduate.
Type: Scholarship.
Value: New Zealand $13,000 per year.
Length of Study: One year.
Frequency: Annual.
Study Establishment: The University of Otago.
Country of Study: New Zealand.
No. of awards offered: Between 40-50.
Application Procedure: Applicants must complete an application form, available from the website.
Closing Date: October 1st.

University of Otago PhD Scholarships
Subjects: All subjects.
Purpose: To fund research towards a PhD degree.
Eligibility: Open to permanent residents or citizens of New Zealand or Australia and to citizens of France and Germany with a minimum qualification of a First Class (Honours) Degree.
Level of Study: Doctorate.
Type: Scholarship.
Value: New Zealand $20,000.
Length of Study: Three years.
Frequency: Annual.
Study Establishment: The University of Otago.
Country of Study: New Zealand.
No. of awards offered: Between 40-50.
Application Procedure: Applicants must complete an application form, available from the website.
Closing Date: October 1st.

University of Otago Prestigious PhD Scholarships

Subjects: All subjects.
Purpose: To fund research towards a PhD degree.
Eligibility: Open to permanent residents or citizens of New Zealand or Australia, and to citizens of France and Germany with a minimum qualification of a First Class (Honours) Degree.
Level of Study: Doctorate.
Type: Scholarship.
Value: New Zealand $25,000.
Length of Study: Three years.
Frequency: Annual.
Study Establishment: The University of Otago.
Country of Study: New Zealand.
No. of awards offered: 10.
Application Procedure: Applicants must complete an application form, available from the website.
Closing Date: October 1st.

UNIVERSITY OF OXFORD

University Offices, Wellington Square, Oxford, Oxfordshire, OX1 2JD, England
Tel: (44) 1865 270000
Fax: (44) 1865 270708
www: http://www.ox.ac.uk
Contact: Ms Clare Woodcock, Information Officer

Artal Scholarships

Subjects: European politics and society and European and comparative law.
Purpose: To provide assistance for those studying an MPhil or MJuris degree.
Eligibility: Open to citizens of Belgium.
Level of Study: Postgraduate.
Type: Scholarship.
Value: UK£6,000.
Frequency: Annual.
Study Establishment: The University of Oxford.
Country of Study: United Kingdom.
No. of awards offered: Up to four.
Application Procedure: Applicants must complete an application form available from the International Office or the website.
Closing Date: January 31st.
Additional Information: Please contact the International Office for further information.

For further information contact:

The International Office, University Offices, Wellington Square, Oxford, OX1 2JD, England
www: http://www.admin.ox.ac.uk/io

Balliol College Dervorguilla Scholarship

Subjects: Arts or sciences.
Eligibility: Open to overseas students only.
Level of Study: Postgraduate.
Type: Scholarship.
Value: College and university fees plus a full maintenance grant.
Length of Study: Two years, with the possibility of renewal for a third year.
Frequency: Annual.
Study Establishment: Balliol College, the University of Oxford.
Country of Study: United Kingdom.
No. of awards offered: Two, one in arts and one in science.
Application Procedure: Applicants must write for details.
Closing Date: January 31st.

For further information contact:

Tutor for Graduate Admissions, Balliol College, Oxford, Oxfordshire OX1 3BJ, England

Balliol College Domus Graduate Scholarships

Subjects: All subjects.
Eligibility: Open to overseas students only.

Type: Scholarship.
Length of Study: Two years, with a possibility of renewal for a third year.
Frequency: Annual.
Study Establishment: The University of Oxford.
Country of Study: United Kingdom.
No. of awards offered: Varies.

For further information contact:

Tutor for Graduate Admissions, Balliol College, Oxford, Oxfordshire OX1 3BJ, England

Balliol College Fawkes Memorial Scholarship in Philosophy

Subjects: Philosophy.
Eligibility: Overseas students only.
Level of Study: Postgraduate.
Type: Scholarship.
Value: To be confirmed.
Length of Study: Two years, renewable for a further two years in the event that the student continues on the DPhil, subject to satisfactory progress.
Study Establishment: Balliol College, University of Oxford.
Country of Study: United Kingdom.
No. of awards offered: One.
Application Procedure: Applicants must contact the Tutor for Graduate Admissions at Balliol College.

For further information contact:

Balliol College, Oxford, Ox1 3BJ, England
Contact: Tutor for Graduate Admissions

Balliol College Foley-Béjar Scholarship

Subjects: All subjects.
Eligibility: Open to Mexican nationals and citizens of Spain and Ireland.
Level of Study: Postgraduate.
Type: Scholarship.
Length of Study: Two years, renewable for a third year.
Study Establishment: Balliol College, University of Oxford.
Country of Study: United Kingdom.
No. of awards offered: One.
Application Procedure: Applicants must contact the Tutor for Graduate Admissions at Balliol College.

For further information contact:

Balliol College, University of Oxford, Oxford, Oxfordshire OX1 3BJ, England
Contact: Tutor for Graduate Admissions

Balliol College Gregory Kulkes Scholarships in Law

Subjects: Law.
Eligibility: Open to students of the European Union only.
Level of Study: Postgraduate.
Type: Scholarship.
Value: To be decided.
Length of Study: Two years, renewable for a third year.
Frequency: Annual.
Study Establishment: Balliol College, University of Oxford.
Country of Study: United Kingdom.
No. of awards offered: Up to two.
Application Procedure: Applicants must contact the tutor for graduate admissions at Balliol College.
Funding: Private.

For further information contact:

Balliol College, Oxford, Oxfordshire OX1 3BJ, England
Contact: Tutor for Graduate Admissions

Balliol College Mark Sadler Scholarship

Subjects: Mathematics.
Eligibility: Home and overseas students.

Level of Study: Postgraduate.
Type: Scholarship.
Length of Study: Up to a maximum of three years.
Study Establishment: Balliol College, University of Oxford.
Country of Study: United Kingdom.
No. of awards offered: One.
Application Procedure: Applicants must contact the Tutor for Graduate Admissions at Balliol College.

For further information contact:

Balliol College, Oxford, OX1 3BJ, England
Contact: Tutor for Graduate Admissions,

Balliol College Marvin Bower Scholarship

Subjects: International relations, politics or economics.
Eligibility: Open to home and European students only.
Type: Scholarship.
Value: UK£2,000.
Length of Study: Two years, with a possibility of renewal for a third year.
Country of Study: United Kingdom.
No. of awards offered: One.
Closing Date: Please contact the College.

For further information contact:

Tutor for Graduate Admissions, Balliol College, Oxford, Oxfordshire OX1 3BJ, England

Balliol College Snell Exhibition

Subjects: All subjects.
Eligibility: Open to graduates of Glasgow University only.
Level of Study: Graduate, Postgraduate.
Value: UK£1,000 per year.
Length of Study: Three years.
Frequency: Annual.
Study Establishment: Balliol College, the University of Oxford.
Country of Study: United Kingdom.
No. of awards offered: One.
Application Procedure: Applicants must contact the Tutor for Graduate Admissions at Balliol College.
Closing Date: Please contact the College.

For further information contact:

Tutor for Graduate Admissions, Balliol College, Oxford, Oxfordshire, OX1 3BJ, England

Balliol College Templeton Scholarship in Management

Subjects: Management.
Eligibility: Open only to overseas students.
Level of Study: Postgraduate.
Type: Scholarship.
Value: UK£2,000.
Length of Study: Two years, renewable for a third year.
Study Establishment: Balliol College, University of Oxford.
Country of Study: United Kingdom.
No. of awards offered: One.
Application Procedure: Applicants must contact the Tutor for Graduate Admissions at Balliol College.

For further information contact:

Balliol College, University of Oxford, Oxford, Oxfordshire, OX1 3BJ, England
Contact: Tutor for Graduate Admissions

Brasenose College John Hicks Foundation Scholarship

Subjects: Economics.
Eligibility: Home and overseas students. Preferred areas of specialization are Money and Banking or Macroeconomics.
Level of Study: Doctorate.
Type: Scholarship.
Value: UK£5,061 per annum, plus some dining rights and guaranteed accommodation for the first year of the course, at normal charge.

Length of Study: Up to three years.
Study Establishment: Brasenose College, University of Oxford.
Country of Study: United Kingdom.
No. of awards offered: One.
Application Procedure: Applicants must contact the Admissions Secretary at Brasenose College.

For further information contact:

Brasenose College, Oxford, OX1 4AJ,
Contact: The Admissions Secretary

Brasenose College Michael Woods Senior Scholarship

Subjects: Philosophy.
Eligibility: Open to applicants reading for the BPhil or DPhil in Philosophy.
Level of Study: Postgraduate.
Type: Scholarship.
Value: UK£1,500 per year plus some dining rights and guaranteed accommodation in the College for the first year of the course, at the normal charge.
Length of Study: Two years
Frequency: Varies.
Study Establishment: Brasenose College, the University of Oxford.
Country of Study: United Kingdom.
Application Procedure: Applicants must write for details.
Closing Date: Please write for details.
Additional Information: This scholarship is not available again before October 2006.

For further information contact:

Tutor for Graduates, Brasenose College, Oxford, Oxfordshire, OX1 4AJ, England

Brasenose Hector Pilling Scholarship

Subjects: Varies: in 2005 the scholarship will be awarded in the ARTS.
Eligibility: Open to graduates of any Commonwealth university, excluding the United Kingdom.
Level of Study: Postgraduate.
Type: Scholarship.
Frequency: Other.
Study Establishment: Brasenose College, the University of Oxford.
Country of Study: United Kingdom.
No. of awards offered: One.
Application Procedure: Applicants must write for details.
Closing Date: Please write for details.
Funding: Private.
Contributor: In conjunction with the University's Clarendon Fund Studentship scheme.
Additional Information: This scholarship is offered in conjunction with the Clarendon Fund in Studentship Scheme.

For further information contact:

University Offices, Wellington Square, Oxford, Oxfordshire, OX1 2JD, England
Email: international.office@admin.ox.ac.uk
Contact: International Office

British Chevening Scholarships (formerly known as Foreign and Commonwealth Office Scholarships and Awards)

Subjects: All subjects.
Purpose: To enable future leaders, decision makers and opinion formers to study in the United Kingdom.
Eligibility: Preference is given to postgraduates or those already established in a career.
Level of Study: Postgraduate.
Type: Scholarship.
Value: Varies.
Length of Study: Usually one year.
Study Establishment: The University of Oxford.
Country of Study: United Kingdom.

Application Procedure: Applicants must apply for information available on request from the British Council in the applicant's home country. Candidates are selected by British diplomatic missions overseas. Applicants must apply independently for admission to the University through the Graduate Admissions Office.
Closing Date: Please write for details.
Funding: Government.
Contributor: The Foreign and Commonwealth Office.
Additional Information: The scholarships are administered by the British Council on behalf of the Foreign Office. Further information is available on request or from the website http://www.britishcouncil.org.

Chevening Oxford-Australia Scholarships
Subjects: A range of disciplines including economics, environmental studies, human rights or law.
Purpose: To assist individuals with overseas study.
Eligibility: Open to Australian nationals.
Level of Study: Postgraduate.
Type: Scholarship.
Value: Up to Australian $34,000, to cover fees & living expenses.
Length of Study: One year.
Frequency: Annual.
Study Establishment: The University of Oxford.
Country of Study: United Kingdom.
No. of awards offered: Two.
Application Procedure: Applicants must write for details or visit the website http://www.rsc.anu.edu.au/oxford.
Closing Date: 21st February.

For further information contact:

Oxford-Australia Scholarships Committee, Research School for Chemistry, Australian National University, Canberra, ACT 0200, Australia
Tel: (61) 2 6125 3578
Fax: (61) 2 6125 4903
Email: jww@rsc.anu.edu.au
Contact: Professor J W White

Christ Church American Friends Scholarship
Subjects: All subjects.
Eligibility: Open to graduate students from the United States of America only.
Level of Study: Postgraduate.
Type: Scholarship.
Value: US$7000.
Length of Study: One year.
Frequency: Annual.
Study Establishment: Christ Church, the University of Oxford.
Country of Study: United Kingdom.
No. of awards offered: Varies.
Application Procedure: Applicants must apply for the scholarship when applying for admission.
Closing Date: Please write for details.
Funding: Private.

For further information contact:

The Tutor for Graduates' Secretary, Christ Church, Oxford, Oxfordshire, OX1 1DP, England

Christ Church Hugh Pilkington Scholarship
Subjects: All subjects.
Eligibility: Open to graduate students from outside the United States.
Level of Study: Postgraduate.
Type: Scholarship.
Value: UK£3,000 per year.
Length of Study: One year.
Frequency: Annual.
Study Establishment: Christ Church, the University of Oxford.
Country of Study: United Kingdom.
Application Procedure: Applicants must write to the Tutor for Graduates' Secretary at Christ Church for further information. Applications should be made when applying for admission.

For further information contact:

Dean's Secretary, Christ Church, Oxford, Oxfordshire OX1 1DP, England

Christ Church Senior Scholarship
Subjects: All subjects.
Purpose: To enable graduate scholars to undertake training or a definite course of literary, educational, scientific or professional study.
Eligibility: Open to candidates who will have been reading for a higher degree in the University of Oxford for at least one year, but not more than two years, by October 1st of the year in which the award is sought.
Level of Study: Postgraduate.
Type: Scholarship.
Value: Rooms and maintenance at Research Council level, subject to deduction of grants from other sources.
Length of Study: Two years, with a possibility of renewal for a further year.
Frequency: Annual.
Study Establishment: Christ Church, the University of Oxford.
Country of Study: United Kingdom.
No. of awards offered: Varies.
Application Procedure: Applicants must write for details. Applications should be made in February.
Additional Information: Normally, the scholarship is held in conjunction with an award from a government agency which pays the university fees.

For further information contact:

Tutor of Graduates' Secretary, Christ Church, Oxford, Oxfordshire, OX1 1DP, England

Clarendon Fund Bursaries
Subjects: All subjects.
Purpose: To enable outstanding candidates who have been accepted for admission to the University to take up their places.
Eligibility: Open to students who are liable for fees at the overseas rate and who are, therefore, not home or European Union students.
Level of Study: Doctorate, Postgraduate.
Type: Bursary.
Value: The financial circumstances of applicants will be taken into account in determining the level of awards. It is expected that most awards will be partial although full scholarships will occasionally be provided.
Frequency: Annual.
Study Establishment: The University of Oxford.
Country of Study: United Kingdom.
No. of awards offered: Approx. 100.
Application Procedure: Applicants must complete the application form available from the International Office. See http://www.admin.ox.ac.uk/io for further information.
Closing Date: The end of January.
Funding: Private.
Contributor: Oxford University Press.
Additional Information: Candidates must apply for an Overseas Research Students (ORS) award if the course they intend to follow makes them eligible.

Corpus Christi College Charles Oldham Graduate Scholarship in Classics
Subjects: Classics.
Eligibility: Overseas, home and EU students.
Level of Study: Postgraduate.
Type: Scholarship.
Value: Full fees, graduate maintenance grant and some dining rights.
Length of Study: Up to three years.
Frequency: Every 3 years (approx.).
Study Establishment: Corpus Christi College.
Country of Study: England.
No. of awards offered: One.
Closing Date: Please write for details.

Funding: Private.
Additional Information: Next election not expected before October 2005.

For further information contact:

Corpus Christi College, Merton Street, Oxford, OX1 4JF, England
Contact: The College Secretary

Corpus Christi College EK Chambers Studentship

Subjects: English literature.
Eligibility: Open to candidates who have studied classics at a UK university.
Level of Study: Postgraduate.
Type: Studentship.
Value: Full fees and graduate maintenance grant plus some dining rights.
Length of Study: Two-three years.
Frequency: Varies.
Study Establishment: Corpus Christi College or Somerville College, the University of Oxford.
Country of Study: United Kingdom.
No. of awards offered: One.
Application Procedure: Applicants must write for details.
Closing Date: Please write for details.

For further information contact:

St Cross Building, Manor Road, Oxford, OX1 3UQ, England
Contact: The Faculty of English

Corpus Christi College Garside Scholarship in Mathematics

Subjects: Mathematics.
Level of Study: Postdoctorate.
Type: Scholarship.
Value: UK£1,650 per annum, plus limited dining rights.
Length of Study: Up to two years.
Frequency: Every two years.
Study Establishment: Corpus Christi College, University of Oxford.
No. of awards offered: One.
Application Procedure: Applicants must contact the College Secretary, Corpus Christi College.
Additional Information: Country: Overseas, home and EU.

For further information contact:

Corpus Christi College, Merton Street, Oxford, OX1 4JF,
Contact: The College Secretary

DFID Shared Scholarship Scheme

Subjects: A subject related to the economic and social development of the student's home country.
Eligibility: Open to students from developing Commonwealth countries. Candidates must not be living or studying in a developed country or be employed by a government department (national or local) or a parastatal organisation. Candidates must certify that they would otherwise be unable to afford the cost of study in the United Kingdom and that they will return to work or study in their home country as soon as their award ends. Candidates should normally be under the age of 35 years at the time the award commences.
Level of Study: Postgraduate.
Type: Scholarship.
Value: University and college fees plus maintenance and return airfare to Great Britain.
Study Establishment: The University of Oxford.
Country of Study: United Kingdom.
No. of awards offered: 3.
Application Procedure: Applicants must complete application forms available on request from the International Office, Wellington Square, or from the website at http://www.admin.ox.ac.uk/io. Applicants must apply separately for admission to Oxford through the Graduate Admissions Office.
Closing Date: May 1st.
Funding: Government.

Dolabani Fund for Syriac Studies

Subjects: Syriac studies.
Purpose: To assist students in meeting the cost of engaging in courses involving Syriac studies at the University and for the provision of grants for the purchase of Syriac manuscripts for the Bodleian Library and the Oriental Institute Library. Also to further Syriac studies within the University and to support students from Syriac churches studying their own tradition in working for formal qualifications of the University.
Eligibility: Open to graduate students of the University who are nationals of the Middle East or the region of the Indian state of Kerala.
Level of Study: Postgraduate.
Type: Grant.
Value: Varies.
Study Establishment: The University of Oxford.
Country of Study: United Kingdom.
No. of awards offered: Varies.
Application Procedure: Applicants must submit a statement of purpose for which the grant is requested and, in the case of graduate students, the name of the applicant's supervisor.
Closing Date: 12th March.
Funding: Private.

For further information contact:

Secretary, Board of the Faculty of Oriental Studies, Oriental Institute, Pusey Lane, Oxford, Oxfordshire, OX1 2LE, England

Dulverton Scholarships

Subjects: All subjects.
Purpose: To provide assistance for students of outstanding academic merit and financial need.
Eligibility: Open to students from Eastern European countries, namely Albania, Armenia, Azerbaijan, Belarus, Bosnia, Bulgaria, Croatia, Czech Republic, Estonia, Georgia, Hungary, Latvia, Lithuania, Macedonia, Moldova, Poland, Romania, the Russian Federation, Slovakia, Slovenia, the Ukraine and Yugoslavia.
Level of Study: Postgraduate.
Value: Full scholarships will cover university and college fees and maintenance for the length of the proposed course of study. Partial scholarships will be awarded on the basis of financial need.
Study Establishment: The University of Oxford.
Country of Study: United Kingdom.
No. of awards offered: Varies.
Application Procedure: Applicants must apply separately for admission to Oxford through the Graduate Admissions Office, and should write for further particulars and an application form. Further information can also be found at http://www.admin.ox.ac.uk/io.
Closing Date: January 31st.
Funding: Private.
Contributor: The Dulverton Trust.

For further information contact:

International Office, University Offices, Wellington Square, Oxford, Oxfordshire, OX1 2JD, England

Exeter College Usher-Cunningham Senior Studentship

Subjects: Alternately awarded for medical science and medieval or modern history.
Purpose: To support graduate study.
Eligibility: Open to graduates of Irish universities only.
Level of Study: Postgraduate.
Type: Studentship.
Value: Home level fees plus maintenance up to the equivalent of a Research Council Award.
Length of Study: Usually awarded for up to three years.
Frequency: Every three years.
Study Establishment: Exeter College, the University of Oxford.
Country of Study: United Kingdom.
No. of awards offered: One.
Application Procedure: Applicants must address enquiries to the Academic Administrator.
Closing Date: Please write for details.

Funding: Private.
Contributor: An endowment.

For further information contact:

Academic Administrator, Exeter College, Oxford, Oxfordshire, OX1 3DP, England

Felix Scholarships
Subjects: All subjects.
Purpose: To enable graduates accepted for entry to Oxford to read for taught graduate courses or for a Master's or DPhil degree by research, who would be unable without financial assistance, to take up their place.
Eligibility: Open to Indian nationals under 30 years of age who must have at least a First Class (Honours) Bachelors Degree from an Indian university or comparable institution. Those who already hold degrees from universities outside India are not eligible to apply.
Level of Study: Doctorate, Postgraduate.
Value: University and college fees plus maintenance costs.
Length of Study: For two years in the first instance, with a possible extension for three years for those initially registered for a DPhil degree.
Study Establishment: The University of Oxford.
Country of Study: United Kingdom.
No. of awards offered: Up to six.
Application Procedure: Applicants must apply separately for admission to Oxford through the Graduate Admissions Office and should write for further details. Applicants for Felix Scholarships are expected to apply for an Overseas Research Student (ORS) award if the course they intend to take makes them eligible.
Closing Date: March 1st.

For further information contact:

International Office, University Offices, Wellington Square, Oxford, Oxfordshire, OX1 2JD, England
www: http://www.admin.ox.ac.uk/io

Freshfields Studentship in Law
Subjects: Law.
Level of Study: Postgraduate.
Type: Studentship.
Value: UK£7,500.
Length of Study: One year.
Frequency: Annual.
Study Establishment: The University of Oxford.
Country of Study: United Kingdom.
No. of awards offered: Two.
Application Procedure: Applicants must contact the International Office for an application form and further details.
Closing Date: June 30th.
Funding: Private.

For further information contact:

The International Office, University Offices, Wellington Square, Oxford, Oxfordshire, OX1 2JD, England
Tel: (44) 1865 270105
Email: international.office@admin.ox.ac.uk
www: http://www.admin.ox.ac.uk/io

Fulbright Oxford University Scholarships
Subjects: All subjects.
Level of Study: Doctorate, Postgraduate.
Value: Round trip travel, a maintenance allowance and approved tuition fees. A candidate gaining three awards ie. the Fulbright, Overseas Research Award (ORS) and Oxford bursary will have adequate funding for two years.
Length of Study: Two-three years.
Study Establishment: The University of Oxford.
Country of Study: United Kingdom.
No. of awards offered: Three.
Application Procedure: Applicants must complete an application form.

Closing Date: October 21st. Those enrolled in United States institutions must file applications with their Fulbright Programme Advisor by the deadline set by the campus advisor.
Funding: Private.
Additional Information: The course must lead to a higher degree and qualify for funding under the Overseas Research Student (ORS) award scheme. Candidates must apply for this award.

For further information contact:

US Student Programs, Institute of International Education (IIE), 809 United Nations Plaza, New York, NY 10017-3580, United States of America
www: www.iee.org

Green College Joan Doll Scholarship
Subjects: Any MSc degree offered at the College.
Level of Study: Graduate.
Type: Scholarship.
Value: College fee.
Length of Study: One year.
Study Establishment: Green College, University of Oxford.
Country of Study: United Kingdom.

For further information contact:

Green College, Oxford, Oxfordshire OX2 6HG,
Contact: The College Secretary

Hertford College Senior Scholarships
Subjects: All subjects.
Eligibility: Restricted to students about to commence a new research degree course or those about to upgrade their current course.
Level of Study: Postgraduate.
Type: Scholarship.
Value: UK£500 per year, plus priority for housing and some dining rights.
Length of Study: Two years.
Study Establishment: Hertford College, the University of Oxford.
Country of Study: United Kingdom.
No. of awards offered: Four - Five.
Application Procedure: Applicants must write to the College for further details.

For further information contact:

College Secretary, Hertford College, Oxford, Oxfordshire, OX1 3BW, England

Hill Foundation Scholarships
Subjects: All subjects.
Eligibility: Open to students from the Russian Federation studying for a postgraduate or a second Bachelor of Arts degree. Candidates should not normally be more than 25 years of age and should be intending to return to Russia at the end of their period of study.
Level of Study: Postgraduate.
Type: Scholarship.
Value: University and college fees, travel to and from the United Kingdom and a grant for maintenance.
Study Establishment: The University of Oxford.
Country of Study: United Kingdom.
No. of awards offered: Up to six.
Application Procedure: Applicants must complete the form for scholarships and bursaries for international students available from the International Office or online at http://www.admin.ox.ac.uk/io.
Closing Date: January 15th.
Funding: Private.
Additional Information: The Foundation particularly wants to encourage applications from candidates for a second BA degree. Further information is available from http://www.hillfoundationscholarships.org.

Hong Kong Oxford Scholarship Fund Bursaries (China)
Subjects: All subjects.
Eligibility: Open to nationals of the People's Republic of China. Students should be planning to return to and benefit their home country on completion of their studies.

Level of Study: Postgraduate.
Value: Up to UK£4,000.
Study Establishment: The University of Oxford.
Country of Study: United Kingdom.
No. of awards offered: Varies.
Application Procedure: Applicants must apply for admission to Oxford through the Graduate Admissions Office and should write for further details. Further information can also be found at http://www.admin.ox.ac.uk/io.
Closing Date: June.

For further information contact:

International Office, University Offices, Wellington Square, Oxford, Oxfordshire, OX1 2JD, England

James Fairfax and Oxford-Australia Fund

Subjects: Oxford-Australia Fund scholarships are open to any discipline whereas James Fairfax Scholarships are intended for those wishing to study in the arts or social sciences.
Level of Study: Postgraduate.
Value: University fees at the home and European Union rate, college fees and a living allowance of the order of Australian $12,000 per year.
Length of Study: Oxford-Australia Fund scholarships are for two years, or in the case of DPhil for three years, and James Fairfax Scholarships will generally be of two years duration.
Study Establishment: The University of Oxford.
Country of Study: United Kingdom.
No. of awards offered: One-two.
Application Procedure: Applicants must write for details or visit the website at http://www.rsc.anu.edu.au/oxford.
Closing Date: February 21st.
Funding: Private.
Contributor: Australian scholars who have studied at Oxford, and in particular, Mr James Fairfax.
Additional Information: Candidates are also expected to apply for an Overseas Research Student (ORS) award if the course they intend to follow makes them eligible.

For further information contact:

Chairman (Oxford Australia Scholarships Committee), Research School of Chemistry, Australian National University, Canberra, ACT ACT 0200, Australia
Tel: (61) 2 6125 3578
Fax: (61) 2 6125 4903
Email: jww@rsc.anv.edu.au
Contact: Professor J W White

James Ingham Halstead Scholarship in Music

Subjects: Music.
Eligibility: Open to graduates of any university who intend to proceed to one of the university's advanced degrees in music eg. M.Litt, M.Phil or DPhil or to graduates who are intending to supplicate for the BMus or DMus.
Level of Study: Doctorate, Postdoctorate, Postgraduate.
Type: Scholarship.
Value: Usually UK£300 per year.
Length of Study: One year, with a possibility of renewal for a further two years subject to reports of satisfactory progress.
Frequency: Annual.
Study Establishment: The University of Oxford.
Country of Study: United Kingdom.
No. of awards offered: Varies.
Application Procedure: Applicants must submit an application which includes their date of birth, a brief statement of their academic career, an example of original work eg. compositions, theses, essays, articles, etc. whether published or not, a brief statement of proposed research and the names of two referees. If applicants submit pieces of research whose purpose and relationship to their main plan of research is not immediately clear a short introduction should be included to set the work in the context of larger aims.
Closing Date: February 28th.
Funding: Private.
Contributor: The James Ingham Halstead Bequest.

Additional Information: Halstead Scholars may qualify for awards supplementary to their financial circumstances and the state of the fund.

For further information contact:

Board of the Faculty of Music, St Aldate's, Oxford, OX1 1DB, England
Contact: Secretary

Jesus College Meyricke Graduate Scholarships

Subjects: All subjects.
Eligibility: Open to graduates of the University of Wales who have been accepted by the College.
Level of Study: Graduate.
Type: Scholarship.
Value: UK£500 per year.
Length of Study: Up to three years.
Study Establishment: Jesus College, the University of Oxford.
Country of Study: United Kingdom.
Application Procedure: Applicants must write for details.

For further information contact:

Tutor for Graduates, Jesus College, Oxford, Oxfordshire, OX1 3DW, England

Jesus College Tarmac Graduate Scholarship

Subjects: Physical and social sciences.
Eligibility: Open to candidates from Poland or the Czech Republic only.
Level of Study: Postgraduate.
Type: Scholarship.
Value: All fees.
Length of Study: Up to three years.
Study Establishment: Jesus College, the University of Oxford.
Country of Study: United Kingdom.
No. of awards offered: One.
Application Procedure: Applicants must contact the Tutor for Graduate Admissions at Jesus College.

For further information contact:

Jesus Colllege, University of Oxford, Oxford, Oxfordshire, OX1 3DW, England
Contact: Tutor for Graduates

Jesus College The Alun Hughes' Graduate Scholarship

Subjects: Polynesia or Micronesia.
Eligibility: Open to applicants who have been accepted by the University of Oxford to undertake research towards a DPhil in the correct subject area.
Level of Study: Doctorate.
Type: Scholarship.
Value: Home and European Union fees.
Length of Study: Up to three years.
Frequency: Every 3 years approx.
Study Establishment: Jesus College, the University of Oxford.
Country of Study: United Kingdom.
No. of awards offered: Normally only one holder at a time.
Application Procedure: Applicants must write for details.
Closing Date: Please write for details.

For further information contact:

Tutor for Graduates, Jesus College, Oxford, Oxfordshire, OX1 3DW, England

Joanna Randall-MacIver Junior Research Fellowship

Subjects: Fine art, music or literature of any nation and of any period.
Eligibility: Open to women of any nationality who have completed their doctorate or are within sight of submission.
Level of Study: Postdoctorate.
Type: Fellowship.
Value: Stipend (varies), plus free board and lodging, plus UK£1,068 research allowance.
Length of Study: One year, renewable for one further year.

Frequency: Other.
Study Establishment: Tenable in rotation at Lady Margaret Hall, Somerville, St Hugh's, St Hilda's, St Anne's.
Country of Study: United Kingdom.
No. of awards offered: One.
Application Procedure: There is no application form, but candidates must obtain further particulars before applying.
Funding: Private.
Contributor: Oxford University.
Additional Information: The fellowship is awarded at five Oxford Colleges in rotation.

For further information contact:

St Hilda's College, Oxford, Oxfordshire OX4 1DY, England
Tel: (44) 1865 276815
Fax: (44) 1865 276816
Contact: Academic Office

Joint Modern History Faculty/St Antony's College Scholarship

Subjects: Modern history.
Eligibility: Open to graduate students reading modern history, who have already completed a Master's degree, from Botswana, Lesotho, Malawi, Mozambique, Namibia, South Africa, Swaziland, Zambia or Zimbabwe.
Level of Study: Doctorate.
Type: Scholarship.
Value: Fees and maintenance.
Length of Study: Three years.
Frequency: Every two years.
Study Establishment: St Antony's College, the University of Oxford.
Country of Study: United Kingdom.
No. of awards offered: One.
Application Procedure: Applicants must apply to DR Hubert Stadler at the address given below.

For further information contact:

Modern History Faculty University of Oxford, Oxford, Oxon, OX1 3BD, England
Contact: Dr Hubert Stadler

K C Wong Scholarships

Subjects: All subjects.
Purpose: To assist students studying at doctorate level.
Eligibility: Open to residents of the People's Republic of China only.
Level of Study: Doctorate.
Value: University and college fees plus maintenance.
Length of Study: Three years.
Study Establishment: The University of Oxford.
Country of Study: United Kingdom.
No. of awards offered: Three.
Application Procedure: Applicants must write for further details and an application form or visit the website at http://www.admin.ox.ac.uk/io.
Closing Date: January 31st.
Funding: Private.
Contributor: The K C Wong Foundation and the University of Oxford.
Additional Information: Applicants for the K C Wong Scholarships are also expected to apply for an Overseas Research Students (ORS) award.

For further information contact:

International Office, University Offices, Wellington Square, Oxford, Oxfordshire, OX1 2JD, England

Karim Rida Said Foundation Scholarships

Subjects: All subjects.
Purpose: To assist students with either a taught Master's degree, a Master's degree by research or for the DPhil degree.
Eligibility: Open to students from Iraq, Jordan, Lebanon, Palestine or Syria.
Level of Study: Doctorate, Postgraduate.

Value: University and college fees plus a maintenance grant for the duration of the student's course.
Frequency: Annual.
Study Establishment: The University of Oxford.
Country of Study: United Kingdom.
No. of awards offered: Varies.
Application Procedure: Applicants must apply separately for admission to Oxford through the Graduate Admissions Office and should write for further details.
Closing Date: April 1st.
Funding: Private.
Contributor: The Karim Rida Said Foundation.
Additional Information: Applicants are expected to apply for an Overseas Research Student (ORS) award if the course they intend to follow makes them eligible.

For further information contact:

International Office, University Offices, Wellington square, Oxford, Oxfordshire OX1 2JD, England

Keble College Gosden Graduate Scholarship

Subjects: All subjects.
Eligibility: Open to students intending to seek ordination in a church in communion with the Church of England.
Level of Study: Postgraduate.
Type: Scholarship.
Value: Up to UK£5,000 per year.
Length of Study: Up to three years.
Study Establishment: Keble College, the University of Oxford.
Country of Study: United Kingdom.
Application Procedure: Applicants must contact the Deputy Academic Administrator at Keble College in the first instance.
Closing Date: March.

For further information contact:

Keble College, Oxford, Oxfordshire, OX1 3PG, England
Email: college.office@keb.ox.ac.uk
Contact: Deputy Academic Administrator

Keble College Gwynne-Jones Scholarship

Subjects: All subjects
Eligibility: Open to nationals of Sierra Leone or the Yoruba speaking people of Nigeria.
Level of Study: Postgraduate.
Type: Scholarship.
Value: Up to UK£4,000 per year.
Length of Study: Up to three years.
Frequency: Varies.
Study Establishment: Keble College, the University of Oxford.
Country of Study: United Kingdom.
No. of awards offered: Varies.
Application Procedure: Applicants must write for details.
Closing Date: May.
Funding: Private.

For further information contact:

Keble College, Oxford, Oxfordshire, OX1 3PG, England
Email: college.office@keb.ox.ac.uk
Contact: Deputy Academic Administrator

Keble College Ian Palmer Graduate Scholarship in Information Technology

Subjects: Computer science and related fields concerning the practical uses of computer systems.
Eligibility: Please write for details.
Level of Study: Postgraduate.
Type: Scholarship.
Value: To the value of college fees.
Length of Study: Up to three years.
Frequency: Other.
Study Establishment: Keble College, the University of Oxford.
Country of Study: United Kingdom.

No. of awards offered: Varies.
Application Procedure: Applicants must write for details.
Closing Date: May.
Funding: Private.

For further information contact:

Keble College, Oxford, Oxfordshire, OX1 3PG, England
Email: college.office@keb.ox.ac.uk
Contact: Deputy Academic Administrator

Keble College Ian Tucker Memorial Bursary
Subjects: All subjects.
Eligibility: Candidates must demonstrate sporting prowess principally in the field of rugby football, together with qualities that will make a contribution to both the College and University.
Type: Bursary.
Value: UK£3,000.
Length of Study: One year.
Frequency: Other.
Study Establishment: Keble College, the University of Oxford.
Country of Study: United Kingdom.
No. of awards offered: Two.
Application Procedure: Applicants must contact the Tutor for Graduates at Keble College.

For further information contact:

Keble College, Oxford, Oxfordshire, OX1 3PG, England
Email: college.office@keb.ox.ac.uk
Contact: Deputy Academic Administrator

Keble College Keble Association Graduate Scholarship
Subjects: All subjects.
Level of Study: Postgraduate.
Type: Scholarship.
Value: UK£2,000.
Length of Study: One year.
Frequency: Annual.
Study Establishment: Keble College, the University of Oxford.
Country of Study: United Kingdom.
No. of awards offered: Two.
Application Procedure: Applicants must write for details.
Closing Date: May.
Funding: Private.

For further information contact:

Keble College, Oxford, Oxfordshire, OX1 3PG, England
Email: college.office@keb.ox.ac.uk
Contact: Deputy Academic Administrator

Keble College Paul Hayes Graduate Scholarship
Subjects: All subjects.
Eligibility: Candidates must demonstrate sporting excellence.
Level of Study: Doctorate, Graduate.
Type: Scholarship.
Value: Up to the value of college fees.
Length of Study: Up to three years.
Frequency: Other.
Study Establishment: Keble College, the University of Oxford.
Country of Study: United Kingdom.
No. of awards offered: One.
Application Procedure: Applicants must contact the Deputy Academic Administrator at Keble College.
Closing Date: May.

For further information contact:

Keble College, Oxford, Oxfordshire, OX1 3PG, England
Email: college.office@keb.ox.ac.uk
Contact: Deputy Academic Administrator

Kellogg College Graduate Studentships
Subjects: All subjects.
Eligibility: Open to part-time DPhil students at Kellogg College.

Level of Study: Doctorate.
Type: Studentship.
Value: Approx. UK£600 per year.
Length of Study: Up to six years.
Frequency: Annual.
Study Establishment: Kellogg College, the University of Oxford.
Country of Study: United Kingdom.
Application Procedure: Applicants must contact the Tutor for Admissions at Kellogg College.

For further information contact:

Tutor for Admissions, Kellogg College, Oxford, Oxfordshire, OX1 2JA, England

Kellogg College Kellogg Scholarships
Subjects: All subjects.
Eligibility: Open only to those offered a place at Kellogg College, Oxford.
Level of Study: Postgraduate.
Type: Scholarship.
Value: Approx. UK£300 per year.
Length of Study: More than two years.
Study Establishment: Kellogg College, the University of Oxford.
Country of Study: United Kingdom.
Application Procedure: Applicants must contact the Tutor for Admissions at Kellogg College in the first instance.

For further information contact:

Tutor for Admissions, Kellogg College, Oxford, Oxfordshire, OX1 2JA, England

Lady Margaret Hall EPA Cephalosporin Research Fellowship
Subjects: Biological, chemical or medical sciences.
Purpose: To provide an opportunity for academic postdoctoral research.
Eligibility: Open to qualified persons who hold, or will have obtained, a doctorate or equivalent degree by the start of tenure, and are engaged in advanced scientific research in Oxford.
Level of Study: Postgraduate.
Type: Fellowship.
Value: Not less than UK£3,000 per year, but may be held with other postdoctoral awards.
Length of Study: Two years, not renewable.
Frequency: Other.
Study Establishment: Lady Margaret Hall, the University of Oxford.
Country of Study: United Kingdom.
No. of awards offered: One.
Closing Date: As advertised.
Additional Information: Terms and conditions may be varied according to the decisions of the governing body. The fellowship may sometimes be offered as a supplementary award.

For further information contact:

Lady Margaret Hall, Norham Gardens, Oxford, Oxfordshire, OX2 6QA, England
Tel: (44) 1865 274300
Fax: (44) 1865 511069
Contact: Principal's Secretary

Lady Margaret Hall Warr-Goodman Graduate Scholarship
Subjects: Any.
Level of Study: Postdoctorate.
Type: Scholarship.
Value: UK£1,000 per annum, plus limited dining rights.
Length of Study: One year, with the possibility of extension for a further year.
Study Establishment: Lady Margaret Hall, University of Oxford.
Application Procedure: Applicants must contact the Tutor for Graduates or the Academic Administrator.

For further information contact:

Lady Margaret Hall, Norham Gardens, Oxford, OX2 6QA,

Linacre College A J Hosier Studentship

Subjects: Husbandry, agricultural economics or statistics and applied agricultural science.
Purpose: To fund graduate study.
Eligibility: Candidates must be honours graduates of a university in the United Kingdom and be citizens of the United Kingdom.
Level of Study: Postgraduate.
Type: Studentship.
Value: UK£4,000 per year which may be divided between more than one person.
Length of Study: One year.
Study Establishment: Linacre College, the University of Oxford.
Country of Study: United Kingdom.
No. of awards offered: Varies.
Application Procedure: Applicants must contact the Tutor for Admissions for further details.

For further information contact:

Tutor for Admissions, Linacre College, Oxford, Oxfordshire, OX1 3JA, England

Linacre College Applied Materials Scholarships

Subjects: Materials science, environmental studies.
Level of Study: Postgraduate.
Type: Scholarship.
Value: Up to UK£2,000 per year.
Length of Study: Up to three years.
Frequency: Varies, not available every year.
Study Establishment: Linacre College, the University of Oxford.
Country of Study: United Kingdom.
No. of awards offered: Up to five.
Application Procedure: Applicants must contact the Tutor for Admissions at Linacre College.

For further information contact:

Linacre College, Oxford, Oxfordshire OX1 3JA, England
www: http://www.linacre.ox.ac.uk

Linacre College Canadian National Scholarship

Subjects: All subjects.
Eligibility: Open to suitably qualified students of Canadian nationality reading or intending to read for a postgraduate degree.
Level of Study: Graduate, Postgraduate.
Type: Scholarship.
Value: Approx. UK£3,800 per year.
Length of Study: One year.
Frequency: May not be available every year.
Study Establishment: Linacre College, the University of Oxford.
Country of Study: United Kingdom.
Application Procedure: Applicants must write for details or visit the website at http://www.linacre.ox.ac.uk.

For further information contact:

The College Secretary, Linacre College, Oxford, Oxfordshire OX1 3DR, England

Linacre College Domus Studentships

Subjects: All subjects.
Purpose: To assist postgraduate study.
Eligibility: Open to students with a good first degree, who intend to begin reading for a higher degree or to current members of Linacre College.
Level of Study: Postgraduate.
Type: Studentship.
Value: UK£250 per year plus priority for accommodation.
Length of Study: Up to three years.
Frequency: Annual.
Study Establishment: Linacre College, the University of Oxford.
Country of Study: United Kingdom.
No. of awards offered: Varies.
Funding: Private.
Contributor: College funds.

For further information contact:

The Tutor for Admissions Linacre College, St Cross Road, Oxford, Oxfordshire OX1 3JA, England

Linacre College EPA Cephalosporin Junior Research Fellowships

Subjects: Biology, biochemistry, medicine, organic chemistry, psychology.
Purpose: To assist postdoctoral research.
Eligibility: Open to persons with a postdoctoral qualification.
Level of Study: Postdoctorate.
Type: Fellowship.
Value: UK£250 per year.
Length of Study: Up to two years.
Frequency: Annual.
Study Establishment: Linacre College, the University of Oxford.
Country of Study: United Kingdom.
No. of awards offered: Three.
Closing Date: January 31st.
Funding: Private.
Contributor: Linacre College.
No. of awards given last year: Three.
No. of applicants last year: 46.

For further information contact:

Linacre College, St Cross Road, Oxford, Oxfordshire OX1 3JA, England
Tel: (44) 1865 271657
Fax: (44) 1865 271668
Email: jane.edwards@linacre.ox.ac.uk
www: http://www.linacre.ox.ac.uk
Contact: College Secretary

Linacre College European Blaschko Visiting Research Scholarship

Subjects: Pharmacology, neuropharmacology.
Purpose: To enable European students to carry out research for one year in the department of Pharmacology or the MRC Anatomical Neuropharmacology Unit.
Eligibility: Open to students with a doctorate or equivalent degree from Europe
Level of Study: Postgraduate.
Type: Scholarship.
Value: College and university fees for visiting student status, stipend and the cost of return travel from the scholars home country.
Length of Study: One year.
Frequency: Annual.
Study Establishment: Linacre College, the University of Oxford.
Country of Study: United Kingdom.
Closing Date: Please write for details.
Funding: Private.

For further information contact:

Department of Pharmacology, Mansfield Road, Oxford, Oxfordshire OX1 3QT, England
Contact: Professor A D Smith

Linacre College Heselton Legal Research Scholarship

Subjects: English or European Union law research degrees.
Purpose: To fund graduate research.
Level of Study: Postgraduate.
Type: Scholarship.
Value: UK£1,000 per year.
Length of Study: One year.
Frequency: Varies.
Study Establishment: Linacre College, the University of Oxford.
Country of Study: United Kingdom.
Application Procedure: Applicants must contact the College Secretary at Linacre College in the first instance, or see http://www.linacre.ox.ac.uk.
Additional Information: This scholarship may not be available every year.

For further information contact:

Linacre College, Oxford, Oxfordshire OX1 3JA, England
Contact: College Secretary

Linacre College Lloyd African Scholarship DFID Shared Scholarships

Subjects: Development studies.
Purpose: To enable a qualified graduate student from an African university to pursue a one year taught Master's course.
Eligibility: Open to qualified graduate students from developing Commonwealth countries.
Level of Study: Postgraduate.
Type: Scholarship.
Value: University and college fees, maintenance and return airfare.
Length of Study: One-two years.
Frequency: Annually or biannually.
Study Establishment: Linacre College, the University of Oxford.
Country of Study: United Kingdom.
No. of awards offered: One.
Application Procedure: Applicants must write for details.
Funding: Private.

For further information contact:

Queen Elizabeth House, St Giles, Oxford, Oxfordshire OX1 3LA, England
Contact: Ms J Steele

Linacre College Mary Blaschko Graduate Scholarship

Subjects: Arts and humanities.
Eligibility: Open to suitably qualified students reading or intending to read for a research degree in the arts and humanities.
Level of Study: Postgraduate, Research.
Type: Scholarship.
Value: UK£2,000 per year.
Length of Study: One-two years.
Frequency: May not be available every year.
Study Establishment: Linacre College, the University of Oxford.
Country of Study: United Kingdom.
No. of awards offered: Two.
Application Procedure: Applicants must write for details. Forms are also available from http://www.linacre.ox.ac.uk.
Funding: Private.

For further information contact:

Tutor for Admissions Linacre College, Oxford, Oxfordshire OX1 3UA, England

Linacre College Norman and Ivy Lloyd Scholarship/DFID Shared Scholarship

Subjects: Environmental change and management.
Purpose: To enable a student from developing Commonwealth countries to undertake the MSc.
Eligibility: Open to nationals of developing Commonwealth countries.
Level of Study: Postgraduate.
Type: Scholarship.
Value: University and college fees plus maintenance and return airfare from the scholar's home country.
Length of Study: One year.
Frequency: Annual.
Study Establishment: Linacre College, the University of Oxford.
Country of Study: United Kingdom.
No. of awards offered: Varies.
Application Procedure: Applicants must write for details.
Closing Date: Please write for details.
Funding: Private.

For further information contact:

Environmental Change Institute, 5 Mansfield Road, Oxford, Oxfordshire OX1 3TB, England
Contact: Dr J Boatman

Linacre College Rausing Scholarships

Subjects: Subjects vary from year to year.
Level of Study: Postgraduate.
Type: Scholarship.
Value: Up to UK£2,000 per year.
Length of Study: Up to three years.
Frequency: Varies, not available every year.
Study Establishment: Linacre College, the University of Oxford.
Country of Study: United Kingdom.
No. of awards offered: Two.
Application Procedure: Applicants must be nominated by the faculty. No separate application is required.

Linares Rivas Scholarship

Subjects: All subjects.
Eligibility: Open to students from Spain, studying at or recently graduated from a Spanish university.
Level of Study: Graduate.
Value: University and college fees and a grant towards living costs.
Length of Study: One year.
Study Establishment: The University of Oxford.
Country of Study: United Kingdom.
No. of awards offered: One.
Application Procedure: Applicants must complete the application form obtainable from the International Office and should visit the website at http://www.admin.ox.ac.uk/io for further information.
Closing Date: January 31st.
Funding: Private.
Contributor: The trustees of the late Lady Consuelo Maria Allen.

For further information contact:

International Office, University Offices, Wellington Square, Oxford, Oxfordshire OX1 2JD, England

Lincoln College Berrow Foundation Scholarships

Subjects: All subjects.
Purpose: To permit graduates of certain Swiss universities to undertake postgraduate study at Oxford.
Eligibility: Open to graduates of the Swiss universities Berne, Geneva, Lausanne, Fribourg, Neuchâtel or the Ecole Polytechnique Fédérale de Lausanne, of Swiss or Lichtenstein Nationality only.
Level of Study: Doctorate, Postgraduate.
Type: Scholarship.
Value: All university and college fees are covered plus maintenance allowance.
Length of Study: Two years, with a possibility of renewal for a further year.
Frequency: Annual.
Study Establishment: Lincoln College, the University of Oxford.
Country of Study: United Kingdom.
No. of awards offered: Up to four.
Application Procedure: Applicants must write for details.
Funding: Private.

For further information contact:

Rector's Office Lincoln College, Oxford, Oxfordshire OX1 3DR, England

Lincoln College Berrow Foundation's Lord Florey Scholarships in Medical, Chemical and Biochemical Sciences

Subjects: Medical, chemical and biochemical sciences.
Eligibility: Open to nationals of Switzerland and Lichtenstein.
Level of Study: Postgraduate.
Type: Scholarship.
Value: Tuition fees and maintenance grant.
Length of Study: Two years, with the possibility of extension for a third year.
Study Establishment: Lincoln College, University of Oxford.
Application Procedure: Applicants must contact the Rector's Office.

For further information contact:

Lincoln College, Oxford, Oxfordshire OX1 3DR,

Lincoln College Erich and Rochelle Endowed Prize in Music

Subjects: Any discipline other than music.
Eligibility: Open to graduate students of exceptional and proven musical ability. The successful candidate will be expected to play a prominent part in the musical life of the college and in particular to act, if requested, as organising secretary of the college's active Music Society.
Level of Study: Postgraduate.
Value: UK£300.
Length of Study: One year only.
Frequency: Annual.
Study Establishment: Lincoln College, the University of Oxford.
Country of Study: United Kingdom.
No. of awards offered: One.
Closing Date: Please write for details.
Funding: Private.

For further information contact:

Admissions Office Lincoln College, Oxford, Oxfordshire OX1 3DR, England

Lincoln College Keith Murray Senior Scholarship

Subjects: All subjects.
Purpose: To permit students from outside the European Union to undertake postgraduate study at Oxford University.
Eligibility: Open to holders of a high first degree who are citizens of any country outside the European Community.
Level of Study: Doctorate, Postgraduate.
Type: Scholarship.
Value: All university and college fees are covered, plus maintenance allowance.
Length of Study: Two years, with the possibility of renewal for a third year.
Frequency: Every two years.
Study Establishment: Lincoln College, the University of Oxford.
Country of Study: United Kingdom,
No. of awards offered: More than one, depending on funds available.
Application Procedure: Applicants must write for details.
Funding: Private.

For further information contact:

The Rector's Office Lincoln College, Oxford, Oxfordshire OX1 3DR, England

Lincoln College Overseas Graduate Entrance Scholarships

Subjects: Crewe Scholarship may be held in any area of study.
Eligibility: Restricted to those offered a place at Lincoln College.
Level of Study: Postgraduate.
Type: Scholarship.
Value: UK£1,500.
Length of Study: One year.
Study Establishment: Lincoln College, the University of Oxford.
Country of Study: United Kingdom.
No. of awards offered: Four.
Application Procedure: For further information contact the Tutor for Graduates, Lincoln College.

For further information contact:

Lincoln College, Oxford, Oxfordshire OX1 3DR, England
Contact: Tutor for Graduates

Lincoln College Overseas Graduate Scholarship

Subjects: All subjects.
Eligibility: Open to those offered a place for graduate study at Lincoln College.
Level of Study: Graduate.

Type: Scholarship.
Value: UK£1,500.
Length of Study: One year.
Frequency: Annual.
Study Establishment: Lincoln College, the University of Oxford.
Country of Study: United Kingdom.
Application Procedure: Applicants must write for details.
Closing Date: Please write for details.

For further information contact:

Admissions Office Lincoln College, Oxford, Oxfordshire OX1 3DR, England

Lincoln College Supperstone Law Scholarship

Subjects: Law.
Eligibility: Open to candidates reading for the BCL or the MJuris, with an emphasis or special interest in European or public law.
Type: Scholarship.
Value: UK£400.
Length of Study: One year.
Study Establishment: Lincoln College, the University of Oxford.
Country of Study: United Kingdom.
No. of awards offered: One.
Application Procedure: Applicants must contact the Admissions Office at Lincoln College.
Closing Date: Please contact the College.

For further information contact:

Admissions Office Lincoln College, Oxford, Oxfordshire OX1 3DR, England

Lincoln College, Kenneth Seward-Shaw Scholarship

Subjects: Law, history, politics, English.
Level of Study: Postgraduate.
Type: Scholarship.
Value: UK£1,500.
Length of Study: One year.
Study Establishment: Lincoln College, University of Oxford.
Application Procedure: Applicants must contact the Admissions Office.

For further information contact:

Lincoln College, Oxford, Oxfordshire OX1 3DR, England
Contact: Admissions Office

Magdalen College Hichens Award

Subjects: MBA.
Level of Study: MBA, Postgraduate.
Type: Scholarship.
Value: Free accommodation in college for the duration of the course.
Length of Study: One year.
Frequency: Annual.
Study Establishment: Magdalen College, the University of Oxford.
Country of Study: United Kingdom.
No. of awards offered: Up to three.
Application Procedure: Applicants must contact the Senior Chemistry Tutor Magdalen College.

For further information contact:

The Senior Chemistry Tutor, Magdalen College, Oxford, Oxfordshire OX1 4AU, England

Magdalen College Perkins Research Studentship

Subjects: Chemistry.
Level of Study: Postgraduate.
Type: Scholarship.
Value: UK£9,000 per year.
Length of Study: One year initially, with possibility of renewal for further two years.
Study Establishment: Magdalen College, the University of Oxford.
Country of Study: United Kingdom.
No. of awards offered: One.

Application Procedure: Applicants must contact the Senior Chemistry Tutor, Magdalen College.

For further information contact:

Magdalen College, University of Oxford, Oxford, Oxon OX1 4AU, England
Contact: The Senior Chemistry Tutor

Mansfield College Elfan Rees Scholarship
Subjects: Alternates between politics and theology.
Level of Study: Postgraduate.
Type: Scholarship.
Value: UK£2,300 per year.
Length of Study: Two years.
Frequency: Every 4 years.
Study Establishment: Mansfield College, the University of Oxford.
Country of Study: United Kingdom.
No. of awards offered: Varies.
Application Procedure: Applicants must write for details.
Funding: Private.
Additional Information: Next available in 2005 for politics.

For further information contact:

Tutor for Graduates Mansfield College, Oxford, Oxfordshire OX1 3TF, England

Merton College Domus Graduate Scholarships A
Subjects: All subjects accepted by the College.
Eligibility: Open to non United Kingdom students.
Level of Study: Graduate.
Type: Scholarship.
Value: Fees, housing and maintenance.
Length of Study: Three years.
Frequency: Annual.
Study Establishment: Merton College, the University of Oxford.
Country of Study: United Kingdom.
No. of awards offered: Two.
Application Procedure: Applicants must write for details.
Closing Date: Please write for details. The deadline is usually in mid February.

For further information contact:

Merton College, Oxford, Oxfordshire OX1 4JD, England
Contact: Secretary for Graduates

Merton College Domus Graduate Scholarships B
Subjects: All subjects accepted by the College.
Eligibility: Open to United Kingdom students who hold a First Class Degree and are still unfunded in September.
Level of Study: Graduate.
Type: Scholarship.
Value: Fees, housing and maintenance.
Length of Study: Three years.
Frequency: Annual.
Study Establishment: Merton College, the University of Oxford.
Country of Study: United Kingdom.
No. of awards offered: Two.
Application Procedure: Applicants must write for details.
Closing Date: Late August.

For further information contact:

Merton College, Oxford, Oxfordshire OX1 4JD, England
Contact: Secretary for Graduates

Merton College Greendale Scholarship
Subjects: All subjects.
Eligibility: Open to nationals and permanent residents of Switzerland who have a degree from a Swiss university.
Level of Study: Postgraduate.
Type: Scholarship.
Value: Fees, housing and maintenance.
Length of Study: Up to three years.

Frequency: Annual.
Study Establishment: Merton College, the University of Oxford.
Country of Study: United Kingdom.
No. of awards offered: One.
Closing Date: Early January although applicants should confirm this with the college.
Funding: Private.

For further information contact:

Merton College, Oxford, Oxfordshire OX1 4JD, England
Contact: Secretary for Graduates

Merton College Leventis Scholarship
Subjects: Greek studies from the Bronze Age to AD 1453.
Eligibility: Open to citizens of Greece or the Republic of Cyprus.
Level of Study: Postgraduate.
Type: Scholarship.
Value: Fees, housing and maintenance.
Length of Study: Three years.
Frequency: Every two years.
Study Establishment: Merton College, the University of Oxford.
Country of Study: United Kingdom.
No. of awards offered: One.
Closing Date: Please contact the College.
Funding: Private.

For further information contact:

Secretary for Graduates, Merton College, Oxford, Oxfordshire OX1 4JD, England

Merton College Reed Foundation Scholarship
Subjects: All subjects except medicine.
Eligibility: Open to nationals of underdeveloped countries, which are decided on a rotational basis.
Type: Scholarship.
Value: Fees, board & lodging, maintenance grant.
Length of Study: Two years.
Frequency: Every two years.
Study Establishment: Merton College, the University of Oxford.
Country of Study: United Kingdom.
No. of awards offered: One.
Application Procedure: Applicants must write for details.
Closing Date: Early January.
Funding: Private.

For further information contact:

Merton College, Oxford, Oxfordshire OX1 4JD, England
Contact: Secretary for Graduates

Michael Wills Scholarships
Subjects: All subjects.
Eligibility: Open to citizens of Germany aged between 21-25 years. Candidates should not already have been studying at a university in the United Kingdom for more than one year at the time of application.
Level of Study: Postgraduate.
Value: University and college fees and a maintenance grant.
Length of Study: Up to two years.
Study Establishment: The University of Oxford.
Country of Study: United Kingdom.
No. of awards offered: One.
Application Procedure: Applicants must apply through the DAAD in Germany.
Closing Date: The end of October.

For further information contact:

Dept 313, DAAD, Kennedyallee 50, Bonn, D-53175, Germany
Tel: (49) 228 882 239
Contact: H Kowalczich

Museveni Scholarship
Subjects: African economics.
Purpose: To support DPhil students from Africa.

Eligibility: Open to nationals of Africa.
Level of Study: Doctorate.
Type: Scholarship.
Value: Up to UK£10,000.
Length of Study: One year.
Study Establishment: The Centre for the Study of African Economies, University of Oxford.
Country of Study: United Kingdom.
No. of awards offered: One.
Application Procedure: Applications must include a copy of the research proposal, a curriculum vitae and details of other applications for funding and/or funding obtained for DPhil studies.

For further information contact:

CSAE, Department of Economics, Manor Road Building, Oxford, Oxfordshire OX1 3UQ, England
www: http://www.economics.ox.ac.uk
Contact: Administrator

New College Reynolds Graduate Studentship in History
Subjects: Modern history.
Level of Study: Graduate.
Type: Scholarship.
Value: Home/EU fees, plus equivalent of an AHRB scholarship.
Length of Study: One year.
Frequency: Annual.
Study Establishment: New College, University of Oxford.
Country of Study: United Kingdom.
No. of awards offered: One.

For further information contact:

New College, Oxford, Oxfordshire OX1 3BN,
Contact: The Bursar

Noon/Chevening/OSI Oxford Scholarships
Subjects: All subjects.
Eligibility: Open to nationals of Pakistan, with preference being given to those who have not previously studied outside Pakistan.
Level of Study: Postgraduate.
Study Establishment: The University of Oxford.
Country of Study: United Kingdom.
No. of awards offered: Varies. There are a small number of full or partial awards.
Application Procedure: Applicants must apply separately for admission to Oxford through the Graduate Admissions Office and should write for further details. Further information can also be found at http://www.admin.ox.ac.uk/io.
Closing Date: April 1st.
Funding: Government, Private.
Contributor: The Noon Educational Foundation, the Foreign and Commonwealth Office the Open Society Institute and the University of Oxford.

For further information contact:

International Office, University Offices, Wellington Square, Oxford, Oxfordshire OX1 2JD, England

Nuffield College Funded Studentships
Subjects: Social sciences.
Purpose: To assist students on a postgraduate degree course.
Eligibility: Open to persons with at least an Upper Second Class (Honours) Degree or equivalent.
Level of Study: Postgraduate.
Type: Studentship.
Value: UK£13,990 (Home + EU students) UK£18,868 (Overseas students).
Length of Study: For the length of the course, subject to satisfactory progress upto four years.
Frequency: Annual.
Study Establishment: Nuffield College, the University of Oxford.
Country of Study: United Kingdom.
No. of awards offered: Varies.

Application Procedure: Applicants must submit a completed Nuffield application form with two pieces of recent academic written work. Applications must be made to the relevant faculty board of the university via the Graduate Admissions Office of the University. Candidates are advised to apply as early as possible.
Additional Information: Requests for information should be addressed to the College Secretary.

For further information contact:

College Secretary, Nuffield College, Oxford, Oxfordshire OX1 1NF, England
Email: glynis.baleham@nuf.ox.ac.uk
www: http://www.hicks.nuf.ox.ac.uk

Nuffield College Prize Research Fellowships
Subjects: Social sciences, political science, economics.
Purpose: To allow young scholars to continue research.
Eligibility: Open to men and women no more than five years beyond first degree graduation, or at a comparable stage in their academic careers.
Level of Study: Postgraduate.
Type: Fellowship.
Value: UK£9,311 per year for Predoctoral Fellows, UK£16,950 per year for Postdoctoral Fellows, plus accommodation or housing allowance, children's allowance and essential travel expenses.
Length of Study: Two years, extendable for one further year provided a doctorate is completed within an appropriate time.
Frequency: Annual.
Study Establishment: Nuffield College, the University of Oxford.
Country of Study: United Kingdom.
No. of awards offered: Three-six.
Application Procedure: Requests for information should be addressed to the PRF Competition Secretary.
Closing Date: End of October.
No. of awards given last year: 4.

For further information contact:

Nuffield College, Oxford, OX1 1NF, England
www: http://www.nuff.ox.ac.uk/

Oppenheimer Fund
Subjects: Any.
Level of Study: Postgraduate.
Value: Up to UK£5,000.
Length of Study: Duration of the student's course, subject to satisfactory progress.
Frequency: Annual.
Study Establishment: University of Oxford.
Country of Study: United Kingdom.
No. of awards offered: One partial award.
Application Procedure: Applicants must contact the Tutor for Graduate Admissions at Balliol College.
Funding: Private.

For further information contact:

International Office, University Offices, Wellington Square, Oxford, OX1 2JD, England
Email: international.office@admin.ox.ac.uk
www: http://www.admin.ox.ac.uk/io/

Oriel College Walter Raleigh Scholarship
Subjects: Environmental studies.
Eligibility: Open to students reading for the MSc course in environmental change and management.
Level of Study: Postgraduate.
Type: Scholarship.
Value: UK£4,000.
Length of Study: One year.
Frequency: Annual.
Study Establishment: Oriel College, the University of Oxford.
Country of Study: United Kingdom.
No. of awards offered: One.

Application Procedure: Applicants must contact the Tutor for Graduates, in the first instance at Oriel College.

For further information contact:

Oriel College, Oxford, OX1 4EW, England

ORISHA (Oxford Research in the Scholarship and Humanities of Africa) Studentships

Subjects: Social and cultural anthropology, archaeology, Egyptology, history, human geography, African literature, politics and international relations and sociology, subject to appropriate supervision being available.

Purpose: To support postgraduate study of Africa in the humanities.

Eligibility: Open to candidates for admission, or those already registered as graduate students. The successful applicant, if not already a member of an Oxford college, may be offered a place at St Antony's College or St Cross College.

Level of Study: Postgraduate.

Type: Studentship.

Value: University fees plus maintenance allowance. University fees will normally be covered at the home rate although in exceptional circumstances supplemental grants may be made in order to meet, or to go some way towards meeting, the difference between the home and overseas fee.

Length of Study: Two years with the possibility of extension for three and occasionally four years.

Frequency: Annual.

Study Establishment: The University of Oxford.

Country of Study: United Kingdom.

No. of awards offered: One.

Application Procedure: Applicants must write to the Secretary of the Interfaculty Committee for African Studies at the University Offices for further details.

Closing Date: February 25th.

OSI (Open Society Institute)/FCO Chevening Scholarships

Subjects: Humanities, social sciences, environmental sciences.

Purpose: To assist candidates studying for a Master's degree in certain subjects or conducting research for nine months as a visiting student.

Eligibility: Open to citizens of central and eastern Europe namely Albania, Belarus, Bosnia, Bulgaria, Croatia, Kazakhstan, Latvia, Lithuania, Macedonia, Moldova, Poland, Romania, Russia, Slovakia, the Ukraine, Uzbekistan and Yugoslavia.

Level of Study: Postgraduate.

Type: Scholarship.

Value: University and college fees, basic maintenance costs, travel to and from Oxford.

Length of Study: One year.

Frequency: Annual.

Study Establishment: The University of Oxford.

Country of Study: United Kingdom.

No. of awards offered: Up to 40.

Application Procedure: Applicants must submit a single application which will serve for both the scholarship and for entry to the university. Application forms and further details are available from the OSI/SOROS Foundation office in the applicants country of residence or from the website, http:// www.soros.org.

Closing Date: November 28th.

Funding: Government, Private.

Contributor: The OSI and the Foreign and Commonwealth Institute.

Additional Information: Students will be selected both on the basis of academic excellence and the potential to become leaders, decision-makers and opinion formers in their own country.

Overseas Research Student (ORS) Awards Scheme

Subjects: All subjects.

Eligibility: Some limitations on type of degree apply; competition is severe.

Level of Study: Doctorate, Postgraduate.

Value: Equivalent to the difference between home and overseas fees.

Length of Study: Renewable for as long as a student is liable for university fees.

Study Establishment: The University of Oxford.

Country of Study: United Kingdom.

No. of awards offered: Varies.

Application Procedure: Applicants must write for further details.

Closing Date: January.

Funding: Government.

Contributor: The British Government.

Additional Information: For further information please see the website.

For further information contact:

International Office, University Offices, Wellington Square, Oxford, Oxfordshire, OX1 2JD, England

Oxford Kobe Scholarships (Japan)

Subjects: All subjects.

Eligibility: Open to citizens of Japan taking up places to study for a graduate degree.

Level of Study: Graduate.

Type: Scholarship.

Value: University and college fees plus a maintenance allowance and the cost of travel to and from Japan at the start and end of the course.

Length of Study: One year, with a possibility of renewal for a further two years.

Frequency: Annual.

Study Establishment: The University of Oxford with one scholarship normally tenable at St Catherine's College.

Country of Study: United Kingdom.

No. of awards offered: Two.

Application Procedure: Applicants must complete the application form obtainable from the International Office and should visit http:// www.admin.ox.ac.uk/io for further information.

Closing Date: December 30th.

For further information contact:

International Office, University Offices, Wellington Square, Oxford, Oxfordshire, OX1 2JD, England

Oxford University Graduate Assistance Fund Awards

Subjects: All subjects.

Purpose: To assist meritorious students to achieve the level of funding necessary to embark on their chosen course or to complete a graduate degree.

Eligibility: Open to United Kingdom and European Union students only.

Level of Study: Doctorate, Postgraduate.

Type: Grant.

Value: Varies.

Frequency: Annual.

Study Establishment: The University of Oxford.

Country of Study: United Kingdom.

No. of awards offered: Varies.

Application Procedure: Applicants must apply as directed on the standard application form for graduate study. For further information see http://www.admin.ox.ac.uk/io.

Oxford University Theological Scholarships (Eastern and Central Europe)

Subjects: Theology.

Purpose: To enable students to pursue further studies in the University's Faculty of Theology.

Eligibility: Open to candidates, normally between the ages of 22 and 40, who will already have, or expect to obtain, a theological degree from a recognised university or theological college. Applications are invited from citizens of Russia, the Ukraine and any other countries of the former Soviet Union, apart from the Baltic States, Slovakia, Slovenia, Croatia, Bosnia, Macedonia, Bulgaria, Albania and Yugoslavia.

Level of Study: Graduate.

Type: Scholarship.

Value: Fees, a maintenance allowance and, where necessary, a return air fare.
Length of Study: Up to one year.
Study Establishment: The Faculty of Theology, the University of Oxford.
Country of Study: United Kingdom.
No. of awards offered: Up to four.
Application Procedure: Applicants must contact Mrs Elizabeth Macallister for further information.
Closing Date: December 31st.
Funding: Government, Private.
Contributor: Member churches of the Council of Churches for Britain and Ireland, the Foreign and Commonwealth Office and Oxford University.
Additional Information: Scholarships are open to members of any Christian denomination.

For further information contact:

Humanities & Social Sciences Division, University of Oxford, 34 St Giles, Oxford, Oxfordshire, OX1 3LH, England
Tel: (44) 1865 270117
Fax: (44) 1865 270553
Email: elizabeth.macallister@admin.ox.ac.uk
Contact: Mrs Elizabeth Macallister

Pembroke College Atkinson Scholarship

Eligibility: Open to male graduates of Melbourne University.
Level of Study: Postgraduate.
Type: Other.
Value: UK£3,500 plus dining rights.
Length of Study: Two years.
Frequency: Annual.
Study Establishment: Pembroke College, the University of Oxford.
Country of Study: United Kingdom.
No. of awards offered: Varies.
Application Procedure: Applicants must write for details.
Funding: Private.

For further information contact:

Pembroke College, Oxford, OX1 1DW, England
Contact: Admissions Secretary

Pembroke College Jose Gregorio Hernandez Award of the Venezuelan National Academy of Medicine

Subjects: Medicine or the biological sciences.
Eligibility: Open to nationals of Venezuela. Students must be nominated by the Venezuelan National Academy of Medicine and then accepted by the General Medical Council.
Level of Study: Postgraduate.
Type: Stipendary.
Value: Varies.
Length of Study: One year, renewable for a further year.
Frequency: Annual.
Study Establishment: Pembroke College, the University of Oxford.
Country of Study: United Kingdom.
No. of awards offered: Varies.
Application Procedure: Applicants must write for details.
Funding: Private.

For further information contact:

Pembroke College, Oxford, OX1 1DW, England
Contact: Admissions Secretary

Pembroke College TEPCO Senior Studentship

Subjects: Open to all subjects, but humanities preferred.
Purpose: To support the completion of a doctoral thesis after AHRB funding has been refused.
Eligibility: Open to nationals from any country.
Level of Study: Postgraduate.
Type: Stipendary.
Value: Up to UK£4,720, plus dining rights.
Length of Study: One year, renewable for a further year.

Frequency: Annual.
Study Establishment: Pembroke College, the University of Oxford.
Country of Study: United Kingdom.
No. of awards offered: Varies.
Application Procedure: Applicants must write for details.
Funding: Private.

For further information contact:

Pembroke College, Oxford, OX1 1DW, England
Contact: Admissions Secretary

Pirie-Reid Scholarships

Subjects: All subjects.
Purpose: To enable persons who would otherwise be prevented by lack of funds to begin a course of study at Oxford.
Level of Study: Postgraduate.
Type: Scholarship.
Value: University and college fees normally at the home rate plus maintenance grant, subject to assessment of income from other sources.
Length of Study: Renewable from year to year, subject to satisfactory progress and continuance of approved full-time study.
Frequency: Annual.
Study Establishment: The University of Oxford.
Country of Study: United Kingdom.
Application Procedure: Applicants must write for application forms. Candidates must apply for admission to the university through the Graduate Admissions Office.
Closing Date: May 1st.
Funding: Private.
Additional Information: Preference will be given to candidates applying from other universities ie. not matriculated at Oxford, and to those domiciled or educated in Scotland. Candidates not fulfilling these criteria are unlikely to be successful.

For further information contact:

Life & Environmental Sciences Divisional Office, 2 South Parks Road, Oxford, Oxfordshire OX1 3UB, England
Email: judith.brown@admin.ox.ac.uk
Contact: Mrs J Brown

Prendergast Bequest

Subjects: All subjects.
Eligibility: Open to applicants born in the Republic of Ireland whose parents are also citizens of the Republic of Ireland. Applicants must already be at the University of Oxford, or have received a firm offer of both faculty and college place, for a one year taught Master's course.
Level of Study: Postgraduate, Undergraduate.
Type: Grant.
Value: Varies, approx. UK£500-2,000 and is means tested.
Length of Study: One year.
Frequency: Varies.
Study Establishment: The University of Oxford.
Country of Study: United Kingdom.
No. of awards offered: Varies.
Application Procedure: Applicants must complete an application form. Further information and application forms are available on written request or from http://www.admin.ox.ac.uk/io.
Closing Date: August.
Funding: Private.

For further information contact:

Prendergast Bequest, University Offices, Wellington Square, Oxford, Oxfordshire OX1 2JD, England
Contact: Secretary to the Board of Management

Queen's College Cyril and Phyllis Long Studentship

Subjects: All subjects.
Eligibility: Overseas students only.
Level of Study: Postgraduate.
Type: Studentship.
Value: Equivalent of a Research Council maintenance grant.

Length of Study: Three years.
Frequency: Annual.
Study Establishment: The Queen's College, the University of Oxford.
Country of Study: United Kingdom.
No. of awards offered: One.
Closing Date: Please write for details.
Funding: Private.

For further information contact:

International Office, University Offices, Wellington Square, Oxford, OX1 2JD, England

Queen's College Florey EPA Scholarship
Subjects: Medical, biological or chemical sciences.
Eligibility: Open to nationals of European Union countries (excluding the United Kingdom and Ireland) Finland, Norway and Sweden.
Level of Study: Postgraduate.
Type: Scholarship.
Value: UK£2,000 per year. Assistance may also be given with fees to a maximum of half the cost.
Length of Study: One year, renewable for a second and third year.
Frequency: Annual.
Study Establishment: The Queen's College, the University of Oxford.
Country of Study: United Kingdom.
No. of awards offered: Varies.
Closing Date: Please contact the organisation.
Funding: Private.

For further information contact:

Tutor for Graduates, The Queen's College, Oxford, Oxfordshire, OX1 4AW, England

Queen's College George Oakes Senior Scholarship
Subjects: Aspects of the culture of the United States of America.
Eligibility: Open to citizens of the United Kingdom.
Level of Study: Postgraduate.
Type: Scholarship.
Value: UK£2,000 per year.
Length of Study: One year, renewable for a second and third year.
Frequency: Other.
Study Establishment: The Queen's College, the University of Oxford.
Country of Study: United Kingdom.
No. of awards offered: One.

For further information contact:

Tutor for Graduates, The Queen's College, Oxford, Oxfordshire, OX1 4AW, England

Queen's College Hastings Senior Scholarship
Subjects: All subjects.
Eligibility: Open to graduates with First Class (Honours) Degrees from the Universities of Bradford, Hull, Leeds, Sheffield or York.
Level of Study: Postgraduate.
Type: Scholarship.
Value: UK£2,000 per year (under review). Assistance may be given with fees if the holder is not eligible for Research Council or British Academy Studentships.
Length of Study: One year, renewable for a second and third year.
Study Establishment: The Queen's College, the University of Oxford.
Country of Study: United Kingdom.
Application Procedure: Applicants must contact the Tutor for Graduates at Queen's College in the first instance.

For further information contact:

Tutor for Graduates, The Queen's College, Oxford, Oxfordshire, OX1 4AW, England

Queen's College Holwell Studentship
Subjects: Religion and theology.
Eligibility: Open to home and overseas students.
Level of Study: Postgraduate.
Type: Studentship.
Value: UK£2,000 per year.
Length of Study: Two years, renewable for a third.
Study Establishment: The Queen's College, the University of Oxford.
Country of Study: United Kingdom.
No. of awards offered: One.

For further information contact:

41 St Giles, Oxford, OX1 3LW, England
Contact: Faculty of Theology

Queen's College Wendell Herbruck Studentship
Subjects: All subjects.
Eligibility: Open to residents of the United States of America who are no older than 26 when appointed. Preference will be given to residents of Ohio.
Level of Study: Postgraduate.
Type: Studentship.
Value: UK£2,000 per year.
Length of Study: One year, renewable for a second and third year.
Frequency: Varies.
Study Establishment: The Queen's College, the University of Oxford.
Country of Study: United Kingdom.
No. of awards offered: Varies.
Application Procedure: Applicants must write for details.
Funding: Private.
Additional Information: The next election is expected for entry in 2005.

For further information contact:

Tutor for Graduates, The Queen's College, Oxford, Oxfordshire, OX1 4AW, England

Regent's Park College (Permanent Private Hall) Asheville Scholarship
Subjects: Theology.
Eligibility: Open to men and women from Baptist seminaries in the United States of America.
Level of Study: Postgraduate.
Type: Scholarship.
Value: Up to UK£1,000 per year.
Length of Study: Up to two years, in the second and third year of the course.
Frequency: Annual.
Study Establishment: Regents Park College (Permanent Private Hall), the University of Oxford.
Country of Study: United Kingdom.
No. of awards offered: Varies.
Application Procedure: Applicants must contact the College for further information.
Funding: Private.

For further information contact:

Regent's Park College, Pusey Street, Oxford, Oxfordshire, OX1 2LB, England

Regent's Park College (Permanent Private Hall) Eastern European Scholarship
Subjects: Theology.
Eligibility: Open to students from Central and Eastern Europe with a preference given, but not restricted to, members of the Baptist denomination.
Level of Study: Postgraduate.
Type: Scholarship.
Value: Up to UK£1,800 per year.
Length of Study: Up to three years.

Frequency: Annual.
Study Establishment: Regent's Park College (Permanent Private Hall), the University of Oxford.
Country of Study: United Kingdom.
No. of awards offered: One.
Application Procedure: Applicants must contact the college for further information.
Funding: Private.

For further information contact:

Regent's Park College, Pusey Street, Oxford, Oxfordshire OX1 2LB, England

Regent's Park College (Permanent Private Hall) Ernest Payne Scholarship

Subjects: Theology.
Eligibility: Open to residents in the United Kingdom who are preparing for Baptist ministry.
Level of Study: Postgraduate.
Type: Scholarship.
Value: Up to UK£1,500 per year towards fees.
Length of Study: Two years, extendable to three.
Frequency: Annual.
Study Establishment: Regent's Park College (Permanent Private Hall), the University of Oxford.
Country of Study: United Kingdom.
No. of awards offered: One.
Application Procedure: Applicants must contact the college for further information.
Funding: Private.

For further information contact:

Regent's Park College, Pusey Street, Oxford, Oxfordshire OX1 2LB, England

Regent's Park College (Permanent Private Hall) Henman Scholarship

Subjects: Theology.
Eligibility: Open to overseas students.
Level of Study: Postgraduate.
Type: Scholarship.
Value: Up to UK£1,800 per year.
Length of Study: Up to three years.
Frequency: Annual.
Study Establishment: Regents Park College (Permanent Private Hall), the University of Oxford.
Country of Study: United Kingdom.
No. of awards offered: Varies.
Application Procedure: Applicants must contact the college for further information.
Funding: Private.

For further information contact:

Regent's Park College, Pusey Street, Oxford, Oxfordshire OX1 2LB, England

Regent's Park College (Permanent Private Hall) J W Lord Scholarship

Subjects: Theology.
Eligibility: Open to men and women preparing to serve Christian churches in India, Hong Kong and China, or otherwise in Asia, Africa, Central and South America and the Caribbean. The award is also available for in service training or sabbatical study for similar candidates.
Level of Study: Postgraduate.
Type: Scholarship.
Value: Up to UK£1,500 per year.
Length of Study: Up to three years.
Frequency: Annual.
Study Establishment: Regent's Park College (Permanent Private Hall), the University of Oxford.
Country of Study: United Kingdom.

No. of awards offered: Varies.
Application Procedure: Applicants must contact the college for further information.
Funding: Private.

For further information contact:

Regent's Park College, Pusey Street, Oxford, Oxfordshire OX1 2LB, England

Regent's Park College (Permanent Private Hall) Organ Scholarship

Subjects: All subjects but with a preference for music.
Eligibility: Open to suitably qualified candidates in any subject, but preference will be given to graduate students in music.
Level of Study: Postgraduate.
Type: Scholarship.
Value: UK£2,000 per year.
Length of Study: Up to three years, renewable annually.
Frequency: Annual.
Study Establishment: Regent's Park College (Permanent Private Hall), the University of Oxford.
Country of Study: United Kingdom.
No. of awards offered: Varies.
Application Procedure: Applicants must contact the college for further information.
Funding: Private.
Additional Information: The scholarship includes duties as musical director and organist at New Road Baptist Church.

For further information contact:

Regent's Park College, Pusey Street, Oxford, Oxfordshire OX1 2LB, England

Regent's Park College Studentships of the Centre for the Study of Christianity and Culture

Subjects: Any area concerning the relation of the Christian faith to culture.
Level of Study: Postgraduate.
Type: Studentship.
Value: College fees.
Length of Study: Up to three years.
Study Establishment: Regent's Park College, (Permanent Private Hall), the University of Oxford.
Country of Study: United Kingdom.

For further information contact:

Regent's Park College, Pusey Street, Oxford, Oxfordshire OX1 2LB, England
Contact: The Tutor for Graduates

Rhodes Scholarships

Subjects: All subjects.
Eligibility: Open to candidates aged 19-25 years, though in Kenya the upper age limit is 27. Rhodes Scholars must have graduated from a university and have resided for several years in their country of origin.
Level of Study: Doctorate, Graduate, Postgraduate.
Type: Scholarship.
Value: University and college fees plus maintenance stipend.
Length of Study: Two-three years.
Frequency: Annual.
Study Establishment: The University of Oxford.
Country of Study: United Kingdom.
No. of awards offered: 90.
Application Procedure: Rhodes Scholars are chosen by local Selection Committees in each constituency. There is no formal written examination as scholars are chosen for their academic all round qualities on the evidence of testimonials from responsible persons and after personal interviews by the Selection Committee concerned. Elections usually take place in November and December and the scholars come into residence the following October. After election, application is made on behalf of scholars for admission to individual colleges and faculties in Oxford and the election is not confirmed by

663

the Rhodes Trustees until the scholar-elect has been accepted for admission by the college.

Funding: Private.

Contributor: The Rhodes Trust.

Additional Information: A separate memorandum explaining the regulations in detail is published for each country and may be obtained from the local secretaries. See http://www.rhodesscholar.org for further information. The annual distribution of awards is as follows: Australia nine, Bermuda one, Commonwealth Caribbean two, Canada 11, Germany four, Hong Kong one, India six, Jamaica one, Kenya two, Malaysia one, New Zealand three, Pakistan two, Singapore one, Southern Africa 10, Uganda one, United States of America 32, Zambia one, Zimbabwe two, Bangladesh one.

For further information contact:

See www.admin.ox.ac.uk/io for details of organising secretaries in each country.

Sasakawa Fund Scholarships

Subjects: All subjects which require some period of study in Japan.

Eligibility: Candidates must be Japanese nationals or students from countries other than Japan whose course at the University of Oxford requires some period of study in Japan.

Level of Study: Doctorate, Graduate.

Type: Scholarship.

Value: Up to UK£5,000.

Length of Study: One year in the first instance, with the possibility of renewal for a maximum of three years, subject to satisfactory progress.

Frequency: Varies.

Study Establishment: The University of Oxford.

Country of Study: United Kingdom.

No. of awards offered: Up to two.

Application Procedure: Applicants from outside the United Kingdom must complete the Scholarships and Bursaries for International Student form available from the International Office or the university website. Applicants from the United Kingdom should contact the Secretary of the Sasakawa Fund.

Closing Date: March 1st.

Additional Information: Applicants must either have been accepted by the University of Oxford to undertake a research degree as a probationer research or DPhil student, or be currently undertaking such a course.

For further information contact:

The Sasakawa Fund, The Oriental Institute, Pusey Lane, Oxford, Oxfordshire OX1 2LE, England

Tel: (44) 1865 278225

Fax: (44) 1865 278190

Contact: Secretary

Scatcherd European Scholarships

Subjects: All subjects.

Eligibility: Open to nationals of any European country, excluding the United Kingdom and Turkey and including the Russian Federation and countries to the West of the Urals. Applicants must be taking up places to read either for a postgraduate degree, a second Bachelor of Arts degree or to spend a period of study as a visiting graduate student at the University of Oxford.

Level of Study: Postgraduate.

Type: Scholarship.

Value: University and college fees plus maintenance grant.

Study Establishment: The University of Oxford.

Country of Study: United Kingdom.

No. of awards offered: More than 10.

Application Procedure: Applicants must complete the application form obtainable from the International Office and should see http://www.admin.ox.ac.uk/io for further information.

Closing Date: 31 January.

For further information contact:

International Office, University Offices, Wellington Square, Oxford, Oxfordshire OX1 2JD, England

Shell Centenary Scholarships and Shell Centenary Chevening Scholarships

Subjects: Applied statistics, biodiversity, conservation and management, computer science, mathematics and foundations of computer science, environmental change and management, environmental geomorphology, economics for development, industrial relations and human resources management, public policy in Latin America, forced migration, criminology and criminal justice.

Purpose: To assist with Master's degrees.

Eligibility: Open to students from countries which are not current or applicant members of the Organisation for Economic Co-operation and Development (OECD) or from the Czech Republic, Hungary, Mexico, Poland, Slovakia or Turkey. Candidates should normally be aged 20-35 years and be intending to return to the home country at the end of the period of study. They should normally already hold a degree of an equivalent standard to a United Kingdom First Class (Honours) Degree or be expecting to obtain such a degree before the start of their proposed course.

Level of Study: Postgraduate.

Value: University and college fees, maintenance and return air travel to the United Kingdom.

Frequency: Annual.

Study Establishment: The University of Oxford.

Country of Study: United Kingdom.

No. of awards offered: Up to nine.

Application Procedure: Applicants must apply separately for admission to Oxford through the Graduate Admissions Office. Please write for further particulars and an application form or visit http://www.admin.ox.ac.uk/io.

Closing Date: January 31st.

Funding: Commercial.

For further information contact:

International Office, University Offices, Wellington Square, Oxford, Oxfordshire OX1 2JD, England

Sir John Rhys Studentship in Celtic Studies

Subjects: Celtic studies.

Purpose: To enable the successful candidate to complete a research programme on which he or she is already engaged.

Eligibility: Open to candidates engaged in graduate research in Celtic studies who need financial support in respect of living expenses, or fees. The award is not intended for those who hold full-time university posts.

Level of Study: Postgraduate.

Type: Studentship.

Value: Normally similar to that of a graduate studentship from a United Kingdom research council. The amount is dependent on the applicant's circumstances.

Length of Study: One year, renewable only in exceptional circumstances.

Frequency: Annual.

Study Establishment: The University of Oxford, normally Jesus College.

Country of Study: United Kingdom.

No. of awards offered: One.

Application Procedure: Applicants must send applications to the Secretary of the Taylor Institution and should include a curriculum vitae, a brief outline of the research proposed, an indication of the size of grant required ie. any necessary expenses in addition to the normal living costs of a graduate student and of other sources of financial support, brief details of any other awards or appointments for which the candidate is applying, the names of two academic referees and the candidate's address for the Easter period if different from the term time address. Applicants who are not already members of the university should apply for admission through the Graduate Admissions Office.

Closing Date: March 1st.

Funding: Private.

Contributor: The Sir John Rhys Fund.

Additional Information: The successful applicant, if not already a member of the University of Oxford, would normally become a member of Jesus College and would be expected to reside in Oxford for the greater part of the academic year.

For further information contact:

41 Wellington Square, Oxford, Oxfordshire OX1 2JF, England
Email: enquiries@modern-languages.ox.ac.uk
Contact: Secretary of the Taylor Institution

Somerville College Graduate Scholarships
Subjects: Humanities and science.
Eligibility: Overseas students only.
Level of Study: Postgraduate.
Type: Scholarship.
Value: College fees only.
Length of Study: Two years, with the possibility of renewal for a third year.
Frequency: Annual.
Study Establishment: Somerville College, the University of Oxford.
Country of Study: United Kingdom.
Application Procedure: Applicants must contact the University's International Office.

Somerville College Janet Watson Bursary
Subjects: All subjects.
Eligibility: Open to graduates from the United States of America who are in need of financial assistance.
Level of Study: Postgraduate.
Type: Bursary.
Value: UK£2,000-3,500 p.a.
Length of Study: One year, with possibility of renewal for second year.
Study Establishment: Somerville College, the University of Oxford.
Country of Study: United Kingdom.
Application Procedure: Applicants must contact the Assistant College Secretary.
Funding: Private.

For further information contact:

Somerville College, Oxford, Oxfordshire OX2 6HD, England
Contact: Assistant College Secretary

Somerville College Levick Sisters Senior Scholarship
Subjects: Philosophy or philology including Sanskrit and Old Norse.
Eligibility: Open to candidates reading for a higher degree.
Level of Study: Postgraduate.
Type: Scholarship.
Length of Study: One year, in the first instance.
Frequency: Annual.
Study Establishment: Somerville College, the University of Oxford.
Country of Study: United Kingdom.
Application Procedure: Applicants must contact the Assistant College Secretary.

For further information contact:

Somerville College, Oxford, Oxfordshire OX2 6HD, England
Contact: Assistant College Secretary

St Anne's College Biegun Warburg Junior Research Fellowship
Subjects: Research in the human and social sciences.
Purpose: To fund research in the human and social sciences.
Eligibility: Open to graduates in their second or subsequent year of research, and to candidates registered for doctorates at other universities.
Level of Study: Doctorate, Postdoctorate.
Type: Fellowship.
Value: UK£10,750 in 2002 (reviewed annually) plus accommodation or living-out allowance.
Length of Study: One year in the first instance, renewable for up to one additional year.
Frequency: Other.
Study Establishment: St Anne's College, the University of Oxford.

Country of Study: United Kingdom.
No. of awards offered: One.
Application Procedure: Further particulars should be requested in August or September one year before the award.
Closing Date: October.

For further information contact:

St Anne's College, Oxford, OX2 6HS, England

St Anne's College Drapers' Company Junior Research Fellowship
Subjects: In specified fields in Mathematics or the Sciences. Next award in 2005: Physics, Mathematics, Computation, Chemistry.
Purpose: To fund research.
Eligibility: Open to graduates in their second or subsequent year of research, and to candidates registered for doctorates at other universities.
Level of Study: Doctorate, Postdoctorate.
Type: Fellowship.
Value: UK£10,750 in 2002 (reviewed annually) plus free accommodation or living allowance.
Length of Study: One year in the first instance, may be renewed for up to one additional year.
Frequency: Other.
Study Establishment: St Anne's College, the University of Oxford.
Country of Study: United Kingdom.
No. of awards offered: One.
Application Procedure: Further particulars should be requested in August or September one year before the award.
Closing Date: October.
Contributor: The Drapers' Company.

For further information contact:

St Anne's College, Oxford, OX2 6HS, England

St Anne's College Ethics Scholarship
Subjects: Philosophy.
Eligibility: Applicants must have an interest in ethics and have been accepted at St Anne's to read for a higher degree of more than one year's duration in philosophy
Level of Study: Postgraduate.
Type: Scholarship.
Value: UK£600 plus fees and maintenance at the level of an AHRB studentship.
Length of Study: One year with the possibility of renewal for a further year.
Frequency: Annual.
Study Establishment: St Anne's College, the University of Oxford.
Country of Study: United Kingdom.
No. of awards offered: One.

For further information contact:

St Anne's College, Oxford, Oxfordshire OX2 6HS, England
Contact: College Secretary

St Anne's College Fulford Junior Research Fellowship
Subjects: In specified fields in the arts.
Purpose: To fund research.
Eligibility: Open to graduates in their second or subsequent year of research, and to candidates registered for doctorates at other universities.
Level of Study: Doctorate, Postdoctorate.
Type: Fellowship.
Value: UK£10,750 in 2002 (reviewed annually) plus free accommodation or living allowance.
Length of Study: One year in the first instance, may be renewed for up to one additional year.
Frequency: Other.
Study Establishment: St Anne's College, the University of Oxford.
Country of Study: United Kingdom.
No. of awards offered: One.

Application Procedure: Further particulars should be requested in August or September one year before the award.
Closing Date: October.

For further information contact:

St Anne's College, Oxford, OX2 6HS, England

St Anne's College Ioma Evans-Pritchard Junior Research Fellowship

Subjects: Varies.
Purpose: To fund research.
Eligibility: Open to graduates who are normally resident in the British Isles and to members of African universities.
Level of Study: Doctorate, Postdoctorate.
Type: Fellowship.
Value: UK£10,750 in 2003 (reveiwed annually) plus free accommodation or living allowance.
Length of Study: One year in the first instance, may be renewed for up to one additional year.
Frequency: Other.
Study Establishment: St Anne's College, the University of Oxford.
Country of Study: United Kingdom.
No. of awards offered: One.
Application Procedure: Further particulars should be requested in August or September one year before the award.
Closing Date: October.

For further information contact:

St Anne's College, Oxford, OX2 6HS, England

St Anne's College Irene Jamieson Research Scholarship

Subjects: Any arts or social science subject offered by the College.
Purpose: To fund graduate research.
Eligibility: EU & UK students.
Level of Study: Postgraduate.
Type: Scholarship.
Value: Equal to the college fee.
Length of Study: One year, renewable for a further year.
Frequency: Annual.
Study Establishment: St Anne's College, the University of Oxford.
Country of Study: United Kingdom.
No. of awards offered: Two.
Application Procedure: For more information contact the College Secretary.

For further information contact:

St Anne's College, Oxford, Oxfordshire OX2 6HS, England
Contact: College Secretary

St Anne's College Kathleen Bourne Junior Research Fellowship

Subjects: French language and literature, or humanities.
Purpose: To fund research in a French subject.
Eligibility: Open to graduates in their second or subsequent year of research, and to candidates registered for doctorates at other universities. Candidates must be from one of the countries or territories of the British Commonwealth, or the Republic of Ireland.
Level of Study: Doctorate, Postdoctorate.
Type: Fellowship.
Value: UK£10,750 in 2002 (reveiwed annually) plus free accommodation or living allowance.
Length of Study: One year in the first instance, may be renewed for up to one additional year.
Frequency: Other.
Study Establishment: St Anne's College, the University of Oxford.
Country of Study: United Kingdom.
No. of awards offered: One.
Application Procedure: Further particulars should be requested in August or September one year before the award.
Closing Date: October.

St Anne's College Olwen Rhys Research Scholarship

Subjects: Medieval romance language or literature.
Purpose: To fund graduate research.
Level of Study: Postgraduate.
Type: Scholarship.
Value: Equal to the college fee.
Length of Study: One year, renewable for a further year.
Frequency: Annual.
Study Establishment: St Anne's College, the University of Oxford.
Country of Study: United Kingdom.
No. of awards offered: One.
Application Procedure: All graduates who have accepted a place at St Anne's by June 20th will automatically be considered without any further application being necessary. For more information contact the College Secretary.

For further information contact:

St Anne's College, Oxford, Oxfordshire OX2 6HS, England
Contact: College Secretary

St Anne's College Overseas Scholarship

Subjects: All subjects offered by the University.
Purpose: To fund graduate research.
Eligibility: Open to graduates of any university who are not United Kingdom or European Community citizens.
Level of Study: Postgraduate.
Type: Scholarship.
Value: Equal to the college fee.
Length of Study: One year, renewable for a further year.
Frequency: Annual.
Study Establishment: St Anne's College, the University of Oxford.
Country of Study: United Kingdom.
No. of awards offered: Three.
Application Procedure: All graduates who have accepted a place at St Anne's by June 14th will automatically be considered without any further application being necessary. For more information contact the College Secretary.

For further information contact:

St Anne's College, Oxford, Oxfordshire OX2 6HS, England
Contact: College Secretary

St Anne's College Una Goodwin Research Scholarship

Subjects: Any science subject offered by the College.
Purpose: To fund graduate research.
Level of Study: Postgraduate.
Type: Scholarship.
Value: Equal to the college fee.
Length of Study: One year, renewable for a further year.
Frequency: Annual.
Study Establishment: St Anne's College, the University of Oxford.
Country of Study: United Kingdom.
No. of awards offered: One.
Application Procedure: For more information contact the College Secretary.
Closing Date: June 20th.

For further information contact:

St Anne's College, Oxford, Oxfordshire OX2 6HS, England
Contact: College Secretary

St Antony's College EFG Bank Group Scholarship

Subjects: All subjects in which the College specialises.
Eligibility: Open to graduate students of Greek nationality who are reading for a higher degree.
Level of Study: Graduate.
Type: Scholarship.
Value: Fees, maintenance and travel costs.
Length of Study: Two years.
Study Establishment: St Antony's College, the University of Oxford.
Country of Study: United Kingdom.

Application Procedure: Applicants must contact the College Secretary.
Funding: Private.

For further information contact:

St Anthony's College, Oxford, Oxfordshire, OX2 6JF, England
Contact: College Secretary

St Antony's College Ismene Fitch Scholarship
Subjects: Humanities.
Eligibility: Open to graduate students of Greek nationality reading for a doctorate in the humanities.
Level of Study: Doctorate.
Type: Scholarship.
Value: Fees and maintenance.
Length of Study: Three years.
Frequency: Every six years.
Study Establishment: St Antony's College, the University of Oxford.
Country of Study: United Kingdom.

For further information contact:

St Anthony's College, Oxford, Oxfordshire OX2 6JF, England
Contact: College Secretary

St Antony's College Ronaldo Falconer Scholarship
Subjects: All subjects in which the college specialises.
Eligibility: Open to graduate students from Costa Rica studying for a higher degree.
Level of Study: Graduate.
Type: Scholarship.
Value: Fees, maintenance and some travel costs.
Length of Study: One-three years depending on the course.
Study Establishment: St Antony's College, the University of Oxford.
Country of Study: United Kingdom.
Application Procedure: Applicants must write for details.
Closing Date: Please write for details.
Additional Information: Address for application: as mentioned above or The Director, Latin American Centre, St Antony's College, Oxford, OX2 6UF, England.

For further information contact:

CIAPA, PO Box 4224, San Jose, Costa Rica
Fax: (506) 224 9280
Email: enquiries@lac.ox.ac.uk
Contact: Dr Ronaldo Cerdas

St Antony's College Sassoon Scholarship
Subjects: All subjects in which the college specialises.
Eligibility: Open to graduate students reading for a doctorate.
Level of Study: Doctorate.
Type: Scholarship.
Value: University and college fees.
Length of Study: Three years.
Frequency: Annual.
Study Establishment: St Antony's College, the University of Oxford.
Country of Study: United Kingdom.

For further information contact:

St Anthony's College, Oxford, Oxfordshire OX2 6JF, England
Contact: College Secretary

St Antony's College Sir John Swire Scholarship
Subjects: All subjects in which the college specialises.
Eligibility: Open to graduate students from North East and South East Asia studying for a higher degree.
Level of Study: Graduate.
Type: Scholarship.
Value: Fees, maintenance and some travel costs.
Length of Study: Two years, with a possibility of renewal for a further year.
Frequency: Varies.
Study Establishment: St Antony's College, the University of Oxford.

Country of Study: United Kingdom.
No. of awards offered: One.
Application Procedure: Applicants must write for details.
Funding: Commercial.

For further information contact:

St Antony's College, Oxford, Oxfordshire OX2 6JF, England
Contact: College Secretary

St Antony's College Swire Centenary and Cathay Pacific Scholarship (Japan)
Subjects: All subjects in which the college specialises.
Eligibility: Open to students from Japan studying for a higher degree.
Level of Study: Graduate.
Type: Scholarship.
Value: Fees, maintenance and some travel costs.
Length of Study: Two years, with a possibility of renewal for a further year.
Frequency: Annual.
Study Establishment: St Antony's College, the University of Oxford.
Country of Study: United Kingdom.
Application Procedure: Applicants must write for details.
Closing Date: Please write for details.
Funding: Commercial.

For further information contact:

John Swire & Sons Japan Limited, Toho Twin Tower Building, 1-5-2 Yurakucho, Chiyodaku, Tokyo, 100-0006, Japan

St Antony's College Swire/Cathay Pacific Scholarship (Hong Kong)
Subjects: All subjects in which the college specialises.
Eligibility: Open to permanent residents of Hong Kong who have completed the majority of their education there.
Level of Study: Graduate.
Type: Scholarship.
Value: Fees, maintenance and some travel costs.
Length of Study: Two years, with a possibility of renewal for a further year.
Frequency: Annual.
Study Establishment: St Antony's College, the University of Oxford.
Country of Study: United Kingdom.
Application Procedure: Applicants must write for details.
Closing Date: Please write for details.
Funding: Commercial.

For further information contact:

John Swire & Sons (HK) Limited, 35/F Two Pacific Place, 88 Queensway, Hong Kong
Contact: Assistant Manager - Group Public Affairs

St Antony's College Swire/Cathay Pacific Scholarship (Republic of Korea)
Subjects: All subjects in which the college specialises.
Eligibility: Open to graduate students from the Republic of Korea studying for a higher degree.
Level of Study: Graduate.
Type: Scholarship.
Value: Fees, maintenance and some travel costs.
Length of Study: Two years, with a possibility of renewal for a further year.
Frequency: Annual.
Study Establishment: St Antony's College, the University of Oxford.
Country of Study: United Kingdom.
Application Procedure: Applicants must write for details.
Closing Date: Please write for details.
Funding: Commercial.

For further information contact:

Personnel & Administration Department, Cathay Pacific Airways Limited, 5th Floor Chase Plaza Building, 34-35 Jung-dong, Choong-ku, Seoul 100-120, Korea, Republic (South)

St Antony's College Swire/Chevening Scholarship (Hong Kong)

Subjects: All subjects in which the College specialises.
Eligibility: Open to graduate students who are permanent residents of Hong Kong and who have completed the majority of their education there.
Level of Study: Graduate.
Type: Scholarship.
Value: Fees, maintenance and some travel costs.
Length of Study: Two years, with a possibility of renewal for a further year.
Frequency: Annual.
Study Establishment: St Antony's College, the University of Oxford.
Country of Study: United Kingdom.
Application Procedure: Applicants must write for details.
Closing Date: Please write for details.
Funding: Commercial.

For further information contact:

John Swire & Sons (HK) Limited, 35/F Two Pacific Place, 88 Queensway, Hong Kong
Contact: Assistant Manager - Group Public Affairs

St Antony's College Wai Seng Senior Research Scholarship

Subjects: Subjects concerning the Asia Pacific region.
Level of Study: Doctorate.
Type: Scholarship.
Value: Fees and maintenance.
Length of Study: Two years.
Frequency: Every two years.
Study Establishment: St Antony's College, the University of Oxford.
Country of Study: United Kingdom.
No. of awards offered: One.

For further information contact:

Asian Studies Centre, St Antony's College, University of Oxford, Oxford, Oxfordshire, OX2 6JF, England
Contact: The Director

St Catherine's College Glaxo Scholarship in Medicine (2nd BM)

Subjects: Medicine.
Eligibility: Open to any student who has a confirmed place on the clinical medicine course (2nd BM) in the Oxford Medical School. Preference will be given to students who are not eligible for full funding eg. graduates who have already completed an Honours Degree before embarking on the pre-clinical course (1st BM) or the fast track graduate medical course.
Value: UK£1,500 per year.
Length of Study: Up to three years.
Study Establishment: St Catherine's College, the University of Oxford.
Country of Study: United Kingdom.

For further information contact:

St Catherine's College, Oxford, Oxfordshire, OX1 3UJ, England
Contact: Academic Registrar

St Catherine's College Graduate Scholarship

Subjects: Arts or Sciences.
Purpose: To assist graduates studying for a research degree, usually in their second year at the University of Oxford.
Eligibility: Candidates from any country may apply.
Level of Study: Postgraduate.
Type: Scholarship.
Value: UK£2,000.
Length of Study: Up to three years.
Frequency: Annual.
Study Establishment: St Catherine's College, the University of Oxford.
Country of Study: United Kingdom.

No. of awards offered: One.
Application Procedure: Please write for details.

For further information contact:

St Catherine's College, Oxford, Oxfordshire, OX1 3UJ, England
Contact: Academic Registrar

St Catherine's College Great Eastern Scholarship

Subjects: All subjects.
Eligibility: Open to Indian nationals.
Level of Study: Graduate.
Type: Scholarship.
Value: UK£2,000 per year.
Length of Study: Up to three years.
Study Establishment: St Catherine's College, the University of Oxford.
Country of Study: United Kingdom.

For further information contact:

St Catherine's College, Oxford, Oxfordshire, OX1 3UJ, England
Contact: Academic Registrar

St Catherine's College Leathersellers' Company Graduate Scholarship

Subjects: The physical or biological sciences, mathematics or engineering.
Eligibility: Open to graduates of any British university who wish to undertake research in the physical or biological sciences, mathematics and engineering. This may be held in conjunction with another award.
Level of Study: Graduate.
Type: Scholarship.
Value: UK£2,000 per year.
Length of Study: Up to three years.
Frequency: Annual.
Study Establishment: St Catherine's College, the University of Oxford.
Country of Study: United Kingdom.
Application Procedure: Applicants must contact the Academic Registrar or visit the website for further information.
Closing Date: April.
Funding: Private.

For further information contact:

St Catherine's College, Manor Road, Oxford, Oxfordshire, OX1 3UJ, England
Contact: Academic Registrar

St Catherine's College Overseas Graduate Scholarship

Subjects: All subjects.
Purpose: To assist graduates studying for a research degree, usually in their first year at the University of Oxford.
Eligibility: Open to qualified individuals who are citizens of non European Union countries.
Level of Study: Postgraduate.
Type: Scholarship.
Value: UK£1,500.
Length of Study: Two years.
Frequency: Varies.
Country of Study: United Kingdom.
No. of awards offered: One.
Application Procedure: Applicants must write for details.

For further information contact:

St Catherine's College, Oxford, Oxfordshire, OX1 3UJ, England
Contact: Academic Registrar

St Cross College F C Osmaston Scholarship

Subjects: Forestry.
Purpose: To support postgraduate study.
Eligibility: Any Country.
Level of Study: Postgraduate.

Type: Scholarship.
Value: UK£500 per year.
Length of Study: Up to three years.
Frequency: Annual.
Study Establishment: St Cross College, the University of Oxford.
Country of Study: United Kingdom.
No. of awards offered: One.

For further information contact:

St Cross College, Oxford, Oxfordshire, OX1 3LZ, England
Tel: (44) 1865 278490
Contact: Tutor for Admissions

St Cross College Paula Soans O'Brian Scholarships

Subjects: All subjects.
Purpose: To support postgraduate study.
Eligibility: Overseas students only.
Level of Study: Postgraduate.
Type: Scholarship.
Value: UK current college fee.
Length of Study: One-three years.
Frequency: Varies.
Study Establishment: St Cross College, the University of Oxford.
Country of Study: United Kingdom.
No. of awards offered: One-two.
Application Procedure: Awarded in conjunction with the University Clasendon Fund Scheme. Separate application to the college is not required.

St Cross College Unilever Scholarship

Subjects: Science, particularly biochemistry or engineering.
Purpose: To support postgraduate study.
Eligibility: Home, EU and overseas students.
Level of Study: Postgraduate.
Type: Scholarship.
Value: Current college fee.
Length of Study: One-three years.
Frequency: Annual.
Study Establishment: St Cross College, the University of Oxford.
Country of Study: United Kingdom.
No. of awards offered: One.
Application Procedure: Applicants must write for details.
Funding: Commercial.
Contributor: Unilever.

For further information contact:

St Cross College, Oxford, Oxfordshire, OX1 3LZ, England
Contact: College Secretary

St Edmund Hall William R Miller Graduate Awards

Subjects: All subjects.
Level of Study: Postgraduate.
Value: Free accommodation.
Length of Study: One year with possible extension for a further year.
Frequency: Annual.
Study Establishment: St Edmund Hall, the University of Oxford.
Country of Study: United Kingdom.
No. of awards offered: Three per year.
Application Procedure: Applicants must contact the Senior Tutor at St Edmund Hall for further information.
Closing Date: May 1st.

For further information contact:

St Edmund Hall, Oxford, Oxfordshire, OX1 4AR, England
Contact: Registrar

St Hilda's College Dame Helen Gardner Scholarship

Subjects: Humanities including literature, languages, ancient or modern history, music, fine art.
Purpose: To support study in the humanities.
Eligibility: Open to women who have been accepted to read for a higher research degree in the humanities at the University of Oxford.

Level of Study: Postgraduate.
Type: Scholarship.
Value: Up to UK£5,000 per years.
Length of Study: One-three years.
Frequency: Every three years.
Study Establishment: St Hilda's College, the University of Oxford.
Country of Study: United Kingdom.
No. of awards offered: One.
Application Procedure: Applicants must write for details.
Funding: Private.
Contributor: Dame Helen Gardner Bequest.

For further information contact:

St Hilda's College, Oxford, Oxfordshire, OX4 1DY, England
Contact: Admissions Secretary

St Hilda's College E P Abraham Junior Research Fellowship

Subjects: Chemistry, medicine or the biological sciences.
Eligibility: Open to women of any nationality who have completed their doctorate, or are within sight of submission.
Level of Study: Postdoctorate.
Type: Fellowship.
Value: UK£11,561 (2001-2002) per year, plus free board and lodging, plus UK£1,068 research allowance.
Length of Study: Two years, renewable for one additional year.
Frequency: Varies.
Study Establishment: St Hilda's College, the University of Oxford.
Country of Study: United Kingdom.
No. of awards offered: One.
Funding: Private.
Contributor: St Hilda's College.

For further information contact:

St Hilda's College, Oxford, Oxfordshire, OX4 1DY, England
Contact: Tutorial Secretary

St Hilda's College Graduate Scholarships

Subjects: All subjects offered by the university.
Eligibility: Open to female graduates from any country who are working towards a higher research degree.
Level of Study: Postgraduate.
Type: Scholarship.
Value: Up to UK£1,000 per year.
Length of Study: One-three years.
Frequency: Annual.
Study Establishment: St Hilda's College, the University of Oxford.
Country of Study: United Kingdom.
No. of awards offered: Varies.
Funding: Private.
Contributor: St Hilda's College.

For further information contact:

St Hilda's College, Oxford, Oxfordshire, OX4 1DY, England
Contact: Admissions Secretary

St Hilda's College Julia Mann Junior Research Fellowship

Subjects: Any subject offered by the university.
Eligibility: Open to women of any nationality who have completed their doctorate or are within sight of submission.
Level of Study: Postdoctorate.
Type: Fellowship.
Value: UK£11,561 (2001-2002) per year, plus free board and lodging, plus UK£1,068 research allowance.
Length of Study: Two years, renewable for one additional year.
Study Establishment: St Hilda's College, the University of Oxford.
Country of Study: United Kingdom.
No. of awards offered: One.
Application Procedure: There is no application form, but candidates must obtain further particulars before applying.
Funding: Private.
Contributor: St Hilda's College.

No. of applicants last year: 43.
Additional Information: The governing body of the college decides in which subject area(s) the award should be advertised in different years.

For further information contact:

St Hilda's College, Oxford, Oxfordshire, OX4 1DY, England
Contact: Tutorial Secretary

St Hilda's College McIlrath Junior Research Fellowship
Subjects: Any subject offered by the University.
Eligibility: Open to women of the United Kingdom or Commonwealth or EIRE who have completed their doctorate or are within sight of submission.
Level of Study: Postgraduate.
Type: One fellowship.
Value: UK£11,561 (2001-2002) per year, plus free board and lodging, plus UK£1,068 research allowance.
Length of Study: Two years, renewable for a third.
Study Establishment: The College, for 2 years, renewable for 1 additional year.
Country of Study: United Kingdom.
Additional Information: The governing body of the college decides in which subject area(s) the award should be advertised in different years.

For further information contact:

St Hilda's College, Oxford, Oxfordshire, OX4 1DY, England
Contact: Tutorial Secretary

St Hilda's College New Zealand Bursaries
Subjects: All subjects offered by the College.
Eligibility: Open to female students who are citizens of New Zealand and who have been accepted for a graduate research degree. Though the main criteria for the award is academic merit, financial circumstances are also considered. Applicants must show evidence of sufficient funding to complete their course.
Level of Study: Postgraduate.
Type: Bursary.
Length of Study: Initially for one year, but may be extended.
Frequency: Annual.
Study Establishment: St Hilda's College, the University of Oxford.
Country of Study: United Kingdom.
No. of awards offered: Varies.
Funding: Private.
Contributor: The Raymond and Sisam Funds.

For further information contact:

St Hilda's College, Oxford, Oxfordshire, OX4 1DY, England
Contact: Admissions Secretary

St Hilda's College Rhodes Visiting Fellowship for Women
Subjects: Any subject offered by the university.
Eligibility: Open to women of postdoctoral academic standing.
Level of Study: Postdoctorate.
Type: Fellowship.
Value: UK£13,223 (2001-2002) per year, plus free board and lodging, or housing allowance; and UK£1,068 research allowance and travel expenses to and from the home Country.
Length of Study: Two years, renewable for one additional year.
Study Establishment: St Hilda's College, the University of Oxford.
Country of Study: United Kingdom.
No. of awards offered: One.
Funding: Private.
Contributor: Rhodes Fellowship Trust.
Additional Information: The fellowship is restricted to specific countries in different years.

For further information contact:

St Hilda's College, Oxford, Oxfordshire, OX4 1DY, England
Contact: Tutorial Secretary

St Hilda's College Schoolmistress Fellowships
Subjects: Any subject offered by the university.
Purpose: To enable a practising teacher to undertake private study in Oxford.
Eligibility: Open to women engaged in sixth form teaching in schools and colleges.
Level of Study: Professional development.
Type: Fellowship.
Value: To cover room and board.
Length of Study: Study periods of up to 4 weeks.
Frequency: Annual.
Study Establishment: St Hilda's College, the University of Oxford.
Country of Study: United Kingdom.
No. of awards offered: Up to six.
Application Procedure: Please write for details.
Funding: Private.
Contributor: St Hilda's College.

For further information contact:

St Hilda's College, Oxford, Oxfordshire, OX4 1DY, England
Contact: College Secretary

St Hilda's College V H Galbraith Fellowship in Medieval Studies
Subjects: Medieval studies in history, history of art and architecture, languages and literature, philosophy, archeology, law or music.
Purpose: To enable a medieval historian to carry out research and teaching at St Hilda's College.
Eligibility: Open to women who have recently completed a doctorate. Preference is for scholars at the start of their career. Teaching as well as research is required.
Level of Study: Postdoctorate.
Type: Fellowship.
Value: UK£13,814 (2001-2002) per year, plus board and lodging, plus UK£1,068 research allowance.
Length of Study: Two years.
Frequency: Dependent on funds available.
Study Establishment: St Hilda's College, the University of Oxford.
Country of Study: United Kingdom.
No. of awards offered: One.
Application Procedure: The award is advertised when funds are available, normally every 3-4 years. Advertised in January for the following October. There is no application form.
Closing Date: Usually early February.
Funding: Private.
Contributor: Galbraith Fund.

For further information contact:

St Hilda's College, Oxford, Oxfordshire OX4 1DY, England
Contact: Tutorial Secretary

St Hugh's College Bursaries for Students from PRC
Subjects: All subjects offered by the College.
Eligibility: Open to nationals of the People's Republic of China.
Level of Study: Postgraduate.
Type: Scholarship.
Value: UK£2,000 per year.
Study Establishment: St Hugh's College, the University of Oxford.
Country of Study: United Kingdom.
Application Procedure: Applicants must contact the Academic Administrator in the first instance.

For further information contact:

St Hugh's College, Oxford, Oxfordshire, OX2 6LE, England
Contact: Academic Administrator

St Hugh's College Graduate Scholarships
Subjects: All subjects by research.
Purpose: To provide financial support to graduates reading for a degree by research.
Eligibility: Open to British nationals and candidates from overseas.
Level of Study: Postgraduate.

Type: Scholarship.
Value: UK£2,000 per year.
Length of Study: One year, with possibility of renewal for a second year.
Frequency: Annual.
Study Establishment: St Hugh's College, the University of Oxford.
Country of Study: United Kingdom.
No. of awards offered: Up to 12.
Application Procedure: Applicants must contact the Academic Administrator in the first instance.

For further information contact:

St Hugh's College, Oxford, Oxfordshire, OX2 6LE, England
Fax: (44) 1865 274912
Contact: Academic Administrator

St John's College Beeston Scholarships

Subjects: All subjects, with special encouragement given to applications in the field of Middle Eastern studies.
Eligibility: Open only to current graduate students of St John's.
Level of Study: Postgraduate.
Type: Scholarship.
Value: Free accommodation, plus UK£500 p.a.
Length of Study: Normally two years.
Study Establishment: St John's College, the University of Oxford.
Country of Study: United Kingdom.
No. of awards offered: One.

For further information contact:

St John's College, Oxford, Oxfordshire, OX1 3JP, England

St John's College Junior Research Fellowship

Subjects: Arts and humanities, engineering, law, mathematics and computer science, medical sciences, natural sciences, theology, social and behavioural sciences.
Purpose: Research.
Level of Study: Doctorate, Postdoctorate.
Type: Fellowship.
Value: UK£16,104 (increase pending).
Length of Study: Three years, renewable for one further year.
Frequency: Annual.
Study Establishment: St John's College, the University of Oxford.
Country of Study: United Kingdom.
Application Procedure: Application form must be completed. Junior Research Fellowships are advertised nationally during the Autumn of the year preceding appointment.
Closing Date: December.

For further information contact:

St John's College, Oxford, Oxfordshire, OX1 3JP, England
Contact: Academic Administrator

St John's College North Senior Scholarships

Subjects: All subjects.
Purpose: Research.
Eligibility: Open only to current graduate students of St John's.
Level of Study: Postgraduate.
Type: Scholarship.
Value: Free accommodation, plus UK£500 p.a.
Length of Study: Up to two years.
Frequency: Annual.
Study Establishment: St John's College, the University of Oxford.
Country of Study: United Kingdom.
No. of awards offered: Two.

For further information contact:

St John's College, Oxford, Oxfordshire, OX1 3JP, England

St Peter's College Bodossaki Foundation Graduate Scholarship in Science

Subjects: Natural sciences.
Eligibility: Open to nationals of Greece.
Level of Study: Postgraduate.

Type: Scholarship.
Value: Up to UK£8,000.
Length of Study: Up to three years.
Study Establishment: St Peter's College, the University of Oxford.
Country of Study: United Kingdom.
Application Procedure: Applicants must contact the Tutor for Graduates at St Peter's College in the first instance.
Funding: Private.
Contributor: The Bodossaki Foundation.

For further information contact:

St Peter's College, Oxford, Oxfordshire, OX1 2DL, England

St Peter's College Leonard J Theberge Memorial Scholarship

Subjects: All subjects offered by the college.
Eligibility: Open to students admitted to the college only. Candidates must be citizens of the United States of America and preference will be given to mature students over 30 or those who have been employed for five years.
Level of Study: Postgraduate.
Type: Scholarship.
Value: A modest contribution to maintenance and personal expenses.
Length of Study: One-two years.
Study Establishment: St Peter's College, the University of Oxford.
Country of Study: United Kingdom.
Application Procedure: Applicants must contact the Tutor for Graduates in the first instance.

For further information contact:

St Peter's College, Oxford, Oxfordshire, OX1 2DL, England
Contact: Tutor for Graduates

Templeton College Barclay DPHIL Scholarship

Subjects: Management Studies.
Eligibility: Open to students from the United Kingdom.
Level of Study: Graduate.
Type: Scholarship.
Value: Up to UK£5,000.
Length of Study: One year.
Frequency: Annual.
Study Establishment: Templeton College, the University of Oxford.
Country of Study: United Kingdom.
No. of awards offered: One.
Application Procedure: Applicants must contact the Academic Administrator.
Funding: Private.

For further information contact:

Templeton College, Oxford, Oxfordshire, OX1 5NY, England
Email: admissions@templeton.ox.ac.uk
www: http://www.templeton.ox.ac.uk
Contact: Academic Administrator

Templeton College Leyland Scholarships

Subjects: Management studies.
Level of Study: Postgraduate.
Type: Scholarship.
Value: Up to UK£1,500.
Length of Study: One year.
Frequency: Annual.
Study Establishment: Templeton College, the University of Oxford.
Country of Study: United Kingdom.
No. of awards offered: Up to three.
Application Procedure: Applicants must contact the Academic Administrator for further information.

For further information contact:

Templeton College, Oxford, Oxfordshire, OX1 5NY, England
Email: admissions@templeton.ox.ac.uk
www: http://www.templeton.ox.ac.uk
Contact: Academic Administrator

Templeton College Rosemary Stewart Scholarship

Subjects: Management studies, healthcare organisation and management.
Eligibility: Open to graduates of any university who would otherwise experience financial difficulty.
Level of Study: Postgraduate.
Type: Scholarship.
Value: UK£3,000 per year.
Length of Study: Up to Three years.
Frequency: Every three years.
Study Establishment: Templeton College, the University of Oxford.
Country of Study: United Kingdom.
No. of awards offered: One.
Application Procedure: Applicants must apply to the Academic Administrator, Templeton College and should visit http://www.templeton.ox.ac.uk for further information.

For further information contact:

Templeton College, University of Oxford, Oxford, Oxon, OX1 5NY, England
Contact: Academic Administrator

Trinity College Birkett Scholarship in Environmental Studies

Subjects: Environmental change and management.
Eligibility: Open to any graduate accepted for the MSc.
Level of Study: Postgraduate.
Type: Scholarship.
Value: UK£2,400.
Length of Study: One year.
Frequency: Annual.
Study Establishment: Trinity College, the University of Oxford.
Country of Study: United Kingdom.
No. of awards offered: Two.
Application Procedure: Please contact the Academic Administrator for details.

For further information contact:

Trinity College, Oxford, OX1 3BH, England
Contact: Academic Administrator

Trinity College Cecil Lubbock Memorial Scholarship

Subjects: Humanities or social sciences.
Type: Scholarship.
Value: Up to UK£5,000.
Length of Study: One-three years, depending on the course.
Study Establishment: Trinity College, the University of Oxford.
Country of Study: United Kingdom.
No. of awards offered: Two.
Application Procedure: Contact the Academic Administrator for details.

For further information contact:

Trinity College, Oxford, OX1 3BH, England
Contact: Academic Administrator

Trinity College Junior Research Fellowship

Subjects: Biological sciences, history, geography, theology and music, law, philosophy, economics, politics, physical sciences, english, classics, modern languages.
Purpose: To promote and encourage research among those at the start of an academic career.
Eligibility: Open to suitably qualified candidates having some research experience (eg., a completed doctoral thesis).
Level of Study: Doctorate, Postdoctorate.
Type: Fellowship.
Value: Approx. UK£16,495 per year.
Length of Study: Three years, not renewable.
Frequency: Annual.
Study Establishment: Trinity College, the University of Oxford.
Country of Study: United Kingdom.
No. of awards offered: One.

Application Procedure: Please write for details.
Closing Date: Early October of the year preceding the start of the appointment.
Additional Information: Subjects vary from year to year.

For further information contact:

Trinity College, Oxford, OX1 3BH, England
Contact: Academic Administrator

Trinity College Max Beloff Scholarship in History

Subjects: History.
Eligibility: Open to candidates intending to read for a research degree in history.
Level of Study: Graduate, Research.
Type: Scholarship.
Value: University and college fees at the home or European Union rate.
Length of Study: Up to three years.
Study Establishment: Trinity College, the University of Oxford.
Country of Study: United Kingdom.
No. of awards offered: One.
Application Procedure: Applicants must write for details.
Closing Date: Please write for details.
Funding: Private.

For further information contact:

Graduate Studies Office, Modern History Faculty, Broad Street, Oxford, Oxfordshire, OX1 3BD, England

Trinity College Sarnia Scholarship

Subjects: Arts.
Eligibility: Restricted to arts candidates who have been accepted by the University of Oxford but who have not obtained funding from other sources.
Type: Scholarship.
Value: University and College fees.
Length of Study: Up to three years.
Study Establishment: Trinity College, the University of Oxford.
Country of Study: United Kingdom.
No. of awards offered: One.
Application Procedure: Applicants must write for details.
Closing Date: Please write for details.
Additional Information: The Scholarship funds one Scholar at a time and is advertised only in the years when it falls vacant.

For further information contact:

Trinity College, Oxford, Oxfordshire, OX1 3BH, England
Contact: Tutor for Graduates

University College Chellgren Scholarship

Subjects: All subjects, but with a preference for those studying economics.
Level of Study: Graduate.
Type: Scholarship.
Value: UK£1,500 per year.
Length of Study: Up to three years.
Study Establishment: The University College, the University of Oxford.
Country of Study: United Kingdom.

For further information contact:

University College, Oxford, Oxfordshire, OX1 4BH, England
Contact: Senior Tutor

University College Loughman Scholarship

Subjects: All subjects.
Eligibility: Preference is given to those who can demonstrate excellence in, and who will make a significant contribution to, college life through non academic pursuits eg. arts, community service, sport etc.
Level of Study: Graduate.
Type: Scholarship.
Value: UK£2,500 per year.

Length of Study: Up to three years.
Study Establishment: University College, the University of London.
Country of Study: United Kingdom.

For further information contact:

University College, Oxford, Oxfordshire, OX1 4BH, England
Contact: Senior Tutor

University College Luis Ugueto Venezuelan Graduate Scholarship

Subjects: All subjects.
Eligibility: Open to Venezuelan nationals only.
Level of Study: Postgraduate.
Type: Scholarship.
Length of Study: Up to three years.
Study Establishment: University College, the University of Oxford.
Country of Study: United Kingdom.
No. of awards offered: One.
Application Procedure: Applicants must apply to the Senior Tutor, University College.

For further information contact:

University College, University of Oxford, Oxford, Oxon, OX1 4BH, England
Contact: Senior Tutor

University College Old Members' Trust Graduate Scholarship

Subjects: All subjects.
Level of Study: Doctorate.
Type: Scholarship.
Value: UK£3,000 per year.
Length of Study: Up to three years.
Study Establishment: University College, the University of Oxford.
Country of Study: United Kingdom.
Funding: Private.

For further information contact:

University College, Oxford, Oxfordshire, OX1 4BH, England
Contact: Senior Tutor

University College Senior Scholarship

Subjects: All subjects.
Level of Study: Postgraduate.
Type: Scholarship.
Value: UK£5,000 per year.
Length of Study: Up to three years.
Study Establishment: University College, the University of Oxford.
Country of Study: United Kingdom.
No. of awards offered: One.
Application Procedure: Applicants must apply to the Senior Tutor at University College.

For further information contact:

University College, University of Oxford, Oxford, Oxfordshire, OX1 4BH, England
Contact: Senior Tutor

Wadham College Brookman Organ Scholarship

Subjects: All subjects.
Level of Study: Postgraduate.
Type: Scholarship.
Value: UK£1,700-2,500 plus benefits.
Length of Study: One year.
Study Establishment: Wadham College, University of Oxford.
Country of Study: United Kingdom.
No. of awards offered: One.
Application Procedure: Applicants must apply to The Registrar, Wadham College.
Closing Date: February.

Additional Information: The award entails certain chapel and choir duties. See http://www.wadham.ox.ac.uk for further information.

For further information contact:

Wadham College University of Oxford, Oxford, Oxfordshire, OX1 3PN, England
Contact: The Registrar

Wadham College Donner Canadian Foundation Scholarship

Subjects: Law (BCL or MJur courses only).
Level of Study: Postgraduate.
Type: Scholarship.
Value: CAN$30,000.
Length of Study: One year.
Study Establishment: Wadham College, University of Oxford.
Country of Study: United Kingdom.
No. of awards offered: One.
Application Procedure: Applicants must apply to the Registrar at Wadham College.
Closing Date: January 31st.
Contributor: Donner Canadian Foundation, Allen E. Gotlieb.
Additional Information: For further information see http://www.wadham.ox.ac.uk.

For further information contact:

Wadham College, University of Oxford, Oxford, Oxfordshire, OX1 3PN, England
Contact: The Registrar

Wadham College Norwegian Scholarship

Subjects: All subjects.
Eligibility: Open to registered students or graduates of Oslo University, who are Norwegian citizens.
Level of Study: Postgraduate.
Type: Scholarship.
Value: Fees and maintenance.
Length of Study: One year.
Frequency: Annual.
Study Establishment: Wadham College, the University of Oxford.
Country of Study: United Kingdom
Application Procedure: Applicants must submit applications in August of each year to the committee for the Norsk Oxford-Stipendium ved Wadham College at the University of Oslo.
Closing Date: August.

Wadham College Senior Scholarship

Subjects: Any.
Level of Study: Postgraduate.
Type: Scholarship.
Value: £500.
Length of Study: One year.
Study Establishment: Wadham College, University of Oxford.
Application Procedure: Contact the Registrar, Wadham College for information.

For further information contact:

Wadham College, Oxford, Oxfordshire OX1 3PN,

Wadham College Stinton Scholarship

Subjects: All subjects.
Level of Study: Postgraduate.
Type: Fellowship.
Value: UK£1,750.
Length of Study: One year.
Study Establishment: Wadham College, University of Oxford.
Country of Study: United Kingdom.
No. of awards offered: One.
Application Procedure: Applicants must apply to the Registrar, Wadham College. For further information see http://www.wadham.ox.ac.uk.
Closing Date: June.

For further information contact:

Wadham College, University of Oxford, Oxford, Oxfordshire, OX1 3PN, England
Contact: The Registrar

Winter Williams Studentship in Law
Subjects: Law.
Level of Study: Doctorate, Postgraduate.
Type: Studentship.
Value: UK£7,500.
Length of Study: Up to three years.
Frequency: Annual.
Study Establishment: The University of Oxford.
Country of Study: United Kingdom.
No. of awards offered: Two.
Application Procedure: Applicants must contact the International Office for an application form and further details.
Closing Date: June 30th.
Funding: Private.

For further information contact:

The International Office, University Offices, Wellington Square, Oxford, Oxfordshire, OX1 2JD, England
Tel: (44) 1865 270105
Email: international.office@admin.ox.ac.uk
www: http://www.admin.ox.ac.uk/io

Wolfson College Stipendiary Junior Research Fellowships
Subjects: Social anthropology, indology (in rotation), history and/or philosophy of science history and philosophy of mathematics (in rotation), humanities (six fields in rotation), intellectual history (as funds permit).
Purpose: To facilitate research in given fields.
Level of Study: Doctorate, Postdoctorate, Postgraduate.
Type: Fellowship.
Value: UK£12,445 per year and single accommodation in college without charge and common table meals (UK£30 per week) in Hall.
Length of Study: Three years.
Frequency: Every three years.
Study Establishment: Wolfson College, the University of Oxford.
Country of Study: United Kingdom.
No. of awards offered: Four-five.
Application Procedure: For information contact the President's Secretary at Wolfson College.
Additional Information: Interview in Oxford required.

For further information contact:

Wolfson College, Oxford, Oxfordshire, OX2 6UD, England

Wolfson College: Norman - Hargreaves-Mawdsley Studentship
Subjects: Eighteenth-century Spanish History, preferably in relation to American colonies.
Eligibility: Open to citizens of any country.
Level of Study: Postgraduate.
Type: Studentship.
Value: UK£2,500 per annum.
Length of Study: Two to three years.
Frequency: Varies - next award in 2000.
Study Establishment: Wolfson College, the University of Oxford.
Country of Study: United Kingdom.
No. of awards offered: One.
Application Procedure: Please contact the Academic Secretary at Wolfson College.

For further information contact:

Wolfson College, Oxford, Oxfordshire OX2 6UD, England
Contact: Academic Secretary

THE UNIVERSITY OF QUEENSLAND

Office of Research & Postgraduate Studies, Cumbrae-Stewart Building Research Road, Brisbane, QLD 4072, Australia
Tel: (61) 7 3365 2033
Fax: (61) 7 3365 4455
Email: OPER@research.uq.edu.au
www: http://www.uq.edu.au
Contact: Director

The University of Queensland is recognised internationally as a premier research institution. The University attracts world class students and staff, and has numerous notable alumni. Its teaching, learning and research activities are underpinned by state of the art computing and it has received numerous awards.

University of Queensland Postdoctoral Research Fellowship
Subjects: All subjects offered by the University.
Purpose: To assist persons wishing to conduct full-time research at the University in any of its disciplines.
Eligibility: Open to candidates of any nationality. Applicants must not have had more than five years of full-time professional experience since the award of a doctoral degree as at June 30th of the year before the fellowship commences. Fellowships may be offered to applicants who do not hold a doctoral degree provided that evidence is given that a doctoral thesis has been submitted by June 30th.
Level of Study: Postdoctorate, Professional development.
Type: Fellowship.
Value: Australian $49,444 - 55,099 per year plus excursion return airfare for the recipient only.
Length of Study: Three years.
Frequency: Annual.
Study Establishment: The University of Queensland.
Country of Study: Australia.
No. of awards offered: Twelve(12).
Application Procedure: Applicants must complete an application form available from the heads of the relevant department or from the Director of Research Services. Application forms are also available from the website.
Closing Date: May 31st of the year preceding the award.
Funding: Government.
Additional Information: Further information is available on request.

University of Queensland Postgraduate Research Scholarships
Subjects: All subjects offered by the University.
Purpose: To support full-time study towards a Master of Philosophy degree or a Doctor of Philosophy degree.
Eligibility: Open to candidates of any nationality who are acceptable as full-time internal students for a research degree at the University. Applicants should hold an Australian First Class Degree, a Master's degree, or the equivalent. Candidates must have a sound knowledge of both written and spoken English.
Level of Study: Research.
Type: Scholarship.
Value: Australian $18,009.
Length of Study: The Master of Philosophy degree is two years, and the Doctor of Philosophy degree is up to three years.
Frequency: Annual.
Study Establishment: The University of Queensland.
Country of Study: Australia.
No. of awards offered: Approx. 100.
Application Procedure: International applicants must apply through the University's International Education Directorate. Australian applicants must apply through the Scholarships Officer.
Closing Date: The deadline for international applicants is August 31st and October 31st for Australian applicants.
Funding: Government.
Additional Information: To assist with tuition fee expenses international students may apply for the International Postgraduate Research Scholarships (IPRS) which are administered through the International

Education Directorate. For more comprehensive information please visit: http://www.uq.edu.auhttp://www.uq.edu.au/studyhttp://www.u-q.edu.au/grad-school.

University of Queensland Travel Scheme for International Collaborative Research

Subjects: All subjects offered by the University.
Purpose: To facilitate visits by scholars from institutions in other countries.
Eligibility: Open to any suitably qualified Scholar actively engaged in academic work at a university or internationally recognised research institution who will be able to contribute substantially to research activity in the department to which he or she is attached at the University of Queensland.
Level of Study: Postdoctorate, Research.
Type: Grant.
Value: Return economy airfare.
Length of Study: Applicants must spend at least four weeks during the semester at the University of Queensland in the year of the award.
Frequency: Annual.
Study Establishment: The University of Queensland.
Country of Study: Australia.
No. of awards offered: Approx. 15.
Application Procedure: Applicants must complete an application form, available from the heads of the relevant department or from the Director of Research Services. Application forms are also available from the website.
Closing Date: August 1st of the year preceding the award year.
Funding: Government.
No. of awards given last year: 12.
No. of applicants last year: 22.
Additional Information: Further information is available on request.

THE UNIVERSITY OF READING

Whiteknights, PO Box 217, Reading, Berkshire, RG6 6AH, England
Tel: (44) 118 378 7430
Fax: (44) 118 378 6248
Email: studentships@reading.ac.uk
www: http://www.rdg.ac.uk
Contact: Student Financial Support Office

The University of Reading offers postgraduate taught and research degree courses in all the traditional subject areas except medical sciences. Other, more vocational courses are also offered. Research work in many areas is of international renown.

BPF Lord Samuel of Wych Cross Memorial Award

Subjects: Land management.
Purpose: To assist students who would otherwise be unable financially to follow the MSc course.
Eligibility: Open to candidates who hold a first degree and are, at the time of the award, ordinarily resident in the United Kingdom.
Level of Study: Postgraduate.
Type: Scholarship.
Value: UK£1,000-2,000.
Length of Study: One year.
Frequency: Annual.
Study Establishment: The University of Reading.
Country of Study: United Kingdom.
No. of awards offered: One-three.
Application Procedure: Applicants must submit a curriculum vitae by invitation to the Director of Full-time Postgraduate Real Estate Programme.
Closing Date: Applications will be invited in May of the intended year of entry.
Funding: Private.
No. of awards given last year: Three.
Additional Information: Scholars must intend to remain resident in the United Kingdom after the term of the scholarship has ended.

For further information contact:

Director of the Postgraduate Real Estate Programme, Department of Real Estate & Planning, The University of Reading, Reading, Berkshire England
Tel: (44) 118 378 6336
Email: n.s.french@reading.ac.uk
Contact: Mr Nick French

University of Reading General Overseas Scholarships

Subjects: All subjects, subject to the availability of appropriate supervision at the University.
Purpose: To enable students to obtain a postdoctoral degree.
Eligibility: Open to applicants from mainland China only.
Level of Study: Doctorate, Postgraduate.
Type: Studentship.
Value: Full tuition fees and maintenance at a rate related to that offered by the relevant United Kingdom Funding Council.
Length of Study: Up to three years.
Frequency: Annual.
Study Establishment: The University of Reading.
Country of Study: United Kingdom.
No. of awards offered: Five.
Application Procedure: Applicants must fulfil the eligibility criteria and express an interest in the scholarships to be considered.
Closing Date: Please contact the University.
Funding: Private.
Contributor: University of Reading.
No. of awards given last year: Three.
No. of applicants last year: 135.

University of Reading Postgraduate Studentship

Subjects: All subjects, subject to the availability of appropriate supervision at the University.
Purpose: To enable students to obtain a doctoral degree.
Eligibility: Open to candidates holding a first degree qualification.
Level of Study: Doctorate, Postgraduate.
Type: Studentship.
Value: The composition fee at the home standard rate plus maintenance award related to the relevant Research Council rate.
Length of Study: Up to three years.
Frequency: Annual.
Study Establishment: The University of Reading.
Country of Study: United Kingdom.
No. of awards offered: Four.
Application Procedure: Applicants must be nominated to the students Financial Support Office. Full details are avaliable at www.reading.ac.uk/studentships.
Closing Date: February of the year of entry.
Funding: Private.
Contributor: The University of Reading.
No. of awards given last year: Four.
No. of applicants last year: 90.
Additional Information: Applications are assessed on the quality of their research proposal and shortlisted applicants will be asked to attend an interview.

University of Reading Research Studentships within the Social Sciences

Subjects: The social sciences.
Purpose: To enable students to obtain a doctoral degree.
Level of Study: Doctorate, Postgraduate.
Type: Scholarship.
Value: Composition fee at the home standard rate plus a maintenance award related to the rate paid by the relevant Research Council.
Length of Study: Up to three years.
Frequency: Annual.
Study Establishment: The University of Reading.
Country of Study: United Kingdom.
No. of awards offered: Up to 10.
Application Procedure: Applicants must complete an application form available from the Faculty office, email faspg@reading.ac.uk.
Closing Date: February of the year of entry.

Funding: Private.
Contributor: The University of Reading.
No. of awards given last year: Four.
No. of applicants last year: 17.

University of Reading Research Studentships: Faculty of Arts and Humanities

Subjects: Research areas within those covered by the Faculty of Arts and Humanities.
Purpose: To enable students to obtain a doctoral degree.
Level of Study: Doctorate, Postgraduate.
Type: Studentship.
Value: Composition fee at the home standard rate plus a maintenance award related to that paid by the relevant United Kingdom Research Council.
Length of Study: Three years.
Frequency: Annual.
Study Establishment: The University of Reading.
Country of Study: United Kingdom.
No. of awards offered: Varies.
Application Procedure: Applicants must complete an application form, available from the Faculty office, email: faspg@reading.ac.uk. Eligible applicants are expected to apply for, and accept if offered, a scholarship from the relevant United Kingdom Research Council or an ORS award.
Closing Date: February of the year of entry.
Funding: Private.

UNIVERSITY OF RHODE ISLAND

College of Business Administration, 210 Flagg Road, Kingston, RI 02881-0802, United States of America
Tel: (1) 401 874 4241
Fax: (1) 401 874 7047
Email: mba@etal.uri.edu
www: http://www.cba.uri.edu/graduate/mba.htm
Contact: Ms Lisa Lancellotta, MBA Co-ordinator

The University of Rhode Island, College of Business Administration offers three AACSB accredited MBA programmes to fit students' needs: the one year full-time MBA, the providence evening part-time MBA and the 18 month executive weekend MBA. The College also offers an MS in Accounting and a PhD in business.

URI Assistantships

Subjects: All subjects.
Purpose: To award degree candidates for services rendered to a department or a particular research project.
Eligibility: Applicants must hold Bachelor's degrees and must have been admitted as degree candidates by the Graduate School.
Level of Study: Graduate, MBA.
Type: Assistantship.
Value: Stipends vary.
Length of Study: Varies.
Frequency: Annual.
Study Establishment: The University of Rhode Island.
Country of Study: United States of America.
No. of awards offered: Varies.
Application Procedure: Applicants must contact the Graduate School.
Closing Date: Please contact the organisation.
Funding: Government.
Additional Information: The duties of those holding assistantships consist of assisting, under supervision, with the instructional or research activity of a department. Assistants will be required to devote a maximum of 20 hours a week to departmental work, not more than 10 hours of which may be in classroom contact.

URI Fellowships

Subjects: All subjects.
Purpose: To recognise scholars' achievement and promise. To enable scholars to pursue graduate study and research full-time without rendering services to the University.

Eligibility: Applicants must be full-time students.
Level of Study: Graduate, MBA.
Type: Competition.
Value: Stipends vary with the nature and tenure of each fellowship. In most instances, fellows have tuition and registration fees paid by the University.
Length of Study: Varies.
Frequency: Annual.
Study Establishment: The University of Rhode Island.
Country of Study: United States of America.
No. of awards offered: Varies.
Application Procedure: Fellows are selected from lists of nominees submitted by department chairpersons.
Closing Date: Please contact the organisation.

UNIVERSITY OF SOUTH AUSTRALIA

Research Services, Mawson Lakes Boulevard, Mawson Lakes, SA 5095, Australia
Tel: (61) 8 8302 3615
Fax: (61) 8 8302 3997
Email: robert.lawrence@unisa.edu.au
www: http://www.unisa.edu.au/orc/resdeg/rbdindex.htm
Contact: Ms Jayne Taylor, Research Degrees Manager

The University of South Australia's mission is to educate professionals, create and apply knowledge and serve the community.

International Postgraduate Research Scholarships (IPRS)

Subjects: Most subjects. Applicants should consult the University for details.
Level of Study: Doctorate, Postgraduate.
Type: Research Scholarship.
Value: Approx. Australian $18,000 per year.
Frequency: Annual.
Study Establishment: The University of South Australia.
Country of Study: Australia.
Application Procedure: Applicants must submit an application form, which can be obtained from the website.
Closing Date: The end of August.
Funding: Government.
Contributor: Department of Education, Science and Training (DEST).
No. of awards given last year: Six.
No. of applicants last year: 140.

UNIVERSITY OF SOUTHAMPTON

Highfield, Southampton, Hampshire, SO17 1BJ, England
Tel: (44) 23 8059 4741
Fax: (44) 23 8059 3037
www: http://www.soton.ac.uk
Contact: Academic Registrar

The University of Southampton was founded as the Hartley Institute in the mid nineteenth-century and was granted its Royal Charter in 1952. Today, the University offers a range of postgraduate and research courses in the following faculties: arts, engineering and applied science, law, mathematics, medicine, health and biological science, science and social sciences.

University of Southampton Studentships

Subjects: All subjects offered by the University.
Purpose: To support research study.
Eligibility: Open to candidates who hold a good Honours Degree and are eligible for admission to the department in which they intend to study.
Level of Study: Postgraduate, Research.
Type: Studentship.
Value: Based on Research Council Studentship rates.
Length of Study: The duration of the course of study and research.
Frequency: Annual.
Study Establishment: The University of Southampton.
Country of Study: United Kingdom.

No. of awards offered: Varies.
Application Procedure: Applicants must make initial enquiries to the head of the academic department in which research is to be undertaken.
Closing Date: Varies. Enquiries should be made by January for the following October.

World Universities Network (WUN) Scholarship Scheme

Subjects: Selected areas within chemistry, engineering sciences, geography, law, ocean and earth science, physics, politics and biological sciences.
Purpose: To support research visits to partner American universities.
Eligibility: Open to candidates currently registered for an MPhil or PhD degree in one of the University of Southampton's departments participating in the WUN scheme.
Level of Study: Postgraduate, Research.
Type: Scholarship.
Value: Up to UK£10,000.
Length of Study: The duration of the research visit, which is normally three months.
Frequency: Annual.
Study Establishment: Partner universities.
Country of Study: United States of America.
No. of awards offered: Varies.
Application Procedure: Applicants must make initial enquiries to the head of the academic department in which they are registered for their research degree.
Closing Date: Varies.
Contributor: The University of Southampton.
No. of awards given last year: Five.
No. of applicants last year: Seven.

UNIVERSITY OF SOUTHERN CALIFORNIA (USC)

University Park, Mail Code 4012, Los Angeles, CA 90089, United States of America
Tel: (1) 213 740 5294
Fax: (1) 213 740 8607
www: http://www.usc.edu/dept/LAS/Faculty/mellon.htm
Contact: Mr Richard Tithecott, Assistant Administrative Director

Located near the heart of Los Angeles, the University of Southern California (USC) is a private research university. It maintains a tradition of academic strength at all levels, from the earliest explorations of the undergraduate to the advanced scholarly research of the postdoctoral Fellow.

Andrew W Mellon Postdoctoral Fellowships in the Humanities

Subjects: The humanities.
Purpose: To encourage junior scholars to develop their research.
Eligibility: Open to Scholars who received their PhD within the past seven years and who do not hold tenure at an academic institution.
Level of Study: Postdoctorate.
Type: Fellowship.
Value: Approx. US$38,000, plus full faculty fringe benefits and modest research expense support.
Frequency: Annual.
Study Establishment: The University of Southern California.
Country of Study: United States of America.
No. of awards offered: One-two.
Application Procedure: This information varies each year so applicants should consult the website. Website being revised.
Funding: Private.
Contributor: The Mellon Foundation.
No. of awards given last year: Two.
No. of applicants last year: 100.

USC College Dissertation Fellowship

Subjects: Arts and humanities, natural sciences, social and behavioural sciences.

Purpose: To provide financial assistance to students who are about to begin, or are in the process of, writing their doctoral dissertation in the College of Letters, Arts and Sciences at USC.
Eligibility: Open to outstanding students of any nationality, who present evidence of achievement and promise as Scholars and have completed all but the dissertation stage of their degree.
Level of Study: Postdoctorate, Postgraduate.
Type: Fellowship.
Value: US$16,000 plus four units of tuition.
Length of Study: One year.
Frequency: Annual.
Study Establishment: The University of Southern California.
Country of Study: United States of America.
No. of awards offered: 37.
Application Procedure: Application dossiers are collated by department.

USC College of Letters, Arts and Sciences Merit Award

Subjects: Arts and humanities, natural sciences and social or behavioural sciences.
Purpose: To provide an opportunity for students working towards a PhD degree who intend to pursue a career in university teaching and research.
Eligibility: Open to outstanding seniors and graduates of any nationality who present evidence of achievement and promise as Scholars.
Level of Study: Graduate.
Type: Fellowship.
Value: US$16,000 per year minimum, plus full tuition and health insurance.
Length of Study: Up to five years. This consists of two years of fellowship and three years of graduate assistantship.
Frequency: Annual.
Study Establishment: The University of Southern California.
Country of Study: United States of America.
No. of awards offered: 100.
Application Procedure: Application forms are available from the USC academic department to which the student is applying for admission.
Closing Date: Varies by department.
No. of awards given last year: 75.

UNIVERSITY OF ST ANDREWS

School of Modern Languages, Buchanan Building, Union Street, St Andrews, Fife, KY16 9PH, Scotland
Contact: Dr William Henry Jackson

Eugène Vinaver Memorial Trust, 45, Albert Street, Durham DH1 4RJ, England. The Eugène Vinaver Trust exists to promote research into Arthurian studies, as defined by the international Arthurian Society. It offers subventions to publishers to facilitate the publication of scholarly works; it also offers grants to portgraduate students pursuing research in the Arthurian field.

Barron Bequest

Subjects: Any field of Arthurian studies.
Purpose: To support postgraduate research in Arthurian studies.
Eligibility: Open to graduates of any university of the British Isles, including those of the Republic of Ireland.
Type: Grant.
Value: Up to UK£1,250 towards academic fees.
Length of Study: One year. Candidates may apply for further years on a basis of parity with applying for the first times.
Frequency: Annual.
Country of Study: United Kingdom, Republic of Ireland.
No. of awards offered: Varies.
Application Procedure: For application details please contact: Dr W. H. Jackson, Arthurian Research Support Fund, School of Modern Languages, University of St. Andrews, Buchanan Building, Union Street, St. Andrews, Fife KY16 9PH, Scotland, e-mail: whj@st-andrews.ac.uk.
Closing Date: April 30th.

Funding: Private.
Contributor: Any university in the British Isles, including those of the Republic of Ireland, except Owens College, University of Manchester.
No. of awards given last year: 3.

UNIVERSITY OF STIRLING

Research Office, Stirling, FK9 4LA, Scotland
Tel: (44) 1786 407041
Fax: (44) 1786 466688
Email: research@stir.ac.uk
www: http://www.stir.ac.uk
Contact: Research Services Officer

The University of Stirling offers the following postgraduate awards: Doctor of Philosophy, Master of Letters and Master of Science, MEd and EdD. The University is organised into four faculties: Arts, Human Science, Management and Natural Sciences. Most research degrees are available on a full-time or part-time basis. Further information is given in the relevant departmental entries.

University of Stirling Research Studentships
Subjects: The arts and human sciences eg. applied social science, psychology, education, nursing and midwifery, management and natural sciences, including aquaculture.
Purpose: To support postgraduate study.
Eligibility: Applicants must also apply to external funding bodies.
Level of Study: Doctorate, Postgraduate.
Type: Studentship.
Value: UK£6,800 per year.
Length of Study: A maximum of three years.
Frequency: Annual.
Study Establishment: The University of Stirling.
Country of Study: Scotland.
No. of awards offered: 12 new studentships per academic year.
Application Procedure: Applicants must complete an application form for the individual faculty. Further information and application forms are available from the relevant faculty office, to which the completed application forms must be returned.
Closing Date: Please consult the relevant faculty office for details.
Funding: Private.
Contributor: The University of Stirling.
No. of awards given last year: 12.
Additional Information: Further information is available on request.

UNIVERSITY OF SUSSEX/ASSOCIATION OF COMMONWEALTH UNIVERSITIES

Postgraduate Office, Sussex House, Falmer, Brighton, East Sussex BN1 9RH, England
Tel: (44) 1273 606755
Fax: (44) 1273 678335
Email: t.o-donnell@sussex.ac.uk
www: http://www.sussex.ac.uk
Contact: Mr Terry O'Donnell

The University of Sussex is one of the United Kingdom's foremost research institutions. The University boasts a distinguished faculty that includes 17 Fellows of the Royal Society and four Fellows of the British Academy. The University has around 20,000 students, 25 per cent of whom are postgraduates.

Geoff Lockwood Scholarship
Subjects: All subjects.
Eligibility: Open to United Kingdom students.
Level of Study: Postgraduate.
Type: Scholarship.
Value: UK£1,000.
Frequency: Annual.
No. of awards offered: One.
Additional Information: Applicants should see the website.

Sasakawa Scholarship
Subjects: Science, economic and environmental policy, internationalism or gender roles in modern society.
Purpose: To educate graduate students with high potential for future leadership in international life as well as in private endeavour.
Eligibility: Applications are usually accepted from students from United Kingdom, China, Eastern Europe or former Soviet Republics.
Level of Study: Postgraduate.
Type: Scholarship.
Value: Fees, maintenance award and return airfare.
Length of Study: One year.
Frequency: Annual.
Study Establishment: Sussex University.
Country of Study: United Kingdom.
No. of awards offered: Three.
Application Procedure: Applicants must complete and submit an application form with transcripts and academic references.

University of Sussex Overseas Development Administration Shared Scholarship Scheme
Subjects: Subjects related to the economic and social development of overseas countries.
Purpose: To help students of high academic calibre in developing Commonwealth countries who would not be eligible for awards to study in the United Kingdom under existing British Government schemes, and would not be able to afford to pay for the cost themselves.
Eligibility: Candidates must be below the age of 35, have sufficient fluency in English, not have studied in the United Kingdom before, be a national of a developing Commonwealth country, not be living in a developed country and not be employed by a government department.
Level of Study: Postgraduate.
Type: Scholarship.
Value: Fees and maintenance grant.
Length of Study: One year.
Frequency: Annual.
Study Establishment: Sussex University.
Country of Study: United Kingdom.
No. of awards offered: Two.
Application Procedure: Applicants must complete and submit an application form with academic transcripts and references.
Closing Date: Usually mid March.
Additional Information: Only applicants from targeted countries are eligible to apply and this information is usually known in the January preceding the start of the academic year. Targeted countries are decided annually. Successful applicants must agree to return to their home country on completion of studies.

University of Sussex Overseas Research Studentships
Subjects: Arts and humanities, education science, english, law, mathematics and computer science, communication and information science, natural sciences or social sciences.
Purpose: To assist overseas students of outstanding merit and research potential.
Eligibility: Open to students applying for research degrees eg. the MPhil or the DPhil who are assessed as liable to the overseas rate of fee. Applicants are allowed to submit an award through only one institution.
Level of Study: Postgraduate.
Type: Scholarship.
Value: Part of tuition fee.
Length of Study: Up to three years.
Frequency: Annual.
Study Establishment: The University of Sussex.
Country of Study: United Kingdom.
No. of awards offered: 15.
Application Procedure: Applicants must complete and submit an application form with academic transcripts and references.
Closing Date: Early April.

University of Sussex/Association of Commonwealth Universities Access Fund Bursaries

Subjects: All subjects.
Eligibility: Open to United Kingdom students.
Level of Study: Postgraduate.
Type: Bursary.
Value: UK£2,000.
Frequency: Annual.
No. of awards offered: 20.
Additional Information: Applicants should visit the website for further details.

University of Sussex/Association of Commonwealth Universities Graduate Teaching Assistantships

Subjects: All subjects.
Eligibility: Applicants must visit the website for full eligibility requirements.
Level of Study: Postgraduate.
Type: Other.
Value: Includes at least a fee waiver but possibly more, depending on whether the student undertakes teaching.
Length of Study: Varies.
Frequency: Annual.
No. of awards offered: 20.
Application Procedure: Applicants must visit the website for details of the application procedure.
Closing Date: Please contact the organisation.

THE UNIVERSITY OF SYDNEY

Research Office, Main Quadrangle A14, Sydney, NSW 2006, Australia
Tel: (61) 2 9351 3250
Fax: (61) 2 9351 4812
Email: scholars@reschols.usyd.edu.au
www: http://www.usyd.edu.au/su/reschols/welcome.html
Contact: Ms Carmen NG, Research Training

The role of the University of Sydney is to create, preserve, transmit, extend and apply knowledge through teaching, research, creative works and other forms of scholarship. In carrying out its role, the University affirms its commitment to the values and goals of institutional autonomy, recognises the importance of ideas and intellectual freedom to pursue critical and open enquiry, as well as social responsibility, tolerance, honesty and respect, as the hallmarks of relationships throughout the University community. It also understands the needs and expectations of those whom it serves and constantly improves the quality and delivery of its services.

Australian Postgraduate Award (APA)

Subjects: All subjects.
Purpose: To enable candidates with exceptional research potential to undertake a higher degree by research.
Eligibility: Open to Australian citizens and permanent residents, and citizens of New Zealand.
Level of Study: Doctorate, Postgraduate, Research.
Type: Scholarship.
Value: Approx. Australian $18,009 per year.
Length of Study: Two years for Master's by research candidates, and three years with a possible six month extension for PhD candidates.
Frequency: Annual.
Study Establishment: The University of Sydney.
Country of Study: Australia.
No. of awards offered: Varies from year to year.
Application Procedure: Applicants must complete a form, available from the Research Office between August and October. Forms can also be downloaded from the website or emailed on request.
Closing Date: October 31st.
Funding: Government.
No. of awards given last year: 147.

International Postgraduate Research Scholarships (IPRS) and University of Sydney International Postgraduate Awards (IPA)

Subjects: All subjects.
Purpose: To support candidates with exceptional research potential.
Eligibility: Open to suitably qualified graduates eligible to commence a higher degree by research. Australia and New Zealand citizens and Australian permanent residents are not eligible to apply.
Level of Study: Doctorate, Postgraduate, Research.
Type: Scholarship.
Value: Tuition fees for IPRS and for IPA approx. Australian $18,009 per year.
Length of Study: Two years for the Master's by research candidates, and three years with a possible six month extension for PhD candidates.
Frequency: Annual.
Study Establishment: The University of Sydney.
Country of Study: Australia.
No. of awards offered: Varies from year to year.
Application Procedure: Applicants must complete an application form, available between May and August from the International Office.
Closing Date: August 31st.
Funding: Government.
No. of awards given last year: 31.

For further information contact:

International Office, Services Building G12, Sydney, NSW 2006, Australia
Tel: (61) 2 9351 4161
Fax: (61) 2 9351 4013
Email: infoschol@io.usyd.edu.au
Contact: International Scholarships Officer

University of Sydney Postgraduate Award (UPA)

Subjects: All subjects.
Purpose: To enable candidates with exceptional research potential to undertake a higher degree by research.
Eligibility: Open to Australian citizens and permanent residents and New Zealand citizens.
Level of Study: Doctorate, Postgraduate, Research.
Type: Scholarship.
Value: Approx. Australian $18,009 per year.
Length of Study: Two years for the Master's by research candidates, and three years with a possible six month extension for PhD candidates.
Frequency: Annual.
Study Establishment: The University of Sydney.
Country of Study: Australia.
No. of awards offered: Varies from year to year.
Application Procedure: Applicants must complete a form, available from the Research Office between August and October. Forms can also be downloaded from the website or emailed on request.
Closing Date: October 31st.
Funding: Government.
No. of awards given last year: 40.

UNIVERSITY OF TORONTO

Admissions & Awards, 315 Bloor Street West, Toronto, ON, M5S 1A3, Canada
Tel: (1) 416 978 7960
Fax: (1) 416 978 7022
Email: ask@adm.utoronto.ca
www: http://www.utoronto.ca
Contact: Grants Management Officer

The University of Toronto, an institution with an impressive history and a future of remarkable promise, was ranked Canada's top research intensive University for the fourth consecutive year by Maclean's magazine and is one of the leading universities of its kind in the world. The University provides its students with access to extraordinary professors and a diverse array of rigorous programmes. Moreover, the University offers students the best of both worlds, as nine colleges offer the experience of a rich liberal arts education within the larger setting of a great research university.

Taylor Statten Memorial Fund

Subjects: Any professional field or career related to youth services such as, but not restricted to, physical and health education, psychology, teaching, the ministry and social work.
Purpose: To assist post Baccalaureate study in any relevant professional field.
Eligibility: Open to graduates of Canadian universities who are under 25 years of age. Candidates should have high academic standing with previous experience in the youth field.
Level of Study: Postgraduate.
Type: Fellowship.
Value: Approx. Canadian $1,500 per year.
Length of Study: One year.
Frequency: Annual.
Study Establishment: Any appropriate university.
Country of Study: Canada.
No. of awards offered. One.
Application Procedure: Application forms should be accompanied by a transcript of the applicant's university record. Applicants are also responsible for ensuring that three letters of recommendation reach the Committee before the deadline. At least two of the letters should be written by university teachers with whom the applicant has studied.
Closing Date: February 28th.
No. of awards given last year: One.

UNIVERSITY OF ULSTER

Research Office, Cromore Road, Coleraine, Co. Londonderry, BT52 1SA, Northern Ireland
Tel: (44) (028) 70324729
Fax: (44) (028) 70324905
www: http://www.ulst.ac.uk & http://www.ulster.ac.uk/researchstudy
Contact: Mrs H Campbell, Administrative Assistant

The University of Ulster's Vision is to be a model of an outstanding regional university with a national and international reputation for quality. The University makes a major contribution to the economic, social and cultural advancement of Northern Ireland as a region within a national and international context and plays a key role in attracting inward investment. Core business activities are teaching and learning, research and technology and knowledge transfer.

Vice - Chancellor's Research Scholarships (VCRS)

Subjects: All subjects.
Purpose: To assist candidates of a high academic standard to complete research degrees (PhD).
Eligibility: All eligible applicants for admission to full-time research studies, as advertised on website.
Level of Study: Postgraduate.
Type: Scholarship.
Value: Fees and maintenance grant.
Length of Study: A maximum of three years.
Frequency: Annual.
Study Establishment: University of Ulster.
Country of Study: United Kingdom.
No. of awards offered: Varies.
Application Procedure: Applicants must complete an application form.
Closing Date: Check website.
Funding: Private.
No. of awards given last year: 50.
No. of applicants last year: 600.
Additional Information: Further information is available on the website.

For further information contact:

Contact: Mrs Hazel Campbell

UNIVERSITY OF WALES, ABERYSTWYTH

Old College, King Street, Aberystwyth, Ceredigion, SY23 2AX, Wales
Tel: (44) 1970 622023
Fax: (44) 1970 622921
Email: pg-admissions@aber.ac.uk
www: http://www.aber.ac.uk
Contact: Dr Rhys Williams, Postgraduate Admissions Officer

Located in beautiful surroundings, the University of Wales provides an ideal learning environment. Information services are among the best in the United Kingdom, and students also enjoy free access to one of the six copyright libraries of Britain, the National Library of Wales, which is adjacent to the University campus.

University of Wales (Aberystwyth) Postgraduate Research Studentships

Subjects: Studies leading to the award of a PhD in any of our 17 academic departments. The university offers a wide range of research opportunities within the faculties of science, social sciences and arts.
Purpose: To enable United Kingdom and European Union students to undertake full-time doctoral study at the University of Wales, Aberystwyth.
Eligibility: Open to United Kingdom and European Union candidates who have obtained at least an Upper Second Class (Honours) Degree or equivalent in their degree examination and who wish to study full-time.
Level of Study: Doctorate, Postgraduate, Research.
Type: Studentship.
Value: United Kingdom fees plus a subsistence allowance based on research council rates.
Length of Study: One year, in the first instance, but usually renewable for up to two additional years subject to satisfactory academic progress.
Frequency: Annual.
Study Establishment: The University of Wales, Aberystwyth.
Country of Study: United Kingdom.
No. of awards offered: Usually 12 per annum.
Application Procedure: Applicants must complete an application form, available from the Postgraduate Admissions Office or from our website: www.aber.ac.uk.
Closing Date: March 1st.
Funding: Private.
Contributor: The University of Wales, Aberystwyth.
No. of awards given last year: 12.
No. of applicants last year: 120.
Additional Information: For all enquiries, please contact the Postgraduate Admissions Office.

UNIVERSITY OF WALES, BANGOR (UWB)

Academic Registry, College Road, Bangor, Gwynedd, LL57 2DG, Wales
Tel: (44) 1248 382025
Fax: (44) 1248 370451
Email: aos057@bangor.ac.uk
www: http://www.bangor.ac.uk
Contact: Dr John C T Perkins, Assistant Registrar

The University of Wales, Bangor (UWB) is the principal seat of learning, scholarship and research in North Wales. It was established in 1884 and is a constituent institution of the Federal University of Wales. The University attaches considerable importance to research training in all disciplines and offers research studentships of a value similar to those of the British public funding bodies.

Llewellyn and Mary Williams Scholarship

Subjects: All biological sciences, including marine biology.
Purpose: To support doctoral studies and research training in the biological sciences.
Eligibility: Open to First Class (Honours) Degree holders who are classified as home or European Community student for fee purposes.

Level of Study: Doctorate, Postgraduate.
Type: Scholarship.
Value: Equal to that of a British Research Council Studentship.
Length of Study: Three years.
Frequency: Dependent on funds available.
Study Establishment: The University of Wales, Bangor.
Country of Study: United Kingdom.
No. of awards offered: One.
Application Procedure: This scholarship is allocated to the School of Biological Sciences every third year. Applicants must contact the Head of School for details.
Closing Date: May 15th.
Funding: Private.
No. of awards given last year: One.
No. of applicants last year: 10.

Mr and Mrs David Edward Memorial Award

Subjects: All subjects offered by the University.
Purpose: To support doctoral studies in any subject area.
Eligibility: Open to holders of a relevant First Class (Honours) Degree or, exceptionally, Upper Second Class (Honours) Degree, who are of any nationality classified as a United Kingdom or European Union student for fee purposes.
Level of Study: Doctorate, Postgraduate.
Type: Other.
Value: No less than that of a Research Council or British Academy Research Studentship, including fees.
Length of Study: One year, renewable for a maximum of a further two years if satisfactory progress is maintained.
Frequency: Dependent on funds available.
Study Establishment: The University of Wales, Bangor.
Country of Study: United Kingdom.
No. of awards offered: One.
Application Procedure: Applicants must complete an application form, available from the Postgraduate Admissions Office at the University.
Closing Date: May 15th.
Funding: Private.
No. of awards given last year: One.
No. of applicants last year: 20.

Sir William Roberts Scholarship

Subjects: Agriculture and agricultural science.
Purpose: To fund research training to PhD level.
Eligibility: Open to candidates classified as 'home based' who have attained a First Class (Honours) Degree or Upper Second Class (Honours) Degree. These scholarships are allocated to the School of Agricultural and Forest Sciences and the School of Biological Sciences.
Level of Study: Doctorate, Postgraduate.
Type: Scholarship.
Value: Equal to that of a British Research Council Research Studentship.
Length of Study: One year, renewable for a maximum of two additional years.
Frequency: Annual.
Study Establishment: The University of Wales, Bangor.
Country of Study: United Kingdom.
No. of awards offered: Two.
Application Procedure: Applicants must contact the relevant Head of School.
Closing Date: June 1st.
Funding: Private.
No. of awards given last year: Two.
No. of applicants last year: 20.

UWB Departmental Research Studentships

Subjects: All subjects offered by the University.
Purpose: To fund research training to PhD level.
Eligibility: Open to candidates classified as United Kingdom and European Union students for fee purposes who have attained a First Class (Honours) Degree or, exceptionally, an Upper Second Class Honours Degree or equivalent.

Level of Study: Doctorate, Postgraduate.
Type: Other.
Value: Equal to that of a British Research Council Studentship.
Length of Study: One year, renewable for a maximum of two additional years.
Frequency: Annual.
Study Establishment: The University of Wales, Bangor.
Country of Study: United Kingdom.
No. of awards offered: 12-15.
Application Procedure: Applicants must contact the relevant department of proposed study. The department will nominate the most worthy eligible students.
Closing Date: April 30th.
Funding: Private.
No. of awards given last year: 11.
No. of applicants last year: 90.

UWB Research Studentships

Subjects: All subjects offered by the University.
Purpose: To support students for the duration of a PhD programme.
Eligibility: Open to recent graduates, classified at the lower European Union rate for payment purposes, who hold a First Class (Honours) Degree or Upper Second Class (Honours) Degree or equivalent in a relevant subject.
Level of Study: Postgraduate.
Type: Studentship.
Value: Equal to that of a British Research Council Studentship.
Length of Study: Three years.
Frequency: Annual.
Study Establishment: The University of Wales, Bangor.
Country of Study: United Kingdom.
No. of awards offered: 10-14.
Application Procedure: Applicants must contact the Senior Postgraduate Tutor in the department of the proposed research programme.
Closing Date: May 15th. Those interested should make enquiries well before this date.
Funding: Government, Private.
Contributor: The UWB Research Committee and local bequests.
No. of awards given last year: 14.
No. of applicants last year: Approx. 100.
Additional Information: In exceptional circumstances an award may be made to an international student classified for the full cost fee. In such a case the student would be required to pay the difference between the full cost fee and the home or European Union fee.

UNIVERSITY OF WALES, LAMPETER

Lampeter, Ceredigion, SA48 7ED, Wales
Tel: (44) (44) 1570 422 351
Fax: (44) (44) 1570 423 423
Email: t.rodervick@lamp.ac.uk
www: http://www.lamp.ac.uk
Contact: R.C. Jarman, Registrar and Secretary

At Lampeter we think of university life as a whole. Research is greatly prized by our academic staff and we can offer a wide range of supervision in the humanities and social sciences. There is simply no other long-established university with our pedigree which operates on such an intimate scale.

Delahaye Memorial Benefaction

Purpose: Awarded by Magdalene College, Cambridge to a graduate of UWL who is accepted to read Honours Theology at Cambridge.
Value: UK£60.

Helen McCormack Turner Memorial Scholarship

Purpose: Awarded annually to a postgraduate student who graduated recently from the University of Wales, Lampeter (i.e. in 2002). The recipient must be less than 25 years of age on 1 August 2002. Awarded to graduates pursing research only (for the degrees of MPhil/PhD).
Value: UK£250.

Herbert Hughes Scholarship

Purpose: Awarded annually to postgraduate or undergraduate students of any discipline who intend to serve in the Ministry of the Church in Wales. (Preference may be given to candidates from the parish of Silian, Ceredigion).
Value: UK£170.

Mary Radcliffe Scholarship

Purpose: Awarded annually to graduates of UWL on results in the final examination for the BA degree, and tenable by a graduate reading Theology.
Value: UK£150.

RHYS Curzon-Jones Scholarship

Purpose: Awarded annually to a postgraduate student of any discipline which is a candidate for Holy Orders in the Church in Wales.
Value: UK£50.

Ridley Lewis Bursary

Purpose: Awarded annually to a postgraduate student funding his/her studies in whole or in part from his/her own resources.
Value: UK£50.

W.D. Llewelyn Memorial Benefaction

Purpose: Tenable for one year and awarded annually to graduates of UWL for further degrees or research at Lampeter or at other universities.
Value: Six awards of UK£100 each.

UNIVERSITY OF WALES, NEWPORT

Caerleon Campus, PO Box 179, Newport, NP18 3YG, Wales
Tel: (44) 1633 430088
Fax: (44) 1633 432006
www: www.wales.ac.uk

The University of Wales College, Newport, has been involved in higher education for more than 80 years, and its roots go back even further to the first Mechanics Institute in the town, which opened in 1841.

Pilcher Senior Research Fellowship

Subjects: Welsh and Celtic Studies.
Purpose: To support a student in advanced research in the fields of Welsh and Celtic Studies.
Level of Study: Postdoctorate.
Type: Fellowship.
Frequency: As needed.
Study Establishment: University of Wales
Country of Study: Wales.
Application Procedure: Please check with the website or the University.
Funding: Private.
Contributor: The late Sophia Margaretta Pilcher.

The Stott Fellowship

Subjects: Welsh and Celtic Studies.
Purpose: To support a student in advanced research in the fields of Welsh and Celtic Studies.
Level of Study: Postgraduate.
Type: Fellowship.
Frequency: As needed.
Study Establishment: University of Wales.
Country of Study: Wales.
Application Procedure: Please check with the website or the university.
Funding: Private.
Contributor: Miss Muriel Stott of Colwyn Bay.

University of Wales Postgraduate Studentship

Subjects: Any as agreed by the University.
Purpose: To support a student with a first class honours degree at the university to progress to postgraduate research.

Level of Study: Doctorate.
Type: Scholarship.
Frequency: Annual.
Study Establishment: University of Wales
Country of Study: Wales.
Application Procedure: Please check with the website of the University.
Funding: Private.
Contributor: Private benefactions.

UNIVERSITY OF WALES, SWANSEA

Singleton Park, Swansea, SA2 8PP, Wales
Tel: (44) 1792 205678
Fax: (44) 1792 295157
www: www2.swan.ac.uk

Founded in 1920, the university stands in Parkland overlooking Swansea Bay on the edge of the Gower Peninsular, Britain's first area of outstanding natural beauty.

Scholarship to Study in France

Subjects: Any subject provided it is studied at an accredited institution in Paris.
Purpose: To support an outstanding postgraduate student to study or carry out research in France for one academic year.
Eligibility: Candidates must be British or French nationals.
Type: Scholarship.
Value: UK£8,000 in Paris, UK£7,500 outside Paris, + registration and tuition fees.
Length of Study: 1 year.
Frequency: Annual.
Study Establishment: French run institutions of higher education or research.
Country of Study: France.
Closing Date: 19th March.
Funding: Private.

UNIVERSITY OF WARWICK

Coventry, CV4 7AL, United Kingdom
Tel: (44) 247 652 3523
Fax: (44) 247 646 1606
Email: pgoffice@warwick.ac.uk
www: www.2.warwick.ac.uk

The University of Warwick offers an exciting range of doctoral, research-based and taught Master's programmes in the Humanities, Sciences, Social Sciences and Medicine. In the 2001 Research Assessment Exercise, Warwick was ranked fifth in the UK for research quality. Postgraduate students make up around 35% of our 18000 students. The University is located in the heart of England, adjacent to the city of Coventry and on the border with Warwickshire.

Argentina Chevening.

Subjects: Applicants should be nationals of Argentina not currently registered at the University.
Level of Study: Postgraduate.
Type: Scholarship.
Value: UK£15,000.
Length of Study: 1 Year.
Frequency: One off.
Study Establishment: Argentina Ministry of Foreign Affairs.
Country of Study: United Kingdom.
No. of awards offered: 2.
Application Procedure: Application form from British Council.
Closing Date: September.
Contributor: University of Warwick, Foreign and Common wealth.

For further information contact:

The British Council, Marcelo T. de Alvear, 590, 4th Floor, 1058, Buenos Aires, Argentina
Email: info@britishcouncil.org

Brazil- Law Chevening

Subjects: Nationals of Brazil not current registered at the University of Warwick.
Level of Study: Postgraduate.
Type: Scholarship.
Value: Cost of Academic fees and full maintenance.
Frequency: One off award.
Study Establishment: The University of Warwick.
Country of Study: United Kingdom.
No. of awards offered: 1.
Application Procedure: Application form.
Contributor: The University of Warwick, British Council.

For further information contact:

The British Council, Eo. Centro Empresarial Varie, SCN Quadra 04, Block B, Torre Oeste Consunto 202, Brasilia, DF, Brazil
Email: brasilia@britishcouncil.org.br
Contact: Irene Taitson

Busary for Postgraduate Study (French Studies)

Subjects: This award is for students applying for the taught MA in French culture and thought, or for the research MA in French Studies.
Purpose: To support students on MAs in French Studies.
Eligibility: Candidates must have accepted a place on the MA; apply to AHRB/ any other source of funding for which they may be eligible.
Level of Study: Postdoctorate.
Type: Scholarship.
Value: Value of home/ EU fees.
Length of Study: 1 year.
Frequency: Annual.
Study Establishment: University of Warwick.
Country of Study: United Kingdom.
No. of awards offered: 4.
Application Procedure: No form. All applications to the MA will automatically be considered.
Closing Date: 14th Feb.
No. of awards given last year: 4.
No. of applicants last year: 5.

Caribbean (Postgraduate Award)

Subjects: Caribbean Nationals (inc. non oommonwoalth countrioc) not currently registered on a Postgraduate course.
Level of Study: Postgraduate.
Type: Scholarship.
Value: UK£6,000.
Length of Study: 1 Year.
Frequency: One off.
Study Establishment: The University of Warwick.
Country of Study: United Kingdom.
No. of awards offered: 1.
Application Procedure: Application form.
Closing Date: 26th May 2004.
Contributor: The University of Warwick.
No. of awards given last year: 1.
Additional Information: Deducted from the academic fees.

Caribbean Undergraduate Award.

Subjects: Any subject, open to prospective undergraduate students, from the Caribbean (including non-commonwealth countries).
Type: One Off Award.
Value: UK£3,000.
Length of Study: 3 Years.
Frequency: One off award.
Country of Study: United Kingdom.
No. of awards offered: 1.
Application Procedure: Application form needs to be filled in.
Closing Date: 5th May 2004.
Funding: International Office.
Contributor: University of Warwick.
Additional Information: The scholarship will be deducted from the successful candidate's Academic fees and is a one-off award, non-renewable after the first year of study.

East Africa (Post Graduate Award)

Subjects: Nationals of Kenya, Tanzania, Uganda not currently registered.
Level of Study: Postgraduate.
Type: Scholarship.
Value: UK£2,000.
Length of Study: 1 Year.
Frequency: One off.
Study Establishment: UK.
Country of Study: United Kingdom.
No. of awards offered: 1.
Application Procedure: Application form.
Closing Date: May 26th 2004.
Contributor: University of Warwick.
No. of awards given last year: 1.

East Africa HEFP Award

Subjects: One off award for 2004, entry open to prospective full-time students of HEFP(Higher Education Foundation Programme) in any subject area.
Eligibility: Eligible to the nationals of East Africa.
Type: Award.
Value: UK£2,000.
Length of Study: 1 Year.
Frequency: One off award.
Country of Study: United Kingdom.
No. of awards offered: One.
Application Procedure: Application form needs to be filled in.
Closing Date: 5th May 2004.
Funding: International Office.
Contributor: International Office.
Additional Information: The scholarship will be deducted from the successful candidate's academic fees and is a one-off award, non-renewable after the first year of study.

East European Scholarship Scheme

Subjects: Available for any subject.
Purpose: To fund a Masters Student at Warwick.
Eligibility: National/resident of Bulgaria, Moldova, Belarus, Romania or Georgia. Not have studied long-term outside these countries. Show potential to make a contribution to home country after graduation. Be registered on or applying for a 1 year taught Master.
Level of Study: Postdoctorate.
Type: Scholarship.
Value: UK£6,470 (2001) -fees + maintenance. Flight allowance given.
Length of Study: 1 year.
Frequency: Annual.
Study Establishment: University of Warwick.
Country of Study: United Kingdom.
No. of awards offered: 10.
Application Procedure: Application forms are distributed by SOROS offices in the relevant countries.
Closing Date: 9th Jan.
Funding: Government, Private.
Contributor: SOROS, FCO.
No. of awards given last year: 10.
Additional Information: Address for Application: Apply to SOROS offices in the relevant country.

Ghana (postgraduate)

Subjects: Nationals of Ghana, not currently registered on a post-graduate course.
Level of Study: Postgraduate.
Type: Scholarship.
Value: UK£2,000.
Length of Study: 1 Year.
Frequency: One off.
Study Establishment: The University of Warwick.
Country of Study: United Kingdom.
No. of awards offered: 1.
Application Procedure: Application form.
Closing Date: May 26th 2004.
Contributor: The University of Warwick.

India U/G Award

Subjects: Applicants must be Indian nationals domiciles of India, not currently registered in an U/G course - One award from an Indian Exam Board; One award for Best A-level or B-Candidate.
Level of Study: .
Type: U/G.
Value: UK£9,000.
Length of Study: 3 years.
Frequency: Renewable for length of study.
Study Establishment: University of Warwick.
Country of Study: United Kingdom.
No. of awards offered: 2.
Application Procedure: Application form.
Closing Date: 5th May 2004.
Contributor: University of Warwick.
Additional Information: Award deducted from academic fees.

India (postgraduate)

Subjects: National of India, not currently registered on a postgraduate course.
Level of Study: Postgraduate.
Type: Ocholarohip.
Value: UK£8,000.
Length of Study: 1 Year.
Frequency: One off.
Study Establishment: University of Warwick.
Country of Study: United Kingdom.
No. of awards offered: 1.
Application Procedure: Application Form.
Closing Date: 26 th May.
Contributor: University of Warwick.
Additional Information: Deducted from academic fees and accommodation expenses.

India Engineering ITM Award for Indian students

Subjects: Applicants should be Indian nationals undertaking their first year of a University of Warwick BENG/MENG degree ATITM.
Value: UK£2,000.
Length of Study: 3/4 years.
Frequency: One off award.
Country of Study: United Kingdom.
No. of awards offered: 1.
Application Procedure: Application forms need to be filled in.
Closing Date: 5th May 2004.
Contributor: University of Warwick.
Additional Information: The Scholarship will be deducted from the successful candidate's academic fees in the second year at Warwick.

India LLb Law Scholarship

Subjects: Applicants should be Indian nationals or Domiciles of India, not currently registered on an undergraduate course.
Level of Study: .
Type: Scholarship.
Value: UK£9,000.
Length of Study: 3 years.
Frequency: Renewable for length of study.
Study Establishment: University of Warwick.
Country of Study: United Kingdom.
No. of awards offered: 1.
Application Procedure: Complete application form.
Closing Date: May 26th 2004.
Contributor: University of Warwick.
Additional Information: Award deducted from academic fees.

India LLM in Dev. Postgraduate.

Subjects: Nationals of India, not registered on a postgraduate course.
Level of Study: Postgraduate.
Type: Scholarship.
Value: UK£8,000.
Length of Study: 1 Year.
Frequency: One off.
Study Establishment: UK.

Country of Study: United Kingdom.
No. of awards offered: 1.
Application Procedure: Application form.
Closing Date: May 26th 2004.
Contributor: The University of Warwick.
Additional Information: Deducted from academic fees and accommodation expenses.

Japan HEFP Award

Subjects: One off award for 2004 entry open to prospective full time students of HEFP(Higher Education Foundation Programme) in any subject.
Level of Study: .
Type: One off award.
Value: UK£2,000.
Length of Study: 1 Year.
Frequency: One off award.
Country of Study: United Kingdom.
No. of awards offered: One.
Application Procedure: Application form. Needs to be filled in.
Closing Date: 5th May 2004.
Funding: International Office.
Contributor: International Office, University of Warwick.
Additional Information: The scholarship will be deducted from the successful candidates academic fees and is a one-off award, non-renewable after the first year of study.

Japan Postgraduate Award

Subjects: Any subject area.
Eligibility: Nationals from Japan.
Type: Scholarship.
Value: UK£5,000 each.
Frequency: One off.
Study Establishment: The University of Warwick.
Country of Study: United Kingdom.
No. of awards offered: 2.
Application Procedure: Application form.
Closing Date: 26th May 2004.
Contributor: The University of Warwick.

Korea Postgraduate MNW Chevening Award

Subjects: Any subject area.
Level of Study: Predoctorate.
Type: Scholarship.
Value: Fees and Maintenance Grant.
Length of Study: One year full time.
Frequency: One off award.
Study Establishment: 2 Awards for study at the University of Warwick.
Country of Study: United Kingdom.
No. of awards offered: 6 altogether (2 for studying at Warwick).
Contributor: The University of Manchester, Nottingham and Warwick British Council.

For further information contact:

MNW Universities Korean Office, Kanganam Office, SEOCHO4 Dong, SEO CHO-GU, South Korea, 137 856,
Tel: 8041308-25

Korea Undergraduate Award

Subjects: Applicants should be nationals of South Korea, not currently registered on an undergraduate course.
Type: Scholarship.
Value: UK£3,000.
Length of Study: 1 Year.
Frequency: One off award.
Study Establishment: University of Warwick.
Country of Study: United Kingdom.
Application Procedure: Application to be completed.
Closing Date: 5th May 2004.
Contributor: University of Warwick.
Additional Information: Award deducted from fees.

Latin Amercia Postgraduate Award.
Subjects: Nationals from one of the countries in this region not currently registered on a postgraduate course at the university.
Type: Scholarship.
Value: UK£5,000.
Frequency: One off award.
Study Establishment: The University of Warwick.
Country of Study: United Kingdom.
No. of awards offered: 1.
Application Procedure: Application Form.
Closing Date: 26th May 2004.
Contributor: The University of Warwick, International Office.

Latin America Undergraduate
Subjects: Applicants should be nationals from one of the countries in Latin America, not currently registered on an U/G course.
Type: Scholarship.
Value: UK£5,000.
Length of Study: 3 Years.
Frequency: One off award.
Study Establishment: University of Warwick.
Country of Study: United Kingdom.
No. of awards offered: 1.
Application Procedure: Application form.
Closing Date: 5th May 2004.
Contributor: University of Warwick.
Additional Information: Award deducted from fees.

Lord Rootes Memorial Fund
Subjects: An individual or society can apply for a grant for a project.
Purpose: To support a student's or society's project.
Eligibility: Must be either a full time or part time postgraduate or undergraduate student on a course of at least 2 years duration or a student society.
Level of Study: Postdoctorate.
Type: Grant.
Value: From UK£200 for individuals to UK£3,000 for groups.
Length of Study: At least 2 years.
Frequency: Annual.
Study Establishment: University of Warwick.
Country of Study: United Kingdom.
No. of awards offered: Variable.
Application Procedure: Application form plus detailed project proposed of up to 6 A4 pages including financial plan.
Closing Date: End of week 1, Spring Term (approx 9 Jan).
Funding: Private.
Contributor: Lord Rootes Memorial Fund.
No. of applicants last year: 34.

M.O.A.C. MSc Studentships
Subjects: Mathematical-biology and biophysical chemistry.
Purpose: To support students working to an MSc in Molecular organisation and Assembly in cells.
Eligibility: Candidates must be graduates in mathematical or physical sciences.
Level of Study: Postgraduate.
Type: Scholarship.
Value: UK£11,385 stipend.
Length of Study: 1 year.
Frequency: Annual.
Study Establishment: University of Warwick.
Country of Study: United Kingdom.
No. of awards offered: 10.
Funding: Private.

M.O.A.C. PhD Studentships
Subjects: Mathematical biology and biophysical chemistry.
Purpose: To support students working to a PhD in Mathematical Biology and Biophysical and Chemistry.
Eligibility: Candidates must be graduates in mathematical or physical sciences.
Level of Study: Postgraduate.
Type: Scholarship.

Value: UK£11,385 stipend.
Length of Study: 3 years.
Frequency: Annual.
Study Establishment: University of Warwick.
Country of Study: United Kingdom.
No. of awards offered: 10.
Funding: Private.

Malaysia Undergraduate
Subjects: Applicants should be Malaysian nationals not currently registered on an undergraduate course.
Type: Scholarship.
Value: UK£2,000.
Length of Study: 3 years.
Frequency: Renewable for length of study.
Study Establishment: University of Warwick.
Country of Study: United Kingdom.
No. of awards offered: 6.
Application Procedure: Application form.
Closing Date: 5th May 2004.
Contributor: University of Warwick.
Additional Information: Award deducted from fees.

Mauritius Postgraduate Award
Subjects: Open to applicants who are nationals of Mauritius not currently registered on a postgraduate course at the University of Warwick.
Type: Scholarship.
Value: UK£2,000.
Length of Study: 1 Year full Time.
Frequency: One off award.
Study Establishment: University of Warwick.
Country of Study: United Kingdom.
No. of awards offered: 1.
Application Procedure: Application form.
Closing Date: 26th May 2004.
Contributor: The University of Warwick, International Office.

Mauritius Undergraduate Award
Subjects: Nationals of Mauritius, not currently registered on an undergraduate course.
Type: Scholarship.
Value: UK£2,500.
Length of Study: 3 Years.
Frequency: Renewable.
Study Establishment: University of Warwick.
Country of Study: United Kingdom.
No. of awards offered: 1.
Application Procedure: Application to complete.
Closing Date: 30th March 2004.
Contributor: University of Warwick.
Additional Information: Award deducted from academic fees.

Mexico Chevening: Chevening/ Brockmann/ Warwick Award.
Subjects: For the Nationals of Mexico, not currently registered at the University of Warwick.
Study Establishment: The University of Warwick.
Country of Study: United Kingdom.
No. of awards offered: 1.
Application Procedure: Application form.
Contributor: The British Council, The Brockmann Foundation, The University of Warwick.

For further information contact:

The British Council, Lope de Vega, No. 316, Col, Chapultepec Morales, Delègacion Miguel Hidalgo, CP 11570, DF, Mexico

Nigeria Postgraduate Award
Subjects: Applicants should be nationals of Nigeria, not currently registered on a postgraduate course at the University of Warwick.

Type: Scholarship.
Value: UK£3,000.
Length of Study: One year full time.
Frequency: One off award.
Study Establishment: The University of Warwick.
Country of Study: United Kingdom.
Application Procedure: Application Form.
Closing Date: 26th May 2004.
Contributor: The University of Warwick.

North America Postgraduate Awards.
Subjects: Applicants should be nationals of the United States or Canada, not currently registered on a postgraduate course at the university.
Type: Scholarship.
Value: UK£3,500.
Length of Study: One year.
Frequency: One off award.
Study Establishment: The University of Warwick.
Country of Study: United Kingdom.
No. of awards offered: 1.
Application Procedure: Application form.
Closing Date: 26th May 2004.
Contributor: The University of Warwick.

Pakistan Undergraduate Award
Subjects: Applicants should be nationals of Pakistan, not currently registered on an undergraduate course.
Type: Scholarship.
Value: UK£1,500.
Length of Study: 1 year.
Frequency: One off award.
Study Establishment: University of Warwick.
Country of Study: United Kingdom.
No. of awards offered: 1.
Application Procedure: Application form.
Closing Date: 5th May 2004.
Contributor: University of Warwick.
Additional Information: Award deducted from candidate's academic fees.

Pakistan Post Graduate Award.
Subjects: Applicants should be nationals of Pakistan, not currently registered on a postgraduate course at the university.
Type: Scholarship.
Length of Study: One year full time.
Frequency: One off award.
Study Establishment: The University of Warwick.
Country of Study: United Kingdom.
Application Procedure: Application form.
Closing Date: 26th May 2004.
Contributor: The University of Warwick.

Psychology Departmental Studentship
Subjects: Available for any Psychology PhD.
Purpose: To support Psychology PhD Students.
Eligibility: Must be registered for a PhD. Must have outstanding academic ability. Must have applied for external funding. Must be a current/new PhD student not in their final year.
Level of Study: Doctorate.
Type: Studentship.
Value: Home fees + UK£9,500 (for overseas fee payers, the overseas portion of the fee is waived).
Length of Study: 3 years.
Frequency: Annual.
Study Establishment: University of Warmick.
Country of Study: United Kingdom.
No. of awards offered: Variable.
Application Procedure: Apply directly to the Department.
Closing Date: 31st January.
Funding: Government.
No. of applicants last year: 10.

Research Studentship in Computer Science.
Subjects: Available for any Computer Science PhD.
Purpose: To support PhD students in Computer Science.
Eligibility: Outstanding academic ability.
Level of Study: Doctorate.
Type: Studentship.
Value: Fees(full or part) and or maintenance based on EPSRC levels.
Length of Study: 3 years.
Frequency: Dependent on funds available.
Study Establishment: University of Warwick.
Country of Study: United Kingdom.
No. of awards offered: 5 in operation at any one time ie no specific annual allocation.
Application Procedure: Department will automatically consider all PhD candidates.
Closing Date: Early application for PhD are advised.
Funding: Government.
No. of awards given last year: 5.

Russia M.E.F.P. Undergraduate Award
Subjects: Applicants should be nationals of Russia, not currently registered on an undergraduate course.
Type: Scholarship.
Value: UK£5,000.
Length of Study: 1 year.
Frequency: One-off Award.
Study Establishment: University of Warwick.
Country of Study: United Kingdom.
No. of awards offered: 1.
Application Procedure: Application form.
Closing Date: 5th May 2004.
Contributor: University of Warwick.
Additional Information: Award deducted from candidate's academic fees.

Russia Postgraduate Chevening Award
Level of Study: Postgraduate.
Type: Scholarship.
Value: U£20,000.
Frequency: One off award.
Study Establishment: University of Warwick.
Country of Study: United Kingdom.
No. of awards offered: 1.
Application Procedure: Application form.
Closing Date: 1st December 2003.
Contributor: University of Warwick.
Additional Information: Tuition fees & Monthly stipend.

Singpore (Undergraduate Award)
Subjects: Nationals of Singpore, not currently registered on an undergraduate course.
Type: Scholarship.
Value: Full fees in student's 1st year.
Length of Study: 1st year.
Frequency: Non-renewable.
Study Establishment: UK.
Country of Study: United Kingdom.
No. of awards offered: 1.
Application Procedure: Application form.
Closing Date: 5th May 2004.
Contributor: University of Warwick.
Additional Information: Full fees 1st year only.

South Africa (Undergraduate)
Subjects: Nationals of South Africa, not currently registered on an undergraduate course.
Type: Scholarship.
Value: UK£2,000.
Length of Study: 3 years.
Frequency: Renewable for 3 years.
Study Establishment: University of Warwick.
Country of Study: United Kingdom.
No. of awards offered: 1.

Application Procedure: Application Form.
Closing Date: 5th May 2004.
Contributor: University of Warwick.
Additional Information: One award, Renewable, up to 3 years Tuition fees.

Sports bursary

Subjects: Available to student on any course who competes at national level, or should potential to do so.
Purpose: To support outstanding sports people.
Eligibility: Candidates should be already competing in their sport at a national standard, or by their presence in national or regional training squads, show the potential to achieve their standard.
Level of Study: Postgraduate.
Type: Bursary.
Value: Approx UK£300. More may be available for exceptional cases.
Length of Study: At least 1 year.
Frequency: Annual.
Study Establishment: University of Warwick.
Country of Study: United Kingdom.
No. of awards offered: Varies. 11 in 2002.
Application Procedure: By letter at the start of the academic year to the Department of Physical Education and sport.
Closing Date: No deadline.
Funding: Government.
No. of awards given last year: 11.
No. of applicants last year: 11.

University of Warwick Music Scholarships

Subjects: Available to students in any subject.
Purpose: To support students with outstanding musical ability.
Eligibility: Should be an undergraduate or postgraduate student. Have applied for admission to the University on a full-time scheme and satisfy the entry requirements.
Level of Study: Postgraduate.
Type: Scholarship.
Value: UK£450 per year (with an additional subsidy on music tution fees).
Length of Study: At least 1 year.
Frequency: Annual.
Study Establishment: University of Warwick.
Country of Study: United Kingdom.
No. of awards offered: Between 2 and 4.
Application Procedure: Application form avaliable online or from the Music Centre Secretary.
Closing Date: 10th Feb in proposed year of entry.
Funding: Private.
No. of awards given last year: 3.
No. of applicants last year: 40.

For further information contact:

Contact: Music Centre Secretary

Vietnam (Undergraduate)

Subjects: Nationals of Vietnam, not currently registered on an undergraduate course.
Type: Scholarship.
Value: UK£2,000.
Length of Study: 3 years.
Frequency: Renewable.
Study Establishment: University of Warwick.
Country of Study: United Kingdom.
No. of awards offered: 2 Awards.
Application Procedure: Application Form.
Closing Date: 5th May 2004.
Contributor: University of Warwick.
Additional Information: Deducted from academic fees.

Vietnam HEFP Award

Subjects: One off Award for 2004 entry open to prospective full-time students off HEFP(Higher Education Foundation Programme) in any subject area.
Value: UK£2,500.

Length of Study: 1 Year.
Frequency: One Off.
Country of Study: United Kingdom.
No. of awards offered: 1.
Application Procedure: Application Form needs to be filled in.
Closing Date: 5th May 2004.
Funding: International Office.
Contributor: International Office, University of Warwick.
Additional Information: The scholarship will be deducted from the successful candidate's Academic fees and is a one-off award, non-renewable after the first year.

Warwick Postgraduate Research Fellowship.

Subjects: Available for PhD students in any department.
Purpose: To support PhD students.
Eligibility: * Be registered for a PhD* Outstanding academic ability.* Have applied for external funding.* Be a current or new PhD student not in their final year.
Level of Study: Doctorate.
Type: Fellowship.
Value: Home fees + UK£9,500 maintenance(2002).
Length of Study: 3 years.
Frequency: Annual.
Study Establishment: University of Warwick.
Country of Study: United Kingdom.
No. of awards offered: 25.
Application Procedure: Application forms can be downloaded from the web and sent to the department.
Closing Date: First round: 31st Jan, Second round: 1st July.
Funding: Government.
No. of awards given last year: 25.
No. of applicants last year: 361.

UNIVERSITY OF WESTERN AUSTRALIA

Nedlands, Perth, WA 6009, Australia
Tel: (61) 8 9380 2490
Fax: (61) 8 9380 1919
Email: medwards@admin.uwa.edu.au
www: http://www.uwa.edu.au
Contact: Ms Margaret Edwards, Senior Administrative Officer

Gledden Postgraduate Studentships

Subjects: Applied science, particularly relating to engineering, mining, surveying and cognate subjects.
Purpose: To enable the holder to conduct research in applied science leading to a higher qualification.
Eligibility: Open to postgraduates with a First Class (Honours) Degree, or its equivalent, in an applied science with research experience included in the degree course. Applicants must be graduates of the University of Western Australia of not more than three years.
Level of Study: Postgraduate.
Type: Studentship.
Value: Australian $22,283 per year tax free, and a thesis allowance of Australian $420 for Master's candidates or Australian $840 for doctoral candidates.
Length of Study: Up to three years and six months.
Frequency: Other.
Study Establishment: The University of Western Australia depending on the approved study plan. Permission may exceptionally be given for part of the research to be conducted at another university or recognised institution in Australia.
Country of Study: Australia.
No. of awards offered: Two or Three.
Closing Date: October 31st of the year preceding tenure.
Funding: Private.
No. of awards given last year: Two.

Gledden Visiting Senior Fellowships

Subjects: Applied science, particularly relating to surveying, engineering, mining and cognate subjects.
Purpose: To provide travel costs or living expenses in order to allow scholars from outside Western Australia to visit the University and contribute to its work and activities in applied science.

Eligibility: Open to graduates from outside Western Australia who have doctoral degrees or qualifications or experience equivalent to doctorate.
Level of Study: Professional development, Research.
Type: Fellowship.
Value: Determined on an individual basis.
Length of Study: From one academic term, which is defined as a minimum of three months, or up to two years.
Frequency: Annual.
Study Establishment: The University of Western Australia.
Country of Study: Australia.
No. of awards offered: Varies.
Application Procedure: Applications are invited by advertisement as and when directed by the Vice-Chancellor of the University.
Closing Date: March 31st.
Funding: Private.

Richard Walter Gibbon Medical Research Fellowship

Subjects: The causes and treatment of cancer and Parkinson's disease.
Purpose: To promote research by facilitating and encouraging students to pursue postgraduate research in the Faculty of Medicine at the University.
Eligibility: Open to Australian residents who are medical graduates of a recognised tertiary institution.
Level of Study: Postgraduate.
Type: Fellowship.
Value: Australian $20,500 per year plus Australian $1,000 for consumables and a Australian $500 travel allowance per year.
Length of Study: Up to three years and six months.
Frequency: Other.
Study Establishment: The University of Western Australia.
Country of Study: Australia.
No. of awards offered: Varies.
Closing Date: October 31st.
Funding: Private.
No. of awards given last year: One.
No. of applicants last year: One.
Additional Information: Except by permission a Fellow may not engage in any work during tenure of the fellowship other than that for which it was awarded. A full report is required at the end of tenure. Resulting publications must acknowledge that the work was done under the Gibbon Fellowship.

Saw Medical Research Fellowship

Subjects: The cause, prevention and cure of disease, primarily diabetes mellitus.
Purpose: To promote personal research.
Eligibility: Candidates do not need to have medical qualifications.
Level of Study: Doctorate.
Type: Fellowship.
Value: Up to Australian $45,000-50,000 per year depending on qualifications.
Length of Study: One year, renewable for a further year.
Frequency: Annual.
Study Establishment: The University of Western Australia.
Country of Study: Australia.
No. of awards offered: Several, determined annually.
Closing Date: August 1st to September 1st.
Funding: Private.
No. of awards given last year: Two.
Additional Information: Except by permission a Fellow may not engage in any work during tenure of the fellowship other than that for which it was awarded. The fellowship may not be held concurrently with other awards.

University of Western Australia Postdoctoral Research Fellowship

Subjects: All areas covered by the University of Western Australia's departments.
Purpose: To provide an appointment to a postdoctoral research Fellow to carry out a research project in a University of Western Australia department, who will bring special new expertise and a high level of relevant experience which is not otherwise available at the University.
Eligibility: Open to all nationalities. Applicants should hold a PhD for all appointments. The appointment of an overseas Fellow is subject to the Australian Department of Immigration and Ethnic Affairs' approval of the University's sponsorship for residence, and the Fellow's successful application for appropriate visa.
Level of Study: Postdoctorate.
Type: Fellowship.
Value: Australian $37,345-40,087 per year plus Australian $3,500-5,000 per year fellowship grant. A relocation grant is also included.
Length of Study: Two years.
Frequency: Annual.
Study Establishment: The University of Western Australia.
Country of Study: Australia.
No. of awards offered: Three.
Application Procedure: Applicants must apply through the University of Western Australia's departments only.
Closing Date: Approx. March 1st.

University of Western Australia Postgraduate Awards

Subjects: All subjects offered by the University.
Purpose: To enable students to conduct research leading to a Master's or doctoral degree.
Eligibility: Open to Australian citizens who are graduates with a minimum of an Upper Second Class (Honours) Degree, or a small number of overseas graduates who possess a First Class (Honours) Degree or equivalent.
Level of Study: Postgraduate.
Type: Studentship.
Value: Australian $17,000 per year tax free plus travel costs, relocation allowance within Australia of up to Australian $1,345 and thesis allowance of Australian $420 for Master's candidates or Australian $840 for doctoral.
Length of Study: Two years for Master's or three years and six months for doctoral candidates.
Frequency: Annual.
Study Establishment: The University of Western Australia.
Country of Study: Australia.
No. of awards offered: Varies.
Application Procedure: Applicants must write for details or obtain information from the university website.
Closing Date: August 31st for overseas applicants and October 31st for Australian applicants.
Funding: Private.
No. of awards given last year: 49.
No. of applicants last year: 450.
Additional Information: Scholarships may not be held concurrently with other awards of a similar nature. Employment is permitted to a maximum of 240 hours in a calendar year and no more than eight hours in any one week.

THE UNIVERSITY OF WESTERN ONTARIO

Centre for Interdisciplinary Studies in Chemical Physics, London, ON N6A 3K7, Canada
Tel: (1) 519 661 4088
Fax: (1) 519 661 3032
Email: ccp@uwo.ca
www: http://www.uwo.ca/ccp
Contact: Director

The University of Western Ontario is a modern, well equipped university offering programmes in all major academic disciplines. With its enrolment of over 25,000 students, Western is the fifth largest Canadian university and the second largest university in Ontario.

University of Western Ontario Senior Visiting Fellowship

Subjects: Current research programmes are focused on problems in condensed matter, properties of isolated atoms and molecules, surface studies and biological applications, X-ray spectroscopy and expert systems.

Purpose: To bring established senior scientists to the Centre for Interdisciplinary Studies in Chemical Physics to work on problems that are interdisciplinary in nature and of interest to Centre members.
Eligibility: Open to senior scientific researchers of established standing. There are no nationality restrictions.
Level of Study: Postdoctorate.
Type: Fellowship.
Value: Varies.
Length of Study: 3-12 months.
Frequency: Annual.
Study Establishment: The Centre.
Country of Study: Canada.
No. of awards offered: Varies.
Application Procedure: Applicants must complete an application form, available on the website.
Closing Date: October of the year preceding tenure.
Funding: Government.
Additional Information: Further details are available on request.

UNIVERSITY OF WESTERN SYDNEY

Office of Research Services, Hawkesbury Campus, Building H3, Locked Bag 1797, Penrith South DC, NSW 1797, Australia
Tel: (61) 2 4570 1463
Fax: (61) 2 4570 1686
Email: t.mills@uws.edu.au
www: http://www.uws.edu.au
Contact: Ms Tracey Mills, Research Scholarships Development Officer

University of Western Sydney Postgraduate Research Award (UWSPRA)
Subjects: All subjects offered by the University.
Purpose: To encourage excellence in research and support postgraduate research students enrolled in Doctor of Philosophy or Master's (Honours) courses at UWS.
Eligibility: Open to students who are enrolled in a full-time postgraduate research degree at the institution. The award holder is not permitted to receive similar funding from another Australian government source or other industry support in the form of a scholarship of equivalent value. Awards are not available to students who already hold a PhD degree or a postgraduate Master's degree in situations where the applicant seeks enrolment in or can only be accepted for a Master's degree.
Level of Study: Doctorate.
Type: Scholarship.
Value: A tax free stipend for each year of the award which will be equivalent to the APA base rate. The candidate will also receive a thesis allowance.
Length of Study: Three years for PhD candidates and two years for Master's candidates from the commencement of the course.
Frequency: Annual.
Study Establishment: The University of Western Sydney.
Country of Study: Australia.
No. of awards offered: 25.
Application Procedure: Applications must be made on the necessary form and submitted to the Office of Research Services with the required support material.
Closing Date: October 31st.
Funding: Government, Private.
Contributor: The University of Western Sydney.
No. of awards given last year: 25.
No. of applicants last year: 200.

UNIVERSITY OF WOLLONGONG

Northfields Avenue, Wollongong, NSW 2522, Australia
Tel: (61) 2 4221 3386
Fax: (61) 2 4221 4338
Email: research_office@uow.edu.au
www: http://www.uow.edu.au
Contact: Mr Tim McDonald, Postgraduate Research Scholarships Officer

The town of Wollongong sits between the dramatic Illawarra escarpment and the Pacific Ocean just one hour away from Sydney, Australia's largest city. The University of Wollongong enjoys a significant international research profile attracting more Australian Research Council funding per student in 2001 than any other Australian university. Over 850 postgraduate students are enrolled of which 30 per cent are overseas students.

University of Wollongong Postgraduate Awards
Subjects: Any research subject offered by the University.
Purpose: To provide financial support for full-time study leading to a Master's or PhD degree.
Eligibility: Open to graduates with at least a First Class (Honours) Degree. Holders of the award must pursue studies on a full-time basis and submit an annual report.
Level of Study: Doctorate, Postgraduate.
Type: Award.
Value: Australian $18,009.
Length of Study: Two years for the Master's or three years for the PhD. Renewals are subject to satisfactory progress.
Frequency: Annual.
Study Establishment: The University of Wollongong.
Country of Study: Australia.
No. of awards offered: Varies.
Application Procedure: Applicants must complete an application form, available from the Office of Research in July and August each year.
Closing Date: October 31st.
Additional Information: Holders of the award must pursue studies on a full-time basis and submit an annual report.

UNIVERSITY OF YORK

Graduate Schools Office, Heslington, York, England
Tel: (44) 1904 432143
Fax: (44) 1904 432092
Email: graduate@york.ac.uk
www: http://www.york.ac.uk/admin/gso/gsp
Contact: Mr Philip Simison

The University of York offers postgraduate degree courses in archaeology, art history, biology, biochemistry, chemistry, communication studies, computer science, economics, educational studies, electronics, English, environment, health sciences, history, language and linguistics, management, mathematics, medieval studies, music, philosophy, physics, politics, psychology, social policy, social work, sociology and women's studies.

University of York Masters Scholarships
Subjects: All subjects.
Purpose: To assist candidates of high academic standards to complete Masters degrees.
Eligibility: Open to full-time candidates for Masters degrees eg. the MA, MSc or MRes.
Level of Study: Postgraduate.
Type: Scholarship.
Value: Fee waiver equivalent to home or European Union fee.
Length of Study: One year.
Frequency: Annual.
Study Establishment: The University of York.
Country of Study: United Kingdom.
No. of awards offered: 14.
Application Procedure: Applicants must complete an application form, available from the Graduate Schools Office.
Closing Date: May 31st.

University of York Research Studentships/Scholarships
Subjects: All subjects.
Purpose: To assist candidates of a high academic standard to complete research degrees.
Eligibility: Open to full-time candidates for research degrees (PhD).
Level of Study: Doctorate, Postgraduate.
Type: Scholarship.

Value: Fees at home or European Union rate plus up to UK£8,000.
Length of Study: Up to three years.
Frequency: Annual.
Study Establishment: The University of York.
Country of Study: United Kingdom.
No. of awards offered: 27.
Application Procedure: Applicants must complete an application form, available from Graduate Schools Office.
Closing Date: May 31st.

University of York Scholarships for Overseas Students

Subjects: All subjects offered by the University.
Purpose: To assist overseas candidates of a high academic standard.
Eligibility: Open to students who have been accepted for registration as a full-time student for a degree, diploma or certificate course of the University of York and are liable to pay tuition fees at the full-cost rate for overseas ie. non European Community students.
Level of Study: Postgraduate.
Type: Scholarship.
Value: Waiver of up to one-third overseas fee.
Length of Study: Up to three years.
Frequency: Annual.
Study Establishment: The University of York.
Country of Study: United Kingdom.
No. of awards offered: 15.
Application Procedure: Applicants must complete an application form, available from the International Office.
Closing Date: May 1st.

US ARMY CENTER OF MILITARY HISTORY

Dissertation Fellowship Committee, Building 35 103 3rd Avenue, Fort Lesley, Washington, DC 20319-5058, United States of America
Tel: (1) 202 685 2108
Fax: (1) 202 685 2077
Email: cmhonline@hgda.army.mil
www: http://www.army.mil/cmh-pg
Contact: Executive Secretary

The US Army Center of Military History is the historical agency for the United States Army.

US Army Center of Military History Dissertation Fellowships

Subjects: For the purposes of this programme, the history of war on land is broadly defined, including such areas as biography, military campaigns, military organisation and administration, policy, strategy, tactics, weaponry, technology, training, logistics and evolution of civil military relations.
Purpose: To support scholarly research and writing among qualified civilian graduate students preparing dissertations in the history of war on land, especially the history of the United States Army.
Eligibility: Open to civilian graduate students of the United States of America who have completed all requirements for a PhD degree except the dissertation by September.
Level of Study: Doctorate.
Type: Fellowship.
Value: US$9,000 stipend, plus access to the Center's facilities and technical expertise.
Frequency: Annual.
Country of Study: Any country.
No. of awards offered: Two.
Application Procedure: Applicants must submit a completed application form, a proposed plan of research, a statement of approval from the academic director of the dissertation, two other letters of recommendation, an official graduate transcript, and a writing sample of approximately 25 pages. Samples should be complete pieces, not fragments of a larger study.
Closing Date: 15th January (each year).
Funding: Government.
Contributor: The United States army.

No. of awards given last year: Two.
No. of applicants last year: 19.
Additional Information: Fellows visit the Center at the beginning and end of the fellowship period. On the first visit, the Fellow meets key individuals at the Center and is consulted on ways that the Center can help him or her. On the second visit, the Fellow presents an oral report on his or her progress. A brief written report and a copy of the completed dissertation are also required. Candidates who have previously held or accepted an equivalent fellowship from any other United States Department of Defense agency are not eligible.

US NAVAL HISTORICAL CENTER

805 Kidder Breese Street, Washington Navy Yard, Washington, DC 20374-5060, United States of America
Tel: (1) 202 433 3940
Fax: (1) 202 433 3593
Email: edward.marolda@navy.mil
www: http://www.history.navy.mil
Contact: Dr Edward J Marolda, Senior Historian

The US Naval Historical Center works to enhance the Navy's effectiveness by preserving, analysing and interpreting its hard earned experience and history for the Navy and the American people.

Rear Admiral John D Hayes Pre-Doctoral Fellowship in US Naval History

Subjects: United States of America naval history.
Purpose: To assist scholars in the research for, or the writing of, doctoral dissertations relating to United States of America naval history.
Eligibility: Open to United States citizens, enrolled in a recognised graduate school, who have completed all the requirements for a PhD except the dissertation, and have an approved topic in the field of United states of America naval history.
Level of Study: Doctorate.
Type: Fellowship.
Value: US$10,000.
Frequency: Annual.
Country of Study: United States of America.
No. of awards offered: One.
Application Procedure: Applicants must submit a completed and signed application with supporting data attached, including a copy of approved an dissertation outline.
Closing Date: February 28th.
Funding: Government.
No. of awards given last year: One.
No. of applicants last year: 15.

Vice Admiral Edwin B Hooper Research Grants

Subjects: United States of America naval history.
Purpose: To assist scholars in the research for or the writing of books or articles.
Eligibility: Applicants must be United States citizens and must hold a PhD from an accredited university, or equivalent attainment as a published author.
Level of Study: Postdoctorate.
Type: Research grant.
Value: US$2,500.
Frequency: Annual.
Country of Study: United States of America.
No. of awards offered: Two.
Application Procedure: Applicants must send a letter stating the purpose and scope of the research project, including a proposed budget, and a completed application. In addition, two letters of recommendation from individuals familiar with the applicant's field of study will be required.
Closing Date: February 28th.
Funding: Government, Private.
Contributor: Non appropriate fund.
No. of awards given last year: Two.
No. of applicants last year: 15.

THE US-UK FULBRIGHT COMMISSION

Fulbright House, 62 Doughty Street, London, WC1N 2JZ, England
Tel: (44) 20 7404 6880
Fax: (44) 20 7404 6834
Email: education@fulbright.co.uk
www: http://www.fulbright.co.uk
Contact: Ms L Ingarfield, British Programme Manager

The US-UK Fulbright Commission has a programme of awards offered annually to citizens of the United Kingdom and United States of America. The United States Educational Advisory Service deals with enquiries from the public on all aspects of United States education including sources of funding for study in the United States of America.

Fulbright 2nd Air Division USAAF Librarianship at Memorial Library, Norwich

Subjects: Library science.
Purpose: To assist the development of the work of the 2nd Air Division Memorial Library in building service links with secondary schools, to develop opportunities for educational work with adults and to oversee their web based initiatives.
Eligibility: Applicants must hold a MLS, MS or MA degree in a relevant field, have a minimum three years of experience of working in a library, particularly a public library, and have strong communication skills.
Level of Study: Professional development.
Value: Approx. UK£22,000(GBP) plus round trip travel for grantee and housing.
Length of Study: One year.
Frequency: Annual.
Study Establishment: Memorial Library, Norwich.
Country of Study: United Kingdom.
No. of awards offered: One.
Application Procedure: Applicants must complete an application form.
Closing Date: August 1st.
Funding: Private.
No. of awards given last year: One.

For further information contact:

3007 Tilden Street, Suite 5M, Washington, DC 20008-3009, United States of America
Contact: Grants Management Officer

Fulbright AstraZeneca Research Scholarship

Subjects: Cell biology, molecular biology, bioinformatics, biochemistry or chemistry.
Purpose: To enable a postdoctoral scientist to carry out research at a top centre in the United States of America.
Eligibility: Open to British scientists.
Level of Study: Postdoctorate.
Type: Scholarship.
Value: UK£15,000 plus round trip travel.
Length of Study: A minimum of 10 months.
Frequency: Annual.
Study Establishment: An approved establishment.
Country of Study: United States of America.
No. of awards offered: One.
Application Procedure: Applicants must complete an application form.
Closing Date: Mid March.
Funding: Private.
No. of awards given last year: One.
No. of applicants last year: Three.
Additional Information: Shortlisted candidates will usually be interviewed in April or May.

Fulbright Co-Sponsored MBA Awards

Subjects: MBA.
Purpose: To enable MBA candidates to participate in United States of America MBA programmes.

Eligibility: Open to European Union citizens normally resident in the United Kingdom. Applicants must hold the minimum of an Upper Second Class (Honours) Degree, have a minimum of two-three years of work experience and be able to demonstrate leadership qualities.
Level of Study: MBA, Postgraduate.
Type: Scholarship.
Value: Tuition fees and maintenance for the first academic year.
Length of Study: Nine months.
Frequency: Annual.
Country of Study: United States of America.
No. of awards offered: Approx. Four.
Application Procedure: Applicants must complete an application form and submit this with two references.
Closing Date: Late January.
Funding: Commercial, Government.
No. of awards given last year: Seven.
No. of applicants last year: 50.
Additional Information: Shortlisted candidates will be interviewed in February.

Fulbright Distinguished Scholar Awards

Subjects: All subjects.
Purpose: To allow outstanding academics or professionals who are established or potential leaders in their field to undertake a period of professional development in the United States of America.
Eligibility: Open to European Union citizens who are normally resident in the United Kingdom, and are planning a minimum stay of 10 months, normally with an affiliation to one academic institution in the United States. Proof of this affiliation and details of its nature are necessary. Medical doctors intending to work with patients in any capacity while in the United States are not eligible. Awards are not available for peripatetic visits or attendance at conferences only.
Level of Study: Professional development.
Type: Fellowship.
Value: UK£15,000, visa paperwork processed and visa paid by the Commission, and health and accident insurance.
Length of Study: A minimum stay of 10 months.
Frequency: Annual.
Country of Study: United States of America.
No. of awards offered: Two.
Application Procedure: Applicants must draw up a detailed project outline and provide evidence that a United States institution will agree to act as host and supervisor. Lecturers and researchers must have an invitation from the host institution. Completed applications should reach the Commission by the deadline and may not be emailed.
Closing Date: Late March.
Funding: Government.
No. of awards given last year: Three.

Fulbright Fellowship in Cancer Research

Subjects: Oncology.
Purpose: To enable a scientist or clinician to carry out research into cancer, to enhance mutual understanding and strengthen relations between the two countries.
Eligibility: Open to scientists or clinicians who are British or European Union citizens resident in the United Kingdom.
Level of Study: Postdoctorate.
Type: Fellowship.
Value: UK£15,000.
Length of Study: 6-12 months.
Frequency: Annual.
Study Establishment: An approved institution.
Country of Study: United States of America.
No. of awards offered: One.
Application Procedure: Applicants must submit a formal application. Application forms and full details of the fellowship are available from the website.
Closing Date: Mid April.
Funding: Government.
No. of awards given last year: One.
Additional Information: Shortlisted candidates will be interviewed.

Fulbright Graduate Student Awards

Subjects: All subjects.

Purpose: To enable students to follow postgraduate study or research in the United Kingdom.

Eligibility: Open to United States of America citizens, normally resident in the United States of America. Applicants must have a minimum grade point average of 3.5 and be able to demonstrate evidence of leadership qualities. Applicants should be adventurous and be able to demonstrate that they will maximise academic, social and cultural opportunities available in the United Kingdom. A full profile of the ideal candidate is available from the website.

Level of Study: MBA, Postgraduate, Research.

Value: Maintenance allowance and approved tuition fees are covered.

Length of Study: Nine months.

Frequency: Annual.

Study Establishment: Any approved Institute of Higher Education.

Country of Study: United Kingdom.

No. of awards offered: Approx. 20.

Application Procedure: Applicants must submit a formal application with four references.

Closing Date: October.

Funding: Commercial, Government, Private.

Contributor: The United States and United Kingdom governments.

No. of awards given last year: 20.

No. of applicants last year: approx. 600.

Additional Information: A telephone interview is required of 48 shortlisted candidates.

For further information contact:

Institute of International Education, 809 United Nations Plaza, New York, NY 10017, United States of America

Tel: (1) 212 984 5466

Fax: (1) 212 984 5465

Contact: Student Program Division

Fulbright Police Studies Fellowship

Subjects: Policing.

Purpose: To enable serving police officers to spend 3-6 months in the United States of America researching an aspect of policing.

Eligibility: Open to British police officers (minimum Inspector level).

Level of Study: Professional development.

Type: Fellowship.

Value: UK£5,000 (includes round trip travel).

Length of Study: Three months.

Frequency: Annual.

Study Establishment: An approved United States of America Institute of Higher Education.

Country of Study: United States of America.

No. of awards offered: Five.

Application Procedure: Applicants must complete a formal application.

Closing Date: March 30th.

Funding: Government.

No. of awards given last year: Two.

No. of applicants last year: Six.

Additional Information: Shortlisted candidates will usually be interviewed in June.

Fulbright Police Studies Fellowships

Subjects: Law enforcement.

Purpose: To enable British police officers or civilian staff to spend time in the United States developing their professional expertise and gaining experience of American policing.

Eligibility: Open to all ranks of police officers and civilian staff. Female and ethnic minority staff are particularly encouraged to apply. Candidates will not follow a degree course, but should have some kind of academic affiliation during the award period. It is not necessary for applicants to confirm an affiliation prior to submitting their application.

Level of Study: Professional development.

Type: Fellowship.

Value: UK£5,000 to cover round trip travel and additional expenses.

Length of Study: A minimum of three months.

Frequency: Annual.

Country of Study: United States of America.

No. of awards offered: 7.

Application Procedure: Applicants must contact the British programme manager at the Fulbright Commission.

Closing Date: Late March.

Funding: Government.

No. of awards given last year: Four.

Fulbright Postgraduate Student Awards

Subjects: All subjects.

Purpose: To enable students to pursue postgraduate study or research in the United States of America.

Eligibility: Open to European Union citizens who are normally resident in the United Kingdom, hold a minimum of an Upper Second Class (Honours) Degree and demonstrate outstanding leadership qualities.

Level of Study: Postgraduate.

Value: Tuition and maintenance for nine months and round trip travel.

Length of Study: A minimum of nine months.

Frequency: Annual.

Study Establishment: An approved Institute of Higher Education.

Country of Study: United States of America.

No. of awards offered: 10-15.

Application Procedure: Applicants must submit a formal application with two references. Applications can be obtained from the British programme manager or by visiting the website.

Closing Date: Usually in early November.

Funding: Government.

No. of awards given last year: 15.

No. of applicants last year: 400.

Additional Information: Shortlisted candidates will be interviewed in mid February.

Fulbright Scholar Grants

Subjects: All subjects.

Purpose: To enable Scholars to carry out lecturing and research in the United Kingdom.

Eligibility: Open to United States of America Scholars who took their first degree more than five years ago. Young academics in their twenties and thirties are actively encouraged to apply.

Level of Study: Postdoctorate, Professional development, Research, Lecture.

Value: UK£15,000 inclusive of round trip travel, pro rata.

Length of Study: Three-Twelve months.

Frequency: Annual.

Study Establishment: An approved Institute of Higher Education.

Country of Study: United Kingdom.

No. of awards offered: Four.

Application Procedure: Applicants must submit a formal application with four references.

Closing Date: August 1st.

Funding: Government.

No. of awards given last year: 5.

For further information contact:

Council for International Exchange of Scholars, 3007 Tilden Street North West, Suite 5M, Washington, DC 20008-3009, United States of America

Tel: (1) 202 686 6245

Email: we1@ciesnet.cies.org

Contact: Grants Management Officer

Fulbright-Chester Schirmer Fellowship in Music Composition

Subjects: Music composition.

Purpose: To enable talented young composers to spend a period of time in the United States extending their artistic expertise and experience and taking an important step in developing an international reputation.

Eligibility: Open to candidates who are establishing a reputation in the United Kingdom as a professional composer, have completed their

graduate education can and show that their work would benefit from exposure to American influences.
Level of Study: Postdoctorate, Professional development, Research.
Type: Fellowship.
Value: Up to UK£12,000, pro rata.
Length of Study: A minimum of four months and a maximum of twelve.
Frequency: Annual.
Country of Study: United Kingdom.
No. of awards offered: One.
Application Procedure: Applicants should submit an initial application, including six copies of a score and tape of two recent and representative works, a full curriculum vitae plus complete work list, a list of recent performances and commissions. An outline of reasons for wishing to visit and work in the United States and benefits likely to result to the composer and his or her music should also be included with references from two professional referees.
Closing Date: Mid March.
Funding: Commercial.
Contributor: Chester Music.
No. of awards given last year: One.

Fulbright-Humphrey Fellowship for Civil Servants
Subjects: Public policy.
Purpose: To enable a British civil servant to spend one year at the Hubert Humphrey Institute of Public Affairs at the University of Minnesota.
Eligibility: Open to British civil servants at Principal Officer level or above.
Level of Study: Professional development.
Type: Fellowship.
Value: US$10,000 plus round trip travel. Confirmation is required that salary will still be paid during the award period.
Length of Study: One year.
Frequency: Annual.
Study Establishment: The Hubert Humphrey Institute of Public Affairs, University of Minnesota.
Country of Study: United States of America.
No. of awards offered: One.
Application Procedure: Applicants must submit a formal application, research proposal and departmental reference.
Closing Date: Usually late November.
Funding: Private.
No. of awards given last year: One.
Additional Information: Shortlisted candidates will usually be interviewed in January.

Fulbright-Robertson Visiting Professorship in British History
Subjects: British history.
Purpose: To enable a British scholar to spend 10 months lecturing in British history at Westminster College, Fulton in Missouri.
Eligibility: Open to Scholars of British history, with one-two years of experience of teaching undergraduates.
Level of Study: Professional development.
Type: Other.
Value: Up to US$40,000 plus round trip travel for the grantee and up to four accompanying dependants.
Length of Study: 10 months.
Frequency: Annual.
Study Establishment: Westminster College, Fulton, Missouri.
Country of Study: United States of America.
No. of awards offered: One.
Application Procedure: Applicants must submit a formal application with two references.
Closing Date: Usually at the end of January.
Funding: Private.
Contributor: Westminster College, Fulton, Missouri.
No. of awards given last year: One.
No. of applicants last year: Three.
Additional Information: Shortlisted candidates will usually be interviewed in March.

US-UK Fulbright Commission Police Research Fellowship.
Subjects: Criminal law.
Purpose: To enable active domestic police officers and police administrators to extend their professional expertise and experience in conducting research into any aspect of policing.
Eligibility: Applicants should ideally hold a Bachelor's degree in criminal justice, police studies or a related discipline within the social sciences.
Level of Study: Professional development.
Value: UK£5,000.
Length of Study: Three months.
Frequency: Annual.
Study Establishment: Institutes of Higher Education or a police force.
Country of Study: United Kingdom.
No. of awards offered: Two.
Application Procedure: Applicants must complete an application form available from the organisation.
Closing Date: August 1st.
Funding: Government.
No. of awards given last year: Two.

For further information contact:

3007 Tilden Street, Suite 5M, Washington, DC 2008-3009, United States of America
Contact: CIES

VATICAN FILM LIBRARY

Mellon Fellowship Program, Pius XII Memorial Library, Saint Louis University, 3650 Lindell Boulevard, St. Louis, MO 63108-3302, United States of America
Tel: (1) (314) 977-3090
Fax: (1) (314) 977-3108
Email: vfl@slu.edu
www: http://www.slu.edu/libraries/vfl

The Vatican Library at Saint Louis University in St. Louis, Missouri, is a microfilm repository for the Vatican Library manuscripts housed in Rome and a research center for medieval and Renaissance manuscripts studies in general. The research collections of the Vatican Film Library contain a wide range of primary source manuscript materials on microfilm, microfiche, and in digital reproduction, in addition to slides and printed facsimile editions, ranging in date from the fifth to the nineteenth centuries, along with a large number of incunabula and early-printed books also on microfilm and microfiche. At the core of these collections are the microfilmed copies of approximately three-quarters of the Vatican Library's Greek, Latin, and Western European vernacular manuscripts, as well as Hebrew, Ethiopic, and Arabic manuscripts. The Patristic age is exceedingly well documented, as is medieval literature in all its forms, particularly in the Romance languages.

Vatican Film Library Mellon Fellowship
Subjects: Classical languages and literature, palaeography, scriptural and patristic studies, history, philosophy and sciences in the Middle Ages and the Renaissance, and early Romance literature. There are also opportunities for supported research in the history of music, manuscript illumination, mathematics and technology, theology, liturgy, Roman and canon law or political theory.
Purpose: To assist scholars wishing to conduct research in the manuscript collections in the Vatican Film Library at Saint Louis University.
Eligibility: Open to candidates who are at postdoctoral level, or graduate students formally admitted to PhD candidacy and working on their dissertation.
Level of Study: Doctorate, Graduate, Postdoctorate, Postgraduate, Predoctorate, Research.
Type: Fellowship.
Value: Travel expenses and Per Diem expenses (currently US$73).
Length of Study: Two-eight weeks.
Study Establishment: The Vatican Film Library.
Country of Study: United States of America.

Application Procedure: Applicants must write, in the first instance, to describe the topic of the planned research and to indicate the exact dates during which support is desired.

Closing Date: March 1st for research in June to August, June 1st for research in September to December and October 1st for research in January to May.

Additional Information: Application to the fellowship program should be initiated by a brief project description accompanied by a list of manuscripts or other archival materials the applicant wishes to consult in the course of his or her research in order that the presence of these materials in the collections and their suitability for the proposed research may be determined. Confirmation of the presence or absence of these materials and their appropriateness for the proposed topic will be sent shortly thereafter. A formal application should then be submitted which shall include a cover letter stating the title and proposed dates of research, a detailed statement of the project proposal of not more than two or three pages in length, a list of the manuscripts or other archival materials to be consulted, a selective bibliography of primary and secondary sources relating to the research topic, and a curriculum vitae. Applications submitted by Ph.D. candidates should also include a letter of recommendation from their advisor with reference to the applicant's palaeographical and language. Further information is available on the website.

VERNE CATT MCDOWELL CORPORATION

PO Box 1336, Albany, OR 97321-0440, United States of America
Tel: (1) 541 926 6829
Contact: Ms Emily Killin, Business Manager

The Verne Catt McDowell Scholarship educates pastoral ministers of the Christian Church (Disciples of Christ) by providing supplementary financial grants to graduate theology students.

Verne Catt McDowell Scholarship
Subjects: Religion, theology or church administration.
Purpose: To provide supplemental financial grants to men and women for graduate theological education for ministry in the Christian Church (Disciples of Christ) denomination.
Eligibility: All scholarship candidates must be ministers ordained or studying to meet the requirements to be ordained as a minister in the Christian Church (Disciples of Christ). Candidates must be members of the Christian Church (Disciples of Christ) denomination. Preference is given to Oregon graduates and United States citizens.
Level of Study: Postgraduate.
Type: Scholarship.
Value: US$350 per school month.
Length of Study: One-three years.
Frequency: Annual.
Study Establishment: A graduate institution of theological education, accredited by the general assembly of the Christian Church (Disciples of Christ).
Country of Study: United States of America.
No. of awards offered: Six.
Application Procedure: Applicants must complete an application form and provide details of qualifications, transcripts, three references and state where they obtained information about the Scholarship. An interview may be requested.
Closing Date: May 1st.
Funding: Private.
Contributor: I A McDowell.
No. of awards given last year: Six.
No. of applicants last year: 12.

VERNON WILLEY TRUST

Guardian Trust, PO Box 9, Christchurch, 8001, New Zealand
Tel: (64) 3 366 6764
Fax: (64) 3 366 7616
Email: alilley@nzgt.co.nz
www: http://www.nzgt.co.nz
Contact: Mr F Cattermole

Vernon Willey Trust Awards
Subjects: The sheep and wool industry of New Zealand.
Purpose: To assist with research and education into the production, processing and marketing of wool and the general development of the industry for the national benefit of New Zealand.
Eligibility: Open to New Zealand citizens, permanent New Zealand residents or overseas researchers working in New Zealand.
Level of Study: Doctorate, Postdoctorate.
Type: Fellowship.
Value: Varies, usually between New Zealand $30,000-35,000.
Length of Study: Up to three years.
Frequency: Dependent on funds available.
Country of Study: New Zealand.
No. of awards offered: One.
Application Procedure: Applicants must complete an application form.
Closing Date: The first week in November.
Funding: Private.
No. of awards given last year: Nil.
No. of applicants last year: Nil.
Additional Information: Applicants for financial grants must satisfy the Committee that their activities are of general or public benefit. The results of the research or studies are expected to be covered by material suitable for publication in recognised scientific or technical journals.

VICTORIA UNIVERSITY

Emmanuel College, 75 Queen's Park Crescent East, Toronto, ON M5S 1K7, Canada
Tel: (1) 416 585 4539
Fax: (1) 416 585 4516
Email: ec.office@utoronto.ca
www: http://www.vicu.utoronto.ca

Emmanuel College, set within Victoria University and the University of Toronto, is the United Church of Canada's largest theological college. The College offers four basic or first professional degrees and five advanced or graduate degrees. About 210 students are currently enrolled. Emmanuel College is one of seven member schools of the Toronto School of Theology.

Bertram Maura Memorial Entrance Scholarship
Subjects: Theology, specifically in the fields of the Old and New Testament.
Purpose: To provide funding to doctoral students.
Eligibility: Open to outstanding doctoral students.
Level of Study: Doctorate.
Type: Scholarship.
Value: Dependent on funds available, but usually Canadian $10,000.
Length of Study: Two years.
Frequency: Annual.
Study Establishment: Emmanuel College.
Country of Study: Canada.
No. of awards offered: Usually 4.
Closing Date: March 31st.
Funding: Private.

Bloor Lands Entrance Scholarship
Subjects: Religion and theology.
Purpose: To assist newly admitted ThD or PhD students with potential for excellence in scholarship demonstrated by high achievement in previous theological studies.
Level of Study: Doctorate.
Type: Scholarship.
Value: Varies dependent on funds available, but usually Canadian $10,000.
Length of Study: Two years.
Frequency: Annual.
Study Establishment: Emmanuel College.
Country of Study: Canada.
No. of awards offered: Usually 3 or 4.
Application Procedure: Admission to the Toronto School of Theology/Emmanuel College must first be granted. Application

is then made care of the Director of Advanced Degree Studies.
Closing Date: March 31st.
Funding: Private.

Finishing Scholarships

Subjects: Religion and theology.
Purpose: To enable a doctoral student to finish his or her dissertation in the year in which the award is made.
Eligibility: Open to doctoral students at the end of the programme.
Level of Study: Doctorate.
Type: Scholarship.
Value: Approx. Canadian $10,000.
Length of Study: One year.
Frequency: Annual.
Study Establishment: Emmanuel College.
Country of Study: Canada.
No. of awards offered: Three.
Closing Date: March 31st.
Funding: Private.

Frank P Fidler Memorial Award

Subjects: Religion and theology.
Purpose: To assist alumni returning for further study.
Eligibility: Applications from those interested in studying the Church's ministry with various types of families in today's changing world are particularly encouraged. Preference is given to graduates returning to Emmanuel to complete a ThM or second basic degree.
Level of Study: Doctorate.
Type: Scholarship.
Value: Varies.
Length of Study: One year.
Frequency: Annual.
Study Establishment: Emmanuel College.
Country of Study: Canada.
No. of awards offered: One.
Closing Date: March 31st.
Funding: Private.

In-Course Scholarships

Subjects: Religion and theology.
Eligibility: Open to doctoral students.
Level of Study: Doctorate.
Type: Scholarship.
Value: Varies.
Length of Study: Two-three years.
Frequency: Annual.
Study Establishment: Emmanuel College.
Country of Study: Canada.
No. of awards offered: Varies from year to year.
Closing Date: March 31st.
Funding: Private.
Additional Information: These scholarships are awarded to students who have demonstrated academic excellence to assist them beyond the residency phase of their studies.

Vernon Hope Emory Entrance Scholarship

Subjects: Religion and theology.
Purpose: To support an outstanding newly admitted ThD or PhD student.
Level of Study: Doctorate.
Type: Scholarship.
Value: Varies according to funds available.
Length of Study: Two years.
Frequency: Annual.
Study Establishment: Emmanuel College.
Country of Study: Canada.
No. of awards offered: One.
Application Procedure: Admission to the Toronto School of Theology/Emmanuel College must be first granted. Application is then made care of the Director of Advanced Degree Studies.
Closing Date: March 31st.
Funding: Private.

Victoria University Graduate Student Assistantships

Subjects: Religion and theology. Graduate students are assigned to work with the Asian Centre and in the fields of Christian education, church and society, ethics, field education, history of Christianity, homiletics, the Old and New Testament, pastoral theology and systematic theology or worship.
Purpose: To provide funding for doctoral students.
Level of Study: Doctorate.
Type: Scholarship.
Value: Canadian $9,300 per year.
Length of Study: Two years.
Frequency: Annual.
Study Establishment: Emmanuel College.
Country of Study: Canada.
No. of awards offered: Usually 12 or 13.
Application Procedure: Admission to the Toronto School of Theology/Emmanuel College must first be granted. Application is then made care of the Director of Advance Degree Studies.
Closing Date: February 28th.
Funding: Private.

VIRGINIA CENTER FOR THE CREATIVE ARTS

154 San Angelo Drive, Amherst, VA 24521, United States of America
Tel: (1) 434 946 7236
Fax: (1) 434 946 7239
Email: vcca@vcca.com
www: http://www.vcca.com
Contact: Ms Suny Monk, Director

The Virginia Center for the Creative Arts is a year round community that provides a supportive environment for superior national and international visual artists, writers and composers, of all cultural and economic backgrounds, to pursue their creative work without distraction in a pastoral residential setting.

Virginia Center for the Creative Arts Fellowships

Subjects: Writing, musical composition, photography or art.
Purpose: To support literary, musical and visual artists during the most crucial creative phase of their work.
Eligibility: Open to artists with professional competence and promise, regardless of age, sex, citizenship or academic background. Writers, visual artists, composers, choreographers, photographers, film makers, interdisciplinary and multimedia artists are all eligible. Admission is through a jury selection process.
Level of Study: Unrestricted.
Type: Residential Fellowships.
Value: Subsidised residence at the Center. No cash stipends or travel allowances are provided.
Length of Study: Two to eight weeks residential fellowships.
Frequency: Annual.
Study Establishment: The Center.
Country of Study: United States of America.
No. of awards offered: Approx. 300.
Application Procedure: Applicants must submit an application form, work samples and letters of reference.
Closing Date: January 15th, May 15th or September 15th.
Funding: Commercial, Government, Private.
No. of awards given last year: 309.
No. of applicants last year: 850.
Additional Information: Type of Award: Residential Fellowships.

THE VITILIGO SOCIETY

125 Kennington Road, London, SE11 6SF, England
Tel: (44) 20 7840 0855
Fax: (44) 20 7840 0866
Email: all@vitiligosociety.org.uk
www: http://www.vitiligosociety.org.uk
Contact: Mr Marion Lesage, Administrative Assistant

The Vitiligo Society was established in 1985 as a patient support group for people who suffer from the skin condition vitiligo, where patches of skin become hypopigmented. This is a chronic, unstable and disfiguring condition which can cause extreme distress and ensuing psychological problems due to loss of self esteem and stigmatisation. The Vitiligo Society exists to further the physical, social and emotional well being of those who are affected by vitiligo. Its mission statement is to promote a positive approach to living with vitiligo and an important aspect of this aim is to support research.

Vitiligo Society Grants

Subjects: Vitiligo related research in areas such as dermatology, psychology and biochemistry.
Purpose: To facilitate research.
Eligibility: Open to research undertaken in the United Kingdom only.
Level of Study: Postgraduate.
Type: A variable number of grants.
Value: Dependent on resources available at the time of application.
Length of Study: No restrictions.
Frequency: Twice a year.
Country of Study: United Kingdom.
No. of awards offered: Varies according to funds available.
Application Procedure: Application forms are available from the website.
Closing Date: March 31st for the May meeting and September 30th for the November meeting.
Contributor: Members of the Vitiligo Society.
No. of awards given last year: One.
No. of applicants last year: Three.
Additional Information: Although it is keen to fund research, applicants should be aware that the Society is quite a small charity and that its resources are limited. Therefore it is not usually possible to support long-term salaries or the purchase of expensive technical equipment.

VITUKI TRAINING

International Postgraduate Course on Hydrology, Pf 27, Budapest, H-1453, Hungary
Tel: (36) 1 215 3043
Fax: (36) 1 215 3043
Email: training@vituki.hu
www: http://www.vituki.hu/ceg/tanf_hmem/index.htm
Contact: Director

Supported by hydraulic, hydromachinery, hydrochemical, hydrobiological, wastewater technological and soil mechanical laboratories, equipment, instrumentation, computer facilities and library, VITUKI is one of the most complex water oriented organisations in Europe. It contains three institutes and a training centre in the fields of hydrology, hydrogeology, hydraulics, water quality and pollution control.

VITUKI Training Financial Support for Course Participants

Subjects: Hydrology based subjects such as mathematics, hydraulics, geosciences, hydrological studies, hydrological processes, observation processing, analysis, forecasting, application, aquatic environment and water management.
Purpose: To make a contribution towards raising the level of hydrological sciences in developing and transitional countries.
Eligibility: Open to nationals of any country who are under 40 years of age. A degree from a recognised institution is required in applied mathematics, mathematical statistics, systems analysis, hydrology, fluid mechanics, geology or meteorology.
Level of Study: Postgraduate.
Type: Grant.
Value: US$8,000.
Length of Study: Four months.
Frequency: Annual.
Study Establishment: The premises of VITUKI in Budapest.
Country of Study: Hungary.
No. of awards offered: Four.
Application Procedure: Applicants must write for details.
Closing Date: December 31st.

Funding: Government.
Contributor: The Hungarian government.
No. of awards given last year: Four.
No. of applicants last year: 40.
Additional Information: The course's finances are essentially based on applicants holding fellowships granted by international organisations, by their own government, or on applicants paying for themselves. The course's admission board may be able to propose fellowship applicants to sponsoring national or international agencies, but awards no fellowships of its own.

VON KARMAN INSTITUTE FOR FLUID DYNAMICS (VKI)

Chausse de Waterloo 72, Rhode-Saint-Genese, B-1640, Belgium
Tel: (32) 2 359 9611
Fax: (32) 2 359 9600
Email: secretariat@vki.ac.be
www: http://www.vki.ac.be

The Von Karman Institute for Fluid Dynamics (VKI) is an international postgraduate training and research centre specialising in the fluid dynamic aspects of aircraft, spacecraft, turbomachines, wind flows and industrial processes.

VKI Fellowship

Subjects: Fluid dynamics.
Purpose: To support the living costs of recipients who attend the VKI post-graduate diploma course.
Eligibility: Open to citizens of NATO countries, with the exception of Canada, Denmark, Greece, the Netherlands and the United Kingdom, who have the equivalent of a five year engineering degree. Applicants must have a working knowledge of English.
Level of Study: Postgraduate.
Type: Fellowship.
Value: Varies.
Length of Study: Nine months.
Frequency: Annual.
Study Establishment: The VKI.
Country of Study: Belgium.
No. of awards offered: Varies.
Application Procedure: Applicants must submit two application forms, one endorsed by the RTO National Delegate (NATO Research and Technology Organisation). Copies of college transcripts and three references are required.
Closing Date: Applications received before March 1st will be given priority.
Funding: Government.
No. of awards given last year: 21.
No. of applicants last year: 52.
Additional Information: Please contact the organisation or visit the website for further details.

W EUGENE SMITH MEMORIAL FUND, INC.

c/o International Center of Photography, 1133, Avenue of the Americas, New York, NY 10036, United States of America
Tel: (1) 212 857 0038
www: http://www.smithfund.org
Contact: Ms Helen Marcus, President

The W Eugene Smith Memorial Fund, Inc. presents a major grant to a photographer whose past work and proposed project follows in the humanistic tradition of Smith. The Funds' grant programme is financed by Nikon, Inc.

Smith (W Eugene) Grant in Humanistic Photography

Subjects: Photojournalism.
Purpose: To support a photographer working on a project in the humanistic tradition of W Eugene Smith, in order to continue to pursue the work.

Eligibility: Open to outstanding photographers of any nationality.
Level of Study: Professional development.
Type: Grant.
Value: One grant for US$30,000 with a possible second grant for US$5,000.
Frequency: Annual.
Country of Study: Any country.
No. of awards offered: Two.
Application Procedure: Applicants must send a stamped (60 cents) addressed envelope for application information.
Closing Date: July 15th, 2004.
Funding: Commercial.
Contributor: Nikon, Inc.
No. of awards given last year: Two.
No. of applicants last year: 182.

WACKER FOUNDATION

8523 Thackery, 1115, Dallas, TX 75225, United States of America
Tel: (1) 214 368 0150
Fax: (1) 214 373 3308
Email: wackerjohn@aol.com
www: http://www.crime-times.org
Contact: Mr John A Wacker, President

The Wacker Foundation funds research and dissemination of research information which targets the proving, diagnosing or treating of biologically based disordered behaviour. Areas of special interest include nutrition, food and chemical intolerance, neurochemistry and genetics.

Wacker Foundation Research Grant
Subjects: Neurology, mental health, biomedicine, biophysics, molecular biology, genetics, neurosciences, toxicology and cognitive sciences.
Value: Varies.
Frequency: Dependent on funds available.
Application Procedure: Applicants must submit a brief letter giving a description of the proposed project and stating the appropriate cost.
Closing Date: There is no deadline.
Funding: Private.

THE WARBURG INSTITUTE

University of London, Woburn Square, London, WC1H 0AB, England
Tel: (44) 20 7862 8949
Fax: (44) 20 7862 8955
Email: warburg@sas.ac.uk
www: http://www.sas.ac.uk/warburg
Contact: E A Witchell, Administrative Assistant

The Warburg Institute is concerned with the interdisciplinary study of the continuities between the ancient Mediterranean civilisations and the cultural and intellectual history of post classical Europe before 1800 AD. Its collections are arranged to encourage research into the processes by which different fields of thought and art interact.

Albin Salton Fellowship
Subjects: The formation of a new world view by pursuing research in to cultural contracts between Europe, the East and the New World in the late medieval, Renaissance and early modern periods.
Purpose: To enable a younger scholar to spend two months at the Warburg Institute.
Eligibility: Applicants must normally be under 35 years of age on October 1st of the academic year prior to which the fellowship is taken up, and have completed at least one year of research towards a doctorate. Post doctoral candidates, if are 35, must normally have been awarded their doctorate within the preceding academic year. If their doctorate was awarded earlier, they should explain the reasons for any interruption in their academic career in a covering letter.
Level of Study: Doctorate, Postdoctorate.
Type: Fellowship.

Value: UK£1,500 for a United Kingdom holder or UK£1,850 for an overseas holder.
Length of Study: Two months.
Frequency: Annual.
Study Establishment: The Warburg Institute.
Country of Study: United Kingdom.
No. of awards offered: One.
Application Procedure: Applications should be made by letter to the Director enclosing a full CV comprising name, date of birth, address (including email address) and present occupation, school and university education, degrees, teaching and research experience, publications; an outline of proposed research (of not more than two pages); particulars of grants received; if any, on the same subject; the names and addresses of three persons who have agreed to write, without further invitation, in support of the application.
Closing Date: 1st December of preceding year.
Funding: Private.
No. of awards given last year: One.
Additional Information: The Fellowship is intended to promote the understanding of those elements of cultural and intellectual history which led to the formation of a new world view, understood in the broadest cultural, political and socio-economic terms, as Europe began to develop contacts with the world outside Europe, and that world came into contact with Europe.

Brian Hewson Crawford Fellowship
Subjects: The classical tradition.
Purpose: To support research into any aspect of the classical tradition.
Eligibility: Fellowships are generally open to younger scholars and preference will normally be given to those under 35 years of age on October 1st 2003. Candidates may be pre or postdoctoral but must have completed at least one year of research on their doctoral dissertation by the time they submit their application. Postdoctoral candidates, if they are over 35, must normally have been awarded their doctorate within the preceding academic year. If their doctorate was awarded before this they should explain the reasons for the interruption in their academic career in a covering letter.
Level of Study: Doctorate, Postdoctorate.
Type: Fellowship.
Value: UK based holders UK£1,500. Overseas holder UK£1,850.
Length of Study: Two months.
Frequency: Annual.
Study Establishment: The Warburg Institute.
Country of Study: United Kingdom.
No. of awards offered: One.
Application Procedure: Applications should be made by letter to the Director enclosing a full CV comprising name, date of birth, address (including email address) and present occupation, school and university education, degrees, teaching and research experience, publications; an outline of proposed research (of not more than two pages); particulars of grants received; if any, on the same subject; the names and addresses of three persons who have agreed to write, without further invitation, in support of the application.
Closing Date: 1st December of the preceding year.
Funding: Private.
No. of awards given last year: One.

Frances A Yates Fellowships
Subjects: Any aspect of intellectual and cultural history with emphasis on the medieval and renaissance. Preference to those areas of knowledge to which same Frances Yates made a contribution.
Purpose: To promote research in any aspect of cultural and intellectual history.
Eligibility: Fellowships are generally for younger Scholars and preference will normally be given to those under 35 years of age on October 1st 2003. Candidates may be pre or postdoctoral but must have completed at least one year of research on their doctoral dissertation by the time they submit their application. Postdoctoral candidates, if they are over 35, must normally have been awarded their doctorate within the preceding academic year. If their doctorate was awarded before this they should explain the reasons for the interruption in their academic career in a covering letter.

Level of Study: Doctorate, Postdoctorate.
Type: Fellowship.
Value: Short-term fellowships are UK£1,500-3,000; overseas holders UK£1,850-3,500.The long-term fellowship is UK£17,000-18,000 p.a.
Length of Study: The long-term fellowship is one-three years, not normally renewable, and short-term fellowships are two-four months, not renewable.
Frequency: Annual.
Study Establishment: The Warburg Institute.
Country of Study: United Kingdom.
No. of awards offered: One long-term fellowship which is not awarded every year and 10 short-term fellowships.
Application Procedure: Applications should be made by letter to the Director enclosing a full CV comprising name, date of birth, address (including email address) and present occupation, school and university education, degrees, teaching and research experience, publications; an outline of proposed research (of not more than two pages); particulars of grants received, if any, on the same subject; the names and addresses of three persons who have agreed to write, without further invitation, in support of the application.
Closing Date: 1st December of preceding year
Funding: Private.
No. of awards given last year: Seven.
Additional Information: Those employed as Professor, Lecturer or equivalent in a university or learned institution may normally hold an award only if they are taking unpaid leave for the whole of the period. The Fellowship may not be held concurrently with another Fellowship or award. The Fellow will be expected to participate in the life of the Institute and to put his/her knowledge at the disposal of the Institute by presenting his/her work in a seminar and by advising the Library and Photographic Collection. The Fellow may teach elsewhere during tenure of the Fellowship only with the express permission of the Director.

Henri Frankfort Fellowship

Subjects: The intellectual and cultural history of the ancient Near and Middle East, with particular reference to society, art, architecture, religion, philosophy and science; the relations between the cultures of Mesopotamia, Egypt and the Aegean and their influence on later civilisations.
Purpose: To promote research.
Eligibility: Fellowships are generally for younger Scholars and preference will normally be given to those under 35 years of age on October 1st 2003. Candidates may be pre or postdoctoral but must have completed at least one year's research on their doctoral dissertation by the time they submit their application. Postdoctoral candidates, if they are over 35, must normally have been awarded their doctorate within the preceding academic year. If their doctorate was awarded before this they should explain the reasons for the interruption in their academic career in a covering letter.
Level of Study: Doctorate, Postdoctorate.
Type: Fellowship.
Value: UK holders UK£1,500-2,250; overseas holders UK£1850-2700.
Length of Study: Two-three months.
Frequency: Annual.
Study Establishment: The Warburg Institute.
Country of Study: United Kingdom.
No. of awards offered: One.
Application Procedure: Applications should be made by letter to the Director enclosing a full CV comprising name, date of birth, address (including email address) and present occupation, school and university education, degrees, teaching and research experience, publications; an outline of proposed research (of not more than two pages); particulars of grants received; if any, on the same subject; the names and addresses of three persons who have agreed to write, without further invitation, in support of the application.
Closing Date: 1st December in the preceding year.
Funding: Private.
No. of awards given last year: One.
Additional Information: This fellowship is not intended to support archaeological excavation.

Mellon Research Fellowships

Subjects: Humanities.
Purpose: To fund a fellowship programme at The Warburg Institute.
Eligibility: Open to Bulgarian, Czech, Hungarian, Polish, Romanian and Slovak Scholars. From 2004-5 open also to Estonian, Latian and Lithuanian candidates. Candidates should not be permanently resident outside these countries. Fellows should have obtained a doctorate or have equivalent experience. The fellowships are intended for younger postdoctoral Scholars and preference will be given to those under 40 years of age.
Level of Study: Postdoctorate.
Type: Fellowship.
Value: The sterling equivalent of US$11,500.
Length of Study: Three months.
Frequency: Annual.
Study Establishment: The Warburg Institute.
Country of Study: England.
No. of awards offered: Three.
Application Procedure: Applications should be made by letter to the Director enclosing a full CV comprising name, date of birth, address (including email address) and present occupation, school and university education, degrees, teaching and research experience, publications; an outline of proposed research (of not more than two pages); particulars of grants received, if any, on the same subject; the names and addresses of 2 or 3 persons who have agreed to write, without further invitation in support of the application.
Closing Date: April 1st in the preceding year.
Funding: Private.
No. of awards given last year: Three.
Additional Information: Fellows will be expected to participate in the life of the Institute and to put their knowledge at the disposal of the Institute by presenting their work in a seminar and by advising the library and photographic collection. Fellows will be required to present a brief written report at the conclusion of their appointment.

Nord/LB Warburg-Wolfenbüttel Research Fellowship

Subjects: Cultural and intellectual history of early modern Europe.
Purpose: To promote research.
Eligibility: Fellowships are generally for younger Scholars and preference will normally be given to those under 35 years of age on October 1st 2002. Candidates may be pre or postdoctoral but must have completed at least one year of research on their doctoral dissertation by the time they submit their application. Postdoctoral candidates, if they are over 35, must normally have been awarded their doctorate within the preceding academic year. If their doctorate was awarded before this they should explain the reasons for the interruption in their academic career in a covering letter.
Level of Study: Doctorate, Postdoctorate.
Type: Fellowship.
Value: Approx. UK£5,000 paid in Euros.
Length of Study: Two months in the United Kingdom and two months in Germany.
Frequency: Annual.
Study Establishment: Warburg Institute and Herzog August Bibliothek Wolfenbüttel.
Country of Study: The United Kingdom and Germany.
No. of awards offered: One.
Application Procedure: Applicants must contact the Secretary and Registrar for further information.
Closing Date: Early December.
Funding: Commercial.
No. of awards given last year: One.

Sophia Fellowship

Subjects: The history of astrology.
Purpose: To promote research into the history of astrological theory, practice, iconography and their relation to other arts and sciences in both Western and non Western societies.
Eligibility: Applicants must normally be 29 years of age or over on October 1st of the academic year prior to which the fellowship is taken up, and must have completed more than one year of postgraduate research when they apply. There is no upper age limit for this fellowship.

Level of Study: Research.
Type: Fellowship.
Value: UK£2,250-3,500 depending on the length of tenure.
Length of Study: Three-four months.
Frequency: Annual.
Study Establishment: The Warburg Institute.
Country of Study: United Kingdom.
No. of awards offered: One.
Application Procedure: Applicants must contact the Secretary and Registrar for further information.
Closing Date: Early December.
Funding: Private.
No. of awards given last year: One.

WARWICK BUSINESS SCHOOL

University of Warwick, Coventry, CV4 7AL, England
Tel: (44) 24 7652 4306
Fax: (44) 24 7652 3719
Email: enquiries@wbs.ac.uk
www: http://www.wbs.ac.uk
Contact: Ms Diana Holton, Assistant Communications Manager

With 300 staff and 4,000 students from 112 countries worldwide, Warwick Business School is an international school and is accredited with management associations in North America, Europe and the United Kingdom. Its high calibre research feeds into top quality teaching on undergraduate, specialist Master's, doctoral and MBA degrees.

Warwick Business School Bursaries (for Doctoral Students)

Subjects: Business, management and social science.
Purpose: To aid outstanding applicants to the doctoral programme to complete their studies.
Eligibility: Warwick Business school accepts applications for entry onto its doctoral programme from suitably qualified students across a range of business, management and social science backgrounds.
Level of Study: Doctorate.
Type: Scholarship.
Value: Approx. UK£3,000.
Frequency: Annual.
Study Establishment: Warwick Business School.
Country of Study: England.
No. of awards offered: Up to 20.
Application Procedure: Applicants must contact the doctoral pro-gramme office for further application details.

Warwick Business School Dean's Bursaries (for MBA Study)

Subjects: MBA.
Purpose: To allow candidates to pursue the full-time MBA course.
Eligibility: Applicants must already have accepted a place on the Warwick MBA by full-time study.
Level of Study: MBA, Professional development.
Type: Scholarship.
Value: Approx. UK£5,000.
Frequency: Annual.
Study Establishment: Warwick Business School.
Country of Study: England.
No. of awards offered: 5-10.
Application Procedure: Applicants must submit a competitive essay to the Business School.

WASHINGTON UNIVERSITY

Graduate School of Arts & Sciences Campus, Box 1187, 1 Brookings Drive, St Louis, MO 63130, United States of America
Tel: (1) 314 935 6818
Fax: (1) 314 935 4887
Email: graduateschool@artsci.wustl.edu
www: http://www.artsci.wustl.edu
Contact: Ms Nancy P Pope, Assistant Dean

Mr and Mrs Spencer T Olin Fellowships for Women

Subjects: All subjects.
Purpose: To encourage women of exceptional promise to prepare for professional careers.
Eligibility: Open to female graduates of a Baccalaureate institution in the United States of America who plan to prepare for a career in higher education or the professions. Applicants must meet the admission requirements of their graduate or professional school at Washington University. Preference will be given to those who wish to study for the highest earned degree in their chosen field, do not already hold an advanced degree, and are not currently enrolled in a graduate or professional degree programme.
Level of Study: Doctorate, Graduate.
Type: Fellowship.
Value: Full tuition and, in some cases, a living expense stipend.
Length of Study: One year, renewable for up to four years, or until the completion of the degree programme, whichever comes first.
Frequency: Annual.
Study Establishment: Washington University.
Country of Study: United States of America.
No. of awards offered: Approx. 10.
Application Procedure: Applicants must complete an application form. Finalists must be interviewed on campus at the expense of the University.
Closing Date: February 1st.
Funding: Private.
Contributor: The Monticello College Foundation.
No. of awards given last year: 14.
No. of applicants last year: 375.
Additional Information: Candidates must also make concurrent ap-plication to the department or school of Washington University in which they plan to study.

Washington University Chancellor's Graduate Fellowship Program for African Americans

Subjects: Any of Washington University's PhD or DSc programmes in arts and sciences, business, engineering or social work.
Purpose: To encourage African Americans who are interested in becoming college or university professors.
Eligibility: Open to African American doctoral candidates. Applicants must meet the admission requirements of their graduate or profes-sional school at Washington University.
Level of Study: Doctorate, Graduate.
Type: Fellowship.
Value: Doctoral candidates will receive full tuition plus US$19,400 stipend and allowances.
Length of Study: Five years, subject to satisfactory academic progress.
Frequency: Annual.
Study Establishment: Washington University.
Country of Study: United States of America.
No. of awards offered: Five-six.
Application Procedure: Applicants must complete an application form. Finalists must be interviewed on the campus at the expense of the university. Applications should be addressed to Assistant Dean Sheri Notaro.
Closing Date: January 25th.
No. of awards given last year: Nine.
No. of applicants last year: 105.
Additional Information: The fellowship includes other Washington University programmes providing final disciplinary training for pro-spective college professors.

WEIZMANN INSTITUTE OF SCIENCE

Feinberg Graduate School, PO Box 26
Rehovot, 76100, Israel
Tel: (972) 8 934 2924
Fax: (972) 8 934 4114
Email: nfinfo@weizmann.ac.il
www: http://www.weizmann.ac.il/feinberg
Contact: Grants Management Officer

The Weizmann Institute of Science is one of the top ranking multi-disciplinary research institutions in the world. Noted for its wide ranging exploration of the sciences and technology, the Institute houses 2,400 scientists, technicians and research students devoted to a better understanding of nature and our place within it.

Weizmann Institute of Science MSc Fellowships

Subjects: Life sciences, including brain research, cell biology, molecular genetics, biochemistry, biophysics, immunology, biological regulation, plant sciences and bioinformatics; chemistry, including physical, theoretical, organic, biological, environmental sciences and energy research and material sciences; physics, including theoretical, experimental, applied, semi-conductor and biological; and mathematics, including pure and applied, computer science or science teaching.
Purpose: To enable study at the Feinberg Graduate School of the Weizmann Institute of Science.
Eligibility: Open to holders of a BSc degree from an accredited Institute of Higher Education in Israel or of an equivalent degree from a recognised overseas university.
Level of Study: Postgraduate.
Type: Fellowship.
Value: Living expenses.
Length of Study: Two years.
Frequency: Annual.
Study Establishment: The Institute.
Country of Study: Israel.
Application Procedure: Applicants must write for details.
Closing Date: June 1st.
Funding: Private.
No. of awards given last year: 230.
No. of applicants last year: 700.

Weizmann Institute of Science PhD Fellowships

Subjects: Life sciences, including brain research, cell biology, molecular genetics, biochemistry, biophysics, immunology, biological regulation, plant sciences and bioinformatics; chemistry, including physical, theoretical, organic, biological, environmental sciences and energy research and material sciences; physics, including theoretical, experimental, applied, semi-conductor and biological; and mathematics, including pure and applied, computer science or science teaching.
Purpose: To enable study at the Feinberg Graduate School of the Weizmann Institute of Science.
Eligibility: Open to holders of an MSc or MD degree.
Level of Study: Doctorate.
Type: Fellowship.
Value: Living expenses.
Length of Study: Four and a half years.
Frequency: Annual.
Study Establishment: The Institute.
Country of Study: Israel.
Application Procedure: Applicants must write for details.
Funding: Private.
No. of awards given last year: 656.
Additional Information: A special programme is offered to students wishing to take a direct BSc to PhD route.

Weizmann Institute of Science Postdoctoral Fellowships Program

Subjects: Life sciences, including brain research, cell biology, molecular genetics, biochemistry, biophysics, immunology, biological regulation, plant sciences and bioinformatics; chemistry, including physical, theoretical, organic, biological, environmental sciences and energy research and material sciences; physics, including theoretical, experimental, applied, semi-conductor and biological; and mathematics, including pure and applied, computer science or science teaching.
Eligibility: Open to holders of a PhD degree.
Level of Study: Postdoctorate.
Type: Fellowship.
Value: Living expenses.
Length of Study: One-three years.

Frequency: Annual.
Study Establishment: The Institute.
Country of Study: Israel.
Application Procedure: Applicants must write for details.
Closing Date: January 1st and May 15th.
Funding: Private.
No. of awards given last year: 204.
No. of applicants last year: 350.

WELLBEING

27 Sussex Place, London, NW1 4SP, England
Tel: (44) 20 7772 6338
Fax: (44) 20 7724 7725
Email: sblackburne.wellbeing@rcog.org.uk
www: http://www.wellbeing.org.uk
Contact: Mrs Sophia Blackburne, Research Grants Administrator

WellBeing is the fund raising and research arm of the Royal College of Obstetricians and Gynaecologists, funding medical and scientific research in hospitals and universities. WellBeing is involved in research into all aspects of pregnancy, birth and the care of the newborn, women's cancers, infertility, period problems, incontinence and the menopause.

WellBeing Project Grants

Subjects: All aspects of pregnancy, birth and the care of newborns, women's gynaecological cancers including screening procedures, diagnostic techniques and treatments, and quality of life issues including infertility, menstruation, incontinence, the menopause and osteoporosis.
Purpose: To fund research projects.
Eligibility: Open to specialists in any obstetrics and gynaecology interrelated field.
Level of Study: Postgraduate, Professional development, Research.
Type: Grant.
Value: A maximum of UK£100,000 over three years, with not more than UK£55,000 in the first year.
Length of Study: One-three years.
Frequency: Annual.
Study Establishment: A hospital or university.
Country of Study: United Kingdom.
No. of awards offered: Varies depending on the amount of disposable income.
Application Procedure: Applicants must write for details or access the website.
Closing Date: May 16th.
Funding: Private, Commercial.
No. of awards given last year: Four.
No. of applicants last year: 106.

WELLCHILD INTERNATIONAL

33 Rodney Road, Cheltenham, Gloucester, GL50 1HX, England
Tel: (44) 1242 530007
Email: info@wellchild.org.uk
www: http://www.wellchild.org.uk
Contact: The Administrator

WellChild is committed to caring for and supporting all sick children, whatever their illness, through research, treatment, prevention and cure, and providing information and advice for all those who care for them.

WellChild Pump-Priming Grants

Subjects: Diseases in children.
Purpose: To enable a student to run a pilot study.
Level of Study: Doctorate, Postdoctorate, Postgraduate.
Type: Grant.
Value: Up to UK£10,000.
Frequency: Annual.
Study Establishment: Accredited institute in United Kingdom.
Country of Study: United Kingdom.

Application Procedure: Download application and guidelines from the website.
Closing Date: 26th September
Funding: Private.
Additional Information: Assessment by peer review and Scientific Medical Advisory Committee.

Wellchild Research Fellowships

Subjects: Diseases in children.
Purpose: To support clinicians working towards the development of their own research projects.
Level of Study: Doctorate, Postdoctorate, Postgraduate.
Type: Fellowship.
Value: Appropriate salary costs.
Length of Study: Up to three years.
Frequency: Annual.
Study Establishment: Accredited institute in United Kingdom.
Country of Study: United Kingdom.
Application Procedure: Download application and guidelines from the website.
Closing Date: 26th September
Funding: Private.
Additional Information: Assessment by peer review and Scientific Medical Advisory Committee.

THE WELLCOME TRUST

The Wellcome Building, 183 Euston Road, London, NW1 2BE, England
Tel: (44) 20 7611 8888
Fax: (44) 20 7611 8545
Email: grantenquiries@wellcome.ac.uk
www: http://www.wellcome.ac.uk
Contact: Grants Information Officer

The Wellcome Trust's mission is to foster and promote research with the aim of improving human and animal health. The Trust funds most areas of biomedical research, although its support for cancer research is limited.

Wellcome Trust Awards, Fellowships and Studentships

Subjects: Biomedical sciences, from the basic sciences related to medicine to the clinical aspects of medicine and veterinary medicine. The Trust also operates a portfolio of schemes to support research in the history of medicine, the public appreciation of sciences or bioethics.
Purpose: To support and maintain the strength of biomedical research by providing individual researchers of the highest quality with the resources they need to pursue their subject.
Eligibility: Open to academic staff in universities, medical and veterinary schools and other Institutes of Higher Education, who are engaged in all types of medical research.
Level of Study: Postdoctorate, Professional development, Research.
Type: Other.
Value: Varies.
Length of Study: Varies.
Frequency: Differs for each funding scheme.
Country of Study: Other.
No. of awards offered: Varies.
Application Procedure: Applicants must submit a written preliminary outline for all schemes except United Kingdom based project and programme grants consisting of a brief curriculum vitae of the applicant including their source of salary, an outline of the proposed research project and the approximate cost of project. Requests for application forms for United Kingdom based project and programme grants must be directed to the appropriate scientific panel of the Trust. Further information on application procedures is available on the website.
Closing Date: Preliminary applications are accepted at any time. Please visit the website for scheme deadlines.
Contributor: Endowment.
Additional Information: The Welcome Trust is one of the most richly endowed of all charitable institutions that fund general medical research in the United Kingdom. The Governors review their policy annually in response to proposals from their advisory panels and professional staff.

WENNER-GREN FOUNDATION FOR ANTHROPOLOGICAL RESEARCH

220 Fifth Avenue, 16th Floor, New York, NY 10001, United States of America
Tel: (1) 212 683 5000
Fax: (1) 212 683 9151
Email: inquiries@wennergren.org
www: http://www.wennergren.org
Contact: Fellowships Office

The Wenner-Gren Foundation for Anthropological Research supports research, conferences, training, archiving and collaboration in all branches of anthropology, including cultural and social anthropology, ethnology, biological and physical anthropology, archaeology and anthropological linguistics, and in closely related disciplines concerned with human origins, development and variation.

Richard Carley-Hunt Postdoctoral Fellowship

Subjects: Anthropology.
Purpose: To aid the write up of research results.
Eligibility: Scholars must be within 10 years of receipt of the PhD.
Level of Study: Postdoctorate.
Type: Fellowship.
Value: Up to US$40,000.
Frequency: Annual.
Additional Information: Qualified Scholars are eligible without regard to nationality or institutional affiliation.

Wenner-Gren Dissertation Fieldwork Grants

Subjects: Anthropology.
Purpose: To aid doctoral dissertation or thesis research
Level of Study: Doctorate.
Type: Grant.
Value: Up to US$25,000.
Frequency: Annual.
Application Procedure: A formal application on up-to-date form should be downloaded from the website.
Closing Date: May 1st and November 1st

Wenner-Gren Post - PhD Grants

Subjects: Anthropology.
Purpose: To support a researcher in postdoctoral fieldwork.
Eligibility: Applicants must have the PhD in hand before they apply.
Level of Study: Postdoctorate.
Type: Grant.
Value: Up to US$25,000.
Frequency: Annual.
Application Procedure: Download on up-to-date form from the website.

WESLEYAN UNIVERSITY

Center for the Humanities, Middletown, CT 06459-0069, United States of America
Tel: (1) 860 685 3044
Fax: (1) 860 685 2171
Email: bkeating@wesleyan.edu
www: http://www.wesleyan.edu
Contact: Ms Brenda Keating, Administrative Assistant

Wesleyan University offers instruction in 41 departments and programmes and 50 major fields of study and awards the Bachelor of Arts and graduate degrees. Master's degrees are awarded in 11 fields of study and doctoral degrees in six. Students may choose from about 960 courses each year and may be asked to devise, with the faculty, some 1,500 individual tutorials and lessons.

Andrew W Mellon Postdoctoral Fellowship

Subjects: Arts, humanities and cultural studies.
Purpose: To promote interdisciplinary interests among younger scholars.
Eligibility: Open to persons who have received their PhD within the last four years.
Level of Study: Postdoctorate.
Type: Fellowship.
Value: US$40,000, plus US$500 reserve.
Frequency: Annual.
Country of Study: Any country.
No. of awards offered: One.
Application Procedure: Applicants must request a brochure detailing the application process. There is no formal application form.
Closing Date: November 15th.
Funding: Private.
No. of awards given last year: One.
No. of applicants last year: 115.
Additional Information: The Fellow must reside in Middletown during the tenure of the fellowship, give one public lecture and teach one course of 20 students.

WEST VIRGINIA UNIVERSITY

PO Box 6070, Morgantown, West Virginia 26506, United States of America
Tel: (1) 304 558 4417
Fax: (1) 304 558 3264
www: http://www.wvu.edu

West Virginia University is located in Morgantown, West Virginia.

Senate Grants for Research & Scholarship

Subjects: Any as approved by the University of West Virginia.
Purpose: To support a postgraduate student in research and other scholarly activities.
Level of Study: Postgraduate.
Type: Scholarship.
Frequency: Annual.
Study Establishment: University of West Virginia
Country of Study: United States of America.
Closing Date: November 3.

WESTERN MICHIGAN UNIVERSITY

1903 West Michigan Avenue, Western Michigan University, Kalamazoo, MI 49008, United States of America
Tel: (1) 269 387 3530
Email: finaid-info@wmich.edu
www: http://www.wmich.edu

Western Michigan University is one of the nation's premier student-centred research universities with an enrollment of more than 26,000 students. WMU is focused on delivering high-quality undergraduate instruction, advancing its growing graduate component and solving real-world problems through research as well as through partnerships with business and government.

Graduate College Doctoral Associateships

Subjects: Any subject as approved by West Michigan University.
Purpose: To support outstanding doctoral students with regular admission to a doctoral program.
Level of Study: Doctorate.
Type: Assistantship.
Frequency: Annual.
Study Establishment: West Michigan University.
Country of Study: United States of America.
Application Procedure: Apply to the Graduate College or download application form from the website. Applications should be sent directly to the department chair or graduate advisor.
Closing Date: February 15th
Additional Information: The associateship requires 20 hours of service per week from the student in the department or related area.

Graduate College Fellowships

Subjects: Any subject as approved by West Michigan University.
Purpose: To support outstanding students with their Master's degree.
Level of Study: Postgraduate.
Type: Fellowship.
Length of Study: 6 months.
Frequency: Annual.
Study Establishment: West Michigan University.
Country of Study: United States of America.
Application Procedure: Apply to the Graduate College or download an application form from the website.
Additional Information: The fellowship requires no service from the student but encourages participation in the professional activities of the department.

Graduate Student Research Fund

Subjects: Any subject as approved by West Michigan University.
Purpose: To support graduate students engaged in independent scholarly research, scientific enquiry, inventive technology and original artistic activity.
Eligibility: The fund is intended to help students pay extraordinary or unusual costs incurred in research programs.
Level of Study: Postgraduate.
Type: Scholarship.
Value: Up to US$600.
Frequency: Annual.
Study Establishment: West Michigan University.
Country of Study: United States of America.

Historically Underrepresented Groups Program

Subjects: Any subject as approved by West Michigan University.
Purpose: To support entering doctoral students from historically underrepresented groups.
Eligibility: Candidates must be from African-American, Hispanic or Native American (with tribal affiliation) heritage.
Level of Study: Doctorate.
Type: Award.
Frequency: Annual.
Study Establishment: West Michigan University.
Country of Study: United States of America.
Application Procedure: Contact the Graduate College Diversity Program.
Closing Date: February 15th

Thurgood Marshall Assistantships

Subjects: Any subject as approved by West Michigan University.
Purpose: To support a student from a historically under represented group to work on their Master's degree.
Eligibility: Proof of heritage may be required.
Level of Study: Postgraduate.
Type: Assistantship.
Value: Partial tuition Scholarship.
Length of Study: 2 years.
Frequency: Annual.
Study Establishment: West Michigan University.
Country of Study: United States of America.
Application Procedure: Apply to the college or download a form from the website.
Closing Date: February 15th

WHATCOM MUSEUM OF HISTORY AND ART

121 Prospect Street, Bellingham, WA 98225, United States of America
Tel: (1) 360 676 6981
Fax: (1) 360 738 7409
Email: museuminfo@cob.org
www: http://www.whatcommuseum.org
Contact: Ms Deanna Zipp, Museum Secretary

Jacobs Research Fund

Subjects: Field research in language, social organisation, political organisation, religion, mythology, music, other arts, psychology and folk science.

Purpose: To support anthropological research, sociocultural or linguistic in content of the indigenous peoples of Canada, mainland United States, including Alaska, and Mexico, with a focus on the Pacific Northwest.

Eligibility: Projects in archaeology, physical anthropology, applied anthropology and applied linguistics are not eligible and archival research is not supported.

Level of Study: Unrestricted.

Type: Grant.

Value: Up to US$1,200.

Length of Study: One year.

Frequency: Annual.

Country of Study: The Pacific Northwest or other regions of the North American Continent.

No. of awards offered: Usually 16.

Application Procedure: Applicants must complete an application form. Further information and application forms are available on written request or from the website.

Closing Date: Please contact the organisation.

Funding: Private.

Contributor: Melville and Elizabeth Jacobs.

Additional Information: The Jacobs Research Fund is an enduring expression of a commitment to the collection and preservation of data documenting the languages, ethnography and literature of indigenous peoples.

WHITEHALL FOUNDATION, INC.

PO Box 3423, Palm Beach, FL 33480
United States of America
Tel: (1) 561 655 4474
Fax: (1) 561 659 4978
Email: email@whitehall.org
www: http://www.whitehall.org
Contact: Ms Catherine Thomas, Corporate Secretary

The Whitehall Foundation, through its programme of grants and grants-in-aid, assists scholarly research in the life sciences. It is the Foundation's policy to assist those dynamic areas of basic biological research that are not heavily supported by Federal agencies or other foundations with specialised missions.

Whitehall Foundation Grants-in-Aid

Subjects: Neurobiology focusing on invertebrate and vertebrate neurobiology, specifically investigations of neural mechanisms involved in sensory, motor and other complex functions of the whole organism as these relate to behaviour.

Purpose: To better understand behavioural output or brain mechanisms of behaviour.

Eligibility: Open to researchers at the assistant professor level who have experienced difficulty in competing for research funds as they have not yet become firmly established. Senior scientists may also apply.

Level of Study: Research.

Type: Research grant one year.

Value: Up to US$30,000.

Length of Study: One year.

Frequency: Annual.

Country of Study: United States of America.

Application Procedure: Applicants must contact the Foundation.

Closing Date: Letter of intent deadline, Jan 15th, April 15th, Oct 15th.

Funding: Private.

Additional Information: For up to date policy, application information and important calendar deadlines please refer to the website.

For further information contact:

www: www.whitehall.org

Whitehall Foundation Research Grants

Subjects: The Foundation's current interest is in the field of neurobiology, defined as follows - invertebrate and vertebrate (exclusive of human beings) neurobiology, specifically investigations of neural mechanisms involved in sensory, motor and other complex functions of the whole organism as these relate to behaviour.

Purpose: To assist scholarly research in dynamic areas of the life sciences that are not already heavily supported by other funding agencies.

Eligibility: Open to scientists of all ages at the PhD or assistant professor level who are affiliated with recognised institutions. Applications are judged on the scientific merit of the proposal and evidence of the competence of the applicant.

Level of Study: Research, must be Asst. Professor or higher to make application.

Type: Research grant - at U.S Institutions only.

Value: US$20,000-75,000 per year. Funds may not be used for purchase of major items of permanent equipment, travel unless it is to unique field areas essential to the research, replacement of PI's regular salary or summer salary, consultant's fees.

Length of Study: Up to three years, with the possibility of renewal.

Frequency: Annual.

Country of Study: United States of America.

Application Procedure: Applications are not accepted from investigators who already have, or expect to receive, substantial support from other sources even though the support may be for an unrelated project. A letter of intent is required prior to application form being sent. There is no deadline for the letter.

Closing Date: Letter of intent deadline, Jan 15th, April 15th, October 1st.

Funding: Private.

No. of awards given last year: 27.

No. of applicants last year: 100+.

Whitehall Foundation Research Grants

Subjects: Neurobiology focusing on invertebrate and vertebrate neurobiology, specifically investigations of neural mechanisms involved in sensory, motor and other complex functions of the whole organism as these relate to behaviour.

Purpose: To better understand behavioural output or brain mechanisms of behaviour.

Eligibility: Open to established scientists of all ages working at accredited institutions in the United States of America. The principal investigator must hold no less than the position of assistant professor, or the equivalent, in order to make an application. The Foundation does not award funds to investigators who have substantial existing or potential support.

Level of Study: Research.

Type: Research grant.

Value: US$30,000-75,000 per year.

Length of Study: Up to three years.

Application Procedure: Please visit web-site @ www.whitehall.org.

Funding: Private.

Additional Information: For up to date policy, application information and important calendar deadlines, please refer to the website.

WILLIAM HONYMAN GILLESPIE SCHOLARSHIP TRUST

Messrs Tod Murray WS, 66 Queen Street, Edinburgh, EH2 4NE, Scotland
Tel: (44) 131 226 4771
Fax: (44) 131 225 3676
Email: maildesk@todsmurray.com
Contact: Trustees

William Honyman Gillespie Scholarships

Subjects: Theology.

Purpose: To allow the recipient to engage in a full-time approved scheme of studies or research.

Eligibility: Open to graduates of a Theological College of one of the Scottish Universities.

Level of Study: Postgraduate.
Type: Scholarship.
Value: UK£1,000 per year.
Length of Study: Two years.
Frequency: Annual.
Study Establishment: An approved university or similar institution.
Country of Study: Any country.
No. of awards offered: Varies, usually one to two.
Application Procedure: Applicants must submit applications through the principal of the theological college of which the applicant is a graduate. Application guidelines are available from the Trust or the candidate's university department.
Closing Date: May 15th.
Funding: Private.
No. of awards given last year: 2.
No. of applicants last year: Two.

WILSON ORNITHOLOGICAL SOCIETY

Fort Collins Science Center, 2150 Centre Avenue, Building C, Fort Collins, CO 80526-8118, United States of America
Tel: (1) 970 226 9466
Email: jim_sedgwick@usgs.gov
www: http://www.ummz.lsa.umich.edu/birds/wos.html
Contact: Administrative Assistant

Founded in 1888 and named after Alexander Wilson, the father of American ornithology, the Wilson Ornithological Society publishes a scientific journal, the Wilson Bulletin, holds annual meetings, provides research awards and maintains an outstanding research library.

George A Hall/Harold F Manfield Award
Subjects: Any aspect of ornithology.
Purpose: To encourage and stimulate research projects on birds, by amateurs and students.
Eligibility: Open to independent researchers without access to funds and facilities available at colleges, universities or governmental agencies. The award is restricted to non professionals.
Level of Study: Postgraduate.
Type: Award.
Value: US$1,000.
Frequency: Annual.
Country of Study: Any country.
No. of awards offered: One.
Application Procedure: An application form must be completed and submitted with three letters of recommendation and a research proposal. Forms are available from the website.
Closing Date: January 15th.
Funding: Private.

Louis Agassiz Fuertes Award
Subjects: Any aspect of ornithology.
Eligibility: Open to all ornithologists, although graduate students and young professionals are preferred. Any avian research is eligible.
Level of Study: Unrestricted.
Type: Award.
Value: US$2,500.
Frequency: Annual.
No. of awards offered: One.
Application Procedure: Application forms are available from the website.

Paul A Stewart Awards
Subjects: Ornithology, especially studies of bird movements based on banding, analysis of recoveries and returns of banded birds, with an emphasis on economic ornithology.
Purpose: To support research projects on birds.
Eligibility: Open to students, amateurs and professionals without preference.
Level of Study: Unrestricted.
Type: Award.
Value: US$500.
Frequency: Annual.

Country of Study: Any country.
No. of awards offered: Up to four.
Application Procedure: An application form must be completed and submitted with three letters of recommendation and a research proposal. Forms are available from the website.
Closing Date: January 15th.
Funding: Private.

WINGATE SCHOLARSHIPS

2nd Floor, 20-22 Stukeley Street, London, WC2B 5LR, England
Email: clark@wingate.org.uk
www: http://www.wingate.org.uk
Contact: Ms Faith Clark, Administrator

Wingate Scholarships are awarded to exceptional individuals, who need financial support to undertake creative or original work of intellectual, scientific, artistic, social or environmental value of great potential or proven excellence and to outstanding musicians for advanced training.

Wingate Scholarships
Subjects: Almost any subject except medical research, fine arts, performing arts (except music), business courses or courses leading to professional qualifications and electives.
Purpose: To fund creative or original work of intellectual, scientific, artistic, social or environmental value and advanced music study.
Eligibility: Open to British, Commonwealth, Irish, Israeli or other European Union country citizens provided that they are, and have been for at least three years, resident in the United Kingdom. Applicants must be over 24 years of age. No upper age limit. No academic qualifications are necessary.
Level of Study: Doctorate, Postdoctorate, Postgraduate, Research.
Type: Scholarship.
Value: Costs of a project which may last for up to three years. This is an average of UK£6,500 total to a maximum in any one year of UK£10,000.
Length of Study: One-three years.
Frequency: Annual.
Study Establishment: Any approved institute.
Country of Study: Any country.
No. of awards offered: Approx. 40-45.
Application Procedure: Applicants must complete application forms, available from the administrator or the website. Applicants must be able to satisfy the Scholarship Committee that they need financial support to undertake the work projected, and show why the proposed work (if it takes the form of academic research) is unlikely to attract Research Council, British Academy or major agency funding.
Closing Date: February 1st.
Funding: Private.
Contributor: HHW Foundation.
No. of awards given last year: 50.
No. of applicants last year: 600.
Additional Information: The scholarships are not intended for professional qualifications, taught courses or electives. Musicians are eligible for advanced training, but apart from that all applicants must have projects which are personal to them and involve either creative or original work.

WINSTON CHURCHILL FOUNDATION OF THE USA

PO Box 1240, Gracie Station, New York, NY 10028, United States of America
Tel: (1) 212 879 3480
Fax: (1) 212 879 3480
Email: churchillf@aol.com
www: http://www.britishcouncil-http://www.usa.org/learning/students/fundingscholarships
Contact: Mr Harold Epstein, Executive Director

The Winston Churchill Foundation of the USA provides scholarships for American students to pursue graduate studies in engineering, mathematics and sciences at Churchill College, the University of Cambridge.

Winston Churchill Scholarship

Subjects: Engineering, mathematics, computer science or natural & physical sciences.
Purpose: To encourage the development of American scientific and technological talent and foster Anglo American ties.
Eligibility: Open to United States of America citizens only. Applicants must be enrolled in one of 75 institutions participating in programme.
Level of Study: Postgraduate.
Type: Scholarship.
Value: Approx. US$27,000.
Length of Study: One year.
Frequency: Annual.
Study Establishment: Churchill College, the University of Cambridge.
Country of Study: United Kingdom.
No. of awards offered: 11.
Application Procedure: Applicants must complete a formal application, available from the liaison person at institutions participating in this programme.
Closing Date: November 15th.
Funding: Private.
No. of awards given last year: 11.
No. of applicants last year: 100.

WINSTON CHURCHILL MEMORIAL TRUST (AUS)

Churchill House, 30 Balmain Crescent, Acton, ACT 2601, Australia
Tel: (61) 2 6247 8333
Fax: (61) 2 6249 8944
Email: churchilltrust@bigpond.com
www: http://www.churchilltrust.com.au
Contact: Ms Margaret Bell, Senior Executive Officer, Finance & Administration

The principal object of the Winston Churchill Memorial Trust (Aus) is to perpetuate and honour the memory of Sir Winston Churchill by awarding memorial fellowships known as Churchill Fellowships.

Churchill Fellowships

Subjects: All subjects.
Purpose: To enable Australians from all walks of life to undertake an overseas investigation project of a kind that is not fully available in Australia.
Eligibility: Normally open to Australian citizens only, over 18 years of age. No prescribed qualifications, academic or otherwise, are needed for eligibility of the award. Merit is the primary test, whether based on past achievement or demonstrated ability for future achievements in any walk of life. The only criteria for the awarding of a fellowship is that the applicant has gone as far as they can go in Australia and now needs to go overseas to obtain information not available within Australia. Those wishing for fellowships only to obtain higher academic or formal qualifications will not be eligible.
Level of Study: Unrestricted.
Type: Fellowship.
Value: Approx. Australian $20,000, return economy air fare to the country or countries to be visited, and a living allowance plus fees if necessary.
Length of Study: 4-10 weeks but this may be longer or shorter depending upon the project.
Frequency: Annual.
Country of Study: Any country.
No. of awards offered: Approx. 100.
Application Procedure: Applicants must complete and submit an application form to the appropriate regional office. For an application form contact the national office or go to the website.
Closing Date: Last day of February.
Funding: Private.
No. of awards given last year: 110.
No. of applicants last year: 862.

Additional Information: Further information is available from the website or call National Office on free call 1800 777 231.

For further information contact:

Varies for each state. Address details are on the website and on printed information.

WINSTON CHURCHILL MEMORIAL TRUST (UK)

15 Queen's Gate Terrace, London, SW7 5PR, England
Tel: (44) 20 7584 9315
Fax: (44) 20 7581 0410
Email: office@wcmt.org.uk
www: www.wcmt.org.uk
Contact: Ms S Matthews, Trust Office Manager

Winston Churchill Tavelling Fellowships

Subjects: Approx. 10 categories of occupation, which vary annually and are representative of culture, social and public service, technology, commerce and industry, agriculture and nature, recreation and adventure.
Purpose: To enable men and women from all walks of life and all ages to travel abroad in pursuit of a worthwhile purpose and so to contribute more to their trade or profession, their community and their country.
Eligibility: Open to British citizens, whose purposes must be covered by one of the categories chosen for the year.
Level of Study: Unrestricted.
Type: Fellowship.
Value: The average award is UK£5,500. This covers all travel, living and equipment expenses by individual assessment. The fellowship scheme does not cover attending courses, academic studies, student grants or gap year projects.
Length of Study: Four-eight weeks.
Frequency: Annual.
Country of Study: Other.
No. of awards offered: Approx. 100.
Application Procedure: Applicants must complete an application form.
Closing Date: September to October.
Funding: Private.
Contributor: The public.
No. of awards given last year: 100.
No. of applicants last year: 100.
Additional Information: 1) Categories are announced at the beginning of June. 2) Awards are announced at the beginning of February. 3) Fellows may travel after 1st April.

THE WISCONSIN HISTORICAL SOCIETY

816 State Street, Madison, WI, 53706
United States of America
Tel: (1) 608 264 6464
Fax: (1) 608 264 6486
www: http://www.shsw.wisc.edu
Contact: State Historian

The Wisconsin Historical Society engages the public with the excitement of discovery, inspires people with new perspectives on the past and illuminates the relevance of history in our lives today.

Alice E Smith Fellowship

Subjects: Wisconsin history.
Level of Study: Research.
Type: Fellowship.
Value: Please contact the organisation.
Frequency: Four times per year.
Country of Study: United States of America.
Application Procedure: Application forms are available from the website.

Amy Louise Hunter Fellowship
Subjects: Wisconsin history.
Level of Study: Research.
Type: Fellowship.
Value: Please contact the organisation.
Country of Study: United States of America.
Application Procedure: Application forms are available from the website.

John C Geilfuss Fellowship
Subjects: Wisconsin's business and economic history.
Level of Study: Research.
Type: Fellowship.
Value: Please contact the organisation.
Country of Study: United States of America.
Application Procedure: Application forms are available from the website.

WOLF FOUNDATION

39 Hamaapilim Street, PO Box 398, Herzlia Bet, 46103, Israel
Tel: (972) 9 955 7120
Fax: (972) 9 954 1253
Email: wolffund@netvision.net.il
www: http://www.aquanet.co.il/wolf
Contact: Mr Yaron Gruder, Director General

The Wolf Foundation was established in 1976 by Doctor Ricardo Wolf (1887-1981), inventor, diplomat and philanthropist, and his wife Francisca Subirana-Wolf (1900-1981), in order to promote science and art for the benefit of mankind.

Wolf Foundation Prizes
Subjects: In science the fields are agriculture, chemistry, mathematics, medicine or physics, and in the arts the fields are architecture, music, painting or sculpture.
Purpose: To recognise the achievements of outstanding scientists and artists in the interest of mankind and friendly relations among people.
Eligibility: There are no eligibility restrictions.
Level of Study: Postgraduate.
Type: Prize.
Value: The prize in each field consists of a diploma and US$100,000.
Frequency: Annual.
Country of Study: Any country.
No. of awards offered: Four prizes in sciences and one in arts.
Application Procedure: Applicants must request an application form.
Closing Date: August 31st.
Funding: Private.
Contributor: The founder, Richard Wolf.

THE WOLFSON FOUNDATION

8 Queen Anne Street, London, W1G 9LD, England
Tel: (44) 20 7323 5730
Fax: (44) 20 7323 3241
Contact: Executive Secretary

The aims of the Wolfson Foundation are the advancement of arts and humanities, science, health and education. Grants are given to back excellence and talent, and provide support for promising projects which may be under funded, particularly for renovation and equipment. The emphasis is on science and technology, research, education, health and the arts.

Wolfson Foundation Grants
Subjects: Medicine and healthcare, including the prevention of disease and the care and treatment of the sick, disadvantaged and disabled, research, science, technology and education, particularly where benefits may accrue to the development of industry or commerce in the United Kingdom, arts and the humanities including libraries, museums, galleries, theatres, academies or historic buildings.

Eligibility: Open to registered charities and to exempt charities such as universities. Eligible applications from registered charities for contributions to appeals will normally be considered only when at least 50 per cent of that appeal has already been raised. Grants to universities for research and scholarship are normally made under the umbrella of designated competitive programmes in which vice chancellors and principals are invited to participate from time to time. Applications from university researchers are not considered outside these programmes. Grants are not made to private individuals.
Level of Study: Postgraduate.
Type: Grant.
Value: The Trustees make several types of grant which are not necessarily independent of each other. Capital Project grants may contribute towards the cost of erecting a new building or extension, or of renovating and refurbishing existing buildings. Equipment Grants supply equipment for specific purposes and/or furnishing and fittings. Recurrent costs are not normally provided.
Frequency: The trustees meet twice a year.
Country of Study: Any country.
No. of awards offered: Varies.
Application Procedure: Applicants must submit in writing a brief outline of the project with one copy of the organisation's most recent audited accounts before embarking on a detailed proposal.
Closing Date: March 1st or September 1st.
Funding: Private.
No. of awards given last year: 194.
No. of applicants last year: 1,200.

THE WOLFSONIAN-FLORIDA INTERNATIONAL UNIVERSITY

1001 Washington Avenue, Miami Beach, FL 33139, United States of America
Tel: (1) 305 535 2613
Fax: (1) 305 531 2133
Email: research@thewolf.fiu.edu
www: http://www.wolfsonian.fiu.edu
Contact: Mr John Mogul, Interim Academic Programmes Officer

The Wolfsonian-Florida International University is a museum and research centre that promotes the examination of modern material culture. Through exhibitions, publications, scholarships, educational programmes and public presentations, the Wolfsonian strives to enhance the understanding of objects as agents and reflections of social, cultural, political and technological change. The collection includes works on paper, furniture, paintings, sculpture, glass, textiles, ceramics, books and many other kinds of objects as agents and reflections of social, cultural, political and technological change.

Wolfsonian FIU Fellowship
Subjects: North American and European decorative propaganda, fine arts and rare books. The United States of America, Great Britain, Germany, Italy and the Netherlands are the countries that are most extensively represented within the Wolfsonian's collection.
Purpose: To conduct research on the Wolfsonian's collection of objects and library materials from the period 1885-1945, including decorative arts, works on paper, books and ephemera.
Eligibility: Wolfsonian Fellowships are granted on the basis of outstanding professional or academic accomplishment and are limited to those with at least a Master's degree. Doctoral candidates may apply for dissertation research related to the Wolfsonian collection.
Level of Study: Doctorate, Postdoctorate, Professional development.
Type: Fellowship.
Value: Approx. US$400 per week, plus travel and accommodation.
Length of Study: Approx. three-five weeks.
Frequency: Annual.
Study Establishment: The Wolfsonian-Florida International University.
Country of Study: United States of America.
No. of awards offered: Varies, approx. five.
Application Procedure: Applicants must complete an application form and submit this with three letters of recommendation. Contact the Academic Programs Co-ordinator for details and application materials.

Closing Date: December 31st.
No. of awards given last year: Five.
No. of applicants last year: 29.

WOMEN BAND DIRECTORS INTERNATIONAL (WBDI)

292 Band Hall, Louisiana State University, Baton Rouge, LA 70803, United States of America
Tel: (1) 225 578 2384
Fax: (1) 225 578 4693
Email: moorhouse@lsu.edu
www: http://www.womenbanddirectors.org
Contact: Ms Linda Moorhouse, Past President WBDI

Women Band Directors International (WBDI) is an organisation in which every woman band director is represented at the international level regardless of the length of her experience or the level at which she works. It is the only international organisation for women band directors.

WBDI Scholarship Awards
Subjects: Music education.
Purpose: To support young college women presently preparing to be band directors.
Eligibility: Open to women band instrumental majors enrolled in a university and working towards a degree in music education.
Level of Study: Unrestricted.
Type: Scholarship.
Value: US$300.
Frequency: Annual.
Country of Study: United States of America.
No. of awards offered: Five.
Application Procedure: Applicants must write for details or download an application form from the website.
Closing Date: December 1st.
Funding: Private.
No. of awards given last year: Five.
No. of applicants last year: 160.

WOMEN'S INTERNATIONAL LEAGUE FOR PEACE AND FREEDOM (WILPF)

PO Box 28, Geneva, CH-2012, Switzerland
Tel: (41) 22 919 7080
Fax: (41) 22 919 7081
Email: wilpf@iprolink.ch
www: http://www.wilpf.int.ch
Contact: Internships Programme

Founded in 1915 to protest against the war then raging in Europe, the Women's International League for Peace and Freedom (WILPF) aims to bring together women of different political and philosophical conviction, united in their determination to study, make known and help abolish the political, social, economic and psychological causes of war and to work for a constructive peace.

WILPF Internship in Disarmament and Economic Justice
Subjects: Disarmament or economic justice, in the context of the United Nations (UN) and international organisations.
Purpose: To focus on the work of the UN and non governmental organisations (NGOs) in their promoting and strengthening efforts for disarmament and the peaceful settlement of conflict, as well as their involvement in economic justice and North-South relations.
Eligibility: The internships are reserved for women in recognition of the fact that women remain largely excluded from positions concerned with questions of foreign policy and international relations, although their presence in these crucial areas is much needed. Priority is given to women between the ages of 25-30 and preference is given to WILPF members. Fluency in oral and written English is essential and Spanish and French speaking skills are an advantage for the work of the interns.

Level of Study: Graduate, Postgraduate, Professional development.
Type: Internship.
Value: Round trip travel from home to Geneva and a small stipend which covers basic living expenses in an expensive city. Accommodation is also provided.
Length of Study: From mid January to mid December.
Frequency: Annual.
Study Establishment: WILPF in Geneva.
Country of Study: Switzerland.
No. of awards offered: One.
Application Procedure: All applications must be submitted in English and should state clearly the internship for which the application is submitted. Applications must include a curriculum vitae, a covering letter giving reasons for wanting to follow the programme, a 1,000-1,500 word essay about a human rights or disarmament issue stating why this is of interest and two recommendations from non family members.
Closing Date: Please contact the organisation for dates.
Funding: Private.

WILPF Internship in Human Rights
Subjects: Human rights in the context of the United Nations (UN) and international organisations.
Purpose: To provide leadership training for young women.
Eligibility: The internships are reserved for women in recognition of the fact that women remain largely excluded from positions concerned with questions of foreign policy and international relations, although their presence in these crucial areas is much needed. Priority is given to women between the ages of 25-30, and preference is given to WILPF members. Fluency in oral and written English is essential and Spanish and French speaking skills are an advantage for the work of the interns.
Level of Study: Graduate, Postgraduate.
Type: Internship.
Value: Round trip travel from home to Geneva and a small stipend which covers basic living expenses in an expensive city. Accommodation is also provided.
Length of Study: From mid January to mid December.
Frequency: Annual.
Study Establishment: WILPF in Geneva.
Country of Study: Switzerland.
No. of awards offered: One.
Application Procedure: All applications must be submitted in English and should state clearly the internship for which the application is submitted. Applications must include a curriculum vitae, a covering letter giving reasons for wanting to follow the programme, a 1,000-1,500 word essay about a human rights or disarmament issue stating why this is of interest and two recommendations from non family members.
Closing Date: Please contact the organisation for dates.
Funding: Private.
Additional Information: The intern follows the annual session of the UN Commission on Human Rights, its working group, the Committee on Economic Social and Cultural Rights and meetings of UN Agencies, as well as participating in non governmental organisation meetings and WILPF activities.

WOMEN'S STUDIO WORKSHOP (WSW)

PO Box 489, Rosendale, NY 12472, United States of America
Tel: (1) 845 658 9133
Fax: (1) 845 658 9031
Email: info@wsworkshop.org
www: http://www.wsworkshop.org
Contact: Ms Ellen Kucera, Public Relations Director

The Women's Studio Workshop (WSW) is an artist run workshop with facilities for printmaking, papermaking, photography, book arts and ceramics. WSW supports the creation of new work through an annual book arts grant programme and an ongoing subsidised fellowship programme. WSW offers studio based educational programming in the above disciplines through its annual Summer Arts Institute.

Gerald R Dodge Foundation Residency for New Jersey Artists

Subjects: Books, printmaking, papermaking, photography and clay.
Purpose: To provide artists with time and resources to create a new body of work, or to edition a new bookwork.
Eligibility: Open to applicants only resident in New Jersey. Emerging artists encouraged to apply.
Level of Study: Unrestricted.
Type: Grant.
Length of Study: Six weeks.
Frequency: Annual.
No. of awards offered: Two.
Application Procedure: Applicants must submit an application form, a one page project description on a separate sheet of paper, a curriculum vitae, ten slides of recent work, a slide script including title, medium, size and date, and a stamped addressed envelope for return of materials. Forms are available from the website.
Closing Date: April 1.
Funding: Private.
No. of awards given last year: 2.

For further information contact:

736 Binnewater Lane, Kingston, New York, NY, 12401, United States of America

Hands-On-Art Visiting Artists Project

Subjects: Artist books.
Purpose: To assist an emerging artist in the creation of a new artist book while also working with school children in WSW's studio based Art-In-Education programme.
Eligibility: Open to all artists. Emerging artists are encouraged to apply.
Level of Study: Unrestricted.
Type: Grant.
Length of Study: Eight weeks.
Frequency: Annual.
No. of awards offered: Two.
Application Procedure: Applicants must apply through a two part application. Artists apply to WSW, WSW juries and then to the NEA. Artists must submit a one page description of their intended artists book project, including details of the medium to be used for printing the book, number of pages, page size, edition size (100 preferred), a structural dummy, materials budget, curriculum vitae, a one page description of relevant work experience with young people, ten slides of recent work and a Stamped Addressed Envelope.
Funding: Government.

For further information contact:

736 Binnewater Lane, Kingston, New York, NY, 12401, United States of America

WSW Artists' Book Residencies

Subjects: Art books.
Purpose: To enable artists to produce a limited edition of a book work at the Women's Studio Workshop.
Level of Study: Unrestricted.
Type: Residency Grant.
Value: A stipend of up to US$2,000. Plus materials of up to US$450 and housing.
Length of Study: Six weeks.
Frequency: Annual.
Study Establishment: WSW.
Country of Study: United States of America.
No. of awards offered: Varies, usually between three to five.
Application Procedure: Applicants must submit an application including a one page description of the proposed project, the medium or media used to print the book, the number of pages, page size, edition number, a structural dummy, a materials budget, a curriculum vitae, 6-10 slides and a stamped addressed envelope for return of materials. Applications are reviewed by past grant recipients and a WSW staff artist. Applicants should write for an application form.
Closing Date: November 15th.
Funding: Government, Private.

Contributor: Private foundations.
No. of awards given last year: Two.
No. of applicants last year: 150.

For further information contact:

722 Binnewater Lane, Kingston, NY 12401, United States of America

WSW Artists' Fellowships

Subjects: Intaglio, water based silkscreen, photography, papermaking or ceramics, letterpress, book arts.
Purpose: To provide a time for artists to explore new ideas in a dynamic and co-operative community of women artists in a rural environment.
Eligibility: Open to women artists only.
Level of Study: Unrestricted.
Type: Fellowship.
Value: The award includes on site housing and unlimited access to the studios. Cost to artists will be US$200 per week, including their own material.
Length of Study: Two-four weeks between September and June.
Frequency: Annual.
Study Establishment: WSW.
Country of Study: United States of America.
No. of awards offered: 10-20.
Application Procedure: Applicants must complete an application form, available on request or online at www.wsworkshop.org.
Closing Date: March 15th or November 1st.
Funding: Government, Private.
Contributor: Private foundations.
No. of awards given last year: 25.
No. of applicants last year: 100.

For further information contact:

722 Binnewater Lane, Kingston, NY, 12401, United States of America

WSW Internships

Subjects: Book arts, papermaking, printmaking, ceramics or photography.
Purpose: To provide opportunities for young artists to continue development of their work in a supportive environment while learning studio skills and responsibilities.
Eligibility: Open to young women artists or students who are aged between 20 and 30.
Level of Study: Unrestricted.
Type: Internship.
Value: US$150 per month plus housing.
Length of Study: Two-six months.
Frequency: Annual.
Study Establishment: WSW.
Country of Study: United States of America.
No. of awards offered: Eight.
Application Procedure: Applicants must submit a curriculum vitae, 10-20 slides, with slide list, three current letters of reference, a letter of interest which addresses the question of why an internship at WSW would be important, and a stamped addressed envelope.
Closing Date: October 15th for the Spring-Summer session which runs from January through to July and April 1st for the Autumn-Winter session which runs from August to December. Oct. 15 for Chili Bowl Internship (Jan-Feb). June 1 for Summer Intern (June-August).
Funding: Government, Private.
Contributor: Private foundations.
No. of awards given last year: Eight.
No. of applicants last year: 65.

For further information contact:

722 Binnewater Lane, Kingston, New York, NY, 12401, United States of America

WSW Production Grants

Subjects: Artists' books.
Purpose: To assist artists working in their own studios with the creation and publication of a book work.

Eligibility: Open to all artists.
Level of Study: Unrestricted.
Type: Grant.
Value: Production costs of up to US$1,000.
Frequency: Annual.
Country of Study: Any country.
No. of awards offered: 2 per year.
Application Procedure: Applicants must submit an application including a one paragraph description of the proposed project, the medium or media used to print the book, the number of pages, page size, edition number, a structural dummy, a materials budget, a curriculum vitae, 6-10 slides and a stamped addressed envelope for return of materials. Applications are reviewed by past grant recipients and a WSW staff artist. Applicants can download an application form from the website.
Closing Date: November 15th.
Funding: Government, Private.
Contributor: Private foundations.
No. of awards given last year: Two.
No. of applicants last year: 100.

For further information contact:

722 Binnewater Lane, Kingston, NY, 12401, United States of America

THE WOODROW WILSON NATIONAL FELLOWSHIP FOUNDATION

CN 5281, Princeton, NJ 08543-5281, United States of America
Tel: (1) 609 542 7007
Fax: (1) 609 542 0066
Email: charlotte@wwnff.org
www: http://www.woodrow.org
Contact: Ms Judith L Pinch

The Woodrow Wilson National Fellowship Foundation, an independent, non-profit organisation, attempts to maximise human potential through education. The Foundation seeks to sponsor excellence in education and thus develop a new generation of leaders.

Andrew W Mellon Fellowships in Humanistic Studies
Subjects: Humanistic studies.
Purpose: To allow exceptionally promising students to prepare for careers of teaching and scholarship in humanistic studies by providing top level, competitive, portable awards, and to contribute to the continuity of teaching and research of the highest order in America's colleges and universities.
Eligibility: Open to college seniors or recent graduates who are United States of America citizens or permanent residents entering into a programme leading to a PhD in the humanities. Applicants must not be enrolled in graduate or professional study, or hold an MA degree.
Level of Study: Doctorate.
Type: Fellowship.
Value: US$17,500 plus tuition and mandated fees.
Length of Study: One year.
Frequency: Annual.
Country of Study: United States of America or Canada.
No. of awards offered: 85.
Application Procedure: Applicants must provide their full name, current address and telephone number, their physical address in March, details of their undergraduate institution, major and year of graduation, the intended discipline in graduate school, details of their mailing address, and United States of America mail or email. These must be provided by mail, phone, fax or email.
Closing Date: Early December.
Funding: Private.
No. of awards given last year: 85.

Charlotte W Newcombe Doctoral Dissertation Fellowships
Subjects: Topics of religious or ethical values in all fields.
Purpose: To encourage new and significant research.

Eligibility: Open to students enrolled in doctoral programmes in the humanities and social sciences at an American university. Students must have completed all predissertation requirements by November 30th.
Level of Study: Doctorate.
Type: Fellowship.
Value: US$17,000.
Frequency: Annual.
Study Establishment: At any appropriate graduate school.
Country of Study: United States of America.
No. of awards offered: 32.
Application Procedure: Applicants must write for details.
Closing Date: Early December.
Funding: Private.
No. of awards given last year: 35.
No. of applicants last year: 450.

Woodrow Wilson Grants in Women's Studies
Subjects: Women's studies, the history, education or psychology of women, and women's health.
Purpose: To assist those writing dissertations.
Eligibility: Open to doctoral candidates at American universities who have completed all the requirements for the degree course, except the dissertation.
Level of Study: Doctorate.
Type: Grant.
Value: Approx. US$3,000-5,000.
Length of Study: One year.
Frequency: Annual.
Country of Study: United States of America.
No. of awards offered: 20.
Application Procedure: Applicants must write for details.
Closing Date: Early November.
Funding: Private.
No. of awards given last year: 25.
No. of applicants last year: 250.

WOODS HOLE OCEANOGRAPHIC INSTITUTION

Education Office, Clark Laboratory MS #31, 360 Woods Hole Road, Woods Hole, MA 02543-1541, United States of America
Tel: (1) 508 289 2950
Fax: (1) 508 457 2188
Email: postdoc@whoi.edu
www: http://www.whoi.edu/education
Contact: Administration Associate & Program Co-ordinator

The Woods Hole Oceanographic Institution is a private, independent, non-profit corporation dedicated to research and higher education at the frontiers of ocean science. Its primary mission is to develop and effectively communicate a fundamental understanding of the processes and characteristics governing how the oceans function and how they interact with the earth as a whole.

Woods Hole Oceanographic Institution Geophysical Fluid Dynamics (GFD) Fellowships
Subjects: Classical fluid dynamics, physical oceanography, meteorology, astrophysics, planetary atmospheres, geological fluid dynamics, hydromagnetics, physics and applied mathematics.
Purpose: To bring together graduate students and researchers from a variety of fields who share a common interest in the non linear dynamics of rotating, stratified fields.
Eligibility: There are no eligibility restrictions.
Level of Study: Graduate.
Type: Fellowship.
Value: Please contact the organisation.
Length of Study: Ten weeks.
Frequency: Annual.
Study Establishment: Woods Hole Oceanographic Institution.
Country of Study: United States of America.
No. of awards offered: Up to 10.

Application Procedure: Application forms may be obtained from the GFD section of the education website or by writing directly to the Fellowship Committee.
Closing Date: February 15th.
Funding: Government.
Contributor: The United States office of Naval Research and the United States National Science Foundation.

Woods Hole Oceanographic Institution Postdoctoral Awards in Marine Policy and Ocean Management

Subjects: Novel proposals in such fields as political science, international affairs, decision theory, economics, diplomacy, management, geography, law, engineering and anthropology will be considered.
Eligibility: Open to Scholars and practitioners from relevant fields in the social sciences, natural sciences, law and management who are interested in applying their disciplinary training and experience to investigations which require a significant component of marine research. Applicants must have completed their doctorate degree or possess equivalent professional qualifications through career experience.
Level of Study: Postdoctorate.
Value: Please contact the organisation.
Length of Study: One year.
Frequency: Annual.
Study Establishment: Woods Hole Oceanographic Institution.
Country of Study: United States of America.
No. of awards offered: Varies.
Closing Date: January 15th for notification in March.
Additional Information: Award recipients in the programme have pursued such studies as the implications of oil exploration along the North eastern coast of the United States of America, problems of international law created by new developments in aquaculture and fish farming, economic benefits of some oceanographic research, a perceptual study of New England fishermen, and oceanic waste disposal.

Woods Hole Oceanographic Institution Postdoctoral Fellowships in Ocean Science and Engineering

Subjects: Oceanography and oceanographic engineering.
Purpose: To further the education and training of recent recipients of doctoral degrees in engineering science or with interests in marine science.
Eligibility: Open to United States citizens and foreign nationals who have earned a PhD degree in biology, physics, microbiology, molecular biology, chemistry, geology, geophysics, oceanography, meteorology, engineering or mathematics. Scientists with more than three years of postdoctoral experience are not eligible.
Level of Study: Postdoctorate.
Type: Fellowship.
Value: Please contact the organisation.
Length of Study: 18 months.
Frequency: Annual.
Study Establishment: Woods Hole Oceanographic Institution.
Country of Study: United States of America.
No. of awards offered: 7-10.
Application Procedure: Applicants must complete and submit an application form with transcripts, reference letters, complete transcripts of undergraduate and graduate records, and a concise statement describing research interests. Further information and application forms may be obtained from the postdoctoral section of the website.
Closing Date: January 15th for notification in March.
Funding: Government, Private.
Additional Information: Award holders work in the laboratory under the general supervision of an appropriate member of the staff, but are expected to work independently on research problems of their own choice.

Woods Hole Oceanographic Institution Postdoctoral Fellowships in the Interdisciplinary Institutes

Subjects: The exploration and characterisation of ocean biodiversity, indicators and assessment of the health of marine ecosystems, development of new sensors, instruments and analyses for ocean biology, the role of the Atlantic Ocean in modes of climate variability,

monitoring to improve climate forecasts, ocean and atmosphere interactions, thermohaline circulation and abrupt climate change. Other topics of investigation include the dynamics of deep earth, crustal accretion processes, gas hydrates, earth-ocean-life interactions, seafloor observatory science and instrumentation, mechanisms providing nutrients to drive primary productivity and the fate of organic matter from primary productivity.
Purpose: To foster interdisciplinary research addressing critical issues within the Institute and encourage research and understanding of the subject area.
Eligibility: Applicants must be new or recent doctoral graduates with an interest in oceanographic sciences or engineering. Usually, scientists with more than three-four years of postdoctoral experience are not considered eligible for these awards.
Level of Study: Postdoctorate.
Type: Fellowship.
Value: Please contact the organisation.
Length of Study: 18 months.
Frequency: Varies.
Study Establishment: The Ocean Life Institute, the Earth and Ocean Exploration Institute, the Coastal Ocean Institute and the Ocean and Climate Change Institute at the Woods Hole Oceanographic Institution.
Country of Study: United States of America.
No. of awards offered: One-two.
Application Procedure: Applicants must contact the Institute directly. In addition to the application form, the application must also include a current curriculum vitae, a minimum of three non Woods Hole Oceanographic Institute recommendations, a concise statement describing research interests, in particular those that the applicant would like to purse at the Woods Hole facility as well as more general career plans, transcripts of the applicant's complete undergraduate and graduate records and a brief synopsis of their doctoral dissertation. Further information and application forms may be obtained through the education section of the website.
Closing Date: January 15th.
Additional Information: Announcement of awards will be made by March 31st.

Woods Hole Oceanographic Institution Research Fellowships in Marine Policy

Subjects: Oceanography, social and behavioural sciences, political science, international relations, economics and law as related to marine policy.
Purpose: To provide support and experience to scientists interested in marine policy issues, to provide opportunities for interdisciplinary application of social sciences and natural sciences to marine policy problems, and to conduct research and convey information necessary for the development of effective local, national and international ocean policy.
Eligibility: Open to citizens of the United States and foreign nationals with a PhD or equivalent professional experience.
Level of Study: Postdoctorate, Professional development.
Type: Fellowship.
Value: Please contact the organisation.
Length of Study: One year.
Frequency: Annual.
Study Establishment: Woods Hole Oceanographic Institution.
Country of Study: United States of America.
No. of awards offered: One.
Application Procedure: Applicants must complete and submit a formal application form with transcripts, three references and a proposal for a research project to undertake whilst at the Institution.
Closing Date: January 15th.
Funding: Government, Private.

Woods Hole Oceanographic Institution/NOAA Cooperative Institute for Climate and Ocean Research Postdoctoral Fellowship

Subjects: Coastal ocean and near shore processes, the ocean's participation in climate and climate variability and marine ecosystem processes analysis.

Purpose: To build ties between WHOI investigators and colleagues at NOAA laboratories and to develop co-operative NOAA funded research at academic institutions in the Northeastern United States of America. The fellowship also aims to further the education and training of recent recipients of doctoral degrees in the marine sciences.

Eligibility: Open to United States citizens and foreign nationals who have earned a PhD degree in biology, physics, microbiology, molecular biology, chemistry, geology, geophysics, oceanography, meteorology, engineering or mathematics. Scientists with more than three years of postdoctoral experience are not eligible.

Level of Study: Postdoctorate.

Type: Fellowship.

Value: Please contact the organisation.

Length of Study: 18 months.

Frequency: Annual.

Study Establishment: Woods Hole Oceanographic Institution.

Country of Study: United States of America.

No. of awards offered: One.

Application Procedure: Applicants must complete and submit an application form with transcripts, reference letters, complete transcripts of undergraduate and graduate records and a concise statement describing research interests. Further information and application forms may be obtained from the education section of the website.

Closing Date: January 15th for notification in March.

Funding: Government.

Contributor: The NOAA.

Additional Information: Award holders work in the laboratory under the general supervision of an appropriate member of the staff, but are expected to work independently on research problems of their own choice.

WORLD CANCER RESEARCH FUND INTERNATIONAL (WCRF)

First Floor, 19 Harley Street, London, W1G 9QJ, England
Tel: (44) 20 7343 4200
Fax: (44) 20 7343 4220
Email: research@wcrf.org.uk
www: http://www.wcrf.org
Contact: Grant Administrator

The World Cancer Research Fund International (WCRF) is the umbrella association for the WCRF global network, providing leadership, policy and strategic guidance for its national members. It administers the research grant programme in the United Kingdom, the Netherlands, Germany and Hong Kong. The WCRF global network is dedicated to the prevention of cancer through healthy diets and associated lifestyles. It aims to develop and strengthen the scientific knowledge of the links between food, nutrition and cancer, and also to raise awareness that healthy diets and associated lifestyles reduce cancer risk.

WCRF International Research Grants

Subjects: Social and preventive medicine, public health, epidemiology, diet and cancer prevention. Preference is given to research on whole body systems and populations, and also to research that is likely to increase scientific and public understanding of how to reduce the risk of cancer through food, nutrition and associated factors. The organisation are also interested in research proposals designed to develop the findings of the expert report entitled Food, Nutrition and the Prevention of Cancer: a global perspective.

Purpose: To fund innovative research science designed to increase knowledge of the effects of diet and nutrition on the origins, causes and prevention of cancer.

Eligibility: Open to qualified researchers of any nationality. Preference is given to applicants from the United Kingdom, Netherlands, Germany, France and China.

Level of Study: Unrestricted.

Type: Research grant.

Value: Up to a maximum of UK£150,000 over four years with a maximum of UK£50,000 in any one year.

Length of Study: One-four years.

Frequency: Annual.

Study Establishment: Universities, medical schools, research institutions and other centres of academic excellence.

Country of Study: Any country.

No. of awards offered: Varies.

Application Procedure: The programme is advertised in Nature July each year. An application pack is available from WCRF International as well as from the website.

Closing Date: Mid September for outline applications and late February for full application forms.

Funding: Private.

Contributor: Public donations.

No. of awards given last year: 9.

No. of applicants last year: 86.

WORLD LEARNING

School for International Training (SIT), Kipling Road, PO Box 676, Brattleboro, VT 05301, United States of America
Tel: (1) 802 257 7751
Fax: (1) 802 258 3500
Email: shonna.thomas@worldlearning.org
www: http://www.worldlearning.org
Contact: Ms Shonna Thomas, Marketing Department

The School for International Training (SIT) at World Learning educates leaders capable of bridging differences between people and nations in an effort to build a more peaceful and sustainable world. Accredited by the New England Association of Schools and Colleges, SIT offers Master's degrees in international and intercultural fields, as well as continuing education opportunities, management development courses, and peace and conflict transformation training.

School for International Training (SIT) Extension

Subjects: Teacher education, organisational management, web based research and instruction, and conflict transformation.

Purpose: To offer continuing education opportunities for professionals through innovative, high quality courses.

Eligibility: Open to persons of any nationality.

Length of Study: One week to one month.

Study Establishment: SIT.

No. of awards offered: Varies.

Application Procedure: Applicants must write for details or visit the website.

Additional Information: Online and on campus intensive formats allow professionals from around the world to engage in reflective learning and practice while working in their chosen fields. For information on deadlines and other aspects of the awards please visit the website at http://www.sit.edu/extension.

School for International Training Master of Arts in Teaching Program

Subjects: Reflection, observation, self evaluation, experiential learning and skills development within a strong learning community.

Purpose: To prepare language teachers committed to professional development and service in their field.

Eligibility: Open to persons of any nationality who are preparing for a language teaching career.

Level of Study: Postgraduate.

Type: Scholarship.

Value: Varies.

Length of Study: A period which includes a time of student teaching and homestay. The programme is offered in a one year or two summer format designed for working professionals.

Frequency: Annual.

Study Establishment: SIT.

Country of Study: Any country.

No. of awards offered: A small number.

Application Procedure: Applicants must complete an institutional financial aid application and should contact Michael Ireland for further details, by email on michael.ireland@worldlearning.org.

Closing Date: Rolling admissions.

Additional Information: Students master technical teaching methodologies through language classroom practice, on campus coursework and a supervised teaching internship. Further information is available on the website http://www.sit.edu/mat.

School for International Training Programmes in Intercultural Service, Leadership and Management

Subjects: International student services, international recruitment, student advising, community education, citizen exchange and educational travel, theory and history of international education, immigration law and practice, advising and management, multicultural organisation development, citizen capacity building, multinational human resource development, and community development and social action, human resource development and training, diversity leadership, programme planning, proposal writing, policy advocacy and training, community development, social action and development management, cultural, political, economic and environmental context of management, strategic planning, management of human and financial resources, marketing and the theory and practice of sustainable development, conflict and identity or conflict analysis.

Purpose: To provide funding for competency based, professional level training for intercultural managers through the following courses: SIT's Master of Arts in International Education, SIT's Master of Arts in Conflict Transformation, SIT's Master of Arts in Intercultural Relations, SIT's Master of Arts in Sustainable Development, SIT's Master of Science in Organisational Management and SIT's Master of Arts in Intercultural Service, Leadership and Management.

Eligibility: Open to persons of any nationality.

Level of Study: Graduate.

Type: Scholarship.

Value: Varies.

Frequency: Annual.

Study Establishment: SIT.

Country of Study: Any country.

No. of awards offered: Varies.

Application Procedure: Applicants must complete an Institutional Financial Aid application and should contact Michael Ireland for further details by email on michael.ireland@worldlearning.org.

Closing Date: Rolling admissions.

Additional Information: Further information is available on the website http://www.sit.edu/degree.html.

WORLD METEOROLOGICAL ORGANIZATION (WMO)

Education & Training Department, 7 bis Avenue de la Paix, Case postale No 2300, Geneva, CH-1211, Switzerland
Tel: (41) 22 730 8111
Fax: (41) 22 734 2326
Email: ipa@www.wmo.ch
www: http://www.wmo.ch
Tel: 41 41 99 OMM CH
Contact: Director

The World Meteorological Organization (WMO) is an inter-governmental organisation with a membership of 185 member states and territories. It originated from the International Meteorological Organization, which was founded in 1873. Set up in 1950, WMO became the specialised agency of the United Nations for meteorology, weather and climate, operational hydrology and related sciences.

WMO Education and Training Fellowships

Subjects: Atmospheric science, meteorology, operational hydrology and related sciences.

Purpose: To educate and train meteorological personnel on individually tailored or group study training programmes.

Eligibility: Open to nationals from WMO member countries. Potential candidates should meet the requirements for academic qualifications, relevant experience, language proficiency, age limits and other specific requirements, as stipulated by the host training institutions concerned.

Level of Study: Professional development.

Type: Fellowship.

Value: According to UN rates.

Length of Study: Varies.

Frequency: Dependent on funds available.

Study Establishment: Dependent on the required training or education.

Country of Study: The applicants home country.

No. of awards offered: Approx. 300.

Application Procedure: Applicants must be designated officially through the permanent representative with WMO, which will normally be the Director of the National Meteorological Service in the requesting country concerned.

Funding: Government.

No. of awards given last year: 310.

No. of applicants last year: 590.

THE WORLD PRESS INSTITUTE (WPI)

1576 Summit Avenue, St Paul, MN 55105
United States of America
Tel: (1) 651 696 6360
Fax: (1) 651 696 6306
Email: wpi@macalester.edu
www: http://www.worldpressinstitute.org
Contact: Mr John Ullmann, Executive Director

The World Press Institute (WPI) makes it possible for qualified international journalists to report on United States government and politics, business, education, communications, social issues, science, technology and culture on the basis of personal experience and knowledge. WPI Fellows travel throughout the United States to meet, interview and live with Americans of all walks of life. WPI gives lectures and training on the role and responsibilities of a free press in democracy and pays all expenses plus a daily per diem.

WPI Fellowship

Subjects: Journalism.

Purpose: To provide the opportunity for international journalists to study the governance, business, communication, education, culture and social issues of the United States and to offer observation and training in the role of a free press in a democracy.

Eligibility: Open to non United States full-time professional journalists with a minimum of five years of experience in print or electronic journalism. Applicants must be fluent in spoken and written English.

Level of Study: Professional development.

Type: Fellowship.

Value: US$25,000.

Length of Study: Four months.

Frequency: Annual.

Study Establishment: Macalester College.

Country of Study: United States of America.

No. of awards offered: 10.

Application Procedure: Applicants must complete application materials available on request or from the website.

Closing Date: December 31st.

Funding: Commercial, Private.

Contributor: Macalester College, the McCormick Tribune Foundation and the Knight Foundation.

No. of awards given last year: 10.

No. of applicants last year: 100-200.

Additional Information: WPI Fellowships are intended for journalists with a strong commitment to long-term careers in print or broadcast journalism. The programme is purposefully difficult and demanding, requiring each participant to work as part of the group.

WORLD STUDIO FOUNDATION

200 Varick Street, Suite 507, New York, NY 10014, United States of America
Tel: (1) 212 366 1317
Email: info@worldstudio.org
www: http://www.worldstudio.org
Contact: Grants Enquiries

Worldstudio Foundation is devoted to encouraging social responsibility in the design arts and professions.

Worldstudio Foundation Scholarship

Subjects: Fine or commercial art, design or architecture, advertising, fashion design, film/video, film/theatre design, graphic design, interior design and photographies.
Purpose: To support a graduate student to pursue artistic study.
Eligibility: Though not a requirement, minority status is a significant factor considered, and applicants must have financial need.
Level of Study: Postgraduate.
Type: Scholarship.
Value: US$100 to US$5,000
Frequency: Annual.
Study Establishment: An accredited university in the U.S.A.
Country of Study: United States of America.
Closing Date: March 19th
Funding: Private.
Contributor: World Studio Foundation.

THE WORSHIPFUL COMPANY OF MUSICIANS

6th Floor, 2 London Wall Buildings, London, EC2M 5PP, England
Tel: (44) 20 7496 8980
Fax: (44) 20 7588 3633
Email: deputyclerk@wcom.org.uk
www: http://www.wcom.org.uk
Contact: Ms Margaret Alford, Deputy Clerk

The Worshipful Company of Musicians supports young musicians particularly in the 'wilderness' years between graduating and setting out on their musical careers.

Allcard Grants

Subjects: Music.
Purpose: To support the advanced training of performers at home or abroad for string, voice or piano accompanists, and wind instruments in exceptional circumstances.
Eligibility: Open to individuals wishing to undertake a relevant training or research programme. The grants are not available for courses leading either to a first degree at a university or to a diploma at a college of music, and only in exceptional circumstances will assistance towards the cost of a fourth or fifth year at a college of music be considered. Grants are not available towards the purchase of instruments. Applicants must have studied at a British institution for at least three years.
Level of Study: Postgraduate.
Type: Grant.
Value: Up to UK£3,000.
Frequency: Annual.
Country of Study: Any country.
No. of awards offered: A limited number.
Application Procedure: Applicants must be nominated by principals or heads of music departments at the Royal Academy of Music, the Royal College of Music, the Guildhall School of Music, the Royal Northern College of Music, the Royal Scottish Academy of Music and Drama, the Welsh College of Music, the Birmingham Conservatoire, the Trinity College of Music, City University, Huddersfield University, Goldsmiths or other university departments.
Closing Date: Applications are to be made after January 1st and before April 30th.
No. of awards given last year: Four.
No. of applicants last year: 30.

Carnwath Scholarship

Subjects: Music.
Purpose: To support young pianists.
Eligibility: Open to any person of either sex permanently resident in the United Kingdom and 21-25 years of age. The scholarship is intended only for the advanced student who has successfully completed a solo performance course at a college of music.
Level of Study: Postgraduate.

Type: Scholarship.
Value: UK£4,150 per year.
Length of Study: Up to two years.
Frequency: Every two years.
Country of Study: United Kingdom.
No. of awards offered: One.
Application Procedure: Applicants must be nominated by principals of the Royal Academy of Music, the Guildhall School of Music and Drama, the Royal Northern College of Music, the Royal Scottish Academy of Music, Trinity College of Music, London College of Music, the Welsh College of Music and Drama, Birmingham School of Music or the Royal College of Music. No application should be made directly to the Worshipful Company of Musicians.
Closing Date: June 1st in the year of the award.

John Clementi Collard Fellowship

Subjects: Music.
Eligibility: Open to professional musicians of standing and experience who show excellence in one or more of the higher branches of musical activity, such as composition, research and performance including conducting.
Level of Study: Postgraduate.
Type: Fellowship.
Value: UK£10,000 per year.
Length of Study: Up to three years.
Frequency: Approx. every three years.
Country of Study: United Kingdom.
No. of awards offered: One.
Application Procedure: Applicants must be nominated by professors of music at Oxford, Cambridge or London Universities, directors of the Royal College of Music, principals of the Royal Academy of Music, the Guildhall School of Music and Drama or the Royal Northern College of Music. No application should be made directly to the Worshipful Company of Musicians.

Maisie Lewis Young Artists Fund

Subjects: Musical performance.
Purpose: To assist young artists of outstanding ability who wish to acquire experience on the professional soloist concert platform.
Eligibility: Open to instrumentalists including organists up to 25 years of age and to singers of up to 30 years of age.
Level of Study: Postgraduate.
Value: Reimbursement of recitalists' expenses.
Frequency: Annual.
Country of Study: United Kingdom.
No. of awards offered: Four-six half recitals per year.
Application Procedure: Applicants must complete an application form, available from January 1st.
Closing Date: May 1st.
No. of awards given last year: Four.
No. of applicants last year: 80.
Additional Information: Auditions are normally held in September.

YALE CENTER FOR BRITISH ART

Public Information, Education and Programs, 1080 Chapel Street, Box 208280, New Haven, CT 06520-8280, United States of America
Tel: (1) 203 432 2850
Fax: (1) 203 432 9628
Email: bacinfo@yale.edu
www: http://www.yale.edu/ycba
Contact: Ms Mary Beth Graham, Acting Programme Co-ordinator

The Yale Center for British Art houses the most comprehensive collection of English paintings, prints, drawings, rare books and sculpture outside the United Kingdom. Given to Yale University by Paul Mellon, the Center's resources illustrate British life and culture from the sixteenth-century to the present.

Yale Center for British Art Fellowships

Subjects: British art from the Elizabethan period onwards.
Purpose: To allow scholars of literature, history, the history of art or related fields to study the Center's holdings of paintings, drawings,

prints, rare books, and manuscripts and to make use of its research facilities.
Eligibility: Open to scholars in Postdoctoral or equivalent research related to British art. Applications are also welcomed from candidates enrolled in doctoral programs who are writing their dissertations (A.B.D.).
Level of Study: Postdoctorate, Predoctorate.
Type: Fellowship.
Value: Cost of travel to and from New Haven, plus accommodation and a living allowance.
Length of Study: One-four months; postdoctorate; 1-2 months for pre-doctorate.
Frequency: Annual.
Study Establishment: The Yale Center for British Art.
Country of Study: United States of America.
No. of awards offered: 15-20.
Application Procedure: Applicants must submit their name, address, telephone number, a curriculum vitae listing professional experience, education and publications, a three-page research proposal and two confidential letters of recommendation. There is no application form.
Closing Date: January 15th.
Funding: Private.
Contributor: The Yale Center for British Art Endowment Fund.
No. of awards given last year: 15.
No. of applicants last year: 30.

YALE UNIVERSITY PRESS

PO Box 209040, New Haven, CT 06520-9040, United States of America
Tel: (1) 203 432 0960
Fax: (1) 203 432 2394
Email: yyp@yalepress3.unipress.yale.edu
www: http://www.yale.edu/yup
Contact: Poetry Editor

Yale Series of Younger Poets

Subjects: Poetry.
Purpose: To select a book length poetry manuscript for publication.
Eligibility: Open to writers who are United States citizens under 40 years of age who have not yet published a book of poetry. Poems must be original, not translations.
Level of Study: Unrestricted.
Type: Prize.
Frequency: Annual.
Country of Study: United States of America.
No. of awards offered: One.
Application Procedure: Applicants must write for more information on entry criteria.
Closing Date: October 1-November 15.
Funding: Commercial.

YEHUDI MENUHIN INTERNATIONAL VIOLIN COMPETITION FOR YOUNG VIOLINISTS

The Royal Academy of Music, Marylebone Road, London, NW1 5HT, England
Tel: (44) 20 7873 7411
Fax: (44) 20 7873 7411
Email: menuhincompetition@geniusoftheviolin.org
www: http://www.geniusoftheviolin.org
Contact: Ms Susanne Barthelmes, Administrator

The Yehudi Menuhin International Violin Competition for Young Violinists is an international competition which is open to applicants of any nationality under the age of 22.

Yehudi Menuhin International Competition for Young Violinists

Subjects: Violin performance.
Eligibility: Open to violinists of any nationality. The maximum age of competitors is 21.

Type: Prize.
Value: Up to UK£5,000.
Frequency: Every two years.
Country of Study: Any country.
No. of awards offered: 9 plus special prizes awarded at the jury's discretion.
Application Procedure: Applicants must submit a completed application form, audition recording, two letters of recommendation, details of education, musical training and concert experience.
Closing Date: Next competition March/April 2006 contact the organisation for details.
Funding: Commercial, Government, Private.
No. of awards given last year: 9.
No. of applicants last year: 180.
Additional Information: The competition is held in London in partnership with the Royal Academy of Music. Competitors are accommodated by host families.

YONSEI UNIVERSITY

Graduate School of International Studies (GSIS), 134 Shinchon-dong, Sodaemoon-ku, Seoul, 120-749, Korea, Republic (South)
Tel: (82) 2 212 33293
Fax: (82) 2 392 3321
Email: gsis@mail.yonsei.ac.kr
www: http://gsis.yonsei.ac.kr
Contact: Jisook Han, Admissions Officer

Yonsei University offers Master's and PhD programmes in English.

Hwa Am Scholarship

Subjects: All subjects.
Purpose: To financially assist students.
Eligibility: Students with promise in the field of international cooperation.
Level of Study: M.A.
Type: Scholarship.
Value: Approx US$840 up to US$1,670.
Length of Study: One semester.
Frequency: Each semester.
Study Establishment: GSIS.
Country of Study: Korea.
No. of awards offered: 2-3.
Application Procedure: Selected by GSIS.
Closing Date: The end of May for autumn entry and the end of November for spring entry.
Funding: Private.
No. of awards given last year: n/a.
No. of applicants last year: n/a.

Incoming Students Award

Subjects: All subjects.
Purpose: To financially assist students.
Eligibility: Incoming students who show outstanding academic potential.
Level of Study: M.A./PhD.
Type: Full scholarship (only for first semester).
Value: Not specified.
Frequency: First semester only.
Length of Study: One semester.
Study Establishment: GSIS.
Country of Study: Korea.
No. of awards offered: Up to 10.
Application Procedure: Selected by GSIS.
Closing Date: The end of May for autumn entry.
Funding: Private.
No. of awards given last year: n/a.
No. of applicants last year: n/a.

International Students Award

Subjects: All subjects.
Purpose: To financially assist students.

Eligibility: Incoming students from respective continents with good academic records and in need of financial support.
Level of Study: Not specified.
Type: Award.
Value: From US$770 up to US$3,077.
Length of Study: One semester
Frequency: Only for first semester.
Study Establishment: GSIS.
Country of Study: Korea.
No. of awards offered: 2-3 from each continent.
Application Procedure: Application Needed.
Closing Date: The end of May for autumn entry.
Funding: Private.
No. of awards given last year: n/a.
No. of applicants last year: n/a.

Korea Foundation Fellowship

Subjects: Korean studies.
Purpose: To financially assist foreign students specializing in Korean studies.
Eligibility: Not available to Korean Nationals.
Level of Study: M.A./PhD.
Type: Fellowship.
Value: About US$3,340 (PhD). US$1,670 (MA).
Length of Study: One semester.
Frequency: Each semester.
Study Establishment: GSIS.
Country of Study: Korea.
No. of awards offered: 3-5.
Application Procedure: Application needed.
Closing Date: The end of May for autumn entry and the end of November for spring entry.
Funding: Private.
No. of awards given last year: n/a.
No. of applicants last year: n/a.

Korea-Japan Cultural Association Scholarship

Subjects: All subjects.
Purpose: To financially assist students.
Eligibility: Japanese students with good academic records.
Type: Scholarship.
Value: US$1,347.
Length of Study: One semester.
Frequency: Each semester.
Study Establishment: GSIS.
Country of Study: Korea.
No. of awards offered: 1-2.
Application Procedure: Selected by KJCAS.
Closing Date: The end of May for autumn entry and the end of November for spring entry.
Funding: Private.
No. of awards given last year: n/a.
No. of applicants last year: n/a.

Kwanjeong Scholarship for Chinese Young Leaders

Subjects: All subjects.
Purpose: To financially assist students.
Eligibility: Incoming or current chinese students with academic and professional promise.
Level of Study: Not specified.
Type: Scholarship.
Value: US$3,330.
Length of Study: One semester.
Frequency: Each semester.
Study Establishment: GSIS.
Country of Study: Korea.
No. of awards offered: Up to 30.
Application Procedure: Application needed.
Closing Date: The end of May for autumn entry and the end of November for spring entry.
Funding: Private.
No. of awards given last year: n/a.
No. of applicants last year: n/a.

Scholarship for Academic Excellence

Subjects: All subjects.
Purpose: To financially assist students.
Eligibility: All students with GPA of over 3.7 and in need of financial aid.
Level of Study: M.A./PhD.
Type: Scholarship.
Value: US$840 up to US$3,340.
Length of Study: One semester.
Frequency: Each semester.
Study Establishment: GSIS.
Country of Study: Korea.
No. of awards offered: Unlimited.
Application Procedure: Financial Aid application reviewed by GSIS.
Closing Date: The end of May for autumn entry and the end of November for spring entry.
Funding: Private.
No. of awards given last year: n/a.
No. of applicants last year: n/a.

Underwood Fellowship

Subjects: All subjects.
Purpose: To financially assist students with high GPA and a commitment to good citizenship.
Eligibility: Not available to Korean Nationals.
Level of Study: M.A.
Type: Fellowship.
Value: Approx US$1,670.
Length of Study: One Semester.
Frequency: Each semester.
Study Establishment: GSIS.
Country of Study: Korea.
No. of awards offered: 3-4.
Application Procedure: To be announced.
Closing Date: The end of May for autumn entry and the end of November for spring entry.
Funding: Private.
No. of awards given last year: n/a.
No. of applicants last year: n/a.

Yonsei University Dean's Award

Subjects: All subjects.
Purpose: To financially assist three or four new foreign students based on academic performance and financial need.
Eligibility: The award is not available to Korean nationals.
Level of Study: MBA.
Type: Scholarship.
Value: US$840 per person.
Length of Study: One semester.
Frequency: Every semester.
Study Establishment: GSIS.
Country of Study: Korea.
No. of awards offered: Three or four.
Application Procedure: Applicants must apply for the academic course as usual and will be automatically considered for the scholarships.
Closing Date: The end of May for Autumn entry, and the end of November for Spring entry.
Funding: Private.
No. of awards given last year: 10.
No. of applicants last year: 80.

YORKSHIRE SCULPTURE PARK

Bretton Hall, West Bretton, Wakefield, Yorkshire, WF4 4LG, United Kingdom
Tel: (44) 1924 830579
Fax: (44) 1924 800044
www: http://ysp.co.uk
Contact: Dr Peter Murray, Administrator

Yorkshire Sculpture park is one of Europe's leading open-air art organisations showing modern and contemporary work by leading UK and international artists.

Feiweles Trust Dance Bursary

Subjects: Dance, music, art, sculpture.
Purpose: To support an artist at the beginning of their career, after training.
Level of Study: Postgraduate.
Type: Bursary.
Value: UK£10,000
Length of Study: 3 months.
Frequency: Annual.
Study Establishment: Workshops within the community.
Country of Study: United Kingdom.
Application Procedure: Send a letter including a paragraph explaining exactly how the bursary would benefit the development of your career, plus a full C.V.
Closing Date: 20th February
Funding: Private.
Contributor: Feiweles Trust.
Additional Information: It is expected that appointed artists will use this bursary experience to develop their own artistic practice. A different art form is supported each year.

For further information contact:

The Feiweles Trust, Yorkshire Sculpture Park, West Bretton, Wakefield, WF4 4LG, United Kingdom

ZONTA INTERNATIONAL FOUNDATION

557 West Randolph Street
Chicago, IL 60661-2206
United States of America
Tel: (1) 312 930 0951
Fax: (1) 312 930 0951
Email: aubides@zonta.org
www: http://www.zonta.org
Tel: 190200 UT
Contact: Ms Ana L Ubides, Programme Co-ordinator

The Zonta International Foundation is a worldwide service organisation of executives in business and the professions working together to advance the status of women.

Amelia Earhart Fellowship Awards

Subjects: Aerospace related science and engineering.
Purpose: To enable women to undertake graduate study.
Eligibility: Open to women of any nationality who have a Bachelor's degree in a qualifying area of science or engineering related to advanced studies in aerospace related science or aerospace related engineering. By the time the fellowship grant is awarded, candidates must have completed one year of aerospace related graduate studies. Applicants must demonstrate a superior academic record with evidence of potential at a recognised university or college and provide evidence of a well defined research programme.
Level of Study: Graduate.
Type: Fellowship.
Value: US$6,000 which may be used for books and fees, tuition or living expenses. Payments are made in equal instalments in September and December.
Frequency: Annual
Study Establishment: Any institution offering accredited graduate courses and degrees in aerospace studies.
Country of Study: Any country.
No. of awards offered: Approx. 35.
Application Procedure: Applicants must submit an application form in English, available from the website, including biographical information, a list of schools attended and degrees received, transcripts of grades and verifications form, employment history, plans for intended study, an essay on academic and professional goals, a photograph and three letters of recommendation from teachers. Information other than transcripts and recommendations must be limited to the space provided on the application form as attachments will not be considered. International applicants must also provide English translations for all non English documents. All applicants will be notified by mid May.
Closing Date: November 15th.
Funding: Private.
No. of awards given last year: 35.
No. of applicants last year: 152.
Additional Information: The Zonta International Amelia Earhart Fellowship Awards were established in 1938 in honour of Amelia Earhart, famed pilot and member of Zonta International.

SUBJECT AND ELIGIBILITY
GUIDE TO AWARDS

AGRICULTURE, FORESTRY AND FISHERY

General
Agronomy
Animal husbandry and animal production
  Sericulture
Horticulture and viticulture
Crop husbandry and crop production
Agriculture and farm management
Agricultural economics
Food science and production
  Meat and poultry
  Dairy
  Fish
  Oenology
  Brewing
  Harvest technology
Soil and water science
  Water management
  Soil conservation
Veterinary medicine
Tropical/Sub-tropical agriculture
Forestry
  Forest soils
  Forest biology
  Forest pathology
  Forest products
  Forest economics
  Forest management
Fishery
  Aquaculture

ARCHITECTURE AND TOWN PLANNING

General
Structural architecture
Architectural restoration
Environmental design
Landscape architecture
Town and community planning
Regional planning

ARTS AND HUMANITIES

General
Interpretation and translation
Writing (authorship)
Native language and literature
Modern languages and literatures
  English
  French
  Spanish
  Germanic languages
  German
  Swedish
  Danish
  Norwegian
  Italian
  Portuguese
  Romance languages
  Modern Greek
  Dutch
  Baltic languages
  Celtic languages
  Finnish
  Russian
  Slavonic languages (others)
  Hungarian
  Fino Ugrian languages
  European languages (others)

Altaic languages
Arabic
Hebrew
Chinese
Korean
Japanese
Indian languages
Iranic languages
African Languages
Amerindian languages
Austronesian and oceanic languages
Classical languages and literatures
  Latin
  Classical Greek
  Sanskrit
Linguistics and philology
  Applied linguistics
  Psycholinguistics
  Grammar
  Semantics and terminology
  Phonetics
  Logopedics
Comparative literature
History
  Prehistory
  Ancient civilisations
  Medieval history
  Modern history
  Contemporary history
Archaeology
Philosophy
  Philosophical schools
  Metaphysics
  Logic
  Ethics

BUSINESS ADMINISTRATION AND MANAGEMENT

General
Business studies
International business
Secretarial studies
Business machine operation
Business computing
Management systems and techniques
Accountancy
Real estate
Marketing and sales management
Insurance management
Finance, banking and investment
Personnel management
Labour/industrial relations
Public administration
Institutional administration
MBA

EDUCATION AND TEACHER TRAINING

General
Nonvocational subjects education
  Education in native language
  Foreign languages education
  Mathematics education
  Science education
  Humanities and social science education
  Physical education
  Literacy education

Vocational subjects education
  Agricultural education
  Art education
  Commerce/business education
  Computer education
  Technology education
  Health education
  Home economics education
  Industrial arts education
  Music education
Pre-school education
Primary education
Secondary education
Adult education
Special education
  Education of the gifted
  Education of the handicapped
  Education of specific learning disabilities
  Education of foreigners
  Education of natives
  Education of the socially disadvantaged
  Bilingual/bicultural education
Teacher trainers education
Higher education teacher training
Educational science
  International and comparative education
  Philosophy of education
  Curriculum
  Teaching and learning
  Educational research
  Educational technology
  Educational and student counselling
  Educational administration
  Educational testing and evaluation
  Distance education

ENGINEERING

General
Surveying and mapping science
Engineering drawing/design
Chemical engineering
Civil, construction and transportation engineering
Environmental and Sanitary Engineering
Safety engineering
Electrical/electronic and telecommunications engineering
Computer engineering
Industrial and management engineering
Metallurgical engineering
Production engineering
Materials engineering
Mining and minerals engineering
Petroleum engineering
Energy engineering
Nuclear engineering
Mechanical/electromechanical engineering
Hydraulic/pneumatic engineering
Sound engineering
Automotive engineering
Measurement/precision engineering

Control engineering (robotics)
Aeronautical and aerospace engineering
Marine engineering and naval architecture
Agricultural engineering
Forestry engineering
Bioengineering and biomedical engineering

FINE AND APPLIED ARTS

General
History and Philosophy of Art
  Aesthetics
Art management
Drawing and painting
Sculpture
Handicrafts
Music
  Musicology
  Music theory and composition
  Conducting
  Singing
  Musical instruments (performance)
  Religious music
  Jazz and popular music
  Opera
Drama
Dancing
Photography
Cinema and television
Design
  Interior design
  Furniture design
  Fashion design
  Textile design
  Graphic design
  Industrial design
  Display and stage design

HOME ECONOMICS

General
Household management
Clothing and sewing
Nutrition
Child care/child development
House arts and environment

LAW

General
History of law
Comparative law
International law
Human rights
Labour law
Maritime law
Law of the air
Notary studies
Civil law
Commercial law
Public law
  Constitutional law
  Administrative law
  Fiscal law
Criminal law
Canon law
Islamic law
European community law

MASS COMMUNICATION AND INFORMATION SCIENCE

General
Journalism
Radio/television broadcasting
Public relations and publicity
Mass communication
Media studies
Communications skills
Library science
Museum studies and conservation
Museum management
Restoration of works of art
Documentation techniques and archiving

MATHEMATICS AND COMPUTER SCIENCE

General
Statistics
Actuarial science
Applied mathematics
Computer science
Artificial intelligence
Systems analysis

MEDICAL SCIENCES

General
Public health and hygiene
  Social/preventive medicine
  Dietetics
  Sports medicine
Health administration
Medicine and surgery
  Anaesthesiology
  Cardiology
  Dermatology
  Endocrinology
  Epidemiology
  Gastroenterology
  Geriatrics
  Gynaecology and obstetrics
  Haematology
  Hepathology
  Nephrology
  Neurology
  Oncology
  Ophthalmology
  Otorhinolaryngology
  Parasitology
  Pathology
  Paediatrics
  Plastic surgery
  Pneumology
  Psychiatry and mental health
  Rheumatology
  Urology
  Virology
  Tropical medicine
  Venereology
Rehabilitation medicine and therapy
Nursing
Medical auxiliaries
Midwifery
Radiology
Treatment techniques
Medical technology
Dentistry and stomatology
  Oral pathology
  Orthodontics
  Periodontics
  Community dentistry
Dental technology
  Prosthetic dentistry
Pharmacy
Biomedicine
Optometry
Podiatry
Forensic medicine and dentistry
Acupuncture
Homeopathy
Chiropractic
Osteopathy
Traditional eastern medicine

NATURAL SCIENCES

General
Biological and life sciences
  Anatomy
  Biochemistry
  Biology
  Histology
  Biophysics and molecular biology
  Biotechnology
  Botany
  Plant pathology
  Embryology and reproduction biology
  Genetics
  Immunology
  Marine biology
  Limnology
  Microbiology
  Neurosciences
  Parasitology
  Pharmacology
  Physiology
  Toxicology
  Zoology
Chemistry
  Analytical chemistry
  Inorganic chemistry
  Organic chemistry
  Physical chemistry
Earth and geological sciences
  Geochemistry
  Geography (Scientific)
  Geology
  Mineralogy and crystallography
  Petrology
  Geophysics and seismology
  Palaeontology
Physics
  Atomic and molecular physics
  Nuclear physics
  Optics
  Solid state physics
  Thermal physics
Astronomy and astrophysics
Atmosphere science/ meteorology
  Arctic studies
  Arid land studies
Oceanography

RECREATION, WELFARE, PROTECTIVE SERVICES

General
Police and law enforcement
Criminology
Fire protection/control
Military science
Civil security
Peace and disarmament
Social welfare and social work
  Public and community services
Vocational counselling
Environmental studies
  Ecology
  Natural resources
  Environmental management
  Wildlife and pest management
Physical education and sports
  Sports management
  Sociology of sports
Leisure studies
Parks and recreation

RELIGION AND THEOLOGY

General
Religious studies
  Christian
  Jewish
  Islam
  Asian religious studies
  Agnosticism and Atheism
  Ancient religions
Religious education
Holy writings
Religious practice
Church administration (pastoral work)
Theological studies
Comparative religion
Sociology of religion
History of religion
Esoteric practices

SERVICE TRADES

General
Hotel and restaurant
Hotel management
Cooking and catering
Retailing
Tourism

SOCIAL AND BEHAVIOURAL SCIENCES

General
  Economics
  Economic history
  Economic and finance policy
  Taxation
  Econometrics
  Industrial and production economics
Political science and government
  Comparative politics
International relations
Sociology
  History of societies
  Comparative sociology
  Social policy
  Social institutions
  Social communication problems
  Futurology
Demography
Anthropology
  Ethnology
  Folklore
Women's studies
Urban Studies
Rural studies
Cognitive sciences
Psychology
  Experimental psychology
  Social and community psychology
  Clinical psychology
  Personality psychology
  Industrial/organisational psychology
  Psychometrics
  Educational psychology
Geography (social and economic)
Development studies
Area and cultural studies
  North African
  Subsahara African
  African studies
  African American
  Native American
  Hispanic American
  American
  Canadian
  Asian
  South Asian
  East Asian
  Southeast Asian
  European (EC)
  Eastern European
  Western European
  Nordic
  Caribbean
  Latin American
  Pacific area
  Aboriginal
  Middle Eastern
  Islamic
  Jewish
Preservation of cultural heritage
Ancient civilisations (Egyptology, Assyriology)

TRADE, CRAFT AND INDUSTRIAL TECHNIQUES

General
Food processing techniques
Building trades
Electrical/electronic equipment and maintenance techniques
Metal trades techniques
Mechanical equipment and maintenance techniques
Wood technology
Heating, air conditioning and refrigeration technology
Leather techniques
Textile techniques
Paper and packaging technology
Graphic arts techniques
  Printing
  Publishing and book trade
Laboratory techniques
Optical technology

TRANSPORT AND COMMUNICATIONS

General
Air transport
Marine transport and nautical science
Railway transport
Road transport
Transport management
Transport economics
Postal services
Telecommunications services

ANY SUBJECT

Any Country

African Nations

Australia

British Commonwealth

Canada

Caribbean Countries

East European Countries

Far East

Indian Sub-Continent

Middle East

New Zealand

United States of America

West European Countries

AGRICULTURE, FORESTRY AND FISHERY

GENERAL

Any Country

African Nations

Australia

British Commonwealth

Canada

Caribbean Countries

East European Countries

Far East

Indian Sub-Continent

AGRONOMY

Middle East

Hubert H Humphrey Fellowship Programme, 609

New Zealand

Wingate Scholarships, 704

South Africa

Hubert H Humphrey Fellowship Programme, 609
Wingate Scholarships, 704

South America

Hubert H Humphrey Fellowship Programme, 609

United Kingdom

Mr and Mrs David Edward Memorial Award, 681
Sir William Roberts Scholarship, 681
Swiss Federal Institute of Technology Scholarships, 598
UWB Departmental Research Studentships, 681
UWB Research Studentships, 681
Wingate Scholarships, 704

United States of America

Swiss Federal Institute of Technology Scholarships, 598

West European Countries

Mr and Mrs David Edward Memorial Award, 681
Sir William Roberts Scholarship, 681
UWB Departmental Research Studentships, 681
UWB Research Studentships, 681
Wingate Scholarships, 704

ANIMAL HUSBANDRY AND ANIMAL PRODUCTION

Any Country

CATIE Scholarships, 605
CQU Postgraduate Research Award, 224
John Hervey, Broadcasters and Smallsreed Awards, 613
Massey Doctoral Scholarship, 408
Perry Postgraduate Scholarships, 490
Perry Postgraduate Scholarships and Research Awards, 491
Teagasc Walsh Fellowships, 599
UFAW Animal Welfare Research Training Scholarships, 616
UFAW Research and Project Awards, 616
UFAW Small Project and Travel Awards, 616
UFAW Vacation Scholarships, 616
University of Bristol Postgraduate Scholarships, 619
University of Stirling Research Studentships, 678

African Nations

Hubert H Humphrey Fellowship Programme, 609
Joint Japan/World Bank Graduate Scholarship Program (JJ/WBGSP), 355

Australia

University of Western Sydney Postgraduate Research Award (UW-SPRA), 689
Wingate Scholarships, 704

British Commonwealth

Joint Japan/World Bank Graduate Scholarship Program (JJ/WBGSP), 355
Wingate Scholarships, 704

Canada

Canadian Window on International Development, 358
IDRC Doctoral Research Awards, 358
Wingate Scholarships, 704

Caribbean Countries

Hubert H Humphrey Fellowship Programme, 609
Joint Japan/World Bank Graduate Scholarship Program (JJ/WBGSP), 355

East European Countries

Hubert H Humphrey Fellowship Programme, 609
Joint Japan/World Bank Graduate Scholarship Program (JJ/WBGSP), 355

Far East

Hubert H Humphrey Fellowship Programme, 609
Joint Japan/World Bank Graduate Scholarship Program (JJ/WBGSP), 355
Swiss Federal Institute of Technology Scholarships, 598

Indian Sub-Continent

Hubert H Humphrey Fellowship Programme, 609
Joint Japan/World Bank Graduate Scholarship Program (JJ/WBGSP), 355
Sir William Roberts Scholarship, 681
Wingate Scholarships, 704

Middle East

Hubert H Humphrey Fellowship Programme, 609
Joint Japan/World Bank Graduate Scholarship Program (JJ/WBGSP), 355

New Zealand

University of Western Sydney Postgraduate Research Award (UW-SPRA), 689
Vernon Willey Trust Awards, 694
Wingate Scholarships, 704

South Africa

Hubert H Humphrey Fellowship Programme, 609
Joint Japan/World Bank Graduate Scholarship Program (JJ/WBGSP), 355
Wingate Scholarships, 704

South America

Hubert H Humphrey Fellowship Programme, 609
Joint Japan/World Bank Graduate Scholarship Program (JJ/WBGSP), 355

United Kingdom

Linacre College A J Hosier Studentship, 655
Mr and Mrs David Edward Memorial Award, 681
Sir William Roberts Scholarship, 681
Swiss Federal Institute of Technology Scholarships, 598
University of Wales (Aberystwyth) Postgraduate Research Studentships, 680
UWB Departmental Research Studentships, 681
UWB Research Studentships, 681
Wingate Scholarships, 704

United States of America

Swiss Federal Institute of Technology Scholarships, 598

West European Countries

Mr and Mrs David Edward Memorial Award, 681
Sir William Roberts Scholarship, 681
UWB Departmental Research Studentships, 681
UWB Research Studentships, 681
Wingate Scholarships, 704

SERICULTURE

Any Country

Perry Postgraduate Scholarships, 490
Perry Postgraduate Scholarships and Research Awards, 491

Australia

Wingate Scholarships, 704

British Commonwealth

Wingate Scholarships, 704

Canada

IDRC Doctoral Research Awards, 358
Wingate Scholarships, 704

Indian Sub-Continent

Wingate Scholarships, 704

New Zealand

Wingate Scholarships, 704

South Africa

Wingate Scholarships, 704

United Kingdom

Wingate Scholarships, 704

West European Countries

Wingate Scholarships, 704

HORTICULTURE AND VITICULTURE

Any Country

Blaxall Valentine Trust Award, 536
CDU Senior Research Fellowship, 230
CDU Three Year Postdoctoral Fellowship, 230
CQU Postgraduate Research Award, 224
FIRST Scholarship Program, 281
Herb Society of America Research Grant, 323
Massey Doctoral Scholarship, 408
Perry Postgraduate Scholarships, 490
Perry Postgraduate Scholarships and Research Awards, 491
Queen Elizabeth the Queen Mother Bursary, 537
RHS Financial Award, 537
Stanley Smith (UK) Horticultural Trust Awards, 594
Teagasc Walsh Fellowships, 599

African Nations

Hubert H Humphrey Fellowship Programme, 609
Joint Japan/World Bank Graduate Scholarship Program (JJ/WBGSP), 355

Australia

University of Western Sydney Postgraduate Research Award (UW-SPRA), 689
Wingate Scholarships, 704

British Commonwealth

Joint Japan/World Bank Graduate Scholarship Program (JJ/WBGSP), 355
Wingate Scholarships, 704

Canada

Canadian Window on International Development, 358
Horticultural Research Institute Grants, 327
IDRC Doctoral Research Awards, 358
Wingate Scholarships, 704

Caribbean Countries

Hubert H Humphrey Fellowship Programme, 609
Joint Japan/World Bank Graduate Scholarship Program (JJ/WBGSP), 355

East European Countries

Hubert H Humphrey Fellowship Programme, 609
Joint Japan/World Bank Graduate Scholarship Program (JJ/WBGSP), 355

Far East

Hubert H Humphrey Fellowship Programme, 609
Joint Japan/World Bank Graduate Scholarship Program (JJ/WBGSP), 355
Osaka Travel Award, 537

Indian Sub-Continent

Hubert H Humphrey Fellowship Programme, 609
Joint Japan/World Bank Graduate Scholarship Program (JJ/WBGSP), 355
Sir William Roberts Scholarship, 681
Wingate Scholarships, 704

Middle East

Hubert H Humphrey Fellowship Programme, 609
Joint Japan/World Bank Graduate Scholarship Program (JJ/WBGSP), 355

New Zealand

University of Western Sydney Postgraduate Research Award (UW-SPRA), 689
Wingate Scholarships, 704

South Africa

Hubert H Humphrey Fellowship Programme, 609
Joint Japan/World Bank Graduate Scholarship Program (JJ/WBGSP), 355
Wingate Scholarships, 704

South America

Hubert H Humphrey Fellowship Programme, 609
Joint Japan/World Bank Graduate Scholarship Program (JJ/WBGSP), 355

United Kingdom

Coke Trust Award, 536
Jerusalem Botanical Gardens Scholarship, 292
Martin McLaren Horticultural Scholarship, 344
Osaka Travel Award, 537
Sir William Roberts Scholarship, 681
Wingate Scholarships, 704

United States of America

Horticultural Research Institute Grants, 327

West European Countries

Sir William Roberts Scholarship, 681
Wingate Scholarships, 704

CROP HUSBANDRY AND CROP PRODUCTION

Any Country

CQU Postgraduate Research Award, 224
Massey Doctoral Scholarship, 408
Perry Postgraduate Scholarships, 490
Perry Postgraduate Scholarships and Research Awards, 491
Teagasc Walsh Fellowships, 599
University of Bristol Postgraduate Scholarships, 619

African Nations

Hubert H Humphrey Fellowship Programme, 609
Joint Japan/World Bank Graduate Scholarship Program (JJ/WBGSP), 355

Use of Fertility Enhancing Food, Forage and Cover Crops in Sustainably Managed Agroecosystems: The Bentley Fellowship, 358
Wingate Scholarships, 704

South America

Hubert H Humphrey Fellowship Programme, 609
Joint Japan/World Bank Graduate Scholarship Program (JJ/WBGSP), 355
Use of Fertility Enhancing Food, Forage and Cover Crops in Sustainably Managed Agroecosystems: The Bentley Fellowship, 358

United Kingdom

Linacre College A J Hosier Studentship, 655
Sir William Roberts Scholarship, 681
University of Wales (Aberystwyth) Postgraduate Research Studentships, 680
UWB Research Studentships, 681
Wingate Scholarships, 704

United States of America

Appraisal Institute Education Trust Scholarship, 91
Fulbright Senior Specialists Program, 245
Horticultural Research Institute Grants, 327

West European Countries

Sir William Roberts Scholarship, 681
UWB Research Studentships, 681
Wingate Scholarships, 704

FOOD SCIENCE AND PRODUCTION

Any Country

AIATSIS Research Grants, 116
BBSRC Research Grants, 129
Massey Doctoral Scholarship, 408
Perry Postgraduate Scholarships, 490
Perry Postgraduate Scholarships and Research Awards, 491
Teagasc Walsh Fellowships, 599
University of Bristol Postgraduate Scholarships, 619

African Nations

Ecosystem Approaches to Human Health Awards, 358
Hubert H Humphrey Fellowship Programme, 609
International Postgraduate Research Scholarships (IPRS), 676
Joint Japan/World Bank Graduate Scholarship Program (JJ/WBGSP), 355

Australia

University of Western Sydney Postgraduate Research Award (UW-SPRA), 689
Wingate Scholarships, 704

British Commonwealth

International Postgraduate Research Scholarships (IPRS), 676
Joint Japan/World Bank Graduate Scholarship Program (JJ/WBGSP), 355
Wingate Scholarships, 704

Canada

Ecosystem Approaches to Human Health Awards, 358
IDRC Doctoral Research Awards, 358
International Postgraduate Research Scholarships (IPRS), 676
Wingate Scholarships, 704

Caribbean Countries

Ecosystem Approaches to Human Health Awards, 358
Hubert H Humphrey Fellowship Programme, 609

International Postgraduate Research Scholarships (IPRS), 676
Joint Japan/World Bank Graduate Scholarship Program (JJ/WBGSP), 355

East European Countries

FEMS Fellowship, 280
Hubert H Humphrey Fellowship Programme, 609
International Postgraduate Research Scholarships (IPRS), 676
Joint Japan/World Bank Graduate Scholarship Program (JJ/WBGSP), 355

Far East

Ecosystem Approaches to Human Health Awards, 358
Hubert H Humphrey Fellowship Programme, 609
International Postgraduate Research Scholarships (IPRS), 676
Joint Japan/World Bank Graduate Scholarship Program (JJ/WBGSP), 355
Swiss Federal Institute of Technology Scholarships, 598

Indian Sub-Continent

Ecosystem Approaches to Human Health Awards, 358
Hubert H Humphrey Fellowship Programme, 609
International Postgraduate Research Scholarships (IPRS), 676
Joint Japan/World Bank Graduate Scholarship Program (JJ/WBGSP), 355
Sir William Roberts Scholarship, 681
Wingate Scholarships, 704

Middle East

Ecosystem Approaches to Human Health Awards, 358
Hubert H Humphrey Fellowship Programme, 609
International Postgraduate Research Scholarships (IPRS), 676
Joint Japan/World Bank Graduate Scholarship Program (JJ/WBGSP), 355

New Zealand

University of Western Sydney Postgraduate Research Award (UW-SPRA), 689
Wingate Scholarships, 704

South Africa

Ecosystem Approaches to Human Health Awards, 358
Hubert H Humphrey Fellowship Programme, 609
International Postgraduate Research Scholarships (IPRS), 676
Joint Japan/World Bank Graduate Scholarship Program (JJ/WBGSP), 355
Wingate Scholarships, 704

South America

Hubert H Humphrey Fellowship Programme, 609
International Postgraduate Research Scholarships (IPRS), 676
Joint Japan/World Bank Graduate Scholarship Program (JJ/WBGSP), 355

United Kingdom

FEMS Fellowship, 280
International Postgraduate Research Scholarships (IPRS), 676
Sir William Roberts Scholarship, 681
Swiss Federal Institute of Technology Scholarships, 598
Wingate Scholarships, 704

United States of America

International Postgraduate Research Scholarships (IPRS), 676
Swiss Federal Institute of Technology Scholarships, 598

West European Countries

FEMS Fellowship, 280
International Postgraduate Research Scholarships (IPRS), 676

Sir William Roberts Scholarship, 681
Wingate Scholarships, 704

MEAT AND POULTRY

Any Country

Perry Postgraduate Scholarships, 490
Perry Postgraduate Scholarships and Research Awards, 491
Teagasc Walsh Fellowships, 599

African Nations

Joint Japan/World Bank Graduate Scholarship Program (JJ/WBGSP), 355

Australia

University of Western Sydney Postgraduate Research Award (UW-SPRA), 689
Wingate Scholarships, 704

British Commonwealth

Joint Japan/World Bank Graduate Scholarship Program (JJ/WBGSP), 355
Wingate Scholarships, 704

Canada

Wingate Scholarships, 704

Caribbean Countries

Joint Japan/World Bank Graduate Scholarship Program (JJ/WBGSP), 355

East European Countries

Joint Japan/World Bank Graduate Scholarship Program (JJ/WBGSP), 355

Far East

Joint Japan/World Bank Graduate Scholarship Program (JJ/WBGSP), 355

Indian Sub-Continent

Joint Japan/World Bank Graduate Scholarship Program (JJ/WBGSP), 355
Wingate Scholarships, 704

Middle East

Joint Japan/World Bank Graduate Scholarship Program (JJ/WBGSP), 355

New Zealand

University of Western Sydney Postgraduate Research Award (UW-SPRA), 689
Vernon Willey Trust Awards, 694
Wingate Scholarships, 704

South Africa

Joint Japan/World Bank Graduate Scholarship Program (JJ/WBGSP), 355
Wingate Scholarships, 704

South America

Joint Japan/World Bank Graduate Scholarship Program (JJ/WBGSP), 355

United Kingdom

Wingate Scholarships, 704

West European Countries

Wingate Scholarships, 704

DAIRY

Any Country

Massey Doctoral Scholarship, 408
Perry Postgraduate Scholarships, 490
Perry Postgraduate Scholarships and Research Awards, 491
Teagasc Walsh Fellowships, 599

African Nations

Joint Japan/World Bank Graduate Scholarship Program (JJ/WBGSP), 355

Australia

University of Western Sydney Postgraduate Research Award (UW-SPRA), 689
Wingate Scholarships, 704

British Commonwealth

Joint Japan/World Bank Graduate Scholarship Program (JJ/WBGSP), 355
Wingate Scholarships, 704

Canada

Wingate Scholarships, 704

Caribbean Countries

Joint Japan/World Bank Graduate Scholarship Program (JJ/WBGSP), 355

East European Countries

Joint Japan/World Bank Graduate Scholarship Program (JJ/WBGSP), 355

Far East

Joint Japan/World Bank Graduate Scholarship Program (JJ/WBGSP), 355

Indian Sub-Continent

Joint Japan/World Bank Graduate Scholarship Program (JJ/WBGSP), 355
Wingate Scholarships, 704

Middle East

Joint Japan/World Bank Graduate Scholarship Program (JJ/WBGSP), 355

New Zealand

University of Western Sydney Postgraduate Research Award (UW-SPRA), 689
Wingate Scholarships, 704

South Africa

Joint Japan/World Bank Graduate Scholarship Program (JJ/WBGSP), 355
Wingate Scholarships, 704

South America

Joint Japan/World Bank Graduate Scholarship Program (JJ/WBGSP), 355

United Kingdom

Wingate Scholarships, 704

West European Countries

Wingate Scholarships, 704

FISH

Any Country
Woods Hole Oceanographic Institution Research Fellowships in Marine Policy, 710

African Nations
Joint Japan/World Bank Graduate Scholarship Program (JJ/WBGSP), 355

Australia
University of Western Sydney Postgraduate Research Award (UW-SPRA), 689
Wingate Scholarships, 704

British Commonwealth
Joint Japan/World Bank Graduate Scholarship Program (JJ/WBGSP), 355
Wingate Scholarships, 704

Canada
Olin Fellowship, 113
Wingate Scholarships, 704

Caribbean Countries
Joint Japan/World Bank Graduate Scholarship Program (JJ/WBGSP), 355

East European Countries
Joint Japan/World Bank Graduate Scholarship Program (JJ/WBGSP), 355

Far East
Joint Japan/World Bank Graduate Scholarship Program (JJ/WBGSP), 355

Indian Sub-Continent
Joint Japan/World Bank Graduate Scholarship Program (JJ/WBGSP), 355
Wingate Scholarships, 704

Middle East
Joint Japan/World Bank Graduate Scholarship Program (JJ/WBGSP), 355

New Zealand
University of Western Sydney Postgraduate Research Award (UW-SPRA), 689
Wingate Scholarships, 704

South Africa
Joint Japan/World Bank Graduate Scholarship Program (JJ/WBGSP), 355
Wingate Scholarships, 704

South America
Joint Japan/World Bank Graduate Scholarship Program (JJ/WBGSP), 355

United Kingdom
Wingate Scholarships, 704

United States of America
Olin Fellowship, 113

West European Countries
Wingate Scholarships, 704

OENOLOGY

Australia
Wingate Scholarships, 704

British Commonwealth
Wingate Scholarships, 704

Canada
Wingate Scholarships, 704

Indian Sub-Continent
Wingate Scholarships, 704

New Zealand
Wingate Scholarships, 704

South Africa
Wingate Scholarships, 704

United Kingdom
Wingate Scholarships, 704

West European Countries
Wingate Scholarships, 704

BREWING

Australia
Wingate Scholarships, 704

British Commonwealth
Wingate Scholarships, 704

Canada
Wingate Scholarships, 704

Indian Sub-Continent
Wingate Scholarships, 704

New Zealand
Wingate Scholarships, 704

South Africa
Wingate Scholarships, 704

United Kingdom
Wingate Scholarships, 704

West European Countries
Wingate Scholarships, 704

HARVEST TECHNOLOGY

Any Country
Perry Postgraduate Scholarships, 490
Perry Postgraduate Scholarships and Research Awards, 491

African Nations
Joint Japan/World Bank Graduate Scholarship Program (JJ/WBGSP), 355

Australia
Wingate Scholarships, 704

WATER MANAGEMENT

New Zealand

University of Western Sydney Postgraduate Research Award (UW-SPRA), 689
Wingate Scholarships, 704

South Africa

International Postgraduate Research Scholarships (IPRS), 676
Joint Japan/World Bank Graduate Scholarship Program (JJ/WBGSP), 355
Wingate Scholarships, 704

South America

Austrian Academy of Sciences Postgraduate Course in Limnology, 121
International Postgraduate Research Scholarships (IPRS), 676
Joint Japan/World Bank Graduate Scholarship Program (JJ/WBGSP), 355

United Kingdom

Hallam Studentships, 558
International Postgraduate Research Scholarships (IPRS), 676
Mr and Mrs David Edward Memorial Award, 681
Silsoe Awards, 249
UWB Departmental Research Studentships, 681
UWB Research Studentships, 681
Wingate Scholarships, 704

United States of America

Earthwatch Education Awards, 264
Horticultural Research Institute Grants, 327
International Postgraduate Research Scholarships (IPRS), 676
Olin Fellowship, 113

West European Countries

Hallam Studentships, 558
International Postgraduate Research Scholarships (IPRS), 676
Mr and Mrs David Edward Memorial Award, 681
Silsoe Awards, 249
UWB Departmental Research Studentships, 681
UWB Research Studentships, 681
Wingate Scholarships, 704

SOIL CONSERVATION

Any Country

BBSRC Research Grants, 129
CATIE Scholarships, 605
CDU Three Year Postdoctoral Fellowship, 230
DEED (Demonstration of Energy-Efficient Developments) Scholarship, 69
Kenneth E Grant Research Scholarship, 589
Massey Doctoral Scholarship, 408
Mott MacDonald Charitable Trust Scholarships, 426
Perry Postgraduate Scholarships, 490
Perry Postgraduate Scholarships and Research Awards, 491
University of Stirling Research Studentships, 678

African Nations

International Postgraduate Research Scholarships (IPRS), 676
Postgraduate Studies in Physical Land Resources Scholarship, 356
Use of Fertility Enhancing Food, Forage and Cover Crops in Sustainably Managed Agroecosystems: The Bentley Fellowship, 358

Australia

Wingate Scholarships, 704

British Commonwealth

International Postgraduate Research Scholarships (IPRS), 676
Postgraduate Studies in Physical Land Resources Scholarship, 356

Wingate Scholarships, 704

Canada

Canadian Window on International Development, 358
International Postgraduate Research Scholarships (IPRS), 676
Use of Fertility Enhancing Food, Forage and Cover Crops in Sustainably Managed Agroecosystems: The Bentley Fellowship, 358
Wingate Scholarships, 704

Caribbean Countries

International Postgraduate Research Scholarships (IPRS), 676
Postgraduate Studies in Physical Land Resources Scholarship, 356
Use of Fertility Enhancing Food, Forage and Cover Crops in Sustainably Managed Agroecosystems: The Bentley Fellowship, 358

East European Countries

International Postgraduate Research Scholarships (IPRS), 676
Natural History Museum Sys-Resource, 461

Far East

International Postgraduate Research Scholarships (IPRS), 676
Postgraduate Studies in Physical Land Resources Scholarship, 356
Use of Fertility Enhancing Food, Forage and Cover Crops in Sustainably Managed Agroecosystems: The Bentley Fellowship, 358

Indian Sub-Continent

International Postgraduate Research Scholarships (IPRS), 676
Postgraduate Studies in Physical Land Resources Scholarship, 356
Use of Fertility Enhancing Food, Forage and Cover Crops in Sustainably Managed Agroecosystems: The Bentley Fellowship, 358
Wingate Scholarships, 704

Middle East

International Postgraduate Research Scholarships (IPRS), 676
Postgraduate Studies in Physical Land Resources Scholarship, 356
Use of Fertility Enhancing Food, Forage and Cover Crops in Sustainably Managed Agroecosystems: The Bentley Fellowship, 358

New Zealand

Wingate Scholarships, 704

South Africa

International Postgraduate Research Scholarships (IPRS), 676
Postgraduate Studies in Physical Land Resources Scholarship, 356
Use of Fertility Enhancing Food, Forage and Cover Crops in Sustainably Managed Agroecosystems: The Bentley Fellowship, 358
Wingate Scholarships, 704

South America

International Postgraduate Research Scholarships (IPRS), 676
Postgraduate Studies in Physical Land Resources Scholarship, 356
Use of Fertility Enhancing Food, Forage and Cover Crops in Sustainably Managed Agroecosystems: The Bentley Fellowship, 358

United Kingdom

Hallam Studentships, 558
International Postgraduate Research Scholarships (IPRS), 676
Mr and Mrs David Edward Memorial Award, 681
Silsoe Awards, 249
University of Wales (Aberystwyth) Postgraduate Research Studentships, 680
UWB Departmental Research Studentships, 681
UWB Research Studentships, 681
Wingate Scholarships, 704

United States of America

Earthwatch Education Awards, 264
International Postgraduate Research Scholarships (IPRS), 676

West European Countries

Hallam Studentships, 558
International Postgraduate Research Scholarships (IPRS), 676
Mr and Mrs David Edward Memorial Award, 681
Natural History Museum Sys-Resource, 461
Silsoe Awards, 249
UWB Departmental Research Studentships, 681
UWB Research Studentships, 681
Wingate Scholarships, 704

VETERINARY MEDICINE

Any Country

CIHR Fellowships Program, 208
Horserace Betting Levy Board Senior Equine Clinical Scholarships, 326
Horserace Betting Levy Board Veterinary Research Training Scholarship, 326
James Houston Scholarship, 634
James M Harris/Sarah W Sweatt Student Travel Grant, 254
John Crawford Scholarship, 634
Massey Doctoral Scholarship, 408
Perry Postgraduate Scholarships, 490
Perry Postgraduate Scholarships and Research Awards, 491
Sir Richard Stapley Educational Trust Grants, 564
UFAW Animal Welfare Research Training Scholarships, 616
UFAW Research and Project Awards, 616
UFAW Small Project and Travel Awards, 616
UFAW Vacation Scholarships, 616
University of Bristol Postgraduate Scholarships, 619
University of Glasgow Postgraduate Research Scholarships, 634
Wellcome Trust Awards, Fellowships and Studentships, 701

African Nations

Hubert H Humphrey Fellowship Programme, 609
Joint Japan/World Bank Graduate Scholarship Program (JJ/WBGSP), 355

Australia

Wingate Scholarships, 704

British Commonwealth

Joint Japan/World Bank Graduate Scholarship Program (JJ/WBGSP), 355
Wingate Scholarships, 704

Canada

Wingate Scholarships, 704

Caribbean Countries

Hubert H Humphrey Fellowship Programme, 609
Joint Japan/World Bank Graduate Scholarship Program (JJ/WBGSP), 355

East European Countries

FEMS Fellowship, 280
Hubert H Humphrey Fellowship Programme, 609
Joint Japan/World Bank Graduate Scholarship Program (JJ/WBGSP), 355

Far East

Hubert H Humphrey Fellowship Programme, 609
Joint Japan/World Bank Graduate Scholarship Program (JJ/WBGSP), 355

Indian Sub-Continent

Hubert H Humphrey Fellowship Programme, 609
Joint Japan/World Bank Graduate Scholarship Program (JJ/WBGSP), 355

Sir William Roberts Scholarship, 681
Wingate Scholarships, 704

Middle East

Hubert H Humphrey Fellowship Programme, 609
Joint Japan/World Bank Graduate Scholarship Program (JJ/WBGSP), 355

New Zealand

Wingate Scholarships, 704

South Africa

Hubert H Humphrey Fellowship Programme, 609
Joint Japan/World Bank Graduate Scholarship Program (JJ/WBGSP), 355
Wingate Scholarships, 704

South America

Hubert H Humphrey Fellowship Programme, 609
Joint Japan/World Bank Graduate Scholarship Program (JJ/WBGSP), 355

United Kingdom

FEMS Fellowship, 280
Harry Steele-Bodger Memorial Travelling Scholarship, 159
Mr and Mrs David Edward Memorial Award, 681
Petsavers Award, 492
Polish Government Postgraduate Scholarships Scheme, 501
Sir William Roberts Scholarship, 681
UWB Departmental Research Studentships, 681
Wingate Scholarships, 704

West European Countries

FEMS Fellowship, 280
Henry Dryerre Scholarship, 548
Karl-Enigk-Stipendium, 556
Mr and Mrs David Edward Memorial Award, 681
Sir William Roberts Scholarship, 681
UWB Departmental Research Studentships, 681
Wingate Scholarships, 704

TROPICAL/SUB-TROPICAL AGRICULTURE

Any Country

CATIE Scholarships, 605
CDU Senior Research Fellowship, 230
CDU Three Year Postdoctoral Fellowship, 230
CQU Postgraduate Research Award, 224
Earthwatch Field Research Grants, 264

African Nations

Hubert H Humphrey Fellowship Programme, 609
Joint Japan/World Bank Graduate Scholarship Program (JJ/WBGSP), 355
Postgraduate Studies in Physical Land Resources Scholarship, 356
TWNSO Grants to Institutions in the South for Joint Research Projects, 602
Use of Fertility Enhancing Food, Forage and Cover Crops in Sustainably Managed Agroecosystems: The Bentley Fellowship, 358

Australia

Wingate Scholarships, 704

British Commonwealth

Joint Japan/World Bank Graduate Scholarship Program (JJ/WBGSP), 355
Postgraduate Studies in Physical Land Resources Scholarship, 356
Wingate Scholarships, 704

Canada

Canadian Window on International Development, 358
IDRC Doctoral Research Awards, 358
Use of Fertility Enhancing Food, Forage and Cover Crops in Sustainably Managed Agroecosystems: The Bentley Fellowship, 358
Wingate Scholarships, 704

Caribbean Countries

Hubert H Humphrey Fellowship Programme, 609
Joint Japan/World Bank Graduate Scholarship Program (JJ/WBGSP), 355
Postgraduate Studies in Physical Land Resources Scholarship, 356
TWNSO Grants to Institutions in the South for Joint Research Projects, 602
Use of Fertility Enhancing Food, Forage and Cover Crops in Sustainably Managed Agroecosystems: The Bentley Fellowship, 358

East European Countries

Hubert H Humphrey Fellowship Programme, 609
Joint Japan/World Bank Graduate Scholarship Program (JJ/WBGSP), 355

Far East

Hubert H Humphrey Fellowship Programme, 609
Joint Japan/World Bank Graduate Scholarship Program (JJ/WBGSP), 355
Postgraduate Studies in Physical Land Resources Scholarship, 356
TWNSO Grants to Institutions in the South for Joint Research Projects, 602
Use of Fertility Enhancing Food, Forage and Cover Crops in Sustainably Managed Agroecosystems: The Bentley Fellowship, 358

Indian Sub-Continent

Hubert H Humphrey Fellowship Programme, 609
Joint Japan/World Bank Graduate Scholarship Program (JJ/WBGSP), 355
Postgraduate Studies in Physical Land Resources Scholarship, 356
Sir William Roberts Scholarship, 681
TWNSO Grants to Institutions in the South for Joint Research Projects, 602
Use of Fertility Enhancing Food, Forage and Cover Crops in Sustainably Managed Agroecosystems: The Bentley Fellowship, 358
Wingate Scholarships, 704

Middle East

Hubert H Humphrey Fellowship Programme, 609
Joint Japan/World Bank Graduate Scholarship Program (JJ/WBGSP), 355
Postgraduate Studies in Physical Land Resources Scholarship, 356
TWNSO Grants to Institutions in the South for Joint Research Projects, 602
Use of Fertility Enhancing Food, Forage and Cover Crops in Sustainably Managed Agroecosystems: The Bentley Fellowship, 358

New Zealand

Wingate Scholarships, 704

South Africa

Hubert H Humphrey Fellowship Programme, 609
Joint Japan/World Bank Graduate Scholarship Program (JJ/WBGSP), 355
Postgraduate Studies in Physical Land Resources Scholarship, 356
TWNSO Grants to Institutions in the South for Joint Research Projects, 602
Use of Fertility Enhancing Food, Forage and Cover Crops in Sustainably Managed Agroecosystems: The Bentley Fellowship, 358
Wingate Scholarships, 704

South America

Hubert H Humphrey Fellowship Programme, 609

Joint Japan/World Bank Graduate Scholarship Program (JJ/WBGSP), 355
Postgraduate Studies in Physical Land Resources Scholarship, 356
TWNSO Grants to Institutions in the South for Joint Research Projects, 602
Use of Fertility Enhancing Food, Forage and Cover Crops in Sustainably Managed Agroecosystems: The Bentley Fellowship, 358

United Kingdom

Mr and Mrs David Edward Memorial Award, 681
Sir William Roberts Scholarship, 681
UWB Departmental Research Studentships, 681
UWB Research Studentships, 681
Wingate Scholarships, 704

West European Countries

Mr and Mrs David Edward Memorial Award, 681
Sir William Roberts Scholarship, 681
UWB Departmental Research Studentships, 681
UWB Research Studentships, 681
Wingate Scholarships, 704

FORESTRY

Any Country

CATIE Scholarships, 605
Earthwatch Field Research Grants, 264
Edmund Niles Huyck Preserve, Inc. Graduate and Postgraduate Grants, 266
Gilbert F White Postdoctoral Fellowship, 515
Hyland R Johns Grant Program, 605
John Z Duling Grant Program, 605
Joseph L Fisher Dissertation Award, 515
Perry Postgraduate Scholarships and Research Awards, 491
St Cross College F C Osmaston Scholarship, 668
Teagasc Walsh Fellowships, 599
Trinity College Junior Research Fellowship, 672
University of Stirling Research Studentships, 678

African Nations

Hubert H Humphrey Fellowship Programme, 609
Joint Japan/World Bank Graduate Scholarship Program (JJ/WBGSP), 355
Use of Fertility Enhancing Food, Forage and Cover Crops in Sustainably Managed Agroecosystems: The Bentley Fellowship, 358

Australia

Wingate Scholarships, 704

British Commonwealth

Joint Japan/World Bank Graduate Scholarship Program (JJ/WBGSP), 355
Wingate Scholarships, 704

Canada

Canadian Forest Service Graduate Supplements, 575
Canadian Forestry Foundation Forest Capital of Canada Award, 204
Canadian Forestry Foundation Forest Education Scholarship, 204
Community Forestry: Trees and People - John G Bene Fellowship, 358
IDRC Doctoral Research Awards, 358
Use of Fertility Enhancing Food, Forage and Cover Crops in Sustainably Managed Agroecosystems: The Bentley Fellowship, 358
Wingate Scholarships, 704

Caribbean Countries

Hubert H Humphrey Fellowship Programme, 609
Joint Japan/World Bank Graduate Scholarship Program (JJ/WBGSP), 355

Use of Fertility Enhancing Food, Forage and Cover Crops in Sustainably Managed Agroecosystems: The Bentley Fellowship, 358

East European Countries

Hubert H Humphrey Fellowship Programme, 609
Joint Japan/World Bank Graduate Scholarship Program (JJ/WBGSP), 355

Far East

Hubert H Humphrey Fellowship Programme, 609
Joint Japan/World Bank Graduate Scholarship Program (JJ/WBGSP), 355
Swiss Federal Institute of Technology Scholarships, 598
Use of Fertility Enhancing Food, Forage and Cover Crops in Sustainably Managed Agroecosystems: The Bentley Fellowship, 358

Indian Sub-Continent

Hubert H Humphrey Fellowship Programme, 609
Joint Japan/World Bank Graduate Scholarship Program (JJ/WBGSP), 355
Sir William Roberts Scholarship, 681
Use of Fertility Enhancing Food, Forage and Cover Crops in Sustainably Managed Agroecosystems: The Bentley Fellowship, 358
Wingate Scholarships, 704

Middle East

Hubert H Humphrey Fellowship Programme, 609
Joint Japan/World Bank Graduate Scholarship Program (JJ/WBGSP), 355
Use of Fertility Enhancing Food, Forage and Cover Crops in Sustainably Managed Agroecosystems: The Bentley Fellowship, 358

New Zealand

Wingate Scholarships, 704

South Africa

Hubert H Humphrey Fellowship Programme, 609
Joint Japan/World Bank Graduate Scholarship Program (JJ/WBGSP), 355
Use of Fertility Enhancing Food, Forage and Cover Crops in Sustainably Managed Agroecosystems: The Bentley Fellowship, 358
Wingate Scholarships, 704

South America

Hubert H Humphrey Fellowship Programme, 609
Joint Japan/World Bank Graduate Scholarship Program (JJ/WBGSP), 355
Use of Fertility Enhancing Food, Forage and Cover Crops in Sustainably Managed Agroecosystems: The Bentley Fellowship, 358

United Kingdom

Mr and Mrs David Edward Memorial Award, 681
Silsoe Awards, 249
Sir William Roberts Scholarship, 681
Swiss Federal Institute of Technology Scholarships, 598
UWB Departmental Research Studentships, 681
UWB Research Studentships, 681
Wingate Scholarships, 704

United States of America

Earthwatch Education Awards, 264
Swiss Federal Institute of Technology Scholarships, 598

West European Countries

Mr and Mrs David Edward Memorial Award, 681
Silsoe Awards, 249
Sir William Roberts Scholarship, 681
UWB Departmental Research Studentships, 681
UWB Research Studentships, 681
Wingate Scholarships, 704

FOREST SOILS

Any Country

Edmund Niles Huyck Preserve, Inc. Graduate and Postgraduate Grants, 266

African Nations

Joint Japan/World Bank Graduate Scholarship Program (JJ/WBGSP), 355

Australia

Wingate Scholarships, 704

British Commonwealth

Joint Japan/World Bank Graduate Scholarship Program (JJ/WBGSP), 355
Wingate Scholarships, 704

Canada

Canadian Forest Service Graduate Supplements, 575
Wingate Scholarships, 704

Caribbean Countries

Joint Japan/World Bank Graduate Scholarship Program (JJ/WBGSP), 355

East European Countries

Joint Japan/World Bank Graduate Scholarship Program (JJ/WBGSP), 355
Natural History Museum Sys-Resource, 461

Far East

Joint Japan/World Bank Graduate Scholarship Program (JJ/WBGSP), 355

Indian Sub-Continent

Joint Japan/World Bank Graduate Scholarship Program (JJ/WBGSP), 355
Sir William Roberts Scholarship, 681
Wingate Scholarships, 704

Middle East

Joint Japan/World Bank Graduate Scholarship Program (JJ/WBGSP), 355

New Zealand

Wingate Scholarships, 704

South Africa

Joint Japan/World Bank Graduate Scholarship Program (JJ/WBGSP), 355
Wingate Scholarships, 704

South America

Joint Japan/World Bank Graduate Scholarship Program (JJ/WBGSP), 355

United Kingdom

Mr and Mrs David Edward Memorial Award, 681
Sir William Roberts Scholarship, 681
UWB Departmental Research Studentships, 681
UWB Research Studentships, 681
Wingate Scholarships, 704

United States of America

Earthwatch Education Awards, 264

West European Countries

Mr and Mrs David Edward Memorial Award, 681
Natural History Museum Sys-Resource, 461
Sir William Roberts Scholarship, 681
UWB Departmental Research Studentships, 681
UWB Research Studentships, 681
Wingate Scholarships, 704

FOREST BIOLOGY

Any Country

BP Conservation Programme Awards, 123
Edmund Niles Huyck Preserve, Inc. Graduate and Postgraduate Grants, 266
University of Stirling Research Studentships, 678

African Nations

Joint Japan/World Bank Graduate Scholarship Program (JJ/WBGSP), 355

Australia

Wingate Scholarships, 704

British Commonwealth

Joint Japan/World Bank Graduate Scholarship Program (JJ/WBGSP), 355
Wingate Scholarships, 704

Canada

Canadian Forest Service Graduate Supplements, 575
Wingate Scholarships, 704

Caribbean Countries

Joint Japan/World Bank Graduate Scholarship Program (JJ/WBGSP), 355

East European Countries

Joint Japan/World Bank Graduate Scholarship Program (JJ/WBGSP), 355
Natural History Museum Sys-Resource, 461

Far East

Joint Japan/World Bank Graduate Scholarship Program (JJ/WBGSP), 355

Indian Sub-Continent

Joint Japan/World Bank Graduate Scholarship Program (JJ/WBGSP), 355
Sir William Roberts Scholarship, 681
Wingate Scholarships, 704

Middle East

Joint Japan/World Bank Graduate Scholarship Program (JJ/WBGSP), 355

New Zealand

Wingate Scholarships, 704

South Africa

Joint Japan/World Bank Graduate Scholarship Program (JJ/WBGSP), 355
Wingate Scholarships, 704

South America

Joint Japan/World Bank Graduate Scholarship Program (JJ/WBGSP), 355

United Kingdom

Mr and Mrs David Edward Memorial Award, 681
Sir William Roberts Scholarship, 681
UWB Departmental Research Studentships, 681
UWB Research Studentships, 681
Wingate Scholarships, 704

United States of America

Earthwatch Education Awards, 264

West European Countries

Mr and Mrs David Edward Memorial Award, 681
Natural History Museum Sys-Resource, 461
Sir William Roberts Scholarship, 681
UWB Departmental Research Studentships, 681
UWB Research Studentships, 681
Wingate Scholarships, 704

FOREST PATHOLOGY

Any Country

Edmund Niles Huyck Preserve, Inc. Graduate and Postgraduate Grants, 266

African Nations

Joint Japan/World Bank Graduate Scholarship Program (JJ/WBGSP), 355

Australia

Wingate Scholarships, 704

British Commonwealth

Joint Japan/World Bank Graduate Scholarship Program (JJ/WBGSP), 355
Wingate Scholarships, 704

Canada

Canadian Forest Service Graduate Supplements, 575
Wingate Scholarships, 704

Caribbean Countries

Joint Japan/World Bank Graduate Scholarship Program (JJ/WBGSP), 355

East European Countries

Joint Japan/World Bank Graduate Scholarship Program (JJ/WBGSP), 355

Far East

Joint Japan/World Bank Graduate Scholarship Program (JJ/WBGSP), 355

Indian Sub-Continent

Joint Japan/World Bank Graduate Scholarship Program (JJ/WBGSP), 355
Sir William Roberts Scholarship, 681
Wingate Scholarships, 704

Middle East

Joint Japan/World Bank Graduate Scholarship Program (JJ/WBGSP), 355

New Zealand

Wingate Scholarships, 704

South Africa

Joint Japan/World Bank Graduate Scholarship Program (JJ/WBGSP), 355
Wingate Scholarships, 704

South America

Joint Japan/World Bank Graduate Scholarship Program (JJ/WBGSP), 355

United Kingdom

Mr and Mrs David Edward Memorial Award, 681
Sir William Roberts Scholarship, 681
UWB Departmental Research Studentships, 681
UWB Research Studentships, 681
Wingate Scholarships, 704

United States of America

Earthwatch Education Awards, 264

West European Countries

Mr and Mrs David Edward Memorial Award, 681
Sir William Roberts Scholarship, 681
UWB Departmental Research Studentships, 681
UWB Research Studentships, 681
Wingate Scholarships, 704

FOREST PRODUCTS

Any Country

Research Student Bursary, 163

African Nations

Joint Japan/World Bank Graduate Scholarship Program (JJ/WBGSP), 355

Australia

Wingate Scholarships, 704

British Commonwealth

Joint Japan/World Bank Graduate Scholarship Program (JJ/WBGSP), 355
Wingate Scholarships, 704

Canada

Canadian Forest Service Graduate Supplements, 575
Wingate Scholarships, 704

Caribbean Countries

Joint Japan/World Bank Graduate Scholarship Program (JJ/WBGSP), 355

East European Countries

Joint Japan/World Bank Graduate Scholarship Program (JJ/WBGSP), 355

Far East

Joint Japan/World Bank Graduate Scholarship Program (JJ/WBGSP), 355

Indian Sub-Continent

Joint Japan/World Bank Graduate Scholarship Program (JJ/WBGSP), 355
Sir William Roberts Scholarship, 681
Wingate Scholarships, 704

Middle East

Joint Japan/World Bank Graduate Scholarship Program (JJ/WBGSP), 355

New Zealand

Wingate Scholarships, 704

South Africa

Joint Japan/World Bank Graduate Scholarship Program (JJ/WBGSP), 355
Wingate Scholarships, 704

South America

Joint Japan/World Bank Graduate Scholarship Program (JJ/WBGSP), 355

United Kingdom

Mr and Mrs David Edward Memorial Award, 681
Sir William Roberts Scholarship, 681
UWB Departmental Research Studentships, 681
UWB Research Studentships, 681
Wingate Scholarships, 704

United States of America

Earthwatch Education Awards, 264

West European Countries

Mr and Mrs David Edward Memorial Award, 681
Sir William Roberts Scholarship, 681
UWB Departmental Research Studentships, 681
UWB Research Studentships, 681
Wingate Scholarships, 704

FOREST ECONOMICS

Any Country

CATIE Scholarships, 605

African Nations

Joint Japan/World Bank Graduate Scholarship Program (JJ/WBGSP), 355

Australia

Wingate Scholarships, 704

British Commonwealth

Joint Japan/World Bank Graduate Scholarship Program (JJ/WBGSP), 355
Wingate Scholarships, 704

Canada

Canadian Forest Service Graduate Supplements, 575
Wingate Scholarships, 704

Caribbean Countries

Joint Japan/World Bank Graduate Scholarship Program (JJ/WBGSP), 355

East European Countries

Joint Japan/World Bank Graduate Scholarship Program (JJ/WBGSP), 355

Far East

Joint Japan/World Bank Graduate Scholarship Program (JJ/WBGSP), 355

Indian Sub-Continent

Joint Japan/World Bank Graduate Scholarship Program (JJ/WBGSP), 355
Sir William Roberts Scholarship, 681
Wingate Scholarships, 704

FOREST MANAGEMENT

FISHERY

Canada

IDRC Doctoral Research Awards, 358
Olin Fellowship, 113
Wingate Scholarships, 704

Caribbean Countries

Hubert H Humphrey Fellowship Programme, 609
Joint Japan/World Bank Graduate Scholarship Program (JJ/WBGSP), 355

East European Countries

Hubert H Humphrey Fellowship Programme, 609
Joint Japan/World Bank Graduate Scholarship Program (JJ/WBGSP), 355

Far East

Austrian Academy of Sciences MSc Course in Limnology and Wetlands Ecosystems, 121
Austrian Academy of Sciences Postgraduate Course in Limnology, 121
Hubert H Humphrey Fellowship Programme, 609
Joint Japan/World Bank Graduate Scholarship Program (JJ/WBGSP), 355

Indian Sub-Continent

Austrian Academy of Sciences MSc Course in Limnology and Wetlands Ecosystems, 121
Austrian Academy of Sciences Postgraduate Course in Limnology, 121
Hubert H Humphrey Fellowship Programme, 609
Joint Japan/World Bank Graduate Scholarship Program (JJ/WBGSP), 355
Wingate Scholarships, 704

Middle East

Hubert H Humphrey Fellowship Programme, 609
Joint Japan/World Bank Graduate Scholarship Program (JJ/WBGSP), 355

New Zealand

Wingate Scholarships, 704

South Africa

Hubert H Humphrey Fellowship Programme, 609
Joint Japan/World Bank Graduate Scholarship Program (JJ/WBGSP), 355
Wingate Scholarships, 704

South America

Austrian Academy of Sciences MSc Course in Limnology and Wetlands Ecosystems, 121
Austrian Academy of Sciences Postgraduate Course in Limnology, 121
Hubert H Humphrey Fellowship Programme, 609
Joint Japan/World Bank Graduate Scholarship Program (JJ/WBGSP), 355

United Kingdom

Mr and Mrs David Edward Memorial Award, 681
UWB Departmental Research Studentships, 681
UWB Research Studentships, 681
Wingate Scholarships, 704

United States of America

Olin Fellowship, 113

West European Countries

Mr and Mrs David Edward Memorial Award, 681
UWB Departmental Research Studentships, 681
UWB Research Studentships, 681

Wingate Scholarships, 704

AQUACULTURE

Any Country

BBSRC Research Grants, 129
CDU Senior Research Fellowship, 230
CDU Three Year Postdoctoral Fellowship, 230
University of Stirling Research Studentships, 678
Woods Hole Oceanographic Institution Research Fellowships in Marine Policy, 710

African Nations

Austrian Academy of Sciences Postgraduate Course in Limnology, 121
Joint Japan/World Bank Graduate Scholarship Program (JJ/WBGSP), 355

Australia

Wingate Scholarships, 704

British Commonwealth

Joint Japan/World Bank Graduate Scholarship Program (JJ/WBGSP), 355
Wingate Scholarships, 704

Canada

Wingate Scholarships, 704

Caribbean Countries

Joint Japan/World Bank Graduate Scholarship Program (JJ/WBGSP), 355

East European Countries

Joint Japan/World Bank Graduate Scholarship Program (JJ/WBGSP), 355
Natural History Museum Sys-Resource, 461

Far East

Austrian Academy of Sciences Postgraduate Course in Limnology, 121
Joint Japan/World Bank Graduate Scholarship Program (JJ/WBGSP), 355

Indian Sub-Continent

Austrian Academy of Sciences Postgraduate Course in Limnology, 121
Joint Japan/World Bank Graduate Scholarship Program (JJ/WBGSP), 355
Wingate Scholarships, 704

Middle East

Joint Japan/World Bank Graduate Scholarship Program (JJ/WBGSP), 355

New Zealand

Wingate Scholarships, 704

South Africa

Henderson Postgraduate Scholarships, 518
Joint Japan/World Bank Graduate Scholarship Program (JJ/WBGSP), 355
Wingate Scholarships, 704

South America

Austrian Academy of Sciences Postgraduate Course in Limnology, 121
Joint Japan/World Bank Graduate Scholarship Program (JJ/WBGSP), 355

United Kingdom

Mr and Mrs David Edward Memorial Award, 681
UWB Departmental Research Studentships, 681
UWB Research Studentships, 681
Wingate Scholarships, 704

West European Countries

Mr and Mrs David Edward Memorial Award, 681
Natural History Museum Sys-Resource, 461
UWB Departmental Research Studentships, 681
UWB Research Studentships, 681
Wingate Scholarships, 704

ARCHITECTURE AND TOWN PLANNING

GENERAL

Any Country

Advanced Fellowships, 71
Architecture Master's Degree Travelling Fellowship, 565
ASCSA Fellowships, 71
BFWG: M H Joseph Prize, 143
Board of Architects of New South Wales Research Grant, 130
Canadian Department of Foreign Affairs Faculty Enrichment Program, 205
Canadian Department of Foreign Affairs Faculty Research Program, 205
Canadian Department of Foreign Affairs Institutional Research Program, 206
Carroll LV Meeks Fellowship, 584
Center for Advanced Study in the Behavioral Sciences Postdoctoral Residential Fellowships, 223
Cintas Fellowships, 101
Cotton Research Fellowships, 261
Edilia and François-Auguste de Montequin Fellowship in Iberian and Latin American Architecture, 585
ERASMUS Prize, 288
FAMSI Research Grant, 287
Foundation Praemium Erasmianum Study Prize, 288
Frederick Douglass Institute Postdoctoral Fellowship, 289
George Pepler International Award, 551
Humanitarian Trust Awards, 329
Interior Architecture Travelling Fellowship, 566
Lindbergh Grants, 230
Matsumae International Foundation Research Fellowship, 408
Neville Chamberlain Scholarship, 618
NUS Graduate Scholarships for ASEAN Nationals, 459
Paul Mellon Centre Grants, 489
Ramsden Bursaries, 586
RIAS Award for Measured Drawing, 537
RIAS John Maclaren Travelling Fellowship, 538
Rosann Berry Fellowship, 585
RSA Annual Student Competition, 542
RSA Art for Architecture, 545
Sir John Burnet Memorial Award, 538
Sir Robert Lorimer Memorial Award, 538
Sir Rowand Anderson Silver Medal, 538
Spiro Kostof Annual Meeting Fellowship, 585
Stroud Bursaries, 586
The Alastair Salvesen Art Scholarship, 541
The John Kinross Memorial Fund Student Scholarships/RSA, 541
Thomas Ross Award, 538
University of Dundee Research Awards, 629
University of Glasgow Postgraduate Research Scholarships, 634
University of Manchester Research Studentships and Scholarships, 642
University of Stirling Research Studentships, 678
Wolf Foundation Prizes, 706
Wolfsonian FIU Fellowship, 706

African Nations

ABCCF Student Grant, 91
Friends of Peterhouse Bursary, 491
Fulbright Postdoctoral Research and Lecturing Awards for Non-US Citizens, 245
Hubert H Humphrey Fellowship Programme, 609
International Postgraduate Research Scholarships (IPRS), 676
Merton College Reed Foundation Scholarship, 658

Australia

Byera Hadley Travelling Scholarships, 130
Friends of Peterhouse Bursary, 491
Fulbright Awards, 119
Fulbright Postdoctoral Fellowships, 119
Fulbright Postdoctoral Research and Lecturing Awards for Non-US Citizens, 245
Fulbright Postgraduate Studentships, 120
Marten Bequest Travelling Scholarships, 222
University of Western Sydney Postgraduate Research Award (UW-SPRA), 689
Wingate Scholarships, 704

British Commonwealth

Friends of Peterhouse Bursary, 491
International Postgraduate Research Scholarships (IPRS), 676
Merton College Reed Foundation Scholarship, 658
Rome Scholarship in Architecture, 156
Sargant Fellowship, 157
Wingate Scholarships, 704

Canada

Friends of Peterhouse Bursary, 491
Fulbright Postdoctoral Research and Lecturing Awards for Non-US Citizens, 245
International Postgraduate Research Scholarships (IPRS), 676
OAS Graduate Academic Studies, 483
Wingate Scholarships, 704

Caribbean Countries

Friends of Peterhouse Bursary, 491
Hubert H Humphrey Fellowship Programme, 609
International Postgraduate Research Scholarships (IPRS), 676
Merton College Reed Foundation Scholarship, 658
OAS Graduate Academic Studies, 483

East European Countries

AHRB Doctoral Awards Scheme, 99
CRF (Caledonian Research Foundation)/RSE European Visiting Research Fellowships, 547
Fulbright Postdoctoral Research and Lecturing Awards for Non-US Citizens, 245
Hubert H Humphrey Fellowship Programme, 609
International Postgraduate Research Scholarships (IPRS), 676
Merton College Reed Foundation Scholarship, 658
Research Preparation Master's Scheme, 99

Far East

Friends of Peterhouse Bursary, 491
Fulbright Postdoctoral Research and Lecturing Awards for Non-US Citizens, 245
Hubert H Humphrey Fellowship Programme, 609
International Postgraduate Research Scholarships (IPRS), 676
Jackson Memorial Fellowship, 310
JACL Scholarship and Award Program, 377
Merton College Reed Foundation Scholarship, 658
NUS Graduate Scholarships for ASEAN Nationals, 459
NUS Research Scholarship, 459
Swiss Federal Institute of Technology Scholarships, 598

Indian Sub-Continent

Friends of Peterhouse Bursary, 491

STRUCTURAL ARCHITECTURE

New Zealand

Wingate Scholarships, 704

South Africa

Hubert H Humphrey Fellowship Programme, 609
International Postgraduate Research Scholarships (IPRS), 676
Wingate Scholarships, 704

South America

Hubert H Humphrey Fellowship Programme, 609
International Postgraduate Research Scholarships (IPRS), 676

United Kingdom

Hallam Studentships, 558
International Postgraduate Research Scholarships (IPRS), 676
Professional Preparation Master's Scheme, 99
RSA Design Directions, 545
Swiss Federal Institute of Technology Scholarships, 598
Wingate Scholarships, 704

United States of America

Horticultural Research Institute Grants, 327
International Postgraduate Research Scholarships (IPRS), 676
Swiss Federal Institute of Technology Scholarships, 598

West European Countries

Hallam Studentships, 558
International Postgraduate Research Scholarships (IPRS), 676
Professional Preparation Master's Scheme, 99
RSA Design Directions, 545
Wingate Scholarships, 704

LANDSCAPE ARCHITECTURE

Any Country

Dumbarton Oaks Fellowships and Junior Fellowships, 262
MacDowell Colony Residencies, 402
Mott MacDonald Charitable Trust Scholarships, 426
Stanley Smith (UK) Horticultural Trust Awards, 594
Urban Design Travelling Fellowship, 566

African Nations

International Postgraduate Research Scholarships (IPRS), 676

Australia

Wingate Scholarships, 704

British Commonwealth

International Postgraduate Research Scholarships (IPRS), 676
Wingate Scholarships, 704

Canada

Horticultural Research Institute Grants, 327
International Postgraduate Research Scholarships (IPRS), 676
Wingate Scholarships, 704

Caribbean Countries

International Postgraduate Research Scholarships (IPRS), 676

East European Countries

International Postgraduate Research Scholarships (IPRS), 676
Professional Preparation Master's Scheme, 99

Far East

International Postgraduate Research Scholarships (IPRS), 676

Indian Sub-Continent

International Postgraduate Research Scholarships (IPRS), 676
Wingate Scholarships, 704

Middle East

International Postgraduate Research Scholarships (IPRS), 676

New Zealand

Wingate Scholarships, 704

South Africa

International Postgraduate Research Scholarships (IPRS), 676
Wingate Scholarships, 704

South America

International Postgraduate Research Scholarships (IPRS), 676

United Kingdom

International Postgraduate Research Scholarships (IPRS), 676
Martin McLaren Horticultural Scholarship, 344
Professional Preparation Master's Scheme, 99
Wingate Scholarships, 704

United States of America

Horticultural Research Institute Grants, 327
International Postgraduate Research Scholarships (IPRS), 676

West European Countries

International Postgraduate Research Scholarships (IPRS), 676
Professional Preparation Master's Scheme, 99
Wingate Scholarships, 704

TOWN AND COMMUNITY PLANNING

Any Country

George Pepler International Award, 551
Massey Doctoral Scholarship, 408
Mott MacDonald Charitable Trust Scholarships, 426
RICS Education Trust Award, 520
University of Dundee Research Awards, 629
University of Stirling Research Studentships, 678
Urban Design Travelling Fellowship, 566

African Nations

Ecosystem Approaches to Human Health Awards, 358
Hubert H Humphrey Fellowship Programme, 609
International Postgraduate Research Scholarships (IPRS), 676

Australia

Wingate Scholarships, 704

British Commonwealth

International Postgraduate Research Scholarships (IPRS), 676
Wingate Scholarships, 704

Canada

Ecosystem Approaches to Human Health Awards, 358
International Postgraduate Research Scholarships (IPRS), 676
Office of Critical Infrastructure Protection and Emergency Preparedness (EPC) Research Fellowship in Honour of Stuart Nesbitt White, 110
TAC Scholarships, 604
Wingate Scholarships, 704

Caribbean Countries

Ecosystem Approaches to Human Health Awards, 358
Hubert H Humphrey Fellowship Programme, 609
International Postgraduate Research Scholarships (IPRS), 676

East European Countries

Hubert H Humphrey Fellowship Programme, 609
International Postgraduate Research Scholarships (IPRS), 676

Far East

Ecosystem Approaches to Human Health Awards, 358
Hubert H Humphrey Fellowship Programme, 609
International Postgraduate Research Scholarships (IPRS), 676
Swiss Federal Institute of Technology Scholarships, 598

Indian Sub-Continent

Ecosystem Approaches to Human Health Awards, 358
Hubert H Humphrey Fellowship Programme, 609
International Postgraduate Research Scholarships (IPRS), 676
Wingate Scholarships, 704

Middle East

Ecosystem Approaches to Human Health Awards, 358
Hubert H Humphrey Fellowship Programme, 609
International Postgraduate Research Scholarships (IPRS), 676

New Zealand

Wingate Scholarships, 704

South Africa

Ecosystem Approaches to Human Health Awards, 358
Hubert H Humphrey Fellowship Programme, 609
International Postgraduate Research Scholarships (IPRS), 676
Wingate Scholarships, 704

South America

Hubert H Humphrey Fellowship Programme, 609
International Postgraduate Research Scholarships (IPRS), 676

United Kingdom

Hallam Studentships, 558
International Postgraduate Research Scholarships (IPRS), 676
Polish Government Postgraduate Scholarships Scheme, 501
Studentship in City and Regional Planning, 219
Swiss Federal Institute of Technology Scholarships, 598
Wingate Scholarships, 704

United States of America

International Postgraduate Research Scholarships (IPRS), 676
Swiss Federal Institute of Technology Scholarships, 598

West European Countries

Hallam Studentships, 558
International Postgraduate Research Scholarships (IPRS), 676
Wingate Scholarships, 704

REGIONAL PLANNING

Any Country

George Pepler International Award, 551
Massey Doctoral Scholarship, 408
Mott MacDonald Charitable Trust Scholarships, 426
University of Dundee Research Awards, 629
Urban Design Travelling Fellowship, 566

African Nations

Hubert H Humphrey Fellowship Programme, 609
International Postgraduate Research Scholarships (IPRS), 676

Australia

Wingate Scholarships, 704

British Commonwealth

International Postgraduate Research Scholarships (IPRS), 676
Wingate Scholarships, 704

Canada

International Postgraduate Research Scholarships (IPRS), 676
Office of Critical Infrastructure Protection and Emergency Preparedness (EPC) Research Fellowship in Honour of Stuart Nesbitt White, 110
TAC Scholarships, 604
Wingate Scholarships, 704

Caribbean Countries

Hubert H Humphrey Fellowship Programme, 609
International Postgraduate Research Scholarships (IPRS), 676

East European Countries

Hubert H Humphrey Fellowship Programme, 609
International Postgraduate Research Scholarships (IPRS), 676

Far East

Hubert H Humphrey Fellowship Programme, 609
International Postgraduate Research Scholarships (IPRS), 676
Swiss Federal Institute of Technology Scholarships, 598

Indian Sub-Continent

Hubert H Humphrey Fellowship Programme, 609
International Postgraduate Research Scholarships (IPRS), 676
Wingate Scholarships, 704

Middle East

Hubert H Humphrey Fellowship Programme, 609
International Postgraduate Research Scholarships (IPRS), 676

New Zealand

Wingate Scholarships, 704

South Africa

Hubert H Humphrey Fellowship Programme, 609
International Postgraduate Research Scholarships (IPRS), 676
Wingate Scholarships, 704

South America

Hubert H Humphrey Fellowship Programme, 609
International Postgraduate Research Scholarships (IPRS), 676

United Kingdom

Hallam Studentships, 558
International Postgraduate Research Scholarships (IPRS), 676
Swiss Federal Institute of Technology Scholarships, 598
Wingate Scholarships, 704

United States of America

International Postgraduate Research Scholarships (IPRS), 676
Minorities and Women Educational Scholarship Program, 91
Swiss Federal Institute of Technology Scholarships, 598

West European Countries

Hallam Studentships, 558
International Postgraduate Research Scholarships (IPRS), 676
Wingate Scholarships, 704

ARTS AND HUMANITIES

GENERAL

Any Country

'Drawn to Art' Fellowship
AAS Northeast Modern Language Association Fellowship, 26

African Nations

Australia

British Commonwealth

Canada

Caribbean Countries

East European Countries

Far East

West European Countries

INTERPRETATION AND TRANSLATION

Any Country

Australia

British Commonwealth

Canada

East European Countries

Far East

Middle East

New Zealand

South Africa

United Kingdom

United States of America

West European Countries

MODERN LANGUAGES AND LITERATURES

Any Country

African Nations

Australia

British Commonwealth

Canada

Caribbean Countries

East European Countries

Far East

Indian Sub-Continent

Middle East

New Zealand

South Africa

South America

United Kingdom

United States of America

Universita' Per Stranieri Di Siena Unstra Grants, 615
Wingate Scholarships, 704

Canada

Universita' Per Stranieri Di Siena Unstra Grants, 615
Wingate Scholarships, 704

Caribbean Countries

Universita' Per Stranieri Di Siena PVS Grants, 614

East European Countries

AHRB Doctoral Awards Scheme, 99
Research Preparation Master's Scheme, 99
Universita' Per Stranieri Di Siena PVS Grants, 614
Universita' Per Stranieri Di Siena Unstra Grants, 615

Far East

Universita' Per Stranieri Di Siena Unstra Grants, 615

Indian Sub-Continent

Universita' Per Stranieri Di Siena PVS Grants, 614
Wingate Scholarships, 704

Middle East

Universita' Per Stranieri Di Siena Unstra Grants, 615

New Zealand

Universita' Per Stranieri Di Siena Unstra Grants, 615
Wingate Scholarships, 704

South Africa

Universita' Per Stranieri Di Siena Unstra Grants, 615
Wingate Scholarships, 704

South America

Universita' Per Stranieri Di Siena PVS Grants, 614

United Kingdom

AHRB Doctoral Awards Scheme, 99
Balsdon Fellowship, 155
Research Preparation Master's Scheme, 99
Rome Awards in Archaeology, History and Letters, 156
Rome Fellowship, 156
Rome Scholarships in Ancient, Medieval and Later Italian Studies, 156
Universita' Per Stranieri Di Siena Unstra Grants, 615
Universita' Per Stranieri Di Siena Socrates Erasmus Students Mobility, 614
University of Kent School of European Culture and Language Scholarships, 637
University of Wales (Aberystwyth) Postgraduate Research Studentships, 680
Wingate Scholarships, 704

United States of America

Universita' Per Stranieri Di Siena Unstra Grants, 615

West European Countries

AHRB Doctoral Awards Scheme, 99
Research Preparation Master's Scheme, 99
Universita' Per Stranieri Di Siena Socrates Erasmus Students Mobility, 614
University of Kent School of European Culture and Language Scholarships, 637
Wingate Scholarships, 704

PORTUGUESE

Any Country

Barron Bequest, 677

Katherine Singer Kovacs Prize, 423
Trinity College Junior Research Fellowship, 672
University of Bristol Postgraduate Scholarships, 619
University of Manchester Research Studentships and Scholarships, 642

Australia

Wingate Scholarships, 704

British Commonwealth

Wingate Scholarships, 704

Canada

Wingate Scholarships, 704

East European Countries

AHRB Doctoral Awards Scheme, 99
Research Preparation Master's Scheme, 99

Indian Sub-Continent

Wingate Scholarships, 704

New Zealand

Wingate Scholarships, 704

South Africa

Wingate Scholarships, 704

United Kingdom

AHRB Doctoral Awards Scheme, 99
Research Preparation Master's Scheme, 99
Wingate Scholarships, 704

West European Countries

AHRB Doctoral Awards Scheme, 99
Research Preparation Master's Scheme, 99
Wingate Scholarships, 704

ROMANCE LANGUAGES

Any Country

Ahmanson and Getty Postdoctoral Fellowships, 606
ASECS (American Society for Eighteenth-Century Studies)/Clark Library Fellowships, 606
Camargo Fellowships, 164
Clark Library Short-Term Resident Fellowships, 606
Clark Predoctoral Fellowships, 607
Clark-Huntington Joint Bibliographical Fellowship, 607
Massey Doctoral Scholarship, 408
University of Bristol Postgraduate Scholarships, 619
University of Glasgow Postgraduate Research Scholarships, 634
USC College Dissertation Fellowship, 677
USC College of Letters, Arts and Sciences Merit Award, 677

Australia

Wingate Scholarships, 704

British Commonwealth

Wingate Scholarships, 704

Canada

Gilbert Chinard Fellowships, 336
Harmon Chadbourn Rorison Fellowship, 336
Wingate Scholarships, 704

East European Countries

AHRB Doctoral Awards Scheme, 99
Research Preparation Master's Scheme, 99

Indian Sub-Continent
Wingate Scholarships, 704

New Zealand
Wingate Scholarships, 704

South Africa
Wingate Scholarships, 704

United Kingdom
AHRB Doctoral Awards Scheme, 99
Research Preparation Master's Scheme, 99
Wingate Scholarships, 704

United States of America
Gilbert Chinard Fellowships, 336
Harmon Chadbourn Rorison Fellowship, 336

West European Countries
AHRB Doctoral Awards Scheme, 99
Research Preparation Master's Scheme, 99
Wingate Scholarships, 704

MODERN GREEK

Any Country
Aristotle University of Thessaloniki Scholarships, 93
M Alison Frantz Fellowship in Post-Classical Studies at the Gennadius Library (formerly known as the Gennadeion Fellowship), 72
Mary Isabel Sibley Fellowship, 497
NEH Fellowships, 72
Trinity College Junior Research Fellowship, 672
University of Glasgow Postgraduate Research Scholarships, 634

Australia
Wingate Scholarships, 704

British Commonwealth
Hector and Elizabeth Catling Bursary, 155
Wingate Scholarships, 704

Canada
1) Thompson (Homer and Dorothy) Fellowship 2) Elisabeth Alfolate Fellowship, 196
Wingate Scholarships, 704

East European Countries
AHRB Doctoral Awards Scheme, 99
Research Preparation Master's Scheme, 99

Indian Sub-Continent
Wingate Scholarships, 704

New Zealand
Wingate Scholarships, 704

South Africa
Wingate Scholarships, 704

United Kingdom
AHRB Doctoral Awards Scheme, 99
Hector and Elizabeth Catling Bursary, 155
Research Preparation Master's Scheme, 99
Wingate Scholarships, 704

West European Countries
AHRB Doctoral Awards Scheme, 99

Research Preparation Master's Scheme, 99
Wingate Scholarships, 704

DUTCH

Any Country
Barron Bequest, 677
University of Manchester Research Studentships and Scholarships, 642

Australia
Wingate Scholarships, 704

British Commonwealth
Wingate Scholarships, 704

Canada
Wingate Scholarships, 704

East European Countries
AHRB Doctoral Awards Scheme, 99
Research Preparation Master's Scheme, 99

Indian Sub-Continent
Wingate Scholarships, 704

New Zealand
Wingate Scholarships, 704

South Africa
Wingate Scholarships, 704

United Kingdom
AHRB Doctoral Awards Scheme, 99
Research Preparation Master's Scheme, 99
Wingate Scholarships, 704

West European Countries
AHRB Doctoral Awards Scheme, 99
Research Preparation Master's Scheme, 99
Wingate Scholarships, 704

BALTIC LANGUAGES

Any Country
M Alison Frantz Fellowship in Post-Classical Studies at the Gennadius Library (formerly known as the Gennadeion Fellowship), 72

Australia
Wingate Scholarships, 704

British Commonwealth
Wingate Scholarships, 704

Canada
Wingate Scholarships, 704

East European Countries
AHRB Doctoral Awards Scheme, 99
Research Preparation Master's Scheme, 99

Indian Sub-Continent
Wingate Scholarships, 704

New Zealand
Wingate Scholarships, 704

South Africa

Wingate Scholarships, 704

United Kingdom

AHRB Doctoral Awards Scheme, 99
Research Preparation Master's Scheme, 99
Wingate Scholarships, 704

United States of America

IREX Individual Advanced Research Opportunities, 366

West European Countries

AHRB Doctoral Awards Scheme, 99
Research Preparation Master's Scheme, 99
Wingate Scholarships, 704

CELTIC LANGUAGES

Any Country

Barron Bequest, 677
Cornwall Heritage Trust Scholarship, 633
Delahaye Memorial Benefaction, 681
Dublin Institute for Advanced Studies Scholarship in Celtic Studies, 262
Helen McCormack Turner Memorial Scholarship, 681
Herbert Hughes Scholarship, 682
Mary Radcliffe Scholarship, 682
McCaig Postgraduate Scholarships, 221
RHYS Curzon-Jones Scholarship, 682
Ridley Lewis Bursary, 682
Sir John Rhys Studentship in Celtic Studies, 664
University of Glasgow Postgraduate Research Scholarships, 634
W.D. Llewelyn Memorial Benefaction, 682

Australia

Wingate Scholarships, 704

British Commonwealth

Wingate Scholarships, 704

Canada

Wingate Scholarships, 704

East European Countries

AHRB Doctoral Awards Scheme, 99
Research Preparation Master's Scheme, 99

Indian Sub-Continent

Wingate Scholarships, 704

New Zealand

Wingate Scholarships, 704

South Africa

Wingate Scholarships, 704

United Kingdom

AHRB Doctoral Awards Scheme, 99
Mr and Mrs David Edward Memorial Award, 681
Research Preparation Master's Scheme, 99
University of Wales (Aberystwyth) Postgraduate Research Studentships, 680
UWB Departmental Research Studentships, 681
UWB Research Studentships, 681
Wingate Scholarships, 704

West European Countries

AHRB Doctoral Awards Scheme, 99

Mr and Mrs David Edward Memorial Award, 681
Research Preparation Master's Scheme, 99
UWB Departmental Research Studentships, 681
UWB Research Studentships, 681
Wingate Scholarships, 704

FINNISH

Any Country

ASF Translation Prize, 88
CIMO Scholarships for Post-graduate Studies at a Finnish University, 225

Australia

Wingate Scholarships, 704

British Commonwealth

Wingate Scholarships, 704

Canada

Wingate Scholarships, 704

East European Countries

AHRB Doctoral Awards Scheme, 99
Research Preparation Master's Scheme, 99

Indian Sub-Continent

Wingate Scholarships, 704

New Zealand

Wingate Scholarships, 704

South Africa

Wingate Scholarships, 704

United Kingdom

AHRB Doctoral Awards Scheme, 99
Research Preparation Master's Scheme, 99
Wingate Scholarships, 704

United States of America

Fulbright Teacher and Administrator Exchange, 294

West European Countries

AHRB Doctoral Awards Scheme, 99
Research Preparation Master's Scheme, 99
Wingate Scholarships, 704

RUSSIAN

Any Country

Aldo and Jeanne Scaglione Prize for Studies in Slavic Languages and Literatures, 422
Andrew W Mellon Postdoctoral Fellowships in the Humanities, 677
Barron Bequest, 677
Kennan Institute Short Term Grants, 385
Queen Mary Research Studentships, 506
University of Bristol Postgraduate Scholarships, 619
University of Glasgow Postgraduate Research Scholarships, 634
University of Manchester Research Studentships and Scholarships, 642
USC College Dissertation Fellowship, 677
USC College of Letters, Arts and Sciences Merit Award, 677

Australia

Wingate Scholarships, 704

British Commonwealth
Wingate Scholarships, 704

Canada
Wingate Scholarships, 704

East European Countries
AHRB Doctoral Awards Scheme, 99
Research Preparation Master's Scheme, 99

Indian Sub-Continent
Wingate Scholarships, 704

New Zealand
Wingate Scholarships, 704

South Africa
Wingate Scholarships, 704

United Kingdom
AHRB Doctoral Awards Scheme, 99
Research Preparation Master's Scheme, 99
Wingate Scholarships, 704

United States of America
IREX Individual Advanced Research Opportunities, 366
IREX John J and Nancy Lee Roberts Fellowship Program, 366
Kennan Institute Research Scholarship, 385

West European Countries
AHRB Doctoral Awards Scheme, 99
Research Preparation Master's Scheme, 99
Wingate Scholarships, 704

SLAVONIC LANGUAGES (OTHERS)

Any Country
Aldo and Jeanne Scaglione Prize for Studies in Slavic Languages and Literatures, 422
Canadian Institute of Ukrainian Studies Research Grants, 207
Helen Darcovich Memorial Doctoral Fellowship, 207
Kennan Institute Short Term Grants, 385
Marusia and Michael Dorosh Master's Fellowship, 207
Neporany Research and Teaching Fellowship, 207
University of Glasgow Postgraduate Research Scholarships, 634

Australia
Wingate Scholarships, 704

British Commonwealth
Wingate Scholarships, 704

Canada
Wingate Scholarships, 704

East European Countries
AHRB Doctoral Awards Scheme, 99
Research Preparation Master's Scheme, 99

Indian Sub-Continent
Wingate Scholarships, 704

New Zealand
Wingate Scholarships, 704

South Africa
Wingate Scholarships, 704

United Kingdom
AHRB Doctoral Awards Scheme, 99
Polish Government Postgraduate Scholarships Scheme, 501
Research Preparation Master's Scheme, 99
Wingate Scholarships, 704

United States of America
IREX Individual Advanced Research Opportunities, 366
IREX John J and Nancy Lee Roberts Fellowship Program, 366
Kennan Institute Research Scholarship, 385
The Kosciuszko Foundation Year Abroad Program at the Jagiellonian University in Krakow, 388

West European Countries
AHRB Doctoral Awards Scheme, 99
Research Preparation Master's Scheme, 99
Wingate Scholarships, 704

HUNGARIAN

Australia
Wingate Scholarships, 704

British Commonwealth
Wingate Scholarships, 704

Canada
Wingate Scholarships, 704

East European Countries
AHRB Doctoral Awards Scheme, 99
Research Preparation Master's Scheme, 99

Indian Sub-Continent
Wingate Scholarships, 704

New Zealand
Wingate Scholarships, 704

South Africa
Wingate Scholarships, 704

United Kingdom
AHRB Doctoral Awards Scheme, 99
Research Preparation Master's Scheme, 99
Wingate Scholarships, 704

United States of America
Fulbright Teacher and Administrator Exchange, 294
IREX Individual Advanced Research Opportunities, 366
IREX John J and Nancy Lee Roberts Fellowship Program, 366

West European Countries
AHRB Doctoral Awards Scheme, 99
Research Preparation Master's Scheme, 99
Wingate Scholarships, 704

FINO UGRIAN LANGUAGES

Any Country
CIMO Scholarships for Post-graduate Studies at a Finnish University, 225

Australia
Wingate Scholarships, 704

British Commonwealth

Wingate Scholarships, 704

Canada

Wingate Scholarships, 704

East European Countries

AHRB Doctoral Awards Scheme, 99
Research Preparation Master's Scheme, 99

Indian Sub-Continent

Wingate Scholarships, 704

New Zealand

Wingate Scholarships, 704

South Africa

Wingate Scholarships, 704

United Kingdom

AHRB Doctoral Awards Scheme, 99
Research Preparation Master's Scheme, 99
Wingate Scholarships, 704

West European Countries

AHRB Doctoral Awards Scheme, 99
Research Preparation Master's Scheme, 99
Wingate Scholarships, 704

EUROPEAN LANGUAGES (OTHERS)

Australia

Wingate Scholarships, 704

British Commonwealth

Wingate Scholarships, 704

Canada

Wingate Scholarships, 704

East European Countries

AHRB Doctoral Awards Scheme, 99
Research Preparation Master's Scheme, 99

Indian Sub-Continent

Wingate Scholarships, 704

New Zealand

Wingate Scholarships, 704

South Africa

Wingate Scholarships, 704

United Kingdom

AHRB Doctoral Awards Scheme, 99
Polish Embassy Scholarship for Polonicum, Warsaw University, Jagiellonian University, Cracow, Silesia University, Katowice, KUL, Lublin, 501
Research Preparation Master's Scheme, 99
University of Wales (Aberystwyth) Postgraduate Research Student-ships, 680
Wingate Scholarships, 704

United States of America

ACLS East European Language Training Grants, 39

West European Countries

AHRB Doctoral Awards Scheme, 99
Research Preparation Master's Scheme, 99
Wingate Scholarships, 704

ALTAIC LANGUAGES

Australia

Wingate Scholarships, 704

British Commonwealth

Wingate Scholarships, 704

Canada

Wingate Scholarships, 704

East European Countries

AHRB Doctoral Awards Scheme, 99
Research Preparation Master's Scheme, 99

Indian Sub-Continent

Wingate Scholarships, 704

New Zealand

Wingate Scholarships, 704

South Africa

Wingate Scholarships, 704

United Kingdom

AHRB Doctoral Awards Scheme, 99
Research Preparation Master's Scheme, 99
Wingate Scholarships, 704

United States of America

ARIT - Bosphorus University Language Fellowships, 70
IREX John J and Nancy Lee Roberts Fellowship Program, 366

West European Countries

AHRB Doctoral Awards Scheme, 99
Research Preparation Master's Scheme, 99
Wingate Scholarships, 704

ARABIC

Any Country

Anthony Parsons Memorial Scholarship, 632
AUC International Graduate Fellowships in Arabic Studies, Middle East Studies and Sociology-Anthropology
AUC Teaching Arabic as a Foreign Language Fellowships, 85
British Academy Ancient Persia Fund, 133
SOAS Bursary, 555
SOAS Research Student Fellowships, 555
University of Manchester Research Studentships and Scholarships, 642

Australia

Wingate Scholarships, 704

British Commonwealth

Wingate Scholarships, 704

Canada

Wingate Scholarships, 704

East European Countries

AHRB Doctoral Awards Scheme, 99
Research Preparation Master's Scheme, 99

Indian Sub-Continent

Wingate Scholarships, 704

New Zealand

Wingate Scholarships, 704

South Africa

Wingate Scholarships, 704

United Kingdom

AHRB Doctoral Awards Scheme, 99
CBRL Research Grant, 244
CBRL Travel Grant, 244
Research Preparation Master's Scheme, 99
Wingate Scholarships, 704

United States of America

ARCE Fellowships, 69
Fulbright Teacher and Administrator Exchange, 294

West European Countries

AHRB Doctoral Awards Scheme, 99
Research Preparation Master's Scheme, 99
Wingate Scholarships, 704

HEBREW

Any Country

Barron Bequest, 677
Jacob Hirsch Fellowship, 72
SOAS Bursary, 555
SOAS Research Student Fellowships, 555
United States Center for Advanced Holocaust Studies Research Fellowships, 608
University of Glasgow Postgraduate Research Scholarships, 634
University of Manchester Research Studentships and Scholarships, 642

Australia

Wingate Scholarships, 704

British Commonwealth

Wingate Scholarships, 704

Canada

JCC Association Scholarships, 378
Wingate Scholarships, 704

East European Countries

AHRB Doctoral Awards Scheme, 99
Research Preparation Master's Scheme, 99

Indian Sub-Continent

Wingate Scholarships, 704

New Zealand

Wingate Scholarships, 704

South Africa

Wingate Scholarships, 704

United Kingdom

AHRB Doctoral Awards Scheme, 99
CBRL Research Grant, 244
CBRL Travel Grant, 244
Research Preparation Master's Scheme, 99
Wingate Scholarships, 704

United States of America

JCC Association Scholarships, 378

West European Countries

AHRB Doctoral Awards Scheme, 99
Research Preparation Master's Scheme, 99
Wingate Scholarships, 704

CHINESE

Any Country

Andrew W Mellon Postdoctoral Fellowships in the Humanities, 677
Massey Doctoral Scholarship, 408
SOAS Bursary, 555
SOAS Research Student Fellowships, 555
USC College of Letters, Arts and Sciences Merit Award, 677

Australia

Wingate Scholarships, 704

British Commonwealth

Wingate Scholarships, 704

Canada

Wingate Scholarships, 704

East European Countries

AHRB Doctoral Awards Scheme, 99
Research Preparation Master's Scheme, 99

Indian Sub-Continent

Wingate Scholarships, 704

New Zealand

Wingate Scholarships, 704

South Africa

Wingate Scholarships, 704

United Kingdom

AHRB Doctoral Awards Scheme, 99
Research Preparation Master's Scheme, 99
Wingate Scholarships, 704

West European Countries

AHRB Doctoral Awards Scheme, 99
Research Preparation Master's Scheme, 99
Wingate Scholarships, 704

KOREAN

Any Country

Andrew W Mellon Postdoctoral Fellowships in the Humanities, 677
Korea Foundation Advanced Research Grant, 386
Korea Foundation Fellowship for Field Research, 386
Korea Foundation Fellowship for Graduate Studies, 386
Korea Foundation Fellowship for Korean Language Training, 386
Korea Foundation Postdoctoral Fellowship, 387
SOAS Bursary, 555
SOAS Research Student Fellowships, 555
USC College Dissertation Fellowship, 677
USC College of Letters, Arts and Sciences Merit Award, 677

Australia

Wingate Scholarships, 704

British Commonwealth

Wingate Scholarships, 704

Canada

Wingate Scholarships, 704

East European Countries

AHRB Doctoral Awards Scheme, 99
Research Preparation Master's Scheme, 99

Indian Sub-Continent

Wingate Scholarships, 704

New Zealand

Wingate Scholarships, 704

South Africa

Wingate Scholarships, 704

United Kingdom

AHRB Doctoral Awards Scheme, 99
Research Preparation Master's Scheme, 99
Wingate Scholarships, 704

West European Countries

AHRB Doctoral Awards Scheme, 99
Research Preparation Master's Scheme, 99
Wingate Scholarships, 704

JAPANESE

Any Country

Andrew W Mellon Postdoctoral Fellowships in the Humanities, 677
Massey Doctoral Scholarship, 408
SOAS Bursary, 555
SOAS Research Student Fellowships, 555
USC College Dissertation Fellowship, 677
USC College of Letters, Arts and Sciences Merit Award, 677

Australia

Wingate Scholarships, 704

British Commonwealth

Wingate Scholarships, 704

Canada

Wingate Scholarships, 704

East European Countries

AHRB Doctoral Awards Scheme, 99
Research Preparation Master's Scheme, 99

Indian Sub-Continent

Wingate Scholarships, 704

New Zealand

Wingate Scholarships, 704

South Africa

Wingate Scholarships, 704

United Kingdom

AHRB Doctoral Awards Scheme, 99
Research Preparation Master's Scheme, 99
Wingate Scholarships, 704

West European Countries

AHRB Doctoral Awards Scheme, 99
Eugen and Ilse Seibold Award, 257

Research Preparation Master's Scheme, 99
Wingate Scholarships, 704

INDIAN LANGUAGES

Any Country

SOAS Bursary, 555
SOAS Research Student Fellowships, 555

Australia

Wingate Scholarships, 704

British Commonwealth

Wingate Scholarships, 704

Canada

SICI India Studies Fellowship Competition, 558
Wingate Scholarships, 704

East European Countries

AHRB Doctoral Awards Scheme, 99
Research Preparation Master's Scheme, 99

Indian Sub-Continent

Wingate Scholarships, 704

New Zealand

Wingate Scholarships, 704

South Africa

Wingate Scholarships, 704

United Kingdom

AHRB Doctoral Awards Scheme, 99
Research Preparation Master's Scheme, 99
Wingate Scholarships, 704

West European Countries

AHRB Doctoral Awards Scheme, 99
Research Preparation Master's Scheme, 99
Wingate Scholarships, 704

IRANIC LANGUAGES

Any Country

British Academy Ancient Persia Fund, 133
SOAS Bursary, 555
SOAS Research Student Fellowships, 555
University of Manchester Research Studentships and Scholarships, 642

African Nations

British School of Archaeology in Iraq Grants, 158

Australia

British School of Archaeology in Iraq Grants, 158
Wingate Scholarships, 704

British Commonwealth

British School of Archaeology in Iraq Grants, 158
Wingate Scholarships, 704

Canada

British School of Archaeology in Iraq Grants, 158
Wingate Scholarships, 704

New Zealand

Wingate Scholarships, 704

South Africa

Wingate Scholarships, 704

United Kingdom

AHRB Doctoral Awards Scheme, 99
Research Preparation Master's Scheme, 99
Wingate Scholarships, 704

West European Countries

AHRB Doctoral Awards Scheme, 99
Research Preparation Master's Scheme, 99
Wingate Scholarships, 704

CLASSICAL LANGUAGES AND LITERATURES

Any Country

Adolfo Omodeo Scholarship, 374
Advanced Fellowships, 71
Aldo and Jean Scaglione Prize for a Translation of a Literary Work, 422
Aldo and Jeanne Scaglione Prize for Comparative Literary Studies, 422
ASCSA Fellowships, 71
ASCSA Summer Sessions, 72
British Academy Larger Research Grants, 134
British Academy Overseas Conference Grants, 134
British Academy Small Personal Research Grants, 134
British Academy Worldwide Congress Grant, 135
Center for Advanced Study in the Behavioral Sciences Postdoctoral Residential Fellowships, 223
Center for Hellenic Studies Junior Fellowships, 223
Charlotte W Newcombe Doctoral Dissertation Fellowships, 709
Corpus Christi College Charles Oldham Graduate Scholarship in Classics, 649
Dumbarton Oaks Fellowships and Junior Fellowships, 262
External Faculty Fellowships, 594
FAMSI Research Grant, 287
Foundation Praemium Erasmianum Study Prize, 288
Frederico Chabod Scholarship, 374
Hugh Le May Fellowship, 519
Jacob Hirsch Fellowship, 72
James Russell Lowell Prize, 423
Lois Roth Award for a Translation of Literary Work, 423
M Alison Frantz Fellowship in Post-Classical Studies at the Gennadius Library (formerly known as the Gennadeion Fellowship), 72
Mary Isabel Sibley Fellowship, 497
Massey Doctoral Scholarship, 408
MLA Prize for a Distinguished Scholarly Edition, 424
MLA Prize for a First Book, 424
MLA Prize for Independent Scholars, 424
NHC Fellowships, 449
Onassis Foreigners' Fellowship Programme Educational Scholarships Category B, 15
Renaissance Society Fellowships, 581
St Anne's College Fulford Junior Research Fellowship, 665
St Anne's College Olwen Rhys Research Scholarship, 666
University of Bristol Postgraduate Scholarships, 619
University of Glasgow Postgraduate Research Scholarships, 634
University of Manchester Research Studentships and Scholarships, 642
University of Otago International Scholarships, 646
USC College Dissertation Fellowship, 677
USC College of Letters, Arts and Sciences Merit Award, 677

African Nations

Corpus Christi College Charles Oldham Graduate Scholarship in Classics, 649

Australia

Corpus Christi College Charles Oldham Graduate Scholarship in Classics, 649
University of Otago Masters Awards, 646
University of Otago PhD Scholarships, 646
University of Otago Prestigious PhD Scholarships, 647
Wingate Scholarships, 704

British Commonwealth

Corpus Christi College Charles Oldham Graduate Scholarship in Classics, 649
Wingate Scholarships, 704

Canada

1) Thompson (Homer and Dorothy) Fellowship 2) Elisabeth Alfolate Fellowship, 196
Corpus Christi College Charles Oldham Graduate Scholarship in Classics, 649
Vatican Film Library Mellon Fellowship, 693
Wingate Scholarships, 704

Caribbean Countries

Corpus Christi College Charles Oldham Graduate Scholarship in Classics, 649

East European Countries

AHRB Doctoral Awards Scheme, 99
Brian Hewson Crawford Fellowship, 697
Corpus Christi College Charles Oldham Graduate Scholarship in Classics, 649
CRF (Caledonian Research Foundation)/RSE European Visiting Research Fellowships, 547
Research Preparation Master's Scheme, 99

Far East

Corpus Christi College Charles Oldham Graduate Scholarship in Classics, 649
JACL Scholarship and Award Program, 377
University of Otago Dr Sulaiman Daud 125th Jubilee International Postgraduate Scholarship, 646

Indian Sub-Continent

Corpus Christi College Charles Oldham Graduate Scholarship in Classics, 649
Wingate Scholarships, 704

Middle East

Corpus Christi College Charles Oldham Graduate Scholarship in Classics, 649

New Zealand

Corpus Christi College Charles Oldham Graduate Scholarship in Classics, 649
University of Otago Masters Awards, 646
University of Otago PhD Scholarships, 646
University of Otago Prestigious PhD Scholarships, 647
Wingate Scholarships, 704

South Africa

Corpus Christi College Charles Oldham Graduate Scholarship in Classics, 649
Wingate Scholarships, 704

South America

Corpus Christi College Charles Oldham Graduate Scholarship in Classics, 649

United Kingdom

AHRB Doctoral Awards Scheme, 99
British Conference Grants, 135

United Kingdom

AHRB Doctoral Awards Scheme, 99
Dover Fund, 581
Dover Fund Grant, 581
Hector and Elizabeth Catling Bursary, 155
Research Preparation Master's Scheme, 99
University of Kent School of European Culture and Language Scholarships, 637
Wingate Scholarships, 704

United States of America

Fulbright Teacher and Administrator Exchange, 294

West European Countries

AHRB Doctoral Awards Scheme, 99
Merton College Leventis Scholarship, 658
Research Preparation Master's Scheme, 99
University of Kent School of European Culture and Language Scholarships, 637
Wingate Scholarships, 704

SANSKRIT

Any Country

SOAS Bursary, 555
SOAS Research Student Fellowships, 555
Somerville College Levick Sisters Senior Scholarship, 665

Australia

Wingate Scholarships, 704

British Commonwealth

Wingate Scholarships, 704

Canada

Wingate Scholarships, 704

East European Countries

AHRB Doctoral Awards Scheme, 99
Research Preparation Master's Scheme, 99

Indian Sub-Continent

Wingate Scholarships, 704

New Zealand

Wingate Scholarships, 704

South Africa

Wingate Scholarships, 704

United Kingdom

AHRB Doctoral Awards Scheme, 99
Research Preparation Master's Scheme, 99
Wingate Scholarships, 704

West European Countries

AHRB Doctoral Awards Scheme, 99
Research Preparation Master's Scheme, 99
Wingate Scholarships, 704

LINGUISTICS AND PHILOLOGY

Any Country

Advanced Fellowships, 71
Aldo and Jeanne Scaglione Prize for French and Francophone Literary Studies, 422

Aldo and Jeanne Scaglione Prize for Studies in Germanic Languages and Literatures, 422
Aldo and Jeanne Scaglione Prize for Studies in Slavic Languages and Literatures, 422
Andrew W Mellon Postdoctoral Fellowships in the Humanities, 677
ASCSA Fellowships, 71
ASCSA Summer Sessions, 72
British Academy Overseas Conference Grants, 134
British Academy Small Personal Research Grants, 134
Camargo Fellowships, 164
CDU Senior Research Fellowship, 230
CDU Three Year Postdoctoral Fellowship, 230
Center for Advanced Study in the Behavioral Sciences Postdoctoral Residential Fellowships, 223
CIMO Scholarships for advanced studies of Finnish Language at a Finnish University, 225
CIMO Scholarships for Post-graduate Studies at a Finnish University, 225
External Faculty Fellowships, 594
FAMSI Research Grant, 287
Fondation Fyssen Postdoctoral Study Grants, 281
Gypsy Lore Society Young Scholar's Prize in Romani Studies, 311
Hugh Le May Fellowship, 519
Jacob Hirsch Fellowship, 72
James Russell Lowell Prize, 423
Kenneth W Mildenberger Prize, 423
M Alison Frantz Fellowship in Post-Classical Studies at the Gennadius Library (formerly known as the Gennadeion Fellowship), 72
Marusia and Michael Dorosh Master's Fellowship, 207
Mina P Shaughnessy Prize, 423
MLA Prize for a Distinguished Bibliography, 423
MLA Prize for a First Book, 424
MLA Prize for Independent Scholars, 424
NEH Fellowships, 72
Neporany Research and Teaching Fellowship, 207
Phillips Fund Grants for Native American Research, 66
Queen Mary Research Studentships, 506
Renaissance Society Fellowships, 581
SOAS Bursary, 555
SOAS Research Student Fellowships, 555
Somerville College Levick Sisters Senior Scholarship, 665
Trinity College Junior Research Fellowship, 672
United States Center for Advanced Holocaust Studies Research Fellowships, 608
University of Essex Scholarships, 632
University of Glasgow Postgraduate Research Scholarships, 634
University of Manchester Research Studentships and Scholarships, 642
University of Otago International Scholarships, 646
University of Stirling Research Studentships, 678
USC College Dissertation Fellowship, 677
USC College of Letters, Arts and Sciences Merit Award, 677

Australia

Universita' Per Stranieri Di Siena Unstra Grants, 615
University of Otago Masters Awards, 646
University of Otago PhD Scholarships, 646
University of Otago Prestigious PhD Scholarships, 647
University of Western Sydney Postgraduate Research Award (UW-SPRA), 689
Wingate Scholarships, 704

British Commonwealth

Universita' Per Stranieri Di Siena Unstra Grants, 615
Wingate Scholarships, 704

Canada

Gilbert Chinard Fellowships, 336
Harmon Chadbourn Rorison Fellowship, 336
Paul Sargent Memorial Linguistic Scholarship Program, 110
Universita' Per Stranieri Di Siena Unstra Grants, 615
Wingate Scholarships, 704

Australia
Universita' Per Stranieri Di Siena Unstra Grants, 615
Wingate Scholarships, 704

British Commonwealth
Universita' Per Stranieri Di Siena Unstra Grants, 615
Wingate Scholarships, 704

Canada
Universita' Per Stranieri Di Siena Unstra Grants, 615
Wingate Scholarships, 704

East European Countries
Research Preparation Master's Scheme, 99
Universita' Per Stranieri Di Siena Unstra Grants, 615

Far East
Universita' Per Stranieri Di Siena Unstra Grants, 615

Indian Sub-Continent
Wingate Scholarships, 704

Middle East
Universita' Per Stranieri Di Siena Unstra Grants, 615

New Zealand
Universita' Per Stranieri Di Siena Unstra Grants, 615
Wingate Scholarships, 704

South Africa
Universita' Per Stranieri Di Siena Unstra Grants, 615
Wingate Scholarships, 704

United Kingdom
Mr and Mrs David Edward Memorial Award, 681
Research Preparation Master's Scheme, 99
Universita' Per Stranieri Di Siena Unstra Grants, 615
Universita' Per Stranieri Di Siena Socrates Erasmus Students Mobility, 614
UWB Departmental Research Studentships, 681
UWB Research Studentships, 681
Wingate Scholarships, 704

United States of America
Fulbright Distinguished Chairs Program, 245
Fulbright Senior Specialists Program, 245
Universita' Per Stranieri Di Siena Unstra Grants, 615

West European Countries
Mr and Mrs David Edward Memorial Award, 681
Research Preparation Master's Scheme, 99
Universita' Per Stranieri Di Siena Socrates Erasmus Students Mobility, 614
UWB Departmental Research Studentships, 681
UWB Research Studentships, 681
Wingate Scholarships, 704

PHONETICS

Any Country
Andrew W Mellon Postdoctoral Fellowships in the Humanities, 677
Camargo Fellowships, 164
University of Manchester Research Studentships and Scholarships, 642

Australia
Universita' Per Stranieri Di Siena Unstra Grants, 615
Wingate Scholarships, 704

British Commonwealth
Universita' Per Stranieri Di Siena Unstra Grants, 615
Wingate Scholarships, 704

Canada
Universita' Per Stranieri Di Siena Unstra Grants, 615
Wingate Scholarships, 704

East European Countries
Research Preparation Master's Scheme, 99
Universita' Per Stranieri Di Siena Unstra Grants, 615

Far East
Universita' Per Stranieri Di Siena Unstra Grants, 615

Indian Sub-Continent
Wingate Scholarships, 704

Middle East
Universita' Per Stranieri Di Siena Unstra Grants, 615

New Zealand
Universita' Per Stranieri Di Siena Unstra Grants, 615
Wingate Scholarships, 704

South Africa
Universita' Per Stranieri Di Siena Unstra Grants, 615
Wingate Scholarships, 704

United Kingdom
Mr and Mrs David Edward Memorial Award, 681
Research Preparation Master's Scheme, 99
Universita' Per Stranieri Di Siena Unstra Grants, 615
UWB Departmental Research Studentships, 681
UWB Research Studentships, 681
Wingate Scholarships, 704

United States of America
Universita' Per Stranieri Di Siena Unstra Grants, 615

West European Countries
Mr and Mrs David Edward Memorial Award, 681
Research Preparation Master's Scheme, 99
UWB Departmental Research Studentships, 681
UWB Research Studentships, 681
Wingate Scholarships, 704

LOGOPEDICS

Australia
Wingate Scholarships, 704

British Commonwealth
Wingate Scholarships, 704

Canada
Wingate Scholarships, 704

East European Countries
Research Preparation Master's Scheme, 99

Indian Sub-Continent
Wingate Scholarships, 704

New Zealand
Wingate Scholarships, 704

South Africa

Wingate Scholarships, 704

United Kingdom

Mr and Mrs David Edward Memorial Award, 681
Research Preparation Master's Scheme, 99
Wingate Scholarships, 704

West European Countries

Mr and Mrs David Edward Memorial Award, 681
Research Preparation Master's Scheme, 99
Wingate Scholarships, 704

COMPARATIVE LITERATURE

Any Country

Adolfo Omodeo Scholarship, 374
Advanced Fellowships, 71
Ahmanson and Getty Postdoctoral Fellowships, 606
Aldo and Jeanne Scaglione Prize for Comparative Literary Studies, 422
Aldo and Jeanne Scaglione Prize for French and Francophone Literary Studies, 422
Aldo and Jeanne Scaglione Prize for Italian Studies, 422
Aldo and Jeanne Scaglione Prize for Studies in Germanic Languages and Literatures, 422
Aldo and Jeanne Scaglione Prize for Studies in Slavic Languages and Literatures, 422
Andrew W Mellon Postdoctoral Fellowships in the Humanities, 677
ASCSA Fellowships, 71
ASCSA Summer Sessions, 72
ASECS (American Society for Eighteenth-Century Studies)/Clark Library Fellowships, 606
British Academy Larger Research Grants, 134
British Academy Overseas Conference Grants, 134
British Academy Small Personal Research Grants, 134
British Academy Worldwide Congress Grant, 135
Camargo Fellowships, 164
Center for Advanced Study in the Behavioral Sciences Postdoctoral Residential Fellowships, 223
Charlotte W Newcombe Doctoral Dissertation Fellowships, 709
ChLA Beiter Scholarships for Graduate Students, 234
ChLA Research Fellowships and Scholarships, 234
Clark Library Short-Term Resident Fellowships, 606
Clark Predoctoral Fellowships, 607
Clark-Huntington Joint Bibliographical Fellowship, 607
CMRS Summer Fellowship, 607
CQU Postgraduate Research Award, 224
External Faculty Fellowships, 594
Fenia and Yaakov Leviant Memorial Prize, 423
Foundation Praemium Erasmianum Study Prize, 288
Frederico Chabod Scholarship, 374
Howard R Marraro Prize, 423
IHS Humane Studies Fellowships, 339
Institute of Irish Studies Senior Visiting Research Fellowship, 344
Jacob Hirsch Fellowship, 72
James Russell Lowell Prize, 423
Katherine Singer Kovacs Prize, 423
Kennan Institute Short Term Grants, 385
M Alison Frantz Fellowship in Post-Classical Studies at the Gennadius Library (formerly known as the Gennadeion Fellowship), 72
Mary Isabel Sibley Fellowship, 497
MLA Prize for a Distinguished Bibliography, 423
MLA Prize for a First Book, 424
MLA Prize for Independent Scholars, 424
NEH Fellowships, 72
NHC Fellowships, 449
Queen Mary Research Studentships, 506
Renaissance Society Fellowships, 581
SOAS Bursary, 555
SOAS Research Student Fellowships, 555

Trinity College Junior Research Fellowship, 672
United States Center for Advanced Holocaust Studies Research Fellowships, 608
University of Essex Scholarships, 632
University of Glasgow Postgraduate Research Scholarships, 634
University of Manchester Research Studentships and Scholarships, 642
USC College Dissertation Fellowship, 677
USC College of Letters, Arts and Sciences Merit Award, 677
William Sanders Scarborough Prize, 424
Yaddo Residency, 243

Australia

Quinn, Nathan and Edmond Scholarships, 149
University of Western Sydney Postgraduate Research Award (UW-SPRA), 689
Wingate Scholarships, 704

British Commonwealth

Quinn, Nathan and Edmond Scholarships, 149
Wingate Scholarships, 704

Canada

Mary McNeill Scholarship in Irish Studies, 344
Quinn, Nathan and Edmond Scholarships, 149
Wingate Scholarships, 704

East European Countries

AHRB Doctoral Awards Scheme, 99
CRF (Caledonian Research Foundation)/RSE European Visiting Research Fellowships, 547
Research Preparation Master's Scheme, 99

Indian Sub-Continent

Quinn, Nathan and Edmond Scholarships, 149
Wingate Scholarships, 704

New Zealand

Quinn, Nathan and Edmond Scholarships, 149
University of Western Sydney Postgraduate Research Award (UW-SPRA), 689
Wingate Scholarships, 704

South Africa

Quinn, Nathan and Edmond Scholarships, 149
Wingate Scholarships, 704

United Kingdom

AHRB Doctoral Awards Scheme, 99
BAAS Short Term Awards, 136
British Conference Grants, 135
CBRL Research Grant, 244
CBRL Travel Grant, 244
CRF (Caledonian Research Foundation)/RSE European Visiting Research Fellowships, 547
Molson Research Awards, 136
Mr and Mrs David Edward Memorial Award, 681
Prix du Québec, 136
Quinn, Nathan and Edmond Scholarships, 149
Regional Agency for the Right to University Study (DSU) Grants, 614
Research Preparation Master's Scheme, 99
Universita' Per Stranieri Di Siena Socrates Erasmus Students Mobility, 614
University of Essex Foundation Scholarships, 632
University of Kent School of European Culture and Language Scholarships, 637
University of Wales (Aberystwyth) Postgraduate Research Studentships, 680
UWB Departmental Research Studentships, 681
UWB Research Studentships, 681
Wingate Scholarships, 704

United States of America

West European Countries

HISTORY

Any Country

African Nations

Australia

British Commonwealth

Canada

East European Countries

Far East

Indian Sub-Continent

New Zealand

South Africa

South America

United Kingdom

United States of America

West European Countries

PREHISTORY

Any Country

Australia

British Commonwealth

Canada

East European Countries

ANCIENT CIVILISATIONS

African Nations

Australia

British Commonwealth

Canada

East European Countries

Indian Sub-Continent

New Zealand

South Africa

United Kingdom

United States of America

West European Countries

CONTEMPORARY HISTORY

Any Country

Australia

British Commonwealth

Canada

East European Countries

Indian Sub-Continent

New Zealand

South Africa

United Kingdom

United States of America

West European Countries

ARCHAEOLOGY

Any Country

PHILOSOPHY

South Africa

Wingate Scholarships, 704

United Kingdom

AHRB Doctoral Awards Scheme, 99
British Conference Grants, 135
CBRL Research Grant, 244
CBRL Travel Grant, 244
CRF (Caledonian Research Foundation)/RSE European Visiting Research Fellowships, 547
ESU Chautauqua Institution Scholarships, 271
Research Preparation Master's Scheme, 99
St Anne's College Ethics Scholarship, 665
University of Essex Foundation Scholarships, 632
University of Kent School of European Culture and Language Scholarships, 637
Wingate Scholarships, 704

United States of America

Fulbright Distinguished Chairs Program, 245
Fulbright Senior Specialists Program, 245
IREX John J and Nancy Lee Roberts Fellowship Program, 366
Kennan Institute Research Scholarship, 385
NEH Fellowship, 75
NEH Postdoctoral Research Award, 75
Vatican Film Library Mellon Fellowship, 693

West European Countries

AHRB Doctoral Awards Scheme, 99
CRF (Caledonian Research Foundation)/RSE European Visiting Research Fellowships, 547
Research Preparation Master's Scheme, 99
University of Kent School of European Culture and Language Scholarships, 637
University of Otago Masters Awards, 646
University of Otago PhD Scholarships, 646
University of Otago Prestigious PhD Scholarships, 647
Wingate Scholarships, 704

PHILOSOPHICAL SCHOOLS

Any Country

Advanced Fellowships, 71
Ahmanson and Getty Postdoctoral Fellowships, 606
Andrew W Mellon Postdoctoral Fellowships in the Humanities, 677
ASECS (American Society for Eighteenth-Century Studies)/Clark Library Fellowships, 606
Camargo Fellowships, 164
Clark Library Short-Term Resident Fellowships, 606
Clark Predoctoral Fellowships, 607
Clark-Huntington Joint Bibliographical Fellowship, 607
Henry Moore Institute Research Fellowship, 322
Kanner Fellowship In British Studies, 607
NEH Fellowships, 72
United States Center for Advanced Holocaust Studies Research Fellowships, 608
University of Dundee Research Awards, 629

Australia

Wingate Scholarships, 704

British Commonwealth

Hector and Elizabeth Catling Bursary, 155
Wingate Scholarships, 704

Canada

Wingate Scholarships, 704

East European Countries

AHRB Doctoral Awards Scheme, 99
Research Preparation Master's Scheme, 99

Indian Sub-Continent

Wingate Scholarships, 704

New Zealand

Wingate Scholarships, 704

South Africa

Wingate Scholarships, 704

United Kingdom

AHRB Doctoral Awards Scheme, 99
Hector and Elizabeth Catling Bursary, 155
Research Preparation Master's Scheme, 99
Wingate Scholarships, 704

West European Countries

AHRB Doctoral Awards Scheme, 99
Research Preparation Master's Scheme, 99
Wingate Scholarships, 704

METAPHYSICS

Any Country

Advanced Fellowships, 71
Andrew W Mellon Postdoctoral Fellowships in the Humanities, 677
Camargo Fellowships, 164
Kanner Fellowship In British Studies, 607
Massey Doctoral Scholarship, 408
NEH Fellowships, 72
University of Dundee Research Awards, 629

Australia

Wingate Scholarships, 704

British Commonwealth

Wingate Scholarships, 704

Canada

Wingate Scholarships, 704

East European Countries

AHRB Doctoral Awards Scheme, 99
Research Preparation Master's Scheme, 99

Indian Sub-Continent

Wingate Scholarships, 704

New Zealand

Wingate Scholarships, 704

South Africa

Wingate Scholarships, 704

United Kingdom

AHRB Doctoral Awards Scheme, 99
Research Preparation Master's Scheme, 99
Wingate Scholarships, 704

West European Countries

AHRB Doctoral Awards Scheme, 99
Research Preparation Master's Scheme, 99
Wingate Scholarships, 704

LOGIC

Any Country

Advanced Fellowships, 71
Andrew W Mellon Postdoctoral Fellowships in the Humanities, 677
Camargo Fellowships, 164
Kanner Fellowship In British Studies, 607
Massey Doctoral Scholarship, 408
NEH Fellowships, 72
University of Dundee Research Awards, 629
University of Manchester Research Studentships and Scholarships, 642

Australia

Wingate Scholarships, 704

British Commonwealth

Wingate Scholarships, 704

Canada

Wingate Scholarships, 704

East European Countries

AHRB Doctoral Awards Scheme, 99
Research Preparation Master's Scheme, 99

Indian Sub-Continent

Wingate Scholarships, 704

New Zealand

Wingate Scholarships, 704

South Africa

Wingate Scholarships, 704

United Kingdom

AHRB Doctoral Awards Scheme, 99
Research Preparation Master's Scheme, 99
Wingate Scholarships, 704

West European Countries

AHRB Doctoral Awards Scheme, 99
Research Preparation Master's Scheme, 99
Wingate Scholarships, 704

ETHICS

Any Country

Advanced Fellowships, 71
AIATSIS Research Grants, 116
Andrew W Mellon Postdoctoral Fellowships in the Humanities, 677
Camargo Fellowships, 164
Charlotte W Newcombe Doctoral Dissertation Fellowships, 709
Delahaye Memorial Benefaction, 681
Helen McCormack Turner Memorial Scholarship, 681
Herbert Hughes Scholarship, 682
Kanner Fellowship In British Studies, 607
Mary Radcliffe Scholarship, 682
Massey Doctoral Scholarship, 408
NEH Fellowships, 72
RHYS Curzon-Jones Scholarship, 682
Ridley Lewis Bursary, 682
United States Center for Advanced Holocaust Studies Research Fellowships, 608
University of Dundee Research Awards, 629
University of Manchester Research Studentships and Scholarships, 642
W.D. Llewelyn Memorial Benefaction, 682

Australia

Wingate Scholarships, 704

British Commonwealth

Wingate Scholarships, 704

Canada

Wingate Scholarships, 704

East European Countries

AHRB Doctoral Awards Scheme, 99
Research Preparation Master's Scheme, 99

Indian Sub-Continent

Wingate Scholarships, 704

New Zealand

Wingate Scholarships, 704

South Africa

Wingate Scholarships, 704

United Kingdom

AHRB Doctoral Awards Scheme, 99
ESU Chautauqua Institution Scholarships, 271
Research Preparation Master's Scheme, 99
Wingate Scholarships, 704

United States of America

NEH Postdoctoral Research Award, 75

West European Countries

AHRB Doctoral Awards Scheme, 99
Research Preparation Master's Scheme, 99
Wingate Scholarships, 704

BUSINESS ADMINISTRATION AND MANAGEMENT

GENERAL

Any Country

AIATSIS Research Grants, 116
Alberta Research Council Karl A Clark Memorial Scholarship, 617
Andrew Mellon Foundation Scholarship, 518
Ashridge Entrepreneurial Bursary, 102
AUC Assistantships, 84
AUC Graduate Merit Fellowships, 84
AUC University Fellowships, 86
Canadian Department of Foreign Affairs Faculty Enrichment Program, 205
Canadian Department of Foreign Affairs Faculty Research Program, 205
Canadian Department of Foreign Affairs Institutional Research Program, 206
Canadian Natural Resources Limited Graduate Scholarship, 620
CDU Three Year Postdoctoral Fellowship, 230
Center for Advanced Study in the Behavioral Sciences Postdoctoral Residential Fellowships, 223
CESC-SSHRC Education Research Initiative, 576
Concordia University Graduate Fellowships, 241
CQU Postgraduate Research Award, 224
David J Azrieli Graduate Fellowship, 241
Delahaye Memorial Benefaction, 681
Equiano Memorial Award, 596
Ernst Meyer Prize, 353

African Nations

Australia

British Commonwealth

Canada

Caribbean Countries

East European Countries

Far East

Indian Sub-Continent

Middle East

New Zealand

South Africa

South America

United Kingdom

United States of America

West European Countries

International Postgraduate Research Scholarships (IPRS), 390
International Postgraduate Research Scholarships (IPRS), 676
Janson Johan Helmich Scholarships and Travel Grants, 376
Mr and Mrs David Edward Memorial Award, 681
Student Awards Agency for Scotland-Postgraduate Students' Allowances Scheme, 596
UWB Departmental Research Studentships, 681
UWB Research Studentships, 681
Wingate Scholarships, 704

BUSINESS STUDIES

Any Country

Ashridge Entrepreneurial Bursary, 102
CQU Postgraduate Research Award, 224
ETS Summer Program in Research for Graduate Students, 266
Golden Key National Honor Society Business Achievement Awards, 305
ISM Doctoral Grants, 340
ISM Senior Research Fellowship Program, 340
Kennan Institute Short Term Grants, 385
La Trobe University Postgraduate Scholarship, 390
LCCIEB Examinations Board Scholarships, 400
Massey Doctoral Scholarship, 408
Templeton College Barclay DPHIL Scholarship, 671
University of Essex Scholarships, 632
University of Glasgow Postgraduate Research Scholarships, 634
University of Kent Canterbury Business School, 636
University of Stirling Research Studentships, 678

African Nations

MCTC Assistance for Courses, 304
MCTC Tuition and Maintenance Scholarships, 304

Australia

University of Western Sydney Postgraduate Research Award (UW-SPRA), 689

Caribbean Countries

MCTC Assistance for Courses, 304
MCTC Tuition and Maintenance Scholarships, 304

East European Countries

MCTC Assistance for Courses, 304
MCTC Tuition and Maintenance Scholarships, 304

Far East

MCTC Assistance for Courses, 304
MCTC Tuition and Maintenance Scholarships, 304

Indian Sub-Continent

MCTC Assistance for Courses, 304
MCTC Tuition and Maintenance Scholarships, 304

Middle East

MCTC Assistance for Courses, 304
MCTC Tuition and Maintenance Scholarships, 304

New Zealand

University of Western Sydney Postgraduate Research Award (UW-SPRA), 689

South Africa

MCTC Assistance for Courses, 304
MCTC Tuition and Maintenance Scholarships, 304

South America

MCTC Assistance for Courses, 304
MCTC Tuition and Maintenance Scholarships, 304

United Kingdom

ESRC 1+3 Awards & +3 Awards, 265
Hallam Studentships, 558
Mr and Mrs David Edward Memorial Award, 681
Polish Government Postgraduate Scholarships Scheme, 501
University of Essex Foundation Scholarships, 632
University of Wales (Aberystwyth) Postgraduate Research Studentships, 680
UWB Departmental Research Studentships, 681
UWB Research Studentships, 681

United States of America

Adelphi University Scholarships, 8
Fulbright Senior Specialists Program, 245

West European Countries

ESRC 1+3 Awards & +3 Awards, 265
Eugen and Ilse Seibold Award, 257
Hallam Studentships, 558
Mr and Mrs David Edward Memorial Award, 681
UWB Departmental Research Studentships, 681
UWB Research Studentships, 681

INTERNATIONAL BUSINESS

Any Country

Ashridge Entrepreneurial Bursary, 102
CDU Senior Research Fellowship, 230
CQU Postgraduate Research Award, 224
Frederick Douglass Institute Postdoctoral Fellowship, 289
Frederick Douglass Institute Predoctoral Dissertation Fellowship, 290
ISM Doctoral Grants, 340
ISM Senior Research Fellowship Program, 340
Kennan Institute Short Term Grants, 385
LCCIEB Examinations Board Scholarships, 400
Massey Doctoral Scholarship, 408
Rhodes University Postdoctoral Fellowship, 519
Thomas Holloway Research Studentship, 536
University of Dundee Research Awards, 629
University of Essex Scholarships, 632
University of Glasgow Postgraduate Research Scholarships, 634
University of Kent Canterbury Business School, 636
University of Stirling Research Studentships, 678

African Nations

Hubert H Humphrey Fellowship Programme, 609

Australia

University of Western Sydney Postgraduate Research Award (UW-SPRA), 689
Wingate Scholarships, 704

British Commonwealth

Wingate Scholarships, 704

Canada

Wingate Scholarships, 704

Caribbean Countries

Hubert H Humphrey Fellowship Programme, 609

East European Countries

Hubert H Humphrey Fellowship Programme, 609

Far East

Hubert H Humphrey Fellowship Programme, 609

South Africa

Hubert H Humphrey Fellowship Programme, 609
MCTC Assistance for Courses, 304
MCTC Tuition and Maintenance Scholarships, 304

South America

Hubert H Humphrey Fellowship Programme, 609
MCTC Assistance for Courses, 304
MCTC Tuition and Maintenance Scholarships, 304

United Kingdom

BSUF May and Ward Scholarships (for British scholars), 158
Hallam Studentships, 558
Polish Government Postgraduate Scholarships Scheme, 501
University of Essex Foundation Scholarships, 632
University of Wales (Aberystwyth) Postgraduate Research Studentships, 680

United States of America

BSUF May and Ward Scholarships (for British scholars), 158

West European Countries

Hallam Studentships, 558

ACCOUNTANCY

Any Country

Ashridge Entrepreneurial Bursary, 102
CQU Postgraduate Research Award, 224
La Trobe University Postgraduate Scholarship, 390
LCCIEB Examinations Board Scholarships, 400
Massey Doctoral Scholarship, 408
Rhodes University Postdoctoral Fellowship, 519
University of Dundee Research Awards, 629
University of Essex Scholarships, 632
University of Glasgow Postgraduate Research Scholarships, 634
University of Manchester Research Studentships and Scholarships, 642
University of Stirling Research Studentships, 678
UNO Graduate Assistantships, 644

African Nations

BP - FCO Chevening - Leeds University Scholarships, 638
Hubert H Humphrey Fellowship Programme, 609
IATF IATA Aviation Training and Development Institute (ATDI) Scholarships, 353

Australia

University of Western Sydney Postgraduate Research Award (UW-SPRA), 689

British Commonwealth

BP - FCO Chevening - Leeds University Scholarships, 638

Caribbean Countries

BP - FCO Chevening - Leeds University Scholarships, 638
Hubert H Humphrey Fellowship Programme, 609
IATF IATA Aviation Training and Development Institute (ATDI) Scholarships, 353

East European Countries

Hubert H Humphrey Fellowship Programme, 609
IATF IATA Aviation Training and Development Institute (ATDI) Scholarships, 353

Far East

BP - FCO Chevening - Leeds University Scholarships, 638
Hubert H Humphrey Fellowship Programme, 609

IATF IATA Aviation Training and Development Institute (ATDI) Scholarships, 353
University of Leeds International Fee Bursary (Vietnam), 641
University of Leeds International Fee Bursary (Vietnam), 641

Indian Sub-Continent

BP - FCO Chevening - Leeds University Scholarships, 638
Hubert H Humphrey Fellowship Programme, 609
IATF IATA Aviation Training and Development Institute (ATDI) Scholarships, 353

Middle East

BP - FCO Chevening - Leeds University Scholarships, 638
Hubert H Humphrey Fellowship Programme, 609
IATF IATA Aviation Training and Development Institute (ATDI) Scholarships, 353

New Zealand

University of Western Sydney Postgraduate Research Award (UW-SPRA), 689

South Africa

BP - FCO Chevening - Leeds University Scholarships, 638
Henderson Postgraduate Scholarships, 518
Hubert H Humphrey Fellowship Programme, 609
IATF IATA Aviation Training and Development Institute (ATDI) Scholarships, 353

South America

BP - FCO Chevening - Leeds University Scholarships, 638
Hubert H Humphrey Fellowship Programme, 609
IATF IATA Aviation Training and Development Institute (ATDI) Scholarships, 353

United Kingdom

BSUF May and Ward Scholarships (for British scholars), 158
ESRC 1+3 Awards & +3 Awards, 265
Hallam Studentships, 558
Mr and Mrs David Edward Memorial Award, 681
University of Essex Foundation Scholarships, 632
University of Wales (Aberystwyth) Postgraduate Research Studentships, 680
UWB Departmental Research Studentships, 681
UWB Research Studentships, 681

United States of America

Accountemps student Scholarship, 371
BSUF May and Ward Scholarships (for British scholars), 158
John L. Carey Scholarship, 372
Minority Accounting Doctoral Scholarship Program, 388

West European Countries

ESRC 1+3 Awards & +3 Awards, 265
Hallam Studentships, 558
Mr and Mrs David Edward Memorial Award, 681
UWB Departmental Research Studentships, 681
UWB Research Studentships, 681

REAL ESTATE

Any Country

Massey Doctoral Scholarship, 408
RICS Education Trust Award, 520

African Nations

Hubert H Humphrey Fellowship Programme, 609

Australia

University of Western Sydney Postgraduate Research Award (UW-SPRA), 689

Caribbean Countries

Hubert H Humphrey Fellowship Programme, 609

East European Countries

Hubert H Humphrey Fellowship Programme, 609

Far East

Hubert H Humphrey Fellowship Programme, 609

Indian Sub-Continent

Hubert H Humphrey Fellowship Programme, 609

Middle East

Hubert H Humphrey Fellowship Programme, 609

New Zealand

University of Western Sydney Postgraduate Research Award (UW-SPRA), 689

South Africa

Hubert H Humphrey Fellowship Programme, 609

South America

Hubert H Humphrey Fellowship Programme, 609

United States of America

Appraisal Institute Education Trust Scholarship, 91

MARKETING AND SALES MANAGEMENT

Any Country

Ashridge Entrepreneurial Bursary, 102
CQU Postgraduate Research Award, 224
Equiano Memorial Award, 596
LCCIEB Examinations Board Scholarships, 400
Massey Doctoral Scholarship, 408
University of Stirling Research Studentships, 678

African Nations

Hubert H Humphrey Fellowship Programme, 609
IATF IATA Aviation Training and Development Institute (ATDI) Scholarships, 353
MCTC Assistance for Courses, 304
MCTC Tuition and Maintenance Scholarships, 304

Australia

University of Western Sydney Postgraduate Research Award (UW-SPRA), 689

Canada

Horticultural Research Institute Grants, 327

Caribbean Countries

Hubert H Humphrey Fellowship Programme, 609
IATF IATA Aviation Training and Development Institute (ATDI) Scholarships, 353
MCTC Assistance for Courses, 304
MCTC Tuition and Maintenance Scholarships, 304

East European Countries

Hubert H Humphrey Fellowship Programme, 609
IATF IATA Aviation Training and Development Institute (ATDI) Scholarships, 353
MCTC Assistance for Courses, 304
MCTC Tuition and Maintenance Scholarships, 304

Far East

Hubert H Humphrey Fellowship Programme, 609
IATF IATA Aviation Training and Development Institute (ATDI) Scholarships, 353
MCTC Assistance for Courses, 304
MCTC Tuition and Maintenance Scholarships, 304

Indian Sub-Continent

Hubert H Humphrey Fellowship Programme, 609
IATF IATA Aviation Training and Development Institute (ATDI) Scholarships, 353
MCTC Assistance for Courses, 304
MCTC Tuition and Maintenance Scholarships, 304

Middle East

Hubert H Humphrey Fellowship Programme, 609
IATF IATA Aviation Training and Development Institute (ATDI) Scholarships, 353
MCTC Assistance for Courses, 304
MCTC Tuition and Maintenance Scholarships, 304

New Zealand

University of Western Sydney Postgraduate Research Award (UW-SPRA), 689

South Africa

Hubert H Humphrey Fellowship Programme, 609
IATF IATA Aviation Training and Development Institute (ATDI) Scholarships, 353
MCTC Assistance for Courses, 304
MCTC Tuition and Maintenance Scholarships, 304

South America

Hubert H Humphrey Fellowship Programme, 609
IATF IATA Aviation Training and Development Institute (ATDI) Scholarships, 353
MCTC Assistance for Courses, 304
MCTC Tuition and Maintenance Scholarships, 304

United Kingdom

BSUF May and Ward Scholarships (for British scholars), 158
ESRC 1 + 3 Awards & + 3 Awards, 265
University of Wales (Aberystwyth) Postgraduate Research Studentships, 680

United States of America

BSUF May and Ward Scholarships (for British scholars), 158
Fulbright Distinguished Chairs Program, 245
Fulbright Senior Specialists Program, 245
Horticultural Research Institute Grants, 327

West European Countries

ESRC 1 + 3 Awards & + 3 Awards, 265

INSURANCE MANAGEMENT

Any Country

Ernst Meyer Prize, 353
Geneva Association, 353
International Association for the Study of Insurance Economics Research Grants, 353
Massey Doctoral Scholarship, 408

African Nations

Hubert H Humphrey Fellowship Programme, 609

Canada

S S Huebner Foundation for Insurance Education Predoctoral Fellowships, 552

Canada

Horticultural Research Institute Grants, 327

Caribbean Countries

Hubert H Humphrey Fellowship Programme, 609
IATF IATA Aviation Training and Development Institute (ATDI) Scholarships, 353
Joint Japan/World Bank Graduate Scholarship Program (JJ/WBGSP), 355

East European Countries

Hubert H Humphrey Fellowship Programme, 609
IATF IATA Aviation Training and Development Institute (ATDI) Scholarships, 353
Joint Japan/World Bank Graduate Scholarship Program (JJ/WBGSP), 355

Far East

Hubert H Humphrey Fellowship Programme, 609
IATF IATA Aviation Training and Development Institute (ATDI) Scholarships, 353
Joint Japan/World Bank Graduate Scholarship Program (JJ/WBGSP), 355
University of Leeds International Fee Bursary (Vietnam), 641
University of Leeds International Fee Bursary (Vietnam), 641

Indian Sub-Continent

Hubert H Humphrey Fellowship Programme, 609
IATF IATA Aviation Training and Development Institute (ATDI) Scholarships, 353
Joint Japan/World Bank Graduate Scholarship Program (JJ/WBGSP), 355

Middle East

Hubert H Humphrey Fellowship Programme, 609
IATF IATA Aviation Training and Development Institute (ATDI) Scholarships, 353
Joint Japan/World Bank Graduate Scholarship Program (JJ/WBGSP), 355

New Zealand

University of Western Sydney Postgraduate Research Award (UW-SPRA), 689

South Africa

Hubert H Humphrey Fellowship Programme, 609
IATF IATA Aviation Training and Development Institute (ATDI) Scholarships, 353
Joint Japan/World Bank Graduate Scholarship Program (JJ/WBGSP), 355

South America

Hubert H Humphrey Fellowship Programme, 609
IATF IATA Aviation Training and Development Institute (ATDI) Scholarships, 353
Joint Japan/World Bank Graduate Scholarship Program (JJ/WBGSP), 355

United Kingdom

BSUF May and Ward Scholarships (for British scholars), 158
ESRC 1+3 Awards & +3 Awards, 265
Hallam Studentships, 558

United States of America

BSUF May and Ward Scholarships (for British scholars), 158
Fulbright Senior Specialists Program, 245
Horticultural Research Institute Grants, 327

West European Countries

ESRC 1+3 Awards & +3 Awards, 265
Hallam Studentships, 558

LABOUR/INDUSTRIAL RELATIONS

Any Country

Ashridge Entrepreneurial Bursary, 102
CQU Postgraduate Research Award, 224
Equiano Memorial Award, 596
Mackenzie King Travelling Scholarships, 402
University of Stirling Research Studentships, 678

African Nations

Hubert H Humphrey Fellowship Programme, 609
Joint Japan/World Bank Graduate Scholarship Program (JJ/WBGSP), 355

Australia

University of Western Sydney Postgraduate Research Award (UW-SPRA), 689

British Commonwealth

Joint Japan/World Bank Graduate Scholarship Program (JJ/WBGSP), 355

Caribbean Countries

Hubert H Humphrey Fellowship Programme, 609
Joint Japan/World Bank Graduate Scholarship Program (JJ/WBGSP), 355

East European Countries

Hubert H Humphrey Fellowship Programme, 609
Joint Japan/World Bank Graduate Scholarship Program (JJ/WBGSP), 355

Far East

Hubert H Humphrey Fellowship Programme, 609
Joint Japan/World Bank Graduate Scholarship Program (JJ/WBGSP), 355

Indian Sub-Continent

Hubert H Humphrey Fellowship Programme, 609
Joint Japan/World Bank Graduate Scholarship Program (JJ/WBGSP), 355

Middle East

Hubert H Humphrey Fellowship Programme, 609
Joint Japan/World Bank Graduate Scholarship Program (JJ/WBGSP), 355

New Zealand

University of Western Sydney Postgraduate Research Award (UW-SPRA), 689

South Africa

Hubert H Humphrey Fellowship Programme, 609
Joint Japan/World Bank Graduate Scholarship Program (JJ/WBGSP), 355

South America

Hubert H Humphrey Fellowship Programme, 609
Joint Japan/World Bank Graduate Scholarship Program (JJ/WBGSP), 355

United Kingdom

BSUF May and Ward Scholarships (for British scholars), 158
Mr and Mrs David Edward Memorial Award, 681

UWB Departmental Research Studentships, 681
UWB Research Studentships, 681

United States of America

BSUF May and Ward Scholarships (for British scholars), 158
Fulbright Distinguished Chairs Program, 245
Fulbright Senior Specialists Program, 245

West European Countries

Mr and Mrs David Edward Memorial Award, 681
UWB Departmental Research Studentships, 681
UWB Research Studentships, 681

PUBLIC ADMINISTRATION

Any Country

CQU Postgraduate Research Award, 224
Equiano Memorial Award, 596
Massey Doctoral Scholarship, 408
Metropolitan Museum of Art Summer Internships for Graduate Students, 419
SSRC Program on Philanthropy and the Non-profit Sector Fellowships, 573
University of Kent Canterbury Business School, 636
University of Manchester Research Studentships and Scholarships, 642

African Nations

Hubert H Humphrey Fellowship Programme, 609
Joint Japan/World Bank Graduate Scholarship Program (JJ/WBGSP), 355
MCTC Assistance for Courses, 304
MCTC Tuition and Maintenance Scholarships, 304

Australia

University of Western Sydney Postgraduate Research Award (UW-SPRA), 689
Wingate Scholarships, 704

British Commonwealth

Joint Japan/World Bank Graduate Scholarship Program (JJ/WBGSP), 355
Wingate Scholarships, 704

Canada

Frank Knox Memorial Fellowships at Harvard University, 109
Wingate Scholarships, 704

Caribbean Countries

Hubert H Humphrey Fellowship Programme, 609
Joint Japan/World Bank Graduate Scholarship Program (JJ/WBGSP), 355
MCTC Assistance for Courses, 304
MCTC Tuition and Maintenance Scholarships, 304

East European Countries

Hubert H Humphrey Fellowship Programme, 609
Joint Japan/World Bank Graduate Scholarship Program (JJ/WBGSP), 355
MCTC Assistance for Courses, 304
MCTC Tuition and Maintenance Scholarships, 304

Far East

Hubert H Humphrey Fellowship Programme, 609
Joint Japan/World Bank Graduate Scholarship Program (JJ/WBGSP), 355
MCTC Assistance for Courses, 304
MCTC Tuition and Maintenance Scholarships, 304

Indian Sub-Continent

Hubert H Humphrey Fellowship Programme, 609
Hubert H Humphrey Fellowships, 610
Joint Japan/World Bank Graduate Scholarship Program (JJ/WBGSP), 355
MCTC Assistance for Courses, 304
MCTC Tuition and Maintenance Scholarships, 304
Wingate Scholarships, 704

Middle East

Hubert H Humphrey Fellowship Programme, 609
Joint Japan/World Bank Graduate Scholarship Program (JJ/WBGSP), 355
MCTC Assistance for Courses, 304
MCTC Tuition and Maintenance Scholarships, 304

New Zealand

University of Western Sydney Postgraduate Research Award (UW-SPRA), 689
Wingate Scholarships, 704

South Africa

Hubert H Humphrey Fellowship Programme, 609
Joint Japan/World Bank Graduate Scholarship Program (JJ/WBGSP), 355
MCTC Assistance for Courses, 304
MCTC Tuition and Maintenance Scholarships, 304
Wingate Scholarships, 704

South America

Hubert H Humphrey Fellowship Programme, 609
Joint Japan/World Bank Graduate Scholarship Program (JJ/WBGSP), 355
MCTC Assistance for Courses, 304
MCTC Tuition and Maintenance Scholarships, 304

United Kingdom

BSUF May and Ward Scholarships (for British scholars), 158
Frank Knox Fellowships at Harvard University, 288
Kennedy Scholarships, 385
Wingate Scholarships, 704

United States of America

Atlantic Fellowships in Public Policy, 139
BSUF May and Ward Scholarships (for British scholars), 158
Charles and Kathleen Manatt Democracy Studies, 372
Fulbright Distinguished Chairs Program, 245
IREX Individual Advanced Research Opportunities, 366

West European Countries

Wingate Scholarships, 704

INSTITUTIONAL ADMINISTRATION

Any Country

CQU Postgraduate Research Award, 224
Equiano Memorial Award, 596
Massey Doctoral Scholarship, 408

African Nations

Hubert H Humphrey Fellowship Programme, 609

Australia

Wingate Scholarships, 704

British Commonwealth

Wingate Scholarships, 704

EDUCATION AND TEACHER TRAINING

GENERAL

Australia

Hastings Center International Visiting Scholars Program, 318

British Commonwealth

Hastings Center International Visiting Scholars Program, 318

Canada

CIC The Bayer, Inc. Award for High School Chemistry Teachers, 233
CIC Union Carbide Award for Chemical Education, 233

Caribbean Countries

Hastings Center International Visiting Scholars Program, 318
MCTC Assistance for Courses, 304
MCTC Tuition and Maintenance Scholarships, 304

East European Countries

Canon Foundation Award, 217
Hastings Center International Visiting Scholars Program, 318
MCTC Assistance for Courses, 304
MCTC Tuition and Maintenance Scholarships, 304

Far East

Canon Foundation Award, 217
Hastings Center International Visiting Scholars Program, 318
MCTC Assistance for Courses, 304
MCTC Tuition and Maintenance Scholarships, 304

Indian Sub-Continent

Hastings Center International Visiting Scholars Program, 318
MCTC Assistance for Courses, 304
MCTC Tuition and Maintenance Scholarships, 304

Middle East

Hastings Center International Visiting Scholars Program, 318
MCTC Assistance for Courses, 304
MCTC Tuition and Maintenance Scholarships, 304

New Zealand

Hastings Center International Visiting Scholars Program, 318

South Africa

Hastings Center International Visiting Scholars Program, 318
MCTC Assistance for Courses, 304
MCTC Tuition and Maintenance Scholarships, 304

South America

Hastings Center International Visiting Scholars Program, 318
MCTC Assistance for Courses, 304
MCTC Tuition and Maintenance Scholarships, 304

United Kingdom

Canon Foundation Award, 217
Hallam Studentships, 558
Hastings Center International Visiting Scholars Program, 318
University of Wales (Aberystwyth) Postgraduate Research Studentships, 680
UWB Departmental Research Studentships, 681
UWB Research Studentships, 681

United States of America

Earthwatch Education Awards, 264
ETS Postdoctoral Fellowships, 266
NIH Research Grants, 450

West European Countries

Canon Foundation Award, 217
Hallam Studentships, 558
Hastings Center International Visiting Scholars Program, 318

UWB Departmental Research Studentships, 681
UWB Research Studentships, 681

HUMANITIES AND SOCIAL SCIENCE EDUCATION

Any Country

ASCSA Summer Sessions, 72
Bernadotte E Schmitt Grants, 49
Equiano Memorial Award, 596
ETS Summer Program in Research for Graduate Students, 266
J Franklin Jameson Fellowship, 49
Jacob Hirsch Fellowship, 72
Renaissance Society Fellowships, 581
University of Stirling Research Studentships, 678

African Nations

International Postgraduate Research Scholarships (IPRS), 676

British Commonwealth

International Postgraduate Research Scholarships (IPRS), 676

Canada

Canadian Window on International Development, 358
International Postgraduate Research Scholarships (IPRS), 676

Caribbean Countries

International Postgraduate Research Scholarships (IPRS), 676

East European Countries

International Postgraduate Research Scholarships (IPRS), 676

Far East

International Postgraduate Research Scholarships (IPRS), 676

Indian Sub-Continent

International Postgraduate Research Scholarships (IPRS), 676

Middle East

International Postgraduate Research Scholarships (IPRS), 676

South Africa

International Postgraduate Research Scholarships (IPRS), 676

South America

International Postgraduate Research Scholarships (IPRS), 676

United Kingdom

All Saints Educational Trust Personal Awards, 19
International Postgraduate Research Scholarships (IPRS), 676
Mr and Mrs David Edward Memorial Award, 681
UWB Departmental Research Studentships, 681
UWB Research Studentships, 681

United States of America

Earthwatch Education Awards, 264
ETS Postdoctoral Fellowships, 266
International Postgraduate Research Scholarships (IPRS), 676
James Madison Fellowship Program, 376

West European Countries

International Postgraduate Research Scholarships (IPRS), 676
Mr and Mrs David Edward Memorial Award, 681
UWB Departmental Research Studentships, 681
UWB Research Studentships, 681

PHYSICAL EDUCATION

Any Country

Massey Doctoral Scholarship, 408
NSCA Challenge Scholarship, 458
NSCA Power Systems Professional Scholarship, 458
NSCA Student Research Grant, 458
University of Glasgow Postgraduate Research Scholarships, 634
University of Manchester Research Studentships and Scholarships, 642
University of Stirling Research Studentships, 678

African Nations

International Postgraduate Research Scholarships (IPRS), 676

British Commonwealth

International Postgraduate Research Scholarships (IPRS), 676

Canada

International Postgraduate Research Scholarships (IPRS), 676
JCC Association Scholarships, 378

Caribbean Countries

International Postgraduate Research Scholarships (IPRS), 676

East European Countries

International Postgraduate Research Scholarships (IPRS), 676

Far East

International Postgraduate Research Scholarships (IPRS), 676

Indian Sub-Continent

International Postgraduate Research Scholarships (IPRS), 676

Middle East

International Postgraduate Research Scholarships (IPRS), 676

South Africa

International Postgraduate Research Scholarships (IPRS), 676

South America

International Postgraduate Research Scholarships (IPRS), 676

United Kingdom

International Postgraduate Research Scholarships (IPRS), 676
Mr and Mrs David Edward Memorial Award, 681
UWB Departmental Research Studentships, 681
UWB Research Studentships, 681

United States of America

ETS Postdoctoral Fellowships, 266
International Postgraduate Research Scholarships (IPRS), 676
JCC Association Scholarships, 378

West European Countries

International Postgraduate Research Scholarships (IPRS), 676
Mr and Mrs David Edward Memorial Award, 681
UWB Departmental Research Studentships, 681
UWB Research Studentships, 681

LITERACY EDUCATION

Any Country

Albert J Harris Award, 364
AUC Writing Center Graduate Fellowships, 86
Dina Feitelson Research Award, 365
Elva Knight Research Grant, 365
ETS Summer Program in Research for Graduate Students, 266
Helen M Robinson Award, 365
International Reading Association Outstanding Dissertation of the Year Award, 365
International Reading Association Teacher as Researcher Grant, 365
Jeanne S Chall Research Fellowship, 365

African Nations

International Postgraduate Research Scholarships (IPRS), 676
Reading/Literacy Research Fellowship, 366

Australia

Reading/Literacy Research Fellowship, 366

British Commonwealth

International Postgraduate Research Scholarships (IPRS), 676
Reading/Literacy Research Fellowship, 366

Canada

International Postgraduate Research Scholarships (IPRS), 676
Valuing Literacy in Canada Doctoral and Postdoctoral Fellowship Supplements, 580

Caribbean Countries

International Postgraduate Research Scholarships (IPRS), 676
Reading/Literacy Research Fellowship, 366

East European Countries

International Postgraduate Research Scholarships (IPRS), 676
Reading/Literacy Research Fellowship, 366

Far East

International Postgraduate Research Scholarships (IPRS), 676
Reading/Literacy Research Fellowship, 366

Indian Sub-Continent

International Postgraduate Research Scholarships (IPRS), 676
Reading/Literacy Research Fellowship, 366

Middle East

International Postgraduate Research Scholarships (IPRS), 676
Reading/Literacy Research Fellowship, 366

New Zealand

Reading/Literacy Research Fellowship, 366

South Africa

International Postgraduate Research Scholarships (IPRS), 676
Norah Taylor Bursary, 591
Reading/Literacy Research Fellowship, 366
SACEE EX-PCE Bursary, 591

South America

International Postgraduate Research Scholarships (IPRS), 676
Reading/Literacy Research Fellowship, 366

United Kingdom

International Postgraduate Research Scholarships (IPRS), 676
Reading/Literacy Research Fellowship, 366

United States of America

ETS Postdoctoral Fellowships, 266
International Postgraduate Research Scholarships (IPRS), 676

West European Countries

International Postgraduate Research Scholarships (IPRS), 676
Reading/Literacy Research Fellowship, 366

VOCATIONAL SUBJECTS EDUCATION

Any Country

LCCIEB Examinations Board Scholarships, 400
Lincoln College Erich and Rochelle Endowed Prize in Music, 657
Snowdon Award, 569

African Nations

Joint Japan/World Bank Graduate Scholarship Program (JJ/WBGSP), 355

Australia

Fulbright Professional Award for Vocational Education and Training, 121
University of Western Sydney Postgraduate Research Award (UW-SPRA), 689

British Commonwealth

Joint Japan/World Bank Graduate Scholarship Program (JJ/WBGSP), 355

Caribbean Countries

Joint Japan/World Bank Graduate Scholarship Program (JJ/WBGSP), 355

East European Countries

Joint Japan/World Bank Graduate Scholarship Program (JJ/WBGSP), 355

Far East

Joint Japan/World Bank Graduate Scholarship Program (JJ/WBGSP), 355

Indian Sub-Continent

Joint Japan/World Bank Graduate Scholarship Program (JJ/WBGSP), 355

Middle East

Joint Japan/World Bank Graduate Scholarship Program (JJ/WBGSP), 355

New Zealand

University of Western Sydney Postgraduate Research Award (UW-SPRA), 689

South Africa

Joint Japan/World Bank Graduate Scholarship Program (JJ/WBGSP), 355
SACEE EX-PCE Bursary, 591

South America

Joint Japan/World Bank Graduate Scholarship Program (JJ/WBGSP), 355

United Kingdom

Hilda Martindale Exhibitions, 324
Smith and Nephew Foundation Postdoctoral Nursing Research Fellowship, 567
Student Awards Agency for Scotland-Postgraduate Students' Allowances Scheme, 596

West European Countries

Student Awards Agency for Scotland-Postgraduate Students' Allowances Scheme, 596

AGRICULTURAL EDUCATION

Any Country

UFAW Animal Welfare Research Training Scholarships, 616
UFAW Research and Project Awards, 616
UFAW Small Project and Travel Awards, 616
UFAW Vacation Scholarships, 616

African Nations

Joint Japan/World Bank Graduate Scholarship Program (JJ/WBGSP), 355

British Commonwealth

Joint Japan/World Bank Graduate Scholarship Program (JJ/WBGSP), 355

Canada

Horticultural Research Institute Grants, 327

Caribbean Countries

Joint Japan/World Bank Graduate Scholarship Program (JJ/WBGSP), 355

East European Countries

Joint Japan/World Bank Graduate Scholarship Program (JJ/WBGSP), 355

Far East

Joint Japan/World Bank Graduate Scholarship Program (JJ/WBGSP), 355

Indian Sub-Continent

Joint Japan/World Bank Graduate Scholarship Program (JJ/WBGSP), 355

Middle East

Joint Japan/World Bank Graduate Scholarship Program (JJ/WBGSP), 355

South Africa

Joint Japan/World Bank Graduate Scholarship Program (JJ/WBGSP), 355

South America

Joint Japan/World Bank Graduate Scholarship Program (JJ/WBGSP), 355

United States of America

Horticultural Research Institute Grants, 327

ART EDUCATION

Any Country

Ebb & Flow Grant, 265
Henry Moore Institute Research Fellowship, 322
Massey Doctoral Scholarship, 408
Metropolitan Museum of Art Roswell L Gilpatric Internship, 418
Metropolitan Museum of Art Six Month Internship, 418
Metropolitan Museum of Art Summer Internships for College Students, 419
Metropolitan Museum of Art Summer Internships for Graduate Students, 419
MICA Fellowship, 407
University of Manchester Research Studentships and Scholarships, 642

African Nations

International Postgraduate Research Scholarships (IPRS), 676

British Commonwealth

International Postgraduate Research Scholarships (IPRS), 676

Canada

International Postgraduate Research Scholarships (IPRS), 676

Caribbean Countries
International Postgraduate Research Scholarships (IPRS), 676

East European Countries
International Postgraduate Research Scholarships (IPRS), 676

Far East
International Postgraduate Research Scholarships (IPRS), 676

Indian Sub-Continent
International Postgraduate Research Scholarships (IPRS), 676

Middle East
International Postgraduate Research Scholarships (IPRS), 676

South Africa
International Postgraduate Research Scholarships (IPRS), 676

South America
International Postgraduate Research Scholarships (IPRS), 676

United Kingdom
International Postgraduate Research Scholarships (IPRS), 676

United States of America
International Postgraduate Research Scholarships (IPRS), 676

West European Countries
International Postgraduate Research Scholarships (IPRS), 676

COMMERCE/BUSINESS EDUCATION

Any Country
CESC-SSHRC Education Research Initiative, 576
White House Historical Association Fellowships, 482

African Nations
Joint Japan/World Bank Graduate Scholarship Program (JJ/WBGSP), 355

British Commonwealth
Joint Japan/World Bank Graduate Scholarship Program (JJ/WBGSP), 355

Canada
CESC-SSHRC Education Research Initiative, 576

Caribbean Countries
Joint Japan/World Bank Graduate Scholarship Program (JJ/WBGSP), 355

East European Countries
Joint Japan/World Bank Graduate Scholarship Program (JJ/WBGSP), 355

Far East
Joint Japan/World Bank Graduate Scholarship Program (JJ/WBGSP), 355

Indian Sub-Continent
Joint Japan/World Bank Graduate Scholarship Program (JJ/WBGSP), 355

Middle East
Joint Japan/World Bank Graduate Scholarship Program (JJ/WBGSP), 355

South Africa
Joint Japan/World Bank Graduate Scholarship Program (JJ/WBGSP), 355

South America
Joint Japan/World Bank Graduate Scholarship Program (JJ/WBGSP), 355

COMPUTER EDUCATION

Any Country
CESC-SSHRC Education Research Initiative, 576
Ebb & Flow Grant, 265
ETS Summer Program in Research for Graduate Students, 266
Massey Doctoral Scholarship, 408

African Nations
International Postgraduate Research Scholarships (IPRS), 676

British Commonwealth
International Postgraduate Research Scholarships (IPRS), 676

Canada
CESC-SSHRC Education Research Initiative, 576
International Postgraduate Research Scholarships (IPRS), 676

Caribbean Countries
International Postgraduate Research Scholarships (IPRS), 676

East European Countries
International Postgraduate Research Scholarships (IPRS), 676

Far East
International Postgraduate Research Scholarships (IPRS), 676

Indian Sub-Continent
International Postgraduate Research Scholarships (IPRS), 676

Middle East
International Postgraduate Research Scholarships (IPRS), 676

South Africa
International Postgraduate Research Scholarships (IPRS), 676

South America
International Postgraduate Research Scholarships (IPRS), 676

United Kingdom
International Postgraduate Research Scholarships (IPRS), 676

United States of America
International Postgraduate Research Scholarships (IPRS), 676

West European Countries
International Postgraduate Research Scholarships (IPRS), 676

TECHNOLOGY EDUCATION

Any Country
Blanche E Woolls Scholarship for School Library Media Service, 125
CESC-SSHRC Education Research Initiative, 576
DEED (Demonstration of Energy-Efficient Developments) Scholarship, 69
Exxon Mobil Teaching Fellowships, 524
Massey Doctoral Scholarship, 408

University of Manchester Research Studentships and Scholarships, 642
University of Stirling Research Studentships, 678

African Nations

Joint Japan/World Bank Graduate Scholarship Program (JJ/WBGSP), 355

British Commonwealth

Joint Japan/World Bank Graduate Scholarship Program (JJ/WBGSP), 355

Canada

CESC-SSHRC Education Research Initiative, 576

Caribbean Countries

Joint Japan/World Bank Graduate Scholarship Program (JJ/WBGSP), 355

East European Countries

Joint Japan/World Bank Graduate Scholarship Program (JJ/WBGSP), 355

Far East

Joint Japan/World Bank Graduate Scholarship Program (JJ/WBGSP), 355

Indian Sub-Continent

Joint Japan/World Bank Graduate Scholarship Program (JJ/WBGSP), 355

Middle East

Joint Japan/World Bank Graduate Scholarship Program (JJ/WBGSP), 355

South Africa

Joint Japan/World Bank Graduate Scholarship Program (JJ/WBGSP), 355

South America

Joint Japan/World Bank Graduate Scholarship Program (JJ/WBGSP), 355

United States of America

Earthwatch Education Awards, 264
ETS Postdoctoral Fellowships, 266

HEALTH EDUCATION

Any Country

AFSP Distinguished Investigation Awards, 45
AFSP Pilot Grants, 46
AFSP Postdoctoral Research Fellowships, 46
AFSP Standard Research Grants, 46
AFSP Young Investigator Award, 46
Allen Foundation Grants, 19
ASBAH Research Grant, 103
Breast Cancer Campaign Project Grants, 132
Massey Doctoral Scholarship, 408
NSCA Challenge Scholarship, 458
NSCA Student Research Grant, 458
University of Manchester Research Studentships and Scholarships, 642

African Nations

Hastings Center International Visiting Scholars Program, 318
Joint Japan/World Bank Graduate Scholarship Program (JJ/WBGSP), 355

Australia

Hastings Center International Visiting Scholars Program, 318

British Commonwealth

Hastings Center International Visiting Scholars Program, 318
Joint Japan/World Bank Graduate Scholarship Program (JJ/WBGSP), 355

Canada

JCC Association Scholarships, 378

Caribbean Countries

Hastings Center International Visiting Scholars Program, 318
Joint Japan/World Bank Graduate Scholarship Program (JJ/WBGSP), 355

East European Countries

FEMS Fellowship, 280
Hastings Center International Visiting Scholars Program, 318
Joint Japan/World Bank Graduate Scholarship Program (JJ/WBGSP), 355

Far East

Hastings Center International Visiting Scholars Program, 318
Joint Japan/World Bank Graduate Scholarship Program (JJ/WBGSP), 355

Indian Sub-Continent

Hastings Center International Visiting Scholars Program, 318
Joint Japan/World Bank Graduate Scholarship Program (JJ/WBGSP), 355

Middle East

Hastings Center International Visiting Scholars Program, 318
Joint Japan/World Bank Graduate Scholarship Program (JJ/WBGSP), 355

New Zealand

Hastings Center International Visiting Scholars Program, 318

South Africa

Hastings Center International Visiting Scholars Program, 318
Joint Japan/World Bank Graduate Scholarship Program (JJ/WBGSP), 355

South America

Hastings Center International Visiting Scholars Program, 318
Joint Japan/World Bank Graduate Scholarship Program (JJ/WBGSP), 355

United Kingdom

FEMS Fellowship, 280
Hastings Center International Visiting Scholars Program, 318
Hospital Savings Association (HSA) Charitable Trust Scholarships, 526
Innovation and Creative Practice Award, 506

United States of America

JCC Association Scholarships, 378
PhRMAF Postdoctoral Fellowships in Health Outcomes Research, 492
PhRMAF Predoctoral Fellowships in Health Outcomes Research, 494
PhRMAF Research Starter Grants in Health Outcomes Research, 495
PhRMAF Sabbatical Fellowships in Health Outcomes Research, 496

West European Countries

FEMS Fellowship, 280
Hastings Center International Visiting Scholars Program, 318

HOME ECONOMICS EDUCATION

United Kingdom

All Saints Educational Trust Personal Awards, 19

United States of America

National Restaurant Association Educational Foundation Professional Development Scholarship for educators., 457

MUSIC EDUCATION

Any Country

Brandon University Graduate Assistantships, 132
Eastman School of Music Graduate Awards, 264
Ebb & Flow Grant, 265
Friends of the Philharmonia Award for Wood Wind Performers, 498
Lady Marga Alexander Memorial Award for Cellists, 498
Massey Doctoral Scholarship, 408
Royal Academy of Music General Bursary Awards, 525
WBDI Scholarship Awards, 707

United Kingdom

Polish Government Postgraduate Scholarships Scheme, 501

PRE-SCHOOL EDUCATION

Any Country

CQU Postgraduate Research Award, 224
Ebb & Flow Grant, 265
Equiano Memorial Award, 596
ETS Summer Program in Research for Graduate Students, 266
Massey Doctoral Scholarship, 408

African Nations

International Postgraduate Research Scholarships (IPRS), 676
Joint Japan/World Bank Graduate Scholarship Program (JJ/WBGSP), 355
MCTC Assistance for Courses, 304
MCTC Tuition and Maintenance Scholarships, 304

Australia

University of Western Sydney Postgraduate Research Award (UW-SPRA), 689

British Commonwealth

International Postgraduate Research Scholarships (IPRS), 676
Joint Japan/World Bank Graduate Scholarship Program (JJ/WBGSP), 355

Canada

CNRS Fellowships, 210
International Postgraduate Research Scholarships (IPRS), 676
JCC Association Scholarships, 378

Caribbean Countries

International Postgraduate Research Scholarships (IPRS), 676
Joint Japan/World Bank Graduate Scholarship Program (JJ/WBGSP), 355
MCTC Assistance for Courses, 304
MCTC Tuition and Maintenance Scholarships, 304

East European Countries

International Postgraduate Research Scholarships (IPRS), 676
Joint Japan/World Bank Graduate Scholarship Program (JJ/WBGSP), 355
MCTC Assistance for Courses, 304
MCTC Tuition and Maintenance Scholarships, 304

Far East

International Postgraduate Research Scholarships (IPRS), 676
Joint Japan/World Bank Graduate Scholarship Program (JJ/WBGSP), 355
MCTC Assistance for Courses, 304
MCTC Tuition and Maintenance Scholarships, 304

Indian Sub-Continent

International Postgraduate Research Scholarships (IPRS), 676
Joint Japan/World Bank Graduate Scholarship Program (JJ/WBGSP), 355
MCTC Assistance for Courses, 304
MCTC Tuition and Maintenance Scholarships, 304

Middle East

International Postgraduate Research Scholarships (IPRS), 676
Joint Japan/World Bank Graduate Scholarship Program (JJ/WBGSP), 355
MCTC Assistance for Courses, 304
MCTC Tuition and Maintenance Scholarships, 304

New Zealand

University of Western Sydney Postgraduate Research Award (UW-SPRA), 689

South Africa

International Postgraduate Research Scholarships (IPRS), 676
Joint Japan/World Bank Graduate Scholarship Program (JJ/WBGSP), 355
MCTC Assistance for Courses, 304
MCTC Tuition and Maintenance Scholarships, 304

South America

International Postgraduate Research Scholarships (IPRS), 676
Joint Japan/World Bank Graduate Scholarship Program (JJ/WBGSP), 355
MCTC Assistance for Courses, 304
MCTC Tuition and Maintenance Scholarships, 304

United Kingdom

International Postgraduate Research Scholarships (IPRS), 676

United States of America

ETS Postdoctoral Fellowships, 266
ETS Sylvia Taylor Johnson Minority Fellowship Educational Measurement, 267
International Postgraduate Research Scholarships (IPRS), 676
JCC Association Scholarships, 378

West European Countries

International Postgraduate Research Scholarships (IPRS), 676

PRIMARY EDUCATION

Any Country

CQU Postgraduate Research Award, 224
Equiano Memorial Award, 596
ETS Summer Program in Research for Graduate Students, 266
Massey Doctoral Scholarship, 408
University of Glasgow Postgraduate Research Scholarships, 634
University of Manchester Research Studentships and Scholarships, 642
University of Stirling Research Studentships, 678

African Nations

International Postgraduate Research Scholarships (IPRS), 676
Joint Japan/World Bank Graduate Scholarship Program (JJ/WBGSP), 355
MCTC Tuition and Maintenance Scholarships, 304

Australia

University of Western Sydney Postgraduate Research Award (UW-SPRA), 689

British Commonwealth

International Postgraduate Research Scholarships (IPRS), 676
Joint Japan/World Bank Graduate Scholarship Program (JJ/WBGSP), 355

Canada

CNRS Fellowships, 210
International Postgraduate Research Scholarships (IPRS), 676

Caribbean Countries

International Postgraduate Research Scholarships (IPRS), 676
Joint Japan/World Bank Graduate Scholarship Program (JJ/WBGSP), 355
MCTC Tuition and Maintenance Scholarships, 304

East European Countries

International Postgraduate Research Scholarships (IPRS), 676
Joint Japan/World Bank Graduate Scholarship Program (JJ/WBGSP), 355
MCTC Tuition and Maintenance Scholarships, 304

Far East

International Postgraduate Research Scholarships (IPRS), 676
Joint Japan/World Bank Graduate Scholarship Program (JJ/WBGSP), 355
MCTC Tuition and Maintenance Scholarships, 304

Indian Sub-Continent

International Postgraduate Research Scholarships (IPRS), 676
Joint Japan/World Bank Graduate Scholarship Program (JJ/WBGSP), 355
MCTC Tuition and Maintenance Scholarships, 304

Middle East

International Postgraduate Research Scholarships (IPRS), 676
Joint Japan/World Bank Graduate Scholarship Program (JJ/WBGSP), 355
MCTC Tuition and Maintenance Scholarships, 304

New Zealand

University of Western Sydney Postgraduate Research Award (UW-SPRA), 689

South Africa

International Postgraduate Research Scholarships (IPRS), 676
Joint Japan/World Bank Graduate Scholarship Program (JJ/WBGSP), 355
MCTC Tuition and Maintenance Scholarships, 304
Norah Taylor Bursary, 591

South America

International Postgraduate Research Scholarships (IPRS), 676
Joint Japan/World Bank Graduate Scholarship Program (JJ/WBGSP), 355
MCTC Tuition and Maintenance Scholarships, 304

United Kingdom

All Saints Educational Trust Personal Awards, 19
International Postgraduate Research Scholarships (IPRS), 676
Mr and Mrs David Edward Memorial Award, 681
Student Awards Agency for Scotland-Postgraduate Students' Allowances Scheme, 596
University of Wales (Aberystwyth) Postgraduate Research Studentships, 680

UWB Departmental Research Studentships, 681
UWB Research Studentships, 681

United States of America

ETS Postdoctoral Fellowships, 266
ETS Sylvia Taylor Johnson Minority Fellowship Educational Measurement, 267
International Postgraduate Research Scholarships (IPRS), 676

West European Countries

International Postgraduate Research Scholarships (IPRS), 676
Mr and Mrs David Edward Memorial Award, 681
Student Awards Agency for Scotland-Postgraduate Students' Allowances Scheme, 596
UWB Departmental Research Studentships, 681
UWB Research Studentships, 681

SECONDARY EDUCATION

Any Country

CQU Postgraduate Research Award, 224
Electrochemical Society Summer Fellowships, 267
Equiano Memorial Award, 596
ETS Summer Program in Research for Graduate Students, 266
Massey Doctoral Scholarship, 408
University of Glasgow Postgraduate Research Scholarships, 634
University of Manchester Research Studentships and Scholarships, 642
University of Stirling Research Studentships, 678

African Nations

International Postgraduate Research Scholarships (IPRS), 676
Joint Japan/World Bank Graduate Scholarship Program (JJ/WBGSP), 355

Australia

University of Western Sydney Postgraduate Research Award (UW-SPRA), 689

British Commonwealth

International Postgraduate Research Scholarships (IPRS), 676
Joint Japan/World Bank Graduate Scholarship Program (JJ/WBGSP), 355

Canada

CNRS Fellowships, 210
International Postgraduate Research Scholarships (IPRS), 676

Caribbean Countries

International Postgraduate Research Scholarships (IPRS), 676
Joint Japan/World Bank Graduate Scholarship Program (JJ/WBGSP), 355

East European Countries

FEMS Fellowship, 280
International Postgraduate Research Scholarships (IPRS), 676
Joint Japan/World Bank Graduate Scholarship Program (JJ/WBGSP), 355

Far East

International Postgraduate Research Scholarships (IPRS), 676
Joint Japan/World Bank Graduate Scholarship Program (JJ/WBGSP), 355

Indian Sub-Continent

International Postgraduate Research Scholarships (IPRS), 676
Joint Japan/World Bank Graduate Scholarship Program (JJ/WBGSP), 355

Middle East

International Postgraduate Research Scholarships (IPRS), 676
Joint Japan/World Bank Graduate Scholarship Program (JJ/WBGSP), 355

New Zealand

University of Western Sydney Postgraduate Research Award (UW-SPRA), 689

South Africa

International Postgraduate Research Scholarships (IPRS), 676
Joint Japan/World Bank Graduate Scholarship Program (JJ/WBGSP), 355
Norah Taylor Bursary, 591
SACEE EX-PCE Bursary, 591

South America

International Postgraduate Research Scholarships (IPRS), 676
Joint Japan/World Bank Graduate Scholarship Program (JJ/WBGSP), 355

United Kingdom

All Saints Educational Trust Personal Awards, 19
FEMS Fellowship, 280
International Postgraduate Research Scholarships (IPRS), 676
Mr and Mrs David Edward Memorial Award, 681
Student Awards Agency for Scotland-Postgraduate Students' Allowances Scheme, 596
University of Wales (Aberystwyth) Postgraduate Research Studentships, 680
UWB Departmental Research Studentships, 681
UWB Research Studentships, 681

United States of America

ETS Postdoctoral Fellowships, 266
ETS Sylvia Taylor Johnson Minority Fellowship Educational Measurement, 267
International Postgraduate Research Scholarships (IPRS), 676
The Walter J. Jensen Fellowship for French Language, Literature, and Culture, 497

West European Countries

FEMS Fellowship, 280
International Postgraduate Research Scholarships (IPRS), 676
Mr and Mrs David Edward Memorial Award, 681
Student Awards Agency for Scotland-Postgraduate Students' Allowances Scheme, 596
UWB Departmental Research Studentships, 681
UWB Research Studentships, 681

ADULT EDUCATION

Any Country

CQU Postgraduate Research Award, 224
Ebb & Flow Grant, 265
Equiano Memorial Award, 596
ETS Summer Program in Research for Graduate Students, 266
Massey Doctoral Scholarship, 408
OISE/UT FUNDING SUPPORT, 477
OISE/UT Graduate Assistantships, 477
Snowdon Award, 569
University of Glasgow Postgraduate Research Scholarships, 634
University of Stirling Research Studentships, 678

African Nations

International Postgraduate Research Scholarships (IPRS), 676
Joint Japan/World Bank Graduate Scholarship Program (JJ/WBGSP), 355

Australia

University of Western Sydney Postgraduate Research Award (UW-SPRA), 689

British Commonwealth

International Postgraduate Research Scholarships (IPRS), 676
Joint Japan/World Bank Graduate Scholarship Program (JJ/WBGSP), 355

Canada

CNRS Fellowships, 210
International Postgraduate Research Scholarships (IPRS), 676

Caribbean Countries

International Postgraduate Research Scholarships (IPRS), 676
Joint Japan/World Bank Graduate Scholarship Program (JJ/WBGSP), 355

East European Countries

International Postgraduate Research Scholarships (IPRS), 676
Joint Japan/World Bank Graduate Scholarship Program (JJ/WBGSP), 355

Far East

International Postgraduate Research Scholarships (IPRS), 676
Joint Japan/World Bank Graduate Scholarship Program (JJ/WBGSP), 355

Indian Sub-Continent

International Postgraduate Research Scholarships (IPRS), 676
Joint Japan/World Bank Graduate Scholarship Program (JJ/WBGSP), 355

Middle East

International Postgraduate Research Scholarships (IPRS), 676
Joint Japan/World Bank Graduate Scholarship Program (JJ/WBGSP), 355

New Zealand

University of Western Sydney Postgraduate Research Award (UW-SPRA), 689

South Africa

International Postgraduate Research Scholarships (IPRS), 676
Joint Japan/World Bank Graduate Scholarship Program (JJ/WBGSP), 355
SACEE EX-PCE Bursary, 591

South America

International Postgraduate Research Scholarships (IPRS), 676
Joint Japan/World Bank Graduate Scholarship Program (JJ/WBGSP), 355

United Kingdom

International Postgraduate Research Scholarships (IPRS), 676
Regional Agency for the Right to University Study (DSU) Grants, 614
Student Awards Agency for Scotland-Postgraduate Students' Allowances Scheme, 596

United States of America

ETS Postdoctoral Fellowships, 266
ETS Sylvia Taylor Johnson Minority Fellowship Educational Measurement, 267
International Postgraduate Research Scholarships (IPRS), 676

West European Countries

International Postgraduate Research Scholarships (IPRS), 676
Regional Agency for the Right to University Study (DSU) Grants, 614

Student Awards Agency for Scotland-Postgraduate Students' Allowances Scheme, 596

SPECIAL EDUCATION

Any Country

CDU Senior Research Fellowship, 230
CDU Three Year Postdoctoral Fellowship, 230
Ebb & Flow Grant, 265
Equiano Memorial Award, 596
ETS Summer Program in Research for Graduate Students, 266
Massey Doctoral Scholarship, 408
OISE/UT FUNDING SUPPORT, 477
OISE/UT Graduate Assistantships, 477
Snowdon Award, 569
University of Manchester Research Studentships and Scholarships, 642
University of Stirling Research Studentships, 678

African Nations

Joint Japan/World Bank Graduate Scholarship Program (JJ/WBGSP), 355

Australia

University of Western Sydney Postgraduate Research Award (UW-SPRA), 689

British Commonwealth

Joint Japan/World Bank Graduate Scholarship Program (JJ/WBGSP), 355

Canada

CNRS Fellowships, 210
JCC Association Scholarships, 378

Caribbean Countries

Joint Japan/World Bank Graduate Scholarship Program (JJ/WBGSP), 355

East European Countries

Joint Japan/World Bank Graduate Scholarship Program (JJ/WBGSP), 355

Far East

Joint Japan/World Bank Graduate Scholarship Program (JJ/WBGSP), 355

Indian Sub-Continent

Joint Japan/World Bank Graduate Scholarship Program (JJ/WBGSP), 355

Middle East

Joint Japan/World Bank Graduate Scholarship Program (JJ/WBGSP), 355

New Zealand

University of Western Sydney Postgraduate Research Award (UW-SPRA), 689

South Africa

Joint Japan/World Bank Graduate Scholarship Program (JJ/WBGSP), 355

South America

Joint Japan/World Bank Graduate Scholarship Program (JJ/WBGSP), 355

United Kingdom

Hallam Studentships, 558

United States of America

ACRES Scholarship, 41
ETS Postdoctoral Fellowships, 266
ETS Sylvia Taylor Johnson Minority Fellowship Educational Measurement, 267
JCC Association Scholarships, 378

West European Countries

Hallam Studentships, 558

EDUCATION OF THE GIFTED

Any Country

Massey Doctoral Scholarship, 408

African Nations

Joint Japan/World Bank Graduate Scholarship Program (JJ/WBGSP), 355

British Commonwealth

Joint Japan/World Bank Graduate Scholarship Program (JJ/WBGSP), 355

Caribbean Countries

Joint Japan/World Bank Graduate Scholarship Program (JJ/WBGSP), 355

East European Countries

Joint Japan/World Bank Graduate Scholarship Program (JJ/WBGSP), 355

Far East

Joint Japan/World Bank Graduate Scholarship Program (JJ/WBGSP), 355

Indian Sub-Continent

Joint Japan/World Bank Graduate Scholarship Program (JJ/WBGSP), 355

Middle East

Joint Japan/World Bank Graduate Scholarship Program (JJ/WBGSP), 355

South Africa

Joint Japan/World Bank Graduate Scholarship Program (JJ/WBGSP), 355

South America

Joint Japan/World Bank Graduate Scholarship Program (JJ/WBGSP), 355

United States of America

ETS Sylvia Taylor Johnson Minority Fellowship Educational Measurement, 267

EDUCATION OF THE HANDICAPPED

Any Country

Apex Foundation Annual Research Grants, 91
ASBAH Research Grant, 103
Ebb & Flow Grant, 265
ETS Summer Program in Research for Graduate Students, 266
Massey Doctoral Scholarship, 408
Snowdon Award, 569
University of Manchester Research Studentships and Scholarships, 642

African Nations

Joint Japan/World Bank Graduate Scholarship Program (JJ/WBGSP), 355

British Commonwealth

Joint Japan/World Bank Graduate Scholarship Program (JJ/WBGSP), 355

Caribbean Countries

Joint Japan/World Bank Graduate Scholarship Program (JJ/WBGSP), 355

East European Countries

Joint Japan/World Bank Graduate Scholarship Program (JJ/WBGSP), 355

Far East

Joint Japan/World Bank Graduate Scholarship Program (JJ/WBGSP), 355

Indian Sub-Continent

Joint Japan/World Bank Graduate Scholarship Program (JJ/WBGSP), 355

Middle East

Joint Japan/World Bank Graduate Scholarship Program (JJ/WBGSP), 355

South Africa

Joint Japan/World Bank Graduate Scholarship Program (JJ/WBGSP), 355

South America

Joint Japan/World Bank Graduate Scholarship Program (JJ/WBGSP), 355

United States of America

ACRES Scholarship, 41
Emblem Club Scholarship Foundation Grant, 268
ETS Postdoctoral Fellowships, 266
ETS Sylvia Taylor Johnson Minority Fellowship Educational Measurement, 267

EDUCATION OF SPECIFIC LEARNING DISABILITIES

Any Country

ASBAH Research Grant, 103
Ebb & Flow Grant, 265
ETS Summer Program in Research for Graduate Students, 266
Massey Doctoral Scholarship, 408
University of Manchester Research Studentships and Scholarships, 642

African Nations

Joint Japan/World Bank Graduate Scholarship Program (JJ/WBGSP), 355
MCTC Assistance for Courses, 304
MCTC Tuition and Maintenance Scholarships, 304

British Commonwealth

Joint Japan/World Bank Graduate Scholarship Program (JJ/WBGSP), 355

Caribbean Countries

Joint Japan/World Bank Graduate Scholarship Program (JJ/WBGSP), 355

MCTC Assistance for Courses, 304
MCTC Tuition and Maintenance Scholarships, 304

East European Countries

Joint Japan/World Bank Graduate Scholarship Program (JJ/WBGSP), 355
MCTC Assistance for Courses, 304
MCTC Tuition and Maintenance Scholarships, 304

Far East

Joint Japan/World Bank Graduate Scholarship Program (JJ/WBGSP), 355
MCTC Assistance for Courses, 304
MCTC Tuition and Maintenance Scholarships, 304

Indian Sub-Continent

Joint Japan/World Bank Graduate Scholarship Program (JJ/WBGSP), 355
MCTC Assistance for Courses, 304
MCTC Tuition and Maintenance Scholarships, 304

Middle East

Joint Japan/World Bank Graduate Scholarship Program (JJ/WBGSP), 355
MCTC Assistance for Courses, 304
MCTC Tuition and Maintenance Scholarships, 304

South Africa

Joint Japan/World Bank Graduate Scholarship Program (JJ/WBGSP), 355
MCTC Assistance for Courses, 304
MCTC Tuition and Maintenance Scholarships, 304
SACEE EX-PCE Bursary, 591

South America

Joint Japan/World Bank Graduate Scholarship Program (JJ/WBGSP), 355
MCTC Assistance for Courses, 304
MCTC Tuition and Maintenance Scholarships, 304

United Kingdom

Mr and Mrs David Edward Memorial Award, 681
UWB Departmental Research Studentships, 681
UWB Research Studentships, 681

United States of America

ACRES Scholarship, 41

West European Countries

Mr and Mrs David Edward Memorial Award, 681
UWB Departmental Research Studentships, 681
UWB Research Studentships, 681

EDUCATION OF FOREIGNERS

Any Country

AUC Arabic Language Fellowships, 84
Equiano Memorial Award, 596
University of Stirling Research Studentships, 678

South Africa

SACEE EX-PCE Bursary, 591

United Kingdom

Mr and Mrs David Edward Memorial Award, 681
UWB Departmental Research Studentships, 681
UWB Research Studentships, 681

United States of America

Fulbright Teacher and Administrator Exchange, 294
Japanese Residencies Program, 480

West European Countries

Mr and Mrs David Edward Memorial Award, 681
UWB Departmental Research Studentships, 681
UWB Research Studentships, 681

EDUCATION OF NATIVES

Any Country

CDU Senior Research Fellowship, 230
CDU Three Year Postdoctoral Fellowship, 230
Equiano Memorial Award, 596

African Nations

International Postgraduate Research Scholarships (IPRS), 676

British Commonwealth

International Postgraduate Research Scholarships (IPRS), 676

Canada

International Postgraduate Research Scholarships (IPRS), 676

Caribbean Countries

International Postgraduate Research Scholarships (IPRS), 676

East European Countries

International Postgraduate Research Scholarships (IPRS), 676

Far East

International Postgraduate Research Scholarships (IPRS), 676

Indian Sub-Continent

International Postgraduate Research Scholarships (IPRS), 676

Middle East

International Postgraduate Research Scholarships (IPRS), 676

South Africa

International Postgraduate Research Scholarships (IPRS), 676
Norah Taylor Bursary, 591
SACEE EX-PCE Bursary, 591

South America

International Postgraduate Research Scholarships (IPRS), 676

United Kingdom

International Postgraduate Research Scholarships (IPRS), 676

United States of America

Fulbright Teacher and Administrator Exchange, 294
International Postgraduate Research Scholarships (IPRS), 676

West European Countries

International Postgraduate Research Scholarships (IPRS), 676

EDUCATION OF THE SOCIALLY DISADVANTAGED

Any Country

CDU Senior Research Fellowship, 230
CDU Three Year Postdoctoral Fellowship, 230
Equiano Memorial Award, 596

ETS Summer Program in Research for Graduate Students, 266
Frederick Douglass Institute Postdoctoral Fellowship, 289

African Nations

Joint Japan/World Bank Graduate Scholarship Program (JJ/WBGSP), 355

British Commonwealth

Joint Japan/World Bank Graduate Scholarship Program (JJ/WBGSP), 355

Caribbean Countries

Joint Japan/World Bank Graduate Scholarship Program (JJ/WBGSP), 355

East European Countries

Joint Japan/World Bank Graduate Scholarship Program (JJ/WBGSP), 355

Far East

Joint Japan/World Bank Graduate Scholarship Program (JJ/WBGSP), 355

Indian Sub-Continent

Joint Japan/World Bank Graduate Scholarship Program (JJ/WBGSP), 355

Middle East

Joint Japan/World Bank Graduate Scholarship Program (JJ/WBGSP), 355

South Africa

Joint Japan/World Bank Graduate Scholarship Program (JJ/WBGSP), 355
Norah Taylor Bursary, 591
SACEE EX-PCE Bursary, 591

South America

Joint Japan/World Bank Graduate Scholarship Program (JJ/WBGSP), 355

United States of America

ACRES Scholarship, 41

BILINGUAL/BICULTURAL EDUCATION

Any Country

CDU Senior Research Fellowship, 230
CDU Three Year Postdoctoral Fellowship, 230
Equiano Memorial Award, 596
Neporany Research and Teaching Fellowship, 207

United Kingdom

Mr and Mrs David Edward Memorial Award, 681
University of Wales (Aberystwyth) Postgraduate Research Studentships, 680
UWB Departmental Research Studentships, 681
UWB Research Studentships, 681

United States of America

Fulbright Teacher and Administrator Exchange, 294

West European Countries

Mr and Mrs David Edward Memorial Award, 681
UWB Departmental Research Studentships, 681
UWB Research Studentships, 681

TEACHER TRAINERS EDUCATION

Any Country

CQU Postgraduate Research Award, 224
Ebb & Flow Grant, 265
Equiano Memorial Award, 596
ETS Summer Program in Research for Graduate Students, 266
Massey Doctoral Scholarship, 408
University of Glasgow Postgraduate Research Scholarships, 634
University of Stirling Research Studentships, 678
Weizmann Institute of Science MSc Fellowships, 700
Weizmann Institute of Science PhD Fellowships, 700

African Nations

Hubert H Humphrey Fellowship Programme, 609
International Postgraduate Research Scholarships (IPRS), 676
MCTC Assistance for Courses, 304
MCTC Tuition and Maintenance Scholarships, 304

Australia

Japanese Government (Monbukagakusho) Scholarships In-Service Training for Teachers Category, 377
Ministry of Foreign Affairs (France) Stage de Nouméa (Three Week Course), 291
Ministry of Foreign Affairs (France) Stage de Paris/Toulon, 291
Ministry of Foreign Affairs (France) Support for FATFA (Federation of the Association of Teachers of French in Australia), 291
University of Western Sydney Postgraduate Research Award (UW-SPRA), 689

British Commonwealth

International Postgraduate Research Scholarships (IPRS), 676

Canada

CNRS Fellowships, 210
International Postgraduate Research Scholarships (IPRS), 676

Caribbean Countries

Hubert H Humphrey Fellowship Programme, 609
International Postgraduate Research Scholarships (IPRS), 676
MCTC Assistance for Courses, 304
MCTC Tuition and Maintenance Scholarships, 304

East European Countries

Hubert H Humphrey Fellowship Programme, 609
International Postgraduate Research Scholarships (IPRS), 676
MCTC Assistance for Courses, 304
MCTC Tuition and Maintenance Scholarships, 304

Far East

Hubert H Humphrey Fellowship Programme, 609
International Postgraduate Research Scholarships (IPRS), 676
MCTC Assistance for Courses, 304
MCTC Tuition and Maintenance Scholarships, 304

Indian Sub-Continent

Hubert H Humphrey Fellowship Programme, 609
International Postgraduate Research Scholarships (IPRS), 676
MCTC Assistance for Courses, 304
MCTC Tuition and Maintenance Scholarships, 304

Middle East

Hubert H Humphrey Fellowship Programme, 609
International Postgraduate Research Scholarships (IPRS), 676
MCTC Assistance for Courses, 304
MCTC Tuition and Maintenance Scholarships, 304

New Zealand

University of Western Sydney Postgraduate Research Award (UW-SPRA), 689

South Africa

Hubert H Humphrey Fellowship Programme, 609
International Postgraduate Research Scholarships (IPRS), 676
MCTC Assistance for Courses, 304
MCTC Tuition and Maintenance Scholarships, 304
Norah Taylor Bursary, 591
SACEE EX-PCE Bursary, 591

South America

Hubert H Humphrey Fellowship Programme, 609
International Postgraduate Research Scholarships (IPRS), 676
MCTC Assistance for Courses, 304
MCTC Tuition and Maintenance Scholarships, 304

United Kingdom

All Saints Educational Trust Personal Awards, 19
International Postgraduate Research Scholarships (IPRS), 676
Mr and Mrs David Edward Memorial Award, 681
Student Awards Agency for Scotland-Postgraduate Students' Allowances Scheme, 596
University of Wales (Aberystwyth) Postgraduate Research Studentships, 680
UWB Departmental Research Studentships, 681
UWB Research Studentships, 681

United States of America

ETS Postdoctoral Fellowships, 266
International Postgraduate Research Scholarships (IPRS), 676
National Restaurant Association Educational Foundation Professional Development Scholarship for educators., 457

West European Countries

International Postgraduate Research Scholarships (IPRS), 676
Mr and Mrs David Edward Memorial Award, 681
Student Awards Agency for Scotland-Postgraduate Students' Allowances Scheme, 596
UWB Departmental Research Studentships, 681
UWB Research Studentships, 681

HIGHER EDUCATION TEACHER TRAINING

Any Country

ASCSA Summer Sessions, 72
Episcopal Church Foundation Graduate Fellowship Program, 273
Equiano Memorial Award, 596
ETS Summer Program in Research for Graduate Students, 266
Massey Doctoral Scholarship, 408
OISE/UT FUNDING SUPPORT, 477
OISE/UT Graduate Assistantships, 477
University of Bristol Postgraduate Scholarships, 619
University of Glasgow Postgraduate Research Scholarships, 634
University of Stirling Research Studentships, 678

African Nations

Hubert H Humphrey Fellowship Programme, 609

Caribbean Countries

Hubert H Humphrey Fellowship Programme, 609

East European Countries

Hubert H Humphrey Fellowship Programme, 609

Far East

Hubert H Humphrey Fellowship Programme, 609

Indian Sub-Continent

Hubert H Humphrey Fellowship Programme, 609

Middle East

Hubert H Humphrey Fellowship Programme, 609

South Africa

Hubert H Humphrey Fellowship Programme, 609
Norah Taylor Bursary, 591
SACEE EX-PCE Bursary, 591

South America

Hubert H Humphrey Fellowship Programme, 609

United Kingdom

Mr and Mrs David Edward Memorial Award, 681
UWB Departmental Research Studentships, 681
UWB Research Studentships, 681

United States of America

ETS Postdoctoral Fellowships, 266
The Walter J. Jensen Fellowship for French Language, Literature, and Culture, 497

West European Countries

Mr and Mrs David Edward Memorial Award, 681
UWB Departmental Research Studentships, 681
UWB Research Studentships, 681

EDUCATIONAL SCIENCE

Any Country

Camargo Fellowships, 164
CDU Senior Research Fellowship, 230
CDU Three Year Postdoctoral Fellowship, 230
CQU Postgraduate Research Award, 224
Equiano Memorial Award, 596
Esther A and Joseph Klingenstein Fellowship Awards, 274
IAU Travel Grant, 354
Klingenstein Summer Institute, 274
University of Bristol Postgraduate Scholarships, 619
University of Glasgow Postgraduate Research Scholarships, 634
University of Sussex Overseas Research Studentships, 678
Weizmann Institute of Science MSc Fellowships, 700
Weizmann Institute of Science PhD Fellowships, 700

African Nations

Hubert H Humphrey Fellowship Programme, 609
Joint Japan/World Bank Graduate Scholarship Program (JJ/WBGSP), 355

Australia

University of Western Sydney Postgraduate Research Award (UW-SPRA), 689

British Commonwealth

Joint Japan/World Bank Graduate Scholarship Program (JJ/WBGSP), 355

Caribbean Countries

Hubert H Humphrey Fellowship Programme, 609
Joint Japan/World Bank Graduate Scholarship Program (JJ/WBGSP), 355

East European Countries

Hubert H Humphrey Fellowship Programme, 609
Joint Japan/World Bank Graduate Scholarship Program (JJ/WBGSP), 355

Far East

Hubert H Humphrey Fellowship Programme, 609

Joint Japan/World Bank Graduate Scholarship Program (JJ/WBGSP), 355

Indian Sub-Continent

Hubert H Humphrey Fellowship Programme, 609
Joint Japan/World Bank Graduate Scholarship Program (JJ/WBGSP), 355

Middle East

Hubert H Humphrey Fellowship Programme, 609
Joint Japan/World Bank Graduate Scholarship Program (JJ/WBGSP), 355

New Zealand

University of Western Sydney Postgraduate Research Award (UW-SPRA), 689

South Africa

Hubert H Humphrey Fellowship Programme, 609
Joint Japan/World Bank Graduate Scholarship Program (JJ/WBGSP), 355

South America

Hubert H Humphrey Fellowship Programme, 609
Joint Japan/World Bank Graduate Scholarship Program (JJ/WBGSP), 355

United Kingdom

ESRC 1 + 3 Awards & + 3 Awards, 265
Hallam Studentships, 558

United States of America

ETS Postdoctoral Fellowships, 266

West European Countries

ESRC 1 + 3 Awards & + 3 Awards, 265
Hallam Studentships, 558

INTERNATIONAL AND COMPARATIVE EDUCATION

Any Country

Camargo Fellowships, 164
Frederick Douglass Institute Predoctoral Dissertation Fellowship, 290

African Nations

University of Sussex Overseas Development Administration Shared Scholarship Scheme, 678

Australia

Wingate Scholarships, 704

British Commonwealth

Wingate Scholarships, 704

Canada

Wingate Scholarships, 704

Far East

University of Sussex Overseas Development Administration Shared Scholarship Scheme, 678

Indian Sub-Continent

University of Sussex Overseas Development Administration Shared Scholarship Scheme, 678
Wingate Scholarships, 704

PHILOSOPHY OF EDUCATION

CURRICULUM

International Postgraduate Research Scholarships (IPRS), 676
Joint Japan/World Bank Graduate Scholarship Program (JJ/WBGSP), 355

South Africa

Hubert H Humphrey Fellowship Programme, 609
International Postgraduate Research Scholarships (IPRS), 676
Joint Japan/World Bank Graduate Scholarship Program (JJ/WBGSP), 355
SACEE EX-PCE Bursary, 591

South America

Hubert H Humphrey Fellowship Programme, 609
International Postgraduate Research Scholarships (IPRS), 676
Joint Japan/World Bank Graduate Scholarship Program (JJ/WBGSP), 355

United Kingdom

International Postgraduate Research Scholarships (IPRS), 676
Mr and Mrs David Edward Memorial Award, 681
UWB Departmental Research Studentships, 681
UWB Research Studentships, 681

United States of America

International Postgraduate Research Scholarships (IPRS), 676

West European Countries

International Postgraduate Research Scholarships (IPRS), 676
Mr and Mrs David Edward Memorial Award, 681
UWB Departmental Research Studentships, 681
UWB Research Studentships, 681

TEACHING AND LEARNING

Any Country

AUC Writing Center Graduate Fellowships, 86
CDU Senior Research Fellowship, 230
CDU Three Year Postdoctoral Fellowship, 230
Dina Feitelson Research Award, 365
ETS Summer Program in Research for Graduate Students, 266
International Reading Association Teacher as Researcher Grant, 365
Jeanne S Chall Research Fellowship, 365
Massey Doctoral Scholarship, 408
OISE/UT FUNDING SUPPORT, 477
OISE/UT Graduate Assistantships, 477
University of Manchester Research Studentships and Scholarships, 642
University of Stirling Research Studentships, 678

African Nations

International Postgraduate Research Scholarships (IPRS), 676

British Commonwealth

International Postgraduate Research Scholarships (IPRS), 676

Canada

International Postgraduate Research Scholarships (IPRS), 676

Caribbean Countries

International Postgraduate Research Scholarships (IPRS), 676

East European Countries

International Postgraduate Research Scholarships (IPRS), 676

Far East

International Postgraduate Research Scholarships (IPRS), 676

Indian Sub-Continent

International Postgraduate Research Scholarships (IPRS), 676

Middle East

International Postgraduate Research Scholarships (IPRS), 676

South Africa

International Postgraduate Research Scholarships (IPRS), 676
Norah Taylor Bursary, 591
SACEE EX-PCE Bursary, 591

South America

International Postgraduate Research Scholarships (IPRS), 676

United Kingdom

ESRC 1 + 3 Awards & + 3 Awards, 265
International Postgraduate Research Scholarships (IPRS), 676
Mr and Mrs David Edward Memorial Award, 681
UWB Departmental Research Studentships, 681
UWB Research Studentships, 681

United States of America

ETS Postdoctoral Fellowships, 266
ETS Sylvia Taylor Johnson Minority Fellowship Educational Measurement, 267
International Postgraduate Research Scholarships (IPRS), 676

West European Countries

ESRC 1 + 3 Awards & + 3 Awards, 265
International Postgraduate Research Scholarships (IPRS), 676
Mr and Mrs David Edward Memorial Award, 681
UWB Departmental Research Studentships, 681
UWB Research Studentships, 681

EDUCATIONAL RESEARCH

Any Country

Albert J Harris Award, 364
CDU Senior Research Fellowship, 230
CDU Three Year Postdoctoral Fellowship, 230
ChLA Beiter Scholarships for Graduate Students, 234
ChLA Research Fellowships and Scholarships, 234
Dina Feitelson Research Award, 365
Elva Knight Research Grant, 365
ETS Summer Program in Research for Graduate Students, 266
Helen M Robinson Award, 365
IAU Travel Grant, 354
International Reading Association Teacher as Researcher Grant, 365
Jeanne S Chall Research Fellowship, 365
Massey Doctoral Scholarship, 408
NSCA Challenge Scholarship, 458
NSCA Power Systems Professional Scholarship, 458
NSCA Student Research Grant, 458
OISE/UT FUNDING SUPPORT, 477
OISE/UT Graduate Assistantships, 477
University of Glasgow Postgraduate Research Scholarships, 634
University of Manchester Research Studentships and Scholarships, 642
University of Stirling Research Studentships, 678
White House Historical Association Fellowships, 482

African Nations

International Postgraduate Research Scholarships (IPRS), 676
Joint Japan/World Bank Graduate Scholarship Program (JJ/WBGSP), 355
Reading/Literacy Research Fellowship, 366
University of Sussex Overseas Development Administration Shared Scholarship Scheme, 678

Australia

Reading/Literacy Research Fellowship, 366
Wingate Scholarships, 704

British Commonwealth

International Postgraduate Research Scholarships (IPRS), 676
Joint Japan/World Bank Graduate Scholarship Program (JJ/WBGSP), 355
Reading/Literacy Research Fellowship, 366
Wingate Scholarships, 704

Canada

International Postgraduate Research Scholarships (IPRS), 676
Wingate Scholarships, 704

Caribbean Countries

International Postgraduate Research Scholarships (IPRS), 676
Joint Japan/World Bank Graduate Scholarship Program (JJ/WBGSP), 355
Reading/Literacy Research Fellowship, 366

East European Countries

International Postgraduate Research Scholarships (IPRS), 676
Joint Japan/World Bank Graduate Scholarship Program (JJ/WBGSP), 355
Reading/Literacy Research Fellowship, 366

Far East

International Postgraduate Research Scholarships (IPRS), 676
Joint Japan/World Bank Graduate Scholarship Program (JJ/WBGSP), 355
Reading/Literacy Research Fellowship, 366
University of Sussex Overseas Development Administration Shared Scholarship Scheme, 678

Indian Sub-Continent

International Postgraduate Research Scholarships (IPRS), 676
Joint Japan/World Bank Graduate Scholarship Program (JJ/WBGSP), 355
Reading/Literacy Research Fellowship, 366
University of Sussex Overseas Development Administration Shared Scholarship Scheme, 678
Wingate Scholarships, 704

Middle East

International Postgraduate Research Scholarships (IPRS), 676
Joint Japan/World Bank Graduate Scholarship Program (JJ/WBGSP), 355
Reading/Literacy Research Fellowship, 366

New Zealand

Reading/Literacy Research Fellowship, 366
Wingate Scholarships, 704

South Africa

International Postgraduate Research Scholarships (IPRS), 676
Joint Japan/World Bank Graduate Scholarship Program (JJ/WBGSP), 355
Reading/Literacy Research Fellowship, 366
Wingate Scholarships, 704

South America

International Postgraduate Research Scholarships (IPRS), 676
Joint Japan/World Bank Graduate Scholarship Program (JJ/WBGSP), 355
Reading/Literacy Research Fellowship, 366

United Kingdom

Hallam Studentships, 558
International Postgraduate Research Scholarships (IPRS), 676
Mr and Mrs David Edward Memorial Award, 681
Polish Embassy Short Visits Grants, 501
Polish Government Postgraduate Scholarships Scheme, 501
Reading/Literacy Research Fellowship, 366

University of Wales (Aberystwyth) Postgraduate Research Studentships, 680
UWB Departmental Research Studentships, 681
UWB Research Studentships, 681
Wingate Scholarships, 704

United States of America

ETS Postdoctoral Fellowships, 266
ETS Sylvia Taylor Johnson Minority Fellowship Educational Measurement, 267
International Postgraduate Research Scholarships (IPRS), 676

West European Countries

Hallam Studentships, 558
International Postgraduate Research Scholarships (IPRS), 676
Mr and Mrs David Edward Memorial Award, 681
Reading/Literacy Research Fellowship, 366
UWB Departmental Research Studentships, 681
UWB Research Studentships, 681
Wingate Scholarships, 704

EDUCATIONAL TECHNOLOGY

Any Country

CDU Senior Research Fellowship, 230
CDU Three Year Postdoctoral Fellowship, 230
ETS Summer Program in Research for Graduate Students, 266
Massey Doctoral Scholarship, 408
University of Stirling Research Studentships, 678

African Nations

Hubert H Humphrey Fellowship Programme, 609
International Postgraduate Research Scholarships (IPRS), 676
Joint Japan/World Bank Graduate Scholarship Program (JJ/WBGSP), 355

British Commonwealth

International Postgraduate Research Scholarships (IPRS), 676
Joint Japan/World Bank Graduate Scholarship Program (JJ/WBGSP), 355

Canada

International Postgraduate Research Scholarships (IPRS), 676

Caribbean Countries

Hubert H Humphrey Fellowship Programme, 609
International Postgraduate Research Scholarships (IPRS), 676
Joint Japan/World Bank Graduate Scholarship Program (JJ/WBGSP), 355

East European Countries

Hubert H Humphrey Fellowship Programme, 609
International Postgraduate Research Scholarships (IPRS), 676
Joint Japan/World Bank Graduate Scholarship Program (JJ/WBGSP), 355

Far East

Hubert H Humphrey Fellowship Programme, 609
International Postgraduate Research Scholarships (IPRS), 676
Joint Japan/World Bank Graduate Scholarship Program (JJ/WBGSP), 355

Indian Sub-Continent

Hubert H Humphrey Fellowship Programme, 609
International Postgraduate Research Scholarships (IPRS), 676
Joint Japan/World Bank Graduate Scholarship Program (JJ/WBGSP), 355

Middle East

Hubert H Humphrey Fellowship Programme, 609
International Postgraduate Research Scholarships (IPRS), 676
Joint Japan/World Bank Graduate Scholarship Program (JJ/WBGSP), 355

South Africa

Hubert H Humphrey Fellowship Programme, 609
International Postgraduate Research Scholarships (IPRS), 676
Joint Japan/World Bank Graduate Scholarship Program (JJ/WBGSP), 355

South America

Hubert H Humphrey Fellowship Programme, 609
International Postgraduate Research Scholarships (IPRS), 676
Joint Japan/World Bank Graduate Scholarship Program (JJ/WBGSP), 355

United Kingdom

International Postgraduate Research Scholarships (IPRS), 676

United States of America

Earthwatch Education Awards, 264
ETS Postdoctoral Fellowships, 266
International Postgraduate Research Scholarships (IPRS), 676

West European Countries

International Postgraduate Research Scholarships (IPRS), 676

EDUCATIONAL AND STUDENT COUNSELLING

Any Country

ETS Summer Program in Research for Graduate Students, 266
Massey Doctoral Scholarship, 408
University of Manchester Research Studentships and Scholarships, 642

African Nations

Hubert H Humphrey Fellowship Programme, 609
International Postgraduate Research Scholarships (IPRS), 676
Joint Japan/World Bank Graduate Scholarship Program (JJ/WBGSP), 355

British Commonwealth

International Postgraduate Research Scholarships (IPRS), 676
Joint Japan/World Bank Graduate Scholarship Program (JJ/WBGSP), 355

Canada

International Postgraduate Research Scholarships (IPRS), 676

Caribbean Countries

Hubert H Humphrey Fellowship Programme, 609
International Postgraduate Research Scholarships (IPRS), 676
Joint Japan/World Bank Graduate Scholarship Program (JJ/WBGSP), 355

East European Countries

Hubert H Humphrey Fellowship Programme, 609
International Postgraduate Research Scholarships (IPRS), 676
Joint Japan/World Bank Graduate Scholarship Program (JJ/WBGSP), 355

Far East

Hubert H Humphrey Fellowship Programme, 609
International Postgraduate Research Scholarships (IPRS), 676

Joint Japan/World Bank Graduate Scholarship Program (JJ/WBGSP), 355

Indian Sub-Continent

Hubert H Humphrey Fellowship Programme, 609
International Postgraduate Research Scholarships (IPRS), 676
Joint Japan/World Bank Graduate Scholarship Program (JJ/WBGSP), 355

Middle East

Hubert H Humphrey Fellowship Programme, 609
International Postgraduate Research Scholarships (IPRS), 676
Joint Japan/World Bank Graduate Scholarship Program (JJ/WBGSP), 355

South Africa

Hubert H Humphrey Fellowship Programme, 609
International Postgraduate Research Scholarships (IPRS), 676
Joint Japan/World Bank Graduate Scholarship Program (JJ/WBGSP), 355

South America

Hubert H Humphrey Fellowship Programme, 609
International Postgraduate Research Scholarships (IPRS), 676
Joint Japan/World Bank Graduate Scholarship Program (JJ/WBGSP), 355

United Kingdom

International Postgraduate Research Scholarships (IPRS), 676

United States of America

International Postgraduate Research Scholarships (IPRS), 676

West European Countries

International Postgraduate Research Scholarships (IPRS), 676

EDUCATIONAL ADMINISTRATION

Any Country

ETS Summer Program in Research for Graduate Students, 266
Massey Doctoral Scholarship, 408
OISE/UT FUNDING SUPPORT, 477
OISE/UT Graduate Assistantships, 477

African Nations

Hubert H Humphrey Fellowship Programme, 609
International Postgraduate Research Scholarships (IPRS), 676
Joint Japan/World Bank Graduate Scholarship Program (JJ/WBGSP), 355
University of Sussex Overseas Development Administration Shared Scholarship Scheme, 678

British Commonwealth

International Postgraduate Research Scholarships (IPRS), 676
Joint Japan/World Bank Graduate Scholarship Program (JJ/WBGSP), 355

Canada

International Postgraduate Research Scholarships (IPRS), 676

Caribbean Countries

Hubert H Humphrey Fellowship Programme, 609
International Postgraduate Research Scholarships (IPRS), 676
Joint Japan/World Bank Graduate Scholarship Program (JJ/WBGSP), 355

East European Countries

Hubert H Humphrey Fellowship Programme, 609

International Postgraduate Research Scholarships (IPRS), 676
Joint Japan/World Bank Graduate Scholarship Program (JJ/WBGSP), 355

Far East

Hubert H Humphrey Fellowship Programme, 609
International Postgraduate Research Scholarships (IPRS), 676
Joint Japan/World Bank Graduate Scholarship Program (JJ/WBGSP), 355
University of Sussex Overseas Development Administration Shared Scholarship Scheme, 678

Indian Sub-Continent

Hubert H Humphrey Fellowship Programme, 609
International Postgraduate Research Scholarships (IPRS), 676
Joint Japan/World Bank Graduate Scholarship Program (JJ/WBGSP), 355
University of Sussex Overseas Development Administration Shared Scholarship Scheme, 678

Middle East

Hubert H Humphrey Fellowship Programme, 609
International Postgraduate Research Scholarships (IPRS), 676
Joint Japan/World Bank Graduate Scholarship Program (JJ/WBGSP), 355

South Africa

Hubert H Humphrey Fellowship Programme, 609
International Postgraduate Research Scholarships (IPRS), 676
Joint Japan/World Bank Graduate Scholarship Program (JJ/WBGSP), 355

South America

Hubert H Humphrey Fellowship Programme, 609
International Postgraduate Research Scholarships (IPRS), 676
Joint Japan/World Bank Graduate Scholarship Program (JJ/WBGSP), 355

United Kingdom

International Postgraduate Research Scholarships (IPRS), 676

United States of America

ETS Sylvia Taylor Johnson Minority Fellowship Educational Measurement, 267
International Postgraduate Research Scholarships (IPRS), 676

West European Countries

International Postgraduate Research Scholarships (IPRS), 676

EDUCATIONAL TESTING AND EVALUATION

Any Country

ASBAH Research Grant, 103
CDU Senior Research Fellowship, 230
CDU Three Year Postdoctoral Fellowship, 230
ETS Summer Program in Research for Graduate Students, 266
OISE/UT Graduate Assistantships, 477
University of Stirling Research Studentships, 678

African Nations

International Postgraduate Research Scholarships (IPRS), 676
Joint Japan/World Bank Graduate Scholarship Program (JJ/WBGSP), 355
University of Sussex Overseas Development Administration Shared Scholarship Scheme, 678

Australia

Wingate Scholarships, 704

British Commonwealth

International Postgraduate Research Scholarships (IPRS), 676
Joint Japan/World Bank Graduate Scholarship Program (JJ/WBGSP), 355
Wingate Scholarships, 704

Canada

International Postgraduate Research Scholarships (IPRS), 676
Wingate Scholarships, 704

Caribbean Countries

International Postgraduate Research Scholarships (IPRS), 676
Joint Japan/World Bank Graduate Scholarship Program (JJ/WBGSP), 355

East European Countries

International Postgraduate Research Scholarships (IPRS), 676
Joint Japan/World Bank Graduate Scholarship Program (JJ/WBGSP), 355

Far East

International Postgraduate Research Scholarships (IPRS), 676
Joint Japan/World Bank Graduate Scholarship Program (JJ/WBGSP), 355
University of Sussex Overseas Development Administration Shared Scholarship Scheme, 678

Indian Sub-Continent

International Postgraduate Research Scholarships (IPRS), 676
Joint Japan/World Bank Graduate Scholarship Program (JJ/WBGSP), 355
University of Sussex Overseas Development Administration Shared Scholarship Scheme, 678
Wingate Scholarships, 704

Middle East

International Postgraduate Research Scholarships (IPRS), 676
Joint Japan/World Bank Graduate Scholarship Program (JJ/WBGSP), 355

New Zealand

Wingate Scholarships, 704

South Africa

International Postgraduate Research Scholarships (IPRS), 676
Joint Japan/World Bank Graduate Scholarship Program (JJ/WBGSP), 355
Wingate Scholarships, 704

South America

International Postgraduate Research Scholarships (IPRS), 676
Joint Japan/World Bank Graduate Scholarship Program (JJ/WBGSP), 355

United Kingdom

International Postgraduate Research Scholarships (IPRS), 676
Wingate Scholarships, 704

United States of America

ETS Postdoctoral Fellowships, 266
ETS Sylvia Taylor Johnson Minority Fellowship Educational Measurement, 267
International Postgraduate Research Scholarships (IPRS), 676

West European Countries

International Postgraduate Research Scholarships (IPRS), 676
Wingate Scholarships, 704

DISTANCE EDUCATION

Any Country

African Nations

British Commonwealth

Caribbean Countries

East European Countries

Far East

Indian Sub-Continent

Middle East

South Africa

South America

ENGINEERING

GENERAL

Any Country

North Dakota Indian Scholarship, 472
NRC Twinning Program, 455
OAS Graduate Academic Studies, 483
Olive Lynn Salembier Scholarship, 588
Past Presidents Scholarships, 589
Renate W Chasman Scholarship, 162
SME Education Foundation Grants Program, 566
Spinal Cord Research Foundation Grants, 485
SWE General Motors Foundation Graduate Scholarship, 589
Swiss Federal Institute of Technology Scholarships, 598
Washington University Chancellor's Graduate Fellowship Program for African Americans, 699
Winston Churchill Scholarship, 705

West European Countries

CERN Doctoral Student Programme, 228
CERN Fellowships, 228
CERN Technical Student Programme, 228
EPSRC Doctoral Training Grants (DTGs), 269
Eugen and Ilse Seibold Award, 257
Fulbright Postdoctoral Research and Lecturing Awards for Non-US Citizens, 143
Hallam Studentships, 558
International Postgraduate Research Scholarships (IPRS), 390
International Postgraduate Research Scholarships (IPRS), 676
Janson Johan Helmich Scholarships and Travel Grants, 376
Royal Academy of Engineering International Travel Grants, 525
Royal Society University Research Fellowships, 544
RSA Design Directions, 545
Sheffield Hallam University Research Studentships, 558
St Anne's College Una Goodwin Research Scholarship, 666
The Bernard Butler Trust Fund, 374
Wingate Scholarships, 704

SURVEYING AND MAPPING SCIENCE

Any Country

DEED (Demonstration of Energy-Efficient Developments) Scholarship, 69
John Moyes Lessells Scholarships, 548
Mott MacDonald Charitable Trust Scholarships, 426
RICS Education Trust Award, 520

African Nations

International Postgraduate Research Scholarships (IPRS), 676

Australia

Fulbright Postgraduate Student Award for Engineering, 120
Fulbright Postgraduate Student Award for Science and Engineering, 120
Wingate Scholarships, 704

British Commonwealth

International Postgraduate Research Scholarships (IPRS), 676
Wingate Scholarships, 704

Canada

Canadian Window on International Development, 358
International Postgraduate Research Scholarships (IPRS), 676
Wingate Scholarships, 704

Caribbean Countries

International Postgraduate Research Scholarships (IPRS), 676

East European Countries

International Postgraduate Research Scholarships (IPRS), 676

Far East

International Postgraduate Research Scholarships (IPRS), 676

Indian Sub-Continent

International Postgraduate Research Scholarships (IPRS), 676
Wingate Scholarships, 704

Middle East

International Postgraduate Research Scholarships (IPRS), 676

New Zealand

Wingate Scholarships, 704

South Africa

International Postgraduate Research Scholarships (IPRS), 676
Wingate Scholarships, 704

South America

International Postgraduate Research Scholarships (IPRS), 676

United Kingdom

International Postgraduate Research Scholarships (IPRS), 676
Wingate Scholarships, 704

United States of America

International Postgraduate Research Scholarships (IPRS), 676

West European Countries

International Postgraduate Research Scholarships (IPRS), 676
Wingate Scholarships, 704

ENGINEERING DRAWING/DESIGN

Any Country

CQU Postgraduate Research Award, 224
DEED (Demonstration of Energy-Efficient Developments) Scholarship, 69
John Moyes Lessells Scholarships, 548
Mott MacDonald Charitable Trust Scholarships, 426

African Nations

International Postgraduate Research Scholarships (IPRS), 676

Australia

Fulbright Postgraduate Student Award for Engineering, 120
Fulbright Postgraduate Student Award for Science and Engineering, 120
Wingate Scholarships, 704

British Commonwealth

International Postgraduate Research Scholarships (IPRS), 676
Wingate Scholarships, 704

Canada

International Postgraduate Research Scholarships (IPRS), 676
TAC Scholarships, 604
Wingate Scholarships, 704

Caribbean Countries

International Postgraduate Research Scholarships (IPRS), 676

East European Countries

International Postgraduate Research Scholarships (IPRS), 676

Far East

International Postgraduate Research Scholarships (IPRS), 676

Indian Sub-Continent

International Postgraduate Research Scholarships (IPRS), 676
Wingate Scholarships, 704

Middle East

International Postgraduate Research Scholarships (IPRS), 676

New Zealand

Wingate Scholarships, 704

South Africa

International Postgraduate Research Scholarships (IPRS), 676
Wingate Scholarships, 704

South America

International Postgraduate Research Scholarships (IPRS), 676

United Kingdom

International Postgraduate Research Scholarships (IPRS), 676
Wingate Scholarships, 704

United States of America

ASNE Scholarships, 81
International Postgraduate Research Scholarships (IPRS), 676
Winston Churchill Scholarship, 705

West European Countries

International Postgraduate Research Scholarships (IPRS), 676
Wingate Scholarships, 704

CHEMICAL ENGINEERING

Any Country

ACS/PRF Scientific Education Grants, 35
ACS/PRF Type AC Grants, 35
ACS/PRF Type B Grants, 36
BP/RSE Research Fellowships, 547
DEED (Demonstration of Energy-Efficient Developments) Scholarship, 69
Exxon Mobil Teaching Fellowships, 524
John Moyes Lessells Scholarships, 548
Massey Doctoral Scholarship, 408
Mott MacDonald Charitable Trust Scholarships, 426
Trinity College Junior Research Fellowship, 672
University of Bristol Postgraduate Scholarships, 619
Welch Foundation Scholarship, 371

African Nations

International Postgraduate Research Scholarships (IPRS), 676

Australia

C T Taylor Studentship for PhD Study, 173
Fulbright Postgraduate Student Award for Engineering, 120
Fulbright Postgraduate Student Award for Science and Engineering, 120
Wingate Scholarships, 704

British Commonwealth

International Postgraduate Research Scholarships (IPRS), 676
Wingate Scholarships, 704

Canada

C T Taylor Studentship for PhD Study, 173
CIC Award for Environmental Improvement, 232
CIC Catalysis Award, 232
CIC Macromolecular Science and Engineering Lecture Award, 232
CIC Medal, 232
CIC Montreal Medal, 232
CIC Union Carbide Award for Chemical Education, 233
CSCT Norman and Marion Bright Memorial Award, 211
International Postgraduate Research Scholarships (IPRS), 676
Wingate Scholarships, 704

Caribbean Countries

International Postgraduate Research Scholarships (IPRS), 676

East European Countries

International Postgraduate Research Scholarships (IPRS), 676
VKI Fellowship, 696

Far East

Huntsman Tioxide Cambridge Scholarship for Postgraduate Study, 179
International Postgraduate Research Scholarships (IPRS), 676
Swiss Federal Institute of Technology Scholarships, 598

Indian Sub-Continent

International Postgraduate Research Scholarships (IPRS), 676
Wingate Scholarships, 704

Middle East

International Postgraduate Research Scholarships (IPRS), 676

New Zealand

C T Taylor Studentship for PhD Study, 173
Wingate Scholarships, 704

South Africa

Huntsman Tioxide Cambridge Scholarship for Postgraduate Study, 179
International Postgraduate Research Scholarships (IPRS), 676
Wingate Scholarships, 704

South America

International Postgraduate Research Scholarships (IPRS), 676

United Kingdom

International Postgraduate Research Scholarships (IPRS), 676
Polish Government Postgraduate Scholarships Scheme, 501
Swiss Federal Institute of Technology Scholarships, 598
Wingate Scholarships, 704

United States of America

ACS/PRF Type G 'Starter' Grants
American Electroplaters and Surface Finishers Society Scholarship, 372
Army Research Laboratory Postdoctoral Fellowship Program, 75
International Postgraduate Research Scholarships (IPRS), 676
NRC Twinning Program, 455
SRC Graduate Fellowship Program, 557
SRC Master's Scholarship Program, 557
SWE General Motors Foundation Graduate Scholarship, 589
Swiss Federal Institute of Technology Scholarships, 598
VKI Fellowship, 696
Winston Churchill Scholarship, 705

West European Countries

International Postgraduate Research Scholarships (IPRS), 676
VKI Fellowship, 696
Wingate Scholarships, 704

CIVIL, CONSTRUCTION AND TRANSPORTATION ENGINEERING

Any Country

CQU Postgraduate Research Award, 224
De Paepe - Willems Award, 364
DEED (Demonstration of Energy-Efficient Developments) Scholarship, 69
John Moyes Lessells Scholarships, 548
Johnson's Wax Research Fellowship, 406

Mott MacDonald Charitable Trust Scholarships, 426
NRC Research Associateships, 456
QUEST Institution of Civil Engineers Continuing Education Award, 346
QUEST Institution of Civil Engineers Overseas Travel Awards, 346
Rees Jeffreys Road Fund Bursaries, 332
RICS Education Trust Award, 520
Structural Engineering Travelling Fellowship, 566
Trinity College Junior Research Fellowship, 672
University of Bristol Postgraduate Scholarships, 619
University of Dundee Research Awards, 629
University of Glasgow Postgraduate Research Scholarships, 634
University of Manchester Research Studentships and Scholarships, 642

African Nations

International Postgraduate Research Scholarships (IPRS), 676
Shell centenary chevening scholarships, 640
Shell Centenary Scholarships, 640
The Bernard Butler Trust Fund, 374

Australia

Fulbright Postgraduate Student Award for Engineering, 120
Fulbright Postgraduate Student Award for Science and Engineering, 120
University of Western Sydney Postgraduate Research Award (UW-SPRA), 689
Wingate Scholarships, 704

British Commonwealth

International Postgraduate Research Scholarships (IPRS), 676
Shell centenary chevening scholarships, 640
Shell Centenary Scholarships, 640
The Bernard Butler Trust Fund, 374
Wingate Scholarships, 704

Canada

International Postgraduate Research Scholarships (IPRS), 676
TAC Scholarships, 604
Wingate Scholarships, 704

Caribbean Countries

International Postgraduate Research Scholarships (IPRS), 676
Shell centenary chevening scholarships, 640
Shell Centenary Scholarships, 640
The Bernard Butler Trust Fund, 374

East European Countries

CERN Doctoral Student Programme, 228
CERN Fellowships, 228
CERN Technical Student Programme, 228
International Postgraduate Research Scholarships (IPRS), 676
The Bernard Butler Trust Fund, 374

Far East

International Postgraduate Research Scholarships (IPRS), 676
Shell centenary chevening scholarships, 640
Shell Centenary Scholarships, 640
Swiss Federal Institute of Technology Scholarships, 598
The Bernard Butler Trust Fund, 374

Indian Sub-Continent

International Postgraduate Research Scholarships (IPRS), 676
Shell centenary chevening scholarships, 640
Shell Centenary Scholarships, 640
The Bernard Butler Trust Fund, 374
Wingate Scholarships, 704

Middle East

International Postgraduate Research Scholarships (IPRS), 676
Shell centenary chevening scholarships, 640

Shell Centenary Scholarships, 640
The Bernard Butler Trust Fund, 374

New Zealand

University of Western Sydney Postgraduate Research Award (UW-SPRA), 689
Wingate Scholarships, 704

South Africa

International Postgraduate Research Scholarships (IPRS), 676
Shell centenary chevening scholarships, 640
Shell Centenary Scholarships, 640
The Bernard Butler Trust Fund, 374
Wingate Scholarships, 704

South America

International Postgraduate Research Scholarships (IPRS), 676
Shell centenary chevening scholarships, 640
Shell Centenary Scholarships, 640
The Bernard Butler Trust Fund, 374

United Kingdom

CERN Doctoral Student Programme, 228
CERN Fellowships, 228
CERN Technical Student Programme, 228
Hallam Studentships, 558
International Postgraduate Research Scholarships (IPRS), 676
QUEST C H Roberts Bequest, 345
Rees Jeffreys Road Fund Bursaries, 332
Rees Jeffreys Road Fund Bursaries, 332
Swiss Federal Institute of Technology Scholarships, 598
The Bernard Butler Trust Fund, 374
Wingate Scholarships, 704
Young Consulting Engineer of the Year, 107

United States of America

ASNE Scholarships, 81
International Postgraduate Research Scholarships (IPRS), 676
NRC Twinning Program, 455
SWE General Motors Foundation Graduate Scholarship, 589
Swiss Federal Institute of Technology Scholarships, 598
Winston Churchill Scholarship, 705

West European Countries

CERN Doctoral Student Programme, 228
CERN Fellowships, 228
CERN Technical Student Programme, 228
Hallam Studentships, 558
International Postgraduate Research Scholarships (IPRS), 676
QUEST C H Roberts Bequest, 345
Rees Jeffreys Road Fund Bursaries, 332
The Bernard Butler Trust Fund, 374
Wingate Scholarships, 704

ENVIRONMENTAL AND SANITARY ENGINEERING

Any Country

AWWA Academic Achievement Award, 87
AWWA Thomas R Camp Scholarship, 87
DEED (Demonstration of Energy-Efficient Developments) Scholarship, 69
John Moyes Lessells Scholarships, 548
Massey Doctoral Scholarship, 408
Mott MacDonald Charitable Trust Scholarships, 426
QUEST Institution of Civil Engineers Overseas Travel Awards, 346
Solids Handling Award, 351
University of Dundee Research Awards, 629
VITUKI Training Financial Support for Course Participants, 696

African Nations

BP - FCO Chevening - Leeds University Scholarships, 638
International Postgraduate Research Scholarships (IPRS), 676
Joint Japan/World Bank Graduate Scholarship Program (JJ/WBGSP), 355
Shell centenary chevening scholarships, 640
Shell Centenary Scholarships, 640

Australia

Fulbright Postgraduate Student Award for Engineering, 120
Fulbright Postgraduate Student Award for Science and Engineering, 120
University of Western Sydney Postgraduate Research Award (UW-SPRA), 689
Wingate Scholarships, 704

British Commonwealth

BP - FCO Chevening - Leeds University Scholarships, 638
International Postgraduate Research Scholarships (IPRS), 676
Joint Japan/World Bank Graduate Scholarship Program (JJ/WBGSP), 355
Shell centenary chevening scholarships, 640
Shell Centenary Scholarships, 640
Wingate Scholarships, 704

Canada

AWWA Abel Wolman Fellowship, 86
AWWA Larson Aquatic Research Support, 87
Canadian Window on International Development, 358
Horticultural Research Institute Grants, 327
International Postgraduate Research Scholarships (IPRS), 676
TAC Scholarships, 604
Wingate Scholarships, 704

Caribbean Countries

BP - FCO Chevening - Leeds University Scholarships, 638
International Postgraduate Research Scholarships (IPRS), 676
Joint Japan/World Bank Graduate Scholarship Program (JJ/WBGSP), 355
Shell centenary chevening scholarships, 640
Shell Centenary Scholarships, 640

East European Countries

CERN Doctoral Student Programme, 228
CERN Fellowships, 228
CERN Technical Student Programme, 228
International Postgraduate Research Scholarships (IPRS), 676
Joint Japan/World Bank Graduate Scholarship Program (JJ/WBGSP), 355
VKI Fellowship, 696

Far East

BP - FCO Chevening - Leeds University Scholarships, 638
International Postgraduate Research Scholarships (IPRS), 676
Joint Japan/World Bank Graduate Scholarship Program (JJ/WBGSP), 355
Shell centenary chevening scholarships, 640
Shell Centenary Scholarships, 640

Indian Sub-Continent

BP - FCO Chevening - Leeds University Scholarships, 638
International Postgraduate Research Scholarships (IPRS), 676
Joint Japan/World Bank Graduate Scholarship Program (JJ/WBGSP), 355
Shell centenary chevening scholarships, 640
Shell Centenary Scholarships, 640
Wingate Scholarships, 704

Middle East

BP - FCO Chevening - Leeds University Scholarships, 638
International Postgraduate Research Scholarships (IPRS), 676

Joint Japan/World Bank Graduate Scholarship Program (JJ/WBGSP), 355
Shell centenary chevening scholarships, 640
Shell Centenary Scholarships, 640

New Zealand

University of Western Sydney Postgraduate Research Award (UW-SPRA), 689
Wingate Scholarships, 704

South Africa

BP - FCO Chevening - Leeds University Scholarships, 638
International Postgraduate Research Scholarships (IPRS), 676
Joint Japan/World Bank Graduate Scholarship Program (JJ/WBGSP), 355
Shell centenary chevening scholarships, 640
Shell Centenary Scholarships, 640
Wingate Scholarships, 704

South America

AWWA Abel Wolman Fellowship, 86
AWWA Larson Aquatic Research Support, 87
BP - FCO Chevening - Leeds University Scholarships, 638
International Postgraduate Research Scholarships (IPRS), 676
Joint Japan/World Bank Graduate Scholarship Program (JJ/WBGSP), 355
Shell centenary chevening scholarships, 640
Shell Centenary Scholarships, 640

United Kingdom

CERN Doctoral Student Programme, 228
CERN Fellowships, 228
CERN Technical Student Programme, 228
International Postgraduate Research Scholarships (IPRS), 676
John Stanley Scholarship, 332
Polish Government Postgraduate Scholarships Scheme, 501
Silsoe Awards, 249
Wingate Scholarships, 704

United States of America

Army Research Laboratory Postdoctoral Fellowship Program, 75
ASNE Scholarships, 81
AWWA Abel Wolman Fellowship, 86
AWWA Holly A Cornell Scholarship, 87
AWWA Larson Aquatic Research Support, 87
Horticultural Research Institute Grants, 327
International Postgraduate Research Scholarships (IPRS), 676
NRC Twinning Program, 455
VKI Fellowship, 696
Winston Churchill Scholarship, 705

West European Countries

CERN Doctoral Student Programme, 228
CERN Fellowships, 228
CERN Technical Student Programme, 228
International Postgraduate Research Scholarships (IPRS), 676
Silsoe Awards, 249
VKI Fellowship, 696
Wingate Scholarships, 704

SAFETY ENGINEERING

Any Country

DEED (Demonstration of Energy-Efficient Developments) Scholarship, 69
John Moyes Lessells Scholarships, 548
Mott MacDonald Charitable Trust Scholarships, 426
University of Manchester Research Studentships and Scholarships, 642

African Nations

International Postgraduate Research Scholarships (IPRS), 676
Joint Japan/World Bank Graduate Scholarship Program (JJ/WBGSP), 355

Australia

Fulbright Postgraduate Student Award for Engineering, 120
Fulbright Postgraduate Student Award for Science and Engineering, 120
Wingate Scholarships, 704

British Commonwealth

International Postgraduate Research Scholarships (IPRS), 676
Joint Japan/World Bank Graduate Scholarship Program (JJ/WBGSP), 355
Wingate Scholarships, 704

Canada

International Postgraduate Research Scholarships (IPRS), 676
TAC Scholarships, 604
Wingate Scholarships, 704

Caribbean Countries

International Postgraduate Research Scholarships (IPRS), 676
Joint Japan/World Bank Graduate Scholarship Program (JJ/WBGSP), 355

East European Countries

CERN Doctoral Student Programme, 228
CERN Fellowships, 228
CERN Technical Student Programme, 228
International Postgraduate Research Scholarships (IPRS), 676
Joint Japan/World Bank Graduate Scholarship Program (JJ/WBGSP), 355

Far East

International Postgraduate Research Scholarships (IPRS), 676
Joint Japan/World Bank Graduate Scholarship Program (JJ/WBGSP), 355

Indian Sub-Continent

International Postgraduate Research Scholarships (IPRS), 676
Joint Japan/World Bank Graduate Scholarship Program (JJ/WBGSP), 355
Wingate Scholarships, 704

Middle East

International Postgraduate Research Scholarships (IPRS), 676
Joint Japan/World Bank Graduate Scholarship Program (JJ/WBGSP), 355

New Zealand

Wingate Scholarships, 704

South Africa

International Postgraduate Research Scholarships (IPRS), 676
Joint Japan/World Bank Graduate Scholarship Program (JJ/WBGSP), 355
Wingate Scholarships, 704

South America

International Postgraduate Research Scholarships (IPRS), 676
Joint Japan/World Bank Graduate Scholarship Program (JJ/WBGSP), 355

United Kingdom

CERN Doctoral Student Programme, 228
CERN Fellowships, 228
CERN Technical Student Programme, 228

International Postgraduate Research Scholarships (IPRS), 676
University of Wales (Aberystwyth) Postgraduate Research Studentships, 680
Wingate Scholarships, 704

United States of America

ASNE Scholarships, 81
International Postgraduate Research Scholarships (IPRS), 676
Winston Churchill Scholarship, 705

West European Countries

CERN Doctoral Student Programme, 228
CERN Fellowships, 228
CERN Technical Student Programme, 228
International Postgraduate Research Scholarships (IPRS), 676
Wingate Scholarships, 704

ELECTRICAL/ELECTRONIC AND TELECOMMUNICATIONS ENGINEERING

Any Country

Building Systems Technology Research Grant, 565
CDU Senior Research Fellowship, 230
CDU Three Year Postdoctoral Fellowship, 230
CQU Postgraduate Research Award, 224
D H Thomas Travel Bursary, 346
DEED (Demonstration of Energy-Efficient Developments) Scholarship, 69
Hudswell Bequest Travelling Fellowships, 346
Hudswell International Research Scholarships, 346
IEE Master's Degree Research Scholarship, 347
IEE Postgraduate Scholarships, 347
IEE Robinson Research Fellowship, 347
IEE Younger Members Conference Bursary, 347
J R Beard Travelling Fund Awards, 347
John Moyes Lessells Scholarships, 548
Johnson's Wax Research Fellowship, 406
KSTU Rector's Grant, 385
Leonard Research Grant, 348
Leslie H Paddle Fellowship, 348
Massey Doctoral Scholarship, 408
Milwaukee Foundation's Frank Rogers Bacon Research Assistantship, 406
Mott MacDonald Charitable Trust Scholarships, 426
NRC Research Associateships, 456
Princess Royal Scholarship, 348
Queen Mary Research Studentships, 506
Robinson Research Scholarship, 348
Trinity College Junior Research Fellowship, 672
TUCS Postgraduate Grant, 606
University of Bristol Postgraduate Scholarships, 619
University of Dundee Research Awards, 629
University of Essex Scholarships, 632
University of Glasgow Postgraduate Research Scholarships, 634

African Nations

International Postgraduate Research Scholarships (IPRS), 676
Shell centenary chevening scholarships, 640
Shell Centenary Scholarships, 640
William Morley Bursary, 349

Australia

Fulbright Postgraduate Student Award for Engineering, 120
Fulbright Postgraduate Student Award for Science and Engineering, 120
University of Western Sydney Postgraduate Research Award (UW-SPRA), 689
Wingate Scholarships, 704

British Commonwealth

International Postgraduate Research Scholarships (IPRS), 676
Shell centenary chevening scholarships, 640
Shell Centenary Scholarships, 640
Wingate Scholarships, 704

Canada

International Postgraduate Research Scholarships (IPRS), 676
Wingate Scholarships, 704

Caribbean Countries

International Postgraduate Research Scholarships (IPRS), 676
Shell centenary chevening scholarships, 640
Shell Centenary Scholarships, 640

East European Countries

CERN Doctoral Student Programme, 228
CERN Fellowships, 228
CERN Technical Student Programme, 228
International Postgraduate Research Scholarships (IPRS), 676

European Union

Master Training Packages (MTP), 631

Far East

International Postgraduate Research Scholarships (IPRS), 676
Shell centenary chevening scholarships, 640
Shell Centenary Scholarships, 640
Swiss Federal Institute of Technology Scholarships, 598

Indian Sub-Continent

International Postgraduate Research Scholarships (IPRS), 676
Shell centenary chevening scholarships, 640
Shell Centenary Scholarships, 640
Wingate Scholarships, 704

Middle East

International Postgraduate Research Scholarships (IPRS), 676
Shell centenary chevening scholarships, 640
Shell Centenary Scholarships, 640

New Zealand

University of Western Sydney Postgraduate Research Award (UW-SPRA), 689
Wingate Scholarships, 704

South Africa

International Postgraduate Research Scholarships (IPRS), 676
Shell centenary chevening scholarships, 640
Shell Centenary Scholarships, 640
Wingate Scholarships, 704

South America

International Postgraduate Research Scholarships (IPRS), 676
Shell centenary chevening scholarships, 640
Shell Centenary Scholarships, 640

United Kingdom

CERN Doctoral Student Programme, 228
CERN Fellowships, 228
CERN Technical Student Programme, 228
Hallam Studentships, 558
International Postgraduate Research Scholarships (IPRS), 676
Lord Lloyd of Kilgerran Memorial Prize, 348
Mr and Mrs David Edward Memorial Award, 681
Swiss Federal Institute of Technology Scholarships, 598
University of Kent Department of Electronics Studentships, 636
UWB Departmental Research Studentships, 681
UWB Research Studentships, 681

William Morley Bursary, 349
Wingate Scholarships, 704

United States of America

Army Research Laboratory Postdoctoral Fellowship Program, 75
ASNE Scholarships, 81
International Postgraduate Research Scholarships (IPRS), 676
NRC Twinning Program, 455
SRC Graduate Fellowship Program, 557
SRC Master's Scholarship Program, 557
SWE General Motors Foundation Graduate Scholarship, 589
Swiss Federal Institute of Technology Scholarships, 598
Winston Churchill Scholarship, 705

West European Countries

CERN Doctoral Student Programme, 228
CERN Fellowships, 228
CERN Technical Student Programme, 228
Hallam Studentships, 558
International Postgraduate Research Scholarships (IPRS), 676
Mr and Mrs David Edward Memorial Award, 681
University of Kent Department of Electronics Studentships, 636
UWB Departmental Research Studentships, 681
UWB Research Studentships, 681
Wingate Scholarships, 704

COMPUTER ENGINEERING

Any Country

CDI Internship, 223
CQU Postgraduate Research Award, 224
DEED (Demonstration of Energy-Efficient Developments) Scholarship, 69
ESRF Postdoctoral Fellowships, 277
Golden Key National Honor Society Information Systems Achievement Awards, 306
John Moyes Lessells Scholarships, 548
KSTU Rector's Grant, 385
Massey Doctoral Scholarship, 408
Mott MacDonald Charitable Trust Scholarships, 426
Queen Mary Research Studentships, 500
Trinity College Junior Research Fellowship, 672
TUCS Postgraduate Grant, 606
University of Bristol Postgraduate Scholarships, 619
University of Essex Scholarships, 632

African Nations

International Postgraduate Research Scholarships (IPRS), 676

Australia

Fulbright Postgraduate Student Award for Engineering, 120
Fulbright Postgraduate Student Award for Science and Engineering, 120
University of Western Sydney Postgraduate Research Award (UW-SPRA), 689
Wingate Scholarships, 704

British Commonwealth

International Postgraduate Research Scholarships (IPRS), 676
Wingate Scholarships, 704

Canada

International Postgraduate Research Scholarships (IPRS), 676
Wingate Scholarships, 704

Caribbean Countries

International Postgraduate Research Scholarships (IPRS), 676

East European Countries

CERN Doctoral Student Programme, 228
CERN Fellowships, 228

CERN Technical Student Programme, 228
International Postgraduate Research Scholarships (IPRS), 676

Far East

International Postgraduate Research Scholarships (IPRS), 676
Swiss Federal Institute of Technology Scholarships, 598

Indian Sub-Continent

International Postgraduate Research Scholarships (IPRS), 676
Wingate Scholarships, 704

Middle East

International Postgraduate Research Scholarships (IPRS), 676

New Zealand

University of Western Sydney Postgraduate Research Award (UWSPRA), 689
Wingate Scholarships, 704

South Africa

International Postgraduate Research Scholarships (IPRS), 676
Wingate Scholarships, 704

South America

International Postgraduate Research Scholarships (IPRS), 676

United Kingdom

CERN Doctoral Student Programme, 228
CERN Fellowships, 228
CERN Technical Student Programme, 228
ESRF Thesis Studentships, 277
Hallam Studentships, 558
International Postgraduate Research Scholarships (IPRS), 676
Mr and Mrs David Edward Memorial Award, 681
Royal Academy of Engineering International Travel Grants, 525
Swiss Federal Institute of Technology Scholarships, 598
University of Kent Department of Electronics Studentships, 636
University of Wales (Aberystwyth) Postgraduate Research Studentships, 680
UWB Departmental Research Studentships, 681
UWB Research Studentships, 681
Wingate Scholarships, 704

United States of America

Army Research Laboratory Postdoctoral Fellowship Program, 75
ASNE Scholarships, 81
International Postgraduate Research Scholarships (IPRS), 676
NRC Twinning Program, 455
SRC Graduate Fellowship Program, 557
SRC Master's Scholarship Program, 557
SWE General Motors Foundation Graduate Scholarship, 589
Swiss Federal Institute of Technology Scholarships, 598
Winston Churchill Scholarship, 705

West European Countries

CERN Doctoral Student Programme, 228
CERN Fellowships, 228
CERN Technical Student Programme, 228
ESRF Thesis Studentships, 277
Hallam Studentships, 558
International Postgraduate Research Scholarships (IPRS), 676
Mr and Mrs David Edward Memorial Award, 681
Royal Academy of Engineering International Travel Grants, 525
University of Kent Department of Electronics Studentships, 636
UWB Departmental Research Studentships, 681
UWB Research Studentships, 681
Wingate Scholarships, 704

INDUSTRIAL AND MANAGEMENT ENGINEERING

Any Country

DEED (Demonstration of Energy-Efficient Developments) Scholarship, 69
John Moyes Lessells Scholarships, 548
Johnson's Wax Research Fellowship, 406
Kenward Memorial Fellowship, 618
KSTU Rector's Grant, 385
Massey Doctoral Scholarship, 408
Mott MacDonald Charitable Trust Scholarships, 426
University of Bristol Postgraduate Scholarships, 619

African Nations

International Postgraduate Research Scholarships (IPRS), 676
Joint Japan/World Bank Graduate Scholarship Program (JJ/WBGSP), 355

Australia

Fulbright Postgraduate Student Award for Engineering, 120
Fulbright Postgraduate Student Award for Science and Engineering, 120
Wingate Scholarships, 704

British Commonwealth

International Postgraduate Research Scholarships (IPRS), 676
Joint Japan/World Bank Graduate Scholarship Program (JJ/WBGSP), 355
Wingate Scholarships, 704

Canada

International Postgraduate Research Scholarships (IPRS), 676
Wingate Scholarships, 704

Caribbean Countries

International Postgraduate Research Scholarships (IPRS), 676
Joint Japan/World Bank Graduate Scholarship Program (JJ/WBGSP), 355

East European Countries

International Postgraduate Research Scholarships (IPRS), 676
Joint Japan/World Bank Graduate Scholarship Program (JJ/WBGSP), 355

Far East

International Postgraduate Research Scholarships (IPRS), 676
Joint Japan/World Bank Graduate Scholarship Program (JJ/WBGSP), 355
Swiss Federal Institute of Technology Scholarships, 598

Indian Sub-Continent

International Postgraduate Research Scholarships (IPRS), 676
Joint Japan/World Bank Graduate Scholarship Program (JJ/WBGSP), 355
Wingate Scholarships, 704

Middle East

International Postgraduate Research Scholarships (IPRS), 676
Joint Japan/World Bank Graduate Scholarship Program (JJ/WBGSP), 355

New Zealand

Wingate Scholarships, 704

South Africa

International Postgraduate Research Scholarships (IPRS), 676
Joint Japan/World Bank Graduate Scholarship Program (JJ/WBGSP), 355

Wingate Scholarships, 704

South America

International Postgraduate Research Scholarships (IPRS), 676
Joint Japan/World Bank Graduate Scholarship Program (JJ/WBGSP), 355

United Kingdom

Hallam Studentships, 558
International Postgraduate Research Scholarships (IPRS), 676
Royal Commission Industrial Fellowships, 534
Swiss Federal Institute of Technology Scholarships, 598
Wingate Scholarships, 704

United States of America

ASNE Scholarships, 81
International Postgraduate Research Scholarships (IPRS), 676
NRC Twinning Program, 455
SWE General Motors Foundation Graduate Scholarship, 589
Swiss Federal Institute of Technology Scholarships, 598
Winston Churchill Scholarship, 705

West European Countries

Hallam Studentships, 558
International Postgraduate Research Scholarships (IPRS), 676
Wingate Scholarships, 704

METALLURGICAL ENGINEERING

Any Country

DEED (Demonstration of Energy-Efficient Developments) Scholarship, 69
John Moyes Lessells Scholarships, 548
University of Manchester Research Studentships and Scholarships, 642
Welch Foundation Scholarship, 371

African Nations

International Postgraduate Research Scholarships (IPRS), 676

Australia

Fulbright Postgraduate Student Award for Engineering, 120
Fulbright Postgraduate Student Award for Science and Engineering, 120
Wingate Scholarships, 704

British Commonwealth

International Postgraduate Research Scholarships (IPRS), 676
Wingate Scholarships, 704

Canada

International Postgraduate Research Scholarships (IPRS), 676
Wingate Scholarships, 704

Caribbean Countries

International Postgraduate Research Scholarships (IPRS), 676

East European Countries

International Postgraduate Research Scholarships (IPRS), 676

Far East

International Postgraduate Research Scholarships (IPRS), 676
Stephen and Anna Hui Fellowship, 333

Indian Sub-Continent

International Postgraduate Research Scholarships (IPRS), 676
Wingate Scholarships, 704

Middle East

International Postgraduate Research Scholarships (IPRS), 676

New Zealand

Wingate Scholarships, 704

South Africa

International Postgraduate Research Scholarships (IPRS), 676
Wingate Scholarships, 704

South America

International Postgraduate Research Scholarships (IPRS), 676

United Kingdom

Hallam Studentships, 558
International Postgraduate Research Scholarships (IPRS), 676
Sheffield Hallam University Research Studentships, 558
Wingate Scholarships, 704

United States of America

American Electroplaters and Surface Finishers Society Scholarship, 372
Army Research Laboratory Postdoctoral Fellowship Program, 75
ASNE Scholarships, 81
International Postgraduate Research Scholarships (IPRS), 676
NRC Twinning Program, 455
Winston Churchill Scholarship, 705

West European Countries

Hallam Studentships, 558
International Postgraduate Research Scholarships (IPRS), 676
Sheffield Hallam University Research Studentships, 558
Wingate Scholarships, 704

PRODUCTION ENGINEERING

Any Country

DEED (Demonstration of Energy-Efficient Developments) Scholarship, 69
John Moyes Lessells Scholarships, 548
Kenward Memorial Fellowship, 618
Massey Doctoral Scholarship, 408
University of Manchester Research Studentships and Scholarships, 642

African Nations

International Postgraduate Research Scholarships (IPRS), 676

Australia

Fulbright Postgraduate Student Award for Engineering, 120
Fulbright Postgraduate Student Award for Science and Engineering, 120
Wingate Scholarships, 704

British Commonwealth

International Postgraduate Research Scholarships (IPRS), 676
Wingate Scholarships, 704

Canada

International Postgraduate Research Scholarships (IPRS), 676
SME Education Foundation Grants Program, 566
Wingate Scholarships, 704

Caribbean Countries

International Postgraduate Research Scholarships (IPRS), 676

East European Countries

International Postgraduate Research Scholarships (IPRS), 676

MATERIALS ENGINEERING

CERN Technical Student Programme, 228
Hallam Studentships, 558
International Postgraduate Research Scholarships (IPRS), 676
Royal Academy of Engineering International Travel Grants, 525
Sheffield Hallam University Research Studentships, 558
Wingate Scholarships, 704

MINING AND MINERALS ENGINEERING

Any Country

Bosworth Smith Trust Fund, 344
DEED (Demonstration of Energy-Efficient Developments) Scholarship, 69
G Vernon Hobson Bequest, 345
John Moyes Lessells Scholarships, 548
Mott MacDonald Charitable Trust Scholarships, 426
Stanley Elmore Fellowships, 345
Trinity College Junior Research Fellowship, 672

African Nations

BP - FCO Chevening - Leeds University Scholarships, 638
International Postgraduate Research Scholarships (IPRS), 676
Shell centenary chevening scholarships, 640
Shell Centenary Scholarships, 640

Australia

Edgar Pam Fellowship, 345
Fulbright Postgraduate Student Award for Engineering, 120
Fulbright Postgraduate Student Award for Science and Engineering, 120
Wingate Scholarships, 704

British Commonwealth

BP - FCO Chevening - Leeds University Scholarships, 638
International Postgraduate Research Scholarships (IPRS), 676
Shell centenary chevening scholarships, 640
Shell Centenary Scholarships, 640
Wingate Scholarships, 704

Canada

Edgar Pam Fellowship, 345
International Postgraduate Research Scholarships (IPRS), 676
Wingate Scholarships, 704

Caribbean Countries

BP - FCO Chevening - Leeds University Scholarships, 638
International Postgraduate Research Scholarships (IPRS), 676
Shell centenary chevening scholarships, 640
Shell Centenary Scholarships, 640

East European Countries

International Postgraduate Research Scholarships (IPRS), 676
Natural History Museum Sys-Resource, 461

Far East

BP - FCO Chevening - Leeds University Scholarships, 638
International Postgraduate Research Scholarships (IPRS), 676
Shell centenary chevening scholarships, 640
Shell Centenary Scholarships, 640
Stephen and Anna Hui Fellowship, 333

Indian Sub-Continent

BP - FCO Chevening - Leeds University Scholarships, 638
International Postgraduate Research Scholarships (IPRS), 676
Shell centenary chevening scholarships, 640
Shell Centenary Scholarships, 640
Wingate Scholarships, 704

Middle East

BP - FCO Chevening - Leeds University Scholarships, 638
International Postgraduate Research Scholarships (IPRS), 676
Shell centenary chevening scholarships, 640
Shell Centenary Scholarships, 640

New Zealand

Edgar Pam Fellowship, 345
Wingate Scholarships, 704

South Africa

BP - FCO Chevening - Leeds University Scholarships, 638
Edgar Pam Fellowship, 345
International Postgraduate Research Scholarships (IPRS), 676
Shell centenary chevening scholarships, 640
Shell Centenary Scholarships, 640
Wingate Scholarships, 704

South America

BP - FCO Chevening - Leeds University Scholarships, 638
International Postgraduate Research Scholarships (IPRS), 676
Shell centenary chevening scholarships, 640
Shell Centenary Scholarships, 640

United Kingdom

Edgar Pam Fellowship, 345
International Postgraduate Research Scholarships (IPRS), 676
Mining Club Award, 345
Polish Government Postgraduate Scholarships Scheme, 501
Wingate Scholarships, 704

United States of America

International Postgraduate Research Scholarships (IPRS), 676
Winston Churchill Scholarship, 705

West European Countries

International Postgraduate Research Scholarships (IPRS), 676
Natural History Museum Sys-Resource, 461
Wingate Scholarships, 704

PETROLEUM ENGINEERING

Any Country

ACS/PRF Scientific Education Grants, 35
ACS/PRF Type AC Grants, 35
ACS/PRF Type B Grants, 36
DEED (Demonstration of Energy-Efficient Developments) Scholarship, 69
Exxon Mobil Teaching Fellowships, 524
John Moyes Lessells Scholarships, 548
Mott MacDonald Charitable Trust Scholarships, 426

Australia

Fulbright Postgraduate Student Award for Engineering, 120
Fulbright Postgraduate Student Award for Science and Engineering, 120
Wingate Scholarships, 704

British Commonwealth

Wingate Scholarships, 704

Canada

Wingate Scholarships, 704

Far East

Stephen and Anna Hui Fellowship, 333

Indian Sub-Continent

Wingate Scholarships, 704

New Zealand

Wingate Scholarships, 704

South Africa

Wingate Scholarships, 704

United Kingdom

Wingate Scholarships, 704

United States of America

SWE General Motors Foundation Graduate Scholarship, 589
Winston Churchill Scholarship, 705

West European Countries

Wingate Scholarships, 704

ENERGY ENGINEERING

Any Country

Alberta Research Council Scholarship, 620
ASHRAE Grants-in-Aid for Graduate Students, 80
Building Systems Technology Research Grant, 565
CDU Senior Research Fellowship, 230
CDU Three Year Postdoctoral Fellowship, 230
DEED (Demonstration of Energy-Efficient Developments) Scholarship, 69
Earthwatch Field Research Grants, 264
John Moyes Lessells Scholarships, 548
Kenward Memorial Fellowship, 618
KSTU Rector's Grant, 385
Mott MacDonald Charitable Trust Scholarships, 426
Trinity College Junior Research Fellowship, 672
University of Manchester Research Studentships and Scholarships, 642

African Nations

Joint Japan/World Bank Graduate Scholarship Program (JJ/WBGSP), 355

Australia

Fulbright Postgraduate Student Award for Engineering, 120
Fulbright Postgraduate Student Award for Science and Engineering, 120
Wingate Scholarships, 704

British Commonwealth

Joint Japan/World Bank Graduate Scholarship Program (JJ/WBGSP), 355
Wingate Scholarships, 704

Canada

Wingate Scholarships, 704

Caribbean Countries

Joint Japan/World Bank Graduate Scholarship Program (JJ/WBGSP), 355

East European Countries

Joint Japan/World Bank Graduate Scholarship Program (JJ/WBGSP), 355
VKI Fellowship, 696

Far East

Joint Japan/World Bank Graduate Scholarship Program (JJ/WBGSP), 355

Indian Sub-Continent

Joint Japan/World Bank Graduate Scholarship Program (JJ/WBGSP), 355
Wingate Scholarships, 704

Middle East

Joint Japan/World Bank Graduate Scholarship Program (JJ/WBGSP), 355

New Zealand

Wingate Scholarships, 704

South Africa

Joint Japan/World Bank Graduate Scholarship Program (JJ/WBGSP), 355
Wingate Scholarships, 704

South America

Joint Japan/World Bank Graduate Scholarship Program (JJ/WBGSP), 355

United Kingdom

Wingate Scholarships, 704

United States of America

ASNE Scholarships, 81
NRC Twinning Program, 455
VKI Fellowship, 696
Winston Churchill Scholarship, 705

West European Countries

VKI Fellowship, 696
Wingate Scholarships, 704

NUCLEAR ENGINEERING

Any Country

AINSE Awards, 116
Alan F Henry/Paul A Greebler Scholarship, 60
DEED (Demonstration of Energy-Efficient Developments) Scholarship, 69
John and Muriel Landis Scholarship Awards, 61
John Moyes Lessells Scholarships, 548
Mott MacDonald Charitable Trust Scholarships, 426
Trinity College Junior Research Fellowship, 672
University of Manchester Research Studentships and Scholarships, 642

Australia

Fulbright Postgraduate Student Award for Engineering, 120
Fulbright Postgraduate Student Award for Science and Engineering, 120
Wingate Scholarships, 704

British Commonwealth

Wingate Scholarships, 704

Canada

Wingate Scholarships, 704

East European Countries

CERN Doctoral Student Programme, 228
CERN Fellowships, 228
CERN Technical Student Programme, 228

Indian Sub-Continent

Wingate Scholarships, 704

New Zealand

Wingate Scholarships, 704

South Africa

Wingate Scholarships, 704

United Kingdom

CERN Doctoral Student Programme, 228
CERN Fellowships, 228
CERN Technical Student Programme, 228
Wingate Scholarships, 704

United States of America

ASNE Scholarships, 81
Everitt P Blizard Scholarship, 61
James F Schumar Scholarship, 61
John Randall Scholarship, 61
NRC Twinning Program, 455
Robert A Dannels Memorial Scholarship, 61
Robert A Dannels Scholarship, 62
Verne R Dapp Memorial Scholarship, 62
Verne R Dapp Scholarship, 62
Walter Meyer Scholarship, 62
Winston Churchill Scholarship, 705

West European Countries

CERN Doctoral Student Programme, 228
CERN Fellowships, 228
CERN Technical Student Programme, 228
Wingate Scholarships, 704

MECHANICAL/ELECTROMECHANICAL ENGINEERING

Any Country

ASHRAE Grants-in-Aid for Graduate Students, 80
BP/RSE Research Fellowships, 547
Building Systems Technology Research Grant, 565
CQU Postgraduate Research Award, 224
DEED (Demonstration of Energy-Efficient Developments) Scholarship, 69
ESRF Postdoctoral Fellowships, 277
Exxon Mobil Teaching Fellowships, 524
Flatman Grants, 349
Jamoc Clayton Awards, 350
James Clayton Lectures, 350
James Clayton Overseas Conference Travel for Senior Engineers, 350
James Clayton Postgraduate Hardship Award, 350
James Watt International Medal, 350
John Moyes Lessells Scholarships, 548
Kenward Memorial Fellowship, 618
KSTU Rector's Grant, 385
Labrow Grants, 350
Massey Doctoral Scholarship, 408
Mott MacDonald Charitable Trust Scholarships, 426
Neil Watson Grants, 350
Queen Mary Research Studentships, 506
Thomas Andrew Common Grants, 351
University of Bristol Postgraduate Scholarships, 619
University of Dundee Research Awards, 629
University of Edinburgh College of Science and Engineering Scholarship, 631
University of Glasgow Postgraduate Research Scholarships, 634
University of Manchester Research Studentships and Scholarships, 642

African Nations

BP - FCO Chevening - Leeds University Scholarships, 638
International Postgraduate Research Scholarships (IPRS), 676
Shell centenary chevening scholarships, 640
Shell Centenary Scholarships, 640

Australia

Fulbright Postgraduate Student Award for Engineering, 120
Fulbright Postgraduate Student Award for Science and Engineering, 120
Wingate Scholarships, 704

British Commonwealth

BP - FCO Chevening - Leeds University Scholarships, 638
International Postgraduate Research Scholarships (IPRS), 676
Shell centenary chevening scholarships, 640
Shell Centenary Scholarships, 640
Wingate Scholarships, 704

Canada

Horticultural Research Institute Grants, 327
International Postgraduate Research Scholarships (IPRS), 676
Spinal Cord Research Foundation Grants, 485
Wingate Scholarships, 704

Caribbean Countries

BP - FCO Chevening - Leeds University Scholarships, 638
International Postgraduate Research Scholarships (IPRS), 676
Shell centenary chevening scholarships, 640
Shell Centenary Scholarships, 640

East European Countries

CERN Doctoral Student Programme, 228
CERN Fellowships, 228
CERN Technical Student Programme, 228
International Postgraduate Research Scholarships (IPRS), 676
Spencer Wilks Scholarship/Fellowship, 351
VKI Fellowship, 696

Far East

BP - FCO Chevening - Leeds University Scholarships, 638
International Postgraduate Research Scholarships (IPRS), 676
Shell centenary chevening scholarships, 640
Shell Centenary Scholarships, 640

Indian Sub-Continent

BP - FCO Chevening - Leeds University Scholarships, 638
International Postgraduate Research Scholarships (IPRS), 676
Shell centenary chevening scholarships, 640
Shell Centenary Scholarships, 640
Wingate Scholarships, 704

Middle East

BP - FCO Chevening - Leeds University Scholarships, 638
International Postgraduate Research Scholarships (IPRS), 676
Shell centenary chevening scholarships, 640
Shell Centenary Scholarships, 640

New Zealand

Wingate Scholarships, 704

South Africa

BP - FCO Chevening - Leeds University Scholarships, 638
International Postgraduate Research Scholarships (IPRS), 676
Shell centenary chevening scholarships, 640
Shell Centenary Scholarships, 640
Wingate Scholarships, 704

South America

BP - FCO Chevening - Leeds University Scholarships, 638
International Postgraduate Research Scholarships (IPRS), 676
Shell centenary chevening scholarships, 640
Shell Centenary Scholarships, 640

United Kingdom

CERN Doctoral Student Programme, 228
CERN Fellowships, 228
CERN Technical Student Programme, 228
International Postgraduate Research Scholarships (IPRS), 676
Spencer Wilks Scholarship/Fellowship, 351
Wingate Scholarships, 704

United States of America

Army Research Laboratory Postdoctoral Fellowship Program, 75
ASME Graduate Teaching Fellowship Program, 80
ASNE Scholarships, 81
Elisabeth M and Winchell M Parsons Scholarship, 81
Horticultural Research Institute Grants, 327
International Postgraduate Research Scholarships (IPRS), 676
Marjorie Roy Rothermel Scholarship, 81
NRC Twinning Program, 455
Spinal Cord Research Foundation Grants, 485
SRC Graduate Fellowship Program, 557
SRC Master's Scholarship Program, 557
SWE General Motors Foundation Graduate Scholarship, 589
VKI Fellowship, 696
Winston Churchill Scholarship, 705

West European Countries

CERN Doctoral Student Programme, 228
CERN Fellowships, 228
CERN Technical Student Programme, 228
International Postgraduate Research Scholarships (IPRS), 676
Spencer Wilks Scholarship/Fellowship, 351
VKI Fellowship, 696
Wingate Scholarships, 704

HYDRAULIC/PNEUMATIC ENGINEERING

Any Country

DEED (Demonstration of Energy-Efficient Developments) Scholarship, 69
Horton (Hydrology) Research Grant, 46
John Moyes Lessells Scholarships, 548
Kenward Memorial Fellowship, 618
KSTU Rector's Grant, 385
Mott MacDonald Charitable Trust Scholarships, 426

African Nations

International Postgraduate Research Scholarships (IPRS), 676
Joint Japan/World Bank Graduate Scholarship Program (JJ/WBGSP), 355

Australia

Fulbright Postgraduate Student Award for Engineering, 120
Fulbright Postgraduate Student Award for Science and Engineering, 120
Wingate Scholarships, 704

British Commonwealth

International Postgraduate Research Scholarships (IPRS), 676
Joint Japan/World Bank Graduate Scholarship Program (JJ/WBGSP), 355
Wingate Scholarships, 704

Canada

Horticultural Research Institute Grants, 327
International Postgraduate Research Scholarships (IPRS), 676
Wingate Scholarships, 704

Caribbean Countries

International Postgraduate Research Scholarships (IPRS), 676
Joint Japan/World Bank Graduate Scholarship Program (JJ/WBGSP), 355

East European Countries

International Postgraduate Research Scholarships (IPRS), 676
Joint Japan/World Bank Graduate Scholarship Program (JJ/WBGSP), 355

Far East

International Postgraduate Research Scholarships (IPRS), 676
Joint Japan/World Bank Graduate Scholarship Program (JJ/WBGSP), 355

Indian Sub-Continent

International Postgraduate Research Scholarships (IPRS), 676
Joint Japan/World Bank Graduate Scholarship Program (JJ/WBGSP), 355
Wingate Scholarships, 704

Middle East

International Postgraduate Research Scholarships (IPRS), 676
Joint Japan/World Bank Graduate Scholarship Program (JJ/WBGSP), 355

New Zealand

Wingate Scholarships, 704

South Africa

International Postgraduate Research Scholarships (IPRS), 676
Joint Japan/World Bank Graduate Scholarship Program (JJ/WBGSP), 355
Wingate Scholarships, 704

South America

International Postgraduate Research Scholarships (IPRS), 676
Joint Japan/World Bank Graduate Scholarship Program (JJ/WBGSP), 355

United Kingdom

International Postgraduate Research Scholarships (IPRS), 676
Wingate Scholarships, 704

United States of America

ASNE Scholarships, 81
Horticultural Research Institute Grants, 327
International Postgraduate Research Scholarships (IPRS), 676
NRC Twinning Program, 455
Winston Churchill Scholarship, 705

West European Countries

International Postgraduate Research Scholarships (IPRS), 676
Wingate Scholarships, 704

SOUND ENGINEERING

Any Country

John Moyes Lessells Scholarships, 548
Kenward Memorial Fellowship, 618

Australia

Fulbright Postgraduate Student Award for Engineering, 120
Fulbright Postgraduate Student Award for Science and Engineering, 120
Wingate Scholarships, 704

British Commonwealth

Wingate Scholarships, 704

Canada

Wingate Scholarships, 704

East European Countries

VKI Fellowship, 696

Indian Sub-Continent

Wingate Scholarships, 704

New Zealand

Wingate Scholarships, 704

South Africa

Wingate Scholarships, 704

United Kingdom

Wingate Scholarships, 704

United States of America

ASNE Scholarships, 81
NRC Twinning Program, 455
VKI Fellowship, 696
Winston Churchill Scholarship, 705

West European Countries

VKI Fellowship, 696
Wingate Scholarships, 704

AUTOMOTIVE ENGINEERING

Any Country

John Moyes Lessells Scholarships, 548
Kenward Memorial Fellowship, 618
KSTU Rector's Grant, 385
Massey Doctoral Scholarship, 408
Trinity College Junior Research Fellowship, 672
University of Bristol Postgraduate Scholarships, 619

African Nations

BP - FCO Chevening - Leeds University Scholarships, 638
International Postgraduate Research Scholarships (IPRS), 676
Shell centenary chevening scholarships, 640
Shell Centenary Scholarships, 640

Australia

Fulbright Postgraduate Student Award for Engineering, 120
Fulbright Postgraduate Student Award for Science and Engineering, 120
Wingate Scholarships, 704

British Commonwealth

BP - FCO Chevening - Leeds University Scholarships, 638
International Postgraduate Research Scholarships (IPRS), 676
Shell centenary chevening scholarships, 640
Shell Centenary Scholarships, 640
Wingate Scholarships, 704

Canada

International Postgraduate Research Scholarships (IPRS), 676
Wingate Scholarships, 704

Caribbean Countries

BP - FCO Chevening - Leeds University Scholarships, 638
International Postgraduate Research Scholarships (IPRS), 676
Shell centenary chevening scholarships, 640
Shell Centenary Scholarships, 640

East European Countries

International Postgraduate Research Scholarships (IPRS), 676

Far East

BP - FCO Chevening - Leeds University Scholarships, 638
International Postgraduate Research Scholarships (IPRS), 676
Shell centenary chevening scholarships, 640
Shell Centenary Scholarships, 640

Indian Sub-Continent

BP - FCO Chevening - Leeds University Scholarships, 638

International Postgraduate Research Scholarships (IPRS), 676
Shell centenary chevening scholarships, 640
Shell Centenary Scholarships, 640
Wingate Scholarships, 704

Middle East

BP - FCO Chevening - Leeds University Scholarships, 638
International Postgraduate Research Scholarships (IPRS), 676
Shell centenary chevening scholarships, 640
Shell Centenary Scholarships, 640

New Zealand

Wingate Scholarships, 704

South Africa

BP - FCO Chevening - Leeds University Scholarships, 638
International Postgraduate Research Scholarships (IPRS), 676
Shell centenary chevening scholarships, 640
Shell Centenary Scholarships, 640
Wingate Scholarships, 704

South America

BP - FCO Chevening - Leeds University Scholarships, 638
International Postgraduate Research Scholarships (IPRS), 676
Shell centenary chevening scholarships, 640
Shell Centenary Scholarships, 640

United Kingdom

Hallam Studentships, 558
International Postgraduate Research Scholarships (IPRS), 676
University of Wales (Aberystwyth) Postgraduate Research Studentships, 680
Wingate Scholarships, 704

United States of America

International Postgraduate Research Scholarships (IPRS), 676
NRC Twinning Program, 455
Winston Churchill Scholarship, 705

West European Countries

Hallam Studentships, 558
International Postgraduate Research Scholarships (IPRS), 676
Wingate Scholarships, 704

MEASUREMENT/PRECISION ENGINEERING

Any Country

ESRF Postdoctoral Fellowships, 277
John Moyes Lessells Scholarships, 548
Kenward Memorial Fellowship, 618
KSTU Rector's Grant, 385

African Nations

International Postgraduate Research Scholarships (IPRS), 676

Australia

Fulbright Postgraduate Student Award for Engineering, 120
Fulbright Postgraduate Student Award for Science and Engineering, 120
Wingate Scholarships, 704

British Commonwealth

International Postgraduate Research Scholarships (IPRS), 676
Wingate Scholarships, 704

Canada

International Postgraduate Research Scholarships (IPRS), 676
Wingate Scholarships, 704

Caribbean Countries

International Postgraduate Research Scholarships (IPRS), 676

East European Countries

International Postgraduate Research Scholarships (IPRS), 676

Far East

International Postgraduate Research Scholarships (IPRS), 676

Indian Sub-Continent

International Postgraduate Research Scholarships (IPRS), 676
Wingate Scholarships, 704

Middle East

International Postgraduate Research Scholarships (IPRS), 676

New Zealand

Wingate Scholarships, 704

South Africa

International Postgraduate Research Scholarships (IPRS), 676
Wingate Scholarships, 704

South America

International Postgraduate Research Scholarships (IPRS), 676

United Kingdom

ESRF Thesis Studentships, 277
International Postgraduate Research Scholarships (IPRS), 676
Wingate Scholarships, 704

United States of America

ASNE Scholarships, 81
International Postgraduate Research Scholarships (IPRS), 676
NRC Twinning Program, 455
Winston Churchill Scholarship, 705

West European Countries

ESRF Thesis Studentships, 277
International Postgraduate Research Scholarships (IPRS), 676
Wingate Scholarships, 704

CONTROL ENGINEERING (ROBOTICS)

Any Country

BP/RSE Research Fellowships, 547
CDU Senior Research Fellowship, 230
CDU Three Year Postdoctoral Fellowship, 230
CQU Postgraduate Research Award, 224
John Moyes Lessells Scholarships, 548
Kenward Memorial Fellowship, 618
KSTU Rector's Grant, 385
Trinity College Junior Research Fellowship, 672

African Nations

International Postgraduate Research Scholarships (IPRS), 676

Australia

Fulbright Postgraduate Student Award for Engineering, 120
Fulbright Postgraduate Student Award for Science and Engineering, 120
University of Western Sydney Postgraduate Research Award (UW-SPRA), 689
Wingate Scholarships, 704

British Commonwealth

International Postgraduate Research Scholarships (IPRS), 676
Wingate Scholarships, 704

Canada

Horticultural Research Institute Grants, 327
International Postgraduate Research Scholarships (IPRS), 676
Wingate Scholarships, 704

Caribbean Countries

International Postgraduate Research Scholarships (IPRS), 676

East European Countries

International Postgraduate Research Scholarships (IPRS), 676

Far East

International Postgraduate Research Scholarships (IPRS), 676

Indian Sub-Continent

International Postgraduate Research Scholarships (IPRS), 676
Wingate Scholarships, 704

Middle East

International Postgraduate Research Scholarships (IPRS), 676

New Zealand

University of Western Sydney Postgraduate Research Award (UW-SPRA), 689
Wingate Scholarships, 704

South Africa

International Postgraduate Research Scholarships (IPRS), 676
Wingate Scholarships, 704

South America

International Postgraduate Research Scholarships (IPRS), 676

United Kingdom

International Postgraduate Research Scholarships (IPRS), 676
University of Wales (Aberystwyth) Postgraduate Research Studentships, 680
Wingate Scholarships, 704

United States of America

Army Research Laboratory Postdoctoral Fellowship Program, 75
ASNE Scholarships, 81
Horticultural Research Institute Grants, 327
International Postgraduate Research Scholarships (IPRS), 676
NRC Twinning Program, 455
Winston Churchill Scholarship, 705

West European Countries

International Postgraduate Research Scholarships (IPRS), 676
Wingate Scholarships, 704

AERONAUTICAL AND AEROSPACE ENGINEERING

Any Country

A Verville Fellowship, 568
Amelia Earhart Fellowship Awards, 716
Daniel and Florence Guggenheim Fellowship, 434
John Moyes Lessells Scholarships, 548
Kenward Memorial Fellowship, 618
KSTU Rector's Grant, 385
National Air and Space Museum Aviation/Space Writers Award, 569
NRC Research Associateships, 456
Queen Mary Research Studentships, 506
Ramsay Fellowship in Naval Aviation History, 569

The Guggenheim Fellowships, 568
Trinity College Junior Research Fellowship, 672
University of Bristol Postgraduate Scholarships, 619
University of Glasgow Postgraduate Research Scholarships, 634
University of Manchester Research Studentships and Scholarships, 642

African Nations

International Postgraduate Research Scholarships (IPRS), 676

Australia

Fulbright Postgraduate Student Award for Engineering, 120
Fulbright Postgraduate Student Award for Science and Engineering, 120
Wingate Scholarships, 704

British Commonwealth

Handley Page Award, 525
International Postgraduate Research Scholarships (IPRS), 676
Wingate Scholarships, 704

Canada

International Postgraduate Research Scholarships (IPRS), 676
Wingate Scholarships, 704

Caribbean Countries

International Postgraduate Research Scholarships (IPRS), 676

East European Countries

International Postgraduate Research Scholarships (IPRS), 676
VKI Fellowship, 696

Far East

International Postgraduate Research Scholarships (IPRS), 676

Indian Sub-Continent

International Postgraduate Research Scholarships (IPRS), 676
Wingate Scholarships, 704

Middle East

International Postgraduate Research Scholarships (IPRS), 676

New Zealand

Wingate Scholarships, 704

South Africa

International Postgraduate Research Scholarships (IPRS), 676
Wingate Scholarships, 704

South America

International Postgraduate Research Scholarships (IPRS), 676

United Kingdom

Handley Page Award, 525
International Postgraduate Research Scholarships (IPRS), 676
Wingate Scholarships, 704

United States of America

ASNE Scholarships, 81
International Postgraduate Research Scholarships (IPRS), 676
NRC Twinning Program, 455
VKI Fellowship, 696
Winston Churchill Scholarship, 705

West European Countries

International Postgraduate Research Scholarships (IPRS), 676
VKI Fellowship, 696
Wingate Scholarships, 704

MARINE ENGINEERING AND NAVAL ARCHITECTURE

Any Country

De Paepe - Willems Award, 364
Froude Research Scholarship in Naval Architecture, 538
John Moyes Lessells Scholarships, 548
Mott MacDonald Charitable Trust Scholarships, 426
Sir William White Postgraduate Scholarship in Naval Architecture, 539
Society of Naval Architects and Marine Engineers Graduate Scholarships, 587
University of Glasgow Postgraduate Research Scholarships, 634
Woods Hole Oceanographic Institution Postdoctoral Fellowships in Ocean Science and Engineering, 710
Woods Hole Oceanographic Institution/NOAA Co-operative Institute for Climate and Ocean Research Postdoctoral Fellowship, 710

Australia

Fulbright Postgraduate Student Award for Engineering, 120
Fulbright Postgraduate Student Award for Science and Engineering, 120
Wingate Scholarships, 704

British Commonwealth

Wingate Scholarships, 704

Canada

Society of Naval Architects and Marine Engineers Graduate Scholarships, 587
Wingate Scholarships, 704

Indian Sub-Continent

Wingate Scholarships, 704

New Zealand

Wingate Scholarships, 704

South Africa

Wingate Scholarships, 704

United Kingdom

Wingate Scholarships, 704

United States of America

ASNE Scholarships, 81
NRC Twinning Program, 455
Society of Naval Architects and Marine Engineers Graduate Scholarships, 587

West European Countries

Wingate Scholarships, 704

AGRICULTURAL ENGINEERING

Any Country

BBSRC Research Grants, 129
DEED (Demonstration of Energy-Efficient Developments) Scholarship, 69
John Moyes Lessells Scholarships, 548
Massey Doctoral Scholarship, 408
Mott MacDonald Charitable Trust Scholarships, 426
QUEST Institution of Civil Engineers Overseas Travel Awards, 346
Teagasc Walsh Fellowships, 599

African Nations

International Postgraduate Research Scholarships (IPRS), 676
Joint Japan/World Bank Graduate Scholarship Program (JJ/WBGSP), 355

Australia

Fulbright Postgraduate Student Award for Engineering, 120
Fulbright Postgraduate Student Award for Science and Engineering, 120
Wingate Scholarships, 704

British Commonwealth

International Postgraduate Research Scholarships (IPRS), 676
Joint Japan/World Bank Graduate Scholarship Program (JJ/WBGSP), 355
Wingate Scholarships, 704

Canada

Canadian Window on International Development, 358
International Postgraduate Research Scholarships (IPRS), 676
Wingate Scholarships, 704

Caribbean Countries

International Postgraduate Research Scholarships (IPRS), 676
Joint Japan/World Bank Graduate Scholarship Program (JJ/WBGSP), 355

East European Countries

International Postgraduate Research Scholarships (IPRS), 676
Joint Japan/World Bank Graduate Scholarship Program (JJ/WBGSP), 355

Far East

International Postgraduate Research Scholarships (IPRS), 676
Joint Japan/World Bank Graduate Scholarship Program (JJ/WBGSP), 355

Indian Sub-Continent

International Postgraduate Research Scholarships (IPRS), 676
Joint Japan/World Bank Graduate Scholarship Program (JJ/WBGSP), 355
Wingate Scholarships, 704

Middle East

International Postgraduate Research Scholarships (IPRS), 676
Joint Japan/World Bank Graduate Scholarship Program (JJ/WBGSP), 355

New Zealand

Wingate Scholarships, 704

South Africa

International Postgraduate Research Scholarships (IPRS), 676
Joint Japan/World Bank Graduate Scholarship Program (JJ/WBGSP), 355
Wingate Scholarships, 704

South America

International Postgraduate Research Scholarships (IPRS), 676
Joint Japan/World Bank Graduate Scholarship Program (JJ/WBGSP), 355

United Kingdom

International Postgraduate Research Scholarships (IPRS), 676
Silsoe Awards, 249
Wingate Scholarships, 704

United States of America

International Postgraduate Research Scholarships (IPRS), 676

West European Countries

International Postgraduate Research Scholarships (IPRS), 676
Silsoe Awards, 249
Wingate Scholarships, 704

FORESTRY ENGINEERING

Any Country

John Moyes Lessells Scholarships, 548

African Nations

Joint Japan/World Bank Graduate Scholarship Program (JJ/WBGSP), 355

Australia

Fulbright Postgraduate Student Award for Engineering, 120
Fulbright Postgraduate Student Award for Science and Engineering, 120
Wingate Scholarships, 704

British Commonwealth

Joint Japan/World Bank Graduate Scholarship Program (JJ/WBGSP), 355
Wingate Scholarships, 704

Canada

Canadian Window on International Development, 358
Wingate Scholarships, 704

Caribbean Countries

Joint Japan/World Bank Graduate Scholarship Program (JJ/WBGSP), 355

East European Countries

Joint Japan/World Bank Graduate Scholarship Program (JJ/WBGSP), 355

Far East

Joint Japan/World Bank Graduate Scholarship Program (JJ/WBGSP), 355

Indian Sub-Continent

Joint Japan/World Bank Graduate Scholarship Program (JJ/WBGSP), 355
Wingate Scholarships, 704

Middle East

Joint Japan/World Bank Graduate Scholarship Program (JJ/WBGSP), 355

New Zealand

Wingate Scholarships, 704

South Africa

Joint Japan/World Bank Graduate Scholarship Program (JJ/WBGSP), 355
Wingate Scholarships, 704

South America

Joint Japan/World Bank Graduate Scholarship Program (JJ/WBGSP), 355

United Kingdom

Wingate Scholarships, 704

West European Countries

Wingate Scholarships, 704

BIOENGINEERING AND BIOMEDICAL ENGINEERING

Any Country

Alberta Heritage Full-Time Studentship, 13
BBSRC Research Grants, 129

Equipment Grants, 319
John Moyes Lessells Scholarships, 548
Queen Mary Research Studentships, 506
Trinity College Junior Research Fellowship, 672
University of Manchester Research Studentships and Scholarships, 642
Welch Foundation Scholarship, 371

African Nations

Hastings Center International Visiting Scholars Program, 318
International Postgraduate Research Scholarships (IPRS), 676

Australia

Fulbright Postgraduate Student Award for Engineering, 120
Fulbright Postgraduate Student Award for Science and Engineering, 120
Hastings Center International Visiting Scholars Program, 318
Wingate Scholarships, 704

British Commonwealth

Hastings Center International Visiting Scholars Program, 318
International Postgraduate Research Scholarships (IPRS), 676
Wingate Scholarships, 704

Canada

International Postgraduate Research Scholarships (IPRS), 676
Spinal Cord Research Foundation Grants, 485
Wingate Scholarships, 704

Caribbean Countries

Hastings Center International Visiting Scholars Program, 318
International Postgraduate Research Scholarships (IPRS), 676

East European Countries

FEMS Fellowship, 280
Hastings Center International Visiting Scholars Program, 318
International Postgraduate Research Scholarships (IPRS), 676
VKI Fellowship, 696

Far East

Hastings Center International Visiting Scholars Program, 318
International Postgraduate Research Scholarships (IPRS), 676
Swiss Federal Institute of Technology Scholarships, 598

Indian Sub-Continent

Hastings Center International Visiting Scholars Program, 318
International Postgraduate Research Scholarships (IPRS), 676
Wingate Scholarships, 704

Middle East

Hastings Center International Visiting Scholars Program, 318
International Postgraduate Research Scholarships (IPRS), 676

New Zealand

Hastings Center International Visiting Scholars Program, 318
Wingate Scholarships, 704

South Africa

Hastings Center International Visiting Scholars Program, 318
International Postgraduate Research Scholarships (IPRS), 676
Wingate Scholarships, 704

South America

Hastings Center International Visiting Scholars Program, 318
International Postgraduate Research Scholarships (IPRS), 676

United Kingdom

FEMS Fellowship, 280
Hastings Center International Visiting Scholars Program, 318

International Postgraduate Research Scholarships (IPRS), 676
Polish Government Postgraduate Scholarships Scheme, 501
Swiss Federal Institute of Technology Scholarships, 598
Wingate Scholarships, 704

United States of America

AHA National Established Investigator Award, 48
Army Research Laboratory Postdoctoral Fellowship Program, 75
International Postgraduate Research Scholarships (IPRS), 676
NRC Twinning Program, 455
Spinal Cord Research Foundation Grants, 485
Swiss Federal Institute of Technology Scholarships, 598
VKI Fellowship, 696
Winston Churchill Scholarship, 705

West European Countries

FEMS Fellowship, 280
Hastings Center International Visiting Scholars Program, 318
International Postgraduate Research Scholarships (IPRS), 676
VKI Fellowship, 696
Wingate Scholarships, 704

FINE AND APPLIED ARTS

GENERAL

Any Country

Adolfo Omodeo Scholarship, 374
Ahmanson and Getty Postdoctoral Fellowships, 606
AIATSIS Research Grants, 116
Alberta Art Foundation Graduate Scholarships in the Department of Art, 620
Andrew Mellon Foundation Scholarship, 518
Arts Council of Northern Ireland General Arts Award, 99
ASECS (American Society for Eighteenth-Century Studies)/Clark Library Fellowships, 606
Austro-American Association of Boston Scholarship, 123
Awards and Schemes for Artists Arts Council England, London, 400
Banff Centre Financial Assistance, 124
Barbara Thom Postdoctoral Fellowship, 329
British Academy Larger Research Grants, 134
Camargo Fellowships, 164
Canada Council Grants for Professional artists, 195
Canada Council Travel Grants, 195
Canadian Department of Foreign Affairs Faculty Enrichment Program, 205
Canadian Department of Foreign Affairs Faculty Research Program, 205
Canadian Department of Foreign Affairs Institutional Research Program, 206
Canadian Institute of Ukrainian Studies Research Grants, 207
Clark-Huntington Joint Bibliographical Fellowship, 607
Concordia University Graduate Fellowships, 241
David J Azrieli Graduate Fellowship, 241
Earthwatch Field Research Grants, 264
Ebb & Flow Grant, 265
Equiano Memorial Award, 596
ERASMUS Prize, 288
Feiweles Trust Dance Bursary, 716
Fine Arts Work Center in Provincetown Fellowships, 281
Foundation Praemium Erasmianum Study Prize, 288
Frederico Chabod Scholarship, 374
Golden Key National Honor Society Art International, 305
Hagley/Winterthur Arts and Industries Fellowship, 312
Hambidge Center Residency Program Scholarships, 313
Hands-On-Art Visiting Artists Project, 708
Harold White Fellowships, 452
Hugh Le May Fellowship, 519
IHS Humane Studies Fellowships, 339

African Nations

Australia

British Commonwealth

Canada

Caribbean Countries

East European Countries

Far East

Indian Sub-Continent

Middle East

New Zealand

Friends of Peterhouse Bursary, 491
Fulbright Postdoctoral Research and Lecturing Awards for Non-US Citizens, 245
Quinn, Nathan and Edmond Scholarships, 149
University of Western Sydney Postgraduate Research Award (UW-SPRA), 689
Wingate Scholarships, 704

South Africa

Friends of Peterhouse Bursary, 491
Fulbright Postdoctoral Research and Lecturing Awards for Non-US Citizens, 245
International Postgraduate Research Scholarships (IPRS), 676
Isie Smuts Research Award, 590
NRF Doctoral Scholarships and Postdoctoral Fellowships for Study Abroad, 456
NRF Scholarships for Doctoral Study, 456
NRF Scholarships for Master's Study, 457
Quinn, Nathan and Edmond Scholarships, 149
Wingate Scholarships, 704
Wolfson Foundation Grants, 706

South America

Friends of Peterhouse Bursary, 491
Fulbright Commission (Argentina) Master's Program, 293
Fulbright Postdoctoral Research and Lecturing Awards for Non-US Citizens, 245
Guggenheim Fellowships to Assist Research and Artistic Creation (Latin America and the Caribbean), 383
International Postgraduate Research Scholarships (IPRS), 676
Merton College Reed Foundation Scholarship, 658
OAS Graduate Academic Studies, 483

United Kingdom

ACW Capital Grants, 100
ACW Inter-Recce, 100
ACW Lottery Film Grants, 101
AHRB Doctoral Awards Scheme, 99
Britich Academy Awards, 133
BSUF May and Ward Scholarships (for British scholars), 158
Canada Memorial Foundation Scholarships, 106
CBRL Research Grant, 244
CBRL Travel Grant, 244
ESU Chautauqua Institution Scholarships, 271
Fulbright Postdoctoral Research and Lecturing Awards for Non-US Citizens, 245
Hallam Studentships, 558
Hilda Martindale Exhibitions, 324
International Postgraduate Research Scholarships (IPRS), 676
International Studio Programme at PS 1, 100
Italian Government Scholarships, 420
Oppenheim-John Downes Trust Grants, 478
Portia Geach Memorial Award, 222
Professional Preparation Master's Scheme, 99
Quinn, Nathan and Edmond Scholarships, 149
Research Preparation Master's Scheme, 99
Rome Scholarships in the Fine Arts, 157
St Anne's College Irene Jamieson Research Scholarship, 666
Tyrone Guthrie Centre at Annaghmakerrig, 100
University of Kent School of Drama, Film and Visual Arts Scholarships, 637
University of Wales (Aberystwyth) Postgraduate Research Studentships, 680
Wingate Scholarships, 704
Wolfson Foundation Grants, 706

United States of America

ACC Fellowship Grants Program, 103
BSUF May and Ward Scholarships (for British scholars), 158
Bush Artist Fellows Program, 164
FACE Croatia, 101

Fellowship for American College Students, 513
Friends of Peterhouse Bursary, 491
Fulbright Distinguished Chairs Program, 245
Fulbright Scholar Program for United States Citizens, 245
Fulbright Senior Specialists Program, 245
GAP (Grants for Artists Projects) Program, 98
Guggenheim Fellowships to Assist Research and Artistic Creation (USA and Canada), 383
Harriet Hale Woolley Scholarships, 612
International Postgraduate Research Scholarships (IPRS), 676
JACL Scholarship and Award Program, 377
Louise Wallace Hackney Fellowship, 63
National Endowment for the Humanities Fellowships, 330
NLAPW Grants for Mature Women, 452
North Dakota Indian Scholarship, 472
OAS Graduate Academic Studies, 483
Richard Rodgers Awards for the Musical Theatre, 23
Twining Humbe Award for Lifetime Aritistic Achievement, 98
UCLA IAC Postdoctoral/Visiting Scholar Fellowships, 607
Worldstudio Foundation Scholarship, 713

West European Countries

AHRB Doctoral Awards Scheme, 99
Fulbright Postdoctoral Research and Lecturing Awards for Non-US Citizens, 245
Hallam Studentships, 558
International Postgraduate Research Scholarships (IPRS), 676
Professional Preparation Master's Scheme, 99
Research Preparation Master's Scheme, 99
St Anne's College Irene Jamieson Research Scholarship, 666
The Metropolitan Museum of Art Annette Kade Art History Fellowship, 418
Tyrone Guthrie Centre at Annaghmakerrig, 100
University of Kent School of Drama, Film and Visual Arts Scholarships, 637
Wingate Scholarships, 704

HISTORY AND PHILOSOPHY OF ART

Any Country

'Drawn to Art' Fellowship
Adolfo Omodeo Scholarship, 374
Advanced Fellowships, 71
Ahmanson and Getty Postdoctoral Fellowships, 606
Albert J Beveridge Grant, 49
Andrew W Mellon Postdoctoral Fellowships in the Humanities, 677
ARIT Humanities and Social Science Fellowships, 70
ASCSA Fellowships, 71
ASCSA Summer Sessions, 72
ASECS (American Society for Eighteenth-Century Studies)/Clark Library Fellowships, 606
Barbara Thom Postdoctoral Fellowship, 329
Bernadotte E Schmitt Grants, 49
British Academy Larger Research Grants, 134
British Academy Overseas Conference Grants, 134
British Academy Small Personal Research Grants, 134
British Academy Visiting Professorships for Overseas Scholars, 135
British Academy Worldwide Congress Grant, 135
Camargo Fellowships, 164
Carroll LV Meeks Fellowship, 584
CDU Senior Research Fellowship, 230
Center for Advanced Study in the Behavioral Sciences Postdoctoral Residential Fellowships, 223
Clark Library Short-Term Resident Fellowships, 606
Clark Predoctoral Fellowships, 607
Clark-Huntington Joint Bibliographical Fellowship, 607
CMRS Summer Fellowship, 607
Collaborative Research Grants, 301
Council of the Institute Awards, 502
Curatorial Research Fellowships, 301
Duquesne University Graduate Assistantship, 263

African Nations

Australia

British Commonwealth

Canada

Caribbean Countries

East European Countries

Far East

Indian Sub-Continent

Middle East

New Zealand

South Africa

South America

United Kingdom

University of Wales (Aberystwyth) Postgraduate Research Studentships, 680
Wingate Scholarships, 704

United States of America

ACC Fellowship Grants Program, 103
ARCE Fellowships, 69
Fulbright Distinguished Chairs Program, 245
Fulbright Senior Specialists Program, 245
Gilbert Chinard Fellowships, 336
Gladys Krieble Delmas Foundation Grants, 303
Harmon Chadbourn Rorison Fellowship, 336
International Postgraduate Research Scholarships (IPRS), 676
IREX Individual Advanced Research Opportunities, 366
Kennan Institute Research Scholarship, 385
Kress Fellowship in the Art and Archaeology of Jordan, 75
National Endowment for the Humanities Fellowships, 330
NEH Fellowship, 75
NEH Postdoctoral Research Award, 75
Sally Kress Tompkins Fellowship, 585
Vatican Film Library Mellon Fellowship, 693

West European Countries

AHRB Doctoral Awards Scheme, 99
International Postgraduate Research Scholarships (IPRS), 676
Professional Preparation Master's Scheme, 99
Research Preparation Master's Scheme, 99
Universita' Per Stranieri Di Siena Socrates Erasmus Students Mobility, 614
Wingate Scholarships, 704

AESTHETICS

Any Country

Adolfo Omodeo Scholarship, 374
Andrew W Mellon Postdoctoral Fellowships in the Humanities, 677
ASCSA Fellowships, 71
British Academy Overseas Conference Grants, 134
British Academy Worldwide Congress Grant, 135
Camargo Fellowships, 164
Duquesne University Graduate Assistantship, 263
Frederico Chabod Scholarship, 374
Henry Moore Institute Research Fellowship, 322
Kanner Fellowship In British Studies, 607

African Nations

International Postgraduate Research Scholarships (IPRS), 676

Australia

Wingate Scholarships, 704

British Commonwealth

International Postgraduate Research Scholarships (IPRS), 676
Wingate Scholarships, 704

Canada

International Postgraduate Research Scholarships (IPRS), 676
Wingate Scholarships, 704

Caribbean Countries

International Postgraduate Research Scholarships (IPRS), 676

East European Countries

AHRB Doctoral Awards Scheme, 99
International Postgraduate Research Scholarships (IPRS), 676
Research Preparation Master's Scheme, 99

Far East

ACC Fellowship Grants Program, 103
International Postgraduate Research Scholarships (IPRS), 676

Indian Sub-Continent

International Postgraduate Research Scholarships (IPRS), 676
Wingate Scholarships, 704

Middle East

International Postgraduate Research Scholarships (IPRS), 676

New Zealand

Wingate Scholarships, 704

South Africa

International Postgraduate Research Scholarships (IPRS), 676
Wingate Scholarships, 704

South America

International Postgraduate Research Scholarships (IPRS), 676

United Kingdom

AHRB Doctoral Awards Scheme, 99
British Conference Grants, 135
International Postgraduate Research Scholarships (IPRS), 676
Research Preparation Master's Scheme, 99
Wingate Scholarships, 704

United States of America

ACC Fellowship Grants Program, 103
International Postgraduate Research Scholarships (IPRS), 676

West European Countries

AHRB Doctoral Awards Scheme, 99
International Postgraduate Research Scholarships (IPRS), 676
Research Preparation Master's Scheme, 99
Wingate Scholarships, 704

ART MANAGEMENT

Any Country

Curatorial Research Fellowships, 301
Massey Doctoral Scholarship, 408
Metropolitan Museum of Art Six Month Internship, 418
Metropolitan Museum of Art Summer Internships for College Students, 419
Metropolitan Museum of Art Summer Internships for Graduate Students, 419
WSW Internships, 708

African Nations

International Postgraduate Research Scholarships (IPRS), 676

Australia

Wingate Scholarships, 704

British Commonwealth

International Postgraduate Research Scholarships (IPRS), 676
Wingate Scholarships, 704

Canada

International Postgraduate Research Scholarships (IPRS), 676
Wingate Scholarships, 704

Caribbean Countries

International Postgraduate Research Scholarships (IPRS), 676

East European Countries

International Postgraduate Research Scholarships (IPRS), 676
Professional Preparation Master's Scheme, 99

Far East

ACC Fellowship Grants Program, 103
Hong Kong Arts Development Council - FCO Chevening - Leeds University Scholarships, 639
International Postgraduate Research Scholarships (IPRS), 676

Indian Sub-Continent

International Postgraduate Research Scholarships (IPRS), 676
Wingate Scholarships, 704

Middle East

International Postgraduate Research Scholarships (IPRS), 676

New Zealand

Wingate Scholarships, 704

South Africa

International Postgraduate Research Scholarships (IPRS), 676
Wingate Scholarships, 704

South America

International Postgraduate Research Scholarships (IPRS), 676

United Kingdom

International Postgraduate Research Scholarships (IPRS), 676
Professional Preparation Master's Scheme, 99
Wingate Scholarships, 704

United States of America

ACC Fellowship Grants Program, 103
Congress Bundestag Youth Exchange for Young Professionals, 223
International Postgraduate Research Scholarships (IPRS), 676

West European Countries

International Postgraduate Research Scholarships (IPRS), 676
Professional Preparation Master's Scheme, 99
Wingate Scholarships, 704

DRAWING AND PAINTING

Any Country

Abbey Harris Mural Fund, 5
Advanced Fellowships, 71
Alberta Art Foundation Graduate Scholarships in the Department of Art, 620
ASCSA Summer Sessions, 72
Banff Centre Financial Assistance, 124
Camargo Fellowships, 164
CDU Senior Research Fellowship, 230
Chautauqua Institution Awards, 231
Cintas Fellowships, 101
Don Freeman Memorial Grant-in-Aid, 586
Ebb & Flow Grant, 265
Elizabeth Greenshields Grant, 268
FAMSI Research Grant, 287
Fine Arts Work Center in Provincetown Fellowships, 281
Foundation Praemium Erasmianum Study Prize, 288
Frederick Douglass Institute Postdoctoral Fellowship, 289
Frederick Douglass Institute Predoctoral Dissertation Fellowship, 290
Gottlieb Foundation Emergency Assistance Grants, 9
Gottlieb Foundation Individual Support Grants, 9
Hambidge Center Residency Program Scholarships, 313
Haystack Scholarship, 319
Jacob Hirsch Fellowship, 72
MacDowell Colony Residencies, 402
Massey Doctoral Scholarship, 408
MICA Fellowship, 407
Pollock-Krasner Foundation Grant, 502
Ragdale Foundation Residencies, 511

Research Student Bursary, 163
Rhodes University Postdoctoral Fellowship, 519
RSA Annual Student Competition, 542
The Alastair Salvesen Art Scholarship, 541
The John Kinross Memorial Fund Student Scholarships/RSA, 541
University of Dundee Research Awards, 629
Virginia Center for the Creative Arts Fellowships, 695
Yaddo Residency, 243

African Nations

International Postgraduate Research Scholarships (IPRS), 676
Royal Over-Seas League Travel Scholarship, 522

Australia

Fulbright Postgraduate Student Award for the Visual and Performing Arts, 120
Marten Bequest Travelling Scholarships, 222
Portia Geach Memorial Award, 222
Royal Over-Seas League Travel Scholarship, 522
University of Western Sydney Postgraduate Research Award (UW-SPRA), 690

British Commonwealth

Hector and Elizabeth Catling Bursary, 155
International Postgraduate Research Scholarships (IPRS), 676
Rome Scholarships in the Fine Arts, 157
Royal Over-Seas League Travel Scholarship, 522
Sargant Fellowship, 157
Wingate Rome Scholarship in the Fine Arts, 157

Canada

International Postgraduate Research Scholarships (IPRS), 676
Royal Over-Seas League Travel Scholarship, 522
Vatican Film Library Mellon Fellowship, 693

Caribbean Countries

International Postgraduate Research Scholarships (IPRS), 676
Royal Over-Seas League Travel Scholarship, 522

East European Countries

AHRB Doctoral Awards Scheme, 99
International Postgraduate Research Scholarships (IPRS), 676
Professional Preparation Master's Scheme, 99

Far East

ACC Fellowship Grants Program, 103
International Postgraduate Research Scholarships (IPRS), 676
Royal Over-Seas League Travel Scholarship, 522

Indian Sub-Continent

International Postgraduate Research Scholarships (IPRS), 676
Royal Over-Seas League Travel Scholarship, 522
USEFI Professional Fellowships in Plastics and Performing Arts, Museum Studies and Arts/Culture Management, 611

Middle East

International Postgraduate Research Scholarships (IPRS), 676
Sharett Scholarship Program, 22

New Zealand

Royal Over-Seas League Travel Scholarship, 522
University of Western Sydney Postgraduate Research Award (UW-SPRA), 689

South Africa

International Postgraduate Research Scholarships (IPRS), 676
Royal Over-Seas League Travel Scholarship, 522

South America

International Postgraduate Research Scholarships (IPRS), 676

United Kingdom

Abbey Fellowships in Painting, 155
Abbey Fellowships in Painting, 155
Abbey Scholarship in Painting, 155
Abbey Scholarship in Painting, 155
AHRB Doctoral Awards Scheme, 99
Arts Council of England Helen Chadwick Fellowship, 155
British School at Rome Fellowship, 100
ESU Chautauqua Institution Scholarships, 271
Friends of Israel Educational Foundation Young Artist Award, 292
Hallam Studentships, 558
Hector and Elizabeth Catling Bursary, 155
International Postgraduate Research Scholarships (IPRS), 676
Polish Government Postgraduate Scholarships Scheme, 501
Portia Geach Memorial Award, 222
Professional Preparation Master's Scheme, 99
Rome Scholarships in the Fine Arts, 157
Royal Over-Seas League Travel Scholarship, 522
Sainsbury Scholarship in Painting and Sculpture, 157
Sargant Fellowship, 157
Sir William Gillies Bequest-Hospitalfield Residencies, 542
University of Wales (Aberystwyth) Postgraduate Research Studentships, 680
Wingate Rome Scholarship in the Fine Arts, 157

United States of America

Abbey Fellowships in Painting, 155
Abbey Fellowships in Painting, 155
Abbey Scholarship in Painting, 155
Abbey Scholarship in Painting, 155
ACC Fellowship Grants Program, 103
Bush Artist Fellows Program, 164
Fulbright Senior Specialists Program, 245
Gerald R Dodge Foundation Residency for New Jersey Artists, 708
International Postgraduate Research Scholarships (IPRS), 676
John F and Anna Lee Stacey Scholarships, 383
NLAPW Grants for Mature Women, 452
Twining Humbe Award for Lifetime Aritistic Achievement, 98
Vatican Film Library Mellon Fellowship, 693

West European Countries

AHRB Doctoral Awards Scheme, 99
Hallam Studentships, 558
International Postgraduate Research Scholarships (IPRS), 676
Professional Preparation Master's Scheme, 99

SCULPTURE

Any Country

Advanced Fellowships, 71
Alberta Art Foundation Graduate Scholarships in the Department of Art, 620
ASCSA Fellowships, 71
ASCSA Summer Sessions, 72
Banff Centre Financial Assistance, 124
Camargo Fellowships, 164
CDU Senior Research Fellowship, 230
Chautauqua Institution Awards, 231
Cintas Fellowships, 101
Ebb & Flow Grant, 265
Elizabeth Greenshields Grant, 268
FAMSI Research Grant, 287
Fine Arts Work Center in Provincetown Fellowships, 281
Foundation Praemium Erasmianum Study Prize, 288
Frink School Bursary, 293
Gilroy Roberts Art of Engraving Fellowship, 303
Gottlieb Foundation Emergency Assistance Grants, 9
Gottlieb Foundation Individual Support Grants, 9
Hambidge Center Residency Program Scholarships, 313
Haystack Scholarship, 319
Henry Moore Institute Research Fellowship, 322

Hugh Last and Donald Atkinson Funds Committee Grants, 581
Jacob Hirsch Fellowship, 72
MacDowell Colony Residencies, 402
MICA Fellowship, 407
NEH Fellowships, 72
Pollock-Krasner Foundation Grant, 502
Ragdale Foundation Residencies, 511
Research Student Bursary, 163
Rhodes University Postdoctoral Fellowship, 519
RSA Annual Student Competition, 542
The Alastair Salvesen Art Scholarship, 541
The John Kinross Memorial Fund Student Scholarships/RSA, 541
University of Dundee Research Awards, 629
Virginia Center for the Creative Arts Fellowships, 695
Yaddo Residency, 243

African Nations

International Postgraduate Research Scholarships (IPRS), 676

Australia

Fulbright Postgraduate Student Award for the Visual and Performing Arts, 120
Marten Bequest Travelling Scholarships, 222
University of Western Sydney Postgraduate Research Award (UW-SPRA), 689

British Commonwealth

Hector and Elizabeth Catling Bursary, 155
International Postgraduate Research Scholarships (IPRS), 676
Rome Scholarships in the Fine Arts, 157
Sargant Fellowship, 157
Wingate Rome Scholarship in the Fine Arts, 157

Canada

International Postgraduate Research Scholarships (IPRS), 676

Caribbean Countries

International Postgraduate Research Scholarships (IPRS), 676

East European Countries

AHRB Doctoral Awards Scheme, 99
International Postgraduate Research Scholarships (IPRS), 676
Professional Preparation Master's Scheme, 99

Far East

ACC Fellowship Grants Program, 103
Hong Kong Arts Development Council - FCO Chevening - Leeds University Scholarships, 639
International Postgraduate Research Scholarships (IPRS), 676

Indian Sub-Continent

International Postgraduate Research Scholarships (IPRS), 676
USEFI Professional Fellowships in Plastics and Performing Arts, Museum Studies and Arts/Culture Management, 611

Middle East

International Postgraduate Research Scholarships (IPRS), 676
Sharett Scholarship Program, 22

New Zealand

University of Western Sydney Postgraduate Research Award (UW-SPRA), 689

South Africa

International Postgraduate Research Scholarships (IPRS), 676

South America

International Postgraduate Research Scholarships (IPRS), 676

United Kingdom

AHRB Doctoral Awards Scheme, 99
British School at Rome Fellowship, 100
ESU Chautauqua Institution Scholarships, 271
Hallam Studentships, 558
Hector and Elizabeth Catling Bursary, 155
International Postgraduate Research Scholarships (IPRS), 676
Polish Government Postgraduate Scholarships Scheme, 501
Professional Preparation Master's Scheme, 99
Rome Scholarships in the Fine Arts, 157
Sainsbury Scholarship in Painting and Sculpture, 157
Sargant Fellowship, 157
Sir William Gillies Bequest-Hospitalfield Residencies, 542
Wingate Rome Scholarship in the Fine Arts, 157

United States of America

ACC Fellowship Grants Program, 103
Bush Artist Fellows Program, 164
Fulbright Senior Specialists Program, 245
Gerald R Dodge Foundation Residency for New Jersey Artists, 708
International Postgraduate Research Scholarships (IPRS), 676
NLAPW Grants for Mature Women, 452
Twining Humbe Award for Lifetime Aritistic Achievement, 98

West European Countries

AHRB Doctoral Awards Scheme, 99
Hallam Studentships, 558
International Postgraduate Research Scholarships (IPRS), 676
Professional Preparation Master's Scheme, 99

HANDICRAFTS

Any Country

Ebb & Flow Grant, 265
Foundation Praemium Erasmianum Study Prize, 288
Hambidge Center Residency Program Scholarships, 313
Haystack Scholarship, 319
Research Student Bursary, 163

African Nations

International Postgraduate Research Scholarships (IPRS), 676

Australia

Fulbright Postgraduate Student Award for the Visual and Performing Arts, 120
Wingate Scholarships, 704

British Commonwealth

International Postgraduate Research Scholarships (IPRS), 676
Wingate Scholarships, 704

Canada

International Postgraduate Research Scholarships (IPRS), 676
Saidye Bronfman Award, 196
Wingate Scholarships, 704

Caribbean Countries

International Postgraduate Research Scholarships (IPRS), 676

East European Countries

AHRB Doctoral Awards Scheme, 99
International Postgraduate Research Scholarships (IPRS), 676
Professional Preparation Master's Scheme, 99

Far East

ACC Fellowship Grants Program, 103
International Postgraduate Research Scholarships (IPRS), 676

Indian Sub-Continent

International Postgraduate Research Scholarships (IPRS), 676
Wingate Scholarships, 704

Middle East

International Postgraduate Research Scholarships (IPRS), 676

New Zealand

Wingate Scholarships, 704

South Africa

International Postgraduate Research Scholarships (IPRS), 676
Wingate Scholarships, 704

South America

International Postgraduate Research Scholarships (IPRS), 676

United Kingdom

AHRB Doctoral Awards Scheme, 99
International Postgraduate Research Scholarships (IPRS), 676
Professional Preparation Master's Scheme, 99
Wingate Scholarships, 704

United States of America

ACC Fellowship Grants Program, 103
Bush Artist Fellows Program, 164
International Postgraduate Research Scholarships (IPRS), 676
Twining Humbe Award for Lifetime Aritistic Achievement, 98

West European Countries

AHRB Doctoral Awards Scheme, 99
International Postgraduate Research Scholarships (IPRS), 676
Janson Johan Helmich Scholarships and Travel Grants, 376
Professional Preparation Master's Scheme, 99
Wingate Scholarships, 704

MUSIC

Any Country

Advanced Fellowships, 71
Ahmanson and Getty Postdoctoral Fellowships, 606
Allcard Grants, 713
Alvin H Johnson 50 Dissertation One Year Fellowship, 59
Arthur Rubinstein International Piano Master Competition, 98
Austro-American Association of Boston Scholarship, 123
Banff Centre Financial Assistance, 124
Brandon University Graduate Assistantships, 132
British Academy Larger Research Grants, 134
Camargo Fellowships, 164
Canada Council Grants for Professional artists, 195
Chautauqua Institution Awards, 231
Clark-Huntington Joint Bibliographical Fellowship, 607
Cleveland Institute of Music Scholarships and Accompanying Fellowships, 238
Ebb & Flow Grant, 265
ESU Music Scholarships, 271
Feiweles Trust Dance Bursary, 716
Foundation Praemium Erasmianum Study Prize, 288
Fromm Foundation Commission, 293
Guilhermina Suggia Gift, 429
Hambidge Center Residency Program Scholarships, 313
Harold White Fellowships, 452
Hinrichsen Foundation Awards, 324
International Beethoven Piano Competition Vienna, 355
International Music Competition of the ARD, 93
International Robert Schumann Competition, 371
J B C Watkins Award, 195
James Ingham Halstead Scholarship in Music, 652
Kanner Fellowship In British Studies, 607

West European Countries

MUSICOLOGY

Any Country

Australia

British Commonwealth

Canada

East European Countries

Far East

Indian Sub-Continent

New Zealand

South Africa

United Kingdom

United States of America

West European Countries

MUSIC THEORY AND COMPOSITION

Any Country

Royal College of Music Scholarships, 527
RPS Composition Prize, 541
Ryan Davies Memorial Fund Scholarship Grants, 552
San Francisco Conservatory Performance Scholarships in Music, 554
Thomas Holloway Research Studentship, 536
United States Center for Advanced Holocaust Studies Research Fellowships, 608
Virginia Center for the Creative Arts Fellowships, 695
Yaddo Residency, 243

Australia

Wingate Scholarships, 704

British Commonwealth

Countess of Munster Musical Trust Awards, 248
Wingate Scholarships, 704

Canada

Ruth Watson Henderson Choral Composition Competition, 236
Sigma Alpha Iota Inter-American Music Awards, 559
Wingate Scholarships, 704

East European Countries

AHRB Doctoral Awards Scheme, 99
Research Preparation Master's Scheme, 99

Far East

ACC Fellowship Grants Program, 103
Hong Kong Arts Development Council - FCO Chevening - Leeds University Scholarships, 639

Indian Sub-Continent

Wingate Scholarships, 704

Middle East

Sharett Scholarship Program, 22

New Zealand

Wingate Scholarships, 704

South Africa

SAMRO Intermediate Bursaries for Composition Study In Southern Africa, 553
SAMRO Overseas Scholarship, 553
Wingate Scholarships, 704

South America

Sigma Alpha Iota Inter-American Music Awards, 559

United Kingdom

AHRB Doctoral Awards Scheme, 99
Countess of Munster Musical Trust Awards, 248
Francis Chagrin Fund, 288
Frank Knox Fellowships at Harvard University, 288
Fulbright-Chester Schirmer Fellowship in Music Composition, 692
Kennedy Scholarships, 385
Mr and Mrs David Edward Memorial Award, 681
Research Preparation Master's Scheme, 99
UWB Departmental Research Studentships, 681
UWB Research Studentships, 681
Wingate Scholarships, 704

United States of America

ACC Fellowship Grants Program, 103
ASCAP Foundation Morton Gould Young Composer Awards, 102
Bush Artist Fellows Program, 164
Commissioning Music/USA, 414
Composer Assistance Program, 58
Harvey Gaul Composition Contest, 499

Margaret Fairbank Jory Copying Assistance Program, 58
NLAPW Grants for Mature Women, 452
Sigma Alpha Iota Inter-American Music Awards, 559
Worldstudio Foundation Scholarship, 713

West European Countries

AHRB Doctoral Awards Scheme, 99
Mr and Mrs David Edward Memorial Award, 681
Research Preparation Master's Scheme, 99
UWB Departmental Research Studentships, 681
UWB Research Studentships, 681
Wingate Scholarships, 704

CONDUCTING

Any Country

Chautauqua Institution Awards, 231
Cleveland Institute of Music Scholarships and Accompanying Fellowships, 238
Eastman School of Music Graduate Awards, 264
Prague Spring International Music Competition, 503
Royal College of Music Scholarships, 527
Ryan Davies Memorial Fund Scholarship Grants, 552
San Francisco Conservatory Performance Scholarships in Music, 554

Australia

Wingate Scholarships, 704

British Commonwealth

Wingate Scholarships, 704

Canada

Leslie Bell Prize, 235
Ruth Watson Henderson Choral Composition Competition, 236
Wingate Scholarships, 704

East European Countries

AHRB Doctoral Awards Scheme, 99

Far East

ACC Fellowship Grants Program, 103

Indian Sub-Continent

Wingate Scholarships, 704

Middle East

Sharett Scholarship Program, 22

New Zealand

Wingate Scholarships, 704

South Africa

Wingate Scholarships, 704

United Kingdom

AHRB Doctoral Awards Scheme, 99
Mr and Mrs David Edward Memorial Award, 681
UWB Departmental Research Studentships, 681
UWB Research Studentships, 681
Wingate Scholarships, 704

United States of America

ACC Fellowship Grants Program, 103

West European Countries

AHRB Doctoral Awards Scheme, 99
Donatella Flick Conducting Competition, 260
Mr and Mrs David Edward Memorial Award, 681

RELIGIOUS MUSIC

Any Country

JAZZ AND POPULAR MUSIC

OPERA

British Commonwealth

ACW Community Touring Night Out, 100
Countess of Munster Musical Trust Awards, 248
Wingate Scholarships, 704

Canada

Wingate Scholarships, 704

East European Countries

AHRB Doctoral Awards Scheme, 99
Research Preparation Master's Scheme, 99

Far East

ACC Fellowship Grants Program, 103

Indian Sub-Continent

Wingate Scholarships, 704

Middle East

ACW Community Touring Night Out, 100
Sharett Scholarship Program, 22

New Zealand

Wingate Scholarships, 704

South Africa

ACW Community Touring Night Out, 100
Wingate Scholarships, 704

South America

ACW Community Touring Night Out, 100

United Kingdom

ACW Community Touring Night Out, 100
AHRB Doctoral Awards Scheme, 99
Countess of Munster Musical Trust Awards, 248
Research Preparation Master's Scheme, 99
Wingate Scholarships, 704

United States of America

ACC Fellowship Grants Program, 103
The Fund for US Artists, 101

West European Countries

AHRB Doctoral Awards Scheme, 99
Research Preparation Master's Scheme, 99
Wingate Scholarships, 704

DRAMA

Any Country

Advanced Fellowships, 71
AIIS Senior Performing and Creative Arts Fellowships, 50
Alfred Bradley Bursary Award, 18
ASCSA Fellowships, 71
ASCSA Summer Sessions, 72
Austro-American Association of Boston Scholarship, 123
Banff Centre Financial Assistance, 124
British Academy Larger Research Grants, 134
British Academy Overseas Conference Grants, 134
British Academy Small Personal Research Grants, 134
British Academy Worldwide Congress Grant, 135
Canada Council Grants for Professional artists, 195
Chautauqua Institution Awards, 231
Ebb & Flow Grant, 265
External Faculty Fellowships, 594
Fine Arts Work Center in Provincetown Fellowships, 281
Foundation Praemium Erasmianum Study Prize, 288

Golden Key National Honor Society Performing Arts Showcase, 306
Jacob Hirsch Fellowship, 72
Kanner Fellowship In British Studies, 607
La Trobe University Postgraduate Scholarship, 390
MacDowell Colony Residencies, 402
Massey Doctoral Scholarship, 408
Mildred and Albert Panowski Playwriting Award, 282
NEH Fellowships, 72
Queen Mary Research Studentships, 506
Rhodes University Postdoctoral Fellowship, 519
Rockefeller Fellowships in Black Performing Arts, 594
Ryan Davies Memorial Fund Scholarship Grants, 552
Society for Theatre Research Awards, 584
The J. Watumull Scholarship for the Study of India, 634
Thomas Holloway Research Studentship, 536
University of Bristol Postgraduate Scholarships, 619
University of Manchester Research Studentships and Scholarships, 642
Yaddo Residency, 243

African Nations

INROADS, 101

Australia

Fulbright Postgraduate Student Award for the Visual and Performing Arts, 120
Marten Bequest Travelling Scholarships, 222
Quinn, Nathan and Edmond Scholarships, 149
University of Western Sydney Postgraduate Research Award (UW-SPRA), 689

British Commonwealth

ACW Community Touring Night Out, 100
Quinn, Nathan and Edmond Scholarships, 149

Canada

Quinn, Nathan and Edmond Scholarships, 149

East European Countries

AHRB Doctoral Awards Scheme, 99
Professional Preparation Master's Scheme, 99
Research Preparation Master's Scheme, 99

Far East

ACC Fellowship Grants Program, 103
INROADS, 101

Indian Sub-Continent

Quinn, Nathan and Edmond Scholarships, 149
USEFI Professional Fellowships in Plastics and Performing Arts, Museum Studies and Arts/Culture Management, 611

Middle East

ACW Community Touring Night Out, 100
Sharett Scholarship Program, 22

New Zealand

Quinn, Nathan and Edmond Scholarships, 149
University of Western Sydney Postgraduate Research Award (UW-SPRA), 689

South Africa

ACW Community Touring Night Out, 100
INROADS, 101
Quinn, Nathan and Edmond Scholarships, 149

South America

ACW Community Touring Night Out, 100
INROADS, 101

United Kingdom

ACW Community Touring Night Out, 100
AHRB Doctoral Awards Scheme, 99
British Conference Grants, 135
Professional Preparation Master's Scheme, 99
Quinn, Nathan and Edmond Scholarships, 149
Research Preparation Master's Scheme, 99
University of Kent School of Drama, Film and Visual Arts Scholarships, 637
University of Wales (Aberystwyth) Postgraduate Research Studentships, 680

United States of America

ACC Fellowship Grants Program, 103
Fulbright Senior Specialists Program, 245
The Fund for US Artists, 101

West European Countries

AHRB Doctoral Awards Scheme, 99
Professional Preparation Master's Scheme, 99
Research Preparation Master's Scheme, 99
University of Kent School of Drama, Film and Visual Arts Scholarships, 637

DANCING

Any Country

Advanced Fellowships, 71
ASCSA Fellowships, 71
ASCSA Summer Sessions, 72
Banff Centre Financial Assistance, 124
British Academy Larger Research Grants, 134
British Academy Overseas Conference Grants, 134
British Academy Small Personal Research Grants, 134
British Academy Worldwide Congress Grant, 135
Canada Council Grants for Professional artists, 195
Chautauqua Institution Awards, 231
Earthwatch Field Research Grants, 264
Ebb & Flow Grant, 265
Feiweles Trust Dance Bursary, 716
Foundation Praemium Erasmianum Study Prize, 288
Golden Key National Honor Society Performing Arts Showcase, 306
Hambidge Center Residency Program Scholarships, 313
J B C Watkins Award, 195
Jacob Hirsch Fellowship, 72
Jacob's Pillow Education Fund Scholarship, 375
Massey Doctoral Scholarship, 408
NEH Fellowships, 72
Queen Mary Research Studentships, 506
Rhodes University Postdoctoral Fellowship, 519
Rockefeller Fellowships in Black Performing Arts, 594
Ryan Davies Memorial Fund Scholarship Grants, 552
The J. Watumull Scholarship for the Study of India, 634
Yaddo Residency, 243

African Nations

INROADS, 101

Australia

Fulbright Postgraduate Student Award for the Visual and Performing Arts, 120
Lady Mollie Askin Ballet Travelling Scholarship, 222
Marten Bequest Travelling Scholarships, 222
University of Western Sydney Postgraduate Research Award (UW-SPRA), 689

British Commonwealth

ACW Community Touring Night Out, 100

East European Countries

AHRB Doctoral Awards Scheme, 99
Professional Preparation Master's Scheme, 99
Research Preparation Master's Scheme, 99

Far East

ACC Fellowship Grants Program, 103
INROADS, 101

Indian Sub-Continent

USEFI Professional Fellowships in Plastics and Performing Arts, Museum Studies and Arts/Culture Management, 611

Middle East

ACW Community Touring Night Out, 100
Sharett Scholarship Program, 22

New Zealand

University of Western Sydney Postgraduate Research Award (UW-SPRA), 689

South Africa

ACW Community Touring Night Out, 100
INROADS, 101

South America

ACW Community Touring Night Out, 100
INROADS, 101

United Kingdom

ACW Community Touring Night Out, 100
AHRB Doctoral Awards Scheme, 99
British Conference Grants, 135
Professional Preparation Master's Scheme, 99
Research Preparation Master's Scheme, 99

United States of America

ACC Fellowship Grants Program, 103
Bush Artist Fellows Program, 164
Fulbright Senior Specialists Program, 245
The Fund for US Artists, 101
UCLA IAC Postdoctoral/Visiting Scholar Fellowships, 607

West European Countries

AHRB Doctoral Awards Scheme, 99
Professional Preparation Master's Scheme, 99
Research Preparation Master's Scheme, 99

PHOTOGRAPHY

Any Country

Alberta Art Foundation Graduate Scholarships in the Department of Art, 620
Banff Centre Financial Assistance, 124
British Academy Larger Research Grants, 134
British Academy Overseas Conference Grants, 134
British Academy Small Personal Research Grants, 134
British Academy Worldwide Congress Grant, 135
Camargo Fellowships, 164
Cintas Fellowships, 101
Hambidge Center Residency Program Scholarships, 313
John Hervey, Broadcasters and Smallsreed Awards, 613
Library Company of Philadelphia and Historical Society of Pennsylvania Research Fellowships in American History and Culture, 398
Light Work Artist-in-Residence Program, 399
MacDowell Colony Residencies, 402
Massey Doctoral Scholarship, 408
MICA Fellowship, 407
Rhodes University Postdoctoral Fellowship, 519

CINEMA AND TELEVISION

DESIGN

Any Country

British Academy Larger Research Grants, 134
British Academy Overseas Conference Grants, 134
British Academy Worldwide Congress Grant, 135
Cintas Fellowships, 101
Foundation Praemium Erasmianum Study Prize, 288
Hagley/Winterthur Arts and Industries Fellowship, 312
Hambidge Center Residency Program Scholarships, 313
Haystack Scholarship, 319
Massey Doctoral Scholarship, 408
MICA Fellowship, 407
MICA International Fellowship Award, 407
University of Dundee Research Awards, 629
Wolfsonian FIU Fellowship, 706

African Nations

International Postgraduate Research Scholarships (IPRS), 676

Australia

Fulbright Postgraduate Student Award for the Visual and Performing Arts, 120
University of Western Sydney Postgraduate Research Award (UW-SPRA), 689
Wingate Scholarships, 704

British Commonwealth

International Postgraduate Research Scholarships (IPRS), 676
Wingate Scholarships, 704

Canada

Frank Knox Memorial Fellowships at Harvard University, 109
International Postgraduate Research Scholarships (IPRS), 676
Wingate Scholarships, 704

Caribbean Countries

International Postgraduate Research Scholarships (IPRS), 676

East European Countries

AHRB Doctoral Awards Scheme, 99
International Postgraduate Research Scholarships (IPRS), 676
Professional Preparation Master's Scheme, 99

Far East

International Postgraduate Research Scholarships (IPRS), 676

Indian Sub-Continent

International Postgraduate Research Scholarships (IPRS), 676
Wingate Scholarships, 704

Middle East

International Postgraduate Research Scholarships (IPRS), 676
Sharett Scholarship Program, 22

New Zealand

University of Western Sydney Postgraduate Research Award (UW-SPRA), 689
Wingate Scholarships, 704

South Africa

International Postgraduate Research Scholarships (IPRS), 676
Wingate Scholarships, 704

South America

International Postgraduate Research Scholarships (IPRS), 676

United Kingdom

AHRB Doctoral Awards Scheme, 99

International Postgraduate Research Scholarships (IPRS), 676
Lord Barnby Foundation Bursaries, 599
Polish Government Postgraduate Scholarships Scheme, 501
Professional Preparation Master's Scheme, 99
RSA Design Directions, 545
Wingate Scholarships, 704

United States of America

Congress Bundestag Youth Exchange for Young Professionals, 223
Fulbright Senior Specialists Program, 245
International Postgraduate Research Scholarships (IPRS), 676
The George & Viola Hoffman Fund, 105

West European Countries

AHRB Doctoral Awards Scheme, 99
International Postgraduate Research Scholarships (IPRS), 676
Janson Johan Helmich Scholarships and Travel Grants, 376
Professional Preparation Master's Scheme, 99
RSA Design Directions, 545
Wingate Scholarships, 704

INTERIOR DESIGN

Any Country

ASID/Joel Polsky-Fixtures Furniture Academic Achievement Award, 80
ASID/Joel Polsky-Fixtures Furniture Prize, 80
ASID/Mabelle Wilhelmina Boldt Memorial Scholarship, 80
Interior Architecture Travelling Fellowship, 566
Massey Doctoral Scholarship, 408
University of Dundee Research Awards, 629

African Nations

International Postgraduate Research Scholarships (IPRS), 676

British Commonwealth

International Postgraduate Research Scholarships (IPRS), 676

Canada

International Postgraduate Research Scholarships (IPRS), 676

Caribbean Countries

International Postgraduate Research Scholarships (IPRS), 676

East European Countries

AHRB Doctoral Awards Scheme, 99
International Postgraduate Research Scholarships (IPRS), 676
Professional Preparation Master's Scheme, 99

Far East

International Postgraduate Research Scholarships (IPRS), 676

Indian Sub-Continent

International Postgraduate Research Scholarships (IPRS), 676

Middle East

International Postgraduate Research Scholarships (IPRS), 676

South Africa

International Postgraduate Research Scholarships (IPRS), 676

South America

International Postgraduate Research Scholarships (IPRS), 676

United Kingdom

AHRB Doctoral Awards Scheme, 99
International Postgraduate Research Scholarships (IPRS), 676
Professional Preparation Master's Scheme, 99
RSA Design Directions, 545

United States of America

International Postgraduate Research Scholarships (IPRS), 676

West European Countries

AHRB Doctoral Awards Scheme, 99
International Postgraduate Research Scholarships (IPRS), 676
Professional Preparation Master's Scheme, 99
RSA Design Directions, 545

FURNITURE DESIGN

Any Country

Haystack Scholarship, 319
Research Student Bursary, 163
University of Dundee Research Awards, 629

African Nations

International Postgraduate Research Scholarships (IPRS), 676

British Commonwealth

International Postgraduate Research Scholarships (IPRS), 676

Canada

International Postgraduate Research Scholarships (IPRS), 676

Caribbean Countries

International Postgraduate Research Scholarships (IPRS), 676

East European Countries

AHRB Doctoral Awards Scheme, 99
International Postgraduate Research Scholarships (IPRS), 676
Professional Preparation Master's Scheme, 99

Far East

International Postgraduate Research Scholarships (IPRS), 676

Indian Sub-Continent

International Postgraduate Research Scholarships (IPRS), 676

Middle East

International Postgraduate Research Scholarships (IPRS), 676

South Africa

International Postgraduate Research Scholarships (IPRS), 676

South America

International Postgraduate Research Scholarships (IPRS), 676

United Kingdom

AHRB Doctoral Awards Scheme, 99
International Postgraduate Research Scholarships (IPRS), 676
Professional Preparation Master's Scheme, 99

United States of America

International Postgraduate Research Scholarships (IPRS), 676

West European Countries

AHRB Doctoral Awards Scheme, 99
International Postgraduate Research Scholarships (IPRS), 676
Professional Preparation Master's Scheme, 99

FASHION DESIGN

Any Country

Cotton Industry War Memorial Trust Scholarships, 599
CSA Adele Filene Travel Award, 243

CSA Stella Blum Research Grant, 243
CSA Travel Research Grant, 244
Massey Doctoral Scholarship, 408
Textile Institute Scholarship, 600
University of Dundee Research Awards, 629

African Nations

International Postgraduate Research Scholarships (IPRS), 676

British Commonwealth

International Postgraduate Research Scholarships (IPRS), 676

Canada

International Postgraduate Research Scholarships (IPRS), 676

Caribbean Countries

International Postgraduate Research Scholarships (IPRS), 676

East European Countries

AHRB Doctoral Awards Scheme, 99
International Postgraduate Research Scholarships (IPRS), 676
Professional Preparation Master's Scheme, 99

Far East

International Postgraduate Research Scholarships (IPRS), 676

Indian Sub-Continent

International Postgraduate Research Scholarships (IPRS), 676

Middle East

International Postgraduate Research Scholarships (IPRS), 676
Sharett Scholarship Program, 22

South Africa

International Postgraduate Research Scholarships (IPRS), 676

South America

International Postgraduate Research Scholarships (IPRS), 676

United Kingdom

AHRB Doctoral Awards Scheme, 99
International Postgraduate Research Scholarships (IPRS), 676
Lord Barnby Foundation Bursaries, 599
Professional Preparation Master's Scheme, 99
RSA Design Directions, 545
Worshipful Company of Weavers' Scholarships, 600

United States of America

International Postgraduate Research Scholarships (IPRS), 676
Worldstudio Foundation Scholarship, 713

West European Countries

AHRB Doctoral Awards Scheme, 99
International Postgraduate Research Scholarships (IPRS), 676
Professional Preparation Master's Scheme, 99
RSA Design Directions, 545

TEXTILE DESIGN

Any Country

Cotton Industry War Memorial Trust Scholarships, 599
CSA Adele Filene Travel Award, 243
CSA Stella Blum Research Grant, 243
CSA Travel Research Grant, 244
Hambidge Center Residency Program Scholarships, 313
Haystack Scholarship, 319
Textile Institute Scholarship, 600
University of Dundee Research Awards, 629

Caribbean Countries

International Postgraduate Research Scholarships (IPRS), 676

East European Countries

AHRB Doctoral Awards Scheme, 99
International Postgraduate Research Scholarships (IPRS), 676
Professional Preparation Master's Scheme, 99

Far East

International Postgraduate Research Scholarships (IPRS), 676

Indian Sub-Continent

International Postgraduate Research Scholarships (IPRS), 676

Middle East

International Postgraduate Research Scholarships (IPRS), 676
Sharett Scholarship Program, 22

New Zealand

University of Western Sydney Postgraduate Research Award (UW-SPRA), 689

South Africa

International Postgraduate Research Scholarships (IPRS), 676

South America

International Postgraduate Research Scholarships (IPRS), 676

United Kingdom

AHRB Doctoral Awards Scheme, 99
Hallam Studentships, 558
International Postgraduate Research Scholarships (IPRS), 676
Professional Preparation Master's Scheme, 99
Royal Commission Industrial Design Studentship, 534
RSA Design Directions, 545

United States of America

International Postgraduate Research Scholarships (IPRS), 676

West European Countries

AHRB Doctoral Awards Scheme, 99
Hallam Studentships, 558
International Postgraduate Research Scholarships (IPRS), 676
Professional Preparation Master's Scheme, 99
RSA Design Directions, 545

DISPLAY AND STAGE DESIGN

Any Country

Banff Centre Financial Assistance, 124

African Nations

International Postgraduate Research Scholarships (IPRS), 676

British Commonwealth

International Postgraduate Research Scholarships (IPRS), 676

Canada

International Postgraduate Research Scholarships (IPRS), 676

Caribbean Countries

International Postgraduate Research Scholarships (IPRS), 676

East European Countries

AHRB Doctoral Awards Scheme, 99
International Postgraduate Research Scholarships (IPRS), 676
Professional Preparation Master's Scheme, 99

Far East

International Postgraduate Research Scholarships (IPRS), 676

Indian Sub-Continent

International Postgraduate Research Scholarships (IPRS), 676

Middle East

International Postgraduate Research Scholarships (IPRS), 676
Sharett Scholarship Program, 22

South Africa

International Postgraduate Research Scholarships (IPRS), 676

South America

International Postgraduate Research Scholarships (IPRS), 676

United Kingdom

AHRB Doctoral Awards Scheme, 99
International Postgraduate Research Scholarships (IPRS), 676
Professional Preparation Master's Scheme, 99

United States of America

International Postgraduate Research Scholarships (IPRS), 676

West European Countries

AHRB Doctoral Awards Scheme, 99
International Postgraduate Research Scholarships (IPRS), 676
Professional Preparation Master's Scheme, 99

HOME ECONOMICS

GENERAL

Any Country

AIATSIS Research Grants, 116
Alberta Research Council Scholarship, 620
Canadian Natural Resources Limited Graduate Scholarship, 620

African Nations

Fulbright Postdoctoral Research and Lecturing Awards for Non-US Citizens, 245
Joint Japan/World Bank Graduate Scholarship Program (JJ/WBGSP), 355
Merton College Reed Foundation Scholarship, 658

Australia

Fulbright Awards, 119
Fulbright Postdoctoral Research and Lecturing Awards for Non-US Citizens, 245
Fulbright Postgraduate Studentships, 120

British Commonwealth

Joint Japan/World Bank Graduate Scholarship Program (JJ/WBGSP), 355
Merton College Reed Foundation Scholarship, 658

Canada

Fulbright Postdoctoral Research and Lecturing Awards for Non-US Citizens, 245
Killam Research Fellowships, 195
Mary A Clarke Memorial Scholarship, Silver Jubilee Scholarship and Fiftieth Anniversary Scholarship, 206
OAS Graduate Academic Studies, 483
Robin Hood Multifoods Scholarship, 206
Ruth Binnie Scholarship, 206

Caribbean Countries

Joint Japan/World Bank Graduate Scholarship Program (JJ/WBGSP), 355
Merton College Reed Foundation Scholarship, 658
OAS Graduate Academic Studies, 483

East European Countries

Fulbright Postdoctoral Research and Lecturing Awards for Non-US Citizens, 245
Joint Japan/World Bank Graduate Scholarship Program (JJ/WBGSP), 355
Merton College Reed Foundation Scholarship, 658

Far East

Fulbright Postdoctoral Research and Lecturing Awards for Non-US Citizens, 245
JACL Scholarship and Award Program, 377
Joint Japan/World Bank Graduate Scholarship Program (JJ/WBGSP), 355
Merton College Reed Foundation Scholarship, 658

Indian Sub-Continent

Fulbright Postdoctoral Research and Lecturing Awards for Non-US Citizens, 245
Joint Japan/World Bank Graduate Scholarship Program (JJ/WBGSP), 355
Merton College Reed Foundation Scholarship, 658

Middle East

Fulbright Postdoctoral Research and Lecturing Awards for Non-US Citizens, 245
Joint Japan/World Bank Graduate Scholarship Program (JJ/WBGSP), 355
Merton College Reed Foundation Scholarship, 658

New Zealand

Fulbright Postdoctoral Research and Lecturing Awards for Non-US Citizens, 245

South Africa

Fulbright Postdoctoral Research and Lecturing Awards for Non-US Citizens, 245
Isie Smuts Research Award, 590
Joint Japan/World Bank Graduate Scholarship Program (JJ/WBGSP), 355

South America

Fulbright Commission (Argentina) Master's Program, 293
Fulbright Postdoctoral Research and Lecturing Awards for Non-US Citizens, 245
Joint Japan/World Bank Graduate Scholarship Program (JJ/WBGSP), 355
Merton College Reed Foundation Scholarship, 658
OAS Graduate Academic Studies, 483

United Kingdom

All Saints Educational Trust Corporate Awards, 19
All Saints Educational Trust Personal Awards, 19
Canada Memorial Foundation Scholarships, 106
Fulbright Postdoctoral Research and Lecturing Awards for Non-US Citizens, 245

United States of America

Fulbright Scholar Program for United States Citizens, 245
JACL Scholarship and Award Program, 377
North Dakota Indian Scholarship, 472
OAS Graduate Academic Studies, 483

West European Countries

Fulbright Postdoctoral Research and Lecturing Awards for Non-US Citizens, 245

CLOTHING AND SEWING

Any Country

Cotton Industry War Memorial Trust Scholarships, 599
CSA Adele Filene Travel Award, 243
CSA Stella Blum Research Grant, 243
CSA Travel Research Grant, 244
Textile Institute Scholarship, 600

United Kingdom

Lord Barnby Foundation Bursaries, 599
Worshipful Company of Weavers' Scholarships, 600

NUTRITION

Any Country

Allen Foundation Grants, 19
Bio-Serv Award in Experimental Animal Nutrition, 79
Cenrium Center for Nutritional Science Award, 79
Conrad A Elvehjem Award for Public Service in Nutrition, 79
E L R Stokstad Award, 79
Earthwatch Field Research Grants, 264
Food-Based Approaches to Micronutrient Malnutrition Program, 603
Mead Johnson Award, 79
Osborne and Mendel Award, 79
University of Otago International Scholarships, 646

African Nations

International Postgraduate Research Scholarships (IPRS), 676
Joint Japan/World Bank Graduate Scholarship Program (JJ/WBGSP), 355

Australia

University of Otago Masters Awards, 646
University of Otago PhD Scholarships, 646
University of Otago Prestigious PhD Scholarships, 647

British Commonwealth

International Postgraduate Research Scholarships (IPRS), 676
Joint Japan/World Bank Graduate Scholarship Program (JJ/WBGSP), 355

Canada

International Postgraduate Research Scholarships (IPRS), 676
Robin Hood Multifoods Scholarship, 206

Caribbean Countries

International Postgraduate Research Scholarships (IPRS), 676
Joint Japan/World Bank Graduate Scholarship Program (JJ/WBGSP), 355

East European Countries

International Postgraduate Research Scholarships (IPRS), 676
Joint Japan/World Bank Graduate Scholarship Program (JJ/WBGSP), 355

Far East

International Postgraduate Research Scholarships (IPRS), 676
Joint Japan/World Bank Graduate Scholarship Program (JJ/WBGSP), 355
University of Otago Dr Sulaiman Daud 125th Jubilee International Postgraduate Scholarship, 646

LAW

GENERAL

African Nations

Australia

British Commonwealth

Canada

HISTORY OF LAW

Any Country

Australia

British Commonwealth

Canada

East European Countries

Indian Sub-Continent

New Zealand

South Africa

United Kingdom

United States of America

West European Countries

COMPARATIVE LAW

Any Country

African Nations

Australia

British Commonwealth

Canada

Caribbean Countries

East European Countries

AHRB Doctoral Awards Scheme, 99
EUI Postgraduate Scholarships, 277
Hastings Center International Visiting Scholars Program, 318
Hubert H Humphrey Fellowship Programme, 609
Research Preparation Master's Scheme, 99

Far East

Hastings Center International Visiting Scholars Program, 318
Hubert H Humphrey Fellowship Programme, 609

Indian Sub-Continent

Hastings Center International Visiting Scholars Program, 318
Hubert H Humphrey Fellowship Programme, 609
Wingate Scholarships, 704

Middle East

Hastings Center International Visiting Scholars Program, 318
Hubert H Humphrey Fellowship Programme, 609

New Zealand

Hastings Center International Visiting Scholars Program, 318
Wingate Scholarships, 704

South Africa

Hastings Center International Visiting Scholars Program, 318
Hubert H Humphrey Fellowship Programme, 609
Wingate Scholarships, 704

South America

Hastings Center International Visiting Scholars Program, 318
Hubert H Humphrey Fellowship Programme, 609

United Kingdom

AHRB Doctoral Awards Scheme, 99
EUI Postgraduate Scholarships, 277
Hastings Center International Visiting Scholars Program, 318
Molson Research Awards, 136
Prix du Québec, 136
Research Preparation Master's Scheme, 99
University of Essex Foundation Scholarships, 632
Wingate Scholarships, 704

United States of America

Fulbright Distinguished Chairs Program, 245
Fulbright Senior Specialists Program, 245
IREX John J and Nancy Lee Roberts Fellowship Program, 366
Kennan Institute Research Scholarship, 385

West European Countries

AHRB Doctoral Awards Scheme, 99
Artal Scholarships, 647
EUI Postgraduate Scholarships, 277
Hastings Center International Visiting Scholars Program, 318
Research Preparation Master's Scheme, 99
Wingate Scholarships, 704

INTERNATIONAL LAW

Any Country

Center for Advanced Study in the Behavioral Sciences Postdoctoral Residential Fellowships, 223
Foundation Praemium Erasmianum Study Prize, 288
Gilbert Murray Trust Junior Awards, 302
Graduate Institute of International Studies (HEI-Geneva) Scholarships, 308
Hague Academy of International Law / Scholarships for Sessions of Courses, 313
Jean Monnet Fellowships, 278

Jennings Randolph Program for International Peace Senior Fellowships, 612
Paul H Nitze School of Advanced International Studies (SAIS) Financial Aid and Fellowships, 130
The Airey Neave Research Fellowships, 12
University Institute of European Studies Postgraduate Scholarships, 616
University of Bristol Postgraduate Scholarships, 619
University of Dundee Research Awards, 629
University of Essex Scholarships, 632
USIP Solicited Grants, 612
USIP Unsolicited Grants, 613
Woods Hole Oceanographic Institution Research Fellowships in Marine Policy, 710

African Nations

Hague Academy of International Law / Doctoral Scholarships, 313
Hastings Center International Visiting Scholars Program, 318
Hubert H Humphrey Fellowship Programme, 609
University of Sussex Overseas Development Administration Shared Scholarship Scheme, 678

Australia

Hastings Center International Visiting Scholars Program, 318
Wingate Scholarships, 704

British Commonwealth

Hastings Center International Visiting Scholars Program, 318
Wingate Scholarships, 704

Canada

Canadian Window on International Development, 358
Viscount Bennett Fellowship, 197
Wingate Scholarships, 704

Caribbean Countries

Hastings Center International Visiting Scholars Program, 318
Hubert H Humphrey Fellowship Programme, 609

East European Countries

AHRB Doctoral Awards Scheme, 99
EUI Postgraduate Scholarships, 277
Hastings Center International Visiting Scholars Program, 318
Hubert H Humphrey Fellowship Programme, 609
Research Preparation Master's Scheme, 99

Far East

Hague Academy of International Law / Doctoral Scholarships, 313
Hastings Center International Visiting Scholars Program, 318
Hubert H Humphrey Fellowship Programme, 609
University of Sussex Overseas Development Administration Shared Scholarship Scheme, 678

Indian Sub-Continent

Hastings Center International Visiting Scholars Program, 318
Hubert H Humphrey Fellowship Programme, 609
University of Sussex Overseas Development Administration Shared Scholarship Scheme, 678
Wingate Scholarships, 704

Middle East

Hastings Center International Visiting Scholars Program, 318
Hubert H Humphrey Fellowship Programme, 609

New Zealand

Hastings Center International Visiting Scholars Program, 318
Wingate Scholarships, 704

South Africa

Hastings Center International Visiting Scholars Program, 318
Hubert H Humphrey Fellowship Programme, 609

Wingate Scholarships, 704

South America

Hague Academy of International Law / Doctoral Scholarships, 313
Hastings Center International Visiting Scholars Program, 318
Hubert H Humphrey Fellowship Programme, 609

United Kingdom

AHRB Doctoral Awards Scheme, 99
EUI Postgraduate Scholarships, 277
Hastings Center International Visiting Scholars Program, 318
Research Preparation Master's Scheme, 99
University of Essex Foundation Scholarships, 632
University of Wales (Aberystwyth) Postgraduate Research Studentships, 680
Wingate Scholarships, 704

United States of America

Fulbright Senior Specialists Program, 245
Germanistic Society of America Fellowships, 301
IREX John J and Nancy Lee Roberts Fellowship Program, 366
Kennan Institute Research Scholarship, 385

West European Countries

AHRB Doctoral Awards Scheme, 99
EUI Postgraduate Scholarships, 277
Hastings Center International Visiting Scholars Program, 318
Research Preparation Master's Scheme, 99
Wingate Scholarships, 704

HUMAN RIGHTS

Any Country

Center for Advanced Study in the Behavioral Sciences Postdoctoral Residential Fellowships, 223
Eli M Oboler Memorial Award, 54
Equiano Memorial Award, 596
Foundation Praemium Erasmianum Study Prize, 288
Giulia Mereu Scholarship, 631
Jean Monnet Fellowships, 278
Jennings Randolph Program for International Peace Senior Fellowships, 612
NHC Fellowships, 449
The Airey Neave Research Fellowships, 12
University of Bristol Postgraduate Scholarships, 619
University of Essex Scholarships, 632
USIP Solicited Grants, 612
USIP Unsolicited Grants, 613
WILPF Internship in Disarmament and Economic Justice, 707
WILPF Internship in Human Rights, 707

African Nations

Hastings Center International Visiting Scholars Program, 318
Hubert H Humphrey Fellowship Programme, 609
Joint Japan/World Bank Graduate Scholarship Program (JJ/WBGSP), 355

Australia

Chevening Oxford-Australia Scholarships, 649
Hastings Center International Visiting Scholars Program, 318
Wingate Scholarships, 704

British Commonwealth

Hastings Center International Visiting Scholars Program, 318
Joint Japan/World Bank Graduate Scholarship Program (JJ/WBGSP), 355
Wingate Scholarships, 704

Canada

Bora Laskin National Fellowship in Human Rights Research, 575

Thérèse F Casgrain Fellowship, 580
Viscount Bennett Fellowship, 197
Wingate Scholarships, 704

Caribbean Countries

Hastings Center International Visiting Scholars Program, 318
Hubert H Humphrey Fellowship Programme, 609
Joint Japan/World Bank Graduate Scholarship Program (JJ/WBGSP), 355

East European Countries

AHRB Doctoral Awards Scheme, 99
EUI Postgraduate Scholarships, 277
Hastings Center International Visiting Scholars Program, 318
Hubert H Humphrey Fellowship Programme, 609
Joint Japan/World Bank Graduate Scholarship Program (JJ/WBGSP), 355
Research Preparation Master's Scheme, 99

Far East

Hastings Center International Visiting Scholars Program, 318
Hubert H Humphrey Fellowship Programme, 609
Joint Japan/World Bank Graduate Scholarship Program (JJ/WBGSP), 355

Indian Sub-Continent

Hastings Center International Visiting Scholars Program, 318
Hubert H Humphrey Fellowship Programme, 609
Joint Japan/World Bank Graduate Scholarship Program (JJ/WBGSP), 355
Wingate Scholarships, 704

Middle East

Hastings Center International Visiting Scholars Program, 318
Hubert H Humphrey Fellowship Programme, 609
Joint Japan/World Bank Graduate Scholarship Program (JJ/WBGSP), 355

New Zealand

Hastings Center International Visiting Scholars Program, 318
Wingate Scholarships, 704

South Africa

Hastings Center International Visiting Scholars Program, 318
Hubert H Humphrey Fellowship Programme, 609
Joint Japan/World Bank Graduate Scholarship Program (JJ/WBGSP), 355
Wingate Scholarships, 704

South America

Hastings Center International Visiting Scholars Program, 318
Hubert H Humphrey Fellowship Programme, 609
Joint Japan/World Bank Graduate Scholarship Program (JJ/WBGSP), 355

United Kingdom

AHRB Doctoral Awards Scheme, 99
ESRC 1+3 Awards & +3 Awards, 265
EUI Postgraduate Scholarships, 277
Hastings Center International Visiting Scholars Program, 318
Research Preparation Master's Scheme, 99
University of Essex Foundation Scholarships, 632
Wingate Scholarships, 704

United States of America

Atlantic Fellowships in Public Policy, 139
Fulbright Senior Specialists Program, 245
IREX John J and Nancy Lee Roberts Fellowship Program, 366
Kennan Institute Research Scholarship, 385

West European Countries

AHRB Doctoral Awards Scheme, 99
ESRC 1+3 Awards & +3 Awards, 265
EUI Postgraduate Scholarships, 277
Hastings Center International Visiting Scholars Program, 318
Research Preparation Master's Scheme, 99
Wingate Scholarships, 704

LABOUR LAW

Any Country

Center for Advanced Study in the Behavioral Sciences Postdoctoral Residential Fellowships, 223
Jean Monnet Fellowships, 278
Massey Doctoral Scholarship, 408
University of Bristol Postgraduate Scholarships, 619
University of Essex Scholarships, 632

African Nations

Hubert H Humphrey Fellowship Programme, 609
Joint Japan/World Bank Graduate Scholarship Program (JJ/WBGSP), 355

Australia

Wingate Scholarships, 704

British Commonwealth

Joint Japan/World Bank Graduate Scholarship Program (JJ/WBGSP), 355
Wingate Scholarships, 704

Canada

Viscount Bennett Fellowship, 197
Wingate Scholarships, 704

Caribbean Countries

Hubert H Humphrey Fellowship Programme, 609
Joint Japan/World Bank Graduate Scholarship Program (JJ/WBGSP), 355

East European Countries

EUI Postgraduate Scholarships, 277
Hubert H Humphrey Fellowship Programme, 609
Joint Japan/World Bank Graduate Scholarship Program (JJ/WBGSP), 355

Far East

Hubert H Humphrey Fellowship Programme, 609
Joint Japan/World Bank Graduate Scholarship Program (JJ/WBGSP), 355

Indian Sub-Continent

Hubert H Humphrey Fellowship Programme, 609
Joint Japan/World Bank Graduate Scholarship Program (JJ/WBGSP), 355
Wingate Scholarships, 704

Middle East

Hubert H Humphrey Fellowship Programme, 609
Joint Japan/World Bank Graduate Scholarship Program (JJ/WBGSP), 355

New Zealand

Wingate Scholarships, 704

South Africa

Hubert H Humphrey Fellowship Programme, 609

Joint Japan/World Bank Graduate Scholarship Program (JJ/WBGSP), 355
Wingate Scholarships, 704

South America

Hubert H Humphrey Fellowship Programme, 609
Joint Japan/World Bank Graduate Scholarship Program (JJ/WBGSP), 355

United Kingdom

EUI Postgraduate Scholarships, 277
University of Essex Foundation Scholarships, 632
Wingate Scholarships, 704

United States of America

Fulbright Senior Specialists Program, 245

West European Countries

EUI Postgraduate Scholarships, 277
Wingate Scholarships, 704

MARITIME LAW

Any Country

Center for Advanced Study in the Behavioral Sciences Postdoctoral Residential Fellowships, 223
Woods Hole Oceanographic Institution Research Fellowships in Marine Policy, 710

African Nations

Hubert H Humphrey Fellowship Programme, 609

Australia

Wingate Scholarships, 704

British Commonwealth

Wingate Scholarships, 704

Canada

Viscount Bennett Fellowship, 197
Wingate Scholarships, 704

Caribbean Countries

Hubert H Humphrey Fellowship Programme, 609

East European Countries

AHRB Doctoral Awards Scheme, 99
Hubert H Humphrey Fellowship Programme, 609
Research Preparation Master's Scheme, 99

Far East

Hubert H Humphrey Fellowship Programme, 609

Indian Sub-Continent

Hubert H Humphrey Fellowship Programme, 609
Wingate Scholarships, 704

Middle East

Hubert H Humphrey Fellowship Programme, 609

New Zealand

Wingate Scholarships, 704

South Africa

Hubert H Humphrey Fellowship Programme, 609
Wingate Scholarships, 704

South America

Hubert H Humphrey Fellowship Programme, 609

United Kingdom

AHRB Doctoral Awards Scheme, 99
Research Preparation Master's Scheme, 99
Wingate Scholarships, 704

West European Countries

AHRB Doctoral Awards Scheme, 99
Research Preparation Master's Scheme, 99
Wingate Scholarships, 704

LAW OF THE AIR

Any Country

Center for Advanced Study in the Behavioral Sciences Postdoctoral Residential Fellowships, 223

African Nations

Hubert H Humphrey Fellowship Programme, 609
IATF Aviation MBA Scholarship, 352
IATF IATA Aviation Training and Development Institute (ATDI) Scholarships, 353

Australia

Wingate Scholarships, 704

British Commonwealth

Wingate Scholarships, 704

Canada

Viscount Bennett Fellowship, 197
Wingate Scholarships, 704

Caribbean Countries

Hubert H Humphrey Fellowship Programme, 609
IATF Aviation MBA Scholarship, 352
IATF IATA Aviation Training and Development Institute (ATDI) Scholarships, 353

East European Countries

AHRB Doctoral Awards Scheme, 99
Hubert H Humphrey Fellowship Programme, 609
IATF Aviation MBA Scholarship, 352
IATF IATA Aviation Training and Development Institute (ATDI) Scholarships, 353
Research Preparation Master's Scheme, 99

Far East

Hubert H Humphrey Fellowship Programme, 609
IATF Aviation MBA Scholarship, 352
IATF IATA Aviation Training and Development Institute (ATDI) Scholarships, 353

Indian Sub-Continent

Hubert H Humphrey Fellowship Programme, 609
IATF Aviation MBA Scholarship, 352
IATF IATA Aviation Training and Development Institute (ATDI) Scholarships, 353
Wingate Scholarships, 704

Middle East

Hubert H Humphrey Fellowship Programme, 609
IATF Aviation MBA Scholarship, 352
IATF IATA Aviation Training and Development Institute (ATDI) Scholarships, 353

New Zealand

Wingate Scholarships, 704

South Africa

Hubert H Humphrey Fellowship Programme, 609
IATF Aviation MBA Scholarship, 352
IATF IATA Aviation Training and Development Institute (ATDI) Scholarships, 353
Wingate Scholarships, 704

South America

Hubert H Humphrey Fellowship Programme, 609
IATF Aviation MBA Scholarship, 352
IATF IATA Aviation Training and Development Institute (ATDI) Scholarships, 353

United Kingdom

AHRB Doctoral Awards Scheme, 99
Research Preparation Master's Scheme, 99
Wingate Scholarships, 704

West European Countries

AHRB Doctoral Awards Scheme, 99
Research Preparation Master's Scheme, 99
Wingate Scholarships, 704

NOTARY STUDIES

Any Country

Center for Advanced Study in the Behavioral Sciences Postdoctoral Residential Fellowships, 223

Canada

Viscount Bennett Fellowship, 197

CIVIL LAW

Any Country

Center for Advanced Study in the Behavioral Sciences Postdoctoral Residential Fellowships, 223
H Thomas Austern Memorial Writing Competition - Food and Drug Law, 282
University of Bristol Postgraduate Scholarships, 619
University of Essex Scholarships, 632

African Nations

International Postgraduate Research Scholarships (IPRS), 676
Joint Japan/World Bank Graduate Scholarship Program (JJ/WBGSP), 355

Australia

Wingate Scholarships, 704

British Commonwealth

International Postgraduate Research Scholarships (IPRS), 676
Joint Japan/World Bank Graduate Scholarship Program (JJ/WBGSP), 355
Wingate Scholarships, 704

Canada

International Postgraduate Research Scholarships (IPRS), 676
Viscount Bennett Fellowship, 197
Wingate Scholarships, 704

Caribbean Countries

International Postgraduate Research Scholarships (IPRS), 676

Joint Japan/World Bank Graduate Scholarship Program (JJ/WBGSP), 355

East European Countries

International Postgraduate Research Scholarships (IPRS), 676
Joint Japan/World Bank Graduate Scholarship Program (JJ/WBGSP), 355

Far East

International Postgraduate Research Scholarships (IPRS), 676
Joint Japan/World Bank Graduate Scholarship Program (JJ/WBGSP), 355

Indian Sub-Continent

International Postgraduate Research Scholarships (IPRS), 676
Joint Japan/World Bank Graduate Scholarship Program (JJ/WBGSP), 355
Wingate Scholarships, 704

Middle East

International Postgraduate Research Scholarships (IPRS), 676
Joint Japan/World Bank Graduate Scholarship Program (JJ/WBGSP), 355

New Zealand

Wingate Scholarships, 704

South Africa

International Postgraduate Research Scholarships (IPRS), 676
Joint Japan/World Bank Graduate Scholarship Program (JJ/WBGSP), 355
Wingate Scholarships, 704

South America

International Postgraduate Research Scholarships (IPRS), 676
Joint Japan/World Bank Graduate Scholarship Program (JJ/WBGSP), 355

United Kingdom

International Postgraduate Research Scholarships (IPRS), 676
University of Essex Foundation Scholarships, 632
Wingate Scholarships, 704

United States of America

Fulbright Senior Specialists Program, 245
International Postgraduate Research Scholarships (IPRS), 676

West European Countries

International Postgraduate Research Scholarships (IPRS), 676
Wingate Scholarships, 704

COMMERCIAL LAW

Any Country

Center for Advanced Study in the Behavioral Sciences Postdoctoral Residential Fellowships, 223
H Thomas Austern Memorial Writing Competition - Food and Drug Law, 282
Massey Doctoral Scholarship, 408
Queen Mary Research Studentships, 506
University Institute of European Studies Postgraduate Scholarships, 616
University of Bristol Postgraduate Scholarships, 619
University of Dundee Research Awards, 629
University of Essex Scholarships, 632
University of Stirling Research Studentships, 678

African Nations

International Postgraduate Research Scholarships (IPRS), 676

University of Sussex Overseas Development Administration Shared Scholarship Scheme, 678

British Commonwealth

International Postgraduate Research Scholarships (IPRS), 676

Canada

International Postgraduate Research Scholarships (IPRS), 676
Viscount Bennett Fellowship, 197

Caribbean Countries

International Postgraduate Research Scholarships (IPRS), 676

East European Countries

International Postgraduate Research Scholarships (IPRS), 676

Far East

International Postgraduate Research Scholarships (IPRS), 676
University of Sussex Overseas Development Administration Shared Scholarship Scheme, 678

Indian Sub-Continent

International Postgraduate Research Scholarships (IPRS), 676
University of Sussex Overseas Development Administration Shared Scholarship Scheme, 678

Middle East

International Postgraduate Research Scholarships (IPRS), 676

South Africa

International Postgraduate Research Scholarships (IPRS), 676

South America

International Postgraduate Research Scholarships (IPRS), 676

United Kingdom

International Postgraduate Research Scholarships (IPRS), 676
Polish Government Postgraduate Scholarships Scheme, 501
University of Essex Foundation Scholarships, 632
University of Wales (Aberystwyth) Postgraduate Research Studentships, 680

United States of America

International Postgraduate Research Scholarships (IPRS), 676

West European Countries

International Postgraduate Research Scholarships (IPRS), 676

PUBLIC LAW

Any Country

Center for Advanced Study in the Behavioral Sciences Postdoctoral Residential Fellowships, 223
Jack Nelson Legal Fellowship, 512
Jean Monnet Fellowships, 278
Lincoln College Supperstone Law Scholarship, 657
NHC Fellowships, 449
Reporters Committee Legal Fellowship, 513
Robert R McCormick Tribune Foundation Journalism Fellowship, 513
Robert R McCormick Tribune Foundation Legal Fellowship, 513
University of Bristol Postgraduate Scholarships, 619
University of Dundee Research Awards, 629
University of Essex Scholarships, 632

African Nations

Hubert H Humphrey Fellowship Programme, 609
International Postgraduate Research Scholarships (IPRS), 676

British Commonwealth

International Postgraduate Research Scholarships (IPRS), 676

Canada

International Postgraduate Research Scholarships (IPRS), 676
Jules and Gabrielle Léger Fellowship, 577
Viscount Bennett Fellowship, 197

Caribbean Countries

Hubert H Humphrey Fellowship Programme, 609
International Postgraduate Research Scholarships (IPRS), 676

East European Countries

EUI Postgraduate Scholarships, 277
Hubert H Humphrey Fellowship Programme, 609
International Postgraduate Research Scholarships (IPRS), 676

Far East

Hubert H Humphrey Fellowship Programme, 609
International Postgraduate Research Scholarships (IPRS), 676

Indian Sub-Continent

Hubert H Humphrey Fellowship Programme, 609
International Postgraduate Research Scholarships (IPRS), 676

Middle East

Hubert H Humphrey Fellowship Programme, 609
International Postgraduate Research Scholarships (IPRS), 676

South Africa

Hubert H Humphrey Fellowship Programme, 609
International Postgraduate Research Scholarships (IPRS), 676

South America

Hubert H Humphrey Fellowship Programme, 609
International Postgraduate Research Scholarships (IPRS), 676

United Kingdom

EUI Postgraduate Scholarships, 277
International Postgraduate Research Scholarships (IPRS), 676
University of Essex Foundation Scholarships, 632

United States of America

Fulbright Senior Specialists Program, 245
International Postgraduate Research Scholarships (IPRS), 676

West European Countries

EUI Postgraduate Scholarships, 277
International Postgraduate Research Scholarships (IPRS), 676

CONSTITUTIONAL LAW

Any Country

Center for Advanced Study in the Behavioral Sciences Postdoctoral
Residential Fellowships, 223
H Thomas Austern Memorial Writing Competition - Food and Drug
Law, 282
Jack Nelson Legal Fellowship, 512
John Philip Immroth Award for Intellectual Freedom, 55
Reporters Committee Legal Fellowship, 513
Robert R McCormick Tribune Foundation Journalism Fellowship, 513
Robert R McCormick Tribune Foundation Legal Fellowship, 513

United Kingdom

Molson Research Awards, 136

United States of America

Fulbright Senior Specialists Program, 245

ADMINISTRATIVE LAW

Any Country

Center for Advanced Study in the Behavioral Sciences Postdoctoral
Residential Fellowships, 223
H Thomas Austern Memorial Writing Competition - Food and Drug
Law, 282

FISCAL LAW

Any Country

Center for Advanced Study in the Behavioral Sciences Postdoctoral
Residential Fellowships, 223

CRIMINAL LAW

Any Country

Center for Advanced Study in the Behavioral Sciences Postdoctoral
Residential Fellowships, 223
University of Bristol Postgraduate Scholarships, 619
University of Dundee Research Awards, 629
University of Essex Scholarships, 632
University of Stirling Research Studentships, 678

African Nations

University of Sussex Overseas Development Administration Shared
Scholarship Scheme, 678

Canada

Viscount Bennett Fellowship, 197

East European Countries

Sasakawa Scholarship, 678

Far East

Sasakawa Scholarship, 678
University of Sussex Overseas Development Administration Shared
Scholarship Scheme, 678

Indian Sub-Continent

University of Sussex Overseas Development Administration Shared
Scholarship Scheme, 678

United Kingdom

Sasakawa Scholarship, 678
University of Essex Foundation Scholarships, 632

United States of America

Fulbright Senior Specialists Program, 245
US-UK Fulbright Commission Police Research Fellowship, 693

CANON LAW

Any Country

Center for Advanced Study in the Behavioral Sciences Postdoctoral
Residential Fellowships, 223

ISLAMIC LAW

Any Country

CDU Three Year Postdoctoral Fellowship, 230
Center for Advanced Study in the Behavioral Sciences Postdoctoral
Residential Fellowships, 223

United States of America

ARCE Fellowships, 69

MASS COMMUNICATION AND INFORMATION SCIENCE

GENERAL

University of Otago Masters Awards, 646
University of Otago PhD Scholarships, 646
University of Otago Prestigious PhD Scholarships, 647
Wingate Scholarships, 704

JOURNALISM

Any Country

AUC Sheikh Kamal Adham Fellowship, 85
CDI Internship, 223
CQU Postgraduate Research Award, 224
Edelstein International Fellowship, 231
Equiano Memorial Award, 596
Felix Morley Journalism Competition, 338
Glenn E and Barbara Hodsdon Ullyot Scholarship, 232
Gordon Cain Fellowship, 232
Herbert Hoover Presidential Library Association Travel Grants, 323
IHS Humane Studies Fellowships, 339
IHS Young Communicators Fellowship, 339
John Hervey, Broadcasters and Smallsreed Awards, 613
NAB Grants for Research in Broadcasting, 435
Nieman Fellowships for Journalists, 471
Paul H Nitze School of Advanced International Studies (SAIS) Financial Aid and Fellowships, 130
Reuters Foundation Environment in the News Research Study Programme, 517
Rhodes University Postdoctoral Fellowship, 519
RTNDF Fellowships, 508
Société de Chimie Industrielle (American Section) Fellowship, 232
University of Glasgow Postgraduate Research Scholarships, 634
WPI Fellowship, 712

African Nations

Hubert H Humphrey Fellowship Programme, 609
International Postgraduate Research Scholarships (IPRS), 676
Joint Japan/World Bank Graduate Scholarship Program (JJ/WBGSP), 355
Reuter Foundation Television Journalism Programme, 516
Reuters Foundation Fellowships, 517
Reuters Foundation Journalism Training, 517
Reuters Foundation Workshops for Photojournalists, 517
Thomson Foundation Scholarship, 603

Australia

University of Western Sydney Postgraduate Research Award (UW-SPRA), 689

British Commonwealth

International Postgraduate Research Scholarships (IPRS), 676
Joint Japan/World Bank Graduate Scholarship Program (JJ/WBGSP), 355

Canada

IAPA Scholarship Fund, Inc., 352
International Postgraduate Research Scholarships (IPRS), 676

Caribbean Countries

Alva Clarke Memorial Fellowship, 516
Hubert H Humphrey Fellowship Programme, 609
IAPA Scholarship Fund, Inc., 352
International Postgraduate Research Scholarships (IPRS), 676
Joint Japan/World Bank Graduate Scholarship Program (JJ/WBGSP), 355
Reuter Foundation Television Journalism Programme, 516
Reuters Foundation Fellowships, 517
Reuters Foundation Workshops for Photojournalists, 517
Thomson Foundation Scholarship, 603

East European Countries

Hubert H Humphrey Fellowship Programme, 609
International Postgraduate Research Scholarships (IPRS), 676

Joint Japan/World Bank Graduate Scholarship Program (JJ/WBGSP), 355
Professional Preparation Master's Scheme, 99
Reuter Foundation Television Journalism Programme, 516
Reuters Foundation Fellowships, 517
Reuters Foundation Journalism Training, 517
Reuters Foundation Workshops for Photojournalists, 517
Thomson Foundation Scholarship, 603

Far East

Hubert H Humphrey Fellowship Programme, 609
International Postgraduate Research Scholarships (IPRS), 676
Joint Japan/World Bank Graduate Scholarship Program (JJ/WBGSP), 355
Reuter Foundation Television Journalism Programme, 516
Reuters Foundation Fellowships, 517
Reuters Foundation Journalism Training, 517
Reuters Foundation Workshops for Photojournalists, 517
Thomson Foundation Scholarship, 603

Indian Sub-Continent

Hubert H Humphrey Fellowship Programme, 609
International Postgraduate Research Scholarships (IPRS), 676
Joint Japan/World Bank Graduate Scholarship Program (JJ/WBGSP), 355
Reuter Foundation Television Journalism Programme, 516
Reuters Foundation Fellowships, 517
Reuters Foundation Journalism Training, 517
Reuters Foundation Workshops for Photojournalists, 517
Thomson Foundation Scholarship, 603

Middle East

Hubert H Humphrey Fellowship Programme, 609
International Postgraduate Research Scholarships (IPRS), 676
Joint Japan/World Bank Graduate Scholarship Program (JJ/WBGSP), 355
Reuter Foundation Television Journalism Programme, 516
Reuters Foundation Fellowships, 517
Reuters Foundation Workshops for Photojournalists, 517
Thomson Foundation Scholarship, 603

New Zealand

University of Western Sydney Postgraduate Research Award (UW-SPRA), 689

South Africa

Hubert H Humphrey Fellowship Programme, 609
International Postgraduate Research Scholarships (IPRS), 676
Joint Japan/World Bank Graduate Scholarship Program (JJ/WBGSP), 355
Reuter Foundation Television Journalism Programme, 516
Reuters Foundation Fellowships, 517
Reuters Foundation Journalism Training, 517
Reuters Foundation Workshops for Photojournalists, 517
SACEE EX-PCE Bursary, 591
Thomson Foundation Scholarship, 603

South America

Hubert H Humphrey Fellowship Programme, 609
IAPA Scholarship Fund, Inc., 352
International Postgraduate Research Scholarships (IPRS), 676
Joint Japan/World Bank Graduate Scholarship Program (JJ/WBGSP), 355
Reuter Foundation Television Journalism Programme, 516
Reuters Foundation Fellowships, 517
Reuters Foundation Workshops for Photojournalists, 517
Thomson Foundation Scholarship, 603

United Kingdom

International Postgraduate Research Scholarships (IPRS), 676
Polish Government Postgraduate Scholarships Scheme, 501
Professional Preparation Master's Scheme, 99

United States of America

West European Countries

RADIO/TELEVISION BROADCASTING

Any Country

African Nations

British Commonwealth

Canada

Caribbean Countries

East European Countries

Far East

Indian Sub-Continent

Middle East

South Africa

South America

United Kingdom

United States of America

West European Countries

PUBLIC RELATIONS AND PUBLICITY

Any Country

African Nations

British Commonwealth

Canada

International Postgraduate Research Scholarships (IPRS), 676

Caribbean Countries

Hubert H Humphrey Fellowship Programme, 609
International Postgraduate Research Scholarships (IPRS), 676

East European Countries

Hubert H Humphrey Fellowship Programme, 609
International Postgraduate Research Scholarships (IPRS), 676

Far East

Hubert H Humphrey Fellowship Programme, 609
International Postgraduate Research Scholarships (IPRS), 676

Indian Sub-Continent

Hubert H Humphrey Fellowship Programme, 609
International Postgraduate Research Scholarships (IPRS), 676

Middle East

Hubert H Humphrey Fellowship Programme, 609
International Postgraduate Research Scholarships (IPRS), 676

South Africa

Hubert H Humphrey Fellowship Programme, 609
International Postgraduate Research Scholarships (IPRS), 676

South America

Hubert H Humphrey Fellowship Programme, 609
International Postgraduate Research Scholarships (IPRS), 676

United Kingdom

International Postgraduate Research Scholarships (IPRS), 676

United States of America

Fulbright Senior Specialists Program, 245
International Postgraduate Research Scholarships (IPRS), 676

West European Countries

International Postgraduate Research Scholarships (IPRS), 676

MASS COMMUNICATION

Any Country

CQU Postgraduate Research Award, 224
Equiano Memorial Award, 596
John Hervey, Broadcasters and Smallsreed Awards, 613
NAB Grants for Research in Broadcasting, 435
University of Stirling Research Studentships, 678

African Nations

Hubert H Humphrey Fellowship Programme, 609
International Postgraduate Research Scholarships (IPRS), 676
MCTC Assistance for Courses, 304
MCTC Tuition and Maintenance Scholarships, 304

Australia

University of Western Sydney Postgraduate Research Award (UW-SPRA), 689

British Commonwealth

International Postgraduate Research Scholarships (IPRS), 676

Canada

BBM Scholarship, 196
Canadian Window on International Development, 358
Frederick T Metcalf Award Program, 110

International Postgraduate Research Scholarships (IPRS), 676
Jim Bourque Scholarship, 92

Caribbean Countries

Hubert H Humphrey Fellowship Programme, 609
International Postgraduate Research Scholarships (IPRS), 676
MCTC Assistance for Courses, 304
MCTC Tuition and Maintenance Scholarships, 304

East European Countries

EMBO Award for Communication in the Life Sciences, 275
Hubert H Humphrey Fellowship Programme, 609
International Postgraduate Research Scholarships (IPRS), 676
MCTC Assistance for Courses, 304
MCTC Tuition and Maintenance Scholarships, 304

Far East

Hubert H Humphrey Fellowship Programme, 609
International Postgraduate Research Scholarships (IPRS), 676
MCTC Assistance for Courses, 304
MCTC Tuition and Maintenance Scholarships, 304

Indian Sub-Continent

Hubert H Humphrey Fellowship Programme, 609
International Postgraduate Research Scholarships (IPRS), 676
MCTC Assistance for Courses, 304
MCTC Tuition and Maintenance Scholarships, 304

Middle East

Hubert H Humphrey Fellowship Programme, 609
International Postgraduate Research Scholarships (IPRS), 676
MCTC Assistance for Courses, 304
MCTC Tuition and Maintenance Scholarships, 304

New Zealand

University of Western Sydney Postgraduate Research Award (UW-SPRA), 689

South Africa

Hubert H Humphrey Fellowship Programme, 600
International Postgraduate Research Scholarships (IPRS), 676
MCTC Assistance for Courses, 304
MCTC Tuition and Maintenance Scholarships, 304

South America

Hubert H Humphrey Fellowship Programme, 609
International Postgraduate Research Scholarships (IPRS), 676
MCTC Assistance for Courses, 304
MCTC Tuition and Maintenance Scholarships, 304

United Kingdom

EMBO Award for Communication in the Life Sciences, 275
Hallam Studentships, 558
International Postgraduate Research Scholarships (IPRS), 676
University of Wales (Aberystwyth) Postgraduate Research Studentships, 680

United States of America

DJ Newspaper Fund Editing Intern Program, 260
Fulbright Distinguished Chairs Program, 245
Fulbright Senior Specialists Program, 245
Ian Axford (New Zealand) Fellowships in Public Policy, 239
International Postgraduate Research Scholarships (IPRS), 676
IREX Short-Term Travel Grants, 367
Robert Bosch Foundation Fellowships, 520

West European Countries

EMBO Award for Communication in the Life Sciences, 275
Hallam Studentships, 558
International Postgraduate Research Scholarships (IPRS), 676

MEDIA STUDIES

Any Country

CQU Postgraduate Research Award, 224
Joyce Tracy Fellowship, 26
Massey Doctoral Scholarship, 408
NAB Grants for Research in Broadcasting, 435
NHC Fellowships, 449
Rhodes University Postdoctoral Fellowship, 519
Thomas Holloway Research Studentship, 536
University of Stirling Research Studentships, 678
University of Sussex Overseas Research Studentships, 678

African Nations

International Postgraduate Research Scholarships (IPRS), 676
MCTC Assistance for Courses, 304
MCTC Tuition and Maintenance Scholarships, 304

Australia

University of Western Sydney Postgraduate Research Award (UW-SPRA), 689

British Commonwealth

International Postgraduate Research Scholarships (IPRS), 676

Canada

International Postgraduate Research Scholarships (IPRS), 676

Caribbean Countries

International Postgraduate Research Scholarships (IPRS), 676
MCTC Assistance for Courses, 304
MCTC Tuition and Maintenance Scholarships, 304

East European Countries

AHRB Doctoral Awards Scheme, 99
International Postgraduate Research Scholarships (IPRS), 676
MCTC Assistance for Courses, 304
MCTC Tuition and Maintenance Scholarships, 304
Research Preparation Master's Scheme, 99

Far East

International Postgraduate Research Scholarships (IPRS), 676
MCTC Assistance for Courses, 304
MCTC Tuition and Maintenance Scholarships, 304

Indian Sub-Continent

International Postgraduate Research Scholarships (IPRS), 676
MCTC Assistance for Courses, 304
MCTC Tuition and Maintenance Scholarships, 304

Middle East

International Postgraduate Research Scholarships (IPRS), 676
MCTC Assistance for Courses, 304
MCTC Tuition and Maintenance Scholarships, 304

New Zealand

University of Western Sydney Postgraduate Research Award (UW-SPRA), 689

South Africa

International Postgraduate Research Scholarships (IPRS), 676
MCTC Assistance for Courses, 304
MCTC Tuition and Maintenance Scholarships, 304
SACEE EX-PCE Bursary, 591

South America

International Postgraduate Research Scholarships (IPRS), 676
MCTC Assistance for Courses, 304
MCTC Tuition and Maintenance Scholarships, 304

United Kingdom

AHRB Doctoral Awards Scheme, 99
ESRC 1 + 3 Awards & + 3 Awards, 265
Hallam Studentships, 558
International Postgraduate Research Scholarships (IPRS), 676
Polish Government Postgraduate Scholarships Scheme, 501
Research Preparation Master's Scheme, 99
University of Wales (Aberystwyth) Postgraduate Research Studentships, 680

United States of America

Fulbright Distinguished Chairs Program, 245
Fulbright Senior Specialists Program, 245
Ian Axford (New Zealand) Fellowships in Public Policy, 239
International Postgraduate Research Scholarships (IPRS), 676

West European Countries

AHRB Doctoral Awards Scheme, 99
ESRC 1 + 3 Awards & + 3 Awards, 265
Hallam Studentships, 558
International Postgraduate Research Scholarships (IPRS), 676
Research Preparation Master's Scheme, 99

COMMUNICATIONS SKILLS

Any Country

CESC-SSHRC Education Research Initiative, 576
CQU Postgraduate Research Award, 224
IHS Humane Studies Fellowships, 339
University of Stirling Research Studentships, 678

African Nations

International Postgraduate Research Scholarships (IPRS), 676

British Commonwealth

International Postgraduate Research Scholarships (IPRS), 676

Canada

BBM Scholarship, 196
CESC-SSHRC Education Research Initiative, 576
International Postgraduate Research Scholarships (IPRS), 676

Caribbean Countries

International Postgraduate Research Scholarships (IPRS), 676

East European Countries

International Postgraduate Research Scholarships (IPRS), 676

Far East

International Postgraduate Research Scholarships (IPRS), 676

Indian Sub-Continent

International Postgraduate Research Scholarships (IPRS), 676

Middle East

International Postgraduate Research Scholarships (IPRS), 676

South Africa

International Postgraduate Research Scholarships (IPRS), 676
SACEE EX-PCE Bursary, 591

South America

International Postgraduate Research Scholarships (IPRS), 676

United Kingdom

CBRL Research Grant, 244
ESRC 1 + 3 Awards & + 3 Awards, 265

Hallam Studentships, 558
International Postgraduate Research Scholarships (IPRS), 676

United States of America

Fulbright Senior Specialists Program, 245
International Postgraduate Research Scholarships (IPRS), 676

West European Countries

ESRC 1+3 Awards & +3 Awards, 265
Hallam Studentships, 558
International Postgraduate Research Scholarships (IPRS), 676

LIBRARY SCIENCE

Any Country

3M/NMRT Professional Development Grant, 52
AALL and West George A Strait Minority Scholarship Endowment, 32
AASL Frances Henne Award, 52
AASL Highsmith Research Grant, 52
AASL Information Technology Pathfinder Award, 52
ALA/Information Today Library of the Future Award, 53
Beta Phi Mu Award, 53
Blanche E Woolls Scholarship for School Library Media Service, 125
Bogle-Pratt International Library Travel Fund, 53
Bound to Stay Bound Book Scholarships, 53
Canadian Institute of Ukrainian Studies Research Grants, 207
Carroll Preston Baber Research Grant, 53
Christopher J Hoy/ERT Scholarship, 53
David Rozkuska Scholarship, 53
Doctoral Dissertation Fellowship, 125
EBSCO ALA Conference Sponsorship, 53
Elizabeth Futas Catalyst for Change Award, 54
Equality Award, 54
Eugene Garfield Doctoral Dissertation Fellowship, 126
Facts on File Grant, 54
Frances Henne/YALSA/VOYA Research Grant, 54
Frank B Sessa Award, 126
Frederick G Melcher Scholarships, 54
Crolior Foundation Award, 54
H W Wilson Library Staff Development Grant, 54
Harold Lancour Scholarship For International Study, 126
Howard Drake Memorial Fund, 341
IALS Visiting Fellowship in Law Librarianship, 341
J Franklin Jameson Fellowship, 49
James F. Connolly Lexisnexis Academic and Library Solutions Scholarship, 33
Jesse H Shera Award for Excellence in Doctoral Research, 55
Jesse H Shera Award for Research, 55
Joseph W Lippincott Award, 55
Ken Haycock Award for Promoting Librarianship, 55
Law Librarians in Continuing Education Courses (Type V), 33
Lester J Cappon Fellowship in Documentary Editing, 467
Lexis/Nexis/GODORT/ALA Documents to the People Award
LexisNexis/John R. Johnson Memorial Scholarship Endowment, 33
Library Degree for Law School Graduates (Type I), 33
Library Degree for Non-Law School Graduates (Type III), 33
Library Research Round Table Research Award, 55
LITA/Christian Larew Memorial Scholarship in Library & Information Technology, 397
LITA/SIRSI Scholarship in Library and Information Technology, 398
Loleta D Fyan Public Library Research Grant, 56
Marshall Cavendish Excellence in Library Programming, 56
Melvil Dewey Medal, 56
New Leaders Travel Grant, 56
Penguin Putnam Books for Young Readers Award, 56
Primark Student Travel Award, 56
Rev Andrew L Bouwhuis Memorial Scholarship, 221
Samuel Lazerow Fellowship for Research in Acquisitions or Technical Services, 57
Sarah Rebecca Reed Award, 126
Schneider Family Book Award, 57

Shirley Olofson Memorial Awards, 57
SIRSI Leader in Library Technology Grant, 57
Sullivan Award for Public Library Administrators Supporting Services to Ch, 57
W. Y. Boyd Literary Award, 57
World Book, Inc. Grant, 221
YALSA/Baker and Taylor Conference Grants, 57

African Nations

Cunningham Memorial International Fellowship, 409
Hubert H Humphrey Fellowship Programme, 609
International Postgraduate Research Scholarships (IPRS), 676
The Guust van Wesemael Literacy Prize, 359

Australia

Cunningham Memorial International Fellowship, 409

British Commonwealth

Cunningham Memorial International Fellowship, 409
International Postgraduate Research Scholarships (IPRS), 676

Canada

Canadian Window on International Development, 358
CLA Dafoe Scholarship, 209
CLA Research and Development Grants, 209
David H Clift Scholarship, 53
H W Wilson Scholarship, 209
International Postgraduate Research Scholarships (IPRS), 676
LITA/LSSI Minority Scholarship in Library and Information Technology, 397
LITA/OCLC Minority Scholarship in Library & Information Technology, 397
Mary V Gaver Scholarship, 56
Miriam L Hornback Scholarship, 56
MLA Continuing Education Grants, 409
MLA Doctoral Fellowship, 409
MLA Research, Development and Demonstration Project Award, 410
MLA Scholarship, 410
MLA Scholarship for Minority Students, 410
NMRT/EBSCO Scholarship, 56
Spectrum Initiative Scholarship Program, 57
Tom C Drewes Scholarship, 57
World Book Graduate Scholarship in Library Science, 209

Caribbean Countries

Cunningham Memorial International Fellowship, 409
Hubert H Humphrey Fellowship Programme, 609
International Postgraduate Research Scholarships (IPRS), 676
The Guust van Wesemael Literacy Prize, 359

East European Countries

AHRB Doctoral Awards Scheme, 99
Cunningham Memorial International Fellowship, 409
Hans-Peter Geh Grant for Conference Participation, 359
Hubert H Humphrey Fellowship Programme, 609
International Postgraduate Research Scholarships (IPRS), 676
Professional Preparation Master's Scheme, 99
The Guust van Wesemael Literacy Prize, 359

Far East

Cunningham Memorial International Fellowship, 409
Hubert H Humphrey Fellowship Programme, 609
International Postgraduate Research Scholarships (IPRS), 676
The Guust van Wesemael Literacy Prize, 359

Indian Sub-Continent

Cunningham Memorial International Fellowship, 409
Hubert H Humphrey Fellowship Programme, 609
International Postgraduate Research Scholarships (IPRS), 676
The Guust van Wesemael Literacy Prize, 359

MUSEUM STUDIES AND CONSERVATION

South America

Hubert H Humphrey Fellowship Programme, 609
International Postgraduate Research Scholarships (IPRS), 676

United Kingdom

AHRB Doctoral Awards Scheme, 99
CBRL Research Grant, 244
CBRL Travel Grant, 244
International Postgraduate Research Scholarships (IPRS), 676
June Baker Trust Awards, 384
Professional Preparation Master's Scheme, 99
Wingate Scholarships, 704

United States of America

Fulbright Senior Specialists Program, 245
International Postgraduate Research Scholarships (IPRS), 676

West European Countries

AHRB Doctoral Awards Scheme, 99
International Postgraduate Research Scholarships (IPRS), 676
Natural History Museum Sys-Resource, 461
Professional Preparation Master's Scheme, 99
Wingate Scholarships, 704

MUSEUM MANAGEMENT

Any Country

Advanced Fellowships, 71
ASCSA Fellowships, 71
J Franklin Jameson Fellowship, 49
Massey Doctoral Scholarship, 408
Metropolitan Museum of Art Roswell L Gilpatric Internship, 418
Metropolitan Museum of Art Six Month Internship, 418
Metropolitan Museum of Art Summer Internships for College Students, 419
Metropolitan Museum of Art Summer Internships for Graduate Students, 419

African Nations

Hubert H Humphrey Fellowship Programme, 609
International Postgraduate Research Scholarships (IPRS), 676

British Commonwealth

International Postgraduate Research Scholarships (IPRS), 676

Canada

International Postgraduate Research Scholarships (IPRS), 676

Caribbean Countries

Hubert H Humphrey Fellowship Programme, 609
International Postgraduate Research Scholarships (IPRS), 676

East European Countries

Hubert H Humphrey Fellowship Programme, 609
International Postgraduate Research Scholarships (IPRS), 676
Natural History Museum Sys-Resource, 461
Professional Preparation Master's Scheme, 99

Far East

Hong Kong Arts Development Council - FCO Chevening - Leeds University Scholarships, 639
Hubert H Humphrey Fellowship Programme, 609
International Postgraduate Research Scholarships (IPRS), 676

Indian Sub-Continent

Hubert H Humphrey Fellowship Programme, 609
International Postgraduate Research Scholarships (IPRS), 676

Middle East

Hubert H Humphrey Fellowship Programme, 609
International Postgraduate Research Scholarships (IPRS), 676

South Africa

Hubert H Humphrey Fellowship Programme, 609
International Postgraduate Research Scholarships (IPRS), 676

South America

Hubert H Humphrey Fellowship Programme, 609
International Postgraduate Research Scholarships (IPRS), 676

United Kingdom

CBRL Research Grant, 244
CBRL Travel Grant, 244
International Postgraduate Research Scholarships (IPRS), 676
Professional Preparation Master's Scheme, 99

United States of America

Fulbright Senior Specialists Program, 245
International Postgraduate Research Scholarships (IPRS), 676
NHPRC Fellowship in Archival Administration, 448

West European Countries

International Postgraduate Research Scholarships (IPRS), 676
Natural History Museum Sys-Resource, 461
Professional Preparation Master's Scheme, 99

RESTORATION OF WORKS OF ART

Any Country

Advanced Fellowships, 71
ASCSA Fellowships, 71
ASCSA Summer Sessions, 72
Henry Moore Institute Research Fellowship, 322
Jacob Hirsch Fellowship, 72
M Alison Frantz Fellowship in Post-Classical Studies at the Gennadius Library (formerly known as the Gennadeion Fellowship), 72
Metropolitan Museum of Art Roswell L Gilpatric Internship, 418
Metropolitan Museum of Art Six Month Internship, 418
Metropolitan Museum of Art Summer Internships for College Students, 419
Metropolitan Museum of Art Summer Internships for Graduate Students, 419
NEH Fellowships, 72

African Nations

International Postgraduate Research Scholarships (IPRS), 676

Australia

Wingate Scholarships, 704

British Commonwealth

International Postgraduate Research Scholarships (IPRS), 676
Wingate Scholarships, 704

Canada

International Postgraduate Research Scholarships (IPRS), 676
Wingate Scholarships, 704

Caribbean Countries

International Postgraduate Research Scholarships (IPRS), 676

East European Countries

International Postgraduate Research Scholarships (IPRS), 676
Professional Preparation Master's Scheme, 99

Far East

Hong Kong Arts Development Council - FCO Chevening - Leeds University Scholarships, 639
International Postgraduate Research Scholarships (IPRS), 676

Indian Sub-Continent

International Postgraduate Research Scholarships (IPRS), 676
Wingate Scholarships, 704

Middle East

International Postgraduate Research Scholarships (IPRS), 676

New Zealand

Wingate Scholarships, 704

South Africa

International Postgraduate Research Scholarships (IPRS), 676
Wingate Scholarships, 704

South America

International Postgraduate Research Scholarships (IPRS), 676

United Kingdom

CBRL Research Grant, 244
CBRL Travel Grant, 244
International Postgraduate Research Scholarships (IPRS), 676
June Baker Trust Awards, 384
Polish Government Postgraduate Scholarships Scheme, 501
Professional Preparation Master's Scheme, 99
Wingate Scholarships, 704

United States of America

Fulbright Senior Specialists Program, 245
International Postgraduate Research Scholarships (IPRS), 676

West European Countries

International Postgraduate Research Scholarships (IPRS), 676
Professional Preparation Master's Scheme, 99
Wingate Scholarships, 704

DOCUMENTATION TECHNIQUES AND ARCHIVING

Any Country

Advanced Fellowships, 71
Albert J Beveridge Grant, 49
ASCSA Fellowships, 71
Bernadotte E Schmitt Grants, 49
Doctoral Dissertation Fellowship, 125
Eugene Garfield Doctoral Dissertation Fellowship, 126
J Franklin Jameson Fellowship, 49
Lester J Cappon Fellowship in Documentary Editing, 467
Littleton-Griswold Research Grant, 49
Metropolitan Museum of Art Roswell L Gilpatric Internship, 418
Metropolitan Museum of Art Six Month Internship, 418
Metropolitan Museum of Art Summer Internships for College Students, 419
Metropolitan Museum of Art Summer Internships for Graduate Students, 419
NEH Fellowships, 72
Research Student Bursary, 163

African Nations

International Postgraduate Research Scholarships (IPRS), 676

Australia

Wingate Scholarships, 704

British Commonwealth

International Postgraduate Research Scholarships (IPRS), 676
Wingate Scholarships, 704

Canada

International Postgraduate Research Scholarships (IPRS), 676
Wingate Scholarships, 704

Caribbean Countries

International Postgraduate Research Scholarships (IPRS), 676

East European Countries

AHRB Doctoral Awards Scheme, 99
International Postgraduate Research Scholarships (IPRS), 676
Professional Preparation Master's Scheme, 99

Far East

International Postgraduate Research Scholarships (IPRS), 676

Indian Sub-Continent

International Postgraduate Research Scholarships (IPRS), 676
Wingate Scholarships, 704

Middle East

International Postgraduate Research Scholarships (IPRS), 676

New Zealand

Wingate Scholarships, 704

South Africa

International Postgraduate Research Scholarships (IPRS), 676
Wingate Scholarships, 704

South America

International Postgraduate Research Scholarships (IPRS), 676

United Kingdom

AHRB Doctoral Awards Scheme, 99
CBRL Research Grant, 244
CBRL Travel Grant, 244
International Postgraduate Research Scholarships (IPRS), 676
Professional Preparation Master's Scheme, 99
University of Wales (Aberystwyth) Postgraduate Research Studentships, 680
Wingate Scholarships, 704

United States of America

Fulbright Senior Specialists Program, 245
International Postgraduate Research Scholarships (IPRS), 676
NHPRC Fellowship in Archival Administration, 448
NHPRC Fellowship in Documentary Editing, 449

West European Countries

AHRB Doctoral Awards Scheme, 99
International Postgraduate Research Scholarships (IPRS), 676
Professional Preparation Master's Scheme, 99
Wingate Scholarships, 704

MATHEMATICS AND COMPUTER SCIENCE

GENERAL

Any Country

Abdus Salam ICTP Fellowships, 5
AIATSIS Research Grants, 116

Royal Society History of Science Meetings, 544
St Anne's College Una Goodwin Research Scholarship, 666
Swiss Federal Institute of Technology Scholarships, 598
University of Essex Foundation Scholarships, 632
University of Wales (Aberystwyth) Postgraduate Research Student-
ships, 680
UWB Departmental Research Studentships, 681
UWB Research Studentships, 681
Wingate Scholarships, 704
Wolfson Foundation Grants, 706

United States of America

AMS Centennial Fellowship, 58
BSUF May and Ward Scholarships (for British scholars), 158
Catching The Dream Scholarships, 221
Congress Bundestag Youth Exchange for Young Professionals, 223
Foundation for Science and Disability Student Grant Fund, 287
Friends of Peterhouse Bursary, 491
Fulbright Scholar Program for United States Citizens, 245
Fulbright Senior Specialists Program, 245
International Postgraduate Research Scholarships (IPRS), 676
JACL Scholarship and Award Program, 377
North Dakota Indian Scholarship, 472
NRC Twinning Program, 455
OAS Graduate Academic Studies, 483
PhRMAF Postdoctoral Fellowships in Informatics, 492
PhRMAF Research Starter Grants in Informatics, 495
PhRMAF Sabbatical Fellowships in Informatics, 496
Renate W Chasman Scholarship, 162
Swiss Federal Institute of Technology Scholarships, 598
Vatican Film Library Mellon Fellowship, 693
Winston Churchill Scholarship, 705

West European Countries

CERN Doctoral Student Programme, 228
CERN Fellowships, 228
CERN Technical Student Programme, 228
EPSRC Doctoral Training Grants (DTGs), 269
EPSRC Postdoctoral Fellowships in Mathematics, 269
Fulbright Postdoctoral Research and Lecturing Awards for Non-US
Citizens, 245
Hallam Studentships, 558
International Postgraduate Research Scholarships (IPRS), 676
James Ellis Research Fellowship, 543
Janson Johan Helmich Scholarships and Travel Grants, 376
Mr and Mrs David Edward Memorial Award, 681
Royal Society University Research Fellowships, 544
St Anne's College Una Goodwin Research Scholarship, 666
University of Otago Masters Awards, 646
University of Otago PhD Scholarships, 646
University of Otago Prestigious PhD Scholarships, 647
UWB Departmental Research Studentships, 681
UWB Research Studentships, 681
Wingate Scholarships, 704

STATISTICS

Any Country

Acadia Graduate Teaching Assistantships, 6
Center for Advanced Study in the Behavioral Sciences Postdoctoral
Residential Fellowships, 223
CESC-SSHRC Education Research Initiative, 576
CIIT - Centers for Health Research Postdoctoral Fellowships, 237
CIIT - Centers for Health Research Predoctoral Traineeships, 237
CQU Postgraduate Research Award, 224
Hugh Kelly Fellowship, 519
Massey Doctoral Scholarship, 408
Pierre Robillard Award, 595
Queen Mary Research Studentships, 506
Rhodes University Postdoctoral Fellowship, 519
Sir James McNeill Foundation Postgraduate Scholarship, 425

Solomon Lefschetz Instructorships, 227
Thomas Holloway Research Studentship, 536
Trinity College Junior Research Fellowship, 672
University of Bristol Postgraduate Scholarships, 619
University of Essex Scholarships, 632
University of Glasgow Postgraduate Research Scholarships, 634
University of Kent Institute of Mathematics and Statistics (IMS)
Studentships, 637
University of Manchester Research Studentships and Scholarships, 642
University of Stirling Research Studentships, 678

African Nations
International Postgraduate Research Scholarships (IPRS), 676

Australia
Wingate Scholarships, 704

British Commonwealth
International Postgraduate Research Scholarships (IPRS), 676
Wingate Scholarships, 704

Canada
CESC-SSHRC Education Research Initiative, 576
International Postgraduate Research Scholarships (IPRS), 676
Wingate Scholarships, 704

Caribbean Countries
International Postgraduate Research Scholarships (IPRS), 676

East European Countries
International Postgraduate Research Scholarships (IPRS), 676
Shell Centenary Scholarships and Shell Centenary Chevening
Scholarships, 664

Far East
International Postgraduate Research Scholarships (IPRS), 676

Indian Sub-Continent
International Postgraduate Research Scholarships (IPRS), 676
Wingate Scholarships, 704

Middle East
International Postgraduate Research Scholarships (IPRS), 676

New Zealand
Wingate Scholarships, 704

South Africa
International Postgraduate Research Scholarships (IPRS), 676
Wingate Scholarships, 704

South America
International Postgraduate Research Scholarships (IPRS), 676

United Kingdom
ESRC 1 + 3 Awards & + 3 Awards, 265
Hallam Studentships, 558
International Postgraduate Research Scholarships (IPRS), 676
Mr and Mrs David Edward Memorial Award, 681
Sheffield Hallam University Research Studentships, 558
University of Essex Foundation Scholarships, 632
UWB Departmental Research Studentships, 681
UWB Research Studentships, 681
Wingate Scholarships, 704

United States of America
ETS Postdoctoral Fellowships, 266
ETS Sylvia Taylor Johnson Minority Fellowship Educational Measure-
ment, 267

Fulbright Senior Specialists Program, 245
International Postgraduate Research Scholarships (IPRS), 676
NRC Twinning Program, 455
Winston Churchill Scholarship, 705

West European Countries

ESRC 1 + 3 Awards & + 3 Awards, 265
Hallam Studentships, 558
International Postgraduate Research Scholarships (IPRS), 676
Mr and Mrs David Edward Memorial Award, 681
Sheffield Hallam University Research Studentships, 558
UWB Departmental Research Studentships, 681
UWB Research Studentships, 681
Wingate Scholarships, 704

ACTUARIAL SCIENCE

Any Country

Center for Advanced Study in the Behavioral Sciences Postdoctoral
Residential Fellowships, 220
Sir James McNeill Foundation Postgraduate Scholarship, 425
The Actuarial Foundation Individual Grants Competition, 7

African Nations

International Postgraduate Research Scholarships (IPRS), 676

British Commonwealth

International Postgraduate Research Scholarships (IPRS), 676

Canada

International Postgraduate Research Scholarships (IPRS), 676

Caribbean Countries

International Postgraduate Research Scholarships (IPRS), 676

East European Countries

International Postgraduate Research Scholarships (IPRS), 676

Far East

International Postgraduate Research Scholarships (IPRS), 676

Indian Sub-Continent

International Postgraduate Research Scholarships (IPRS), 676

Middle East

International Postgraduate Research Scholarships (IPRS), 676

South Africa

International Postgraduate Research Scholarships (IPRS), 676

South America

International Postgraduate Research Scholarships (IPRS), 676

United Kingdom

International Postgraduate Research Scholarships (IPRS), 676
Mr and Mrs David Edward Memorial Award, 681

United States of America

ETS Postdoctoral Fellowships, 266
Fulbright Senior Specialists Program, 245
International Postgraduate Research Scholarships (IPRS), 676
Winston Churchill Scholarship, 705

West European Countries

International Postgraduate Research Scholarships (IPRS), 676
Mr and Mrs David Edward Memorial Award, 681

APPLIED MATHEMATICS

Any Country

Center for Advanced Study in the Behavioral Sciences Postdoctoral
Residential Fellowships, 223
CIIT - Centers for Health Research Postdoctoral Fellowships, 237
CIIT - Centers for Health Research Predoctoral Traineeships, 237
CQU Postgraduate Research Award, 224
Hugh Kelly Fellowship, 519
Massey Doctoral Scholarship, 408
NERC Postdoctoral Research Fellowships, 460
Queen Mary Research Studentships, 506
Rhodes University Postdoctoral Fellowship, 519
Sir James McNeill Foundation Postgraduate Scholarship, 425
SISSA Fellowships, 367
Solomon Lefschetz Instructorships, 227
Trinity College Junior Research Fellowship, 672
University of Bristol Postgraduate Scholarships, 619
University of Dundee Research Awards, 629
University of Essex Scholarships, 632
University of Glasgow Postgraduate Research Scholarships, 634
University of Kent Institute of Mathematics and Statistics (IMS)
Studentships, 637
University of Manchester Research Studentships and Scholarships, 642
University of Stirling Research Studentships, 678
University of Western Ontario Senior Visiting Fellowship, 688
Weizmann Institute of Science MSc Fellowships, 700
Weizmann Institute of Science PhD Fellowships, 700
Weizmann Institute of Science Postdoctoral Fellowships Program, 700
Woods Hole Oceanographic Institution Postdoctoral Fellowships in
Ocean Science and Engineering, 710
Woods Hole Oceanographic Institution/NOAA Co-operative Institute
for Climate and Ocean Research Postdoctoral Fellowship, 710

African Nations

International Postgraduate Research Scholarships (IPRS), 676

Australia

University of Western Sydney Postgraduate Research Award (UW-
SPRA), 689
Wingate Scholarships, 704

British Commonwealth

International Postgraduate Research Scholarships (IPRS), 676
Wingate Scholarships, 704

Canada

International Postgraduate Research Scholarships (IPRS), 676
Wingate Scholarships, 704

Caribbean Countries

International Postgraduate Research Scholarships (IPRS), 676

East European Countries

International Postgraduate Research Scholarships (IPRS), 676

Far East

International Postgraduate Research Scholarships (IPRS), 676

Indian Sub-Continent

International Postgraduate Research Scholarships (IPRS), 676
Wingate Scholarships, 704

Middle East

International Postgraduate Research Scholarships (IPRS), 676

New Zealand

University of Western Sydney Postgraduate Research Award (UW-
SPRA), 689
Wingate Scholarships, 704

South Africa

International Postgraduate Research Scholarships (IPRS), 676
Wingate Scholarships, 704

South America

International Postgraduate Research Scholarships (IPRS), 676

United Kingdom

Hallam Studentships, 558
International Postgraduate Research Scholarships (IPRS), 676
Mr and Mrs David Edward Memorial Award, 681
Polish Government Postgraduate Scholarships Scheme, 501
University of Essex Foundation Scholarships, 632
University of Wales (Aberystwyth) Postgraduate Research Studentships, 680
UWB Departmental Research Studentships, 681
UWB Research Studentships, 681
Wingate Scholarships, 704

United States of America

Army Research Laboratory Postdoctoral Fellowship Program, 75
ASNE Scholarships, 81
ETS Postdoctoral Fellowships, 266
Fannie and John Hertz Foundation Fellowships, 280
Fulbright Senior Specialists Program, 245
International Postgraduate Research Scholarships (IPRS), 676
NRC Twinning Program, 455
Winston Churchill Scholarship, 705

West European Countries

Hallam Studentships, 558
International Postgraduate Research Scholarships (IPRS), 676
Mr and Mrs David Edward Memorial Award, 681
UWB Departmental Research Studentships, 681
UWB Research Studentships, 681
Wingate Scholarships, 704

COMPUTER SCIENCE

Any Country

Acadia Graduate Teaching Assistantships, 6
AUC Graduate Merit Fellowships, 84
AUC Laboratory Instruction Graduate Fellowships in Engineering and Computer Science, 85
BP/RSE Research Fellowships, 547
Center for Advanced Study in the Behavioral Sciences Postdoctoral Residential Fellowships, 223
Computer Science Overseas Research Student (ORS) Award, 631
Computing Laboratory Bursary, 635
CQU Postgraduate Research Award, 224
DEED (Demonstration of Energy-Efficient Developments) Scholarship, 69
ESRF Postdoctoral Fellowships, 277
ETS Summer Program in Research for Graduate Students, 266
Golden Key National Honor Society Information Systems Achievement Awards, 306
Hugh Kelly Fellowship, 519
Keble College Ian Palmer Graduate Scholarship in Information Technology, 653
KSTU Rector's Grant, 385
Lydia I Pickup Memorial Scholarship, 588
Massey Doctoral Scholarship, 408
Microsoft Corporation Scholarships, 588
NCAR Postdoctoral Appointments in the Advanced Study Program, 439
NFB Computer Science Scholarship, 440
Queen Mary Research Studentships, 506
Research Student Bursary, 163
Research Studentship in Computer Science., 686
Rhodes University Postdoctoral Fellowship, 519

Sigma Xi Grants-in-Aid of Research, 563
Thomas Holloway Research Studentship, 536
TUCS Postgraduate Grant, 606
University of Bristol Postgraduate Scholarships, 619
University of Dundee Research Awards, 629
University of Essex Scholarships, 632
University of Glasgow Postgraduate Research Scholarships, 634
University of Manchester Research Studentships and Scholarships, 642
University of Stirling Research Studentships, 678
Weizmann Institute of Science MSc Fellowships, 700
Weizmann Institute of Science PhD Fellowships, 700
Weizmann Institute of Science Postdoctoral Fellowships Program, 700

African Nations

International Postgraduate Research Scholarships (IPRS), 676

Australia

University of Western Sydney Postgraduate Research Award (UW-SPRA), 689
Wingate Scholarships, 704

British Commonwealth

International Postgraduate Research Scholarships (IPRS), 676
Wingate Scholarships, 704

Canada

International Postgraduate Research Scholarships (IPRS), 676
Lydia I Pickup Memorial Scholarship, 588
Wingate Scholarships, 704

Caribbean Countries

International Postgraduate Research Scholarships (IPRS), 676

East European Countries

CERN Doctoral Student Programme, 228
CERN Fellowships, 228
CERN Technical Student Programme, 228
International Postgraduate Research Scholarships (IPRS), 676
Shell Centenary Scholarships and Shell Centenary Chevening Scholarships, 664

European Union

Computer Science EPSRC Studentships EU Postgraduates, 631

Far East

International Postgraduate Research Scholarships (IPRS), 676
University of Leeds International Fee Bursary (Vietnam), 641
University of Leeds International Fee Bursary (Vietnam), 641

Indian Sub-Continent

International Postgraduate Research Scholarships (IPRS), 676
Wingate Scholarships, 704

Middle East

International Postgraduate Research Scholarships (IPRS), 676

New Zealand

University of Western Sydney Postgraduate Research Award (UW-SPRA), 689
Wingate Scholarships, 704

South Africa

International Postgraduate Research Scholarships (IPRS), 676
Wingate Scholarships, 704

South America

International Postgraduate Research Scholarships (IPRS), 676

United Kingdom

CERN Doctoral Student Programme, 228
CERN Fellowships, 228
CERN Technical Student Programme, 228
EPSRC Quota for Computer Science, 635
Hallam Studentships, 558
International Postgraduate Research Scholarships (IPRS), 676
Sheffield Hallam University Research Studentships, 558
University of Essex Foundation Scholarships, 632
University of Wales (Aberystwyth) Postgraduate Research Studentships, 680
UWB Departmental Research Studentships, 681
Wingate Scholarships, 704

United States of America

Army Research Laboratory Postdoctoral Fellowship Program, 75
ASNE Scholarships, 81
ETS Postdoctoral Fellowships, 266
Fannie and John Hertz Foundation Fellowships, 280
Foundation for Science and Disability Student Grant Fund, 287
Fulbright Distinguished Chairs Program, 215
Fulbright Senior Specialists Program, 245
International Postgraduate Research Scholarships (IPRS), 676
NRC Twinning Program, 455
Olive Lynn Salembier Scholarship, 588
PhRMAF Postdoctoral Fellowships in Informatics, 492
PhRMAF Research Starter Grants in Informatics, 495
PhRMAF Sabbatical Fellowships in Informatics, 496
Winston Churchill Scholarship, 705

West European Countries

CERN Doctoral Student Programme, 228
CERN Fellowships, 228
CERN Technical Student Programme, 228
EPSRC Quota for Computer Science, 635
Hallam Studentships, 558
International Postgraduate Research Scholarships (IPRS), 676
Sheffield Hallam University Research Studentships, 558
UWB Departmental Research Studentships, 681
Wingate Scholarships, 704

ARTIFICIAL INTELLIGENCE

Any Country

BP/RSE Research Fellowships, 547
Center for Advanced Study in the Behavioral Sciences Postdoctoral Residential Fellowships, 223
Computer Science Overseas Research Student (ORS) Award, 631
CQU Postgraduate Research Award, 224
International School of Crystallography Grants, 367
Keble College Ian Palmer Graduate Scholarship in Information Technology, 653
Queen Mary Research Studentships, 506
Thomas Holloway Research Studentship, 536
University of Bristol Postgraduate Scholarships, 619
University of Essex Scholarships, 632
University of Manchester Research Studentships and Scholarships, 642
University of Sussex Overseas Research Studentships, 678

African Nations

International Postgraduate Research Scholarships (IPRS), 676

Australia

University of Western Sydney Postgraduate Research Award (UW-SPRA), 689
Wingate Scholarships, 704

British Commonwealth

International Postgraduate Research Scholarships (IPRS), 676
Wingate Scholarships, 704

Canada

International Postgraduate Research Scholarships (IPRS), 676
Wingate Scholarships, 704

Caribbean Countries

International Postgraduate Research Scholarships (IPRS), 676

East European Countries

CERN Fellowships, 228
International Postgraduate Research Scholarships (IPRS), 676

European Union

Computer Science EPSRC Studentships EU Postgraduates, 631

Far East

International Postgraduate Research Scholarships (IPRS), 676

Indian Sub-Continent

International Postgraduate Research Scholarships (IPRS), 676
Wingate Scholarships, 704

Middle East

International Postgraduate Research Scholarships (IPRS), 676

New Zealand

University of Western Sydney Postgraduate Research Award (UW-SPRA), 689
Wingate Scholarships, 704

South Africa

International Postgraduate Research Scholarships (IPRS), 676
Wingate Scholarships, 704

South America

International Postgraduate Research Scholarships (IPRS), 676

United Kingdom

CERN Fellowships, 228
Hallam Studentships, 558
International Postgraduate Research Scholarships (IPRS), 676
Sheffield Hallam University Research Studentships, 558
University of Essex Foundation Scholarships, 632
University of Wales (Aberystwyth) Postgraduate Research Studentships, 680
Wingate Scholarships, 704

United States of America

Army Research Laboratory Postdoctoral Fellowship Program, 75
ASNE Scholarships, 81
International Postgraduate Research Scholarships (IPRS), 676
NRC Twinning Program, 455
Winston Churchill Scholarship, 705

West European Countries

CERN Fellowships, 228
Hallam Studentships, 558
International Postgraduate Research Scholarships (IPRS), 676
Sheffield Hallam University Research Studentships, 558
Wingate Scholarships, 704

SYSTEMS ANALYSIS

Any Country

Center for Advanced Study in the Behavioral Sciences Postdoctoral Residential Fellowships, 223
Computer Science Overseas Research Student (ORS) Award, 631
CQU Postgraduate Research Award, 224

MEDICAL SCIENCES

GENERAL

African Nations

Australia

British Commonwealth

Canada

Caribbean Countries

East European Countries

RCOG USA/British Isles Visiting Fellowship, 531
Regent's Park College (Permanent Private Hall) J W Lord Scholarship, 663
Royal College of Surgeons, New York Travelling Fellowships, 533
Royal Society History of Science Meetings, 544
Silsoe Awards, 249
Sir Charles Hastings and Charles Oliver Hawthorne Grants, 153
Smith and Nephew Foundation Postdoctoral Nursing Research Fellowship, 567
Wolfson Foundation Grants, 706

United States of America

AACR - Thomas J. Bardoo Science Education Awards for Undergraduate Students, 28
AACR Minority Serving Institutions Faculty Award in Cancer Research, 28
AHA National Established Investigator Award, 48
AHA National Scientist Development Grant, 48
Alcohol Beverage Medical Research Foundation Research Project Grant, 14
American Otological Society Research Grants, 64
American Otological Society Research Training Fellowships, 64
BSUF May and Ward Scholarships (for British scholars), 158
Catching The Dream Scholarships, 221
CFF Research Programmes in Cystic Fibrosis, 252
CFF Training Programmes in Cystic Fibrosis, 252
Colin L Powell Minority Postdoctoral Fellowship in Tropical Disease Research, 442
Diversity Program in Neuroscience, 68
Diversity Program in Neuroscience Postdoctoral Fellowship, 68
Fellowship for American College Students, 513
Foundation for Science and Disability Student Grant Fund, 287
Fulbright Scholar Program for United States Citizens, 245
Fulbright Senior Specialists Program, 245
Ian Axford (New Zealand) Fellowships in Public Policy, 239
International Postgraduate Research Scholarships (IPRS), 390
International Postgraduate Research Scholarships (IPRS), 676
ISN Visiting Scholars Program, 368
JACL Scholarship and Award Program, 377
John E Fogarty International Research Scientist Development Award, 382
John P Utz Postdoctoral Fellowship in Medical Mycology, 442
Joseph Collins Foundation Grants, 384
National Headache Foundation Research Grant, 443
New Investigator Fellowships Training Initiative (NIFTI), 286
NFID New Investigator Matching Grants, 442
NFID Postdoctoral Fellowship in Nosocomial Infection Research and Training, 442
NOF Scholar's, Foundation and Mazess Research Grants, 454
North Dakota Indian Scholarship, 472
Open Gate Research Grant, 478
Parker B Francis Fellowship Program, 486
PhRMAF Medical Student Fellowships, 492
PhRMAF Postdoctoral Fellowships in Health Outcomes Research, 492
PhRMAF Predoctoral Fellowships in Health Outcomes Research, 494
PhRMAF Research Starter Grants in Health Outcomes Research, 495
PhRMAF Sabbatical Fellowships in Health Outcomes Research, 496
Postdoctoral Training Programme in Addiction and Mental Health, 225
Promotion of Doctoral Studies (PODS), 286
RCOG USA/British Isles Visiting Fellowship, 531
Research Grants, 272
RSNA Research Fellow Program, 509
RSNA Scholars Program, 510
Scholarships for Émigrés in the Health Professions, 379
The Robert Wood Johnson Health & Society Scholars Program., 521
Vatican Film Library Mellon Fellowship, 693

West European Countries

BHF Research Awards, 147
DEL Postgraduate Studentships and Bursaries for Study in Northern Ireland, 255
Eugen and Ilse Seibold Award, 257

Fulbright Postdoctoral Research and Lecturing Awards for Non-US Citizens, 245
Hastings Center International Visiting Scholars Program, 318
Health Services Research Fellowships, 320
Henry Dryerre Scholarship, 548
International Postgraduate Research Scholarships (IPRS), 390
International Postgraduate Research Scholarships (IPRS), 676
ISN Visiting Scholars Program, 368
John Fyffe Memorial Fellowship, 148
MRC Collaborative/Industrial Collaborative Studentships, 411
MRC Masters Studentships, 411
MRC Research Studentships, 412
Queen's College Florey EPA Scholarship, 662
Rink Research Fellowship Scheme, 543
Royal Society University Research Fellowships, 544
Silsoe Awards, 249
University of Otago Masters Awards, 646
University of Otago PhD Scholarships, 646
University of Otago Prestigious PhD Scholarships, 647

PUBLIC HEALTH AND HYGIENE

Any Country

AACR Scholar-in-Training Awards, 29
AFSP Distinguished Investigation Awards, 45
AFSP Pilot Grants, 46
AFSP Postdoctoral Research Fellowships, 46
AFSP Standard Research Grants, 46
AFSP Young Investigator Award, 46
AMFAR Basic Research Grant, 88
AMFAR Clinical Research Fellowship, 88
Barbers Company Clinical Nursing Scholarship, 527
BNF/Nestlé Bursary Scheme, 153
CBS Transfusion Medicine Fellowship Awards, 198
Center for Advanced Study in the Behavioral Sciences Postdoctoral Residential Fellowships, 223
CIHR Fellowships Program, 208
Colt Foundation PhD Fellowship, 238
Denis Burkitt Study Awards, 154
Health Services Research Fellowships, 320
HRB Project Grants-General, 320
IARC Postdoctoral Fellowships for Training in Cancer Research, 352
Meningitis Research Foundation Project Grant, 416
Meningitis Research Foundation Small Project Grant, 416
Meningitis Trust Research Award, 417
Population Council Fellowships in Population and Social Sciences, 502
Postgraduate Research Bursaries, 272
Research Student Bursary, 163
Roche Research Foundation, 521
Sigma Xi Grants-in-Aid of Research, 563
Sir Allan Sewell Visiting Fellowship, 310
Special Travel Allowances, 201
Susan G Komen Breast Cancer Foundation Dissertation Research Award, 597
Susan G Komen Breast Cancer Foundation Postdoctoral Fellowship in Breast Cancer Research, Public Health or Epidemiology, 597
The Commonwealth Fund / Harvard University Fellowship in Minority Health Policy, 239
The Pedro Zamora Public Policy Fellowship, 12
University of Bristol Postgraduate Scholarships, 619
University of Glasgow Postgraduate Research Scholarships, 634
University of Manchester Research Studentships and Scholarships, 642
Visiting Scientist Awards, 201
WCRF International Research Grants, 711

African Nations

ABCCF Student Grant, 91
Ecosystem Approaches to Human Health Awards, 358
Hubert H Humphrey Fellowship Programme, 609
International Postgraduate Research Scholarships (IPRS), 676
Joint Japan/World Bank Graduate Scholarship Program (JJ/WBGSP), 355

Australia

Asthma Foundation of New South Wales Medical Research Project Grant, 111
Biomedical (Dora Lush) and Public Health Postgraduate Scholarships, 443
Biomedical and Medical Postgraduate Research Scholarships, 111
Career Development Awards, 444
Howard Florey Centenary Fellowship, 444
New South Wales Cancer Council Research Programme Grant, 464
New South Wales Cancer Council Research Project Grants, 464
NHMRC Medical and Dental and Public Health Postgraduate Research Scholarships, 445
Public Health Fellowship, 445
Sidney Sax Fellowship (Overseas Public Health), 445
Training Scholarship for Indigenous Health Research., 445

British Commonwealth

International Postgraduate Research Scholarships (IPRS), 676
Joint Japan/World Bank Graduate Scholarship Program (JJ/WBGSP), 355

Canada

Alcohol Beverage Medical Research Foundation Research Project Grant, 14
Canadian Window on International Development, 358
CBS Postdoctoral Fellowship (PDF), 197
CBS Research and Development Program Individual Grants, 197
CBS Research and Development Program Major Equipment Grants, 198
CNRS Fellowships, 210
Dr Sydney Segal Research Grants, 205
Ecosystem Approaches to Human Health Awards, 358
Frank Knox Memorial Fellowships at Harvard University, 109
Idea Grants, 214
International Postgraduate Research Scholarships (IPRS), 676
PAHO Grants, 485
Research Planning Grants, 214
Researcher Travel Grant, 214

Caribbean Countries

Ecosystem Approaches to Human Health Awards, 358
Hubert H Humphrey Fellowship Programme, 609
International Postgraduate Research Scholarships (IPRS), 676
Joint Japan/World Bank Graduate Scholarship Program (JJ/WBGSP), 355
PAHO Grants, 485

East European Countries

Hubert H Humphrey Fellowship Programme, 609
International Postgraduate Research Scholarships (IPRS), 676
Joint Japan/World Bank Graduate Scholarship Program (JJ/WBGSP), 355

Far East

Ecosystem Approaches to Human Health Awards, 358
Hubert H Humphrey Fellowship Programme, 609
International Postgraduate Research Scholarships (IPRS), 676
Joint Japan/World Bank Graduate Scholarship Program (JJ/WBGSP), 355

Indian Sub-Continent

Ecosystem Approaches to Human Health Awards, 358
Hubert H Humphrey Fellowship Programme, 609
International Postgraduate Research Scholarships (IPRS), 676
Joint Japan/World Bank Graduate Scholarship Program (JJ/WBGSP), 355

Middle East

ABCCF Student Grant, 91
Ecosystem Approaches to Human Health Awards, 358
Hubert H Humphrey Fellowship Programme, 609

International Postgraduate Research Scholarships (IPRS), 676
Joint Japan/World Bank Graduate Scholarship Program (JJ/WBGSP), 355

New Zealand

Training Scholarship for Indigenous Health Research., 445

South Africa

Ecosystem Approaches to Human Health Awards, 358
Hubert H Humphrey Fellowship Programme, 609
International Postgraduate Research Scholarships (IPRS), 676
Joint Japan/World Bank Graduate Scholarship Program (JJ/WBGSP), 355

South America

Hubert H Humphrey Fellowship Programme, 609
International Postgraduate Research Scholarships (IPRS), 676
Joint Japan/World Bank Graduate Scholarship Program (JJ/WBGSP), 355

United Kingdom

Alzheimers Society Research Grants, 22
Brackenbury Grant, 151
Hospital Savings Association (HSA) Charitable Trust Scholarships, 526
Innovation and Creative Practice Award, 506
International Postgraduate Research Scholarships (IPRS), 676

United States of America

Alcohol Beverage Medical Research Foundation Research Project Grant, 14
Australian-American Health Policy Fellowships, 239
Fulbright Senior Specialists Program, 245
Ian Axford (New Zealand) Fellowships in Public Policy, 239
International Postgraduate Research Scholarships (IPRS), 676
IREX Individual Advanced Research Opportunities, 366
IREX John J and Nancy Lee Roberts Fellowship Program, 366
National Research Service Award Mental Health and Adjustment in the Life Course, 399
NBRC/AMP Gareth B Gish, MS RRT Memorial Postgraduate Recognition Award, 29
NIH Research Grants, 450
PAHO Grants, 485
Parker B Francis Respiratory Research Grant, 30
PhRMAF Postdoctoral Fellowships in Health Outcomes Research, 492
PhRMAF Predoctoral Fellowships in Health Outcomes Research, 494
PhRMAF Research Starter Grants in Health Outcomes Research, 495
PhRMAF Sabbatical Fellowships in Health Outcomes Research, 496
William F Miller, MD Postgraduate Education Recognition Award, 30

West European Countries

Health Services Research Fellowships, 320
International Postgraduate Research Scholarships (IPRS), 676

SOCIAL/PREVENTIVE MEDICINE

Any Country

AACR Career Development Awards in Cancer Research, 28
AACR Research Fellowships, 28
AFSP Distinguished Investigation Awards, 45
AFSP Pilot Grants, 46
AFSP Postdoctoral Research Fellowships, 46
AFSP Standard Research Grants, 46
AFSP Young Investigator Award, 46
AMFAR Basic Research Grant, 88
AMFAR Clinical Research Fellowship, 88
ASBAH Research Grant, 103
BackCare Research Grants, 123
Barbers Company Clinical Nursing Scholarship, 527

African Nations

Australia

British Commonwealth

Canada

Caribbean Countries

East European Countries

Far East

Indian Sub-Continent

Middle East

New Zealand

South Africa

South America

United Kingdom

United States of America

Ian Axford (New Zealand) Fellowships in Public Policy, 239
International Postgraduate Research Scholarships (IPRS), 676
National Research Service Award Mental Health and Adjustment in the Life Course, 399
New Investigator Fellowships Training Initiative (NIFTI), 286
Promotion of Doctoral Studies (PODS), 286
Research Grants, 272

West European Countries

Hastings Center International Visiting Scholars Program, 318
International Postgraduate Research Scholarships (IPRS), 676

DIETETICS

Any Country

AICR Investigator Initiator Grants, 49
Barbers Company Clinical Nursing Scholarship, 527
Bio-Serv Award in Experimental Animal Nutrition, 79
BNF/Nestlé Bursary Scheme, 153
Cenrium Center for Nutritional Science Award, 79
Conrad A Elvehjem Award for Public Service in Nutrition, 79
Denis Burkitt Study Awards, 154
E L R Stokstad Award, 79
Mead Johnson Award, 79
Osborne and Mendel Award, 79
Queen Elizabeth the Queen Mother Fellowship Award, 514
Research into Ageing Prize Studentships, 515
Research into Ageing Programme Grants, 515
Research Student Bursary, 163
Royal Irish Academy Award in Nutritional Sciences, 540

African Nations

Joint Japan/World Bank Graduate Scholarship Program (JJ/WBGSP), 355

British Commonwealth

Joint Japan/World Bank Graduate Scholarship Program (JJ/WBGSP), 355

Caribbean Countries

Joint Japan/World Bank Graduate Scholarship Program (JJ/WBGSP), 355

East European Countries

Joint Japan/World Bank Graduate Scholarship Program (JJ/WBGSP), 355

Far East

Joint Japan/World Bank Graduate Scholarship Program (JJ/WBGSP), 355

Indian Sub-Continent

Joint Japan/World Bank Graduate Scholarship Program (JJ/WBGSP), 355

Middle East

Joint Japan/World Bank Graduate Scholarship Program (JJ/WBGSP), 355

New Zealand

National Heart Foundation of New Zealand Fellowships, 447
National Heart Foundation of New Zealand Limited Budget Grants, 447
National Heart Foundation of New Zealand Maori Cardiovascular Research Fellowship, 447
National Heart Foundation of New Zealand Project Grants, 447
National Heart Foundation of New Zealand Travel Grants

South Africa

Joint Japan/World Bank Graduate Scholarship Program (JJ/WBGSP), 355

South America

Joint Japan/World Bank Graduate Scholarship Program (JJ/WBGSP), 355

United Kingdom

NOS Project Grants, 455
PWSA (UK) Research Grants, 503

SPORTS MEDICINE

Any Country

Barbers Company Clinical Nursing Scholarship, 527
Colt Foundation PhD Fellowship, 238
NSCA Challenge Scholarship, 458
NSCA Student Research Grant, 458
OREF Career Development Award, 483
OREF Prospective Clinical Research, 483
OREF Research Grants, 484
OREF Resident Research Award, 484
Queen Elizabeth the Queen Mother Fellowship Award, 514
Research into Ageing Prize Studentships, 515
Research into Ageing Programme Grants, 515
Research Student Bursary, 163
SOM Research Grant, 588
University of Bristol Postgraduate Scholarships, 619
University of Glasgow Postgraduate Research Scholarships, 634
University of Stirling Research Studentships, 678

African Nations

International Postgraduate Research Scholarships (IPRS), 676
Joint Japan/World Bank Graduate Scholarship Program (JJ/WBGSP), 355

British Commonwealth

International Postgraduate Research Scholarships (IPRS), 676
Joint Japan/World Bank Graduate Scholarship Program (JJ/WBGSP), 355

Canada

Fellowship in Health Services Research, 483
Idea Grants, 214
International Postgraduate Research Scholarships (IPRS), 676
OREF Clinical Research Award, 483
Research Planning Grants, 214
Researcher Travel Grant, 214

Caribbean Countries

International Postgraduate Research Scholarships (IPRS), 676
Joint Japan/World Bank Graduate Scholarship Program (JJ/WBGSP), 355

East European Countries

International Postgraduate Research Scholarships (IPRS), 676
Joint Japan/World Bank Graduate Scholarship Program (JJ/WBGSP), 355

Far East

International Postgraduate Research Scholarships (IPRS), 676
Jackson Memorial Fellowship, 310
Joint Japan/World Bank Graduate Scholarship Program (JJ/WBGSP), 355

Indian Sub-Continent

International Postgraduate Research Scholarships (IPRS), 676
Joint Japan/World Bank Graduate Scholarship Program (JJ/WBGSP), 355

Middle East

International Postgraduate Research Scholarships (IPRS), 676

Joint Japan/World Bank Graduate Scholarship Program (JJ/WBGSP), 355

South Africa

International Postgraduate Research Scholarships (IPRS), 676
Joint Japan/World Bank Graduate Scholarship Program (JJ/WBGSP), 355

South America

International Postgraduate Research Scholarships (IPRS), 676
Joint Japan/World Bank Graduate Scholarship Program (JJ/WBGSP), 355

United Kingdom

Duke of Edinburgh Prize for Sports Medicine, 345
International Postgraduate Research Scholarships (IPRS), 676
Sir Robert Atkins Award, 345

United States of America

Fellowship in Health Services Research, 483
International Postgraduate Research Scholarships (IPRS), 676
New Investigator Fellowships Training Initiative (NIFTI), 286
OREF Clinical Research Award, 483
Promotion of Doctoral Studies (PODS), 286
Research Grants, 272

West European Countries

International Postgraduate Research Scholarships (IPRS), 676

HEALTH ADMINISTRATION

Any Country

AFSP Distinguished Investigation Awards, 45
AFSP Pilot Grants, 46
AFSP Postdoctoral Research Fellowships, 46
AFSP Standard Research Grants, 46
AFSP Young Investigator Award, 46
Barbers Company Clinical Nursing Scholarship, 527
Center for Advanced Study in the Behavioral Sciences Postdoctoral Residential Fellowships, 223
Health Services Research Fellowships, 320
HRB Project Grants-General, 320
La Trobe University Postgraduate Scholarship, 390
Massey Doctoral Scholarship, 408
Population Council Fellowships in Population and Social Sciences, 502
Press Ganey Best Practices Research Program, 504
Roche Research Foundation, 521
Savoy Foundation Post Doctoral and Clinical Research Fellowships, 555
Savoy Foundation Research Grants, 555
Savoy Foundation Studentships, 555
Sir Allan Sewell Visiting Fellowship, 310
Templeton College Rosemary Stewart Scholarship, 672
The Pedro Zamora Public Policy Fellowship, 12
University of Bristol Postgraduate Scholarships, 619
University of Glasgow Postgraduate Research Scholarships, 634

African Nations

ABCCF Student Grant, 91
Hastings Center International Visiting Scholars Program, 318
Hubert H Humphrey Fellowship Programme, 609
International Postgraduate Research Scholarships (IPRS), 676
Joint Japan/World Bank Graduate Scholarship Program (JJ/WBGSP), 355

Australia

Fulbright Awards, 119
Harkness Fellowships in Health Care Policy, 239
Hastings Center International Visiting Scholars Program, 318
New South Wales Cancer Council Research Project Grants, 464

British Commonwealth

Hastings Center International Visiting Scholars Program, 318
International Postgraduate Research Scholarships (IPRS), 676
Joint Japan/World Bank Graduate Scholarship Program (JJ/WBGSP), 355

Canada

Albert W. Dent Graduate Student Scholarship, 287
CNRS Fellowships, 210
Foster G. McGaw Graduate Student Scholarship, 287
Idea Grants, 214
International Postgraduate Research Scholarships (IPRS), 676
Office of Critical Infrastructure Protection and Emergency Preparedness (EPC) Research Fellowship in Honour of Stuart Nesbitt White, 110
PAHO Grants, 485
Research Planning Grants, 214
Researcher Travel Grant, 214

Caribbean Countries

Hastings Center International Visiting Scholars Program, 318
Hubert H Humphrey Fellowship Programme, 609
International Postgraduate Research Scholarships (IPRS), 676
Joint Japan/World Bank Graduate Scholarship Program (JJ/WBGSP), 355
PAHO Grants, 485

East European Countries

Hastings Center International Visiting Scholars Program, 318
Hubert H Humphrey Fellowship Programme, 609
International Postgraduate Research Scholarships (IPRS), 676
Joint Japan/World Bank Graduate Scholarship Program (JJ/WBGSP), 355

Far East

Hastings Center International Visiting Scholars Program, 318
Hubert H Humphrey Fellowship Programme, 609
International Postgraduate Research Scholarships (IPRS), 676
Joint Japan/World Bank Graduate Scholarship Program (JJ/WBGSP), 355

Indian Sub-Continent

Hastings Center International Visiting Scholars Program, 318
Hubert H Humphrey Fellowship Programme, 609
International Postgraduate Research Scholarships (IPRS), 676
Joint Japan/World Bank Graduate Scholarship Program (JJ/WBGSP), 355

Middle East

ABCCF Student Grant, 91
Hastings Center International Visiting Scholars Program, 318
Hubert H Humphrey Fellowship Programme, 609
International Postgraduate Research Scholarships (IPRS), 676
Joint Japan/World Bank Graduate Scholarship Program (JJ/WBGSP), 355

New Zealand

Harkness Fellowships in Health Care Policy, 239
Hastings Center International Visiting Scholars Program, 318

South Africa

Hastings Center International Visiting Scholars Program, 318
Hubert H Humphrey Fellowship Programme, 609
International Postgraduate Research Scholarships (IPRS), 676
Joint Japan/World Bank Graduate Scholarship Program (JJ/WBGSP), 355

South America

Hastings Center International Visiting Scholars Program, 318
Hubert H Humphrey Fellowship Programme, 609

International Postgraduate Research Scholarships (IPRS), 676
Joint Japan/World Bank Graduate Scholarship Program (JJ/WBGSP), 355

United Kingdom

Harkness Fellowships in Health Care Policy, 239
Hastings Center International Visiting Scholars Program, 318
Hospital Savings Association (HSA) Charitable Trust Scholarships, 526
International Postgraduate Research Scholarships (IPRS), 676

United States of America

Albert W. Dent Graduate Student Scholarship, 287
Congress Bundestag Youth Exchange for Young Professionals, 223
Foster G. McGaw Graduate Student Scholarship, 287
Ian Axford (New Zealand) Fellowships in Public Policy, 239
International Postgraduate Research Scholarships (IPRS), 676
PAHO Grants, 485
PhRMAF Postdoctoral Fellowships in Health Outcomes Research, 492
PhRMAF Sabbatical Fellowships in Health Outcomes Research, 496

West European Countries

Hastings Center International Visiting Scholars Program, 318
Health Services Research Fellowships, 320
International Postgraduate Research Scholarships (IPRS), 676

MEDICINE AND SURGERY

Any Country

AACR Scholar-in-Training Awards, 29
BackCare Research Grants, 123
Barbers Company Clinical Nursing Scholarship, 527
BJA/Royal College of Anaesthetists Project and Fellowship Grants, 150
BMRP for Inflammatory Bowel Disease Grants, 160
British Journal of Surgery Research Bursaries, 150
CAMS Scholarship, 235
Career development program, 395
CCFF Scholarships, 200
CCFF Visiting Scientist Awards, 201
CIHR Fellowships Program, 208
Collaborative Career Development Fellowship in Stem Cell Research, 410
Cooley's Anemia Foundation Research Fellowship Grant, 242
Daland Fellowships in Clinical Investigation, 65
Dr Hadwen Trust for Humane Research Grants, 261
Equipment Grants, 319
Ethicon Foundation Fund, 533
Fellowships in Biomedicine, 557
FRAXA Grants and Fellowships, 289
Glenn/AFAR Scholarships for Research in the Biology of Aging, 44
Humanitarian Trust Awards, 329
Hypertension Trust Studentship, 331
ICS Scholarship, 357
ISH Postdoctoral Award, 285
Islamic Organisation for Medical Sciences Prize, 389
John of Arderne Medal, 549
Linacre College EPA Cephalosporin Junior Research Fellowships, 655
Lionel College Memorial Fellowship in Otolaryngology, 533
Lister Institute Research Prizes, 400
Lord Dowding Fund for Humane Research, 401
Medical Insurance Agency Prize, 550
Meningitis Research Foundation Project Grant, 416
Meningitis Research Foundation Small Project Grant, 416
Meningitis Trust Research Award, 417
Michael Geisman Memorial Fellowship Grant, 484
National Marfan Foundation Research Grant, 452
NORD Clinical Research Grants, 454

NORD/ROSCOE BRADY Lysosomal Storage Diseases Fellowships, 454
Norman Tanner Medal and Prize (1st Prize) Glaxo Travelling Fellowship (2nd Prize), 550
Novartis Foundation Symposium Bursaries, 475
OREF Career Development Award, 483
OREF Prospective Clinical Research, 483
OREF Research Grants, 484
OREF Resident Research Award, 484
Osteogenesis Imperfecta Foundation Seed Research Grant, 484
Postgraduate Research Bursaries, 272
Queen Mary Research Studentships, 506
RESTRACOMP Research Fellowship, 327
Roche Research Foundation, 521
Savoy Foundation Post Doctoral and Clinical Research Fellowships, 555
Savoy Foundation Research Grants, 555
Savoy Foundation Studentships, 555
Sigma Theta Tau International Association of Perioperative Registered Nurses Foundation Grant, 559
Sigma Xi Grants-in-Aid of Research, 563
Sir Richard Stapley Educational Trust Grants, 661
Translational Research Program, 396
UICC International Fellowships for Beginning Investigators (ACSBI), 370
University of Bristol Postgraduate Scholarships, 619
University of Glasgow Postgraduate Research Scholarships, 634
University of Manchester Research Studentships and Scholarships, 642
WellBeing Project Grants, 700
Wellcome Trust Awards, Fellowships and Studentships, 701

Australia

Asthma Foundation of New South Wales Medical Research Project Grant, 111
Biomedical and Medical Postgraduate Research Scholarships, 111
Foundation for High Blood Pressure Research Postdoctoral Fellowship, 285
NHMRC Medical and Dental and Public Health Postgraduate Research Scholarships, 445

Canada

CCFF Research Grants, 200
CSCI/RCPSC/PAIRO Canadian Specialty Resident Research Awards, 212
CTS Fellowships, 213
Fellowship in Health Services Research, 483
Leslie Bernstein Grant, 24
Leslie Bernstein Investigator Development Grant, 24
Leslie Bernstein Resident Research Grants, 24
OREF Clinical Research Award, 483
Postdoctoral Training Programme in Addiction and Mental Health, 225
Research Planning Grants, 214

South Africa

Henderson Postgraduate Scholarships, 518

United Kingdom

Breast Cancer Research Grant, 132
British Lung Foundation Project Grants, 151
Hypertension Trust Fellowship, 331
Moynihan Travelling Fellowship/Dinwoody Trust Travelling Scholarships, 107
Polish Government Postgraduate Scholarships Scheme, 501
Royal College of Surgeons, New York Travelling Fellowships, 533
Sue McCarthy Travelling Scholarship, 321

United States of America

AFAR Research Grants, 43
AFAR/Pfizer Research Grants in Metabolic Control and Late Life Diseases, 43
AHA National Established Investigator Award, 48

Beeson Career Development Award, 43
Ellison Medical Foundation/AFAR Senior Postdoctoral Research Program, 44
Fellowship in Health Services Research, 483
Glenn/AFAR Research Grant Program for Postdoctoral Fellows, 44
Leslie Bernstein Grant, 24
Leslie Bernstein Investigator Development Grant, 24
Leslie Bernstein Resident Research Grants, 24
Merck/AFAR Junior Investigator Award in Geriatric Clinical Pharmacology, 44
OREF Clinical Research Award, 483
Postdoctoral Training Programme in Addiction and Mental Health, 225
RPS FAR Medical Student Geriatric Scholars Program, 44

ANAESTHESIOLOGY

Any Country

BackCare Research Grants, 123
Barbers Company Clinical Nursing Scholarship, 527
BJA/Royal College of Anaesthetists Project and Fellowship Grants, 150
National Heart Research Fund Medical Research Grant, 448
NORD Clinical Research Grants, 454
Queen Elizabeth the Queen Mother Fellowship Award, 514
Queen Mary Research Studentships, 506
Research into Ageing Prize Studentships, 515
Research into Ageing Programme Grants, 515
University of Bristol Postgraduate Scholarships, 619

United Kingdom

Resuscitation Council Research Fellowships, 516
Resuscitation Council Research Grants, 516

United States of America

AFAR Research Grants, 43
Beeson Career Development Award, 43
FAER Research Education Grant, 283
FAER Research Fellowship Grant, 283
FAER Research Starter Grants, 283
FAER Research Training Grant (RTG), 283

CARDIOLOGY

Any Country

AHAF National Heart Foundation, 47
Barbers Company Clinical Nursing Scholarship, 527
BHF Overseas Visiting Fellowships, 147
Cooley's Anemia Foundation Research Fellowship Grant, 242
GlaxoSmithKline Collaborative Research Projects, 304
Hypertension Trust Studentship, 331
Lister Institute Research Prizes, 400
National Heart Foundation of New Zealand Senior Fellowship, 448
National Heart Research Fund Medical Research Grant, 448
National Marfan Foundation Research Grant, 452
NHF Grant, 446
NORD Clinical Research Grants, 454
Queen Elizabeth the Queen Mother Fellowship Award, 514
Queen Mary Research Studentships, 506
Research into Ageing Prize Studentships, 515
Research into Ageing Programme Grants, 515
Research Student Bursary, 163
Services to Academia, 304
The ACCF/Pfizer Postdoctoral Fellowship Awards in Cardiovascular Medicine, 475
University of Bristol Postgraduate Scholarships, 619

Australia

National Heart Foundation of Australia Career Development Fellowship, 446

National Heart Foundation of Australia Clinical Research Fellowship, 446
National Heart Foundation of Australia Overseas Research Fellowships, 446
National Heart Foundation of Australia Postgraduate Biomedical Research Scholarship, 446
National Heart Foundation of Australia Postgraduate Clinical Research Scholarship, 447
National Heart Foundation of Australia Postgraduate Public Health Research Scholarship, 447
National Heart Foundation of Australia Research Grants-in-Aid, 447

Canada

Alcohol Beverage Medical Research Foundation Research Project Grant, 14

East European Countries

BHF Clinical Science Fellowships, 146
BHF Intermediate Research Fellowships, 146
BHF Junior Research Fellowships, 147
BHF PhD Studentships, 147
BHF Senior Research Fellowships, 147
BHF Travelling Fellowships, 147

New Zealand

National Heart Foundation of New Zealand Fellowships, 447
National Heart Foundation of New Zealand Limited Budget Grants, 447
National Heart Foundation of New Zealand Maori Cardiovascular Research Fellowship, 447
National Heart Foundation of New Zealand Project Grants, 447
National Heart Foundation of New Zealand Travel Grants

United Kingdom

BHF Clinical Science Fellowships, 146
BHF Intermediate Research Fellowships, 146
BHF Junior Research Fellowships, 147
BHF PhD Studentships, 147
BHF Senior Research Fellowships, 147
BHF Travelling Fellowships, 147
Geoffrey Holt, Ivy Powell and Edith Walsh Grants, 151
Hypertension Trust Fellowship, 331
Resuscitation Council Research Fellowships, 516
Resuscitation Council Research Grants, 516
Sue McCarthy Travelling Scholarship, 321

United States of America

AFAR Research Grants, 43
AHA National Established Investigator Award, 48
AHA National Scientist Development Grant, 48
Alcohol Beverage Medical Research Foundation Research Project Grant, 14
Beeson Career Development Award, 43
RSNA Institutional Clinical Fellowship in Cardiovascular Imaging, 509

West European Countries

BHF Clinical Science Fellowships, 146
BHF Intermediate Research Fellowships, 146
BHF Junior Research Fellowships, 147
BHF PhD Studentships, 147
BHF Senior Research Fellowships, 147
BHF Travelling Fellowships, 147

DERMATOLOGY

Any Country

Barbers Company Clinical Nursing Scholarship, 527
CERIES Research Award, 227
DEBRA UK Research Grant Scheme, 254
LEPRA Grants, 150

ENDOCRINOLOGY

Any Country

Australia

New South Wales Cancer Council Research Programme Grant, 464
New South Wales Cancer Council Research Project Grants, 464

Canada

Alcohol Beverage Medical Research Foundation Research Project Grant, 14

United Kingdom

DRWF Research Fellowship, 258
NOS Project Grants, 455
PWSA (UK) Research Grants, 503

United States of America

ADA Career Development Awards, 41
ADA Clinical Research Grants, 42

EPIDEMIOLOGY

Any Country

Research into Ageing Programme Grants, 515
Stroke Research Awards, 596
The Pfizer/AGS Foundation Junior Faculty Scholars Program, 476
University of Bristol Postgraduate Scholarships, 619
Wilson-Fulton and Robertson Awards in Ageing Research, Cecille Gould Memorial Fund Award in Cancer Research, Richard Shepherd Fellowship, 44

Canada

Alcohol Beverage Medical Research Foundation Research Project Grant, 14

South Africa

Zerilda Steyn Memorial Trust, 11

United Kingdom

Alzheimers Society Research Grants, 22
NOS Project Grants, 455
REMEDI Research Grants, 512

United States of America

AFAR Research Grants, 43
Alcohol Beverage Medical Research Foundation Research Project Grant, 14
Beeson Career Development Award, 43
Ellison Medical Foundation/AFAR Senior Postdoctoral Research Program, 44
Ian Axford (New Zealand) Fellowships in Public Policy, 239
Merck/AFAR Junior Investigator Award in Geriatric Clinical Pharmacology, 44
NIH Research Grants, 450
RPS FAR Medical Student Geriatric Scholars Program, 44

GYNAECOLOGY AND OBSTETRICS

Any Country

BackCare Research Grants, 123
Barbers Company Clinical Nursing Scholarship, 527
Fellowships in Biomedicine, 557
Lalor Foundation Postdoctoral Fellowships, 391
Lister Institute Research Prizes, 400
Meningitis Research Foundation Project Grant, 416
Meningitis Research Foundation Small Project Grant, 416
Michael Geisman Memorial Fellowship Grant, 484
MRC Royal College of Obstetricians and Gynaecologists (RCOG) Training Fellowship, 412
NORD Clinical Research Grants, 454
Osteogenesis Imperfecta Foundation Seed Research Grant, 484
Queen Mary Research Studentships, 506
RCOG Bernhard Baron Travelling Scholarships, 530
RCOG Eden Travelling Fellowship, 530
RCOG Edgar Gentilli Prize, 530
RCOG Ethicon Travel Awards, 530
RCOG Green-Armytage and Spackman Travelling Scholarship, 530
RCOG Harold Malkin Prize, 530
RCOG Overseas Fund, 531
UICC International Cancer Research Technology Transfer Fellowships (ICRETT), 369
University of Bristol Postgraduate Scholarships, 619
University of Dundee Research Awards, 629
University of Manchester Research Studentships and Scholarships, 642
WellBeing Project Grants, 700

Australia

New South Wales Cancer Council Research Programme Grant, 464
New South Wales Cancer Council Research Project Grants, 464

Canada

ACOG/3M Pharmaceuticals Research Awards in Lower Genital Infections, 36

ACOG/Berlex Laboratories Research Award in PMS/PMDD, 37
ACOG/Berlex Laboratories Research Award in PMS/PMDD, 37
ACOG/Cytyc Corporation Research Award for the Prevention of Cervical Cancer, 37
ACOG/Kenneth Gottesfeld-Charles Hohler Memorial Foundation Research Award in Ultrasound, 37
ACOG/Organon, Inc. Research Award in Contraception, 38
ACOG/Ortho-McNeil Academic Training Fellowships in Obstetrics and Gynaecology, 38
ACOG/Solvay Pharmaceuticals Research Award in Menopause, 38
Warren H Pearse/Wyeth Pharmaceuticals Women's Health Policy Research Award, 38

United Kingdom

Endometriosis Millennium Fund Award, 530
Katherine Bishop Harman Grant, 152
Nichols Fellowship, 550
NOS Project Grants, 455
RCOG Research Prize, 531
RCOG USA/British Isles Visiting Fellowship, 531
RCOG William Blair-Bell Memorial Lectureships in Obstetrics and Gynaecology, 531
RCOG/Wyeth Historical Lecture, 531
REMEDI Research Grants, 512
Tim Chard Case History, 531

United States of America

ACOG/3M Pharmaceuticals Research Awards in Lower Genital Infections, 36
ACOG/Berlex Laboratories Research Award in PMS/PMDD, 37
ACOG/Berlex Laboratories Research Award in PMS/PMDD, 37
ACOG/Cytyc Corporation Research Award for the Prevention of Cervical Cancer, 37
ACOG/Kenneth Gottesfeld-Charles Hohler Memorial Foundation Research Award in Ultrasound, 37
ACOG/Organon, Inc. Research Award in Contraception, 38
ACOG/Ortho-McNeil Academic Training Fellowships in Obstetrics and Gynaecology, 38
ACOG/Solvay Pharmaceuticals Research Award in Menopause, 38
AFAR Research Grants, 43
Beeson Career Development Award, 43
RCOG USA/British Isles Visiting Fellowship, 531
Warren H Pearse/Wyeth Pharmaceuticals Women's Health Policy Research Award, 38

HAEMATOLOGY

Any Country

Barbers Company Clinical Nursing Scholarship, 527
Career development program, 395
CBS Graduate Fellowship Program, 197
CBS Transfusion Medicine Fellowship Awards, 198
Cooley's Anemia Foundation Research Fellowship Grant, 242
Friends of Jose Carreras International Leukemia Foundation Fellowship, 292
Gordon Piller Studentships, 395
ICR Research Studentships, 342
Lady Tata Memorial Trust Scholarships, 391
Leukaemia Research Fund Clinical Research Training Fellowships, 395
Leukaemia Research Fund Clinical Training Fellowship, 395
Leukaemia Research Fund Grant Programme, 395
Lister Institute Research Prizes, 400
LRFC Awards, 396
Meningitis Research Foundation Project Grant, 416
Meningitis Research Foundation Small Project Grant, 416
NORD Clinical Research Grants, 454
Queen Elizabeth the Queen Mother Fellowship Award, 514
Queen Mary Research Studentships, 506
Research into Ageing Prize Studentships, 515
Research into Ageing Programme Grants, 515

Translational Research Program, 396
UICC International Cancer Research Technology Transfer Fellowships (ICRETT), 369
University of Bristol Postgraduate Scholarships, 619
University of Dundee Research Awards, 629

Australia

New South Wales Cancer Council Research Programme Grant, 464
New South Wales Cancer Council Research Project Grants, 464

Canada

Alcohol Beverage Medical Research Foundation Research Project Grant, 14
CBS Postdoctoral Fellowship (PDF), 197
CBS Research and Development Program Individual Grants, 197
CBS Research and Development Program Major Equipment Grants, 198
CBS Research Fellowship In Hemostasis (RFH), 198
CBS Small Projects Fund, 198

United Kingdom

REMEDI Research Grants, 512

United States of America

AFAR Research Grants, 43
Alcohol Beverage Medical Research Foundation Research Project Grant, 14
Beeson Career Development Award, 43

HEPATHOLOGY

Any Country

AGA Elsevier Research Initiative Award, 283
AGA June and Donald O Castell, MD Esophageal Clinical Research Award, 284
AGA Merck Clinical Research Career Development Award, 284
AGA Miles and Shirley Fiterman Foundation Basic Research Awards, 284
AGA Miles and Shirley Fiterman Foundation Clinical Research in Gastroenterology or Hepatology/Nutrition Awards, 284
AGA R Robert and Sally D Funderburg Research Scholar Award in Gastric Biology Related to Cancer, 284
AGA Research Scholar Awards, 285
AGA Student Research Fellowship Awards, 285
Barbers Company Clinical Nursing Scholarship, 527
CLDF Research Grant, 234
Cooley's Anemia Foundation Research Fellowship Grant, 242
Lister Institute Research Prizes, 400
NORD Clinical Research Grants, 454

Canada

Alcohol Beverage Medical Research Foundation Research Project Grant, 14
Canadian Liver Foundation Graduate Studentships, 209
Canadian Liver Foundation Operating Grant, 209

United States of America

AFAR Research Grants, 43
AGA Astra Zeneca Fellowship/Faculty Transition Awards, 283
Alcohol Beverage Medical Research Foundation Research Project Grant, 14
Beeson Career Development Award, 43

NEPHROLOGY

Any Country

ASN-ASP Junior Development Grant in Geriatric Nephrology, 82
Barbers Company Clinical Nursing Scholarship, 527
Carl W Gottschalk Research Scholar Award, 82

ISN Travel Grants, 368
Lister Institute Research Prizes, 400
LSA Medical Research Grant, 402
M James Scherbenske Grant (formerly the ASN Career Enhancement Grant), 83
NORD Clinical Research Grants, 454
RFA Grants, 500

African Nations
ISN Fellowship Awards, 368

Australia
Australian Kidney Foundation Medical Research Grants & Scholarships, 116
Australian Kidney Foundation Seeding and Equipment Grants, 117
ISN Visiting Scholars Program, 368

British Commonwealth
ISN Fellowship Awards, 368

Canada
ISN Visiting Scholars Program, 368

Caribbean Countries
ISN Fellowship Awards, 368

East European Countries
ISN Fellowship Awards, 368
ISN Visiting Scholars Program, 368

Far East
ISN Fellowship Awards, 368
ISN Visiting Scholars Program, 368

Indian Sub-Continent
ISN Fellowship Awards, 368

Middle East
ISN Fellowship Awards, 368
ISN Visiting Scholars Program, 368

New Zealand
ISN Visiting Scholars Program, 368

South Africa
ISN Fellowship Awards, 368
ISN Visiting Scholars Program, 368

South America
ISN Fellowship Awards, 368

United Kingdom
ASN-ASP Junior Development Grant in Geriatric Nephrology, 82
Elizabeth Wherry and Charlotte Eyck Grants, 151
ISN Visiting Scholars Program, 368
NKRF Research Project Grants, 451
NKRF Senior Fellowships, 451
NKRF Special Project Grants, 451
NKRF Studentships, 451
NKRF Training Fellowships, 451

United States of America
AFAR Research Grants, 43
Beeson Career Development Award, 43
ISN Visiting Scholars Program, 368

West European Countries
ISN Visiting Scholars Program, 368

NEUROLOGY

Any Country

AFSP Distinguished Investigation Awards, 45
AFSP Pilot Grants, 46
AFSP Postdoctoral Research Fellowships, 46
AFSP Standard Research Grants, 46
AFSP Young Investigator Award, 46
AHAF Alzheimer's Disease Research Grant, 47
AHAF National Heart Foundation, 47
Alzheimer's Research Trust Clinical Research Training Fellowship, 21
Alzheimer's Research Trust Emergency Support Grant, 21
Alzheimer's Research Trust Network Project Co-operation Grant
Alzheimer's Research Trust PhD Studentships, 21
Alzheimer's Research Trust Pilot Project Grant, 21
Alzheimer's Research Trust Research Equipment Grant, 22
Alzheimer's Research Trust Research Fellowships, 22
Alzheimer's Research Trust Research Major Programme Project Grants, 22
ASBAH Research Grant, 103
Ataxia Research Grant, 436
Ataxia UK Research Studentships, 111
Ataxia UK Travel Award, 112
BackCare Research Grants, 123
Barbers Company Clinical Nursing Scholarship, 527
Batten Disease Support and Research Association Research Grant Awards, 124
Cerebra Research Grant, 227
Charles B Wilson Brain Tumor Research Excellence Grant, 436
CLDF Research Grant, 234
CRPF Research Grant, 236
Epilepsy Research Foundation Research Grant, 273
Fellowships in Biomedicine, 557
FRAXA Grants and Fellowships, 289
French Foundation Fellowships, 313
GlaxoSmithKline Collaborative Research Projects, 304
HDA Research Project Grants, 330
HDA Studentship, 330
Henry R Viets Medical/Graduate Student Research Fellowship, 431
Herbert H Jasper Fellowship, 224
Institute for the Study of Aging Grants Program, 340
Jackie Deakin Dystonia Prize Essay Competition, 263
Jeanne Timmins Costello Fellowships, 426
Lister Institute Research Prizes, 400
LSA Medical Research Grant, 402
MDA Grant Programs, 428
Meningitis Research Foundation Project Grant, 416
Meningitis Research Foundation Small Project Grant, 416
Meningitis Trust Research Award, 417
Migraine Trust Grants, 419
MND Research Project and Pump Pricing Grants, 426
Multiple Sclerosis Society of Great Britain and Northern Ireland Research Grants, 428
NABTC/NABTT Research Grant, 436
NARSAD Distinguished Investigator Awards, 434
NARSAD Independent Investigator Awards, 434
NARSAD Young Investigator Awards, 434
National Multiple Sclerosis Society Pilot Research Grants, 453
National Multiple Sclerosis Society Postdoctoral Fellowships, 453
National Multiple Sclerosis Society Research Grants, 453
NORD Clinical Research Grants, 454
Oligo Brain Tumor Fund, 437
Osserman/Sosin/McClare Research Fellowship, 431
Parkinson's Disease Foundation International Research Grants Program, 486
PDF Postdoctoral Fellowships, 487
PDF Summer Fellowships, 487
Postgraduate Research Bursaries, 272
Preston Robb Fellowship, 426
Project Grant, 112
PSP Research Grants, 505
Queen Elizabeth the Queen Mother Fellowship Award, 514
Queen Mary Research Studentships, 506

Research into Ageing Prize Studentships, 515
Research into Ageing Programme Grants, 515
RSM Presidents Prize, 551
Satellite Meeting at Major Symposium on Related Disorders, 112
Savoy Foundation Post Doctoral and Clinical Research Fellowships, 555
Savoy Foundation Research Grants, 555
Savoy Foundation Studentships, 555
Services to Academia, 304
Stroke Research Awards, 596
TSA Research Grants, 604
UICC International Cancer Research Technology Transfer Fellowships (ICRETT), 369
UICC International Fellowships for Beginning Investigators (ACSBI), 370
University of Bristol Postgraduate Scholarships, 619
University of Manchester Research Studentships and Scholarships, 642
Wacker Foundation Research Grant, 697
Whitehall Foundation Grants-in-Aid, 703
Whitehall Foundation Research Grants, 703
Whitehall Foundation Research Grants, 703
William P. VanWagenen Fellowship, 34

African Nations

William P. VanWagenen Fellowship, 34

Australia

William P. VanWagenen Fellowship, 34

British Commonwealth

William P. VanWagenen Fellowship, 34

Canada

Alcohol Beverage Medical Research Foundation Research Project Grant, 14
JP Cordeau Fellowship, 225
Spinal Cord Research Foundation Grants, 485
William P. VanWagenen Fellowship, 34

Caribbean Countries

William P. VanWagenen Fellowship, 34

East European Countries

Linacre College European Blaschko Visiting Research Scholarship, 655
William P. VanWagenen Fellowship, 34

Far East

William P. VanWagenen Fellowship, 34

Indian Sub-Continent

William P. VanWagenen Fellowship, 34

Middle East

William P. VanWagenen Fellowship, 34

New Zealand

William P. VanWagenen Fellowship, 34

South Africa

William P. VanWagenen Fellowship, 34

South America

William P. VanWagenen Fellowship, 34

United Kingdom

Alzheimers Society Research Grants, 22
Doris Hillier Grant, 151

Guillain-Barré Syndrome Support Group Research Fellowship, 311
Linacre College European Blaschko Visiting Research Scholarship, 655
MND PhD Studentship Award, 426
PDS Research Project Grant, 487
PDS Studentships and Junior/Senior Fellows, 487
REMEDI Research Grants, 512
Vera Down Grant, 153
William P. VanWagenen Fellowship, 34

United States of America

AFAR Research Grants, 43
Alcohol Beverage Medical Research Foundation Research Project Grant, 14
Beeson Career Development Award, 43
Diversity Program in Neuroscience, 68
Diversity Program in Neuroscience Postdoctoral Fellowship, 68
National Multiple Sclerosis Society Junior Faculty Awards, 452
NIH Research Grants, 450
NREF Research Fellowship, 34
NREF Young Clinician Investigator Award, 34
Spinal Cord Research Foundation Grants, 485

West European Countries

Linacre College European Blaschko Visiting Research Scholarship, 655

ONCOLOGY

Any Country

AACR Career Development Awards in Cancer Research, 28
AACR Gertrude B Elion Cancer Research Award, 28
AACR Research Fellowships, 28
AACR Scholar-in-Training Awards, 29
AACR Women in Cancer Research Brigid G Leventhal Scholar Awards, 29
Action Cancer Project Grant, 6
Action Cancer Research Grants, 6
Action Cancer Research Studentship, 6
AICR Investigator Initiator Grants, 49
Barbers Company Clinical Nursing Scholarship, 527
Breast Cancer Campaign Project Grants, 132
Cancer Research Clinical Research Fellowships, 216
Cancer Research Society, Inc. (Canada) Research Grants, 216
Cancer Research UK, 216
Cancer Research UK LRI Graduate Studentships, 217
Cancer Research UK LRI Research Fellowships, 217
CANSA Research Grants, 215
Career development program, 395
CBCRI Feasibility Grants, 199
CBCRI Research Grants Competition, 199
CBCRI Special Programs/Idea Grants, 199
CBCRI Special Programs/Streams of Excellence Grants, 199
Charles B Wilson Brain Tumor Research Excellence Grant, 436
ESSO Fellowships, 276
Fellowships in Biomedicine, 557
GlaxoSmithKline Collaborative Research Projects, 304
Gordon Piller Studentships, 395
IARC Postdoctoral Fellowships for Training in Cancer Research, 352
ICR Research Studentships, 342
Leukaemia Research Fund Clinical Research Training Fellowships, 395
Leukaemia Research Fund Clinical Training Fellowship, 395
Leukaemia Research Fund Grant Programme, 395
Lister Institute Research Prizes, 400
LRFC Awards, 396
Melville Trust for Care and Cure of Cancer Research Fellowships, 415
Melville Trust for Care and Cure of Cancer Research Grants, 415
NABTC/NABTT Research Grant, 436
NCIC Research Grants to Individuals, 438
NCIC Research Scientist Awards, 438

Neuroblastoma Society Research Grants, 463
NORD Clinical Research Grants, 454
OFAS Grants, 479
ONS Foundation Research Awards, 477
Prostate Research Campaign UK (Research Grants), 505
Queen Mary Research Studentships, 506
Ruth Estrin Goldberg Memorial for Cancer Research, 552
Services to Academia, 304
Susan G Komen Breast Cancer Foundation Postdoctoral Fellowship in Breast Cancer Research, Public Health or Epidemiology, 597
Sylvia Lawler Prize, 551
Translational Research Program, 396
UICC International Cancer Research Technology Transfer Fellowships (ICRETT), 369
UICC International Fellowships for Beginning Investigators (ACSBI), 370
UICC Translational Cancer Research Fellowships (TCRF), 370
UICC Yamagiwa-Yoshida Memorial International Cancer Study Grants, 371
University of Bristol Postgraduate Scholarships, 619
University of Dundee Research Awards, 629
University of Manchester Research Studentships and Scholarships, 642
WCRF International Research Grants, 711
WellBeing Project Grants, 700
Wilson-Fulton and Robertson Awards in Ageing Research, Cecille Gould Memorial Fund Award in Cancer Research, Richard Shepherd Fellowship, 44

African Nations

UICC Trish Greene International Oncology Nursing Fellowships, 370

Australia

Cancer Council South Australia Research Grants, 216
New South Wales Cancer Council Research Programme Grant, 464
New South Wales Cancer Council Research Project Grants, 464
Richard Walter Gibbon Medical Research Fellowship, 688

British Commonwealth

UICC Trish Greene International Oncology Nursing Fellowships, 370

Canada

AACR Minority Serving Institutions Faculty Award in Cancer Research, 28
Alcohol Beverage Medical Research Foundation Research Project Grant, 14
CCS Feasibility Grants, 437
CTCRI Best Knowledge Synthesis grants RFA, 214
Idea Grants, 214
NCIC Clinical Research Fellowships, 437
NCIC Equipment Grants for New Investigators, 437
NCIC Post-PhD and Post-MD Research Fellowships, 437
NCIC Research Grants for New Investigators, 438
NCIC Research Studentships, 438
NCIC Travel Awards for Senior Level PhD Students, 439
Research Planning Grants, 214
Researcher Travel Grant, 214
Student Research Grant, 214

Caribbean Countries

UICC Trish Greene International Oncology Nursing Fellowships, 370

East European Countries

Fulbright Fellowship in Cancer Research, 691
UICC Trish Greene International Oncology Nursing Fellowships, 370

Far East

UICC Asia-Pacific Cancer Society Training Grants (APCASOT), 369
UICC International Cancer Technology Transfer Fellowships (ICRETT) for Bilateral Exchanges Between Indonesia and the Netherlands, 370
UICC Trish Greene International Oncology Nursing Fellowships, 370

Indian Sub-Continent

UICC Trish Greene International Oncology Nursing Fellowships, 370

Middle East

UICC Trish Greene International Oncology Nursing Fellowships, 370

South Africa

CANSA Travel and Subsistence (Study) Grants, 215
Lady Cade Memorial Fellowship, 215
UICC Trish Greene International Oncology Nursing Fellowships, 370

South America

UICC Trish Greene International Oncology Nursing Fellowships, 370

United Kingdom

British Lung Foundation Project Grants, 151
Fulbright Fellowship in Cancer Research, 691
Helen Tomkinson and Albert McMaster Grant, 152
Paterson 4 Year Studentship, 489
PhD Studentship, 489
Prostate Research Campaign UK (Research Grants), 505
T P Gunton Grant, 153

United States of America

AACR - Minority Scholar Awards in Cancer Research, 27
AACR - Thomas J. Bardoo Science Education Awards for Undergraduate Students, 28
AACR Minority Serving Institutions Faculty Award in Cancer Research, 28
AFAR Research Grants, 43
AHNS Career Development Award, 46
AHNS Pilot Research Grant, 46
Alcohol Beverage Medical Research Foundation Research Project Grant, 14
Beeson Career Development Award, 43
BTS Research Grant, 131
Damon Runyon Cancer Research Foundation Fellowship Award, 252
Damon Runyon Scholar Award, 253
Surgeon Scientist Career Development Award, 47
The Damon Runyon-Lilly Clinical Investigator Award, 253
The Young Investigator Award, 47

West European Countries

Fulbright Fellowship in Cancer Research, 691
Paterson 4 Year Studentship, 489
PhD Studentship, 489

OPHTHALMOLOGY

Any Country

AHAF Macular Degeneration Research, 47
AHAF National Glaucoma Research, 47
Barbers Company Clinical Nursing Scholarship, 527
Lister Institute Research Prizes, 400
LSA Medical Research Grant, 402
MRC Patient Oriented Clinician Scientist Fellowship, 412
MRC Royal College of Surgeons of Edinburgh Training Fellowship, 412
National Marfan Foundation Research Grant, 452
NORD Clinical Research Grants, 454
Ophthalmology Travelling Fellowship, 550
Pilot Project Grants Program, 304
Queen Elizabeth the Queen Mother Fellowship Award, 514
Research into Ageing Prize Studentships, 515
Research into Ageing Programme Grants, 515
Royal College of Ophthalmologists Clinical Research Fellowships The Keeler Scholarship., 531
Royal College of Ophthalmologists Travel Awards Ethicon Foundation Fund., 532

Royal College of Ophthalmologists Travel Awards The Dorey Bequest., 532
Sigma Xi Grants-in-Aid of Research, 563
University of Bristol Postgraduate Scholarships, 619
University of Manchester Research Studentships and Scholarships, 642

Canada

Alcohol Beverage Medical Research Foundation Research Project Grant, 14
E A Baker Fellowship/Grant, 210

United Kingdom

Guide Dogs Ophthalmic Research Fellowship Grant, 310
Guide Dogs Ophthalmic Research Grant, 311
Iris Fund Grants for Research and Equipment (Ophthalmology), 373
John William Clark Grant, 152
Middlemore Grant, 153
Royal College of Ophthalmologists Clinical Research Fellowships The Pharmacia Ophthalmic Fellowship, 532
Royal College of Ophthalmologists Travel Awards Sir William Lister Award, 532

United States of America

AFAR Research Grants, 43
Alcohol Beverage Medical Research Foundation Research Project Grant, 14
Beeson Career Development Award, 43
Heed Fellowship Stipend, 321
Prevent Blindness America Investigator Award, 504

OTORHINOLARYNGOLOGY

Any Country

ATA Scientific Research Grants, 83
Barbers Company Clinical Nursing Scholarship, 527
Karl Storz Travelling Scholarship, 550
Lionel College Memorial Fellowship in Otolaryngology, 533
Lister Institute Research Prizes, 400
Meningitis Research Foundation Small Project Grant, 416
Michael Geisman Memorial Fellowship Grant, 484
NORD Clinical Research Grants, 454
Osteogenesis Imperfecta Foundation Seed Research Grant, 484

United Kingdom

Norman Gamble Fund and Research Prize, 550

United States of America

AFAR Research Grants, 43
Beeson Career Development Award, 43

PARASITOLOGY

Any Country

Barbers Company Clinical Nursing Scholarship, 527
Lister Institute Research Prizes, 400
NORD Clinical Research Grants, 454

African Nations

AHRI African Fellowship, 94
International Postgraduate Research Scholarships (IPRS), 676

British Commonwealth

International Postgraduate Research Scholarships (IPRS), 676

Canada

International Postgraduate Research Scholarships (IPRS), 676

Caribbean Countries

International Postgraduate Research Scholarships (IPRS), 676

East European Countries

FEMS Fellowship, 280
International Postgraduate Research Scholarships (IPRS), 676
Natural History Museum Sys-Resource, 461

Far East

International Postgraduate Research Scholarships (IPRS), 676

Indian Sub-Continent

International Postgraduate Research Scholarships (IPRS), 676

Middle East

International Postgraduate Research Scholarships (IPRS), 676

South Africa

International Postgraduate Research Scholarships (IPRS), 676

South America

International Postgraduate Research Scholarships (IPRS), 676

United Kingdom

FEMS Fellowship, 280
International Postgraduate Research Scholarships (IPRS), 676
NOS Project Grants, 455

United States of America

Beeson Career Development Award, 43
International Postgraduate Research Scholarships (IPRS), 676

West European Countries

FEMS Fellowship, 280
International Postgraduate Research Scholarships (IPRS), 676
Karl-Enigk-Stipendium, 556
Natural History Museum Sys-Resource, 461

PATHOLOGY

Any Country

AHAF National Heart Foundation, 47
Association of Clinical Pathologists Intercalated BSc Scholarship, 105
Barbers Company Clinical Nursing Scholarship, 527
BMRP for Inflammatory Bowel Disease Grants, 160
Career development program, 395
CBS Transfusion Medicine Fellowship Awards, 198
CCFF Fellowships, 200
CCFF Studentships, 201
Gillson Scholarship in Pathology, 584
Lister Institute Research Prizes, 400
Meningitis Research Foundation Project Grant, 416
Meningitis Research Foundation Small Project Grant, 416
NARSAD Distinguished Investigator Awards, 434
NARSAD Independent Investigator Awards, 434
NARSAD Young Investigator Awards, 434
NORD Clinical Research Grants, 454
Queen Elizabeth the Queen Mother Fellowship Award, 514
Queen Mary Research Studentships, 506
Research into Ageing Prize Studentships, 515
Research into Ageing Programme Grants, 515
Special Travel Allowances, 201
University of Bristol Postgraduate Scholarships, 619
University of Manchester Research Studentships and Scholarships, 642
Visiting Scientist Awards, 201

African Nations

International Postgraduate Research Scholarships (IPRS), 676

Australia

New South Wales Cancer Council Research Programme Grant, 464
New South Wales Cancer Council Research Project Grants, 464

British Commonwealth

International Postgraduate Research Scholarships (IPRS), 676

Canada

Alcohol Beverage Medical Research Foundation Research Project Grant, 14
CBS Postdoctoral Fellowship (PDF), 197
CBS Research and Development Program Individual Grants, 197
CBS Research and Development Program Major Equipment Grants, 198
CTS Fellowships, 213
International Postgraduate Research Scholarships (IPRS), 676

Caribbean Countries

International Postgraduate Research Scholarships (IPRS), 676

East European Countries

International Postgraduate Research Scholarships (IPRS), 676

Far East

International Postgraduate Research Scholarships (IPRS), 676

Indian Sub-Continent

International Postgraduate Research Scholarships (IPRS), 676

Middle East

International Postgraduate Research Scholarships (IPRS), 676

South Africa

International Postgraduate Research Scholarships (IPRS), 676

South America

International Postgraduate Research Scholarships (IPRS), 676

United Kingdom

British Lung Foundation Project Grants, 151
International Postgraduate Research Scholarships (IPRS), 676
PDS Research Project Grant, 487
PDS Studentships and Junior/Senior Fellows, 487
Resuscitation Council Research Grants, 516

United States of America

AFAR Research Grants, 43
Alcohol Beverage Medical Research Foundation Research Project Grant, 14
Beeson Career Development Award, 43
Hilgenfeld Foundation Grant, 324
International Postgraduate Research Scholarships (IPRS), 676

West European Countries

International Postgraduate Research Scholarships (IPRS), 676

PAEDIATRICS

Any Country

ASBAH Research Grant, 103
BackCare Research Grants, 123
Barbers Company Clinical Nursing Scholarship, 527
Cerebra Research Grant, 227
Charles H Hood Foundation Child Health Research Grant, 231
Food-Based Approaches to Micronutrient Malnutrition Program, 603
FRAXA Grants and Fellowships, 289
ICR Research Studentships, 342
LSA Medical Research Grant, 402

Meningitis Research Foundation Project Grant, 416
Meningitis Research Foundation Small Project Grant, 416
Meningitis Trust Research Award, 417
Michael Geisman Memorial Fellowship Grant, 484
Neuroblastoma Society Research Grants, 463
NORD Clinical Research Grants, 454
Osteogenesis Imperfecta Foundation Seed Research Grant, 484
Postgraduate Research Bursaries, 272
Queen Mary Research Studentships, 506
RESTRACOMP Research Fellowship, 327
Savoy Foundation Post Doctoral and Clinical Research Fellowships, 555
Savoy Foundation Research Grants, 555
Savoy Foundation Studentships, 555
Thrasher Research and Field Demonstration Project Grants, 603
Translational Research Program, 396
UICC International Cancer Research Technology Transfer Fellowships (ICRETT), 369
University of Bristol Postgraduate Scholarships, 619
University of Dundee Research Awards, 629
University of Manchester Research Studentships and Scholarships, 642

African Nations

Heinz Visiting and Travelling Fellowships, 533
Sally Mugabe Memorial Cambridge DFID Scholarship for Postgraduate Study, 189

Australia

Heinz Visiting and Travelling Fellowships, 533
New South Wales Cancer Council Research Programme Grant, 464
New South Wales Cancer Council Research Project Grants, 464

Canada

CNRS Fellowships, 210
CTS Fellowships, 213
Dr Sydney Segal Research Grants, 205
Duncan L Gordon Fellowships, 327
Heinz Visiting and Travelling Fellowships, 533

Indian Sub-Continent

Heinz Visiting and Travelling Fellowships, 533

New Zealand

Heinz Visiting and Travelling Fellowships, 533

South Africa

Heinz Visiting and Travelling Fellowships, 533

United Kingdom

Birth Defects Foundation Full and Small Grants, 129
British Lung Foundation Project Grants, 151
Heinz Visiting and Travelling Fellowships, 533
NOS Project Grants, 455
PWSA (UK) Research Grants, 503
REMEDI Research Grants, 512
Resuscitation Council Research Fellowships, 516
WellChild Pump-Priming Grants, 700
Wellchild Research Fellowships, 701

United States of America

Beeson Career Development Award, 43
New Investigator Fellowships Training Initiative (NIFTI), 286
Promotion of Doctoral Studies (PODS), 286
Research Grants, 272

PLASTIC SURGERY

Any Country

BAPS Student Bursaries, 138
BAPS Travelling Bursary, 138

Barbers Company Clinical Nursing Scholarship, 527
Meningitis Research Foundation Project Grant, 416
Meningitis Research Foundation Small Project Grant, 416
NORD Clinical Research Grants, 454
Paton/Maser Memorial Fund, 138
Plastic Surgery Basic Research Grant, 500
Plastic Surgery Research Fellowship Award, 500
PSEF Scientific Essay Contest, 500

African Nations

BAPS Fellowship, 138

Canada

Leslie Bernstein Grant, 24
Leslie Bernstein Investigator Development Grant, 24
Leslie Bernstein Resident Research Grants, 24

Far East

BAPS Fellowship, 138

Indian Sub-Continent

BAPS Fellowship, 138

Middle East

BAPS Fellowship, 138

United States of America

Beeson Career Development Award, 43
Leslie Bernstein Grant, 24
Leslie Bernstein Investigator Development Grant, 24
Leslie Bernstein Resident Research Grants, 24

PNEUMOLOGY

Any Country

Barbers Company Clinical Nursing Scholarship, 527
Fungal Research Trust Travel Grants, 295
NORD Clinical Research Grants, 454

Canada

Alcohol Beverage Medical Research Foundation Research Project Grant, 14
CNRS Fellowships, 210
CTS Fellowships, 213
Parker B Francis Fellowship Program, 486

United Kingdom

British Lung Foundation Project Grants, 151
H C Roscoe Grant, 152
The James Trust, 152

United States of America

Alcohol Beverage Medical Research Foundation Research Project Grant, 14
Beeson Career Development Award, 43
Parker B Francis Fellowship Program, 486

PSYCHIATRY AND MENTAL HEALTH

Any Country

AFSP Distinguished Investigation Awards, 45
AFSP Pilot Grants, 46
AFSP Postdoctoral Research Fellowships, 46
AFSP Standard Research Grants, 46
AFSP Young Investigator Award, 46
Alzheimer's Research Trust PhD Studentships, 21
BackCare Research Grants, 123
Barbers Company Clinical Nursing Scholarship, 527

Australia

CDRF Project Grants, 236
CDRF Research Fellowship, 236
Metro A Ogryzlo International Fellowship, 97

Canada

Alcohol Beverage Medical Research Foundation Research Project Grant, 14
Arthritis Society Industry Program, 97
Arthritis Society Research Fellowships, 97
Arthritis Society Research Grants, 97
Fellowship in Health Services Research, 483
Geoff Carr Lupus Fellowship, 97
OREF Clinical Research Award, 483

Caribbean Countries

Metro A Ogryzlo International Fellowship, 97

East European Countries

CDRF Project Grants, 236
CDRF Research Fellowship, 236
Metro A Ogryzlo International Fellowship, 97

Far East

Metro A Ogryzlo International Fellowship, 97

Indian Sub-Continent

Metro A Ogryzlo International Fellowship, 97

Middle East

Metro A Ogryzlo International Fellowship, 97

New Zealand

Metro A Ogryzlo International Fellowship, 97

South Africa

Metro A Ogryzlo International Fellowship, 97

South America

Metro A Ogryzlo International Fellowship, 97

United Kingdom

arc Clinical Research Fellowships, 94
'arc Clinician Scientist Fellowship, 94
arc Educational Project Grants, 95
arc Educational Research Fellowships, 95
arc Educational Travel/Training Bursaries, 95
arc Equipment Grants, 95
arc Non-clinical Career Development Fellowships, 95
arc PhD Studentships, 96
arc Postgraduate Training Bursaries, 96
arc Programme Grants, 96
arc Project Grants, 96
arc Senior Research Fellowships, 96
arc Travelling Fellowships, 96
CDRF Project Grants, 236
CDRF Research Fellowship, 236
Doris Hillier Grant, 151
NOS Project Grants, 455
REMEDI Research Grants, 512

United States of America

AFAR Research Grants, 43
Alcohol Beverage Medical Research Foundation Research Project Grant, 14
Beeson Career Development Award, 43
CDRF Project Grants, 236
CDRF Research Fellowship, 236
Fellowship in Health Services Research, 483
OREF Clinical Research Award, 483

West European Countries

CDRF Project Grants, 236
CDRF Research Fellowship, 236
Metro A Ogryzlo International Fellowship, 97

UROLOGY

Any Country

ASBAH Research Grant, 103
Barbers Company Clinical Nursing Scholarship, 527
CRPF Research Grant, 236
ICR Research Studentships, 342
Lalor Foundation Postdoctoral Fellowships, 391
Lister Institute Research Prizes, 400
NORD Clinical Research Grants, 454
Prostate Research Campaign UK (Research Grants), 505
Queen Elizabeth the Queen Mother Fellowship Award, 514
Queen Mary Research Studentships, 506
Research into Ageing Prize Studentships, 515
Research into Ageing Programme Grants, 515
Royal Society of Medicine Travelling Fellowship, 551
WellBeing Project Grants, 700

Australia

Australian Kidney Foundation Medical Research Grants & Scholarships, 116
Australian Kidney Foundation Seeding and Equipment Grants, 117

Canada

Spinal Cord Research Foundation Grants, 485

United Kingdom

Prostate Research Campaign UK (Research Grants), 505

United States of America

AFAR Research Grants, 43
Beeson Career Development Award, 43
Spinal Cord Research Foundation Grants, 485

VIROLOGY

Any Country

Barbers Company Clinical Nursing Scholarship, 527
Career development program, 395
CBS Transfusion Medicine Fellowship Awards, 198
GlaxoSmithKline Collaborative Research Projects, 304
Lister Institute Research Prizes, 400
NARSAD Distinguished Investigator Awards, 434
NARSAD Independent Investigator Awards, 434
NARSAD Young Investigator Awards, 434
NORD Clinical Research Grants, 454
Queen Mary Research Studentships, 506
Services to Academia, 304
Translational Research Program, 396
University of Dundee Research Awards, 629
Wilson-Fulton and Robertson Awards in Ageing Research, Cecille Gould Memorial Fund Award in Cancer Research, Richard Shepherd Fellowship, 44

Canada

CBS Postdoctoral Fellowship (PDF), 197
CBS Research and Development Program Individual Grants, 197
CBS Research and Development Program Major Equipment Grants, 198

East European Countries

FEMS Fellowship, 280

United Kingdom

British Lung Foundation Project Grants, 151
FEMS Fellowship, 280
H C Roscoe Grant, 152

United States of America

Beeson Career Development Award, 43

West European Countries

FEMS Fellowship, 280

TROPICAL MEDICINE

Any Country

Barbers Company Clinical Nursing Scholarship, 527
Earthwatch Field Research Grants, 264
Fungal Research Trust Travel Grants, 295
Lister Institute Research Prizes, 400
Meningitis Research Foundation Project Grant, 416
Meningitis Research Foundation Small Project Grant, 416
Meningitis Trust Research Award, 417
NORD Clinical Research Grants, 454

African Nations

AHRI African Fellowship, 94

United States of America

Beeson Career Development Award, 43
Colin L Powell Minority Postdoctoral Fellowship in Tropical Disease Research, 442

VENEREOLOGY

Any Country

Barbers Company Clinical Nursing Scholarship, 527
Lister Institute Research Prizes, 400
NORD Clinical Research Grants, 454
Queen Elizabeth the Queen Mother Fellowship Award, 514
Research into Ageing Prize Studentships, 515
Research into Ageing Programme Grants, 515

United States of America

Beeson Career Development Award, 43

REHABILITATION MEDICINE AND THERAPY

Any Country

Alberta Heritage Full-Time Studentship, 13
Ataxia UK Research Studentships, 111
Ataxia UK Travel Award, 112
BackCare Research Grants, 123
Barbers Company Clinical Nursing Scholarship, 527
CCFF Fellowships, 200
CIHR Fellowships Program, 208
CRPF Research Grant, 236
DEBRA UK Research Grant Scheme, 254
Equipment Grants, 319
HDA Research Project Grants, 330
Meningitis Research Foundation Project Grant, 416
Meningitis Research Foundation Small Project Grant, 416
Michael Geisman Memorial Fellowship Grant, 484
MND Research Project and Pump Pricing Grants, 426
National Heart Research Fund Medical Research Grant, 448
Osteogenesis Imperfecta Foundation Seed Research Grant, 484
Postgraduate Research Bursaries, 272
Project Grant, 112
Queen Elizabeth the Queen Mother Fellowship Award, 514

Research into Ageing Prize Studentships, 515
Research into Ageing Programme Grants, 515
Roche Research Foundation, 521
Satellite Meeting at Major Symposium on Related Disorders, 112
Savoy Foundation Post Doctoral and Clinical Research Fellowships, 555
Savoy Foundation Research Grants, 555
Savoy Foundation Studentships, 555
Sigma Theta Tau International/Rehabilitation Nursing Foundation Grant, 562
SOM Research Grant, 588
Special Travel Allowances, 201
Spinal Cord Injury Research Foundation Grants, 593
UICC International Fellowships for Beginning Investigators (ACSBI), 370
UICC Translational Cancer Research Fellowships (TCRF), 370
University of Manchester Research Studentships and Scholarships, 642

African Nations

International Postgraduate Research Scholarships (IPRS), 676

Australia

Sir Robert Menzies Memorial Research Scholarships in the Allied Health Sciences, 565
University of Western Sydney Postgraduate Research Award (UW-SPRA), 689

British Commonwealth

International Postgraduate Research Scholarships (IPRS), 676

Canada

Alberta Heritage Health Research Studentship, 13
CCFF Senior Scientist Research Training Award, 200
CPCRS Research Grants, 211
CTS Fellowships, 213
International Postgraduate Research Scholarships (IPRS), 676
Spinal Cord Research Foundation Grants, 485

Caribbean Countries

International Postgraduate Research Scholarships (IPRS), 676

East European Countries

International Postgraduate Research Scholarships (IPRS), 676

European Union

Clinical Research Training Fellowship in Nursing and Midwifery, 319

Far East

International Postgraduate Research Scholarships (IPRS), 676
UICC International Cancer Technology Transfer Fellowships (ICRETT) for Bilateral Exchanges Between Indonesia and the Netherlands, 370

Indian Sub-Continent

International Postgraduate Research Scholarships (IPRS), 676

Middle East

International Postgraduate Research Scholarships (IPRS), 676

New Zealand

National Heart Foundation of New Zealand Fellowships, 447
National Heart Foundation of New Zealand Limited Budget Grants, 447
National Heart Foundation of New Zealand Maori Cardiovascular Research Fellowship, 447
National Heart Foundation of New Zealand Project Grants, 447
National Heart Foundation of New Zealand Travel Grants
University of Western Sydney Postgraduate Research Award (UW-SPRA), 689

South Africa

International Postgraduate Research Scholarships (IPRS), 676

South America

International Postgraduate Research Scholarships (IPRS), 676

United Kingdom

Alzheimers Society Research Grants, 22
British Lung Foundation Project Grants, 151
Doris Hillier Grant, 151
Guillain-Barré Syndrome Support Group Research Fellowship, 311
International Postgraduate Research Scholarships (IPRS), 676
MND PhD Studentship Award, 426
Owen Shaw Award, 159
PDS Research Project Grant, 487
PDS Studentships and Junior/Senior Fellows, 487
REMEDI Research Grants, 512

United States of America

AHA National Established Investigator Award, 48
AHA National Scientist Development Grant, 48
AMBUCS Scholarship, 372
Damon Runyon Cancer Research Foundation Fellowship Award, 252
Damon Runyon Scholar Award, 253
FPT Research Grants, 286
International Postgraduate Research Scholarships (IPRS), 676
McMillan Doctoral Scholarships, 286
New Investigator Fellowships Training Initiative (NIFTI), 286
NIH Research Grants, 450
Prevent Blindness America Investigator Award, 504
Promotion of Doctoral Studies (PODS), 286
Research Grants, 272
Spinal Cord Research Foundation Grants, 485

West European Countries

International Postgraduate Research Scholarships (IPRS), 676

NURSING

Any Country

AACN - Datex Ohmeda Grant, 31
AACN Clinical Practice Grant, 32
AACN Critical Care Grant, 32
AACN Mentorship Grant, 32
AACN Sigma Theta Tau Critical Care Grant, 32
AAHN Student Research Award, 30
AFSP Distinguished Investigation Awards, 45
AFSP Pilot Grants, 46
AFSP Postdoctoral Research Fellowships, 46
AFSP Standard Research Grants, 46
AFSP Young Investigator Award, 46
Alberta Heritage Full-Time Studentship, 13
American Nurses Foundation Research Grant, 32
Barbers Company Clinical Nursing Scholarship, 527
CCFF Studentships, 201
CDU Senior Research Fellowship, 230
CDU Three Year Postdoctoral Fellowship, 230
CIHR Fellowships Program, 208
CQU Postgraduate Research Award, 224
Equipment Grants, 319
La Trobe University Postgraduate Scholarship, 390
Massey Doctoral Scholarship, 408
Meningitis Trust Research Award, 417
MND Research Project and Pump Pricing Grants, 426
Myasthenia Gravis Nursing Research Fellowship, 431
ONS Foundation Research Awards, 477
Post doctoral award to honor Cadet Nurse Corps, 30
Postgraduate Research Bursaries, 272
Queen Elizabeth the Queen Mother Fellowship Award, 514
RCN Grants, 529

RCN Scholarships Fund, 529
Research into Ageing Programme Grants, 515
Research Student Bursary, 163
Roche Research Foundation, 521
Rosemary Berkel Crisp Research Award, 559
Sigma Theta Tau International Association of Perioperative Registered Nurses Foundation Grant, 559
Sigma Theta Tau International Research Grant Opportunities, 560
Sigma Theta Tau International/American Association of Critical Care Nurses, 560
Sigma Theta Tau International/American Association of Diabetes Educators Grant, 560
Sigma Theta Tau International/American Nephrology Nurses Association Grant, 560
Sigma Theta Tau International/American Nurses Foundation Grant, 561
Sigma Theta Tau International/Emergency Nurses Association Foundation Grant, 561
Sigma Theta Tau International/Oncology Nursing Society Grant, 562
Sir Allan Sewell Visiting Fellowship, 310
Special Travel Allowances, 201
University of Dundee Research Awards, 629
University of Glasgow Postgraduate Research Scholarships, 631
University of Manchester Research Studentships and Scholarships, 642
University of Stirling Research Studentships, 678
Virginia Henderson/Sigma Theta Tau International Clinical Research Grant, 563

African Nations

ABCCF Student Grant, 91
Hastings Center International Visiting Scholars Program, 318
Hubert H Humphrey Fellowship Programme, 609
International Postgraduate Research Scholarships (IPRS), 676

Australia

Hastings Center International Visiting Scholars Program, 318
Sir Robert Menzies Memorial Research Scholarships in the Allied Health Sciences, 565
University of Western Sydney Postgraduate Research Award (UWSPRA), 689

British Commonwealth

Hastings Center International Visiting Scholars Program, 318
International Postgraduate Research Scholarships (IPRS), 676

Canada

Alberta Heritage Health Research Studentship, 13
CNF Scholarships and Fellowships, 210
CNRS Fellowships, 210
CNRS Research Grants, 210
CTS Fellowships, 213
Dr Sydney Segal Research Grants, 205
International Postgraduate Research Scholarships (IPRS), 676
Research Planning Grants, 214

Caribbean Countries

Hastings Center International Visiting Scholars Program, 318
Hubert H Humphrey Fellowship Programme, 609
International Postgraduate Research Scholarships (IPRS), 676

East European Countries

Hastings Center International Visiting Scholars Program, 318
Hubert H Humphrey Fellowship Programme, 609
International Postgraduate Research Scholarships (IPRS), 676

European Union

Clinical Research Training Fellowship in Nursing and Midwifery, 319

Far East

Hastings Center International Visiting Scholars Program, 318
Hubert H Humphrey Fellowship Programme, 609
International Postgraduate Research Scholarships (IPRS), 676

Indian Sub-Continent

Hastings Center International Visiting Scholars Program, 318
Hubert H Humphrey Fellowship Programme, 609
International Postgraduate Research Scholarships (IPRS), 676

Middle East

ABCCF Student Grant, 91
Hastings Center International Visiting Scholars Program, 318
Hubert H Humphrey Fellowship Programme, 609
International Postgraduate Research Scholarships (IPRS), 676

New Zealand

Hastings Center International Visiting Scholars Program, 318
University of Western Sydney Postgraduate Research Award (UW-SPRA), 689

South Africa

DENOSA Bursaries, Scholarships and Grants, 254
Hastings Center International Visiting Scholars Program, 318
Hubert H Humphrey Fellowship Programme, 609
International Postgraduate Research Scholarships (IPRS), 676

South America

Hastings Center International Visiting Scholars Program, 318
Hubert H Humphrey Fellowship Programme, 609
International Postgraduate Research Scholarships (IPRS), 676

United Kingdom

Alzheimers Society Research Grants, 22
British Lung Foundation Project Grants, 151
Hastings Center International Visiting Scholars Program, 318
HSA Charitable Trust Awards For Health Care Assistants
HSA Charitable Trust Scholarships for Nurses and Midwives, 528
Innovation and Creative Practice Award, 506
International Postgraduate Research Scholarships (IPRS), 676
Johnson & Johnson/Ethicon Nurses Education Trust Fund, 528
MND PhD Studentship Award, 426
Mr and Mrs David Edward Memorial Award, 681
NQS Project Grants, 455
Nuffield Trust/RCN Travelling Fellowships, 528
PDS Research Project Grant, 487
PDS Studentships and Junior/Senior Fellows, 487
RCN Educational Scholarships. Hettie C. Hopkins Care of the Elderly Nursing Scholarship, 529
RCN Educational Scholarships. The Allen Iswlyn Giles Memorial Nursing Scholarship, 529
RCN Margaret Parkinson Scholarships, 529
Resuscitation Council Research Fellowships, 516
Resuscitation Council Research Grants, 516
Smith and Nephew Foundation Nursing Research Studentship, 567
Smith and Nephew Foundation Postdoctoral Nursing Research Fellowship, 567
UWB Departmental Research Studentships, 681
UWB Research Studentships, 681

United States of America

AORN Doctoral Degree Scholarship, 90
AORN Master's Degree Scholarship, 90
Ian Axford (New Zealand) Fellowships in Public Policy, 239
International Postgraduate Research Scholarships (IPRS), 676
Nurses' Educational Funds Fellowships and Scholarships, 475
PhRMAF Postdoctoral Fellowships in Health Outcomes Research, 492
PhRMAF Predoctoral Fellowships in Health Outcomes Research, 494
PhRMAF Research Starter Grants in Health Outcomes Research, 495
PhRMAF Sabbatical Fellowships in Health Outcomes Research, 496
Scholarships for Émigrés in the Health Professions, 379
Sigma Theta Tau International Small Research Grants, 560
Sigma Theta Tau International/Association of Operating room Nurses Foundation Grant, 561

Sigma Theta Tau International/Glaxo Wellcome New Investigator Mentor Grant, 561
Sigma Theta Tau International/Glaxo Wellcome Prescriptive Practice Grant, 562
Sigma Theta Tau International/Mead Johnson Nutritionals Perinatal Grant, 562

West European Countries

Hastings Center International Visiting Scholars Program, 318
International Postgraduate Research Scholarships (IPRS), 676
Mr and Mrs David Edward Memorial Award, 681
UWB Departmental Research Studentships, 681
UWB Research Studentships, 681

MEDICAL AUXILIARIES

Any Country

Barbers Company Clinical Nursing Scholarship, 527
Equipment Grants, 319
Roche Research Foundation, 521

African Nations

International Postgraduate Research Scholarships (IPRS), 676

British Commonwealth

International Postgraduate Research Scholarships (IPRS), 676

Canada

International Postgraduate Research Scholarships (IPRS), 676

Caribbean Countries

International Postgraduate Research Scholarships (IPRS), 676

East European Countries

International Postgraduate Research Scholarships (IPRS), 676

Far East

International Postgraduate Research Scholarships (IPRS), 676

Indian Sub-Continent

International Postgraduate Research Scholarships (IPRS), 676

Middle East

International Postgraduate Research Scholarships (IPRS), 676

South Africa

International Postgraduate Research Scholarships (IPRS), 676

South America

International Postgraduate Research Scholarships (IPRS), 676

United Kingdom

International Postgraduate Research Scholarships (IPRS), 676

United States of America

International Postgraduate Research Scholarships (IPRS), 676

West European Countries

International Postgraduate Research Scholarships (IPRS), 676

MIDWIFERY

Any Country

Barbers Company Clinical Nursing Scholarship, 527
CQU Postgraduate Research Award, 224
Equipment Grants, 319

RADIOLOGY

South Africa

International Postgraduate Research Scholarships (IPRS), 676

South America

International Postgraduate Research Scholarships (IPRS), 676

United Kingdom

BIR Travel Bursary, 149
International Postgraduate Research Scholarships (IPRS), 676
Mr and Mrs David Edward Memorial Award, 681
NOS Project Grants, 455
UWB Departmental Research Studentships, 681
UWB Research Studentships, 681

United States of America

Damon Runyon Cancer Research Foundation Fellowship Award, 252
International Postgraduate Research Scholarships (IPRS), 676
Prevent Blindness America Investigator Award, 504
RSNA Educational Scholar Program, 508
RSNA Holman Pathway Research Seed Grant, 509
RSNA Institutional Clinical Fellowship in Cardiovascular Imaging, 509
RSNA Medical Student Departmental Grant Program, 509
RSNA Medical Student/Scholar Assistant Program, 509
RSNA Research Fellowship in Basic Radiologic Sciences, 510
RSNA Research Resident Program, 510

West European Countries

International Postgraduate Research Scholarships (IPRS), 676
Mr and Mrs David Edward Memorial Award, 681
UWB Departmental Research Studentships, 681
UWB Research Studentships, 681

TREATMENT TECHNIQUES

Any Country

AFSP Distinguished Investigation Awards, 45
AFSP Pilot Grants, 46
AFSP Postdoctoral Research Fellowships, 46
AFSP Standard Research Grants, 46
AFSP Young Investigator Award, 46
ATA Scientific Research Grants, 83
BackCare Research Grants, 123
Barbers Company Clinical Nursing Scholarship, 527
BMRP for Inflammatory Bowel Disease Grants, 160
Breast Cancer Campaign Project Grants, 132
BRPS Research Grants, 154
Career development program, 395
CCFF Fellowships, 200
CCFF Studentships, 201
Cooley's Anemia Foundation Research Fellowship Grant, 242
CRPF Research Grant, 236
CSMLS Founders' Fund Award, 213
DEBRA UK Research Grant Scheme, 254
Equipment Grants, 319
FRAXA Grants and Fellowships, 289
GlaxoSmithKline Collaborative Research Projects, 304
HDA Studentship, 330
Institute for the Study of Aging Grants Program, 340
Institutional Fellowship in Radiological Informatics, 508
Meningitis Research Foundation Project Grant, 416
Meningitis Research Foundation Small Project Grant, 416
Meningitis Trust Research Award, 417
Michael Geisman Memorial Fellowship Grant, 484
National Heart Research Fund Medical Research Grant, 448
NORD Clinical Research Grants, 454
NORD/ROSCOE BRADY Lysosomal Storage Diseases Fellowships, 454
OREF Career Development Award, 483
OREF Prospective Clinical Research, 483
OREF Research Grants, 484

OREF Resident Research Award, 484
Osteogenesis Imperfecta Foundation Seed Research Grant, 484
Postgraduate Research Bursaries, 272
Roche Research Foundation, 521
Services to Academia, 304
SOM Research Grant, 588
Special Travel Allowances, 201
Spinal Cord Injury Research Foundation Grants, 593
Stroke Research Awards, 596
Translational Research Program, 396
UICC International Fellowships for Beginning Investigators (ACSBI), 370
UICC Translational Cancer Research Fellowships (TCRF), 370

African Nations

International Postgraduate Research Scholarships (IPRS), 676

Australia

New South Wales Cancer Council Research Programme Grant, 464
New South Wales Cancer Council Research Project Grants, 464
Sir Robert Menzies Memorial Research Scholarships in the Allied Health Sciences, 565
University of Western Sydney Postgraduate Research Award (UWSPRA), 689

British Commonwealth

International Postgraduate Research Scholarships (IPRS), 676

Canada

Fellowship in Health Services Research, 483
International Postgraduate Research Scholarships (IPRS), 676
OREF Clinical Research Award, 483
Spinal Cord Research Foundation Grants, 485

Caribbean Countries

International Postgraduate Research Scholarships (IPRS), 676

East European Countries

International Postgraduate Research Scholarships (IPRS), 676

Far East

International Postgraduate Research Scholarships (IPRS), 676
UICC International Cancer Technology Transfer Fellowships (ICRETT) for Bilateral Exchanges Between Indonesia and the Netherlands, 370

Indian Sub-Continent

International Postgraduate Research Scholarships (IPRS), 676

Middle East

International Postgraduate Research Scholarships (IPRS), 676

New Zealand

University of Western Sydney Postgraduate Research Award (UWSPRA), 689

South Africa

International Postgraduate Research Scholarships (IPRS), 676

South America

International Postgraduate Research Scholarships (IPRS), 676

United Kingdom

Alzheimers Society Research Grants, 22
British Lung Foundation Project Grants, 151
International Postgraduate Research Scholarships (IPRS), 676
Nathaniel Bishop Harman Award, 153
NOS Project Grants, 455
Owen Shaw Award, 159

PDS Research Project Grant, 487
PDS Studentships and Junior/Senior Fellows, 487
Resuscitation Council Research Fellowships, 516
Resuscitation Council Research Grants, 516

United States of America

Damon Runyon Scholar Award, 253
Fellowship in Health Services Research, 483
International Postgraduate Research Scholarships (IPRS), 676
National Headache Foundation Research Grant, 443
OREF Clinical Research Award, 483
Prevent Blindness America Investigator Award, 504
Spinal Cord Research Foundation Grants, 485

West European Countries

International Postgraduate Research Scholarships (IPRS), 676

MEDICAL TECHNOLOGY

Any Country

Barbers Company Clinical Nursing Scholarship, 527
Breast Cancer Campaign Project Grants, 132
BRPS Research Grants, 154
Career development program, 395
CCFF Fellowships, 200
CCFF Studentships, 201
Cooley's Anemia Foundation Research Fellowship Grant, 242
Equipment Grants, 319
GlaxoSmithKline Collaborative Research Projects, 304
HDA Studentship, 330
Institutional Fellowship in Radiological Informatics, 508
Meningitis Research Foundation Project Grant, 416
Meningitis Research Foundation Small Project Grant, 416
Meningitis Trust Research Award, 417
MND Research Project and Pump Pricing Grants, 426
NORD Clinical Research Grants, 454
Queen Elizabeth the Queen Mother Fellowship Award, 514
Queen Mary Research Studentships, 506
Research into Ageing Prize Studentships, 515
Research into Ageing Programme Grants, 515
Roche Research Foundation, 521
Savoy Foundation Post Doctoral and Clinical Research Fellowships, 555
Savoy Foundation Studentships, 555
Services to Academia, 304
Special Travel Allowances, 201
Translational Research Program, 396
UICC International Fellowships for Beginning Investigators (ACSBI), 370

African Nations

Hastings Center International Visiting Scholars Program, 318

Australia

Hastings Center International Visiting Scholars Program, 318

British Commonwealth

Hastings Center International Visiting Scholars Program, 318

Canada

CCFF Senior Scientist Research Training Award, 200
Quebec CE Fund Grants, 213

Caribbean Countries

Hastings Center International Visiting Scholars Program, 318

East European Countries

Hastings Center International Visiting Scholars Program, 318

Far East

Hastings Center International Visiting Scholars Program, 318
UICC International Cancer Technology Transfer Fellowships (ICRETT) for Bilateral Exchanges Between Indonesia and the Netherlands, 370

Indian Sub-Continent

Hastings Center International Visiting Scholars Program, 318

Middle East

Hastings Center International Visiting Scholars Program, 318

New Zealand

Hastings Center International Visiting Scholars Program, 318

South Africa

Hastings Center International Visiting Scholars Program, 318

South America

Hastings Center International Visiting Scholars Program, 318

United Kingdom

Alzheimers Society Research Grants, 22
Birth Defects Foundation Full and Small Grants, 129
British Lung Foundation Project Grants, 151
Hastings Center International Visiting Scholars Program, 318
MND PhD Studentship Award, 426
Resuscitation Council Research Fellowships, 516
Resuscitation Council Research Grants, 516

United States of America

Ian Axford (New Zealand) Fellowships in Public Policy, 239
Prevent Blindness America Investigator Award, 504

West European Countries

Hastings Center International Visiting Scholars Program, 318

DENTISTRY AND STOMATOLOGY

Any Country

AADR Student Research Fellowships, 29
Barbers Company Clinical Nursing Scholarship, 527
BDA / Dentsply Scholarship Fund, 139
CAMS Scholarship, 235
CIHR Fellowships Program, 208
Colyer Prize, 549
DCF Biennial Research Award, 255
DDF Scholarship for the Development of a Research Technique for Dentistry/Dental Research, 591
Equipment Grants, 319
Michael Geisman Memorial Fellowship Grant, 484
National Association of Dental Assistants Annual Scholarship Award, 435
NORD Clinical Research Grants, 454
Osteogenesis Imperfecta Foundation Seed Research Grant, 484
Queen Mary Research Studentships, 506
Roche Research Foundation, 521
Sir Richard Stapley Educational Trust Grants, 564
University of Bristol Postgraduate Scholarships, 619
University of Dundee Research Awards, 629
University of Glasgow Postgraduate Research Scholarships, 634
University of Manchester Research Studentships and Scholarships, 642
Winifred E Preedy Postgraduate Bursary, 115

Australia

NHMRC Medical and Dental and Public Health Postgraduate Research Scholarships, 445

Canada

United Kingdom

United States of America

ORAL PATHOLOGY

Any Country

ORTHODONTICS

Any Country

PERIODONTICS

Any Country

COMMUNITY DENTISTRY

Any Country

DENTAL TECHNOLOGY

Any Country

United States of America

PROSTHETIC DENTISTRY

Any Country

PHARMACY

Any Country

African Nations

Australia

BIOMEDICINE

Australia

Biomedical (Dora Lush) and Public Health Postgraduate Scholarships, 443
Burnet Fellowships, 443
C J Martin Fellowships (Overseas Biomedical), 444
Hastings Center International Visiting Scholars Program, 318
NHMRC/INSERM Exchange Fellowships, 445
Peter Doherty Fellowships, 445

British Commonwealth

Hastings Center International Visiting Scholars Program, 318
International Postgraduate Research Scholarships (IPRS), 676

Canada

Alcohol Beverage Medical Research Foundation Research Project Grant, 14
CTS Fellowships, 213
International Postgraduate Research Scholarships (IPRS), 676
Research Planning Grants, 214

Caribbean Countries

Hastings Center International Visiting Scholars Program, 318
International Postgraduate Research Scholarships (IPRS), 676

East European Countries

FEMS Fellowship, 280
Fogarty International Research Collaboration Award (FIRCA), 382
Hastings Center International Visiting Scholars Program, 318
International Postgraduate Research Scholarships (IPRS), 676

Far East

Hastings Center International Visiting Scholars Program, 318
International Postgraduate Research Scholarships (IPRS), 676

Indian Sub-Continent

Hastings Center International Visiting Scholars Program, 318
International Postgraduate Research Scholarships (IPRS), 676

Middle East

Fogarty International Research Collaboration Award (FIRCA), 382
Hastings Center International Visiting Scholars Program, 318
International Postgraduate Research Scholarships (IPRS), 676

New Zealand

Hastings Center International Visiting Scholars Program, 318

South Africa

Hastings Center International Visiting Scholars Program, 318
International Postgraduate Research Scholarships (IPRS), 676

South America

Fogarty International Research Collaboration Award (FIRCA), 382
Hastings Center International Visiting Scholars Program, 318
International Postgraduate Research Scholarships (IPRS), 676

United Kingdom

Alzheimers Society Research Grants, 22
British Lung Foundation Project Grants, 151
FEMS Fellowship, 280
Hastings Center International Visiting Scholars Program, 318
International Postgraduate Research Scholarships (IPRS), 676
MND PhD Studentship Award, 426
MRC Collaborative/Industrial Collaborative Studentships, 411
MRC Research Studentships, 412

United States of America

AFAR Research Grants, 43
Alcohol Beverage Medical Research Foundation Research Project Grant, 14

Fogarty International Research Collaboration Award (FIRCA), 382
International Postgraduate Research Scholarships (IPRS), 676
MARC Faculty Predoctoral Fellowships, 449
NIGMS Fellowship Awards for Minority Students, 449
NIGMS Fellowship Awards for Students With Disabilities, 450
NIGMS Postdoctoral Awards, 450
NIGMS Research Project Grants, 450
NIGMS Research Supplements for Underrepresented Minorities, 450
Prevent Blindness America Investigator Award, 504

West European Countries

FEMS Fellowship, 280
Fogarty International Research Collaboration Award (FIRCA), 382
Hastings Center International Visiting Scholars Program, 318
International Postgraduate Research Scholarships (IPRS), 676
MRC Collaborative/Industrial Collaborative Studentships, 411
MRC Research Studentships, 412

OPTOMETRY

Any Country

Barbers Company Clinical Nursing Scholarship, 527
CIHR Fellowships Program, 208
NORD Clinical Research Grants, 454
PhD Studentships within Clinical Investigation and Visual Function Research Group, 219
Roche Research Foundation, 521
University of Bristol Postgraduate Scholarships, 619

Australia

Sir Robert Menzies Memorial Research Scholarships in the Allied Health Sciences, 565

United States of America

Prevent Blindness America Investigator Award, 504

PODIATRY

Any Country

BackCare Research Grants, 123
Barbers Company Clinical Nursing Scholarship, 527
NORD Clinical Research Grants, 454
Roche Research Foundation, 521

African Nations

International Postgraduate Research Scholarships (IPRS), 676

Australia

University of Western Sydney Postgraduate Research Award (UW-SPRA), 689

British Commonwealth

International Postgraduate Research Scholarships (IPRS), 676

Canada

International Postgraduate Research Scholarships (IPRS), 676

Caribbean Countries

International Postgraduate Research Scholarships (IPRS), 676

East European Countries

International Postgraduate Research Scholarships (IPRS), 676

Far East

International Postgraduate Research Scholarships (IPRS), 676

Indian Sub-Continent

International Postgraduate Research Scholarships (IPRS), 676

Middle East

International Postgraduate Research Scholarships (IPRS), 676

New Zealand

University of Western Sydney Postgraduate Research Award (UW-SPRA), 689

South Africa

International Postgraduate Research Scholarships (IPRS), 676

South America

International Postgraduate Research Scholarships (IPRS), 676

United Kingdom

International Postgraduate Research Scholarships (IPRS), 676

United States of America

International Postgraduate Research Scholarships (IPRS), 676

West European Countries

International Postgraduate Research Scholarships (IPRS), 676

FORENSIC MEDICINE AND DENTISTRY

Any Country

Barbers Company Clinical Nursing Scholarship, 527
NORD Clinical Research Grants, 454
Roche Research Foundation, 521
University of Dundee Research Awards, 629
University of Glasgow Postgraduate Research Scholarships, 634

African Nations

International Postgraduate Research Scholarships (IPRS), 676

British Commonwealth

International Postgraduate Research Scholarships (IPRS), 676

Canada

International Postgraduate Research Scholarships (IPRS), 676

Caribbean Countries

International Postgraduate Research Scholarships (IPRS), 676

East European Countries

International Postgraduate Research Scholarships (IPRS), 676

Far East

International Postgraduate Research Scholarships (IPRS), 676

Indian Sub-Continent

International Postgraduate Research Scholarships (IPRS), 676

Middle East

International Postgraduate Research Scholarships (IPRS), 676

South Africa

International Postgraduate Research Scholarships (IPRS), 676

South America

International Postgraduate Research Scholarships (IPRS), 676

United Kingdom

C H Milburn Grant, 151
International Postgraduate Research Scholarships (IPRS), 676

United States of America

International Postgraduate Research Scholarships (IPRS), 676

West European Countries

International Postgraduate Research Scholarships (IPRS), 676

ACUPUNCTURE

Any Country

BackCare Research Grants, 123
Barbers Company Clinical Nursing Scholarship, 527
Breast Cancer Campaign Project Grants, 132
Roche Research Foundation, 521

HOMEOPATHY

Any Country

Barbers Company Clinical Nursing Scholarship, 527
Breast Cancer Campaign Project Grants, 132
Roche Research Foundation, 521

CHIROPRACTIC

Any Country

BackCare Research Grants, 123
Barbers Company Clinical Nursing Scholarship, 527
CIHR Fellowships Program, 208
CRPF Research Grant, 236
Roche Research Foundation, 521

African Nations

International Postgraduate Research Scholarships (IPRS), 676

British Commonwealth

International Postgraduate Research Scholarships (IPRS), 676

Canada

International Postgraduate Research Scholarships (IPRS), 676

Caribbean Countries

International Postgraduate Research Scholarships (IPRS), 676

East European Countries

International Postgraduate Research Scholarships (IPRS), 676

Far East

International Postgraduate Research Scholarships (IPRS), 676

Indian Sub-Continent

International Postgraduate Research Scholarships (IPRS), 676

Middle East

International Postgraduate Research Scholarships (IPRS), 676

South Africa

International Postgraduate Research Scholarships (IPRS), 676

South America

International Postgraduate Research Scholarships (IPRS), 676

United Kingdom

International Postgraduate Research Scholarships (IPRS), 676

United States of America

International Postgraduate Research Scholarships (IPRS), 676

West European Countries

International Postgraduate Research Scholarships (IPRS), 676

OSTEOPATHY

Any Country

BackCare Research Grants, 123
Barbers Company Clinical Nursing Scholarship, 527
Roche Research Foundation, 521

Canada

Alcohol Beverage Medical Research Foundation Research Project Grant, 14
Canadian Osteopathic Educational Trust Fund Financial Assistance, 211

United States of America

Alcohol Beverage Medical Research Foundation Research Project Grant, 14
AOA Research Grants, 63

TRADITIONAL EASTERN MEDICINE

Any Country

Barbers Company Clinical Nursing Scholarship, 527
Roche Research Foundation, 521

Australia

University of Western Sydney Postgraduate Research Award (UW-SPRA), 689

New Zealand

University of Western Sydney Postgraduate Research Award (UW-SPRA), 689

United Kingdom

Alzheimers Society Research Grants, 22

NATURAL SCIENCES

GENERAL

Any Country

AACR Scholar-in-Training Awards, 29
AIATSIS Research Grants, 116
Alberta Research Council Karl A Clark Memorial Scholarship, 617
Andrew Mellon Foundation Scholarship, 518
Andrew Stratton Scholarship, 632
ARC Discovery Projects Australian Research Fellow/Queen Elizabeth II Fellow (ARF/QEII), 118
ARC Discovery Projects Postdoctoral Fellow (APD), 118
ARC Projects - Professional Fellow (APF), 119
ASCSA Research Fellow in Environmental Studies, 71
ASCSA Research Fellow in Faunal Studies, 71
ASCSA Research Fellow in Geoarchaeology, 71
Association for Women in Science Educational Foundation Predoctoral Awards, 104
Balliol College Dervorguilla Scholarship, 647
BIAL Award, 127
Biochemical Society General Travel Fund, 129
BP Conservation Programme Awards, 123
Carnegie Institution of Washington Fellowships, 220
CCFF Scholarships, 200
CCFF Visiting Scientist Awards, 201
Claude McCarthy Fellowships, 465
Colt Foundation PhD Fellowship, 238
Concordia University Graduate Fellowships, 241
CRPF Research Grant, 236
DAAD Leibniz Scholarships for Doctoral Candidates and post-Docs, 298

Danish Cancer Society Scientific Award, 253
Daphne Jackson Fellowship, 253
David J Azrieli Graduate Fellowship, 241
Delahaye Memorial Benefaction, 681
Dorothy Hodgkin Fellowships, 542
Downing College Research Fellowships, 623
Earthwatch Field Research Grants, 264
Edmund Niles Huyck Preserve, Inc. Graduate and Postgraduate Grants, 266
Foulkes Foundation Fellowship, 282
Franklin Research Grant Program, 65
Fund for UFO Research Grants, 295
G M McKinley Research Fund, 505
Girton College Research Fellowships, 625
GlaxoSmithKline Collaborative Research Projects, 304
Griffith University Postgraduate Research Scholarships, 310
Heinrich Wieland Prize, 388
Helen McCormack Turner Memorial Scholarship, 681
Herbert Hughes Scholarship, 682
HFSP Long-Term Fellowships, 361
HFSP Short Term Fellowships, 362
Honda Prize, 325
HSS Travel Grant, 324
Hugh Kelly Fellowship, 519
Humanitarian Trust Awards, 329
ICGEB Long-Term Postdoctoral Fellowship Programme, 355
ICGEB Short-Term Postdoctoral Fellowship Programme, 355
IFER Fellowship for Alternatives in Scientific Research, 360
IFT Graduate Fellowships, 343
Israel International Schloarship, 145
J Lawrence Angel Fellowship in Human Skeletal Studies, 72
Lady Margaret Hall EPA Cephalosporin Research Fellowship, 654
Leverhulme Trust Senior Research Fellowships, 543
Lincoln College Erich and Rochelle Endowed Prize in Music, 657
Lindbergh Grants, 230
Lord Dowding Fund for Humane Research, 401
Mary Radcliffe Scholarship, 682
Matsumae International Foundation Research Fellowship, 408
McDonnell Graduate Fellowship in the Space Sciences, 408
Monash International Postgraduate Research Scholarship (MIPRS), 424
Monash University Silver Jubilee Postgraduate Scholarship, 425
National Marfan Foundation Research Grant, 452
NEH Fellowships, 72
NERC Advanced Research Fellowships, 460
NERC Postdoctoral Research Fellowships, 460
NFB Howard Brown Rickard Scholarship, 441
Novartis Foundation Symposium Bursaries, 475
NRC Research Associateships, 456
NRF Fellowships for Postdoctoral Research, 456
Oliver Gatty Studentship, 626
Pembroke College Graduate Awards, 626
Perry Postgraduate Scholarships and Research Awards, 491
Predoctoral Fellowship Programme ICGEB International PhD Course, 356
Predoctoral Fellowship Programme ICGEB JNU PhD Course in Molecular Biology, 356
Queen Mary Research Studentships, 506
Ralph Brown Expedition Award, 535
Rhodes University Postgraduate Scholarship, 519
RHYS Curzon-Jones Scholarship, 682
Ridley Lewis Bursary, 682
Roche Research Foundation, 521
Royal Irish Academy European Exchange Fellowship, 540
Royal Society Conference Grants, 543
Royal Society Industry Fellowships Scheme, 544
Royal Society Research Grants Scheme, 544
Scottish Executive / RSE Support Research Fellowships, 549
Scottish Executive Personal Research Fellowships, 549
SEG Scholarships, 587
Shell Centenary Scholarships at Cambridge (Non-OECD Countries), 190
Shirtcliffe Fellowship, 465

African Nations

Australia

British Commonwealth

Canada

Caribbean Countries

East European Countries

Far East

West European Countries

BIOLOGICAL AND LIFE SCIENCES

Any Country

African Nations

Australia

British Commonwealth

Canada

Caribbean Countries

East European Countries

Far East

Indian Sub-Continent

Middle East

New Zealand

South Africa

South America

United Kingdom

BIOLOGY

Canada

IDRC Doctoral Research Awards, 358
Postdoctoral Training Programme in Addiction and Mental Health, 225
Research Planning Grants, 214
Spinal Cord Research Foundation Grants, 485
Use of Fertility Enhancing Food, Forage and Cover Crops in Sustainably Managed Agroecosystems: The Bentley Fellowship, 358

Caribbean Countries

EMBO World Programme Fellowships, 276
Use of Fertility Enhancing Food, Forage and Cover Crops in Sustainably Managed Agroecosystems: The Bentley Fellowship, 358

East European Countries

Natural History Museum Sys-Resource, 461
Olga Kennard Research Fellowship Scheme, 543

Far East

Austrian Academy of Sciences MSc Course in Limnology and Wetlands Ecosystems, 121
Austrian Academy of Sciences Postgraduate Course in Limnology, 121
EMBO World Programme Fellowships, 276
University of Otago Dr Sulaiman Daud 125th Jubilee International Postgraduate Scholarship, 646
Use of Fertility Enhancing Food, Forage and Cover Crops in Sustainably Managed Agroecosystems: The Bentley Fellowship, 358

Indian Sub-Continent

Austrian Academy of Sciences MSc Course in Limnology and Wetlands Ecosystems, 121
Austrian Academy of Sciences Postgraduate Course in Limnology, 121
EMBO World Programme Fellowships, 276
Use of Fertility Enhancing Food, Forage and Cover Crops in Sustainably Managed Agroecosystems: The Bentley Fellowship, 358

Middle East

EMBO World Programme Fellowships, 276
Use of Fertility Enhancing Food, Forage and Cover Crops in Sustainably Managed Agroecosystems: The Bentley Fellowship, 358

New Zealand

University of Otago Masters Awards, 646
University of Otago PhD Scholarships, 646
University of Otago Prestigious PhD Scholarships, 647
University of Western Sydney Postgraduate Research Award (UW-SPRA), 689

South Africa

EMBO World Programme Fellowships, 276
Use of Fertility Enhancing Food, Forage and Cover Crops in Sustainably Managed Agroecosystems: The Bentley Fellowship, 358

South America

Austrian Academy of Sciences MSc Course in Limnology and Wetlands Ecosystems, 121
Austrian Academy of Sciences Postgraduate Course in Limnology, 121
EMBO World Programme Fellowships, 276
Use of Fertility Enhancing Food, Forage and Cover Crops in Sustainably Managed Agroecosystems: The Bentley Fellowship, 358

United Kingdom

Dax Copp Travelling Fellowship, 341
ESRF Thesis Studentships, 277
Fulbright AstraZeneca Research Scholarship, 691
Llewellyn and Mary Williams Scholarship, 680
Martin McLaren Horticultural Scholarship, 344
Mr and Mrs David Edward Memorial Award, 681

NERC Advanced Course Studentships, 459
NERC Research Studentships, 460
Polish Government Postgraduate Scholarships Scheme, 501
University of Essex Foundation Scholarships, 632
University of Wales (Aberystwyth) Postgraduate Research Studentships, 680
UWB Departmental Research Studentships, 681
UWB Research Studentships, 681

United States of America

AFAR Research Grants, 43
AHA National Established Investigator Award, 48
AHA National Scientist Development Grant, 48
APS Conference Student Award, 66
APS Minority Travel Fellowship Awards, 66
Beeson Career Development Award, 43
Caroline tum Suden/Frances Hellebrandt Professional Opportunity Awards, 67
Earthwatch Education Awards, 264
Ellison Medical Foundation/AFAR Senior Postdoctoral Research Program, 44
Fulbright Senior Specialists Program, 245
Glenn/AFAR Research Grant Program for Postdoctoral Fellows, 44
MARC Faculty Predoctoral Fellowships, 449
NIGMS Fellowship Awards for Minority Students, 449
NIGMS Fellowship Awards for Students With Disabilities, 450
NIGMS Postdoctoral Awards, 450
NIGMS Research Project Grants, 450
NIGMS Research Supplements for Underrepresented Minorities, 450
NIH Research Grants, 450
NRC Twinning Program, 455
PhRMAF Postdoctoral Fellowships in Pharmacology-Morphology, 493
Postdoctoral Training Programme in Addiction and Mental Health, 225
Procter and Gamble Professional Opportunity Awards, 67
Spinal Cord Research Foundation Grants, 485
Washington University Chancellor's Graduate Fellowship Program for African Americans, 699
William T Porter Fellowship Award, 67

West European Countries

ESRF Thesis Studentships, 277
Eugen and Ilse Seibold Award, 257
Llewellyn and Mary Williams Scholarship, 680
Mr and Mrs David Edward Memorial Award, 681
Natural History Museum Sys-Resource, 461
Olga Kennard Research Fellowship Scheme, 543
University of Otago Masters Awards, 646
University of Otago PhD Scholarships, 646
University of Otago Prestigious PhD Scholarships, 647
UWB Departmental Research Studentships, 681
UWB Research Studentships, 681

HISTOLOGY

Any Country

BBSRC Research Grants, 129
Health Research Board PhD training sites, 319
HRB Postdoctoral Research Fellowships, 320
HRB Project Grants-General, 320
HRB Research Project Grants North-South Co-operation, 320
HRB Summer Student Grants, 320
Lister Institute Research Prizes, 400
Massey Doctoral Scholarship, 408
Meningitis Research Foundation Project Grant, 416
Meningitis Research Foundation Small Project Grant, 416
Muscular Dystrophy Research Grants, 429
Savoy Foundation Post Doctoral and Clinical Research Fellowships, 555
Savoy Foundation Studentships, 555
University of Otago International Scholarships, 646

BIOPHYSICS AND MOLECULAR BIOLOGY

Canada

Alcohol Beverage Medical Research Foundation Research Project Grant, 14
IDRC Doctoral Research Awards, 358
Postdoctoral Training Programme in Addiction and Mental Health, 225
Spinal Cord Research Foundation Grants, 485

Caribbean Countries

EMBO World Programme Fellowships, 276

East European Countries

EMBO Award for Communication in the Life Sciences, 275
FEMS Fellowship, 280
The Laboratory of Molecular Biology (LMB) Newton Cambridge Scholarships, 182

Far East

EMBO World Programme Fellowships, 276
University of Otago Dr Sulaiman Daud 125th Jubilee International Postgraduate Scholarship, 646

Indian Sub-Continent

EMBO World Programme Fellowships, 276

Middle East

EMBO World Programme Fellowships, 276

New Zealand

University of Otago Masters Awards, 646
University of Otago PhD Scholarships, 646
University of Otago Prestigious PhD Scholarships, 647
University of Western Sydney Postgraduate Research Award (UW-SPRA), 689

South Africa

EMBO World Programme Fellowships, 276

South America

EMBO World Programme Fellowships, 276

United Kingdom

Alzheimers Society Research Grants, 22
British Lung Foundation Project Grants, 151
EMBO Award for Communication in the Life Sciences, 275
ESRF Thesis Studentships, 277
FEMS Fellowship, 280
M.O.A.C. MSc Studentships, 685
M.O.A.C. PhD Studentships, 685
MND PhD Studentship Award, 426
Mr and Mrs David Edward Memorial Award, 681
PDS Research Project Grant, 487
PDS Studentships and Junior/Senior Fellows, 487
University of Essex Foundation Scholarships, 632
University of Wales (Aberystwyth) Postgraduate Research Studentships, 680
UWB Departmental Research Studentships, 681
UWB Research Studentships, 681

United States of America

AHA National Established Investigator Award, 48
AHA National Scientist Development Grant, 48
Alcohol Beverage Medical Research Foundation Research Project Grant, 14
Beeson Career Development Award, 43
Fannie and John Hertz Foundation Fellowships, 280
MARC Faculty Predoctoral Fellowships, 449
NIGMS Fellowship Awards for Minority Students, 449
NIGMS Fellowship Awards for Students With Disabilities, 450
NIGMS Postdoctoral Awards, 450
NIGMS Research Project Grants, 450

NIGMS Research Supplements for Underrepresented Minorities, 450
NRC Twinning Program, 455
PhRMAF Postdoctoral Fellowships in Pharmacology-Morphology, 493
Postdoctoral Training Programme in Addiction and Mental Health, 225
Spinal Cord Research Foundation Grants, 485
Washington University Chancellor's Graduate Fellowship Program for African Americans, 699

West European Countries

EMBO Award for Communication in the Life Sciences, 275
ESRF Thesis Studentships, 277
FEMS Fellowship, 280
Mr and Mrs David Edward Memorial Award, 681
The Laboratory of Molecular Biology (LMB) Newton Cambridge Scholarships, 182
University of Otago Masters Awards, 646
University of Otago PhD Scholarships, 646
University of Otago Prestigious PhD Scholarships, 647
UWB Departmental Research Studentships, 681
UWB Research Studentships, 681

BIOTECHNOLOGY

Any Country

BBSRC Research Grants, 129
Career development program, 395
Electrochemical Society Summer Fellowships, 267
EMBO Long-Term Fellowships in Molecular Biology, 275
EMBO Restart Fellowship, 275
EMBO Short-Term Fellowships in Molecular Biology, 275
EMBO Young Investigator, 276
Foulkes Foundation Fellowship, 282
FRAXA Grants and Fellowships, 289
Fungal Research Trust Travel Grants, 295
GlaxoSmithKline Collaborative Research Projects, 304
HRB Postdoctoral Research Fellowships, 320
HRB Project Grants-General, 320
HRB Research Project Grants North-South Co-operation, 320
HRB Summer Student Grants, 320
Hugh Kelly Fellowship, 519
ICGEB Long-Term Postdoctoral Fellowship Programme, 355
ICGEB Short-Term Postdoctoral Fellowship Programme, 355
Institute for the Study of Aging Grants Program, 340
International School of Crystallography Grants, 367
Massey Doctoral Scholarship, 408
Meningitis Research Foundation Project Grant, 416
Meningitis Research Foundation Small Project Grant, 416
Muscular Dystrophy Research Grants, 429
NARSAD Distinguished Investigator Awards, 434
NARSAD Independent Investigator Awards, 434
NARSAD Young Investigator Awards, 434
NRC Research Associateships, 456
Perry Postgraduate Scholarships, 490
Predoctoral Fellowship Programme ICGEB JNU PhD Course in Molecular Biology, 356
Promega Biotechnology Research Award, 78
Queen Elizabeth the Queen Mother Fellowship Award, 514
Queen Mary Research Studentships, 506
Research into Ageing Prize Studentships, 515
Research into Ageing Programme Grants, 515
Rhodes University Postdoctoral Fellowship, 519
Savoy Foundation Post Doctoral and Clinical Research Fellowships, 555
Savoy Foundation Studentships, 555
Services to Academia, 304
Sigma Xi Grants-in-Aid of Research, 563
Teagasc Walsh Fellowships, 599
UFAW Animal Welfare Research Training Scholarships, 616
UFAW Research and Project Awards, 616
UFAW Small Project and Travel Awards, 616
UFAW Vacation Scholarships, 616
University of Dundee Research Awards, 629

PLANT PATHOLOGY

University of Otago Prestigious PhD Scholarships, 647
University of Western Sydney Postgraduate Research Award (UW-SPRA), 689
Wingate Scholarships, 704

British Commonwealth

Wingate Scholarships, 704

Canada

IDRC Doctoral Research Awards, 358
Wingate Scholarships, 704

Caribbean Countries

EMBO World Programme Fellowships, 276

East European Countries

EMBO Award for Communication in the Life Sciences, 275

Far East

EMBO World Programme Fellowships, 276
University of Otago Dr Sulaiman Daud 125th Jubilee International Postgraduate Scholarship, 646

Indian Sub-Continent

EMBO World Programme Fellowships, 276
Wingate Scholarships, 704

Middle East

EMBO World Programme Fellowships, 276

New Zealand

University of Otago Masters Awards, 646
University of Otago PhD Scholarships, 646
University of Otago Prestigious PhD Scholarships, 647
University of Western Sydney Postgraduate Research Award (UW-SPRA), 689
Wingate Scholarships, 704

South Africa

EMBO World Programme Fellowships, 276
Wingate Scholarships, 704

South America

EMBO World Programme Fellowships, 276

United Kingdom

EMBO Award for Communication in the Life Sciences, 275
Llewellyn and Mary Williams Scholarship, 680
Martin McLaren Horticultural Scholarship, 344
Mr and Mrs David Edward Memorial Award, 681
NERC Advanced Course Studentships, 459
NERC Research Studentships, 460
University of Kent Research School of Biosciences, 637
University of Wales (Aberystwyth) Postgraduate Research Studentships, 680
UWB Departmental Research Studentships, 681
UWB Research Studentships, 681
Wingate Scholarships, 704

United States of America

Earthwatch Education Awards, 264

West European Countries

EMBO Award for Communication in the Life Sciences, 275
Llewellyn and Mary Williams Scholarship, 680
Mr and Mrs David Edward Memorial Award, 681
University of Kent Research School of Biosciences, 637
University of Otago Masters Awards, 646
University of Otago PhD Scholarships, 646

University of Otago Prestigious PhD Scholarships, 647
UWB Departmental Research Studentships, 681
UWB Research Studentships, 681
Wingate Scholarships, 704

EMBRYOLOGY AND REPRODUCTION BIOLOGY

Any Country

BackCare Research Grants, 123
BBSRC Research Grants, 129
Childrens Medical Research Institute Graduate Scholarships and Postgraduate Fellowships, 234
Childrens Medical Research Institute Postdoctoral Fellowship, 235
EMBO Long-Term Fellowships in Molecular Biology, 275
EMBO Restart Fellowship, 275
EMBO Short-Term Fellowships in Molecular Biology, 275
EMBO Young Investigator, 276
Foulkes Foundation Fellowship, 282
Health Research Board PhD training sites, 319
HRB Project Grants-General, 320
HRB Research Project Grants North-South Co-operation, 320
HRB Summer Student Grants, 320
Lalor Foundation Postdoctoral Fellowships, 391
Lister Institute Research Prizes, 400
LSRF Three Year Postdoctoral Fellowships, 399
Massey Doctoral Scholarship, 408
Perry Postgraduate Scholarships, 490
Queen Mary Research Studentships, 506
Rhodes University Postdoctoral Fellowship, 519
Sigma Xi Grants-in-Aid of Research, 563
UFAW Animal Welfare Research Training Scholarships, 616
UFAW Research and Project Awards, 616
UFAW Small Project and Travel Awards, 616
UFAW Vacation Scholarships, 616
University of Otago International Scholarships, 646
University of Stirling Research Studentships, 678
Weizmann Institute of Science MSc Fellowships, 700
Weizmann Institute of Science PhD Fellowships, 700
Weizmann Institute of Science Postdoctoral Fellowships Program, 700
WellBeing Project Grants, 700
Wellcome Trust Awards, Fellowships and Studentships, 701

African Nations

EMBO World Programme Fellowships, 276
Hastings Center International Visiting Scholars Program, 318

Australia

Childrens Medical Research Institute Postgraduate Scholarship, 235
Hastings Center International Visiting Scholars Program, 318
University of Otago Masters Awards, 646
University of Otago PhD Scholarships, 646
University of Otago Prestigious PhD Scholarships, 647

British Commonwealth

Hastings Center International Visiting Scholars Program, 318

Caribbean Countries

EMBO World Programme Fellowships, 276
Hastings Center International Visiting Scholars Program, 318

East European Countries

EMBO Award for Communication in the Life Sciences, 275
Hastings Center International Visiting Scholars Program, 318

Far East

EMBO World Programme Fellowships, 276
Hastings Center International Visiting Scholars Program, 318

University of Otago Dr Sulaiman Daud 125th Jubilee International Postgraduate Scholarship, 646

Indian Sub-Continent

EMBO World Programme Fellowships, 276
Hastings Center International Visiting Scholars Program, 318

Middle East

EMBO World Programme Fellowships, 276
Hastings Center International Visiting Scholars Program, 318

New Zealand

Hastings Center International Visiting Scholars Program, 318
University of Otago Masters Awards, 646
University of Otago PhD Scholarships, 646
University of Otago Prestigious PhD Scholarships, 647

South Africa

EMBO World Programme Fellowships, 276
Hastings Center International Visiting Scholars Program, 318

South America

EMBO World Programme Fellowships, 276
Hastings Center International Visiting Scholars Program, 318

United Kingdom

EMBO Award for Communication in the Life Sciences, 275
Hastings Center International Visiting Scholars Program, 318
Llewellyn and Mary Williams Scholarship, 680
Mr and Mrs David Edward Memorial Award, 681
University of Wales (Aberystwyth) Postgraduate Research Studentships, 680
UWB Departmental Research Studentships, 681
UWB Research Studentships, 681

United States of America

Fulbright Senior Specialists Program, 245

West European Countries

EMBO Award for Communication in the Life Sciences, 275
Hastings Center International Visiting Scholars Program, 318
Llewellyn and Mary Williams Scholarship, 680
Mr and Mrs David Edward Memorial Award, 681
University of Otago Masters Awards, 646
University of Otago PhD Scholarships, 646
University of Otago Prestigious PhD Scholarships, 647
UWB Departmental Research Studentships, 681
UWB Research Studentships, 681

GENETICS

Any Country

AFSP Distinguished Investigation Awards, 45
AFSP Pilot Grants, 46
AFSP Postdoctoral Research Fellowships, 46
AFSP Standard Research Grants, 46
AFSP Young Investigator Award, 46
AHAF Alzheimer's Disease Research Grant, 47
AHAF Macular Degeneration Research, 47
Alzheimer's Research Trust Clinical Research Training Fellowship, 21
Alzheimer's Research Trust Emergency Support Grant, 21
Alzheimer's Research Trust Network Project Co-operation Grant
Alzheimer's Research Trust PhD Studentships, 21
Alzheimer's Research Trust Pilot Project Grant, 21
Alzheimer's Research Trust Research Equipment Grant, 22
Alzheimer's Research Trust Research Fellowships, 22
Alzheimer's Research Trust Research Major Programme Project Grants, 22
ASBAH Research Grant, 103
Ataxia Research Grant, 436

Ataxia UK Research Studentships, 111
Ataxia UK Travel Award, 112
BBSRC Research Grants, 129
BMRP for Inflammatory Bowel Disease Grants, 160
Cancer Research Clinical Research Fellowships, 216
Cancer Research UK LRI Graduate Studentships, 217
Cancer Research UK LRI Research Fellowships, 217
Career development program, 395
CGD Research Trust Grants, 237
Childrens Medical Research Institute Graduate Scholarships and Postgraduate Fellowships, 234
Childrens Medical Research Institute Postdoctoral Fellowship, 235
CRPF Research Grant, 236
Direct Research on Ataxia-Telangiectasia, 3
EMBO Long-Term Fellowships in Molecular Biology, 275
EMBO Restart Fellowship, 275
EMBO Short-Term Fellowships in Molecular Biology, 275
EMBO Young Investigator, 276
Foulkes Foundation Fellowship, 282
FRAXA Grants and Fellowships, 289
Fungal Research Trust Travel Grants, 295
GlaxoSmithKline Collaborative Research Projects, 304
Health Research Board PhD training sites, 319
HRB Postdoctoral Research Fellowships, 320
HRB Project Grants-General, 320
HRB Research Project Grants North-South Co-operation, 320
HRB Summer Student Grants, 320
IARC Postdoctoral Fellowships for Training in Cancer Research, 352
ICGEB Long-Term Postdoctoral Fellowship Programme, 355
ICGEB Short-Term Postdoctoral Fellowship Programme, 355
ICR Research Studentships, 342
Institute for the Study of Aging Grants Program, 340
L S B Leakey Foundation General Research Grant, 389
La Trobe University Postgraduate Scholarship, 390
Lister Institute Research Prizes, 400
LSA Medical Research Grant, 402
LSRF Three Year Postdoctoral Fellowships, 399
March of Dimes Research Grants, 404
Massey Doctoral Scholarship, 408
Meningitis Research Foundation Project Grant, 416
Meningitis Research Foundation Small Project Grant, 416
Michael Geisman Memorial Fellowship Grant, 484
MND Research Project and Pump Pricing Grants, 426
Muscular Dystrophy Research Grants, 429
NARSAD Distinguished Investigator Awards, 434
NARSAD Young Investigator Awards, 434
National Marfan Foundation Research Grant, 452
NERC Advanced Research Fellowships, 460
NERC Postdoctoral Research Fellowships, 460
NHF Grant, 446
NORD Clinical Research Grants, 454
Osteogenesis Imperfecta Foundation Seed Research Grant, 484
Perry Postgraduate Scholarships and Research Awards, 491
Predoctoral Fellowship Programme ICGEB International PhD Course, 356
Predoctoral Fellowship Programme ICGEB JNU PhD Course in Molecular Biology, 356
Project Grant, 112
Queen Elizabeth the Queen Mother Fellowship Award, 514
Queen Mary Research Studentships, 506
Research into Ageing Prize Studentships, 515
Research into Ageing Programme Grants, 515
RFA Grants, 500
Rhodes University Postdoctoral Fellowship, 519
Satellite Meeting at Major Symposium on Related Disorders, 112
Savoy Foundation Post Doctoral and Clinical Research Fellowships, 555
Savoy Foundation Studentships, 555
Services to Academia, 304
Sigma Xi Grants-in-Aid of Research, 563
Teagasc Walsh Fellowships, 599
Translational Research Program, 396
TSA Research Grants, 604

University of Otago Prestigious PhD Scholarships, 647
UWB Departmental Research Studentships, 681
UWB Research Studentships, 681

IMMUNOLOGY

Any Country

AACR Scholar-in-Training Awards, 29
Abbott Laboratories Award in Clinical and Diagnostic Immunology, 76
AHAF Macular Degeneration Research, 47
ANRF Research Grants, 94
BBSRC Research Grants, 129
BMRP for Inflammatory Bowel Disease Grants, 160
Cancer Research Clinical Research Fellowships, 216
Cancer Research UK LRI Graduate Studentships, 217
Career development program, 395
CBS Graduate Fellowship Program, 197
CBS Transfusion Medicine Fellowship Awards, 198
CGD Research Trust Grants, 237
CRPF Research Grant, 236
EMBO Long-Term Fellowships in Molecular Biology, 275
EMBO Restart Fellowship, 275
EMBO Short-Term Fellowships in Molecular Biology, 275
EMBO Young Investigator, 276
Foulkes Foundation Fellowship, 282
Fungal Research Trust Travel Grants, 295
Gordon Piller Studentships, 395
Health Research Board PhD training sites, 319
HRB Postdoctoral Research Fellowships, 320
HRB Project Grants-General, 320
HRB Research Project Grants North-South Co-operation, 320
HRB Summer Student Grants, 320
IARC Postdoctoral Fellowships for Training in Cancer Research, 352
ICGEB Long-Term Postdoctoral Fellowship Programme, 355
Leukaemia Research Fund Clinical Research Training Fellowships, 395
Leukaemia Research Fund Clinical Training Fellowship, 395
Leukaemia Research Fund Grant Programme, 395
Lister Institute Research Prizes, 400
LSRF Three Year Postdoctoral Fellowships, 399
Meningitis Research Foundation Project Grant, 416
Meningitis Research Foundation Small Project Grant, 416
Muscular Dystrophy Research Grants, 429
NARSAD Distinguished Investigator Awards, 434
NARSAD Independent Investigator Awards, 434
NARSAD Young Investigator Awards, 434
National Multiple Sclerosis Society Research Grants, 453
NORD Clinical Research Grants, 454
NRC Research Associateships, 456
Predoctoral Fellowship Programme ICGEB International PhD Course, 356
Predoctoral Fellowship Programme ICGEB JNU PhD Course in Molecular Biology, 356
Queen Elizabeth the Queen Mother Fellowship Award, 514
Queen Mary Research Studentships, 506
Research into Ageing Prize Studentships, 515
Research into Ageing Programme Grants, 515
Rhodes University Postdoctoral Fellowship, 519
Savoy Foundation Post Doctoral and Clinical Research Fellowships, 555
Savoy Foundation Studentships, 555
Sigma Xi Grants-in-Aid of Research, 563
The Pfizer Fellowships in Rheumatology / Immunology., 476
Translational Research Program, 396
University of Dundee Research Awards, 629
University of Essex Scholarships, 632
University of Manchester Research Studentships and Scholarships, 642
University of Otago International Scholarships, 646
University of Stirling Research Studentships, 678
Weizmann Institute of Science MSc Fellowships, 700
Weizmann Institute of Science PhD Fellowships, 700

Weizmann Institute of Science Postdoctoral Fellowships Program, 700
WellBeing Project Grants, 700
Wellcome Trust Awards, Fellowships and Studentships, 701
Wilson-Fulton and Robertson Awards in Ageing Research, Cecille Gould Memorial Fund Award in Cancer Research, Richard Shepherd Fellowship, 44

African Nations

EMBO World Programme Fellowships, 276

Australia

New South Wales Cancer Council Research Programme Grant, 464
New South Wales Cancer Council Research Project Grants, 464
University of Otago Masters Awards, 646
University of Otago PhD Scholarships, 646
University of Otago Prestigious PhD Scholarships, 647
University of Western Sydney Postgraduate Research Award (UW-SPRA), 689

Canada

CBS Postdoctoral Fellowship (PDF), 197
CBS Research and Development Program Individual Grants, 197
CBS Research and Development Program Major Equipment Grants, 198
Eli Lilly and Company Research Award, 77

Caribbean Countries

EMBO World Programme Fellowships, 276

East European Countries

EMBO Award for Communication in the Life Sciences, 275
FEMS Fellowship, 280

Far East

EMBO World Programme Fellowships, 276
University of Otago Dr Sulaiman Daud 125th Jubilee International Postgraduate Scholarship, 646

Indian Sub-Continent

EMBO World Programme Fellowships, 276

Middle East

EMBO World Programme Fellowships, 276

New Zealand

University of Otago Masters Awards, 646
University of Otago PhD Scholarships, 646
University of Otago Prestigious PhD Scholarships, 647
University of Western Sydney Postgraduate Research Award (UW-SPRA), 689

South Africa

EMBO World Programme Fellowships, 276

South America

EMBO World Programme Fellowships, 276

United Kingdom

Alzheimers Society Research Grants, 22
EMBO Award for Communication in the Life Sciences, 275
FEMS Fellowship, 280
Llewellyn and Mary Williams Scholarship, 680
Mr and Mrs David Edward Memorial Award, 681
University of Essex Foundation Scholarships, 632
University of Wales (Aberystwyth) Postgraduate Research Studentships, 680
UWB Departmental Research Studentships, 681
UWB Research Studentships, 681

United States of America

AFAR Research Grants, 43
AFAR/Pfizer Research Grants in Metabolic Control and Late Life Diseases, 43
Beeson Career Development Award, 43
Eli Lilly and Company Research Award, 77
MARC Faculty Predoctoral Fellowships, 449
NIGMS Fellowship Awards for Minority Students, 449
NIGMS Fellowship Awards for Students With Disabilities, 450
NIGMS Postdoctoral Awards, 450
NIGMS Research Project Grants, 450
NIGMS Research Supplements for Underrepresented Minorities, 450
NIH Research Grants, 450
Washington University Chancellor's Graduate Fellowship Program for African Americans, 699

West European Countries

EMBO Award for Communication in the Life Sciences, 275
FEMS Fellowship, 280
Llewellyn and Mary Williams Scholarship, 680
Mr and Mrs David Edward Memorial Award, 681
University of Otago Masters Awards, 646
University of Otago PhD Scholarships, 646
University of Otago Prestigious PhD Scholarships, 647
UWB Departmental Research Studentships, 681
UWB Research Studentships, 681

MARINE BIOLOGY

Any Country

BBSRC Research Grants, 129
Bermuda Biological Station for Research Grant In Aid, 125
CDU Senior Research Fellowship, 230
CDU Three Year Postdoctoral Fellowship, 230
Earthwatch Field Research Grants, 264
EMBO Long-Term Fellowships in Molecular Biology, 275
EMBO Restart Fellowship, 275
EMBO Short-Term Fellowships in Molecular Biology, 275
EMBO Young Investigator, 276
Hudson River Research Grants, 328
Hudson River Travel Grants, 328
Hugh Kelly Fellowship, 519
Mount Desert Island New Investigator Award, 427
NERC Advanced Research Fellowships, 460
NERC Postdoctoral Research Fellowships, 460
NRC Research Associateships, 456
Queen Mary Research Studentships, 506
Rhodes University Postdoctoral Fellowship, 519
Sigma Xi Grants-in-Aid of Research, 563
Tibor T Polgar Fellowship, 328
UFAW Research and Project Awards, 616
University of Dundee Research Awards, 629
University of Essex Scholarships, 632
University of Manchester Research Studentships and Scholarships, 642
University of Otago International Scholarships, 646
University of Stirling Research Studentships, 678
Woods Hole Oceanographic Institution Research Fellowships in Marine Policy, 710
Woods Hole Oceanographic Institution/NOAA Co-operative Institute for Climate and Ocean Research Postdoctoral Fellowship, 710

African Nations

EMBO World Programme Fellowships, 276

Australia

Noel and Kate Monkman Postgraduate Award, 376
University of Otago Masters Awards, 646
University of Otago PhD Scholarships, 646
University of Otago Prestigious PhD Scholarships, 647
Wingate Scholarships, 704

British Commonwealth

Wingate Scholarships, 704

Canada

IDRC Doctoral Research Awards, 358
Wingate Scholarships, 704

Caribbean Countries

EMBO World Programme Fellowships, 276

East European Countries

EMBO Award for Communication in the Life Sciences, 275
FEMS Fellowship, 280
Natural History Museum Sys-Resource, 461

Far East

EMBO World Programme Fellowships, 276
University of Otago Dr Sulaiman Daud 125th Jubilee International Postgraduate Scholarship, 646

Indian Sub-Continent

EMBO World Programme Fellowships, 276
Wingate Scholarships, 704

Middle East

EMBO World Programme Fellowships, 276

New Zealand

University of Otago Masters Awards, 646
University of Otago PhD Scholarships, 646
University of Otago Prestigious PhD Scholarships, 647
Wingate Scholarships, 704

South Africa

EMBO World Programme Fellowships, 276
Henderson Postgraduate Scholarships, 518
Wingate Scholarships, 704

South America

EMBO World Programme Fellowships, 276

United Kingdom

EMBO Award for Communication in the Life Sciences, 275
FEMS Fellowship, 280
Llewellyn and Mary Williams Scholarship, 680
Mr and Mrs David Edward Memorial Award, 681
NERC Advanced Course Studentships, 459
NERC Research Studentships, 460
Polish Government Postgraduate Scholarships Scheme, 501
University of Essex Foundation Scholarships, 632
University of Wales (Aberystwyth) Postgraduate Research Studentships, 680
UWB Departmental Research Studentships, 681
UWB Research Studentships, 681
Wingate Scholarships, 704

United States of America

Earthwatch Education Awards, 264
NRC Twinning Program, 455
Woods Hole Oceanographic Institution Postdoctoral Fellowships in the Interdisciplinary Institutes, 710

West European Countries

EMBO Award for Communication in the Life Sciences, 275
FEMS Fellowship, 280
Llewellyn and Mary Williams Scholarship, 680
Mr and Mrs David Edward Memorial Award, 681
Natural History Museum Sys-Resource, 461
University of Otago Masters Awards, 646

University of Otago PhD Scholarships, 646
University of Otago Prestigious PhD Scholarships, 647
UWB Departmental Research Studentships, 681
UWB Research Studentships, 681
Wingate Scholarships, 704

LIMNOLOGY

Any Country

BBSRC Research Grants, 129
Earthwatch Field Research Grants, 264
Edmund Niles Huyck Preserve, Inc. Graduate and Postgraduate Grants, 266
Massey Doctoral Scholarship, 408
NERC Advanced Research Fellowships, 460
NERC Postdoctoral Research Fellowships, 460
Sigma Xi Grants-in-Aid of Research, 563
University of Otago International Scholarships, 646

African Nations

Austrian Academy of Sciences MSc Course in Limnology and Wetlands Ecosystems, 121
Austrian Academy of Sciences Postgraduate Course in Limnology, 121
Institute of Limnology Postgraduate Training Fellowships, 122

Australia

University of Otago Masters Awards, 646
University of Otago PhD Scholarships, 646
University of Otago Prestigious PhD Scholarships, 647

East European Countries

FEMS Fellowship, 280

Far East

Austrian Academy of Sciences MSc Course in Limnology and Wetlands Ecosystems, 121
Austrian Academy of Sciences Postgraduate Course in Limnology, 121
Institute of Limnology Postgraduate Training Fellowships, 122
University of Otago Dr Sulaiman Daud 125th Jubilee International Postgraduate Scholarship, 646

Indian Sub-Continent

Austrian Academy of Sciences MSc Course in Limnology and Wetlands Ecosystems, 121
Austrian Academy of Sciences Postgraduate Course in Limnology, 121
Institute of Limnology Postgraduate Training Fellowships, 122

New Zealand

University of Otago Masters Awards, 646
University of Otago PhD Scholarships, 646
University of Otago Prestigious PhD Scholarships, 647

South America

Austrian Academy of Sciences MSc Course in Limnology and Wetlands Ecosystems, 121
Austrian Academy of Sciences Postgraduate Course in Limnology, 121
Institute of Limnology Postgraduate Training Fellowships, 122

United Kingdom

FEMS Fellowship, 280
Llewellyn and Mary Williams Scholarship, 680
Mr and Mrs David Edward Memorial Award, 681
NERC Advanced Course Studentships, 459
NERC Research Studentships, 460
UWB Departmental Research Studentships, 681
UWB Research Studentships, 681

United States of America

Earthwatch Education Awards, 264
NRC Twinning Program, 455

West European Countries

FEMS Fellowship, 280
Llewellyn and Mary Williams Scholarship, 680
Mr and Mrs David Edward Memorial Award, 681
University of Otago Masters Awards, 646
University of Otago PhD Scholarships, 646
University of Otago Prestigious PhD Scholarships, 647
UWB Departmental Research Studentships, 681
UWB Research Studentships, 681

MICROBIOLOGY

Any Country

Abbott-ASM Lifetime Achievement Award, 76
ASBAH Research Grant, 103
ASM Graduate Microbiology Teaching Award, 76
Aventis Pharmaceuticals Award, 76
BBSRC Research Grants, 129
BD Award for Research in Clinical Microbiology, 77
bioMérieux Sonnenwirth Award for Leadership in Clinical Microbiology, 77
BMRP for Inflammatory Bowel Disease Grants, 160
Career development program, 395
CDU Senior Research Fellowship, 230
CDU Three Year Postdoctoral Fellowship, 230
Dade MicroScan Young Investigator Award, 77
Edmund Niles Huyck Preserve, Inc. Graduate and Postgraduate Grants, 266
EMBO Long-Term Fellowships in Molecular Biology, 275
EMBO Restart Fellowship, 275
EMBO Short-Term Fellowships in Molecular Biology, 275
EMBO Young Investigator, 276
ESRF Postdoctoral Fellowships, 277
Foulkes Foundation Fellowship, 282
Fungal Research Trust Travel Grants, 295
GlaxoSmithKline Collaborative Research Projects, 304
Health Research Board PhD training sites, 319
HRB Postdoctoral Research Fellowships, 320
HRB Project Grants-General, 320
HRB Research Project Grants North-South Co-operation, 320
HRB Summer Student Grants, 320
Hugh Kelly Fellowship, 519
ICGEB Long-Term Postdoctoral Fellowship Programme, 355
La Trobe University Postgraduate Scholarship, 390
Lister Institute Research Prizes, 400
LSRF Three Year Postdoctoral Fellowships, 399
Massey Doctoral Scholarship, 408
Meningitis Research Foundation Project Grant, 416
Meningitis Research Foundation Small Project Grant, 416
Meningitis Trust Research Award, 417
NARSAD Distinguished Investigator Awards, 434
NARSAD Independent Investigator Awards, 434
NARSAD Young Investigator Awards, 434
NERC Advanced Research Fellowships, 460
NERC Postdoctoral Research Fellowships, 460
NRC Research Associateships, 456
Predoctoral Fellowship Programme ICGEB International PhD Course, 356
Predoctoral Fellowship Programme ICGEB JNU PhD Course in Molecular Biology, 356
Procter and Gamble Award in Applied and Environmental Microbiology, 78
Queen Mary Research Studentships, 506
Rhodes University Postdoctoral Fellowship, 519
Royal Irish Academy Award in Microbiology, 539
Royal Irish Academy Award in Nutritional Sciences, 540
Services to Academia, 304

MND PhD Studentship Award, 426
Mr and Mrs David Edward Memorial Award, 681
PDS Research Project Grant, 487
PDS Studentships and Junior/Senior Fellows, 487
UWB Departmental Research Studentships, 681
UWB Research Studentships, 681
William P. VanWagenen Fellowship, 34

United States of America

AFAR Research Grants, 43
Alcohol Beverage Medical Research Foundation Research Project Grant, 14
Beeson Career Development Award, 43
Diversity Program in Neurosciences, 68
FPT Research Grants, 286
McMillan Doctoral Scholarships, 286
NIH Research Grants, 450
NRC Twinning Program, 455
NREF Research Fellowship, 34
NREF Young Clinician Investigator Award, 34
Postdoctoral Training Programme In Addiction and Mental Health, 223
Promotion of Doctoral Studies (PODS), 286
Spinal Cord Research Foundation Grants, 485
Washington University Chancellor's Graduate Fellowship Program for African Americans, 699

West European Countries

EMBO Award for Communication in the Life Sciences, 275
Mr and Mrs David Edward Memorial Award, 681
University of Otago Masters Awards, 646
University of Otago PhD Scholarships, 646
University of Otago Prestigious PhD Scholarships, 647
UWB Departmental Research Studentships, 681
UWB Research Studentships, 681

PARASITOLOGY

Any Country

BBSRC Research Grants, 129
BMRP for Inflammatory Bowel Disease Grants, 160
Edmund Niles Huyck Preserve, Inc. Graduate and Postgraduate Grants, 266
EMBO Long-Term Fellowships in Molecular Biology, 275
EMBO Restart Fellowship, 275
EMBO Short-Term Fellowships in Molecular Biology, 275
EMBO Young Investigator, 276
Health Research Board PhD training sites, 319
HRB Postdoctoral Research Fellowships, 320
HRB Project Grants-General, 320
HRB Research Project Grants North-South Co-operation, 320
HRB Summer Student Grants, 320
ICGEB Long-Term Postdoctoral Fellowship Programme, 355
Lister Institute Research Prizes, 400
Massey Doctoral Scholarship, 408
NERC Advanced Research Fellowships, 460
NERC Postdoctoral Research Fellowships, 460
Predoctoral Fellowship Programme ICGEB International PhD Course, 356
Predoctoral Fellowship Programme ICGEB JNU PhD Course in Molecular Biology, 356
Sigma Xi Grants-in-Aid of Research, 563
UFAW Animal Welfare Research Training Scholarships, 616
University of Dundee Research Awards, 629
University of Otago International Scholarships, 646
University of Stirling Research Studentships, 678
Wellcome Trust Awards, Fellowships and Studentships, 701

African Nations

EMBO World Programme Fellowships, 276

Australia

University of Otago Masters Awards, 646
University of Otago PhD Scholarships, 646
University of Otago Prestigious PhD Scholarships, 647

Canada

IDRC Doctoral Research Awards, 358

Caribbean Countries

EMBO World Programme Fellowships, 276

East European Countries

EMBO Award for Communication in the Life Sciences, 275
FEMS Fellowship, 280
Natural History Museum Sys-Resource, 461

Far East

EMBO World Programme Fellowships, 276
University of Otago Dr Sulaiman Daud 125th Jubilee International Postgraduate Scholarship, 646

Indian Sub-Continent

EMBO World Programme Fellowships, 276

Middle East

EMBO World Programme Fellowships, 276

New Zealand

University of Otago Masters Awards, 646
University of Otago PhD Scholarships, 646
University of Otago Prestigious PhD Scholarships, 647

South Africa

EMBO World Programme Fellowships, 276

South America

EMBO World Programme Fellowships, 276

United Kingdom

EMBO Award for Communication in the Life Sciences, 275
FEMS Fellowship, 280
Llewellyn and Mary Williams Scholarship, 680
Mr and Mrs David Edward Memorial Award, 681
NERC Advanced Course Studentships, 459
NERC Research Studentships, 460
University of Wales (Aberystwyth) Postgraduate Research Studentships, 680
UWB Departmental Research Studentships, 681
UWB Research Studentships, 681

West European Countries

EMBO Award for Communication in the Life Sciences, 275
FEMS Fellowship, 280
Karl-Enigk-Stipendium, 556
Llewellyn and Mary Williams Scholarship, 680
Mr and Mrs David Edward Memorial Award, 681
Natural History Museum Sys-Resource, 461
University of Otago Masters Awards, 646
University of Otago PhD Scholarships, 646
University of Otago Prestigious PhD Scholarships, 647
UWB Departmental Research Studentships, 681
UWB Research Studentships, 681

PHARMACOLOGY

Any Country

A J Clark Studentship, 154
AACR Scholar-in-Training Awards, 29

African Nations

Australia

British Commonwealth

Canada

Caribbean Countries

East European Countries

Far East

Indian Sub-Continent

Middle East

New Zealand

South Africa

South America

United Kingdom

United States of America

AFAR Research Grants, 43
AFPE Clinical Pharmacy Post-Pharm D Fellowships in the Biomedical Research Sciences Program, 45
AFPE Gateway Research Scholarship Program, 45
AFPE Predoctoral Fellowships, 45
Alcohol Beverage Medical Research Foundation Research Project Grant, 14
International Postgraduate Research Scholarships (IPRS), 676
MARC Faculty Predoctoral Fellowships, 449
Merck/AFAR Junior Investigator Award in Geriatric Clinical Pharmacology, 44
NIGMS Fellowship Awards for Minority Students, 449
NIGMS Fellowship Awards for Students With Disabilities, 450
NIGMS Postdoctoral Awards, 450
NIGMS Research Project Grants, 450
NIGMS Research Supplements for Underrepresented Minorities, 450
NIH Research Grants, 450
PhRMA Medical Student Research Fellowships, 492
PhRMAF Medical Student Fellowships, 492
PhRMAF Postdoctoral Fellowships in Health Outcomes Research, 492
PhRMAF Postdoctoral Fellowships in Informatics, 492
PhRMAF Postdoctoral Fellowships in Pharmaceutics, 493
PhRMAF Postdoctoral Fellowships in Pharmacology-Morphology, 493
PhRMAF Postdoctoral Fellowships in Pharmacology/Toxicology, 493
PhRMAF Predoctoral Fellowships in Health Outcomes Research, 494
PhRMAF Predoctoral Fellowships in Pharmaceutics, 494
PhRMAF Predoctoral Fellowships in Pharmacology/Toxicology, 494
PhRMAF Research Starter Grants in Health Outcomes Research, 495
PhRMAF Research Starter Grants in Informatics, 495
PhRMAF Research Starter Grants in Pharmaceutics, 495
PhRMAF Research Starter Grants in Pharmacology/Toxicology, 496
PhRMAF Sabbatical Fellowships in Health Outcomes Research, 496
PhRMAF Sabbatical Fellowships in Informatics, 496
PhRMAF Sabbatical Fellowships in Pharmaceutics, 496
PhRMAF Sabbatical Fellowships in Pharmacology/Toxicology, 497
Postdoctoral Training Programme in Addiction and Mental Health, 225

West European Countries

EMBO Award for Communication in the Life Sciences, 275
International Postgraduate Research Scholarships (IPRS), 676
Linacre College European Blaschko Visiting Research Scholarship, 655
Llewellyn and Mary Williams Scholarship, 680
Mr and Mrs David Edward Memorial Award, 681
University of Otago Masters Awards, 646
University of Otago PhD Scholarships, 646
University of Otago Prestigious PhD Scholarships, 647
UWB Departmental Research Studentships, 681

PHYSIOLOGY

Any Country

AHAF National Heart Foundation, 47
BBSRC Research Grants, 129
BMRP for Inflammatory Bowel Disease Grants, 160
Colt Foundation PhD Fellowship, 238
EMBO Long-Term Fellowships in Molecular Biology, 275
EMBO Restart Fellowship, 275
EMBO Short-Term Fellowships in Molecular Biology, 275
EMBO Young Investigator, 276
Health Research Board PhD training sites, 319
HRB Postdoctoral Research Fellowships, 320
HRB Project Grants-General, 320
HRB Research Project Grants North-South Co-operation, 320
HRB Summer Student Grants, 320
Lister Institute Research Prizes, 400
LSRF Three Year Postdoctoral Fellowships, 399
Massey Doctoral Scholarship, 408
Meningitis Research Foundation Project Grant, 416

Meningitis Research Foundation Small Project Grant, 416
MND Research Project and Pump Pricing Grants, 426
Mount Desert Island New Investigator Award, 427
Muscular Dystrophy Research Grants, 429
NARSAD Distinguished Investigator Awards, 434
NARSAD Independent Investigator Awards, 434
NARSAD Young Investigator Awards, 434
NERC Advanced Research Fellowships, 460
NERC Postdoctoral Research Fellowships, 460
NHF Grant, 446
NSCA Challenge Scholarship, 458
NSCA Power Systems Professional Scholarship, 458
NSCA Student Research Grant, 458
Queen Elizabeth the Queen Mother Fellowship Award, 514
Research into Ageing Prize Studentships, 515
Research into Ageing Programme Grants, 515
Rhodes University Postdoctoral Fellowship, 519
Savoy Foundation Post Doctoral and Clinical Research Fellowships, 555
Savoy Foundation Studentships, 555
Sigma Xi Grants-in-Aid of Research, 563
UFAW Animal Welfare Research Training Scholarships, 616
UFAW Research and Project Awards, 616
UFAW Small Project and Travel Awards, 616
UFAW Vacation Scholarships, 616
University of Bristol Postgraduate Scholarships, 619
University of Dundee Research Awards, 629
University of Manchester Research Studentships and Scholarships, 642
University of Otago International Scholarships, 646
Weizmann Institute of Science MSc Fellowships, 700
Weizmann Institute of Science PhD Fellowships, 700
Weizmann Institute of Science Postdoctoral Fellowships Program, 700
Wellcome Trust Awards, Fellowships and Studentships, 701

African Nations

EMBO World Programme Fellowships, 276

Australia

University of Otago Masters Awards, 646
University of Otago PhD Scholarships, 646
University of Otago Prestigious PhD Scholarships, 647

Canada

Alcohol Beverage Medical Research Foundation Research Project Grant, 14
Spinal Cord Research Foundation Grants, 485

Caribbean Countries

EMBO World Programme Fellowships, 276

East European Countries

EMBO Award for Communication in the Life Sciences, 275

Far East

EMBO World Programme Fellowships, 276
University of Otago Dr Sulaiman Daud 125th Jubilee International Postgraduate Scholarship, 646

Indian Sub-Continent

EMBO World Programme Fellowships, 276

Middle East

EMBO World Programme Fellowships, 276

New Zealand

University of Otago Masters Awards, 646
University of Otago PhD Scholarships, 646
University of Otago Prestigious PhD Scholarships, 647

Roche Research Foundation, 521
Royal Society of Chemistry Journals Grants for International Authors, 546
Royal Society of Chemistry Research Fund, 546
Royal Society of Chemistry Visits to Developing Countries, 547
Services to Academia, 304
Sigma Xi Grants-in-Aid of Research, 563
Société de Chimie Industrielle (American Section) Fellowship, 232
St Hilda's College E P Abraham Junior Research Fellowship, 669
University of Bristol Postgraduate Scholarships, 619
University of Dundee Research Awards, 629
University of Edinburgh College of Science and Engineering Scholarship, 631
University of Glasgow Postgraduate Research Scholarships, 634
University of Manchester Research Studentships and Scholarships, 642
University of Otago International Scholarships, 646
University of Western Ontario Senior Visiting Fellowship, 688
USC College Dissertation Fellowship, 677
USC College of Letters, Arts and Sciences Merit Award, 677
Weizmann Institute of Science MSc Fellowships, 700
Weizmann Institute of Science PhD Fellowships, 700
Weizmann Institute of Science Postdoctoral Fellowships Program, 700
Woods Hole Oceanographic Institution Postdoctoral Fellowships in Ocean Science and Engineering, 710
Woods Hole Oceanographic Institution/NOAA Co-operative Institute for Climate and Ocean Research Postdoctoral Fellowship, 710
World Universities Network (WUN) Scholarship Scheme, 677

African Nations

ABCCF Student Grant, 91
Corday-Morgan Memorial Fund, 546
International Postgraduate Research Scholarships (IPRS), 676
Lindemann Trust Fellowships, 271
TWAS Prizes, 601
TWAS Prizes to Young Scientists in Developing Countries, 601
TWAS Research Grants, 601
TWOWS Postgraduate Fellowships for Women from Sub-Saharan Africa and Least Developed Countries (LDC) at Centres of Excellence in the South, 602

Australia

Corday-Morgan Memorial Fund, 546
Fulbright Postgraduate Student Award for Science and Engineering, 120
Lindemann Trust Fellowships, 271
University of Otago Masters Awards, 646
University of Otago PhD Scholarships, 646
University of Otago Prestigious PhD Scholarships, 647
University of Western Sydney Postgraduate Research Award (UW-SPRA), 689
Wingate Scholarships, 704

British Commonwealth

British (General) Fellowship, 511
Corday-Morgan Memorial Fund, 546
International Postgraduate Research Scholarships (IPRS), 676
Lindemann Trust Fellowships, 271
Magdalen College Perkins Research Studentship, 657
Wingate Scholarships, 704

Canada

AWWA Larson Aquatic Research Support, 87
CIC Award for Environmental Improvement, 232
CIC Catalysis Award, 232
CIC Macromolecular Science and Engineering Lecture Award, 232
CIC Medal, 232
CIC Montreal Medal, 232
CIC Pestcon Graduate Scholarship, 233
CIC Union Carbide Award for Chemical Education, 233
Corday-Morgan Memorial Fund, 546
Cottrell College Science Awards, 514

Cottrell Scholars Awards, 514
International Postgraduate Research Scholarships (IPRS), 676
Lindemann Trust Fellowships, 271
Research Corporation (USA) Research Opportunity Awards, 514
Wingate Scholarships, 704

Caribbean Countries

International Postgraduate Research Scholarships (IPRS), 676
TWAS Prizes, 601
TWAS Prizes to Young Scientists in Developing Countries, 601
TWAS Research Grants, 601

East European Countries

EPSRC Doctoral Training Grants (DTGs), 269
International Postgraduate Research Scholarships (IPRS), 676

Far East

Corday-Morgan Memorial Fund, 546
International Postgraduate Research Scholarships (IPRS), 676
Lindemann Trust Fellowships, 271
Swiss Federal Institute of Technology Scholarships, 598
TWAS Prizes, 601
TWAS Prizes to Young Scientists in Developing Countries, 601
TWAS Research Grants, 601

Indian Sub-Continent

Corday-Morgan Memorial Fund, 546
International Postgraduate Research Scholarships (IPRS), 676
Lindemann Trust Fellowships, 271
TWAS Prizes, 601
TWAS Prizes to Young Scientists in Developing Countries, 601
TWAS Research Grants, 601
Wingate Scholarships, 704

Middle East

ABCCF Student Grant, 91
International Postgraduate Research Scholarships (IPRS), 676
TWAS Prizes, 601
TWAS Prizes to Young Scientists in Developing Countries, 601
TWAS Research Grants, 601

New Zealand

Corday-Morgan Memorial Fund, 546
Lindemann Trust Fellowships, 271
University of Otago Masters Awards, 646
University of Otago PhD Scholarships, 646
University of Otago Prestigious PhD Scholarships, 647
University of Western Sydney Postgraduate Research Award (UW-SPRA), 689
Wingate Scholarships, 704

South Africa

Corday-Morgan Memorial Fund, 546
Henderson Postgraduate Scholarships, 518
International Postgraduate Research Scholarships (IPRS), 676
Lindemann Trust Fellowships, 271
TWAS Prizes, 601
TWAS Prizes to Young Scientists in Developing Countries, 601
TWAS Research Grants, 601
Wingate Scholarships, 704

South America

AWWA Larson Aquatic Research Support, 87
International Postgraduate Research Scholarships (IPRS), 676
TWAS Prizes, 601
TWAS Prizes to Young Scientists in Developing Countries, 601
TWAS Research Grants, 601

United Kingdom

Alzheimers Society Research Grants, 22
British (General) Fellowship, 511

Corday-Morgan Memorial Fund, 546
EPSRC Doctoral Training Grants (DTGs), 269
EPSRC Grant for School of Physical Sciences, 635
ESRF Thesis Studentships, 277
Hallam Studentships, 558
International Postgraduate Research Scholarships (IPRS), 676
Lindemann Trust Fellowships, 271
Mr and Mrs David Edward Memorial Award, 681
Sheffield Hallam University Research Studentships, 558
Swiss Federal Institute of Technology Scholarships, 598
UWB Departmental Research Studentships, 681
Wingate Scholarships, 704

United States of America

ACS/PRF Type G 'Starter' Grants
AFAR Research Grants, 43
Army Research Laboratory Postdoctoral Fellowship Program, 75
AWWA Larson Aquatic Research Support, 87
Cottrell College Science Awards, 514
Cottrell Scholars Awards, 514
Fannie and John Hertz Foundation Fellowships, 280
Fulbright Senior Specialists Program, 245
International Postgraduate Research Scholarships (IPRS), 676
MARC Faculty Predoctoral Fellowships, 449
McDonnell Center Astronaut Fellowships in the Space Sciences, 408
NIGMS Fellowship Awards for Minority Students, 449
NIGMS Fellowship Awards for Students With Disabilities, 450
NIGMS Postdoctoral Awards, 450
NIGMS Research Project Grants, 450
NIGMS Research Supplements for Underrepresented Minorities, 450
NRC Twinning Program, 455
Research Corporation (USA) Research Opportunity Awards, 514
Swiss Federal Institute of Technology Scholarships, 598
Washington University Chancellor's Graduate Fellowship Program for African Americans, 699
Winston Churchill Scholarship, 705

West European Countries

EPSRC Doctoral Training Grants (DTGs), 269
EPSRC Grant for School of Physical Sciences, 635
ESRF Thesis Studentships, 277
Hallam Studentships, 558
International Postgraduate Research Scholarships (IPRS), 676
Janson Johan Helmich Scholarships and Travel Grants, 376
Mr and Mrs David Edward Memorial Award, 681
Queen's College Florey EPA Scholarship, 662
Sheffield Hallam University Research Studentships, 558
University of Otago Masters Awards, 646
University of Otago PhD Scholarships, 646
University of Otago Prestigious PhD Scholarships, 647
UWB Departmental Research Studentships, 681
Wingate Scholarships, 704

ANALYTICAL CHEMISTRY

Any Country

BP/RSE Research Fellowships, 547
CDU Senior Research Fellowship, 230
CDU Three Year Postdoctoral Fellowship, 230
GlaxoSmithKline Collaborative Research Projects, 304
JILA Postdoctoral Research Associateship and Visiting Fellowships, 379
Massey Doctoral Scholarship, 408
NRC Research Associateships, 456
Queen Mary Research Studentships, 506
Rhodes University Postdoctoral Fellowship, 519
Services to Academia, 304
Sigma Xi Grants-in-Aid of Research, 563
Teagasc Walsh Fellowships, 599
University of Bristol Postgraduate Scholarships, 619
University of Manchester Research Studentships and Scholarships, 642

African Nations

IFS Research Grant, 360
International Postgraduate Research Scholarships (IPRS), 676

Australia

Fulbright Postgraduate Student Award for Science and Engineering, 120
University of Western Sydney Postgraduate Research Award (UW-SPRA), 689

British Commonwealth

Hector and Elizabeth Catling Bursary, 155
International Postgraduate Research Scholarships (IPRS), 676

Canada

AWWA Larson Aquatic Research Support, 87
CIC Catalysis Award, 232
CSCT Norman and Marion Bright Memorial Award, 211
International Postgraduate Research Scholarships (IPRS), 676

Caribbean Countries

IFS Research Grant, 360
International Postgraduate Research Scholarships (IPRS), 676

East European Countries

International Postgraduate Research Scholarships (IPRS), 676

Far East

IFS Research Grant, 360
International Postgraduate Research Scholarships (IPRS), 676

Indian Sub-Continent

IFS Research Grant, 360
International Postgraduate Research Scholarships (IPRS), 676

Middle East

IFS Research Grant, 360
International Postgraduate Research Scholarships (IPRS), 676

New Zealand

University of Western Sydney Postgraduate Research Award (UW-SPRA), 689

South Africa

IFS Research Grant, 360
International Postgraduate Research Scholarships (IPRS), 676

South America

AWWA Larson Aquatic Research Support, 87
IFS Research Grant, 360
International Postgraduate Research Scholarships (IPRS), 676

United Kingdom

Alzheimers Society Research Grants, 22
Hector and Elizabeth Catling Bursary, 155
International Postgraduate Research Scholarships (IPRS), 676
Mr and Mrs David Edward Memorial Award, 681
UWB Departmental Research Studentships, 681
UWB Research Studentships, 681

United States of America

American Nuclear Society Undergraduate Scholarship, 60
AWWA Larson Aquatic Research Support, 87
International Postgraduate Research Scholarships (IPRS), 676
James R Vogt Scholarship, 102
NRC Twinning Program, 455
Washington University Chancellor's Graduate Fellowship Program for African Americans, 699

West European Countries

International Postgraduate Research Scholarships (IPRS), 676
Mr and Mrs David Edward Memorial Award, 681
UWB Departmental Research Studentships, 681
UWB Research Studentships, 681

INORGANIC CHEMISTRY

Any Country

ACS/PRF Type AC Grants, 35
ACS/PRF Type B Grants, 36
BP/RSE Research Fellowships, 547
CDU Senior Research Fellowship, 230
CDU Three Year Postdoctoral Fellowship, 230
GlaxoSmithKline Collaborative Research Projects, 304
JILA Postdoctoral Research Associateship and Visiting Fellowships, 379
Massey Doctoral Scholarship, 408
NRC Research Associateships, 456
Queen Mary Research Studentships, 506
Rhodes University Postdoctoral Fellowship, 519
Services to Academia, 304
Sigma Xi Grants-in-Aid of Research, 563
University of Bristol Postgraduate Scholarships, 619
University of Dundee Research Awards, 629
University of Manchester Research Studentships and Scholarships, 642
Weizmann Institute of Science MSc Fellowships, 700
Weizmann Institute of Science PhD Fellowships, 700
Weizmann Institute of Science Postdoctoral Fellowships Program, 700

African Nations

International Postgraduate Research Scholarships (IPRS), 676

Australia

Fulbright Postgraduate Student Award for Science and Engineering, 120

British Commonwealth

Hector and Elizabeth Catling Bursary, 155
International Postgraduate Research Scholarships (IPRS), 676

Canada

International Postgraduate Research Scholarships (IPRS), 676

Caribbean Countries

International Postgraduate Research Scholarships (IPRS), 676

East European Countries

International Postgraduate Research Scholarships (IPRS), 676

Far East

International Postgraduate Research Scholarships (IPRS), 676

Indian Sub-Continent

International Postgraduate Research Scholarships (IPRS), 676

Middle East

International Postgraduate Research Scholarships (IPRS), 676

South Africa

International Postgraduate Research Scholarships (IPRS), 676

South America

International Postgraduate Research Scholarships (IPRS), 676

United Kingdom

Alzheimers Society Research Grants, 22
Hector and Elizabeth Catling Bursary, 155

International Postgraduate Research Scholarships (IPRS), 676
Mr and Mrs David Edward Memorial Award, 681
UWB Departmental Research Studentships, 681
UWB Research Studentships, 681

United States of America

ACS/PRF Type G 'Starter' Grants
International Postgraduate Research Scholarships (IPRS), 676
NRC Twinning Program, 455
Washington University Chancellor's Graduate Fellowship Program for African Americans, 699

West European Countries

International Postgraduate Research Scholarships (IPRS), 676
Mr and Mrs David Edward Memorial Award, 681
UWB Departmental Research Studentships, 681
UWB Research Studentships, 681

ORGANIC CHEMISTRY

Any Country

ACS/PRF Type AC Grants, 35
ACS/PRF Type B Grants, 36
BBSRC Research Grants, 129
BP/RSE Research Fellowships, 547
CQU Postgraduate Research Award, 224
GlaxoSmithKline Collaborative Research Projects, 304
Heinrich Wieland Prize, 388
Ichikizaki Fund for Young Chemists, 212
JILA Postdoctoral Research Associateship and Visiting Fellowships, 379
Linacre College EPA Cephalosporin Junior Research Fellowships, 655
Massey Doctoral Scholarship, 408
Novartis Foundation Symposium Bursaries, 475
NRC Research Associateships, 456
Queen Mary Research Studentships, 506
Rhodes University Postdoctoral Fellowship, 519
Services to Academia, 304
Sigma Xi Grants-In-Aid of Research, 563
University of Bristol Postgraduate Scholarships, 619
University of Dundee Research Awards, 629
University of Manchester Research Studentships and Scholarships, 642
Weizmann Institute of Science MSc Fellowships, 700
Weizmann Institute of Science PhD Fellowships, 700
Weizmann Institute of Science Postdoctoral Fellowships Program, 700

African Nations

IFS Research Grant, 360
International Postgraduate Research Scholarships (IPRS), 676

Australia

Fulbright Postgraduate Student Award for Science and Engineering, 120
University of Western Sydney Postgraduate Research Award (UWSPRA), 689

British Commonwealth

International Postgraduate Research Scholarships (IPRS), 676

Canada

AWWA Larson Aquatic Research Support, 87
International Postgraduate Research Scholarships (IPRS), 676

Caribbean Countries

IFS Research Grant, 360
International Postgraduate Research Scholarships (IPRS), 676

East European Countries

International Postgraduate Research Scholarships (IPRS), 676

Far East

IFS Research Grant, 360
International Postgraduate Research Scholarships (IPRS), 676

Indian Sub-Continent

IFS Research Grant, 360
International Postgraduate Research Scholarships (IPRS), 676

Middle East

IFS Research Grant, 360
International Postgraduate Research Scholarships (IPRS), 676

New Zealand

University of Western Sydney Postgraduate Research Award (UW-SPRA), 689

South Africa

IFS Research Grant, 360
International Postgraduate Research Scholarships (IPRS), 676

South America

AWWA Larson Aquatic Research Support, 87
IFS Research Grant, 360
International Postgraduate Research Scholarships (IPRS), 676

United Kingdom

Alzheimers Society Research Grants, 22
Hickinbottom/Briggs Fellowship, 546
International Postgraduate Research Scholarships (IPRS), 676
Mr and Mrs David Edward Memorial Award, 681
UWB Departmental Research Studentships, 681
UWB Research Studentships, 681

United States of America

ACS/PRF Type G 'Starter' Grants
AWWA Larson Aquatic Research Support, 87
International Postgraduate Research Scholarships (IPRS), 676
NRC Twinning Program, 455
Washington University Chancellor's Graduate Fellowship Program for African Americans, 699

West European Countries

International Postgraduate Research Scholarships (IPRS), 676
Mr and Mrs David Edward Memorial Award, 681
UWB Departmental Research Studentships, 681
UWB Research Studentships, 681

PHYSICAL CHEMISTRY

Any Country

ACS/PRF Type AC Grants, 35
ACS/PRF Type B Grants, 36
BP/RSE Research Fellowships, 547
GlaxoSmithKline Collaborative Research Projects, 304
JILA Postdoctoral Research Associateship and Visiting Fellowships, 379
Massey Doctoral Scholarship, 408
NRC Research Associateships, 456
Queen Mary Research Studentships, 506
Rhodes University Postdoctoral Fellowship, 519
Services to Academia, 304
Sigma Xi Grants-in-Aid of Research, 563
University of Bristol Postgraduate Scholarships, 619
University of Dundee Research Awards, 629
University of Manchester Research Studentships and Scholarships, 642

Weizmann Institute of Science MSc Fellowships, 700
Weizmann Institute of Science PhD Fellowships, 700
Weizmann Institute of Science Postdoctoral Fellowships Program, 700
Welch Foundation Scholarship, 371

African Nations

International Postgraduate Research Scholarships (IPRS), 676

Australia

Fulbright Postgraduate Student Award for Science and Engineering, 120

British Commonwealth

International Postgraduate Research Scholarships (IPRS), 676

Canada

International Postgraduate Research Scholarships (IPRS), 676

Caribbean Countries

International Postgraduate Research Scholarships (IPRS), 676

East European Countries

International Postgraduate Research Scholarships (IPRS), 676

Far East

International Postgraduate Research Scholarships (IPRS), 676

Indian Sub-Continent

International Postgraduate Research Scholarships (IPRS), 676

Middle East

International Postgraduate Research Scholarships (IPRS), 676

South Africa

International Postgraduate Research Scholarships (IPRS), 676

South America

International Postgraduate Research Scholarships (IPRS), 676

United Kingdom

Alzheimers Society Research Grants, 22
International Postgraduate Research Scholarships (IPRS), 676
Mr and Mrs David Edward Memorial Award, 681
UWB Departmental Research Studentships, 681
UWB Research Studentships, 681

United States of America

ACS/PRF Type G 'Starter' Grants
International Postgraduate Research Scholarships (IPRS), 676
NRC Twinning Program, 455
PhRMAF Research Starter Grants in Pharmaceutics, 495
Washington University Chancellor's Graduate Fellowship Program for African Americans, 699

West European Countries

International Postgraduate Research Scholarships (IPRS), 676
Mr and Mrs David Edward Memorial Award, 681
UWB Departmental Research Studentships, 681
UWB Research Studentships, 681

EARTH AND GEOLOGICAL SCIENCES

Any Country

AAC Research Grants, 25
ACS/PRF Scientific Education Grants, 35
ACS/PRF Type AC Grants, 35
ACS/PRF Type B Grants, 36

American Association of Petroleum Geologists Foundation Grants-in-Aid, 35
ASCSA Research Fellow in Environmental Studies, 71
ASCSA Research Fellow in Geoarchaeology, 71
Association for Women in Science Educational Foundation Predoctoral Awards, 104
BFWG: Johnstone and Florence Stoney Studentship, 143
Canadian Natural Resources Limited Graduate Scholarship, 620
CDU Senior Research Fellowship, 230
CDU Three Year Postdoctoral Fellowship, 230
Downing College Research Fellowships, 623
Earthwatch Field Research Grants, 264
ESRF Postdoctoral Fellowships, 277
Horton (Hydrology) Research Grant, 46
HRF Graduate Fellowships, 328
Hudson River Graduate Fellowships, 328
L S B Leakey Foundation General Research Grant, 389
Linacre College Applied Materials Scholarships, 655
McDonnell Graduate Fellowship in the Space Sciences, 408
NCAR Postdoctoral Appointments in the Advanced Study Program, 439
NERC Advanced Research Fellowships, 460
NERC Postdoctoral Research Fellowships, 460
NSF Division of Earth Sciences, 457
Queen Mary Research Studentships, 506
SEG Scholarships, 587
Sigma Xi Grants-in-Aid of Research, 563
Smithsonian Institution Graduate Student Fellowships, 567
Smithsonian Institution Senior Fellowships, 568
Trent R Dames and William W Moore Fellowship, 79
University of Bristol Postgraduate Scholarships, 619
University of Dundee Research Awards, 629
University of Glasgow Postgraduate Research Scholarships, 634
University of Manchester Research Studentships and Scholarships, 642
University of Otago International Scholarships, 646
University of Stirling Research Studentships, 678
University of Western Ontario Senior Visiting Fellowship, 688
USC College Dissertation Fellowship, 677
USC College of Letters, Arts and Sciences Merit Award, 677
W Frank Blair Award, 233
Weizmann Institute of Science MSc Fellowships, 700
Weizmann Institute of Science PhD Fellowships, 700
Weizmann Institute of Science Postdoctoral Fellowships Program, 700
Woods Hole Oceanographic Institution Geophysical Fluid Dynamics (GFD) Fellowships, 709
Woods Hole Oceanographic Institution Postdoctoral Fellowships in Ocean Science and Engineering, 710
Woods Hole Oceanographic Institution/NOAA Co-operative Institute for Climate and Ocean Research Postdoctoral Fellowship, 710
World Universities Network (WUN) Scholarship Scheme, 677

African Nations

ABCCF Student Grant, 91
International Postgraduate Research Scholarships (IPRS), 676
Postgraduate Studies in Physical Land Resources Scholarship, 356
TWAS Fellowship for Postdoctoral Research and Advanced Training, 600
TWAS Grants for Scientific Meetings in Developing Countries, 600
TWAS Prizes to Young Scientists in Developing Countries, 601
TWOWS Postgraduate Fellowships for Women from Sub-Saharan Africa and Least Developed Countries (LDC) at Centres of Excellence in the South, 602

Australia

C T Taylor Studentship for PhD Study, 173
Fulbright Postgraduate Student Award for Science and Engineering, 120
University of Otago PhD Scholarships, 646
University of Otago Prestigious PhD Scholarships, 647
University of Western Sydney Postgraduate Research Award (UW-SPRA), 689
Wingate Scholarships, 704

British Commonwealth

International Postgraduate Research Scholarships (IPRS), 676
Postgraduate Studies in Physical Land Resources Scholarship, 356
Wingate Scholarships, 704

Canada

C T Taylor Studentship for PhD Study, 173
GSA Research Grants, 296
International Postgraduate Research Scholarships (IPRS), 676
Office of Critical Infrastructure Protection and Emergency Preparedness (EPC) Research Fellowship in Honour of Stuart Nesbitt White, 110
Wingate Scholarships, 704

Caribbean Countries

International Postgraduate Research Scholarships (IPRS), 676
Postgraduate Studies in Physical Land Resources Scholarship, 356
TWAS Fellowship for Postdoctoral Research and Advanced Training, 600
TWAS Grants for Scientific Meetings in Developing Countries, 600
TWAS Prizes to Young Scientists in Developing Countries, 601

East European Countries

International Postgraduate Research Scholarships (IPRS), 676
Natural History Museum Sys-Resource, 461

Far East

International Postgraduate Research Scholarships (IPRS), 676
Postgraduate Studies in Physical Land Resources Scholarship, 356
Swiss Federal Institute of Technology Scholarships, 598
TWAS Fellowship for Postdoctoral Research and Advanced Training, 600
TWAS Grants for Scientific Meetings in Developing Countries, 600
TWAS Prizes to Young Scientists in Developing Countries, 601
University of Otago Dr Sulaiman Daud 125th Jubilee International Postgraduate Scholarship, 646

Indian Sub-Continent

International Postgraduate Research Scholarships (IPRS), 676
Postgraduate Studies in Physical Land Resources Scholarship, 356
TWAS Fellowship for Postdoctoral Research and Advanced Training, 600
TWAS Grants for Scientific Meetings in Developing Countries, 600
TWAS Prizes to Young Scientists in Developing Countries, 601
Wingate Scholarships, 704

Middle East

ABCCF Student Grant, 91
International Postgraduate Research Scholarships (IPRS), 676
Postgraduate Studies in Physical Land Resources Scholarship, 356
TWAS Fellowship for Postdoctoral Research and Advanced Training, 600
TWAS Grants for Scientific Meetings in Developing Countries, 600
TWAS Prizes to Young Scientists in Developing Countries, 601

New Zealand

C T Taylor Studentship for PhD Study, 173
University of Otago PhD Scholarships, 646
University of Otago Prestigious PhD Scholarships, 647
University of Western Sydney Postgraduate Research Award (UW-SPRA), 689
Wingate Scholarships, 704

South Africa

Henderson Postgraduate Scholarships, 518
International Postgraduate Research Scholarships (IPRS), 676
Postgraduate Studies in Physical Land Resources Scholarship, 356
TWAS Fellowship for Postdoctoral Research and Advanced Training, 600
TWAS Grants for Scientific Meetings in Developing Countries, 600

Mr and Mrs David Edward Memorial Award, 681
NERC Advanced Course Studentships, 459
NERC Research Studentships, 460
UWB Departmental Research Studentships, 681
UWB Research Studentships, 681

United States of America

ACS/PRF Type G 'Starter' Grants
Fannie and John Hertz Foundation Fellowships, 280
GSA Research Grants, 296
International Postgraduate Research Scholarships (IPRS), 676
NRC Twinning Program, 455
Washington University Chancellor's Graduate Fellowship Program for African Americans, 699

West European Countries

Albert Maucher Prize, 256
International Postgraduate Research Scholarships (IPRS), 676
Mr and Mrs David Edward Memorial Award, 681
Natural History Museum Sys-Resource, 461
UWB Departmental Research Studentships, 681
UWB Research Studentships, 681

GEOGRAPHY (SCIENTIFIC)

Any Country

AAG Dissertation Research Grants, 104
AAG General Research Fund, 104
CEPS Fellowship, 433
Earthwatch Field Research Grants, 264
Hugh Kelly Fellowship, 519
Massey Doctoral Scholarship, 408
Monica Cole Research Grant, 534
NERC Advanced Research Fellowships, 460
NERC Postdoctoral Research Fellowships, 460
Queen Mary Research Studentships, 506
Sigma Xi Grants-in-Aid of Research, 563
Thomas Holloway Research Studentship, 536
University of Bristol Postgraduate Scholarships, 619
University of Dundee Research Awards, 629
University of Edinburgh College of Science and Engineering Scholarship, 631
University of Manchester Research Studentships and Scholarships, 642
University of Stirling Research Studentships, 678
Violet Cressey-Marcks Fisher Travel Scholarship, 535
Warren Nystrom Fund Awards, 105
Weizmann Institute of Science Postdoctoral Fellowships Program, 700

African Nations

International Postgraduate Research Scholarships (IPRS), 676
Postgraduate Studies in Physical Land Resources Scholarship, 356

Australia

Fulbright Postgraduate Student Award for Science and Engineering, 120

British Commonwealth

International Postgraduate Research Scholarships (IPRS), 676
Postgraduate Studies in Physical Land Resources Scholarship, 356

Canada

Geomatics for Informed Decisions (GEOIDE) Networks of Centres of Excellence Graduate Supplement Program, 576
GSA Research Grants, 296
IDRC Doctoral Research Awards, 358
International Postgraduate Research Scholarships (IPRS), 676

Caribbean Countries

International Postgraduate Research Scholarships (IPRS), 676
Postgraduate Studies in Physical Land Resources Scholarship, 356

East European Countries

International Postgraduate Research Scholarships (IPRS), 676
Natural History Museum Sys-Resource, 461

Far East

International Postgraduate Research Scholarships (IPRS), 676
Postgraduate Studies in Physical Land Resources Scholarship, 356

Indian Sub-Continent

International Postgraduate Research Scholarships (IPRS), 676
Postgraduate Studies in Physical Land Resources Scholarship, 356

Middle East

International Postgraduate Research Scholarships (IPRS), 676
Postgraduate Studies in Physical Land Resources Scholarship, 356

South Africa

International Postgraduate Research Scholarships (IPRS), 676
Postgraduate Studies in Physical Land Resources Scholarship, 356

South America

International Postgraduate Research Scholarships (IPRS), 676
Postgraduate Studies in Physical Land Resources Scholarship, 356

United Kingdom

International Postgraduate Research Scholarships (IPRS), 676
NERC Advanced Course Studentships, 459
NERC Research Studentships, 460
Polish Government Postgraduate Scholarships Scheme, 501
University of Wales (Aberystwyth) Postgraduate Research Studentships, 680

United States of America

GSA Research Grants, 296
International Postgraduate Research Scholarships (IPRS), 676
NRC Twinning Program, 455

West European Countries

International Postgraduate Research Scholarships (IPRS), 676
Natural History Museum Sys-Resource, 461

GEOLOGY

Any Country

Acadia Graduate Teaching Assistantships, 6
ACS/PRF Scientific Education Grants, 35
ACS/PRF Type AC Grants, 35
Alberta Research Council Scholarship, 620
American Association of Petroleum Geologists Foundation Grants-in-Aid, 35
ASCSA Research Fellow in Geoarchaeology, 71
BP/RSE Research Fellowships, 547
CEPS Fellowship, 433
Claude Harris Leon Foundation Postdoctoral Fellowship Award, 238
Earthwatch Field Research Grants, 264
G Vernon Hobson Bequest, 345
Gladys W Cole Memorial Research Award, 296
Hugh Kelly Fellowship, 519
L S B Leakey Foundation General Research Grant, 389
NERC Advanced Research Fellowships, 460
NERC Postdoctoral Research Fellowships, 460
Queen Mary Research Studentships, 506
Rhodes University Postdoctoral Fellowship, 519
Sigma Xi Grants-in-Aid of Research, 563
Thomas Holloway Research Studentship, 536
University of Bristol Postgraduate Scholarships, 619
University of Edinburgh College of Science and Engineering Scholarship, 631

University of Manchester Research Studentships and Scholarships, 642

University of Stirling Research Studentships, 678

Weizmann Institute of Science Postdoctoral Fellowships Program, 700

African Nations

BP - FCO Chevening - Leeds University Scholarships, 638
International Postgraduate Research Scholarships (IPRS), 676
Lindemann Trust Fellowships, 271
Postgraduate Studies in Physical Land Resources Scholarship, 356
Shell centenary chevening scholarships, 640
Shell Centenary Scholarships, 640

Australia

Edgar Pam Fellowship, 345
Fulbright Postgraduate Student Award for Science and Engineering, 120
Lindemann Trust Fellowships, 271

British Commonwealth

BP - FCO Chevening - Leeds University Scholarships, 638
Hector and Elizabeth Catling Bursary, 155
International Postgraduate Research Scholarships (IPRS), 676
Lindemann Trust Fellowships, 271
Postgraduate Studies in Physical Land Resources Scholarship, 356
Shell centenary chevening scholarships, 640
Shell Centenary Scholarships, 640

Canada

Edgar Pam Fellowship, 345
GSA Research Grants, 296
IDRC Doctoral Research Awards, 358
International Postgraduate Research Scholarships (IPRS), 676
Lindemann Trust Fellowships, 271

Caribbean Countries

BP - FCO Chevening - Leeds University Scholarships, 638
International Postgraduate Research Scholarships (IPRS), 676
Postgraduate Studies in Physical Land Resources Scholarship, 356
Shell centenary chevening scholarships, 640
Shell Centenary Scholarships, 640

East European Countries

International Postgraduate Research Scholarships (IPRS), 676
Natural History Museum Sys-Resource, 461

Far East

BP - FCO Chevening - Leeds University Scholarships, 638
International Postgraduate Research Scholarships (IPRS), 676
Lindemann Trust Fellowships, 271
Postgraduate Studies in Physical Land Resources Scholarship, 356
Shell centenary chevening scholarships, 640
Shell Centenary Scholarships, 640
Stephen and Anna Hui Fellowship, 333

Indian Sub-Continent

BP - FCO Chevening - Leeds University Scholarships, 638
International Postgraduate Research Scholarships (IPRS), 676
Lindemann Trust Fellowships, 271
Postgraduate Studies in Physical Land Resources Scholarship, 356
Shell centenary chevening scholarships, 640
Shell Centenary Scholarships, 640

Middle East

BP - FCO Chevening - Leeds University Scholarships, 638
International Postgraduate Research Scholarships (IPRS), 676
Postgraduate Studies in Physical Land Resources Scholarship, 356
Shell centenary chevening scholarships, 640
Shell Centenary Scholarships, 640

New Zealand

Edgar Pam Fellowship, 345
Lindemann Trust Fellowships, 271

South Africa

BP - FCO Chevening - Leeds University Scholarships, 638
Edgar Pam Fellowship, 345
International Postgraduate Research Scholarships (IPRS), 676
Lindemann Trust Fellowships, 271
Postgraduate Studies in Physical Land Resources Scholarship, 356
Shell centenary chevening scholarships, 640
Shell Centenary Scholarships, 640

South America

BP - FCO Chevening - Leeds University Scholarships, 638
International Postgraduate Research Scholarships (IPRS), 676
Postgraduate Studies in Physical Land Resources Scholarship, 356
Shell centenary chevening scholarships, 640
Shell Centenary Scholarships, 640

United Kingdom

Edgar Pam Fellowship, 345
Hector and Elizabeth Catling Bursary, 155
International Postgraduate Research Scholarships (IPRS), 676
Lindemann Trust Fellowships, 271
Mr and Mrs David Edward Memorial Award, 681
NERC Advanced Course Studentships, 459
NERC Research Studentships, 460
Polish Government Postgraduate Scholarships Scheme, 501
University of Wales (Aberystwyth) Postgraduate Research Studentships, 680

United States of America

ACS/PRF Type G 'Starter' Grants
Fannie and John Hertz Foundation Fellowships, 280
GSA Research Grants, 296
International Postgraduate Research Scholarships (IPRS), 676
Norwegian Thanksgiving Fund Scholarship, 474
NRC Twinning Program, 455
Washington University Chancellor's Graduate Fellowship Program for African Americans, 699

West European Countries

Albert Maucher Prize, 256
International Postgraduate Research Scholarships (IPRS), 676
Mr and Mrs David Edward Memorial Award, 681
Natural History Museum Sys-Resource, 461

MINERALOGY AND CRYSTALLOGRAPHY

Any Country

BP/RSE Research Fellowships, 547
ESRF Postdoctoral Fellowships, 277
International School of Crystallography Grants, 367
L S B Leakey Foundation General Research Grant, 389
Queen Mary Research Studentships, 506
Rhodes University Postdoctoral Fellowship, 519
Sigma Xi Grants-in-Aid of Research, 563
University of Bristol Postgraduate Scholarships, 619
University of Manchester Research Studentships and Scholarships, 642
Weizmann Institute of Science MSc Fellowships, 700
Weizmann Institute of Science PhD Fellowships, 700
Weizmann Institute of Science Postdoctoral Fellowships Program, 700

African Nations

International Postgraduate Research Scholarships (IPRS), 676

Australia

Fulbright Postgraduate Student Award for Science and Engineering, 120
University of Western Sydney Postgraduate Research Award (UW-SPRA), 689

British Commonwealth

Hector and Elizabeth Catling Bursary, 155
International Postgraduate Research Scholarships (IPRS), 676

Canada

GSA Research Grants, 296
International Postgraduate Research Scholarships (IPRS), 676

Caribbean Countries

International Postgraduate Research Scholarships (IPRS), 676

East European Countries

International Postgraduate Research Scholarships (IPRS), 676
Natural History Museum Sys-Resource, 461

Far East

International Postgraduate Research Scholarships (IPRS), 676
Stephen and Anna Hui Fellowship, 333

Indian Sub-Continent

International Postgraduate Research Scholarships (IPRS), 676

Middle East

International Postgraduate Research Scholarships (IPRS), 676

New Zealand

University of Western Sydney Postgraduate Research Award (UW-SPRA), 689

South Africa

International Postgraduate Research Scholarships (IPRS), 676

South America

International Postgraduate Research Scholarships (IPRS), 676

United Kingdom

ESRF Thesis Studentships, 277
Hector and Elizabeth Catling Bursary, 155
International Postgraduate Research Scholarships (IPRS), 676
Polish Government Postgraduate Scholarships Scheme, 501

United States of America

Fannie and John Hertz Foundation Fellowships, 280
GSA Research Grants, 296
International Postgraduate Research Scholarships (IPRS), 676
NRC Twinning Program, 455

West European Countries

ESRF Thesis Studentships, 277
International Postgraduate Research Scholarships (IPRS), 676
Natural History Museum Sys-Resource, 461

PETROLOGY

Any Country

American Association of Petroleum Geologists Foundation Grants-in-Aid, 35
BP/RSE Research Fellowships, 547
NERC Advanced Research Fellowships, 460
NERC Postdoctoral Research Fellowships, 460
Rhodes University Postdoctoral Fellowship, 519

Sigma Xi Grants-in-Aid of Research, 563
University of Manchester Research Studentships and Scholarships, 642

Australia

Fulbright Postgraduate Student Award for Science and Engineering, 120

British Commonwealth

Hector and Elizabeth Catling Bursary, 155

Canada

GSA Research Grants, 296

East European Countries

Natural History Museum Sys-Resource, 461

Far East

Stephen and Anna Hui Fellowship, 333

United Kingdom

Hector and Elizabeth Catling Bursary, 155
NERC Advanced Course Studentships, 459
NERC Research Studentships, 460

United States of America

GSA Research Grants, 296

West European Countries

Natural History Museum Sys-Resource, 461

GEOPHYSICS AND SEISMOLOGY

Any Country

Abdus Salam ICTP Fellowships, 5
ACS/PRF Scientific Education Grants, 35
ACS/PRF Type AC Grants, 35
ACS/PRF Type B Grants, 36
American Association of Petroleum Geologists Foundation Grants-in-Aid, 35
BP/RSE Research Fellowships, 547
CEPS Fellowship, 433
Dublin Institute for Advanced Studies Scholarship in Astronomy, Astrophysics and Geophysics, 262
Earthwatch Field Research Grants, 264
JILA Postdoctoral Research Associateship and Visiting Fellowships, 379
NERC Advanced Research Fellowships, 460
NERC Postdoctoral Research Fellowships, 460
Rhodes University Postdoctoral Fellowship, 519
SEG Scholarships, 587
University of Bristol Postgraduate Scholarships, 619
University of Edinburgh College of Science and Engineering Scholarship, 631
University of Manchester Research Studentships and Scholarships, 642
Weizmann Institute of Science MSc Fellowships, 700
Weizmann Institute of Science PhD Fellowships, 700
Weizmann Institute of Science Postdoctoral Fellowships Program, 700

African Nations

BP - FCO Chevening - Leeds University Scholarships, 638
International Postgraduate Research Scholarships (IPRS), 676
Lindemann Trust Fellowships, 271
Shell centenary chevening scholarships, 640
Shell Centenary Scholarships, 640

Australia

Fulbright Postgraduate Student Award for Science and Engineering, 120
Lindemann Trust Fellowships, 271

United Kingdom

CERN Doctoral Student Programme, 228
CERN Fellowships, 228
CERN Technical Student Programme, 228
ESRF Thesis Studentships, 277

United States of America

ASNE Scholarships, 81
NRC Twinning Program, 455

West European Countries

CERN Doctoral Student Programme, 228
CERN Fellowships, 228
CERN Technical Student Programme, 228
ESRF Thesis Studentships, 277

SOLID STATE PHYSICS

Any Country

Abdus Salam ICTP Fellowships, 5
BP/RSE Research Fellowships, 547
ESRF Postdoctoral Fellowships, 277
International School of Crystallography Grants, 367
JILA Postdoctoral Research Associateship and Visiting Fellowships, 379
SISSA Fellowships, 367
Thomas Holloway Research Studentship, 536
Weizmann Institute of Science MSc Fellowships, 700
Weizmann Institute of Science PhD Fellowships, 700
Weizmann Institute of Science Postdoctoral Fellowships Program, 700
Welch Foundation Scholarship, 371

East European Countries

CERN Doctoral Student Programme, 228
CERN Fellowships, 228
CERN Technical Student Programme, 228

United Kingdom

CERN Doctoral Student Programme, 228
CERN Fellowships, 228
CERN Technical Student Programme, 228
ESRF Thesis Studentships, 277
University of Wales (Aberystwyth) Postgraduate Research Studentships, 680

United States of America

ASNE Scholarships, 81
NRC Twinning Program, 455

West European Countries

CERN Doctoral Student Programme, 228
CERN Fellowships, 228
CERN Technical Student Programme, 228
ESRF Thesis Studentships, 277

THERMAL PHYSICS

Any Country

JILA Postdoctoral Research Associateship and Visiting Fellowships, 379
Weizmann Institute of Science MSc Fellowships, 700
Weizmann Institute of Science PhD Fellowships, 700
Weizmann Institute of Science Postdoctoral Fellowships Program, 700

African Nations

International Postgraduate Research Scholarships (IPRS), 676

British Commonwealth

International Postgraduate Research Scholarships (IPRS), 676

Canada

International Postgraduate Research Scholarships (IPRS), 676

Caribbean Countries

International Postgraduate Research Scholarships (IPRS), 676

East European Countries

CERN Fellowships, 228
International Postgraduate Research Scholarships (IPRS), 676

Far East

International Postgraduate Research Scholarships (IPRS), 676

Indian Sub-Continent

International Postgraduate Research Scholarships (IPRS), 676

Middle East

International Postgraduate Research Scholarships (IPRS), 676

South Africa

International Postgraduate Research Scholarships (IPRS), 676

South America

International Postgraduate Research Scholarships (IPRS), 676

United Kingdom

CERN Fellowships, 228
International Postgraduate Research Scholarships (IPRS), 676
University of Wales (Aberystwyth) Postgraduate Research Studentships, 680

United States of America

ASNE Scholarships, 81
International Postgraduate Research Scholarships (IPRS), 676
NRC Twinning Program, 455

West European Countries

CERN Fellowships, 228
International Postgraduate Research Scholarships (IPRS), 676

ASTRONOMY AND ASTROPHYSICS

Any Country

Abdus Salam ICTP Fellowships, 5
Association for Women in Science Educational Foundation Predoctoral Awards, 104
Carnegie Institution of Washington Fellowships, 220
Daphne Jackson Fellowship, 253
Downing College Research Fellowships, 623
Dublin Institute for Advanced Studies Scholarship in Astronomy, Astrophysics and Geophysics, 262
European Young Investigator (EVRYI) Awards, 487
Fund for UFO Research Grants, 295
IAU Travel Grant, 354
Institute for Advanced Study Postdoctoral Residential Fellowships, 338
Isaac Newton Studentship, 626
Jansky Postdoctorals, 455
JILA Postdoctoral Research Associateship and Visiting Fellowships, 379
McDonnell Graduate Fellowship in the Space Sciences, 408
NCAR Postdoctoral Appointments in the Advanced Study Program, 439
NRC Research Associateships, 456
PPARC Postdoctoral Fellowships, 488

PPARC Research Grants in Astronomy and Particle Physics, 488
PPARC Royal Society Industry Fellowships, 488
PPARC Senior Research Fellowships, 488
Queen Mary Research Studentships, 506
SAO Predoctoral Fellowships, 567
Sigma Xi Grants-in-Aid of Research, 563
SISSA Fellowships, 367
Smithsonian Institution Graduate Student Fellowships, 567
Smithsonian Institution Senior Fellowships, 568
University of Bristol Postgraduate Scholarships, 619
University of Glasgow Postgraduate Research Scholarships, 634
University of Manchester Research Studentships and Scholarships, 642
USC College Dissertation Fellowship, 677
USC College of Letters, Arts and Sciences Merit Award, 677
Weizmann Institute of Science MSc Fellowships, 700
Weizmann Institute of Science PhD Fellowships, 700
Woods Hole Oceanographic Institution Geophysical Fluid Dynamics (GFD) Fellowships, 709

African Nations

Lindemann Trust Fellowships, 271
TWAS Fellowship for Postdoctoral Research and Advanced Training, 600
TWOWS Postgraduate Fellowships for Women from Sub-Saharan Africa and Least Developed Countries (LDC) at Centres of Excellence in the South, 602

Australia

Lindemann Trust Fellowships, 271
University of Western Sydney Postgraduate Research Award (UW-SPRA), 689
Wingate Scholarships, 704

British Commonwealth

Lindemann Trust Fellowships, 271
Wingate Scholarships, 704

Canada

Cottrell College Science Awards, 514
Cottrell Scholars Awards, 514
Lindemann Trust Fellowships, 271
Research Corporation (USA) Research Opportunity Awards, 514
Wingate Scholarships, 704

Caribbean Countries

TWAS Fellowship for Postdoctoral Research and Advanced Training, 600

East European Countries

CERN Fellowships, 228
PPARC Postgraduate Studentships, 488

Far East

Lindemann Trust Fellowships, 271
TWAS Fellowship for Postdoctoral Research and Advanced Training, 600

Indian Sub-Continent

Lindemann Trust Fellowships, 271
TWAS Fellowship for Postdoctoral Research and Advanced Training, 600
Wingate Scholarships, 704

Middle East

TWAS Fellowship for Postdoctoral Research and Advanced Training, 600

New Zealand

Lindemann Trust Fellowships, 271

University of Western Sydney Postgraduate Research Award (UW-SPRA), 689
Wingate Scholarships, 704

South Africa

Henderson Postgraduate Scholarships, 518
Lindemann Trust Fellowships, 271
TWAS Fellowship for Postdoctoral Research and Advanced Training, 600
Wingate Scholarships, 704

South America

ESO Fellowship, 276
TWAS Fellowship for Postdoctoral Research and Advanced Training, 600

United Kingdom

CERN Fellowships, 228
Goldsmiths Company Science for Society Courses, 307
Lindemann Trust Fellowships, 271
PPARC Daphne Jackson Memorial Fellowships, 488
PPARC Postgraduate Studentships, 488
University of Wales (Aberystwyth) Postgraduate Research Studentships, 680
Wingate Scholarships, 704

United States of America

Cottrell College Science Awards, 514
Cottrell Scholars Awards, 514
Fannie and John Hertz Foundation Fellowships, 280
Fulbright Senior Specialists Program, 245
McDonnell Center Astronaut Fellowships in the Space Sciences, 408
Norwegian Thanksgiving Fund Scholarship, 474
NRC Twinning Program, 455
Research Corporation (USA) Research Opportunity Awards, 514
Winston Churchill Scholarship, 705

West European Countries

CERN Fellowships, 228
ESO Fellowship, 276
PPARC Postgraduate Studentships, 488
Wingate Scholarships, 704

ATMOSPHERE SCIENCE/METEOROLOGY

Any Country

AAC Research Grants, 25
Abdus Salam ICTP Fellowships, 5
Association for Women in Science Educational Foundation Predoctoral Awards, 104
BFWG: Johnstone and Florence Stoney Studentship, 143
Daphne Jackson Fellowship, 253
Downing College Research Fellowships, 623
Earthwatch Field Research Grants, 264
McDonnell Graduate Fellowship in the Space Sciences, 408
NCAR Postdoctoral Appointments in the Advanced Study Program, 439
NERC Advanced Research Fellowships, 460
NERC Postdoctoral Research Fellowships, 460
Queen Mary Research Studentships, 506
Sigma Xi Grants-in-Aid of Research, 563
University of Manchester Research Studentships and Scholarships, 642
University of Stirling Research Studentships, 678
Weizmann Institute of Science MSc Fellowships, 700
Weizmann Institute of Science PhD Fellowships, 700
WMO Education and Training Fellowships, 712
Woods Hole Oceanographic Institution Geophysical Fluid Dynamics (GFD) Fellowships, 709
Woods Hole Oceanographic Institution Postdoctoral Fellowships in Ocean Science and Engineering, 710

Woods Hole Oceanographic Institution/NOAA Co-operative Institute for Climate and Ocean Research Postdoctoral Fellowship, 710

African Nations

INM Fellowship for Curso Internacional de Técnico en Meteorologia General Applicada, 351
INM Short-term Fellowship, 351
TWAS Fellowship for Postdoctoral Research and Advanced Training, 600
TWOWS Postgraduate Fellowships for Women from Sub-Saharan Africa and Least Developed Countries (LDC) at Centres of Excellence in the South, 602

Australia

Wingate Scholarships, 704

British Commonwealth

Wingate Scholarships, 704

Canada

Wingate Scholarships, 704

Caribbean Countries

TWAS Fellowship for Postdoctoral Research and Advanced Training, 600

East European Countries

INM Fellowship for Curso Internacional de Técnico en Meteorologia General Applicada, 351
INM Short-term Fellowship, 351

Far East

TWAS Fellowship for Postdoctoral Research and Advanced Training, 600

Indian Sub-Continent

TWAS Fellowship for Postdoctoral Research and Advanced Training, 600
Wingate Scholarships, 704

Middle East

INM Fellowship for Curso Internacional de Técnico en Meteorologia General Applicada, 351
INM Short-term Fellowship, 351
TWAS Fellowship for Postdoctoral Research and Advanced Training, 600

New Zealand

Wingate Scholarships, 704

South Africa

Henderson Postgraduate Scholarships, 518
TWAS Fellowship for Postdoctoral Research and Advanced Training, 600
Wingate Scholarships, 704

South America

INM Fellowship for Curso Internacional de Técnico en Meteorologia General Applicada, 351
INM Short-term Fellowship, 351
TWAS Fellowship for Postdoctoral Research and Advanced Training, 600

United Kingdom

NERC Advanced Course Studentships, 459
NERC Research Studentships, 460
University of Wales (Aberystwyth) Postgraduate Research Studentships, 680
Wingate Scholarships, 704

United States of America

Fannie and John Hertz Foundation Fellowships, 280
NRC Twinning Program, 455
Winston Churchill Scholarship, 705

West European Countries

Janson Johan Helmich Scholarships and Travel Grants, 376
Wingate Scholarships, 704

ARCTIC STUDIES

Any Country

AAC Research Grants, 25
Earthwatch Field Research Grants, 264
NERC Advanced Research Fellowships, 460
NERC Postdoctoral Research Fellowships, 460
University of Stirling Research Studentships, 678

United Kingdom

NERC Advanced Course Studentships, 459
NERC Research Studentships, 460
University of Wales (Aberystwyth) Postgraduate Research Studentships, 680

United States of America

Norwegian Thanksgiving Fund Scholarship, 474
NRC Twinning Program, 455

ARID LAND STUDIES

Any Country

Earthwatch Field Research Grants, 264
NERC Advanced Research Fellowships, 460
NERC Postdoctoral Research Fellowships, 460
University of Stirling Research Studentships, 678
W Frank Blair Award, 233

United Kingdom

NERC Advanced Course Studentships, 459
NERC Research Studentships, 460

United States of America

NRC Twinning Program, 455

OCEANOGRAPHY

Any Country

Association for Women in Science Educational Foundation Predoctoral Awards, 104
Bermuda Biological Station for Research Grant In Aid, 125
Daphne Jackson Fellowship, 253
Downing College Research Fellowships, 623
Earthwatch Field Research Grants, 264
Horton (Hydrology) Research Grant, 46
NCAR Postdoctoral Appointments in the Advanced Study Program, 439
NERC Advanced Research Fellowships, 460
NERC Postdoctoral Research Fellowships, 460
Queen Mary Research Studentships, 506
Rhodes University Postdoctoral Fellowship, 519
University of Stirling Research Studentships, 678
Weizmann Institute of Science MSc Fellowships, 700
Weizmann Institute of Science PhD Fellowships, 700
Woods Hole Oceanographic Institution Geophysical Fluid Dynamics (GFD) Fellowships, 709
Woods Hole Oceanographic Institution Postdoctoral Awards in Marine Policy and Ocean Management, 710

RECREATION, WELFARE, PROTECTIVE SERVICES

GENERAL

East European Countries

Fulbright Postdoctoral Research and Lecturing Awards for Non-US Citizens, 245
Hubert H Humphrey Fellowship Programme, 609
International Postgraduate Research Scholarships (IPRS), 676
Merton College Reed Foundation Scholarship, 658

Far East

Friends of Peterhouse Bursary, 491
Fulbright Postdoctoral Research and Lecturing Awards for Non-US Citizens, 245
Hubert H Humphrey Fellowship Programme, 609
International Postgraduate Research Scholarships (IPRS), 676
Jackson Memorial Fellowship, 310
JACL Scholarship and Award Program, 377
Merton College Reed Foundation Scholarship, 658

Indian Sub-Continent

Friends of Peterhouse Bursary, 491
Fulbright Postdoctoral Research and Lecturing Awards for Non-US Citizens, 245
Hubert H Humphrey Fellowship Programme, 609
International Postgraduate Research Scholarships (IPRS), 676
Merton College Reed Foundation Scholarship, 658
Wingate Scholarships, 704

Middle East

Friends of Peterhouse Bursary, 491
Fulbright Postdoctoral Research and Lecturing Awards for Non-US Citizens, 245
Hubert H Humphrey Fellowship Programme, 609
International Postgraduate Research Scholarships (IPRS), 676
Merton College Reed Foundation Scholarship, 658

New Zealand

Friends of Peterhouse Bursary, 491
Fulbright Postdoctoral Research and Lecturing Awards for Non-US Citizens, 245
Wingate Scholarships, 704

South Africa

Friends of Peterhouse Bursary, 491
Fulbright Postdoctoral Research and Lecturing Awards for Non-US Citizens, 245
Hubert H Humphrey Fellowship Programme, 609
International Postgraduate Research Scholarships (IPRS), 676
Isie Smuts Research Award, 590
Wingate Scholarships, 704

South America

Friends of Peterhouse Bursary, 491
Fulbright Commission (Argentina) Master's Program, 293
Fulbright Postdoctoral Research and Lecturing Awards for Non-US Citizens, 245
Hubert H Humphrey Fellowship Programme, 609
International Postgraduate Research Scholarships (IPRS), 676
Merton College Reed Foundation Scholarship, 658
OAS Graduate Academic Studies, 483

United Kingdom

BSUF May and Ward Scholarships (for British scholars), 158
Canada Memorial Foundation Scholarships, 106
Fulbright Postdoctoral Research and Lecturing Awards for Non-US Citizens, 245
Hilda Martindale Exhibitions, 324
International Postgraduate Research Scholarships (IPRS), 676
UWB Departmental Research Studentships, 681
UWB Research Studentships, 681
Wingate Scholarships, 704

United States of America

BSUF May and Ward Scholarships (for British scholars), 158
Friends of Peterhouse Bursary, 491
Fulbright Scholar Program for United States Citizens, 245
International Postgraduate Research Scholarships (IPRS), 676
JACL Scholarship and Award Program, 377
North Dakota Indian Scholarship, 472
OAS Graduate Academic Studies, 483
UCLA IAC Postdoctoral/Visiting Scholar Fellowships, 607

West European Countries

Fulbright Postdoctoral Research and Lecturing Awards for Non-US Citizens, 245
International Postgraduate Research Scholarships (IPRS), 676
UWB Departmental Research Studentships, 681
UWB Research Studentships, 681
Wingate Scholarships, 704

POLICE AND LAW ENFORCEMENT

Any Country

Equiano Memorial Award, 596

United Kingdom

Fulbright Police Studies Fellowship, 692
Fulbright Police Studies Fellowships, 692

United States of America

Fulbright Senior Specialists Program, 245

CRIMINOLOGY

Any Country

Center for Advanced Study in the Behavioral Sciences Postdoctoral Residential Fellowships, 223
Equiano Memorial Award, 596
Humanitarian Trust Awards, 329
United States Center for Advanced Holocaust Studies Research Fellowships, 608
University of Essex Scholarships, 632
University of Glasgow Postgraduate Research Scholarships, 634
University of Manchester Research Studentships and Scholarships, 642
University of Stirling Research Studentships, 678

Australia

CRC Grants, 250
University of Western Sydney Postgraduate Research Award (UWSPRA), 689
Wingate Scholarships, 704

British Commonwealth

Wingate Scholarships, 704

Canada

Doctoral Awards, 576
Standard Research Grants, 580
Wingate Scholarships, 704

East European Countries

Shell Centenary Scholarships and Shell Centenary Chevening Scholarships, 664

Indian Sub-Continent

Wingate Scholarships, 704

Caribbean Countries

Hubert H Humphrey Fellowship Programme, 609
International Postgraduate Research Scholarships (IPRS), 676
MCTC Assistance for Courses, 304
MCTC Tuition and Maintenance Scholarships, 304

East European Countries

Hubert H Humphrey Fellowship Programme, 609
International Postgraduate Research Scholarships (IPRS), 676
MCTC Assistance for Courses, 304
MCTC Tuition and Maintenance Scholarships, 304

Far East

Hubert H Humphrey Fellowship Programme, 609
International Postgraduate Research Scholarships (IPRS), 676
MCTC Assistance for Courses, 304
MCTC Tuition and Maintenance Scholarships, 304

Indian Sub-Continent

Hubert H Humphrey Fellowship Programme, 609
International Postgraduate Research Scholarships (IPRS), 676
MCTC Assistance for Courses, 304
MCTC Tuition and Maintenance Scholarships, 304
Wingate Scholarships, 704

Middle East

Hubert H Humphrey Fellowship Programme, 609
International Postgraduate Research Scholarships (IPRS), 676
MCTC Assistance for Courses, 304
MCTC Tuition and Maintenance Scholarships, 304

New Zealand

University of Western Sydney Postgraduate Research Award (UW-SPRA), 689
Wingate Scholarships, 704

South Africa

Hubert H Humphrey Fellowship Programme, 609
International Postgraduate Research Scholarships (IPRS), 676
MCTC Assistance for Courses, 304
MCTC Tuition and Maintenance Scholarships, 304
Wingate Scholarships, 704
Zerilda Steyn Memorial Trust, 11

South America

Hubert H Humphrey Fellowship Programme, 609
International Postgraduate Research Scholarships (IPRS), 676
MCTC Assistance for Courses, 304
MCTC Tuition and Maintenance Scholarships, 304

United Kingdom

ESRC 1 + 3 Awards & + 3 Awards, 265
General Social Care Council Postgraduate Bursary, 296
Hallam Studentships, 558
International Postgraduate Research Scholarships (IPRS), 676
Mr and Mrs David Edward Memorial Award, 681
University of Wales (Aberystwyth) Postgraduate Research Studentships, 680
UWB Departmental Research Studentships, 681
UWB Research Studentships, 681
Wingate Scholarships, 704

United States of America

Adelphi University Scholarships, 8
Congress Bundestag Youth Exchange for Young Professionals, 223
CSWE Doctoral Fellowships in Social Work for Ethnic Minority Students Preparing for Leadership Roles in Mental Health and/or Substance Abuse, 247
CSWE Doctoral Fellowships in Social Work for Ethnic Minority Students Specialising in Mental Health, 248

CSWE Minority Fellowship Program, 248
Fulbright Senior Specialists Program, 245
Ian Axford (New Zealand) Fellowships in Public Policy, 239
International Postgraduate Research Scholarships (IPRS), 676
IREX Short-Term Travel Grants, 367
JCC Association Scholarships, 378
Robert Bosch Foundation Fellowships, 520
Washington University Chancellor's Graduate Fellowship Program for African Americans, 699
Whitney Young Fellowships, 599

West European Countries

ESRC 1 + 3 Awards & + 3 Awards, 265
General Social Care Council Postgraduate Bursary, 296
Hallam Studentships, 558
International Postgraduate Research Scholarships (IPRS), 676
Mr and Mrs David Edward Memorial Award, 681
UWB Departmental Research Studentships, 681
UWB Research Studentships, 681
Wingate Scholarships, 704

PUBLIC AND COMMUNITY SERVICES

Any Country

ASBAH Research Grant, 103
CQU Postgraduate Research Award, 224
Memorial Foundation for Jewish Culture International Scholarship Programme for Community Service, 416
SSRC Program on Philanthropy and the Non-profit Sector Fellowships, 573

African Nations

Hubert H Humphrey Fellowship Programme, 609
International Postgraduate Research Scholarships (IPRS), 676
MCTC Assistance for Courses, 304
MCTC Tuition and Maintenance Scholarships, 304

British Commonwealth

International Postgraduate Research Scholarships (IPRS), 676

Canada

Doctoral Awards, 576
International Postgraduate Research Scholarships (IPRS), 676
JCC Association Scholarships, 378

Caribbean Countries

Hubert H Humphrey Fellowship Programme, 609
International Postgraduate Research Scholarships (IPRS), 676
MCTC Assistance for Courses, 304
MCTC Tuition and Maintenance Scholarships, 304

East European Countries

Hubert H Humphrey Fellowship Programme, 609
International Postgraduate Research Scholarships (IPRS), 676
MCTC Assistance for Courses, 304
MCTC Tuition and Maintenance Scholarships, 304

Far East

Hubert H Humphrey Fellowship Programme, 609
International Postgraduate Research Scholarships (IPRS), 676
MCTC Assistance for Courses, 304
MCTC Tuition and Maintenance Scholarships, 304

Indian Sub-Continent

Hubert H Humphrey Fellowship Programme, 609
International Postgraduate Research Scholarships (IPRS), 676
MCTC Assistance for Courses, 304
MCTC Tuition and Maintenance Scholarships, 304

Middle East

Hubert H Humphrey Fellowship Programme, 609
International Postgraduate Research Scholarships (IPRS), 676
MCTC Assistance for Courses, 304
MCTC Tuition and Maintenance Scholarships, 304

South Africa

Hubert H Humphrey Fellowship Programme, 609
International Postgraduate Research Scholarships (IPRS), 676
MCTC Assistance for Courses, 304
MCTC Tuition and Maintenance Scholarships, 304

South America

Hubert H Humphrey Fellowship Programme, 609
International Postgraduate Research Scholarships (IPRS), 676
MCTC Assistance for Courses, 304
MCTC Tuition and Maintenance Scholarships, 304

United Kingdom

International Postgraduate Research Scholarships (IPRS), 676

United States of America

Congress Bundestag Youth Exchange for Young Professionals, 223
International Postgraduate Research Scholarships (IPRS), 676
JCC Association Scholarships, 378

West European Countries

International Postgraduate Research Scholarships (IPRS), 676

VOCATIONAL COUNSELLING

Any Country

Equiano Memorial Award, 596

United States of America

Ian Axford (New Zealand) Fellowships in Public Policy, 239

ENVIRONMENTAL STUDIES

Any Country

Alberta Law Foundation Graduate Scholarship, 620
American Association of Petroleum Geologists Foundation Grants-in-Aid, 35
ASCSA Research Fellow in Environmental Studies, 71
CDU Senior Research Fellowship, 230
CDU Three Year Postdoctoral Fellowship, 230
Center for Advanced Study in the Behavioral Sciences Postdoctoral Residential Fellowships, 223
Earthwatch Field Research Grants, 264
Edmund Niles Huyck Preserve, Inc. Graduate and Postgraduate Grants, 266
George A Hall/Harold F Manfield Award, 704
Gilbert F White Postdoctoral Fellowship, 515
Honda Prize, 325
Hudson River Expedited Grants, 328
Hudson River Graduate Fellowships, 328
Hudson River Research Grants, 328
Hudson River Travel Grants, 328
Joseph L Fisher Dissertation Award, 515
Lindbergh Grants, 230
Louis Agassiz Fuertes Award, 704
NCAR Postdoctoral Appointments in the Advanced Study Program, 439
NERC Advanced Research Fellowships, 460
NERC Postdoctoral Research Fellowships, 460
Oriel College Walter Raleigh Scholarship, 659
Paul A Stewart Awards, 704

Reuters Foundation Environment in the News Research Study Programme, 517
RFF Fellowships in Environmental Regulatory Implementation, 515
Rhodes University Postdoctoral Fellowship, 519
Sigma Xi Grants-in-Aid of Research, 563
Tibor T Polgar Fellowship, 328
University of Bristol Postgraduate Scholarships, 619
University of Dundee Research Awards, 629
University of Essex Scholarships, 632
University of Glasgow Postgraduate Research Scholarships, 634
University of Manchester Research Studentships and Scholarships, 642
University of Stirling Research Studentships, 678
University of Sussex Overseas Research Studentships, 678
Woods Hole Oceanographic Institution Research Fellowships in Marine Policy, 710

African Nations

Corpus Christi ACE Scholarship for Postgraduate Study, 176
Ecosystem Approaches to Human Health Awards, 358
Hastings Center International Visiting Scholars Program, 318
Hubert H Humphrey Fellowship Programme, 609
IFS Research Grant, 360
International Postgraduate Research Scholarships (IPRS), 676
Shell Centenary Scholarships (Developing Countries of the Commonwealth), 190

Australia

Fulbright Postgraduate Student Award for Science and Engineering, 120
Hastings Center International Visiting Scholars Program, 318
Wingate Scholarships, 704

British Commonwealth

Hastings Center International Visiting Scholars Program, 318
International Postgraduate Research Scholarships (IPRS), 676
Wingate Scholarships, 704

Canada

Canadian Window on International Development, 358
Community Forestry: Trees and People - John G Bene Fellowship, 358
Ecosystem Approaches to Human Health Awards, 358
Horticultural Research Institute Grants, 327
IDRC Doctoral Research Awards, 358
International Postgraduate Research Scholarships (IPRS), 676
Wingate Scholarships, 704

Caribbean Countries

Ecosystem Approaches to Human Health Awards, 358
Hastings Center International Visiting Scholars Program, 318
Hubert H Humphrey Fellowship Programme, 609
IFS Research Grant, 360
International Postgraduate Research Scholarships (IPRS), 676

East European Countries

Corpus Christi ACE Scholarship for Postgraduate Study, 176
Hastings Center International Visiting Scholars Program, 318
Hubert H Humphrey Fellowship Programme, 609
International Postgraduate Research Scholarships (IPRS), 676
Natural History Museum Sys-Resource, 461
OSI (Open Society Institute)/FCO Chevening Scholarships, 660
Shell Centenary Cambridge Scholarships (Countries outside of the Commonwealth), 189
Shell Centenary Scholarships (Developing Countries of the Commonwealth), 190
Shell Centenary Scholarships and Shell Centenary Chevening Scholarships, 664

Far East

Croucher Foundation Fellowships and Scholarships, 251
Ecosystem Approaches to Human Health Awards, 358
Hastings Center International Visiting Scholars Program, 318

ECOLOGY

British Commonwealth

International Postgraduate Research Scholarships (IPRS), 676
Wingate Scholarships, 704

Canada

IDRC Doctoral Research Awards, 358
International Postgraduate Research Scholarships (IPRS), 676
Wingate Scholarships, 704

Caribbean Countries

International Postgraduate Research Scholarships (IPRS), 676

East European Countries

Corpus Christi ACE Scholarship for Postgraduate Study, 176
International Postgraduate Research Scholarships (IPRS), 676
Natural History Museum Sys-Resource, 461

Far East

International Postgraduate Research Scholarships (IPRS), 676

Indian Sub-Continent

Corpus Christi ACE Scholarship for Postgraduate Study, 176
International Postgraduate Research Scholarships (IPRS), 676
Wingate Scholarships, 704

Middle East

International Postgraduate Research Scholarships (IPRS), 676

New Zealand

Wingate Scholarships, 704

South Africa

International Postgraduate Research Scholarships (IPRS), 676
Wingate Scholarships, 704

South America

International Postgraduate Research Scholarships (IPRS), 676

United Kingdom

International Postgraduate Research Scholarships (IPRS), 676
Mr and Mrs David Edward Memorial Award, 681
NERC Advanced Course Studentships, 459
NERC Research Studentships, 460
University of Essex Foundation Scholarships, 632
University of Wales (Aberystwyth) Postgraduate Research Student-ships, 680
UWB Departmental Research Studentships, 681
UWB Research Studentships, 681
Wingate Scholarships, 704

United States of America

Congress Bundestag Youth Exchange for Young Professionals, 223
Earthwatch Education Awards, 264
Fulbright Senior Specialists Program, 245
International Postgraduate Research Scholarships (IPRS), 676
Welder Wildlife Foundation Fellowship, 520
Woods Hole Oceanographic Institution Postdoctoral Fellowships in the Interdisciplinary Institutes, 710

West European Countries

International Postgraduate Research Scholarships (IPRS), 676
Mr and Mrs David Edward Memorial Award, 681
Natural History Museum Sys-Resource, 461
UWB Departmental Research Studentships, 681
UWB Research Studentships, 681
Wingate Scholarships, 704

NATURAL RESOURCES

Any Country

Alberta Law Foundation Graduate Scholarship, 620
American Association of Petroleum Geologists Foundation Grants-in-Aid, 35
AWWA Thomas R Camp Scholarship, 87
Canadian Embassy (USA) Faculty Enrichment Program, 202
CDU Senior Research Fellowship, 230
CDU Three Year Postdoctoral Fellowship, 230
Earthwatch Field Research Grants, 264
Edmund Niles Huyck Preserve, Inc. Graduate and Postgraduate Grants, 266
Hudson River Expedited Grants, 328
Hudson River Graduate Fellowships, 328
Hudson River Research Grants, 328
Hudson River Travel Grants, 328
Rhodes University Postdoctoral Fellowship, 519
Sigma Xi Grants-in-Aid of Research, 563
Tibor T Polgar Fellowship, 328
University of Calgary Faculty of Law Graduate Scholarship, 622
University of Stirling Research Studentships, 678

African Nations

International Postgraduate Research Scholarships (IPRS), 676

Australia

Fulbright Postgraduate Student Award for Science and Engineering, 120
Wingate Scholarships, 704

British Commonwealth

International Postgraduate Research Scholarships (IPRS), 676
Wingate Scholarships, 704

Canada

AWWA Abel Wolman Fellowship, 86
IDRC Doctoral Research Awards, 358
International Postgraduate Research Scholarships (IPRS), 676
Wingate Scholarships, 704

Caribbean Countries

International Postgraduate Research Scholarships (IPRS), 676

East European Countries

International Postgraduate Research Scholarships (IPRS), 676
Natural History Museum Sys-Resource, 461

Far East

International Postgraduate Research Scholarships (IPRS), 676

Indian Sub-Continent

International Postgraduate Research Scholarships (IPRS), 676
Wingate Scholarships, 704

Middle East

International Postgraduate Research Scholarships (IPRS), 676

New Zealand

Wingate Scholarships, 704

South Africa

International Postgraduate Research Scholarships (IPRS), 676
Wingate Scholarships, 704

South America

AWWA Abel Wolman Fellowship, 86
International Postgraduate Research Scholarships (IPRS), 676

United Kingdom

International Postgraduate Research Scholarships (IPRS), 676
Mr and Mrs David Edward Memorial Award, 681
UWB Departmental Research Studentships, 681
UWB Research Studentships, 681
Wingate Scholarships, 704

United States of America

AWWA Abel Wolman Fellowship, 86
Congress Bundestag Youth Exchange for Young Professionals, 223
Earthwatch Education Awards, 264
Fulbright Senior Specialists Program, 245
International Postgraduate Research Scholarships (IPRS), 676

West European Countries

International Postgraduate Research Scholarships (IPRS), 676
Mr and Mrs David Edward Memorial Award, 681
Natural History Museum Sys-Resource, 461
UWB Departmental Research Studentships, 681
UWB Research Studentships, 681
Wingate Scholarships, 704

ENVIRONMENTAL MANAGEMENT

Any Country

AWWA Academic Achievement Award, 87
CDU Senior Research Fellowship, 230
CDU Three Year Postdoctoral Fellowship, 230
CQU Postgraduate Research Award, 224
Earthwatch Field Research Grants, 264
Hudson River Expedited Grants, 328
Hudson River Graduate Fellowships, 328
Hudson River Research Grants, 328
Hudson River Travel Grants, 328
March of Dimes Research Grants, 404
NERC Advanced Research Fellowships, 460
NERC Postdoctoral Research Fellowships, 460
Rhodes University Postdoctoral Fellowship, 519
Sigma Xi Grants-in-Aid of Research, 563
Stanley Smith (UK) Horticultural Trust Awards, 594
Tibor T Polgar Fellowship, 328
UFAW Animal Welfare Research Training Scholarships, 616
UFAW Research and Project Awards, 616
UFAW Small Project and Travel Awards, 616
UFAW Vacation Scholarships, 616
University of Calgary Faculty of Law Graduate Scholarship, 622
University of Kent Anthropology Bursaries, 636
University of Stirling Research Studentships, 678

African Nations

Corpus Christi ACE Scholarship for Postgraduate Study, 176
Hubert H Humphrey Fellowship Programme, 609
International Postgraduate Research Scholarships (IPRS), 676

Australia

Fulbright Postgraduate Student Award for Science and Engineering, 120
University of Western Sydney Postgraduate Research Award (UW-SPRA), 689
Wingate Scholarships, 704

British Commonwealth

ACU Quality of Life Awards, 106
International Postgraduate Research Scholarships (IPRS), 676
Linacre College Norman and Ivy Lloyd Scholarship/DFID Shared Scholarship, 656
Wingate Scholarships, 704

Canada

AWWA Abel Wolman Fellowship, 86
CIC Award for Environmental Improvement, 232
Horticultural Research Institute Grants, 327

IDRC Doctoral Research Awards, 358
International Postgraduate Research Scholarships (IPRS), 676
Wingate Scholarships, 704

Caribbean Countries

Hubert H Humphrey Fellowship Programme, 609
International Postgraduate Research Scholarships (IPRS), 676

East European Countries

Corpus Christi ACE Scholarship for Postgraduate Study, 176
Hubert H Humphrey Fellowship Programme, 609
International Postgraduate Research Scholarships (IPRS), 676
Natural History Museum Sys-Resource, 461

Far East

Hubert H Humphrey Fellowship Programme, 609
International Postgraduate Research Scholarships (IPRS), 676

Indian Sub-Continent

Corpus Christi ACE Scholarship for Postgraduate Study, 176
Hubert H Humphrey Fellowship Programme, 609
International Postgraduate Research Scholarships (IPRS), 676
Wingate Scholarships, 704

Middle East

Hubert H Humphrey Fellowship Programme, 609
International Postgraduate Research Scholarships (IPRS), 676

New Zealand

University of Western Sydney Postgraduate Research Award (UW-SPRA), 689
Wingate Scholarships, 704

South Africa

Hubert H Humphrey Fellowship Programme, 609
International Postgraduate Research Scholarships (IPRS), 676
Wingate Scholarships, 704

South America

AWWA Abel Wolman Fellowship, 86
Hubert H Humphrey Fellowship Programme, 609
International Postgraduate Research Scholarships (IPRS), 676

United Kingdom

International Postgraduate Research Scholarships (IPRS), 676
Mr and Mrs David Edward Memorial Award, 681
NERC Advanced Course Studentships, 459
NERC Research Studentships, 460
University of Wales (Aberystwyth) Postgraduate Research Studentships, 680
UWB Departmental Research Studentships, 681
UWB Research Studentships, 681
Wingate Scholarships, 704

United States of America

AWWA Abel Wolman Fellowship, 86
AWWA Holly A Cornell Scholarship, 87
Congress Bundestag Youth Exchange for Young Professionals, 223
Earthwatch Education Awards, 264
Fulbright Senior Specialists Program, 245
Horticultural Research Institute Grants, 327
International Postgraduate Research Scholarships (IPRS), 676

West European Countries

International Postgraduate Research Scholarships (IPRS), 676
Mr and Mrs David Edward Memorial Award, 681
Natural History Museum Sys-Resource, 461
UWB Departmental Research Studentships, 681
UWB Research Studentships, 681
Wingate Scholarships, 704

WILDLIFE AND PEST MANAGEMENT

Any Country

CDU Senior Research Fellowship, 230
CDU Three Year Postdoctoral Fellowship, 230
Earthwatch Field Research Grants, 264
Hudson River Expedited Grants, 328
Hudson River Graduate Fellowships, 328
Hudson River Research Grants, 328
Hudson River Travel Grants, 328
Paul A Stewart Awards, 704
Sigma Xi Grants-in-Aid of Research, 563
Tibor T Polgar Fellowship, 328
UFAW Animal Welfare Research Training Scholarships, 616
UFAW Research and Project Awards, 616
UFAW Small Project and Travel Awards, 616
UFAW Vacation Scholarships, 616
University of Stirling Research Studentships, 678

African Nations

Hubert H Humphrey Fellowship Programme, 609
International Postgraduate Research Scholarships (IPRS), 676

Australia

Wingate Scholarships, 704

British Commonwealth

International Postgraduate Research Scholarships (IPRS), 676
Wingate Scholarships, 704

Canada

IDRC Doctoral Research Awards, 358
International Postgraduate Research Scholarships (IPRS), 676
Wingate Scholarships, 704

Caribbean Countries

Hubert H Humphrey Fellowship Programme, 609
International Postgraduate Research Scholarships (IPRS), 676

East European Countries

Hubert H Humphrey Fellowship Programme, 609
International Postgraduate Research Scholarships (IPRS), 676

Far East

Hubert H Humphrey Fellowship Programme, 609
International Postgraduate Research Scholarships (IPRS), 676

Indian Sub-Continent

Hubert H Humphrey Fellowship Programme, 609
International Postgraduate Research Scholarships (IPRS), 676
Wingate Scholarships, 704

Middle East

Hubert H Humphrey Fellowship Programme, 609
International Postgraduate Research Scholarships (IPRS), 676

New Zealand

Wingate Scholarships, 704

South Africa

Hubert H Humphrey Fellowship Programme, 609
International Postgraduate Research Scholarships (IPRS), 676
Wingate Scholarships, 704

South America

Hubert H Humphrey Fellowship Programme, 609
International Postgraduate Research Scholarships (IPRS), 676

United Kingdom

International Postgraduate Research Scholarships (IPRS), 676
Mr and Mrs David Edward Memorial Award, 681
UWB Departmental Research Studentships, 681
UWB Research Studentships, 681
Wingate Scholarships, 704

United States of America

Congress Bundestag Youth Exchange for Young Professionals, 223
Earthwatch Education Awards, 264
Fulbright Senior Specialists Program, 245
International Postgraduate Research Scholarships (IPRS), 676
Welder Wildlife Foundation Fellowship, 520

West European Countries

International Postgraduate Research Scholarships (IPRS), 676
Mr and Mrs David Edward Memorial Award, 681
UWB Departmental Research Studentships, 681
UWB Research Studentships, 681
Wingate Scholarships, 704

PHYSICAL EDUCATION AND SPORTS

Any Country

Acadia Graduate Teaching Assistantships, 6
CQU Postgraduate Research Award, 224
John Hervey, Broadcasters and Smallsreed Awards, 613
Research Student Bursary, 163
Rhodes University Postdoctoral Fellowship, 519
University of Bristol Postgraduate Scholarships, 619
University of Essex Scholarships, 632
University of Exeter Sports Scholarships, 633
University of Glasgow Postgraduate Research Scholarships, 634
University of Manchester Research Studentships and Scholarships, 642
University of Otago International Scholarships, 646
University of Stirling Research Studentships, 678

African Nations

International Postgraduate Research Scholarships (IPRS), 676

Australia

University of Otago PhD Scholarships, 646
University of Otago Prestigious PhD Scholarships, 647

British Commonwealth

International Postgraduate Research Scholarships (IPRS), 676

Canada

International Postgraduate Research Scholarships (IPRS), 676
JCC Association Scholarships, 378

Caribbean Countries

International Postgraduate Research Scholarships (IPRS), 676

East European Countries

International Postgraduate Research Scholarships (IPRS), 676

Far East

International Postgraduate Research Scholarships (IPRS), 676
University of Otago Dr Sulaiman Daud 125th Jubilee International Postgraduate Scholarship, 646

Indian Sub-Continent

International Postgraduate Research Scholarships (IPRS), 676

Middle East

International Postgraduate Research Scholarships (IPRS), 676

New Zealand

University of Otago PhD Scholarships, 646
University of Otago Prestigious PhD Scholarships, 647

South Africa

International Postgraduate Research Scholarships (IPRS), 676

South America

International Postgraduate Research Scholarships (IPRS), 676

United Kingdom

Hallam Studentships, 558
International Postgraduate Research Scholarships (IPRS), 676
Mr and Mrs David Edward Memorial Award, 681
University of Essex Foundation Scholarships, 632
University of Wales (Aberystwyth) Postgraduate Research Studentships, 680
UWB Departmental Research Studentships, 681
UWB Research Studentships, 681

United States of America

AAC Mountaineering Fellowship Fund Grants, 25
International Postgraduate Research Scholarships (IPRS), 676
JCC Association Scholarships, 378

West European Countries

Hallam Studentships, 558
International Postgraduate Research Scholarships (IPRS), 676
Mr and Mrs David Edward Memorial Award, 681
University of Otago PhD Scholarships, 646
University of Otago Prestigious PhD Scholarships, 647
UWB Departmental Research Studentships, 681
UWB Research Studentships, 681

SPORTS MANAGEMENT

Any Country

CQU Postgraduate Research Award, 224
Massey Doctoral Scholarship, 408
University of Bristol Postgraduate Scholarships, 619
University of Stirling Research Studentships, 678

African Nations

International Postgraduate Research Scholarships (IPRS), 676

British Commonwealth

International Postgraduate Research Scholarships (IPRS), 676

Canada

International Postgraduate Research Scholarships (IPRS), 676
JCC Association Scholarships, 378

Caribbean Countries

International Postgraduate Research Scholarships (IPRS), 676

East European Countries

International Postgraduate Research Scholarships (IPRS), 676

Far East

International Postgraduate Research Scholarships (IPRS), 676

Indian Sub-Continent

International Postgraduate Research Scholarships (IPRS), 676

Middle East

International Postgraduate Research Scholarships (IPRS), 676

South Africa

International Postgraduate Research Scholarships (IPRS), 676

South America

International Postgraduate Research Scholarships (IPRS), 676

United Kingdom

International Postgraduate Research Scholarships (IPRS), 676
Mr and Mrs David Edward Memorial Award, 681
University of Wales (Aberystwyth) Postgraduate Research Studentships, 680
UWB Departmental Research Studentships, 681
UWB Research Studentships, 681

United States of America

Congress Bundestag Youth Exchange for Young Professionals, 223
International Postgraduate Research Scholarships (IPRS), 676
JCC Association Scholarships, 378

West European Countries

International Postgraduate Research Scholarships (IPRS), 676
Mr and Mrs David Edward Memorial Award, 681
UWB Departmental Research Studentships, 681
UWB Research Studentships, 681

SOCIOLOGY OF SPORTS

Any Country

CQU Postgraduate Research Award, 224
University of Stirling Research Studentships, 678

African Nations

International Postgraduate Research Scholarships (IPRS), 676

British Commonwealth

International Postgraduate Research Scholarships (IPRS), 676

Canada

International Postgraduate Research Scholarships (IPRS), 676
JCC Association Scholarships, 378

Caribbean Countries

International Postgraduate Research Scholarships (IPRS), 676

East European Countries

International Postgraduate Research Scholarships (IPRS), 676

Far East

International Postgraduate Research Scholarships (IPRS), 676

Indian Sub-Continent

International Postgraduate Research Scholarships (IPRS), 676

Middle East

International Postgraduate Research Scholarships (IPRS), 676

South Africa

International Postgraduate Research Scholarships (IPRS), 676

South America

International Postgraduate Research Scholarships (IPRS), 676

United Kingdom

ESRC 1 + 3 Awards & +3 Awards, 265
International Postgraduate Research Scholarships (IPRS), 676
Mr and Mrs David Edward Memorial Award, 681

University of Wales (Aberystwyth) Postgraduate Research Student-
ships, 680
UWB Departmental Research Studentships, 681
UWB Research Studentships, 681

United States of America

International Postgraduate Research Scholarships (IPRS), 676
JCC Association Scholarships, 378

West European Countries

ESRC 1+3 Awards & +3 Awards, 265
International Postgraduate Research Scholarships (IPRS), 676
Mr and Mrs David Edward Memorial Award, 681
UWB Departmental Research Studentships, 681
UWB Research Studentships, 681

LEISURE STUDIES

Any Country

Research Student Bursary, 163
University of Stirling Research Studentships, 678

African Nations

International Postgraduate Research Scholarships (IPRS), 676

British Commonwealth

International Postgraduate Research Scholarships (IPRS), 676

Canada

International Postgraduate Research Scholarships (IPRS), 676
JCC Association Scholarships, 378

Caribbean Countries

International Postgraduate Research Scholarships (IPRS), 676

East European Countries

International Postgraduate Research Scholarships (IPRS), 676

Far East

International Postgraduate Research Scholarships (IPRS), 676

Indian Sub-Continent

International Postgraduate Research Scholarships (IPRS), 676

Middle East

International Postgraduate Research Scholarships (IPRS), 676

South Africa

International Postgraduate Research Scholarships (IPRS), 676

South America

International Postgraduate Research Scholarships (IPRS), 676

United Kingdom

International Postgraduate Research Scholarships (IPRS), 676
Mr and Mrs David Edward Memorial Award, 681
UWB Departmental Research Studentships, 681

United States of America

International Postgraduate Research Scholarships (IPRS), 676
JCC Association Scholarships, 378

West European Countries

International Postgraduate Research Scholarships (IPRS), 676
Mr and Mrs David Edward Memorial Award, 681
UWB Departmental Research Studentships, 681

PARKS AND RECREATION

Any Country

Stanley Smith (UK) Horticultural Trust Awards, 594

African Nations

International Postgraduate Research Scholarships (IPRS), 676

British Commonwealth

International Postgraduate Research Scholarships (IPRS), 676

Canada

International Postgraduate Research Scholarships (IPRS), 676
JCC Association Scholarships, 378

Caribbean Countries

International Postgraduate Research Scholarships (IPRS), 676

East European Countries

International Postgraduate Research Scholarships (IPRS), 676

Far East

International Postgraduate Research Scholarships (IPRS), 676

Indian Sub-Continent

International Postgraduate Research Scholarships (IPRS), 676

Middle East

International Postgraduate Research Scholarships (IPRS), 676

South Africa

International Postgraduate Research Scholarships (IPRS), 676

South America

International Postgraduate Research Scholarships (IPRS), 676

United Kingdom

International Postgraduate Research Scholarships (IPRS), 676
Polish Government Postgraduate Scholarships Scheme, 501
University of Wales (Aberystwyth) Postgraduate Research Student-
ships, 680

United States of America

Ian Axford (New Zealand) Fellowships in Public Policy, 239
International Postgraduate Research Scholarships (IPRS), 676
JCC Association Scholarships, 378

West European Countries

International Postgraduate Research Scholarships (IPRS), 676

RELIGION AND THEOLOGY

GENERAL

Any Country

Ahmanson and Getty Postdoctoral Fellowships, 606
AIATSIS Research Grants, 116
Andrew W Mellon Postdoctoral Fellowships in the Humanities, 677
ARIT Humanities and Social Science Fellowships, 70
ASCSA Summer Sessions, 72
ASECS (American Society for Eighteenth-Century Studies)/Clark
Library Fellowships, 606
Bertram Maura Memorial Entrance Scholarship, 694
Bloor Lands Entrance Scholarship, 694
British Academy Larger Research Grants, 134

RELIGIOUS STUDIES

Any Country

Australia

British Commonwealth

Canada

Bishop Thomas Hoyt Jr Fellowship, 338
Ministry Fellowship, 294
Wingate Scholarships, 704

East European Countries

AHRB Doctoral Awards Scheme, 99
CRF (Caledonian Research Foundation)/RSE European Visiting Research Fellowships, 547
Research Preparation Master's Scheme, 99

Indian Sub-Continent

Wingate Scholarships, 704

New Zealand

Wingate Scholarships, 704

South Africa

Wingate Scholarships, 704

United Kingdom

AHRB Doctoral Awards Scheme, 99
All Saints Educational Trust Personal Awards, 19
CBRL Research Grant, 244
CBRL Travel Grant, 244
CRF (Caledonian Research Foundation)/RSE European Visiting Research Fellowships, 547
Mr and Mrs David Edward Memorial Award, 681
Research Preparation Master's Scheme, 99
UWB Departmental Research Studentships, 681
UWB Research Studentships, 681
Wingate Scholarships, 704

United States of America

ARCE Fellowships, 69
Bishop Thomas Hoyt Jr Fellowship, 338
Fellowship Programme for Émigrés Pursuing Careers in Jewish Education, 378
Fulbright Senior Specialists Program, 245
Ministry Fellowship, 294

West European Countries

AHRB Doctoral Awards Scheme, 99
CRF (Caledonian Research Foundation)/RSE European Visiting Research Fellowships, 547
Mr and Mrs David Edward Memorial Award, 681
Research Preparation Master's Scheme, 99
UWB Departmental Research Studentships, 681
UWB Research Studentships, 681
Wingate Scholarships, 704

CHRISTIAN

Any Country

Advanced Fellowships, 71
Ahmanson and Getty Postdoctoral Fellowships, 606
Andrew W Mellon Postdoctoral Fellowships in the Humanities, 677
ASECS (American Society for Eighteenth-Century Studies)/Clark Library Fellowships, 606
Bross Prize, 162
Clark Library Short-Term Resident Fellowships, 606
Clark Predoctoral Fellowships, 607
Clark-Huntington Joint Bibliographical Fellowship, 607
Gibson Studentship, 625
Harvard University, Center for the Study of World Religions, Senior Fellowship, 318
M Alison Frantz Fellowship in Post-Classical Studies at the Gennadius Library (formerly known as the Gennadeion Fellowship), 72

NEH Fellowships, 72
University of Stirling Research Studentships, 678

Australia

Wingate Scholarships, 704

British Commonwealth

Wingate Scholarships, 704

Canada

Wingate Scholarships, 704

East European Countries

AHRB Doctoral Awards Scheme, 99
Research Preparation Master's Scheme, 99

Indian Sub-Continent

Wingate Scholarships, 704

New Zealand

Wingate Scholarships, 704

South Africa

Wingate Scholarships, 704

United Kingdom

AHRB Doctoral Awards Scheme, 99
All Saints Educational Trust Personal Awards, 19
Mr and Mrs David Edward Memorial Award, 681
Research Preparation Master's Scheme, 99
UWB Departmental Research Studentships, 681
UWB Research Studentships, 681
Wingate Scholarships, 704

West European Countries

AHRB Doctoral Awards Scheme, 99
Mr and Mrs David Edward Memorial Award, 681
Research Preparation Master's Scheme, 99
UWB Departmental Research Studentships, 681
UWB Research Studentships, 681
Wingate Scholarships, 704

JEWISH

Any Country

Advanced Fellowships, 71
Ahmanson and Getty Postdoctoral Fellowships, 606
Andrew W Mellon Postdoctoral Fellowships in the Humanities, 677
ASECS (American Society for Eighteenth-Century Studies)/Clark Library Fellowships, 606
Bernard and Audre Rapoport Fellowships, 50
Clark Library Short-Term Resident Fellowships, 606
Clark Predoctoral Fellowships, 607
Clark-Huntington Joint Bibliographical Fellowship, 607
Delahaye Memorial Benefaction, 681
Ethel Marcus Memorial Fellowship, 50
Harvard University, Center for the Study of World Religions, Senior Fellowship, 318
Helen McCormack Turner Memorial Scholarship, 681
Herbert Hughes Scholarship, 682
Israel International Schloarship, 145
Jacob Hirsch Fellowship, 72
Loewenstein-Wiener Fellowship Awards, 51
M Alison Frantz Fellowship in Post-Classical Studies at the Gennadius Library (formerly known as the Gennadeion Fellowship), 72
Marguerite R Jacobs Memorial Award, 51
Mary Radcliffe Scholarship, 682
Memorial Foundation for Jewish Culture Grants for Jewish Research and Publication, 415

ISLAM

ASIAN RELIGIOUS STUDIES

University of Manchester Research Studentships and Scholarships, 642

University of Stirling Research Studentships, 678

Australia

Wingate Scholarships, 704

British Commonwealth

Wingate Scholarships, 704

Canada

Wingate Scholarships, 704

East European Countries

AHRB Doctoral Awards Scheme, 99
Research Preparation Master's Scheme, 99

Indian Sub-Continent

Wingate Scholarships, 704

New Zealand

Wingate Scholarships, 704

South Africa

Wingate Scholarships, 704

United Kingdom

AHRB Doctoral Awards Scheme, 99
Research Preparation Master's Scheme, 99
Wingate Scholarships, 704

West European Countries

AHRB Doctoral Awards Scheme, 99
Research Preparation Master's Scheme, 99
Wingate Scholarships, 704

AGNOSTICISM AND ATHEISM

Any Country

Andrew W Mellon Postdoctoral Fellowships in the Humanities, 677
Harvard University, Center for the Study of World Religions, Senior Fellowship, 318

Australia

Wingate Scholarships, 704

British Commonwealth

Wingate Scholarships, 704

Canada

Wingate Scholarships, 704

East European Countries

AHRB Doctoral Awards Scheme, 99
Research Preparation Master's Scheme, 99

Indian Sub-Continent

Wingate Scholarships, 704

New Zealand

Wingate Scholarships, 704

South Africa

Wingate Scholarships, 704

United Kingdom

AHRB Doctoral Awards Scheme, 99

Research Preparation Master's Scheme, 99
Wingate Scholarships, 704

West European Countries

AHRB Doctoral Awards Scheme, 99
Research Preparation Master's Scheme, 99
Wingate Scholarships, 704

ANCIENT RELIGIONS

Any Country

Advanced Fellowships, 71
Andrew W Mellon Postdoctoral Fellowships in the Humanities, 677
ASCSA Fellowships, 71
ASCSA Summer Sessions, 72
FAMSI Research Grant, 287
Harvard University, Center for the Study of World Religions, Senior Fellowship, 318
Jacob Hirsch Fellowship, 72
M Alison Frantz Fellowship in Post-Classical Studies at the Gennadius Library (formerly known as the Gennadeion Fellowship), 72
Mary Isabel Sibley Fellowship, 497
NEH Fellowships, 72
SOAS Bursary, 555

Australia

Wingate Scholarships, 704

British Commonwealth

Hector and Elizabeth Catling Bursary, 155
Wingate Scholarships, 704

Canada

Wingate Scholarships, 704

East European Countries

AHRB Doctoral Awards Scheme, 99

Indian Sub-Continent

Wingate Scholarships, 704

New Zealand

Wingate Scholarships, 704

South Africa

Wingate Scholarships, 704

United Kingdom

AHRB Doctoral Awards Scheme, 99
Hector and Elizabeth Catling Bursary, 155
Wingate Scholarships, 704

United States of America

ARCE Fellowships, 69

West European Countries

AHRB Doctoral Awards Scheme, 99
Wingate Scholarships, 704

RELIGIOUS EDUCATION

Any Country

Dempster Fellowship, 295
Equiano Memorial Award, 596

African Nations

International Postgraduate Research Scholarships (IPRS), 676

British Commonwealth

International Postgraduate Research Scholarships (IPRS), 676

Canada

International Postgraduate Research Scholarships (IPRS), 676
Ministry Fellowship, 294

Caribbean Countries

International Postgraduate Research Scholarships (IPRS), 676

East European Countries

International Postgraduate Research Scholarships (IPRS), 676

Far East

International Postgraduate Research Scholarships (IPRS), 676

Indian Sub-Continent

International Postgraduate Research Scholarships (IPRS), 676

Middle East

International Postgraduate Research Scholarships (IPRS), 676

South Africa

International Postgraduate Research Scholarships (IPRS), 676

South America

International Postgraduate Research Scholarships (IPRS), 676

United Kingdom

All Saints Educational Trust Personal Awards, 19
CBRL Research Grant, 244
CBRL Travel Grant, 244
International Postgraduate Research Scholarships (IPRS), 676
Mr and Mrs David Edward Memorial Award, 681
UWB Departmental Research Studentships, 681
UWB Research Studentships, 681

United States of America

Fellowship Programme for Émigrés Pursuing Careers in Jewish Education, 378
International Postgraduate Research Scholarships (IPRS), 676
Ministry Fellowship, 294

West European Countries

International Postgraduate Research Scholarships (IPRS), 676
Mr and Mrs David Edward Memorial Award, 681
UWB Departmental Research Studentships, 681
UWB Research Studentships, 681

HOLY WRITINGS

Any Country

Council of the Institute Awards, 502
Gibson Studentship, 625
Israel International Schloarship, 145
SOAS Bursary, 555
SOAS Research Student Fellowships, 555

Australia

Wingate Scholarships, 704

British Commonwealth

Wingate Scholarships, 704

Canada

Wingate Scholarships, 704

Indian Sub-Continent

Wingate Scholarships, 704

New Zealand

Wingate Scholarships, 704

South Africa

Wingate Scholarships, 704

United Kingdom

CBRL Research Grant, 244
CBRL Travel Grant, 244
UWB Research Studentships, 681
Wingate Scholarships, 704

United States of America

ARCE Fellowships, 69

West European Countries

UWB Research Studentships, 681
Wingate Scholarships, 704

RELIGIOUS PRACTICE

Any Country

SOAS Bursary, 555
SOAS Research Student Fellowships, 555

Canada

Ministry Fellowship, 294

United Kingdom

CBRL Research Grant, 244
CBRL Travel Grant, 244
Mr and Mrs David Edward Memorial Award, 681
UWB Departmental Research Studentships, 681
UWB Research Studentships, 681

United States of America

Fellowship Programme for Émigrés Pursuing Careers in Jewish Education, 378
Ministry Fellowship, 294

West European Countries

Mr and Mrs David Edward Memorial Award, 681
UWB Departmental Research Studentships, 681
UWB Research Studentships, 681

CHURCH ADMINISTRATION (PASTORAL WORK)

Canada

Ministry Fellowship, 294

United Kingdom

CBRL Research Grant, 244
CBRL Travel Grant, 244
Hilda Martindale Exhibitions, 324
Mr and Mrs David Edward Memorial Award, 681
UWB Departmental Research Studentships, 681
UWB Research Studentships, 681

United States of America

Ministry Fellowship, 294
Verne Catt McDowell Scholarship, 694

West European Countries

THEOLOGICAL STUDIES

Any Country

African Nations

Australia

British Commonwealth

Canada

Caribbean Countries

East European Countries

Indian Sub-Continent

Middle East

New Zealand

South Africa

South America

United Kingdom

United States of America

West European Countries

COMPARATIVE RELIGION

Any Country

Australia

British Commonwealth

Canada

East European Countries

SOCIOLOGY OF RELIGION

HISTORY OF RELIGION

SOAS Bursary, 555
SOAS Research Student Fellowships, 555
University of Bristol Postgraduate Scholarships, 619
W.D. Llewelyn Memorial Benefaction, 682

Australia
Wingate Scholarships, 704

British Commonwealth
Wingate Scholarships, 704

Canada
Wingate Scholarships, 704

East European Countries
AHRB Doctoral Awards Scheme, 99
Research Preparation Master's Scheme, 99

Indian Sub-Continent
Wingate Scholarships, 704

New Zealand
Wingate Scholarships, 704

South Africa
Wingate Scholarships, 704

United Kingdom
AHRB Doctoral Awards Scheme, 99
CBRL Research Grant, 244
CBRL Travel Grant, 244
Mr and Mrs David Edward Memorial Award, 681
Regent's Park College Studentships of the Centre for the Study of Christianity and Culture, 663
Research Preparation Master's Scheme, 99
UWB Departmental Research Studentships, 681
UWB Research Studentships, 681
Wingate Scholarships, 704

United States of America
Fritz Stern Dissertation Prize, 299
Thyssen Heideking Fellowship, 300

West European Countries
AHRB Doctoral Awards Scheme, 99
Kade-Heideking Fellowship, 300
Mr and Mrs David Edward Memorial Award, 681
Research Preparation Master's Scheme, 99
UWB Departmental Research Studentships, 681
UWB Research Studentships, 681
Wingate Scholarships, 704

ESOTERIC PRACTICES

East European Countries
CRF (Caledonian Research Foundation)/RSE European Visiting Research Fellowships, 547

United Kingdom
CBRL Research Grant, 244
CBRL Travel Grant, 244
CRF (Caledonian Research Foundation)/RSE European Visiting Research Fellowships, 547

West European Countries
CRF (Caledonian Research Foundation)/RSE European Visiting Research Fellowships, 547

SERVICE TRADES

GENERAL

Any Country
AIATSIS Research Grants, 116
CDU Three Year Postdoctoral Fellowship, 230
CQU Postgraduate Research Award, 224
Field Psych Trust Grant, 281
Massey Doctoral Scholarship, 408
Southern Cross University Postgraduate Research Scholarships, 592
University of Dundee Research Awards, 629

African Nations
Fulbright Postdoctoral Research and Lecturing Awards for Non-US Citizens, 245
International Postgraduate Research Scholarships (IPRS), 676
Merton College Reed Foundation Scholarship, 658

Australia
Fulbright Awards, 119
Fulbright Postdoctoral Fellowships, 119
Fulbright Postdoctoral Research and Lecturing Awards for Non-US Citizens, 245

British Commonwealth
International Postgraduate Research Scholarships (IPRS), 676
Merton College Reed Foundation Scholarship, 658

Canada
Fulbright Postdoctoral Research and Lecturing Awards for Non-US Citizens, 245
International Postgraduate Research Scholarships (IPRS), 676
OAS Graduate Academic Studies, 483

Caribbean Countries
International Postgraduate Research Scholarships (IPRS), 676
Merton College Reed Foundation Scholarship, 658
OAS Graduate Academic Studies, 483

East European Countries
Fulbright Postdoctoral Research and Lecturing Awards for Non-US Citizens, 245
International Postgraduate Research Scholarships (IPRS), 676
Merton College Reed Foundation Scholarship, 658

Far East
Fulbright Postdoctoral Research and Lecturing Awards for Non-US Citizens, 245
International Postgraduate Research Scholarships (IPRS), 676
Merton College Reed Foundation Scholarship, 658

Indian Sub-Continent
Fulbright Postdoctoral Research and Lecturing Awards for Non-US Citizens, 245
International Postgraduate Research Scholarships (IPRS), 676
Merton College Reed Foundation Scholarship, 658

Middle East
Fulbright Postdoctoral Research and Lecturing Awards for Non-US Citizens, 245
International Postgraduate Research Scholarships (IPRS), 676
Merton College Reed Foundation Scholarship, 658

New Zealand
Fulbright Postdoctoral Research and Lecturing Awards for Non-US Citizens, 245

South Africa

Fulbright Postdoctoral Research and Lecturing Awards for Non-US Citizens, 245
International Postgraduate Research Scholarships (IPRS), 676
Isie Smuts Research Award, 590

South America

Fulbright Commission (Argentina) Master's Program, 293
Fulbright Postdoctoral Research and Lecturing Awards for Non-US Citizens, 245
International Postgraduate Research Scholarships (IPRS), 676
Merton College Reed Foundation Scholarship, 658
OAS Graduate Academic Studies, 483

United Kingdom

Canada Memorial Foundation Scholarships, 106
Fulbright Postdoctoral Research and Lecturing Awards for Non-US Citizens, 245
Hallam Studentships, 558
Hilda Martindale Exhibitions, 334
International Postgraduate Research Scholarships (IPRS), 676

United States of America

Congress Bundestag Youth Exchange for Young Professionals, 223
Fulbright Scholar Program for United States Citizens, 245
International Postgraduate Research Scholarships (IPRS), 676
OAS Graduate Academic Studies, 483

West European Countries

Fulbright Postdoctoral Research and Lecturing Awards for Non-US Citizens, 245
Hallam Studentships, 558
International Postgraduate Research Scholarships (IPRS), 676
Janson Johan Helmich Scholarships and Travel Grants, 376

HOTEL AND RESTAURANT

Any Country

University of Dundee Research Awards, 629

African Nations

International Postgraduate Research Scholarships (IPRS), 676

British Commonwealth

International Postgraduate Research Scholarships (IPRS), 676

Canada

International Postgraduate Research Scholarships (IPRS), 676

Caribbean Countries

International Postgraduate Research Scholarships (IPRS), 676

East European Countries

International Postgraduate Research Scholarships (IPRS), 676

Far East

International Postgraduate Research Scholarships (IPRS), 676

Indian Sub-Continent

International Postgraduate Research Scholarships (IPRS), 676

Middle East

International Postgraduate Research Scholarships (IPRS), 676

South Africa

International Postgraduate Research Scholarships (IPRS), 676

South America

International Postgraduate Research Scholarships (IPRS), 676

United Kingdom

International Postgraduate Research Scholarships (IPRS), 676

United States of America

Congress Bundestag Youth Exchange for Young Professionals, 223
International Postgraduate Research Scholarships (IPRS), 676
National Restaurant Association Educational Foundation Professional Development Scholarship for educators., 457

West European Countries

International Postgraduate Research Scholarships (IPRS), 676

HOTEL MANAGEMENT

Any Country

University of Dundee Research Awards, 629

African Nations

Hubert H Humphrey Fellowship Programme, 609
International Postgraduate Research Scholarships (IPRS), 676

British Commonwealth

International Postgraduate Research Scholarships (IPRS), 676

Canada

International Postgraduate Research Scholarships (IPRS), 676

Caribbean Countries

Hubert H Humphrey Fellowship Programme, 609
International Postgraduate Research Scholarships (IPRS), 676

East European Countries

Hubert H Humphrey Fellowship Programme, 609
International Postgraduate Research Scholarships (IPRS), 676

Far East

Hubert H Humphrey Fellowship Programme, 609
International Postgraduate Research Scholarships (IPRS), 676

Indian Sub-Continent

Hubert H Humphrey Fellowship Programme, 609
International Postgraduate Research Scholarships (IPRS), 676

Middle East

Hubert H Humphrey Fellowship Programme, 609
International Postgraduate Research Scholarships (IPRS), 676

South Africa

Hubert H Humphrey Fellowship Programme, 609
International Postgraduate Research Scholarships (IPRS), 676

South America

Hubert H Humphrey Fellowship Programme, 609
International Postgraduate Research Scholarships (IPRS), 676

United Kingdom

International Postgraduate Research Scholarships (IPRS), 676

United States of America

Congress Bundestag Youth Exchange for Young Professionals, 223
International Postgraduate Research Scholarships (IPRS), 676
National Restaurant Association Educational Foundation Professional Development Scholarship for educators., 457

West European Countries

International Postgraduate Research Scholarships (IPRS), 676

COOKING AND CATERING

United States of America

Congress Bundestag Youth Exchange for Young Professionals, 223

United States of America

National Restaurant Association Educational Foundation Professional Development Scholarship for educators., 457

RETAILING

African Nations

International Postgraduate Research Scholarships (IPRS), 676

British Commonwealth

International Postgraduate Research Scholarships (IPRS), 676

Canada

International Postgraduate Research Scholarships (IPRS), 676

Caribbean Countries

International Postgraduate Research Scholarships (IPRS), 676

East European Countries

International Postgraduate Research Scholarships (IPRS), 676

Far East

International Postgraduate Research Scholarships (IPRS), 676

Indian Sub-Continent

International Postgraduate Research Scholarships (IPRS), 676

Middle East

International Postgraduate Research Scholarships (IPRS), 676

South Africa

International Postgraduate Research Scholarships (IPRS), 676

South America

International Postgraduate Research Scholarships (IPRS), 676

United Kingdom

International Postgraduate Research Scholarships (IPRS), 676

United States of America

Congress Bundestag Youth Exchange for Young Professionals, 223
International Postgraduate Research Scholarships (IPRS), 676

West European Countries

International Postgraduate Research Scholarships (IPRS), 676

TOURISM

Any Country

AIATSIS Research Grants, 116
CDU Senior Research Fellowship, 230
CDU Three Year Postdoctoral Fellowship, 230
CQU Postgraduate Research Award, 224
Massey Doctoral Scholarship, 408
Research Student Bursary, 163
University of Kent Anthropology Bursaries, 636

African Nations

Hubert H Humphrey Fellowship Programme, 609
International Postgraduate Research Scholarships (IPRS), 676
MCTC Assistance for Courses, 304
MCTC Tuition and Maintenance Scholarships, 304

Australia

University of Western Sydney Postgraduate Research Award (UW-SPRA), 689

British Commonwealth

International Postgraduate Research Scholarships (IPRS), 676

Canada

International Postgraduate Research Scholarships (IPRS), 676

Caribbean Countries

Hubert H Humphrey Fellowship Programme, 609
International Postgraduate Research Scholarships (IPRS), 676
MCTC Assistance for Courses, 304
MCTC Tuition and Maintenance Scholarships, 304

East European Countries

Hubert H Humphrey Fellowship Programme, 609
International Postgraduate Research Scholarships (IPRS), 676
MCTC Assistance for Courses, 304
MCTC Tuition and Maintenance Scholarships, 304

Far East

Hubert H Humphrey Fellowship Programme, 609
International Postgraduate Research Scholarships (IPRS), 676
MCTC Assistance for Courses, 304
MCTC Tuition and Maintenance Scholarships, 304

Indian Sub-Continent

Hubert H Humphrey Fellowship Programme, 609
International Postgraduate Research Scholarships (IPRS), 676
MCTC Assistance for Courses, 304
MCTC Tuition and Maintenance Scholarships, 304

Middle East

Hubert H Humphrey Fellowship Programme, 609
International Postgraduate Research Scholarships (IPRS), 676
MCTC Assistance for Courses, 304
MCTC Tuition and Maintenance Scholarships, 304

New Zealand

University of Western Sydney Postgraduate Research Award (UW-SPRA), 689

South Africa

Hubert H Humphrey Fellowship Programme, 609
International Postgraduate Research Scholarships (IPRS), 676
MCTC Assistance for Courses, 304
MCTC Tuition and Maintenance Scholarships, 304

South America

Hubert H Humphrey Fellowship Programme, 609
International Postgraduate Research Scholarships (IPRS), 676
MCTC Assistance for Courses, 304
MCTC Tuition and Maintenance Scholarships, 304

United Kingdom

Hallam Studentships, 558
International Postgraduate Research Scholarships (IPRS), 676

United States of America

Congress Bundestag Youth Exchange for Young Professionals, 223
International Postgraduate Research Scholarships (IPRS), 676

West European Countries

Hallam Studentships, 558
International Postgraduate Research Scholarships (IPRS), 676

SOCIAL AND BEHAVIOURAL SCIENCES

GENERAL

Any Country

ACLS Charles A Ryskamp Research Fellowships, 39
ACLS/Andrew W Mellon Fellowships for Junior Faculty, 40
AIATSIS Research Grants, 116
Alberta Heritage Clinical Fellowships, 12
Alberta Heritage Clinical Investigatorships, 12
Alberta Heritage Full-Time Fellowships, 13
Alberta Heritage Full-Time Studentship, 13
Alberta Heritage Medical Scholarships, 13
Alberta Heritage Medical Scientist Awards, 13
Alberta Heritage Part-Time Fellowships, 14
Alberta Heritage Part-Time Studentship, 14
Andrew Mellon Foundation Scholarship, 518
Anne Cummins Scholarship, 580
ARIT Humanities and Social Science Fellowships, 70
ASCSA Summer Sessions, 72
AUC Graduate Merit Fellowships, 84
AUC Ryoichi Sasakawa Young Leaders Graduate Scholarship, 85
AUC University Fellowships, 86
Behavioral Sciences Research Training Fellowship, 272
British Academy Overseas Conference Grants, 134
British Academy Small Personal Research Grants, 134
British Academy Visiting Professorships for Overseas Scholars, 135
British Academy Worldwide Congress Grant, 135
British Academy/ACU Grants for International Collaboration, 106
Camargo Fellowships, 164
Canadian Department of Foreign Affairs Faculty Enrichment Program, 205
Canadian Department of Foreign Affairs Faculty Research Program, 205
Canadian Department of Foreign Affairs Institutional Research Program, 206
Canadian Institute of Ukrainian Studies Research Grants, 207
Center for Advanced Study in the Behavioral Sciences Postdoctoral Residential Fellowships, 223
CESC-SSHRC Education Research Initiative, 576
Charles G Koch Summer Fellowship, 338
Clark Library Short-Term Resident Fellowships, 606
Concordia University Graduate Fellowships, 241
DAAD Leibniz Scholarships for Doctoral Candidates and post-Docs, 298
David J Azrieli Graduate Fellowship, 241
Downing College Research Fellowships, 623
Eli Ginzberg Award, 325
Equiano Memorial Award, 596
ERASMUS Prize, 288
ETS Summer Program in Research for Graduate Students, 266
Field Psych Trust Grant, 281
Foundation Praemium Erasmianum Study Prize, 288
Franklin Research Grant Program, 65
Frederick Douglass Institute Postdoctoral Fellowship, 289
Frederick Douglass Institute Predoctoral Dissertation Fellowship, 290
George Walford International Essay Prize (GWIEP), 296
Gilbert F White Postdoctoral Fellowship, 515
Gordon Allport Intergroup Relations Prize, 582
Grant Notley Memorial Postdoctoral Fellowship, 617
Griffith University Postgraduate Research Scholarships, 310
Health Services Research Fellowships, 320
Helen Darcovich Memorial Doctoral Fellowship, 207
Heritage Population Health Investigators, 14

Hobart Houghton Research Fellowship, 518
HRF Graduate Fellowships, 328
HSS Travel Grant, 324
Hudson River Graduate Fellowships, 328
Hugh Le May Fellowship, 519
IHS Humane Studies Fellowships, 339
IHS Liberty & Society Summer Seminars, 339
Institute for Advanced Studies in the Humanities Visiting Research Fellowships, 337
Institute for Advanced Study Postdoctoral Residential Fellowships, 338
Irish Research Funds, 373
J D Stout Fellowship, 595
J Franklin Jameson Fellowship, 49
Jeanne Humphrey Block Dissertation Award, 322
Jennings Randolph Program for International Peace Senior Fellowships, 612
John M Olin Institute for Strategic Studies Predoctoral and Postdoctoral Fellowships in National Security, 316
Joseph L Fisher Dissertation Award, 515
Kennan Institute Short Term Grants, 385
Korea Foundation Advanced Research Grant, 386
Korea Foundation Fellowship for Field Research, 386
Korea Foundation Fellowship for Graduate Studies, 386
Korea Foundation Fellowship for Korean Language Training, 386
Korea Foundation Postdoctoral Fellowship, 387
La Trobe University Postgraduate Scholarship, 390
Library Resident Research Fellowships, 65
Lincoln College Erich and Rochelle Endowed Prize in Music, 657
March of Dimes Research Grants, 404
Marusia and Michael Dorosh Master's Fellowship, 207
Monash International Postgraduate Research Scholarship (MIPRS), 424
Monash University Silver Jubilee Postgraduate Scholarship, 425
Neporany Research and Teaching Fellowship, 207
NRF Fellowships for Postdoctoral Research, 456
Nuffield College Funded Studentships, 659
Nuffield College Prize Research Fellowships, 659
NUS Graduate Scholarships for ASEAN Nationals, 459
Pembroke College Graduate Awards, 626
PhD Studentships in Social Sciences, 219
Queen Mary Research Studentships, 506
Rhodes University Postgraduate Scholarship, 519
Royal Irish Academy European Exchange Fellowship, 540
Russell Sage Foundation Visiting Scholar Appointments, 551
Sabbatical Fellowship for the Humanities and Social Sciences, 66
School for International Training Master of Arts in Teaching Program, 711
Scottish Executive / RSE Support Research Fellowships, 549
Scottish Executive Personal Research Fellowships, 549
Sigma Xi Grants-in-Aid of Research, 563
Sir Allan Sewell Visiting Fellowship, 310
Sir Richard Stapley Educational Trust Grants, 564
SOAS Bursary, 555
SOAS Research Student Fellowships, 555
Southern Cross University Postgraduate Research Scholarships, 592
SSRC Africa Program Advanced Research Grants, 570
SSRC International Dissertation Field Research Fellowship Program, 572
SSRC Program on Philanthropy and the Non-profit Sector Fellowships, 573
SSRC Program on the Corporation as a Social Institution Fellowships, 573
SSRC Sexuality Research Fellowship Program, 574
SSRC Summer Institute on International Migration, 574
SSSS Student Research Grant Award, 583
St John's College Junior Research Fellowship, 671
Stanley G French Graduate Fellowship, 242
Studying Diverse Lives, 322
Thank-Offering to Britain Fellowships, 135
Trinity College Cecil Lubbock Memorial Scholarship, 672
Trinity College Junior Research Fellowship, 672
University of Dundee Research Awards, 629

African Nations

Australia

British Commonwealth

Canada

Caribbean Countries

East European Countries

Far East

West European Countries

ECONOMICS

Any Country

African Nations

Australia

British Commonwealth

Canada

International Postgraduate Research Scholarships (IPRS), 676
Mr and Mrs David Edward Memorial Award, 681
University of Otago PhD Scholarships, 646
University of Otago Prestigious PhD Scholarships, 647
UWB Departmental Research Studentships, 681
UWB Research Studentships, 681
Wingate Scholarships, 704

ECONOMIC HISTORY

Any Country

AIER Summer Fellowship, 49
Arthur H Cole Grants-in-Aid, 265
Camargo Fellowships, 164
Center for Advanced Study in the Behavioral Sciences Postdoctoral Residential Fellowships, 223
CMRS Summer Fellowship, 607
Dissertation Year Fellowships, 315
Frederick Douglass Institute Postdoctoral Fellowship, 289
Frederick Douglass Institute Predoctoral Dissertation Fellowship, 290
Gordon Cain Fellowship, 232
Harry S Truman Library Institute Dissertation Year Fellowships, 314
Harry S Truman Library Institute Research Grants, 314
Harry S Truman Library Institute Scholar's Award, 315
Harvard/Newcomen Postdoctoral Award, 470
Herbert Hoover Presidential Library Association Travel Grants, 323
IHS Summer Graduate Research Fellowship, 339
Institute of European History Fellowships, 342
John C Geilfuss Fellowship, 706
Library Company of Philadelphia and Historical Society of Pennsylvania Research Fellowships in American History and Culture, 398
Library Company of Philadelphia Program in Early American Economy and Society, 398
NHC Fellowships, 449
Paul H Nitze School of Advanced International Studies (SAIS) Financial Aid and Fellowships, 130
Queen Mary Research Studentships, 506
Research Grants, 272
Rhodes University Postdoctoral Fellowship, 519
Rockefeller Archive Center Research Grant Program, 522
Roosevelt Institute Research Grant, 289
Russell Sage Foundation Visiting Scholar Appointments, 551
Scholar's Award, 315
University of Bristol Postgraduate Scholarships, 619
University of Essex Scholarships, 632
University of Manchester Research Studentships and Scholarships, 642
University of Stirling Research Studentships, 678

African Nations

International Postgraduate Research Scholarships (IPRS), 676

Australia

Wingate Scholarships, 704

British Commonwealth

International Postgraduate Research Scholarships (IPRS), 676
Wingate Scholarships, 704

Canada

International Postgraduate Research Scholarships (IPRS), 676
Wingate Scholarships, 704

Caribbean Countries

International Postgraduate Research Scholarships (IPRS), 676

East European Countries

CRF (Caledonian Research Foundation)/RSE European Visiting Research Fellowships, 547
International Postgraduate Research Scholarships (IPRS), 676

Far East

International Postgraduate Research Scholarships (IPRS), 676
University of Leeds International Fee Bursary (Vietnam), 641
University of Leeds International Fee Bursary (Vietnam), 641

Indian Sub-Continent

International Postgraduate Research Scholarships (IPRS), 676
Wingate Scholarships, 704

Middle East

International Postgraduate Research Scholarships (IPRS), 676

New Zealand

Wingate Scholarships, 704

South Africa

International Postgraduate Research Scholarships (IPRS), 676
Wingate Scholarships, 704

South America

International Postgraduate Research Scholarships (IPRS), 676

United Kingdom

CBRL Research Grant, 244
CBRL Travel Grant, 244
CRF (Caledonian Research Foundation)/RSE European Visiting Research Fellowships, 547
ESRC 1 + 3 Awards & + 3 Awards, 265
International Postgraduate Research Scholarships (IPRS), 676
Molson Research Awards, 136
Mr and Mrs David Edward Memorial Award, 681
Prix du Québec, 136
University of Essex Foundation Scholarships, 632
University of Wales (Aberystwyth) Postgraduate Research Studentships, 680
UWB Departmental Research Studentships, 681
UWB Research Studentships, 681
Wingate Scholarships, 704

United States of America

ARCE Fellowships, 69
Fritz Stern Dissertation Prize, 299
Fulbright Distinguished Chairs Program, 245
Fulbright Senior Specialists Program, 245
International Postgraduate Research Scholarships (IPRS), 676
Newcomen Society Dissertation Fellowship in Business and American Culture, 471
Thyssen Heideking Fellowship, 300

West European Countries

CRF (Caledonian Research Foundation)/RSE European Visiting Research Fellowships, 547
ESRC 1 + 3 Awards & + 3 Awards, 265
International Postgraduate Research Scholarships (IPRS), 676
Kade-Heideking Fellowship, 300
Mr and Mrs David Edward Memorial Award, 681
UWB Departmental Research Studentships, 681
UWB Research Studentships, 681
Wingate Scholarships, 704

ECONOMIC AND FINANCE POLICY

Any Country

Center for Advanced Study in the Behavioral Sciences Postdoctoral Residential Fellowships, 223
Dissertation Year Fellowships, 315
Harry S Truman Library Institute Dissertation Year Fellowships, 314
Harry S Truman Library Institute Research Grants, 314
Harry S Truman Library Institute Scholar's Award, 315

Jean Monnet Fellowships, 278
Massey Doctoral Scholarship, 408
Paul H Nitze School of Advanced International Studies (SAIS) Financial Aid and Fellowships, 130
Queen Mary Research Studentships, 506
Research Grants, 272
Scholar's Award, 315
Thomas Holloway Research Studentship, 536
University of Bristol Postgraduate Scholarships, 619
University of Dundee Research Awards, 629
University of Essex Scholarships, 632
University of Manchester Research Studentships and Scholarships, 642
University of Stirling Research Studentships, 678

African Nations

Hubert H Humphrey Fellowship Programme, 609
International Postgraduate Research Scholarships (IPRS), 676

Australia

Wingate Scholarships, 704

British Commonwealth

International Postgraduate Research Scholarships (IPRS), 676
Wingate Scholarships, 704

Canada

International Postgraduate Research Scholarships (IPRS), 676
S S Huebner Foundation for Insurance Education Predoctoral Fellowships, 552
Wingate Scholarships, 704

Caribbean Countries

Hubert H Humphrey Fellowship Programme, 609
International Postgraduate Research Scholarships (IPRS), 676

East European Countries

EUI Postgraduate Scholarships, 277
Hubert H Humphrey Fellowship Programme, 609
International Postgraduate Research Scholarships (IPRS), 676

Far East

Hubert H Humphrey Fellowship Programme, 609
International Postgraduate Research Scholarships (IPRS), 676
University of Leeds International Fee Bursary (Vietnam), 641
University of Leeds International Fee Bursary (Vietnam), 641
University of Leeds International Fee Bursary (Vietnam), 641

Indian Sub-Continent

Hubert H Humphrey Fellowship Programme, 609
International Postgraduate Research Scholarships (IPRS), 676
Wingate Scholarships, 704

Middle East

Hubert H Humphrey Fellowship Programme, 609
International Postgraduate Research Scholarships (IPRS), 676

New Zealand

Wingate Scholarships, 704

South Africa

Hubert H Humphrey Fellowship Programme, 609
International Postgraduate Research Scholarships (IPRS), 676
Wingate Scholarships, 704

South America

Hubert H Humphrey Fellowship Programme, 609
International Postgraduate Research Scholarships (IPRS), 676

United Kingdom

CBRL Research Grant, 244
CBRL Travel Grant, 244
ESRC 1 + 3 Awards & + 3 Awards, 265
EUI Postgraduate Scholarships, 277
International Postgraduate Research Scholarships (IPRS), 676
Molson Research Awards, 136
Mr and Mrs David Edward Memorial Award, 681
University of Essex Foundation Scholarships, 632
University of Wales (Aberystwyth) Postgraduate Research Studentships, 680
UWB Departmental Research Studentships, 681
UWB Research Studentships, 681
Wingate Scholarships, 704

United States of America

Fulbright Distinguished Chairs Program, 245
Fulbright Senior Specialists Program, 245
International Postgraduate Research Scholarships (IPRS), 676
IREX Short-Term Travel Grants, 367
S S Huebner Foundation for Insurance Education Predoctoral Fellowships, 552

West European Countries

ESRC 1 + 3 Awards & + 3 Awards, 265
EUI Postgraduate Scholarships, 277
International Postgraduate Research Scholarships (IPRS), 676
Mr and Mrs David Edward Memorial Award, 681
UWB Departmental Research Studentships, 681
UWB Research Studentships, 681
Wingate Scholarships, 704

TAXATION

Any Country

AIER Summer Fellowship, 49
Center for Advanced Study in the Behavioral Sciences Postdoctoral Residential Fellowships, 223
Rhodes University Postdoctoral Fellowship, 519
University of Bristol Postgraduate Scholarships, 619
University of Stirling Research Studentships, 678

African Nations

Hubert H Humphrey Fellowship Programme, 609
International Postgraduate Research Scholarships (IPRS), 676

Australia

Wingate Scholarships, 704

British Commonwealth

International Postgraduate Research Scholarships (IPRS), 676
Wingate Scholarships, 704

Canada

Alcohol Beverage Medical Research Foundation Research Project Grant, 14
International Postgraduate Research Scholarships (IPRS), 676
Wingate Scholarships, 704

Caribbean Countries

Hubert H Humphrey Fellowship Programme, 609
International Postgraduate Research Scholarships (IPRS), 676

East European Countries

Hubert H Humphrey Fellowship Programme, 609
International Postgraduate Research Scholarships (IPRS), 676

Far East

Hubert H Humphrey Fellowship Programme, 609
International Postgraduate Research Scholarships (IPRS), 676

Indian Sub-Continent

Hubert H Humphrey Fellowship Programme, 609
International Postgraduate Research Scholarships (IPRS), 676
Wingate Scholarships, 704

Middle East

Hubert H Humphrey Fellowship Programme, 609
International Postgraduate Research Scholarships (IPRS), 676

New Zealand

Wingate Scholarships, 704

South Africa

Hubert H Humphrey Fellowship Programme, 609
International Postgraduate Research Scholarships (IPRS), 676
Wingate Scholarships, 704

South America

Hubert H Humphrey Fellowship Programme, 609
International Postgraduate Research Scholarships (IPRS), 676

United Kingdom

International Postgraduate Research Scholarships (IPRS), 676
University of Wales (Aberystwyth) Postgraduate Research Studentships, 680
UWB Departmental Research Studentships, 681
UWB Research Studentships, 681
Wingate Scholarships, 704

United States of America

Alcohol Beverage Medical Research Foundation Research Project Grant, 14
International Postgraduate Research Scholarships (IPRS), 676

West European Countries

International Postgraduate Research Scholarships (IPRS), 676
UWB Departmental Research Studentships, 681
UWB Research Studentships, 681
Wingate Scholarships, 704

ECONOMETRICS

Any Country

Center for Advanced Study in the Behavioral Sciences Postdoctoral Residential Fellowships, 223
CESC-SSHRC Education Research Initiative, 576
Jean Monnet Fellowships, 278
Paul H Nitze School of Advanced International Studies (SAIS) Financial Aid and Fellowships, 130
Queen Mary Research Studentships, 506
University of Bristol Postgraduate Scholarships, 619
University of Dundee Research Awards, 629
University of Essex Scholarships, 632
University of Manchester Research Studentships and Scholarships, 642
University of Stirling Research Studentships, 678

African Nations

International Postgraduate Research Scholarships (IPRS), 676

Australia

University of Western Sydney Postgraduate Research Award (UW-SPRA), 689

Wingate Scholarships, 704

British Commonwealth

International Postgraduate Research Scholarships (IPRS), 676
Wingate Scholarships, 704

Canada

Alcohol Beverage Medical Research Foundation Research Project Grant, 14
CESC-SSHRC Education Research Initiative, 576
International Postgraduate Research Scholarships (IPRS), 676
Wingate Scholarships, 704

Caribbean Countries

International Postgraduate Research Scholarships (IPRS), 676

East European Countries

EUI Postgraduate Scholarships, 277
International Postgraduate Research Scholarships (IPRS), 676

Far East

International Postgraduate Research Scholarships (IPRS), 676

Indian Sub-Continent

International Postgraduate Research Scholarships (IPRS), 676
Wingate Scholarships, 704

Middle East

International Postgraduate Research Scholarships (IPRS), 676

New Zealand

University of Western Sydney Postgraduate Research Award (UW-SPRA), 689
Wingate Scholarships, 704

South Africa

International Postgraduate Research Scholarships (IPRS), 676
Wingate Scholarships, 704

South America

International Postgraduate Research Scholarships (IPRS), 676

United Kingdom

Alzheimers Society Research Grants, 22
ESRC 1+3 Awards & +3 Awards, 265
EUI Postgraduate Scholarships, 277
International Postgraduate Research Scholarships (IPRS), 676
Mr and Mrs David Edward Memorial Award, 681
University of Essex Foundation Scholarships, 632
UWB Departmental Research Studentships, 681
UWB Research Studentships, 681
Wingate Scholarships, 704

United States of America

Alcohol Beverage Medical Research Foundation Research Project Grant, 14
International Postgraduate Research Scholarships (IPRS), 676

West European Countries

ESRC 1+3 Awards & +3 Awards, 265
EUI Postgraduate Scholarships, 277
International Postgraduate Research Scholarships (IPRS), 676
Mr and Mrs David Edward Memorial Award, 681
UWB Departmental Research Studentships, 681
UWB Research Studentships, 681
Wingate Scholarships, 704

INDUSTRIAL AND PRODUCTION ECONOMICS

Any Country

Center for Advanced Study in the Behavioral Sciences Postdoctoral Residential Fellowships, 223
Houblon-Norman Fellowships/George Fellowships, 327
KSTU Rector's Grant, 385
Thomas Holloway Research Studentship, 536

African Nations

Hubert H Humphrey Fellowship Programme, 609
International Postgraduate Research Scholarships (IPRS), 676

Australia

Wingate Scholarships, 704

British Commonwealth

International Postgraduate Research Scholarships (IPRS), 676
Wingate Scholarships, 704

Canada

International Postgraduate Research Scholarships (IPRS), 676
S S Huebner Foundation for Insurance Education Predoctoral Fellowships, 552
Wingate Scholarships, 704

Caribbean Countries

Hubert H Humphrey Fellowship Programme, 609
International Postgraduate Research Scholarships (IPRS), 676

East European Countries

Hubert H Humphrey Fellowship Programme, 609
International Postgraduate Research Scholarships (IPRS), 676

Far East

Hubert H Humphrey Fellowship Programme, 609
International Postgraduate Research Scholarships (IPRS), 676

Indian Sub-Continent

Hubert H Humphrey Fellowship Programme, 609
International Postgraduate Research Scholarships (IPRS), 676
Wingate Scholarships, 704

Middle East

Hubert H Humphrey Fellowship Programme, 609
International Postgraduate Research Scholarships (IPRS), 676

New Zealand

Wingate Scholarships, 704

South Africa

Hubert H Humphrey Fellowship Programme, 609
International Postgraduate Research Scholarships (IPRS), 676
Wingate Scholarships, 704

South America

Hubert H Humphrey Fellowship Programme, 609
International Postgraduate Research Scholarships (IPRS), 676

United Kingdom

ESRC 1+3 Awards & +3 Awards, 265
International Postgraduate Research Scholarships (IPRS), 676
Mr and Mrs David Edward Memorial Award, 681
University of Wales (Aberystwyth) Postgraduate Research Studentships, 680
UWB Departmental Research Studentships, 681
UWB Research Studentships, 681
Wingate Scholarships, 704

United States of America

International Postgraduate Research Scholarships (IPRS), 676
NRC Twinning Program, 455
S S Huebner Foundation for Insurance Education Predoctoral Fellowships, 552

West European Countries

ESRC 1+3 Awards & +3 Awards, 265
International Postgraduate Research Scholarships (IPRS), 676
Mr and Mrs David Edward Memorial Award, 681
UWB Departmental Research Studentships, 681
UWB Research Studentships, 681
Wingate Scholarships, 704

POLITICAL SCIENCE AND GOVERNMENT

Any Country

ABF Fellowships in Law and Social Science, 35
Acadia Graduate Teaching Assistantships, 6
Ahmanson and Getty Postdoctoral Fellowships, 606
AIATSIS Research Grants, 116
ASECS (American Society for Eighteenth-Century Studies)/Clark Library Fellowships, 606
Association for Women in Science Educational Foundation Predoctoral Awards, 104
British Academy Overseas Conference Grants, 134
British Academy Small Personal Research Grants, 134
British Academy Worldwide Congress Grant, 135
Camargo Fellowships, 164
Canadian Embassy (USA) Senior Fellowship Program, 202
CDI Internship, 223
CDU Senior Research Fellowship, 230
CDU Three Year Postdoctoral Fellowship, 230
Celso Furtado Award, 602
Center for Advanced Study in the Behavioral Sciences Postdoctoral Residential Fellowships, 223
Clark Predoctoral Fellowships, 607
Clark-Huntington Joint Bibliographical Fellowship, 607
Dissertation Year Fellowships, 315
Downing College Research Fellowships, 623
Equiano Memorial Award, 596
Foundation Praemium Erasmianum Study Prize, 288
Frederick Douglass Institute Postdoctoral Fellowship, 289
Frederick Douglass Institute Predoctoral Dissertation Fellowship, 290
Gilbert F White Postdoctoral Fellowship, 515
Graduate Institute of International Studies (HEI-Geneva) Scholarships, 308
Grant Notley Memorial Postdoctoral Fellowship, 617
Harry S Truman Library Institute Dissertation Year Fellowships, 314
Harry S Truman Library Institute Research Grants, 314
Harry S Truman Library Institute Scholar's Award, 315
Herbert Hoover Presidential Library Association Travel Grants, 323
HFG Dissertation Fellowship, 314
HFG Research Program, 314
IHS Summer Graduate Research Fellowship, 339
Institute of Irish Studies Senior Visiting Research Fellowship, 344
Joseph L Fisher Dissertation Award, 515
Kennan Institute Short Term Grants, 385
Lincoln College, Kenneth Seward-Shaw Scholarship, 657
M Alison Frantz Fellowship in Post-Classical Studies at the Gennadius Library (formerly known as the Gennadeion Fellowship), 72
MA/Msc Studentship in European Studies, 218
Mansfield College Elfan Rees Scholarship, 658
Marusia and Michael Dorosh Master's Fellowship, 207
NHC Fellowships, 449
Nuffield College Prize Research Fellowships, 659
Paul H Nitze School of Advanced International Studies (SAIS) Financial Aid and Fellowships, 130
PhD Studentship in European Studies, 218
PhD Studentship in Political Theory, 631
Queen Mary Research Studentships, 506

COMPARATIVE POLITICS

Institute of Irish Studies Senior Visiting Research Fellowship, 344
Jean Monnet Fellowships, 278
Paul H Nitze School of Advanced International Studies (SAIS) Financial Aid and Fellowships, 130
PhD Studentship in Political Theory, 631
Queen Mary Research Studentships, 506
University of Bristol Postgraduate Scholarships, 619
University of Dundee Research Awards, 629
University of Essex Scholarships, 632
University of Stirling Research Studentships, 678

African Nations

International Postgraduate Research Scholarships (IPRS), 676

Australia

Wingate Scholarships, 704

British Commonwealth

International Postgraduate Research Scholarships (IPRS), 676
Wingate Scholarships, 704

Canada

International Postgraduate Research Scholarships (IPRS), 676
Jules and Gabrielle Léger Fellowship, 577
Mary McNeill Scholarship in Irish Studies, 344
Wingate Scholarships, 704

Caribbean Countries

International Postgraduate Research Scholarships (IPRS), 676

East European Countries

EUI Postgraduate Scholarships, 277
International Postgraduate Research Scholarships (IPRS), 676
Young Scholars Forum, 300

Far East

International Postgraduate Research Scholarships (IPRS), 676

Indian Sub-Continent

International Postgraduate Research Scholarships (IPRS), 676
Wingate Scholarships, 704

Middle East

International Postgraduate Research Scholarships (IPRS), 676

New Zealand

Wingate Scholarships, 704

South Africa

International Postgraduate Research Scholarships (IPRS), 676
Wingate Scholarships, 704

South America

International Postgraduate Research Scholarships (IPRS), 676

United Kingdom

Balliol College Marvin Bower Scholarship, 648
CBRL Research Grant, 244
CBRL Travel Grant, 244
ESRC 1 + 3 Awards & + 3 Awards, 265
EUI Postgraduate Scholarships, 277
International Postgraduate Research Scholarships (IPRS), 676
University of Essex Foundation Scholarships, 632
University of Wales (Aberystwyth) Postgraduate Research Studentships, 680
Wingate Scholarships, 704
Young Scholars Forum, 300

United States of America

ARCE Fellowships, 69
Émigré Memorial German Internship Programs, 268
Fritz Stern Dissertation Prize, 299
Fulbright Senior Specialists Program, 245
International Postgraduate Research Scholarships (IPRS), 676
IREX Individual Advanced Research Opportunities, 366
IREX John J and Nancy Lee Roberts Fellowship Program, 366
IREX Short-Term Travel Grants, 367
Mary McNeill Scholarship in Irish Studies, 344
NRC Twinning Program, 455
Thyssen Heideking Fellowship, 300
Young Scholars Forum, 300

West European Countries

Balliol College Marvin Bower Scholarship, 648
ESRC 1 + 3 Awards & + 3 Awards, 265
EUI Postgraduate Scholarships, 277
International Postgraduate Research Scholarships (IPRS), 676
Kade-Heideking Fellowship, 300
Wingate Scholarships, 704
Young Scholars Forum, 300

INTERNATIONAL RELATIONS

Any Country

British Academy Overseas Conference Grants, 134
British Academy Small Personal Research Grants, 134
British Academy Worldwide Congress Grant, 135
Canadian Embassy (USA) Senior Fellowship Program, 202
CDI Internship, 223
Center for Advanced Study in the Behavioral Sciences Postdoctoral Residential Fellowships, 223
Downing College Research Fellowships, 623
Equiano Memorial Award, 596
Foundation Praemium Erasmianum Study Prize, 288
Frederick Douglass Institute Postdoctoral Fellowship, 289
Frederick Douglass Institute Predoctoral Dissertation Fellowship, 290
Gilbert Murray Trust Junior Awards, 302
Harry S Truman Library Institute Research Grants, 314
Harvard University Graduate Student Associate Program, 316
HFG Dissertation Fellowship, 314
HFG Research Program, 314
Institute of Current World Affairs Fellowships, 342
Jean Monnet Fellowships, 278
Joseph L Fisher Dissertation Award, 515
Kennan Institute Short Term Grants, 385
M Alison Frantz Fellowship in Post-Classical Studies at the Gennadius Library (formerly known as the Gennadeion Fellowship), 72
Mackenzie King Travelling Scholarships, 402
Marusia and Michael Dorosh Master's Fellowship, 207
Otto Klineberg Intercultural and International Relations Award, 582
Paul H Nitze School of Advanced International Studies (SAIS) Financial Aid and Fellowships, 130
Program on US-Japan Relations Advanced Research Fellowships, 317
Research Grants, 272
Rhodes University Postdoctoral Fellowship, 519
Rockefeller Archive Center Research Grant Program, 522
SAIIA Bradlow Fellowship, 592
Sir Patrick Sheehy Scholarships, 190
SOAS Bursary, 555
SOAS Research Student Fellowships, 555
Theodore Lentz Fellowship in Peace and Conflict Resolution Research, 393
Theodore Lentz Postdoctoral or Sabbatical Fellowship in Peace and Conflict Resolution Research, 224
University of Bristol Postgraduate Scholarships, 619
University of Dundee Research Awards, 629
University of Essex Scholarships, 632
University of Glasgow Postgraduate Research Scholarships, 634

SOCIOLOGY

HISTORY OF SOCIETIES

IDRC Doctoral Research Awards, 358
International Postgraduate Research Scholarships (IPRS), 676
Joshua Feigenbaum Award, 325
Research Planning Grants, 214
Wingate Scholarships, 704

Caribbean Countries

Hastings Center International Visiting Scholars Program, 318
International Postgraduate Research Scholarships (IPRS), 676
Joshua Feigenbaum Award, 325

East European Countries

EUI Postgraduate Scholarships, 277
Hastings Center International Visiting Scholars Program, 318
International Postgraduate Research Scholarships (IPRS), 676
Joshua Feigenbaum Award, 325

Far East

Hastings Center International Visiting Scholars Program, 318
International Postgraduate Research Scholarships (IPRS), 676
Joshua Feigenbaum Award, 325
University of Sussex Overseas Development Administration Shared
Scholarship Scheme, 678

Indian Sub-Continent

Hastings Center International Visiting Scholars Program, 318
International Postgraduate Research Scholarships (IPRS), 676
Joshua Feigenbaum Award, 325
University of Sussex Overseas Development Administration Shared
Scholarship Scheme, 678
Wingate Scholarships, 704

Middle East

Hastings Center International Visiting Scholars Program, 318
International Postgraduate Research Scholarships (IPRS), 676
Joshua Feigenbaum Award, 325

New Zealand

Hastings Center International Visiting Scholars Program, 318
Joshua Feigenbaum Award, 325
Wingate Scholarships, 704

South Africa

Hastings Center International Visiting Scholars Program, 318
International Postgraduate Research Scholarships (IPRS), 676
Joshua Feigenbaum Award, 325
Wingate Scholarships, 704

South America

Hastings Center International Visiting Scholars Program, 318
International Postgraduate Research Scholarships (IPRS), 676
Joshua Feigenbaum Award, 325

United Kingdom

ESRC 1+3 Awards & +3 Awards, 265
EUI Postgraduate Scholarships, 277
Fulbright-Humphrey Fellowship for Civil Servants, 693
Hastings Center International Visiting Scholars Program, 318
International Postgraduate Research Scholarships (IPRS), 676
Joshua Feigenbaum Award, 325
Molson Research Awards, 136
Mr and Mrs David Edward Memorial Award, 681
PDS Research Project Grant, 487
PDS Studentships and Junior/Senior Fellows, 487
Prix du Québec, 136
University of Essex Foundation Scholarships, 632
University of Kent School of Physical Sciences., 638
UWB Departmental Research Studentships, 681
UWB Research Studentships, 681
Wingate Scholarships, 704

United States of America

Alcohol Beverage Medical Research Foundation Research Project
Grant, 14
ARCE Fellowships, 69
Fulbright Senior Specialists Program, 245
International Postgraduate Research Scholarships (IPRS), 676
National Research Service Award Mental Health and Adjustment in
the Life Course, 399
NIH Research Grants, 450

West European Countries

ESRC 1+3 Awards & +3 Awards, 265
EUI Postgraduate Scholarships, 277
Hastings Center International Visiting Scholars Program, 318
International Postgraduate Research Scholarships (IPRS), 676
Mr and Mrs David Edward Memorial Award, 681
University of Kent School of Physical Sciences., 638
UWB Departmental Research Studentships, 681
UWB Research Studentships, 681
Wingate Scholarships, 704

SOCIAL INSTITUTIONS

Any Country

Center for Advanced Study in the Behavioral Sciences Postdoctoral
Residential Fellowships, 223
FAMSI Research Grant, 287
HRB Research Project Grants North-South Co-operation, 320
HRB Summer Student Grants, 320
M Alison Frantz Fellowship in Post-Classical Studies at the Gennadius
Library (formerly known as the Gennadeion Fellowship), 72
University of Bristol Postgraduate Scholarships, 619
University of Essex Scholarships, 632
University of Manchester Research Studentships and Scholarships,
642
University of Stirling Research Studentships, 678

African Nations

International Postgraduate Research Scholarships (IPRS), 676

Australia

Wingate Scholarships, 704

British Commonwealth

International Postgraduate Research Scholarships (IPRS), 676
Wingate Scholarships, 704

Canada

Alcohol Beverage Medical Research Foundation Research Project
Grant, 14
International Postgraduate Research Scholarships (IPRS), 676
Wingate Scholarships, 704

Caribbean Countries

International Postgraduate Research Scholarships (IPRS), 676

East European Countries

International Postgraduate Research Scholarships (IPRS), 676

Far East

International Postgraduate Research Scholarships (IPRS), 676

Indian Sub-Continent

International Postgraduate Research Scholarships (IPRS), 676
Wingate Scholarships, 704

Middle East

International Postgraduate Research Scholarships (IPRS), 676

New Zealand

Wingate Scholarships, 704

South Africa

International Postgraduate Research Scholarships (IPRS), 676
Wingate Scholarships, 704

South America

International Postgraduate Research Scholarships (IPRS), 676

United Kingdom

ESRC 1 + 3 Awards & + 3 Awards, 265
International Postgraduate Research Scholarships (IPRS), 676
Mr and Mrs David Edward Memorial Award, 681
University of Essex Foundation Scholarships, 632
UWB Departmental Research Studentships, 681
UWB Research Studentships, 681
Wingate Scholarships, 704

United States of America

Alcohol Beverage Medical Research Foundation Research Project Grant, 14
ARCE Fellowships, 69
Fulbright Senior Specialists Program, 245
International Postgraduate Research Scholarships (IPRS), 676
NIH Research Grants, 450

West European Countries

ESRC 1 + 3 Awards & + 3 Awards, 265
International Postgraduate Research Scholarships (IPRS), 676
Mr and Mrs David Edward Memorial Award, 681
UWB Departmental Research Studentships, 681
UWB Research Studentships, 681
Wingate Scholarships, 704

SOCIAL COMMUNICATION PROBLEMS

Any Country

BackCare Research Grants, 123
Center for Advanced Study in the Behavioral Sciences Postdoctoral Residential Fellowships, 223
HRB Research Project Grants North-South Co-operation, 320
HRB Summer Student Grants, 320
John L. Stanley Award, 325
Joshua Feigenbaum Award, 325
NCAR Postdoctoral Appointments in the Advanced Study Program, 439
Robert K. Merton Award, 326
University of Bristol Postgraduate Scholarships, 619
University of Essex Scholarships, 632
University of Manchester Research Studentships and Scholarships, 642
University of Stirling Research Studentships, 678

African Nations

International Postgraduate Research Scholarships (IPRS), 676
Joshua Feigenbaum Award, 325

Australia

Joshua Feigenbaum Award, 325
Wingate Scholarships, 704

British Commonwealth

International Postgraduate Research Scholarships (IPRS), 676
Joshua Feigenbaum Award, 325
Wingate Scholarships, 704

Canada

Alcohol Beverage Medical Research Foundation Research Project Grant, 14
International Postgraduate Research Scholarships (IPRS), 676

Joshua Feigenbaum Award, 325
Wingate Scholarships, 704

Caribbean Countries

International Postgraduate Research Scholarships (IPRS), 676
Joshua Feigenbaum Award, 325

East European Countries

International Postgraduate Research Scholarships (IPRS), 676
Joshua Feigenbaum Award, 325

Far East

International Postgraduate Research Scholarships (IPRS), 676
Joshua Feigenbaum Award, 325

Indian Sub-Continent

International Postgraduate Research Scholarships (IPRS), 676
Joshua Feigenbaum Award, 325
Wingate Scholarships, 704

Middle East

International Postgraduate Research Scholarships (IPRS), 676
Joshua Feigenbaum Award, 325

New Zealand

Joshua Feigenbaum Award, 325
Wingate Scholarships, 704

South Africa

International Postgraduate Research Scholarships (IPRS), 676
Joshua Feigenbaum Award, 325
Wingate Scholarships, 704

South America

International Postgraduate Research Scholarships (IPRS), 676
Joshua Feigenbaum Award, 325

United Kingdom

ESRC 1 + 3 Awards & + 3 Awards, 265
International Postgraduate Research Scholarships (IPRS), 676
Joshua Feigenbaum Award, 325
Mr and Mrs David Edward Memorial Award, 681
University of Essex Foundation Scholarships, 632
UWB Departmental Research Studentships, 681
UWB Research Studentships, 681
Wingate Scholarships, 704

United States of America

Alcohol Beverage Medical Research Foundation Research Project Grant, 14
Fulbright Senior Specialists Program, 245
International Postgraduate Research Scholarships (IPRS), 676
NIH Research Grants, 450

West European Countries

ESRC 1 + 3 Awards & + 3 Awards, 265
International Postgraduate Research Scholarships (IPRS), 676
Mr and Mrs David Edward Memorial Award, 681
UWB Departmental Research Studentships, 681
UWB Research Studentships, 681
Wingate Scholarships, 704

FUTUROLOGY

Any Country

Dublin Institute for Advanced Studies Scholarship in Celtic Studies, 262
Equiano Memorial Award, 596
John L. Stanley Award, 325
Joshua Feigenbaum Award, 325
Robert K. Merton Award, 326

DEMOGRAPHY

ANTHROPOLOGY

African Nations

Australia

British Commonwealth

Canada

East European Countries

Far East

Indian Sub-Continent

New Zealand

South Africa

United Kingdom

British Conference Grants, 135
British Institute in Eastern Africa Graduate Attachments, 148
British Institute in Eastern Africa Research Grants, 148
CBRL Research Grant, 244
CBRL Travel Grant, 244
Emslie Horniman Anthropological Scholarship Fund, 526
ESRC 1+3 Awards & +3 Awards, 265
Hector and Elizabeth Catling Bursary, 155
Prix du Québec, 136
Sasakawa Scholarship, 678
William Wyse Studentship in Social Anthropology, 627
Wingate Scholarships, 704

United States of America

ACC Fellowship Grants Program, 103
Alcohol Beverage Medical Research Foundation Research Project Grant, 14
ARCE Fellowships, 69
Council of American Overseas Research Centers (CAORC) Senior (Postdoctoral) Fellowships, 74
Earthwatch Education Awards, 264
Fulbright Senior Specialists Program, 245
GMF Research Fellowships Program, 301
Ian Axford (New Zealand) Fellowships in Public Policy, 239
IREX Individual Advanced Research Opportunities, 366
IREX John J and Nancy Lee Roberts Fellowship Program, 366
IREX Short-Term Travel Grants, 367
Kennan Institute Research Scholarship, 385
Mary McNeill Scholarship in Irish Studies, 344
NIH Research Grants, 450
NRC Twinning Program, 455
UCLA IAC Postdoctoral/Visiting Scholar Fellowships, 607
Washington University Chancellor's Graduate Fellowship Program for African Americans, 699

West European Countries

ESRC 1+3 Awards & +3 Awards, 265
University of Otago PhD Scholarships, 646
University of Otago Prestigious PhD Scholarships, 647
William Wyse Studentship in Social Anthropology, 627
Wingate Scholarships, 704

ETHNOLOGY

Any Country

AIATSIS Research Grants, 116
ASCSA Fellowships, 71
Center for Advanced Study in the Behavioral Sciences Postdoctoral Residential Fellowships, 223
CIMO Scholarships for Post-graduate Studies at a Finnish University, 225
Earthwatch Field Research Grants, 264
External Faculty Fellowships, 594
Fondation Fyssen Postdoctoral Study Grants, 281
Institute of Irish Studies Senior Visiting Research Fellowship, 344
Jacobs Research Fund, 703
M Alison Frantz Fellowship in Post-Classical Studies at the Gennadius Library (formerly known as the Gennadeion Fellowship), 72
NEH Fellowships, 72

Australia

Wingate Scholarships, 704

British Commonwealth

Wingate Scholarships, 704

Canada

1) Thompson (Homer and Dorothy) Fellowship 2) Elisabeth Alfolate Fellowship, 196

Mary McNeill Scholarship in Irish Studies, 344
Wingate Scholarships, 704

Far East

ACC Fellowship Grants Program, 103

Indian Sub-Continent

Wingate Scholarships, 704

New Zealand

Wingate Scholarships, 704

South Africa

Wingate Scholarships, 704

United Kingdom

CBRL Research Grant, 244
CBRL Travel Grant, 244
ESRC 1+3 Awards & +3 Awards, 265
Wingate Scholarships, 704

United States of America

ACC Fellowship Grants Program, 103
ARCE Fellowships, 69
Earthwatch Education Awards, 264
IREX John J and Nancy Lee Roberts Fellowship Program, 366
Mary McNeill Scholarship in Irish Studies, 344

West European Countries

ESRC 1+3 Awards & +3 Awards, 265
Wingate Scholarships, 704

FOLKLORE

Any Country

AIATSIS Research Grants, 116
ASCSA Fellowships, 71
Center for Advanced Study in the Behavioral Sciences Postdoctoral Residential Fellowships, 223
CIMO Scholarships for Post-graduate Studies at a Finnish University, 225
Earthwatch Field Research Grants, 264
External Faculty Fellowships, 594
Institute of Irish Studies Senior Visiting Research Fellowship, 344
Jacobs Research Fund, 703
M Alison Frantz Fellowship in Post-Classical Studies at the Gennadius Library (formerly known as the Gennadeion Fellowship), 72
NEH Fellowships, 72

Australia

Wingate Scholarships, 704

British Commonwealth

Wingate Scholarships, 704

Canada

Mary McNeill Scholarship in Irish Studies, 344
Wingate Scholarships, 704

Far East

ACC Fellowship Grants Program, 103

Indian Sub-Continent

Wingate Scholarships, 704

New Zealand

Wingate Scholarships, 704

South Africa

Wingate Scholarships, 704

United Kingdom

CBRL Research Grant, 244
CBRL Travel Grant, 244
ESRC 1 + 3 Awards & + 3 Awards, 265
Wingate Scholarships, 704

United States of America

ACC Fellowship Grants Program, 103
ARCE Fellowships, 69
Earthwatch Education Awards, 264
IREX John J and Nancy Lee Roberts Fellowship Program, 366
Mary McNeill Scholarship in Irish Studies, 344

West European Countries

ESRC 1 + 3 Awards & + 3 Awards, 265
Wingate Scholarships, 704

WOMEN'S STUDIES

Any Country

ABF Fellowships in Law and Social Science, 35
Advanced Fellowships, 71
Ahmanson and Getty Postdoctoral Fellowships, 606
AIATSIS Research Grants, 116
ASCSA Fellowships, 71
ASECS (American Society for Eighteenth-Century Studies)/Clark Library Fellowships, 606
British Academy Overseas Conference Grants, 134
British Academy Small Personal Research Grants, 134
British Academy Worldwide Congress Grant, 135
Camargo Fellowships, 164
Center for Advanced Study in the Behavioral Sciences Postdoctoral Residential Fellowships, 223
Clark Library Short-Term Resident Fellowships, 606
Clark Predoctoral Fellowships, 607
Clark-Huntington Joint Bibliographical Fellowship, 607
Downing College Research Fellowships, 623
External Faculty Fellowships, 594
Foundation Praemium Erasmianum Study Prize, 288
Frederick Douglass Institute Postdoctoral Fellowship, 289
Frederick Douglass Institute Predoctoral Dissertation Fellowship, 290
Henry A Murray Dissertation Award Program, 322
HFG Dissertation Fellowship, 314
HFG Research Program, 314
Jeanne Humphrey Block Dissertation Award, 322
Kennan Institute Short Term Grants, 385
La Trobe University Postgraduate Scholarship, 390
Library Company of Philadelphia and Historical Society of Pennsylvania Research Fellowships in American History and Culture, 398
M Alison Frantz Fellowship in Post-Classical Studies at the Gennadius Library (formerly known as the Gennadeion Fellowship), 72
Marusia and Michael Dorosh Master's Fellowship, 207
NEH Fellowships, 72
NHC Fellowships, 449
OISE/UT FUNDING SUPPORT, 477
OISE/UT Graduate Assistantships, 477
Research Student Bursary, 163
Rockefeller Archive Center Research Grant Program, 522
Russell Sage Foundation Visiting Scholar Appointments, 551
United States Center for Advanced Holocaust Studies Research Fellowships, 608
University of Bristol Postgraduate Scholarships, 619
University of Dundee Research Awards, 629
University of Essex Scholarships, 632
University of Glasgow Postgraduate Research Scholarships, 634
University of Manchester Research Studentships and Scholarships, 642
University of Otago International Scholarships, 646

Wolfsonian FIU Fellowship, 706
Woodrow Wilson Grants in Women's Studies, 709

African Nations

Hastings Center International Visiting Scholars Program, 318
Hubert H Humphrey Fellowship Programme, 609
International Postgraduate Research Scholarships (IPRS), 676
MCTC Assistance for Courses, 304
MCTC Tuition and Maintenance Scholarships, 304
Sally Mugabe Memorial Cambridge DFID Scholarship for Postgraduate Study, 189
University of Sussex Overseas Development Administration Shared Scholarship Scheme, 678

Australia

Hastings Center International Visiting Scholars Program, 318
University of Otago PhD Scholarships, 646
University of Otago Prestigious PhD Scholarships, 647
University of Western Sydney Postgraduate Research Award (UWSPRA), 689
Wingate Scholarships, 704

British Commonwealth

Hastings Center International Visiting Scholars Program, 318
Hector and Elizabeth Catling Bursary, 155
International Postgraduate Research Scholarships (IPRS), 676
Wingate Scholarships, 704

Canada

Alcohol Beverage Medical Research Foundation Research Project Grant, 14
Gilbert Chinard Fellowships, 336
Harmon Chadbourn Rorison Fellowship, 336
Idea Grants, 214
IDRC Doctoral Research Awards, 358
International Postgraduate Research Scholarships (IPRS), 676
Postdoctoral Training Programme in Addiction and Mental Health, 225
Research Planning Grants, 214
Thérèse F Casgrain Fellowship, 580
Wingate Scholarships, 704

Caribbean Countries

Hastings Center International Visiting Scholars Program, 318
Hubert H Humphrey Fellowship Programme, 609
International Postgraduate Research Scholarships (IPRS), 676
MCTC Assistance for Courses, 304
MCTC Tuition and Maintenance Scholarships, 304

East European Countries

Hastings Center International Visiting Scholars Program, 318
Hubert H Humphrey Fellowship Programme, 609
International Postgraduate Research Scholarships (IPRS), 676
MCTC Assistance for Courses, 304
MCTC Tuition and Maintenance Scholarships, 304
Menzies Centre for Australian Studies Visiting Fellowships European, 417
Sasakawa Scholarship, 678

Far East

Hastings Center International Visiting Scholars Program, 318
Hubert H Humphrey Fellowship Programme, 609
International Postgraduate Research Scholarships (IPRS), 676
MCTC Assistance for Courses, 304
MCTC Tuition and Maintenance Scholarships, 304
Sasakawa Scholarship, 678
University of Otago Dr Sulaiman Daud 125th Jubilee International Postgraduate Scholarship, 646
University of Sussex Overseas Development Administration Shared Scholarship Scheme, 678

Indian Sub-Continent

Hastings Center International Visiting Scholars Program, 318
Hubert H Humphrey Fellowship Programme, 609
International Postgraduate Research Scholarships (IPRS), 676
MCTC Assistance for Courses, 304
MCTC Tuition and Maintenance Scholarships, 304
University of Sussex Overseas Development Administration Shared
Scholarship Scheme, 678
Wingate Scholarships, 704

Middle East

Hastings Center International Visiting Scholars Program, 318
Hubert H Humphrey Fellowship Programme, 609
International Postgraduate Research Scholarships (IPRS), 676
MCTC Assistance for Courses, 304
MCTC Tuition and Maintenance Scholarships, 304

New Zealand

Hastings Center International Visiting Scholars Program, 318
University of Otago PhD Scholarships, 646
University of Otago Prestigious PhD Scholarships, 647
University of Western Sydney Postgraduate Research Award (UW-
SPRA), 689
Wingate Scholarships, 704

South Africa

Hastings Center International Visiting Scholars Program, 318
Hubert H Humphrey Fellowship Programme, 609
International Postgraduate Research Scholarships (IPRS), 676
MCTC Assistance for Courses, 304
MCTC Tuition and Maintenance Scholarships, 304
Wingate Scholarships, 704

South America

Hastings Center International Visiting Scholars Program, 318
Hubert H Humphrey Fellowship Programme, 609
International Postgraduate Research Scholarships (IPRS), 676
MCTC Assistance for Courses, 304
MCTC Tuition and Maintenance Scholarships, 304

United Kingdom

British Conference Grants, 135
ESRC 1+3 Awards & +3 Awards, 265
Hastings Center International Visiting Scholars Program, 318
Hector and Elizabeth Catling Bursary, 155
International Postgraduate Research Scholarships (IPRS), 676
Mr and Mrs David Edward Memorial Award, 681
Sasakawa Scholarship, 678
University of Essex Foundation Scholarships, 632
UWB Departmental Research Studentships, 681
UWB Research Studentships, 681
Wingate Scholarships, 704

United States of America

AAUW Eleanor Roosevelt Teacher Fellowships, 4
AAUW University Scholar-in-Residence, 4
Alcohol Beverage Medical Research Foundation Research Project
Grant, 14
ARCE Fellowships, 69
Fulbright Distinguished Chairs Program, 245
Fulbright Senior Specialists Program, 245
Gilbert Chinard Fellowships, 336
Harmon Chadbourn Rorison Fellowship, 336
Ian Axford (New Zealand) Fellowships in Public Policy, 239
International Postgraduate Research Scholarships (IPRS), 676
IREX Individual Advanced Research Opportunities, 366
IREX John J and Nancy Lee Roberts Fellowship Program, 366
IREX Short-Term Travel Grants, 367
Kennan Institute Research Scholarship, 385
Postdoctoral Training Programme in Addiction and Mental Health, 225
UCLA IAC Postdoctoral/Visiting Scholar Fellowships, 607

University of New Hampshire Postdoctoral Fellowships For Research
on Family Violence, 645

West European Countries

ESRC 1+3 Awards & +3 Awards, 265
Hastings Center International Visiting Scholars Program, 318
International Postgraduate Research Scholarships (IPRS), 676
Menzies Centre for Australian Studies Visiting Fellowships European,
417
Mr and Mrs David Edward Memorial Award, 681
University of Otago PhD Scholarships, 646
University of Otago Prestigious PhD Scholarships, 647
UWB Departmental Research Studentships, 681
UWB Research Studentships, 681
Wingate Scholarships, 704

URBAN STUDIES

Any Country

AIATSIS Research Grants, 116
ASCSA Fellowships, 71
British Academy Overseas Conference Grants, 134
British Academy Small Personal Research Grants, 134
British Academy Worldwide Congress Grant, 135
Center for Advanced Study in the Behavioral Sciences Postdoctoral
Residential Fellowships, 223
Downing College Research Fellowships, 623
Eli Ginzberg Award, 325
Equiano Memorial Award, 596
External Faculty Fellowships, 594
Frederick Douglass Institute Postdoctoral Fellowship, 289
Frederick Douglass Institute Predoctoral Dissertation Fellowship, 290
Gypsy Lore Society Young Scholar's Prize in Romani Studies, 311
HFG Dissertation Fellowship, 314
HFG Research Program, 314
J B Harley Research Fellowships in the History of Cartography, 374
John L. Stanley Award, 325
Joseph L Fisher Dissertation Award, 515
Joshua Feigenbaum Award, 325
Kennan Institute Short Term Grants, 385
M Alison Frantz Fellowship in Post-Classical Studies at the Gennadius
Library (formerly known as the Gennadeion Fellowship), 72
MA/Msc Studentship in European Studies, 218
PhD Studentship in European Studies, 218
Queen Mary Research Studentships, 506
Robert K. Merton Award, 326
Rockefeller Archive Center Research Grant Program, 522
Russell Sage Foundation Visiting Scholar Appointments, 551
University of Bristol Postgraduate Scholarships, 619
University of Glasgow Postgraduate Research Scholarships, 634
University of Kent Sociology and Social and Public Policy Student-
ships, 638
University of Manchester Research Studentships and Scholarships,
642
Wolfsonian FIU Fellowship, 706

African Nations

Ecosystem Approaches to Human Health Awards, 358
Hubert H Humphrey Fellowship Programme, 609
International Postgraduate Research Scholarships (IPRS), 676
Joshua Feigenbaum Award, 325

Australia

Joshua Feigenbaum Award, 325
Wingate Scholarships, 704

British Commonwealth

International Postgraduate Research Scholarships (IPRS), 676
Joshua Feigenbaum Award, 325
Wingate Scholarships, 704

Canada

Alcohol Beverage Medical Research Foundation Research Project Grant, 14
Ecosystem Approaches to Human Health Awards, 358
IDRC Doctoral Research Awards, 358
International Postgraduate Research Scholarships (IPRS), 676
Joshua Feigenbaum Award, 325
Wingate Scholarships, 704

Caribbean Countries

Ecosystem Approaches to Human Health Awards, 358
Hubert H Humphrey Fellowship Programme, 609
International Postgraduate Research Scholarships (IPRS), 676
Joshua Feigenbaum Award, 325

East European Countries

Hubert H Humphrey Fellowship Programme, 609
International Postgraduate Research Scholarships (IPRS), 676
Joshua Feigenbaum Award, 325

Far East

Ecosystem Approaches to Human Health Awards, 358
Hubert H Humphrey Fellowship Programme, 609
International Postgraduate Research Scholarships (IPRS), 676
Joshua Feigenbaum Award, 325

Indian Sub-Continent

Ecosystem Approaches to Human Health Awards, 358
Hubert H Humphrey Fellowship Programme, 609
International Postgraduate Research Scholarships (IPRS), 676
Joshua Feigenbaum Award, 325
Wingate Scholarships, 704

Middle East

Ecosystem Approaches to Human Health Awards, 358
Hubert H Humphrey Fellowship Programme, 609
International Postgraduate Research Scholarships (IPRS), 676
Joshua Feigenbaum Award, 325

New Zealand

Joshua Feigenbaum Award, 325
Wingate Scholarships, 704

South Africa

Ecosystem Approaches to Human Health Awards, 358
Hubert H Humphrey Fellowship Programme, 609
International Postgraduate Research Scholarships (IPRS), 676
Joshua Feigenbaum Award, 325
Wingate Scholarships, 704

South America

Hubert H Humphrey Fellowship Programme, 609
International Postgraduate Research Scholarships (IPRS), 676
Joshua Feigenbaum Award, 325

United Kingdom

British Conference Grants, 135
ESRC 1 + 3 Awards & + 3 Awards, 265
International Postgraduate Research Scholarships (IPRS), 676
Joshua Feigenbaum Award, 325
Wingate Scholarships, 704

United States of America

Alcohol Beverage Medical Research Foundation Research Project Grant, 14
ARCE Fellowships, 69
Fulbright Senior Specialists Program, 245
Ian Axford (New Zealand) Fellowships in Public Policy, 239
International Postgraduate Research Scholarships (IPRS), 676
IREX Individual Advanced Research Opportunities, 366

IREX John J and Nancy Lee Roberts Fellowship Program, 366
Kennan Institute Research Scholarship, 385
UCLA IAC Postdoctoral/Visiting Scholar Fellowships, 607

West European Countries

ESRC 1 + 3 Awards & + 3 Awards, 265
International Postgraduate Research Scholarships (IPRS), 676
Wingate Scholarships, 704

RURAL STUDIES

Any Country

AIATSIS Research Grants, 116
ASCSA Fellowships, 71
British Academy Overseas Conference Grants, 134
British Academy Small Personal Research Grants, 134
British Academy Worldwide Congress Grant, 135
Center for Advanced Study in the Behavioral Sciences Postdoctoral Residential Fellowships, 223
CQU Postgraduate Research Award, 224
Downing College Research Fellowships, 623
Earthwatch Field Research Grants, 264
Joseph L Fisher Dissertation Award, 515
Kennan Institute Short Term Grants, 385
M Alison Frantz Fellowship in Post-Classical Studies at the Gennadius Library (formerly known as the Gennadeion Fellowship), 72
Rockefeller Archive Center Research Grant Program, 522
University of Glasgow Postgraduate Research Scholarships, 634
University of Manchester Research Studentships and Scholarships, 642

African Nations

Hubert H Humphrey Fellowship Programme, 609
International Postgraduate Research Scholarships (IPRS), 676
University of Sussex Overseas Development Administration Shared Scholarship Scheme, 678

Australia

Wingate Scholarships, 704

British Commonwealth

International Postgraduate Research Scholarships (IPRS), 676
Wingate Scholarships, 704

Canada

Alcohol Beverage Medical Research Foundation Research Project Grant, 14
IDRC Doctoral Research Awards, 358
International Postgraduate Research Scholarships (IPRS), 676
Wingate Scholarships, 704

Caribbean Countries

Hubert H Humphrey Fellowship Programme, 609
International Postgraduate Research Scholarships (IPRS), 676

East European Countries

Hubert H Humphrey Fellowship Programme, 609
International Postgraduate Research Scholarships (IPRS), 676

Far East

Hubert H Humphrey Fellowship Programme, 609
International Postgraduate Research Scholarships (IPRS), 676
University of Sussex Overseas Development Administration Shared Scholarship Scheme, 678

Indian Sub-Continent

Hubert H Humphrey Fellowship Programme, 609
International Postgraduate Research Scholarships (IPRS), 676

COGNITIVE SCIENCES

PSYCHOLOGY

Alcohol Beverage Medical Research Foundation Research Project Grant, 14
Heritage Health Research Career Renewal Awards, 14
Idea Grants, 214
International Postgraduate Research Scholarships (IPRS), 676
Joshua Feigenbaum Award, 325
Postdoctoral Training Programme in Addiction and Mental Health, 225
Research Planning Grants, 214
Wingate Scholarships, 704

Caribbean Countries

International Postgraduate Research Scholarships (IPRS), 676
Joshua Feigenbaum Award, 325

East European Countries

International Postgraduate Research Scholarships (IPRS), 676
Joshua Feigenbaum Award, 325

Far East

International Postgraduate Research Scholarships (IPRS), 676
Joshua Feigenbaum Award, 325
University of Otago Dr Sulaiman Daud 125th Jubilee International Postgraduate Scholarship, 646

Indian Sub-Continent

International Postgraduate Research Scholarships (IPRS), 676
Joshua Feigenbaum Award, 325
Wingate Scholarships, 704

Middle East

International Postgraduate Research Scholarships (IPRS), 676
Joshua Feigenbaum Award, 325

New Zealand

Joshua Feigenbaum Award, 325
University of Otago PhD Scholarships, 646
University of Otago Prestigious PhD Scholarships, 647
University of Western Sydney Postgraduate Research Award (UW-SPRA), 689
Wingate Scholarships, 704

South Africa

International Postgraduate Research Scholarships (IPRS), 676
Joshua Feigenbaum Award, 325
Wingate Scholarships, 704

South America

International Postgraduate Research Scholarships (IPRS), 676
Joshua Feigenbaum Award, 325

United Kingdom

Alzheimers Society Research Grants, 22
British Conference Grants, 135
ESRC 1+3 Awards & +3 Awards, 265
Hallam Studentships, 558
International Postgraduate Research Scholarships (IPRS), 676
Joshua Feigenbaum Award, 325
Mr and Mrs David Edward Memorial Award, 681
PDS Research Project Grant, 487
PDS Studentships and Junior/Senior Fellows, 487
University of Essex Foundation Scholarships, 632
UWB Departmental Research Studentships, 681
UWB Research Studentships, 681
Wingate Scholarships, 704

United States of America

Alcohol Beverage Medical Research Foundation Research Project Grant, 14

ETS Postdoctoral Fellowships, 266
Fulbright Distinguished Chairs Program, 245
Fulbright Senior Specialists Program, 245
International Postgraduate Research Scholarships (IPRS), 676
IREX Individual Advanced Research Opportunities, 366
IREX John J and Nancy Lee Roberts Fellowship Program, 366
IREX Short-Term Travel Grants, 367
Kennan Institute Research Scholarship, 385
National Research Service Award Mental Health and Adjustment in the Life Course, 399
NIH Research Grants, 450
NRC Twinning Program, 455
Postdoctoral Training Programme in Addiction and Mental Health, 225
UCLA IAC Postdoctoral/Visiting Scholar Fellowships, 607
University of New Hampshire Postdoctoral Fellowships For Research on Family Violence, 645
Washington University Chancellor's Graduate Fellowship Program for African Americans, 699

West European Countries

ESRC 1+3 Awards & +3 Awards, 265
Hallam Studentships, 558
International Postgraduate Research Scholarships (IPRS), 676
Mr and Mrs David Edward Memorial Award, 681
University of Otago PhD Scholarships, 646
University of Otago Prestigious PhD Scholarships, 647
UWB Departmental Research Studentships, 681
UWB Research Studentships, 681
Wingate Scholarships, 704

EXPERIMENTAL PSYCHOLOGY

Any Country

Center for Advanced Study in the Behavioral Sciences Postdoctoral Residential Fellowships, 223
D Scott Rogo Award for Parapsychological Literature, 485
Eileen J Garrett Scholarship, 485
NARSAD Distinguished Investigator Awards, 434
NARSAD Independent Investigator Awards, 434
NARSAD Young Investigator Awards, 434
Parapsychology Foundation Grant, 400
UFAW Research and Project Awards, 616
UFAW Small Project and Travel Awards, 616
UFAW Vacation Scholarships, 616
University of Bristol Postgraduate Scholarships, 619
University of Dundee Research Awards, 629
University of Essex Scholarships, 632

African Nations

International Postgraduate Research Scholarships (IPRS), 676

Australia

Wingate Scholarships, 704

British Commonwealth

International Postgraduate Research Scholarships (IPRS), 676
Wingate Scholarships, 704

Canada

International Postgraduate Research Scholarships (IPRS), 676
Wingate Scholarships, 704

Caribbean Countries

International Postgraduate Research Scholarships (IPRS), 676

East European Countries

International Postgraduate Research Scholarships (IPRS), 676

Far East

International Postgraduate Research Scholarships (IPRS), 676

SOCIAL AND COMMUNITY PSYCHOLOGY

MCTC Tuition and Maintenance Scholarships, 304
Wingate Scholarships, 704

South America

Hubert H Humphrey Fellowship Programme, 609
International Postgraduate Research Scholarships (IPRS), 676
Joshua Feigenbaum Award, 325
MCTC Assistance for Courses, 304
MCTC Tuition and Maintenance Scholarships, 304

United Kingdom

Alzheimers Society Research Grants, 22
ESRC 1+3 Awards & +3 Awards, 265
International Postgraduate Research Scholarships (IPRS), 676
Joshua Feigenbaum Award, 325
Mr and Mrs David Edward Memorial Award, 681
PDS Research Project Grant, 487
PDS Studentships and Junior/Senior Fellows, 487
University of Essex Foundation Scholarships, 632
UWB Departmental Research Studentships, 681
UWB Research Studentships, 681
Wingate Scholarships, 704

United States of America

International Postgraduate Research Scholarships (IPRS), 676
National Research Service Award Mental Health and Adjustment in
the Life Course, 399
NIH Research Grants, 450
NRC Twinning Program, 455
Washington University Chancellor's Graduate Fellowship Program for
African Americans, 699

West European Countries

ESRC 1+3 Awards & +3 Awards, 265
International Postgraduate Research Scholarships (IPRS), 676
Mr and Mrs David Edward Memorial Award, 681
UWB Departmental Research Studentships, 681
UWB Research Studentships, 681
Wingate Scholarships, 704

CLINICAL PSYCHOLOGY

Any Country

Albert Ellis Institute Clinical Fellowship, 12
BackCare Research Grants, 123
Center for Advanced Study in the Behavioral Sciences Postdoctoral
Residential Fellowships, 223
Health Research Board PhD training sites, 319
HRB Project Grants-General, 320
NARSAD Distinguished Investigator Awards, 434
NARSAD Independent Investigator Awards, 434
OISE/UT FUNDING SUPPORT, 477
OISE/UT Graduate Assistantships, 477
Queen Elizabeth the Queen Mother Fellowship Award, 514
Research into Ageing Prize Studentships, 515
Research into Ageing Programme Grants, 515
Research Student Bursary, 163
Thomas Holloway Research Studentship, 536
University of Dundee Research Awards, 629
University of Essex Scholarships, 632
University of Manchester Research Studentships and Scholarships,
642

African Nations

International Postgraduate Research Scholarships (IPRS), 676

Australia

New South Wales Cancer Council Research Programme Grant, 464
New South Wales Cancer Council Research Project Grants, 464

University of Western Sydney Postgraduate Research Award (UW-
SPRA), 689

British Commonwealth

International Postgraduate Research Scholarships (IPRS), 676

Canada

International Postgraduate Research Scholarships (IPRS), 676

Caribbean Countries

International Postgraduate Research Scholarships (IPRS), 676

East European Countries

International Postgraduate Research Scholarships (IPRS), 676

Far East

International Postgraduate Research Scholarships (IPRS), 676

Indian Sub-Continent

International Postgraduate Research Scholarships (IPRS), 676

Middle East

International Postgraduate Research Scholarships (IPRS), 676

New Zealand

University of Western Sydney Postgraduate Research Award (UW-
SPRA), 689

South Africa

International Postgraduate Research Scholarships (IPRS), 676

South America

International Postgraduate Research Scholarships (IPRS), 676

United Kingdom

Alzheimers Society Research Grants, 22
International Postgraduate Research Scholarships (IPRS), 676
Mr and Mrs David Edward Memorial Award, 681
PDS Research Project Grant, 407
PDS Studentships and Junior/Senior Fellows, 487
PWSA (UK) Research Grants, 503
University of Essex Foundation Scholarships, 632
UWB Departmental Research Studentships, 681
UWB Research Studentships, 681

United States of America

International Postgraduate Research Scholarships (IPRS), 676
MFP Mental Health and Substance Abuse Services, 69
NIH Research Grants, 450
University of New Hampshire Postdoctoral Fellowships For Research
on Family Violence, 645
Washington University Chancellor's Graduate Fellowship Program for
African Americans, 699

West European Countries

International Postgraduate Research Scholarships (IPRS), 676
Mr and Mrs David Edward Memorial Award, 681
UWB Departmental Research Studentships, 681
UWB Research Studentships, 681

PERSONALITY PSYCHOLOGY

Any Country

BackCare Research Grants, 123
Center for Advanced Study in the Behavioral Sciences Postdoctoral
Residential Fellowships, 223
University of Essex Scholarships, 632
University of Stirling Research Studentships, 678

African Nations

International Postgraduate Research Scholarships (IPRS), 676

British Commonwealth

International Postgraduate Research Scholarships (IPRS), 676

Canada

International Postgraduate Research Scholarships (IPRS), 676

Caribbean Countries

International Postgraduate Research Scholarships (IPRS), 676

East European Countries

International Postgraduate Research Scholarships (IPRS), 676

Far East

International Postgraduate Research Scholarships (IPRS), 676

Indian Sub-Continent

International Postgraduate Research Scholarships (IPRS), 676

Middle East

International Postgraduate Research Scholarships (IPRS), 676

South Africa

International Postgraduate Research Scholarships (IPRS), 676

South America

International Postgraduate Research Scholarships (IPRS), 676

United Kingdom

Alzheimers Society Research Grants, 22
ESRC 1 + 3 Awards & + 3 Awards, 265
International Postgraduate Research Scholarships (IPRS), 676
Mr and Mrs David Edward Memorial Award, 681
PWSA (UK) Research Grants, 503
University of Essex Foundation Scholarships, 632
UWB Departmental Research Studentships, 681
UWB Research Studentships, 681

United States of America

International Postgraduate Research Scholarships (IPRS), 676
NIH Research Grants, 450

West European Countries

ESRC 1 + 3 Awards & + 3 Awards, 265
International Postgraduate Research Scholarships (IPRS), 676
Mr and Mrs David Edward Memorial Award, 681
UWB Departmental Research Studentships, 681
UWB Research Studentships, 681

INDUSTRIAL/ORGANISATIONAL PSYCHOLOGY

Any Country

BackCare Research Grants, 123
Center for Advanced Study in the Behavioral Sciences Postdoctoral Residential Fellowships, 223
University of Essex Scholarships, 632

African Nations

Hubert H Humphrey Fellowship Programme, 609
International Postgraduate Research Scholarships (IPRS), 676

British Commonwealth

International Postgraduate Research Scholarships (IPRS), 676

Canada

International Postgraduate Research Scholarships (IPRS), 676

Caribbean Countries

Hubert H Humphrey Fellowship Programme, 609
International Postgraduate Research Scholarships (IPRS), 676

East European Countries

Hubert H Humphrey Fellowship Programme, 609
International Postgraduate Research Scholarships (IPRS), 676

Far East

Hubert H Humphrey Fellowship Programme, 609
International Postgraduate Research Scholarships (IPRS), 676

Indian Sub-Continent

Hubert H Humphrey Fellowship Programme, 609
International Postgraduate Research Scholarships (IPRS), 676

Middle East

Hubert H Humphrey Fellowship Programme, 609
International Postgraduate Research Scholarships (IPRS), 676

South Africa

Hubert H Humphrey Fellowship Programme, 609
International Postgraduate Research Scholarships (IPRS), 676

South America

Hubert H Humphrey Fellowship Programme, 609
International Postgraduate Research Scholarships (IPRS), 676

United Kingdom

ESRC 1 + 3 Awards & + 3 Awards, 265
International Postgraduate Research Scholarships (IPRS), 676
Mr and Mrs David Edward Memorial Award, 681
University of Essex Foundation Scholarships, 632
UWB Departmental Research Studentships, 681
UWB Research Studentships, 681

United States of America

International Postgraduate Research Scholarships (IPRS), 676
National Research Service Award Mental Health and Adjustment in the Life Course, 399

West European Countries

ESRC 1 + 3 Awards & + 3 Awards, 265
International Postgraduate Research Scholarships (IPRS), 676
Mr and Mrs David Edward Memorial Award, 681
UWB Departmental Research Studentships, 681
UWB Research Studentships, 681

PSYCHOMETRICS

Any Country

Center for Advanced Study in the Behavioral Sciences Postdoctoral Residential Fellowships, 223
ETS Summer Program in Research for Graduate Students, 266
University of Essex Scholarships, 632

United Kingdom

Alzheimers Society Research Grants, 22
Mr and Mrs David Edward Memorial Award, 681
University of Essex Foundation Scholarships, 632
UWB Departmental Research Studentships, 681
UWB Research Studentships, 681

United States of America

NIH Research Grants, 450

University of New Hampshire Postdoctoral Fellowships For Research on Family Violence, 645

West European Countries

Mr and Mrs David Edward Memorial Award, 681
UWB Departmental Research Studentships, 681
UWB Research Studentships, 681

EDUCATIONAL PSYCHOLOGY

Any Country

BackCare Research Grants, 123
Center for Advanced Study in the Behavioral Sciences Postdoctoral Residential Fellowships, 223
Equiano Memorial Award, 596
John L. Stanley Award, 325
Joshua Feigenbaum Award, 325
OISE/UT FUNDING SUPPORT, 477
OISE/UT Graduate Assistantships, 477
University of Bristol Postgraduate Scholarships, 619
University of Dundee Research Awards, 629
University of Essex Scholarships, 632
University of Stirling Research Studentships, 678

African Nations

Hubert H Humphrey Fellowship Programme, 609
Joshua Feigenbaum Award, 325

Australia

Joshua Feigenbaum Award, 325
Wingate Scholarships, 704

British Commonwealth

Joshua Feigenbaum Award, 325
Wingate Scholarships, 704

Canada

Joshua Feigenbaum Award, 325
Wingate Scholarships, 704

Caribbean Countries

Hubert H Humphrey Fellowship Programme, 609
Joshua Feigenbaum Award, 325

East European Countries

Hubert H Humphrey Fellowship Programme, 609
Joshua Feigenbaum Award, 325

Far East

Hubert H Humphrey Fellowship Programme, 609
Joshua Feigenbaum Award, 325

Indian Sub-Continent

Hubert H Humphrey Fellowship Programme, 609
Joshua Feigenbaum Award, 325
Wingate Scholarships, 704

Middle East

Hubert H Humphrey Fellowship Programme, 609
Joshua Feigenbaum Award, 325

New Zealand

Joshua Feigenbaum Award, 325
Wingate Scholarships, 704

South Africa

Hubert H Humphrey Fellowship Programme, 609
Joshua Feigenbaum Award, 325

Wingate Scholarships, 704

South America

Hubert H Humphrey Fellowship Programme, 609
Joshua Feigenbaum Award, 325

United Kingdom

ESRC 1+3 Awards & +3 Awards, 265
Joshua Feigenbaum Award, 325
Mr and Mrs David Edward Memorial Award, 681
PWSA (UK) Research Grants, 503
University of Essex Foundation Scholarships, 632
UWB Departmental Research Studentships, 681
UWB Research Studentships, 681
Wingate Scholarships, 704

West European Countries

ESRC 1+3 Awards & +3 Awards, 265
Mr and Mrs David Edward Memorial Award, 681
UWB Departmental Research Studentships, 681
UWB Research Studentships, 681
Wingate Scholarships, 704

GEOGRAPHY (SOCIAL AND ECONOMIC)

Any Country

AAG General Research Fund, 104
ABF Fellowships in Law and Social Science, 35
Ahmanson and Getty Postdoctoral Fellowships, 606
AIAR Annual Professorship, 73
AIATSIS Research Grants, 116
ASCSA Fellowships, 71
ASCSA Summer Sessions, 72
Association for Women in Science Educational Foundation Predoctoral Awards, 104
British Academy Overseas Conference Grants, 134
British Academy Small Personal Research Grants, 134
British Academy Worldwide Congress Grant, 135
Center for Advanced Study in the Behavioral Sciences Postdoctoral Residential Fellowships, 223
CQU Postgraduate Research Award, 224
Downing College Research Fellowships, 623
Earthwatch Field Research Grants, 264
Gypsy Lore Society Young Scholar's Prize in Romani Studies, 311
J B Harley Research Fellowships in the History of Cartography, 374
John L. Stanley Award, 325
Joseph L Fisher Dissertation Award, 515
Joshua Feigenbaum Award, 325
Kennan Institute Short Term Grants, 385
M Alison Frantz Fellowship in Post-Classical Studies at the Gennadius Library (formerly known as the Gennadeion Fellowship), 72
Population Council Fellowships in Population and Social Sciences, 502
Queen Mary Research Studentships, 506
Rhodes University Postdoctoral Fellowship, 519
Robert K. Merton Award, 326
St Anne's College Biegun Warburg Junior Research Fellowship, 665
University of Bristol Postgraduate Scholarships, 619
University of Dundee Research Awards, 629
University of Glasgow Postgraduate Research Scholarships, 634
University of Manchester Research Studentships and Scholarships, 642
University of Otago International Scholarships, 646
University of Stirling Research Studentships, 678
USC College Dissertation Fellowship, 677
USC College of Letters, Arts and Sciences Merit Award, 677
Violet Cressey-Marcks Fisher Travel Scholarship, 535
Warren Nystrom Fund Awards, 105
Woods Hole Oceanographic Institution Postdoctoral Awards in Marine Policy and Ocean Management, 710

DEVELOPMENT STUDIES

AREA AND CULTURAL STUDIES

African Nations

Australia

British Commonwealth

Canada

Caribbean Countries

East European Countries

Far East

Indian Sub-Continent

Middle East

New Zealand

South Africa

South America

United Kingdom

United Kingdom

AHRB Doctoral Awards Scheme, 99
British Institute in Eastern Africa Graduate Attachments, 148
British Institute in Eastern Africa Research Grants, 148
Research Preparation Master's Scheme, 99

West European Countries

AHRB Doctoral Awards Scheme, 99
Research Preparation Master's Scheme, 99

AFRICAN AMERICAN

Any Country

Albert J Beveridge Grant, 49
Center for Advanced Study in the Behavioral Sciences Postdoctoral Residential Fellowships, 223
Equiano Memorial Award, 596
Frederick Douglass Institute Postdoctoral Fellowship, 289
Frederick Douglass Institute Predoctoral Dissertation Fellowship, 290
Huggins Quarles Award, 190
Library Company of Philadelphia and Historical Society of Pennsylvania Research Fellowships in American History and Culture, 398
Wolfsonian FIU Fellowship, 706

East European Countries

AHRB Doctoral Awards Scheme, 99
Research Preparation Master's Scheme, 99

United Kingdom

AHRB Doctoral Awards Scheme, 99
Research Preparation Master's Scheme, 99

United States of America

ACLS/SSRC/NEH International and Area Studies Fellowships, 41
Fulbright Distinguished Chairs Program, 245
Fulbright Senior Specialists Program, 245
SSRC-Mellon Mays Fellowships, 574
Syracuse University African American Fellowship, 598

West European Countries

AHRB Doctoral Awards Scheme, 99
Research Preparation Master's Scheme, 99

NATIVE AMERICAN

Any Country

Albert J Beveridge Grant, 49
Center for Advanced Study in the Behavioral Sciences Postdoctoral Residential Fellowships, 223
Jacobs Research Fund, 703
Library Company of Philadelphia and Historical Society of Pennsylvania Research Fellowships in American History and Culture, 398

East European Countries

AHRB Doctoral Awards Scheme, 99
Research Preparation Master's Scheme, 99

United Kingdom

AHRB Doctoral Awards Scheme, 99
Research Preparation Master's Scheme, 99

United States of America

ACLS/SSRC/NEH International and Area Studies Fellowships, 41
Fulbright Senior Specialists Program, 245
SSRC-Mellon Mays Fellowships, 574

West European Countries

AHRB Doctoral Awards Scheme, 99

Research Preparation Master's Scheme, 99

HISPANIC AMERICAN

Any Country

Albert J Beveridge Grant, 49
Center for Advanced Study in the Behavioral Sciences Postdoctoral Residential Fellowships, 223
Library Company of Philadelphia and Historical Society of Pennsylvania Research Fellowships in American History and Culture, 398

East European Countries

AHRB Doctoral Awards Scheme, 99
Research Preparation Master's Scheme, 99

United Kingdom

AHRB Doctoral Awards Scheme, 99
Research Preparation Master's Scheme, 99

United States of America

ACLS/SSRC/NEH International and Area Studies Fellowships, 41
Fulbright Senior Specialists Program, 245
SSRC-Mellon Mays Fellowships, 574

West European Countries

AHRB Doctoral Awards Scheme, 99
Research Preparation Master's Scheme, 99

AMERICAN

Any Country

AAS American Society for Eighteenth-Century Studies Fellowships, 25
Albert J Beveridge Grant, 49
Canadian Embassy (USA) Senior Fellowship Program, 202
Center for Advanced Study in the Behavioral Sciences Postdoctoral Residential Fellowships, 223
Donald Groves Fund, 62
Joyce Tracy Fellowship, 26
Kate B and Hall J Peterson Fellowships, 27
Library Company of Philadelphia and Historical Society of Pennsylvania Research Fellowships in American History and Culture, 398
Library Company of Philadelphia Program in Early American Economy and Society, 398
University of Essex Scholarships, 632
Wolfsonian FIU Fellowship, 706

East European Countries

AHRB Doctoral Awards Scheme, 99
Research Preparation Master's Scheme, 99

United Kingdom

AHRB Doctoral Awards Scheme, 99
BAAS Short Term Awards, 136
Queen's College George Oakes Senior Scholarship, 662
Research Preparation Master's Scheme, 99
University of Essex Foundation Scholarships, 632

United States of America

AAS National Endowment for the Humanities Visiting Fellowships, 26
ACLS/SSRC/NEH International and Area Studies Fellowships, 41
Fulbright Distinguished Chairs Program, 245
Fulbright Senior Specialists Program, 245
SSRC-Mellon Mays Fellowships, 574

West European Countries

AHRB Doctoral Awards Scheme, 99
Research Preparation Master's Scheme, 99

EAST ASIAN

Any Country

Bernadotte E Schmitt Grants, 49
Center for Advanced Study in the Behavioral Sciences Postdoctoral Residential Fellowships, 223
Korea Foundation Advanced Research Grant, 386
Korea Foundation Fellowship for Field Research, 386
Korea Foundation Fellowship for Graduate Studies, 386
Korea Foundation Fellowship for Korean Language Training, 386
Korea Foundation Postdoctoral Fellowship, 387
SAIIA Bradlow Fellowship, 592

African Nations

International Postgraduate Research Scholarships (IPRS), 676

British Commonwealth

International Postgraduate Research Scholarships (IPRS), 676

Canada

Canadian Window on International Development, 358
International Postgraduate Research Scholarships (IPRS), 676

Caribbean Countries

International Postgraduate Research Scholarships (IPRS), 676

East European Countries

AHRB Doctoral Awards Scheme, 99
International Postgraduate Research Scholarships (IPRS), 676
Research Preparation Master's Scheme, 99

Far East

ACC Fellowship Grants Program, 103
International Postgraduate Research Scholarships (IPRS), 676

Indian Sub-Continent

International Postgraduate Research Scholarships (IPRS), 676

Middle East

International Postgraduate Research Scholarships (IPRS), 676

South Africa

International Postgraduate Research Scholarships (IPRS), 676

South America

International Postgraduate Research Scholarships (IPRS), 676

United Kingdom

AHRB Doctoral Awards Scheme, 99
Bernard Buckman Scholarship, 555
International Postgraduate Research Scholarships (IPRS), 676
Research Preparation Master's Scheme, 99

United States of America

ACC Fellowship Grants Program, 103
International Postgraduate Research Scholarships (IPRS), 676

West European Countries

AHRB Doctoral Awards Scheme, 99
Bernard Buckman Scholarship, 555
International Postgraduate Research Scholarships (IPRS), 676
Research Preparation Master's Scheme, 99

SOUTHEAST ASIAN

Any Country

Bernadotte E Schmitt Grants, 49
CDU Senior Research Fellowship, 230

CDU Three Year Postdoctoral Fellowship, 230
Center for Advanced Study in the Behavioral Sciences Postdoctoral Residential Fellowships, 223
Harold White Fellowships, 452
SAIIA Bradlow Fellowship, 592

African Nations

International Postgraduate Research Scholarships (IPRS), 676

British Commonwealth

International Postgraduate Research Scholarships (IPRS), 676

Canada

Canadian Window on International Development, 358
International Postgraduate Research Scholarships (IPRS), 676

Caribbean Countries

International Postgraduate Research Scholarships (IPRS), 676

East European Countries

AHRB Doctoral Awards Scheme, 99
International Postgraduate Research Scholarships (IPRS), 676
Research Preparation Master's Scheme, 99

Far East

ACC Fellowship Grants Program, 103
International Postgraduate Research Scholarships (IPRS), 676

Indian Sub-Continent

International Postgraduate Research Scholarships (IPRS), 676

Middle East

International Postgraduate Research Scholarships (IPRS), 676

South Africa

International Postgraduate Research Scholarships (IPRS), 676

South America

International Postgraduate Research Scholarships (IPRS), 676

United Kingdom

AHRB Doctoral Awards Scheme, 99
International Postgraduate Research Scholarships (IPRS), 676
Research Preparation Master's Scheme, 99

United States of America

ACC Fellowship Grants Program, 103
International Postgraduate Research Scholarships (IPRS), 676

West European Countries

AHRB Doctoral Awards Scheme, 99
International Postgraduate Research Scholarships (IPRS), 676
Research Preparation Master's Scheme, 99

EUROPEAN (EC)

Any Country

ASCSA Summer Sessions, 72
Austro-American Association of Boston Scholarship, 123
Bernadotte E Schmitt Grants, 49
Camargo Fellowships, 164
Center for Advanced Study in the Behavioral Sciences Postdoctoral Residential Fellowships, 223
Irish Research Funds, 373
NEH Fellowships, 72
Paul H Nitze School of Advanced International Studies (SAIS) Financial Aid and Fellowships, 130

SSRC Berlin Programme for Advanced German and European Studies, 570

University for Foreigners Scholarships, 615

Wolfsonian FIU Fellowship, 706

Canada

SSRC Berlin Programme for Advanced German and European Studies, 570

East European Countries

AHRB Doctoral Awards Scheme, 99

Research Preparation Master's Scheme, 99

United Kingdom

AHRB Doctoral Awards Scheme, 99

Italian Government Scholarships, 420

Research Preparation Master's Scheme, 99

United States of America

Fritz Halbers Fellowship, 394

SSRC Berlin Programme for Advanced German and European Studies, 570

West European Countries

AHRB Doctoral Awards Scheme, 99

Fritz Halbers Fellowship, 394

Research Preparation Master's Scheme, 99

EASTERN EUROPEAN

Any Country

Advanced Fellowships, 71

ASCSA Summer Sessions, 72

Bernadotte E Schmitt Grants, 49

Canadian Institute of Ukrainian Studies Research Grants, 207

Center for Advanced Study in the Behavioral Sciences Postdoctoral Residential Fellowships, 223

Helen Darcovich Memorial Doctoral Fellowship, 207

Institute of European History Fellowships, 342

Kennan Institute Short Term Grants, 385

M Alison Frantz Fellowship in Post-Classical Studies at the Gennadius Library (formerly known as the Gennadeion Fellowship), 72

Marusia and Michael Dorosh Master's Fellowship, 207

NEH Fellowships, 72

Neporany Research and Teaching Fellowship, 207

Paul H Nitze School of Advanced International Studies (SAIS) Financial Aid and Fellowships, 130

United States Center for Advanced Holocaust Studies Research Fellowships, 608

University of Essex Scholarships, 632

Wolfsonian FIU Fellowship, 706

East European Countries

AHRB Doctoral Awards Scheme, 99

Elisabeth Barker Fund, 135

FACE Croatia, 101

Kosciuszko Foundation Tuition Scholarships, 388

Research Preparation Master's Scheme, 99

United Kingdom

AHRB Doctoral Awards Scheme, 99

Polish Government Postgraduate Scholarships Scheme, 501

Research Preparation Master's Scheme, 99

University of Essex Foundation Scholarships, 632

United States of America

ACLS Dissertation Fellowships in East European Studies, 39

ACLS East European Language Training Grants, 39

ACLS Fellowships for Postdoctoral Research in East European Studies, 39

FACE Croatia, 101

GMF Research Fellowships Program, 301

IREX Individual Advanced Research Opportunities, 366

IREX John J and Nancy Lee Roberts Fellowship Program, 366

IREX Short-Term Travel Grants, 367

Kennan Institute Research Scholarship, 385

Kosciuszko Foundation Tuition Scholarships, 388

The George & Viola Hoffman Fund, 105

West European Countries

AHRB Doctoral Awards Scheme, 99

Elisabeth Barker Fund, 135

Research Preparation Master's Scheme, 99

WESTERN EUROPEAN

Any Country

Advanced Fellowships, 71

ASCSA Research Fellow in Environmental Studies, 71

ASCSA Research Fellow in Faunal Studies, 71

ASCSA Research Fellow in Geoarchaeology, 71

Austro-American Association of Boston Scholarship, 123

Bernadotte E Schmitt Grants, 49

Center for Advanced Study in the Behavioral Sciences Postdoctoral Residential Fellowships, 223

Institute of European History Fellowships, 342

Irish Research Funds, 373

M Alison Frantz Fellowship in Post-Classical Studies at the Gennadius Library (formerly known as the Gennadeion Fellowship), 72

NEH Fellowships, 72

Onassis Foreigners' Fellowship Programme Educational Scholarships Category B, 15

Paul H Nitze School of Advanced International Studies (SAIS) Financial Aid and Fellowships, 130

United States Center for Advanced Holocaust Studies Research Fellowships, 608

University of Essex Scholarships, 632

Wolfsonian FIU Fellowship, 706

Canada

Gilbert Chinard Fellowships, 336

Harmon Chadbourn Rorison Fellowship, 336

East European Countries

AHRB Doctoral Awards Scheme, 99

Research Preparation Master's Scheme, 99

United Kingdom

AHRB Doctoral Awards Scheme, 99

Research Preparation Master's Scheme, 99

University of Essex Foundation Scholarships, 632

United States of America

Émigré Memorial German Internship Programs, 268

Gilbert Chinard Fellowships, 336

GMF Research Fellowships Program, 301

Harmon Chadbourn Rorison Fellowship, 336

West European Countries

AHRB Doctoral Awards Scheme, 99

Research Preparation Master's Scheme, 99

NORDIC

Any Country

Bernadotte E Schmitt Grants, 49

Center for Advanced Study in the Behavioral Sciences Postdoctoral Residential Fellowships, 223

University of Essex Scholarships, 632

Canada

Ministry of Education, Science and Culture (Iceland) Scholarships in Icelandic Studies, 420

East European Countries

AHRB Doctoral Awards Scheme, 99
Ministry of Education, Science and Culture (Iceland) Scholarships in Icelandic Studies, 420
Research Preparation Master's Scheme, 99

Far East

Ministry of Education, Science and Culture (Iceland) Scholarships in Icelandic Studies, 420

United Kingdom

AHRB Doctoral Awards Scheme, 99
Ministry of Education, Science and Culture (Iceland) Scholarships in Icelandic Studies, 420
Research Preparation Master's Scheme, 99
University of Essex Foundation Scholarships, 632

United States of America

Ministry of Education, Science and Culture (Iceland) Scholarships in Icelandic Studies, 420
Norwegian Thanksgiving Fund Scholarship, 474

West European Countries

AHRB Doctoral Awards Scheme, 99
Ministry of Education, Science and Culture (Iceland) Scholarships in Icelandic Studies, 420
Research Preparation Master's Scheme, 99

CARIBBEAN

Any Country

Albert J Beveridge Grant, 49
Center for Advanced Study in the Behavioral Sciences Postdoctoral Residential Fellowships, 223
Equiano Memorial Award, 596
Frederick Douglass Institute Postdoctoral Fellowship, 289
Frederick Douglass Institute Predoctoral Dissertation Fellowship, 290
Huggins-Quarles Award, 480
University of Essex Scholarships, 632

Canada

Canadian Window on International Development, 358

East European Countries

AHRB Doctoral Awards Scheme, 99
Research Preparation Master's Scheme, 99

United Kingdom

AHRB Doctoral Awards Scheme, 99
Research Preparation Master's Scheme, 99
University of Essex Foundation Scholarships, 632

West European Countries

AHRB Doctoral Awards Scheme, 99
Research Preparation Master's Scheme, 99

LATIN AMERICAN

Any Country

Albert J Beveridge Grant, 49
Center for Advanced Study in the Behavioral Sciences Postdoctoral Residential Fellowships, 223
FAMSI Research Grant, 287

Frederick Douglass Institute Postdoctoral Fellowship, 289
Frederick Douglass Institute Predoctoral Dissertation Fellowship, 290
Paul H Nitze School of Advanced International Studies (SAIS) Financial Aid and Fellowships, 130
SAIIA Bradlow Fellowship, 592
University of Essex Scholarships, 632

Canada

Canadian Window on International Development, 358

East European Countries

AHRB Doctoral Awards Scheme, 99
Shell Centenary Scholarships and Shell Centenary Chevening Scholarships, 664

United Kingdom

AHRB Doctoral Awards Scheme, 99
Anglo-Brazilian Society Scholarship, 89
British Academy 44th International Congress of Americanists Fund, 133
University of Essex Foundation Scholarships, 632

United States of America

British Academy 44th International Congress of Americanists Fund, 133

West European Countries

AHRB Doctoral Awards Scheme, 99

PACIFIC AREA

Any Country

Center for Advanced Study in the Behavioral Sciences Postdoctoral Residential Fellowships, 223
Jesus College The Alun Hughes' Graduate Scholarship, 652
St Antony's College Wai Seng Senior Research Scholarship, 668

East European Countries

AHRB Doctoral Awards Scheme, 99
Research Preparation Master's Scheme, 99

United Kingdom

AHRB Doctoral Awards Scheme, 99
Research Preparation Master's Scheme, 99

United States of America

CFR International Affairs Fellowship Programme in Japan, 246

West European Countries

AHRB Doctoral Awards Scheme, 99
Research Preparation Master's Scheme, 99

ABORIGINAL

Any Country

AIATSIS Research Grants, 116
CDU Senior Research Fellowship, 230
CDU Three Year Postdoctoral Fellowship, 230
Center for Advanced Study in the Behavioral Sciences Postdoctoral Residential Fellowships, 223
Harold White Fellowships, 452

African Nations

International Postgraduate Research Scholarships (IPRS), 676

British Commonwealth

International Postgraduate Research Scholarships (IPRS), 676

South America

Hubert H Humphrey Fellowship Programme, 609
International Postgraduate Research Scholarships (IPRS), 676

United Kingdom

CBRL Research Grant, 244
CBRL Travel Grant, 244
International Postgraduate Research Scholarships (IPRS), 676
UWB Research Studentships, 681
Wingate Scholarships, 704

United States of America

ACC Fellowship Grants Program, 103
David Baumgardt Memorial Fellowship, 394
Earthwatch Education Awards, 264
Fritz Halbers Fellowship, 394
Fulbright Senior Specialists Program, 245
Ian Axford (New Zealand) Fellowships in Public Policy, 239
International Postgraduate Research Scholarships (IPRS), 676
IREX John J and Nancy Lee Roberts Fellowship Program, 366
Norwegian Ministry of Foreign Affairs Travel Grants, 474
UCLA IAC Postdoctoral/Visiting Scholar Fellowships, 607

West European Countries

David Baumgardt Memorial Fellowship, 394
Fritz Halbers Fellowship, 394
International Postgraduate Research Scholarships (IPRS), 676
Natural History Museum Sys-Resource, 461
UWB Research Studentships, 681
Wingate Scholarships, 704

ANCIENT CIVILISATIONS (EGYPTOLOGY, ASSYRIOLOGY)

Any Country

Advanced Fellowships, 71
ASCSA Fellowships, 71
ASCSA Research Fellow in Environmental Studies, 71
ASCSA Research Fellow in Faunal Studies, 71
ASCSA Research Fellow in Geoarchaeology, 71
ASCSA Summer Sessions, 72
ASOR Mesopotamian Fellowship, 73
Downing College Research Fellowships, 623
External Faculty Fellowships, 594
FAMSI Research Grant, 287
Frances M Schwartz Fellowship, 62
Grants for ANS Summer Seminar in Numismatics, 63
J Lawrence Angel Fellowship in Human Skeletal Studies, 72
Jacob Hirsch Fellowship, 72
NEH Fellowships, 72
NHC Fellowships, 449
Shaykh Hamad Fellowship in Islamic Numismatics, 63
SOAS Research Student Fellowships, 555

African Nations

British School of Archaeology in Iraq Grants, 158

Australia

British School of Archaeology in Iraq Grants, 158
Wingate Scholarships, 704

British Commonwealth

British School of Archaeology in Iraq Grants, 158
Wingate Scholarships, 704

Canada

British School of Archaeology in Iraq Grants, 158
Wingate Scholarships, 704

East European Countries

AHRB Doctoral Awards Scheme, 99
Research Preparation Master's Scheme, 99

Far East

British School of Archaeology in Iraq Grants, 158

Indian Sub-Continent

British School of Archaeology in Iraq Grants, 158
Wingate Scholarships, 704

New Zealand

British School of Archaeology in Iraq Grants, 158
Wingate Scholarships, 704

South Africa

British School of Archaeology in Iraq Grants, 158
Wingate Scholarships, 704

United Kingdom

AHRB Doctoral Awards Scheme, 99
British School of Archaeology in Iraq Grants, 158
CBRL Research Grant, 244
CBRL Travel Grant, 244
Research Preparation Master's Scheme, 99
Wingate Scholarships, 704

United States of America

IREX John J and Nancy Lee Roberts Fellowship Program, 366

West European Countries

AHRB Doctoral Awards Scheme, 99
Research Preparation Master's Scheme, 99
Wingate Scholarships, 704

TRADE, CRAFT AND INDUSTRIAL TECHNIQUES

GENERAL

Any Country

AIATSIS Research Grants, 116
Concordia University Graduate Fellowships, 241
David J Azrieli Graduate Fellowship, 241
Dorothy Hodgkin Fellowships, 542
Honda Prize, 325
Leverhulme Trust Senior Research Fellowships, 543
Matsumae International Foundation Research Fellowship, 408
Royal Society Industry Fellowships Scheme, 544
Stanley G French Graduate Fellowship, 242

African Nations

Merton College Reed Foundation Scholarship, 658

Australia

Coral Sea Business Administration Scholarship, 119
Fulbright Awards, 119
Fulbright Postgraduate Studentships, 120

British Commonwealth

Merton College Reed Foundation Scholarship, 658

Canada

J W McConnell Memorial Fellowships, 241
OAS Graduate Academic Studies, 483

Caribbean Countries

Merton College Reed Foundation Scholarship, 658
OAS Graduate Academic Studies, 483

East European Countries

Merton College Reed Foundation Scholarship, 658

Far East

Jackson Memorial Fellowship, 310
JACL Scholarship and Award Program, 377
Merton College Reed Foundation Scholarship, 658

Indian Sub-Continent

Merton College Reed Foundation Scholarship, 658

Middle East

Merton College Reed Foundation Scholarship, 658

South Africa

Isie Smuts Research Award, 590

South America

Fulbright Commission (Argentina) Master's Program, 293
Merton College Reed Foundation Scholarship, 658
OAS Graduate Academic Studies, 483

United Kingdom

BSUF May and Ward Scholarships (for British scholars), 158
Canada Memorial Foundation Scholarships, 106
Hilda Martindale Exhibitions, 324

United States of America

BSUF May and Ward Scholarships (for British scholars), 158
Congress Bundestag Youth Exchange for Young Professionals, 223
Early American Industries Association Research Grants Program, 263
JACL Scholarship and Award Program, 377
North Dakota Indian Scholarship, 472
OAS Graduate Academic Studies, 483

West European Countries

Janson Johan Helmich Scholarships and Travel Grants, 376
Royal Society University Research Fellowships, 544

FOOD PROCESSING TECHNIQUES

African Nations

Hubert H Humphrey Fellowship Programme, 609

Caribbean Countries

Hubert H Humphrey Fellowship Programme, 609

East European Countries

Hubert H Humphrey Fellowship Programme, 609

Far East

Hubert H Humphrey Fellowship Programme, 609

Indian Sub-Continent

Hubert H Humphrey Fellowship Programme, 609

Middle East

Hubert H Humphrey Fellowship Programme, 609

South Africa

Hubert H Humphrey Fellowship Programme, 609

South America

Hubert H Humphrey Fellowship Programme, 609

United States of America

Congress Bundestag Youth Exchange for Young Professionals, 223
National Restaurant Association Educational Foundation Professional Development Scholarship for educators., 457

BUILDING TRADES

United States of America

Congress Bundestag Youth Exchange for Young Professionals, 223

United States of America

Early American Industries Association Research Grants Program, 263

ELECTRICAL/ELECTRONIC EQUIPMENT AND MAINTENANCE TECHNIQUES

Any Country

KSTU Rector's Grant, 385

United States of America

Congress Bundestag Youth Exchange for Young Professionals, 223

METAL TRADES TECHNIQUES

Any Country

KSTU Rector's Grant, 385

United States of America

Congress Bundestag Youth Exchange for Young Professionals, 223
Early American Industries Association Research Grants Program, 263

MECHANICAL EQUIPMENT AND MAINTENANCE TECHNIQUES

Any Country

KSTU Rector's Grant, 385

United States of America

Congress Bundestag Youth Exchange for Young Professionals, 223
Early American Industries Association Research Grants Program, 263

WOOD TECHNOLOGY

United Kingdom

UWB Research Studentships, 681

United States of America

Congress Bundestag Youth Exchange for Young Professionals, 223
Early American Industries Association Research Grants Program, 263

West European Countries

UWB Research Studentships, 681

HEATING, AIR CONDITIONING AND REFRIGERATION TECHNOLOGY

Any Country

ASHRAE Grants-in-Aid for Graduate Students, 80

Canadian Department of Foreign Affairs Faculty Research Program, 205
Canadian Department of Foreign Affairs Institutional Research Program, 206
Concordia University Graduate Fellowships, 241
David J Azrieli Graduate Fellowship, 241
Matsumae International Foundation Research Fellowship, 408
Rees Jeffreys Road Fund Bursaries, 332
Stanley G French Graduate Fellowship, 242

African Nations

ABCCF Student Grant, 91
Friends of Peterhouse Bursary, 491
Fulbright Postdoctoral Research and Lecturing Awards for Non-US Citizens, 245
Hubert H Humphrey Fellowship Programme, 609
International Postgraduate Research Scholarships (IPRS), 676
Merton College Reed Foundation Scholarship, 658

Australia

Coral Sea Business Administration Scholarship, 119
Friends of Peterhouse Bursary, 491
Fulbright Awards, 119
Fulbright Postdoctoral Fellowships, 119
Fulbright Postdoctoral Research and Lecturing Awards for Non-US Citizens, 245
Fulbright Postgraduate Studentships, 120
Wingate Scholarships, 704

British Commonwealth

Friends of Peterhouse Bursary, 491
International Postgraduate Research Scholarships (IPRS), 676
Merton College Reed Foundation Scholarship, 658
Wingate Scholarships, 704

Canada

Friends of Peterhouse Bursary, 491
Fulbright Postdoctoral Research and Lecturing Awards for Non-US Citizens, 245
International Postgraduate Research Scholarships (IPRS), 676
J W McConnell Memorial Fellowships, 241
NSERC Postdoctoral Fellowships, 462
NSERC Postgraduate Scholarships, 462
OAS Graduate Academic Studies, 483
TAC Scholarships, 604
Wingate Scholarships, 704

Caribbean Countries

Friends of Peterhouse Bursary, 491
Hubert H Humphrey Fellowship Programme, 609
International Postgraduate Research Scholarships (IPRS), 676
Merton College Reed Foundation Scholarship, 658
OAS Graduate Academic Studies, 483

East European Countries

Fulbright Postdoctoral Research and Lecturing Awards for Non-US Citizens, 245
Hubert H Humphrey Fellowship Programme, 609
International Postgraduate Research Scholarships (IPRS), 676
Merton College Reed Foundation Scholarship, 658

Far East

Friends of Peterhouse Bursary, 491
Fulbright Postdoctoral Research and Lecturing Awards for Non-US Citizens, 245
Hubert H Humphrey Fellowship Programme, 609
International Postgraduate Research Scholarships (IPRS), 676
Merton College Reed Foundation Scholarship, 658

Indian Sub-Continent

Friends of Peterhouse Bursary, 491

Fulbright Postdoctoral Research and Lecturing Awards for Non-US Citizens, 245
Hubert H Humphrey Fellowship Programme, 609
International Postgraduate Research Scholarships (IPRS), 676
Merton College Reed Foundation Scholarship, 658
Wingate Scholarships, 704

Middle East

ABCCF Student Grant, 91
Friends of Peterhouse Bursary, 491
Fulbright Postdoctoral Research and Lecturing Awards for Non-US Citizens, 245
Hubert H Humphrey Fellowship Programme, 609
International Postgraduate Research Scholarships (IPRS), 676
Merton College Reed Foundation Scholarship, 658

New Zealand

Friends of Peterhouse Bursary, 491
Fulbright Postdoctoral Research and Lecturing Awards for Non-US Citizens, 245
Wingate Scholarships, 704

South Africa

Friends of Peterhouse Bursary, 491
Fulbright Postdoctoral Research and Lecturing Awards for Non-US Citizens, 245
Hubert H Humphrey Fellowship Programme, 609
International Postgraduate Research Scholarships (IPRS), 676
Isie Smuts Research Award, 590
Wingate Scholarships, 704

South America

Friends of Peterhouse Bursary, 491
Fulbright Commission (Argentina) Master's Program, 293
Fulbright Postdoctoral Research and Lecturing Awards for Non-US Citizens, 245
Hubert H Humphrey Fellowship Programme, 609
International Postgraduate Research Scholarships (IPRS), 676
Merton College Reed Foundation Scholarship, 658
OAS Graduate Academic Studies, 483

United Kingdom

BSUF May and Ward Scholarships (for British scholars), 158
Canada Memorial Foundation Scholarships, 106
ESRC 1+3 Awards & +3 Awards, 265
Fulbright Postdoctoral Research and Lecturing Awards for Non-US Citizens, 245
Hilda Martindale Exhibitions, 324
International Postgraduate Research Scholarships (IPRS), 676
Kennedy Scholarships, 385
Rees Jeffreys Road Fund Bursaries, 332
Rees Jeffreys Road Fund Research Grants, 512
Wingate Scholarships, 704

United States of America

BSUF May and Ward Scholarships (for British scholars), 158
Congress Bundestag Youth Exchange for Young Professionals, 223
Friends of Peterhouse Bursary, 491
Fulbright Scholar Program for United States Citizens, 245
Ian Axford (New Zealand) Fellowships in Public Policy, 239
International Postgraduate Research Scholarships (IPRS), 676
North Dakota Indian Scholarship, 472
OAS Graduate Academic Studies, 483

West European Countries

ESRC 1+3 Awards & +3 Awards, 265
Fulbright Postdoctoral Research and Lecturing Awards for Non-US Citizens, 245
International Postgraduate Research Scholarships (IPRS), 676
Janson Johan Helmich Scholarships and Travel Grants, 376
Rees Jeffreys Road Fund Bursaries, 332

Rees Jeffreys Road Fund Research Grants, 512
Wingate Scholarships, 704

AIR TRANSPORT

African Nations
Hubert H Humphrey Fellowship Programme, 609

African Nations
International Postgraduate Research Scholarships (IPRS), 676

British Commonwealth
Handley Page Award, 525
International Postgraduate Research Scholarships (IPRS), 676

Canada
International Postgraduate Research Scholarships (IPRS), 676

Caribbean Countries
Hubert H Humphrey Fellowship Programme, 609
International Postgraduate Research Scholarships (IPRS), 676

East European Countries
Hubert H Humphrey Fellowship Programme, 609
International Postgraduate Research Scholarships (IPRS), 676

Far East
Hubert H Humphrey Fellowship Programme, 609
International Postgraduate Research Scholarships (IPRS), 676

Indian Sub-Continent
Hubert H Humphrey Fellowship Programme, 609
International Postgraduate Research Scholarships (IPRS), 676

Middle East
Hubert H Humphrey Fellowship Programme, 609
International Postgraduate Research Scholarships (IPRS), 676

South Africa
Hubert H Humphrey Fellowship Programme, 609
International Postgraduate Research Scholarships (IPRS), 676

South America
Hubert H Humphrey Fellowship Programme, 609
International Postgraduate Research Scholarships (IPRS), 676

United Kingdom
Handley Page Award, 525
International Postgraduate Research Scholarships (IPRS), 676

United States of America
Congress Bundestag Youth Exchange for Young Professionals, 223
International Postgraduate Research Scholarships (IPRS), 676

West European Countries
International Postgraduate Research Scholarships (IPRS), 676

MARINE TRANSPORT AND NAUTICAL SCIENCE

Any Country
De Paepe - Willems Award, 364
Woods Hole Oceanographic Institution Research Fellowships in Marine Policy, 710

African Nations
Hubert H Humphrey Fellowship Programme, 609

Caribbean Countries
Hubert H Humphrey Fellowship Programme, 609

East European Countries
Hubert H Humphrey Fellowship Programme, 609

Far East
Hubert H Humphrey Fellowship Programme, 609

Indian Sub-Continent
Hubert H Humphrey Fellowship Programme, 609

Middle East
Hubert H Humphrey Fellowship Programme, 609

South Africa
Hubert H Humphrey Fellowship Programme, 609

South America
Hubert H Humphrey Fellowship Programme, 609

United States of America
Congress Bundestag Youth Exchange for Young Professionals, 223

RAILWAY TRANSPORT

Any Country
CQU Postgraduate Research Award, 224
Mott MacDonald Charitable Trust Scholarships, 426

African Nations
Hubert H Humphrey Fellowship Programme, 609
International Postgraduate Research Scholarships (IPRS), 676

British Commonwealth
International Postgraduate Research Scholarships (IPRS), 676

Canada
International Postgraduate Research Scholarships (IPRS), 676

Caribbean Countries
Hubert H Humphrey Fellowship Programme, 609
International Postgraduate Research Scholarships (IPRS), 676

East European Countries
Hubert H Humphrey Fellowship Programme, 609
International Postgraduate Research Scholarships (IPRS), 676

Far East
Hubert H Humphrey Fellowship Programme, 609
International Postgraduate Research Scholarships (IPRS), 676

Indian Sub-Continent
Hubert H Humphrey Fellowship Programme, 609
International Postgraduate Research Scholarships (IPRS), 676

Middle East
Hubert H Humphrey Fellowship Programme, 609
International Postgraduate Research Scholarships (IPRS), 676

South Africa
Hubert H Humphrey Fellowship Programme, 609
International Postgraduate Research Scholarships (IPRS), 676

South America
Hubert H Humphrey Fellowship Programme, 609
International Postgraduate Research Scholarships (IPRS), 676

United Kingdom

International Postgraduate Research Scholarships (IPRS), 676

United States of America

Congress Bundestag Youth Exchange for Young Professionals, 223
International Postgraduate Research Scholarships (IPRS), 676

West European Countries

International Postgraduate Research Scholarships (IPRS), 676

ROAD TRANSPORT

Any Country

Mott MacDonald Charitable Trust Scholarships, 426
Rees Jeffreys Road Fund Bursaries, 332

African Nations

Hubert H Humphrey Fellowship Programme, 609
International Postgraduate Research Scholarships (IPRS), 676
Joint Japan/World Bank Graduate Scholarship Program (JJ/WBGSP), 355

British Commonwealth

International Postgraduate Research Scholarships (IPRS), 676
Joint Japan/World Bank Graduate Scholarship Program (JJ/WBGSP), 355

Canada

International Postgraduate Research Scholarships (IPRS), 676
TAC Scholarships, 604

Caribbean Countries

Hubert H Humphrey Fellowship Programme, 609
International Postgraduate Research Scholarships (IPRS), 676
Joint Japan/World Bank Graduate Scholarship Program (JJ/WBGSP), 355

East European Countries

Hubert H Humphrey Fellowship Programme, 609
International Postgraduate Research Scholarships (IPRS), 676
Joint Japan/World Bank Graduate Scholarship Program (JJ/WBGSP), 355

Far East

Hubert H Humphrey Fellowship Programme, 609
International Postgraduate Research Scholarships (IPRS), 676
Joint Japan/World Bank Graduate Scholarship Program (JJ/WBGSP), 355

Indian Sub-Continent

Hubert H Humphrey Fellowship Programme, 609
International Postgraduate Research Scholarships (IPRS), 676
Joint Japan/World Bank Graduate Scholarship Program (JJ/WBGSP), 355

Middle East

Hubert H Humphrey Fellowship Programme, 609
International Postgraduate Research Scholarships (IPRS), 676
Joint Japan/World Bank Graduate Scholarship Program (JJ/WBGSP), 355

South Africa

Hubert H Humphrey Fellowship Programme, 609
International Postgraduate Research Scholarships (IPRS), 676
Joint Japan/World Bank Graduate Scholarship Program (JJ/WBGSP), 355

South America

Hubert H Humphrey Fellowship Programme, 609
International Postgraduate Research Scholarships (IPRS), 676
Joint Japan/World Bank Graduate Scholarship Program (JJ/WBGSP), 355

United Kingdom

International Postgraduate Research Scholarships (IPRS), 676
Rees Jeffreys Road Fund Bursaries, 332
Rees Jeffreys Road Fund Bursaries, 332
Rees Jeffreys Road Fund Research Grants, 512

United States of America

Congress Bundestag Youth Exchange for Young Professionals, 223
International Postgraduate Research Scholarships (IPRS), 676

West European Countries

International Postgraduate Research Scholarships (IPRS), 676
Rees Jeffreys Road Fund Bursaries, 332
Rees Jeffreys Road Fund Research Grants, 512

TRANSPORT MANAGEMENT

Any Country

Mott MacDonald Charitable Trust Scholarships, 426
Trinity College Birkett Scholarship in Environmental Studies, 672

African Nations

Hubert H Humphrey Fellowship Programme, 609
International Postgraduate Research Scholarships (IPRS), 676

Australia

Wingate Scholarships, 704

British Commonwealth

International Postgraduate Research Scholarships (IPRS), 676
Wingate Scholarships, 704

Canada

International Postgraduate Research Scholarships (IPRS), 676
TAC Scholarships, 604
Wingate Scholarships, 704

Caribbean Countries

Hubert H Humphrey Fellowship Programme, 609
International Postgraduate Research Scholarships (IPRS), 676

East European Countries

Hubert H Humphrey Fellowship Programme, 609
International Postgraduate Research Scholarships (IPRS), 676

Far East

Hubert H Humphrey Fellowship Programme, 609
International Postgraduate Research Scholarships (IPRS), 676

Indian Sub-Continent

Hubert H Humphrey Fellowship Programme, 609
International Postgraduate Research Scholarships (IPRS), 676
Wingate Scholarships, 704

Middle East

Hubert H Humphrey Fellowship Programme, 609
International Postgraduate Research Scholarships (IPRS), 676

New Zealand

Wingate Scholarships, 704

South Africa

Hubert H Humphrey Fellowship Programme, 609
International Postgraduate Research Scholarships (IPRS), 676
Wingate Scholarships, 704

South America

Hubert H Humphrey Fellowship Programme, 609
International Postgraduate Research Scholarships (IPRS), 676

United Kingdom

ESRC 1+3 Awards & +3 Awards, 265
International Postgraduate Research Scholarships (IPRS), 676
Rees Jeffreys Road Fund Bursaries, 332
Silsoe Awards, 249
Wingate Scholarships, 704

United States of America

Congress Bundestag Youth Exchange for Young Professionals, 223
International Postgraduate Research Scholarships (IPRS), 676

West European Countries

ESRC 1+3 Awards & +3 Awards, 265
International Postgraduate Research Scholarships (IPRS), 676
Silsoe Awards, 249
Wingate Scholarships, 704

TRANSPORT ECONOMICS

Any Country

Mott MacDonald Charitable Trust Scholarships, 426
Rees Jeffreys Road Fund Bursaries, 332

African Nations

Hubert H Humphrey Fellowship Programme, 609
International Postgraduate Research Scholarships (IPRS), 676

British Commonwealth

International Postgraduate Research Scholarships (IPRS), 676

Canada

International Postgraduate Research Scholarships (IPRS), 676
TAC Scholarships, 604

Caribbean Countries

Hubert H Humphrey Fellowship Programme, 609
International Postgraduate Research Scholarships (IPRS), 676

East European Countries

Hubert H Humphrey Fellowship Programme, 609
International Postgraduate Research Scholarships (IPRS), 676

Far East

Hubert H Humphrey Fellowship Programme, 609
International Postgraduate Research Scholarships (IPRS), 676

Indian Sub-Continent

Hubert H Humphrey Fellowship Programme, 609
International Postgraduate Research Scholarships (IPRS), 676

Middle East

Hubert H Humphrey Fellowship Programme, 609
International Postgraduate Research Scholarships (IPRS), 676

South Africa

Hubert H Humphrey Fellowship Programme, 609
International Postgraduate Research Scholarships (IPRS), 676

South America

Hubert H Humphrey Fellowship Programme, 609
International Postgraduate Research Scholarships (IPRS), 676

United Kingdom

ESRC 1+3 Awards & +3 Awards, 265
International Postgraduate Research Scholarships (IPRS), 676
Rees Jeffreys Road Fund Bursaries, 332
Rees Jeffreys Road Fund Bursaries, 332
Rees Jeffreys Road Fund Research Grants, 512

United States of America

Congress Bundestag Youth Exchange for Young Professionals, 223
International Postgraduate Research Scholarships (IPRS), 676

West European Countries

ESRC 1+3 Awards & +3 Awards, 265
International Postgraduate Research Scholarships (IPRS), 676
Rees Jeffreys Road Fund Bursaries, 332
Rees Jeffreys Road Fund Research Grants, 512

POSTAL SERVICES

African Nations

Hubert H Humphrey Fellowship Programme, 609

Caribbean Countries

Hubert H Humphrey Fellowship Programme, 609

East European Countries

Hubert H Humphrey Fellowship Programme, 609

Far East

Hubert H Humphrey Fellowship Programme, 609

Indian Sub-Continent

Hubert H Humphrey Fellowship Programme, 609

Middle East

Hubert H Humphrey Fellowship Programme, 609

South Africa

Hubert H Humphrey Fellowship Programme, 609

South America

Hubert H Humphrey Fellowship Programme, 609

United States of America

Congress Bundestag Youth Exchange for Young Professionals, 223

TELECOMMUNICATIONS SERVICES

Any Country

Equiano Memorial Award, 596
Mott MacDonald Charitable Trust Scholarships, 426

African Nations

Hubert H Humphrey Fellowship Programme, 609
International Postgraduate Research Scholarships (IPRS), 676

British Commonwealth

International Postgraduate Research Scholarships (IPRS), 676

Canada

Canadian Wireless Telecommunications Association (CWTA) Graduate Scholarship, 109

INDEX OF AWARDS

INDEX OF DISCONTINUED AWARDS

AAUW Educational Foundation
AAUW Educational Foundation Scholar-in-Residence

Academy of Sciences of the Czech Republic
UNESCO-ROSTE Long-term Postgraduate Training Course

Alberta Heritage Foundation for Medical Research (AHFMR)
Alberta Heritage Dental Fellowships

American Academy of Child and Adolescent Psychiatry
James Comer Minority Research Fellowship for Medical Students

American Accounting Association (AAA)
AAA Fellowship Programme in Accounting
Arthur H Carter Scholarship

American Antiquarian Society (AAS)
Richard F and Virginia P Morgan Fellowship

American Association for Cancer Research (AACR)
AACR American Cancer Society Award for Research Excellence in Cancer Epidemiology and Prevention
AACR Bruce F Cain Memorial Award
AACR G H A Clowes Memorial Award
AACR Gerald B Grindley Memorial Scholar-in-Training
AACR Joseph H Burchenal AACR Clinical Research Award
AACR Peczoller International Award for Cancer Research
AACR Richard and Hinda Rosenthal Foundation Award
AACR Susan G Komen Breast Cancer Foundation Career Development Award

American College of Obstetricians and Gynecologists (ACOG)
ACOG/Ethicon Research Award for Innovations in Gynecological Surgery
ACOG/Merck Award for Research in Migraine Management in Women's Healthcare
ACOG/Novartis Pharmaceuticals Fellowship for Research in Osteoporosis of the Postmenopausal Woman
ACOG/Parke-Davis Research Award to Advance the Management of Women's Healthcare
ACOG/Pharmacia Corporation Research Award on Overactive Bladder
ACOG/Searle Research Award in Gynecologic Infections and their Complications
ACOG/Tambrands Research Award in Menstrual Health

American Council of Learned Societies (ACLS)
Abe Fellowship Program

American Educational Research Association (AERA)
AERA Fellowship

American Library Association (ALA)
ASCLA Research Grant
G K Hall Award for Library Literature
Herbert and Virginia White Award for Promoting Librarianship
Louise Giles Minority Scholarship
Shirley Crawford Minority Scholarship

American Nuclear Society (ANS)
Alvin M Weinberg Medal

American Numismatic Society (ANS)
ANS Fellowship in Roman Studies

American Psychiatric Association
APA/Glaxo Wellcome Fellowship

American Research Center in Egypt (ARCE)
Egyptian Development Fellowships

American School of Classical Studies at Athens (ASCSA)
Samuel H Kress Joint Athens-Jerusalem Fellowship

American Schools of Oriental Research (ASOR)
NEH Postdoctoral Fellowships
USIA Junior Fellowships

American Society for Microbiology (ASM)
Vector Laboratories Young Investigator Award

American Society for Nutritional Sciences
Borden Award in Nutrition

American Society of Hypertension
American Society of Hypertension/Hoechst Marion Roussel Clinical Fellowship in Hypertension

Anglo-German Foundation for the Study of Industrial Society
Anglo-German Foundation for the Study of Industrial Society Research Grant

Arc of the United States
Arc of the United States Research Grant

Architects Registration Council of the United Kingdom
Architects Registration Council Education Fund Award

Arthritis Foundation
Arthritis Foundation Biomedical Science Grant
Arthritis Foundation Clinical Science Grant

Arts Council of Ireland
Arts Council of Ireland Apprentice/Assistant Scheme for Visual Artists
Arts Council of Ireland Architectural Research Bursary
Arts Council of Ireland Artists in Residence (Schools)
Arts Council of Ireland Artists in Residence (Youthwork)
Arts Council of Ireland Arts Educators' Awards
Arts Council of Ireland Awards for Play Directors
Arts Council of Ireland Awards to Choreographers
Arts Council of Ireland Awards to Designers for the Stage
Arts Council of Ireland Awards to Professional Dance Teachers
Arts Council of Ireland Awards to Professional Dancers
Arts Council of Ireland Bursaries for Advanced Instrumentalists and Singers
Arts Council of Ireland Bursaries in Literature
Arts Council of Ireland Bursary in Contemporary Architectural Criticism
Arts Council of Ireland Choreographers Bursary
Arts Council of Ireland Composers Commission Scheme
Arts Council of Ireland Composers' Bursaries
Arts Council of Ireland Conductors Study Awards
Arts Council of Ireland Dance Commission Scheme
Arts Council of Ireland Dance Project Scheme
Arts Council of Ireland Film and Video Awards
Arts Council of Ireland Materials/Equipment Grants and Documentation Grants
Arts Council of Ireland Opera Commissioning Scheme
Arts Council of Ireland Opera Training Awards
Arts Council of Ireland Play Directors in Residence
Arts Council of Ireland Playwrights Commissioning Scheme
Arts Council of Ireland Postgraduate Scholarships for Architecture
Arts Council of Ireland Studio Rental Assistance Grant
Arts Council of Ireland Studio Rental Assistance Grants
Arts Council of Ireland Travel Awards to Creative Artists
Arts Council of Ireland Visual Arts Bursaries
Arts Council of Ireland Visual Arts Postgraduate Scholarships

Arts Council of Northern Ireland
Alice Berger Hammerschlag Trust Award
Arts Council Printmaker in Residence at Belfast Print Workshop
Bass Ireland Arts Awards
Bursary in Contemporary Visual Arts Criticism
George Campbell Memorial Travel Award
Milliken Brothers Award
Thomas Dammann Junior Memorial Trust

Arts Council of Wales
ACW Artform Development Scheme
ACW Arts for All
ACW Awards for Advanced Study in Music
ACW Awards for Career Development of Individual Visual Artists and Craftspeople
ACW Awards for Individual Visual Artists and Craftspeople
ACW Barclays Stage Partners
ACW Dance and Drama Development and Training Awards
ACW Dance and Drama Group Sponsored Training Initiatives
ACW Director Training
ACW Grants for Artists
ACW Grants for Visual Artists Exhibition Spaces and Grants for Visual Arts Studio Groups
ACW Grants to Dancers
ACW Grants to Periodicals, The Franchise Scheme
ACW Grants to Publishers

ACW Individual Craftspeople Awards
ACW Individual Professional Visual Artists Awards
ACW Inter-link
ACW Literature Projects Fund
ACW Masterclass/Industrial Experience Grants
ACW Music Projects Grants
ACW New Music Commission Support
ACW New Visual Artists
ACW Performing Arts Events Programme
ACW Performing Arts Projects
ACW Pilot Training Grants Scheme
ACW Playwright's Bursaries
ACW Playwrighting Commissions and Writers On Attachment
ACW Production Grants for Individual Books
ACW Special Project Grants
ACW Trainee Director and Associate Director Bursaries
ACW Training Grants to Individuals
ACW Translation Grants
ACW Visiting Arts Fund
ACW Visual Arts Project Fund
ACW Writers on Tour and Literature Residencies
ACW Writers' Bursaries, Enabling Grants and Travel Awards
ACW Writers' Critical Service
ACW Writers' Mentoring
ACW Young Welsh Singers Competition

Arts International
Artists Exploration Fund
Arts International Arts Presenters Exploration Fund
Fund for US Artists at International Festivals and Exhibitions

Association of Universities and Colleges of Canada (AUCC)
CIBC Youthvision Graduate Research Award Program

Asthma Society of Canada
Asthma Society of Canada Research Grants

Atlantic Salmon Federation (ASF)
Bensinger-Liddell Salmon Fellowship

Australian-American Fulbright Commission
Fulbright Postgraduate Student Award for Aboriginal and Torres Strait
   Islander People
Fulbright Postgraduate Student Award to undertake an MBA

British Association of Plastic Surgeons (BAPS)
BAPS European Travelling Scholarship

British Council
British Marshall Scholarships

British Institute of Radiology (BIR)
Flude Memorial Prize

British Pharmacological Society
British Pharmacological Society Intercalated Awards

British School at Rome (BSR)
Henry Moore Sculpture Fellowship at the BSR

Broadcast Education Association (BEA)
Broadcasters' Association Shane Media Scholarships

**Cambridge Commonwealth Trust, Cambridge Overseas Trust
   and Associated Trusts**
CEU Soros Cambridge Scholarships
Charles Wallace Bangladesh and Pakistan Trusts DFID Scholarships
Charles Wallace Pakistan Trust Bursaries
Monash Scholarship
Nedbank and Old Mutual Cambridge Scholarships
President Aylwin Studentship

Canada Council for the Arts
Canada Council Arts Grants 'A'
Canada Council Arts Grants 'B'
Canada Council Short-Term Grants
Glenn Gould Foundation

Canadian Cystic Fibrosis Foundation (CCFF)
CCFF/Canadian Institutes of Health Research (CIHR) Fellowships

Canadian Forestry Foundation
Canadian Forestry Foundation Trees and People (TAP) Award

Canadian Home Economics Association (CHEA)
Nestlé Canada, Inc. Scholarship

Canadian Society for Chemical Engineering (CSChE)
J E Zajic Postgraduate Scholarship in Biochemical Engineering of the
   CSCHE

Canadian Society for Chemical Technology
CSCT NOVA Chemicals Limited Award for Chemistry teaching in
   Community and Technical Colleges

Canadian Society for Clinical Investigation (CSCI)
CSCI/Schering Research Fellowship
Schering Travelling Fellowships

Canadian Thoracic Society (CTS)
CTS Scholarships

Cancer Research Society, Inc.
Cancer Research Society, Inc. (Canada) Predoctoral Fellowships

CEU Graduate School of Business
Demján Scholarship

Charles Darwin University (CDU)
Deputy Chancellors Postdoctoral Research
NTU One Year Postdoctoral Fellowship

Chemical Heritage Foundation (CHF)
Eugene Garfield Fellowship

CIIT - Centers for Health Research
CIIT - Centers for Health Research Postdoctoral Traineeships

Clive and Vera Ramaciotti Foundations
Ramaciotto Travel Awards

College of Occupational Therapists
Agnes Storar/Constance Owens Fund
Farrer-Brown Professional Development Fund
HAS Charitable Trust
Lord Byers Memorial Fund
Margaret Dawson Fund
Pressalit Fellowship Award
Rompa Quality of Life Award
Speechmark Bursary

Council for British Archaeology (CBA)
British Archaeological Research Grants

Council for British Research in the Levant (CBRL)
British School of Archaeology in Jerusalem Research and Travel
   Grants
Jerusalem Scholarship

Council for International Exchange of Scholars (CIES)
NATO Advanced Research Fellowships and Institutional Grants

Cranfield University, School of Management
Cranfield University, School of Management Executive MBA
   Programme (Part-time)
Jean Monnet Chevening Scholarships/Entente Cordiale Scholarships
McKinsey MBA Scholarship

Department of Education and Science (Ireland)
Irish Government Scholarship

Deutsche Forschungsgemeinschaft (DFG)
Gerhard Hess Programme

Diabetes UK
British Diabetic Association Group Grant
Diabetes Development Project

Economic and Social Research Council (ESRC)
ESRC Research Studentships
MBA Programme

Edward Boyle Memorial Trust
Edward Boyle Medical Elective Bursaries
Edward Boyle Music Award

Engineering and Physical Sciences Research Council (EPSRC)
EPSRC Advanced Course and Research Master Studentships
EPSRC Standard Research Studentships
EPSRC Studentships

Epilepsy Foundation (EF)
EF International Clinical Research Fellowship

Eurotox
Eurotox Merit Award
Eurotox Young Scientist's Award
Gerhard Zbinden Memorial Lecture

Finnish Institute in London Trust
Finnish Institute Award

Foundation for Digestive Health and Nutrition
ADHF TAP Pharmaceuticals, Inc. Outcomes Research Awards
AGA Student Abstract Prizes
ASGE Endoscopic Research and Outcomes and Effectiveness Awards
Wilson-Cook Endoscopic Research Career Development Awards

Frederick Douglass Institute for African and African-American Studies
Frederick Douglass Institute for African and African-American Studies Fellowships for Graduate Study

French Embassy, Linguistic Section
Ministry of Foreign Affairs (France) Stage de la Réunion (One Month Scholarships)

Fulbright Foundation (UK)
British-American Chamber of Commerce Awards

German Academic Exchange Service (DAAD)
Berlin - European Metropolis of the Third Millennium
Contemporary German Literature Grant
DAAD Fulbright Grants
DAAD Grants for Canadians
DAAD Guest Lectureships
DAAD Information Visits
DAAD Learn German in Germany for Faculty
DAAD Program for International Lawyers
DAAD Research Grants for Recent PhD Recipients and PhD Candidates
DAAD Temporary Teaching Assignments for Highly Qualified Academics at German Universities
Munich University Summer Training in European and German Law (MUST)
NSF (National Science Foundation)-DAAD Grants for the Natural, Engineering and Social Sciences

Getty Grant Program, J Paul Getty Trust
Central and Eastern European Fellowships in the History of Art and the Humanities

Glaucoma Research Foundation
Clinician-Scientist Fellowship

Grains Research and Development Corporation (GRDC)
GRDC Postdoctoral Fellowships

Grimsby International Singers Competition
Alec Redshaw Memorial Awards

Grundy Educational Trust
Grundy Educational Trust Award

Harvard University
MacArthur Fellowships on Transnational Security Issues

Health Research Council of New Zealand (HRC)
HRC Postdoctoral Fellowship

Henry A Murray Research Center
Radcliffe Institute Fellowships

Howard Hughes Medical Institute (HHMI)
HHMI Predoctoral Fellowships

Huntington's Disease Association
Huntington's Disease Association Research Grant

Imperial College of Science, Technology and Medicine
Concrete Structures Bursaries

Indiana Historical Society
Indiana Historical Society Graduate Fellowships in History

INSEAD
Danone MBA Scholarship
Eric Salmon & Partners Scholarship
Estée Lauder INSEAD Scholarship
IAF Diversity Scholarship for Africa
INSEAD A T Kearney Scholarship
INSEAD Alumni Fund (IAF) Scholarships for Central and Eastern European Countries
INSEAD Gesellschaft Deutschland Scholarship
INSEAD Lister Vickery Memorial Award
Minute Maid Company Scholarship

Institute for Advanced Studies in the Humanities
European Enlightenment Project Fellowships

Institute for Humane Studies (IHS)
IHS Donald Bogie Prize
IHS Eberhard Student Writing Competition
IHS John M Olin Fellowships
IHS Summer Faculty Fellowships
Institute for Humane Studies Assistance Fund for Professionals
R C Hoiles and IHS Postdoctoral Fellowships

Institute of Orthopaedics
Institute of Orthopaedics Fellowship in Paediatric Orthopaedic Surgery

Institution of Electrical Engineers (IEE)
IEE Bursaries for IEE Vacation Schools, Technical Seminars and Workshops
IEE Conference International Bursary
IEE Management Scholarship
IEE Measurement Prize

International Centre for Diarrhoeal Disease Research (ICDDR)
ICDDR Health Research Training Fellowship

International Foundation of Employee Benefit Plans (IFEBP)
IFEBP Grants for Research

International Human Frontier Science Program Organization (HFSP)
HFSP Research Grants

International Human Frontier Science Program Organization (HFSP)
HFSP Long-term Fellowship
HFSP Short-term Fellowships

International Institute for Management Development (IMD)
President's Scholarship

International Institute for Population Sciences (IIPS)
IIPS Diploma in Population Studies

International Mathematical Union (IMU)
IMU Visiting Mathematician Programme
International Mathematical Union Fellowship

International Research and Exchange Board (IREX)
IREX Mongolia Research Fellowship Program
IREX Russian/US Young Leadership Fellows for Public Service Program
IREX Starr Collaborative Research Grants Program

International Telecommunication Union (ITU)
International Telecommunication Union Fellowship

King Edward VII British-German Foundation
King Edward VII Scholarships

Kosciuszko Foundation
Kosciuszko Foundation Fellowships and Grants for Polish Citizens
Kosciuszko Foundation Sembrich Voice Competition
Summer Study Abroad Programs in Polish Language and Culture

Marcel Hicter Foundation
Council of Europe Travel Bursary Scheme

Medical Research Council (MRC)
MRC NHS Special Fellowships in Health Services Research
MRC Research Fellowship in Clinical Psychology
MRC Research Training Fellowship
MRC Royal College of Physicians and Pathologists Training Fellowships

MRC Travelling Fellowships
MRC/PPARC Research Training Fellowship

Meet The Composer, Inc.
Meet The Composer New Residencies

Menzies Centre for Australian Studies
Northcote Visiting Scholarship Scheme
Sir Robert Menzies Centre for Australian Studies Visiting Fellowships
Visual Arts Fellowship

Minnesota Historical Society (MHS)
MHS Research Grant

Monash University
Logan Research Fellowships

Musicians Benevolent Fund (MBF)
Emily English Scholarship
Professor Charles Leggett Trust

National Association for Core Curriculum, Inc.
Bossing-Edwards Research Scholarship Award

National Cancer Institute of Canada (NCIC)
Terry Fox New Frontiers Initiative

National Federation of the Blind (NFB)
NFB Frank Walton Horn Memorial Scholarship
NFB Humanities Scholarship
NFB Lora E Dunetz Scholarship
NFB Melva T Owen Memorial Scholarship

National Health and Medical Research Council (NHMRC)
Eccles Awards - No longer avaliable.
NHMRC Public Health Travelling Fellowships
R Douglas Wright Awards

National Heart Foundation of Australia
Warren McDonald International Fellowship

National Historical Publications and Records Commission (NHPRC)
NHPRC Documentary Editing and Archival and Records Management Grants

National Osteoporosis Society (NOS)
NOS Fellowships

National Research Council (NRC) Office for Central Europe and Eurasia
COBASE Collaboration in Basic Science and Engineering

National Research Foundation (NRF)
NRF Scholarships for Study towards an Honours Degree

National Restaurant Association Educational Foundation
H J Heinz Fellowship Program
National Restaurant Association Educational Foundation Graduate Degree Scholarship
National Restaurant Association Graduate Degree Fellowships
National Restaurant Association Industry Assistance Grants
National Restaurant Association ProMgmt Undergraduate Scholarship Program

National University of Singapore (NUS)
Lee Foundation and Tan Sri Dr Runme Shaw Foundation Fellowships in Orthopaedic Surgery
Mobil-NUS Postgraduate Medical Research Scholarship

Natural Sciences and Engineering Research Council of Canada (NSERC)
NSERC Chairs in the Management of Technological Change
NSERC Equipment Grants
NSERC EWR Steacie Memorial Fellowships
NSERC International Opportunity Fund
NSERC NATO Science Fellowships
NSERC New Faculty Support Grants
NSERC Project Research Grants
NSERC Strategic Project Grants (SPG)

New Energy and Industrial Technology Development Organisation (NEDO)
International Joint Research Grant Programme (NEDO Grant)

North Atlantic Treaty Organization (NATO)
NATO Euro-Atlantic Partnership Council Fellowships Programme (NATO-EPAC)

North West Cancer Research Fund
Reginald Bellis Bequest

Ontario Arts Council (OAC)
OAC Literature Grants to Periodicals Program for Organizations

Organization of American Historians (OAH)
Jamestown Scholars: New Dissertation Fellowships from the National Park Service and OAH
Merle Curti Award in American Intellectual History

Philadelphia Museum of Art
Arts Education Development Project (Program Advancement Grants)

Prevent Blindness America
Fight for Sight Postdoctoral Research Fellowships
Fight for Sight Student Research Fellowships

Purina Mills, Inc.
Purina Mills Research Fellowships

Queen's University of Belfast
Musgrave Research Studentships
Queen's University of Belfast Visiting Fellowships
Queen's University of Belfast Visiting Studentships

Radcliffe Institute for Advanced Study
Berkshire Summer Fellowship
Bunting Institute Affiliation
Bunting Institute Biomedical Research Fellowship
Bunting Institute Peace Fellowship
Bunting Institute Science Scholars Fellowship
Marian Cabot Putnam Fellowship

Radio and Television News Directors Foundation (RTNDF)
RTNDF Scholarships

Research Corporation (USA)
Research Corporation (USA) Research Innovation Awards

Reuters Foundation
Reuter Foundation Next Generation Graphics Awards for News Graphics Journalists
Reuters Foundation University Fellowship
Robert Mauthner Memorial Fellowship

Royal College of Midwives
Emma-Jane Award

Royal College of Nursing (RCN)
Alun Islwyn Giles Memorial Nursing Scholarship

Royal College of Obstetricians and Gynaecologists (RCOG)
RCOG Green-Armytage Anglo American Lectureship
RCOG Medical Student Prizes
RCOG Menopause Travel Award

Royal Holloway, University of London
Royal Holloway, University of London Masters Studentship
University of London Awards

Royal Irish Academy
Royal Irish Academy National Committee for Biochemistry Travel Bursary Scheme
Royal Irish Academy Senior Visiting Fellowships

Royal Pharmaceutical Society of Great Britain
Leverhulme Scholarships
Redwood Scholarship, Ransom Fellowship, Rammell Studentship, Lewis Edwards Memorial Scholarship, Jacob Bell Memorial Scholarship
Victor Reed Scholarships

Royal Philharmonic Society (RPS)
Kathleen Ferrier Awards and Decca Prize

Royal Society of Edinburgh (RSE)
Wellcome Trust-RSE Senior Research Fellowship

Scottish Opera
John Noble Bursary Award

Scripps Howard Foundation
Ellen B Scripps Fellowships
Robert P Scripps Graphic Arts Grants
Scripps Howard Foundation Scholarships
Scripps Howard Foundation Special Grants

Shastri Indo-Canadian Institute (SICI)
Shastri Indo-Canadian Institute Language Training Fellowship
Shastri Indo-Canadian Institute Summer Programme
Shastri Indo-Canadian Institute Women and Development
  Fellowships

Sheffield Hallam University
Sheffield Hallam University Research Bursary

Skidmore, Owings and Merrill Foundation
CIAU (Chicago Institute for Architecture and Urbanism) Award

Smith and Nephew Foundation
Smith and Nephew Foundation Medical Research Fellowships
Smith and Nephew Nursing Research Scholarships

Social Science Research Council (SSRC)
Public Policy Research on Contemporary Hispanic Issues Summer
  Workshop on Statistical Research Methods
SSRC China Program Fellowships for Dissertation Research Abroad
SSRC China Program Fellowships for Postdoctoral Research
SSRC International Migration Program Dissertation Fellowships
SSRC International Migration Program Postdoctoral Fellowships
SSRC International Migration Program Summer Dissertation
  Workshop
SSRC International Predissertation Field Research Fellowships
SSRC Japan Program Advanced Research Grants
SSRC Japan Program Grants for Research Planning Activities
SSRC Korea Program Advanced Research Grants
SSRC Korea Program Dissertation Fellowships
SSRC Korea Program Grants for Planning Activities
SSRC Latin America and Caribbean Program Advanced Research
  Grants
SSRC Latin America and the Caribbean Program Dissertation
  Fellowships
SSRC Latin American Program Research and Training Fellowship on
  Collective Memory of Repression: Comparative Perspectives on
  Democratization Processes in Latin America's Southern Core
SSRC MacArthur Foundation Dissertation Fellowships
SSRC MacArthur Foundation Postdoctoral Fellowships
SSRC Near and Middle East Program Advanced Research
  Fellowships in the Social Sciences and Humanities
SSRC Near and Middle East Program Dissertation Research
  Fellowships in the Social Sciences and Humanities
SSRC Program on the Arts Dissertation Fellowship
SSRC Religion and Immigration Predoctoral Fellowships
SSRC Research Planning Grants
SSRC Southeast Asia Program Vietnam Advanced Research Grants
SSRC Southeast Asia Program Vietnam Dissertation Field Research
  Fellowships

**Social Sciences and Humanities Research Council of Canada
  (SSHRC)**
Canadian Tobacco Control Research Initiative Planning Grants
Canadian Tobacco Control Research Initiative: Better Practices in
  Tobacco Control Grants
Federalism and Federations Program Research Grants
Federalism and Federations Program: New Patterns of Interactions,
  Interests and Community Research Grants
INE Collaborative Research Initiatives
INE Research Alliances
INE Research Grants
National Research Network on the Human Dimensions of Biosphere
  Greenhouse Gas Management: Research Directorship Grant
National Research Network on the Human Dimensions of Biosphere
  Greenhouse Gas Management: Research Node Grants
Ocean Management National Research Network Initiative
Valuing Literacy in Canada Strategic Partnership Development Grants
Valuing Literacy in Canada Strategic Research Grants

Society of Orthopaedic Medicine
Society of Orthopaedic Medicine PGDip/MSc Award

South African Dental Association
Lever Pond's Postgraduate Fellowship

Stanford Humanities Center
Shared Research Group Fellowships for Postdoctoral Scholars
Shared Research Group Fellowships for Senior Scholars

Textile Institute
Lee 400 Educational Trust

United States Center for Advanced Holocaust Studies
Pearl Resnick Post Doctoral Fellowship

United States Educational Foundation in India (USEFI)
USEFI Fellowships in Educational Administration

University of Cambridge
Cambridge Overseas Bursaries in Social Anthropology
Cropwood Fellowship Programme
Frazer Studentship in Social Anthropology

University of Cambridge, Judge Institute of Management
Browns Restaurant Scholarships

University of Kent
University of Kent at Canterbury Second English Scholarship

University of Leeds
Arab-British Chamber Charitable Foundation Scholarship
ARUP-Leeds University FCO Chevening Scholarship
Guinness-Leeds University FCO Chevening Scholarships
Iceland - Leeds University FCO Chevening Scholarships
International Fee Bursaries (Brazil)
International Fee Bursaries (India)
International Fee Bursaries (Indonesia)
International Fee Bursaries (Malaysia)
International MBA Fee Bursaries
Jordan-Leeds University-Chevening Scholarship
Marks and Spencer - Leeds University- FCO Chevening Scholarships
Rothmans-Leeds University FCO Chevening Scholarships
Unilever Thai Holdings - Leeds University - FCO Chevening
  Scholarships
University of Leeds Fee Scholarship

University of New England (UNE)
UNE Research Scholarships

University of Oxford
A J Hosier Studentship
Balliol College Sir Edward Heath Scholarship
Balliol College The Eddie Dinshaw Scholarship
Brasenose College Senior Germaine Scholarship
Brasenose Senior Germaine Scholarship
Christ Church DFID Shared Scholarship
Citibank/Chevening Scholarships
Donald Tovey Memorial Prize
Gordon Milburn Junior Research Fellowship
Hall-Houghton Studentship in Biblical Studies
Janet Watson Bursary
Jesus College Graduate Scholarship
Jesus College Old Member's Graduate Scholarship
Joanna Randall-MacIver Junior Research Fellowship
Korea Foundation Scholarship in Korean Studies
Law Scholarships for Students from Israel
Linacre College Lloyd African Scholarships/DFID Shared
  Scholarship
Linacre College Unipart Scholarship
Lincoln College Dresdner Kleinwort Benson Senior Scholarships
Lincoln College Overseas Graduate Entrance Scholarship The Paul
  Shuffrey Scholarship
Merton College Graduate Entrance Scholarships
Merton College Senior Scholarships
New Century Scholarships
Nuffield College Guardian Research Fellowship
Nuffield College Gwilym Gibbon Research Fellowships
Nuffield College ODA Shared Scholarship
Oxford Overseas Bursaries
Peter Jenks Vietnam Scholarship
Plant Sciences Department Claridge Druce Scholarship
Queen's College ODA Shared Scholarship
Radhakrishnan/British Chevening Scholarships
Somerville College Margaret Pelly Scholarship, in association with the
  OPTIMA project
Somerville College Ruth Adler Scholarship

St Anne's College Research Scholarship
St Anne's College Schoolteacher Fellowship
St Antony's College Fay and Geoffrey Elliott Graduate Studentship in Russian and East European Studies
St Antony's College Rothschild Scholarship in Economics
St Hugh's College Dorothea Gray Scholarship
St Hugh's College Rawnsley Studentship
St Hugh's College William Thomas and Gladys Willing Scholarship
St Hugh's College Yates Senior Scholarship
Templeton College MBA Scholarship
Trinity College Kandiah Thirunavukkarasu Graduate Scholarship
University of Oxford E K Chambers Studentship in English Literature
University of Oxford Graduate Studentships in the Modern History Faculty
Varley-Gradwell Travelling Fellowship in Insect Ecology
Violet Vaughan Morgan Commonwealth Studentship in English Literature
Wolfson College Department for International Development Shared Scholarship Scheme (formerly ODASSS)
Wolfson College Graduate Studentships
Wolfson College ODA Shared Scholarship
Wolfson College The Hargreaves-Mawdsley Studentship

University of Reading
Otway Cave Scholarship

University of Regina
Regina Graduate Scholarships
Regina Teaching Assistantships

University of Stirling
University of Stirling MBA Programme

University of York
University of York Postgraduate Student Bursaries

US-UK Fulbright Commission
Academic Administrator in Veterinary Education
Fulbright Calvin Klein/Harvey Nichols Award in Fashion Design
Fulbright Fellowship in Securities Law
Fulbright Louise Buchanan Fellowship in Cancer Research
Fulbright TEB Clarke Fellowship in Screenwriting
Fulbright Zurich Business Research Award
Fulbright-RCVS Fellowship
Royal Society Fulbright Scholarships
Royal Society-Fulbright Postdoctoral Science Fellowship Programme to the USA

Van Slyke Society
Van Slyke Society Research Grant in Critical and point-of-care Testing

Wenner-Gren Foundation for Anthropological Research
Wenner-Gren Foundation Anthropological Research Grants

World Without War Council, Inc. (WWWC)
WWWC Americans and World Affairs Fellows Program

Yale Center for British Art
Andrew W Mellon Fellowship

INDEX OF AWARDING ORGANISATIONS